The New York Times 2002

ALMANAC

●

Edited by John W. Wright

WITH EDITORS AND REPORTERS OF

The Times

PENGUIN REFERENCE

PENGUIN REFERENCE BOOKS
Published by the Penguin Group
Penguin Putnam Inc., 375 Hudson Street,
New York, New York 10014, U.S.A.
Penguin Books Ltd, 27 Wrights Lane,
London W8 5TZ, England
Penguin Books Australia Ltd,
Ringwood, Victoria, Australia
Penguin Books Canada Ltd,
10 Alcorn Avenue,
Toronto, Ontario, Canada M4V 3B2
Penguin Books (N.Z.) Ltd,
182–190 Wairau Road,
Auckland 10, New Zealand

Penguin Books Ltd, Registered Offices:
Harmondsworth, Middlesex, England

Published in 2001 by
Penguin Reference Books,
a member of Penguin Putnam Inc.

10 9 8 7 6 5 4 3 2 1

ISBN 0 14 10.0235 0
ISSN 1523-7079

Printed in the United States of America
Set in Utopia and Optima

Designed by Virginia Norey

Please direct all comments to:

The New York Times Almanac
122 East 42nd Street
New York, New York 10168

CONTRIBUTORS AND STAFF

General Editor
John W. Wright

Executive Editor
John Rosenthal

Senior Editors and Writers
Bryan Bunch, John Connelly, Jeffrey Hacker, Alan Joyce, John Major, Allison Paxton Paine, Lincoln Paine, Patricia Szczerba, Jenny Tesar

Contributing Editors
Abigail Elbow, Alice Finer, Glen Gendzel, Deborah Kaple, Jerold Kappes, Michael Kaufman, Thomas LaRosa, Steven Lichtman, David Major, Lisa Renaud

Researchers and Fact Checkers
Grant Flowers, William T. LeGro, Susan McMichaels, Robert L. Spring, Johanna Stoberock, Victoria Vine

Data Entry
Arlene Jacks, Dorothy Green

The New York Times
Thomas K. Carley, President, News Services; Nancy Lee, Vice President, Business Development; Mitchel Levitas, Editorial Director, Book Development

Editors
Laura Chang, Renee Murawski, David Rampe, David Stout

Correspondents
Lawrence K. Altman, James Barron, Barry Bearak, Pam Belluck, Alex Berenson, Dana Candey, Francis X. Clines, Alan Cowell, Steven Erlanger, Howard W. French, Joel Greenberg, Linda Greenhouse, David Johnston, Gina Kolata, Clifford Krauss, Warren E. Leary, Steve Lohr, Alison Mitchell, Seth Mydans, Floyd Norris, Norimitsu Onishi, Andrew C. Revkin, James Risen, Kevin Sack, David E. Sanger, Eric Schmitt, Katharine Q. Seelye, Thom Shanker, Andrew Ross Sorkin, Alessandra Stanley, James Sterngold, Richard W. Stevenson, Sheryl Gay Stolberg, Ginger Thompson, Patrick E. Tyler, Louis Uchitelle, Don Van Natta Jr., Nicholas Wade, John Noble Wilford.

Maps
Steve Hadermeyer, John Papasian

CONTENTS

AMERICA ATTACKED:
UNCONVENTIONAL WAR ON TWO FRONTS

Like the day on which John F. Kennedy was assassinated in 1963 or the day on which Pearl Harbor was attacked in 1941, Sept. 11 was one of those days that divide things into "before" and "after." What happened in less than two hours on that morning was unthinkable, almost indescribable. Four commercial jetliners were commandeered by small teams of terrorists armed with ordinary box cutters and a ruthless understanding of how to turn planes into fiery missiles that could destroy quintessential symbols of American wealth and power.

The next day the Bush Administration singled out Osama bin Laden's terrorist organization as responsible for the attacks. Washington also demanded that the Taliban rulers of Afghanistan, who had long sheltered his terrorist training camps, turn him over or face military attack. After cobbling together a fragile coalition of allies that included NATO countries, Russia, China, India and even Muslim Pakistan, the U.S. launched a retaliatory air war.

Then, unexpectedly, a spate of biological attacks in Florida, Washington, New York City and New Jersey unnerved the nation. No one claimed credit for the refined spores of anthrax contained in ordinary envelopes, but soon postal workers in Washington and New Jersey were infected. Anthrax also killed a hospital worker in Manhattan, though it was not immediately clear how she would have been exposed to the highly dangerous, inhaled form of the disease. The source of the attacks was unknown by early November, prompting a remarkable plea from the baffled F.B.I. for help from the public, along with a million dollar reward for information.

Fears of a fresh terrorist assault rose in October as an initial surge of confidence and patriotic unity began to fade. Although 88 percent of those questioned in a *New York Times*/CBS News poll taken in late October applauded the attacks on Afghanistan and put President Bush's approval rating at 87 percent, only 18 percent of the public said it had a "great deal" of confidence in the ability of the U.S. government to protect against future terrorist attacks.

By Oct. 29, when a coalition of civil liberties groups said it would file a lawsuit demanding that the government identify everyone who had been taken into custody and explain what charges they were facing, the F.B.I. was detaining more than 1,000 people. But no one had been arrested as a suspected conspirator.

●

THE ATTACKS   On the morning of Sept. 11, President George W. Bush was in Sarasota, Florida, speaking to children about education. Informed of the attacks, he left hastily, and as the brutal efficiency of the hijackers became clear, Air Force One took a circuitous route back to Washington, moving the president to command posts in Louisiana and Nebraska before returning to the capital.

One of the hijacked planes—American Airlines Flight 11, which had veered off its Boston-to-Los Angeles route and barreled over New York at more than 500 miles an hour—took aim at the north tower of the World Trade Center, to be followed less than 20 minutes later by United Airlines Flight 175, also headed from Boston to Los Angeles. It smashed into the second tower. A third jet, Ameri-

can Airlines Flight 77, flying from Dulles Airport outside Washington to Los Angeles, slammed into the Pentagon. The fourth, United Airlines Flight 93, on the way from Newark to San Francisco, went down in Pennsylvania after passengers apparently fought with the terrorists. Its original target was believed to be another national symbol in Washington—perhaps the White House or the U.S. Capitol.

The twin towers collapsed less than two hours after they were hit, consumed by jet engine fuel in a meltdown that left thousands of tons of smoldering debris at what came to be called "ground zero." Desperate employees plunged to their deaths from blown-out windows hundreds of feet in the air. Mayor Rudolph W. Giuliani warned on Sept. 11 that the death toll from the attack on the trade center, an enormous city-within-a-city, would be "more than any of us can bear." Hundreds of emergency rescue workers—firefighters, police officers and paramedics—had clambered into the two buildings, lugging hoses and heavy equipment and looking for injured people to carry out. At last count 343 firefighters did not make it, devastating entire fire companies throughout the city; the police said that more than 70 officers were missing. At the Pentagon, an estimated 125 perished. A total of 266 crew and passengers aboard the four airliners also died. By Oct. 31, the toll of victims at the trade center was estimated at 4,295.

On Sept. 14, the F.B.I. released the names of 19 suspected hijackers; some had studied to be pilots at flight schools in Florida. Washington's case against bin Laden was largely circumstantial, though NATO officials said on Oct. 2 that the United States had provided "clear and compelling proof" that bin Laden and his radical Islamic organization, Al Qaeda (the Base), were behind the attacks.

THE AFTERMATH   In countless ways, the rhythms and rituals of American life changed overnight. Within hours of the attacks, the police began checking trucks heading into New York City. Guards checked concert-goers' briefcases at temples of high culture; backpacks were barred at ballparks. Some lawmakers called for a reassessment of intelligence activities and an end to the perennial turf wars that thwart the exchange of secret information while others in and out of Congress sought ways to determine how an open society could defend itself without compromising individual liberties.

President Bush got credit for making the right political moves and sounding the right spirit of resolve in bringing the "evildoers" to "justice" while deploring scattered vigilante attacks on middle easterners in several American cities. The President's prime-time speech to a joint session of Congress on Sept. 20 was widely considered the high point of the administration's efforts to rally public opinion here and abroad. In his speech, Mr. Bush also announced the creation of a new executive agency of Homeland Security and appointed Gov. Tom Ridge of Pennsylvania to plow through bureaucratic roadblocks that threatened to slow the defense of things that had never had to be defended before—not only border crossings, but power plants, bridges and reservoirs. Airline passengers paid attention to what they carried in carry-on luggage as airport guards confiscated nail clippers and other seemingly innocuous items that now were deemed potential onboard weapons. National Guard troops were pressed into service to patrol major airports.

The economy, which had been sliding toward recession before Sept. 11, stumbled badly. After a four-day suspension of trading—the longest since the Great Depression—the Dow Jones industrial average tumbled 14.3 percent, making it one of the worst weeks in Wall Street history. By mid-October, the stock market had largely recovered, then sagged again as some economists said a "doomsday scenario" for a full-scale financial meltdown would linger for some time. Unemployment jumped to 5.4 percent in October, the highest in five years. Over 400,000 workers lost their jobs.

The airlines—grounded for almost a week after Sept. 11—appealed for federal assistance. After passenger traffic plunged dramatically, Congress approved a $15 billion bailout package on Sept. 21. The House and Senate also agreed to set up an open-ended fund for victims of the attacks in New York and Washington.

THE DIPLOMATIC COALITION   The attacks reshuffled the diplomatic deck. Russia, scarred by its own war against rebels in Chechnya in the 1990's—a decade after its humiliating withdrawal from Afghanistan—opened its airspace for American warplanes. "Not only is the cold war over," Secretary of State Colin Powell said on October 18, "the post-cold-war period is over." Prime Minister Tony Blair of Great Britain took the lead among NATO allies. Among Muslim countries, which were understandably ambivalent about aiding the United States, the shakiest was also the most essential: Pakistan. Its president and former military ruler, General Pervez Musharraf, agreed to allow American use of Pakistani bases after receiving assurances of billions of dollars in American aid and the end of Washington's trade embargo, imposed when Pakistan exploded a nuclear weapon.

Large anti-American protests in Islamabad and other cities were tightly controlled by police, but as America's bombing war continued, General Musharraf urged a quick end to the campaign. As the Islamic holy month of Ramadan approached, Defense Secretary Donald H. Rumsfeld pledged to continue the assault, now bolstered by small numbers of American ground troops who helped coordinate the bombing of Taliban positions with opposition forces of the anti-Taliban Northern Alliance.

Though Pakistan was clearly the focus of the Muslim role in the allied coalition, internal tensions also were apparent in Egypt and Saudi Arabia, the latter an even more lukewarm partner. Indeed, both Pakistan and Saudi Arabia had contributed enormous sums to support bin Laden and the Taliban during the Soviet occupation of Afghanistan in the 1980's. The C.I.A. itself had funneled weapons and money to Pakistan, whose intelligence agencies worked closely with the Taliban leadership—and still do, according to some reports.

THE MILITARY RESPONSE   President Bush declared war on terrorism hours after the jetliners hit their targets at the World Trade Center and the Pentagon. But the actual military response did not begin until Oct. 7, when the United States and Great Britain launched a barrage against Afghanistan. Bombers, fighter planes and cruise missiles pounded bin Laden's training camps and knocked out what the Pentagon described as the military strongholds of his Taliban protectors.

Three million pounds of explosives blasted Afghanistan in the first month of the campaign as the Pentagon tried to block the Taliban's supply lines. Soon after the air attacks began, ground forces of the opposition Northern Alliance went on the offensive but without notable success. Secretary of Defense Donald Rumsfeld cautioned that organizing effective resistance in the south would not be easy—the Taliban are "survivors," he said. "It would be unwise to think that the outcome is determined—it's not." By the end of October, small units of American ground troops were reported with units of the Northern Alliance, bolstering their forces and coordinating air attacks on Taliban targets.

But the American air war was not without problems. Bombs went astray and on two occasions badly damaged a compound used by the International Committee of the Red Cross in Kabul. Destroying tanks one at a time, bombing caves or uncovering Taliban troops nestled in villages made for increasingly gloomy military assessments that air power could prevail. Pentagon officials said that documents collected in a daring ground sweep of buildings in Kandahar on Oct. 19 did not yield the intelligence bonanza Washington had hoped for.

ANTHRAX TERROR   For many Americans the military campaign was overshadowed by widespread fears caused by the first biological weapon attack on the U.S. The means of delivery was deceptively simple, frightening and effective: letters sent through the Postal Service containing, in several cases, finely ground spores of the deadly germ anthrax. Anthrax claimed its first victim on Oct. 5, an employee of a South Florida tabloid publisher. On Oct. 10, officials in New York announced that an anthrax-laden letter had infected an assistant to the NBC anchor Tom Brokaw, who had opened an envelope addressed to him in mid-September.

An envelope containing at least a tablespoon of anthrax was mailed to Senate majority leader, Tom Daschle. On Oct. 15, an aide opened the envelope, releasing a puff of spore-laden powder. Fearing contamination throughout the Capitol, the House of Representative shut down for four days, but the Senate voted not to follow suit. Tests on Oct. 17 showed that 31 workers on Capitol Hill had been exposed to anthrax spores from the letter addressed to Daschle. At the *New York Post*, which received a similar letter, an editorial assistant was found to have cutaneous anthrax. Also infected was an assistant to CBS anchor Dan Rather. Eventually, anthrax turned up in mail processing facilities in New York, New Jersey and Washington and in a smaller sorting center that handles letters addressed to the White House.

The anthrax attacks involved small numbers; by Nov. 2, there had been four deaths among 10 people known to be infected with inhalation anthrax, the most severe form of the disease, and seven known incidents of cutaneous (skin) anthrax. During the entire 20th century, the United States had recorded only 18 cases of inhalation anthrax. "It's a weapon of mass hysteria—not mass destruction," one scientist said. Anxiety levels climbed higher and higher as disease investigators in "moon suits" were kept busy, though they chased many false alarms.

Still, the federal government and the Centers for Disease Control acknowledged that scientists and ▾

civilian officials had fumbled on the germ-warfare front, largely because they had never had to cope with anything like it before. For example, they ignored the possibility that postal workers might have been infected as tainted envelopes whizzed through fast-moving mail sorting machinery. Even the postmaster general said that he could not absolutely guarantee the safety of the mails.

On Oct. 29, about a month after the first tainted letters had passed through a huge mail processing center in midtown Manhattan, more anthrax was discovered in Washington—at the State Department, the Justice Department and in a federal building housing the Voice of America. But officials said they still had no idea where the deadly spores had come from and they could not conclude initially whether the anthrax bacteria was home-grown or foreign-made.

By far the public's biggest bio-terrorist scare came on Oct. 31, when a 61-year-old hospital stockroom employee in New York City died. Kathy T. Nguyen, a Vietnamese immigrant who lived alone in the Bronx, was the city's first victim of inhalation anthrax and the first victim who did not work for a news organization or in a federal installation. She died before health officials could speak to her about where she had been in early to mid-October, when she was most likely exposed. Initial tests on the supply room were negative. The mystery remained. To make matters worse, the F.B.I. admitted publicly on Nov. 2 after weeks of investigation that it was stymied in the frantic search to find the source of the anthrax attack.

THE OUTLOOK There were signs of edginess as the crisis entered its eighth bleak week. Popular support for President Bush remained strong even as public confidence in the country's ability to protect itself against further terrorist attacks—in whatever form and place, no one knew—dropped sharply. By then, the Bush administration's rapid response to the deadliest single attack on the American mainland rapidly had devolved into a drawn-out military and diplomatic struggle. Allied strategists seemed to favor the course they had followed from the start: step up the bombing, support internal opponents of the Taliban, and in the process hope to destroy Osama bin Laden's network and his Taliban protectors. But after only weeks of bombing, a small presence of allied ground troops, and a faltering effort to create a post-Taliban coalition government in Afghanistan, it was too soon for optimism in a new species of unconventional war that many worried would go on for years.

— *James Barron*
Nov. 5, 2001

Late Breaking News

Israeli Army Occupies West Bank Despite U.S. Protests

The violent struggles between Palestinian gunmen and the Israeli army continued throughout October. After Israel's right-wing minister of tourism, Rehavam Zeevi, was assassinated by two Palestinians (Oct. 17), Israel greatly widened the war by sending troops, tanks and helicopter gunships into Bethlehem and eight other cities and towns in the West Bank (Oct. 19-21). Ignoring pleas from Pres. Bush to withdraw from Palestinian territory, the Israelis pushed ahead even further (Oct. 24). Bowing to intense U.S. pressure, Israel finally began to withdraw (Oct. 28) but deadly attacks by armed Palestinians halted the movement. At the end of the month Israeli Foreign Minister Shimon Peres announced a plan (Oct. 30) to meet with Yasir Arafat, a move that would most likely deepen the divisions in Israel's fractured government.

Breakthrough in Irish Peace Process

The events of Sept. 11 had a serious impact on the deadlocked Irish peace plan. According to some observers, the I.R.A. became fearful that Irish-American support was eroding and that the time had come for action. On October 23, 2001, the I.R.A. declared that it had begun to dismantle its arsenal of weapons, heeding a call from its political arm, Sinn Fein, and expressing hope that the move would "save the peace process" in Northern Ireland. British Prime Minister Tony Blair quickly responded with a promise to meet some I.R.A. demands, including the withdrawal of some troops. The next day, Britain began dismantling three high-tech military watchtowers and one base, and announced that it would no longer seek to extradite or prosecute people at large facing charges related to the Protestant-Catholic conflict. Despite renewed optimism among politicians, however, Irish citizens were skeptical that an end to the decades-old conflict was any closer at hand.

The Nobel Prizes, 2001

PEACE
United Nations and **Kofi Annan**, 63, (Ghana), the U.N.'s Secretary General since January 1, 1997, in equal portions, for "their work for a better organized and more peaceful world."

PHYSICS
Eric A. Cornell (U.S.), **Carl E. Wieman** (U.S.), and **Wolfgang Ketterle** (Germany), "for the achievement of Bose-Einstein condensation in dilute gases of alkali atoms, and for early fundamental studies of the properties of the condensates."

PHYSIOLOGY OR MEDICINE
Leland H. Hartwell, 61, (U.S.), **R. Timothy Hunt**, 58, (U.K.), and **Paul M. Nurse**, 52 (U.K.), "for their discoveries of key regulators of the cell cycle."

CHEMISTRY
William S. Knowles, 84, (U.S.) and **Ryoji Noyori**, 63, (Japan), for their work on chirally catalysed hydrogenation reactions." **K. Barry Sharpless**, 60 (U.S.), "for his work on chirally catalysed oxidation reactions."

ECONOMIC SCIENCES
George A. Akerlof, 61, (U.S.), **A. Michael Spence**, 58, (U.S.), and **Joseph E. Stiglitz**, 58, (U.S.), "for their analyses of markets with asymmetric information."

LITERATURE
V.S. Naipaul, 69, (U.K., born Trinidad) "for having united perceptive narrative and incorruptible scrutiny in works that compel us to see the presence of suppressed histories."

NOVEMBER

1 With the U.S. presidential election less than a week away, Al Gore spends the day in Florida warning voters that Bush's proposals on Social Security would threaten their retirement.

2 On the campaign trail, Bush acknowledges the truth of reports that he had been arrested for drunk driving 24 years ago.

The Democrats release a new TV ad that bluntly questions Bush's capability to be president.

3 Gore and Bush trade attacks on each other with Gore mocking Bush's gaffe that Social Security was not a federal program, and Bush asserting that the Clinton Administration had left America "undefended against missile attack."

4 Pres. Clinton vetoes a bill renewing the authority of the nation's intelligence agencies because it contains what he calls "a badly flawed provision" that would make it a crime for a government official to disclose classified information.

6 Gore finishes his campaign with a 30-hour, seven-city assault and pointedly portrays himself as more vigorous than his rival.

George W. Bush ends his campaign with symbolic appearances in Tennessee and Arkansas, the home states of Gore and Clinton.

7 About 100 million Americans go to the polls on Election Day and, in the closest election in U.S. history, George W. Bush appears to defeat Al Gore for President as Florida moves into the Republican column early in the morning.

Hillary Rodham Clinton is a very strong winner in the New York Senate race and becomes the only First Lady in U.S. History to win public office.

8 After a tumultuous night there is no clear winner in the presidential election. Gore holds a slim lead in the national popular vote, but Bush holds a lead of 1,700 votes out of 6 million cast in Florida; Florida law requires a machine recount.

Four Palestinian teenagers and one Israeli woman are killed as new violence breaks out in the West Bank and Gaza Strip, on the eve of a meeting between Pres. Clinton and Yasir Arafat.

9 Israeli helicopter gunships attack a vehicle carrying a Palestinian militia leader, killing him and two women in the first planned killing of a Palestinian leader since violent clashes began six weeks ago. (See "Major News Stories.")

10 In the U.S. presidential election, unofficial machine recount results cut Bush's lead in Florida to 327 votes, but Republicans still demand a concession from Gore.

11 As several Florida counties prepare for a manual vote recount, Bush files suit in federal court to stop them.

13 Philippine President Estrada is impeached on corruption charges. (See "Major News Stories.")

Israel faces its worst recent one-day death toll when two Israeli soldiers and two civilians are killed in two separate attacks.

14 Pres. Clinton requests $750 million in emergency aid for Israel.

15 Gore pledges an end to all legal challenges if Bush agrees to a statewide manual recount in Florida, but Florida Secretary of State Katherine Harris rejects all hand recounts and Bush refuses Gore's offer. Republican Congressional leaders speculate publicly about how they could help deliver Florida's electoral votes to Bush.

Israeli helicopters attack Palestinian targets and Israeli soldiers shoot and kill eight Palestinians and wound dozens more.

16 The Florida Supreme Court rules that hand recounts may continue; Republicans return to federal court, claiming recounts are unconstitutional.

Pres. Clinton arrives in Hanoi, Vietnam, becoming the first U.S. president to visit since Richard Nixon in 1969.

17 Yasir Arafat orders gunmen in Palestinian-controlled territories to cease fire in his first public repudiation of the escalating violence.

18 Initial results from overseas ballots triple Bush's lead in Florida, but confusion over postmarks throws many of these ballots into dispute; Republican lawmakers in Florida announce plans to name a pro-Bush slate of electors if Gore ultimately claims victory.

20 The Florida Supreme Court sharply questions lawyers from both parties, offering little hint of how it will ultimately rule.

Peruvian President Fujimori formally resigns, ending a tumultuous, scandal-filled decade in power. (See "Major News Stories.")

21 The Florida Supreme Court extends the state's vote certification deadline to November 27 and rules that the results of manual recounts submitted by that morning must be included in the final tally. The court sets no clear standards for determining voter intent, however.

China agrees to stop selling missile components and equipment to countries developing nuclear weapons, in return for which the U.S. will waive sanctions for the past sale of such material.

22 Russia announces its intent to withdraw from a 1995 agreement limiting sales of tanks and other weapons to Iran.

Yemeni officials identify the bombers of the U.S. destroyer Cole as two Saudi Arabian citizens, with possible links to Osama bin Laden.

25 Talks in The Hague on the Kyoto Protocol, an international global warming treaty, collapse due to last-minute disagreements between European and American negotiators.

26 Katherine Harris declares Bush the winner of Florida's electoral votes, but Democrats immediately head to court to contest the certification.

27 New Jersey state documents show that at least 8 of every 10 automobile searches by state troopers on the New Jersey Turnpike in the last decade involved minority drivers; the state attorney general cites this as evidence of a systematic process of racial profiling.

30 November proves to be the worst month for the Nasdaq composite index since the October 1987 crash; the index is down 48.5 percent from its record high in March, dropped 22.9 percent in November alone, and is at its lowest level since August 1999. (See "Major News Stories.")

DECEMBER

1 In an unprecedented hearing at the Supreme Court, lawyers for Bush and Gore present their arguments. Gore's campaign suffers two major legal blows in the Florida courts: the state Supreme Court refuses an appeal to begin an immediate recount of 14,000 disputed ballots, and also refuses to order a new election in Palm Beach County.

In Chile, former dictator Gen Augusto Pinochet is charged with kidnapping his opponents in 1973 and is ordered to be placed under house arrest.
3   PepsiCo agrees to buy Quaker Oats for $13.4 billion in stock, giving Pepsi control of the popular Gatorade brand.
4   Reacting to public fears about mad cow disease, European Union agricultural ministers ban the use of animal feed laced with animal products and take steps that may lead to the slaughter of two million cattle. (See "Major News Stories.")

Pres. Clinton creates a the largest U.S. nature preserve, 84 million acres, around the northwestern Hawaiian Islands.
5   Republicans reject demands by Democrats for committee co-chairmanships and other forms of power sharing in an evenly divided U.S. Senate.
6   U.N. Secretary General Kofi Annan announces an end to the two-year war between Ethiopia and Eritrea.
7   Yasir Arafat appears on television holding a submachine gun, in an apparent attempt to regain favor with Palestinians who believe he has compromised their interests.
8   Gore loses two lawsuits to throw out almost 25,000 absentee ballots in Martin and Seminole Counties, but his hopes are revived by a 4-to-3 Florida Supreme Court ruling that orders the immediate recount of disputed ballots across the state and adds votes from previous recounts to the certified Florida totals.

The Palestinian movement Fatah and other Islamic groups call for a "day of rage" to honor the anniversary of the first Palestinian uprising in 1987; 10 people are killed in the West Bank and East Jerusalem. (See "Major News Stories.")
9   The recount in Florida is abruptly halted when the U.S. Supreme Court issues a stay until it can hear an appeal from the Bush camp.

Ehud Barak resigns as Israel's prime minister, forcing a new election in early February.
10   In a dramatic televised return to Israel, former Prime Minister Benjamin Netanyahu announces his intention to reclaim the leadership of the Likud party and the office of prime minister.

In Johannesburg, negotiators from 122 nations agree on a global ban on 12 highly toxic chemicals, a group of persistent organic pollutants known as the "dirty dozen."
12   A bitterly divided U.S. Supreme Court puts an end to recounts, the Florida Supreme Court rejects the Gore team's suit to throw out absentee ballots, and the Florida House of Representatives votes in favor of a pro-Bush slate of electors.

The Marine Corps grounds its fleet of Osprey aircraft after one crashes, killing all four marines on board; the crash is the fourth in the program since 1991 and the second this year.
13   Gore delivers a gracious concession speech and Bush makes his first speech as president-elect, both of them urging unity.

Clinton engages in debate with hard-line lawmakers in the National Assembly of Northern Ireland who oppose his peace plan for the country.
14   President-elect Bush claims he will be "aggressive" in seeking Democrats for high-ranking administration jobs.

The F.T.C. approves the merger of America Online and Time Warner, under strict conditions meant to ensure competition.
15   The last working reactor at Chernobyl power station in the Ukraine is shut down.

Stocks tumble, with the Nasdaq, Dow and S&P 500 indices all falling over 2 percent.

16   President-elect Bush names Colin Powell to be secretary of state; he will be the first African-American to hold this position.
18   Bush receives 271 Electoral College votes, Al Gore 266, one fewer than expected, because an elector in Washington D.C. leaves her ballot blank.
19   Israel's Likud Party nominates Ariel Sharon for prime minister after Netanyahu withdraws.

President-elect Bush visits Bill Clinton at the White House to discuss foreign policy; later, Bush meets with Al Gore for a brief, "cordial" meeting.
20   Pres. Clinton welcomes Israeli and Palestinian negotiators to the White House in hopes of reaching a settlement before he leaves office.
21   Israeli officials state that they are now actively hunting down and killing Palestinians suspected of planning attacks on Israeli citizens.
22   Pres.-elect Bush announces his selection of John Ashcroft as Attorney General; Democratic leaders promise to challenge the nomination.

U.N. members reach an agreement to reduce American dues in the organization, a move which promises to reduce friction between the U.N. and lawmakers in Washington.
23   A democratic coalition supporting Yugoslav president Vojislav Kostunica wins a landslide victory in Serbian parliamentary elections, officially marking the collapse of the Milosevic regime.
26   Seven employees of a Wakefield, Mass. Internet consulting company are shot and killed by 42-year-old software tester Michael McDermott, who was apparently upset that his wages were being garnisheed to pay back taxes.
28   The Israeli Army seals off the entire West Bank and Gaza Strip after Palestinian bombs kill two Israelis. (See "Major News Stories.")

The U.S. Census Bureau announces the first result of the 2000 Census: the national population is 281,421,906 people, a 13.2 percent increase in 10 years and 6 million above recent predictions.

President-elect Bush names Donald Rumsfeld to be Secretary of Defense, the same position he held in the Ford administration.
29   Technology stocks continue their nosedive, as the Nasdaq plunges over 80 points to finish the year down 39.3 percent. (See "Major News Stories.")
30   Five powerful terrorist bombs kill 14 people and injure 100 more in the Philippine capital of Manila.

JANUARY

1   Yasir Arafat travels to Washington for a hastily arranged meeting with Pres. Clinton. Earlier in the day, a car bomb injures 30 people in the Israeli town of Netanya and hundreds of Palestinians march through Ramallah to commemorate the 36th anniversary of the founding of Arafat's Fatah movement. (See "Major News Stories.")
3   Hillary Clinton is sworn in as a U.S. Senator, earning a place in history as the only former First Lady to hold public office.

The Fed slashes interest rates one-half point, suggesting concern that the economy is stalling but also boosting the Nasdaq 324.83 points, a one-day record for the index.
4   The chief rabbis of Israel state that Jewish law forbids giving up sovereignty over Jerusalem's Temple Mount, one of the terms offered in Clinton's latest peace proposal.
5   The U.S. Senate votes to give Democrats and Republicans equal seats on committees.
8   Thousands of Israelis gather in Jerusalem to protest the American peacekeeping plan, which would divide the city between Arabs and Jews.

9 Linda Chavez, Bush's nominee for Secretary of Labor, withdraws herself from consideration amid criticism of her alleged employment of an illegal immigrant.

Astronomers announce they have discovered two new planetary systems with features unlike anything previously seen, including what may be a planet 17 times as massive as Jupiter.

11 The U.S. Army confirms that American soldiers killed unarmed civilians in the Korean War, but that the deaths were not deliberate.

12 Scientists announce that they have successfully inserted a jellyfish gene into a monkey egg, fertilized it, and gave birth to a healthy monkey.

13 A major earthquake measuring 7.6 on the Richter scale kills hundreds of people in El Salvador and Guatemala.

15 Scientists announce that they have used a particle accelerator to smash gold atoms together to produce the highest-density matter ever created in an experiment.

16 Congolese President Laurent D. Kabila is shot and killed by his bodyguard.

A tanker runs aground in the Galapagos islands and begins to leak its 243,000 gallons of fuel.

17 As the financial crisis worsens, California begins a program of rolling blackouts affecting hundreds of thousands of people. (See "Major News Stories.")

Two independent teams of U.S. scientists report that they have slowed light to a stop, stored it, and released it again. (See "Major News Stories.")

18 Judge Ronnie White testifies against John Ashcroft, asserting that Ashcroft willfully distorted White's record in opposing his nomination to a seat on federal court.

Jesse Jackson admits to fathering a child out of wedlock with an employee of his organization.

20 In his final hours in office, Pres. Clinton issues pardons to more than 100 people, including a fugitive businessman. (See "Major News Stories.")

George W. Bush is sworn in as the 43rd President of the United States.

21 Pope John Paul II names a record-breaking 37 new cardinals, including three Americans.

American officials report that Iraq has rebuilt factories near Baghdad long suspected of producing chemical and biological weapons

22 Pres. Bush moves to block federal aid to overseas groups that provide abortion counseling.

23 Five members of the banned Falun Gong spiritual group set themselves on fire in Beijing's Tiananmen Square to protest their suppression by China's government; one person dies.

Pres. Bush announces his commitment to providing more federal money to religious-based social service organizations.

26 The most powerful earthquake in 50 years strikes the Indian state of Gujarat, killing at least 7,000 people.

Two companies announce that they have decoded the genome of rice, raising hopes for improvement of a food that is a worldwide staple.

28 U.S. government officials say that in the final hours of Clinton's presidency, almost two dozen people—many with personal connections to Clinton—had their pardon applications moved to the front of the line, in many cases bypassing review by the Justice Department and the F.B.I. (See "Major News Stories.")

29 Pres. Bush signs two executive orders increasing governmental involvement in religious-based community groups.

FEBRUARY

1 Drawing more votes to defeat his nomination than any Attorney General candidate since 1925, John Ashcroft wins Senate confirmation in a 58-to-42 vote.

2 Under fire for receiving gifts worth hundreds of thousands of dollars during his presidency and for his plans to rent expensive office space in Manhattan, Clinton announces that he and Hillary will pay for $86,000 in gifts received in 2000 and that his foundation will share the cost of office space.

5 Russian Defense Minister Igor Sergeyev warns that Russia may resort to a new arms race if the U.S. moves ahead with plans to build a national missile shield.

6 Ariel Sharon becomes Israel's new prime minister by the largest margin in the nation's history. (See "Major News Stories.")

7 After firing several shots on the sidewalk outside the White House, a former I.R.S. employee is shot in the leg by Secret Service agents.

8 A Congressional committee investigating Clinton's pardon of Marc Rich discovers that Rich's ex-wife, Denise, pledged nearly $1 million to Clinton's presidential library.

9 The U.S. Navy nuclear submarine Greeneville smashes into a Japanese fishing boat, killing nine of the 35 crew and passengers when the boat sinks. (See "Major News Stories.")

10 *The New York Times* reports that two rival teams of U.S. scientists analyzing the human genome have found that there may be as few as 30,000 human genes, far fewer than previously thought. (See "Major News Stories.")

12 The NASA spacecraft NEAR Shoemaker lands on the asteroid Eros, ending a yearlong orbit and becoming the first man-made instrument to land on such a body.

13 A 6.6-magnitude earthquake hits El Salvador, killing at least 100 people and injuring more than 1,000.

14 A Palestinian bus driver plows into a crowd of Israeli soldiers and civilians in Tel Aviv, killing eight and injuring 20.

16 American and British planes attack Iraqi targets, an action Pres. Bush defends as a necessary response to recent Iraqi provocations.

18 Scientists at Ohio State University's Byrd Polar Research Center report that the ice cap atop Mt. Kilimanjaro is melting and could disappear within 15 years.

20 Robert Hanssen, a senior FBI counterintelligence agent, is arrested on charges of spying for Russia for 15 years. (See "Major News Stories.")

21 New reports reveal that Hillary Clinton's brother, Hugh, was paid almost $400,000 for lobbying for a presidential pardon for two felons, a businessman convicted of mail fraud and perjury and a cocaine trafficker. (See "Major News Stories.")

22 In his first news conference, Pres. Bush promotes his tax cut and education program, and also expresses strong concerns that China may be helping to build radar sites that defend Iraq against Western warplanes.

23 In Borneo after six days of fighting between migrants and indigenous tribesmen, at least 200 are dead and tens of thousands have fled.

24 Serbia's new government arrests Slobodan Milosevic's former secret police chief on charges of murder, and hints that Milosevic and his family may be brought in soon.

26 Israeli Labor Party leaders accept Ariel Sharon's invitation to join a coalition government.

27   Bill Clinton waives executive privilege and declares he will not prevent his former aides from testifying about his last-minute pardons.
28   An earthquake measuring 6.8 on the Richter scale hits the U.S. Pacific Northwest, causing no deaths but injuring hundreds and causing damage estimated in the billions of dollars in Seattle and other nearby cities.

MARCH
1   In accordance with a strict interpretation of Islamic law banning all idols, the Islamic Taliban movement begins demolishing statues across Afghanistan, including two enormous ancient stone Buddhas in Bamiyan Province.
2   Napster agrees to prevent users of its service from exchanging thousands of copyrighted songs identified by major record companies.
5   After complaining of chest pains, Vice Pres. Dick Cheney is hospitalized to clear a partially-blocked artery. (See "Major News Stories.")
7   New Census results show that the U.S. Hispanic population has grown about 60 percent in 10 years, making it roughly equal to blacks as the largest minority.
In meetings with South Korean Pres. Kim Dae Jung, Pres. Bush says he will not follow through on the Clinton Administration's plans to hold missile talks with North Korea.
8   The Bush administration announces that despite warnings from NATO allies about increased Albanian insurgency in the region, the U.S. will not allow its peacekeeping troops to cross from Kosovo into Serbia.
9   A 14-year-old Florida boy, convicted of murdering a 6-year-old girl when he was 12, is sentenced to life in prison.
11   In England twenty-five more farms are reported to have foot-and-mouth disease, bringing the total to 164 since it was first reported in February. (See "Major News Stories.")
13   Pres. Bush reneges on a campaign pledge and says his administration will not regulate carbon dioxide emissions in U.S. power plants.
The U.S. bans imports of European animals and animal products, citing concern over the spread of foot-and-mouth disease.
16   New skirmishes erupt as Albanian insurgents step up their campaign to reclaim Albanian parts of Macedonia. (See "Major News Stories.")
19   California is hit again with rolling blackouts after a heat wave strikes and two major power generators fail. (See "Major News Stories.")
20   E.P.A. administrator Christie Whitman announces the agency will withdraw regulations approved by the Clinton administration that would have reduced the permissible standard for arsenic in drinking water by 80 percent.
In Washington Pres. Bush and Prime Minister Ariel Sharon meet to discuss the future of the Israel-U.S. relationship and the current conflict.
21   Because of the arrest of an F.B.I. agent charged with spying for Moscow for over 15 years, the Bush administration orders several Russian diplomats to leave the U.S. and says that 40 or more will be asked to leave in the coming months.
Paleontologists in Africa say they have discovered a 3.5 million-year-old skull that is apparently from a new branch of the human family tree, raising questions about theories of a single line of human descent. (See "Major News Stories.")
22   Russia's Mir space station, launched in 1986, makes its final descent to Earth, breaking up in the atmosphere and crashing into the Pacific Ocean between New Zealand and Chile.

Very near a school where a similar incident took place two weeks earlier, an 18-year-old opens fire on a San Francisco high school, seriously wounding two students. (See "Major News Stories.")
Responding to concerns that the America Bar Association has increasingly taken a liberal stance on major issues, the White House ends the organization's privileged role in evaluating candidates for federal judgeships.
23   A report from Britain's Ministry of Agriculture projects that the number of sites affected by the foot-and-mouth epidemic will soon rise by 70 each day and could exceed 4,000 by June.
24   *The New York Times* reveals evidence from researchers that cloning animals may have negative side effects, including defective organs or severe developmental problems like obesity.
25   Macedonian forces begin their offensive against Albanian rebels in Tetovo, reclaiming several villages. (See "Major News Stories.")
Mass graves containing over 200 bodies are found in the Burundi capital Bujumbura, apparently the result of fighting between Hutu rebels and government forces that began in February.
26   In Hebron, a Palestinian sniper kills an Israeli baby girl and wounds her father, leading to fighting and the sealing of the town by Israeli troops.
27   In the latest attempt to keep California's electricity producers in business, state power regulators approve the largest rate increase in California history. (See "Major News Stories.")
28   Ariel Sharon orders Israeli helicopters to attack training camps and bases of Yasir Arafat's personal security forces after a Palestinian suicide bomber kills himself and two Israeli teenagers.
29   Fugitive anti-abortion activist James C. Kopp, charged with killing a doctor in 1998, is arrested in western France.
30   U.S. researchers report promising results from experiments using stem cells from bone marrow to repair animal heart tissue.
31   Serbian special forces commandos storm the residence of Slobodan Milosevic before dawn; after an exchange of gunfire, police serve Milosevic with an arrest warrant which he refuses to acknowledge. (See "Major News Stories.")

APRIL
1   A Chinese fighter jet collides with a U.S. Navy spy plane near the Chinese coast; the U.S. plane makes an emergency landing on Hainan island and the crew is taken into Chinese custody. (See "Major News Stories.")
After several violent displays, including a threat to kill himself and his family, Slobodan Milosevic is arrested peacefully in Belgrade.
2   The McCain-Feingold campaign finance bill passes the Senate 59-41, though Republican leaders promise a fight in the House.
An Iraqi helicopter gunship is used to assassinate a member of the Islamic Jihad group in the Gaza Strip, the first such killing since Ariel Sharon took office; and in Bethlehem at least six people are killed when intense fighting breaks out after the slaying of an Israeli soldier by Palestinians.
3   A U.S.-China standoff escalates as China refuses to return the crew of the downed American spy plane until the U.S. issues a full apology for the incident and agrees to cancel all surveillance flights off the Chinese coast.
Vice Pres. Cheney casts tie-breaking vote in the Senate, halting an attempt by Democrats to shift money from Bush's tax cut plan to Medicare.
5   The Bush administration issues a new statement of "regret" over the recent collision.

6 California's largest utility files for bankruptcy, faulting the state government for not acting quickly enough to resolve the energy crisis.

10 U.S. stock markets post broad gains and the Dow Jones closes above 10,000 for the first time in nearly a month, but financial analysts warn against too much economic optimism.

The U.S. announces that it has submitted a formal statement of regret to the Chinese government.

11 In Johannesburg, South Africa 43 spectators are killed and over 100 injured in a stampede at a packed soccer stadium.

12 China accepts the U.S.'s latest letter of regret and releases all 24 crew members; the downed spy plane, however, remains in China.

The mayor of Cincinnati declares a state of emergency and institutes a street curfew after racially-charged violence spreads in the wake of the recent shooting of a black teenager by police.

13 The Pentagon produces a videotape of a previous encounter between a Chinese fighter jet and an American spy plane, which it says is evidence of a pattern of dangerous and aggressive flying by the Chinese military.

15 In its first action against the Syrian Army since 1996, Israel responds to recent Hezbollah attacks with strikes at Syrian radar sites, killing one Syrian soldier and wounding four.

16 The E.P.A. announces that it will leave in place a Clinton Administration rule that would protect thousands of acres of U.S. wetlands.

17 Following a harsh rebuke from U.S. Secretary of State Colin Powell, the Israeli Army withdraws from positions it had occupied in the Gaza Strip less than 24 hours earlier.

18 Stock prices surge when the Federal Reserve cuts interest rates by half a percentage point for the fourth time in less than four months.

In a 5-4 decision, the Supreme Court rules that race is a reasonable consideration in Congressional redistricting, if it is not the "dominant and controlling" one. (See "Major News Stories.")

19 U.S. Navy officials announce that the captain of the submarine that sank a Japanese fishing boat in February will not be court-martialled, instead receiving a letter of reprimand.

20 At Pres. Bush's first major international meeting, the Summit of the Americas in Quebec, he promises to make the expansion of economic and political connections in Latin America his first priority. Violent protests take place along its perimeter.

A private plane carrying American missionaries is mistakenly shot down by a Peruvian Air Force jet searching for drug traffickers.

23 White House officials reveal that Pres. Bush will offer advanced weapons and warships to Taiwan, while keeping the controversial Aegis radar defense system off the table.

24 Former Japanese health and welfare minister Junichiro Koizumi is elected leader of the Liberal Democratic party, putting him in line to become Japans' ninth Prime Minister in ten years.

In a 5-4 decision the Supreme Court rules that police officers may make a full custodial arrest of someone breaking even a minor law without violating constitutional restrictions on unreasonable seizure. (See "Major News Stories.")

25 Former U.S. Senator Bob Kerry, who won the Medal of Honor for his Vietnam military service, admits that he led a combat mission in 1969 that resulted in the killing of 13 to 20 unarmed civilians, mostly women and children.

The journal *Nature* reports that an international team of paleontologists has discovered a feathered dinosaur fossil that may be the strongest evidence of an evolutionary link between dinosaurs and modern birds.

26 Officials of the New York City Police Department reveal to *The New York Times* that the four officers who killed unarmed African immigrant Amadou Diallo will not be disciplined, since internal investigating panels found that they had not violated police guidelines.

27 After a federal judge declined a request by Puerto Rico to block military training on the island of Vieques earlier in the week, the U.S. Navy resumes bombing exercises, prompting an escalation of protests by residents and U.S. politicians. (See "Major News Stories.")

29 U.S. astronomers say they have detected patterns in the glow from primordial gases that gives them a picture of the universe's infancy.

30 Vice Pres. Dick Cheney declares that the Bush administration strategy in the ongoing energy crisis will be to increase the energy supply instead of limiting demand.

MAY

1 Pres. Bush calls for a new relationship with Russia that would include an expansive missile defense system and cuts in nuclear arsenals.

In Birmingham, Ala. a jury of eight whites and four blacks convict Thomas E. Blanton or murdering four black girls in a 1963 church bombing. (See "Major News Stories.")

2 A grand jury in Manhattan indicts the former heads of two giant auction houses, Sotheby's and Christie's, on federal antitrust charges stemming from a conspiracy to fix fees.

3 For the first time the U.S. is voted off the U.N. Human Rights Commission.

Florida lawmakers reach agreement to ban punch-card ballot machines, to provide money for new equipment and to require hand counts in disputed elections.

4 The Labor Dept. reports a loss of 223,000 jobs in April, the largest since 1991.

In Athens, Pope John Paul II expresses "deep regret" for his church's misdeeds against the Greek Orthodox Church. (See "Major News Stories.")

6 In Damascus Pope John Paul II makes a bold bid to cut through centuries of division by becoming the first pope ever to set foot in a mosque.

7 The Pentagon says that Secty. of Defense Rumsfeld will propose a sweeping overhaul of its space programs, sharply increasing the importance of outer space in strategic military planning.

9 In a show of unity, House Republicans pass a budget resolution allowing for tax cuts of $1.35 trillion over 11 years and $2 trillion in spending in the next fiscal year. Democrats denounce the budget as dishonest.

In a soccer stadium in Accra, Ghana, over 123 people are killed in a stampede resulting from police firing tear gas into the unruly crowd.

10 The F.B.I. says it has discovered thousands of pages of interview reports and other materials about the Oklahoma City bombing that were never given to Timothy J. McVeigh's defense lawyers. (See "Major News Stories.")

11 Attorney General Ashcroft announces that McVeigh's execution will be delayed until June 11.

12 As Pres. Bush prepares to unveil his plan to curb what he calls an energy "crisis," *The New York Times* reports that the energy industry has already raised production significantly because of higher prices.

Russian and American archaeologists announce they have discovered an ancient civilization that thrived in Central Asia more than 4,000 years ago. (See "Major News Stories.")

13 Voters in Italy elect the party of conservative media baron Silvio Berlusconi to run the national government, ending five years of center-left rule.

14 The U.S. Supreme Court rules, 8–0, that federal law does not allow a "medical necessity" exception to the prohibition of marijuana.

15 The Federal Reserve lowers interest rates again, this time by half a percentage point, saying its decision was driven by the deteriorating outlook for business. (See "Major News Stories.")

16 The Bush administration releases its energy plan that calls for more drilling, the possibility of renewed nuclear power, and conservation.

18 A Palestinian suicide bomber kills at least five Israelis and wounds over 100 at a shopping mall in Netanya. Israeli jets retaliate by bombing the West Bank and Gaza Strip for the first time since the 1967 war. (See "Major News Stories.")

20 *The New York Times* reports that a Bush administration review has recommended that the U.S. not accept a draft agreement to enforce the treaty banning germ weapons.

23 Senator James M. Jeffords of Vermont tells his aides that he plans to leave the Republican Party and become an independent, a move that would give Democrats control of the Senate. (See "Major News Stories.")

26 With many Democrats joining with almost all Republicans, both houses of Congress pass the $1.35 trillion tax cut. (See "Major News Stories.")

29 In Federal District Court in New York, a jury convicts four men of conspiring with Osama bin Laden in a terrorist plot to bomb U.S. embassies in Kenya and Tanzania in 1998.

In Los Angeles, Pres. Bush meets with Gov. Gray Davis of California and they clash sharply over the wisdom of capping the price of electricity.

31 Lawyers for Timothy J. McVeigh ask the federal judge who sentenced him to death to grant a stay of execution because the government failed to produce thousands of pages of evidence. (See "Major News Stories.")

JUNE

1 Outside a Tel Aviv beach club, a suicide bomber kills at least 17 people and injures scores more. (See "Major News Stories.")

The royal family of Nepal are shot in their palace, allegedly by the Crown Prince who then shoots himself. (See "Major News Stories.")

2 Yasir Arafat denounces the attack in Tel Aviv and calls for cease-fire.

3 The Pentagon says Defense Secty. Donald H. Rumsfeld has ordered all contacts with the Chinese armed forces to cease.

Alejandro Toledo, the son of a poor sheep herder, wins Peru's presidential election. (See "Major News Stories.")

4 The U.S. Supreme Court overturns the death sentence of a retarded man in Texas.

5 As Republican control of the Senate abruptly ends, Pres. Bush reaches out to Democrats and moderates in his party.

The Bush administration announces it is sending George Tenet, the director of central intelligence, to Israel in an effort to maintain calm.

6 A much-anticipated report requested by the White House from the National Academy of Sciences declares that global warming is a real problem that is getting worse.

Pres. Bush announces that the U.S. will restart negotiations with North Korea on a broad range of issues including the exporting of missiles.

8 Prime Minister Tony Blair and the Labor Party sweep to a huge victory in Great Britain's national election.

Voters in Ireland, one of the European Union's greatest success stories, reject the plan to expand the E.U. by 12 members.

9 For a second day tropical storm Allison continues to batter southeast Texas leaving at least 15 people dead and $1 billion in damages.

11 Timothy J. McVeigh is executed by lethal injection in the federal prison in Terre Haute, Ind. (See "Major News Stories.")

Pres. Bush makes it clear that while he embraces the recent report from the National Academy of Sciences his administration will reject the Kyoto accord on global warming.

The U.S. Supreme Court rules 5-to-4 that police use of thermal imaging to search homes requires a search warrant. The Court also rules 6-to-3 that public schools must open their doors to after-school religious activities. (See "Major News Stories.")

12 After six days of intensive mediation by the U.S., the Israelis and Palestinians reluctantly accept a cease-fire proposal.

Pres. Bush begins his first trip to Europe; in Spain he calls the ABM treaty "a relic," and emphasizes his opposition to the Kyoto global warming accord.

13 The Bush administration says it will halt all military exercises and aerial bombing runs on the Puerto Rican island of Vieques by May 2003.

The leaders of Germany and France publicly contradict Pres. Bush's assertion that there was a "new receptivity" to the missile shield plan.

15 Speaking in Warsaw, Pres. Bush calls for an Atlantic Alliance that would stretch all the way to Russia's borders.

16 Pres. Bush meets Russian Pres. Putin in Slovenia and at a news conference Putin urges Bush not to act alone on building a missile shield.

17 Gov. Rick Perry of Texas vetoes legislation that would have banned the execution of the mentally retarded.

18 Russia's Pres. Vladimir Putin says that if the U.S. proceeds with its plan to construct a missile shield, Russia would upgrade its nuclear arsenal to be sure it could overwhelm such a shield.

19 Atty. Gen. John Ashcroft notifies Congress that he has named a team of lawyers to explore the possibility of settling the Justice Dept.'s lawsuit against the tobacco industry.

20 A *New York Times*/CBS News Poll shows Pres. Bush's standing as a leader has diminished considerably with his job approval rating dropping to 53 percent.

The New York Times reports that Arthur Andersen has settled a civil fraud suit brought by the S.E.C. and has agreed to pay a $7 mil. penalty, the largest ever assessed against an accounting firm.

In Houston, Texas Andrea Yates drowns her five young children in a bathtub, supposedly as a result of post-partum depression.

21 A federal grand jury in Washington, D.C. returns a 46-count indictment charging 13 Saudis and a Lebanese man in the truck bombing at the Khobar Towers in Saudi Arabia that killed 19 U.S. airmen and wounded 400 others in 1996.

23 The Yugoslav cabinet committs itself to sending Slobodan Milosevic to the U.N. tribunal in the Hague to face trial on war crimes charges.

A powerful earthquake hits southern Peru killing over 300 people and destroying hundreds of houses and buildings.

25 The U.S. Supreme Court rules (5 to 4) that immigrants who had pleaded guilty to crimes before 1996 do not face automatic deportation.

U.S. troops in Macedonia escort hundreds of armed Albanian rebels away from a town and a huge riot erupts over the action. (See "Major News Stories.")

26 In Washington, Pres. Bush meets with Prime Minister Sharon of Israel who repeats his requirement for peace, 10 days without violence.

27 For the sixth time this year the Federal Reserve cuts its benchmark interest rate, this time by a quarter of a percentage point and signals that its campaign to revive the flagging economy may be entering its final stages. (See "Major News Stories.")

After a three-day special session the U.N. General Assembly approves a declaration outlining how the world should fight the AIDS epidemic.

28 A federal appeals court finds that Microsoft repeatedly abused its monopoly power but it throws out a lower court's order that the company be broken up. (See "Major News Stories.")

Slobodan Milosevic is jailed in The Hague, Netherlands to await trial by the U.N. war crimes tribunal. (See "Major News Stories.")

29 Vice Pres. Cheney says doctors will implant a sophisticated heart pacemaker and defibrillator; this will be his third significant procedure since he was elected. (See "Major News Stories.")

30 Doctors in Washington, D.C. successfully implant a pacemaker in Vice Pres. Dick Cheney's chest. (See "Major News Stories.")

JULY

1 First Minister David Trimble of Northern Ireland resigns his post because of the I.R.A.'s refusal to disarm, casting the peace process into uncertainty. (See "Major News Stories.")

2 The Bush administration scales back its plans to drill for oil and gas in the Gulf of Mexico.

3 Slobodan Milosevic appears before an international tribunal in The Hague and dismisses the court with disdain as an "illegal organ."

Surgeons in Louisville, Ky. announce that they have placed the fully implantable artificial heart in a human being. (See "Major News Stories.")

5 Pres. Bush telephones Pres. Jiang Zemin of China to "build a better relationship" but he brings up the secret arrests of U.S. citizens and green card holders by Chinese security forces.

6 The U.S. Dept. of Labor reports that the nation's employers cut 114,000 jobs in June, refuting reports that the economy was recovering.

Robert P. Hanssen, the former F.B.I. agent, pleads guilty to charges that he had spied for Russia since 1985 in exchange for the government not to seek the death penalty.

8 The Comcast Corp. seeks to become the nation's biggest cable television company by making an unsolicited offer to acquire AT&T's cable operation for $44.5 billion in stock.

9 *The New York Times* reports that for the first time in the 20-year history of the popular 401(k) retirement savings plan, the average account lost money in 2000.

10 Scientists at a Virginia fertility clinic announce they have created human embryos expressly for medical experiments.

12 The effort to overhaul the campaign finance law collapses in the House of Representatives in a procedural battle with Speaker J. Dennis Hastert saying he has "no plan to bring up this bill now."

13 The Olympic Committee announces that the 2008 Summer Games will be held in Beijing.

14 Peace talks, led by Prime Minister Tony Blair and Irish Prime Minister Bertie Ahern, aimed at rescuing the Northern Ireland treaty end without a breakthrough. (See "Major News Stories.")

16 Russia and China sign a treaty of "friendship and cooperation," committing them to oppose the U.S. plan for a missile shield.

17 In a speech at the World Bank headquarters in Washington, Pres. Bush calls for a major change in the way rich nations help poorer countries, proposing that up to 50 percent of aid be given as direct grants rather than loans.

19 After an investigation into the death of a health volunteer the federal government suspends almost all of the $300 million in funding given to Johns Hopkins for medical research.

20 As the leaders of the world's largest industrialized nations meet in Genoa, Italy, tens of thousands of anti-globalization protesters riot and one is shot to death by police.

21 As protests continue in Genoa, with as many as 50,000 demonstrators in and through the streets, the major allies of the U.S. tell Pres. Bush they intend to ratify the Kyoto Protocol on global warming without American participation.

22 Pres. Bush and Russian Pres. Putin announce they have agreed to link discussions of U.S. plans to deploy a missile defense system with the prospect of large cuts in nuclear arsenals.

Pres. Abdurraham Wahid of Indonesia declares a state of emergency although he is on the verge of being ousted by Parliament and the military.

23 In Bonn, Germany 178 nations ratify a compromise agreement to formally require industrialized countries to cut emissions of gases linked to global warming.

In the most peaceful transfer of power in Indonesia's history, Megawati Sukarnoputri is sworn in as president moments after the legislature voted to end Pres. Wahid's tenure.

Pres. Bush meets with Pope John Paul II outside Rome and hears the pontiff condemn research using cells from human embryos.

24 In Kosovo, Pres. Bush tells thousands of cheering troops that "America's contribution is essential, both militarily and politically," a major change in his position before his election.

A Chinese court convicts two Chinese citizens with permanent residency in the U.S. of spying for Taiwan and sentences them to 10 years in prison. One is released and deported the next day.

26 Despite stormy opposition from the Bush administration the Senate votes overwhelmingly (70-30) to support efforts to impose strict safety standards on Mexican trucks seeking access to roads in the U.S.

27 The House votes 219 to 189 to require the Bush administration to keep in place Clinton-imposed restrictions on the amount of arsenic allowed in drinking water.

The Dept. of Commerce announces that economic growth nearly halted in the second quarter meaning it was now in its weakest condition since early 1993. (See "Major News Stories.")

28 Secty. of State Colin L. Powell ends his first meeting with China's leaders sounding upbeat but admitting little progress regarding China's opposition to U.S. plans for a missile shield.

31 *The New York Times* reports that EPA administrator Christie Whitman has agreed to go ahead with the Clinton plan to require G.E. to dredge PCB pollution from the Hudson River.

By a wide margin the House of Representatives votes to completely ban human cloning including for medical research.

AUGUST

1 The House of Representatives passes Pres. Bush's energy plan to promote production and

conservation, including allowing drilling in the Arctic National Wildlife Refuge in Alaska.
2   The House passes a bill creating new federal rights for millions in managed health care plans, including access to specialists but limiting the right to sue insurance companies.

At the Hague, the Bosnian Serb general, Radislav Korstic, is found guilty of genocide by an international court for his role in the execution of 7,000 unarmed Mulsim men near Srebrenica in 1995.
6   The I.R.A. agrees to a new method of destroying its arsenal that British and Irish leaders call "significant." (See "Major News Stories.")
7   David Trimble, leader of the Protestant faction, rejects the I.R.A. arms offer.
9   Pres. Bush addresses the nation on TV to announce he will allow federal taxpayer money to be used for research into stem cells for human embryos but limiting it to cells already extracted. (See "Major News Stories.")

In a downtown Jerusalem restaurant a suicide bomber blows himself up, killing 15 others, including six children, and wounding about 130. (See "Major News Stories.")
15   NATO decides to send 400 British troops to Macedonia to disarm the ethnic Albanian rebels. (See "Major News Stories.")
19   *The New York Times* reports that the world economy has slowed to a crawl as the U.S., Europe, Japan and some major developing countries undergo a rare simultaneous slump.
21   A senior Bush administration official says the U.S. has told Russia it has until November to agree to changes in the Antiballistic Missile Treaty or the U.S. will withdraw from the accord.

The I.M.F. agrees to provide Argentina with $8 billion in emergency aid to stabilize its economy.
22   The Bush administration releases budget projections showing that surpluses outside the Social Security system will dwindle to almost nothing over the next several years.
23   A top Chinese official openly admits that his country is facing a serious AIDS epidemic.
27   Congressional budget analysts warn that the economic downturn and the Bush tax-cut package would force the federal government to spend $9 billion from the Social Security surplus.
29   The Commerce Dept. reports that the U.S. economy grew more slowly in the second quarter than at any time in eight years.
31   At a U.N. conference on intolerance held in South Africa, Yasir Arafat denounces Israel as a racist colonial power just one hour after aides say Palestinians would reject a planned proposal labeling Israel a racist state.

SEPTEMBER
1   The Bush administration says it will drop its objections to China's nuclear missile buildup in the hope of overcoming China's opposition to the U.S. missile defense plan.
3   The U.S. and Israel walk out of the U.N. meeting on racism being held in South Africa, denouncing a proposed condemnation of Israel.
4   Pres. Bush and Senate Democratic leaders say they have agreed not to tap the Social Security program to pay the government's other bills.
5   In Belfast, Protestant extremists detonate a bomb near a girls' Catholic school as children are heading to class. (See "Major News Stories.")
6   The Bush administration announces it will no longer seek the breakup of Microsoft to settle the antitrust case, abandoning the central claim of the lawsuit. (See "Major News Stories.")

7   The U.S. jobless rate jumps to 4.9 percent, the biggest rise since 1995. (See "Major News Stories.")
10   A panel of scientific experts reports that new lines of human embryonic stem cells will be necessary if the science is to fulfill its potential. (See "Major News Stories.")
11   In the worst terrorist attack in U.S. history, hijackers crash two U.S. airliners into New York's World Trade Center, causing an inferno that destroys both buildings within two hours, killing thousands. A third hijacked plane crashes into the Pentagon, and a fourth crashes in western Pennsylvania. (See pages iv-v)
12   Federal authorities link the hijackers to Osama bin Laden. Cell phone conversations from passengers aboard the fourth plane indicate that the hijackers intended to crash it into the White House, but several passengers joined forces to overwhelm the hijackers.
13   Pres. Bush pins responsibility for the World Trade Center attacks on Osama bin Laden, vowing a military response against terrorist networks around the world and nations that harbor them.
14   The F.B.I. releases the names of 19 men believed to be the hijackers of the four U.S. airplanes used in the Sept. 11 attacks. All 19 are men of Middle Eastern descent, most of them had been living in the U.S. for several years, and at least nine had studied to be pilots at Florida flight schools.

With one dissenting vote, both houses of Congress vote to give Pres. Bush "all necessary and appropriate force" to respond to the terrorist attacks.
15   Pres. Bush tells the military to prepare for a protracted war against terrorists and the countries that support them.

Sec. of State Colin Powell asks Saudi Arabia to sever diplomatic relations with the Taliban, which has harbored Osama bin Laden and allowed him to operate training camps in Afghanistan.

Pakistan pledges cooperation but warns that military action would need U.N. support.
17   Wall Street reopens for the first time since Sept. 11. Government and business leaders persuade investors not to panic, but sell-offs send the Dow plummeting by more than 7 percent.

The Federal Reserve cuts its benchmark rate to 3 percent.

Pres. Bush says he wants Osama bin Laden "dead or alive." He calls up 35,000 military reservists to patrol American harbors and airspace.

The Taliban demands to see "convincing evidence" that Osama bin Laden is responsible for the September 11 attacks and refuses to turn him over to U.S. authorities.
18   The Justice Department asks for authority to detain and arrest immigrants suspected of crimes. Drawing the greatest ire of civil liberties advocates is a rule that would allow the government to detain legal immigrants indefinitely without arresting them for any specific crime.

Pres. Bush and Congress agree to bail out the airline industry, which announced 44,000 layoffs in the days following the terrorist attacks.

Palestinian leader Yasir Arafat orders his troops to cease fire, and says he wants to join the U.S. efforts to wipe out terrorism. Israel pulls its tanks and troops out of Palestinian-controlled areas.
19   Pres. Bush orders heavy bombers and other aircraft to take position within striking distance of Afghanistan and he insists the Taliban turn over Osama bin Laden.
20   In an address to a joint meeting of Congress, Pres. Bush pledges an attack on Afghanistan

unless it surrenders bin Laden now, and he warns of a long campaign against terrorism.

21   The Bush administration says it will waive economic sanctions against Pakistan in exchange for cooperation and support of military actions.

Both houses of Congress overwhelmingly pass a $15 billion package to bail out the ailing airlines industry. They also agree to set up an open-ended federal fund to compensate victims of the attacks.

The Dow declines 14.3 percent, ending one of the worst weeks in stock market history.

23   The Bush administration says it plans to make public evidence linking Osama bin Laden to the terror attacks in an effort to persuade Muslim nations that a military response is justified.

Democratic leaders say they favor a federal takeover of airport security.

24   Pres. Bush orders an immediate freeze on all assets in the U.S. of suspected terrorist groups and individuals and he gives the treasury secretary broad new powers to impose sanctions on banks around the world that provide them access to the international finance system.

Pres. Vladimir V. Putin offers the U.S. broad support for anti-terrorist operations in Afghanistan.

25   At a Senate Finance Committee meeting, Federal Reserve chairman Alan Greenspan and former treasury secretary Robert E. Rubin say they oppose further cuts in the capital gains tax and reducing corporate taxes.

27   Speaking to a crowd of airline workers at O'Hare Airport in Chicago, Pres. Bush announces that the federal government will take on a larger role in airport security and that more than 4,000 National Guard troops will begin protecting the nation's 420 commercial airports.

28   The U.N. Security Council unanimously adopts a U.S.-sponsored resolution requiring all 189 member states to crack down on terrorists and to cooperate in a campaign against them.

30   The administration says that Pres. Bush has approved a secret effort to strengthen several groups opposing the Taliban ruler of Afghanistan.

(For Late Breaking News, see page vi.)

Obituaries November 1, 2000–October. 31, 2001

Aaliyah (Aaliyah Dana Houghton), 22, U.S. rhythm and blues singer and actress whose albums each sold millions of copies. Her first musical success came at age 14. She also appeared in several movies. In a small plane crash, Abaco Island, the Bahamas, Aug. 25, 2001.

Adams, Douglas, 49, British author whose best-selling novels, beginning with *The Hitchhiker's Guide to the Galaxy,* satirized science fiction as well as technology and politics. Of a heart attack, May 11, 2001, Santa Barbara, Calif.

Adler, Mortimer, 98, New York-born high school and college dropout who went on to found the "Great Books" program with Robert Hutchins at the Univ. of Chicago; author of many popular books on philosophy and education. Of old age, San Mateo, Calif., June 28, 2001.

Ahrens, Edward, 85, Chicago-born scientist whose research led to understanding of the role of saturated and unsaturated fats on cholesterol levels and the need for dietary change. Cause undisclosed, Princeton, N.J., Dec. 9, 2000.

Amado, Jorge, 88, Brazil's most popular novelist, whose 32 books often champion the poor and women (notably *Dona Flor and Her Two Husbands*), many translated worldwide. Of diabetes-related heart and lung failure, Salvador, Brazil, Aug. 6, 2001.

Ammons, A.R. 75, highly-acclaimed U.S. poet whose many prizes include the 1993 National Book Award; highly regarded teacher at Cornell University. Of cancer, Ithaca, N.Y., Feb. 25, 2001.

Anthony, Earl, 63, U.S. pro bowler, the first man to win $1 million; winner of 41 Professional Bowlers Assoc. titles and six P.B.A. national championships. After a fall, Aug. 14, 2001.

Antley, Chris, 34, U.S. jockey, winner of 3,480 races including two Kentucky Derbys (1991,1999), who struggled with weight and drug problems. Of a drug overdose, Pasadena, Calif., Dec. 3, 2000.

Atkins, Chet, 77, Tennessee-born guitarist whose performing style helped create the Nashville Sound and whose producing skill made Nashville the country music capital. Of cancer, Nashville, Tenn., June 30, 2001.

Aumont, Jean-Pierre, 90, French actor in numerous Hollywood movies, including *Lili* in 1953, often

as the romantic lead; appeared in even more French films in a 65-year career, notably in Truffaut's *Day for Night.* Of old age, St. Tropez, Jan. 30, 2001.

Balthus (Balthasar Klossowski), 92, European painter and stage designer born in Paris to Polish parents; known for his sometimes erotic portraits and agitated still lifes. Of old age, at his chalet near Gstaad, Switzerland, Feb. 18, 2001.

Barnard, Christiaan, 78, South African surgeon who performed first human heart transplant, Dec. 3, 1967, paving the way for what is now a standard procedure. Of an asthma attack, Cyprus, Sept. 2, 2001.

Basov, Nikolai, 78, Russian scientist, co-winner of 1964 Nobel Prize in Physics for research that led to development of lasers. Cause, date and place of death undisclosed.

Birenda, Bir Bikram Shah Dev, 55, king of Nepal since 1972, a popular leader who accepted democratic reforms; assassinated with his wife and other members of the royal family by his son, the crown prince, who later died from self-inflicted gunshot wounds. Katmandu, June 1, 2001.

Borge, Victor, 91, Danish-born maestro of comedy and the piano, whose ebullient routines of music, wordplay and pratfalls entertained millions on TV, Broadway and worldwide. Of old age, Greenwich, Conn., Dec. 23, 2000.

Boudreau, Lou, 84, baseball Hall of Famer, best known as the shortstop whiz who also managed the Cleveland Indians and led them to the 1948 World Championship; at age 24 in 1941, the youngest manager in major league history. Of heart failure, Olympia Fields, Ill., Aug. 10, 2001.

Brooks, Gwendolyn, 83, U.S. poet who wrote of everyday lives with deep compassion, transforming her native Chicago South Side into "Bronzeville," her vision of the black experience; awarded 1950 Pulitzer Prize and 1995 National Medal of Arts. Cause undisclosed, Chicago, Dec. 3, 2000.

Brown, Les, 88, Pennsylvania-born musician, leader of his "Band of Renown," the last of the 1940's big bands; composed hit song "Sentimental Journey"; longtime associate of Bob Hope on radio and TV. Of old age, Los Angeles, Jan. 4, 2001.

Buckey, Peggy McMartin, 74, U.S. educator accused of child molestation at family-owned school along with her son in two headline trials; charges were dropped due to weak evidence and lack of corroboration of children's lurid stories. Cause undisclosed, Torrance, Calif., Dec. 15, 2000.

Caras, Roger, 72, U.S. champion of animal rights; president of the A.S.P.C.A. 1991-99, well-known as announcer for the Westminster Kennel Club Dog Show. Of heart attack complications, Towson, Md., Feb. 18, 2001.

Coca, Imogene, 92, pixie TV comic best known for her partnership with Sid Caesar on the 1950's *Your Show of Shows*, where she brought down the house nationwide every Saturday night with her endearing mugging in hilarious skits that ranged from the latest movie parody to elaborate dance spectacles. Of natural causes, Westport, Conn., June 2, 2001.

Como, Perry, 88, Pennsylvania barber who became one of the nation's best-loved and enduring singers, first on radio and recordings, then on long-running TV variety shows that featured his relaxed and friendly style. Of natural causes, Jupiter, Fla., May 12, 2001.

Corso, Gregory, 70, U.S. poet, one of the Beat Generation with Allen Ginsberg and Jack Kerouac; rough stylist in the manner of Whitman. Of prostate cancer, Robbinsdale, Minn., Jan 17, 2001.

Dagmar (Virginia Ruth Egnor), 79, U.S. actress and 1950's TV personality whose tall, curvy figure and low-cut gowns made her single stage name familiar to viewers of *Broadway Open House*, an early forerunner of late-night comedy shows. Cause undisclosed, Ceredo, W. Va., Oct. 9, 2001.

De La Beckwith, Byron, 80, convicted in 1994 of the 1963 murder of civil rights leader Medgar Evers; two 1964 Mississippi juries failed to convict. Of heart disease, Jackson, Miss., Jan. 21, 2001.

Donahue, Troy, 65, U.S. movie star who was a teen heartthrob in movies of the 1950's and 60's such as *A Summer Place* and *Parrish*. Of a heart attack, Santa Monica, Calif., Sept. 2, 2001.

Downey, Morton Jr., 67, U.S. TV personality and a singer like his father; turned to political causes and found fame in the 1980's as host of a bruising talk show featuring his insults and chain-smoking. Of lung cancer, Los Angeles, March 12, 2001.

Earnhardt, Dale, 49, legendary U.S. race car champion who died when his familiar black stock car crashed into a wall at the Daytona 500; intense winner of seven Winston Cups. Daytona Beach, Fla., Feb. 18, 2001.

Eisenberg, Arlene, 66, Brooklyn-born writer of best-selling *What to Expect* books about pregnancy and motherhood in collaboration with her daughters. Of breast cancer, New York, Feb. 8, 2001.

Epstein, Julius, 91, screenwriter from New York's Lower East Side, best known for the Oscar-winning *Casablanca*, written with his twin brother, Philip; author of more than 50 movies in a 50-year career. Of natural causes, Los Angeles, Dec. 30, 2000.

Evans, Dale, 88, Texas-born actress and songwriter, the "queen" to husband Roy Rogers's "king" of westerns in movies and TV; sang the couple's theme song, "Happy Trails to You." Of old age, Apple Valley, Calif., Feb. 7, 2001.

Evans, Rowland, 79, U.S. political pundit, the urbane half of Evans and Novak journalism team, whose inside conservative views achieved wide attention in newspaper columns and on TV. Of esophageal cancer, Washington, March 23, 2001.

Francis, Arlene, 93, TV and radio personality best known for the elegant diction and gowns with which she graced *What's My Line?*, the popular 50's and 60's TV show. Of Alzheimer's disease, San Francisco, May 31, 2001.

Gebel-Williams, Gunther, 66, German-born animal trainer who became an international circus star for 50 years; never brutal or forceful, he made trust the foundation of his relationship to his animals, especially the big cats lions, tigers and leopards. Of cancer, Venice, Fla., July 19, 2001.

Gonzalez, Henry, 84, Texas Democrat who served in the House of Representatives for 37 years, a fighter for public housing and the integrity of the banking industry, as well as civil rights, growing out of his Mexican-American heritage. Cause undisclosed, San Antonio, Nov. 28, 2000.

Graham, Katharine, 84, *Washington Post* publisher who took over newspaper after her husband's suicide and with the aid of a crack editorial staff turned it into a national power with exposés of the *Pentagon Papers* and the Watergate scandal; awarded 1998 Pulitzer Prize for her memoir, *Personal History*. Of head injuries after a fall, Boise, Idaho, July 17, 2001.

Greco, José, 82, Italian-born, Brooklyn-raised dancer who made the staccato style of Spanish dancing familiar to millions via Broadway, TV and touring shows in the U.S. and Europe. Cause undisclosed, Lancaster, Pa., Dec. 31, 2000.

Greenberg, Joseph, 85, U.S. linguist whose effort to work out the historical relationships among most of the world's 5,000 languages is regarded as a monumental work. Of cancer, May 7, 2001, Stanford, Calif.

Groza, Lou ("The Toe"), 76, Ohio-born Hall of Fame football player with Cleveland Browns 1946-67 as place-kicker and tackle; his 263 field goals led to nickname; 1954 Player of the Year. Of a heart attack, Middleburg, Ohio, Nov. 29, 2000.

Hanna, William, 90, U.S. film animator, who with partner Joseph Barbera created memorable cartoon characters such as "Tom and Jerry," as well as TV's "Flintstones" and "Yogi Bear." Of natural causes, North Hollywood, Calif., March 22, 2001.

Herblock (Herbert Lawrence Block), 91, Chicago-born cartoonist whose incisive observations of the national scene over seven decades made him one of the most highly respected journalists of the 20th century; winner of three Pulitzer Prizes. Of old age, Washington, D.C., Oct. 7, 2001.

Hewlett, William, 87, U.S. engineer, co-founder of Hewlett-Packard, the trailblazer of Silicon Valley and leading computer company; his hands-on approach became the model for many organizations. Well-known for philanthropic work. Of natural causes, Portola Valley, Calif., Jan. 12, 2001.

Hibbler, Al, 85, Mississippi-born blind jazz singer who started out with Duke Ellington's 1940's band and went on to record several hit singles, most memorably "Unchained Melody," in his characteristically husky vibrato. Cause undisclosed, Chicago, April 24, 2001.

Horwich, Frances R., 93, "Miss Frances" of *Ding Dong School*, the warm, friendly 1950's TV teacher to the nation's children, she led the way for later shows such as *Sesame Street*. Cause and place undisclosed, July 25, 2001.

Hoyle, Sir Fred, 86, British scientist who coined the term "Big Bang" as a mocking name for the origin of the universe, a theory he disagreed with, though his opposition provoked much study leading to general acceptance of the theory. After a stroke, Bournemouth, England, Aug. 20, 2001.

Husseini, Faisal, 60, Palestinian leader who led the fight against occupation of the West Bank and Gaza Strip; respected by Israelis for his advocacy of a peaceful solution in the Middle East. Of a heart attack, Kuwait, May 31, 2001.

Jackson, Levi, 74, football star at Yale, in 1948 the first African American elected captain there, noted in headlines nationwide; later served as

Ford Motor Co. vice president. Of congestive heart failure, Detroit, Dec. 7, 2000.

Jiménez, Marcos Pérez, 87, Venezuelan leader of vicious, corrupt military junta that ruled autocratically (1952-58) with U.S. approval because of rich oil supply until popular uprising. Of undisclosed causes, Madrid, Sept. 20, 2001.

Johnson, J.J. (James Louis), 77, dominant jazz musician, consummate bebop trombonist, whose technique was widely imitated; after playing in classic "Birth of the Cool" recordings, composed numerous large-scale works and film scores. A suicide after surviving cancer, Indianapolis, Feb. 4, 2001.

Jones, Jimmy, 94, leading horse trainer for 60 years, many of them with renowned Calumet Farms; trained eight Kentucky Derby winners, including Citation, 1948 Triple Crown winner. Of old age, Maryville, Mo., Sept. 2, 2001.

Kabila, Laurent, 62, president of Congo; wily and ruthless leader whose ouster of Mobutu in 1997 led to high expectations for his nation that were never fulfilled. Assassinated, Kinshasa, Jan. 17, 2001.

Kael, Pauline, 82, influential U.S. film critic whose *New Yorker* reviews (1968-91) brought a passionate intellectual style to movie reviewing; often went overboard in praise or damnation: yes to *The Godfather* or Brando in *Last Tango in Paris*; no to *The Sound of Music* and *Dances with Wolves*. Cause undisclosed, Great Barrington, Mass., Sept. 3, 2001.

Ketcham, Hank, 81, U.S. cartoonist whose "Dennis the Menace" has remained a playfully naughty 4-year-old entertaining millions worldwide for 50 years. Of natural causes, Carmel, Calif., June 1, 2001.

Kiam, Victor, 74, U.S. enterpreneur who bought the Remington Company and became its TV salesman because he liked its razors so much. After several heart attacks, Stamford, Conn., May 27, 2001.

Kramer, Stanley, 87, New York-born filmmaker whose works focus on social issues such as racial discrimination, juvenile delinquency and privacy of political beliefs; most notable are *High Noon*, *The Defiant Ones* and *Judgment at Nuremberg*. Of pneumonia, Los Angeles, Feb. 19, 2001.

Lapidus, Morris, 98, Russian-born, Brooklyn-raised architect whose childhood memory of Coney Island's Luna Park inspired the gaudy, colorful style he brought to South Florida hotels, most notably the Fontainebleu and Eden Roc. Of natural causes, Miami Beach, Jan. 18, 2001.

Lardner, Ring Jr., 85, U.S. writer blacklisted in 1947 for refusing to admit to congress his Communist Party membership; Academy Award winner for screenplays of *Woman of the Year* and *M*A*S*H*. Cause undisclosed, New York, October 31, 2000.

Le Clercq, Tanaquil, 71, Paris-born U.S. ballerina, fourth wife and elegant muse to George Balanchine, for whom he created numerous roles, before her sparkling career was cut short by polio in 1956, after which she became an inspiring teacher. Of pneumonia, New York, Dec. 31, 2000.

Lewis, John, 80, U.S. jazz pianist, the soul of the Modern Jazz Quartet, the group that married Bach with bebop and brought "cool" jazz into the concert hall; his many compositions include the classic "Django" and some film scores. Cause undisclosed, New York, March 29, 2001

Lindbergh, Anne Morrow, 94, U.S. writer best known for her 1955 best seller, *Gift from the Sea*, inspirational reflections on women's lives and goals; a 1930's celebrity with aviator husband, Charles Lindbergh. Of old age after several strokes, Passumpsic, Vt., Feb. 7, 2001.

Lindsay, John V., 79, New York City mayor (1966-73). A glamorous figure during a time of social unrest, strikes and "white flight" who left "Fun City"

near bankruptcy. Liberal Republican congressman 1959-65. Of Parkinson's and pneumonia complications, Hilton Head, S.C., Dec. 19, 2000.

Livingston, Jay, 86, U.S. songwriter of such pop hits as "Buttons and Bows," "Mona Lisa" and "Que Sera', Sera'" (all Oscar winners) with partner Ray Evans. Cause undisclosed, Los Angeles, Oct. 17, 2001.

Ludlum, Robert, 73, U.S. actor turned writer of 21 fast-paced novels that sold more than 290 million copies, most of them international thrillers beginning with *The Scarlatti Inheritance* (1971). Of a heart attack, Naples Fla., March 12, 2001.

Maas, Peter, 72, best-selling New York-born writer who specialized in organized crime and corruption, notably headlining the Mafia in *The Valachi Papers* and police graft in *Serpico*. Cause undisclosed, New York, Aug. 23, 2001.

Mansfield, Mike, 98, Montana Democrat who served in the House 1942-52, then in the Senate for 24 years, becoming majority leader in 1961; ambassador to Japan 1977-87, longer than anyone else in the position. His thoughtful manner belied his strong influence on foreign policy and significant legislation such as civil rights. Of old age, Washington D.C., Oct. 5, 2001.

Masoud, Ahmad Shah, 48, Afghan leader of anti-Taliban forces called the Northern Alliance; his fame was won successfully fighting the Soviets in the 80's. Assassinated by men posing as journalists, Khwaja Bahouddin, Afghanistan, Sept. 15, 2001.

Masters, William H., 85, Cleveland-born physician who, with Virginia E. Johnson, wrote several best-selling studies of human sexual behavior, which built on Kinsey's work and helped millions. Of Parkinson's disease, Tucson, Ariz. Feb. 16, 2001.

Mathews, Eddie, 69, Hall of Fame third baseman for the Braves, in Boston, Milwaukee and Atlanta; hit 512 home runs in 17 seasons. Of pneumonia, San Diego, Feb. 18, 2001.

McGuire, Al, 72, New York basketball coach who went from playing for St. John's and a brief pro career to head winning teams at Marquette, 1964-77; later a colorful TV commentator; 1992 Hall of Famer. Of leukemia, Milwaukee, Jan 26, 2001.

McGuire, Dorothy, 83, U.S. actress who often portrayed warmly resolute women, most notably in such films as *A Tree Grows in Brooklyn*, *Gentlemen's Agreement* and *Friendly Persuasion*. Of heart failure, Santa Monica, Calif., Sept. 14, 2001.

McKay, John, 77, coach of winning football teams at U.S.C. 1960-75; headed NFL Tampa Bay Buccaneers 1976-84. Of diabetic kidney failure, Tampa, Fla., June 10, 2001.

McTaggart, David, 69, Canadian environmentalist who transformed Greenpeace into a forceful movement worldwide, beginning with commando-like raids on French atomic testing in 1972. Of auto crash injuries, Perugia, Italy, March 23, 2001.

Moakley, Joe, 74, Massachusetts Democrat, congressman since 1972 who never apologized for his drive to bring federal money for public works to his district and hometown, Boston. Of leukemia, Bethesda Naval Hospital, Md., May 28, 2001.

Néel, Louis, 95, French scientist, co-winner 1970 Nobel Prize in Physics for discoveries about magnetic fields that led to advancements in electronics and information storage. Of natural causes, Brive-Corrèze, France, Nov. 17, 2000.

Oakes, John B., 87, U.S. journalist and the liberal voice of *The New York Times* editorials 1961-76; cousin to the newspaper's owners; brought the popular "op-ed" page to the Times. After a stroke, New York, April 5, 2001.

Olson, Barbara, 45, U.S. conservative political commentator and author of a bitter attack on

Hillary Clinton, *Hell to Pay*, after serving as chief counsel to Republican committee investigating Clinton travel office firings. Died in hijacked plane that crashed into the Pentagon, Sept. 11, 2001.

Paz Estenssoro, Victor, 93, Bolivian political leader who served as president four times after leading a revolution against a military junta in 1952; known for toughness and authoritarian measures. Of circulatory problems, Tarija, Bolivia, June 7, 2001.

Phillips, John, 65, U.S. songwriter and a founder of the Mamas and the Papas, whose first hit, "California Dreamin'," typified their hippie sentiments; a rehabilitated drug and alcohol addict. Of heart failure, Los Angeles, March 18, 2001.

Quine, W.V., 92, Harvard philosopher and logician who championed an empirical view of knowledge that depends solely on language; best-known essay, "Two Dogmas of Empiricism," challenged tenets of logical positivism. Of old age, Boston, Dec. 25, 2000.

Quinn, Anthony, 86, Mexican-born actor best known for his role as Zorba the Greek on stage and screen; first a star in Fellini's *La Strada*; Oscar winner for *Viva Zapata!* and *Lust for Life*. Of respiratory failure, Boston, June 3, 2001.

Ramone, Joey (b. Jeffrey Hyman), 49, U.S. entertainer, lead singer of the Ramones, the 1970's band that gave birth to punk rock with its headlong music and comic-book lyrics. Of lymphatic cancer, New York, April 15, 2001.

Reagan, Maureen, 60, daughter of Pres. Ronald Reagan and actress Jane Wyman, she unsuccessfully ran for Congress and served as a Republican political operative who sometimes disagreed with the party's conservative agenda. Of melanoma, Sacramento, Calif., Aug. 8, 2001.

Richler, Mordecai, 70, Canadian writer whose articles and novels depict contemporary Montreal life, often targeting his Jewish roots and Quebec separatism; *The Apprenticeship of Duddy Kravitz*, a study of adolescent ambition, brought wider fame. Of kidney cancer, Montreal, July 3, 2001.

Robards, Jason, 78, intense U.S. actor best known for his strong portrayals of O'Neill characters, most notably Hickey in *The Iceman Cometh*; Oscar winner for *All the President's Men* and *Julia*. Of cancer, Bridgeport, Conn., Dec. 26, 2000.

Rogers, William P., 87, New York lawyer who served as Pres. Eisenhower's attorney general and Pres. Nixon's secretary of state; overshadowed by Henry Kissinger in early 1970's. Of congestive heart failure, Bethesda Md., Jan. 2, 2001.

Ruff, Charles, 61, U.S. attorney who successfully defended Pres. Clinton in his impeachment trial; legal skills evident in Watergate investigations and defenses of such political figures as John Glenn. Of a heart attack, Washington, Nov. 19, 2000.

Shannon, Claude, 84, U.S. computer scientist, the first to devise the system of manipulating 1's and 0's at the heart of modern computer theory and the basis for the worldwide communication system. Of Alzheimer's disease, Medford, Mass., Feb. 24, 2001

Shull, Clifford G., 85, U.S. scientist, co-winner 1994 Nobel Prize in Physics for development of ways to bounce neutrons off substances to analyze their molecular structure. Of natural causes, Medford, Mass., March 31, 2001.

Simon, Herbert A., 84, awarded 1978 Nobel Prize in economics for theories that recognized rational constraints on individual decision making, stemming from his pioneer computer studies. Of surgical complications, Pittsburgh, Feb. 9, 2001.

Sinopoli, Giuseppe, 54, highly acclaimed Italian concert and opera conductor; wide-ranging interests included degrees in medicine and archaeology. Of a heart attack while conducting *Aida* in Berlin, April 21, 2001.

Sothern, Ann, 92, U.S. movie and TV actress who moved from Broadway to numerous B pictures; best known for *A Letter to Three Wives* (1949). Produced her own 1950's TV shows, *Private Secretary* and *The Ann Sothern Show*. Of old age, Ketchum, Idaho, March 15, 2001.

St. Clair, James, 80, U.S. lawyer who represented Pres. Nixon in Watergate hearings before the Supreme Court. Cause undisclosed, Westwood, Mass., March 10, 2001.

Stanley, Kim, 76, U.S. actress whose "Method" sensitivity won Broadway audiences in the 1950's in Inge's plays *Picnic* and *Bus Stop*. Depression prevented stardom, though acclaimed films include *The Goddess* and *Seance on a Wet Afternoon*. Cause undisclosed, Santa Fe, N.M., Aug. 20, 2001.

Staples, Roebuck (Pops), 85, Mississippi-born gospel singer who with his children formed the Staple Singers, the Rock and Roll Hall of Fame group whose best-selling recordings brought the good news of uplift and peace to millions. Of natural causes, Dolton, Ill., Dec. 19, 2000.

Stargell, Willie, 61, U.S. baseball star who brought Pittsburgh Pirates to a 1979 World Series win with his powerful bat and enthusiastic leadership; won home run title twice; elected to Hall of Fame. Of a stroke, Wilmington N.C., April 9, 2001.

Stassen, Harold E., 93, Republican politician whose success as Minnesota governor at age 31 led to nine attempts to win the party's presidential nomination from 1948 to 1988; oversaw foreign aid and disarmament matters in Eisenhower administration. Of old age, Bloomington, Minn., March 4, 2001.

Stern, Isaac, 81, U.S. (b. Ukraine) violinist whose rich tone and passionate approach to music became a touchstone for generations of players and music lovers. In 1960 he became a hero with his crusade to save Carnegie Hall from the wrecker's ball. Of heart failure, New York, Sept. 22, 2001.

Storr, Anthony, 80, British psychiatrist who wrote several popular books, such as *The Integrity of the Personality*, which deal with interpersonal relations, as well as books on Freud and Jung; a notable TV commentator. Of a heart attack at an after-dinner speech, Oxford, England, March 17, 2001.

Szulc, Tad, 74, Polish-born newsman best known for his reporting to *The New York Times* about plans to invade Cuba that resulted in the 1961 Bay of Pigs disaster; author of several books, including biographies of John Paul II and Fidel Castro. Of cancer, Washington, D.C., May 21, 2001.

Trenet, Charles, 87, popular French singer and composer in the "chanson" tradition of Piaf and Brel; his "La Mer" became the familiar "Beyond the Sea." After a stroke, Paris, Feb. 18, 2001.

Trout, Robert, 91, U.S. radio and TV journalist since 1930's, mostly for CBS; known for the ease with which he covered events, from the abdication of Edward VIII and D-Day to Churchill's funeral; first described Pres. Roosevelt's radio talks as "fireside chats." Of old age, New York, Nov. 14, 2000.

Van Thieu, Nguyen, 76, president of South Vietnam during the most tumultous years of the Vietnam War; fled the country as the North Vietnamese overran the South on April 21, 1975. A wily though cautious man, his leadership style aided his rise to power as well as the chaos that surrounded his fall, following which he resided in London and Boston. Cause undisclosed, Boston, Sept. 29, 2001.

Walston, Ray, 86, New Orleans-born actor who became a Tony-winning Broadway star playing the Devil in *Damn Yankees*; went on to movie and TV fame, best known for *My Favorite Martian*. Cause undisclosed, Beverly Hills, Calif., Jan. 1, 2001.

Welty, Eudora, 92, beloved U.S. writer of short stories and novels, notably "Why I Live at the P.O."; 1973 Pulitzer Prize for *The Optimist's Daughter* among many other honors. Of old age, Jackson, Miss., July 23, 2001.

Wheelwright, George W. III, 97, U.S. scientist, sometime painter and rancher, co-founder with Edwin Land of Polaroid Corp.; traveled widely to popularize and market products stemming from their development of polarized lenses. Of natural causes, Tiburon, Calif., March 1, 2001.

Williams, Hosea, 74, Georgia civil rights fighter alongside Rev. Martin Luther King Jr. in the 1960's; in the front lines of the bloody 1965 Selma march, which turned TV headlines into national legislation. Of cancer, Atlanta, Nov. 16, 2000.

Woodcock, Leonard, 89, U.S. labor leader who rose to United Auto Workers presidency in 1970, winning significant gains from General Motors; as Pres. Carter's envoy he re-established relations with China; appointed ambassador in 1979. Of old age, Ann Arbor, Mich., Jan 16, 2001.

Woodling, Gene, 78, steady left fielder for the New York Yankees whose dependable bat helped the team win five World Series 1949-53. After a 1997 stroke, Wadsworth, Ohio, June 2, 2001.

Younger, Tank (Paul), 73, trailblazing black football player, he starred at Grambling and with L.A. Rams and went to the Pro Bowl five times. After a long illness, Inglewood, Calif., Sept. 15, 2001.

Zatopek, Emil, 78, Czech runner whose awkward style belied his record-breaking performances, most notably his three 1952 Olympic gold medals in the 5,000 and 10,000 meters and the marathon, still a unique achievement. After a stroke, Prague, Nov., 22, 2000.

Major News Stories of 2001

By Correspondents of The New York Times

NATIONAL NEWS

President Bush Takes Command

When George Bush and members of his administration look back at their first year in office, Sept. 11, 2001, is the stark dividing line. Priorities changed, agendas altered dramatically. It was the day, Mr. Bush said, when he found his mission.

In his first eight months, he seemed to be looking for a unifying theme for his presidency. Shortly after his inauguration when, for the first time, his words found presidential loft, he set out to create what he called a new tone in Washington. He invited Democratic leaders to the White House and found common ground with liberals like Senator Ted Kennedy on a program to increase the Federal role in education.

But the bipartisan bonhomie did not last. By late spring, sharp differences had cropped up. When Senator James Jeffords of Vermont, a moderate Republican, shocked the White House by becoming an independent, control of the Senate switched to the Democrats. Suddenly the Democrats had the power to bottle up legislation they did not like, and there was seething at both ends of Pennsylvania Avenue.

Mr. Bush meanwhile, seemed unsure of his role. His verbal gaffes continued, giving fodder to late-night television comics. His aides worried that he did not seem sufficiently presidential. Mr. Bush sought out bigger issues. When he had to make a decision, in early August, about whether the government would permit research on human stem cells, which offer great medical promise but raised a host of ethical issues about the eventual cloning of humans, he delved deeply into the issue. He struck a compromise that was notable less for its details than for the fact that it seemed to engage him intellectually.

Abroad, allies were suspicious. Mr. Bush came to office determined to restore America's ability to act in its own interests, but he found that difficult. Quickly, he learned that he could not withdraw American troops from peacekeeping missions in the Balkans without fracturing the alliance with NATO, and after declaring during the campaign that he opposed the financial bailouts of countries that mismanaged their economies, he participated in two, for Turkey and Argentina.

Relations with China turned especially rocky on April 1, when an American surveillance plane was hit by a Chinese fighter that had come too close. The Chinese pilot was killed; the American crew landed their crippled craft in China but spent more than a week in detention as furious negotiations took place to win their release. The incident made Mr. Bush realize that he was headed toward trouble with the world's most populous nation, and soon he dropped his campaign talk that China was a strategic competitor, muted his criticisms of its human rights record, and began trying to rebuild a strained relationship.

He insisted, however, that the 1972 Anti-Ballistic Missile Treaty, which limited his ability to conduct tests of his missile-defense program, was an outdated relic of the Cold War. He began negotiations with Russia, but threatened that if an agreement could not be worked out he would simply withdraw from the treaty. Europeans muttered about American unilateralism.

That was the situation on Sept. 10, when Mr. Bush left Washington for a two-day trip to Florida to visit schools and make the case for his education bill, which was stuck in Congress.

When he went to sleep that night in a resort in Longboat Key, Mr. Bush thought his biggest problem in the months ahead would be the deteriorating economy. The next morning he took a short drive to an elementary school in Sarasota, and heard vague news of what seemed to be an accident at the World Trade Center. Fifteen minutes later, as he sat in a class with second-graders, his chief of staff, Andy Card, whispered the news: A second jetliner had hit the other tower, "and America is under attack." Mr. Bush blanched, but stayed in his seat. Half an hour later, he fumbled for the right message of sympathy and a promise to hunt down the hijackers, whom he called "folks." His agents whisked him into Air Force One, and as chaos reigned in Washington, where another jet hit the Pentagon, Mr. Bush grappled with the reality that he was about to become a wartime president.

It took a few days for the role to fit the man. But he got off to a swift start: within days he introduced what became the "Bush doctrine." It states that not only would America pursue the terrorists, it would treat any government or country that harbored the terrorists with the same military force reserved for those who Mr. Bush now daily called "evil-doers." By the weekend after the attack, he had come up with a two-phased plan at Camp David: Attack the terrorists in Afghanistan and the Taliban government that supports them, then worry about whether to widen the war to Iraq or other states suspected of terrorist acts. Early the next week he said he wanted Osama bin Laden, the head of the al Qaeda terrorist network, "dead or alive," a comment that sounded a bit like a scene from an old Western, and caused some consternation among the allies.

Mr. Bush hit his stride with a war message to a joint session of Congress, a speech that had almost Churchillian moments as he described America's war aims — the elimination of terrorism with a "global reach"— and his resolve that "We will rally the world to this cause, by our efforts and by our courage. We will not tire, we will not falter, and we will not fail." From that moment on, he seemed to grow into his presidency. He stayed relentlessly on message: That America would not negotiate with terrorists, that he had given the Taliban leadership time to hand over Mr. bin Laden, that they had "chosen unwisely." Invoking wartime secrecy, he refused to talk about operational details, even as he met with his national security council every morning to plot strategy, and to figure out how to put a post-Taliban government in place.

By the end of the year, he was emerging as a stronger leader in the eyes of the rest of the world. He traveled to China, using an Asian summit meeting to bolster the coalition of nations involved in counter-terrorism. His poll ratings soared. He seemed decisive. But as his vice president, Dick Cheney, said, "There will be good days and bad days along the way," and it was still an open question how the man who had to remake his presidency overnight would deal with the bad days.

—*David E. Sanger*

The Invaluable but Vulnerable Dick Cheney

In the early days of President George W. Bush's administration, Vice President Dick Cheney was portrayed as the omnipotent chief operating officer in Mr. Bush's corporate-style government. Mr. Cheney, 60, a former White House chief of staff, Secretary of Defense, and president of a large oil-services company, vetted Mr. Bush's Cabinet selections. A former Republican congressman from Wyoming with impeccable conservative credentials, Mr. Cheney played the role of supreme power broker between the White House and Capitol Hill. Mr. Cheney and his boss seemed tethered at the hip, starting with the intelligence and national-security briefings Mr. Bush received in the Oval Office each morning.

After six months in office, though, Mr. Cheney proved he was mortal in more ways than one. On June 30, doctors successfully implanted a sophisticated pacemaker and defibrillator in Mr. Cheney's chest, his third significant cardiac procedure since his election as vice president.

A far-reaching energy report drafted by an interagency task force that he led drew sharp criticism for seeming too in favor of oil, coal, and natural gas interests, at the expense of conservation measures, which Mr. Cheney dismissed as mere "personal virtue."

By August, Mr. Cheney was feuding with the General Accounting Office, an investigative arm of Congress, for refusing to disclose the names of outside officials who met with the energy task force. And Mr. Cheney's own energy habits came under scrutiny, when the White House asked Congress to shift the electricity bill for the official vice presidential mansion, an estimated $186,000 in 2001, to the Navy.

Still, Mr. Cheney had become one of the most influential vice presidents in history, largely through presidential design. Mr. Bush entrusted Mr. Cheney with so much, from rounding up votes on the administration's tax-cut bill to overseeing an anti-terrorism commission, not just because of the vice president's experience and judgment, but also because Mr. Cheney had no presidential ambitions of his own. During the September 11 attacks on the Pentagon and the World Trade Center, Mr. Cheney found himself in an even more active role, with President Bush far from the White House at the time. From a secure area beneath the White House, Mr. Cheney advised the president to stay away from Washington for his own safety, and orchestrated the administration's first response to the terrorist attacks.

Mr. Cheney and his aides said all along that he would play an even more effective role behind the scenes once other Cabinet officers were settled in and took the lead on matters from national missile defense to tax policy.

—*Eric Schmitt*

Bush and Republicans Win Big Tax Cut

After years of partisan gridlock over how to apportion the federal budget surplus, and months of debate over how to address the slowing economy, Congress passed the largest tax cut in two decades on May 26.

President Bush, who had made a big tax cut the centerpiece of his campaign and of his legislative agenda after he took office, signed the bill on June 7, calling it "the first major achievment of a new era."

The bill encountered intense opposition from Democrats as it moved through the House and the Senate. Democrats said it would eat up too much of the surplus at a time when the nation had other issues to address, including the growing financial strains on Social Security and Medicare. And they said it would provide too much of its benefits to the wealthy at the expense of lower and middle income people.

But the measure enjoyed overwhelming support among Republicans. It also won qualified but critical support from Alan Greenspan, the Federal Reserve chairman, who said the surplus would be so big that the nation could pay off nearly all of its debt in the next decade and still have plenty left over for a substantial tax reduction.

Most of all, though, the tax cut plan picked up political momentum as the economy decelerated. Although Mr. Bush's original proposal contained no provision for an immediate tax cut to stimulate the economy in 2001, he supported bipartisan calls to amend it to put money back into the pockets of taxpayers almost immediately.

The final measure cut taxes by $1.35 trillion over 10 years. It provided for all households that had paid federal income taxes for the 2000 tax year to get rebate checks in the summer of 2001 — up to $600 for married couples and up to $300 for single people. The rebates were to total $38 billion.

The measure called for phased-in reductions in all income tax rates. It also called for a gradual doubling of the child credit to $1,000 from $500, gave a tax break to married couples with two incomes, increased contribution limits for individual retirement accounts and 401(k) retirement plans and gradually repealed the federal tax on large estates.

But to keep the tax cut within the size approved by Congress for the 10 years covered by the budget plan, the bill relied on what even its supporters acknowledged was a gimmick. It called for the entire tax cut to be repealed after 2010, returning the tax code in 2011 to where it stood before Mr. Bush signed the legislation.

Even before 2001 ended, however, the tax cut ran into budget problems, opening the door to calls by some Democrats to rethink whether all its provisions should be allowed to take effect in coming years.

On Aug. 22, the White House released new projections showing that the budget surplus outside of Social Security had all but disappeared for the next several years. It attributed the decline the projected surplus largely to the slowing economy, but Democrats said the tax cut was the deciding factor in putting the government at risk of dipping into the Social Security surplus in coming years, a step both parties had vowed not to take.

—*Richard W. Stevenson*

Bush v. Gore and Other Supreme Court Cases

Of the 79 decisions the Supreme Court issued during its term, which began Oct. 2, 2000 and ended June 28, 2001, there was one that far overshadowed all others. In *Bush v. Gore*, decided by a vote of 5 to 4 late on the night of Dec. 12, the court ended the 2000 presidential election by declaring that there could be no further recounting of votes in Florida, where George W. Bush then held a minuscule lead in the contest for the state's decisive 25 electoral votes.

Everything about the court's role in the post-election period was unusual and heatedly contested. In light of the Supreme Court's usual effort to remain aloof from the political fray, few people expected the justices to become involved in the first place. But they did so not once but twice, acting both times at the request of lawyers representing the Republican nominee.

In the first case, *Bush v. Palm Beach County Canvassing Board*, decided Dec. 4, the court heard Governor Bush's challenge to a decision of the Florida Supreme Court that extended by 12 days the state's deadline for certifying the vote. That decision favored Vice President Al Gore's effort to keep recounts going in several counties where the Democratic nominee had the best hope of closing the gap. The Bush lawyers appealed on the ground that federal election law as well as the Constitution barred state courts from changing election procedures that had been established by the state legislature. Without explicitly endorsing these arguments, the justices unanimously vacated the Florida Supreme Court's decision and instructed that court to explain more fully the basis for its action.

The Florida court then issued a second decision on Dec. 8 that also favored Vice President Gore, this one ordering a statewide manual recount of ballots that when counted by machine had not shown any choice for president. The Bush campaign appealed immediately in the case that became *Bush v. Gore*. On Dec. 9, the justices ordered a temporary stay of the recount just as it was getting underway, the 5-to-4 vote revealing for the first time the deep split within the court.

The case was argued on Dec. 11 and decided the following day with an unusual unsigned opinion that had the support of Justices Anthony M. Kennedy, Sandra Day O'Connor, Antonin Scalia, Clarence Thomas, and Chief Justice William H. Rehnquist. The opinion declared that variations from county to county in the rules for counting the ballots amounted to a violation of the constitutional guarantee of equal protection. There was no time to fix the problem, the majority said, so the recount that the court itself had suspended three days earlier could not resume. Justices John Paul Stevens, David H. Souter, Ruth Bader Ginsburg and Stephen G. Breyer each wrote vigorous dissenting opinions.

The election was over; six days later, the Electoral College chose George W. Bush by a vote of 271 to 266. The debate continues, not only over the court's role but also over the implications of the majority's equal protection analysis..

It was not only in *Bush v. Gore* that the court showed itself to be deeply split. One-third of the term's decisions, 29 out of 79, were by votes of 5 to 4, an unusually large proportion.

The term marked the seventh consecutive year without turnover on the court, a period of stability unmatched since the early 19th century. But stability did not mean predictability, and the term contained its share of surprises. Criminal defendants fared unexpectedly well from this conservative court. For example, in *Kyllo v. United States*, decided June 11, the court ruled that the police need a search warrant before aiming a thermal imaging device at a private home. Such devices are used to detect patterns of heat suggestive of an indoor marijuana-growing operation. In *City of Indianapolis v. Edmond*, decided Nov. 28, the court ruled out using narcotics-detecting dogs at police roadblocks set up to catch drunk drivers.

It was an important term for immigration law, with two decisions rejecting current federal immigration policy. In *Immigration and Naturalization Service v. St. Cyr*, decided June 25, the court ruled that immigrants who had pleaded guilty to crimes that made them deportable retained rights that the government argued Congress had abolished, to seek administrative waivers of deportation and to take a further appeal to federal court. In *Zadvydas v. Davis*, decided June 28,2000, the court ruled that the government cannot keep deportable aliens in indefinite detention for lack of a country willing to take them.

In a free speech case, the court ruled in *Good News Club v. Milford Central School* on June 11 that public schools must open their doors to after-hours religious activities on the same basis as any other after-school activity.

The court ruled in *Board of Trustees of the University of Alabama v. Garrett* on Feb. 21 that state employees who face job discrimination on account of disability cannot sue for damages under the Americans with Disabilities Act. That decision continued the court's recent trend of finding states immune from the full reach of federal policy.

—Linda Greenhouse

Furor Over Clinton's Last-Minute Pardons

An American president's decision to grant pardons just before leaving office often elicts questions and controversy. But President Bill Clinton's pardon of a fugitive commodities trader named Marc Rich, issued just hours before he left the White House on Jan. 20, 2001, triggered a Federal criminal investigation, Congressional hearings, and intensive media coverage that overshadowed the first weeks of the new Bush Administration.

On a frenzied final morning in the Oval Office, Mr. Clinton granted 140 pardons and 36 prison commutations to a group that included Whitewater figure Susan McDougal, two felons who paid Mr. Clinton's brother-in-law a lobbying fee of $434,000, and the president's own half-brother, Roger.

But the decision to pardon Mr. Rich, a billionaire who fled the United States in 1983 to escape an indictment on charges of tax fraud, racketeering, and illegal oil trading with Iran, embroiled the former president in a scandal with the familiar theme of money and politics that threatened to tarnish his legacy.

Mr. Rich was accused of evading $48 million in taxes, making his one of the largest tax evasion cases in American history. The pardon stunned and angered United States law enforcement officials and was criticized even by some of Mr. Clinton's most ardent supporters.

Although Mr. Rich had renounced his American citizenship and had lived in Switzerland since 1983, he retained some influential allies in the United States. Critics questioned whether he had, in effect, bought his pardon.

His former wife, Denise Rich, who had given more than $1.3 million to the Democratic Party since 1993 and $450,000 to the Clinton Presidential Library to be built in Little Rock, Ark., wrote Mr. Clinton asking him to pardon her former husband.

Mr. Rich hired the former White House counsel Jack Quinn, who personally asked Mr. Clinton to pardon Mr. Rich and his partner, Pincus Green. Israeli Prime Minister Ehud Barak also personally asked Mr. Clinton to pardon Mr. Rich.

House and Senate committees held hearings that examined the circumstances surrounding the pardon. On Feb. 14, the United States attorney in New York, Mary Jo White, opened a criminal investigation. A grand jury subpoenaed bank records and took witness testimony. Ms. Rich agreed to cooperate with Federal prosecutors under a grant of immunity. Her lawyers said she had done nothing wrong.

At a hearing before a House committee on Feb. 14, the Justice Department's top pardon attorney, Roger C. Adams, testified that presidential aides misled pardon authorities about Mr. Rich's fugitive status. Mr. Adams said the White House had not informed him that Mr. Rich was a fugitive. Instead, the aides said Mr. Rich was "living abroad," Mr. Adams said.

As the furor intensified, Mr. Clinton defended himself in a 1,638-word op-ed piece published in *The New York Times* on Feb. 18. The former president said his decision to pardon Mr. Rich was based solely on the merits.

"The suggestion that I granted the pardons because Mr. Rich's former wife, Denise, made political contributions and contributed to the Clinton Library foundation is utterly false," Mr. Clinton wrote. "There was absolutely no quid pro quo. Indeed, other friends and financial supporters sought pardons in cases which, after careful consideration based on the information available to me, I determined I could not grant."

In late February, Ms. White's office expanded its criminal inquiry to investigate the activities of Roger Clinton, Mr. Clinton's half-brother. Roger Clinton sought clemency for about 10 people but was not paid for his efforts, according to an aide to the former president. Roger Clinton himself denied any wrongdoing.

It was also revealed that President Clinton had granted a pardon and commuted the prison sentence for two wealthy felons who had paid lobbying fees to Hugh Rodham, a Miami lawyer and the brother of Senator Hillary Rodham Clinton of New York. Mr. Rodham was paid $434,000 for his asstance in obtaining a prison commutation for Carlos Vignali, a convicted cocaine trafficker from California, and a pardon for Almon Glenn Braswell, a businessman convicted of mail fraud and perjury in 1983. After his role was revealed in the media, Mr. Rodham pledged to return the fees.

Mr. and Mrs. Clinton issued a statement saying they were "deeply disturbed" to learn of the payment. And Senator Clinton told reporters that she had played no role in any of the pardons granted by her husband.

Although some members of Congress called for Mr. Clinton to testify about the Rich pardon, the former president was never required to do so. By late August, the U.S. Attorney's Office was still investigating.

—Don Van Natta Jr.

Jeffords Bolts the G.O.P. and Democrats Gain Control of the Senate

Senator James M. Jeffords of Vermont hardly seemed the type to set off a political earthquake. For more than a quarter-century, he had served in the House and the Senate, a camera-shy, moderate Republican in an increasingly conservative party. He stayed in the G.O.P. fold when he could but voted with Democrats when he could not.

It was a tenable balancing act until the election of a Republican president, George W. Bush, and a Senate evenly split between the two parties. Now, every Senate vote was critical and Mr. Jeffords found himself inescapably in the limelight—most particularly when the Senate took up a federal budget plan and Mr. Bush's pet $1.6 trillion, 10-year tax cut proposal.

Mr. Jeffords tried to secure a promise of full financing for special-education programs he had long championed. When he could not, he became one of a handful of centrists from both parties who forced the President to tweak and scale back the tax cut, to $1.35 trillion.

Shortly before his vote against Mr. Bush's tax plan, on May 10, he began suffering slights and whispers that policies dear to him might suffer because of his apostasy. The White House did not invite him to a ceremony honoring a Vermont teacher.

And on May 24, after weeks of quiet courtship from Democrats, his years of party loyalty came to an end. Home in Vermont, he read off a roll call of Republicans who had served his state before him. "I became a Republican not because I was born into the party," said Mr. Jeffords, 67, "but because of the fundamental principles that these and many Republicans stood for: moderation, tolerance, fiscal responsibility."

Yet times had changed, he said: "Increasingly, I find myself in disagreement with my party." He said he was becoming an independent and would caucus with the Democrats.

The decision echoed well beyond Vermont, upending the fragile balance of power in the Senate and catapulting the Democrats into the majority. For the first time since the end of 1994, the Democrats took full control, assuming the committee chairmanships and the ability to set the legislative agenda.

Some Republicans called Mr. Jeffords a traitor. Others agonized over the health of their party. Democrats gave Mr. Jeffords an ovation.

Still, when the Democrats used their new majority status to put forward a patients' bill of rights, there was Mr. Jeffords sponsoring a competing version supported by Mr. Bush. As Mr. Jeffords had said in Vermont, "I have changed my party label, but I have not changed my beliefs."

—*Alison Mitchell*

Oklahoma City Bomber Is Put to Death

Timothy J. McVeigh, the man convicted of killing 168 people in the Oklahoma City bombing, was executed on June 11 at the federal prison in Terre Haute, Ind.

Mr. McVeigh, 33, the first federal prisoner to be put to death since 1963, was killed by lethal injection with three drugs.

Watching Mr. McVeigh die in Indiana were 10 people from Oklahoma City whose relatives or friends had been killed in the bombing of the Alfred P. Murrah federal building on April 19, 1995, considered at the time the most heinous terrorist crime in American history. Some 232 other victims and victims' relatives were watching on closed circuit television from Oklahoma City, able to look directly into Mr. McVeigh's face as he died.

Mr. McVeigh, who was convicted of the bombing in 1997, had said he attacked the federal building in retaliation for federal government raids near Waco, Tex., and at Ruby Ridge, Idaho.

He was supposed to be executed a month earlier, on May 16. But on May 10, the federal government disclosed that the Federal Bureau of Investigation had failed to turn over to defense lawyers more than 4,000 pages of documents concerning the bombing investigation. Attorney General John Ashcroft postponed the execution until June to give defense lawyers time to examine the evidence.

Government officials said the failure to provide the documents was an oversight and that the evidence was not material to Mr. McVeigh's defense. Ultimately, a judge agreed and refused to stay the execution.

The execution was carried out in clinical fashion, with Mr. McVeigh strapped to a gurney and the lethal drugs pumped into his body through a tube in his leg. The 10 journalists who witnessed it through windows stood after Mr. McVeigh was wheeled into the death chamber he tried to make eye contact with each reporter and also with his lawyers.

He could not see the witnesses from Oklahoma City, who were behind tinted glass, but he squinted in their direction. Witnesses in Oklahoma City said he seemed to be looking directly into the camera. He died with his eyes open.

Mr. McVeigh did not have any last words, but at his request, prison officials distributed a poem that he had copied by hand onto a sheet of notebook paper. The poem, called "Invictus" and written in 1875 by William Ernest Henley, is popular with rebellious teenagers. It read in part:

"Out of the night that covers me
Black as the Pit from pole to pole
I thank whatever Gods may be
For my unconquerable soul"

—*Pam Belluck*

Ex-Klansman Is Convicted In 1963 Church Bombing

It took nearly 38 years. But on May 1, a jury in Birmingham, Ala., convicted Thomas E. Blanton Jr. of murdering four black girls in the bombing of the 16th Street Baptist Church, one of the most brutal and galvanizing events of the civil rights era.

The four girls — Denise McNair, 11, and Carole Robertson, Addie Mae Collins, and Cynthia Wesley, all 14 — were killed in the church basement on Sept. 15, 1963, as they prepared for a Sunday morning service.

Mr. Blanton, a former Ku Klux Klansman and virulent segregationist, was one of four men identified by the Federal Bureau of Investigation as suspects shortly after the bomb detonated. None was tried at the time, ostensibly because the director of the F.B.I., J. Edgar Hoover, believed it would be impossible to win convictions with circumstantial evidence and an all-white jury in the Jim Crow South. Authorities on that period also surmise that Mr. Hoover may have feared embarrassing disclosures about the involvement of F.B.I. informants who were members of the Klan.

The presumed ringleader in the church bombing, Robert Chambliss, was eventually tried and convicted in 1977, and died in prison eight years later. Another suspect, Herman Cash, died in 1994 without ever being tried. In July, after Mr. Blanton's conviction, the final suspect, Bobby Frank Cherry, was ruled mentally incompetent to stand trial after several psychiatric examinations.

Mr. Blanton, 62, who is appealing his conviction, was sentenced to life in prison. Though the prosecution, led by United States Attorney Doug Jones, was handicapped by the passage of time and the deaths of numerous witnesses, the jury of eight whites and four blacks spent barely two hours in deliberations following a two-week trial. The critical evidence against Mr. Blanton included secretly recorded F.B.I. audiotapes that captured Mr. Blanton speaking generically about his role in various bombings.

—*Kevin Sack*

Police Confront Charges From the Outside, Discontent From Within

When Cincinnati exploded in several nights of violent protests in April after a white police officer fatally shot an unarmed black man, Timothy Thomas, onlookers expressed shock. The city had been among the leaders in driving down the statistics of violent crime in the 1990's. But the spark was a separate issue, long simmering since the 1960's, in which African-American residents accused the predominantly white police force of racial profiling and excessive use of force.

City by city, fresh grievances erupted, along with new police scandals,even as crime remained relatively low. In Seattle, similar complaints of racial profiling were lodged against the police.

In New York City, the criminal phase of the racially charged two-year-long case involving Amadou Diallo ended on Jan. 31, when the Justice Department said it would not prosecute the four police officers who killed him two years earlier. Three months after that decision, on April 26, Police Commissioner Bernard B. Kerik decided not to discipline the officers, who shot Mr. Diallo, an unarmed street vendor from West Africa, 41 times in the vestibule of his Bronx apartment. The officers, who were acquitted of criminal charges in a state trial on Feb. 25, 2000, said they confronted him because they thought he resembled a rape suspect.

On July 12, another case involving New York police ended when Abner Louima, a Haitian immigrant tortured by police officers in a station house bathroom in 1997, settled a civil lawsuit against the city and its main police union for a total of $8.75 million. It was the most the city has ever paid to settle a claim of police brutality.

In August, 17 precinct officers were disciplined after the automobile deaths of a four people allegedly struck down by an off-duty policeman, Joseph Gray, accused of drinking with other officers in a parking lot near a precinct house.

In Los Angeles and Miami, questions arose about the corruptibility and competence of police officers as scandal stories swept the city and morale plummeted. Investigators delved into allegedly falsified police testimony and blue wall conspiracies. Miami prosecutors focused on repeated instances of questionable shootings of unarmed civilians.

As if in response, police began showing signs of resentment. "De-policing" suddenly became an issue as the Cincinnati police union, determined to avoid further accusations of racism, backed off its "pro-active" policing routines, with the result that violent crime shot up in black neighborhoods. A similar tactic was evident in Seattle.

In Detroit, a federal investigation into alleged police abuses was followed by a flood of resignations, with experienced officers opting for less controversial suburban forces. At the same time, urban police departments faced increasing difficulty in attracting recruits from their own cities. Salary scales for police were considered too low and the aggravation factor too high by young job seekers, even those from families where joining the force has been a tradition. One of the more respected members of the Seattle high command, John Diaz, an assistant chief, renounced any ambitions to rise to Seattle police chief, citing the "insane" pressures of the post. He summarized the growing disgruntlement with the policeman's lot in life: "No one wants the job."

—*Francis X. Clines*

Two California Schools Shaken by Gunfire

A backpack filled with textbooks. And a gun. An incomprehensibly angry young man. High schools students taunting, teasing, flirting between classes. A strange popping sound. Then bloodshed, death and tears.

Not so long ago shooting sprees were not a part of high school's hazards, but after the killings at Columbine High School near Littleton, Colo., in 1999, they occur with alarming persistence. In the 2000-2001 school year, two high schools in the hardscrabble San Diego suburbs of Santee and El Cajon were scarred by shootings. On March 5, Charles Andrew Williams, then 15, was charged with killing two students and wounding 13 other people at Santana High School in Santee.

Mr. Williams, reportedly a victim of bullying, calmly squeezed off about 30 random shots before police surrounded him in a bathroom, disarmed him and led him to jail. His .22 caliber handgun had been reloaded and the hammer was cocked.

"Everyone was yelling and screaming except him," said Officer Jack Smith of the San Diego Sheriff's Department, who helped make the arrest. "One kid was shouting, 'He shot me! He shot me!' But the kid was completely calm."

Less than three weeks later, on March 22, a shooting took place at Granite Hills High School, in El Cajon. A student, Jason Anthony Hoffman, 18, was arrested and charged with pulling up to the school in his car, hunting down an assistant principal and opening fire. He missed the administrator, but hit and wounded five other people, none of whom died.

Mr. Hoffman was a big, intimidating student who was described as generally well-mannered, but with a temper. He had just been rejected in an effort to enlist in the Navy.

—*James Sterngold*

Protests in Puerto Rico Briefly Halt Navy Drills

For more than six decades, the United States Navy has used the eastern tip of the tiny Puerto Rican island of Vieques for mock bombings, invasions and other drills. But now, the people who make the island their home want the military to stop using their turf for target practice.

The issue has become a politically charged feud between the people and leaders of Vieques and the United States military since a Puerto Rican security guard was killed on the firing range by an errant bomb in 1999. Since then, thousands of people have held sit-ins, marches and candlelight vigils at the entrance of Camp Garcia, the Navy's main training area.

Although the military has been reluctant to pull out because the island provides the Navy with the ability to conduct naval, aerial and amphibious exercises, the White House on June 14 called for ending exercises there by May 2003. But island residents say the bombings, which are conducted about four miles from inhabited areas, have subjected them to unnecessary hazards and pressed for amore expedient withdrawal.

Celebrities and mainland politicians joined in the conflict, with some arrested for protesting on the grounds. The Rev. Al Sharpton, the civil rights activist; Robert F. Kennedy Jr., the environmental lawyer; Dennis Rivera, the labor leader from New York; and Jacqueline Jackson, the wife of the Rev. Jesse Jackson; were all arrested and jailed for trespassing at Camp Garcia.

In a nonbinding, symbolic referendum vote on July 29, 68 percent of those who went to the polls on the island were in favor of an immediate military withdraw. Thirty percent of the voters favored letting the military stay indefinitely, and 1.7 percent supported the Navy staying only until 2003.

The referendum drew 80.6 percent of the island's 5,893 registered voters, and Gov. Sila Maria Calderon, who pushed for the referendum, sent the results to President Bush and Congressional leaders. It is unlikely, however, that much will change before 2003.

After the referendum results were announced, the Navy said it would continue its training. The bombing resumed on Aug. 2.

—*Dana Canedy*

F.B.I. Blunders Lead to Major Overhaul

In late June, Louis J. Freeh stepped down as Director of the Federal Bureau of Investigation, after serving eight years of his 10-year term in which he had become the most powerful Director in recent memory, next only to J. Edgar Hoover. But Mr. Freeh left the bureau reeling from a series of embarrassing lapses and missteps.

During his tenure, Mr. Freeh had presided over an aggressive expansion, cultivating lawmakers with control over the F.B.I.'s budget and jurisdiction. As a result, the bureau's spending grew expansively by 58 percent, to more than $3.4 billion a year. Under Mr. Freeh, more than 5,000 agents and 4,000 technical and analytical employees were hired. In response to threats of terrorism, he extended the F.B.I.'s overseas reach, doubling to 44 the number of F.B.I. offices abroad.

But his accomplishments were all but undone by managerial blunders in bread-and-butter areas. The mistakes buffeted the F.B.I. senior echelons, ignited a furor in Congress, and left top officials at the Justice Department, the F.B.I.'s parent agency, wondering how to clean up the troubled agency after Mr. Freeh's departure.

Lawmakers in both political parties lashed out at the F.B.I. as ineptly run, poorly disciplined and unwilling to admit mistakes. Republicans and Democrats demanded tighter supervision and more checks on the F.B.I.'s independence.

For his part, Attorney General John Ashcroft ordered the Justice Department's Inspector General to investigate, and hired a management consulting firm to examine administrative practices at the F.B.I. In his first speech at F.B.I. headquarters, on July 16, Mr. Ashcroft bluntly informed bureau employees that the F.B.I.'s failings had eroded public trust.

In reality, fissures in the F.B.I.'s facade of professionalism had been apparent for some time. On Feb. 18, Robert P. Hanssen, a senior F.B.I. counterintelligence agent, was unmasked as a Russian spy. The case sent shock waves through the ranks of agents, many of whom said they felt outraged and betrayed. But the Hanssen case was only the start.

On May 11, Justice Department officials admitted that thousands of pages of F.B.I. investigative reports in the Oklahoma City bombing case had never been turned over to defense lawyers for Timothy J. McVeigh, who had been convicted of the bombing and was to be executed on May 16. The belated discovery forced Mr. Ashcroft, a death penalty proponent, to postpone the execution for a month—a decision that disrupted the aura of procedural regularity that had surrounded the first federal execution in 38 years. By the end of their search, F.B.I. officials discovered more than 4,000 pages of interview reports, pho-

tographs and other material that should have been turned over to defense lawyers.

Mr. McVeigh's lawyers sought to delay the execution. On June 6, Richard P. Matsch, the federal judge who had presided over the case, said he was shocked by the F.B.I.'s conduct, but swept aside the defense request for a postponement, saying the missing documents were immaterial to Mr. McVeigh's defense. Mr. McVeigh died by lethal injection on June 11.

The F.B.I.'s problems did not end there. On May 3, F.B.I. officials acknowledged that agents had failed to turn over secretly recorded audiotapes and other evidence to Alabama officials in the early 1970's, when the state reopened its investigation into one of the most horrific crimes of the civil rights era, the 1963 bombing of the 16th Street Baptist Church in Birmingham. Four black girls died in the blast.

The tapes played an important role in the May 1 conviction of Thomas E. Blanton Jr., a former Ku Klux Klansman who had remained free for 24 years after state prosecutors, who were unaware of the tapes, concluded they did not have enough evidence.

At times, the breakdowns at the F.B.I. seemed to be cropping up everywhere. F.B.I. officials announced on July 17 that an inventory had found 449 firearms and 184 laptop computers had been stolen or were unaccounted for, including at least one laptop and possibly three others that contained classified data. The missing firearms included some automatic weapons and one handgun later determined to have been used in a homicide.

On July 5, President Bush named Robert S. Mueller III, a veteran prosecutor, to succeed Mr. Freeh. Lawmakers anxious for a leadership change applauded the appointment of Mr. Mueller, a former Marine Corps officer who headed the Justice Department's criminal division during the presidency of George H.W. Bush.. After two uncontentious days of hearings, the Senate voted unanimously to confirm Mr. Mueller, who promised that he would bring a stringent new management style and greater accountability to the agency.

—*David Johnston*

F.B.I. Agent Arrested as Russian Spy

Seldom has there been a more bizarre espionage case than that of the F.B.I. agent Robert P. Hanssen, who pleaded guilty on July 6 to spying for Moscow. The Hanssen story included a stripper and a conservative Catholic organization, and centered on an aloof man described by one psychiatrist who interviewed him as driven by his inner "demons" to betray the nation's secrets.

In what officials described as the most serious case of espionage in the history of the Federal Bureau of Investigation, Mr. Hanssen, then 56, was arrested on Feb. 18 and charged with having spied for Moscow since 1985. But after he pleaded guilty (accepting a sentence of life in prison with no parole as prosecutors agreed not to seek the death penalty), Mr. Hanssen told his debriefers that he actually began spying for the first time in 1979, soon after he began working in F.B.I. counter-intelligence in New York. He said he broke off his spying activities in 1981, but then resumed in 1985. He continued until 1992, stopped again, and then started again in 1999. He then spied from

1999 until his arrest in a wooded Virginia park, where he had just dropped off a bag of classified documents.

Moscow paid Mr. Hanssen $600,000 in cash and diamonds, and he was promised another $800,000, which the Russians told him was being held in a bank in Moscow.

Mr. Hanssen's worst betrayals were committed in 1985. He told Moscow about the existence of a secret eavesdropping tunnel that the F.B.I. and the National Security Agency had dug underneath the Soviet embassy in Washington. He also compromised three K.G.B. officers who were spying for the United States. Two of those agents were later executed.

Prompted by the Hanssen case, the Bush Administration demanded that Russia withdraw approximately 50 intelligence officers from its embassy and missions in the United States. The United States complained that the Russians had returned to Cold War levels of intelligence staffing in America. Russia responded by demanding that four Central Intelligence Agency officers be pulled out of the C.I.A.'s much smaller station in Moscow. The episode was the most serious burst of diplomatic reprisals between the two nations since the mid-1980's.

Mr. Hanssen's behavior during his life as a spy was remarkable. Outwardly, he was a devout and traditional Catholic, a member of a conservative Catholic organization called Opus Dei. The father of six children, he lived modestly with his family in suburban Vienna, Va.

He expressed very conservative political views to friends and collegues. But secretly, he was Moscow's longest-serving mole, searching for ways to spend the proceeds of his espionage. A former Washington stripper, Priscilla Sue Galey, now living in Columbus, Ohio, has said publicly that Mr. Hanssen spent thousands of dollars on her over several years in an attempt to help her improve her life but never sought a romantic relationship with her.

—*James Risen*

Rolling Blackouts Cause Upheaval in California

When the San Francisco area suffered a brief blackout on a broiling summer day in 2000, it was dismissed as a fluke. But by the fall power utilities were reporting worsening shortages of electricity. And the simmering troubles burst into a full crisis by January, when California was hit with several rolling blackouts and the governor acknowledged that the problem would require a reworking of the entire energy system.

California's energy crisis took a huge financial and political toll. Gov. Gray Davis, who was expected to be reelected easily, found his approval ratings plummeting. The state's budget swung from a huge surplus to a potentially big deficit. The state's largest utility, Pacific Gas and Electric, was forced to file for bankruptcy. And ratepayers were saddled with increases of as much 40 percent in their bills.

After weeks of close calls, the first blackout this year hit on January 17 at 11:40 a.m. and ran for three hours in Central and Northern California. There were more blackouts in January and sporadic blackouts in March and then, for the last time, on May 8.

Experts blamed California's three year old experiment in electricity deregulation as a principal cause of the crisis. The plan forced the big utilities to sell most of their generating plants. By pitting power generators against the utilities that distributed the electricity the deregulation plan intended to create a competitive market and lower prices. But, in fact, there was little incentive for generators to build new plants, despite growing demand in a state with a rapidly growing population. In addition, while wholesale prices could rise and fall, the prices that the utilities could charge their customers were capped by regulators. When consumer demand began to outstrip supplies, prices shot well above what the utilities could charge. Elected officials accused the generators of price gouging and the utilities were caught in a desperate downward cycle of growing losses.

By mid-year, the utilities complained they had sustained more than $12 billion in losses. In April, Pacific Gas and Electric filed for bankruptcy. Southern California Edison said it was teetering on the brink, and narrowly avoided bankruptcy when it worked out a rescue plan with the state in September. State officials sought refunds from the generators on charges they manipulated prices, but eventually won only modest rebates. But adding to public anger was the speed with which the situation turned around. The state government was forced to pay more than $10 billion as the principal buyer of power when the utilities ran into financial trouble. The state was left to sell the power to consumers through the utilities at less than it paid. When regulators balked at the governor's plan for selling bonds to cover those costs, the state's budget was hit hard.

But after the state spent billions more lining up long-term contracts to insure an adequate supply of power, prices began to plummet due to relatively cool summer temperatures, conservation and the rapid construction of some new power plants. By July, the state found itself in the embarrassing position of having to sell back to the market at low prices surplus power it had purchased at exorbitant prices. But experts expect the state to be saddled with the costs of the crisis for a decade or more.

—*James Sterngold*

U.S. BUSINESS AND THE ECONOMY

U.S. Economy Slows Dramatically

The boom faded suddenly in the late summer of 2000. The bubbles that had played so important a role in fueling the boom gave way, deflating the economy. Stock prices plunged and thousands of companies that had been investing heavily to expand their facilities pulled back. And then terrorists struck on September 11, and the economy, in response, spiraled toward recession.

For nearly five years the gross domestic product, measuring the rising value of the nation's output of goods and services, had surged. The late 1990's were reminiscent of the prosperity that had bathed country in the 1960's, the last great period of strong economic growth and rising productivity. And then, starting in July of 2000, the economy unwound.

Growth slowed from an annual rate of nearly 6 percent in the second quarter to less than 2 percent for the next four quarters. By the third quarter, July through September of 2001, the G.D.P. was expanding at a rate barely above zero, and the nation braced for more hard months, which came when terrorists crashed airliners into the World Trade Center and the Pentagon, destroying the former and damaging the latter.

This downturn was different, even before the terrorism. In nearly every previous downturn since World War II, the economy had quickly deteriorated into a recession, during which the G.D.P. contracted for at least six months. But only two of these lasted as long as 16 months and then prosperity quickly returned. This time, the economy bounced along the bottom for a full year and many forecasters warned that the weak growth could continue without a recession into the next year without a formal recession ever developing.

There were other differences. Strong consumer demand and rising inflation preceded virtually all of the previous post-war recessions. The Federal Reserve responded by raising interest rates to discourage borrowing and spending. The rising rates became too restrictive and the economy toppled into recession, which the Fed then cured by pulling down rates.

This time interest rates never got very high. Instead, expectations collapsed. The new information technologies had promised rising productivity and rising profits — and stock prices rose exuberantly in anticipation of the windfall. Productivity did improve and profits did rise, but in hindsight neither grew enough to justify the stock market surge. The stock market bubble, however, played a big role in financing business investment in equipment and computers and this spending contributed mightily to the unusually strong economic growth.

When profits failed to meet expectations, the expectations gave way. Hundreds of companies formed to exploit the Internet — the famous dot-coms — never made a profit, and the Nasdaq, where the shares of many high-tech companies were traded, finally plunged, precipitating the slowdown in economic growth. The Nasdaq went from a peak of just over 5000 in March of 2000 to below 1800 in 2001.

The Fed responded by cutting interest rates sharply in 2001. The rate cuts helped to sustain consumer spending and the housing industry, and strength in these sectors kept the economy from slipping into recession. But with profits shrinking, corporate America continued to shrink investment, despite the lower rates. Weak exports and weak economies in Asia and Europe contributed to the American slowdown.

The big question in the first week of September was whether the prolonged slowdown would undermine the consumer. Layoffs had proliferated and the unemployment rate had gradually risen from a low of 3 percent in the late summer of 2000 to 4.9 percent a year later. By the standards of the past 20 years, that was still low unemployment. Tens of millions Americans, holding jobs, told pollsters they remained optimistic.

That optimism faded quickly when terrorists on September 11 destroyed the World Trade Center and damaged the Pentagon. The psychological impact of the attacks and the uncertainty concerning the future did considerable damage to the economy. Consumers pulled back, business executives froze new investment and a barely growing economy finally began to contract, moving the nation toward recession in the year's final months.

—*Louis Uchitelle*

The Disappearing Dot-Coms

If there was still any question about whether the dot-com industry would survive in 2001, the answer was a resounding no. Indeed, the industry became even more stigmatized in 2001 with its own moniker: dot-bomb. Dot-com's like Etoys had already declared bankruptcy in 2000, proving that even the best funded and most inventive companies were virtually always be doomed if they could not turn a profit. Still, Amazon.com managed to stay in business without turning a profit in 2001 by significantly scaling back its ambitious plans and aligning itself with more traditional businesses like Toys R Us to supply some its products and leverage better known retail brands.

Most dot-coms were not as lucky as Amazon.com, which has the deepest pockets of just about any company in the industry. Kozmo.com, the Internet retailer that started in New York three years ago and was one of the first dot-coms to promise online deliveries to people's homes, shuttered its virtual doors in April. It burnt through about $250 million in three years - including money invested by Amazon.com. Kozmo.com, an ingenious idea to deliver everything from videos to snacks to electronics within an hour, was the victim of its own rush to expand its business nationwide using a business plan that never made much sense. Likewise, Webvan, an Internet site that allowed customers to order groceries that would then be delivered to the home went belly-up.

Among the other biggest casualties of the Internet age was Inside.com, an Internet news site that covered the media and was backed by some top names in journalism. Unable to turn a profit, Inside.com was sold to a joint venture run by Primedia and Steven Brill, but even that partnership was unable to change the site's fortunes. In October, Primedia and Mr. Brill dissolved their relationship and took Inside.com offline. With the dot-com world imploding, *The Industry Standard*, a magazine — on paper and online — also went under without revenue from its free spending dot-com advertisers.

Despite the gloom and doom, one dot-com industry sector that proved somewhat resilient was the online ticket reservation business. Companies like Expedia, which Microsoft sold this year to USA Network and Priceline, which scaled back it other businesses, were doing extremely well until the drop off in travel following the terrorist attacks on September 11.

—*Andrew Ross Sorkin*

Economic Slowdown Ends Stock Market Mania

In 2000, the stock market's long-running party ended suddenly and badly. One year later, investors discovered that the hangover, for the market and the economy, would run long and deep.

When the Nasdaq composite index plunged in April 2000, losing one-third of its value in weeks, many investors thought damage from the sell-off would be confined mainly to companies whose primary business was selling products or services over the Internet. Outside the technology industry, the spillover from the crash was expected to be minor. Even within the industry, larger, more profitable companies, like Intel and Cisco Systems, were expected to continue to grow.

But by the fall of 2000, the crisis had spread. Communications companies which had spent tens of billions of dollars to build new fiber-optic networks found that they had badly overestimated demand for data transmission. Facing spiraling losses, sometimes even bankrutpcy, they cut back on spending on equipment from companies like Cisco and Nortel Networks.

Chip makers like Intel, computer manufacturers like Dell, and software companies such as Oracle also reported slowing sales, as Wall Street discovered that much of the growth in corporate investment on technology had been tied to the now-burst Internet bubble. The slump worsened in early 2001, and many once-profitable technology companies began reporting losses. Overall economic growth, which had been driven by technology spending, also slowed sharply.

In the early months of 2001, stocks moved lower, even though the Federal Reserve repeatedly lowered short-term interest rates in an effort to help the faltering economy. The selling culminated in a mini-crash from mid-March to early April.

By then, many technology stocks had fallen 70, 80, or even 90 percent from the highs they had reached the previous year. For most other stocks, the damage was not nearly as severe, but because technology stocks had become such a large part of the overall market during the boom, broader market indexes had also fallen sharply. The Standard & Poor's 500, which includes the largest publicly traded American companies, fell from its high of 1,527.46 in March 2000 to 1,103.25 on April 2001, a drop of 28 percent.

Stocks recovered broadly during the spring as investors bet that lower interest rates would stimulate growth. Continued strong consumer spending and falling energy prices added to Wall Street's optimism. But as spring turned into summer with no revival in technology spending or overall economic growth, stocks wilted again. In July, a series of dismal profit reports from big companies led investors to worry that corporate America might begin a wide round of layoffs in the fall, depressing consumer confidence and spending and putting the United States into a full-blown recession. This time the losses were not confined to technology. Brokerage firms, automakers, retailers, and other economically sensitive stocks were hit. By Sep. 10, the S&P 500 had given back all of its spring gains and stood at 1,092.54.

The terrorist attacks of Sep. 11 only added to the gloom in the markets. The destruction of the World Trade Center, which killed some 6,000 people, many of whom worked in the securities industry, deeply shocked Wall Street. The attack forced Lehman Brothers and Merrill Lynch, two major securities firms, out of their headquarters and led to a four-day shutdown of U.S. securities markets, the longest since the Depression.

Even after markets reopened and the initial fears faded, investors confronted an economy that seemed much more fragile than it had only days before. Stocks fell sharply in the first week of trading after the attacks, with the Dow Jones industrial average of 30 large companies dropping 14 percent, its biggest weekly fall since 1933.

Many professional investors worried that without a large package of new spending or tax cuts from the federal government, the economy might slide into a long and deep recession. From their highs in 2000, the Dow and S&P had fallen more than one-third, and the Nasdaq had dropped a staggering 70 percent, the biggest slide in a major American index since the Depression. More than $5 trillion in shareholder wealth had disappeared. Not everyone was gloomy, of course. Plenty of investors remained bullish for the long run, arguing that with government help, the United States could grow strongly again as soon as mid-2002. But in just 18 months, the prevailing mood on Wall Street had swung from mania to deep anxiety.

—*Alex Berenson*

Fear of Regulators Slows the Pace of Mergers

If 2000 was the year of the mega-merger, 2001 was the year of the derailed merger. Two of the world's largest planned industrial mergers were foiled by regulators over worries that consolidation may be going too far. General Electric's last-minute $45 billion bid for Honeywell International was blocked by European regulators, despite receiving approval in Washington. Likewise, United Airlines abandoned its proposed $4.3 billion takeover of US Airways because of opposition from regulators in the United States.

The regulatory climate in Washington and in Brussels, where the European Commission is based, weighed heavily on the types of deals corporations attempted in 2001. The type of industry shifting mergers, like America Online's acquisition of Time Warner in 2000, virtually disappeared in 2001. Instead, companies sought somewhat smaller, more strategic mergers with a high likelihood of regulatory approval.

Consolidation in the fast-growing energy sector was popular, but media and telecommunication mergers were perhaps the most intriguing. The large cable operator, Comcast, made a hostile $44.5 billion takeover offer for AT&T's cable business in July in an attempt to become the nation's largest cable operator. General Motors put its satellite television business, Hughes Electronics and its DirecTV unit, up for sale. Among the bidders were Rupert Murdoch's News Corp. and satellite operator EchoStar Communications. While General Motors has yet to pick a suitor, the regulatory climate has weighed heavily on General Motors' board. The offer from EchoStar is higher than News Corp.'s offer, but the board is likely to choose News Corp.'s bid because combining with EchoStar could raise the ire of regulators in Washington.

Among the smaller deals this year, General Electric's $2 billion acquisition of U.S. Spanish-language broadcaster Telemundo Communications Group in October, marked an important shift in the market's perception of G.E.'s commitment to its NBC television business. Vivendi Universal also made a deal that was once unthinkable. It acquired the online music-sharing site MP3.com for $372 million in May despite having filed a copyright infringement lawsuit against MP3.com less than a year ago, which MP3.com later settled for $53.4 million.

One of the reason's companies were wary to do deals in 2001 was the stock market's almost knee-jerk reaction to pummel the merging companies' stocks. The hardest hit deal was Hewlett-Packard's proposed $25 billion acquisition of Compaq. The day the transaction was announced, investors beat both companies stock down. At its day's low of $10.75, Compaq shares sold for less than at any time since July 30, 1996. "Two losers don't make a winner," said Bob Djurdjevic, the president of Annex Research, echoing the sentiments of other investors.

One deal that investors seemed to respond positively to was PepsiCo's $13.4 billion acquisition of

Quaker Oats in December. The transaction gave PepsiCo control of Quaker's much-coveted Gatorade sports drink brand.

—Andrew Ross Sorkin

S.E.C. Charges Arthur Andersen With Fraud

Arthur Andersen, one of the Big Five accounting firms, suffered twin blows to its reputation as the Securities and Exchange Commission first brought civil fraud charges against a partner in the firm and then filed similar charges against the entire firm in a different case. It was the first time in more than a decade that the commission had filed such charges against a major accounting firm.

On June 19, Andersen settled the charges, which stemmed from audits of Waste Management Inc., whose $1.43 billion restatement of earnings in 1998 was said by the commission to be the largest ever. The firm agreed to pay a fine of $7 million.

According to the S.E.C., Andersen's auditors uncovered problems with Waste Management's profit reports in the early 1990's. In early 1994, while auditing Waste Management's 1993 results, the accounting firm identified $128 million in misstatements relating to that year and prior periods, the S.E.C. said, and asked Waste Management to change its reports to eliminate those earnings, an action that would have reduced reported profit by 12 percent. In addition, it found other bad accounting practices that the S.E.C. said led to other overstatements of profit that Andersen did not quantify.

When Waste Management refused to make changes, Andersen concluded that the overstatements were not material, a decision that was crucial since the audit opinion states that financial reports "present fairly, in all material respects," the company's financial position.

The S.E.C. suit noted that by backing down, Andersen had left itself in a difficult position.

"Unless the auditor stands up to management" the first time it discovers incorrect accounting, the commission said in its order, "the auditor ultimately will find itself in an untenable position: it either must continue issuing unqualified audit reports on materially misstated financial statements and hope that its conduct will not be discovered or it must force a restatement or qualify its report and thereby subject itself to the liability that likely will result from the exposure of its role in the prior issuance of the materially misstated financial statements."

In the end, Waste Management and its auditors did pay $220 million to settle shareholder suits.

A month before the Waste Management charges were settled, the S.E.C. filed civil fraud allegations against a partner in Arthur Andersen who had audited the books of the Sunbeam Corporation, which later restated its earnings and said that its former chief executive, Albert J. Dunlap, had overseen an accounting fraud. The auditor denied the charges, and Andersen, which was not sued, said it was supporting him.

—Floyd Norris

Microsoft Wins Antitrust Appeal But Still Faces Sanctions

Microsoft gained valuable ground in its antitrust battle with the government in 2001. But the company also lost its last hope of escaping sanctions that promise to outlaw some of Microsoft's bare-knuckled business tactics.

The big legal step came on June 28, when a federal appeals court threw out a lower court's order in June 2000 that Microsoft should be split in two. The appeals court also sharply criticized Judge Thomas Penfield Jackson for his comments to reporters about Microsoft's chairman William H. Gates and other company executives. Judge Jackson told one reporter that Mr. Gates had a "Napoleonic concept of himself" and, with another, he compared Microsoft's incriminating e-mails to intercepted conversations by drug traffickers who "never figure out that they shouldn't be saying certain things on the phone." The appeals court found his indiscretions "deliberate, repeated, egregious and flagrant."

But while they upbraided Judge Jackson personally and disagreed with him on a few points to law, the appeals court judges agreed with him that Microsoft was a monopolist that had repeatedly violated the nation's antitrust laws.

A few weeks later, on July 11, Microsoft nodded toward the appeals court ruling and announced that it would offer personal computer makers more freedom to choose what software and services they feature on top of Windows XP operating system the new version of Microsoft's monopoly product, which went on sale Oct. 25. The company's rivals and critics called the move a grudging half-step toward acknowledging that the appeals court ruling meant Microsoft would have to change its bullying ways.

The Bush administration made its first move in the case on Sept. 6, saying it would not seek a breakup of the company and would not pursue the charge that Microsoft necessarily violated the law by bundling its Internet browsing software with Windows. The appeals court had not prevented the government and 18 states suing Microsoft from seeking a breakup order, but it had repeatedly suggested that such a drastic step seemed extreme.

Yet the Justice Department also said that it would seek sanctions based on the conduct remedies ordered by Judge Jackson, which, at the time, were intended as an interim remedy until a breakup plan was implemented. Those conduct remedies included requiring Microsoft to offer "unbundled" versions of Windows without a browser and Internet media player, for example allowing PC companies to select add-on feature from Microsoft or rivals. The remedies also included forcing Microsoft to openly share technical information with other software companies.

A new federal district court judge, Colleen Kollar-Kotelly, inherited the Microsoft case, and on Sept. 28 she ordered the sides to begin another round of settlement talks. Four previous efforts had failed. And the two sides began far apart, with a Microsoft lawyer characterizing the initial proposals as potentially "devastating" to the company. Judge Kollar-Kotelly set a deadline of Nov. 2, for the two sides to reach a settlement. Then, on Oct. 9, the Supreme Court decided not to hear Microsoft's appeal, removing any hope the company had that it could escape punishment.

Without a last-minute settlement, hearings on what sanctions to impose on Microsoft were scheduled to begin in the spring of 2002 three-and-a-half years and a few generations of technology removed from the beginning of the trial on Oct. 19, 1998.

—Steve Lohr

INTERNATIONAL NEWS STORIES

Hopes for Peace Wither as Hundreds Die In Mideast

The Israeli-Palestinian conflict descended into a maelstrom of violence that defied attempts to reach a cease-fire and resume peace negotiations. By October 2001, a year into the Palestinian uprising, nearly 600 Palestinians and 200 Israelis had died in a grinding war of attrition. It followed last-ditch negotiations on core issues toward a permanent peace settlement. These issues, including the fate of Palestinian refugees, Jewish settlements and Jerusalem, had been left unresolved at a summit meeting at Camp David in July 2000.

The negotiations, based on guidelines proposed by President Clinton, ran out of time as new elections in Israel swept Ariel Sharon to a landslide victory over the incumbent prime minister, Ehud Barak. The hawkish Mr. Sharon rode to power on a wave of anxieties of an Israeli public shaken by months of violence. The months preceding the early February vote shattered hopes for peace among many Israelis and Palestinians: In the West Bank town of Ramallah, a Palestinian mob lynched two Israeli reserve soldiers who had blundered into the city. Television images of the killing shocked Israel, and it responded with a helicopter strikes on Ramallah and Gaza.

At a meeting in Egypt in Oct. 2000 between President Clinton, Mr. Barak and Yasir Arafat, the Israelis and Palestinians agreed to a truce, but it quickly unravelled in a series of Palestinian shootings and bombings and Israeli missile strikes on Palestinian towns. Using helicopter gunships, the Israelis assassinated a Palestinian paramilitary commander, beginning a policy of pinpoint killings that led to the deaths of more than three dozen suspected militants. After a roadside bomb tore through a schoolbus near the Israeli settlement of Kfar Darom in the Gaza Strip, killing two people, the Israelis hit back with massive airborne bombardments across the Gaza Strip.

With peace efforts collapsing and his parliamentary support eroded, Mr. Barak agreed to the new elections. Working to build a broad-based coalition, Mr. Sharon brought the vanquished Labor party into his cabinet, including Shimon Peres, an architect of the Oslo peace accords with the Palestinians, as Foreign Minister, and Binyamin Ben-Eliezer, as Minister of Defense.

But the inauguration of the hybrid government brought no new diplomatic initiatives. Israeli troops shot stone-throwing youths, Palestinian gunmen killed Israeli settlers in drive-by shootings, and Islamic militants carried out suicide attacks in Israeli cities, causing Israeli air and missile strikes on Palestinian targets. In daily gun-battles, Palestinians fired at Israeli positions and settlements, and the Israelis shelled Palestinian towns and refugee camps. The death toll on both sides continued to climb. The Israeli army blockaded Palestinian cities and villages.

The Sharon government ratcheted up the Israeli military responses to Palestinian violence. In the Gaza Strip, Palestinian attacks were met with armored thrusts into refugee camps and the demolition of dozens of homes. After mortars were fired into Israel in April, an Israeli force entered a swath of Gaza Strip territory in an operation that one general said could last "days, weeks, months." The troops were withdrawn the next day under strong American pressure, but raids into Palestinian-held areas later became commonplace in both the West Bank and Gaza Strip.

Another threshold was crossed in May when the Israelis used F-16 warplanes in the West Bank for the first time since the 1967 Middle East war. They bombed targets in Nablus and Ramallah after a suicide bomber killed six Israelis and wounded more than 100 in an attack in Netanya. The Israeli strikes killed 11 Palestinian officers. On June 1, a Palestinian bomber killed 21 Israelis, many of them teenage girls, in an explosion outside a beachfront disco in Tel Aviv. The attack led to the first public call by Mr. Arafat for an immediate and unconditional cease-fire since the start of the Palestinian uprising.

George J. Tenet, the director of American central intelligence, secured the agreement of both sides to a cease-fire plan that was to have been a prelude to the resumption of peace talks. Guidelines for a return to the negotiating table had been laid out in a report submitted in May by a fact-finding committee headed by the former American Senator George J. Mitchell. The report recommended an immediate cessation of violence and a resumption of security cooperation, followed by a cooling off period and confidence-building measures, including the cessation of Israeli settlement activity.

The cease-fire never took hold. More violence ensued, and on Aug. 10, a Hamas suicide bomber killed 15 people in a crowded pizzeria in downtown Jerusalem, prompting an Israeli takeover of Orient House, the headquarters of the Palestine Liberation Organization in East Jerusalem and symbol of Palestinian aspirations for a state with Jerusalem as its capital. The Israelis sent tanks farther into Palestinian-held territory, and a senior Palestinian official, Mustafa Zibri, head of the radical Popular Front for the Liberation of Palestine, was assassinated in a helicopter strike on his office.

After the terrorist attacks in New York and Washington, the Bush administration worked hard to put together a coalition including Arab nations to fight Islamic terrorists. Washington brought intense pressure on the Israelis and Palestinians to abide by a cease-fire, and Mr. Bush called the creation of a Palestinian state part of the long-term vision for peace in the region.

—Joel Greenberg

Moderates in Northern Ireland Lose Influence to Hard-Liners

A defining image for Northern Ireland in 2001 was forged on the rainswept Ardoyne Road in north Belfast when a crowd of Protestants tried to blockade an all-girls primary school, forcing Roman Catholic girls as young as four to run a gauntlet between columns of armored police cars to reach class. A pipe-bomb was thrown. Insults were hurled. Parents were spat upon.

In the end, the Protestants and Catholics resolutely looked away from each other. But the moment was significant because this was the year when the optimism generated by the 1998 Good Friday peace accord finally gave way to the hard-liners in both camps who opposed the peace deal from the very beginning.

British national elections on June 7 strengthened both hard-line Protestants led by the Rev. Ian Paisley, and Sinn Fein, the political wing of the Irish Republican Army. For the first time, voters frustrated by the snail-like pace of peace talks, swung towards the extremes and away from the relative centrist Protestant and Catholic parties that had overseen the peace process. The moderates lost out.

Indeed, frustrated by the I.R.A.'s persistent refusal to set a timetable for disarmament, David Trimble, the province's first minister, quit on July 1, sparking a protracted constitutional crisis that led to direct rule from London being restored for 24-hour periods, a technical maneuver to prevent the total collapse of the Catholic-Protestant home rule government that was the centerpiece of the 1998 peace agreement. For reasons of health, John Hume, the head of the more moderate Catholic Social Democratic and Labor Party, resigned in September. The resignations meant that Northern Ireland's two winners of the 1998 Nobel Peace Prize had both pulled back from office.

Yet, the long-running, on-off discussions optimistically titled a peace process somehow lumbered along, despite such obstacles as a car bombing in London ascribed to the breakaway Real I.R.A., which is not heeding the province's broader cease-fire.

That same month, March, the I.R.A. itself said it would resume disarmament talks with an international commission supervising the turnover of guerrilla weaponry. That was not enough to prevent Mr. Trimble's subsequent resignation, but a sense of gathering crisis did persuade the British and Irish government to produce a new set of peace proposals covering the contentious issues left unresolved by the Good Friday agreement: these included disarmament of paramilitary forces like the I.R.A., the structure of a new police force and the dismantling of the British military presence.

In August, moreover, both the I.R.A. and the international commission announced that they had agreed on a mechanism to "put I.R.A. arms completely and verifiably beyond use." Without a firm commitment to a timetable for disarmament, however, Mr. Trimble's Ulster Unionists objected. The constitutional crisis caused by Mr. Trimble's resignation and the impasse in negotiations continued in tandem, even though the I.R.A. first withdrew its offer, then later pledged to renew negotiations with the commission.

For United States officials, the I.R.A.'s negotiating maneuvers were greatly overshadowed by events far from Northern Ireland, when three men arrested in Colombia in August and were accused of being I.R.A. members acting as military instructors to a Colombian guerrilla group known as FARC. Washington has given Colombia money and military assistance to combat drug trafficking by the rebels and regards them as a dangerous terrorist group. The idea of a link between the Colombian guerrillas and the I.R.A. seriously damaged Sinn Fein's standing in the United States as a player in the peace process.

The I.R.A. and Sinn Fein both sought to distance themselves from the three men's activities, and the I.R.A. said it "sent no one to Colombia to train or to engage in any military cooperation with any group." The Americans, however, left no doubt that they saw things differently. Richard N. Haass, President Bush's special envoy to Northern Ireland, said publicly of the three men: ``They were not there for their vacations, they were not there for an exchange of views on negotiation techniques in the peace process, but for discussion with FARC on matters that come under the rubric of terrorism."

—*Alan Cowell*

(See "Late Breaking News" for update.)

Pope John Paul Pursues Peace With Orthodox Church

Some predicted that having passed the age of 80, his health visibly flagging, John Paul II would slow down after closing the 2000 Holy Year that marked the 2,000th anniversary of birth of Jesus. A few cardinals hinted that he might retire. Instead, the pope in 2001 kept climbing new summits, elevating 44 men to the college of cardinals, an unprecedented number that cemented his stamp on the institution that will someday select his successor.

The veteran of nearly 100 papal voyages also traveled to new places, groundbreaking journeys that reflected his longstanding dream of reconciling Roman Catholicism and the Eastern Orthodox Church, divided since the schism of 1054. In May, on a pilgrimage following the path of St. Paul to Greece, Syria and Malta, the pope tried to woo the Greek Orthodox Church, one of the most conservative, by expressing "deep regret" for the misdeeds of Catholics throughout the centuries, including the crusaders' sack of Constantinople in 1204; it is a historic grievance of the Greek Church. Archbishop Christodoulos rewarded his Roman Catholic guest for that long-awaited gesture by lifting an Orthodox taboo against joint prayer and reciting the Lord's prayer with him.

John Paul II came at least physically closer to his dream of visiting Russia with a five-day trip to neighboring Ukraine in June, for which he overlooked the fierce objections of the Orthodox Church in Moscow and its affiliate in Ukraine. His trip had at times clashing goals: the pope wanted to celebrate the rebirth of the Ukrainian Greek Catholic church, which follows Eastern rites but is loyal to Rome, after decades of Soviet oppression. But he also hoped to soften the resistance of the Russian Orthodox Church, which views the pope's support for Ukraine's five million Greek Catholics as one of the chief obstacles to reconciliation. Metropolitan Vladimir, head of the Ukrainian Orthodox Church that is loyal to Moscow, declined to meet with the pope. But Moscow did not break off relations with Rome, as some had threatened, and the pope's brinksmanship seemed to pay off, or at least he did not close off any of his options.

But with time and his physical strength running out, the 81-year-old pope was in no mood to wait and see how the Ukraine trip played out over time. He quickly made another trip to two other former Soviet republics with Orthodox and Catholic populations, Kazakhstan and Armenia, in September. Some in the Vatican whisper that the pope is spending too much time on the uphill battle to win over the Orthodox Church, neglecting perhaps more pressing issues within the Roman Catholic Church. But the Polish pope has a strong messianic streak, and he realizes his successor may not share the same vision.

—*Alessandra Stanley*

Foot-and-Mouth Devastates Britain

Barely had Britain shaken off the stigma of mad cow disease from the 1990's than its herds confronted yet another scourge in 2001: foot-and-mouth disease. Even before the authorities' first acknowledgment of the disease on Feb. 21, the nonfatal illness had begun its rampage in many parts of the land, including important tourist areas such as the Lake District in the northwest and Devon in the southwest.

As a result, exports and movements of farm animals were banned. Footpaths were closed. Untold thousands of Americans and other visitors canceled vacations to Britain, and the cost to farming and tourism was estimated at almost $3 billion. Almost four million animals from around 9,000 farms were slaughtered. The outbreak was the worst in more than 30 years.

Unlike mad cow disease, a form of which can kill humans, foot-and-mouth is found mainly in cloven-hooved animals such as pigs, sheep, goats, and cows, and its incidence among humans is extremely rare. It is not usually fatal to the animals (or humans) but causes blistering on animals' hooves and mouths, weight loss and temporary lameness. It is highly contagious and can be transmitted on a light breeze or on the clothing or car-tires of people who have been in contact with infected animals.

But its main threat is economic: infected animals are unfit for market, cost money to tend while they recover, and nations where the disease has been identified lose their access to export markets. Both the European Union and the United States halted imports of British meat products and animals.

After a brief debate about whether the disease could be contained through vaccination —a move that would have had longer-term repercussions for British meat exporters and would have led to the slaughter of many animals anyway—the British authorities made their decision. They resolved to combat the disease by destroying not just infected animals but also uninfected animals from areas surrounding farms where the disease had been confirmed.

Such was the extent of the challenge in digging burial pits and incinerating carcasses that the British Army was called out within weeks of the outbreak. Prime Minister Tony Blair said the army's logistical effort was greater than it had been to transport British soldiers during the Persian Gulf war against Iraqi forces in 1990-91.

While there are no known biological or clinical links between foot-and-mouth and mad cow disease, the two outbreaks did share some characteristics: both bore serious economic consequences for Britain's shrinking farm businesses, and both carried political freight. Indeed, the foot-and-mouth outbreak forced Mr. Blair to postpone a general election for one month because of the political risk of holding the vote when many rural Britons, traditionally mistrustful of Mr. Blair's Labor Party, were locked in combat with the disease.

When he did call an election for June 7, which he won resoundingly, Mr. Blair insisted that the fight against the disease was "in the home stretch." That turned out to be a premature assessment. As the year wore on, hundreds of thousands more animals were slaughtered and the disease continued to flare in new areas, even as farmers and the government traded accusations over who was to blame for its continued spread.

Government officials said farmers and rural workers had been lax in following disinfection regulations supposed to the stop the disease from spreading. But farmers said government inspectors and haulers transporting carcasses had themselves flouted the regulations.

Part of the blame lay with the structure of the British meat industry. European regulations have made it too expensive for small, local abbatoirs to stay in business, so animals were routinely transported hundreds of miles to bigger slaughterhouses. Additionally, truckloads of sheep for sale also traveled long distances to market, as sellers looked for the best prices.

This constant movement of animals meant that, by the time the government announced the disease among pigs at a slaughterhouse in Essex on Feb. 21, it had already spread undetected among sheep from a farm nearby. And they, in turn, had been transported around the country for two to three weeks before restrictions were imposed on animal movements. According to David Tyson, president of the British Veterinary Association, this meant that, from the beginning, farmers and authorities were playing "a catch-up job."

—Alan Cowell

U.S. Submarine Accidentally Sinks Japanese Fishing Vessel

The *U.S.S. Greeneville*, a nuclear attack submarine, steamed out of Pearl Harbor around midday on Feb. 9 leaving a third of its crew behind for training and with no mission beyond taking 16 civilians on a demonstration cruise. At the same time, the *Ehime Maru*, a trawler used for training students at a Japanese fisheries school, left Honolulu for the last portion of a teaching cruise. It steamed into the hazy afternoon until, about 10 miles south of Diamond Head, two loud bumps began a nightmare that put a chill in United States relations with Japan.

Within seconds, water and oil were swirling around the ankles of the Japanese crew. The bow lifted, the lights went out and in less than five minutes, as one student frantically clambered up a mast slipping under the swells, the 190-foot *Ehime Maru* had sunk. Twenty-six people were saved, while nine people, including four students, were lost.

The *Greeneville* surfaced and then turned around in a futile effort to help after realizing it had caused the disaster.

Officials at the Japanese school and in the government expressed outrage. The anger deepened when it came out that the *Greeneville* was not only sailing just for the sake of its visitors, but that several of them had been seated at the controls when the accident occurred.

The submarine had done what is called an emergency main ballast blow, in which it dives to about 400 feet then dramatically roars to the surface. Although the Navy insisted that the civilians had all been closely supervised when at the controls, it admitted that the crew had failed to realize the *Ehime Maru* was so close.

The Navy held an inquiry in which top officials uncovered a series of lapses. The skipper, Commander Scott Waddle, conceded that he had rushed through routine safety procedures. He said he had spent 80 seconds scanning through the periscope and had seen no approaching ships. The procedure is supposed to take three minutes.

He admitted that a video monitor that tracks other vessels in the vicinity was not working, but that he had ordered no special precautions. A paper chart where the crew is supposed to pencil in information on nearby vessels was not updated. And a sonar officer said he saw the *Ehime Maru* approaching, but that because the commander had not spotted it with the periscope, he assumed the instruments were wrong, overruled the computer and manually placed it at a greater distance.

On April 23, the Navy found Commander Waddle had committed two violations of the service's code, dereliction of duty and subjecting a vessel to hazard, but it did not order a court martial. Commander Waddle was forced to retire, but with his full rank and his full pension.

Four other officers — including the ship's executive officer, the chief of staff of the submarine fleet, the chief of boat and the sonar supervisor — were admonished. The Japanese government said the process had been fair, but some civilians objected.

"The punishment is absolutely not one that the families can accept," said Moriuki Kato, governor of Ehime Prefecture in Japan, where the students lived.

—*James Sterngold*

U.S. Spy Plane Collides With Chinese Jet

An April 1 collision between a Chinese jet fighter and a U.S. surveillance plane over the South China Sea killed the Chinese pilot, resulted in the 11-day detention of the 24-member American crew, and bruised relations between the two nations.

The American plane, an EP-3E Aires II, was flying in international airspace conducting its usual mission —sucking up electronic communications from the Chinese military—when an F-8 jet fighter scrambled to intercept it.

What happened next is still in dispute. The Chinese maintain that the propeller-driven U.S. plane swerved into the Chinese fighter. In rebuttal, the Pentagon released a videotape that it said showed the Chinese pilot, lieutenant commander Wang Wei, on a previous mission flying so dangerously close to an American plane that the high-pressure "wash" spitting from his engine actually thumped the U.S. aircraft.

But on April 1, two planes struck each other, and the Chinese pilot fell into the sea. Although the American airplane was badly damaged, Lt. Shane Osborn wrestled it safely down to an emergency landing at a Chinese military airfield on Hainan Island.

During the harrowing descent, the crew attempted to destroy hardware and software that enabled the plane to intercept and analyze Chinese communications, smashing some gear by ax and sledgehammer and dumping manuals through a hatch on the fuselage. The Pentagon assumes, however, that the Chinese gleaned useful information while the plane remained in Chinese custody.

The United States Government expressed regret for the collision, the loss of the Chinese pilot and the emergency entry into Chinese airspace during the crash-landing. But U.S. officials insisted that it was not an apology, and that the recklessness of the Chinese pilot was wholly to blame.

After the U.S. crew returned home to a hero's welcome, the U.S. asked to repair the $80 million plane and fly it away. But the Chinese said no.

Thus, the recovery of the EP-3E turned into an international encounter all its own, as the top-secret U.S. intelligence plane was chopped into pieces and hauled away from a Chinese military runway in the belly of a commercial Russian cargo plane. To close out the drama, the Chinese demanded $1 million for the care of the crew and expenses incurred during the three months it held the plane and helped engineer its return.

The U.S. did its own calculations and sent $34,567, which the Chinese angrily rejected.

—*Thom Shanker*

Japan's New Prime Minister Pledges Many Reforms

For years, Junichiro Koizumi had been an also-ran in campaigns to lead Japan's long-ruling Liberal Democratic Party. So even when he began to emerge in the spring as a surprising front-runner in the campaign for prime minister, few in the country's establishment seemed to take his candidacy seriously.

Running the classic insurgent's race, Mr. Koizumi, a former health and postal services minister, called himself an "oddball," and pointedly refused to curry favor with the Liberal Democratic Party barons who have long dominated Japanese politics. He focused his campaign instead on the disgruntled rank and file, urging them to "Change the L.D.P. to Change Japan."

Despite campaign slogans such as "reform with no sacred cows," which heralded painful changes in an economy already hurt by 11 years of near-consecutive recession, Mr. Koizumi's popularity within his own party quickly spread to the broader public, and in his third run for prime minister, he won a landslide victory.

He became premier on April 26, and enjoyed unprecedented standing in opinion polls, with support levels hovering at 75 percent and above. The prime minister's popularity has also paid off for his party. In July elections to the upper house of parliament that were seen as an early referendum on the new Government, the ruling party made strong gains. That reversed years of steady decline at the polls that had forced it to team up with several smaller parties in coalitions to stay in power.

For many Japanese, Mr. Koizumi, with a mop of wavy hair, direct speech and confident manner, seemed almost to embody change. His reform agenda, meanwhile, was sweeping in its themes but, according to many critics, often short on detail.

The new prime minister pledged himself to fiscal austerity to rein in Japan's ballooning public debt. Toward this end, he has promised to sharply limit the issuance of Government bonds, and put an end to the country's huge public works spending. For years that was an important source of patronage for the Liberal Democratic Party.

At the same time, Mr. Koizumi's Government has pushed for reforms of the banking sector, even saying that many banks must be allowed to fail if Japan's economy is to return to strong growth. Since the collapse of the country's financial bubble, private banks have accumulated huge amounts of non-performing debts, but have been protected from collapse by extraordinarily low interest rates, and by loose accounting rules that economists say have masked the extent of the problem.

From the start, Mr. Koizumi faced the likelihood of bitter resistance from the mainstream of his party, which has maintained deep ties with banking, construction and other industries that were expected to be hit hard hit by his program. But in his first months in office, even before any major reforms could be enacted, pressures grew on him. The economy weakened significantly, and when unemployment reached a record 5 percent in August, the Government began facing strong public calls to help the jobless and strengthen the safety net.

—Howard W. French

The Balkan War Spills Into Macedonia

Macedonia managed to escape the wars that erupted over the greater part of Tito's Yugoslavia after it broke up in 1989. Its luck ran out in March 2001, as an insurgency of ethnic Albanian militants, supplied and supported by bordering Kosovo, rose up to fight for equal rights for Macedonia's ethnic Albanian minority.

Small and poor, Macedonia is dominated by Slavs, who make up perhaps two-thirds of the population, while ethnic Albanians make up one quarter to one third. No one knows just how much, and that has been part of the problem.

The situation is different than in Kosovo, where Slobodan Milosevic had allowed little ethnic Albanian control over a province where they represented a huge majority. Instead, the Macedonians have always recognized ethnic Albanian political parties, which have taken part in government coalitions. And Albanians have shared in the proceeds of the smuggling that keeps much of the Macedonian economy alive.

But longstanding Albanian demands had stalled for such things as equal status, the use of Albanian as an official language, and better representation in the police. And NATO's defeat of the Serbs in Kosovo in 1999—and the victory of the Kosovo Liberation Army—created a new legitimacy for armed struggle that the Macedonian government was slow to understand.

Important members of the Kosovo Liberation Army were born in Macedonia and moved easily across the mountainous border. The new insurgency, known as the National Liberation Army, had the same initials in Albanian as the Kosovo Liberation Army, and nearly identical red and gold shoulder patches. Isolated attacks on Macedonian policemen beginning in January quickly spread, and the Macedonian government responded in haste. It relied on its badly organized police and tiny army to defeat an insurgency that quickly grew in Albanian-dominated areas.

NATO troops were slow to try to cut off the border to the movement of weapons, ammunition and armed Albanians, and the new Bush administration held back from a new commitment in the Balkans. Leaders of the European Union and NATO worked hard to patch together a solution. While the Macedonian president, Boris Trajkovski, was amenable, the more nationalist government balked at quick concessions and the fighting grew.

Albanian insurgents essentially took over as much as a third of the country and some Macedonians joined anti-Albanian vigilante groups. Human rights abuses grew on both sides, in a pattern familiar to the region. The government seemed to be losing the war. In mid-August, after intense negotiations under international auspices, both sides signed an agreement to improve Albanian rights and pledged to preserve a cease-fire.

The rebels said they would disarm and disband in return for an amnesty. And NATO troops, led by Britain, entered Macedonia to disarm the rebels. But NATO governments were insisting that their troops would not stay beyond a limited period, put at 30 days, and would not "make peace," but simply collect the arms the rebels handed over.

Skeptical Macedonians remembered that NATO had made a similar deal with the Albanians fighting in Kosovo, who promised to disarm but failed to do so. The skeptics wondered whether the Albanians in Macedonia were any more sincere, and if not what NATO would do about it.

—Steven Erlanger

The Fall of Slobodan Milosevic

Slobodan Milosevic sat at last in the Hague, awaiting trial on war crimes charges for his part in the 1999 Kosovo war. It was an extraordinary fall for a proud man who once ran Serbia uncontested.

Mr. Milosevic, who considered his battle for Kosovo against NATO's might the act of a patriot, not a war criminal, said he did not recognize the authority of the Hague. But if Mr. Milosevic had not decided to call an early election and put his own job as Yugoslav president up for direct vote, he would probably still be president in Belgrade.

Vojislav Kostunica, a shy constitutional lawyer known for his personal honesty, ran against Mr. Milosevic in the Yugoslav presidential election. A moderate nationalist from the Serbian heartland, Mr. Kostunica was a bridge over which Serbs unhappy with Mr. Milosevic, the loss of Kosovo and international isolation could safely cross into open opposition.

In the first round, on Sept. 24, 2000, Mr. Kostunica and the coalition of opposition parties that supported him claimed he had won just over 50 percent of the vote, making a runoff unnecessary. Mr. Milosevic, however, insisted that Mr. Kostunica had won less than 50 percent.

Mr. Kostunica refused to yield. The anti-Milosevic campaign received millions of dollars of aid from Washington and the European Union. But it was the Serbs themselves, somewhat to their own surprise, who rose up to defend their vote.

In a growing series of demonstrations and strikes, most importantly at a coal mine at Kolubara, they demanded that Mr. Milosevic go. Despite orders, the army and police refused to crack down on the protesters, and Mr. Milosevic resigned on Oct. 6.

The Serbian government, where real power lies, was pressed to call new elections, and on Dec. 23 the opposition coalition, still known as the Democratic Opposition of Serbia, won a large victory. The party leader, Zoran Djindjic, became Serbian prime minister.

The strains between Mr. Djindjic and Mr. Kostunica, who had years earlier quit the Democratic Party to form his own group, increased markedly, especially over the issue of Mr. Milosevic. Both men had vowed not to send Mr. Milosevic to the Hague, but pressure to arrest Mr. Milosevic grew from the United States and from within the Democratic Opposition coalition.

Washington threatened to withhold economic aid if Mr. Milosevic was not arrested by the end of March; on March 30, without telling Mr. Kostunica, Mr. Djindjic and the police moved to arrest Mr. Milosevic, but failed, producing an embarrassing standoff that lasted until the early hours of April 1. Milosevic supporters went to his defense and he threatened to kill himself, sometimes putting a gun to his mouth.

But after promises from Mr. Kostunica and Mr. Djindjic that he would not be shipped to the Hague, Mr. Milosevic surrendered, and was taken to Belgrade's Central Prison. Still, pressure on Belgrade to hand him over to the International Tribunal in the Hague continued to mount, with Washington again threatening to withhold aid and refusing to attend an international donors' conference. Mr. Kostunica, who had pledged to keep Mr. Milosevic from going to the Hague, had to bend.

On June 28, on the eve of the conference, Mr. Djindjic and the Serbian government moved, again without telling Mr. Kostunica. They shipped Mr. Milosevic to the Hague, and Washington duly attended the conference, which pledged some $1.2 billion in aid to Serbia, much of it already committed by the European Union. As one Serbian government adviser said: "Milosevic became too expensive to keep."

Many Serbs were happy to be rid of Milosevic; others were humiliated. But Belgrade basked in Western approval, even as Kosovo continued to remain under international control, its status undetermined. Despite promises of aid, Serbia remains poor, its economy badly lagging and its politicians more interested in business and squabbling than in reform. Many Serbs still consider Mr. Milosevic a hero. But in The Hague, the tribunal prosecutor, Carla del Ponte, said she was also preparing to add his role in the Bosnian war to the indictment against Mr. Milosevic.

—*Steven Erlanger*

Putin Takes Control in Russia

Vladimir V. Putin was just another apparatchik and a KGB lieutenant colonel who joined Russia's democratic revolution as the Soviet Union was falling apart in 1991. Today most Russians are still puzzling over the circumstances that led to his rise when Russia's first democratically elected president, Boris N. Yeltsin, went canvassing among his circle of aides for a successor, and announced his choice on the last day of 2000.

In his memoir, Mr. Yeltsin said that one thing he admired about Mr. Putin was the fierce loyalty he showed when his superiors were under political attack, and that trait could yet prove useful to Mr. Yeltsin if the money laundering and kickback investigations by Swiss authorities should ever threaten him while Mr. Putin is in office.

In other ways, Mr. Putin has moved on from the Yeltsin era, tackling an array of economic and political reform issues—the tax code, customs reform, judicial reform—that were all but neglected during Mr. Yeltsin's time. Putting in long hours, broken by swimming and judo exercises, Mr. Putin has cut a far more robust profile than his predecessor. He is a deft politician who has tamed unruly governors; built an effective majority in parliament, where he bargains with faction leaders, including Communists, an anathema for Mr. Yeltsin.

But also under Mr. Putin, Russia continues to prosecute a relentless military campaign in the rebellious republic of Chechnya, where hundreds of thousands of civilians remain displaced by indiscriminate bombing. At the same time he has broken the political power of Russia's oligarchs, singling out two of the most visible, Vladimir Gusinsky and Boris Berezovsky, for special treatment.

In April, acting on the Kremlin's behalf, the state-controlled gas monopoly, Gazprom, took control of Mr. Gusinsky's media empire, including the country's only independent television network, NTV. Mr. Berezovsky was stripped of his control of ORT, the main state television channel. Both men went into exile, though they are struggling to regain influence. The crackdown on media barons has incited fears that Mr. Putin is rebuilding Soviet-style central authority by setting limits on democratic institutions.

But the most important surprise is that since his election and inauguration in May 2000, Mr. Putin has maintained enviably high approval ratings, even while the Russian economy is only 60 percent of what it was a decade ago, poverty is rampant in the countryside, and population and health are declining.

Internationally, Mr. Putin traveled extensively, playing Russia's weak hand creatively by binding Moscow more closely to Europe and to China, with whom Russia signed a treaty of friendship and military cooperation in July. This has given Mr. Putin leverage with President George W. Bush, whom Mr. Putin met for the first time in June at a summit in Slovenia on critical issues as missile defense, NATO expansion, proliferation of nuclear technologies, and weapons sales to Iran and other so-called rogue states.

—*Patrick E. Tyler*

Indonesia Again Gets a New President

Indonesia got its fourth president in three turbulent years as the legislature flexed its new-found muscles and voted out Abdurrahman Wahid after just 21 months in office. He was replaced by the long-time president-in-waiting, Megawati Sukarnoputri, his vice president.

Fears quickly arose that this conservative politician, the daughter of Indonesia's founder, Sukarno, would begin to roll back the liberal reforms that had begun to flourish since the ousting in 1998 of Mr. Sukarno's successor, Suharto. The great burst of reforms came during the interim presidency of B.J. Habibie, who followed Mr. Suharto.

When Mr. Wahid took office in October 1999, he was seen as the flower of the reform movement, a tolerant, democratic-minded Moslem leader who appointed Indonesia's first civilian defense minister. But Mr. Wahid was not born to be a president. Quirky, impulsive, unfocused, pugnacious, he kept right on, as Indonesia's leader, acting as a gadfly and provocateur.

He liked to pad around the palace barefoot. He often dozed during public ceremonies. Most damaging politically, he refused to cut the deals and make the compromises he needed considering his sliver-thin power base.

The legislature, made up almost entirely of his opponents, went after him. In January 2001, it began a long impeachment process by passing a censure motion based on two corruption charges. The poorly substantiated charges were widely understood to be a pretext and they faded from view.

But the process continued in the next months. Mr. Wahid brushed aside these moves, inflaming his opponents. The face-off came on July 23 when Mr. Wahid issued a pre-dawn decree suspending the legislature and calling for new elections. He already knew the armed forces would not enforce it; indeed, army tanks had surrounded his palace as a warning to him. The military bloc in the legislature joined in the vote later that day to remove him and replace him with Mrs. Megawati.

The new president's style could not be more different than that of Mr. Wahid, who was silent, slow-moving, and more interested in preservation of the status quo than in change. But the problems confronting her were the same, and intractable as ever—a nearly bankrupt economy, a poverty-ridden population, two armed separatist movements. And she was surrounded, just as Mr. Wahid had been, by political enemies already looking ahead to the next election in 2004.

—Seth Mydans

President Estrada Ousted in Philippines

This was the year that "people power" lost its mystique. Fifteen years after its first incarnation, when Filipinos rose up with near-religious democratic fervor to oust Ferdinand E. Marcos from the presidency, "people power" was redefined as a calculated tool of politics.

Its first reincarnation came in response to the failure of the democratic process to remove President Joseph Estrada by impeachment on corruption charges. Huge crowds filled the streets in conscious imitation of the uprising of 1986. The Supreme Court followed with a ruling that Mr. Estrada had lost legitimacy because the people no longer supported him. Then the military stepped in, in what some participants called a "soft coup," to usher Mr. Estrada from office on Jan. 20, 2001.

Filipinos congratulated themselves, saying, "We did it again." They explained their little hop over legal process by saying, in effect, that they had to sidestep democracy in order to save it.

The second replay came on May 1 when Mr. Estrada's supporters stormed Malacanang Palace in an apparent attempt to oust his successor, Gloria Macapagal Arroyo. It was a different crowd, poorer, tougher, more violent.

This time, the military stayed loyal and the uprising was crushed. But Filipinos began to ask themselves what genie they had let out of the bottle in the name of people power. The potency of street protests and the decisive role of the military put Philippine democracy in a new perspective. The message to future presidents: watch your back.

There was a postscript. On July 10, Mr. Estrada was arraigned on a capital charge of plunder for stealing $76 million during his presidency. It was unlikely that he would face execution, but his trial was expected to drag on for years.

—Seth Mydans

Royal Family Massacred in Nepal

On June 1, much of Nepal's royal family was massacred as they gathered to eat dinner at Narayanhity Palace in the capital city, Katmandu. Among the 10 victims to die from bullet wounds were King Birendra, a beloved figure in the tiny Himalayan nation, and his wife, Queen Aishwarya.

The killer, according to an official inquiry panel, was their son Dipendra, the 29-year-old crown prince, whose suicide attempt finally ended the shooting spree and put him in a coma. His motive remains something of a mystery, though palace insiders have said that his parents had prohibited his marriage to the woman he loved.

In the immediate aftermath of the murders, no news of the tragedy was broadcast on state-run television and radio for 15 hours. With information difficult to come by, rumors spread at a wild pace.

Then, in another bizarre episode, Dipendra, while brain dead, was named king on June 2 by an advisory board to the monarchy. While the board members were aware that the prince was the chief suspect in the killings, they decided they had no choice in the matter: the rules of succession could not be bypassed.

At the same time, Birendra's brother, Gyanendra, was named regent, the de facto king. People were reluctant to believe that their popular crown prince could have committed so ghastly a crime. They took to the streets in protest, many of them openly speaking of conspiracy theories that blamed Gyanendra, who had not been in Katmandu on the calamitous night. Curfews had to be imposed to keep the peace.

Before dawn on June 4, Dipendra died. His reign had lasted a mere 40 hours, all of them spent in a coma. Gyanendra was elevated to the throne, which led to rioting and another curfew.

Some measure of normality returned to Nepal, a nation of 23 million located between India and China, only after the inquiry panel released its report on June 14. Investigators concluded that Dipendra was high on whiskey and drugs when he did the shooting.

—Barry Bearak

Assassination of President Kabila Changes Political Focus in Congo

President Laurent Kabila, the once obscure guerilla fighter who deposed the longtime dictator Mobutu Sese Seko in 1997, was assassinated in Kinshasa on Jan. 16, 2001, by a bodyguard who shot him inside his own office.

Mr. Kabila, who was in his mid-60's, is said to have died immediately. But the government acknowledged his death only on Jan. 18, a day after naming his 29-year-old son, Maj. Gen. Joseph Kabila, as the new president.

Months later, the government had still not produced any conclusive report on who killed Mr. Kabila. But there was no shortage of motives. Mr. Kabila, who had promised democracy and stability, brought even greater repression and disorder to Congo. His former patrons, the Rwandans and Ugandans, had backed Congolese rebels since August 1998, while he had gained the support of Zimbabwe and Angola.

Throughout his term, Mr. Kabila seemed more interested in clinging to power. He blocked efforts by United Nations and African officials to start talks that might end the war or diminish his authority. The Angolans were said to have become increasingly frustrated by his obstinacy.

His death produced dramatic diplomatic changes for Congo. It was not clear whose orders he was following, but Joseph Kabila immediately pulled Congo out of its isolation. He visited Washington, which had strained relations with Kinshasa, as well as several capitals in Europe.

At home, he liberalized the currency and diamond markets, and allowed a small degree of political openness. He mended relations with the United Nations force in the Congo. So marked was the contrast with his father that the West, including the new Bush Administration, began taking a harder line against Rwanda and Uganda, long-time favorites of Western institutions like the World Bank. Whether Joseph Kabila was more interested in the good of the Congo than staying in power remained unclear.

—Norimitsu Onishi

Fujimori and Spy Chief Flee Peru

Alberto K. Fujimori's 10-year regime collapsed in a series of scandals, forcing him to flee to Japan and submit his resignation by fax. In his place Alejandro Toledo, Mr. Fujimori's old nemesis, rose to power in July 2001 completing a rags to riches story and heralding a new chapter in Peru's combustible political history.

In between this stunning turn of events, an eight-month transitional government led by interim President Valentin Paniagua, began a process of cleaning up the armed forces and courts as well as shepherding the country through another turbulent political campaign and presidential election in April and May.

Mr. Paniagua's reform efforts were aided by the weekly broadcasting of videotapes captured from Mr. Fujimori's intelligence chief, Vladimiro Montesinos, before he fled Peru in a yacht destined for Ecuador and finally Venezuela. The videotapes showed Mr. Montesinos, a long time collaborator of the C.I.A., handing out bribes and making deals with many of the nation's top military officers, media executives, politicians and businessmen.

The television broadcasts of the tapes provided a turbulent backdrop to two rounds of presidential elections that produced a close finish between Mr. Toledo and former President Alan Garcia. The campaign revolved around Mr. Toledo's personal scandals, including reports he used cocaine and had refused to recognize an illegitimate daughter and past allegations that Mr. Garcia had taken kickbacks as president in the 1980's.

Mr. Toledo, a former shoeshine boy who was educated in the United States, won the narrow victory and held a symbolic inaugural ceremony in the Inca ruins of Machu Picchu in July. As a former official with the World Bank, Mr. Toledo offered a populist vision for the poor but promised to follow fiscal conservatism to protect Peru's creditworthiness. Mr. Garcia said he had matured, and did well enough to catapult himself back in Peruvian politics as a major figure who would now lead the opposition and probably run for president again.

Mr. Montesinos was finally captured in Venezuela with the help of the F.B.I. shortly before Mr. Toledo took power. Investigators found that had amassed more than $250 million in foreign bank accounts. Prosecutors said they hoped to convict him on charges of money-laundering, gun-running, bribing officials and leading a death squad. They hinted that the only way he could avoid a life-sentence was if he gave them information that could lead to the extradition and conviction of Mr. Fujimori.

Mr. Fujimori remained in a luxury apartment in Tokyo through the year, occasionally giving interviews to the local press and appearing at social functions with influential Japanese. The Japanese government stood by Mr. Fujimori, who had been the first ethnic Japanese ever elected as leader of a country other than Japan. His parents had been born in Japan, so Mr. Fujimori was able to claim dual citizenship, which appeared to protect him from extradition. Peruvian prosecutors said that if they could not extradite him, they would press to have him tried in Japan.

—Clifford Krauss

After Seven Decades, Mexico Elects Outsider as President

Breaking 71 years of entrenched rule, Vicente Fox became the first president of Mexico to be elected from the political opposition. His come-from-behind victory on July 2, 2000 —propelled by the nation's fervent hopes for democratic change, and managed by marketing masters — ended the authoritarian dominance of the Institutional Revolutionary Party.

That party, forged at the end of the Mexican Revolution, had been the world's longest-ruling political machine.

And within hours of his inauguration, which followed in December, Mr. Fox promised constituents a modern-day revolution, pledging to lift 40 million Mexicans out of poverty and to wipe out decades of corruption.

Mr. Fox, a son of ranchers, learned about the long reach of poverty in Mexico when, without a college degree, he joined Coca-Cola as a route supervisor in the 1960's, and covered five states in six years. After transferring to Mexico City, he rose through the ranks to become the president of Coca-Cola's Latin America division.

Still, corporate life did not satisfy the strapping Mr. Fox, called the Marlboro Man of Mexico for his rugged appearance and penchant for boots and cowboy hats. After joining the conservative National Action Party, he ran for governor of his home state, Guanajuato, in 1991, and lost, blaming fraud. The loss only ignited his popularity and solidified Mr. Fox's determination to bring down the government party. He was elected governor six years later in a sweeping victory.

At the start of his presidential campaign, Mr. Fox hired marketing wizards and ordered them to sell him like a brand of toothpaste. And in a move that created lingering distrust in his party, the candidate distanced himself from colleagues in the party and won alliances with leaders of diverse political camps.

The divorced father of four adult children, Mr. Fox was inaugurated as Mexico's first single president. A Roman Catholic, he clashed with church leaders when he later married his former spokeswoman, Marta Sahagun.

The marriage briefly revived the political honeymoon between Mr. Fox and the public, which had become unhappy with Mr. Fox's performance. Political differences divided and paralyzed the cabinet. The president's Indian Rights Bill, whose passage was crucial to winning peace with the Zapatista rebels in Chiapas, had been severely weakened by his party's leaders in Congress.

President Fox stirred accusations of political favoritism when he appointed a committee of wealthy businessmen to reform Mexico's most prized government institution, the state run oil company, Pemex. And Mexicans from all classes and education levels protested the president's plan to impose new taxes on food and medicine.

Mr. Fox, who boasts himself a dreamer, did seem to make strides on one of his grandest visions. In his first visit to the United States as president-elect, he capitalized on his status as Mexico's most democratically elected leader to press for agreements on issues that had roiled relations for decades.

He told Washington that he wanted the border to be open to a freer flow of goods and workers. Saying that undocumented Mexican immigrants should not have to live in shadows of shame, Mr. Fox calls them national heroes and asked Washington to acknowledge the value of Mexican labor to the United States economy. And he has campaigned for immigration reforms that would include expanded guest worker programs and a legal status for the three million Mexicans working in the United States.

Mr. Fox has also appealed to immigrants to channel part of the money that they send back to their homeland into projects that would generate jobs, and thereby to help the government stem the flow of migration to the United States. Mexico receives some $8 billion in remittances each year, making immigrants the third largest source of foreign income, behind oil and tourism.

President Fox raised Mexico's international prominence when he became the first official state visitor to Washington under the administration of President George W. Bush, who said the United States had no more important partner than Mexico.

New feelings of trust among law enforcement officials on both sides resulted in the arrest and extradition of several important drug traffickers. And in Washington, Congress took up a measure to exempt Mexico from the annual process of certifying that Mexico is cooperating in the war against drugs, an evaluation that Latin Americans have long resented.

—Ginger Thompson

Chile's Pinochet Avoids Trial

Chile's retired General Augusto Pinochet was arrested and briefly put under house arrest on charges that he was involved in the murders and disappearances of scores of dissidents by a death squad in 1973, but prosecution of the case stalled through 2001 in a thicket of legal procedures and politics.

The former dictator's lawyers found a winning legal tack by arguing that their 85-year-old client was not mentally fit to stand trial, and their appeal gained support among the political establishment and military. Still, the formal charging of the man who ruled Chile with an iron fist from 1973 to 1990 was a watershed in the development of civilian democracy in Chile.

The charges brought against General Pinochet in late 2000 were reduced by a court in March, from the allegation that he was the mastermind of the death squad to his being an accessory who covered up its crimes. After that, the legal battle centered on the defense argument that General Pinochet, who suffers from diabetes and wears a pacemaker, could not properly defend himself because of memory problems caused by a series of minor strokes he suffered while he was under house arrest under a Spanish warrant in Britain in 1999.

When an appeals court in July agreed with the defense argument, there was little protest or celebration since most of Chile wanted to put memories of the 1973-1990 dictatorship into the past. The final outcome was something of a compromise. General Pinochet was not acquitted and his role in political life was finally ended, but he was very likely to escape a humiliating trial, although more legal problems are still possible due to over 200 criminal complaints filed against him.

President Ricardo Lagos, the first Socialist to govern the country since General Pinochet ousted Salvador Allende, did not overtly interfere in the case.

—Clifford Krauss

SCIENCE AND MEDICINE

Bush Endorses Limited Research on Stem Cells

Science and politics collided this year in the debate over whether taxpayers should finance research on human embryonic stem cells. In August, in his first televised address to the nation, President Bush announced that he would permit the government to pay for certain stem cell studies. But, saying he had moral qualms about the work, he imposed strict limits on it.

Stem cells, the human body's primordial master cells, can grow into any cell or tissue in the body. Scientists hope to use them to create replacement body parts for the sick or injured—insulin-producing cells to treat diabetes, for example, or nerve cells that could help victims of spinal cord injuries walk.

But stem cell research leaves many people, including religious conservatives, deeply uneasy, because the cells are extracted from human embryos, which are destroyed by the experiments. Proponents of stem cell studies argue that the embryos, typically left over from in vitro fertilization attempts, would be discarded anyway. But opponents say the work is tantamount to murder.

President Bush was confronted with the stem cell issue as soon as he took office in January. His predecessor, Bill Clinton, had issued a rule that would have allowed federally funded scientists to work on embryonic stem cells so long as the government did not pay for the actual extraction. But Mr. Bush had made a campaign promise not to permit taxpayers to finance any stem cell studies, and his conservative supporters demanded he live up to it.

So Mr. Bush put a hold on the Clinton rule, saying he would review it. Throughout the late spring and early summer, the president's political advisers urged him to reject stem cell research outright. But many of Mr. Bush's fellow Republicans, notably Senator Orrin Hatch of Utah and Senator Bill Frist of Tennessee, came out in favor of the work. And patients, desperate for cures, waged an intense campaign to build public support.

At the same time, the stem cell issue became tangled up with a related one, human cloning. Through a process known as therapeutic cloning, scientists say they could create human embryos that would yield stem cells that are a perfect tissue match for patients. In July, however, the House of Representatives passed a bill that would make any type of cloning, whether for reproduction or research, a crime; Mr. Bush supported that bill.

The following month, on Aug. 9, Mr. Bush issued a delicately-crafted compromise on stem cell research that, he said, would encourage the work but discourage the further destruction of embryos—lines where, in Mr. Bush's words, "the life-and-death decision has already been made." He decided to confine public financing to 64 self-sustaining colonies, or lines, of stem cells that had already been extracted from human embryos—lines where, in Mr. Bush's words, "the life-and-death decision has already been made."

But rather than settle the controversy, Mr. Bush's announcement only inflamed it. Scientists and patients raised questions about the quality of the 64 lines, and the administration eventually acknowledged that only two dozen of them were fully developed and available for research. Congress began hearings to determine whether the policy should be expanded.

—Sheryl Gay Stolberg

The Human Genome Comes Into Focus

The two rival teams of biologists who announced in June 2000 they had decoded the human genome took a second step in February 2001. They published their first interpretations of the genome, both sides agreeing that the DNA in the genome contained instructions for about 30,000 different genes.

The number was surprisingly small, both in relation to the general estimate of 100,000 genes that had long prevailed in the textbooks, and also in comparison with the genes already found in the two smaller animals whose genomes had been decoded in pilot projects. The roundworm has 20,000 genes and the fruitfly 13,000.

One team was an international consortium of academic centers led by the National Institutes of Health, a Washington agency, and the Wellcome Trust, a London-based medical philanthropy. The other team, a last minute entrant in the race, was Celera Genomics of Rockville, Maryland, a company headed by Dr. J. Craig Venter and allied with Applied Biosystems, the principal maker of the instruments used to decode the sequence of units in DNA molecules.

The smaller than expected number of human genes led biologists to surmise that human complexity must be achieved in other ways besides the mere number of genes, such as by a more elaborate interaction between the protein products of the genes.

The human genome is expected to become the infrastructure of the 21st century's medicine because, at least in principle, it should allow scientists to catalog the genes for every working part in the human body, including the variant versions that are the basis of most human disease, and to devise genetic level therapies.

Because of the genome's importance, the consortium's scientists believe it should be made freely available to researchers around the world, and have made their version freely accessible through GenBank, a computer data base run by the National Institutes of Health. Celera charges a subscription for access to its version of the genome.

Since both the consortium's scientists and Celera agreed that 30,000 or so was the correct number of human genes, the two sides, often at loggerheads, seemed to have reached consensus on a major issue. But extent of agreement turned out to be much less than met the eye. In August, scientists at the Genomics Institute of the Novartis Research Foundation in San Diego reported that the two sets of 30,000 genes found by the two teams were not the same but overlapped only partially. The San Diego and other scientists suggested the real number of human genes was at least 40,000.

The swiftly changing estimate of the human gene complement illustrated how far biologists had to go in understanding the most basic feature of the genome.

A distinctive feature to emerge from the first glimpses of the human genome is that much of it consists of what is called repetitive DNA, long stretches where the same sequence of DNA units is repeated over and over. These repeated units are of no functional importance to the human cell, so far as is known, because they do not code for proteins or the control segments that govern the operation of genes. Nonetheless, some 75 percent of the genome consists of this apparently useless DNA.

Many parts of the genome seem to have arisen by a large scale duplication of existing regions, some of them containing large numbers of genes. Chromosome 19, for instance, has sections borrowed from 16 of the other human chromosomes. The genome is packaged into 23 pairs of chromosomes, with one member of every pair being inherited from each parent. The genes in the duplicated sections have changed in the course of evolution but still bear a family resemblance to their originals. This sectional duplication seems to have been a motive force in evolution since the extra genes have been free to evolve and assume new roles in the cell.

The consortium scientists argued in their analysis of the genome that some 200 human genes had somehow been acquired directly from bacteria, since they had no known counterparts in higher animals. But this contention was strongly criticized by other scientists and the consortium did not rush to defend its view.

In May, a complicated dispute erupted between the two teams when the consortium scientists accused Celera of having essentially cribbed both the consortium's data and its method of assembling the analyzed snippets of DNA into a complete sequence. Celera had made no secret of having used the consortium's publicly accessible data to supplement its own, but insisted vigorously that it had used its own method of assembling the two sets of data.

Celera has analyzed the genome of the mouse, and the consortium is following suit, because comparing the human genome with that of another mammal is expected to yield important insights. Both the genes and their control regions are likely to have remained fairly similar in both genomes, whereas the repetitive units in both have been free to diverge because they perform no useful function. By lining the two genomes up, biologists hope to see the important regions of each stand out through the similarity of their DNA sequences.

—Nicholas Wade

Human Family Tree Grows More Complex

New discoveries have given the human family tree more branches and deeper roots.

Paleontologists led by Dr. Meave G. Leakey found a 3.5 million-year-old skull from what they say is an entirely new branch of early human relatives. The new genus and species was named Kenyanthropus platyops, or flat-faced man of Kenya.

Judging by the age and look of the skull, the discoverers said it now seemed that the fossil species commonly known as Lucy, or Australopithecus afarensis, which lived at the same time, was not alone on the African plain. Lucy may not even be a direct human ancestor after all. Several aspects of the new skull seemed to anticipate the look of later hominids.

So scientists found themselves contemplating a family tree, once drawn with a trunk straight and true, that looks more like a tangle of branches of uncertain relationship, false starts and dead ends.

Other fossil hunters, in Ethiopia, found bones and teeth of forest-dwelling creatures who lived as long as 5.8 million years ago, close to the fateful evolutionary split between the lineage leading to modern humans and the one that produced chimpanzees. Molecular studies indicate the divergence occurred 5.5 million to 6.5 million years ago.

Yohannes Haile-Selassie, a doctoral candidate who discovered the bones, said the species, tentatively named Ardipithecus ramidus kadabba, "was phylogenetically close to the common ancestor of chimpanzees and humans."

Of particular importance is the evidence that these early hominids lived in a relatively wet and cool forest. In that case, the crucial development of upright walking, considered a definitive characteristic of hominids, presumably occurred in a wooded habitat and not as an adaptation to life on the treeless savanna, as had been supposed.

—*John Noble Wilford*

U.S. Abandons Global Warming Treaty

In 2001, global warming vaulted from the realm of science and international policy to the hot seat of politics, largely through decisions made by a newly elected president who questioned the climate experts' growing consensus that humans were contributing to the problem.

In March, President Bush abandoned a campaign pledge to cut power plants' releases of carbon dioxide, the main heat-trapping gas, and rejected the Kyoto Protocol, a climate treaty negotiated by the Clinton administration that would, if enacted, require industrial powers to cut emissions.

The decisions bolstered his standing with conservative Republicans but caused Mr. Bush's first significant dip in opinion polls and prompted moderate Republicans and Democrats to criticize his environmental policies sharply.

Mr. Bush's actions came even as evidence mounted that emissions of heat-trapping gases from smokestacks and tailpipes were a significant cause of warming.

In January, the Intergovernmental Panel on Climate Change, a group of hundreds of scientists from around the world, issued its third assessment of the climate issue in 10 years and concluded that the link to human actions was stronger than ever.

In February, other scientists reported that the buildup of greenhouse gases released by smokestacks and vehicles was probably linked to the accelerating melting of the snowcap on Mount Kilimanjaro and glaciers in the Andes.

In April, oceanographers found a firm relationship between the human influence on the atmosphere and a warming of the oceans.

The Bush administration, which remained skeptical, in May asked the National Academy of Sciences for its critique of the intergovernmental body's conclusions. The academy panel strongly endorsed the international panel's main conclusions.

Last July, after four years of debate, almost all of the world's nations, with the United States on the sidelines, agreed to a rulebook for the Kyoto Protocol. But the treaty still faced further hurdles before it could be ratified, mainly because the withdrawal of the United States made its ratification more difficult and its efficacy more questionable.

The United States is the largest emitter of greenhouse gases, responsible for about a fourth of all human emissions. Japan was one of several large industrial countries that agreed to the treaty rules but said that it would be reluctant to approve the treaty without American participation.

Under pressure to rejoin international talks from both Republicans and Democrats in Congress, the Bush administration said it would come up with an alternative to the climate treaty later in the year.

—*Andrew C. Revkin*

A Space Station Falls; Another Rises

Space exploration in 2001 was marked by the rise and fall of two space stations, and a determined tourist linked to both.

After 15 years as a symbol of Russia's proud space program, the massive Mir space station was brought down from the sky in flaming pieces to crash into the Pacific Ocean. Russia, short on money, could no longer afford to support Mir and also contribute a major share to the International Space Station.

Led by the United States, the 16 nations constructing the new station moved to make up for past delays with a flurry of flights that almost monthly added major components to the orbital outpost and filled it with supplies. Missions by American shuttles and Russian rockets added a huge solar-power wing, the Destiny science module, scientific equipment, a robotic arm for outside work and an airlock for space walks to end the preliminary phase of building the $60 billion station.

In the midst of this busy construction period, the new station got a visit from the first space tourist, a California business executive named Dennis Tito. Mr. Tito, a former NASA engineer who made a fortune as a financial consultant, had agreed to pay Russia up to $20 million for a visit to Mir to fulfill his lifelong dream of going into space. Rather than lose this needed money, Russian officials said they would let Mr. Tito visit the new station instead, setting up a heated dispute with NASA and the other partners who said it was too early for civilian visitors.

After intense negotiations, in which Mr. Tito agreed to pay for anything he might break, he was allowed to visit the station for eight days in May with a Russian crew, but restricted in what he could do or touch.

Like the Russians, NASA also found that it was having money problems because of the station. The agency discovered that its share of space station construction costs, capped by Congress at $25 billion, had exceeded the budget by more than $4 billion. NASA officials said the cost overrun could force it to cut staffing and some research functions when the station is completed in 2004.

—*Warren E. Leary*

Doctors Test New Self-Contained Mechanical Heart

Robert Tools, a 59-year-old man with end-stage heart failure, became the first recipient of a self-contained artificial heart at Jewish Hospital in Louisville on July 2.

Fifty days later, Mr. Tools, a former telephone company technical librarian, spoke publicly about his experience with the AbioCor device. He said that it was "not easy" to adjust to the lack of a heartbeat, the constant whirring sound and its weight in his chest. With its energy coil, battery and controller, the AbioCor weighs more than four pounds, more than a healthy heart.

Yet Mr. Tools emphasized his gratitude for the whirring, saying that "As long as I can hear the sound, I know I am here."

On Sept. 13, a 70-year-old retired businessman, Tom Christerson, became the second to receive the AbioCor.

Officials of the device's maker, Abiomed of Danvers, Mass., said they hoped the implant could allow recipients to resume healthy lives. But tests are needed in more people before the AbioCor can gain federal approval for marketing.

The AbioCor differs significantly from the much larger, air-driven Jarvik-7 artificial heart that was tested in the early 1980's. One recipient, William J. Schroeder, lived for 620 days on the Jarvik-7, though for much of the time he was handicapped by a severe stroke from a clot that formed in the device and floated to his brain.

Unlike a normal heart in which the two main chambers, the right and left ventricles, pump blood in unison to the lungs and body, respectively, the AbioCor alternates the pumping. One time it pumps blood that is returned from the rest of the body to become oxygen rich in the lungs. Then the device pumps the oxygenated blood to the body, and continues alternating.

Though the initial phase of the testing was successful, complications like blood clots and infections could arise at any time. Another unknown is how long the AbioCor will last. Eventually, the recipients might choose to have a heart transplant to replace the device.

—*Lawrence K. Altman*

Volunteer Dies in Medical Experiment at Johns Hopkins

Ellen Roche, a healthy 24-year-old woman, died on June 2, a month after she inhaled the chemical hexamethonium as part of a research study at Johns Hopkins University. The chemical had destroyed her lungs.

The death prompted an inquiry by the federal government, which for several days suspended all federally financed research involving human subjects at the university, and raised questions about protections for study volunteers. After its own review, Johns Hopkins, considered one of the nation's top research institutions, said on July 16 that it bore full responsibility for Ms. Roche's death.

The study's principal investigator, Dr. Alkis Togias, wanted to give the chemical to healthy volunteers to investigate a hypothesis on the causes of asthma. But the chemical's safety had never been established. Dr. Togias, an associate professor of clinical immunology, missed published articles indicating that the chemical may be dangerous to inhale. And he had brushed off what, in retrospect, may have been warning signs that the chemical was dangerous. Just before Ms.

Roche inhaled the chemical, another volunteer had developed a persistent cough and shortness of breath. Ms. Roche was the third study subject to inhale the chemical.

In its investigation, the federal Office for Human Research Protections determined that the committees that oversee studies involving human subjects, the institutional review boards, were understaffed and overworked at Hopkins. It said that the review board had erred in not questioning the proposal to give volunteers hexamethonium and for allowing the chemical to be called a "medication" in the consent document signed by the volunteers.

But medical experts were divided on whether the dangers of the inhaled hexamethonium could have been foreseen. Hopkins officials said that while they would improve their process for reviewing medical studies, the chemical's dangers were apparent only with hindsight.

In August, Johns Hopkins came under federal investigation again, for an experiment designed to test how well different levels of repair in Baltimore rental housing worked to reduce lead in the blood of inner-city children.

—*Gina Kolata*

New Cholesterol Guidelines Take Bolder Approach

In May, a federal panel issued new guidelines on cholesterol that make many more Americans candidates for cholesterol-lowering drugs, increasing the number who should be taking those drugs to 36 million, from 13 million under the old guidelines.

The older, 1993 guidelines were much more conservative but were issued in "a different era," said Dr. Michael Lauer, who directs clinical research in cardiology for the Cleveland Clinic Foundation. It was before a series of large studies showed that vigorous cholesterol lowering, with a class of drugs called statins, could prevent heart attacks in people who had never had one but whose cholesterol levels were elevated.

These drugs slash cholesterol levels by blocking a liver enzyme needed to synthesize cholesterol. In August one statin medication, Baycol, was recalled after being linked to 31 deaths, but as a class the statins are considered very safe, with no side effects for most people.

"We didn't even know back in 1993 that all these people need aggressive cholesterol lowering therapy," said Dr. James I. Cleeman, coordinator of the group that issued the guidelines, the National Cholesterol Education Program of the National Heart, Lung, and Blood Institute. "We do know that now," he added.

According to the new guidelines, anyone whose cholesterol levels push their chances of having a heart attack to at least 20 percent should be treated as aggressively as patients who already had a heart attack.

The guidelines do not exclude lowering cholesterol with changes in diet and weight loss. But, medical experts said, most people cannot lose weight and dietary changes have at best fairly minor effects on cholesterol levels. And many people do not follow the diet, doctors said.

"For many people, they can't get on the diet, they can't stick to the diet," Dr. Lauer said. "The medications are very well tolerated and they result in dramatic reductions in cholesterol levels. They should be used."

—*Gina Kolata*

AIDS is Still Spreading, After 20 Years

Twenty years after it was first recognized, AIDS has killed or infected an estimated 58 million people in a pandemic that rivals the worst in history. In June, the United Nations General Assembly held a special session on AIDS, the first ever devoted to a health issue.

H.I.V., the AIDS virus, affects countries and regions in differing patterns. For example, in the United States, an estimated 1 million people have AIDS, have died from it, or are infected with H.I.V. The American epidemic has shifted from one primarily affecting white gay men to one affecting more women and minority groups. About 40,000 new infections have occurred in each of recent years.

In other countries, particularly in Africa, AIDS is primarily spread through heterosexual intercourse, and in some areas AIDS is affecting more women than men. In Africa, the world's worst affected region, about 22 million people have died, an additional 25 million are infected, and 12 million children have been orphaned. Amid the dismal statistics, a few encouraging signs have emerged: countries like Uganda and Senegal that have instituted strong prevention programs have slowed the rate of spread.

A huge worry is Asia, where H.I.V. apparently is quietly spreading in heavily populated countries like India and China. For example, after years of denials, Chinese officials in August admitted the country was facing a serious H.I.V. epidemic affecting an estimated 600,000 people. Many experts believe the figure is much higher and that China faces the potential of a widespread epidemic affecting 20 million people by 2010, largely through transmission of H.I.V. by injecting drug use, tainted blood or medical equipment and prostitution.

The U.N. issued a strong call for prevention and sought $9 billion to fight H.I.V. globally. Though drug companies have lowered the cost of AIDS drugs to impoverished countries, most health officials stressed that only a vaccine will stop the pandemic.

—Lawrence K. Altman

A Fine-Feathered Dinosaur

Paleontologists discovered what they say is the most persuasive evidence so far that feathers predated the origin of birds and that modern birds are descendants of dinosaurs.

Other dinosaur remains with featherlike traces have been unearthed in recent years, but nothing as complete as the 130 million-year-old specimen found by American and Chinese scientists in Liaoning Province of northeastern China. The well-preserved skeleton resembles that of a duck with a reptilian tail, altogether about three feet long. Etched in the rock like a filigree decoration surrounding the skeleton are imprints of downy fibers, tufts and filaments of the primitive feathers.

"This is the specimen we've been waiting for," said Dr. Mark A Norell, a paleontologist at the American Museum of Natural History. It and other recent discoveries of birdlike dinosaurs and dinosaurlike birds encouraged support for the theory of a dinosaur-bird ancestral link. A few dissenters argue that birds evolved from some earlier, yet undiscovered, reptile.

In other research, a paleontologist at Ohio University has done what amounts to some reconstructive surgery on dinosaur faces. Comparing dinosaur skulls and the physiology of their closest living relatives, Dr. Lawrence M. Witmer concluded that scientists have been wrong about the position of the nostrils through which the huge reptiles breathed, smelled, regulated body temperature and generally nosed around the Mesozoic landscape.

The fleshy nostrils, he said, were near the tip of the dinosaur's long snout and near the mouth, not higher up and closer to the eyes, as had been widely thought for more than a century. The research, said Dr. Witmer, shows that in this regard "dinosaurs are like almost all other animals today."

The "nose job" does more than alter ideas about how dinosaurs looked. The position of the nostrils could be important in understanding how dinosaurs found food and detected menacing predators or desirable mates and how they atained such enormous sizes.

—John Noble Wilford

Signs of a Lost Asian Culture Revealed

The end of the cold war opened vast stretches of Central Asia to exploration by the world's archaeologists. One result, announced in May, was what appears to be the discovery of a previously unrecognized ancient civilization that thrived more than 4,000 years ago.

Archaeologists of the former Soviet Union had already uncovered traces of this desert society, long vanished. As early as 2300 B.C. in what is now Turkmenistan, people built large oasis communities with imposing mud-brick buildings and fortifications. They herded sheep and grew grain in irrigated fields. They had bronze axes, fine ceramics, alabaster carvings and jewelry of gold and semiprecious stones.

Soviet archaeologists gave the culture the prosaic name of the Bactria Margiana Archaeology Complex, or BMAC (pronounced BEE-mack), after the ancient Greek names of two regions it encompasses. As the findings became more widely known, all that seemed lacking for this society to meet most definitions of a true ancient civilization was evidence of a writing system.

Dr. Fredrik T. Hiebert of the University of Pennsylvania thinks his new excavations have turned up that evidence: a tiny stone object inscribed with mystifying symbols that look like an early form of writing.

The thumbnail-size object, with at most five characters on it, was found in ancient ruins at Anau, a site in Turkmenistan near the border with Iran. Writing experts agreed that the symbols seemed to be unlike contemporary scripts in Egypt, Mesopotamia, Iran or the Indus River valley.

On closer study, some scholars questioned whether this was truly writing, and others said the inscription resembled Chinese writing, which deepened the mystery. There is no clear evidence for Chinese writing before about 1300 B.C.—1,000 years after the presumed date of the ruins and the stone object. Even more puzzling, the inscription is said to look like a Chinese script not used until 200 B.C. Only more digging is likely to solve the mystery.

—John Noble Wilford

Calendar of the Year

UNDERSTANDING CALENDARS

The day Earth turns at a fairly steady pace about the imaginary line that defines the North and South Poles. This line through the poles is called Earth's *axis*. Each turn about the axis, called a *rotation*, takes slightly less than 24 hours. Since Earth is also traveling around the Sun, however, the time from noon to noon is longer than the time it takes for one rotation—about 3 minutes and 56 seconds longer, or almost exactly 24 hours. The time from noon to noon changes slightly during the year, depending on where Earth is in its path. If you average all the days in a year, the mean time from noon to noon is exactly 24 hours.

The year All the nine planets of the solar system travel in nearly circular paths, called *orbits*, around the Sun. Each trip around the Sun is called a *revolution*. The planets all revolve in the same direction, which can be observed from Earth by noting the position the Sun has among the background stars, which are traditionally grouped into constellations. (Since you can't see the Sun and stars at the same time, you can observe where the Sun rises or sets each day and then note the stars that appear in the same region.) Over the course of a year, the Sun appears to pass through the 12 constellations that make up the zodiac.

Earth's trip around the Sun, reflected in the Sun's trip through the zodiac, takes about 365.25 days. This varies slightly from time to time, so astronomers add or delete a second in some years to keep their records in tune with Earth's motion. (see also "Precession of the equinoxes" below).

Seasons The seasons mark the change in the pattern of daylight over the course of the year. Because the Earth is tilted with respect to its path around the Sun, different parts receive different amounts of sunlight during Earth's annual orbit, the time we know as a year. Between late September (around the 21st) and late March, Earth's Northern Hemisphere is tilted away from the Sun. This period constitutes the fall and winter seasons for the Northern Hemisphere, during which there are fewer than 12 hours of daylight each day. For the rest of the year, spring and summer, the Northern Hemisphere is tilted toward the Sun, and daylight hours constitute more than half of each day. In the Southern Hemisphere, this situation is reversed: spring and summer last from late September to late March, while fall and winter make up the other half of the year.

At the points of transition from long days and short nights to short days and long nights and vice versa, the *equinoxes* occur—the two days of the year when periods of daylight and darkness are equal. The *vernal equinox*, marking the first day of spring, takes place on or around March 21 in the Northern Hemisphere, while the *autumnal equinox*, marking the beginning of fall, is on or around September 21. Officially, summer begins on the day of the longest daytime during the year, about June 21 in the Northern Hemisphere, called the *summer solstice*. The *winter solstice*, about December 21 in the Northern Hemisphere, has the shortest amount of daylight and the longest night of the year. The word *solstice* means "standing still Sun." These two days are so called because the apparent movement of where the Sun rises or sets reaches its extreme positions on the solstices and then reverses direction.

Precession of the equinoxes Ancient Greek astronomers determined that the direction of Earth's axis is constantly, but very slowly, changing in a regular pattern. The kind of change is similar to the way a spinning top slowly leans one way then another as its axis changes direction. This movement of the Earth is caused by several factors, the most dominant being one called *precession*. The precession of the Earth results from its not being a perfect sphere. Earth's diameter is about 27 miles greater from one side of the equator to the other than it is from one pole to the other. (Earth is oblate, or fat around the middle, as a result of its rotation.)

Picture Earth without considering its revolution. Keep Earth's center in the same place mentally, and think about how the axis changes position during precession. Any point on Earth's axis (except the center of the planet) moves in a slow circle as a result of precession. This movement is so slow that it takes 26,000 years for a point to return to its original spot. In the meantime, the axis gradually changes its position in relation to the stars. While what we call the North Star (officially known as Polaris) is currently positioned above the North Pole about one degree off center, over time the axis will shift, so that about A.D. 15,000 the star Vega will be above the North Pole within about four degrees of that axis. By about A.D. 28,000, Polaris will have returned to its present position.

As the precession continues, one of its effects is to change the times of the year that seasons occur. Our calendar is corrected for this; if it were not, the vernal equinox would, over 13,000 years, shift from around March 21 to about September 21, the date at which the autumnal equinox is now. For this reason, the precession of the Earth is generally known as the precession of the equinoxes.

Although the precession of the equinoxes is slow, it can be easily observed. The year of about 365.25 days is the time it takes from one vernal equinox to the next. Because of the precession of the equinoxes, however, the time it takes the Sun to appear in the same position with respect to the

Solar Phenomena: The Seasons, 2002

Solar phenomenon	Month	Day	Hour	Min
Perigee[1]	Jan.	2	14	–
Vernal equinox	Mar.	20	19	16
Summer solstice	June	21	13	24
Apogee[2]	July	6	04	–
Autumnal equinox	Sept.	23	04	5
Winter solstice	Dec.	22	01	14

Note: Shown in Universal time (UT). To convert to local time, see "Timing Planetary Phenomena." 1. Sun closest to the Earth (91.4 million miles). 2. Sun farthest from the Earth (94.5 million miles). **Source:** U.S. Naval Observatory, *Astronomical Phenomena for the Year 2002* (2000)

stars is 20 minutes, 24 seconds longer than the period from one equinox to the next. For this reason, accurate star maps have to specify both the date and the year for which they are intended.

Lunar Calendar

There is some evidence that very early humans (c. 25,000 B.C.) used marks on bone to indicate the passage of time, which they may have measured by the Moon's phases. A calendar for the year can be based upon the Moon's phases, which gives a year of 12 periods from new moon to new moon (hence the word *month*) lasting about 354 days. This is about 11 days shorter than the time it takes Earth to revolve around the Sun. The Chinese, who still use a version of this calendar, resolve the discrepancy by inserting extra months at fixed intervals to bring the lunar and solar years into alignment. The Chinese year is divided into months that are either 29 or 30 days long, since the time from new moon to new moon is approximately 29.5 days. The New Year begins at the first new moon over China between Jan. 21 and Feb. 19, and is celebrated for a four-day period. Each year has both a number and a name. The year 2002, or 4639 in the Chinese era, is the Year of the Horse.

Solar Calendar

The ancient Egyptians were the first people known to have instituted a solar calendar. In actuality, their calendar might be called a stellar calendar, since the year began with the rising of Sirius (the brightest star in the sky) at the same place the Sun rises, which generally happened at the same time the Nile flooded. The Egyptians determined that a year was 365 days, about one-quarter of a day short of the true solar year, so gradually the Egyptian calendar no longer coincided with the seasons. Historical records reveal when the Egyptian calendar and the rising of Sirius coincided, from which astronomers inferred that the Egyptian calendar must have been instituted in either 4241 B.C. or 2773 B.C. The Egyptian calendar had 12 months of 30 days and five days of festival, a system adopted by various early cultures, although some continued to use lunar calendars.

Julian Calendar

In 46 B.C., Julius Caesar realized that various parts of the land controlled by Rome used different calendars, so he asked the astronomer Sosigenes to develop a uniform calendar. Sosigenes proposed that since the year was 365.25 days long (though not exactly), a 365-day calendar be kept with one day added (a leap day) every fourth year. When Caesar introduced the new system, he also added days to the year 46 B.C. to bring the seasons in line with the calendar. With a total of 445 days, 46 B.C. is the longest calendar year on record. A year at that time began in what we call March, and the months were numbered. *September, October, November,* and *December* derive from this system

and mean "seventh," "eighth," "ninth," and "tenth" months respectively.

There was a little further adjustment of the calendar, however, by Augustus Caesar, the first Roman emperor. The name of the fifth month was changed from Quintilis to July to honor Julius Caesar, and Augustus named the sixth month August after himself. So that August would not be shorter than 31-day July, Augustus borrowed a day from February.

Because of the Roman Empire's great sphere of influence, the Julian calendar became the ordinary calendar of Western nations.

Julian Day Count

A year after the Gregorian calendar was first instituted, Joseph Justus Scaliger developed a system of counting days instead of years, which is still used by astronomers. Called the Julian Day Count (after his father Julius Caesar Scaliger), it begins with 1 on Jan. 1, 4713 B.C. On this date, the Julian calendar, the lunar calendar, and the Roman tax system (which had its own calendar) all coincided—something that won't happen again until A.D. 3267. Each day within such a 7,980-year period is numbered.

Gregorian Calendar

From at least A.D. 730, it was known that the solar year—measured from vernal equinox to vernal equinox—was somewhat short of 365.25 days. Each century the solar year gets about half a second shorter. In 1990 the solar year was calculated at 365 days, 5 hours, 48 minutes, and 45.5 seconds long, not 365¼ days, which is what the Julian calendar assumes. Because the date of Easter was slipping, Pope Gregory XIII instituted calendar reform in 1582. He proclaimed that the day following Oct. 4 would be Oct. 15, which dropped 10 days from the year. Furthermore, on the advice of astronomer Christoph Clavius, the new calendar would be kept in line by omitting the leap year in century years unless they were divisible by 400. Thus 1900 was not a leap year in the Gregorian calendar, but 2000 was.

Most Roman Catholic countries and some other Western countries adopted the new system, but England did not. Finally, in 1752, England and its colonies adopted the Gregorian calendar, but they had to drop 11 days to fit common Western practice. It was at this time that New Year's Day in England was moved from Mar. 25 to Jan. 1, changing the number of the year for the almost three months affected. Thus George Washington was born according to the Julian calendar on Feb. 11, 1731, but he came to celebrate his birthday on Feb. 22, 1732 according to the Gregorian calendar.

Because the solar year is shortening, astronomers today keep the Gregorian calendar in line by making a one-second adjustment, as needed, usually on Dec. 31 at midnight, whenever the error's accumulation nears one second.

When Did the Third Millennium Begin?

Did the third millennium begin on January 1, 2000, January 1, 2001, or an entirely different day? The answer depends on how you count your years. If you believe that our calendar began in the year 1, rather than the year 0, then a thousand years did not pass until the end of the year 1000, and the third millennium didn't start until 2001.

But by that logic, the 1990s wouldn't have begun until 1991, and would have included the year 2000. Yet we routinely consider years ending in 0 to be the first year of a decade rather than the last, so why should it be any different for millennia? Also, calendars are an inexact science and plenty of shifting of days, months, and years, have been perpetrated over the years by kings, emperors, and popes. The Jewish calendar counted more than 3,700 years before Western calendars counted their first, while the Chinese celebrated the third millennium more than 1,600 years ago.

Perpetual Calendar, 1775–2050

A perpetual calendar lets you find the day of the week for any date in any year. Since January 1 may fall on any of the seven days of the week, and may be a leap or non-leap year, 14 different calendars are possible. The number next to each year corresponds to one of the 14 calendars. For example, in 1776, calendar 9 (a leap year in which Jan. 1 fell on a Monday) was used; July 4 of that year was a Thursday. Calendar 2 was used in 2001; Calendar 3 will be used in 2002.

Year	No.	Year	No.	Year	No.	Year	No.	Year	No.	Year	No.	Year	No.
1775	1	1815	1	1855	2	1895	3	1935	3	1975	4	2015	5
1776	9	1816	9	1856	10	1896	11	1936	11	1976	12	2016	13
1777	4	1817	4	1857	5	1897	6	1937	6	1977	7	2017	1
1778	5	1818	5	1858	6	1898	7	1938	7	1978	1	2018	2
1779	6	1819	6	1859	7	1899	1	1939	1	1979	2	2019	3
1780	14	1820	14	1860	8	1900	2	1940	9	1980	10	2020	11
1781	2	1821	2	1861	3	1901	3	1941	4	1981	5	2021	6
1782	3	1822	3	1862	4	1902	4	1942	5	1982	6	2022	7
1783	4	1823	4	1863	5	1903	5	1943	6	1983	7	2023	1
1784	12	1824	12	1864	13	1904	13	1944	14	1984	8	2024	9
1785	7	1825	7	1865	1	1905	1	1945	2	1985	3	2025	4
1786	1	1826	1	1866	2	1906	2	1946	3	1986	4	2026	5
1787	2	1827	2	1867	3	1907	3	1947	4	1987	5	2027	6
1788	10	1828	10	1868	11	1908	11	1948	12	1988	13	2028	14
1789	5	1829	5	1869	6	1909	6	1949	7	1989	1	2029	2
1790	6	1830	6	1870	7	1910	7	1950	1	1990	2	2030	3
1791	7	1831	7	1871	1	1911	1	1951	2	1991	3	2031	4
1792	8	1832	8	1872	9	1912	9	1952	10	1992	11	2032	12
1793	3	1833	3	1873	4	1913	4	1953	5	1993	6	2033	7
1794	4	1834	4	1874	5	1914	5	1954	6	1994	7	2034	1
1795	5	1835	5	1875	6	1915	6	1955	7	1995	1	2035	2
1796	13	1836	13	1876	14	1916	14	1956	8	1996	9	2036	10
1797	1	1837	1	1877	2	1917	2	1957	3	1997	4	2037	5
1798	2	1838	2	1878	3	1918	3	1958	4	1998	5	2038	6
1799	3	1839	3	1879	4	1919	4	1959	5	1999	6	2039	7
1800	4	1840	11	1880	12	1920	12	1960	13	2000	14	2040	8
1801	5	1841	6	1881	7	1921	7	1961	1	2001	2	2041	3
1802	6	1842	7	1882	1	1922	1	1962	2	2002	3	2042	4
1803	7	1843	1	1883	2	1923	2	1963	3	2003	4	2043	5
1804	8	1844	9	1884	10	1924	10	1964	11	2004	12	2044	13
1805	3	1845	4	1885	5	1925	5	1965	6	2005	7	2045	1
1806	4	1846	5	1886	6	1926	6	1966	7	2006	1	2046	2
1807	5	1847	6	1887	7	1927	7	1967	1	2007	2	2047	3
1808	13	1848	14	1888	8	1928	8	1968	9	2008	10	2048	11
1809	1	1849	2	1889	3	1929	3	1969	4	2009	5	2049	6
1810	2	1850	3	1890	4	1930	4	1970	5	2010	6	2050	7
1811	3	1851	4	1891	5	1931	5	1971	6	2011	7		
1812	11	1852	12	1892	13	1932	13	1972	14	2012	8		
1813	6	1853	7	1893	1	1933	1	1973	2	2013	3		
1814	7	1854	1	1894	2	1934	2	1974	3	2014	4		

1

```
JANUARY              FEBRUARY             MARCH
S  M  T  W  T  F  S  S  M  T  W  T  F  S  S  M  T  W  T  F  S
 1  2  3  4  5  6  7              1  2  3              1  2  3
 8  9 10 11 12 13 14  4  5  6  7  8  9 10  4  5  6  7  8  9 10
15 16 17 18 19 20 21 11 12 13 14 15 16 17 11 12 13 14 15 16 17
22 23 24 25 26 27 28 18 19 20 21 22 23 24 18 19 20 21 22 23 24
29 30 31             25 26 27 28          25 26 27 28 29 30 31

APRIL                MAY                  JUNE
S  M  T  W  T  F  S  S  M  T  W  T  F  S  S  M  T  W  T  F  S
                  1        1  2  3  4  5              1  2  3
 2  3  4  5  6  7  8  6  7  8  9 10 11 12  4  5  6  7  8  9 10
 9 10 11 12 13 14 15 13 14 15 16 17 18 19 11 12 13 14 15 16 17
16 17 18 19 20 21 22 20 21 22 23 24 25 26 18 19 20 21 22 23 24
23 24 25 26 27 28 29 27 28 29 30 31       25 26 27 28 29 30
30

JULY                 AUGUST               SEPTEMBER
S  M  T  W  T  F  S  S  M  T  W  T  F  S  S  M  T  W  T  F  S
                  1        1  2  3  4  5              1  2
 2  3  4  5  6  7  8  6  7  8  9 10 11 12  3  4  5  6  7  8  9
 9 10 11 12 13 14 15 13 14 15 16 17 18 19 10 11 12 13 14 15 16
16 17 18 19 20 21 22 20 21 22 23 24 25 26 17 18 19 20 21 22 23
23 24 25 26 27 28 29 27 28 29 30 31       24 25 26 27 28 29 30
30 31

OCTOBER              NOVEMBER             DECEMBER
S  M  T  W  T  F  S  S  M  T  W  T  F  S  S  M  T  W  T  F  S
 1  2  3  4  5  6  7              1  2  3              1  2
 8  9 10 11 12 13 14  4  5  6  7  8  9 10  3  4  5  6  7  8  9
15 16 17 18 19 20 21 11 12 13 14 15 16 17 10 11 12 13 14 15 16
22 23 24 25 26 27 28 18 19 20 21 22 23 24 17 18 19 20 21 22 23
29 30 31             25 26 27 28 29 30    24 25 26 27 28 29 30
                                          31
```

2

```
JANUARY              FEBRUARY             MARCH
S  M  T  W  T  F  S  S  M  T  W  T  F  S  S  M  T  W  T  F  S
    1  2  3  4  5  6              1  2  3              1  2  3
 7  8  9 10 11 12 13  4  5  6  7  8  9 10  4  5  6  7  8  9 10
14 15 16 17 18 19 20 11 12 13 14 15 16 17 11 12 13 14 15 16 17
21 22 23 24 25 26 27 18 19 20 21 22 23 24 18 19 20 21 22 23 24
28 29 30 31          25 26 27 28          25 26 27 28 29 30 31

APRIL                MAY                  JUNE
S  M  T  W  T  F  S  S  M  T  W  T  F  S  S  M  T  W  T  F  S
 1  2  3  4  5  6  7        1  2  3  4  5              1  2
 8  9 10 11 12 13 14  6  7  8  9 10 11 12  3  4  5  6  7  8  9
15 16 17 18 19 20 21 13 14 15 16 17 18 19 10 11 12 13 14 15 16
22 23 24 25 26 27 28 20 21 22 23 24 25 26 17 18 19 20 21 22 23
29 30                27 28 29 30 31       24 25 26 27 28 29 30

JULY                 AUGUST               SEPTEMBER
S  M  T  W  T  F  S  S  M  T  W  T  F  S  S  M  T  W  T  F  S
 1  2  3  4  5  6  7           1  2  3  4                    1
 8  9 10 11 12 13 14  5  6  7  8  9 10 11  2  3  4  5  6  7  8
15 16 17 18 19 20 21 12 13 14 15 16 17 18  9 10 11 12 13 14 15
22 23 24 25 26 27 28 19 20 21 22 23 24 25 16 17 18 19 20 21 22
29 30 31             26 27 28 29 30 31    23 24 25 26 27 28 29
                                          30

OCTOBER              NOVEMBER             DECEMBER
S  M  T  W  T  F  S  S  M  T  W  T  F  S  S  M  T  W  T  F  S
    1  2  3  4  5  6              1  2  3                    1
 7  8  9 10 11 12 13  4  5  6  7  8  9 10  2  3  4  5  6  7  8
14 15 16 17 18 19 20 11 12 13 14 15 16 17  9 10 11 12 13 14 15
21 22 23 24 25 26 27 18 19 20 21 22 23 24 16 17 18 19 20 21 22
28 29 30 31          25 26 27 28 29 30    23 24 25 26 27 28 29
                                          30 31
```

3

JANUARY

S	M	T	W	T	F	S
		1	2	3	4	5
6	7	8	9	10	11	12
13	14	15	16	17	18	19
20	21	22	23	24	25	26
27	28	29	30	31		

FEBRUARY

S	M	T	W	T	F	S
					1	2
3	4	5	6	7	8	9
10	11	12	13	14	15	16
17	18	19	20	21	22	23
24	25	26	27	28		

MARCH

S	M	T	W	T	F	S
					1	2
3	4	5	6	7	8	9
10	11	12	13	14	15	16
17	18	19	20	21	22	23
24	25	26	27	28	29	30
31						

APRIL

S	M	T	W	T	F	S
	1	2	3	4	5	6
7	8	9	10	11	12	13
14	15	16	17	18	19	20
21	22	23	24	25	26	27
28	29	30				

MAY

S	M	T	W	T	F	S
			1	2	3	4
5	6	7	8	9	10	11
12	13	14	15	16	17	18
19	20	21	22	23	24	25
26	27	28	29	30	31	

JUNE

S	M	T	W	T	F	S
						1
2	3	4	5	6	7	8
9	10	11	12	13	14	15
16	17	18	19	20	21	22
23	24	25	26	27	28	29
30						

JULY

S	M	T	W	T	F	S
	1	2	3	4	5	6
7	8	9	10	11	12	13
14	15	16	17	18	19	20
21	22	23	24	25	26	27
28	29	30	31			

AUGUST

S	M	T	W	T	F	S
				1	2	3
4	5	6	7	8	9	10
11	12	13	14	15	16	17
18	19	20	21	22	23	24
25	26	27	28	29	30	31

SEPTEMBER

S	M	T	W	T	F	S
1	2	3	4	5	6	7
8	9	10	11	12	13	14
15	16	17	18	19	20	21
22	23	24	25	26	27	28
29	30					

OCTOBER

S	M	T	W	T	F	S
		1	2	3	4	5
6	7	8	9	10	11	12
13	14	15	16	17	18	19
20	21	22	23	24	25	26
27	28	29	30	31		

NOVEMBER

S	M	T	W	T	F	S
					1	2
3	4	5	6	7	8	9
10	11	12	13	14	15	16
17	18	19	20	21	22	23
24	25	26	27	28	29	30

DECEMBER

S	M	T	W	T	F	S
1	2	3	4	5	6	7
8	9	10	11	12	13	14
15	16	17	18	19	20	21
22	23	24	25	26	27	28
29	30	31				

4

JANUARY

S	M	T	W	T	F	S
			1	2	3	4
5	6	7	8	9	10	11
12	13	14	15	16	17	18
19	20	21	22	23	24	25
26	27	28	29	30	31	

FEBRUARY

S	M	T	W	T	F	S
						1
2	3	4	5	6	7	8
9	10	11	12	13	14	15
16	17	18	19	20	21	22
23	24	25	26	27	28	

MARCH

S	M	T	W	T	F	S
						1
2	3	4	5	6	7	8
9	10	11	12	13	14	15
16	17	18	19	20	21	22
23	24	25	26	27	28	29
30	31					

APRIL

S	M	T	W	T	F	S
		1	2	3	4	5
6	7	8	9	10	11	12
13	14	15	16	17	18	19
20	21	22	23	24	25	26
27	28	29	30			

MAY

S	M	T	W	T	F	S
				1	2	3
4	5	6	7	8	9	10
11	12	13	14	15	16	17
18	19	20	21	22	23	24
25	26	27	28	29	30	31

JUNE

S	M	T	W	T	F	S
1	2	3	4	5	6	7
8	9	10	11	12	13	14
15	16	17	18	19	20	21
22	23	24	25	26	27	28
29	30					

JULY

S	M	T	W	T	F	S
		1	2	3	4	5
6	7	8	9	10	11	12
13	14	15	16	17	18	19
20	21	22	23	24	25	26
27	28	29	30	31		

AUGUST

S	M	T	W	T	F	S
					1	2
3	4	5	6	7	8	9
10	11	12	13	14	15	16
17	18	19	20	21	22	23
24	25	26	27	28	29	30
31						

SEPTEMBER

S	M	T	W	T	F	S
	1	2	3	4	5	6
7	8	9	10	11	12	13
14	15	16	17	18	19	20
21	22	23	24	25	26	27
28	29	30				

OCTOBER

S	M	T	W	T	F	S
			1	2	3	4
5	6	7	8	9	10	11
12	13	14	15	16	17	18
19	20	21	22	23	24	25
26	27	28	29	30	31	

NOVEMBER

S	M	T	W	T	F	S
						1
2	3	4	5	6	7	8
9	10	11	12	13	14	15
16	17	18	19	20	21	22
23	24	25	26	27	28	29
30						

DECEMBER

S	M	T	W	T	F	S
	1	2	3	4	5	6
7	8	9	10	11	12	13
14	15	16	17	18	19	20
21	22	23	24	25	26	27
28	29	30	31			

5

JANUARY

S	M	T	W	T	F	S
				1	2	3
4	5	6	7	8	9	10
11	12	13	14	15	16	17
18	19	20	21	22	23	24
25	26	27	28	29	30	31

FEBRUARY

S	M	T	W	T	F	S
1	2	3	4	5	6	7
8	9	10	11	12	13	14
15	16	17	18	19	20	21
22	23	24	25	26	27	28

MARCH

S	M	T	W	T	F	S
1	2	3	4	5	6	7
8	9	10	11	12	13	14
15	16	17	18	19	20	21
22	23	24	25	26	27	28
29	30	31				

APRIL

S	M	T	W	T	F	S
			1	2	3	4
5	6	7	8	9	10	11
12	13	14	15	16	17	18
19	20	21	22	23	24	25
26	27	28	29	30		

MAY

S	M	T	W	T	F	S
					1	2
3	4	5	6	7	8	9
10	11	12	13	14	15	16
17	18	19	20	21	22	23
24	25	26	27	28	29	30
31						

JUNE

S	M	T	W	T	F	S
	1	2	3	4	5	6
7	8	9	10	11	12	13
14	15	16	17	18	19	20
21	22	23	24	25	26	27
28	29	30				

JULY

S	M	T	W	T	F	S
			1	2	3	4
5	6	7	8	9	10	11
12	13	14	15	16	17	18
19	20	21	22	23	24	25
26	27	28	29	30	31	

AUGUST

S	M	T	W	T	F	S
						1
2	3	4	5	6	7	8
9	10	11	12	13	14	15
16	17	18	19	20	21	22
23	24	25	26	27	28	29
30	31					

SEPTEMBER

S	M	T	W	T	F	S
		1	2	3	4	5
6	7	8	9	10	11	12
13	14	15	16	17	18	19
20	21	22	23	24	25	26
27	28	29	30			

OCTOBER

S	M	T	W	T	F	S
				1	2	3
4	5	6	7	8	9	10
11	12	13	14	15	16	17
18	19	20	21	22	23	24
25	26	27	28	29	30	31

NOVEMBER

S	M	T	W	T	F	S
1	2	3	4	5	6	7
8	9	10	11	12	13	14
15	16	17	18	19	20	21
22	23	24	25	26	27	28
29	30					

DECEMBER

S	M	T	W	T	F	S
		1	2	3	4	5
6	7	8	9	10	11	12
13	14	15	16	17	18	19
20	21	22	23	24	25	26
27	28	29	30	31		

6

JANUARY

S	M	T	W	T	F	S
					1	2
3	4	5	6	7	8	9
10	11	12	13	14	15	16
17	18	19	20	21	22	23
24	25	26	27	28	29	30
31						

FEBRUARY

S	M	T	W	T	F	S
	1	2	3	4	5	6
7	8	9	10	11	12	13
14	15	16	17	18	19	20
21	22	23	24	25	26	27
28						

MARCH

S	M	T	W	T	F	S
	1	2	3	4	5	6
7	8	9	10	11	12	13
14	15	16	17	18	19	20
21	22	23	24	25	26	27
28	29	30	31			

APRIL

S	M	T	W	T	F	S
				1	2	3
4	5	6	7	8	9	10
11	12	13	14	15	16	17
18	19	20	21	22	23	24
25	26	27	28	29	30	

MAY

S	M	T	W	T	F	S
						1
2	3	4	5	6	7	8
9	10	11	12	13	14	15
16	17	18	19	20	21	22
23	24	25	26	27	28	29
30	31					

JUNE

S	M	T	W	T	F	S
		1	2	3	4	5
6	7	8	9	10	11	12
13	14	15	16	17	18	19
20	21	22	23	24	25	26
27	28	29	30			

JULY

S	M	T	W	T	F	S
				1	2	3
4	5	6	7	8	9	10
11	12	13	14	15	16	17
18	19	20	21	22	23	24
25	26	27	28	29	30	31

AUGUST

S	M	T	W	T	F	S
1	2	3	4	5	6	7
8	9	10	11	12	13	14
15	16	17	18	19	20	21
22	23	24	25	26	27	28
29	30	31				

SEPTEMBER

S	M	T	W	T	F	S
			1	2	3	4
5	6	7	8	9	10	11
12	13	14	15	16	17	18
19	20	21	22	23	24	25
26	27	28	29	30		

OCTOBER

S	M	T	W	T	F	S
					1	2
3	4	5	6	7	8	9
10	11	12	13	14	15	16
17	18	19	20	21	22	23
24	25	26	27	28	29	30
31						

NOVEMBER

S	M	T	W	T	F	S
	1	2	3	4	5	6
7	8	9	10	11	12	13
14	15	16	17	18	19	20
21	22	23	24	25	26	27
28	29	30				

DECEMBER

S	M	T	W	T	F	S
			1	2	3	4
5	6	7	8	9	10	11
12	13	14	15	16	17	18
19	20	21	22	23	24	25
26	27	28	29	30	31	

7

JANUARY

S	M	T	W	T	F	S
						1
2	3	4	5	6	7	8
9	10	11	12	13	14	15
16	17	18	19	20	21	22
23	24	25	26	27	28	29
30	31					

FEBRUARY

S	M	T	W	T	F	S
		1	2	3	4	5
6	7	8	9	10	11	12
13	14	15	16	17	18	19
20	21	22	23	24	25	26
27	28					

MARCH

S	M	T	W	T	F	S
		1	2	3	4	5
6	7	8	9	10	11	12
13	14	15	16	17	18	19
20	21	22	23	24	25	26
27	28	29	30	31		

APRIL

S	M	T	W	T	F	S
					1	2
3	4	5	6	7	8	9
10	11	12	13	14	15	16
17	18	19	20	21	22	23
24	25	26	27	28	29	30

MAY

S	M	T	W	T	F	S
1	2	3	4	5	6	7
8	9	10	11	12	13	14
15	16	17	18	19	20	21
22	23	24	25	26	27	28
29	30	31				

JUNE

S	M	T	W	T	F	S
			1	2	3	4
5	6	7	8	9	10	11
12	13	14	15	16	17	18
19	20	21	22	23	24	25
26	27	28	29	30		

JULY

S	M	T	W	T	F	S
					1	2
3	4	5	6	7	8	9
10	11	12	13	14	15	16
17	18	19	20	21	22	23
24	25	26	27	28	29	30
31						

AUGUST

S	M	T	W	T	F	S
	1	2	3	4	5	6
7	8	9	10	11	12	13
14	15	16	17	18	19	20
21	22	23	24	25	26	27
28	29	30	31			

SEPTEMBER

S	M	T	W	T	F	S
				1	2	3
4	5	6	7	8	9	10
11	12	13	14	15	16	17
18	19	20	21	22	23	24
25	26	27	28	29	30	

OCTOBER

S	M	T	W	T	F	S
						1
2	3	4	5	6	7	8
9	10	11	12	13	14	15
16	17	18	19	20	21	22
23	24	25	26	27	28	29
30	31					

NOVEMBER

S	M	T	W	T	F	S
		1	2	3	4	5
6	7	8	9	10	11	12
13	14	15	16	17	18	19
20	21	22	23	24	25	26
27	28	29	30			

DECEMBER

S	M	T	W	T	F	S
				1	2	3
4	5	6	7	8	9	10
11	12	13	14	15	16	17
18	19	20	21	22	23	24
25	26	27	28	29	30	31

8

JANUARY

S	M	T	W	T	F	S
1	2	3	4	5	6	7
8	9	10	11	12	13	14
15	16	17	18	19	20	21
22	23	24	25	26	27	28
29	30	31				

FEBRUARY

S	M	T	W	T	F	S
			1	2	3	4
5	6	7	8	9	10	11
12	13	14	15	16	17	18
19	20	21	22	23	24	25
26	27	28	29			

MARCH

S	M	T	W	T	F	S
				1	2	3
4	5	6	7	8	9	10
11	12	13	14	15	16	17
18	19	20	21	22	23	24
25	26	27	28	29	30	31

APRIL

S	M	T	W	T	F	S
1	2	3	4	5	6	7
8	9	10	11	12	13	14
15	16	17	18	19	20	21
22	23	24	25	26	27	28
29	30					

MAY

S	M	T	W	T	F	S
		1	2	3	4	5
6	7	8	9	10	11	12
13	14	15	16	17	18	19
20	21	22	23	24	25	26
27	28	29	30	31		

JUNE

S	M	T	W	T	F	S
					1	2
3	4	5	6	7	8	9
10	11	12	13	14	15	16
17	18	19	20	21	22	23
24	25	26	27	28	29	30

JULY

S	M	T	W	T	F	S
1	2	3	4	5	6	7
8	9	10	11	12	13	14
15	16	17	18	19	20	21
22	23	24	25	26	27	28
29	30	31				

AUGUST

S	M	T	W	T	F	S
			1	2	3	4
5	6	7	8	9	10	11
12	13	14	15	16	17	18
19	20	21	22	23	24	25
26	27	28	29	30	31	

SEPTEMBER

S	M	T	W	T	F	S
						1
2	3	4	5	6	7	8
9	10	11	12	13	14	15
16	17	18	19	20	21	22
23	24	25	26	27	28	29
30						

OCTOBER

S	M	T	W	T	F	S
	1	2	3	4	5	6
7	8	9	10	11	12	13
14	15	16	17	18	19	20
21	22	23	24	25	26	27
28	29	30	31			

NOVEMBER

S	M	T	W	T	F	S
				1	2	3
4	5	6	7	8	9	10
11	12	13	14	15	16	17
18	19	20	21	22	23	24
25	26	27	28	29	30	

DECEMBER

S	M	T	W	T	F	S
						1
2	3	4	5	6	7	8
9	10	11	12	13	14	15
16	17	18	19	20	21	22
23	24	25	26	27	28	29
30	31					

9

JANUARY
S	M	T	W	T	F	S
			1	2	3	4
7	8	9	10	11	12	13
14	15	16	17	18	19	20
21	22	23	24	25	26	27
28	29	30	31			

FEBRUARY
S	M	T	W	T	F	S
				1	2	3
4	5	6	7	8	9	10
11	12	13	14	15	16	17
18	19	20	21	22	23	24
25	26	27	28	29		

MARCH
S	M	T	W	T	F	S
				1	2	3
3	4	5	6	7	8	9
10	11	12	13	14	15	16
17	18	19	20	21	22	23
24	25	26	27	28	29	30
31						

APRIL
S	M	T	W	T	F	S
	1	2	3	4	5	6
7	8	9	10	11	12	13
14	15	16	17	18	19	20
21	22	23	24	25	26	27
28	29	30				

MAY
S	M	T	W	T	F	S
			1	2	3	4
5	6	7	8	9	10	11
12	13	14	15	16	17	18
19	20	21	22	23	24	25
26	27	28	29	30	31	

JUNE
S	M	T	W	T	F	S
						1
2	3	4	5	6	7	8
9	10	11	12	13	14	15
16	17	18	19	20	21	22
23	24	25	26	27	28	29
30						

JULY
S	M	T	W	T	F	S
	1	2	3	4	5	6
7	8	9	10	11	12	13
14	15	16	17	18	19	20
21	22	23	24	25	26	27
28	29	30	31			

AUGUST
S	M	T	W	T	F	S
				1	2	3
4	5	6	7	8	9	10
11	12	13	14	15	16	17
18	19	20	21	22	23	24
25	26	27	28	29	30	31

SEPTEMBER
S	M	T	W	T	F	S
1	2	3	4	5	6	7
8	9	10	11	12	13	14
15	16	17	18	19	20	21
22	23	24	25	26	27	28
29	30					

OCTOBER
S	M	T	W	T	F	S
		1	2	3	4	5
6	7	8	9	10	11	12
13	14	15	16	17	18	19
20	21	22	23	24	25	26
27	28	29	30	31		

NOVEMBER
S	M	T	W	T	F	S
					1	2
3	4	5	6	7	8	9
10	11	12	13	14	15	16
17	18	19	20	21	22	23
24	25	26	27	28	29	30

DECEMBER
S	M	T	W	T	F	S
1	2	3	4	5	6	7
8	9	10	11	12	13	14
15	16	17	18	19	20	21
22	23	24	25	26	27	28
29	30	31				

10

JANUARY
S	M	T	W	T	F	S
6	7	1	2	3	4	5
6	7	8	9	10	11	12
13	14	15	16	17	18	19
20	21	22	23	24	25	26
27	28	29	30	31		

FEBRUARY
S	M	T	W	T	F	S
					1	2
3	4	5	6	7	8	9
10	11	12	13	14	15	16
17	18	19	20	21	22	23
24	25	26	27	28		

MARCH
S	M	T	W	T	F	S
					1	2
3	4	5	6	7	8	9
10	11	12	13	14	15	16
17	18	19	20	21	22	23
24	25	26	27	28	29	30
31						

APRIL
S	M	T	W	T	F	S
	1	2	3	4	5	6
7	8	9	10	11	12	13
14	15	16	17	18	19	20
21	22	23	24	25	26	27
28	29	30				

MAY
S	M	T	W	T	F	S
			1	2	3	
4	5	6	7	8	9	10
11	12	13	14	15	16	17
18	19	20	21	22	23	24
25	26	27	28	29	30	31

JUNE
S	M	T	W	T	F	S
1	2	3	4	5	6	7
8	9	10	11	12	13	14
15	16	17	18	19	20	21
22	23	24	25	26	27	28
29	30					

JULY
S	M	T	W	T	F	S
		1	2	3	4	5
6	7	8	9	10	11	12
13	14	15	16	17	18	19
20	21	22	23	24	25	26
27	28	29	30	31		

AUGUST
S	M	T	W	T	F	S
					1	2
3	4	5	6	7	8	9
10	11	12-13	14	15	16	
17	18	19	20	21	22	23
24	25	26	27	28	29	30
31						

SEPTEMBER
S	M	T	W	T	F	S
	1	2	3	4	5	6
7	8	9	10	11	12	13
14	15	16	17	18	19	20
21	22	23	24	25	26	27
28	29	30				

OCTOBER
S	M	T	W	T	F	S
			1	2	3	4
5	6	7	8	9	10	11
12	13	14	15	16	17	18
19	20	21	22	23	24	25
26	27	28	29	30	31	

NOVEMBER
S	M	T	W	T	F	S
						1
2	3	4	5	6	7	8
9	10	11	12	13	14	15
16	17	18	19	20	21	22
23	24	25	26	27	28	29
30						

DECEMBER
S	M	T	W	T	F	S
	1	2	3	4	5	6
7	8	9	10	11	12	13
14	15	16	17	18	19	20
21	22	23	24	25	26	27
28	29	30	31			

11

JANUARY
S	M	T	W	T	F	S
			1	2	3	4
5	6	7	8	9	10	11
12	13	14	15	16	17	18
19	20	21	22	23	24	25
26	27	28	29	30	31	

FEBRUARY
S	M	T	W	T	F	S
						1
2	3	4	5	6	7	8
9	10	11	12	13	14	15
16	17	18	19	20	21	22
23	24	25	26	27	28	29

MARCH
S	M	T	W	T	F	S
1	2	3	4	5	6	7
8	9	10	11	12	13	14
15	16	17	18	19	20	21
22	23	24	25	26	27	28
29	30	31				

APRIL
S	M	T	W	T	F	S
			1	2	3	4
5	6	7	8	9	10	11
12	13	14	15	16	17	18
19	20	21	22	23	24	25
26	27	28	29	30		

MAY
S	M	T	W	T	F	S
					1	2
3	4	5	6	7	8	9
10	11	12	13	14	15	16
17	18	19	20	21	22	23
24	25	26	27	28	29	30
31						

JUNE
S	M	T	W	T	F	S
	1	2	3	4	5	6
7	8	9	10	11	12	13
14	15	16	17	18	19	20
21	22	23	24	25	26	27
28	29	30				

JULY
S	M	T	W	T	F	S
			1	2	3	4
5	6	7	8	9	10	11
12	13	14	15	16	17	18
19	20	21	22	23	24	25
26	27	28	29	30	31	

AUGUST
S	M	T	W	T	F	S
						1
2	3	4	5	6	7	8
9	10	11	12	13	14	15
16	17	18	19	20	21	22
23	24	25	26	27	28	29
30	31					

SEPTEMBER
S	M	T	W	T	F	S
		1	2	3	4	5
6	7	8	9	10	11	12
13	14	15	16	17	18	19
20	21	22	23	24	25	26
27	28	29	30			

OCTOBER
S	M	T	W	T	F	S
				1	2	3
4	5	6	7	8	9	10
11	12	13	14	15	16	17
18	19	20	21	22	23	24
25	26	27	28	29	30	31

NOVEMBER
S	M	T	W	T	F	S
1	2	3	4	5	6	7
8	9	10	11	12	13	14
15	16	17	18	19	20	21
22	23	24	25	26	27	28
29	30					

DECEMBER
S	M	T	W	T	F	S
		1	2	3	4	5
6	7	8	9	10	11	12
13	14	15	16	17	18	19
20	21	22	23	24	25	26
27	28	29	30	31		

12

JANUARY
S	M	T	W	T	F	S
			1	2	3	
4	5	6	7	8	9	10
11	12	13	14	15	16	17
18	19	20	21	22	23	24
25	26	27	28	29	30	31

FEBRUARY
S	M	T	W	T	F	S
1	2	3	4	5	6	7
8	9	10	11	12	13	14
15	16	17	18	19	20	21
22	23	24	25	26	27	28
29						

MARCH
S	M	T	W	T	F	S
	1	2	3	4	5	6
7	8	9	10	11	12	13
14	15	16	17	18	19	20
21	22	23	24	25	26	27
28	29	30	31			

APRIL
S	M	T	W	T	F	S
				1	2	3
4	5	6	7	8	9	10
11	12	13	14	15	16	17
18	19	20	21	22	23	24
25	26	27	28	29	30	

MAY
S	M	T	W	T	F	S
						1
2	3	4	5	6	7	8
9	10	11	12	13	14	15
16	17	18	19	20	21	22
23	24	25	26	27	28	29
30	31					

JUNE
S	M	T	W	T	F	S
		1	2	3	4	5
6	7	8	9	10	11	12
13	14	15	16	17	18	19
20	21	22	23	24	25	26
27	28	29	30			

JULY
S	M	T	W	T	F	S
				1	2	3
4	5	6	7	8	9	10
11	12	13	14	15	16	17
18	19	20	21	22	23	24
25	26	27	28	29	30	31

AUGUST
S	M	T	W	T	F	S
1	2	3	4	5	6	7
8	9	10	11	12	13	14
15	16	17	18	19	20	21
22	23	24	25	26	27	28
29	30	31				

SEPTEMBER
S	M	T	W	T	F	S
			1	2	3	4
5	6	7	8	9	10	11
12	13	14	15	16	17	18
19	20	21	22	23	24	25
26	27	28	29	30		

OCTOBER
S	M	T	W	T	F	S
					1	2
3	4	5	6	7	8	9
10	11	12	13	14	15	16
17	18	19	20	21	22	23
24	25	26	27	28	29	30
31						

NOVEMBER
S	M	T	W	T	F	S
	1	2	3	4	5	6
7	8	9	10	11	12	13
14	15	16	17	18	19	20
21	22	23	24	25	26	27
28	29	30				

DECEMBER
S	M	T	W	T	F	S
			1	2	3	4
5	6	7	8	9	10	11
12	13	14	15	16	17	18
19	20	21	22	23	24	25
26	27	28	29	30	31	

13

JANUARY
S	M	T	W	T	F	S
					1	2
3	4	5	6	7	8	9
10	11	12	13	14	15	16
17	18	19	20	21	22	23
24	25	26	27	28	29	30
31						

FEBRUARY
S	M	T	W	T	F	S
	1	2	3	4	5	6
7	8	9	10	11	12	13
14	15	16	17	18	19	20
21	22	23	24	25	26	27
28	29					

MARCH
S	M	T	W	T	F	S
		1	2	3	4	5
6	7	8	9	10	11	12
13	14	15	16	17	18	19
20	21	22	23	24	25	26
27	28	29	30	31		

APRIL
S	M	T	W	T	F	S
					1	2
3	4	5	6	7	8	9
10	11	12	13	14	15	16
17	18	19	20	21	22	23
24	25	26	27	28	29	30

MAY
S	M	T	W	T	F	S
1	2	3	4	5	6	7
8	9	10	11	12	13	14
15	16	17	18	19	20	21
22	23	24	25	26	27	28
29	30	31				

JUNE
S	M	T	W	T	F	S
			1	2	3	4
5	6	7	8	9	10	11
12	13	14	15	16	17	18
19	20	21	22	23	24	25
26	27	28	29	30		

JULY
S	M	T	W	T	F	S
					1	2
3	4	5	6	7	8	9
10	11	12	13	14	15	16
17	18	19	20	21	22	23
24	25	26	27	28	29	30
31						

AUGUST
S	M	T	W	T	F	S
	1	2	3	4	5	6
7	8	9	10	11	12	13
14	15	16	17	18	19	20
21	22	23	24	25	26	27
28	29	30	31			

SEPTEMBER
S	M	T	W	T	F	S
				1	2	3
4	5	6	7	8	9	10
11	12	13	14	15	16	17
18	19	20	21	22	23	24
25	26	27	28	29	30	

OCTOBER
S	M	T	W	T	F	S
						1
2	3	4	5	6	7	8
9	10	11	12	13	14	15
16	17	18	19	20	21	22
23	24	25	26	27	28	29
30	31					

NOVEMBER
S	M	T	W	T	F	S
		1	2	3	4	5
6	7	8	9	10	11	12
13	14	15	16	17	18	19
20	21	22	23	24	25	26
27	28	29	30			

DECEMBER
S	M	T	W	T	F	S
				1	2	3
4	5	6	7	8	9	10
11	12	13	14	15	16	17
18	19	20	21	22	23	24
25	26	27	28	29	30	31

14

JANUARY
S	M	T	W	T	F	S
						1
2	3	4	5	6	7	8
9	10	11	12	13	14	15
16	17	18	19	20	21	22
23	24	25	26	27	28	29
30	31					

FEBRUARY
S	M	T	W	T	F	S
		1	2	3	4	5
6	7	8	9	10	11	12
13	14	15	16	17	18	19
20	21	22	23	24	25	26
27	28					

MARCH
S	M	T	W	T	F	S
		1	2	3	4	5
6	7	8	9	10	11	12
13	14	15	16	17	18	19
20	21	22	23	24	25	26
27	28	29	30	31		

APRIL
S	M	T	W	T	F	S
					1	2
3	4	5	6	7	8	9
10	11	12	13	14	15	16
17	18	19	20	21	22	23
24	25	26	27	28	29	30

MAY
S	M	T	W	T	F	S
1	2	3	4	5	6	7
8	9	10	11	12	13	14
15	16	17	18	19	20	21
22	23	24	25	26	27	28
29	30	31				

JUNE
S	M	T	W	T	F	S
			1	2	3	4
5	6	7	8	9	10	11
12	13	14	15	16	17	18
19	20	21	22	23	24	25
26	27	28	29	30		

JULY
S	M	T	W	T	F	S
					1	2
3	4	5	6	7	8	9
10	11	12	13	14	15	16
17	18	19	20	21	22	23
24	25	26	27	28	29	30
31						

AUGUST
S	M	T	W	T	F	S
	1	2	3	4	5	6
7	8	9	10	11	12	13
14	15	16	17	18	19	20
21	22	23	24	25	26	27
28	29	30	31			

SEPTEMBER
S	M	T	W	T	F	S
				1	2	3
4	5	6	7	8	9	10
11	12	13	14	15	16	17
18	19	20	21	22	23	24
25	26	27	28	29	30	

OCTOBER
S	M	T	W	T	F	S
						1
2	3	4	5	6	7	8
9	10	11	12	13	14	15
16	17	18	19	20	21	22
23	24	25	26	27	28	29
30	31					

NOVEMBER
S	M	T	W	T	F	S
		1	2	3	4	5
6	7	8	9	10	11	12
13	14	15	16	17	18	19
20	21	22	23	24	25	26
27	28	29	30			

DECEMBER
S	M	T	W	T	F	S
				1	2	3
4	5	6	7	8	9	10
11	12	13	14	15	16	17
18	19	20	21	22	23	24
25	26	27	28	29	30	31

HOLIDAYS AND HOLY DAYS

▶ FEDERAL HOLIDAYS IN THE U.S.

Congress and the president have designated 10 days as federal holidays. Although these are so widely observed as to be considered "national" holidays, they technically apply only to federal employees and the District of Columbia. It is up to the individual states to designate their own holidays. When a federal holiday falls on a Saturday or a Sunday, it is observed on the preceding Friday or the following Monday.

New Year's Day (January 1)   The observance of the New Year dates back to pre-Christian times when rites were performed to ensure the return of spring.

Martin Luther King, Jr., Day (Third Monday in January)   Before his assassination in 1968, Martin Luther King, Jr., was the foremost civil rights leader of the 1950s and 1960s, and in 1964 he won the Nobel Peace Prize. In 1983, Congress set aside this day to celebrate his life and accomplishments.

Washington's Birthday (Third Monday in February)   Originally celebrated on the actual birthday of America's first president (February 22), this holiday was officially moved in 1971 to the third Monday in February to create a three-day weekend. It is sometimes known as Presidents' Day, because the birthday of Abraham Lincoln (Feb. 12) is so close.

Memorial Day (Last Monday in May)   Memorial Day (also known as Decoration Day) honors soldiers fallen in battle. Dating from the Civil War, it is traditionally marked with parades and memorial services.

Independence Day (Fourth of July)   The most important U.S. holiday, Independence Day commemorates the signing of the Declaration of Independence on July 4, 1776, an event that marked America's birth as a free nation. The holiday was first observed in 1777 and is celebrated with fireworks, parades, and oratory.

Labor Day (First Monday in September)   The idea of Peter J. McGuire, president of the United Brotherhood of Carpenters and Joiners of America, the official observance of a day celebrating the American worker was signed into law on June 28, 1894.

Columbus Day (Second Monday in October)   On Oct. 12, 1492, Christopher Columbus and his crew landed in the Bahama Islands after sailing across the Atlantic. First celebrated in 1792, Columbus Day was not officially recognized until 1909. Its observance is of special national pride to Italian-Americans who claim the Genoese Columbus for their own.

Veterans' Day (Nov. 11)   Armistice Day, which marked the end of World War I on Nov. 11, 1918, was made a legal holiday in 1938. The name was changed to Veterans' Day in 1954 to honor all of America's veterans.

Thanksgiving (Fourth Thursday in November)   Thanksgiving Day was first observed in Plymouth Colony (Massachusetts) in 1621, the year in which the Pilgrims landed in the New World and gave thanks for their first harvest and for the new land they had colonized. President Lincoln proclaimed Thanksgiving a national holiday in 1863.

Christmas is celebrated December 25.   (See also "Christian Holy Days.")

▶ U.S. MINOR HOLIDAYS AND OCCASIONS

April Fool's Day (April 1)   A day for practical jokes, the origins of April Fool's Day are obscure, but it bears some resemblance to an ancient Roman festival honoring the goddess of nature.

Arbor Day (Last Friday in April)   Dedicated to trees and their preservation. Its observance is meant to encourage preservation of the environment. Internationally it is observed on December 22.

Armed Forces Day (Third Saturday in May)   A day to honor of the members of the United States Armed Forces.

Citizenship Day (September 17)   First observed by presidential proclamation in 1952, Citizenship Day falls on the same day as the old Constitution Day, which it replaces, but the name of which is still in use.

Daylight Saving Time   The idea of moving clocks ahead one hour to capture more daylight on summer evenings dates back to colonial times—Benjamin Franklin first suggested it in a 1784 essay—but it did not become a nationwide practice until the Uniform Time Act of 1966 (effective April of 1967). During World War I, World War II, and the energy crisis of 1973–74, the U.S. adopted daylight saving time all year round to save money on fuel. Daylight saving time is not observed in Hawaii, the Eastern time zone portion of Indiana, most of Arizona (except on the Navajo Indian Reservation) or in the territories of American Samoa, Guam, Puerto Rico, and the Virgin Islands. By law, daylight saving time begins at 2 A.M. on the first Sunday in April and ends at 2 A.M. on the last Sunday in October, when clocks are turned back one hour. Remember to "Spring ahead, Fall back."

Election Day (Tuesday after first Monday in November)   In years evenly divisible by four, presidential elections are held; in years evenly divisible by two, elections for all members of the House of Representatives and for one-third of the members of the Senate are held.

Father's Day (Third Sunday in June)   Father's Day was first observed in West Virginia in 1908, but it was not until 1972 that the president signed a Congressional resolution designating its official observance. Father's Day is a uniquely American institution.

Flag Day (June 14)   The first observance of Flag Day was in 1877, the centenary of the adoption of the Flag Resolution, which adopted the design of the American flag flown today. President Truman signed the Flag Day Bill in 1949.

Important Dates in the U.S. and Canada, 2001–06

Event	2001	2002	2003	2004	2005	2006
New Year's Day[2]	Jan. 1	Jan. 1	Jan. 1	Jan. 1	Jan. 1	Jan. 1
Martin Luther King Day[2]	Jan. 15	Jan. 21	Jan. 20	Jan. 19	Jan. 17	Jan. 16
Groundhog Day	Feb. 2	Feb. 2	Feb. 2	Feb. 2	Feb. 2	Feb. 2
St. Valentine's Day	Feb. 14	Feb. 14	Feb. 14	Feb. 14	Feb. 14	Feb. 14
Susan B. Anthony Day	Feb. 15	Feb. 15	Feb. 15	Feb. 15	Feb. 15	Feb. 15
Washington's Birthday[2]	Feb. 19	Feb. 18	Feb. 17	Feb. 16	Feb. 21	Feb. 20
Mardi Gras	Feb. 27	Feb. 12	Mar. 4	Feb. 24	Feb. 9	Feb. 28
St. Patrick's Day	Mar. 17	Mar. 17	Mar. 17	Mar. 17	Mar. 17	Mar. 17
April Fool's Day	Apr. 1	Apr. 1	Apr. 1	Apr. 1	Apr. 1	Apr. 1
Daylight Saving begins	Apr. 1	Apr. 7	Apr. 6	Apr. 4	Apr. 3	Apr. 2
Arbor Day	Apr. 27	Apr. 26	Apr. 25	Apr. 30	Apr. 29	Apr. 28
National Teacher Day	May 8	May 7	May 6	May 4	May 3	May 2
Mother's Day[2]	May 13	May 12	May 11	May 9	May 8	May 14
Armed Forces Day	May 19	May 18	May 17	May 15	May 21	May 20
Victoria Day[3]	May 21	May 20	May 19	May 24	May 23	May 22
National Maritime Day	May 22	May 22	May 22	May 22	May 22	May 22
Memorial Day[2]	May 28	May 27	May 26	May 31	May 30	May 29
Flag Day	June 14	June 14	June 14	June 14	June 14	June 14
Father's Day	June 17	June 16	June 15	June 20	June 19	June 18
Canada Day[3]	July 1	July 1	July 1	July 1	July 1	July 1
Independence Day[2]	July 4	July 4	July 4	July 4	July 4	July 4
Labor Day[2,3]	Sept. 3	Sept. 2	Sept. 1	Sept. 6	Sept. 5	Sept. 4
Citizenship Day	Sept. 17	Sept. 17	Sept. 17	Sept. 17	Sept. 17	Sept. 17
Columbus Day[2]	Oct. 8	Oct. 14	Oct. 13	Oct. 11	Oct. 10	Oct. 9
Thanksgiving Day[3] (Can.)	Oct. 8	Oct. 14	Oct. 13	Oct. 11	Oct. 10	Oct. 9
United Nations Day	Oct. 24	Oct. 24	Oct. 24	Oct. 24	Oct. 24	Oct. 24
Daylight Saving ends	Oct. 28	Oct. 27	Oct. 26	Oct. 31	Oct. 30	Oct. 29
Halloween	Oct. 31	Oct. 31	Oct. 31	Oct. 31	Oct. 31	Oct. 31
Election Day (U.S.)	Nov. 6	Nov. 5	Nov. 4	Nov. 2	Nov. 8	Nov. 7
Veterans'(Armistice) Day[2]	Nov. 11	Nov. 11	Nov. 11	Nov. 11	Nov. 11	Nov. 11
Remembrance Day[3]	Nov. 11	Nov. 11	Nov. 11	Nov. 11	Nov. 11	Nov. 11
Thanksgiving Day[2] (U.S.)	Nov. 22	Nov. 28	Nov. 27	Nov. 25	Nov. 24	Nov. 23
Christmas Day[2,3]	Dec. 25	Dec. 25	Dec. 25	Dec. 25	Dec. 25	Dec. 25
Boxing Day[3]	Dec. 26	Dec. 26	Dec. 26	Dec. 26	Dec. 26	Dec. 26
Kwanzaa[4]	Dec. 26	Dec. 26	Dec. 26	Dec. 26	Dec. 26	Dec. 26
New Year's Eve	Dec. 31	Dec. 31	Dec. 31	Dec. 31	Dec. 31	Dec. 31

1. Leap year; February has 29 days. 2. Federal holiday in U.S. 3. Federal holiday in Canada. 4. First day of seven-day holiday.

Groundhog Day (February 2) On this day the groundhog peeks out of his burrow to look for his shadow. If he sees his shadow, six weeks of winter will follow; if he doesn't, spring is just around the corner.

Halloween (October 31) All Hallow's Eve (the day before the feast of All Saints in the Christian calendar) began as a pagan custom honoring the dead and a celebration of autumn. The wearing of costumes can be traced back to medieval religious practice in which parishioners dressed as saints and angels and paraded through the churchyard. The modern practice of "trick or treat" is of American origin with no apparent historical basis.

Kwanzaa (or Kwanza) This secular celebration by African-Americans commemorates their African heritage and emphasizes the role of family and community. It begins on Dec. 26 and lasts for seven days; on each day one candle of a candelabrum is lighted. Kwanzaa was developed by Maulana Karenga and was first observed in 1966.

Mother's Day (Second Sunday in May) Conceived by Anne M. Jarvis of Philadelphia, where it was first observed, as a day for children to pay tribute to their mothers, this was declared a national holiday by presidential proclamation in 1914.

National Maritime Day (May 22) Designated by presidential proclamation in 1935, this commemorates the anniversary of the departure of the SS *Savannah* on the first successful transoceanic voyage of a steam-powered vessel, in 1819. It is also a day of remembrance of merchant mariners who died in defense of their country.

National Teacher Day (Tuesday of first full week in May) This is a day when students and communities around the country honor their teachers and the teaching profession.

St. Patrick's Day (March 17) A day in honor of Ireland's patron saint, St. Patrick's Day is a religious, political, and social event rolled into one. In Ireland, St. Patrick is honored by church ceremonies and a three-day period of devotion. In the United States, March 17 is celebrated with parades and the "wearing of the green."

St. Valentine's Day (February 14) Originally an occasion to honor two Christian saints martyred by the Roman Emperor Claudius (214–270), since the Middle Ages St. Valentine's Day has been dedicated to lovers, probably because it is believed to be the day that birds choose their mates.

Susan B. Anthony Day (February 15) Anthony (1820–1906) was one of the first women's rights advocates, working especially for equal suffrage—that is, the right to vote. She was a co-founder and later president of the National Woman Suffrage Association.

United Nations Day (October 24) This commemorates the ratification of the United Nations Charter on this date in 1945 by the five permanent members of the Security Council and a majority of the other Charter signatories.

▶**CHRISTIAN HOLY DAYS**

Christmas is the celebration of Christ's birth. The exact date of his birth is unknown, but the date of December 25 was probably chosen because it coincided with the ancient mid-winter celebrations honoring pagan deities. The 12 days of Christmas fall between Christmas and Epiphany (January 6), the day the Wise Men visited the Christ child.

Advent, a religious season that begins on the Sunday nearest Nov. 30 and lasts until Christmas, both celebrates the birth of Jesus and anticipates His second coming. At one time Advent was a solemn season observed by fasting, but this is no longer the case.

Easter is the most important holy day in the Christian religion. It is the celebration of Christ's Resurrection from the dead, which gave Christians the hope of salvation and eternal life. Although Easter is only one day, the full observance of the holy day spans from Septuagesima Sunday (70 days before Easter Sunday), which may fall as early as January, to Pentecost, which can occur as late as June.

Easter always falls on the first Sunday after the first full moon after the vernal equinox on March 21. Thus, Easter can fall no earlier than March 23 (if the first full moon is a Saturday March 22) and no later than April 24 (if the first full moon is a Sunday, April 17).

Mardi Gras (Shrove Tuesday; Fat Tuesday) Originally a day of penance, the last day before the beginning of Lent is now celebrated with feasting and merrymaking.

Ash Wednesday derives its name from the rite of burning the palms carried on the Palm Sunday of the year before and using the ashes to mark worshippers' foreheads with a cross.

Lent, a 40-day period of fasting and penitence beginning on Ash Wednesday and ending on Easter Sunday, Lent is traditionally observed by fasting, performing acts of charity, and by giving up certain pleasures and amusements.

Palm Sunday, the Sunday before Easter, celebrates Jesus' triumphant entry into Jerusalem where palm branches were spread before Him to honor His path.

Holy (Maundy) Thursday, is the anniversary of the Last Supper. The traditional services mark three events that occurred during the week before Jesus was crucified: He washed the feet of his 12 disciples; He instituted the Eucharist (the sacrament of Holy Communion); and He was arrested and imprisoned.

Good Friday marks the day of Christ's Crucifixion. The holy day is observed with fasting, mourning, and penitence.

Holy Saturday is the day that anticipates the Resurrection. In the Catholic church, special vigils are held on Holy Saturday evening.

Easter Sunday marks the day of Christ's Resurrection. Many worshippers celebrate the holy day with sunrise services, a custom believed to be inspired by the example of Mary Magdalene, who went to Christ's tomb "early, while it was yet dark."

Pentecost (literally, "fiftieth day") is the end of the full ecclesiastical observance of Easter. It takes place on the seventh Sunday after Easter Sunday and commemorates the descent of the Holy Spirit upon the Apostles.

The Annunciation This holy day marks the archangel Gabriel's announcement to Mary that she would conceive and give birth to Jesus. It is celebrated by Roman Catholics on March 25; it is not observed by Protestant denominations.

Trinity Sunday The Sunday after Pentecost, this occasion honors the Father, Son, and Holy Spirit. It was declared a part of the church calendar in 1334 by Pope John XXII and is observed by Roman Catholics and by some Protestant denominations.

Corpus Christi This feast celebrates the presence of the body (*corpus*) of Christ in the Eucharist. At one time this was the principal feast of the church year, but today it is observed only by Catholic churches. Corpus Christi is celebrated on the Thursday following Trinity Sunday.

All Saints' Day, celebrated on November 1, honors all of the Christian saints. In America, many churches mark the Sunday nearest November 1 as a day to pay tribute to those who have died during the year. All Saints' Day is observed primarily by Roman Catholics.

Calendar of Christian Holy Days

Year A.D.	Ash Wednesday	Good Friday	Easter Sunday	Pentecost	Trinity Sunday
2000	March 8	April 21	April 23	June 11	June 18
2001	February 28	April 13	April 15	June 3	June 10
2002	February 13	March 29	March 31	May 19	May 26
2003	March 5	April 18	April 20	June 8	June 15
2004	February 25	April 9	April 11	May 30	June 6
2005	February 10	March 25	March 27	May 15	May 22
2006	March 1	April 14	April 16	June 4	June 11
2007	February 21	April 6	April 8	May 27	June 3

Holy Days of Obligation are feast days in the Catholic calendar observed by attendance at Mass and rest from unnecessary work. Six holy days of obligation are observed in the United States:

1. Solemnity of Mary, Jan. 1 (formerly, Christ's circumcision, the first shedding of his blood, was commemorated on this day).

2. Ascension (of Jesus to Heaven), 40 days after Easter

3. Assumption of the Blessed Virgin into Heaven, Aug. 15

4. All Saints Day, Nov. 1

5. Mary's Immaculate Conception (honoring the Mother of God as the only person conceived without original sin), Dec. 8

6. Christmas, Dec. 25

▶ **THE JEWISH CALENDAR**

The months of the Jewish year are Tishri, Heshvan, Kislev, Tebet, Shebat, Adar, Nisan, Iyar, Sivan, Tammuz, Ab, and Elul. The Jewish era dates from the year of the creation (*anno mundii* or A.M.), which is equal to 3761 B.C.), thus 5762 began in 2001 and ends in 2002 of the Gregorian calendar. (Tishri, the first month of the Jewish year, falls in either September or October of the Gregorian calendar.)

Because the Jewish calendar is a blend of solar and lunar calendars, there are intercalated months to keep the lunar and solar years in alignment. (Intercalation is the insertion of an extra day, month, or other unit—February 29 in a leap year, for example—into a calendar). The intercalated month is called Adar Sheni or Veadar—Second Adar.

▶ **JEWISH HOLY DAYS**

Sabbath is the first and most important Jewish holy day, occurring each week from sundown Friday to sundown Saturday. It is a day of rest and spiritual growth, given to men and women so they will remember the sweetness of freedom and keep it. Sabbath takes precedence over all other observances.

Rosh Hashanah (New Year) held to be the birthday of the world, is also called the Day of Judgment and Remembrance, and the day of the shofar—a ram's horn—which is blown to remind Jews of Abraham's willingness to sacrifice his son Isaac. The holiday takes place on the first and second days of Tishri (in September or October).

Yom Kippur (Day of Atonement) concludes the 10 days of repentance that Rosh Hashanah begins and takes place from sundown on the ninth day of Tishri until sundown on the 10th.

The observance begins with the recitation of the most famous passage in the Jewish liturgy—*Kol Nidre*—which nullifies unfulfilled vows made in the past year. The entire day is spent praying and fasting.

Sukkoth (Tabernacles) is a harvest festival celebrated from the 15th through the 22nd of Tishri. Sukkoth also commemorates the journey of the Jewish people through the wilderness to the land of Israel. Jewish families take their meals this week in a roughly constructed *sukkah* (booth)—a reminder of an agricultural society, of the Exodus, and of how precarious and fragile life can be. On the Simchath Torah, the 23rd of Tishri, a congregation finishes reading the last book of the Torah and immediately starts again with the first.

Hanukkah (Chanukah, Feast of Dedication; Festival of Lights) The importance of the eight-day feast, which begins on the 25th day of Kislev, is its commemoration of the first war in human history fought in the cause of religious freedom. The Maccabees vanquished not just the military threat to Judaism, but the internal forces for assimilation into the Hellenistic culture of Israel's rulers. Jews light candles for eight nights to mark a miracle: a day's supply of oil, found in the recaptured Temple, which according to religious myth, burned for eight days.

Purim (Feast of Lots) set on the 14th day of Adar, is another celebration of survival, noting the events described in the Book of Esther. At Purim, Jews rejoice at Queen Esther's and her cousin Mordecai's defeat of Haman, the Persian King Ahaseurus's advisor who plotted to slaughter all the Persian Jews around 400 B.C.

Pesach (Passover) beginning on the 15th day of Nisan and lasting seven days, commemorates the exodus of the Hebrews from Egypt in about 1300 B.C. The name, Passover, also recalls God's sparing (passing over) the Jewish firstborn during the plagues upon the land brought by God through Moses. The holiday is marked by eating only unleavened foods, participating in a *seder*, or special meal, and reading the *Haggadah*, the story of the Hebrews' deliverance from Egypt.

Shabuoth (Feast of Weeks) is observed on the sixth or seventh day of Sivan. Originally an agricultural festival, Shabuoth is a celebration of the revelation of the Torah at Mt. Sinai, by which God established his covenant with the Jewish people.

Calendar of Jewish Holy Days, 5761–67

Year-AM	Rosh Hashanah[1]	Yom Kippur	Sukkoth[1]	Hanukkah[1]	Purim	Pesach[1]	Shabuoth[1]
5761	Sept. 30, 2000	Oct. 9, 2000	Oct. 14, 2000	Dec. 22, 2000	Mar. 9, 2001	Apr. 8, 2001	May 28, 2001
5762	Sept. 18, 2001	Sept. 27, 2001	Oct. 2, 2001	Dec. 10, 2001	Feb. 26, 2002	Mar. 28, 2002	May 17, 2002
5763	Sept. 7, 2002	Sept. 16, 2002	Sept. 21, 2002	Nov. 30, 2002	Mar. 18, 2003	Apr. 17, 2003	June 6, 2003
5764	Sept. 27, 2003	Oct. 6, 2003	Oct. 11, 2003	Dec. 20, 2003	Mar. 7, 2004	Apr. 6, 2004	May 26, 2004
5765	Sept. 16, 2004	Sept. 25, 2004	Sept. 30, 2004	Dec. 8, 2004	Mar. 25, 2005	Apr. 24, 2005	June 13, 2005
5766	Oct. 4, 2005	Oct. 13, 2005	Oct. 18, 2005	Dec. 26, 2005	Mar. 14, 2006	Apr. 13, 2006	June 2, 2006
5767	Sept. 23, 2006	Oct. 2, 2006	Oct. 7, 2006	Dec. 15, 2996	Mar. 4, 2007	Apr. 3, 2007	May 23, 2007

Note: The Jewish day begins and ends at sundown. Thus, all holidays begin at sundown of the day preceding the date shown.
1. Multi-day holiday; first day of holiday shown. **Source:** B'nai B'rith. www.bnaibrith.org.

►THE ISLAMIC CALENDAR

The 12 months of the Islamic year are: Muharram, Safar, Rab'i I, Rab'i II, Jomada I, Jomada II, Rajab, Sha'ban, Ramadan, Shawwal, Dhu al-Qa'dah, Dhu al-Hijja. The Islamic calendar is based on a lunar year of 12 months of 30 and 29 days (alternating every month) and the year is equal to 354 days. It runs in cycles of 30 years, of which the 2nd, 5th, 7th, 10th, 13th, 16th, 18th, 21st, 24th, 26th, and 29th are leap years. Leap years have 355 days, the extra day being added to the last month, Dhu al-Hijja. There are no intercalated months or leap years, so the Islamic year does not keep a constant relationship to the solar year—which dictates the seasons—and months occur about 10 or 11 days earlier than in the year before.

The caliph Abu Bakr adopted A.D. 622, the year of the *hejira* (Mohammed's migration from Mecca to Medina), as the first year of Islam. However, dating of the Muslim era varies throughout the Islamic world. In some countries, the year of the Muslim era is obtained by subtracting 622 from the Gregorian year; A.D. 2002 equals 1380 A.H. (anno hegirae, in the year of the hejira).

Other countries (Saudi Arabia, Yemen, and the principalities of the Persian Gulf) continue to use a purely lunar year. To approximate the Muslim era equivalent of the Gregorian year, subtract 622 (the year of hejira in the Gregorian calendar) from the current year, and multiply the result by 1.031 (days in the year of the Gregorian calendar divided by days in the lunar year): 2002 A.D. = (2002-622) x 1.031 = 1423 A.H. The accompanying calendar uses this method of calculation.

►MUSLIM HOLY DAYS

Ramadan the ninth month of the Islamic calendar, is the Islamic faith's holiest period. To honor the month in which the Koran was revealed, all adult Muslims of sound body and mind fast, eschewing food, water, or even a kiss between the hours of sunrise and sunset. Exempted from the fast are women in menstruation or childbirth bleeding, the chronically ill, or people on a journey, all of whom must make up the fast days at a later date.

Id al-Fitr This day of feasting is celebrated at the end of Ramadan. To mark the fast's break, worshippers also attend an early morning service, Salat-ul-'Id, at which they give alms in staple foodstuffs or their monetary value.

Id al-Adha The Feast of Sacrifice takes place on the 10th day of Dhu al-Hijja, the last month of the year and the season of the haj, or pilgrimage. The day begins with a service in the mosques or other places of gathering, and for those who are not pilgrims, continues with the ritual slaughter of a sheep in commemoration of God's ransom of Abraham's son from sacrifice. At least a third of the meat of the animal is to be given in charity.

Fridays At noontime, Muslims attend mosque or comparable gathering places to say the congregational Friday prayer that ends the week. While Friday is the holy day of the weekly Muslim calendar, it is not a Sabbath comparable to Christian Sundays or Jewish Saturdays, and there are no restrictions on work or other worldly enterprises.

►THE HINDU YEAR

The Hindu year consists of 12 months: Caitra, Vaisakha, Jyaistha, Asadha, Sravana, Bhadrapada, Asvina, Karttika, Margasivsa, Pansa, Magha, and Phalguna. Calendrically, holidays are of two types, lunar and solar. Solar holidays in the Hindu calendar include:

Mesasamkranti The beginning of the new astrological year, when the Sun enters the constellation Aries.

Makaraj-Samkranti The winter solstice, when the sun enters the constellation Capricorn.

Mahavisuva Day is New Year's Eve.

Principal holidays determined by the lunar year are:

Ramanavami (Caitra 9), celebrates the birth of Rama, in Hindu folklore, the epitome of chivalry, courage, and obedience to sacred law. Considered an incarnation of Vishnu, his name is synonymous with God.

Rathayatra (Asadha 2), the pilgrimage of the chariot festival of Orissa.

Janmastami (Sravana 8), The birthday of Krishna, an incarnation of the supreme deity, Vishnu, celebrated as a philosopher-king and hero.

Dasahra (Asvina 7-10), commemorates Rama's victory over the demon Ravana.

Laksmipuja (Asvina 15), honors Laksmi, goddess of good fortune.

Dipavali (Karttika 15), festival of lights and exchanging of presents.

Mahasivaratri (Magha 13), which honors the god Shiva, one of the three supreme Hindu gods. Shiva, whose name means "Auspicious One," is a god of both reproduction and destruction.

Calendar of Muslim Holy Days

Year A.H. (A.D.)	New Year's Day 1 Muharram	1 Ramadan	Id al-Fitr, 1 Shawwal	Id al-Adha, 10 Dhu al-Hijja
1420 (1999-2000)	April 18, 1999	Dec. 9, 1999	Jan. 8, 2000	Mar. 17, 2000
1421 (2000-01)	April 6, 2000	Nov. 27, 2000	Dec. 27, 2000	Mar. 10, 2001
1422 (2001-02)	March 26, 2001	Nov. 17, 2001	Dec. 16, 2001	Feb. 23, 2002
1423 (2002-03)	March 15, 2002	Nov. 6, 2002	Dec. 6, 2002	Feb. 12, 2003
1424 (2003-04)	March 4, 2003	Oct. 27, 2003	Nov. 25, 2003	Feb. 1, 2004
1425 (2004-05)	Feb. 22, 2004	Oct. 15, 2004	Nov. 14, 2004	Jan. 21, 2005
1426 (2005-06)	Feb. 10, 2005	Oct. 5, 2005	Nov. 3, 2005	Jan. 11, 2006

Note: The Islamic calendar is based on calculation and depends on actual sighting of the moon. Therefore the dates above are estimates. For exact dates, contact your local masjid, organization, or scholar.
Source: *Islamic Calendar* (www.assirat.org/Hcal). Copyright © 2000 Dar Assirat. All rights reserved.

Chinese Years, 1900–2019

Year of the Rat	1900	1912	1924	1936	1948	1960	1972	1984	1996	2008
. . . Ox	1901	1913	1925	1937	1949	1961	1973	1985	1997	2009
. . . Tiger	1902	1914	1926	1938	1950	1962	1974	1986	1998	2010
. . . Hare (Rabbit)	1903	1915	1927	1939	1951	1963	1975	1987	1999	2011
. . . Dragon	1904	1916	1928	1940	1952	1964	1976	1988	2000	2012
. . . Snake	1905	1917	1929	1941	1953	1965	1977	1989	2001	2013
. . . Horse	1906	1918	1930	1942	1954	1966	1978	1990	2002	2014
. . . Sheep(Goat)	1907	1919	1931	1943	1955	1967	1979	1991	2003	2015
. . . Monkey	1908	1920	1932	1944	1956	1968	1980	1992	2004	2016
. . . Rooster	1909	1921	1933	1945	1957	1969	1981	1993	2005	2017
. . . Dog	1910	1922	1934	1946	1958	1970	1982	1994	2006	2018
. . . Pig	1911	1923	1935	1947	1959	1971	1983	1995	2007	2019

Months of the Year

Gregorian	Hebrew	Hindu	Muslim
January	Shebat	Magha	Muharram
February	Adar	Phalguna	Safar
March	Nisan	Caitra	Rab'i I
April	Iyar	Vaisakha	Rab'i II
May	Sivan	Jyaistha	Jomada I
June	Tammuz	Asadha	Jomada II
July	Ab	Sravana	Rajab
August	Elul	Bhadrapada	Sha'ban
September	Tishri	Asvina	Ramadan
October	Heshvan	Karttika	Shawwal
November	Kislev	Margasivsa	Dhu al-Qa'dah
December	Tebet	Pansa	Dhu al-Hijja

Note: The months of the traditional (lunar) Muslim calendar occur at different times every year. Months in italics indicate the first month of the year in the respective calendars.

Astrological Calendar

Dates	Sign
January 20 - February 18	Aquarius, the water bearer
February 19-March 20	Pisces, the fishes
March 21-April 19	Aries, the ram
April 20-May 20	Taurus, the bull
May 21-June 20	Gemini, the twins
June 21-July 22	Cancer, the crab
July 23-August 22	Leo, the lion
August 23-September 22	Virgo, the virgin
September 23-October 22	Libra, the scales
October 23-November 21	Scorpio, the scorpion
November 22-December 21	Sagittarius, the archer
December 22-January 19	Capricorn, the goat

Birthstones

Month	Stone
January	Garnet
February	Amethyst
March	Aquamarine, Bloodstone
April	Diamond
May	Emerald
June	Alexandrite, Moonstone, Pearl
July	Ruby
August	Peridot, Sardonyx
September	Sapphire
October	Opal, Tourmaline
November	Topaz
December	Turquoise, Lapis Lazuli

Wedding Anniversaries

Anniversary	Type of gift	Anniversary	Type of gift
1st	Paper	14th	Ivory
2nd	Cotton	15th	Crystal
3rd	Leather	20th	China
4th	Fruit, flowers	25th	Silver
5th	Wood	30th	Pearl
6th	Sugar	35th	Coral
7th	Copper, wool	40th	Ruby
8th	Bronze, pottery	45th	Sapphire
9th	Pottery, willow	50th	Gold
10th	Tin	55th	Emerald
11th	Steel	60th	Diamond
12th	Silk, linen	70th	Platinum
13th	Lace		

ASTRONOMICAL EVENTS, 2002

The main astronomical events included in this section are the phases of the Moon, the Moon's perigee (when it is closest to the Earth) and apogee (when it is farthest away), lunar and solar eclipses, and the visibility of the planets.

▶PHASES OF THE MOON

The relative position of the Earth, Moon, and Sun affect what, if any, part of the Moon we can see illuminated by the Sun during our night. A new moon occurs when the Moon is precisely aligned between the Earth and the Sun, making the Moon invisible from the Earth. When the Moon is at first quarter (90° from the Sun relative to the Earth), its sunlit part appears in the shape of a D (in the Southern Hemisphere, a backward D). A full moon, when the Moon shows an almost fully illuminated face, occurs when the Moon is 180° around the sky from the Sun. The last quarter (or third quarter) occurs when the Moon is again moving toward a position between the Earth and the Sun, and it appears as a backward D (a normal D in the Southern Hemisphere). Intermediate phases are the crescent moon—between the new Moon and first quarter, and between the last quarter and new Moon; and the gibbous moon, occurring between the half and the full Moon. The full cycle from one phase through all

Phases of the Moon, 2002

	New moon				First quarter				Full moon				Last quarter		
Month	d	h	m	Month	d	h	m	Month	d	h	m	Month	d	h	m
												Jan.	06	03	55
Jan.	13	13	29	Jan.	21	17	46	Jan.	28	22	50	Feb.	04	13	33
Feb.	12	07	41	Feb.	20	12	02	Feb.	27	09	17	Mar.	06	01	24
Mar.	14	02	02	Mar.	22	02	28	Mar.	28	18	25	Apr.	04	15	29
Apr.	12	19	21	Apr.	20	12	48	Apr.	27	03	00	May	04	07	16
May	12	10	45	May	19	19	42	May	26	11	51	June	03	00	05
June	10	23	46	June	18	00	29	June	24	21	42	July	02	17	19
July	10	10	26	July	17	04	47	July	24	09	07	Aug.	01	10	22
Aug.	08	19	15	Aug.	15	10	12	Aug.	22	22	29	Aug.	31	02	31
Sept.	07	03	10	Sept.	13	18	08	Sept.	21	13	59	Sept.	29	17	03
Oct.	06	11	18	Oct.	13	05	33	Oct.	21	07	20	Oct.	29	05	28
Nov.	04	20	34	Nov.	11	20	52	Nov.	20	01	34	Nov.	27	15	46
Dec.	04	07	34	Dec.	11	15	49	Dec.	19	19	10	Dec.	27	00	31

Note: Shown in Universal Time (UT). To convert to local time, see "Timing Planetary Phenomena."
Source: U.S. Naval Observatory, *Astronomical Phenomena for the Year 2002* (2000).

the other phases takes about 29.53 days and is called a *lunation*.

▶ VISIBILITY OF THE PLANETS, 2002

Mercury can only be seen low in the east before sunrise, or low in the west after sunset (about the time of the beginning or end of twilight). It is visible in the mornings between the following approximate dates: Feb. 3-March 29, June 6-July 13, and Oct. 5-31. The planet is brighter at the end of each period, (the best conditions in northern latitudes occur in mid-October, and in southern latitudes from mid-February to mid-March). It is visible in the evenings between the following approximate dates: Jan. 1-22, April 16-May 17, July 29-Sept. 21, and Dec. 1-31. The planet is brighter at the beginning of each period, (the best conditions in northern latitudes occur from late April to early May, and in southern latitudes from mid-August to mid-September.

Venus is too close to the Sun for observation until late February when it appears as a brilliant object in the evening sky. During the last week of October it again becomes too close to the Sun for observation until the end of the first week of November, when it reappears in the morning sky. Venus is in conjunction with Saturn on May 7, with Mars on May 10, and with Jupiter on June 3.

Mars can be seen in the evening sky in Aquarius at the beginning of the year. It moves into Pisces during the second week of January, into Aries in late February, Taurus in early April, and into Gemini from late May. It becomes too close to the Sun for observation during the second half of June, reappearing in the morning sky from late September in Leo. It then continues into Virgo in the first week of October and into Libra from mid-December. Mars is in conjunction with Saturn on May 4, Venus on May 10, and Jupiter on July 3.

Jupiter is at opposition on Jan. 1, when it can be seen throughout the night in Gemini. Its eastward elongation gradually decreases, and from late March it can be seen only in the evening sky. In early July, it becomes too close to the Sun for observation. It reappears in the morning sky in early August in Cancer. Its westward elongation gradually increases until by mid-November it can

Visibility of the Planets, 2002

Planet	Morning Twilight	Evening Twilight
Venus	Nov. 7–Dec. 31	Feb. 25–Oct. 26
Mars	Sept. 25–Dec. 31	Jan. 1–June 24
Jupiter	Aug. 3–Dec. 31	Jan. 1– July 6
Saturn	June 28–Dec. 17	Jan. 1–May 22
		Dec. 17–Dec. 31

Source: U.S. Naval Observatory, *Astronomical Phenomena for the Year 2002* (2000).

be seen for more than half the night. Jupiter is in conjunction with Venus on June 3 and with Mars on July 3.

Saturn is in Taurus at the beginning of the year. It can be seen for more than half the night until late February, after which it can be seen only in the evening sky. Its eastward elongation gradually decreases, and in the second half of May, it becomes too close to the Sun for observation. It reappears in the morning sky in late June and passes into Orion at the beginning of September and Taurus in the second half of November. It is at opposition on December 17, when it can be seen throughout the night. For the remainder of the year, its eastward elongation gradually decreases and is visible for the greater part of the night. Saturn is in conjunction with Mars on May 4, Venus on May 7, and Mercury on July 2.

Uranus is visible in the evening sky in Capricorn for the first three weeks of January. It then becomes too close to the Sun for observation until the second week of March, when it reappears in the morning sky. It is at opposition on August 20, and from mid-November it can be seen only in the evening sky.

Neptune is visible as an evening star for the first week of January in Capricorn, and remains in this constellation throughout the year. It then becomes too close to the Sun for observation until a few days after mid-February, when it reappears in the morning sky. It is at opposition on Aug. 2, and after early November, it can only be seen in the evening sky.

Do not confuse

(1) Mars with Saturn from late April to mid-May, when Saturn is the brighter object. (2) Venus with Mars in the first half of May and again from late November to the end of December, with Saturn in the first half of May, and with Jupiter in the first week of June. On all occasions, Venus is the brighter object. (3) Mercury with Saturn in late June to early July, and with Mars in the first half of October.   On both occasions, Mercury is the brighter object.

►TIMING PLANETARY PHENOMENA

The times for astronomical data shown here are expressed in Universal Time (UT) which is the standard time of the Greenwich meridian (0° of longitude) also known as Greenwich mean time (GMT). To convert to local time, determine your longitude and subtract 1 hour for every 15° of longitude west of 0°; or add 1 hour for every 15° longitude east of 0°.

The first new moon of 2002 occurs Jan. 13 at 1319 hours in UT. The equivalent time in New York (74°W) is 5 hours earlier, or Jan. 13 at 0819 hours (8:19 A.M.); in Chicago (87°W), 6 hours earlier, or Jan. 13 at 7:19 A.M.; in Denver (105°W), 7 hours earlier, or Jan. 13 at 6:19 P.M.; and in San Francisco (122°W), 8 hours earlier, or Jan 13 at 5:19 A.M. (To obtain the P.M. equivalent of UT times later than 1200, subtract 12.) Note that local clock times may differ from these standard times, especially in summer when clocks are often advanced by 1 hour.

►ECLIPSES
Eclipses of the Moon

A lunar eclipse occurs when the Sun, Earth, and Moon are in a straight line and the shadow of the Earth falls on the Moon. There are three kinds of lunar eclipse. A *total eclipse* occurs when the Moon passes completely into the Earth's total umbra, or shadow, so the Sun cannot be seen from the Moon. A *partial eclipse* occurs when only part of the Earth's umbra falls across the Moon and the Sun is partially visible from some places on the Moon. A *penumbral eclipse* occurs when only the Earth's penumbra (partial shadow) shades the Moon; and from the Moon one's view of the Sun would be only partially blocked by the Earth. It is usually difficult to detect a penumbral eclipse from the Earth.

During 2002, there will be three penumbral eclipses of the Moon. (All times shown in universal time (UT). To convert to local time, see *Timing Planetary Phenomena*.)

May 26, 2002–Penumbral eclipse.

Moon enters penumbra 10:12.7, *Middle of eclipse* 12:03.3, *Moon leaves penumbra* 13:53.8, Penumbral magnitude of the eclipse: 0.715. The beginning of the umbral phase will be visible in most of North America except the northeast, Central America, western South America, extreme northeast Russia, eastern Asia, and Australia. The end

will be visible in southwestern Alaska, Asia except the extreme north, and Australia.

June 24, 2002–Penumbral Eclipse.   *Moon enters penumbra* 20:18.4, *Middle of eclipse* 21:27.1, *Moon leaves penumbra* 22:35.4, Penumbral magnitude of the eclipse: 0.235. The beginning of the umbral phase will be visible in Australia, Indonesia, southern and western Asia, Europe except the extreme north, Africa, extreme eastern South America, and Antarctica. The end will be visible in Africa, Europe except the extreme north, most of South America except the northwest, Antarctica, western Australia, and southwest Asia.

November 19–20, 2002–Penumbral Eclipse.

Moon enters penumbra Nov. 19, 23:32.0, *Middle of eclipse* Nov. 20, 1:46.5, *Moon leaves penumbra* Nov. 20, 4:01.1, Penumbral magnitude of the eclipse: 0.886. The beginning of the penumbral phase will be visible in North America except the western part, Africa, Europe, Greenland, Central America, South America except the southern tip, and extreme western Asia. The end will be visible in North America, the Arctic, Central America, South America, Greenland, Europe, northern and western Russia, the western Middle East, western Africa, and the Antarctic Peninsula.

Eclipses of the Sun

A solar eclipse occurs when the Moon passes between the Earth and the Sun; there are three types.   A total eclipse occurs when the Moon's shadow completely covers the Sun and the sky turns dark.   Total eclipses occur along a narrow path (typically 100-200 miles wide) called the track of totality and last only a few minutes at any point on the track. A partial eclipse occurs when the Moon covers only a portion of the Sun. A total eclipse may be only partial in less than optimum viewing locations. An annular (ring-shaped) eclipse occurs when the Moon is too far from the Earth to completely cover the Sun, so that at the height of the eclipse, a ring of light surrounds the Moon.

In 2002, there will be one total and one annular eclipse of the Sun; only the annular eclipse will be visible from the U.S.

June 10–11–Annular Eclipse.   *Eclipse begins* June 10, 20:51.8; *central eclipse at local apparent noon* June 10, 23:48.2; *eclipse ends* 2:36.6. It will be visible over the U.S. and northern Mexico, Canada except for its extreme northeastern sections, Eastern Asia, Japan, Indonesia, Northern Australia, and the Pacific Ocean. The best viewing spots in the U.S. will be along a path from Michigan to western Texas.

December 4, 2002–Total Eclipse.   *Eclipse begins* 4:51.3; *central eclipse at local apparent noon* 7:38.7; *eclipse ends* 10:11.0. It will be visible in Africa except the north, parts of Antarctica, Indonesia, Australia, the South Island of New Zealand, and the southeast Atlantic Ocean. The best viewing spots for the maximum eclipse will be in central Australia and western Africa.

The United States of America shares the North American continent with Canada, Mexico, and the Central American nations. The 48 conterminous states lie in a broad land mass from approximately 24°N to 49°N from south to north, and 67°W to 124°W from east to west. It is bordered on the north by Canada, on the south by Mexico and the Gulf of Mexico, on the east by the Atlantic Ocean, and on the west by the Pacific Ocean. The two nonconterminous states of Alaska and Hawaii are located to the northwest on the North American continent, and in the Pacific Ocean Basin approximately 2,400 miles southwest of the state of California, respectively.

▶ POLITICAL-GEOGRAPHIC DIVISIONS
The Bureau of the Census groups the states in a number of divisions and sub-divisions.

Northeast
New England Maine, New Hampshire, Vermont, Massachusetts, Rhode Island, Connecticut.
Middle Atlantic New York, New Jersey, Pennsylvania.

Midwest
East North Central Ohio, Indiana, Illinois, Michigan, Wisconsin.
West North Central Minnesota, Iowa, Missouri, North Dakota, South Dakota, Nebraska, Kansas.

South
South Atlantic Delaware, Maryland, District of Columbia, Virginia, West Virginia, North Carolina, South Carolina, Georgia, Florida.
East South Central Kentucky, Tennessee, Alabama, Mississippi.
West South Central Arkansas, Louisiana, Oklahoma, Texas.

Pacific
Mountain Montana, Idaho, Wyoming, Colorado, New Mexico, Arizona, Utah, Nevada.
Pacific Washington, Oregon, California, Alaska, Hawaii.

▶ PHYSIOGRAPHIC REGIONS
The physiographic regions, or the primary geological features and landforms, of the United States are:

Atlantic and Gulf Coast Plains
These run from the islands of southern New England, Cape Cod, and Long Island, through New Jersey, Delaware, Maryland, Virginia, North Carolina, South Carolina, Georgia, Florida, Alabama, Mississippi, Louisiana, Texas; includes lower Mississippi Valley in Arkansas, Missouri, Tennessee.

Appalachian System
The Appalachian System is divided into five parts:
New England White Mountains (New Hampshire), Green Mountains (Vermont), Champlain Lowland and Hudson Valley (Vermont, New York), Catskill Mountains (New York).
The Piedmont Pennsylvania, Virginia, North Carolina, South Carolina, Georgia, Alabama.
Great Smoky and Blue Ridge Mountains Pennsylvania (Poconos), [discontinuous], Virginia, North Carolina, Georgia.
Ridge and Valley Pennsylvania, West Virginia, Virginia, Kentucky, Tennessee, Alabama.
Appalachian Plateau Pennsylvania, Ohio, West Virginia, Kentucky, Tennessee, Alabama.

Canadian (or Laurentian) Shield
This region covers much of eastern Canada and extends into the U.S. in two places:
Adirondack Mountains New York.
Superior Upland Upper Michigan, Wisconsin, Minnesota.

Central Lowland
The Central Lowland includes most of the U.S. interior, and is divided into four parts:
Interior Lowlands Ohio, Kentucky, Tennessee.
Mississippi Great Lakes Basin Ohio, Indiana, Illinois, Michigan, Wisconsin, Iowa, North Dakota, South Dakota.
Interior Highlands Ozark Mountains: Missouri, Arkansas, Oklahoma; Ouachita Mountains: Arkansas, Oklahoma.
Great Plains North Dakota, South Dakota, Nebraska, Kansas, Oklahoma, Texas, Montana, Wyoming, Colorado, New Mexico.

Cordilleran Province
Rocky Mountains New Mexico, Colorado, Wyoming, Montana.

Intermontane Range
This range is divided into four sections:
Colorado Plateau Colorado, Utah, New Mexico, Arizona (including Grand Canyon).
Basin and Range Plateau Nevada, Utah (including Wasatch Range).
Desert Basin and Range California (including Death Valley), Arizona.
Snake and Columbia River Basins Idaho, Washington, Oregon.

U.S. Geographic Extremes

Because the Aleutian Islands wrap around the Greenwich Meridian, Alaska technically contains both the easternmost and westernmost points in the United States.

Extreme	Contiguous 48 states (Long. or Lat.)	U.S. (Long. or Lat.)[1]
North	Northwest Angle Inlet, Minn. 49° 23' N	Point Barrow, Alaska, 71° 23' N
South	Key West, Fla. 24° 33' N	Ka Lae, Hawaii 18° 55' N
East	West Quoddy Head, Maine, 66° 57' W	Pochnoi Point, Alaska, 179° 52' E
West	Capa Alava, Wash. 124° 44' W	Amatignak Island, Alaska 179° 09' W

1. U.S. states only; does not include U.S. territories and possessions. **Source:** U.S. Geological Survey, *Elevations and Distances in the United States*, online edition. http://mapping.usgs.gov/mac/isb/pubs/booklets/elvadist/elvadist.html.

Pacific Coastlands

This region is divided into four sections, three oriented north-south, the other east-west.

Cascade Mountains and Sierra Nevada Washington, Oregon, California, Nevada.

Puget Sound, Willamette Valley, and Central Valley Washington, Oregon, California.

Coast Ranges Washington, Oregon, California.

Los Angeles Extension Tehachapi Mountains (east-west), San Gabriel Mountains, and San Bernardino Mountains.

▶ NATIONAL PARK SYSTEM

The National Park System of the U.S. began in March 1872 with the establishment of the Yellowstone National Park in the Territories of Montana and Wyoming, "as a public park or pleasuring ground for the benefit and enjoyment of the people" and was placed "under exclusive control of the Secretary of the Interior." The founding of Yellowstone began a worldwide national park movement and today more than 100 countries contain some 1,200 national parks or equivalent preserves.

President Woodrow Wilson created the National Park Service as a bureau within the Department of the Interior in 1916, and charged it with protecting the 35 national parks and monuments then in existence. Today, the U.S. National Park System comprises 382 areas covering more than 84 million acres (3 percent of total U.S. area) in 49 states (there are no areas in Delaware), the District of Columbia, Guam, Puerto Rico, Saipan, and the Virgin Islands. Additions to the National Park System are generally made through acts of Congress, and national parks can be created only through such acts. But under the Antiquities Act of 1906, the President has authority to proclaim national monuments on lands already under Federal jurisdiction.

The diversity of the parks managed by the National Park Service (NPS) is reflected in the variety of titles given to them. Although the system is best known for its scenic National Parks, more than half the areas of the National Park System preserve places, and commemorate persons, events, and activities important in the nation's history. Brief definitions of each type of park follow, together with the number of areas and total Federal acreage. An additional 11 areas such as the White House, the National Mall, etc., totaling 37,723 acres of Federal land were without designation.

National battlefields/battlefield parks/battlefield site/military parks

cover a variety of areas associated with U.S. military history (Antietam National Battlefield, Maryland). (1 battlefield site, 1 acre; 9 military parks, 35,170 acres; 11 battlefields, 11,877 acres; 3 battlefield parks, 8,060 acres)

National Capital Parks

include more than 346 sites (The Ellipse; Lafayette Park) throughout the Washington, D.C., area. (6,482 acres)

National historical parks

are areas of greater physical extent and complexity than historic sites (Nez Perce, Idaho). (40; 114,727 acres)

National historic sites

include areas of prehistoric and modern historical interest (Tuskegee Institute, Mississippi), archaeological sites, historic structures and the like. Because it is of importance to both the U.S. and Canada, St. Croix Island (22 acres) is designated an International Historic Site. (77; 20,122 acres)

National lakeshores/seashores

(Cape Cod NS, Massachusetts; Pictured Rocks NL, Michigan) preserve shoreline areas and offshore islands while providing water-oriented recreation. (4 lakeshores, 145,644 acres; 10 seashores, 478,283 acres)

National memorial

designates an area or structure that is commemorative in nature (Mt. Rushmore, South Dakota). (28; 8,041 acres)

National monuments

are intended to preserve at least one nationally significant resource (Rainbow Bridge, Utah). They are usually smaller than national parks and lack the diversity of attractions. (72; 1,880,658 acres)

National parks

contain a variety of resources and encompass large land and water areas (Grand Canyon, Arizona) to help provide adequate protection of resources. (56; 49,689,002 acres)

National parkways

are ribbons of land flanking roadways (Natchez Trace, Mississippi, Alabama and Tennessee) that offer an opportunity for leisurely driving through areas of scenic interest. (4; 164,039 acres)

National preserves

serve primarily to protect certain resources (Big Thicket, Texas). Activities like hunting and fishing or mineral extraction may be permitted. (17; 21,445,909 acres)

National recreation areas

were originally areas surrounding reservoirs (Lake Mead, Nevada and Arizona), but now include other lands and waters set aside for recreational use. (18; 3,403,577 acres)

National reserves

are similar to the preserves, but are administered by state or local authorities (City of Rocks, Idaho). (2; 10,933 acres)

National rivers/wild and scenic riverways

preserve ribbons of land bordering free-flowing streams that have not been dammed, channelized, or otherwise altered (Delaware River, Pennsylvania and New Jersey). Activities such as hiking, boating and hunting may be permitted. (6 National Rivers; 311,093 acres; 9 National Wild & Scenic Riverways; 72,780 acres)

National scenic trails

are usually long-distance footpaths winding through areas of natural beauty (Appalachian Trail, Maine to Georgia). (3; 157,938 acres)

National wilderness areas

are designated under the Wilderness Act of 1964, which provides that "there shall be no commercial enterprise and no permanent road within any wilderness area . . . and (except for emergency uses) no temporary road, no use of motor vehicles, motorized equipment or motorboats, no landing of aircraft, no other form of mechanical transport, and no structure or installation." Wilderness areas are usually part of other larger entities.

In addition to the National Park System, there are three groups of areas that are closely linked in importance and purpose to NPS-managed areas.

Affiliated areas

(designated by Act of Congress, 1970) are areas in the U.S. and Canada that preserve significant areas outside the National Park System but that rely on NPS assistance.

U.S. National Parks: Acreage, Visits, and Overnight Stays, 1990-2000

National Park, State	Acres under Federal protection, 2000	Visits ('000s)			Overnight stays ('000s)		
		1990	1999	2000	1990	1999	2000
Acadia, Maine	45,852	2,413	2,602	2,469	223	159	146
Arches, Utah	76,353	621	870	786	58	49	46
Badlands, South Dakota	232,822	1,326	950	1,106	35	50	54
Big Bend, Texas	775,279	257	328	262	215	218	186
Biscayne, Florida	170,956	573	443	393	29	N.A.	N.A.
Black Canyon of the Gunnison, Colorado	27,705	(1)	200	192	(1)	12	14
Bryce Canyon , Utah	35,833	863	1,082	1,099	144	150	145
Canyonlands, Utah	337,570	277	446	402	78	111	108
Capitol Reef, Utah	240,573	562	680	613	48	41	42
Carlsbad Caverns, New Mexico	46,427	747	514	469	(x)	(x)	(x)
Channel Islands, California	79,019	144	607	483	32	164	101
Crater Lake, Oregon	183,224	385	418	427	45	66	73
Cugyahoga Valley, Ohio	19,371	(1)	(1)	3,325	(1)	(1)	6
Death Valley, California-Nevada	3,236,771	(1)	1,228	1,179	(1)	240	225
Denali, Alaska	4,724,735	547	387	364	118	124	121
Dry Tortugas, Florida	61,481	19	74	84	25	38	41
Everglades, Florida	1,398,617	958	1,074	995	128	99	106
Gates of the Arctic, Alaska	7,266,102	1	8	12	5	7	1
Glacier Bay, Alaska	3,222,698	204	443	385	36	40	44
Glacier, Montana	1,013,153	1,987	1,685	1,729	330	335	309
Grand Canyon, Arizona	1,180,863	3,777	4,575	4,460	908	1,132	1085
Grand Teton, Wyoming	307,620	1,588	2,680	2,590	597	578	532
Great Basin, Nevada	77,180	65	90	81	44	33	32
Great Smoky Mountain, Tennessee-North Carolina	520,977	8,152	10,284	10,176	463	454	421
Guadalupe Mountains, Texas	86,190	193	220	199	18	24	20
Haleakala, Hawaii	28,969	1,261	1,963	1,620	19	24	24
Hawaii Volcanoes, Hawaii	207,643	1,097	1,503	1,515	112	121	110
Hot Springs, Arkansas	4,880	1,123	1,384	1,338	8	7	4
Isle Royale, Michigan	539,282	23	23	21	56	64	61
Joshua Tree, California	954,270	(1)	1,316	1,234	(1)	254	245
Katmai, Alaska	3,611,495	41	51	72	12	25	29
Kenai Fjords, Alaska	601,839	66	291	255	1	5	4
Kings Canyon, California	461,845	1,063	560	529	302	241	217
Kobuk Valley, Alaska	1,669,813	3	6	3	(x)	(x)	(x)
Lake Clark, Alaska	2,226,630	10	6	6	1	3	2
Lassen Volcanic, California	106,367	461	354	375	113	84	79
Mammoth Cave, Kentucky	52,003	1,925	1,711	1,749	98	93	89
Mesa Verde, Colorado	51,891	611	636	452	159	127	82
Mount Rainier, Washington	235,625	1,327	1,291	1,345	184	163	196
North Cascades, Washington	504,575	456	21	26	97	15	19
Olympic, Washington	913,517	2,795	3,364	3,328	404	399	506
Petrified Forest, Arizona	93,532	845	667	605	1	2	2
Redwood, California	77,715	348	370	383	16	70	59
Rocky Mountain, Colorado	265,363	2,647	3,186	3,185	209	250	232
Saguaro, Arizona	87,156	(1)	749	765	(1)	2	2
Sequoia, California	402,334	1,064	873	839	345	274	252
Shenandoah, Virginia	197,060	1,772	1,339	1,420	323	273	284
Theodore Roosevelt, North Dakota	69,702	461	431	432	26	29	28
Virgin Island, U.S. Virgin Islands	12,913	665	425	704	173	173	215
Voyageurs, Minnesota	133,044	224	229	227	47	18	18
Wind Cave, South Dakota	28,295	586	762	669	11	11	10
Wrangell-St. Elias, Alaska	7,661,519	36	29	28	3	7	2
Yellowstone, Montana-Wyoming	2,219,789	2,824	3,131	2,838	1,345	1,239	1,191
Yosemite, California	759,530	3,125	3,494	3,401	2,220	1,551	1,633
Zion, Utah	143,035	2,102	2,450	2,432	292	237	243
Total National Parks	**49,689,002**	**54,619**	**64,503**	**66,076**	**10,156**	**9,886**	**9,696**
Total National Parks System[2]	**84,327,466**	**255,655**	**287,125**	**285,891**	**17,625**	**16,283**	**15,726**

Note: (x) = less than 1,000. Visit and overnight stay data often varies from year to year because of special events such as anniversaries and natural disasters. 1. Area was not a National Park in year shown. 2. Includes National Historic Sites, National Memorials, National Seashores, National Parkways, and other areas under the jurisdiction of the National Park Service. **Source:** *U.S. National Park Service Statistical Abstract 2000* (2001).

Wild and Scenic Rivers System (designated by Act of Congress, 1968) preserves undeveloped rivers as free-flowing streams accessible for public use. Wild rivers are free of dams and generally accessible only by trails; scenic rivers have relatively primitive shorelines and are largely undeveloped but may be accessible by road.

State Parks and Recreation Areas by State, 1999

State	Areas	Total Acreage	Visitors ('000s) Day	Visitors ('000s) Total[1]	Revenues ('000s)	Revenues as percent of operating expenditures
Total U.S.	5,660	12,915,624	704,980	766,842	$650,864	43.4%
Alabama	23	49,710	4,781	5,923	26,160	90.9
Alaska	138	3,291,118	3,147	3,855	2,106	39.3
Arizona	28	58,526	1,555	2,180	4,521	31.9
Arkansas	66	51,292	5,800	6,460	13,311	50.0
California	263	1,375,779	70,798	76,736	68,535	31.3
Colorado	236	346,149	8,481	9,508	12,040	58.1
Connecticut	130	180,088	7,581	7,959	3,726	35.5
Delaware	25	20,039	3,777	3,977	6,654	34.3
Florida	145	512,538	13,295	14,645	25,766	48.9
Georgia	64	73,145	14,605	15,344	19,823	45.4
Hawaii	67	24,589	15,000	15,071	275	4.9
Idaho	27	43,048	2,057	2,354	3,182	39.7
Illinois	384	411,156	41,291	41,891	951	2.1
Indiana	33	177,886	15,984	18,652	29,266	73.0
Iowa	174	63,171	13,997	14,736	3,265	31.5
Kansas	24	52,300	4,713	7,100	3,998	53.1
Kentucky	49	43,310	6,442	7,575	47,755	68.2
Louisiana	56	36,119	940	1,469	2,819	20.8
Maine	168	94,604	2,189	2,454	1,931	29.2
Maryland	98	295,135	10,122	10,780	13,847	41.7
Massachusetts	236	287,163	12,506	13,497	5,570	18.1
Michigan	95	265,176	22,413	27,745	17,724	64.4
Minnesota	79	245,083	7,504	8,407	10,705	44.7
Mississippi	29	24,327	3,631	4,277	6,706	36.9
Missouri	85	136,791	16,526	17,709	6,766	23.0
Montana	355	54,494	1,266	1,507	1,571	31.5
Nebraska	85	133,044	7,915	9,368	13,232	74.5
Nevada	24	132,565	2,511	2,666	1,822	25.0
New Hampshire	84	74,471	4,101	4,361	9,845	208.6
New Jersey	115	343,419	14,609	15,019	7,840	29.0
New Mexico	31	90,693	1,890	4,725	3,623	24.5
New York	651	1,015,758	57,664	61,960	58,924	47.0
North Carolina	57	158,339	12,869	13,269	3,440	14.1
North Dakota	31	20,046	923	1,068	923	42.2
Ohio	73	204,871	57,000	60,220	25,180	41.5
Oklahoma	51	71,586	14,235	15,546	21,234	52.5
Oregon	224	94,331	36,683	38,752	14,548	41.8
Pennsylvania	117	283,383	34,303	36,019	12,080	18.9
Rhode Island	74	8,748	5,980	6,332	3,684	82.3
South Carolina	58	81,572	8,262	9,564	15,265	65.1
South Dakota	86	96,099	6,219	6,843	7,522	79.4
Tennessee	108	285,594	30,517	31,834	26,192	54.0
Texas	122	628,207	19,778	21,446	26,028	53.3
Utah	54	113,799	5,914	6,958	7,707	37.4
Vermont	66	83,617	434	834	5,623	106.5
Virginia	61	75,447	4,934	5,520	7,258	47.3
Washington	263	262,226	46,006	48,138	10,368	27.5
West Virginia	47	195,565	7,609	8,249	17,364	63.3
Wisconsin	65	128,578	12,498	14,181	11,438	67.7
Wyoming	36	120,930	1,727	2,158	751	17.3

1. Includes overnight visitors.   **Source:** National Association of State Park Directors (Tucson, Ariz.), *2000 Annual Information Exchange.*

National Trails System (designated by National Trails System Act of 1968) includes trails in both urban and rural settings for persons of all ages, interests, skills, and physical abilties. The Appalachian Trail and the Pacific Crest were the first two trails designated under the National Trails System. Today, there are more than 800 trails, in every state, Puerto Rico, and the District of Columbia, totaling more than 9,000 miles in length.

Source: National Park Service, *The National Parks: Index 1999-2001.*

▶**RIVERS AND LAKES**
Major Navigable Waterways of the United States The U.S inland and intracoastal waterway system handles over 500 million tons of traffic each year, carried by a fleet of more than 5,000 towboats and 31,000 barges on over 11,000 miles of primary channels. Ninety percent of these channels have depths of between 9 and 14 feet. Maintenance and improvement of the waterways—including channel dredging, bridge and levee maintenance, and the construction of canals and locks—are in large measure the re-

sponsibility of the U.S. Army Corps of Engineers. The 522-mile New York State Barge Canal System is the only major nonFederal waterway in the country.

Mississippi River System The major inland river transportation network is the Mississippi River and its tributaries. This north-south-oriented system includes the Mississippi River, the Ohio River System, the Illinois Waterway, and the Arkansas and Missouri rivers, among others. In this system there are about 7,000 miles of heavily used, improved navigable channels, 85 percent of which have at least nine-foot navigable channel depths.

Intracoastal Waterways At its mouth, the Mississippi River is intersected by the Gulf Intracoastal Waterway (GIWW), which parallels the Gulf Coast for 1,180 miles from St. Marks River, Florida, to Brownsville, Texas, at the Mexican border. The GIWW is intersected by a number of river systems in addition to the Mississippi, including the Mobile River, the Apalachicola, and the Houston Ship Channel.

This network of major inland and coastal waterways connects some of the largest Gulf Coast ports—New Orleans, La.; Houston, Beaumont and Corpus Christi, Tex.; and Mobile, Ala.—with some of the largest inland ports—St. Louis, Mo.; Pittsburgh, Pa.; Huntington, W. Va.; Cincinnati, Ohio; Memphis, Tenn; and Chicago, Ill. The 40-foot controlling depth of the Mississippi River between the Gulf of Mexico and Baton Rouge allows ocean shipping to join the barge traffic, making this segment especially vital to both the domestic and foreign commerce of the United States.

The Atlantic Intracoastal Waterway provides 1,329 miles of protected channels for commercial and recreational navigation along the Atlantic Coast from Key West, Fla., to Norfolk, Va. Partially protected segments of the waterway continue north from Norfolk along the Delmarva Peninsula, the New Jersey coast, and Long Island. Among the major Atlantic Coast ports located along this waterway are Miami, Savannah, Baltimore, Philadelphia, and New York/New Jersey.

Pacific Coast In comparison with the Mississippi River system and the intracoastal waterways of the Atlantic and Gulf coasts, the inland and coastal waterways of the Pacific are few. Shallow draft waterways include the Columbia-Snake Waterway and the Willamette River above Portland, Oreg.; the Sacramento River above Sacramento, Calif.; the San Joaquin River above Stockton, Calif.; and a few short navigable rivers stretching along the Washington and Oregon coasts.

The accompanying table shows the major navigable rivers in the United States, their total length,

the distance commercially navigable, the body of water they flow into, and the head of navigation—the upriver point beyond which commercial ships cannot pass—and the states through or by which the rivers pass, from source to mouth.

Great Lakes and St. Lawrence Seaway The Great Lakes have been crucial to the development of the United States. They were the highways along which people and finished goods moved west, and along which raw materials such as lumber, minerals, and grains were transported to eastern markets. Later, the cities of the Great Lakes, such as Chicago, Duluth, Detroit, and Buffalo, became important centers of finance, industry, and trade in their own right. So important was the maritime trade of the Lakes that in the 1890s, Chicago was the fourth-largest port in the world, despite being closed by ice for as many as five months a year.

An early obstacle to Great Lakes navigation was the fact that the lakes are not all at the same elevation: there is a difference of 354 feet between the level of the westernmost Lake Superior and easternmost Lake Ontario, and there is another 246 feet descent from Lake Ontario down the St. Lawrence River where it empties into the Atlantic Ocean. (It is 2,342 miles from Duluth, Minnesota, at the western end of Lake Superior, to the mouth of the St. Lawrence.)

The first canal (1799) was built on the St. Mary's River between Lake Superior and Lake Huron. (Today, there are two Sault Sainte Marie [or Soo] Canals—along the 70-mile river.) In 1825, the United States opened the way between the upper Lakes (all but Lake Ontario) and the Atlantic via the 175-mile Erie Canal between Buffalo, on Lake Erie, and Albany, on the Hudson River north of New York City. Canada followed with the 27-mile Welland Canal (1833) connecting Welland on Lake Erie and St. Catharine's on Lake Ontario.

The most ambitious undertaking was the construction of the St. Lawrence Seaway, a joint Canadian-American effort to open the entire length of the St. Lawrence and the Great Lakes to oceangoing navigation. Started in 1955 and opened to navigation in 1959, the seaway's system of canals and locks allows ships of up to 730 feet in length and 27 feet draft to sail the entire 2,342 miles from the mouth of the St. Lawrence to Duluth, Minn., at the western end of Lake Superior. The seaway also provides hydroelectric power for Canada and the United States.

The Panama Canal One of the great engineering feats of the world, the 44-mile Panama Canal bisects the continents of North and South America, making it possible for ships to sail between the Atlantic and Pacific oceans without rounding

	The Great Lakes					
	Area		Depth		Height above sea level	
Lake	(sq. mi)	(sq. km)	(feet)	(meters)	(feet)	(meters)
Erie	9,940	25,745	210	64	571	174
Huron	23,010	59,596	750	229	577	176
Michigan	22,400	58,016	923	281	577	176
Ontario	7,540	19,529	802	244	246	75
Superior	31,820	82,414	1,333	406	600	183

Source: U.S. Environmental Protection Agency and Environment Canada, *The Great Lakes: An Environmental Atlas and Resource Book* (1987).

the treacherous Cape Horn at the tip of South America. The U.S. government began construction of the canal in 1904, and it was opened to commercial navigation Aug. 15, 1914. For inter-ocean shippers, the savings in distance and time afforded by the canal are enormous. A ship sailing from New York to San Francisco via the Panama Canal travels a distance of 5,264 miles, a savings of more than 7,800 miles—or about 20 days— over the 13,100-mile route around Cape Horn. The minimum depth of the canal is 41 feet, the minimum width 300 feet, and the highest elevation above sea level 85 feet.

The Canal Zone, a 10-mile-wide strip of land around the canal in the Republic of Panama was acquired in 1903 by the United States, who governed it until 1979. The Panama Canal Treaty of 1977 abolished the Canal Zone as an independent political entity, but the canal's maintenance and operation remained the responsibility of the U.S. Panama Canal Commission until 1999, when the Republic of Panama assumed full responsibility.

Land Cover and Use, by State, 1997 (thousands of acres)

State	Total surface area[1]	Federal land area	Developed[2]	Rural cropland	Rural pastureland	Rural rangeland	Rural forestland
				Non-Federal land areas			
United States	1,941,827	452,913	104,812	374,690	119,144	402,976	398,409
Alabama	33,424	2,240	2,410	2,919	3,527	68	21,073
Arizona	72,964	30,634	1,675	1,204	67	32,114	4,262
Arkansas	34,037	3,997	1,501	7,582	5,453	73	14,765
California	101,510	48,584	5,687	9,561	1,065	17,457	14,295
Colorado	66,625	24,145	1,706	8,860	1,269	23,855	3,729
Connecticut	3,195	143	897	199	107	-	1,729
Delaware	1,534	321	238	472	23	-	347
Florida	37,534	6,938	5,449	2,719	4,177	3,193	12,255
Georgia	37,741	3,177	4,238	4,661	2,853	-	21,216
Hawaii	4,163	446	186	244	89	946	1,514
Idaho	53,488	34,120	811	5,500	1,253	6,478	3,942
Illinois	36,059	1,252	3,262	23,954	2,525	-	3,631
Indiana	23,158	858	2,356	13,358	1,818	-	3,638
Iowa	36,017	663	1,803	25,262	3,554	-	2,084
Kansas	52,661	1,064	2,882	26,460	2,213	15,179	1,290
Kentucky	25,863	1,815	1,955	5,151	5,613	-	10,440
Louisiana	31,377	5,063	1,693	5,568	2,376	280	13,114
Maine	20,966	1,457	747	419	82	-	17,633
Maryland	7,870	1,832	1,291	1,598	454	-	2,331
Massachusetts	5,339	477	1,549	271	114	-	2,657
Michigan	37,349	4,385	3,764	8,439	2,004	-	16,238
Minnesota	54,010	6,484	2,361	21,328	3,423	-	14,830
Mississippi	30,527	2,632	1,656	5,296	3,699	-	16,019
Missouri	44,614	2,766	2,653	13,710	10,947	98	12,118
Montana	94,110	28,150	881	15,086	3,495	37,016	5,279
Nebraska	49,510	1,139	1,268	19,421	1,976	22,864	799
Nevada	70,763	60,315	416	711	271	8,300	297
New Hampshire	5,941	1,000	642	132	92	-	3,875
New Jersey	5,216	679	1,849	574	109	-	1,625
New Mexico	77,823	26,603	1,325	1,842	207	40,276	4,915
New York	31,361	1,495	3,373	5,375	2,627	-	17,533
North Carolina	33,709	5,284	4,181	5,539	1,980	-	15,678
North Dakota	45,251	2,834	1,152	24,991	1,105	10,551	443
Ohio	26,445	781	3,797	11,504	1,980	-	6,984
Oklahoma	44,738	2,230	1,997	9,709	7,933	13,974	7,254
Oregon	62,161	32,088	1,296	3,800	1,905	9,556	12,295
Pennsylvania	28,995	1,204	4,336	5,245	1,812	-	15,306
Rhode Island	813	154	205	20	24	-	381
South Carolina	19,939	1,857	2,325	2,542	1,182	-	10,958
South Dakota	49,358	3,991	1,035	16,738	2,078	21,764	532
Tennessee	26,974	2,020	2,618	4,566	4,985	-	11,736
Texas	171,052	7,062	8,984	26,762	15,807	95,323	10,627
Utah	54,339	36,079	760	1,676	695	10,720	1,830
Vermont	6,154	659	346	601	342	-	4,118
Virginia	27,087	4,604	2,805	2,879	3,071	-	13,030
Washington	44,035	13,478	2,214	6,689	1,200	5,744	12,666
West Virginia	15,508	1,385	986	848	1,503	-	10,472
Wisconsin	35,920	3,142	2,543	10,537	2,882	-	13,634
Wyoming	62,603	29,184	716	2,171	1,181	27,150	995

Note: U.S. Totals exclude Alaska and the District of Columbia. 1. Includes water area and minor land cover and uses not shown separately. 2. Includes urban and built-up areas in units of 10 acres or greater, and rural tranportation areas.
Source: U.S. Department of Agriculture, National Resource and Conservation Service and Iowa State University, *Statistical Laboratory, Summary Report,* 1997 National Resources Inventory, December, 1999.

Major Navigable Rivers in the U.S.

Ultimate outflow/river	Length (miles)	Navigable length (miles)	Mouth to head of navigation	States/provinces (from source to mouth)
ATLANTIC OCEAN				
St. Lawrence	760	760	Gulf of St. Lawrence to Lake Ontario	N.Y.; Ontario, Quebec (Canada)
Cape Cod Canal	17	17	Sandwich to Buzzards Bay, Mass.	Mass.
Connecticut	407	52	Long Island Sound to Hartford, Conn.	N.H., Vt., Mass., Conn.
Hudson	306	134	New York Bay to Troy Lock, N.Y. New York State Barge Canal links to Lake Erie (353 mi. Troy to Buffalo), and to Lakes Champlain, Ontario, Cayuga, Seneca.	N.Y.
Delaware	367	77	Delaware Bay to Trenton, N.J.	N.Y., Pa., N.J., Del.
Chesapeake and Delaware Canal	14	14	Delaware Bay to Chesapeake Bay	Del., Md.
Potomac	287	101	Chesapeake Bay to Washington, D.C.	Va., Md., D.C.
James	340	87	Chesapeake Bay to Richmond, Va.	Va.
Roanoke	410	112	Atlantic Ocean to Altavista, N.C.	Va., N.C.
Cape Fear	202	111	Atlantic Ocean to Fayetteville, N.C.	N.C.
Savannah	314	181	Atlantic Ocean to Augusta, Ga.	S.C., Ga.
Saint Johns	285	160	Atlantic Ocean to Lake Harney	Fla.
GULF OF MEXICO				
Chattahoochee	436	194	Apalachicola River to Columbus, Ga.	Ga., Ala.
Apalachicola	90	90	Gulf of Mexico to Chattahoochee, Fla.	Fla.
Mobile	45	45	Mobile Bay to confluence of Alabama and Tombigbee rivers	Ala.
Alabama	318	305	Mobile River to Montgomery, Ala.	Ala.
Tombigbee	362	362	Mobile River to Amory, Miss. Linked to Tennessee River by Tennessee-Tombigbee Waterway (253 mi.)	Miss., Ala.
Black Warrior	217	217	Tombigbee River to Birmingham, Ala.	Ala.
Houston Ship Channel	57	57	Galveston Bay to Houston, Tex.	Tex.
Rio Grande[1]	1,885	13	Gulf of Mexico to Brownsville, Tex.	Colo., N.Mex., Tex., Mexico
MISSISSIPPI RIVER SYSTEM				
Mississippi	2,348	1,807	Gulf of Mexico to Minneapolis, Minn.,	Minn., Wis., Iowa, Ill., Mo., Ky., Tenn., Ark., Miss., La
EASTERN TRIBUTARIES OF THE MISSISSIPPI				
Illinois	273	273	Mississippi River to Joliet. Also linked to Mississippi by Illinois and Mississippi Canal (La Salle to Rockport); and to Lake Michigan (at Chicago, Calumet, East Chicago Gary) by Illinois Waterway	Ill.
Ohio	981	981	Mississippi River to Pittsburgh, Pa.	Pa., Ohio, W.Va., Ind., Ky., Ill.
Monongahela	129	129	Ohio River to Fairmont, W.Va.	W.Va., Pa.
Allegheny	325	72	Ohio River to East Brady, Pa.	N.Y., Pa.
Kanawha	97	91	Ohio River to Charleston, W.Va.	W.Va.
Kentucky	259	82	Ohio River to Beattyville, Ky.	Ky.
Green	360	103	Ohio River to Bowling Green, Ky.	Ky.
Cumberland	694	387	Ohio River to Burnside, Ky.	Ky., Tenn.
Tennessee	652	648	Ohio River to Knoxville, Tenn.	Tenn., Ala., Miss., Ky.
Yazoo	169	165	Mississippi River to Greenwood, Miss.	Miss.
WESTERN TRIBUTARIES OF THE MISSISSIPPI				
Missouri	2,315	735	Mississippi River to Ponca, Nebr.	Mont., N.Dak., S.Dak., Nebr., Iowa, Kans., Mo.
Arkansas	1,396	448	McClellan-Kerr Arkansas River System from Mississippi River to Catoosa, Okla., incorporates sections of White, Arkansas, Verdigris rivers.	Colo., Kans., Okla., Ark.,
Ouachita[2]	605	351	Mississippi River to Camden, Ark.	Ark., La.
Red	1,018	236	Mississippi River to Shreveport, La.	N.Mex., Tex., Okla., Ark., La.
Atchafalaya[3]	220	220	Atchafalaya Bay to Mississippi River	La.
PACIFIC OCEAN				
San Joaquin	340	103	Sacramento River to Hills Ferry, Calif.	Calif.
Sacramento	374	163	San Francisco Bay to Chico Landing, Calif.	Calif.
Columbia	1,210	285	Pacific Ocean to Pasco, Wash.	British Col. (Can.), Wash., Oreg.
Snake	1,083	192	Columbia River to Johnson Bar Landing,	Wyo., Idaho, Oreg., Wash.
Willamette	294	133	Columbia River to Harrisburg, Oreg.	Oreg.

Note: All distances given in nautical miles except for the Mississippi River and its tributaries: 1 nautical mile = 1.151 statute miles. 1. In Mexico known as the Río Bravo or Río Bravo del Norte. 2. Lower 57 miles known as the Black River. 3. Flows from the Mississippi River to the Gulf of Mexico.
Source: National Oceanic and Atmospheric Administration, *Distances Between United States Ports, 1987* (1987).

Extreme Elevations of States and Outlying Areas

State	Highest Point Name	Feet	Meters	Lowest Point Name	Feet	Meters
United States	Mount McKinley, Alaska	20,320	6,198	Death Valley, Calif.	-282	-86
Alabama	Cheaha Mountain	2,405	733	Gulf of Mexico	Sea level	
Alaska	Mount McKinley	20,320	6,198	Pacific Ocean	Sea level	
Arizona	Humphreys Peak	12,633	3,853	Colorado River	70	21
Arkansas	Magazine Mountain	2,753	840	Ouachita River	55	17
California	Mount Whitney	14,494	4,419	Death Valley	-282	-86
Colorado	Mount Elbert	14,433	4,402	Arkansas River	3,315	1,011
Connecticut	Mount Frissell, South slope	2,380	726	Long Island Sound	Sea level	
Delaware	Ebright Rd., New Castle Co.	448	137	Atlantic Ocean	Sea level	
Dist of Columbia	Tenleytown	410	125	Potomac River	1	0.3
Florida	Sec.30,T6N,R20W, Walton Co.	345	105	Atlantic Ocean	Sea level	
Georgia	Brasstown Bald	4,784	1,459	Atlantic Ocean	Sea level	
Hawaii	Mauna Kea	13,806	4,208	Pacific Ocean	Sea level	
Idaho	Borah Peak	12,662	3,862	Snake River	710	217
Illinois	Charles Mound	1,235	377	Mississippi River	279	85
Indiana	Franklin Township, Wayne Co.	1,257	383	Ohio River	320	98
Iowa	Sec. 29, T100N, R41W Osceola Co.	1,670	509	Mississippi River	480	146
Kansas	Mount Sunflower	4,039	1,232	Verdigris River	679	207
Kentucky	Black Mountain	4,139	1,262	Mississippi River	257	78
Louisiana	Driskill Mountain	535	163	New Orleans	-8	-2
Maine	Mount Katahdin	5,267	1,606	Atlantic Ocean	Sea level	
Maryland	Backbone Mountain	3,360	1,025	Atlantic Ocean	Sea level	
Massachusetts	Mount Greylock	3,487	1,064	Atlantic Ocean	Sea level	
Michigan	Mount Arvon	1,979	604	Lake Erie	571	174
Minnesota	Eagle Mountain, Cook Co.	2,301	702	Lake Superior	600	183
Mississippi	Woodall Mountain	806	246	Gulf of Mexico	Sea level	
Missouri	Taum Sauk Mountain	1,772	540	St. Francis River	230	70
Montana	Granite Peak	12,799	3,904	Kootenai River	1,800	549
Nebraska	Johnson Township, Kimball Co.	5,424	1,653	Missouri River	840	256
Nevada	Boundary Peak	13,140	4,007	Colorado River	479	146
New Hampshire	Mount Washington	6,288	1,918	Atlantic Ocean	Sea level	
New Jersey	High Point	1,803	550	Atlantic Ocean	Sea level	
New Mexico	Wheeler Peak	13,161	4,014	Red Bluff Reservoir	2,842	867
New York	Mount Marcy	5,344	1,630	Atlantic Ocean	Sea level	
North Carolina	Mount Mitchell	6,684	2,039	Atlantic Ocean	Sea level	
North Dakota	White Butte, Slope Co.	3,506	1,069	Red River	750	229
Ohio	Campbell Hill	1,549	472	Ohio River	455	139
Oklahoma	Black Mesa	4,973	1,517	Little River	289	88
Oregon	Mount Hood	11,239	3,428	Pacific Ocean	Sea level	
Pennsylvania	Mount Davis	3,213	980	Delaware River	Sea level	
Rhode Island	Jerimoth Hill	812	248	Atlantic Ocean	Sea level	
South Carolina	Sassafras Mountain	3,560	1,086	Atlantic Ocean	Sea level	
South Dakota	Harney Peak	7,242	2,209	Big Stone Lake	966	295
Tennessee	Clingmans Dome	6,643	2,026	Mississippi River	178	54
Texas	Guadalupe Peak	8,749	2,668	Gulf of Mexico	Sea level	
Utah	Kings Peak	13,528	4,126	Beaverdam Creek	2,000	610
Vermont	Mount Mansfield	4,393	1,340	Lake Champlain	95	29
Virginia	Mount Rogers	5,729	1,747	Atlantic Ocean	Sea level	
Washington	Mount Rainier	14,410	4,395	Pacific Ocean	Sea level	
West Virginia	Spruce Knob	4,861	1,483	Potomac River	240	73
Wisconsin	Timms Hill	1,951	595	Lake Michigan	579	177
Wyoming	Gannett Peak	13,804	4,210	Belle Fourche River	3,099	945
Puerto Rico	Cerro de Punta	4,390	1,339	Atlantic Ocean	Sea level	
Amer. Samoa	Lata Mountain	3,160	964	Pacific Ocean	Sea level	
Guam	Mount Lamlam	1,332	405	Pacific Ocean	Sea level	
Virgin Islands	Crown Mountain	1,556	475	Atlantic Ocean	Sea level	

Note: Sec. denotes section; T, township; R, range; N, north; W, west.
Source: U.S. Geological Survey, *Elevations and Distances in the United States* (2000).

U.S. History

DOCUMENTS OF
U.S. HISTORY

▶THE DECLARATION OF INDEPENDENCE

After a year of war with Britain, American patriots were driven to make the final break in 1776. On June 7, before the Continental Congress in Philadelphia, Richard Henry Lee of Virginia proposed a declaration that the colonies "are, and of right ought to be, free and independent States." A committee of five, headed by Thomas Jefferson, was appointed to draw up the formal Declaration of Independence on June 10. The committee brought its version, mainly the work of Jefferson, back to Congress on June 28. Congress voted unanimously to declare independence on July 2, and after making several changes in the Jefferson committee's draft, they unanimously adopted the Declaration of Independence on July 4. Copies of the Declaration were dispatched to the states for approval. Charles Carroll of Maryland was the last surviving signer of the Declaration when he died on November 14, 1832. The original document is on display today at the National Archives in Washington, D.C.

In Congress, July 4, 1776,
THE UNANIMOUS DECLARATION
OF THE
THIRTEEN UNITED STATES
OF AMERICA,

When in the Course of human events, it becomes necessary for one people to dissolve the political bands which have connected them with another, and to assume among the Powers of the earth, the separate and equal station to which the Laws of Nature and of Nature's God entitle them, a decent respect to the opinions of mankind requires that they should declare the causes which impel them to the separation.

We hold these truths to be self-evident, that all men are created equal, that they are endowed by their Creator with certain unalienable Rights, that among these are Life, Liberty and the pursuit of Happiness. That to secure these rights, Governments are instituted among Men, deriving their just powers from the consent of the governed. That whenever any Form of Government becomes destructive of these ends, it is the Right of the People to alter or to abolish it, and to institute new Government, laying its foundation on such principles and organizing its powers in such form, as to them shall seem most likely to effect their Safety and Happiness. Prudence, indeed, will dictate that governments long established should not be changed for light and transient causes; and accordingly all experience hath shown, that mankind are more disposed to suffer, while evils are sufferable, than to right themselves by abolishing the forms to which they are accustomed. But when a long train of abuses and usurpations, pursuing invariably the same Object evinces a design to reduce them under absolute Despotism, it is their right, it is their duty, to throw off such Government, and to provide new Guards for their future security. Such has been the patient sufferance of these Colonies; and such is now the ne-

cessity which constrains them to alter their former Systems of Government. The history of the present King of Great Britain is a history of repeated injuries and usurpations, all having in direct object the establishment of an absolute Tyranny over these States. To prove this, let Facts be submitted to a candid world.

He has refused his Assent to Laws, the most wholesome and necessary for the public good.

He has forbidden his Governors to pass Laws of immediate and pressing importance, unless suspended in their operation till his Assent should be obtained; and when so suspended, he has utterly neglected to attend to them.

He has refused to pass other Laws for the accommodation of large districts of people, unless those people would relinquish the right of Representation in the Legislature, a right inestimable to them and formidable to tyrants only.

He has called together legislative bodies at places unusual, uncomfortable, and distant from the depository of their Public Records, for the sole purpose of fatiguing them into compliance with his measures.

He has dissolved Representative Houses repeatedly, for opposing with manly firmness his invasions on the rights of the people.

He has refused for a long time, after such dissolutions, to cause others to be elected; whereby the Legislative Powers, incapable of Annihilation, have returned to the People at large for their exercise; the State remaining in the mean time exposed to all the dangers of invasion from without, and convulsions within.

He has endeavoured to prevent the population of these States; for that purpose obstructing the Laws of Naturalization of Foreigners; refusing to pass others to encourage their migration hither, and raising the conditions of new Appropriations of Lands.

He has obstructed the Administration of Justice, by refusing his Assent to Laws for establishing Judiciary Powers.

He has made Judges dependent on his Will alone, for the tenure of their offices, and the amount and payment of their salaries.

He has erected a multitude of New Offices, and sent hither swarms of Officers to harass our People, and eat out their substance.

He has kept among us, in times of peace, Standing Armies without the Consent of our legislature.

He has affected to render the Military independent of and superior to the Civil Power.

He has combined with others to subject us to a jurisdiction foreign to our constitution, and unacknowledged by our laws; giving his Assent to their acts of pretended legislation:

For quartering large bodies of armed troops among us:

For protecting them, by a mock Trial, from Punishment for any Murders which they should commit on the Inhabitants of these States:

For cutting off our Trade with all parts of the world:

For imposing taxes on us without our consent:

For depriving us in many cases, of the benefits of Trial by Jury:

For transporting us beyond Seas to be tried for pretended offences:

For abolishing the free System of English Laws in a neighbouring Province, establishing therein an Arbitrary government, and enlarging its Boundaries so as to render it at once an example and fit instrument for introducing the same absolute rule into these Colonies:

For taking away our Charters, abolishing our most valuable Laws, and altering fundamentally the forms of our Government:

For suspending our own legislature, and declaring themselves invested with Power to legislate for us in all cases whatsoever.

He has abdicated Government here, by declaring us out of his Protection and waging War against us.

He has plundered our seas, ravaged our Coasts, burnt our towns, and destroyed the lives of our people.

He is at this time transporting large armies of foreign mercenaries to compleat the works of death, desolation and tyranny, already begun with circumstances of Cruelty & perfidy scarcely paralleled in the most barbarous ages, and totally unworthy of the Head of a civilized nation.

He has constrained our fellow Citizens taken Captive on the high Seas to bear Arms against their Country, to become the executioners of their friends and Brethren, or to fall themselves by their Hands.

He has excited domestic insurrections amongst us, and has endeavoured to bring on the inhabitants of our frontiers, the merciless Indian Savages, whose known rule of warfare, is an undistinguished destruction of all ages, sexes and conditions.

In every stage of these Oppressions We have Petitioned for Redress in the most humble terms: Our repeated Petitions have been answered only by repeated injury. A prince, whose character is thus marked by every act which may define a Tyrant, is unfit to be the ruler of a free People.

Nor have We been wanting in attention to our British brethren. We have warned them from time to time of attempts by their legislature to extend an unwarrantable jurisdiction over us. We have reminded them of the circumstances of our emigration and settlement here. We have appealed to their native justice and magnanimity, and we have conjured them by the ties of our common kindred to disavow these usurpations, which would inevitably interrupt our connections and correspondence. They too have been deaf to the voice of justice and of consanguinity. We must, therefore, acquiesce in the necessity, which denounces our Separation and hold them, as we hold the rest of mankind, Enemies in War, in Peace Friends.

We, therefore, the Representatives of the United States of America, in General Congress, Assembled, appealing to the Supreme Judge of the world for the rectitude of our intentions, do, in the Name, and by Authority of the good People of these Colonies, solemnly publish and declare, That these United Colonies are, and of Right ought to be Free and Independent States; that they are Absolved from all Allegiance to the British Crown, and that all political connection between them and the State of Great Britain, is and ought to be totally dissolved; and that as Free and Independent States, they have full Power to levy War, conclude Peace, contract Alliances, establish Commerce, and to do all other Acts and Things which Independent States may of right do. And for the support of this Declaration, with a firm reliance on the Protection of Divine Providence, we mutually pledge to each other our Lives, our Fortunes and our sacred Honor.

▶ THE U.S. CONSTITUTION

During and after the Revolution, the United States was governed by the Continental Congress under the Articles of Confederation, which delegated very limited powers to the national government and reserved the rest to the states. Economic chaos, political confusion, and widespread dissatisfaction with the lack of central authority peaked after Shays' Rebellion in 1786. George Washington lent his prestige to the call for a convention to consider a new form of government. Congress endorsed the plan on February 21, 1787, "for the sole and express purpose of revising the Articles of Confederation." All states but Rhode Island sent delegates to the convention, which opened in Philadelphia on May 14. The delegates moved at once to discard the Articles, draw up a new Constitution, and conduct their meetings in secrecy, while Washington presided and James Madison took notes. A long summer of debate and compromise finally produced the document that most of the delegates signed on September 17. Congress ordered the Constitution sent to the states for ratification on September 28, requiring approval by at least nine of them to validate the new charter. Whether the Constitution would be adopted was in doubt until June 21, 1788, when New Hampshire became the ninth state to ratify it. The Constitution went into effect on March 4, 1789. All of the original thirteen states eventually ratified the Constitution, ending with Rhode Island on May 29, 1790. The U.S. Constitution remains the world's oldest written constitution.

Preamble

We, the People of the United States, in Order to form a more perfect Union, establish Justice, insure domestic Tranquillity, provide for the common defence, promote the general Welfare, and secure the Blessings of Liberty to ourselves and our Posterity, do ordain and establish this Constitution for the United States of America.

Article I

Section 1 All legislative powers herein granted shall be vested in a Congress of the United States, which shall consist of a Senate and House of Representatives.

Section 2 [1] The House of Representatives shall be composed of members chosen every second year by the people of the several States, and the electors in each State shall have the qualifications requisite for electors of the most numerous branch of the State legislature.

[2] No person shall be a Representative who shall not have attained to the age of twenty-five years, and been seven years a citizen of the United States, and who shall not, when elected, be an inhabitant of that State in which he shall be chosen.

[3] Representatives and direct taxes shall be apportioned among the several States which may be included within this Union, according to their respective numbers, which shall be determined by adding to the whole number of free persons, including those bound to service for a term of years, and excluding Indians not taxed, three-fifths of all other persons. The actual enumeration shall be made within three years after the first meeting of the Congress of the United States, and within every subsequent term of ten years, in such manner as they shall by law direct. The number of Representatives shall not exceed one for every thirty thousand, but each State shall have at least one Representative; and until such enumeration shall be made, the State of New Hampshire shall

Signers of the Declaration of Independence

Delegate	State	Born/Died	Delegate	State	Born/Died
Adams, John	Massachusetts	1735–1826	Lynch, Thomas, Jr.	South Carolina	1749–1779
Adams, Samuel	Massachusetts	1722–1803	McKean, Thomas	Delaware	1734–1817
Bartlett, Josiah	New Hampshire	1729–1795	Middleton, Arthur	South Carolina	1742–1787
Braxton, Carter	Virginia	1736–1797	Morris, Lewis	New York	1726–1798
Carroll, Charles	Maryland	1737–1832	Morris, Robert	Pennsylvania	1734–1806
Chase, Samuel	Maryland	1741–1811	Morton, John	Pennsylvania	1724–1777
Clark, Abraham	New Jersey	1726–1794	Nelson, Thomas Jr.	Virginia	1738–1789
Clymer, George	Pennsylvania	1739–1813	Paca, William	Maryland	1740–1799
Ellery, William	Rhode Island	1727–1820	Paine, Robert Treat	Massachusetts	1731–1814
Floyd, William	New York	1734–1821	Penn, John	North Carolina	1741–1788
Franklin, Benjamin	Pennsylvania	1706–1790	Read, George	Delaware	1733–1798
Gerry, Elbridge	Massachusetts	1744–1814	Rodney, Caesar	Delaware	1728–1784
Gwinnett, Button	Georgia	1732–1777	Ross, George	Pennsylvania	1730–1779
Hall, Lyman	Georgia	1724–1790	Rush, Benjamin	Pennsylvania	1745–1813
Hancock, John	Massachusetts	1737–1793	Rutledge, Edward	South Carolina	1749–1800
Harrison, Benjamin	Virginia	1726–1791	Sherman, Roger	Connecticut	1721–1793
Hart, John	New Jersey	? –1779	Smith, James	Pennsylvania	1713–1806
Hewes, Joseph	North Carolina	1730–1779	Stockton, Richard	New Jersey	1730–1781
Heyward, Thomas, Jr.	South Carolina	1746–1809	Stone, Thomas	Maryland	1743–1787
Hooper, William	North Carolina	1742–1790	Taylor, George	Pennsylvania	1716–1781
Hopkins, Stephen	Rhode Island	1707–1785	Thornton, Matthew	New Hampshire	1714–1803
Hopkinson, Francis	New Jersey	1737–1791	Walton, George	Georgia	1741–1804
Huntington, Samuel	Connecticut	1731–1796	Whipple, William	New Hampshire	1730–1785
Jefferson, Thomas	Virginia	1743–1826	Williams, William	Connecticut	1731–1811
Lee, Richard Henry	Virginia	1732–1794	Wilson, James	Pennsylvania	1742–1798
Lee, Francis Lightfoot	Virginia	1734–1797	Witherspoon, John	New Jersey	1723–1794
Lewis, Francis	New York	1713–1803	Wolcott, Oliver	Connecticut	1726–1797
Livingston, Philip	New York	1716–1778	Wythe, George	Virginia	1726–1806

be entitled to choose three; Massachusetts, eight; Rhode Island and Providence Plantations, one; Connecticut, five; New York, six; New Jersey, four; Pennsylvania, eight; Delaware, one; Maryland, six; Virginia, ten; North Carolina, five; South Carolina, five; and Georgia, three.

[4] When vacancies happen in the representation from any State, the executive authority thereof shall issue writs of election to fill such vacancies.

[5] The House of Representatives shall choose their Speaker and other officers, and shall have the sole power of impeachment.

Section 3 [1] The Senate of the United States shall be composed of two Senators from each State, chosen by the legislature thereof for six years; and each Senator shall have one vote.

[2] Immediately after they shall be assembled in consequence of the first election, they shall be divided as equally as may be into three classes. The seats of the Senators of the first class shall be vacated at the expiration of the second year, of the second class at the expiration of the fourth year, and of the third class at the expiration of the sixth year, so that one-third may be chosen every second year; and if vacancies happen by resignation or otherwise during the recess of the legislature of any State, the executive thereof may make temporary appointments until the next meeting of the legislature, which shall then fill such vacancies.

[3] No person shall be a Senator who shall not have attained to the age of thirty years, and been nine years a citizen of the United States, and who shall not, when elected, be an inhabitant of that State for which he shall be chosen.

[4] The Vice-President of the United States shall be President of the Senate, but shall have no vote, unless they be equally divided.

[5] The Senate shall choose their other officers and also a President pro tempore in the absence of the Vice-President, or when he shall exercise the office of President of the United States.

[6] The Senate shall have the sole power to try all impeachments. When sitting for that purpose, they shall be on oath or affirmation. When the President of the United States is tried, the Chief Justice shall preside; and no person shall be convicted without the concurrence of two-thirds of the members present.

[7] Judgment in cases of impeachment shall not extend further than to removal from office, and disqualification to hold and enjoy any office of honor, trust, or profit under the United States; but the party convicted shall, nevertheless, be liable and subject to indictment, trial, judgment, and punishment, according to law.

Section 4 [1] The times, places, and manner of holding elections for Senators and Representatives shall be prescribed in each State by the legislature thereof; but the Congress may at any time by law make or alter such regulations, except as to the places of choosing Senators.

[2] The Congress shall assemble at least once in every year, and such meeting shall be on the first Monday in December, unless they shall by law appoint a different day.

Section 5 [1] Each House shall be the judge of the elections, returns, and qualification of its own members, and a majority of each shall constitute a quorum to do business; but a smaller number may adjourn from day to day, and may be authorized to compel the attendance of absent members, in such manner, and under such penalties, as each House may provide.

[2] Each House may determine the rules of its proceedings, punish its members for disorderly behavior, and with the concurrence of two-thirds, expel a member.

[3] Each House shall keep a journal of its proceedings, and from time to time publish the

same, excepting such parts as may in their judgment require secrecy, and the yeas and nays of the members of either House on any question shall, at the desire of one-fifth of those present, be entered on the journal.

[4] Neither House, during the session of Congress, shall, without the consent of the other, adjourn for more than three days, nor to any other place than that in which the two Houses shall be sitting.

Section 6 [1] The Senators and Representatives shall receive a compensation for their services, to be ascertained by law and paid out of the Treasury of the United States. They shall, in all cases except treason, felony, and breach of the peace, be privileged from arrest during their attendance at the session of their respective Houses, and in going to and returning from the same; and for any speech or debate in either House they shall not be questioned in any other place.

[2] No Senator or Representative shall, during the time for which he was elected, be appointed to any civil office under the authority of the United States, which shall have been created, or the emoluments whereof shall have been increased during such time; and no person holding any office under the United States shall be a member of either House during his continuance in office.

Section 7 [1] All bills for raising revenue shall originate in the House of Representatives; but the Senate may propose or concur with amendments as on other bills.

[2] Every bill which shall have passed the House of Representatives and the Senate shall, before it becomes a law, be presented to the President of the United States; if he approves he shall sign it, but if not he shall return it, with his objections, to that House in which it shall have originated, who shall enter the objections at large on their journal and proceed to reconsider it. If after such reconsideration two-thirds of that House shall agree to pass the bill, it shall be sent, together with the objections, to the other House, by which it shall likewise be reconsidered, and if approved by two-thirds of that House it shall become a law. But in all such cases the vote of both Houses shall be determined by yeas and nays, and the names of the persons voting for and against the bill shall be entered on the journal of each House respectively. If any bill shall not be returned by the President within ten days (Sundays excepted) after it shall have been presented to him, the same shall be a law, in like manner as if he had signed it, unless the Congress by their adjournment prevent its return, in which case it shall not be a law.

[3] Every order, resolution or vote to which the concurrence of the Senate and House of Representatives may be necessary (except on a question of adjournment) shall be presented to the President of the United States; and before the same shall take effect shall be approved by him, or being disapproved by him, shall be repassed by two-thirds of the Senate and House of Representatives, according to the rules and limitations prescribed in the case of a bill.

Section 8 [1] The Congress shall have power to lay and collect taxes, duties, imposts and excises, to pay the debts and provide for the common defense and general welfare of the United States; but all duties, imposts and excises shall be uniform throughout the United States;

[2] To borrow money on the credit of the United States;

[3] To regulate commerce with foreign nations, and among the several States, and with the Indian tribes;

[4] To establish an uniform rule of naturalization, and uniform laws on the subject of bankruptcies throughout the United States;

[5] To coin money, regulate the value thereof, and of foreign coin, and fix the standard of weights and measures;

[6] To provide for the punishment of counterfeiting the securities and current coin of the United States;

[7] To establish post offices and post roads;

[8] To promote the progress of science and useful arts by securing for limited times to authors and inventors the exclusive right to their respective writings and discoveries;

[9] To constitute tribunals inferior to the Supreme Court;

[10] To define and punish piracies and felonies committed on the high seas and offenses against the law of nations.

[11] To declare war, grant letters of marque and reprisal, and make rules concerning captures on land and water;

[12] To raise and support armies, but no appropriation of money to that use shall be for a longer term than two years;

[13] To provide and maintain a navy;

[14] To make rules for the government and regulation of the land and naval forces;

[15] To provide for calling forth the militia to execute the laws of the Union, suppress insurrections, and repel invasions;

[16] To provide for organizing, arming and disciplining the militia, and for governing such part of them as may be employed in the service of the United States, reserving to the States respectively the appointment of the officers, and the authority of training the militia according to the discipline prescribed by Congress;

[17] To exercise exclusive legislation in all cases whatsoever over such district (not exceeding ten miles square) as may, by cession of particular States and the acceptance of Congress, become the seat of the Government of the United States, and to exercise like authority over all places purchased by the consent of the legislature of the State in which the same shall be, for the erection of forts, magazines, arsenals, dockyards, and other needful buildings;

[18] To make all laws which shall be necessary and proper for carrying into execution the foregoing powers, and all other powers vested by this Constitution in the Government of the United States, or in any department or officer thereof.

Section 9 [1] The migration or importation of such persons as any of the States now existing shall think proper to admit shall not be prohibited by the Congress prior to the year one thousand eight hundred and eight, but a tax or duty may be imposed on such importation, not exceeding ten dollars for each person.

[2] The privilege of the writ of habeas corpus shall not be suspended, unless when in cases of rebellion or invasion the public safety may require it.

[3] No bill of attainder or ex post facto law shall be passed.

[4] No capitation or other direct tax shall be laid, unless in proportion to the census or enumeration hereinbefore directed to be taken.

[5] No tax or duty shall be laid on articles exported from any State.

[6] No preference shall be given by any regulation of commerce or revenue to the ports of one State

over those of another; nor shall vessels bound to or from one State be obliged to enter, clear or pay duties in another.

[7] No money shall be drawn from the Treasury but in consequence of appropriations made by law; and a regular statement and account of the receipts and expenditures of all public money shall be published from time to time.

[8] No title of nobility shall be granted by the United States; and no person holding any office of profit or trust under them shall, without the consent of the Congress, accept of any present, emolument, office, or title of any kind whatever from any king, prince, or foreign state.

Section 10 [1] No State shall enter into any treaty, alliance, or confederation; grant letters of marque and reprisal; coin money, emit bills of credit, make anything but gold and silver coin a tender in payment of debts; pass any bill of attainder, ex post facto law or law impairing the obligation of contracts, or grant any title of nobility.

[2] No State shall, without the consent of the Congress, lay any imposts or duties on imports or exports, except what may be absolutely necessary for executing its inspection laws; and the net produce of all duties and imposts, laid by any State on imports or exports, shall be for the use of the Treasury of the United States; and all such laws shall be subject to the revision and control of the Congress.

[3] No State shall, without the consent of Congress, lay any duty of tonnage, keep troops and ships of war in time of peace, enter into any agreement or compact with another State or with a foreign power, or engage in war, unless actually invaded or in such imminent danger as will not admit of delay.

Article II

Section 1 [1] The executive power shall be vested in a President of the United States of America. He shall hold his office during the term of four years, and together with the Vice-President, chosen for the same term, be elected as follows:

[2] Each State shall appoint, in such manner as the legislature thereof may direct, a number of Electors, equal to the whole number of Senators and Representatives to which the State may be entitled in the Congress; but no Senator or Representative, or person holding an office of trust or profit under the United States shall be appointed an Elector.

[3] The Electors shall meet in their respective States and vote by ballot for two persons, of whom one at least shall not be an inhabitant of the same State with themselves. And they shall make a list of all the persons voted for, and of the number of votes for each; which list they shall sign and certify, and transmit sealed to the seat of government of the United States, directed to the President of the Senate. The President of the Senate shall, in the presence of the Senate and House of Representatives, open all the certificates, and the votes shall then be counted. The person having the greatest number of votes shall be the President, if such number be a majority of the whole number of Electors appointed; and if there be more than one who have such majority, and have an equal number of votes, then the House of Representatives shall immediately choose by ballot one of them for President; and if no person have a majority, then from the five highest on the list the said House shall in like manner choose the President. But in choosing the President the votes shall be taken by States, the representation from each State having one vote; a quorum for this purpose shall consist of a member or members from two-thirds of the States, and a majority of all the States shall be necessary to a choice. In every case, after the choice of the President, the person having the greatest number of votes of the Electors shall be the Vice-President. But if there should remain two or more who have equal votes, the Senate shall choose from them by ballot the Vice-President.

[4] The Congress may determine the time of choosing the Electors and the day on which they shall give their votes, which day shall be the same throughout the United States.

[5] No person except a natural-born citizen, or citizen of the United States at the time of the adoption of this Constitution, shall be eligible to the office of President; neither shall any person be eligible to that office who shall not have attained to the age of thirty-five years, and been fourteen years a resident within the United States.

[6] In case of the removal of the President from office, or of his death, resignation, or inability to discharge the powers and duties of the said office, the same shall devolve on the Vice-President, and the Congress may by law provide for the case of removal, death, resignation, or inability, both of the President and Vice-President, declaring what officer shall then act as President, and such officer shall act accordingly until the disability be removed or a President shall be elected.

[7] The President shall, at stated times, receive for his services a compensation, which shall neither be increased nor diminished during the period for which he shall have been elected, and he shall not receive within that period any other emolument from the United States or any of them.

[8] Before he enter on the execution of his office he shall take the following oath or affirmation:

"I do solemnly swear (or affirm) that I will faithfully execute the office of President of the United States, and will to the best of my ability preserve, protect, and defend the Constitution of the United States."

Section 2 [1] The President shall be Commander-in-Chief of the Army and Navy of the United States, and of the militia of the several States when called into the actual service of the United States; he may require the opinion, in writing, of the principal officer in each of the executive departments, upon any subject relating to the duties of their respective offices, and he shall have power to grant reprieves and pardons for offenses against the United States, except in cases of impeachment.

[2] He shall have power, by and with the advice and consent of the Senate, to make treaties, provided two-thirds of the Senators present concur; and he shall nominate, and, by and with the advice and consent of the Senate, shall appoint ambassadors, other public ministers and consuls, judges of the Supreme Court, and all other officers of the United States whose appointments are not herein otherwise provided for, and which shall be established by law; but the Congress may by law vest the appointment of such inferior officers, as they think proper, in the President alone, in the courts of law, or in the heads of departments.

[3] The President shall have power to fill up all vacancies that may happen during the recess of the Senate, by granting commissions which shall expire at the end of their next session.

Section 3 He shall from time to time give to the Congress information of the state of the Union, and recommend to their consideration such measures as he shall judge necessary and expedient; he may, on extraordinary occasions, convene both Houses, or either of them, and in case of disagreement between them with respect to the time of adjournment, he may adjourn them to such time as he shall think proper; he shall receive ambassadors and other public ministers; he shall take care that the laws be faithfully executed, and shall commission all the officers of the United States.

Section 4 The President, Vice-President and all civil officers of the United States shall be removed from office on impeachment for and conviction of treason, bribery, or other high crimes and misdemeanors.

Article III

Section 1 The judicial power of the United States shall be vested in one Supreme Court, and in such inferior courts as the Congress may from time to time ordain and establish. The judges, both of the Supreme and inferior courts, shall hold their offices during good behavior, and shall, at stated times, receive for their services a compensation which shall not be diminished during their continuance in office.

Section 2 [1] The judicial power shall extend to all cases, in law and equity, arising under this Constitution, the laws of the United States, and treaties made, or which shall be made, under their authority; to all cases affecting ambassadors, other public ministers, and consuls; to all cases of admiralty and maritime jurisdiction; to controversies to which the United States shall be a party; to controversies between two or more States; between a State and citizens of another State; between citizens of different States; between citizens of the same State claiming lands under grants of different States, and between a State, or the citizens thereof, and foreign states, citizens, or subjects.

[2] In all cases affecting ambassadors, other public ministers and consuls, and those in which a State shall be party, the Supreme Court shall have original jurisdiction. In all the other cases before mentioned the Supreme Court shall have appellate jurisdiction, both as to law and fact, with such exceptions and under such regulations as the Congress shall make.

[3] The trial of all crimes, except in cases of impeachment, shall be by jury; and such trial shall be held in the State where the said crimes shall have been committed; but when not committed within any State, the trial shall be at such place or places as the Congress may by law have directed.

Section 3 [1] Treason against the United States shall consist only in levying war against them, or in adhering to their enemies, giving them aid and comfort. No person shall be convicted of treason unless on the testimony of two witnesses to the same overt act, or on confession in open court.

[2] The Congress shall have power to declare the punishment of treason, but no attainder of treason shall work corruption of blood or forfeiture except during the life of the person attained.

Article IV

Section 1 Full faith and credit shall be given in each State to the public acts, records, and judicial proceedings of every other State. And the Congress may by general laws prescribe the manner in which such acts, records, and proceedings shall be proved, and the effect thereof.

Section 2 [1] The citizens of each State shall be entitled to all privileges and immunities of citizens in the several States.

[2] A person charged in any State with treason, felony, or other crime, who shall flee from justice, and be found in another State, shall, on demand of the executive authority of the State from which he fled, be delivered up, to be removed to the State having jurisdiction of the crime.

[3] No person held to service or labor in one State, under the laws thereof, escaping into another, shall, in consequence of any law or regulation therein, be discharged from such service or labor, but shall be delivered up on claim to the party to whom such service or labor may be due.

Section 3 [1] New States may be admitted by the Congress into this Union; but no new State shall be formed or erected within the jurisdiction of any other State; nor any State be formed by the junction of two or more States or parts of States, without the consent of the legislatures of the States concerned as well as of the Congress.

[2] The Congress shall have power to dispose of and make all needful rules and regulations respecting the territory or other property belonging to the United States; and nothing in this Constitution shall be so construed as to prejudice any claims of the United States or of any particular State.

Section 4 The United States shall guarantee to every State in this Union a republican form of government, and shall protect each of them against invasion, and on application of the legislature, or of the executive (when the legislature cannot be convened), against domestic violence.

Article V

The Congress, whenever two-thirds of both Houses shall deem it necessary, shall propose amendments to this Constitution, or, on the application of the legislatures of two-thirds of the several States, shall call a convention for proposing amendments, which in either case shall be valid to all intents and purposes as part of this Constitution, when ratified by the legislatures of three-fourths of the several States, or by conventions in three-fourths thereof, as the one or the other mode of ratification may be proposed by the Congress; provided that no amendment which may be made prior to the year one thousand eight hundred and eight shall in any manner affect the first and fourth clauses in the Ninth Section of the First Article; and that no State, without its consent, shall be deprived of its equal suffrage in the Senate.

Article VI

[1] All debts contracted and engagements entered into, before the adoption of this Constitution, shall be as valid against the United States under this Constitution as under the Confederation.

[2] This Constitution, and the laws of the United States which shall be made in pursuance thereof, and all treaties made, or which shall be made, under the authority of the United States, shall be the supreme law of the land; and the judges in every State shall be bound thereby, anything in the Constitution or laws of any State to the contrary notwithstanding.

[3] The Senators and Representatives before mentioned and the members of the several State legislatures, and all executive and judicial officers both of the United States and of the several States, shall be bound by oath or affirmation to support

this Constitution; but no religious test shall ever be required as a qualification to any office or public trust under the United States.

Article VII
The ratification of the conventions of nine States shall be sufficient for the establishment of this Constitution between the States so ratifying the same.

Amendments to the Constitution
[The first 10 amendments, known collectively as The Bill of Rights, were adopted in 1791.]

Amendment I
Congress shall make no law respecting an establishment of religion, or prohibiting the free exercise thereof; or abridging the freedom of speech or of the press; or the right of the people peaceably to assemble, and to petition the government for a redress of grievances.

Amendment II
A well-regulated militia being necessary to the security of a free State, the right of the people to keep and bear arms shall not be infringed.

Amendment III
No soldier shall, in time of peace, be quartered in any house without the consent of the owner, nor in time of war, but in a manner to be prescribed by law.

Amendment IV
The right of the people to be secure in their persons, houses, papers, and effects, against unreasonable searches and seizures, shall not be violated, and no warrants shall issue but upon probable cause, supported by oath or affirmation, and particularly describing the place to be searched, and the persons or things to be seized.

Amendment V
No person shall be held to answer for a capital, or otherwise infamous crime, unless on a presentment or indictment of a grand jury, except in cases arising in the land or naval forces, or in the militia, when in actual service in time of war or public danger; nor shall any person be subject for the same offense to be twice put in jeopardy of life or limb; nor shall be compelled in any criminal case to be a witness against himself, nor be deprived of life, liberty or property, without due process of law; nor shall private property be taken for public use without just compensation.

Amendment VI
In all criminal prosecutions, the accused shall enjoy the right to a speedy and public trial, by an impartial jury of the State and district wherein the crime shall have been committed, which district shall have been previously ascertained by law, and to be informed of the nature and cause of the accusation; to be confronted with the witnesses against him; to have compulsory process for obtaining witnesses in his favor, and to have the assistance of counsel for his defense.

Amendment VII
In suits at common law, where the value in controversy shall exceed twenty dollars, the right of trial by jury shall be preserved, and no fact tried by a jury shall be otherwise re-examined in any court of the United States, than according to the rules of the common law.

Amendment VIII
Excessive bail shall not be required, nor excessive fines imposed, nor cruel and unusual punishments inflicted.

Amendment IX
The enumeration in the Constitution of certain rights shall not be construed to deny or disparage others retained by the people.

Amendment X
The powers not delegated to the United States by the Constitution, nor prohibited by it to the States, are reserved to the States respectively, or to the people.

Amendment XI   [Adopted Jan. 8, 1798]
The judicial power of the United States shall not be construed to extend to any suit in law or equity, commenced or prosecuted against one of the United States by citizens of another State, or by citizens or subjects of any foreign state.

Amendment XII   [Adopted Sept. 25, 1804]
[1] The Electors shall meet in their respective States and vote by ballot for President and Vice-President, one of whom, at least, shall not be an inhabitant of the same State with themselves; they shall name in their ballots the person voted for as President, and in distinct ballots the person voted for as Vice-President, and they shall make distinct lists of all persons voted for as President and of all persons voted for as Vice-President, and of the number of votes for each; which lists they shall sign and certify, and transmit sealed to the seat of the government of the United States, directed to the President of the Senate. The President of the Senate shall, in the presence of the Senate and House of Representatives, open all the certificates and the votes shall then be counted. The person having the greatest number of votes for President shall be the President, if such number be a majority of the whole number of Electors appointed; and if no person have such majority, then from the persons having the highest numbers not exceeding three on the list of those voted for as President, the House of Representatives shall choose immediately, by ballot, the President. But in choosing the President the votes shall be taken by States, the representation from each State having one vote; a quorum for this purpose shall consist of a member or members from two-thirds of the States, and a majority of all the States shall be necessary to a choice. And if the House of Representatives shall not choose a President whenever the right of choice shall devolve upon them, before the fourth day of March next following, then the Vice-President shall act as President, as in the case of the death or other constitutional disability of the President.
[2] The person having the greatest number of votes as Vice-President shall be the Vice-President, if such number be a majority of the whole number of Electors appointed; and if no person have a majority, then from the two highest numbers on the list the Senate shall choose the Vice-President; a quorum for the purpose shall consist of two-thirds of the whole number of Senators, and a majority of the whole number shall be necessary to a choice. But no person constitutionally ineligible to the office of President shall be eligible to that of Vice-President of the United States.

Amendment   XIII   [Adopted Dec. 18, 1865]
Section 1 Neither slavery nor involuntary servi-

tude, except as a punishment for crime whereof the party shall have been duly convicted, shall exist within the United States, or any place subject to their jurisdiction.

Section 2 Congress shall have power to enforce this article by appropriate legislation.

Amendment XIV   [Adopted July 28, 1868]

Section 1 All persons born or naturalized in the United States, and subject to the jurisdiction thereof, are citizens of the United States and of the State wherein they reside. No State shall make or enforce any law which shall abridge the privileges or immunities of citizens of the United States; nor shall any State deprive any person of life, liberty or property, without due process of law; nor deny to any person within its jurisdiction the equal protection of the laws.

Section 2 Representatives shall be apportioned among the several States according to their respective numbers, counting the whole number of persons in each State, excluding Indians not taxed. But when the right to vote at any election for the choice of Electors for President and Vice-President of the United States, Representatives in Congress, the executive and judicial officers of a State, or the members of the legislature thereof, is denied to any of the male inhabitants of such State, being twenty-one years of age, and citizens of the United States, or in any way abridged except for participation in rebellion or other crime, the basis of representation therein shall be reduced in the proportion which the number of such male citizens shall bear to the whole number of male citizens twenty-one years of age in such State.

Section 3 No person shall be a Senator or Representative in Congress, or elector of President and Vice-President, or hold any office, civil or military, under the United States or under any State, who, having previously taken an oath as a member of Congress, or as an officer of the United States, or as a member of any State legislature, or as an executive or judicial officer of any State, to support the Constitution of the United States, shall have engaged in insurrection or rebellion against the same, or given aid or comfort to the enemies thereof. But Congress may, by a vote of two-thirds of each House, remove such disability.

Section 4 The validity of the public debt of the United States, authorized by law, including debts incurred for payment of pensions and bounties for services in suppressing insurrection or rebellion, shall not be questioned. But neither the United States nor any State shall assume or pay any debt or obligation incurred in aid of insurrection or rebellion against the United States, or any claim for the loss or emancipation of any slave; but all such debts, obligations, and claims shall be held illegal and void.

Section 5 The Congress shall have power to enforce, by appropriate legislation, the provisions of this article.

Amendment XV   [Adopted Mar. 30, 1870]

Section 1 The right of citizens of the United States to vote shall not be denied or abridged by the United States or by any State on account of race, color, or previous condition of servitude.

Section 2 The Congress shall have power to enforce this article by appropriate legislation.

Amendment XVI   [Adopted Feb. 25, 1913]

The Congress shall have power to lay and collect taxes on incomes, from whatever source derived, without apportionment among the several States, and without regard to any census or enumeration.

Amendment XVII   [Adopted May 31, 1913]

Section 1 The Senate of the United States shall be composed of two Senators from each State, elected by the people thereof, for six years; and each Senator shall have one vote. The electors in each State shall have the qualifications requisite for electors of the most numerous branch of the State legislatures.

Section 2 When vacancies happen in the representation of any State in the Senate, the executive authority of such State shall issue writs of election to fill such vacancies: Provided, that the legislature of any State may empower the executive thereof to make temporary appointments until the people fill the vacancies by election as the legislature may direct.

Section 3 This amendment shall not be so construed as to affect the election or term of any Senator chosen before it becomes valid as part of the Constitution.

Amendment XVIII   [Adopted Jan. 29, 1919]

Section 1 After one year from the ratification of this article the manufacture, sale or transportation of intoxicating liquors within, the importation thereof into, or the exportation thereof from the United States and all territory subject to the jurisdiction thereof, for beverage purposes, is hereby prohibited.

Section 2 The Congress and the several States shall have concurrent power to enforce this article by appropriate legislation.

Section 3 This article shall be inoperative unless it shall have been ratified as an amendment to the Constitution by the legislatures of the several States, as provided in the Constitution, within seven years from the date of the submission hereof to the States by the Congress.

Amendment XIX   [Adopted Aug. 26, 1920]

Section 1 The right of citizens of the United States to vote shall not be denied or abridged by the United States or by any State on account of sex.

Section 2 Congress shall have power to enforce this article by appropriate legislation.

Amendment XX   [Adopted Feb. 6, 1933]

Section 1 The terms of the President and Vice-President shall end at noon on the 20th day of January, and the terms of Senators and Representatives at noon on the 3d day of January, of the years in which such terms would have ended if this article had not been ratified; and the terms of their successors shall then begin.

Section 2 The Congress shall assemble at least once in every year, and such meeting shall begin at noon on the 3d day of January, unless they shall by law appoint a different day.

Section 3 If, at the time fixed for the beginning of the term of the President, the President-elect shall have died, the Vice-President-elect shall become President. If a President shall not have been chosen before the time fixed for the beginning of his term or if the President-elect shall have failed to qualify, then the Vice-President-elect shall act as President until a President shall have qualified; and the Congress may by law provide for the case wherein neither a President-elect nor a Vice-President-elect shall have qualified, declaring who shall then act as President, or the manner in which one who is to act shall be selected, and such person shall act accordingly until a President or Vice-President shall have qualified.

Section 4 The Congress may by law provide for the case of the death of any of the persons from whom the House of Representatives may choose a President whenever the right of choice shall have devolved upon them, and for the case of death of any of the persons from whom the Senate may choose a Vice-President whenever the right of choice shall have devolved upon them.

Section 5 Sections 1 and 2 shall take effect on the 15th day of October following the ratification of this article.

Section 6 This article shall be inoperative unless it shall have been ratified as an amendment to the Constitution by the legislatures of three-fourths of the several States within seven years from the date of its submission.

Amendment XXI [Adopted Dec. 5, 1933]

Section 1 The eighteenth article of amendment to the Constitution of the United States is hereby repealed.

Section 2 The transportation or importation into any State, territory, or possession of the United States for delivery or use therein of intoxicating liquors, in violation of the laws thereof, is hereby prohibited.

Section 3 This article shall be inoperative unless it shall have been ratified as an amendment to the Constitution by conventions in the several States, as provided in the Constitution, within seven years from the date of the submission hereof to the States by the Congress.

Amendment XXII [Adopted Feb. 26, 1951]

Section 1 No person shall be elected to the office of President more than twice, and no person who has held the office of President, or acted as President, for more than two years of a term to which some other person was elected President shall be elected to the office of President more than once. But this Article shall not apply to any person holding the office of President when this Article was proposed by the Congress, and shall not prevent any person who may be holding the office of President, or acting as President, during the term within which this Article becomes operative from holding the office of President or acting as President during the remainder of such term.

Section 2 This article shall be inoperative unless it shall have been ratified as an amendment to the Constitution by the legislatures of three-fourths of the several States within seven years from the date of its submission to the States by the Congress.

Amendment XXIII [Adopted Apr. 3, 1961]

Section 1 The District constituting the seat of Government of the United States shall appoint in such manner as the Congress may direct:

A number of electors of President and Vice-President equal to the whole number of Senators and Representatives in Congress to which the District would be entitled if it were a State, but in no event more than the least populous State; they shall be in addition to those appointed by the States, but they shall be considered, for the purposes of the election of President and Vice-President, to be electors appointed by a State; and they shall meet in the District and perform such duties as provided by the twelfth article of amendment.

Section 2 The Congress shall have power to enforce this article by appropriate legislation.

Amendment XXIV [Adopted Jan. 23, 1964]

Section 1 The right of citizens of the United States to vote in any primary or other election for President or Vice-President, for electors for President or Vice-President, or for Senator or Representative in Congress, shall not be denied or abridged by the United States or any State by reason of failure to pay any poll tax or other tax.

Section 2 The Congress shall have power to enforce this article by appropriate legislation.

Amendment XXV [Adopted Feb. 10, 1967]

Section 1 In case of the removal of the President from office or of his death or resignation, the Vice-President shall become President.

Section 2 Whenever there is a vacancy in the office of the Vice-President, the President shall nominate a Vice-President who shall take office upon confirmation by a majority vote of both Houses of Congress.

Section 3 Whenever the President transmits to the President pro tempore of the Senate and the Speaker of the House of Representatives his written declaration that he is unable to discharge the powers and duties of his office, and until he transmits to them a written declaration to the contrary, such powers and duties shall be discharged by the Vice-President as Acting President.

Section 4 Whenever the Vice-President and a majority of either the principal officers of the executive departments or of such other body as Congress may by law provide, transmit to the President pro tempore of the Senate and the Speaker of the House of Representatives their written declaration that the President is unable to discharge the powers and duties of his office, the Vice-President shall immediately assume the powers and duties of the office as Acting President.

Thereafter, when the President transmits to the President pro tempore of the Senate and the Speaker of the House of Representatives his written declaration that no inability exists, he shall resume the powers and duties of his office unless the Vice-President and a majority of either the principal officers of the executive department or of such other body as Congress may by law provide, transmit within four days to the President pro tempore of the Senate and the Speaker of the House of Representatives their written declaration that the President is unable to discharge the powers and duties of his office. Thereupon Congress shall decide the issue, assembling within forty-eight hours for that purpose if not in session. If the Congress, within twenty-one days after receipt of the latter written declaration, or, if Congress is not in session, within twenty-one days after Congress is required to assemble, determines by two-thirds vote of both Houses that the President is unable to discharge the powers and duties of his office, the Vice-President shall continue to discharge the same as Acting President; otherwise the President shall resume the powers and duties of his office.

Amendment XXVI [Adopted June 30, 1971]

Section 1 The right of citizens of the United States, who are eighteen years of age or older, to vote shall not be denied or abridged by the United States or by any State on account of age.

Section 2 The Congress shall have power to enforce this article by appropriate legislation.

Amendment XXVII [Adopted May 18, 1992]

No law, varying the compensation for the services of the Senators and Representatives, shall take effect until an election of Representatives shall have intervened.

▶THE EMANCIPATION PROCLAMATION

On July 22, 1862, Abraham Lincoln read to his cabinet a preliminary draft of an emancipation proclamation. Secretary of State William Seward suggested that the proclamation not be issued until a military victory had been won. The battle of Antietam gave Lincoln his desired opportunity, and on Sept. 22, he read to his cabinet a second draft of the proclamation. After some changes this was issued as a preliminary proclamation; the formal and definite proclamation came Jan. 1, 1863.

A Proclamation.

Whereas on the 22nd day of September, A.D. 1862, a proclamation was issued by the President of the United States, containing among other things, the following, to wit:

"That on the 1st day of January, A.D. 1863, all persons held as slaves within any State or designated part of a State the people whereof shall then be in rebellion against the United States shall be then, thenceforward, and forever free; and the executive government of the United States, including the military and naval authority thereof, will recognize and maintain the freedom of such persons and will do no act or acts to repress such persons, or any of them, in any efforts they may make for their actual freedom.

"That the executive will on the 1st day of January aforesaid, by proclamation, designate the States and parts of States, if any, in which the people thereof, respectively, shall then be in rebellion against the United States; and the fact that any State or the people thereof shall on that day be in good faith represented in the Congress of the United States by members chosen thereto at elections wherein a majority of the qualified voters of such States shall have participated shall, in the absence of strong countervailing testimony, be deemed conclusive evidence that such State and the people thereof are not then in rebellion against the United States."

Now, therefore, I, Abraham Lincoln, President of the United States, by virtue of the power in me vested as Commander-in-Chief of the Army and Navy of the United States in time of actual armed rebellion against the authority and government of the United States, and as a fit and necessary war measure for suppressing said rebellion, do, on this 1st day of January, A.D. 1863, and in accordance with my purpose so to do, publicly proclaimed for the full period of one hundred days from the first day above mentioned, order and designate as the States and parts of States wherein the people thereof, respectively, are this day in rebellion against the United States the following, to wit:

Arkansas, Texas, Louisiana (except the parishes of St. Bernard, Plaquemines, Jefferson, St. John, St. Charles, St. James, Ascension, Assumption, Terrebonne, Lafourche, St. Mary, St. Martin, and Orleans, including the city of New Orleans), Mississippi, Alabama, Florida, Georgia, South Carolina, North Carolina, and Virginia (except the forty-eight counties designated as West Virginia, and also the counties of Berkeley, Accomac, Northhampton, Elizabeth City, York, Princess Anne, and Norfolk, including the cities of Norfolk and Portsmouth), and which excepted parts are for the present left precisely as if this proclamation were not issued.

And by virtue of the power and for the purpose aforesaid, I do order and declare that all persons held as slaves within said designated States and parts of States are, and henceforward shall be, free; and that the Executive Government of the United States, including the military and naval authorities thereof, will recognize and maintain the freedom of said persons.

And I hereby enjoin upon the people so declared to be free to abstain from all violence, unless in necessary self-defense; and I recommend to them that, in all cases when allowed, they labor faithfully for reasonable wages.

And I further declare and make known that such persons of suitable condition will be received into the armed service of the United States to garrison forts, positions, stations, and other places, and to man vessels of all sorts in said service.

And upon this act, sincerely believed to be an act of justice, warranted by the Constitution upon military necessity, I invoke the considerate judgment of mankind and the gracious favor of Almighty God.

▶THE GETTYSBURG ADDRESS

Abraham Lincoln's most famous and most eloquent words were delivered on Nov. 19, 1863, at the dedication of the cemetery that held the remains of the 45,000 soldiers who fell at the Battle of Gettysburg, a significant Union victory.

"Fourscore and seven years ago our fathers brought forth on this continent, a new nation, conceived in Liberty, and dedicated to the proposition that all men are created equal.

"Now we are engaged in a great civil war, testing whether that nation or any nation so conceived and so dedicated, can long endure. We are met on a great battle-field of that war. We have come to dedicate a portion of that field, as a final resting place for those who here gave their lives that that nation might live. It is altogether fitting and proper that we should do this.

"But, in a larger sense, we can not dedicate—we can not consecrate—we can not hallow—this ground. The brave men, living and dead, who struggled here, have consecrated it, far above our poor power to add or detract. The world will little note, nor long remember what we say here, but it can never forget what they did here. It is for us the living, rather, to be dedicated here to the unfinished work which they who fought here have thus far so nobly advanced. It is rather for us to be here dedicated to the great task remaining before us—that from these honored dead we take increased devotion to that cause for which they gave the last full measure of devotion—that we here highly resolve that these dead shall not have died in vain—that this nation, under God, shall have a new birth of freedom—and that government of the people, by the people, for the people, shall not perish from the earth."

▶PLEDGE OF ALLEGIANCE

The original version of the Pledge of Allegiance appeared in the September 8, 1892, issue of *Youth's Companion* magazine. Authorship was in dispute between magazine staffers Francis Bellamy and James B. Upham until 1939, when the United States Flag Association declared Bellamy the author, and the Library of Congress concurred in 1957. Congress mandated two wording changes in the original version by substituting "the flag of the United States of America" for "my flag" in 1923, and adding "under God" in 1954. Public schools throughout the United States made the daily Pledge of Allegiance obligatory, and students who refused were expelled until the Supreme Court ruled in *West Virginia Board of Education v. Barnette* (1943) that the First Amendment protected the "right of silence" as well as freedom of speech.

"I pledge allegiance to the flag of the United States of America, and to the Republic, for which it stands, one nation, under God, indivisible, with liberty and justice for all."

CHRONOLOGY OF U.S. HISTORY

c. 1000 Viking explorer Leif Ericson explores North American coast and founds temporary colony called Vinland.

1492 On first voyage to America, Christopher Columbus lands at San Salvador island in Bahamas.

1493 Pope Alexander VI divides New World between Spain and Portugal.

1497 John Cabot claims Newfoundland for King Henry VII of England.

1499 Florentine merchant Amerigo Vespucci visits New World and begins writing popular accounts of his voyages.

1506 Columbus dies poor and embittered, convinced he found a new route to Asia and refusing to believe he discovered new continent.

1507 German mapmaker Martin Waldseemüller, after reading Vespucci's descriptions of the New World, names it "America" after him.

1513 Juan Ponce de León discovers Florida. Vasco Nuñez de Balboa crosses Panama and sights Pacific Ocean.

1519 Hernán Cortés lands in Mexico.

1520 Ferdinand Magellan, leader of the first expedition to circumnavigate the globe, discovers the South American straits that bear his name. In 1521, he is killed in the Philippines by natives.

1522 Cortés captures Mexico City and conquers Aztec empire.

1524 Giovanni de Verrazano, commissioned by King Francis I of France, discovers New York harbor and Hudson River.

1534 Jacques Cartier of France explores coast of Newfoundland and Gulf of St. Lawrence.

1536 Traveling overland from Gulf of Mexico, Alvar Núñez Cabeza de Vaca reaches Gulf of California.

1539 Fernando de Soto conquers Florida and begins three-year trek across Southeast.

1540 Francisco Vásquez de Coronado explores Southwest, discovering Grand Canyon and introducing horses to North America.

1541 Coronado discovers Mississippi River.

1542 João Rodrígues Cabrilho explores coast of California, missing San Francisco Bay.

1565 Don Pedro Menéndez de Aviles founds first permanent European settlement in North America at St. Augustine, Florida.

1572 Sir Francis Drake of England makes first voyage to America, landing in Panama.

1576 English explorer Martin Frobisher searches for Northwest Passage.

1577 Drake begins voyage of plunder around the world.

1579 Drake lands north of San Francisco Bay and claims region for Queen Elizabeth I.

1584 Sir Walter Raleigh discovers Roanoke Island. He names land Virginia, after Queen Elizabeth.

1585 Raleigh establishes England's first American colony at Roanoke.

1586 Drake evacuates surviving Roanoke settlers.

1587 Raleigh resettles Roanoke with 150 new colonists. Virginia Dare first child of English parents born in America.

1591 Relief expedition returns to the Roanoke colony; all settlers disappeared without trace.

1602 Captain Bartholomew Gosnold, first Englishman to set foot in New England, explores Cape Cod and Martha's Vineyard.

1603 Samuel de Champlain of France explores St. Lawrence Seaway, later founds Quebec.

1607 First permanent English settlement in America established at Jamestown, Virginia. Only 32 of original 105 colonists survive first winter.

1608 Captain John Smith imprisoned by Indians and saved by Pocahontas, daughter of Chief Powhatan.

1609 Henry Hudson sets out in search of Northwest Passage. Champlain sails into Great Lakes.

1611 Hudson cast adrift by mutinous crewmen to die in bay named after him.

1612 First Dutch trading post appears on Manhattan Island.

1616 Smallpox epidemic decimates Indian tribes from Maine to Rhode Island.

1619 Dutch traders bring first African slaves to Virginia for sale. Americans hold first election when Virginia planters vote for House of Burgesses.

1620 Pilgrims and others arrive in Plymouth, Massachusetts, aboard *Mayflower*. They draw up the Mayflower Compact.

1622 Most of Virginia colony wiped out in an Indian attack.

1624 King James I revokes Virginia's charter and makes it royal colony.

1626 The Dutch colony of New Amsterdam founded on Manhattan Island, bought from Indians for about $24.

1630 John Winthrop sets sail for Massachusetts with 900 Puritans and others, beginning Great Migration to New England.

1632 King Charles I of England grants Lord Baltimore charter to establish colony in Maryland.

1634 Massachusetts adopts representative government. Jean Nicolet of France begins trading with Indians in Wisconsin.

1635 Roger Williams, banished from Massachusetts, founds dissident colony of Rhode Island.

1636 New Englanders massacre hundreds of Indians in Pequot War. Harvard College established.

1638 First Swedish colony founded in Delaware.

1639 "Oath of a Free Man" the first English document printed in America. First public school appears in Dorchester, first post office in Boston, and Connecticut writes first colonial constitution.

1644 Indians make last unsuccessful attempt to expel English settlers from Virginia. First American ship built in Boston.

1647 Margaret Brent of Maryland first American woman to demand right to vote. Massachusetts passes first compulsory education law. First witchcraft execution occurs in Hartford, Conn.

1648 Boston shoemakers and coopers establish first American labor unions.

1651 Parliament passes first Navigation Act regulating colonial trade.

1652 Rhode Island first colony to outlaw slavery. First American coins minted in Boston.

1654 Jacob Barsimon, first American Jew, arrives in New Amsterdam, followed by 23 more Jews from Brazil.

1655 Dutch colonists capture Swedish colony in Delaware. Lady Deborah Moody of Long Island first American woman to vote.

1656 First Quakers arrive in America; imprisoned in Boston, beaten, and deported.

1659 Massachusetts hangs two Quakers on Boston Common.

1660 Parliament forbids Americans to export goods to countries other than England. Massachusetts outlaws celebration of Christmas.

1661 Virginia becomes the first colony to recognize slavery as legal.

1662 Connecticut granted royal charter. Massachusetts appoints official press censors and institutes half-way covenant.

1663 Parliament requires colonial imports from Europe to pass first through England. King Charles II grants charters to Carolina and Rhode Island

1664 New Amsterdam captured by Richard Nicolls, who renames it New York. New Jersey established.

1670 Charles Town, later called Charleston, first permanent settlement in Carolina.

1672 Parliament tightens trade restrictions on colonies and appoints American customs collectors.

1673 French explorers Jacques Marquette and Louis Joliet paddle down Mississippi River to Arkansas. Regular mail service begins between Boston and New York. Dutch forces recapture New York.

1674 Treaty of Westminster restores New York to England. King Louis XIV of France sends Sieur de La Salle to explore Mississippi River.

1675 Thousands die in King Philip's War between New Englanders and five Indian tribes.

1676 Bacon's Rebellion overthrows government of Virginia and burns down Jamestown.

1680 New Hampshire separated from Massachusetts and made royal colony.

1681 King Charles II names William Penn proprietor of Pennsylvania.

1682 Penn founds Philadelphia. Sieur de La Salle claims North American interior for France, naming it Louisiana.

1683 First German-Americans, group of Mennonites, arrive in Philadelphia.

1684 King Charles II revokes Massachusetts charter.

1686 King James II appoints Sir Edmund Andros governor-general of Dominion of New England, dissolving colonial governments.

1688 Quakers publish first anti-slavery tracts in Pennsylvania.

1689 Andros surrenders to Boston mobs and colonial self-government is reestablished. Jacob Leisler seizes power in New York uprising. King William's War begins in America.

1690 Massachusetts issues first colonial paper money. American campaigns against French Canada fail. French and Indians burn Schenectady, N.Y.

1691 Jacob Leisler surrenders and is hanged. Massachusetts rechartered with religious freedom.

1692 Witchcraft hysteria breaks out in Salem, Mass., leading to 20 executions.

1693 College of William and Mary chartered, the second college in America.

1695 New York City organizes public relief for poor and homeless.

1696 Parliament places more commercial restrictions on colonies. American merchants join slave trade.

1697 Treaty of Ryswick ends King William's War.

1701 Antoine de la Mothe Cadillac establishes French outpost at Detroit, Michigan. Yale College founded. Delaware separated from Pennsylvania.

1702 Queen Anne's War breaks out.

1704 *Boston News-Letter* first regularly published newspaper in America.

1710 German Migration to America begins. British and American forces capture Port Royal, Nova Scotia.

1711 Anglo-American attack on Quebec fails. Tuscarora Indian War breaks out in North Carolina.

1712 Militia quell slave rebellion in New York City. Pennsylvania prohibits importing slaves.

1713 Treaty of Utrecht ends Queen Anne's War.

1716 First American theater built in Williamsburg, Va. Slavery introduced to French Louisiana.

1718 Jean Baptiste le Moyne founds French city of New Orleans.

1721 Sir Robert Walpole loosens colonial trade restrictions with policy of "salutary neglect."

1722 France declares New Orleans capital of Louisiana.

1723 America's first business corporation chartered in Connecticut.

1724 France expels all Jews from Louisiana.

1728 First American synagogue built in New York City.

1729 North and South Carolina receive royal charters.

1731 Benjamin Franklin founds first American library in Philadelphia.

1732 King George II grants charter to Georgia. Only Catholic church in colonial America opens in Philadelphia. Benjamin Franklin begins publishing *Poor Richard's Almanac*. George Washington born in Virginia.

1733 Parliament passes the Molasses Act, taxing imports from non-British sugar islands.

1734 Beginning of Great Awakening, widespread religious revival.

1735 French begin settling in Illinois.

1737 Boston holds its first public celebration of St. Patrick's Day.

1739 War of Jenkin's Ear begins. South Carolina slaves mount Stono Rebellion. French explorers Pierre and Paul Mallet discover Rocky Mountains.

1741 Danish navigator Vitus Bering, hired by Peter the Great of Russia, explores coast of Alaska. *American Magazine*, first in colonies, begins publishing in Philadelphia. Slave insurrection panic sweeps New York City.

1742 First sugar cane planted in Louisiana.

1744 King George's War breaks out.

1745 British and Americans capture Fort Louisbourg on Cape Breton Island. French and Indians raid Maine.

1748 Treaty of Aix-la-Chapelle ends King George's War and returns Fort Louisbourg to France.

1751 Parliament forbids New England colonies to issue paper money.

1752 Benjamin Franklin conducts famous kite experiment. Liberty bell is cracked in Philadelphia.

1753 Governor Dinwiddie of Virginia sends George Washington into Ohio country to demand withdrawal of French. First steam engine arrives in America.

1754 Washington skirmishes with French patrol, touching off French and Indian War. Franklin presents Albany Plan of Union for colonies.

1755 Quakers withdraw from Pennsylvania assembly rather than vote for military spending. Washington leads retreat from Battle of the Wilderness.

1758 British and American forces lose Battle of Ticonderoga, but capture Louisbourg and Fort Duquesne. New Jersey sets aside first Indian reservation for Onami tribe.

1759 General Wolfe defeats General Montcalm as British capture Quebec. Both generals fall in battle.

1760 After fall of Montreal, all of New France surrenders to Britain. King George III crowned in England.

1762 King Louis XV of France secretly cedes Louisiana to Spain.

1763 Treaty of Paris ends French and Indian War. France cedes Canada to Britain. King George

III prohibits Americans to settle in West. Conspiracy of Pontiac threatens frontier.

1764 Parliament passes Sugar Act and forbids all colonies to issue paper money. French settlers found St. Louis. "Paxton Boys" march on Philadelphia. In Boston, James Otis protests, "no taxation without representation."

1765 Parliament passes Stamp Act (tax on newspapers, legal documents, etc.) and Quartering Act (requiring housing of British soldiers in homes). Sons of Liberty organize resistance and non-importation throughout colonies. Stamp Act Congress meets in New York.

1766 Parliament repeals the Stamp Act, but passes Declaratory Act affirming its right to pass laws binding on colonies. Chief Pontiac makes peace.

1767 Parliament enacts Townshend Duties and suspends New York assembly for resisting Quartering Act.

1768 "Regulators" rebel in North Carolina. Boston riots against Townshend Duties.

1769 Daniel Boone explores Kentucky. Father Junipero Serra founds San Diego, first Spanish mission in California. Gaspar de Portola sails into San Francisco Bay.

1770 Five Americans perish in Boston Massacre (Mar. 5). Parliament repeals Townshend Duties, except tax on tea.

1772 Rhode Island mob burns British revenue ship *Gaspee*. Boston appoints first Committee of Correspondence.

1773 Parliament passes Tea Act, leading to Boston Tea Party (Dec. 16).

1774 Parliament passes "Intolerable Acts" punishing colonists for Tea Party. Boston is occupied by British forces. First Continental Congress meets in Philadelphia.

1775 American Revolution begins with Battle of Lexington and Concord (Apr. 19). Second Continental Congress appoints George Washington as commander of Continental Army. British win Battle of Bunker Hill. First abolition society organized in Pennsylvania.

1776 Tom Paine's *Common Sense* published. Declaration of Independence signed. Congress adopts name, "United States of America." British occupy New York City. Washington crosses Delaware to win Battle of Trenton, N.J.

1777 Americans win battles at Princeton and Saratoga. British occupy Philadelphia. Congress adopts Stars and Stripes flag and endorses Articles of Confederation. Washington's army spends winter at Valley Forge, Pa.

1778 France makes alliance with U.S. and declares war on Britain. When French fleet arrives, British evacuate Philadelphia.

1779 Congress offers to make peace in exchange for independence. British withdraw from New York City.

1780 Pennsylvania first state to abolish slavery. British occupy Charleston, S.C. Washington quells Continental Army mutiny. Benedict Arnold defects to British.

1781 French and American victory at Battle of Yorktown ends the American Revolution. Articles of Confederation take effect. Los Angeles founded by Spanish missionaries.

1782 Parliament votes for peace with U.S. Negotiations in Paris lead to provisional Anglo-American peace treaty. Virginia permits owners to free their slaves. First English Bible printed in America.

1783 Massachusetts, Connecticut, and Rhode Island abolish slavery. Treaty of Paris signed (Sept.

3), officially ending American Revolution . Washington retires to Mount Vernon, Va.

1784 Congress ratifies Treaty of Paris. Spain closes Mississippi River to American trade. First bale of American cotton shipped to Britain.

1785 First state university chartered in Georgia.

1786 Virginia proclaims religious freedom. Shays's Rebellion put down in Massachusetts. Annapolis Convention calls for revising Articles of Confederation. New Jersey abolishes slavery.

1787 Convention in Philadelphia writes Constitution. Congress passes Northwest Ordinance and submits Constitution for state approval.

1788 Constitution ratified by New Hampshire (June 21), the ninth state to do so thereby marking its final approval.

1789 Constitution takes effect (March 4). George Washington wins first presidential election unopposed. Federal government begins meeting in New York City. Congress enacts first Federal tariff.

1790 First antislavery petitions are submitted to Congress. Temporary capital moved to Philadelphia. Pope Pius VI appoints John Carroll first Catholic bishop in U.S. First U.S. census lists population at 3,929,625.

1791 Congress sets up First Bank of the United States and first internal revenue law, a tax on whiskey. Vermont enters union as 14th state. Bill of Rights takes effect. Pres. Washington selects site of new U.S. capital on the Potomac River.

1792 New York stock traders begin meeting under a tree on Wall Street. Pres. Washington is unanimously reelected. Construction begins on White House.

1793 Eli Whitney invents cotton gin. Congress passes first Fugitive Slave Act. Pres. Washington holds first official cabinet meeting and lays cornerstone for Capitol. Britain begins confiscating American ships trading with France.

1794 Pres. Washington defeats Whiskey Rebellion in Pennsylvania. U.S. and Britain sign Jay's Treaty. Ohio Indians defeated at Battle of Fallen Timbers.

1795 Georgia stung by scandal of Yazoo land frauds. Senate ratifies Jay's Treaty with Britain.

1796 Pres. Washington delivers "Farewell Address." France begins to confiscate ships trading with Britain.

1797 France insults American diplomats in XYZ Affair. Spanish begin building Mission San Juan Capistrano in California.

1798 Georgia last state to abolish slave trade. Congress passes Alien and Sedition Acts. U.S. renounces alliance with France as unofficial naval war breaks out.

1799 Russian-American trading company set up in Alaska. New York abolishes slavery.

1800 Library of Congress founded. Convention of 1800 signed, ending quasi-war between U.S. and France. Spain secretly cedes Louisiana to France. Congress begins meeting in Washington.

1801 Election of Thomas Jefferson results in first transfer of executive power between rival parties. Congress takes jurisdiction over District of Columbia. Tripoli pirates declare war on U.S.

1802 U.S. Military Academy established at West Point, N.Y.

1803 Louisiana Purchase from France doubles size of the U.S. Federal outpost founded at Fort Dearborn, Illinois, future site of Chicago.

1804 Lewis and Clark expedition sets out from St. Louis. Alexander Hamilton killed in duel with Aaron Burr.

1805 Barbary War with Tripoli ends.

1806   Congress authorizes construction of Cumberland Road. Noah Webster's first dictionary published.

1807   Britain and France enact blockades in Europe, confiscating American trading ships. British attack USS *Chesapeake*. Embargo Act forbids all American exports.

1808   Congress declares end to African slave trade.

1809   Embargo Act replaced with Non-Intercourse Act, outlawing exports to Britain and France. First steamboat sea voyage made from New York City to Philadelphia.

1810   Pres. Madison annexes West Florida.

1811   Worst earthquake in U.S. history rocks Ohio-Mississippi valleys. Russians settle at Ft. Ross, California. First Bank of the United States fails to obtain recharter. Gen. William Henry Harrison defeats Indians at Battle of Tippecanoe.

1812   War of 1812 begins by close vote in Congress. New England resists war. British clamp blockade on U.S. ports, capture Detroit, and repel American attack on Canada at Queenstown.

1813   Americans regain Detroit, attack Toronto and Ft. George in Canada, but surrender to British at Beaver Dams, Ontario. Captain Oliver H. Perry wins control of the Great Lakes. British and Indians burn Buffalo, N.Y.

1814   British destroy Fort Oswego, N.Y., and set fire to Washington, D.C. Francis Scott Key writes "The Star Spangled Banner." New Englanders opposed to war meet secretly at Hartford Convention. First textile mill established at Waltham, Mass. Treaty of Ghent ends War of 1812.

1815   General Andrew Jackson routs British at Battle of New Orleans, before news arrives that War of 1812 is over.

1816   Congress charters Second Bank of the U.S.

1817   Rush-Bagot Treaty between Britain and U.S. demilitarizes Great Lakes. New York Stock and Exchange Board organized. Work begins on Erie Canal. Indian attack starts Seminole War in Florida.

1818   Cumberland Road opens. Congress adopts present format for American flag. Canadian boundary dispute with Britain settled.

1819   Panic of 1819 plunges South and West into depression. U.S. obtains Florida from Spain in Adams-Onís Treaty, settling border of Louisiana. *Savannah* makes first successful trans-Atlantic crossing under steam power.

1820   Missouri Compromise solves crisis over admission of Missouri as slave state. Abolitionists begin colonizing freed slaves to Africa.

1821   First Catholic cathedral in U.S. built in Baltimore.

1822   Denmark Vesey and 36 others executed for organizing rebel slave conspiracy in Charleston, S.C.

1823   Monroe Doctrine, masterminded by Secy. of State John Quincy Adams, announced by Pres. Monroe.

1824   Russia and U.S. settle territorial disputes in Pacific Northwest. First presidential nominating convention held in Utica, N.Y.

1825   John Quincy Adams chosen president in infamous "Corrupt Bargain" with Henry Clay, who becomes Secy. of State. Erie Canal opened. Mexico invites Americans to settle in Texas.

1826   Anti-Mason party organized. John Adams and Thomas Jefferson die on 50th anniversary of Declaration of Independence. Jedediah Smith leads first overland expedition to California.

1827   U.S. and Britain agree to joint occupation of Pacific Northwest.

1828   Congress passes protectionist "Tariff of Abominations" over Southern protests.

1829   Mexico refuses Pres. Jackson's offer to buy Texas.

1830   Webster-Hayne Debate in U.S. Senate reveals sectional tension. Church of Latter-Day Saints (the Mormons) founded by Joseph Smith in Fayette, N.Y. Mexico forbids further American immigration to Texas.

1831   Nat Turner leads bloodiest of all slave rebellions, killing 57 whites in Virginia.

1832   Black Hawk War fought in Illinois and Wisconsin. First nationwide Democratic Party convention held in Baltimore. Pres. Jackson vetoes bill to recharter national bank. South Carolina nullifies "Tariff of Abominations."

1833   Massachusetts last state to end tax support for churches. Congress lowers tariff and passes "Force Bill" to pressure South Carolina, which rescinds nullification. American Anti-Slavery Society organized.

1834   Whig party organized by Senators Henry Clay and Daniel Webster in opposition to Pres. Jackson. Anti-abolitionist riots break out in New York and Philadelphia.

1835   Samuel Morse invents telegraph. National debt completely paid off. Pres. Jackson survives first attempt to assassinate a president. Second Seminole War begins in Florida.

1836   Samuel Colt invents revolver. Texas declares independence from Mexico and requests U.S. annexation. Mexican army captures Alamo, but Texans are victorious at San Jacinto.

1837   Panic of 1837 begins lengthy depression.

1838   Joshua Giddings of Ohio is first abolitionist elected to Congress. Trans-Atlantic steamship service established. Congress blocks abolitionist petitions with "Gag Rule."

1839   Abner Doubleday of Cooperstown, N.Y., codifies rules of baseball. Congress outlaws dueling in Washington, D.C.

1840   "Log Cabin Campaign" between William Henry Harrison and Martin Van Buren begins era of mass political participation. Liberty Party founded by abolitionists in Albany, N.Y.

1841   First emigrant train of 48 covered wagons arrives in California. Pres. Harrison dies after month in office. First Japanese immigrant arrives in New Bedford, Mass.

1842   Webster-Ashburton Treaty settles Canada boundary disputes between U.S. and Britain. U.S. accidentally seizes California, then returns it with apology to Mexico.

1843   End of Second Seminole War. B'Nai B'rith founded in New York. Mormons begin practicing polygamy.

1844   Baptists first church to split North and South over slavery. Samuel Morse sends first telegraph message. James K. Polk, first "Dark horse" candidate, elected President.

1845   "Potato Famine" begins massive Irish immigration. U.S. annexes Texas, over Mexican protests. U.S. Naval Academy opens at Annapolis, Md.

1846   Mexican War begins when U.S. troops are attacked in disputed Texas territory. American settlers in California stage Bear Flag Revolt. Oregon Treaty gives U.S. sole possession of Pacific Northwest up to 49th parallel. First recorded baseball game played in Hoboken, N.J.

1847   Wilmot Proviso, forbidding slavery expansion, passes House and sets off wave of panic in South. General Winfield Scott conquers Mexico

City. Brigham Young leads Mormons to Utah. Abraham Lincoln of Illinois arrives in Congress.

1848   Treaty of Guadalupe-Hidalgo ends Mexican War, ceding Southwest to U.S. Revolution of 1848 begins wave of German immigration. New York-Chicago telegraph line completed. Chicago Board of Trade established. Free Soil party organized. Gold discovered in California. First Chinese immigrants arrive in San Francisco. Lucretia Mott and Elizabeth Cady Stanton hold first Women's Rights Convention in Seneca Falls, N.Y.

1849   Gold Rush brings hundreds of thousands to California. Elizabeth Blackwell first American woman to receive medical degree.

1850   Sen. Henry Clay's Compromise of 1850 solves crisis over slavery expansion. Clayton-Bulwer Treaty pledges Anglo-American cooperation in building any Central American canal. John C. Calhoun of South Carolina delivers last address to Senate.

1851   Y.M.C.A. established. Northern mobs resist Fugitive Slave Act. Maine is first state to pass prohibition laws. *New York Times* founded. Herman Melville's *Moby Dick* published.

1852   Harriet Beecher Stowe's *Uncle Tom's Cabin* published.

1853   U.S. buys Gila River valley from Mexico in Gadsden Purchase. Native American, or "Know-Nothing," party founded. Commodore Matthew C. Perry opens trade with Japan.

1854   Congress passes Kansas-Nebraska Act, setting off mass protests across North. Republican Party founded. U.S. threatens to seize Cuba from Spain in Ostend Manifesto.

1855   "Bleeding Kansas" fighting begins as pro-slavery and anti-slavery settlers hold rival state conventions. First railroad train crosses Mississippi River at Rock Island, Ill., into Davenport, Iowa.

1856   Cong. Preston Brooks of South Carolina beats Sen. Charles Sumner of Massachusetts unconscious on Senate floor. John Brown leads Pottawatomie massacre in Kansas. First Republican national convention nominates John C. Frémont for president in Pittsburgh, Pa.

1857   New York-St. Louis railroad completed. Supreme Court hands down controversial *Dred Scott* decision protecting slavery. Panic of 1857 sends North into depression.

1858   Lincoln-Douglas Debates dramatize issue of slavery expansion in Illinois race for Senate. First trans-Atlantic telegraph cable laid.

1859   John Brown's raid on Harper's Ferry arsenal to launch abolitionist war against slavery ends in his capture and execution. Slave insurrection panic sweeps South. Comstock Silver Lode discovered in Nevada. First producing oil well in U.S. flows in Titusville, Pa.

1860   Democratic Party splits into Northern and Southern wings. South Carolina is first state to secede from Union after victory of Abraham Lincoln. Crittenden Compromise fails to preserve Union. Pony Express begins mail delivery between California and Missouri.

1861   Civil War begins with attack on Ft. Sumter in South Carolina (Apr. 12). Pres. Lincoln calls for 75,000 volunteers to put down rebellion. Jefferson Davis of Mississippi elected Pres. of Confederate States of America. New York-San Francisco telegraph link completed. Yale awards first American Ph.D. Congress enacts first Federal income tax.

1862   Congress issues "greenbacks," subsidizes transcontinental railroad, abolishes slavery in District of Columbia, and passes Homestead Act. Pres. Lincoln issues Emancipation Proclamation after Battle of Antietam, bloodiest of Civil War.

1863   Emancipation Proclamation takes effect (Jan. 1). Union victories at Vicksburg, Miss., and Gettysburg, Pa., signal turning point of Civil War. West Virginia secedes from Virginia and rejoins Union. Hundreds killed in New York City draft riot. Pres. Lincoln proclaims Thanksgiving national holiday.

1864   Pres. Lincoln names General Ulysses S. Grant as commander of Union armies. General William T. Sherman destroys Atlanta and conducts "March to the Sea." Confederate army of General Robert E. Lee crippled in Wilderness Campaign. Cheyenne and Arapaho Indians slaughtered in Sand Creek Massacre in Colorado.

1865   General Lee surrenders to General Grant at Appomattox Court House, Virginia (Apr. 9). Pres. Lincoln assassinated by John Wilkes Booth in Washington, D.C. (Apr. 14). Confederacy dissolved, ending Civil War. Pres. Johnson proclaims amnesty for most rebels. Slavery outlawed by adoption of Thirteenth Amendment. Ku Klux Klan founded in Pulaski, Tenn.

1866   In the struggle over Reconstruction policy, Congress overrides Pres. Johnson's vetoes of Civil Rights Act and New Freedmen's Bureau Bill. Whites riot in New Orleans to protest black suffrage. Grand Army of the Republic organized by Union veterans.

1867   Congress takes control of Reconstruction in the South by passing First Reconstruction Act over Pres. Johnson's veto and Tenure of Office Act. U.S. purchases Alaska from Russia for $7.2 million (2¢ an acre). Farmers organize Patrons of Husbandry, beginning Granger movement.

1868   For violating Tenure of Office Act of 1867, Pres. Johnson is impeached in the House (Feb. 24), but acquitted in the Senate by a single vote (May 16). U.S. and China sign Burlingame Treaty to allow immigration. Fourteenth Amendment grants equal citizenship and protection to freedmen (July 28). Half a million black votes help elect Gen. Ulysses S. Grant to the presidency. The typewriter invented.

1869   "Hard Money" prevails when Congress passes Public Credit Act, promising repayment of government debts in gold. Transcontinental railroad completed when Union Pacific and Central Pacific lines meet at Promontory Point, Utah (May 10). Jay Gould and James Fisk cause financial panic by trying to corner gold market on "Black Friday" (Sept. 24). Knights of Labor national union organized. National Women's Suffrage Association formed in New York. Wyoming Territory grants first U.S. women's suffrage.

1870   Fifteenth Amendment guarantees right to vote for all U.S. citizens, though only Wyoming and Utah territories allow women's suffrage (Mar. 30). Congress passes first Ku Klux Act to enforce Fifteenth Amendment. First black senator and black congressman are elected.

1871   Congress passes second Ku Klux Act to enforce Fourteenth Amendment in the South. Tammany Hall ring overthrown in New York City when *New York Times* begins publishing exposé of Boss William Marcy Tweed. Most of Chicago destroyed in the Great Fire (Oct. 8-11). Anti-Chinese race riots in Los Angeles. Illinois enacts first railroad regulations.

1872   Liberal Republicans bolt from Pres. Grant and nominate newspaperman Horace Greeley for president. Crédit Mobilier scandal implicates Vice Pres. Schuyler Colfax and embarrasses Grant administration. Yellowstone National Park created. Susan B. Anthony arrested for leading suffragists to the polls. Montgomery Ward opens for business in Chicago.

1873 Silver withdrawn from money supply in the "Crime of '73." Congressmen raise their own salaries 50%, retroactive for two years, and double president's pay in "Salary Grab" Act. Panic of 1873, triggered by failure of Jay Cooke's banking house, begins depression of 1870s. New York Stock Exchange forced to close for ten days. Great Bonanza silver lode discovered in Nevada. San Francisco installs first cable cars.

1874 Granger movement begins passing railroad regulations in Midwestern states. Women's Christian Temperance Union founded in Cleveland, Ohio. Democrats recapture Congress for first time since Civil War. Greenback Party formed in Indianapolis. Black rioters attack courthouse in Vicksburg, Miss. Chautauqua movement begins bringing educational speakers to rural communities across the country.

1875 Congress passes Specie Resumption Act to reduce money supply by redeeming greenbacks for gold, and Civil Rights Act to guarantee equal rights for freedmen. Whiskey Ring scandal casts further pall on Grant administration. Archbishop John McCloskey of New York first American bishop. *Aristides* wins first Kentucky Derby at Churchill Downs, Ky.

1876 U.S. awards patent to Alexander Graham Bell for the telephone. Gen. George A. Custer and 265 men are massacred by Sioux Indians at Little Big Horn, Montana (June 25). Centennial of the United States celebrated. Democrat Samuel Tilden outpolls Republican candidate Rutherford B. Hayes as presidential election is thrown into the House (Nov. 7). Professional baseball's National League established. Kappa Alpha opens first college fraternity house at Williams College. Central Park in New York completed.

1877 Congress appoints Electoral Commission to solve impasse over disputed 1876 election (Jan. 29). House votes 185 to 184 to declare Rutherford B. Hayes President-elect, three days before his inauguration (Mar. 2). Reconstruction officially ends with withdrawal of Federal troops from the South (Apr. 24). Pres. Hayes sends in troops as Great Railroad Strike paralyzes much of the country (July 17). Anti-Chinese riots break out in San Francisco. Colorado silver rush begins.

1878 Sen. A. A. Sargent introduces Women's Suffrage Amendment in Congress. Greenback-Labor Party formed in Toledo, Ohio. Limited coinage of silver resumes with Bland-Allison Act. Democrats win control of both houses of Congress for first time since 1858. American Bar Association organized in Saratoga, N.Y. Edison Electric begins operating in New York City. New Haven, Conn., sets up first commercial telephone network.

1879 U.S. resumes specie payments for greenbacks. Pres. Hayes battles with Congress over use of Federal troops in elections. F.W. Woolworth opens his first store in Utica, N.Y. First Church of Christ, Scientist, founded in Boston. Thomas Edison invents light bulb. California adopts state constitution forbidding employment of Chinese labor. Henry George's radical social critique, *Progress and Poverty*, becomes best-seller.

1880 Pres. Hayes declares U.S. must control any Isthmian canal. U.S. and China agree to Chinese Exclusion Treaty (Nov. 17). National Farmers' Alliance organized in Chicago. American branch of Salvation Army founded in Philadelphia, Pa. Census lists U.S. population over 50 million for first time (50,155,783).

1881 Pres. Garfield assassinated by Charles Guiteau in Washington, D.C. (July 2—dies Sept. 19). Chester A Arthur becomes President. (Sept. 20). Clara Barton creates American Red Cross. Booker T. Washington founds Tuskegee Institute for black education in Alabama. Russian Jews begin immigrating to U.S. to escape pogroms.

1882 John D. Rockefeller organizes Standard Oil trust, first such combination. Congress passes first Chinese Exclusion Act (May 10), and legislates first immigration restrictions: no paupers, convicts, or mental defectives (Aug. 3). Knights of Columbus founded with permission from Roman Catholic Church.

1883 Congress passes Pendleton Act, requiring civil service competition for Federal jobs. Brooklyn Bridge opened in New York. Supreme Court strikes down Civil Rights Act of 1875. New York-Chicago telephone service begins. Ohio River floods devastate Cincinnati. U.S. Navy builds its first steel ships. Railroads agree on Standard Time zones for North America.

1884 "Mugwumps" bolt Republican Party. Statue of Liberty cornerstone laid (Aug. 5). Belva A. Lockwood of Equal Rights Party first woman candidate for president. Grover Cleveland of New York first Democrat elected president since Civil War. Home Insurance Building of Chicago first skyscraper in the world. Moses Fleetwood Walker first black professional baseball player.

1885 Washington Monument completed after 36 years of construction. U.S. Marines land in Panama (Apr. 24). Senate refuses to ratify treaty for building a canal across Nicaragua. Congress outlaws building fences on public lands in the West. Josiah Strong's best-seller *Our Country* argues for American imperialism.

1886 Knights of Labor rail strike sets off national wave of strikes for eight-hour day. Haymarket Riot in Chicago leads to execution of seven anarchists. Statue of Liberty in New York Harbor dedicated (Oct. 28). American Federation of Labor (AFL) founded in Columbus, Ohio. Indian wars end with capture of Geronimo.

1887 Congress creates Interstate Commerce Commission, first Federal regulatory agency, but with weak enforcement powers. Congress distributes reservation land to Indians, also bans opium imports. First electric trolley line built in Richmond, Va. U.S. Navy leases base at Pearl Harbor, Hawaii. First American golf club founded in Foxburg, Pa.

1888 Snow falls for 36 hours in New York, killing 400 people in "Great Blizzard of '88" (Mar. 12). First secret ballot election in Louisville, Ky. George Eastman brings first Kodak camera to the market. National Geographic Society founded in Washington, D.C. Edward Bellamy's utopian novel, *Looking Backward*, a sensational best-seller.

1889 Four new states—N.D., S.D., Mont., Wash.—all admitted in one day (Feb. 22). Oklahoma Land Rush results when former Indian territory opens for settlement (Apr. 22). Johnstown Flood claims thousands of lives in Pennsylvania (May 31). Kansas passes first antitrust law. Jane Addams founds Hull House in Chicago. First "All-American" college football players chosen. Tower Building, first New York skyscraper, completed.

1890 Congress passes Sherman Antitrust Act (July 2) and Sherman Silver Purchase Act. Wyoming admitted as first state with women's suffrage (July 10). Sioux uprising ends at Battle of Wounded Knee (Dec. 29). Yosemite National Park created. Mississippi leads South in disfranchising black voters. Jacob Riis's *How the Other Half Lives* awakens Americans to urban poverty. First Army-Navy football game played—Navy 24, Army 0.

1891 Ex-Pres. Cleveland denounces "dangerous and reckless experiment" of silver coinage. New Orleans mob lynches 11 Italian immigrants. People's, or Populist, Party organized in Cincinnati. U.S. and Chile nearly go to war over death of two American sailors in Valparaiso (Oct. 16). Dr. James A. Naismith invents basketball in Springfield, Mass. Thomas Edison patents first American-made motion picture camera.

1892 Populist candidate James B. Weaver of Iowa receives over a million votes for president. Violent strikes break out among steel workers in Homestead, Pa., and silver miners in Coeur d'Alene, Idaho. Chinese immigrants forced to register with Federal government. First gasoline-powered American automobile built in Chicopee, Mass. Boll weevil first appears in Texas.

1893 U.S. gold reserve falls below $100 million (Apr. 21). Panic of 1893, touched off by New York stock market crash (June 27), begins second-worst depression in U.S. history. Congress repeals Sherman Silver Purchase Act (Oct. 30). Hawaii requests U.S. annexation. Mormon Temple dedicated in Salt Lake City, Utah. Thousands perish in Louisiana cyclone. Frank Lloyd Wright completes first solo project, the Winslow home in Chicago.

1894 Coxey's Army of unemployed march on Washington, D.C. (Apr. 30). U.S. Treasury issues two $50 million bond offerings to shore up dwindling gold reserves. Congress enacts first peace-time Federal income tax, denounced as "socialism, communism, devilism" (Aug. 27). Pullman strike paralyzes railroads across the country. Thomas Edison exhibits his kinetoscope.

1895 Billionaire banker J.P. Morgan bails out U.S. Treasury, faced with a gold drain. "Silver Democrats" appeal for unlimited silver coinage as way out of depression. Supreme Court rules income tax unconstitutional (May 20). Venezuelan boundary dispute brings U.S. and Britain close to war. Cuban insurrection against Spanish rule begins, winning American sympathy. National Association of Manufacturers formed in Cincinnati. First professional football game played in Latrobe, Pa.

1896 Supreme Court approves segregation (*Plessy vs. Ferguson*). William Jennings Bryan, "Silver Democrat" of Nebraska, wins nomination with "Cross of Gold" speech (July 7). Gold discovered in Klondike, Alaska, defusing the money question (Aug. 16). American athletes sweep nine of 12 events at first International Olympics. Henry Ford builds his first automobile. First American motion pictures appear in theaters. "The Yellow Kid," first comic strip, begins running in *New York World*.

1897 U.S. and Britain consent to arbitration of boundary disputes in Olney-Pauncefote Convention (Jan. 11). Venezuelan boundary dispute ends with Britain accepting arbitration. Klondike gold rush to Alaska moves into full swing. U.S. offers to mediate Cuban rebellion, lodges official complaint against Spanish brutality. "Yellow press" newspapers keep up constant assault on Spain. First American subway completed in Boston.

1898 After mysterious explosion of battleship *Maine* in Havana harbor (Feb. 15), Spanish-American War breaks out (Apr. 21). Commodore George Dewey destroys Spanish fleet at Manila Bay (May 1) and U.S. takes Manila (Aug. 13). After Battle of San Juan Hill (July 1), Spanish garrison at Santi-

ago, Cuba, surrenders (July 17). U.S. takes Cuba, Puerto Rico, Guam, Wake Island, and Philippines from Spain in Treaty of Paris (Dec. 10). Senate agrees to annex Hawaii.

1899 Philippine Revolt against U.S. rule erupts. Secy. of State John Hay issues Open Door notes to European powers and Japan, requesting no spheres of influence in China (Sept. 6). U.S. and Germany agree to partition Samoan Islands (Dec. 2). Congress investigates incompetence in War Department, revealed during Spanish-American War.

1900 "Hard Money" triumphs as U.S. returns to single gold standard (Mar. 14). Puerto Rico and Hawaii become U.S. territories by acts of Congress (Apr. 12 & Apr. 30). U.S. troops relieve foreign legations under siege in Peking, China, during Boxer Rebellion (Aug. 14). Olds Company opens first Detroit auto factory. Carrie Nation leads hatchet-wielding women into Kansas saloons to smash liquor barrels.

1901 J.P. Morgan creates U.S. Steel, first billion-dollar corporation. U.S. retains control over Cuba with Platt Amendment. Pres. McKinley shot by anarchist Leon Czolgosz in Buffalo, N.Y. (Sept. 6—dies Sept. 14). Hay-Pauncefote Treaty secures British approval for a U.S.-built canal in Panama (Nov. 18). First great Texas oil strike made near Beaumont, Tex. Pres. Roosevelt promises to "speak softly and carry a big stick."

1902 End of Philippine Insurrection. Reclamation Act initiates Federal policy of conservation of natural resources (June 17). Congress declares Philippines an unorganized territory and its inhabitants are not U.S. citizens (July 1). First Rose Bowl football game played. Pres. Roosevelt helps mediate Pennsylvania coal strike.

1903 U.S. prevails over Canada in Alaskan boundary dispute. Pres. Roosevelt helps Panama gain independence from Colombia, then negotiates treaty to build Panama Canal. Orville and Wilbur Wright conduct first powered flight near Kitty Hawk, N.C. (Dec. 17). *The Great Train Robbery*, first feature-length motion picture, released. Wisconsin holds first primary elections. Ford Motor Company formed. Boston defeats Pittsburgh in first baseball World Series.

1904 Supreme Court upholds antitrust dissolution of Northern Securities company (Mar. 14). Pres. Roosevelt wins reelection and says he will not run again (Nov. 8). "Roosevelt Corollary" to Monroe Doctrine justifies U.S. intervention to keep other powers out of Western hemisphere. First New York City subway opened. New York state enacts first speed limit: 20 mph on open roads. Deaf, dumb, and blind, Helen Keller graduates from Radcliffe College.

1905 Supreme Court disallows limits on length of working day. Industrial Workers of the World, a radical labor union, formed in Chicago. Pres. Roosevelt mediates Treaty of Portsmouth, ending Russo-Japanese War. U.S. takes control of Santo Domingo trade. Black leaders hold Niagara Falls Conference, calling for equal rights.

1906 San Francisco destroyed by earthquake and fire (Apr. 18-19). Responding to consumer pressure, Congress passes Pure Food and Drug Act and Meat Inspection Act. Race riot breaks out in Atlanta (Sept. 22). Japan protests segregation of Asian students in California schools (Oct. 25). Pres. Roosevelt first American to win the Nobel Peace Prize, and first sitting president to leave U.S. on visit to Panama.

1907 Panic of 1907 triggers crash on Wall Street (Mar. 13) and run on banks across the country.

Pres. Roosevelt orders exclusion of Japanese laborers (Mar. 14). U.S. Navy's "Great White Fleet" embarks on tour around the world. Congress outlaws corporate contributions to political campaigns. Hundreds killed in coal mine explosions in Monongah, W. Va., and Jacobs Creek, Pa. All-time record 1,285,349 immigrants arrive in one year.

1908 U.S. and Japan conclude "Gentleman's Agreement" limiting immigration. Ford Model T appears on the market (Oct. 1). Root-Takahira Agreement promises U.S. and Japan will respect each other's interests in Pacific. Pres. Roosevelt appoints National Conservation Commission. Federal Bureau of Investigation established. New York City outlaws women smoking in public.

1909 Robert E. Peary plants American flag at North Pole (Apr. 6). Pres. Taft opens 700,000 acres for settlement in the West. W.E.B. DuBois founds National Association for the Advancement of Colored People (NAACP), advocating racial equality. U.S. troops land in Nicaragua.

1910 Theodore Roosevelt calls for "New Nationalism" in a speech at Ossawatomie, Kans. *Los Angeles Times* building destroyed by terrorist bomb (Oct. 1). Glacier National Park created. Mann Act cracks down on "white slave" trade. Boy Scouts of America chartered. Ballinger-Pinchot controversy reveals major differences over conservation policy in Taft administration.

1911 Sen. Robert M. LaFollette of Wisconsin founds National Progressive Republican League to promote reform (Jan. 21). Pres. Taft orders U.S. troops to border during Mexican Revolution. Supreme Court upholds antitrust breakups of Standard Oil and American Tobacco. Calbraith P. Rodgers makes first transcontinental airplane flight. U.S. bankers take control of Nicaragua's finances. Steel magnate Andrew Carnegie donates $125 million for philanthropic purposes.

1912 *Titanic* sinks on maiden voyage from England (Apr. 15). Progressive, or "Bull Moose," Party founded by Theodore Roosevelt, who survives an assassination attempt by John Schrank in Milwaukee (Oct. 14). Massachusetts adopts first minimum wage law. U.S. Marines land in Honduras, Cuba, Nicaragua, and Santo Domingo. Textile strike in Lawrence, Mass.

1913 Sixteenth Amendment empowers Federal government to collect income taxes (Feb. 25), and Seventeenth Amendment allows for popular election of U.S. senators (May 31). Congress creates Federal Reserve system. Ford Motor Company introduces assembly line. John D. Rockefeller donates $100 million to philanthropic Rockefeller Foundation. Grand Central Station opens in New York City.

1914 Pres. Wilson nearly goes to war with Mexico over arrests of American sailors in Tampico. U.S. Navy shells Vera Cruz and lands Marines in retaliation (Apr. 21). U.S. declares neutrality in World War I (Aug. 4). Congress passes Clayton Act, toughening antitrust standards. Congress proclaims Mother's Day.

1915 *Birth of a Nation*, first movie blockbuster. Pres. Wilson strongly protests German sinking of *Lusitania* with 128 Americans aboard (May 7). U.S. Marines land in Haiti (July 28). Ku Klux Klan revived in Atlanta, Ga. Coast-to-coast long distance telephone service begins.

1916 House-Grey Memorandum warns Germany that refusal to negotiate may bring U.S. into World War I. Gen. John Pershing chases Pancho Villa into Mexico after border raid on Columbus, N.Mex. (Mar. 15). Britain blacklists U.S. firms doing business with Germany. U.S. acquires Virgin Islands from Denmark for $25 million. Pres. Wilson wins reelection with slogan, "He Kept Us Out of War" (Nov. 7). Jeanette Rankin of Montana first woman elected to Congress. Louis D. Brandeis first Jewish member of Supreme Court. Margaret Sanger opens first birth control clinic in Brooklyn, N.Y. National Park Service created.

1917 Germany resumes unrestricted submarine warfare, leading U.S. to sever diplomatic relations (Feb. 3). Gen. John Pershing withdraws from Mexico. Zimmerman Telegram, intercepted by British intelligence and made public, reveals German overtures to Mexico in case of war (Feb. 24). U.S. merchant ships armed for self-defense against German submarines (Mar. 13). After Pres. Wilson proclaims "the world must be made safe for democracy," Congress declares war on Germany (Apr. 6) and Austria-Hungary (Dec. 7). Prohibition begins as wartime conservation measure. Race riot breaks out in East St. Louis.

1918 Pres. Wilson announces U.S. war aims in "Fourteen Points" speech (Jan. 8). U.S. troops join Allied intervention in Russian Revolution (Aug. 2). Congress passes Sedition Act. Over a million U.S. troops participate in month-long Meuse-Argonne campaign (Sept. 26-Nov. 11). Republicans win control of Congress, a rebuke to Pres. Wilson . Armistice Day ends World War I (Nov. 11) as mass celebrations break out across the country. Pres. Wilson goes to Europe for peace conference. Supreme Court approves draft laws and strikes down child labor laws. Influenza epidemic takes hundreds of thousands American lives.

1919 Eighteenth Amendment establishes Prohibition (Jan. 29). Strike wave sweeps country, triggering "Red Scare." American Communist Party organized in Chicago. Race riots in Washington, D.C., and Chicago. Pres. Wilson suffers incapacitating stroke during nationwide speaking tour (Sept. 26). Volstead Act implements national Prohibition enforcement. Versailles Treaty, including League of Nations, rejected by Senate (Nov. 19). Grand Canyon National Park created. New York-Chicago daily airmail service begins.

1920 Attorney General A. Mitchell Palmer stages "Palmer Raids," arresting and deporting thousands of radicals and immigrants. Sacco and Vanzetti are arrested for murder in Braintree, Mass. Supreme Court upholds Prohibition. Nineteenth Amendment establishes women's suffrage (Aug. 26). National League of Women Voters organized. Wall Street rocked by a terrorist bomb, killing 30 bystanders (Sept. 16). First regular radio broadcasts begin in East Pittsburgh, Pa. Pres. Wilson receives Nobel Peace Prize. U.S. population, more urban than rural for first time, tops 100 million (105,710,620).

1921 Pres. Harding, promising a "return to normalcy," takes office. U.S. negotiates separate peace with Germany, Austria, and Hungary. Ku Klux Klan spreads terror in the South. International disarmament conference meets in Washington, D.C. Jack Dempsey defeats Georges Carpentier in first million-dollar prize fight.

1922 Washington Conference concludes with nine international treaties to limit naval arms race, relax tensions in the Pacific, and protect China. Supreme Court upholds women's suffrage. Lincoln Memorial dedicated in Washington, D.C. (May 30). Pres. Harding vetoes "Bonus Bill" for World War I veterans. Congress passes joint resolution in favor of Jewish homeland in Palestine (Sept. 21). First commercial radio show broadcast in New York.

1923 Last U.S. occupation troops leave Germany (Jan. 10). Senate begins investigating corruption in

Veterans Bureau and Teapot Dome oil leases (Oct. 25). Pres. Harding dies mysteriously of "apoplexy" in San Francisco (Aug. 2). Pres. Coolidge's address to Congress, calling for economy in government, first radio broadcast of a presidential speech (Dec. 6). Oklahoma declares martial law to crack down on Ku Klux Klan. Yankee Stadium opens.

1924 Congress provides bonuses for World War I veterans over Pres. Coolidge's veto. Congress passes Immigration Act, imposing strict national quota system. European powers accept Dawes Plan for repayment of war debts and reparations. U.S. Marines withdraw from Santo Domingo. Coast-to-coast air mail service begins. Tornados wreak havoc in Midwest.

1925 Tennessee outlaws teaching evolution in school, leading to the Scopes Trial in Dayton, Tenn. (July 10-21). Ku Klux Klan marches on Washington, D.C. (Aug. 8) Nellie Tayloe Ross of Wyoming first woman governor. Florida land boom draws hordes of speculators. Colonel Billy Mitchell suspended from U.S. Army for advocating stronger air force. Chicago gang wars break out as Al Capone consolidates bootlegging operations.

1926 Secy. Treasury of Andrew Mellon's drastic tax cuts approved. Admiral Richard E. Byrd and Floyd Bennett first to fly over North Pole (May 9). Henry Ford institutes 8-hour day and 5-day work week at Ford Motor Company factories. Hurricane sweeps Florida, killing 372 people. Book of the Month Club founded. U.S. Marines return to Nicaragua.

1927 Charles Lindbergh completes non-stop solo flight from New York to Paris (May 20-21), returns home to huge welcoming crowds. Sacco and Vanzetti executed in Massachusetts, despite international protests. *The Jazz Singer* with Al Jolson becomes first "talkie" motion picture (Oct. 6). Holland Tunnel in New York opened. Mississippi River floods causes $300 million damage. Ford Model A unveiled. Mechanical cotton picker invented. New York-London commercial telephone service begins.

1928 U.S. joins fourteen countries in signing Kellogg-Briand Pact for the "outlawry of war" (Aug. 27). Clark Memorandum disavows future U.S. interventions in Latin America. Pres. Coolidge refuses to aid American farmers mired in agricultural depression. Walt Disney creates "Steamboat Willie," first Mickey Mouse cartoon. George Eastman demonstrates color motion picture technology. Republicans promise "a chicken in every pot, a car in every garage."

1929 St. Valentine's Day Massacre claims six lives in Chicago gang wars. Young Plan replaces Dawes Plan for payment of war debts and reparations. Albert B. Fall, former secretary of the Interior, found guilty in Teapot Dome scandal. Stock market crash on "Black Tuesday" (Oct. 29) ushers in Great Depression.

1930 Wave of bank failures sweeps U.S., wiping out millions of savings accounts and leading to private hoarding of gold. U.S., Britain, and Japan sign London Naval Treaty limiting naval arms race (Apr. 22). Hawley-Smoot Tariff raises barriers to world trade, worsening Depression. Congress creates Veteran's Administration (July 3).

1931 World War I veterans are offered "Bonus Loans" to combat Depression. "Star Spangled Banner" becomes national anthem. "Scottsboro Boys" arrested for rape in Alabama. Empire State Building, tallest building in the world, opens in New York City. Pres. Hoover declares moratorium on international debt and reparations payments.

1932 Stimson Doctrine announces U.S. disapproval of Japanese invasion of China. Congress approves Reconstruction Finance Corporation to help recovery. Norris-LaGuardia act restricts use of injunctions against labor strikes. Franklin D. Roosevelt, promising a "New Deal" for Americans, elected president in Democratic landslide. Stock market drops to 10% of its 1929 value; national income cut in half. "Bonus Army" of poor veterans marches on Washington, D.C. Amelia Earhart first woman to fly solo across the Atlantic.

1933 Giuseppe Zangara kills Chicago Mayor Anton J. Cermak in a Miami, Fla., motorcade, narrowly missing president-elect Franklin D. Roosevelt (Feb. 15). Banks are closed for four days by presidential order (Mar. 5). During "Hundred Days" (Mar. 9-June 16), Pres. Roosevelt pushes New Deal through Congress, conducts first "Fireside Chat" on radio, and takes U.S. off gold standard. Beer and wine made legal again (Mar. 22). Congress passes National Industrial Recovery Act (June 16). U.S. recognizes Soviet Union (Nov. 16). U.S. Marines withdraw from Nicaragua. Frances Perkins, Sec. of Labor, becomes first woman cabinet member.

1934 Dust storms inundate Southwest, driving "Okies" and "Arkies" to California. General strike paralyzes San Francisco (July 16). John Dillinger, public enemy number one, killed by FBI agents (July 22). Sen. Gerald P. Nye of North Dakota begins investigating role of U.S. munitions manufacturers in World War I. U.S. releases Cuba from Platt Amendment. U.S. troops withdrawn from Haiti.

1935 Supreme Court invalidates National Industrial Recovery Act. Pres. Roosevelt pushes more "Second New Deal" legislation through Congress, notably the Wagner Act protecting unions, Social Security Act, and "Soak the Rich" Wealth Tax Act. Sen. Huey P. Long of Louisana assassinated (Sept. 8). Congress of Industrial Organization (CIO) formed (Nov. 9). Congress passes first Neutrality Act. Alcoholics Anonymous founded.

1936 Congress passes second Neutrality Act. France, Britain, and U.S. sign New London Naval Treaty (Mar. 25). U.S. declares neutrality in Spanish Civil War (Aug. 7). CIO auto workers begin sitdown strikes in Flint, Mich. (Dec. 30). *Life* magazine begins publishing. Jesse Owens wins four gold medals at "Nazi Olympics" in Berlin.

1937 Congress passes third Neutrality Act. Pres. Roosevelt proposes controversial "court-packing" plan. German dirigible *Hindenburg* explodes and burns in Lakehurst, N.J. (May 6). Pres. Roosevelt angers isolationists with "Quarantine Speech" (Oct. 5). Japanese planes sink U.S. Navy gunboat *Panay* in China (Dec. 12). Slow recovery ends abruptly as Depression worsens.

1938 Republican gains in Congress signal end of New Deal. Pres. Roosevelt calls for military buildup (Jan. 28). Mexico seizes U.S.-owned oil wells (Mar. 18). Rep. Martin Dies of Texas begins House Un-American Activities Committee (HUAC) investigations of Communists and Fascists. Howard Hughes sets record for around-the-world flight in less than four days (July 14). "Invasion from Mars" radio broadcast by Orson Welles causes widespread panic (Oct. 30). Hurricane devastates Atlantic coast, killing 700 people.

1939 Supreme Court upholds Tennessee Valley Authority. Pan Am begins first regular trans-Atlantic passenger service. U.S. declares neutrality in World War II (Sept. 5). Congress passes fourth Neutrality Act, approving Pres. Roosevelt's request for "cash-and-carry" arms sales to belligerents. Nylon stockings appear on the market.

1940   As World War II engulfs Europe, Pres. Roosevelt announces U.S. has moved from "neutrality" to "non-belligerency" (June 10). U.S. and Britain conclude Destroyers-for-Bases deal. Congress enacts a peacetime draft (Sept. 16) and massive increases in military spending. Over 16 million men register for draft as Pres. Roosevelt's embargo on strategic exports takes effect. Roosevelt, reelected to an unprecedented third term, calls for U.S. to become "the arsenal of democracy" (Dec. 20).

1941   Congress appropriates $7 billion in Lend-Lease aid to Britain. German submarine sinks merchant ship *Robin Moor*, first U.S. casualty of war (May 21). Roosevelt responds by declaring "unlimited national emergency" (May 27), freezing German and Italian assets in U.S. (June 14), and promising aid to Soviet Union (June 24). Roosevelt freezes Japanese assets in retaliation for invasion of Indochina (July 25). Pres. Roosevelt and Prime Minister Winston Churchill issue Atlantic Charter (Aug. 12). U.S. Navy is ordered to "shoot on sight" at German warships (Sept. 11). "America has been attacked, the shooting has started," Pres. Roosevelt informs the country (Oct. 27). Japanese planes attack Pearl Harbor, Hawaii, killing 2,400 U.S. servicemen and civilians (Dec. 7). U.S. declares war on Japan (Dec. 10) and on Germany and Italy (Dec. 11).

1942   Roosevelt creates War Production Board, calls for mass mobilization, and puts New Deal on hold. U.S. troops land in North Ireland, first to arrive in Europe (Jan. 26). Pres. Roosevelt approves internment of Japanese-Americans for duration of war (Feb. 20). Japanese submarine shells an oil refinery in Santa Barbara, Calif. (Feb. 23). Maj. James H. Doolittle stages carrier-launched bombing raid on Tokyo (Apr. 18). U.S. forces surrender in Philippines (May 6), but win major naval victories over Japan in Coral Sea (May 4-8) and at Midway (June 3-6). U.S. offensive begins in Pacific with invasion of Guadalcanal Island (Aug. 7). First all-U.S. bombing attack launched against German forces at Rouen, France (Aug. 17). Congress approves "Victory Tax" on wartime incomes. Allies land 400,000 men in North Africa (Nov. 7-8). Eight German saboteurs apprehended in New York; six executed. Cocoanut Grove nightclub fire in Boston kills 492.

1943   Congress appropriates $100 billion for war effort. Roosevelt and Churchill demand "unconditional surrender" at Casablanca conference in Morocco (Jan. 24). U.S. Marines drive last Japanese from Guadalcanal (Feb. 9). U.S. troops defeated in first battle with Germans at Kasserine Pass, Tunisia (Feb. 20). Pres. Roosevelt declares wage-and-price freeze to stem inflation. U.S. and Britain invade Sicily (July 10) and Italy proper (Sept. 3). Roosevelt and Churchill meet with Chiang Kai-Shek of China in Cairo, Egypt (Nov. 22), and with Josef Stalin of Soviet Union in Teheran, Iran (Dec. 4-6). Gen. Dwight D. Eisenhower named Supreme Commander of Allied forces in Europe. Congress approves Federal income tax withholding. Race riots in Detroit and Harlem kill 40.

1944   U.S. and British planes begin around-the-clock bombing of Berlin. Allied forces land at Anzio, Italy (Jan. 22). Congress approves $1.35 billion for United Nations Relief and Reconstruction Agency, first U.S. foreign aid (Mar. 29). Allied forces enter Rome (June 5) as reconquest of Europe begins with D-Day invasion of Normandy (June 6). Allied breakout from Normandy sends German forces reeling across France (July 25). Postwar financial arrangements made at an international conference in Bretton Woods, N.H. (July 1-22). Plans for United Nations made at Dumbarton Oaks conference (Aug. 21-Oct. 7). Gen. Douglas MacArthur begins reconquest of Philippines with landings at Leyte Gulf (Oct. 20). Congress passes Servicemen's Readjustment Act, known as "GI Bill of Rights." Roosevelt wins fourth term.

1945   Roosevelt, Churchill, and Stalin meet for last time at Yalta in Soviet Crimea to begin postwar planning (Feb. 4-11). Allied forces cross Rhine River and drive into heart of Germany (Mar. 7). U.S. air raids destroy Tokyo (Mar. 10-11). Pres. Roosevelt dies suddenly of cerebral hemorrhage in Warm Springs, Ga. (Apr. 12). United Nations Conference begins meeting in San Francisco (Apr. 24). Germany surrenders, ending war in Europe (May 7). Fifty nations sign U.N. Charter (June 26). First atomic explosion occurs in test at Alamagordo, N.Mex. (July 16). Pres. Truman meets with Churchill and Stalin at Potsdam, Germany (July 17-Aug. 2). Atomic bombs dropped on Hiroshima (Aug. 6) and Nagasaki (Aug. 9); Japan surrenders (Aug. 14), ending World War II. Council of Allied Foreign Ministers meets in London, unable to agree on peace treaty (Dec. 16-27). Television channels are allotted for commercial use. Empire State Building hit by B-25 bomber in heavy fog.

1946   Strike wave sweeps U.S., idling 4.6 million U.S. workers. Congress passes Employment Act, committing Federal government to postwar economic management. Winston Churchill warns Americans about Communist expansion with "Iron Curtain" speech at Westminster College in Fulton, Mo. (Mar. 5). Pres. Truman seizes control of railroads and coal mines during strikes. Paris Peace Conference ends in failure (July 29-Oct. 15). U.S. presents Baruch Plan for international control of atomic energy, grants independence to Philippines (July 4), and agrees to loan Britain $3.5 billion for postwar reconstruction. Congress creates Atomic Energy Commission. U.N. General Assembly begins meeting in New York.

1947   Council of Foreign Ministers meets in Moscow, again unable to agree on peace treaty (Mar. 10-Apr. 24). Pres. Truman announces Truman Doctrine, promising aid to countries threatened by subversion (May 12). Secy. of State George C. Marshall announces Marshall Plan for postwar reconstruction of Europe (June 5). Republican-dominated Congress restricts union organizing with Taft-Hartley Act. House Committee on Un-American Activities (HUAC) begins investigating Communism in Hollywood (Oct. 20). Texas City, Tex., wiped out when a munitions ship explodes, killing over 500 people. Jackie Robinson of Brooklyn Dodgers breaks color line in baseball.

1948   Postwar inflation keeps prices rising fast. Congress approves $5.3 billion for Marshall Plan aid to Europe with Foreign Assistance Act. U.S. recognizes new state of Israel (May 14) and admits 205,000 war refugees from Europe. Britain and U.S. begin airlifting supplies into West Berlin after Soviets cut off all traffic into city (June 26). Pres. Truman orders peacetime draft and desegregation of U.S. armed forces. HUAC charges Alger Hiss with spying for Soviet Union. Pres. Truman wins upset reelection victory over New York Gov. Thomas E. Dewey. Idlewild International Airport, world's largest, opens in New York.

1949   Pres. Truman calls for "Fair Deal" domestic programs and "Point Four" foreign aid programs. U.S., Canada, and 10 Western European nations sign treaty that will lead to North Atlantic Treaty Organization (NATO). Berlin Airlift ends when Soviets finally lift blockade (May 12). Pres. Truman announces Soviet atomic bomb test (Sept. 23). Eleven U.S. Communist leaders convicted of conspiring to overthrow government. Steel strike idles half a million workers nationwide (Oct. 1-Nov. 11). *Lucky Lady II* of U.S. Air Force completes first non-stop around-the-world flight.

1950   Sen. Joseph R. McCarthy of Wisconsin issues his first accusations of Communists in government at a speech in Wheeling, W. Va. North Korea invades South Korea, beginning Korean War (June 25). Pres. Truman orders U.S. intervention (June 27), obtains U.N. support (July 7), asks Congress for a $10 billion rearmament program (July 20), and calls up reserves (Aug. 4). Inchon landing begins rout of North Korean invaders (Sept. 15). U.N. troops recapture Seoul (Sept. 26) and invade North Korea (Oct. 7). Congress passes Internal Security Act, requiring registration of Communist organizations, over Pres. Truman's veto (Sept. 23). Puerto Rican nationalists nearly assassinate Pres. Truman in Washington (Nov. 11). After China intervenes in the Korean War, Pres. Truman proclaims a national emergency (Dec. 16).

1951   Gen. Dwight D. Eisenhower comes out of retirement to accept command of Allied forces in Europe (Apr. 4). Julius and Ethel Rosenberg sentenced to death for spying (Apr. 5). Pres. Truman removes Gen. Douglas MacArthur from command in Korea for insubordination (Apr. 11). MacArthur returns to the U.S., greeted by exultant crowds, to deliver address to Congress. Missouri River floods devastate Kansas City, causing over $1 billion in damages (July 11–25). U.S. concludes a mutual defense pact with Australia and New Zealand, and signs a peace treaty with Japan (Sept. 8). Congress passes the Mutual Security Act, providing $7 billion for foreign aid and military cooperation with pro-U.S. nations. CBS transmits first color television broadcast from New York.

1952   Pres. Truman seizes steel mills paralyzed by strikes (Apr. 8). U.S., Britain, and France sign a peace treaty with West Germany (May 26). Construction begins on USS *Nautilus*, first atomic submarine. Supreme Court upholds barring subversives from teaching in schools. Sen. Richard M. Nixon of California, Republican candidate for Vice President, delivers "Checkers Speech" on national television to explain his "secret slush fund." Republicans win control of White House and both houses of Congress for first time since 1928. U.S. announces first successful hydrogen bomb test at Eniwetok Atoll in Marshall Islands (Nov. 16).

1953   Thirteen more Communist leaders are convicted of conspiring to overthrow the government. Julius and Ethel Rosenberg are executed in Ossining, N.Y. (June 19). Pres. Eisenhower lifts wage and price controls, increases U.S. support for French war effort in Indochina, negotiates armistice ending Korean War (June 27). Congress creates Department of Health, Education, and Welfare (Apr. 1). U.S. pledges aid to Spain in exchange for military bases (Sept. 26). Major Chuck Yeager of the U.S. Air Force sets new air speed record in rocket-powered X-1 jet plane.

1954   Secy. of State John Foster Dulles vows "massive retaliation" against Soviet aggression (Jan. 12). Foreign Ministers Conference in Berlin fails to achieve reunification of Germany (Jan. 25-Feb. 18). Puerto Rican nationalists shoot five Congressmen on the floor of the House of Representatives (Mar. 1). U.S. negotiates the Southeast Asia Treaty Organization (SEATO) security pact (Sept. 8). Supreme Court orders school

desegregation in the *Brown* decision (May 17). CIA helps overthrow the Arbenz government in Guatemala (June 29). Congress passes Communist Control Act. Senate censures Sen. Joseph McCarthy. France announces that U.S. has paid for most of the Indochina war. New York Stock Exchange prices finally reattain 1929 levels.

1955   Pres. Eisenhower promises to use atomic weapons in case of war and conducts first televised press conference. U.S., Soviet Union, and Allies agree on Austrian peace treaty to end occupation. Summit conference of U.S., British, French, and Soviet leaders in Switzerland produces "Spirit of Geneva." Supreme Court orders school desegregation to proceed "with all deliberate speed." Pres. Eisenhower hospitalized for three weeks following heart attack. Interstate Commerce Commission orders desegregation on interstate trains and buses. AFL and CIO labor federations merge to form the AFL-CIO, with 15 million members. Dr. Jonas Salk perfects polio vaccine. Dr. Martin Luther King, Jr., leads bus boycott in Montgomery, Ala.

1956   Pres. Eisenhower refuses to intervene against Soviet invasion of Hungary and exerts pressure on Allies to withdraw from Suez. Congressmen signing Southern Manifesto promise "massive resistance" to school desegregation. Atomic Energy Commission approves commercial nuclear power plants. Congress passes Highway Act, appropriating $32 billion for construction of a vast nationwide road system. TWA and United airliners collide in midair and crash into Grand Canyon, killing 128 people (June 30). First trans-Atlantic telephone cable begins operating. Grace Kelly marries Prince Rainier III of Monaco.

1957   Pres. Eisenhower announces Eisenhower Doctrine, promising aid to any Middle Eastern country threatened by Communism. McClellan Committee begins investigating corruption and racketeering in International Brotherhood of Teamsters union. Sen. J. Strom Thurmond of South Carolina sets all-time filibuster record (24 hours, 27 minutes) with speech against civil rights (Aug. 30). Congress eventually approves the first Civil Rights Act since Reconstruction (Sept. 9). Pres. Eisenhower sends troops to Little Rock, Ark., to enforce Federal desegregation order (Sept. 24). First underground atomic test conducted in Nevada (Sept. 19).

1958   In response to Soviet launch of Sputnik, U.S. launches Explorer I, first American satellite; Congress creates National Aeronautics and Space Administration (NASA) and passes National Defense Education Act. Vice President Nixon nearly killed by angry mob in Caracas, Venezuela. At request of weak government in Beirut, Pres. Eisenhower orders U.S. Marines to land in Lebanon (July 15). Nuclear submarine *Nautilus* performs first undersea crossing of North Pole (Aug. 5). Presidential assistant Sherman Adams forced to resign in scandal over accepting favors (Sept. 22).

1959   Fidel Castro's takeover of Cuba begins rapid deterioration of U.S.-Cuba relations (Jan. 1). Alaska becomes 49th state (Jan. 3), and Hawaii becomes 50th state (Aug. 21). Joint U.S.-Canada St. Lawrence Seaway project completed. Congress passes the Landrum-Griffin Act to suppress racketeering in labor unions. Vice Pres. Richard M. Nixon holds impromptu "kitchen debate" in Moscow with Soviet Premier Nikita Khrushchev. Charles Van Doren testifies that his victory on the "$64,000 Question" TV game show was fixed.

1960   U.S. and Japan conclude new security treaty (Jan. 19). Black students stage first sit-in at a Woolworth's lunch counter in Greensboro, N.C. (Feb. 1). U-2 spy plane, with American pilot Francis Gary Powers, is shot down over the Soviet Union (May 1). Congress passes second Civil Rights Act since Reconstruction. Congress investigates "payola" in the radio industry, leading to the arrest of Alan Freed, "father of rock 'n' roll." After Cuba rejects American protests over confiscated property, Pres. Eisenhower imposes trade embargo. John F. Kennedy and Richard M. Nixon hold first televised presidential campaign debates. Kennedy wins election by 0.3% of popular vote, closest presidential election since 1884 (Nov. 8).

1961   Pres. Eisenhower breaks diplomatic relations with Cuba, warns Americans to beware of "military-industrial complex." CIA-backed Bay of Pigs invasion fails to overthrow Castro regime in Cuba (Apr. 17). Commander Alan B. Shephard, Jr., U.S. Navy, first American in space on Mercury rocket (May 5). Soviet construction of Berlin Wall creates temporary crisis (Aug. 13). Pres. Kennedy creates Peace Corps and Alliance for Progress. American families advised to build nuclear fallout shelters. "Freedom Rides" civil rights protests broken up by riots in Anniston and Birmingham, Ala. American Medical Association reports link between smoking and heart disease. National Council of Churches endorses birth control for families.

1962   Lt. Col. John H. Glenn, Jr., first American to orbit Earth. Pres. Kennedy convinces steel companies to rescind price increases. U.S. conducts first successful test of sea-launched long-range ballistic missile with nuclear warhead. Pres. Kennedy sends U.S. marshals to protect James H. Meredith, a black student at University of Mississippi. U.S. extends a $100 million emergency loan to the United Nations. Threat of nuclear war during Cuban Missile Crisis averted when Soviet Union agrees to withdraw missiles from Cuba (Oct. 22-28). Rachel Carson's *Silent Spring* draws attention to environmental crisis.

1963   Pres. Kennedy proposes the Medicare program. U.S., Great Britain, and the Soviet Union conclude the Nuclear Test-Ban Treaty outlawing atmospheric testing (July 25). "Hot line" between Washington and Moscow put in place. Civil rights movement reaches a climax with mass demonstrations in Birmingham, Ala., and epic March on Washington, where Martin Luther King delivers his "I Have a Dream" speech (Aug. 28). Pres. Kennedy is assassinated in Dallas, Tex., by Lee Harvey Oswald (Nov. 22), who is murdered by Jack Ruby (Nov. 24).

1964   Pres. Johnson, taking up Pres. Kennedy's cause, calls for a "War on Poverty." Supreme Court orders states to redraw Congressional boundaries to ensure fair representation. Alaska declared disaster area after major earthquake rocks Anchorage (Mar. 28). Mississippi "Freedom Summer" begins with murder of three civil rights workers (June 22). Pres. Johnson pushes landmark Civil Rights and Economic Opportunity acts through Congress. After alleged North Vietnamese attack on U.S. Navy destroyers, Congress passes Tonkin Gulf Resolution giving Pres. Johnson free hand in Vietnam (Aug. 7). Warren Commission reports there was no conspiracy to assassinate Pres. Kennedy (Sept. 27). The Rev. Martin Luther King Jr. wins Nobel Peace Prize.

1965   Pres. Johnson calls for the "Great Society." Black nationalist Malcolm X is assassinated in New York City (Feb. 21). Pres. Johnson orders U.S. Marines into South Vietnam (Mar. 8) and into Santo Domingo (Apr. 38). U.S. troops authorized to undertake offensive operations in South Vietnam (June 8). Martin Luther King leads civil rights marches from Selma to Montgomery, Ala., and in white neighborhoods of Chicago. Congress approves Medicare (July 30) and Voting Rights Act (Aug. 6). The Watts Riot in Los Angeles leaves 34 dead and over $200 million in damage (Aug. 11-16), accelerating wave of ghetto riots. Tornadoes sweep Midwest, killing 271 and injuring 5,000.

1966   Pres. Johnson orders first B-52 strategic bombing raids on North Vietnam (Apr. 12). Supreme Court rules police must advise suspects of their rights. Cesar Chavez leads United Farm Workers strike and boycott against California grape growers. Stokeley Carmichael of Student Non-Violent Coordinating Committee demands "Black Power." Congress enacts safety standards for automobiles. Edward W. Brooke of Massachusetts is first black Senator since Reconstruction. U.S. troops in Vietnam increase from 215,000 to over 400,000.

1967   Green Bay defeats Kansas City in first ever Super Bowl. Hundreds of thousands of anti-war protesters march on Washington (Apr. 15 & Oct. 21-22). Pres. Johnson announces U.S. troop level will reach 525,000 by end of 1968. Worst race riot in U.S. history erupts in Detroit (July 23), leaving 43 dead, while riot in Newark, N.J., (July 12) kills another 26. Sen. Eugene McCarthy (D-Minn.) announces antiwar candidacy for president (Nov. 30). U.S. agrees to refrain from placing nuclear weapons in space and joins General Agreement on Tariffs and Trade (GATT). Albert DeSalvo, the "Boston Strangler," sentenced to life in prison. Thurgood Marshall becomes first black justice on Supreme Court.

1968   North Korea seizes USS *Pueblo*, holding 82 crewmen hostage (Jan. 23). North Vietnam and Viet Cong launch massive Tet Offensive (Jan. 30). Pres. Johnson makes surprise announcement that he will not seek re-election (Mar. 31). Martin Luther King assassinated by James Earl Ray in Memphis, Tenn. (Apr. 4). Washington-Hanoi peace talks begin in Paris (May 10). After winning California primary, Sen. Robert F. Kennedy of New York murdered by Sirhan Sirhan in Los Angeles (June 5). U.S. signs Nuclear Non-Proliferation Treaty. Democratic Convention in Chicago marred by riots and police violence against antiwar demonstrators. Shirley Chisholm of New York is the first black woman elected to Congress. Apollo VIII completes first moon orbit.

1969   Oil spill off Santa Barbara, Calif., draws attention to need for environmental protection (Feb. 5). Pres. Nixon asks Congress to fund Anti-Ballistic Missile program (ABM) as "safeguard" for strategic defense. U.S. losses in Vietnam exceed losses in Korean War. Sen. Edward M. Kennedy (D-Mass.) drives off a bridge at Chappaquiddick, Mass., killing Mary Jo Kopechne (July 18). Neil Armstrong and Buzz Aldrin of Apollo XI are first men to walk on the moon (July 20). Hurricane Camille claims over 300 victims in the South. Trial of Chicago Eight (later Chicago Seven, after Bobby Seale tried separately) begins. Woodstock music festival near Bethel, N.Y., draws 400,000 young fans (Aug. 15-18). Vietnam Moratorium and "March Against Death" antiwar demonstrations draw hundreds of thousands to Washington. U.S. and the Soviet Union begin Strategic Arms Limitation Talks (SALT) in Helsinki, Finland.

1970   Pres. Nixon calls for "Vietnamization" to decrease U.S. involvement in war. U.S. bombing

of North Vietnam escalates dramatically; nationwide protests break out when U.S. invades Cambodia (Apr. 29). Four students are killed and nine wounded by National Guard units at Kent State University in Ohio (May 4). SALT negotiations reopen in Vienna, Austria. Lt. William L. Calley court martialed for massacre of 102 civilians in My Lai South Vietnam (Nov. 12). Supreme Court upholds new 18-year-old voting age (Dec. 21). Congress creates Environmental Protection Agency, passes Water Quality Improvement Act, Air Quality Control Act, and Occupational Safety and Health Act.
1971   Pres. Nixon proposes Federal revenue sharing with states. Charles Manson and three women followers convicted for Tate-LaBianca murders in Los Angeles (Jan. 25). Major earthquake rocks Southern California, killing 64 and injuring over 1,000 (Feb. 9). Supreme Court approves busing to achieve school integration. Indian occupation of Alcatraz Island in San Francisco Bay comes to an end. Prison riot in Attica, N.Y., kills 43 inmates and guards. *New York Times* begins publishing "Pentagon Papers," top-secret history of Vietnam War (June 13). U.S. devalues dollar (Dec. 18). U.S. troops in Vietnam reach 139,000; U.S. air attacks are heaviest since 1968.
1972   Nixon first president to visit China (Feb. 21–28) and the Soviet Union (May 22–30). Airlines begin screening passengers to prevent hijackings. Congress passes Equal Rights Amendment and submits it to states for ratification. Gov. George Wallace of Alabama shot and seriously wounded by Arthur Bremer while campaigning for president in Laurel, Md. (May 15). Five men arrested for breaking into Democratic National Committee headquarters at the Watergate complex in Washington (June 17). Federal grand jury indicts five burglars and two former White House aides in Watergate trial (Sept. 15). Pres. Nixon angers farmers with the "Great Grain Robbery," a secret deal to sell wheat at discount to Soviet Union. National Security Advisor Henry Kissinger announces "peace is at hand" in Vietnam in time for Pres. Nixon to carry 49 states in election. U.S. troops in Vietnam fall to 69,000 as Nixon orders resumption of heavy bombing of North Vietnam (Dec. 18).
1973   Supreme Court disallows state restrictions on abortions (*Roe vs. Wade*). U.S. signs Paris peace accords ending Vietnam War (Jan. 27). Trial of Watergate burglars reveals conspiracy to conceal White House involvement. Top presidential aides H.R. Haldeman, John Ehrlichman, John Dean, and Attorney General Richard Kleindienst resign amid charges of White House cover-up (Apr. 30). Sen. Sam Ervin of North Carolina chairs Senate investigation of Watergate scandal on national television (May 17–Nov. 15). Pres. Nixon fires Watergate Special Prosecutor Archibald Cox and others in "Saturday Night Massacre" (Oct. 20). Vice President Spiro Agnew resigns after threat of prosecution for tax evasion (Oct. 10). Gasoline prices skyrocket after Arab nations embargo oil exports to U.S. in retaliation for U.S. aid to Israel in Yom Kippur War (Oct. 17). Pres. Nixon turns over first White House tapes, which include mysterious 18 1/2 minute gap (Nov. 26). Gerald R. Ford of Michigan sworn in as first vice president chosen under 25th Amendment (Dec. 6). Indians defy Federal authority in Wounded Knee, S.D.
1974   Arab oil embargo of U.S. lifted (Mar. 18). Supreme Court rules that Pres. Nixon must submit all White House tapes to Special Prosecutor Leon Jaworski (July 24). House Judiciary Committee votes three articles of impeachment (July 24–30). Pres. Nixon releases transcripts of tapes

that show he ordered cover-up (Aug. 5). Citing "political" difficulties, Pres. Nixon resigns (Aug. 8), elevating Vice President Ford to presidency (Aug. 9). Pres. Ford shocks nation by pardoning Nixon for all crimes (Sept. 8). Pres. Ford meets with Soviet Premier Leonid Brezhnev in Vladivostock to approve SALT treaty (Nov. 23–24). Newspaper heiress Patty Hearst kidnapped in Berkeley, Calif., by radical Symbionese Liberation Army.
1975   Nixon aides convicted of obstructing justice in Watergate investigation (Jan. 1). Last Americans evacuate Saigon as South Vietnam falls to North Vietnamese invasion (Apr. 30). Cambodia seizes USS *Mayaguez* (May 12), and Pres. Ford orders rescue operation (May 14). Apollo-Soyuz, joint Soviet-American space mission, achieves link-up in space (July 17). Lynette "Squeaky" Fromme and Sarah Jane Moore attempt to assassinate Pres. Ford in separate California incidents (Sept. 5 & Sept. 22). Congress votes to admit women to Army, Navy, and Air Force academies. House Democrats dismantle seniority system. Church Committee discovers CIA helped overthrow Salvador Allende of Chile and plotted to assassinate Fidel Castro of Cuba.
1976   Congress repeatedly overrides Pres. Ford's vetoes of bills providing for jobs, health, education, and welfare programs. Supreme Court upholds death penalty (July 3). Bicentennial of U.S. celebrated coast to coast. Jimmy Carter defeats Pres. Ford in November elections, as voters hold Ford responsible for pardoning Richard Nixon. Justice Department begins probing South Korean bribery of Congressmen and other officials. NASA's Viking I and Viking II space probes land on Mars and transmit scientific data, along with color photographs, back to Earth. "Legionnaire's Disease" breaks out at American Legion convention in Philadelphia, eventually claiming 29 victims. Hundreds of West Point cadets found to have cheated on exams.
1977   Pres. Carter pardons Vietnam War draft evaders, threatens to reduce foreign aid for countries violating human rights, calls for "moral equivalent of war" in energy conservation, and signs Panama Canal treaty (Sept. 7). U.S. declares 200-mile sovereignty zone in Atlantic and Pacific oceans to exclude foreign fishing vessels. Power blackout sets off arson and looting spree in New York City (July 13–14). Oil begins flowing through the Alaska pipeline. Pres. Carter accuses oil industry of "the biggest rip-off in history" (Oct. 13). ABC mini-series *Roots*, draws 130 million viewers.
1978   Pres. Carter postpones production of neutron bomb. California voters approve Proposition 13, reducing property taxes and setting off a nationwide "taxpayers' revolt." Supreme Court gives limited approval to affirmative action programs, but disallows quotas for college admissions (June 28). In private talks with Anwar Sadat and Menachem Begin, Pres. Carter mediates peace between Egypt and Israel with landmark Camp David Accords (Sept. 17). Nearly one thousand American followers of the Rev. Jim Jones commit mass suicide in Jonestown, Guiana, after cult members murder Rep. Leo Ryan of California and others (Nov. 18). House investigations of John F. Kennedy and Martin Luther King assassinations conclude that conspiracies were probable in both cases (Dec. 30). Federal loan guarantees rescue New York City from financial crisis.
1979   U.S. resumes diplomatic relations with China (Jan 1). Worst nuclear accident in U.S. history takes place at Three Mile Island power plant near Harrisburg, Pa. Pres. Carter and Premier

Brezhnev sign SALT II treaty in Vienna (June 18). The Shah of Iran and Anastasio Somoza of Nicaragua, both U.S.-supported dictators, flee revolutions in their countries. Iranian militants seize U.S. Embassy in Teheran, taking 66 American hostages and demanding return of the Shah from U.S. (Nov. 4). Iranians release 13 American hostages, all blacks or women. Pres. Carter deports illegal Iranian students, freezes Iranian assets, and bars oil imports from Iran. Pope John Paul II visits U.S. Inflation reaches highest level in 33 years as Organization of Petroleum Exporting Countries (OPEC) doubles price of oil.

1980   Canadian embassy officials help six Americans escape from Iran (Jan. 29). In response to Soviet invasion of Afghanistan, Pres. Carter embargoes grain and high technology exports to Soviet Union, approves arms sales to China, and secures U.S. boycott of Olympics in Moscow. Congress grants Pres. Carter's request for Crude Oil Windfall Profits Tax and for resumption of Selective Service draft registration. Pres. Carter's secret rescue mission for American hostages in Iran fails when a U.S. Navy helicopter crashes in desert, killing eight servicemen (Apr. 24). Mt. St. Helens erupts in Washington state, killing 26 people and causing $2.7 billion in damage (May 18). Banking and trucking industries deregulated. FBI's "Abscam" operation implicates over 30 public officials, including a Senator and seven Congressmen, for accepting bribes.

1981   Minutes after Pres. Reagan is sworn in, Iran releases 52 American hostages after 444 days in captivity. Pres. Reagan shot by John Hinckley in Washington (Mar. 30), but makes full recovery. *Columbia* completes first successful space shuttle mission (Apr. 12–14). Federal air traffic controllers go on strike and lose jobs when Pres. Reagan fires all 13,000 of them. Sandra Day O'Connor unanimously confirmed as first woman justice of Supreme Court. Pres. Reagan lifts grain embargo against Soviet Union, but imposes new sanctions after Poland declares martial law. Congress accepts Pres. Reagan's plans for tax cuts, lower domestic spending, and major defense buildup. U.S. sends military advisors and aid to El Salvador.

1982   Ending 13-year antitrust suit, AT&T agrees to surrender control of local Bell System phone companies in return for expansion into new business pursuits (Jan. 8). Pres. Reagan calls for "New Federalism," transferring programs to state and local control. Unemployment exceeds 10% for first time since Great Depression, and Federal budget deficit exceeds $100 billion a year for first time ever. After a decade, Equal Rights Amendment fails falling three states short of ratification.

1983   Inflation slows as oil prices decline sharply. Congress admits internment of Japanese-Americans during World War II was unjust, and agrees to bail out the Social Security system. National Commission on Excellence in Education reports U.S. is a "nation at risk" because of inferior elementary and secondary schools. Sally Ride is first American woman astronaut, aboard space shuttle *Challenger*. Pres. Reagan strongly condemns Soviet Union for shooting down Korean airliner with 269 people aboard (Sept. 1). U.S. Marines join multinational peacekeeping force in Beirut, Lebanon, where Muslim terrorists kill 240 of them in suicide bombing (Oct. 23). U.S. invades Grenada to overthrow Cuban-backed regime (Oct. 25). Pres. Reagan calls for large-scale funding of Strategic Defense Initiative, or "Star Wars."

1984   Economic recovery begins as unemployment falls, inflation rate declines, economic growth accelerates, and U.S. dollar soars on international markets. Pres. Reagan orders U.S. Marines out of Lebanon (Feb. 7). The Rev. Jesse Jackson mounts first major challenge by black candidate for major party nomination. Rep. Geraldine Ferraro, (D-N.Y.) becomes first woman to receive major party nomination for vice president. Soviet bloc countries boycott Olympics in Los Angeles. Pres. Reagan wins landslide re-election over Democratic challenger Walter Mondale.

1985   Pres. Reagan calls for more tax and budget cuts to sustain economic growth (Feb. 4–6). Despite worldwide protests from Jewish organizations, Pres. Reagan delivers address at Bitburg cemetery in West Germany, where Nazi SS troops are buried (May 5). Muslim terrorists hijack TWA airliner (June 14), kill one American hostage, then release rest in Beirut (June 30). Palestinian terrorists kill an American hostage aboard hijacked Italian cruise ship *Achille Lauro* (Oct. 9). Pres. Reagan and Soviet Premier Mikhail Gorbachev hold their first summit meeting in Geneva (Nov. 19–21). Pres. Reagan signs Gramm-Rudman Act, requiring automatic spending cuts if Congress cannot reduce burgeoning Federal deficit.

1986   Space shuttle *Challenger* explodes in midair over Florida, killing six astronauts and a civilian passenger (Jan. 28). Investigations reveal NASA relaxed safety regulations to speed up launch date. U.S. Navy repels attack by Libyan forces during maneuvers in Gulf of Sidra (Mar. 24). Pres. Reagan blames Libya for death of two Americans in terrorist bombing of West Berlin disco, then orders retaliatory air raids on Tripoli and Benghazi (Apr. 14). Second Reagan-Gorbachev summit in Reykjavik, Iceland, reaches impasse over arms control and "Star Wars" (Oct. 12). Congress approves sweeping revision of U.S. tax structure. Democrats regain control of Senate. Pres. Reagan denies trading arms for hostages as Iran-Contra scandal breaks (Nov. 19). Wall Street financier Ivan Boesky fined $100 million for illegal insider trading on stock market.

1987   Pres. Reagan submits first trillion-dollar U.S. budget to Congress as national debt mounts steadily. Stock market closes above 2000 for first time in U.S. history. Tower Commission inquiry into Iran-Contra affair criticizes White House staff and Pres. Reagan's "management style." U.S.-Japan trade war erupts. After Pres. Reagan orders U.S. Navy into Persian Gulf to escort Kuwaiti oil tankers, an Iraqi warplane accidentally attacks USS *Stark*, killing 37 sailors (May 27). Bernhard Goetz acquitted of major charges in New York City "Subway Vigilante" shootings. Stock market crashes 508 points in one day, an all-time record, jolting markets around the world (Oct. 16). Third Reagan-Gorbachev summit in Washington produces agreement to dismantle medium-range missiles in Europe (Dec. 8).

1988   U.S. pressure on ruler Mañuel Noriega to step down plunges Panama into economic turmoil. After Iran lays mines in Persian Gulf, U.S. Navy warships and planes destroy two Iranian oil platforms and repel Iranian counterattacks (Apr. 18–19). USS *Vincennes* accidentally shoots down Iranian passenger plane, killing 290 people (July 3). George Bush becomes first sitting vice president elected president since 1836. Terrorist bomb aboard Pan Am Flight 103 kills all 259 aboard, mostly Americans, and 11 on the ground in Lockerbie, Scotland (Dec. 21). Drexel Burnham Lambert agrees to pay all-time record $650 million penalty for securities fraud (Dec. 21).

1989   Exxon Valdez supertanker spills over 11 million gallons of oil off Alaska coast (Mar. 24). HUD scandal reveals fraud, mismanagement, and influence-peddling under Reagan administration. Speaker of the House Jim Wright and Democartic majority whip Tony Coelho resign over ethics violations. Supreme Court upholds the right to burn U.S. flag. President Bush signs $300 billion savings-and-loan bailout (Aug. 9). Severe earthquake, second worst in U.S. history, inflicts $6 billion damage and leaves 62 dead in San Francisco Bay area (Oct. 17). L. Douglas Wilder of Virginia is the first black elected governor (Nov. 7). After Panama declares a "state of war" with the U.S., Pres. Bush sends 24,000 U.S. troops to overthrow the Noriega regime and install a popularly elected government (Dec. 20).

1990   After Iraq invades Kuwait (Aug. 2), U.S. launches Operation Desert Shield: more than 200,000 U.S. troops move into Saudi Arabia and the navy blockades all oil exports from Iraq and all imports except food. Pres. Bush refuses any compromise with Iraq's dictator, Saddam Hussein, and works with UN Security Council to condemn invasion and impose stringent economic sanctions.   Bush and Gorbachev meet twice: U.S. agrees to some economic aid, grants USSR most favored nation trade status, also secures agreement that Iraq must withdraw from Kuwait. Pres. Bush breaks campaign pledge of "no new taxes." A major flaw in the $1.5 bil. Hubble Space Telescope is discovered shortly after its deployment. Drexel Burnham Lambert defaults on $100 mil. in loans; Michael Milken, head of junk bond department, is fined $600 mil. and sentenced to jail.

1991   U.S. Operation Desert Storm quickly and decisively drives Iraq's armed forces out of Kuwait. The ground war lasts only 100 hours. Bush and Gorbachev sign first nuclear arms reduction treaty (July 31) as U.S.S.R. continues to crumble. U.S. establishes diplomatic relations with former Soviet republics, Estonia, Latvia, and Lithuania. Unemployment rate rises to highest level in a decade. Interest rates are cut to lowest levels in 20 years. Senate's confirmation of Clarence Thomas's nomination to the Supreme Court is delayed by Anita Hill's luridly detailed charges (Oct. 6) of sexual harassment 10 years earlier. Oliver North and John Poindexter are exonerated in connection with the Iran-contra scandal. Four white Los Angeles policemen indicted for videotaped beating of black motorist Rodney King.

1992   The Americans with Disabilities Act, the most sweeping anti-discrimination legislation since the Civil Rights Act of 1964 guarantees equal access for the disabled (Jan. 26). Pres. Bush and Russian Pres. Boris Yeltsin issue joint statement officially ending the Cold War (Feb.1). Riots erupt in Los Angeles minutes after an all-white jury acquits four L.A. police officers of beating Rodney King (April 29-May 4). More than 50 people are killed, 2,000 injured, and over 7,000 arrested. Billionaire-populist Ross Perot enters the presidential race as a third-party candidate. Federal Reserve cuts discount rate to 3%, its lowest rate since 1963, after unemployment skyrockets to 7.8%, its highest level since 1983 (July 2). Bill Clinton defeats George Bush and Ross Perot to become the 42nd President (Nov. 3). Pres. Bush commits at least 28,000 U.S. troops to protect the delivery of relief supplies to war- and famine-torn Somalia (Dec. 3). IBM announces it will cut 25,000 more jobs in 1993 in the wake of $6 billion losses, the biggest loss ever for an American cor-

poration. Pres. Bush pardons six Reagan Administration officials for their involvement in the Iran-Contra scandal.

1993   More than 120 nations, including the U.S. and Russia, agree to ban production, stockpiling, and use of all chemical weapons and to destroy them all within 10 years. Hillary Rodham Clinton becomes the first First Lady to have an office in the White House. She chairs a committee to overhaul the nation's health care system. Sears Roebuck and Co. closes 113 stores, eliminates 50,000 jobs, and ceases publication of the Sears Catalog after 97 years (Jan. 25). Family Leave Act guarantees workers up to 12 weeks of unpaid leave for medical emergencies (Feb. 4). A powerful car bomb rips through the parking garage at New York's World Trade Center, killing 7, and injuring about 1,000 (Feb. 26). Four agents from the Federal Bureau of Alcohol, Tobacco and Firearms are killed in a bloody gunfight at the Waco, Texas compound of religious cult leader David Koresh, beginning a 51-day standoff that ends when Koresh orders his followers to set the buildings on fire, resulting in a conflagration that kills him and 86 of his followers (April 19). "The worst storm of the century" according to the National Weather Service pelts the mid-Atlantic and Northeast with as much as 40 inches of snow, killing at least 104 people. The Supreme Court rules (9-0) that public school systems must permit religious groups to use their buildings after hours if they allow community groups to do so. Law enforcement officials raid a suspected bomb factory in New York City, uncovering a highly organized terrorist group plotting to bomb the UN, federal office buildings, and the Lincoln and Holland tunnels, and to assassinate prominent politicians. Eight suspects are arrested, all said to be Muslim extremists (June 24). The Supreme Court rules (5-4) that legislative districts drawn to increase black representation can violate the constitutional rights of white voters. Pres. Clinton signs the Brady Bill, requiring gun purchasers to wait five days before taking possession to give sellers and law enforcement officials time to check the buyers' backgrounds.   The U.S. and Europe sign the General Agreement of Tariffs and Trade (GATT), reducing tariffs substantially on trade in more industries in more countries than any other pact in history. The Pentagon rules that gays and lesbians may serve in the military, but may not proclaim their sexual orientation. Astronauts restore full vision to the Hubble Space Telescope.

1994   Federated Department Stores acquires R.H. Macy & Company, creating the largest department store chain in America. Iran-contra prosecutor Lawrence E. Walsh finds no evidence that President Ronald Reagan or Vice President George Bush broke the law. All four of the men on trial for the World Trade Center bombing are found guilty of all charges against them and are each sentenced to 240 years in prison. Rodney King wins $3.8 mil. in damages for his 1991 beating by the L.A. police. L.A. police charge former football star O.J. Simpson with murdering his ex-wife Nicole Brown and Ron Goldman. Simpson leads police on a bizarre 60-mile low-speed car chase (televised live on all major networks) before surrendering to police (June 17). The dollar dips below 100 Japanese yen, a post-World War II low (June 21). Major league baseball players' strike results in the cancellation of the World Series for the first time ever (Aug. 11). The number of inmates in U.S. prisons tops one million, giving the U.S.

the highest incarceration rate in the world. Republicans take control of both Houses of Congress for the first time in 40 years (Nov. 8).

1995 The Congressional Accountability Act ends Congress's exemption from laws against workplace harassment and discrimination. The Dow Jones industrial average tops the 4,000 mark (Feb. 23). A federal judge issues an injunction against major league baseball owners for unfair labor practices, ending the longest players' strike in sports history. A massive car bomb blows up a Federal building in Oklahoma City, killing 169 people, including 15 children in a day-care center (April 19). Authorities apprehend Timothy McVeigh (April 21) as a prime suspect. The Supreme Court (5-4) overturns term limits on Congressional offices in 23 states. The Supreme Court (5-4) rules that affirmative action programs can only survive constitutional scrutiny if they are "narrowly tailored" to accomplish a "compelling governmental interest." Pres. Clinton announces full diplomatic recognition of Vietnam (July 11). The Walt Disney Company acquires Capital Cities/ABC. A federal grand jury indicts Timothy J. McVeigh and Terry L. Nichols on charges of blowing up the Oklahoma City Federal Building. The Chase Manhattan Corporation merges with the Chemical Banking Corporation, creating the largest bank in the nation. The League of Women Voters reports that the Motor Voter Law has increased voter registration by a record five million Americans in just eight months. Sheik Omar Abdel Rahman and nine of his militant Muslim followers are convicted of conspiring to blowup the United Nations and assassinate political leaders. A mostly black Los Angeles jury finds O.J. Simpson not guilty of murdering his ex-wife Nicole Brown Simpson and Ron Goldman. (Oct. 3). Pres. Clinton dispatches 20,000 U.S. troops to Bosnia as part of an international deployment to enforce the Dayton peace agreements to end the four-year civil war in the Balkans.

1996 After the second government shutdown in a month, Congress votes to return hundreds of thousands of workers to their jobs and to reopen nonessential government offices that had closed for three weeks in the budget impasse. Pres. Clinton offers a plan to balance the budget within seven years, as Republicans had demanded, but promising smaller tax cuts (Jan. 5-6). The Hubble Space Telescope returns the first-ever images of Pluto, and pictures showing the existence of more than 50 billion galaxies, or five times the number previously thought to exist. According to the new information, the Sun is one of 100 billion stars in the Milky Way. Congress approves a vast bill rewriting laws governing the telecommunications industries, deregulating cable television, increasing competition among local phone companies, and requiring a v-chip in new televisions to screen out violence (Feb. 1). Conservative columnist Pat Buchanan shocks Bob Dole and the Republican party by winning the New Hampshire primary (Feb. 20). The Liggett Group becomes the first U.S. cigarette manufacturer to break ranks and agree to a settlement in a giant classs action suit against the tobacco industry (Mar. 13). Pres. Clinton signs the line-item veto, which allows the president to invalidate certain bills without negating entire packages of legislation. (Apr. 9). Pres. Clinton signs legislation allowing workers to take their health insurance with them when they change or leave jobs and to restrict insurers' ability to deny policies to workers with preexisting medical conditions. The worst drought since the Dust Bowl era of the 1930s plagues the southwest, bankrupting 10,000 farmers in Oklahoma alone. Ark. Gov. Jim Guy Tucker and James and Susan McDougal, three former business partners of Pres. Clinton, are convicted of felonies in connection with the failed Madison Guaranty Savings and Loan. The Census Bureau reports that the gap between the richest 20 percent of Americans and everybody else has reached postwar high (June 18). A truck bomb blows up a housing complex in Saudi Arabia, killing 19 U.S. soldiers and wounding 300 others (June 25). TWA Flight 800 explodes in midair and crashes into the Atlantic Ocean, killing all 230 aboard (July 17). A pipe bomb blows up in Atlanta's Olympic Park during the Olympics, killing one woman and injuring more than 100 (July 27). Pres. Clinton signs welfare reform legislation, ending more than 60 years of Federal cash assistance and replacing it with a system of block grants to the states (July 31). Hurricane Fran batters the southeast coast, killing 22 people and causing $1 billion worth of damage (Sept. 4–7). Pres. Clinton signs the Defense of Marriage Act, denying Federal recognition to same-sex marriages, (Sept. 21). Pres. Clinton defeats Bob Dole and Ross Perot to win re-election (Nov. 5).

1997 The U.S. economy continues to grow, driving unemployment below 5 percent for the first time in 24 years. The Dow Jones Industrial Average breaks 7,000 in Feb., and 8,000 in July. Mergers and acquisitions by major corporations reach record levels: notably Dean Witter and Morgan Stanley, Lockheed Martin and Northrup Grumman, World Com and MCI. Madeleine Albright becomes the first woman Sec. of State. A civil jury finds O.J. Simpson liable in the killings of his ex-wife and her friend and orders Simpson to pay $33.5 million in damages to their families. The Senate unanimously approves a very broad investigation into White House and Congressional campaign fundraising (March 11). Comet Hale-Bopp, with its brilliant 31-million-mile tail, makes continuous appearances from March to May. Police in San Diego County find the bodies of 39 members of a cult called Heaven's Gate who committed suicide together when Comet Hale-Bopp appeared (March 26). The Senate approves (74-26) the Chemical Weapons Convention prohibiting the production and storage of poison gas. The Supreme Court rules unanimously that a sitting president can be sued for actions outside the scope of his official duties thereby allowing the Paula Jones sexual harassment suit to proceed. After a five-week trial, Timothy J. McVeigh is found guilty on all 11 counts of murder and conspiracy in the 1995 bombing of the Federal building in Oklahoma City that killed 168 (June 2); he is sentenced to death. The tobacco industry agrees to pay $368.5 bil. over 25 years to compensate states for the cost of smoking-related illnesses. The Supreme Court rules (5-4) that the Constitution allows public school teachers to work in parochial schools that need remedial or supplemental classes. Mars Pathfinder, a robotic spacecraft, arrives on Mars (July 4), and sends back panoramic pictures of the landscape. IBM Computer, Deep Blue, defeats world chess champion Garry Kasparov. Atty. General Janet Reno absolves Pres. Clinton of criminal wrongdoing because the Justice Department found no credible evidence he broke any campaign finance laws. The Hubble Space Telescope returns pictures of a star as bright as 10 million suns. An Iowa woman gives birth to seven babies, the most ever born alive in the U.S. (Nov. 19). The Dept. of Agriculture issues sweeping regulations outlining what can legally be labeled as organic. A jury in Denver convicts Terry L. Nichols of conspiring to bomb the Oklahoma City Federal Building and of involuntary manslaughter (but not murder). The judge later sentences him to life in prison. Thirty of Wall Street's largest brokerage firms agree to pay $900 million to end a civil suit contending they conspired for years to fix prices on the Nasdaq stock market.

1998 Pres. Clinton becomes the first sitting President ever to submit as a defendant in a civil court challenge when he defends himself against charges that he sexually harassed Paula Jones when he was Governor of Arkansas (Jan. 17) In his testimony under oath, and later in a national television address (Jan. 26), Clinton also denies having sexual relations with White House intern Monica Lewinsky, an allegation raised by Jones' lawyers. Texas executes Karla Faye Tucker, a convicted murderer, the first woman put to death there since the Civil War. Students at schools in Jonesboro, Ark. (March 24) and Springfield, Ore. (May 21) open fire on classmates and teachers killing four in Arkansas and three in Oregon, and injuring dozens of others. The F.D.A. approves Viagra for male impotence. SBC Communications acquires Ameritech Corp. for $62 bil., creating the nation's largest local phone company. The Senate votes overwhelmingly to expand NATO to include Poland, Hungary, and the Czech Republic (April 30). Astronomers detect a titanic explosion in the outer reaches of the cosmos rivaled only by the Big Bang (May 6). Pres. Clinton signs legislation to overhaul the I.R.S. and make it more friendly to citizens. The Federal Government and 20 state Attorneys General file two broad, aggressive antitrust lawsuits against Microsoft, accusing it of attempting to control access to the Internet. Pictures from the Hubble Space Telescope show the first image of a planet outside our solar system (May 28). Scientists break the code of the tuberculosis bacterium, a germ that kills more people in the world than any other infectious agent. Pres. Clinton extends the moratorium on oil drilling off most of U.S. ocean coastlines for 10 more years. The Supreme Court (6-3) overturns the Line Item Veto. Dow Corning Corp. agrees to pay $3.2 billion to thousands of women claiming injury from silicone breast implants. In exchange for immunity from Federal prosecution, Monica Lewinsky testifies that she and Pres. Clinton had a sexual affair in the White House. Two powerful bombs explode minutes apart outside the U.S. Embassies in Kenya and Tanzania, killing at least 190 people and wounding nearly 5,000, mostly in Nairobi (Aug. 7). Pres. Clinton testifies that he had an "inappropriate" relationship with former White House intern Monica Lewinsky. Later he goes on national TV to confess he had lied in January. (Aug. 17). The U.S. retaliates for the bombings of its Embassies by deploying about 75 U.S. cruise missiles on targets near Kabul in Afghanistan and in Khartoum. The Republican-controlled House Judiciary Committee votes along party lines to recommend a formal impeachment investigation against Pres. Clinton. Surprisingly, the President's standing improves in the polls, which reveal that a majority of Americans disapprove of the Judiciary Committee's handling of the matter. Pres. Clinton announces a budget surplus of about $70 bil., the first since 1969 and the largest on record. The National Center for Health Statistics reports that AIDS deaths in the U.S. decreased by 46 percent in 1997, the steepest one-year drop ever. Democrats surpris-

ingly pick up five seats in mid-term elections for the House, indicating distaste for the drive to impeach Pres. Clinton (Nov. 3). Nevertheless, the Republican-controlled House Judiciary Committee forges ahead with impeachment proceedings. The nation's four largest cigarette makers agree to pay $206 billion to resolve all remaining state claims over health costs related to smoking. The settlement does not shield them from punitive damages and class action suits (Nov. 23). The House Judiciary Committee recommends four articles of impeachment against Pres. Clinton; the full House, strictly along party lines, approves two of the articles: perjury and obstruction of justice (Dec. 19).

1999 The top two Salt Lake City organizers of the 2002 Winter Olympics resign after investigators discover they bribed International Olympic Committee members in the city's bid for the games. In the first presidential impeachment trial in 131 years, Pres. Clinton's lawyers assert unequivocally that he did not commit perjury and he did not obstruct justice (Jan. 19).. Republicans reject an attempt by Senate Democrats to press for a bipartisan censure resolution to rebuke the president (Feb. 7) rather than proceed with the impeachment trial. The full Senate votes to acquit Pres. Clinton on both articles of impeachment, falling short of even a majority vote on either charge (Feb. 12). Pres. Clinton announces he will send nearly 4,000 troops to Kosovo as part of a NATO peacekeeping force (Feb. 13). NATO forces begin dropping bombs and cruise missiles on Serbian forces occupying Kosovo (Mar. 24). Astronomers announce the detection of three large planets around a solar-type star, Upsilon Andromedae, 44 light-years away, the first solid evidence that our solar system is no singular phenomenon in the universe (April 15). In the deadliest school massacre in U.S. history, two teenagers in Littleton, Colo. kill 12 students and one teacher and wound at least 20 others with guns and explosives. (April 20). The Supreme Court unanimously strikes down a 65-year-old ban on broadcast advertising of casino gambling. Texas Gov. George W. Bush declares he will not accept Federal matching funds because his $37 mil. campaign war chest allows him to far outspend his rivals for the Republican presidential nomination. The FCC relaxes rules that had prevented a single company from owning two stations in the nation's largest cities. The Kansas Board of Education votes to delete virtually any mention of evolution from the state's science curriculum (Aug. 11). Viacom Inc. acquires CBS Corp. for $37.3 billion. A Federal judge in Charlotte, N.C. rules that forced integration of the Charlotte-Mecklenburg School District is no longer necessary, ending the court-ordered busing first approved by the Supreme Court in 1971 (Sept. 10). MCI Worldcom Inc. acquires the Sprint Corp. for $108 billion. The FCC substantially loosens rules that had kept one company from controlling too much of the cable industry, allowing AT&T to own more than a third of the nation's TV, phone, and high-speed Internet service franchises. Pres. Clinton says he will use administrative actions that bypass Congressional opposition to permanently protect at least 40 million acres of Federal forest land from road building, logging, and mining. The Senate (51-48) rejects a treaty banning all underground nuclear testing, dealing Pres. Clinton a humbling defeat on one of his key policy aims. For the fourth straight year, Senate Republicans kill legislation to reform the nation's campaign finance system (Oct. 19). For the first time, Dow

Jones adds stocks from the high-yielding but more volatile Nasdaq stock exchange (Microsoft and Intel) to its Industrial Average. Congress repeals the 1933 Glass-Steagall Act, which had prevented the securities, banking, and insurance industries from expanding into one another's businesses (Nov. 4). The White House agrees to a deal with Congressional Republicans that will release $1 billion in dues the U.S. owes to the U.N. as long as none of the funds go to organizations promoting abortion rights. A meeting of the World Trade Organization thrusts Seattle into turmoil, as thousands of demonstrators storm the city to protest the WTO's secretive practices and its policies on the environment and international labor (Nov. 29-Dec. 4). A federal grand jury in New Mexico indicts Wen Ho Lee, a nuclear weapons engineer, on 59 counts of illegally removing highly classified material from the Los Alamos weapons laboratory (Dec. 10). Pres. Jimmy Carter officially hands over control of the Panama Canal to Panamanian Pres. Mireya Moscoso (Dec. 14).

2000 The Clinton Administration decides that 6-year-old Cuban refugee Elián González should be sent back to his father in Cuba (Jan 5). America Online announces it will buy Time Warner for $165 bil. in the biggest merger in history (Jan 10). The U.S. government concedes that workers making nuclear weapons have been exposed to dangerous radiation and chemicals (Jan 28). Illinois Gov. George Ryan halts all executions in his state citing a "shameful record of convicting innocent people and putting them on death row." (Jan 31). Four white New York City police officers are acquitted of all charges in the shooting of African immigrant Amadou Diallo (Feb 25). Two New York City police officers are convicted of covering up a brutal assault on Abner Louima (Mar 6). Al Gore wins all of "Super Tuesday's" 13 primaries and George W. Bush nine, virtually assuring their nominations (Mar 7). Two of the nation's largest and oldest newspaper companies, the Tribune Co. and the Times Mirror Co. merge (Mar 13). The Supreme Court rules (5-4) that the F.D.A. never received Congressional authority to regulate tobacco products (Mar 21). Thousands of demonstrators clog the streets of Washington, D.C. protesting the effects of the global economy (Apr 16). Armed U.S. immigration agents break into the house where Elián González has been held and take the 6-year-old boy by force. (Apr 22). The Supreme Court (5-4) invalidates a federal law permitting victims of rape, domestic violence, etc. to sue their attackers in federal court (May 15). In a victory for the Clinton Administration, the Senate narrowly rejects a measure to set a deadline for withdrawing U.S. ground troops from Kosovo (May 18). The Labor Dept. reports that 116,000 jobs were lost in May, the largest drop in eight years (June 2). A Federal judge orders the breakup of Microsoft, saying the severe remedy was necessary because the software giant "has proved untrustworthy in the past" (June 7). NASA announces that images from the Mars Global Surveyor suggest a relatively recent water flow on the planet (June 21). Two rival groups of scientists announce that they have deciphered the human genome (June 26). The Supreme Court rules that the government cannot prohibit doctors from performing the so-called "partial-birth abortion," and that the Boy Scouts of America have a constitutional right to exclude gay members (June 28). U.S. and Vietnam sign a treaty allowing free trade between them for the first time since the end of the Vietnam War (June 13). Germany's largest phone company agrees to acquire U.S. cellular communications company VoiceStream for $50.7 bil., the first acquisition of a U.S. telecommunications company by a foreign corporation (June 23). A federal judge tells the Napster online music service to stop permitting the exchange of copyrighted material (June 26). Demand for electricity soars in California and the state nearly runs out of power (Aug. 2). Al Gore picks Connecticut Senator Joseph Lieberman to be his running mate, the first time a Jew will be on the ticket of a major party (Aug. 7). Facing lawsuits and a federal investigation, the Firestone tire company admits that millions of tires seemed prone to flinging off their treads and announces it will replace the 6.5 million tires still on the road (Aug. 9). The U.S. government agrees to drop virtually its entire case against Wen-Ho Lee, the Chinese-American scientist the F.B.I. had accused of stealing nuclear weapons secrets (Sept. 10). The independent prosecutor in the Whitewater investigation concludes that there is insufficient evidence to show that Bill or Hillary Clinton committed any crimes (Sept. 20). The F.D.A. approves the marketing of the abortion-inducing pill RU486 (Sept. 28). The U.S. Navy destroyer Cole, refueling in Yemen, is rocked by a terrorist bomb, killing 17 sailors (Oct. 12). U.S. pharmacy chains and drug manufacturers begin withdrawing cold remedies and appetite suppressants containing the ingredient phenylpropanolamine, or PPA, which scientists have linked to a slight risk of stroke in young women (Nov. 6). Hillary Rodham Clinton wins the New York Senate race, becoming the only First Lady in U.S. History to hold public office (Nov. 7). Vice Pres. Al Gore holds a slim lead in the national popular vote for president, but the Electoral College is not decided because Florida's outcome is too close to call. Gov. George W. Bush holds a lead of 1,700 votes in Florida and Florida law requires a machine recount (Nov. 8). Bush's lead in Florida falls to about 300 and a manual recount is begun in several counties (Nov. 9). Bush files suit in federal court to stop all manual recounts; Gore's campaign asserts that all votes should be counted. (Nov. 11). Florida officials declare Bush to be the winner of Florida's electoral votes but Democrats head to state court to contest the certification (Nov. 26). The New Jersey attorney general reveals evidence of a systematic process of racial profiling by police officers (Nov. 27). The U.S. Supreme Court reaffirms the Fourth Amendment prohibition against unlawful searches and seizures in a ruling that bars police roadblocks to check for drugs (Nov. 28). For the first time in history the U.S. Supreme Court hears arguments relating to a presidential election (Dec. 1). Pres. Clinton issues an executive order creating the largest U.S. nature preserve, encompassing 84 million acres around the northwestern Hawaiian Islands (Dec. 4). The Florida Supreme Court orders the immediate recount of disputed ballots across the state (Dec. 8). A bitterly divided U.S. Supreme Court (5-4) ends the Florida recounts, handing the state, and thus the election, to Bush. (Dec. 12). Gore concedes the following day. Seven employees of a Wakefield, Mass. Internet consulting company are shot and killed by 42-year-old software tester Michael McDermott (Dec. 26). The U.S. Census Bureau announces that the national population is 281,421,906 people, a 13.2 percent increase in 10 years and more than 6 million above recent predictions (Dec. 28).

BIOGRAPHIES OF U.S. PRESIDENTS

1. George Washington (1789–97)

Born in Westmoreland County, Virginia, on Feb. 22, 1732, the first president, with a love for the land, trained as a surveyor in his teens. At age 16 he went to live with his brother Lawrence, who built Mount Vernon. Lawrence died only four years later, leaving his property to George, who went on to become one of Virginia's foremost landowners, ultimately acquiring more than 100,000 acres in Virginia and what is now West Virginia. In 1753 Washington joined the French and Indian War as an officer in the Virginia militia and fought bravely if poorly. The war provided Washington with the beginnings of his anti-British sentiments, exposing him to the arrogance of his British commanders. Upon returning to plantation life, and marrying Martha Custis, in 1759, Washington's resentment of the British was further fueled by their commercial restrictions. With the passage of the Stamp Act of 1765, Washington joined opposition to imperial rule in the Virginia House of Burgesses, becoming ever more active in resisting the British. He went as a delegate to the Continental Congress, which chose him to command the Continental Army when war with Britain broke out in 1775. Washington proved an uncommonly resourceful general, keeping his ragtag army together through years of defeat, retreat, and hard winters to outlast the British and finally prevail at Yorktown in 1781. Here, as in all his life, Washington earned respect for his judgment, dignity, and bearing. Retiring to Mount Vernon after the war, the general quashed suggestions that he assume military dictatorship of the fledgling republic, not wanting to subvert the very principles for which the Americans had fought. But because of his belief in a strong central government, Washington felt compelled to return to public life to salvage his country from the chaotic Articles of Confederation. In 1787 he presided over the Constitutional Convention in Philadelphia, which framed the presidency with him in mind, the only president ever elected unanimously in the electoral college (twice).

Washington's renowned judgment equaled the task of setting presidential precedent, for, as he wrote, "It is devoutly wished on my part, that these precedents may be fixed on true principles." His first act as president was to urge adoption of the Bill of Rights. Other notable achievements included national unity, quelling the Whiskey Rebellion, bolstering the treasury with a national bank, settling Jay's Treaty of commerce with Britain, and maintaining neutrality in the French Revolution. Washington successfully implemented executive power and quieted fears and suspicions of executive tyranny. But he regretted the rivalry between Thomas Jefferson and Alexander Hamilton, which led to the birth of political parties in his own cabinet; Washington feared that allegiance to "factions" would someday eclipse the guiding light of patriotism. After refusing a third term in 1796, Washington in his Farewell Address warned against party spirit, sectionalism, and "entangling alliances" with other nations. He died on Dec. 14, 1799, "first in war, first in peace, and first in the hearts of his countrymen," as his friend Henry Lee eulogized him.

2. John Adams (1797–1801)

A fifth-generation American directly descended from a Mayflower passenger, John Adams was born on Oct. 30, 1735, in Braintree, Massachusetts. At Harvard Adams considered the ministry but turned to law. He joined his cousin Sam Adams as an early opponent of the Stamp Act of 1765, organizing the Sons of Liberty and defending Americans accused of smuggling. Yet he also defended the British soldiers brought to trial for the Boston Massacre in 1770. In the Revolution, Adams persuaded the Continental Congress to commission George Washington as commander in chief, declare independence, and put stars and stripes on the flag. He wrote the Massachusetts state constitution in 1779 and negotiated peace with Britain in 1782. The first vice president, Adams called that position the "most insignificant office that ever the invention of man contrived or his imagination conceived."

Elected president as a Federalist in 1796, Adams retained Washington's cabinet, but Alexander Hamilton turned the party against him for refusing to make war on France. Adams built up the navy and kept the peace, but disaffecting the Federalists and signing the Alien and Sedition Acts (1798) politically weakened "His Rotundity." Adams lost the 1800 election to the increasingly popular Thomas Jefferson. The first president to reside in the White House, Adams lived to be 90, able to see his son John Quincy Adams elected the sixth president in 1824. John Adams died on the same day that Thomas Jefferson did: July 4, 1826, the 50th anniversary of the Declaration of Independence they both signed.

3. Thomas Jefferson (1801–09)

Thomas Jefferson was born on Apr. 13, 1743, in Albemarle County, Virginia, son of a self-made Virginian who died when Jefferson was 14. Jefferson graduated from William and Mary in 1762, began practicing law in 1767, and joined the Virginia House of Burgesses in 1769. With his pen Jefferson sharply criticized British rule, winning a place on Virginia's Committee of Correspondence to keep in touch with patriots in other colonies. His writings amassed great respect, earning him the right, as a delegate to the Continental Congress in 1776, to draft the Declaration of Independence. He then returned to Virginia as wartime governor, narrowly escaping capture when British troops destroyed his home. Congress sent Jefferson to Europe in 1784; he was minister to France during the Constitutional Convention and the early French Revolution, an event that affected him profoundly. As secretary of state under Washington, Jefferson's faith in democracy and states' rights clashed repeatedly with Alexander Hamilton's pursuit of central executive power. Jefferson resigned in 1793 and led opposition to the Federalists, whom Jefferson called "monarchists in principle." As vice president after 1796, Jefferson speeded the Federalists' downfall by secretly authoring the Kentucky Resolutions, critical of the Alien and Sedition Acts.

The House of Representatives chose Jefferson (ironically, with Hamilton's support) over Aaron Burr, whose electoral votes for president equaled his in 1800. "We are all Republicans—we are all Federalists," appealed Jefferson in his inaugural address, easing the transfer of power. In his first term, Jefferson slashed the budget, lowered taxes, reduced the national debt, and sent marines to fight Barbary pirates. Despite some concern over his constitutional authority to make the acquisition, Jefferson's greatest feat was the Louisiana Purchase from France in 1803, which doubled the size of the United States. "The less said about the constitutional difficulties, the better," wrote Jefferson, sending Lewis and Clark to explore the new lands. In his second term, Jefferson's unpopular Embargo Act (1807) was an attempt to avoid war with Britain or France, but it ruined American merchants. Retiring to Monticello in 1809, Jefferson busied himself with inventions and designing the University of Virginia. He died on the 50th anniversary of the Declaration of Independence, July 4, 1826. His broad interests spanned music, science, architecture, agronomy, and the classics, as well as politics and government.

4. James Madison (1809–17)

James Madison was born to a wealthy family on Mar. 16, 1751, in Port Conway, Virginia. A Princeton graduate, Madison attended the first Virginia state convention in 1776, drafting a bill that guaranteed religious liberty. As the youngest member of the Continental Congress in 1780, he led the movement to revise the Articles of Confederation. At the Constitutional Convention in Philadelphia in 1787, Madison's Virginia Plan became the pivot of discussion. Madison, dubbed the Father of the Constitution, tirelessly directed debate and applied his political wisdom. His voluminous notes provide the best record of the convention. Madison helped ratify the Constitution by coauthoring *The Federalist* (1787–88) with John Jay and Alexander Hamilton. A four-term congressman, Madison drafted the Bill of Rights and cofounded the Democratic-Republican party. In 1794 he married a young and ebullient widow, Dolley Payne Todd, an especially popular first lady. Madison led the opposition to the Federalists' Alien and Sedition Acts with the Virginia Resolutions, arguing the acts were unconstitutional attacks on liberty. Jefferson chose Madison as his secretary of state and later as his successor. Madison easily won the election of 1808. Britain and France preyed on American shipping throughout Madison's first term. Pushed by war hawks in Congress, Madison asked for a declaration of war to defend American rights against British outrages. Reelected despite numerous American defeats in the War of 1812, Madison barely escaped Washington as the British burned the White House. Yet he persisted in "Mr. Madison's War" until the Peace of Ghent (1814) and belated victory at New Orleans (1815) vindicated him. War expenses forced Madison to recharter the national bank and raise the tariff, contrary to his Jeffersonian principles. But by 1817 Madison could retire confident of secure independence, surging nationalism, and the total collapse of his Federalist opponents who had opposed the war. He died on June 28, 1836, having outlived all the Founding Fathers. Madison's presidency pales beside his greatest contributions—the Constitution and the Bill of Rights.

5. James Monroe (1817–25)

The last Revolutionary hero and member of the "Virginia Dynasty" to become president, James Monroe was born on Apr. 28, 1758, in Westmoreland County, Virginia. He left the College of William and Mary to answer the call to arms in 1775. Wounded at Trenton, Monroe fought courageously and rose to lieutenant colonel under Gen. Washington. He learned law as an aide to Thomas Jefferson, who helped Monroe into Congress and

the Senate. Much diplomatic experience followed Monroe's appointment as minister to France in 1794. Governor of Virginia from 1799 to 1802, Monroe returned to Europe to negotiate the Louisiana Purchase and later served in Britain and Spain. James Madison appointed him secretary of state in 1811 and secretary of war in 1814. Chosen to succeed Madison, Monroe won the 1816 election and presided over the Era of Good Feeling, a period marked by minimal sectional or partisan discord. Monroe bought Florida from Spain in 1819, and his popularity survived the Panic of 1819 as well as rancorous debates over the admission of Missouri as a slave state. Monroe toured the nation to jubilant crowds, winning reelection with all but one electoral vote in 1820. John Quincy Adams, his secretary of state, suggested Monroe proclaim American opposition to European encroachment in the Western Hemisphere, which he did in 1823; decades later this became known as the Monroe Doctrine. After retiring, Monroe became a regent of the University of Virginia (1826) and a member of the Virginia constitutional convention of 1829. Because of lack of attention over the years, his private affairs had suffered greatly, and Monroe discovered he was lapsing into bankruptcy. He sold his plantation and died all but penniless on Independence Day, July 4, 1831.

6. John Quincy Adams (1825–29)

The first president's son to become president, John Quincy Adams was born on July 11, 1767, in Braintree, Massachusetts. A true child of the Revolution, Adams watched the Battle of Bunker Hill while holding his mother's hand, and he spent his teens in Europe with his father, John Adams, on diplomatic missions for the new nation. He entered Harvard in 1785, already an experienced diplomat fluent in seven languages. After a brief career as a Boston lawyer, Adams was minister to Holland in 1794 and to Prussia in 1797. As a Federalist, Adams was elected to the Senate in 1803, but after supporting Thomas Jefferson, he had to resign. James Madison made Adams minister to Russia in 1809, in time to witness Napoleon's invasion. Then Adams helped negotiate the Peace of Ghent (1814) before serving as ambassador to England, the second of three Adams generations to hold that post. James Monroe recalled Adams from Europe—where he had spent most of his life—to appoint him secretary of state in 1817, and in that post, Adams purchased Florida from Spain, patched relations with Britain, and conceived the Monroe Doctrine.

Running for president in 1824, Adams was beaten by Andrew Jackson in both popular and electoral votes; but with Henry Clay's support, the House of Representatives chose Adams for president. No one ever became president with less than Adams's 31 percent of the vote, yet he refused to conciliate his foes or even act like a politician. Adams posed above politics and made no effort to deal with Congress or use patronage. Consequently, elaborate plans for internal improvements and national academies came to naught. Adams, like his father, failed to win a second term, as Jackson gained revenge at the polls in 1828. Massachusetts rescued Adams from despair by sending him to Congress in 1830, and "Old Man Eloquent" remained a powerful antislavery leader until he collapsed on the floor of the House at age 80; he died in the Speaker's Room on Feb. 23, 1848. John Quincy Adams, who considered himself a failure as president, worked for the first 11 presidents and numbers among the most important architects of early American foreign policy.

7. Andrew Jackson (1829–37)

Born to Scotch-Irish immigrants in Waxhaw, South Carolina, on Mar. 15, 1767, Andrew Jackson was the first first-generation American to become president, as well as the first president from the western frontier and the first of seven to be born in a log cabin. Orphaned at 15, he was by then already a Revolutionary veteran, a former prisoner of war, and scarred by the saber of a British officer whose boots he refused to clean. Jackson read law and made his way to the Tennessee frontier, marrying Rachel Donelson Robards in 1791. She neglected to divorce her first husband, but Jackson challenged to a duel anyone who questioned his marriage, once even killing a man on the field of honor. Jackson's frontier law practice prospered, and Tennessee elected him its first congressman in 1796. He served only briefly in the Senate; Washington so disgusted the rough-hewn Jackson that he resigned. Back in Tennessee, Jackson became a respected judge and honorary major general of the militia. In the War of 1812, Jackson led troops to victory at the Battle of New Orleans (1815), his men routing British invaders twice their number.

"Old Hickory" was now a national icon, reentering the Senate in 1823 and running for president as a hero above party. Jackson won more popular and electoral votes than anyone in 1824 but lost when the election was thrown into the House and Henry Clay supported John Quincy Adams. Vowing revenge against the politicians, Jackson swept to victory in 1828 as the "people's choice" reform candidate. Jackson's wife died on the eve of his inauguration. As president, Jackson aggrandized the power of his office on behalf of the common man by expanding suffrage, rotating officeholders (the "spoils system"), and economizing in government. Under Jackson the Federal government completely paid off the national debt. Jackson vetoed Federal road-building and banking—yet he asserted Federal authority by ordering troops to South Carolina in the Nullification Crisis of 1832–33. The Whig party arose in opposition to "King Andrew I," especially to his high-handed veto of the national bank, but voters endorsed Jackson's war on privilege by reelecting him in 1832. In his second term, Jackson seized land from the Native Americans, ignoring the Supreme Court, and he recognized Texas in hopes of taking more land from Mexico. He became the first president to ride a train (1833) and to survive an assassination attempt (1835). After placing his friend Martin Van Buren in the White House, Jackson retired to the Hermitage, his plantation in Tennessee. He remained quite influential behind the scenes, persuading the Democrats to discard Van Buren and nominate James K. Polk in 1844. Jackson finally succumbed to dropsy and old wounds on June 8, 1845.

8. Martin Van Buren (1837–41)

The first president to have played no part in the Revolution, Martin Van Buren was born to a Dutch family in Kinderhook, New York, on Dec. 5, 1782. Apprenticed to a lawyer at 14, Van Buren took to law and politics—so well, in fact, that he came to be called the Little Magician. By 1821 staunch party loyalty elevated him to the Senate, where Van Buren led northern supporters of

Andrew Jackson and guided his victory in 1828. Brief service as New York governor ended when Jackson appointed him secretary of state in 1829. Van Buren helped build the Democratic party, and Jackson made him vice president in 1832. As Jackson's heir apparent, Van Buren won the 1836 election, but two months after he took office, the Panic of 1837 launched a severe depression that spoiled his presidency. "Martin Van Ruin" responded by creating the independent treasury system, but his lack of popularity was beyond repair. He made enemies in the North by protecting slavery and in the South by refusing to annex Texas. Though the self-made son of an innkeeper, Van Buren was cast by his opponents as an aristocrat. In 1844 Van Buren lost the Democratic nomination when Jackson abandoned him over the Texas issue. Then, in 1848 Van Buren guaranteed a Democratic defeat by founding the Free Soil party and running for president, which split the decisive New York vote. Van Buren died a Unionist on July 24, 1862, the only president whose life touched both the Revolution and the Civil War.

9. William Henry Harrison (1841)

Son of a signatory of the Declaration of Independence and grandfather of a president, William Henry Harrison was born in Charles City County, Virginia, on Feb. 9, 1773. Campaign legend held that his birthplace was a log cabin, but in fact it was a plantation mansion. Harrison left medical school to join the army and fight Native Americans in the Northwest in 1791. After an illustrious military career, he served in Congress (1816–19), the U.S. Senate (1825–28), and as ambassador to Colombia (1828–29) before falling victim to Andrew Jackson's spoils system. Harrison fit Whig designs of defeating Jacksonians with a war hero of their own and received the Whig nomination to face Martin Van Buren in 1840. Harrison's campaign sidestepped issues to cast him as a plain frontiersman who guzzled hard cider while Van Buren sipped champagne. In the first modern election full of hoopla and hype, "Tippecanoe and Tyler Too"—the Whig slogan—linked Harrison's most famous victory with his obscure running mate. A huge turnout gave Harrison the victory at age 67, the oldest president until Ronald Reagan. Harrison delivered a record 8,500-word inaugural address hatless and coatless on a drizzly winter day. He caught a cold from which he never recovered and succumbed to pneumonia on Apr. 4, 1841. He was the first president to die in the White House—where he lived for only 31 days. His grandson, Benjamin Harrison, was the 23rd president.

10. John Tyler (1841–45)

The first vice president to become president by succession, the first president to see impeachment proposed against him, and the only president to change parties in office, John Tyler was born on Mar. 29, 1790, in Charles City County, Virginia. He was a Virginia legislator, congressman, senator, and governor before the Whigs chose him as William Henry Harrison's running mate in 1840. Though a strict constructionist and states' rights advocate, Tyler earned the Whigs' favor by opposing Andrew Jackson. But as president after Harrison's death, "His Accidency" earned their ire by vetoing, in mid-1842, two tariff bills vital to the Whig party. Eventually, his cabinet resigned and his party expelled him. Outraged members of Congress called for his impeachment. On July 10, 1842, John Minor Botts, a Whig representative from Richmond, Va., proposed the appointment of a special committee to investigate Tyler's conduct in office with an eye toward impeachment. The proposal was defeated on Jan. 10, 1843, by a vote of 127 to 83. This was the first time presidential impeachment proceedings were introduced in Congress. Tyler concluded the Webster-Ashburton Treaty (1842), which adjusted the northeastern boundary of the United States, and the Texas annexation (1845), but without popular or partisan support, he was powerless and decided against running for reelection. A veto on his last day in office became the first ever to be overridden. Tyler died on Jan. 18, 1862, awaiting his seat in the Confederate Congress.

11. James Knox Polk (1845–49)

The first dark-horse president, James Knox Polk was born in Mecklenburg County, North Carolina, on Nov. 2, 1795. A star orator in Tennessee politics, Polk idolized Andrew Jackson. "Young Hickory" took Jackson's old seat in Congress in 1825 and was reelected seven times. Polk was Speaker of the House from 1835 to 1839 and governor of Tennessee until 1841. He lost two bids for reelection, and his political career seemed over when the Democrats nominated him for president in 1844. Polk's name had not even appeared on the first seven ballots, but the deadlocked convention latched onto Polk as a pro-expansion dark horse. In the election he defeated Henry Clay by 1.5 percent of the vote on a platform that ignored slavery. From his inaugural address onward, Polk pursued expansion in the West. In 1846, he bluffed the British into believing the United States would go to war over Oregon, extracting a treaty for it. When Mexico attacked U.S. troops in disputed Texas territory, Polk called it an invasion and got a declaration of war. The ensuing Mexican War (1846–48) won California and the Southwest for the United States in the Treaty of Guadalupe-Hidalgo. Polk declined a second term, having fulfilled the nation's "Manifest Destiny" to span the continent. The last strong president before Abraham Lincoln, Polk added a million square miles to the United States. But the issue of slavery in the new territories split the Democrats and soon the whole country. "The presidency is not a bed of roses," complained Polk, who left the White House totally exhausted and died three months later, on June 15, 1849.

12. Zachary Taylor (1849–50)

Zachary Taylor, the first president to have no previous political experience, was born on Nov. 24, 1784, in Montebello, Virginia. His father was a colonel in the Revolutionary War, and Taylor—along with four brothers—served as a professional soldier for nearly 40 years. After distinguished service against the British and Native Americans, Gen. Taylor's finest hour came during the Mexican War, when he captured Monterrey and smashed Gen. Santa Ana's much larger army at the Battle of Buena Vista (1847). Though Taylor had never held office or even voted, the Whigs eagerly nominated "Old Rough and Ready" for president in 1848; Taylor, like William Henry Harrison, was an apolitical war hero above the slavery controversy. He won the election when the new Free Soil party siphoned off Democratic votes, but Taylor took office with Congress in chaos over the admission of California as a free state. Taylor opposed the Compromise of 1850 and probably would have vetoed it, but he died suddenly of acute indigestion on July 9, 1850. (A

long, hot Fourth of July at Washington Monument ceremonies had no doubt contributed to his weakened state.) Backers of the compromise rejoiced that Taylor's death saved the Union. Taylor was both the last of eight slave owners and the last Whig to be elected president.

13. Millard Fillmore (1850–53)

Born in a log cabin on Jan. 7, 1800, Millard Fillmore was the son of a poor farmer in Locke Township, New York. Apprenticed to a cloth maker in his youth, Fillmore struggled for an education and got a job teaching even though he never attended college. Clerking for a judge taught Fillmore enough law to join the bar at age 23, and he became a prosperous New York attorney. Fillmore entered politics as an Anti-Mason and was a four-term congressman when the Whigs made him Zachary Taylor's vice president in 1848. Dignified good looks were Fillmore's main political asset; he was quite unprepared for the presidency when Taylor died suddenly in 1850. Fillmore delayed civil war another decade by signing the Compromise of 1850, but he lost the nomination in 1852 when the Whigs turned to Gen. Winfield Scott, yet another genial war hero and their last candidate. In 1856 Fillmore ran again for president as candidate of the American, or "Know Nothing," party. Fillmore hoped to unite the country behind anti-Catholicism and nativism, submerging the slavery issue, but he carried only Maryland. Though a Unionist in the Civil War, Fillmore denounced Abraham Lincoln and remained sharply critical of Republicans until his death on Mar. 8, 1874.

14. Franklin Pierce (1853–57)

Son of a Revolutionary War hero, Franklin Pierce was born in Hillsboro, New Hampshire, on Nov. 23, 1804—the first president born in the 19th century. A leader of Jacksonian Democrats in Congress in the 1830s, Pierce had been absent from national politics for a decade when the deadlocked Democratic convention nominated him for president on the 49th ballot in 1852. A dark horse candidate, Pierce won enough southern votes to defeat Gen. Winfield Scott, his Mexican War commander, becoming the youngest president as of that date. Pierce greatly hastened the coming of the Civil War by signing the Kansas-Nebraska Act (1854), which repealed the Missouri Compromise and reopened the dangerous issue of slavery expansion. He continually appeased the South by backing proslavery ruffians in "Bleeding Kansas," encouraging slavery expansionists who coveted Cuba, and buying the land known as the Gadsden Purchase from Mexico for a southern railroad. As a result Pierce's party lost elections to Republicans who charged that "slave power" controlled the White House. In 1856 Pierce became the only elected president to be denied his own party's renomination. During the Civil War, Pierce criticized the Emancipation Proclamation and was nearly lynched by angry New Englanders. He died a forgotten, depressed alcoholic, in Concord, New Hampshire, on Oct. 8, 1869, the only president from New Hampshire.

15. James Buchanan (1857–61)

Considered one of the worst presidents because of his lack of good judgment and moral courage, and also the only bachelor president, James Buchanan was born in Mercersburg, Pennsylvania, on Apr. 23, 1791. A lawyer and veteran of the War of 1812, Buchanan compiled more than 40 years of public service as legislator and diplomat.

The Democrats nominated Buchanan in 1856 largely because he was in England during the Kansas-Nebraska debate and thus remained untainted by either side of the issue. Millard Fillmore's "Know-Nothing" candidacy helped Buchanan defeat John C. Frémont, the first Republican candidate for president. Buchanan favored "popular sovereignty" over slavery in the territories and was the last of the Doughfaces, or northern politicians submissive to the South. Few Americans shared Buchanan's faith that the Supreme Court's Dred Scott decision (1857) would end conflict over slavery expansion "speedily and finally." When it did not, Buchanan tried to close the issue himself by urging that Kansas be admitted as a slave state—an even worse miscalculation. Democrats deserted him, and Republicans won the House in 1858, but Buchanan's vetoes and southern votes in the Senate stalemated the government. He inadvertently helped Abraham Lincoln win in 1860 by refusing to conciliate his own party. The secession crisis paralyzed Buchanan, who denied both the southern right to secede and the Federal government's right to do anything about it; he was relieved to hand Lincoln the reins. Buchanan died on June 1, 1868. On the day before, he predicted that "history will vindicate my memory," but historians continue mainly to denigrate him.

16. Abraham Lincoln (1861–65)

A largely unpopular president until he was assassinated (the first assassinated president), Abraham Lincoln was born in a log cabin in Hodgenville, Kentucky, on Feb. 12, 1809. He accumulated barely a year's total education while growing up, though he did learn to write and developed a fondness for reading. Family moves took him to Indiana and then to Illinois by the time he was 21. At age 19 Lincoln had worked his way down the Mississippi and came away appalled at slavery. He served in the Black Hawk War (1832) before losing an election for the state legislature. A failed storekeeper, Lincoln worked odd jobs while he taught himself law, sometimes walking 20 miles to borrow books. He finally made the state legislature in 1834 as a Whig, and in 1842 married Mary Todd, having canceled their engagement once before.

Elected to Congress in 1846, Lincoln denounced James K. Polk for precipitating the Mexican War. He returned to his Springfield, Ill., law practice after only one term. But the repeal of the Missouri Compromise shocked Lincoln back into politics, and he helped organize the Illinois Republicans. An unsuccessful candidate for the Senate in 1858, Lincoln drew national attention in debates with Stephen A. Douglas, the nation's leading Democrat. Lincoln was rewarded with his party's nomination for president in 1860, the least objectionable candidate among several more prominent Republicans. He defeated three opponents in the election, though his name did not even appear on the ballot in the South. As Southern states left the Union, Lincoln preached conciliation and promised no harm to slavery—but he vowed to crush secession and forced the issue at Ft. Sumter. After early reverses in the Civil War, Lincoln decided slavery had to be abolished altogether to restore the Union, and he issued the Emancipation Proclamation (1862). Lincoln's management of the war was thwarted by incompetent generals, feuding politicians, and his own inexperience, which matched that of his troops. Yet, like them, Lincoln learned on the job, settling

on Ulysses S. Grant as his top general by 1864. The powers of the presidency expanded dramatically under Lincoln, who stretched the Constitution on behalf of the war effort. Lincoln defeated Gen. George McClellan for reelection in 1864, vowing to "bind up the nation's wounds." Before he had the chance, Lincoln was shot on Good Friday, five days after the war's end, by John Wilkes Booth, an arch-Confederate. Lincoln died the next morning, on Apr. 15, 1865. His martyrdom spurred the vengefulness of Reconstruction, ironically against Lincoln's own wishes. Millions of Americans lined the 1,700-mile route of Lincoln's funeral train, their mournful cries resounding all the way back to Illinois. Lincoln's prestige has grown with time, until many have come to regard him as the greatest president.

17. Andrew Johnson (1865–69)

The first president to be impeached, Andrew Johnson was born in Raleigh, North Carolina, on Dec. 29, 1808, the son of a poor laborer. No president could claim humbler origins: Johnson's father died when he was three, his mother worked as a washerwoman, and he never attended a day of school in his life. As a teenager he ran away to Tennessee, opened a successful tailor's shop, and got elected mayor of Greeneville by age 21. A fiery Democratic stump speaker, Johnson's attacks on Whigs and rich planters won him a seat in the state legislature in 1835 and in Congress in 1843, made him governor in 1853, and took him to the Senate in 1857. Alone among 22 southern senators, Johnson stayed loyal to the Union in 1861, though a mob of Virginians nearly lynched him for it. Lincoln appointed Johnson military governor of Tennessee, and he was nominated for vice president on the "National Union" ticket in 1864. Suddenly made president by Lincoln's assassination, Johnson vowed to carry on Lincoln's policy of leniency toward the South, but radical Republican opposition and his own coarse ineptitude led to serious clashes with Congress. Johnson vetoed 29 bills and was overridden 15 times, more than any other president to that time. A former slave owner, Johnson resisted Republican efforts to aid the freedmen. His only victory was the unpopular purchase of Alaska in 1867. Congress systematically stripped him of power until Johnson fought back by removing his disloyal secretary of war, Edwin M. Stanton. Impeached in the House for defying the Tenure of Office Act, Johnson was tried in the Senate and acquitted by a single vote on May 26, 1868. Few presidents were so stymied in office. Tennessee helped vindicate Johnson by making him the only former president elected to the Senate, he died a few months later, on July 31, 1875.

18. Ulysses S. Grant (1869–77)

A better general than president, Ulysses Simpson Grant was born in Point Pleasant, Ohio, on Apr. 27, 1822. Having barely passed West Point's height requirement for entrance, Grant attended the academy and graduated in the middle of his class in 1843. Fifty of Grant's classmates fought with or against him as Civil War generals. He served under Gen. Zachary Taylor in the Mexican War before marrying his sweetheart, Julia Dent, in 1848. Assigned to isolated posts after 1852, Grant grew bored away from his family and reportedly turned to heavy drinking. Finally resigning from the army in 1854, he went to Missouri, only to fail in farming and real estate. When the Civil War began, Grant was working in his younger brother's leather shop in Galena, Ill. He received a commission and rose rapidly to brigadier general. U.S. Grant acquired the nickname Unconditional Surrender for his string of western victories, notably at Vicksburg and Chattanooga in 1863. Once Abraham Lincoln made him supreme commander in 1864, Grant opened a relentless offensive that quickly ended the war. He personally accepted Gen. Robert E. Lee's surrender at Appomattox in 1865. After feuding with Andrew Johnson, Grant joined the Republicans and was elected president in 1868. Grant pressed radical Reconstruction in the South with mixed results. Corruption—notably the Jay Gould (1869), Crèdit Mobilier (1872), and Whiskey Ring (1875) scandals—marred Grant's presidency; nevertheless, he easily won reelection in 1872. The Panic of 1873 triggered a deep economic depression that dissuaded Grant from a third term in 1876. Reconsidering in 1880, he sought the Republican nomination again and nearly succeeded. Afterward Grant retired and went bankrupt. To provide for his family, he began writing his memoirs. Developing cancer, Grant valiantly hung on to finish the project, which would earn him some literary fame and his family half a million dollars. He died on July 23, 1885, just four days after completing his autobiography.

19. Rutherford B. Hayes (1877–81)

Rutherford Birchard Hayes was born a frail child on Oct. 4, 1822, in Delaware, Ohio, where he was raised by his mother. After attending Harvard Law School, he set up a successful Cincinnati law practice in 1849. Hayes defended fugitive slaves and helped found the Ohio Republicans. In 1852 he married Lucy Ware Webb, the first college graduate first lady. A decorated Civil War veteran, Hayes was wounded five times and promoted to general. From 1868 to 1876 he served as governor of Ohio. Republicans turned to Hayes as a scandal-free hero in 1876 and nominated him for president. He lost the election to Samuel Tilden of the Democrats, but Republicans in Congress disputed enough state vote totals to connive "Rutherfraud" into office with the support of southern Democrats. Hayes's first acts were to appoint an ex-Confederate to his cabinet and to withdraw Federal troops from the South. He never overcame the resulting stigma of political bargain, and facing a Democratic Congress, Hayes seemed destined for a weak presidency. Yet he put the nation back on the gold standard, put down railroad strikes, reformed the civil service, and banished liquor from the White House before keeping his promise to serve only one term. Hayes viewed the return of prosperity and Republican majorities in Congress as personal triumphs. He worked quietly for charitable causes until his death on Jan. 17, 1893.

20. James A. Garfield (1881)

The last log cabin president, James Abram Garfield was born near Orange, Ohio, on Nov. 19, 1831, and like Rutherford B. Hayes, Garfield was raised by his mother. Garfield graduated from Williams College in 1856, became a classics professor, president of Hiram College, a lawyer, and at age 30 the youngest Union general in the Civil War. Garfield left the battlefield in 1864 to enter Congress, where he remained until the Republicans nominated him for president in 1880, a dark-horse compromise between Grant and James G. Blaine. Garfield defeated Gen. Winfield Scott Hancock of the Democrats by 0.1 percent of the vote in a campaign stressing tariffs. Republicans im-

mediately swarmed to Garfield, demanding patronage for their rival "Stalwart" and "Half-Breed" factions. After only four months in office, Garfield was shot in a train station by Charles J. Guiteau, a disappointed Stalwart office-seeker. Garfield died 80 days later, on Sept. 19, 1881, the second presidential assassination ending the second-shortest presidency. When hordes of Republican hopefuls had besieged the White House begging for jobs, Garfield had exclaimed: "My God! What is there in this place that a man should ever want to get in it?"

21. Chester A. Arthur (1881–85)

Chester Alan Arthur was born a preacher's son on Oct. 5, 1829, in Fairfield, Vermont. He grew up in Vermont and in New York to become an ardent abolitionist like his father. A true machine politician, Arthur worked for Republican candidates in New York and enjoyed several patronage jobs during the Civil War. Ulysses S. Grant appointed him collector of the port of New York in 1871, and Arthur prospered there until 1879, when Rutherford B. Hayes removed him in the name of reform. In 1880 "Half-Breed" Republicans nominated Arthur for vice president in a conciliatory gesture to his "Stalwart" faction. "The office of Vice President is a greater honor than I ever dreamed of attaining," he said. But Arthur acceded to the presidency on Sept. 19, 1881, when another Stalwart assassinated James A. Garfield. Perhaps shamed into supporting civil service reform, Arthur signed the Pendleton Act (1883) and rooted out post office graft. Democrats in Congress thwarted the rest of Arthur's initiatives; Republicans, whose calls for spoils Arthur ignored, denied him renomination in 1884. He lost a Senate race in New York and died two years later, on Nov. 18, 1886. Arthur was the last of three presidents in the single year 1881.

22, 24. Grover Cleveland (1885–89; 1893–97)

The only president to serve two nonconsecutive terms, Stephen Grover Cleveland was a minister's son, born in Caldwell, New Jersey, on Mar. 18, 1837. The family moved to New York, where Cleveland's uncle made him a lawyer. He showed scant interest in politics until Buffalo elected him mayor in 1881, and the next year Cleveland became governor. His war on corrupt Tammany Hall made Cleveland the perfect Democratic reform candidate for president in 1884. During the election campaign, backers of James G. Blaine, the Republican candidate, accused Cleveland of fathering an illegitimate child. He admitted it and won anyway—by 0.3 percent of the vote—but not before the Republicans came up with the immortal campaign chant "Ma! Ma! Where's my Pa? / Gone to the White House, / Ha! Ha! Ha!" The first Democratic president after the Civil War, Cleveland pushed for civil service reform and lower tariffs. In the first White House wedding, Cleveland married Frances Folsom in 1886. Cleveland cast over 300 vetoes—more than twice the combined total of all previous presidents. He cut Civil War pensions, seized 81 million acres of unused land from railroads, and signed the Interstate Commerce Act (1887). Defeated in the 1888 election, Cleveland claimed there was "no happier man in the United States"; yet four years later he won a rematch with Benjamin Harrison. Back in the White House, Cleveland underwent a secret operation to remove his cancerous upper jaw. His tight-money policies did nothing to help the depression after the Panic of 1893. Cleveland sent Federal troops to break up the Pullman strike (1894) and supported William McKinley, a Republican, for president in 1896. "I have tried so hard to do right," Cleveland said on his deathbed on June 24, 1908.

23. Benjamin Harrison (1889–93)

Benjamin Harrison was born on Aug. 20, 1833, at the North Bend, Ohio, farm of his grandfather William Henry Harrison, the ninth president. He took up the law in Indiana before joining the Union Army in 1862. Harrison finished the Civil War a brigadier general and returned to Indiana, where he was a prominent Republican, defeated for governor in 1876 but elected senator in 1881. A colorless compromise candidate for president, Harrison won the 1888 election despite receiving fewer popular votes than Grover Cleveland. Harrison bowed to the "Billion Dollar Congress" of free-spending Republicans who escalated Civil War pensions, transportation subsidies, naval construction, and spoils patronage. The McKinley Tariff, the Sherman Anti-Trust Act, the Sherman Silver Purchase Act (all 1890), and Secretary of State James G. Blaine's vigorous foreign policy were hallmarks of Harrison's administration, which oversaw the admission of six new states. Democrats won back Congress in 1890 and the White House in 1892, when Harrison lost to Cleveland in their rematch. A legal expert, Harrison taught at Stanford University and defended Venezuela in a boundary dispute with Britain before his death, on Mar. 13, 1901. Harrison referred to the White House as "my jail."

25. William McKinley (1897–1901)

The last Civil War veteran to become president, William McKinley was born in Niles, Ohio, on Jan. 29, 1843, son of an iron founder. A college dropout, McKinley was a post office clerk when the Civil War began. He volunteered as a private and mustered out as a 22-year-old major. McKinley studied law and was elected to Congress in 1876. A longtime Republican floor leader, he authored the record-high McKinley Tariff of 1890, before losing his seat that same year. Ohio millionaire Marcus Hanna, McKinley's political manager, engineered two governor's terms for him and funded McKinley's run for the presidency in 1896. William Jennings Bryan opposed him on a free-silver platform, but McKinley's dignified front porch campaign stressed sound money, tariffs, and the "full dinner pail." He won the election with the first popular majority since Grant's reelection. Strongly probusiness, McKinley raised the tariff still higher and reluctantly led the country into the Spanish-American War (1898). By acquiring the Philippines and other islands, the country became a world power under McKinley, who went on to proclaim the open-door policy in China. McKinley defeated Bryan by an even larger margin in 1900 and was enjoying great popularity when anarchist Leon Czolgosz shot him in Buffalo, N.Y. McKinley died two weeks later, on Sept. 14, 1901.

26. Theodore Roosevelt (1901–09)

Theodore Roosevelt was born in New York City on Oct. 27, 1858, the only president born there. A small, sickly child plagued by asthma, Roosevelt overcame a pampered youth to live the "strenuous life:" he boxed, hiked, hunted, rode horses, and climbed the Matterhorn. After graduating Phi Beta Kappa from Harvard in 1880, he attended Columbia Law School and became the youngest member of New York's legislature. Rich men of his day did not consider politics a suitable avocation, but Roosevelt desperately wanted "to be of the governing class." His first wife, Alice Hathaway Lee, died on the same day his mother died in 1884. Roosevelt wrote books and ran a cattle ranch in North Dakota until he married Edith Kermit Carow in 1886 and they moved to Oyster Bay, N.Y. During the Spanish-American War, Roosevelt left a job at the Navy Department in 1898 to lead the Rough Riders volunteer regiment in Cuba, achieving glory in the Battle of San Juan Hill. Elected governor of New York immediately upon returning home, Roosevelt was named William McKinley's running mate, in 1900. Roosevelt learned of McKinley's death while on a mountain-climbing expedition.

The youngest president at 42, "T.R." promised a Square Deal to close the gap between capital and labor. He mounted well-publicized campaigns against big business and successfully arbitrated major strikes. "Teddy's" popularity soared when he humbled billionaire J.P. Morgan in the Northern Securities case, and a record plurality re-elected him in 1904. Roosevelt signed progressive laws to regulate railroads, inspect food and drugs, and create more than 150 million acres of national parks and forests. No less vigorous in foreign policy, Roosevelt's corollary to the Monroe Doctrine asserted the country would intervene to prevent European involvement in Latin America. For helping to end the Russo-Japanese War, Roosevelt became the first American to win the Nobel Prize, but he considered the Panama Canal his greatest achievement. Roosevelt kept his pledge not to seek a third term in 1908—but in 1912 he ran against his chosen successor, William Howard Taft. Denied his party's nomination, Roosevelt survived an assassination attempt and won more than four million votes as the Progressive, or Bull Moose, candidate. During World War I, Roosevelt bitterly denounced the neutrality policy of Woodrow Wilson, who then denied Roosevelt's request to lead troops in France. While laying plans for another run at the White House, Roosevelt died suddenly of a cardiac embolism on Jan. 6, 1919. "No president has ever enjoyed himself as much as I have," he once said.

27. William Howard Taft (1909–13)

By far the largest president at over 330 pounds, William Howard Taft was born in Cincinnati, Ohio, on Sept. 15, 1857. He graduated from Yale in 1878, then followed his father into law and Republican politics: "I always had my plate right side up when offices were falling," Taft wrote. William McKinley sent him to govern the Philippines in 1900, and Theodore Roosevelt appointed him secretary of war in 1904. Taft traveled around the world as Roosevelt's personal emissary, becoming T.R.'s chosen successor in 1908. As president, Taft tried to carry on Roosevelt's policies, but he wrecked the Republican party by alienating progressives from conservative "Stand-Patters" over tariff and conservation issues. Taft initiated the income tax and pursued antitrust suits against big business—but generally he sided with wealthy interests. An infuriated Roosevelt challenged Taft unsuccessfully for the Republican nomination in 1912, then outpolled him in the election, giving Woodrow Wilson the victory. With eight electoral votes, Taft suffered the worst-ever defeat for an incumbent president. But the better part of his career lay ahead: Taft, always more comfortable as a jurist, taught law at Yale until he was appointed chief justice of the United States in

1921. He served with distinction, alternating a liberal nationalism in economic affairs with political and social conservatism. Taft died on Mar. 8, 1930. Never nostalgic for the White House, Taft once said, "I don't remember that I ever was president."

28. Woodrow Wilson (1913–21)

Born on Dec. 28, 1856, in Staunton, Virginia, the son of a Presbyterian minister, Thomas Woodrow Wilson grew up in Virginia, Georgia, South Carolina, and North Carolina—the first southern president since Andrew Jackson. Probably dyslexic, Wilson was slow to read; yet he became the most highly educated president. Graduated from Princeton in 1879, Wilson studied law before taking a Ph.D. in political science at Johns Hopkins in 1886. He taught at Bryn Mawr and Wesleyan University before Princeton appointed him professor in 1890. Wilson attracted the attention of Democratic bosses after he was elected Princeton's president in 1902, and they persuaded him to run for New Jersey governor in 1910. A strong progressive, Wilson won easily—and then turned on party bosses by sponsoring anti-machine reforms. In 1912 the Democrats nominated Wilson for president on the 46th ballot, and he won, with Theodore Roosevelt and William Howard Taft splitting the Republican vote.

Wilson's expert knowledge of government and strong party leadership pushed the Underwood Tariff, the Federal Reserve Act, the Federal Trade Commission, and the Clayton Antitrust Act through Congress by 1914. Restoring competition to the monopoly-plagued economy was the goal of Wilson's "New Freedom," until war in Europe made neutrality his top priority. German attacks on Allied ships carrying Americans strained Wilson's commitment, but he was narrowly reelected in 1916 on the slogan "He Kept Us Out of the War." After Germany spurned Wilson's mediation and resumed attacks on Allied shipping, Congress declared war at Wilson's behest in April 1917. World War I would "make the world safe for democracy," Wilson vowed, and he issued "Fourteen Points" for a just peace. After the armistice in November 1918, Wilson became the first president to visit Europe, when he attended the Paris peace conference that produced the Versailles Treaty. Wilson's dream of "peace without vengeance" was frustrated at Versailles, where he compromised away his Fourteen Points to obtain the League of Nations for collective security. In July 1919, Wilson returned home to face hostile Republicans in the Senate, where his treaty languished. On a nationwide speaking tour, Wilson collapsed from exhaustion in Colorado and suffered a paralytic stroke in October 1919. Wilson, all but incapacitated, refused to compromise as the Senate rejected the Versailles Treaty. Wilson's second wife, Edith Bolling Galt, whom he married in 1915, shielded the disabled president from the press and politicians until the end of his term in 1921. Woodrow Wilson died in his sleep on Feb. 3, 1924, frustrated by his own country's refusal to join the League of Nations.

29. Warren G. Harding (1921–23)

The first president born after the Civil War, Warren Gamaliel Harding was born in Blooming Grove, Ohio, which earlier had been named Corsica, on Nov. 2, 1865. He taught, studied law, and sold insurance before following his father into the newspaper business. Marriage to Florence De-Wolfe, a wealthy widow, in 1891 helped finance Harding's paper, the Marion Star. A staunch Republican, Harding's probusiness editorials got him elected state senator and lieutenant governor. Although defeated for governor in 1910, Harding was elected senator four years later. Republicans turned to him in 1920 as a compromise candidate for president, the "best of the second-raters"; his good looks were expected to win over women first-time voters. Elected by an unprecedented 61 percent majority, Harding promised a return to "normalcy" for Americans tired of war and Woodrow Wilson. Harding's administration featured higher tariffs, lower taxes, and immigration restriction—but perhaps most notably, pervasive corruption and incompetence by Harding's crooked appointees. Harding was disturbed by the dishonesty of "my God-damn friends," two of whom committed suicide to avoid prosecution. While visiting San Francisco, Harding died suddenly of an embolism on Aug. 2, 1923. Scandals involving secret love affairs, official graft, and the vast Teapot Dome swindle erupted soon thereafter. Mrs. Harding zealously tracked down Harding's letters and destroyed them, leaving him the most enigmatic president, and certainly one of the worst.

30. Calvin Coolidge (1923–29)

The only president to share the nation's birthday, John Calvin Coolidge was born in Plymouth, Vermont, on July 4, 1872. Descended from a long line of New Englanders, he graduated from Amherst in 1895, practiced law in Massachusetts, and entered Republican politics in 1899. Coolidge rose slowly through a succession of state offices until he was elected governor of Massachusetts in 1918. Acclaimed for crushing the Boston police strike in 1919, Coolidge became the unexpected Republican vice-presidential nominee in 1920. After Warren G. Harding's death while still in office, Coolidge's own father swore him in as the new president. "Silent Cal" was the butt of jokes for his laconic utterances, but his minimalist approach to government fit the public mood, and he restored respectability to the White House, tainted by Harding's corrupt appointees and all-night poker parties. Instead of the whiskey that once flowed freely there, ice water in paper cups was served to visitors. Coolidge, untouched by leftover scandals, won the election in his own right in 1924. Pronouncing that the "business of America is business," he ushered in the heady years of Coolidge Prosperity, as the stock market soared higher and higher. Coolidge ignored foreign affairs and made frugality his trademark, slashing the budget at the expense of farmers and veterans, even driving out a White House cook who could not abide Coolidge's cost cutting. "It's a pretty good idea to get out when they still want you," Coolidge said, surprising the nation at the peak of his success by declining to run again in 1928. A popular president, Coolidge was safely out of politics when the Great Depression arrived. He died on Jan. 5, 1933, on the eve of the New Deal.

31. Herbert Hoover (1929–33)

Born in West Branch, Iowa, on Aug. 10, 1874, Herbert Clark Hoover was the first president from west of the Mississippi. Orphaned at eight and raised by Quaker relatives in Iowa and Oregon, Hoover joined the first graduating class of Stanford University in 1895. He became a world-famous mining engineer and a multimillionaire by age 40. In World War I, Hoover helped rescue

Americans stranded in Europe, distributed food supplies to occupied Belgium, and convinced the nation to save food ("Hooverize") for the war effort. Hoover was Woodrow Wilson's economic adviser at Versailles, and he organized relief for famine-struck Russia during the revolution. Joining the Republicans in 1919, Hoover earned prominence as the secretary of commerce in the 1920s and was elected president in 1928—the only electoral victory of his life. He promised a "chicken in every pot," but a few months later, the Wall Street crash brought on the Great Depression. Paralyzed by his conservative instincts, Hoover could not halt the spread of bank failures, bankruptcy, unemployment, and despair. Government should not get involved, he believed, and public relief would ruin American morals—so Hoover called for a balanced budget while promising the return of prosperity. He sent tanks to disperse veterans begging for pensions, and shantytowns across the country were dubbed Hoovervilles. Massively defeated by Franklin D. Roosevelt in 1932, Hoover called the New Deal "socialistic, collectivistic, fascistic and communistic." For decades Americans blamed Hoover for the depression and criticized his hard-hearted refusal to help the needy. Hoover lived another 31 years, the longest postpresidential lifespan, and he salvaged his reputation with more relief work after World War II. In retirement Hoover chaired two bipartisan commissions on government reorganization, issuing many important recommendations for Federal reform. Boulder Dam on the Colorado River was renamed to honor Hoover before he died, at age 90, on Oct. 20, 1964.

32. Franklin D. Roosevelt (1933–45)

The only president elected more than twice, Franklin Delano Roosevelt was born to a wealthy Hyde Park, New York, family on Jan. 30, 1882. He followed his cousin, Theodore Roosevelt, into Harvard and Columbia Law School—but not into the Republican party. F.D.R. was a Democratic state senator, assistant secretary of the navy, and nominee for vice president in 1920. Paralyzed by polio in 1921, Roosevelt learned to walk with braces and canes. As governor of New York after 1928, he pioneered unemployment relief in the Great Depression, earning him the Democratic nomination for president in 1932. Herbert Hoover, brooding and baffled by the depression, posed little challenge to the beaming, magnetic Roosevelt, who won the election by 23 million to 16 million votes. F.D.R. promised vague but bold experimentation ("above all, try something"), and as he took office in the worst inaugural crisis since Abraham Lincoln's, he assured Americans they had "nothing to fear but fear itself." F.D.R.'s first 100 days set a breakneck pace as compliant congressmen approved his New Deal for relief and recovery. Major landmarks were the National Industrial Recovery Act, the Agricultural Adjustment Act, the Tennessee Valley Authority, the Works Progress Administration, the National Labor Relations Act (Wagner Act), and the Social Security Act (1933–35). Though often contradictory and ineffective, the New Deal established the Federal government's responsibility for protecting farmers, workers, and the unemployed while actively regulating the economy to prevent another crash. F.D.R.'s high-profile "fireside chats," public works projects, and Social Security programs overcame despair and restored public confidence in the economy and government.

Reelected by a huge margin in 1936, Roosevelt proved incapable of ending the depression, as he ran afoul of the "nine old men" on the Supreme Court. Almost as many Americans called Roosevelt a Communist as praised him for rescuing the common man. Despite alienating many voters with his court-packing plan and "soak the rich" taxes, F.D.R. won an unprecedented third term in 1940. As war loomed in Europe, F.D.R. used his mastery of public opinion to lead Americans away from isolation, helping Britain with the destroyers-for-bases deal (1940) and Lend-Lease Act (1941) even before Pearl Harbor. World War II then occupied F.D.R.'s full attention as he shelved the New Deal and orchestrated the mammoth war effort. Roosevelt crisscrossed the globe to meet with Allied leaders and kept close personal control of diplomacy and grand strategy. He rallied a powerful sense of national purpose in the war, winning his fourth election in 1944. Together with Winston Churchill and Josef Stalin, F.D.R. planned a postwar peace of UN cooperation. Just after the Yalta Conference, Roosevelt died suddenly of a cerebral hemorrhage on Apr. 12, 1945, days before the war's end. His wife of 40 years, Eleanor Roosevelt, easily the most influential first lady, led her husband's campaign on behalf of disadvantaged Americans and continued it long after his death.

33. Harry S Truman (1945–53)

A plain midwestern farmer and World War I artilleryman, Harry S Truman (the S does not stand for a middle name) was born on May 8, 1884, in Lamar, Missouri. After his Kansas City haberdashery failed, Truman entered politics as a Democrat in the 1920s, and the local Pendergast machine arranged his election to the Senate as a New Dealer in 1934. National attention came to Truman when he headed a congressional committee investigating government waste during World War II. When Franklin D. Roosevelt needed a new vice president in 1944, he chose Truman. After only a few weeks in office, Truman had the presidency thrust upon him by Roosevelt's sudden death in April 1945. "Pray for me, boys," he told his first press conference. Utterly unprepared, Truman did not even know about the atomic bomb project, but he vowed to carry on Roosevelt's policies. Truman proved a remarkably capable chief executive. In his first four months, Truman approved the United Nations, accepted the German surrender, met with Allied leaders at Potsdam, and ordered atomic bombs dropped on Japan. As the Cold War commenced, Truman talked tough with the Soviets, accusing them of breaking agreements and intimidating helpless neighbors. In 1947 he proclaimed the Truman Doctrine, promising U.S. aid to threatened countries, and the Marshall Plan to aid European recovery and contain communism. The next year Truman ordered the Berlin airlift when the Soviets cut off West Berlin, and he promised to help Third World countries with the Point Four program. No less assertive at home, Truman made progress on civil rights, subdued restive unions, and prevented the Republican-controlled Congress from dismantling the New Deal—a specter that he effectively raised to win surprise reelection in 1948. Truman committed the country to the NATO alliance in 1949 and sent troops to South Korea when Communist armies invaded in 1950. But as Congress rejected Truman's ambitious Fair Deal domestic program and the Korean War bogged down, Truman's last years were barren. He had more vetoes overridden than all presidents but Andrew Johnson, and his poll ratings were lower than all but

Jimmy Carter's. Truman, who initially raised fears of subversion with his loyalty program, could not quell the Red Scare that swept his party from power in 1952, as Republicans hammered away on the theme that Democrats were "soft on communism." Truman was convinced that he saved the world from communism, prevented World War III, and could have won another term if he chose to run in 1952. "He did his damndest" was the only eulogy Harry Truman desired on his death, on Dec. 26, 1972. Out of favor when he left office, Truman gained rising respect after his death.

34. Dwight D. Eisenhower (1953–61)

The last war hero president, Dwight David Eisenhower was born in Denison, Texas, on Oct. 14, 1890, and grew up poor in Kansas. A military history buff, Eisenhower graduated with the 1915 class of West Point that produced 59 generals. He married Mamie Doud, his wife of 52 years, and spent World War I as a tank-training instructor. Eisenhower, only a major at age 40, rose rapidly during World War II, promoted past 350 senior officers to become commander of U.S. forces in Europe in 1942. By the end of 1944, he was the first U.S. five-star general and Supreme Allied Commander, taking the German surrender in May 1945. By that point a global celebrity, Eisenhower was army chief of staff until 1948, when he resigned to become president of Columbia University. Pres. Truman named him to command NATO forces in 1950, but two years later, Eisenhower retired again to take the Republican nomination and run for president against Adlai E. Stevenson.

"Ike" became perhaps the most popular president in U.S. history, though many questioned his lax work habits, detached management style, and baffling speeches. Prominent millionaires in Eisenhower's cabinet and archconservatives such as Sec. of State John Foster Dulles seemed to have free rein, and Eisenhower acquiesced in Sen. Joe McCarthy's wild charges of subversion. His administration stockpiled atomic weapons and promised "massive retaliation" against Soviet aggression—yet did nothing when the Red Army rolled into Hungary in 1956. Eisenhower did end the Korean War, concluded several alliance agreements, and cut the defense budget. The "Eisenhower Doctrine" promised U.S. aid to Middle Eastern countries fighting communism. When Britain, France, and Israel invaded the Suez Canal in 1956, Eisenhower led UN condemnation and forced them to withdraw, though he sent U.S. Marines into Lebanon two years later. He began heavy U.S. involvement in Vietnam by backing the French and then the puppet Diem regime. At home Eisenhower promised to scale back the government—yet he expanded Social Security; created the Department of Health, Education, and Welfare; and spent billions on public housing and freeways. He pointedly stressed religious devotion. The Supreme Court's *Brown* decision, which Eisenhower deeply regretted, inaugurated the civil rights movement. Eisenhower defeated Stevenson again in 1956, but Soviet domination of space, revolution in Cuba, embarrassment over the Soviets' shooting down of a U.S. spy plane, and his own ill health marred his second term. Eisenhower reluctantly sent paratroopers to enforce desegregation in Little Rock, Ark., in 1957. Democrats controlled Congress for all but two years of Eisenhower's presidency. In retirement Eisenhower approved of U.S. intervention in Vietnam and counseled presidents until his death on Mar. 28, 1969.

35. John F. Kennedy (1961–63)

The youngest man elected president, the only Roman Catholic, and the first born in the 20th century, John Fitzgerald Kennedy was born in Brookline, Massachusetts, on May 29, 1917, to a family of Irish politicos. His father, Joseph P. Kennedy, was ambassador to England and one of the richest men in America. Kennedy attended Dexter and Choate Academies, the London School of Economics, and Princeton before graduating from Harvard in 1940. A patrol boat commander in World War II, Kennedy was decorated for bravery in saving the lives of wounded crew members. Kennedy's father arranged his election to Congress, where he served three undistinguished terms before entering the Senate in 1952. In 1953, he married wealthy socialite Jacqueline Bouvier, and in 1957, he won the Pulitzer Prize for *Profiles in Courage*, a study of principled politicians. In 1960, running on a platform that lambasted Republicans for insufficient anticommunism and "vigor," Kennedy became the first candidate to utilize the presidential primary system to defeat three prominent opponents for the Democratic nomination. In the general election, Kennedy edged sitting vice president Richard M. Nixon by the narrowest of margins: 118,000 votes out of 69 million cast. The campaign was the first to feature televised presidential debates, in which Kennedy's poise, polish, and charisma were an invaluable asset.

During the campaign, Kennedy had pledged a New Frontier, but his social programs languished in Congress. Undaunted, he plunged into foreign affairs, his primary interest. Just after taking office, he approved the disastrous Bay of Pigs invasion, and a year later, he terrified the world by confronting the Soviets over the presence of their missiles in Cuba. He visited the Berlin Wall and expressed solidarity with Germans under the Russian gun. But he also set up the Washington-Moscow hotline, and signed the Nuclear Test Ban Treaty (1963).

Thousands of U.S. troops went to Vietnam as Kennedy escalated the commitment to containing communism. Kennedy vastly increased spending for defense and space programs, vowing to put a man on the Moon. He also engineered a $10 billion tax cut that eventually brought prosperity and increased revenues. As racial unrest spread, Kennedy cautiously supported the civil rights movement, introducing sweeping legislation that would not pass in his lifetime—nor would his plans for aid to education and medical care for the elderly reach fruition before his death. In a Dallas, Tex., motorcade on Nov. 22, 1963, he was fatally shot. Kennedy's alleged assassin, Lee Harvey Oswald, a left-wing ex-marine, was in turn murdered by Jack Ruby two days later. While doubts persisted that Oswald acted alone, Kennedy's martyrdom helped realize his legislative legacy, and subsequent revelation of his many peccadilloes have not tarnished the "Kennedy myth."

36. Lyndon B. Johnson (1963–69)

The eighth vice president to succeed by death of a president, Lyndon Baines Johnson was born on his father's Texas ranch near Stonewall on Aug. 27, 1908. He worked his way through Southwest Texas State Teachers College, taught briefly, then took a job in Washington—where he would live for all but two years until he left the White House. Government fascinated Johnson, and he reveled in making connections, marrying heiress Claudia Alta "Lady Bird" Taylor after a two-month courtship in 1934. An ardent New Dealer, Johnson won election to Congress as a Democrat in 1937. Reelected three times without opposition, Johnson became the first congressman to volunteer for combat in World War II, winning a Silver Star before returning to Washington. In 1948, on his second try, "Landslide Lyndon" was elected to the Senate by just 87 votes. Hard work and Texas oil money made Johnson the youngest Senate majority leader by 1955. A huge man, Johnson's powers of persuasion were legendary, but he failed in his bid for the Democratic nomination for president in 1960. Johnson accepted John F. Kennedy's offer of the vice presidency and campaigned hard in the South to aid their narrow victory. Made president a thousand days later by the tragedy in Dallas, Johnson vowed to continue Kennedy's programs, pushing them through Congress with surprising ease. Notable were the Civil Rights Act outlawing segregation and the Equal Opportunity Act, which declared "war on poverty." After less than a year in office, Johnson defeated Barry Goldwater by the biggest plurality in history.

Now president in his own right, Johnson unveiled plans for a Great Society free from poverty and discrimination and passed the Education Act, Medical Care Act, and the Voting Rights Act in 1965. But Johnson came to grief in Vietnam, where he broke his 1964 campaign promise not to send "American boys to fight Asian wars." Earlier administrations committed the U.S. to defending South Vietnam, but Johnson intervened massively to prove American credibility to allies and enemies alike. Following the Tonkin Gulf incident (1964), Johnson steadily expended American power and lives in Vietnam, but victory, or a means to achieve it, never came within reach—despite the presence of over half a million U.S. troops by 1968. Johnson's presidency unraveled as American losses mounted, antiwar protests grew strident, race riots exploded in inner cities across the nation, and the government developed a credibility gap. Virtually a prisoner of the White House, Johnson faced a war he could neither win nor leave behind and a nation more deeply divided than at any time since the Civil War. In March 1968 Johnson effectively resigned by announcing he would not seek another term. He retired to his sprawling Texas ranch and stayed out of politics until his death, on Jan. 22, 1973.

37. Richard M. Nixon (1969–74)

The only president to resign from office, Richard Milhous Nixon was born in Yorba Linda, California, to a poor Quaker family on Jan. 9, 1913. A graduate of Whittier College and Duke University Law School, Nixon married Thelma "Pat" Ryan in 1940, saw noncombat service in World War II, and rode into Congress on the Republican wave of 1946. He gained fame in the anti-Communist trial of Alger Hiss before entering the Senate in 1950. Dwight D. Eisenhower made Nixon his running mate in 1952, but Nixon was nearly forced to resign for accepting questionable contributions. He appealed for national exoneration in the televised "Checkers" speech. A well-traveled vice president, Nixon almost lost his life to hostile Latin American mobs in 1958, and he waged an impromptu debate in Moscow with Soviet premier Nikita Khrushchev in 1959. Eisenhower's obvious successor in 1960, Nixon narrowly lost the election to John F. Kennedy, and when he lost a California gubernatorial race in 1962, his career seemed over. Yet he practiced law in New York until the Republicans nominated him again in 1968. To a nation riven by the Vietnam

War, Nixon promised "law and order," appealing to calm and unity against a background of riots, assassinations, and protest. Nixon defeated Hubert H. Humphrey with the smallest victor's share of the vote since 1912.

Vowing to "bring us together," Nixon tried to thwart the bureaucracy and Democrats in Congress by centralizing executive power. To control inflation, he ordered wage-price controls and devalued the dollar for the first time since the depression. Seeking "peace with honor" in Vietnam, Nixon built up the South Vietnamese army and withdrew U.S. troops—while massively escalating bombing of North Vietnam. Antiwar protests reached fever pitch when the United States invaded Cambodia in 1970. Nixon responded with appeals to the "silent majority," attacks on press freedom, and clandestine harassment of administration critics. High points of his first administration were the Apollo moon landing in 1969, Nixon's pathbreaking visit to China in 1972, and the first Strategic Arms Limitation Treaty with the Soviet Union. Twelve days after announcing "peace is at hand" in Vietnam, Nixon was reelected by a landslide, carrying an unprecedented 49 states. During the campaign five burglars were arrested in the Democratic party headquarters, and by early 1973, they were linked to the White House. The ensuing "Watergate" scandal exposed the Nixon administration's rampant corruption, illegality, and deceit. Nixon himself downplayed the scandal as mere politics, but when his aides resigned in disgrace, Nixon's role in ordering an illegal cover-up came to light in the press, courts, and congressional investigations. Nixon evaded taxes, accepted illicit campaign contributions, ordered secret bombings, and harassed opponents with executive agencies, wiretaps, and break-ins. Vice Pres. Spiro T. Agnew resigned in October 1973 for accepting bribes, but Nixon hung on to power, claiming, "I am not a crook," as the House began impeachment proceedings. Subpoenas and Supreme Court orders forced Nixon to release tapes of his White House conversations authorizing the Watergate cover-up. Ultimately, he resigned to avoid impeachment for obstruction of justice, abuse of power, and contempt of Congress. Claiming to have lost his "political base," Nixon announced his resignation on national television on Aug. 9, 1974. He never admitted wrongdoing, though he later conceded errors of judgment. Saved by a blanket pardon from Gerald R. Ford, his second vice president, Nixon retired to California, later moving to New Jersey. He dedicated the remainder of his life to unsullying his name, while becoming a foreign policy adviser to presidents until his death at the age of 81 in 1994.

38. Gerald R. Ford (1974–77)

The only vice president and president never elected to either office, Gerald Rudolph Ford was born in Omaha, Nebraska, on July 14, 1913. An Eagle Scout, he grew up in Michigan and attended the University of Michigan on a football scholarship, playing on the national championship teams of 1932 and 1933. After graduating in 1935, Ford coached football and boxing at Yale while attending law school. In the navy he earned 10 battle stars in the Pacific during World War II. Ford was elected to Congress in 1948 as a Republican. He would be reelected 12 times, never by less than 60 percent. His solid conservative record elevated him to House Republican minority leader by 1965. For supporting Richard M. Nixon, Ford was rewarded with the vice presidency in December

1973, replacing Spiro T. Agnew under the 25th Amendment. "I do not think the public would stand for it," Ford said at his confirmation hearings, when asked if he would ever pardon Nixon. For eight months Ford stayed loyal to Nixon, until his resignation made Ford the new president on Aug. 9, 1974. Ford announced "our long national nightmare is over," but a month later he shocked the nation by giving Nixon a blanket pardon. Ford denied any deal had been made, but his public standing never recovered. He struggled with huge Democratic majorities in Congress to stem soaring inflation and unemployment, casting 66 vetoes in all. In the Mayaguez incident, Ford sent the marines to rescue 39 Americans captured by Cambodia.

Breaking a 1973 pledge, Ford decided to seek reelection, and while campaigning, he survived two assassination attempts by California women. Ford was far behind Jimmy Carter in the polls, but he carried four more states than Carter in the election—which Ford lost by 57 electoral votes. It was the first defeat of an incumbent president since Herbert Hoover's.

39. Jimmy Carter (1977–81)

James Earl Carter, the first deep-southerner elected president in 128 years, was born in Plains, Georgia, on Oct. 1, 1924. He grew up on a farm with no plumbing or electricity but realized his dream of attending the U.S. Naval Academy. Carter graduated in 1946 and married Rosalynn Smith. He joined the submarine fleet and studied nuclear physics, leaving the Navy in 1953 to run the family peanut business. He was elected to the Georgia state senate in 1962. Defeated for governor in 1966, Carter campaigned constantly for the next four years, winning on his second try in 1970. Carter reorganized the government and hired more blacks, declaring that the "time for racial discrimination is over." A month before leaving office in 1974, Carter was the first Democrat to announce his candidacy for president in 1976, again campaigning constantly. "Jimmy Who?" burst into headlines by winning narrow pluralities over nine rivals in early primaries. Carter's grinning, homespun style and earnest vows of honesty ("I will never lie to you") struck a chord with voters after Watergate. Carter won the nomination and defeated incumbent Gerald R. Ford by 2 percent of the vote. Lack of Washington connections helped his candidacy but not his presidency, for Carter never shook his image as the provincial amateur. Democratic majorities in Congress ignored Carter's pleas for tax reform and a long-range energy policy. Transportation deregulation, environmental protection, and new departments of energy and education were Carter's main domestic achievements.

But as Federal spending mounted and oil prices doubled, most Americans blamed Carter for runaway inflation. His 20 percent approval rating in August 1979 was the lowest ever recorded. In foreign affairs Carter obtained a Panama Canal treaty, normalized relations with China, and mediated the Camp David peace accords between Israel and Egypt. He moved toward closer relations with the Soviet Union, signing the SALT II treaty in 1979, but the Soviet invasion of Afghanistan led Carter to embargo grain sales to the USSR and to order a boycott of the 1980 Moscow Olympics. The Carter Doctrine announced the United States would defend the Persian Gulf, where ironically, Carter soon met his downfall in the Iran hostage crisis. Early public support for Carter's restraint gradually withered under the glare of relentless media coverage. Carter himself became a hostage of Iran, trapped in the White House as Edward Kennedy nearly deprived him of the Democratic nomination. In April 1980, Carter approved a military rescue mission whose tragic failure reinforced his image of incompetence and weakness, which Republican candidate Ronald Reagan exploited, winning the election in a landslide. Carter left the White House discredited, his informal style ridiculed as inappropriate. In later years he won recognition as a trustworthy international negotiator.

40. Ronald Reagan (1981–89)

Ronald Wilson Reagan was born in Tampico, Illinois, on Feb. 6, 1911. Reagan was a radio sports announcer when he made his first movie in 1937. Over 50 more films would follow in Reagan's prolific Hollywood career. In 1940 he married actress Jane Wyman, who divorced him in 1948. During World War II, Reagan made propaganda films for the U.S. Army, and after the war he became president of the Screen Actors Guild. Then a Democrat, Reagan assailed Communists in Hollywood. He married Nancy Davis, another actress, in 1952. As his movie career waned, Reagan espoused conservative causes, switching to the Republican party in 1960. Reagan made a dramatic speech at the end of the 1964 campaign, and despite his total lack of experience he was elected governor of California in 1966 by a million votes. As governor, Reagan broke all promises by raising taxes, increasing spending, and expanding the state government—yet he easily won reelection in 1970. He made unsuccessful runs for the Republican presidential nomination in 1968 and 1976 before winning it in 1980. He swept past Jimmy Carter in the crushing "Reagan Revolution" of 1980, carrying 44 states and making huge Republican gains in Congress.

"Reaganomics" promised to cut taxes and social spending while vastly increasing the defense budget and somehow balancing the budget. Congress was unmoved until Mar. 20, 1981, when a crazed youth named John Hinckley shot Reagan twice in the chest. Reagan's good humor and rapid recovery charmed Americans—especially the press, which had questioned his age and health. Reagan then prevailed over Congress to pass mammoth tax cuts. The national debt began its meteoric rise under Reagan as defense spending outweighed cuts in social programs. By 1986 the U.S. had become a net borrower for the first time since World War I, but falling oil prices slowed inflation and rekindled economic growth, for which Reagan took credit. Calling the Soviet Union an "evil empire," Reagan built up the armed forces, deployed U.S. nuclear missiles in Europe, and began the Strategic Defense Initiative. He sent U.S. Marines to Lebanon, where 240 of them died in a terrorist attack. To halt the spread of communism, Reagan ordered the invasion of Grenada and isolated the Sandinista government of Nicaragua. Reelected by another landslide in 1984, with the economy booming and his public esteem high, Reagan seemed headed for an even more successful second term. He ordered bombing raids on Libya and met with Soviet leader Mikhail Gorbachev, eventually producing historic arms control agreements. But in 1987 Reagan's invincible popularity finally succumbed to the Iran-Contra scandal: White House staff had secretly sold arms to Iran in hopes of freeing American hostages held in Lebanon, using the profits illegally to fund Contra fighters in Nicaragua. Many top Reagan aides had to resign, but more damaging was the president's apparent loss of control over his own administration.

Reagan left office with the highest approval rating of any departing president since FDR. In retirement he was knighted by Queen Elizabeth. As the Iran-Contra trials continued in 1990, Reagan was ordered to testify under oath about his role in the scandal; he responded 130 times with "I don't recall" or "I don't remember." In 1995, he revealed he was suffering from Alzheimer's disease.

41. George H. Bush (1989–93)

The first sitting vice president elected president in over 150 years, George Herbert Walker Bush was born in Milton, Massachusetts, on June 12, 1924. His father was former U.S. Senator Prescott Sheldon Bush (R-Conn., 1952-63) As a Navy pilot during World War II, Bush was shot down over the Pacific and rescued at sea. He married Barbara Pierce, a Smith College student, on Jan. 6, 1945, and graduated Phi Beta Kappa in economics from Yale in 1948. Bush spurned an offer from his millionaire father's Wall Street firm to pursue a career in the Texas oil fields that eventually made him a millionaire in his own right.

Running on a conservative anti-Communist and anti-civil rights platform, Bush won the Republican nomination for Senate in 1964 and again in 1970, but lost the general election both times. In between, he was elected to Congress from a wealthy suburban Houston district. Presidents Richard Nixon and Gerald Ford rewarded the Republican party loyalist with appointed offices, including U.S. ambassador to the United Nations (1971), chairman of the Republican National Committee (1973), and director of the CIA (1976). After losing the Republican presidential nomination to Ronald Reagan in 1980, Bush accepted Reagan's offer to join him on the winning ticket.

One of the few members of Reagan's staff to emerge unscathed by the Iran-Contra affair, Bush bested Bob Dole for the Republican nomination in 1988. With Reagan's endorsement, Bush defeated Massachusetts governor Michael S. Dukakis, renewing the Reagan pledge of "no new taxes" and vowing to uphold the Reagan legacy of less government, strong defense, and family values. He declared war on "this scourge" of drugs by creating an office of National Drug Control Policy within the White House. Bush's first official act was to proclaim January 20 as the "National Day of Prayer."

Bush suffered early criticism for lack of leadership. For months, many key administration posts went unfilled, and the Senate rejected John Tower as Bush's nominee for defense secretary. But Bush struck back with major initiatives, including major arms control proposals and two summit meetings with Soviet premier Mikhail Gorbachev. In December 1989, Bush ordered the invasion of Panama to protect U.S. citizens and overthrow the regime of Gen. Manuel Noriega.

As one eastern bloc country after another opted for democracy in 1989 and 1990, Bush enjoyed the highest public approval rating of any postwar president. This popularity gave him the political leverage to renege on his campaign pledge of "no new taxes." His popularity rose to record levels when he ordered Operation Desert Storm to liberate Kuwait from Iraqi occupation. But it later became apparent that Bush had ordered a cease-fire much too early, allowing Saddam Hussein to retain power in Iraq.

Throughout 1991, as the Soviet Union was crumbling, Bush acted quickly and decisively to support those republics seeking independence, and to provide food and medical supplies where needed. He and Gorbachev declared an end to the arms race by signing the first nuclear arms reduction pact in July.

Bush had less success on the domestic front. In spring of 1992, his approval rating dipped below 40 percent, reflecting the deepening economic recession that drove unemployment levels to their highest level in a decade. Bush was challenged first in the primaries and then in the general election by opponents who made the economy the central issue of their campaigns. Bush survived a vicious attack from the right wing of his party to win the Republican nomination. But unable to get the economy on course, Bush lost to Bill Clinton in a three-way race that saw independent candidate Ross Perot capture nearly 20 percent of the vote. It marked only the 10th time that an incumbent president had been unseated.

42. Bill Clinton (1993–2001)

William Jefferson Clinton was born in tiny Hope, Arkansas, on Aug. 19, 1946. His father, William Jefferson Blythe 3d, was killed before his son was born, leaving his wife, Virginia, to raise their son alone. Four years later, she married Roger Clinton; Bill assumed his stepfather's surname. After graduating from Georgetown University, Bill Clinton went to Oxford University on a Rhodes scholarship and then to Yale Law School, where he met Hillary Rodham, whom he married in 1973.

Clinton was elected Arkansas attorney general in 1976, and two years later became the nation's youngest governor in 40 years. In 1980 he became the nation's youngest ex-governor, a victim of the Reagan Republican landslide. But in 1982, Clinton won his old job back, and over the next decade helped Arkansas to transform its economy. He became a leading figure among the so-called New Democrats, who called for welfare reform, smaller government, and other Reagan-like ideas.

In 1992, Clinton emerged as a shaky frontrunner among six Democratic hopefuls for the presidential nomination. Allegations that he had extramarital affairs, dodged the draft during the Vietnam War, and smoked marijuana threatened to derail his campaign early. But as the candidate with the most money and the best-articulated campaign strategy—creating more jobs—Clinton was able to stay in the race the longest, fending off all rivals long before the Democratic convention.

In a three-way race that saw billionaire populist Ross Perot enter, withdraw, and then re-enter the field as an independent, Clinton garnered 366 of the 538 electoral votes, despite winning only 43 percent of the popular vote. Incumbent George Bush captured 37 percent, and Perot 19 percent, of the 104 million votes cast.

Clinton entered office hoping that a Democratic president and a Democratic Congress could untangle the gridlock that had paralyzed Washington for 12 years. But his first act as president, a pledge to end the ban on lesbians and gay men in the armed forces, met with heavy resistance from top military leaders. And his economic stimulus package fell to defeat in the face of a remarkable Republican filibuster in the Senate.

During his second 100 days, he signed the family leave bill, lifted restrictions on abortion counseling at federally funded clinics, and laid the groundwork for the North American Free Trade Agreement. The passage of his first budget—with Vice Pres. Al Gore casting the deciding vote in the Senate—started the nation on the road to recovery from the burden of the enormous deficits created by the Reagan and Bush administrations. In the ensuing economic prosperity, the 5 to 8 percent increase on the tax rates of the wealthiest Americans as well as a surge in capital gains taxes from the booming stock markets generated so much income for the Treasury that deficits turned to surpluses by 1998.

Clinton had several early successes on the foreign policy front, assuring the stability of Russia's government through a coup attempt, and negotiating a peace treaty between Israel and the PLO that recognized Palestinian self-rule in Gaza and part of the West Bank. Clinton's handling of the escalating conflict in Bosnia (placing the issue in the hands of the U.N.) allowed him to avoid engagement while placing the responsibility for inaction squarely on the European nations. And his brinksmanship with North Korea resulted in Pyongyang's agreement to dismantle nuclear reactors that could be used to produce ammunition for nuclear weapons.

On the domestic front, however, Clinton still found little support for his programs. A complex, poorly presented plan (devised by a committee headed by First Lady Hillary Rodham Clinton) called for guaranteed health coverage to all Americans, regardless of pre-existing conditions or ability to pay. But it also promised a huge government bureaucracy that opponents claimed would be less efficient than the post office. Politicians of all stripes responded with half a dozen rival plans, with the end result that no reform took place.

Throughout 1993, Clinton's approval ratings sagged, and in the 1994 midterm elections, the GOP won control of both Houses of Congress for the first time in more than 40 years. New House Speaker Newt Gingrich moved to center stage, proclaiming a Republican revolution, and Clinton barely raised a contrary voice or a veto threat as the House raced through the provisions of the Contract with America. Republicans in Congress also flexed their new muscles in 1995 by opening hearings on the Clintons' controversial investment in a land deal known as Whitewater.

As he prepared for a second term, Clinton's approval ratings rebounded. He took centrist positions on issues like abortion and affirmative action. He took pains to avoid being branded "liberal," signing the Republican welfare bill that ended 60-year-old guarantees for poor people. And he stood up to the aggressive Republican majority on the issue of how quickly to reduce the $4.5 trillion Federal deficit. This stalemate forced brief shutdowns of the Federal government in November 1995 and January 1996, which Clinton managed to blame on Gingrich.

Clinton's successes in foreign policy also buoyed him in 1995 and 1996 as he oversaw the peaceful election of a new president in Haiti, secured $20 billion in emergency loans to rescue Mexico from economic disaster, and established full diplomatic relations with Vietnam.

With the stock market soaring, unemployment falling, and inflation firmly in check, Clinton won reelection almost effortlessly against aging Senator Bob Dole, whose campaign lacked vigor and focus.

Clinton's second term began with modest goals. He remained on the defensive against a Republican Congress determined to pass tax cuts for the wealthy while cutting social programs. The Whitewater scandal, however, came back to haunt him in an unexpected way. Failing to uncover anything directly implicating the President or Mrs. Clinton in connection with the land deal, independent counsel Kenneth Starr expanded his inquiry far beyond its original scope and unearthed evidence of an affair between Clinton and a young White House intern, Monica Lewinsky. Clinton emphatically denied the allegation, but after becoming the first sitting president ever subpoenaed to testify before a federal grand jury, Clinton later admitted that he had had an "inappropriate" relationship with Monica Lewinsky.

Clinton's admission did little to hurt his approval ratings, which remained high, some said, because of the strong economy. In the 1998 elections, Democrats gained five seats in the House. Despite polls indicating that an overwhelming majority of Americans wanted Congress to drop the Lewinsky matter, the Republican-controlled House approved two articles of impeachment articles—perjury and obstruction of justice—against Clinton, making him the first president impeached since Andrew Johnson in 1868. The month-long Senate trial was filled with legal wrangling on all sides, but in the end, not even a simple majority could be mustered for either impeachment article, far short of the two-thirds needed for conviction.

Clinton appeared chastened, but not humbled, by the Lewinsky incident. The day after his acquittal, he sent 4,000 troops to Kosovo as part of a NATO peacekeeping force, and after a month of bitter debate, Congress approved more than $12 billion to fund the action. Many analysts doubted that NATO could halt Serbian aggression in the province without sending ground troops, but the alliance continued air strikes for 72 days until Serbian Pres. Slobodan Milosevic finally agreed to withdraw all military forces from Kosovo. An international peacekeeping force of 50,000 troops began policing Kosovo under the U.N. flag.

On the domestic front, Clinton and the Republican Congress battled over the a much-larger-than-expected budget surplus, the first since 1969. Clinton proposed shoring up Social Security and expanding Medicare to cover prescription drugs, which the Congress refused to pass, while the Republicans approved a $792 billion tax cut, which Clinton vetoed. The stalemate had one positive result, though: with money going to neither Republican tax cuts nor Clinton Administration spending proposals, the surplus went to paying off the most important component of the national debt: the $3.6 trillion in Treasury bonds. The two sides did get together to overturn major sections of the 1933 Glass-Steagall Act, which had prevented the securities, banking, and insurance industries from expanding into one another's businesses.

With Hillary running for a New York Senate seat and Al Gore distancing himself from the Clinton administration in his own bid for president, Bill Clinton spent much of his final year on a global "farewell tour" trying to shore up his legacy. In June, Clinton successfully shepherded a bill through Congress granting China permanent trade status. A September meeting with Chinese president Jiang Zemin, however, failed to produce any new agreements on missile exports, Tibet, or Taiwan. Throughout 2000, Clinton focused heavily on rekindled violence in Israel and Palestine. But despite a major summit at Camp David, frequent meetings with Palestinian leader Yasir Araft and Israeli Prime Minister Ehud Barak failed to produce any real breakthroughs.

Clinton used his power to make appointments during Congressional recess by appointing the first black judge to the U.S. Appeals Court in Richmond, Va. He also granted federal protection to large areas of land, including one that created the nation's largest nature preserve around the northwestern Hawaiian islands.

The Whitewater investigation officially came to a close in 2000. Clinton also reached a settlement with independent counsel Robert W. Ray on the Lewinsky case, bringing that investigation to an end on the condition that Clinton would admit to giving false testimony under oath, surrender his law license for five years, pay a fine to the Arkansas Bar Association and agree not to seek reimbursement of legal fees.

Clinton continued to steal the spotlight even after he left office. He and Hillary came under fire for taking thousands of dollars worth of gifts and furniture with them, including some items that were allegedly White House property. Hillary's brother Hugh Rodham was found to have accepted $400,000 in return for lobbying for presidential pardons for two felons. Most troubling, however, was Clinton's last-minute pardon of fugitive businessman Marc Rich, wanted for years on charges of tax evasion and illegal business deals with Iran.

43. George W. Bush (2001–)

The election of George Walker Bush was unusual in several ways. Like John Qunicy Adams, the only other son of a president to win the White House, Bush lost the popular vote (by more than 400,000 votes to Vice Pres. Al Gore). And he didn't capture a majority in the Electoral College until five weeks after the election, when the U.S. Supreme Court , largely along party lines, voted 5-4 to suspend recounts in Florida, which Bush appeared to win by fewer than 1,000 votes.

Bush was born on July 6, 1946 in New Haven, Connecticut. He identified himself as a native of Texas after his family moved there when he was almost two. His wealthy family connections helped him to land a spot at Yale University, where he continued his undistinguished academic career, and had several run-ins with the police over drunken pranks.

In 1968, at the height of the Vietnam War, Bush entered the Texas National Guard and spent two years learning to fly. In 1973 he attended Harvard Business School, received an M.B.A. in 1975, and returned to Texas to enter the oil business. He married Laura Welch, a Texas schoolteacher in 1977.

His first bid for public office, a 1978 campaign for a Congressional seat, ended in defeat. After the campaign, Bush returned to his oil business, amassing a great personal fortune even while his business steadily lost money until it was bought out in 1986. Meanwhile, in the summer of 1985, Bush's parents set up a meeting between him and evangelist Billy Graham, which led the younger Bush to a more serious practice of Christianity. A year later, concerned about the effect that excessive drinking and often-boisterous behavior were having on his wife and daughters, Bush swore off alcohol.

After cashing out of his oil company, Bush headed for Washington, D.C. in 1987 to work for his father's presidential campaign. In 1989, the younger Bush joined a family friend in purchasing the Texas Rangers baseball team, paying his share with funds borrowed against oil company stock.

In 1994, against the advice of friends and family, Bush made a surprising leap into the race for governor of Texas, challenging the popular incumbent Ann Richards. Despite his lack of political experience, Bush's down-home style won him the office with 54 percent of the vote. In 1998, he won again with 69 percent of the vote, becoming the first Texas governor elected to a second consecutive four-year term. That same year, he and his partners sold the Rangers, with the Governor realizing a profit of more than $14 million.

Though he was initially reluctant to run for president until his term as governor ended, advisers convinced him that the time was right in 2000. He was in an excellent financial position after the sale of the Rangers and the Republican party lacked any single strong candidate. Before he had even committed to the race, he was the clear favorite in the polls, and huge sums of money flowed into his campaign treasury from corporations and wealthy Republicans. Soon, however, Senator John McCain of Arizona emerged as a strong competitor in an unusually close primary race. After stating that he would rather be "underestimated than feared," Bush lost the New Hampshire primary to McCain but in a bruising, bitter fight, Bush came back to win South Carolina. The two remained neck-and-neck until Super Tuesday, when Bush won 9 of the 13 state primaries and effectively clinched the party nomination.

For vice president, Bush tapped Dick Cheney, secretary of defense under his father. Bush's campaign promised to restore dignity to the White House and pledged a huge tax cut intended to give a large part of the current and projected budget surplus back to the taxpayers. Throughout the race, Bush took pains to portray himself as a consensus-builder who would bring bipartisanship to Washington, but he was dogged by the public perception that he was a poor speaker and lacked comprehension of major issues.

After months of both candidates jockeying for the support of moderate and undecided voters, election night turned out to be closer than anyone anticipated. TV networks called the race for Gore on election night. Early the next morning, after an errror was detected in the Florida ballot counts, the networks projected Bush as the winner. Finally, around 4:30 a.m., they claimed that the race was in fact too close to call.

The next 36 days brought an unprecedented struggle over Florida ballots, both sides battling in the media and in state and federal court over buttefly ballots, dimpled chads, and the correct procedures for conducting recounts. Although Gore unquestionably won the national popular vote, Florida (with its 25 votes in the Electoral College) held the key to the election. After two recounts and the counting of absentee ballots, Bush led in Florida by fewer than 1,000 votes out of six million cast, but allegations of confusing ballots, defective voting machines and illegal barring of many voters threw the process into chaos. Bush remained calm, almost aloof during this time as his supporters continued to assert that he had won the election. The race finally ended on December 12, when the U.S. Supreme Court ordered an end to the recounts, delivering Florida and the White House to Bush. Gore conceded the next day.

For additional information about the first year of the Bush presidency, see Part I: "The Almanac of the Year."

Presidential Elections, 1796–2000

George Washington of Virginia ran unopposed for president in 1789 and 1792. He received 69 and 132 electoral votes in those years, respectively. John Adams of Massachusetts was elected vice-president in both years, receiving 34 and 77 electoral votes.

1796

Party	Candidate	Popular vote	Per- cent	Elec- toral vote
Federalist	John Adams (Mass.)	N.A.	N.A.	71
	and Thomas Pinckney (S.C.)	N.A.	N.A.	59
Democratic-	Thomas Jefferson (Va.)	N.A.	N.A.	68
Republican	and Aaron Burr (N.Y.)	N.A.	N.A.	30

Key Issues Washington set a precedent by refusing to run for a third term. Though the Founders hoped to avoid parties, factions developed around Hamilton and Jefferson during Washington's first term. Hamilton's Federalists supported a strong central government that would play a major role in the national economy and represent the commercial interests of the north. Jefferson's Republicans advocated states' rights and the agrarian interests of the south. Regional Influences Though led by Hamilton, the Federalists nominated the more moderate Adams. Jefferson's strength in the south was balanced by Adams's power in the north. Eleven Federalist electors in New Hampshire failed to vote for Pinckney, their party's vice-presidential nominee, giving the position to Jefferson.

1800

Party	Candidate	Popular vote	Per- cent	Elec- toral vote
Democratic-	Thomas Jefferson (Va.)	N.A.	N.A.	73
Republican	and Aaron Burr (N.Y.)	N.A.	N.A.	73
Federalist	John Adams (Mass.)	N.A.	N.A.	65
	and Charles C. Pinckney (S.C.)	N.A.	N.A.	64
Federalist	John Jay (N.Y.)	N.A.	N.A.	1

Key Issues Adams divided the Federalists by keeping the U.S. out of war with France over seizures of American ships by the French. In the meantime the Republicans under Jefferson organized nationally. They accused the Federalists of aristocratic and monarchical leanings, citing large taxes levied to maintain a standing army and navy, the Alien and Sedition Acts seeking to silence the administration's critics, and suppression of the Whiskey Rebellion. Regional Influences The Republicans again carried the South, but also won New York through the efforts of vice-presidential nominee Burr. The election was thrown into the House when Jefferson and Burr received an equal number of electoral votes. With Hamilton's support, Jefferson won the election in the Federalist-dominated House.

1804

Party	Candidate	Popular vote	Per- cent	Elec- toral vote
Democratic-	Thomas Jefferson (Va.)	N.A.	N.A.	162
Republican	and George Clinton (N.Y.)	N.A.	N.A.	162
Federalist	Charles C. Pinckney (S.C.)	N.A.	N.A.	14
	and Rufus King (N.Y.)	N.A.	N.A.	14

Key Issues In 1804 Vice-President Burr, a northern Republican, joined with a group of northeastern Federalists in a plot to unite New York and New England in a separate nation. The plot was exposed, discrediting the Federalists. Jefferson, already popular for his personal qualities as well as the Louisiana Purchase, swept to an easy victory. Regional Influences Jefferson lost only three states, and even swept all of New England with the exception of Connecticut.

1808

Party	Candidate	Popular vote	Per- cent	Elec- toral vote[1]
Democratic-	James Madison (Va.)	N.A.	N.A.	122
Republican	and George Clinton (N.Y.)	N.A.	N.A.	113
Federalist	Charles C. Pinckney (S.C.)	N.A.	N.A.	47
	and Rufus King (N.Y.)	N.A.	N.A.	47

Key Issues Jefferson reinforced the two-term precedent by refusing to run for a third term. Madison, his chosen successor, easily won the Republican nomination and the presidency. Regional Influences Pinckney and the Federalists regained most of the New England votes lost four years earlier and increased their strength in Congress due to commercial opposition to the embargo imposed by Jefferson on the export of American goods to warring European nations.

[1]Clinton received six electoral votes for president. Madison and James Monroe of Virginia both received three electoral votes for vice-president.

1812

Party	Candidate	Popular vote	Per- cent	Elec- toral vote
Democratic-	James Madison (Va.)	N.A.	N.A.	128
Republican	and Elbridge Gerry (Mass.)	N.A.	N.A.	131
Federalist	DeWitt Clinton (N.Y.)	N.A.	N.A.	89
	and Jared Ingersoll (Pa.)	N.A.	N.A.	86

Key Issues The election was a referendum on Madison's bid for a declaration of war against Great Britain in response to Britain's attempts to block the sale of southern raw materials in European markets. A vote for Madison was a vote for war, a vote for Clinton a vote for peace. Regional Influences Commercial interests in the northeast opposed war with Great Britain. The original 13 states were evenly split in the election, favoring Madison 90-89. New England, except Vermont, voted for Clinton, as did a majority of the Middle Atlantic states. The South voted unanimously for Madison. But all of the western states voted for Madison and thus for war.

1816

Party	Candidate	Popular vote	Per- cent	Elec- toral vote
Democratic-	James Monroe (Va.)	N.A.	N.A.	183
Republican	and D. D. Tompkins (N.Y.)	N.A.	N.A.	183
Federalist	Rufus King (N.Y.)	N.A.	N.A.	34
	and John E. Howard (Md.)	N.A.	N.A.	22

Key Issues Nationalism triumphed after the war with Britain, a time of national and economic growth that saw establishment of an expanded standing army, central bank, Federal tariff and large internal improvements despite opposition from northeastern Federalists. Regional Influences Monroe, Madison's chosen successor, won a landslide victory that seemed to validate Madison's nationalistic program, which called for a stronger standing army, a protective tariff, uniform currency and a nationwide system of roads and canals, including the Cumberland Road. The Federalists won only three states, all in New England.

1820

Party	Candidate	Popular vote	Per- cent	Elec- toral vote
Democratic-	James Monroe (Va.)	N.A.	N.A.	231
Republican	and D.D. Tompkins (N.Y.)	N.A.	N.A.	218
Democratic- Republican	John Q. Adams (Mass.)	N.A.	N.A.	1

Key Issues The election was held at the height of the "Era of Good Feelings," though sectional differences over slavery earlier in the year led to the Missouri Compromise, which in its final version resulted in the admittance of Missouri as a slave state with the provision that it allow free Negroes of other states to retain their freedom while in Missouri. The Federalists ceased to exist as a functioning party by the time of the election and failed to run a candidate against Monroe. **Regional Influences** Monroe ran unopposed for reelection. One elector from New Hampshire voted for Adams so that only Washington would hold the honor of being elected to the presidency by a unanimous vote.

1824

Party	Candidate	Popular vote	Per cent	Electoral vote
Democratic-Republican	John Q. Adams (Mass.)	113,122	30.92	84
Democratic-Republican	Andrew Jackson (Tenn.)	151,271	41.34	99
Democratic-Republican	William H. Crawford (Ga.)	40,876	11.17	41
Democratic-Republican	Henry Clay (Ky.)	47,531	12.99	37
Other		13,053	3.57	—
	Total Vote	365,833		
	Jackson Plurality	38,149		

Key Issues Personalities dominated an election in which all four candidates ran as Democratic-Republicans. Crawford, Monroe's treasury secretary, won the nomination of the party's congressional caucus. But few attended the caucus and most electors were chosen by state legislatures. Crawford later suffered a stroke and was not a serious candidate. John C. Calhoun of South Carolina ran unopposed for vice-president. **Regional Influences** Each candidate represented his region Adams the commercial northeast, Crawford the cotton south, Clay and Jackson the agrarian west. Jackson, a hero of the War of 1812 and battles against Indians, won a clear plurality of the popular vote and was the only candidate with support outside his home region. But no candidate won a majority of the electoral vote and the election was decided in the House, where Speaker Clay's support gave the victory to Adams.

1828

Party	Candidate	Popular vote	Per cent	Electoral vote
Democratic-Republican	Andrew Jackson (Tenn.) and John C. Calhoun (S.C.)	642,553	55.97	178 171
National-Republican	John Q. Adams (Mass.) and Richard Rush (Pa.)	500,987	43.63	83 83
Other		4,568	0.40	—
	Total Vote	1,148,018		
	Jackson Plurality	141,656		

Key Issues Personalities again overshadowed issues. The Jackson campaign catered to popular prejudices, portraying the contest as one between democracy and aristocracy. The Jackson coalition was a forerunner of the modern Democratic Party and reestablished two-party politics in the U.S. **Regional Influences** Jackson won the south and west easily, and appealed to discontented laborers in the north. Adams carried only New England, New Jersey, Maryland and Delaware.

1832

Party	Candidate	Popular vote	Per cent	Electoral vote
Democrat	Andrew Jackson (Tenn.) and Martin Van Buren (N.Y.)	701,780	54.23	219 189
National-Republican	Henry Clay (Ky.) and John Sergeant (Pa.)	484,205	37.42	49 49
Anti-Masonic	William Wirt (Md.) and Amos Ellmaker (Pa.)	100,715	7.78	7 7
Independent	John Floyd (Va.) and Henry Lee (Mass.)	—		11 11
Other		7,273	0.56	—
	Total Vote	1,293,973		
	Jackson Plurality	217,575		

Key Issues The Anti-Masons, the first third-party in American politics, began in opposition to secret societies in particular and privileged groups in general, but were at heart an anti-Jackson party. The two established parties followed the Anti-Masons lead by holding national nominating conventions to select a presidential nominee. While Jackson's opposition to the Bank of the United States was made an issue by the two major parties, the election was more a referendum on Jackson himself.

Regional Influences Anti-Masonic strength was concentrated in rural sections of New England and the Middle Atlantic states. In those states National-Republicans and Anti-Masons supported the same ticket. With the forces against him divided, Jackson won easily. Clay won only half of the New England states, Wirt won only Vermont. Jackson captured Maine and New Hampshire. In South Carolina, where electors still were chosen by the legislature, nullificationists cast their ballots for Floyd.

1836

Party	Candidate	Popular vote	Per cent	Electoral vote
Democrat	Martin Van Buren (N.Y.) and Richard M. Johnson (Ky.)	764,716 147	50.83	170
Whig	William Henry Harrison (Ohio)	550,816	36.63	73
Whig	Hugh L. White (Tenn.)	146,107	9.72	26
Whig	Daniel Webster (Mass.)	41,201	2.74	14
	Willie P. Mangum (N.C.)			11
Other		1,234	0.08	—
	Total Vote	1,503,534		
	Van Buren Plurality	213,360		

Key Issues Jackson's heavy-handed tactics, especially in his successful battle against the national bank, led the National-Republicans to rename themselves Whigs, after the 18th Century British party that tried to lessen the power of the crown. But lacking effective national leadership and divided along sectional lines, the anti-Jackson forces could not agree on a single candidate or platform and instead ran three regional candidates. **Regional Influences** Whig strategy was to throw the election into the House, where they could unite around a single candidate. Webster was to win New England, Harrison the west and Lawson the south. Van Buren, forced on the Democrats by Jackson, foiled the plan by picking up enough states throughout the nation to win by a slim majority. Johnson fell one electoral vote short of a majority for vice-president and was selected by the Senate. The South Carolina legislature cast its votes for Mangum.

1840

Party	Candidate	Popular vote	Per cent	Electoral vote
Whig	William Henry Harrison (Ohio) and John Tyler (Va.)	1,275,390	52.88	234
Democrat	Martin Van Buren (N.Y.)	1,128,854	46.81	60
Liberty	James G. Birney (N.Y.)	6,797	0.28	—
Other		767	0.03	—
	Total Vote	2,411,808		
	Harrison Plurality	146,536		

Key Issues With the country still reeling from the Panic of 1837, the Democrats were on the defensive. Though differences prevented them from writing a platform, the Whigs rallied around Harrison. In a campaign notable for its absence of issues, the Whigs turned the tables on Jackson's party. Harrison, despite his wealthy origins, was portrayed as the "log-cabin, hard-cider candidate" opposing the allegedly aristocratic Van Buren. The Democrats left the selection of a vice-presidential candidate to each state. **Regional Influences** Van Buren won only seven states, just one outside of the south or west. Harrison was long associated with the west and Tyler was a conservative Southerner and friend of Henry Clay. For the first time, active two-party politics was established across the nation. The 68-year-old Harrison caught a severe cold after delivering a lengthy Inaugural Address in the rain and died one month into his term.

1844

Party	Candidate	Popular vote	Per cent	Electoral vote
Democrat	James K. Polk (Tenn.) and George M. Dallas (Pa.)	1,339,494	49.54	170
Whig	Henry Clay (Ky.) and Theodore Frelinghuysen (N.J.)	1,300,004	48.08	
Abolitionist	James G. Birney (N.Y.)	62,103	2.30	—
Other		2,058	0.08	—
	Total Vote	2,703,659		
	Polk Plurality	39,490		

Key Issues Manifest Destiny, the goal of a U.S. stretching from the Atlantic to the Pacific, was the central issue because of the question of the annexation of Texas. With the election approaching, opponents of slavery lead the Senate to reject a treaty between Texas and the Tyler Administration that would have preserved Texan slavery and made it a U.S. territory. The two leading presidential candidates, Clay and Van Buren, sought to smother the slavery issue by ignoring it. But Polk snatched the Democratic nomination with his clear and vocal advocacy of annexation of Texas and general territorial expansion. **Regional Influences** Expansionism was immensely popular, especially in the south and west, where memories of the depression following 1837 added to the attraction of new, vast, and open public lands. Support for manifest destiny more than made up for anti-slavery sentiment elsewhere and Polk won a narrow plurality but a clear victory.

1848

Party	Candidate	Popular vote	Percent	Electoral vote
Whig	Zachary Taylor (La.) and Millard Fillmore (N.Y.)	1,361,393	47.28	163
Democrat	Lewis Cass (Mich.) and William O. Butler (Ky.)	1,223,460	42.49	127
Free Soil	Martin Van Buren (N.Y.) and Charles Francis Adams (Mass.)	291,501	10.12	—
Other		2,830	0.10	—
	Total Vote	2,879,184		
	Taylor Plurality	137,933		

Key Issues The Wilmot Proviso, calling for a ban on extension of slavery into territories acquired in the Mexican War, dominated the election. But both major parties evaded the issue. Slavery foes banded together to form the Free Soil Party, which won no electoral votes but drew enough popular support away from the Democrats to throw the election to "Old Rough and Ready," Zachary Taylor, a slave-holder. Taylor died in July 1850. **Regional Influences** Both major parties balanced their tickets with a Northerner and Southerner. Free Soilers were mostly Northern Democrats, anti-slavery Whigs and abolitionists. There was no distinct pattern in the Electoral College following a lackluster campaign. Free Soil strength in New York gave the state and the election to the Whigs.

1852

Party	Candidate	Popular vote	Percent	Electoral vote
Democrat	Franklin Pierce (N.H.) and William R. D. King (Ala.)	1,607,510	50.84	254
Whig	Winfield Scott (Va.) and William A. Graham (N.C.)	1,386,942	43.87	42
Free Soil	John P. Hale (N.H.) and George Washington Julian (Ind.)	155,210	4.91	—
Other		12,168	0.38	—
	Total Vote	3,161,830		
	Pierce Plurality	220,568		

Key Issues The election was a referendum on the Compromise of 1850, in which Congress voted to admit California as a free state, create the territories of New Mexico and Utah with no restriction on slavery, abolish the slave trade in the District of Columbia, purchase disputed land from Texas on behalf of New Mexico, and toughen the Fugitive Slave Act. The Democrats strongly endorsed the Compromise, but the bitterly divided Whigs only vaguely accepted it. **Regional Influences** The Democrats won a resounding electoral victory, capturing 27 states to the four taken by the Whigs Massachusetts, Vermont, Kentucky and Tennessee. Free Soilers returned to the Democrats and the Whigs never again were a political force in a nation which believed the slave question was behind it.

1856

Party	Candidate	Popular vote	Percent	Electoral vote
Democrat	James Buchanan (Pa.) and John C. Breckinridge (Ky.)	1,836,072	45.28	174
Republican	John C. Frémont (Calif.) and William L. Dayton (N.J.)	1,342,345	33.11	114
Whig	Millard Fillmore (N.Y.) and Andrew J. Donelson (Tenn.)	873,053	21.53	8
Other		3,177	0.08	—
	Total Vote	4,054,647		
	Buchanan Plurality	493,727		

Key Issues The Democrats firmly endorsed "popular sovereignty" even though it led to great turmoil in the territory of Kansas. But they chose as their nominee Buchanan, largely because he had been out of the country and was untainted by "Bleeding Kansas" battle, which pitted supporters and foes of slavery trying to organize the territory into a slave or free state. The Republicans, a new party of northern Whigs and Democrats committed to the containment of slavery ran Fremont, a popular general and explorer. **Regional Influences** Frémont carried all but five of the free states. But Buchanan won all of the south in addition to the five northern states and was elected. Fillmore, supported by the Know-Nothings and Whig remnants, only won Maryland but strongly challenged the Democrats in the south.

1860

Party	Candidate	Popular vote	Percent	Electoral vote
Republican	Abraham Lincoln (Ill.) and Hannibal Hamlin (Maine)	1,865,908	39.82	180
Democrat	Stephen A. Douglas (Ill.) and Herschel V. Johnson (Ga.)	1,380,202	29.46	12
Democrat	John C. Breckinridge (Ky.) and Joseph Lane (Oreg.)	848,019	18.09	72
Constitutional Union and Other	John Bell (Tenn.) Edward Everett (Mass.)	590,901	12.61	39
		531	0.01	—
	Total Vote	4,685,561		
	Lincoln Plurality	485,706		

Key Issues Sectional differences over slavery came to a head in 1860. The Democrats could not agree on a candidate and split into northern and southern factions. The Northerners backed Douglas and popular sovereignty, the Southerners Breckinridge and Federal protection of slavery in the territories. The Republicans, virtually all Northerners, were a pro-tariff, nationalistic party that opposed the extension of slavery but did not seek to overturn it where it already existed. Bell, the candidate of Whigs and Know-Nothings who backed Fillmore in 1856, were a compromise party expressing support for preservation of the Union. **Regional Influences** In effect there were two separate contests in 1860 Lincoln versus Douglas in the north, Breckinridge versus Bell in the south. Free states outnumbered slave states and cast half again as many electoral votes. Lincoln won every northern state except New Jersey and, though not even on the ballot in 10 southern states, was elected president. Breckinridge captured 11 of the 15 southern states. The four southern states won by Douglas and Bell were in the upper south.

1864

Party	Candidate	Popular vote	Percent	Electoral vote
Republican	Abraham Lincoln (Ill.) and Andrew Johnson (Tenn.)	2,218,388	55.02	212
Democrat	George B. McClellan (N.Y.) and George H. Pendleton (Ohio)	1,812,807	44.96	21
	Total Vote	4,031,887		
	Lincoln Plurality	405,581		

Key Issues Lincoln's renomination was not assured. Radical Republicans thought he was not aggressive enough in his conduct of the war or plans for the eventual peace, but moderation ultimately prevailed. The Republicans ran as the Union Party and nominated Johnson, a pro-Union Democrat, for vice-president. The Democrats ran a peace campaign, calling the war a failure. But McClellan, a popular general, broke with his party's platform and denied the war was a failure, denouncing members of his party who seemed to advocate peace at any price. He opposed emancipation as a goal of the war. **Regional Influences** Military victories around election time helped the embattled incumbent. Lincoln won a convincing popular and electoral victory with the support of middle-class professionals, farmers, laborers and the strongly pro-Union voters who voted for Bell four years earlier. McClellan was strongest in areas carried by Breckinridge four years before. Eleven Confederate states did not participate in the election.

1868

Party	Candidate	Popular vote	Percent	Electoral vote
Republican	Ulysses S. Grant (Ohio) and Schuyler Colfax (Ind.)	3,013,650	52.66	214
Democrat	Horatio S. Seymour (N.Y.) and Francis P. Blair (Mo.)	2,708,744	47.34	80
Other		46	—	—
	Total Vote	5,722,440		
	Grant Plurality	304,906		

Key Issues The Republicans waved the "bloody shirt" of the war and ran on their program of Radical Reconstruction. While calling for Negro suffrage in the south, the Republicans asserted it was a matter for individual northern states to decide for themselves. Democrats ran against Reconstruction, declaring that the question of Negro suffrage should be decided by individual southern states as well. **Regional Influences** Despite Grant's popularity, the Republicans were just able to win the election. Seymour carried only eight states, though he did well in the states won by Grant. Without black votes in the South, Grant would not have received a majority of the popular vote. The votes of the "unreconstructed" states of Mississippi, Texas and Virginia were not counted.

1872

Party	Candidate	Popular vote	Percent	Electoral vote
Republican	Ulysses S. Grant (Ohio) and Henry Wilson (Mass.)	3,598,235	55.63	286
Liberal Republican/ Democrat	Horace Greeley (N.Y.) and Benjamin Gratz Brown (Mo.)	2,834,761	43.83	—
Straight Democrat	Charles O'Conor (N.Y.)	18,602	—	—
	Other	16,081	0.25	—
	Total Vote	6,467,679		
	Grant Plurality	763,474		

Key Issues Liberal Republicans broke with Grant over corruption in his administration, high tariffs and continued Radical Reconstruction. They nominated Greeley, editor of the *New York Tribune*. The Democrats endorsed Greeley and the Liberal platform. But the great scandals of the Grant administration were not yet revealed and the Republicans again waved the bloody shirt to victory. **Regional Influences** Greeley carried only two states in the lower South and four border states. He died shortly after the election (Nov. 29, 1872) and his electoral votes went to other candidates: Thomas Hendricks, Indiana, 42; Benjamin Gratz Brown, Missouri, 18; Charles J. Jenkins, Georgia, 2; and David Davis, Illinois, 1.

> *"Great men are not chosen president, firstly because great men are rare in politics; secondly, because the method of choice does not bring them to the top; thirdly, because they are not, in quiet times, absolutely necessary."*
> –English jurist, historian, and diplomat James Bryce,
> *The American Commonwealth* (1888)

1876

Party	Candidate	Popular vote	Percent	Electoral vote
Republican	Rutherford B. Hayes (Ohio) and William A. Wheeler (N.Y.)	4,034,311	47.95	185
Democrat	Samuel J. Tilden (N.Y.) and Thomas A. Hendricks (Ind.)	4,288,546	50.97	184
Greenback	Peter Cooper (N.Y.)	75,973	0.90	—
Other		14,271	0.17	—
	Total Vote	8,413,101		
	Tilden Plurality	254,235		

Key Issues The Republicans were in trouble as 1876 approached due to rampant corruption in the Grant administration and the economic depression that followed the Panic of 1873. Hayes, a three-term Ohio governor known for his unassailable integrity, was nominated to run against the favored Democrat, Tilden, a New York reform governor whose reputation was made in opposition to the Tweed political machine. Both men espoused conservative economics. Cooper and the Greenbacks advocated currency expansion. **Regional Influences** As Election Day approached, Tilden could count on winning all of the south except for the three states still controlled by Republican carpetbaggers: South Carolina, Louisiana, and Florida. He seemed assured of victory when those states appeared to vote for him along with several northern states, including New York and New Jersey. But Republicans claimed South Carolina, Louisiana and Florida for Hayes, arguing that thousands of blacks who would have voted for Hayes were barred from voting there. Election boards in those Republican-controlled states gave Hayes the needed majority, and thus the election. In the uproar that followed Congress set up an Election Commission to validate the returns. The commission voted strictly along party lines, eight to seven, to give the election to Hayes. Despite charges that Republicans stole the election, Hayes later was inaugurated peaceably after he let it be known that as president he would end military reconstruction by withdrawing Federal troops from the south and that he would restore "efficient local government" to the south.

1880

Party	Candidate	Popular vote	Percent	Electoral vote
Republican	James A. Garfield (Ohio) and Chester A. Arthur (N.Y.)	4,461,158	48.27	214
Democrat	Winfield S. Hancock (Pa.) and William H. English (Ind.)	4,444,260	48.25	155
Greenback	James B. Weaver (Iowa) and Benjamin J. Chambers (Tex.)	305,997	3.32	—
Other		14,005	0.15	—
	Total Vote	9,210,420		
	Garfield Plurality	1,898		

Key Issues With the war and Reconstruction behind, no major issues arose over which the major parties disagreed. The Democrats, the party of secession 20 year earlier, nominated General Hancock to help combat the stigma of treason. Garfield made a protectionist tariff central to his campaign. **Regional Influences** The balance between Republican strength in the Midwest and west and Democratic strength in the south resulted in a plurality of less than 2,000 for Garfield out of more than 9 million votes cast. Four months into his term Garfield was shot by a disappointed office-seeker.

1884

Party	Candidate	Popular vote	Percent	Electoral vote
Democrat	Grover Cleveland (N.Y.) and Thomas A. Hendricks (Ind.)	4,874,621	48.50	219
Republican	James G. Blaine (Maine) and John A. Logan (Ill.)	4,848,936	48.25	182
Greenback	Benjamin F. Butler (Mass.)	175,096	1.74	—
Prohibition	John P. St. John (Kans.)	147,482	1.47	—
Other		3,619	0.04	—
	Total Votes	10,049,754		
	Cleveland Plurality	25,685		

Key Issues The private lives and morals of the candidates were the focus of a campaign notable for mudslinging. Blaine was accused of accepting bribes from a railroad company for whom he obtained a Federal grant and Republicans taunted Cleveland for fathering a son out of wedlock. Still, Cleveland, known for his independence and integrity in public life, attracted the votes of many liberal Republicans and reformers unable to stomach Blaine, a Radical Republican leader. **Regional Influences** Cleveland carried all of the southern states as well as the key swing states of Indiana, New Jersey, Connecticut and New York, becoming the first Democrat elected president since the Civil War. Cleveland carried his home state of New York and its 36 electoral votes by less than 1,200 votes.

1888

Party	Candidate	Popular vote	Per-cent	Elec-toral vote
Republican	Benjamin Harrison (Ind.) and Levi P. Morton (N.Y.)	5,443,892	47.82	233
Democrat	Grover Cleveland (N.Y.) and Allen G. Thurman (Ohio)	5,534,488	48.62	168
Prohibition	Clinton B. Fisk (N.J.)	249,813	2.19	—
Union Labor	Alson J. Streeter (Ill.)	146,602	1.29	—
Other		8,519	0.07	—
	Total Votes	11,383,320		
	Cleveland Plurality	90,596		

Key Issues Cleveland made tariff reform central to his administration, seeking to lower existing high tariffs. The Republicans campaigned on the need to maintain high wages by keeping a high tariff on imported goods. **Regional Influences** Despite the emphasis on the tariff, Cleveland still carried such manufacturing states as New Jersey and Connecticut as well as most of the south. But though Cleveland won 90,000 more popular votes than Harrison, the Republican carried the pro-tariff swing states of Indiana and New York by slight margins to win the election in the electoral college in one of the most corrupt campaigns in history.

1892

Party	Candidate	Popular vote	Per-cent	Elec-toral vote
Democrat	Grover Cleveland (N.Y.) and Adlai E. Stevenson (Ill.)	5,551,883	46.05	277
Republican	Benjamin Harrison (Indiana) and Whitelaw Reid (N.Y.)	5,179,244	42.96	145
Populist	James B. Weaver (Iowa) and James G. Field (Virginia)	1,024,280	8.50	22
Prohibition	John Bidwell (California)	270,770	2.25	—
Other		29,920	0.25	
	Total Votes	12,056,097		
	Cleveland Plurality	372,639		

Key Issues Cleveland and Harrison again fought a battle over the tariff, which the Republicans drastically raised in 1890. Both men were out of touch with the growing agrarian and populist discontent. Weaver, campaigning for free silver, became the first third-party candidate to gain electoral votes since the war. **Regional Influences** Cleveland improved upon his 1884 and 1888 showings to win the most decisive presidential victory in 20 years. This time he carried the swing states of New York, New Jersey, Connecticut and Indiana as well as the traditionally Republican states of Illinois, California and Wisconsin.

1896

Party	Candidate	Popular vote	Per-cent	Elec-toral vote
Republican	William McKinley (Ohio) and Garret A. Hobart (N.J.)	7,108,480	51.01	271
Democrat/ Populist	William J. Bryan (Nebr.) and Democrat Arthur Sewall (Me.) and Populist Thomas E. Watson (Ga.)	6,511,495	46.73	176 149
National Democrat	John M. Palmer (Ill.)	133,435	0.96	—
Prohibition	Joshua Levering (Md.)	125,072	0.90	—
Other		57,256	0.41	—
	Total Votes	13,935,738		
	McKinley Plurality	596,985		

Key Issues The Democrats absorbed Populist energies and abandoned the conservatism of Cleveland by nominating Bryan and adopting key elements of the Populist program, especially the call for free silver. The pro-tariff and pro-gold Republicans led by McKinley and Mark Hanna outspent the Democrats by almost 12 to 1. In losing, Bryan amassed more votes than any victorious candidate before him. **Regional Influences** Bryan did not carry a single state north of Virginia or east of Missouri. His hold on the agricultural south and west was broken by Republican victories in Maryland, Delaware, West Virginia, Kentucky, California and Oregon. Bryan, failing to appeal to labor, carried no industrial or urban states.

1900

Party	Candidate	Popular vote	Per-cent	Elec-toral vote
Republican	William McKinley (Ohio) and Theodore Roosevelt (N.Y.)	7,218,039	51.67	292
Democrat	William J. Bryan (Nebr.) and Adlai E. Stevenson (Ill.)	6,358,345	45.51	155
Prohibition	John C. Woolley (Ill.)	209,004	1.50	—
Social Democrat	Eugene V. Debs (Ind.)	86,935	0.62	—
Other		98,147	0.70	—
	Total Vote	13,970,470		
	McKinley Plurality	859,694		

Key Issues Imperialism in the Philippines joined free silver and the tariff as the key issues in a replay of the 1896 election. Bryan tried to unite the silver interests in the west and south with supporters of the gold standard in a coalition against imperialism, which the Democratic platform called the "paramount issue" of the campaign. But voters did not desert McKinley in a time of prosperity. **Regional Influences** Bryan carried only the Solid South and four silver states in the west, and was defeated in the silver states of Kansas, South Dakota, Utah and Wyoming as well as his home state of Nebraska. Both houses of Congress were led by significant Republican majorities.

1904

Party	Candidate	Popular vote	Per-cent	Elec-toral vote
Republican	Theodore Roosevelt (N.Y.) and Charles W. Fairbanks (Ind.)	7,626,593	56.41	336
Democrat	Alton B. Parker (N.Y.) and Henry G. Davis (W. Va.)	5,082,898	37.60	140
Socialist	Eugene V. Debs (Ind.)	402,489	2.98	—
Prohibition	Silas C. Swallow (Pa.)	258,596	1.91	—
Other		148,388	1.10	—
	Total Votes	13,518,964		
	Roosevelt Plurality	2,543,695		

Key Issues Roosevelt stole the mantle of reform from the Democrats with his campaigns against the "malefactors of great wealth." The Democrats turned to the right by nominating the lackluster Parker, a judge with close ties to Wall Street. Parker turned his back on Bryan Democrats by renouncing free silver. **Regional Influences** Roosevelt won a landslide victory based largely on his own personality and popularity. The Democrats won only 13 states, none outside the south.

1908

Party	Candidate	Popular vote	Per-cent	Elec-toral vote
Republican	William H. Taft (Ohio) and James S. Sherman (N.Y.)	7,662,258	51.58	321
Democrat	William J. Bryan (Nebr.) and John W. Kern (Ind.)	6,406,801	43.05	162
Socialist	Eugene V. Debs (Ind.)	420,380	2.82	—
Prohibition	Eugene W. Chafin (Ill.)	252,821	1.70	—
Other		126,474	0.85	—
	Total Vote	14,882,734		
	Taft Plurality	1,269,457		

Key Issues The immensely popular Roosevelt declined to run. Taft, his secretary of war and handpicked successor, debated Bryan over who was better qualified to complete TR's progressive program. Bryan abandoned silver and courted labor but ran a lackluster losing campaign. **Regional Influences** Bryan again carried the South. But the appeal of Roosevelt's reform programs helped the Republicans to do well in the west and Taft's background as a Yale graduate and Federal jurist enabled him to carry the east as well.

1912

Party	Candidate	Popular vote	Per-cent	Electoral vote
Democrat	Woodrow Wilson (N.J.) and Thomas Marshall (Ind.)	6,293,152	41.84	435
Progressive	Theodore Roosevelt (N.Y.) and Hiram Johnson (Calif.)	4,119,207	27.39	88
Republican	William H. Taft (Ohio) and James S. Sherman (N.Y.)	3,486,333	23.18	8
Socialist	Eugene V. Debs (Ind.)	900,369	5.99	—
Other		241,902	1.61	—
	Total Vote	15,040,963		
	Wilson Plurality	2,173,945		

Key Issues Taft's conservatism and political ineptitude led Roosevelt to challenge him within the party from the left. Unable to wrest the nomination from Taft, Roosevelt ran a third-party campaign. The election boiled down to a contest between Roosevelt and Wilson and their respective conceptions of progressivism. Roosevelt's "New Nationalism" called for strong Federal regulations to control the trusts and big businesses. Wilson's "New Freedom" sought instead to revive competition through vigorous application of anti-trust laws. The Progressives advocated a broad array of social reforms to be implemented by the Federal government while the Democrats emphasized the primacy of the states in such matters. **Regional Influences** Though he amassed fewer votes than did Bryan in 1908, Wilson took advantage of the split in the Republican ranks to win a decisive plurality of the vote. He did best in traditional Democratic states, but was able to win most traditionally Republican states as well. Roosevelt won only 6 states, including California, which he carried by fewer than 200 votes. Taft carried Utah and Vermont. The Democrats also won control of both houses of Congress, their best overall performance since the Civil War.

1916

Party	Candidate	Popular vote	Per-cent	Electoral vote
Democrat	Woodrow Wilson (N.J.) and Thomas Marshall (Ind.)	9,126,300	49.24	277
Republican	Charles Evans Hughes (N.Y.) and Charles W. Fairbanks (Ind.)	8,546,789	46.11	254
Socialist	Allen L. Benson (N.Y.)	589,924	3.18	—
Prohibition	James F. Hanly (Ind.)	221,030	1.19	—
Other		50,979	0.28	—
	Total Vote	18,535,022		
	Wilson Plurality	579,511		

Key Issues The campaign was a referendum on Wilson's first term, his program of domestic reform, and his policy toward the war in Europe. He ran a peace campaign with the slogan "He kept us out of war" and attracted the votes of many Bull Moosers. Voters who felt Wilson was either too harsh or too lenient toward Germany tended to vote Republican. Irish-American and German-American extremists, virulently opposed to aiding Great Britain, embarrassed Hughes with their vocal support. A coalition of labor, farmers, reformers, and intellectuals won the election for Wilson. **Regional Influences** Hughes, a former reform governor of New York who left the Supreme Court to challenge Wilson, carried all of the east except New Hampshire and all of the Old Northwest except Ohio. But the South was again solid for the Democrats and so was every state west of the Mississippi except Minnesota, Iowa, South Dakota and Oregon, which Wilson lost by close margins. The electoral vote was the closest since 1876.

1920

Party	Candidate	Popular vote	Per-cent	Electoral vote
Republican	Warren G. Harding (Ohio) and Calvin Coolidge (Mass.)	16,133,314	60.30	404
Democrat	James M. Cox (Ohio) and Franklin D. Roosevelt (N.Y.)	9,140,884	34.17	127
Socialist	Eugene V. Debs (Ind.)	913,664	3.42	—
Farmer-Labor	Parley P. Christensen (Utah)	264,540	0.99	—
Other		301,384	1.13	—
	Total Vote	26,753,786		
	Harding Plurality	6,992,430		

Key Issues The voters turned against Wilsonian progressivism and internationalism by electing Harding, a vacuous party hack who promised a "return to normalcy" after the turbulent years of domestic reform and world war. The undistinguished Cox ran in support of the League of Nations and little else. **Regional Influences** Harding carried every state outside of the south, except Tennessee. The Republicans added to their majorities in both houses of Congress, regained in 1918.

1924

Party	Candidate	Popular vote	Per-cent	Electoral vote
Republican	Calvin Coolidge (Mass.) and Charles G. Dawes (Ohio)	15,717,553	54.00	382
Democrat	John W. Davis (N.Y.) and Charles W. Bryan (Nebr.)	8,386,169	28.84	136
Progressive Socialist	Robert M. LaFollette (Wis.) and Burton K. Wheeler (Mont.)	4,814,050	16.56	13
Other		158,187	0.55	—
	Total Vote	29,075,959		
	Coolidge Plurality	7,331,384		

Key Issues The country "kept cool with Coolidge" as the Democrats could not overcome prosperity or themselves. Davis, a conservative Wall Street lawyer, was a compromise nominee selected by a bitterly divided party after 103 ballots. Reformers, labor and farmers flocked to the LaFollette candidacy. **Regional Influences** All 12 of the Democratic states were from the south. LaFollette's 13 electoral votes came from his home of Wisconsin.

1928

Party	Candidate	Popular vote	Per-cent	Electoral vote
Republican	Herbert C. Hoover (Calif.) and Charles E. Curtis (Kans.)	21,411,911	58.20	444
Democrat	Alfred E. Smith (N.Y.) and Joseph T. Robinson (Ark.)	15,000,185	40.77	87
Socialist	Norman Thomas (N.Y.)	266,453	0.72	—
Worker's	William Z. Foster (Ill.)	48,170	0.13	—
Other		63,565	0.17	—
	Total Vote	36,790,364		
	Hoover Plurality	6,411,806		

Key Issues Booze, bigotry, Tammany, and prosperity did in the Democrats. Rural America would not vote for an anti-Prohibition, big-city, Catholic machine politician, despite Smith's success as governor of New York, especially while the Republicans could convincingly cite the success of their economic leadership. **Regional Influences** The solid south was shattered as Hoover Democrats gave Republicans the states of Virginia, North Carolina, Tennessee, Florida and Texas for the first time since Reconstruction. Smith lost his own state and every western and border state. But Smith set the stage for the New Deal coalition with the votes of urban ethnics, he carried the nation's 12 largest cities, all of which had been won by the Republicans four years earlier. The Democrats also won votes in the traditionally Republican west among farmers unsure about prosperity.

1932

Party	Candidate	Popular vote	Per-cent	Electoral vote
Democrat	Franklin D. Roosevelt (N.Y.) and John Nance Garner (Tex.)	22,825,016	57.42	472
Republican	Herbert C. Hoover (Calif.) and Charles E. Curtis (Kans.)	15,758,397	39.64	59
Socialist	Norman Thomas (N.Y.)	883,990	2.22	—
Communist	William Z. Foster (Ill.)	102,221	0.26	—
Other		179,758	0.45	—
	Total Vote	39,749,382		
	Roosevelt Plurality	7,066,619		

Key Issues The Democrats won by blaming the Republicans for the Great Depression. Roosevelt was the first presidential nominee of a major party to address his nominating convention, pledging to help "the forgotten man at the bottom of the economic pyramid." In a vague and contradictory platform, the Democrats promised to balance the Federal budget by drastically reducing expenses and vowed to spend Federal dollars to attack the nation's economic woes. **Regional Influences** Roosevelt lost only six states, Maine, New Hampshire, Vermont, Connecticut, Delaware, and Pennsylvania, carrying all of the agricultural West and South. He put the finishing touches on the New Deal coalition by also improving upon Smith's margins of victory in the nation's big cities.

1936

Party	Candidate	Popular vote	Per-cent	Electoral vote
Democrat	Franklin D. Roosevelt (N.Y.) and John Nance Garner (Tex.)	27,747,636	60.79	523
Republican	Alfred M. Landon (Kans.) and Frank Knox (Ill.)	16,679,543	36.54	8
Union	William Lemke (N.Dak.)	892,492	1.96	—
Socialist	Norman Thomas (N.Y.)	187,785	0.41	—
Other		134,847	0.30	—
	Total Vote	45,642,303		
	Roosevelt Plurality	11,068,093		

Key Issues Despite intense opposition to the New Deal, its great public appeal was confirmed in the most one-sided election since 1820 and sweeping victories for the Democrats in Congress. The populist forces of the late Huey Long coalesced around Lemke but failed to gather widespread support. **Regional Influences** Roosevelt carried every state except Maine and Vermont. The New Deal coalition was at its height as every large city voted overwhelmingly for FDR. The middle-class, farmers in the west and south, big-city ethnics, labor and reform intellectuals flocked to the Democrats. Northern Blacks also began to vote heavily Democratic for the first time.

1940

Party	Candidate	Popular vote	Per-cent	Electoral vote
Democrat	Franklin D. Roosevelt (N.Y.) and Henry A. Wallace (Iowa)	27,263,448	54.70	449
Republican	Wendell L. Willkie (Ind.) and Charles L. McNary (Oreg.)	22,336,260	44.82	82
Socialist	Norman Thomas (N.Y.)	116,827	0.23	—
Prohibition	Roger W. Babson (Mass.)	58,685	0.12	—
Other		65,223	0.13	—
	Total Vote	49,840,443		
	Roosevelt Plurality	4,927,188		

Key Issues With war raging in Europe the electorate turned its attention from domestic to foreign affairs. The international scene led the Democrats to break with tradition and renominate FDR for a third term. The Republicans turned to businessman and political neophyte Willkie, a charismatic former Democrat. Willkie's internationalism and the pledge of both candidates to keep the U.S. out of the war minimized the role of foreign policy in the campaign. **Regional Influences** Willkie carried only 10 states, mostly in the Midwest. But Roosevelt's percentage of the popular vote was markedly down from 1936.

1944

Party	Candidate	Popular vote	Per-cent	Electoral vote
Democrat	Franklin D. Roosevelt (N.Y.) and Harry S Truman (Mo.)	25,611,936	53.39	432
Republican	Thomas E. Dewey (N.Y.) and John W. Bricker (Ohio)	22,013,372	45.89	99
Socialist	Norman Thomas (N.Y.)	79,100	0.16	—
Prohibition	Claude A. Watson (Calif.)	74,733	0.16	—
Other		195,778	0.41	—
	Total Vote	47,974,819		
	Roosevelt Plurality	3,598,564		

Key Issues With both candidates supporting New Deal social legislation and an international organization to maintain the peace after the war, the nation chose to let FDR lead America into the post-war era. Big-city bosses and southern conservatives, with FDR's private support, ousted Wallace from the ticket in favor of Truman. **Regional Influences** Roosevelt won 36 states and the Democrats improved their control over Congress and the nation's statehouses. The Republicans only won a handful of western and New England states.

1948

Party	Candidate	Popular vote	Per-cent	Electoral vote
Democrat	Harry S Truman (Mo.) and Alben W. Barkley (Ky.)	24,105,587	49.51	303
Republican	Thomas E. Dewey (N.Y.) and Earl Warren (Calif.)	21,970,017	45.12	189
States' Rights	Strom Thurmond (S.C.) and Fielding L. Wright (Miss.)	1,169,134	2.40	39
Progressive	Henry A. Wallace (Iowa) and Glen H. Taylor (Idaho)	1,157,057	2.38	—
Other		290,647	0.60	—
	Total Vote	48,692,442		
	Truman Plurality	2,135,570		

Key Issues The Republicans were sure of victory after 16 years of Democratic rule and the desertion of the Democrats by conservative Southern Dixiecrats and the ultra-liberal Wallace faction. But Dewey's dour personality and Truman's intense whistle-stop campaign against the "do-nothing, good-for-nothing" Republican Eightieth Congress resulted in one of the biggest upsets in presidential history. **Regional Influences** Dewey captured all of the Middle Atlantic and New England states, except Massachusetts and Connecticut, along with the Dakotas, Nebraska and Kansas in the Midwest and Oregon in the northwest. Thurmond won South Carolina, Mississippi, Alabama and Louisiana in the Deep South.

1952

Party	Candidate	Popular vote	Per-cent	Electoral vote
Republican	Dwight D. Eisenhower (Kans.) and Richard M. Nixon (Calif.)	33,936,137	55.13	442
Democrat	Adlai E. Stevenson (Ill.) and John J. Sparkman (Ala.)	27,314,649	44.38	89
Progressive	Vincent W. Hallinan (Calif.)	140,416	0.23	—
Prohibition	Stuart Hamblen (Calif.)	73,413	0.12	—
Other		86,503	0.14	—
	Total Vote	61,551,118		
	Eisenhower Plurality	6,621,485		

Key Issues Popular war hero Eisenhower swept to victory after uniting the internationalist and isolationist factions of the Republican party. He routed the Democrats by promising to kick out alleged crooks and communists in Washington, wage a more aggressive fight against communists worldwide and "go to Korea," implying that he had a plan to end the war there. **Regional Influences** Stevenson, who appealed to northern liberals as well as southern states' rights Democrats, carried only nine states in the south. The Republicans also won slight majorities in both houses of Congress and were in control of the national government for the first time in 20 years.

1956

Party	Candidate	Popular vote	Percent	Electoral vote
Republican	Dwight D. Eisenhower (Kans.) and Richard M. Nixon (Calif.)	35,585,247	57.37	457
Democrat	Adlai E. Stevenson (Ill.) and Estes Kefauver (Tenn.)	26,030,172	41.97	73
Constitution/ States' Rights	T. Coleman Andrews (Va.)	108,055	0.17	—
Socialist-Labor	Eric Hass (New York)	44,300	0.07	—
Other		257,600	0.42	—
	Total Vote	62,025,372		
	Eisenhower Plurality	9,555,073		

Key Issues Eisenhower won an easy victory in a rematch of the 1952 election. His popularity did not translate into victories for his party elsewhere, as Democrats increased their control of Congress, regained in 1954, and their hold on the nation's governorships. **Regional Influences** Winning even more handsomely than he did in 1952, Eisenhower lost only seven southern states.

1960

Party	Candidate	Popular vote	Percent	Electoral vote
Democrat	John F. Kennedy (Mass.) and Lyndon B. Johnson (Tex.)	34,221,344	49.72	303
Republican	Richard M. Nixon (Calif.) and Henry Cabot Lodge (Mass.)	34,106,671	49.55	219
Socialist-Labor	Eric Hass (N.Y.)	47,522	0.07	—
Other		337,175	0.48	15
Unpledged		116,248	0.17	—
	Total Vote	68,828,960		
	Kennedy Plurality	114,673		

Key Issues Kennedy called for the government to play a larger role in stimulating the national economy in order to fund domestic social programs as well as to sustain a defense build-up and keep ahead militarily of the Soviet Union. The election was the first in which there were nationally televised debates between the two candidates. Kennedy's slick television performance played a role in his narrow triumph. **Regional Influences** The Democrats won a thin victory by narrowly defeating the Republicans in the Middle Atlantic states, the Deep South, Illinois and Texas. Nixon carried most of the Midwest, border and western states. Conservative Democratic Senator Harry F. Byrd of Virginia received 15 electoral votes: all eight of Mississippi's, six of Alabama's, and one of Oklahoma's eight.

1964

Party	Candidate	Popular vote	Percent	Electoral vote
Democrat	Lyndon B. Johnson (Tex.) and Hubert H. Humphrey (Minn.)	43,126,584	61.05	486
Republican	Barry M. Goldwater (Ariz.) and William E. Miller (N.Y.)	27,177,838	38.47	52
Socialist-Labor	Eric Hass (N.Y.)	45,187	0.06	—
Socialist Workers	Clifton DeBerry (N.Y.)	32,701	0.05	—
Other		258,794	0.37	—
	Total Vote	70,641,104		
	Johnson Plurality	15,948,746		

Key Issues Johnson ran for election in his own right on the basis of his Great Society domestic programs. The reactionary Goldwater campaigned against the New Deal and for the bombing of North Vietnam. **Regional Influences** Johnson won all but six states—Goldwater's home state of Arizona and five states in the Deep South—in the biggest popular and electoral landslide since 1936. Forty new Northern Democrats were elected to the House on LBJ's coattails.

1968

Party	Candidate	Popular vote	Percent	Electoral vote
Republican	Richard M. Nixon (Calif.) and Spiro T. Agnew (Md.)	31,785,148	43.42	301
Democrat	Hubert H. Humphrey (Minn.) and Edmund S. Muskie (Maine)	31,274,503	42.72	191
American Independent	George C. Wallace (Ala.) and Curtis LeMay (Ohio)	901,151	13.53	46
Socialist-Labor	Henning A. Blomen (Mass.)	52,591	0.07	—
Other		189,977	0.20	—
	Total Vote	73,203,370		
	Nixon Plurality	510,645		

Key Issues With the country divided over Vietnam, Humphrey failed to emerge from the shadow of the unpopular Johnson, while the previously hawkish Nixon pledged to end the war and hinted that he had a secret plan to do so. Wallace attacked Federal encroachment on states' rights, desegregation, "pointy-headed" intellectuals and the Administration's timidity in Vietnam, in an effort to capture blue-collar votes. **Regional Influences** Barely more than 500,000 votes separated Nixon and Humphrey, but the Republican edge in the Electoral College was comfortable and the combined anti-Democratic vote amounted to a repudiation of the Johnson-Humphrey Administration. Humphrey's strength was in the eastern seaboard states. Wallace won five states in the Deep South.

1972

Party	Candidate	Popular vote	Percent	Electoral vote
Republican	Richard M. Nixon (Calif.) and Spiro T. Agnew (Md.)	47,170,179	60.69	520
Democrat	George S. McGovern (S.Dak.) and R. Sargent Shriver (Md.)	29,171,791	37.53	17
American Independent	John G. Schmitz (Calif.)	1,090,673	1.40	—
People's	Benjamin Spock	78,751	0.10	—
Other		216,196	0.28	(1)
	Total Vote	77,727,590		
	Nixon Plurality	17,998,388		

Key Issues Seeking to create a Republican majority by converting Wallace Democrats, Nixon pursued a "Southern strategy" of denouncing busing, the welfare state, the media and intellectuals. McGovern was unable to overcome an image of radicalism furthered by Republican charges that he was the candidate of "acid, abortion, and amnesty." **Regional Influences** The GOP's Southern strategy was aided by an assassination attempt on Wallace that knocked him out of the race. Nixon lost only Massachusetts and the District of Columbia, but Democrats added to their majority in the Senate and maintained control of the House.

[1] The Libertarian slate of John Hospers and Theodora Nathan received 1 electoral vote from a Republican elector in Virginia.

1976

Party	Candidate	Popular vote	Percent	Electoral vote
Democrat	Jimmy Carter (Ga.) and Walter F. Mondale (Minn.)	40,830,763	50.06	297
Republican	Gerald R. Ford (Mich.) and Robert Dole (Kans.)	39,147,793	48.00	240[1]
Independent	Eugene J. McCarthy (Minn.)	756,691	0.93	—
Libertarian	Roger MacBride (Va.)	173,011	0.21	—
Other		647,631	0.79	—
	Total Vote	81,555,889		
	Carter Plurality	1,682,970		

Key Issues In the wake of Watergate, Carter ran a moralistic campaign as a political outsider. Vague on issues, he railed against the Washington bureaucracy and vowed to lead "a government that is as good and honest and decent . . . as filled with love as are the American people." He also promised Americans that he would never lie to them. **Regional Influences** Ford nearly overcame a huge early deficit in the polls. But Carter's background as a southern moderate enabled him to eke out a victory through wins in northern, southern and border states.

[1]Ronald Reagan received one electoral vote from an elector in Washington.

1980

Party	Candidate	Popular vote	Percent	Electoral vote
Republican	Ronald Reagan (Calif.) and George Bush (Tex.)	43,901,812	50.75	489
Democrat	Jimmy Carter (Ga.) and Walter F. Mondale (Minn.)	35,483,820	41.02	49
Independent	John B. Anderson (Ill.) and Patrick J. Lucey (Wis.)	5,719,722	6.61	—
Libertarian	Edward E. Clark (Calif.)	921,188	1.06	—
Other		486,754	0.56	—
	Total Vote	86,513,296		
	Reagan Plurality	8,417,992		

Key Issues Inflation, an energy shortage, the taking of American hostages by Iran and a strong primary challenge from Edward Kennedy of Massachusetts weakened Carter. Reagan, promising to get government "off the backs fo the American people," pledged to cut taxes, increase defense spending, and balance the Federal budget. Anderson, a Republican, ran as an independent to the left of both Carter and Reagan. **Regional Influences** Reagan swept to a landslide win in the Electoral College as Carter carried only six states and the Washington, D.C.

1984

Party	Candidate	Popular vote	Percent	Electoral vote
Republican	Ronald Reagan (Calif.) and George Bush (Tex.)	54,450,603	58.78	525
Democrat	Walter F. Mondale (Minn.) and Geraldine Ferraro (N.Y.)	37,573,671	40.56	13
Libertarian	David Bergland (Calif.)	227,949	0.25	—
Other		570,343	0.61	—
	Total Vote	92,628,458		
	Reagan Plurality	16,876,932		

Key Issues The economy was flying after emerging in late 1983 from the worst economic downturn since the Great Depression. Reagan, whose commercials proclaimed it was "morning in America," ridiculed Mondale as an old-fashioned "tax-and-spend, gloom-and-doom" Democrat. Controversy over her husband's finances blunted Ferraro's appeal as the first woman on a major party ticket. **Regional Influences** Mondale carried only his home state of Minnesota and the District of Columbia as Reagan won the greatest electoral victory in American history and the fifth highest share of the popular vote.

1988

Party	Candidate	Popular vote	Percent	Electoral vote
Republican	George Bush (Tex.) and J. Danforth Quayle (Ind.)	48,881,011	53.37	426
Democrat	Michael S. Dukakis (Mass.) and Lloyd Bentsen (Tex.)	41,828,350	45.67	111[1]
Libertarian	Ron Paul (Texas)	431,499	0.47	—
New Alliance	Lenora Fulani (New York)	218,159	0.24	—
Other		226,852	0.25	—
	Total Vote	91,585,871		
	Bush Plurality	7,052,661		

Key Issues Trailing Dukakis by 17 points in early summer, Bush made an issue of his opponent's "liberalism," depicting the Massachusetts governor as soft on crime. Bush made a household name out of Willie Horton, a black Massachusetts prison inmate who raped a woman while on a prison furlough. Bush also called Dukakis a card-carrying member of the American Civil Liberties Union and said that he didn't share the same values as the American people. Dukakis' failure to respond to those charges and to shed the "liberal" label until late in the campaign ultimately doomed his candidacy, despite Bush's links to the Iran-Contra scandal and to Panama's drug-running leader, Gen. Mañuel Noriega. **Regional Influences** Dukakis won the District of Columbia and only 10 states: Washington, Oregon, Hawaii, New York, Minnesota, Wisconsin, Iowa, New York, West Virginia, Rhode Island, and his home state of Massachusettts. Bush easily captured the formerly Democratic "solid South."

[1]Bentsen received one electoral vote for President.

1992

Party	Candidate	Popular vote	Percent	Electoral vote
Democrat	Bill Clinton (Ark.) and Al Gore (Tenn.)	44,908,233	42.95	370
Republican	George Bush (Tex.) and J. Danforth Quayle (Ind.)	39,102,282	37.40	168
Independent	Ross H. Perot (Tex.) and James H. Stockdale (Calif.)	19,721,433	18.86	—
Other		820,788	0.79	
	Total Vote	104,552,736		
	Clinton Plurality	5,805,951		

Key Issues Bush's approval ratings were sky high as little as 13 months before the election, but a flagging economy and a national debt that wouldn't go away spelled his downfall in a three-way race that saw billionaire Ross Perot capture more votes than any third-party candidate since Theodore Roosevelt in 1912. Excitement for Perot, who entered the race in March, quit in July, and re-entered the campaign in October, brought a record 102 million people to the polls. Clinton ran especially strong among women, who supported his stances in favor of abortion rights and a strong defense of the environment. **Regional Influences** Perot's presence prevented either major party candidate from capturing an outright majority in every state except New York, Maryland, Arkansas (all of which went for Clinton) and Mississippi (which supported Bush). But Clinton won pluralities in California, Georgia, Illinois, Massachusetts, Michigan, Minnesota, Missouri, New Jersey, Ohio, Pennsylvania, Tennessee, Washington, and Wisconsin. The only states with double-digit electoral votes in Bush's column were Florida, Indiana, North Carolina, Texas, and Virginia.

1996

Party	Candidate	Popular vote	Percent	Electoral vote
Democrat	Bill Clinton (Ark.) and Al Gore (Tenn.)	47,402,357	49.24	379
Republican	Bob Dole (Kans.) and Jack Kemp (N.Y.)	39,198,755	40.71	159
Reform	Ross H. Perot and Patrick Choate	8,085,402	8.40	—
Green	Ralph Nader	684,902	0.71	—
Libertarian	Harry Browne	485,798	0.50	—
Other		420,009	0.44	—
	Total Vote	96,277,223		
	Clinton Plurality	8,203,602		

[1]Other includes write-ins and "none of the above."

Key Issues Clinton easily won re-election, campaigning on the strong economy and declining crime rates. Less than half of the voting age population went to the polls, the lowest number since 1924. Among those who did vote, Clinton ran strong with women, Asian-Americans, and Hispanics, and captured about half of the voters who described themselves as Independents. Dole's refusal to contravene his own party's strict stand against abortion hurt him dearly among women, who overwhelmingly chose Clinton. Perot's presence in the race prevented Clinton from winning an outright majority, but was not nearly as influential as it had been four years earlier. **Regional Influences** The president carried 31 states, including New York, California, Florida, Illinois, and Pennsylvania. Dole won 19 states, including Texas, Virginia, North Carolina, Georgia, and Indiana, as well as his home state of Kansas.

2000

Party	Candidate	Popular vote	Percent	Electoral vote
Republican	George W. Bush (Tex.) and Dick Cheney (Wyo.)	50,455,156	47.87	271
Democrat	Al Gore (Tenn.) and Joe Lieberman (Conn.)	50,992,335	48.38	266[1]
Green	Ralph Nader and Winona LaDuke	2,882,897	2.74	--
Reform	Pat Buchanan and Ezola Foster	448,892	0.42	--
Libertarian	Harry Browne	384,429	0.36	--
Other		232,932	0.23	--
	Total Vote	105,396,641		
	Gore Plurality	537,179		

1. One elector from the District of Columbia abstained.

▶THE ELECTORAL COLLEGE

The Electoral College is the body of electors chosen by all of the states that ultimately is responsible for selecting the president of the United States. The Framers did not want the nation's Chief Executive chosen by either the national legislature or the people directly. Instead they set up the Electoral College, under Article II, sections 2 and 3 of the Constitution to provide for indirect election of the president: "Each State shall appoint, in such manner as the legislature thereof may direct, a number of Electors, equal to the whole number of Senators and Representatives to which the State may be entitled in the Congress; but no Senator or Representative, or person holding an office of trust or profit under the United States, shall be appointed an Elector."

Electors were supposed to be distinguished, enlightened citizens who would cast a disinterested vote for president. From the start, however, electors have been instruments of partisan passions.

At first, most state legislatures were responsible for choosing electors. By 1828, however, all states except South Carolina allowed electors to be chosen by direct popular election. (In South Carolina, the legislature continued to select electors until the Civil War.) When electors began to be selected by popular vote, parties presented slates of candidates for presidential electors who were tacitly pledged to support the party's nominees for president and vice president. This is how the practice began of states voting as a unit. Subsequently, many states passed laws requiring their electors to vote as a bloc. Where it is not required by law, it is customary for all of a state's electors to vote for the candidate receiving a plurality of the popular vote in that state. The names of the candidates for electors may or may not appear on the ballot alongside the names of the candidates to whom they are pledged. Voters really vote for presidential electors, though, even when they seem to be casting a ballot for a presidential candidate.

The presidential electors chosen by the voters in November meet in their state capitals on the first Monday after the second Wednesday in December to cast their vote for president and vice president. The results of this balloting are sent to the president of the U.S. Senate, the directors of the U.S. General Services Administration, the state's secretary of state, and to the judge of the Federal District Court of the district in which the electors gathered. Sealed state ballots are opened and counted at a joint session of Congress on January 6 following the election year.

Originally electors voted for two individuals for president on a single ballot. The winner of a majority of the vote was elected president, the runner-up vice-president. The Framers fully expected there to be many elections in which no candidate would gain a majority of the vote and the president would have to be selected by the House of Representatives, where each state delegation would cast a single vote. But in 1789 and 1792 every elector voted for George Washington. In both years John Adams was the runner-up and, thus, vice president.

Problems inherent in this system became apparent once Washington was no longer a candidate.

Voter Turnout in Presidential Elections, 1928–2000

Year	Total Vote	Voting Age Population		Registered Voters	
		Number	Percent Voting	Number[1]	Percent Voting
1928	36,879,414	71,185,000	51.8%	N/A	N/A
1932	39,816,522	75,768,000	52.6	N/A	N/A
1936	45,646,817	80,354,000	56.8	N/A	N/A
1940	49,815,312	84,728,000	58.8	N/A	N/A
1944	48,025,684	95,573,000	56.1	N/A	N/A
1948	48,833,680	95,573,000	51.1	N/A	N/A
1952	61,551,919	99,929,000	61.6	N/A	N/A
1956	62,033,908	104,515,000	59.4	N/A	N/A
1960	68,838,204	109,159,000	63.06	N/A	N/A
1964	70,644,592	114,090,000	61.92	73,715,818	95.83%
1968	73,211,875	120,328,186	60.84	81,658,180	89.65
1972	77,718,554	140,776,000	55.21	97,328,541	79.85
1976	81,555,789	152,309,190	53.55	105,037,986	77.64
1980	86,515,221	164,597,000	52.56	113,043,734	76.53
1984	92,652,680	174,466,000	53.11	124,150,614	74.63
1988	91,594,693	182,778,000	50.11	126,379,628	72.48
1992	104,405,155	189,529,000	55.09	133,821,178	78.01
1996	96,456,345	196,511,000	49.08	146,211,960	65.97
2000	105,586,274	205,815,000	51.30	156,421,311	67.50

Source: Federal Election Commission. www.fec.gov

In 1796, Adams and Thomas Jefferson finished first and second in the balloting and were elected president and vice president, respectively, despite being fierce foes. By 1800, two formal parties had evolved which nominated a single candidate for both president and vice president. A Federalist elector purposely failed to vote for the party's vice presidential nominee, Thomas Pinckney, in order to assure a potential majority for Adams. But overzealous Republican electors all voted for both Jefferson and the party's vice presidential nominee, Aaron Burr. Both men received the same majority of the electoral vote and the election had to be decided by the House, where Jefferson won. This led to adoption of the Twelfth Amendment to the Constitution, implemented in 1804, which requires electors to cast separate ballots for president and vice president. If no candidate achieves a majority of the electoral vote for vice president, the position is filled by the Senate with each sena-

The 2000 Presidential Election

State	REPUBLICAN George W. Bush/ Dick Cheney Popular Vote	Percent	Electoral Vote	DEMOCRAT Al Gore/ Joseph Lieberman Popular Vote	Percent	Electoral Vote	GREEN Ralph Nader/ Winona LaDuke Popular Vote	Percent
Alabama	941,173	56.48	9	692,611	41.57	—	18,323	1.10
Alaska	167,398	58.62	3	79,004	27.67	—	28,747	10.07
Arizona	781,652	51.02	8	685,341	44.73	—	45,645	2.98
Arkansas	472,940	51.31	6	422,768	45.86	—	13,421	1.46
California	4,567,429	41.65	—	5,861,203	53.45	54	418,707	3.82
Colorado	883,748	50.75	8	738,227	42.39	—	91,434	5.25
Connecticut	561,094	38.44	—	816,015	55.91	8	64,452	4.42
Delaware	137,288	41.90	—	180,068	54.96	3	8,307	2.54
Dist. of Columbia	18,073	8.95	—	171,923	85.16	2[1]	10,576	5.24
Florida	2,912,790	48.85	25	2,912,253	48.84	—	97,488	1.63
Georgia	1,419,720	54.67	13	1,116,230	42.98	—	13,432	0.52
Hawaii	137,845	37.46	—	205,286	55.79	4	21,623	5.88
Idaho	336,937	67.17	4	138,637	27.64	—	12,292	2.45
Illinois	2,019,421	42.58	—	2,589,026	54.60	22	103,759	2.19
Indiana	1,245,836	56.65	12	901,980	41.01	—	18,531	0.84
Iowa	634,373	48.22	—	638,517	48.54	7	29,374	2.23
Kansas	622,332	58.04	6	399,276	37.24	—	36,086	3.37
Kentucky	872,492	56.50	8	638,898	41.37	—	23,192	1.50
Louisiana	927,871	52.55	9	792,344	44.88	—	20,473	1.16
Maine	286,616	43.97	—	319,951	49.09	4	37,127	5.70
Maryland	813,797	40.28	—	1,140,782	56.46	10	53,768	2.66
Massachusetts	878,502	32.50	—	1,616,487	59.8	12	173,564	6.42
Michigan	1,953,139	46.15	—	2,170,418	51.28	18	84,165	1.99
Minnesota	1,109,659	45.50	—	1,168,266	47.91	10	126,696	5.20
Mississippi	572,844	57.62	7	404,614	40.70	—	8,122	0.82
Missouri	1,189,924	50.42	11	1,111,138	47.08	—	38,515	1.63
Montana	240,178	58.44	3	137,126	33.36	—	24,437	5.95
Nebraska	433,862	62.25	5	231,780	33.25	—	24,540	3.52
Nevada	301,575	49.52	4	279,978	45.98	—	15,008	2.46
New Hampshire	273,559	48.07	4	266,348	46.80	—	22,198	3.90
New Jersey	1,284,173	40.29	—	1,788,850	56.13	15	94,554	2.97
New Mexico	286,417	47.85	—	286,783	47.91	5	21,251	3.55
New York	2,403,374	35.23	—	4,107,697	60.21	33	244,030	3.58
North Carolina	1,631,163	56.03	14	1,257,692	43.20	—	0	0.00
North Dakota	174,852	60.66	3	95,284	33.06	—	9,486	3.29
Ohio	2,350,363	49.99	21	2,183,628	46.44	—	117,799	2.51
Oklahoma	744,337	60.31	8	474,276	38.43	—	0	0.00
Oregon	713,577	46.52	—	720,342	46.96	7	77,357	5.04
Pennsylvania	2,281,127	46.43	—	2,485,967	50.60	23	103,392	2.10
Rhode Island	130,555	31.91	—	249,508	60.99	4	25,052	6.12
South Carolina	785,937	56.84	8	565,561	40.90	—	20,200	1.46
South Dakota	190,700	60.30	3	118,804	37.56	—	0	0.00
Tennessee	1,061,949	51.15	11	981,720	47.28	—	19,781	0.95
Texas	3,799,639	59.30	32	2,433,746	37.98	—	137,994	2.15
Utah	515,096	66.83	5	203,053	26.34	—	35,850	4.65
Vermont	119,775	40.70	—	149,022	50.63	3	20,374	6.92
Virginia	1,437,490	52.47	13	1,217,290	44.44	—	59,398	2.17
Washington	1,108,864	44.58	—	1,247,652	50.16	11	103,002	4.14
West Virginia	336,475	51.92	5	295,497	45.59	—	10,680	1.65
Wisconsin	1,237,279	47.61	—	1,242,987	47.83	11	94,070	3.62
Wyoming	147,947	67.76	3	60,481	27.70	—	4,625	2.12
Total	50,455,156	47.87%	271	50,992,335	48.38%	266	2,882,897	2.74%

1. One elector from the District of Columbia abstained. **Source:** Federal Election Commission. www.fec.gov

Campaign Contribution Limits for Individuals and PACs

Recipient	Individual contributor	Multi-candidate committee	Other political committee
Each candidate or candidate committee	$1,000	$5,000	$1,000
National party committee	20,000	15,000	20,000
Other political committee	5,000	5,000	5,000
Total per calendar year	**$25,000**	**no limit**	**no limit**

tor casting a single ballot. This has happened only once, when the Senate selected Richard M. Johnson after he fell one electoral vote short of a majority for vice president in 1836.

Today, 270 votes are required to reach a majority in the Electoral College. There have been two elections in which no candidate received a majority of the electoral vote. In 1824, no candidate achieved a majority of the vote, and in 1876, disputed results in several states prevented either Rutherford B. Hayes or Samuel J. Tilden from achieving a majority. John Quincy Adams and Hayes won those contests, respectively. A candidate also can be elected president despite losing the popular vote. This occurred, again in 1824 and 1876, when the House selected Adams and Hayes, though they lost the popular vote to Andrew Jackson and Tilden, respectively; in 1888, when Benjamin Harrison was elected over Grover Cleveland despite receiving a minority of the popular vote; and in 2000, when George W. Bush lost the popular vote by more than 400,000 votes to Al Gore, but won enough states for an Electoral College victory.

▶THE FEDERAL ELECTION CAMPAIGN ACT

In 1971 Congress passed the Federal Election Campaign Act to reform various aspects of campaign financing. The law was amended and strengthened in 1974 and 1976, and the Federal Election Commission (FEC) was established to administer the law, which affects candidates for the U.S. House of Representatives, the U.S. Senate, and the presidency, as well as the political committees that support them. The act requires disclosure of sources and uses of funds for Federal elections, provides public financing for presidential elections, and sets limits on campaign contributions. The specific requirements of each of these three parts of the act are detailed below.

Public disclosure Candidates for Federal office and the political committees that support them must register and file periodic disclosures of their campaign finance activities with the Clerk of the House, the Secretary of the Senate, or the FEC. These reports are available to the public within 48 hours of their disclosure. A candidate is defined as one who has raised or spent more than $5,000 in any given year in campaigning for Federal office. A political committee is defined as a club, committee, association, or organization that receives contributions or makes expenditures of more than $1,000 to a Federal candidate in any calendar year. In recent years they have come to be called PACs, for Political Action Committee.

Public financing Public financing is provided for eligible presidential candidates in primary and general elections, and for national party committees for the nominating conventions. Financing is given in the form of matching payments to primary candidates, public grants to

nominees in the general election, and public grants to the national party committees for the conventions. The money for public financing is raised by the Presidential Election Campaign Fund, which collects three dollars from the tax payment of every taxpayer who checks off this box on his or her Federal income tax return.

Contribution limits and prohibitions In Federal elections the act prohibits contributions from the treasuries of national banks, corporations, and labor organizations; contributions from government contractors; contributions from foreign nationals (green card holders); cash contributions in excess of $100 per person; and contributions supplied by one person in the name of another person.

Additionally, the act sets contribution limits as shown in the accompanying table.

POLITICAL OFFICE HOLDERS

▶THE VICE PRESIDENCY

Unlike the office of the president, that of the vice president has sometimes been left vacant after the death of the vice president, or his assumption of higher office on the death of the president. Until adoption of the 25th Amendment to the Constitution in 1967, there was no provision to fill a vacancy in the vice presidency. Under the amendment, the president must name a vice president when the office is vacant, and the nominee must pass a majority vote of approval in both houses of Congress. Gerald Ford, Richard Nixon's choice to replace Spiro Agnew after the latter's resignation in 1973, was the first vice president to gain the office under the amendment. The second was Nelson Rockefeller, whom Ford nominated to the position after he became president upon Nixon's resignation the following year. While the 25th Amendment does not supersede the presidential order of succession, it decreases the likelihood of the office's ever falling to the Speaker of the House or a sitting cabinet member.

▶PRESIDENTIAL ORDER OF SUCCESSION

Article II of the Constitution gives to Congress the power to determine the presidential order of succession should both the president and vice president die, become incapacitated or be disqualified from office. The present law, passed in 1947, puts the Speaker of the House first in line to the presidency, followed by the president pro tempore of the Senate. The order of succession then goes through the members of the Cabinet, in the order in which the executive departments were established:

(1) Secretary of State, (2) Secretary of the Treasury, (3) Secretary of Defense, (4) Attorney Gen-

eral, (5) Secretary of the Interior, (6) Secretary of Agriculture, (7) Secretary of Commerce, (8) Secretary of Labor, (9) Secretary of Health and Human Services, (10) Secretary of Housing and Urban Development, (11) Secretary of Transportation, (12) Secretary of Energy, (13) Secretary of Education, (14) Secretary of Veterans' Affairs. The following sentence, composed of words using the first letter (or letters) of each cabinet department, is often used as a mnemonic device to remember the order: See The Dog Jump In A Circle; Leave HEr HOme To ENtertain EDucated Veterans. (State, Treasury, Defense, Justice, Interior, Agriculture, Commerce, Labor, HEalth and Human Services, HOusing and Urban Development, Transportation, ENergy, EDucation, Veterans Affairs.

Until the 1970 legislation removing the Postmaster General from the Cabinet and establishing an in-

Vice Presidents of the United States

Name	Party	Tenure	State, birth-death
1. John Adams	Fed.	1789–97	Mass., 1735–1826
2. Thomas Jefferson	D-R	1797–1801	Va., 1743–1826
3. Aaron Burr	D-R	1801–05	N.Y., 1756–1836
4. George Clinton	D-R	1805–13†	N.Y., 1739–1812
5. Elbridge Gerry	D-R	1813–17†	Mass., 1744–1814
6. Daniel D. Tompkins	D-R	1817–25	N.Y., 1774–1825
7. John C. Calhoun	D-R	1825–33[1]	S.C., 1782–1850
8. Martin Van Buren	D	1833–37	N.Y., 1782–1862
9. Richard M. Johnson	D	1837–41[2]	Ky., 1780–1850
10. John Tyler	Whig	1841[3]	Va., 1790–1862
11. George M. Dallas	D	1845–49	Pa., 1792–1864
12. Millard Fillmore	Whig	1849–50[4]	N.Y., 1800–74
13. William R. King	D	1853–57†	Ala., 1786–1853
14. John C. Breckenridge	D	1857–61	Ky., 1821–75
15. Hannibal Hamlin	R	1861–65	Maine, 1809–91
16. Andrew Johnson	D	1865[5]	Tenn., 1808–75
17. Schuyler Colfax	R	1869–73	Ind., 1823–85
18. Henry Wilson	R	1873–77†	Mass., 1812–75
19. William A. Wheeler	R	1877–81	N.Y., 1819–87
20. Chester A. Arthur	R	1881[6]	N.Y., 1829–86
21. Thomas A. Hendricks	D	1885†	Ind., 1819–85
22. Levi P. Morton	R	1889–93	N.Y., 1824–1920
23. Adlai E. Stevenson	D	1893–97	Ill., 1835–1914
24. Garret A. Hobart	R	1897–1901†	N.J., 1844–99
25. Theodore Roosevelt	R	1901[7]	N.Y., 1858–1919
26. Charles W. Fairbanks	R	1905–09	Ind., 1852–1918
27. James S. Sherman	R	1909–13†	N.Y., 1855–1912
28. Thomas R. Marshall	D	1913–21	Ind., 1854–1925
29. Calvin Coolidge	R	1921–23[8]	Mass., 1872–1933
30. Charles G. Dawes	R	1925–29	Ill., 1865–1951
31. Charles Curtis	R	1929–33	Kans., 1860–1936
32. John Nance Garner	D	1933–41	Tex., 1868–1967
33. Henry A. Wallace	D	1941–45	Iowa, 1888–1965
34. Harry S Truman	D	1945[9]	Mo., 1884–1972
35. Alben W. Barkley	D	1949–53	Ky., 1877–1956
36. Richard M. Nixon	R	1953–61	Calif., 1913–95
37. Lyndon B. Johnson	D	1961–63[10]	Tex., 1908–73
38. Hubert H. Humphrey	D	1965–69	Minn., 1911–78
39. Spiro T. Agnew	R	1969–73[11]	Md., 1918–96
40. Gerald R. Ford	R	1973–74[12]	Mich., 1913–
41. Nelson A. Rockefeller	R	1974–77[13]	N.Y., 1908–79
42. Walter F. Mondale	D	1977–81	Minn., 1928–
43. George Bush	R	1981–89	Tex., 1924–
44. J. Danforth Quayle	R	1989–93	Ind., 1947–
45. Albert Gore	D	1993–2001	Tenn., 1948–
46. Richard Cheney	R	2001–	Wyo., 1941–

Notes: Fed. = Federalist. D = Democrat. D-R = Democratic-Republican. R = Republican. † = Died in office. 1. Resigned to become senator from South Carolina (1832-43). 2. Voted in by senate after no candidate for vice president gained a majority in the electoral college. 3. Became president after Benjamin Harrison's death. 4. Became president after Zachary Taylor's death. 5. Nominated by Republicans to run with Abraham Lincoln on the Union ticket; became president after Lincoln's assassination. 6. Became president after James Garfield's assassination. 7. Became president after William McKinley's assassination. 8. Became president after Warren Harding's death. 9. Became president after Franklin D. Roosevelt's death. 10. Became president after John F. Kennedy's assassination. 11. Resigned while under investigation for receiving kickbacks as governor of Maryland; first vice president named under terms of the 25th amendment; assumed presidency after Richard Nixon resigned. 13. Named vice president by Ford.

Speakers of the U.S. House of Representatives

Name	Party	State	Dates in Office
1. Frederick A.C. Muhlenberg	D-R	Pa.	1789–91
2. Jonathan Trumbull	Fed.	Conn.	1791–93
3. Frederick A. C. Muhlenberg	D-R	Pa.	1793–95
4. Jonathan Dayton	Fed.	N.J.	1795–97
5. George Dent	Fed.	Md.	1797–99
6. Theodore Sedgwick	Fed.	Mass.	1799–1801
7. Nathaniel Macon	D-R	N.C.	1801–07
8. Joseph B. Varnum	D-R	Mass.	1807–11
9. Henry Clay	D-R	Ky.	1811–14
10. Langdon Cheves	D-R	S.C.	1814–15
11. Henry Clay	D-R	Ky.	1815–20
12. John W. Taylor	D-R	N.Y.	1820–21
13. Philip Barbour	D-R	Va.	1821–23
14. Henry Clay	D-R	Ky.	1822–23
15. John W. Taylor	D-R	N.Y.	1825–27
16. Andrew Stevenson	D	Va.	1827–34
17. John Bell	D	Tenn.	1834–35
18. James K. Polk	D	Tenn.	1835–39
19. Robert M.T. Hunter	NP	Va.	1839–41
20. John White	Whig	Ky.	1841–43
21. John W. Jones	D	Va.	1843–45
22. John W. Davis	D	Ind.	1845–47
23. Robert C. Winthrop	Whig	Mass.	1847–49
24. Howell Cobb	D	Ga.	1849–51
25. Linn Boyd	D	Ky.	1851–55
26. Nathaniel Banks	R	Mass.	1855–57
27. James L. Orr	D	S.C.	1857–59
28. William Pennington	Whig	N.J.	1859–61
29. Galusha A. Grow	R	Pa.	1861–63
30. Schuyler Colfax	R	Ind.	1863–69
31. James G. Blaine	R	Maine	1869–75
32. Michael C. Kerr	D	Ind.	1875–76
33. Samuel J. Randall	D	Pa.	1876–81
34. J. Warren Keifer	R	Ohio	1881–83
35. John G. Carlisle	D	Ky.	1883–89
36. Thomas B. Reed	R	Maine	1889–91
37. Charles F. Crisp	D	Ga.	1891–95
38. Thomas B. Reed	R	Maine	1895–99
39. David B. Henderson	R	Iowa	1899–1903
40. Joseph G. Cannon	R	Ill.	1903–11
41. Champ Clark	D	Mo.	1911–19
42. Frederick H. Gillett	R	Mass.	1919–25
43. Nicholas Longworth	R	Ohio	1925–31
44. John Nance Garner	D	Tex.	1931–33
45. Henry T. Rainey	D	Ill.	1933–34
46. Joseph W. Byrns	D	Tenn.	1935–36
47. William B. Bankhead	D	Ala.	1936–39
48. Sam Rayburn	D	Tex.	1940–46
49. Joseph W. Martin Jr.	R	Mass.	1947–49
50. Sam Rayburn	D	Tex.	1949–52
51. Joseph W. Martin Jr.	R	Mass.	1953–54
52. Sam Rayburn	D	Tex.	1955–61
53. John W. McCormack	D	Mass.	1962–71
54. Carl B. Albert	D	Okla.	1971–76
55. Thomas P. O'Neill Jr.	D	Mass.	1977–87
56. James C. Wright Jr.	D	Tex.	1987–89
57. Thomas S. Foley	D	Wash.	1989–95
58. Newt Gingrich	R	Ga.	1995–99
59. J. Dennis Hastert	R	Ill.	1999–

Notes: D = Democrat. Fed. = Federalist. R = Republican.

dependent Postal Service, the Postmaster General was fifth in line to the presidency. The heads of new departments are automatically added to the line of succession as the new departments are created.

A Cabinet member must be a natural-born U.S. citizen and at least 35 years old in order to become acting president. If a Cabinet member next-in-line to fill a presidential vacancy were not yet 35, the presidency would pass to the next Cabinet member in the order of succession who had attained that age.

Cabinet Members

Washington Administration (1789-97)

Secretary of State	Thomas Jefferson	1789–93
	Edmund Randolph	1794–95
	Timothy Pickering	1795–97
Secretary of Treasury	Alexander Hamilton	1789–95
	Oliver Wolcott	1795–97
Secretary of War	Henry Knox	1789–94
	Timothy Pickering	1795–96
	James McHenry	1796–97
Attorney General	Edmund Randolph	1789–93
	William Bradford	1794–95
	Charles Lee	1795–97
Postmaster General	Samuel Osgood	1789–91
	Timothy Pickering	1791–94
	Joseph Habersham	1795–97

John Adams Administration (1797–1801)

Secretary of State	Timothy Pickering	1797–1800
	John Marshall	1800–1801
Secretary of Treasury	Oliver Wolcott	1797–1800
	Samuel Dexter	1800–1801
Secretary of War	James McHenry	1797–1800
	Samuel Dexter	1800–1801
Attorney General	Charles Lee	1797–1801
Postmaster General	Joseph Habersham	1797–1801
Secretary of Navy	Benjamin Stoddert	1798–1801

Jefferson Administration (1801–09)

Secretary of State	James Madison	1801–09
Secretary of Treasury	Samuel Dexter	1801
	Albert Gallatin	1801–09
Secretary of War	Henry Dearborn	1801–09
Attorney General	Levi Lincoln	1801–05
	Robert Smith	1805
	John Breckinridge	1805–06
	Caesar Rodney	1807–09
Postmaster General	Joseph Habersham	1801
	Gideon Granger	1801–09
Secretary of Navy	Robert Smith	1801–09

Madison Administration (1809–17)

Secretary of State	Robert Smith	1809–11
	James Monroe	1811–17
Secretary of Treasury	Albert Gallatin	1809–13
	George Campbell	1814
	Alexander Dallas	1814–16
	William Crawford	1816–17
Secretary of War	William Eustis	1809–17
	John Armstrong	1813–14
	James Monroe	1814–15
	William Crawford	1815–17
Attorney General	Caesar Rodney	1809–11
	William Pinkney	1811–14
	Richard Rush	1814–17
Postmaster General	Gideon Granger	1809–14
	Return Meigs	1814–17
Secretary of Navy	Paul Hamilton	1809–13
	William Jones	1813–14
	Benjamin Crowninshield	1814–17

Monroe Administration (1817–25)

Secretary of State	John Quincy Adams	1817–25
Secretary of Treasury	William Crawford	1817–25
Secretary of War	George Graham	1817
	John C. Calhoun	1817–25
Attorney General	Richard Rush	1817
	William Wirt	1817–25
Postmaster General	Return Meigs	1817–23
	John McLean	1823–25
Secretary of Navy	Benjamin Crowninshield	1817–18
	Smith Thompson	1818–23
	Samuel Southard	1823–25

John Quincy Adams Administration (1825–29)

Secretary of State	Henry Clay	1825–25
Secretary of Treasury	Richard Rush	1825–25
Secretary of War	James Barbour	1825–29
	Peter Porter	1828–29
Attorney General	William Wirt	1825–29
Postmaster General	John McLean	1825–29
Secretary of Navy	Samuel Southard	1825–29

Jackson Administration (1829–37)

Secretary of State	Martin Van Buren	1829–33
	Edward Livingston	1831–33
	Louis McLane	1833–34
	John Forsyth	1834–37
Secretary of Treasury	Samuel Ingham	1829–31
	Louis McLane	1831–33
	William Duane	1833
	Roger B. Taney	1833–34
	Levi Woodbury	1834–37
Secretary of War	John H. Eaton	1829–31
	Lewis Cass	1831–37
	Benjamin Butler	1837
Attorney General	John M. Berrien	1829–31
	Roger B. Taney	1831–33
	Benjamin Butler	1833–37
Postmaster General	William Barry	1829–35
	Amos Kendall	1835–37
Secretary of Navy	John Branch	1829–31
	Levi Woodbury	1831–34
	Mahlon Dickerson	1834–37

Van Buren Administration (1837–41)

Secretary of State	John Forsyth	1837–41
Secretary of Treasury	Levi Woodbury	1837–41
Secretary of War	Joel Poinsett	1837–41
Attorney General	Benjamin Butler	1837–38
	Felix Grundy	1838–40
	Henry D. Gilpin	1840–41
Postmaster General	Amos Kendall	1837–40
	John M. Niles	1840–41
Secretary of Navy	Mahlon Dickerson	1837–38
	James Paulding	1838–41

William Harrison Administration (1841)

Secretary of State	Daniel Webster	1841
Secretary of Treasury	Thomas Ewing	1841
Secretary of War	John Bell	1841
Attorney General	John J. Crittenden	1841
Postmaster General	Francis Granger	1841
Secretary of Navy	George Badger	1841

Tyler Administration (1841–45)

Secretary of State	Daniel Webster	1841–43
	Hugh S. Legaré	1843
	Abel P. Upshur	1843–44
	John C. Calhoun	1844–45
Secretary of Treasury	Thomas Ewing	1841
	Walter Forward	1841–43
	John C. Spencer	1843–44
	George Bibb	1844–45
Secretary of War	John Bell	1841
	John C. Spencer	1841–43
	James M. Porter	1843–44
	William Wilkins	1844–45
Attorney General	John J. Crittenden	1841
	Hugh S. Legaré	1841–43
	John Nelson	1843–45
Postmaster General	Francis Granger	1841
	Charles Wickliffe	1841
Secretary of Navy	George Badger	1841
	Abel P. Upshur	1841
	David Henshaw	1843–44
	Thomas Gilmer	1844
	John Y. Mason	1844–45

Polk Administration (1845–49)

Secretary of State	James Buchanan	1845–49
Secretary of Treasury	Robert J. Walker	1845–49
Secretary of War	William L. Marcy	1845–49
Attorney General	John Y. Mason	1845–46
	Nathan Clifford	1846–48
	Isaac Toucey	1848–49
Postmaster General	Cave Johnson	1845–49
Secretary of Navy	George Bancroft	1845–46
	John Y. Mason	1846–49

Taylor Administration (1849–50)

Secretary of State	John M. Clayton	1849–50
Secretary of Treasury	William Meredith	1849–50
Secretary of War	George Crawford	1849–50
Attorney General	Reverdy Johnson	1849–50
Postmaster General	Jacob Collamer	1849–50
Secretary of Navy	William Preston	1849–50
Secretary of Interior	Thomas Ewing	1849–50

Fillmore Administration (1850–53)

Secretary of State	Daniel Webster	1850–52
	Edward Everett	1852–53
Secretary of Treasury	Thomas Corwin	1850–53
Secretary of War	Charles Conrad	1850–53
Attorney General	John J. Crittenden	1850–53
Postmaster General	Nathan Hall	1850–52
	Sam D. Hubbard	1852–53
Secretary of Navy	William A. Graham	1852–53
	John P. Kennedy	1852–53
Secretary of Interior	Thomas McKennan	1850
	Alexander Stuart	1850–53

Pierce Administration (1853–57)

Secretary of State	William L. Marcy	1853–57
Secretary of Treasury	James Guthrie	1853–57
Secretary of War	Jefferson Davis	1853–57
Attorney General	Caleb Cushing	1853–57
Postmaster General	James Campbell	1853–57
Secretary of Navy	James C. Dobbin	1853–57
Secretary of Interior	Robert McClelland	1853–57

Buchanan Administration (1857–61)

Secretary of State	Lewis Cass	1857–60
	Jeremiah S. Black	1860–61
Secretary of Treasury	Howell Cobb	1857–60
	Philip Thomas	1860–61
	John A. Dix	1861
Secretary of War	John B. Floyd	1857–61
	Joseph Holt	1861
Attorney General	Jeremiah S. Black	1857–60
	Edwin M. Stanton	1860–61
Postmaster General	Aaron W. Brown	1857–59
	Joseph Holt	1859–61
	Horatio King	1861
Secretary of Navy	Isaac Toucey	1857–61
Secretary of Interior	Jacob Thompson	1857–61

Lincoln Administration (1861–65)

Secretary of State	William H. Seward	1861–65
Secretary of Treasury	Salmon P. Chase	1861–65
	William P. Fessenden	1864–65
	Hugh McCulloch	1865
Secretary of War	Simon Cameron	1861–62
	Edwin M. Stanton	1862–65
Attorney General	Edward Bates	1861–64
	James Speed	1864–65
Postmaster General	Horatio King	1861
	Montgomery Blair	1861–64
	William Dennison	1864–65
Secretary of Navy	Gideon Welles	1861–65
Secretary of Interior	Caleb B. Smith	1861–63
	John P. Usher	1863–65

Andrew Johnson Administration (1865–69)

Secretary of State	William H. Seward	1865–69
Secretary of Treasury	Hugh McCulloch	1865–69
Secretary of War	Edwin M. Stanton	1865–67
	Ulysses S. Grant	1867–68
	Lorenzo Thomas	1868
	John M. Schofield	1868–69
Attorney General	James Speed	1865–66
	Henry Stanbery	1866–68
	William M. Evarts	1868–69
Postmaster General	William Dennison	1865–66
	Alexander Randall	1866–69
Secretary of Navy	Gideon Welles	1865–69
Secretary of Interior	John P. Usher	1865
	James Harlan	1865–66
	Orville H. Browning	1866–69

Grant Administration (1869–77)

Secretary of State	Elihu B. Washburne	1869
	Hamilton Fish	1869–77
Secretary of Treasury	George S. Boutwell	1869–73
	William Richardson	1873–74
	Benjamin Bristow	1874–76
	Lot M. Morrill	1876–77
Secretary of War	John A. Rawlins	1869
	William T. Sherman	1869
	William W. Belknap	1869–76
	Alphonso Taft	1876

	James D. Cameron	1876–77
Attorney General	Ebenezer Hoar	1869–70
	Amos T. Ackerman	1870–71
	G. H. Williams	1871–75
	Edwards Pierrepont	1875–76
	Alphonso Taft	1876–77
Postmaster General	John A. J. Creswell	1869–74
	James W. Marshall	1874
	Marshall Jewell	1874–76
	James N. Tyner	1876–77
Secretary of Navy	Adolph E. Borie	1869
	George M. Robeson	1869–77
Secretary of Interior	Jacob D. Cox	1869–70
	Columbus Delano	1870–75
	Zachariah Chandler	1875–77

Hayes Administration (1877–81)

Secretary of State	William M. Evarts	1877–81
Secretary of Treasury	John Sherman	1877–81
Secretary of War	George W. McCrary	1877–79
	Alex Ramsey	1879–81
Attorney General	Charles Devens	1877–81
Postmaster General	David M. Key	1877–80
	Horace Maynard	1880–81
Secretary of Navy	Richard W. Thompson	1877–80
	Nathan Goff, Jr.	1881
Secretary of Interior	Carl Schurz	1877–81

Garfield Administration (1881)

Secretary of State	James G. Blaine	1881
Secretary of Treasury	William Windom	1881
Secretary of War	Robert T. Lincoln	1881
Attorney General	Wayne MacVeagh	1881
Postmaster General	Thomas L. James	1881
Secretary of Navy	William H. Hunt	1881
Secretary of Interior	Samuel J. Kirkwood	1881

Arthur Administration (1881–85)

Secretary of State	F. T. Frelinghuysen	1881–85
Secretary of Treasury	Charles J. Folger	1881–84
	Walter Q. Gresham	1884
	Hugh McCulloch	1884–85
Secretary of War	Robert T. Lincoln	1881–85
Attorney General	Benjamin H. Brewster	1881–85
Postmaster General	Timothy O. Howe	1881–83
	Walter Q. Gresham	1883–84
	Frank Hatton	1884–85
Secretary of Navy	William H. Hunt	1881–82
	William E. Chandler	1882–85
Secretary of Interior	Samuel J. Kirkwood	1881–82
	Henry M. Teller	1882–85

Cleveland Administration (1885–89)

Secretary of State	Thomas F. Bayard	1885–89
Secretary of Treasury	Daniel Manning	1885–87
	Charles S. Fairchild	1887–89
Secretary of War	William C. Endicott	1885–89
Attorney General	Augustus H. Garland	1885–89
Postmaster General	William F. Vilas	1885–88
	Don M. Dickinson	1888–89
Secretary of Navy	William C. Whitney	1885–89
Secretary of Interior	Lucius Q. C. Lamar	1885–88
	William F. Vilas	1888–89
Secretary of Agriculture	Norman J. Colman	1889

Benjamin Harrison Administration (1889–93)

Secretary of State	James G. Blaine	1889–92
	John W. Foster	1892–93
Secretary of Treasury	William Windom	1889–91
	Charles Foster	1891–93
Secretary of War	Redfield Proctor	1889–91
	Stephen B. Elkins	1891–93
Attorney General	William H. H. Miller	1889–91
Postmaster General	John Wanamaker	1889–93
Secretary of Navy	Benjamin F. Tracy	1889–93
Secretary of Interior	John W. Noble	1889–93
Secretary of Agriculture	Jeremiah M. Rusk	1889–93

Cleveland Administration (1893–97)

Secretary of State	Walter Q. Gresham	1893–95
	Richard Olney	1895–97
Secretary of Treasury	John G. Carlisle	1893–97
Secretary of War	Daniel S. Lamont	1893–97
Attorney General	Richard Olney	1893–95
	James Harmon	1895–97
Postmaster General	Wilson S. Bissell	1893–95
	William L. Wilson	1895–95
Secretary of Navy	Hilary A. Herbert	1893–97
Secretary of Interior	Hoke Smith	1893–96
	David R. Francis	1896–97
Secretary of Agriculture	Julius S. Morton	1893–97

McKinley Administration (1897–1901)

Secretary of State	John Sherman	1897–98
	William R. Day	1898
	John Hay	1898–1901
Secretary of Treasury	Lyman J. Gage	1897–1901
Secretary of War	Russell A. Alger	1897–99
	Elihu Root	1899–1901
Attorney General	Joseph McKenna	1897–98
	John W. Griggs	1898–1901
	Philander C. Knox	1901
Postmaster General	James A. Gary	1897–98
	Charles E. Smith	1898–1901
Secretary of Navy	John D. Long	1897–1901
Secretary of Interior	Cornelius N. Bliss	1897–99
	Ethan A. Hitchcock	1899–1901
Secretary of Agriculture	James Wilson	1897–1901

Theodore Roosevelt Administration (1901–09)

Secretary of State	John Hay	1901–05
	Elihu Root	1905–09
	Robert Bacon	1909
Secretary of Treasury	Lyman J. Gage	1901–02
	Leslie M. Shaw	1902–07
	George B. Cortelyou	1907–09
Secretary of War	Elihu Root	1901–04
	William H. Taft	1904–08
	Luke E. Wright	1908–09
Attorney General	Philander C. Knox	1901–04
	William H. Moody	1904–06
	Charles J. Bonaparte	1906–09
Postmaster General	Charles E. Smith	1901–02
	Henry C. Payne	1902–04
	Robert J. Wynne	1904–05
	George B. Cortelyou	1905–07
	George von L. Meyer	1907–09
Secretary of Navy	John D. Long	1901–02
	William H. Moody	1902–04
	Paul Morton	1904–05
	Charles J. Bonaparte	1905–06
	Victor H. Metcalf	1906–08
	Truman H. Newberry	1908–09
Secretary of Interior	Ethan A. Hitchcock	1901–07
	James R. Garfield	1907–09

Secretary of Agriculture	James Wilson	1901–09
Secretary of Labor and Commerce	George B. Cortelyou	1903–04
	Victor H. Metcalf	1904–06
	Oscar S. Straus	1906–09
	Charles Nagel	1909

Taft Administration (1909–13)

Secretary of State	Philander C. Knox	1909–13
Secretary of Treasury	Franklin MacVeagh	1909–13
Secretary of War	Jacob M. Dickinson	1909–11
	Henry L. Stimson	1911–13
Attorney General	George W. Wickersham	1909–13
Postmaster General	Frank H. Hitchcock	1909–13
Secretary of Navy	George von L. Meyer	1909–13
Secretary of Interior	Richard A. Ballinger	1909–11
	Walter Fisher	1911–13
Secretary of Agriculture	James Wilson	1909–13
Secretary of Labor and Commerce	Charles Nagel	1909–13

Wilson Administration (1913–21)

Secretary of State	William J. Bryan	1913–15
	Robert Lansing	1915–20
	Bainbridge Colby	1920–21
Secretary of Treasury	William G. McAdoo	1913–18
	Carter Glass	1918–20
	David F. Houston	1920–21
Secretary of War	Lindley M. Garrison	1913–16
	Newton D. Baker	1916–21
Attorney General	James C. McReynolds	1913–14
	Thomas W. Gregory	1914–19
	A. Mitchell Palmer	1919–21
Postmaster General	Albert S. Burleson	1913–21
Secretary of Navy	Josephus Daniels	1913–21
Secretary of Interior	Franklin K. Lane	1913–20
	John B. Payne	1920–21
Secretary of Agriculture	David F. Houston	1913–20
	Edwin T. Meredith	1920–21
Secretary of Commerce	William C. Redfield	1913–19
Secretary of Labor	William B. Wilson	1913–21

Harding Administration (1921–23)

Secretary of State	Charles E. Hughes	1921–23
Secretary of Treasury	Andrew Mellon	1921–23
Secretary of War	John W. Weeks	1921–23
Attorney General	Harry M. Daugherty	1921–23
Postmaster General	Will H. Hays	1921–22
	Hubert Work	1922–23
	Harry S. New	1923
Secretary of Navy	Edwin Denby	1921–23
Secretary of Interior	Albert B. Fall	1921–23
	Hubert Work	1923
Secretary of Agriculture	Henry C. Wallace	1921–23
Secretary of Commerce	Herbert C. Hoover	1921–23
Secretary of Labor	James J. Davis	1921–23

Coolidge Administration (1923–29)

Secretary of State	Charles E. Hughes	1923–25
	Frank B. Kellogg	1925–29
Secretary of Treasury	John W. Weeks	1923–25
	Dwight F. Davis	1925–29
Attorney General	Henry M. Daugherty	1923–24
	Harlan F. Stone	1923–25
	John G. Sargent	1925–29
Postmaster General	Harry S. New	1923–29
Secretary of Navy	Edwin Denby	1923–24
	Curtis D. Wilbur	1924–29
Secretary of Interior	Hubert Work	1923–28
	Roy O. West	1928–29

Secretary of Agriculture	Henry C. Wallace	1923–24
	Howard M. Gore	1924–25
	William M. Jardine	1925–29
Secretary of Commerce	Herbert C. Hoover	1923–28
	William F. Whiting	1928–29
Secretary of Labor	James J. Davis	1923–29

Hoover Administration (1929–33)

Secretary of State	Henry L. Stimson	1929–33
Secretary of Treasury	Andrew Mellon	1929–32
	Ogden L. Mills	1932–33
Secretary of War	James W. Good	1929
	Patrick J. Hurley	1929–33
Attorney General	William D. Mitchell	1929–33
Postmaster General	Walter F. Brown	1929–33
Secretary of Navy	Charles F. Adams	1929–33
Secretary of Interior	Ray L. Wilbur	1929–33
Secretary of Agriculture	Arthur M. Hyde	1929–33
Secretary of Commerce	Robert P. Lamont	1929–32
	Roy D. Chapin	1932–33
Secretary of Labor	James J. Davis	1929–30
	William N. Doak	1930–33

Franklin D. Roosevelt Administration (1933–45)

Secretary of State	Cordell Hull	1933–44
	Edward R. Stettinius, Jr.	1944–45
Secretary of Treasury	William H. Woodin	1933–34
	Henry Morgenthau, Jr.	1934–45
Secretary of War	George H. Dern	1933–36
	Henry A. Woodring	1936–40
	Henry L. Stimson	1940–45
Attorney General	Homer S. Cummings	1933–39
	Frank Murphy	1939–40
	Robert H. Jackson	1940–41
	Francis Biddle	1941–45
Postmaster General	James A. Farley	1933–40
	Frank C. Walker	1940–45
Secretary of Navy	Claude A. Swanson	1933–40
	Charles Edison	1940
	Frank Knox	1940–44
	James V. Forrestal	1944–45
Secretary of Interior	Harold L. Ickes	1933–45
Secretary of Agriculture	Henry A. Wallace	1933–40
	Claude R. Wickard	1940–45
Secretary of Commerce	Daniel C. Roper	1933–39
	Harry L. Hopkins	1939–40
	Jesse Jones	1940–45
	Henry A. Wallace	1945
Secretary of Labor	Frances Perkins	1933–45

Truman Administration (1945–53)

Secretary of State	Edward R. Stettinius, Jr.	1945
	James F. Byrnes	1945–47
	George C. Marshall	1947–49
	Dean G. Acheson	1949–53
Secretary of Treasury	Fred M. Vinson	1945–46
	John W. Snyder	1946–53
Secretary of War	Robert P. Patterson	1945–47
	Kenneth C. Royall	1947
Attorney General	Tom C. Clark	1945–49
	J. Howard McGrath	1949–52
	James P. McGranery	1952–53
Postmaster General	Frank C. Walker	1945
	Robert E. Hannegan	1945–47
	Jesse M. Donaldson	1947–53
Secretary of Navy	James V. Forrestal	1945–47
Secretary of Interior	Harold L. Ickes	1945–46
	Julius A. Krug	1946–49
	Oscar L. Chapman	1949–53
Secretary of Agriculture	Clinton P. Anderson	1945–48
	Charles F. Brannan	1948–53

Secretary of Commerce	Henry A. Wallace	1945–46
	W. Averell Harriman	1946–48
	Charles W. Sawyer	1948–53
Secretary of Labor	Lewis B. Schwellenbach	1945–48
	Maurice J. Tobin	1948–53
Secretary of Defense	James V. Forrestal	1947–49
	Louis A. Johnson	1949–50
	George C. Marshall	1950–51
	Robert A. Lovett	1951–53

Eisenhower Administration (1953–61)

Secretary of State	John Foster Dulles	1953–59
	Christian A. Herter	1959–61
Secretary of Treasury	George M. Humphrey	1953–57
	Robert B. Anderson	1957–61
Attorney General	Herbert Brownell, Jr.	1953–58
	William P. Rogers	1958–61
Postmaster General	Arthur E. Summerfield	1953–61
Secretary of Interior	Douglas McKay	1953–56
	Fred A. Seaton	1956–61
Secretary of Agriculture	Ezra T. Benson	1953–61
Secretary of Commerce	Sinclair Weeks	1953–58
	Lewis L. Strauss	1958–59
	Frederick H. Mueller	1959–61
Secretary of Labor	Martin P. Durkin	1953
	James P. Mitchell	1953–61
Secretary of Defense	Charles E. Wilson	1953–57
	Neil H. McElroy	1957–59
	Thomas S. Gates, Jr.	1959–61
Secretary of Health, Education, and Welfare	Oveta Culp Hobby	1953–55
	Marion B. Folsom	1955–58
	Arthur S. Flemming	1958–61

Kennedy Administration (1961–63)

Secretary of State	Dean Rusk	1961–63
Secretary of Treasury	C. Douglas Dillon	1961–63
Attorney General	Robert F. Kennedy	1961–63
Postmaster General	J. Edward Day	1961–63
	John A. Gronouski	1963
Secretary of Interior	Stewart L. Udall	1961–63
Secretary of Agriculture	Orville L. Freeman	1961–63
Secretary of Commerce	Luther H. Hodges	1961–63
Secretary of Labor	Arthur J. Goldberg	1961–62
	W. Willard Wirtz	1962–63
Secretary of Defense	Robert S. McNamara	1961–63
Secretary of Health, Education, and Welfare	Abraham A. Ribicoff	1961–62
	Anthony J. Celebrezze	1962–63

Lyndon Johnson Administration (1963–69)

Secretary of State	Dean Rusk	1963–69
Secretary of Treasury	C. Douglas Dillon	1963–65
	Henry H. Fowler	1965–69
Attorney General	Robert F. Kennedy	1963–64
	Nicholas Katzenbach	1965–66
	Ramsey Clark	1967–69
Postmaster General	John A. Gronouski	1963–65
	Lawrence F. O'Brien	1965–68
	Marvin Watson	1968–69
Secretary of Interior	Stewart L. Udall	1963–69
Secretary of Agriculture	Orville L. Freeman	1963–69
Secretary of Commerce	Luther H. Hodges	1963–64
	John T. Connor	1964–67
	Alexander B. Trowbridge	1967–68
	Cyrus R. Smith	1968–69
Secretary of Labor	W. Willard Wirtz	1963–69
Secretary of Defense	Robert F. McNamara	1963–68
	Clark Clifford	1968–69
Secretary of Health, Education, and Welfare	Anthony J. Celebrezze	1963–65
	John W. Gardner	1965–68
	Wilbur J. Cohen	1968–69

Secretary of Housing & Urban Development	Robert C. Weaver	1966–69
	Robert C. Wood	1969
Secretary of Transportation	Alan S. Boyd	1967–69

Nixon Administration (1969–74)

Secretary of State	William P. Rogers	1969–73
	Henry A. Kissinger	1973–74
Secretary of Treasury	David M. Kennedy	1969–70
	John B. Connally	1971–72
	George P. Shultz	1972–74
	William E. Simon	1974
Attorney General	John N. Mitchell	1969–72
	Richard G. Kleindienst	1973–73
	Elliot L. Richardson	1973
	William B. Saxbe	1973–74
Postmaster General	Winton M. Blount	1969–71
Secretary of Interior	Walter J. Hickel	1969–70
	Rogers Morton	1971–74
Secretary of Agriculture	Clifford M. Hardin	1969–71
	Earl L. Butz	1971–74
Secretary of Commerce	Maurice H. Stans	1969–72
	Peter G. Peterson	1972–73
	Frederick B. Dent	1973–74
Secretary of Labor	George P. Shultz	1969–70
	James D. Hodgson	1970–73
	Peter J. Brennan	1973–74
Secretary of Defense	Melvin R. Laird	1969–73
	Elliot L. Richardson	1973
	James R. Schlesinger	1973–74
Secretary of Health, Education, and Welfare	Robert H. Finch	1969–70
	Elliot L. Richardson	1970–73
	Caspar W. Weinberger	1973–74
Secretary of Housing & Urban Development	George Romney	1969–73
	James T. Lyon	1973–74
Secretary of Transportation	John A. Volpe	1969–73
	Claude S. Brinegar	1973–74

Ford Administration (1974–77)

Secretary of State	Henry A. Kissinger	1974–77
Secretary of Treasury	William E. Simon	1974–77
Attorney General	William Saxbe	1974–75
	Edward Levi	1975–77
Secretary of Interior	Rogers Morton	1974–75
	Stanley K. Hathaway	1975
	Thomas Kleppe	1975–77
Secretary of Agriculture	Earl L. Butz	1974–76
	John A. Knebel	1976–77
Secretary of Commerce	Frederick B. Dent	1974–75
	Rogers Morton	1975–76
	Elliot L. Richardson	1976–77
Secretary of Labor	Peter J. Brennan	1974–75
	John T. Dunlop	1975–76
	W. J. Usery	1976–77
Secretary of Defense	James R. Schlesinger	1974–75
	Donald Rumsfeld	1975–77
Secretary of Health, Education, and Welfare	Caspar Weinberger	1974–75
	Forrest D. Mathews	1975–77
Secretary of Housing & Urban Development	James T. Lynn	1974–75
	Carla A. Hills	1975–77
Secretary of Transportation	William T. Coleman	1975–77

Carter Administration (1977–81)

Secretary of State	Cyrus R. Vance	1977–80
	Edmund Muskie	1980–81
Secretary of Treasury	W. Michael Blumenthal	1977–79
	G. William Miller	1979–81
Attorney General	Griffin Bell	1977–79
	Benjamin R. Civiletti	1979–81

Secretary of Interior	Cecil D. Andrus	1977–81
Secretary of Agriculture	Robert Bergland	1977–81
Secretary of Commerce	Juanita M. Kreps	1977–79
	Philip M. Klutznick	1979–81
Secretary of Labor	F. Ray Marshall	1977–81
Secretary of Defense	Harold Brown	1977–81
Secretary of Health, Education, and Welfare	Joseph A. Califano	1977–79
	Patricia R. Harris	1979–80
Secretary of Health & Human Services[1]	Patricia R. Harris	1980–81
Secretary of Housing & Urban Development	Patricia R. Harris	1977–79
	Moon Landrieu	1979–81
Secretary of Transportation	Brock Adams	1977–79
	Neil E. Goldschmidt	1979–81
Secretary of Energy	James R. Schlesinger	1977–79
	Charles W. Duncan	1979–81
Secretary of Education[1]	Shirley M. Hufstedler	1980–81

1. The Dept. of Health, Education, and Welfare was split into the Dept. of Education and the Dept. of Health and Human Services on May 4, 1980.

Reagan Administration (1981–89)

Secretary of State	Alexander M. Haig	1981–82
	George P. Shultz	1982–89
Secretary of Treasury	Donald Regan	1981–85
	James A. Baker, III	1985–89
Secretary of Defense	Caspar Weinberger	1981–87
	Frank Carlucci	1987–89
Attorney General	William F. Smith	1981–85
	Edwin A. Meese, III	1985–88
	Richard L. Thornburgh	1988–89
Secretary of Interior	James Watt	1981–83
	William P. Clark, Jr.	1983–85
	Donald P. Hodel	1985–89
Secretary of Agriculture	John Block	1981–86
	Richard E. Lyng	1986–89
Secretary of Commerce	Malcolm Baldridge	1981–89
Secretary of Labor	Raymond Donovan	1981–85
	William E. Brock	1985–89
Secretary of Health & Human Services	Richard Schweiker	1981–83
	Margaret Heckler	1983–85
	Otis R. Bowen	1985–89
Secretary of Housing & Urban Development	Samuel Pierce	1981–89
Secretary of Transportation	Drew Lewis	1981–83
	Elizabeth Dole	1983–89
Secretary of Energy	James Edwards	1981–82
	Donald P. Hodel	1982–85
	John S. Herrington	1985–89
Secretary of Education	Terrel H. Bell	1981–85
	William J. Bennett	1985–89

George Bush Administration (1989–93)

Secretary of State	James A. Baker III	1989–92
	Lawrence Eagleburger	1992–93
Secretary of Treasury	Nicholas F. Brady	1989–93
Secretary of Defense	Dick Cheney	1989–93
Attorney General	Richard L. Thornburgh	1989–91
	William P. Barr	1991–93
Secretary of Interior	Manuel Lujan	1989–93
Secretary of Agriculture	Clayton K. Yeutter	1989–91
	Edward Madigan	1991–93
Secretary of Commerce	Robert A. Mosbacher	1989–91
	Barbara Franklin	1991–93
Secretary of Labor	Elizabeth Hanford Dole	1989–90
	Lynn Martin	1990–93
Secretary of Health & Human Services	Louis Sullivan	1989–93
Secretary of Housing & Urban Development	Jack F. Kemp	1989–93

Secretary of Transportation	Samuel K. Skinner	1989–91
	Andrew Card	1991–93
Secretary of Energy	James D. Watkins	1989–93
Secretary of Education	Lauro D. Cavazos	1989–90
	Lamar Alexander	1990–93
Secretary of Veterans' Affairs	Edward J. Derwinski	1989–92
	Anthony J. Principi	1992–93

Clinton Administration (1993–2001)

Secretary of State	Warren M. Christopher	1993–97
	Madeleine K. Albright	1997–2001
Secretary of Treasury	Lloyd Bentsen	1993–94
	Robert E. Rubin	1994–99
	Lawrence H. Summers	1999–2001
Secretary of Defense	Les Aspin	1993–94
	William Perry	1994–97
	William S. Cohen	1997–2001
Attorney General	Janet Reno	1993–2001
Secretary of Interior	Bruce Babbitt	1993–2001
Secretary of Agriculture	Mike Espy	1993–94
	Dan Glickman	1995–2001
Secretary of Commerce	Ronald H. Brown	1993–96
	Mickey Kantor	1996–97
	William M. Daley	1997–2000
	Norman Y. Mineta	2000–2001
Secretary of Labor	Robert B. Reich	1993–97
	Alexis M. Herman	1997–2001
Secretary of Health & Human Services	Donna E. Shalala	1993–2001
Secretary of Housing & Urban Development	Henry G. Cisneros	1993–97
	Andrew M. Cuomo	1997–2001
Secretary of Transportation	Federico F. Peña	1993–97
	Rodney E. Slater	1997–2001
Secretary of Energy	Hazel O'Leary	1993–97
	Federico F. Peña	1997–98
	Bill Richardson	1998–2001
Secretary of Education	Richard W. Riley	1993–2001
Secretary of Veterans' Affairs	Jesse Brown	1993–97
	Hershel Gober, acting	1997–98
	Togo D. West Jr.	1998–99
	Hershel Gober, acting	1999–2001

George W. Bush Administration (2001–)

Secretary of State	Colin Powell	2001–
Secretary of Treasury	Paul O'Neill	2001–
Secretary of Defense	Donald Rumsfeld	2001–
Attorney General	John Ashcroft	2001–
Secretary of Interior	Gale Norton	2001–
Secretary of Agriculture	Ann Veneman	2001–
Secretary of Commerce	Donald Evans	2001–
Secretary of Labor	Elaine Chao	2001–
Secretary of Health & Human Services	Tommy Thompson	2001–
Secretary of Housing & Urban Development	Mel Martinez	2001–
Secretary of Transportation	Norman Mineta	2001–
Secretary of Energy	Spencer Abraham	2001–
Secretary of Education	Rod Paige	2001–
Secretary of Veterans' Affairs	Anthony Principi	2001–

THE U.S. SUPREME COURT

►IMPORTANT SUPREME COURT DECISIONS

Marbury v. Madison (1803)   The Court struck down a law "repugnant to the constitution" for the first time and set the precedent for judicial review of acts of Congress. In a politically ingenious ruling on the Judiciary Act of 1789, Chief Justice John Marshall asserted the Supreme Court's power "to say what the law is," while avoiding a confrontation with President Thomas Jefferson. Not until the *Dred Scott* case of 1857 would another Federal law be ruled unconstitutional.

Fletcher v. Peck (1810)   The Court ruled that Georgia could not deprive land speculators of their title, even though the previous owners had obtained the land from the state through fraud and bribery. Arising from the infamous Yazoo land frauds of 1795, this decision followed the Constitution's obligation of contracts clause and was the first time the Court invalidated a state law.

Dartmouth College v. Woodward (1819) The Court encouraged business investment with this decision by treating corporate charters as fully protected contracts. Not even the state legislatures that originally granted them charters to private corporations, unless they retained the power to do so. Dartmouth College remained a private institution despite New Hampshire's attempt to take it over. This decision, which opened the way for abuse of corporate privileges, would later be modified in the *Charles River Bridge* (1837) and *Munn v. Illinois* (1877) cases.

McCulloch v. Maryland (1819)   "Broad," as opposed to "strict," construction of the Constitution received high court approval in Chief Justice John Marshall's opinion upholding the constitutionality of the national bank against a Maryland challenge. This ruling enhanced Federal governmental authority by liberally interpreting the power of Congress to make laws "necessary and proper" for its specified powers. At a time when states were trying to tax the Bank of the United States out of existence, this decision also forbade such state interference with the Federal government. "The power to tax," Marshall wrote, "involves the power to destroy."

Cohens v. Virginia (1821)   With this ruling, the Court reiterated its power to hear appeals from state courts, and affirmed the national supremacy of Federal judicial power. Virginia's conviction of the Cohens for selling lottery tickets in violation of state law was upheld, but so too was the Cohens' right to appeal to the Court, which Virginia had challenged. Critics of judicial "consolidationalism" were reminded of the Court's comprehensive powers as the ultimate appellate court for all Americans.

Gibbons v. Ogden (1824)   In a dispute arising from a New York ferry monopoly, the Court ruled that states could not restrain interstate commerce in any way, and that congressional power to regulate interstate commerce "does not stop at the jurisdictional lines of the several states." The decision helped prevent interstate trade wars, quite common under the Articles of Confederation, from breaking out under the Constitution. Chief Justice Marshall's opinion also confirmed the broad potential power of the Constitution's commerce clause.

Charles River Bridge v. Warren Bridge (1837) A key decision for economic development, this case arose when state-chartered proprietors of a Boston toll bridge objected that a new state-chartered bridge across the Charles River would put them out of business. Chief Justice Roger B. Taney, in his first constitutional ruling, held that state charters implied no vested rights and that ambiguities must be construed in favor of the public, which would benefit from the new toll-free bridge. This decision balanced private property rights against the public welfare.

Dred Scott v. Sanford (1857)   Dred Scott, a Missouri slave, sued for his liberty after his owner took him into free territory. The Court ruled that Congress could not bar slavery in the territories. Scott remained a slave because the Missouri Compromise of 1820, prohibiting slavery from part of the Louisiana Purchase, violated the Fifth Amendment by depriving slave owners of their right to enjoy property without due process of law. Scott himself could not even sue, for he was held to be property, not a citizen. This decision sharpened sectional conflict by sweeping away legal barriers to the expansion of slavery.

Ex Parte Milligan (1866)   President Abraham Lincoln's suspension of some civil liberties during the Civil War was attacked in this decision, which upheld the right of *habeas corpus*. The Court ruled that the president could not hold military tribunals in areas remote from battle and where civil courts were open and functioning. Milligan's conviction by such a Civil War tribunal in Indianapolis, was overturned. The Constitution, admonished the Court, applies "at all times, and under all circumstances."

Slaughter-House Cases (1873)   In its first ruling on the Fourteenth Amendment, the Court held that Louisiana's grant of a butcher monopoly did not violate the privileges and immunities of competitors, nor deny them equal protection of the laws, nor deprive them of property without due process. Only a few rights deriving from "Federal citizenship" were subject to Federal protection, while states still protected most civil and property rights. Federal protection of civil rights, even for former slaves, was very narrowly interpreted in this ruling. But this decision broadly upheld business regulation by states until

Chief Justices of the United States

Chief Justice	Tenure[1]	Appointed by
John Jay	1789–1795	George Washington
John Rutledge[3]	1795	George Washington
Oliver Ellsworth	1796–1800	George Washington
John Marshall[4]	1801–35	John Adams
Roger B. Taney	1836–64	Andrew Jackson
Salmon P. Chase	1864–73	Abraham Lincoln
Morrison R. Waite	1874–88	Ulysses S. Grant
Melville W. Fuller	1888–1910	Grover Cleveland
Edward D. White	1910–21	William Howard Taft
William Howard Taft[5]	1921–30	Warren G. Harding
Charles Evans Hughes[2]	1930–41	Herbert Hoover
Harlan F. Stone[2]	1941–46	Franklin D. Roosevelt
Fred M. Vinson	1946–53	Harry S Truman
Earl Warren	1953–69	Dwight D. Eisenhower
Warren E. Burger	1969–87	Richard M. Nixon
William H. Rehnquist[2]	1987–	Ronald Reagan

1. Dates are for tenure as Chief Justice. For complete tenure on Supreme Court, see "Supreme Court Justices." 2. Served as Associate Justice prior to appointment as Chief Justice. 3. Served one term, but appointment not confirmed by Senate. 4. Longest tenure as Chief Justice. 5. Formerly served as 27th president of the United States.

Santa Clara Co. v. Southern Pacific Railroad Co. (1886) applied the Fourteenth Amendment to defense of corporate property rights.

Munn v. Illinois (1877)   This decision, in one of the "Granger Cases," enabled states to regulate private property in the public interest when the public had an interest in that property. The Court held that Illinois laws setting maximum rates for grain storage

did not violate the Fourteenth Amendment's ban on deprivation of property without due process of law, and did not restrain interstate commerce. But for the next half century, the Court imposed the burden of proof on the states for their regulatory laws.

Civil Rights Cases (1883)   Racial equality was postponed 80 years by this decision, which struck down the Civil Rights Act of 1875 and allowed for

Justices of the Supreme Court of the United States, 1789–2001

Name	Tenure	Appointed by	Name	Tenure	Appointed by
Baldwin, Henry	1830–44	Andrew Jackson	Livingston, H. Brockholst	1806–23	Thomas Jefferson
Barbour, Philip P.	1836–41	Andrew Jackson			
Black, Hugo L.	1937–71	Franklin D. Roosevelt	Lurton, Horace H.	1910–14	William Howard Taft
Blackmun, Harry A.	1970–94	Richard M. Nixon	Marshall, John[1]	1801–35	John Adams
Blair, John	1789–96	George Washington	Marshall, Thurgood	1967–92	Lyndon B. Johnson
Blatchford, Samuel	1882–93	Chester A. Arthur	Matthews, Stanley	1881–89	James A. Garfield
Bradley, Joseph P.	1870–92	Ulysses S. Grant	McKenna, Joseph	1898–1925	William McKinley
Brandeis, Louis D.	1916–39	Woodrow Wilson	McKinley, John	1837–52	Martin Van Buren
Brennan, William J., Jr.	1956–90	Dwight D. Eisenhower	McLean, John	1829–61	Andrew Jackson
Brewer, David J.	1889–1910	Benjamin Harrison	McReynolds, James C.	1914–41	Woodrow Wilson
Breyer, Stephen G.	1994–	Bill Clinton	Miller, Samuel F.	1862–90	Abraham Lincoln
Brown, Henry B.	1890–1906	Benjamin Harrison	Minton, Sherman	1949–56	Harry S Truman
Burger, Warren E.[1]	1969–86	Richard M. Nixon	Moody, William H.	1906–10	Theodore Roosevelt
Burton, Harold H.	1945–58	Harry S Truman	Moore, Alfred	1799–1804	John Adams
Butler, Pierce	1922–39	Warren G. Harding	Murphy, Frank	1940–49	Franklin D. Roosevelt
Byrnes, James F.	1941–42	Franklin D. Roosevelt	Nelson, Samuel	1845–72	John Tyler
Campbell, John A.	1853–61	Franklin Pierce	O'Connor, Sandra Day	1981–	Ronald Reagan
Cardozo, Benjamin N.	1932–38	Herbert Hoover	Paterson, William	1793–1806	George Washington
Catron, John	1837–65	Martin Van Buren	Peckham, Rufus W.	1895–1910	Grover Cleveland
Chase, Salmon P.[1]	1864–73	Abraham Lincoln	Pitney, Mahlon	1912–22	William Howard Taft
Chase, Samuel	1796–1811	George Washington	Powell, Lewis F., Jr.	1972–87	Richard M. Nixon
Clark, Tom C.	1949–67	Harry S Truman	Reed, Stanley F.	1938–57	Franklin D. Roosevelt
Clarke, John H.	1916–22	Woodrow Wilson	Rehnquist, William H.[1]	1972–	Richard M. Nixon
Clifford, Nathan	1858–81	James J. Buchanan	Roberts, Owen J.	1930–45	Herbert Hoover
Curtis, Benjamin R.	1851–57	Millard Fillmore	Rutledge, John[1]	1789–91	George Washington
Cushing, William	1789–1810	George Washington		1795	George Washington
Daniel, Peter V.	1841–60	Martin Van Buren	Rutledge, Wiley B.	1943–49	Franklin D. Roosevelt
Davis, David	1862–77	Abraham Lincoln	Sanford, Edward T.	1923–30	Warren G. Harding
Day, William R.	1903–22	Theodore Roosevelt	Scalia, Antonin	1986–	Ronald Reagan
Douglas, William O.[2]	1939–75	Franklin D. Roosevelt	Shiras, George	1892–1903	Benjamin Harrison
Duval, Gabriel	1811–36	James Madison	Souter, David H.	1990–	George Bush
Ellsworth, Oliver[1]	1796–1800	George Washington	Stevens, John Paul	1975–	Gerald R. Ford
Field, Stephen J.	1863–97	Abraham Lincoln	Stewart, Potter	1959–81	Dwight D. Eisenhower
Fortas, Abe	1965–69	Lyndon B. Johnson	Stone, Harlan F.[1]	1925–46	Calvin Coolidge
Frankfurter, Felix	1939–62	Franklin D. Roosevelt	Story, Joseph	1811–45	James Madison
Fuller, Melville W.[1]	1888–1910	Grover Cleveland	Strong, William	1870–80	Ulysses S. Grant
Ginsburg, Ruth Bader	1993–	Bill Clinton	Sutherland, George	1922–38	Warren G. Harding
Goldberg, Arthur J.	1962–65	John F. Kennedy	Swayne, Noah H.	1862–81	Abraham Lincoln
Gray, Horace	1881–1902	Chester A. Arthur	Taft, William Howard[1,5]	1921–30	Warren G. Harding
Grier, Robert C.	1846–70	James K. Polk	Taney, Roger B.[1]	1836–64	Andrew Jackson
Harlan, John Marshall	1877–1911	Rutherford B. Hayes	Thomas, Clarence	1991–	George Bush
Harlan, John Marshall[3]	1955–71	Dwight D. Eisenhower	Thompson, Smith	1823–43	James Monroe
Harrison, Robert H.	1789–90	George Washington	Todd, Thomas	1807–26	Thomas Jefferson
Holmes, Oliver Wendell	1902–32	Theodore Roosevelt	Trimble, Robert	1826–28	John Quincy Adams
Hughes, Charles Evans[1,4]	1910–16	William Howard Taft	Van Devanter, Willis	1910–37	William Howard Taft
	1930–41	Herbert Hoover	Vinson, Fred M.[1]	1946–53	Harry S Truman
Hunt, Ward	1872–82	Ulysses S. Grant	Waite, Morrison R.[1]	1874–88	Ulysses S. Grant
Iredell, James	1790–99	George Washington	Warren, Earl[1]	1953–69	Dwight D. Eisenhower
Jackson, Howell E.	1893–95	Benjamin Harrison	Washington, Bushrod	1798–1829	John Adams
Jackson, Robert H.	1941–54	Franklin D. Roosevelt	Wayne, James M.	1835–67	Andrew Jackson
Jay, John[1]	1789–95	George Washington	White, Byron R.	1962–93	John F. Kennedy
Johnson, Thomas	1791–93	George Washington	White, Edward D.[1]	1894–1921	Grover Cleveland
Johnson, William	1804–34	Thomas Jefferson	Whittaker, Charles E.	1957–62	Dwight D. Eisenhower
Kennedy, Anthony M.	1987–	Ronald Reagan	Wilson, James	1789–98	George Washington
Lamar, Joseph R.	1911–16	William Howard Taft	Woodbury, Levi	1845–51	James K. Polk
Lamar, Lucius Q. C.	1888–93	Grover Cleveland	Woods, William B.	1880–87	Rutherford B. Hayes

Note: Dates reflect complete tenure on the Supreme Court, including tenure as Chief Justice. 1. See "Chief Justices of the United States" for dates of tenure and appointment as Chief Justice. 2. Longest-serving justice. 3. The two Harlans were grandfather and grandson. 4. Stepped down as Associate Justice to run for president in 1916; later appointed Chief Justice. 5. Formerly served as 27th U.S. president private segregation. The Fourteenth Amendment's guarantee of equal protection, the Court ruled, applied against state action—but not against private individuals, whose discrimination unaided by the states was beyond Federal control. Segregation of public facilities was approved soon afterward in *Plessy v. Ferguson* (1896).

United States v. E.C. Knight Co. (1895)
The first ruling on the Sherman Antitrust Act of 1890, this decision curtailed Federal regulation of monopolies by placing national manufacturers beyond the reach of the Constitution's commerce clause. Only the actual interstate commerce of monopolies, not their production activities, was subject to Federal control. The Court's distinction between production and commerce impeded Federal regulation of manufacturing until *National Labor Relations Board v. Jones & Laughlin Steel Corp.* (1937).

Plessy v. Ferguson (1896)
The "separate but equal" doctrine supporting public segregation by law received the Court's approval in this ruling, which originated with segregated railroad cars in Louisiana. The Court held that as long as equal accommodations were provided, segregation was not discrimination and did not deprive blacks of equal protection of the laws under the Fourteenth Amendment. This decision was overturned in *Brown v. Board of Education* (1954).

Lochner v. New York (1905)
This decision struck down a New York law placing limits on maximum working hours for bakers. The law violated the Fourteenth Amendment by restricting individual "freedom of contract" to buy and sell labor, and was an excessive use of state police power, the Court held. The ruling was soon modified in *Muller v. Oregon* (1908), which approved state-regulated limits on women's labor after the Court used sociological and economic data to consider the health and morals of women workers.

Standard Oil Co. of New Jersey v. United States (1911)
Federal efforts to break up monopolies under the Sherman Antitrust Act had to follow the "rule of reason," according to this ruling. Only those combinations in restraint of trade which were contrary to the public interest, and therefore unreasonable, were illegal. Although the Taft administration's prosecution of Standard Oil was upheld, breaking up one of the nation's leading monopolies, further antitrust suits were impaired by this decision, which facilitated the 1920s merger movement.

Schenk v. United States (1919)
The Court unanimously held that World War I limits on freedom of speech did not violate the First Amendment—if the speech in question represented a "clear and present danger." That famous doctrine of Justice Oliver Wendell Holmes, which approved the arrest of a draft resister for handing out pamphlets to soldiers in wartime, became an important standard for interpreting the First Amendment. But in subsequent cases of this period, the Court added that the mere "bad tendency" of speech to cause danger could be grounds for censorship.

Schechter Poultry Corp. v. United States (1935)
At the height of its assault on the New Deal, the Court struck down the National Industrial Recovery Act in the famous "Sick Chicken Case." The NIRA was found to delegate excessive legislative regulatory powers to the executive without constitutional authority, and to regulate commerce within states in violation of the commerce clause.

Schechter's kosher chicken supply house in New York did not have to abide by the NIRA's rigid industry codes, the Court ruled.

National Labor Relations Board v. Jones & Laughlin Steel Corp. (1937)
Under pressure from the public and President Franklin D. Roosevelt, the Court abruptly reversed itself and began approving New Deal legislation. In this case, laws protecting unions and barring "unfair labor practices" were upheld by the "stream of commerce" doctrine that employers who sold their goods and obtained their raw materials through interstate commerce were subject to Federal regulation. This ruling overturned *U.S. v. E.C. Knight Co.* (1895) and became the basis for the expansive understanding of the commerce power.

West Virginia Board of Education v. Barnette (1943)
The Court reversed its earlier ruling in *Minersville School District v. Gobitis* (1940), which had required Jehovah's Witnesses to salute the flag in school. In this case, also brought against a Jehovah's Witness, the Court recognized that refusing to salute the flag did not violate anyone's rights, and that the First Amendment protected the "right of silence" as well as freedom of speech.

Korematsu v. United States (1944)
President Franklin D. Roosevelt's Executive Order No. 9066, which approved the West Coast evacuation and internment of 120,000 Japanese-Americans during World War II, was upheld on the grounds of "military necessity" in this ruling. The Court was reluctant to interfere with executive authority in time of national emergency. But in *Ex parte Endo* (1944), the Court held that persons of proven loyalty should not be interned. In August 1988, Congress made a formal apology to former internees and appropriated $1.25 billion in compensation for the 60,000 survivors.

Dennis v. United States (1951)
At the height of the postwar "Red Scare," the Court upheld the conviction of 11 American Communist leaders under the Smith Act of 1940, which made it a crime to belong to organizations teaching or advocating the violent overthrow of the government. The "clear and present danger" doctrine could be disregarded, the Court held, if "the gravity of the 'evil,' discounted by its improbability, justifies such invasion of free speech as is necessary to avoid the evil." Over 100 Communists were indicted as a result, effectively destroying the Communist Party as a political force.

Youngstown Sheet and Tube Co. v. Sawyer (1952)
During the Korean War, when President Harry S Truman seized steel plants to keep them operating despite a strike, the Court held that his action was an unconstitutional usurpation of legislative authority. Only an act of Congress, not the president's inherent executive powers or military powers as commander-in-chief, could justify such a sizeable confiscation of property, despite the wartime emergency.

Brown v. Board of Education of Topeka (1954)
Chief Justice Earl Warren led the Court unanimously to decide that segregated schools violated the equal protection clause of the Fourteenth Amendment. The "separate but equal" doctrine of *Plessy v. Ferguson* (1896) was overruled after a series of cases dating back to *Missouri ex. rel. Gaines v. Canada* (1938) had already limited it. "Separate educational facilities are inherently unequal," held the Court. Efforts to desegregate southern schools after the *Brown* decision met with massive resistance for many years.

Baker v. Carr (1962) Overrepresentation of rural districts in state legislatures, which effectively disfranchised millions of voters, led the Court to abandon its traditional non-interference in drawing legislative boundaries. Tennessee citizens deprived of full representation by "arbitrary and capricious" malapportionment were denied equal protection under the Fourteenth Amendment, ruled the Court. All states eventually reapportioned their legislatures in conformance with the "one man, one vote" doctrine of *Reynolds v. Sims* (1964).

Gideon v. Wainwright (1963) Reversing an earlier ruling in *Betts v. Brady* (1942), the Court held that the Sixth Amendment guaranteed access to qualified counsel, which was "fundamental to a fair trial." Gideon was entitled to a retrial because Florida failed to provide him with an attorney. After this decision, states were required to furnish public defenders for indigent defendants in felony cases. In *Argersinger v. Hamlin* (1972), the ruling was extended to all cases that might result in imprisonment.

Heart of Atlanta Motel, Inc. v. United States (1964) The Court upheld Title II of the Civil Rights Act of 1964, outlawing private discrimination in public accommodations, as a legitimate exertion of Federal power over interstate commerce. Congress had "ample power" to forbid racial discrimination in facilities that affected commerce by serving interstate travelers. The Heart of Atlanta Motel was located on two interstate highways, so the Court could sidestep the *Civil Rights Cases* (1883) protection of private discrimination to overrule it.

Griswold v. Connecticut (1965) In striking down an 1879 Connecticut law against the use of contraceptives, the Court established a "right to privacy" that was implied by, though not specifically enumerated in the First, Third, Fourth, Fifth, Ninth, and Fourteenth Amendments. The case is most notable for laying the groundwork for other legal challenges invoking this newfound right to privacy. Foremost among them is the 1973 *Roe v. Wade* decision allowing women to choose abortion.

South Carolina v. Katzenbach (1966) Federal intervention on behalf of voting rights was upheld in this decision. South Carolina sued the Attorney General, contending that the 1965 Voting Rights Act encroached on the reserved powers of the states, treated the states unequally, and violated separation of powers. Chief Justice Warren ruled that the Fifteenth Amendment gave Congress broad powers to "use any rational means to effectuate the constitutional prohibition of racial discrimination in voting." After this decision, blacks registered and voted in massive numbers in the South.

Miranda v. Arizona (1966) Expanding upon *Gideon v. Wainwright* (1963) and *Escobedo v. Illinois* (1964), the Court set forth stringent interrogation procedures for criminal suspects to protect their Fifth Amendment freedom from self-incrimination. Miranda's confession to kidnapping and rape was obtained without counsel and without his having been advised of his right to silence, so it was ruled inadmissable as evidence. This decision obliged police to advise suspects of their rights upon taking them into custody.

New York Times Co. v. United States (1971) When the *New York Times* and the *Washington Post* published the top-secret "Pentagon Papers" in 1971, revealing government duplicity in the Vietnam War, the Nixon administration obtained an injunction against the *Times* on grounds of national security. But in a brief *per curiam* opinion, the Court observed that in this case, the government had not met the "heavy burden of showing justification" for "prior restraint" on freedom of the press.

Roe v. Wade (1973) In a controversial ruling, the Court held that state laws restricting abortion were an unconstitutional invasion of a woman's right to privacy. Only in the last trimester of pregnancy, when the fetus achieved viability outside the womb, might states regulate abortion—except when the life or health of the mother was at stake. In *Planned Parenthood of Central Missouri v. Danforth* (1976), the Court added that wives did not need their husbands' consent to obtain abortions.

United States v. Nixon (1974) In a unanimous ruling, the Court held that the secret White House recordings of President Richard M. Nixon's conversations with aides were subject to subpoena in the Watergate coverup trial. Nixon's claim to "executive privilege" was rejected as invalid because military and national security issues were not at stake, and Chief Justice Warren Burger cited *Marbury v. Madison* (1803) to assert the Court's primacy in constitutional issues. Once the tapes were released, documenting Nixon's obstruction of justice, the president resigned to avoid impeachment.

University of California Regents v. Bakke (1978) Twice refused admission to medical school, Bakke sued the University of California for giving "affirmative action" preference to less-qualified black applicants. In an ambiguous 5-4 ruling, the Court agreed that Bakke's right to equal protection had been denied, that he should be admitted, and that affirmative action quotas should be discarded. But at the same time, the Court recognized race as "a factor" in admissions and hiring. Affirmative action could continue as long as rigid quotas did not constitute, in effect, "reverse discrimination."

Immigration and Naturalization Service v. Chadha (1983) The legislative veto, contained in hundreds of Federal statutes since 1932, was disallowed in this decision. Congress exceeded its constitutional powers when it blocked the Attorney General's suspension of a deportation order for Jagdish Rai Chadha, a Kenyan student who overstayed his visa. The Court held that the Immigration and Nationality Act's legislative veto provision violated the constitutional separation of powers. Chief Justice Burger recognized that Congress would prefer to delegate authority to the executive branch and reserve the right to veto administrative regulations, but "we have not found a better way to preserve freedom" than the separation of powers.

Bowers v. Hardwick (1986) In a controversial 5-4 decision applauded by fundamentalists but protested by gay activists, the Court ruled that the constitutional right to privacy does not protect homosexual relations, even between consenting adults in their own homes. Georgia's law against oral and anal sex, passed in 1816, could be applied to homosexuals (the Court declined to rule on whether heterosexuals might also be prosecuted). The decision raised fears of bedroom patrols and sexual surveillance, despite a right to privacy in intimate personal matters established in cases dating back to the 1920s. Justice Byron White ruled that "none of the rights announced in those cases bears any resemblance to the claimed constitutional right of homosexuals to engage in acts of sodomy."

Bush v. Gore (2000) (See Part I: "Major News Stories of the Year.")

The Federal Government

In their desire to create a government based on an elaborate system of "checks and balances," the Founding Fathers divided the sources of power into three separate and distinct branches of government—the legislative, the judicial, and the executive. The fundamental purpose, organization, and workings of these three branches are set down in the first three articles of the Constitution. Despite the passing of more than two centuries, the creation of dozens of departments, agencies, and commissions, the ongoing employment of almost 2.5 million civilian workers, and the presence of a standing peacetime military force of some 1.5 million, this structure remains essentially unchanged.

Below is a list of every major body within the Federal Government. Wherever possible, a Web home page is included. Every entry mentions the date each entity was founded and summarizes its official function. (The primary source of this information is the National Archives and Records Administration, Office of the Federal Register, *U.S. Government Manual*.)

THE JUDICIAL BRANCH

▶SUPREME COURT OF THE UNITED STATES
United States Supreme Court Building; 1 First St. NE, Washington, D.C. 20543. (202) 479-3000. Created by Judiciary Act of September 24, 1789 in accordance with Article III, Section 1 of the Constitution. Comprised of the chief justice and a number of associate justices to be fixed by Congress. Justices (including the chief justice) are chosen by the president with the advice and consent of the Senate and have lifetime tenure. Court terms begin the first Monday of October and usually last until the end of June. In recent years, the Court has seen the size of its docket nearly double (from 4,212 in 1970 to close to 8,000 in 1997), but it has heard fewer and fewer of these cases (see the accompanying table).

▶LOWER COURTS
U.S. Courts of Appeals
These intermediate appellate courts were created by act of March 3, 1891, to relieve the Supreme Court of having to reconsider all trials originally decided by Federal courts. Decisions of these courts are final except when law provides for direct review by the Supreme Court. Each of the 50 states is assigned to one of the following judicial circuits that compose the Court of Appeals system.

District of Columbia Circuit: Washington, D.C.
First Circuit: Maine, Massachusetts, New Hampshire, Rhode Island, Puerto Rico.

The Supreme Court, 2001

Name	Appointed by	Born	Law school
William H. Rehnquist (chief justice)	Nixon, 1972 Reagan, 1986	1924	Stanford
John Paul Stevens	Ford, 1975	1920	Northwestern
Sandra Day O'Connor	Reagan, 1981	1930	Stanford
Antonin Scalia	Reagan, 1986	1936	Harvard
Anthony M. Kennedy	Reagan, 1987	1936	Harvard
David H. Souter	Bush, 1990	1939	Harvard
Clarence Thomas	Bush, 1991	1948	Yale
Ruth Bader Ginsburg	Clinton, 1993	1933	Columbia
Stephen G. Breyer	Clinton, 1994	1945	Yale

Cases Before U.S. Supreme Court, U.S. Courts of Appeals, and U.S. District Courts, 1970–98

Status	1970	1980	1990	1995	1996	1997	1998
U.S. Supreme Court[1]							
Total cases on docket	4,212	5,144	6,316	7,565	7,602	7,692	8,083
Cases argued	151	154	125	90	90	96	90
Number of signed opinions	109	123	112	75	80	91	75
U.S. Courts of Appeals[2]							
Cases commenced	11,662	23,200	40,898	49,671	51,524	52,571	53,328
Cases terminated	10,699	20,887	38,520	50,085	49,359	51,295	51,348
Cases disposed of[3]	6,139	10,607	21,006	28,187	26,988	26,287	24,917
Median months to final disposition[4]	8.2	8.9	10.1	10.5	10.3	11.1	11.5
U.S. District Courts[2]							
Civil cases commenced[5]	87,300	168,800	217,900	239,013	272,681	265,151	261,252
Trials[5, 6]	8,000	10,100	9,200	7,700	7,500	7,400	N.A.
Percent reaching trial	10.0%	6.5%	4.3%	3.4%	3.1%	3.0%	N.A.
Criminal cases commenced[5, 7]	38,100	28,000	46,500	44,200	47,100	48,700	N.A.
Defendants disposed of	36,400	36,600	56,500	55,300	59,500	62,100	N.A.
Not convicted	8,200	8,000	9,800	9,000	8,500	7,500	N.A.
Convicted	28,200	28,600	46,700	46,300	51,000	54,500	N.A.

1. Statutory term of court begins first Monday in October. 2. For year ending June 30. 3. Terminated on the merits after hearing or submission. Beginning 1980, data not comparable with earlier years due to changes in criteria. 4. Prior to 1985, the figure is from filing of complete record to final disposition; beginning 1985, figure is from filing notice of appeal to final disposition. 5. Figures rounded in source. 6. A trial is defined as a contested proceeding (other than a hearing on a motion) before either court or jury in which evidence is introduced and final judgment sought. 7. Excludes transfers.   **Source:** Office of the Clerk, Supreme Court of the United States, unpublished data; Administrative Office of the U.S. Courts, *Annual Report of the Director*.

Second Circuit: Connecticut, New York, Vermont
Third Circuit: Delaware, New Jersey, Pennsylvania, Virgin Islands
Fourth Circuit: Maryland, North Carolina, South Carolina, Virginia, West Virginia
Fifth Circuit: Louisiana, Mississippi, Texas
Sixth Circuit: Kentucky, Michigan, Ohio, Tennessee
Seventh Circuit: Illinois, Indiana, Wisconsin
Eighth Circuit: Arkansas, Iowa, Minnesota, Missouri, Nebraska, North Dakota, South Dakota
Ninth Circuit: Alaska, Arizona, California, Guam, Hawaii, Idaho, Montana, Nevada, Northern Mariana Islands, Oregon, Washington
Tenth Circuit: Colorado, Kansas, New Mexico, Oklahoma, Utah, Wyoming
Eleventh Circuit: Alabama, Florida, Georgia
Federal Circuit

U.S. District Courts   These are trial courts of general Federal jurisdiction. There are 89 courts in the 50 states, including at least one in each state and the District of Columbia. Each court has from 2 to 28 federal district judgeships, depending on the amount of work within the territory. Overall, there are 610 permanent district judges in the 50 states, 15 in the District of Columbia and seven in Puerto Rico. Usually one judge is required to decide a case, but in some limited cases it is required that three judges be called together to comprise the court.

Administrative Office of the U.S. Courts   One Columbus Circle NE, Washington, D.C.   20544. (202)-502-2600.   www.uscourts.gov. Created by act of Aug. 7, 1939. Its areas of primary concern are administering courts, supervising probation office, and overseeing administration of bankruptcy courts, magistrate offices, and public defender's offices.

Federal Judicial Center   Thurgood Marshall Federal Judiciary Building, One Columbus Circle NE, Washington,   D.C.   20002-8003.   (202)-502-4000. www.fjc.gov. Created by act of Dec. 20, 1967. Its mission is to further the development and adoption of improved judicial administration in U.S. courts. The Chief Justice of the Supreme Court is the permanent chairman of the center's Board of Directors.

United States Sentencing Commission.   Suite 2-500, South Lobby, One Columbus Circle NE, Washington,   D.C.   20002-8002.   (202)-502-4500. www.ussc.gov. Created by the Sentencing Reform Act of 1984. Establishes sentencing guidelines (including forms and severity of punishment) for federal offenses.

THE LEGISLATIVE BRANCH

Architect of the Capitol   U.S. Capitol Building, Washington, D.C. 20515. (202) 228-1793. www.aoc.gov. First Architect appointed in 1793 by President. Permanent authority for care of Capitol established by Act of August 15, 1876. Responsible for care and maintenance of Capitol building and grounds, Library of Congress buildings, and U.S. Supreme Court building. Operates Senate and House restaurants. Maintains, operates, and cares for House and Senate office buildings. Plans future construction, renovation, reconstruction, and alterations to existing buildings.

U.S. Botanic Garden   Director's Office: 245 First Street SW, Washington, D.C. 20024. (202) 225-8333. www.aoc.gov. Conservatory: Maryland Avenue-First to Second Streets SW; Washington, D.C. 20024. (202) 225-6646. Created in 1820. Collects, cultivates, and grows vegetable and plant matter of this and other countries for exhibition and display. Provides study materials on vegetable and plant matter for students, botanists, horticulturists, floriculturists, and garden clubs.

General Accounting Office (GAO)   441 G Street NW Washington, D.C. 20548. (202) 512-3000. www.gao.gov. Created in 1921 by Budget and Accounting Act. Provides legal, accounting, auditing, and claims settlement services for Congress. Facilitates more efficient government operations.

Government Printing Office (GPO)   732 North Capitol Street NW, Washington, D.C. 20401. (202) 512-0000. www.access.gpo.gov. Created June 23, 1860 by Congressional Joint Resolution 25. Provides printing and binding services for Congress and the departments and establishments of the Federal Government. Furnishes blank paper, ink, and supplies to all agencies. Prepares and distributes catalogs and Government publications.

Library of Congress   101 Independence Ave. SE Washington, D.C. 20540. (202) 707-5000. http://lcweb.loc.gov. Created by law of April 24, 1800. Librarian appointed by the President. Buys books necessary for use by Congress and/or other governmental agencies. National library of the United States. Develops and maintains national book classification systems such as the Library of Congress and Dewey Decimal systems. Maintains and publishes The National Union Catalogs.

Congressional Budget Office (CBO)   Second and D Streets SW Washington, D.C. 20515. (202) 226-2600. www.cbo.gov. Created by Congressional Budget Act of 1974. Provides Congress with basic budget data. Analyzes and evaluates alternative fiscal and budgetary policy options and programs and makes recommendations to Congress. Publishes annual report on the budget.

How A Bill Becomes Law

Usually bills are raised in any of the various committees of the Senate or House of Representatives. If the bill is supported by a majority of the committee, it is brought to the floor of the house in which it originated, and voted upon. If it gains majority support in the full Senate or House, the other house of Congress votes on it. If the bill is passed in both the Senate and House, it is sent to the President, who may either sign it, veto it, or not act on it.

If the president signs it or refuses to act within 10 days and the Congress is still in session, the bill becomes law. If the president vetoes it, it is returned to the Senate and the House for another vote; a two-thirds majority in each house is then required to overturn the presidential veto. However, if the president refuses to act on a bill and Congress adjourns before the end of the 10-day period, the legislation is dead. This is known as a pocket veto.

Occasionally, bills are raised on the floor of the Senate or the House, in which case the first step of committee voting is avoided and the legislation process begins with the full Senate or House Vote. All other processes remain the same.

How to Contact Your Senator or Representative

To contact any Senator, call (202)-224-3121. More information about the Senate is available on the Internet at **www.senate.gov.** To reach a Representative, call (202)-225-3121. More information about the House is available on the Internet at **www.house.gov**

The 107th Congress of the United States

The upper house of the U.S. Congress, the Senate, is composed of 100 members: two from each state. Members are elected to six-year terms. One-third of the Senate faces re-election every two years. Senators must have been U.S. citizens for at least nine years and must be at least 30 years old. In the table below, the senior senator is listed first.

The lower house of government is known as the House of Representatives, and is composed of 435 members. The number of representatives from each state is determined by population every 10 years; every state is entitled to at least one representative. The entire House faces re-election every two years. Representatives must have been U.S. citizens for at least seven years and must be at least 25 years old.

In addition to state representatives, there are delegates from the District of Columbia, American Samoa, Guam, and the Virgin Islands, and a resident commissioner from Puerto Rico. They may take part in floor debates, but they may not vote.

Senate Offices

President	Dick Cheney (R)
Majority Leader	Thomas A. Daschle (D)
Majority Whip	Harry Reid (D)
Minority Leader	Trent Lott (R)
Minority Whip	Don Nickles (R)

House Offices

Speaker	Dennis Hastert (R)
Majority Leader	Dick Armey (R)
Majority Whip	Tom DeLay (R)
Minority Leader	Richard Gephardt (D)
Minority Whip	Nancy Pelosi (D)

Alabama
Richard C. Shelby (R)
Jeff Sessions (R)

Alaska
Ted Stevens (R)
Frank H. Murkowski (R)

Arizona
John McCain (R)
Jon Kyl (R)

Arkansas
Tim Hutchinson (R)
Blanche Lincoln (D)

California
Dianne Feinstein (D)
Barbara Boxer (D)

Colorado
Ben Nighthorse Campbell (R)
Wayne A. Allard (R)

Connecticut
Christopher J. Dodd (D)
Joseph I. Lieberman (D)

Delaware
Joseph R. Biden Jr. (D)
Thomas R. Carper (D)

Florida
Bob Graham (D)
Bill Nelson (D)

Georgia
Max Cleland (D)
Zell Miller (D)

Hawaii
Daniel K. Inouye (D)
Daniel K. Akaka (D)

Idaho
Larry E. Craig (R)
Mike Crapo (R)

Illinois
Peter Fitzgerald (R)
Richard J. Durbin (D)

Indiana
Richard G. Lugar (R)
Evan Bayh (D)

Iowa
Chuck Grassley (R)
Tom Harkin (D)

Kansas
Pat Roberts (R)
Sam Brownback (R)

Kentucky
Mitch McConnell (R)
Jim Bunning (R)

Louisiana
John B. Breaux (D)
Mary Landrieu (D)

Maine
Olympia J. Snowe (R)
Susan Collins (R)

Maryland
Paul S. Sarbanes (D)
Barbara A. Mikulski (D)

Massachusetts
Edward M. Kennedy (D)
John F. Kerry (D)

Michigan
Carl Levin (D)
Debbie Stabenow (D)

Minnesota
Paul Wellstone (DFL)
Mark Dayton (DFL)

Mississippi
Thad Cochran (R)
Trent Lott (R)

Missouri
Christopher S. Bond (R)
Jean Carnahan (D)

Montana
Max Baucus (D)
Conrad R. Burns (R)

Nebraska
Charles Hagel (R)
Ben Nelson (D)

Nevada
Harry Reid (D)
John Ensign (R)

New Hampshire
Bob Smith (R)
Judd Gregg (R)

New Jersey
Robert Torricelli (D)
Jon Corzine (D)

New Mexico
Pete V. Domenici (R)
Jeff Bingaman (D)

New York
Charles Schumer (D)
Hillary Rodham Clinton (D)

North Carolina
Jesse Helms (R)
John Edwards (D)

North Dakota
Kent Conrad (D)
Byron L. Dorgan (D)

Ohio
Mike DeWine (R)
George Voinovich (R)

Oklahoma
Don Nickles (R)
James Inhofe (R)

Oregon
Ron Wyden (D)
Gordon Smith (R)

Pennsylvania
Arlen Specter (R)
Rick Santorum (R)

Rhode Island
Jack Reed (D)
Lincoln Chafee (R)

South Carolina
Strom Thurmond (R)
Ernest F. Hollings (D)

South Dakota
Thomas A. Daschle (D)
Tim Johnson (D)

Tennessee
Fred Thompson (R)
William H. Frist (R)

Texas
Phil Gramm (R)
Kay Bailey Hutchison (R)

Utah
Orrin G. Hatch (R)
Robert F. Bennett (R)

Vermont
Patrick J. Leahy (D)
James M. Jeffords (I)

Virginia
John W. Warner (R)
George Allen (R)

Washington
Patty Murray (D)
Maria Cantwell (D)

West Virginia
Robert C. Byrd (D)
John D. Rockefeller IV (D)

Wisconsin
Herb Kohl (D)
Russell D. Feingold (D)

Wyoming
Craig Thomas (R)
Mike Enzi (R)

THE HOUSE OF REPRESENTATIVES

District	City	Representative
Alabama		
1st	Mobile	Sonny Callahan (R)
2nd	Montgomery	Terry Everett (R)
3rd	Anniston	Bob Riley (R)
4th	Jasper	Robert B. Aderholt (R)
5th	Huntsville	Robert E. (Bud) Cramer Jr. (D)
6th	Birmingham	Spencer Bachus (R)
7th	Tuscaloosa	Earl F. Hilliard (D)
Alaska		
1st	At-Large	Don Young (R)
Arizona		
1st	Tempe	Jeff Flake (R)
2nd	Phoenix	Ed Pastor (D)
3rd	Flagstaff	Bob Stump (R)
4th	Scottsdale	John B. Shadegg (R)
5th	Tucson	Jim Kolbe (R)
6th	Mesa	J.D. Hayworth (R)
Arkansas		
1st	Jonesboro	Marion Berry (D)
2nd	Little Rock	Vic Snyder (D)
3rd	Fort Smith	Vacant
4th	Pine Bluff	Mike Ross (D)
California		
1st	Fairfield	Mike Thompson (D)
2nd	Chico	Wally Herger (R)
3rd	Sacramento	Doug Ose (R)
4th	Roseville	John T. Doolittle (R)
5th	Sacramento	Robert T. Matsui (D)
6th	Marin County	Lynn C. Woolsey (D)
7th	Richmond	George Miller (D)
8th	San Francisco	Nancy Pelosi (D)
9th	Oakland	Barbara Lee (D)
10th	Walnut Creek	Ellen O. Tauscher (D)
11th	Stockton	Richard W. Pombo (R)
12th	San Mateo	Tom Lantos (D)
13th	Hayward	Fortney Pete Stark (D)
14th	Palo Alto	Anna G. Eshoo (D)
15th	Sunnyvale	Michael M. Honda (D)
16th	San Jose	Zoe Lofgren (D)
17th	Monterey	Sam Farr (D)
18th	Modesto	Gary A.Condit (D)
19th	Fresno	George P. Radanovich (R)
20th	Fresno	Calvin M. Dooley (D)
21st	Bakersfield	William M. Thomas (R)
22nd	Santa Barbara	Lois Capps (D)
23rd	Simi Valley	Elton Gallegly (R)
24th	Thousand Oaks	Brad Sherman (D)
25th	Santa Clarita	Howard "Buck" McKeon (R)
26th	Van Nuys	Howard L. Berman (D)
27th	Pasadena	Adam B. Schiff (D)
28th	Claremont	David Dreier (R)
29th	Hollywood	Henry A. Waxman (D)
30th	Boyle Heights	Xavier Becerra (D)
31st	Alhambra	Hilda L. Solis (D)
32nd	Culver City	Diane E. Watson (D)
33rd	E. Los Angeles	Lucille Roybal-Allard (D)
34th	La Puente	Grace F. Napolitano (D)
35th	Watts	Maxine Waters (D)
36th	Rolling Hills	Jane Harman (D)
37th	Compton	Juanita Millender-McDonald(D)
38th	Long Beach	Stephen Horn (R)
39th	Fullerton	Edward R. Royce (R)
40th	Redlands	Jerry Lewis (R)
41st	Ontario	Gary G. Miller (R)
42nd	San Bernardino	Joe Baca (D)
43rd	Riverside	Ken Calvert (R)
44th	Moreno Valley	Mary Bono (R)
45th	Huntington Beach	Dana Rohrabacher (R)
46th	Anaheim	Loretta Sanchez (D)
47th	Irvine	Christopher Cox (R)
48th	San Clemente	Ron Packard (R)
49th	San Diego	Darrell E. Issa (R)
50th	Chula Vista	Bob Filner (D)
51st	Escondido	Randy "Duke" Cunningham (R)
52nd	El Cajon	Duncan Hunter (R)
Colorado		
1st	Denver	Diana DeGette (D)
2nd	Boulder	Mark Udall (D)
3rd	Pueblo	Scott McInnis (R)
4th	Greeley	Bob Schaffer (R)
5th	Colorado Springs	Joel Hefley (R)
6th	Lakewood	Thomas G. Tancredo (R)
Connecticut		
1st	Hartford	John B. Larson (D)
2nd	New London	Rob Simmons (R)
3rd	New Haven	Rosa L. DeLauro (D)
4th	Stamford	Christopher Shays (R)
5th	Waterbury	James H. Maloney (D)
6th	New Britain	Nancy L. Johnson (R)
Delaware		
1st	At-Large	Michael N.Castle (R)
Florida		
1st	Pensacola	Joe Scarborough (R)
2nd	Tallahassee	Allen Boyd (D)
3rd	Jacksonville	Corrine Brown (D)
4th	Jacksonville	Ander Crenshaw (R)
5th	Gainesville	Karen L.Thurman (D)
6th	Ocala	Cliff Stearns (R)
7th	New Smyrna Beach	John L.Mica (R)
8th	Orlando	Ric Keller (R)
9th	Clearwater	Michael Bilirakis (R)
10th	St. Petersburg	C.W. Bill Young (R)
11th	Tampa	Jim Davis (D)
12th	Lakeland	Adam H. Putnam (R)
13th	Sarasota	Dan Miller (R)
14th	Fort Myers	Porter J. Goss (R)
15th	Melbourne	Dave Weldon (R)
16th	West Palm Beach	Mark Foley (R)
17th	Miami	Carrie P.Meek (D)
18th	Miami Beach	Ileana Ros-Lehtinen (R)
19th	Boca Raton	Robert Wexler (D)
20th	Pembroke Pines	Peter Deutsch (D)
21st	Hialeah	Lincoln Diaz-Balart (R)
22nd	Fort Lauderdale	E. Clay Shaw Jr. (R)
23rd	Fort Lauderdale	Alcee L.Hastings (D)
Georgia		
1st	Savannah	Jack Kingston (R)
2nd	Albany	Sanford D. Bishop (D)
3rd	Columbus	Mac Collins (R)
4th	DeKalb County	Cynthia A. McKinney (D)
5th	Atlanta	John Lewis (D)
6th	Alfaretta-Roswell	Johnny Isakson (R)
7th	Rome	Bob Barr (R)
8th	Macon	Saxby Chambliss (R)
9th	LaFayette	Nathan Deal (R)
10th	Augusta	Charlie Norwood (R)
11th	Athens	John Linder (R)
Hawaii		
1st	Honolulu	Neil Abercrombie (D)
2nd	Outer Islands	Patsy T. Mink (D)
Idaho		
1st	Boise	C. L. "Butch" Otter (R)
2nd	Pocatello	Michael K. Simpson (R)

District City	Representative	District City	Representative
Illinois		7th Baltimore	Elijah E. Cummings (D)
1st Chicago, south	Bobby L. Rush (D)	8th Rockville	Constance A. Morella (R)
2nd Lake Calumet	Jesse L. Jackson Jr. (D)	**Massachusetts**	
3rd Oak Lawn	William O. Lipinski (D)	1st Pittsfield	John W. Olver (D)
4th Chicago	Luis V. Gutierrez (D)	2nd Springfield	Richard E. Neal (D)
5th Chicago, north	Rod R. Blagojevich (D)	3rd Worcester	James P. McGovern (D)
6th Des Plaines	Henry J. Hyde (R)	4th Brookline	Barney Frank (D)
7th Chicago, loop	Danny K. Davis (D)	5th Lowell	Martin T. Meehan (D)
8th Schaumburg	Philip M. Crane (R)	6th Salem	John F. Tierney (D)
9th Evanston	Janice D. Schakowsky (D)	7th Lexington	Edward J. Markey (D)
10th Waukegan	Mark Steven Kirk (R)	8th Cambridge	Michael E. Capuano (D)
11th Joliet	Jerry Weller (R)	9th Boston	Stephen P. Lynch (D)
12th Belleville	Jerry F. Costello (D)	10th Quincy	William D. Delahunt (D)
13th Oak Brook	Judy Biggert (R)	**Michigan**	
14th Batavia	J. Dennis Hastert (R)	1st Upper Peninsula	Bart Stupak (D)
15th Bloomington	Thomas W. Ewing (R)	2nd Muskegon	Peter Hoekstra (R)
16th Rockford	Donald A. Manzullo (R)	3rd Grand Rapids	Vernon J. Ehlers (R)
17th Moline	Lane Evans (D)	4th Houghton Lake	Dave Camp (R)
18th Peoria	Ray LaHood (R)	5th Saginaw	James A. Barcia (D)
19th Decatur	David D. Phelps (D)	6th Kalamazoo	Fred Upton (R)
20th Springfield	John Shimkus (R)	7th Jackson	Nick Smith (R)
Indiana		8th Lansing	Mike Rogers (R)
1st Gary	Peter J. Visclosky (D)	9th Flint	Dale E. Kildee (D)
2nd Muncie	Mike Pence (R)	10th Port Huron	David E. Bonior (D)
3rd South Bend	Tim Roemer (D)	11th Bloomfield Hills	Joe Knollenberg (R)
4th Fort Wayne	Mark E. Souder (R)	12th Sterling Heights	Sander M. Levin (D)
5th Kokomo	Steve Buyer (R)	13th Ann Arbor	Lynn N. Rivers (D)
6th Indianapolis	Dan Burton (R)	14th Detroit	John Conyers Jr. (D)
7th Terre Haute	Brian D. Kerns (R)	15th Detroit	Carolyn C. Kilpatrick (D)
8th Evansville	John N. Hostettler (R)	16th Dearborn	John D. Dingell (D)
9th Bloomington	Baron P. Hill (D)	**Minnesota**	
10th Indianapolis	Julia Carson (D)	1st Rochester	Gil Gutknecht (IR)
Iowa		2nd Willmar	Mark R. Kennedy (IR)
1st Cedar Rapids	James A. Leach (R)	3rd Bloomington	Jim Ramstad (IR)
2nd Waterloo	Jim Nussle (R)	4th St. Paul	Betty McCollum (DFL)
3rd Ames	Leonard L. Boswell (D)	5th Minneapolis	Martin Olav Sabo (DFL)
4th Des Moines	Greg Ganske (R)	6th Stillwater	Bill Luther (DFL)
5th Sioux City	Tom Latham (R)	7th St. Cloud	Colin C. Peterson (DFL)
Kansas		8th Duluth	James L. Oberstar (DFL)
1st Dodge City	Jerry Moran (R)	**Mississippi**	
2nd Topeka	Jim Ryun (R)	1st Oxford	Roger F. Wicker (R)
3rd Kansas City	Dennis Moore (D)	2nd Vicksburg	Bennie G. Thompson (D)
4th Wichita	Todd Tiahrt (R)	3rd Meridian	Charles W. "Chip" Pickering (R)
Kentucky		4th Jackson	Ronnie Shows (D)
1st Paducah	Ed Whitfield (R)	5th Pascagoula	Gene Taylor (D)
2nd Owensboro	Ron Lewis (R)	**Missouri**	
3rd Louisville	Anne M. Northrup (R)	1st St. Louis	William Lacy Clay (D)
4th Covington	Ken Lucas (D)	2nd Kirkwood	W. Todd Akin (R)
5th Somerset	Harold Rogers (R)	3rd St. Louis	Richard A. Gephardt (D)
6th Lexington	Ernie Fletcher (R)	4th Jefferson City	Ike Skelton (D)
Louisiana		5th Kansas City	Karen McCarthy (D)
1st Metairie	David Vitter (R)	6th St. Joseph	Sam Graves (R)
2nd New Orleans	William J. Jefferson (D)	7th Springfield	Roy Blunt (R)
3rd Houma	W.J. (Billy) Tauzin (R)	8th Cape Girardeau	Jo Ann Emerson (R)
4th Shreveport	Jim McCrery (R)	9th Hannibal	Kenny C. Hulshof (R)
5th Alexandria	John Cooksey (R)	**Montana**	
6th Baton Rouge	Richard H. Baker (R)	1st At-Large	Dennis R. Rehberg (R)
7th Lake Charles	Christopher John (D)	**Nebraska**	
Maine		1st Lincoln	Doug Bereuter (R)
1st Portland	Thomas H. Allen (D)	2nd Omaha	Lee Terry (R)
2nd Bangor	John Elias Baldacci (D)	3rd Grand Island	Bill Barrett (R)
Maryland		**Nevada**	
1st Annapolis	Wayne T. Gilchrest (R)	1st Las Vegas	Shelley Berkley (D)
2nd Towson	Robert L. Ehrlich Jr. (R)	2nd Reno	Jim Gibbons (R)
3rd Baltimore	Benjamin L. Cardin (D)	**New Hampshire**	
4th Landover	Albert Russell Wynn (D)	1st Manchester	John E. Sununu (R)
5th Bowie	Steny H. Hoyer (D)	2nd Concord	Charles F. Bass (R)
6th Hagerstown	Roscoe G. Bartlett (R)		

District City	Representative	District City	Representative
New Jersey		3rd Dayton	Tony P. Hall (D)
1st Camden	Robert E. Andrews (D)	4th Lima	Michael G. Oxley (R)
2nd Atlantic City	Frank A. LoBiondo (R)	5th Sandusky	Paul E. Gillmor (R)
3rd Cherry Hill	Jim Saxton (R)	6th Portsmouth	Ted Strickland (D)
4th Trenton	Christopher H. Smith (R)	7th Marysville	David L. Hobson (R)
5th Ridgewood	Marge Roukema (R)	8th Hamilton	John A. Boehner (R)
6th New Brunswick	Frank Pallone Jr. (D)	9th Toledo	Marcy Kaptur (D)
7th Union	Mike Ferguson (R)	10th Cleveland	Dennis Kucinich (D)
8th Paterson	Bill Pascrell Jr. (D)	11th Shaker Heights	Stephanie Tubbs Jones (D)
9th Hackensack	Steven R. Rothman (D)	12th Columbus	Patrick J. Tiberi (R)
10th Newark	Donald M. Payne (D)	13th Oberlin	Sherrod Brown (D)
11th Morristown	Rodney P. Frelinghuysen (R)	14th Akron	Tom Sawyer (D)
12th Princeton	Rush D. Holt (D)	15th Columbus	Debra Pryce (R)
13th Jersey City	Robert Menendez (D)	16th Canton	Ralph Regula (R)
New Mexico		17th Youngstown	James A. Traficant Jr. (D)
1st Albuquerque	Heather Wilson (R)	18th Steubenville	Robert W. Ney (R)
2nd Picacho	Joseph R. Skeen (R)	19th Ashtabula	Steven C. LaTourette (R)
3rd Santa Fe	Tom Udall (D)	**Oklahoma**	
New York		1st Tulsa	Steve Largent (R)[1]
1st Centereach	Felix J. Grucci Jr. (R)	2nd Muskogee	Brad Carson (D)
2nd Babylon	Steve Israel (D)	3rd Marietta	Wes Watkins (R)
3rd Westbury	Peter T. King (R)	4th Norman	J.C. Watts Jr. (R)
4th Garden City	Carolyn McCarthy (D)	5th Oklahoma City	Ernest J. Istook (R)
5th Queens	Gary L. Ackerman (D)	6th Cheyenne	Frank D. Lucas (R)
6th Jamaica	Gregory W. Meeks (D)	**Oregon**	
7th Flushing	Joseph Crowley (D)	1st Portland	David Wu (D)
8th Manhattan, West	Jerrold Nadler (D)	2nd Medford	Greg Walden (R)
9th Brooklyn	Anthony D. Weiner (D)	3rd Portland	Earl Blumenauer (D)
10th Brooklyn Heights	Edolphus Towns (D)	4th Eugene	Peter A. DeFazio (D)
11th Flatbush	Major R. Owens (D)	5th Salem	Darlene Hooley (D)
12th Brooklyn	Nydia M. Velázquez (D)	**Pennsylvania**	
13th Staten Island	Vito Fossella (R)	1st Philadelphia	Robert A. Brady (D)
14th Manhattan, East	Carolyn B. Maloney (D)	2nd West Philadelphia	Chaka Fattah (D)
15th Harlem	Charles B. Rangel (D)	3rd NE Philadelphia	Robert A. Borski (D)
16th Bronx	José E. Serrano (D)	4th Beaver	Melissa A. Hart (R)
17th Yonkers	Eliot L. Engel (D)	5th State College	John Peterson (R)
18th White Plains	Nita M. Lowey (D)	6th Reading	Tim Holden (D)
19th Poughkeepsie	Sue W. Kelly (R)	7th Swarthmore	Curt Weldon (R)
20th Newburgh	Benjamin A. Gilman (R)	8th Bucks County	James C. Greenwood (R)
21st Albany	Michael R. McNulty (D)	9th Altoona	Bill Shuster (R)
22nd Saratoga Springs	John E. Sweeney (R)	10th Scranton	Don Sherwood (R)
23rd Utica	Sherwood L. Boehlert (R)	11th Wilkes-Barre	Paul E. Kanjorski (D)
24th Watertown	John M. McHugh (R)	12th Johnstown	John P. Murtha (D)
25th Syracuse	James T. Walsh (R)	13th Villanova	Joseph M. Hoeffel (D)
26th Kingston	Maurice D. Hinchey (D)	14th Pittsburgh	William J. Coyne (D)
27th Seneca Falls	Thomas M. Reynolds (R)	15th Allentown	Patrick J. Toomey (R)
28th Rochester	Louise McIntosh Slaughter (D)	16th Lancaster	Joseph R. Pitts (R)
29th Niagara Falls	John J. LaFalce (D)	17th Harrisburg	George W. Gekas (R)
30th Buffalo	Jack Quinn (R)	18th McKeesport	Michael F. Doyle (D)
31st Corning	Amo Houghton (R)	19th York	Todd Russell Platts (R)
North Carolina		20th Washington	Frank Mascara (D)
1st Greenville	Eva M. Clayton (D)	21st Erie	Phil English (R)
2nd Raleigh	Bob Etheridge (D)	**Rhode Island**	
3rd Outer Banks	Walter B. Jones (R)	1st Providence	Patrick J. Kennedy (D)
4th Raleigh-Durham	David E. Price (D)	2nd Warwick	James R. Langevin (D)
5th Winston-Salem	Richard Burr (R)	**South Carolina**	
6th Greensboro	Howard Coble (R)	1st Charleston	Henry E. Brown Jr. (R)
7th Wilmington	Mike McIntyre (D)	2nd Columbia	Vacant
8th Fayetteville	Robin Hayes (R)	3rd Anderson	Lindsey O. Graham (R)
9th Charlotte	Sue Wilkins Myrick (R)	4th Spartanburg	Jim DeMint (R)
10th Hickory	Cass Ballenger (R)	5th Rock Hill	John M. Spratt Jr. (D)
11th Asheville	Charles H. Taylor (R)	6th Florence	James E. Clyburn (D)
12th Charlotte	Melvin L. Watt (D)	**South Dakota**	
North Dakota		1st At-Large	John R. Thune (R)
1st At-Large	Earl Pomeroy (D)	**Tennessee**	
Ohio		1st Kingsport	William L. Jenkins (R)
1st Cincinnati	Steve Chabot (R)	2nd Knoxville	John J. Duncan Jr. (R)
2nd Indian Hill	Rob Portman (R)	3rd Chattanooga	Zach Wamp (R)

District City	Representative	District City	Representative
4th Shelbyville	Van Hilleary (R)	**Virginia**	
5th Nasvhille	Bob Clement (D)	1st Newport News	Jo Ann Davis (R)
6th Murfreesboro	Bart Gordon (D)	2nd Virginia Beach	Edward L. Schrock (R)
7th Memphis	Ed Bryant (R)	3rd Norfolk	Robert C. Scott (D)
8th Jackson	John S. Tanner (D)	4th Portsmouth	J. Randy Forbes (R)
9th Memphis	Harold E. Ford Jr. (D)	5th Charlottesville	Virgil H. Goode Jr. (D)
Texas		6th Roanoke	Bob Goodlatte (R)
1st Texarkana	Max Sandlin (D)	7th Richmond	Eric Cantor (R)
2nd Lufkin	Jim Turner (R)	8th Alexandria	James P. Moran (D)
3rd North Dalllas	Sam Johnson (R)	9th Blacksburg	Rick Boucher (D)
4th Tyler	Ralph M. Hall (D)	10th Arlington	Frank R. Wolf (R)
5th Dallas	Pete Sessions (R)	11th Fairfax	Thomas M. Davis (R)
6th Waxahachie	Joe Barton (R)	**Washington**	
7th Houston	John Abney Culberson (R)	1st Redmond	Jay Inslee (D)
8th College Station	Kevin Brady (R)	2nd Everett	Rick Larsen (D)
9th Beaumont	Nick Lampson (D)	3rd Olympia	Brian Baird (D)
10th Austin	Lloyd Doggett (D)	4th Yakima	Doc Hastings (R)
11th Waco	Chet Edwards (D)	5th Spokane	George R. Nethercutt Jr. (R)
12th Fort Worth	Kay Granger (R)	6th Tacoma	Norman D. Dicks (D)
13th Amarillo	Mac Thornberry (R)	7th Seattle	Jim McDermott (D)
14th Victoria	Ron Paul (R)	8th Bellevue	Jennifer Dunn (R)
15th McAllen	Rubén Hinojosa (D)	9th Renton	Adam Smith (D)
16th El Paso	Silvestre Reyes (D)	**West Virginia**	
17th Abilene	Charles W. Stenholm (D)	1st Wheeling	Alan B. Mollohan (D)
18th Houston	Sheila Jackson-Lee (D)	2nd Charleston	Shelley Moore Capito (R)
19th Lubbock	Larry Combest (R)	3rd Huntington	Nick J. Rahall, II (D)
20th San Antonio	Charles A. Gonzalez (D)	**Wisconsin**	
21st Midland	Lamar S. Smith (R)	1st Kenosha	Paul Ryan (R)
22nd Brazoria	Tom DeLay (R)	2nd Madison	Tammy Baldwin (D)
23rd Laredo	Henry Bonilla (R)	3rd Eau Claire	Ron Kind (D)
24th Arlington	Martin Frost (D)	4th Milwaukee	Gerald D. Kleczka (D)
25th Pasadena	Ken Bentsen (D)	5th Wauwatosa	Thomas M. Barrett (D)
26th Irving	Richard K. Armey (R)	6th Oshkosh	Thomas Petri (R)
27th Corpus Christi	Solomon P. Ortiz (D)	7th Wausau	David R. Obey (D)
28th San Antonio	Ciro D. Rodriguez (D)	8th Green Bay	Mark Green (R)
29th Houston	Gene Green (D)	9th Sheboygan	F. James Sensenbrenner Jr. (R)
30th Dallas	Eddie Bernice Johnson (D)	**Wyoming**	
Utah		1st At Large	Barbara Cubin (R)
1st Ogden	James V. Hansen (R)	**NON-VOTING REPRESENTATIVES**	
2nd Salt Lake City	Jim Matheson (D)	American Samoa	Eni F. H. Faleomavaega (D)
3rd Provo	Chris Cannon (R)	District of Columbia	Eleanor Holmes Norton (D)
Vermont		Guam	Robert A. Underwood (D)
1st At-Large	Bernard Sanders (I)	Puerto Rico	Aníbal Acevedo-Vilá (D)
		Virgin Islands	Donna M. Christian-Green (D)

Note: D = Democrat; DFL = Democratic-Farmer-Labor (Minn.); I= Independent; IR = Independent Republican (Minn.); R = Republican. 1. Rep. Largent announced his resignation, effective Nov. 29, 2001. **Source:** Clerk of the U.S. House of Representatives.

Congressional Reapportionment, 2000

As a result of population shifts reported in the 2000 Census, a total of eight states will gain representatives (four of them will gain two), while 10 states will lose representatives (two states will lose two each). States cannot have fewer than one representative, so even though North Dakota experienced a much lower growth rate than New York, it cannot lose its sole member of Congress, whereas New York will lose two representatives. The table below shows states gaining and losing representation in 2002. Reapportionment of districts will take effect in time for the November 2002 elections.

States Gaining Representatives

Arizona	+2	California	+1
Florida	+2	Colorado	+1
Georgia	+2	Nevada	+1
Texas	+2	North Carolina	+1

Source: U.S. Census Bureau.

States Losing Representatives

New York	-2	Michigan	-1
Pennsylvania	-2	Mississippi	-1
Connecticut	-1	Ohio	-1
Illinois	-1	Oklahoma	-1
Indiana	-1	Wisconsin	-1

THE EXECUTIVE BRANCH

►**EXECUTIVE OFFICE OF THE PRESIDENT**
White House Office   1600 Pennsylvania Ave. NW, Washington, DC 20500 (202) 456-1414. www.whitehouse.gov. Serves president in performance of duties incident to his office. Maintains communication with Congress, individual members of Congress, heads of executive agencies, media, and public.

Office of the Vice President of the United States   Old Executive Office Building, Washington, DC 20501. (202) 456-2326. www.whitehouse.gov. Vice president participates in cabinet meetings and is, by statute, a member of National Security Council and board of regents of the Smithsonian Institution; serves as president of Senate; empowered to succeed to presidency pursuant to Article II and the 20th and 25th amendments to the Constitution.

Council of Economic Advisers   Old Executive Office Building, Washington, DC 20502. (202) 395-5084. www.whitehouse.gov/WH/EOP/ CEA/html. Created by Employment Act of 1946. Council's three members—appointed by president—analyze the various segments of the economy, appraise and assess existing economic programs, recommend new economic programs, and assist in preparation President's economic reports to Congress.

Council on Environmental Quality   722 Jackson Place NW, Washington DC 20503. (202) 395-5750. www.whitehouse.gov/ceq/. Old Executive Office Building, Room 360, Washington DC 20501. (202) 456-6224. Created by National Environmental Policy Act of 1969. Recommends national policies to improve quality of environment. Analyzes environmental changes and trends. Assesses and evaluates existing environmental programs. Assists president in compiling annual environmental quality report to Congress.

National Security Council (NSC)   Old Executive Office Building, Washington DC 20506. (202) 456-1414. Created by National Security Act of 1947. Chaired by president. Members include vice president and secretaries of state and defense. Chairman of Joint Chiefs of Staff is statutory military adviser; CIA director is intelligence adviser. Advises president on integration of domestic, foreign, and military policies relating to national security.

Office of Administration   Old Executive Office Building, 725 17th St. NW, Washington, DC 20503. (202) 395-6963. Created December 12, 1977. Provides administrative services to all units within executive office except those in direct support of president.

Office of Management and Budget (OMB)   Executive Office Building, Washington, DC 20503. (202 -395-3080. www.whitehouse.gov/ OMB/. Created July 1, 1970. Assists president in reviewing and assessing efficiency of structure and management of executive branch. Expands interagency cooperation. Assists president in preparing Government's budget and fiscal program. Supervises, controls, and administers the budget. Coordinates departmental advice and makes recommendations to president based on this advice. Plans, conducts, and promotes evaluation efforts to help president assess program objectives, performance, and efficiency. Keeps president informed of work planned and performed by the various Government agencies.

Office of National Drug Control Policy   Executive Office of the President, Washington, DC 20500. (202) 395-6700. www.whitehousedrugpolicy.gov. Created by National Narcotics Leadership Act of 1988. Coordinates Federal, state and local efforts to control illegal drug abuse and devises national strategies to ensure that national anti-drug activities are carried out effectively.

Office of Policy Development   Old Executive Office Building, Washington, D.C. 20502. Comprised of the *Domestic Policy Council* (202-456-2216) and *National Economic Council* (202-456-6630), which are responsible for advising and assisting the president in the formulation, coordination, and implementation of domestic and economic policy.

Office of Science and Technology Policy   Old Executive Office Building, Washington, DC 20500. (202) 395-7347. www.whitehouse.gov/

The Cabinet

The president is the administrative head of the executive branch of the Federal Government. A creation of custom and tradition dating back to George Washington's administration, the Cabinet functions at the pleasure of the president. Its purpose is to advise the president on any subject on which he requests information. The Cabinet is composed of the heads of the 14 executive departments and certain other executive officials to whom the president accords cabinet rank. In the Bush Administration, Cabinet-level rank has been accorded to the officials listed below (as of September 26, 2001)

President George W. Bush
Vice President Dick Cheney

Office	Officer
Secretary of State	Colin Powell
Secretary of the Treasury	Paul O'Neill
Secretary of Defense	Donald Rumsfeld
Attorney General (Dept. of Justice)	John Ashcroft
Secretary of the Interior	Gale Norton
Secretary of Agriculture	Ann Veneman
Secretary of Commerce	Donald Evans
Secretary of Labor	Elaine Chao
Secretary of Health and Human Services	Tommy Thompson
Secretary of Housing and Urban Development	Melquiades Martinez
Secretary of Transportation	Norman Mineta
Secretary of Energy	Spencer Abraham
Secretary of Education	Roderick Paige
Secretary of Veterans Affairs	Anthony Principi
White House Chief of Staff	Andrew Card
Administrator, Environmental Protection Agency	Christine Todd Whitman
Director, Office of Management and Budget	Mitch Daniels
U.S. Trade Representative	Robert Zoelick
Director, Office of National Drug Control Policy	John Walters
Director of Homeland Security	Tom Ridge

Source: White House Press Office.

ostp.html. Created May 11, 1976. Serves as source of scientific, engineering, and technological analysis and expertise for president with respect to public policy in areas of economy, national security, health, foreign relations, and environment. Appraises sale, quality, and effectiveness of U.S. efforts in science and technology.

Office of the U.S. Trade Representative
600 17th St. NW, Washington, DC 20508. (202)-395-3230. Created as Office of the Special Representative for Trade Negotiations, Jan. 15, 1963. Congress made it agency of executive office under Trade Act of 1974. Sets and administers overall trade policy. Representative is chief U.S. representative for all activities of the General Agreement on Tariffs and Trade (GATT) and at discussions, meetings, and negotiations in most conferences in which trade and commodity are issues.

▶DEPARTMENT OF AGRICULTURE (USDA)
14th St. and Independence Ave. SW, Washington, DC 20250. (202) 720-2791. www.usda.gov. Created May 15, 1862; incorporated into Cabinet, Feb. 8, 1889. Improves and maintains farm income, develops agricultural markets abroad, curbs poverty, hunger, and malnutrition. Through inspection and grading services, safeguard standards of quality in the nation's food supply. The dept. was reorganized in 1994 into eight program or mission areas: *Rural Development, Alternative Agricultural Research & Commercialization Center, Marketing & Regulatory Programs, Food Safety, Food Nutrition & Consumer Services, Farm & Foreign Agriculture Services, Research Education & Economics,* and *Natural Resources & Environment.* Each program area may be further divided into more specific agencies, such as the Rural Housing Service or the Food Safety and Inspection Service.

▶DEPARTMENT OF COMMERCE
14th St. between Constitution and Pennsylvania Avenues NW, Washington, DC 20230. (202) 482-2000. www.doc.gov. Created Feb. 14, 1903 as part of Dept. of Commerce and Labor. Redesignated Dept. of Commerce Mar. 4, 1913. Promotes international trade, economic growth, and technological advancement through encouragement of competitive free-enterprise system, prevention of unfair trade, granting of patents, promotion of tourism, and assistance in the growth of minority businesses. The department is divided into 12 operating units; only the major agencies are described in detail below.

Bureau of the Census
www.census.gov. Created Mar. 6, 1902 by act of Congress. Collects, tabulates, and publishes census statistics about America, its people, and its economy. Statistics are used by Congress, president, and public to aid development and evaluation of public policy. Population and housing censuses are performed every 10 years. Censuses of agriculture, state and local governments, manufacturers, mineral industries, distributive trades, and construction and transportation industries are performed every five years. Special censuses are performed on demand from state and local governments.

Economic Development Administration (EDA)
Created by Public Works and Economic Development Act of 1965. Promotes new jobs, protects existing jobs, and stimulates job growth in areas where unemployment is high or incomes are low.

International Trade Administration (ITA)
www.ita.gov. Created Jan. 2, 1980. Promotes world trade and strengthens U.S. position in relation to world trade and investment.

Minority Business Development Agency (MBDA)
www.mbda.gov. Created Nov. 1, 1979. Promotes minority business. Ensures effective, equitable, and competitive participation by minority business in free enterprise system.

National Oceanic and Atmospheric Administration (NOAA)
www.noaa.gov. Created Oct. 3, 1970. Investigates and maps oceans of world. Discovers, utilizes, and conserves living resources of oceans. Monitors and predicts conditions of atmosphere, sun, and oceans; warns against deterioration of these conditions arising from natural and man-made events and circumstances. Provides weather reports and forecasts. Forecasts floods, hurricanes, and other weather-related natural disasters.

Technology Administration
Created by Congress in 1988 and includes the Office of Technology, National Technical Information Service, and the National Institute of Standards and Technology. Works with U.S. industries to promote competitiveness and to maximize the impact of technology on economic growth.

▶DEPARTMENT OF DEFENSE (DOD)
The Pentagon, Washington, DC 20301-1155. (703) 545-6700. www.defenselink.mil. Created by National Security Act Amendments of 1949. Provides necessary military forces to deter war and protect security of the country. The three armed forces departments and the Organization of the Joint Chiefs of Staff comprise the military side of the Defense Dept. (Additional information can be found later in "National Defense.")

Organization of the Joint Chiefs of Staff
Consists of Chairman of Joint Chiefs of Staff, the chiefs of staff of the three armed forces departments, and the Commandant of the Marine Corps. Advises and assists president and secretary of defense on most military issues. Assists president and secretary of defense in planning, direction, and allocation of strategic resources. Compares strengths and capabilities of American forces with those of potential adversaries.

Department of the Air Force
www.af.mil. Created Sept. 18, 1947 by National Security Act of 1947. Works in conjunction with other armed forces to protect peace and security of the U.S. Focuses on air missions and protecting American interests from invasion by air.

Department of the Army
www.army.mil. U.S. Army created June 14, 1775 by Continental Congress. Dept. of the Army created 1947 by National Security Act of 1947. Organizes, trains, and equips active and reserve forces to protect peace, security, welfare, and defense of the U.S. Its mission focuses on land operations and maneuvers.

Department of the Navy
www.navy.mil. U.S. Navy created Oct. 13, 1775, by Continental Congress. Dept. of the Navy created Apr. 30, 1798. Protects U.S. from attack by sea. Encompasses Marine Corps. Maintains freedom of the seas.

▶DEPARTMENT OF EDUCATION
400 Maryland Ave. SW, Washington, DC 20202. (800) USA-LEARN. www. ed.gov. Created Oct. 17, 1979, by Dept. of Education Organization Act. Es-

tablishes policy for, administers, and coordinates almost all Federal assistance to education.

▶DEPARTMENT OF ENERGY (DOE)

1000 Independence Ave. SW, Washington, DC 20585. (202) 586-5000. www.doe.gov. Created Oct. 1, 1977, by Dept. of Energy Organization Act. Coordinates and administrates energy functions of Federal Government, including research and development of energy technology, marketing Federal power, energy conservation, nuclear weapons, and energy regulation.

▶DEPARTMENT OF HEALTH AND HUMAN SERVICES (HHS)

200 Independence Ave. SW, Washington, DC 20201. (202) 619-0257. www.dhhs.gov. Created Apr. 11, 1953, as Dept. of Health, Education, and Welfare. Re-designated Dept. of Health and Human Services Oct. 17, 1979, by Dept. of Education Organization Act. Advises president in formulation of public policy regarding health, welfare, and income and security programs. The department is divided into 12 major administrations and agencies; only the major agencies are described in detail below

Administration for Children and Families (ACF) www.acf.gov. Created April 15, 1991. Administers child welfare services, foster care and child care programs, the Head Start Program, and other family preservation and support services.

Centers for Disease Control and Prevention (CDC) www.cdc.gov. Reorganized, Nov. 9, 1995. Responsible for protecting the public health by preventing and controlling diseases.

Food and Drug Administration (FDA) www.fda.gov. Created by Agriculture Appropriation Act of 1931; reorganized Nov. 9, 1995. Protects the health of the nation against impure and unsafe foods, drugs, cosmetics, and other hazards.

Health Care Financing Administration (HCFA) www.hcfa.gov. Created Mar. 8, 1977. Oversees Medicare and Medicaid Health Insurance and grant programs. (See the section on "Social Insurance Programs" for additional information about these programs).

National Institutes of Health (NIH) www.nih.gov. Reorganized, Nov. 1995. The principal biomedical research agency of the Federal Government, its mission is to employ science in the pursuit of knowledge to improve human health conditions.

Substance Abuse and Mental Health Services Administration www.samhsa.gov. Disseminates accurate and up-to-date information on and provides leadership in the prevention and treatment of addictive and mental disorders.

▶DEPARTMENT OF HOUSING AND URBAN DEVELOPMENT (HUD)

451 Seventh St. SW, Washington, DC 20410. (202) 708-1422. www.hud.gov. Created Nov. 9, 1965, by Dept. of Housing and Urban Development Act. Administers mortgage programs to help families become homeowners. Fosters construction of new housing and renovation of existing rental housing. Provides aid for low-income families who cannot afford their rent. Enacts programs to prevent housing discrimination. Encourages strong private sector housing industry.

THE EXECUTIVE BRANCH 133

▶DEPARTMENT OF THE INTERIOR

1849 C St. NW, Washington, DC 20240. (202) 208-3171. www.doi.gov. Created Mar. 3, 1849. Principal U.S. conservation agency. Directs use and conservation of public lands and natural resources; administers over 500 million acres of Federal land and has trust responsibilities for approximately 50 million acres, mostly Indian reservations. Prescribes use of land and water resources, fish and wildlife, national parks and historic places, and mineral resources; aids in preservation of American Indian reservation communities.

United States Fish and Wildlife Service www.fws.gov. Conserves and protects fish and wildlife and their habitats. Assesses environmental impact of pesticides, thermal pollution, hydroelectric dams, and nuclear power sites.

National Park Service www.nps.gov. Created Aug. 25, 1916. Administers, protects, and maintains diverse system of national parks, monuments, historic areas, and recreation areas; encourages understanding of the historic value of these sites through lectures, tours, and exhibits.

U.S. Geological Survey www.usgs.gov. Created Mar. 3, 1879. Identifies and classifies land, water, energy, and mineral resources. Investigates potential hazards such as earthquakes and volcanoes. Conducts topographic mapping.

Bureau of Indian Affairs www.usgs.gov/doi/bureau-indian-affairs.html. Created 1824 as part of Dept. of War. Transferred to Dept. of Interior in 1849. Trains American Indian and Alaska native peoples to manage their own affairs under trust relationship to Federal Government. Facilitates public and private aid to advancement of these peoples.

Bureau of Land Management (BLM) www.blm.gov. Created July 16, 1946, by consolidation of the General Land Office and the Grazing Service. Manages 270 million acres of public lands primarily in Far West and in Alaska. Resources in these lands include timber, oil, gas, hard minerals, and wildlife habitats.

▶DEPARTMENT OF JUSTICE

950 Pennsylvania Ave. NW, Washington, DC 20530. (202) 514-2000. www.usdoj.gov. Created June 22, 1870. Enforces the law in the public interest. Ensures fair competition in free enterprise system; enforces drug, immigration, and naturalization laws; Conducts all Supreme Court suits in which U.S. is party or is concerned. Advises president on legal matters.

Federal Bureau of Investigation (FBI) www.fbi.gov. Created 1908. Principal investigative bureau of Justice Dept. Investigates violations of Federal law. Areas of primary concern are organized crime (including drug trafficking), terrorism, white-collar crime, and foreign counterintelligence.

Bureau of Prisons Imprisons and rehabilitates criminals convicted of Federal crimes and sentenced to serve time in Federal prison.

United States Marshals Service Provides security and support to Federal court system. Apprehends Federal fugitives. Ensures safety of Federal witnesses. Executes court orders and arrest warrants. Maintains custody, manages, and sells property seized from criminals.

Immigration and Naturalization Service (INS) Created Mar. 3, 1891. Controls immigration into U.S. by facilitating entry to qualified persons and denying admission to unqualified aliens. Deports illegal aliens already in U.S. Encourages and facilitates naturalization and citizenship.

Drug Enforcement Administration (DEA) Created July 1973. Investigates interstate drug-trafficking. Enforces Government regulations regarding manufacture, distribution, sale, and dispensing of controlled substances;

▶**DEPARTMENT OF LABOR** 200 Constitution Ave NW, Washington, DC 20210. (202) 693-5000. www.dol.gov. Created Mar. 4, 1913. Improves welfare and working conditions of wage earners. Guarantees minimum wages and overtime pay as well as unemployment insurance and workers' compensation. Prevents employment discrimination. Protects pension rights. Provides for job training programs. Pays special attention to labor-related needs of minority workers, old and young, women, and disabled people.

Employment and Training Administration (ETA) www.doleta.gov. Provides employment security through unemployment insurance, worker dislocation programs, and Federal-state employment service system. Trains or retrains and finds employment for disadvantaged workers through Job Training Partnership Act (JTPA).

Pension and Welfare Benefits Administration (PWBA) www.dol.gov/dol/pwba/. Created Sept. 2, 1974, by Employment Retirement Income Security Act of 1974 (ERISA). Requires private pension and welfare plan administrators to give participants summaries of pension and welfare plans. Keeps summaries on file. Regulates financial operations of pension and welfare plans.

Occupational Safety and Health Administration (OSHA) www.osha.gov. Created 1970 by Occupational Safety and Health Act. Promotes safety and health standards in workplace. Issues regulations, conducts investigations, issues citations, and proposes penalties for violations of health standards and regulations.

Bureau of Labor Statistics (BLS) www.bls.gov. Data-gathering agency. Collects, processes, interprets, and distributes data involving employment, unemployment, wages, family income and expenditures, worker's compensation, industrial relations, productivity, and technological change.

Veteran's Employment and Training Service (VETS) Maximizes training and employment opportunities for veterans and disabled. Ensures that legislation involving veterans is carried out by local public employment services and by private enterprise.

▶**DEPARTMENT OF STATE** 2201 C Street NW; Washington, D.C. 20520. (202) 647-4000. www.state.gov. Created July 27, 1789, as Dept. of Foreign Affairs. Renamed Dept. of State Sept. 15, 1789. Advises president on foreign policy. Formulates and executes policy to protect and defend American interests overseas. Negotiates treaties and agreements with foreign countries. Oversees and administers overseas information and cultural programs, including Voice of America and Fulbright scholarship program.

United States Mission to the United Nations Represents U.S. at U.N.. Carries out U.S. foreign policy as it relates to U.N.

Foreign Service Maintains relations with more than 140 nations around world. Reports to State Dept. on developments relating to safety and welfare of U.S., its citizens, and their interests. Ambassadors to each country are personal representatives of the president and have full responsibility for carrying out U.S. foreign policy within the country. Ambassadors negotiate agreements between host country and U.S., explain and administer U.S. foreign policy, and maintain relations with government and public of host country.

▶**DEPARTMENT OF TRANSPORTATION** 400 Seventh St. SW, Washington, DC 20590. (202) 366-4000. www.dot.gov. Created Oct. 15, 1966. Establishes nation's comprehensive transportation policy. Several umbrella administrations are responsible for highway planning, development, and construction; urban mass transit; railroads; aviation; and the safety of waterways, ports, highways, and oil and gas pipelines.

United States Coast Guard www.uscg. mil. Created Jan. 28, 1915. Included in Dept. of Transportation Apr. 1, 1967. Coast Guard is at all times a branch of armed forces and a service with Dept. of Transportation except when operating as part of Navy during war. Primary maritime law enforcement agency for U.S. Suppresses drug smuggling and trafficking. Licenses marine vessels. Administers and inspects violations of safety standards for design, construction, equipment and maintenance of commercial marine vessels and offshore structures in U.S. waters. Provides search and rescue functions for saving lives and property in U.S. waters. Operates ice-breaking vessels to facilitate marine transportation.

Federal Aviation Administration (FAA) www.faa.gov. Created 1958 by Federal Aviation Act. Included in Dept. of Transportation in 1967. Regulates air commerce in effort to promote safety and secure national defense interests. Directs use of navigable U.S. airspace. Develops and operates system of air traffic control for both civil and military aircraft. Regulates aircraft noise.

Federal Highway Administration (FHWA) www.fhwa.dot.gov. Included in Dept. of Transportation in 1967 by Dept. of Transportation Act. Promotes highway safety. Provides aid for construction and maintenance of state and Federal highway systems.

Federal Railroad Administration (FRA) www.fra.dot.gov. Created by Dept. of Transportation Act of 1966. Administers and enforces railroad safety regulations such as track maintenance, inspection and equipment standards, and operating practices.

National Highway Traffic Safety Administration www.nhtsa.dot.gov. Created by Highway Safety Act of 1970. Research and development programs are aimed at reducing number of highway collisions, reducing severity of injuries and economic loss involved in highway accidents, and reducing fatalities resulting from highway crashes.

Federal Transit Administration www.fta. dot.gov. Created July 1, 1968. Improves equipment and methods used in urban mass transit. Encourages planning of cost-effective mass transit systems. Provides economic and technical assistance for mass transit programs.

Maritime Administration (MARAD) www. marad.dot.gov. Created May 24, 1950. Included in Dept. of Transportation Aug. 6, 1981, by Maritime

Act of 1981. Constructs or supervises construction of U.S. flag merchant ships for Federal government. Generates business for U.S. ships. Develops ports and facilities for maritime transport.

Saint Lawrence Seaway Development Corporation www.dot.gov/slsdc/. Created May 13, 1954. Owns, develops, maintains, and operates St. Lawrence Seaway between Montreal and Lake Erie within territorial limits of U.S. Provides safe and efficient waterway for maritime commerce.

Research and Special Programs Administration www.rspa.dot.gov. Created Sept. 23, 1977. Responsible for transportation of hazardous materials and pipeline safety. Oversees Office of Hazardous Materials Safety.

Bureau of Transportation Statistics www.bts.gov. Created by Transportation Efficiency Act of 1991. Compiles, analyzes, and disseminates statistics and other information on the nation's transportation systems.

Surface Transportation Board www.stb.dot.gov. Created by ICC Termination Act of 1995. A bipartisan adjudicatory body whose three members are appointed by the President with the Senate's consent. It judges disputes over the various laws pertaining to interstate surface transportation.

▶DEPARTMENT OF THE TREASURY
1500 Pennsylvania Ave. NW, Washington, DC 20220. (202) 622-2000. www.treas.gov. Created Sept. 2, 1789. Formulates and recommends economic, financial, tax, and fiscal policies. Acts as financial agent for U.S. Government. Manufactures coins and currency.

Money Men

The first U.S. paper money was printed in 1862. Until then, state banks printed their own notes, but there were no federal bills. The Secretary of the Treasury selects the designs shown on United States currency and coinage. In 1862, Treasury Secretary Salmon Chase put his face on the first U.S. notes in an attempt to further his political ambitions. To this day, he remains on the front of the $10,000 bill, though it is no longer in circulation. Federal law prohibits portraits of living persons from appearing on Government Securities. Therefore, the portraits on our currency notes and coins are of deceased persons whose places in history the American people know well. The basic designs of all denominations of U.S. paper currency in circulation today were selected in 1928.

Note	Portrait, Importance
$ 1	George Washington, 1st President
$ 2	Thomas Jefferson, 3rd President
$ 5	Abraham Lincoln, 16th President
$ 10	Alexander Hamilton, 1st Sec. of Treasury
$ 20	Andrew Jackson, 7th President
$ 50	Ulysses Grant, 18th President
$100	Ben Franklin, Statesman
$500[1]	William McKinley, 25th President
$1000[1]	Grover Cleveland, 22nd/24th President
$5000[1]	James Madison, 4th President
$10,000[1]	Salmon Chase, Sec. of Treasury in 1862
$100,000[2]	Woodrow Wilson, 28th President

1. No longer in circulation. 2. This note never appeared in general circulation, and was only used in transactions between Federal Reserve Banks. **Source:** U.S. Bureau of Engraving and Printing. www.moneyfactory.com

Bureau of Alcohol, Tobacco and Firearms www.atf.treas.gov/. Created July 1, 1972. Enforces and administers laws regulating production, use, distribution, and sale of alcohol and tobacco products, firearms, and explosives. Bureau's objectives are to eliminate illegal trafficking, possession and use of firearms and explosives, to suppress illegal alcohol and tobacco trafficking, and to ensure safety of storage facilities for explosives.

United States Customs Service www.customs.treas.gov/. Created Mar. 3, 1927 as Bureau of Customs. Re-designated Customs Service Apr. 4, 1973. Collects revenue from imports. Enforces customs treaties. Assesses and collects customs duties, excise taxes, fees, and penalties on imported merchandise. Seizes contraband including narcotics and illegal drugs. Processes people, mail, carriers, and cargo in and out of U.S. Apprehends violators of U.S. customs regulations and related laws including copyright, patent, and trademark, and import quotas. Suppresses traffic of illegal narcotics, pornography, counterfeit monetary instruments; quarantines animals, plants, and foods.

Bureau of Engraving and Printing www.bep.treas.gov/. Created July 11, 1862. Designs, prints, and finishes Federal Reserve notes, U.S. postage stamps, identification cards, and Treasury securities. Inhibits counterfeiting of these documents.

Internal Revenue Service (IRS) www.irs.gov. Created July 1, 1862. Administers and enforces internal revenue laws except those relating to alcohol, tobacco, firearms, and explosives. Determines, assesses, and collects Federal tax revenues from public. Encourages, assesses, and enforces compliance with tax laws.

United States Mint www.usmint.treas.gov/. Mint of the United States created Apr. 2, 1792. Bureau of the Mint created Feb. 12, 1873. Renamed United States Mint Jan. 9, 1984. Manufactures and distributes coins for circulation through Federal Reserve Banks. Mints foreign coins. Processes gold and silver bullion. Manufactures national medals, proof coin sets, and commemorative coins for sale to public.

Bureau of the Public Debt www.publicdebt.treas.gov/. Created June 30, 1940. Manages public debt. Offers public debt securities. Audits retired securities and interest coupons. Maintains accounting control over public debt receipts and expenditures, securities, and interest costs. Adjudicates claims of lost, stolen, or destroyed securities.

United States Secret Service www.treas.gov.usss/. Protects president and vice president (and president-elect and vice president-elect) of U.S. and their families. Protects former presidents and their wives until their death. Protects distinguished foreign visitors and U.S. officials abroad at direction of president. Detects and apprehends counterfeiters. Suppresses forgery of government securities and documents.

Office of Thrift Supervision (OTS) 1700 G St., NW, Washington, DC 20552. (202) 906-6913. www.ots.treas.gov. Created by the Financial Institutions Reform, Recovery and Enforcement Act, Aug. 9, 1989. Established by Congress as part of a reorganization of the thrift regulatory structure, the OTS has authority to charter Federal thrift institutions, and to serve as the primary regulator of

Federal and state chartered thrifts belonging to the Savings Association Insurance Fund (SAIF).

▶DEPARTMENT OF VETERANS AFFAIRS

810 Vermont Ave. NW, Washington, DC 20420. (202) 273-4800. www.va.gov. Created by Dept. of Veterans Affairs Act of 1988; predecessor Veterans Administration created 1930. Administers benefit programs for veterans and their families, including military-related death or disability compensation, pensions, education and rehabilitation, home loan guaranty, medical care programs, and the National Cemetery System.

Veterans Health Administration Provides hospital, nursing home, and outpatient care to eligible veterans. Operates over 100 medical centers, nearly 400 outpatient clinics, over 100 nursing home care units and many Vietnam Veteran Outreach Centers.

Veterans Benefit Administration Has responsibility for claims for disability compensation and pension, specially adapted housing and automobiles, special clothing allowances, and emergency officers' retirement pay, survivors' claims for death compensation, dependency and indemnity compensation, burial and plot allowance claims, and reimbursement for headstones.

▶INDEPENDENT ESTABLISHMENTS & GOVERNMENT CORPORATIONS

African Development Foundation 1400 Eye St. NW, Washington, DC 20005. (202) 673-3916. www.adf.gov. Created in 1984 by African Development Foundation Act. Nonprofit Government corporation. Through grants, loans, and loan guarantees, aids self-help efforts by poor people in African countries.

AMTRAK (National Railroad Passenger Corporation) 60 Massachusetts Ave. NE, Washington, DC 20002. (202) 906-3000. www. amtrak.com. Created by Rail Passenger Service Act of 1970. Develops, operates, and improves inter-city rail passenger service to create national rail transportation system.

Central Intelligence Agency (CIA) Washington, DC 20505. (703) 482-1100. www.cia.gov. Created by National Security Act of 1947. Under direction of president and National Security Council. Advises NSC on intelligence matters of national security. Collects, evaluates, and disseminates intelligence information relating to national security and to drug production and trafficking. Collects, produces, and disseminates counterintelligence and foreign intelligence here (in conjunction with FBI) and abroad. Conducts special activities as directed by president. Protects security of its activities, information, and personnel by necessary and appropriate means.

Commodity Futures Trading Commission (CFTC) 1155 21st St. NW, Washington, DC 20581. (202) 418-5000. www.cftc.gov/. Created May 14, 1973 by Commodity Futures Act of 1973. Regulates trading on the 11 U.S. futures exchanges. Regulates activities of commodity exchange members, public brokerage houses, commodity trading advisers, and other related employees.

Consumer Product Safety Commission (CPSC) East-West Towers, 4330 East-West Highway, Bethesda, Md. 20814. www.cpsc.gov. (301) 504-0580. Created May 14, 1973 by Consumer Product Safety Act. Protects public from unreasonable risk of injury from consumer products. Develops, enforces, and evaluates safety standards for consumer products.

Corporation for National Community Service 1201 New York Ave. NW, Washington, DC 20525. (202) 606-5000. www.nationalcorps. org. Created by National and Community Service Act of 1993. Incorporates programs previously administered by ACTION. Administers agencies such as AmeriCorps and AmeriCorps VISTA, which encourage and provide national and community service by volunteers, schools, and retired and senior volunteers.

Defense Nuclear Facilities Safety Board 625 Indiana Ave. NW, Suite 700, Washington, D.C. 20004. (202) 694-7000. www.dnfsb.gov. Created by Atomic Energy Act of 1954; established as independent agency Sept. 29, 1988. Reviews and evaluates standards for defense nuclear facilities of the Department of Energy. Investigates practices that may imperil public health and safety.

Environmental Protection Agency (EPA) 401 M St. SW, Washington, DC 20460. (888)-372-8255. www.epa.gov. Created Dec. 2, 1970. Protects and enhances environment. Controls and reduces pollution of air and water. Regulates solid-waste disposal and use of pesticides, radiation, and toxic substances.

Equal Employment Opportunity Commission (EEOC) 1801 L St. NW, Washington, DC 20507. (202) 663-4900. www.eeoc.gov. Created July 2, 1965, by Title VII of Civil Rights Act of 1964. Protects against discrimination based on race, color, handicap, religion, sex, age, and national origin in hiring, promoting, firing, wages, testing, training, apprenticeship, and all other terms and conditions of employment.

Export-Import Bank of the United States 811 Vermont Ave. NW, Washington, DC 20571. (800) 565-EXIM. www.exim.gov. Created Feb. 2, 1934. Facilitates and aids exports of U.S. goods and services through loans, loan guarantees, and insurance to exporters and private banks.

Farm Credit Administration 1501 Farm Credit Drive, McLean, Va. 22102-5090. (703) 883-4056. www.fca.gov. Created by Farm Credit Act of 1971. Regulates and examines programs, banks, associations, and organizations of the Farm Credit System, which provides credit to farmers, ranchers, producers of farm products, rural home owners, and associations and organizations of farmers, ranchers, and farm-equipment producers.

Federal Communications Commission (FCC) 445 12th St. SW, Washington, DC 20554. (888) 225-5322. www.fcc.gov. Created by Communications Act of 1934. Regulates interstate and foreign communications by radio, television, wire, and cable. Oversees development of broadcast services and the rapid and efficient provision of telephone and telegraph services nationwide.

Federal Deposit Insurance Corporation (FDIC) 550 17th St. NW, Washington, DC 20429. (202) 393-8400. www.fdic.gov. Created June 16, 1933, by Federal Reserve Act. Protects money supply by insuring deposits in and reviewing operations of state-chartered banks that are not members of the Federal Reserve System. Assumed responsibility for insuring savings and loan institutions formerly insured by defunct Federal Savings and Loan Insurance Corp. (FSLIC) in 1989.

Federal Election Commission (FEC) 999 E St. NW, Washington, DC 20463. (800) 424-9530. www.fec.gov. Created by Federal Election Campaign Act of 1971. Provides public funding for presidential elections. Ensures public disclosure of campaign finance activities. Administers and enforces contribution and spending limits for Federal elections. (See also "U.S. Presidential Elections.")

Federal Emergency Management Agency (FEMA) 500 C St. SW, Washington, DC 20472. (202) 646-4600. www.fema.gov Created Mar. 31, 1979. Provides single point of accountability for all Federal emergency preparedness, mitigation, and response activities. Facilitates most efficient use of resources in cases of natural or man-made emergencies.

Federal Housing Finance Board 1777 F St. NW, Washington, DC 20006. (202) 408-2500. www.fhfb.gov. Created August 9, 1989. Responsible for the administration and enforcement of the Federal Home Loan Bank Act, ensuring that banks carry out their housing finance and community investment mission

Federal Labor Relations Authority (FLRA) 607 14th St. NW, Washington, DC 20424 (202) 482-6560. www.flra.gov. Created Jan. 1, 1979. Protects rights of Federal employees to organize, bargain collectively, and participate in labor organizations. Oversees rights and obligations of Federal employees and the labor organizations that represent them.

Federal Maritime Commission 800 North Capitol St. NW, Washington, D.C. 20573-0001. (202) 523-5707. www.fmc.gov. Created August 12, 1961. Regulates waterborne foreign commerce, insures that U.S. international trade is open to all nations on fair and equitable terms, and protects against unauthorized, concerted activity in U.S. waterborne commerce.

Federal Mediation and Conciliation Service 2100 K. St. NW, Washington, D.C. 20427. (202) 606-8100. www.fmcs.gov. Created in 1947 by Labor Management Relations Act. Promotes development of stable labor management relations. Prevents or minimizes work stoppages by helping to settle disputes and by advocating collective bargaining, mediation, and arbitration.

Federal Reserve System Board of Governors of Federal Reserve System. 20th St. and Constitution Ave. NW, Washington, DC 20551. (202) 452-3000. www.federalreserve.gov. Created Dec. 23, 1913, by Federal Reserve Act. Central Bank of U.S. Administers and creates national credit and monetary policy. Regulates money supply. Maintains soundness of banking industry. (See also the section on "The U.S. Economy").

Federal Trade Commission (FTC) Pennsylvania Ave. at Sixth St. NW, Washington, DC 20580. (202) 326-2222. www.ftc.gov. Created in 1914 by Federal Trade Commission Act and Clayton Act. Maintains free and fair competition in free enterprise system. Breaks up monopolies. Seeks to prevent corruption, restraints on trade, and unfair trade practices.

General Services Administration (GSA) General Service Building, 18th and F Sts. NW, Washington, DC 20405. (202) 708-5082. www.gsa.gov. Created July 1, 1949, by Federal Property and Administrative Services Act of 1949. Establishes policy for and manages Government property and records, construction of buildings, distribution of supplies, and other Government services. Its services are divided among four service agencies: the *Information Resources Management Services*, the *Federal Supply Service*, the *Public Buildings Service (PBS)*, and the *Federal Property Resources Service (FPRS)*.

Inter-American Foundation 901 North Stuart St., Arlington, Va. 22203. (703) 306-4301. www.iaf.gov. Created by Congress in 1969. Supports social and economic development in Latin America and Caribbean. Makes grants to self-help organizations for the poor.

National Aeronautics and Space Administration (NASA) 300 E. Street SW, Washington, DC 20546. (202) 358-0000. www.nasa. gov. Created by National Aeronautics and Space Act of 1958. Develops, constructs, tests, and operates vehicles for in-flight research within and outside Earth's atmosphere. Disseminates information about space exploration and agency's activities.

National Archives and Records Administration (NARA) 8601 Adelphi Rd., College Park, Md. 20740-6001. (301) 713-6800. www.nara. gov. Created Oct. 19, 1984. Establishes policy for managing records of U.S. Government and making them available to public. Maintains 11 regional archives and 14 Federal records centers, as well as 11 presidential libraries or collections.

National Capital Planning Commission 801 Pennsylvania Ave. NW, Suite 301, Washington, D.C. 20576. (202) 482-7200. www.ncpc.gov. Created as a park planning agency by act of June 6, 1924. Serves as the central planning agency for development activities for Federal lands in the National Capital region in and around Washington.

National Credit Union Administration (NCUA) 1775 Duke St., Alexandria, Va. 22314-3428. (703) 518-6300. www.ncua.gov. Created Mar. 10, 1970. Charters, insures, supervises, and examines Federal credit unions. Administers National Credit Union Share Insurance Fund. Supplies emergency loans to credit unions through Central Liquidity Facility.

National Foundation on the Arts and the Humanities 1100 Pennsylvania Ave. NW, Washington, DC 20506. Created in 1965. Its three divisions encourage and support national progress in humanities and arts. The *National Endowment for the Arts (NEA)* (202-682-5400) fosters professional excellence in arts. The *National Endowment for the Humanities (NEH)* (202-606-8400; www.neh.gov) is an independent grant-making agency that supports research, education, and public programs in humanities. The *Institute of Museum and Library Services (IMS)* (202-606-8536; www.imls.gov) assists museums in maintaining, increasing, and improving services to public.

National Labor Relations Board (NLRB) 1099 14th Street NW, Washington, DC 20570. (202) 273-1000. www.nlrb.gov. Created by National Labor Relations Act of 1935 (also known as Wagner Act). Administers Federal labor law. Safeguards employees' rights to organize, conducts elections to determine whether workers want unions as their bargaining representative, and prevents or remedies unfair labor practices.

National Mediation Board 1301 K Street NW, Suite 250 East, Washington, DC 20572. (202) 692-

5000. www.nmb.gov. Created June 21, 1934, by amendment to Railway Labor Act. Resolves and investigates representation disputes in railroad and airline industries that could interrupt flow of commerce and endanger national economy.

National Science Foundation (NSF) 4201 Wilson Blvd., Arlington, Va. 22230. (703) 306-1234. www.nsf.gov. Created by National Science Foundation Act of 1950. Promotes progress of science and engineering through support of research and education programs.

National Transportation Safety Board (NTSB) 490 L'Enfant Plaza SW, Washington, DC 20594. (202) 314-6000. www.ntsb.gov. Created Apr. 1, 1975, by Independent Safety Board Act of 1974. Ensures safe operation of all types of transportation in U.S. Investigates accidents, conducts studies, and makes policy recommendations to government agencies, transportation industry, and others.

Nuclear Regulatory Commission (NRC) Washington, DC 20555. (301) 415-7000. www.nrc. gov. Created by Energy Reorganization Act of 1974. Licenses and regulates uses of civilian nuclear energy to protect public health and environment. Sets licensing regulations, issues licenses for, and inspects construction, ownership, and operation of nuclear reactors and other nuclear materials.

Office of Personnel Management (OPM) 1900 E St. NW, Washington, DC 20415. (202) 606-1800. www.opm.gov. Created Jan. 1, 1979. Recruits, examines, trains, and promotes people for Government jobs, regardless of race, religion, sex, political influence, and other nonmerit factors. Provides direct benefits, including health and life insurance, to employees and to retired employees and their survivors.

Overseas Private Investment Corporation (OPIC) 1100 New York Ave. NW, Washington, DC 20527. (202) 336-8400. www.opic.gov. Established as an independent agency in 1998. Promotes economic growth in developing countries by encouraging U.S. private investment in those nations.

Peace Corps 1111 20th St. NW, Washington, DC 20526. (202) 692-2000. www.peacecorps.gov. Created by Peace Corps Act of 1961. Promotes world peace and friendship. Helps people of other countries develop manpower by bringing U.S. volunteers abroad to participate in public works programs. Emphasis placed on helping the poorest areas of countries served by the Peace Corps.

Pension Benefit Guaranty Corporation (PBGC) 1200 K St. NW, Washington, DC 20005. (202) 326-4000. www.pbgc.gov. Created Sept. 2, 1974, by Title IV of Employee Retirement Income Security Act of 1974. Guarantees payment of nonforfeitable pension benefits in covered private sector defined benefit pension plans.

Postal Rate Commission 1333 H St. NW, Washington, DC 20268-0001. (202) 789-6800. www.prc.gov. Created Aug. 12, 1970, by Postal Reorganization Act. Recommends changes in postal rates, fees, services, programs, studies, and mail classification schedules. Hears complaints about postal rates, services, and fees.

Securities and Exchange Commission (SEC) 450 Fifth St. NW, Washington, DC 20549. (202) 942-4150. www.sec.gov. Created July 2, 1934 by Securities Exchange Act of 1934. Provides fullest possible disclosure to the public of securities sales, operations, and registrations. Protects public against malpractice in securities and financial markets.

Selective Service System National Headquarters, Arlington, Va. 22209-2425. (703) 605-4000. www.sss.gov. Created June 24, 1948, by Military Selective Service Act. Requires registration, and maintains list of males age 18-26 eligible to serve in armed forces in case of national security emergency.

Small Business Administration (SBA) 409 Third St. SW, Washington, DC 20416. (202) 205-6600. www.sba.gov. Created by Small Business Act of 1953. Aids, counsels, makes loans to, and protects interests of small businesses; ensures that they receive a fair amount of Government purchases and contracts.

Social Security Administration 6401 Security Blvd., Baltimore, Md. 21235. (410) 965-1234. www.ssa.gov. Created July 16, 1946; made independent agency by Social Security Independence Act of 1994. Manages the nation's social insurance program, consisting of retirement, survivors, and disability insurance programs, commonly known as Social Security. Also administers the Supplemental Security Income program for the aged, blind, and disabled. Studies poverty and recommends solutions. Assigns Social Security numbers to all U.S. workers.

Tennessee Valley Authority (TVA) 400 West Summit Hill Dr., Knoxville, Tenn. 37902. (865) 632-2101. 1 Massachusetts Ave. NW, Washington, DC 20444-0001. (202)-898-2999. www.tva.gov. Created May 18, 1933. Government-owned corporation. Conducts resource development programs for advancement of growth in Tennessee Valley region. Controls floods, develops navigation, produces electric power, develops fertilizer, improves recreation, and develops forestry and wildlife.

United States Agency for International Development (AID) 1300 Pennsylvania Ave. NW, Washington, DC 20523-0001. (202) 712-0000. www.info.usaid.gov. Established as independent agency in 1998. Administers foreign economic and humanitarian assistance programs in the developing world, Central and Eastern Europe, and the countries of the former Soviet Union.

United States Commission on Civil Rights 624 Ninth St. NW, Washington, DC 20425. (202) 376-8177. www.usccr.gov. Created by Civil Rights Act of 1957. Collects and studies information on discrimination based on race, color, religion, age, sex, handicap, or national origin. Assures equal protection in voting rights and enforcement of civil rights laws. Promotes equal opportunity in education, employment, and housing.

United States International Trade Commission 500 E St. SW, Washington, DC 20436. (202) 205-2000. www.usitc.gov. Created Sept. 8, 1916. Furnishes studies, reports, and recommendations regarding international trade and tariffs to president, Congress, and other government agencies.

United States Postal Service 475 L'Enfant Plaza SW, Washington, DC 20260-0010. (202) 268-2000. www.usps.gov. Created Aug. 12, 1970, by Postal Reorganization Act. Provides mail processing and delivery service to individuals and businesses in U.S. Protects mail from loss or theft and apprehends violators of postal laws.

FEDERAL EMPLOYEES AND BUDGET

		Budget (millions)		
Year	Number of employees[1]	Receipts	Outlays	Surplus or deficit (-)
1901	239,476	$588	$525	$63
1910	388,708	676	694	-18
1920	655,265	6,649	6,358	291
1930	601,319	4,058	3,320	738
1940	1,042,420	6,548	9,468	-2,920
1945	3,816,310	45,159	92,712	-47,553
1950	1,960,708	39,443	42,562	-3,119
1960	2,398,704	92,492	92,191	301
1970	2,984,574	192,807	195,649	-2,842
1980	2,875,866	517,112	590,947	-73,835
1990	3,128,267	1,031,969	1,253,198	-221,229
1995	2,920,277	1,351,830	1,515,837	-164,007
1996	2,847,392	1,453,062	1,560,572	-107,510
1997	2,787,137	1,579,292	1,601,282	-21,990
1998	2,789,532	1,721,798	1,652,619	69,179
1999	2,749,239	1,827,454	1,702,875	124,579
2000	2,708,101	2,025,218	1,789,562	236,982
2001[2]	N.A.	2,136,946	1,8562,38	280,708

The Federal Government: Employees and Budget, 1901–2001

1. Paid civilians only. 2. Projected. **Source:** Office of Management and Budget, *Budget of the United States Government, FY 2002.*

▶ FEDERAL JOBS AND SALARIES

As of March 31, 2000 (the latest year available), there were 1,671,438 full-time non-postal Federal civilian employees. Nearly 97 percent of the Federal civilian workforce was employed in the United States; 12,605 (0.8 percent) worked in U.S. territories, and 40,444 (2.4 percent) worked in foreign countries. The majority of government employees worked in metropolitan statistical areas, led by the Washington, D.C., MSA, with 267,959, or 16.0 percent of the total.

Four executive departments accounted for nearly 70 percent of the Federal civilian workforce. The Department of Defense employed 647,287 civilians (38.7 percent of the total), Veterans Affairs employed 191,958 (11.5 percent), the Treasury 150,624 (9.0 percent), and Justice 121,422 (7.3 percent).

Federal Government civilian employees are paid according to a number of different systems: the General Schedule (GS), Federal Wage Systems, and other acts and administratively determined systems. Overall, the average salary for full-time civilian government employees was $50,429. Employees under the General Schedule on average earned more than those on Federal Wage Systems ($49,428 to $37,082), but not as much as employees covered by other acts and administrative determinations, who averaged $66,248. Average salaries by major geographic areas were: United States, $50,616; Washington, D.C. area, $63,969; foreign countries, $46,452; and U.S. territories, $39,359.

White-Collar Employees
General Schedule   The number of white-collar employees has been declining for four years. General schedule employment declined by 18,284 workers between 1999 and 2000, a drop of nearly 1.5 percent over the previous year. There are 15 grades broadly defined in terms of responsibility, difficulty, and qualifications; within each grade there are 10 steps. Within-grade advancement occurs on a fixed schedule, though employees demonstrating "high-quality performance" can receive "quality step increases." In all, General Schedule employees make up more than three-quarters of all civilians employed by the Government.

Foreign Service Personnel and Veterans Affairs
There were 4,224 Foreign Service Officers in 2000, with an average salary of $80,789. Non-officers in the foreign service numbered 7,235 and averaged $53,868 in salary. The pay system of the Department of Veterans Affairs covered 7,174 physicians and dentists with an average salary of $100,304; 236 podiatrists and optometrists ($89,795); 30,563 nurses ($54,739); and 1,141 physicians' assistants ($65,689).

Executive Schedule (EX) and Senior Executive Service (ES)
The very top executives in the executive branch are paid under a system known as the Executive Schedule (EX). Broadly speaking, the five Executive Schedule levels include the following job titles: level I, cabinet members; level II, deputy secretaries of major departments; level III, presidential advisors, chief administrators of major independent agencies, and under secretaries; level IV, assistant secretaries, deputy under secretaries, and general counsels. in executive departments; and level V, deputy assistant secretaries, administrators, commissioners, and directors. Executive Schedule employment was 447, with an average salary of $126,765. The Senior Executive Service (ES) covers most managerial and policy positions in the executive branch that do not require Senate confirmation. In 2000, there were 7,044 employees covered by ES; salaries averaged $126,994.

Special rates
The Government has difficulty recruiting and retaining qualified personnel in certain occupations and for certain locations with higher competitive salaries. To alleviate this problem, the Office of Personnel Management has the authority to establish special rates for certain white-collar positions. The number of white-collar employees receiving special-rate salaries varies from year to year; in 2000, it was 138,455.

Blue-Collar Employees
As of March 31, 2000, the federal government employed 205,215 workers (12.3 percent of the civilian Government workforce) in blue-collar (trades and labor) occupations. Most of these (200,879 or 97.9 percent) were employed in the United States; 11,478, or 5.6 percent worked in and around the Washington, D.C. metro area. The Department of Defense employed 151,624, or 73.9 percent of all blue-collar government workers.

Blue-collar pay rates are governed by federal Wage Systems and determined on a prevailing rate basis by pay locality. The worldwide average salary for the blue-collar workforce in 2000 was $37,082. Salaries were highest in the United States (where they averaged $37,228) and lowest in foreign countries, (where they averaged just

$29,635). Blue-collar salaries averaged $38,047 in the Washington D.C. metropolitan area, but only $30,191 in U.S. territories and possessions.

▶THE BUDGET SURPLUS

After 30 years of annual budget deficits, the Federal Government in early 2001 found itself in the unusual position of counting budget surpluses. The surplus in 2000 was $236.4 billion, and was projected to increase to $304 million in the year 2006. That was before the September 11 attacks on the World Trade Center, which hastened a long-feared economic recession, and caused economists to predict a budget deficit for 2001. But even three years of record surpluses have done little to dent the immense federal debt run up by the government during the 1980s. In 2000, the gross federal debt was $5.6 trillion, or more than five times

what it was in 1980 (see the U.S. Economy for an explanation of the difference between deficits and the debt). In fact, the annual interest on the national debt alone ($223 billion in 2000) is nearly as much as the 2000 surplus. Moreover, the surpluses seem a lot smaller if you don't include Social Security, which both political parties have agreed to hold above budgetary wrangling. If you protect

Salaries of Federal Officials

In 1999, Congress voted to double the next president's salary from $200,000 to $400,000. Less noticed was the fact that legislators were due for their own 3.4 percent cost of living raise. The following salaries took effect in 2001, and will automatically increase each year with the cost of living unless Congress actively votes against a raise.

Branch/Official	Salary
Executive branch	
President	$400,000
Vice President	186,300
Legislative branch	
Senate	
President pro tempore,	$161,200
Majority and Minority Leaders	161,200
Senators	145,100
House of Representatives	
Speaker of the House	$186,300
Minority and majority leaders	161,200
Representatives	145,100
Judicial branch	
Chief Justice	$186,300
Associate justices	178,300
Circuit judges	153,900
District judges	145,100
Bankruptcy and magistrate judges	133,492

Source: Office of Personnel Management; Administrative Office of the U.S. Courts.

Federal Government Pay Systems, 2000

Grade	Employees	Mean Salary
General Schedule		
GS-1	589	$15,485
GS-2	1,864	17,896
GS-3	12,753	20,460
GS-4	54,789	23,659
GS-5	111,546	27,066
GS-6	85,289	30,515
GS-7	124,811	33,590
GS-8	47,830	37,906
GS-9	123,621	40,350
GS-10	15,367	45,798
GS-11	173,576	49,181
GS-12	199,230	59,098
GS-13	157,095	70,958
GS-14	70,063	84,447
GS-15	37,673	101,302
Total	**1,216,096**	**$49,428**
Senior Level (SL)	477	$93,137-122,400[1]
Executive Schedule (EX)		
Level I	17	$157,000
Level II	33	141,300
Level III	91	130,200
Level IV	283	122,400
Level V	23	114,500
Total	**447**	**$126,765**
Senior Executive Service (ES)		
ES-1	768	$106,200
ES-2	850	111,200
ES-3	1,012	116,300
ES-4	2688	122,200
ES-5	1167	122,400
ES-6	559	122,400
Total	**7,044**	**$126,994**

Note: As of March 31. 1. Mean salary not available. Salary range shown. **Source:** U.S. Office of Personnel Management, *Pay Structure of the Federal Civil Service 2000*, (2001).

U.S. Federal Employment, 1992–2000

Description	1992	1998	1999	2000
Executive branch civilian employment[1]	2,226,778	1,855,796	1,819,636	1,877,643
U.S. Postal Service[2]	792,049	871,520	866,393	860,777
Military personnel on active duty[3]	1,847,600	1,442,289	1,421,443	1,420,495
Department of Defense	1,808,131	1,406,830	1,385,703	1,384,338
Department of Transportation (Coast Guard)	39,469	35,459	35,740	36,157
Total executive branch employment	**4,866,427**	**4,169,605**	**4,108,133**	**4,065,253**
Legislative branch	38,509	30,474	30,353	31,157
Judicial branch	27,987	31,742	32,196	32,184
Total federal employment	**4,932,923**	**4,231,821**	**4,170,682**	**4,128,596**

1. Excludes Postal Service employees. 2. Includes Postal Rate Commission. 3. Excludes reserve components.
Source: Office of Management and Budget, *Budget of the United States Government, FY 2002*.

Government Employment and Population, 1961–2000

| | Government employment | | | | | |
Fiscal year	Federal executive branch[1] ('000s)	Total Federal personnel ('000s)	State and local governments ('000s)	All governmental units ('000s)	Executive branch employment as a percent of all governmental units[1]	Executive branch employment per 1,000 population[1]
1962	2,485	5,354	6,549	11,903	20.9%	13.3%
1965	2,496	5,215	7,696	12,911	19.3	12.8
1970[2]	2,944	6,085	9,822	15,907	18.5	14.4
1975	2,848	5,061	11,937	16,998	16.8	13.2
1980[2]	2,821	4,965	13,375	18,340	15.4	12.4
1985	3,008	5,256	13,519	18,775	16.0	12.6
1990[2]	3,067	5,234	15,219	20,453	15.0	12.3
1995	2,858	4,475	16,484	20,959	13.6	10.9
1996	2,786	4,354	16,662	21,016	13.3	10.5
1997	2,725	4,226	16,858	21,084	12.9	10.2
1998	2,727	4,196	17,137	21,333	12.8	10.1
1999	2,687	4,135	17,501	21,636	12.4	9.8
2000[2]	2,645	4,092	17,793	21,885	12.1	9.6

1. Civilian employment only, including full-time permanent, temporary, part-time, and intermittent employees in the executive branch, including the Postal Service, and beginning in 1970, includes various disadvantaged worker-trainee programs. 2. Includes temporary employees in the decennial census. **Source:** Office of Management and Budget, *Budget of the United States Government, FY 2002.*

Federal Government Employment and Outlays, by Branch and Agency, 1999–2002

| | | Outlays (millions of dollars) | | | |
| | | Actual | | Estimated | |
Agency	Employment 2000[1]	1999	2000	2001	2002
Legislative branch	31,157	$2,609	2,911	3,086	3,268
Judicial branch	32,186	3,790	4,086	4,300	4,856
Executive branch[2]:	1,814,300	—	—	—	—
Executive Office of the President	N.A.	417	283	289	309
Department of Agriculture	95,100	62,834	283	289	309
Department of Commerce	113,300	5,036	7,807	5,549	5,182
Department of Defense[3] (military functions)	660,300	261,380	281,223	283,915	303,449
Department of Defense (civil functions)	N.A.	32,014	32,684	34,400	35,402
Department of Education	4,600	32,269	33,900	36,652	45,230
Department of Energy	15,600	16,048	15,010	16,739	17,245
Department of Health and Human Services	60,500	359,702	382,626	430,466	468,787
Dept. of Housing and Urban Development	10,100	32,734	30,828	37,299	34,791
Department of the Interior	67,300	7,815	8,029	8,687	9,275
Department of Justice	122,800	18,317	19,554	20,689	22,527
Department of Labor	16,300	32,461	31,355	38,220	42,042
Department of State	27,300	6,456	6,850	9,302	9,700
Department of Transportation	63,000	41,831	45,964	50,611	54,861
Department of the Treasury	143,700	386,697	391,246	388,549	381,539
Department of Veterans Affairs	202,600	43,168	47,087	45,235	51,480
Environmental Protection Agency	17700	6,750	7,238	7,495	7,596
General Services Administration	14,000	-46	28	603	-223
National Aeronautics & Space Administration (NASA)	18,400	13,664	13,442	13,777	14,248
Office of Personnel Management	2,800	47,515	48,660	50,978	53,351
Small Business Administration	4,300	57	-421	-971	687
Social Security Administration (off-budget)	62,400	379,213	396,169	421,901	441,092
Totals[4, 5]	1,877,643	$1,702,875	$1,788,826	$1,856,238	$1,960,564

Note: Outlays are the measure of Government spending—payments to liquidate obligations (other than the repayment of debt), net of cash, and offsetting collections. Outlays are generally recorded on a cash basis, but also include many cash-equivalent transactions and interest accrued on public issues of the public debt. 1. Employment figures exclude developmental positions under the Worker-Trainee Opportunity Program; participants in the Cooperative Education Program; disadvantaged summer and part-time workers under such Office of Personnel Management programs as Summer Aides, stay-in-school, and junior fellowship; and certain statutory exemptions. Figures for executive branch rounded at source. 2. Civilian employment. 3. By law (10 U.S.C. Chapter 4, section 140b) the Department of Defense is exempt from full-time equivalent employment controls. Data shown are estimated. 4. Employment totals do not include FDIC or U.S. Postal Service. 5. Outlay totals do not account for undistributed offsetting receipts.
Source: Office of Management and Budget, *Budget of the United States Government, FY 2002.*

Medicare and federal pension trust funds too—an issue that was hotly debated in Washington in the summer of 2001—whatever surplus there might have been is almost negligible.

►GLOSSARY OF FEDERAL BUDGET TERMS

Budget authority The term budget authority means the authority provided by law to incur financial obligations that result in immediate or future outlays involving government funds or to collect offsetting receipts.

Budget deficit/surplus A budget deficit occurs when government outlays exceed government receipts; a surplus occurs when receipts exceed outlays. The budget surplus in 2000 was a record $236.9 billion; the record deficit was $290.4 billion in 1992.

Fiscal year The Federal Government's fiscal year begins Oct. 1 and ends Sept. 30 of the next calendar year; so, FY 2001 began Oct. 1, 2001, and ends Sept. 30, 2002.

Intergovernmental expenditure/revenue Amounts paid to or received from other governments either in the form of shared revenues and grants-in-aid, as reimbursements for performance of general government activities or for specific services such as care of prisoners for the paying government, or in lieu of taxes.

Off-budget/on-budget Some presentations in the Federal budget distinguish on-budget totals from off-budget totals. On-budget totals reflect the transactions of all Federal Government entities except those excluded from the budget totals by law, the two Social Security trust funds (old-age and survivors insurance and the Federal disability insurance trust funds), and the Postal Service fund. Off-budget totals reflect the transactions of government entities excluded from the on-budget totals by law.

Offsetting collections Offsetting collections are collections from the public that result from business-type or market-oriented activities and collections; examples include proceeds from the sale of electric power by the Tennessee Valley Authority, voluntary medical insurance premiums paid to the supplementary medical insurance trust fund, and the sale of postage stamps.

Outlays Budget outlays are expenditures and net lending of funds under budget authority during the fiscal year. They constitute the spending side of the budget and are compared to receipts in calculating the budget surplus or deficit.

Receipts Budget receipts constitute the income side of the budget and are composed almost entirely of taxes or other compulsory payments to the government. They are compared to outlays in calculating the budget surplus or deficit.

The Congressional Budget Process

On or before	Action to be completed
First Monday in February	President submits his budget. Congressional committees have six weeks to submit views and estimates to Budget Committees.
February 15	Congressional Budget Office submits report to budget committees.
April 1	Senate budget committee reports concurrent resolution on the budget.
April 15	Congress completes action on concurrent resolution on the budget.
May 15	Annual appropriation bills may be considered in the House.
June 10	House Appropriations Committee reports last annual appropriations bill.
June 15	Congress completes action on reconciliation legislation.
June 30	House completes action on annual appropriation bills.
October 1	Fiscal year begins.

1. A concurrent resolution sets levels for new budget authority and outlays, direct loan obligations, primary loan guarantee commitments, the amount by which Federal revenues should be increased or decreased, the budget surplus or deficit, the public debt, and so on. **Source:** Committee on Ways and Means, U.S. House of Representatives, *Overview of Entitlement Programs,* (annual).

Federal Government Receipts By Source, 1934–2001 (billions of dollars)

Year	Individual income taxes	Corporation income taxes[1]	Social insurance & retirement receipts	Excise taxes	Other[2]	Total
1934	$0.4	$0.3	[3]	$1.4	$0.8	**3.0**
1940	0.9	1.2	$1.8	2.0	0.7	**6.5**
1950	15.8	10.4	4.3	7.6	1.4	**39.4**
1960	40.7	21.5	14.7	11.7	3.9	**92.5**
1970	90.4	32.8	44.3	15.7	9.5	**192.8**
1980	244.1	64.6	157.8	24.3	26.3	**517.1**
1990	466.9	93.5	380.0	35.3	56.2	**1,032.0**
1995	590.2	157.0	484.5	57.5	62.6	**1,351.8**
1996	656.4	171.8	509.4	54.0	61.4	**1,453.1**
1997	737.5	182.3	539.4	56.9	63.2	**1,579.3**
1998	828.6	188.7	571.8	57.7	75.0	**1,721.8**
1999	879.5	184.7	611.8	70.4	81.0	**1,827.5**
2000	1,004.5	207.3	652.9	68.9	91.8	**2,025.2**
2001[4]	1,072.9	213.1	689.7	71.1	90.1	**2,136.9**

1. Beginning in 1990 includes trust fund receipts for the hazardous substance Superfund. 2. Includes estate and gift taxes, customs duties and fees, federal reserve deposits, and other. 3. Less than $100 million. 4. Estimate.
Source: Office of Management and Budget, *Budget of the United States Government, FY 2002*

Trust fund In the Federal budget, a trust fund means only that the law requires that funds must be accounted for separately and used only for specified purposes. The largest trust funds are those for civil service and military retirement, Social Security, Medicare, and unemployment insurance. These are financed largely by Social Security taxes and contributions and payments from the general fund. There are also major trust funds for transportation and bank deposit insurance which are financed by user charges.

User charges These are charges for services rendered, collected in the form of taxes, such as highway excise taxes to fund the highway trust fund.

Outlays by Budget Enforcement Act Category, 1970–2001 (billions)

Category	1970	1980	1990	1995	1999	2000	2001[1]
Total Outlays	**$195.6**	**$590.9**	**$1,253.2**	**$1,515.8**	**$1,702.9**	**$1,788.8**	**$1,856.2**
Discretionary outlays	120.3	276.3	500.6	544.9	572.0	614.8	649.4
National defense	81.9	134.6	300.1	273.6	275.5	295.0	299.6
Non-defense, international	4.0	12.8	19.1	20.1	19.5	21.3	24.1
Non-defense, domestic	34.4	128.9	181.4	251.2	277.0	298.6	325.7
Mandatory outlays	**61.0**	**262.1**	**568.2**	**738.8**	**901.1**	**950.8**	**1,000.5**
Social Security	29.6	117.1	246.5	333.3	387.0	406.0	430.0
Deposit Insurance	-0.5	-0.4	57.9	-17.9	-5.3	-3.1	-1.0
Means-tested entitlements[2]	10.1	45.0	94.1	181.6	211.9	226.3	241.4
Other	30.4	120.4	206.4	286.3	348.0	364.0	377.7
Undistributed offsetting receipts[3]	-8.6	-19.9	-36.7	-44.5	-40.4	-42.6	-47.7
Net interest	14.4	52.5	184.4	232.2	229.7	223.2	206.4

1. Estimate. 2. Includes Medicaid, food stamps, family support assistance (AFDC), supplemental security income (SSI), child nutrition programs, earned income tax credits, and veterans' pensions. 3. Includes asset sales.
Source: Office of Management and Budget, *Budget of the United States Government, FY 2002.*

Budget Outlays and Percent Distribution, by Function, 1970–2000

Function	1970	1980	1990	1995	1999	2000
			Millions of dollars			
National defense	**$81,692**	**$133,995**	**$299,331**	**$272,066**	**$274,873**	**$294,494**
Human resources	**75,349**	**313,374**	**619,329**	**923,765**	**1,058,722**	**1,115,262**
Education, training, employment and social services	8,634	31,843	38,755	54,263	56241	59,201
Health	5,907	23,169	57,716	115,418	141,074	154,534
Medicare	6,213	32,090	98,102	159,855	190,447	197,113
Income Security	15,655	86,540	147,076	220,493	237,707	247,895
Social Security	30,270	118,547	248,623	335,846	390,041	409,436
Veterans benefits & services	8,669	21,185	29,058	37,890	43,212	47,083
Physical resources	**15,574**	**65,985**	**126,039**	**59,142**	**81,930**	**84,665**
Energy	997	10,156	3,341	4,936	912	1060
Natural resources and environment	3,065	13,858	17,080	21,915	23,968	25,031
Commerce and housing credit	2,112	9,390	67,600	-17,808	2,647	3,211
Transportation	7,008	21,329	29,485	39,350	42,533	46,854
Community and regional development	2,392	11,252	8,498	10,641	11,870	10,629
Net interest	**14,380**	**52,538**	**184,380**	**232,169**	**229,735**	**223,218**
Other functions	**17,286**	**44,996**	**60,734**	**73,150**	**98,060**	**113,768**
International affairs	4,330	12,714	13,764	16,434	15,243	17,216
General science, space, & technology	4,511	5,832	14,444	16,724	18,125	18,637
Agriculture	5,166	8,839	11,958	9,778	23,011	36,641
Administration of justice	959	4,584	9,993	16,216	25,924	27,820
General government	2,320	13,028	10,575	13,998	15,757	13,454
Total[1]	**$195,649**	**$590,947**	**$1,253,198**	**$1,515,837**	**$1,702,875**	**$1,788,826**
			As percentage of total			
National defense	**41.8%**	**22.7%**	**23.9%**	**17.9%**	**16.1%**	**16.5%**
Human resources	**38.5**	**53.0**	**49.4**	**60.9**	**62.2**	**62.3**
Physical resources	**8.0**	**11.2**	**10.1**	**3.9**	**4.8**	**4.7**
Net interest	**7.4**	**8.9**	**14.7**	**15.3**	**13.5**	**12.5**
Other functions	**8.8**	**7.6**	**4.8**	**4.8**	**5.8**	**6.4**

1. Includes undistributed offsetting receipts not shown separately.
Source: Office of Management and Budget, *Budget of the United States Government, FY 2002.*

Federal Government Finances, 2000–02

Category	2000 Actual	2001 Estimate	2002 Estimate
RECEIPTS, TOTAL	**$2,025,218**	**$2,136,946**	**$2,191,734**
Individual income taxes, total	1,004,462	1,072,927	1,078,789
Corporation income taxes, total	207,289	213,069	218,786
Social insurance and retirement receipts, total	652,852	689,656	725,798
Employment and general retirement:	620,451	655,505	689,531
Old-age and survivors insurance (Off-budget)	411,677	430,916	453,853
Disability insurance (Off-budget)	68,907	72,954	77,067
Hospital insurance	135,529	147,228	154,098
Railroad retirement:	4,338	4,407	4,513
Unemployment insurance:	27,640	29,560	31,946
Deposits by States[1]	20,701	22,405	24,601
Federal unemployment receipts[1]	6,871	7,105	7,257
Railroad unemployment receipts[1]	68	50	88
Other retirement:	4,761	4,591	4,321
Federal employees' retirement—employee share	4,691	4,523	4,259
Non-Federal employees retirement[2]	70	68	62
Excise taxes, total	**68,865**	**71,148**	**74,020**
Federal funds, total	22,692	23,984	24,916
Alcohol taxes	8,140	7,688	7,810
Tobacco taxes	7,221	7,548	8,140
Transportation fuels tax	819	779	743
Telephone and teletype services	5,670	5,914	6,295
Ozone depleting chemicals and products	125	94	65
Other Federal fund excise taxes	717	1,961	1,863
Trust funds, total	46,173	47,164	49,104
Highway	34,972	35,431	36,539
Airport and airway	9,739	10,414	11,183
Aquatic resources	342	352	392
Black lung disability insurance	518	555	570
Inland waterway	101	93	93
Hazardous substance superfund	2	0	0
Oil spill liability	182	0	0
Vaccine injury compensation	133	134	137
Leaking underground storage tank	184	185	190
Estate and gift taxes, total	**29,010**	**31,072**	**28,699**
Customs duties, total	**19,914**	**21,442**	**22,537**
Miscellaneous Receipts	**42,826**	**37,632**	**43,105**
Miscellaneous taxes	99	104	109
United Mine Workers of America combined benefit fund	155	149	143
Deposit of earnings, Federal Reserve System	32,293	26,599	31,800
Defense cooperation	12	6	6
Fees for permits and regulatory and judicial services	7,664	8,919	9,189
Fines, penalties, and forfeitures	2,422	1,923	1,880
Gifts and contributions	260	286	183
Refunds and recoveries	−79	−354	−298
OUTLAYS, TOTAL	**$1,788,826**	**$1,856,238**	**$1,960,564**
National defense, total	294,494	299,136	319,193
Department of Defense—Military, total	281,223	283,915	303,449
Military Personnel	75,950	72,089	79,334
Operation and Maintenance	105,870	110,415	113,246
Procurement	51,696	52,734	56,131
Research, Development, Test, and Evaluation	37,606	37,962	42,656
Military Construction	5,109	5,198	4,792
Family Housing	3,413	3,683	3,815
Other	1,579	1,834	3,475
Atomic energy defense activities	12,161	13,746	14,317
Defense-related activities	1,110	1,475	1,427
International affairs, total	**17,216**	**17,461**	**21,000**
International development and humanitarian assistance	6,518	7,027	7,247
International security assistance	6,387	6,320	6,701
Conduct of foreign affairs	4,709	6,721	7,187
Foreign information and exchange activities	817	860	818
International financial programs	−1,215	−3,467	−953
General science, space and technology, total	**18,637**	**19,726**	**20,798**
General science and basic research	6,210	6,851	7,440
Space flight, research, and supporting activities	12,427	12,875	13,358
Energy, total	**−1,060**	**−655**	**−322**
Energy supply	−2,118	−1,744	−1,493
Energy conservation	666	743	798

Category	2000 Actual	2001 Estimate	2002 Estimate
Emergency energy preparedness	162	162	167
Energy information, policy, and regulation	230	184	206
Natural resources and environment, total	**25,031**	**27,370**	**27,494**
Water resources	5,081	5,431	4,993
Conservation and land management	5,901	6,808	6,796
Recreational resources	3,419	3,808	4,140
Pollution control and abatement	7,402	7,666	7,753
Other natural resources	3,228	3,657	3,812
Agriculture, total	**36,641**	**25,922**	**18,622**
Farm income stabilization	33,452	22,096	14,673
Agricultural research and services	3,189	3,826	3,949
Commerce and housing credit, total	**3,211**	**−768**	**6,946**
Mortgage credit	−3,335	1,295	−2,965
Postal Service	2,129	2,689	3,205
Deposit insurance	−3,051	−986	−652
Other advancement of commerce	7,468	−3,766	7,358
Transportation, total	**46,854**	**51,079**	**55,038**
Ground transportation	31,697	34,458	37,400
Air transportation	10,571	11,970	13,121
Water transportation	4,394	4,357	4,622
Other transportation	192	294	−105
Community and regional development, total	**10,629**	**10,572**	**11,743**
Community development	5,480	5,549	5,681
Area and regional development	2,538	2,757	2,828
Disaster relief and insurance	2,611	2,266	3,234
Education, training, employment, and social services, total	**59,201**	**65,251**	**76,602**
Elementary, secondary, and vocational education	20,578	23,508	26,151
Higher education	10,116	9,605	15,614
Research and general education aids	2,532	3,029	3,043
Training and employment	6,772	8,128	9,044
Other labor services	1,199	1,405	1,461
Social services	18,004	19,576	21,289
Health, total	**154,534**	**175,306**	**201,501**
Health care services	136,231	154,238	177,345
Health research and training	15,979	18,547	21,509
Consumer and occupational health and safety	2,324	2,521	2,647
Medicare, total	**197,113**	**219,258**	**229,903**
Income security, total	**247,895**	**262,617**	**275,675**
General retirement and disability insurance (excluding social security)	4,975	5,594	4,664
Federal employee retirement and disability	77,152	81,176	84,398
Unemployment compensation	23,012	27,808	30,749
Housing assistance	28,800	30,972	32,465
Food and nutrition assistance	32,483	35,005	36,589
Other income security	81,473	82,062	86,810
Social security, total	**409,436**	**433,623**	**455,119**
Veterans benefits and services, total	**47,083**	**45,363**	**51,582**
Income security for veterans	24,872	22,377	26,043
Veterans education, training and rehabilitation	1,342	1,690	1,952
Hospital and medical care for veterans	19,516	20,797	21,781
Veterans housing	342	−987	327
Other veterans benefits and services	1,011	1,486	1,479
Administration of justice, total	**27,820**	**29,430**	**32,283**
Federal law enforcement activities	11,617	12,698	13,202
Federal litigative and judicial activities	7,762	8,235	9,042
Federal correctional activities	3,707	4,238	4,280
Criminal justice assistance	4,734	4,259	5,759
General government, total	**13,454**	**16,834**	**16,308**
Legislative functions	2,222	2,402	2,685
Executive direction and management	631	682	830
Central fiscal operations	8,345	9,513	9,762
General property and records management	225	902	417
Central personnel management	184	171	174
General purpose fiscal assistance	2,084	2,431	2,320
Other general government	2,241	2,119	1,513
Deductions for offsetting receipts	−2,478	−1,386	−1,393
Net interest, total	**223,218**	**206,369**	**188,131**

1 Deposits by States cover the benefit part of the program. Federal unemployment receipts cover administrative costs at both the Federal and State levels. Railroad unemployment receipts cover both the benefits and administrative costs of the program for the railroads. 2 Represents employer and employee contributions to the civil service retirement and disability fund for covered employees of Government-sponsored, privately owned enterprises and the District of Columbia municipal government.
Source: Office of Management and Budget, *Budget of the United States Government, FY 2002*

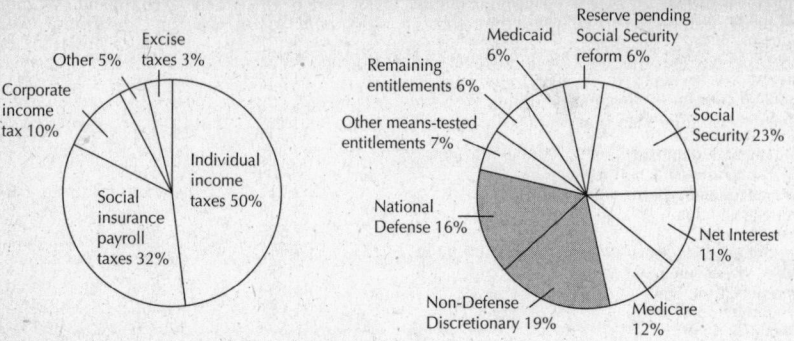

Federal Government Dollar, Fiscal Year 2002

Revenues: $2,192 billion

Outlays $1,960 billion

Revenues pie chart:
- Other 5%
- Excise taxes 3%
- Corporate income tax 10%
- Social insurance payroll taxes 32%
- Individual income taxes 50%

Outlays pie chart:
- Medicaid 6%
- Reserve pending Social Security reform 6%
- Remaining entitlements 6%
- Other means-tested entitlements 7%
- National Defense 16%
- Social Security 23%
- Net Interest 11%
- Medicare 12%
- Non-Defense Discretionary 19%

Note: Gray-shaded areas are discretionary outlays. All other outlays are mandatory.
Source: Office of Management and Budget, *Budget of the United States Government, FY 2002.*

Federal Budget Outlays for National Defense Functions, 1962–2001 (billions of dollars)

Function	1962	1970	1980	1990	1999	2000	2001[1]
Military personnel	$16,331	$29,032	$40,897	$75,622	$69,503	$75,950	$72,089
Percent of defense budget	31.2%	35.4%	30.5%	25.2%	25.2%	25.8%	24.1%
Operations & maintenance	$11,594	$21,609	$44,788	$88,340	$96,418	$105,870	$110,415
Procurement	14,532	21,584	29,021	80,972	48,826	51,696	52,734
Research, development, test and evaluation	6,319	7,166	13,127	37,458	37,363	37,606	37,962
Military construction	1,347	1,168	2,450	5,080	5,521	5,109	5,198
Family housing	259	614	1,680	3,501	3,692	3,413	3,683
Other	−271	−1,050	−1,050	−1,218	57	1,579	1,834
Total outlays[2]	$52,345	$81,692	$133,995	$299,331	$274,873	$294,494	$299,136

1. Estimate. 2. Includes atomic energy defense activities and other defense-related activities not shown separately.
Source: Office of Management and Budget, *Budget of the United States Government, FY 2002.*

NATIONAL DEFENSE

In 2000, the United States spent nearly $295 billion to keep 1.4 million people in active military service and to build and maintain the greatest arsenal of weapons ever known.

Since the end of World War II, a large percentage of people and material have been committed to regions around the world that the Government has determined are vital to U.S. interests. Between 1961 and 1980, the defense budget averaged around $200 billion annually (in 1982 constant dollars)—even during the Vietnam War. In 1981, however, the Reagan administration began a massive defense buildup which swelled successive defense budgets to unprecedented peacetime levels and in the process helped to quadruple the annual federal deficit in less than five years.

When the Cold War ended, the defense budget started to recede from its all-time high of $303 billion in 1989. But since 1998, the amount spent on the military has been increasing again; by 2002, the defense budget is expected to top $300 million again. This is an extraordinary sum in peacetime, but the U.S. remains committed to maintaining active duty and reserve forces sufficient for quick and effective response to crises around the world, and is equipped to fight significant wars on two fronts should such a situation arise.

The defense establishment The earliest precursor to the Department of Defense was the War Department, established by Congress in 1789; a separate Navy Department was created in 1798. These were merged under the National Security Act of 1947 and subsequent amendments. By 1949 the secretary of defense was established as the principal assistant to the president on defense matters in charge of the Defense Department.

The Department of Defense (DoD) is a cabinet-level organization responsible for providing the military forces needed to deter war and protect the security of the United States. The major elements of these forces are the Army, Navy, Air Force, and Marine Corps. Under the president, who is also the commander-in-chief, the secretary of defense exercises direction, authority and control over the Department of Defense, which includes the three military departments, the Joint

Chiefs of Staff and Joint Staff, nine unified and specified commands, 14 defense agencies, and seven DoD field activities.

The four armed services are subordinate to the military departments, which are responsible for recruiting, training and equipping their forces. The Marine Corps is the second armed service in the Department of the Navy. (A fifth armed service, the U.S. Coast Guard, reports to the Department of Transportation in peacetime and to the Department of the Navy in wartime.)

Chain of command Operational command of U.S. combat forces is assigned to the nation's unified and specified commands. The chain of command runs from the president to the secretary of defense, through the Joint Chiefs of Staff to the commanders-in-chief of the unified and specified commands. (The four service secretaries are not part of this chain of command.) A *unified command* is composed of forces from two or more services, has a broad and continuing mission and is normally organized on a geographical basis. A *specified command* also has a broad and continuing mission but is organized on a functional basis and is normally made up of forces from a single service.

▶U.S. ARMY

In peacetime, the primary mission of the continental U.S. armies is to train reserves and national guard, plan for mobilization, and coordinate domestic emergency relief efforts. The

Chairmen of the Joint Chiefs of Staff, 1949–2001

General of the Army Omar N. Bradley, USA	1949–53
Adm. Arthur W. Radford, USN	1953–57
Gen. Nathan F. Twining, USAF	1957–60
Gen. Lyman L. Lemnitzer, USA	1960–62
Gen. Maxwell D. Taylor, USA	1962–64
Gen. Earle G. Wheeler, USA	1964–70
Adm. Thomas H. Moorer, USN	1970–74
Gen. George S. Brown, USAF	1974–78
Gen. David C. Jones, USAF	1978–82
Gen. John W. Vessey Jr., USA	1982–85
Adm. William J. Crowe, USN	1985–89
Gen. Colin L. Powell, USA	1989–93
Gen. John Shalikashvili, USA	1993–97
Gen. H. Hugh Shelton, USA	1997–2001
Gen. Richard B. Myers, USAF	2001-present

Defense Establishment Employees, 2000

Branch	Active Duty[1] Officers	Active Duty[1] Enlisted	Active Duty[1] Total	Civilian employees
Army[2]	76,667	401,414	482,170	248,285
Navy[2]	53,550	315,471	373,193	195,698
Marine Corps	17,938	155,383	173,321	(N.A.)
Air Force	69,023	282,356	355,654	161,184
Total DoD	217,178	1,154,624	1,384,338	714,663

Note: As of September 30, 2000. 1. Includes Academy Cadets and Midshipmen, not shown separately. 2. Includes Marine Corps civilian personnel. Source: U.S. Dept. of Defense, *Selected Manpower Statistics, Fiscal Year 2000* (2001). www.defenselink.mil.

Military Personnel on Active Duty, 1789–2000

Year/War	Total	Year/War	Total	Year/War	Total
1789	718	1870	50,348	*Korean Conflict (1950-53)*	
1795	5,296	1880	37,894	*1950*	1,460,261
1801	7,108	1890	38,666	*1951*	3,249,455
1810	11,554			*1952*	3,635,912
		Spanish-American War (1898)		*1953*	3,555,067
War of 1812 (1812-15)		*1898*	235,785		
1812	12,631			1960	2,476,435
1813	25,152	1900	139,344		
1814	46,858	1915	174,112	*Vietnam Conflict (1964-73)*	
1815	40,885			*1964*	2,687,409
		World War I (1917-18)		*1965*	2,655,389
1820	15,113	*1917*	643,833	*1966*	3,094,058
1830	11,942	*1918*	2,897,167	*1967*	3,376,880
1840	21,616			*1968*	3,547,902
		1919	1,172,602	*1969*	3,460,162
Mexican War (1846-48)		1920	343,302	*1970*	3,066,294
1846	39,165	1930	255,648		
1847	57,761	1940	458,365	1975	2,128,120
1848	60,308			1980	2,050,627
		World War II (1941-46)		1985	2,151,032
1850	20,824	*1941*	1,801,101		
1860	27,958	*1942*	3,858,791	*Operation Desert Storm (1990-91)*	
		1943	9,044,745	*1990*	2,043,705
Civil War (1861-65)		*1944*	11,451,719	*1991*	1,985,555
1861	217,112	*1945*	12,123,455		
1862	673,124	*1946*	3,030,088	1995	1,518,224
1863	960,061			2000	1,384,338
1864	1,031,724				
1865	1,062,848				

Note: Figures in italics are wartime years. Totals exclude Coast Guard.
Source: Bureau of the Census, *Statistical History of the U.S.* (1976) and U.S. Dept. of Defense, unpublished statistics.

largest unit is a numbered *army,* such as the Fifth Army. (In time of war, two or three armies may be brought under a single command in an *army group.*) An *army* is made up of two or more corps plus a headquarters (HQ) unit; a *corps* is made up of two to five divisions and an HQ.

There are 18 active and 10 reserve divisions in the U.S. Army combat forces. The *division* is a self-sufficient force, typically consisting of three *brigades* (each comprising three to five battalions) and various combat support elements. A *brigade* is made up of two or more regiments or battalions; a *regiment,* of subordinate units such as battalions, companies or squadrons; a *battalion,* of four or more companies; a *company* of several platoons; and a *platoon* of four squads. A *squad* consists of about 10 soldiers.

Major U.S. Army Forces

Unit	Headquarters
Forces Command	**Ft. McPherson, Ga.**
Central Command/Third U.S. Army	Ft. McPherson, Ga.
First U.S. Army	Ft. Gillem, Ga.
Fifth U.S. Army	Ft. Sam Houston, Texas
I Corps	Ft. Lewis, Wash.
III Corps, "Phantom Corps"	Ft. Hood, Texas
4th Infantry Division (mech.), "The Ivy Division"	Ft. Hood, Texas
1st Cavalry Division	Ft. Hood, Texas
III Corps Artillery	Ft. Sill, Oklahoma
13th Corps. Support Command	Ft. Hood, Texas
XVIII Airborne Corps	Ft. Bragg, N.C.
10th Mountain Division (Light Infantry)	Ft. Drum, N.Y.
3rd Infantry Division (mech.)	Ft. Stewart, Ga.
82nd Airborne Division, "All American"	Ft. Bragg, N.C.
101st Airborne Division (air assault), "Screaming Eagles"	Ft. Campbell, Kentucky
XVIII Airborne Corps Artillery	Ft. Bragg, N.C.
1st Corps Support Command	Ft. Bragg, N.C.
National Training Center	Ft. Irwin, Calif.
U.S. Army Europe (7th Army)	**Heidelberg, Germany**
V Corps	Heidelberg, Germany
3rd Infantry Division (mech.), "Rock of the Marne"	Würzburg, Germany
1st Armored Division, "Old Ironsides"	Bad Kreuznach, Germany
1st Personnel Command	Schwetzingen, Germany
3rd Corps Support Command	Wiesbaden, Germany
21st Theater Army Area Command	Kaiserslautern, Germany
Seventh Army Training Command	Grafenwöhr, Germany
U.S. Army Pacific	**Ft. Shafter, Hawaii**
U.S. Army, Japan/ 9th Theater Army Area Command	Camp Zama, Japan
U.S. Army, Alaska	Ft. Wainwright, Alaska
25th Infantry Division (light)/U.S. Army Hawaii	Schofield Barracks,Hawaii
8th Army	**Seoul, South Korea**
2nd Infantry Division, "Indianhead"	Uijonbu, South Korea
19th Theater Army Area Command	Taegu, South Korea
U.S. Army South	**Ft. Clayton, Panama**
Military Police Command	Ft. Clayton, Panama
Army Materiel Command	**Alexandria, Va.**
Army Special Operations Command	**Ft. Bragg, N.C.**
Army Training and Doctrine Command	**Ft. Monroe, Va.**
Army Intelligence and Security Command	**Ft. Belvoir, Va.**
Information Systems Command	**Ft. Huachuca, Ariz.**
Criminal Investigation Command	**Ft. Belvoir, Va.**
Corps of Engineers	**Washington, D.C.**
Medical Command	**Ft. Sam Houston, Tex.**
National Guard divisions:	
28th Infantry Division, "Keystone"	Harrisburg, Pa.
29th Infantry Division (light), "Blue and Grey"	Ft. Belvoir, Va.
34th Infantry Division	St. Paul, Minn.
35th Infantry Division (mech.), "Santa Fe"	Ft. Leavenworth, Kansas
38th Infantry Division, "Cyclone"	Indianapolis, Ind.
40th Infantry Division (mech.), "Sunshine"	Los Alamitos, Calif.
42nd Infantry Division, "Rainbow"	Troy, N.Y.
49th Armored Division, "Lone Star"	Austin, Texas

Source: U.S. Army Force Command.

▶U.S. MARINE CORPS

Marine Corps organization emphasizes the close integration of air-ground operations for service with the U.S. fleet and for the conduct of land operations essential to the prosecution of a naval campaign. All Marines serve "at the pleasure of the president," and the Corps's mission includes "performing such other duties as the President may direct."

The smallest tactical unit of Marine Corps infantry is the *fire team*, which consists of 4 Marines. A *squad* is made up of three fire teams, and there are three squads to a *platoon*, three platoons to a *company*, three companies to a *battalion*, three battalions to a *regiment*, three regiments to a *brigade*, and three brigades to a *division*.

These components are organized into three basic organizational structures called *Marine air-*

ground task forces, or MAGTFs. The largest— about 47,500 personnel—is the *Marine Expeditionary Force* (MEF), which consists of a Marine air wing (330 planes), a Marine division, and a force service support group. The *Marine Expeditionary Brigade* (MEB) consists of a Marine air group (150 planes), a regimental landing group and a brigade service support group—about 15,000 personnel. The smallest and most responsive Marine force, the *Marine Expeditionary Unit*

U.S. Service Academies

U.S. Military Academy, West Point, N.Y. 10996; (Founded, 1802).

U.S. Naval Academy, Annapolis, Md. 21402; (1845).

U.S. Air Force Academy, Colorado Springs, Colo. 80840; (1954).

U.S. Coast Guard Academy, New London, Conn. 06320; (1876).

U.S. Merchant Marine Academy, Kings Point, N.Y. 11024; (1943).

Major Naval Operating Forces

Name	Headquarters
Pacific Fleet	Pearl Harbor, Hawaii
Third Fleet	San Diego, Calif.
Seventh Fleet	Yokosuka, Japan
Atlantic Fleet	Norfolk, Va.
Second Fleet	Norfolk, Va.
U.S. Naval Forces Europe	London, England
Sixth Fleet	Gaeta, Italy
Military Sealift Command	Washington, D.C.
Naval Reserve Force	New Orleans, La.
Mine Warfare Command	Ingleside, Texas
Operational and Test	Norfolk, Va.
Evaluation Force	
Naval Forces Southern Command	Rodman, Panama
Naval Forces Central Command	Manama, Bahrain
Fifth Fleet	Manama, Bahrain
Naval Special Warfare Command	Coronado, Calif.

Source: U.S. Dept. of Defense, *Defense Almanac.* www.defenselink.mil.

Major Coast Guard Commands

Name	Headquarters
Coast Guard Headquarters	Washington, D.C.
Atlantic Area	Portsmouth, Va.
1st District	Boston, Mass.
5th District	Portsmouth, Va.
7th District	Miami, Fla.
8th District	New Orleans, La.
9th District	Cleveland, Ohio
Pacific Area	Alameda, Calif.
13th District	Seattle, Wash.
14th District	Honolulu, Hawaii
17th District	Juneau, Alaska

Source: U.S. Coast Guard.

Major Marine Corps Commands

Name	Headquarters
Fleet Marine Force, Atlantic	Camp Lejeune, N.C.
Fleet Marine Force, Pacific	Camp H.M. Smith, Hawaii
Marine Corps Combat Development Command	Quantico, Va.
Marine Corps Systems Command	Quantico, Va.
I Marine Expeditionary Force	Camp Pendleton,Calif.
II Marine Expeditionary Force	Camp Lejeune, N.C.
III Marine Expeditionary Force	Camp Butler, Okinawa, Japan
Marine Corps Air Ground Combat Center	Twentynine Palms, Calif.
Marine Reserve Forces	New Orleans, La.

Source: U.S. Dept. of Defense, *Defense Almanac.* www.defenselink.mil.

Major Air Force Units

Name	Headquarters/Location
Air Combat Command	Langley AFB, Hampton, Va.
Air Force Materiel Command	Wright-Patterson AFB, Dayton, Ohio
Air Force Space Command	Peterson AFB, Colorado Spring, Colo.
Air Force Special Operations Command	Hurlburt Field, Fort Walton Beach, Fla.
Air Mobility Command	Scott AFB, Belleville, Ill.
Air Education and Training Command	Randolph AFB, San Antonio, Texas
Pacific Air Forces	Hickam AFB, Honolulu, Hawaii
U.S. Air Forces, Europe	Ramstein AB, Ramstein, Germany

Note: AB = air base; AFB = air force base; RAF = Royal Air Force (UK).   **Source:** U.S. Dept. of Defense, *Defense Almanac*, www.defenselink.mil

(MEU), consists of about 2,500 personnel and is made up of a helicopter squadron, a battalion landing team, and a unit service support group. MEUs are sea-based, can be airlifted and they are equipped and trained to be self-sustaining in the field for up to 15 days.

▶U.S. NAVY

The ships of the U.S. Navy are organized into the Pacific Fleet, the Atlantic Fleet, and U.S. Naval Forces Europe. These are composed of numbered fleets which consist of *carrier battle groups, battleship surface action groups* and one or more *underway replenishment groups*. Smaller subdivisions of naval forces are the *flotilla* consisting of two or more squadrons; a *squadron*, of two or more divisions; and a *division*, normally made up of four ships.

A naval *task force* designates a collection of ships under a single command designed to accomplish a particular tactical or strategic purpose. An *amphibious squadron* consists of amphibious assault ships, amphibious transport docks, dock landing ships and tank landing ships, and transports troops and equipment necessary for an assault landing from the sea.

▶U.S. COAST GUARD

The Coast Guard is a branch of the armed forces of the United States at all times. What distinguishes it from the other services is that it is part of the Department of Transportation—not Defense—except during wartime, or at the direction of the president, when it operates as part of the Navy. A successor to the Revenue Marine established in 1790, its primary function is to enforce federal maritime law.

▶U.S. AIR FORCE

The Air Force is organized into a number of commands. Within commands concerned with the strategic or tactical operation of aircraft, the primary subdivisions are indicated by the term air force prefaced by a number, as the Eighth Air Force. Such an *air force* is comprised of wings; a *wing* consists of two or more groups or squadrons; a *group* consists of two or more squadrons; and a *squadron* is made up of two or more flights. A *flight* is the basic tactical unit and consists of four or more planes.

▶SPECIAL OPERATIONS FORCES (SOF)

A unified command whose elements are drawn from the four major services, the special operations forces are designated to achieve military objectives of a limited and specific nature. Among the various elements of the SOF are: *Army* special forces; Rangers; psychological operations, civil affairs, and special operations aviation units; *Navy* SEAL and SEAL delivery vehicle teams; and *Air Force* Twenty-third Air Force special operations force.

U.S. Service and Casualties in Major Wars and Conflicts

War or conflict	Number serving	Battle deaths	Other deaths	Wounds not mortal
Revolutionary War (1775–83)				
Army	N.A.	4,044	N.A.	6,004
Navy	N.A.	342	N.A.	114
Marines	N.A.	49	N.A.	70
Total	N.A.	4,435	N.A.	6,188
War of 1812 (1812–15)				
Army	N.A.	1,950	N.A.	4,000
Navy	N.A.	265	N.A.	439
Marines	N.A.	45	N.A.	66
Total	286,730	2,260	N.A.	4,505
Mexican War (1846–48)				
Army	N.A.	1,721	11,550	4,102
Navy	N.A.	1	N.A.	3
Marines	N.A.	11	N.A.	47
Total	78,718	1,733	11,550	4,152
Civil War (1861–65)[1]				
Army	2,128,948	138,154	221,374	280,040
Navy	84,415[2]	2,112	2,411	1,710
Marines	—	148	312	131
Total	2,213,363	140,414	224,097	281,881
Spanish-American War (1898)				
Army	280,564	369	2,061	1,594
Navy	22,875	10	0	47
Marines	3,321	6	0	21
Total	306,760	385	2,061	1,662
World War I (1917–1918)				
Army	4,057,101	50,510	55,868	193,663
Navy	599,051	431	6,856	819
Marines	78,839	2,461	390	9,520
Total	4,734,991	53,402	63,114	204,002
World War II (1941–46)				
Army	11,260,000	234,874	83,400	565,861
Navy	4,183,466	36,950	25,664	37,778
Marines	669,100	19,733	4,778	67,207
Total	16,112,566	291,557	113,842	670,846
Korean Conflict (1950–53)				
Army	2,834,000	27,709	806	77,596
Navy	1,177,000	468	939	1,576
Marines	424,000	4,267	1,261	23,744
Air Force	1,285,000	1,302	243	368
Total	5,720,000	33,746	3,249	103,284
Vietnam Conflict (1964–73)				
Army	4,368,000	30,905	7,275	96,802
Navy	1,842,000	1,631	925	4,178
Marines	794,000	13,081	1,754	51,392
Air Force	1,740,000	1,738	842	931
Total	8,744,000	47,355	10,796	153,303
Operation Desert Storm (1990–91)[3]				
Army	246,682	98	105	N.A.
Navy	98,652	6	14	N.A.
Marines	71,254	24	26	N.A.
Air Force	50,571	20	6	N.A.
Total	467,159	148	151	467

Note: N.A. = not available. Prior to World War I, dates are approximate. Actual period covered for World War I: Apr. 6, 1917-Nov. 11, 1918; World War II: Dec. 7, 1941-Dec. 31, 1946; Korea: June 25, 1950-July 27, 1953; Vietnam: Aug. 4, 1964-Jan. 27, 1973. 1. Union Forces only; authoritative statistics for Confederate forces not available. Estimates of the number who served range from 600,000 to 1.5 million. *The Final Report of the Provost Marshal General, 1863-1866* indicated 133,821 Confederate deaths (74,524 battle and 59,297 other) based upon incomplete returns. In addition, an estimated 26,000-31,000 Confederate prisoners died in prisons. 2. Includes Navy and Marines. 3. DMDC, Sept. 9, 1991. Deployment figures changed continuously throughout the operation and have since, and have depended on, among other things, the timely reporting and posting of data.
Source: U.S. Dept. of Defense, *Defense Almanac.* www.defenselink.mil.

▶RESERVE FORCES

The United States has always relied on reserve forces that can be called to active duty or mobilized to deal with emergencies beyond the capacities of active forces. The reserve forces constitute the initial and primary augmentation of active forces in any emergency requiring rapid expansion of those forces.

There are seven reserve components: Army National Guard, Army Reserve, Naval Reserve, Marine Corps Reserve, Air National Guard, Air Force Reserve, and Coast Guard Reserve. All National Guard and Reserve personnel are assigned to one of three categories: the Ready Reserve, the Standby Reserve, or the Retired Reserve. All National Guard members are in the Ready Reserve.

U.S. Armed Forces Worldwide, 2000

Region/Area	Army	Navy	Marine Corps	Air Force	Total
U.S., total[1]	378,571	312,756	143,934	291,260	1,126,521
Continental U.S.	345,343	187,575	135,516	270,319	938,753
Alaska	6,218	92	21	9,426	15,757
Hawaii	15,483	7,998	5,960	4,489	33,930
Guam	40	1,490	5	1,731	3,266
Johnston Atoll	210	0	0	19	229
Puerto Rico	796	1,997	28	75	2,896
Transients	10,455	11,639	2,404	5,201	29,699
Afloat	0	101,962	0	0	101,962
Europe, total[1]	70,251	10,843	3,441	32,876	117,411
Belgium[2]	916	95	33	510	1,554
Bosnia and Herzegovina	5,675	30	2	1	5,708
Croatia	130	0	7	1	138
Germany[2]	53,995	276	271	14,661	69,203
Greece[2]	63	248	188	179	678
Greenland[2]	0	0	0	125	125
Hungary	350	0	18	7	375
Iceland[2]	1	988	54	593	1,636
Italy[2]	2,341	4,692	131	4,026	11,190
Macedonia, Former Yugoslav Republic	345	0	0	2	347
Netherlands[2]	359	12	13	275	659
Portugal[2]	15	54	7	929	1,005
Russia	19	4	65	13	101
Serbia (includes Kosovo)	5,395	0	6	26	5,427
Spain[2]	36	1,625	86	260	2,007
Turkey[2]	184	18	45	1,759	2,006
United Kingdom[2]	383	1,249	165	9,410	11,207
Afloat	0	1,512	2,255	0	3,767
NATO, Total	(58,678)	(9,285)	(1,070)	(32,818)	(101,851)
East Asia and Pacific, total[1]	29,368	29,389	20,660	22,030	101,447
Australia	11	71	22	71	175
Japan	1,787	5,496	19,682	13,194	40,159
Korea	27,481	318	97	8,669	36,565
Singapore	6	85	278	42	411
Thailand	39	9	453	25	526
Afloat	0	23,307	45	0	23,352
North Africa, Near East and South Asia, total[1]	3,477	16,556	398	8,953	29,384
Bahrain	33	734	155	27	949
Diego Garcia	3	598	0	24	625
Egypt	354	33	42	70	499
Kuwait	2,235	10	36	2,321	4,602
Oman	2	60	10	179	251
Saudi Arabia	770	325	63	5,895	7,053
United Arab Emirates	0	7	8	387	402
Afloat	0	14,772	0	0	14,772
Sub-Saharan Africa, total	42	3	160	19	224
Western Hemisphere, total[1]	3,922	3,548	1,280	2,036	10,786
Canada	8	56	9	83	156
Colombia	166	8	24	26	224
Cuba (Guantanamo)	7	441	239	1	688
Honduras	156	2	14	179	351
Peru	5	11	404	5	425
Afloat	0	3,068	0	0	3,068
Worldwide, total[1]	482,170	373,193	173,321	355,654	1,384,338
Ashore	482,170	228,572	171,021	355,654	1,237,417
Afloat	0	144,621	2,300	0	146,921

Note: Note: As of Sept. 30, 2000. 1. Includes other countries not shown separately. 2. Member of NATO Europe.
Source: U.S. Dept. of Defense. *Defense Almanac.* www.defenselink.mil.

The Ready Reserve consists of the Selected Reserve, the Individual Ready Reserve, and the Inactive National Guard. Some reservists are organized in units, others train as individuals. All are subject to orders for active duty in time of war or national emergency.

In addition, members of the Selected Reserve may be ordered to active duty under implementation of the presidential call-up authority, under which the president can activate up to 200,000 members of the Selected Reserve involuntarily, for operational missions, for not more than 90 days, without declaring a national emergency.

▶NUCLEAR FORCES

Nuclear forces are classified as either strategic or nonstrategic. The strategic triad—a cornerstone of post-World War II U.S. defense—is composed of land-based missile forces, including intercontinental ballistic missiles (ICBMs); submarine-launched ballistic missiles (SLBMs); and manned aircraft of the strategic bomber force. Nonstrategic nuclear weapons are shorter-range weapons that can be deployed on the battlefield and include sea-launched cruise missiles, artillery-fired atomic projectiles, and dual-capable (conventional and nuclear) aircraft.

Top 10 Defense Contractors, 2000

Company	Awards (billions)
1. Lockheed Martin Corporation	$15.1
2. Boeing Company	12.0
3. Raytheon Company	6.3
4. General Dynamics Corp.	4.2
5. Northrop Grumman Corporation	3.1
6. Litton Industries	2.7
7. United Technologies Corporation	2.1
8. TRW Inc.	2.0
9. General Electric Company Inc.	1.6
10. Science Applications International	1.5

Source: U.S. Dept. of Defense, *Defense Almanac*. www.defenselink.mil.

Guard and Reserve Forces, 2000

Status	Army National Guard	Army Reserve	Naval Reserve	Marine Corps Reserve	Air National Guard	Air Force Reserve	Total DoD	Coast Guard Reserve
Selected Reserve								
Officers	29,663	38,956	18,691	3,544	13,346	16,664	120,864	1,015
Warrant Officers	7,737	2,883	243	424	—	—	11,287	189
Enlisted	315,644	165,053	67,997	35,698	93,019	55,676	733,087	6,761
Total	353,044	206,892	86,931	39,666	106,365	72,340	865,238	7,965
Individual Ready Reserve/Inactive National Guard								
Officers	406	32,771	13,740	2,841	—	10,171	59,929	184
Warrant Officers	68	2,641	15	86	—	—	2,810	38
Enlisted	3,738	126,260	83,389	57,261	—	40,133	310,781	4,550
Total	4,212	161,672	97,144	60,188	—	50,304	373,520	4,772
Total Ready Reserve								
Officers	30,069	71,727	32,431	6,385	13,346	26,835	180,793	1,199
Warrant Officers	7,805	5,524	258	510	—	—	14,097	227
Enlisted	319,382	291,313	151,386	92,959	93,019	95,809	1,043,868	11,311
Total	**357,256**	**368,564**	**184,075**	**99,854**	**106,365**	**122,644**	**1,238,758**	**12,737**

Note: As of September 30. **Source:** U.S. Dept. of Defense, *Selected Manpower Statistics, Fiscal Year 2000* (2001). www.defenselink.mil.

Minorities in Uniform, 2000

Service	Black Americans Number	Black Americans Percent	Hispanic Americans Number	Hispanic Americans Percent	Other[1] Number	Other[1] Percent	Total Number	Total Percent
Officers, Total	**18,309**	**8.5%**	**8,269**	**3.8%**	**11,150**	**5.2%**	**37,728**	**17.5%**
Army	9,162	12.0	3,105	4.1	4,075	5.3	16,342	21.4
Navy	3,524	6.7	2,732	5.2	2,653	5.0	8,909	16.9
Marines	1,341	7.5	914	5.1	599	3.3	2,854	15.9
Air Force	4,282	6.3	1,518	2.2	3,823	5.6	9,623	14.1
Enlisted, Total	**254,509**	**22.3%**	**99,297**	**8.7%**	**73,888**	**6.5%**	**427,694**	**37.5%**
Army	115,240	29.2	34,232	8.7	26,388	6.7	175,860	44.6
Navy	62,974	20.3	29,630	9.5	27,568	8.9	120,172	38.7
Marines	25,023	16.4	20,174	13.2	7,185	4.7	52,382	34.4
Air Force	51,272	18.2	15,261	5.4	12,747	4.5	79,280	28.1
DoD Total	**272,818**	**20.1%**	**107,566**	**7.9%**	**85,038**	**6.3%**	**465,422**	**34.4%**

Note: As of September 5, 2000. 1. Includes Native Americans, Alaskan Natives, and Pacific Islanders.
Source: U.S. Dept. of Defense, *Defense 2000*. www.defenselink.mil.

Women in Uniform: Female Active Duty Military Personnel 1945-2000

Year	Total DoD	Army Officers	Army Enlisted	Navy Officers	Navy Enlisted	Marine Corps. Officers	Marine Corps. Enlisted	Air Force Officers	Air Force Enlisted
1945	266,256	62,775	93,095	19,188	72,833	809	17,556	N.A.	N.A.
1950	22,069	4,431	6,551	2,447	2,746	45	535	1,532	3,782
1960	31,550	4,263	8,279	2,711	5,360	123	1,488	3,675	5,651
1970	41,479	5,248	11,476	2,888	5,795	299	2,119	4,667	8,987
1975	96,868	4,594	37,701	3,676	17,498	345	2,841	4,981	25,232
1980	171,418	7,609	61,729	4,877	30,103	487	6,219	8,493	51,901
1985	211,606	10,828	68,419	6,913	45,690	654	9,041	11,927	58,134
1990	227,018	12,404	71,217	7,808	52,099	677	8,679	13,331	60,803
1995	196,116	10,786	57,260	7,899	47,931	690	7,403	12,068	52,079
1999	195,917	10,506	60,283	7,758	41,399	888	9,274	11,841	53,968
2000	200,468	10,791	62,491	7,816	42,750	932	9,525	11,819	54,344

Source: U.S. Dept. of Defense, *Selected Manpower Statistics,* Fiscal Year 2000 (2001). www.defenselink.mil.

Major Weapon Systems and Combat Forces, 1980-2001

Weapon or force	1980	1990	1999	2000	2001
STRATEGIC (NUCLEAR) FORCES					
Land-based ICBMs					
Minuteman	1,000	950	500	500	500
Peacekeeper	0	50	50	50	50
Heavy bombers[1]					
B-52	241	154	56	56	56
B-1	0	90	74	80	82
B-2 (stealth bomber)	0	0	13	16	16
Submarine-Launched Ballistic Missiles[2]					
Poseidon (C-3 and C-4)[3]	336	368	0	0	0
Trident (C-4 and D-5)	0	216	432	432	432
GENERAL PURPOSE FORCES					
Active land forces					
Army divisions	16	18	10	10	10
Marine Corps divisions	3	3	3	3	3
Army Separate brigades[4]	8	8	3	3	3
Army Special Forces groups	2	5	7	7	7
Army Ranger regiment	0	1	1	1	1
Active tactical air forces (PAA/squadrons)					
Air Force attack and fighter aircraft	1,608/74	1,722/76	936/49	936/47	906/45
Navy attack and fighter aircraft	696/60	622/57	432/36	432/36	432/36
Marine Corps attack and fighter aircraft	329/25	334/24	308/21	308/21	308/21
Naval forces					
Strategic forces ships	48	39	18	18	18
Battle forces ships	384	412	256	259	259
Support forces ships	41	65	25	25	25
Reserve forces ships	6	31	18	16	15
Total battle forces deployable	479	547	317	318	317
Coastal defense, mine warfare, and other	52	19	22	22	22
AIRLIFT AND SEALIFT FORCES					
Intertheater airlift (PMAI)[5]					
C-5	70	109	104	104	104
C-141	234	234	136	104	88
KC-10	0	57	54	54	54
C-17	0	0	37	46	58
Intratheater airlift (PMAI)[5]					
C-130[6]	482	460	425	425	418
Sealift ships[7]					
Tankers, active	21	28	10	10	10
Cargo, active	23	40	49	52	57
Ready Reserve Force (RRF)	24	96	87	87	87

Note: PMAI = primary mission aircraft inventory. 1. Excludes backup and attrition reserve aircraft. 2. Number operational. 3. C-3 missiles were removed from Poseidon submarines in September of 1992. 4. Includes the Eskimo scout group and the armored cavalry regiments. 5. Excludes development/test and training aircraft. 6. Excludes Dept. of Navy aircraft. 7. Includes fast sealift ships, afloat prepositioned force ships, and common user (charter) ships. **Source:** U.S. Dept. of Defense, *Defense Almanac.* www.defenselink.mil.

Department of Defense Contract Awards, Payroll, and Civilian and Military Personnel by State, 1999

State	Payroll[1] ('000s)	Contract awards[2] ('000s)	Personnel[3] Military	Civilian
Alabama	$2,352,073	$2,676,744	11,272	20,955
Alaska	860,085	609,981	15,684	4,247
Arizona	1,930,868	4,171,941	21,240	8,117
Arkansas	759,624	246,056	4,888	3,570
California	11,394,822	17,371,558	109,697	64,086
Colorado	2,359,477	2,441,790	29,247	11,118
Connecticut	538,141	3,169,394	4,412	2,593
Delaware	325,720	91,749	3,898	1,370
District of Columbia	1,172,812	1,611,954	13,240	12,651
Florida	6,722,007	6,806,055	50,731	26,322
Georgia	4,800,915	4,112,571	62,714	30,678
Hawaii	2,422,172	984,849	32,354	16,318
Idaho	391,225	155,987	4,326	1,411
Illinois	2,440,230	1,315,580	35,674	12,988
Indiana	891,445	1,648,349	991	9,266
Iowa	264,615	419,385	443	1,514
Kansas	1,117,979	887,380	16,354	5,457
Kentucky	1,877,023	1,386,786	36,149	8,734
Louisiana	1,347,434	1,441,713	15,246	7,815
Maine	571,235	686,364	2,136	5,520
Maryland	3,587,843	5,466,503	29,859	32,101
Massachusetts	796,956	4,714,942	2,535	6,970
Michigan	848,183	1,167,864	1,085	7,664
Minnesota	432,807	1,212,291	862	2,418
Mississippi	1,394,084	1,537,891	12,069	9,434
Missouri	1,590,805	4,602,627	17,184	9,516
Montana	299,768	98,006	3,663	1,113
Nebraska	654,882	225,887	7,988	3,323
Nevada	791,005	276,131	7,721	2,068
New Hampshire	254,100	359,907	376	1,028
New Jersey	1,521,093	2,850,762	7,116	14,549
New Mexico	1,103,992	614,173	11,642	6,915
New York	1,787,150	3,289,418	20,532	11,365
North Carolina	4,519,786	1,039,620	86,594	16,311
North Dakota	391,365	149,102	7,499	1,638
Ohio	2,136,432	2,592,556	7,668	23,544
Oklahoma	2,259,156	1,139,932	25,234	20,187
Oregon	544,143	304,320	933	2,908
Pennsylvania	2,175,764	3,864,543	3,261	25,772
Rhode Island	458,669	312,187	3,415	4,352
South Carolina	2,426,677	868,545	38,289	9,495
South Dakota	258,432	93,948	3,171	1,264
Tennessee	1,101,582	1,092,565	2,679	4,939
Texas	8,811,306	8,666,461	108,835	39,993
Utah	976,733	532,906	4,844	12,419
Vermont	95,849	213,552	125	525
Virginia	11,169,951	12,240,573	80,132	78,973
Washington	3,951,370	2,296,094	32,398	22,322
West Virginia	261,333	109,157	614	1,713
Wisconsin	435,727	644,452	578	3,119
Wyoming	234,371	62,038	3,496	932
Total U.S.	$101,811,216	$114,875,139	1,014,166	633,600

1. Payroll estimates cover active duty military and direct hire civilian personnel, including Army Corps of Engineers. 2. Military awards for supplies, services and construction; expenditures relating to awards may extend over several years. Net value of contracts of over $25,000 for work in each state; the state in which the prime contractor is located is not necessarily the state in which the subcontracted work is done.
Source: U.S. Dept. of Defense, *Selected Manpower Statistics, Fiscal Year 2000 (2001)*. www.defenselink.mil.

Active Duty, Monthly Basic Pay Table

Pay Grade	Army Rank	Years of Service			
		2	10	20	26
	Commissioned Officers				
0-10	General, Admiral	N.A.	N.A.	$11,049	$11,142
0-9	Lieut. General, Vice-Admiral	N.A.	N.A.	9,664	10,356
0-8	Maj. General, Rear Admiral	$7,062	$7,820	9,157	9,383
0-7	Brig. General, Commodore	6,068	6,716	8,281	8,323
0-6	Colonel, Captain	4,627	5,189	6,617	7,310
0-5	Lt. Colonel, Commander	3,955	4,584	5,790	5,965
0-4	Major, Lt. Commander	3,457	4,410	4,987	4,987
0-3	Captain, Lieutenant	2,991	3,993	4,292	4,292
0-2	1st Lieutenant, Lieut. (J.G.)	2,621	3,185	3,185	3,185
0-1	2nd Lieutenant, Ensign	2,079	2,513	2,513	2,513
	Warrant Officers				
W-5	Chief Warrant Officer	N.A.	N.A.	$4,641	$5,120
W-4	Chief Warrant Officer	$2,892	$3,477	4,168	4,591
W-3	Chief Warrant Officer	2,650	3,084	3,670	4,045
W-2	Chief Warrant Officer	2,315	2,751	3,281	3,503
W-1	Warrant Officer	2,044	2,523	3,019	3,019
	Enlisted Personnel				
E-9	Sgt. Major, Master C.P.O.	N.A.	$3,127	$3,602	$4,061
E-8	Master Sgt., Senior C.P.O.	N.A.	2,698	3,138	3,613
E-7	Sgt.1st Class, Chief Petty Officer	$1,999	2,379	2,759	3,250
E-6	Staff Sgt., Petty Officer 1st Class	1,740	2,123	2,368	2,370
E-5	Sergeant, Petty Officer 2d Class	1,549	1,930	2,008	2,008
E-4	Corporal, Petty Officer 3d Class	1,424	1,653	1,653	1,653
E-3	Pvt. 1st Class, Seaman	1,307	1,385	1,385	1,385
E-2	Private, Seaman	1,169	1,169	1,169	1,169
E-1	Recruit, Seaman Recruit	1,043	1,043	1,043	1,043

Note: Effective Jan. 1, 2001. Numbers rounded to nearest dollar. N.A.: Not Applicable
Source: U.S. Department of Defense. http://pay2000.dtic.mil/

SOCIAL INSURANCE PROGRAMS

In order to provide a "safety net" for the disadvantaged, the elderly, and the disabled, the Federal Government administers a range of social insurance and social assistance programs. Many of these programs are administered by the Social Security Administration, which became an independent Government agency in 1995. But many cabinet-level departments, other independent Government agencies, and state government human services agencies also run programs such as food stamps (Dept. of Agriculture), public housing (Dept. of Housing and Urban Development),

Social Insurance Programs: Beneficiaries and Payments, 1999

Program	Beneficiaries ('000s)	Benefits (billions)
OASDI	44,500	$415,100
Medicare	39,532	N.A.
Medicaid[1]	40,649	142,318
Food Stamps	17,200	14,985
Welfare	5,781	N.A.
Supplemental Security Insurance[2]	6,641	30,959

Note: OASDI = Old Age, Survivors, and Disability Insurance; 1. Figure for 1998. 2. Figure for 1999.
Sources: Social Security Administration; Administration on Children and Families; Health Care Financing Administration.

and programs for veterans (Dept. of Veterans Affairs).

Social insurance programs were not developed all at once to fulfill a specific agenda of national need. Rather they are a hodgepodge of legislation passed (and often altered) over the years to meet the needs of particular groups of citizens at particular times. In what the Government calls "social insurance programs," certain risks—injury, disability, unemployment, old age, and death—are lumped together. "Premiums," usually in the form of a payroll tax, are paid by employees and/or their employers. The benefit is paid, regardless of other financial resources (other than earnings), when one of those "risks" occurs.

▶ SOCIAL SECURITY

The Depression proved that the traditional support systems—the family, private charities, and local government—failed in nationwide economic hard times. Many old people had exhausted their savings and were destitute; in fact, during the Depression less than 10 percent of the aged left estates large enough to be probated. This led to the enactment of one of the most comprehensive pieces of legislation ever passed by Congress, the Social Security Act.

Signed into law by Franklin Roosevelt on August 14, 1935, the Social Security Act established two social insurance programs: a Federal system of old-age benefits for retired workers in commerce and industry and a federal-state system of unemployment insurance. The law also provided for Federal matching grants-in-aid to states to help them assist the needy aged, the blind, and children. Today, in the words of former Social Security Commissioner Dorcas R. Hardy, it is "the most

SOCIAL SERVICE
PROGRAMS INFORMATION

Information about social service programs can be obtained from the following government agencies:

Aid to Families with Dependent Children (AFDC) This program was abolished under the Welfare Reform Act of 1996. It was replaced with the Temporary Assistance to Needy Families (TANF) program. Information is available from the Administration for Children and Families, U.S. Dept. of Health and Human Services. (202)-401-9200. www.acf.dhhs.gov

Black lung program Office of Workers Compensation Programs, U.S. Dept. of Labor. (202)-693-0046. www.dol.gov/dol/esa/public/owcp-org.htm

Food Stamps Food and Consumer Service, U.S. Dept. of Agriculture. (703) 305-2276. www.usda.gov/fcs/fcs.htm

Head Start Administration for Children and Families, U.S. Dept. of Health and Human Services. (202)-401-9200. www.acf.dhhs.gov

Medicaid Health Care Financing Administration, U.S. Dept. of Health and Human Services. (410) 786-3151. www.ssa.gov/hcfa/hcfahp2.html

Medicare (HI) Health Care Financing Administration, U.S. Dept. of Health and Human Services. (410) 786-3151. www.ssa.gov/hcfa/hcfahp2.html

Social Security (OASDI) Social Security Administration. (410) 965-7700. www.ssa.gov/

Special nutrition programs Food and Consumer Service, U.S. Dept. of Agriculture. (703) 305-2276. www.usda.gov/fcs/fcs.htm

Supplemental Security Income (SSI) Social Security Administration. (410) 965-7700. www.ssa.gov

Temporary disability insurance Office of Workers Compensation Programs, U.S. Dept. of Labor. (202)-219-7503. www.dol.gov/dol/esa/public/owcp-org.htm

Unemployment insurance Office of Workers Compensation Programs, U.S. Dept. of Labor. (202)-219-7503. www.dol.gov/dol/esa/public/owcp-org.htm

Veterans' benefits U.S. Dept. of Veterans Affairs. (202) 273-5700. www.va.gov

fits. The amount deducted from paychecks increased steadily from 1983 before levelling off in 1990 at 7.65 percent. Employers must contribute the same amount. Self-employed workers, who are both employee and employer, pay both shares, or a total of 15.3 percent. Contributions are limited to the first $76,200 of earnings although Medicare taxes continue at a rate of 1.45 percent each for employer and employee (twice that amount for the self-employed) for all earnings above that amount.

Old Age, Survivors and Disability Insurance (OASDI)

This program's basic principles are that benefits are related to earnings in covered work, benefits are paid regardless of income from savings, pensions, etc. and universal compulsory coverage is to assure a base of economic security. Monthly benefits are payable at age 65 to workers who are eligible, and lump sum payments are made to the estates of workers who die before reaching 65. The addition of disability insurance in 1956 and hospital insurance in 1965 broadened the program's scope, and in 1972 Congress authorized provisions for cost-of-living increases. The 1983 amendments improved the program's financial footing with tax rate increases in self-employment tax rates, and taxing up to one-half of benefits for certain upper-income beneficiaries.

To receive Social Security benefits, generally you must have worked for 10 years in a job in which you contributed to the Social Security fund. Your social security benefit is not directly dependent on the number of years you worked. Rather it is based on your average earnings over your working lifetime. The average recipient receives benefits equivalent to 42 percent of an average working year's earnings. Because Social Security is designed to benefit low-income workers, people in upper-income brackets generally receive a lower percentage of their working year's earnings when they collect their benefits. However, you can still earn money while collecting Social Security. Recipients under age 65 may earn up to $10,800 before their benefits are reduced; after that amount, $1 is withheld for every $2 earned). Recipients between 65 and 69 may earn up to $17,000, after which $1 is withheld for every $3 earned. Recipients over age 70 may earn any amount of money while collecting Social Security benefits.

complex Government program that God and Congress ever created."

The first payments of monthly benefits were made in 1940. Major changes in the scope of Social Security were made in 1956, when the program was broadened through the addition of disability insurance; in 1965, through the addition of Medicare and Medicaid; in 1970, when the black lung program was developed to provide benefits to coal miners (and their survivors) who suffer from pneumoconiosis (black lung disease); in 1974, when social security insurance was taken over by the Social Security Administration; and in 1972 Congress authorized provisions for cost-of-living increases. In 1983, amendments provided for the taxing of up to one-half of benefits for certain upper-income beneficiaries.

Workers and their employers each contribute an equal amount to the Social Security program to pay for retirement, disability, and Medicare bene-

OASDI Beneficiaries and Benefit Payments, 1999

Type of Beneficiaries	Number ('000s)	Total benefits (billions)	Average monthly benefit
Retired workers	27,800	$22.3	$804
Dependents of retired workers	3,200	1.3	406
Disabled workers	4,900	3.7	754
Dependents of disabled workers	1,600	0.4	250
Survivors of deceased workers	7,000	4.9	774
Total monthly beneficiaries	**44,500**	**$385**	**N.A.**

Note: OASDI = old-age, survivors and disability insurance.
Source: Social Security Administration, *Fact Sheet on OASDI*

Approximate Monthly Retirement, Disability, and Survivor Benefits

Worker's age, 2000	Worker's family	Insured worker's earnings, 1999				
		$20,000	$30,000	$40,000	$50,000	$72,600 or more
Retirement Benefits[1]						
45	Retired worker only	$841	$1,107	$1,352	$1,477	$1,774
	Worker and spouse[2]	1,261	1,660	2,028	2,215	2,661
55	Retired worker only	841	1,107	1,352	1,475	1,713
	Worker and spouse[2]	1,261	1,660	2,028	2,215	1,569
65	Retired worker only	769	1,014	1,224	1,307	1,433
	Worker and spouse[2]	1,153	1,521	1,836	1,960	2,149
Disability Benefits[3]						
25	Disabled worker only	$841	$1,107	$1,352	$1,477	$1,726
	Disabled, with dependents[4]	1,261	1,661	2,028	2,215	2,589
35	Disabled worker only	841	1,107	1,352	1,477	1,734
	Disabled, with dependents[4]	1,261	1,661	2,028	2,215	2,602
45	Disabled worker only	841	1,107	1,352	1,477	1,715
	Disabled, with dependents[4]	1,261	1,661	2,028	2,215	2,573
55	Disabled worker only	841	1,107	1,352	1,464	1,633
	Disabled, with dependents[4]	1,261	1,661	2,028	2,196	2,450
64	Disabled worker only	787	1,038	1,255	1,340	1,468
	Disabled, with dependents[4]	1,181	1,557	1,883	2,010	2,202
Survivor benefits[5]						
35	Spouse and 1 child [6]	$1,260	$1,660	$2,028	$2,214	$2,614
	Spouse and 2 children[7]	1,459	2,008	2,366	2,585	3,050
	1 child only	630	830	1,014	1,107	1,307
	Spouse at age 60	601	792	966	1,056	1,246
45	Spouse and 1 child [6]	1,260	1,660	2,028	2,214	2,580
	Spouse and 2 children[7]	1,459	2,008	2,366	2,585	3,010
	1 child only	630	830	1,014	1,107	1,290
	Spouse at age 60	601	792	966	1,056	1,229
55	Spouse and 1 child [6]	1,260	1,660	2,028	2,196	2,500
	Spouse and 2 children[7]	1,459	2,008	2,366	2,562	2,858
	1 child only	630	830	1,014	1,098	1,225
	Spouse at age 60	601	792	966	1,046	1,168

Note: Assumes steady earnings; actual benefits depend on the pattern of past and future earnings. 1. If worker retires at normal retirement age with steady lifetime earnings. 2. Spouse is assumed to be the same age as the worker. Spouse may qualify for a higher retirement benefit based on his or her own work record. 3. For workers with steady earnings and disabled in 1998. 4. Includes spouse and child, the maximum family benefit. 5. For workers with steady earnings who died in 1999. 6. Benefits are the same for two children if no parent survives or if the surviving parent has substantial earnings. 7. Equals maximum family benefit.
Source: Social Security Administration, Social Security: Understanding the Benefits (2000).

Medicare: Recipients and Benefits, 1975–2000

Category	1975	1980	1985	1990	1995	1999	2000[1]
Hospital Insurance (HI)							
Total enrolled ('000s)	23,842	27,540	30,065	33,363	37,015	38,844	39,332
Aged	21,795	24,572	27,121	30,050	32,649	33,585	33,886
Disabled	2,047	2,968	2,944	3,313	4,366	5,259	5,445
Total Beneficiaries ('000s)	5,362	6,664	6,840	6,989	8,000	7,040[2]	7,130[2]
Aged	4,906	5,943	6,168	6,314	7,080	6,230[2]	6,310[2]
Disabled	456	721	672	675	920	810[2]	820[2]
Average annual benefit	$434	$863	$1,587	$1,970	$3,063	$3,324	$3,282
Aged	432	853	1,563	1,947	3,078	3,367	3,324
Disabled	460	948	1,808	2,176	2,955	3,049	3,021
Supplementary Medical Insurance (SMI)							
Total enrolled	23,339	27,120	29,721	32,333	35,496	36,960	37,390
Aged	21,504	24,422	27,049	29,426	31,622	32,379	32,660
Disabled	1,835	2,698	2,672	2,907	3,874	4,582	4,730
Total Beneficiaries	12,108	17,703	22,132	26,004	29,774	26,782[2]	27,197[2]
Aged	11,311	16,034	20,199	23,820	26,681	23,297[2]	23,582[2]
Disabled	797	1,669	1,933	2,184	3,093	3,485[2]	3,615[2]
Average annual benefit	$161	$374	$734	$1,282	$1,788	$2,142	$2,451
Aged	153	348	705	1,250	1,728	2,104	2,656
Disabled	259	610	1,022	1,603	2,282	2,412	2,422

1. Estimate.   2. Beneficiary numbers for 1999 and 2000 include only those receiving care under Fee For Service programs. A small number of beneficiaries who received benefits under managed care programs are not included in this figure.
Source: Health Care Financing Administration, Division of Budget, unpublished data, 2000.

You may start collecting Social Security as early as age 62, but you will receive only 80 percent of the amount you would have received if you retired at age 65. The normal retirement age will be increased gradually from 65 to 67, beginning in the year 2003. See the accompanying table for approximate monthly retired, disabled, and survivor benefits.

If you become disabled—defined as having a physical or mental impairment that permanently prevents you from doing any substantial work (i.e. worth more than $500 a month)—you are eligible for additional benefits after six months. See the accompanying table for examples of disability benefits.

Additional benefits are also paid to the survivors of workers eligible for Social Security. Widows and widowers over the age of 60, children under the age of 18, and certain other survivors each generally receive amounts equivalent to 75 percent to 100 percent of the worker's Social Security benefit. There is, however, a per-family benefit limit, usually equal to 150-180 percent of the worker's benefit rate.

The OASDI programs are financed from taxes collected on earnings in covered jobs from employees and employers, which are deposited in two separate trust funds. The money received by the trust funds can be used only to pay OASDI benefits and operating expenses.

Medicare

The Social Security Amendments of 1965 established two contributory health insurance programs designed to provide assistance for medical expenses for the aged and disabled. The first is a compulsory program of hospital insurance (HI) which provides basic protection against the costs of inpatient hospital services and related post-hospital care, including home health services, part-time nursing care, and physical therapy. This is commonly referred to as Part B. Persons reaching age 65 without qualifying for HI may voluntarily enroll by paying a monthly premium. In 2000, HI paid all hospital bills for the first 60 days after the patient paid a deductible of $776. After day 60, the patient was responsible for a co-payment of $194 per day. For nursing homes, the first 20 days have no deductible, but $97 a day thereafter, up to 100 days.

The second health program, called Part B, is supplementary medical insurance (SMI) coverage, a voluntary program in which enrolled individuals pay a monthly premium. The program's coverage includes physician's and surgeon's services, outpatient services, laboratory tests, ambulance services, surgical dressings, home health services, and comprehensive outpatient services. The premium is $45.50 per month after the patient has paid the deductible ($100); Part B pays for 80 percent of covered services.

As with OASDI, hospital insurance is financed by a tax on earnings: of the 7.65 percent tax on earnings (FICA) deducted from employee paychecks, 1.65 percent is for hospital insurance and 6 percent is for OASDI.

Supplemental Security Insurance Beneficiaries and Benefits, 1975–98

| | Beneficiaries | | | | Benefits (millions) | | | |
| | | | State Supplement | | | | State Supplement | |
Year	Total[1]	Federal SSI	Federally admin- istered	State admin- istered	Total	Federal SSI	Federally admin- istered	State admin- istered
Total								
1975	4,359,625	3,893,419	1,684,018	303,391	$5,878.2	$4,313.5	$1,402.5	$162.2
1980	4,194,100	3,682,411	1,684,765	249,474	7,941.7	5,866.4	1,848.3	226.1
1990	4,888,180	4,412,131	2,058,273	285,530	16,598.7	12,893.8	3,239.2	465.7
1995	6,575,753	6,194,493	2,517,805	299,603	27,627.7	23,919.4	3,117.9	590.4
1997	6,564,613	6,211,867	2,372,479	656,970	29,052.1	25,457.4	2,913.2	681.5
1998	6,649,465	6,289,070	2,411,707	660,685	30,216.3	26,404.8	3,003.4	808.1
Aged								
1975	2,333,685	2,024,765	843,917	184,679	$2,604.8	$1,843.0	$ 673.5	$ 88.3
1980	1,838,381	1,533,366	702,763	134,555	2,734.3	1,860.2	756.8	117.2
1990	1,484,160	1,256,623	649,530	115,890	3,736.1	2,521.4	1,038.0	176.7
1995	1,479,415	1,314,720	663,390	114,451	4,467.1	3,374.8	864.5	227.9
1997	1,395,845	1,251,374	619,516	130,652	4,532.0	3,479.9	823.6	228.4
1998	1,369,206	1,225,578	617,984	138,225	4,424.9	3,327.9	838.4	258.6
Blind								
1975	75,315	68,375	31,376	4,933	$130.9	$ 92.4	$34.8	$3.7
1980	79,139	68,945	36,214	3,649	190.1	131.5	54.3	4.2
1990	84,109	74,781	40,334	3,042	334.1	238.4	90.5	5.2
1995	84,273	77,064	38,695	3,577	375.3	298.2	69.2	8.0
1997	81,449	74,926	36,050	4,543	374.9	302.7	65.2	7.0
1998	81,029	74,623	36,193	4,635	366.5	291.0	67.1	8.3
Disabled								
1975	11,950,625	1,800,279	808,725	113,504	$3,142.5	$2,378.1	$ 694.2	$ 70.2
1980	2,276,130	2,080,100	945,788	104,367	5,013.9	3,874.7	1,037.1	102.2
1990	3,319,911	3,080,727	1,368,409	166,598	12,520.6	10,134.0	2,110.6	275.9
1995	5,010,326	4,802,709	1,815,720	179,542	22,782.1	20,246.4	2,184.2	347.9
1997	5,078,995	4,885,567	1,716,913	281,274	24,006.3	21,685.4	2,024.4	296.4
1998	5,190,815	4,988,869	1,757,530	310,000	25,304.7	22,785.9	2,098.9	420.9

1. Total beneficiaries includes some people who receive both Federal SSI and a state supplement.
Source: Social Security Administration, *Social Security Bulletin, Annual Statistical Supplement.*

(Medicaid, a separate program that helps the financially needy of all ages pay for health care, is not a part of Social Security. It is discussed in "Other Income Support Programs," below).

Supplemental Security Income (SSI)

In 1974, Congress replaced the federal-state programs for needy aged (over 65 years old), blind, and disabled people with a single Federal Supplementary Security Income program. SSI eligibility depends on whether you work and in what state you live. In addition, SSI recipients may have no more than $2,000 in assets ($3,000 for married couples), though houses and cars are not usually counted as assets in this equation. The qualifying standards for disability benefits are the same as those used for the Social Security disability insurance program. More than 6.6 million people received SSI benefits in 1998; the basic monthly Federal benefit is the same in all states: $458 for one person and $687 for a couple. States have the option of supplementing Federal SSI under their own programs administered. More than 2.4 million persons received state supplements in 1998; the average payment was about $100.

Black Lung Program

Established by the Federal Coal Mine Health and Safety Act of 1969, this provides monthly cash benefits to coal miners who are totally disabled because of "black lung" disease (pneumoconiosis) and to survivors of miners who die from this disease. Benefits are paid mostly out of a trust fund financed by an excise tax on coal. The number of beneficiaries continues to decline as older beneficiaries are dying in greater numbers than new claimants are entering the program. A total of 94,488 miners, widows, and their dependents received a total of $459.06 million in 1998, down from $1.0 billion in 1985, when 294,846 people were receiving benefits.

Social Security and You

While Social Security benefits are automatic for all people who hold a Social Security card and who are eligible for programs, the Social Security Administration (SSA) recommends that workers check the agency's records of their earnings every three to five years. If their records are not accurate—the SSA says that 1 percent of eligible wages are not credited to workers' records—your benefits could be lower than you deserve.

To find out what your earnings are, pick up a Personal Earnings and Benefit Estimate Statement (PEBES). This, as well as free booklets detailing eligibility requirements and benefit payments, is available at any of the more than 1,300 local SSA offices nationwide. They are also available by calling 1-800-234-5SSA, 1-800-772-1212, or on the Internet at www.ssa.gov.

▶OTHER INCOME SUPPORT PROGRAMS
Welfare

The Social Security Act of 1935 included a provision authorizing Aid to Families with Dependent Children (AFDC), commonly known as "welfare." Benefits were limited to families with children under 18. But in the much-ballyhooed 1996 welfare reform effort, the Federal Government ended more than 60 years of guaranteed assistance to the needy, and replaced it with a system of block grants to the states, who could use the money to enact their own welfare programs. The Temporary Assistance to Needy Families (TANF) Block Grant replaced AFDC on July 1, 1997. TANF gives states broad discretion to determine eligibility and benefit levels. However, families may not receive benefits for longer than 60 months, unwed teenage parents must stay in school and live at home, and people convicted of drug-related felonies are banned from receiving TANF or Food Stamp benefits. In addition, non-working adults must participate in community service within two months of receiving benefits, and must find work within two years. Parents with children under age 1 are exempt from the work requirements (under age 6 if child care is not available).

Welfare reform has succeeded in reducing the number of people receiving Government assistance. In 1999, the total number of people receiving welfare benefits had dropped to 7.2 million, its lowest level in 30 years. That's a 50 percent drop from the all-time high of 14.4 million reached in March, 1994. The President's Council of Economic Advisers said that nearly half of the decline in the welfare rolls can be attributed to the growth of the economy. Another 30 percent, the Council said, resulted from welfare reform. Reform has most benefited white families. they made up 38 percent of all welfare families in 1990, but only 30.5 percent in 1999. Over the same period, the percentage of welfare families that were black declined only from 40 percent to 38.3 percent, while the percentage of Hispanic families increased dramatically, from 16.6 percent to 24.5 percent.

Medicaid

Enacted jointly with Medicare in 1965, Medicaid provides Federal matching funds to states to help pay the cost of medical care and services for low-income persons. Payments are made to suppliers of the care and service. To be eligible for matching funds, a state Medicaid program must cover all persons who receive assistance under TANF. (Most SSI recipients are also covered.) In 1998, 40.6 million aged, blind, disabled, or poor persons with families received Medicaid benefits at a total cost to state and federal governments of $142 billion. Medicaid may also pay the premiums for supplementary medical insurance and the deductible and co-insurance cost of hospital insur-

Welfare Beneficiaries and Benefits, 1970–99

| | Average monthly beneficiaries ('000s) | | | Benefits | |
Year	Recipients	Families	Children	Total (millions)	Average monthly benefit
1970	7,429	1,909	5,494	$ 4,082	$178
1975	11,067	3,269	7,821	8,153	208
1980	10,597	3,574	7,220	11,540	269
1985	10,813	3,692	7,165	14,580	329
1990	11,460	3,974	7,755	18,539	389
1995	13,652	4,876	9,274	22,032	377
1996	12,649	4,553	8,673	20,295	371
1997	10,381	3,734	N.A.	N.A.	359
1998	8,358	3,027	N.A.	N.A.	358
1999	7,018	2,582	N.A.	N.A.	357

Note: "Welfare" refers to the Aid to Families with Dependent Children (AFDC) program through 1996; in 1997, AFDC was renamed Temporary Assistance to Needy Families (TANF), and many more restrictions were added. **Source:** Administration for Children and Families, unpublished data.

ance. Medicaid also covers some medical services that Medicare does not.

Food Stamps

By providing eligible applicants with coupons to buy food, this program enables families in need to purchase a nutritionally adequate diet. In general, a household is considered eligible if it has less than $2,000 in liquid assets, or if 30 percent of its countable cash income is insufficient to purchase an adequate low-cost diet as defined by the U.S. Department of Agriculture (USDA) "Thrifty Food Plan." The Food Stamp Act of 1964 set eligibility requirements for food stamp program participants and provides coupons through state and local agencies that are used to buy food in approved retail stores. States delegate varying degrees of authority to counties and cities, but the Federal Government finances 100 percent of the state-issued food benefits and part of the state's administrative costs. The Omnibus Budget Reconciliation Act of 1982 tightened eligibility and authorized pilot projects in which recipients lose their stamps if they don't work at least 20 hours a week.

Federal Food Assistance Programs, 1970–2000

Program	1970	1980	1990	1995	1999	2000
Participants (millions)						
Participants (millions)						
Food stamps	4.3	21.1	20.1	26.6	18.2	17.2
National school lunch program[1]	22.4	26.6	24.1	25.7	26.9	27.2
School breakfast[1]	0.5	3.6	4.1	6.3	7.4	7.5
Women-infants-children[2]	—	1.9	4.5	6.9	7.3	7.2
Child and adult care[3]	0.1	0.7	1.5	2.4	2.7	2.7
Federal cost (millions)						
Food stamps	$4,624	$8,721	$14,187	$22,765	$15,755	$14,985
National school lunch program[1]	300	2,279	3,214	4,466	5,314	5,489
School breakfast[2]	11	288	596	1,048	1,345	1,393
Women-infants-children	—	584	1,637	2,516	2,853	2,947
Child and adult care[3]	6	207	720	1,296	1,436	1,485

1. Average monthly participation during school year. Covers public and private elementary and secondary schools and residential child care institutions. Costs do not include the value of USDA donated commodities. 2. WIC serves pregnant and postpartum women, infants, and children up to age five. 3. Provides year-round subsidies to feed preschool children in child care centers and family day care programs. Certain care centers serving disabled or elderly adults also receive meal subsidies.
Source: U.S. Dept. of Agriculture, Annual Historical Review of Food and Nutrition Service Programs, annual, and unpublished data.

Medicaid Recipients and Vendor Payments, 1975–98

Year	Aged	Blind	Disabled	Dependent children under 21	Adults in families with dependent children	Other/ Unknown	Total
Recipients ('000s)							
1975	3,615	109	2,355	9,598	4,529	1,800	22,207
1981	3,367	86	2,993	9,581	5,187	1,364	21,980
1985	3,061	80	2,937	9,757	5,518	1,239	21,814
1990	3,202	83	3,635	11,220	6,010	1,105	25,255
1995	4,119	92	5,767	17,164	7,604	1,536	36,282
1997	3,954	(1)	6,129	15,269	6,797	1,429	33,579
1998	3,964	(1)	6,638	18,309	7,908	3,176	40,649
Medical Vendor Payments (millions of dollars)							
1975	$4,358	$93	$3,052	$2,186	$2,062	$ 492	$12,242
1981	9,926	154	9,301	3,508	3,763	552	27,204
1985	14,096	249	13,203	4,414	4,746	798	37,508
1990	21,508	434	23,969	9,100	8,590	1,258	64,859
1995	36,527	848	48,570	17,976	13,511	2,709	120,141
1997	37,721	(1)	54,129	15,666	12,298	3,737	123,551
1998	40,602	(1)	60,375	20,459	14,833	3,702	142,318
Payments Per Capita							
1975	$1,205	$ 850	$1,296	$ 228	$ 455	$ 273	$ 556
1981	2,948	1,784	3,108	366	725	405	1,238
1985	4,605	3,104	4,496	452	860	658	1,719
1990	6,717	5,212	6,595	811	1,429	1,062	2,568
1995	8,868	9,256	8,422	1,047	1,777	1,762	3,311
1997	9,539	(1)	8,832	1,026	1,809	2,615	3,679
1998	10,243	(1)	9,095	1,117	1,876	1,166	3,501

Note: Figures are in current dollars. A small number of recipients are in more than one category. 1. Figures for blind were combined with those for the disabled in 1997. **Source:** Health Care Financing Administration, 2082 Report (2000).

Special nutrition programs

The USDA administers a number of programs designed to help safeguard the health and well-being of the nation's children by assisting the states in providing adequate meals to all children at a moderate cost. The programs include the National School Lunch Program, the School Breakfast Program, the Summer Food Service Program, the Child Care Food Program, the Special Milk Program, and the Special Supplemental Food Program for Women, Infants, and Children (WIC) Program. The nutrition program for the elderly requires no income test, but preference is given to those with the greatest need.

Housing subsidies

The Federal Government has traditionally provided housing aid directly to lower-income households in the form of rental and mortgage-interest subsidies. The primary purposes are to improve housing quality and to reduce housing costs for lower-income households. Other goals include promoting residential construction, expanding housing opportunities for disadvantaged groups and groups with special housing needs, promoting neighborhood preservation and revitalization, increasing homeownership, and empowering the poor to become homeowners.

Most housing aid is targeted to very-low-income renters through two basic types of rental assistance programs. Project-based aid is typically tied to projects specifically produced for lower-income households through new construction or substantial renovation. Almost all project-based aid is provided through production-oriented programs, including the public-housing program, the section 8 new construction and substantial rehabilitation program, and the section 236 mortgage-interest-subsidy program (administered by the Department of Housing and Urban Development), and the section 515 mortgage-interest-subsidy program administered by the Farmers Home Administration.

Household-based subsidies that permit renters to choose from standard housing units in the existing private housing stock. Rental assistance programs generally reduce tenants' rent payments to 30 percent of their income, with the Government paying the balance of the contract rents.

The Federal Government also assists some lower- and moderate-income households in becoming homeowners by making long-term commitments to reduce their mortgage interest. These generally reduce mortgage payments, property taxes, and insurance costs to a fixed percentage of income, ranging from 20 percent to 28 percent.

The total number of households receiving assistance has increased substantially, from 3.2 million in 1977 to 5.7 million in 1995. Total outlays for housing aid rose from $2.9 billion in 1977 to an estimated 26.0 billion in 1996; outlays per unit rose from $1,160 to $5,480 over the same period.

Housing for the homeless

HUD funding for homeless programs is made available to state and local governments, Indian tribes, and non-profit organizations. The specific programs are the Emergency Shelter Grants (ESG) Program, the Supportive Housing Demonstration Program, the Shelter-Plus-Care Homeless Rental Housing Assistance, and the HUD-Owned Single Property Disposition Program.

Head Start

Head Start provides a wide range of services to children of low-income families (and their families) up to the age of five. Its goals are to improve the social competence, learning skills, and health and nutrition status of low-income children so that they can begin school on an equal footing with their more advantaged peers. The services include cognitive and language development, medical, dental, and mental health services (including screening and immunizations), and nutritional and social services. Parental involvement is extensive, through both volunteer participation and employment of parents as Head Start staff. At least 90 percent of Head Start children come from families with incomes at or below the poverty line, and at least 10 percent of enrollment slots in each state must be available to disabled children. In 1999, more than 830,000 children were served in Head Start programs, at a total

Head Start Participation and Funding, 1966–2000

Year	Enrollment	Appropriations
1966	733,000	$198,900,000
1970	477,400	325,700,000
1980	376,300	735,000,000
1990	540,930	1,552,000,000
1995	750,696	3,534,128,000
1996	752,077	3,569,329,000
1997	793,809	3,980,546,000
1998	822,316	4,347,433,000
1999	826,016	4,658,151,448
2000	857,664	5,267,000,000

1. Estimate. **Source:** U.S. Dept of Health and Human Services, Administration for Children and Families. www.acf.hhs.gov.

U.S. Weighted Average Poverty Thresholds by Family Size, 1960–2000

| Year | Maximum yearly family income | | | | | | |
	1 person	2 people	3 people	4 people	5 people	6 people	7 people
1960	$1,490	$1,924	$2,359	$3,022	$3,560	$4,002	$4,921[1]
1970	1,954	2,525	3,099	3,968	4,680	5,260	6,468[1]
1980	4,190	5,363	6,565	8,414	9,966	11,269	12,761
1990	6,652	8,509	10,419	13,359	15,792	17,839	20,241
1995	7,763	9,933	12,158	15,569	18,408	20,804	23,552
1996	7,995	10,233	12,516	16,036	18,952	21,389	24,268
1997	8,183	10,473	12,802	16,400	19,380	21,886	24,802
1998	8,316	10,634	13,003	16,660	19,680	22,228	25,257
1999	8,501	10,869	13,290	17,029	20,127	22,727	25,912
2000	8,794	11,239	13,738	17,603	21,819	23,528	26,754

1. Seven or more people. **Source:** U.S. Bureau of the Census, *Current Population Survey* (2001).

Federal cost of $4.7 billion, or an average cost of $5,147 per child. More than 55 percent of Head Start families have incomes of less than $9,000 per year, and 72.7 percent have yearly incomes of less than $12,000. Since 1980, the children served by Head Start have grown younger, less black, and more Hispanic. Five-year-olds made up 21 percent of the Head Start population in 1980; in 1998 they constituted only 6 percent. Meanwhile, four-year-olds increased from 55 to 59 percent. In 1980, 19 percent of Head Start children were Hispanic; in 1998, 26 percent were Hispanic, while black Head Start children declined from 42 to 36 percent over the same period.

Poverty income guidelines
The poverty income guidelines are used to determine whether a person or family is eligible for assistance under a particular federal program. The poverty threshold is established each year by increasing the previous year's threshold by the change in the Consumer Price Index. The original poverty threshold was devised in 1960 and was equal to three times the amount of money to buy the cheapest "nutritionally adequate" diet as dictated by the Department of Agriculture.

Unemployment Compensation
The Social Security Act provided an inducement to states to enact unemployment insurance laws, and by 1937 all 48 states, the territories of Alaska and Hawaii, and the District of Columbia had passed such laws. All contributions collected under state laws are deposited in the unemployment trust fund of the U.S. Treasury, but each state maintains a separate account. A state may withdraw money from its account only to pay benefits. Each state has major responsibility for the content and development of its unemployment insurance law. Nationwide, Unemployment covers about 125 million workers.

Workers must be ready, able and willing to work and must be registered for work at a state public employment office. A worker's benefit is based on his or her employment in covered work over a prior performance period. No state can deny benefit to a claimant if he or she refuses to accept a new job under substandard labor conditions or where he or she would be required to join a company union.

In the first quarter of 2000, 4.2 million people made initial unemployment claims, 2.2 were receiving benefits, and 583,000 exhausted their compensation. The average weekly benefit was $194 and the average duration of benefit was 14.5 weeks, making the average total benefit $2,820. The weekly benefit varies from state to state, but the general formula is designed to compensate for between 50 percent and 70 percent of average weekly pretax wage, up to a state-determined minimum.

Workers' compensation
Social insurance began in the United States with worker's compensation. A law covering Federal civilian employees was passed in 1908; the first state compensation law to be held constitutional was enacted in 1911. These laws made industry responsible for the compensation of workers (or their survivors) injured or killed while on the job. A worker incurring an occupational injury is compensated regardless of fault or blame in the accident. A separate Federal program enacted in 1969 protects coal miners (see "Black lung program" below).

Workers' compensation is almost exclusively financed by employers on the principle that the cost of work-related accidents is part of the expense of production. Every state except Texas mandates coverage under workers' compensation for private employees. Certain categories of workers, usually domestic, agricultural, and casual laborers, are often exempted from this requirement. Employers can use private insurance companies or can qualify as self-insurers. Workers' compensation covered 124 million workers in 1999, or about 86 percent of the civilian labor force. The cash benefit for temporary total disability, permanent, total or partial disability, or death of a breadwinner is usually about 66.7 percent of weekly earnings at the time of the accident. Most state laws pay temporary disability benefits for as long as the disability lasts and the condition has not been stabilized to the point where no further improvement can result from medical treatment. Total benefit payments under workers' compensation programs in 1999 were $43.4 billion, up from $42.3 billion in 1998, but down from $45.3 billion in 1993.

Permanent partial disability compensation for specific, or "schedule" injuries (for clearly measurable matters) is generally subject to different (usually lower) dollar maximums and is determined without regard to loss of earning power. Compensation for "nonschedule" injuries (injuries to head, back, nervous system) is the difference between wages before and after impairment. Death benefits are related to earnings and graduated by the number of dependents. Medical benefits are furnished without limit as to time or amount for accidental injuries. Temporary Disability Insurance provides coverage against the risk of lost wages due to short-term nonoccupational disability. The Federal Unemployment Tax Act permits states where employees make contributions under the unemployment insurance program to use some or all of those contributions for disability benefits. It is estimated that about two-thirds of the nation's wage and salary earners in private employment have some protection through various voluntary and governmental group arrangements. In general the benefit amount for a week is intended to replace at least half the weekly wage loss for a maximum of 26 to 39 weeks per year.

▶VETERANS' BENEFITS
The tradition of veterans' benefits dates to the 18th century when the Continental Congress provided disability pensions for veterans of the Revolutionary War. Today, the Department of Veterans Affairs (DVA) offers a wide range of services and benefits to eligible veterans, their dependents, and their survivors.

While the veteran population as a whole is decreasing in numbers (from about 29.5 million in 1975 to o 24.4 million in 2000), the number of veterans age 65 or older is increasing rapidly. The use and cost of medical care are expected to grow more rapidly over the next several years than those of other veterans' benefits and services. Compensation and pension caseloads are decreasing steadily due to beneficiary deaths, terminations for excess incomes, and age limitation for dependents. The number of trainees under the Montgomery GI bill will increase as more veterans become eligible.

Veterans who have incurred injuries or illness while in service are entitled to service-connected compensation. The amounts are determined by disability ratings. Death compensation or dependency and indemnity compensation is paid to survivors of veterans who died as a result of service-connected causes.

War veterans who have become permanently and totally disabled from non-service-connected causes, and to survivors of war veterans may receive means-tested veterans' pensions. Benefits are based on family size, and the pensions provide a floor of income.

Medical programs   The VA operates 172 hospital centers, 132 nursing homes, 40 domiciliaries, and 398 outpatient clinics. In 2000, the VA expected to treat about 673,000 patients in VA hospitals and another 111,000 in nursing homes. The VA extends free priority care to service-connected disabled veterans, to veterans in special categories, and to needy non-service-connected veterans. As facilities and other resources permit, the VA provides care to non-service-connected veterans with incomes that exceed the mandatory care income limits.

Housing and loan programs   Since 1944, the VA has guaranteed more than 16.2 million loans totaling over $661 billion. The maximum guaranty is as follows: 50 percent of the loan amount for loans of $45,000 or less; $22,500 for loans between $45,001 and $56,250; the lesser of $36,000 or 40 percent of the loan for loans between $56,251 and $144,000; and the lesser of $46,000 or 25 percent of the loan for loans in excess of $144,000.

Other veterans' programs   Since 1944, when the Montgomery GI Bill became law, more than 20 million veterans and military personnel have benefited from its education and training programs. Contributions are required, and veterans can receive a basic educational benefit of up to $400 per month for 36 months while in an educational program. The total cost of this program is more than $73 billion.

The Veterans Job Training Act program provides payments to defray training costs of employers who hire certain veterans of the Korean conflict or Vietnam era who have been unemployed for long periods of time.

Veterans Benefits and Services: Outlays and Recipients, 1975–2000

Fiscal year	Compensation and pensions	Readjustment, education, job training	Medical programs	Housing loans
Outlays (millions)				
1975	$ 7,860	$4,593	$3,665	N.A.
1980	11,688	2,342	6,515	N.A.
1985	14,714	1,059	9,547	N.A.
1990	15,241	278	12,134	N.A.
1995	18,966	1,124	15,981	N.A.
1996	17,170	1,106	16,372	32,609
1997	19,389	1,167	17,149	27,042
1998	19,700	1,429	17,441	37,906
1999	21,800	N.A.	18,300	54,000
2000	21,500	N.A.	19,400	23,300
Recipients ('000s)				
1975	4,855	2,804	1,985	290
1980	4,646	1,232	2,671	297
1985	4,005	491	2,963	179
1990	3,614	329	3,018	196
1995	3,332	476	2,859	263
1996	2,253	297	2,937	321
1997	2,200	297	3,142	261
1998	2,700	297	3,431	344
1999	2,700	288	3,600	486
2000	2,700	279	3,800	200

Source: Facts About the Depratment of Veterans Affairs (1975-2000).

THE INTERNAL REVENUE SERVICE

Founded in 1862, the Internal Revenue Service (I.R.S.) is the office of the Department of the Treasury charged with collecting Federal taxes. The Constitution empowers Congress to levy excise taxes and--in emergencies--to raise direct taxes. Congress's right to levy taxes on the income of individuals and corporations was contested throughout the 19th century, but that authority was written into the Constitution with the passage of the 16th Amendment in 1913. Today, the source of most of the Federal Government's revenues are the individual income tax, corporate income tax, excise taxes, estate taxes, and gift taxes. The I.R.S. is responsible for these taxes as well as for collecting employee and employer payments for social insurance and retirement insurance (see "Social Insurance Programs").

In 1998, Congress enacted a major overhaul of the I.R.S. in hopes of transforming the agency from a menacing symbol of Government authority into a resource for taxpayers trying to cope with the increasingly bewildering tax code. The legislation established an outside board with broad authority to supervise the I.R.S.'s operations, and perhaps more important, shifted the burden of proof in tax dispute cases to the I.R.S. (previously, taxpayers had to prove their innocence). Initial reaction to the legislation was overwhelmingly favorable. But tax experts correctly predicted the law would give scofflaws greater incentive to cheat on their taxes. Property seizures dropped by 98 percent between 1997 and 1999, garnishments of bank accounts and paychecks were a quarter of their level two years earlier, and tax liens, which insure that back taxes are paid when properties are sold, were down by 67 percent.

But the most damaging change was the anti-harassment section of the legislation, which tax collectors say is thwarting them from collecting taxes from delinquent filers. Several I.R.S. agents said they no longer pursued outstanding tax bills vigorously because they feared losing their jobs under the anti-harassment policy. In 1998, the I.R.S. gave up on collecting back taxes from just 98 taxpayers; in 2000, the agency wrote off $2.5 billion in back taxes owed by more than 650,000 delinquent taxpayers. In the first three months of 2001, the I.R.S. abandoned efforts to collect an additional $890 million from other delinquent filers.

The decline in aggressive pursuit of tax cheats actually began even before the new law went into effect. In 1996, the I.R.S. audited 2.13 million of the 155 million tax returns filed, a rate of 1.38 percent. Two years later, the agency examined only half as many returns (1.36 million, out of a total of 161 million filed, or 0.8 percent). Almost all of the decrease in audits came in individual returns. The I.R.S. audited just under 2 million individual returns in 1996; that number dropped to 1.2 million in 1998 and 1.1 million in 1999. The agency also eased up on corporate tax filings. In 1996, it audited 69,650 corporate returns (2.67 percent); corporate audits fell to 54,051 returns (2.1 percent) in 1998 and 39,099 returns (1.55 percent) in 1999.

The shift can also be seen in the number and distribution of I.R.S. employees. Total I.R.S. employment dropped from 102,082 in 1996 to 97,375 in 1998, but that's only half the story. The number of tax collectors dropped 34 percent from 17,610 to 11,621, while the number of auditors and tax examiners fell 22 percent, from 27,433 to 21,458. Meanwhile, the I.R.S.'s customer service staff skyrocketed from 1,777 employees in 1996 to a whopping 12,216 in 1997, and then nearly doubled again to 21,328, in 1998. That's a 1,300 percent increase in just two years.

For now, the shift in emphasis hasn't hurt the Federal coffers. Total I.R.S. tax collections (as well as tax per capita) reached all-time highs in 1998 and again in 1999 (See the accompanying table). Meanwhile, the cost of collecting all that money, dropped from an all-time high of 60 cents per $1000 in 1993 to 43 cents in 1998 and 1999, about the same as it was in 1967. One example of the I.R.S.'s economical use of resources: it examined 35.7 percent of the 9,000 returns filed by corpora-

Tax Returns Processed, 1990–99

Type of return	Number of returns ('000s)				
	1990	1995	1996	1998	1999
Individual income tax (Form 1040 series)	112,492	116,298	120,745	123,000	125,227
Individual estimated tax (Form 1040ES)	38,188	35,475	38,634	42,413	39,228
Fiduciary (Form 1041 series)	2,702	3,187	3,310	3,388	3,390
Fiduciary estimated tax (Form 1041ES)	651	583	815	1,028	914
Partnership (Form 1065)	1,741	1,572	1,770	1,826	1,966
Corporation (Forms 1120 series, 1066)	4,311	4,781	5,158	5,311	5,403
Estate tax (Forms 706, 706NA)	59	83	97	109	117
Gift tax (Form 709)	146	215	251	258	286
Employment taxes (Forms 94X series, CT-1, 1042)	28,914	29,006	28,918	29,274	29,048
Exempt organizations (Forms 990 series, 4720, 5227)	484	560	607	676	677
Employee plans (Form 5500 series)	1,016	1,262	1,337	1,662	1,414
Excise taxes (Forms 720, 730, 2290, 11C)	840	787	821	815	762
Supplemental documents (1040X, 2688, 4868, 7004, 1041A)	10,170	11,937	14,048	14,695	15,873
Total tax returns	201,715	205,747	216,510	224,453	224,305

Source: Internal Revenue Service, 1999 Data Book (2001).

Tax Rate Schedules, 2001

Taxable income	What you pay
Single Individual	
$0-$27,050	15% of sum over $0
$27,050- $65,550	$4,057.50 + 27.5% of sum over $27,050
$65,550-$136,750	14,645.00 + 30.5% of sum over $65,550
$136,750 - $297,350	36,361.00 + 35.5% of sum over $136,750
over $297,350	93,374.00 + 39.1% of sum over$297,350
Heads of Households	
$0- $36,250	15% of sum over $0
$36,250- $93,650	$5,437.50 + 27.5% of sum over $36,250
$93,650- $151,650	21,222.50 + 30.5% of sum over $93,650
$151,650- $297,350	38,912.50 + 35.5% of sum over $151,650
over $297,350	90,636.00 + 39.1% of sum over $297,350
Married individuals filing jointly, or qualifying widow(er)	
$0- $45,200	15% of sum over $0
$45,200- $109,250	$6,780.00+ 27.5% of sum over $45,200
$109,250- $166,500	24,393.75 + 30.5% of sum over $109,250
$166,500- $297,350	41,855.00 + 35.5% of sum over $166,500
over $297,350	88,306.75 + 39.1% of sum over $297,350
Married, Filing Separate Return	
$0- $22,600	15% of sum over $0
$22,600- $54,625	$3,390.00 + 27.5% of sum over $22,600
$54,625- $83,250	12,196.88+ 30.5% of sum over $54,625
$83,250- $148,675	20,927.50 + 35.5% of sum over $83,250
over $148,675	44,153.38 + 39.1% of sum over $148,675

Note: Preliminary figures, subject to review by the Office of Management & Budget. Source: Internal Revenue Service.

tions with total revenues of $250 million or more, resulting in $11.1 billion in additional taxes and penalties, or more than $455,000 per audit. The other closely monitored group of tax returns is from estates valued at $5 million or more. There were 4,200 such returns filed in 1999; the I.R.S. examined 33.8 percent of them, resulting in $665.6 million in additional taxes and penalties ($472,584 per examination).

▶ TAX CHANGES IN 2001

In 2001, President Bush persuaded Congress to pass a tax cut that reduces the top four income tax rates—39.6%, 36%, 31%, and 28%—by half a percentage point. But the most immediate consequence of the tax cut was a $300 check that the government mailed out to individual taxpayers and $600 to families as an advance against a lower tax bill in April, 2002.

For the 2002 tax year, the top tax brackets are each reduced by another half a percentage point, and the limits on tax-free contribution to retirement accounts increases. In addition, the estate tax exemption rises from $675,000 to $1 million, and the top estate tax rate is cut from 55 percent to 50 percent.

▶ PRINCIPAL DEDUCTIONS

Taxes: Taxpayers who pay a state and/or local tax may deduct this amount from their Federal tax payment. In addition, in Alabama, Iowa, Louisiana, Missouri, Oklahoma, Oregon, and Utah, taxpayers may deduct their Federal income tax before calculating their state tax payments.

Personal exemptions: Taxpayers are allowed to claim personal exemptions for the taxpayer and each dependent claimed in filing income tax. Congress determines the amount (since 1990, pegged to the inflation rate) allowable for deductions on personal and other exemptions. Because the personal exemption is the same for a single person as for a married couple, the tax schedule effectively dissuades people from getting married. For several years, politicians have discussed eliminating the so-called marriage tax penalty, but to date have not remedied this situation.

Interest expenses: The most common interest deduction is on home mortgages, thus making the cost of owning a home more affordable to most Americans. Although politically very popular, the mortgage deduction is what experts call an "upside-down" subsidy because the more a tax-

Returns Filed and Examined, and Additional Taxes and Penalties, 1998–99

Type of return	Total returns filed, 1997[1]	Total returns examined, 1998	Percent examined	Additional taxes and penalties (thousands)[2]	Average tax and penalty per return[3]
All returns, total	163,253,100	1,228,406	0.75%	$19,467,559	—
Individual, total	122,546,900	1,100,273	0.90	4,458,474	$16,622
1040A, income under $25,000	44,323,300	600,949	1.36	1,444,961	9,837
Non 1040A, income under $25,000	13,109,600	76,215	0.58	222,402	11,413
Non 1040A, income $25,000-$50,000	28,831,900	103,340	0.36	253,771	7,436
Non 1040A, income $50,000-$100,000	20,873,000	77,698	0.37	247,686	8,852
Non 1040A, income $100,000 and over	7,025,000	80,038	1.14	1,183,346	28,620
Schedule C—receipts under $25,000	2,546,800	68,450	2.69	167,151	8,555
Schedule C—receipts $25,000-$100,000	3,267,300	42,391	1.30	228,973	9,175
Schedule C—receipts $100,000 and over	1,876,000	44,945	2.40	648,968	18,554
Schedule F—receipts under $100,000	417,000	2,832	0.68	8,615	8,802
Schedule F—receipts $100,000 and over	277,000	3,415	1.23	52,601	31,217
Corporation, total	2,523,100	39,099	1.55	12,841,329	57,418
No balance sheet	293,900	1,969	0.67	147,210	28,729
Under $250,000	1,506,300	6,865	0.46	104,427	14,006
$250,000-$1 million	429,600	7,226	1.68	110,247	15,194
$1 million-$ 5 million	187,700	9,253	4.93	235,987	25,744
$5 million-$10 million	28,700	2,955	10.30	121,804	40,518
$10 million-$50 million	30,900	4,604	14.90	392,656	83,621
$50 million-$100 million	7,700	1,270	16.49	199,558	149,491
$100 million-$250 million	7,700	1,450	18.83	338,481	217,247
$250 million and over	9,000	3,213	35.70	11,091,431	455,265
Form 1120F	21,600	294	1.36	99,528	315,905
Fiduciary	3,397,600	6,382	0.19	87,910	19,539
Estate, total	110,100	9,319	8.46	1,057,654	116,993
Gross estate under $1 million	59,900	2,863	4.78	101,564	37,047
Gross estate $1 million-$5 million	46,000	5,035	10.95	290,514	59,130
Gross estate $5 million and over	4,200	1,421	33.83	665,576	472,584
Gift	261,200	2,369	0.91	346,061	146,208
Employment	29,131,500	24,105	0.08	422,583	10,182
Excise	821,900	12,562	1.53	151,569	10,030
Miscellaneous taxable[4]	—	339		57,963	21,340
Partnerships	1,861,000	7,991	0.43	—	—
S-Corporations	2,599,800	21,169	0.81	—	—

Note: Totals may not add due to rounding. 1. Calendar year. 2. Recommended. 3. Includes only returns reviewed by revenue agents. Additional taxes and penalties were recovered through reviews of individual returns by tax auditors and service centers. 4. Includes taxable small business corporations (1120S). **Source:** Internal Revenue Service, *1999 Data Book* (2001).

payer earns, the greater the tax cut yielded. In recent years, 20 percent of the tax savings from home mortgage interest has gone to taxpayers earning more than $200,000.

Medical expenses: Although almost all medical expenses are deductible, it is difficult to take a deduction because your combined expenses for the year must total 7.5 percent of your adjusted gross income. So, for someone with an adjusted gross income of $25,000, medical expenses would have to exceed $1,875 not covered by any medical insurance.

▶ **ELECTRONIC FILING**

The number of people filing their tax returns electronically has jumped dramatically in the 1990s. Just over 4 million individuals filed electronically in 1990; by 1993, that number had tripled to 12.3 million. The number more than doubled again, to 29.4 million in 1999.

▶ **CHECK BOXES**

In 1999, just under 15 million people checked the little box authorizing the I.R.S. to send a portion of their tax to the Presidential Election Campaign

Fund. That meant $61.0 million went to that fund. Since 1972, more than $1 billion has gone to public financing of presidential elections.

Internal Revenue Collections, Costs, and Tax Per Capita, 1960–99

Fiscal year	Collections ('000s)	Cost of collecting- $100	Tax per capita
1960	91,774,803	$ 0.40	$ 507.97
1965	114,434,634	0.52	588.95
1970	195,722,096	0.45	955.31
1975	293,822,726	0.54	1,375.84
1980	519,375,273	0.44	2,275.66
1985	742,871,541	0.48	3,098.99
1990	1,056,365,652	0.52	4,222.00
1995	1,375,731,835	0.54	5,216.70
1996	1,486,546,674	0.49	5,584.11
1997	1,623,272,071	0.44	6,039.43
1998	1,769,408,739	0.43	6,521.50
1999	1,904,151,888	0.43	6,957.79

Note: In current dollars.
Source: Internal Revenue Service, *1999 Data Book* (2001).

Internal Revenue Collections, 1999

Type of return	Gross collections	Refunds[1]	Net collections Amount	Net collections Percent of total
Corporation income taxes	$216,324,889,000	$34,061,844,000	$182,263,045,000	10.6%
Individual income taxes[2]	1,002,185,76,000	146,951,967,000	855,233,798,000	49.8
Employment taxes, total	598,669,865,000	3,999,304,000	594,670,561,000	34.6
Estate and gift taxes	28,385,607,000	654,267,000	27,731,340,000	1.6
Excise taxes	58,585,763,000	1,666,745,000	56,919,018,000	3.3
Grand total	**$1,904,151,888,000**	**$187,334,127,000**	**$1,716,817,761,000**	**100.0%**

1. Excludes excise taxes paid to the Customs Service and Bureau of Alcohol, Tobacco and Firearms. Does not include interest paid on refunds.
2. Includes Presidential Election Campaign Fund contributions of $61.0 million. **Source:** Internal Revenue Service, *1999 Data Book* (2001).

I.R.S. Collections by Principal Sources, 1961–99 (thousands of dollars)

Year	Total Internal Revenue collections	Corporate income & profits tax	Individual income tax	Employment taxes	Estate and gift taxes	Excise taxes
1961	$94,401,086	$21,764,940	$46,153,001	$12,502,451	$ 1,916,392	$12,064,302
1970	195,722,096	35,036,983	103,651,585	37,449,188	3,680,076	15,904,264
1980	519,375,273	72,379,610	287,547,782	128,330,480	6,498,381	24,619,021
1990	1,056,365,652	110,016,539	540,228,408	367,219,321	11,761,939	27,139,445
1995	1,375,731,835	174,422,173	675,779,337	465,405,305	15,144,394	44,980,627
1996	1,486,546,674	189,054,791	745,313,276	492,365,178	17,591,817	42,221,611
1997	1,623,272,071	204,492,336	825,020,880	528,596,833	20,356,401	44,805,621
1998	1,769,408,739	213,270,011	928,065,856	557,799,193	24,630,962	45,642,716
1999	1,904,151,888	216,324,889	1,002,185,765	598,669,865	28,385,607	58,585,763

Note: In current dollars. **Source:** Internal Revenue Service, *1999 Data Book* (2001).

Average Itemized Deductions By Income Level, 2000

Adjusted gross income ranges	Percent itemizing deductions	Average deduction for: Medical	Taxes	Gifts	Interest	Total
0- $15,000	3.56%	$7,500	$1,963	$1,350	$5,958	$11,522
$15,000- $30,000	14.64	5,137	2,200	1,619	5,866	10,627
$30,000- $50,000	36.66	4,992	2,991	1,774	6,247	11,770
$50,000-$100,000	69.58	5,950	4,918	2,282	7,544	15,228
$100,000-$200,000	90.49	10,494	9,262	3,727	10,806	23,500
$200,000 or more	92.46	32,259	36,592	19,454	21,735	64,996

Note: 2000 data based on tax returns for the 1999 tax year. **Source:** Research Institute of America, *Federal Taxes Weekly Alert,* July, 2001.

THE U.S. POSTAL SERVICE

With nearly 800,000 employees moving more than 200 billion pieces of mail annually, the U.S. Postal Service provides one of the most vital Government services. What most people don't realize is that it's done at a cost to the consumer significantly less than in any other industrial nation, and that for first-class mail, the on-time delivery rate is still over 95 percent for local mail and 90 percent for cross-country.

First established by the Continental Congress in 1775, the Postal Service was made part of the Federal system in the Constitution and the office of postmaster general established in George Washington's very first cabinet. In 1969, however, in response to vociferous complaints of mismanagement, waste, unreliable service, and staggering financial losses, the Nixon administration reorganized the service as an independent establishment within the executive branch. The Postal Service Act of 1969 removed the postmaster general from the cabinet and created a self-supporting postal corporation owned by the Federal Government and vested power in an 11-member Board of Governors, nine of whom are appointed by the president with the consent of the Senate; these in turn appoint the postmaster general who serves as the CEO of the postal-service; the 11th member of the board is chosen by the other 10 and serves as deputy postmaster general.

Finally, the 1969 law established an independent Postal Rate Commission of five members, appointed by the president, to recommend postal rates and classifications for adoption by the Board of Governors. Under this agreement, the Postal Service turned a profit five times in the early 1980s. But between 1989 and 1994, the Postal Service lost money every year. A 1995 hike in the price of stamps helped create record-level profits in 1995, 1996, and 1997, more than wiping out the $2.6 billion lost between 1993 and 1994. But this didn't stop the Board of Governors from approving a one-cent hike in the price of stamps in 1999 and another one-cent hike two years later. Measured in constant dollars, the real cost of a stamp in 2001 was 7 cents, a penny less than in 1971. But most complaints about stamp price increases result not from the price of the stamp, but from the hassle of obtaining stamps in the new denominations.

Postage rates If you know the weight of a package, you can determine the amount of postage you will need before going to the post office. Point your browser to http://postcalc.usps.gov.

In 2000, the Postal Service delivered a record 208 billion pieces of mail, and delivers more mail each day than Federal Express delivers all year. If the Postal Service were privately held, its $62.2 billion in revenues would rank it in the top 10 on the list of Fortune 500 companies and the top 30 companies in the world.

Domestic Postage Rates

Weight up to	Rate	Weight up to	Rate	Weight up to	Rate
1 oz.	$0.34	6 oz.	$1.49	11 oz.	2.64
2 oz.	0.57	7 oz.	1.72	12 oz.	2.87
3 oz.	0.80	8 oz.	1.95	13 oz.	3.10
4 oz.	1.03	9 oz.	2.18	over 13 oz.:	
5 oz.	1.26	10 oz.	2.41	UsePriority Mail	

Post cards   21 cents. Post cards cannot exceed 4.25" x 6", nor be smaller than 3.5" x 5".
Priority mail   Priority mail is a zone-based domestic service providing two-day delivery to all major parts of the U.S.

Weight up to	Rate	Weight up to	Rate
1 lb.	$3.50	4 lbs.	$6.45
2 lbs.	3.95	5 lbs.	7.70
3 lbs.	5.20	5-70 lbs.	8.10-103.20

For packages weighing more than five pounds, rates depend on the zone. The maximum weight is 70 pounds.
Express mail   is an overnight delivery service available every day of the year for items up to 70 lbs. in weight and 108 in. in combined length and girth. The post office will pick up packages to be sent by express mail a $10.25 fee (per pickup, not per package). Call 1-800-222-1811.

Weight up to	Rate	Weight up to	Rate
8 oz.	$12.45	3 lbs.	$19.15
2 lbs.	16.25	4-70 lbs.	22.05-121.30

Parcel Post   This is a zone-based class of mail for sending books, circulars, catalogs, other printed matter, and merchandise-weighing not more than 70 pounds. Parcel Post must measure 130 inches or less in combined length and girth. A regular package up to a pound is $3.42; the maximum rate is $40.43 for a 70-pound package sent to zone 8. Oversized parcels are charged approximately double the maximum rates.

Source: U.S. Postal Service. www.usps.gov

International Postage Rates

Type/ Weight up to	Canada	Mexico	Europe	Australia, Japan & New Zealand	All other countries
Airmail letters					
1.0 oz	$0.60	$0.60	$0.80	$0.80	$0.80
2.0 oz	0.85	0.85	1.60	1.70	1.55
3.0 oz	1.10	1.25	2.40	2.60	2.30
4.0 oz	1.35	1.65	3.20	3.50	3.05
8.0 oz	2.35	3.25	6.40	7.10	6.05
Postcards	0.50	0.50	0.70	0.70	0.70

Source: U.S. Postal Service. www.usps.gov

Volume and Revenue of Mail by Type, 1990–2000

Type of Service	Millions of pieces				Revenues (millions)	
	1990	1996	1999	2000	1999	2000
First-class	89,269	98,216	101,936	103,526	$34,933	$35,516
Priority mail	518	937	1,189	1,222	4,533	4,837
Express mail	59	58	69	71	942	996
Mailgrams	14	4	4	4	2	1
Periodicals	10,682	10,126	10,274	10,365	2,115	2,171
Third-class	63,725	71,686	85,662	90,057	14,436	15,193
Parcel Post	663	949	1,043	1,128	1,828	1,912
International surface	166	104	103	79	194	180
International air	632	949	927	1,021	1,434	1,477
U.S. Postal Service	538	360	382	363	N.A.	N.A.
Free for the blind	35	50	53	47	N.A.	N.A.
Total mail	166,301	183,439	201,643	207,882	$60,418	$62,284

Source: U.S. Postal Service, 2000 Annual Report.

Postal Abbreviations for States and Territories

State	Abb.	State	Abb.
Alabama	AL	Nevada	NV
Alaska	AK	New Hampshire	NH
Arizona	AZ	New Jersey	NJ
Arkansas	AR	New Mexico	NM
California	CA	New York	NY
Colorado	CO	North Carolina	NC
Connecticut	CT	North Dakota	ND
Delaware	DE	Ohio	OH
District of	DC	Oklahoma	OK
Columbia		Oregon	OR
Florida	FL	Pennsylvania	PA
Georgia	GA	Rhode Island	RI
Hawaii	HI	South Carolina	SC
Idaho	ID	South Dakota	SD
Illinois	IL	Tennessee	TN
Indiana	IN	Texas	TX
Iowa	IA	Utah	UT
Kansas	KS	Vermont	VT
Kentucky	KY	Virginia	VA
Louisiana	LA	Washington	WA
Maine	ME	West Virginia	WV
Maryland	MD	Wisconsin	WI
Massachusetts	MA	Wyoming	WY
Michigan	MI	American Samoa	AS
Minnesota	MN	Guam	GU
Mississippi	MS	Northern Mariana	CM
Missouri	MO	Islands	
Montana	MT	Puerto Rico	PR
Nebraska	NE	Virgin Islands	VI

Postal Service Employees and Offices, 1990–2000

Category	1990	2000
Employees		
Headquarters (Washington, D.C.)	2,291	2,279
Field support units	5,691	5,566
Inspection services (field)	4,259	4,190
Area offices	N.A.	1,597
Postmasters	26,995	26,121
Supervisors, managers	43,458	38,797
Professional, administrative, and technical personnel	9,793	9,959
Clerks	290,380	281,956
Nurses	286	191
Mailhandlers	51,123	60,851
City delivery carriers	236,081	241,079
Motor vehicle operators	7,308	9,347
Rural delivery carriers (full-time)	42,252	57,111
Special delivery messengers	2,012	0
Building and equipment maintenance personnel	33,323	42,284
Vehicle maintenance personnel	4,874	5,546
Total career employees	760,668	787,538
Non-career employees	26,829	29,572
Offices, stations and branches	40,067	38,060
Post offices	28,959	27,876
Stations and branches	11,108	10,184
Classified stations and branches	5,008	5,802
Contract stations and branches	4,397	2,833
Community post offices	1,703	1,549

Source: U.S. Postal Service, 2000 Annual Report.

Despite the advent of overnight delivery services, fax machines, the total volume of mail continues to grow faster than the Postal Service loses market share. In 1988, the Postal Service delivered 77 percent of all business and personal correspondence, which was then a $25.9 billion business. In 1996, the Postal Service's share of that market had slipped to 59 percent, but the total amount of correspondence had nearly doubled, to $48 billion. In other words, the Postal Service lost millions of potential customers but nevertheless increased its revenues from $19.9 billion to $28.3 billion.

Zip Codes   There are about 42,000 separate ZIP codes in the U.S.; the number is constantly changing. A national ZIP code directory is available in every post office. Directory assistance telephone operators can also provide ZIP code information. You can also find ZIP codes for almost any address at **www.cedar.buffalo.edu/adserv.html**, a site run by the State University of New York at Buffalo. The site also shows maps of the surrounding area.

The price of a first-class letter is 19 cents in Mexico, 24 cents in Australia, 36 cents in Italy, 40 cents in France and Great Britain, 50 cents in Germany, 52 cents in Switzerland, 74 cents in Japan, and 34 cents in the U.S.

States, Territories, and Possessions

This section, a compilation of history and statistics about the 50 United States, the District of Columbia, and U.S. territories and possessions, includes a brief history of each state and territory; its official motto and other emblems; a summary of geographic, demographic, and economic facts; and a list of prominent natives, places, and dates.

Statistical sources include the U.S. Census Bureau's 2000 decennial census and *The Statistical Abstract* (annual); the Council of State Government's *Book of the States* and *State Elective Officials and the Legislatures*; and the Bureau of Economic Analysis's *Survey of Current Business*.

The headings for demographic statistics in the paragraphs on People and Language conform to U.S. Census Bureau usage, except "Black" is used as short for Black or African American, "Indian" is used for American Indian and Alaska Native, and "Pacific Islander" is used for Native Hawaiian and other Pacific Islander. Note that Hispanics may be of any race.

Estimates of the Resident Population by State, 1990-2000

State	Population ('000s)		Change 1990 to 2000	
	2000 Census	1990 Census	Number	Percent
United States	281,422	248,710	32,712	13.2%
Alabama	4,447	4,041	407	10.1
Alaska	627	550	77	14.0
Arizona	5,131	3,665	1,465	40.0
Arkansas	2,673	2,351	323	13.7
California	33,872	29,760	4,112	13.8
Colorado	4,301	3,294	1,007	30.6
Connecticut	3,406	3,287	118	3.6
Delaware	784	666	117	17.6
District of Columbia	572	607	-35	-5.7
Florida	15,982	12,938	3,044	23.5
Georgia	8,186	6,478	1,708	26.4
Hawaii	1,212	1,108	103	9.3
Idaho	1,294	1,007	287	28.5
Illinois	12,419	11,431	989	8.6
Indiana	6,080	5,544	536	9.7
Iowa	2,926	2,777	150	5.4
Kansas	2,688	2,478	211	8.5
Kentucky	4,042	3,685	356	9.7
Louisiana	4,469	4,220	249	5.9
Maine	1,275	1,228	47	3.8
Maryland	5,296	4,781	515	10.8
Massachusetts	6,349	6,016	333	5.5
Michigan	9,938	9,295	643	6.9
Minnesota	4,919	4,375	544	12.4
Mississippi	2,845	2,573	271	10.5
Missouri	5,595	5,117	478	9.3
Montana	902	799	103	12.9
Nebraska	1,711	1,578	133	8.4
Nevada	1,998	1,202	796	66.3
New Hampshire	1,236	1,109	127	11.4
New Jersey	8,414	7,730	684	8.9
New Mexico	1,819	1,515	304	20.1
New York	18,976	17,990	986	5.5
North Carolina	8,049	6,629	1,421	21.4
North Dakota	642	639	3	0.5
Ohio	11,353	10,847	506	4.7
Oklahoma	3,451	3,146	305	9.7
Oregon	3,421	2,842	579	20.4
Pennsylvania	12,281	11,882	399	3.4
Rhode Island	1,048	1,003	45	4.5
South Carolina	4,012	3,487	525	15.1
South Dakota	755	696	59	8.5
Tennessee	5,689	4,877	812	16.7
Texas	20,852	16,987	3,865	22.8
Utah	2,233	1,723	510	29.6
Vermont	609	563	46	8.2
Virginia	7,079	6,187	891	14.4
Washington	5,894	4,867	1,027	21.1
West Virginia	1,808	1,793	15	0.8
Wisconsin	5,364	4,892	472	9.6
Wyoming	494	454	40	8.9

Note: Includes armed forces residing in each state.
Source: U.S. Bureau of the Census, 2001. www.census.gov

▶ALABAMA

The memory of the Native American presence is particularly strong in Alabama. Trade with the Northeast via the Ohio River valley began during the Burial Mound Period (1000 B.C.–A.D. 700) and continued until European contact. Meso-American influence is evident in the agrarian Mississippian culture that followed. Pressured by white settlers in the early 19th century, the Creeks warred against the U.S. government until defeated by General Andrew Jackson.

The cradle of the Confederacy during the Civil War, Alabama was at stage center in the civil rights movement of the 1950s and 1960s. Although cotton is still a major crop, the northern part of the state around Birmingham is a major industrial area with abundant coal, iron ore, limestone, and electricity from the TVA. Increasingly urban—70 percent of the population lived in rural areas 50 years ago, compared with less than 40 percent today—Alabama's economy is progressing slowly, although it still ranks near last in taxes and in money spent on education.

Name Probably after Alabama tribe. **Nickname** Yellowhammer State, Heart of Dixie. **Capital** Montgomery. **Entered union** Dec. 14, 1819 (22nd). **Motto** "We dare defend our rights."
Emblems **Bird** Yellowhammer. **Dance** Square dance. **Game bird** Wild turkey. **Fish** Tarpon. **Fossil** *Basilosaurus oetoides*. **Mineral** Hematite. **Nut** Pecan. **Song** "Alabama." **Stone** Marble. **Tree** Southern (longleaf) pine.
Land Total area 51,705 sq. mi. (29th), incl. 938 sq. mi. inland water. **Borders** Tenn., Ga., Fla., Gulf of Mexico, Miss. **Rivers** Alabama, Chattahoochee, Mobile, Tennessee, Tennessee-Tombigbee Waterway, Tensaw, Tombigbee. **Lakes** Guntersville, Pickwick, Wheeler, Wilson (all formed by Tennessee Valley Authority [TVA]); Dannelly Res., Martin, Lewis Smith, Weiss. **Mountains** Cumberland, Lookout, Raccoon, Sand.
Elected officials Gov. Don Siegelman (D, term exp. 2003) Lt. Gov. Steve Windom (R). Sec. State Jim Bennett (R). Atty. Gen. William Pryor (R).
People (2000) 4,447,100 (23rd). **Race/Hispanic Origin** (2000): White 71.1%. Black 26.0%. Indian 0.5%. Asian 0.7%. Other 0.7%. Two or more races 1.0%. Hispanic 1.7%.
Cities (2000) Birmingham 242,820. Montgomery 201,568. Mobile 198,915. Huntsville 158,216. Tuscaloosa 77,906. Hoover 62,742. Dothan 57,737. Decatur 53,929. Auburn 42,987. Gadsden 38,978.

Business Gross State Product, 1997: $103.11 bil. (25th). **Leading Sectors of GSP** (1997): Manufacturing 21.45%; Services 16.64%; Government 15.26%. *Fortune* **500 Companies** (2000): 7: SCI Systems, Saks, Caremark Rx, Healthsouth, Southtrust Corp., Regions Financial, Amsouth Bancorp.

Famous natives Hank Aaron, baseball player. Tallulah Bankhead, actress. William B. Bankhead, politician. Hugo L. Black, jurist. Wernher von Braun (b. Germany), rocket scientist. Nat "King" Cole, singer. Red Eagle (William Weatherfield), Creek leader. W.C. Handy, musician. Frank M. Johnson, Jr., jurist. Helen Keller, author. Coretta Scott (Mrs. Martin Luther) King, reformer. Harper Lee, author. Joe Louis, boxer. Jesse Owens, runner. Leroy Robert "Satchell" Paige, baseball player. Walker Percy, author. George Wallace, politician. Hank Williams, singer.

Noteworthy places Alabama Deep Sea Fishing Rodeo, Dauphin Island. Alabama Space and Rocket Center, U.S. Space Camp, Huntsville. Battleship USS *Alabama*, Mobile. Birmingham Museum of Art. First White House of the Confederacy, Montgomery. Horseshoe Bend Natl. Military Park. Mound State Monument Archaeological Museum, Moundville. Museum of Natural History, Univ. Alabama, Tuscaloosa. Point Clear (resort). Russell Cave Natl. Monument. Tuskegee Institute.

Memorable events Humans first inhabit Russell Cave c. 6000 B.C. Temple Mound culture flourishes around Moundville, A.D. 1200–1500. First Europeans in Mobile Bay 1519. Hernando de Soto's battle with Tuscaloosa possibly bloodiest encounter ever between Europeans and Native Americans in U.S. 1540. Spanish at Mobile Bay 1599. Pierre Le Moyne, sieur d'Iberville, establishes first permanent colony at Mobile 1711. Treaty of Paris gives Mobile to Britain 1763. U.S. control recognized 1783. Chickasaws, Choctaws, and Cherokees cede lands to U.S. 1805. First Baptist Church established 1808. Gen. Andrew Jackson defeats Creek Indian Confederacy at Horseshoe Bend 1814. Cotton principal cash crop 1820s. Beginning of coal and iron mining and steel manufacturing 1850s. Alabama secedes from Union; first capital of Confederate States of America at Montgomery 1861. Battle of Mobile Bay 1864. Readmitted to Union 1868. Booker T. Washington founds Tuskegee Institute 1881. Destruction of cotton crops by boll weevils leads to diversification of rural economy 1915. Tennessee Valley Authority enacted by Congress 1933. Montgomery bus boycott 1955. Freedom march from Selma to Montgomery 1965.

Tourist information (800) ALABAMA. **www.state.al.us.**

▶**ALASKA**

One-fifth the size of the entire lower 48 states, Alaska is a vast, geographically varied wilderness. The coast from the Bering Sea to the Arctic was originally inhabited by Eskimos and Aleuts, while inland and to the south were Athapascans and people of the Northwest Indian culture. Russian fur traders in the 1740s were the first Europeans to recognize the region's commercial potential, and the Russian Orthodox faith is still found in the old territorial capital of Sitka (New Archangel).

Russia sold Alaska to the United States in 1867 for $7.2 million—2 cents an acre—and Alaska experienced successive booms in furs, fishing and whaling, and gold. Discovery of oil on the North Slope near Prudhoe Bay in 1968 and completion

Population Density of U.S. States, 1980–99

State	Population per square mile		
	1980	1990	1999
U.S. Total	**64.1**	**70.4**	**77.4**
Alabama	76.7	79.6	86.1
Alaska	0.7	1.0	1.1
Arizona	23.9	32.3	42.0
Arkansas	43.9	45.1	49.0
California	151.7	191.0	212.5
Colorado	27.9	31.8	39.1
Connecticut	641.4	678.5	677.4
Delaware	304.0	340.8	385.4
District of Columbia	10,397.9	9,884.4	8452.8
Florida	180.7	239.9	280.2
Georgia	94.3	111.8	134.5
Hawaii	150.2	172.5	184.6
Idaho	11.4	12.2	15.1
Illinois	205.6	205.6	218.2
Indiana	153.1	154.6	165.7
Iowa	52.1	49.7	51.4
Kansas	28.9	30.3	32.4
Kentucky	92.1	92.8	99.7
Louisiana	96.5	96.9	100.4
Maine	36.5	39.8	40.6
Maryland	431.4	489.1	529.1
Massachusetts	732.0	767.6	787.9
Michigan	163.0	163.6	173.6
Minnesota	51.2	55.0	60.0
Mississippi	53.7	54.9	59.0
Missouri	71.4	74.3	79.4
Montana	5.4	5.5	6.1
Nebraska	20.4	20.5	21.7
Nevada	7.3	10.9	16.5
New Hampshire	102.6	123.7	133.9
New Jersey	992.7	1,044.3	1097.6
New Mexico	10.7	12.5	14.3
New York	371.8	381.0	385.3
North Carolina	120.7	136.1	157.0
North Dakota	9.5	9.3	9.2
Ohio	263.7	264.9	274.9
Oklahoma	44.1	45.8	48.9
Oregon	27.4	29.6	34.5
Pennsylvania	264.7	265.1	267.6
Rhode Island	906.4	960.3	948.2
South Carolina	103.6	115.8	129.0
South Dakota	9.1	9.2	9.7
Tennessee	111.4	118.3	133.0
Texas	54.3	64.9	76.5
Utah	17.8	21.0	25.9
Vermont	55.3	60.8	64.2
Virginia	135.0	156.3	173.6
Washington	62.1	73.1	86.5
West Virginia	81.0	74.5	75.0
Wisconsin	86.6	90.1	96.7
Wyoming	4.8	4.7	4.9

Note: Persons per square mile for all years calculated on the basis of land area data from the 1990 census.
Source: *Statistical Abstract of the United States*, 2001.

of an 800-mile trans-Alaska pipeline a decade later made oil production the centerpiece of the state's economy in the 1980s. Although the population has grown by more than 10 percent during the 1990s, the number of people per square mile remains below 1.5. In recent years, tourism based on the state's extraordinary beauty, has grown substantially and now many Alaskans oppose proposed oil exploration at the Arctic National Wildlife Refuge. The memory of the *Exxon Valdez* oil spill into Prince William Sound in 1989 has had a powerful effect.

Name From Aleut *alaska* and Eskimo *alakshak*, both meaning "mainland." **Nickname** "The Last Frontier." **Capital** Juneau. **Entered union** Jan. 3, 1959 (49th). **Motto** "North to the future."
Emblems **Bird** Willow ptarmigan. **Fish** King salmon. **Flower** Forget-me-not. **Gem** Jade. **Marine mammal** Bowhead whale. **Mineral** Gold. **Song** "Alaska's Flag." **Sport** Mushing (dog-team racing). **Tree** Sitka spruce.
Land **Total area** 591,004 sq. mi. (1st), incl. 20,171 sq. mi. inland water. **Borders** Arctic Ocean (Chukchi Sea, Beaufort Sea), Yukon, British Columbia, Pacific Ocean, Bering Strait. **Rivers** Colville, Porcupine, Noatak, Yukon, Susitna, Copper, Kobuk, Koyukuk, Kuskokwim, Tanana. **Mountains** Alaska Range (Mt. McKinley 20,320 ft., highest in North America), Aleutian Range, Brooks Range, Kuskokwim, St. Elias. **Other notable features** Aleutian Islands, Alexander Archipelago, Kodiak Island, Nunivak Island, Point Barrow (71°23'N), Pribilof Islands, Seward Peninsula, St. Lawrence Island.
Elected officials Gov. Tony Knowles (D, term exp. 2002). Lt. Gov. Fran Ulmer (D). Atty. Gen. Bruce M. Botelho (D).
People (2000) 626,932 (48th). **Race/Hispanic Origin** (2000): White 69.3%. Black 3.5%. Indian 15.6%. Asian 4.0%. Pacific Islander 0.5%. Other 1.6%. Two or more races 5.4%. Hispanic 4.1%.
Cities (2000) Anchorage 260,283. Juneau 30,711. Fairbanks 30,224. Sitka 8,835. Ketchikan 7,922. Kenai 6,942. Kodiak 6,334. Bethel 5,471. Wasilla 5,469. Barrow 4,581.
Business **Gross State Product,** 1997: $24.49 bil. (45th). **Leading Sectors of GSP** (1997): Mining 21.10%; Government 19.75%; Transportation & public utilities 15.60%. *Fortune* 500 **Companies** (2000): 0.
Famous natives Aleksandr Baranov (b. Russia), first governor of Russian America. Vitus Bering (b. Denmark), explorer. Ernest Gruening (b. N.Y.), governor. Carl Ben Eielson, bush pilot. Walter Hickel (b. Kans.), governor.
Noteworthy places Aniakchak Natl. Monument. Bering Land Bridge Natl. Preserve. Cape Krusenstern Natl. Monument. Denali Natl. Park (formerly Mt. McKinley Natl. Park). Gates of the Arctic Natl. Park. Glacier Bay Natl. Park. Katmai Natl. Park (Valley of Ten Thousand Smokes). Kenai Fjords Natl. Park. Klondike Gold Rush Natl. Hist. Park. Kobuk Valley Natl. Park. Lake Clark Natl. Park. Little Diomede Island—2.5 mi. from Big Diomede Island (Russia). Sitka Natl. Hist. Park. St. Michael's Cathedral, Sitka. Wrangell–St. Elias Natl. Park.
Memorable events Earliest migration from Asia to Americas across Bering Sea land bridge, c. 15,000 years ago. Alaska inhabited by Tlingits, Tinnehs, Aleuts, and Eskimos. Peter the Great sponsors expedition to find land opposite Siberia 1728. Bering expedition lands near Mt. Elias; begins Pacific Northwest fur trade with Europe and Asia 1741. Russians establish first European settlement at Three Saints Bay 1784. Russian-American Company chartered 1799. Baranov's massacre of Tlingits at Sitka 1802. Gold discovered at Stikine Creek (1861), Juneau (1880), Fortymile Creek (1886), Nome (1898), Fairbanks (1903). Russians sell Alaska to U.S. for $7.2 million 1867. First salmon cannery established 1878. Japanese

occupy Agattu, Attu, and Kiska islands 1942–43. Alaskans vote for statehood 1946. Statehood 1959. Earthquake destroys Anchorage, Northwest Panhandle, and Cook Inlet; tsunami wipes out Valdez; coast sinks 32 ft. at Kodiak and Seward and rises 16 ft. at Cordova 1964. Oil discovered on North Slope 1968. Alaska Native Claims Settlement Act gives Alaska's Native Americans 44 million acres for native landholdings 1971. Completion of 789-mi. pipeline to Valdez 1977. Population growth of 32.8% highest in U.S. 1980–86. *Exxon Valdez* spills 10 million gallons of oil into Prince William Sound off Valdez — worst oil spill in U.S. history 1989.
Tourist information 1-907-929-2200. **www.state.ak.us.**

▶ARIZONA

The Hopi village of Oraibi is the oldest continuously inhabited town in the United States, and today vast tracts of Arizona are reserved for Apaches, Hopis, Navajos, Papagos and other Native Americans. Last of the 48 conterminous states admitted to the union, Arizona was sparsely settled until the advent of air conditioning in the postwar years made it habitable and a popular destination for retirees. More recently, there has been a boom in manufacturing and light industry, and in the last decade, population growth has been among the highest in the nation. Mexican-Americans are an important political force.

As in most southwestern states, water scarcity is a major problem. Arizona draws 2.8 million acre-feet of water from the Colorado River, whose water it shares with 5 other states and Mexico.
Name Probably from the Pima or Papago for "place of small springs." **Nickname** Grand Canyon State. **Capital** Phoenix. **Entered union** Feb. 14, 1912 (48th). **Motto** *Ditat deus* (God enriches).
Emblems **Bird** Cactus wren. **Flower** Blossom of the saguaro cactus. **Gemstone** Turquoise. **Official neck wear** Bolo tie. **Songs** "Arizona March Song," "Arizona." **Tree** Palo verde.
Land **Total area** 114,000 sq. mi. (6th), incl. 492 sq. mi. inland water. **Borders** Utah, Colo., N.Mex., Sonora, Baja California Norte, Calif., Nev. **Rivers** Colorado, Gila, Little Colorado, Salt, Zuni. **Lakes** Havasu, Mead, Mohave, Powell, Roosevelt, San Carlos. **Mountains** Black, Gila, Hualpai, Mohawk, San Francisco Peaks (Humphreys Peak 12,633 ft.). **Other notable features** Grand Canyon, Kaibab Plateau, Painted and Sonoran Deserts, Petrified Forest.
Elected officials Gov. Jane Dee Hull (R, term exp. 2003). Atty. Gen. Janet Napolitano (D). Sec. State Betsy Bayless (R).
People (2000) 5,130,632 (20th). **Race/Hispanic Origin** (2000): White 75.5%. Black 3.1%. Indian 5.0%. Asian 1.8%. Pacific Islander 0.1%. Other 11.6%. Two or more races 2.9%. Hispanic 25.3%.
Cities (2000) Phoenix 1,321,045. Tucson 486,699. Mesa 396,375. Glendale 218,812. Scottsdale 202,705. Chandler 176,581. Tempe 158,625. Gilbert 109,697. Peoria 108,364. Yuma 77,515.
Business **Gross State Product,** 1997: $121.24 bil. (24th). **Leading Sectors of GSP** (1997): Services 20.60%; Finance, insurance, and real estate 19.41%; Manufacturing 14.69%. *Fortune* 500 **Companies** (2000): 5: Avnet, Allied Waste Industries, Phelps Dodge, Pinnacle West Capital, Microage.
Famous natives Bruce Babbitt, politician. Cesar Chavez, labor leader. Cochise, Apache chief. Andrew Ellicott Douglass (b. Vt.), dendrochronologist. Wyatt Earp (b. Ill.), lawman. Barry Goldwater, politician. Goyathlay (Geronimo), Apache chieftain. Carl T. Hayden, congressman. Eusebio Kino

(b. Italy), missionary. Sandra Day O'Connor, jurist. William H. Rehnquist, jurist. Linda Ronstadt, singer. Morris Udall, politician.

Noteworthy Places   Canyon de Chelly Natl. Monument. Casa Grande Ruins Natl. Monument. Chiricahua Natl. Monument. Ft. Bowie. Grand Canyon Natl. Park. Heard Museum, Phoenix. London Bridge, Lake Havasu City. Montezuma Castle Natl. Monument. Navajo Natl. Monument. Organ Pipe Cactus Natl. Monument. Painted Desert. Petrified Forest Natl. Park. Pipe Spring Natl. Monument. Saguaro Natl. Monument. Slot canyons, Upper and Lower Antelope Canyons, near Page. Sunset Crater Natl. Monument. Taliesin West, near Scottsdale. Tonto Natl. Monument. Tumacacori Natl. Monument. Tuzigoot Natl. Monument. Walnut Canyon Natl. Monument. Wupatki Natl. Monument.

Memorable events   Apaches and Navajos absorb Pueblos c. A.D. 1000. Alvar Núñez Cabeza de Vaca, first Spanish explorer 1536. Marcos de Niza 1539. Ruled as part of New Spain 1598–1821. First missionaries among Hopis 1638. Tubac first European settlement 1752. Tucson founded 1776. Apaches wipe out settlements under Mexican control, except Tucson 1821. Northern part ceded to U.S. following Mexican War 1848. Area south of Gila River to U.S. after Gadsden Purchase 1853. Territory 1863. Southern Pacific Railroad reaches Tucson 1880. Apaches subjugated 1886. Congress refuses to grant statehood 1906. Roosevelt Dam and Reservoir built on Salt River 1911. Native Americans given right to vote 1948. Glen Canyon Dam built on Colorado River 1964. Population growth of 24.3 percent is second highest in U.S., 1990–97.

Tourist information   (888) 520-3433. www.state.az.us.

▶**ARKANSAS**

First inhabited by bluff dwellers 10,000 years ago, the Boston and Ouachita mountains of western Arkansas are the only mountains between the Appalachians and the Rockies. By the time of the Hernando De Soto expedition of 1541, Arkansas was inhabited by a variety of peoples: the agrarian Quapaws to the south, the Caddo to the west and south, the Osage to the north, and the Chickasaw and Choctaw in the northeast. The Arkansas Post, the first permanent settlement in the Mississippi Valley, became the pillar of the French claim to the region that became the Louisiana Purchase.

Not fully part of the deep south, and cut off geographically from the Midwest, Arkansas has developed slowly. Although cotton was a mainstay of the economy and Arkansas joined the Confederacy during the Civil War, it was the first southern state to have integrated public colleges after World War II, a fact overshadowed by Gov. Orville Faubus's resistance to the integration of the Little Rock public schools. In recent years, Arkansas has attracted manufacturing and industry, but has one of the highest rural populations and ranks low in services, income, and education attainment.

Name From term for Quapaw tribe given by other Indians. **Nickname** Land of Opportunity. **Capital** Little Rock. **Entered union** June 15, 1836 (25th). **Motto** *Regnat populus* (Let the people rule). **Emblems Bird** Mockingbird. **Flower** Apple blossom. **Gem** Diamond. **Song** "Arkansas." **Tree** Pine. **Land Total area** 53,187 sq. mi. (27th), incl. 1,109 sq. mi. inland water. **Borders** Mo., Tenn, Miss., La., Tex., Okla. **Rivers** Arkansas, Mississippi, Ouachita, Red, St. Francis, White. **Lakes** Beaver,

Bull Shoals, Chicot, Dardanelle, Greers Ferry, Greeson, Norfolk, Ouachita. **Other notable features** Ozark Mts.

Elected officials   Gov. Mike Huckabee (R, term exp. 2003). Lt. Gov. Winthrop P. Rockefeller (R). Sec. State Sharon Priest (D). Atty. Gen. Mark Pryor (D).

People   (2000) 2,673,400 (33rd). **Race/Hispanic Origin** (2000): White 80.0%. Black 15.7%. Indian 0.7%. Asian 0.8%. Pacific Islander 0.1%. Other 1.3%. Two or more races 1.3%. Hispanic 3.2%.

Cities   (2000) Little Rock 183,133. Fort Smith 80,268. North Little Rock 60,433. Fayetteville 58,047. Jonesboro 55,515. Pine Bluff 55,085. Springdale 45,798. Conway 43,167. Rogers 38,829. Hot Springs 35,750.

Business   Gross State Product, 1997: $58.48 bil. (32nd). **Leading Sectors of GSP** (1997): Manufacturing 23.95%; Services 15.15%; Government 11.94%. *Fortune* **500 Companies** (2000): 5: Wal-Mart Stores, Dillard's, Tyson Foods, Alltel, Murphy Oil.

Famous natives   Maya Angelou, author. Linda Bloodworth-Thomason, television producer/director. Glen Campbell, singer. Hattie W. Caraway, first woman senator. Johnny Cash, singer. Eldridge Cleaver, author. Bill Clinton, U.S. president. William Fulbright (b. Mo.), politician. Alan Ladd, actor. Douglas MacArthur, general. Dick Powell, actor. Brooks Robinson, baseball player. Winthrop Rockefeller (b. N.Y.), politician/philanthropist. Edward Durrell Stone, architect. C. Vann Woodward, historian.

Noteworthy places   Arkansas Post Natl. Monument (first permanent French settlement in lower Mississippi Valley). Buffalo Natl. River. Crater of Diamonds State Park, Murfreesboro. Eureka Springs. Ft. Smith Natl. Hist. Site. Hot Springs Natl. Park. Pea Ridge Natl. Military Park.

Memorable Events   Bluff-dwellers present c. A.D. 500, followed by mound-building cultures. Hernando de Soto explores for Spain 1541. Jacques Marquette and Louis Jolliet explore for France 1673. René-Robert de La Salle meets Quapaws 1682. Henri de Tonti founds Arkansas Post on Arkansas River 1686. Ceded from France to Spain 1782; to France 1800; to U.S. 1803. Territory 1819. Admitted to Union as slave state, under terms of 1820 Missouri Compromise, 1836. Secedes from Union 1861. Fall of Little Rock to Union army 1863. Readmitted to Union 1868. Bauxite discovered 1887. Oil production begins 1920s. Federal troops called to Little Rock to ensure high school desegregation 1957. Winthrop Rockefeller (b. N.Y.) first Republican governor since Reconstruction 1966. McClellan-Kerr Arkansas River Navigation System links Arkansas and Oklahoma to Mississippi River system 1971. Governor Bill Clinton Elected U.S. President 1992.

Tourist information   (800) NATURAL or (800) 482-8999. www.state.ar.us.

▶**CALIFORNIA**

Before the arrival of Europeans, no area of comparable size in North America was home to a greater variety of languages and cultures than what is now California, and today the state's population is more diverse than that of any other. In 2001, non-Hispanic whites became a minority of California's population; by 2040, demographers project that the majority of Californians will be Hispanic.

The largest state by population since the 1960s, California gained seven Congressional representatives in the 1990 Census redistricting, and one more in 2000. By some estimates, California is the sixth largest economic power in the world.

Despite these attractions, and the state's rugged terrain and dramatic vistas, California has problems. The state's position as a leader in agriculture masks an alarming lack of water. It already draws off 4.4 million acre-feet annually from the Colorado River, mostly for irrigating the Imperial Valley—a desert when settlers crossed it 150 years ago. Almost the entire flow of the San Joaquin River is similarly diverted for the Central Valley. This inefficient use of water leaves less and less for consumption by people, whose numbers have leaped from 15 million in 1960 to over 32 million today.

Of more immediate concern is the threat of earthquakes. California has already suffered eight major earthquakes in this century. The 1906 quake destroyed San Francisco, and the Loma Prieta earthquake on October 17, 1989—one of the most powerful quakes in U.S. history—killed 67 people, left 48,000 people homeless and resulted in $10 billion of property damage. Like surfers waiting for the perfect wave, scientists are still bracing for "the big one."

Name Probably from mythical island in García Ordoñez de Montalvo's 16th-century romance, *The Deeds of Esplandián.* **Nickname** Golden State. **Capital** Sacramento. **Entered union** Sept. 9, 1850 (31st). **Motto** "Eureka" (I have found it). **Emblems Animal** California grizzly bear (extinct). **Bird** California valley quail. **Fish** California golden trout. **Flower** Golden poppy. **Fossil** California saber-toothed cat. **Gemstone** Benitoite. **Insect** California dog-face butterfly. **Marine mammal** California gray whale. **Mineral** Gold. **Reptile** California desert tortoise. **Rock** Serpentine. **Song** "I Love You, California." **Tree** California redwood. **Land** Total area 158,706 sq. mi. (3rd), incl. **2,407** sq. mi. inland water. **Borders** Oreg., Nev., Ariz., Baja California Norte, Pacific Ocean. **Rivers** American, Colorado, Colorado River Aqueduct, Eel, Friant-Kern Canal, Klamath, Russian, Sacramento, Salinas, San Joaquin. **Lakes** Clear, Goose, Honey, Mono, Owens, Salton Sea, Shasta, Tahoe. **Mountains** Coast Ranges, Klamath, Lassen Peak, Sierra Nevada (Mt. Whitney 14,494 ft.). **Other notable features** Catalina Islands, Death Valley (282 ft. below sea level), San Francisco Bay, San Joaquin Valley.

Elected officials Gov. Gray Davis (D term exp. 2003). Lt. Gov. Cruz Bustamante (D) Sec. State Bill Jones (R). Atty. Gen. Bill Lockyer (D).

People (2000) 33,871,648 (1st). **Race/Hispanic Origin** (2000): White 59.5%. Black 6.7%. Indian 1.0%. Asian 10.9%. Pacific Islander 0.3%. Other 16.8%. Hispanic 32.4%.

Cities (2000) Los Angeles 3,694,820. San Diego 1,223,400. San Jose 894,943. San Francisco 776,733. Long Beach 461,522. Fresno 427,652. Sacramento 407,018. Oakland 399,484. Santa Ana 337,977. Anaheim 328,014.

Business Gross State Product, 1997: $1.043 tril. (1st). **Leading Sectors of GSP** (1997): Finance, insurance, and real estate 22.97%; Services 22.94%; Manufacturing 14.15%. *Fortune* **500 Companies** (2000): 55: including Hewlett-Packard, Chevron, McKesson HBOC, Intel, Safeway, Ingram Micro, Wells Fargo, Walt Disney, PG&E Corp., Bergen Brunswig, Cisco Systems, Sun Microsystems, Occidental Petroleum, Solectron, Gap, Edison International, Pacificare Health Systems, Tenet Healthcare, Fluor, Oracle, Gateway, Applied Materials, Computer Sciences, Wellpoint Health Networks, Unocal, Health Net, Northrop Grumman, Apple Computer, Sempra Energy, Charles Schwab.

Famous natives Ansel Adams, photographer. Dave Brubeck, musician. Luther Burbank (b. Mass.), horticulturist. John Cage, composer. Joe DiMaggio, baseball player. Robert Frost, poet. Ernest and Julio Gallo (b. Italy), vintners. Pancho Gonzales, tennis player. Samuel Ichiye Hayakawa, politician/educator. William Randolph Hearst, publisher. Steve Jobs, computer scientist. Billie Jean King, tennis player. Allen Lockheed, aviator. Jack London, author. Paul Masson (b. France), vintner. Marilyn Monroe, actress. John Muir (b. Scotland), naturalist. Richard M. Nixon, U.S. president. John Northrop, aviator. Adlai Stevenson, politician. John Steinbeck, author. Levi Strauss (b. Germany), clothier. Edward Teller (b. Hungary), nuclear physicist. Shirley Temple, actress. Earl Warren, politician/jurist.

Noteworthy places Big Sur, Monterey. Cabrillo Natl. Monument. California Academy of Sciences, San Francisco. California Palace of the Legion of Honor, San Francisco. Channel Islands Natl. Park. Devils Postpile Natl. Monument. Death Valley Natl. Monument. Disneyland. Fine Arts Museum of San Francisco. Fishermen's Wharf, San Francisco. Hollywood. Huntington Library and Botanical Gardens, San Marino. J. Paul Getty Museum, Malibu. Joshua Tree Natl. Monument. Kings Canyon Natl. Park. Lassen Volcanic Natl. Park. Lava Beds Natl. Monument. Los Angeles Co. Museum of Art. Muir Woods Natl. Monument. Mt. Palomar Observatory. Natl. Maritime Museum, San Francisco. Natural History Museum, Los Angeles. Natural History Museum of San Diego. Norton Simon Museum of Art at Pasadena. Pinnacles Natl. Monument. Redwood Natl. Park. Rosicrucian Egyptian Museum, San José. San Diego Museum of Art. San Diego Museum of Man. San Diego Zoo. San Francisco Museum of Modern Art. Sequoia Natl. Park. Southwest Museum (Casa de Adobe), Los Angeles. Yosemite Natl. Park.

Memorable events João Rodrigues Cabrilho lands at San Diego Bay 1542. Francis Drake lands north of San Francisco Bay 1579. Junípero Serra founds missions at San Diego (1769), Monterey (1770), San Luis Obispo (1772), and San Juan Capistrano (1776). California declares allegiance to independent Mexico 1821. First wagon train from Missouri 1841. Gold discovered north of Los Angeles 1842. California declares itself independent republic 1846. Gold found at John Sutter's mill; nine days later, by Treaty of Guadalupe Hidalgo, Mexico cedes California to U.S. 1848. Announcement of gold discovery brings 80,000 'Forty-niners. Gold rush peaks 1852. Transcontinental telegraph completed 1861. Transcontinental railway completed 1869. U.S. Congress enacts Chinese Exclusion Act, prohibiting immigration of Chinese laborers 1882, 1892, and 1902; Act repealed 1943. San Francisco earthquake kills 452, destroys 28,000 buildings 1906. Webb Alien Land Law prohibits Japanese from holding land 1913. Los Angeles has one car for every three people, twice national average, 1925. Dust Bowl immigrants 1930. Hollywood produces bulk of movies for U.S. theaters, which number more than banks 1940. Most populous state 1963. Proposition 13 limits property tax, 1978. Loma Prieta earthquake registers 7.1 on Richter scale — second most powerful in U.S. history; 67 dead, 48,000 homeless, and $10 billion in property damage, 1989. Riots in Los Angeles kill 60 and cause $1 billion in damage, 1992.

Tourist information (800) TO-CALIF. **www.state.ca.us.**

►COLORADO

The native peoples of Colorado were the Plains Indians (Arapahoe and Cheyenne) to the east and Great Basin Indians (Utes) to the west. This pre-Columbian division of the land is reflected today in Colorado's economy, which is a mix of agriculture and technology in the east and mining and ski tourism in the mountains. During the oil price shocks of the 1970s, shale-oil production on the Western Slope created a boom comparable to Colorado's silver and lead boom in the late 19th century. During the 1990s, strong job growth has attracted many young people: the population has increased by more than 18 percent, while the percentage of people over 65 has fallen to 10 percent, one of the lowest in the nation. While a state of great natural beauty, it must cope with a high altitude that almost doubles the effect of auto emissions. Economic development means in large part resource extraction and requires more and more water, whose limited supply poses a great question for the future.

Name For Spanish for the color red. **Nickname** Centennial State. **Capital** Denver. **Entered union** Aug. 1, 1876 (38th). **Motto** *Nil sine numine* (Nothing without providence).

Emblems **Animal** Rocky Mountain bighorn sheep. **Bird** Lark bunting. **Flower** Rocky Mountain Columbine. **Gem** Aquamarine. **Song** "Where the Columbines Grow." **Tree** Colorado blue spruce.

Land **Total area** 104,091 sq. mi. (8th), incl. **496** sq. mi. inland water. **Borders** Wyo., Nebr., Kans., N.Mex., Ariz., Utah. **Rivers** Arkansas, Colorado, Green, Platte, Rio Grande. **Lakes** Blue Mesa, Dillon, Granby. **Mountains** Front Range, Laramie, Sangre de Cristo, San Juan, Sawatch Range (Mt. Elbert 14,443 ft.).

Elected officials Gov. Bill Owens (R, term exp. 2003). Lt. Gov. Joe Rogers (R). Sec. State Donetta Davidson (R). Atty. Gen. Ken Salazar (D).

People (2000) 4,301,261 (24th). **Race/Hispanic Origin** (2000): White 82.8%. Black 3.8%. Indian 1.0%. Asian 2.2%. Pacific Islander 0.1%. Other 7.2%. Two or more races 2.8%. Hispanic 17.1%.

Cities (2000) Denver 554,636. Colorado Springs 360,890. Aurora 276,393. Lakewood 144,126. Fort Collins 118,652. Arvada 102,153. Pueblo 102,121. Westminster 100,940. Boulder 94,673. Thornton 82,384.

Business **Gross State Product,** 1997: $126.08 bil. (22nd). **Leading Sectors of GSP** (1997): Services 22.09%; Finance, insurance, and real estate 17.36%; Government 12.60%. **Fortune 500 Companies** (2000): 4: Qwest Communications, Transmontaigne, Ball, Western Gas Resources.

Famous natives Charlie Bent (b. Va.), trapper. "Unsinkable" Molly Brown, *Titanic* survivor. Scott Carpenter, astronaut. Lon Chaney, actor. Jack Dempsey, boxer. Mamie Eisenhower, first lady. Douglas Fairbanks, actor. Scott Hamilton, ice skater. Anne Parrish, novelist. Lowell Thomas, journalist. Byron R. White, jurist.

Noteworthy Places Black Canyon of the Gunnison National Park. Buffalo Bill grave site, Evergreen. Central City Opera House. Colorado Springs Fine Arts Center. Denver Art Museum. Denver Mint. Denver Museum of Natural History. Dinosaur Natl. Monument. Florissant Fossil Beds Natl. Monument. Garden of the Gods, Colorado Springs. Great Sand Dunes Natl. Monument. Hovenweep Natl. Monument. Mesa Verde Natl. Park. Molly Brown House, Denver. Pikes Peak. Red Rocks Amphitheater. Rocky Mountain Natl. Park, Aspen. Rocky Mountain Natl. Park. U.S. Air Force Academy, Colorado Springs. U.S. Olympic Headquarters, Colorado Springs. Yucca House Natl. Monument.

Memorable events Pueblos build cliff dwellings near Mesa Verde through 1200s. Arapahos and Cheyennes settle area after 13th century. France abandons claims 1763. Juan de Uribarri explores area 1786. Spain restores area to France 1801. To United States as part of Louisiana Purchase 1803. Zebulon Pike explores for United States 1806. Kit Carson and other scouts explore and trade with Native Americans 1810s–20s. Native Americans form alliance at Brent's Fork 1840. John Frémont's explorations 1842–53. Present territorial limits after Mexican War 1848. First permanent settlement at San Luis 1851. Gold found west of Denver—"Pike's Peak or Bust"—1858. Mineral springs bring first tourists 1861. Homestead Act encourages farming 1862. U.S. Army kills 400 Cheyenne at Sand Creek Massacre 1864. Utes and Cheyennes fight white settlement through 1870s. John Wesley Powell and nine others navigate Colorado River from the Green River branch in Wyoming to the end of Grand Canyon in Arizona 1869. Railroad link to Denver 1870. Silver and lead discoveries 1875. Uranium discovered near Grand Junction 1946. U.S. Air Force Academy founded Denver 1954; to Colorado Springs 1958. Shale oil boom on Western Slope 1974 and 1979. Accumulation of nuclear waste threatens suspension of operations at Rocky Flats 1988.

Tourist information (800) COLORADO. www.state.co.us.

►CONNECTICUT

Called the "arsenal of the nation" during the Revolution, Connecticut remained in modern times the leader among the 50 states in defense-contract dollars per capita. In recent years, this has caused a serious dislocation in the economy as the nation downsizes its military capabilities. Still, as home to over a dozen *Fortune* 500 companies (including several major insurance companies), and with easy access to New York City, Connecticut remains the state with the highest per capita income in the country.

Severe budget deficits in 1991 forced passage of a state income tax and helped to reveal the disparities in wealth between the very rich suburbs and the decaying industrial cities such as Bridgeport. As the economy is being retooled, population has actually declined slightly.

Name From Mahican word meaning "beside the long tidal river." **Nicknames** Constitution State, Nutmeg State. **Capital** Hartford. **Entered union** Jan. 9, 1788 (5th). **Motto** *Qui transtulit sustinet* (He who transplanted still sustains).

Emblems **Animal** Sperm whale. **Bird** American robin. **Flower** Mountain laurel. **Hero** Nathan Hale. **Insect** European praying mantis. **Mineral** Garnet. **Ship** USS *Nautilus*. **Song** "Yankee Doodle." **Tree** White oak.

Land **Total area** 5,018 sq. mi. (48th), incl. **146** sq. mi. inland water. **Borders** Mass., R.I., Long Island Sound, N.Y. **Rivers** Connecticut, Housatonic, Mianus, Naugatuck, Thames. **Lakes** Bantam, Barkhamstead, Candlewood, Waramaug. **Other notable features** Berkshire Hills, Long Island Sound.

Elected officials Gov. John G. Rowland (R, term exp. 2003). Lt. Gov. M. Jodi Rell (R). Sec. State Susan Bysiewicz (D). Atty. Gen. Richard Blumenthal (D).

People (2000) 3,405,565 (29th). **Race/Hispanic Origin** (2000): White 81.6%. Black 9.1%. Indian 0.3%. Asian 2.4%. Other 4.3%. Two or more races 2.2%. Hispanic 9.4%.
Cities (2000) Bridgeport 139,529. New Haven 123,626. Hartford 121,578. Stamford 117,083. Waterbury 107,271. Norwalk 82,951. Danbury 74,848. New Britain 71,538. West Hartford 63,589. Greenwich 61,101.
Business **Gross State Product,** 1997: $134.57 bil. (21st). **Leading Sectors of GSP** (1997): Finance, insurance, and real estate 28.97%; Services 21.69%; Manufacturing 16.73%. *Fortune* **500 Companies** (2000): 13: General Electric, Aetna, United Technologies, Tosco, Xerox, Hartford Financial Services, Union Carbide, Northeast Utilities, Praxair, Pitney Bowes, Oxford Health Plans, Ames Department Stores, Emcor Group.
Famous natives Benedict Arnold, traitor. P.T. Barnum, showman. Lyman Beecher, theologian. John Brown, abolitionist. Samuel Colt, inventor. Jonathan Edwards, theologian. Charles Goodyear, inventor. Nathan Hale, patriot. Katharine Hepburn, actress. Charles Ives, composer. J.P. Morgan, financier. Ralph Nader, consumer advocate. Frederick Law Olmsted, landscape architect. Harriet Beecher Stowe, author. John Trumbell, artist. Noah Webster, lexicographer. Eli Whitney, inventor.
Noteworthy places Charles Ives Center, Danbury. Eugene O'Neill Memorial Theater Center, Waterford. Gilette Castle. Housatonic State Park. Mark Twain House, Hartford. Mystic Marinelife Aquarium. Mystic Seaport. Norwalk Maritime Center. U.S. Coast Guard Academy. USS *Nautilus*, New London. Wadsworth Atheneum, Hartford. Whitney Museum of Modern Art, Stamford. Yale Center for British Art, New Haven. Yale University, New Haven.
Memorable events Adriaen Block claims for Dutch 1614. First English settlement in Windsor 1633. Royal charter of 1662 hidden in Charter Oak 1687. *Hartford Courant*, oldest continuously published newspaper in U.S., first published 1764. Samuel Colt develops six-shooter 1835. Horace Wells uses first anesthesia 1844. Elias Howe invents sewing machine 1845. U.S. Coast Guard Academy founded New London 1876. First woman governor elected in her own right, Ella T. Grasso, 1974.
Tourist information (800) CT-BOUND. www.state.ct.us.

▶**DELAWARE**
The du Pont family has enjoyed a political and economic prominence in Delaware unmatched in the history of the other 49 states. Seven generations ago E.I. du Pont de Nemours and Co. was founded as a gunpowder mill, then grew into a monopoly, and in the wake of World War I, diversified into today's giant, with interests in banking, media, and real estate. Only half the size of Los Angeles County, Delaware was called the corporate state by Ralph Nader's "raiders" in 1973. Its liberal incorporation laws have led more than half the *Fortune* 500 companies to incorporate there. (A total of more than 170,000 corporations are incorporated in Delaware). It was one of the few states to prosper even during the recessions of the early 1980s and early 1990s.
   Name For Thomas West, Lord De La Warre, colonial governor of Virginia. **Nicknames** First State, Diamond State. **Capital** Dover. **Entered union** Dec. 7, 1787 (1st). **Motto** "Liberty and Independence."

Emblems **Bird** Blue hen chicken. **Fish** Weakfish. **Flower** Peach blossom. **Insect** Ladybug. **Rock** Sillimanite. **Song** "Our Delaware." **Tree** American holly.
Land Total area 2,044 sq. mi. (49th), incl. 112 sq. mi. inland water. **Borders** Pa., N.J., Atlantic Ocean, Md. **Rivers** Chesapeake & Delaware Canal, Delaware, Nanticoke.
Elected officials Gov. Ruth Ann Minner (D, term exp. 2005). Lt. Gov. John Carney (D). Sec. State Harriet Smith Windsor (D). Atty. Gen. M. Jane Brady (R).
People (2000) 783,600 (45th). **Race/Hispanic Origin** (2000): White 74.6%. Black 19.2%. Indian 0.3%. Asian 2.1%. Other 2.0%. Two or more races 1.7%. Hispanic 4.8%.
Cities (2000) Wilmington 72,664. Dover 32,135. Newark 28,547. Milford 6,732. Seaford 6,699. Middletown 6,161. Elsmere 5,800. Smyrna 5,679. New Castle 4,862. Georgetown 4,643.
Business **Gross State Product,** 1997: $31.59 bil. (41st). **Leading Sectors of GSP** (1997): Finance, insurance, and real estate 39.09%; Manufacturing 19.34%; Services 14.19%. *Fortune* **500 Companies** (2000): 3: E.I. DuPont Nemours, MBNA, Conectiv.
Famous natives Valerie Bertinelli, actress. John Dickinson (b. Md.), Penman of the Revolution. Eleuthère I. du Pont, manufacturer. Pierre S. ("Pete") du Pont, politician. Morgan Edwards, founder of Brown University (R.I.). Thomas Macdonough, navy officer. Howard Pyle, illustrator. Edward R. Squibb, physician/manufacturer. Christopher Ward, historian.
Noteworthy places Brandywine Zoo, Wilmington. Delaware Art Museum, Wilmington. Delaware State Museum, Dover. Dover Downs International Speedway. Grand Opera House, Wilmington. Hagley Museum, Wilmington. Rehoboth Beach.
Memorable events Dutch arrive 1631. Swedes establish first permanent settlement at Wilmington 1638. Captured by Dutch 1655. To England 1664. Part of territory granted to William Penn 1682. Breaks off from Pennsylvania; first to ratify Constitution 1787. E.I. du Pont de Nemours Co. founded 1802. Railroad connects Wilmington to Philadelphia and Baltimore 1838. Though slave state, sides with Union during Civil War 1861–65. Delaware last state to abolish whipping post (last used 1952) 1972.
Tourist information (800) 441-8846. www.state.de.us.

▶**DISTRICT OF COLUMBIA**
Chosen as the site for the nation's capital by George Washington, Washington, D.C., was carved out of land ceded by Maryland and Virginia. Although under Federal jurisdiction, the District has petitioned for statehood as New Columbia. In 1961 Congress enacted the 23rd Amendment granting citizens of D.C. the right to vote in Presidential elections for the first time, and 10 years later gave the District a nonvoting delegate to the House of Representatives. The District's largest employer is the federal government, and printing is the largest industry. Pres. John F. Kennedy called it a city of "Southern efficiency and Northern charm," but since his time, the city has become a leading patron of the arts. The problems of any large city are made worse by the city's largely transient population of government workers. The city, as the seat of the U.S. Government is a mecca for tourists from around the

world, and more than 17 million people visit it each year.

Name After Christopher Columbus; Columbia was commonly used for the United States before 1800. **Nickname** None. **Capital** Washington. **Became capital** Dec. 1, 1800. **Motto** *Justitia omnibus* (Justice for all).

Emblems **Bird** Wood thrush. **Flower** American beauty rose. **Tree** Scarlet oak.

Land **Total area** 69 sq. mi., incl. 6 sq. mi. inland water. **Borders** Md., Va. **Rivers** Anacostia, Potomac.

Elected officials Mayor Anthony A. Williams (D, term exp. 2003).

People (2000) 572,059 (N.A.). **Race/Hispanic Origin** (2000): White 30.8%. Black 60.0%. Indian 0.3%. Asian 2.7%. Pacific Islander 0.1%. Other 3.8%. Two or more races 2.4%. Hispanic 7.9%.

Business **Gross State Product,** 1997: $52.37 bil. (N.A.). **Leading Sectors of GSP** (1997): Government 37.12%; Services 32.40%; Finance, insurance, and real estate 18.20%. *Fortune* 500 **Companies** (2000): 2: Fannie Mae, Danaher.

Famous natives Edward Albee, playwright. Carl Bernstein, journalist. John Foster Dulles, politician. Duke Ellington, composer. J. Edgar Hoover, FBI director. Marjorie Kinnan Rawlings, novelist. John Philip Sousa, composer.

Noteworthy places The Capitol. Chesapeake & Ohio Canal Natl. Hist. Park. Corcoran Gallery of Art. Dumbarton Oaks. FDR Memorial. Folger Shakespeare Library. Freer Gallery of Art. Hirshhorn Museum. Jefferson Memorial. Kennedy Center. Korean War Veterans Memorial. Library of Congress. Lincoln Memorial. Natl. Air and Space Museum. Natl. Gallery of Art. Natl. Museum of African Art. Natl. Museum of American Art. Natl. Museum of American History. Natl. Museum of Natural History. Natl. Portrait Gallery. Naval Observatory. Navy Memorial Museum. Renwick Gallery. Smithsonian Institution. Vietnam Veterans Memorial. Washington Monument. Washington Zoo. White House. Woodrow Wilson House.

Memorable events Originally part of Maryland. Congress approves plan to secure land for seat of Federal Government, no more than 10 miles square, on land in Virginia and Maryland 1787. George Washington commissions Pierre Charles l'Enfant to lay out city 1791. Government moves 1800. British sail up the Potomac and burn capital 1814. Virginia reclaims its half of District 1846. President Abraham Lincoln assassinated 1865. Coxey's Army marches on Washington 1894. The Bonus Army—17,000 veterans—marches on Washington 1932. Led by Martin Luther King, Jr., 200,000 march for Civil Rights 1963. One hundred thousand protest Vietnam War 1971. Democratic party headquarters at Watergate burglarized by men linked to President Richard M. Nixon's reelection effort 1972. Congress grants limited self-rule; mayor and city council elected 1975.

Tourist information 1-202-789-7000.
www.dc.gov.

▶**FLORIDA**

A vast network of swamps, rivers, and lakes, much of Florida is barely above sea level. Florida is home to Disney World, Cypress Gardens, the wealth-laden resort of Palm Beach, the *National Enquirer*, and the Okefenokee Swamp. The pleasant climate and proximity to the Caribbean and Latin America have attracted tourists, large populations of the elderly (almost 19 percent of the population is over 65) and immigrants. Over the last two decades, it has been one of the fastest-growing states. The

growth has brought with it, however, attendant increases in drug trafficking, racial disturbances, and environmental damage to such wildlife as the crocodile, alligator, and the Florida panther.

Name By Juan Ponce de León for Pascua Florida (Easter festival of the flowers). **Nickname** Sunshine State. **Capital** Tallahassee. **Entered union** Mar. 3, 1845 (27th). **Motto** "In God We Trust". **Poet laureate** Dr. Edmund Skellings.

Emblems **Animal** Florida panther. **Beverage** Orange juice. **Bird** Mockingbird. **Flower** Orange blossom. **Freshwater fish** Florida largemouth bass. **Gem** Moonstone. **Marine mammals** Dolphin, manatee. **Saltwater fish** Atlantic sailfish. **Shell** Horse conch. **Song** "Old Folks at Home" ("Swanee River"). **Stone** Agatized coral. **Tree** Sabal palmetto palm.

Land **Total area** 58,664 sq. mi. (22nd), incl. 4,511 sq. mi. inland water. **Borders** Ga., Atlantic Ocean, Gulf of Mexico, Ala. **Rivers** Apalachicola, Caloosahatchee, Indian, Kissimmee, Perdido, St. Johns, St. Mary's, Suwanee, Withlacoochee. **Lakes** Apopka, George, Okeechobee, Seminole. **Other notable features** Everglades, Florida Keys, Okefenokee Swamp.

Elected officials Gov. John Ellis "Jeb" Bush (R, term exp. 2003). Lt. Gov. Frank T. Brogan (R). Sec. State Katherine Harris (R). Atty. Gen. Robert A. Butterworth (D).

People (2000) 15,982,378 (4th). **Race/Hispanic Origin** (2000): White 78.0%. Black 14.6%. Indian 14.6%. Asian 0.3%. Pacific Islander 0.1%. Other 3.0%. Two or more races 2.4%. Hispanic 16.8%.

Cities (2000) Jacksonville 735,617. Miami 362,470. Tampa 303,447. St. Petersburg 248,232. Hialeah 226,419. Orlando 185,951. Fort Lauderdale 152,397. Tallahassee 150,624. Hollywood 139,357. Pembroke Pines 137,427.

Business **Gross State Product,** 1997: $380.61 bil. (5th). **Leading Sectors of GSP** (1997): Services 23.96%; Finance, insurance, and real estate 22.01%; Government 12.23%. *Fortune* 500 **Companies** (2000): 12: AutoNation, Tech Data, Publix Super Markets, Winn-Dixie Stores, Office Depot, FPL Group, Ryder System, Lennar, Spherion, Darden Restaurants, Jabil Circuit, Hughes Supply.

Famous natives Mary Bethune, educator/reformer. Faye Dunaway, actress. Chris Evert, tennis player. Zora Neale Hurston, writer. James Weldon Johnson, lawyer/novelist. Osceola, Seminole chief. Sidney Poitier, actor. A. Philip Randolph, labor leader. Edmund Kirby Smith, Confederate general. Joseph Warren "Vinegar Joe" Stillwell, army officer. Ben Vereen, actor/singer.

Noteworthy places Biscayne Natl. Park. Castillo de San Marcos, St. Augustine. Everglades Natl. Park. Florida State Museum, Gainesville. Ft. Jefferson Natl. Monument. Ft. Matanzas Natl. Monument. Kennedy Space Center, Cape Canaveral. Ringling Museum, Sarasota. St. Augustine. Walt Disney World/EPCOT Center, Orlando.

Memorable events Juan Ponce de León claims Florida for Spain 1513. French stake claim for Florida 1562; build Ft. Caroline 1564. Pedro Menéndez de Avilés founds St. Augustine, first permanent European settlement in U.S. 1565. Spain cedes Florida to United States 1819. Seminole War 1835–42. State secedes from Union 1861. Readmitted 1868. Carl Fisher begins to develop Miami Beach as resort 1912. Florida's first paper mill opens expanding forest industry 1931. More than 100,000 Cuban refugees enter United States, most through Florida, during Mariel boat lift 1980. Army Corps of Engineers announce plans to let Kissimmee River, canalized in 1971, return to natural course to Lake Okeechobee; the largest back-to-nature project ever undertaken in U.S. 1990. Hurricane Andrew causes $10 billion in damage to South Florida 1992. **Tourist information** (888) 735-2872. **www.state.fl.us.**

▶ **GEORGIA**
The largest state east of the Mississippi River, Georgia is diverse in its terrain, embracing the woods of the Blue Ridge Mountains to the north and the alligators of the Okefenokee Swamp in the south. Though two-thirds of the population are urban dwellers, Georgia's farms rank at or near the top in poultry production and are leading producers of pecans, cattle, hogs, and peanuts. Atlanta, the largest city in the South, elected Andrew Young the first black member of the U.S. Congress and Maynard Jackson the first black mayor from the South since Reconstruction. Today divisions linger in Georgia, the cities favoring a progressive stance and the rural areas clinging to some of the ways of the Old South. Some of those divisions came to a peaceful resolution in early 2001, when the state redesigned its flag to reduce the size and prominence of the Confederate cross.

Name For King George II of England 1732. **Nicknames** Empire State of the South, Peach State. **Capital** Atlanta. **Entered union** Jan. 2, 1788 (4th). **Motto** "Wisdom, justice, moderation." **Emblems Bird** Brown thrasher. **Fish** Largemouth bass. **Flower** Cherokee rose. **Fossil** Shark tooth. **Gem** Quartz. **Insect** Honeybee. **Songs** "Georgia," "Georgia on My Mind." **Tree** Live oak. **Wildflower** Azalea.
Land Total area 58,910 sq. mi. (21st), incl. 854 sq. mi. inland water. **Borders** Tenn., N.C., S.C., Atlantic Ocean, Fla., Ala. **Rivers** Altamaha, Apalachicola, Chattahoochee, Flint, Ocmulgee, Oconee, Savannah, Suwanee. **Lakes** Clark Hill, Harding, Hartwell, Seminole, Sidney Lanier, Sinclair, Walter F. George, West Point Lake. **Other notable features** Blue Ridge Mountains (Mount Enotah 4,784 ft.), Okefenokee Swamp.
Elected officials Gov. Roy Barnes (D, term exp. 2003). Lt. Gov. Mark Taylor (D). Sec. State Cathy Cox (D). Atty. Gen. Thurbert E. Baker (D).
People (2000) 8,186,453 (10th). **Race/Hispanic Origin** (2000): White 65.1%. Black 28.7%. Indian 0.3%. Asian 2.1%. Pacific Islander 0.1%. Two or more races 1.4%. Hispanic 5.3%.
Cities (2000) Atlanta 416,474. Augusta 199,775. Columbus 186,291. Savannah 131,510. Athens 101,489. Macon 97,255. Roswell 79,334. Albany 76,939. Marietta 58,748. Warner Robins 48,804.
Business Gross State Product, 1997: $229.47 bil. (10th). **Leading Sectors of GSP** (1997): Services 18.49%; Manufacturing 17.45%; Finance, insurance, and real estate 16.46%. **Fortune 500 Companies** (2000): 15: Home Depot, United Parcel Service, Bellsouth, Southern, Georgia-Pacific, Coca-Cola, Delta Air Lines, Coca-Cola Enterprises, AFLAC, Suntrust Banks, Genuine Parts, First Data, Flowers Industries, Cox Communications, Mohawk Industries.
Famous natives James Brown, singer. Erskine Caldwell, author. James Earl ("Jimmy") Carter, U.S. president. Ray Charles, musician. Ty Cobb, baseball player. James Dickey, poet. Martin Luther King, Jr., minister/reformer. Sidney Lanier, author. Little Richard, musician. Carson McCullers, author. Alexander McGillivray, Creek chief. Margaret Mitchell, author. Elijah Muhammad, religious leader. Flannery O'Connor, author. Burt

Reynolds, actor. Jackie Robinson, baseball player. Tomochichi, Yamacraw chief. Ted Turner (b. Ohio), businessman. Joanne Woodward, actress. **Noteworthy places** Chickamauga and Chattanooga Natl. Military Park. Confederate Memorial, Stone Mountain. Ft. Frederica Natl. Monument. Ft. Pulaski Natl. Monument. High Museum of Art, Atlanta. Martin Luther King Natl. Hist. Site., Atlanta. Ocmulgee Natl. Monument. Okefenokee Swamp. Savannah Historic District. **Memorable events** Hernando de Soto explores region 1540. Cotton gin invented 1793. Georgia expels Cherokee Indian tribes on Trail of Tears 1832–38. Secedes from Union 1860. Gen. William T. Sherman's 60,000 troops cut 60-mi. swathe in their "march to the sea" 1864. Formula for Coca-Cola developed by chemist in search of cure for hangover 1886. Cyclone kills 1,000 in Charleston, S.C., and Savannah 1893. Franklin D. Roosevelt dies at the Little White House, Warm Springs 1945. First state to give vote to 18-year-olds 1948. Emory University designated to receive $100-million philanthropic gift from Robert W. Woodruff 1979. Dept. of Justice rules that state's process for electing superior court judges violates 1965 Voting Rights Act 1990. Summer Olympics held in Atlanta 1996.
Tourist information (800) VISIT-GA. **www.state.ga.us.**

▶ **HAWAII**
What the air conditioner did for the Sunbelt, the jetliner has done for Hawaii, the last state to enter the Union. Because of the jet, Hawaii is a possible vacation spot for millions and welcomes 20 times the air travelers of 25 years ago. Tourism is Hawaii's key industry, attracting more than 6.5 million visitors to the state each year. Recent economic problems in Japan have had a negative effect on Hawaii's tourism numbers, and the state economy has suffered greatly as a result. Thousands of miles from both California and mainland Asia, Hawaii was originally peopled by Polynesian seafarers around A.D. 500 and has the richest ethnic mix of any state, with the lowest percentage of whites and highest percentages of Asians. It was partly fear of this diversity that stalled its statehood. A link between the United States and Asia, Hawaii is the center of U.S. defense in the Pacific and is home to 100,000 veterans, three-quarters of them veterans of Vietnam. Hawaii produces large quantities of pineapples and sugar cane, and efforts are under way to harness thermal electric power from Mauna Loa volcano.

Name Of unknown origin, perhaps from Hawaii Loa, traditional discoverer of islands, or from Hawaiki, the traditional Polynesian homeland. **Nicknames** Aloha State, Paradise of the Pacific. **Capital** Honolulu. **Entered union** Aug. 21, 1959 (50th). **Motto** *Ua mau ke ea o ka aina i ke pono* (The life of the land is perpetuated in righteousness). **Emblems Bird** Nene (Hawaiian goose). **Fish** Humuhumunukunukuapuaa (reef triggerfish). **Flower** Pua aloalo (hibiscus). **Song** "Hawaii Ponoi." **Tree** Kukui (candlenut).
Land Total area 6,470 sq. mi. (47th), incl. 45 sq. mi. inland water. Surrounded by Pacific Ocean. **Rivers** Kaukonahua Stream, Wailuku Stream. **Lakes** Halulu, Kolekole, Salt Lake, Waiia Res. **Other notable features** Pearl Harbor. Hualalai, Kilauea, Mauna Kea (13,796 ft.), and Mauna Loa volcanoes. **Main islands** Hawaii, Kauai, Lanai, Maui, Molokai, Oahu.

Elected officials Gov. Benjamin J. Cayetano (D, term exp. 2002). Lt. Gov/Sec. State, Mazie K. Hirono (D). Atty. Gen. Earl I. Anzai (D).
People (2000) 1,211,537 (42nd). **Race/Hispanic Origin** (2000): White 24.3%. Black 1.8%. Indian 0.3%. Asian 41.6%. Pacific Islander 9.4%. Other 1.3%. Two or more races 21.4%. Hispanic 7.2%.
Cities (2000) Honolulu 371,657. Hilo 40,759. Kailua 36,513. Kaneohe 34,970. Waipahu 33,108. Pearl City 30,976. Waimalu 29,371. Mililani Town 28,608. Kahului 20,146. Kihei 16,749.
Business   Gross State Product, 1997: $38.02 bil. (40th). **Leading Sectors of GSP** (1997): Finance, insurance, and real estate 22.36%; Services 22.13%; Government 21.13%. **Fortune 500 Companies** (2000): 0.
Famous natives Bernice P. Bishop, philanthropist. Sanford B. Dole, statehood advocate. Charlotte (b. Ohio) and Luther Halsey Gulick, Camp Fire Girls founders. Don Ho, singer. Daniel J. Inouye, politician. Duke Kahanamoku, swimmer. Victoria Kaiulani, last heiress presumptive to Hawaiian throne. Kamehameha I, king. Kamehameha III, king. Liliuokalani, queen. Bette Midler, singer.
Noteworthy places Bernice P. Bishop Museum, Honolulu. Diamond Head. Haleakala Natl. Park, Maui. Hawaii Volcanoes Natl. Park (Kilauea and Mauna Loa), Hawaii. Iolani Palace, Honolulu. Kaloko-Honokohau Natl. Hist. Park, Molokai. Natl. Cemetery of the Pacific and USS *Arizona* Memorial. Polynesian Cultural Center, Laiea. Pu'uhonua o Honaunau Natl. Hist. Park, Hawaii.
Memorable events Polynesians first arrive 6th century. Second wave of Polynesians arrive 10th century. Captain James Cook first European to visit islands 1778; killed on Hawaii 1779. Sugar production begins 1835. Land reform ends feudal system 1848. Monarchy rule ends in revolution 1893. Becomes U.S. Territory 1900. Japanese attack Pearl Harbor 1941. Statehood 1959.
Tourist information (800) 464-2924.
www.state.hi.us.

▶ IDAHO
Home to some of the most isolated and rugged country in the United States, Idaho's diversified economy has traditionally been based on lumber and potatoes (more than 13 billion pounds in 1993). In the 1980s these were augmented by a number of small high-tech industries fleeing the high cost of business in California. During the 1990s the population has grown rapidly (20 percent by 1997).
Name Means "gem of the mountains." **Nickname** Gem State. **Capital** Boise. **Entered union** July 3, 1890 (43rd). **Motto** *Esto perpetua* (May it last forever).
Emblems   Bird Mountain bluebird. **Flower** Syringa. **Gem** Star garnet. **Horse** Appaloosa. **Song** "Here We Have Idaho." **Tree** Western white pine.
Land   Total area 83,564 sq. mi. (13th), incl. 1,152 sq. mi. inland water. **Borders** British Columbia, Mont., Wyo., Utah, Nev., Oreg., Wash. **Rivers** Bear, Clearwater, Payette, Salmon, Snake. **Lakes** American Falls Res., Coeur d'Alene, Pend Oreille. **Mountains** Bitterroot Range, Centennial, Clearwater, Salmon River, Sawtooth Range (Castle Peak 11,820 ft.), Wasatch Range. **Other notable features** Grand Canyon of the Snake River.
Elected officials Gov. Dirk Kempthorne (R, term exp. 2003). Lt. Gov. Jack Riggs, M.D. (R). Sec. State Pete T. Cenarrusa (R). Atty. Gen. Alan G. Lance (R).
People (2000) 1,293,953 (39th). **Race/Hispanic Origin** (2000): White 91.0%. Black 0.4%. Indian

1.4%. Asian 0.9%. Pacific Islander 0.1%. Other 4.2%. Two or more races 2.0%. Hispanic 7.9%.
Cities (2000) Boise City 185,787. Nampa 51,867. Pocatello 51,466. Idaho Falls 50,730. Meridian 34,919. Coeur d'Alene 34,514. Twin Falls 34,469. Lewiston 30,904. Caldwell 25,967. Moscow 21,291.
Business   Gross State Product, 1997: $29.15 bil. (43rd). **Leading Sectors of GSP** (1997): Manufacturing 19.93%; Services 16.67%; Government 13.29%. **Fortune 500 Companies** (2000): 3: Albertson's, Boise Cascade, Micron Technology.
Famous natives Joseph, Nez Percé chief. Ezra Taft Benson, politician. Gutzon Borglum, sculptor. Frank Church, politician. Ezra Pound, poet. Harmon Killebrew, baseball player. Jerry Kramer, football player. Sacagawea (Bird Woman), Shoshone interpreter. Lana Turner, actress.
Noteworthy places Craters of the Moons Natl. Monument. Hell's Canyon Natl. Recreation Area. Nez Percé Natl. Hist. Park. Sawtooth Natl. Recreation Area. Sun Valley ski resort. Yellowstone Natl. Park.
Memorable events Lewis and Clark expedition 1805. Becomes part of U.S. when Idaho Treaty concluded with Britain 1846. Gold Rush 1860. Nez Percé War 1877. Statehood 1890. World's first breeder reactor built at Idaho Falls, 1951. Snake River opened to navigation, linking Lewiston to Pacific Ocean at Astoria, Oregon, 1975. New Teton River Dam collapses as it is being filled for first time; 10 dead, $400 million in damage 1976.
Tourist information (800) 635-7820.
www.state.id.us.

▶ ILLINOIS
The Illinois economy is enormously productive and diverse. While Chicago is a leader in world finance and trade, the southern part of the state has rich farmlands (the state is second to Iowa in corn and soybean exports) and mineral deposits (both coal and gas — there are especially rich coal deposits in the southeast region around Cairo, known as Little Egypt). Manufacturing centers on Chicago, Rockford—the state's second-largest city—and Springfield, the capital. Chicago is also a major transportation hub with extensive rail networks, an international port serving ships from both the Atlantic and Gulf of Mexico, and the largest airport in the country.
Name Corruption of *iliniwek* ("tribe of the superior men"), natives of region at time of earliest French explorations. **Nickname** Prairie State. **Capital** Springfield. **Entered union** Dec. 3, 1818 (21st). **Motto** "State sovereignty—national unity." **Slogan** "Land of Lincoln."
Emblems   Animal White-tailed deer. **Bird** Cardinal. **Flower** Violet. **Insect** Monarch butterfly. **Mineral** Fluorite. **Song** "Illinois." **Tree** White oak.
Land   Total area 56,345 sq. mi. (24th), incl. 700 sq. mi. inland water. **Borders** Wis., Lake Michigan, Ind., Ky., Mo., Iowa. **Rivers** Fox, Illinois, Illinois Waterway, Kankakee, Kaskaskia, Mississippi, Ohio, Rock, Vermillion, Wabash. **Lakes** Carlyle, Crab Orchard. **Other notable features** Charles Mound (1,235 ft.), Little Egypt.
Elected officials Gov. George H. Ryan (R, term exp. 2003). Lt. Gov. Corinne G. Wood (R). Sec. State Jesse White (D). Atty. Gen. Jim Ryan (R).
People (2000) 12,419,293 (5th). **Race/Hispanic Origin** (2000): White 73.5%. Black 15.1%. Indian 0.2%. Asian 3.4%. Other 5.8%. Two or more races 1.9%. Hispanic 12.3%.
Cities (2000) Chicago 2,869,016. Rockford 150,115. Aurora 142,990. Naperville 128,358. Peo-

ria 112,936. Springfield 111,454. Joliet 106,221. Elgin 94,487. Waukegan 87,901. Cicero 85,616.
Business   Gross State Product, 1997: $393.53 bil. (4th). **Leading Sectors of GSP** (1997): Services 20.93%; Finance, insurance, and real estate 20.19%; Manufacturing 18.21%. *Fortune* **500 Companies** (2000): 39: including State Farm Insurance, Sears Roebuck, Motorola, Allstate, Bank One Corp., Walgreen, Sara Lee, Caterpillar, UAL, McDonald's, Abbott Laboratories, Deere, Archer Daniels Midland, Household International, Illinois Tool Works, Smurfit-Stone Container, Navistar International, Exelon, Aon, Baxter International.
Famous natives   Jane Addams, reformer (Nobel Peace Prize, 1930). Ernie Banks, baseball player. Saul Bellow, author (Nobel Prize, 1976). Harry A. Blackmun, jurist. Ray Bradbury, author. Gwendolyn Brooks, poet. William Jennings Bryan, politician. Edgar Rice Burroughs, novelist. St. Frances Xavier Cabrini (b. Italy). Clarence Darrow, lawyer. Miles Davis, musician. John Dos Passos, novelist. Enrico Fermi (b. Italy), nuclear physicist (Nobel Prize, 1938). Robert Louis ("Bob") Fosse, choreographer. Milton Friedman, economist (Nobel Prize, 1976). Benny Goodman, musician. Ernest Hemingway, novelist. Charlton Heston, actor. William Holden, actor. Abraham Lincoln, U.S. President (b. Kentucky). Vachel Lindsay, poet. Archibald MacLeish, poet. Ludwig Mies van der Rohe (b. Germany), architect. Charles W. Post, cereal manufacturer. Ronald Reagan, U.S. president. Carl Sandburg, poet. Albert G. Spalding, merchant. John Paul Stevens, jurist. Gloria Swanson, actress.
Noteworthy places   Art Institute of Chicago. Crab Orchard Wildlife Refuge. Dickson Mounds Museum, Lewistown. Field Museum of Natural History, Chicago. Ft. Chartres. Ft. Kaskaskia. Ft. Massac. Frank Lloyd Wright Historic District, Oak Park. Illinois State Museum, Springfield. Lincoln Home Natl. Hist. Park, Springfield. Mormon Settlement, Nauvoo. Morton Arboretum, Lisle. Museum of Science and Industry, Chicago. Shawnee Natl. Forest. Starved Rock State Park.
Memorable events   French missionary explorers Jacques Marquette and Louis Jolliet in Illinois 1673. Cahokia first European settlement 1699. Territory to England after French and Indian War 1763. Chicago founded by Jean-Baptiste Point du Sable 1779. Illinois and Michigan Canal links Lake Michigan and Mississippi River 1848. Lincoln-Douglas Debates at Springfield 1860. Half of Chicago destroyed by great fire 1871. Terrorist bombing leaves nine dead and 130 wounded in Haymarket affair, Chicago 1886. Columbia Exposition, Chicago 1893. First successful nuclear chain reaction created at University of Chicago 1942. Riots at Democratic National Convention in Chicago 1968. Sears Tower, world's tallest building (1,454 ft.), completed in Chicago 1973. Mississippi and Illinois rivers flood and cause $1.5 billion in damage 1993.
Tourist information   (800) 2-CONNECT.
www.state.il.us.

▶**INDIANA**
Indiana is strong in both farms and manufacturing. Its southern half has large coal deposits and produces most of the limestone quarried in the United States. To the north the fertile land helps make Indiana one of the primary farm-belt states. Indiana is also very much a part of the industrial Midwest, where unemployment is always a threat, especially in the heavily industrial areas of Gary and Indianapolis (the latter of which has developed into a center for high-tech industries

through the 1980s and 1990s). These geographic divisions have parallels in the political history of the state, which during the Civil War was Union in the north and Confederate in the south.
Name   For the land of Indians by early settlers, who found many distinct tribes living in region. **Nickname** Hoosier State. **Capital** Indianapolis. **Entered union** Dec. 11, 1816 (19th). **Motto** "The Crossroads of America."
Emblems   **Bird** Cardinal. **Flower** Peony. **Poem** "Indiana." **Song** "On the Banks of the Wabash, Far Away." **Stone** Indiana limestone. **Tree** Tulip tree.
Land   Total area 36,185 sq. mi. (38th), incl. 253 sq. mi. inland water. **Borders** Lake Michigan, Mich., Ohio, Ky., Ill. **Rivers** Kankakee, Ohio, Tippecanoe, Wabash, White, Whitewater. **Lakes** Freeman, Shafer.
Elected officials   Gov. Frank O'Bannon (D, term exp. 2005). Lt. Gov. Joseph Kernan (D). Sec. State Sue Anne Gilroy (R). Atty. Gen. Steve Carter (R).
People   (2000) 6,080,485 (14th). Race/Hispanic Origin (2000): White 87.5%. Black 8.4%. Indian 0.3%. Asian 1.0%. Other 1.6%. Two or more races 1.2%. Hispanic 3.5%.
Cities   (2000) Indianapolis 791,926. Fort Wayne 205,727. Evansville 121,582. South Bend 107,789. Gary 102,746. Hammond 83,048. Bloomington 69,291. Muncie 67,430. Anderson 59,734. Terre Haute 59,614.
Business   Gross State Product, 1997: $161.70 bil. (15th). **Leading Sectors of GSP** (1997): Manufacturing 31.02%; Services 15.88%; Finance, insurance, and real estate 13.2%. *Fortune* **500 Companies** (2000): 5: Eli Lilly, Anthem Insurance, Conseco, Cummins Engine, Nisource.
Famous natives   Larry Bird, basketball player. Hoagy Carmichael, composer. Eugene V. Debs, politician/organizer. Theodore Dreiser, author. Benjamin Harrison, U.S. president. Jimmy Hoffa, union leader. Michael Jackson, singer. David Letterman, comedian. Carole Lombard, actress. Cole Porter, composer. Ernie Pyle, journalist. Knute Rockne (b. Norway), football coach. Paul Samuelson, economist (Nobel Prize, 1960). Booth Tarkington, author. Kurt Vonnegut, author. Wendell L. Willkie, politician. Wilbur Wright, aviator.
Noteworthy places   Ernie Pyle birthplace, Dana. George Rogers Clark Natl. Hist. Park, Vincennes. Benjamin Harrison home, Indianapolis. Hoosier Natl. Forest. Indiana Dunes Natl. Lakeshore. Indianapolis Motor Speedway and Museum. Indianapolis Museum of Art. New Harmony village. Notre Dame Univ., South Bend. Old state capital, Corydon. Wilbur Wright State Memorial, Millville. Wyandotte Cave. Tippecanoe sites.
Memorable events   Mound Builders present c. A.D. 1000. René-Robert Cavelier de La Salle explores for French 1679–87. French near Vincennes from c. 1700. French cede territory to British 1763. Gen. Ambrose Clark captures Ft. Vincennes 1779. Territory ceded to U.S. 1783; included in Northwest Territory 1787. Miamis defeat U.S. twice in 1790. Gen. Anthony Wayne defeats Miamis at Battle of Fallen Timbers 1794. Territory included in Indiana Territory 1800. Gen. William Henry Harrison defeats Tecumseh's Indian Confederation at Tippecanoe 1811. Statehood 1816. Studebaker wagon company founded in South Bend 1852. U.S. Steel establishes mill at company-built town of Gary 1906. First Indianapolis 500 run 1911. Only a dozen companies producing cars, down from a pre-World War I peak of 375, 1920. Studebaker, last Indiana-based car maker, closes 1963.
Tourist information   (800) 289-6646.
www.state.in.us.

▶**IOWA**

Iowa lies between the two great rivers of the central United States, the Mississippi and the Missouri, with a quarter of the nation's richest and deepest topsoil. Iowa's farmers lead the country in the production of corn, and Iowa is also a big producer of hogs, cattle, and other livestock. With about 75 percent of Iowans employed in agriculture-related industries and 90 percent of the land farmed, Iowa can be deeply affected by natural disasters such as droughts and floods. Yet more than 100 *Fortune* 500 companies have production facilities in this farm state. Industrial production has risen since World War II. Iowans send abroad a quarter of the food they produce. As a result, this traditionally Republican state is better attuned to world developments than one might suspect.

Name For Iowa tribe. **Nickname** Hawkeye State. **Capital** Des Moines. **Entered union** Dec. 28, 1846 (29th). **Motto** "Our liberties we prize and our rights we will maintain."

Emblems **Bird** Eastern goldfinch. **Flower** Wild rose. **Song** "The Song of Iowa." **Stone** Geode. **Tree** Oak.

Land **Total area** 56,275 sq. mi. (25th), incl. 310 sq. mi. inland water. **Borders** Minn., Wis., Ill., Mo., Nebr., S.Dak. **Rivers** Big Sioux, Des Moines, Mississippi, Missouri. **Lakes** Okoboji, Rathburn Res., Red Rock, Saylorville Res., Spirit, Storm. **Other notable features** Ocheyedan Mound (1,675 ft.).

Elected officials Gov. Tom Vilsack (D, term exp. 2003). Lt. Gov. Sally Pederson (D). Sec. State Chet Culver (D). Atty. Gen. Thomas J. Miller (D).

People (2000) 2,926,324 (30th). **Race/Hispanic Origin** (2000): White 93.9%. Black 2.1%. Indian 0.3%. Asian 1.3%. Other 1.3%. Two or more races 1.1%. Hispanic 2.8%.

Cities (2000) Des Moines 198,682. Cedar Rapids 120,758. Davenport 98,359. Sioux City 85,013. Waterloo 68,747. Iowa City 62,220. Council Bluffs 58,268. Dubuque 57,686. Ames 50,731. West Des Moines 46,403.

Business **Gross State Product,** 1997: $80.48 bil. (29th). **Leading Sectors of GSP** (1997): Manufacturing 24.38%; Services 15.32%; Finance, insurance, and real estate 14.77%. *Fortune* **500 Companies** (2000): 2: Principal Financial, Maytag.

Famous natives Norman E. Borlaug, agronomist (Nobel Peace Prize, 1970). William F. ("Buffalo Bill") Cody, scout/showman. George Gallup, pollster. Josiah B. Grinnell (b. Vt.), abolitionist. Herbert Hoover, U.S. president. Harry L. Hopkins, politician. John L. Lewis, labor leader. John R. Mott, religious leader. Billy Sunday, baseball player/evangelist. John Wayne, actor. Meredith Wilson, composer. Grant Wood, painter.

Noteworthy places Amana Colonies. Davenport Art Gallery. Des Moines Art Center. Effigy Mounds Natl. Monument, Marquette. Ft. Dodge Hist. Museum. Herbert Hoover birthplace and library, West Branch. Natl. Rivers Hall of Fame, Dubuque. Putnam Museum, Davenport.

Memorable events Mound Builders present c. A.D. 1000. Jacques Marquette and Louis Jolliet claim land for France 1673. Part of Louisiana Purchase 1803. Part of Missouri Territory 1812–21. Black Hawk Wars 1832, 1834–37. First permanent settlement at Dubuque 1833. Organized as Iowa Territory (incl. parts of Minnesota, North Dakota, and South Dakota) 1838. Statehood 1846. Capital moved from Iowa City to Des Moines 1857. Fifty percent of Iowa's farms foreclosed during depression 1929–35. Iowa's urban population exceeds rural for first time 1960. Population loss of 7.9 percent in the 1980s. Floods cause $2.2 billion in damage 1993.

Tourist information (800) 345-IOWA. www.state.ia.us.

▶**KANSAS**

Kansas burst on the American scene as the territory called Bleeding Kansas, seething with conflict over the spread of slavery. Victorious New England abolitionists imprinted the state with the Puritan ethic. They were early supporters of prohibition, partly to discourage foreign newcomers. Kansas suffered enormously during the Great Depression and "Dust Bowl" days of the 1930s but rebounded strongly during the war. Wichita's aircraft industries, vital to the war effort, helped the Kansas economy to remain strong in the postwar years as family farming declined dramatically. Today Kansas remains a primary producer of wheat, cattle, and other agricultural products. Its manufacturing base still includes extensive aircraft industries, and it leads the states in the production of helium. The geographic center of the continental U.S. is near Lebanon.

Name For Kansa or Kaw, "people of the south wind." **Nickname** Sunflower State. **Capital** Topeka. **Entered union** Jan. 29, 1861 (34th). **Motto** *Ad astra per aspera* (To the stars through adversity).

Emblems **Animal** American buffalo. **Bird** Western meadowlark. **Flower** Wild native sunflower. **March** "The Kansas March." **Song** "Home on the Range." **Tree** Cottonwood.

Land **Total area** 82,277 sq. mi. (14th), incl. 499 sq. mi. inland water. **Borders** Nebr., Mo., Okla., Colo. **Rivers** Arkansas, Kansas, Missouri, Republican, Saline, Smoky Hill, Solomon. **Lakes** Kanapolis, Malvern, Perry, Pomona, Tuttle Creek, Waconda. **Other notable features** Flint Hills.

Elected officials Gov. Bill Graves (R, term exp. 2003). Lt. Gov. Gary Sherrer (R). Sec. State Ron Thornburgh (R). Atty. Gen. Carla J. Stovall (R).

People (2000) 2,688,418 (32nd). **Race/Hispanic Origin** (2000): White 86.1%. Black 5.7%. Indian 0.9%. Asian 1.7%. Other 3.4%. Two or more races 2.1%. Hispanic 7.0%.

Cities (2000) Wichita 344,284. Overland Park 149,080. Kansas City 146,866. Topeka 122,377. Olathe 92,962. Lawrence 80,098. Shawnee 47,996. Salina 45,679. Manhattan 44,831. Hutchinson 40,787.

Business **Gross State Product,** 1997: $71.74 bil. (31st). **Leading Sectors of GSP** (1997): Manufacturing 17.82%; Services 17.14%; Government 13.60%. *Fortune* **500 Companies** (2000): 2: Sprint, Yellow.

Famous natives "Buffalo Bill" Cody. Walter Chrysler, carmaker. Robert Dole, politician. Amelia Earhart, aviator. Dwight David Eisenhower (b. Tex.), general/U.S. president. Dennis Hopper, actor. William Inge, playwright. Nancy Landon Kassebaum, politician. Alf Landon, politician. Edgar Lee Masters, poet. James Naismith, inventor of basketball. Carry Nation (b. Ky.), prohibitionist. Charlie ("Bird") Parker, musician. Damon Runyon, writer. Gale Sayers, football player. William Allen White, the Sage of Emporia, editor.

Noteworthy places Agricultural Hall of Fame, Kansas City. Dodge City. Eisenhower Center, Abilene. Ft. Larned. Ft. Leavenworth. Ft. Riley. Ft. Scott. John Brown's Cabin, Osawatomie. Kansas Cosmosphere and Space Discovery Center, Hutchinson. Kansas State Historical Society Museum, Topeka. Wichita Art Museum.

Memorable events   First major expedition to region under Francisco Vásquez de Coronado 1540–41. La Salle claims territory including Kansas for France 1682. Part of Louisiana Purchase 1803. Area visited by Meriwether Lewis and George Rogers Clark (1803), Zebulon Pike (1806), and Stephen H. Long (1819). Santa Fe Trail crosses Kansas 1821. Fts. Leavenworth (1827), Scott (1842), and Riley (1853) established to protect pioneers on Santa Fe and Oregon trails. Organized as Territory by Kansas-Nebraska Act 1854, which repealed Missouri Compromise of 1820. "Bleeding Kansas" scene of free vs. slave rivalry 1854–56. Statehood 1861. Introduction of winter wheat makes Kansas leading U.S. wheat producer 1870. Airplane manufacturing starts in Wichita 1919. World-famous Menninger Foundation for mental health founded 1919. "Dust Bowl" drought drives thousands of farmers off the land, especially in western Kansas, 1934–35. Murder of Clutter family by Richard E. Hickock and Perry E. Smith at Holcomb (later the subject of Truman Capote's *In Cold Blood*,) 1959.
Tourist information   (800) 252-6727. **www.accesskansas.org.**

▶**KENTUCKY, COMMONWEALTH OF**
First pioneered by English immigrants in the mid-17th century, Kentucky's golden age as a choice frontier destination in the early 1800s was brought to an end by the Civil War. During the Civil War, the Bluegrass gentry supported the Confederacy, while the Appalachian backwoods men enlisted in the Union Army. Many took advantage of their uniforms to settle old accounts, and the social order was often threatened before the turn of the century. Though the state is known today for its bourbon and horse breeding, many Kentuckians make their living from the land as tobacco farmers or coal miners. The Appalachian part of the state in the east delivers about 20 percent of the nation's coal, but its economic problems remain acute, despite vast expenditures during the "war on poverty."

Name   Corruption of the Iroquois *kenta-ke* (meadow land) or Wyandot *kah-ten-tah-teh* (land of tomorrow). **Nickname** Bluegrass State. **Capital** Frankfort. **Entered union** June 1, 1792 (15th). **Motto** "United we stand, divided we fall."
Emblems   **Bird** Cardinal. **Colors** Blue and gold. **Fish** Bass. **Flower** Goldenrod. **Song** "My Old Kentucky Home." **Tree** Tulip poplar. **Wild animal** Gray squirrel.
Land   Total area 40,409 sq. mi. (37th), incl. 740 sq. mi. inland water. **Borders** Ind., Ohio, W.Va., Va., Tenn., Mo., Ill. **Rivers** Cumberland, Kentucky, Licking, Ohio, Tennessee. **Lakes** Barkley, Barren River Res., Dewey, Grayson Res., Laurel Res., Nolin Res., Rough Res. **Mountains** Appalachian (Black Mt. 4,145 ft.), Cumberland. **Other notable features** Tennessee Valley.
Elected officials   Gov. Paul E. Patton (D, term exp. 2003). Lt. Gov. Stephen L. Henry, M.D. (D). Sec. State John Y. Brown III (D). Atty. Gen. A.B. Chandler (D).
People   (2000) 4,041,769 (25th). **Race/Hispanic Origin** (2000): White 90.1%. Black 7.3%. Indian 0.2%. Asian 0.7%. Other 0.6%. Two or more races 1.1%. Hispanic 1.5%.
Cities   (2000)   Lexington-Fayette   260,512. Louisville 256,231. Owensboro 54,067. Bowling Green 49,296. Covington 43,370. Hopkinsville 30,089. Frankfort 27,741. Henderson 27,373. Richmond 27,152. Jeffersontown 26,633.

Business   **Gross State Product,** 1997: $100.08 bil. (26th). **Leading Sectors of GSP** (1997): Manufacturing 27.34%; Services 15.21%; Government 13.23%. **Fortune 500 Companies** (2000): 4: Humana, Ashland, Tricon Global Restaurants, Lexmark International.
Famous natives   Muhammad Ali, boxer. Alben W. Barkley, politician. Daniel Boone (b. Pa.), frontiersman. Louis D. Brandeis, jurist. Kit Carson, frontiersman. Henry Clay, politician. Jefferson Davis, president of Confederate States of America. D.W. Griffith, director. John Marshall Harlan, jurist. Abraham Lincoln, U.S. president. Col. Harland Sanders, entrepreneur. Frederick M. Vinson, jurist. Robert Penn Warren, author.
Noteworthy places   Abraham Lincoln birthplace, Hodgenville. Churchill Downs, Louisville. George S. Patton, Jr. Military Museum, Fort Knox. J.B. Speed Art Museum, Louisville. Land Between the Lakes Natl. Rec. Area. Mammoth Cave Natl. Park. My Old Kentucky Home, Bardstown. Old Ft. Harrod State Park.
Memorable events   English enter territory through Cumberland Gap 1750. Territory included in area ceded by French 1763. Daniel Boone leads expeditions into region 1769. First settlement Harrodsburg 1774. Daniel Boone blazes Wilderness Trail through Cumberland Gap, establishes Ft. Boonesborough 1775. Organized as a county of Virginia 1776. British support Indian resistance ("Dark and Bloody Wars") until George Rogers Clark captures British forts in Indiana and Illinois 1778. Included as part of United States after Revolution 1783. Virginia approves separate statehood, achieved 1792. First steamboat reaches Louisville from New Orleans 1815. Invaded by Confederate armies 1862. Kentucky Derby first run at Louisville 1875. State has highest per capita income of southern states 1900; ranks last among all 48 states in per capita income 1940. Farm population decreases by 76%, and total number of farms by 53%, 1945–80.
Tourist information   (800) 225-TRIP or (800) 255-PARK. **www.kydirect.net.**

▶**LOUISIANA**
European influences and ethnic diversity distinguish Louisiana from the rest of the nation. When Louisiana entered the Union in 1812, it brought with it a French legal system and a bilingualism that still survive. African-Americans, Cajuns and Creoles have contributed to its distinctive music and cuisine. The state has rich farmland, more oil and gas reserves than any other state but Texas, and in New Orleans an international port that serves the most extensive river system in North America.

The "devil's bargain" with the petrochemical industry struck by charismatic populist governor Huey Long (assassinated in 1935) brought needed jobs to the state. But the environmental impact of 100 loosely regulated petrochemical plants on the Mississippi River between New Orleans and Baton Rouge is being assessed only now. The state's reliance on the petroleum industry was felt when a downturn in oil prices in the 1980s led to massive unemployment. Economic diversification is under way, especially in field of tourism.

Name   For King Louis XIV. **Nickname** Pelican State. **Capital** Baton Rouge. **Entered union** Apr. 30, 1812 (18th). **Motto** "Union, justice, confidence."
Emblems   **Bird** Eastern brown pelican. **Colors** Gold, white, and blue. **Crustacean** Crawfish. **Dog** Catahoula leopard. **Flower** Magnolia. **Fossil** Pet-

rified palmwood. **Gem** Agate. **Insect** Honeybee. **Songs** "Give Me Louisiana," "You Are My Sunshine." **Tree** Bald cypress.
Land   Total area 47,751 sq. mi. (31st), incl. 3,230 sq. mi. inland water. **Borders** Ark., Miss., Gulf of Mexico, Tex. **Rivers** Atchafalaya, Mississippi, Ouachita, Pearl, Red, Sabine. **Lakes** Bistineau, Borgne, Caddo, Catahoula, Grand, Maurepas, Pontchartrain, Salvador, White. **Other notable features** Bayou Barataria, Bayou Bodcau, Bayou D'Arbonne, Driskill Mt. (535 ft.).
Elected officials   Gov. Mike Foster Jr. (D, term exp. 2004). Lt. Gov. Kathleen B. Blanco (D). Sec. State W. Fox McKeithen (R). Atty. Gen. Richard Ieuyob (D).
People   (2000) 4,468,976 (22nd). **Race/Hispanic Origin** (2000): White 63.9%. Black 32.5%. Indian 0.6%. Asian 1.2%. Other 0.7%. Two or more races 1.1%. Hispanic 2.4%.
Cities   (2000) New Orleans 484,674. Baton Rouge 227,818. Shreveport 200,145. Lafayette 110,257. Lake Charles 71,757. Kenner 70,517. Bossier City 56,461. Monroe 53,107. Alexandria 46,342. New Iberia 32,623.
Business   Gross State Product, 1997: $124.35 bil. (23rd). **Leading Sectors of GSP** (1997): Services 16.19%; Mining 15.92%; Manufacturing 15.73%. *Fortune* **500 Companies** (2000): 1: Entergy.
Famous natives   Louis "Satchmo" Armstrong, jazz musician. Pierre Beauregard, Confederate general. Terry Bradshaw, football player. Braxton Bragg, Confederate general. Truman Capote, author. Clyde Cessna, aviator. Michael DeBakey, surgeon. Fats Domino, singer. Lillian Hellman, author. Mahalia Jackson, singer. Jean Baptiste Le Moyne, sieur de Bienville (b. Canada), founded New Orleans. Jerry Lee Lewis, singer. Huey P. Long, senator. Ferdinand Joseph La Menthe "Jelly Roll" Morton, musician. Leonidas K. Polk, clergyman/Confederate general. Henry Miller Shreve (b. NJ), riverboat captain. Edward D. White, Jr., jurist.
Noteworthy places   Avery Island. Cabildo, New Orleans. French Quarter, New Orleans. Garden District, New Orleans. Hodges Gardens, Natchitoches. Jean Lafitte Natl. Hist. Park, Chalmette. Kent House Museum, Alexandria. Longfellow-Evangeline State Commemorative Area, St. Martinsville. Louisiana Maritime Museum, Baton Rouge. New Orleans Museum of Art.
Memorable events   Area first visited by Alonso Alvarez de Piñeda 1519. Claimed by René-Robert Cavelier de La Salle for France 1682. New Orleans founded 1718. French crown colony 1731. Four thousand Acadians (Cajuns) from Nova Scotia forcibly transported by British to Louisiana and settled in Bayou Teche 1755. Lands west of Mississippi given to Spain for help in French and Indian War 1763. Lands east of Mississippi ceded to Britain 1763. Same lands retroceded to France 1800. Jefferson negotiates Louisiana Purchase; U.S. acquires 885,000 sq. mi. for $15 million 1803. Statehood 1812. Andrew Jackson beats British at Battle of New Orleans 1815. State secedes 1861. Surrenders to Union forces 1862. Readmitted to Union 1868. Petroleum discovered 1901. Huey "The Kingfish" Long elected to Senate 1928; assassinated 1935. Racial designation law of 1970 repealed 1983.
Tourist information   (800) 33-GUMBO. www.state.la.us.

▶**MAINE**
Down-Easters—the original Puritans as well as the later French Canadians—are distinct from the New Englanders of Maine's economically more vital sister states. Their land, especially the coast, is rugged, and the living everywhere is hard. Maine touches only one other state, and it has an end-of-the-line feel to it. Lumbering, fishing, and potato farming were the traditional industries. More than half of the state is still unorganized territory largely owned by paper companies. In the 18th century, canneries, textiles, and shoe factories developed. Recently Maine's economy has combined light industry and tourism that is moving it into the mainstream. The modern Maine entrepreneur, often an out-of-stater, seeks an economy based on small industries and more in keeping with Maine's independent spirit.
   Name Either for Maine in France or to distinguish mainland from islands in the Gulf of Maine. **Nickname** Pine Tree State. **Capital** Augusta. **Entered union** Mar. 15, 1820 (23rd). **Motto** *Dirigo* (I direct).
Emblems   Animal Moose. **Bird** Chickadee. **Fish** Landlocked salmon. **Flower** White pinecone and tassel. **Insect** Honeybee. **Mineral** Tourmaline. **Song** "State of Maine Song." **Tree** Eastern white pine.
Land   Total area 33,265 sq. mi. (39th), incl. 2,270 sq. mi. inland water. **Borders** Quebec, New Brunswick, Atlantic Ocean, N.H. **Rivers** Alagash, Androscoggin, Aroostock, Kennebec, Machias, Penobscot, Piscataqua, Salmon Falls, St. John. **Lakes** Chamberlain, Chesuncook, Grand, Moosehead, Rangeley, Sebago. **Other notable features** Longfellow Mts. (Mt. Katahadin 5,268 ft.), Mt. Desert Island, Penobscot Bay.
Elected officials   Gov. Angus S. King, Jr. (I, term exp. 2003). Sec. State Dan A. Gwadowsky (D). Atty. Gen. G. Steven Rowe (D).
People   (2000) 1,274,923 (40th). **Race/Hispanic Origin** (2000): White 96.9%. Black 0.5%. Indian 0.6%. Asian 0.7%. Other 0.2%. Two or more races 1.0%. Hispanic 0.7%.
Cities   (2000) Portland 64,249. Lewiston 34,690. Bangor 31,473. South Portland 23,324. Auburn 23,203. Brunswick 21,172. Biddeford 20,942. Sanford 20,806. Augusta 18,560. Scarborough 16,970.
Business   Gross State Product, 1997: $30.16 bil. (42nd). **Leading Sectors of GSP** (1997): Services 19.23%; Finance, insurance, and real estate 19.16%; Manufacturing 17.09%. *Fortune* **500 Companies** (2000): 0.
Famous natives   Cyrus H.K. Curtis, publisher. Hannibal Hamlin, politician. Sarah Orne Jewett, novelist. Henry Wadsworth Longfellow, poet. Sir Hiram and Hudson Maxim, inventors. Edna St. Vincent Millay, poet. Edmund S. Muskie, politician. John Knowles Paine, composer. Kenneth Roberts, novelist. Edward Arlington Robinson, poet. Nelson Rockefeller, politician. Marguerite Yourcenar (b. France), author.
Noteworthy places   Acadia National Park, Mt. Desert Island. Allagash National Wilderness Waterway. Boothbay Railway Museum Campobello-Longfellow House, Portland. Maine Maritime Museum, Bath. Portland Art Museum Roosevelt-Campobello Intl. Park, Campobello Island. St. Croix Island Natl. Monument.
Memorable events   Vikings explore coast c. A.D.1000. Bartholomew Gosnold sails along coast 1602. French settlers at St. Croix River 1604. Included in grant to Plymouth Company 1606. Monhegan Island and Saco settled 1622. Annexed to Massachusetts Colony 1652. French attack northern territory intermittently through 1713. Statehood 1820. Border with Canada settled 1842.

First state prohibition law enacted 1851. Penobscot and Passamaquoddy tribes file claim against state for $300 million compensation for land seized in violation of 1790 Indian Non-Intercourse Act, 1972; settled for $81.5 million 1980. **Tourist information**   (800) 533-9595. **www.state.me.us.**

▶MARYLAND

Maryland wraps like a fishhook from the Atlantic Ocean around the fish-rich Chesapeake Bay and into the Cumberland Mountains in the northwest. Baltimore—full of urban problems but newly redeveloped with urban homesteading and shopsteading—holds the center. The suburbs of Baltimore and Washington seem far removed from the Delmarva (**del**aware, **mar**yland, **virginia**) peninsula with its watermen hanging on to an older way of life. Terrain, cultures, and history are a border state's mix of North and South. Founded as a haven for Catholics, Maryland's population is still 20 percent Catholic.

Name For Henrietta Maria, queen consort of Charles I. **Nicknames** Old Line State, Free State. **Capital** Annapolis. **Entered union** Apr. 28, 1788 (7th). **Motto** *Fatti maschii, parole femine* (Manly deeds, womanly words).

Emblems **Bird** Baltimore oriole. **Dog** Chesapeake Bay retriever. **Fish** Rockfish. **Flower** Black-eyed Susan. **Fossil** *Ecphora quadricostata* (extinct snail). **Insect** Baltimore checkerspot butterfly. **Song** "Maryland, My Maryland." **Sport** Jousting. **Tree** White oak.

Land **Total area** 10,460 sq. mi. (42nd), incl. 623 sq. mi. inland water. **Borders** Pa., Del., Atlantic Ocean, Va., D.C., W.Va. **Rivers** Chester, Choptank, Nanticoke, Patapsco, Patuxent, Pocomoke, Potomac, Susquehanna. **Other notable features** Allegheny Mts., Blue Ridge Mts., Chesapeake Bay.

Elected officials Gov. Parris N. Glendening (D, term exp. 2003). Lt. Gov. Kathleen Kennedy Townsend (D). Sec. State John T. Willis (D). Atty. Gen. J. Joseph Curran, Jr. (D).

People (2000) 5,296,486 (19th). **Race/Hispanic Origin** (2000): White 64.0%. Black 27.9%. Indian 0.3%. Asian 4.0%. Other 1.8%. Two or more races 2.0%. Hispanic 4.3%.

Cities (2000). Baltimore 651,154. Frederick 52,767. Gaithersburg 52,613. Bowie 50,269. Rockville 47,388. Hagerstown 36,687. Annapolis 35,838. College Park 24,657. Salisbury 23,743. Cumberland 21,518.

Business **Gross State Product,** 1997: $153.80 bil. (16th). **Leading Sectors of GSP** (1997): Services 23.58%; Finance, insurance, and real estate 22.20%; Government 17.22%. **Fortune 500 Companies** (2000): 7: Lockheed Martin, Marriott International, Crestline Capital, Sodexho Marriott Services, Black & Decker, Allegheny Energy, Constellation Energy.

Famous natives Russell Baker, journalist. Benjamin Banneker, surveyor. Eubie Blake, pianist. Rachel Carson, biologist/author. Stephen Decatur, navy officer. Frederick Douglass, abolitionist. Billie Holiday, singer. Johns Hopkins, financier/philanthropist. Francis Scott Key, lawyer/poet. Thurgood Marshall, jurist. H.L. Mencken, writer. Charles Willson Peale, artist. William Pinckney, statesman. James Rouse, urban planner. Babe Ruth, baseball player. Upton Sinclair, author. Roger B. Taney, jurist. Harriet Tubman, abolitionist. John Waters, filmmaker.

Noteworthy places Aberdeen Proving Ground. Antietam Natl. Battlefield, Sharpsburg.

Assateague Island Natl. Seashore. Natl. Aquarium in Baltimore. Baltimore Museum of Art. Baltimore Museum of Industry. Calvert Marine Museum, Solomons. Chesapeake & Ohio Canal Natl. Hist. Park. Chesapeake Bay Maritime Museum, St. Michaels. Ft. McHenry Natl. Monument, Baltimore. Harpers Ferry Natl. Hist. Park. Liberty ship *John W. Brown*, Baltimore. St. Marys City. State House, Annapolis. U.S. Naval Academy, Annapolis. USS *Constellation*, Baltimore. Walters Art Gallery, Baltimore.

Memorable events John Smith explores area 1608. William Claiborne sets up trading post on Kent Island 1631. Land granted to Cecilius Calvert, Lord Baltimore, 1632. Leonard Calvert and 200 Roman Catholic settlers land on Blakistone Island 1634. Mason Dixon Line establishes northern boundary of state 1763–67; later identified as boundary between slave and nonslave states. Francis Scott Key composes "The Star Spangled Banner" after British fail to take Ft. McHenry 1814. U.S. Naval Academy founded Annapolis 1845. State under federal military control during Civil War 1861–65. First state to adopt income tax 1938. Alabama Gov. George C. Wallace shot while campaigning in Democratic presidential primary 1972.

Tourist Information (800) MD-IS-FUN. **www.state.md.us.**

▶MASSACHUSETTS, COMMONWEALTH OF

Massachusetts is rich in the history of the early American republic. The Boston Tea Party, the "shot heard 'round the world" from Lexington and Concord, and the Battle of Bunker Hill are American folklore. So is the feast of Thanksgiving, first celebrated by the Puritans at Plymouth. Fishing, trade, textiles, and leather industries were the backbone of Massachusetts's 19th-century economy. In the 1980s, Boston's Route 128 became the East Coast counterpart to California's Silicon Valley, with some of the nation's most advanced computer and electronic research and manufacturing. The state's "economic miracle" of the 1980s ended abruptly, and Massachusetts endured a severe downturn during the recession of the early 1990s. It recently rebounded, along with most of the nation.

A staple of the Massachusetts scene is education, in which the state is a national leader. Boston alone boasts such institutions as Harvard University (founded 1636), M.I.T., Northeastern, Brandeis, Boston University, Boston College, Wellesley, and Tufts. To the west are the University of Massachusetts, Amherst, Williams, Smith, and Mt. Holyoke.

Name For Massachuset tribe, whose name means "at or about the great hill." **Nickname** Bay State. **Capital** Boston. **Entered union** Feb. 6, 1788 (6th). **Motto** *Ense petit placidam sub libertate quietem* (By the sword we seek peace, but peace only under liberty).

Emblems **Beverage** Cranberry juice. **Bird** Chickadee. **Building & monument stone** Granite. **Dog** Boston terrier. **Explorer rock** Dighton Rock. **Fish** Cod. **Flower** Mayflower. **Folk song** "Massachusetts." **Gem** Rhodonite. **Heroine** Deborah Samson. **Historical rock** Plymouth Rock. **Horse** Morgan. **Insect** Ladybug. **Marine mammal** Right whale. **Mineral** Babingtonite. **Poem** "Blue Hills of Massachusetts." **Rock** Roxbury pudding stone. **Song** "All Hail to Massachusetts." **Stone** Granite. **Tree** American elm.

Land **Total area** 8,284 sq. mi. (45th), incl. 460 sq. mi. inland water. **Borders** Vt., N.H., Atlantic

Ocean, R.I., Conn., N.Y. **Rivers** Cape Cod Canal, Connecticut, Merrimack, Taunton. **Other notable features** Buzzard's Bay, Cape Ann, Cape Cod, Cape Cod Bay, Connecticut Valley, Elizabeth Islands, Martha's Vineyard, Monomoy Island, Nantucket Island.

Elected officials Gov. Jane Swift (R, term exp. 2003). Lt. Gov. (vacant). Sec. of Commonwealth William Francis Galvin (D). Atty. Gen. Thomas Reilly (D).

People (2000) 6,349,097 (13th). **Race/Hispanic Origin** (2000): White 84.5%. Black 5.4%. Indian 0.2%. Asian 3.8%. Other 3.7%. Two or more races 2.3%. Hispanic 2.3%.

Cities (2000) Boston 589,141. Worcester 172,648. Springfield 152,082. Lowell 105,167. Cambridge 101,355. Brockton 94,304. New Bedford 93,768. Fall River 91,938. Lynn 89,050. Quincy 88,025.

Business Gross State Product, 1997: $221.01 bil. (11th). **Leading Sectors of GSP** (1997): Services 26.45%; Finance, insurance, and real estate 24.30%; Manufacturing 14.66%. *Fortune* **500 Companies** (2000): 13: FleetBoston Financial, Raytheon, Liberty Mutual Insurance Group, Mass. Mutual Life Insurance, Staples, Gillette, TJX, EMC, John Hancock Financial Services, State Street Corp., BJ's Wholesale Club, Thermo Electron, Allmerica Financial.

Famous natives John Adams, U.S. president. John Quincy Adams, U.S. president. Samuel Adams, patriot. Horatio Alger, clergyman/author. Susan B. Anthony, suffragette. Clara Barton, nurse. Leonard Bernstein, composer. George Herbert Walker Bush, U.S. president. John ("Johnny Appleseed") Chapman, pioneer. Richard Cardinal Cushing, prelate. Bette Davis, actress. Emily Dickinson, poet. Ralph Waldo Emerson, author. Marshall Field, merchant. R. Buckminster Fuller, inventor/engineer. John Hancock, patriot. Oliver Wendell Holmes, jurist. Winslow Homer, painter. John F. Kennedy, U.S. president. Jack Kerouac, author. Cotton Mather, theologian. Samuel Eliot Morison, historian. Samuel Morse, inventor. Thomas P. "Tip" O'Neill, congressman. Edgar Allan Poe, poet/author. Paul Revere patriot/silversmith. Louis Sullivan, architect. Henry David Thoreau, author.

Noteworthy places Addison Gallery of American Art, Andover. Arnold Arboretum, Boston. Arthur M. Sackler Museum, Cambridge. Berkshires Museum, Pittsfield. Boston Museum of Fine Arts. Boston Natl. Hist. Park (incl. Bunker Hill, Charlestown Navy Yard, Old North Church). Busch-Reisinger Museum, Cambridge. Cape Cod Natl. Seashore. Clark Art Institute, Williamsburg. Fogg Art Museum, Boston. Gardner Art Museum, Boston. Hancock Shaker Village. Lowell Natl. Hist. Park. Minute Man Natl. Hist. Park, Lexington and Concord. Nantucket Hist. Society. Old Sturbridge Village. Peabody Museum, Salem. Plimoth Plantation, Plymouth. Tanglewood Music Festival, Lenox. *U.S.S. Constitution* ("Old Ironsides"), Charlestown. Walden Pond. Woods Hole Oceanographic Institute. Worcester Art Museum.

Memorable events Pilgrims land at Plymouth 1620. First Thanksgiving celebrated 1621. Harvard College founded 1636. Region acquires province of Maine 1652. Colonists battle Wampanoags in King Philip's War 1655–56. Boston Massacre 1770. Boston Tea Party protests taxation 1773. Battles at Lexington, Concord, and Bunker Hill 1775. Shays's Rebellion 1785–86. Maine becomes a separate state 1820. Massachusetts receives influx of Irish immigrants fleeing famine 1845. Textile workers' strike at Lawrence brings International Workers of the World (IWW) to prominence in East 1912. Cape Cod Canal completed 1914. International protest follows trial and execution of anarchists Nicola Sacco and Bartolomeo Vanzetti for robbery and murder 1920; names cleared by governor's proclamation 1970. Eleven robbers steal $2.7 million from Brink's North Terminal Garage 1950. Martha's Vineyard and Nantucket symbolically vote to secede from state 1973.

Tourist information (800) 227-MASS. **www.state.ma.us.**

▶**MICHIGAN**
The automobile is the single commodity with which Michigan is most identified, and it is the home of the big three automakers, General Motors, Ford, and Chrysler. More than 50 percent of Michiganders live in the southeastern corner of the state, where the car industry flourishes. In the Upper Peninsula, across the Straits of Mackinac, lumber and copper have been the principal commodities from the 19th century, and the northern part of the Lower Peninsula boasts rich farmland. Michigan's boundaries include parts of four of the five Great Lakes, and it has more coastline than any state except Alaska. Michigan has had an outstanding reputation in higher education, and the University of Michigan at Ann Arbor and Michigan State are helping to foster the state's high-tech industries. But the state's heavy reliance on auto manufacturing makes the state vulnerable to economic downturns, as well as the general contraction of the American industry.

Name From the Fox *mesikami*, "large lake." **Nicknames** Wolverine State, Lake State. **Capital** Lansing. **Entered union** Jan. 26, 1837 (26th). **Motto** *Si quaeris peninsulam amoenam circumspice* (If you are looking for a beautiful peninsula, look around you).

Emblems Bird Robin. **Fish** Trout. **Flower** Apple blossom. **Gem** Chlorastrolite. **Insect** Dragonfly. **Song** "Michigan, My Michigan." **Stone** Petoskey stone. **Tree** White pine.

Land Total area 58,527 sq. mi. (23rd), incl. 1,573 sq. mi. inland water. **Borders** Lake Superior, Ontario, Lake Huron, Lake Erie, Ohio, Ind., Lake Michigan, Wisc. **Rivers** Brule, Detroit, Kalamazoo, Menominee, Montreal, Muskegon, St. Joseph, St. Mary's. **Lakes** Burt, Higgins, Houghton, Huron, Manistique, Michigan, Mullett, St. Clair, Superior. **Other notable features** Isle Royale, Mt. Curwood (1,980 ft.), Saginaw Bay, Traverse Bay, Whitefish Bay.

Elected officials Gov. John R. Engler (R, term exp. 2003). Lt. Gov. Dick Posthumus (R). Sec. State Candice S. Miller (R). Atty. Gen. Jennifer Granholm (D).

People (2000) 9,938,444 (8th). **Race/Hispanic Origin** (2000): White 80.2%. Black 14.2%. Indian 0.6%. Asian 1.8%. Other 1.3%. Two or more races 1.9%. Hispanic 3.3%.

Cities (2000) Detroit 951,270. Grand Rapids 197,800. Warren 138,247. Flint 124,943. Sterling Heights 124,471. Lansing 119,128. Ann Arbor 114,024. Livonia 100,545. Dearborn 97,775. Westland 86,602.

Business Gross State Product, 1997: $272.61 bil. (9th). **Leading Sectors of GSP** (1997): Manufacturing 25.76%; Services 18.94%; Finance, insurance, and real estate 15.35%. *Fortune* **500 Companies** (2000): 19: General Motors, Ford Motor, Kmart, Delphi Automotive, Dow Chemical, Lear, Whirlpool, CMS Energy, Masco, Kellogg, Federal-Mogul, DTE

Energy, Arvinmeritor, United Auto Group, Kelly Services, Pulte, Comerica, Steelcase, Borders Group.
Famous natives   Ralph J. Bunche, statesman (Nobel Peace Prize, 1950). Paul de Kruif, bacteriologist. Thomas Dewey, politician. Herbert H. Dow (b. Canada), chemical manufacturer. Edna Ferber, author. Gerald Ford (b. Neb.) U.S. president. Henry Ford, industrialist. Edgar Guest, journalist/poet. Robert Ingersoll, industrialist. Will Kellogg, businessman/philanthopist. Charles A. Lindbergh, aviator. Madonna, singer. Antoine de La Mothe, sieur de Cadillac (b. France), founded Detroit. Pontiac, Ottawa chief. William Upjohn, drug manufacturer.
Noteworthy places   Detroit Historical Society. Detroit Institute of Arts. Dossin Great Lakes Museum, Detroit. Great Lakes Indian Interpretive Museum, Detroit. Greenfield Village, Dearborn. Historic Ft. Wayne, Detroit. Isle Royale Natl. Park. Mackinac Island. Pictured Rocks Natl. Lakeshore, Lake Superior. Sleeping Bear Dunes Natl. Lakeshore, Lake Superior.
Memorable events   French explorers in region 1634. Jacques Marquette settles Sault Ste. Marie 1668. Detroit founded as French military post 1701. Region ceded to England 1763; to United States 1783. Included in Northwest Territory but British maintain control until 1796. Michigan Territory 1805. First steamboat on Great Lakes reaches Detroit 1818. Statehood 1837. First state to outlaw capital punishment 1846. Republican party organized at Jackson 1854. Canals at Sault Ste. Marie link Lakes Superior and Huron 1855. Ransom E. Olds and Henry Ford, working independently, develop gasoline-powered car 1896. United Auto Workers first to use sit-down strike successfully in contract negotiations 1935. Race riot, one of the worst in U.S. history, leaves 43 dead and $200 million in damages in Detroit 1967. Congress authorizes $1.5 billion in federal loan guarantees to bail out Chrysler Corporation 1979.
Tourist information   (800) 543-2YES.
www.state.mi.us.

▶ MINNESOTA

A land of at least 10,000 lakes, Minnesota is a magnet for those who love the outdoors. It is also home to the largest Scandinavian populations in the United States. Originally exploited for its wealth of lumber and iron—the Mesabi Range still produces much of the nation's iron ore—Minnesota also has highly developed agribusinesses (especially dairy products), manufacturing, and transportation industries. Minneapolis and St. Paul are at the north end of the Mississippi River system, and Duluth at the westernmost point of Lake Superior is the largest U.S. inland port. Minnesota has one of the best state school systems.
   Name From the Sioux *minisota*, "sky-tinted waters." **Nicknames** North Star State, Gopher State, Land of 10,000 Lakes. **Capital** St. Paul. **Entered union** May 11, 1858 (32rd). **Motto** *L'étoile du nord* (Star of the north).
Emblems   **Bird** Common loon. **Beverage** Milk. **Fish** Walleye. **Flower** Pink and white lady's slipper. **Gem** Lake Superior agate. **Grain** Wild rice. **Mushroom** Morel, or sponge mushroom. **Song** "Hail, Minnesota!." **Tree** Red pine.
Land   Total area 84,402 sq. mi. (12th), incl. 4,854 sq. mi. inland water. **Borders** Manitoba, Ontario, Lake Superior, Wisc., Iowa, S.Dak., N.Dak. **Rivers** Minnesota, Mississippi, Red River of the North, St. Croix. **Lakes** Itasca, Lake of the Woods, Leech, Mille Lacs, Red, Winnibigoshish. **Other notable features** Mesabi Range.

Elected officials   Gov. Jesse Ventura (Independence Party of Minnesota, term exp. 2003). Lt. Gov. Mae Schunk (Independent) Sec. State Mary Kiffmeyer (R). Atty. Gen. Mike Hatch (D).
People   (2000) 4,919,479 (21st). **Race/Hispanic Origin** (2000): White 89.4%. Black 3.5%. Indian 1.1%. Asian 2.9%. Other 1.3%. Two or more races 1.7%. Hispanic 2.9%.
Cities   (2000) Minneapolis 382,618. St. Paul 287,151. Duluth 86,918. Rochester 85,806. Bloomington 85,172. Brooklyn Park 67,388. Plymouth 65,894. Eagan 63,557. Coon Rapids 61,607. Burnsville 60,220.
Business   Gross State Product, 1997: $149.39 bil. (18th). **Leading Sectors of GSP** (1997): Services 19.97%; Manufacturing 18.92%; Finance, insurance, and real estate 18.42%. *Fortune* 500 **Companies** (2000): 16: Target, UnitedHealth Group, Supervalu, Minnesota Mining & Mfg., Best Buy, Xcel Energy, Northwest Airlines, U.S. Bancorp, St. Paul Cos., Cenex Harvest States, General Mills, Medtronic, Nash Finch, Hormel Foods, ADC Telecommunications, Lutheran Brotherhood.
Famous natives   Warren Burger, jurist. Bob Dylan, musician. F. Scott Fitzgerald, novelist. Judy Garland, actress. J. Paul Getty, businessman. Garrison Keillor, humorist. Sinclair Lewis, author (Nobel Prize, 1930). Paul Manship, sculptor. William and Charles Mayo, surgeons. Eugene McCarthy, politician. Walter F. Mondale, politician. Charles Schulz, cartoonist. Richard W. Sears, merchant.
Noteworthy places   Boundary Waters Canoe Area. Grand Portage Natl. Monument. International Falls. Lake Itasca State Park (headwaters of Mississippi). Mall of America. Mayo Clinic, Rochester. Minneapolis Institute of Arts. Minnehaha Falls, Minneapolis. Minnesota Zoo, Apple Valley. Pipestone Natl. Monument. Tyrone Guthrie Theater, Minneapolis. Voyageurs Natl. Park. Walker Art Center, Minneapolis.
Memorable events   Pierre Esprit Radisson and Médard Chouart des Groselliers visit area 1654–60. René-Robert de La Salle and Louis Hennepin explore upper Mississippi 1680. Daniel Greysolon, sieur de Duluth, claims region for France 1679. Area east of Mississippi to Britain 1763; to United States 1783. Western region of state as part of Louisiana Purchase 1803. Britain cedes northern strip to United States 1818. Ft. Snelling built 1820. Northern border settled by Ashburton Treaty 1842. Minnesota Territory created 1849. Statehood 1858. Sioux driven from state after uprising led by Chief Little Crow 1862. Iron ore deposits discovered in Mesabi Range 1890. Democratic party merges with Farmer-Labor party 1944.
Tourist information   (800) 657-3700.
www.state.mn.us.

▶ MISSISSIPPI

Mississippi's rank as the poorest state in the nation can be traced to the Civil War. Before the Civil War, Mississippi was the fifth-wealthiest state in the nation. The war cost the state 30,000 men. Plantation owners who survived the war were virtually bankrupted by the emancipation of the slaves, and Union troops under Sherman and others left widespread destruction in their wake. The increasingly harsh race-laws passed around 1900 also cost the state in the emigration of almost half a million (75 percent blacks, 25 percent whites) in the 1940s. Compounding all this was the fact that until World War II, Mississippi had virtually no urban center such as Jackson to attract or sustain major industry. In race relations particularly, Mississippi has made vast improvements, and there have been substantial gains in education and the attraction of out-of-state companies, especially light industry.

Name From the Ojibwa *misi sipi*, "great river." **Nickname** Magnolia State. **Capital** Jackson. **Entered union** Dec. 10, 1817 (20th). **Motto** *Virtute et armis* (By virtue and arms).

Emblems **Beverage** Milk. **Bird** Mockingbird. **Fish** Largemouth or black bass. **Flower** Magnolia. **Fossil** Prehistoric whale. **Insect** Honeybee. **Mammal** White-tailed deer. **Song** "Go, Mississippi." **Stone** Petrified wood. **Tree** Magnolia. **Waterfowl** Wood duck. **Water mammal** Porpoise.

Land Total area 47,689 sq. mi. (32nd), incl. 456 sq. mi. inland water. **Borders** Tenn., Ala., Gulf of Mexico, La., Ark. **Rivers** Big Black, Mississippi, Pearl, Tennessee, Yazoo. **Lakes** Arkabutla, Grenada, Ross Barnett Res., Sardis. **Other notable features** Pontotoc Ridge.

Elected officials Gov. Ronnie Musgrove (D, term exp. 2004). Lt. Gov. Amy Tuck (D). Sec. State Eric Clark (D). Atty. Gen. Mike Moore (D).

People (2000) 2,844,658 (31st). **Race/Hispanic Origin** (2000): White 61.4%. Black 36.3%. Indian 0.4%. Asian 0.7%. Other 0.5%. Two or more races 0.7%. Hispanic 1.4%.

Cities (2000) Jackson 184,256. Gulfport 71,127. Biloxi 50,644. Hattiesburg 44,779. Greenville 41,633. Meridian 39,968. Tupelo 34,211. Southaven 28,977. Vicksburg 26,407. Pascagoula 26,200.

Business **Gross State Product**, 1997: $58.31 bil. (33rd). **Leading Sectors of GSP** (1997): Manufacturing 22.63%; Services 16.68%; Government 14.93%. *Fortune* **500 Companies** (2000): 1: Worldcom.

Famous natives Medgar Evers, civil rights leader. William Faulkner, novelist. Shelby Foote, historian. Jim Henson, puppeteer. B.B. King, musician. Elvis Presley, singer. Leontyne Price, opera singer. Jerry Rice, football player. John C. Stennis, politician. Conway Twitty, singer. Muddy Waters, musician. Eudora Welty, novelist. Ben Ames Williams, novelist. Tennessee Williams, playwright. Richard Wright, author.

Noteworthy places Delta Blues Museum, Clarksdale. Natchez Trace Natl. Parkway. Seafood Industry Museum, Biloxi. Tupelo Natl. Battlefield. Vicksburg Natl. Military Park.

Memorable events Hernando de Soto's expedition travels through Mississippi 1540–41. René-Robert Cavelier de La Salle claims Mississippi valley for France 1682. Pierre Le Moyne, sieur d'Iberville builds Ft. Maurepas on Biloxi Bay 1699. Natchez (Ft. Rosalie) established 1716. France cedes territory to Britain 1763. Mississippi Territory (including presentday Alabama) created 1798. Statehood (Natchez first capital) 1817. Secedes from Union; Jefferson Davis becomes president of Confederacy 1861. Siege of Vicksburg 1863. Petroleum discovered 1939. Gov. Ross R. Barnett found guilty of contempt in preventing desegregation of University of Mississippi; James H. Meredith first black enrolled at University of Mississippi 1962. Civil rights leader Medgar Evers assassinated in Jackson and buried in Arlington National Cemetery 1963. White civil rights workers James Cheney, Andrew Goodman, and Michael Schwener killed 1964.

Tourist information (800) WARMEST. www.state.ms.us.

▶MISSOURI

Missouri is remarkable for the number and variety of its neighbors—southern states (Arkansas, Kentucky, and Tennessee), midwestern states (Illinois and Iowa), and Plains states (Oklahoma, Nebraska, and Kansas). For Missouri, geography was destiny. Still one of the country's most important inland ports, St. Louis was founded at the confluence of the Missouri and Mississippi rivers and became the gateway to the West; and Independence (now part of metropolitan Kansas City) got its start provisioning wagons for the Oregon and Santa Fe trails. The Pony Express from St. Joseph to Sacramento began in 1860, and the first attempt at airmail service was tried in St. Louis in 1911. While farming and livestock are still important to the state's economy, manufacturing and services are now the biggest sectors.

Name From the Iliniwek *missouri*, "owner of big canoes." **Nickname** Show Me State. **Capital** Jefferson City. **Entered union** Aug. 10, 1821 (24th). **Motto** *Salus populi suprema lex esto* (The welfare of the people shall be the supreme law).

Emblems **Bird** Bluebird. **Flower** Hawthorne. **Insect** Honeybee. **Mineral** Galena. **Rock** Mozarkite. **Song** "Missouri Waltz." **Tree** Dogwood.

Land Total area 69,697 sq. mi. (19th), incl. 752 sq. mi. inland water. **Borders** Iowa, Ill., Ky., Tenn., Ark., Okla., Kans., Nebr. **Rivers** Des Moines, Mississippi, Missouri, Osage, St. Francis. **Lakes** Bull Shoals, Clearwater, Lake of the Ozarks, Lake of the Woods, Table, Wappapella. **Other notable features** Ozark Mts. (Taum Sauk Mt. 1,772 ft.).

Elected officials Gov. Roger B. Wilson (D, term exp. 2001). Sec. State Rebecca McDowell Cook (D). Atty. Gen. Jeremiah W. Nixon (D).

People (2000) 5,595,211 (17th). **Race/Hispanic Origin** (2000): White 84.9%. Black 11.2%. Indian 0.4%. Asian 1.1%. Pacific Islander 0.1%. Other 0.8%. Two or more races 1.5%. Hispanic 2.1%.

Cities (2000) Kansas City 441,545. St. Louis 348,189. Springfield 151,580. Independence 113,288. Columbia 84,531. St. Joseph 73,990. Lee's Summit 70,700. St. Charles 60,321. St. Peters 51,381. Florissant 50,497.

Business **Gross State Product,** 1997: $152.10 bil. (17th). **Leading Sectors of GSP** (1997): Manufacturing 20.51%; Services 19.61%; Finance, insurance, and real estate 14.87%. *Fortune* **500 Companies** (2000): 13: Utilicorp United, Emerson Electric, May Department Stores, Anheuser-Busch, Farmland Industries, Premcor, Express Scripts, Graybar Electric, Leggett & Platt, Ameren, Trans World Airlines, Interstate Bakeries, Charter Communications.

Famous natives Thomas Hart Benton, painter. Yogi Berra, baseball player. George Caleb Bingham (b. Va.), painter. Omar Bradley, general. Adophus Busch (b. Germany), brewer. George Washington Carver, botanist. Walter Cronkite, journalist. Walt Disney, film producer. T.S. Eliot, poet. Walker Evans, photographer. Langston Hughes, poet. Jesse James, outlaw. Marianne Moore, poet. Reinhold Niebuhr, theologian. J.C. Penny, businessman. John J. "Black Jack" Pershing, soldier. Joseph Pulitzer (b. Hungary), publisher. Ginger Rogers, dancer. Casey Stengel, baseball player. Virgil Thompson, composer. Harry S Truman, U.S. president. Mark Twain, writer. Tom Watson, golfer. Shelley Winters, actress.

Noteworthy places Churchill Memorial, Gateway Arch, St. Louis. George Washington Carver Natl. Monument, Diamond. Harry S Truman Library, Independence. Mark Twain Area,

Hannibal. Nelson-Atkins Museum of Art, Kansas City. Pony Express Museum, St. Joseph. St. Louis Art Museum. Wilson's Creek Natl. Battlefield. Cahokia Mounds State Historic Site, near St. Louis. **Memorable events** French miners and hunters settle at Ste. Genevieve 1735. Pierre Laclade settles St. Louis 1765. New Madrid earthquakes (8.6 on Richter scale) rock buildings as far away as Baltimore 1811-12. Statehood 1821. Missouri legislature split over secesssion: minority party adopts secession ordinance; Missouri admitted to Confederacy; majority party remains loyal to Union 1861. Jesse James killed by fellow gang member at St. Joseph 1882. Lake of the Ozarks formed after completion of Bagnell Dam on Missouri River 1931. Winston Churchill delivers "iron curtain" speech at Fulton 1952. Gateway Arch, 630 ft. high, opens at St. Louis 1964. St. Louis population declines 53 percent 1950–90. Floods cause $3 billion in damage 1993.
Tourist information   (800) 877-1234. **www.state.mo.us.**

▶**MONTANA**
Mountains account for only the western two-fifths of "Big Sky Country," where copper mining, lumber, and tourism are the chief industries. The eastern portion of the state is part of the Great Plains, devoted to agriculture and ranching. For many years Montana was in the grip of the Anaconda Copper Mining Company, which virtually owned the state government and took most its profits out of the state. After Anaconda's demise in the 1970s, Montana developed some of the most stringent environmental laws in the West. In recent years, many famous Hollywood stars, as well as media mogul Ted Turner, have bought large tracts of land in Western Montana.
Name From Spanish *montaña*, "mountainous." **Nicknames** Treasure State, Big Sky Country. **Capital** Helena. **Entered union** Nov. 8, 1889 (41st). **Motto** *Oro y plata* (Gold and silver).
Emblems **Bird** Western meadowlark. **Fish** Blackspotted cutthroat trout. **Flower** Bitterroot. **Gems** Yogo sapphire, Montana agate. **Grass** Bluebunch wheatgrass. **Song** "Montana." **State ballad** "Montana Melody." **Tree** Ponderosa pine.
Land **Total area** 147,046 sq. mi. (4th), incl. 1,658 sq. mi. inland water. **Borders** British Columbia, Alberta, Saskatchewan, N.Dak., S.Dak., Wyo., Idaho. **Rivers** Kootenai, Milk, Missouri, Musselshell, Powder, Yellowstone. **Lakes** Bighorn, Canyon Ferry, Elwell, Flathead, Ft. Peck. **Mountains** Absaroka Range, Beartooth Range (Granite Peak 12,799 ft.), Big Belt, Bitterroot Range, Centennial, Crazy, Lewis Range, Little Belt. **Other notable features** Continental Divide, Missoula Valley.
Elected officials Gov. Judy Martz (R, term exp. 2005). Lt. Gov. Karl Ohs (R). Sec. State Bob Brown (R). Atty. Gen. Mike McGrath (D).
People (2000) 902,195 (44th). **Race/Hispanic Origin** (2000): White 90.6%. Black 0.3%. Indian 6.2%. Asian 0.5%. Pacific Islander 0.1%. Other 0.6%. Two or more races 1.7%. Hispanic 2.0%.
Cities (2000) Billings 89,847. Missoula 57,053. Great Falls 56,690. Butte-Silver Bow 34,606. Bozeman 27,509. Helena 25,780. Kalispell 14,223. Havre 9,621. Anaconda-Deer Lodge County 9,417. Miles City 8,487.
Business **Gross State Product,** 1997: $19.16 bil. (47th). **Leading Sectors of GSP** (1997): Services 19.69%; Government 15.68%; Finance, insurance, and real estate 13.53%. *Fortune* **500 Companies** (2000): 0.

Famous natives Gary Cooper, actor. Marcus Daly (b. Ireland), mine owner. Chet Huntley, journalist. Myrna Loy, actress. Mike Mansfield (b. N.Y.), politician/diplomat. Jeanette Rankin, politician/reformer. Charles M. Russell, artist.
Noteworthy places Big Hole Natl. Battlefield. Bob Marshall Wilderness. Charles M. Russell Museum, Great Falls. Custer Battlefield Natl. Monument. Ft. Union Trading Post Natl. Hist. Site. Lewis and Clark Caverns State Park. Museum of the Plains Indian, Browning. Natl. Bison Range. Waterton-Glacier International Peace Park. World Museum of Mining, Butte. Yellowstone Natl. Park.
Memorable events French explorers and trappers visit region 1740s. Large part of state in Louisiana Purchase 1803. Lewis and Clark expedition 1805–6. Ft. Benton first permanent settlement 1846. Western part of state included in Washington Territory 1853 and 1859; eastern part in Nebraska (1854) and Dakota (1861) territories. Gold discovered at Bannack (1862) and Alder Gulch (1863). Organized as Montana Territory 1864. Dakota and Cheyenne defeat U.S. troops under Gen. William Armstrong Custer at Battle of Little Bighorn 1876. Under Chief Joseph, Nez Percé beat U.S. Army at Big Hole Basin 1877. Marcus Daly discovers copper near Butte 1880s. Statehood 1889. Homesteaders enter state 1909. Ft. Peck Dam completed 1940. Anaconda Copper Mining, dominant in Montana industry and politics since 1915, closes mining operations at Butte 1983. Elizabeth Prophet (Guru Ma) convinces 3,000 disciples of the Church Universal and Triumphant to await nuclear cataclysm in underground shelters in Paradise Valley while state bureaucrats worried over sewage facilities 1990.
Tourist information (800) VISIT-MT, (800) 548-3390. **www.state.mt.us.**

▶**NEBRASKA**
Although set aside as Indian territory in 1834 and made off-limits to white settlement, thousands of whites crossed the region along the Independence, Mormon, and Oregon trails. Eventually Congress opened the land to settlement, which accelerated after the Homestead Act of 1862 and the coming of the railroads. The newcomers took up ranching and farming under hard conditions. The winter of 1886–87 killed thousands of cattle and drove many large-scale ranchers into bankruptcy, while the dust bowl of the 1930s spurred a mass exodus. Significant industry did not develop until World War II, when many war-related industries and army airfields moved to the center of the country. Nebraska is among the leading agricultural states, especially in the production of corn for grain and livestock. A state constitutional amendment passed in 1982 prevents the sale of farmlands and ranch lands from being sold to any-one other than a Nebraska family farm corporation.
Name From the Oto *nebrathka*, "flat water." **Nickname** Cornhusker State. **Capital** Lincoln. **Entered union** Mar. 1, 1867 (37th). **Motto** "Equality before the law."
Emblems **Bird** Western meadowlark. **Flower** Goldenrod. **Fossil** Mammoth. **Gem** Blue agate. **Grass** Little blue stem. **Insect** Honeybee. **Mammal** White-tailed deer. **Rock** Prairie agate. **Soil** Soils of the Holdrege series. **Song** "Beautiful Nebraska." **Tree** Western cottonwood.
Land **Total area** 77,355 sq. mi. (15th), incl. 711 sq. mi. inland water. **Borders** S.Dak., Iowa, Mo., Kans., Colo., Wyo. **Rivers** Missouri, North Platte, Republican, South Platte. **Lakes** Harlan Co. Res.,

Lewis and Clark Lake. **Other notable features** Pine Ridge, Sand Hills.
Elected officials Gov. Mike Johanns (R, term exp. 2003). Lt. Gov. David I. Maurstad (R). Sec. State John A. Gale (R). Atty. Gen. Don Stenberg (R).
People (2000) 1,711,263 (38th). **Race/Hispanic Origin** (2000): White 89.6%. Black 4.0%. Indian 0.9%. Asian 1.3%. Other 2.8%. Two or more races 1.4%. Hispanic 5.5%.
Cities (2000) Omaha 390,007. Lincoln 225,581. Bellevue 44,382. Grand Island 42,940. Kearney 27,431. Fremont 25,174. Hastings 24,064. North Platte 23,878. Norfolk 23,516. Columbus 20,971.
Business **Gross State Product,** 1997: $48.81 bil. (36th). **Leading Sectors of GSP** (1997): Services 17.75%; Finance, insurance, and real estate 15.22%; Government 14.22%. *Fortune* **500 Companies** (2000): 5: Berkshire Hathaway, Conagra, Union Pacific, Peter Kiewitt Sons', Mutual of Omaha Insurance.
Famous natives Fred Astaire, dancer. Marlon Brando, actor. William Jennings Bryan, politician. Johnny Carson (b. Iowa), comedian. Willa Cather (b. Va.), author. Loren Eiseley, anthropologist. The Rev. Edward J. Flanagan (b. Ireland), reformer. Henry Fonda, actor. Rollin Kirby, cartoonist. Melvin Laird, politician. Harold Lloyd, actor. Mahpiua Luta (Red Cloud), Oglala Sioux chief. Malcolm X, religious leader. Roscoe Pound, educator.
Noteworthy places Agate Fossil Beds Natl. Monument. Arbor Lodge State Park, Nebraska City. Boys Town, Omaha. Buffalo Bill Ranch State Hist. Park. Chimney Rock Hist. Site. Homestead Natl. Monument, Beatrice. Oregon Trail. Pioneer Village, Minden. Scotts Bluff Natl. Monument. Stuhr Museum of the Prairie Pioneer, Grand Island.
Memorable events Acquired as part of Louisiana Purchase 1803. Separate territory created by Kansas-Nebraska Act 1854. Size reduced after creation of Colorado and Dakota territories 1861. Statehood 1867. To encourage tree planting, becomes first state to observe Arbor Day 1872. Adopts unicameral legislature 1937. Oil discovered 1939. Population peaks at 1,605,000 1984–85.
Tourist information (800) 228-4307.
www.state.ne.us.

▶ **NEVADA**
Set in the Great Basin desert, Nevada is one of the most barren places in North America, and the state receives less rainfall than any other. First explored by Europeans in 1776, it was 75 years before anyone thought of establishing a town in the area, and it did not last a decade. Miners came to Nevada early, but the discovery of the Comstock Lode in 1859 brought thousands. To add free-state congressional votes, Nevada was hustled into the Union in 1864, three years before its boundaries were settled. That boom was over by the 1870s, and it took more gold and silver strikes in the early 1900s, as well as the discovery of copper, to get the economy rolling again. The mainstay of the economy since World War II has been the gambling industry, which generates virtually half of all tax revenues. During the 1990s, Nevada has been the fastest growing state in the union, with skyrocketing tourism fueling much of the growth.
Name From Spanish, meaning "snow-covered sierra." **Nicknames** Sagebrush State, Silver State. **Capital** Carson City. **Entered union** Oct. 31, 1864 (36th). **Motto** "All for our country."
Emblems **Animal** Desert bighorn sheep. **Bird** Mountain bluebird. **Flower** Sagebrush. **Fossil**

Icthyosaur. **Grass** Indian ricegrass. **Metal** Silver. **Song** "Home Means Nevada." **Tree** Single-leaf piñon.
Land **Total area** 110,561 sq. mi. (7th), incl. 667 sq. mi. inland water. **Borders** Oreg., Idaho, Utah, Ariz., Calif. **Rivers** Colorado, Humboldt. **Lakes** Pyramid, Walker, Winnemucca. **Other notable features** Black Rock Desert, Carson Sink, Humboldt Salt Marsh, Mojave Desert.
Elected officials Gov. Kenny Guinn (R, term exp. 2003). Lt. Gov. Lorraine Hunt (R). Sec. State Dean Heller (R). Atty. Gen. Frankie Sue Del Papa (D).
People (2000) 1,998,257 (35th). **Race/Hispanic Origin** (2000): White 75.2%. Black 6.8%. Indian 1.3%. Asian 4.5%. Pacific Islander 0.4%. Other 8.0%. Two or more races 3.8%. Hispanic 19.7%.
Cities (2000) Las Vegas 478,434. Reno 180,480. Henderson 175,381. North Las Vegas 115,488. Sparks 66,346. Carson City 52,457. Elko 16,708. Boulder City 14,966. Mesquite 9,389. Fallon 7,536.
Business **Gross State Product,** 1997: $57.41 bil. (34th). **Leading Sectors of GSP** (1997): Services 32.52%; Finance, insurance, and real estate 18.77%; Government 9.91%. *Fortune* **500 Companies** (2000): 3: Park Place Entertainment, Harrah's Entertainment, MGM Mirage.
Famous natives Andre Agassi, tennis player. Walter Van Tilburg Clark (b. Me.), author. Sarah Winnemucca Hopkins, interpeter/teacher. John William MacKay, miner. William Morris Stewart (b. N.Y.), lawyer/senator.
Noteworthy places Death Valley Natl. Monument. Las Vegas. Lehman Caves Natl. Monument. Valley of the Fire State Park, Overton.
Memorable events Francisco Tomás Garcés explores area 1775–76. Jedediah Smith, trader, crosses region 1826–27. Old Spanish Trail (1830) and California Trail (1833) cross region. John Frémont explores area 1843–45. To United States after Mexican War 1846. Genoa, first settlement in Nevada, founded as Mormon Station 1849. Gold of Comstock Lode discovered 1859. Organized as separate territory 1861. Statehood 1864. Nevada legalizes gambling 1931. Hoover Dam built on Colorado River 1935. Nuclear tests begun at Yucca Flats 1951. Population grows more than 550 percent 1950–88, and 25 percent in 1990s.
Tourist information (800) NEVADA8.
www.state.nv.us.

▶ **NEW HAMPSHIRE**
New Hampshire has a disproportionate influence on presidential elections because by state law its primary must fall at least one week before any other state's (though Iowa's caucuses can come earlier). Through independence the mainstays of the economy were fishing, trade, and farming. Boston proved more suitable for trade, and New Hampshire's stubborn land was outproduced by the more fertile valleys to the south and west. The state's economy receded until the beginning of the Industrial Revolution, when there was tremendous growth in textile-producing mill towns in the Merrimack River Valley. The mills began to close after World War I, and the economy faltered again. Improvement came as high-tech firms from Boston sought refuge in New Hampshire's favorable tax climate. The state's economy was pummeled by the severe New England recession in the early 1990s, but has rebounded since.
Name For English county of Hampshire. **Nickname** Granite State. **Capital** Concord. **Entered union** June 21, 1788 (9th). **Motto** "Live free or die."

Emblems **Amphibian** Spotted newt. **Bird** Purple finch. **Flower** Purple lilac. **Gem** Smoke quartz. **Insect** Ladybug. **Mineral** Beryl. **Song** "Old New Hampshire." **Tree** White birch.
Land **Total area** 9,279 sq. mi. (44th), incl. 286 sq. mi. inland water. **Borders** Quebec, Maine, Atlantic Ocean, Mass., Vt. **Rivers** Connecticut, Merrimack, Piscataqua, Saco, Salmon Falls. **Lakes** First Connecticut, Francis, Newfound, Ossipee, Sunapee, Winnipesaukee. **Other notable features** Isles of Shoals, White Mts. (Mt. Washington 6,288 ft., highest peak in Northeast).
Elected officials Gov. Jeanne Shaheen (D, two-year term exp. 2003). Sec. State William Gardner (D). Atty. Gen. Philip McLaughlin (D).
People (2000) 1,235,786 (41st). **Race/Hispanic Origin** (2000): White 96.0%. Black 0.7%. Indian 0.2%. Asian 1.3%. Other 0.6%. Two or more races 1.1%. Hispanic 1.7%.
Cities (2000) Manchester 107,006. Nashua 86,605. Concord 40,687. Derry 34,021. Rochester 28,461. Salem 28,112. Dover 26,884. Merrimack 25,119. Londonderry 23,236. Hudson 22,928.
Business **Gross State Product,** 1997: $38.11 bil. (39th). **Leading Sectors of GSP** (1997): Manufacturing 24.99%; Finance, insurance, and real estate 21.98%; Services 18.38%. *Fortune* 500 **Companies** (2000): 0.
Famous natives Salmon P. Chase, jurist. Ralph Adams Cram, architect. Mary Baker Eddy, founder, Church of Christ, Scientist. Daniel Chester French, sculptor. Horace Greeley, journalist. Sarah Buell Hale, author. Franklin Pierce, U.S. president. Augustus Saint-Gaudens (b. Ireland), sculptor. Alan Shepard, astronaut. Daniel Webster, politician. Eleazar Wheelock (b. Conn.), Dartmouth founder.
Noteworthy places Currier Gallery of Art, Manchester. The Flume (gorge). Franconia Notch. Isles of Shoals. Lake Winnipesaukee. Mt. Washington. Shaker Village, Canterbury. St. Gaudens Natl. Hist. Site. Strawbery Bank. White Mountains Natl. Forest.
Memorable events Martin Pring sails along coast 1603. Champlain explores area 1604. John Smith visits Isles of Shoals 1614. Included in king's grant to John Mason and Sir Ferdinando Gorges 1622. First settlers at Little Harbor, near Portsmouth 1623. Made separate royal province 1679, though under Massachusetts governor 1699–1741. Rogers's Rangers halt Indian raids 1759. New Hampshire patriots seize British fort at Portsmouth and drive out Royal governor 1775. Province relinquishes claims to New Connecticut (Vermont) 1782. First textile mill built 1803. Treaty of Portsmouth ends Russo-Japanese War 1905. Bretton Woods conference leads to establishment of International Monetary Fund 1944. First state to adopt lottery to support public education 1963.
Tourist information (800) FUN-IN-NH. www.state.nh.us.

▶ **NEW JERSEY**
With the entire state population classified as living in metro areas, New Jersey is the most densely populated state, 15 times the national average. The image survives of New Jersey as a chemical-industrial wasteland south of New York Harbor. Pharmaceuticals and chemicals are in fact New Jersey's leading products, but the next most important industry is tourism, because of the money tourists spend at the gaming tables of Atlantic City. What earns New Jersey its nickname, the Garden State, is its extensive small-scale agriculture, which produces tomatoes, dairy products, asparagus, blueberries, corn, and poultry.
New Jersey lies on a plain between Philadelphia and New York City, two larger neighbors that have overshadowed New Jersey on the national scene since colonial days. Yet during the Revolution, more than 100 battles were fought on New Jersey soil, and today the overwhelming majority of containerized shipping in the Port of New York and New Jersey is shipped from New Jersey terminals. Per capita income is always among the top five in the nation.
Name After English Channel Island of Jersey. **Nickname** Garden State. **Capital** Trenton. **Entered union** Dec. 18, 1787 (3rd). **Motto** "Liberty and prosperity."
Emblems **Animal** Horse. **Bird** Eastern goldfinch. **Flower** Violet. **Insect** Honeybee. **Memorial tree** Dogwood. **Tree** Red oak.
Land **Total area** 7,787 sq. mi. (46th), incl. 319 sq. mi. inland water. **Borders** N.Y., Atlantic Ocean, Del., Pa. **Rivers** Delaware, Hackensack, Hudson, Passaic. **Lakes** Greenwood, Hopatcong, Round Valley Res., Spruce Run. **Other notable features** Delaware Water Gap, Kittatinny Mts., Palisades, Pine Barrens, Ramapo Mts.
Elected officials Gov. Donald T. DiFrancesco (R, term exp. 2002). Sec. State DeForest B. Soaries, Jr. (R). Atty. Gen. John J. Farmer, Jr. (R).
People (2000) 8,414,350 (9th). **Race/Hispanic Origin** (2000): White 72.6%. Black 13.6%. Indian 0.2%. Asian 5.7%. Other 5.4%. Two or more races 2.5%. Hispanic 13.3%.
Cities (2000) Newark 273,546. Jersey City 240,055. Paterson 149,222. Elizabeth 120,568. Edison 97,687. Woodbridge 97,203. Dover 89,706. Hamilton 87,109. Trenton 85,403. Camden 79,904.
Business **Gross State Product,** 1997: $294.06 bil. (8th). **Leading Sectors of GSP** (1997): Finance, insurance, and real estate 23.41%; Services 21.89%; Manufacturing 13.96%. *Fortune* 500 **Companies** (2000): 22: Lucent Technologies, Merck, Johnson & Johnson, Honeywell International, Prudential Insurance Co. of America, Pharmacia, American Home Products, Toys "R" Us, Schering-Plough, Ingersoll-Rand, American Standard, Chubb, Public Service Enterprise Group, Automatic Data Processing, Campbell Soup, Engelhard, GPU, Foster Wheeler, Pathmark Stores, Becton Dickinson, Quest Diagnostics, Summit Bancorp.
Famous natives Count Basie, jazz musician. William J. Brennan, jurist. Aaron Burr, politician. Grover Cleveland, U.S. president. James Fenimore Cooper, novelist/historian. Stephen Crane, author. Thomas Edison, inventor. Albert Einstein (b. Germany), nuclear physicist. Waldo Frank, author. Joyce Kilmer, poet. Jerry Lewis, actor. Jack Nicholson, actor. Zebulon Pike, explorer. Molly Pitcher, Revolutionary War heroine. Paul Robeson, actor/singer. Walter Schirra, astronaut. Frank Sinatra, singer. Alfred Stieglitz, photographer. Meryl Streep, actress. Aaron Montgomery Ward, merchant. William Carlos Williams, poet.
Noteworthy places Atlantic City. Cape May Historic District. Edison Natl. Hist. Site, West Orange. Lakehurst Naval Air Station. Liberty State Park, Jersey City. Morristown Natl. Hist. Park. Newark Museum. Palisades Interstate Park. Pine Barrens wilderness area. Princeton University. Walt Whitman House, Camden.
Memorable events Giovanni de Verrazano explores 1524. Hudson explores up Hudson River 1609. Dutch settlers establish Ft. Nassau 1623. New Jersey taken over by British and organized as

colony under Sir George Carteret 1665. Major battles of Revolution at Trenton (1776), Princeton (1777), and Monmouth (1778). Women given vote at Elizabethtown 1800. Voting rights restricted to men 1807. Adopts state constitution 1844. Passenger ship *Morro Castle* burns off Asbury Park; 134 die 1934. Dirigible *Hindenburg* explodes while mooring at Lakehurst; 36 die 1937. New Jersey Turnpike linking New York City and Philadelphia opens 1952. Five days of race riots in Newark leave 26 dead 1967. Gambling legalized in Atlantic City 1978. State enacts strictest gun legislation in United States 1990.
Tourist information   (800) JERSEY7, ext. 7963. **www.state.nj.us.**

▶ NEW MEXICO
The development problem of the western states is shared by New Mexico, which of all states has the smallest percentage of its area covered by water. Rich in other resources, it is the uranium capital of the world. The state mineral tax brings in a large percentage of state revenues, some of which goes into permanent endowments. Distribution of wealth in New Mexico remains uneven, but Hispanics, who tend to register as Democrats, vote in roughly the same ways as Anglos. A higher percentage of Native Americans live in New Mexico than in any other state.

Today, mining's influence on the state economy has waned in favor of service industry jobs. Despite the enormous governmental investment in research at Los Alamos, where the atom bomb was born, the highly classified nature of this work limits the development of related industry.
Name By Spanish explorers after Mexico. **Nickname** Land of Enchantment. **Capital** Santa Fe. **Entered union** Jan. 6, 1912 (47th). **Motto** *Crescit eundo* (It grows as it goes).
Emblems   Animal Black bear. **Bird** Roadrunner (chaparral bird). **Fish** Cutthroat trout. **Flower** Yucca. **Fossil** *Coelphysis* dinosaur. **Gem** Turquoise. **Songs** "O, Fair New Mexico," "Así es Nuevo Mejico." **Tree** Piñon. **Vegetables** Frijole, chili.
Land   Total area 121,593 sq. mi. (5th), incl. 258 sq. mi. inland water. **Borders** Colo., Okla., Tex., Chihuahua, Ariz. **Rivers** Gila, Pecos, Rio Grande, Zuni. **Lakes** Conchas Res., Eagle Nest, Elephant Butte Res., Navajo Res., Ute Res. **Mountains** Chuska, Guadalupe, Sacramento, San Andres, Sangre de Cristo. **Other notable features** Carlsbad Caverns, Continental Divide, Staked Plain.
Elected officials   Gov. Gary E. Johnson (R), term exp. 2003). **Lt. Gov.** Walter D. Bradley (R). **Sec. State** Rebecca Vigil-Giron (D). **Atty. Gen.** Patricia Madrid (D).
People   (2000) 1,819,046 (36th). **Race/Hispanic Origin** (2000): White 66.8%. Black 1.9%. Indian 9.5%. Asian 1.1%. Pacific Islander 0.1%. Other 17.0%. Two or more races 3.6%. Hispanic 42.1%.
Cities   (2000) Albuquerque 448,607. Las Cruces 74,267. Santa Fe 62,203. Rio Rancho 51,765. Roswell 45,293. Farmington 37,844. Alamogordo 35,582. Clovis 32,667. Hobbs 28,657. Carlsbad 25,625.
Business   Gross State Product, 1997: $45.24 bil. (37th). **Leading Sectors of GSP** (1997): Manufacturing 17.43%; Services 17.22%; Government 17.12%. *Fortune* **500 Companies** (2000): 0.
Famous natives   William "Billy the Kid" Bonney (b. N.Y.), outlaw. Peter Hurd, artist. Archbishop Jean Baptiste Lamy (b. France), missionary. Georgia O'Keeffe (b. Wis.), artist. Popé, Tewa Pueblo chief. Harrison Schmitt, astronaut.

Noteworthy places   Aztec Ruins Natl. Monument. Bandelier Natl. Monument. Capulin Mt. Natl. Monument. Carlsbad Caverns Natl. Park. Chaco Culture Natl. Hist. Park. El Morro Natl. Monument. Ft. Union Natl. Monument. Gila Cliff Dwellings Natl. Monument. Museum of New Mexico, Santa Fe. Pecos Mission. Salinas Mission. Santa Fe Opera. Wheelwright Museum of the American Indian, Santa Fe. White Sands Natl. Monument.
Memorable events   Marcos de Niza enters Zuni country 1539. Juan de Oñate establishes first Spanish settlement on Rio Grande near Espanola 1598. Santa Fe founded; becomes capital of New Mexico 1710. Santa Fe Trail from Independence, Missouri, completed; Mexico secedes from Spain 1821. Manuel Armijo suppresses revolt against Mexican rule (1837); defeats invasion from Republic of Texas (1841). Land annexed by United States after Mexican-American War 1848. Organized as territory with Arizona and part of Colorado 1850. Lincoln County War pits cattlemen against merchants 1878–81. Statehood; 17 killed in raid by Pancho Villa 1912. Los Alamos selected as first research and development facility for nuclear weapons 1942. First atom bomb exploded at Alamogordo Air Base 1945.
Tourist information   (800) 545-2040. **www.state.nm.us.**

▶ NEW YORK
New York's greatest and most inviting asset has always been its strategic location and long arteries into the hinterland. New York Bay is one of the great natural harbors of the world, and the broad Hudson River is one of the most fortunately placed. After the opening of the Erie Canal between the Hudson and Lake Erie in 1825, New York City became the trading center for the Midwest as well as the Hudson Valley and the Atlantic Coast. Buffalo also experienced a boom, becoming a major Great Lakes industrial port. New York is still the first state in number of manufacturing establishments and employees. Wall Street alone employs half a million people.

Although New York's population grew by nearly half a million people between 1980 and 1990, its relatively slow rate of growth resulted in a loss of three congressional seats—an indication of the change in the state's political clout. As its place among the 50 states has fallen by some measures, New York City's worldwide importance in business, culture, and communications has risen.
Name For Duke of York, later James II, of England. **Nickname** Empire State. **Capital** Albany. **Entered union** July 26, 1788 (11th). **Motto** *Excelsior* (Higher).
Emblems   Animal Beaver. **Beverage** Milk. **Bird** Bluebird. **Fish** Brook or speckled trout. **Flower** Rose. **Fossil** Prehistoric crab (*Eurypterus remipes*). **Fruit** Apple. **Gem** Garnet. **Song** "I Love New York." **Tree** Sugar maple.
Land   Total area 49,108 sq. mi. (30th), incl. 1,731 sq. mi. inland water. **Borders** Lake Ontario, Ontario, Quebec, Vt., Mass., Conn., Atlantic Ocean, N.J., Pa., Lake Erie. **Rivers** Allegheny, Delaware, Genesee, Hudson, Mohawk, New York State Barge Canal, Niagara, St. Lawrence, Susquehanna. **Lakes** Cayuga, Champlain, Chautauqua, Erie, George, Oneida, Ontario, Seneca. **Mountains** Adirondack (Mt. Marcy 5,344 ft.), Allegheny, Berkshire Hills, Catskill, Kittatinny, Ramapo. **Other notable features** Hudson Valley, Mohawk Valley, Niagara Falls, Palisades, Thousand Islands.

Elected officials Gov. George E. Pataki (R, term exp. 2003). Lt. Gov. Mary Donohue (R). Sec. State Randy A. Daniels (D). Atty. Gen. Eliot Spitzer (D).
People (2000) 18,976,457 (3rd). **Race/Hispanic Origin** (2000): White 67.9%. Blac, 15.9%. Indian 0.4%. Asian 5.5%. Other 7.1%. Two or more races 3.1%. Hispanic 15.1%.
Cities (2000) New York 8,008,278. Buffalo 292,648. Rochester 219,773. Yonkers 196,086. Syracuse 147,306. Albany 95,658. New Rochelle 72,182. Mount Vernon 68,381. Schenectady 61,821. Utica 60,651.
Business Gross State Product, 1997: $651.65 bil. (2nd). **Leading Sectors of GSP** (1997): Finance, insurance, and real estate 31.19%; Services 22.75%; Manufacturing 11.42%. ***Fortune* 500 Companies** (2000): 55: including Citigroup, International Business Machines, AT&T, Verizon Communications, Philip Morris, J.P. Morgan Chase, Texaco, American International Group, Morgan Stanley Dean Witter, Merrill Lynch, TIAA-CREF, Goldman Sachs Group, MetLife, Pfizer, International Paper, Lehman Brothers Holdings, American Express, New York Life Insurance, Bristol-Myers Squibb, Loews, Pepsico, Viacom, Eastman Kodak, Arrow Electronics, Amerada Hess, Bear Stearns, Marsh & McLennan, Consolidated Edison, Colgate-Palmolive, Guardian Life Insurance Co. of America.
Famous natives Woody Allen, director. John Jacob Astor (b. Germany), merchant. Humphrey Bogart, actor. George Burns, actor. Aaron Copland, composer. Agnes De Mille, choreographer. George Eastman, camera inventor. Millard Fillmore, U.S. president. Lou Gehrig, baseball player. George Gershwin, composer. Julia Ward Howe, reformer. Washington Irving, author. Henry James, author. Vince Lombardi, football coach. Groucho Marx, comedian. Herman Melville, author. Ogden Nash, poet/humorist. Eugene O'Neill, playwright. Otetiani "Red Jacket", Seneca chief. Channing E. Phillips, minister/reformer. John D. Rockefeller, industrialist. Norman Rockwell, illustrator. Richard Rodgers, composer. Franklin Delano Roosevelt, U.S. president. Theodore Roosevelt, U.S. president. Jonas Salk, physician. Elizabeth Ann Seton, first American saint. Elizabeth Cady Stanton, suffragette. James Johnson Sweeney, art critic. Martin Van Buren, U.S. president. Mae West, actress. E.B. White, author. Walt Whitman, poet.
Noteworthy places Albright-Knox Gallery of American Art, Buffalo. American Merchant Marine Museum, Kings Point. Baseball Hall of Fame, Cooperstown. Bear Mt. State Park. Buffalo Museum of Science. Corning Glass Center, Corning. Erie Canal Museum, Syracuse. Farmers' Museum, Cooperstown. Fenimore House, Cooperstown. Franklin D. Roosevelt Natl. Hist. Site, Hyde Park. Ft. Stanwix Natl. Monument, Rome. Ft. Ticonderoga. Hudson Valley. Mohawk Valley. Niagara Falls. Palisades Interstate Park. Saratoga Natl. Hist. Park. Vanderbilt Museum, Hyde Park. U.S. Military Academy, West Point. Women's Rights Natl. Hist. Park, Seneca Falls. **New York City** American Academy of Arts & Sciences. American Museum of Natural History. Bronx Zoo. Brooklyn Botanical Garden. Brooklyn Museum. Cathedral of St. John the Divine. Cooper-Hewitt Museum. Federal Hall. Fraunces Tavern. Frick Collection. Guggenheim Museum. Hispanic Society of America. Jewish Museum. Lincoln Center for the Performing Arts. Metropolitan Museum of Art. Museum of Modern Art. Museum of the American Indian. N.Y. Public Library. N.Y. Stock Exchange.

Rockefeller Center. South Street Seaport Museum. Statue of Liberty. United Nations.
Memorable events Giovanni de Verrazano sails into New York Bay 1524. Samuel de Champlain sails down the St. Lawrence River 1603. Henry Hudson sails up Hudson River 1609. Dutch establish Ft. Orange (Albany) 1614. Peter Minuit buys Manhattan Island and founds colony of New Amsterdam 1625. British take New Amsterdam and name it New York 1664. Ethan Allen takes Ft. Ticonderoga 1775. George Washington inaugurated president New York City 1789. U.S. Military Academy founded West Point 1802. Erie Canal opened 1825. Statue of Liberty dedicated 1886. New York City includes Manhattan, Bronx, Queens, Brooklyn, and Staten Island 1898. President William McKinley assassinated in Buffalo 1901. UN headquarters established at New York City 1945. St. Lawrence Seaway opened 1959. One-fourth of New York City below poverty level 1984.
Tourist information (800) CALL-NYS. **www.state.ny.us.**

▶ NORTH CAROLINA
At the time of the Revolution, tobacco and rice plantations dominated the economy of the eastern part of the state, which in turn dominated the legislature. Next to last to ratify the Constitution, North Carolina was the last Southern state to secede from the Union. The Civil War cost North Carolina dearly; reconstruction was short-lived, and blacks were effectively disenfranchised again by the turn of the century. Since World War II, the state has grown increasingly prosperous, especially in the "academic triangle" that encloses the University of North Carolina at Chapel Hill, Duke, and North Carolina State. The traditional industries of textiles, furniture, and tobacco still lead, partly because of diversification within them. North Carolina benefits from the general Sunbelt boom and from an influx of foreign capital; it maintains a healthy manufacturing sector, and has enjoyed steady economic growth in the 1990s.
Name For King Charles I (Carolus is Latin for Charles). **Nicknames** Tarheel State, Old North State. **Capital** Raleigh. **Entered union** Nov. 21, 1789 (12th). **Motto** *Esse quam videri* (To be rather than to seem).
Emblems Bird Cardinal. **Fish** Channel bass. **Flower** Dogwood. **Insect** Honeybee. **Precious stone** Emerald. **Reptile** Eastern box turtle. **Rock** Granite. **Shell** Scotch bonnet. **Song** "The Old North State." **Tree** Pine.
Land Total area 52, 669 sq. mi. (28th), incl. 3,826 sq. mi. inland water. **Borders** Va., Atlantic Ocean, S.C., Tenn., Georgia. **Rivers** Pee Dee, Roanoke, Yadkin. **Lakes** Buggs Island, High Rock, Mattamuskeet, Norman, Waccamaw. **Mountains** Black, Blue Ridge, Great Smoky, Unaka. **Other notable features** Great Dismal Swamp, Mount Mitchell, Outer Banks, Pamlico Sound.
Elected officials Gov. Michael F. Easley (D, term exp. 2005). Lt. Gov. Beverly Purdue (D). Sec. State Elaine Marshall (D). Atty. Gen. Roy Cooper (D).
People (2000) 8,049,313 (11th). **Race/Hispanic Origin** (2000): White 72.1%. Black 21.6%. Indian 1.2%. Asian 1.4%. Other 2.3%. Two or more races 1.3%. Hispanic 4.7%.
Cities (2000) Charlotte 540,828. Raleigh 276,093. Greensboro 223,891. Durham 187,035. Winston-Salem 185,776. Fayetteville 121,015. Cary 94,536. High Point 85,839. Wilmington 75,838. Asheville 68,889.

Business   Gross State Product, 1997: $218.89 bil. (12th). **Leading Sectors of GSP** (1997): Manufacturing 26.48%; Services 15.69%; Finance, insurance, and real estate 15.10%. *Fortune* **500 Companies** (2000): 13: Bank of America Corp., Duke Energy, First Union Corp., Lowe's, R.J. Reynolds Tobacco, Wachovia Corp., Sonic Automotive, VF, B.F. Goodrich, BB&T Corp., Nucor, Progress Energy, Jefferson-Pilot.

Famous natives   Benjamin Newton Duke and James Buchanan Duke, industrialists/philanthropists. Richard J. Gatling, inventor. Billy Graham, minister. Andy Griffith, actor. O. Henry, writer. Andrew Johnson, U.S. president. William Rufus King, politician. Charles Kuralt, journalist. Meadowlark Lemon, athlete. Dolley Madison, First Lady. Thelonius Monk, musician. Edward R. Murrow, journalist. James Knox Polk, U.S. president. Moses Waddell, Confederate general. Thomas Wolfe, author.

Noteworthy places   Bennett Place. Blue Ridge Natl. Parkway. Cape Hatteras and Cape Lookout Natl. Seashore. Carl Sandburg home, Hendersonville. Ft. Raleigh. Great Smoky Mountains Natl. Park. Great Smoky Mountains Natl. Hist. Park. Guilford Courthouse Natl. Military Park. Mint Museum, Charlotte. Moores Creek Natl. Battlefield. North Carolina Maritime Museum, Beaufort. North Carolina Museum of Art, Raleigh. Roanoke Island. Wright Brothers Natl. Memorial, Kitty Hawk.

Memorable events   Part of Carolina grant given to eight noblemen by Charles II 1663. Culpepper's Rebellion in reaction to unfair tax collection policies 1677. Tuscarora lose war against European immigrants 1713. Proprietors sell rights to Crown; becomes royal province 1729. Mecklenburg Declaration (1775), forerunner of Declaration of Independence. Becomes first colony to sanction explicitly declaration of independence from Britain in Apr. 1776. Gen. Charles Cornwallis wins Battle of Guilford Courthouse, but British lose control of colony 1781. Ratifies Constitution 1789. Gives up claims to western territories, now part of Tennessee 1790. Establishes first state university system in United States 1829. Cherokees driven out of North Carolina to Oklahoma 1838. Secedes 1861. Readmitted to Union 1868. American Tobacco Company founded 1890. Wright brothers launch first successful airplane at Kitty Hawk 1903. Confrontation between Ku Klux Klan and anti-Klan demonstrators leaves five dead; 12 Klansmen charged with first-degree murder 1979.

Tourist information   (800) VISIT-NC. www.ncgov.com.

▶**NORTH DAKOTA**
The first permanent settlers in North Dakota were Scots-Canadians who settled at Pembina on the Red River near the Canadian border, and who traded primarily with Winnipeg and St. Paul. The arrival of the Northern Pacific Railway in 1872 created a surge of huge farms, many of which were wiped out by drought and harsh winters in the 1880s. There followed a huge influx of Norwegians and Germans whose influence is still very apparent today. North Dakota's economy is heavily agricultural and leads the nation in production of wheat. Farming is centered in the fertile Red River of the North Valley, with livestock throughout the rest of the state.

Name For northern section of Dakota territory; *dakota* is Sioux word for "allies." **Nicknames**

Sioux State, Peace Garden State, Flickertail State. **Capital** Bismarck. **Entered union** Nov. 2, 1889 (39th). **Motto** "Liberty and union, now and forever, one and inseparable."

Emblems   Beverage Milk. **Bird** Western meadowlark. **Fish** Northern pike. **Flower** Wild prairie rose. **Fossil** Teredo petrified wood. **Grass** Western wheatgrass. **March** "Spirit of North Dakota." **Song** "North Dakota Hymn." **Tree** American elm.

Land   Total area 70,703 sq. mi. (17th), incl. 1,403 sq. mi. inland water. **Borders** Saskatchewan, Manitoba, Minn., S.Dak., Mont. **Rivers** Missouri, Red River of the North. **Lakes** Ashtabula, Devils, Oahe, Sakakawea. **Other notable features** Geographical center of North America, Missouri Plateau, Red River Valley, Rolling Drift Prairie.

Elected officials   Gov. John Hoeven (R, term exp. 2004). Lt. Gov. Jack Dalrymple (R). Sec. State Alvin A. Jaegar (R). Atty. Gen. Wayne Stenehjem (R).

People   (2000) 642,200 (47th). **Race/Hispanic Origin** (2000): White 92.4%. Black 0.6%. Indian 4.9%. Asian 0.6%. Other 0.4%. Two or more races 1.2%. Hispanic 1.2%.

Cities   (2000) Fargo 90,599. Bismarck 55,532. Grand Forks 49,321. Minot 36,567. Mandan 16,718. Dickinson 16,010. Jamestown 15,527. West Fargo 14,940. Williston 12,512. Wahpeton 8,586.

Business   Gross State Product, 1997: $15.79 bil. (49th). **Leading Sectors of GSP** (1997): Services 18.42%; Government 15.44%; Finance, insurance, and real estate 13.48%. *Fortune* **500 Companies** (2000): 0.

Famous natives   Angie Dickinson, actress. John Bernard Flannagan, sculptor. Louis L'Amour, novelist. Peggy Lee, singer. Roger Maris, baseball player. Eric Sevareid, broadcaster. Vihjalmur Stefansson (b. Canada), ethnologist. Lawrence Welk, entertainer.

Noteworthy places   Ft. Abraham Lincoln State Park. Ft. Union Trading Post Natl. Hist. Site. International Peace Garden. Knife River Indian Villages Natl. Hist. Site. Theodore Roosevelt Natl. Park, the Badlands.

Memorable events   Pierre Gaultier de Varennes, sieur de Vérendrye first European to visit area 1738. United States acquires half of territory in Louisiana Purchase 1803. Meriwether Lewis and William Clark expedition builds Ft. Mandan 1804–5. First permanent settlement at Pembina 1812. Britain cedes western half of state to United States 1818. Missouri River steamboats reach territory 1838. First railroad arrives 1873. Statehood 1889. First state to hold presidential primary 1912. Garrison Dam completed forming Lake Sakakawea; gambling (blackjack) legalized 1981. Red River floods, devastating agriculture, 1997.

Tourist information   (800) HELLO-ND. www.discovernd.com.

▶**OHIO**
The first settlements in Ohio were Marietta, in 1788, and Cincinnati in 1789, on the Ohio River, but significant migration into the state didn't occur until after the War of 1812. Shipping flourished in the 1820s and 1830s thanks to a network of canals connecting the Ohio and Lake Erie. Since 1959 the St. Lawrence Seaway has helped keep Ohio among the top five exporting states. Heavy industry also flourished in the northern cities that had access to coal and iron ore from the Lake Superior region. The 1870s saw the development of a manufacturing base that later became an integral part of the automotive industry. Al-

though Ohio's economy has traditionally been well balanced between agriculture, industry, mining, and trade, the recession of the early 1980s weakened manufacturing, triggered flight from the industrial cities, and saw a dramatic shift to a service economy and to high-tech industry.

Name From the Iroquois *oheo*, "beautiful." **Nickname** Buckeye State. **Capital** Columbus. **Entered union** Mar. 1, 1803 (17th). **Motto** "With God, all things are possible."

Emblems **Beverage** Tomato juice. **Bird** Cardinal. **Flower** Scarlet carnation. **Gem** Ohio flint. **Insect** Ladybug. **Song** "Beautiful Ohio." **Tree** Buckeye.

Land Total area 41,330 sq. mi. (35th), incl. 326 sq. mi. inland water. **Borders** Mich., Lake Erie, Pa., W.Va., Ky., Ind. **Rivers** Cuyahoga, Maumee, Miami, Muskingum, Ohio, Sandusky, Scioto. **Lakes** Berlin Res., Dillon Res., Erie, Mosquito Res., St. Mary's.

Elected officials Gov. Bob Taft (R, term exp. 2003). Lt. Gov. Maureen O'Connor (R). Sec. State. J. Kenneth Blackwell (R). Atty. Gen. Betty D. Montgomery (R).

People (2000) 11,353,140 (7th). **Race/Hispanic Origin** (2000): White 85.0%. Black 11.5%. Indian 0.2%. Asian 1.2%. Other 0.8%. Two or more races 1.4%. Hispanic 1.9%.

Cities (2000) Columbus 711,470. Cleveland 478,403. Cincinnati 331,285. Toledo 313,619. Akron 217,074. Dayton 166,179. Parma 85,655. Youngstown 82,026. Canton 80,806. Lorain 68,652.

Business **Gross State Product,** 1997: $320.51 bil. (7th). **Leading Sectors of GSP** (1997): Manufacturing 26.16%; Services 18.03%; Finance, insurance, and real estate 15.90%. *Fortune* 500 **Companies** (2000): 29: including Kroger, Procter & Gamble, Cardinal Health, Federated Department Stores, TRW, Nationwide Insurance Enterprise, Goodyear Tire & Rubber, American Electric Power, Dana, Limited, National City Corp., Eaton, Keycorp, Cinergy, FirstEnergy, Progressive, NCR, Owens-Illinois, Parker Hannifin, Sherwin-Williams.

Famous natives Sherwood Anderson, writer. Neil Armstrong, astronaut. George Bellows, artist. Ambrose Bierce, author. George Armstrong Custer, army officer. Paul Laurence Dunbar, poet. Thomas A. Edison, inventor. James A. Garfield, U.S. president. John Glenn, astronaut/politician. Ulysses S. Grant, U.S. president/general. Zane Grey, author. Warren G. Harding, U.S. president. Benjamin Harrison, U.S. president. Rutherford B. Hayes, U.S. president. Bob Hope, entertainer. William McKinley, U.S. president. Annie Oakley, markswoman. Ransom Eli Olds, carmaker. Eddie Rickenbacker, pilot. William Sherman, army officer. William Howard Taft, U.S. president/chief justice. Art Tatum, pianist. Tecumseh, Shawnee chief. James Thurber, humorist. Orville Wright, airplane inventor.

Noteworthy places Air Force Museum, Dayton. Cleveland Museum of Art. Cleveland Museum of Natural History. Columbus Museum of Art. Great Lakes Historical Society Museum, Vermilion. Mound City Group Natl. Monument, Chillicothe. Neil Armstrong Air and Space Museum, Wapakoneta. Ohio River Museum, Marietta. Pro Football Hall of Fame, Canton. Toledo Museum of Art.

Memorable events Hopewell Mound-Builders present throughout state prior to arrival of Miamis, Shawnees, Wyandots, and Delawares. Conflicting claims by France, Virginia, Connecticut, and New York 1609–1786. René-Roger Cavelier de La Salle visits region 1669–70. To Britain 1763. To United States after 1783. Becomes part of North-

west Territory 1787. First settlement at Marietta 1788. Gen. "Mad" Anthony Wayne beats Tecumseh at Battle of Fallen Timbers 1794. Enters Union 1803. Harrison beats Tecumseh at Battle of Tippecanoe 1811. Oliver Hazard Perry beats British fleet at Battle of Put-in-Bay 1813. Ohio and Erie Canal completed 1832. Dayton flood kills 400 in Miami River Valley; damage put at $100 million 1913. Carl B. Stokes elected mayor of Cleveland, first black mayor of major U.S. city 1967. Four students protesting Vietnam War killed by National Guard at Kent State University 1970.

Tourist information (800) BUCKEYE. www.state.oh.us.

▶OKLAHOMA

French trappers entered the region of Oklahoma in the 1700s. In 1830 the land was designated the Indian Country, set aside for members of the Cherokees, Chickasaw, Choctaw, Creek, and Seminole deported from the southeast by the Indian Removal Act of 1830. These "Five Civilized Tribes," among others, fared well until the Civil War. They supported the Confederacy (some were actually slave-holders), and in 1868 Col. George Armstrong Custer led a massacre of Cheyenne at the Battle of the Washita. Twenty years later the government abrogated its treaty commitments and opened the territory to settlement. Today the state has a distinctly southern character. The region bordering the Red River is known as "Little Dixie," and as many as two-thirds of all Oklahomans consider themselves born-again Christians.

Oklahoma has a diversified economy. The state led the country in oil and gas production through the 1920s. Agriculture was hit heavily by the dust bowl of the 1930s, and thousands of "Okies" fled west. While agriculture and petroleum are still vital to the economy, manufacturing is increasingly important. The state is crossed by two of the country's longest rivers. The Arkansas links Catoosa (near Tulsa) to the Gulf of Mexico and the Mississippi River system; but the Red River is not navigable in Oklahoma, and dissolved salts make it useless for agriculture, industry or residential purposes.

Name From the Choctaw *okla humma*, "land of the red people." **Nickname** Sooner State. **Capital** Oklahoma City. **Entered union** Nov. 16, 1907 (46th). **Motto** *Labor omnia vincit* (Work overcomes all obstacles).

Emblems **Animal** American buffalo. **Bird** Scissor-tailed flycatcher. **Colors** Green and white. **Fish** White bass. **Floral emblem** Mistletoe. **Grass** Indian grass. **Poem** "Howdy Folks." **Reptile** Collared lizard (mountain boomer). **Song** "Oklahoma!" **Stone** Barite rose (rose rock). **Tree** Redbud. **Waltz** "Oklahoma Wind."

Land Total area 69,956 sq. mi. (18th), incl. 1,301 sq. mi. inland water. **Borders** Kans., Mo., Ark., Tex., N.Mex., Colo. **Rivers** Arkansas, Canadian, Cimarron, Red. **Lakes** Canton, Lake o' the Cherokees, Oologah, Texoma. **Other notable features** Ouachita Mts., Ozark Plateau, Staked Plain, Wichita Mts.

Elected officials Gov. Frank Keating (R, term exp. 2003). Lt. Gov. Mary Fallin (R). Sec. State Mike Hunter (R). Atty. Gen. Drew Edmondson (D).

People (2000) 3,450,654 (27th). **Race/Hispanic Origin** (2000): White 76.2%. Black 7.6%. Indian 7.9%. Asian 1.4%. Pacific Islander 0.1%. Other 2.4%. Two or more races 4.5%. Hispanic 5.2%.

Cities (2000) Oklahoma City 506,132. Tulsa 393,049. Norman 95,694. Lawton 92,757. Broken Arrow 74,859. Edmond 68,315. Midwest City 54,088. Enid 47,045. Moore 41,138. Stillwater 39,065.

Business **Gross State Product,** 1997: $76.64 bil. (30th). **Leading Sectors of GSP** (1997): Services 17.63%; Manufacturing 16.98%; Government 15.77%. *Fortune* **500 Companies** (2000) 5: Phillips Petroleum, Williams, Oneok, Kerr-McGee, OGE Energy.

Famous natives Ralph Ellison, author. Woody Guthrie, reformer/musician. Patrick J. Hurley, diplomat. Karl Jansky, electrical engineer. Mickey Mantle, baseball player. Wiley Post, aviator. Tony Randall, actor. Oral Roberts, evangelist. Will Rogers, humorist. Maria Tallchief, ballerina. Jim Thorpe, athlete.

Noteworthy places American Indian Hall of Fame, Anadarko. Chisholm Trail Museum, Kingfisher. Ft. Gibson Stockade, Muskogee. Natl. Cowboy Hall of Fame, Oklahoma City. Ouachita Natl. Forest. Pioneer Woman Museum, Ponca City. Will Rogers Memorial, Claremore.

Memorable events Francisco Vásquez de Coronado expedition in territory 1541. Except for panhandle, becomes part of Louisiana purchase 1803. Region made Indian Territory (not organized) in 1830 and becomes home of "Five Civilized Tribes"—Cherokee, Choctaw, Chickasaw, Creek, and Seminole—after they left the southeast on Trail of Tears 1828–46. United States acquires panhandle with annexation of Texas 1845. Territory opened to homesteaders 1889. Commercial oil well at Bartlesville 1897. Indian Territory and Oklahoma Territory merged and granted statehood 1907. Gov. John C. Walton impeached after declaring martial law to quell violence 1923. McClellan-Kerr Arkansas River Navigation system links Oklahoma to Mississippi, making Catoosa (Tulsa) major inland port 1971. Timothy McVeigh blows up Federal Building in Oklahoma City, killing 168 people 1995.

Tourist information (800) 652-6552. www.state.ok.us.

▶**OREGON**

Although the Lewis and Clark expedition reached the mouth of the Columbia River in 1805, interest in the area was kindled by the Hudson's Bay Company and later by Jason Lee, a Methodist minister who settled near Salem in 1834. After the decline of the fur trade, lumbering became the most important industry in Oregon. Though lumbering and related industries are still leading employers—the state is the leading grower of Christmas trees—Oregon has benefited from the arrival of smaller computer and electronics firms leaving California in search of a more favorable business climate. Traditionally progressive, it is one of most active states in the environmental protection movement. Only one-third of the population is affiliated with an organized religion.

Name Unknown origin, first applied to Columbia River. **Nickname** Beaver State. **Capital** Salem. **Entered union** Feb. 14, 1859 (33rd). **Motto** "She flies with her own wings." **Poet laureate** William E. Stafford.

Emblems **Animal** Beaver. **Bird** Western meadowlark. **Dance** Square dance. **Fish** Chinook salmon. **Flower** Oregon grape. **Insect** Swallowtail butterfly. **Song** "Oregon, My Oregon." **Stone** Thunderegg. **Tree** Douglas fir.

Land **Total area** 97,073 sq. mi. (10th), incl. 889 sq. mi. inland water. **Borders** Wash., Idaho, Nev., Calif., Pacific Ocean. **Rivers** Columbia, Snake, Willamette. **Mountains** Cascade Range, Coast Range, Klamath. **Other notable features** Willamette Valley.

Elected officials Gov. John A. Kitzhaber (D, term exp. 2003). Sec. State Bill Bradbury (D). Atty. Gen. Hardy Myers (D).

People (2000) 3,421,399 (28th). **Race/Hispanic Origin** (2000): White 86.6%. Black 1.6%. Indian 1.3%. Asian 3.0%. Pacific Islander 0.2%. Other 4.2%. Two or more races 3.1%. Hispanic 8.0%.

Cities (2000) Portland 529,121. Eugene 137,893. Salem 136,924. Gresham 90,205. Beaverton 76,129. Hillsboro 70,186. Medford 63,154. Springfield 52,864. Bend 52,029. Corvallis 49,322.

Business **Gross State Product,** 1997: $98.37 bil. (27th). **Leading Sectors of GSP** (1997): Manufacturing 25.08%; Services 17.31%; Finance, insurance, and real estate 15.15%. *Fortune* **500 Companies** (2000): 2: Nike, Willamette Industries.

Famous natives In-mut-too-yah-lat-lat (Joseph), Nez Percé chief. Ursula LeGuin (b. Calif.), author. Edwin Markham, poet. Dr. John McLoughlin, fur trader, "Father of Oregon". Linus Pauling, chemist. John Reed, author. William Simon U'Ren (b. Wis.), lawyer/reformer.

Noteworthy places Bonneville Dam, Columbia River. Columbia River Gorge. Columbia River Museum, Astoria. Crater Lakes Natl. Park. Ft. Clatsop Natl. Monument. Hells Canyon. High Desert Museum, Bend. John Day Fossil Beds Natl. Monument. Mt. Hood. Oregon Caves Natl. Monument. Oregon Dunes Natl. Recreation Area. Point Perpetua. Timberline Lodge.

Memorable events Sir Francis Drake turns away from fogbound coast of Pacific Northwest 1578. Capt. James Cook visits 1778. Mouth of Columbia River explored by Capt. Robert Gray, who claims region for U.S. 1792. Meriwether Lewis and George Rogers Clark expedition arrives at mouth of Columbia 1805. Claims to Oregon Territory, from California border to Alaska and east to Montana and Wyoming, relinquished by Spain (1819), Russia (1825), and Britain (1846). First settlers arrive Willamette Valley 1843. Organized as territory 1848. Statehood 1859. Railroad arrives 1883. Bonneville Dam completed 1937. Following severe rain and snow that claim 40 lives, Oregon declared disaster area 1964. First state to enact "bottle law" 1972. Snake River opened to navigation, linking Astoria to Lewiston, Idaho, 1975.

Tourist information (800) 547-7842. www.state.or.us.

▶**PENNSYLVANIA, COMMONWEALTH OF**

William Penn and his Quakers encouraged settlement and religious tolerance, and Pennsylvania was the first state to abolish slavery. In the late colonial period, Philadelphia was the cultural capital of the colonies. The first Continental Congress convened there in 1774, and it was for a decade the U.S. capital. With access to both the Great Lakes and to the Atlantic, Pennsylvanians took a lead in opening up the Midwest. Its resources include large coal deposits—which contribute to its ironmaking capabilities—lumber, textiles, and leather. Leadership in these sectors lasted well into the 20th century, when Pennsylvania lost ground to Sunbelt states. As in many states, there has been growth in tourist and service industries, though machinery production and trade continue to expand significantly.

Name For Adm. William Penn, father of William Penn, founder of commonwealth. **Nickname** Keystone State. **Capital** Harrisburg. **Entered union** Dec. 12, 1787 (2nd). **Motto** "Virtue, liberty and independence."

Emblems **Animal** White-tailed deer. **Beautification and conservation plant** Penngift crown vetch. **Beverage** Milk. **Bird** Ruffed grouse. **Dog** Great Dane. **Fish** Brook trout. **Flower** Mountain laurel. **Insect** Firefly. **Tree** Hemlock.

Land Total area 45,308 sq. mi. (33rd), incl. 420 sq. mi. inland water. **Borders** N.Y., N.J., Del., Md., W.Va., Ohio, Lake Erie. **Rivers** Allegheny, Delaware, Juniata, Monongahela, Ohio, Schuylkill, Susquehanna. **Lakes** Allegheny Res., Erie, Pymatuning Res., Shenango Res. **Mountains** Allegheny, Kittatinny, Laurel Hills, Pocono.

Elected officials Gov. Mark Schweiker (R). Sec. Commonwealth Kim Pizzingrilli (R). Atty. Gen. D. Michael Fisher (R).

People (2000) 12,281,054 (6th). **Race/Hispanic Origin** (2000): White 85.4%. Black 10.0%. Indian 0.1%. Asian 1.8%. Other 1.5%. Two or more races 1.2%. Hispanic 3.2%.

Cities (2000) Philadelphia 1,517,550. Pittsburgh 334,563. Allentown 106,632. Erie 103,717. Upper Darby 81,821. Reading 81,207. Scranton 76,415. Bethlehem 71,329. Lower Merion 59,850. Bensalem 58,434.

Business **Gross State Product,** 1997: $339.94 bil. (6th). **Leading Sectors of GSP** (1997): Services 21.85%; Manufacturing 20.04%; Finance, insurance, and real estate 18.99%. *Fortune* **500 Companies** (2000): 25: including USX, ALCOA, Cigna, Rite Aid, Sunoco, Amerisource Health, H.J. Heinz, PPG Industries, Comcast, PNC Financial Services Group, Crown Cork & Seal, Aramark, Unisys, Rohm & Haas, Lincoln National, Mellon Financial Corp., PPL, Air Products & Chemicals, IKON Office Solutions, Hershey Foods.

Famous natives Louisa May Alcott, author. Maxwell Anderson, playwright. James Buchanan, U.S. president. Alexander Calder, sculptor. Andrew Carnegie (b. Scotland), industrialist/philanthropist. Mary Cassatt, painter. Wilt Chamberlain, basketball player. Bill Cosby, comedian/philanthropist. Stephen Foster, songwriter. Benjamin Franklin (b. Mass.), inventor/statesman. Robert Fulton, inventor. Milton S. Hershey, chocolatier. George C. Marshall, statesman. Andrew W. Mellon, financier/philanthropist. Robert E. Peary, explorer. Betsy Ross, patriot. Andy Warhol, artist. Johnny Weismuller, swimmer/actor. Benjamin West, painter.

Noteworthy places Academy of Natural Sciences, Philadelphia. Carnegie Institute, Pittsburgh. Delaware Water Gap Natl. Recreation Area. Ft. Necessity Natl. Battlefield. Franklin Institute, Philadelphia. Gettysburg Battlefield. Hugh Moore Hist. Park and Museums, Easton. Independence Natl. Hist. Park, Philadelphia. Liberty Bell, Carpenters Hall, Philadelphia. Pennsylvania Academy of Fine Arts, Philadelphia. Pennsylvania Dutch Country. Philadelphia Museum of Art. Pine Creek Gorge. Rodin Museum, Philadelphia. Valley Forge Natl. Hist. Park.

Memorable events Cornelis Jacobssen sails into Delaware Bay 1614. Swedes settle at Tinicum Island 1643. Charles II grants proprietary charter to William Penn 1681. First U.S. hospital established, in Philadelphia, 1751. Mason-Dixon Line establishes southern boundary of state 1763–67—later boundary between slave and nonslave states. Declaration of Independence (1776) and Constitution (1787) signed in Philadelphia. Becomes first state to abolish slavery 1780. Bank of North America becomes first bank chartered in United States 1781. Philadelphia capital of United States 1790–1800. First iron furnace in U.S. 1792. First oil well in the world driven near Titusville 1859. Battle of Gettysburg turning point in Civil War; Lincoln's Gettysburg Address 1863. Centennial Exhibition at Philadelphia 1876. Johnstown flood—worst in U.S. history—kills 2,200 people 1889. Pinkerton detectives kill 12 strikers at Homestead steel works near Pittsburgh 1892. Twenty coal miners killed during strike for eight-hour day and other concessions 1897. More than 500 injured during three-day race riot in Philadelphia 1964. Partial meltdown at Three Mile Island forces closure of nuclear reactor 1979. Storage tank spills 713,000 gallons diesel fuel into Monongahela River, disrupting water supplies in Pennsylvania, West Virginia, and Ohio 1988.

Tourist information (800) VISIT-PA. www.state.pa.us.

▶ **RHODE ISLAND AND PROVIDENCE PLANTATIONS**

Giovanni de Verrazano was the first European to record visiting the area of Narragansett Bay, the prominent inlet that almost splits the eastern third of the state from the rest. The first settlers were followers of Roger Williams, who left the restrictive religious atmosphere of the Puritan Massachusetts Bay Colony to found Providence in 1636. Rhode Island is the site of the first U.S. Baptist church, at Providence, and at Newport the first Quaker meetinghouse and the first synagogue. It was the last of the 13 original colonies to ratify the Constitution, the centralized federalism of which many Rhode Islanders objected to. The development of 19th-century Rhode Island was influenced by immigration and the Industrial Revolution; the state's leading manufacturers are still silver, jewelry and textiles. Although it ranks 43rd in population, Rhode Island is second in population density (behind New Jersey) at 947.6 people per square mile.

Name For Rhode Island in Narragansett Bay, named in turn for Mediterranean island of Rhodes. **Nicknames** Ocean State, Little Rhody. **Capital** Providence. **Entered union** May 29, 1790 (13th). **Motto** "Hope."

Emblems **Bird** Rhode Island red. **Flower** Violet. **Mineral** Bowenite. **Rock** Cumberlandite. **Song** "Rhode Island." **Tree** Red maple.

Land Total area 1,212 sq. mi. (50th), incl. 157 sq. mi. inland water. **Borders** Mass., Atlantic Ocean, Conn. **Rivers** Blackstone, Pawcatuck, Providence, Sakonnet. **Other notable features** Block Island, Narragansett Bay, Aquidneck Island.

Elected officials Gov. Lincoln Almond (R, term exp. 2003). Lt. Gov. Charles Fogarty (D). Sec. State Edward S. Inman III (D). Atty. Gen. Sheldon Whitehouse (D).

People (2000) 1,048,319 (43rd). **Race/Hispanic Origin** (2000): White 85.0%. Black 4.5%. Indian 0.5%. Asian 2.3%. Pacific Islander 0.1%. Other 5.0%. Two or more races 2.7%. Hispanic 8.7%.

Cities (2000) Providence 193,618. Warwick 85,808. Cranston 79,269. Pawtucket 72,958. East Providence 48,688. Woonsocket 43,224. Coventry 33,668. North Providence 32,411. Cumberland 31,840. West Warwick 29,581.

Business **Gross State Product,** 1997: $27.81 bil. (44th). **Leading Sectors of GSP** (1997): Finance, insurance, and real estate 24.96%; Services 21.91%; Manufacturing 15.63%. *Fortune* **500 Companies** (2000): 3: CVS, Textron, Hasbro.

Famous natives George M. Cohan, actor/producer. Nathanael Greene, army officer. Galway

Kinell, poet. Metacomet (King Philip), Wampanoag chief. Oliver H. Perry and Matthew C. Perry, naval officers. Gilbert Stuart, portraitist. **Noteworthy places** Brown University, Providence. First Baptist Church in North America (1638), Providence. Hoffenreffer Museum of Anthropology, Bristol. John Carter Brown Library, Providence. Rhode Island School of Design, Providence. Nathanael Greene homestead, Coventry. Museum of Yachting, Newport. Newport mansions. Tennis Hall of Fame, Newport. Touro Synagogue (oldest extant in North America), Newport. **Memorable events** Roger Williams, expelled from Massachusetts Bay Colony, settles in Providence 1636. Other religious exiles settle in Portsmouth (1638), Newport (1639), and Warwick (1642). King Philip's War 1675–76. First Quaker meetinghouse in North America founded 1699. First colony to renounce allegiance to Britain 1776. Last colony to ratify Constitution 1790. Dorr's Rebellion achieves liberalization of state constitution, which had remained unchanged since 1663, 1842. America's Cup Race held in Newport for first time 1930. Newport Bridge across Narragansett Bay completed 1969. *Australia II* first non-U.S. boat to win America's Cup in 132 years 1983.
Tourist information (800) 556-2484.
www.state.ri.us.

▶**SOUTH CAROLINA**
South Carolina's early economy was based on rice—its plantations worked by slaves—though tobacco later played a major role. As was true in North Carolina, many settlers made their way into the back country where they eked out a living as tenant farmers. During the Revolution, Ft. Charlotte was the first British installation to fall to Colonial troops, and at the outbreak of the Civil War, Ft. Sumter was the first Union installation to fall to Confederate forces. While agriculture remained a staple of the state's economy through the close of the 19th century, textile manufacture took over in the early 20th century. The postwar era has seen the rapid expansion of the chemical and paper industries, as well as large-scale development of the Atlantic Coast ports of Charleston, Georgetown, and Port Royal.

Name For King Charles II (Carolus is Latin for Charles). **Nickname** Palmetto State. **Capital** Columbia. **Entered union** May 23, 1788 (8th). **Motto** *Animis opibusque parati* (Prepared in mind and deed); *Dum spiro spero* (While I breathe I hope). **Poet laureate** Helen von Kolnitz Hyer.
Emblems **Animal** White-tailed deer. **Beverage** Milk. **Bird** Carolina wren. **Dance** Shag. **Dog** Boykin spaniel. **Fish** Striped bass. **Flower** Yellow jessamine. **Fruit** Peach. **Shell** Lettered olive. **Song** "Carolina." **Stone** Blue granite. **Tree** Palmetto. **Wild game Bird** Wild turkey.
Land Total area 31,113 sq. mi. (40th), incl. 910 sq. mi. inland water. **Borders** N.C., Atlantic Ocean, Ga. **Rivers** Catawba, Congaree, Edisto, Pee Dee, Savannah, Tugaloo, Wateree. **Lakes** Greenwood, Hartwell, Keowee, Marion, Murray, Santee Res., Wylie. **Other notable features** Blue Ridge Mts., Congaree Swamp, Sea Islands.
Elected officials Gov. Jim Hodges (D, term exp. 2003). Lt. Gov. Bob Peeler (R). Sec. State Jim Miles (R). Atty. Gen. Charles Condon (R).
People (2000) 4,012,012 (26th). **Race/Hispanic Origin** (2000): White 67.2%. Black 29.5%. Indian 0.3%. Asian 0.9%. Other 1.0%. Two or more races 1.0%. Hispanic 2.4%.

Cities (2000) Columbia 116,278. Charleston 96,650. North Charleston 79,641. Greenville 56,002. Rock Hill 49,765. Mount Pleasant 47,609. Spartanburg 39,673. Sumter 39,643. Hilton Head Island 33,862. Florence 30,248.
Business Gross State Product, 1997: $93.26 bil. (28th). **Leading Sectors of GSP** (1997): Manufacturing 24.97%; Services 15.68%; Government 14.82%. *Fortune* **500 Companies** (2000): 1: Scana.
Famous natives James F. Byrnes, politician/jurist. John C. Calhoun, politician. Dizzy Gillespie, musician. Althea Gibson, athlete. DuBose Heyward, author. Andrew Jackson, U.S. president. Eartha Kitt, singer. James Longstreet, army officer. Francis Marion, army officer/politician. Charles C. Pinckney and Thomas Pinckney, diplomats. Edward Rutledge and John Rutledge, politicians. Strom Thurmond, politician.
Noteworthy places Charleston Museum (1773, oldest in United States). Congaree Swamp Natl. Monument. Cowpens Natl. Battlefield. Ft. Moultrie, Ft. Johnson, and Ft. Sumter Natl. Monument, Charleston. Hilton Head Island. Kings Mountain Natl. Military Park. Ninety-Six Natl. Hist. Site, Greenwood. Patriots Point Maritime Museum, Charleston. Sea Islands. Spoleto Music Festival, Charleston.
Memorable events Spanish visit 1521. French Huguenots at Port Royal 1562. Included in Carolina grant by Charles II 1663. Charleston founded 1680. Becomes royal province 1729. Ratifies Constitution 1787. *Best Friend of Charleston*, first American steam locomotive built for passenger use 1833. First state to secede from Union Dec. 20, 1860. Confederate forces attack Ft. Sumter Apr. 12, 1861. Secession repealed 1865. Readmitted to Union 1868. Cyclone kills 1,000 in Savannah, Georgia, and Charleston 1893. Savannah River nuclear plant begins production near Aiken 1951; closed for safety reasons 1988. Hurricane Hugo kills 24 and causes $700 million in property damage 1989. BMW opens plant in Spartanburg 1994.
Tourist information (800) SC-SMILE or 1-803-734-0122.
www.state.sc.us.

▶**SOUTH DAKOTA**
The United States did not organize the Dakota Territory until 1861, and even then interest in the region was scant until gold was discovered in 1874. The majority of those who remained after the gold rush turned to cattle ranching, which was a mainstay of the economy through the first half of the 20th century. The manufacturing base was developed after four major dams were built on the Missouri River in the 1930s. They provided hydroelectric power and increased irrigation along the Missouri, which cuts the state in half. Concerned especially over the abrogation of 19th-century treaties, the American Indian Movement (AIM) took over the courthouse at Wounded Knee for 10 weeks in 1973. While U.S. courts have found in favor of the Sioux in several cases concerning the earlier treaties, many maintain that the settlements were insufficient.

Name For southern section of Dakota territory; *dakota* is Sioux word for "allies." **Nicknames** Coyote State, Sunshine State. **Capital** Pierre. **Entered union** Nov. 2, 1889 (40th). **Motto** "Under God the people rule."
Emblems **Animal** Coyote. **Bird** Chinese ring-necked pheasant. **Fish** Walleye. **Flower** Pasque .

Land Total area 77,116 sq. mi. (16th), incl. 1,164 sq. mi. inland water. **Borders** N.Dak., Minn., Iowa, Nebr., Wyo., Mont. **Rivers** Cheyenne, James, Missouri, Moreau, White. **Lakes** Belle Fourche Res., Big Stone, Traverse. **Other notable features** Badlands, Black Hills (Harney Peak 7,242 ft.).

Elected officials Gov. Bill Janklow (R, term exp. 2003). Lt. Gov. Carole Hillard (R). Sec. State Joyce Hazeltine (R). Atty. Gen. Mark Barnett (R).

People (2000) 754,844 (46th). **Race/Hispanic Origin** (2000): White 88.7%. Black 0.6%. Indian 8.3%. Asian 0.6%. Other 0.5%. Two or more races 1.3%. Hispanic 1.4%.

Cities (2000) Sioux Falls 123,975. Rapid City 59,607. Aberdeen 24,658. Watertown 20,237. Brookings 18,504. Mitchell 14,558. Pierre 13,876. Yankton 13,528. Huron 11,893.Vermillion 9,765.

Business **Gross State Product,** 1997: $20.19 bil. (46th). **Leading Sectors of GSP** (1997): Finance, insurance, and real estate 20.51%; Services 16.51%; Manufacturing 13.34%. **Fortune 500 Companies** (2000): 2: IBP, Northwestern.

Famous natives Tom Brokaw, journalist. Martha "Calamity" Jane Burk (b. Mo.), frontierswoman. Alvin Hansen, economist. Hubert H. Humphrey, politician. Ernest O. Lawrence, physicist (Nobel Prize, 1939). George McGovern, politician. Ta-sunko-witko (Crazy Horse), Oglala Sioux chief. Tatanka Iyotake (Sitting Bull), Sioux chief.

Noteworthy places Badlands Natl. Park. Crazy Horse State Memorial, Custer. Custer State Park. Ft. Sisseton. Geographical center of the United States. Jewel Cave Natl. Monument. Mount Rushmore. Natl. Memorial. Wind Cave Natl. Park.

Memorable events French visit region 1742–43. To United States in Louisiana Purchase 1803. Ft. Pierre first permanent settlement 1817. Part of Dakota Territory 1861. Gold discovered in Black Hills 1874. Divided from North Dakota; statehood 1889. U.S. troops massacre Sioux at Battle of Wounded Knee 1890.

Tourist information (800) SDAKOTA. www.state.sd.us.

▶**TENNESSEE**

At first claimed by Virginia and later by North Carolina, Tennessee had its first great pioneer in Daniel Boone, who traversed the region in the 1760s. Political attitudes in the 18th century were shaped by the land, with the cotton and tobacco growers in the fertile western part of the state favoring slavery and the backwoods people of the eastern hills opposed to it. The Cherokees were removed to Oklahoma by the federal government in the 1830s. The state was captured by Union troops in 1862 and put under the governorship of Andrew Johnson, later a U.S. president.

Its economy was radically altered in the 1930s and 1940s by the creation of the Tennessee Valley Authority, which provided abundant energy for industry, and to a lesser extent by the location of the government's first uranium enrichment facility at Oak Ridge during World War II. The state's leading industries are textiles, food processing, and chemicals, and there is considerable lead and coal mining in the east.

Name For Tenase, principal village of Cherokees. **Nickname** Volunteer State. **Capital** Nashville. **Entered union** June 1, 1796 (16th). **Motto** "Agriculture and commerce." **Slogan** "Tennessee—America at its best." **Poet laureate** Richard M. ("Pek") Gunn.

Emblems **Animal** Raccoon. **Bird** Mockingbird. **Folk dance** Square dance. **Cultivated flower** Iris.

Gem Tennessee pearl. **Insects** Ladybug, firefly. **Poem** "Oh Tennessee, My Tennessee." **Public school song** "My Tennessee." **Rock** Limestone agate. **Songs** "When It's Iris Time in Tennessee," "The Tennessee Waltz," My Homeland, Tennessee," "Rocky Top." **Tree** Tulip poplar. **Wildflower** Passion flower.

Land Total area 42,144 sq. mi. (34th), incl. 989 sq. mi. inland water. **Borders** Ky., Va., N.C., Ga., Ala., Miss., Ark., Mo. **Rivers** Clinch, Cumberland, Mississippi, Tennessee. **Lakes** Boone, Center Hill, Cherokee, Dale Hollow, Douglass, J. Percy Priest, Watauga. **Other notable features** Cumberland Mts., Great Smoky Mts., Tennessee Valley, Unaka Mts.

Elected officials Gov. Don Sundquist (R, term exp. 2003). Lt. Gov. John S. Wilder (D). Sec. State Riley C. Darnell (D). Atty. Gen. Paul Summers (D).

People (2000) 5,689,283 (16th). **Race/Hispanic Origin** (2000): White 80.2%. Black 16.4%. Indian 0.3%. Asian 1.0%. Other 1.0%. two or more races 1.1%. Hispanic 2.2%.

Cities (2000) Memphis 650,100. Nashville-Davidson 569,891. Knoxville 173,890. Chattanooga 155,554. Clarksville 103,455. Murfreesboro 68,816. Jackson 59,643. Johnson City 55,469. Kingsport 44,905. Franklin 41,842.

Business **Gross State Product,** 1997: $147.00 bil. (20th). **Leading Sectors of GSP** (1997): Manufacturing 21.28%; Services 20.31%; Finance, insurance, and real estate 14.44%. **Fortune 500 Companies** (2000): 6: FedEx, HCA, UnumProvident, Eastman Chemical, Dollar General, AutoZone.

Famous natives James Agee, author. Davy Crockett, frontiersman. David Farragut, naval officer. Aretha Franklin, singer. Morgan Freeman, actor. Al Gore, (b. Washington, D.C.), politician. Cordell Hull, statesman (Nobel Peace Prize, 1945). Dolly Parton, singer. Sikawyi (Sequoya), Cherokee scholar. Alvin York, soldier.

Noteworthy places American Museum of Science and Energy, Oak Ridge. Andrew Johnson Natl. Hist. Site, Greenville. Chickamauga and Chattanooga Natl. Military Park. Cumberland Natl. Hist. Park. Ft. Donelson Natl. Military Park. Grand Old Opry, Nashville. Great Smoky Mountains Natl. Park. The Hermitage (Andrew Jackson home), Nashville. Lookout Mountain, Chattanooga. The Parthenon, Nashville. Shiloh Natl. Military Park, Pittsburgh Landing. Stones River Natl. Battlefield, Murfreesboro.

Memorable events De Soto expedition passes through region 1540. French claim territory as part of Louisiana; English claim territory as part of Carolina grant 1663. French claim given up after French and Indian War 1763. State of Franklin established in what is now eastern Tennessee 1784–87. Organized as Territory South of the Ohio 1790. Statehood 1796. Secedes from Union 1861. Battles of Shiloh (1862), Chattanooga (1863), Stones River (1863), and Nashville (1864). Readmitted to Union 1866. Clarence Darrow defends John T. Scopes for violating ban on teaching evolution in public schools; loses case 1925. Congress creates Tennessee Valley Authority 1933. First operational nuclear reactor at Oak Ridge 1943. Martin Luther King assassinated at Memphis 1968. World's Fair held in Knoxville 1982.

Tourist information (800) 836-6200. www.state.tn.us.

▶**TEXAS**

The land that is Texas today was originally part of Spain's holdings in Mexico. After Mexico won independence, the new government invited U.S. citizens to settle there. After many clashes between the Mexican and Anglo cultures, Texas broke away and for 10 years was an independent country before becoming a state in 1845. Modern Texas was made by oil, discovered at Spindletop in 1901, and the state's economy has been tied to the oil market ever since. After World War II, the Texas economy soared, bringing both prosperity and an unprecedented population boom. With the oil glut of the early 1980s, growth came to a halt, causing a drastic realignment of economic priorities. Unemployment jumped more than 20 percent during the 1980s, and remained higher than the national average in 1990, a year that saw many bank failures. The economy has been forced to diversify; currently the petroleum industry accounts for only 7 percent of state revenues, down from 25 percent a decade before. Texas has enormous resources ranging from cotton, cattle, and timber to aerospace, computers, and electronics. The largest of the 48 conterminous states, Texas's image as a state of wide-open spaces is understandable, but fully 80 percent of its people live in metropolitan areas, and Dallas, Houston, and San Antonio are among the nation's 10 largest cities. Twenty-five percent of the population is Hispanic; the majority of those are Mexican-American.

Name From the Caddo *tavshas*, "friends." **Nickname** Lone Star State. **Capital** Austin. **Entered union** Dec. 29, 1845 (28th). **Motto** "Friendship." **Emblems Bird** Mockingbird. **Dish** Chili. **Flower** Bluebonnet. **Gem** Topaz. **Grass** Sideoats grama. **Songs** "Texas, Our Texas," "The Eyes of Texas." **Stone** Palmwood. **Tree** Pecan.
Land Total area 266,807 sq. mi. (2nd), incl. 4,790 sq. mi. inland water. **Borders** Okla., Ark., La., Gulf of Mexico, Tamaulipas, Coahuila, Chihuahua, N.Mex. **Rivers** Brazos, Colorado, Natchez, Red, Rio Grande, Sabine, Trinity. **Lakes** Sam Rayburn Res., Texoma, Toledo Bend Res. **Other notable features** Balcones Escarpment, Diablo Sierra, Edwards Plateau, Guadalupe Mts., Staked Plain, Stockton Plateau.
Elected officials Gov. Rick Perry (R, term exp. 2003). Lt. Gov. Bill Ratliff (R). Sec. State Henry Cuellar (D). Atty. Gen. John Cornyn (R).
People (2000) 20,851,820 (2nd). **Race/Hispanic Origin** (2000): White 71.0%. Black 11.5%. Indian 0.6%. Asian 2.7%. Pacific Islander 0.1%. Other 11.7%. Two or more races 2.5%. Hispanic 32.0%.
Cities (2000) Houston 1,953,631. Dallas 1,188,580. San Antonio 1,144,646. Austin 656,562. El Paso 563,662. Fort Worth 534,694. Arlington 332,969. Corpus Christi 277,454. Plano 222,030. Garland 215,768.
Business Gross State Product, 1997: $601.64 bil. (3rd). **Leading Sectors of GSP** (1997): Services 18.49%; Manufacturing 15.78%; Finance, insurance, and real estate 14.54%. *Fortune* **500 Companies** (2000): 45: including Exxon Mobil, Enron, SBC Communications, Compaq Computer, J.C. Penney, Conoco, Dell Computer, Dynegy, Reliant Energy, TXU, El Paso, AMR, Sysco, Electronic Data Systems, Valero Energy, Fleming, Ultramar Diamond Shamrock, Kimberly-Clark, Halliburton, Waste Management.
Famous natives Stephen Austin (b. Va.), pioneer. James "Jim" Bowie (b. Ky.), army officer. Carol Burnett, comedian. J. Frank Dobie, folklorist. Dwight D. Eisenhower, U.S. president/general. Samuel Houston (b. Va.), president Republic of Texas/governor State of Texas. Howard Hughes,

industrialist/aviator. Lyndon Baines Johnson, U.S. president. Janis Joplin, singer. Barbara Jordan, politician. Audie Murphy, soldier/actor. Chester Nimitz, navy officer. Katherine Anne Porter, author. Samuel T. Rayburn, politician. Mildred "Babe" Didrikson Zaharias, athlete.
Noteworthy places The Alamo, San Antonio. Alibates Flint Quarries Natl. Monument. Big Bend Natl. Park. Ft. Davis. Galveston Historical Foundation. Guadalupe Mountains Natl. Park. Houston Museum of Fine Arts. Lyndon B. Johnson Natl. Hist. Park, Johnson City. Lyndon B. Johnson Space Center, Houston. Old Stone Ft., Nacogdoches. Padre Island Natl. Seashore. San Antonio Missions Natl. Hist. Park. Texas Ranger Museum, Waco.
Memorable events Alonzo Alvarez de Piñeda sails along coast 1519. Estevanico blazes trail through West Texas 1539. Spanish establish settlement at Ysleta near El Paso 1682. René-Robert Cavalier de La Salle attempts to found colony on Matagorda Bay, establishing claim to region for France 1685. Effective Spanish occupation 1715. United States acquires French claim to region with Louisiana Purchase 1803. United States relinquishes claim to Spain 1819. Americans move into region in early 19th century. Mexico, of which Texas is a province, wins independence from Spain 1821. Declaration of Independence from Mexico; Santa Anna victor at Battle of the Alamo; Sam Houston victor at Battle of San Jacinto; founding of Republic of Texas 1836. Texas granted statehood by United States 1845. Secedes from Union 1861; readmitted 1870. Hurricane kills 6,000 at Galveston 1900. NASA Space Center opens at Houston 1962. Pres. Kennedy assassinated at Dallas 1963. Price of oil plunges during 1980s, crippling state economy.
Tourist information (800) 888-8TEX, ext. 728. www.state.tx.us.

▶**UTAH**
In the middle of the Great Basin between the Rocky Mountains and the Sierra Nevada, Utah was an arid and uninviting region. After Joseph Smith, the founder of the Church of Jesus Christ of Latter-day Saints (Mormons), was shot in Illinois, Brigham Young led his people west, ultimately to the Salt Lake Valley in 1847. The chief obstacle to statehood was polygamy, which the church eventually renounced. There was an influx of non-Mormons after the discovery of silver in 1863, but Mormons still comprise two-thirds of the state's population, and the state remains conservative in outlook. Although the federal government is a major employer, government policy has lately been challenged by increased concern over the issues of chemical weapons testing, the MX missile, and disposal of nuclear waste from the Rocky Mountain Arsenal in neighboring Colorado.
Name For Ute Indians. **Nicknames** Beehive State, Mormon State. **Capital** Salt Lake City. **Entered Union** Jan. 4, 1896 (45th). **Motto:** "Industry."
Emblems Animal Elk. **Bird** California Gull. **Emblem** Beehive **Fish** Rainbow Trout **Flower** Sego lily. **Gem** Topaz. **Song** "Utah, We Love Thee." **Tree** Blue spruce.
Land Total area 84,899 sq. mi. (11th), incl. 2,826 sq. mi. inland water. **Borders** Idaho, Wyo., Colo., Ariz., Nev. **Rivers** Bear, Colorado, Green, Sevier. **Lakes** Bear, Great Salt, Utah. **Mountains** La Sal, Uinta (Kings Peak 13,528 ft.) Wasatch Range. **Other notable features** Great Salt Lake Desert (Bonneville Salt Flats) Kaibab Plateau.

Elected officials Gov. Michael O. Leavitt (R, term exp. 2005). Lt. Gov./Sec. State Olene Walker (R). Atty. Gen. Mark Shurtleff (R).
People (2000) 2,233,169 (34th). **Race/Hispanic Origin** (2000): White 89.2%. Black 0.8%. Indian 1.3%. Asian 1.7%. Pacific Islander 0.7%. Other 4.2%. Two or more races 2.1%. Hispanic 9.0%.
Cities (2000) Salt Lake City 181,743. West Valley City 108,896. Provo 105,166. Sandy 88,418. Orem 84,324. Ogden 77,226. West Jordan 68,336. Layton 58,474. Taylorsville 57,439. St. George 49,663.
Business Gross State Product, 1997: $55.42 bil. (35th). **Leading Sectors of GSP** (1997): Services 19.37%; Finance, insurance, and real estate 16.46%; Manufacturing 15.52%. *Fortune 500* **Companies** (2000): 0.
Famous natives Maud Adams, actress. John Moses Browning, inventor. Philo Farnsworth, engineer. Merlin Olsen, football player/actor. Ivy Baker Priest, U.S. treasurer. Brigham Young (b. Vt.), religious leader. Loretta Young, actress.
Noteworthy places Arches Natl. Park. Bryce Canyon Natl. Park. Canyonlands Natl. park. Capitol Reef Natl. Park. Cedar Breaks Natl. Monument. Dinosaur Natl. Monument. Flaming Gorge Dam Natl. Monument. Great Salt Lake. Lake Powell Natl. Monument. Monument Valley. Mormon Tabernacle, Salt Lake City. Natural Bridges Natl. Monument. Promontory Point. Rainbow Bridge Natl. Monument. Temple Square, Salt Lke City. Timpanogas Cave Natl. Monument. Zion Natl. Park.
Memorable events First visted probably by explorers from Coronado expedition 1540. Silvestre Vélez de Escalante and Francisco Atanasio Dominguez explore for Spain 1776. James Bridger discovers Great Salt Lake 1824. Led by Brigham Young, Mormons reach Great Salt Lake 1847. United States acquires Utah region from Mexico 1848. Mormons organize state of Deseret 1849; Congress refuses to recognize and instead organizes Territory of Utah 1850. Silver discovered at Little Cottonwood Canyon 1868. First transcontinental railroad completed with driving of golden spike at Promontory Point 1869. Mormon church renounces polygamy 1890, paving way to statehood 1896. Uranium discovered near Moab 1952. Winter Olympics to be held in Salt Lake City 2002.
Tourist Information (800) 200-1160. www.utah.gov.

▶**VERMONT**
Originally claimed by both New Hampshire and New York, Vermont's independence was asserted by Ethan Allen. His Green Mountain Boys rid the state of New Yorkers in 1770, fought well against the British in the Revolution, and declared the independent republic of New Connecticut in 1777. Allen was eventually overthrown, and Vermont joined the Union in 1791.
Vermont traditionally has strong ties to Canada, and there was an influx of French-Canadians as Vermont began to develop its manufacturing base in the mid-19th century. Vermont's politics have always been characterized by tolerance and progressivism. As New Connecticut, it abolished slavery and allowed universal male suffrage. Vermont's environmental concerns focus on acid rain and the degree to which development (especially by the tourist industry) should infringe on the state's remaining unspoiled land.
Name From French *vert mont*, "green mountain." **Nickname** Green Mountain State. **Capital** Montpelier. **Entered Union** Mar. 4, 1791 (14th). **Motto** "Freedom and unity."

Emblems Animal Morgan horse. **Beverage** Milk. **Bird** Hermit thrush. **Cold-Water Fish** Brook trout. **Flower** Red Clover. **Insect** Honeybee. Song "Hail, Vermont!" **Tree** Sugar Maple. **Warm-Water Fish** Walleye pike.
Land Total Area 9,614 sq. mi. (43rd), incl. 341 sq. mi. inland water. **Borders** Quebec, N.H., Mass., N.Y. **Rivers** Connecticut, Lamoille, Otter Creek, Poultney, White, Winooski. **Lakes** Bomoseen, Champlain, Memphremagog, Willoughby. **Other Notable Features** Grand Isle, Green Mts. (Mt. Mansfield 4,393 ft.), Taconic Mts.
Elected officials Gov. Howard Dean, M.D. (D, two-year term exp. 2003). Lt. Gov. Douglas Racine (D). Sec. State Deborah Markowitz (D). Atty. Gen. William H. Sorrell (D).
People (2000) 608,827 (49th). **Race/Hispanic Origin** (2000): White 96.8%. Black 0.5%. Indian 0.4%. Asian 0.9%. Other 0.2%. Two or more races 1.2%. Hispanic 0.9%.
Cities (2000) Burlington 38,889. Essex 18,626. Rutland 17,292. Colchester 16,986. South Burlington 15,814. Bennington 15,737. Brattleboro 12,005. Hartford 10,367. Milton 9,479. Barre 9,291.
Business Gross State Product, 1997: $15.21 bil. (50th). **Leading Sectors of GSP** (1997): Services 21.05%; Finance, insurance, and real estate 18.07%; Manufacturing 17.95%. *Fortune 500* **Companies** (2000): 0.
Famous natives Ethan Allen (b. Conn.), army officer. Chester A. Arthur, U.S. President. Calvin Coolidge, U.S. president. John Deere, industrialist. George Dewey, naval officer. John Dewey, philosopher. Stephen Douglas, politician. James Fisk, financier. Robert Frost (b. Calif.), poet. Rudy Vallee, singer.
Noteworthy places Bennington Battleground/Monument. Calvin Coolidge Homestead, Plymouth. Maple Grove Maple Museum, Rock of Ages Tourist Center, Graniteville. Shelburne Museum. St. Johnsbury. Vermont Marble Exhibit, Proctor.
Memorable events Samuel de Champlain explores for France 1609. First French settlement at Ste. Anne 1666. First English settlers build Ft. Drummer near Brattleboro 1724. Bennington settled 1761. Ethan Allen organizes Green Mountain Boys 1764. Green Mountain Boys capture Ft. Ticonderoga and Ft. Crown Point 1775. Gen. John Stark defeats British general John Burgoyne near Bennington; constitution abolishes slavery and grants universal male suffrage 1777. Claims to area relinquished by Massachusetts (1781), New Hampshire (1782), and New York (1790). First state admitted after original 13 1791. MacDonough defeats British Lake Champlain fleet 1814. Canal between Hudson River and Lake Champlain gives Vermont direct access to port of New York 1823. Confederate soldiers steal $400,000 from St. Albans bank 1864. Blue law repealed, allowing stores to open on Sundays 1982.
Tourist Information (800) VERMONT. www.state.vt.us.

▶**VIRGINIA, COMMONWEALTH OF**
The first successful English settlement in America was at Jamestown in 1607. The differences between the Virginia colonists and those of Massachusetts were pronounced, and the commercial southern planter class shared little of their New England counterparts' religious zeal. Virginia bred its own strain of independence, and it was the fiery Patrick Henry who heralded the American Revolution with the cry "Give me liberty or give me death." Seven of the first 12 presidents

were from Virginia. With an economy very dependent on labor-intensive tobacco in the mid-19th century, Virginia seceded from the Union over the slavery issue, despite the misgivings of many, including Robert E. Lee. After the war Virginia developed an increasingly diversified industrial and manufacturing base that survives today, with food products, tobacco, and chemicals leading the way. Despite the dramatic decline of the American merchant marine, Virginia's shipbuilding industry in Newport News flourished in the 1980s, thanks to the Pentagon's commitment to a 600-ship navy. Norfolk is also one of the country's leading commercial ports.

Name For Elizabeth I, called Virgin Queen. **Nicknames** Old Dominion, Mother of Presidents, Mother of States. **Capital** Richmond. **Entered union** June 25, 1788 (10th). **Motto** *Sic semper tyrannis* (Thus always to tyrants).

Emblems **Beverage** Milk. **Bird** Cardinal. **Dog** Foxhound. **Flower** Dogwood. **Shell** Oyster. **Song** "Carry Me Back to Old Virginia." **Tree** Dogwood. **Land** Total area 40,767 sq. mi. (36th), incl. 1,063 sq. mi. inland water. **Borders** Md., D.C., Atlantic Ocean, N.C., Tenn., Ky., W.Va. **Rivers** James, Potomac, Rappahannock, Roanoke, Shenandoah, York. **Lakes** Buggs Island, Claytor, Gaston, Leesville. **Mountains** Allegheny, Blue Ridge, Cumberland, Unaka. **Other notable features** Great Dismal Swamp, Shenandoah Valley.

Elected officials Gov. James S. Gilmore III (R, term exp. 2002). Lt. Gov. John H. Hager (R). Sec. Commonwealth Anne P. Petera (R). Atty. Gen. Randolph Beales (R).

People (2000) 7,078,515 (12th). **Race/Hispanic Origin** (2000): White 72.3%. Black 19.6%. Indian 0.3%. Asian 3.7%. Pacific Islander 0.1%. Other 2.0%. Two or more races 2.0%. Hispanic 4.7%.

Cities (2000) Virginia Beach 425,257. Norfolk 234,403. Chesapeake 199,184. Richmond 197,790. Newport News 180,150. Hampton 146,437. Alexandria 128,283. Portsmouth 100,565. Roanoke 94,911. Lynchburg 65,269.

Business **Gross State Product,** 1997: $211.33 bil. (13th). **Leading Sectors of GSP** (1997): Services 20.54%; Finance, insurance, and real estate 18.24%; Government 18.18%. *Fortune* **500 Companies** (2000): 16: Freddie Mac, Circuit City Stores, General Dynamics, US Airways Group, Dominion Resources, CSX, AES, Gannett, Norfolk Southern, Nextel Communications, Capital One Financial, Smithfield Foods, Pittston, USA Education, Owens & Minor, Universal.

Famous natives Richard E. Byrd, explorer/aviator. William Clark, explorer. Jerry Falwell, evangelist. William Henry Harrison, U.S. president. Patrick Henry, Revolutionary patriot. Thomas Jefferson, U.S. president. Joseph E. Johnston, Confederate general. John Paul Jones (b. Scotland), navy officer. Robert E. Lee, Confederate general. Meriwether Lewis, explorer. James Madison, U.S. president. John Marshall, jurist. Cyrus Hall McCormick, inventor. James Monroe, U.S. president. Walter Reed, doctor. Pat Robertson, evangelist/politician. Bill "Bojangles" Robinson, dancer. George C. Scott, actor. Thomas Sumter, army officer. Zachary Taylor, U.S. president. John Tyler, U.S. president. Booker T. Washington, educator. George Washington, U.S. president. Woodrow Wilson, U.S. president.

Noteworthy places Appomattox Courthouse Natl. Hist Park. Arlington Natl. Cemetery. Booker T. Washington Natl. Monument, Roanoke. Colonial Natl. Hist. Park (incl. Jamestown, Yorktown &

Williamsburg). Fredericksburg and Spotsylvania Natl. Military Park. George Washington birthplace, Frederick Co. Harpers Ferry Natl. Hist. Site. The Mariners' Museum, Newport News. Monticello, Charlottesville. Mount Vernon. Petersburg Natl. Battlefield. Robert E. Lee Memorial, Lexington. Shenandoah Natl. Park. Virginia Beach. Virginia Museum of Fine Arts. Wolf Trap Farm for the Performing Arts, Reston.

Memorable events John Smith founds Jamestown, first permanent settlement in North America, 1607. John Rolfe marries Pocahontas, daughter of Powhatan, leader of so-called Powhatan Confederacy 1614. First English women arrive at Jamestown; House of Burgesses established 1619. Northampton Declaration first resistance to taxation without representation 1653. College of William and Mary founded 1693. First state to establish Committee of Correspondence 1773. American Revolution ends with Charles Cornwallis's surrender to George Washington at Yorktown 1781. Nat Turner's slave revolt 1831. State secedes from Union 1861. Civil War ends with Robert E. Lee's surrender to Ulysses S. Grant at Appomattox Courthouse 1865. Readmitted to Union 1870. Norfolk Naval Base founded 1917. John D. Rockefeller, Jr. restores Colonial Williamsburg 1926. E. Claiborne Robins donates $50 million to University of Richmond 1969. Douglas Wilder becomes nation's first black governor 1989.

Tourist information (800) VISIT-VA. www.state.va.us.

▶WASHINGTON

The northwest corner of the continental U.S. was originally the locus of a rich Native American culture noted today primarily for its ornately carved canoes and totem poles. In 1792, Boston merchant Capt. Robert Gray began a trade in sea otter pelts; but the first permanent settlers in the region did not establish themselves for almost 50 years. Agriculture and lumbering were, and remain, mainstays of the state's economy—the farming regions in the east, rich in dairy products, fruit and wheat, and the lumber industry in the western part of the state rely heavily on exports to the Far East. This geographic split reflects the weather patterns: eastern Washington rarely gets more than 10 inches of rain in a year, while on the Pacific coast almost 40 inches is the average.

Since World War I, Puget Sound has been a center of heavy industry and shipbuilding, and 60 percent of the population is concentrated in the region. Boeing maintains one of the country's largest airplane-manufacturing plants in the Seattle-Tacoma area, and Microsoft, the world's leading software company, is located in Redmond. The industrial work force was open to progressive and sometimes radical unionism, and the International Workers of the World (Wobblies) had their national headquarters at Seattle. Before statehood the territorial government pioneered women's suffrage, but Congress declared the women's right to vote unconstitutional.

Name For George Washington. **Nickname** Evergreen State. **Capital** Olympia. **Entered union** Nov. 11, 1889 (42nd). **Motto** *Alki* (By and by).

Emblems **Bird** Willow goldfinch. **Fish** Steelhead trout. **Flower** Western rhododendron. **Gem** Petrified wood. **Song** "Washington, My Home." **Tree** Western hemlock.

Land Total area 68,138 sq. mi. (20th), incl. 1,627 sq. mi. inland water. **Borders** British Columbia, Idaho, Oreg., Pacific Ocean. **Rivers** Chehalis, Columbia, Pend Oreille, Snake, Yakima. **Lakes** Baker, Bank, Chelan, Franklin D. Roosevelt, Ross, Rufus Woods. **Mountains** Cascade Range, Coast Range, Kettle River Range, Olympic. **Other notable features** Puget Sound, San Juan Islands, Strait of Juan de Fuca.

Elected officials   Gov. Gary Locke (D, term exp. 2001). Lt. Gov. Brad Owen (D). Sec. State Sam Reed (D). Atty. Gen. Christine Gregoire (D).

People   (2000) 5,894,121 (15th). **Race/Hispanic Origin** (2000): White 81.8%. Black 3.2%. Indian 1.6%. Asian 5.5%. Pacific Islander 0.4%. Other 3.9%. Two or more races 3.6%. Hispanic 7.5%.

Cities   (2000) Seattle 563,374. Spokane 195,629. Tacoma 193,556. Vancouver 143,560. Bellevue 109,569. Everett 91,488. Federal Way 83,259. Kent 79,524. Yakima 71,845. Bellingham 67,171.

Business   Gross State Product, 1997: $172.25 bil. (14th). **Leading Sectors of GSP** (1997): Services 21.61%; Finance, insurance, and real estate 18.20%; Government 14.25%. *Fortune* **500 Companies** (2000): 11: Boeing, Costco Wholesale, Microsoft, Weyerhauser, Washington Mutual, Paccar, Avista, Safeco, Nordstrom, Puget Energy, Airborne Freight.

Famous natives   Harry L. "Bing" Crosby, singer. Merce Cunningham, choreographer. Bill Gates, businessman. Jimi Hendrix, guitarist. Henry M. "Scoop" Jackson, politician. Robert Joffrey, choreographer. Gary Larson, cartoonist. Edward R. Murrow, reporter (b. North Carolina). Theodore Roethke (b. Mich.), poet. Marcus Whitman (b. N.Y.), missionary/pioneer.

Noteworthy places   Grand Coulee Dam. Klondike Gold Rush Natl. Hist. Park, Seattle. Mount Rainier Natl. Park. Mount Saint Helens Natl. Monument. North Cascades Natl. Park. Olympic Natl. Park. San Juan Islands Natl. Hist. Park. Seattle Art Museum.

Memorable events   Sir Francis Drake skirts coast of Pacific Northwest 1579. Juan de Fuca sails into straits now bearing his name. Bruno de Heceta lands at Hoh River 1775. Capt. James Cook arrives 1778. Capt. Robert Gray discovers mouth of Columbia River, which he names for his ship; George Vancouver explores Puget Sound 1792. Lewis and Clark expedition winters at Columbia River 1805. Marcus Whitman, Protestant Mission Board, settles near Walla Walla 1836. Territorial status 1853. Northern Pacific railroad reaches Puget Sound 1883. Alaska-Yukon-Pacific Exposition at Seattle 1909. Grand Coulee Dam, largest concrete hydroelectric dam in United States, completed 1941. Hanford works atomic energy plant opens 1943. Upholding treaty provisions from Washinton's days as a territory, a decision awards Native Americans half the catch of Northwest salmon and steelhead 1974. Mt. Saint Helens erupts, killing 61, 1980. Washington Public Power Supply System (known as "whoops") defaults on $8.25 billion bond issue 1983. Reports linking growth-enhancing chemical Alar to cancer generate $140 million loss for Washington's apple growers 1988.

Tourist information   (800) 544-1800. access.wa.gov.

▶WEST VIRGINIA

When Virginia seceded in 1861, its western counties reorganized and in 1863 were admitted to the Union as a separate state. Despite the rugged terrain, through which transportation has always been difficult, farming remained the backbone of the economy until the close of the 19th century, when coal mining and other extractive industries

developed. After World War II, the manufacturing base developed to include steel and chemical manufacturing. Even with vast natural resources, West Virginia has long been one of the poorest states in the union. Population losses since the 1950s have been pronounced, and the 8 percent loss between 1980 and 1990 was the highest in the country. There is low participation in the workforce by women and educational achievement is well below the national average.

Name for western part of Virginia. **Nickname** Mountain State. **Capital** Charleston. **Entered union** June 20, 1863 (35th). **Motto** *Montani semper liberi* (Mountaineers are always free).

Emblems   Animal Black bear. **Bird** Cardinal. **Colors** Old gold and blue. **Fish** Brook trout. **Flower** *Rhododendron maximum* (big laurel). **Fruit** Apple. **Songs** "The West Virginia Hills," "West Virginia, My Home Sweet Home," "This Is My West Virginia." **Tree** Sugar maple.

Land   Total area 24,231 sq. mi. (41st), incl. 112 sq. mi. inland water. **Borders** Ohio, Pa., Md., Va., Ky. **Rivers** Big Sandy, Guayandotte, Kanawha, Little Kanawha, Monongahela, Ohio, Potomac. **Lakes** Summersville Dam. **Mountains** Allegheny, Blue Ridge, Cumberland.

Elected officials   Gov. Robert E. Wise, Jr. (D, term exp. 2005). Lt. Gov. Earl Ray Tomblin (D). Sec. State Joe Manchin III (D). Atty. Gen. Darrell V. McGraw (D).

People   (2000) 1,808,344 (37th). **Race/Hispanic Origin** (2000): White 95.0%. Black 3.2%. Indian 0.2%. Asian 0.5%. Other 0.2%. Two or more races 0.9%. Hispanic 0.7%.

Cities   (2000) Charleston 53,421. Huntington 51,475. Parkersburg 33,099. Wheeling 31,419. Morgantown 26,809. Weirton 20,411. Fairmont 19,097. Beckley 17,254. Clarksburg 16,743. Martinsburg 14,972.

Business   Gross State Product, 1997: $38.23 bil. (38th). **Leading Sectors of GSP** (1997): Manufacturing 17.48%; Services 16.83%; Government 14.05%. *Fortune* **500 Companies** (2000): 0.

Famous natives   Newton D. Baker, politician. Pearl Buck, novelist (Nobel Prize, 1938). John W. Davis, politician. Dwight Whitney Morrow, lawyer/diplomat. Michael Owens, manufacturer. Walter Reuther, labor leader. Cyrus Vance, statesman. Jerry West, basketball player. Charles "Chuck" Yeager, pilot.

Noteworthy places   Cass Scenic Railroad. Harpers Ferry Natl. Hist. Park. Monongahela Natl. Forest. New River Gorge Bridge. Science and Cultural Center, Charleston.

Memorable events   First permanent settlement by Morgan Morgan at Mill Creek 1731. Coal discovered on Coal River 1742. Wheeling Convention repudiates act of secession; forms new state of Kanahwa 1861. Enters Union as West Virginia 1863. Population peaks at 2.5 million 1950. Unemployment jumps 8.6% to 18.0%, highest in nation, 1980–83.

Tourist information   (800) CALL-WVA. www.state.wv.us.

▶WISCONSIN

The indigenous people of the region had a largely agricultural economy, but the fur trade drew Europeans into the region. Native resistance to white settlement was strong and not overcome until the Black Hawk Wars of 1832. In the early 19th century, German, Scandinavian, and Dutch farmers migrated to the region in large numbers. Many social welfare policies now common to the nation as a whole—including aid to dependent children, workmen's compensation, and old-age assistance—were pioneered in Wisconsin. Although manufacturing accounts for the lion's share of Wisconsin's profits, agriculture is extremely important, and the state is the nation's leading producer of dairy products. There are major shipping facilities at Superior, Green Bay, and Milwaukee.

Name From the Ojibwa *wishkonsing*, "place of the bearer." **Nickname** Badger State. **Capital** Madison. **Entered union** May 29, 1848 (30th). **Motto** "Forward."

Emblems   Animal Badger. **Bird** Robin. **Domestic animal** Dairy cow. **Fish** Muskellunge. **Flower** Wood violet. **Insect** Honeybee. **Mineral** Galena. **Rock** Red granite. **Soil** Antigo silt loam. **Song** "On, Wisconsin!" **Symbol of peace** Mourning dove. **Tree** Sugar maple. **Wildlife animal** White-tailed deer.

Land   Total area 56,153 sq. mi. (26th), incl. 1,727 sq. mi. inland water. **Borders** Minn., Lake Superior, Mich., Lake Michigan, Ill., Iowa. **Rivers** Black, Chippewa, Menominee, Mississippi, St. Croix, Wisconsin. **Lakes** Chippewa, Du Bay, Mendota, Michigan, Superior, Winnebago. **Other notable features** Apostle Islands, Door Peninsula, Green Bay.

Elected officials   Gov. Scott McCallum (R, term exp. 2003). Lt. Gov. Margaret A. Farrow (R). Sec. State Douglas La Follette (D). Atty. Gen. James Doyle (D).

People   (2000) 5,363,675 (18th). **Race/Hispanic Origin** (2000): White 88.9%. Black 5.7%. Indian 0.9%. Asian 1.7%. Other 1.6%. Two or more races 1.2%. Hispanic 3.6%.

Cities   (2000) Milwaukee 596,974. Madison 208,054. Green Bay 102,313. Kenosha 90,352. Racine 81,855. Appleton 70,087. Waukesha 64,825. Oshkosh 62,916. Eau Claire 61,704. West Allis 61,254.

Business   Gross State Product, 1997: $147.33 bil. (19th). **Leading Sectors of GSP** (1997): Manufacturing 27.75%; Services 16.76%; Finance, insurance, and real estate 16.24%. *Fortune 500* **Companies** (2000): 10: Johnson Controls, Northwestern Mutual, Manpower, Rockwell International, Firstar Corp., Kohl's, American Family Insurance Group, Shopko Stores, Aid Association for Lutherans, Wisconsin Energy.

Famous natives   King Camp Gillette, inventor/businessman. Eric Heiden, speed skater. Harry Houdini (b. Hungary), magician. Robert La Follette, politician. Liberace (Wladziu Valentino), pianist. Alfred Lunt, actor. Joseph R. McCarthy, politician. Spencer Tracy, actor. Thorstein Veblen, economist. Orson Welles, director. Laura Ingalls Wilder, novelist. Thornton Wilder, author. Frank Lloyd Wright, architect.

Noteworthy places   Apostle Island Natl. Lakeshore. Chequamegon Natl. Forest. Circus World Museum, Baraboo. Door County Peninsula. Ice Age Natl. Scientific Reserve. Manitowoc Maritime Museum. Milwaukee Art Museum. Milwaukee Public Museum. Nicolet Natl. Forest. Old Wade House and Carriage Museum, Greenbush. Old World Wisconsin, Eagle. Villa Louis, Prairie du Chien. Wisconsin Dells.

Memorable events   Jean Nicolet lands at Green Bay 1634. French establish mission and trading post near Ashland 1634. British take control of region 1763. Land ceded to United States 1787, but U.S. control not established until after War of 1812. Becomes independent Territory 1836. Statehood 1848. More than 800 die in forest fire near Peshtigo 1871. First hydroelectric plant completed at Appleton 1882. Ringling Brothers circus formed at Baraboo 1884. First state to enact income tax 1911. Milwaukee transfers more than 11,000 students between city and surburban schools 1986.

Tourist information   800-432-TRIP or 800-372-2737.   **www.wisconsin.gov/state/home.**

▶WYOMING

Tens of thousands of migrants traveled through the region along the Óregon Trail, but few settled the land until Ft. Laramie was built in 1834. Territorial status came in 1869. Wyoming was the first state to give the vote to women, and in 1925 Nellie Tayloe Ross became the first woman governor following the death of her husband. Cattle ranching is the traditional mainstay of the economy. The state ranks second in uranium output, petroleum and coal production have become increasingly important. Wyoming is best known for its natural wonders. Yellowstone National Park—the site of Old Faithful—is the oldest and largest national park in the country. Following a decade-long mining boom in the 1970s and 1980s, Wyoming's population declined, and it has fallen behind even Alaska in total population. Although the population has increased in the 1990s, there are still no more than five people per square mile.

Name From the Delaware *maugh-wau-wa-ma,* "large plains" or "mountains and valleys alternating." **Nickname** Equality State. **Capital** Cheyenne. **Entered union** July 10, 1890 (44th). **Motto** "Equal rights."

Emblems   Bird Meadowlark. **Flower** Indian paintbrush. **Gem** Jade. **Song** "Wyoming." **Tree** Cottonwood.

Land   Total area 97,809 sq. mi. (9th), incl. 820 sq. mi. inland water. **Borders** Mont., S.Dak., Nebr., Colo., Utah, Idaho. **Rivers** Bighorn, Green, North Platte, Powder, Snake, Yellowstone. **Lakes** Bighorn, Yellowstone. **Mountains** Absaroka, Bighorn, Black Hills, Laramie, Owl Creek, Teton Range, Wind River Range, Wyoming Range.

Elected officials   Gov. Jim Geringer (R, term exp. 2003). Sec. State Joseph B. Meyer (R). Atty. Gen. Hoke MacMillan (R).

People   (2000) 493,782 (50th). **Race/Hispanic Origin** (2000): White 92.1%. Black 0.8%. Indian 2.3%. Asian 0.6%. Pacific Islander 0.1%. Other 2.5%. Two or more races 1.8%. Hispanic 6.4%.

Cities   (2000) Cheyenne 53,011. Casper 49,644. Laramie 27,204. Gillette 19,646. Rock Springs 18,708. Sheridan 15,804. Green River 11,808. Evanston 11,507. Riverton 9,310. Cody 8,835.

Business   Gross State Product, 1997: $17.56 bil. (48th). **Leading Sectors of GSP** (1997): Mining 31.39%; Transportation & public utilities 13.17%; Government 12.56%. *Fortune* 500 **Companies** (2000): 0.

Famous natives   James Bridger (b. Va.), pioneer. J.C. Penney, businessman. Jackson Pollock, painter. Nellie Tayloe Ross (b. Mo.), politician.

Noteworthy places   Bighorn Canyon Natl. Rec. Area. Buffalo Bill Museum, Cody. Devil's Tower Natl. Monument. Ft. Bridger State Park. Ft. Laramie Natl. Hist. Site. Fossil Butte Natl. Monument. Grand Teton Natl. Park. Medicine Wheel Natl. Hist. Landmark, near Lovell. Natl. Elk Refuge. Yellowstone Natl. Park (Old Faithful).

Memorable events   Part of Louisiana Territory claimed for France 1682. Pierre Gaultier de Varennes, sieur de Vérendrye explores region for France 1743. Region to United States with

Louisiana Purchase 1803. John Colter crosses area of Yellowstone 1807–08. Indian Wars follow massacre of army detachments 1854 and 1866. Wyoming Territory organized 1868. Women's suffrage adopted permanently (first instance in United States); Union Pacific railroad crosses state 1869. Yellowstone, world's first national park, opens 1872. White mob kills 28 Chinese miners and burns Chinatown in Rock Springs 1885. Statehood 1890. Nellie Tayloe Ross first woman governor 1925. First Intercontinental Ballistic Missile (ICBM) base opens near Cheyenne 1951. Fires consume 1.6 million acres of land in and around Yellowstone Park 1988.

Tourist information   (800) CALL-WYO.
www.state.wy.us.

Revenues and Expenditures of State Governments, 1999

State	Revenues		Expenditures	
	Total ('000s)	Per capita (rank)	Total ('000s)	Per capita (rank)
Alabama	$15,501,093	$3,547 (42)	$14,701,938	$3,364 (35)
Alaska	7,312,896	11,795 (1)	6,140,559	9,904 (1)
Arizona	15,121,888	3,165 (49)	14,278,357	2,988 (46)
Arkansas	10,361,000	4,062 (29)	8,943,119	3,506 (31)
California	154,016,720	4,647 (17)	133,672,890	4,033 (16)
Colorado	14,158,140	3,491 (43)	13,148,371	3,242 (37)
Connecticut	16,437,468	5,008 (11)	15,213,482	4,635 (7)
Delaware	4,540,445	6,022 (3)	3,940,802	5,227 (3)
Florida	49,208,745	3,256 (47)	42,458,875	2,810 (49)
Georgia	27,638,537	3,549 (41)	23,203,145	2,979 (47)
Hawaii	6,646,380	5,609 (5)	6,265,729	5,288 (2)
Idaho	4,870,426	3,890 (32)	4,230,335	3,379 (33)
Illinois	43,294,450	3,570 (38)	38,313,971	3,159 (39)
Indiana	19,149,062	3,222 (48)	18,613,822	3,132 (41)
Iowa	11,629,027	4,053 (30)	10,320,512	3,597 (27)
Kansas	8,687,125	3,273 (46)	8,370,653	3,154 (40)
Kentucky	16,853,110	4,255 (23)	14,777,655	3,731 (22)
Louisiana	17,785,900	4,068 (28)	15,705,909	3,592 (28)
Maine	5,887,528	4,699 (16)	4,864,878	3,883 (21)
Maryland	19,612,674	3,792 (35)	17,593,437	3,402 (32)
Massachusetts	28,119,894	4,554 (20)	28,030,302	4,539 (8)
Michigan	46,724,414	4,737 (14)	38,798,045	3,933 (19)
Minnesota	25,089,186	5,253 (8)	20,387,584	4,269 (11)
Mississippi	10,700,917	3,865 (33)	9,926,812	3,585 (29)
Missouri	19,504,680	3,567 (39)	16,524,873	3,022 (44)
Montana	3,725,321	4,219 (24)	3,511,965	3,977 (17)
Nebraska	5,575,535	3,347 (45)	5,183,613	3,111 (42)
Nevada	7,572,930	4,186 (25)	6,103,167	3,374 (34)
New Hampshire	4,024,270	3,351 (44)	3,594,322	2,993 (45)
New Jersey	39,149,997	4,808 (13)	32,058,406	3,937 (18)
New Mexico	8,756,881	5,033 (10)	8,089,399	4,649 (6)
New York	102,241,862	5,619 (4)	92,583,501	5,088 (4)
North Carolina	34,063,932	4,452 (21)	26,830,081	3,507 (30)
North Dakota	2,935,592	4,630 (18)	2,674,523	4,218 (12)
Ohio	51,273,137	4,555 (19)	41,113,309	3,652 (26)
Oklahoma	11,935,084	3,554 (40)	10,655,464	3,173 (38)
Oregon	15,666,106	4,724 (15)	13,964,746	4,211 (13)
Pennsylvania	49,481,716	4,126 (26)	44,236,777	3,688 (24)
Rhode Island	5,478,183	5,528 (6)	4,378,203	4,418 (9)
South Carolina	14,566,262	3,748 (36)	14,482,992	3,727 (23)
South Dakota	2,885,858	3,937 (31)	2,271,671	3,099 (43)
Tennessee	16,903,668	3,082 (50)	15,889,978	2,898 (48)
Texas	71,648,633	3,575 (37)	54,761,328	2,732 (50)
Utah	8,742,192	4,104 (27)	7,809,598	3,666 (25)
Vermont	3,054,762	5,143 (9)	2,602,588	4,381 (10)
Virginia	26,138,391	3,803 (34)	22,739,177	3,308 (36)
Washington	28,737,067	4,993 (12)	24,229,780	4,209 (14)
West Virginia	8,034,281	4,446 (22)	7,335,784	4,060 (15)
Wisconsin	28,334,130	5,397 (7)	20,465,757	3,898 (20)
Wyoming	3,092,259	6,442 (2)	2,372,933	4,944 (5)
United States	$1,152,869,754	$4,236 (N.A.)	$998,365,117	$3,668 (N.A.)

Source: U.S. Bureau of the Census, Governments Division, *State Government Finances.*

STATE GOVERNMENT FINANCES

▶REVENUES AND EXPENDITURES

Revenues

Revenue of state governments from all sources in 1999 was $1.15 trillion, a 5 percent increase over the year before. Taxes accounted for 43.4 percent, or $500 billion of the total state general revenue. Another 22 percent of state revenues came from the federal government. Sales taxes and gross re-ceipts accounted for about another 22 percent, while individual income taxes made up 15 percent of general revenue. Charges were responsible for 6.9 percent of state revenues.

Expenditures

State government expenditures in 1998 totaled $998.4 billion, an increase of 7.3 percent from the amount spent in 1998. State general expenditures amounted to $889.5 billion, 7.5 percent more than in 1998. The leading expenditure categories, by function, were education services (31 percent), public welfare programs (20 percent), highways (6 percent) and health and hospitals (6 percent).

State Tax Collections Per Capita, By Type, 2000

State	Total taxes[1]	Property taxes	Sales taxes	Licenses	Income taxes Individual	Income taxes Corporate
United States	$1,921.46	$39.15	$898.26	$116.79	$692.4	$115.09
Alabama	1,447.78	40.44	725.97	121.80	465.79	54.66
Alaska	2,270.24	71.15	219.70	146.21	N.A.	699.34
Arizona	1,578.90	57.83	905.06	50.71	446.71	101.97
Arkansas	1,821.86	180.25	883.85	97.02	549.87	88.64
California	2,474.28	98.34	874.48	108.96	1,168.37	196.00
Colorado	1,644.88	N.A.	629.81	69.77	845.55	77.88
Connecticut	2,986.65	N.A.	1,484.05	107.24	1,166.80	125.27
Delaware	2,720.94	N.A.	369.24	991.68	935.94	306.69
Florida	1,552.79	47.72	1,197.02	94.17	N.A.	74.01
Georgia	1,650.44	5.88	701.90	57.04	777.45	87.02
Hawaii	2,752.49	N.A.	1,693.64	91.55	878.48	62.13
Idaho	1,837.20	N.A.	815.30	167.35	746.11	97.27
Illinois	1,834.95	4.38	874.39	126.47	614.94	182.08
Indiana	1,661.77	0.61	828.34	40.35	617.28	152.06
Iowa	1,771.98	N.A.	847.00	168.33	646.01	73.34
Kansas	1,809.73	18.08	863.31	88.08	692.46	101.34
Kentucky	1,903.77	96.18	868.98	132.93	668.42	75.82
Louisiana	1,457.24	5.57	832.12	109.67	354.05	49.68
Maine	2,087.25	23.96	934.17	105.40	844.69	117.69
Maryland	1,954.97	48.34	823.49	71.59	870.99	81.40
Massachusetts	2,544.12	0.02	796.94	70.99	1,424.13	205.75
Michigan	2,289.73	171.30	984.53	121.58	723.49	239.73
Minnesota	2,711.37	1.91	1,173.95	198.60	1,127.62	163.30
Mississippi	1,656.30	0.48	1,106.26	98.01	353.88	80.05
Missouri	1,531.94	3.29	720.55	102.88	634.52	47.45
Montana	1,563.70	242.61	381.19	136.51	572.23	110.59
Nebraska	1,742.02	2.55	844.50	110.86	686.00	81.82
Nevada	1,860.25	46.41	1,578.36	181.40	N.A.	N.A.
New Hampshire	1,372.47	383.33	449.51	115.36	53.39	252.61
New Jersey	2,156.74	0.36	974.48	93.88	856.31	160.12
New Mexico	2,057.77	19.17	1,103.29	113.11	484.24	87.59
New York	2,199.35	N.A.	701.24	51.13	1,222.27	146.05
North Carolina	1,890.36	0.00	748.73	113.36	881.75	122.90
North Dakota	1,825.56	3.87	1,020.01	135.75	309.28	121.80
Ohio	1,733.12	1.99	797.90	137.30	725.90	55.54
Oklahoma	1,695.86	N.A.	631.91	243.78	618.58	56.26
Oregon	1,737.79	0.03	212.68	176.84	1,197.59	118.98
Pennsylvania	1,829.40	9.56	851.75	185.11	551.30	138.17
Rhode Island	1,941.12	0.90	956.72	86.58	790.77	71.38
South Carolina	1,590.57	3.16	807.79	93.51	609.56	56.62
South Dakota	1,228.39	N.A.	970.25	156.92	N.A.	59.78
Tennessee	1,360.38	N.A.	1,020.40	157.93	31.69	107.91
Texas	1,315.19	N.A.	1,065.30	182.85	N.A.	N.A.
Utah	1,781.64	N.A.	861.60	61.85	739.51	77.83
Vermont	2,415.84	664.74	774.11	112.22	709.56	72.98
Virginia	1,786.83	4.81	614.83	72.58	964.74	79.95
Washington	2,132.19	288.03	1,643.04	103.15	N.A.	N.A.
West Virginia	1,848.80	1.96	995.44	96.36	534.04	120.44
Wisconsin	2,357.16	16.25	959.16	128.26	1,109.74	109.58
Wyoming	1,951.57	205.35	965.20	180.62	N.A.	N.A.

1. Includes other taxes not shown separately. **Source:** U.S. Bureau of the Census, *State Government Tax Collections, 2000*.

Summary of State Government Finances, 1995–99

Item	Amount (millions) 1995	1999	Item	Amount (millions) 1995	1999
TOTAL REVENUES	**$903,756**	**$1,152,870**	General expenditure	$733,503	$889,475
General Revenue	739,016	906,076	Intergovernmental expenditure	240,978	304,933
Intergovernmental revenue	215,558	253,692	Direct expenditure	492,525	584,542
Taxes	399,148	499,943	**General expenditure, by function:**		
Sales and gross receipts	222,934	239,367	Education	249,670	276,737
Individual income	125,610	172,764	Public Welfare	194,854	182,238
Corporation net income	29,075	30,766	Hospitals	29,139	29,535
Other Taxes	21,528	31,309	Health	30,865	24,857
Current charges	64,774	79,308	Highways	57,374	56,242
Miscellaneous general revenue	59,536	73,133	Police protection	6,451	7,810
Utility revenue	3,845	4,356	Correction	26,069	30,770
Liquor stores revenue	3,073	3,599	Natural resources	12,534	13,601
Insurance trust revenue	157,821	238,838	Parks and recreation	3,403	3,843
			Governmental administration	26,078	32,558
TOTAL EXPENDITURES	**$836,894**	**$998,365**	Interest on general debt	24,485	27,785
Intergovernmental expenditure	240,978	304,933	Other and unallocable	72,648	31,267
Direct expenditure	595,916	693,432	Utility expenditure	7,586	8,779
Current operation	396,035	476,968	Liquor stores expenditure	2,522	2,967
Capital outlay	57,829	68,509	Insurance trust expenditure	93,282	97,144
Insurance benefits and repayments	93,282	97,144			
Assistance and subsidies	23,511	22,229	**Debt at end of fiscal year**	427,239	510,486
Interest on debt	25,259	28,582			
Exhibit: Salaries and wages	125,432	148,236	**Cash and Security holdings**	**$1,388,527**	**$2,265,945**

Source: U.S. Bureau of the Census, Governments Division, *State Government Finances.*

State Government Individual Income Taxes, 2001

State	Taxable income rate range	Taxable income brackets Lowest: amount under	Highest: amount over	State	Taxable income rate range	Taxable income brackets Lowest: amount under	Highest: amount over
Alabama[1,2]	2.0-5.0%	$ 500	$ 3,000	Missouri[1,2]	1.5–6.0%	$1,000	$9,000
Arizona	2.87-5.04	10,000	150,000	Montana	2.0–11.0	2,099	73,000
Arkansas	1.0-7.0	2,999	25,000	Nebraska	2.51–6.68	2,400	26,500
California	1.0-9.3	10,264	45,833	New Hampshire	5.0% on dividend and interest income over $2,400		
Colorado	4.63% on modified federal tax liability						
Connecticut	3.0-4.5	16,000	16,000	New Jersey	1.4-6.37	20,000	75,001
Delaware	2.2-5.95	5,000	60,000	New Mexico	1.7-8.2	5,500	65,000
Dist. of Columbia	5.0-9.5	10,000	20,000	New York[2]	4.0-6.85	8,000	20,000
Georgia	1.0-6.0	750	7,000	North Carolina	6.0-7.75	12,750	60,000
Hawaii	1.6-8.75	3,000	60,000	North Dakota	14% of federal income tax liability		
Idaho[2]	1.9-8.1	1,022	20,442	Ohio[2]	0.691-6.987	5,000	200,000
Illinois	3.0% on taxable net income			Oklahoma[1]	0.5-6.75	1,000	10,000
Indiana[2]	3.4% of federal adjusted gross income			Oregon[1,2]	5.0-9.0	2,450	6,100
Iowa[1]	0.36-8.98	1,148	51,660	Pennsylvania[2]	2.8% on taxable income		
Kansas	3.5-6.45	15,000	30,000	Rhode Island	26% of modified federal tax liability		
Kentucky	2.0-6.0	3,000	8,000	South Carolina	2.5-7.0	2,340	11,700
Louisiana[1]	2.0-6.0	10,000	50,000	Tennessee	6.0% on interest and dividend income		
Maine	2.0-8.5	4,150	16,500	Utah[1]	2.3-7.0	750	3,750
Maryland[2]	2.0-4.85	1,000	3,000	Vermont	24% of federal income tax liability		
Massachusetts	5.6% of taxable income			Virginia	2.0-5.75	3,000	17,000
Michigan[2]	4.2% of federal adjusted gross income			West Virginia	3.0-6.5	10,000	60,000
Minnesota	5.35-7.85	17,570	57,710	Wisconsin	4.73-6.75	7,790	116,890
Mississippi	3.0-5.0	10,000	10,000				

Note: Rates and brackets shown are for single taxpayers. Brackets for married taxpayers filing jointly are double those shown, except in Maryland, where they are the same. Alaska, Florida, Nevada, South Dakota, Texas, Washington, and Wyoming have no state income tax. 1. State with a provision that allows the taxpayer to deduct fully the federal income tax payment. 2. States in which one or more local governments levy a local income tax. **Source:** Government of the District of Columbia, Dept. of Finance and Revenue, *Tax Rates and Tax Burdens in the District of Columbia: A Nationwide Comparison* (January, 2001)

Composition of State Legislatures, 2000–01

State or other jurisdiction	Senate Demo-crats	Senate Repub-licans	Senate Total	House Demo-crats	House Repub-licans	House Total
Alabama	23	12	35	69	36	105
Alaska	5	15	20	14	26	40
Arizona	14	16	30	20	40	60
Arkansas	29	6	35	74	23	100
California	24	15	40[2]	47	32	80[1]
Colorado	15	20	35	25	40	65
Connecticut	19	17	36	96	55	151
Delaware	13	8	21	15	26	41
Florida	15	24	40[2]	47	73	120
Georgia	33	22	56[2]	102	78	180
Hawaii	23	2	25	38	12	51[2]
Idaho	4	31	35	12	58	70
Illinois	27	32	59	62	56	118
Indiana	19	31	50	53	47	100
Iowa	20	30	50	44	56	100
Kansas	13	27	40	48	77	125
Kentucky	18	20	38	64	35	100[2]
Louisiana	28	11	39	75	30	105
Maine	19	15	35[1]	81	69	151[1]
Maryland	32	15	47	106	35	141
Massachusetts	32	8	40	128	29	160[1,2]
Michigan	15	23	38	52	58	110
Minnesota	40	26	67[1]	63	70	134[1]
Mississippi	34	18	52	86	33	122[1]
Missouri	18	16	34	86	76	163[1]
Montana	18	32	50	41	59	100
Nebraska	Nonpartisan		49	Unicameral		
Nevada	9	12	21	28	14	42
New Hampshire	12	12	24	153	244	400[1,2]
New Jersey	16	24	40	32	48	80
New Mexico	25	17	42	40	30	70
New York	23	36	61[2]	98	52	150
North Carolina	35	15	50	66	54	120
North Dakota	18	31	49	34	63	98[2]
Ohio	12	21	33	39	59	99[2]
Oklahoma	33	15	48	61	40	101
Oregon	13	17	30	25	35	60
Pennsylvania	20	30	50	100	103	203
Rhode Island	42	8	50	85	12	100[1,2]
South Carolina	24	22	46	57	67	124
South Dakota	13	22	35	19	51	70
Tennessee	18	15	33	61	38	99
Texas	15	16	31	78	71	150[2]
Utah	11	18	29	21	54	75
Vermont	17	13	30	77	67	150[1]
Virginia	20	20	40	47	52	100[1]
Washington	27	22	49	49	49	98
West Virginia	29	5	34	75	25	100
Wisconsin	17	16	33	44	55	99
Wyoming	10	20	30	17	43	60
Dist. of Columbia[3]	11	2	13	Unicameral		
Amer. Samoa	Nonpartisan		18	Nonpartisan		20
Guam	3	12	15	Unicameral		
N. Mariana Isl.	0	7	9[1,2]	6	11	18[1]
Puerto Rico	19	8	28[1]	37	16	54[1]
U.S. Virgin Isl.	6	2	15[1]	Unicameral		
Total	1,048	950	2,083[4]	2,897	2,582	5,528[5]

Note: As of December, 1999. Numbers in bold indicates the party in the majority. 1. Includes one or more Independent or other third-party legislator . 2. Includes one or more vacancy. 3. Council of the District of Columbia. 4. Includes 68 nonpartisans (from Nebraska and American Samoa), 11 Independent or other third-party legislators, and six vacancies. 5. Includes 20 nonpartisans (from American Samoa), 19 Independent or other third-party legislators, and 14 vacancies.
Source: Council of State Governments, *State Elective Officials and the Legislatures*, 2000

Salaries of Major State Administrative Officials, 2000–01

State	Governor	Lieutenant governor	Secretary of state	Attorney general
Alabama	$94,655	$48,870	$66,722	$124,951
Alaska	81,648	$76,176	([1])	83,292
Arizona	95,000	([2])	70,000	90,000
Arkansas	68,448	33,083	42,780	57,040
California	165,000	123,750	123,750	140,250
Colorado	90,000	68,500	68,500	80,000
Connecticut[3]	78,000	55,000	50,000	60,000
Delaware	107,000	47,900	95,500	105,200
Florida	117,240	112,304	116,056	116,056
Georgia[3]	111,480	72,812	89,538	102,211
Hawaii	94,780	90,041	([1])	85,302
Idaho	95,500	25,250	77,500	85,500
Illinois	140,200	107,200	123,700	123,700
Indiana	77,200	64,000	66,000	79,400
Iowa	104,352	73,047	82,940	99,379
Kansas	91,742	Waived	71,270	81,958
Kentucky	97,068	82,521	82,521	82,521
Louisiana	95,000	85,008	85,000	85,000
Maine	70,000	([4])	48,298[5]	62,670
Maryland	120,000	100,000	70,000	100,000
Massachusetts	135,000	120,000	120,000	122,500
Michigan	151,245	100,671	124,900	124,900
Minnesota	120,303	66,168	66,168	93,981
Mississippi	101,800	60,000	75,000	90,800
Missouri	112,755	68,188	90,471	97,899
Montana[3]	83,672	53,407	62,848	66,756
Nebraska	65,000	47,000	52,000	64,500
Nevada	117,000	50,000	80,000	110,000
New Hampshire	93,263	([4])	74,372	83,256
New Jersey[3]	130,000[6]	([4])	100,225	100,225
New Mexico	90,000	65,000	65,000	72,500
New York	179,000	151,500	120,800	151,500
North Carolina[3]	107,132	94,552	94,552	94,552
North Dakota	76,884	63,180	58,260	65,753
Ohio[3]	119,225	57,637	82,347	85,509
Oklahoma	101,140	75,530	65,000	94,349
Oregon	88,300	([2])	67,900	72,800
Pennsylvania	135,559	113,870	97,603	112,785
Rhode Island	95,000	80,000	80,000	85,000
South Carolina[3]	106,078	46,545	92,007	92,007
South Dakota	89,898	65,2707	61,090	76,357
Tennessee	87,276	49,500	120,000	112,068
Texas	115,345	([8])	112,352	92,217
Utah	93,000	72,300	([1])	78,200
Vermont	88,026	46,030	69,493	83,491
Virginia[3]	110,000	32,000	76,346	97,500
Washington	132,000[(9)]	69,000	75,900	120,000
West Virginia	99,000	([4])	65,000	75,000
Wisconsin	115,699	60,182	54,610	112,274
Wyoming	95,000	([2])	77,000	78,500

1. Lieutenant governor also serves as secretary of state. 2. Secretary of state also serves as lieutenant governor. 3. Data for officials other than governor is for 1998-99. 4. No lieutenant governor. Speaker or President of the Senate next in line of succession to the governorship. 5. Minimum salary; maximum salary is $70,886.6. Governor voluntary accepts a reduced salary of $85,000. 7. Annual salary for duties as presiding officer of the Senate. 8. In Texas, the salary of the Lieutenant Governor is the same as a Senator when serving as President of the Senate ($7,200/year) and the same as Governor when serving as Governor. 9. Annually returns $31,000 of salary to general fund. **Source:** Council of State Governments, *The Book of the States*, 2000-2001.

U.S. TERRITORIES AND POSSESSIONS

The United States administers a number of overseas territories and commonwealth states under a variety of circumstances. The provisions of the Northwest Ordinance of 1787 established the system under which territories of the United States can achieve statehood. In order to elect a territorial legislature and send a nonvoting delegate to Congress, a territory must contain 5,000 inhabitants of voting age; it is eligible for statehood when the population numbers 60,000.

▶ AMERICAN SAMOA
Territory of American Samoa
Geography Location: seven islands (Tutuila, Ta'u, Olosega, Ofu, Aunun, Rose, Swain's) in southern central Pacific Ocean. **Boundaries:** Hawaii about 2,300 mi. (3,700 km) to NNE, Cook Islands to E, Tonga to SW, Western Samoa to W. **Total area:** 76.1 sq. mi. (199 sq km). **Coastline:** 72 mi. (116 km). **Comparative area:** slightly larger than Washington, DC. **Land use:** 5% arable land; 10% permanent crops; 0% meadows and pastures; 70% forest and woodland; 15% other. **Major cities:** (1980 census) Pago Pago (capital) 3,075.

People Population: 67,084 (July 2001 est.) **Nationality:** noun—American Samoan(s); adjective—American Samoan. **Ethnic groups:** 89% Samoan (Polynesian), 2% Caucasian, 4% Tongan, 5% other. **Languages:** Samoan (closely related to Hawaiian and other Polynesian languages) and English; most people are bilingual. **Religions:** 50% Christian Congregationalist, 20% Roman Catholic, 30% mostly Protestant denominations and other.

Government Type: unincorporated and unorganized territory of U.S. **Constitution:** ratified 1966, in effect 1967. **National holiday:** Flag Day, Apr. 17 (1900). **Heads of Government:** Tauese P. Sunia, Governor (since Jan. 1997). **Structure:** executive—governor is popularly elected to four-year term and exercises authority under direction of U.S. Secretary of Interior; legislative—bicameral legislature (Fono) with 18 member Senate chosen by county councils to serve four-year terms and House of Representatives with 20 members popularly elected to serve two-year terms, plus a nonvoting delegate from Swain's Island; judicial—High Court with chief justice and associate justices appointed by U.S. Secretary of Interior.

Economy Monetary unit: U.S. dollar. **Budget:** (1996-97 est.) income: $121 mil.; expend.: 127 mil. **GDP:** $500 mil.; $8,000 per capita (2000 est.). **Chief crops:** bananas, coconuts, vegetables, taro, breadfruit, yams, copra, pineapples, papayas. **Natural resources:** pumice and pumicite. **Major industries:** tuna canneries, handicrafts. **Labor force:** 14,400 (1996) 33% government, 34% tuna canneries, 33% other. **Exports:** $500 mil. (1998); 93% canned tuna. **Imports:** $471 mil. (1996); 56% material for canneries, 8% food, 7% petroleum products, 6% machinery and parts. **Major trading partners:** (1992) *exports:* 99.6% U.S.; *imports:* 62% U.S., 9% Japan, 11% Australia, 7% New Zealand, 4% Fiji, 7% other.

American Samoa consists of seven islands between 14° and 15°S, and 168° and 171°W. It was first peopled by Polynesians in the first millennium B.C. The first European to visit the islands was Louis Antoine de Bougainville, who came in 1768 and called them "The Islands of the Navigators," in recognition of the islanders' seamanship. American whalers and missionaries began visiting the islands in the 1830s, and the United States secured trading privileges by treaty in 1878. In 1889, the United States, Britain, and Germany established tripartite control of the islands. The High Chiefs of Tutuila ceded the islands of Tutuila and Aunun to the United States in 1900, and the High Chiefs of the Manu'a islands ceded those of Tau, Ofu, Olosega, and Rose in 1904. Swain's Island became part of American Samoa in 1925.

The islands have been administered by Department of Interior since 1904. American Samoa is an unincorporated and unorganized territory of the United States, with its own government but under the plenary authority of the Department of the Interior.

▶ BAKER AND HOWLAND ISLANDS
About 1,600 mi. (2,575 km) southwest of Hawaii and 1,000 miles west of Jarvis Island are Baker Island (0°14'N, 176°28'W) and Howland Island (0°48'N, 176°38'W, 40 miles north of Baker). Discovered in 1842, the two coral atolls were worked for guano until about 1890. Great Britain claimed them in 1889, but the U.S. made them territories in 1935 and sent colonists to them. With an area about of about 1 sq. mi. each, neither is inhabited today. Both are unincorporated territories administered by the U.S. Fish and Wildlife Service as part of the National Wildlife Refuge.

▶ GUAM
Territory of Guam
Geography Location: southernmost and largest of Mariana Islands in western North Pacific Ocean; Agaña 13°28'N, 144°45'E. **Boundaries:** Tokyo, Japan about 1,350 mi. (2,170 km) to N, Honolulu, Hawaii 3,300 mi. (5,955 km) to ENE; Federated States of Micronesia to S, Philippines to W across Philippine Sea. **Total area:** 209 sq. mi. (541 sq km). **Coastline:** 78 mi. (125.5 km). **Comparative area:** Three times size of Washington, D.C. **Land use:** 18% forest and woodland; 15% meadows and pastures; 11% arable land; 11% permanent crops; 45% other. **Major cities:** Agaña (capital).

People Population: 157,557 (July 2001 est.) **Nationality:** noun—Guamanian(s); adjective—Guamanian. **Ethnic groups:** 47% Chamorro, 25% Filipino, 10% Caucasian, 18% Chinese, Japanese, Korean, other. **Languages:** English, Chamorro, and Japanese. **Religions:** 85% Roman Catholic, 15% other.

Government Type: organized, unincorporated territory of U.S. **Constitution:** Organic Act of Aug. 1, 1950. **National holiday:** Guam Discovery Day, first Monday in Mar. **Heads of Government:** Carl Gutierrez, governor (since Nov. 8, 1994). **Structure:** executive—governor elected to 4-year term; legislative—unicameral; Senate has 15 members elected for 2-year terms; judicial—U.S. District Court, Guam Superior Court.

Economy Monetary unit: U.S. dollar. **Budget:** (2000) *revenue:* $605.3 mil.; *expend.:* $654.2 mil. **GDP:** $3.2 bil., $21,000 per capita (2000 est.). **Chief crops:** fruits, copra, vegetables, eggs; relatively undeveloped with most food imported.

Livestock: poultry, pigs, cows. **Natural resources:** fishing (largely undeveloped), tourism (especially from Japan). **Major industries:** U.S. military, tourism, construction, transshipment services, concrete products, printing and publishing, food processing, textiles. **Labor force:** 60,000 (2000 est.) ; 40% private services, 26% government, 24% trade, 10% industry. **Exports:** $75.7 mil. (f.o.b. 1999) mostly transshipments of refined petroleum products, construction materials, fish, food and beverage products. **Imports:** $203 mil. (f.o.b. 1999); petroleum and petroleum products; food, manufactured goods. **Major trading partners:** *exports:* 25% U.S., 63% Trust Territory of the Pacific Islands, 12% other; *imports:* 23% U.S., 19% Japan, 58% other.

Guam was inhabited by Chamorros from the Malay Peninsula as early as 1500 B.C. The first European to stop at Guam was Ferdinand Magellan in 1521. Spanish colonization began with the arrival of Jesuit missionaries in 1668. By 1700 pestilence and insurrection had reduced the Chamorro population from 50,000 to about 2,000. Guam was ceded to the United States in 1899. In 1941 it was occupied by Japan—the only inhabited territory of the U.S. to be seized by enemy forces during World War II. It was retaken by the Americans in 1944. Though unincorporated, the Congressionally approved Guam Organic Act provides for a republican form of government with executive, legislative, and judicial branches.

More than one million tourists visit Guam annually, but the impact of military downsizing will nevertheless cause new economic problems.

▶ **JARVIS ISLAND, KINGMAN REEF, AND PALMYRA ATOLL**
Jarvis Island (0°23'S, 160°02'W, about 1,510 mi. S of Hawaii), Kingman Reef (6°24'N, 162°22'W, about 1,070 mi. SSW of Hawaii), and Palmyra Atoll (5°52'N, 162°05'W, about 1,100 mi. SSW of Hawaii) in the Line Island group.

Discovered in 1798, Kingman Reef (0.4 sq. mi.; 1 sq km) was annexed by the U.S. in 1922, and used as an aviation station during the 1930s. Discovered in 1802, Palmyra Atoll consists of about 50 islets with a combined area of four square miles. It was annexed by the Kingdom of Hawaii in 1862, by Great Britain in 1889, and claimed by the U.S. in 1912. Privately owned, it is administered by the Department of the Navy, as is Kingman Reef. Jarvis Island was claimed by the U.S. in 1857, annexed by Great Britain in 1889, and reclaimed by the U.S. in 1935. Its rich guano deposits were worked by U.S. and British companies in the late 19th century.

▶ **JOHNSTON ATOLL**
Geography Location: Johnston Island and Sand Island (uninhabited) in central Pacific Ocean. **Boundaries:** Honolulu, Hawaii about 825 mi. (1,330 km) to ENE, Marshall Islands to SW. **Total area:** 1.1 sq. mi. (2.8 sq km). **Coastline:** 6.21 mi. (10 km). **Comparative area:** about 4.7 times size of The Mall in Washington, DC. **Land use:** 0% arable land; 0% permanent crops; 0% meadows and pastures; 0% forest and woodland; 100% other. **Major cities:** none.
People Population: 970 (Jan. 2001), all U.S. government personnel and contractors.
Government Type: unincorporated territory of U.S.

Johnston Atoll (16°45N, 169°32'W) , 820 miles SW of Hawaii) includes Johnston, Hikina, and Akan Islands, with a total area of 1.1 square miles. Claimed by the U.S. in 1858, Johnston Atoll is manned and administered by the U.S. Defense Special Weapons Agency and managed jointly as a National Wildlife Refuge by the DSWA and the Fish and Wildlife Service.

▶ **MIDWAY ISLANDS**
Geography Location: Sand Island and Eastern Island in northern Pacific Ocean; 28°15'N, 177°25'W. **Boundaries:** Honolulu, Hawaii about 1,460 mi. (2,350 km) to SE, Marshall Islands to SW. **Total area:** 2.0 sq. mi. (5.2 sq km). **Coastline:** 9.3 mi. (15.0 km). **Comparative area:** about nine times size of The Mall in Washington, DC. **Land use:** 0% arable land; 0% permanent crops; 0% meadows and pastures; 0% forest and woodland; 100% other. **Major cities:** none.
People Population: 150 U.S. Fish and Wildlife Service personnel (July, 2001 est.). No indigenous population. **Nationality:** noun—Midway Islander(s); adjective—Midway Island. **Languages:** English. **Religions:** Christianity.
Government Type: unincorporated territory of U.S.
Economy Monetary unit: U.S. dollar. **Major industries:** support of National Wildlife Refuge activities.

Midway Atoll consists of Eastern Island and Sand Island. Although they are part of the Leeward Islands—the westernmost islands of the Hawaiian chain—they are not part of the state of Hawaii. They were the site of the Battle of Midway, June 1942, a turning point in the Pacific theater of World War II. The islands continued to serve as a naval station until 1993; since 1996, it has been managed by the U.S. Fish and Wildlife Service as a National Wildlife Refuge open to the public for snorkeling, scuba diving, and sportfishing.

▶ **NAVASSA**
Located in the Caribbean between the islands of Jamaica and Haiti and 100 mi (160km) south of the U.S. Naval Base at Guantánamo, Cuba, Navassa was claimed by the U.S. in 1856. It is uninhabited except for a lighthouse under U.S. Coast Guard administration. The island is about 2 sq. mi. (5.2 sq km).

▶ **NORTHERN MARIANA ISLANDS**
Commonwealth of the Northern Mariana Islands (CNMI)
Geography Location: Fourteen major islands (including Saipan, Rota, and Tinian) in western central Pacific Ocean. Saipan 15°13'N, 145°44'E. **Boundaries:** Japan to N; Honolulu, Hawaii about 3,500 mi. (5,635 km) to E; Guam to SW; Philippines to W across Philippine Sea. **Total area:** 293 sq. mi. (759 sq km). **Coastline:** undetermined. **Comparative area:** slightly more than 2.5 times size of Washington, D.C. **Land use:** 19% meadows and pastures, 21% arable land, 60% other. **Major cities:** (1990 census) Saipan (capital) 38,896.
People Population: 74,612 (July 2001 est.) **Nationality:** undetermined. **Ethnic groups:** Chamorro majority; Carolinians, other Micronesians; Caucasian, Japanese, Chinese, Korean. **Languages:** English, Chamorro, Carolinian; 86 percent speak a language other than English at home. **Religions:** Christian (Roman Catholic majority); some traditional beliefs.

Government Type: commonwealth associated with U.S. **Constitution:** Covenant Agreement effective Nov. 3, 1986. **National holiday:** Commonwealth Day, Jan. 8. **Heads of Government:** Pedro P. Tenorio, governor (since January, 1998). **Structure:** executive—governor elected by popular vote; legislative—bicameral legislature (nine-member Senate elected for four-year term, 15-member House of Representatives elected for two-year term; judiciary—U.S. District Court, Commonwealth Trial Court, Commonwealth Appeals Court.

Economy **Monetary unit:** U.S. dollar. **Budget:** (1996) *revenues:* $221 mil. *expend:* 213 mil. **GDP:** $900 mil., $12,500 per capita (2000). **Chief crops:** coconuts, fruits, vegetables. **Livestock:** cattle. **Natural resources:** arable land, fish. **Major industries:** tourism, construction, light industry, handicrafts. **Labor force:** 7,476 total indigenous labor force, 2,699 unemployed, 22,560 foreign workers (1995). **Exports:** $N.A. garments. **Imports:** $N.A. food, construction equipment and materials, petroleum products. **Major trading partners:** U.S., Japan.

Running north from the island of Guam across a 600-mile-long archipelago in the Pacific Island group known as Micronesia, the islands of the Northern Marianas (CNMI) were originally settled by Pacific argonauts as early as 1500 B.C. Ferdinand Magellan landed at Saipan in 1521, introducing Western culture to the region. The Spanish took control of the archipelago in 1565 and ruled until 1898, when Germany took over the islands. After World War I, the League of Nations mandated the Marianas to Japan, who developed extensive sugar processing works on Saipan. Allied forces took the Marianas in 1944.

In 1947, the islands were included in the United Nations Trust Territory of the Pacific and placed under U.S. administration. In 1976, the CNMI adopted its own constitution. A mutually approved Covenant to Establish a Commonwealth was implemented by the Marianas and the United States in 1986. The Northern Marianas are subject to provisions of U.S. law, except regarding customs, minimum wages, immigration, and taxation. The people are, as a rule, U.S. citizens. The CNMI benefits from substantially from United States assistance.

▶**PUERTO RICO**
Commonwealth of Puerto Rico
Geography **Location:** large island of Puerto Rico, together with Vieques, Culebra, and many smaller islands, in northeastern Caribbean Sea. San Juan 18° 29′N, 66° 08′W **Boundaries:** Atlantic Ocean to N, Virgin Islands to E, Caribbean Sea to S, Dominican Republic 50 mi. (80 km) to W. **Total land area:** 3,459 sq. mi. (8,959 sq km). **Coastline:** 311 mi. (501 km). **Comparative area:** slightly less than three times size of Rhode Island. **Land use:** 26% pastures; 16% forest and woodland; 5% permanent crops; 4% arable land; 49% other; **Major cities:** (2000 Census) San Juan (capital) 421,958, Bayamón 203,499, Carolina 168,164, Ponce 155,038, Caguas 88,680

People **Population:** 3,808,610 (2000 Census). **Nationality:** noun—Puerto Rican(s); adjective—Puerto Rican. **Ethnic groups:** almost entirely Hispanic. **Languages:** Spanish (official), English. **Religions:** mostly Christian, 85% Roman Catholic, 15% Protestant denominations and other.

Government Type: commonwealth associated with U.S. **Constitution:** effective July 25, 1952. **National holiday:** U.S. Independence Day, July 4. **Heads of Government:** Sila Calderon, governor, since Jan. 2001. **Structure:** executive—governor elected by direct vote to four-year term; legislative—bicameral legislature (Senate with 28 members, House of Representatives with 54 members, all elected by popular vote to four-year terms); judiciary—Supreme Court appointed by governor.

Economy **Monetary unit:** U.S. dollar. **Budget:** (FY99/00) *income:* $6.7 bil.; *expend.:* $9.6 bil. **GDP:** $38.1 bil., $9,800 per capita (1999 est.). **Chief crops:** sugarcane, coffee, pineapples, plantains, bananas (imports a large share of food needs). **Livestock:** cattle, chickens. **Natural resources:** copper, nickel; potential for crude oil. **Major industries:** manufacturing of pharmaceuticals, electronics, apparel, food products, instruments, tourism. **Labor force:** (2000): industry 20%, services 77%, 9.5% unemployed. **Exports:** $38.5 bil. (f.o.b. 2000): pharmaceuticals, electronics, apparel, canned tuna, rum, beverage concentrates, medical equipment, tourism. **Imports:** $27 bil. (c.i.f. 2000); chemicals, machinery and equipment, clothing, food, fish, petroleum products. **Major trading partners:** (1999 est.) *exports:* 88% U.S; *imports:* 60% U.S.

Puerto Rico was initially peopled by the Igneri and Taíno tribes. The island's first European visitor was Christopher Columbus, who landed on the island in 1493. In 1508, Juan Ponce de Léon led the first settlers to San Juan, and by 1514 the Taíno population had dropped from an estimated 30,000 to 4,000. In the 17th and 18th centuries, Puerto Rico was invaded by both English and Danish forces, and though San Juan was captured or burned several times, the Spanish maintained control.

The Spanish constitution granted Puerto Ricans citizenship in 1812, but a revolution was put down in 1868. Spain granted Puerto Rico self-government in 1897 but this was repealed when sovereignty was transferred to the U.S. after the Spanish-American War. Despite early attempts to Americanize Puerto Rico, including an effort to make English the official language and granting citizenship in 1917, the Popular Democratic Party, founded in 1938, brought about a change in political status from that of a U.S. colony to an autonomous commonwealth in 1952.

Governed under the Puerto Rican Federal Relations Act and a constitution modeled on that of the U.S., Puerto Rico is nonetheless an autonomous political entity in voluntary association with the U.S. Despite dramatic increases in industrial development since the 1950s, Puerto Rico suffered from net outward migration until 1988.

Puerto Ricans remain almost equally divided between those who favor statehood and those who favor maintaining commonwealth status, with those seeking independence constituting a vocal but small minority. The statehood-minded argue that limited citizenship is disadvantageous since it allows them to be drafted into the U.S. military but they cannot vote in national elections. The other side fears the burden of full U.S. taxes. In the most recent balloting on the issue, held December 13, 1998, 50.2 percent of Puerto Ricans voted for "none of the above," an option that maintained Puerto Rico's commonwealth status; 46.5 percent voted for statehood, while 2.5 percent preferred independence.

▶VIRGIN ISLANDS
Virgin Islands of the United States
Geography **Location:** three main inhabited islands (St. Croix, St. Thomas and St. John) and about 50 smaller islands, mostly uninhabited, in northeastern Caribbean Sea. Charlotte Amalie 18°22'N, 64°56'W. **Boundaries:** British Virgin Islands to N, Netherlands Antilles to E, Caribbean Sea to S, Puerto Rico about 40 mi. (64 km) to W. **Total area:** 136 sq. mi. (352 sq km). **Coastline:** 117 mi. (188 km). **Comparative area:** twice the size of Washington, DC. **Land use:** 26% meadows and pastures; 15% arable land; 6% permanent crops; 6% forest and woodland; 47% other. **Major cities:** (1990 census) Charlotte Amalie (capital) 12,331; Christiansted 2,555; Frederiksted 1,064. **People Population:** 122,211 (July 2001). **Nationality:** noun—Virgin Islander(s); adjective—Virgin Islander. **Ethnic groups:** 74% West Indian (45% born in Virgin Islands, 29% born elsewhere in West Indies), 13% U.S. mainland, 5% Puerto Rican, 8% other; 80% black, 15% white, 5% other; 14% of Hispanic origin. **Languages:** English (official), Spanish, Creole. **Religions:** 42% Baptist, 34% Roman Catholic, 17% Episcopalian, 7% other.

Government **Type:** organized, unincorporated territory of U.S. **Constitution:** Revised Organic Act of July 22, 1954 serves as constitution. **National holiday:** Transfer Day (from Denmark to U.S.), Mar. 31. **Heads of Government:** Dr. Charles Wesley Turnbull, governor (since Jan. 1999). **Structure:** executive—governor elected to four-year term; unicameral legislature—senate with 15 members elected to two-year terms; judiciary—two U.S. district courts.

Economy **Monetary unit:** U.S. dollar. **Budget:** (1992) *income:* $364.4 mil.; *expend.:* $364.4 mil. **GDP:** $1.8 bil., $15,000 per capita (2000). **Chief crops:** fruit, vegetables, sorghum. **Livestock:** Senepol cattle. **Natural resources:** sun, sand, sea, surf. **Major industries:** tourism, petroleum refining, watch assembly, rum distilling, construction, pharmaceuticals, textiles, electronics. **Labor force:** 47,443 (1990); 79% services, 20% industry, 1.2% agriculture; 4.9% unemployment. **Exports:** $N.A.; refined petroleum products to U.S. **Imports:** $N.A.; 82% crude petroleum for refining. **Major trading partners:** *exports:* U.S., Puerto Rico; imports: U.S., Puerto Rico.

The Virgin Islands of the United States (USVI) consists of more than 50 islands located about 40 miles east of Puerto Rico, and about 1,730 east-

southeast of Miami. Excavations have revealed evidence of human habitation in the Virgin Islands from as early as A.D. 100. By 1493, when Christopher Columbus landed in the islands—which he named for the virgin martyr St. Ursula—they were inhabited by Carib Indians who were driven out by the Spanish in 1555.

In 1672, St. Thomas was settled by the Danish West India Company. The Danes laid claim to St. John in 1683 and purchased St. Croix from the French in 1773. The United States purchased the Virgin Islands from Denmark for $25 million in 1917, and they were made a territory under the jurisdiction of the Navy. U.S. citizenship was granted in 1927, and the Department of the Interior assumed administration of the islands in 1931. The first governor elected by popular vote was installed in 1970, and an independent constitution was voted down by the electorate 1979.

The primary industry is tourism, which accounts for 70 percent of GDP and employs 70 percent of the work force. Inernational business and financial services are increasingly important.

▶WAKE ISLANDS
Geography **Location:** three islands (Wake, Wilkes, and Peale) in North Pacific Ocean; Wake 19°18'N, 166°36'E. **Boundaries:** Honolulu, Hawaii 2,3000 mi. (3,700 km) to E, Marshall Islands to S, Guam about 1,280 mi. (2,060 km) to W. **Total area:** 2.5 sq. mi. (6.5 sq km). **Coastline:** 12 mi. (19.3 km) **Comparative area:** about 11 times size of the Mall in Washington, D.C. **Land use:** 0% arable land; 0% permanent crops; 0% meadows and pastures; 0% forest and woodland; 100% other. **Major cities:** none. **People Population:** no indigenous inhabitants; temporary population of 123 civilian contractors and one U.S. Army civilian. (Jan. 2001). **Government Type:** unincorporated territory of U.S., administered by U.S. Air Force.

The Wake Island group was first discovered by British captain William Wake in 1796. It was chartered by Capt. Charles Wilkes's surveying expedition, which was accompanied by a naturalist named Peale. Annexed by the United States in 1898, Wake became a civil aviation station in the 1930s, and was captured by the Japanese shortly after Pearl Harbor. It was retaken in 1944. Formerly an important commercial aviation base, it is now used only by some commercial cargo planes and for emergency landings.

Resident Population of U.S. Territories, 1960–2020 (in thousands)							
Territory	1960	1970	1980	1990	2000	2010[1]	2020[1]
Puerto Rico	2,358	2,7122	3,210	3,537	3,916	4,088	4,196
Guam	67	86	107	134	155	184	211
Virgin Islands	33	63	100	104	121	133	144
American Samoa	20	27	32	47	65	81	95
Northern Mariana Islands	9	12	17	44	72	99	123

1. Projected. **Source:** U.S. Census Bureau, International Data Base.

Cities and Counties in the U.S.

Included here is basic information about population change, cost of living, and government finances in major U.S. cities, metropolitan statistical areas, and counties. In addition, there are brief descriptions of the 50 largest cities—from Albuquerque to Wichita. Statistical sources include the U.S. Census Bureau's decennial census, *City Government Finances, County Government Finances,* and the *Statistical Abstract of the United States* (all annual publications).

►FORMS OF LOCAL GOVERNMENT

In addition to the one federal and 50 state governments, the Bureau of the Census recognizes five basic types of organized local government. In addition to these, which are authorized in state constitutions and statutes, some local governments operate under a "home-rule charter" the form and organization of which are specified by locally approved charters rather than by general or special state law. The number of local governments and officials continues to skyrocket even as the size of the federal bureaucracy shrinks. In 1997, there were a total of 87,453 state and local governments compared with 85,006 five years earlier.

Counties

County governments are established to provide general government; and include those governments designated as boroughs in Alaska, parishes in Louisiana, and counties in the other states. In 1997, there were 3,043 county governments; the most common forms are:

Council-commission A county government without a chief executive but with an elected governing body that shares administrative responsibility with officials elected or appointed to specific positions.

Council-administrator A county government with an elected governing body responsible for overall policy, and an appointed administrator (sometimes called a county manager, county commissioner, or county judge) responsible for administration. The powers of the administrator under this form of government may vary widely.

Council-elected executive A county government with an elected governing body and an elected chief executive—sometimes called a president or a chairperson of the board. The powers of the executive under this form of government may vary widely.

Municipalities

Municipal governments are established to provide general government for a specific concentration of population in a defined area and include those governments designated as cities, villages, boroughs (except in Alaska), and towns (except in the six New England states, Minnesota, New York and Wisconsin). In 1997, there were 19,372 municipal governments; the most common forms are:

Mayor-council A municipal government with an elected mayor and an elected council or other governing body. In some mayor-council municipalities, the mayor is the chief executive, with

broad powers. In some other mayor-council cities, the mayor has limited powers.

Council-manager A municipal government with an elected council or other governing body responsible for overall policy, and an appointed manager responsible for administration. The council may select a chairperson from among their own number who may be designated as the mayor.

Commission A municipal government with an elected board of commissioners responsible for overall policy. Each commissioner is responsible for administration of one or more departments of the municipal government. The board may select a chairperson from among their own number who may be designated as the mayor.

Towns

Township governments are established to provide general government for areas defined without regard to population concentration and include those governments designated as towns in Connecticut, Maine (including organized plantations), Massachusetts, Minnesota, New Hampshire (including organized locations), New York, Rhode Island, Vermont, and Wisconsin, and townships in other states. In 1997, there were 16,629 township governments; the most common forms are:

Town meeting A township government in which an annual town meeting of resident voters makes basic policy. An elected board (often called "a board of selectmen" or "township supervisors") is responsible for day-to-day administration of the township.

Representative town meeting A township government in which a town meeting composed of elected representatives of the resident voters makes basic policy. This form of government is usually found in more populous towns or townships. An elected board (often called "a board of selectmen" or "township supervisors") is responsible for day-to-day administration of the township.

School districts

School district governments are organized local entities providing public elementary, secondary and/or higher education which, under state law, have sufficient administrative and fiscal autonomy to qualify as separate governments. Excludes "dependent public school systems" of county, township or state governments. In 1997, there were 13,726 school district governments.

Special district governments

All organized local entities other than the four categories listed above, authorized by state law to provide only one or a limited number of designated functions, and with sufficient administrative and fiscal autonomy to qualify as separate governments; known by a variety of titles, including districts, authorities, boards, commissions, etc., as specified in the state legislation. In 1997, there were 34,683 special district governments.

Source: U.S. Bureau of the Census.

THE 50 LARGEST CITIES, 2000

Between 1990 and 2000, the westward movement of the U.S. population again revealed its strength as three cities in the so-called Rust Belt (Buffalo, Cincinnati, Pittsburgh, and Toledo) fell from the list of the 50 largest cities in the U.S. They were replaced by Colorado Springs, Las Vegas, Mesa, Ariz., and Wichita, Kansas.

Among the largest cities in the U.S., however, no city came close to Las Vegas in terms of population growth. Between 1990 and 2000, its population increased from 258,295 to 478,434, leapfrogging more than 30 cities in going from the 63rd largest city to the 32nd.

Following are brief descriptions of the 50 largest cities in the U.S. according to numbers from the 2000 Census. They are set forth in alphabetical order. Several tables showing the growth of major cities in America follow this section. See also the section on Metropolitan Statistical Areas (MSAs) later in this chapter.

▶ ALBUQUERQUE, NEW MEXICO

Seventy million years ago, earthquakes and volcanoes pushed the land that is now Albuquerque above the sea, forming the Rio Grande Valley and a ring of mountain ranges. Even today, the 10,000 foot-high Sandia Mountains are rising slowly and the Rio Grande Valley continues gradually to deepen. During the Ice Age, Sandia Man roamed the area hunting mastodon and buffalo, and some 3,000 years ago, the Anasazi built stone and adobe cities which still stand. The 1530s marked the arrival of Spanish conquistadors and missionaries.

Founded as a Spanish Villa in 1706, when 35 families moved to the land along the Rio Grande, Albuquerque was named by Don Francisco Cuervo y Valdez in honor of the Duke of Albuquerque, King Phillip's Viceroy of New Spain. Indian raids arrested the villa's expansion, and 100 years after its founding, its population numbered a mere 2,200. Benefitting from their proximity to the Santa Fe Trail, the people farmed, raised cattle, marketed wool and adobe for building, and ran trading posts, military supply depots, saloons, hotels, and mercantile businesses. The introduction of the railroad in 1880 spurred Albuquerque's growth, and the 1940 population of 35,000 has since grown more than tenfold.

Today, Albuquerque occupies a central position along the Rio Grande Research Corridor, which stretches from Los Alamos to Las Cruces, and is home to the University of New Mexico and such major high-tech installments as GTE Communications, UNISYS, GE, and Sandia National Laboratories. Albuquerque's cultural and historical attractions include the Albuquerque Museum, the Indian Pueblo Culture Center, the Maxwell Museum of Anthropology, the National Atomic Museum, and Petroglyph National Monument.
Population 448,607 (2000). Rank: 35th. Race/Hispanic Origin (2000): White 71.6%. Black 3.1%. Indian 3.9%. Asian 2.2%. Pacific Islander 0.1%. Other 14.8%. Two or more races 4.3%. Hispanic 39.9%.
Location: 35°05'N, 106°47'W. County: Bernalillo.
Terrain and climate Elev.: 5,300 ft. Area: 127.2 sq. mi. (329.4 sq km). Avg. daily min. temp.: Jan.: 22.3°F/-5.3°C; avg. daily max. July: 92.8°F/33.7°C.

Avg. annual: rainfall, 8.12"; snowfall, 11"; clear days, 71; precipitation days, 135.
Government Form: mayor and council. Mayor Jim Baca. Election: Oct. 2001. Municipal tel. number: (505) 768-3000.
Visitor info: (505) 842-9918 or (800) 284-2282.
www.abqcvb.org

▶ ATLANTA, GEORGIA

Atlanta, the capital and largest city of Georgia, lies at the base of the Blue Ridge Mountains, near the Chattahoochee River. First settled in 1836, the area became the terminus for the Georgia Railroad in 1845 and took the name Atlanta. The population grew to 15,000 by 1861, and during the Civil War, Atlanta became a strategic Confederate depot and collection point for recruits, establishing it as one of the most important cities of the Confederacy and making it a vital objective during Gen. William Tecumseh Sherman's infamous "March to the Sea" in 1864. After two months of bitter battle, Sherman took the city on Sept. 1 and burned most of it to the ground. After the war, the ravaged city was rebuilt; it became the state capital in 1868.

The leading city of the so-called "New South," Atlanta is a the chief commercial hub of the southeastern United States. Atlanta is nicknamed the "City Without Limits" because there are no major rivers, mountains, or coastlines to retard its burgeoning growth into the ever-expanding suburbs. Several *Fortune* 500 Companies have their headquarters in Atlanta (including Coca-Cola and United Parcel Service) as do CNN and the U.S. Centers for Disease Control. Hartsfield Atlanta International (the major hub for Delta Airlines) is the world's second busiest airport, giving rise to the saying, "whether you're going to heaven or hell, you still have to change planes in Atlanta."

The city is also an important educational and cultural center, home to more than 30 institutions of higher learning, including Georgia Tech, Emory University, and Morehouse and Spelman Colleges. The Jimmy Carter Presidential Library is here, as is the grave of the Rev. Martin Luther King Jr.

The 1996 Summer Olympics thrust Atlanta into the international spotlight, and helped fuel the city's economic future. The Olympiad added hundreds of thousands of jobs (most of them permanent) and an estimated $500 million in construction to Atlanta's economy. It also brought Centennial Olympic Park and Turner Field to the downtown landscape.
Population 416,474 (2000). Rank: 39th. Race/Hispanic Origin (2000): White 33.2%. Black 61.4%. Indian 0.2%. Asian 1.9%. Other 2.0%. Two or more races 1.3%. Hispanic 4.5%.
Location: 33°50'N, 84°24'W. County: Fulton.
Terrain and climate Elev.: 1,034 ft. Area: 131.2 sq. mi. (339.80 sq km). Avg. daily min. temp.: Jan.: 32.6°F/0.3°C; avg. daily max. July: 87.9°F/31°C. Avg. annual: rainfall, 48.61"; snowfall, 2"; clear days, 108; precipitation days, 116.
Government Form: mayor and council. Mayor William Craig Campbell. Election: Nov. 2001. Municipal tel. number: (404) 330-6100.
Visitor info: (404) 222-6688.
www.ci.atlanta.ga.us

▶ AUSTIN, TEXAS

Austin, the capital of Texas, lies about 80 miles northeast of San Antonio on the banks of the Colorado River. First inhabited by nomadic Indian tribes, the area had as its first permanent European settler Jacob Harrell, in 1835, who established the town of Waterloo. In 1839, it was chosen as the site of the Texas Republic's capital and was renamed after Stephen F. Austin, who brought the first Anglo settlers to Texas in the 1820s. After 1845, when Texas gained admission into the Union, Austin began to flourish, and by 1930 it had grown into a major regional center with a population of 75,000.

Originally a business and distribution center serving the farmers of the Blackland Prairies to the east, Austin's farmers produce cotton, maize, corn, livestock, and poultry. Traditional industries such as meat packing, canning, and furniture manufacturing have been outstripped by the high-tech companies that have helped to nearly double the population since 1970. The city's economic landscape has for decades been defined by the state government (responsible for 131,000 jobs, or one-fourth of Austin's workforce). The University of Texas, founded in 1881 in Austin, boasts the highest endowment of any U.S. university—a legacy of the Texas oil fields. As the University developed into a first-class institution (with 50,000 students) feeding the city's cultural and economic life, and with the influx of electronics and computer companies, Austin has prospered into a metropolis of national, even worldwide, scope.

In recent years, the university's academic excellence and Austin's reputation for liberalism and progressivism (coffeehouses are more common than cowboy hats) have attracted both the arts and high-tech companies such as Dell Computer, Motorola, 3M, IBM, and Texas Instruments.
Population 656,562 (2000). Rank: 16th. Race/Hispanic Origin (2000): White 65.4%. Black 10.0%. Indian 0.6%. Asian 4.7%. Pacific Islander 0.1%. Other 16.2%. Two or more races 3.0%. Hispanic 30.5%.
Location: 30°20'N, 97°45W. Counties: Travis, Williamson
Terrain and climate Elev.: 570 ft. Area: 232 sq. mi. (600.9 sq km). Avg. daily min. temp.: Jan.: 38.8°F/3.8°C; avg. daily max. July: 95.4°F/35.2°C. Avg. annual: rainfall, 31.50"; snowfall, 1"; clear days, 115; precipitation days, 82.
Government Form: council and manager. Mayor Kirk Watson. Election: May 2003. Municipal tel. number: (512) 499-2000.
Visitor info: (800) 926-ACVB or (512) 478-0098. www.ci.austin.tx.us

▶ **BALTIMORE, MARYLAND**
One of America's most active seaports since Colonial days and chartered in 1729 as a major conduit of tobacco exportation, Baltimore was named after the founder of the colony of Maryland, George Calvert, Lord Baltimore. By the time of the Revolutionary War, it earned fame as an important commercial and maritime center, and ships sailing from Baltimore plied their trade with northern Europe, the Mediterranean, and the Caribbean. Chartered as a city in 1797, Baltimore's commercial activity began to surge, spurred by its burgeoning iron and copper industries, its proximity to the nation's capital, and the arrival of the Baltimore and Ohio Railroad, which developed links to the Midwest. However, the deep, divisive passions of the Civil War stunted growth and it would take years before the city recovered.

A fire in 1904 destroyed almost every building in the downtown area, providing impetus for needed revitalization. The two world wars renewed demands for Baltimore's port facilities and fostered development of a solid heavy industrial base. After World War II, however, the city's infra-structure aged and decayed. Today, Baltimore remains a large port and industrial city with one of the largest steel plants in the world (Bethlehem Steel's Sparrow Point works). Much of the city has been rebuilt through urban renewal efforts, including the nationally acclaimed Inner Harbor Project, and Oriole Park at Camden Yards. The population seems to have stabilized after a loss of almost 20 percent in 1960.

Among the city's historic sites is Fort McHenry, where Francis Scott Key wrote "The Star-Spangled Banner." Baltimore is home to St. Mary's Seminary and University (1791), Johns Hopkins University (1876), and the University of Baltimore (1925), among other noted institutions of higher learning.
Population 651,154 (2000). Rank: 17th. Race/Hispanic Origin (2000): White 31.6%. Black 64.3%. Indian 0.3%. Asian 1.5%. Other 0.7%. Two or more races 1.5%. Hispanic 1.7%.
Location: 39°18'N, 76°37'W. County: independent city within Baltimore County.
Terrain and climate Elev.: 155 ft. Area: 80.3 sq. mi. (208 sq km). Avg. daily min. temp.: Jan.: 24.3°F/-4.2°C; avg. daily max. July: 87.1°F/30.6°C. Avg. annual: rainfall, 43.39"; snowfall, 22"; clear days, 106; precipitation days, 112.
Government Form: mayor and council. Mayor Martin O'Malley. Election: Nov. 2001. Municipal tel. number: (410) 396-3100.
Visitor info: (410) 837-4636 or (800) 282-6632. www.ci.baltimore.md.us

▶ **BOSTON, MASSACHUSETTS**
Named for the English port from which many Puritan immigrants to America came, Boston was first settled in 1630 under the leadership of John Winthrop. As the capital of the Massachusetts Bay Colony, it quickly became the cultural and mercantile capital of the New England colonies. Bostonians never wholly embraced British authority, and they provided the earliest challenges to British rule in their reaction to the Stamp Act (1765) and the Boston Tea Party (1783). The colonists killed in the Boston Massacre (1770) were the first to fall in the years immediately preceding the American Revolution.

With the end of the Revolution, Boston merchants found themselves shut out of English ports by prohibitive tariffs, and in their quest for new markets for American goods opened American trade to the Orient and India. In the 19th century, Boston benefitted early from the industrial revolution, and from several waves of immigration, particularly blacks from the southern states, and Irish and Italians from Europe.

Although Boston's preeminence in trade and industry did not survive the 19th century, it continues to be a major center for banking and financial services. Since World War II its suburbs have flourished as a center of research and development and of the computer industry—Route 128 was the East Coast's answer to California's Silicon Valley during the 1980s—spurring investment in downtown Boston. As the gateway to New England and the birthplace of the Revolution, Boston is also a center for tourism.

Perhaps most important to its identity is Boston's wealth of educational, cultural, and religious tolerance. Harvard University (across the Charles River in Cambridge, 1636) is the country's oldest, and Roxbury Latin (1645) the country's oldest privately endowed secondary school. Today Boston is home to more than 30 colleges and universities, as well as to some of the finest cultural institutions in the country, including the American Academy of Arts and Sciences (1780),

the Massachusetts Historical Society (1791), the Boston Athenaeum (1807), the Boston Public Library (the nation's first, 1854), the Boston Museum of Fine Arts (1870), and the Boston Symphony (1881). Boston is also home to three major medical schools and 27 hospitals including the world famous Massachusetts General and Brigham and Women's.
Population 589,141 (2000). **Rank:** 20th. Race/Hispanic Origin (2000): White 54.5%. Black 25.3%. Indian 0.4%. Asian 7.5%. Pacific Islander 0.1%. Other 7.8%. Two or more races 4.4%. Hispanic 14.4%.
Location: 42°20'N, 71°05'W. County: Suffolk.
Terrain and climate Elev.: 10 ft. Area: 47.2 sq. mi. (122.2 sq km). Avg. daily min. temp.: Jan.: 22.8°F/-5.1°C; avg. daily max. July: 81.8°F/27.6°C. Avg. annual: rainfall, 43.81"; snowfall, 42"; clear days, 99; precipitation days, 128.
Government Form: mayor and council. Mayor Thomas M. Menino. Election: Nov. 2001. Municipal tel. number: (617) 635-4000.
Visitor info: 888-733-2678 or (617) 536-4100. www.ci.boston.ma.us

►CHARLOTTE, NORTH CAROLINA

An area of lush green foothills lying at the southernmost tip of the Carolina Piedmont, Charlotte has long been a crossroads city and an important distribution point for the surrounding farmlands. About 250 years ago, Scotch-Irish settlers retracing old Catawba Indian trading routes established a settlement where the paths crossed, and in 1762 it was named Charlotte, after the new bride of King George III. Remembering Gen. Cornwallis's reference to Charlotte as a "hornet's nest" while his army briefly occupied it during the American Revolution, the city adopted the symbol as its emblem.

The discovery of a 17-pound gold nugget in 1799 triggered a gold rush, and although the mines dotting the landscape boosted business, the California gold rush in the mid-1800s lured away prospectors, putting Charlotte on its future course as a top cotton producer. A leading city of the Confederacy in the Civil War, Charlotte hosted the last full meeting of the Confederate cabinet in 1865. The Queen City's second population surge has occurred over the past 20 years, as Charlotte has become an international banking center, with two of the country's top 25 banks making their headquarters there (including the Bank of America, the nation's second largest). It is also the home of Duke Energy, the largest electric utility in the U.S.

Recently, the city's economic base has diversified beyond the production of chemicals, foodstuffs, machinery, metals, and textiles, and matured into a major center of world trade and technology, with more than 160 multinational companies engaging in such businesses as microelectronics, insurance, machining, and biomedical supplies. Located equidistant from the northwestern, midwestern, and southern Florida markets, Charlotte remains a key distribution conduit. A mid-sized city at the heart of a rapidly expanding metropolitan region, Charlotte ranks as the nation's fifth largest urban area with a population of over five million living within a 100-mile radius of the city. The Charlotte Hornets, the Carolina Panthers, and the Charlotte Motor Speedway are all sources of the city's legendary civic pride and boosterism.
Population 540,828 (2000). **Rank:** 26th. Race/Hispanic Origin (2000): White 58.3%. Black 32.7%. Indian 0.3%. Asian 3.4%. Pacific Islander 0.1%. Other 3.6%. Two or more races 1.7%. Hispanic 7.4%.

Location: 35°16'N, 80°46'W. County: Mecklenburg.
Terrain and climate Elev.: 665 ft. Area: 152.1 sq. mi. (393.9 sq km). Avg. daily min. temp.: Jan.: 30.7°F/-0.7°C; avg. daily max. July: 88.3°F/31.2°C. Avg. annual: rainfall, 43.16"; snowfall, 6"; clear days, 111; precipitation days, 111.
Government Form: council and manager. Mayor Patrick McCrory. Election: Nov. 2001. Municipal tel. number: (704) 336-2241.
Visitor Info: (704) 331-2700 or (800) 231-4636. www.ci.charlotte.nc.us.

►CHICAGO, ILLINOIS

Chicago extends roughly 26 miles along the southwestern shoreline of Lake Michigan. The city has historically been a major transportation hub and gateway to the Great Plains, and continues to be one today with major air, rail, and highway hubs. Nineteen trunk-line railroad routes converge at Chicago, linking it with every major U.S. and Canadian city. The city has three major airports, including O'Hare, the busiest in the nation. It is also the terminus for major interstate highways running east-west and north-south.

Historically, Chicago's rise parallels the growth of the American republic to the west. Chicago was first settled in 1779, when Jean Baptiste Point de Sable built a house on the site. In 1803, federal troops built a stockade named Fort Dearborn, but by 1830 only 12 families had settled in the area. In the 1830s, however, the population grew rapidly as Americans spread westward, and the city of Chicago was incorporated in 1837 with a population of 4,170. Chicago then began to grow into a bustling Great Lakes port, connected to the Mississippi via a system of rivers and canals.

Chicago has maintained its strategic importance despite changes in transportation technology and remains today a prosperous city. Over the years, Chicago has been noted as a hotbed of labor reform, the center of violent organized crime gang wars during the prohibition era, and a prime example of the good and the bad of American city machine politics. But despite its checkered past, it has grown into the wealthiest and most vibrant city in the Midwest with hardly a sign of the rust belt malaise plaguing many of its sister cities. Chicago has grown into a financial center with three of the nation's four largest futures exchanges and the world's largest listed stock options exchange.

Chicago also far outstrips other Midwestern cities in cultural, entertainment, recreational and commercial facilities. Major attractions include the Museum of Science and Industry, the Field Museum of Natural History, the Chicago Historical Society, the Lincoln Park Zoo, the Chicago Lyric Opera Company, the Chicago Symphony Orchestra, and the Chicago Art Institute. Downtown Chicago currently has three of the fifteen tallest man-made structures in the world—the Sears Tower (1,454 ft. high), the John Hancock Building (1,127 ft.), and the Amoco Building (1,136 ft.). It is also home to the world's tallest apartment complex, the 70-story Lake Point Tower, and the world's largest commercial building, the Merchandise Mart.
Population 2,896,016 (2000). **Rank:** 3rd. Race/Hispanic Origin (2000): White 42.0%. Black 36.8%. Indian 0.4%. Asian 4.3%. Pacific Islander 0.1%. Other 13.6%. Two or more races 2.9%. Hispanic 26.0%.
Location: 41°53'N, 87°40'W. County: Cook.
Terrain and climate Elev.: 623 ft. Area: 228.1 sq. mi. (590.8 sq km). Avg. daily min. temp.: Jan.: 13.6°F/-10.2°C; avg. daily max. July: 83.3°F/28.5°C.

Avg. annual: rainfall, 33.34"; snowfall, 40"; clear days, 94; precipitation days, 123.
Government Form: mayor and council. Mayor Richard M. Daley. Election: March, 2003. Municipal tel. number: (312) 744-4000.
Visitor info: (312) 744-2400 or 800-226-6632.
www.ci.chi.il.us

▶CLEVELAND, OHIO

The heart of the largest metropolitan area in Ohio, Cleveland was founded in 1796 and named after Moses Cleaveland, a surveyor with the Connecticut Land Company, which administered the state of Connecticut's lingering claim on 3.5 million acres of what is now Ohio (the Western Reserve). A frontier village at the mouth of the Cuyahoga River on Lake Erie, Cleveland was transformed into the business and manufacturing center of northern Ohio by the opening of the Erie Canal in 1825, and the Ohio and Erie Canal, which linked Cleveland with Portsmouth on the Ohio River. When the Soo Locks opened Lake Superior to trade with the Lower Lakes in 1855, Cleveland became a major shipping center for ore, lumber, copper, coal, and farm produce.

During the Civil War, the city's iron ore and coal deposits were mined for steel production and commercial activity increased to meet the Union's increased demands for heavy machinery, railroad equipment, and ships. In the postwar years, Cleveland's mills and factories expanded even further to satisfy the increased needs of the new cities and farms springing up in the wake of westward migration.

Although heavy manufacturing still employs about 20 percent of the city's workforce, the national trend toward a service economy had a severe impact on the local economy, and the population of the Cleveland metropolitan area declined from a high of 2.8 million in 1970 to only 1.8 million today. Nonetheless, Cleveland is still home to many large industrial companies. There are also many medical and industrial research firms, most notably the world-famous Cleveland Clinic and NASA's Lewis Research Center.

Cleveland's industrial strength manifests itself in its flourishing cultural institutions, including the Cleveland Play House, the oldest repertory house in the nation, the world-famous Cleveland Orchestra, the Cleveland Institute of Art, the Cleveland Museum of Natural History, Western Reserve Historical Society, the Cleveland Health Museum, the Allen Memorial Medical Library, and the Cleveland Zoo.
Population 478,403 (2000). Rank: 33rd. Race/Hispanic Origin (2000): White 41.5%. Black 51.0%. Indian 0.3%. Asian 1.3%. Other 3.6%. Two or more races 2.2%. Hispanic 7.3%.
Location: 41°28'N, 81°43'W. County: Cuyahoga.
Terrain and climate Elev.: 805 ft. Area: 79 sq. mi. (204.6 sq km). Avg. daily min. temp.: Jan.: 18.5°F/-7.5°C; avg. daily max. July: 81.7°F/27.6°C. Avg. annual: rainfall, 35.40"; snowfall, 52"; clear days, 70; precipitation days, 156.
Government Form: mayor and council. Mayor Michael R. White. Election: Nov. 2001. Municipal tel. number: (216) 664-2000.
Visitor info: (800) 321-1004 or (216) 621-4110.
www.travelcleveland.com

▶COLORADO SPRINGS, COLORADO

Colorado's second-largest city lies on the eastern edge of the Rocky Mountains, some 60 miles south of Denver. Most of the city is nestled among rolling hills with views of the 14,110-foot Pikes Peak to the west. General William Jackson Palmer was the first to recognize the area's natural beauty when he founded the city in 1871. In its early years, it was popular with Europeans, especially Britons, and the city acquired the nickname Little London.

The city's first big boom came during the 1890s, when gold was discovered in nearby Cripple Creek in 1891. The gold rush ended in 1917, when the U.S. began coining money with silver. Since the beginning of World War II, the military has been a major presence in Colorado Springs, beginning with the establishment of Fort Carson in 1942 and continuing with the location of the Air Force Academy, several Air Force bases, and the North American Aerospace Defense Command (NORAD) over the years since then.

The city's manufacturing base experienced record growth during the 1960s and 70s due to Colorado Springs' low cost of living and sunny weather patterns (the city has hundreds of clear days and receives less snow than Denver or Minneapolis). Semiconductors, electronic equipment, computers, and plastics are among the major manufacturing industries.

Leading an expansion of the service industry in the Pikes Peak region, the United States Olympic Committee has its headquarters in Colorado Springs, as well as its Olympic Training Center, the world's premier multi-sport training facility.

Colorado Springs also prides itself on its extremely clean air. According to local officials, the city's pollen counts are among the lowest in the country, providing relief to people suffering from asthma, nasal allergies, and other respiratory ailments.
Population 360,890 (2000). Rank: 48th. Race/Hispanic Origin (2000): White 80.7%. Black 6.6%. Indian 0.9%. Asian 2.8%. Pacific Islander 0.2%. Other 5.0%. Two or more races 3.9%. Hispanic 12.0%.
Location: 38°48'N, 104°42'W. County: El Paso.
Terrain and climate Elev. 6,145 ft. Area 183.2 sq. mi. (474.5 sq km). Avg. daily min. temp.: Jan.: 16.1°F/-8.8°C; avg. daily max. July: 86.5°F/30.3°C. Avg. annual: rainfall, 16.24"; snowfall, 51"; clear days, 129; precipitation days, 98.
Government Form: council and manager. Mayor Lou Makepeace. Election: April 2003. Municipal tel. number: (719) 385-CITY.
Visitor info: (800) PIKES PEAK.
www.springsgov.com

▶COLUMBUS, OHIO

The Ohio legislature designated a site along the banks of the Scioto River in the center of the state as the capital in 1812, and named it Columbus in honor of the famous explorer of the New World. From the first, the city exploited its status as the seat of government and its prime location in the middle of the nation's growing network of roads, canals and highways. Incorporated in 1834, Columbus became a thriving hub of agricultural trade.

Between 1850 and 1900, its population grew from 17,800 to over 100,000. Because of the many carriage factories, in the 19th century Columbus was known as the "Buggy Capital of the World." Five railroads passed through the city, so banks soon began to spring up, making Columbus a financial center for the surrounding farm counties.

As in the 19th century, Columbus's modern economy is built on government, agriculture, local finance, and education. In 1950, to counter the trend of suburbanization, the city developed a policy of annexation of surrounding communities. Because it is less reliant on heavy industry than other midwestern cities, it has weathered the decline of the rust belt better than most and it remains a bustling metropolis. In the 1980s, the city realized the creation of more than $780 million in new development and about 100,000 new jobs.

Ohio State University, one of the nation's largest universities, opened as the Ohio Agricultural and Mechanical College in 1870, and the city today has a rich academic community that includes the Ohio Dominican College (whose origins date to 1868), the Columbus College of Art and Design and the Ohio Institute of Technology. Business leaders and politicians have joined in an effort to make the city a center for the arts, refurbishing three theaters and building a complex of three more.

Population 711,470 (2000). **Rank:** 15th. Race/Hispanic Origin (2000): White 67.9%. Black 24.5%. Indian 0.3%. Asian 3.4%. Pacific Islander 0.1%. Other 1.2%. Two or more races 2.6%. Hispanic 2.5%.
Location: 39°57'N, 83°01'W. **Counties:** Fairfield, Franklin.
Terrain and climate Elev.: 833 ft. Area: 186.8 sq. mi. (483.8 sq km). Avg. daily min. temp.: Jan.: 19.4°F/-7°C; avg. daily max. July: 84.4°F/29.1°C. Avg. annual: rainfall, 36.97"; snowfall, 28"; clear days, 75; precipitation days, 136.
Government Form: mayor and city council. Mayor Michael Coleman. Election: Nov. 2003. Municipal tel. number: (614) 645-7671.
Visitor info: (800) 354-2657 or (614) 221-6623. www.ci.columbus.oh.us

▶DALLAS, TEXAS

First settled in 1841 by John Neely Bryan, a Tennessee trader and lawyer, Dallas stretches about 30 miles east of Forth Worth on the Trinity River. Named in 1846 after James K. Polk's vice president, George Mifflin Dallas, it was chartered as a city in 1871. Though it grew substantially with the arrival of railroads in 1872, the population numbered a mere 92,000 in 1910.

Located in the heart of the northern Texas oil belt, Dallas today thrives on a diverse economic base, which, in addition to oil and natural gas, includes production of brick clay and the raw materials for Portland cement, and cotton, grains, fruits, beef, dairy cattle, hogs, sheep and poultry from the farms that surround the city. One of the largest inland cotton markets, and a leading distributor of farm goods and machinery, Dallas also serves as the southwest's banking center with major banks, insurance companies, and the Federal Reserve Bank for the Eleventh District. Key manufacturing industries include aerospace, electronics, transportation equipment, machinery, food and related products, and apparel. Among its leading high-tech employers are Texas Instruments and Electronic Data Systems.

Some of Dallas's distinguished universities are Southern Methodist, Southwestern Medical School of the University of Texas, the Dallas Theological Seminary and Graduate School of Theology, and the Baylor University Schools of Dentistry and Nursing. The Dallas Symphony Orchestra, the Dallas Theater Center, the Dallas Civic Opera, the Dallas Historical Society Museum in the Texas Hall of State, and the Dallas Garden Center, contribute to the city's rich cultural life. Fair Park, the site of the annual State Fair of Texas, remains the most widely attended state fair in the country.

Population 1,188,580 (2000). **Rank:** 8th. Race/Hispanic Origin (2000): White 50.8%. Black

25.9%. Indian 0.5%. Asian 2.7%. Other 17.2%. Two or more races 2.7%. Hispanic 35.6%.
Location: 32°50'N, 96°50'W. **Counties:** Collin, Dallas, Denton, Kaufman, Rockwall.
Terrain and climate Elev.: 596 ft. Area: 331.4 sq. mi. (858.3 sq km). Avg. daily min. temp.: Jan.: 33.9°F/1°C; avg. daily max. July: 97.8°F/36.5°C. Avg. annual: rainfall, 34.16"; snowfall, 3"; clear days, 138; precipitation days, 79.
Government Form: council and manager. Mayor Ronald Kirk. Election: May 2003. Municipal tel. number: (214) 670-4054.
Visitor info: (800) CDALLAS www.ci.dallas.tx.us

▶DENVER, COLORADO

Denver was born during the great "Pikes Peak or Bust" gold rush of 1859 when small flakes of placer gold were found where the South Platte River meets Cherry Creek. In its first few years, the city survived a flood, several major fires, Indian attacks, and an invasion by Confederate soldiers during the Civil War. With the discovery of more gold in the Rocky Mountains, Denver became a boom town. Saloons, gambling halls, and wagon trains lined the mud-filled streets and just about every outlaw, desperado, and lawman in the West made at least one visit to the city. The turn of the century brought respectability and the wealth of the mountains was poured into parks, fountains, tree-lined streets, and elaborate mansions.

During the oil crisis of the late 1970s and early 80s, Denver experienced a second boom when it became a corporate center for oil-from-shale companies working the Western Slope of the Rockies. Then one of the fastest-growing cities in the United States, in 1983, it doubled its office space as part of a five-year building campaign that added 16 skyscrapers, a $76 million pedestrian mall, and an $80 million performing arts center. Expansion was slowed by the energy glut of the mid-1980s, but it has rebounded dramatically in the 1990s and the population grew by close to 10,000 per year in the first few years of the 1990s.

In 1993, the Colorado Rockies baseball team drew more than four million fans to a converted football stadium. And in 1995, after countless setbacks stemming from problems with its automated baggage system, the much-heralded Denver International Airport finally opened its doors, thus completing the final chapter of a vastly overbudget boondoggle.

Denver's population is among the youngest in the nation, and the youthful flavor of the city is very evident. Denver leads the nation in movie attendance and has more sporting goods stores per resident than any city in the world. The city's 205 parks are so active that a speed limit was recently instituted—for bicycles.

Population 554,636 (2000). **Rank:** 25th. Race/Hispanic Origin (2000): White 65.3%. Black 11.1%. Indian 1.3%. Asian 2.8%. Pacific Islander 0.1%. Other 15.6%. Two or more races 3.7%. Hispanic 31.7%.
Location: 39°45'N, 105°00'W. **County:** Denver.
Terrain and climate Elev.: 5,280 ft. Area: 106.8 sq. mi. (276.6 sq km). Avg. daily min. temp.: Jan.: 15.9°F/-8.9°C; avg. daily max. July: 88°F/31°C. Avg. annual: rainfall, 15.31"; snowfall, 60"; clear days, 115; precipitation days, 88.
Government Form: mayor and council. Mayor Wellington E. Webb. Election: May 2003. Municipal tel. number: (720) 865-9000.
Visitor info: (800) 645-3446 or (303) 892-1112. www.denver.org

▶DETROIT, MICHIGAN
Founded in 1701 by Antoine de La Mothe, sieur de Cadillac, Detroit lies on the Detroit River between Lake Erie and Lake Huron. Named Fort Pontchartrain-du-Détroit (of the strait), the oldest permanent settlement on the Great Lakes flourished as a trading post for trappers, under French control (to 1760), then British (to 1796) and then American.

The first steamboat reached Detroit from Buffalo in 1818, but it was the easy access to eastern markets via the Erie Canal in 1825 that allowed Detroit to exploit the abundant natural resources in the Michigan peninsula and fostered its emergence as a modern industrial giant in the post-Civil War years. Tenth among cities in the value of its manufactures by 1899, Detroit's main exports included iron ore, copper, lead, salt, and fish. The development of the automotive industry, which eventually became centered in Detroit, propelled Detroit to number three by the 1920s. While Detroit is the home of General Motors, Chrysler, and Ford, recently the automotive industry has been as much a curse as a blessing, for every setback to any of the "Big Three" is felt throughout the Motor City.

Despite the fact that it still ranks high in industrial manufacturing, Detroit has been plagued by urban decline. The relatively low standard of living among the predominantly black inhabitants ignited riots in the 1940s and 1960s, and the city's crime rate is today among the highest in the nation. However, it was Detroit blacks who gave rise to one of the most sensational expressions of popular culture in the 1960s. Founded in 1960, the Tamla Motown label propelled the Jackson 5, the Supremes, and Stevie Wonder—among others—to world renown, and in the process created one of the largest black-owned businesses in the country.

The city's rich and diverse cultural institutions include the Detroit Institute of Arts (which contains one of the largest collections of American art in the world in addition to extensive European holdings), the Detroit Symphony, the Cranbrook Academy of Art, and the 1,000-acre Belle Isle Park, situated on an island in the Detroit River and featuring beaches, a yacht basin, a zoo, an aquarium, and a botanical gardens. In 2000, Detroit became the first U.S. city to see its population drop below one million.
Population 951,270 (2000). Rank: 10th. Race/Hispanic Origin (2000): White 12.3%. Black 81.6%. Indian 0.3%. Asian 1.0%. Other 2.5%. Two or more races 2.3%. Hispanic 5.0%.
Location: 42°23'N, 83°05'W. County: Wayne.
Terrain and climate Elev.: 581 ft. Area: 135.6 sq. mi. (351.2 sq km). Avg. daily min. temp.: Jan.: 16.1°F/-8.8°C; avg. daily max. July: 83.1°F/28.3°C. Avg. annual: rainfall, 30.97"; snowfall, 39"; clear days, 75; precipitation days, 133.
Government Form: mayor and council. Mayor Dennis Archer. Election: Nov. 2001. Municipal tel. number: (313) 224-3270.
Visitor info: (800) DETROIT or (313) 202-1800. www.ci.detroit.mi.us

▶EL PASO, TEXAS
The largest Texas city bordering Mexico, El Paso sits in the western part of the state on the northern bank of the Rio Grande across from Juarez. A major port of entry, with the biggest commercial and manufacturing base in the area, the city encompasses a region of mines, oil fields, livestock ranches, and farms (principal crops: pecans, fruit, cotton, alfalfa, onions, lettuce, chiles). Important industries include metals smelting and refining, oil and gas refining, textiles, meat packing, and food processing. The city is also home to the University of Texas, at El Paso.

In 1536, Alvar Núñez Cabeza de Vaca crossed the Rio Grande, becoming the first European to set foot in the area, but settlement did not follow until 1659, with the establishment of both El Paso del Norte on the southern bank of the Rio Grande, and the Mission of Guadalupe. In 1682, settlers from New Mexico founded Ysleta, an area within the current city limits of El Paso, but permanent settlement did not begin until the arrival of Juan Maria Ponce de Leon in 1827. Incorporated as a city in 1873, El Paso grew into a major industrial center with the introduction of the railroads in 1881.

El Paso's access to sources of cheap labor complemented its mining, refining, and agricultural activities and helped build the city's manufacturing base. In recent years, however, the movement of manufacturing back to Mexico, where labor costs are far less, has created some concern for that portion of the economy. El Paso's proximity to Juarez, Mexico, makes it a vibrant tourist haven, and its pleasant climate, combined with its position on the immigration route from Latin America, have made El Paso one of the fastest-growing cities in the U.S. El Paso also has the highest percentage of citizens with Hispanic ancestry of any American city with over half a million people.
Population 563,662 (2000). Rank: 23rd. Race/Hispanic Origin (2000): White 73.3%. Black 3.1%. Indian 0.8%. Asian 1.1%. Pacific Islander 0.1%. Other 18.2%. Two or more races 3.4%. Hispanic 76.6%.
Location: 31°50'N, 106°30'W. County: El Paso.
Terrain and climate Elev.: 3,700 ft. Area: 239.7 sq. mi. (620.8 sq km). Avg. daily min. temp.: Jan.: 30.4°F/-0.8°C; avg. daily max. July: 95.3°F/35.1°C. Avg. annual: rainfall, 7.82"; snowfall, 5"; clear days, 194; precipitation days, 45.
Government Form: mayor and council. Mayor: Raymond C. Caballero. Election: May 2003. Municipal tel. number: (915) 541-4145.
Visitor info: (800) 351-6024 or (915) 534-0653. www.ci.el-paso.tx.us

▶FORT WORTH, TEXAS
Named in 1849 after Gen. William J. Worth, commander of the U.S. Army in Texas, Forth Worth originally served to protect settlers from Indian attacks. It grew slowly mainly as a stopover on the cattle drives along the Chisholm Trail until the Texas and Pacific Railroad reached the city in 1871. Stockyards sprang up, making Fort Worth a conduit of cattle shipping, and with the building of a grain elevator, it developed into a milling center as well. By the turn of the century, it had also emerged as a flourishing meat packing market. Oil was discovered in 1917, bringing prosperity and transforming the city into a major refining center with a dozen operating facilities. The two world wars introduced military installations (particularly airfields) to the area. Fort Worth is the sixth largest city in Texas, boasting the state's three finest art museums and a network of parks with total acreage second only to Chicago's.
Population 534,694 (2000). Rank: 27th. Race/Hispanic Origin (2000): White 59.7%. Black 20.3%. Indian 0.6%. Asian 2.6%. Pacific Islander 0.1%. Other 14.0%. Two or more races 2.7%. Hispanic 29.8%.
Location 32°45'N, 97°25'W. County: Tarrant.
Terrain and climate Elev.: 670 ft. Area: 258.5 sq. mi. (670.3 sq km). Avg. daily min. temp.: Jan.: 33.9°F/1°C; avg. daily max. July: 97.8°F/36.5°C. Avg. annual: rainfall, 29.45"; snowfall, 1.4"; clear days, 137; precipitation days, 78.
Government Form: council and manager. Mayor Kenneth Barr. Election: May 2003. Municipal tel. number: (817) 871-8900.

Visitor info: 800-433-5747 or (817) 336-8791. http://ci.fort-worth.tx.us

▶ FRESNO, CALIFORNIA

Fresno grew up around a train station established in 1872 for what became the Southern Pacific Railway. The city was incorporated in 1874. With the introduction of irrigation to the fertile San Joaquin Valley in the 1880s, the small city thrived at the center of a healthy agricultural economy. Today Fresno County is the number one producer of agricultural products in the nation—and the world—and averages more than $2 billion a year in the production and processing of 200 commercial crops, including grapes (for wine and raisins), melon, cotton, alfalfa, barley, grains, cattle, sheep, and poultry.

Fresno's population grew 63 percent between 1980 and 1990, and in the 1980s it was the ninth fastest growing city in the United States and by far the fastest growing of the nation's 50 largest cities.

Located in central California, Fresno—the name is Spanish for ash tree—is a gateway to the Sierra Nevadas, and it is less than 90 minutes from three national parks—Kings Canyon (55 miles), Sequoia (85 miles) and Yosemite (92 miles). Among the attractions to be found within the city limits are the Fresno Art Museum, the Fresno Zoo, the Kearney Mansion Museum (restored home of Theo Kearney, "Raisin King of California"), the Fresno Metropolitan Museum, and the Discovery Center. There are also 10 colleges and universities including a campus of California State University and Fresno City College.

Population 427,652 (2000). Rank: 37th. Race/Hispanic Origin (2000): White 50.2%. Black 8.4%. Indian 1.6%. Asian 11.2%. Pacific Islander 0.1%. Other 23.4%. Two or more races 5.2%. Hispanic 39.9%.

Location 36°47'N, 119°50'W. County: Fresno.

Terrain and climate Elev. 328 ft.; Area: 99.4 sq. mi. (257 sq. km). Avg. daily min. temp. Jan.: 37.4°/3°C; avg. daily max. July: 98°.7F/37°C. Avg. annual rainfall: 10"; snowfall 0"; clear days: 200; precipitation days: 44.

Government Form: council manager. Mayor: Alan Autrey. Election: Nov. 2004. Municipal tel. number: (559) 498-1560.

Visitor info: (559) 233-0836 or (800) 788-0836. www.ci.fresno.ca.us

▶ HONOLULU, HAWAII

First visited by Europeans in 1794, Honolulu, meaning "sheltered harbor," has attracted droves of visitors ever since. Situated on Oahu Island, it benefits from a large bay fully protected by coral reefs and its large port facilities. Because of its hospitable climate, the beaches of Waikiki, its majestic mountains, and exotic locale, tourism is Honolulu's major industry; several million visitors come annually, mainly from the U.S. mainland and the Far East, particularly from Japan.

The defense industry is the second mainstay of Honolulu's economy, as the U.S. has long maintained major installations around the island, including the naval base at Pearl Harbor, Hickam Air Force Base, and the U.S. Army's Schofield Barracks and Fort Shafter. Honolulu also serves as the center for Hawaii's export crops—sugar, pineapple, and molasses—and is the principal port for the import of much of the island state's necessities.

Population 371,657 (2000). Rank: 46th. Race/Hispanic Origin (2000): White 19.7%. Black 1.6%. Indian 0.2%. Asian 55.9%. Pacific Islander 6.8%. Other 0.9%. Two or more races 14.9%. Hispanic 4.4%.

Location: 21°19'N, 157°52'W. County: Honolulu.

Terrain and climate Elev.: 15 ft. Area: 25.3 sq. mi. (65.52 sq km). Avg. daily min. temp.: Jan.: 65.3°F/18.5°C; avg. daily max. July: 87.1°F/30.6°C. Avg. annual rainfall: 23.47"; snowfall: 0"; clear days: 90; precipitation days: 102.

Government Form: mayor and council. Mayor Jeremy Harris. Election: Nov. 2004. Municipal tel. number: (808) 523-4141.

Visitor info: (808) 923-1811. www.co.honolulu.hi.us

▶ HOUSTON, TEXAS

On August 30, 1836, brothers August C. and John K. Allen founded this city and named it after Sam Houston, the first president of the Republic of Texas. The Allens paid just over $1.40 per share for 6,642 acres of land near the headwaters of Buffalo Bayou about 50 miles inland from the Gulf of Mexico. Houston's proximity to Stephen Austin's central Texas colonies gave it great potential as a marketing and distribution site. Incorporated in 1837, the city served as capital of the Republic of Texas until 1840. When the first railroad in Texas began operating out of Houston in 1853, the city developed into a major agricultural center while the discovery of oil in southeast Texas at Spindletop in 1901, and the opening of the man-made Houston Ship Channel in 1914, stimulated petroleum refining and metal fabricating. During World War II, petrochemical production began on a large scale, and with the building of NASA's $761 million complex in the early 1960s (now known as the Johnson Space Center), Houston took center stage as the main player in manned spacecraft.

A major corporate and international business center—more than a dozen *Fortune* 500 companies are based here—present-day Houston has successfully limited its dependence on the energy economy. The Port of Houston is the eighth largest in the world in terms of tonnage handled; the city is also home to four of the nation's 10 major liquid gas pipelines. The presence of the Texas Medical Center also makes Houston a vital U.S. center for the practice and progress of modern high-tech medicine. The Center's 39 institutions occupy in excess of 550 acres and employ more than 50,000 workers. Houston's total health employment exceeds 100,000.

Population 1,953,631 (2000). Rank: 4th. Race/Hispanic Origin (2000): White 49.3%. Black 25.3%. Indian 0.4%. Asian 5.3%. Pacific Islander 0.1%. Other 16.5%. Two or more races 3.1%. Hispanic 37.4%.

Location: 29°50'N, 95°20'W. Counties: Fort Bend, Harris, Montgomery.

Terrain and climate Elev.: 49 ft. Area: 572.7 sq. mi. (1,483.3 sq km). Avg. daily min. temp.: Jan.: 40.8°F/4.8°C; avg. daily max. July: 93.6°F/34.2°C. Avg. annual rainfall: 44.77"; snowfall: 0"; clear days: 94; precipitation days: 107.

Government Form: mayor and council. Mayor Lee P. Brown. Election: Nov. 2001. Municipal tel. number: (713) 247-1000.

Visitor info: (800) 365-7575 or (713) 227-3100. www.cityofhouston.gov

▶ INDIANAPOLIS, INDIANA

Indianapolis, the capital of Indiana and a major commercial center in the country's heartland, is intersected by more highways than any other in the nation, earning it the name, the "Crossroads of America." Fifty percent of America's population is within a day's drive of the city, a geographic asset that makes it a focal point of transportation and manufacturing.

The first European-American settlement, established in 1820 where Fall Creek meets the White River, was chosen as the location of Indiana's capital in 1825. The state government created jobs triggering an expanding population that further swelled with the routing of the National Road (U.S. 40) in 1830. Development mushroomed in 1839 with the building of the Central Canal on the White River, providing a vital transportation link and the necessary water power to run factories, sawmills, and paper mills. Maintenance of the canal, however, proved impossible, and the town declined until the introduction of the railroad. By 1853, railroad lines fed into Indianapolis from every corner of the nation and at one point, nearly 200 trains passed through daily. At the turn of the century, Indianapolis had emerged as a sophisticated city with sidewalks and streetcars. The city's economy prospered during the early stages of the automotive industry, producing more than 50 types of car—including the Duesenberg, the Marmon, and the Stutz—before Detroit gained ascendancy.

Having survived the decline in heavy industry and the flight of the affluent to the suburbs, Indianapolis remains a hub of manufacturing and transportation, with a bustling wheat, soybean, and livestock market. Key industries include electronics, metal fabrication, pharmaceuticals, and transportation equipment. Downtown Indianapolis has enjoyed a renaissance with the construction of a convention center, the Hoosier Dome, Market Square Arena, and the refurbishment of Union Station. But the city's premier attraction remains the Indianapolis 500, the annual Memorial Day weekend auto race, first held in 1911.

Population   791,926   (2000).   Rank: - 12th. Race/Hispanic Origin (2000): White 69.3%. Black 25.3%. Indian 0.3%. Asian 1.4%. Pacific Islander 0.0%. Other 2.0%. Two or more races 1.6%. Hispanic 3.9%.

Location   39°42'N, 86°10'W. County: Marion.

Terrain and climate   Elev.: 808 ft. Area: 352 sq. mi. (911.7 sq km). Avg. daily min. temp.: Jan.: 17.8°F/-7.8°C; avg. daily max. July: 85.2°F/29.5°C. Avg. annual rainfall: 39.12"; snowfall: 21"; clear days: 90; precipitation days: 122.

Government   Form: mayor   and   council. Mayor: Bart Peterson. Election: Nov. 2003. Municipal tel. number: (317) 327-3200.

Visitor info: 800-323-4639 or (317) 237-5200. www.indygov.org

▶**JACKSONVILLE, FLORIDA**

The first Europeans to visit the area were French Huguenots who in 1564 established a colony at Fort Caroline on the Saint Johns River in northeast Florida. The Spanish destroyed the fort in the following year. Permanent settlement began in 1816, and in 1822 Jacksonville was laid out and named for then Maj. Gen. Andrew Jackson, who had led the U.S. campaign to take Florida from the Spanish. Growth was slow until after the Civil War. After World War II, several large naval bases were located here and by 1960 the population was over 200,000. In 1968, the population jumped to more than 500,000 when it was consolidated with Duval County, and Jacksonville became one of the largest cities by area in the U.S.

Florida's largest city, Jacksonville is a major regional center for commerce, industry, finance, and medicine. After years of improvements on its harbor, 25 miles west from the mouth of the Saint Johns, it has grown into a major port of entry and it is the primary distribution center for the region. Jacksonville has also emerged as a leading resort with extensive recreational and convention facilities. Among its amenities are the Haydon Burns Library, the Cummer Gallery of Art, the Jacksonville Art Museum, the Jacksonville Zoological Park, the Saint Johns River Park, and Fort Caroline National Memorial, site of the first European colony in Florida. Among its leading educational institutions are Jacksonville University and the University of Northern Florida.

Population   735,617   (2000).   Rank: 14th. Race/Hispanic Origin (2000): White 64.5%. Black 29.0%. Indian 0.3%. Asian 2.8%. Pacific Islander 0.1%. Other 1.3%. Two or more races 2.0%. Hispanic 4.2%.

Location: 30°15'N, 81°38'W. County: Duval.

Terrain and climate   Elev.: 31 ft. Area: 840 sq. mi. (1,967.6 sq km). Avg. daily min. temp.: Jan.: 41.7°F/ °C; avg. daily max. July: 90.7°F/29.5°C. Avg. annual rainfall: 52.77"; snowfall: 0"; clear days: 98; precipitation days: 116.

Government   Form: mayor and council. Mayor John A. Delaney. Election: May 2003. Municipal tel. number: (904) 630-1776.

Visitor info: (800) 733-2668 or (904) 798-9111. www.ci.jax.fl.us

▶**KANSAS CITY, MISSOURI**

Kansas City was begun as a trading outpost by the French fur trader François Chouteau in 1821. In 1833, the town of Westport was founded nearby, and in 1850 the City of Kansas received its first charter. (Its name was changed to Kansas City in 1889.)

Situated at the confluence of the Kansas and Missouri rivers, Kansas City prospered early on as a river port and as the terminus of the Santa Fe and Oregon trails. With the arrival of the railroad in 1866, Kansas City's status as a major commercial hub was assured. Thanks to its central location and the development of excellent and diversified transportation and storage facilities, Kansas City is one of the nation's key markets for agricultural and livestock products, as well as for the distribution of heavy agricultural machinery. The Kansas City Board of Trade is one of the largest grain and commodities trading markets in the world. Other major industries are greeting card publishing, telecommunications, and high-tech manufacturing, especially instrument landing systems for airplanes. Kansas City is also home to the 10th Federal Reserve Bank.

An early oasis of culture in the midst of an unsettled, untamed prairie (the city once boasted two opera houses), Kansas City remains a mecca of the arts, with cultural offerings like the Kansas City Art Institute, the Nelson Atkins Museum of Art, the Kansas City Symphony, the Lyric Opera, and the Missouri Repertory Theatre. The city's beginnings are preserved in the Lone Jack Civil War Museum and Missouri Town 1855, and it is the site of the annual American Royal Livestock, Horse Show, and Rodeo, held as part of the annual convention of the Future Farmers of America. Among its institutes of higher learning are Rockhurst College (1916), the University of Missouri-Kansas City, and the DeVry Institute of Technology.

Population   441,545   (2000).   Rank: 36th. Race/Hispanic Origin (2000): White 60.7%. Black 31.2%. Indian 0.5%. Asian 1.9%. Pacific Islander 0.1%. Other 3.2%. Two or more races 2.4%. Hispanic 6.9%.

Location: 39°07'N, 94°38'W. Counties: Cass, Clay, Jackson, and Platte.

Terrain and climate   Elev.: 744 ft. Area: 316.4 sq. mi. (819.5 sq km). Avg. daily min. temp.: Jan.: 17.2°F/-8.2°C; avg. daily max. July: 88.5°F/31.3°C. Avg. annual rainfall: 29.27"; snowfall: 5.9"; clear days: 132; precipitation days: 97.

Government   Form: council and manager. Mayor Kay Barnes. Election Apr. 2003. Municipal tel. number: (816) 513-3600.
Visitor info: (800) 767-7700 or (816) 221-5242. www.kcmo.org

▶ **LAS VEGAS, NEVADA**

Las Vegas was originally settled by Mormons in 1855, but its modern history began in 1931, when Nevada legalized gambling and liberalized marriage and divorce laws. From then until 1978 (when Atlantic City re-opened its casinos), Las Vegas prospered while it enjoyed a monopoly on casino gambling in the U.S. Since 1980, it has been one of America's fastest-growing cities, more than doubling in size between 1980 and 1996. There were 164,674 people living in Las Vegas in 1980; by 1996 the city's population had climbed to 376,906. The 2000 Census has the city's population nearing the 500,000 mark. Las Vegas is growing so fast, it prints phone books twice a year.

To be sure, gambling has fueled this growth—gaming revenues topped $6 billion in 1997—but the city's expansion has come even as dozens of other cities across the country have legalized casino gambling on riverboats, at Native American reservations, or even in the French Quarter of New Orleans. Las Vegas has thrived because of a mix of gambling, nightlife, shopping, and an unequivocal commitment to excess. Since 1993, five major resorts have been torn down, only to make way for newer, bigger properties. The nation's 10 biggest hotels (including the 5,000-room MGM Grand) are all here. Over the past decade, the city has built hotels replicating New York City, Paris, Venice (complete with canals through the desert landscape), and the pyramids of Egypt.

More than 30 million visitors (including 3 million conventioneers) travel to Las Vegas each year. With all this tourism have come tens of thousands of new jobs and new housing (an average of 578 new homes per month). Because the city is laid out in a desert, there are few geographical barriers to limit urban expansion, except the availability of drinking water. The city is beginning to confront problems of urban sprawl such as traffic, air pollution, and distribution of resources such as schools and water.
Population   478,434 (2000). Rank: 32nd. Race/Hispanic Origin (2000): White 69.9%. Black 10.4%. Indian 0.7%. Asian 4.8%. Pacific Islander 0.4%. Other 9.7%. Two or more races 4.1%. Hispanic 23.6%.
Location: 36° 05'N, 115°10'W. County: Clark.
Terrain and climate   Elev.: 2,162 ft. Area: 83.3 sq. mi. (215.7 sq km). Avg. daily min. temp.: Jan.: 33.6°F/0.9°C; avg. daily max. July: 105.9°F/41.1°C. Avg. annual rainfall: 4"; snowfall: 1"; clear days: 211; precipitation days: 26.
Government   Form: Council and manager. Mayor Oscar B. Goodman. Election: June 2003. Municipal tel. number (702) 229–6501.
Visitor info: (702) 892–7575. www.ci.las-vegas.nv.us

▶ **LONG BEACH, CALIFORNIA**

Originally the site of an Indian trading camp, by the end of the 18th century the area of what is now Long Beach was part of the Spanish Ranchos Los Alamitos and Cerritos. In 1881, William E. Willmore began development of the land as a resort (which he named for himself). When first incorporated in 1888, the town was named Long Beach after its 8.5 miles of Pacific beachfront. Content to remain a resort community, Long Beach saw its fortunes rewritten in 1921 when extensive petroleum deposits were discovered at Signal Hill. To-

day, industry is a major presence in Long Beach—especially ship repair, transportation, oil refining, and marine research; in addition, the Navy maintains a large base and dry dock.

Among the cultural and recreational attractions Long Beach boasts are its own Museum of Art, the Terrace Theater, home of the Long Beach Symphony Orchestra, and the Long Beach Community Playhouse. Popular tourist attractions include Los Cerritos (a Spanish adobe house which dates to 1844), the Aquarium of the Pacific, and the magnificent ocean liner *Queen Mary* which today serves as a floating maritime museum, convention center, and hotel. Long Beach is also the site of a Formula 1 Grand Prix every spring. Disneyland is in nearby Anaheim.
Population: 461,522 (2000). Rank: 34th. Race/Hispanic Origin (2000): White 45.2%. Black 14.9%. Indian 0.8%. Asian 12.0%. Pacific Islander 1.2%. Other 20.6%. Two or more races 5.3%. Hispanic 35.8%.
Location: 33°46'N, 118°10'W. County: Los Angeles.
Terrain and climate   Elev.: 35 ft. Area: 49.8 sq. mi. (129 sq km). Avg. daily min. temp.: Jan.: 44.3°F/6.8°C; avg. daily max. July: 83°F/28.3°C. Avg. annual rainfall: 12"; snowfall: 0"; clear days: 143; precipitation days: 35.
Government   Form: council and manager. Mayor Beverly O'Neill. Election: April 2002. Municipal tel. number: (562) 570-6801.
Visitor info: (800) 4LB-STAY or (562) 436-3645. www.ci.long-beach.ca.us

▶ **LOS ANGELES, CALIFORNIA**

In pre-Spanish days, the area of Los Angeles was inhabited by approximately 4,000 Indians representing some 30 tribes. The village of Yang-na, with a population of 300, was located in what is now downtown Los Angeles, in the vicinity of Alameda and Commercial Streets. In October of 1542, João Rodrigues Cabrilho, a Portuguese explorer in the employ of Spain, became the first European to set foot on Los Angeles soil, but 200 years passed before a land expedition under the command of Gaspar de Portola crossed the territory on the way from Monterey to San Diego, in 1769.

The establishment of the Mission of San Gabriel (destined to become the largest of the Franciscan Missions) followed and in 1781, the Spanish Governor Felipe Neve founded the city of El Pueblo de Nuestra Señora de los Angeles de Porciuncula ("The Village of Our Lady of the Angels") as part of a plan to colonize California. Spanish rule continued until 1822 when Spain relinquished her holdings in western America, prompting California to pledge her allegiance to the Mexican empire. With the Treaty of Guadalupe Hidalgo (1848) the U.S. acquired all of California from Mexico and in 1850 Los Angeles was incorporated as a city. Introduction of the Southern Pacific Railroad in 1876 sparked a 12-year land boom, promoting the city's growth. By 1892, Los Angeles thrived as a center of oil production and in 1899 work began on the largest man-made deep-water facility in the world. Emerging as the motion picture capital of the world by 1910, industry accelerated in the 1920s and today L.A. ranks as one of the three great industrial cities in the country.

A thriving metropolis, Los Angeles boasts one of the finest highway systems in the world, handling about 6 million cars registered in its five-county area—a car for every two people, the highest ratio in the world. Three transcontinental railway systems terminate in L.A., about 40 certified air carriers fly to all parts of the world, its harbors have 46 miles of waterfront, and the city has the largest trucking center in the west. L.A. remains the world's movie mecca, teeming with studios, stars, and the starstruck.

Los Angelenos live with daily problems of smog, traffic jams, spectacular traffic accidents, and the ever-present threats of mud slides, fires, floods, high winds, and earthquakes. But the year-round sunshine, and the number of beaches and mountain areas, all within an easy drive, tend to ameliorate one's anxiety.

Population 3,694,820 (2000). Rank: 2nd. Race/Hispanic Origin (2000): White 46.9%. Black 11.2%. Indian 0.8%. Asian 10.0%. Pacific Islander 0.2%. Other 25.7%. Two or more races 5.2%. Hispanic 46.5%.

Location: 34°00'N, 118°10'W. County: Los Angeles.

Terrain and climate Elev.: 104 ft. Area: 465.9 sq. mi. (1206.7 sq km). Avg. daily min. temp.: Jan.: 47.3°F/8.5°C; avg. daily max. July: 75.3°F/24°C. Avg. annual rainfall: 14.85"; snowfall: 0"; clear days: 143; precipitation days: 35.

Government Form: mayor and council. Mayor James K. Hahn. Election: April 2004. Municipal tel. number: (213) 485-2121.

Visitor info: (800) 228-2450 or (213) 624-7300. www.ci.la.ca.us

▶MEMPHIS, TENNESSEE

The first settlers in the area of Memphis arrived on the bluffs overlooking the Mississippi River more than 1,000 years ago. The Chickasaw forcibly displaced these people and then lived there for eight centuries until 1838, when the U.S. government scattered the entire tribe to Oklahoma and parts further west so its citizens could develop the land. The Spanish explorer Hernando de Soto first set eyes on the bluffs in 1541. Other explorers passed through over the next century and in 1739 the French built Fort Assumption. The French, Spanish, and the Chickasaw fought over the land for the balance of the 18th century until it became a part of the U.S. in 1797. The area's original American owners, Gen. James Winchester, Judge John Overton, and Gen. Andrew Jackson (who later sold his share and went on to become President), established the town in 1819, and named it Memphis, after the ancient Egyptian city on the Nile.

Riverboatmen gave young Memphis a reputation for brawls and bawdiness, while mosquitoes gave it a history of yellow fever epidemics, which in the 1880s claimed more than half the city's population and jeopardized its charter. A sewage system, the first of its kind, helped finally conquer the epidemic. Between the river traffic and cotton crops, the city prospered, attracting Irish and German immigrants, and by the 20th century was on its way to becoming the unofficial capital of the mid-south. Elvis Presley, who expanded the city's rhythm and blues tradition to become the world's first rock-and-roll idol, remains the city's most enduring contribution to popular culture. In 1991, the Lorraine Motel, where civil rights leader Dr. Martin Luther King Jr. was assassinated in 1968, was opened as the National Civil Rights Museum. In recent years the city's central location has helped it to attract major corporations, most notably FedEx and Northwest Airlines.

Population 650,100 (2000). Rank: 18th. Race/Hispanic Origin (2000): White 34.4%. Black 61.4%. Indian 0.2%. Asian 1.5%. Pacific Islander 0.0%. Other 1.5%. Two or more races 1.0%. Hispanic 3.0%.

Location: 35°07'N, 90°00'W. County: Shelby.

Terrain and climate Elev.: 307 ft. Area: 264.1 sq. mi. (684 sq km). Avg. daily min. temp.: Jan.: 30.9°F/-0.6°C; avg. daily max. July: 91.5°F/33°C. Avg. annual rainfall: 51.57"; snowfall: 6"; clear

days: 118; precipitation days: 106.

Government Form: mayor and council. Mayor: Willie Herenton. Election: Oct. 2003. Municipal tel. number: (901) 576-6000.

Visitor info: 800-873-6282 or (901) 543-5300. www.ci.memphis.tn.us

▶MESA, ARIZONA

Just 15 miles east of Phoenix is Mesa, a one-time suburb that has quickly climbed onto the list of the nation's largest cities. Arizona's third largest city grew by 24.5 percent between 1990 and 1998. There are solid reasons for Mesa's growth: low costs of doing business; a reasonable tax structure; a skilled and well-educated workforce; low crime rate; superior schools; affordable housing; and an abundant water supply. Founded in 1878 and incorporated in 1883, Mesa is the Spanish word for "table top," describing a flat-topped, raised area. The first settlers built homes and farms on a mesa above the surrounding area.

Population 396,375 (2000). Rank: 42nd. Race/Hispanic Origin (2000): White 81.7%. Black 2.5%. Indian 1.7%. Asian 1.5%. Pacific Islander 0.2%. Other 9.7%. Two or more races 2.8%. Hispanic 19.7%.

Location: 33°N, 112°W. County: Maricopa.

Terrain and climate Elev.: 1,241 ft. Area: 124.62 sq. mi. Avg. daily min temp.: Jan.: 35.6°F/2°C; avg. daily max. July: 104.3°F/40.16°C. Avg. annual: rainfall, 7.52"; snowfall, 0"; clear days, 320; precipitation days, 45.

Government Form: mayor and city council. Mayor Keno Hawker. Election: Nov. 2004. Municipal tel. number: (480) 644-2388.

Visitor info: (480) 827-4700. www.ci.mesa.az.us

▶MIAMI, FLORIDA

Miami, the most southerly major city in the continental U.S., sits about two degrees north of the Tropic of Cancer, a location that has made it a long-standing resort haven. Miami in the 1980s also thrived as a major hub of commerce and as a population center for Latin American immigrants, particularly those arriving from Cuba, whose ambition and business acumen contributed to the city's prosperity. While tourists still generate over 60 percent of the area's economic activity, many other areas of enterprise, such as construction, light industry, and agriculture (limes, tomatoes, avocados, mangoes and beans) have flourished.

Miami (whose name is thought to derive from the Indian mayami, meaning "big water"), dates back to the 16th century when Native Americans occupied the southern part of Florida. Fort Dallas, built near the mouth of the Miami River in 1836 as a base of war against the Seminoles, became the first permanent European-American settlement. The building of the Florida East Coast Railroad, coinciding with Miami's incorporation as a city in 1896 (population 343), offered ready access to the area. Resort hotels quickly cropped up and Miami, along with the rest of Florida, enjoyed great success. In 1926, a severe hurricane submerged much of its land under water, abruptly ending Miami's prosperity, but the city managed to steadily grow by draining and developing swampland. After World War II, new resorts rose up, and Miami thrived both as a haven for older retirees and a refuge for a substantial number of Cubans fleeing Castro's repressive regime. In 2000, the city attracted national media attention during the Elian Gonzalez controversy. Gonzalez, a five-year-old Cuban refugee, became the center of a custody battle between Cuba and the U.S. when he survived a raft crossing from Cuba to Florida, but his mother did not.

Today Miami bills itself as the "Gateway of the Americas," where the value of exports and imports has increased by over 20 percent a year for the last decade and foreign banking has expanded rapidly.

Population   362,470   (2000).   Rank: 47th. Race/Hispanic Origin (2000): White 66.6%. Black 22.3%. Indian 0.2%. Asian 0.7%. Other 5.4%. Two or more races 4.7%. Hispanic 65.8%.
Location: 25°45'N, 80°15'W. County: Dade.
Terrain and climate   Elev.: 12 ft. Area: 34.3 sq. mi. (88.8 sq km). Avg. daily min. temp.: Jan.: 59.2°F/15.1°C; avg. daily max. July: 88.7°F/31.5°C. Avg. annual rainfall: 57.55"; snowfall: 0"; clear days: 76; precipitation days: 129.
Government   Form: council and manager. Mayor: Joe Carollo. Election: Nov. 2001. Municipal tel. number: (305) 250-5300.
Visitor info: (800) 933-8448 or (305) 539-3000. www.ci.miami.fl.us

▶ MILWAUKEE, WISCONSIN

During the 1670s the French explorers Jacques Marquette and Louis Joliet were the first Europeans to visit the site of present-day Milwaukee, an area on the western shore of Lake Michigan at the confluence of the Menomonee and Kinnickinnic Rivers. In 1795, Jacques Vicau of the North West Company established a trading post and in 1818, Solomon Laurent Juneau, the first permanent settler, founded Milwaukee (from the Indian term millioke, meaning "beautiful land"). From the 1840s on, large numbers of German immigrants came to the city, making up over 60 percent of the 1850 population; today, an estimated one-third of the city's residents are of German descent.

A flourishing agricultural center, Milwaukee had by the Civil War become the largest wheat market in the world. Its industrial base expanded after the war and by 1940 the city ranked fourth in manufacturing among U.S. cities. Still one of the most vigorous producers of durable goods, especially automotive parts, construction and road building equipment, diesel and gasoline engines, tractors, and outboard motors, Milwaukee also emerged as a major meat-packing center. Reflecting its German heritage, the city developed a thriving brewing industry with several of the largest beer-producing companies in the U.S. (though almost all have since disappeared). A major Great Lakes and international port, Milwaukee handles several international steamship lines.
Population   596,974   (2000).   Rank: 19th. Race/Hispanic Origin (2000): White 50.0%. Black 37.3%. Indian 0.9%. Asian 2.9%. Pacific Islander 0.1%. Other 6.1%. Two or more races 2.7%. Hispanic 12.0%.
Location: 43°09'N, 87°58'W. County: Milwaukee.
Terrain and climate   Elev.: 581 ft. Area: 95.8 sq. mi. (248.1 sq km). Avg. daily min. temp.: Jan.: 11.3°F/-11.5°C; avg. daily max. July: 79.8°F/26.5°C. Avg. annual rainfall: 30.94"; snowfall: 45"; clear days: 96; precipitation days: 122.
Government   Form: mayor   and   council. Mayor: John O. Norquist. Election: Apr. 2004. Municipal tel. number: (414) 286-3200.
Visitor info: (800) 554-1448 or (414) 273-3950. www.milwaukee.org

▶ MINNEAPOLIS, MINNESOTA

With an average annual temperature of 45° F, Minneapolis is the second coldest city in the U.S. But despite its arctic winters, it is one of the most desirable cities in the U.S. It sits astride the Mississippi River, near the headwaters of the Minnesota

River, about 350 miles northwest of Chicago. While it is the largest commercial metropolis in the north between Milwaukee and Seattle, no single industry dominates, although many large computer and electronics companies make Minneapolis their home. A regional banking center and the site of the Federal Reserve Bank for the Ninth District, Minneapolis has the world's largest cash grain exchange, the world's four largest wheat-flour-milling companies, and provides the upper Midwest with truck, barge, and air transport.

In 1682 Father Louis Hennepin, the French priest who explored the Mississippi, was the first European to set eyes on the Falls of St. Anthony, the future site of Minneapolis. Unsettled until Fort Snelling was built in 1819 to protect the fur traders from the Sioux and Chippewa, the town of St. Anthony began growing up on one side of the Mississippi and a second settlement sprang up on the other. The two were consolidated in 1872; the new name was a hybrid of the Indian word minne, meaning "water," and the Greek word for "city," polis. Minneapolis blossomed on the basis of its flour and lumber milling. By century's end, the forests to the north had been depleted, but flour milling continues as a thriving industry to this day.

Long considered a center of progressive political and social thinking, it is a mecca of education and culture. Minneapolis contains the main campus of the University of Minnesota, and boasts the Minnesota Orchestra and the Minneapolis Institute of the Arts. A haven for outdoor enthusiasts, the park system numbers 153 parks encompassing 6,000 acres, and with 12 lakes within its city limits, Minneapolis has 10 percent of its surface covered by water. Despite all this, the city has been steadily losing population (160,000 since 1950) to suburban areas.

Population   382,618   (2000).   Rank: 45th. Race/Hispanic Origin (2000): White 65.1%. Black 18.0%. Indian 2.2%. Asian 6.1%. Pacific Islander 0.1%. Other 4.1%. Two or more races 4.4%. Hispanic 7.6%.
Location: 44°58'N, 93°20'W. County: Hennepin.
Terrain and climate   Elev.: 828 ft. Area: 55.1 sq. mi. (142.7 sq km). Avg. daily min. temp.: Jan.: 2.4°F/-16.4°C; avg. daily max. July: 83.4°F/28.5°C. Avg. annual rainfall: 26.36"; snowfall: 46"; clear days: 100; precipitation days: 113.
Government   Form: mayor   and   council. Mayor: Sharon Sayles Belton. Election: Nov. 2001. Municipal tel. number: (612) 673-2100.
Visitor info: (800) 445-7412 or (612) 661-4700. www.ci.minneapolis.mn.us

▶ NASHVILLE, TENNESSEE

In the winter of 1779–80, settlers from North Carolina, led by James Robertson, arrived at a place on the Cumberland River called Big Salt Lick, and built forts on both sides of the river, one of which they named Nashborough, after Gen. Francis Nash of the Revolutionary Army. Adopting the name Nashville in 1784, the settlement was chartered as a city in 1806, became state capital in 1843, and prospered until the Civil War as the northern terminus of the Natchez Trace, a 500-mile road to Natchez, Mississippi. The site of one of the war's last major battles in December 1864, the city underwent a long period of rebuilding and by the end of the century, the population reached 81,000. The city continued to grow, doubling in population by World War II, and has experienced even greater expansion since that time.

While best known as a major center of both the recording and music-publishing industries, Nashville enjoys a widely diversified economic foundation and serves as a distribution and marketing point for the upper southern region of the U.S. Several religious organizations and their publishing operations are headquartered here, and the city is home to more than a dozen institutions of higher learning, including Vanderbilt University, Fisk University, and Tennessee State University. With a growing base of manufacturing, especially in the automotive sector, and with the insurance and banking industries firmly entrenched, Nashville leaders project a prosperous future. As home of the Grand Ole Opry, Nashville has also developed into a regional tourist and convention attraction. A full-scale replica of the Greek temple the Parthenon is a noted site.

Population 569,891 (2000). Rank: 22nd. Race/Hispanic Origin (2000): White 67.0%. Black 25.9%. Indian 0.3%. Asian 2.3%. Pacific Islander 0.1%. Other 2.4%. Two or more races 2.0%. Hispanic 4.6%.

Location: 36°12'N, 86°46'W. County: Davidson.

Terrain and climate Elev.: 605 ft. Area: 479.5 sq. mi. (1241.9 sq km). Avg. daily min. temp.: Jan.: 27.8°F/-2.3°C; avg. daily max. July: 89.8°F/32.1°C. Avg. annual rainfall: 48.49"; snowfall: 10.7"; clear days: 103; precipitation days: 119.

Government Form: mayor and council. Mayor: Bill Purcell. Election: Aug. 2003. Municipal tel. number: (615) 862-6000.

Visitor info: 1–800-657-6910 or (615) 259-4755. www.nashville.org

▶ NEW ORLEANS, LOUISIANA

Founded in 1718 by Jean Baptiste le Moyne and named Ville d'Orléans after the regent of France, the city of New Orleans is one of the nation's most distinctive cities. Situated only 110 miles from the mouth of the Mississippi River, it has long been a major international port (it ranks second in the nation today), and thanks to overlapping waves of French, Spanish, African-American, and Anglo-American immigrants, it has one of the most richly textured cultures of any city in North America. It is geographically distinct, too, in that much of it is below sea level; the almost constant threat of flooding is mitigated by an intricate network of canals and levees.

After half a century under French rule, New Orleans became the capital of Spanish Louisiana in 1763. It was briefly under French rule again (1800–1803) before being acquired by the United States as part of the Louisiana Purchase. Although Louisiana was admitted as a state in 1815, New Orleans continues to reflect its Spanish and French heritage in its architecture, cuisine, and its flamboyant Mardi Gras celebration in the days leading up to the beginning of Lent. African-American traditions are strong here, too, and Dixieland jazz—long heralded as a uniquely American music—is a fusion of African and European styles.

In addition to being a major port for the export of cotton, rice, petroleum products, iron, steel, and corn, and the import of sugar, bananas, coffee, bauxite, and molasses, New Orleans is a major center for offshore drilling in the Gulf of Mexico. In recent years its industrial sector, with an emphasis on aerospace research and technology, petroleum refinement, and shipbuilding, has been strong.

A major tourist attraction in its own right, the city includes among its special points of interest St. Louis Cathedral, the French Market, Preservation Hall and Dixieland Hall, and the Presbytère—all in the French Quarter—as well as the celebrated residential architecture of the Garden District, the New Orleans Museum of Art, the Confederate Museum, and Audubon Park Zoo. Among its educational institutions are Tulane University, Sophie Newcomb College, and Dillard University.

Population 484,674 (2000). Rank: 31st. Race/Hispanic Origin (2000): White 28.1%. Black 67.3%. Indian 0.2%. Asian 2.3%. Pacific Islander 0.0%. Other 0.9%. Two or more races 1.3%. Hispanic 3.1%.

Location: 30°00'W., 90°05'W. Parish: Orleans.

Terrain and climate Elev.: 30 ft. Area: 199.4 sq. mi. (516.4 sq km). Avg. daily min. temp.: Jan.: 43°F/6.1°C; avg. daily max.: July: 90.7°F/32.6°C. Avg. annual rainfall: 59.74"; snowfall: 0.2"; clear days: 109; precipitation days: 113.

Government Form: mayor and council. Mayor: Marc H. Morial. Election: March 2002. Municipal tel. number: (504) 565-6000.

Visitor info: (504) 566-5011. www2.new-orleans.la.com

▶ NEW YORK CITY, NEW YORK

Even before the arrival of Europeans in North America, the waters that today make New York one of the world's foremost ports—and the foremost city in the United States—were the scene of lively trade between the predominant Algonquian tribes in the region. The city's modern history dates to 1524 when the Florentine explorer, Giovanni de Verrazano, sailed into New York Bay. In 1609, Henry Hudson, an English navigator sailing for the Dutch East India Company, explored the river that bears his name today. In 1625, the Dutch West India Company purchased Manhattan and established Nieuw Amsterdam, which quickly became a profitable trading post. Dutch settlers soon expanded beyond the original colony settling Breukelen, Nieuw Harlem, Bronx, and Staaten Eylandt. Taken by the British in 1664 (the Dutch briefly regained control in 1673-74), and renamed for the Duke of York, the town continued to prosper.

As resentment of British authority grew, New York became a seat of colonial discontent, participating in actions against the Stamp Act (1763) and tea tax (1773). But after the Battle of Long Island and Washington's retreat in August 1776, the British held New York through the end of the war. Yet Washington was inaugurated President at Federal Hall (today the site of the second Federal Reserve Bank) on Wall Street, and from 1789-90 New York was the nation's capital.

Industry and trade expanded dramatically after the opening of the Erie Canal from Troy (150 miles up the Hudson River) and Buffalo (350 miles west of Troy) gave New York direct access to the raw materials and the markets of the Great Lakes states. In the mid-19th century, New York became the primary port of immigration to the U.S. and many of the millions of immigrants who came to America carved out distinctly ethnic neighborhoods throughout the city in a patchwork that survives to the present.

In 1898, an act of the state legislature created "Greater New York," and today New York's population is greater than that of Los Angeles and Chicago (the second and third largest cities in the country) combined. Even if they were separate cities, four of New York boroughs would rank in the top 10—Brooklyn fourth (2.3 million), Queens fifth (1.9 million), Manhattan eighth (1.5 million), and the Bronx ninth (1.2 million).

New York's attractions are seemingly innumerable—enough to draw over 17 million visitors annually—but they include 150 museums, 400 art galleries, dozens of Broadway theaters, and scores of concert halls, clubs, and dance halls. In addition, there are close to 1,000 landmark buildings, more than 50 landmark interiors, and more than

50 historic districts. (A list of attractions can be found under "New York State.") The city leads the nation in the arts, fashion, advertising, banking and financial services, publishing, broadcasting, and certain service industries; it is also the home of the General Assembly of the United Nations. There are 87 colleges and universities here, including Columbia University, New York University, Long Island University, Brooklyn College, Fordham University, the Pratt Institute of Technology, the Juilliard School, and the School of Visual Arts. Manufactured goods include apparel, chemicals, metal products, and printing.

New York City was the site of the worst terrorist attack in U.S. history on Sept. 11, 2001, when two hijacked commercial jets crashed into the twin towers of the World Trade Center, causing the complete collapse of both buildings and killing over 6,000 people.
Population 8,008,278 (2000). Rank: 1st. Race/Hispanic Origin (2000): White 44.7%. Black 26.6%. Indian 0.5%. Asian 9.8%. Pacific Islander 0.1%. Other 13.4%. Two or more races 4.9%. Hispanic 27.0%.
Location: 40°45'N, 74°00'W. Counties: Bronx, Kings, New York, Queens, and Richmond.
Terrain and climate Elev.: 87 ft. Area: 301.5 sq. mi. (780.9 sq km). Avg. daily min. temp.: Jan.: 25.6°F/-3.5°C; avg. daily max. July: 85.3°F/29.6°C. Avg. annual rainfall: 44.12"; snowfall: 29"; clear days: 107; precipitation days: 121.
Government Form: mayor and council. Mayor: Rudolph Giuliani. Election: Nov. 2001. Municipal tel. number: (212) 788-3000.
Visitor info: (212) 484-1200.
http://home.nyc.gov

▶ OAKLAND, CALIFORNIA

The first European-American to settle present-day Oakland was Dom Luis Maria Peralta, who established the 44,000-acre settlement called Rancho San Antonio in 1820. Its first real growth began with the establishment of ferry service to San Francisco in 1852, though the ferry's importance was overshadowed by Oakland's selection as the western terminus of the first transcontinental railroad in 1869. The city remained in the economic shadow of its more sophisticated neighbor across the Bay until the San Francisco earthquake of 1906 drove 100,000–150,000 people to Oakland for shelter. An estimated 65,000 of these are thought to have settled there permanently, providing an impetus for a long period of growth as an international port and industrial center.

A major commercial and cultural center with a container port ranked 10th in the world, Oakland is also the major northern hub of the California freeway system, which is integrated into the Bay Area Rapid Transit (BART) system. It has also become the premier biotechnology center in the region, and it is home to regional and international headquarters for firms in finance, medicine, telecommunications, international trade, and heavy industry.

Long a primarily industrial urban center, Oakland has pumped hundreds of millions of dollars into development of its downtown area and the Jack London waterfront—named for the author who spent his youth on the Oakland docks. Oakland embraces a racially and culturally diverse populace. Oakland sustained heavy damage in the 1989 Loma Prieta earthquake. Two years later, almost to the day, the worst fire in California history leveled more than 1,000 buildings in the Oakland Hills neighborhood, killing 14 people and inflicting more than $1.5 billion in damage.
Population 399,484 (2000). Rank: 41st.

Race/Hispanic Origin (2000): White 31.3%. Black 35.7%. Indian 0.7%. Asian 15.2%. Pacific Islander 0.5%. Other 11.7%. Two or more races 5.0%. Hispanic 21.9%.
Location: 37°50'N, 122°18'W. County: Alameda.
Terrain and climate Elev.: 42 ft. Area: 53.9 sq. mi. (139.6 sq km). Avg. daily min. temp.: Jan.: 43.4°F/6.3°C; avg. daily max. July: 70.6°F/29.6°C. Avg. annual rainfall: 18.03"; snowfall: N.A.; clear days: N.A; precipitation days: N.A.
Government Form: council and manager. Mayor: Jerry Brown. Election: Nov. 2002. Municipal tel. number: (510) 238-3611.
Visitor info: (800) 262-5526 or (510) 839-9000.
www.oaklandnet.com

▶ OKLAHOMA CITY, OKLAHOMA

Oklahoma City quite literally sprang up during the Great Land Rush of 1889 and, by presidential proclamation, opened for European-American settlement officially on April 22 of that year. At day's end, approximately 10,000 settlers had moved in—the greatest one-day non-annexation population increase in the history of cities. Oklahoma became a state in 1907 and Oklahoma City its capital in 1910, by which time the population had swelled to about 64,000. Since then, it has become Oklahoma's largest city, its leading commercial center, and home to the National Cowboy Hall of Fame.

Oklahoma City's economy, based on oil and livestock, thrives on petroleum production, meat processing, and the breeding of stocker and feeder cattle. The city hosts a flourishing printing and publishing industry and manufactures a diversity of products including automobiles, electronic equipment, computers, communications switches, and oil well supplies. As a vital banking center serving the central and western regions of the state, Oklahoma City boasts a Federal Reserve branch bank. On a somewhat less positive note, Oklahoma City reportedly sparked the "go-go" banking syndrome that characterized the 1970s oil boom, when Penn Square Bank's ill-advised oil patch loans nearly devastated the U.S. banking system.

Oklahoma City was the site of one of the deadliest terrorist bombings in U.S. history on April 19, 1995, when a 5,000-pound car bomb ripped a huge hole in the Alfred Murrah Federal Building, killing 169 people, including 15 children in a day care center within the building.
Population 506,132 (2000). Rank: 29th. Race/Hispanic Origin (2000): White 68.4%. Black 15.4%. Indian 3.5%. Asian 3.5%. Pacific Islander 0.1%. Other 5.3%. Two or more races 3.9%. Hispanic 10.1%.
Location: 35°25'N, 97°30'W. Counties: Canadian, Cleveland, McClain, Oklahoma.
Terrain and climate Elev.: 1,304 ft. Area: 604 sq. mi. (1,564.4 sq km). Avg. daily min. temp.: Jan.: 25.2°F/-3.7°C; avg. daily max. July: 93.5°F/34.1°C. Avg. annual: rainfall, 30.89"; snowfall, 9"; clear days, 141; precipitation days, 81.
Government Form: council and manager. Mayor: Kirk Humphries. Election: March 2002. Municipal tel. number: (405) 297-2424.
Visitor info: (800) 225-5652 or (405) 297-8910.
www.okccvb.org

▶ OMAHA, NEBRASKA

Permanent settlement in what is now Omaha began with a fur-trading post established shortly after the Lewis and Clark expedition passed through the area in 1804. In 1820, the government built Ft. Atkinson, and the surrounding community became a major stop on both the Mormon and the Lewis and Clark trails, and was incorporated as a city in 1854. After strong lobbying by citizens of Council Bluffs, Iowa, just across the Missouri River to the east, Omaha (the name means "above all others on the stream") became the eastern terminus of the Union-Pacific transcontinental railroad, the country's first, in 1869. Within six years, the population grew to 39,000 and by the turn of the century, it had passed the 100,000 mark.

As a major transportation hub of the Midwest— Omaha today boasts seven major railroads and the recently expanded Port of Omaha services a dozen barge lines—the city became a major distribution center for meat and grain, living up to its motto "We feed the world" (ConAgra is based here). Its major food products include pasta, potato chips, coffee, pancake mixes, frozen dinners, and Omaha steaks. With dozens of *Fortune* 500 manufacturing operations, and a healthy publishing industry (roughly one out of every four manufacturers is either a publisher or printer), Omaha's diversified economy also has strong roots in insurance (Mutual of Omaha), communications, direct mail/telemarketing, and sophisticated medical facilities are centered at the medical schools of Creighton University and the University of Nebraska. Since 1989 employment in the metro area has grown by 15 percent, while the unemployment rate, one of the lowest in the nation, has been less than 3 percent for several years.

Among its performing arts institutions are the Omaha Symphony, Opera/Omaha, the Omaha Ballet, the Orpheum Theater, and the Omaha Community Playhouse. Museums and historic sites include the Boys Town Hall of Fame, the Henry Doorly Zoo and Aquarium, the Great Plains Black Museum, the historic ships *U.S.S. Hazard* and *U.S.S. Marlin*, and the Old Market, a mixed-use National Historic District on the Missouri River. **Population** 390,007 (2000). Rank: 44th. Race/Hispanic Origin (2000): White 78.4%. Black 13.3%. Indian 0.7%. Asian 1.7%. Pacific Islander 0.1%. Other 3.9%. Two or more races 1.9%. Hispanic 7.5%.
Location: 41°15'N, 95°55'W. County: Douglas.
Terrain and climate Elev.: 982 ft. Area: 99.3 sq. mi. (257.2 sq km). Avg. daily min. temp.: Jan.: 10.2°F/-12.1°C; avg. daily max. July: 88.5°F/31.3°C. Avg. annual rainfall: 30.34"; snowfall: 32"; clear days: 113; precipitation days: 99.
Government Form: mayor and council. Mayor: Mike Fahey. Election: May 2005. Municipal tel. number: (402) 444-5000.
Visitor info: (800) 332-1819 or (402) 444-4660.
www.ci.omaha.ne.us

▶PHILADELPHIA, PENNSYLVANIA

In 1632, a small contingent of Swedes and Finns came to the land where the Schuylkill River meets the Delaware and founded New Sweden. In 1655, Peter Stuyvesant seized New Sweden for the Dutch, inciting conflict with the British until the Dutch relinquished their rights to the territory in 1673. Nine years later, William Penn established a town between the Schuylkill and the Delaware Rivers, named it Philadelphia, "the city of brotherly love," and in two years it evolved into an active settlement of about 2,500 people, most of them Quakers.

In the mid-1700s, Benjamin Franklin began shaping the destiny of Philadelphia by presiding over the founding of the University of Pennsylvania, the Pennsylvania Hospital, and a fire insurance company (the last two were firsts for the young nation). Under his guidance, Philadelphia

became the premier colonial city for the arts and the home of many famous educators, scientists, mathematicians, authors, and painters. In addition, a total of 17 libraries were founded at this time. The meeting place of the Continental Congress and the site of the signing of the Declaration of Independence, Philadelphia was the nation's capital from 1790 to 1800, when the federal government moved permanently to Washington, D.C.

Throughout the 19th century, the influx first of Irish and German, then Jewish, Italian, Polish, and Slavic immigrants from Europe, and blacks from the South, helped build the city's industrial base. Today, Philadelphia ranks high among U.S. cities in oil refining; other principal industries are electrical machinery, automobile and truck bodies, petrochemicals, metalworking, and scientific instruments. But many other businesses have left the city and unemployment and poverty have taken a heavy toll in recent years. Since 1990, the city has lost almost 7 percent of its population.
Population 1,517,550 (2000). Rank: 5th. Race/Hispanic Origin (2000): White 45.0%. Black 43.2%. Indian 0.3%. Asian 4.5%. Other 4.8%. Two or more races 2.2%. Hispanic 8.5%.
Location: 40°00'N, 75°10'W. County: Philadelphia.
Terrain and climate Elev.: 28 ft. Area: 136 sq. mi. (352.2 sq km). Avg. daily min. temp.: Jan.: 23.8°F/-4.5°C; avg. daily max. July: 86.1°F/30°C. Avg. annual rainfall: 41.42"; snowfall: 20"; clear days: 92; precipitation days: 116.
Government Form: mayor and council. Mayor: John F. Street. Election: Nov. 2003. Municipal tel. number: (215) 686-1776.
Visitor info: (215) 636-1666.
www.phila.gov

▶PHOENIX, ARIZONA

Arizona's capital and its largest city sits in the Salt River Valley in a former desert that has become a prosperous agricultural area because of a network of irrigated dams located northeast of the city. Long a resort area owing to its mild climate, Phoenix has recently emerged as a lively commercial and agricultural center as well. A flourishing high-tech haven attracting businesses engaged in electronics, communications, and research and development, the city also has a strong manufacturing base that includes airplane parts, electronic equipment, agricultural chemicals, radios, air conditioners, and leather goods. Among its agricultural products are lettuce, melons, vegetables, grapefruit, oranges, lemons, and olives.

While Phoenix benefits from modern irrigation efforts, the Hohokam Indian people dug the area's first irrigation ditches in the 3rd century, B.C. and developed an extensive network of canals that lasted until their culture's decline in A.D. 1400. The area was not resettled until 1864, when a hay camp was established to supply Camp McDowell 30 miles away. Jack Weilling and "Lord Darrell" Dupa rebuilt the old Indian irrigation ditches in 1867, and named the site Phoenix, after the mythical bird that rose from its own ashes. The settlement grew as a trading post, was incorporated as a city in 1881, became capital of the territory in 1889 and the state capital when Arizona was admitted to the Union in 1912.

With the westward exodus from the snowbelt states, and the perfecting of air conditioning to make the summer heat bearable, the small 1950s resort city of 106,818 people has since swelled almost tenfold. In the 1980s, Phoenix's population grew 24.5 percent from 789,704 to just under a million. Growth between 1990 and 2000 was even faster (34 percent).

Population 1,321,045 (2000). Rank: 6th. Race/Hispanic Origin (2000): White 71.1%. Black 5.1%. Indian 2.0%. Asian 2.0%. Pacific Islander 0.1%. Other 16.4%. Two or more races 3.3%. Hispanic 34.1%.
Location: 33°30'N, 112°04'W. County: Maricopa.
Terrain and climate Elev.: 1,117 ft. Area: 375 sq. mi. (971.3 sq km). Avg. daily min. temp.: Jan.: 44.4°F/6.8°C; avg. daily max. July: 107.5°F/41°C. Avg. annual rainfall: 7.11"; snowfall: 0"; clear days: 214; precipitation days: 34.
Government Form: Mayor and council. Mayor: Skip Rimsza. Election: Sept. 2003. Municipal tel. number: (602) 262-6011.
Visitor info: (602) 254-6500.
www.ci.phoenix.az.us

▶ PORTLAND, OREGON

Portland's renowned beauty is a result of its unique natural setting, which offers a view of the Cascade Mountains and Mt. Hood to the east, Mt. Adams to the northeast, and Mt. St. Helens and Mt. Rainier to the north. Eleven bridges span the Willamette River, which divides the city into east and west sections.

Indian traders traveling between Oregon City and Vancouver carved out an acre of land by the Willamette River 12 miles north of Oregon City, which became known as The Clearing. In 1884 William Overton claimed the 640 acres surrounding the area, which he then sold to Asa Lovejoy and Francis W. Pettygrove, who set out to build a city. Winning a coin toss, Pettygrove named the city-to-be after his hometown in Maine.

As a vital port of entry (the coast's only freshwater port) with a large inland harbor, Portland is a leader in the shipping of lumber, flour, and grain, and has blossomed into Oregon's largest city. Main industries also include paper and pulp, mining, high-technology equipment, and aerospace. Portland enjoys a flourishing arts community and its residents partake of the beaches and ski slopes within easy driving distance.
Population 529,121 (2000). Rank: 28th. Race/Hispanic Origin (2000): White 77.9%. Black 6.6%. Indian 1.1%. Asian 6.3%. Pacific Islander 0.4%. Other 3.5%. Two or more races 4.1%. Hispanic 6.8%.
Location: 45°35'N, 122°40'W. Counties: Clackamas, Multnomah, Washington.
Terrain and climate Elev.: 39 ft. Area: 113.9 sq. mi. (295 sq km). Avg. daily min. temp.: Jan.: 33.5°F/0.8°C; avg. daily max. July: 79.5°F/26.3°C. Avg. annual rainfall: 37.39"; snowfall: 7"; clear days: 69; precipitation days: 152.
Government Form: commission. Mayor: Vera Katz. Election: May 2004. Municipal tel. number: (503) 823-4000.
Visitor info: (800) 962-3700 or (503) 275-8355.
www.ci.portland.or.us

▶ SACRAMENTO, CALIFORNIA

The capital of California and its seventh largest city, Sacramento sits 75 miles northeast of San Francisco at the confluence of the American and Sacramento rivers. A wholesale and retail center for the surrounding rich farmland, the city includes among its main commercial enterprises food processing and canning, and one of the world's largest almond-shelling plants.

Receiving a land grant from the Mexican government in 1839, Swiss-American John Augustus Sutter founded a colony called New Helvetia, and when Fort Sutter was constructed in 1844, it became one of California's chief trading posts. Established soon after the discovery of gold in 1848,

Sacramento grew to 7,000 residents by 1850, became state capital in 1854, and in 1863 was incorporated as a city.

The "Gateway to the Goldfields," "Old Sacramento" became a pivotal point of commerce in the 1860s, connected to the mining towns by the American River, and transporting produce from the farms and orchards lining the banks of the Sacramento River. Sailors stopping in San Francisco visited Sacramento to replenish their stocks of fresh produce and to entertain themselves in the saloons and gambling halls. The wealthy lived in great mansions by the river and the cobblestone streets, gaslights, and wood sidewalks imbued the town with a touch of civility. Today's Sacramento, appreciated for its subtle, quiet charms, boasts 120 parks, hiking and biking trails along the American River Parkway, a large collection of art galleries, two symphony orchestras, ballet, theater and opera companies, and a number of jazz clubs and coffee houses.
Population 407,018 (2000). Rank: 40th. Race/Hispanic Origin (2000): White 48.3%. Black 15.5%. Indian 1.3%. Asian 16.6%. Pacific Islander 0.9%. Other 11.0%. Two or more races 6.4%. Hispanic 21.6%.
Location: 38°33'N, 121°30'W. County: Sacramento.
Terrain and climate Elev.: 25 ft. Area: 97.3 sq. mi. (252 sq km). Avg. daily min. temp.: Jan.: 37.9°F/3.2°C; avg. daily max. July: 93.3°F/34°C. Avg. annual rainfall: 17.87"; snowfall: 0.1"; clear days: 193; precipitation days: 57.
Government Form: council and manager. Mayor: Heather Fargo. Election: Nov. 2004. Municipal tel. number: (916) 264-5704.
Visitor info: 800-292-2334 or (916) 264-7777.
www.sacto.org

▶ SAN ANTONIO, TEXAS

San Antonio, the third largest city in Texas, lies in the state's south-central region at the edge of the Gulf Coastal Plain 140 miles from the Gulf of Mexico. Its economy thrives on agriculture, livestock, and the activity of the wholesale traders who dominate the commerce of southwestern Texas and northern Mexico. It is also a regional leader in biotechnology. Adding further stimulus to the economy are five major military installations—Fort Sam Houston, Randolph Air Force Base, Kelly Air Force Base, Lackland Air Force Base, and Brooks Air Force Base. The military contributes approximately $3 billion annually to the area economy.

The founding of the mission of San Antonio de Valero (later known as the Alamo) and the Presidio of San Antonio in 1718 represented the area's first permanent settlement. When 56 settlers from the Canary Islands joined the original coterie of ranchmen, missionaries, and soldiers, they formed the first municipal organization in Texas, called the villa of San Fernando de Bexar, which became a city in 1809, and suffered under Mexican rule until the battle of San Jacinto in 1836. With the influx of American pioneers and German immigrants (following Texas's statehood in 1845), the population grew to over 96,000 by 1910, and has since increased nearly tenfold. By 1998 it had reached 1.1 million, up 22 percent since 1990.

Today San Antonio is a popular haven for vacationers, with over 10 million visitors per year. San Antonio's attractions include the Alamo and its four sister missions, the Riverwalk along the San Antonio River, Breckenridge Park (home of one of America's largest zoos), Sea World of Texas; La Villita, the Tower of the Americas, and the Spanish Governor's Palace.

Population 1,144,646 (2000). Rank: 9th. Race/Hispanic Origin (2000): White 67.7%. Black 6.8%. Indian 0.8%. Asian 1.6%. Pacific Islander 0.1%. Other 19.3%. Two or more races 3.7%. Hispanic 58.7%.
Location: 29°30'N, 98°30'W. County: Bexar.
Terrain and climate Elev.: 701 ft. Area: 304.5 sq. mi. (788.7 sq km). Avg. daily min. temp.: Jan.: 39°F/3.8°C; avg. daily max. July: 96.3°F/35.7°C. Avg. annual rainfall: 29.13"; snowfall: 0.5"; clear days: 110; precipitation days: 81.
Government Form: council and manager. Mayor: Ed Garza. Election: May 2003. Municipal tel. number: (210) 207-7060.
Visitor info: (800) 447-3372 or (210) 270-8700.
www.ci.sat.tx.us

▶ SAN DIEGO, CALIFORNIA

Sixty years after João Rodrigues Cabrilho first sailed into San Diego Bay, Sebastian Vizcaino embarked from Spain with three ships to explore the coast of California, and in November 1602 anchored on the lee of what is now known as Point Loma. When he finished charting the bay two days later, he changed its original name, San Miguel, to San Diego, in honor of the saint San Diego de Alcalal de Henares, In 1769, Father Junipero Serra established California's first mission, the Mission San Diego de Alcala.

Compared to its sister cities to the north—Los Angeles and San Francisco—San Diego developed slowly, despite its large and hospitable harbor. In 1887, the city became the southern terminus for the Santa Fe Railroad, but floods soon washed out the tracks and trackbeds, and the railroad was rebuilt to terminate in L.A. which had a new manmade harbor. This put San Diego at an almost insurmountable disadvantage. With its industrial development stunted, San Diego welcomed the establishment of a U.S. Navy base during World War I; since then, about a quarter of the Navy's seagoing vessels and roughly 20 percent of the Marine Corps' forces have been located there. Jonas Salk's work on polio and the emergence of the University of California at San Diego have earned the city the reputation as a premier biomedical research center, luring billions of dollars in development and research grants.

San Diego, a picturesque city with many tourist attractions, enjoys an average of 350 days of sunshine, enticing both residents and visitors to its 70 beaches and the parks, resorts, and health spas lining its great bay. Coronado Island is a popular attraction. Balboa Park, host to international expositions in 1915 and 1935, contains the San Diego Zoo, one of the finest in the nation. The pleasure boats berthed at the city's numerous yacht clubs offer a curious contrast to the naval warships moored nearby. San Diego was the site of the 1992 America's Cup yacht races.
Population 1,223,400 (2000). Rank: 7th. Race/Hispanic Origin (2000): White 60.2%. Black 7.9%. Indian 0.6%. Asian 13.6%. Pacific Islander 0.5%. Other 12.4%. Two or more races 4.8%. Hispanic 25.4%.
Location: 32°43'N, 117°10'W. County: San Diego.
Terrain and climate Elev.: 13 ft. Area: 329 sq. mi. (852.1 sq km). Avg. daily min. temp.: Jan.: 48.4°F/9.1°C; avg. daily max. July: 75.6°F/24.2°C. Avg. annual rainfall: 9.32"; snowfall: 0"; clear days: 150; precipitation days: 41.
Government Form: council and manager. Mayor: Dick Murphy. Election: Nov. 2004. Municipal tel. number: (619) 236-5555.
Visitor info: (619) 236-1212.
www.ci.san-diego.ca.us

▶ SAN FRANCISCO, CALIFORNIA

Located near the Golden Gate, the strait between San Francisco Bay and the Pacific Ocean, fogbound San Francisco hid from some of the greatest European navigators to explore the West Coast. João Rodrigues Cabrilho discovered the Farrallon Islands just off the coast in 1542 and Sir Francis Drake landed a few miles north of the Golden Gate in 1579. Yet it was another 200 years before Don Gasper de Portola sailed into the Bay, followed six years later by Don Juan Manuel Ayala who established a town and mission.

Neither the Spanish nor (after 1821) the Mexican governments were very keen on capitalizing on San Francisco's temperate and strategic location, and when Captain John Montgomery raised the American flag there on July 9, 1846, the community consisted of only 840 people. The discovery of gold at Sutter's mill in 1848, and the gold rush of 1849—which brought 40,000 of the hopeful to California, most by ship—catapulted San Francisco onto the world map, and the following year it was incorporated as a city.

San Francisco continued to prosper as a major transportation and industrial center, but in 1906 an earthquake registering 8.6 on the Richter scale claimed 452 lives, 28,000 buildings, and losses totalling approximately $350 million. San Francisco rose from the ashes to become a thriving, multifaceted, cosmopolitan city and one of the country's leaders in world trade. Another major earthquake, measuring 7.1 on the Richter scale, struck on Oct. 17, 1989, causing extensive damage and 67 deaths in the region, but did not devastate the city as thoroughly as the 1906 tremor.

San Francisco today is a port of call for more than 40 steamship lines which import approximately $25 billion worth of goods from more than 300 ports around the world. A major international financial center, it is the headquarters of three of the nation's largest banks, the 12th Federal Reserve District, and the Pacific Stock Exchange. There are also more than 650 insurance companies, and the city is a haven for venture capitalists and entrepreneurs: more than 90 percent of its businesses have fewer than 25 employees. There are also several U.S. military installations in the area.

Well known for its spirit of individualism, San Francisco was a haven for the beat movement of the 1950s, and the capital of the hippie movement of the 1960s was the Haight-Ashbury district. Its more traditional arts institutions include the San Francisco Ballet, the San Francisco Opera, the San Francisco Symphony, and the American Conservatory Theater. Among its leading educational institutions are the University of San Francisco, the Heald Institute of Technology, the University of California, the San Francisco Art Institute, the San Francisco Conservatory of Music, and the San Francisco College of Mortuary Science. Among its many museums are the National Maritime Historic Park, the Fine Arts Museum, and the California Palace of the Legion of Honor. Other attractions include its historic cable cars (first used in 1873), Chinatown, and Fisherman's Wharf.
Population 776,733 (2000). Rank: 13th. Race/Hispanic Origin (2000): White 49.7%. Black 7.8%. Indian 0.4%. Asian 30.8%. Pacific Islander 0.5%. Other 6.5%. Two or more races 4.3%. Hispanic 14.1%.
Location: 37°47'N, 122°30'W. County: San Francisco.
Terrain and climate Elev.: 155 ft. Area: 46.4 sq. mi. (120.2 sq km). Avg. daily min. temp.: Jan.: 41.5°F/5.2°C; avg. daily max. July: 71°F/21°C. Avg. annual rainfall: 19.71"; snowfall: 0"; clear days: 162; precipitation days: 67.

Government Form: mayor and council. Mayor: Willie L. Brown Jr. Election: Nov. 2003. Municipal tel. number: (415) 554-6141.
Visitor info: (415) 391-2000
www.ci.sf.ca.us

▶SAN JOSE, CALIFORNIA

Located at the southern end of San Francisco Bay, about 45 miles south of San Francisco, San Jose was the first non-religious European community founded in California. Pueblo de San Jose de Guadalupe was settled in 1777 by enterprising farmers who sought to make themselves and the region independent of Mexico and the Spanish mission network for their supplies. Fruit and olive trees, hides, tallow, livestock, grain, and lively retail activity all contributed to San Jose's early prosperity, and it was the first state capital (1849–52).

San Jose remained an agricultural center until World War II, when industry and technology began to expand. The rapid growth of innovative industry over the last 20 years, taking its lead from research and development begun at nearby Stanford University in the 1930s, changed the area dramatically. With the revolution in high technology, Santa Clara County became known as Silicon Valley, excelling in the production of information systems, personal computers, peripherals, and fostering a burgeoning semi-conductor industry. At the same time, financial services, real estate, construction, and retail industries all flourished.

More than 2,600 high-tech companies employing 250,000 people are located in San Jose, and one-third of the labor force works in manufacturing, a very high proportion in post-industrial America. Santa Clara County has the highest median family income in California, and median housing prices in San Jose are perennially among the highest in the nation.
Population 894,943 (2000). Rank: 11th. Race/Hispanic Origin (2000): White 47.5%. Black 3.5%. Indian 0.8%. Asian 26.9%. Pacific Islander 0.4%. Other 15.9%. Two or more races 5.0%. Hispanic 30.2%.
Location: 37°20'N, 121°53'W. County: Santa Clara.
Terrain and climate Elev.: 65 ft. Area: 169.2 sq. mi. (438.2 sq km). Avg. daily min. temp.: Jan.: 41.1°F/5°C; avg. daily max.: July: 81.5°F/27.5°C. Avg. annual rainfall: 13.86"; snowfall: 0"; clear days: N.A.; precipitation days: N.A.
Government Form: council and manager. Mayor: Ron Gonzales. Election: Nov. 2002. Municipal tel. number: (408) 277-4237.
Visitor info: (800) SAN JOSE or (408) 295-9600.
www.ci.san-jose.ca.us

▶SEATTLE, WASHINGTON

Located on the protected waters of Puget Sound, Seattle was the first European-American settlement established in the Pacific Northwest north of the Columbia River. Starting out at Alki Point in 1851, the settlers moved to what is now known as Pioneer Square. Befriended by the Suquamish Chief Sealth (Seattle is a loose approximation of his name), the people turned to lumber harvesting and log milling, which formed the backbone of the city's economy.

With the completion of the Great Northern Railway in 1893 and the Alaska gold rush of 1897, when Seattle became "the Gateway to the Klondike," the city was transformed into a metropolis of merchants and entrepreneurs. Even as gold fever abated, and despite a devastating fire in 1899, the city prospered as a major port to the Orient and as an industrial center. In 1909 Seattle was the site of the Alaska-Yukon-Pacific Exposition. The completion of the Panama Canal in 1914 brought even more business to the already bustling port. Two years later, a small company began building two-seater biplanes; in time the little company became Boeing, the world's largest producer of commercial planes, and the largest employer (more than 80,000 people) in the Seattle area. In 2001, the company stunned the Emerald City by announcing that it was moving its corporate headquarters (and 500 jobs) to Chicago.

Endowed with spectacular natural beauty, with the broad expanse of Puget Sound before it, and the snow-capped peaks of the Cascade Mountains and Mt. Rainier visible to the south and east, the Seattle area offers a wide variety of outdoor activities, from skiing and hiking to fishing and boating. A second international exposition, the Seattle World's Fair in 1962, helped establish the city's reputation as a center of technology, trade, industry, and tourism. In 1974 Bill Gates and Paul Allen founded Microsoft and Seattle has since been seen as the hub of the computer world. The leading cultural programs are put on by the Seattle Symphony Orchestra, the Seattle Opera Association, and the Seattle Repertory Theater. Other attractions include the Seattle Art Museum, Pioneer Square, Pike Place Market, the historic ships on Lake Union, and Woodland Park and Zoo, as well as the many events at the 74-acre Seattle Convention Center, whose buildings (including the famed Space Needle), and park-like grounds and fountains are legacies of the World's Fair. Among the 20 universities and colleges in the area are the University of Washington and Seattle Pacific University.
Population 563,374 (2000). Rank: 24th. Race/Hispanic Origin (2000): White 70.1%. Black 8.4%. Indian 1.0%. Asian 13.1%. Pacific Islander 0.5%. Other 2.4%. Two or more races 4.5%. Hispanic 5.3%.
Location: 47°41'N, 122°15'W. County: King.
Terrain and climate Elev.: 450 ft. Area: 83.6 sq. mi. (216.5 sq km). Avg. daily min. temp.: Jan.: 34.3°F/1.2°C; avg. daily max.: July: 75.2°F/24°C. Avg. annual rainfall: 38.85"; snowfall: 15"; clear days: 57; precipitation days: 160.
Government Form: mayor and council. Mayor: Paul Schell. Election: Nov. 2001. Municipal tel. number: (206) 684-4000.
Visitor info: (206) 461-5840.
www.cityofseattle.net

▶ST. LOUIS, MISSOURI

St. Louis is one of the nation's major centers of transportation, manufacturing, commerce, and education. With abundant water and electric power, a workforce of over a million people in the metropolitan area, and a location in an area rich in mineral resources, St. Louis ranks as one of the top 10 industrial areas in the country. It is also one of the nation's busiest river ports, the third-largest rail center, the eighth-largest trucking center, and has the sixth-busiest airport. Aircraft, automobiles, printing, beer, and chemicals are among the principal products. The metropolitan area boasts five universities, 23 colleges, and seven junior colleges. St. Louis University, oldest west of the Mississippi, founded in 1818, and Washington University are world famous for their medical schools and research programs and their Nobel Prize winners.

For the 40 years after its founding in 1764 by Pierre Laclade, St. Louis was a French settlement and trading post, outfitting fur trading expeditions up the Missouri River. With the Louisiana Purchase in 1803, St. Louis came under American control. The city was incorporated in 1823 with a population of almost 5,000. The first steamboat docked at St. Louis in 1817 and steamboats then became a vital part of the city's growth. Fueled by settlers from the East and by waves of Irish and German immigrants attracted by the prosperity of the river trade, the city's population grew rapidly. In 1870, St. Louis had 311,000 people, and it was the country's third largest city after New York and Philadelphia. The population continued to grow to a peak of 856,800 in 1950, but the post-World War II flight to the suburbs hit St. Louis hard, reducing its population by almost half.

The downtown St. Louis area has many landmarks and historic buildings. The Old Cathedral, completed in 1834, and the Old Courthouse, where the Dred Scott case was first tried, have been preserved as part of the Jefferson National Expansion Memorial. Atop the famous Gateway Arch, the observation room provides a panoramic view of the city. Kiel Auditorium contains a 3,500-seat opera house and a 10,000-seat convention hall. Forest Park, site of the 1904 Louisiana Purchase Exposition (also known as the St. Louis World's Fair), contains the St. Louis Zoo, McDonnell Planetarium, and the Jewel Box, an all-glass floral display house. St. Louis is also the home of the Missouri Botanical Gardens, which features the Climatron—a geodesic dome with rare orchids and other tropical plants—and the largest Japanese garden in the United States. The St. Louis Symphony (founded in 1880) is the country's second oldest and is housed in the Powell Symphony Hall.

Population 348,189 (2000). Rank: 49th. Race/Hispanic Origin (2000): White 43.8%. Black 51.2%. Indian 0.3%. Asian 2.0%. Other 0.8%. Two or more races 1.9%. Hispanic 2.0%.
Location: 38°40'N, 90°12'W. County: independent city.
Terrain and climate Elev.: 564 ft. Area: 61.4 sq. mi. (159 sq km). Avg. daily min. temp.: Jan.: 19.9°F/-6.7°C; avg. daily max. July: 89°F/31°C. Avg. annual rainfall: 33.91"; snowfall: 18"; clear days: 105; precipitation days: 108.
Government Form: mayor and council. Mayor: Francis Slay. Election: Mar. 2005. Municipal tel. number: (314) 622-3201.
Visitor info: (800) 888-3861 or (314) 421-1023.
http://stlouis.missouri.org

▶ TUCSON, ARIZONA
The first European to travel through the area that is now Tucson was the Jesuit missionary Eusebio Kino, in 1692. In 1700 the mission of San Xavier del Bac was established among the Papago Indians nearby. It was not until 1776, however, that the Spanish established a permanent settlement, taking its name from the Papago Stjukshon (or *Chuk Shon*), meaning "village of the dark spring at the foot of the mountain." Tucson remained under Spanish and Mexican control until acquired by the U.S. government as part of the Gadsden Purchase in 1853. During the Civil War it was under Confederate control, but from 1867 to 1877 it was the territorial capital.

Despite the arrival of the Southern Pacific railroad in 1880 and the discovery of extensive copper deposits in southern Arizona, neither the city's location nor its natural resources much stimulated its economy. It was best known as a winter and health resort, and as a commercial hub for the surrounding agricultural and mining industries. In 1950, the population was only 45,500.

The last half-century has seen a dramatic change. One of the many beneficiaries of the exodus from the industrial states to the Sunbelt, Tucson's population has grown almost tenfold in that period, and in the last decade Tucson added 20,000 manufacturing jobs. Surrounded by a wealth of natural beauty, the city is still appealing to retirees and tourists, as is reflected in the many golf courses, ranches, and resorts in and around Tucson. It is ringed by four mountain ranges: the Rincon, Santa Catalina, Tucson, and Santa Rita. Other natural wonders include Sabino Canyon (which has the only year-round stream in the region), the Saguaro National Monument (a preserve for Saguaro cacti), and Tucson Mountain Park, home of the Arizona-Sonora Desert Museum. The University of Arizona is located in Tucson, and the Davis-Mothan Air Force Base and Kitts Peak Observatory are nearby.

Population 486,699 (2000). Rank: 30th. Race/Hispanic Origin (2000): White 70.2%. Black 4.3%. Indian 2.3%. Asian 2.5%. Pacific Islander 0.2%. Other 16.8%. Two or more races 3.8%. Hispanic 35.7%.
Location: 32°14'N, 110°59'W. County: Pima.
Terrain and climate Elev.: 2,584 ft. Area: 125 sq. mi. (324.8 sq km). Avg. daily min. temp.: Jan.: 38.1°F/3.3°C; avg. daily max. July: 98.5°F/3.3°C. Avg. annual rainfall: 11.14"; snowfall: 2"; clear days: 198; precipitation days: 50.
Government Form: council and manager. Mayor: Robert Walkup. Election: Nov. 2002. Municipal tel. number: (520) 791-4201.
Visitor info: (520) 624-1817 or (800) 638-8350.
www.ci.tucson.az.us

▶ TULSA, OKLAHOMA
Tulsa was first settled by Indian nations forced out of the South Atlantic States by the Indian Removal Act of 1830. The name they chose for their new home was Tulsey Town, a corruption of *Tullahassee*, meaning "old town." The name Tulsa was made official with the establishment of a post office in 1879. In 1900, Tulsa's population numbered less than 2,000, but the discovery of extensive oil fields at the turn of the century, beginning with the Glenn Pool and Red Fork strikes, started Tulsa on the way from a small Indian settlement to a sizable metropolis. By 1907, its population had increased to 7,298, and by 1920 it was 10 times that. Soon Tulsa was "the Oil Capital of the World."

While still heavily involved in the oil and gas industry—it remains the home of about 500 oil-related companies—modern Tulsa is a far more diverse city than its oil patch origins. Among Tulsa's top employers are regional, national and international firms involved in aviation and aerospace, energy, computer technology, insurance, telecommunications, health care, and electronic equipment. The Port of Catoosa, which opened in 1972 after the completion of the 445-mile Arkansas-Mississippi Waterway, is a major inland port which provides Tulsa with a direct link to the Mississippi River system and the Gulf of Mexico.

While growing in business, Tulsa has preserved the cultural heritage of its early oil barons and workers as well as that of its original Indian settlers. Thomas Gilcrease, a Creek Indian, became a millionaire with the Glenn Pool oil strike, and founded the Thomas Gilcrease Institute of American History and Art, devoted to the American Indian. The Tulsa Opera Company was founded in the early 1900s, and along with the city's philharmonic, ballet, and theaters, it gives Tulsa just cause to lay claim to being the cultural capital of Oklahoma. Tulsans also honor their roots through rodeos and regional music festivals. In addition, representatives of the state's 65 Indian tribes gather in Tulsa each summer for their annual powwow. Among Tulsa's colleges and universities are the University of Tulsa and Oral Roberts University.

Population 393,049 (2000). Rank: 43rd. Race/Hispanic Origin (2000): White 70.1%. Black 15.5%. Indian 4.7%. Asian 1.8%. Pacific Islander 0.1%. Other 3.5%. Two or more races 4.4%. Hispanic 7.2%.

Location: 36°10'N, 96°00'W. Counties: Osage, Tulsa.

Terrain and climate Elev.: 676 ft. Area: 186.1 sq. mi. (482 sq km). Avg. daily min. temp.: Jan.: 24.8°F/-4°C; avg. daily max. July: 93.9°F/34.3°C. Avg. annual rainfall: 38.77"; snowfall: 9"; clear days: 127; precipitation days: 90.

Government Form: commission. Mayor: M. Susan Savage. Election: Apr. 2002. Municipal tel. number: (918) 596-7411.

Visitor info: (918) 585-1201 or (800) 558-3311. www.tulsachamber.com

▶VIRGINIA BEACH, VIRGINIA

Throughout much of its history—which dates to the the landing of the Jamestown colonists at Point Henry in 1607—Virginia Beach was overshadowed by its northern neighbor, Norfolk, which with its magnificent harbor was long the home of many shipping and naval enterprises at the mouth of Chesapeake Bay. But Virginia Beach has seen remarkable change in the last two decades.

In 1970, Virginia Beach's population was 172,000, only slightly more than half that of Norfolk. By 1990, it had grown 128 percent, to 393,000, and surpassing Norfolk as the state's largest city, a distinction it still holds today, though growth cooled to a 8.2 percent between 1990 and 2000. Local initiative accounts for most of this growth: in the same period Norfolk's population fell 10 percent. A dominant presence is the U.S. Navy, which has three bases—Oceana Naval Air Station, Little Creek Naval Amphibious Base, and the Dam Neck Fleet Training Center—and which together with the U.S. Army's Fort Story employs 36,000 military and civilian personnel.

With 38 miles of Atlantic shoreline, 28 miles of public beaches, and the Seashore State Park— 2,700 acres of shady upland woods, cypress swamps, and Spanish moss—the city continues to depend on tourism as a major factor in its economy, attracting 2.5 million visitors a year. The city's main industries, which include marine and engineering services, construction, communications, and electronics, occupy 10 industrial/business parks, including four built by the Virginia Beach Development Authority.

Among Virginia Beach's outstanding historic and recreational attractions are the Virginia Marine Science Museum, the Adam Thoroughgood House (c. 1680, one of the oldest brick houses in North America), the Old Cape Henry Lighthouse, authorized by the first Congress in 1790, and the statue of Admiral Compte de Grasse whose defeat of the British at the Battle of the Virginia Capes brought about the defeat of Gen. Cornwallis at Yorktown and the end of the American Revolution in 1781.

Population 425,257 (2000). Rank: 38th. Race/Hispanic Origin (2000): White 71.4%. Black 19.0%. Indian 0.4%. Asian 4.9%. Pacific Islander 0.1%. Other 1.5%. Two or more races 2.7%. Hispanic 4.2%.

Location: 36°54'N, 75°58'W. County: independent city.

Terrain and climate Elev.: 12 ft. Area: 225.9 sq. mi. (585.1 sq km). Avg. daily min. temp.: Jan.: 31.7°F/-0.1°C; avg. daily max. July: 86.9°F/30.5°C.

Avg. annual rainfall: 45.22"; snowfall: 7"; clear days: 110; precipitation days: 115.

Government Form: council and manager. Mayor: Meyera E. Oberndorf. Election: May 2004. Municipal tel. number: (757) 427-4581.

Visitor info: (800) VA-BEACH (822-3224). www.virginia-beach.va.us

▶WASHINGTON, D.C.

[*For description, see District of Columbia entry in "States, Territories, and Possessions."*]

Population 572,059 (2000). Rank: 21st. Race/Hispanic Origin (2000): White 30.8%. Black 60.0%. Indian 0.3%. Asian 2.7%. Pacific Islander 0.1%. Other 3.8%. Two or more races 2.4%. Hispanic 7.9%.

Location: 38°52'N, 77°00'W. County: independent city.

Terrain and climate Elev.: 30 ft. Area: 62.7 sq. mi. (162.4 sq km). Avg. daily min. temp.: Jan.: 27.5°F/-2.5°C; avg. daily max. July: 87.9°F/31°C. Avg. annual rainfall: 39"; snowfall: 16"; clear days: 101; precipitation days: 111.

Government Form: mayor and council. Mayor: Anthony A. Williams. Election: Nov. 2002. Municipal tel. number: (202) 727-2980.

Visitor info: (202) 789-7000. www.dc.gov

▶WICHITA, KANSAS

Initially settled by Indians during the Civil War who had migrated from Oklahoma, Wichita, which takes its name from the Indian tribe, was officially founded in 1864 as a trading post along the Chisholm Trail, an important cattle route, and was incorporated in 1871. In 1872 the Santa Fe Rail Line reached the city, further cementing its role as a major cattle shipping center, although by 1875 cattle movement was obstructed by farmers' fences, and flour milling and retail trade began to flourished. The discovery of oil nearby in 1915 and the pioneering of aircraft manufacture in the 1920s quickly brought industrial growth to the city, and Wichita is now dominated by aircraft and aerospace equipment manufacture (including Beech Aircraft Corp., Cessna Aircraft Co., Gates Learjet Corp., and the Boeing Military Airplane company), along with oil refining, grain processing and storage, and livestock marketing.

Wichita is home to Friends University (1898), Kansas Newman College (formerly Sacred Heart College, 1933), and Wichita State University (1895). McDonnell Air Force Base is located nearby. Culturally, the city features the Wichita Art Museum (housing one of the country's largest American art collections), the Kansas Coliseum, and the Wichita Symphony Orchestra.

Population 344,284 (2000). Rank: 50th. Race/Hispanic Origin (2000): White 75.2%. Black 11.4%. Indian 1.2%. Asian 4.0%. Pacific Islander 0.1%. Other 5.1%. Two or more races 3.1%. Hispanic 9.6%.

Location: 37°42'N, 97°20'W. County: Sedgwick.

Terrain and climate Elev.: 387.1 ft. Area: 140.2 sq. mi. (363.1sq km). Avg. daily min. temp.: Jan.: 19.2°F/-7.1°C; avg. daily max. July: 92.8°F/33.8°C. Avg. annual rainfall: 29"; snowfall: 16"; clear days: 279; precipitation days: 86.

Government Form: council and manager. Mayor: Bob Knight. Election: Apr. 2003. Municipal tel. number: 316-268-4331.

Visitor info: (800) 288-9424 or (316) 265-2800. www.ci.wichita.ks.us

CITIES IN AMERICA

The number of large U.S. cities continues to grow. The 2000 Census recorded 243 cities with populations over 100,000, up from 199 such places in 1990.

The number of very large cities also continues to grow. In 1990, the only cities with more than a million residents were New York, Los Angeles, Chicago, Houston, Philadelphia, Detroit, Dallas, and San Diego. In the 2000 Census, Detroit's population dropped below a million (mostly from flight to the suburbs), but Phoenix, and San Antonio topped a million.

New York, the nation's largest city, grew by 685,000 people between Censuses, with most of that growth coming in the latter half of the decade. Meanwhile, Los Angeles, which declined in population early in the decade, grew by an overall 479,000 people.

Major U.S. Cities: Population, Population Change, Population Density, and Land Area, 1970–2000

City (Rank, 2000)	Population ('000s) 1970	1980	1990	2000	Percent change 1990-2000	Population per sq. mi. 1990	Land area (sq.mi.) 1990
Abilene, Texas (197)	90	98	107	116	8.7%	1,035	103.1
Akron, Ohio (82)	275	237	223	217	-2.7	3,586	62.2
Albuquerque, N.Mex. (35)	245	332	385	449	16.6	2,909	132.2
Alexandria, Va. (170)	111	103	111	128	15.4	7,267	15.3
Allentown, Pa. (219)	110	104	105	107	1.5	5,949	17.7
Amarillo, Texas (120)	127	149	158	174	10.2	1,793	87.9
Anaheim, Calif. (56)	166	219	266	328	23.1	6,014	44.3
Anchorage , Alaska[1] (66)	48	174	226	260	15.0	133	1,697.7
Ann Arbor, Mich. (199)	100	108	110	114	4.0	4,231	25.9
Arlington, Texas (54)	90	160	262	333	27.2	2,814	93.0
Arvada, Colo. (235)	N.A.	N.A.	89	102	14.5	N.A.	N.A.
Athens-Clarke County, Ga.[1] (237)	N.A.	N.A.	46	101	121.9	N.A.	N.A.
Atlanta, Ga. (40)	495	425	394	416	5.7	2,990	131.8
Augusta-Richmond County, Ga.[1] (91)	N.A.	N.A.	45	200	347.5	N.A.	N.A.
Aurora, Colo. (62)	75	159	222	276	24.4	1,676	132.5
Aurora, Ill. (151)	N.A.	N.A.	100	143	43.6	N.A.	N.A.
Austin, Texas (16)	254	346	466	657	41.0	2,138	217.8
Bakersfield, Calif. (70)	70	106	175	247	41.3	1,904	91.8
Baltimore, Md. (17)	905	787	736	651	-11.5	9,108	80.8
Baton Rouge, La. (75)	166	220	220	228	3.8	2,969	74.0
Bayamon, Puerto Rico (86)	N.A.	N.A.	202	203	0.7	N.A.	N.A.
Beaumont, Texas (200)	118	118	114	114	-0.4	1,427	80.1
Bellevue, Wash. (210)			87	110	26.1		
Berkeley, Calif. (231)	114	103	103	103	0.0	9,783	10.5
Birmingham, Ala. (72)	301	284	266	243	-8.7	1,791	148.5
Boise City, Idaho (108)	75	102	126	186	47.8	2,726	46.1
Boston, Mass. (20)	641	563	574	589	2.6	11,860	48.4
Bridgeport, Conn. (156)	157	143	142	140	-1.5	8,855	16.0
Brownsville, Texas (155)	N.A.	N.A.	99	140	41.2	N.A.	N.A.
Buffalo, N.Y. (59)	463	358	328	293	-10.8	8,083	40.6
Burbank, Calif. (243)	N.A.	N.A.	94	100	7.1	N.A.	N.A.
Cambridge, Mass. (238)	N.A.	N.A.	96	101	5.8	N.A.	N.A.
Cape Coral, Fla. (234)	N.A.	N.A.	75	102	36.4	N.A.	N.A.
Carolina , Puerto Rico (125)	N.A.	N.A.	162	168	3.5	N.A.	N.A.
Carrollton, Texas (209)	N.A.	N.A.	82	110	33.4	N.A.	N.A.
Cedar Rapids, Iowa (185)	111	110	109	121	11.0	2,033	53.5
Chandler, Ariz. (116)	N.A.	N.A.	91	177	95.0	N.A.	N.A.
Charlotte, N.C. (26)	241	315	396	541	36.6	2,272	174.3
Chattanooga, Tenn. (132)	120	170	152	156	2.0	1,288	118.4
Chesapeake, Va. (93)	90	114	152	199	31.1	446	340.7
Chicago, Ill. (3)	3,369	3,005	2,784	2,896	4.0	12,251	227.2
Chula Vista, Calif. (122)	68	84	135	174	28.4	4,661	29.0
Cincinnati, Ohio (55)	454	385	364	331	-9.0	4,717	77.2
Clarksville, Tenn. (228)	N.A.	N.A.	75	103	37.0	N.A.	N.A.
Clearwater, Fla. (212)	N.A.	N.A.	99	109	10.1	N.A.	N.A.
Cleveland, Ohio (33)	751	574	506	478	-5.4	6,565	77.0
Colorado Springs, Colo. (49)	136	215	281	361	28.4	1,535	183.2
Columbia, S.C. (195)	114	101	98	116	18.6	884	117.1
Columbus, Ga.[1] (106)	155	169	179	186	3.9	827	216.1
Columbus, Ohio (15)	540	565	633	711	12.4	3,315	190.9
Concord, Calif. (181)	85	104	111	122	9.4	3,773	29.5
Coral Springs, Fla. (190)	N.A.	N.A.	79	118	48.0	N.A.	N.A.
Corona, Calif. (174)	N.A.	N.A.	76	125	64.2	N.A.	N.A.
Corpus Christi, Texas (61)	205	232	257	277	7.8	1,907	135.0

City (Rank, 2000)	Population ('000s)				Percent change 1990-2000	Population per sq. mi. 1990	Land area (sq.mi.) 1990
	1970	1980	1990	2000			
Costa Mesa, Calif. (213)	N.A.	N.A.	96	109	12.8%	N.A.	N.A.
Dallas, Texas (8)	844	905	1,007	1,189	18.0	2,943	342.4
Daly City, Calif. (227)			92	104	12.3		
Dayton, Ohio (126)	243	194	182	166	-8.7	3,310	55.0
Denver, Colo.[1] (25)	515	493	468	555	18.6	3,051	153.3
Des Moines, Iowa (95)	201	191	193	199	2.8	2,567	75.3
Detroit, Mich. (10)	1,514	1,203	1,028	951	-7.5	7,410	138.7
Downey, Calif. (216)	N.A.	N.A.	91	107	17.4	N.A.	N.A.
Durham, N.C. (105)	95	101	137	187	36.9	1,972	69.3
El Monte, Calif. (196)	70	79	106	116	9.2	11,175	9.5
El Paso, Texas (23)	322	425	515	564	9.4	2,100	245.4
Elizabeth, N.J. (186)	113	106	110	121	9.6	8,929	12.3
Erie, Pa. (226)	129	119	109	104	-4.6	4,944	22.0
Escondido, Calif. (164)	37	64	109	134	22.9	3,048	35.6
Eugene, Oreg. (160)	79	106	113	138	22.4	2,962	38.0
Evansville, Ind. (182)	139	130	126	122	-3.7	3,102	40.7
Fayetteville, N.C. (184)	N.A.	N.A.	76	121	59.9	N.A.	N.A.
Flint, Mich. (175)	193	160	141	125	-11.2	4,161	33.8
Fontana, Calif. (167)	N.A.	N.A.	88	129	47.3	N.A.	N.A.
Fort Collins, Colo. (189)	N.A.	N.A.	88	119	35.2	N.A.	N.A.
Fort Lauderdale, Fla. (134)	140	153	149	152	2.0	4,753	31.4
Fort Wayne, Ind. (85)	178	172	173	206	18.9	2,762	62.7
Fort Worth, Texas (27)	393	385	448	535	19.5	1,592	281.1
Fremont, Calif. (87)	101	132	173	203	17.3	2,250	77.0
Fresno, Calif. (37)	166	217	354	428	20.7	3,573	99.1
Fullerton, Calif. (173)	86	102	114	126	10.4	5,160	22.1
Garden Grove, Calif. (127)	121	123	143	165	15.5	7,974	17.9
Garland, Texas (83)	81	139	181	216	19.4	3,150	57.4
Gary, Ind. (230)	175	152	117	103	-11.9	2,322	50.2
Gilbert town, Ariz. (208)	N.A.	N.A.	29	110	275.8	N.A.	N.A.
Glendale, Ariz. (81)	36	97	148	219	47.7	2,837	52.2
Glendale, Calif. (100)	133	139	180	195	8.3	5,882	30.6
Grand Prairie, Texas (172)	N.A.	N.A.	100	127	27.9	N.A.	N.A.
Grand Rapids, Mich. (96)	198	182	189	198	4.6	4,273	44.3
Green Bay, Wisc. (233)	N.A.	N.A.	96	102	6.1	N.A.	N.A.
Greensboro, N.C. (78)	144	156	184	224	22.0	2,304	79.8
Hampton, Va. (147)	121	123	134	146	9.5	2,583	51.8
Hartford, Conn. (183)	158	136	140	122	-13.0	8,077	17.3
Hayward, Calif. (154)	93	94	111	140	25.6	2,560	43.5
Henderson, Nevada (118)	N.A.	N.A.	65	175	170.1	N.A.	N.A.
Hialeah, Fla. (76)	102	145	188	226	20.4	9,772	19.2
Hollywood, Fla. (157)	107	121	122	139	14.5	4,464	27.3
Honolulu, Hawaii[2] (47)	325	365	365	372	1.7	4,400	85.7
Houston, Texas (4)	1,234	1,595	1,631	1,954	19.8	3,021	539.9
Huntington Beach, Calif. (103)	116	171	182	190	4.4	6,871	26.4
Huntsville, Ala. (130)	139	143	160	158	-1.0	973	164.4
Independence, Mo. (202)	112	112	112	113	0.9	1,436	78.2
Indianapolis , Ind. (12)	737	701	742	792	6.7	2,022	361.7
Inglewood, Calif. (204)	90	94	110	113	2.7	11,952	9.2
Irvine, Calif. (150)	(3)	62	110	143	29.7	2,607	42.3
Irving, Texas (102)	97	110	155	192	23.6	2,293	67.6
Jackson, Miss. (111)	154	203	197	184	-6.3	1,804	109.0
Jacksonville, Fla. (14)	504	541	635	736	15.8	837	758.7
Jersey City, N.J. (73)	260	224	229	240	5.0	15,337	14.9
Joliet, Ill. (221)	N.A.	N.A.	77	106	38.2	N.A.	N.A.
Kansas City, Kans. (146)	168	161	150	147	-1.9	1,390	107.8
Kansas City, Mo. (36)	507	448	435	442	1.5	1,397	311.5
Knoxville, Tenn. (119)	175	175	165	174	5.3	2,135	77.2
Lafayette, La. (207)	N.A.	N.A.	94	110	16.7	N.A.	N.A.
Lakewood, Colo. (148)	93	114	126	144	14.0	3,100	40.8
Lancaster, Calif. (188)	N.A.	N.A.	97	119	22.0	N.A.	N.A.
Lansing, Mich. (187)	131	130	127	119	-6.4	3,755	33.9
Laredo, Texas (117)	69	91	123	177	43.7	3,739	32.9
Las Vegas, Nevada (32)	126	165	258	478	85.2	3,100	83.3
Lexington-Fayette, Ky. (65)	108	204	225	261	15.6	792	284.5
Lincoln, Neb. (77)	150	172	192	226	17.5	3,033	63.3
Little Rock, Ark. (112)	132	159	176	183	4.2	1,709	102.9
Livonia, Mich. (242)	110	105	101	101	-0.3	2,823	35.7
Long Beach, Calif. (34)	359	361	429	462	7.5	8,586	50.0
Los Angeles, Calif. (2)	2,812	2,969	3,485	3,695	6.0	7,426	469.3
Louisville, Ky. (67)	362	299	269	256	-4.8	4,341	62.1
Lowell, Mass. (222)	94	92	103	105	1.7	7,506	13.8

City (Rank, 2000)	Population ('000s)				Percent change 1990-2000	Population per sq. mi. 1990	Land area (sq.mi.) 1990
	1970	1980	1990	2000			
Lubbock, Texas (92)	149	174	186	200	7.2%	1,789	104.1
Madison, Wisc. (84)	172	171	191	208	8.8	3,300	57.8
Manchester, N.H. (218)	N.A.	N.A.	100	107	7.5	N.A.	N.A.
McAllen, Texas (220)	N.A.	N.A.	84	106	26.7	N.A.	N.A.
Memphis, Tenn. (18)	624	646	610	650	6.5	2,384	256.0
Mesa, Ariz. (43)	63	152	288	396	37.6	2,653	108.6
Mesquite, Texas (176)	55	67	101	125	22.7	2,369	42.8
Miami, Fla. (48)	335	347	359	362	1.1	10,074	35.6
Milwaukee, Wisc. (19)	717	636	628	597	-5.0	6,537	96.1
Minneapolis, Minn. (46)	434	371	368	383	3.9	6,706	54.9
Mobile, Ala. (94)	190	200	196	199	1.3	1,663	118.0
Modesto, Calif. (104)	62	107	165	189	14.6	5,458	30.2
Montgomery, Ala. (89)	133	178	187	202	7.7	1,389	135.0
Moreno Valley, Calif. (152)	.(3)	(3)	119	142	19.9	2,418	49.1
Naperville, Ill. (169)	N.A.	N.A.	85	128	50.4	N.A.	N.A.
Nashville-Davidson, Tenn.[1] (22)	426	456	511	570	11.6	1,032	473.3
New Haven, Conn. (179)	138	126	130	124	-5.2	6,922	18.9
New Orleans, La. (31)	593	558	497	485	-2.5	2,751	180.7
New York, N.Y. (1)	7,896	7,072	7,323	8,008	9.4	23,701	309.0
Newark, N.J. (64)	382	329	275	274	-0.6	11,554	23.8
Newport News, Va. (115)	138	145	170	180	5.9	2,510	68.3
Norfolk, Va. (74)	308	267	261	234	-10.3	4,856	53.8
North Las Vegas, Nevada (198)	N.A.	N.A.	48	115	142.1	N.A.	N.A.
Norwalk, Calif. (229)	N.A.	N.A.	94	103	9.6	N.A.	N.A.
Oakland, Calif. (42)	362	339	372	399	7.3	6,640	56.1
Oceanside, Calif. (128)	40	77	128	161	25.4	3,164	40.5
Oklahoma City, Okla. (29)	368	404	445	506	13.8	731	608.2
Omaha, Neb. (45)	347	314	336	390	16.1	3,336	100.7
Ontario, Calif. (131)	64	89	133	158	18.6	3,624	36.8
Orange, Calif. (168)	77	91	111	129	16.4	4,741	23.3
Orlando, Fla. (107)	99	128	165	186	12.9	2,448	67.3
Overland Park, Kans. (143)	78	82	112	149	33.4	2,007	55.7
Oxnard, Calif. (124)	71	108	142	170	19.8	5,843	24.4
Palmdale, Calif. (194)	N.A.	N.A.	69	117	69.5	N.A.	N.A.
Pasadena, Calif. (163)	113	118	132	134	1.8	5,724	23.0
Pasadena, Texas (153)	90	113	119	142	18.7	2,726	43.8
Paterson, N.J. (142)	145	138	141	149	5.9	16,693	8.4
Pembroke Pines, Fla. (161)	N.A.	N.A.	65	137	110.0	N.A.	N.A.
Peoria, Ariz. (214)	N.A.	N.A.	51	108	114.1	N.A.	N.A.
Peoria, Ill. (203)	127	124	114	113	-0.5	2,776	40.9
Philadelphia, Pa. [1] (5)	1,949	1,688	1,586	1,518	-4.3	11,734	135.1
Phoenix, Ariz. (6)	584	790	983	1,321	34.3	2,342	419.9
Pittsburgh, Pa. (53)	520	424	370	335	-9.5	6,649	55.6
Plano, Texas (79)	18	72	129	222	72.5	1,929	66.3
Pomona, Calif. (141)	87	93	132	149	13.5	5,770	22.8
Ponce, Puerto Rico (133)	N.A.	N.A.	159	155	-2.6	N.A.	N.A.
Portland, Oreg. (28)	380	368	437	529	21.0	3,508	124.7
Portsmouth, Va. (241)	111	105	104	101	-3.2	3,139	33.1
Providence, R.I. (121)	179	157	161	174	8.0	8,707	18.5
Provo, Utah (223)	N.A.	N.A.	87	105	21.1	N.A.	N.A.
Pueblo, Colo. (236)	N.A.	N.A.	99	102	3.5	N.A.	N.A.
Raleigh, N.C. (63)	123	150	208	276	32.8	2,395	88.1
Rancho Cucamonga,Calif. (171)	(3)	55	101	128	26.0	2,682	37.8
Reno, Nevada (114)	73	101	134	180	34.8	2,328	57.5
Richmond, Va. (97)	249	219	203	198	-2.6	3,374	60.1
Riverside, Calif. (68)	140	171	227	255	12.7	2,916	77.7
Rochester, N.Y. (80)	295	242	232	220	-5.1	6,435	35.8
Rockford, Ill. (140)	147	140	139	150	7.7	3,110	45.0
Sacramento, Calif. (41)	257	276	369	407	10.2	3,836	96.3
Salem, Oreg. (162)	69	89	108	137	27.0	2,595	41.5
Salinas, Calif. (138)	59	80	109	151	38.9	5,839	18.6
Salt Lake City, Utah (113)	176	163	160	182	13.6	1,467	109.0
San Antonio, Texas (9)	654	786	936	1,145	22.3	2,810	333.0
San Bernardino, Calif. (110).	107	119	164	185	12.9	2,980	55.1
San Diego, Calif. (7)	697	876	1,111	1,223	10.2	3,428	324.0
San Francisco, Calif. [1] (13)	716	679	724	777	7.3	15,502	46.7
San Jose, Calif. (11)	460	629	782	895	14.4	4,568	171.3
San Juan , Puerto Rico (39)	N.A.	N.A.	427	422	-1.1	N.A.	N.A.
Santa Ana, Calif. (52)	156	204	294	338	15.1	10,842	27.1
Santa Clara, Calif. (232)	N.A.	N.A.	94	102	9.3	N.A.	N.A.
Santa Clarita, Calif. (137)	(3)	(3)	111	151	36.6%	2,733	40.5
Santa Rosa, Calif. (144)	50	83	113	148	30.3	3,362	33.7

City (Rank, 2000)	Population ('000s) 1970	1980	1990	2000	Percent change 1990-2000	Population per sq. mi. 1990	Land area (sq.mi.) 1990
Savannah, Ga. (166)	118	142	138	132	-4.4	2,204	62.6
Scottsdale, Ariz. (88)	68	89	130	203	55.8	706	184.4
Seattle, Wash. (24)	531	494	516	563	9.1	6,154	83.9
Shreveport, La. (90)	182	206	199	200	0.8	2,013	98.6
Simi Valley, Calif. (206)	60	78	100	111	11.1	3,034	33.0
Sioux Falls, SD (178)	72	81	101	124	23.0	2,236	45.1
South Bend, Ind. (215)	126	110	106	108	2.2	2,897	36.4
Spokane, Wash. (99)	171	171	177	196	10.4	3,169	55.9
Springfield, Ill. (205)	92	100	105	111	5.9	2,474	42.5
Springfield, Mass. (135)	164	152	157	152	-3.1	4,890	32.1
Springfield, Mo. (136)	120	133	140	152	7.9	2,068	68.0
St. Louis, Mo. (50)	622	453	397	348	-12.2	6,405	61.9
St. Paul, Minn. (60)	310	270	272	287	5.5	5,157	52.8
St. Petersburg, Fla. (69)	216	239	239	248	4.0	4,059	59.2
Stamford, Conn. (191)	109	102	108	117	8.4	2,865	37.7
Sterling Heights, Mich. (177)	61	109	118	124	5.7	3,215	36.6
Stockton, Calif. (71)	110	150	211	244	15.6	4,013	52.6
Sunnyvale, Calif. (165)	96	107	117	132	12.4	5,353	21.9
Syracuse, N.Y. (145)	197	170	164	147	-10.1	6,528	25.1
Tacoma, Wash. (101)	154	159	177	194	9.6	3,677	48.1
Tallahassee, Fla. (139)	73	82	125	151	20.7	1,972	63.3
Tampa, Fla. (58)	278	272	280	303	8.4	2,577	108.7
Tempe, Ariz. (129)	64	107	142	159	11.8	3,590	39.5
Thousand Oaks, Calif. (192)	36	77	104	117	12.1	2,104	49.6
Toledo, Ohio (57)	383	355	333	314	-5.8	4,132	80.6
Topeka, Kans. (180)	125	119	120	122	2.1	2,173	55.2
Torrance, Calif. (159)	135	130	133	138	3.6	6,487	20.5
Tucson, Ariz. (30)	263	331	405	487	20.1	2,594	156.3
Tulsa, Okla. (44)	330	361	367	393	7.0	2,001	183.5
Vallejo, Calif. (193)	72	80	109	117	6.9	3,613	30.2
Vancouver, Wash. (149)	N.A.	N.A.	46	144	209.5	N.A.	N.A.
Ventura, Calif. (240)	N.A.	N.A.	93	101	9.0	N.A.	N.A.
Virginia Beach, Va. (38)	172	262	393	425	8.2	1,583	248.3
Waco, Texas (201)	95	101	104	114	9.8	1,367	75.8
Warren, Mich. (158)	179	161	145	138	-4.6	4,226	34.3
Washington, D.C. (21)	757	638	607	572	-5.7	9,883	61.4
Waterbury, Conn. (217)	108	103	109	107	-1.6	3,815	28.6
West Covina, Calif. (224)	N.A.	N.A.	96	105	9.4	N.A.	N.A.
West Valley City, Utah (211)	N.A.	N.A.	87	109	25.2	N.A.	N.A.
Westminster, Colo. (239)	N.A.	N.A.	75	101	35.3	N.A.	N.A.
Wichita Falls, Texas (225)	N.A.	N.A.	96	104	8.2	N.A.	N.A.
Wichita, Kans. (51)	277	280	304	344	13.2	2,640	115.1
Winston-Salem, N.C. (109)	134	132*	143	186	29.5	2,018	71.1
Worcester, Mass. (123)	177	162	170	173	1.7	4,520	37.6
Yonkers, N.Y. (98)	204	195	188	196	4.3	10,403	18.1

Note: Cities over 100,000 population. 1. Represents the portion of a consolidated city not within one or more separately incorporated areas. 2. Data represent the census designated place of Honolulu, as delineated by the State of Hawaii. 3. Not incorporated
Source: U.S. Bureau of the Census, Statistical Abstract of the United States 1990 (1990), and Release (2001).

Cities, by Population Size, 1960–90

Population size	Number of Cities 1960	1970	1980	1990	Population (mil.) 1960	1970	1980	1990	Percent of Total 1960	1970	1980	1990
Total	18,088	18,666	19,097	19,262	115.9	131.9	140.3	152.9	100%	100%	100%	100%
1 million +	5	6	6	8	17.5	18.8	17.5	20.0	15.1	14.2	12.5	13.0
500,000-1 million	16	20	16	15	11.1	13.0	10.9	10.1	9.6	9.8	7.8	6.6
250,000-500,000	30	30	33	41	10.8	10.5	11.8	14.2	9.3	7.9	8.4	9.3
100,000-250,000	79	97	114	131	11.4	13.9	16.6	19.1	9.8	10.5	11.8	12.5
50,000-100,000	180	232	250	309	12.5	16.2	17.6	21.2	10.8	12.2	12.3	13.9
25,000-50,000	366	455	526	567	12.7	15.7	18.4	20.0	11.0	11.9	13.1	13.0
10,000-25,000	978	1,127	1,260	1,290	15.1	17.6	19.8	20.3	13.1	13.3	14.1	13.3
<10,000	16,434	16,699	16,892	16,901	24.9	26.4	28.0	28.2	21.5	20.0	20.0	18.4

Source: U.S. Bureau of the Census, Statistical Abstract of the United States (annual).

Resident Population of Major U.S Cities by Race and Hispanic Origin, 2000

Geographic area	Total population	Black	American Indian	Asian	Native Hawaiian	Some other race	Two or more races	Hispanic or Latino (any race)
Abilene, Texas	115,930	8.8%	0.6%	1.3%	0.1%	8.7%	2.4%	19.4%
Akron, Ohio	217,074	28.5	0.3	1.5	-	0.4	2.1	1.2
Albuquerque, N.Mex.	448,607	3.1	3.9	2.2	0.1	14.8	4.3	39.9
Alexandria, Va.	128,283	22.5	0.3	5.7	0.1	7.4	4.3	14.7
Allentown, Pa.	106,632	7.8	0.3	2.3	0.1	13.4	3.6	24.4
Amarillo, Texas	173,627	6.0	0.8	2.1	-	11.3	2.3	21.9
Anaheim, Calif.	328,014	2.7	0.9	12.0	0.4	24.2	5.0	46.8
Anchorage, Alaska	260,283	5.8	7.3	5.5	0.9	2.2	6.0	5.7
Ann Arbor, Mich.	114,024	8.8	0.3	11.9	-	1.2	3.1	3.3
Arlington, Texas	332,969	13.7	0.5	6.0	0.1	8.9	2.9	18.3
Arlington, Va.	189,453	9.3	0.3	8.6	0.1	8.3	4.3	18.6
Arvada, Colo.	102,153	0.7	0.7	2.2	0.1	3.1	2.3	9.8
Athens, Ga.	101,489	27.3	0.2	3.1	-	3.1	1.4	6.3
Atlanta, Ga.	416,474	61.4	0.2	1.9	-	2.0	1.2	4.5
Augusta, Ga.	199,775	49.8	0.3	1.5	0.1	1.0	1.8	2.8
Aurora, Colo.	276,393	13.4	0.8	4.4	0.2	8.1	4.2	19.8
Aurora, Ill.	142,990	11.1	0.4	3.1	-	14.5	2.9	32.6
Austin, Texas	656,562	10.0	0.6	4.7	0.1	16.2	3.0	30.5
Bakersfield, Calif.	247,057	9.2	1.4	4.3	0.1	18.7	4.4	32.5
Baltimore, Md.	651,154	64.3	0.3	1.5	-	0.7	1.5	1.7
Baton Rouge, La.	227,818	50.0	0.2	2.6	-	0.5	1.0	1.7
Beaumont, Texas	113,866	45.8	0.2	2.5	-	3.5	1.5	7.9
Bellevue, Wash.	109,569	2.0	0.3	17.4	0.2	2.5	3.2	5.3
Berkeley, Calif.	102,743	13.6	0.5	16.4	0.1	4.6	5.6	9.7
Birmingham, Ala.	242,820	73.5	0.2	0.8	-	0.6	0.8	1.6
Boise City, Idaho	185,787	0.8	0.7	2.1	0.2	1.7	2.4	4.5
Boston, Mass.	589,141	25.3	0.4	7.5	0.1	7.8	4.4	14.4
Bridgeport, Conn.	139,529	30.8	0.5	3.3	0.1	14.8	5.6	31.9
Brownsville, Texas	139,722	0.4	0.4	0.5	-	14.7	2.3	91.3
Buffalo, N.Y.	292,648	37.2	0.8	1.4	-	3.7	2.5	7.5
Burbank, Calif.	100,316	2.1	0.5	9.2	0.1	9.9	6.0	24.9
Cambridge, Mass.	101,355	11.9	0.3	11.9	0.1	3.2	4.6	7.4
Cape Coral, Fla.	102,286	2.0	0.3	0.9	0.1	2.2	1.6	8.3
Carrollton, Texas	109,576	6.3	0.5	10.9	0.1	7.7	2.7	19.5
Cedar Rapids, Iowa	120,758	3.7	0.3	1.8	0.1	0.6	1.8	1.7
Chandler, Ariz.	176,581	3.5	1.2	4.2	0.1	10.8	3.0	21.0
Charlotte, N.C.	540,828	32.7	0.3	3.4	0.1	3.6	1.7	7.4
Chattanooga, Tenn.	155,554	36.1	0.3	1.5	0.1	1.0	1.3	2.1
Chesapeake, Va.	199,184	28.5	0.4	1.8	0.1	0.7	1.6	2.0
Chicago, Ill.	2,896,016	36.8	0.4	4.3	0.1	13.6	2.9	26.0
Chula Vista, Calif.	173,556	4.6	0.8	11.0	0.6	22.1	5.8	49.6
Cincinnati, Ohio	331,285	42.9	0.2	1.5	-	0.6	1.7	1.3
Clarksville, Tenn.	103,455	23.2	0.5	2.2	0.3	2.6	3.3	6.0
Clearwater, Fla.	108,787	9.8	0.3	1.6	0.1	2.5	1.8	9.0
Cleveland, Ohio	478,403	51.0	0.3	1.3	-	3.6	2.2	7.3
Colorado Springs, Colo.	360,890	6.6	0.9	2.8	0.2	5.0	3.9	12.0
Columbia, S.C.	116,278	46.0	0.3	1.7	0.1	1.4	1.4	3.0
Columbus, Ga.	186,291	43.7	0.4	1.5	0.1	1.9	1.9	4.5
Columbus, Ohio	711,470	24.5	0.3	3.4	0.1	1.2	2.6	2.5
Concord, Calif.	121,780	3.0	0.8	9.4	0.5	9.7	5.9	21.8
Coral Springs, Fla.	117,549	9.2	0.2	3.5	0.1	3.0	2.5	15.5
Corona, Calif.	124,966	6.4	0.9	7.5	0.3	17.5	5.3	35.7
Corpus Christi, Texas	277,454	4.7	0.6	1.3	0.1	18.6	3.1	54.3
Costa Mesa, Calif.	108,724	1.4	0.8	6.9	0.6	16.6	4.3	31.8
Dallas, Texas	1,188,580	25.9	0.5	2.7	-	17.2	2.7	35.6
Daly City, Calif.	103,621	4.6	0.4	50.7	0.9	11.3	6.2	22.3
Dayton, Ohio	166,179	43.1	0.3	0.6	-	0.7	1.8	1.6
Denver, Colo.	554,636	11.1	1.3	2.8	0.1	15.6	3.7	31.7
Des Moines, Iowa	198,682	8.1	0.4	3.5	-	3.5	2.2	6.6
Detroit, Mich.	951,270	81.6	0.3	1.0	-	2.5	2.3	5.0
Downey, Calif.	107,323	3.8	0.9	7.7	0.2	29.1	4.9	57.9
Durham, N.C.	187,035	43.8	0.3	3.6	-	4.7	1.9	8.6
East Los Angeles, Calif.	124,283	0.4	1.3	0.8	0.1	54.0	4.2	96.8
El Monte, Calif.	115,965	0.8	1.4	18.5	0.1	39.3	4.3	72.4
El Paso, Texas	563,662	3.1	0.8	1.1	0.1	18.2	3.4	76.6
Elizabeth, N.J.	120,568	20.0	0.5	2.3	-	15.5	5.9	49.5
Erie, Pa.	103,717	14.2	0.2	0.7	-	1.9	2.3	4.4
Escondido, Calif.	133,559	2.3	1.2	4.5	0.2	19.2	4.8	38.7
Eugene, Oreg.	137,893	1.3	0.9	3.6	0.2	2.2	3.7	5.0

Geographic area	Total population	Black	American Indian	Asian	Native Hawaiian	Some other race	Two or more races	Hispanic or Latino (any race)
Evansville, Ind.	121,582	10.9%	0.2%	0.7%	-	0.5%	1.4%	1.1%
Fayetteville, N.C.	121,015	42.4	1.1	2.2	0.2%	2.5	2.8	5.7
Flint, Mich.	124,943	53.3	0.6	0.4	-	1.1	3.1	3.0
Fontana, Calif.	128,929	11.8	1.1	4.4	0.3	31.9	5.4	57.7
Fort Collins, Colo.	118,652	1.0	0.6	2.5	0.1	3.6	2.5	8.8
Fort Lauderdale, Fla.	152,397	28.9	0.2	1.0	-	1.8	3.8	9.5
Fort Wayne, Ind.	205,727	17.4	0.4	1.6	-	2.9	2.3	5.8
Fort Worth, Texas	534,694	20.3	0.6	2.6	0.1	14.0	2.7	29.8
Fremont, Calif.	203,413	3.1	0.5	37.0	0.4	5.5	5.8	13.5
Fresno, Calif.	427,652	8.4	1.6	11.2	0.1	23.4	5.2	39.9
Fullerton, Calif.	126,003	2.3	0.7	16.1	0.2	14.8	4.0	30.2
Garden Grove, Calif.	165,196	1.3	0.8	30.9	0.7	15.4	4.1	32.5
Garland, Texas	215,768	11.9	0.6	7.3	0.1	12.0	2.9	25.6
Gary, Ind.	102,746	84.0	0.2	0.1	-	2.0	1.7	4.9
Gilbert, Ariz.	109,697	2.4	0.6	3.6	0.1	4.8	2.8	11.9
Glendale, Ariz.	218,812	4.7	1.5	2.7	0.1	12.0	3.5	24.8
Glendale, Calif.	194,973	1.3	0.3	16.1	0.1	8.6	10.1	19.7
Grand Prairie, Texas	127,427	13.5	0.8	4.4	0.1	15.9	3.3	33.0
Grand Rapids, Mich.	197,800	20.4	0.7	1.6	0.1	6.6	3.2	13.1
Green Bay, Wisc.	102,313	1.4	3.3	3.8	-	3.7	2.0	7.1
Greensboro, N.C.	223,891	37.4	0.4	2.8	-	2.1	1.7	4.4
Hampton, Va.	146,437	44.7	0.4	1.8	0.1	1.0	2.4	2.8
Hartford, Conn.	121,578	38.1	0.5	1.6	0.1	26.5	5.4	40.5
Hayward, Calif.	140,030	11.0	0.8	19.0	1.9	16.8	7.5	34.2
Henderson, Nevada	175,381	3.8	0.7	4.0	0.4	3.2	3.5	10.7
Hialeah, Fla.	226,419	2.4	0.1	0.4	-	5.5	3.6	90.3
Hollywood, Fla.	139,357	12.1	0.3	2.0	0.1	4.0	3.3	22.5
Honolulu, Hawaii	371,657	1.6	0.2	55.9	6.8	0.9	14.9	4.4
Houston, Texas	1,953,631	25.3	0.4	5.3	0.1	16.5	3.1	37.4
Huntington Beach, Calif.	189,594	0.8	0.6	9.3	0.2	5.8	3.9	14.7
Huntsville, Ala.	158,216	30.2	0.5	2.2	0.1	0.7	1.8	2.0
Independence, Mo.	113,288	2.6	0.6	0.7	0.5	1.4	2.3	3.7
Indianapolis, Ind.	791,926	25.3	0.3	1.4	-	2.0	1.6	3.9
Inglewood, Calif.	112,580	47.1	0.7	1.1	0.4	27.4	4.2	46.0
Irvine, Calif.	143,072	1.4	0.2	29.8	0.1	2.5	4.8	7.4
Irving, Texas	191,615	10.2	0.6	8.2	0.1	13.4	3.2	31.2
Jackson, Miss.	184,256	70.6	0.1	0.6	-	0.2	0.7	0.8
Jacksonville, Fla.	735,617	29.0	0.3	2.8	0.1	1.3	2.0	4.2
Jersey City, N.J.	240,055	28.3	0.4	16.2	0.1	15.1	5.8	28.3
Joliet, Ill.	106,221	18.2	0.3	1.1	-	9.0	2.1	18.4
Kansas City, Kans.	146,866	30.1	0.8	1.7	-	8.6	3.0	16.8
Kansas City, Mo.	441,545	31.2	0.5	1.9	0.1	3.2	2.4	6.9
Knoxville, Tenn.	173,890	16.2	0.3	1.5	-	0.7	1.6	1.6
Lafayette, La.	110,257	28.5	0.2	1.4	-	0.6	1.0	1.9
Lakewood, Colo.	144,126	1.5	1.1	2.7	0.1	4.9	2.6	14.5
Lancaster, Calif.	118,718	16.0	1.0	3.8	0.2	11.1	5.0	24.1
Lansing, Mich.	119,128	21.9	0.8	2.8	0.1	4.5	4.6	10.0
Laredo, Texas	176,576	0.4	0.4	0.5	-	13.9	2.5	94.1
Las Vegas, Nevada	478,434	10.4	0.7	4.8	0.4	9.7	4.1	23.6
Lexington-Fayette, Ky.	260,512	13.5	0.2	2.5	-	1.2	1.6	3.3
Lincoln, Neb.	225,581	3.1	0.7	3.1	0.1	1.8	2.0	3.6
Little Rock, Ark.	183,133	40.4	0.3	1.7	-	1.3	1.3	2.7
Livonia, Mich.	100,545	0.9	0.2	1.9	-	0.3	1.1	1.7
Long Beach, Calif.	461,522	14.9	0.8	12.0	1.2	20.6	5.3	35.8
Los Angeles, Calif.	3,694,820	11.2	0.8	10.0	0.2	25.7	5.2	46.5
Louisville, Ky.	256,231	33.0	0.2	1.4	-	0.7	1.7	1.9
Lowell, Mass.	105,167	4.2	0.2	16.5	-	6.5	3.9	14.0
Lubbock, Texas	199,564	8.7	0.6	1.5	-	14.3	2.0	27.5
Madison, Wisc.	208,054	5.8	0.4	5.8	-	1.7	2.3	4.1
Manchester, N.H.	107,006	2.1	0.3	2.3	-	1.8	1.7	4.6
McAllen, Texas	106,414	0.6	0.4	1.9	-	15.8	2.7	80.3
Memphis, Tenn.	650,100	61.4	0.2	1.5	-	1.5	1.0	3.0
Mesa, Ariz.	396,375	2.5	1.7	1.5	0.2	9.7	2.8	19.7
Mesquite, Texas	124,523	13.3	0.6	3.7	0.1	6.4	2.3	15.7
Metairie, La.	146,136	6.8	0.3	2.8	-	1.9	1.7	7.3
Miami, Fla.	362,470	22.3	0.2	0.7	-	5.4	4.7	65.8
Milwaukee, Wisc.	596,974	37.3	0.9	2.9	0.1	6.1	2.7	12.0
Minneapolis, Minn.	382,618	18.0	2.2	6.1	0.1	4.1	4.4	7.6
Mobile, Ala.	198,915	46.3	0.2	1.5	-	0.5	1.0	1.4
Modesto, Calif.	188,856	4.0	1.2	6.0	0.5	12.7	5.9	25.6
Montgomery, Ala.	201,568	49.6	0.2	1.1	-	0.4	1.0	1.2

Geographic area	Total population	Black	American Indian	Asian	Native Hawaiian	Some other race	Two or more races	Hispanic or Latino (any race)
Moreno Valley, Calif.	142,381	19.9%	0.9%	5.9%	0.5%	20.1%	5.8%	38.4%
Naperville, Ill.	128,358	3.0	0.1	9.6	-	0.8	1.2	3.2
Nashville-Davidson, Tenn..	569,891	25.9	0.3	2.3	0.1	2.4	2.0	4.6
New Haven, Conn.	123,626	37.4	0.4	3.9	0.1	10.9	3.9	21.4
New Orleans, La.	484,674	67.3	0.2	2.3	-	0.9	1.3	3.1
New York, N.Y.	8,008,278	26.6	0.5	9.8	0.1	13.4	4.9	27.0
Bronx borough	1,332,650	35.6	0.9	3.0	0.1	24.7	5.8	48.4
Brooklyn borough	2,465,326	36.4	0.4	7.5	0.1	10.1	4.3	19.8
Manhattan borough	1,537,195	17.4	0.5	9.4	0.1	14.1	4.1	27.2
Queens borough	2,229,379	20.0	0.5	17.6	0.1	11.7	6.1	25.0
Staten Island borough	443,728	9.7	0.2	5.7	-	4.1	2.7	12.1
Newark, N.J.	273,546	53.5	0.4	1.2	-	14.0	4.4	29.5
Newport News, Va.	180,150	39.1	0.4	2.3	0.1	1.8	2.8	4.2
Norfolk, Va.	234,403	44.1	0.5	2.8	0.1	1.7	2.5	3.8
North Las Vegas, Nevada	115,488	19.0	0.8	3.2	0.5	15.8	4.7	37.6
Norwalk, Calif.	103,298	4.6	1.2	11.5	0.4	32.7	4.7	62.9
Oakland, Calif.	399,484	35.7	0.7	15.2	0.5	11.7	5.0	21.9
Oceanside, Calif.	161,029	6.3	0.9	5.5	1.3	14.5	5.2	30.2
Oklahoma City, Okla.	506,132	15.4	3.5	3.5	0.1	5.3	3.9	10.1
Omaha, Neb.	390,007	13.3	0.7	1.7	0.1	3.9	1.9	7.5
Ontario, Calif.	158,007	7.5	1.1	3.9	0.4	34.1	5.3	59.9
Orange, Calif.	128,821	1.6	0.8	9.3	0.2	13.8	3.8	32.2
Orlando, Fla.	185,951	26.9	0.3	2.7	0.1	5.4	3.5	17.5
Overland Park, Kans.	149,080	2.5	0.3	3.8	-	1.2	1.4	3.8
Oxnard, Calif.	170,358	3.8	1.3	7.4	0.4	40.4	4.7	66.2
Palmdale, Calif.	116,670	14.5	1.0	3.8	0.2	20.4	5.2	37.7
Paradise, Nevada	186,070	6.6	0.8	6.5	0.6	8.4	4.7	23.5
Pasadena, Calif.	133,936	14.4	0.7	10.0	0.1	16.0	5.4	33.4
Pasadena, Texas	141,674	1.6	0.7	1.8	-	21.3	3.1	48.2
Paterson, N.J.	149,222	32.9	0.6	1.9	0.1	27.6	6.2	50.1
Pembroke Pines, Fla.	137,427	13.3	0.2	3.8	-	3.7	3.5	28.2
Peoria, Ariz.	108,364	2.8	0.7	1.9	0.1	7.1	2.5	15.4
Peoria, Ill.	112,936	24.8	0.2	2.3	-	1.2	2.2	2.5
Philadelphia, Pa.	1,517,550	43.2	0.3	4.5	-	4.8	2.2	8.5
Phoenix, Ariz.	1,321,045	5.1	2.0	2.0	0.1	16.4	3.3	34.1
Pittsburgh, Pa.	334,563	27.1	0.2	2.7	-	0.7	1.6	1.3
Plano, Texas	222,030	5.0	0.4	10.2	-	3.9	2.3	10.1
Pomona, Calif.	149,473	9.6	1.3	7.2	0.2	34.9	5.0	64.5
Portland, Oreg.	529,121	6.6	1.1	6.3	0.4	3.5	4.1	6.8
Portsmouth, Va.	100,565	50.6	0.5	0.8	0.1	0.6	1.6	1.7
Providence, R.I.	173,618	14.5	1.1	6.0	0.2	17.6	6.1	30.0
Provo, Utah	105,166	0.5	0.8	1.8	0.8	5.1	2.4	10.5
Pueblo, Colo.	102,121	2.4	1.7	0.7	0.1	15.2	3.7	44.1
Raleigh, N.C.	276,093	27.8	0.4	3.4	-	3.2	1.9	7.0
Rancho Cucamonga, Calif.	127,743	7.9	0.7	6.0	0.3	13.3	5.4	27.8
Reno, Nevada	180,480	2.6	1.3	5.3	0.6	9.3	3.6	19.2
Richmond, Va.	197,790	57.2	0.2	1.2	0.1	1.5	1.5	2.6
Riverside, Calif.	255,166	7.4	1.1	5.7	0.4	21.0	5.1	38.1
Rochester, N.Y.	219,773	38.5	0.5	2.2	-	6.6	3.8	12.8
Rockford, Ill.	150,115	17.4	0.3	2.2	-	4.8	2.5	10.2
Sacramento, Calif.	407,018	15.5	1.3	16.6	0.9	11.0	6.4	21.6
Salem, Oreg.	136,924	1.3	1.5	2.4	0.5	7.9	3.4	14.6
Salinas, Calif.	151,060	3.3	1.3	6.2	0.3	38.7	5.1	64.1
Salt Lake City, Utah	181,743	1.9	1.3	3.6	1.9	8.5	3.5	18.8
San Antonio, Texas	1,144,646	6.8	0.8	1.6	0.1	19.3	3.7	58.7
San Bernardino, Calif.	185,401	16.4	1.4	4.2	0.4	27.1	5.3	47.5
San Diego, Calif.	1,223,400	7.9	0.6	13.6	0.5	12.4	4.8	25.4
San Francisco, Calif.	776,733	7.8	0.4	30.8	0.5	6.5	4.3	14.1
San Jose, Calif.	894,943	3.5	0.8	26.9	0.4	15.9	5.0	30.2
Santa Ana, Calif.	337,977	1.7	1.2	8.8	0.3	40.6	4.6	76.1
Santa Clara, Calif.	102,361	2.3	0.5	29.3	0.4	6.9	5.0	16.0
Santa Clarita, Calif.	151,088	2.1	0.6	5.2	0.1	8.5	3.9	20.5
Santa Rosa, Calif.	147,595	2.2	1.4	3.8	0.3	10.3	4.4	19.2
Savannah, Ga.	131,510	57.1	0.2	1.5	0.1	0.9	1.3	2.2
Scottsdale, Ariz.	202,705	1.2	0.6	2.0	0.1	2.3	1.7	7.0
Seattle, Wash.	563,374	8.4	1.0	13.1	0.5	2.4	4.5	5.3
Shreveport, La.	200,145	50.8	0.3	0.8	-	0.4	1.0	1.6
Simi Valley, Calif.	111,351	1.3	0.7	6.3	0.1	6.5	3.7	16.8
Sioux Falls S. Dak.	123,975	1.8	2.1	1.2	0.1	1.2	1.7	2.5
South Bend, Ind.	107,789	24.6	0.4	1.2	0.1	4.9	2.8	8.5
Spokane, Wash.	195,629	2.1	1.8	2.2	0.2	0.9	3.4	3.0

Geographic area	Total population	Black	American Indian	Asian	Native Hawaiian	Some other race	Two or more races	Hispanic or Latino (any race)
Spring Valley, Nevada	117,390	5.3%	0.6%	11.2%	0.5%	5.1%	4.7%	13.8%
Springfield, Ill.	111,454	15.3	0.2	1.5	-	0.5	1.5	1.2
Springfield, Mass.	152,082	21.0	0.4	1.9	0.1	16.4	4.0	27.2
Springfield, Mo.	151,580	3.3	0.8	1.4	0.1	0.9	2.0	2.3
St. Louis, Mo.	348,189	51.2	0.3	2.0	-	0.8	1.9	2.0
St. Paul, Minn.	287,151	11.7	1.1	12.4	0.1	3.8	3.9	7.9
St. Petersburg, Fla.	248,232	22.4	0.3	2.7	0.1	1.1	2.2	4.2
Stamford, Conn.	117,083	15.4	0.2	5.0	-	6.5	3.1	16.8
Sterling Heights, Mich.	124,471	1.3	0.2	4.9	-	0.3	2.5	1.3
Stockton, Calif.	243,771	11.2	1.1	19.9	0.4	17.3	6.8	32.5
Sunnyvale, Calif.	131,760	2.2	0.5	32.3	0.3	7.2	4.3	15.5
Sunrise Manor, Nevada	156,120	12.9	1.0	5.4	0.5	10.1	4.7	26.0
Syracuse, N.Y.	147,306	25.3	1.1	3.4	-	2.2	3.6	5.3
Tacoma, Wash.	193,556	11.2	2.0	7.6	0.9	2.9	6.3	6.9
Tallahassee, Fla.	150,624	34.2	0.2	2.4	0.1	1.0	1.7	4.2
Tampa, Fla.	303,447	26.1	0.4	2.2	0.1	4.2	2.9	19.3
Tempe, Ariz.	158,625	3.7	2.0	4.7	0.3	8.5	3.3	17.9
Thousand Oaks, Calif.	117,005	1.1	0.5	5.9	0.1	4.5	2.8	13.1
Toledo, Ohio	313,619	23.5	0.3	1.0	-	2.3	2.6	5.5
Topeka, Kans.	122,377	11.7	1.3	1.1	-	4.1	3.3	8.9
Torrance, Calif.	137,946	2.2	0.4	28.6	0.3	4.6	4.7	12.8
Tucson, Ariz.	486,699	4.3	2.3	2.5	0.2	16.8	3.8	35.7
Tulsa, Okla.	393,049	15.5	4.7	1.8	0.1	3.5	4.4	7.2
Vallejo, Calif.	116,760	23.7	0.7	24.2	1.1	7.9	6.6	15.9
Vancouver, Wash.	143,560	2.5	1.0	4.5	0.5	2.9	3.8	6.3
Ventura, Calif.	100,916	1.4	1.2	3.0	0.2	11.1	4.3	24.3
Virginia Beach, Va.	425,257	19.0	0.4	4.9	0.1	1.5	2.7	4.2
Waco, Texas	113,726	22.6	0.5	1.4	0.1	12.4	2.3	23.6
Warren, Mich.	138,247	2.7	0.4	3.1	-	0.3	2.2	1.4
Washington, D.C.	572,059	60.0	0.3	2.7	0.1	3.8	2.4	7.9
Waterbury, Conn.	107,271	16.3	0.4	1.5	0.1	10.9	3.7	21.8
West Covina, Calif.	105,080	6.4	0.8	22.7	0.2	21.2	4.9	45.7
West Valley City, Utah	108,896	1.1	1.2	4.3	2.9	8.7	3.5	18.5
Westminster, Colo.	100,940	1.2	0.7	5.5	0.1	5.5	2.8	15.2
Wichita Falls, Texas	104,197	12.4	0.9	2.2	0.1	6.4	3.0	14.0
Wichita, Kans.	344,284	11.4	1.2	4.0	0.1	5.1	3.1	9.6
Winston-Salem, N.C.	185,776	37.1	0.3	1.1	-	4.3	1.6	8.6
Worcester, Mass.	172,648	6.9	0.4	4.9	0.1	7.2	3.4	15.1
Yonkers, N.Y	196,086	16.6	0.4	4.9	-	13.4	4.4	25.9

Note: Black includes African-American. Native American includes Alaska Native. Native Hawaiian includes other Pacific Islander. Cities with populations over 100,000 as of April 1, 2000. **Source:** U.S. Bureau of the Census, Press Release, 2001.

Population Change in the 75 Largest U.S. Cities, 1980–2000

City (2000 Rank)	Population 1980	Population 1990	Population 2000	Percent change, 1980–2000	Change, 1990–2000 Number	Change, 1990–2000 Percent
Albuquerque, N.Mex (35)	332,920	384,736	448,607	15.6%	63,871	16.6%
Anaheim, Calif. (56)	219,494	266,406	328,014	21.4	61,608	23.1
Anchorage, Alaska (66)	174,731	226,338	260,283	29.5	33,945	15.0
Arlington, Texas (54)	160,113	261,721	332,969	63.5	71,248	27.2
Atlanta, Ga. (40)	425,022	394,017	416,474	-7.3	22,457	5.7
Aurora, Colo. (62)	158,588	222,103	276,393	40.1	54,290	24.4
Austin, Texas (16)	345,890	465,622	656,562	34.6	190,940	41.0
Bakersfield, Calif. (70)	N.A.	174,820	247,057	N.A.	72,237	41.3
Baltimore, Md. (17)	786,741	736,014	651,154	-6.4	-84,860	-11.5
Baton Rouge, La. (75)	220,394	219,531	227,818	-0.4	8,287	3.8
Birmingham, Ala. (72)	284,413	265,968	242,820	-6.5	-23,148	-8.7
Boston, Mass. (20)	562,994	574,283	589,141	2.0	14,858	2.6
Buffalo, N.Y (59)	357,870	328,123	292,648	-8.3	-35,475	-10.8
Charlotte, N.C (26)	315,474	395,934	540,828	25.5	144,894	36.6
Chicago, Ill. (3)	3,005,072	2,783,726	2,896,016	-7.4	112,290	4.0
Cincinnati, Ohio (55)	385,409	364,040	331,285	-5.5	-32,755	-9.0
Cleveland, Ohio (33)	573,822	505,616	478,403	-11.9	-27,213	-5.4
Colorado Springs, Colo. (49)	215,105	281,140	360,890	30.7	79,750	28.4
Columbus, Ohio (15)	565,021	632,910	711,470	12.0	78,560	12.4

City (2000 Rank)	Population			Percent change,	Change, 1990–2000	
	1980	1990	2000	1980–2000	Number	Percent
Corpus Christi, Texas (61)	232,134	257,453	277,454	10.9%	20,001	7.8%
Dallas, Texas (8)	904,599	1,006,877	1,188,580	11.3	181,703	18.0
Denver, Colo. (25)	492,686	467,610	554,636	-5.1	87,026	18.6
Detroit, Mich. (10)	1,203,368	1,027,974	951,270	-14.6	-76,704	-7.5
El Paso, Texas (23)	425,259	515,342	563,662	21.2	48,320	9.4
Fort Worth, Texas (27)	385,164	447,619	534,694	16.2	87,075	19.5
Fresno, Calif. (37)	217,491	354,202	427,652	62.9	73,450	20.7
Honolulu, Hawaii. (47)	365,048	365,272	371,657	0.1	6,385	1.7
Houston, Texas (4)	1,595,138	1,630,553	1,953,631	2.2	323,078	19.8
Indianapolis, Ind. (12)	711,539	741,952	791,926	4.3	49,974	6.7
Jacksonville, Fla. (14)	571,003	635,230	735,617	17.9	100,387	15.8
Jersey City, N.J. (73)	223,532	228,537	240,055	2.2	11,518	5.0
Kansas City, Mo. (36)	448,028	435,146	441,545	-2.9	6,399	1.5
Las Vegas, Nev. (32)	164,674	258,295	478,434	56.9	220,139	85.2
Lexington-Fayette, Ky. (65)	204,165	225,366	260,512	10.4	35,146	15.6
Long Beach, Calif. (34)	361,498	429,433	461,522	18.8	32,089	7.5
Los Angeles, Calif. (2)	2,968,528	3,485,557	3,694,820	17.4	209,422	6.0
Louisville, Ky. (67)	298,694	269,063	256,231	-9.9	-12,832	-4.8
Memphis, Tenn. (18)	646,174	610,337	650,100	-5.5	39,763	6.5
Mesa, Ariz. (43)	152,404	288,091	396,375	89.0	108,284	37.6
Miami, Fla. (48)	346,681	358,548	362,470	3.4	3,922	1.1
Milwaukee, Wis. (19)	636,297	628,088	596,974	-1.3	-31,114	-5.0
Minneapolis, Minn. (46)	370,951	368,383	382,618	-0.7	14,235	3.9
Nashville, Tenn. (22)	477,811	510,784	569,891	6.9	59,107	11.6
New Orleans, La. (31)	557,927	496,938	484,674	-10.9	-12,264	-2.5
New York, N.Y. (1)	7,071,639	7,322,564	8,008,278	3.5	685,714	9.4
Newark, N.J. (64)	329,248	275,221	273,546	-16.4	-1,675	-0.6
Norfolk, Va. (74)	266,979	261,229	234,403	-2.2	-26,826	-10.3
Oakland, Calif. (42)	339,337	372,242	399,484	9.7	27,242	7.3
Oklahoma City, Okla. (29)	404,014	444,719	506,132	10.1	61,413	13.8
Omaha, Nebr. (45)	313,939	335,795	390,007	7.0	54,212	16.1
Philadelphia, Pa. (5)	1,688,210	1,585,577	1,517,550	-6.1	-68,027	-4.3
Phoenix, Ariz. (6)	789,704	983,403	1,321,045	24.5	337,642	34.3
Pittsburgh, Pa. (53)	423,959	369,879	334,563	-12.8	-35,316	-9.5
Portland, Oreg. (28)	368,148	437,319	529,121	18.8	91,802	21.0
Raleigh, N.C. (63)	150,255	207,951	276,093	38.4	68,142	32.8
Riverside, Calif. (68)	170,591	226,505	255,166	32.8	28,661	12.7
Sacramento, Calif. (41)	275,741	369,365	407,018	34.0	37,653	10.2
San Antonio, Texas (9)	785,940	935,933	1,144,646	19.1	208,713	22.3
San Diego, Calif. (7)	875,538	1,110,549	1,223,400	26.8	112,851	10.2
San Francisco, Calif. (13)	678,974	723,959	776,733	6.6	52,774	7.3
San Jose, Calif. (11)	629,400	782,248	894,943	24.3	112,695	14.4
San Juan, Puerto Rico (39)	N.A.	426,832	421,958	N.A.	-4,874	-1.1
Santa Ana, Calif. (52)	204,023	293,742	337,977	44.0	44,235	15.1
Seattle, Wash. (24)	493,846	516,259	563,374	4.5	47,115	9.1
St. Louis, Mo. (50)	452,801	396,685	348,189	-12.4	-48,496	-12.2
St. Paul, Minn. (60)	270,320	272,235	287,151	0.7	14,916	5.5
St. Petersburg, Fla. (69)	238,647	238,629	248,232	-0.0	9,603	4.0
Stockton, Calif. (71)	148,283	210,943	243,771	42.3	32,828	15.6
Tampa, Fla. (58)	271,577	280,015	303,447	3.1	23,432	8.4
Toledo, Ohio (57)	354,635	332,943	313,619	-6.1	-19,324	-5.8
Tucson, Ariz. (30)	330,537	405,390	486,699	22.6	81,309	20.1
Tulsa, Okla. (44)	360,919	367,302	393,049	1.8	25,747	7.0
Virginia Beach, Va. (38)	262,199	393,069	425,257	49.9	32,188	8.2
Washington, D.C (21)	638,432	606,900	572,059	-4.9	-34,841	-5.7
Wichita, Kans. (51)	279,838	304,011	344,284	8.6	40,273	13.2

Source: U.S. Bureau of the Census, 2000.

Population of the 50 Largest Cities, 1950–2000

2000 Rank, City	1950	1960	1970[1]	1980[1]	1990	2000	Population change, 1990–2000
1. New York, N.Y.	7,891,957	7,781,984	7,896,000	7,072,000	7,322,564	8,008,278	685,714
2. Los Angeles, Calif.	1,970,358	2,479,015	2,812,000	2,969,000	3,485,557	3,694,820	209,422
3. Chicago, Ill.	3,620,962	3,550,404	3,369,000	3,005,000	2,783,726	2,896,016	112,290
4. Houston, Texas	596,163	938,219	1,234,000	1,595,000	1,630,864	1,953,631	323,078
5. Philadelphia, Pa.	2,071,605	2,002,512	1,949,000	1,688,000	1,585,577	1,517,550	-68,027
6. Phoenix, Ariz.	(2)	439,170	584,000	790,000	984,309	1,321,045	337,642
7. San Diego, Calif.	334,387	573,224	697,000	876,000	1,110,623	1,223,400	112,851
8. Dallas, Texas	434,462	679,684	844,000	905,000	1,007,618	1,188,580	181,703
9. San Antonio, Texas	408,442	587,718	654,000	786,000	935,393	1,144,646	208,713
10. Detroit, Mich.	1,849,568	1,670,144	1,514,000	1,203,000	1,027,974	951,270	-76,704
11. San Jose, Calif.	(2)	(2)	460,000	629,000	782,224	894,943	112,695
12. Indianapolis, Ind.[3]	427,173	476,258	737,000	701,000	731,278	791,926	49,974
13. San Francisco, Calif.	775,357	742,855	716,000	679,000	723,959	776,733	52,774
14. Jacksonville, Fla.[3]	204,517	(2)	504,000	541,000	635,230	735,617	100,387
15. Columbus, Ohio	375,901	471,316	540,000	565,000	632,945	711,470	78,560
16. Austin, Texas	(2)	(2)	254,000	346,000	472,020	656,562	190,940
17. Baltimore, Md.	949,708	939,024	905,000	787,000	736,014	651,154	-84,860
18. Memphis, Tenn.	396,000	497,524	624,000	646,000	618,652	650,100	39,763
19. Milwaukee, Wisc.	637,392	741,324	717,000	636,000	628,088	596,974	-31,114
20. Boston, Mass.	801,444	697,197	641,000	563,000	574,283	589,141	14,858
21. Washington, D.C.	802,178	763,956	757,000	638,000	606,900	572,059	-34,841
22. Nashville, Tenn.[3]	(2)	(2)	426,000	456,000	488,366	569,891	59,107
23. El Paso, Texas	(2)	276,687	322,000	425,000	515,342	563,662	48,320
24. Seattle, Wash.	467,591	557,087	531,000	494,000	516,259	563,374	47,115
25. Denver, Colo.	415,786	493,887	515,000	493,000	467,610	554,636	87,026
26. Charlotte, N.C.	(2)	(2)	241,000	315,000	419,558	540,828	144,894
27. Fort Worth, Texas	278,778	356,268	393,000	385,000	447,619	534,694	87,075
28. Portland, Oreg.	373,628	372,676	380,000	368,000	485,975	529,121	91,802
29. Oklahoma City, Okla.	243,504	324,253	368,000	404,000	444,724	506,132	61,413
30. Tucson, Ariz.	(2)	(2)	263,000	331,000	415,444	486,699	81,309
31. New Orleans, La.	570,445	627,525	593,000	558,000	496,938	484,674	-12,264
32. Las Vegas, Nev.	(2)	(2)	(2)	(2)	258,295	478,434	220,139
33. Cleveland, Ohio	914,808	876,050	751,000	574,000	505,616	478,403	-27,213
34. Long Beach, Calif.	250,767	344,168	359,000	361,000	429,321	461,522	32,089
35. Albuquerque, N.Mex.	(2)	(2)	245,000	332,000	384,619	448,607	63,871
36. Kansas City, Mo.	456,622	475,539	507,000	448,000	434,829	441,545	6,399
37. Fresno, Calif.	(2)	(2)	166,000	217,000	354,091	427,652	73,450
38. Virginia Beach, Va.	(2)	(2)	172,000	262,000	393,089	425,257	32,188
39. Atlanta, Ga.	332,314	487,455	495,000	425,000	394,017	416,474	22,457
40. Sacramento, Calif.	(2)	(2)	257,000	276,000	369,365	407,018	37,653
41. Oakland, Calif.	384,575	367,548	362,000	339,000	372,242	399,484	27,472
42. Mesa, Ariz.	(2)	(2)	(2)	(2)	288,091	396,375	108,284
43. Tulsa, Okla.	(2)	261,685	330,000	361,000	367,302	393,049	25,747
44. Omaha, Neb.	251,117	301,598	347,000	314,000	335,795	390,007	54,212
45. Minneapolis, Minn.	521,718	482,872	434,000	371,000	368,383	382,618	14,235
46. Honolulu, Hawaii[4]	248,034	294,194	325,000	365,000	365,272	371,657	6,385
47. Miami, Fla.	249,276	291,688	335,000	347,000	358,548	362,470	3,922
48. Colorado Springs, Colo.	(2)	(2)	(2)	(2)	281,140	360,890	79,750
49. St. Louis, Mo.	856,796	750,026	622,000	453,000	396,685	348,189	-48,496
50. Wichita, Kans.	(2)	(2)	(2)	279,838	304,011	344,284	40,273

Note: 1. Figure rounded in source. 2. City was not one of the 50 largest that year. 3. City is part of a consolidated city-county government; populations of the other incorporated places in the county have been excluded from the population totals shown here. 4. Not incorporated as a city, but recognized for census purposes as large urban places. Honolulu CDP is coextensive with Honolulu Judicial District within the City and County of Honolulu. **Source:** U.S. Bureau of the Census, 2001

25 Fastest-Growing Major Cities in the U.S., 1990–2000

City	Population		Change, 1990–2000		Overall rank, 2000
	1990	2000	Number	Percent	
1. Augusta, Ga.	44,639	199,775	155,136	347.5%	91
2. Gilbert, Ariz.	29,188	109,697	80,509	275.8	208
3. Vancouver, Wash.	46,380	143,560	97,180	209.5	149
4. Henderson, Nev.	64,942	175,381	110,439	170.1	118
5. North Las Vegas, Nev.	47,707	115,488	67,781	142.1	198
6. Athens, Ga.	45,734	101,489	55,755	121.9	237
7. Peoria, Ariz.	50,618	108,364	57,746	114.1	214
8. Pembroke Pines, Fla.	65,452	137,427	71,975	110.0	161
9. Chandler, Ariz.	90,533	176,581	86,048	95.0	116
10. Las Vegas, Nevada	258,295	478,434	220,139	85.2	32
11. Plano, Texas	128,713	222,030	93,317	72.5	79
12. Palmdale, Calif.	68,842	116,670	47,828	69.5	194
13. Corona, Calif.	76,095	124,966	48,871	64.2	174
14. Fayetteville, N.C.	75,695	121,015	45,320	59.9	184
15. Scottsdale, Ariz.	130,069	202,705	72,636	55.8	88
16. Naperville, Ill.	85,351	128,358	43,007	50.4	169
17. Coral Springs, Fla.	79,443	117,549	38,106	48.0	190
18. Boise City, Idaho	125,738	185,787	60,049	47.8	108
19. Glendale, Ariz.	148,134	218,812	70,678	47.7	81
20. Fontana, Calif.	87,535	128,929	41,394	47.3	167
21. Laredo, Texas	122,899	176,576	53,677	43.7	117
22. Aurora, Ill.	99,581	142,990	43,409	43.6	151
23. Bakersfield, Calif.	174,820	247,057	72,237	41.3	70
24. Brownsville, Texas	98,962	139,722	40,760	41.2	155
25. Austin, Texas	465,622	656,562	190,940	41.0	16

Note: Cities over 100,000 population.   Source: U.S. Bureau of the Census.

25 Fastest-Declining Major U.S. Cities, 1990–2000

City	Population		Change, 1990–2000		Overall rank, 2000
	1990	2000	Number	Percent	
1. Hartford, Conn.	139,739	121,578	-18,161	-13.0%	183
2. St. Louis, Miss.	396,685	348,189	-48,496	-12.2	50
3. Gary, Ind.	116,646	102,746	-13,900	-11.9	230
4. Baltimore, Md.	736,014	651,154	-84,860	-11.5	17
5. Flint, Mich.	140,761	124,943	-15,818	-11.2	175
6. Buffalo, N.Y.	328,123	292,648	-35,475	-10.8	59
7. Norfolk, Va.	261,229	234,403	-26,826	-10.3	74
8. Syracuse, N.Y.	163,860	147,306	-16,554	-10.1	145
9. Pittsburgh, Penn.	369,879	334,563	-35,316	-9.5	53
10. Cincinnati, Ohio	364,040	331,285	-32,755	-9.0	55
11. Dayton, Ohio	182,044	166,179	-15,865	-8.7	126
12. Birmingham, Ala.	265,968	242,820	-23,148	-8.7	72
13. Detroit, Mich.	1,027,974	951,270	-76,704	-7.5	10
14. Lansing, Mich.	127,321	119,128	-8,193	-6.4	187
15. Jackson, Miss.	196,637	184,256	-12,381	-6.3	111
16. Toledo, Ohio	332,943	313,619	-19,324	-5.8	57
17. Washington, D.C.	606,900	572,059	-34,841	-5.7	21
18. Cleveland, Ohio	505,616	478,403	-27,213	-5.4	33
19. New Haven, Conn.	130,474	123,626	-6,848	-5.2	179
20. Rochester, N.Y.	231,636	219,773	-11,863	-5.1	80
21. Milwaukee, Wis.	628,088	596,974	-31,114	-5.0	19
22. Louisville, Ky.	269,063	256,231	-12,832	-4.8	67
23. Erie, Penn.	108,718	103,717	-5,001	-4.6	226
24. Warren, Mich.	144,864	138,247	-6,617	-4.6	158
25. Savannah, Ga.	137,560	131,510	-6,050	-4.4	166

Note: Cities over 100,000 population.   Source: U.S. Bureau of the Census.

CITY FINANCES

▶ TAX BURDENS AND PROGRESSIVITY IN MAJOR U.S. CITIES

Tax rates differ widely not only from state to state and city to city, but also from one income level to another. Any tax system in which the percentage of taxes paid rises with the income level is said to be *progressive.* A system where the percentage tax burden is the same at all income levels is said to be *proportional.* And a system in which the percentage of taxes paid decreases as income rises is said to be *regressive.* Because progressivity is measured as the ratio of one tax rate to another, progressivity does not necessarily reflect the actual tax burden.

State and Local Taxes for Families by Income Level in Selected Cities, 2000

City	$25,000 Percent[1]	Amount	$50,000 Percent[1]	Amount	$75,000 Percent[1]	Amount	$100,000 Percent[1]	Amount
Albuquerque, N.Mex.	7.5%	$1,879	7.2%	$3,613	8.2%	$6,169	8.7%	$8,743
Anchorage, Alaska	3.7	931	3.3	1,665	3.4	2,544	3.2	3,167
Atlanta, Ga.	6.7	1,679	7.7	3,847	8.8	6,586	9.2	9,201
Baltimore, Md.	7.2	1,792	10.7	5,352	11.3	8,461	11.3	11,264
Billings, Mont.	5.3	1,331	6.5	3,269	7.9	5,930	8.7	8,679
Birmingham, Ala.	10.0	2,512	8.2	4,093	8.3	6,189	8.1	8,117
Boise City, Idaho	5.4	1,338	7.2	3,593	8.8	6,632	9.4	9,369
Boston, Mass.	8.2	2,041	9.1	4,569	9.7	7,300	9.8	9,781
Bridgeport, Conn.	21.7	5,420	20.1	10,054	22.5	16,910	22.4	22,442
Burlington, Vt.	6.8	1,705	7.8	3,915	8.7	6,496	9.4	9,360
Charleston, W.Va.	8.2	2,057	7.5	3,750	8.5	6,360	9.0	8,952
Charlotte, N.C.	7.9	1,967	8.2	4,125	9.0	6,781	9.6	9,575
Cheyenne, Wyo.	4.6	1,142	3.1	1,563	3.3	2,485	3.3	3,300
Chicago, Ill.	8.4	2,110	8.0	4,016	8.5	6,386	8.4	8,403
Columbia, S.C.	6.4	1,607	7.9	3,954	9.1	6,837	9.7	9,662
Columbus, Ohio	8.8	2,189	8.6	4,312	9.3	6,996	9.7	9,694
Denver, Colo.	5.0	1,257	5.3	2,632	6.1	4,611	6.4	6,416
Des Moines, Iowa	8.4	2,102	8.9	4,452	9.8	7,379	10.3	10,287
Detroit, Mich.	9.3	2,330	9.2	4,587	9.7	7,264	9.7	9,728
Fargo, N. Dak.	7.9	1,964	6.9	3,442	7.2	5,422	7.4	7,385
Honolulu, Hawaii	8.8	2,205	8.7	4,340	9.5	7,141	9.7	9,709
Houston, Tex.	6.8	1,707	5.2	2,584	5.4	4,040	5.2	5,202
Indianapolis, Ind.	8.0	2,003	7.4	3,676	7.6	5,696	7.5	7,526
Jackson, Miss.	7.4	1,849	7.3	3,661	8.3	6,208	8.7	8,733
Jacksonville, Fla.	5.0	1,262	4.6	2,282	5.0	3,726	4.9	4,852
Kansas City, Mo.	9.3	2,326	8.7	4,344	9.1	6,852	9.4	9,377
Las Vegas, Nev.	6.1	1,522	4.4	2,200	4.4	3,316	4.2	4,217
Little Rock, Ark.	8.5	2,127	7.9	3,928	8.7	6,491	9.0	8,986
Los Angeles, Calif.	9.2	2,288	8.3	4,175	10.1	7,543	11.1	11,122
Louisville, Ky.	10.6	2,650	10.3	5,153	10.6	7,965	10.7	10,746
Manchester, N.H.	9.4	2,362	8.8	4,391	8.9	6,685	8.5	8,469
Memphis, Tenn.	7.3	1,831	5.0	2,516	5.1	3,810	4.9	4,914
Milwaukee, Wis.	8.4	2,099	9.8	4,896	10.6	7,948	10.7	10,708
Minneapolis, Minn.	6.0	1,511	8.4	4,216	9.7	7,273	10.1	10,110
New Orleans, La.	5.7	1,434	6.3	3,136	7.5	5,605	7.7	7,658
New York, N.Y.	8.1	2,013	10.5	5,244	12.2	9,161	12.9	12,920
Newark, N.J.	14.1	3,531	12.6	6,295	12.9	9,656	12.7	12,724
Oklahoma City, Okla.	8.8	2,207	7.9	3,941	8.7	6,507	8.8	8,756
Omaha, Nebr.	6.7	1,663	7.1	3,544	8.1	6,084	8.6	8,635
Philadelphia, Pa.	12.1	3,020	13.4	6,713	13.3	9,959	12.9	12,944
Phoenix, Ariz.	5.9	1,478	5.2	2,594	5.9	4,438	6.3	6,329
Portland, Maine	10.0	2,502	11.2	5,623	12.8	9,617	13.2	13,216
Portland, Oreg.	7.1	1,770	8.0	3,988	8.8	6,614	9.0	9,003
Providence, R.I.	11.3	2,814	11.8	5,921	12.3	9,198	12.8	12,836
Salt Lake City, Utah	8.4	2,093	8.6	4,281	9.1	6,795	9.1	9,054
Seattle, Wash.	8.5	2,113	6.3	3,133	6.3	4,738	6.0	6,048
Sioux Falls, S.Dak.	6.9	1,719	4.8	2,424	4.9	3,673	4.7	4,692
Virginia Beach, Va.	8.2	2,048	8.0	3,988	8.5	6,391	8.7	8,661
Washington, D.C.	8.6	2,146	8.7	4,335	9.9	7,455	10.5	10,459
Wichita, Kans.	5.4	1,356	6.4	3,192	7.6	5,687	8.1	8,104
Wilmington, Del.	5.4	1,361	6.9	3,471	7.7	5,763	7.9	7,866
51 city average[2]	8.0%	$2,007	8.0%	$4,019	8.8%	$6,584	9.0%	$8,982

Note: Tax burdens computed for a family of four. The four major taxes compared are the individual income tax, real property taxes on residential property, general sales and use taxes, and various automobile taxes, including the gasoline tax, registration fees, excise taxes, and personal property taxes. 1. Percentage of income. 2. Average of the largest city in each state plus the District of Columbia.
Source: Government of the District of Columbia, Dept. of Finance and Revenue, *Tax Rates and Tax Burdens in the District of Columbia: A Nationwide Comparison* (2001).

Several factors contribute to the progressivity of a tax system. A graduated individual income tax rate combined with exemptions and credits to lessen the regressiveness of the property tax will increase the progressivity of a tax system. Progressivity can be lessened by a lack of an individual income tax as well as by reliance on regressive taxes such as the sales tax and certain automobile taxes. The upper and lower income levels chosen for comparison also affect progressiveness.

Tax Progressivity of U.S. Cities, 2000

Most progressive	Index	Least progressive	Index
Boise City, Idaho	0.544	Seattle, Wash.	1.455
Billings, Mont.	0.659	Cheyenne, Wyo.	1.479
Minneapolis	0.570	Las Vegas, Nev.	1.531
New York City	0.586	Sioux Falls, S.D.	1.564
Wichita, Kans.	0.636	Memphis, Tenn.	1.578
Average progressivity[1]			**0.929**

Note: An index of less than 1.000 indicates a progressive tax system; an index of greater than one indicates a regressive tax system. A proportional system is indicated by an index of 1.000. 1. The average of the largest city in each state plus the District of Columbia. **Source:** Government of the District of Columbia, *Tax Rates and Tax Burdens in the District of Columbia:* (2001).

20 Best-Paid U.S. Mayors, 2001

Rank, Mayor	City	Salary
1. Richard M. Daley	Chicago	$170,000
2. Rudolph Giuliani	New York	165,000
3. Lee P. Brown	Houston	160,500
4. Dennis Archer	Detroit	157,300
5. James K. Hahn	Los Angeles	147,390
6. Sharpe James	Newark, N.J.	147,000
7. Willie L. Brown Jr.	San Francisco	146,891
8. John A. Delaney	Jacksonville	127,230
9. Martin O'Malley	Baltimore	125,000
10. Thomas M. Menino	Boston	125,000
11. John O. Norquist	Milwaukee	115,851
12. John Spencer	Yonkers, N.Y.	115,000
13. Paul Schell	Seattle	112,731
14. John F. Street	Philadelphia	110,000
14. Willie W. Herenton	Memphis	110,000
14. Dick A. Greco	Tampa, Fla.	110,000
17. Michael E. Coleman	Columbus, Ohio	107,087
18. Wellington E. Webb	Denver	103,056
19. William A. Johnson Jr.	Rochester, N.Y	102,678
20. Jeremy Harris	Honolulu	102,000

Note: This table is based on information submitted by the cities and therefore is unable to rank mayor's salaries for cities that did not voluntarily provide it. **Source:** U.S. Conference of Mayors.

The Cost of Living Index in Selected U.S. Cities, 2000

Urban area	Composite index (100%)	Grocery items (16%)	Housing (28%)	Utilities (8%)	Transportation (10%)	Health care (5%)	Misc. goods & services (33%)
Atlanta, Ga.	102.7	101.5	108.2	93.5	103.7	106.7	100.0
Baltimore, Md.	95.7	93.9	89.0	116.3	101.6	93.8	95.9
Boston, Mass.	132.2	114.1	172.8	130.4	114.4	130.4	112.8
Chicago, Ill.	N.A.	N.A.	N.A.	N.A.	N.A.	N.A.	N.A.
Cincinnati, Ohio	98.3	99.7	91.3	108.7	97.3	92.9	102.3
Cleveland, Ohio	108.2	105.9	107.7	128.5	107.6	116.6	103.8
Dallas, Texas	99.0	97.3	97.6	97.4	103.3	99.0	100.0
Denver, Colo.	108.6	111.8	119.7	88.5	107.5	128.7	99.6
Detroit, Mich.	107.8	110.2	121.6	99.4	107.1	113.9	96.3
Fort Worth, Texas	94.9	96.3	89.1	90.0	98.5	94.9	99.1
Houston, Texas	95.2	93.8	84.4	103.4	106.5	111.1	97.2
Indianapolis, Ind.	96.9	97.1	100.1	98.3	91.8	97.6	95.2
Kansas City, Mo.	99.4	101.0	91.3	105.3	104.9	100.8	102.1
Los Angeles-Long Beach, Calif.	145.8	112.5	234.1	109.1	112.4	122.0	109.7
Miami, Fla.	104.9	106.1	98.0	111.5	109.4	121.0	104.8
Milwaukee-Waukesha, Wisc.	104.2	99.4	112.2	118.7	102.5	100.2	97.5
Minneapolis, Minn.	111.8	100.5	115.0	118.1	113.5	131.2	109.7
Nassau-Suffolk, N.Y.	140.3	124.3	175.2	149.6	112.6	146.2	123.8
New York (Manhattan), N.Y.	241.5	142.8	494.5	173.9	119.7	180.3	137.3
Norfolk-Va. Beach-Newport News , Va.	98.3	100.3	91.4	121.9	100.6	101.5	96.4
Orlando, Fla.	99.0	104.4	93.6	104.2	95.6	108.8	99.2
Philadelphia, Pa.	120.9	105.1	145.2	126.0	116.5	101.2	111.0
Phoenix-Mesa, Ariz.	100.7	103.5	99.4	96.9	107.3	117.5	96.9
Pittsburgh, Pa.	108.1	100.8	112.1	135.0	100.7	96.3	105.8
Portland, Oreg.	106.4	104.2	108.1	88.2	113.4	123.7	105.7
Riverside, Calif.	107.3	107.7	104.4	115.5	111.2	119.1	104.7
Sacramento, Calif.	118.3	118.7	129.8	113.4	117.9	147.2	105.4
San Antonio, Texas	91.3	87.3	86.5	86.5	86.9	94.1	99.4
San Diego, Calif.	124.5	121.9	153.0	120.0	121.3	124.3	103.6
San Francisco, Calif.	189.4	121.8	357.2	142.5	128.9	169.4	112.6
Seattle-Tacoma, Wash.	103.3	112.7	101.1	75.0	107.0	122.4	103.3
St. Louis, Mo.	97.3	94.9	90.8	96.6	102.1	105.0	101.6
Tampa-St. Petersburg, Fla.	100.7	103.3	98.3	99.9	101.4	102.3	101.2
Washington, D.C.	114.0	112.3	128.2	90.2	111.5	119.3	108.5

Note: : Metropolitan areas with more than 1.5 million population. Percentage figures in parentheses show relative weight of component indexes used in calculating composite cost of living index. Figures are averages for second quarter 2000 through first quarter 2001. **Source:** American Chamber of Commerce Researchers Association, *ACCRA Cost of Living Index* (2001).

METROPOLITAN STATISTICAL AREAS (MSAs)

Because population patterns don't conform strictly to city boundaries, statisticians have devised a way of measuring city populations to include people who live around an urban area but whose address is outside the city limits. Known as Metropolitan Statistical Areas (or MSAs), these measures give a much more accurate reflection of how many people actually live in the area than do city population figures. For example, the city of Boston is relatively small: just 589,000 people lived in Boston proper, according to the 2000 Census, making it the 20th-largest city in America. But the Boston metropolitan area, which includes suburbs ranging from Rhode Island to New Hampshire, is the seventh-largest in the country, with a total population of 5.5 million within an hour's commute of the Hub. On the other hand, the population of San Diego proper was more than 1.2 million in 2000, making it the seventh-largest city in the U.S., but the entire San Diego metro area was only 2.8 million, or 17th-largest in the country.

The United States Office of Management and Budget (OMB) first defined metropolitan areas in 1949, subsequently changed the designation to "standard metropolitan area," "standard metropolitan statistical area," and finally "metropolitan statistical area" in 1983.

Defining MSAS, CMSAs, and PMSAs

Currently, the OMB distinguishes between MSAs, consolidated metropolitan statistical areas (CMSAs), and primary metropolitan statistical areas (PMSAs).

Metropolitan Statistical Areas (MSAs) are defined as an area that includes at least one city with 50,000 or more inhabitants, or a Census Bureau-defined urbanized area (of at least 50,000 inhabitants) and a total metropolitan population of at least 100,000. An MSA includes the county in which the central city is located plus any adjacent counties in which at least 50 percent of the population lives in the urbanized area. Additional "outlying counties" are included in the MSA if they meet specified requirements of commuting to the central counties and other selected requirements of metropolitan character (such as population density and percent urban). In New England, MSAs are defined in terms of cities and towns rather than counties.

Consolidated Metropolitan Statistical Areas (PMSAs) are defined as MSAs with populations of one million or more that also contain separate component areas that can each be identified as smaller urban areas, or *Primary Metropolitan Statistical Areas (PMSAs)*. For example, the New York CMSA includes the Primary MSAs of Nassau and Suffolk Counties on Long Island, Bergen and Passaic Counties in Northern New Jersey, and Bridgeport and Milford Counties in Connecticut. PMSAs, like the CMSAs that contain them, are composed of entire counties, except in New England where they are composed of cities and towns.

The 2000 Census counted 280 MSAs in the U.S (down from 284 in 1990), including 20 CMSAs. Although MSAs take up only about 16 percent of the country's land area, they are home to more than 75 percent of all Americans.

According to the 2000 Census, the U.S. population living in all metropolitan areas totaled 229,192,836, an increase of more than 36 million people (19.3 percent) since 1990. That's a significant increase over the previous decade, when MSAs grew by only 11.6 percent. The 1950 Census indicated that there were 14 metropolitan areas of at least one million population; these areas had a combined population of about 45 million people, or less than 30 percent of the national total. By the 1990 Census, the number of MSAs with a million people had grown to 39, with a combined population of 124.8 million people, or 50.2 percent of the U.S. total. By 2000, there were an even 50 MSAs with more than a million people, with a total population of 164.0 million people, or 58.2 percent of the national total.

Population of Metropolitan Statistical Areas, 1990–2000

Metropolitan Statistical Area	1990	2000	Change 1990–2000 Number	Change 1990–2000 Percent	CMSA/MSA rank 1990	CMSA/MSA rank 2000
Abilene, Tex. MSA	119,655	126,555	6,900	5.8	235	230
Aguadilla, P.R. MSA	128,172	146,424	18,252	14.2	N.A.	210
Albany, Ga. MSA	112,561	120,822	8,261	7.3	248	238
Albany-Schenectady-Troy, N.Y. MSA	861,424	875,583	14,159	1.6	48	57
Albuquerque, N.Mex. MSA	589,131	712,738	123,607	21.0	77	62
Alexandria, La. MSA	131,556	126,337	-5,219	-4.0	210	231
Allentown-Bethlehem-Easton, Pa. MSA	595,081	637,958	42,877	7.2	58	66
Altoona, Pa. MSA	130,542	129,144	-1,398	-1.1	219	226
Amarillo, Tex. MSA	187,547	217,858	30,311	16.2	164	160
Anchorage, Alaska MSA	226,338	260,283	33,945	15.0	143	140
Anniston, Ala. MSA	116,034	112,249	-3,785	-3.3	241	249
Appleton-Oshkosh-Neenah, Wis. MSA	315,121	358,365	43,244	13.7	114	117
Asheville, N.C. MSA	191,774	225,965	34,191	17.8	171	157
Athens, Ga. MSA	126,262	153,444	27,182	21.5	182	198
Atlanta, Ga. MSA	2,959,950	4,112,198	1,152,248	38.9	12	11
Auburn-Opelika, Ala. MSA	87,146	115,092	27,946	32.1	N.A.	244
Augusta-Aiken, Ga.-S.C. MSA	395,065	477,441	62,257	15.0	91	87
Austin-San Marcos, Tex. MSA	846,227	1,249,763	403,536	47.7	52	38
Bakersfield, Calif. MSA	543,477	661,645	118,168	21.7	68	65

Metropolitan Statistical Area	1990	2000	Change 1990–2000 Number	Percent	CMSA/MSA rank 1990	2000
Baton Rouge, La. MSA	528,264	602,894	74,630	14.1	71	70
Bangor, Maine MSA	91,629	90,864	-765	-0.8	268	267
Beaumont-Port Arthur, Tex. MSA	361,226	385,090	23,864	6.6	102	107
Bellingham, Wash. MSA	127,780	166,814	39,034	30.5	221	188
Benton Harbor, Mich. MSA	161,378	162,453	1,075	0.7	177	192
Billings, Mont. MSA	113,419	129,352	15,933	14.0	246	225
Biloxi-Gulfport-Pascagoula, Miss. MSA	312,368	363,988	51,620	16.5	156	114
Binghamton, N.Y. MSA	264,497	252,320	-12,177	-4.6	127	143
Birmingham, Ala. MSA	840,140	921,106	80,966	9.6	46	55
Bismarck, N.Dak. MSA	83,831	94,719	10,888	13.0	273	264
Bloomington, Ind. MSA	108,978	120,563	11,585	10.6	251	239
Bloomington-Normal, Ill. MSA	129,180	150,433	21,253	16.5	220	203
Boise City, Idaho MSA	295,851	432,345	136,494	46.1	154	97
Boston-Worcester-Lawrence, Mass.-N.H.-Maine-Conn. CMSA	5,455,403	5,819,100	363,697	6.7	7	7
Boston, Mass.-N.H. PMSA	3,227,707	3,406,829	179,122	5.5	N.A.	N.A.
Brockton, Mass. PMSA	236,409	255,459	19,050	8.1	N.A.	N.A.
Fitchburg-Leominster, Mass. PMSA	138,165	142,284	4,119	3.0	N.A.	N.A.
Lawrence, Mass.-N.H. PMSA	353,232	396,230	42,998	12.2	N.A.	N.A.
Lowell, Mass.-N.H. PMSA	280,578	301,686	21,108	7.5	N.A.	N.A.
Manchester, N.H. PMSA	173,783	198,378	24,595	14.2	N.A.	N.A.
Nashua, N.H. PMSA	168,233	190,949	22,716	13.5	N.A.	N.A.
New Bedford, Mass. PMSA	175,641	175,198	-443	-0.3	N.A.	N.A.
Portsmouth-Rochester, N.H.-Maine PMSA	223,271	240,698	17,427	7.8	N.A.	N.A.
Worcester, Mass.-Conn. PMSA	478,384	511,389	33,005	6.9	N.A.	N.A.
Brownsville-Harlingen-San Benito, Tex. MSA	260,120	335,227	75,107	28.9	129	122
Bryan-College Station, Tex. MSA	121,862	152,415	30,553	25.1	229	200
Buffalo-Niagara Falls, N.Y. CMSA	1,189,288	1,170,111	-19,177	-1.6	33	43
Burlington, Vt. MSA	151,506	169,391	17,885	11.8	212	186
Canton-Massillon, Ohio MSA	394,106	406,934	12,828	3.3	93	101
Casper, Wyo. MSA	61,226	66,533	5,307	8.7	283	279
Cedar Rapids, Iowa MSA	168,767	191,701	22,934	13.6	174	173
Champaign-Urbana, Ill. MSA	173,025	179,669	6,644	3.8	172	178
Charleston-N. Charleston, S.C. MSA	506,875	549,033	42,158	8.3	73	77
Charleston, W.Va. MSA	250,454	251,662	1,208	0.5	134	144
Charlotte-Gastonia-Rock Hill, N.C.-S.C. MSA	1,162,093	1,499,293	337,200	29.0	34	34
Charlottesville, Va. MSA	131,107	159,576	28,469	21.7	214	194
Chattanooga, Tenn.-Ga. MSA	424,347	465,161	40,814	9.6	82	90
Cheyenne, Wyo. MSA	73,142	81,607	8,465	11.6	281	275
Chicago-Gary-Kenosha, Ill.-Ind.-Wis. CMSA	8,239,820	9,157,540	917,720	11.1	3	3
Chicago, Ill. PMSA	7,410,858	8,272,768	861,910	11.6	N.A.	N.A.
Gary, Ind. PMSA	604,526	631,362	26,836	4.4	N.A.	N.A.
Kankakee, Ill. PMSA	96,255	103,833	7,578	7.9	N.A.	N.A.
Kenosha, Wis. PMSA	128,181	149,577	21,396	16.7	N.A.	N.A.
Chico-Paradise, Calif. MSA	182,120	203,171	21,051	11.6	167	167
Cincinnati-Hamilton, Ohio-Ky.-Ind. CMSA	1,817,571	1,979,202	161,631	8.9	23	24
Cincinnati, Ohio-Ky.-Ind. PMSA	1,526,092	1,646,395	120,303	7.9	N.A.	N.A.
Hamilton-Middletown, Ohio PMSA	291,479	332,807	41,328	14.2	N.A.	N.A.
Clarksville-Hopkinsville, Tenn.-Ky. MSA	169,439	207,033	37,594	22.2	173	166
Cleveland-Akron, Ohio CMSA	2,859,644	2,945,831	86,187	3.0	13	16
Akron, Ohio PMSA	657,575	694,960	37,385	5.7	N.A.	N.A.
Cleveland-Lorain-Elyria, Ohio PMSA	2,202,069	2,250,871	48,802	2.2	N.A.	N.A.
Colorado Springs, Colo. MSA	397,014	516,929	119,915	30.2	90	81
Columbia, Mo. MSA	112,379	135,454	23,075	20.5	249	221
Columbia, S.C. MSA	453,331	536,691	83,360	18.4	79	80
Columbus, Ga.-Ala. MSA	260,860	274,624	13,764	5.3	136	138
Columbus, Ohio MSA	1,345,450	1,540,157	194,707	14.5	29	33
Corpus Christi, Tex.	349,894	380,783	30,889	8.8	105	109
Corvallis, Oreg. MSA	70,811	78,153	7,342	10.4	N.A.	277
Cumberland, Md.-W.Va. MSA	101,643	102,008	365	0.4	259	259
Dallas-Fort Worth, Tex. CMSA	4,037,282	5,221,801	1,184,519	29.3	9	9
Dallas, Tex. PMSA	2,676,248	3,519,176	842,928	31.5	N.A.	N.A.
Fort Worth-Arlington, Tex. PMSA	1,361,034	1,702,625	341,591	25.1	N.A.	N.A.
Danville, Va. MSA	108,711	110,156	1,445	1.3	252	253
Davenport-Rock Island-Moline, Iowa-Ill. MSA	350,861	359,062	8,201	2.3	104	116
Dayton-Springfield, Ohio MSA	951,270	950,558	-712	-0.1	44	53
Daytona Beach, Fla. MSA	399,413	493,175	93,762	23.5	96	83
Decatur, Ala. MSA	131,556	145,867	14,311	10.9	211	211
Decatur, Ill. MSA	117,206	114,706	-2,500	-2.1	239	246

Metropolitan Statistical Area	1990	2000	Change 1990–2000 Number	Percent	CMSA/MSA rank 1990	2000
Denver-Boulder-Greeley, Colo. CMSA	1,980,140	2,581,506	601,366	30.4	22	19
Boulder-Longmont, Colo. PMSA	225,339	291,288	65,949	29.3	N.A.	N.A.
Denver, Colo. PMSA	1,622,980	2,109,282	486,302	30.0	N.A.	N.A.
Greeley, Colo. PMSA	131,821	180,936	49,115	37.3	N.A.	N.A.
Des Moines, Iowa MSA	392,928	456,022	63,094	16.1	94	91
Detroit-Ann Arbor-Flint, Mich. CMSA	5,187,171	5,456,428	269,257	5.2	6	8
Ann Arbor, Mich. PMSA	490,058	578,736	88,678	18.1	N.A.	N.A.
Detroit, Mich. PMSA	4,266,654	4,441,551	174,897	4.1	N.A.	N.A.
Flint, Mich. PMSA	430,459	436,141	5,682	1.3	N.A.	N.A.
Dothan, Ala. MSA	130,964	137,916	6,952	5.3	215	219
Dover, Del. MSA	110,993	126,697	15,704	14.1	N.A.	229
Dubuque, Iowa MSA	86,403	89,143	2,740	3.2	271	269
Duluth-Superior, Minn.-Wis. MSA	239,971	243,815	3,844	1.6	140	149
Eau Claire, Wis. MSA	137,543	148,337	10,794	7.8	204	206
El Paso, Tex. MSA	591,610	679,622	88,012	14.9	66	64
Elkhart-Goshen, Ind. MSA	156,198	182,791	26,593	17.0	183	176
Elmira, N.Y. MSA	95,195	91,070	-4,125	-4.3	266	266
Enid, Okla. MSA	56,735	57,813	1,078	1.9	284	280
Erie, Pa. MSA	275,572	280,843	5,271	1.9	124	137
Eugene-Springfield, Oreg. MSA	282,912	322,959	40,047	14.2	119	125
Evansville-Henderson, Ind.-Ky. MSA	278,990	296,195	17,205	6.2	121	133
Fargo-Moorhead, N.Dak.-Minn. MSA	153,296	174,367	21,071	13.7	185	182
Fayetteville, N.C. MSA	274,566	302,963	28,397	10.3	125	131
Fayetteville-Springdale-Rogers, Ark. MSA	210,908	311,121	100,213	47.5	247	130
Flagstaff, Ariz.-Utah MSA	101,760	122,366	20,606	20.2	N.A.	237
Florence, Ala. MSA	131,327	142,950	11,623	8.9	213	213
Florence, S.C. MSA	114,344	125,761	11,417	10.0	245	233
Fort Collins-Loveland, Colo. MSA	186,136	251,494	65,358	35.1	165	145
Fort Myers-Cape Coral, Fla. MSA	335,113	440,888	105,775	31.6	110	95
Fort Pierce-Port St. Lucie, Fla. MSA	251,071	319,426	68,355	27.2	133	127
Fort Smith, Ark.-Okla. MSA	175,911	207,290	31,379	17.8	169	165
Fort Walton Beach, Fla. MSA	143,776	170,498	26,722	18.6	198	184
Fort Wayne, Ind. MSA	456,281	502,141	45,860	10.1	100	82
Fresno, Calif. MSA	755,580	922,516	166,936	22.1	59	54
Gadsden, Ala. MSA	99,840	103,459	3,619	3.6	260	257
Gainesville, Fla. MSA	181,596	217,955	36,359	20.0	155	159
Glens Falls, N.Y. MSA	118,539	124,345	5,806	4.9	238	234
Goldsboro, N.C. MSA	104,666	113,329	8,663	8.3	N.A.	247
Grand Forks, N.Dak.-Minn. MSA	103,181	97,478	-5,703	-5.5	282	262
Grand Junction, Colo. MSA	93,145	116,255	23,110	24.8	N.A.	243
Grand Rapids-Muskegon-Holland, Mich. MSA	937,891	1,088,514	150,623	16.1	57	48
Great Falls, Mont. MSA	77,691	80,357	2,666	3.4	279	276
Green Bay, Wis. MSA	194,594	226,778	32,184	16.5	158	156
Greensboro—Winston-Salem—High Point, N.C. MSA	1,050,304	1,251,509	201,205	19.2	45	37
Greenville, N.C. MSA	107,924	133,798	25,874	24.0	N.A.	222
Greenville-Spartanburg-Anderson, S.C. MSA	830,563	962,441	131,878	15.9	62	52
Harrisburg-Lebanon-Carlisle, Pa. MSA	587,986	629,401	41,415	7.0	67	67
Hartford, Conn. MSA	1,157,585	1,183,110	25,525	2.2	36	42
Hattiesburg, Miss. MSA	98,738	111,674	12,936	13.1	N.A.	250
Hickory-Morganton-Lenoir, N.C. MSA	292,409	341,851	49,442	16.9	148	120
Honolulu, Hawaii MSA	836,231	876,156	39,925	4.8	51	56
Houma, La. MSA	182,842	194,477	11,635	6.4	166	170
Houston-Galveston-Brazoria, Tex. CMSA	3,731,131	4,669,571	938,440	25.2	10	10
Brazoria, Tex. PMSA	191,707	241,767	50,060	26.1	N.A.	N.A.
Galveston-Texas City, Tex. PMSA	217,399	250,158	32,759	15.1	N.A.	N.A.
Houston, Tex. PMSA	3,322,025	4,177,646	855,621	25.8	N.A.	N.A.
Huntington-Ashland, W.Va.-Ky.-Ohio MSA	312,529	315,538	3,009	1.0	115	128
Huntsville, Ala. MSA	293,047	342,376	49,329	16.8	141	119
Indianapolis, Ind. MSA	1,380,491	1,607,486	226,995	16.4	31	29
Iowa City, Iowa MSA	96,119	111,006	14,887	15.5	265	251
Jackson, Mich. MSA	149,756	158,422	8,666	5.8	191	195
Jackson, Miss. MSA	395,396	440,801	45,405	11.5	92	96
Jackson, Tenn. MSA	90,801	107,377	16,576	18.3	278	254
Jacksonville, Fla. MSA	906,727	1,100,491	193,764	21.4	47	46
Jacksonville, N.C. MSA	149,838	150,355	517	0.3	190	204
Jamestown, N.Y. MSA	141,895	139,750	-2,145	-1.5	202	217
Janesville-Beloit, Wis. MSA	139,510	152,307	12,797	9.2	203	201
Johnson City-Kingsport-Bristol, Tenn.-Va. MSA	436,047	480,091	44,044	10.1	81	85

Metropolitan Statistical Area	1990	2000	Change 1990–2000 Number	Change 1990–2000 Percent	CMSA/MSA rank 1990	CMSA/MSA rank 2000
Johnstown, Pa. MSA	241,247	232,621	-8,626	-3.6	138	155
Jonesboro, Ark. MSA	68,956	82,148	13,192	19.1	N.A.	274
Joplin, Mo. MSA	134,910	157,322	22,412	16.6	207	196
Kalamazoo-Battle Creek, Mich. MSA	429,453	452,851	23,398	5.4	146	92
Kansas City, Mo.-Kans. MSA	1,582,875	1,776,062	193,187	12.2	25	26
Killeen-Temple, Tex. MSA	255,301	312,952	57,651	22.6	131	129
Knoxville, Tenn. MSA	585,960	687,249	101,289	17.3	65	63
Kokomo, Ind. MSA	96,946	101,541	4,595	4.7	263	260
La Crosse, Wis.-Minn. MSA	116,401	126,838	10,437	9.0	262	228
Lafayette, La. MSA	344,953	385,647	40,694	11.8	153	106
Lafayette, Ind. MSA	161,572	182,821	21,249	13.2	218	175
Lake Charles, La. MSA	168,134	183,577	15,443	9.2	175	174
Lakeland-Winter Haven, Fla. MSA	405,382	483,924	78,542	19.4	87	84
Lancaster, Pa. MSA	422,822	470,658	47,836	11.3	85	89
Lansing-East Lansing, Mich. MSA	432,674	447,728	15,054	3.5	83	93
Laredo, Tex. MSA	133,239	193,117	59,878	44.9	208	171
Las Cruces, N.Mex. MSA	135,510	174,682	39,172	28.9	206	181
Las Vegas, Nev.-Ariz. MSA	852,737	1,563,282	710,545	83.3	53	32
Lawrence, Kans. MSA	81,798	99,962	18,164	22.2	275	261
Lawton, Okla. MSA	111,486	114,996	3,510	3.1	250	245
Lewiston-Auburn, Maine MSA	93,679	90,830	-2,849	-3.0	269	268
Lexington, Ky. MSA	405,936	479,198	73,262	18.0	106	86
Lima, Ohio MSA	154,340	155,084	744	0.5	184	197
Lincoln, Nebr. MSA	213,641	250,291	36,650	17.2	151	147
Little Rock-North Little Rock, Ark. MSA	513,117	583,845	70,728	13.8	72	74
Longview-Marshall, Tex. MSA	193,801	208,780	14,979	7.7	176	164
Los Angeles-Riverside-Orange County, Calif. CMSA	14,531,529	16,373,645	1,842,116	12.7	2	2
Los Angeles-Long Beach, Calif. PMSA	8,863,164	9,519,338	656,174	7.4	N.A.	N.A.
Orange County, Calif. PMSA	2,410,556	2,846,289	435,733	18.1	N.A.	N.A.
Riverside-San Bernardino, Calif. PMSA	2,588,793	3,254,821	666,028	25.7	N.A.	N.A.
Ventura, Calif. PMSA	669,016	753,197	84,181	12.6	N.A.	N.A.
Louisville, Ky.-Ind. MSA	948,829	1,025,598	76,769	8.1	43	50
Lubbock, Tex. MSA	222,636	242,628	19,992	9.0	147	151
Lynchburg, Va. MSA	193,928	214,911	20,983	10.8	200	161
Macon, Ga. MSA	290,909	322,549	31,640	10.9	120	126
Madison, Wis. MSA	367,085	426,526	59,441	16.2	99	98
Mansfield, Ohio MSA	174,007	175,818	1,811	1.0	223	179
Mayaguez, P.R. MSA	237,143	253,347	16,204	6.8	N.A.	142
McAllen-Edinburg-Mission, Tex. MSA	383,545	569,463	185,918	48.5	95	75
Medford-Ashland, Oreg. MSA	146,389	181,269	34,880	23.8	196	177
Melbourne-Titusville-Palm Bay, Fla. MSA	398,978	476,230	77,252	19.4	89	88
Memphis, Tenn.-Ark.-Miss. MSA	1,007,306	1,135,614	128,308	12.7	41	44
Merced, Calif. MSA	178,403	210,554	32,151	18.0	168	163
Miami-Fort Lauderdale, Fla. CMSA	3,192,582	3,876,380	683,798	21.4	11	12
Fort Lauderdale, Fla. PMSA	1,255,488	1,623,018	367,530	29.3	N.A.	N.A.
Miami, Fla. PMSA	1,937,094	2,253,362	316,268	16.3	N.A.	N.A.
Milwaukee-Racine, Wis. CMSA	1,607,183	1,689,572	82,389	5.1	24	27
Milwaukee-Waukesha, Wis. PMSA	1,432,149	1,500,741	68,592	4.8	N.A.	N.A.
Racine, Wis. PMSA	175,034	188,831	13,797	7.9	N.A.	N.A.
Minneapolis-St. Paul, Minn.-Wis. MSA	2,538,834	2,968,806	429,972	16.9	16	15
Missoula, Mont. MSA	78,687	95,802	17,115	21.8	N.A.	263
Mobile, Ala. MSA	476,923	540,258	63,335	13.3	78	79
Modesto, Calif. MSA	370,522	446,997	76,475	20.6	97	94
Monroe, La. MSA	142,191	147,250	5,059	3.6	201	209
Montgomery, Ala. MSA	292,517	333,055	40,538	13.9	117	123
Muncie, Ind. MSA	119,659	118,769	-890	-0.7	234	242
Myrtle Beach, S.C. MSA	144,053	196,629	52,576	36.5	N.A.	169
Naples, Fla. MSA	152,099	251,377	99,278	65.3	186	146
Nashville, Tenn. MSA	985,026	1,231,311	246,285	25.0	40	39
New London-Norwich, Conn.-R.I. MSA	290,734	293,566	2,832	1.0	126	134
New Orleans, La. MSA	1,285,270	1,337,726	52,456	4.1	32	35
New York-Northern New Jersey-Long Island, N.Y.-N.J.-Conn.-Pa. PMSA	19,549,649	21,199,865	1,650,216	8.4	1	1
Bergen-Passaic, N.J. PMSA	1,278,440	1,373,167	94,727	7.4	N.A.	N.A.
Bridgeport, Conn. PMSA	443,722	459,479	15,757	3.6	N.A.	N.A.
Danbury, Conn. PMSA	193,597	217,980	24,383	12.6	N.A.	N.A.
Dutchess County, N.Y. PMSA	259,462	280,150	20,688	8.0	N.A.	N.A.
Jersey City, N.J. PMSA	553,099	608,975	55,876	10.1	N.A.	N.A.
Middlesex-Somerset-Hunterdon, N.J. PMSA	1,019,835	1,169,641	149,806	14.7	N.A.	N.A.

Metropolitan Statistical Area	1990	2000	Change 1990–2000 Number	Change 1990–2000 Percent	CMSA/MSA rank 1990	CMSA/MSA rank 2000
Monmouth-Ocean, N.J. PMSA	986,327	1,126,217	139,890	14.2	N.A.	N.A.
Nassau-Suffolk, N.Y. PMSA	2,609,212	2,753,913	144,701	5.5	N.A.	N.A.
New Haven-Meriden, Conn PMSA	530,180	542,149	11,969	2.3	N.A.	N.A.
New York, N.Y. PMSA	8,546,846	9,314,235	767,389	9.0	N.A.	N.A.
Newark, N.J. PMSA	1,915,928	2,032,989	117,061	6.1	N.A.	N.A.
Newburgh, N.Y.-Pa. PMSA	335,613	387,669	52,056	15.5	N.A.	N.A.
Stamford-Norwalk, Conn. PMSA	329,935	353,556	23,621	7.2	N.A.	N.A.
Trenton, N.J. PMSA	325,824	350,761	24,937	7.7	N.A.	N.A.
Waterbury, Conn.	221,629	228,984	7,355	3.3	N.A.	N.A.
Norfolk-Virginia Beach-Newport News, Va.-N.C. MSA	1,443,244	1,569,541	126,297	8.8	28	31
Ocala, Fla. MSA	194,833	258,916	64,083	32.9	157	141
Odessa-Midland, Tex. MSA	225,545	237,132	11,587	5.1	236	152
Oklahoma City, Okla. MSA	958,839	1,083,346	124,507	13.0	42	49
Omaha, Nebr.-Iowa MSA	639,580	716,998	77,418	12.1	63	61
Orlando, Fla. MSA	1,224,852	1,644,561	419,709	34.3	37	28
Owensboro, Ky. MSA	87,189	91,545	4,356	5.0	270	265
Panama City, Fla. MSA	126,994	148,217	21,223	16.7	222	207
Parkersburg-Marietta, W.Va.-Ohio MSA	149,169	151,237	2,068	1.4	192	202
Pensacola, Fla. MSA	344,406	412,153	67,747	19.7	107	100
Peoria-Pekin, Ill. MSA	339,172	347,787	8,215	2.4	108	118
Philadelphia-Wilmington-Atlantic City, Pa.-N.J.-Del.-Md. CMSA	5,892,937	6,188,463	295,526	5.0	5	6
Atlantic-Cape May, N.J. PMSA	319,416	354,878	35,462	11.1	N.A.	N.A.
Philadelphia, Pa.-N.J. PMSA	4,922,175	5,100,931	178,756	3.6	N.A.	N.A.
Vineland-Millville-Bridgeton, N.J. PMSA	138,053	146,438	8,385	6.1	N.A.	N.A.
Wilmington-Newark, Del.-Md. PMSA	513,293	586,216	72,923	14.2	N.A.	N.A.
Phoenix-Mesa, Ariz. MSA	2,238,480	3,251,876	1,013,396	45.3	20	14
Pine Bluff, Ark. MSA	85,487	84,278	-1,209	-1.4	272	272
Pittsburgh, Pa. MSA	2,394,811	2,358,695	-36,116	-1.5	19	22
Pittsfield, Mass. MSA	88,695	84,699	-3,996	-4.5	277	271
Pocatello, Idaho MSA	66,026	75,565	9,539	14.4	N.A.	278
Ponce, P.R. MSA	342,660	361,094	18,434	5.4	N.A.	115
Portland, Maine MSA	221,095	243,537	22,442	10.2	150	150
Portland-Salem, Oreg.-Wash. CMSA	1,793,476	2,265,223	471,747	26.3	27	23
Portland-Vancouver, Oreg.-Wash. PMSA	1,515,452	1,918,009	402,557	26.6	N.A.	N.A.
Salem, Oreg. PMSA	278,024	347,214	69,190	24.9	N.A.	N.A.
Providence-Fall River-Warwick, R.I.-Mass. MSA	1,134,350	1,188,613	54,263	4.8	35	40
Provo-Orem, Utah MSA	263,590	368,536	104,946	39.8	128	112
Pueblo, Colo. MSA	123,051	141,472	18,421	15.0	226	215
Punta Gorda, Fla. MSA	110,975	141,627	30,652	27.6	N.A.	214
Raleigh-Durham-Chapel Hill, N.C. MSA	855,545	1,187,941	332,396	38.9	54	41
Rapid City, S.Dak. MSA	81,343	88,565	7,222	8.9	276	270
Reading, Pa. MSA	336,523	373,638	37,115	11.0	109	110
Redding, Calif. MSA	147,036	163,256	16,220	11.0	194	190
Reno, Nev. MSA	254,667	339,486	84,819	33.3	132	121
Richland-Kennewick-Pasco, Wash. MSA	150,033	191,822	41,789	27.9	189	172
Richmond-Petersburg, Va. MSA	865,640	996,512	130,872	15.1	49	51
Roanoke, Va. MSA	224,477	235,932	11,455	5.1	144	153
Rochester, Minn. MSA	106,470	124,277	17,807	16.7	256	235
Rochester, N.Y. MSA	1,062,470	1,098,201	35,731	3.4	39	47
Rockford, Ill. MSA	329,676	371,236	41,560	12.6	118	111
Rocky Mount, N.C. MSA	133,235	143,026	9,791	7.3	N.A.	212
Sacramento-Yolo, Calif. CMSA	1,481,102	1,796,857	315,755	21.3	26	25
Sacramento, Calif. PMSA	1,340,010	1,628,197	288,187	21.5	N.A.	N.A.
Yolo, Calif. PMSA	141,092	168,660	27,568	19.5	N.A.	N.A.
Saginaw-Bay City-Midland, Mich. MSA	399,320	403,070	3,750	0.9	88	102
Salinas, Calif. MSA	355,660	401,762	46,102	13.0	103	103
Salt Lake City-Ogden, Utah MSA	1,072,227	1,333,914	261,687	24.4	38	36
San Angelo, Tex. MSA	98,458	104,010	5,552	5.6	261	256
San Antonio, Tex. MSA	1,324,749	1,592,383	267,634	20.2	30	30
San Diego, Calif. MSA	2,498,016	2,813,833	315,817	12.6	15	17
San Francisco-Oakland-San Jose, Calif. CMSA	6,253,311	7,039,362	786,051	12.6	4	5
Oakland, Calif. PMSA	2,082,914	2,392,557	309,643	14.9	N.A.	N.A.
San Francisco, Calif. PMSA	1,603,678	1,731,183	127,505	8.0	N.A.	N.A.
San Jose, Calif. PMSA	1,497,577	1,682,585	185,008	12.4	N.A.	N.A.
Santa Cruz-Watsonville, Calif. PMSA	229,734	255,602	25,868	11.3	N.A.	N.A.
Santa Rosa, Calif. PMSA	388,222	458,614	70,392	18.1	N.A.	N.A.
Vallejo-Fairfield-Napa, Calif. PMSA	451,186	518,821	67,635	15.0	N.A.	N.A.

Metropolitan Statistical Area	1990	2000	Change 1990–2000 Number	Percent	CMSA/MSA rank 1990	2000
San Juan-Caguas-Arecibo, P.R. CMSA	2,270,808	2,450,292	179,484	7.9	N.A.	20
Arecibo, P.R. PMSA	155,005	174,300	19,295	12.4	N.A.	N.A.
Caguas, P.R. PMSA	279,501	308,365	28,864	10.3	N.A.	N.A.
San Juan-Bayamon, P.R. PMSA	1,836,302	1,967,627	131,325	7.2	N.A.	N.A.
San Luis Obispo-Atascadero-Pasa Robles, Calif. MSA	217,162	246,681	29,519	13.6	N.A.	148
Santa Barbara-Santa Maria-Lompoc, Calif. PMSA	369,608	399,347	29,739	8.0	98	104
Santa Fe, N.Mex. MSA	117,043	147,635	30,592	26.1	240	208
Sarasota-Bradenton, Fla. MSA	489,483	589,959	100,476	20.5	123	73
Savannah, Ga. MSA	258,060	293,000	34,090	13.5	137	135
Scranton-Wilkes-Barre-Hazleton, Pa. MSA	638,466	624,776	-13,690	-2.1	55	68
Seattle-Tacoma-Bremerton, Wash. CMSA	2,970,328	3,554,760	584,432	19.7	14	13
Bremerton, Wash. PMSA	189,731	231,969	42,238	22.3	N.A.	N.A.
Olympia, Wash. PMSA	161,238	207,355	46,117	28.6	N.A.	N.A.
Seattle-Bellevue-Everett, Wash. PMSA	2,033,156	2,414,616	381,460	18.8	N.A.	N.A.
Tacoma, Wash. PMSA	586,203	700,820	114,617	19.6	N.A.	N.A.
Sharon, Pa. MSA	121,003	120,293	-710	-0.6	231	240
Sheboygan, Wis. MSA	103,877	112,646	8,769	8.4	257	248
Sherman-Denison, Tex. MSA	95,021	110,595	15,574	16.4	267	252
Shreveport-Bossier City, La. MSA	376,330	392,302	15,972	4.2	111	105
Sioux City, Iowa-Nebr. MSA	115,018	124,130	9,112	7.9	244	236
Sioux Falls, S.Dak. MSA	139,236	172,412	33,176	23.8	224	183
South Bend, Ind. MSA	247,052	265,559	18,507	7.5	135	139
Spokane, Wash. MSA	361,364	417,939	56,575	15.7	101	99
Springfield, Ill. MSA	189,550	201,437	11,887	6.3	161	168
Springfield, Mass. MSA	587,884	591,932	4,048	0.7	70	72
Springfield, Mo. MSA	264,346	325,721	61,375	23.2	139	124
St. Cloud, Minn. MSA	148,976	167,392	18,416	12.4	159	187
St. Joseph, Mo. MSA	97,715	102,490	4,775	4.9	274	258
St. Louis, Mo.-Ill. MSA	2,492,525	2,603,607	111,082	4.5	17	18
State College, Pa. MSA	123,786	135,758	11,972	9.7	225	220
Steubenville-Weirton, Ohio-W.Va. MSA	142,523	132,008	-10,515	-7.4	199	223
Stockton-Lodi, Calif. MSA	480,628	563,598	82,970	17.3	76	76
Sumter, S.C. MSA	102,637	104,646	2,009	2.0	N.A.	255
Syracuse, N.Y. MSA	742,177	732,117	-10,060	-1.4	61	60
Tallahassee, Fla. MSA	233,598	284,539	50,941	21.8	142	136
Tampa-St. Petersburg-Clearwater, Fla. MSA	2,067,959	2,395,997	328,038	15.9	21	21
Terre Haute, Ind. MSA	147,585	149,192	1,607	1.1	216	205
Texarkana, Tex.-Texarkana, Ark. MSA	120,132	129,749	9,617	8.0	233	224
Toledo, Ohio MSA	614,128	618,203	4,075	0.7	64	69
Topeka, Kans. MSA	160,976	169,871	8,895	5.5	179	185
Tucson, Ariz. MSA	666,880	843,746	176,866	26.5	60	58
Tulsa, Okla. MSA	708,954	803,235	94,281	13.3	56	59
Tuscaloosa, Ala. MSA	150,522	164,875	14,353	9.5	188	189
Tyler, Tex. MSA	151,309	174,706	23,397	15.5	187	180
Utica-Rome, N.Y. MSA	316,633	299,896	-16,737	-5.3	113	132
Victoria, Tex. MSA	74,361	84,088	9,727	13.1	280	273
Visalia-Tulare-Porterville, Calif. MSA	311,921	368,021	56,100	18.0	116	113
Waco, Tex. MSA	189,123	213,517	24,394	12.9	162	162
Washington-Baltimore, D.C.-Md.-Va.-W.Va. CMSA	4,223,485	4,923,153	699,668	16.6	8	4
Baltimore, Md. PMSA	2,382,172	2,552,994	170,822	7.2	N.A.	N.A.
Hagerstown, Md. PMSA	121,393	131,923	10,530	8.7	N.A.	N.A.
Washington, D.C.-Md.-Va.-W.Va. PMSA	4,223,485	4,923,153	699,668	16.6	N.A.	N.A.
Waterloo-Cedar Falls, Iowa MSA	123,798	128,012	4,214	3.4	195	227
Wausau, Wis. MSA	115,400	125,834	10,434	9.0	242	232
West Palm Beach-Boca Raton, Fla. MSA	863,518	1,131,184	267,666	31.0	50	45
Wheeling, W.Va.-Ohio MSA	159,301	153,172	-6,129	-3.8	180	199
Wichita Falls, Tex. MSA	130,351	140,518	10,167	7.8	228	216
Wichita, Kans. MSA	485,270	545,220	59,950	12.4	75	78
Williamsport, Pa. MSA	118,710	120,044	1,334	1.1	237	241
Wilmington, N.C. MSA	171,269	233,450	62,181	36.3	232	154
Yakima, Wash. MSA	188,823	222,581	33,758	17.9	163	158
York, Pa. MSA	339,574	381,751	42,177	12.4	86	108
Youngstown-Warren, Ohio MSA	600,895	594,746	-6,149	-1.0	74	71
Yuba City, Calif. MSA	122,643	139,149	16,506	13.5	227	218
Yuma, Ariz. MSA	106,895	160,026	53,131	49.7	254	193

Note: CMSA = consolidated metropolitan statistical area; MSA = metropolitan statistical area; PMSA = primary metropolitan statistical area; N.A. = not applicable. **Source:** U.S. Bureau of the Census release, 2001.

Population of U.S. Metropolitan Areas by Race and Hispanic Origin, 1990

Rank/Metropolitan area	Total	White	Black	American Indian	Asian or Pacific Islander	Other race	Hispanic origin[1]
1. New York-Northern New Jersey-Long Island, N.Y.-N.J.-Conn. CMSA	18,087,251	12,699,119	3,289,465	46,191	873,213	1,179,263	2,777,951
New York, N.Y. PMSA	8,546,846	4,826,081	2,250,026	29,711	556,399	884,629	1,889,662
Nassau-Suffolk, N.Y. PMSA	2,609,212	2,305,434	193,967	4,636	62,399	42,776	165,238
Newark, N.J. PMSA	1,824,321	1,279,952	422,802	3,144	52,898	65,525	188,299
Bergen-Passaic, N.J. PMSA	1,278,440	1,043,437	106,108	2,221	66,743	59,931	147,868
Middlesex-Somerset-Hunterdon, N.J. PMSA	1,019,835	865,158	70,670	1,420	56,804	25,783	71,695
Monmouth-Ocean, N.J. PMSA	986,327	895,986	59,264	1,327	19,098	10,652	36,357
Jersey City, N.J. PMSA	553,099	380,612	79,770	1,460	36,777	54,480	183,465
Bridgeport-Milford, Conn. PMSA	443,722	371,493	45,826	806	6,577	19,020	44,741
Orange County, N.Y. PMSA	307,647	273,600	22,223	824	3,549	7,451	21,535
Stanford, Conn. PMSA	202,557	171,834	20,767	203	5,570	4,183	13,732
Danbury, Conn. PMSA	187,867	175,780	5,398	301	4,355	2,033	7,136
Norwalk, Conn. PMSA	127,378	109,752	12,644	138	2,044	2,800	8,223
2. Los Angeles-Anaheim-Riverside, Calif. CMSA	14,531,529	9,388,957	1,229,809	87,487	1,339,048	2,486,228	4,779,118
Los Angeles-Long Beach, Calif. PMSA	8,863,164	5,035,103	992,974	45,508	954,485	1,835,094	3,351,242
Riverside-San Bernardino, Calif. PMSA	2,588,793	1,930,095	178,525	24,905	100,792	354,476	686,096
Anaheim-Santa Ana, Calif. PMSA	2,410,556	1,894,593	42,681	12,165	249,192	211,925	564,828
Oxnard-Ventura, Calif. PMSA	669,016	529,166	15,629	4,909	34,579	84,733	176,952
3. Chicago-Gary-Lake County Ill.-Ind-Wis. CMSA	8,065,633	5,772,110	1,547,725	15,758	256,050	473,990	893,422
Chicago, Ill. PMSA	6,069,974	4,098,747	1,332,919	11,550	229,492	397,266	734,827
Gary-Hammond, Ind. PMSA	604,526	460,532	117,142	1,108	3,716	22,028	48,384
Lake County, Ill. PMSA	516,418	450,666	34,771	1,198	12,588	17,195	38,570
Joliet, Ill. PMSA	389,650	335,284	38,382	737	4,887	10,360	20,721
Aurora-Elgin, Ill. PMSA	356,884	307,694	19,216	693	4,698	24,583	45,340
Kenosha, Wis. PMSA	128,181	119,187	5,295	472	669	2,558	5,580
4. San Francisco-Oakland-San Jose, Calif. CMSA	6,253,311	4,334,064	537,753	40,847	926,961	413,686	970,403
Oakland, Calif. PMSA	2,082,914	1,372,818	303,826	14,230	269,566	122,474	273,087
San Francisco, Calif. PMSA	1,603,678	1,058,796	122,494	7,232	329,599	85,557	233,274
San Jose, Calif. PMSA	1,497,577	1,032,190	56,211	9,269	261,466	138,441	314,564
Vallejo-Fairfield-Napa, Calif. PMSA	451,186	325,761	47,043	3,898	47,044	27,440	61,458
Santa Rosa-Petaluma, Calif. PMSA	388,222	351,650	5,547	4,397	10,774	15,854	41,223
Santa Cruz, Calif. PMSA	229,734	192,849	2,632	1,821	8,512	23,920	46,797
5. Philadelphia-Wilmington-Trenton Pa.-N.J.-Del.-Md. CMSA	5,899,345	4,540,541	1,100,347	11,307	123,458	123,692	225,868
Philadelphia, Pa.-N.J. PMSA	4,856,881	3,717,175	929,907	8,335	104,595	96,869	173,980
Wilmington, Del.-N.J.-Md. PMSA	578,587	477,243	85,641	1,128	7,737	6,838	13,875
Trenton, N.J. PMSA	325,824	244,656	61,481	533	9,992	9,162	19,665
Vineland-Millville-Bridgeton, N.J. PMSA	138,053	101,467	23,318	1,311	1,134	10,823	18,348
6. Detroit-Ann Arbor, Mich. CMSA	4,665,236	3,569,087	975,199	17,961	69,454	33,535	90,947
Detroit, Mich. PMSA	4,382,299	3,332,697	943,479	16,885	57,730	31,508	85,216
Ann Arbor, Mich. PMSA	282,937	236,390	31,720	1,076	11,724	2,027	5,731
7. Boston-Lawrence-Salem, Mass.-N.H. CMSA	4,171,643	3,708,228	239,059	7,542	121,405	95,409	193,199
Boston, Mass. PMSA	2,870,669	2,499,859	209,970	5,250	95,044	60,546	128,883
Lawrence-Haverhill, Mass.-N.H. PMSA	393,516	359,052	7,363	857	5,146	21,098	36,300
Lowell, Mass.-N.H. PMSA	273,067	248,937	3,598	388	14,251	5,893	12,193
Salem-Gloucester, Mass. PMSA	264,356	257,396	2,448	305	2,347	1,860	5,506

Rank/Metropolitan area	Total	White	Black	Asian or American Indian	Pacific Islander	Other race	Hispanic origin[1]
Brockton, Mass. PMSA	189,478	168,133	13,770	445	2,158	4,972	7,044
Nashua, N.H. PMSA	180,557	174,851	1,910	297	2,459	1,040	3,273
8. Washington, D.C.-Md.-Va. MSA	3,923,574	2,577,933	1,041,934	11,036	202,437	90,234	224,786
9. Dallas-Fort Worth, Tex. CMSA	3,885,415	2,924,673	554,616	18,972	97,578	289,576	518,917
Dallas, Tex. PMSA	2,553,362	1,854,577	410,766	12,635	67,195	208,189	368,884
Fort Worth-Arlington, Tex. PMSA	1,332,053	1,070,096	143,850	6,337	30,383	81,387	150,033
10. Houston-Galveston-Brazoria, Tex. CMSA	3,711,043	2,507,455	665,378	11,029	132,131	395,050	772,295
Houston, Tex. PMSA	3,301,937	2,188,370	611,243	9,465	126,601	366,258	707,536
Galveston-Texas City, Tex. PMSA	217,399	164,210	38,154	752	3,569	10,714	30,962
Brazoria, Tex. PMSA	191,707	154,875	15,981	812	1,961	18,078	33,797
11. Miami-Fort Lauderdale, Fla. CMSA	3,192,582	2,438,598	591,440	5,700	43,437	113,407	1,061,846
Miami-Hialeah, Fla. PMSA	1,937,094	1,413,015	397,993	3,066	26,307	96,713	953,407
Fort Lauderdale-Hollywood-Pompano Beach, Fla. PMSA	1,255,488	1,025,583	193,447	2,634	17,130	16,694	108,439
12. Atlanta, Ga. MSA	2,833,511	2,020,017	736,153	5,532	51,486	20,323	57,169
13. Cleveland-Akron-Lorain, Ohio CMSA	2,759,823	2,261,217	441,940	5,133	28,187	23,346	52,997
Cleveland, Ohio PMSA	1,831,122	1,435,768	355,619	3,038	20,528	16,169	33,921
Akron, Ohio PMSA	657,575	583,900	65,091	1,357	6,180	1,047	3,815
Lorain-Elyria, Ohio PMSA	271,126	241,549	21,230	738	1,479	6,130	15,261
14. Seattle-Tacoma, Wash. CMSA	2,559,164	2,211,710	123,266	32,071	164,286	27,831	75,555
Seattle, Wash. PMSA	1,972,961	1,713,068	81,056	23,727	135,251	19,859	54,993
Tacoma, Wash. PMSA	586,203	498,642	42,210	8,344	29,035	7,972	20,562
15. San Diego, Calif. MSA	2,498,016	1,672,256	159,306	20,066	198,311	248,077	510,781
16. Minneapolis-St. Paul, Minn.-Wis. MSA	2,464,124	2,270,360	89,710	23,956	65,204	14,894	37,448
17. St. Louis, Mo.-Ill. MSA	2,444,099	1,985,500	423,182	4,947	23,686	6,784	26,014
18. Baltimore, Md. MSA	2,382,172	1,709,309	616,065	6,444	42,634	7,720	30,160
19. Pittsburgh-Beaver Valley, Pa. CMSA	2,242,798	2,041,897	178,857	2,257	16,174	3,613	12,852
Pittsburgh, Pa. PMSA	2,056,705	1,867,138	168,382	2,054	15,797	3,334	11,728
Beaver County, Pa. PMSA	186,093	174,759	10,475	203	377	279	1,124
20. Phoenix, Ariz. MSA	2,122,101	1,799,420	74,257	38,017	36,294	174,113	345,498
21. Tampa-St. Petersburg-Clearwater, Fla. MSA	2,067,959	1,827,492	185,503	5,467	23,055	26,442	139,248
22. Denver-Boulder, Colo. CMSA	1,848,319	1,599,734	97,755	13,884	42,642	94,304	226,200
Denver, Colo. PMSA	1,622,980	1,389,544	95,796	12,571	37,134	87,935	211,005
Boulder-Longmont, Colo. PMSA	225,339	210,190	1,959	1,313	5,508	6,369	15,195
23. Cincinnati-Hamilton, Ohio-Ky.-Ind. CMSA	1,744,124	1,521,061	203,607	2,457	14,260	2,739	9,376
Cincinnati, Ohio-Ky.-Ind. PMSA	1,452,645	1,246,169	190,473	2,078	11,601	2,324	7,909
Hamilton-Middleton, Ohio, PMSA	291,479	274,892	13,134	379	2,659	415	1,467
24. Milwaukee-Racine, Wis. CMSA	1,607,183	1,335,470	214,182	8,522	19,786	29,223	60,340
Milwaukee, Wis. PMSA	1,432,149	1,183,372	197,183	8,001	18,782	24,811	51,306
Racine, Wis. PMSA	175,034	152,098	16,999	521	1,004	4,412	9,034
25. Kansas City, Mo.-Kans. MSA	1,566,280	1,320,564	200,508	7,631	17,444	20,133	45,227
26. Sacramento, Calif. MSA	1,481,102	1,170,505	101,940	17,021	114,520	77,116	172,374
27. Portland-Vancouver, Oreg.-Wash. CMSA	1,477,895	1,350,155	41,671	13,603	52,030	20,436	49,921
Portland, Oreg. PMSA	1,239,842	1,124,963	38,695	11,307	46,360	18,517	44,049
Vancouver, Wash. PMSA	238,053	225,192	2,976	2,296	5,670	1,919	5,872
28. Norfolk-Virginia Beach-Newport News, Va. MSA	1,396,107	947,160	398,093	4,679	35,205	10,970	32,329
29. Columbus, Ohio MSA	1,377,419	1,184,770	164,602	2,880	21,059	4,108	11,363
30. San Antonio, Tex. MSA	1,302,099	978,505	88,778	4,648	16,058	214,110	620,290
31. Indianapolis, Ind. MSA	1,249,822	1,061,142	172,326	2,510	10,081	3,763	11,084
32. New Orleans, La. Msa	1,238,816	770,406	430,470	3,615	21,380	12,945	53,226
33. Buffalo-Niagara Falls, N.Y. CMSA	1,189,288	1,037,211	121,956	7,611	11,026	11,484	24,347
Buffalo, N.Y. PMSA	968,532	831,903	109,852	5,600	10,220	10,957	22,249
Niagara Falls, N.Y. PMSA	220,756	205,308	12,104	2,011	806	527	2,098

Rank/Metropolitan area	Total	White	Black	American Indian	Asian or Pacific Islander	Other race	Hispanic origin[1]
34. Charlotte-Gastonia-Rock Hill, N.C.-S.C. PMSA	1,162,093	911,904	231,654	4,107	11,304	3,124	10,671
35. Providence-Pawtucket-Fall River, R.I.-Mass. CMSA	1,141,510	1,055,370	37,106	3,782	20,050	25,202	47,467
Providence, R.I. PMSA	654,854	590,671	30,526	3,079	14,522	16,056	31,453
Pawtucket-Woonsocket-Attleboro, R.I.-Mass. PMSA	329,384	310,677	5,494	535	3,987	8,691	13,949
Fall River, Mass.-R.I. PMSA	157,272	154,022	1,086	168	1,541	455	2,065
36. Hartford-New Britain-Middletown, Conn. CMSA	1,085,837	933,568	94,925	1,826	15,845	39,673	75,627
Hartford, Conn. PMSA	767,841	641,345	81,550	1,365	12,201	31,380	58,362
New Britain, Conn. PMSA	148,188	132,519	6,574	190	1,937	6,968	13,387
Middletown, Conn. PMSA	90,320	82,829	5,454	143	1,163	731	2,059
Bristol, Conn. PMSA	79,488	76,875	1,347	128	544	594	1,819
37. Orlando, Fla. MSA	1,072,748	888,913	133,308	3,199	20,474	26,854	96,418
38. Salt Lake City-Ogden, Utah MSA	1,072,227	1,000,082	10,464	8,337	25,598	27,746	61,964
39. Rochester, N.Y. MSA	1,002,410	875,886	93,819	2,870	13,978	15,857	31,238
40. Nashville, Tenn. MSA	985,026	818,424	152,349	2,121	10,012	2,120	7,665
41. Memphis, Tenn.-Ariz.-Miss.-MSA	981,747	570,511	399,011	1,791	8,178	2,256	7,986
42. Oklahoma City, Okla. MSA	958,839	777,589	101,082	45,720	17,742	16,706	34,152
43. Louisville, Ky.-Ind. MSA	953,662	818,898	124,761	1,576	5,640	1,787	5,765
44. Dayton-Springfield, Ohio MSA	951,270	811,393	126,238	1,915	9,278	2,446	7,254
45. Greensboro-Winston-Salem-High Point, N.C. MSA	942,091	747,835	182,284	3,196	6,381	2,395	7,096
46. Birmingham, Ala. MSA	907,810	655,609	245,726	1,506	4,014	955	3,989
47. Jacksonville, Fla. MSA	906,727	701,911	181,265	2,587	15,362	5,602	22,479
48. Albany-Schenectady-Troy N.Y. MSA	874,304	815,315	41,112	1,560	10,789	5,528	15,840
49. Richmond-Petersburg, Va. MSA	865,640	595,714	252,340	2,705	11,864	3,017	9,327
50. West Palm Beach-Boca Raton-Delray Beach, Fla. MSA	863,518	732,231	107,705	1,211	9,020	13,351	66,613
51. Honolulu, Hawaii MSA	836,231	264,372	25,875	3,532	526,459	15,993	56,884
52. Austin, Tex. MSA	781,572	600,023	72,254	2,827	18,770	87,698	159,942
53. Las Vegas, Nev. MSA	741,459	602,658	70,738	6,416	26,043	35,604	82,904
54. Raleigh-Durham, N.C. MSA	735,480	533,056	183,447	1,933	13,834	3,210	9,019
55. Scranton-Wilkes-Barre, Pa. MSA	734,175	720,692	7,660	580	3,827	1,416	5,640
56. Tulsa, Okla. MSA	708,954	590,612	58,186	48,196	6,563	5,397	14,534
57. Grand Rapids, Mich. MSA	688,399	623,787	41,311	3,394	7,831	12,076	22,631
58. Allentown-Bethehem-Easton, Pa.-N.J. MSA	686,688	649,890	13,466	688	7,293	15,351	28,885
59. Fresno, Calif. MSA	667,490	422,839	33,423	7,119	57,239	146,870	236,634
60. Tucson, Ariz. MSA	666,880	524,976	20,795	20,330	11,964	88,815	163,262
61. Syracuse, N.Y. MSA	659,864	605,924	39,095	3,948	7,740	3,157	8,926
62. Greenville-Spartanburg, S.C. MSA	640,861	522,632	111,334	959	4,617	1,319	5,120
63. Omaha, Nebr.-Iowa MSA	618,262	550,758	51,426	3,159	6,374	6,545	16,371
64. Toledo, Ohio MSA	614,128	526,555	69,717	1,423	6,146	10,287	20,382
65. Knoxville, Tenn. MSA	604,816	561,535	36,400	1,505	4,540	836	3,232
66. El Paso, Tex. MSA	591,610	452,512	22,110	2,590	6,485	107,913	411,619
67. Harrisburg-Lebanon-Carlisle, Pa. MSA	587,986	536,738	39,472	737	6,251	4,788	10,239
68. Bakersfield, Calif. MSA	543,477	378,479	30,131	7,026	16,541	111,300	151,995
69. New Haven-Meriden, Conn. MSA	530,180	441,831	64,220	947	8,430	14,752	32,907
70. Springfield, Mass. MSA	529,519	457,749	35,081	864	5,397	30,428	47,635
71. Baton Rouge, La. MSA	528,264	363,692	156,509	902	5,657	1,504	7,532
72. Little Rock-North Little Rock, Ark. MSA	513,117	404,808	101,862	1,870	3,347	1,230	4,164
73. Charleston, S.C. MSA	506,875	343,776	153,227	1,613	6,113	2,146	7,512
74. Youngstown-Warren, Ohio MSA	492,619	432,024	54,902	785	1,958	2,950	7,400
75. Wichita, Kans. MSA	485,270	423,784	36,979	5,160	9,109	10,238	19,793
76. Stockton, Calif. MSA	480,628	353,169	27,094	5,085	59,690	35,590	112,673
77. Alburquerque, N. Mex. MSA	480,577	369,445	13,199	16,296	7,386	74,251	178,310
78. Mobile, Ala. MSA	476,923	339,418	130,512	2,570	3,619	804	4,186
79. Columbia, S.C. MSA	453,331	307,454	137,906	1,013	4,820	2,138	5,949
80. Worcester, Mass. MSA	436,905	408,123	9,553	891	7,967	10,371	20,009

Rank/Metropolitan area	Total	White	Black	American Indian	Asian or Pacific Islander	Other race	Hispanic origin[1]
81. Johnson City-Kinsport-Bristol, Tenn.-Va. MSA	436,047	424,751	8,925	766	1,247	358	1,690
82. Chattanooga, Tenn.-Ga. MSA	433,210	370,586	58,218	891	2,825	690	2,539
83. Lansing-East Lansing, Mich. MSA	432,674	381,371	31,365	2,655	8,320	8,963	16,963
84. Flint, Mich. MSA	430,459	336,651	84,257	3,132	2,902	3,517	8,877
85. Lancaster, Pa. MSA	422,822	397,815	10,038	484	4,652	9,833	15,639
86. York, Pa. MSA	417,848	399,694	11,911	501	2,471	3,271	6,381
87. Lakeland-Winter Haven, Fla. MSA	405,382	341,952	54,385	1,158	2,486	5,401	16,600
88. Saginaw-Bay City-Midland, Mich. MSA	399,320	346,643	38,810	1,975	2,504	9,388	17,715
89. Melbourne-Titusville-Palm Bay, Fla. MSA	398,978	358,391	31,417	1,369	5,379	2,422	12,261
90. Colorado Springs, Colo. MSA	397,014	341,400	28,593	3,242	9,841	13,938	34,473
91. Augusta, Ga.-S.C. MSA	396,809	264,801	123,482	941	5,438	2,147	5,620
92. Jackson, Miss. MSA	395,396	224,999	167,899	346	1,754	398	1,944
93. Canton, Ohio MSA	394,106	365,675	25,187	1,015	1,558	671	2,854
94. Des Moines, Iowa MSA	392,928	368,386	14,952	1,015	6,218	2,357	6,614
95. McAllen-Edinburg-Mission, Tex. MSA	383,545	286,858	806	668	1,088	94,125	326,972
96. Daytona Beach, Fla. MSA	370,712	328,530	33,455	915	2,739	5,073	14,840
97. Modesto, Calif. MSA	370,522	297,315	6,450	4,039	19,223	43,495	80,897
98. Santa Barbara-Santa Maria-Lompoc, Calif. MSA	369,608	285,461	10,402	3,351	16,429	53,965	98,199
99. Madison, Wis. MSA	367,085	344,617	10,511	1,201	8,666	2,090	5,744
100. Fort Wayne, Ind. MSA	363,811	326,568	30,380	1,056	2,769	3,038	6,628
101. Spokane, Wash. MSA	361,364	341,874	5,105	5,539	6,569	2,277	6,994
102. Beaumont-Port Arthur, Tex. MSA	361,226	264,365	84,665	890	5,687	5,619	15,241
103. Salinas-Seaside-Monterey, Calif. MSA	355,660	227,008	22,849	3,017	27,856	74,930	119,570
104. Davenport-Rock Island-Mcline, Iowa-Ill. MSA	350,861	322,805	19,115	902	2,502	5,537	13,134
105. Corpus Christi, Tex. MSA	349,894	265,002	13,659	1,394	2,646	67,193	181,860
106. Lexington-Fayette, Ky. MSA	348,428	305,725	37,212	561	4,037	893	3,117
107. Pensacola, Fla. MSA	344,406	277,620	55,893	3,347	6,021	1,525	6,236
108. Peoria, Ill. MSA	339,172	309,325	25,142	587	2,759	1,359	3,642
109. Reading, Pa. MSA	336,523	314,561	10,003	333	2,746	8,880	17,174
110. Fort Myers-Cape Coral, Fla. MSA	335,113	306,200	22,184	672	1,894	4,163	15,094
111. Shreveport, La. MSA	334,341	213,610	116,892	863	2,023	951	4,394
112. Atlantic City, N.J. MSA	319,416	260,185	44,398	778	5,389	8,666	17,972
113. Utica-Rome, N.Y. MSA	316,633	297,746	13,849	613	2,314	2,111	6,174
114. Appleton-Oshkosh-Neenah, Wis. MSA	315,121	306,775	932	2,796	3,805	813	2,280
115. Huntington-Ashland, W.Va.-Ky.-Ohio MSA	312,529	304,244	6,751	372	937	225	1,274
116. Visalia-Tulare-Porterville, Calif. MSA	311,921	204,835	4,618	3,992	13,319	85,157	120,893
117. Montgomery, Ala. MSA	292,517	184,414	105,196	622	1,782	503	2,124
118. Rockford, Ill. MSA	283,719	251,783	23,383	697	3,136	4,720	9,836
119. Eugene-Springfield, Oreg. MSA	282,912	269,798	2,107	3,207	5,557	2,243	6,852
120. Macon-Warner-Robins, Ga. MSA	281,103	180,383	97,294	571	1,941	914	2,832
121. Evansville, Ind.-Ky. MSA	278,990	260,832	16,115	477	1,237	329	1,321
122. Salem, Oreg. MSA	278,024	255,212	2,332	4,041	4,746	11,693	21,027
123. Sarasota, Fla. MSA	277,776	262,836	12,073	483	1,430	954	5,882
124. Erie, Pa. MSA	275,572	257,879	14,304	438	1,411	1,540	3,364
125. Fayetteville, N.C. MSA	274,566	170,069	87,496	4,425	5,769	6,807	13,298
126. New London-Norwich, Conn.-R.I. MSA	266,819	245,933	12,077	1,433	3,549	3,827	8,517
127. Binghamton, N.Y. MSA	264,497	254,447	4,647	450	3,990	963	2,845
128. Provo-Orem, Utah MSA	263,590	253,596	374	1,913	3,958	3,749	8,488
129. Brownsville-Harlington, Tex. MSA	260,120	214,424	825	413	750	43,708	212,995
130. Poughkeepsie, N.Y. MSA	259,462	229,194	21,788	374	5,826	2,280	9,765
131. Killeen-Temple, Tex. MSA	255,301	181,144	49,687	1,405	7,201	15,864	31,238
132. Reno, Nev. MSA	254,667	225,095	5,680	4,921	9,824	9,147	22,959
133. Fort Pierce, Fla. MSA	251,071	214,278	30,709	526	1,565	3,993	10,680
134. Charleston, W.Va. MSA	250,454	234,518	13,919	292	1,450	275	1,042

Rank/Metropolitan area	Total	White	Black	American Indian	Asian or Pacific Islander	Other race	Hispanic origin[1]
135. South Bend-Mishawaka, Ind. MSA	247,052	216,984	24,190	846	2,507	2,525	5,201
136. Columbus, Ga.-Ala. MSA	243,072	144,326	91,484	765	3,107	3,390	7,388
137. Savannah, Ga. MSA	242,622	152,513	86,228	515	2,412	954	2,951
138. Johnstown, Pa. MSA	241,247	236,459	3,836	152	527	273	1,216
139. Springfield, Mo. MSA	240,593	233,186	3,784	1,471	1,600	552	1,991
140. Duluth, Minn.-Wis. MSA	239,971	232,507	1,276	4,487	1,342	359	1,153
141. Huntsville, Ala. MSA	238,912	184,197	48,116	1,601	4,232	766	2,984
142. Tallahassee, Fla. MSA	233,598	158,398	70,227	568	2,788	1,617	5,679
143. Anchorage, Alaska MSA	226,338	182,736	14,544	14,569	10,910	3,579	9,258
144. Roanoke, Va. MSA	224,477	194,645	27,602	281	1,602	347	1,359
145. Portsmouth-Dover-Rochester, N.H.-Maine MSA	223,578	218,216	2,285	414	2,136	527	1,994
146. Kalamazoo, Mich. MSA	223,411	197,427	19,879	1,017	3,168	1,920	3,950
147. Lubbock, Tex. MSA	222,636	176,037	17,154	686	2,722	26,037	51,011
148. Hickory-Morganton, N.C. MSA	221,700	201,558	17,540	417	1,673	512	1,449
149. Waterbury, Conn. MSA	221,629	196,680	15,414	538	1,576	7,421	16,384
150. Portland, Maine MSA	215,281	211,376	1,188	562	1,867	208	1,257
151. Lincoln, Nebr. MSA	213,641	202,663	4,659	1,207	3,367	1,745	3,938
152. Bradenton, Fla. MSA	211,707	190,328	16,400	501	1,227	3,251	9,424
153. Lafayette, La. MSA	208,740	154,146	51,378	440	1,915	861	3,115
154. Boise City, Idaho MSA	205,775	198,888	958	1,382	2,887	1,660	5,556
155. Gainesville, Fla. MSA	204,111	158,479	38,982	443	4,656	1,551	7,205
156. Biloxi-Gulfport, Miss. MSA	197,125	156,255	35,055	595	4,495	725	3,488
157. Ocala, Fla. MSA	194,833	167,094	24,844	638	945	1,312	5,860
158. Green Bay, Wis. MSA	194,594	186,621	1,012	3,869	2,522	570	1,525
159. St. Cloud, Minn. MSA	190,921	188,080	738	637	1,171	295	910
160. Bremerton, Wash. MSA	189,731	171,063	5,107	3,211	8,282	2,068	6,169
161. Springfield, Ill. MSA	189,550	173,114	14,373	319	1,391	353	1,311
162. Waco, Tex. MSA	189,123	146,100	29,520	563	1,384	11,556	23,643
163. Yakima, Wash. MSA	188,823	139,514	1,938	8,405	1,922	37,044	45,114
164. Amarillo, Tex. MSA	187,547	158,517	9,788	1,355	3,216	14,671	25,390
165. Fort Collins-Loveland, Colo. MSA	186,136	175,971	1,114	1,063	2,777	5,211	12,227
166. Houma-Thibodaux, La. MSA	182,842	147,453	26,735	6,814	1,370	470	2,625
167. Chico, Calif. MSA	182,120	165,200	2,361	3,241	5,170	6,148	13,606
168. Merced, Calif. MSA	178,403	120,280	8,523	1,516	15,128	32,956	58,107
169. Fort Smith, Ark.-Okla. MSA	175,911	155,580	6,831	9,054	3,755	691	2,120
170. New Bedford, Mass. MSA	175,641	161,018	4,623	504	841	8,655	7,347
171. Asheville, N.C. MSA	174,821	158,979	14,336	486	765	255	1,173
172. Champaign-Urbana-Rantoul, Ill. MSA	173,025	146,506	16,559	331	8,033	1,596	3,485
173. Clarksville-Hopkinsville, Tenn.-Ky. MSA	169,439	128,583	34,801	688	2,712	2,655	5,567
174. Cedar Rapids, Iowa MSA	168,767	163,164	3,334	363	1,401	505	1,591
175. Lake Charles, La. MSA	168,134	128,181	38,445	387	590	531	1,847
176. Longview-Marshall, Tex. MSA	162,431	122,270	35,975	670	635	2,881	3,053
177. Benton Harbor, Mich. MSA	161,378	133,259	24,872	685	1,487	1,075	2,683
178. Olympia, Wash. MSA	161,238	148,221	2,864	2,498	6,101	1,554	4,873
179. Topeka, Kans. MSA	160,976	141,189	13,365	1,836	1,179	3,407	7,785
180. Wheeling, W.Va.-Ohio MSA	159,301	155,313	3,196	145	546	101	569
181. Muskegon, Mich. MSA	158,983	133,931	21,617	1,338	555	1,542	3,623
182. Athens, Ga. MSA	156,267	124,076	29,003	257	2,352	579	2,011
183. Elkhart-Goshen, Ind. MSA	156,198	146,505	7,106	453	997	1,137	2,932
184. Lima, Ohio MSA	154,340	140,402	12,379	252	749	558	1,483
185. Fargo-Moorhead, N.Dak.-Minn. MSA	153,296	149,004	446	1,497	1,396	953	1,879
186. Naples, Fla. MSA	152,099	139,073	6,986	428	584	5,028	20,734
187. Tyler, Tex. MSA	151,309	113,676	31,572	520	638	4,903	8,986
188. Tuscaloosa, Ala. MSA	150,522	109,398	39,377	253	1,264	230	948
189. Richland-Kennewick-Pasco, Wash. MSA	150,033	129,749	2,395	1,124	3,115	13,650	19,940
190. Jacksonville, N.C. MSA	149,838	111,939	29,808	939	2,994	4,158	8,035
191. Jackson, Mich. MSA	149,756	135,557	11,983	655	653	908	2,303
192. Parkersburg-Marietta, W.Va.-Ohio MSA	149,169	146,698	1,567	242	520	142	479
193. Manchester, N.H. MSA	147,809	144,159	1,133	278	1,442	797	2,415
194. Redding, Calif. MSA	147,036	137,977	1,081	3,954	2,684	1,340	5,652
195. Waterloo-Cedar Falls, Iowa MSA	146,611	136,236	8,584	237	1,137	417	984
196. Medford, Oreg. MSA	146,389	140,188	340	1,863	1,429	2,569	5,949

Rank/Metropolitan area	Total	White	Black	American Indian	Asian or Pacific Islander	Other race	Hispanic origin[1]
197. Anderson, S.C. MSA	145,196	120,384	24,151	173	340	148	559
198. Fort Walton Beach, Fla. MSA	143,776	125,191	13,007	776	3,658	1,144	4,427
199. Steubenville-Weirton, Ohio-W. Va. MSA	142,523	136,078	5,591	237	439	178	710
200. Lynchburg, Va. MSA	142,199	110,847	30,079	277	743	253	923
201. Monroe, La. MSA	142,191	96,870	44,096	239	740	246	1,194
202. Jamestown-Dunkirk, N.Y. MSA	141,895	136,311	2,405	558	545	2,076	4,055
203. Janesville-Beloit, Wis. MSA	139,510	130,803	6,638	369	985	715	1,754
204. Eau Claire, Wis. MSA	137,543	134,056	269	617	2,400	204	611
205. Battle Creek, Mich. MSA	135,982	118,737	14,383	696	1,068	1,098	2,583
206. Las Cruces, N. Mex. MSA	135,510	123,434	2,172	1,009	1,164	7,731	76,448
207. Joplin, Mo. MSA	134,910	130,093	1,327	2,452	751	287	1,150
208. Laredo, Tex. MSA	133,239	93,657	156	201	484	38,741	125,069
209. Greeley, Colo. MSA	131,821	117,247	567	785	1,133	12,089	27,502
210. Decatur, Ala. MSA	131,556	113,685	14,879	2,434	389	169	686
211. Alexandria, La. MSA	131,556	92,989	36,805	564	908	290	1,526
212. Burlington, Vt. MSA	131,439	128,580	814	299	1,465	281	1,171
213. Florence, Ala. MSA	131,327	114,380	16,263	302	289	93	500
214. Charlottesville, Va. MSA	131,107	109,049	18,895	148	2,623	392	1,384
215. Dothan, Ala. MSA	130,964	100,878	27,801	526	1,201	558	1,679
216. Terre Haute, Ind. MSA	130,812	122,933	6,029	338	1,176	336	1,063
217. Anderson, Ind. MSA	130,669	119,734	9,870	299	415	351	885
218. Lafayette-West Lafayette, Ind. MSA	130,598	122,013	2,660	320	4,821	784	2,078
219. Altoona, Pa. MSA	130,542	128,840	1,073	118	380	131	431
220. Bloomington-Normal, Ill. MSA	129,180	121,057	5,563	203	1,624	733	1,671
221. Bellingham, Wash. MSA	127,780	119,229	650	4,014	2,363	1,524	3,718
222. Panama City, Fla. MSA	126,994	109,570	13,713	949	2,229	533	2,256
223. Mansfield, Ohio MSA	126,137	115,078	9,981	223	578	277	903
224. Sioux Falls, S. Dak. MSA	123,809	120,454	754	1,680	714	207	648
225. State College, Pa. MSA	123,786	116,552	2,801	179	3,841	413	1,350
226. Pueblo, Colo. MSA	123,051	104,304	2,253	991	729	14,774	44,090
227. Yuba City, Calif. MSA	122,643	95,062	3,478	2,616	10,996	10,491	17,320
228. Wichita Falls, Tex. MSA	122,378	102,427	11,221	903	1,851	5,976	10,555
229. Bryan-College Station, Tex. MSA	121,862	94,866	13,672	274	4,313	8,737	16,713
230. Hagerstown, Md. MSA	121,393	112,828	7,245	241	793	286	905
231. Sharon, Pa. MSA	121,003	114,479	5,882	115	393	134	506
232. Wilmington, N.C. MSA	120,284	94,895	24,097	435	616	241	924
233. Texarkana, Tex.-Texarkana, Ark. MSA	120,132	92,342	26,423	560	405	402	1,644
234. Muncie, Ind. MSA	119,659	111,232	7,167	274	641	345	853
235. Abilene, Tex. MSA	119,655	100,237	7,547	450	1,449	9,972	17,511
236. Odessa, Tex. MSA	118,934	91,309	5,557	647	662	20,759	37,315
237. Williamsport, Pa. MSA	118,710	115,040	2,816	219	469	166	641
238. Glens Falls, N.Y. MSA	118,539	115,157	2,352	214	392	424	1,789
239. Decatur, Ill. MSA	117,206	102,197	14,135	157	506	211	540
240. Santa Fe, N. Mex. MSA	117,043	96,454	711	2,948	941	15,989	50,947
241. Anniston, Ala. MSA	116,034	92,873	21,578	296	869	418	1,282
242. Wausau, Wis. MSA	115,400	112,189	89	490	2,499	133	470
243. Pascagoula, Miss. MSA	155,243	90,114	23,581	254	1,115	179	1,060
244. Sioux City, Iowa-Nebr. MSA	115,018	107,579	1,953	1,999	1,624	1,863	3,728
245. Florence, S.C. MSA	114,344	69,501	44,276	145	307	115	508
246. Billings, Mont. MSA	113,419	107,921	511	3,235	612	1,140	3,158
247. Fayetteville-Springdale, Ariz. MSA	113,409	108,743	1,676	1,486	1,043	461	1,526
248. Albany, Ga. MSA	112,561	60,041	51,522	281	498	219	928
249. Columbia, Mo. MSA	112,379	100,055	8,377	394	3,129	424	1,226
250. Lawton, Okla. MSA	111,486	79,666	19,908	5,153	3,065	3,694	6,923
251. Bloomington, Ind. MSA	108,978	102,752	2,835	216	2,713	462	1,367
252. Danville, Va. MSA	108,711	73,817	34,350	117	325	102	515
253. Burlington, N.C. MSA	108,213	86,373	20,822	303	487	228	736
254. Yuma, Ariz. MSA	106,895	80,702	3,056	1,429	1,393	20,315	43,388
255. Midland, Tex. MSA	106,611	86,977	8,281	414	888	10,051	22,780
256. Rochester, Minn. MSA	106,470	101,880	788	295	3,237	270	970
257. Sheboygan, Wis. MSA	103,877	100,389	430	357	2,061	640	1,688
258. Fitchburg-Leominster, Mass. MSA	102,797	95,540	2,356	196	1,789	2,916	7,312
259. Cumberland, Md.-W.Va. MSA	101,643	98,821	2,270	71	391	90	420
260. Gadsden, Ala. MSA	99,840	85,274	13,799	250	419	98	331

Rank/Metropolitan area	Total	White	Black	American Indian	Asian or Pacific Islander	Other race	Hispanic origin[1]
261. San Angelo, Tex. MSA	98,458	79,533	4,136	373	998	13,418	25,501
262. La Crosse, Wis. MSA	97,904	94,319	438	340	2,667	140	640
263. Kokomo, Ind. MSA	96,946	91,410	4,408	246	508	374	1,178
264. Kankakee, Ill. MSA	96,255	80,194	14,399	150	644	868	1,946
265. Iowa City, Iowa MSA	96,119	89,649	1,979	176	3,837	478	1,435
266. Elmira, N.Y. MSA	95,195	88,370	5,245	211	690	679	1,441
267. Sherman-Denison, Tex. MSA	95,021	85,553	6,565	1,046	412	1,445	2,795
268. Bangor, Maine MSA	88,745	86,328	467	1,008	798	144	509
269. Lewiston-Auburn, Maine MSA	88,141	86,799	443	197	514	188	559
270. Owensboro, Ky. MSA	87,189	83,168	3,619	101	229	72	312
271. Dubuque, Iowa MSA	86,403	85,367	354	77	437	168	437
272. Pine Bluff, Ark. MSA	85,487	47,878	36,877	227	352	153	427
273. Bismarck, N.Dak. MSA	83,831	81,306	79	2,016	286	144	435
274. St. Joseph, Mo. MSA	83,083	79,378	2,635	273	266	531	1,709
275. Lawrence, Kans. MSA	81,798	72,885	3,324	2,161	2,581	847	2,138
276. Rapid City, S.Dak. MSA	81,343	72,769	1,288	5,835	933	518	1,777
277. Pittsfield, Mass. MSA	79,250	76,597	1,702	142	548	261	770
278. Jackson, Tenn. MSA	77,982	53,423	24,170	66	253	70	376
279. Great Falls, Mont. MSA	77,691	72,345	1,061	3,072	792	421	1,398
280. Victoria, Tex. MSA	74,361	59,251	4,906	208	257	9,739	25,372
281. Cheyenne, Wyo. MSA	73,142	66,280	2,218	528	821	3,295	7,310
282. Grand Forks, N.Dak. MSA	70,683	66,766	1,446	1,244	881	346	1,053
283. Casper, Wyo. MSA	61,226	59,323	458	404	280	761	2,252
284. Enid, Okla. MSA	56,735	52,403	2,020	1,234	587	491	1,086

1. Hispanic persons may be of any race.   **Source:** U.S Bureau of the Census, Press Release CB91-229

Population Change in the Top 100 Metropolitan Statistical Areas, 1990–2000

Since the 1990 Census, the Census Bureau has changed the boundaries of several dozen metropolitan statistical areas (MSAs), merging some areas within others and separating some areas out of larger MSAs. For example, Washington D.C. and Baltimore, Md. are now considered one consolidated metropolitan statistical area rather than two. As a result, population statistics before and after 1990 are not directly comparable for more than 75 MSAs.

Metropolitan Statistical Area	Population 1990	Population 2000	Change, 1990–2000 Number	Change, 1990–2000 Percent
1. New York–Northern New Jersey–Long Island, N.Y.–N.J.–Conn.–Pa. CMSA	19,549,649	21,199,865	1,650,216	8.4%
2. Los Angeles–Riverside–Orange County, Calif. CMSA	14,531,529	16,373,645	1,842,116	12.7
3. Chicago–Gary–Kenosha, Ill.–Ind.–Wisc. CMSA	8,239,820	9,157,540	917,720	11.1
4. Washington–Baltimore, D.C.–Md.–Va.–WV CMSA	6,727,050	7,608,070	881,020	13.1
5. San Francisco–Oakland–San Jose, Calif. CMSA	6,253,311	7,039,362	786,051	12.6
6. Philadelphia–Wilmington–Atlantic City, Pa.–N.J.–Del.–Md. CMSA	5,892,937	6,188,463	295,526	5.0
7. Boston–Worcester–Lawrence, Mass.–N.H.–Maine–Conn. CMSA	5,455,403	5,819,100	363,697	6.7
8. Detroit–Ann Arbor–Flint, Mich. CMSA	5,187,171	5,456,428	269,257	5.2
9. Dallas–Fort Worth, Texas CMSA	4,037,282	5,221,801	1,184,519	29.3
10. Houston–Galveston–Brazoria, Texas CMSA	3,731,131	4,669,571	938,440	25.2
11. Atlanta, Ga. MSA	2,959,950	4,112,198	1,152,248	38.9
12. Miami–Fort Lauderdale, Fla. CMSA	3,192,582	3,876,380	683,798	21.4
13. Seattle–Tacoma–Bremerton, Wash. CMSA	2,970,328	3,554,760	584,432	19.7
14. Phoenix–Mesa, Ariz. MSA	2,238,480	3,251,876	1,013,396	45.3
15. Minneapolis–St. Paul, Minn.–Wisc. MSA	2,538,834	2,968,806	429,972	16.9
16. Cleveland–Akron, Ohio CMSA	2,859,644	2,945,831	86,187	3.0
17. San Diego, Calif. MSA	2,498,016	2,813,833	315,817	12.6
18. St. Louis, Mo.–Ill. MSA	2,492,525	2,603,607	111,082	4.5
19. Denver–Boulder–Greeley, Colo. CMSA	1,980,140	2,581,506	601,366	30.4
20. San Juan–Caguas–Arecibo, Puerto Rico CMSA	2,270,808	2,450,292	179,484	7.9
21. Tampa–St. Petersburg–Clearwater, Fla. MSA	2,067,959	2,395,997	328,038	15.9
22. Pittsburgh, Pa. MSA	2,394,811	2,358,695	-36,116	-1.5
23. Portland–Salem, Oreg.–Wash. CMSA	1,793,476	2,265,223	471,747	26.3
24. Cincinnati–Hamilton, Ohio–KY–Ind. CMSA	1,817,571	1,979,202	161,631	8.9
25. Sacramento–Yolo, Calif. CMSA	1,481,102	1,796,857	315,755	21.3
26. Kansas City, Mo.–Kans. MSA	1,582,875	1,776,062	193,187	12.2
27. Milwaukee–Racine, Wisc. CMSA	1,607,183	1,689,572	82,389	5.1
28. Orlando, Fla. MSA	1,224,852	1,644,561	419,709	34.3
29. Indianapolis, Ind. MSA	1,380,491	1,607,486	226,995	16.4
30. San Antonio, Texas MSA	1,324,749	1,592,383	267,634	20.2

Metropolitan Statistical Area	Population 1990	Population 2000	Change, 1990–2000 Number	Change, 1990–2000 Percent
31. Norfolk–Virginia Beach–Newport News, Va.–N.C. MSA	1,443,244	1,569,541	126,297	8.8
32. Las Vegas, Nev.–Ariz. MSA	852,737	1,563,282	710,545	83.3%
33. Columbus, Ohio MSA	1,345,450	1,540,157	194,707	14.5
34. Charlotte–Gastonia–Rock Hill, N.C.–S.C. MSA	1,162,093	1,499,293	337,200	29.0
35. New Orleans, La. MSA	1,285,270	1,337,726	52,456	4.1
36. Salt Lake City–Ogden, Utah MSA	1,072,227	1,333,914	261,687	24.4
37. Greensboro–Winston-Salem–High Point, N.C. MSA	1,050,304	1,251,509	201,205	19.2
38. Austin–San Marcos, Texas MSA	846,227	1,249,763	403,536	47.7
39. Nashville, Tenn. MSA	985,026	1,231,311	246,285	25.0
40. Providence–Fall River–Warwick, R.I.–Mass. MSA	1,134,350	1,188,613	54,263	4.8
41. Raleigh–Durham–Chapel Hill, N.C. MSA	855,545	1,187,941	332,396	38.9
42. Hartford, Conn. MSA	1,157,585	1,183,110	25,525	2.2
43. Buffalo–Niagara Falls, N.Y. MSA	1,189,288	1,170,111	-19,177	-1.6
44. Memphis, Tenn.–Ark.–Miss. MSA	1,007,306	1,135,614	128,308	12.7
45. West Palm Beach–Boca Raton, Fla. MSA	863,518	1,131,184	267,666	31.0
46. Jacksonville, Fla. MSA	906,727	1,100,491	193,764	21.4
47. Rochester, N.Y. MSA	1,062,470	1,098,201	35,731	3.4
48. Grand Rapids–Muskegon–Holland, Mich. MSA	937,891	1,088,514	150,623	16.1
49. Oklahoma City, Okla. MSA	958,839	1,083,346	124,507	13.0
50. Louisville, Ky.–Ind. MSA	948,829	1,025,598	76,769	8.1
51. Richmond–Petersburg, Va. MSA	865,640	996,512	130,872	15.1
52. Greenville–Spartanburg–Anderson, S.C. MSA	830,563	962,441	131,878	15.9
53. Dayton–Springfield, Ohio MSA	951,270	950,558	-712	-0.1
54. Fresno, Calif. MSA	755,580	922,516	166,936	22.1
55. Birmingham, Ala. MSA	840,140	921,106	80,966	9.6
56. Honolulu, Hawaii MSA	836,231	876,156	39,925	4.8
57. Albany–Schenectady–Troy, N.Y. MSA	861,424	875,583	14,159	1.6
58. Tucson, Ariz. MSA	666,880	843,746	176,866	26.5
59. Tulsa, Okla. MSA	708,954	803,235	94,281	13.3
60. Syracuse, N.Y. MSA	742,177	732,117	-10,060	-1.4
61. Omaha, Neb.-Iowa MSA	639,580	716,998	77,418	12.1
62. Albuquerque, NM MSA	589,131	712,738	123,607	21.0
63. Knoxville, Tenn. MSA	585,960	687,249	101,289	17.3
64. El Paso, Texas MSA	591,610	679,622	88,012	14.9
65. Bakersfield, Calif. MSA	543,477	661,645	118,168	21.7
66. Allentown–Bethlehem–Easton, Pa. MSA	595,081	637,958	42,877	7.2
67. Harrisburg–Lebanon–Carlisle, Pa. MSA	587,986	629,401	41,415	7.0
68. Scranton–Wilkes-Barre–Hazleton, Pa. MSA	638,466	624,776	-13,690	-2.1
69. Toledo, Ohio MSA	614,128	618,203	4,075	0.7
70. Baton Rouge, LA MSA	528,264	602,894	74,630	14.1
71. Youngstown–Warren, Ohio MSA	600,895	594,746	-6,149	-1.0
72. Springfield, Mass. MSA	587,884	591,932	4,048	0.7
73. Sarasota–Bradenton, Fla. MSA	489,483	589,959	100,476	20.5
74. Little Rock–North Little Rock, Ark. MSA	513,117	583,845	70,728	13.8
75. McAllen–Edinburg–Mission, Texas MSA	383,545	569,463	185,918	48.5
76. Stockton–Lodi, Calif. MSA	480,628	563,598	82,970	17.3
77. Charleston–North Charleston, S.C. MSA	506,875	549,033	42,158	8.3
78. Wichita, Kans. MSA	485,270	545,220	59,950	12.4
79. Mobile, Ala. MSA	476,923	540,258	63,335	13.3
80. Columbia, S.C. MSA	453,331	536,691	83,360	18.4
81. Colorado Springs, Colo. MSA	397,014	516,929	119,915	30.2
82. Fort Wayne, Ind. MSA	456,281	502,141	45,860	10.1
83. Daytona Beach, Fla. MSA	399,413	493,175	93,762	23.5
84. Lakeland–Winter Haven, Fla. MSA	405,382	483,924	78,542	19.4
85. Johnson City–Kingsport–Bristol, Tenn.–Va. MSA	436,047	480,091	44,044	10.1
86. Lexington, Ky. MSA	405,936	479,198	73,262	18.0
87. Augusta–Aiken, Ga.–S.C. MSA	415,184	477,441	62,257	15.0
88. Melbourne–Titusville–Palm Bay, Fla. MSA	398,978	476,230	77,252	19.4
89. Lancaster, Pa. MSA	422,822	470,658	47,836	11.3
90. Chattanooga, Tenn.–Ga. MSA	424,347	465,161	40,814	9.6
91. Des Moines, Iowa MSA	392,928	456,022	63,094	16.1
92. Kalamazoo–Battle Creek, Mich. MSA	429,453	452,851	23,398	5.4
93. Lansing–East Lansing, Mich. MSA	432,674	447,728	15,054	3.5
94. Modesto, Calif. MSA	370,522	446,997	76,475	20.6
95. Fort Myers–Cape Coral, Fla. MSA	335,113	440,888	105,775	31.6
96. Jackson, Miss. MSA	395,396	440,801	45,405	11.5
97. Boise City, Idaho MSA	295,851	432,345	136,494	46.1
98. Madison, Wisc. MSA	367,085	426,526	59,441	16.2
99. Spokane, Wash. MSA	361,364	417,939	56,575	15.7
100. Pensacola, Fla. MSA	344,406	412,153	67,747	19.7

Note: CMSA = consolidated metropolitan statistical area; MSA = metropolitan statistical area. For component areas see "Population of Metropolitan Statistical Areas, 1990-2000." **Source:** U.S. Bureau of the Census, 2001.

25 Fastest-Growing Metropolitan Statistical Areas, 1990-2000

Metropolitan Statistical Area	Population		Change, 1990–2000	
	1990	2000	Number	Percent
1. Las Vegas, Nev.-Ariz. MSA	852,737	1,563,282	710,545	83.3%
2. Naples, Fla. MSA	152,099	251,377	99,278	65.3
3. Yuma, Ariz. MSA	106,895	160,026	53,131	49.7
4. McAllen–Edinburg–Mission, Texas MSA	383,545	569,463	185,918	48.5
5. Austin–San Marcos, Texas MSA	846,227	1,249,763	403,536	47.7
6. Fayetteville–Springdale–Rogers, Ark. MSA	210,908	311,121	100,213	47.5
7. Boise City, Idaho MSA	295,851	432,345	136,494	46.1
8. Phoenix–Mesa, Ariz. MSA	2,238,480	3,251,876	1,013,396	45.3
9. Laredo, Texas MSA	133,239	193,117	59,878	44.9
10. Provo–Orem, Utah MSA	263,590	368,536	104,946	39.8
11. Atlanta, Ga. MSA	2,959,950	4,112,198	1,152,248	38.9
12. Raleigh–Durham–Chapel Hill, N.C. MSA	855,545	1,187,941	332,396	38.9
13. Myrtle Beach, S.C. MSA	144,053	196,629	52,576	36.5
14. Wilmington, N.C. MSA	171,269	233,450	62,181	36.3
15. Fort Collins–Loveland, Colo. MSA	186,136	251,494	65,358	35.1
16. Orlando, Fla. MSA	1,224,852	1,644,561	419,709	34.3
17. Reno, Nev. MSA	254,667	339,486	84,819	33.3
18. Ocala, Fla. MSA	194,833	258,916	64,083	32.9
19. Auburn–Opelika, Ala. MSA	87,146	115,092	27,946	32.1
20. Fort Myers–Cape Coral, Fla. MSA	335,113	440,888	105,775	31.6
21. West Palm Beach–Boca Raton, Fla. MSA	863,518	1,131,184	267,666	31.0
22. Bellingham, Wash. MSA	127,780	166,814	39,034	30.5
23. Denver–Boulder–Greeley, Colo. CMSA	1,980,140	2,581,506	601,366	30.4
24. Colorado Springs, Colo. MSA	397,014	516,929	119,915	30.2
25. Dallas–Fort Worth, Texas CMSA	4,037,282	5,221,801	1,184,519	29.3

Note: CMSA= consolidated metropolitan statistical area; MSA = metropolitan statistical area. For component areas see "Population of Metropolitan Statistical Areas, 1990-2000." **Source:** U.S. Bureau of the Census.

24 Fastest-Declining Metropolitan Statistical Areas, 1990–2000

Metropolitan Statistical Area	Population		Change, 1990–2000	
	1990	2000	Number	Percent
1. Steubenville–Weirton, Ohio–W.Va. MSA	142,523	132,008	-10,515	-7.4
2. Grand Forks, N.Dak,–Minn. MSA	103,181	97,478	-5,703	-5.5
3. Utica–Rome, N.Y. MSA	316,633	299,896	-16,737	-5.3
4. Binghamton, N.Y. MSA	264,497	252,320	-12,177	-4.6
5. Pittsfield, Mass. MSA	88,695	84,699	-3,996	-4.5
6. Elmira, N.Y. MSA	95,195	91,070	-4,125	-4.3
7. Alexandria, La. MSA	131,556	126,337	-5,219	-4.0
8. Wheeling, W.Va.–Ohio MSA	159,301	153,172	-6,129	-3.8
9. Johnstown, Pa. MSA	241,247	232,621	-8,626	-3.6
10. Anniston, Ala. MSA	116,034	112,249	-3,785	-3.3
11. Lewiston–Auburn, Maine MSA	93,679	90,830	-2,849	-3.0
12. Scranton–Wilkes-Barre–Hazleton, Pa. MSA	638,466	624,776	-13,690	-2.1
13. Decatur, Ill. MSA	117,206	114,706	-2,500	-2.1
14. Buffalo–Niagara Falls, N.Y. MSA	1,189,288	1,170,111	-19,177	-1.6
15. Jamestown, N.Y. MSA	141,895	139,750	-2,145	-1.5
16. Pittsburgh, Pa. MSA	2,394,811	2,358,695	-36,116	-1.5
17. Pine Bluff, Ark. MSA	85,487	84,278	-1,209	-1.4
18. Syracuse, N.Y. MSA	742,177	732,117	-10,060	-1.4
19. Altoona, Pa. MSA	130,542	129,144	-1,398	-1.1
20. Youngstown–Warren, Ohio MSA	600,895	594,746	-6,149	-1.0
21. Bangor, Maine MSA	91,629	90,864	-765	-0.8
22. Muncie, Ind. MSA	119,659	118,769	-890	-0.7
23. Sharon, Pa. MSA	121,003	120,293	-710	-0.6
24. Dayton–Springfield, Ohio MSA	951,270	950,558	-712	-0.1

Note: MSA = metropolitan statistical area. Only 24 MSA's declined in population between 1990 and 2000. **Source:** U.S. Bureau of the Census release, 1998.

COUNTIES IN AMERICA

In 2001 there were 3,141 counties in the United States. While only 50 percent of Americans live in cities, almost every American lives in a county. Counties were originally the creation of state governments, which saw them as the local arm of state authority, with special responsibility for rural areas. Counties were intended more for the administrative convenience of the state than to meet the immediate needs of county residents and were not designed to have the intimate relationship with, or understanding of, the needs of localities theoretically characteristic of municipalities. But most states have loosened the reins on county governments in recent years, giving them more authority to meet the needs of population centers that have pushed beyond municipal limits. (Note that in Louisiana, counties are called parishes, and in Alaska and New York City, they are known as boroughs.)

Like cities and metropolitan areas, the fastest-growing counties are in the southern and western United States. Seven of the 10 fastest-growing counties in 2000 were in Colorado or Georgia; the other three were in Virginia, Utah and Idaho.

The counties with the largest numerical increase in population between 1990 and 2000 are all in the western U.S.: Maricopa County, Ariz. (950,048), Los Angeles County, Calif. (656,174), Clark County, Nevada (634,306), Harris County, Texas (582,379), and Orange County, Calif. (435,733).

In addition, most of the counties with greatest growth are those in or around major metropolitan areas. Colorado's Douglas and Elbert Counties, which border both the Denver and Colorado Springs metropolitan areas, ranked 1 and 3 in population growth between 1990 and 2000. Both more than doubled over that period. Forsyth County, Ga. (within the Atlanta metropolitan area) was the second-fastest-growing county, increasing by 123.2 percent.

The 50 Largest Counties, 1980–90

Rank, 1990/County	Population 1990	Population 1980	Change 1980–90 Number	Change 1980–90 Percent	Rank 1980
1. Los Angeles County, Calif.	8,863,164	7,477,238	1,385,926	18.5%	1
2. Cook County, Ill.	5,105,067	5,253,628	-148,561	-2.8	2
3. Harris County, Texas	2,818,199	2,409,547	408,652	17.0	3
4. San Diego County, Calif.	2,498,016	1,861,846	636,170	34.2	8
5. Orange County, Calif.	2,410,556	1,932,921	477,635	24.7	6
6. Kings County, N.Y.	2,300,664	2,231,028	69,636	3.1	5
7. Maricopa County, Ariz.	2,122,101	1,509,175	612,926	40.6	12
8. Wayne County, Mich.	2,111,687	2,337,843	-226,156	-9.7	4
9. Queens County, N.Y.	1,951,598	1,891,325	60,273	3.2	7
10. Dade County, Fla.	1,937,094	1,625,509	311,585	19.2	10
11. Dallas County, Texas	1,852,810	1,556,419	296,391	19.0	11
12. Philadelphia County, Pa.	1,585,577	1,688,210	-102,633	-6.1	9
13. King County, Wash.	1,507,319	1,269,898	237,421	18.7	20
14. Santa Clara County, Calif.	1,497,577	1,295,071	202,506	15.6	18
15. New York County, N.Y.	1,487,536	1,428,285	59,251	4.1	15
16. San Bernardino County, Calif.	1,418,380	895,016	523,364	58.5	30
17. Cuyahoga County, Ohio	1,412,140	1,498,400	-86,260	-5.8	13
18. Middlesex County, Mass.	1,398,468	1,367,034	31,434	2.3	16
19. Allegheny County, Pa.	1,336,449	1,450,195	-113,746	-7.8	14
20. Suffolk County, N.Y.	1,321,864	1,284,231	37,633	2.9	19
21. Nassau County, N.Y.	1,287,348	1,321,582	-34,234	-2.6	17
22. Alameda County, Calif.	1,279,182	1,105,379	173,803	15.7	22
23. Broward County, Fla.	1,255,488	1,018,257	237,231	23.3	23
24. Bronx County, N.Y.	1,203,789	1,168,972	34,817	3.0	21
25. Bexar County, Texas	1,185,394	988,971	196,423	19.9	26
26. Riverside County, Calif.	1,170,413	663,199	507,214	76.5	52
27. Tarrant County, Texas	1,170,103	860,880	309,223	35.9	34
28. Oakland County, Mich.	1,083,592	1,011,793	71,799	7.1	25
29. Sacramento County, Calif.	1,041,219	783,381	257,838	32.9	40
30. Hennepin County, Minn.	1,032,431	941,411	91,020	9.7	29
31. St. Louis County, Mo.	993,529	974,180	19,349	2.0	27
32. Erie County, N.Y.	968,532	1,015,472	-46,940	-4.6	24
33. Franklin County, Ohio	961,437	869,126	92,311	10.6	32
34. Milwaukee County, Wis.	959,275	964,988	-5,713	-0.6	28
35. Westchester County, N.Y.	874,866	866,599	8,267	1.0	33
36. Hamilton County, Ohio	866,228	873,203	-6,975	-0.8	31
37. Palm Beach County, Fla.	863,518	576,758	286,760	49.7	70
38. Hartford County, Conn.	851,783	807,766	44,017	5.4	37
39. Pinellas County, Fla.	851,659	728,531	123,128	16.9	45
40. Honolulu County, Hawaii	836,231	762,565	73,666	9.7	43
41. Hillsborough County, Fla.	834,054	646,939	187,115	28.9	57
42. Fairfield County, Conn.	827,645	807,143	20,502	2.5	38
43. Shelby County, Tenn	826,330	777,113	49,217	6.3	41
44. Bergen County, N.J.	825,380	845,385	-20,005	-2.4	36
45. Fairfax County, Va.	818,584	595,754	222,830	37.4	66
46. New Haven County, Conn.	804,219	761,325	42,894	5.6	44
47. Contra Costa County, Calif.	803,732	656,331	147,401	22.5	54
48. Marion County, Tenn.	797,159	765,233	31,926	4.2	42
49. DuPage County, Ill.	781,666	658,858	122,808	18.6	53
50. Essex County, N.J.	778,206	851,304	-73,098	-8.6	35

Source: U.S. Bureau of the Census release, 1991.

The 75 Largest Counties, 1990–2000

Rank, 2000/County	Population, 1990	Population, 2000	Change, 1990-2000	Percent Change
1. Los Angeles County, Calif.	8,863,164	9,519,338	656,174	7.4%
2. Cook County, Ill.	5,105,067	5,376,741	271,674	5.3
3. Harris County, Texas	2,818,199	3,400,578	582,379	20.7
4. Maricopa County, Ariz.	2,122,101	3,072,149	950,048	44.8
5. Orange County, Calif.	2,410,556	2,846,289	435,733	18.1
6. San Diego County, Calif.	2,498,016	2,813,833	315,817	12.6
7. Kings County, N.Y.	2,300,664	2,465,326	164,662	7.2
8. Miami-Dade County, Fla.	1,937,094	2,253,362	316,268	16.3
9. Queens County, N.Y.	1,951,598	2,229,379	277,781	14.2
10. Dallas County, Texas	1,852,810	2,218,899	366,089	19.8
11. Wayne County, Mich.	2,111,687	2,061,162	-50,525	-2.4
12. King County, Wash.	1,507,319	1,737,034	229,715	15.2
13. San Bernardino County, Calif.	1,418,380	1,709,434	291,054	20.5
14. Santa Clara County, Calif.	1,497,577	1,682,585	185,008	12.4
15. Broward County, Fla.	1,255,488	1,623,018	367,530	29.3
16. Riverside County, Calif.	1,170,413	1,545,387	374,974	32.0
17. New York County, N.Y.	1,487,536	1,537,195	49,659	3.3
18. Philadelphia County, Pa.	1,585,577	1,517,550	-68,027	-4.3
19. Middlesex County, Mass.	1,398,468	1,465,396	66,928	4.8
20. Tarrant County, Texas	1,170,103	1,446,219	276,116	23.6
21. Alameda County, Calif.	1,279,182	1,443,741	164,559	12.9
22. Suffolk County, N.Y.	1,321,864	1,419,369	97,505	7.4
23. Cuyahoga County, Ohio	1,412,140	1,393,978	-18,162	-1.3
24. Bexar County, Texas	1,185,394	1,392,931	207,537	17.5
25. Clark County, Nev.	741,459	1,375,765	634,306	85.5
26. Nassau County, N.Y.	1,287,348	1,334,544	47,196	3.7
27. Bronx County, N.Y.	1,203,789	1,332,650	128,861	10.7
28. Allegheny County, Pa.	1,336,449	1,281,666	-54,783	-4.1
29. Sacramento County, Calif.	1,041,219	1,223,499	182,280	17.5
30. Oakland County, Mich.	1,083,592	1,194,156	110,564	10.2
31. Palm Beach County, Fla.	863,518	1,131,184	267,666	31.0
32. Hennepin County, Minn.	1,032,431	1,116,200	83,769	8.1
33. Franklin County, Ohio	961,437	1,068,978	107,541	11.2
34. St. Louis County, Mo.	993,529	1,016,315	22,786	2.3
35. Hillsborough County, Fla.	834,054	998,948	164,894	19.8
36. Fairfax County, Va.	818,584	969,749	151,165	18.5
37. Erie County, N.Y.	968,532	950,265	-18,267	-1.9
38. Contra Costa County, Calif.	803,732	948,816	145,084	18.1
39. Milwaukee County, Wis.	959,275	940,164	-19,111	-2.0
40. Westchester County, N.Y.	874,866	923,459	48,593	5.6
41. Pinellas County, Fla.	851,659	921,482	69,823	8.2
42. DuPage County, Ill.	781,666	904,161	122,495	15.7
43. Salt Lake County, Utah	725,956	898,387	172,431	23.8
44. Shelby County, Tenn.	826,330	897,472	71,142	8.6
45. Orange County, Fla.	677,491	896,344	218,853	32.3
46. Bergen County, N.J.	825,380	884,118	58,738	7.1
47. Fairfield County, Conn.	827,645	882,567	54,922	6.6
48. Honolulu County, Hawaii	836,231	876,156	39,925	4.8
49. Montgomery County, Md.	757,027	873,341	116,314	15.4
50. Marion County, Ind.	797,159	860,454	63,295	7.9
51. Hartford County, Conn.	851,783	857,183	5,400	0.6
52. Hamilton County, Ohio	866,228	845,303	-20,925	-2.4
53. Pima County, Ariz.	666,880	843,746	176,866	26.5
54. New Haven County, Conn.	804,219	824,008	19,789	2.5
55. Fulton County, Ga.	648,951	816,006	167,055	25.7
56. Travis County, Texas	576,407	812,280	235,873	40.9
57. Prince George's County, Md.	729,268	801,515	72,247	9.9
58. Fresno County, Calif.	667,490	799,407	131,917	19.8
59. Essex County, N.J.	778,206	793,633	15,427	2.0
60. Macomb County, Mich.	717,400	788,149	70,749	9.9
61. Duval County, Fla.	672,971	778,879	105,908	15.7
62. San Francisco County, Calif.	723,959	776,733	52,774	7.3
63. Baltimore County, Md.	692,134	754,292	62,158	9.0
64. Ventura County, Calif.	669,016	753,197	84,181	12.6
65. Worcester County, Mass.	709,705	750,963	41,258	5.8
66. Middlesex County, N.J.	671,780	750,162	78,382	11.7
67. Montgomery County, Pa.	678,111	750,097	71,986	10.6
68. Monroe County, N.Y.	713,968	735,343	21,375	3.0
69. Essex County, Mass.	670,080	723,419	53,339	8.0
70. San Mateo County, Calif.	649,623	707,161	57,538	8.9
71. Pierce County, Wash.	586,203	700,820	114,617	19.6
72. Mecklenburg County, N.C.	511,433	695,454	184,021	36.0
73. Jefferson County, Ky.	664,937	693,604	28,667	4.3
74. Suffolk County, Mass.	663,906	689,807	25,901	3.9
75. El Paso County, Texas	591,610	679,622	88,012	14.9

Source: U.S. Bureau of the Census, 2001

The American People Today

The United States is the third most populous nation in the world, ranking behind only China and India. The 2000 Census reported a total U.S. population of 281,421,806, a growth rate of 13.2 percent over the last decade. There were just under 250 million people in 1990; the U.S. population has increased by more than 100 million since 1960, and has doubled since 1940.

The single most noteworthy characteristic of the U.S. population continues to be the "Baby Boom Generation," the 75 million people born between 1946 and 1964. During these years the crude birth rate soared to as high as 24 live births per 1,000 population (compared to 20 or so in the years before World War II). Fertility rates, too, which had stood at about 75 live births per 1,000 women aged 15-44, jumped to as high as 121. As a result the population grew at an annual rate of between 1.4 percent and 1.8 percent.

The Baby Boom produced a generation of Americans much more populous than any other; the result has been that this generation attracts a great deal of attention as it passes through statistical age categories. Demographers sometimes refer to Baby Boomers, somewhat inelegantly perhaps, as the "Pig in the Python" in order to explain how this group has continued to distort the normal contours of the general body of the population. During the 1950's, their numbers required great capital outlays for new schools, and in the 1960's, for expanding colleges and universities. In the 1970's, they jammed the labor market causing higher unemployment rates, but helped the economy by increasing consumption and expanding the housing market.

The most troubling aspect of the 2000 Census is its stark revelation that the American population is very rapidly growing older. In 1970, 9.8 percent of the population was 65 or over; by 2000, 12.6 percent were. In 2030, the Census Bureau projects that fully 20 percent of Americans will be 65 or over.

The impact of this change on the Social Security system cannot be taken too seriously. In 2013, the first Baby Boomers turn 67 (the aging of the population has forced a deferral of the traditional retirement age from 65), and will begin collecting Social Security instead of paying into the fund. Ordinarily, this wouldn't be a remarkable fact. But the generation that followed the Baby Boom—the so-called Baby Bust generation, also known as Generation X—was unusually small. By 1968 the population growth rate had sunk to 1.0 percent; the birth rate to fewer than 18 live births per 1,000 population, and fertility rates to about 85 live births per woman 15-44. As a result, the ratio of people working and paying into Social Security to those receiving payments will shrink dramatically. Today, that ratio is only 3.5-1, but by 2030 it will be closer to 2-1.

In the pages that follow, we have attempted to create a statistical portrait of the population. Note that the Census Bureau updates some information more often than every 10 years with annual population estimates.

THE CENSUS

Article I, section 2 of the U.S. Constitution requires Congress to undertake a census of the population every 10 years for the purpose of apportioning seats in the House of Representatives. Today the decennial census is also used to apportion federal and state funds totalling as much as $100 billion a year, so it is vitally important to local governments and individuals throughout the country. City and county planners, health care administrators, as well as the entire marketing and advertising industries are all strongly dependent on census data for their day-to-day operations. So it's not surprising that the 2000 census, officially taken on April 1, was the largest undertaking of its kind in our history. The first results—state population figures—were released in December 2000, as required by law.

▶ **HIGHLIGHTS OF THE 2000 CENSUS**
Population growth   The resident U.S. population grew from 248.7 million people in 1990 to 281.4 million in 2000. For the first time in the 20th century, every state gained population. The total increase (32.7 million) is the largest numerical increase ever between censuses, though by percentage of total population (13.1), it still ranks below the 28 million person jump caused by the Baby Boom between 1950 and 1960 (an 18.5 percent increase), and far below the 35.1 percent increase between 1790 and 1800.

State and regional growth   The greatest growth occurred in the West and South. The five fastest-growing states were all in the West: Nevada (which grew an astounding 66.3 percent since 1990), Arizona (40.0 percent), Colorado (30.6 percent), Utah (29.6 percent), and Idaho (28.5 percent). Overall, the West grew by 10.4 million people to a total of 63.2 million, or an increase of 19.7 percent. The South increased by 14.8 million, or 17.3 percent. Georgia was the fastest-growing state in the South, increasing by 26.4 percent.

The Midwest grew by 7.9 percent, while the Northeast experienced 5.5 percent growth. Minnesota, up 12.4 percent, was the fastest-growing state in the Midwest, while New Hampshire, which also grew by 12.4 percent, led the Northeast. The state with the lowest population growth was North Dakota, which increased only 0.5 percent. Still, that's a turnaround for the Peace Garden State, which lost 13,917 people between 1980 and 1990.

The center of U.S. population—the exact spot where an imaginary map of the U.S. would balance perfectly if all 281 million residents were of equal weight—was approximately 2.8 miles east of a town called Edgar Springs, Mo. This point is approximately 12.1 miles south and 32.5 miles west of Steelville, Mo., which was the 1990 center of population.

U.S. Resident Population and Population Change by State, 1990–2000

State	1990 Population	1990 Rank	2000 Population	2000 Rank	Change, 1990–2000 Number	Change, 1990–2000 Percent
United States	248,709,873	—	281,421,906	—	32,712,033	13.2%
Alabama	4,040,587	(22)	4,447,100	(23)	406,513	10.1
Alaska	550,043	(49)	626,932	(48)	76,889	14.0
Arizona	3,665,228	(24)	5,130,632	(20)	1,465,404	40.0
Arkansas	2,350,725	(33)	2,673,400	(33)	322,675	13.7
California	29,760,021	(1)	33,871,648	(1)	4,111,627	13.8
Colorado	3,294,394	(26)	4,301,261	(24)	1,006,867	30.6
Connecticut	3,287,116	(27)	3,405,565	(29)	118,449	3.6
Delaware	666,168	(46)	783,600	(45)	117,432	17.6
District of Columbia[1]	606,900	—	572,059	—	-34,841	-5.7
Florida	12,937,926	(4)	15,982,378	(4)	3,044,452	23.5
Georgia	6,478,216	(11)	8,186,453	(10)	1,708,237	26.4
Hawaii	1,108,229	(41)	1,211,537	(42)	103,308	9.3
Idaho	1,006,749	(42)	1,293,953	(39)	287,204	28.5
Illinois	11,430,602	(6)	12,419,293	(5)	988,691	8.6
Indiana	5,544,159	(14)	6,080,485	(14)	536,326	9.7
Iowa	2,776,755	(30)	2,926,324	(30)	149,569	5.4
Kansas	2,477,574	(32)	2,688,418	(32)	210,844	8.5
Kentucky	3,685,296	(23)	4,041,769	(25)	356,473	9.7
Louisiana	4,219,973	(21)	4,468,976	(22)	249,003	5.9
Maine	1,227,928	(38)	1,274,923	(40)	46,995	3.8
Maryland	4,781,468	(19)	5,296,486	(19)	515,018	10.8
Massachusetts	6,016,425	(13)	6,349,097	(13)	332,672	5.5
Michigan	9,295,297	(8)	9,938,444	(8)	643,147	6.9
Minnesota	4,375,099	(20)	4,919,479	(21)	544,380	12.4
Mississippi	2,573,216	(31)	2,844,658	(31)	271,442	10.5
Missouri	5,117,073	(15)	5,595,211	(17)	478,138	9.3
Montana	799,065	(44)	902,195	(44)	103,130	12.9
Nebraska	1,578,385	(36)	1,711,263	(38)	132,878	8.4
Nevada	1,201,833	(39)	1,998,257	(35)	796,424	66.3
New Hampshire	1,109,252	(40)	1,235,786	(41)	126,534	11.4
New Jersey	7,730,188	(9)	8,414,350	(9)	684,162	8.9
New Mexico	1,515,069	(37)	1,819,046	(36)	303,977	20.1
New York	17,990,455	(2)	18,976,457	(3)	986,002	5.5
North Carolina	6,628,637	(10)	8,049,313	(11)	1,420,676	21.4
North Dakota	638,800	(47)	642,200	(47)	3,400	0.5
Ohio	10,847,115	(7)	11,353,140	(7)	506,025	4.7
Oklahoma	3,145,585	(28)	3,450,654	(27)	305,069	9.7
Oregon	2,842,321	(29)	3,421,399	(28)	579,078	20.4
Pennsylvania	11,881,643	(5)	12,281,054	(6)	399,411	3.4
Rhode Island	1,003,464	(43)	1,048,319	(43)	44,855	4.5
South Carolina	3,486,703	(25)	4,012,012	(26)	525,309	15.1
South Dakota	696,004	(45)	754,844	(46)	58,840	8.5
Tennessee	4,877,185	(17)	5,689,283	(16)	812,098	16.7
Texas	16,986,510	(3)	20,851,820	(2)	3,865,310	22.8
Utah	1,722,850	(35)	2,233,169	(34)	510,319	29.6
Vermont	562,758	(48)	608,827	(49)	46,069	8.2
Virginia	6,187,358	(12)	7,078,515	(12)	891,157	14.4
Washington	4,866,692	(18)	5,894,121	(15)	1,027,429	21.1
West Virginia	1,793,477	(34)	1,808,344	(37)	14,867	0.8
Wisconsin	4,891,769	(16)	5,363,675	(18)	471,906	9.6
Wyoming	453,588	(50)	493,782	(50)	40,194	8.9

1. If the District of Columbia were included with the states, it would have ranked 48th in 1990 and 49th in 2000.
Source: U.S. Bureau of the Census, 2001.

Congressional representation Because each state's number of representatives in Congress is based on its population, the population shift to the South and West will bring with it a corresponding shift in representation. A total of eight states will gain representatives (four of them will gain two), while 10 states will lose representatives (two states will lose two each). States cannot have fewer than one representative, so even though North Dakota experienced a much lower growth rate than New York, it cannot lose its sole member of Congress, whereas New York will lose two representatives.

Gainers		Losers	
Arizona	+2	New York	-2
Florida	+2	Pennsylvania	-2
Georgia	+2	Connecticut	-1
Texas	+2	Illinois	-1
California	+1	Indiana	-1
Colorado	+1	Michigan	-1
Nevada	+1	Mississippi	-1
Norh Carolina	+1	Ohio	-1
		Oklahoma	-1
		Wisconsin	-1

State Urban and Rural Percentage of Land Area and Population, 1980–90

State	Land area, 1990 Sq. miles	Land area, 1990 Urban	Land area, 1990 Rural	Population 1980 Urban	Population 1980 Rural	Population 1990 Urban	Population 1990 Rural
U.S. total	3,536,278	2.5%	97.5%	73.7%	26.3%	75.2%	24.8%
Alabama	50,750.2	5.3	94.7	60.0	40.0	60.4	39.6
Alaska	570,373.5	0.1	99.9	64.5	35.5	67.5	32.5
Arizona	113,642.2	1.8	98.2	83.8	16.2	87.5	12.5
Arkansas	52,075.3	2.3	97.7	51.6	48.4	53.5	46.5
California	155,973.2	5.2	94.8	91.3	8.7	92.6	7.4
Colorado	103,728.8	1.3	98.7	80.6	19.4	82.4	17.6
Connecticut	4,845.4	25.9	74.1	78.8	21.2	79.1	20.9
Delaware	1,954.6	10.7	89.3	70.7	29.3	73.0	27.0
Dist. of Columbia	61.4	100.0	0.0	100.0	0.0	100.0	0.0
Florida	55,937.2	9.5	90.5	84.3	15.7	84.8	15.2
Georgia	57,918.7	4.9	95.1	62.3	37.7	63.2	36.8
Hawaii	6,423.4	10.0	90.0	86.5	13.5	89.0	11.0
Idaho	82,751.0	0.4	99.6	54.0	46.0	57.4	42.6
Illinois	55,593.3	5.5	94.5	83.0	17.0	84.6	15.4
Indiana	35,870.1	5.0	95.0	64.2	35.8	64.9	35.1
Iowa	55,874.9	2.0	98.0	58.6	41.4	60.6	39.4
Kansas	81,823.0	1.1	98.9	66.7	33.3	69.1	30.9
Kentucky	39,732.3	2.7	97.3	50.8	49.2	51.8	48.2
Louisiana	43,566.1	3.7	96.3	68.6	31.4	68.1	31.9
Maine	30,864.5	2.3	97.7	47.5	52.5	44.6	55.4
Maryland	9,774.6	16.1	83.9	80.3	19.7	81.3	18.7
Massachusetts	7,838.0	27.4	72.6	83.8	16.2	84.3	15.7
Michigan	56,809.2	4.7	95.3	70.7	29.3	70.5	29.5
Minnesota	79,616.5	2.3	97.7	66.8	33.2	69.9	30.1
Mississippi	46,913.7	2.4	97.6	47.3	52.7	47.1	52.9
Missouri	68,898.1	2.74	97.3	68.1	31.9	68.7	31.3
Montana	145,556.3	0.2	99.8	52.9	47.1	52.5	47.5
Nebraska	76,877.7	0.5	99.5	62.7	37.3	66.1	33.9
Nevada	109,805.5	0.9	99.1	85.3	14.7	88.3	11.7
New Hampshire	8,969.4	5.7	94.3	52.2	47.8	51.0	49.0
New Jersey	7,418.8	32.7	67.3	89.0	11.0	89.4	10.6
New Mexico	121,364.5	0.7	99.3	72.2	27.8	73.0	27.0
New York	47,223.8	7.2	92.8	84.6	15.4	84.3	15.7
North Carolina	48,718.1	4.6	95.4	48.0	52.0	50.4	49.6
North Dakota	68,994.3	0.2	99.8	48.8	51.2	53.3	46.7
Ohio	40,952.6	8.8	91.2	73.3	26.7	74.1	25.9
Oklahoma	68,678.5	2.7	97.3	67.3	32.7	67.7	32.3
Oregon	96,002.5	0.9	99.1	67.9	32.1	70.5	29.5
Pennsylvania	44,819.6	6.7	93.3	69.3	30.7	68.9	31.1
Rhode Island	1,045.0	28.5	71.5	87.0	13.0	86.0	14.0
South Carolina	30,111.1	4.7	95.3	54.1	45.9	54.6	45.4
South Dakota	75,896.0	0.3	99.7	46.4	53.6	50.0	50.0
Tennessee	41,219.5	5.7	94.3	60.4	39.6	60.9	39.1
Texas	261,914.3	2.9	97.1	79.6	20.4	80.3	19.7
Utah	82,168.1	0.9	99.1	84.4	15.6	87.0	13.0
Vermont	9,249.3	1.5	98.5	33.8	66.2	32.2	67.8
Virginia	39,597.8	5.5	94.5	66.0	34.0	69.4	30.6
Washington	66,658.1	2.7	97.3	73.6	26.4	76.4	23.6
West Virginia	24,086.6	1.6	98.4	36.2	63.8	36.1	63.9
Wisconsin	54,313.7	2.9	97.1	64.2	35.8	65.7	34.3
Wyoming	97,104.6	0.2	99.8	62.8	37.2	65.0	35.0

Source: U.S. Bureau of the Census, 1991.

Since 1960, California's representatives have increased from 38 to 53, Florida's have more than doubled from 12 to 25, and Texas's have grown from 23 to 32. Over the same period, New York has lost a total of 12 representatives while Illinois has lost 5.

Urban and rural population growth Since the 1920 census, more than one half of all Americans have lived in an urban area, which can be loosely defined as a place of 2,500 or more inhabitants. During the 1980's, the population of urban areas grew by 20 million people, from 167.1 to 187.1 million people, an increase of 12 percent. By 1990, the proportion of the U.S. population living in urban areas reached 75.2 percent, up from 73.7 percent in 1980. California had the higest proportion of urban population, at 92.6 percent. In comparison, the country's rural population grew by 3.6 percent, from 59.5 million in 1980 to 61.7 million in 1990. Only 11 states, however, had increased percentages of rural population in the 1980s (see the accompanying table) even though 32 states recorded an increase in the number of rural residents. Vermont had the highest rural percentage of population: 67.8 percent.

U.S. Population by State, 1790–1990

State	1790	1800	1810	1820	1830	1840	1850
Total U.S.	3,929,214	5,308,483	7,239,881	9,638,453	12,860,702	17,063,353	23,191,876
Alabama	—	1,250	9,046	127,901	309,527	590,756	771,623
Alaska	—	—	—	—	—	—	—
Arizona	—	—	—	—	—	—	—
Arkansas	—	—	1,062	14,273	30,388	97,574	209,897
California	—	—	—	—	—	—	92,597
Colorado	—	—	—	—	—	—	—
Connecticut	237,946	251,002	261,942	275,248	297,675	309,978	370,792
Delaware	59,096	64,273	72,674	72,749	76,748	78,085	91,532
District of Columbia	—	8,144	15,471	23,336	30,261	33,745	51,687
Florida	—	—	—	—	34,730	54,477	87,445
Georgia	82,548	162,686	252,433	340,989	516,823	691,392	906,185
Hawaii	—	—	—	—	—	—	—
Idaho	—	—	—	—	—	—	—
Illinois	—	—	12,282	55,211	157,445	476,183	851,470
Indiana	—	5,641	24,520	147,178	343,031	685,866	988,416
Iowa	—	—	—	—	—	43,112	192,214
Kansas	—	—	—	—	—	—	—
Kentucky	73,677	220,955	406,511	564,317	687,917	779,828	982,405
Louisiana	—	—	76,556	153,407	215,739	352,411	517,762
Maine	96,540	151,719	228,705	298,335	399,455	501,793	583,169
Maryland	319,728	341,548	380,546	407,350	447,040	470,019	583,034
Massachusetts	378,787	422,845	472,040	523,287	610,408	737,699	994,514
Michigan	—	—	4,762	8,896	31,369	212,267	397,654
Minnesota	—	—	—	—	—	—	6,077
Mississippi	—	7,600	31,306	75,448	136,621	375,651	606,526
Missouri	—	—	19,783	66,586	140,455	383,702	682,044
Montana	—	—	—	—	—	—	—
Nebraska	—	—	—	—	—	—	—
Nevada	—	—	—	—	—	—	—
New Hampshire	141,885	183,858	214,460	244,161	269,328	284,574	317,976
New Jersey	184,139	211,149	245,562	277,575	320,823	373,306	489,555
New Mexico	—	—	—	—	—	—	61,547
New York	340,120	589,051	959,049	1,372,812	1,918,608	2,428,921	3,097,394
North Carolina	393,751	478,103	555,500	638,829	737,987	753,419	869,039
North Dakota	—	—	—	—	—	—	—
Ohio	—	45,365	230,760	581,434	937,903	1,519,467	1,980,329
Oklahoma	—	—	—	—	—	—	—
Oregon	—	—	—	—	—	—	12,093
Pennsylvania	434,373	602,365	810,091	1,049,458	1,348,233	1,724,033	2,311,786
Rhode Island	68,825	69,122	76,931	83,059	97,199	108,830	147,545
South Carolina	249,073	345,591	415,115	502,741	581,185	594,398	668,507
South Dakota	—	—	—	—	—	—	—
Tennessee	35,691	105,602	261,727	422,832	681,904	829,210	1,002,717
Texas	—	—	—	—	—	—	212,592
Utah	—	—	—	—	—	—	11,380
Vermont	85,425	154,465	217,895	235,981	280,652	291,948	314,120
Virginia[2]	747,610	880,200	974,600	1,065,366	1,211,405	1,239,797	1,421,661
Washington	—	—	—	—	—	—	1,201
West Virginia	—	—	—	—	—	—	—
Wisconsin	—	—	—	—	—	30,945	305,391
Wyoming	—	—	—	—	—	—	—

Population growth in metropolitan areas

The 2000 census revealed that more than 80 percent of all U.S. residents (226.0 million) lived in metropolitan areas, while just under 30 percent (84.1 million) lived in metro areas of 5 million people or more. Metro areas with populations between 2.0 million and 5.0 million grew the fastest: they increased by a total of 20 percent. Metro areas with more than 1 million but fewer than 2 million people grew by 17.7 percent. Nonmetropolitan areas grew slowest: a total of 10.2 percent between 1990 and 2000. That's better than the previous decade, however, when nonmetropolitan areas grew by only 3.9 percent.

The 10 fastest-growing metropolitan areas were all in the South or the West. Las Vegas, which leaped from 852,737 to 1.5 million, grew by an astounding 83.3 percent. Napels, Fla. was second, with 65.3 percent growth. Yuma, Ariz. (49.7), McAllen-Edinburg Mission, Texas (48.5) and Austin-San Marcos, Texas (47.7) rounded out the top five.

Race and Hispanic origin

Since 1960, each Census has approached the issue of race in slightly different ways. The most important change for the 2000 Census was the ability of respondents to classify themselves as members of

State	1860	1870	1880	1890	1900	1910	1920
Total U.S.	31,443,321	38,558,371	50,189,209	62,979,766	76,212,168	92,228,496	106,021,537
Alabama	964,201	996,992	1,262,505	1,513,401	1,828,697	2,138,093	2,348,174
Alaska	—	—	33,426	32,052	63,592	64,356	55,036
Arizona	—	9,658	40,440	88,243	122,931	204,354	334,162
Arkansas	435,450	484,471	802,525	1,128,211	1,311,564	1,574,449	1,752,204
California	379,994	560,247	864,694	1,213,396	1,485,053	2,377,549	3,426,861
Colorado	34,277	39,864	194,327	413,249	539,700	799,024	939,629
Connecticut	460,147	537,454	622,700	746,258	908,420	1,114,756	1,380,631
Delaware	112,216	125,015	146,608	168,493	184,735	202,322	223,003
District of Columbia	75,080	131,700	177,624	230,392	278,718	331,069	437,571
Florida	140,424	187,748	269,493	391,422	528,542	752,619	968,470
Georgia	1,057,286	1,184,109	1,542,180	1,837,353	2,216,331	2,609,121	2,895,832
Hawaii	—	—	—	—	154,001	191,874	255,881
Idaho	—	14,999	32,610	88,548	161,772	325,594	431,866
Illinois	1,711,951	2,539,891	3,077,871	3,826,352	4,821,550	5,638,591	6,485,280
Indiana	1,350,428	1,680,637	1,978,301	2,192,404	2,516,462	2,700,876	2,930,390
Iowa	674,913	1,194,020	1,624,615	1,912,297	2,231,853	2,224,771	2,404,021
Kansas	107,206	364,399	996,096	1,428,108	1,470,495	1,690,949	1,769,257
Kentucky	1,155,684	1,321,011	1,648,690	1,858,635	2,147,174	2,289,905	2,416,630
Louisiana	708,002	726,915	939,946	1,118,588	1,381,625	1,656,388	1,798,509
Maine	628,279	626,915	648,936	661,086	694,466	742,371	768,014
Maryland	687,049	780,894	934,943	1,042,390	1,188,044	1,295,346	1,449,661
Massachusetts	1,231,066	1,457,351	1,783,085	2,238,947	2,805,346	3,366,416	3,852,356
Michigan	749,113	1,184,059	1,636,937	2,093,890	2,420,982	2,810,173	3,668,412
Minnesota	172,023	439,706	780,773	1,310,283	1,751,394	2,075,708	2,387,125
Mississippi	791,305	827,922	1,131,597	1,289,600	1,551,270	1,797,114	1,790,618
Missouri	1,182,012	1,721,295	2,168,380	2,679,185	3,106,665	3,293,335	3,404,055
Montana	—	20,595	39,159	142,924	243,329	376,053	548,889
Nebraska	28,841	122,993	452,402	1,062,656	1,066,300	1,192,214	1,296,372
Nevada	6,857	42,491	62,266	47,355	42,335	81,875	77,407
New Hampshire	326,073	318,300	346,991	376,530	411,588	430,572	443,083
New Jersey	672,035	906,096	1,131,116	1,444,933	1,883,669	2,537,167	3,155,900
New Mexico	93,516	91,874	119,565	160,282	195,310	327,301	360,350
New York	3,880,735	4,382,759	5,082,871	6,003,174	7,268,894	9,113,614	10,385,227
North Carolina	992,622	1,071,361	1,399,750	1,617,949	1,893,810	2,206,287	2,559,123
North Dakota	—	2,405	36,909	190,983	319,146	577,056	646,872
Ohio	2,339,511	2,665,260	3,198,062	3,672,329	4,157,545	4,767,121	5,759,394
Oklahoma	—	—	—	258,657	790,371	1,657,155	2,028,283
Oregon	52,465	90,923	174,768	317,704	413,536	672,765	783,389
Pennsylvania	2,906,215	3,521,951	4,282,891	5,258,113	6,302,115	7,665,111	8,720,017
Rhode Island	174,620	217,353	276,531	345,506	428,556	542,610	604,397
South Carolina	703,708	705,606	995,577	1,151,149	1,340,316	1,515,400	1,683,724
South Dakota	4,837	11,776	98,268	348,600	401,570	583,888	636,547
Tennessee	1,109,801	1,258,520	1,542,359	1,767,518	2,020,616	2,184,789	2,337,885
Texas	604,215	818,579	1,591,749	2,235,527	3,048,710	3,896,542	4,663,228
Utah	40,273	86,786	143,963	210,779	276,749	373,351	449,396
Vermont	315,098	330,551	332,286	332,422	343,641	355,956	352,428
Virginia[2]	1,596,318	1,225,163	1,512,565	1,655,980	1,854,184	2,061,612	2,309,187
Washington	11,594	23,955	75,116	357,232	518,103	1,141,990	1,356,621
West Virginia	—	442,014	618,457	762,794	958,800	1,221,119	1,463,701
Wisconsin	775,881	1,054,670	1,315,497	1,693,330	2,069,042	2,333,860	2,632,067
Wyoming	—	9,118	20,789	62,555	92,531	145,965	194,402

more than one race. In previous censuses, someone who was part black and part white had to choose one race or the other on Census forms. For the 2000 Census, however, people with more than one race in their heritage were permitted to identify all their racial backgrounds. More than 6.8 million people identified themselves as being of more than one race. Because it is impossible to know how people of more than one race identified themselves in the past, racial data from the 2000 Census is not strictly comparable with those from previous censuses.

The United States remains overwhelmingly white, though less so than in the past. There were 211 million white people in the U.S. in 2000, and 5 million more who were white and at least one other race. The white-only population was 75.1 percent of the total U.S. population in 2000, down from 80.3 percent 10 years earlier. In 1970, the white population of the U.S. was 87.5 percent of the total.

The black-only population was 34.7 million in 2000, up from just under 30 million in 1990. Another 1.8 million people were black and at least one other race. The black-only population is 12.3 percent of the total, up slightly from 12.1 in 1990 and 11.1 percent in 1970.

The Asian population increased from 6.9 million in 1990 to 10.2 million (Asian-only) in 2000. Another 1.6 million people considered themselves Asian and at least one other race. The Asian-only population represented 3.6 percent of the total, up from 2.8 in 1990. For 2000, the Census Bureau separated out Native Hawaiian and other Pacific Islander from the Asian population for the first time.

State	1930	1940	1950	1960	1970	1980[1]	1990
Total U.S.	123,202,624	132,164,569	151,325,798	179,323,175	203,302,031	226,542,203	248,709,873
Alabama	2,646,248	2,832,961	3,061,743	3,266,740	3,444,354	3,894,025	4,040,587
Alaska	59,278	72,524	128,643	226,167	302,583	401,851	550,043
Arizona	435,573	499,261	749,587	1,302,161	1,775,399	2,716,546	3,665,228
Arkansas	1,854,482	1,949,387	1,909,511	1,786,272	1,923,322	2,286,357	2,350,725
California	5,677,251	6,907,387	10,586,223	15,717,204	19,971,069	23,667,764	29,760,021
Colorado	1,035,791	1,123,296	1,325,089	1,753,947	2,209,596	2,889,735	3,294,394
Connecticut	1,606,903	1,709,242	2,007,280	2,535,234	3,032,217	3,107,564	3,287,116
Delaware	238,380	266,505	318,085	446,292	548,104	594,338	666,168
District of Columbia	486,869	663,091	802,178	763,956	756,668	638,432	606,900
Florida	1,468,211	1,897,414	2,771,305	4,951,560	6,791,418	9,746,961	12,937,926
Georgia	2,908,506	3,123,723	3,444,578	3,943,116	4,587,930	5,462,982	6,478,216
Hawaii	368,300	422,770	499,794	632,772	769,913	964,691	1,108,229
Idaho	445,032	524,873	588,637	667,191	713,015	944,127	1,006,749
Illinois	7,630,654	7,897,241	8,712,176	10,081,158	11,110,285	11,427,409	11,430,602
Indiana	3,238,503	3,427,796	3,934,224	4,662,498	5,195,392	5,490,214	5,544,159
Iowa	2,470,939	2,538,268	2,621,073	2,757,537	2,825,368	2,913,808	2,776,755
Kansas	1,880,999	1,801,028	1,905,299	2,178,611	2,249,071	2,364,236	2,477,574
Kentucky	2,614,589	2,845,627	2,944,806	3,038,156	3,220,711	3,660,324	3,685,296
Louisiana	2,101,593	2,363,880	2,683,516	3,257,022	3,644,637	4,206,116	4,219,973
Maine	797,423	847,226	913,774	969,265	993,722	1,125,043	1,227,928
Maryland	1,631,526	1,821,244	2,343,001	3,100,689	3,923,897	4,216,933	4,781,468
Massachusetts	4,249,614	4,316,721	4,690,514	5,148,578	5,689,170	5,737,093	6,016,425
Michigan	4,842,325	5,256,106	6,371,766	7,823,194	8,881,826	9,262,044	9,295,297
Minnesota	2,563,953	2,792,300	2,982,483	3,413,864	3,806,103	4,075,970	4,375,099
Mississippi	2,009,821	2,183,796	2,178,914	2,178,141	2,216,994	2,520,770	2,573,216
Missouri	3,629,367	3,784,664	3,954,653	4,319,813	4,677,623	4,916,762	5,117,073
Montana	537,606	559,456	591,024	674,767	694,409	786,690	799,065
Nebraska	1,377,963	1,315,834	1,325,510	1,411,330	1,485,333	1,569,825	1,578,385
Nevada	91,058	110,247	160,083	285,278	488,738	800,508	1,201,833
New Hampshire	465,293	491,524	533,242	606,921	737,681	920,610	1,109,252
New Jersey	4,041,334	4,160,165	4,835,329	6,066,782	7,171,112	7,365,011	7,730,188
New Mexico	423,317	531,818	681,187	951,023	1,017,055	1,303,302	1,515,069
New York	12,588,066	13,479,142	14,830,192	16,782,304	18,241,391	17,558,165	17,990,455
North Carolina	3,170,276	3,571,623	4,061,929	4,556,155	5,084,411	5,880,095	6,628,637
North Dakota	680,845	641,935	619,636	632,446	617,792	652,717	638,800
Ohio	6,646,697	6,907,612	7,946,627	9,706,397	10,657,423	10,797,603	10,847,115
Oklahoma	2,396,040	2,336,434	2,233,351	2,328,284	2,559,463	3,025,487	3,145,585
Oregon	953,786	1,089,684	1,521,341	1,768,687	2,091,533	2,633,156	2,842,321
Pennsylvania	9,631,350	9,900,180	10,498,012	11,319,366	11,800,766	11,864,720	11,881,643
Rhode Island	687,497	713,346	791,896	859,488	949,723	947,154	1,003,464
South Carolina	1,738,765	1,899,804	2,117,027	2,382,594	2,590,713	3,120,729	3,486,703
South Dakota	692,849	642,961	652,740	680,514	666,257	690,768	696,004
Tennessee	2,616,556	2,915,841	3,291,718	3,567,089	3,926,018	4,591,023	4,877,185
Texas	5,824,715	6,414,824	7,711,194	9,579,677	11,198,655	14,225,513	16,986,510
Utah	507,847	550,310	688,862	890,627	1,059,273	1,461,037	1,722,850
Vermont	359,611	359,231	377,747	389,881	444,732	511,456	562,758
Virginia	2,421,851	2,677,773	3,318,680	3,966,949	4,651,448	5,346,797	6,187,358
Washington	1,563,396	1,736,191	2,378,963	2,853,214	3,413,244	4,132,353	4,866,692
West Virginia	1,729,205	1,901,974	2,005,552	1,860,421	1,744,237	1,950,186	1,793,477
Wisconsin	2,939,006	3,137,587	3,434,575	3,951,777	4,417,821	4,705,642	4,891,769
Wyoming	225,565	250,742	290,529	330,066	332,416	469,557	453,588

Note: Excludes military and overseas population. Wherever possible, 1980 state boundaries are used in calculating populations of regions, areas, and territories prior to their statehoods. 1. 1980 figures are revised estimates issued by the Census Bureau in 1987. 2. The figures for Virginia through 1860 are from the 1960 census; in the 1980 summary, the Census Bureau gave separate figures for West Virginia between 1790 and 1860, even though it did not become a state until 1863. Since the result diminishes Virginia's population by over 300,000 in 1850 and 1860, a crucial period, we decided to keep the earlier breakdowns. Sources: U.S. Bureau of the Census, 1980 Census of Population: U.S. Summary, Number of Inhabitants (1981), and Release (1990).

People of Hispanic origin may be of any race. Hispanics or Latinos continue to be the fastest-growing segment of the population, primarily because of immigration and high birth rates. The Hispanic or Latino population grew 53 percent between 1980 and 1990 and another 58 percent between 1990 and 2000. Hispanics now make up 12.5 percent of the U.S. population, up from 9.0 percent in 1990 and 6.4 percent in 1980.

Undercounting the U.S. population in the 1990 and 2000 Censuses

The Census Bureau estimates it undercounted the original 1990 Census by about 1.6 percent nationwide. The Bureau concluded that it failed to enumerate 8 million people, and double-counted about 4 million others. That's a net difference of just over 4 million people, or a little more than the population within the Los Angeles city limits. The adjusted 1990 figures were based on a second detailed survey of 170,000 households conducted several months after the original census was completed.

Undercount in the 2000 Census

State	Count		Undercount	
	Official	Adjusted	Number	Percent
United States	248,709,873	252,730,369	4,020,496	1.6%
Alabama	4,040,587	4,113,810	73,223	1.8
Alaska	550,043	561,276	11,233	2.0
Arizona	3,665,228	3,754,666	89,438	2.4
Arkansas	2,350,725	2,392,596	41,871	1.8
California	29,760,021	30,597,578	837,557	2.7
Colorado	3,294,394	3,363,637	69,243	2.1
Connecticut	3,287,116	3,308,343	21,227	0.6
Delaware	666,168	678,385	12,217	1.8
District of Columbia	606,900	628,309	21,409	3.4
Florida	12,937,926	13,197,755	259,829	2.0
Georgia	6,478,216	6,620,641	142,425	2.2
Hawaii	1,108,229	1,129,170	20,941	1.9
Idaho	1,006,749	1,029,283	22,534	2.2
Illinois	11,430,602	11,544,319	113,717	1.0
Indiana	5,544,159	5,572,057	27,898	0.5
Iowa	2,776,755	2,788,332	11,577	0.4
Kansas	2,477,574	2,495,014	17,440	0.7
Kentucky	3,685,296	3,746,044	60,748	1.6
Louisiana	4,219,973	4,314,085	94,112	2.2
Maine	1,227,928	1,237,130	9,202	0.7
Maryland	4,781,468	4,882,452	100,984	2.1
Massachusetts	6,016,425	6,045,224	28,799	0.5
Michigan	9,295,297	9,361,308	66,011	0.7
Minnesota	4,375,099	4,394,610	19,511	0.4
Mississippi	2,573,216	2,629,548	56,332	2.1
Missouri	5,117,073	5,148,974	31,901	0.6
Montana	799,065	818,348	19,283	2.4
Nebraska	1,578,385	1,588,712	10,327	0.7
Nevada	1,201,833	1,230,709	28,876	2.3
New Hampshire	1,109,252	1,118,632	9,380	0.8
New Jersey	7,730,188	7,774,461	44,273	0.6
New Mexico	1,515,069	1,563,579	48,510	3.1
New York	17,990,455	18,262,491	272,036	1.5
North Carolina	6,628,637	6,754,567	125,930	1.9
North Dakota	638,800	643,033	4,233	0.7
Ohio	10,847,115	10,921,741	74,626	0.7
Oklahoma	3,145,585	3,202,963	57,378	1.8
Oregon	2,842,321	2,896,472	54,151	1.9
Pennsylvania	11,881,643	11,916,783	35,140	0.3
Rhode Island	1,003,464	1,004,815	1,351	0.1
South Carolina	3,486,703	3,559,547	72,844	2.0
South Dakota	696,004	702,864	6,860	1.0
Tennessee	4,877,185	4,964,261	87,076	1.8
Texas	16,986,510	17,472,538	486,028	2.8
Utah	1,722,850	1,753,188	30,338	1.7
Vermont	562,758	569,100	6,342	1.1
Virginia	6,187,358	6,313,836	126,478	2.0
Washington	4,866,692	4,958,320	91,628	1.8
West Virginia	1,793,477	1,819,363	25,886	1.4
Wisconsin	4,891,769	4,921,871	30,102	0.6
Wyoming	453,588	463,629	10,041	2.2

Source: U.S. Bureau of the Census, 2001. www.census.gov/dmd/pdf/understate.pdf

Ironically, the greatest undercount was in the government's backyard: Washington, D.C., where an estimated 3.4 percent of the population was not counted. Among the states New Mexico had the greatest undercount as a percentage of state population (3.1 percent), while California suffered the greatest numerical undercount: 837,557 people, the equivalent of more than one seat in ~~gress. Texas was undercounted by 2.8 percent, ~~28, nearly one Congressional district.

Low-income minorities were particularly undercounted: Blacks by 4.4 percent nationwide — nearly 1.4 million, equal to the population of Philadelphia; American Indians by 4.5 percent; Asian and Pacific Islanders by 2.3 percent; and Hispanics by 5 percent — nearly 1.2 million, as if the entire state of Nevada had not been counted. Geography also played a role: the South and West, where people are generally less trusting of the federal government, had undercount rates often twice that of the Midwest and Northeast, which

Portrait of the U.S. Population, April 1, 2000

Characteristic	Number	Percent
Total population	281,421,906	100.0%
SEX		
Male	138,053,563	49.1
Female	143,368,343	50.9
AGE		
Under 18 years	6,042,435	2.1
18 years and over	209,128,094	74.3
21 years and over	196,899,193	70.0
65 years and over	34,991,753	12.4
Median age	35.3	—
RACE		
One race, total	274,595,678	97.6
White only	211,460,626	75.1
Black only	34,658,190	12.3
American Indian and Alaska Native only	2,475,956	0.9
Asian only	10,242,998	3.6
Native Hawaiian and other Pacific Islander only	398,835	0.1
Other race	15,359,073	5.5
Two or more races, total	6,826,228	2.4
Hispanic or Latino (of any race)	35,305,818	12.5
HOUSEHOLD TYPE		
Total households	105,480,101	100.0%
Family households (families)	71,787,347	68.1
With own children under 18 years	34,588,368	32.8
Married-couple family	54,493,232	51.7
With own children under 18 years	24,835,505	23.5
Female householder[1]	12,900,103	12.2
With own children under 18 years	7,561,874	7.2
Nonfamily households	33,692,754	31.9
Householder living alone	27,230,075	25.8
65 years and over	9,722,857	9.2
Average household size (people)	2.59	—
Average family size (people)	3.14	—
HOUSING OCCUPANCY		
Total housing units	115,904,641	100.0%
Occupied housing units	105,480,101	91.0
Vacant housing units	10,424,540	9.0
For seasonal, recreational or occasional use	3,578,718	3.1
Homeowner vacancy rate (percent)		1.7
Rental vacancy rate (percent)		6.8
HOUSING TENURE		
Occupied housing units	105,480,101	100.0%
Owner-occupied	69,815,753	66.2
Renter-occupied	35,664,348	33.8

1. No husband present. **Source:** U.S. Bureau of the Census, 2001

U.S. Population by Region, 1990-2000

Region	1990 Census	2000 Census
United States	**248,790,925**	**281,421,906**
Northeast	**50,828,313**	**53,594,378**
New England	13,206,943	13,922,517
Middle Atlantic	37,621,370	39,671,861
Midwest	**59,669,320**	**64,392,776**
East North Central	42,009,114	45,155,037
West North Central	17,660,206	19,237,739
South	**85,455,793**	**100,236,820**
South Atlantic	43,571,473	51,769,160
East South Central	15,179,959	17,022,810
West South Central	26,704,361	31,444,850
West	**52,837,499**	**63,197,932**
Mountain	13,658,794	18,172,295
Pacific	39,178,705	45,025,637

Source: U.S. Census Bureau.

Population Growth by Region, 1790-2000 (in thousands)

Year	Northeast	Midwest[1]	South[2]	West
1790	1,968	N.A.	1,961	N.A.
1800	2,636	51	2,622	N.A.
1810	3,487	292	3,461	N.A.
1820	4,360	859	4,419	N.A.
1830	5,542	1,610	5,708	N.A.
1840	6,761	3,352	6,951	N.A.
1850	8,627	5,404	8,983	179
1860	10,594	9,097	11,133	619
1870	12,299	12,981	12,288	991
1880	14,507	17,364	16,517	1,801
1890	17,407	22,410	20,028	3,134
1900	21,047	26,333	24,524	4,309
1910	25,869	29,889	29,389	7,082
1920	29,662	34,020	33,126	9,214
1930	34,427	38,594	37,858	12,324
1940	35,977	40,143	41,666	14,379
1950	39,478	44,461	47,197	20,190
1960	44,678	51,619	54,973	28,053
1970	49,041	56,572	62,795	34,804
1980	49,135	58,866	75,372	43,172
1990	50,809	59,669	85,446	52,786
2000	53,594	64,393	100,237	63,198

1. Called North Central prior to 1980. 2. Includes black slave population through 1860.
Source: U.S. Bureau of Census, *The Statistical History of the U.S.* (1976) and 2000 Census of the U.S. www.census.gov.

include such ethnically diverse states as New York, Michigan, Illinois, and Massachusetts.

To prevent the kind of undercounts that plagued the 1990 Census, the Bureau planned in 2000 to use statistical sampling methods to enumerate the hardest-to-count 10 percent of the population, and to conduct a follow-up survey of 750,000 households, which would point out inaccuracies in the initial count. But because census numbers are used to apportion Congressional districts and because blacks and Hispanics (who tend to vote Democratic) made up a significant portion of the 1990 undercount, Republicans in Congress challenged the plan, fearing that an accurate count of the country's minorities would erode GOP numbers. In August 1998 a federal court struck down the use of sampling, saying it violated 1957 and 1976 federal laws governing the census, and in July 1999 the Supreme Court rejected the Clinton administration's appeal of the decision.

As a result, the Census Bureau had to spe additional $1.7 billion (over the $5 billi geted) to count each and every person

U.S. Population, Population Density, and Area of Residence, 1790–1990

Year	Total population	Percent increase	Population per square mile	Percent urban	Percent rural
1790	3,929,214	N.A.	4.5	5.1%	94.9%
1800	5,308,483	35.1%	6.1	6.1	93.9
1810	7,239,881	36.4	4.3	7.3	92.7
1820	9,638,453	33.1	5.5	7.2	92.8
1830	12,866,020	33.5	7.4	8.8	91.2
1840	17,069,453	32.7	9.8	10.8	89.2
1850	23,191,876	35.9	7.9	15.3	84.7
1860	31,443,321	35.6	10.6	19.8	80.2
1870	39,818,449	26.6	13.4	25.7	74.3
1880	50,155,783	26.0	16.9	28.2	71.8
1890	62,947,714	25.5	21.2	35.1	64.9
1900	75,994,575	20.7	25.6	39.6	60.4
1910	91,972,266	21.0	31.0	45.6	54.4
1920	105,710,620	14.9	35.6	51.2	48.8
1930	122,775,046	16.1	41.2	56.1	43.9
1940	131,669,275	7.2	44.2	56.5	43.5
1950	150,697,361	14.5	50.7	64.0	36.0
1960	179,323,175	18.5	50.6	69.9	30.1
1970	203,302,031	13.4	57.4	73.5	26.5
1980	226,545,805	11.4	64.0	73.7	26.3
1990	248,709,873	9.8	70.3	75.2	24.8

Source: U.S. Bureau of Census, *The Statistical History of the U.S.* (1976); *The Statistical Abstract of the United States* (annual).

even those who didn't want to cooperate with pollsters; because of this additional cost, the size of the follow-up survey had to be cut to 314,000 interviews. By comparing this survey with results from traditional census-taking methods, the Census Bureau estimated in early 2001 that at least 6.4 million people were not counted in the 2000 census and at least 3.1 million were counted twice. The undercount rate of aproximately 1.2 percent was better than the 1.6 percent undercount in 1990, but controversy over the uncounted millions continued throughout 2001. In March, 2001, the Census Bureau announced that it would recommend the use of unadjusted numbers for re-drawing Congressional districts; several large cities planned to sue for the release of detailed data about regional and local undercounts, and there was still a possibility that adjusted census figures would be used to allocate other federal and state resources later in the year.
Source: U.S. Bureau of the Census Executive Steering Committee for Accuracy and Coverage Evaluation Policy; www.census.gov.

U.S. POPULATION BY RACE AND HISPANIC ORIGIN

It is important to note that the Census Bureau's classification of the population by race, in its words, "reflects common usage not an attempt to define biological stock." Only since 1960, however, have the Census Bureau's race figures been based on self-identification, and only since 1980 has the Bureau reported statistics on Native Americans, Asians, and persons of Hispanic origin.

The people of the United States are predominantly white, accounting for an estimated 75.1 percent of the total population in 2000 (down from 84.1 percent in 1990). This dominance has been true since colonial days, although even then the indigenous peoples and the African slaves were significant racial minorities. In fact as slave labor became essential to the Southern economy so many slaves were brought here that just before the Civil War blacks constituted 15 percent of the U.S. population.

After the war, the proportion of whites rapidly increased as millions of immigrants from northern Europe settled throughout the country. The relentless movement of the population westward deprived the Native Americans of their lands and—with the assistance of several bloody wars—helped to reduce their numbers to a small fraction of what they were estimated to have been only a century before.

The black population, which represented between 9 and 12 percent of the total for many decades, remained the only significant minority group until the 1960's, when a surge of new immigrants from Puerto Rico, Mexico, and Cuba made the Hispanic presence felt. So rapid and strong an impression did these groups make that the Census Bureau created a new population category, "Hispanic Origin." Since some Hispanics are black, some white, and still others Indian, this designation has nothing to do with race.

During the 1970's and 1980's, the arrival of several million Asians again caused a noticeable change in the composition of the population. The 1990 census was the first one to include a separate category for Asians and Pacific Islanders; in previous years, they had been included together with American Indians, Aleuts, and Eskimos in the "other races" grouping.

The 2000 Census took an even more expansive approach. For the first time, it allowed people to identify themselves by more than one race. Although the vast majority of Americans (97.6 percent) still consider themselves of one race, a total of 6.8 million people said they were members of two or more races (2.4 percent). The most common mix was white and American Indian or Alaska Native; just over a million people identified themselves as such. Another 868,395 said they were a mix of white and Asian, and 784,764 said they were white and black or African-American. Another 2.2 million people said they were white and some other race. A total of 410,285 people identified themselves as members of three races, 38,408 said they were of four races, 8,637 were of five races, and 823 people were of six races.

The 2000 Census was also the first to separate out "Native Hawaiian and Other Pacific Islander" from the Asian category. his new caegory includes people who indicated their races as Guamanian, Chamorro, Samoan, Tahitian, Mariana Islander, or Chuukese. The 2000 Census also includes an "Other race" category, which includes people who did not identify their race, or who wrote in races such as Moroccan, South African, or Belizean.

This category also includes people who wrote in a Hispanic origin (e.g. Mexican, Cuban) instead of a race.

As a result of the expanded race categories, data from the 2000 Census is not directly comparable with information from previous censuses. Wherever possible, we have tried to provide two sets of race statistics for 2000: a) those who consider themselves members only of the race (i.e. white only or black only) and b) the aforementioned members of the race plus those who consider themselves members of the race and at least one other race as well (i.e. white and Asian, or black and Native American).

▶ THE BLACK POPULATION

Ever since the Founding Fathers reached their famous "compromise" declaring a slave the equivalent of three-fifths of a person, the black population has had a less-than-equal standing in

Resident Population of the U.S., by Race and Hispanic Origin, 1990–2000

The 2000 Census was the first to allow people to identify themselves as of more than one race. In the table below, the fourth and fifth columns include people who described themselves only as the race shown. The last two columns includes all of those people, as well as people who described themselves as the race indicated, in addition to at

least one other race. For example, 10.2 million Amerricans described themeselves as Asian alone, but an additional 1.7 million described themselves as part Asian and part some other race. Thus, a total of 11.9 million people may be considered at least partly Asian. Note that persons of Hispanic origin may be of any race.

Race/ Hispanic origin	1990		2000			
	Number	Percent	Race shown only	Percent	Race shown alone or in combination with other race(s)	Percent
Total population	**248,709,873**	**100.0%**	**281,421,906**	**100.0%**	**281,421,906**	**100.0%**
White	199,686,070	80.3	211,460,626	75.1	216,930,975	77.1
Black (African-American)	29,986,060	12.1	34,658,190	12.3	36,419,434	12.9
American Indian and Alaska Native	1,959,234	0.8	2,475,956	0.9	4,119,301	1.5
Asian	6,908,638	2.8	10,242,998	3.6	11,898,828	4.2
Native Hawaiian and other Pacific Islander	365,024	0.1	398,835	0.1	874,414	0.3
Other race	9,804,847	3.9	15,359,073	5.5	18,521,486	6.6
Two or more races	N.A.	N.A.	6,826,228	2.4	N.A.	N.A.
Hispanic origin[1]	22,354,059	9.0	35,305,818	12.5	35,305,818	12.5

1. Persons of Hispanic origin may be of any race.   **Source:** U.S. Bureau of the Census.

Change in the Resident Population, by Race and Hispanic Origin, 1980–2000

Race/ Hispanic origin	Change, 1980-90		Change, 1990-2000			
	Number	Percent change	Number (race only)	Percent change	Race alone or in combination with other race(s)	Percent change
Total population	**22,164,068**	**9.8%**	**32,713,033**	**13.2%**	**32,713,033**	**13.2%**
White	11,314,448	6.0	11,774,556	5.9	17,244,905	8.6
Black (African-American)	3,491,035	13.2	4,672,130	15.6	6,433,374	21.5
American Indian and Alaska Native	538,834	37.9	516,722	26.4	2,160,067	110.3
Asian	3,773,223	107.8	3,334,360	18.3	4,990,190	72.2
Native Hawaiian and other Pacific Islander	(1)	(1)	33,811	9.3	509,390	139.5
Other race	N.A.	N.A.	5,554,226	56.6	8,716,639	88.9
Hispanic origin[2]	7,745,386	53.0	12,951,759	57.9	12,951,759	57.9

1. Native Hawaiian and other Pacific Islander included with Asian from 1980-90. 2. Persons of Hispanic origin may be of any race.
Source: U.S. Bureau of the Census.

relation to the majority of Americans. Over the last two centuries, the struggle for equality, even in a nation pledged to that ideal, has proven long, hard, and in many cases, intractable, as so many contemporary facts and figures in this book make all too evident. From higher infant mortality rates and poverty rates to lower life expectancy and family income levels, the black population continues to suffer the effects of two centuries of slavery and one of institutionalized segregation.

According to the 2000 Census, 34,658,190 Americans identified themselves as black only. They represented 12.3 pecent of all Americans. An additional 1,761,244 were black and at least

Resident Population of States by Race and Hispanic Origin, 2000

State	Total population	One race only					Two or more races	Hispanic or Latino origin
		White	Black or African American	American Indian & Alaska Native	Asian	Other race		
United States	281,421,906	75.1%	12.3%	0.9%	3.6%	5.5%	2.4%	12.5%
Alabama	4,447,100	71.1	26.0	0.5	0.7	0.7	1.0	1.7
Alaska	626,932	69.3	3.5	15.6	4.0	1.6	5.4	4.1
Arizona	5,130,632	75.5	3.1	5.0	1.8	11.6	2.9	25.3
Arkansas	2,673,400	80.0	15.7	0.7	0.8	1.5	1.3	3.2
California	33,871,648	59.5	6.7	1.0	10.9	16.8	4.7	32.4
Colorado	4,301,261	82.8	3.8	1.0	2.2	7.2	2.8	17.1
Connecticut	3,405,565	81.6	9.1	0.3	2.4	4.3	2.2	9.4
Delaware	783,600	74.6	19.2	0.3	2.1	2.0	1.7	4.8
District of Columbia	572,059	30.8	60.0	0.3	2.7	3.8	2.4	7.9
Florida	15,982,378	78.0	14.6	0.3	1.7	3.0	2.4	16.8
Georgia	8,186,453	65.1	28.7	0.3	2.1	2.4	1.4	5.3
Hawaii	1,211,537	24.3	1.8	0.3	41.6	1.3	21.4	7.2
Idaho	1,293,953	91.0	0.4	1.4	0.9	4.2	2.0	7.9
Illinois	12,419,293	73.5	15.1	0.2	3.4	5.8	1.9	12.3
Indiana	6,080,485	87.5	8.4	0.3	1.0	1.6	1.2	3.5
Iowa	2,926,324	93.9	2.1	0.3	1.3	1.3	1.1	2.8
Kansas	2,688,418	86.1	5.7	0.9	1.7	3.4	2.1	7.0
Kentucky	4,041,769	90.1	7.3	0.2	0.7	0.6	1.1	1.5
Louisiana	4,468,976	63.9	32.5	0.6	1.2	0.7	1.1	2.4
Maine	1,274,923	96.9	0.5	0.6	0.7	0.2	1.0	0.7
Maryland	5,296,486	64.0	27.9	0.3	4.0	1.8	2.0	4.3
Massachusetts	6,349,097	84.5	5.4	0.2	3.8	3.7	2.3	6.8
Michigan	9,938,444	80.2	14.2	0.6	1.8	1.3	1.9	3.3
Minnesota	4,919,479	89.4	3.5	1.1	2.9	1.3	1.7	2.9
Mississippi	2,844,658	61.4	36.3	0.4	0.7	0.5	0.7	1.4
Missouri	5,595,211	84.9	11.2	0.4	1.1	0.8	1.5	2.1
Montana	902,195	90.6	0.3	6.2	0.5	0.6	1.7	2.0
Nebraska	1,711,263	89.6	4.0	0.9	1.3	2.8	1.4	5.5
Nevada	1,998,257	75.2	6.8	1.3	4.5	8.0	3.8	19.7
New Hampshire	1,235,786	96.0	0.7	0.2	1.3	0.6	1.1	1.7
New Jersey	8,414,350	72.6	13.6	0.2	5.7	5.4	2.5	13.3
New Mexico	1,819,046	66.8	1.9	9.5	1.1	17.0	3.6	42.1
New York	18,976,457	67.9	15.9	0.4	5.5	7.1	3.1	15.1
North Carolina	8,049,313	72.1	21.6	1.2	1.4	2.3	1.3	4.7
North Dakota	642,200	92.4	0.6	4.9	0.6	0.4	1.2	1.2
Ohio	11,353,140	85.0	11.5	0.2	1.2	0.8	1.4	1.9
Oklahoma	3,450,654	76.2	7.6	7.9	1.4	2.4	4.5	5.2
Oregon	3,421,399	86.6	1.6	1.3	3.0	4.2	3.1	8.0
Pennsylvania	12,281,054	85.4	10.0	0.1	1.8	1.5	1.2	3.2
Rhode Island	1,048,319	85.0	4.5	0.5	2.3	5.0	2.7	8.7
South Carolina	4,012,012	67.2	29.5	0.3	0.9	1.0	1.0	2.4
South Dakota	754,844	88.7	0.6	8.3	0.6	0.5	1.3	1.4
Tennessee	5,689,283	80.2	16.4	0.3	1.0	1.0	1.1	2.2
Texas	20,851,820	71.0	11.5	0.6	2.7	11.7	2.5	32.0
Utah	2,233,169	89.2	0.8	1.3	1.7	4.2	2.1	9.0
Vermont	608,827	96.8	0.5	0.4	0.9	0.2	1.2	0.9
Virginia	7,078,515	72.3	19.6	0.3	3.7	2.0	2.0	4.7
Washington	5,894,121	81.8	3.2	1.6	5.5	3.9	3.6	7.5
West Virginia	1,808,344	95.0	3.2	0.2	0.5	0.2	0.9	0.7
Wisconsin	5,363,675	88.9	5.7	0.9	1.7	1.6	1.2	3.6
Wyoming	493,782	92.1	0.8	2.3	0.6	2.5	1.8	6.4

Note: The Native Hawaiian and other Pacific Islander population, which totaled 0.1 percent nationally, is not shown separately. This category accounted for 9.4 percent of the population in Hawaii, 0.7 percent in Utah, 0.5 percent in Alaska, 0.4 percent in Nevada and Washington, 0.3 percent in California, and 0.2 percent in Oregon, and 0.1 percent in 15 other states. Persons of Hispanic origin may be of any race. Source: U.S. Census Bureau, Census 2000 (2001).

one other race (most often white), making a total of 36,419,434 people (12.9 pecent of the population) at least partly black. The black-only population grew by 15.6 percent between the last two censuses, significantly faster than the overall population, which increased only by 13.2 percent. The number of people who are black or partly black has increased even faster: 6.4 million, or 21.5 percent from 1990-2000.

Most black Americans (54.8 percent of the black-only population) continue to live in the South, where they made up 18.9 percent of the population in 2000. Blacks constituted 11.4 percent of the population in the Northeast, 10.1 percent in the Midwest, and just 4.9 percent in the West (down from 5.4 percent in 1990). The black population of the U.S. remains highly concentrated. The 10 states with the largest number of blacks (see the accompanying table) had 58 percent of all blacks in America (but only 49 percent of the total U.S. population). Blacks constituted more than 50 percent of the population in 96

Black Population of the U.S., 1790-2000

Year	Number ('000s)	Percent of total population	Year	Number ('000s)	Percent of total population	Year	Number ('000s)	Percent of total population
1790	757	19.3%	1920	10,463	9.9%	1995	33,116	12.6%
1800	1,002	18.9	1930	11,891	9.7	1996	33,537	12.6
1850	3,639	15.7	1940	12,866	9.8	1997	33,989	12.7
1860	4,442	14.1	1950	15,042	10.0	1998	34,427	12.7
1870	4,880	12.7	1960[1]	18,872	10.5	1999	34,862	12.8
1880	6,581	13.1	1970	22,581	11.1	2000		
1890	7,489	11.9	1980	26,683	11.8	Black only	34,658	12.3
1900	8,834	11.6	1985	28,994	12.1	Black only or	36,419	12.9
1910	9,828	10.7	1990	30,517	12.3	with other race(s)		

Note: Decennial census figures are as of April 1. Figures for 1995-99 are as of July 1. 1. Includes Alaska and Hawaii for first time.
Source: U.S. Bureau of the Census, The Black Population 2000. (2001). www.census.gov.

Ten States With Largest Black Populations, 2000

Rank, State	Black only		Black only or in combination with other race(s)	
	Number	Percent	Number	Percent
1. New York	3,014,385	15.9%	3,234,165	17.0%
2. Texas	2,404,566	11.5	2,513,041	7.4
3. Georgia	2,349,542	28.7	2,493,057	12.0
4. Florida	2,335,505	14.6	2,471,730	15.5
5. California	2,263,882	6.7	2,393,425	29.2
6. Illinois	1,876,875	15.1	1,937,671	15.6
7. North Carolina	1,737,545	21.6	1,776,283	22.1
8. Maryland	1,477,411	27.9	1,525,036	28.8
9. Louisiana	1,451,944	32.5	1,474,613	14.8
10. Michigan	1,412,742	14.2	1,468,317	32.9

Note: States ranked by Black-only population. Source: U.S. Bureau of the Census, The Black Population 2000. (2001). www.census.gov.

Ten States with Highest Percentage of Black Population, 2000

Rank, State	Total Population	Black only		Black only or in combination with other race(s)	
		Number	Percent	Number	Percent
1. Mississippi	2,573,216	1,033,809	36.3%	1,041,708	36.6%
2. Louisiana	4,219,973	1,451,944	32.5	1,468,317	32.9
3. South Carolina	3,486,703	1,185,216	29.5	1,200,901	29.9
4. Georgia	6,478,216	2,349,542	28.7	2,393,425	29.2
5. Maryland	4,781,468	1,477,411	27.9	1,525,036	28.8
6. Alabama	4,040,587	1,155,930	26.0	1,168,998	26.3
7. North Carolina	6,628,637	1,737,545	21.6	1,776,283	22.1
8. Virginia	6,187,358	1,390,293	19.6	1,441,207	20.4
9. Delaware	666,168	150,666	19.2	157,152	20.1
10. Tennessee	17,990,455	932,809	16.4	953,349	16.8

Note: States ranked by Black-only population. New York ranks 10th (17.0 percent) when states are ranked by percentage of blacks-only or blacks in combination with other races. Source: U.S. Bureau of the Census, The Black Population 2000 (2001). www.census.gov.

counties; 95 of these counties were in the South (St. Louis City, Mo. was the only non-Southern county with a majority black population) and almost all of them were nonmetropolitan counties (with the exceptions of Baltimore City and Prince George's County, Md.). New York and Chicago alone accounted for 9 percent of the total Black population. Among places with 100,000 or more in population, Gary, Indiana had the highest percentage of blacks, with 85 percent, followed by Detroit, Mich., which was 83 percent black.

Significant differences between the races also exist in other demographic categories, most notably in the high rates of divorce and single-motherhood for blacks. In 1999, more black families were headed by a single parent than by a married couple. Between 1970 and 1999, the percentage of black families headed by a female with no husband present jumped from 33.0 percent to 45.1 percent. Meanwhile, the percentage of black married-couple families declined from 64.3 percent in 1970 to 47.1 percent in 1999. Some

Black Population of Metropolitan Areas, 1980–90

Rank/Metropolitan area	1980	1990	Population change, 1980–90 Number	Percent
1. New York-Northern New Jersey-Long Island, N.Y.-N.J.-Conn. CMSA	2,825,102	3,289,465	464,363	16.4%
2. Chicago-Gary-Lake County, Ill.-Ind.-Wis. CMSA	1,557,287	1,547,725	-9,562	-0.6
3. Los Angeles-Anaheim-Riverside, Calif. CMSA	1,059,124	1,229,809	170,685	16.1
4. Philadelphia-Wilmington-Trenton, Pa.-N.J.-Del.-Md. CMSA	1,032,882	1,100,347	67,465	6.5
5. Washington, D.C.-Md.-Va. MSA	870,657	1,041,934	171,277	19.7
6. Detroit-Ann Arbor, Mich. CMSA	921,168	975,199	54,031	5.9
7. Atlanta, Ga. MSA	525,676	736,153	210,477	40.0
8. Houston-Galveston-Brazoria, Tex. CMSA	564,838	665,378	100,540	17.8
9. Baltimore, Md. MSA	560,952	616,065	55,113	9.8
10. Miami-Fort Lauderdale, Fla. CMSA	394,042	591,440	197,398	50.1
11. Dallas-Fort Worth, Tex. CMSA	419,030	554,616	135,586	32.4
12. San Francisco-Oakland,San Jose, Calif. CMSA	468,477	537,753	69,276	14.8
13. Cleveland-Akron-Lorain, Ohio CMSA	425,861	441,940	16,079	3.8
14. New Orleans, La. MSA	409,076	430,470	21,394	5.2
15. St. Louis, Mo.-Ill. MSA	407,918	423,182	15,264	3.7
16. Memphis, Tenn-Ark.-Miss. MSA	364,253	399,011	34,758	9.5
17. Norfolk-Virginia Beach-Newport News, Va. MSA	326,102	398,093	71,991	22.1
18. Richmond-Petersburg, Va. MSA	221,456	252,340	30,884	13.9
19. Birmingham, Ala. MSA	240,271	245,726	5,455	2.3
20. Boston-Lawrence-Salem, Mass.-N.H. MSA	176,265	239,059	62,794	35.6
21. Charlotte-Gastonia-Rock Hill, N.C.-S.C. MSA	194,056	231,654	37,598	19.4
22. Milwaukee-Racine, Wis. CMSA	164,571	214,182	49,611	30.1
23. Cincinnati-Hamilton, Ohio-Ky.-Ind. CMSA	185,728	203,607	17,879	9.6
24. Kansas City, Mo.-Kans. MSA	180,161	200,508	20,347	11.3
25. Tampa-St. Petersburg-Clearwater, Fla. MSA	148,465	185,503	37,038	24.9
26. Raleigh-Durham, N.C. MSA	146,624	183,447	36,823	25.1
27. Greensboro-Winston-Salem-High Point, N.C. MSA	162,134	182,284	20,150	12.4
28. Jacksonville, Fla. MSA	156,025	181,265	25,240	16.2
29. Pittsburgh-Beaver Valley, Pa. CMSA	181,644	178,857	-2,787	-1.5
30. Indianapolis, Ind. MSA	157,254	172,326	15,072	9.6
31. Jackson, Miss. MSA	149,457	167,899	18,442	12.3
32. Columbus, Ohio MSA	137,287	164,602	27,315	19.9
33. San Diego, Calif. MSA	104,452	159,306	54,854	52.5
34. Baton Rouge, La. MSA	137,581	156,509	18,928	13.8
35. Charleston, S.C. MSA	133,478	153,227	19,749	14.8
36. Nashville, Tenn. MSA	137,348	152,349	15,001	10.9
37. Columbia, S.C. MSA	117,906	137,906	20,000	17.0
38. Orlando, Fla. MSA	90,595	133,308	42,713	47.1
39. Mobile, Ala. MSA	126,835	130,512	3,677	2.9
40. Dayton-Springfield, Ohio MSA	118,294	126,238	7,944	6.7
41. Louisville, Ky.-Ind. MSA	120,610	124,761	4,151	3.4
42. Augusta, Ga.-S.C. MSA	106,729	123,482	16,753	15.7
43. Seattle-Tacoma, Wash. CMSA	87,976	123,266	35,290	40.1
44. Buffalo-Niagara Falls, N.Y. CMSA	113,975	121,956	7,981	7.0
45. Shreveport, La. MSA	110,478	116,892	6,414	5.8
46. Greenville-Spartanburg, S.C. MSA	97,561	111,334	13,773	14.1
47. West Palm Beach-Boca Raton-Delray Beach, Fla. MSA	77,576	107,705	30,129	38.8
48. Montgomery, Ala. MSA	94,494	105,196	10,702	11.3
49. Sacramento, Calif. MSA	61,594	101,940	40,346	65.5
50. Little Rock-North Little Rock, Ark. MSA	90,783	101,862	11,079	12.2

Note: Figures are from the 1990 Census. Figures from the 2000 Census willbe available in 2002. Source: U.S. Bureau of the Census.

Black Population in the Largest U.S. Cities, 2000

City	Total Population		Black-only population			Black only or in combination with other race(s) population		
	Rank	Number	Rank	Number	Percent black	Rank	Number	Percent black
New York, N.Y.	1	8,008,278	1	2,129,762	26.6%	1	2,274,049	28.4%
Los Angeles, Calif.	2	3,694,820	7	415,195	11.2	6	444,635	12.0
Chicago, Ill.	3	2,896,016	2	1,065,009	36.8	2	1,084,221	37.4
Houston, Texas	4	1,953,631	5	494,496	25.3	5	505,101	25.9
Philadelphia, Pa.	5	1,517,550	4	655,824	43.2	4	672,162	44.3
Phoenix, Ariz.	6	1,321,045	60	67,416	5.1	53	76,065	5.8
San Diego, Calif.	7	1,223,400	36	96,216	7.9	32	109,470	8.9
Dallas, Texas	8	1,188,580	11	307,957	25.9	11	314,678	26.5
San Antonio, Texas	9	1,144,646	48	78,120	6.8	45	84,250	7.4
Detroit, Mich.	10	951,270	3	775,772	81.6	3	787,687	82.8
Baltimore, Md.	17	651,154	6	418,951	64.3	7	424,449	65.2
Memphis, Tenn.	18	650,100	8	399,208	61.4	8	402,367	61.9
Washington, D.C.	21	572,059	9	343,312	60.0	9	350,455	61.3
New Orleans, La.	31	484,674	10	325,947	67.3	10	329,171	67.9

Source: U.S. Bureau of Census, *The Black Population 2000* (2001). www.census.gov.

660,000 black families (7.8 percent) were headed by a man with no wife present. (See also "The U.S. Economy" for information about black employment, income, wealth and poverty.)

▶ THE HISPANIC POPULATION

The term Hispanic refers to people of Spanish or Latin American origin. American Hispanics are of diverse backgrounds. The vast majority trace their roots to Mexico (58.5 percent), followed by Puerto Rico (9.6 percent) Cuba (3.5 percent) and the Dominican Republic (2.2 percent). A mere 0.3 percent of Hispanic-Americans are from Spain. (These figures do not include Puerto Ricans living in Puerto Rico, which is a U.S. territory, but for which a separate census is issued. In recent years, the flow of Puerto Ricans to U.S. cities has been reversed, with more Puerto Ricans emigrating from the mainland to the island than the other way around.)

Contrary to popular opinion, Spanish-speaking countries are not culturally homogeneous, but varied and complex. They incorporate Spanish and other European influences, as well as Indian and African traits. In the Caribbean area, Panama, and the coasts of Venezuela, Colombia, Ecuador, and sections of Peru, African culture has left a strong legacy. In Mexico, most of Central America, and the Andean countries, diverse Indian cultures have had a major impact. Latin-American society varies greatly according to social class and vast differences exist between urban and rural areas. Since American Hispanics come from different countries and social backgrounds, they do not compose a uniform, cohesive population group.

U.S. Hispanics are of many races. In some areas, intermingling has made it impossible to distinguish one race from another, but in others, races are clearly defined. In Argentina, for example, there is a white majority of 85 percent—mostly of Italian, German, or English extraction. Cuba, the Dominican Republic, Panama, Venezuela, and the coastal areas of Colombia, Ecuador, and Peru all have significant black populations. In Bolivia, about one-half of the population is Indian and a third is mestizo (of mixed white and Indian ancestry). Both Peru and Cuba have concentrations of persons of Chinese ancestry and Peru has a growing Japanese population. In Mexico, birthplace of the majority of most Hispanic-Americans, about 55 percent of the population is mestizo, 30 percent is Indian, and 15 percent is white.

Despite their diversity, the Hispanic peoples are united by many factors, among them language, religion, customs, and attitudes toward self, family, and society. In the United States, these factors vary in importance according to the degree to which an individual has assimilated into the mainstream. For example, although language has traditionally been an important unifying factor, large numbers of second-generation Hispanics are English-dominant. About 85 percent of U.S. Hispanics speak English. Although the Spanish language continues to exert a strong emotional pull among U.S. Hispanics, it is difficult to assess to what extent Spanish will remain a unifying force among future generations.

Growth of the Hispanic population The Hispanic population is one of the fastest-growing segments of the U.S. population. Between 1980 and 2000, the number of Hispanics more than doubled, from 14.6 million to 35.3 million, according to the Census Bureau. Hispanics currently represent 12.5 percent of the U.S. population. According to numbers from the 2000 Census, the Hispanic population for the first time outnumbered the black-alone population (35.3 million to 34.7 million), although blacks alone or in combination with other races outnumbered Hispanics by just over one million. The Census Bureau predicts that Hispanics will become the largest U.S. minority group by any reckoning in the 2010 Census.

The Hispanic population increased by 57.9 percent overall between 1990 and 2000. Mexicans increased by 52.9 percent, Puerto Ricans increased by 24.9 percent, and Cubans increased by 18.9 percent. The "other Hispanic" category, which includes people from Spain, people from all other

Hispanic Population in the Largest U.S. Cities, 2000

City	Total Population Rank	Number	Hispanic population Rank	Number	Percent Hispanic
New York, N.Y.	1	8,008,278	1	2,160,554	27.0%
Los Angeles, Calif.	2	3,694,820	2	1,719,073	46.5
Chicago, Ill.	3	2,896,016	3	753,644	26.0
Houston, Texas	4	1,953,631	4	730,865	37.4
Philadelphia, Pa.	5	1,517,550	24	128,928	8.5
Phoenix, Ariz.	6	1,321,045	6	449,972	34.1
San Diego, Calif.	7	1,223,400	9	310,752	25.4
Dallas, Texas	8	1,188,580	8	422,587	35.6
San Antonio, Texas	9	1,144,646	5	671,394	58.7
Detroit, Mich.	10	951,270	72	47,167	5.0
El Paso, Texas	23	563,662	7	431,875	76.6
San Jose, Calif.	11	894,943	10	269,989	30.2

Source: U.S. Bureau of Census, The Hispanic Population 2000 (2001). www.census.gov.

Resident Hispanic Population by Region and Origin, 2000

	Total, U.S. Number	Northeast Number	Percent	Midwest Number	Percent	South Number	Percent	West Number	Percent
All Hispanics	35,305,818	5,254,087	14.9%	3,124,532	8.8%	11,586,696	32.8%	15,340,503	43.4%
Mexican	20,640,711	479,169	2.3	2,200,196	10.7	6,548,081	31.7	11,413,265	55.3
Puerto Rican	3,406,178	2,074,574	60.9	325,363	9.6	759,305	22.3	246,936	7.2
Cuban	1,241,685	168,959	13.6	45,305	3.6	921,427	74.2	105,994	8.5
Other Hispanic	10,017,244	2,531,385	25.3	553,668	5.5	3,357,883	33.5	3,574,308	35.7

Source: U.S. Bureau of the Census, The Hispanic Population 2000 (2001). www.census.gov.

Spanish-speaking countries in Latin America, and people who did not specify a detailed origin beyond "Hispanic," was the fastest-growing group of Hispanics, increasing by by 96.9 percent.

The rapid growth of the Hispanic population is due primarily to immigration. For example, the number of people of Mexican background living in the U.S. more than doubled between 1980 and 1990, due in large part to the Immigration and Reform Control Act of 1986, which allowed Mexicans and other immigrants living illegally in the United States to obtain legal U.S. citizenship. (See the section on immigration later in this chapter). Hispanics also have higher fertility rates than do the non-Hispanic population. In 1998, the overall fertility rate per 100,000 women ages 15-44 was 65.0, but for Hispanic women, it was 102.8. Mexican-American women had the highest fertility rates of all: 116.6 births per 100,000 women aged 15-44, or approximately double the rate for Cuban-American women.

Half of all Hispanics lived in two states in 2000: California and Texas. Hispanics represented 24.3 percent of the population in the West; they constituted more than 25 percent of the populations of Arizona, California, New Mexico, and Texas. Mexicans were the biggest component of Hispanic populations in the South and West, but there were fewer than half a million Mexicans in the northeast. The majority of Hispanics in the northeast were of Puerto Rican origin. Over a million Puerto Ricans lived in New York alone; another half million lived in New Jersey and Connecticut. The vast majority of Cubans (67 percent) lived in Florida, where they represented 5.2 percent of the entire state population. The heaviest concentration of

States With Largest Hispanic Population, 2000

State	Hispanic population	Total population	Percentage Hispanic
1. California	33,871,648	10,966,556	32.4%
2. Texas	20,851,820	6,669,666	32.0
3. New York	18,976,457	2,867,583	15.1
4. Florida	15,982,378	2,682,715	16.8
5. Illinois	12,419,293	1,530,262	12.3
6. Arizona	5,130,632	1,295,617	25.3
7. New Jersey	8,414,350	1,117,191	13.3
8. New Mexico	1,819,046	765,386	42.1
9. Colorado	4,301,261	735,601	17.1
10. Washington	5,894,121	441,509	7.5

Note: Ranked by number of Hispanics. Nevada which is 19.7 percent Hispanic, has a total of 393,970 Hispanics.
Source: U.S. Bureau of the Census, The Hispanic Population 2000 (2001). www.census.gov.

Hispanics in America is East Los Angeles, Calif., where 120,307 of the 124,283 residents (96.8 percent) are Hispanic. Laredo, Texas, is close behind, with a population that is 94.1 percent Hispanic.

▶THE ASIAN AND NATIVE HAWAIIAN/OTHER PACIFIC ISLANDER POPULATION

In 1970 the Census Bureau counted about 1.5 million Asians and Pacific Islanders living in the U.S. By the 1980 census that figure had more than doubled to 3.4 million, thanks in large part to the more than 400,000 Southeast Asian refugees who came to America between 1975-80 under the Refugee Resettlement Program. By the 1990 Cen-

Hispanic Population of Metropolitan Areas, 1980–90

Rank/Metropolitan area	1980	1990	Population change, 1980–90 Number	Percent
1. Los Angeles-Anaheim-Riverside, Calif. CMSA	2,755,914	4,779,118	2,023,204	73.4%
2. New York-Northern New Jersey-Long Island, N.Y.-N.J.-Conn. CMSA	2,050,998	2,777,951	726,953	35.4
3. Miami-Fort Lauderdale, Fla. CMSA	621,309	1,061,846	440,537	70.9
4. San Francisco-Oakland, San Jose, Calif. CMSA	660,190	970,403	310,213	47.0
5. Chicago-Gary-Lake County, Ill.-Ind.-Wis. CMSA	632,443	893,422	260,979	41.3
6. Houston-Galveston-Brazoria, Tex. CMSA	448,460	772,295	323,835	72.2
7. San Antonio, Tex. MSA	481,511	620,290	138,779	28.8
8. Dallas-Fort Worth, Tex. CMSA	247,823	518,917	271,094	109.4
9. San Diego, Calif. MSA	275,177	510,781	235,604	85.6
10. El Paso, Tex. MSA	297,001	411,619	114,618	38.6
11. Phoenix, Ariz. MSA	199,003	345,498	146,495	73.6
12. McAllen-Edinburg-Mission, Tex. MSA	230,212	326,972	96,760	42.0
13. Fresno, Calif. MSA	150,790	236,634	85,844	56.9
14. Denver-Boulder, Colo. CMSA	173,687	226,200	52,513	30.2
15. Philadelphia-Wilmington-Trenton, Pa.-N.J.-Del.-Md. CMSA	147,902	225,868	77,966	52.7
16. Washington, D.C.-Md.-Va. MSA	94,968	224,786	129,818	136.7
17. Brownsville-Harlingen, Tex. MSA	161,654	212,995	51,341	31.8
18. Boston-Lawrence-Salem, Mass.-N.H. CMSA	92,463	193,199	100,736	108.9
19. Corpus Christi, Tex. MSA	158,119	181,860	23,741	15.0
20. Albuquerque, N.Mex. MSA	154,620	178,310	23,690	15.3
21. Sacramento, Calif. MSA	105,665	172,374	66,709	63.1
22. Tucson, Ariz. MSA	111,418	163,262	51,844	46.5
23. Austin, Tex. MSA	94,367	159,942	65,575	69.5
24. Bakersfield, Calif. MSA	87,026	151,995	64,969	74.7
25. Tampa-St. Petersburg-Clearwater, Fla. MSA	80,265	139,248	58,983	73.5

Note: Figures are from the 1990 Census. Figures from the 2000 Census willbe available in 2002. **Source:** U.S. Bureau of the Census.

Asian Population of the U.S., 1980–90

Group	1980 Census Number	Percent	1990 Census Number	Percent	Population change, 1980–90 Number	Percent
Asian Indian	361,531	0.2%	815,447	0.3%	453,916	125.6%
Chinese	806,040	0.4	1,645,472	0.7	839,432	104.1
Filipino	774,652	0.3	1,406,770	0.6	632,118	81.6
Guamanian	32,158	0.0	49,345	0.0	17,187	53.4
Hawaiian	166,814	0.1	211,014	0.1	44,200	26.5
Japanese	700,974	0.3	847,562	0.3	146,588	20.9
Korean	354,593	0.2	798,849	0.3	444,256	125.3
Samoan	41,948	0.0	62,964	0.0	21,016	50.1
Vietnamese	261,729	0.1	614,547	0.2	352,818	134.8
Other Asian or Pacific Islander	N.A.	N.A.	821,692	0.3	N.A.	N.A.
Total Asian or Pacific Islander	**3,500,439**[1]	**1.5%**	**7,273,662**	**2.9%**	**3,773,223**	**107.8%**

Note: N.A. = Not available from 1980 tabulations. 1. Figures for 1980 are not strictly comparable with those for 1990. The total for 1980 includes only the nine specific groups listed. **Source:** U.S. Bureau of the Census.

sus, their numbers had doubled yet again, with Koreans and Vietnamese responsible for the majority of the increase.

The 2000 Census was the first to consider Native Hawaiians and Other Pacific Islanders (Guamanians, Chamorros, and Samoans) separately from Asians. A total of 874,414 people identified themselves as at least partly Native Hawaiian. Unlike other races, the majority of Native Hawaiians (475,579) were also members of at least one other race. Only 398,835 people identified themselves as Native Hawaiian and Other Pacific Islander alone.

Contrast that with the Asian population: 11,898,828 people said they were Asian or partly

Asian in 2000. Of these, 10,242,998 (86.1 percent) said they were Asian only, while only 1,655,830 were Asian and another race. Chinese are still the largest group of Asians in the U.S., followed closely by Filipinos and Japanese.

▶ THE AMERICAN INDIAN AND ALASKA NATIVE POPULATION

This race was known as the American Indian, Eskimo, and Aleut population for the 1990 Census, which reported a total of 1,959,234 American Indians living in the United States (of these, 85,698 were Eskimos and Aleuts, a.k.a. Alaska Natives). For the 2000 Census, 2,475,956 people identified themselves as American Indian or Alaska Native

Ten States With Largest Asian Population, 2000

Rank, State	Total Population	Asian only		Asian only or in combination with other race(s)	
		Number	Percent	Number	Percent
1. California	33,871,648	3,697,513	10.9%	4,155,685	12.3%
2. New York	18,976,457	1,044,976	5.5	1,169,200	6.2
3. Texas	20,851,820	562,319	2.7	644,193	3.1
4. Hawaii	1,211,537	503,868	41.6	703,232	58.0
5. New Jersey	8,414,350	480,276	5.7	524,356	6.2
6. Illinois	12,419,293	423,603	3.4	473,649	3.8
7. Washington	5,894,121	322,335	5.5	395,741	6.7
8. Florida	15,982,378	266,256	1.7	333,013	2.1
9. Virginia	7,078,515	261,025	3.7	304,559	4.3
10. Massachusetts	6,349,097	238,124	3.8	264,814	4.2
United States	281,421,906	10,242,998	3.6	11,898,828	4.2

Source: Ranked by number of Asian-only population. Nevada (4.5 percent), Alaska (4.0 percent), and Maryland (4.0 percent) ranked sixth through eighth by percentage of Asians. **Source**: U.S. Bureau of the Census, *The Asian Population 2000* (2001). www.census.gov.

Population of Selected Reservations and Trust Lands, 1990

Rank/Reservation or Trust Land	Total population	American Indian, Eskimo or Aleut	
		Population	Percent of total
1. Navajo and Trust Lands, Ariz., N.Mex., Utah	148,451	143,405	96.6%
2. Pine Ridge and Trust Lands, Nebr.-S.Dak.	12,215	11,182	91.5
3. Fort Apache, Ariz.	10,394	9,825	94.5
4. Gila River, Ariz.	9,540	9,116	95.6
5. Papago, Ariz.	8,730	8,480	97.1
6. Rosebud and Trust Lands, S.Dak.	9,696	8,043	83.0
7. San Carlos, Ariz.	7,294	7,110	97.5
8. Zuni Pueblo, Ariz.-N.Mex.	7,412	7,073	95.4
9. Hopi and Trust Lands, Ariz.	7,360	7,061	95.9
10. Blackfeet, Mont.	8,549	7,025	82.2
11. Turtle Mountain and Trust Lands, N.Dak.-S.Dak.	7,106	6,772	95.3
12. Yakima and Trust Lands, Wash.	27,668	6,307	22.8
13. Osage, Okla.[1]	41,645	6,161	14.8
14. Fort Peck, Mont.	10,595	5,782	54.6
15. Wind River, Wyo.	21,851	5,676	26.0
16. Eastern Cherokee, N.C.	6,527	5,388	82.5
17. Flathead, Mont.	21,259	5,130	24.1
18. Cheyenne River, S.Dak.	7,743	5,100	65.9
19. Standing Rock, N.Dak.-S.Dak.	7,956	4,870	61.2
20. Crow and Trust Lands, Mont.	6,370	4,724	74.2
21. Mississippi Choctaw and Trust Lands, Miss.	4,073	3,932	96.5
22. Colville, Wash.	6,957	3,788	54.4
23. Laguna Pueblo and Trust Lands, N.Mex.	3,731	3,634	97.4
24. Red Lake, Minn.	3,699	3,602	97.4
25. Northern Cheyenne and Trust Lands, Mont.-S.Dak.	3,923	3,542	90.3

Note: Ranked by total American Indian, Eskimo, or Aleut population. 1. The Osage Reservation is coextensive with Osage County. **Source**: U.S. Bureau of the Census.

only, and another 1,643,345 said they were this race and at least one other race. That makes for a total of 4,119,301 people who consider themselves at least partly American Indian or Alaska Native.

Not surprisingly, the state with the greatest percentage of American Indians and Alaska natives is Alaska, where people of this race constitute 15.6 percent of the population. New Mexico is second, with 9.5 percent, followed by South Dakota (8.3 percent) and Oklahoma (7.9 percent). The state with the most American Indians and Alaska Natives is California (333,346). Oklahoma is second, with 273,230, Arizona is third, with 255,879, and New Mexico is fourth, with 173,483. Washington, which had 102,940 Native Americans and Alaska Natives in 1990, saw this population drop to 93,301 for the 2000 Census. Meanwhile, the American Indian and Alaska Native population of Texas skyrocketed from 95,682 in 1990 to 118,362 in 2000. Almost half of all American Indians and Alaska Natives (1.2 million) live in the West. Only 162,558 American Indians and Alaska Natives live in the Northeast. Note: all the statistics cited in this paragraph refer to people who identified themselves as members of one race only.

States With Largest American Indian or Alaska Native Population, 2000

Rank, State	Total Population	American Indian or Alaska Native only		American Indian or Alaska Native only or in combination with other race(s)	
		Number	Percent	Number	Percent
1. California	33,871,648	333,346	1.0%	627,562	1.9%
2. Oklahoma	3,450,654	273,230	7.9	391,949	11.4
3. Arizona	5,130,632	255,879	5.0	292,552	5.7
4. New Mexico	1,819,046	173,483	9.5	191,475	10.5
5. Texas	20,851,820	118,362	0.6	215,599	1.0
6. North Carolina	8,049,313	99,551	1.2	131,736	1.6
7. Alaska	626,932	98,043	15.6	119,241	19.0
8. Washington	5,894,121	93,301	1.6	158,940	2.7
9. New York	18,976,457	82,461	0.4	171,581	0.9
10. South Dakota	754,844	62,283	8.3	68,281	9.0
United States	281,421,906	2,475,956	0.9	4,119,301	1.5

Note: Ranked by American Indian or Alaska Native-only population. Montana (6.2 percent), North Dakota (4.9 percent), Wyoming (2.3 percent), and Idaho (1.4 percent) ranked fifth, seventh, eight, and tenth respectively by percentage.
Source: U.S. Bureau of the Census, *The American Indian or Alaska Native Population 2000* (2001). www.census.gov.

The 1990 census reported that only 437,431 members of the American Indian, Eskimo, and Aleut populations lived inside federally "identified areas." There were 554 such areas in 1997, according to the federal government's Bureau of Indian Affairs. These areas include reservations that the federal government recognizes as territory in which American Indian tribes have jurisdiction (state governments are lands held in trust by state governments for the use and benefit of a given tribe), and "trust lands" that are held in trust by the federal government but that consist of property associated with a particular tribe or reservation. The Bureau of Indian Affairs counted 314 reservations in 1997.

U.S. POPULATION BY AGE AND SEX

▶ THE POPULATION BY AGE

With birth rates and fertility rates declining rapidly since 1965 it should come as no surprise that the average age of the U.S. population has been increasing almost as quickly. It will continue to rise for the foreseeable future in part because of the aging members of the Baby Boom generation.

During the Baby Boom years of the 1950s and 1960s, the median age of the population actually

Number of Persons and Percent of Total Population, by Age Group, 1960–2050 (numbers in thousands)

Age in Years	1960	1970	1980	1990	2000	2010	2050
Under 5	20,341	17,166	16,458	18,849	18,987	20,012	27,106
Percent	11.3%	8.4%	7.2%	7.6%	6.9%	6.7%	6.9%
5-13	32,965	36,672	31,095	31,996	36,043	35,605	47,804
Percent	18.2	17.9	13.7	12.8	13.1	12.0	12.1
14-17	11,219	15,924	16,142	13,311	15,752	16,894	21,207
Percent	6.2	7.8	7.1	5.3	5.7	5.7	5.4
18-24	16,128	24,712	30,350	26,826	26,258	30,138	36,333
Percent	8.9	12.1	13.3	10.8	9.6	10.1	9.2
25-34	22,919	25,323	37,626	43,139	37,233	38,292	49,365
Percent	12.7	12.3	16.5	17.3	13.6	12.9	12.5
35-44	24,221	23,150	25,868	37,766	44,659	38,521	47,393
Percent	13.4	11.3	11.4	15.1	16.3	12.9	12.0
45-64	36,203	41,999	44,515	46,280	60,992	78,848	85,862
Percent	20.0	20.5	19.5	18.6	22.2	26.5	21.8
65 & over	16,675	20,107	25,704	31,235	34,709	39,408	78,859
Percent	9.2	9.8	11.3	12.5	12.6	13.2	20.0
85 & over	940	1,430	2,269	3,057	4,259	5,671	18,223
Percent	0.5	0.7	1.0	1.2	1.6	1.9	4.6
100 & over	3	5	15	37	72	131	834
Percent	-	-	-	-	-	-	0.2
Total U.S. population	180,671	205,052	227,757	249,402	274,634	297,716	393,931
Median age	29.4	27.9	30.0	33.0	35.7	37.2	38.1

1. Figures for 1990 are estimated. Figures for 2000 and after are the projections the Census Bureau calls the "middle" or "most likely" series.   Source: U. S. Bureau of the Census, *Projections of the Population of the U.S., by Age, Sex, and Race: 1995 to 2050* (1996).

Resident Population of States, by Age, 1999 (numbers in thousands)

State	Resident population	Under 5 years	5-17 years	18-24 years	25-44 years	45-64 years	65 years and over	Median age
United States	272,691	18,942	51,263	26,019	34,540	59,191	34,540	35.5
Alabama	4,370	291	775	440	1,307	989	568	36.0
Alaska	620	50	147	71	179	138	35	30.9
Arizona	4,778	386	949	460	1,365	991	629	34.5
Arkansas	2,551	178	483	251	706	572	361	36.0
California	33,145	2,499	6,424	3,319	10,707	6,548	3,648	33.6
Colorado	4,056	288	777	393	1,223	967	408	35.7
Connecticut	3,282	218	610	256	1,010	719	469	37.0
Delaware	754	50	132	69	243	160	98	35.9
District of Columbia	519	27	68	46	184	122	72	37.6
Florida	15,111	952	2,618	1,236	4,238	3,325	2,742	38.7
Georgia	7,788	580	1,477	774	2,543	1,653	761	34.0
Hawaii	1,185	80	209	120	345	270	162	36.9
Idaho	1,252	93	258	144	341	274	142	33.5
Illinois	12,128	878	2,304	1,143	3,705	2,603	1,496	35.2
Indiana	5,943	414	1,115	576	1,787	1,308	743	35.4
Iowa	2,869	183	537	282	797	642	428	36.9
Kansas	2,654	184	515	271	768	562	354	35.4
Kentucky	3,961	259	706	405	1,183	914	493	36.1
Louisiana	4,372	314	876	481	1,247	953	501	34.1
Maine	1,253	67	223	111	385	292	175	37.8
Maryland	5,172	347	963	442	1,698	1,125	597	35.7
Massachusetts	6,175	392	1,076	513	1,996	1,338	560	36.5
Michigan	9,864	655	1,906	928	2,995	2,157	1,224	35.5
Minnesota	4,776	322	950	454	1,443	1,022	585	35.4
Mississippi	2,769	202	550	302	795	582	335	33.7
Missouri	5,468	363	1,036	520	1,611	1,192	746	36.1
Montana	883	53	171	89	231	221	117	37.8
Nebraska	1,666	115	329	170	467	356	228	35.5
Nevada	1,809	143	348	156	545	409	207	35.3
New Hampshire	1,201	74	231	98	401	253	145	35.9
New Jersey	8,143	543	1,460	673	2,532	1,827	1,108	37.0
New Mexico	1,740	131	364	176	489	379	200	34.5
New York	18,197	1,214	3,227	1,619	5,644	4,063	2,430	36.4
North Carolina	7,651	534	1,407	709	2,352	1,694	955	35.5
North Dakota	634	39	121	69	175	138	92	36.2
Ohio	11,257	740	2,104	1,065	3,359	2,487	1,501	36.1
Oklahoma	3,358	233	649	343	926	759	449	35.8
Oregon	3,316	220	608	312	952	790	435	36.9
Pennsylvania	11,994	712	2,140	1,025	3,515	2,702	1,899	37.9
Rhode Island	991	62	179	84	308	203	154	36.6
South Carolina	3,886	253	702	393	1,189	875	473	35.5
South Dakota	733	50	148	78	198	153	105	35.4
Tennessee	5,484	367	974	520	1,674	1,268	681	36.2
Texas	20,044	1,640	4,080	2,100	6,034	4,174	2,016	33.0
Utah	2,130	210	497	301	572	363	186	26.7
Vermont	594	32	107	53	188	140	73	37.2
Virginia	6,873	451	1,214	673	2,241	1,519	775	35.4
Washington	5,756	390	1,096	558	1,775	1,280	657	35.5
West Virginia	1,807	101	303	179	496	455	273	38.9
Wisconsin	5,250	332	1,016	508	1,556	1,146	691	36.0
Wyoming	480	30	96	54	127	116	56	36.1

Note: Includes armed forces residing in each state. Figures as of July 1, 1999. Source: U.S. Bureau of the Census, Population Division, Current Population Reports. www.census.gov/population.

declined, the only time it has done so. Since then, however, the steady decline in the percentage of young people, especially those under 18 years of age (from 34.1 percent in 1970, to 25.6 percent in 1990), combined with the increase of those between 25 and 44 (they were 23.6 percent of the population in 1970, but 32.6 percent in 1990) has driven the median age from 28.0 in 1970 to 33.0 in 1990. A five-year increase in 20 years is unprecedented in U.S. history, but what's more revealing is that we will most likely duplicate that feat over the next 20 years. By 1999, the median age of the U.S. population had already increased to 35.5.

The other major factor in the so-called "graying of America" is the increased life expectancy for older people. In 1950, the over-65 population totalled 7 percent of all Americans and numbered nine million. In 1990, 31.7 million Americans (12.3 percent of the population) were over 65; this represents a 24.1 percent increase since 1980 and a 1,000 percent increase since 1900. In 2000, there were 35 million people over 65.

As the population ages, 65 no longer seems old to most people. Especially when millions more people are living past the age of 80. There were 7 million people 80 or older in 1990, 3 million age 85 or older, nearly a million 90 years or older, and 36,000 people over the age of 100. By 2000, there were 16.7 million people over the age of 75 and 4.2 million age 85 or more.

Over the first decade of the 21st century, the over-65 population will grow another 10-12 per-cent—but between 2010 and 2030 the projected increases jump to 31.2 percent and 25.6 percent as the Baby Boom generation finally becomes senior citizens. In the year 2030, an estimated 21 percent of the population, or 65 million Americans, will be 65 years old or older.

Florida, and to a lesser degree, Pennsylvania, have long had the highest concentrations of retirees, but in the 1990s, several states saw dramatic growth in their over-65 population. Nevada's senior population grew by 55 percent between 1990 and 1998, while Alaska's increased 49 percent and Arizona's jumped 29 percent. Hawaii experienced 27 percent growth, Utah saw a 22 percent increase, and Colorado and New Mexico both had increases of 21 percent.

▶ THE POPULATION BY SEX

In 2000, according to the Census Bureau, there were 39.0 million men and 47.1 million women 18 years and over who had never married or who were currently widowed, separated, or divorced—a ratio of 83 unmarried men per 100 unmarried women. The popular interpretation of these figures—that there is a shortage of eligible men—fails to consider that women are more likely to live longer (and so be counted among the widowed) and less likely to remarry after a divorce. In fact, the surplus of women can be entirely attributed to the fact that there are seven million more widows than widowers over the age of 65. But during the peak marrying ages, unmarried men actually outnumber unmarried women: among persons between the ages of 18 and 24 there were 112 unmarried men for every 100 unmarried women; in the 25-to-34 age group, there were 120 men for every 100 women; and men 35-44 outnumber women 109 to 100. It's not until the 45-to-64 group that the reversal begins (68 unmarried men for every 100 available women), and among the 65-and-over there is a dramatic change, with only 32 unmarried men for every 100 unmarried women.

Characteristics of Persons 65 or Older, 1998

Characteristic	Total	Male	Female
Total (millions)	**32.4**	**13.7**	**18.7**
Percent distribution	**100.0%**	**42.1%**	**57.9%**
Marital status:			
Single	3.8%	3.6%	4.0%
Married	57.7	75.9	44.3
Spouse absent	2.4	2.3	2.5
Widowed	31.8	14.0	44.9
Divorced	6.7	6.5	6.8
Family status:			
In families1	67.3	80.4	57.7
Non-family householders	31.2	17.5	41.2
Secondary individuals	1.5	2.0	1.0
Living arrangements:			
Spouse present	55.3	73.6	41.8
Living alone	30.0	16.4	40.1
Living with someone else	14.7	10.0	18.1
Labor force participation:			
Employed	12.0	18.4	8.7
Unemployed	0.4	0.5	0.3
Not in labor force	87.7	83.1	91.1
Percent below poverty level	10.5	7.2	12.8

1. Excludes those living in unrelated subfamilies.
Source: U.S. Bureau of the Census, *Statistical Abstract of the United States* (annual)

Growth of the Over-65 Population, 1900–2050

Year	Population 65 and over		Population 85 and over	
	Number ('000s)	Percent of total population	Number ('000s)	Percent of total population
1900	3,099	4.1%	N.A.	N.A.
1910	3,986	4.3	N.A.	N.A.
1920	4,929	4.7	N.A.	N.A.
1930	6,705	5.5	N.A.	N.A.
1940	9,031	6.9	N.A.	N.A.
1950	12,397	8.1	N.A.	N.A.
1960	16,675	9.2	940	0.5%
1970	20,107	9.8	1,430	0.7
1980	25,549	11.3	2,269	1.0
1990	31,242	12.5	3,080	1.2
2000	34,992	12.8	4,240	1.5
2010	39,408	13.2	5,671	1.9
2020	53,220	16.5	6,460	2.0
2030	69,379	20.0	8,455	2.4
2040	75,233	20.3	13,552	3.7
2050	78,859	20.0	18,223	4.6

Note: Prior to 1960, the Census Bureau did not count persons over 85 separately. Figures for 2010 through 2050 are Census Bureau projections based on their "most likely" series of estimates.
Source: U.S. Bureau of the Census, *Population Projections of the U.S by Age, Sex, Race, and Hispanic Origin.*

U.S. Population by Sex: Totals and Ratio of Males to Females, 1920–2000

Year	Male ('000s)	Female ('000s)	Males per 100 females			
			All ages	14-24	25-44	65+
1920	53,900	51,810	104.0	97.3	105.1	101.3
1930	62,137	60,638	102.5	98.4	101.8	100.5
1940	66,062	65,608	100.7	98.9	98.5	95.5
1950	74,833	75,864	98.6	98.2	96.4	89.6
1960	88,331	90,992	97.1	98.7	95.7	82.8
1970	98,926	104,309	94.8	98.7	95.5	72.1
1980	110,053	116,493	94.5	101.9	97.4	67.6
1990	122,049	127,875	95.1	104.6	98.9	67.2
1995	128,293	134,510	95.4	104.7	98.6	70.7
1999	133,277	139,414	95.6	104.8	98.8	69.1
2000[1]	134,511	140,619	95.7	102.4	97.2	74.1

1. Preliminary. 2. Persons aged 15-24. **Source:** U.S. Bureau of the Census, *Statistical Abstract of the United States* (annual)

Births and Deaths in the U.S., 1910–99

Year	Live births ('000s)	Birth rate[1]	Deaths[2] ('000s)	Death rate[1]
1910	2,777	30.1	N.A.	14.7
1920	2,950	27.7	N.A.	13.0
1930	2,618	21.3	N.A.	11.3
1940	2,559	19.4	1,417	10.8
1950	3,632	24.1	1,452	9.6
1955	4,097	25.0	1,529	9.3
1960	4,258	23.7	1,712	9.5
1965	3,760	19.5	1,828	9.4
1970	3,731	18.4	1,921	9.5
1975	3,144	14.6	1,893	8.8
1980	3,612	15.9	1,990	8.8
1985	3,761	15.8	2,086	8.8
1990	4,158	16.7	2,148	8.6
1995	3,892	14.8	2,309	8.8
1996	3,899	14.7	2,311	8.7
1997	3,882	14.5	2,294	8.6
1998	3,946	14.6	2,331	8.6
1999[3]	3,965	14.5	2,396	8.8

1. Per 1,000 total population. 2. Excludes fetal deaths. 3. Provisional. **Source:** U.S. National Center for Health Statistics, *Vital Statistics of the United States,* (annual) and *National Vital Statistics Report,* June 26, 2001.

Marriages and Divorces in the U.S., 1920–99

Year	Marriages ('000s)	Rate per 1,000 population	Divorces ('000s)	Rate per 1,000 population
1920	1,274	12.0	171	1.6
1930	1,127	9.2	19.6	1.6
1940	1,596	12.1	264	2.0
1950	1,667	11.1	385	2.6
1955	1,531	9.3	377	2.3
1960	1,523	8.5	393	2.2
1965	1,800	9.3	479	2.5
1970	2,163	10.6	708	3.5
1975	2,153	10.0	1,036	4.8
1980	2,390	10.0	1,036	4.8
1985	2,413	10.1	1,190	5.0
1990	2,448	9.8	1,175	4.7
1995	2,336	8.9	1,169	4.4
1996	2,344	8.8	1,150	4.3
1997	2,384	8.9	1,163	4.3
1998	2,244	8.4	1,135	4.2
1999	2,358	8.6	N.A.	4.1[1]

1. Based on reports from only 46 states; California, Colorado, Indiana, and Louisiana no longer report divorce data. **Source:** U.S. National Center for Health Statistics, *Vital Statistics of the United States* (annual) and *National Vital Statistics Report,* Feburary 22, 2001

VITAL STATISTICS

The National Center for Health Statistics does a month-by-month tracking of four sets of numbers which both it and the Census Bureau refer to as "vital": births, deaths, marriages, and divorces.

Births An estimated 3.96 million babies were born in the U.S. in 1999, up slightly from 3.94 million the year before. But the crude birth rate (the number of live births per 1,000 total population) declined slightly to 14.5, matching the record low set in 1997. The fertility rate (the number of births per 1,000 women aged 15-44) was 65.9, just slightly higher than the 20-year low of 65.0 recorded in 1997.

Deaths An estimated 2.40 million people died in 1999, up from 2.33 million in 1998. The crude

death rate increased from 8.65 to 8.77 per 1,000 population. Two influenza outbreaks played a large part in reversing the century-long trend of declining death rates. In 1910, by comparison, the death rate was 14.7. (For infant mortality figures and for information about death rates by cause see the section, "Health and Medicine.")

In 1999 there were 1,569,000 more births than deaths; this figure is called the natural increase, meaning the growth in population without immigration (which has accounted for close to 700,000 people per year in recent years).

Marriages An estimated 2.36 million couples married during 1999, a slight increase from 1998 levels; the marriage rate of 8.6 per 1,000 people was up slightly from the 30-year-low recorded in 1998. In addition to getting married in fewer numbers, people are getting married at a later age In 1960, for example, about 40 percent of all 19-year-old women were married, but by 1990 only 11 percent were. Also in 1960, about 92 percent of all women were married before they reached age 30, but by 1990 only 81 percent were. Moreover, between 1970 and 2000, the proportion of 30-year-olds who had never married more than tripled. In 2000, nearly 20 percent of 30-year-olds were never-married, up from less than 6 percent in 1970.

Divorces The National Center for Health Statistics stopped publishing numbers of divorces in 2000 because four states no longer report divorce

statistics. The latest available year for which data is available is 1998, when an estimated 1.13 million divorces were granted, down slightly from the previous year. The divorce rate per 1,000 population was 4.2, its lowest rate in more than 20 years. The divorce rate peaked in 1979 at 5.3 per 1,000 population. (In that year there were 22.8 divorced women for every 1,000 married women, up from 9.2 in 1960. While the divorce rate has stabilized, the ratio of divorced persons to married persons (with spouse present) has skyrocketed. Between

Births, Deaths, and Marriages in the U.S., By Month, 1999

Month	Births Number	Births Rate per 1,000 population	Deaths Number	Deaths Rate per 1,000 population	Marriages Number	Marriages Rate per 1,000 population
January	322,000	14.0	231,000	10.0	130,000	6.0
February	298,000	14.3	208,000	10.0	141,000	7.2
March	330,000	14.3	223,000	9.6	159,000	7.3
April	319,000	14.3	199,000	8.9	163,000	7.8
May	332,000	14.3	195,000	8.4	205,000	8.8
June	328,000	14.6	176,000	7.9	242,000	10.8
July	353,000	15.2	190,000	8.2	219,000	9.5
August	355,000	15.3	186,000	8.0	229,000	9.9
September	345,000	15.4	176,000	7.9	242,000	10.8
October	336,000	14.5	199,000	8.6	230,000	9.9
November	317,000	14.1	194,000	8.6	200,000	8.9
December	330,000	14.2	218,000	9.4	198,000	8.5

Note: Figures are provisional. **Source:** U.S. National Center for Health Statistics, *Monthly Vital Statistics Report*, (February 22, 2001).

Marital Status of the Population by Sex and Age, 2000 (numbers in thousands)

Sex and Age	Total	Never married Number	Never married Percent	Married Number	Married Percent	Widowed Number	Widowed Percent	Divorced Number	Divorced Percent	Separated Number	Separated Percent
MALE											
Total 15+	103,114	32,253	31.3%	56,501	54.8%	2,604	2.5%	8,572	8.3%	1,818	1.8%
15-19	10,295	10,140	98.5	69	0.7	3	0.0	29	0.3	51	0.5
20-24	9,208	7,710	83.7	1,252	13.6	0	0.0	101	1.1	70	0.8
25-29	8,942	4,625	51.7	3,658	40.9	9	0.1	342	3.8	170	1.9
30-34	9,621	2,899	30.1	5,640	58.6	15	0.2	712	7.4	205	2.1
35-39	11,032	2,241	20.3	6,945	63.0	42	0.4	1,308	11.9	269	2.4
40-44	11,103	1,740	15.7	7,365	66.3	54	0.5	1,467	13.2	316	2.8
45-49	9,654	1,156	12.0	6,675	69.1	53	0.5	1,381	14.3	230	2.4
50-54	8,235	541	6.6	6,352	77.1	104	1.3	996	12.1	148	1.8
55-59	6,105	347	5.7	4,567	74.8	158	2.6	838	13.7	110	1.8
60-64	5,032	265	5.3	3,896	77.4	171	3.4	549	10.9	78	1.6
65-69	4,376	227	5.2	3,350	76.6	285	6.5	376	8.6	77	1.8
70-74	3,673	121	3.3	2,821	76.8	382	10.4	249	6.8	62	1.7
75+	5,837	242	4.1	3,914	67.1	1,327	22.7	225	3.9	33	0.6
FEMALE											
Total 15+	110,660	27,763	25.1%	56,501	51.1%	11,061	10.0%	11,309	10.2%	2,661	2.4%
15-19	9,807	9,401	95.9	276	2.8	10	0.1	35	0.4	52	0.5
20-24	9,233	6,720	72.8	2,110	22.9	11	0.1	168	1.8	164	1.8
25-29	9,326	3,627	38.9	4,676	50.1	18	0.2	575	6.2	289	3.1
30-34	9,896	2,172	21.9	6,290	63.6	63	0.6	904	9.1	341	3.4
35-39	11,288	1,610	14.3	7,481	66.3	131	1.2	1,486	13.2	429	3.8
40-44	11,382	1,341	11.8	7,562	66.4	172	1.5	1,706	15.0	422	3.7
45-49	10,094	1,008	10.0	6,765	67.0	309	3.1	1,616	16.0	279	2.8
50-54	8,647	598	6.9	5,668	65.6	416	4.8	1,604	18.5	242	2.8
55-59	6,763	377	5.6	4,451	65.8	578	8.5	1,133	16.8	148	2.2
60-64	5,487	229	4.2	3,479	63.4	863	15.7	738	13.5	105	1.9
65-69	4,976	175	3.5	2,855	57.4	1,277	25.7	520	10.4	59	1.2
70-74	4,771	188	3.9	2,302	48.2	1,778	37.3	386	8.1	60	1.3
75+	8,988	317	3.5	2,587	28.8	5,435	60.5	438	4.9	72	0.8

Note: Totals may not add up due to independent rounding.
Source: U.S. Bureau of the Census, *America's Families and Living Arrangements 2000* (2001). www.census.gov.

1970 and 2000, the proportion nearly quadrupled, from 47 divorced per 1,000 married to 175 per 1,000. For blacks, the rise was even greater, going from 83 per 1,000 to 330 per 1,000 in the same period.

In 2000, there were 19.9 million currently divorced persons in the U.S., 9.8 percent of the total adult population over 18. There are more divorced women (11.3 million) than men (8.6 million) because women are less likely to remarry.

Percent of Population Never Married, by Age and Sex, 1960–2000

Age	1960	1970	1980	1990	1995	2000
			MEN			
Total: 15 and over	23.2%	28.1%	29.6%	29.9%	31.0%	31.3%
15-17	98.8	99.4	99.4	99.8	99.3	98.7
18	94.6	95.1	97.4	98.5	97.7[1]	98.2
19	87.1	89.9	90.9	95.3	(¹)	(¹)
20-24	53.1	54.7	68.8	79.3	80.7	83.7
25-29	20.8	19.1	33.1	45.2	51.0	51.7
30-34	11.9	9.4	15.9	27.0	28.2	30.1
35-39	8.8	7.2	7.8	14.7	20.3	20.3
40-44	7.3	6.3	7.1	10.5	14.0	15.7
45-54	7.4	7.5	6.1	6.3	8.1	9.4
55-64	8.0	7.8	5.3	5.8	5.0	5.5
65 and over	7.7	7.5	4.9	4.2	4.2	4.2
			WOMEN			
Total: 15 and over	17.3%	22.1%	22.5%	22.8%	23.5%	25.1%
15-17	93.2	97.3	97.0	98.5	98.9	97.9
18	75.6	82.0	88.0	92.0	91.7[1]	93.0
19	59.7	68.8	77.6	88.7	(¹)	(¹)
20-24	28.4	35.8	50.2	62.8	66.7	72.8
25-29	10.5	10.5	20.9	31.1	35.3	38.9
30-34	6.9	6.2	9.5	16.4	19.0	21.9
35-39	6.1	5.4	6.2	10.4	12.6	14.3
40-44	6.1	4.9	4.8	8.0	8.7	11.8
45-54	7.0	4.9	4.7	5.0	6.1	8.6
55-64	8.0	6.8	4.5	3.9	4.3	4.9
65 and over	8.5	7.7	5.9	4.9	4.2	3.6

1. Population aged 18-19 included under 18.
Source: U.S. Bureau of the Census, *America's Families and Living Arrangements 2000* (2001). www.census.gov.

Marital Status, by Race and Hispanic Origin, 1970–2000

Year and Race	Total	Never married Number	Percent	Married Number	Percent	Widowed Number	Percent	Divorced Number	Percent	Separated Number	Percent
All Races											
1970	132,507	21,443	16.2%	94,999	71.7%	11,784	8.9%	4,282	3.2%	N.A.	N.A.
1980	159,528	32,342	20.3	104,564	65.5	12,734	8.0	9,886	6.2	N.A.	N.A.
1990	181,849	40,361	22.2	112,552	61.9	13,810	7.6	15,125	8.3	N.A.	N.A.
2000	201,762	48,213	23.9	115,655	57.3	13,655	6.8	19,828	9.8	4,412	2.2%
White											
1970	118,179	18,444	15.6	85,784	72.6	10,280	8.7	3,671	3.1	N.A.	N.A.
1980	139,480	26,405	18.9	93,800	67.2	10,938	7.8	8,338	6.0	N.A.	N.A.
1990	155,454	31,633	20.3	99,450	64.0	11,730	7.5	12,640	8.1	N.A.	N.A.
2000	168,140	36,017	21.4	101,159	60.2	11,529	6.9	16,507	9.8	2,928	1.7
Black											
1970	12,972	2,668	20.6	8,310	64.1	1,427	11.0	567	4.4	N.A.	N.A.
1980	16,638	5,070	30.5	8,545	51.4	1,627	9.8	1,396	8.4	N.A.	N.A.
1990	20,320	7,141	35.1	9,302	45.8	1,730	8.5	2,146	10.6	N.A.	N.A.
2000	24,016	9,451	39.4	8,818	36.7	1,692	7.0	2,765	11.5	1,290	5.4
Hispanic											
1970	5,066	943	18.6	3,637	71.8	286	5.6	200	3.9	N.A.	N.A.
1980	7,888	1,901	24.1	5,176	65.6	350	4.4	460	5.8	N.A.	N.A.
1990	13,560	3,694	27.2	8,365	61.7	548	4.0	952	7.0	N.A.	N.A.
2000	21,109	5,907	28.0	11,864	56.2	881	4.2	1,619	7.7	838	4.0
Asian and Pacific Islander											
2000	7,859	2,241	28.5	4,792	61.0	332	4.2	360	4.6	135	1.7

Note: Note: Only those people 15 years old and over are included. Hispanic persons may be of any race.
Source: U.S. Bureau of the Census, *America's Families and Living Arrangements 2000* (2001). www.census.gov.

Median Age at First Marriage, by Sex, 1890-2000

Year	Male	Female	Year	Male	Female
1890	26.1	22.0	1991	26.3	24.1
1900	25.9	21.9	1992	26.5	24.4
1910	25.1	21.6	1993	26.5	24.5
1920	24.6	21.2	1994	26.7	24.5
1930	24.3	21.3	1995	26.9	24.5
1940	24.3	21.5	1996	27.1	24.8
1950	22.8	20.3	1997	26.8	25.0
1960	22.8	20.3	1998	26.7	25.0
1970	23.2	20.8	1999	26.9	25.1
1980	24.7	22.0	2000	26.8	25.1
1990	26.1	23.9			

Source: U.S. Bureau of the Census, *America's Families and Living Arrangements 2000* (2001). www.census.gov.

Black-White Married Couples in the U.S., 1960-2000 (thousands)

Year	Total married couples	Total black-white couples	Husband black, wife white	Wife black, husband white
1960	40,491	51	25	26
1970	44,598	65	41	24
1980	49,714	167	122	45
1990	53,256	211	150	61
1995	54,937	328	206	122
1997	54,666	311	201	110
1998	55,305	330	210	120
1999	55,849	364	240	124
2000	56,497	363	268	95

Source: U.S. Bureau of the Census, *America's Families and Living Arrangements 2000* (2001). www.census.gov.

Divorced Persons per 1,000 Married Persons by Sex and Race 1960-2000

Sex/race	All races	White	Black	Hispanic[1]
Both sexes:				
1960	35	33	62	N.A.
1970	47	44	83	61
1980	100	92	203	98
1990	142	133	282	129
1995	161	152	303	152
1996	167	156	344	151
1998	175	168	336	150
2000	175	166	330	145
Male:				
1960	28	27	45	N.A.
1970	35	32	62	40
1980	79	74	149	64
1990	118	112	208	103
1995	134	130	212	130
1996	142	134	266	127
1998	150	144	253	127
2000	151	145	257	120
Female:				
1960	42	38	78	N.A.
1970	60	56	104	81
1980	120	110	258	132
1990	166	153	358	155
1995	187	173	397	174
1996	192	178	425	173
1998	200	187	422	172
2000	200	187	406	168

Note: Persons 18 years and over. Per 1,000 married persons with spouse present. 1. Persons of Hispanic origin may be of any race.
Source: U.S. Bureau of the Census, *America's Families and Living Arrangements 2000* (2001). www.census.gov

Percent of First Marriages Ending in Separation or Divorce by Length of Marriage and Age of Wife

Length of Marriage (years)	Percent ending in separation or divorce				
		Wife's age at first marriage			
	Total	Under 18	18-19	20-24	25 and over
1	3%	4%	4%	2%	2%
2	7	10	9	6	5
3	12	17	15	10	08
4	16	23	20	14	11
5	20	29	24	17	15
6	23	34	28	19	17
7	26	39	32	22	19
8	29	42	35	25	20
9	31	45	37	27	22
10	33	48	40	29	24
11	35	49	42	31	26
12	38	52	44	33	29
13	39	54	46	33	30
14	41	57	47	35	31
15	43	59	49	36	35

Source: National Center for Health Statistics, *Advance Data: First Marriage Dissolution, Divorce, and Remarriage: United States,* May 31, 2001.

▶FERTILITY RATES OF AMERICAN WOMEN

Population experts predict future trends by studying many factors including the crude birth rate (see "Vital Statistics") and the all-important fertility rates. The *general fertility rate* measures the ratio of live births to the total number of women aged 15 to 44. (Until 1990, the Census Bureau had reported based on the number of women 18 to 44, thus projecting a higher fertility rate but discounting the high number of teenage pregnancies.)

The *total fertility rate* is the number of births 1,000 women aged 10 to 50 would have in their lifetimes if, at each year of age, they experienced the birth rates occurring to women of that age in the specified calendar year. The total fertility rate is sometimes defined in the popular media as the number of *likely* births one woman will have in her lifetime; they do this by dividing by 1,000.

The total fertility rate is most helpful in measuring long term trends, especially in determining

A recent study by the National Center for Health Statistics revealed that 43 percent of all first marriages end in separation or divorce within 15 years. One in five ends in the first five years, and one in three ends within 10 years (see the accompanying table). The report also showed a link between the age of the woman and the duration of a marriage. Fifty-nine percent of first marriages involving women under 18 ended in separation or divorce within 15 years, compared with 36 percent of marriages where the bride was 20 or older.

whether or not the nation is sustaining a level of reproduction necessary for maintaining current population levels. That level, generally regarded as 2,100 per 1,000 women, has not been achieved in the U.S. since 1971. But since 1990, the figure has hovered just below that number.

Fertility rates in 1999 were highest among women in their 20s. The fertility rate for women 20-24 was 111.0; for women 25-29 it was 117.6. Black women (70.1) had higher fertility rates overall than white women (65.1), Asian or Pacific Islander women (65.6), or even American Indian women (69.7). Women of Hispanic origin had an overall fertility rate of 102.0; Mexican women had the highest fertility rates of all (111.6), while the rate for Cuban women (51.2) was well below the national average.

One clear indication that women are having children much later in life is the increasing fertility rate of women over 35. Since 1978, fertility rates of women 35-49 have more than doubled.

▶ WOMEN AND CHILDBEARING: CURRENT TRENDS

Unmarried women   According to the Census Bureau's Current Population Survey, approximately 1.1 million unmarried women gave birth in 1998; one million of these births were to never-married women, while 143,000 were to widowed or divorced women. Births out of wedlock represented 31 percent of all births in 1998, and 86 percent of all births to teenagers. Among black

women, the majority of births (67 percent) were out of wedlock. That compares with 38 percent for hispanic women and 22 percent with non-Hispanic white women.

Births to teenagers   Every year in the U.S., almost 500,000 teenagers give birth. Most of these women are unmarried. In 1998, more than 460,000 teenagers gave birth, up dramatically from 288,000 in 1994. The rate of teenage births, however, is beginning to decline. The birth rate for women aged 15-19 hit a 20-year high of 62.1 in 1991, but has declined every year since then, to 48.0 in 1998.

New mothers in the labor force   Being a stay-at-home mother is a luxury most American families can no loner afford. In June, 1998, 59 percent of women with children under the age of one were in the labor force. That's nearly double the rate in 1976 (31 percent), and up from 54 percent in 1992. Even more women go back to work after their children turn one year old; 73 percent of all mothers (regardless of their children's ages) were in the labor force in 1998.

▶ ADOPTION

Between 1973 and 1994, the percent of ever-married women who have ever adopted a child declined from 2.1 percent to 1.3 percent, according to National Surveys of Family Growth from those years. The National Center for Health Statistics attributed the drop to several factors, including the legalization of abortion in 1973 and the development of new reproductive technologies that have reduced the number of unwanted pregnancies. Almost all of the decrease since 1973 has come in unrelated children; the percent of women adopting their nieces, nephews, stepchildren, boyfriend's children, or other related (blood or otherwise) children has held steady.

Perhaps the greatest shift has come in the number of children available for adoption. Before 1973, never-married women under the age of 45 relinquished 8.7 percent of their children for adoption. In 1995, they gave up less than 1 percent. Almost all of this decrease has come among never-married white women, who relinquished nearly 20 percent of their children before 1973. Never-married black women have consistently kept their babies: Only 1.5 percent relinquished their children before 1973, and only 1.1 percent did between 1982 and 1988 (1995 figures were unavailable).

Fertility Rates of U.S. Women, 1930-99

Year	General fertility rate	Total fertility rate	Year	General fertility rate	Total fertility rate
1930	89.2	2,600	1985	66.3	1,844
1935	77.2	2,250	1990	70.9	2,081
1940	79.9	2,301	1991	69.2	2,073
1945	85.9	2,491	1992	68.9	2,073
1950	106.2	3,091	1993	67.6	2,065
1955	118.3	3,574	1994	66.7	2,036
1960	118.0	3,654	1995	65.6	2,019
1965	96.6	2,928	1996	65.3	2,027
1970	87.9	2,480	1997	65.0	2,032
1975	66.0	1,774	1998	65.6	2,058
1980	68.4	1,840	1999	65.9	2,075

Source: U.S. National Center for Health Statistics, *National Vital Statistics Report*, April 17, 2001.

Women and Childbearing in the U.S, by Age, 1976-2000

Characteristic	1976	1980	1990	1995	1999	2000[1]
Total number of women, 18-44 years old ('000s)[2]	41,618	45,652	58,381	60,225	60,082	60,133
Births per 1,000 women						
All women 15-44 years old[3]	67.2	68.4	70.9	65.6	65.9	67.6
15-19 years	N.A.	53.0	59.9	56.8	49.6	48.7
20-24 years	93.22	115.1	116.5	109.8	111.0	112.5
25-29 years	104.8	112.9	120.2	112.2	117.8	121.7
30-34 years	56.4	61.9	80.8	82.5	89.6	94.2
35-39 years	22.6	19.8	31.7	34.3	38.3	40.3
40-44 years	6.5	3.9	5.5	6.6	7.4	7.9

1. Preliminary. 2. Figures for 1976 and later includes women 18-44 years old. 3. Women 18-19 included with women 20-24 years old.
Source: U.S. National Center for Health Statistics, *National Vital Statistics Report*, July 24, 2001.

In 1995, there were 37.4 million ever-married women between the ages of 18 and 44. Of these, 9.9 million, or 26.4 percent, had considered adoption, 1.6 million had taken steps toward adoption, and 472,000 were currently looking to adopt a child. According to the Survey, steps toward adoption include contacting an adoption agency or lawyer, placing a newspaper ad, or having previously adopted a child.

HOUSEHOLDS AND FAMILIES

Since the very first census in 1790, the Federal Government has not only attempted to count every individual, it has also tried to determine where those individuals live and with whom. While the definition of *household* has changed somewhat over the years, it has remained a central element in understanding the basic structure of American society. Since 1970, changes in the size and composition of the household unit have revealed the extent of social change more clearly than any other measure. Note that data on households and families is from the Census Bureau's annual Current Population Survey, not from the decennial census.

▶ HOUSEHOLDS

Virtually all Americans are part of a household. As of March 2000, the Census Bureau determined that 274 million persons belonged to a household, even if that household consisted of only one person. A small number of people in institutions or in unique group living arrangements do not belong to households. According to the official Census Bureau definition, a household consists of all persons who occupy a housing unit. A house, an apartment or other group of rooms, or a single room, is regarded as a housing unit when it is occupied or intended for occupancy as separate living quarters; that is when the occupants do not live and eat with any other persons in the structure and there is direct access from the outside or through a common hall.

There are two major categories of households identified by the Census Bureau: family and nonfamily. A family or family household requires the presence of at least two persons, the householder (i.e. the person in whose name the housing unit is owned or rented) and one or more additional family members related to the householder through birth, adoption or marriage. A nonfamily household consists of a householder who either lives alone or exclusively with persons who are not related to the householder. Since 1970 the rapid growth of nonfamily households has led to a continuous increase in the number of households and a fall in the average number of persons in each. In 2000, there were 104.7 million households in the U.S., the largest number ever, with an average of 2.62 persons in each. This continues a trend begun during the 1970s when the number of households increased by more than 20 percent and over 17.3 million units, nearly double the growth of the 1940s and 1950s and over 60 percent more than the relatively explosive 1960s. The most significant change helping to ignite this surge was the unprecedented increase in the number of nonfamily households, which grew by 77.7 percent in the 1970s and 28.4 percent during the 1980s.

Several factors help to account for this change, including the rapid rise in the divorce rate, as well as an increase in the number of young single people living on their own and deciding to postpone marriage. In 2000, nearly 27 million people, or one in 10, lived alone. The most recent Census Bureau figures indicate that the trend is abating, however. The number of people living alone grew 59 percent during the 1970s, 21 percent during the 1980s, but only 16 percent from 1990 to 2000.

An additional 4.7 million unmarried-couple households were another large segment of the nonfamily population. Unmarried couples made up only a small percentage of all U.S. couples, but their numbers have continued to skyrocket since their sudden appearance on the American social landscape during the 1970s. There were only 523,000 unmarried couples living together in 1970, but their numbers had tripled to 1.6 million in 1980. A growing number of unmarried couples (1.7 million in 2000) have children under 15 years old in their households. This doesn't necessarily mean more children are being born out of wedlock, however, since this category includes children from previous marriages living with an un-remarried

U.S. Households, Number and Size, 1940–2000

Year	Number of households ('000s)	Average number per household All ages	Under 18 years	18 years and older
1940	34,949	3.67	1.14	2.53
1950	43,544	3.37	1.06	2.31
1960[1]	52,799	3.33	1.21	2.12
1970	63,401	3.14	1.09	2.05
1980	80,776	2.76	0.79	1.97
1990	93,347	2.63	0.69	1.94
1995	98,990	2.65	0.71	1.93
1996	99,627	2.65	0.71	1.94
1997	101,018	2.64	0.71	1.93
1998	102,528	2.62	0.70	1.92
1999	103,874	2.61	0.69	1.92
2000	104,705	2.62	0.69	1.93

1. Alaska and Hawaii included for first time. **Source:** U.S. Bureau of the Census, *The Statistical History of the U.S.* (1976); *America's Families and Living Arrangements 2000* (2001). www.census.gov.

Unmarried Couple Households, 1960–2000

Year	Total	Without children under 15	With children under 15
1960	439,000	242,000	197,000
1970	523,000	327,000	196,000
1980	1,589,000	1,159,000	431,000
1990	2,856,000	1,966,000	891,000
1995	3,668,000	2,349,000	1,319,000
1996	3,958,000	2,516,000	1,442,000
1997	4,130,000	2,660,000	1,470,000
1998	4,236,000	2,716,000	1,520,000
1999	4,486,000	2,981,000	1,505,000
2000	4,736,000	3,061,000	1,675,000

Note: Figures may not add to total due to rounding. **Source:** *America's Families and Living Arrangements: 2000* (2001).

parent. As currently defined by the Census Bureau, an unmarried-couple household is two persons of the opposite sex who share living quarters. Although a close personal relationship is implied, other types—including tenancy—are included. But no more than two unrelated adults are present in an unmarried-couple household although children under age 15 may be present.

Despite all the attention given to the growth of nonfamily households, the fact remains that the overwhelming majority of Americans—228 million in 2000—live in some kind of family situation. This is not to say that the size and structure of the family hasn't undergone major revamping in recent decades but rather to emphasize its inherent strength as the basic social unit despite the presence of powerful forces for change.

▶FAMILIES

In 2000 there were 72.0 million families in the U.S., up from 51.6 million in 1970. But the 21st century American family bears less and less resemblance to the 20th century family. Perhaps the greatest change is the drop in the percentage of nuclear families: married couples with their own children. These types of households represented 45 percent of the total in 1960; in 2000, they dropped below 25 for the first time (23.5 percent). Market researchers who once assumed the family consisted of four members now base their assumptions on families of three, reflecting a steady, dramatic decline in the average family size, from 3.58 in 1970 to 3.17 in 2000. These numbers indicate a growing number of families opting not to have children. They constituted 44.1 percent of all families in 1970, but since 1990, they have outnumbered families with children. In 2000, 37.5 million families had children under 18, compared to 38.1 million without children.

More important, perhaps, the proportion of married-couple families declined from 86.9 percent of all family households in 1970 to 76.8 percent in 2000, while the number of family households headed by females with no husbands present soared from 5.5 million, or 10.7 percent of all family households in 1970, to 12.8 million, or 17.6 percent in 2000. (A startling 47.2 percent of black families were headed by single women in 2000, up from 28.0 percent in 1970.)

Households and Families: Growth and Change, 1960–2000

Type of unit	1960	1970	1980	1990	2000	1980–90	1990-2000
	Number ('000s)					Percent change	
All Households	**52,799**	**63,401**	**80,776**	**93,347**	**104,705**	**15.5%**	**12.2%**
Average size	3.33	3.14	2.76	2.63	2.62	—	—
Families	**45,111**	**51,586**	**59,550**	**66,090**	**72,025**	**11.0%**	**9.0%**
Average size	3.67	3.58	3.29	3.17	3.17	—	—
Married couple	39,329	44,755	49,112	52,317	55,311	6.5	5.7
Male householder[1]	1,275	1,239	1,733	2,884	4,028	66.4	39.7
Female householder[1]	4,507	5,591	8,705	10,890	12,687	25.1	16.5
Unrelated subfamilies	**207**	**130**	**360**	**534**	**571**	**48.3%**	**6.9%**
Married couple	75	27	20	68	37	N.A.[2]	N.A.[2]
Father-child[1]	47	11	36	45	57	N.A.[2]	N.A.[2]
Mother-child[1]	85	91	304	421	477	38.5	13.3
Related subfamilies	**1,514**	**1,150**	**1,150**	**2,403**	**2,983**	**109.0%**	**24.1%**
Married couple	871	617	582	871	1,149	49.7	31.9
Father-child[1]	115	48	54	153	201	183.0	31.4
Mother-child[1]	528	484	512	1,378	1,633	169.1	18.5
Nonfamily households	**7,895**	**11,945**	**21,226**	**27,257**	**32,680**	**28.4%**	**19.9%**
Male householder	2,716	4,063	8,807	11,606	14,641	31.8	26.2
Female householder	5,179	7,882	12,419	15,651	18,039	26.0	15.3
One person	6,896	10,851	18,296	22,999	26,724	25.7	16.2

1. No spouse present. 2. Not shown; base less than 75,000.
Source: U.S. Bureau of the Census, *America's Families and Living Arrangements 2000* (2001). www.census.gov.

Families: Number, Average Size and Percent Distribution by Number of Children, 1970–2000

Year	Number of families ('000s)	Average size of family	None	1	2	3	4 or more
			Percent distribution by number of own children under 18				
1970	51,586	3.58	44.1%	18.2%	17.4%	10.6%	9.8%
1980	59,550	3.29	47.9	20.9	19.3	7.8	4.1
1985	62,706	3.23	50.4	20.9	18.6	7.2	3.0
1990	66,090	3.17	51.1	20.5	18.5	7.0	2.8
1995	69,305	3.19	50.5	20.3	19.1	7.3	2.8
1996	69,594	3.20	50.9	20.2	19.0	7.1	2.9
1997	70,241	3.19	50.6	20.4	18.9	7.3	2.8
1998	70,880	3.19	51.0	20.3	18.5	7.6	2.7
1999	71,535	3.18	51.6	20.0	18.3	7.3	2.8
2000	72,025	3.17	50.4	21.5	18.5	6.9	2.8

Source: U.S. Bureau of the Census, *America's Families and Living Arrangements 2000* (2001)). www.census.gov.

Living Arrangements of Children Under 18, by Race, 1970–2000

Arrangement	1970 Number ('000s)	Percent	1980 Number ('000s)	Percent	1990 Number ('000s)	Percent	2000 Number ('000s)	Percent
All children								
Children under 18	69,162	100.0%	63,427	100.0%	64,137	100.0%	72,012	100.0%
Living with:								
Two parents	58,939	85.2	48,624	76.7	46,503	72.5	49,795	69.1
One Parent	8,199	11.9	12,466	19.7	15,867	24.7	19,220	26.7
Mother only	7,452	10.8	11,406	18.0	13,874	21.6	16,162	22.4
Father only	748	1.1	1,060	1.7	1,993	3.1	3,058	4.2
Other relatives	1,547	2.2	1,949	3.1	1,421	2.2	2,160	3.0
Nonrelatives only	477	0.7	388	0.6	346	0.5	837	1.2
White children								
Children under 18	58,791	100.0%	52,242	100.0%	51,390	100.0%	56,455	100.0%
Living with:								
Two parents	52,624	89.5	43,200	82.7	40,593	79.0	42,497	75.3
One Parent	5,110	8.7	7,901	15.1	9,869	19.2	12,192	21.6
Mother only	4,581	7.8	7,059	13.5	8,321	16.2	9,765	17.3
Father only	528	0.9	842	1.6	1,549	3.0	2,427	4.3
Other relatives	695	1.2	887	1.7	708	1.4	1,132	2.0
Nonrelatives only	362	0.6	254	0.5	220	0.4	634	1.1
Black children								
Children under 18	9,422	100.0%	9,375	100.0%	10,018	100.0%	11,412	100.0%
Living with:								
Two parents	5,508	58.5	3,956	42.2	3,781	37.7	4,286	37.6
One Parent	2,995	31.8	4,297	45.8	5,484	54.7	6,080	53.3
Mother only	2,783	29.5	4,117	43.9	5,132	51.2	5,596	49.0
Father only	213	2.3	180	1.9	353	3.5	484	4.2
Other relatives	822	8.7	999	10.7	655	6.5	879	7.7
Nonrelatives only	97	1.0	123	1.3	98	1.0	167	1.5
Hispanic children								
Children under 18	4,006	100.0%	5,459	100.0%	7,174	100.0%	11,613	100.0%
Living with:								
Two parents	3,111	77.7	4,116	75.4	4,789	66.8	7,561	65.1
One Parent	N.A.	N.A.	1,152	21.1	2,154	30.0	3,425	29.5
Mother only	N.A.	N.A.	1,069	19.6	1,943	27.1	2,919	25.4
Father only	N.A.	N.A.	83	1.5	211	2.9	506	4.4
Other relatives	N.A.	N.A.	183	3.4	177	2.5	431	3.7
Nonrelatives only	N.A.	N.A.	8	0.1	54	0.8	196	1.7

Note: N.A.= Not available. Hispanic children may be of any race. Excludes persons under 18 years who were maintaining households or family groups and spouses. **Source:** U.S. Bureau of the Census, *America's Families and Living Arrangements 2000* (2001).

A related development, recently turned into a political issue by those advocating "family values," has been the rising number of single-parent situations. More than 31 percent of families with children under 18 were headed by a single parent in 2000, up from only 13 percent in 1970. The vast majority (82.5 percent) of these single-parent families were headed by women. The number of households headed by never-married women with children continues to grow. There were 248,000 such households in 1970; in 2000, there were 4.2 million of them, more even than the 3.4 million households headed by divorced women with children.

According to the Census Bureau, the period between 1990 and 2000 has seen a general stabilizing of these trends; in the past 10 years, the percentage of married couple families and single-parent families has remained constant. The one startling change has been the growth of single-parent homes headed by fathers. In 2000, they numbered 2.0 million, up from 1.8 million in 1998.

Another important though less vital sign of change is the growth in the number of so-called *subfamilies*. These are families who live in a household and are either related or not to the householder; the Census Bureau describes a *related*

subfamily as a married couple with or without children, or one parent with one or more single (never married) children under 18, living in a household and related to the person who maintains the household. They are not counted in the total number of families. Related subfamilies have nearly tripled since 1980 and now stand at 2.9 million.

An *unrelated subfamily* is a group of two persons or more who are related to one another by birth, marriage, or adoption, but who are not related to the householder. Unrelated subfamilies numbered 571,000 in 2000.

▶ SINGLE PARENTS AND GROWN CHILDREN LIVING AT HOME

Among the social changes that have taken place over the last 20 years, two of the most revealing are where children live, and how soon young people get to live on their own. Since 1970, the percentage of children under 18 living with only one parent has more than doubled. In 2000, 27 percent lived with only one parent, as compared to just under 12 percent in 1970. This increase reflects not only a soaring divorce rate, but a startling increase in the number of children born to unwed mothers, especially among blacks. The numbers of households headed by unmarried black women and divorced black women were equal in 1970. In 2000, never-married black mother households outnumbered divorced-mother black households by nearly four to one. Since 1990, more than half of all black children, one-fifth of white children, and 29 percent of Hispanic children under the age of 18 have lived with one parent only, usually the mother.

Inflation, soaring housing costs, stagnant wage rates, and postponement of marriage have helped to keep young adults of both sexes living at home with their parents for an increasingly long period. In 1970, 8.0 percent of 25-to-34-year-olds lived with their parents. By 1996, that number increased to nearly 12.3 percent, though it retreated to 10.6 pecent in 2000. Because they marry younger, women aged 25-34 were much less likely (8.3 percent in 2000) as men (12.9 percent) to live with their parents. In 1996, a whopping 16.0 percent of men 25-34 lived at home.

▶ LIVING WITH GRANDPARENTS
In 2000, the Census Bureau found that 3.8 million (5.3 percent of the nation's 72 million) children under age 18 lived in the home of their grandparents. This is up from 3.2 percent in 1970 and 3.6 percent in 1980, but down from the all-time high of 5.7 percent in 1996. A total of 3.8 million children under 18 lived with grandparents in 2000, down from 4.1 million in 1996. Of those children,

nearly half lived there with their mothers. Some 5.7 percent (247,000) lived there with their fathers, down from 6.0 percent in 1998. An additional 13.8 percent (531,000) lived with both parents in a grandparent's home, up slightly over the previous year. The remaining 35.3 percent (1,359,000) lived with their grandparents with neither parent present, up from 33.9 percent in 1999.

Source: U.S. Bureau of the Census, *America's Families and Living Arrangements 2000* (2001)

HOUSING

According to the Census Bureau's biannual American Housing Survey, there were 102.8 million occupied housing units in the U.S. in 1999, the latest year for which data are available. Of these units, 68.8 million (66.9 percent) were occupied by homeowners, while the remaining 34.0 million (33.1 percent) were occupied by renters.

Housing units   The American ideal of the intact nuclear family may be somewhat tarnished in these days of high divorce rates and growing single-parent households, but U.S. housing patterns

Characteristics of Occupied Housing Units 1993-99

Characteristic	1993 Units ('000)	1993 Percent of units	1995 Units ('000)	1995 Percent of units	1997 Units ('000)	1997 Percent of units	1999 Units ('000)	1999 Percent of units
Total occupied units	**94,724**	**100.0%**	**97,693**	**100.0%**	**99,487**	**100.0%**	**102,803**	**100.0%**
Owner occupied	61,252	64.7	63,544	65.0	65,487	65.8	68,796	66.9
Renter occupied	33472	35.3	34,150	35.0	34,000	34.1	31,007	30.2
Units in structure								
Single, detached	58,918	62.2%	60,826	62.3%	62,111	62.4%	64,536	62.8%
Single, attached	5,375	5.7	5,545	5.7	5,840	5.9	6,963	6.8
2 to 4	9,279	9.8	9,299	9.5	8,973	9.0	8,572	8.3
5 to 9	4,724	5.0	4,803	4.9	4,852	4.9	4,847	4.7
10 to 19	4,190	4.4	4,342	4.4	4,264	4.3	4,416	4.3
20 to 49	3,154	3.3	3,244	3.3	6,903	6.9	3,343	3.2
50 or more	3,429	3.6	3,470	3.6	N.A.	N.A.	3,341	3.2
Mobile home or trailer	5,655	5.9	6,164	6.3	6,544	6.6	6,785	6.6
Size								
Size of unit (sq. ft.)	1,725	N.A.	1,732	N.A.	1,750	N.A.	1,730	N.A.
Size of lot (acres)	0.43	N.A.	0.43	N.A.	0.35	N.A.	0.34	N.A.
Number of bedrooms								
One	11,279	11.9%	11,777	12.1%	12,399	12.5%	11,986	11.7%
Two	28,965	30.6	29,146	29.8	28,899	29.0	29,166	28.4
Three	38,504	40.6	40,302	41.2	40,597	40.8	43,103	41.9
Four or more	14,848	15.7	15,421	15.8	17,153	17.2	17,689	17.2
Number of bathrooms								
None	526	0.6%	465	0.5%	750	0.8%	676	0.7
One	43,944	46.4	43,777	44.8	44,223	44.4	42,838	41.7
One and a half	14,740	15.6	14,780	15.1	14,987	15.1	16,189	15.8
Two or more	35,515	37.5	38,671	39.6	39,527	39.7	43,100	41.9
Median age (years)	28	N.A.	28	N.A.	30	N.A.	31	N.A.
Mortgage status[1]								
None, owned free and clear	24,068	39.3%	24,518	38.6%	25,453	38.9%	25,604	37.2%
One mortgage	32,302	52.7	34,730	54.7	29,210	44.6	28,960	42.1
Two mortgages	3,975	6.5	4,244	6.7	6,345	9.7	6,884	10.0
Three or more mortgages	71	0.1	52	0.1	444	0.7	415	0.6
Median years remaining	19	N.A.	20	N.A.	21	N.A.	20	N.A.
Median amount outstanding	$48,357	N.A.	$48,466	N.A.	$52,543	N.A.	$63,939	N.A.

1. In this category, figures are perecentages of owner-occupied units only, which represent approximately two-thirds of all occupied units. Not all homeowners reported their mortgage status.
Source: U.S. Bureau of the Census, *American Housing Surveys* 1993, 1995, 1997, and 1999.

still reflect traditional values. Nearly two of every three occupied homes (64.5 million) were detached single unit structures. Mobile homes or trailers, numbering 6.7 million, are not included in those totals. Another 7.0 million were attached single-unit structures such as a brownstone or row house. Cooperatives and condominiums, totaling more than 4.9 million, are counted separately since they may include any number of dwellings.

Homeownership Rates, 1890–2000

Year	Homeownership rate	Year	Homeownership rate
1890	47.8%	1980	64.4%
1900	46.7	1990	64.2
1910	45.9	1995[1]	64.7
1920	45.6	1996[1]	65.4
1930	47.8	1997[1]	65.7
1940	43.6	1998[1]	66.3
1950	55.0	1999[1]	66.8
1960	61.9	2000[1]	67.4
1970	62.9		

1. Figures from 1890-1990 are from the decennial census, which counts every home. Figures from 1995-2000 are from the Census Bureau's annual *Housing Vacancy Survey*, which uses statistical samples. **Source:** U.S. Census Bureau.

Size of housing units The size of the American house decreased slightly for the first time in a decade. The median size of all single, detached one-family houses (including mobile homes) was 1,729 square feet in 1999, down from 1,750 in 1997; for owner-occupied houses, the figure was 1,794 square feet, also down from 1,825. About 19 percent of single houses (13.6 million) had more than 2,500 square feet, and 11.7 percent (8.3 million) had less than 1,000 square feet. The biggest houses are the newest ones: homes built in the past four years had a median area of 1,939 square feet. Although the typical American family is growing smaller, the typical American house is growing larger. The vast majority of houses in 1999 (76.1 percent) had between four and seven rooms; most houses (59.1 percent) had three or more bedrooms, and 41.9 percent had two or more bathrooms.

Equipment and fuel More houses had air conditioning (82.8 percent) than a dishwasher (56.1 percent), a washing machine (78.3 percent), or clothes dryer (74.4 percent). Natural gas was the fuel of choice for most houses: it heated 56.7 percent of houses. Electricity heated 30.3 percent, while 9.7 percent of houses had oil furnaces. Oil is most popular in the Northeast, where it is used to heat 37.7 percent of all houses; outside the Northeast, fewer than 4 percent of houses use oil heat.

Homeownership Rates in the U.S. by Age, Race, and Hispanic Origin, 1982–2000

Characteristic	1982	1985	1990	1995	1998	1999	2000
U.S., total	**64.8%**	**63.9%**	**63.9%**	**64.7%**	**66.3%**	**66.8%**	**67.4%**
By age							
Under 25	19.3	17.2	15.7	15.9	18.2	19.9	21.7
Under 35	41.2	39.9	38.5	38.6	39.3	39.7	40.8
35 to 44	70.0	68.1	66.3	65.2	66.9	67.2	67.9
45 to 54	77.4	75.9	75.2	75.2	75.7	76.0	76.5
55 to 64	80.0	79.5	79.3	79.5	80.9	81.0	80.3
65 and over	74.4	74.8	76.3	78.1	79.3	80.1	80.4
By race and origin							
White	N.A.	N.A.	N.A.	68.7	70.0	70.5	71.1
Black	N.A.	N.A.	N.A.	42.7	45.6	46.3	47.2
Asian	N.A.	N.A.	N.A.	50.8	52.6	53.1	52.8
Hispanic (all races)	N.A.	N.A.	N.A.	42.0	44.7	45.5	46.3

Source: U.S. Bureau of the Census, *2000 Housing Vacancy Survey*, 2001.

Average Sales Prices of New One-Family Houses, by Region, 1965–2000

Year	Northeast	Midwest	South	West	United States Amount	United States Annual percent increase
1965	$22,900	$22,800	$18,900	$23,200	$21,500	N.A.
1970	32,800	28,000	24,000	26,900	26,600	N.A.
1975	47,000	43,400	39,600	44,300	42,600	N.A.
1980	80,300	74,400	69,100	89,400	76,400	6.4%
1985	121,900	95,400	88,900	111,800	100,800	3.3
1990	190,500	133,000	123,500	180,600	149,800	0.7
1995	216,600	157,200	142,000	169,800	158,700	2.7
1996	226,100	158,900	144,200	186,200	166,400	4.9
1997	234,100	173,000	151,400	198,200	176,200	5.9
1998	240,100	179,200	159,700	200,500	181,900	3.2
1999	249,200	187,000	173,500	222,000	195,800	7.6
2000	277,400	199,100	179,300	239,500	207,200	5.8

Note: Figures are in current dollars. **Source:** U.S. Bureau of the Census, *New One-Family Houses Sold* (March 2001).

Gas heats 65.0 percent of the houses in the West and and 78.5 percent of the houses in the Midwest. Electricity heats 51.5 percent of houses in the South.

Growth of housing   In 1999, the median age of all housing structures in the U.S. was 31 years (i.e. built in 1968). Only 8.8 million units built before 1919 were still in use. This reflects the extraordinary growth of the housing industry during the 1970s and 80s, when 35.4 million of the 99.5 million extant units were built. By comparison, only 18.1 million of the housing units still in use were built between 1920 and 1950.

Home ownership   Low mortgage rates, a strong economy, and low unemployment continued to push homeownership rates to record levels. More than two-thirds of householders (67.4%) owned their own homes in 2000, up from 63.9 percent in 1990. (See the accompanying table). Of particular note is the increase in homeownership by those under 25 (21.7 percent in 2000, up from 15.9 percent five years earlier) and over 65 (80.4 percent, up from 78.1 percent in 1995). The growth in elderly homeownership rates reflects the growing independence of people over 65.

The overall increase in homeownership follows a decade—the 1980s—in which skyrocketing home prices prevented many people from buying homes.

Existing One-Family Houses Sold and Median Sales Price, by Region, 1970–2000

	Houses Sold ('000s)					Median Sales Price				
Year	United States	Northeast	Midwest	South	West	United States	Northeast	Midwest	South	West
1970	1,612	251	501	568	292	$23,000	$25,700	$20,100	$20,100	$24,300
1975	2,476	370	701	862	543	35,300	39,300	30,100	30,100	39,600
1980	2,973	403	806	1,092	672	62,200	60,800	51,900	51,900	89,300
1985	3,134	561	806	1,063	704	75,500	88,900	58,900	58,900	95,400
1990	3,219	458	809	1,193	759	92,000	126,400	75,300	75,300	129,600
1995	3,888	547	945	1,433	964	110,500	126,700	94,800	94,800	141,000
1997	4,382	607	1,005	1,596	1,117	121,800	131,800	107,000	107,000	155,200
1998	4,970	662	1,130	1,868	1,309	128,400	135,900	114,300	114,300	164,800
1999	5,205	656	1,148	2,015	1,386	133,300	139,000	119,600	119,600	173,900
2000	5,113	645	1,115	1,992	1,362	139,000	139,400	123,600	123,600	183,000

Source: National Association of Realtors, *Home Sales* (May 2001).

Median Sales Prices of Existing Single-Family Homes for Selected Metropolitan Areas, 1985–2001

Metropolitan area	1985	1990	1995	2000	2001[1]
Atlanta, Ga.	$66,200[2]	$86,400	$97,500	$131,200	$136,00
Baltimore, Md.	72,600	105,900	111,300	153,000	147,00
Boston, Mass.	134,200	174,100	179,000	314,200	345,00
Chicago, Ill.	81,100	116,800	147,900	171,800	184,00
Cincinnati, Ohio-Ky.-Tenn.	60,200	79,800	100,400	126,700	127,00
Cleveland, Ohio	64,400	80,600	104,700	N.A.	N.A.
Dallas, Texas	94,000	89,500	96,400	122,500	122,00
Denver, Colo.	84,300	86,400	127,300	196,800	210,00
Detroit, Mich.	51,700	76,700	98,200	N.A.	N.A.
Honolulu, Hawaii	N.A.	N.A.	349,000	295,000	280,00
Houston, Texas	78,600	70,700	79,200	116,100	118,00
Kansas City, Mo.-Kans.	61,400	74,100	91,700	127,400	130,00
Las Vegas, Nev.	N.A.	N.A.	113,500	137,440	142,00
Los Angeles area, Calif.	125,200	212,100	179,900	215,900	224,00
Miami-Hialeah, Fla.	80,500	89,300	107,100	144,600	152,00
Milwaukee, Wis.	67,500	84,400	114,700	140,700	142,00
Minneapolis-St. Paul, Minn.-Wis.	75,200	88,700	106,800	151,440	140,00
New Orleans, La.	N.A.	N.A.	87,000	112,000	111,00
New York City area, N.Y.	134,000	174,900	169,700	230,200	236,00
Philadelphia, Pa-N.J.	74,000	108,700	118,700	125,200	123,00
Phoenix, Ariz.	74,800	84,000	96,800	134,400	135,00
Pittsburgh, Pa.	N.A.	70,100	82,100	93,600	90,600
St. Louis, Mo.-Ill.	65,700	76,700	87,700	108,440	98,100
San Diego, Calif.	107,400	183,200	171,600	269,400	284,700
San Francisco Bay area, Calif.	145,100	259,300	254,400	454,600	484,300
Seattle, Wash.	N.A.	142,000	159,000	230,100	235,700
Tampa-St. Petersburg-Clearwater, Fla.	58,400	71,440	78,300	110,800	118,500
Washington, D.C.-Md.-Va.	97,100	150,500	156,500	182,600	191,200
U.S. average	N.A.	N.A.	$112,900	$139,000	$139,700

1. First quarter only. 2. Figure is for 1984.   **Source:** National Association of Realtors, *Home Sales* (May 2001).

The decline in homeownership rates in the 1980s was the first in 50 years.

Married couple families had the highest rates of homeownership (82.4 percent in 2000). Single people were less likely to own their own homes, especially single men. Their homeownership rate in 2000 (47.8 percent) was lower than the rate for single women (53.0 percent). Homeownership rates are consistently highest in the Midwest (72.6 percent in 2000) and South (69.6 percent) and lowest in the Northeast (63.4 percent) and West (61.7 percent).

Housing costs   According to the most recent annual survey by the Chicago Title Insurance Company, the median price of a single-family home in 1999 was $175,400, up 4.5 percent from $167,900 in 1998. First-time buyers paid a median price of $150,300; they constituted 44.7 percent of all home buyers. Buyers who previously owned a home paid a median price of $195,000, up 3.1 percent from the previous year. San Francisco was by far the most expensive place to buy a house: the median price was $348,100 for all homes in the Bay Area (up

Fair Market Monthly Rents for Existing Housing for Selected Metropolitan Areas, 2001-02

Metropolitan area	2001			2002		
	1 Bedroom	2 Bedrooms	3 Bedrooms	1 Bedroom	2 Bedrooms	3 Bedrooms
Albuquerque, N.M	$473	$592	$816	$505	$632	$871
Atlanta, Ga.	682	795	1,060	720	839	1,119
Austin-San Marcos, Tex.	615	819	1,137	645	858	1,192
Baltimore, Md.	542	661	875	542	661	875
Boston, Mass.	782	979	1,223	782	979	1,223
Charlotte, N.C.	585	659	869	585	659	869
Chicago, Ill.	661	788	985	711	848	1,060
Cincinnati, Ohio	416	557	746	416	557	746
Cleveland-Lorain-Elyria, Ohio	521	645	820	555	687	874
Colorado Springs, Colo.	486	647	902	486	647	902
Columbus, Ohio	471	605	768	471	605	768
Dallas, Tex.	609	781	1,080	647	830	1,146
Denver, Colo.	575	765	1,062	625	832	1,154
Detroit, Mich.	551	666	833	598	723	904
El Paso, Tex.	451	534	739	451	534	739
Fort Lauderdale, Fla.	580	718	999	609	754	1,049
Fort Worth-Arlington, Tex.	491	637	889	521	675	943
Fresno, Calif.	433	517	720	433	517	720
Honolulu, Hawaii	713	839	1,134	713	839	1,134
Houston, Tex.	495	640	892	529	684	954
Indianapolis, Ind.	465	559	700	465	559	700
Jacksonville, Fla.	530	638	843	530	638	843
Kansas City, Mo.	496	597	826	526	633	875
Las Vegas, Nev.	603	718	999	636	757	1,054
Los Angeles-Long Beach, Calif.	618	782	1,055	618	782	1,055
Memphis, Tenn.	462	542	753	462	542	753
Miami, Fla.	579	722	991	616	768	1,054
Milwaukee-Waukeshau, Wis.	504	633	794	504	633	794
Minneapolis-St. Paul, Minn.	549	702	950	580	742	1,004
Nashville, Tenn.	520	641	873	520	641	873
New Orleans, La.	423	527	717	423	527	717
New York, N.Y.[1]	836	949	1,187	836	949	1,187
Oakland, Calif.	785	985	1,350	921	1,155	1,583
Oklahoma City, Okla.	366	474	659	422	547	760
Orange County, Calif.	792	980	1,364	845	1,046	1,455
Philadelphia, Pa	611	755	945	657	812	1,016
Phoenix-Mesa, Ariz.	523	656	913	544	683	950
Pittsburgh, Pa.	476	574	719	476	574	719
Portland-Vancouver, Oreg.-Wash.	592	730	1,015	592	730	1,015
Sacramento, Calif.	515	645	894	547	685	950
Saint Louis, Mo.	400	519	676	429	556	724
Salt Lake City, Utah	520	660	918	550	698	971
San Antonio, Tex.	434	561	781	461	596	829
San Diego, Calif.	670	839	1,167	716	896	1,247
San Francisco, Calif.	1,154	1,459	2,001	1,154	1,459	2,001
San Jose, Calif.	1,058	1,308	1,792	1,199	1,481	2,030
Seattle-Bellevue-Everett, Wash.	639	809	1,123	639	809	1,123
Tampa-St. Petersburg, Fla.	524	649	862	557	690	917
Tucson, Ariz.	470	625	869	470	625	869
Tulsa, Okla.	402	527	733	427	559	778
Washington, D.C.-Md.-Va.	735	863	1,176	773	907	1,236
West Palm Beach-Boca Raton, Fla.	591	731	971	628	777	1,032

Note: Figures are projections made in the year prior to date shown. 1. Figures include areas outside Manhattan. **Source:** U.S. Dept. of Housing and Urban Development, Office of the Federal Housing Commissioner, *Fair Market Rents*, April 28, 2000 and Jan. 2, 2001.

more than 10 percent from the year before and 20 percent in 1997). That's more than double the median price in Atlanta ($151,600), Philadelphia ($144,000), and Denver ($156,300) and more than $100,000 over the medians in Chicago ($175,400), Los Angeles ($223,000) and even New York City ($192,700). Surprisingly, median sales prices in Washington D.C. ($203,400) and in Boston ($209,200) were both higher than in New York City. Housing prices in Memphis, Tenn. were cheapest of the 20 metropolitan areas surveyed; the median sales price was $110,000.

Average monthly mortgage payments for all homeowners rose from $1,212 in 1998 to $1,240 in 1999. These payments represented 32.3 percent of owners's incomes, about the same as the year before, but way up from 1976, when only 24.0 percent went to mortgage payments. Payments were higher among repeat buyers, but first-time buyers paid a larger percentage of their incomes toward their mortgages. Low interest rates were responsible for the popularity of fixed-rate mortgages, in which the consumer locks into a monthly payment for the life of the loan. Fixed-rate mortgages were the choice of 80 percent of mortgage buyers in 1999, up from 69 percent two years earlier, and up from and 55 percent as recently as 1995.

Adjustable, or variable rate mortgages, in which the monthly payment rises and falls based on the prevailing national interest rates, usually feature lower interest rates (as much as 3 percentage points) for the first several years, and higher rates toward the end of the loan. They were responsible for 14.3 percent of all mortgages in 1999, down from 23.4 percent in 1997, and the all-time high of 36.2 percent in 1995.

The average mortgage length was 28.5 years for first-time home buyers and 27.3 years for repeat buyers. Both numbers are down slightly from the year before. Meanwhile, the average down payment as a percentage of the purchase price continues to decline. In 1976, 26.9 percent of buyers put 10 percent or less down on a home purchase. In 1998, that number had skyrocketed to 50.7 percent. The average down payment was 19.5 percent, down from 25.2 percent in 1976.

Housing and the poor   Two studies published in 1998, one by the Dept. of Housing and Urban Development, and one by the Center on Budget and Policy Priorities, revealed that despite the strong economic growth of the recent years, the housing problems of the poor have grown worse. A severe shortage of affordable apartments has existed all around the nation for several years, forcing 4.4 million poor families to pay more than half their income on rent, usually 60 percent, or more than double what the government calls affordable rent.

The major reasons for this development are stagnating wages for the unskilled, rising real estate values, and the government's failure to supply enough subsidized housing. The number of new subsidized units fell to 70,000 a year during the Reagan-Bush years, down from 260,000 during the Carter Administration. In 1995, when the Republicans took over Congress, the government actually stopped expanding the pool of subsidized housing for the first time in modern history.

About 15 million households currently qualify for federal housing assistance, but only 4.5 million families get it. Of those, about one-third live in conventional housing projects, while the rest receive subsidies that allow them to live in private housing. In each case, the tenants contribute 30 percent of their income toward the rent and the government provides the rest.

Moving   Approximately 43 million Americans (16 percent) move from one home to another every year, according to the Census Bureau's Current Population Reports. Most of those moves (9.0 percent in 2000) were in the same county; only 3.1 percent were from one state to another.

▶**THE HOMELESS**
Although homeless people have become a common sight in almost every community, their plight is always surrounded by some kind of controversy, one that is fueled by a wide range of opinions, some based on fact and others on stereotypes. The often shrill debate about just who the homeless are and what can or should be done for them has been hampered by a lack of re-

Characteristics of Recent Home Buyers, 1976–99						
Item	1976	1980	1990	1995	1998	1999
Median purchase price	$43,340	$68,714	$131,200	$147,700	$167,900	$175,400
First-time buyers	37,670	61,450	106,000	128,300	142,200	150,300
Repeat buyers	50,090	75,750	149,400	164,300	189,800	195,700
Average monthly mortgage payment	$329	$599	$1,127	$1,062	$1,212	$1,240
First-time buyers	313	N.A.	N.A.	988	1,069	1,090
Repeat buyers	342	N.A.	N.A.	1,125	1,343	1,360
As percent of income	24.0%	32.4%	33.8%	32.6%	32.3%	32.3%
Percent buying:						
New houses	15.1%	22.4%	21.2%	21.5%	21.2%	22.7%
Existing houses	84.9	77.6	78.8	78.5	78.8	77.3
Single-family houses	88.8	82.4	83.8	83.1	82.3	83.0
Condominiums	11.2	17.6	13.1	14.0	14.7	13.5
For the first time	44.8	32.9	41.9	46.2	46.2	44.7
Down payment as percentage of sales price	25.2%	28.0%	23.3%	20.4%	19.3%	19.5%
First-time buyers	18.0	20.5	15.7	13.3	12.8	12.6
Repeat buyers	30.8	32.7	28.9	26.8	24.9	25.5
Average age (in years)						
First-time buyers	28.1	28.3	30.5	32.1	32.2	32.0
Repeat buyers	35.9	36.4	39.1	40.7	41.1	41.4

Source: Chicago Title and Trust Company, *Who's Buying Homes in America* (annual).

liable information on everything from the causes of homelessness to the actual number of people living on the streets or in shelters.

The number of homeless Because homelessness is a temporary circumstance, it is nearly impossible to measure the number of homeless. In 1990, the Census Bureau made the first comprehensive federal effort to count the homeless, and identified a total of 228,621 homeless persons on the night of March 21-22. In 2000, the Census Bureau counted 280,527 homeless, but said it would not release detailed statistics on the number of homeless by city and state because it believed the 1990 numbers it published had been inaccurate.

No one believes that any count of the homeless gives an accurate picture of the problem. A 1999 study by the Department of Housing and Urban Development counted 470,000 homeless people on an average night in February, 1996, but suggested that this represented only about a quarter of all the people who were homeless at any time during the year. But the counts begin to provide insight into homelessness. Of those counted, 66 percent were single, and 69 percent were male. The vast majority were white (41 percent) or black (40 percent); only 11 percent of homeless people were Hispanic. More than half of the homeless counted in 1996 had suffered from mental illness at some point (39 percent within the past month). About a quarter had had problems with drug addiction in the past month, while 38 percent said they had been addicted to alcohol. Not surprisingly, most homeless said that insufficient income (30 percent of those surveyed) or lack of a job (24 percent) were the biggest impediments to finding housing.

On the positive side, the 1996 count found that the average homeless person had been without housing for an average of 32 months, down from 39 in 1987. And 30 percent had been homeless for three months or less, up from only 21 percent in 1987. Hunger was down too: only 28 percent of homeless said they "sometimes or often don't get enough to eat," down from 38 percent nine years earlier.

New York (44,794) and Los Angeles (26,554) had by far the most homeless people. The next biggest concentration of homeless were in Philadelphia (14,123) and Boston (13,483). The study also found that homeless populations don't correspond directly to a city's population or even to its population below the poverty line. Chicago, with a total population of 2.7 million, had almost the same number of homeless (13,307) as San Francisco (12,410 homeless among the total population of 735,315). Homeless as a percentage of the number of people below the poverty line was 1.59 in Chicago, 1.98 in Los Angeles, 2.30 in Philadelphia, 2.89 in Boston, 2.99 in New York, and 8.60 in San Francisco. Put another way, for every hundred poor people, there were five times as many homeless in San Francisco as in Chicago.

Federal funding The various federal government programs to assist the homeless are grouped under the Stewart B. McKinney Homeless Assistance Act, which became law in July 1987. The act includes 16 different provisions for emergency shelter, food, health care, mental health care, housing, educational programs, job training, and other community services. Federal agencies providing services specifically for the homeless include the Federal Emergency Management Agency, and Departments of Agriculture, Education, Health and Human Services, Housing and Urban Development, Labor, and Veterans' Affairs. An additional 34 programs, ranging from Medicaid and the Supplemental Security Income program to the Public and Indian housing program and the Ryan White CARE Act, provide general assistance to low-income people, including the homeless. The number of homeless people that these non-homeless-specific programs serve, however, is impossible to determine.

Since 1994, the federal government has budgeted more than $1 billion in funding for the McKinney program. Nevertheless, states and cities still foot the major part of the bill for caring for the homeless.

Funding for Federal Homeless Assistance Programs, 1995-98

Agency and Program	Budget (millions)			
	1995	1996	1997	1998
Dept. of Agriculture				
Homeless Children Nutrition Program	$1.7	$1.7	$2.1	$1.9
Dept. of Education				
Education for Homeless Children and Youth	28.8	23.0	25.0	28.8
Federal Emergency Management Agency				
Emergency Food and Shelter Program	130.0	100.0	100.0	100.0
Dept. of Health and Human Services				
Health Care for the Homeless	65.4	65.5	69.3	71.3
Projects for Assistance in Transition from Homelessness	29.5	20.0	20.0	23.0
Runaway and Homeless Youth Programs	54.1	64.2	66.6	73.5
Dept. of Housing and Urban Development				
Emergency Shelter Grants	155.0	115.0	115.0	165.0
Single-Room Occupancy Moderate Rehabilitation	N.A.	N.A.	10.1	23.5
Shelter Plus Care	162.0	89.0	61.0	116.9
Supportive Housing Program	602.0	577.0	620.0	574.2
Dept. of Labor				
Homeless Veterans Reintegration Project	N.A.	N.A.	N.A.	3.0
Dept. of Veterans' Affairs				
Domiciliary Care for Homeless Veterans	38.9	41.1	37.2	38.5
Homeless Chronically Mentally Ill Veterans	32.3	32.1	32.0	36.4
Homeless Providers Grant and Per Diem Program	6.3	6.3	6.1	5.9
Total	**$1,306.0**	**$1,134.9**	**$1,164.4**	**$1,261.9**

Source: General Accounting Office: *Report to Congressional Committee: Homelessness*, February, 1999.

IMMIGRATION

Over the last four centuries the mingling of peoples from all parts of the world has been a vital element in the formation of the United States both as a land of opportunity and in its emergence as a world power. In one relatively brief period between 1880 and 1920 the massive influx of more than 20 million European immigrants provided the continuous labor supply necessary to transform the nation from an agricultural society to an industrialized one with extraordinary rapidity.

Over the next 40 years, however, the flow of immigration slowed dramatically as the government decided to close the doors to most foreign groups. Motivated at first by a disconcerting kind of nativism, the nation's anti-immigration sentiments were later bolstered by the Great Depression and the need to provide work for those already living here. World War II and the subsequent national readjustment limited immigration for several decades.

Since 1960 a steadily increasing number of immigrants—both legal and illegal—has had a very noticeable impact on both the size and ethnic composition of the American population. The startling upsurge in the number of Asians and Hispanic immigrants during the 1970s, '80s, and '90s has been caused by a variety of factors from wars and political upheaval to the mundane fact of geographical proximity in the case of Mexico. Approximately 700,000 new legal immigrants are arriving annually and well over half are from those two ethnic backgrounds.

In 1998, total immigration hit a 10-year low of 660,477. Many demographers argue that if the immigration rate continues to fall, the effect on

Immigration as a Percentage of Total Population Growth, 1901–98

Period	Percent	Period	Percent
1901-10	39.6%	1950-54	10.6%
1911-20	17.7	1955-59	10.7
1921-30	15.0	1960-64	12.5
1931-34	-0.1	1965-69	19.7
1935-39	3.2	1970-80	19.4
1940-44	7.4	1981-90	32.8
1945-49	10.2	1991-98	37.0

Source: U.S. Dept. of Justice, *1998 Statistical Yearbook of the Immigration and Naturalization Service* (2000).

The Statue of Liberty

The Statue of Liberty was conceived and designed by Frederic Auguste Bartholdi (with Gustave Eiffel's help) and given to the U.S. by the French government in honor of the centennial of American independence in 1876. Funded by subscriptions from the French people it was dedicated by President Grover Cleveland in 1886 and became a national monument in 1924.

Measuring 151 feet (46 m) to the top of her torch, Miss Liberty still stands guard over the entrance to New York harbor, the inscription on its base a poignant reminder of the vision Americans once had of their country:

Give me your tired, your poor
Your huddled masses yearning to breathe free,
The wretched refuse of your teeming shore,
Send these, the homeless, tempest-tost to me:
I lift my lamp beside the golden door.

U.S. Immigration Rate by Decade, 1820–1998

Period	Total immigrants	Rate per 1,000 U.S. population
1820-30	151,824	1.2
1831-40	599,125	3.9
1841-50	1,713,251	8.4
1851-60	2,598,214	9.3
1861-70	2,314,824	6.4
1871-80	2,812,191	6.2
1881-90	5,246,613	9.2
1891-1900	3,687,564	5.3
1901-10	8,795,386	10.4
1911-20	5,735,811	5.7
1921-30	4,107,209	3.5
1931-40	528,431	0.4
1941-50	1,035,039	0.7
1951-60	2,515,479	1.5
1961-70	3,321,677	1.7
1971-80	4,493,314	2.1
1981-90	7,338,062	2.9
1991-98[1]	7,605,066	2.8
Total 1820-1998	64,599,082	N.A.

1. Includes more than 2 million aliens adjusting under the legalization provisions of the Immigration and Control Act (IRCA) of 1986. **Source:** U.S. Dept. of Justice, *1998 Statistical Yearbook of the Immigration and Naturalization Service* (2000).

Percent of Immigrants Admitted by Region, 1955–98

Region	Total, 1955-96	1955-64	1965-74	1975-84	1985-94	1995	1998
Europe	**49.0%**	50.2%	29.8%	13.4%	11.0%	17.8%	13.7%
Asia	**8.6**	7.7	22.4	43.3	32.2	37.2	33.3
Africa	**0.9**	0.7	1.5	2.4	2.6	5.9	6.2
Oceania	**0.4**	0.4	0.7	0.8	0.5	0.7	0.6
North America[1]	**36.0**	35.9	39.6	33.6	48.0	32.1	38.3
Caribbean	7.2	7.0	18.0	15.1	11.0	13.4	11.4
Central America	2.5	2.4	2.5	3.7	6.6	4.4	5.4
Other North America[1]	26.2	26.4	19.0	14.8	30.5	14.3	21.5
South America	**5.2**	5.1	6.0	6.6	6.6	6.3	6.9

Note: Data are for fiscal years. 1. Includes more than 2 million illegal immigrants from Mexico granted permanent legal residence under the 1986 Immigration Reform & Control Act. **Source:** U.S. Dept. of Justice, *1998 Statistical Yearbook of the Immigration and Naturalization Service* (2000).

American population growth could be severe. With the dramatic decline in its birth rates and fertility rates, the U.S. might very well begin to experience negative population growth by the year 2030; by 2020 immigration will add more popula-

tion than natural increase will. According to the Office of Population Research at Princeton University, the U.S. will need 464,000 immigrants each year over the next century just to keep total population in 2100 at the same size as in 1980.

Top 20 Countries of Birth for U.S. Immigrants, and Major Categories of Admission, 1998

| Country of birth | Total immigrants[1] | Percent of total | Category of admission | | | | |
			Relative preferences	Occupational preferences	Immediate relatives	Refugees and asylees	IRCA legalization[2]
All countries	**660,477**	**100.0%**	**191,480**	**77,517**	**283,368**	**54,645**	**955**
1. Mexico	131,575	19.9	55,140	3,586	71,731	41	691
2. China, mainland	36,884	5.6	14,718	8,496	12,740	898	1
3. India	36,482	5.5	15,375	9,533	11,058	373	1
4. Philippines	34,466	5.2	13,582	3,904	16,883	16	3
5. Dominican Republic	20,387	3.1	9,315	265	10,729	18	9
6. Vietnam	17,649	2.7	6,857	96	5,139	4,921	-
7. Cuba	17,375	2.6	802	48	882	14,915	-
8. Jamaica	15,146	2.3	6,047	649	8,421	2	8
9. El Salvador	14,590	2.2	3,968	2,427	7,907	129	48
10. Korea	14,268	2.2	4,336	4,765	5,130	2	1
11. Haiti	13,449	2.0	5,828	225	6,767	537	12
12. Pakistan	13,094	2.0	4,249	1,422	5,953	130	1
13. Colombia	11,836	1.8	2,657	709	8,249	171	15
14. Russia	11,529	1.7	60	1,348	6,147	2,225	1
15. Canada	10,190	1.5	913	5,016	3,906	6	3
16. Peru	10,154	1.5	2,487	906	6,113	338	2
17. United Kingdom	9,011	1.4	828	3,815	4,074	9	6
18. Bangladesh	8,621	1.3	2,073	547	3,002	159	-
19. Poland	8,469	1.3	3,770	1,661	2,454	54	9
20. Iran	7,883	1.2	2,146	797	3,784	754	14

1. Total includes Amerasians, Soviet and Indochinese parolees, foreign government officials, special immigrants, and admissions from nonpreference "underrepresented countries," suspension of deportation, and private law not shown separately. 2. Under the Immigration Reform and Control Act (IRCA) of 1986, illegal aliens with temporary resident status became eligible for permanent legal residence.
Source: U.S. Dept. of Justice, *1998 Statistical Yearbook of the Immigration and Naturalization Service* (2000).

Top 20 Metropolitan Areas of Intended Residence for U.S. Immigrants, 1995–98

| Rank, 1997 and Metropolitan area | Immigrants | | | | | |
| | 1995 | | 1997 | | 1998 | |
	Number	Percent of total	Number	Percent of total	Number	Percent of total
1. New York, N.Y.	111,687	15.5%	107,434	13.5%	81,417	12.3%
2. Los Angeles-Long Beach, Calif.	54,669	7.6	62,314	7.8	60,220	9.1
3. Chicago, Ill.	31,730	4.4	35,386	4.4	31,033	4.7
4. Miami, Fla.	30,935	4.3	45,707	5.7	29,242	4.4
5. Washington D.C.-MD-Va.	25,717	3.6	31,444	3.9	25,639	3.9
6. San Francisco, Calif.	15,773	2.2	16,892	2.1	14,553	2.2
7. Orange County, Calif.	18,187	2.5	18,190	2.3	14,291	2.2
8. Oakland, Calif.	12,011	1.7	15,723	2.0	13,499	2.0
9. Houston, Tex.	14,379	2.0	17,439	2.2	13,189	2.0
10. Boston-Lawrence-Lowell Mass.	16,750	2.3	13,937	1.7	12,854	2.0
11. San Jose, Calif.	12,855	1.8	17,374	2.2	11,811	1.8
12. Riverside-San Bernardino, Calif.	9,385	1.3	9,788	1.2	10,227	1.5
13. Fort Lauderdale, Fla.	8,373	1.2	10,646	1.3	9,954	1.5
14. Detroit, Mich.	9,899	1.4	10,019	1.3	9,852	1.5
15. San Diego, Calif.	12,077	1.7	14,758	1.8	9,836	1.5
16. Dallas, Tex.	9,843	1.4	11,061	1.4	9,641	1.5
17. Newark, N.J.	11,162	1.5	10,801	1.4	9,551	1.4
18. Seattle-Bellevue-Everett, Wash.	9,652	1.3	10,692	1.3	9,497	1.4
19. Philadelphia, Pa.-N.J.	11,440	1.6	10,858	1.4	9,197	1.4
20. Bergen-Passaic, N.J.	9,385	1.3	9,788	1.2	8,645	1.3
Total, all metropolitan areas[1]	**720,461**	**100.0%**	**798,378**	**100.0%**	**660,477**	**100.0%**

1. Includes other MSAs not shown separately.
Source: U.S. Dept. of Justice, *1998 Statistical Yearbook of the Immigration and Naturalization Service* (2000).

Immigration to the U.S. by Country of Last Residence, 1820–1998

Since 1820, Germany has sent more immigrants to the U.S. than has any other country, but Mexico is gaining fast. Nearly six million people immigrated to the U.S. from Mexico between 1820 and 1998, 60 percent of them since 1981. The vast majority of Mexican immigrants in 1989-91 were already living illegally in the U.S. and granted permanent legal residence under the 1986 Immigration Reform and Control Act. But the tide of Mexican immigration shows few signs of abating. More immigrants to the United States came from Mexico than from the next three countries combined in 1998. This table ranks the top 10 nations by the total number of U.S. immigrants since 1820.

Country	1820–1998 Number	Percent of total	1981–90 Number	Percent of total	1991–98 Number	Percent of total
All Countries	**64,599,082**	**100.0%**	**7,338,062**	**100.0%**	**7,605,066**	**100.0%**
Germany	7,156,257	11.1	91,961	1.2	72,792	1.0
Mexico	5,819,966	9.0	1,655,843	22.6	1,931,237	25.4
Italy	5,431,454	8.4	67,254	1.0	58,346	0.8
United Kingdom	5,247,821	8.1	14,667	0.2	125,671	1.6
Ireland	4,779,998	7.4	31,969	0.4	54,865	0.7
Canada	4,453,149	6.9	156,938	2.1	157,564	2.1
Former USSR	3,830,033	5.9	57,677	0.8	386,327	5.1
Austria	1,842,722	2.8	18,340	0.2	20,515	0.3
Hungary	1,675,324	2.6	6,545	0.1	14,113	0.2
Philippines	1,460,421	2.3	548,764	7.5	433,768	5.7

1. Austria and Hungary not counted separately for all years. 2. Norway and Sweden not counted separately for all years.
Source: U.S. Dept. of Justice, *1998 Statistical Yearbook of the Immigration and Naturalization Service* (2000).

Estimated Number of U.S. Immigrants, by Region and Selected Country of Last Residence, 1820–1998

Region/country	Total 1820–1998	1998	Region/country	Total 1820–1998	1998
Europe	**38,233,062**	**92,911**	Korea	778,899	13,691
Austria[1]	1,842,722	610	Philippines	1,460,421	33,176
Belgium	216,297	557	Turkey	445,354	4,016
Czechoslovakia[2]	153,307	931	Vietnam	699,918	16,534
Denmark	375,548	447	Other Asia	1,647,611	49,543
France	816,650	2,961			
Germany	7,156,257	6,923	**North America**	**16,844,829**	**298,156**
Greece	721,464	1,183	Canada	4,453,149	14,295
Hungary[1]	1,675,324	825	Mexico	5,819,966	130,661
Ireland	4,779,998	907	Caribbean	**3,525,703**	**72,948**
Italy	5,431,454	1,966	Cuba	885,421	15,415
Netherlands	385,193	1,036	Dominican Republic	810,201	20,267
Norway[3]	758,026	327	Haiti	375,938	13,316
Poland	751,823	8,202	Jamaica	568,624	14,819
Portugal	521,697	1,523	Other Caribbean	885,519	9,131
Romania	244,106	4,833	Central America	**1,242,394**	**35,368**
Soviet Union	3,830,033	28,984	El Salvador	453,717	14,329
Spain	299,825	1,185	Other Central America	788,677	21,039
Sweden[3]	1,257,133	1,017			
Switzerland	369,046	1,090	**South America**	**1,693,441**	**44,884**
United Kingdom	5,247,821	10,170	Argentina	153,699	1,649
Yugoslavia[4]	183,538	7,264	Colombia	399,892	11,618
Other Europe	224,297	9,970	Ecuador	215,798	6,840
			Other South America	924,052	24,777
Asia	**8,365,931**	**212,799**	**Other America**	**110,176**	**N.A.**
China[5]	1,262,050	41,034			
Hong Kong	398,277	7,379	**Africa**	**614,375**	**37,494**
India	751,349	34,288	**Oceania**	**250,206**	**4,403**
Iran	233,860	4,945	**Not specified**	**290,679**	**14,714**
Israel	170,506	2,546	**All countries**	**64,599,082**	**660,477**
Japan	517,686	5,647			

Note: Because of changes in boundaries and government, figures for many countries, especially those in Asia, are not available for all years or were not reported separately for all years, and are therefore not strictly comparable throughout. Data for many countries are included with countries to which they belonged prior to World War I. 1. Data for Austria and Hungary not reported separately for all years. Total does not include 846,076 immigrants whose country of last residence is listed as Austria-Hungary. 2. Includes both Czech and Slovak Republics. 3. Data for Norway and Sweden not reported separately for all years. Total does not include 60,255 immigrants whose country of last residence is listed as Norway-Sweden. 4. Since 1922, includes immigrants from the Serb, Croat, and Slovene Kingdom. 5. Beginning in 1957, China includes Taiwan.
Source: U.S. Dept. of Justice, *1998 Statistical Yearbook of the Immigration and Naturalization Service* (2000).

Naturalization Rates for U.S. Immigrants by Nation, 1977–95

Almost half of the people who immigrated to the U.S. in 1977 had become a naturalized U.S. citizen by 1995. The following table shows immigrants by country from 1977 and the number and percentage that had been naturalized by 1995.

Region and country of birth	Immigrants admitted, 1977	Naturalizations through 1995 Number	Naturalizations through 1995 Rate	Region and country of birth	Immigrants admitted, 1977	Naturalizations through 1995 Number	Naturalizations through 1995 Rate
All countries	**352,070**	**161,438**	**45.9%**	Ghana	392	238	60.7%
				Kenya	418	257	61.5
Europe	**54,867**	**17,591**	**32.1%**	Morocco	366	182	49.7
Austria	342	61	17.8	Nigeria	570	231	40.5
Belgium	300	67	22.3	South Africa	1,331	856	64.3
Czechoslovakia	504	263	52.2	Tanzania	256	175	68.4
Denmark	362	55	15.2	Uganda	200	119	59.5
Finland	231	40	17.3	Other Africa	1,275	701	55.0
France	1,283	391	30.5				
Germany	4,899	824	16.8	**Oceania**	**2,927**	**735**	**25.1%**
Greece	6,577	2,208	33.6	Australia	1,016	90	8.9
Hungary	771	405	52.5	Fiji	551	274	49.7
Ireland	1,076	297	27.6	New Zealand	449	97	21.6
Italy	5,843	1,131	19.4	Tonga	349	98	28.1
Netherlands	828	152	18.4	Western Samoa	369	136	36.9
Norway	283	32	11.3	Other Oceania	193	40	20.7
Poland	3,468	1,656	47.8				
Portugal	6,964	2,051	29.5	**North America**	**142,313**	**54,068**	**38.0%**
Romania	1,620	1,097	67.7	Canada	9,000	1,626	18.1
Soviet Union	4,535	2,965	65.4	Mexico	30,967	6,869	22.2
Spain	2,086	427	20.5	Caribbean, total	89,885	39,662	44.1%
Sweden	485	66	13.6	Anguilla	354	136	38.4
Switzerland	485	161	33.2	Antigua-Barbuda	614	307	50.0
United Kingdom	8,981	2,032	22.6	Bahamas, The	238	61	25.6
Yugoslavia	2,256	959	42.5	Barbados	2,134	1,037	48.6
Other Europe	688	251	36.5	British Virgin Islands	367	78	21.3
				Cuba	57,023	26,668	46.8
Asia	**119,226**	**72,318**	**60.7%**	Dominica	392	194	49.5
Bangladesh	460	317	68.9	Dominican Republic	8,955	2,561	28.6
Burma (Myanmar)	776	528	68.0	Grenada	1,023	529	51.7
China, People's Republic	14,421	9,444	65.5	Haiti	4,268	1,841	43.1
Cyprus	410	210	51.2	Jamaica	7,896	3,587	45.4
Hong Kong	3,146	2,404	76.4	St. Kitts & Nevis	699	349	49.9
India	15,033	8,877	59.1	St. Lucia	408	202	49.5
Indonesia	658	330	50.2	St. Vincent & Grenadines	456	224	49.1
Iran	3,404	1,855	54.5	Trinidad & Tobago	4,516	1,722	38.1
Iraq	1,996	1,260	63.1	Other Caribbean	542	166	30.6
Israel	2,078	1,332	64.1	Central America	12,381	5,890	47.6%
Japan	3,602	601	16.7	Belize	660	285	43.2
Jordan	2,187	1,379	63.1	Costa Rica	1,221	471	38.6
Korea	19,824	11,745	59.2	El Salvador	3,402	1,688	49.6
Lebanon	3,900	2,551	65.4	Guatemala	2,825	1,291	45.7
Macau	248	182	73.4	Honduras	1,228	640	52.1
Malaysia	387	231	59.7	Nicaragua	1,351	679	50.3
Pakistan	2,563	1,655	64.6	Panama	1,694	836	49.4
Philippines	31,686	20,094	63.4	Other North America	80	21	26.3
Singapore	226	119	52.7				
Sri Lanka	314	194	61.8	**South America**	**25,024**	**12,198**	**48.7%**
Syria	1,342	857	63.9	Argentina	2,136	995	46.6
Taiwan	2,460	1,922	78.1	Bolivia	576	344	59.7
Thailand	3,009	1,202	39.9	Brazil	1,128	299	26.5
Turkey	1,546	623	40.3	Chile	2,047	958	46.8
Vietnam	2,724	1,911	70.2	Colombia	6,138	3,126	50.9
Yemen	284	159	56.0	Ecuador	4,063	1,319	32.5
Other Asia	542	336	62.0	Guyana	4,115	2,439	59.3
				Peru	3,158	1,902	60.2
Africa	**7,713**	**4,528**	**58.7%**	Uruguay	947	529	55.9
Cape Verde	647	263	40.6	Venezuela	485	175	36.1
Egypt	1,964	1,319	67.2	Other South America	231	112	48.5
Ethiopia	294	187	63.6				

Source: U.S. Dept. of Justice, *1996 Statistical Yearbook of the Immigration and Naturalization Service* (1997).

▶ELIGIBILITY

Prior to 1875 anyone from any foreign country could enter the U.S. freely and take up permanent residence here. Over the next 60 years, however, Congress passed laws restricting immigration on the basis of morality (no prostitutes or convicts), race (the Chinese Exclusion Act of 1882 was the first), and national origin (immigrants from Southern and Central Europe as well as Asia were severely limited during the 1920s). In 1952 Congress passed the Immigration and Nationality Act which reaffirmed national origin as the central criterion for eligibility and in 1965, the Hart-Cellar

Immigration Act established a preferential system for skilled workers and relatives of U.S. citizens, but restricted the total number of immigrants to 270,000 each year. However, the number of exceptions to this limit was far greater even than the 270,000 limit. An average of more than 700,000 immigrants legally entered the U.S. each year during the 1980s (not counting illegal aliens naturalized under provisions of the 1986 Immigration Reform and Control Act).

In 1992, the 270,000 limit was replaced with a sliding cap that is even less restrictive than previous immigration laws. The 1990 Immigration Act

Foreign-Born Population by State, 1980-90

	1980			1990		
	Total population	Foreign-born population	Percent foreign-born	Total population	Foreign-born population	Percent foreign-born
United States	226,545,805	14,079,906	6.2%	248,709,873	19,767,316	7.9%
Alabama	3,893,888	39,002	1.0	4,040,587	43,533	1.1
Alaska	401,851	16,216	4.0	550,043	24,814	4.5
Arizona	2,718,215	162,806	6.0	3,665,228	278,205	7.6
Arkansas	2,286,435	22,371	1.0	2,350,725	24,867	1.1
California	23,667,902	3,580,033	15.1	29,760,021	6,458,825	21.7
Colorado	2,889,964	114,130	3.9	3,294,394	142,434	4.3
Connecticut	3,107,576	267,806	8.6	3,287,116	279,383	8.5
Delaware	594,338	18,829	3.2	666,168	22,275	3.3
District of Columbia	638,333	40,559	6.4	606,900	58,887	9.7
Florida	9,746,324	1,058,732	10.9	12,937,926	1,662,601	12.9
Georgia	5,463,105	91,480	1.7	6,478,216	173,126	2.7
Hawaii	964,691	137,016	14.2	1,108,229	162,704	14.7
Idaho	943,935	23,404	2.5	1,006,749	28,905	2.9
Illinois	11,426,518	823,696	7.2	11,430,602	952,272	8.3
Indiana	5,490,224	101,802	1.9	5,544,159	94,263	1.7
Iowa	2,913,808	47,659	1.6	2,776,755	43,316	1.6
Kansas	2,363,679	47,891	2.0	2,477,574	62,840	2.5
Kentucky	3,660,777	34,562	0.9	3,685,296	34,119	0.9
Louisiana	4,205,900	85,502	2.0	4,219,973	87,407	2.1
Maine	1,124,660	43,402	3.9	1,227,928	36,296	3.0
Maryland	4,216,975	195,581	4.6	4,781,468	313,494	6.6
Massachusetts	5,737,037	500,982	8.7	6,016,425	573,733	9.5
Michigan	9,262,078	417,152	4.5	9,295,297	355,393	3.8
Minnesota	4,075,970	107,474	2.6	4,375,099	113,039	2.6
Mississippi	2,520,638	23,527	0.9	2,573,216	20,383	0.8
Missouri	4,916,686	85,616	1.7	5,117,073	83,633	1.6
Montana	786,690	18,319	2.3	799,065	13,779	1.7
Nebraska	1,569,825	31,001	2.0	1,578,385	28,198	1.8
Nevada	800,493	53,784	6.7	1,201,833	104,828	8.7
New Hampshire	920,610	40,961	4.4	1,109,252	41,193	3.7
New Jersey	7,364,823	757,822	10.3	7,730,188	966,610	12.5
New Mexico	1,302,894	52,405	4.0	1,515,069	80,514	5.3
New York	17,558,072	2,388,938	13.6	17,990,455	2,851,861	15.9
North Carolina	5,881,766	78,358	1.3	6,628,637	115,077	1.7
North Dakota	652,717	14,818	2.3	638,800	9,388	1.5
Ohio	10,797,630	302,185	2.8	10,847,115	259,673	2.4
Oklahoma	3,025,290	56,294	1.9	3,145,585	65,489	2.1
Oregon	2,633,105	107,805	4.1	2,842,321	139,307	4.9
Pennsylvania	11,863,895	401,016	3.4	11,881,643	369,316	3.1
Rhode Island	947,154	84,001	8.9	1,003,464	95,088	9.5
South Carolina	3,121,820	46,080	1.5	3,486,703	49,964	1.4
South Dakota	690,768	9,599	1.4	696,004	7,731	1.1
Tennessee	4,591,120	48,369	1.1	4,877,185	59,114	1.2
Texas	14,229,191	856,213	6.0	16,986,510	1,524,436	9.0
Utah	1,461,037	50,451	3.5	1,722,850	58,600	3.4
Vermont	511,456	20,995	4.1	562,758	17,544	3.1
Virginia	5,346,818	177,318	3.3	6,187,358	311,809	5.0
Washington	4,132,156	239,060	5.8	4,866,692	322,144	6.6
West Virginia	1,949,644	21,980	1.1	1,793,477	15,712	0.9
Wisconsin	4,705,767	125,297	2.7	4,891,769	121,547	2.5
Wyoming	469,557	9,607	2.0	453,588	7,647	1.7

Source: U.S. Bureau of the Census, 1999.

limited the total number of immigrants to 700,000 from 1992 to 1995, and to 675,000 thereafter. The Act increased the number of openings for immigrants with valuable employment skills from 54,000 to 140,000 each year, and reserved 55,000

openings each year for immigrants from under-represented countries. In addition, the new law introduced a sliding scale for admitting family-sponsored immigrants. As in previous years, there is no limit to the number of immediate family

Selected Characteristics of Foreign-Born Population, 2000

The foreign-born population of the United States consists of naturalized citizens and more recent immigrants who have not obtained citizenship. As the following table illustrates, the foreign-born population is heavily represented in the West (18.1 percent of the population in the West was not born here) and the Northeast (12.3 percent) and lowest in the Midwest (4.8 percent). Note that race data for foreign-born residents has not been updated since 1999. See the accompanying table for race data.

Characteristic	Total U.S. population ('000s)	Foreign-born population Total number ('000s)	As percent of U.S. population	Naturalized citizens ('000s)	Not citizens ('000s)
Total Population	274,087	28,379	10.4%	10,622	17,758
Age					
0 to 4 years	19,607	289	1.5	54	235
5 to 9 years	20,379	659	3.2	62	597
10 to 14 years	20,328	1,059	5.2	142	917
15 to 19 years	20,102	1,612	8.0	210	1,402
20 to 24 years	18,441	2,366	12.8	366	2,000
25 to 29 years	18,268	2,902	15.9	610	2,292
30 to 34 years	19,518	3,233	16.6	878	2,355
35 to 44 years	44,805	6,235	13.9	2,428	3,807
45 to 54 years	36,631	4,289	11.7	2,135	2,154
55 to 64 years	23,387	2,621	11.2	1,549	1,072
65 to 74 years	17,796	1,778	10.0	1,195	582
75 to 84 years	11,685	965	8.3	695	269
85 years and over	3,140	373	11.9	297	75
Sex					
Male	133,933	14,200	10.6	5,077	9,123
Female	140,154	14,179	10.1	5,544	8,635
Educational Attainment					
Not a high school graduate	27,853	7,397	26.6	2,331	5,066
High school graduate or some college	102,531	9,218	9.0	4,454	4,765
Bachelors degree	29,840	3,615	12.1	1,835	1,780
Graduate/Professional degree	15,006	2,162	14.4	1,168	995
Economic Status					
Employed	134,338	16,532	12.3	6,499	10,033
Unemployed	6,116	852	13.9	221	631
Not in labor force	68,613	8,714	12.7	3,582	5,133
Below poverty	32,258	4,751	14.7	968	3,783
Region of Residence					
Northeast	52,038	6,420	12.3	2,642	3,778
Midwest	63,595	3,036	4.8	1,165	1,870
South	95,928	7,596	7.9	2,782	4,815
West	62,526	11,327	18.1	4,033	7,294

Source: U.S. Bureau of the Census, Current Population Survey, March 2000.

Foreign-Born Population by Sex and Race, 1990-99

Characteristic	1990[1]	1995	1998	1999
Total	19,846,000	22,978,000	25,145,000	25,831,000
Percent of U.S. population	8.0%	8.7%	9.3%	9.5%
By sex				
Male	9,737,000	11,173,000	12157,000	12,472,000
Female	10,109,000	11805,000	12988,000	13,360,000
By race				
White	13,428,000	14,930,000	16,167,000	16,575,000
Black	1,705,000	2117,000	2,425,000	2,517,000
American Indian, Eskimo, Aleut	86,000	120,000	143,000	150,000
Asian and Pacific Islander	4,627,000	5,811,000	6,410,000	6,589,000
Hispanic Origin[2]	7,997,000	9,532,000	10,713,000	11,103,000

1. Figures are from the April 1990 Census. All other figures are as of July 1 of the year shown. 2. People of Hispanic origin may be of any race. Source: U.S. Bureau of the Census, Foreign-Born Resident Population Estimates of the U.S., 1990-99, (2000). www.census.gov.

members admitted each year. However, beginning in 1995, the number of immediate family members admitted in the previous year is subtracted from 480,000 to determine the number of family-sponsored immigrants eligible for admission. The family-sponsored limit may not go below 226,000 in any year, however.

▶ THE FOREIGN-BORN POPULATION

The strong increase in the number of immigrants since the 1970s has helped to reshape the makeup of American society. The percentage of the population that was born outside this country continues to increase. In 2000, according to the Census Bureau, 28.4 million U.S. residents (10.4 percent

Foreign-Born Population by Place of Birth, 1990

Place of Birth	Number	Percent	Place of Birth	Number	Percent
All Foreign-born persons	**21,631,601**	**100.0%**	**North America**	**8,524,594**	**39.4%**
			Canada	870,850	4.0
Europe	**4,812,117**	**22.2%**	Caribbean, total	1,986,835	9.2
Austria	94,398	0.4	Antigua-Barbuda	12,452	0.1
Belgium	41,111	0.2	Bahamas	24,341	0.1
Czechoslovakia	90,042	0.4	Barbados	44,311	0.2
Denmark	37,657	0.2	Cuba	750,609	3.5
Estonia	9,251	0.0	Dominican Republic	356,971	1.7
Finland	23,547	0.1	Grenada	18,183	0.1
France	162,934	0.8	Haiti	229,108	1.1
Germany	1,163,004	5.4	Jamaica	343,458	1.6
Greece	189,267	0.9	Trinidad/Tobago	119,221	0.6
Hungary	112,419	0.5	Other Caribbean	88,181	0.4
Ireland	177,420	0.8	Central America	5,650,374	26.1
Italy	639,518	3.0	Belize	31,222	0.1
Latvia	26,380	0.1	Costa Rica	48,264	0.2
Lithuania	30,344	0.1	El Salvador	472,885	2.2
Netherlands	104,216	0.5	Guatemala	232,977	1.1
Norway	46,240	0.2	Honduras	114,603	0.5
Poland	397,014	1.8	Mexico	4,447,439	20.6
Portugal	218,525	1.0	Nicaragua	171,950	0.8
Romania	92,627	0.4	Panama	124,695	0.6
Spain	103,518	0.5	Other Central America	6,339	0.0
Sweden	57,166	0.3	Other North America	16,535	0.1
Switzerland	43,991	0.2			
United Kingdom	764,627	3.5	**South America**	**1,107,000**	**5.1%**
Yugoslavia	144,563	0.7	Argentina	97,422	0.5
Other Europe	42,338	0.2	Bolivia	33,637	0.2
			Brazil	94,023	0.4
Soviet Union	**336,889**	**1.6%**	Chile	61,212	0.3
			Colombia	303,918	1.4
Asia	**5,412,127**	**25.0%**	Ecuador	147,867	0.7
Afghanistan	28,988	0.1	Guyana	122,554	0.6
Cambodia	119,581	0.6	Peru	152,315	0.7
China	543,208	2.5	Uruguay	21,628	0.1
Hong Kong	152,263	0.7	Venezuela	51,571	0.2
India	463,132	2.1	Other South America	20,853	0.1
Indonesia	50,388	0.2			
Iran	216,963	1.0	**Africa**	**400,691**	**1.9%**
Iraq	45,936	0.2	Cape Verde	14,821	0.1
Israel	97,006	0.4	Egypt	68,662	0.3
Japan	421,921	2.0	Ethiopia	37,422	0.2
Jordan	33,019	0.2	Ghana	21,714	0.1
Korea (South)	663,465	3.1	Kenya	15,871	0.1
Laos	172,925	0.8	Morocco	21,529	0.1
Lebanon	91,037	0.4	Nigeria	58,052	0.3
Malaysia	34,906	0.2	Senegal	2,369	0.0
Myanmar	20,441	0.1	South Africa	38,163	0.2
Pakistan	93,663	0.4	Other Africa	122,088	0.6
Philippines	997,745	4.6			
Saudi Arabia	17,312	0.1	**Oceania**	**122,137**	**0.6%**
Syria	37,654	0.2	Australia	52,469	0.2
Taiwan	253,719	1.2	Fiji	16,269	0.1
Thailand	119,862	0.6	New Zealand	18,039	0.1
Turkey	65,244	0.3	Tonga	11,040	0.1
Vietnam	556,311	2.6	Western Samoa	12,638	0.1
Other Asia	115,438	0.5	Other Oceania	11,682	0.1
			Not reported	**916,046**	**4.2%**

Note: The foreign-born population includes 1,864,285 persons who were born abroad of American parents.
Source: U.S. Bureau of the Census, 1990 Census Special Tabulations (1992).

Foreign-Born Population by Region of Birth, 1850–2000

Year	Total population	Foreign-born population	Percent foreign-born	Europe	Asia	Africa	Oceania	Latin America	North America
1850[1]	23,191,876	2,244,602	9.7%	2,031,867	1,135	551	588	20,773	147,711
1860[1]	31,443,321	4,138,697	13.2	3,807,062	36,796	526	2,140	38,315	249,970
1870	38,558,371	5,567,229	14.4	4,941,049	64,565	2,657	4,028	57,871	493,467
1880	50,155,783	6,679,943	13.3	5,751,823	107,630	2,204	6,859	90,073	717,286
1890	62,622,250	9,249,547	14.8	8,030,347	113,383	2,207	9,353	107,307	980,938
1900	75,994,575	10,341,276	13.6	8,881,548	120,248	2,538	8,820	137,458	1,179,922
1910	91,972,266	13,515,886	14.7	11,810,115	191,484	3,992	11,450	279,514	1,209,717
1920	105,710,620	13,920,692	13.2	11,916,048	237,950	16,126	14,626	588,843	1,138,174
1930	122,775,046	14,204,149	11.6	11,784,010	275,665	18,326	17,343	791,840	1,310,369
1940	131,669,275	11,594,896	8.8	N.A.	N.A.	N.A.	N.A.	N.A.	N.A.
1950	150,216,110	10,347,395	6.9	N.A.	N.A.	N.A.	N.A.	N.A.	N.A.
1960	179,325,671	9,738,091	5.4	7,256,311	490,996	35,355	34,730	908,309	952,500
1970	203,210,158	9,619,302	4.7	5,740,891	824,887	80,143	41,258	1,803,970	812,421
1980	226,545,805	14,079,906	6.2	5,149,572	2,539,777	199,723	77,577	4,372,487	853,427
1990	248,709,873	19,767,316	7.9	4,350,403	4,979,037	363,819	104,145	8,407,837	753,917
2000	274,087,000	28,379,000	10.4	4,355,000	7,246,000	N.A.	N.A.	14,407,000	N.A.

1. In 1850 and 1860, information on nativity was not collected for slaves. The data in the table assume, as was done in 1870 census reports, that all slaves in 1850 and 1860 were native, even though 0.2 percent were foreign-born. 2. Numbers for 2000 rounded at source. **Source:** U.S. Bureau of the Census.

of the total population) were foreign-born. The last time the figure was higher was in 1930, when 11.6 percent of the population was born in another country. More than half of the foreign-born population in America came from Latin America (14.4 million); of these, fully half (7 million) listed Mexico as their birthplace. Another 25.5 percent of the foreign-born population was from Asia. The remainder were divided between Europe (15.3 percent) and other regions (8.1 percent).

Most foreign-born residents come to the U.S. and stay. In 2000, naturalized citizens constituted more than one-third of the foreign-born population. More than 80 percent of foreign-born people who arrived before 1970 are now U.S. citizens. The percentage is 61.9 percent for foreign-born persons arrriving during the 1970s, 38.9 percent for immigrants arriving during the 1980s, and 8.9 percent for those immigrating in the 1990s.

SEX IN AMERICA

Pollsters scrutinize every angle of American life, including what goes on beyond closed bedroom doors. The research ranges from the statistical—like the survey done by the National Center for Health Statistics—to the anecdotal, such as reader polls taken by popular magazines. Here's a summary of the two most serious studies, one conducted by the federal government, the other by a leading university.

▶WOMEN AND SEX
The National Survey of Family Growth is conducted periodically by the National Center for Health Statistics, with a national sample of women aged 15 to 44 years old. The most recent report, issued in May 1997, used data compiled in 1995. Questions concerned marriage and sexual activity. Some findings from the report:

- 75 percent of all married women had pre-marital intercourse; only 12 percent of women waited until marriage to have sex for the first time.
- 52 percent of women aged 20-44 had their first intercourse by age 18, and 75 percent were sexually experienced by age 20, up from 40 percent and 60 percent respectively in 1988.
- Nearly 14 percent of women aged 20-24 had sex before age 15.; the median age at first intercourse for these women was 16.6 years old.
- 28 percent of women had an unintended birth; poor women and non-Hispanic black women were most likely to have had an unplanned birth.
- 20.4 percent of women reported having involuntary intercourse at some time in their lives; more than one-fourth of these women were under 15 when they were forced to have sex.
- 47 percent of unmarried women reported having just one sexual partner in the past year; 11.2 percent had two partners, and 34.5 percent said they had no partners. But over their lifetimes, women of all marital statuses reported many more sexual partners. More than half of all women had three or more sexual partners in their lifetimes.
- 64.2 percent of women currently use contraceptives; the remaining 35.8 percent are divided among women who are pregnant, seeking to have children, or abstinent. Only 5.2 percent of women admitted having unprotected sex. Among women using contraceptives, sterilization (27.7 percent) was the most popular method, followed by the pill (26.9 percent) and the condom (20.4). Women under the age of 30 were most likely to use the pill.

▶SEX PARTNERS AND FREQUENCY OF INTERCOURSE
The National Opinion Research Center at the University of Chicago (NORC) periodically conducts a study of the sexual behavior of adults. The Center interviews a nationwide representative sample of about 1,500 adults to collect accurate data on a wide range of topics dealing with sex. Here are some of the survey's primary findings.

Cohabitation As premarital sex becomes more commonplace and the average age at first marriage grows older, the number of couples living together out of wedlock continues to spiral. Just over 1.1 percent of all couples were living together in 1960; in 1997 (the latest year for which data are available), the rate was 7.0 percent. In 1988, 23.4 percent of married couples had lived together before marrying; by 1994, 28.0 percent had. Cohabiting was most popular among younger couples: 9.4 percent of people 18-29 were cohabiting in 1998, and 43.7 percent had cohabited with their current spouse before marriage. The exact same percentage of 30-39-year-olds cohabited before marriage, but only 7.6 percent of the people in this age group were currently cohabiting in 1998.

Extramarital sex Numbers regarding sex out of wedlock are usually unreliable, since most people are reluctant to admit their affairs to interviewers. The percentage of currently married people admitting to extramarital sex within the last year (3.6 percent in 1998) has fluctuated very little since 1988. More people were willing to admit having an affair at one point in their lives. In 1991, 14.6 percent of people who had ever been married admitted having at least one affair while married; in 1998, 16.5 percent said they had had extramarital sex. These figures are much higher than the one-year numbers because they include married people as well as those who are separated and divorced, perhaps as a result of one of these affairs. Men (4.9 percent in the last year, and 20.8 percent ever) were more likely than women (2.5 percent 13.4 respectively) to admit extramarital activity.

Gender of sex partners For the same reasons, many people are also reluctant to admit homosexual behavior. The percentage of sexually active adults admitting to homosexual behavior within the last year has remained steady at between 2 and 3.5 percent since 1988, but the actual number is probably somewhat higher. A smaller percentage (never more than 1 percent) of people claim to have had sex with partners of both genders. Men who attend church regularly (3.7 percent) were more likely to have had a same sex partner than those who attended church occasionally (3.0 percent) or rarely (3.5 percent).

Number of sex partners The average number of sex partners per person has remained fairly constant over the past few years. A majority of adults have had only one sexual partner in the past five years, and more than two-thirds had only one partner in the past year. Adults in 2000 had an average of 1.14 partners in the last 12 months, and 2.74 partners in the past five years.

Frequency of sexual intercourse Americans had intercourse an average of 62.5 times a year in 2000. That's up from 59.1 times a year in 1998, but not significantly different from data from surveys dating back to 1989. Not surprisingly, married people aged 18-29 had the most sex—99.3 times a year (or twice a week); unmarried people over 70 had the least sex: an average of 3.6 times annually. Just under 19 percent of adults had no sex at all in 2000, and 11 percent have not had sex for the past five years.

Frequency of Sexual Intercourse by Age, Race, and Marital Status 1996-2000

		By Race		By Age					
Marital Status	All Adults	White	Black	18-29	30-39	40-49	50-59	60-69	70+
1996, Total	**65.3**	**61.2**	**64.7**	**83.7**	**79.7**	**63.4**	**47.4**	**28.1**	**9.8**
Married	N.A.	N.A.	N.A.	111.4	82.4	63.4	51.5	32.0	14.9
Unmarried	N.A.	N.A.	N.A.	71.8	76.9	63.4	43.5	23.7	6.4
1998, Total	**59.1**	**60.2**	**62.7**	**82.6**	**78.6**	**63.6**	**47.4**	**27.4**	**9.8**
Married	66.1	N.A.	N.A.	111.6	85.7	69.2	53.8	32.5	16.2
Unmarried	N.A.	N.A.	N.A.	69.1	65.6	49.8	31.2	15.7	2.6
2000, Total	**62.5**	**61.2**	**70.8**	**N.A.**	**N.A.**	**N.A.**	**N.A.**	**N.A.**	**N.A.**
Married	N.A.	N.A.	N.A.	99.3	84.2	71.7	54.8	30.7	16.9
Unmarried	N.A.	N.A.	N.A.	75.2	67.6	48.9	34.1	13.1	3.6

Source: National Opinion Research Center (NORC) *General Social Survey,* 1996, 1998, 2000.

Number of Sexual Partners by Adults, 1991-2000

	Number of sexual partners							
Year	None	1	2	3	4	5–9	10+	Mean
				Last 12 months				
1991	18.4	71.2	5.9	1.9	0.8	1.4	0.4	1.12
1996	15.1	72.2	6.1	3.2	1.6	1.3	0.5	1.36
1998	17.4	70.7	6.0	2.2	1.5	1.4	0.4	1.24
2000	18.9	69.2	5.9	2.9	1.8	1.6	0.3	1.14
				Last five years				
1991	11.3	60.3	8.3	6.7	3.3	6.0	4.2	2.70
1996	10.0	57.8	10.2	7.2	4.7	6.4	3.4	2.83
1998	11.2	59.0	9.2	6.0	4.7	5.7	2.9	2.50
2000	11.3	58.1	9.9	6.4	4.3	6.0	3.3	2.74

Source: National Opinion Research Center (NORC) *General Social Surveys,* 1991-2000.

Agriculture

In recent years, U.S. agriculture has become an integral part of the global economy. American farmers currently produce over 40 percent of the world's corn, 44 percent of its soybeans, and 10 percent of its wheat. Much of this they export to all parts of the world, but especially to Asia and Latin America. In 1990, U.S. agricultural exports totaled $39.5 billion, but by 2000, they were nearly $52 billion. About 27 percent of that total was in grains and feeds; 23 percent was in animals and animal products.

This is a far cry from the small nation of "embattled farmers" who launched the American Revolution. In the early years of the Republic, agriculture, while vital (involving 95 percent of the population), remained relatively small-scale and in economic terms primitive, with the exception of large plantations in the South devoted to cotton, tobacco, and rice. The Civil War brought higher food prices and increased mechanization throughout the farming industry. It also led to federal legislation aimed at encouraging farming; the Homestead Act of 1862 and the Morrill Land Grant College Act were especially important. The decision to build a transcontinental rail system—undertaken by private enterprise abetted by government grants—opened up large areas of the Great Plains to farming, and the railroad companies recruited immigrants to buy and farm the land the government had given the companies.

In the early 20th century, machinery gradually replaced animal power. World War I stimulated agriculture, but the stimulus led to overproduction, which, with the coming of peace, depressed prices and land values. This decline both contributed to and was intensified by the Great Depression, one of the most paralyzing aspects of which was a near total cessation of world agricultural trade. The plight of farmers during the 1930's prompted considerable government remedies, including various forms of credit, price supports, rural electrification, and serious efforts at soil conservation. World War II again gave impetus to agriculture.

After the war, new machinery, new chemicals, and hybrid crops, more resistant to weather and biological enemies significantly increased crop yields. By the end of the 1940's, the United States had become the world's largest single producer of wheat, corn, and soybeans. One byproduct of this success was the creation of huge surpluses. U.S. agriculture proved a potent force in the world economy and in foreign policy, and in 1954, Public Law 480 provided for the export of surplus grains to poorer nations both to prevent starva-

Percent of U.S. Agricultural Exports by Region and Selected Nation, 1980–2000

Category	1980	1990	2000
Total agricultural exports (billions)	$41.2	$39.5	$51.6
Percent by region and nation			
Asia	36.5%	44.8%	43.4%
Japan	14.9	20.6	18.1
Korea, South	4.4	6.7	5.0
Taiwan	2.7	4.2	3.9
China	5.6	2.1	3.3
Hong Kong	1.1	1.8	2.5
Western Europe	31.4	18.7	13.0
European Union	29.6	18.0	12.1
Latin America	15.0	13.0	20.9
Mexico	6.0	6.5	12.7
Canada	4.7	10.7	14.8
Africa	5.5	4.9	4.5

Source: U.S. Dept. of Agriculture, *Agricultural Statistics*, annual

U.S. Farms, Acreage and Population, 1850–2000

Year	Farms ('000s)	Acreage Total ('000s)	Per farm	Percent of US	Farm Population Total ('000s)	Percent of US
1850	1,449	293,561	203	15.6%	—	—
1860	2,044	407,213	199	21.4	—	—
1870	2,660	407,735	153	21.4	—	—
1880	4,009	536,082	134	28.2	21,973	43.8%
1890	4,565	623,219	137	32.7	24,771	42.3
1900	5,740	841,202	147	37.0	29,835	41.9
1910	6,366	881,431	139	38.8	32,077	34.9
1920	6,454	958,677	149	42.2	31,974	30.1
1930	6,295	990,112	157	43.6	30,529	24.9
1940	6,102	1,065,114	175	46.8	30,547	23.2
1950	5,388	1,161,420	216	51.1	23,048	15.3
1960	3,962	1,176,946	297	49.5[1]	15,635	8.7
1970	2,954	1,102,769	373	47.0[2]	9,712	4.8
1980	2,440	1,039,000	426	44.8	6,051	2.7
1990	2,146	987,000	460	42.7	4,801	1.9
1995	2,196	963,000	438	N.A.	N.A.	N.A.
1996	2,191	959,000	438	N.A.	N.A.	N.A.
1997	2,191	956,000	436	N.A.	N.A.	N.A.
1998	2,191	954,000	435	N.A.	N.A.	N.A.
1999	2,192	947,000	432	N.A.	N.A.	N.A.
2000	2,172	943,000	434	N.A.	N.A.	N.A.

Note: Acreage figures after 1980 rounded in source. 1. Figure for 1959. 2. Figure for 1969.   Source: U.S. Bureau of the Census, *Statistical History of the United States* (1970); *Statistical Abstract of the United States.*

tion and stimulate economic development, and to alleviate the pressures on the domestic agriculture sector caused by the surpluses.

Since 1960, the number of American farms has declined as small units lose out to huge agribusinesses owned by corporations. Between 1980 and 1999, the number of farms fell from 2.44 million to 2.17 million, (a decline of 11 percent) while average acreage per farm rose from 426 to 434. Overall, the total land area devoted to farming dropped from 1.04 billion acres to 943 million, a decline of 9 percent. Meanwhile, improved technology has made farming less labor intensive, so the total farm population has also declined precipitously, and is now less than 2 percent of the total popula-

tion, down from 42 percent at the turn of the century, and 15 percent in 1950. The surpluses created by expanded and more efficient production required governments to prop up prices, often at the consumer's expense. Complaints that these programs, initiated in the country during the 1930's to help farmers, have become wasteful and counterproductive, have led to some cuts by recent congressional actions. In 1996, Congress repealed price guarantees on most major crops, to become fully effective by 2002. But this plan failed.

The worldwide nature of agricultural progress—the "green revolution"—has increased competition for markets, in some cases hurting farmers

Farms—Number and Acreage, by State, 1980–2000

State	Number of Farms (000's)			Acreage (millions)			Acreage per farm		
	1980	1990	2000	1980	1990	2000	1980	1990	2000
U.S. total	2,440	2,146	2,172	1,039	987	943	426	460	434
Alabama	59	47	47	12	10	9	207	215	191
Alaska	(z)	1	1	2	1	1	3,378	1,707	1,586
Arizona	8	8	8	38	36	27	5,080	4,641	3,580
Arkansas	59	47	48	17	16	15	280	330	304
California	81	85	68	34	31	28	417	382	318
Colorado	27	27	29	36	33	32	1,358	1,249	1,090
Connecticut	4	4	4	(z)	(z)	(z)	117	108	92
Delaware	4	3	3	1	1	1	186	207	223
Florida	39	41	44	11	11	10	344	266	234
Georgia	59	48	50	15	13	11	254	260	222
Hawaii	4	5	6	2	2	1	458	357	253
Idaho	24	22	25	15	14	12	623	628	486
Illinois	107	83	78	29	28	28	269	342	355
Indiana	87	68	64	17	16	16	193	240	242
Iowa	119	104	95	34	34	33	284	322	345
Kansas	75	69	64	48	48	48	644	694	742
Kentucky	102	93	90	15	14	14	143	152	151
Louisiana	37	32	30	10	9	8	273	278	275
Maine	8	7	7	2	1	1	195	201	187
Maryland	18	15	12	3	2	2	157	148	169
Massachusetts	6	6	8	1	1	1	116	100	93
Michigan	65	54	52	11	11	10	175	200	200
Minnesota	104	89	79	30	30	28	291	337	382
Mississippi	55	40	43	15	13	11	265	325	258
Missouri	120	108	109	31	30	30	261	281	275
Montana	24	25	28	62	61	57	2,601	2,449	2,054
Nebraska	65	37	54	48	47	48	734	826	859
Nevada	3	3	3	9	9	7	3,100	3,560	2,267
New Hampshire	3	3	3	1	(z)	(z)	160	163	135
New Jersey	9	8	10	1	1	1	109	107	86
New Mexico	14	14	15	47	45	44	3,467	3,296	2,895
New York	47	39	38	9	8	8	200	218	203
North Carolina	93	62	57	12	10	9	126	156	161
North Dakota	40	34	30	42	41	39	1,043	1,209	1,300
Ohio	95	83	80	16	16	15	171	188	186
Oklahoma	72	70	85	35	33	34	481	471	400
Oregon	35	37	40	18	18	17	517	488	430
Pennsylvania	62	53	59	9	8	8	145	153	131
Rhode Island	1	1	1	(z)	(z)	(z)	87	95	86
South Carolina	34	25	24	6	5	5	188	208	196
South Dakota	39	35	33	45	44	44	1,169	1,266	1,354
Tennessee	96	87	90	14	12	12	142	139	130
Texas	196	196	226	138	132	130	705	673	575
Utah	14	13	16	12	11	12	919	856	748
Vermont	8	7	7	2	1	1	226	222	197
Virginia	58	46	49	10	9	9	169	193	178
Washington	38	37	40	16	16	16	429	432	383
West Virginia	22	21	21	4	4	4	191	180	178
Wisconsin	93	80	77	19	16	16	200	220	210
Wyoming	9	9	9	35	35	35	3,846	3,899	3,761

Note: z= Fewer than 500,000 acres.   Source: U.S. Dept. of Agriculture, *Farm Numbers and Land in Farms*.

who depend upon exporting a large share of their crop. Nevertheless, the U.S. continues to export agricultural products worth over $50 billion a year, almost half of the total to Asia. The 1997-98 financial crisis there drove down the price of all major commodities, and led to a decline in farm exports. Today's farmers face a difficult future. Record crops from 1996 to 1998 also pushed prices down, in some cases as low as during the Depression. Severe drought in the Southwest and part of the Southeast during 2000 also caused hardship. As a result, government subsidies have risen from $7.3 billion in 1996 to $22.7 billion in 2000. Further consolidation in the industry threatened to force even more family farmers from the business, and to continue the trend of agribusinesses swallowing up land once individually owned and farmed.

U.S. Agricultural Exports: Principal Commodities by Value and Percentage of Agriculture Exports, 1990–2000

Category	1980 Value (billions)	Percent	1990 Value (billions)	Percent	2000 Value (billions)	Percent
Total agricultural exports	$41.2	100.0%	$39.5	100.0%	$51.6	100.0%
Commodities						
Grains and feeds	$19.1	46.4%	$14.4	36.5%	$13.7	26.6%
Oilseeds and products	9.4	22.8	5.7	14.4	8.6	16.6
Animals and animal products	3.8	9.2	6.7	16.9	11.8	23.0
Cotton	2.9	7.0	2.8	7.0	1.9	3.6
Tobacco, unmanufactured	1.3	3.3	1.4	3.6	1.2	2.4
Fruits and preparations	1.3	3.3	2.4	6.0	3.5	6.7
Vegetables and preparations	1.2	2.9	2.2	5.6	4.5	8.7
Nuts and preparations	0.8	1.9	1.0	2.5	1.3	2.6
Other	1.5	3.6	2.9	7.3	5.1	9.9

Source: U.S. Dept. of Agriculture, *Agricultural Statistics*, annual.

U.S. Production of Leading Farm Products as Percent of World Total, 1995–2000

Product	U.S. production (millions of metric tons) 1995	1999	2000	As percent of world total 1995	1999	2000
Total production						
Corn	188.0	240.0	253.0	36.5%	39.6%	43.4%
Soybeans	59.0	72.0	75.0	47.4	45.3	44.1
Wheat	59.0	63.0	61.0	11.0	10.7	10.5
Cotton[1]	19.7	13.9	17.0	23.0	16.4	19.5
Rice, milled	5.6	6.6	6.0	1.5	1.6	1.5
Amount exported						
Corn	52.7	49.4	50.5	72.4%	67.5%	69.8%
Wheat	33.7	29.5	30.0	33.9	26.2	28.1
Soybeans	23.1	26.5	26.5	72.4	57.2	54.6
Cotton[1]	9.4	4.3	6.8	33.0	18.3	24.8
Rice, milled	3.1	2.6	2.8	14.8	10.4	12.2

1. Millions of bales. **Source:** U.S. Dept. of Agriculture, Foreign Agricultural Service, *Foreign Agricultural Commodity Circular Series*.

Top Agricultural States by Farm Marketings, 1999

Rank, State	Farm marketings (millions)	Crops	Livestock and products	Principal commodities
1. California	$24,801	$18,067	$6,714	Dairy products, grapes, greenhouse, cattle
2. Texas	13,052	4,572	8,480	Cattle, cotton, greenhouse, broilers
3. Iowa	9,718	5,004	4,712	Corn, hogs, soybeans, cattle
4. Nebraska	8,555	3,130	5,425	Cattle, corn, soybeans, hogs
5. Kansas	7,616	2,607	5,009	Cattle, wheat, corn, sorghum grain
6. Florida	7,068	5,702	1,363	Oranges, greenhouse, sugarcane, dairy products
7. Minnesota	7,061	3,513	3,548	Dairy products, soybeans, corn, hogs
8. Illinois	6,757	5,233	1,524	Corn, soybeans, hogs, cattle
9. North Carolina	6,688	2,838	3,850	Broilers, hogs, greenhouse, tobacco
10. Wisconsin	5,596	1,447	4,149	Dairy products, cattle, corn, potatoes

Source: U.S. Dept. of Agriculture, Economic Research Service, *United States and State Farm Income*, September, 2000.

Crime and Punishment

▶SERIOUS CRIME

Serious crime is the Justice Department's measure of the total number of violent crimes (murder, rape, robbery, and assault) plus property crimes (burglary, larceny/theft, motor vehicle theft, and arson). The number of serious crimes in the U.S. has decreased every year for the past seven years, from an all-time high of close to 15 million in 1991 to just over 11.6 million in 1999.

The number of violent crimes peaked at 1.93 million in 1992, and has declined every year since then, to 1.43 million in 1999. That's still significantly higher, however, than the 1.04 million violent crimes recorded in 1975. There were 15,530 murders reported to police in the U.S. in 1999, down 21 percent from 1990. Guns were the weapon of choice, accounting for more than two-thirds of all homicides; handguns alone accounted for more than half of all murders.

Property crime reached its all-time high in 1991, at 12.96 million total offenses reported to police. It too has decreased every year, and totaled 10.2 million in 1999, lower than in 1975. The number of burglaries has dropped 31.7 percent, from 3.07 million in 1990 to under 2.1 million in 1999.

The surging economy in 1999 and a thriving job market were major reasons for the steadily declining number of serious crimes, especially the crimes of robbery, burglary, and motor vehicle theft, which have experienced some of the biggest drops. But it does not necessarily explain the equally impressive drop in the number of murders, which experts say is due to the aging of the population, as well as more police and better policing techniques. In addition, tougher sentencing laws have increased the number of people in prison. Note, however, that these explanations do not account for the nearly 80 percent increase in the number of aggravated assaults since 1978. Assaults have de-

clined slightly from the all-time high of 1.14 million reached in 1994, but were still higher in 1999 (916,380) than they were in 1989 (951,710).

The number of forcible rapes is up 59 percent since 1975, but a portion of this significant jump is most likely the result of more women reporting this crime to police, rather than an increase in the number of incidents. Since 1992, the number of rapes reported dropped from 109,060 to 89,110.

The crime rate   Raw numbers of crime do not necessarily tell the whole story. To account for population growth, criminologists use the crime rate per 100,000 population to compare crime statistics from different years. Because the population continues to grow, the rate of crime is dropping even more precipitously than the raw number of crimes. The total number of serious crimes fell nearly 20 percent since 1990, but the rate dropped 26.7 percent. In other words, the likelihood that you will become a victim of crime is dropping even more quickly than the number of crimes committed.

The murder rate in 1999 was 5.7 per 100,000 population, the lowest since 1967 and a 9 percent drop from 1997. Other significant declines have come in property crime. There were 524.7 violent crimes for every 100,000 people in 1999, down 7.5 percent from the year before. Meanwhile, property crimes per 100,000 inhabitants fell from 5,088.5 in 1990 to 3,742.1 in 1999, a drop of 26.5 percent.

The largest states, of course, had the most numbers of crimes. But the rate of crime was by far the greatest in Florida (6,205 serious crimes per 100,000 residents) and New Mexico (5,962.1). Both states have the reputation of being tough on crime, and both have the death penalty, yet these measures have apparently had little impact on crime. Meanwhile, New York, supposedly one of

Serious Crime in the U.S., 1975–99

Crime	1975	1980	1990	1995	1998	1999	Percent change, 1990-99
Number of Offenses Reported to Police							
Violent crime	1,039,710	1,344,520	1,820,130	1,798,790	1,533,890	1,430,690	-21.4%
Murder	20,510	23,040	23,440	21,610	16,970	15,530	-33.7
Forcible rape	56,090	82,990	102,560	97,470	93,140	89,110	-13.1
Robbery	470,500	565,840	639,270	580,510	447,190	409,670	-35.9
Aggravated assault	492,620	672,650	1,054,860	1,099,210	976,580	916,380	-13.1
Property crime	10,252,700	12,063,700	12,655,500	12,063,900	10,951,800	10,204,500	-19.4%
Burglary	3,265,300	3,795,200	3,073,900	2,593,000	2,332,700	2,099,700	-31.7
Larceny/theft	5,977,700	7,136,900	7,945,700	7997700	7,376,300	6,957,400	-12.4
Motor vehicle theft	1,009,600	1,131,700	1,635,900	1,472,400	1,242,800	1,147,300	-29.9
Total serious crimes	11,292,400	13,408,300	14,475,600	13,867,100	12,485,700	11,635,100	-19.6%
Rate per 100,000 inhabitants							
Violent crime	487.8	596.6	731.8	684.6	567.5	524.7	-28.3%
Murder	9.6	10.2	9.4	8.2	6.3	5.7	-39.4
Forcible rape	26.3	36.8	41.2	37.1	34.5	32.7	-20.6
Robbery	220.8	251.1	257.0	220.9	165.4	150.2	-41.6
Aggravated assault	231.1	298.5	424.1	418.3	361.3	336.1	-20.7
Property crime	4,810.7	5,353.3	5,088.5	4,951.3	4,051.8	3,742.1	-26.5%
Burglary	1,532.1	1,684.1	1,235.9	987.1	863.0	770.0	-37.7
Larceny/theft	2,804.8	3,167.0	3,194.8	3,043.8	2,729.0	2,551.4	-20.1
Motor vehicle theft	473.7	502.2	657.8	560.4	459.8	420.7	-36.0
Total serious crimes	5,298.5	5,950.0	5,820.3	5,275.9	4,619.3	4,266.8	-26.7%

Note: Totals may not add up due to independent rounding. **Source:** Federal Bureau of Investigation, *Uniform Crime Reports: Crime in the United States 1999*, www.fbi.gov/ucr/99cius.htm

Serious Crime per 100,000 Population, by State, 1999

State	All serious crime	Violent crime				Property crime		
		Murder	Forcible rape	Robbery	Aggra- vated assault	Burglary	Larceny/ theft	Motor vehicle theft
U.S.	4,266.8	5.7	32.7	150.2	336.1	770.0	2,551.4	420.7
Alabama	4,412.3	7.9	34.6	121.2	326.5	884.4	2,737.2	300.5
Alaska	4,363.2	8.6	83.5	91.4	448.0	611.8	2,690.5	429.4
Arizona	5,896.5	8.0	28.9	152.5	361.6	1,034.4	3,510.5	800.5
Arkansas	4,042.8	5.6	27.8	79.3	312.5	850.3	2,506.0	261.2
California	3,805.0	6.0	28.2	181.1	411.7	675.3	1,994.2	508.3
Colorado	4,063.4	4.6	41.4	75.3	219.2	665.2	2,693.0	364.8
Connecticut	3,389.3	3.3	19.9	123.5	198.9	588.0	2,111.5	344.2
Delaware[1]	4,835.0	3.2	70.2	197.9	462.7	695.6	3,001.9	403.6
Dist. of Columbia[2]	8,067.1	46.4	47.8	644.3	889.2	976.3	4,181.3	1,281.7
Florida	6,205.5	5.7	46.3	211.6	590.5	1,200.3	3,534.5	616.7
Georgia	5,148.5	7.5	29.8	166.4	330.3	917.2	3,182.3	515.2
Hawaii	4,837.5	3.7	29.9	88.1	113.3	795.0	3,414.2	393.2
Idaho	3,149.3	2.0	33.3	17.8	191.8	610.3	2,142.5	151.6
Illinois	4,506.6	7.7	34.2	219.4	471.2	712.3	2,632.1	429.7
Indiana	3,765.9	6.6	27.0	109.3	231.7	714.5	2,335.4	341.4
Iowa	3,224.0	1.5	27.2	36.6	214.7	593.0	2,172.0	179.0
Kansas[3]	4,438.7	6.0	40.1	77.1	259.5	824.2	3,003.8	227.9
Kentucky[3]	2,878.1	5.4	26.3	80.0	189.0	610.9	1,748.7	217.9
Louisiana	5,746.8	10.7	33.1	173.6	515.2	1,092.7	3,425.2	496.2
Maine[3]	2,875.0	2.2	19.1	19.4	71.6	601.1	2,026.5	135.2
Maryland	4,919.2	9.0	30.0	263.7	440.7	835.8	2,848.0	492.0
Massachusetts	3,262.5	2.0	26.9	96.0	426.0	533.8	1,762.7	415.0
Michigan	4,324.8	7.0	49.2	143.0	375.7	777.9	2,396.1	575.8
Minnesota[4]	3,597.2	2.8	42.7	82.0	146.5	580.1	2,465.2	278.0
Mississippi	4,269.8	7.7	41.7	111.6	188.2	1,051.2	2,380.6	488.7
Missouri	4,578.7	6.6	26.3	130.7	336.6	776.8	2,881.3	420.3
Montana[3]	4,069.9	2.6	28.3	25.8	149.7	428.5	3,220.2	214.7
Nebraska	4,108.3	3.6	24.8	75.9	325.9	609.7	2,741.8	326.5
Nevada	4,653.7	9.1	52.1	232.7	276.1	973.6	2,386.2	723.8
New Hampshire[3]	2,281.9	1.5	28.7	21.4	44.9	307.9	1,764.8	112.7
New Jersey	3,400.1	3.5	17.3	174.9	216.1	577.2	1,976.9	434.2
New Mexico	5,962.1	9.8	54.3	148.2	622.2	1,234.5	3,426.0	467.0
New York	3,279.3	5.0	19.6	240.8	323.5	512.3	1,858.1	320.2
North Carolina	5,175.4	7.2	28.2	158.0	348.7	1,286.9	3,012.2	334.3
North Dakota	2,393.1	1.6	22.4	8.8	34.1	368.6	1,794.2	163.4
Ohio	3,996.4	3.5	36.7	128.0	148.2	773.1	2,558.8	348.2
Oklahoma	4,683.9	6.9	40.9	82.9	377.5	1,026.6	2,787.8	361.3
Oregon	5,002.0	2.7	36.8	86.2	249.3	806.7	3,409.3	411.1
Pennsylvania	3,113.7	4.9	27.3	155.7	232.5	467.2	1,898.9	327.1
Puerto Rico	2,105.3	14.6	5.7	252.8	91.6	592.4	776.9	371.3
Rhode Island	3,581.9	3.6	39.5	79.5	164.0	639.9	2,248.6	406.9
South Carolina	5,324.4	6.6	40.8	148.2	651.4	1,019.8	3,085.7	371.7
South Dakota	2,644.7	2.5	45.8	14.1	105.0	444.1	1,915.8	117.5
Tennessee	4,693.9	7.1	44.0	156.8	487.0	936.6	2,601.8	460.5
Texas	5,031.8	6.1	38.0	146.7	369.5	949.7	3,062.6	459.2
Utah	4,976.5	2.1	37.8	54.4	181.3	685.1	3,669.3	346.6
Vermont	2,817.3	2.9	22.9	10.9	77.1	595.5	1,954.5	153.5
Virginia	3,373.9	5.7	25.0	101.1	182.8	471.6	2,326.4	261.2
Washington	5,255.5	3.0	47.1	100.9	226.3	949.5	3,341.5	587.3
West Virginia[5]	2,720.6	4.4	18.6	36.6	291.0	570.2	1,591.6	208.2
Wisconsin	3,296.4	3.4	20.1	84.7	137.6	488.2	2,299.1	263.2
Wyoming	3,454.8	2.3	28.5	15.4	186.0	489.4	2,609.0	124.2

Note: Offense totals are based on all reporting agencies and estimates for unreported areas. 1. An aggregated Delaware state total for forcible rape for 1999 was supplied by the Delaware State Bureau of Investigation. 2. Includes offenses reported by the Zoological Police. 3. Limited data for 1999 were available for Illinois, Kansas, Kentucky, Maine, Montana, and New Hampshire; therefore, it was necessary that their crime counts be estimated. 4. Forcible rape figures furnished by the state Uniform Crime Reporting Program administered by the Minnesota Department of Public Safety are not comparable to those for previous years. 5. Due to reporting changes, data are not comparable to previous years' data.
Source: Federal Bureau of Investigation, *Uniform Crime Reports: Crime in the United States 1999*. www.fbi.gov/ucr/99cius.htm

the most dangerous states, was at 3,279.3 crimes per 100,000 residents, significantly below the national average. The most dangerous place to live, however, was the nation's capital, with 8,067.1 serious crimes per 100,000 residents, nearly double the national average. By metropolitan area, Miami (8,744.7) Albuquerque (7,652.0), West Palm Beach (7,197) and Tucson (6,938.4) topped the list of dangerous cities, yet even these cities averaged a 10 percent drop in crime rate from 1998.

Serious Crime Per 100,000 Population, by Metropolitan Area, 1999

Metropolitan area	All serious crime	Murder	Forcible rape	Robbery	Aggravated assault	Total violent crime[1]	Total property crime[2]
Albuquerque, N. Mex	7,652.0	11.0	45.3	283.6	680.1	1,020.0	6,632.0
Atlanta, Ga.	5,734.9	8.4	32.3	232.9	343.6	617.2	5,117.7
Austin-San Marcos, Texas	4,900.7	3.5	32.8	101.4	249.3	387.0	4,513.8
Bergen-Passaic, N.J.	2,615.3	2.1	8.1	102.4	136.8	249.5	2,365.7
Birmingham, Ala.	3,990.8	11.1	35.3	151.4	271.5	469.2	3,521.6
Boston, Mass.-N.H.	3,046.5	1.8	21.6	108.4	335.7	467.5	2,579.0
Burlington, Vt.	3,698.8	4.0	20.0	22.7	140.8	187.5	3,511.3
Columbus, Ohio	6,115.5	5.9	58.1	245.8	178.8	488.6	5,626.9
Dallas, Texas	5,895.2	7.7	38.0	243.0	415.9	704.5	5,190.7
Denver, Colo.	4,178.4	5.8	36.0	99.2	199.8	340.8	3,837.6
Des Moines, Iowa	4,254.4	4.3	29.0	71.1	164.8	269.2	3,985.2
Detroit, Mich.	4,960.5	11.1	44.5	227.6	479.0	762.2	4,198.3
El Paso, Texas	5,469.3	2.5	36.7	106.0	514.3	659.5	4,809.8
Fort Lauderdale, Fla.	5,555.3	4.5	31.1	192.0	409.5	637.1	4,918.2
Ft. Worth-Arlington, Texas	5,240.6	6.3	41.7	141.6	311.1	500.7	4,740.0
Fresno, Calif.	5,352.3	5.5	33.9	191.0	568.6	799.0	4,553.3
Green Bay, Wis.	3,199.3	3.2	24.9	25.4	144.6	198.2	3,001.1
Greensboro, N.C.	5,524.3	6.7	32.8	174.3	363.5	577.2	4,947.1
Greenville, N.C.	6,659.9	4.8	31.7	167.4	480.8	684.7	5,975.2
Hartford, Conn.	3,674.6	3.6	19.7	136.8	156.7	316.8	3,357.8
Honolulu, Hawaii	4,925.0	4.3	27.1	104.7	117.6	253.6	4,671.3
Houston, Texas	5,173.2	8.1	34.6	260.4	448.7	751.9	4,421.4
Indianapolis, Ind.	4,010.7	8.8	35.3	188.7	356.9	589.6	3,421.0
Jacksonville, Fla.	6,131.7	8.5	54.9	182.2	601.4	847.0	5,284.7
Miami, Fla.	8,744.7	9.2	45.4	411.4	785.4	1,251.4	7,493.3
Middlesex-Somerset, N.J.	2,399.9	1.4	11.0	65.2	120.7	198.3	2,201.6
Minneapolis-St. Paul, Minn.[4]	4,268.7	2.9	46.8	127.4	187.0	364.2	3,904.5
Monmouth-Ocean, N.J.	2,455.7	1.6	12.8	57.0	126.9	198.3	2,257.4
Newark, N.J.	3,931.9	6.8	20.2	304.3	282.2	613.5	3,318.4
New Orleans, La.	6,151.4	16.0	38.2	296.8	490.1	841.1	5,310.3
New York, N.Y.	3,853.5	7.9	20.9	428.2	489.3	946.4	2,907.1
Oakland, Calif.	4,862.2	6.0	32.3	223.1	362.8	624.3	4,237.9
Oklahoma City, Okla.	6,223.3	7.6	53.9	123.5	353.9	538.9	5,684.4
Omaha, Nebr.-Iowa	5,379.4	5.6	40.5	154.2	578.0	778.4	4,601.0
Orange County, Calif.	2,767.5	3.3	17.2	102.8	195.0	318.3	2,449.1
Orlando, Fla.	6,908.3	5.2	49.6	218.5	716.0	989.3	5,919.0
Philadelphia, Pa.-N.J.[3]	4,131.6	7.7	31.8	290.9	347.1	677.5	3,454.0
Phoenix-Mesa, Ariz.	6,283.3	9.7	28.8	182.8	353.6	574.9	5,708.4
Pittsburgh, Pa.	2,625.3	4.3	20.7	104.4	176.9	306.3	2,319.0
Portland, Oreg.	5,215.5	2.9	45.0	120.7	342.9	511.5	4,704.0
Providence, R.I.	3,619.0	3.6	37.7	82.1	174.2	297.6	3,321.5
Raleigh-Durham, N.C.	5,822.8	5.5	26.3	212.9	299.6	544.3	5,278.5
Riverside, Calif.	3,851.7	6.3	34.6	139.6	400.2	580.8	3,271.0
Rochester, N.Y.	3,705.4	3.5	20.0	103.2	126.9	253.6	3,451.8
Sacramento, Calif.	4,362.9	5.5	30.4	172.1	317.5	525.6	3,837.3
Salt Lake City-Ogden, Utah	5,614.7	2.9	40.3	71.8	223.8	338.8	5,275.9
San Antonio, Texas[3]	5,973.6	7.3	47.0	118.2	329.6	502.0	5,471.6
San Diego, Calif.	3,463.5	3.8	28.7	122.9	351.4	506.9	2,956.7
San Francisco, Calif.	4,086.8	4.9	22.8	240.8	277.8	546.3	3,540.5
San Jose, Calif.	2,887.1	2.2	29.7	67.2	345.8	444.9	2,442.3
Seattle-Bellevue, Everett, Wash.	5,746.6	4.0	44.1	134.6	211.1	393.8	5,352.8
Syracuse, N.Y.	3,234.8	1.6	19.4	90.1	220.7	331.9	2,902.9
Tampa-St. Petersburg, Fla.	6,347.1	5.2	50.8	237.1	634.6	927.7	5,419.4
Tucson, Ariz.	6,938.4	7.5	42.4	186.6	421.3	657.8	6,280.6
Tulsa, Okla.	5,031.5	7.4	42.1	127.9	539.0	716.4	4,315.1
West Palm Beach, Fla.	7,197.4	5.5	43.2	243.8	548.1	840.7	6,356.7

Note: 1. Violent crimes are offenses of murder, forcible rape, robbery, and aggravated assault. 2. Property crimes are offenses of burglary, larceny-theft, and motor vehicle theft. Data are not included for the property crime of arson. 3. Due to changes in reporting practices, annexations, and/or incomplete data, figures are not comparable to previous years' data. 4. Forcible rape figures furnished by the state Uniform Crime Reporting Program administered by the Minnesota Department of Public Safety are not comparable to previous years.
Source: Federal Bureau of Investigation, *Uniform Crime Reports: Crime in the United States 1999*. www.fbi.gov/ucr/99cius.htm

New Orleans, with 16.0 homicides per 100,000 residents, was the murder capital of the United States for the third straight year in 1999 (though down significantly from the 31.9 recorded in 1996). Richmond, Va. and Baltimore were second, with 14.5 per 100,000 residents, and Birmingham, Ala. and Detroit had 11.1 murders per 100,000 people. The rate in New York City was 7.9.

Violent crime in other nations   Although every recent official report and news story about crime has emphasized the continuing decline of serious crime, it is helpful to keep in mind that the U.S. remains far and away the most violent industrialized nation. Over the past 20 years, about 20,000 murders have been committed here each year (or 8 to 10 murders a year per 100,000 popula-

Crimes per 100,000 Population in Metropolitan Areas, 1993–99

Metropolitan area	All serious crimes[2]			Violent crimes[1]		
	1993	1998	1999	1993	1998	1999
Albuquerque	7,547.8	8,500.4	7,652.0	1,273.6	1,064.7	1,020.0
Atlanta	7,594.5	6,362.9	5,734.9	923.8	720.3	617.2
Austin	7,584.5	4,891.7	4,900.7	528.2	398.7	387.0
Baltimore	7,275.4	6,234.4	N.A.	1,356.1	1,064.9	N.A.
Bergen-Passaic, N.J.	N.A.	2,728.4	2,615.3	N.A.	260.2	249.5
Birmingham, Ala.	N.A.	4,326.3	3,990.8	N.A.	511.1	469.2
Boston	4,844.6	3,077.9	3,046.5	777.1	450.0	467.5
Charlotte	7,277.0	6,630.3	N.A.	1,204.5	946.7	N.A.
Columbus	6,012.8	6,320.0	6,115.5	682.2	495.4	488.6
Dallas	7,290.9	5,934.3	5,895.2	946.3	728.4	704.5
Denver	6,090.8	4,594.8	4,178.4	731.7	383.5	340.8
Detroit	N.A.	5,701.2	4,960.5	N.A.	850.7	762.2
El Paso	7,827.7	5,431.2	5,469.3	1,031.1	668.4	659.5
Fort Lauderdale	8,904.1	5,511.0	5,555.3	1,005.4	655.3	637.1
Fort Worth	6,880.9	5,240.8	5,240.6	824.6	519.5	500.7
Fresno	8,099.6	5,934.2	5,352.3	1,084.6	872.3	799.0
Greensboro, N.C.	N.A.	5,768.8	5,524.3	N.A.	575.8	577.2
Hartford, Conn.	N.A.	3,770.6	3,674.6	N.A.	325.5	316.8
Honolulu	6,442.9	5,424.8	4,925.0	285.6	267.7	253.6
Houston	N.A.	5,201.7	5,173.2	N.A.	749.1	751.9
Indianapolis	N.A.	4,685.4	4,010.7	N.A.	693.6	589.6
Jacksonville, Fla.	8,598.0	6,613.8	6,131.7	1,419.9	958.4	847.0
Los Angeles-Long Beach, Calif.	7,049.6	4,331.1	N.A.	1,682.5	1,017.0	N.A.
Miami, Fla.	13,500.4	9,831.8	8,744.7	2,136.2	1,281.0	1,251.4
Middlesex, N.J.	N.A	2,681.9	2,399.9	N.A	215.2	198.3
Minneapolis	N.A.	4,699.4	4,268.7	N.A.	400.4	364.2
Monmouth-Ocean, N.J.	N.A.	2,734.6	2,455.7	N.A.	210.5	198.3
Newark, N.J.	N.A.	4,243.8	3,931.9	N.A.	671.5	613.5
New Orleans	8,511.7	6,742.2	6,151.4	1,312.7	939.2	841.1
New York City	7,532.9	4,207.9	3,853.5	1,865.6	1,037.2	946.4
Norfolk, Va.	N.A.	4,912.8	N.A.	N.A.	461.1	N.A.
Oakland, Calif.	7,329.6	5,813.8	4,862.2	1,137.5	738.5	624.3
Oklahoma City	7,692.7	6,755.8	6,223.3	828.2	613.1	538.9
Orange County, Calif.	N.A.	3,049.5	2,767.5	N.A.	350.8	318.3
Philadelphia	4,355.3	N.A.	4,131.6	N.A.	N.A.	677.5
Phoenix	7,787.9	7,060.4	6,283.3	806.8	603.1	574.9
Pittsburgh	3,111.2	2,712.0	2,625.3	393.4	311.0	306.3
Portland, Oreg.	6,244.5	5,743.0	5,215.5	711.8	565.5	511.5
Providence, R.I.	N.A	3,562.1	3,619.0	N.A.	312.3	297.6
Raleigh, N.C.	N.A.	5,709.6	5,822.8	N.A.	560.9	544.3
Riverside, Calif.	N.A.	4,464.4	3,851.7	N.A.	647.7	580.8
Rochester, N.Y.	N.A.	3,902.2	3,705.4	N.A.	281.7	253.6
Sacramento	7,038.4	5,288.2	4,362.9	815.6	589.5	525.6
Salt Lake City	N.A.	6,170.0	5,614.7	N.A.	380.0	338.8
San Antonio	8,450.9	6,118.7	5,973.6	629.7	430.4	502.0
San Diego	6,160.5	3,951.2	3,463.5	873.8	602.0	506.9
San Francisco	6,697.5	4,503.6	4,086.8	1,088.1	630.1	546.3
San Jose, Calif.	4,640.3	3,400.1	2,887.1	524.7	491.9	444.9
Seattle	6,588.1	6,208.4	5,746.6	569.8	436.4	393.8
Syracuse, N.Y.	N.A.	3,577.3	3,234.8	N.A.	325.4	331.9
Tucson, Ariz.	9,219.9	7,566.1	6,938.4	754.2	745.8	657.8
Tulsa, Okla.	5,484.1	5,121.0	5,031.5	801.0	711.6	716.4
Washington, D.C.	5,462.4	4,516.6	N.A.	771.4	526.6	N.A.

1. Violent crimes are offenses of murder, forcible rape, robbery, and aggravated assault. 2. Property crimes are offenses of burglary, larceny-theft, and motor vehicle theft. Data are not included for the property crime of arson.
Source: Federal Bureau of Investigation, *Uniform Crime Reports: Crime in the United States 1999.* www.fbi.gov/ucr/99cius.htm

tion). By comparison, the murder rate is about 0.5 per 100,000 in Japan, 1.1 per 100,000 in France, and 3.4 per 100,000 in Germany.

In 1999, the Bureau of Justice Statistics released a detailed comparison of crime rates in the U.S and England. Although violent crime is increasing in England while it is decreasing in the U.S., the rates of murder, rape, and robbery are still significantly higher in this country than in the U.K. The U.S. murder rate is six times as high as England's, the number of rapes per 100,000 population is three times as high, and the robbery rate is 40 percent higher. It is interesting to note, however, that the rate of assault is 13 percent higher in England, while the rates for burglary and motor vehicle theft are about double U.S. rates.

Homicide, Guns, and Young People

Murders by youthful offenders have followed the same downward trend evidenced in the population at large, but still remain alarmingly high. The rate of homicides by 14-17-year-olds dropped from an all-time high of 24.4 per 100,000 in 1993 to about 9.2 murders per 100,000 population in 1998. But that's still almost double the rate in 1984, when the rate was 4.8 per 100,000. Similarly, the homicide rate for 18-24-year-olds was 31 per 100,000 in 1998, down from highs of more than 40 in 1991 and 1993, but still considerably higher than the 22 in 1985. Over the period 1976-98, the number of nongun homicides by offenders aged 14-24 has declined slightly, while the number of murders involving guns has more than doubled. By comparison, the number of gun homicides by offenders over the age of 25 has actually declined by more than 3,000 since 1976.

▶CRIME VICTIMS

Crime victimization statistics are a second measure of the so-called crime rate. Unlike reported crime statistics (above), which are based on reports to law enforcement authorities, crime victimization statistics are based on Bureau of Justice Statistics interviews with a sampling of people about their personal experience with crime. (The BJS does not ask about or keep statistics on homicides because it is impossible to question the victim).

In 1999, the rate of criminal victimization dropped to its lowest level since the BJS began keeping statistics in 1973. Violent crime was down 33 percent since 1992, while property crime declined 39 percent over the same period. Interestingly, preliminary BJS data shows a further 15 percent drop in violent crime in 2000, while advance data from the FBI Uniform Crime Report suggests that violent crime rates remained stable. More than one year's figures will be needed to determine whether crime continues to fall.

As the accompanying table shows, the victims of most kinds of crime are most likely to be black, young, poor, urban, and except for rape and domestic violence, male. People with family incomes of less than $7,500 were the most likely to be victimized by crime, especially violent crime. In general, the poorer a person is, the more likely he or she is to be the victim of a crime. And while senior citizens often feel most vulnerable to crime, it is teenagers who are most likely to be victimized by all kinds of crime. Children 12-19 years old are almost 20 times as likely to be the victims of violent crime as people over the age of 65.

Crime Rates in the U.S. and England, 1981-96

Year	Murder U.S.	England	Rape U.S.	England	Robbery U.S.	England	Assault U.S.	England	Burglary U.S.	England	Motor Vehicle Theft U.S.	England
1981	9.83	1.13	70.59	4.19	258.75	40.86	289.73	197.49	1,649.47	1,447.36	474.72	670.09
1985	7.95	1.24	72.83	7.19	208.54	54.94	302.94	237.62	1,287.30	1,733.71	461.97	734.98
1990	9.42	1.32	80.86	12.04	257.03	71.15	424.13	351.26	1,235.94	1,979.19	657.75	971.51
1995	8.22	1.44	72.73	18.90	220.95	131.31	418.33	392.63	987.61	2,391.90	560.48	981.18
1996	7.41	1.31	70.79	21.77	202.44	142.35	388.19	439.60	942.95	2,239.15	525.93	948.83

Note: Statistics for England include Wales. Rates are crimes per 100,000 residents.
Source: U.S. Bureau of Justice Statistics, *Crime and Justice in the U.S. and England and Wales, 1981-96.*

Criminal Victimization Rates, 1992-99

Crime	Victimizations ('000s) 1992	1998	1999	Victimization rate per 1,000 persons 1992	1998	1999
All crimes[1]	42,834	31,307	28,780	N.A.	N.A.	N.A.
Violent crimes[1]	10,249	8,116	7,357	49.0	36.6	32.8
Simple assault	6,053	5,224	4,660	28.9	23.5	20.8
Aggravated assault	2,317	1,674	1,503	11.1	7.5	6.7
Robbery	1,272	886	810	6.1	4.0	3.6
Rape/sexual assault	607	333	383	2.9	1.5	1.7
Personal theft[2]	369	296	208	1.8	1.3	0.9
Property crime	32,217	22,895	21,215	325.3	217.4	198.0
Property thefts	24,579	17,703	16,495	248.2	168.1	153.9
Household burglary	5,803	4,054	3,652	58.6	38.5	34.1
Motor vehicle theft	1,835	1,138	1,068	18.5	10.8	10.0

Note: Rates per 1,000 people ages 12 or older. 1. The National Crime Victimization Survey cannot measure murder because it is impossible to question the victim. 2. Includes pocket picking, purse snatching, and attempted purse snatching.
Source: Bureau of Justice Statistics Bulletin, *Criminal Victimization 1999*, www.ojp.usdoj.gov/bjs/abstract/cv99.htm

Rates of Violent Crime and Personal Theft, by Sex, Age, Race, Hispanic Origin, Income, Residence, Marital Status and Region, 1999

Characteristic	Total	Crimes of violence[1]			Theft
		Rape/Sexual assault	Robbery	Assault	
By sex					
Male	37.0	0.4	5.0	31.6	0.9
Female	28.8	3.0	2.3	23.6	0.9
By age					
12-15	74.4	4.0	6.7	63.7	3.1
16-19	77.4	6.9	8.2	62.3	1.5
20-24	68.5	4.3	7.7	56.4	1.0
25-34	36.3	1.7	4.1	30.5	1.2
35-49	25.2	0.8	2.8	21.6	0.4
50-64	14.4	0.2	1.9	12.3	0.6
65+	3.8	0.1	0.7	3.0	0.6
By race					
White	31.9	1.6	3.1	27.2	0.8
Black	41.6	2.6	7.7	31.3	1.3
Other	24.5	1.7	2.5	20.3	1.5
By Hispanic Origin					
Hispanic	33.8	1.9	5.6	26.3	1.5
Non-Hispanic	32.4	1.7	3.4	27.3	0.9
Family Income					
Less than $7,500	57.5	4.3	8.1	45.1	1.9
$7,500-$14,999	44.5	1.6	6.9	35.9	1.1
$15,000-$24,999	35.3	3.2	4.8	27.2	0.8
$25,000-$34,999	37.9	1.2	3.1	33.7	1.2
$35,000-$49,999	30.3	1.6	3.5	25.3	0.5
$50,000-$74,999	33.3	1.5	2.2	29.7	0.4
$75,000 or more	22.9	0.8	1.8	20.3	1.2
By Residence					
Urban	39.8	2.3	6.7	30.9	1.6
Suburban	32.8	1.6	2.8	28.4	0.9
Rural	24.9	1.3	1.7	22.0	0.2
By Marital Status					
Never married	60.6	3.9	7.2	49.5	1.6
Married	14.4	0.3	1.1	12.9	0.4
Divorced/separated	53.6	2.9	5.8	45.0	1.2
Widowed	6.0	0.0	1.9	4.1	1.0
By Region					
Northeast	29.6	1.5	3.6	24.5	1.0
Midwest	35.5	1.6	3.2	30.8	1.0
South	30.2	1.8	3.3	25.1	0.7
West	36.9	1.9	4.6	30.4	1.2

Note: Rates per 1,000 people ages 12 or older. 1. The National Crime Victimization Survey cannot measure murder because it is impossible to question the victim. **Source:** Bureau of Justice Statistics Bulletin, *Criminal Victimization 1999*, www.ojp.usdoj.gov/bjs/abstract/cv99.htm

▶ LAW ENFORCEMENT

As of October 1999, there were 637,551 sworn police officers in the United States (down from 641,208 the year before) and an additional 261,567 civilians employed in police departments. This translates into 2.5 full-time police officers for every 1,000 residents. Including full-time civilian employees, the ratio was 3.6 per 1,000. In cities with more than 250,000 residents, the ratio averaged 3.2 law enforcement employees per 1,000 residents. The ratio was 2.6 and 2.7 in rural and suburban counties.

Overall, civilians made up 29 percent of the law enforcement workforce in 1999. Suburban and rural police departments employed roughly two civilians for every three sworn officers, while big cities employed close to four officers for each civilian. Northeastern states have the greatest number of sworn officers (2.8 officers per 1,000 inhabitants); the West has the fewest (1.8). By sex, 89 percent of sworn officers nationally and in cities collectively is male, but civilian police employees are overwhelmingly female (64 percent on average).

Arrests Nationwide, law enforcement agencies made an estimated 14 million arrests in 1999 for all criminal infractions except traffic violations. This represents a rate of 5,317 arrests per 100,000 population. In cities with populations of 250,000 or more, the arrest rate was 6,401.7 per 100,000; it was 4,205 per 100,000 for suburban counties, and 4,308 per 100,000 for rural counties. The greatest number of arrests were for drug abuse and driving under the influence of drugs or alcohol (1.5 million each), simple assault (1.3 million) and larceny or theft (1.2 million).

By age, 6 percent of all people arrested nationwide in 1999 were under 15; 17 percent were under 18; 32 percent were under 21; and 45 percent were under 25. By sex, 78 percent of all those arrested were males. Females were most often arrested for larceny/theft. By race, 69 percent of all those arrested were white, 29 percent were black, and 2 percent were of other races.

Arrests in the U.S., 1984–99

Crime	1984	1989	Total Arrests 1995	1998	1999	Rate per 100,000
Violent crime	400,877	487,673	619,230	481,278	420,156	244.5
Murder	15,126	16,146	16,701	12,335	9,727	5.7
Forcible rape	28,565	27,461	26,561	21,922	18,759	10.9
Robbery	115,522	123,317	137,811	87,129	73,619	42.8
Aggravated assault	241,664	320,749	438,157	359,892	318,051	185.1
Property crime	1,431,812	1,600,947	1,620,704	1,292,825	1,091,917	635.5
Burglary	338,737	320,470	292,315	233,435	192,570	112.1
Larceny/theft	981,812	1,102,112	1,164,371	940,243	794,201	462.2
Motor vehicle theft	96,975	165,317	149,053	107,003	94,335	54.9
Arson	14,288	13,048	14,965	12,144	10,811	6.3
All serious crimes	1,832,689	2,088,620	2,239,934	1,774,103	1,512,073	880.0
Other crimes	6,995,758	7,902,737	9,167,354	8,517,214	7,624,221	N.A.
Total arrests	**8,828,447**	**9,991,357**	**11,407,288**	**10,291,317**	**9,136,294**	**5,317.0**

Note: Based on a survey of 8,546 law enforcement agencies representing approximately 171,831,000 inhabitants. The number of agencies surveyed and the populations they represent changes from year to year.
Source: Federal Bureau of Investigation, *Uniform Crime Reports: Crime in the United States 1999*, www.fbi.gov/ucr/99cius.htm

Arrests by Race, 1999

Offense charged	Total	White Number	Percent	Black Number	Percent	Other[1] Number	Percent
All arrests	9,100,050	6,283,294	69.0	2,600,510	28.6	216,246	2.3
Violent crime	**419,473**	**248,120**	**59.2**	**162,264**	**38.7**	**9,089**	**2.2**
Murder	9,716	4,460	45.9	5,029	51.8	227	2.4
Forcible rape	18,716	11,510	61.5	6,775	36.2	431	2.3
Robbery	73,542	32,257	43.9	40,040	54.4	1,245	1.7
Aggravated assault	317,499	199,893	63.0	110,420	34.8	7,186	2.2
Property crime	**1,089,567**	**715,705**	**65.7**	**342,451**	**31.4**	**31,411**	**2.9**
Burglary	192,246	131,832	68.6	56,119	29.2	4,295	2.2
Larceny/theft	792,386	524,128	66.1	244,085	30.8	24,173	3.0
Motor vehicle theft	94,161	51,176	54.9	39,694	42.2	2,741	2.9
Arson	10,774	8,019	74.4	2,553	23.7	202	1.9
All serious crimes	**1,509,040**	**963,825**	**63.9**	**504,715**	**33.4**	**40,500**	**2.7**

Note: Based on a survey of 8,545 law enforcement agencies representing 171,823,000 inhabitants. 1. Includes American Indian, Alaskan Native, Asian, and Pacific Islander.
Source: Federal Bureau of Investigation, *Uniform Crime Reports: Crime in the United States 1999*, www.fbi.gov/ucr/99cius.htm

Arrests and Convictions for Crimes Committed in the U.S., 1996

As the following table demonstrates, the number of police and the number of prisons have very little effect on the number of crimes committed because people who commit crimes have very little expectation of getting caught. Except for murder, most felonies rarely even result in an arrest, and result in a conviction even more infrequently. These statistics indicate neither a shortage of police nor leniency by judges, but simply the difficulty of solving a crime after it has been committed and proving who did it.

Offense	Number of crimes reported to police	Number of adults arrested	Arrests as percent of number of crimes	Number of felony convictions	Convictions as percent of number arrested	Convictions as percent of number of crimes
Murder[1]	19,650	16,161	82.2%	11,430	70.7%	58.1%
Robbery	537,050	106,178	19.8	42,831	40.3	8.0
Aggravated assault	1,029,810	445,005	43.2	69,522	15.6	6.7
Burglary	2,501,500	229,745	9.2	93,197	40.6	3.7
Motor vehicle theft	1,395,200	102,578	7.4	17,794	17.3	1.3
Drug trafficking	N.A.	322,393	N.A.	212,504	65.9	N.A.

1. Includes non-negligent manslaughter. **Source:** Bureau of Justice Statistics Bulletin, *Felony Sentences in State Courts, 1996*, January, 1999.

▶CORRECTIONS

The United States has more people in prison (as well as more people in prison per capita) than any other western industrialized nation. In 2000 the Bureau of Justice Statistics reported a record 1.38 million inmates in federal and state prisons. However, the state prison population seems to be levelling off: it rose only 1.3 percent during 2000, the smallest annual growth rate since 1979. In contrast, the federal prison population grew 11 percent in 2000, mainly due to mandatory drug sentences and the takeover of prisoners in the District of Columbia. Since 1980 the number of sentenced inmates per 100,000 residents has risen from 139 to 478.

During 2000, four states experienced double-digit growth in their prison populations. Idaho and North Dakota reported the largest increases (14.1 percent), followed by Mississippi (10.9 percent) and Vermont (10.5 percent). The states with the largest declines were the District of Columbia (down 13.8 percent), Massachusetts (down 5.6 percent) and New Jersey (down 5.4 percent).

The states with the highest incarceration rates (number of prisoners sentenced to more than one year per 100,000 residents) were all in the South. Louisiana led the way with 801 prisoners per 100,000 residents, followed by Texas (730), Mississippi (688), and Oklahoma (685). The lowest rates were found in four of the coldest states: Minnesota (128), Maine (129), North Dakota (158), and New Hampshire (185). The national average was 478, and the highest incarceration rate in the country was in the nation's capital, where 971 of every 100,000 residents were in prison.

Prison and race   Blacks have made up the majority of the increase in the prison population. Between 1990 (the last year in which white prisoners outnumbered blacks) and 2000, the number of blacks behind bars jumped from 360,000 to 610,300, an increase of 69 percent. Meanwhile, the white prison population grew 27 percent, from 370,900 in 1990 to 471,000 in 2000. Black males have the highest incarceration rates (3,457 per 100,000 residents in 2000) while white females have the lowest (34 per 100,000 residents). Put another way, about 3.5 percent of all black males are in prison. In the 25-29 age group, nearly 10 percent of black males are in prison.

Jails and prisons   Although the terms tend to be used synonymously, "jails" and "prisons" differ in the types of inmates they house, their locations, their physical size and their programs. Jails are locally administered facilities that house inmates after arraignment, prisoners serving terms of less than one year, and prisoners who cannot be housed in state prisons due to overcrowding.

Prisons are administered by either state or federal government authority. Typically they hold convicted offenders sentenced to terms of confinement for more than one year. They tend to be

Prisoners in the U.S. by System, Sex, and Race, 1980-2000

Year	By system			By sex and race[1]			
	Total	Federal	State	White male	Black male	White female	Black female
Number							
1980	329,821	24,363	305,458	159,500	140,600	5,900	6,300
1985	502,507	40,223	462,284	242,700	210,500	10,800	10,200
1990	773,919	65,526	708,393	350,700	340,300	20,200	19,700
1995	1,125,874	100,250	1,025,624	487,400	509,800	30,500	31,900
1997	1,242,153	112,973	1,129,180	541,700	548,900	36,300	35,500
1998	1,300,573	123,041	1,177,532	N.A.	N.A.	N.A.	N.A.
1999	1,366,721	135,246	1,228,455	403,700	558,700	27,100	38,300
2000	1,381,892	145,416	1,236,476	436,500	572,900	34,500	37,400
Rate (Prisoners per 100,000 resident population)							
1980	139	9	130	168	1,111	6	45
1985	201	14	187	246	1,559	10	68
1990	292	20	272	338	2,234	19	117
1995	411	32	379	449	3,095	27	176
1997	445	35	410	491	3,253	32	192
1998	461	38	423	N.A.	N.A.	N.A.	N.A.
1999	476	42	434	417	3,408	27	212
2000	477	45	432	449	3,457	34	205

Note: Prisoners sentenced to more than one year. N/A = not available. 1. Prisoners of other races not shown.
Source: Bureau of Justice Statistics Bulletin, *Prisoners in 2000* (2001).

Jail Population, 1985-2000

Age and sex	1985	1990	1995	1999	2000
Number of inmates at midyear	**256,615**	**405,320**	**507,044**	**605,943**	**621,149**
Adults	254,986	403,019	499,300	596,485	613,534
Male	235,909	365,821	448,000	528,998	543,120
Female	19,077	37,198	51,300	67,487	70,414
Juveniles	1,629	2,301	7,800	9,458	7,615
Held as adults	—	—	5,900	8,598	6,126
Held as juveniles	1,629	2,301	1,800	860	1,489
Average daily population	**265,010**	**408,075**	**509,828**	**607,978**	**618,319**

Note: As of June 30 of each year. The average daily population is the sum of the number of inmates in a jail each day for a year, divided by 365. Juveniles are persons defined by state statute as being under a certain age, usually 18, and subject initially to juvenile court authority even if tried as adults. In 1994, the definition was changed to include all persons under age 18.
Source: Bureau of Justice Statistics, *Prison and Jail Inmates at Midyear 2000* (2001), www.ojp.usdoj.gov/bjs/abstract/pjim00.htm

located away from dense population centers, and they are usually larger than jails and have more rehabilitation programs.

Costs of prisons
According to the Criminal Justice Institute, total U.S. expenditures for adult correctional facilities was $34.1 billion in 2000. In state prisons, the average cost per inmate was $57.92 per day in 2000.

Total U.S. prison capital costs increased from $538 million in 1980 to $2.8 billion in 2000. Operating costs surged from $3.1 billion in 1980. to $31.4 billion in 2000. In California, where over 20 new prisons were built during this period, expenditures on prisons rose from $336 million to $4 billion, with capital expenditures increasing by over 1,400 percent (in constant dollars). In Texas, capital expenditures rose over 1,500 percent.

Probation and Parole
When an offender is convicted, the primary sentencing alternatives are incarceration or probation. Once imprisoned,

Number of Prisoners and Incarceration Rates by State, 1999–2000

Region and jurisdiction	Total prisoners			Total sentenced to more than one year		Incarceration rate, 2000
	2000	1999	Percent change, 1999–2000	2000	1999	
U.S. total	1,381,892	1,363,701	1.3%	1,321,137	1,304,074	478
Federal	145,416	135,246	7.5	125,044	114,275	45
State	1,236,476	1,228,455	0.7	1,196,093	1,189,799	432
Alabama[1]	26,225	24,658	—	24,123	24,109	549
Alaska[2]	4,173	3,949	5.7	2,128	2,325	341
Arizona	26,510	25,986	2.0	25,412	23,944	515
Arkansas	11,915	11,415	4.4	11,851	11,336	458
California	163,001	163,067	0.0	160,412	160,517	474
Colorado	16,833	15,670	7.4	16,833	15,670	403
Connecticut[2]	18,355	18,639	-1.5	13,155	13,032	398
Delaware[2]	6,921	6,983	-0.9	3,937	3,730	513
District of Columbia[2]	7,456	8,652	-13.8	5,008	6,730	971
Florida	71,319	69,596	2.5	71,318	69,594	462
Georgia	44,232	42,091	5.1	44,141	42,008	550
Hawaii[2]	5,053	4,903	3.1	3,553	3,817	302
Idaho[4]	5,526	4,842	14.1	5,526	4,842	430
Illinois[3]	45,281	44,660	1.4	45,281	44,660	371
Indiana	20,125	19,309	4.2	20,081	19,016	335
Iowa[3]	7,955	7,232	10.0	7,955	7,232	276
Kansas[3]	8,344	8,567	-2.6	8,344	8,567	312
Kentucky	14,919	15,317	-2.6	14,919	15,317	373
Louisiana	35,047	34,066	2.9	35,047	34,066	801
Maine	1,679	1,716	-2.2	1,635	1,663	129
Maryland	23,538	23,095	1.9	22,490	22,184	429
Massachusetts	10,722	11,356	-5.6	9,479	10,282	252
Michigan	47,718	46,617	2.4	47,718	46,617	480
Minnesota	6,238	5,969	4.5	6,238	5,955	128
Mississippi	20,241	18,247	10.9	19,239	17,410	688
Missouri	27,323	26,155	4.5	27,299	26,133	494
Montana	3,105	2,951	5.2	3,105	2,951	348
Nebraska	3,895	3,688	5.6	3,816	3,632	228
Nevada	10,012	9,494	5.5	9,921	9,413	518
New Hampshire	2,257	2,257	0.0	2,257	2,257	185
New Jersey[3]	29,784	31,493	-5.4	29,784	31,493	362
New Mexico	5,342	5,124	4.3	4,887	4,730	279
New York[4]	70,198	72,899	-3.7	70,198	72,899	383
North Carolina	31,266	31,123	0.5	27,043	26,672	347
North Dakota	1,076	943	14.1	994	866	158
Ohio[3]	45,833	46,842	-2.2	45,833	46,842	406
Oklahoma[3]	23,181	22,393	3.5	23,181	22,393	685
Oregon	10,630	9,860	7.8	10,603	9,840	316
Pennsylvania	36,847	36,525	0.9	36,844	36,525	307
Rhode Island[2]	3,286	3,003	9.4	1,966	1,908	197
South Carolina	21,778	22,008	-1.0	21,017	21,228	532
South Dakota	2,616	2,506	4.4	2,613	2,498	353
Tennessee[3,4]	22,166	22,502	-1.5	22,166	22,502	399
Texas[4]	157,997	163,190	-3.2	150,107	154,865	730
Utah[4]	5,630	5,322	5.8	5,526	5,164	254
Vermont[2]	1,697	1,536	10.5	1,313	1,178	218
Virginia	30,168	29,789	1.3	29,643	29,088	422
Washington	14,915	14,590	2.2	14,666	14,558	251
West Virginia	3,856	3,532	9.2	3,795	3,532	211
Wisconsin	20,612	20,415	1.0	20,013	19,699	376
Wyoming	1,680	1,713	-1.9	1,680	1,713	349

Note: The incarceration rate is equal to the number of prisoners sentenced to more than 1 year per 100,000 residents. 1. Counts for 1999 were for fiscal year ending 9/30. 2. Includes jail population. 3. Includes some inmates sentenced to one year or less. 4. Reporting changed in 1999; percents calculated on counts adjusted for comparable reporting. **Source:** Bureau of Justice Statistics Bulletin, *Prisoners in 2000* (2001).

Lifetime Likelihood of Going to Prison by Age, Sex, Race, and Hispanic Origin

One of every 20 people in the U.S. (5.1 percent) will serve time in a prison during their lifetime, according to a March, 1997, BJS report, if 1991 incarceration rates do not change dramatically. Men (9.0 percent) are much more likely than women (1.1 percent) to be incarcerated in prison at least once during their life, and black men (28.5 percent) are six times as likely as white men (4.4 percent) to be imprisoned. Sixteen percent of Hispanic men are likely to be imprisoned.

Category	Percent expected to go to prison at some time, by age[1]						
	Birth	20	25	30	35	40	45
Total	5.1%	4.5%	3.1%	2.1%	1.4%	0.9%	0.6%
By Sex							
Male	9.0	7.9	5.5	3.7	2.5	1.6	1.0
Female	1.1	1.0	0.8	0.6	0.3	0.2	0.1
By Race/Hispanic origin							
White (non-Hispanic)	2.5%	2.3%	1.7%	1.2%	0.9%	0.6%	0.4%
Male	4.4	4.1	3.0	2.1	1.5	1.1	0.8
Female	0.5	0.5	0.4	0.3	0.2	0.1	0.1
Black (non-Hispanic)	16.2	14.1	9.6	6.0	3.6	2.0	1.2
Male	28.5	25.3	17.3	10.8	6.5	3.6	2.1
Female	3.6	3.5	2.8	1.9	1.1	0.6	0.4
Hispanic	9.4	8.7	6.4	4.9	3.8	2.3	1.6
Male	16.0	14.8	11.1	8.6	6.8	4.3	3.0
Female	1.5	1.5	1.2	0.9	0.6	0.4	0.2

1. Among those not previously incarcerated.
Source: Bureau of Justice Statistics *Lifetime Likelihood of Going to State or Federal Prison*, March, 1997.

the offender may become eligible for parole, a form of conditional release. The explosion in the prison population has understandably led to a corresponding increase in the number of prisoners released on probation or parole. At the end of 1999, according to the Bureau of Justice Statistics, a record 6.3 million people (3.1 percent of all U.S. adult residents) were under "correctional supervision" in the United States: in jail, in prison, on probation, or on parole. More than half this population (over 3.8 million) were on probation; another 725,500 were on parole.

▶ CAPITAL PUNISHMENT

The United States is the only Western industrialized nation that allows capital punishment. In the period 1930–99, 4,457 executions were carried out under state or federal authority. The majority of those (3,859) occurred in the years before the Supreme Court ruled capital punishment unconstitutional in 1972. The Court reinstated the death penalty in 1976; since then, an additional 598 executions have been carried out; all but three were males. Another 3,527 prisoners were on death row at the end of 1999 (all of whom had been convicted of murder). The 98 prisoners executed in 1999 had been on death row an average of 11 years and 11 months, up from an average of 6 years in 1984. Among all prisoners executed between 1977 and 1999, the average time between their most recent sentence and execution was almost 10 years (9.5 years for white prisoners, 10.5 for black prisoners).

A positive aspect of this long delay is that it allows some death row prisoners to prove their innocence before they face the death chamber. According to the Death Penalty Information Center in Washington, D.C., at least 96 prisoners were released from death row in 22 states since 1973 because they were improperly convicted or because evidence of their innocence was discovered after they were sentenced to death. Put another way, for every seven executions since 1976, one wrongly condemned inmate has been set free.

Prisoners Executed by Race, 1930–99

Year	Total	White	Black	Other
1930-39	1,667	827	816	24
1940-49	1,284	490	781	13
1950-59	717	336	376	5
1960-67	191	98	93	0
Total, 1930-67	**3,859**	**1,751**	**2,066**	**42**
1977-79	3	3	0	0
1980-89	117	68	49	0
1990	23	16	7	0
1995	56	33	22	1
1996	45	31	14	0
1997	74	45	27	2
1998	68	48	18	2
1999	98	61	33	4
Total, 1977-99	**598**	**374**	**213**	**11**
Total, 1930-99	**4,457**	**2,125**	**2,279**	**53**

Note: Executions under civil authority only. Does not include 160 executions carried out under military authority since 1930. There were no executions carried out between 1968 and 1977. **Source:** Bureau of Justice Statistics, *Sourcebook of Criminal Justice Statistics*, www.albany.edu/sourcebook/ and *Capital Punishment 1999* (2000), www.ojp.usdoj.gov/bjs/abstract/cp99.htm.

Seventeen states have carried out 100 or more executions since 1930; as of 1998, 12 states and the District of Columbia did not authorize the death penalty for any crime. In Maine, Minnesota, and Wisconsin, there has been no death penalty statute in force since 1930, and Alaska and Hawaii have never had death penalty statutes. The death penalty was either abolished or declared unconstitutional in Michigan (1963), Iowa and West Virginia (1965), the District of Columbia (1973), Rhode Island (1979), Oregon (1981), and Massachusetts (1984). Kansas abolished the death penalty in 1973, but restored it in July, 1994. New York abolished it in 1984, but restored it in 1995. And South Dakota abolished the death penalty in 1915, restored it in 1939, abolished it again 1977, and restored it again 1979.

Prisoners Executed by System, 1930–99

System	Number executed Since 1930	Since 1977	In 1999	On death row, 1999[1]	Method of execution	Minimum age authorized for execution
Alabama	154	19	2	180	Electrocution	16
Alaska	0	0	0	0	No death penalty statute	
Arizona	57	19	7	116	Gas; injection	none
Arkansas	139	21	4	40	Electrocution; injection	14
California[2]	299	7	2	553	Gas; injection	18
Colorado	48	1	0	4	Injection	18
Connecticut	21	0	0	6	Injection	18
Delaware	22	10	2	17	Injection; hanging	16
District of Columbia	40	0	0	0	No death penalty statute	
Federal system	33	0	0	19	Injection	18
Florida	214	44	1	365	Electrocution	16
Georgia	389	23	1	116	Electrocution	17
Hawaii	0	0	0	0	No death penalty statute	
Idaho[2]	4	1	0	21	Injection; firing squad	none
Illinois	102	12	1	156	Injection	18
Indiana	48	7	1	43	Injection	16
Iowa	18	0	0	0	No death penalty statute	
Kansas[3]	15	0	0	3	Injection	18
Kentucky[2]	105	2	1	39	Electrocution; injection	16
Louisiana[2]	158	25	1	85	Injection	none
Maine	0	0	0	0	No death penalty statute	
Maryland	71	3	1	17	Injection	18
Massachusetts	27	0	0	0	No death penalty statute	
Michigan	0	0	0	0	No death penalty statute	
Minnesota	0	0	0	0	No death penalty statute	
Mississippi[2]	158	4	0	60	Injection	16
Missouri[2]	103	41	9	83	Gas; injection	16
Montana[2]	8	2	1	6	Injection	none
Nebraska	7	3	0	9	Electrocution	18
Nevada	37	8	1	86	Injection	16
New Hampshire	1	0	0	0	Hanging; injection	17
New Jersey	74	0	0	14	Injection	18
New Mexico	8	0	0	4	Injection	18
New York[4]	329	0	0	5	Injection	18
North Carolina	278	15	4	202	Injection	17
North Dakota	0	0	0	0	No death penalty statute	
Ohio	173	1	1	199	Electrocution; injection	18
Oklahoma	79	19	6	139	Injection	16
Oregon	21	2	0	25	Injection	18
Pennsylvania	155	3	1	230	Injection	none
Rhode Island	0	0	0	0	No death penalty statute	
South Carolina	186	24	4	65	Electrocution; injection	none
South Dakota[2]	1	0	0	3	Injection	none
Tennessee	93	0	0	100	Electrocution; injection	18
Texas	496	199	35	460	Injection	17
Utah[2]	19	6	1	10	Firing squad; injection	none
Vermont	4	0	0	0	No death penalty statute	
Virginia	165	73	14	31	Electrocution; injection	14
Washington	50	3	1	13	Hanging; injection	18
West Virginia	40	0	0	0	No death penalty statute	
Wisconsin	0	0	0	0	No death penalty statute	
Wyoming	8	1	0	2	Gas; injection	14
Total U.S.	4,457	598	98	3,527		

Note: 1. As of December 31. 2. State authorizes capital punishment for selected crimes other than murder. 3. Death penalty restored in 1994; no executions yet carried out. 4. Death penalty restored in 1995; no executions yet carried out.
Source: Bureau of Justice Statistics Bulletin, *Capital Punishment 1999* (2000), www.ojp.usdoj.gov/bjs/ abstract/cp99.htm

Race and capital punishment Apart from the broad question of whether it is right for the state to take the life of an individual, the three major issues of concern to those opposed to capital punishment are whether it is a deterrent to crime, whether it violates the Eighth Amendment to the Constitution, prohibiting "cruel and unusual punishment" (the U.S. is the only industrialized democracy in the world that hasn't abolished it), and whether it is used fairly with respect to race.

Historically, blacks have been more likely to be executed than whites in proportion both to the general population and to the prison population. In the 1940s, for example, blacks made up less than 10 percent of the population, but more than 60 percent of prisoners executed were black. That's beginning to change, however. Since 1930, 51 percent of prisoners executed have been black, and since 1977, blacks constituted only 36 percent of executions (although they made up 48 percent of the prison population).

Economy and Business

THE U.S. ECONOMY

▶ **GROSS NATIONAL PRODUCT AND GROSS DOMESTIC PRODUCT**

The goal of an economic system is to transform resources into final products by business enterprises for consumption by society. This includes manufacturing goods such as cars, bread, furniture, and so on, and providing services such as health care, education, and motion pictures. The most commonly used measures associated with this goal are Gross National Product (G.N.P.) and Gross Domestic Product (G.D.P.). G.N.P. is the total national output of goods and services valued at market prices. G.N.P. in this broad context measures the output attributable to the factors of production—labor and property—supplied by a country's residents. G.N.P. differs from "national income" mainly in that G.N.P. includes allowances for depreciation and for indirect business taxes (sales and property taxes). G.D.P. is the measure of the output of production attributable to all factors of production (labor and property)

physically located within a country. G.D.P., therefore, excludes net property income from abroad (such as the earnings of U.S. nationals working overseas), which is included in the G.N.P.

The word *final* serves to exclude intermediate goods sold to producers and used to make finished products eventually sold to consumers in the market. Auto parts such as batteries and tires are examples of intermediate goods and are included in G.N.P. or G.D.P. only through the price of a car when it is sold. G.N.P. and G.D.P., in terms of expenditure categories, comprise purchases of goods and services by consumers and government, gross private domestic investment (or business purchases), and net exports.

The assessment of G.N.P. and G.D.P. in current dollars is referred to as a nominal measure. Nominal measures may be misleading because G.N.P. and G.D.P. can appear to rise as average prices rise with inflation. An alternative method is to evaluate G.N.P. and G.D.P. by measuring the value of goods and services using constant prices for a given year; the government currently uses 1996 as the base year. Assessments based on constant prices are referred to as real measures because they indicate the change in quantity of output produced by the economy.

G.D.P. in Current and Constant (1996) Dollars, 1960–2000 (billions)

Item	1960	1970	1980	1990	1995	1999	2000
CURRENT DOLLARS							
Gross domestic product (G.D.P.)	$527.4	$1,039.7	$2,795.6	$5,803.2	$7,400.5	$9,299.2	$9,963.1
Personal consumption expenditures	332.3	648.9	1,762.9	3,831.5	4,969.0	6,268.7	6,757.3
Durable goods	43.3	85.0	214.2	467.6	589.7	761.3	820.3
Nondurable goods	152.9	272.0	696.1	1,246.1	1,497.3	1,845.5	2,010.0
Services	136.1	292.0	852.7	2,117.8	2,882.0	3,661.9	3,927.0
Gross private domestic investment	78.9	152.4	477.9	861.7	1,143.8	1,650.1	1,832.7
Fixed investment	75.7	150.4	484.2	847.2	1,110.7	1,606.8	1,778.2
Change in private inventories	3.2	2.0	-6.3	14.5	33.0	43.3	54.5
Net exports of goods and services	2.4	1.2	-14.9	-71.4	-84.3	-254.0	-370.7
Exports	25.3	57.0	278.9	557.2	818.6	990.2	1,097.3
Imports	22.8	55.8	293.8	628.6	902.8	1,244.2	1,468.0
Government consumption	113.8	237.1	569.7	1,181.4	1,372.0	1,634.4	1,743.7
Federal	65.9	116.4	245.3	508.4	521.5	568.6	595.2
National defense	55.2	90.9	169.6	374.9	350.6	365.0	377.0
State and local	47.9	120.7	324.4	673.0	850.5	1,065.8	1,148.6
CONSTANT (1996) DOLLARS							
Gross domestic product (G.D.P.)	$2,376.7	$3,578.0	$4,900.9	6,707.9	$7,543.8	$8,875.8	$9,318.5
Personal consumption expenditures	1,510.8	2,317.5	3,193.0	4,474.5	5,075.6	5,978.8	6,294.3
Gross private domestic investment	272.8	436.2	655.3	907.3	1,140.6	1,669.7	1,839.8
Net exports of goods and services	—	—	—	-56.5	-78.4	-322.4	-412.4
Exports	87.5	159.3	334.8	575.7	808.2	1,033.0	1,126.3
Imports	108.0	223.1	324.8	632.2	886.6	1,355.3	1,538.7
Government consumption	661.3	931.1	1,020.9	1,387.3	1,406.4	1,536.1	1,579.2

Source: U.S. Bureau of Economic Analysis, *National Income and Product Accounts of the United States* (online edition: ww.bea.doc.gov).

▶DEFINITIONS OF OUTPUT, INCOME, AND EXPENDITURE TERMS

Capital consumption adjustment Used for corporations, nonfarm sole proprietorships, and partnerships, this is the difference between capital consumption claimed on income tax returns and capital consumption allowances measured at straight-line depreciation, consistent service lives, and replacement cost. The tax return data are valued at historical costs and reflect changes over time in service lives and depreciation patterns as permitted by tax regulations.

Consumer expenditure Consumer expenditure statistics presented in the accompanying tables are arrived at from the findings of the Consumer Expenditure Survey program, designed to provide a continuous flow of data on the buying habits of American consumers, necessary for future revisions of the Consumer Price Index. One group of 5,000 consumers in 85 urban areas around the country keeps diaries of expenditures on small, frequently purchased items, such as food and beverages, tobacco, housekeeping supplies, nonprescription drugs, and personal care products and services. Another 5,000 consumers are interviewed quarterly for information about large expenditures, such as those for property, automobiles and major appliances, or expenditures occurring on a fairly regular basis, such as rent, utilities, and insurance premiums.

Disposable personal income is that income after personal tax and nontax payments; this is the income available to persons for spending and saving. Personal tax and nontax payments are tax payments (except personal contributions for social insurance, net of refunds) by persons that are not chargeable to business expense, and also include certain personal payments to general government that are treated like taxes. Personal taxes include income, estate, gift, and personal property taxes and motor vehicle licenses. Nontax payments include passport fees, fines and penalties, donations, and tuitions and fees paid to schools and hospitals operated mainly by government.

Family income The term *family* refers to a group of two or more persons related by birth, marriage, or adoption who reside together; all such persons are considered as members of one family. Family income refers to the sum of all income of the family members.

Gross domestic product (G.D.P.) see "Gross National Product and Gross Domestic Product," above.

Gross Domestic Product (G.D.P.), by Industry, in Current and Constant (1996) Dollars, 1987-99 (billions)

Industry	Current dollars			Constant (1992) dollars		
	1987	1990	1999	1987	1990	1999
Gross Domestic Product (G.D.P.)	$4,742.5	$5,803.2	$9,299.2	$6,113.3	$6,707.9	$8,875.8
All Private industries	4,081.4	4,996.7	8,140.8	5,212.0	5,736.8	7,860.7
Agriculture, forestry, and fisheries	88.9	108.3	125.4	110.3	118.5	150.9
Farms	65.1	79.6	74.2	78.8	84.2	106.3
Agricultural services	23.8	28.7	51.2	31.8	34.6	44.4
Mining	92.2	111.9	111.8	98.5	105.8	121.9
Construction	219.3	248.7	416.4	278.4	290.7	361.1
Manufacturing	888.6	1,040.6	1,500.8	1,046.3	1,102.3	1,529.4
Durable goods	516.8	586.6	877.8	541.0	585.1	970.5
Nondurable goods	371.8	454.0	623.1	512.0	520.2	566.9
Transportation and public utilities	426.2	490.9	779.6	460.4	525.0	752.3
Transportation	158.8	177.4	303.4	162.4	180.6	272.4
Communications	125.5	148.1	260.2	132.6	155.2	264.6
Electric, gas, and sanitary services	141.9	165.4	216.0	165.8	190.0	216.3
Wholesale trade	308.9	376.1	643.3	353.5	395.1	709.3
Retail trade	434.5	507.8	856.4	512.1	559.5	847.3
Finance, insurance, and real estate	829.7	1,010.3	1,792.1	1,169.1	1,250.6	1,692.1
Depository institutions	143.9	171.3	305.3	220.6	244.0	255.0
Nondepository institutions	17.9	23.3	45.3	22.4	26.3	52.5
Security and commodity brokers	41.3	42.3	152.1	41.5	42.0	207.8
Insurance carriers	43.6	64.6	165.0	109.8	112.2	142.6
Insurance agents, brokers, and service	30.4	37.7	56.9	66.3	61.4	50.5
Real estate	531.4	665.7	1,034.0	685.6	763.4	973.5
Services	789.9	1,071.5	1,986.9	1,181.0	1,361.9	1,772.6
Hotels and other lodging places	37.1	46.3	83.5	52.1	55.2	67.3
Personal services	31.0	38.0	58.2	44.0	46.4	53.1
Business services	145.0	203.9	510.8	187.1	241.3	463.5
Auto repair, services, and parking	40.8	50.3	86.8	57.1	61.9	78.3
Motion pictures	13.7	17.7	29.8	19.1	21.2	27.2
Amusement and recreation services	26.2	36.5	78.7	37.1	45.0	70.7
Health services	230.6	314.4	514.2	392.3	423.2	463.5
Legal services	61.8	82.7	125.1	97.8	108.8	111.9
Educational services	31.3	39.6	71.1	47.7	50.3	61.2
Social services	21.0	30.1	61.3	31.4	38.0	53.0
Other services	103.3	149.2	272.8	153.0	191.3	241.9
Government	661.0	806.6	1,158.4	938.0	1,008.2	1,070.4
Federal	258.9	300.2	375.4	369.5	384.7	352.6
State and local	402.1	506.4	783.0	569.2	624.1	717.7

Source: U.S. Bureau of Economic Analysis, *National Income and Product Accounts of the United States* (online edition: ww.bea.doc.gov).

Gross national product (G.N.P.) see "Gross National Product and Gross Domestic Product," above.

Gross state product (GSP) is the gross market value of the goods and services attributable to labor and property located in a state. It is the state counterpart of the nation's G.D.P.

Household income A household includes related family members and all unrelated persons, if any—such as lodgers, foster children, wards, or employees—who share a house, an apartment, or a single room when it is occupied or intended for occupancy as separate living quarters by that household; that is, when the members of the household do not live and eat with any other persons in the structure and there is direct access from the outside or through a common hall. Household income, therefore, is the sum of all income of household members. The *householder* (which replaced the term *head of household* beginning with the 1980 Current Population Survey) is the person in whose name the home is owned or rented. In the case of joint ownership, one person in each household is designated as the householder for statistical purposes.

Inventory valuation adjustment This represents the difference between the book value of inventories used in production and the cost of replacing them.

Mean vs. median income Mean (or average) income refers to the sum of all incomes of a group divided by the number of incomes in that group. Median income is the middle income when they are arranged in order of size—that is, there are the same number of incomes above and below the median. For example, consider incomes of $2,000, $3,000, $4,000, $15,000 and $95,000: the mean income is the sum of these divided by five, or $23,800; the median income is $4,000.

Money income This refers to income received (exclusive of certain money receipts such as capital gains) before payments for such things as personal income taxes, Social Security, union dues, and Medicare deductions. Money income

National Income, by Type of Income, 1960-2000 (billions of current dollars)

Type of Income	1960	1970	1980	1990	1995	1999	2000
National income	$427.5	$837.5	$2,243.0	$4,642.1	$5,876.7	$7,469.7	$8,002.0
Compensation of employees	296.4	617.2	1,651.7	3,351.0	4,202.5	5,299.8	5,638.2
Wages and salaries	272.8	551.5	1,377.4	2,754.6	3,441.1	4,475.1	4,769.4
Government	49.2	117.1	261.2	516.8	622.7	724.4	760.9
Other	223.7	434.3	1,116.2	2,237.9	2,818.4	3,750.7	4,008.5
Supplements to wages, salaries	23.6	65.7	274.3	596.4	761.4	824.6	868.8
Employer contributions for social insurance	9.3	23.8	88.9	206.5	264.5	323.6	344.8
Other labor income	14.4	41.9	185.4	390.0	497.0	501.0	524.0
Proprietors' income[1,2]	51.9	79.8	177.6	381.0	497.7	663.5	710.4
Farm	11.4	14.3	13.1	31.1	22.2	25.3	22.6
Nonfarm	40.4	65.5	164.5	349.9	475.5	638.2	687.8
Rental income of persons[1]	16.2	20.3	31.3	49.1	117.9	143.4	140.0
Corporate profits[1,2]	52.3	81.6	198.5	408.6	668.8	856.0	946.2
Corporate profits[2]	51.4	74.0	209.3	388.6	650.2	813.9	912.7
Profits before tax	51.5	80.6	251.4	401.5	668.5	823.0	925.6
Profits tax liability	22.7	34.4	84.8	140.6	211.0	255.9	284.2
Profits after tax	28.8	46.2	166.6	260.9	457.5	567.1	641.4
Dividends	13.4	24.3	64.1	165.6	254.2	370.7	397.0
Undistributed profits	15.5	21.9	102.6	95.3	203.3	196.4	244.4
Inventory valuation adjustment	-.2	-6.6	-42.1	-12.9	-18.3	-9.1	-12.9
Capital consumption adjustment	1.0	7.6	-10.8	19.9	18.6	42.1	33.5
Net interest	10.7	38.4	183.9	452.4	389.8	507.1	567.2

1. With capital consumption adjustment. 2. With inventory valuation adjustment.
Source: U.S. Bureau of Economic Analysis, *National Income and Product Accounts of the United States* (online edition: ww.bea.doc.gov).

Percent Distribution of National Income, by Type, 1960-2000

Type of income	1960	1970	1980	1990	1995	1999	2000
National income, total	100.0%	100.0%	100.0%	100.0%	100.0%	100.0%	100.0%
Compensation of employees	69.3	73.7	73.6	72.2	71.5	71.5	70.5
Wages and salaries	63.8	65.8	61.4	59.3	58.6	58.6	59.6
Supplements to wages, salaries	5.5	7.8	12.2	12.8	13.0	13.0	10.9
Proprietors' income[1]	12.1	9.5	7.9	8.2	8.5	8.5	8.9
Farm	2.7	1.7	0.6	0.7	0.4	0.4	0.3
Non-farm	9.4	7.8	7.3	7.5	8.1	8.1	8.6
Rental income of persons[2]	3.8	2.4	1.4	1.1	2.0	2.0	1.8
Corporate profits[1]	12.2	9.7	8.8	8.8	11.4	11.4	11.8
Profits before tax	12.0	9.6	11.2	8.6	11.4	11.4	11.6
Profits after tax	6.7	5.5	7.4	5.6	7.8	7.8	8.0
Net interest	2.5	4.6	8.2	9.8	6.6	6.6	7.1

1. With inventory valuation and capital consumption adjustments (not shown separately). 2. With capital consumption adjustment (not shown separately). **Source:** U.S. Bureau of the Census, based on data from U.S. Bureau of Economic Analysis, *National Income and Product Accounts of the United States* (online edition: ww.bea.doc.gov).

does not include income in the form of noncash benefits such as food stamps, health benefits, and subsidized housing; rent-free housing and goods produced and consumed on farms; or the use of business transportation and facilities, full or partial payments by business for retirement programs, medical and educational expenses, and so on. These elements should be considered when comparing income levels. None of the aggregate income concepts (G.N.P., national income, or personal income) is exactly comparable with money income, although personal income is the closest.

National income, the aggregate of labor and property earnings derived from the current production of goods and services, is the sum of employee compensation, proprietors' income, rental income, corporate profits, and net interest. It measures the total factor costs of the goods and services produced by the economy. Income is measured before deduction of taxes.

Personal income is the current income received by persons from all sources minus their personal contributions for social insurance. *Persons* include individuals (including owners of unincorporated

Per Capita Personal Income by State, 1970–2000

State	Personal income (rank)				
	1970	1980	1990	1999[1]	2000[1]
Alabama	$2,960 (49)	$7,720 (48)	$15,225 (43)	$22,946 (44)	$23,471 (45)
Alaska	5,071 (2)	13,863 (1)	21,047 (10)	28,523 (18)	30,064 (16)
Arizona	3,810 (27)	9,328 (31)	16,542 (36)	25,307 (36)	25,578 (38)
Arkansas	2,841 (50)	7,457 (50)	14,032 (50)	22,114 (48)	22,257 (48)
California	4,777 (8)	11,792 (4)	21,821 (9)	29,819 (14)	32,275 (9)
Colorado	4,058 (17)	10,710 (14)	19,224 (19)	31,678 (7)	32,949 (8)
Connecticut	5,077 (1)	12,246 (3)	26,375 (1)	39,167 (1)	40,640 (1)
Delaware	4,611 (9)	10,614 (15)	21,696 (7)	30,685 (10)	31,255 (13)
District of Columbia	5,013 (3)	12,487 (2)	25,628 (2)	38,228 (2)	37,383 (3)
Florida	3,980 (20)	9,894 (22)	19,106 (20)	28,023 (19)	28,145 (24)
Georgia	3,395 (38)	8,395 (38)	17,378 (29)	27,198 (24)	27,940 (25)
Hawaii	4,995 (4)	10,860 (11)	21,333 (8)	27,842 (21)	28,221 (23)
Idaho	3,503 (35)	8,569 (37)	15,317 (42)	23,445 (41)	24,180 (42)
Illinois	4,587 (10)	10,986 (9)	20,494 (12)	31,278 (8)	32,259 (10)
Indiana	3,789 (30)	9,307 (32)	17,174 (31)	26,092 (31)	27,011 (32)
Iowa	3,839 (25)	9,505 (28)	16,959 (34)	25,727 (34)	26,723 (34)
Kansas	3,794 (29)	9,877 (23)	17,988 (23)	26,633 (27)	27,816 (28)
Kentucky	3,150 (44)	8,079 (42)	15,088 (44)	23,161 (43)	24,294 (41)
Louisiana	3,090 (47)	8,761 (35)	14,761 (46)	22,792 (46)	23,334 (46)
Maine	3,409 (37)	8,259 (39)	17,167 (32)	24,960 (38)	25,623 (37)
Maryland	4,519 (12)	10,889 (10)	22,483 (6)	32,166 (6)	33,872 (6)
Massachusetts	4,547 (11)	10,745 (13)	23,203 (4)	35,733 (4)	37,992 (2)
Michigan	4,145 (14)	10,273 (16)	18,710 (21)	27,844 (20)	29,612 (18)
Minnesota	4,012 (19)	10,149 (17)	19,374 (17)	30,622 (11)	32,101 (11)
Mississippi	2,608 (51)	6,915 (51)	12,710 (51)	20,506 (51)	20,993 (51)
Missouri	3,825 (26)	9,341 (30)	17,656 (26)	26,187 (30)	27,445 (29)
Montana	3,554 (34)	8,825 (34)	15,042 (45)	22,314 (47)	22,569 (47)
Nebraska	3,799 (28)	9,096 (33)	17,624 (27)	27,437 (22)	27,829 (27)
Nevada	4,889 (5)	11,577 (6)	20,124 (13)	30,351 (12)	30,529 (15)
New Hampshire	3,910 (23)	9,854 (26)	20,671 (11)	30,905 (9)	33,332 (7)
New Jersey	4,835 (7)	11,703 (5)	24,925 (3)	36,106 (3)	36,983 (4)
New Mexico	3,163 (43)	8,222 (40)	14,441 (47)	22,063 (49)	22,203 (49)
New York	4,866 (6)	11,003 (8)	23,132 (5)	33,946 (5)	34,547 (5)
North Carolina	3,255 (40)	8,067 (43)	16,664 (35)	26,220 (29)	27,194 (31)
North Dakota	3,145 (45)	7,825 (47)	15,324 (41)	23,518 (39)	25,068 (39)
Ohio	4,052 (18)	9,872 (25)	18,125 (22)	27,081 (26)	28,400 (20)
Oklahoma	3,456 (36)	9,444 (29)	15,584 (38)	22,801 (45)	23,517 (44)
Oregon	3,913 (21)	9,938 (19)	17,437 (28)	27,135 (25)	28,350 (21)
Pennsylvania	4,061 (16)	9,989 (18)	19,365 (18)	28,676 (17)	29,539 (19)
Rhode Island	4,086 (15)	9,646 (27)	19,691 (15)	29,720 (15)	29,685 (17)
South Carolina	3,027 (48)	7,624 (49)	15,421 (40)	23,496 (40)	24,321 (40)
South Dakota	3,215 (41)	7,866 (46)	15,538 (39)	25,107 (37)	26,115 (36)
Tennessee	3,168 (42)	8,123 (41)	16,295 (37)	25,581 (35)	26,239 (35)
Texas	3,651 (32)	9,922 (20)	17,219 (30)	26,525 (28)	27,871 (26)
Utah	3,324 (39)	8,003 (45)	14,204 (48)	23,356 (42)	23,907 (43)
Vermont	3,616 (33)	8,583 (36)	17,691 (25)	25,892 (33)	26,901 (33)
Virginia	3,771 (31)	9,918 (21)	19,996 (14)	29,484 (16)	31,162 (14)
Washington	4,188 (13)	10,755 (12)	19,583 (16)	30,295 (13)	31,528 (12)
West Virginia	3,098 (46)	8,041 (44)	14,177 (49)	20,888 (50)	21,915 (50)
Wisconsin	3,912 (22)	9,874 (24)	17,720 (24)	27,412 (23)	28,232 (22)
Wyoming	3,841 (24)	11,414 (7)	17,061 (33)	26,003 (32)	27,230 (30)
U.S. average	**$4,072**	**$10,029**	**$19,142**	**$28,518**	**$29,676**

1. Preliminary, subject to review when numbers from the 2000 Census become available..
Source: Bureau of Economic Analysis, Survey of Current Business, (monthly). www.bea.doc.gov.

firms), nonprofit institutions serving individuals, private trust funds, and private noninsured welfare funds. Personal income includes transfers (payments not resulting from current production) from government and business, such as Social Security benefits and public assistance, but excludes transfers among persons. Also included are certain nonmonetary types of income: estimated net rental value to owner-occupants of their homes, the value of services furnished without payment by financial intermediaries, and food and fuel produced and consumed on farms.

Poverty level is an estimate of the income necessary to purchase what society defines as a mini-

Per Capita Personal Income by Metropolitan Area, 1970–99

Metropolitan Statistical Area (ranked by 1998 income)	1970	1980	1990	1995	1999
United States	**$4,095**	**$10,183**	**$19,584**	**$23,562**	**$28,546**
Metropolitan portion	4,347	10,785	20,800	24,966	30,317
Nonmetropolitan portion	3,158	7,997	14,771	17,961	21,372
Highest per capita income, 1999					
1. San Francisco, Calif.[1]	6,206	15,833	31,516	37,593	$49,695
2. San Jose, Calif.[1]	4,983	13,614	26,186	32,768	46,649
3. New Haven-Bridgeport-Stamford-Danbury-Waterbury, Conn.[1]	5,442	13,252	29,149	35,911	45,267
4. Naples, Fla.	5,368	12,435	27,934	36,632	44,862
5. West Palm Beach-Boca Raton, Fla.	4,900	13,144	30,201	36,065	41,907
6. Bergen-Passaic, N.J.[1]	5,483	13,295	28,401	33,281	40,623
7. Middlesex-Somerset-Hunterdon, N.J.[1]	4,910	12,767	26,946	32,381	39,969
8. Seattle-Bellevue-Everett, Wash.[1]	4,686	12,686	24,036	29,299	39,880
9. Trenton, N.J.[1]	4,858	12,136	26,373	31,685	39,626
10. New York, N.Y.[1]	5,391	11,842	25,836	31,220	38,814
11. Nassau-Suffolk, N.Y.[1]	5,305	12,938	27,796	32,227	38,751
12. Newark, N.J. [1]	5,140	12,145	26,267	31,552	38,715
13. Washington, D.C.-Md.-Va.-W.Va.[1]	5,175	12,884	26,809	31,798	38,403
14. Boulder-Longmont, Colo.[1]	4,284	11,603	22,213	29,243	37,523
15. Boston-Worcester-Lawrence-Lowell-Brockton, Mass.-N.H.	4,515	10,806	23,559	28,520	36,285
16. Denver, Colo.[1]	4,561	12,110	22,053	28,087	36,058
17. Sarasota-Bradenton, Fla.	4,428	11,737	24,750	29,690	35,679
18. Oakland, Calif.[1]	4,985	12,783	24,451	28,842	35,666
19. Reno, Nev.	5,327	13,418	23,623	29,301	35,343
20. Minneapolis-St. Paul, Minn.-Wisc.	4,666	11,840	22,868	28,241	35,250
21. Hartford, Conn.	4,924	12,033	25,378	28,936	35,109
22. Chicago, Ill.[1]	5,000	12,053	23,002	28,525	34,743
23. Dallas, Texas[1]	4,403	11,727	21,710	27,040	34,690
24. Barnstable-Yarmouth, Mass.	4,636	11,025	23,436	27,712	34,470
25. Anchorage, Alaska	6,102	16,154	26,235	29,533	33,813
Lowest per capita income, 1999					
1. McAllen-Edinburg-Mission, Texas	$1,952	$5,365	$9,335	$11,334	$13,339
2. Brownsville-Harlingen-San Benito, Texas	2,178	5,765	9,947	12,294	14,112
3. Laredo, Texas	2,267	5,483	9,437	12,130	14,280
4. Las Cruces, N.Mex.	2,985	6,906	12,667	15,153	17,003
5. El Paso, Texas	2,990	6,556	12,391	14,687	17,216
6. Sumter, S.C.	2,638	6,476	13,152	15,484	18,238
7. Merced, Calif.	3,806	9,522	15,166	15,593	18,367
8. Yuma, Ariz.	3,432	8,227	13,497	17,995	18,452
9. Provo-Orem, Utah	2,714	6,606	12,043	15,664	18,793
10. Visalia-Tulare-Porterville, Calif.	3,623	9,424	14,849	16,586	19,329
11. Auburn-Opelika, Ala.	2,685	7,408	14,247	17,560	19,696
12. Bakersfield, Calif.	3,933	11,080	16,576	17,924	19,886
13. Goldsboro, N.C.	3,071	7,158	14,202	17,606	20,050
14. Pine Bluff, Ark.	2,826	7,712	14,051	17,178	20,141
15. Pocatello, Idaho	3,326	8,723	14,165	17,445	20,252
16. Hattiesburg, Miss.	2,796	7,279	13,500	17,065	20,256
17. Anniston, Ala.	2,808	7,650	14,871	18,130	20,492
18. Gadsden, Ala.	2,934	8,015	14,655	18,236	20,518
19. Huntington-Ashland, W.Va.-Ky.-Ohio	3,158	8,313	14,752	17,652	20,533
20. Houma, La.	2,866	9,441	13,156	16,688	20,547
21. Cumberland, Md.-W.Va.	3,306	8,159	14,688	17,236	20,700
22. Fresno, Calif.	3,906	10,807	16,709	18,523	20,776
23. Yakima, Wash.	3,439	8,993	15,657	18,362	20,811
24. Danville, Va.	2,942	8,013	14,709	17,721	20,833
25. Jamestown, N.Y.	3,666	8,545	15,200	18,087	20,877

Note: in current dollars. 1. Primary Metropolitan Statistical Area.
Source: U.S. Bureau of Economic Analysis, Survey of Current Business, online edition. www.bea.doc.gov.

mally acceptable standard of living. Families and unrelated individuals are classified as being above or below the poverty level according to their money income as a group and the number of people in the group (e.g. in 1990; a family of four with total money income below $13,359 lived below the poverty level). Classification is based on the poverty index originated by the Social Security Administration in 1964 and revised in 1969 and 1980. The poverty index is based solely on money income and does not reflect the fact that many low-income persons receive non-cash benefits such as

Per Capita Money Income, by Race and Hispanic Origin, 1970-99

Year	Current dollars				Constant (1999) dollars			
	All races	White	Black	Hispanic[1]	All races	White	Black	Hispanic[1]
1970	$3,177	$3,354	$1,869	N.A.	$12,816	$13,530	$ 7,539	N.A.
1975	4,818	5,072	2,972	$2,847	14,283	15,036	8,810	$ 8,440
1980	7,787	8,233	4,804	4,865	15,763	16,666	9,725	9,848
1985	11,013	11,671	6,840	6,613	17,052	18,071	10,591	10,239
1990	14,387	15,265	9,017	8,424	18,339	19,458	11,494	10,738
1995	17,227	18,304	10,982	9,300	18,832	20,009	12,005	10,167
1996	18,136	19,181	11,899	10,048	19,257	20,367	12,635	10,669
1997	19,241	20,425	12,351	10,773	19,972	21,201	12,820	11,182
1998	20,120	21,394	12,957	11,434	20,564	21,867	13,243	11,687
1999	21,181	22,375	14,397	11,621	21,181	22,375	14,397	11,621

Note: N.A. = Not available. 1. Hispanic persons may be of any race.
Source: U.S. Bureau of the Census, Current Population Survey. www.census.gov/hhes/income/histinc.

Median Income of Families by Race and Hispanic Origin, 1999

Characteristic	Number of families ('000s)				Median family income			
	All races[1]	White	Black	Hispanic[2]	All races[1]	White	Black	Hispanic[2]
All families	72,031	60,256	8,664	7,561	$48,950	$51,224	$31,778	$31,663
Type of family								
Married-couple families	55,315	48,794	4,144	5,133	56,676	57,089	50,656	37,132
Wife in paid labor force	34,265	29,852	2,936	2,848	66,529	67,208	59,111	47,652
Wife not in paid labor force	21,050	18,942	1,208	2,285	38,626	39,023	29,629	26,256
Male Householder[3]	4,028	3,082	706	658	37,396	39,240	33,796	30,425
Female Householder[3]	12,687	8,380	3,814	1,769	23,732	26,529	18,244	18,701
Number of earners								
No earners	9,321	7,912	1,144	711	21,789	23,813	10,326	10,863
One earner	21,333	16,894	3,437	2,629	32,383	35,696	20,913	20,840
Two earners	32,235	27,653	3,240	2,998	60,802	61,878	60,439	40,249
Three earners	6,766	5,756	670	822	74,899	75,073	68,169	53,054
Four or more earners	2,376	2,041	173	401	91,186	91,667	77,274	72,998

Note: 1. Includes other races not shown separately. 2. Hispanic persons may be of any race. 3. Spouse absent.
Source: U.S. Bureau of the Census, Current Population Reports: Money Income in the United States, 1999. www.census.gov

Persons Below Poverty Level, by Race, 1960-2000

Year	Number below poverty level (millions)					Percent below poverty level				
	All races[1]	White	Black	Hispanic[2]	Asian	All races[1]	White	Black	Hispanic[2]	Asian
1960	39.9	28.3	N.A.	N.A.	N.A.	22.2%	17.8%	N.A.	N.A.	N.A.
1970	25.4	17.5	7.5	N.A.	N.A.	12.6	9.9	33.5%	N.A.	N.A.
1980	29.3	19.7	8.6	3.5	N.A.	13.0	10.2	32.5	25.7%	N.A.
1990	33.6	22.3	9.8	6.0	0.9	13.5	10.7	31.9	28.1	12.2%
1995	36.4	24.4	9.9	8.6	1.4	13.8	11.2	29.3	30.3	14.6
1996	36.5	24.6	9.7	8.7	1.5	13.7	11.2	28.4	29.4	14.5
1997	35.6	24.4	9.1	8.3	1.4	13.3	11.0	26.5	27.1	14.0
1998	34.5	23.5	9.1	8.1	1.3	12.7	10.5	26.1	25.6	12.5
1999	32.3	21.9	8.4	7.4	1.2	11.8	9.8	23.6	22.8	10.7
2000	31.1	21.3	7.9	7.2	1.2	11.3	9.4	22.1	21.2	10.8

1. Includes other races not shown separately. 2. People of Hispanic origin may be of any race.
Source: U.S. Bureau of the Census, Poverty in The United States, 2000 (2001).

Per Capita Personal Income by County, 1999

Rank/County	Per capita income 1999	Percent of national average
Highest per capita income		
1. New York, New York	$81,665	286.1%
2. Pitkin, Colorado	65,573	229.7
3. Teton, Wyoming	59,632	208.9
4. Marin, California	57,982	203.1
5. Fairfield, Connecticut	56,643	198.4
6. Somerset, New Jersey	52,078	182.4
7. Westchester, New York	51,033	178.8
8. Arlington, Virginia	50,118	175.6
9. Morris, New Jersey	49,957	175.0
10. Alexandria City, Virginia	49,609	173.8
11. San Francisco, California	49,464	173.3
12. Bergen, New Jersey	48,017	168.2
13. Fairfax-Fairfax City- Falls Church, Virginia	47,241	165.5
14. San Mateo, California	47,146	165.2
15. Santa Clara, California	46,649	163.4
16. Nantucket, Massachusetts	46,354	162.4
17. Sherman, Texas	46,027	161.2
18. Montgomery, Maryland	45,595	159.7
19. Fulton, Georgia	45,473	159.3
20. Lake, Illinois	45,341	158.8
21. Collier, Florida	44,862	157.2
22. Hunterdon, New Jersey	44,833	157.1
23. DuPage, Illinois	44,793	156.9
24. King, Washington	44,719	156.7
25. Montgomery, Pennsylvania	44,446	155.7
Lowest per capita income		
1. Loup, Nebraska	$ 4,896	17.2
2. McPherson, Nebraska	6,940	24.3
3. Starr, Texas	8,588	30.1
4. Edwards, Texas	8,996	31.5
5. Keya Paha, Nebraska	9,993	35.0
6. Ziebach, South Dakota	10,390	36.4
7. Arthur, Nebraska	10,655	37.3
8. Presidio, Texas	10,739	37.6
9. Maverick, Texas	10,826	37.9
10. Todd, South Dakota	10,920	38.3
11. Sioux, North Dakota	11,023	38.6
12. Sioux, Nebraska	11,147	39.0
13. Shannon, South Dakota	11,280	39.5
14. Zavala, Texas	11,351	39.8
15. Gilliam, Oregon	11,518	40.3
16. Blaine, Nebraska	11,576	40.6
17. Jefferson, Mississippi	11,892	41.7
18. Sherman, Oregon	12,035	42.2
19. Slope, North Dakota	12,097	42.4
20. Elliott, Kentucky	12,279	43.0
21. Zapata, Texas	12,494	43.8
22. Lake, Tennessee	12,556	44.0
23. Willacy, Texas	12,746	44.7
24. Union, Florida	12,751	44.7
25. Mora, New Mexico	12,763	44.7

Source: U.S. Bureau of Economic Analysis, *Survey of Current Business* (online edition: www.bea.doc.gov).

Percent of Persons Below Poverty Level, by State, 1980–2000

State	1980	1990	2000
United States	**13.0%**	**13.5%**	**11.3%**
Alabama	21.2	19.2	14.1
Alaska	9.6	11.4	8.0
Arizona	12.8	13.7	12.1
Arkansas	21.5	19.6	18.0
California	11.0	13.9	12.9
Colorado	8.6	13.7	7.9
Connecticut	8.3	6.0	6.3
Delaware	11.8	6.9	8.7
District of Columbia	20.9	21.1	14.8
Florida	16.7	14.4	10.7
Georgia	13.9	15.8	11.3
Hawaii	8.5	11.0	9.7
Idaho	14.7	14.9	13.0
Illinois	12.3	13.7	11.6
Indiana	11.8	13.0	8.4
Iowa	10.8	10.4	7.1
Kansas	9.4	10.3	9.5
Kentucky	19.3	17.3	11.8
Louisiana	20.3	23.6	17.4
Maine	14.6	13.1	8.3
Maryland	9.5	9.9	7.6
Massachusetts	9.5	10.7	10.1
Michigan	12.9	14.3	10.1
Minnesota	8.7	12.0	5.9
Mississippi	24.3	25.7	12.9
Missouri	13.0	13.4	7.8
Montana	13.2	16.3	15.9
Nebraska	13.0	10.3	8.8
Nevada	8.3	9.8	8.2
New Hampshire	7.0	6.3	4.8
New Jersey	9.0	9.2	8.1
New Mexico	20.6	20.9	16.8
New York	13.8	14.3	13.4
North Carolina	15.0	13.0	12.2
North Dakota	15.5	13.7	10.0
Ohio	9.8	11.5	10.2
Oklahoma	13.9	15.6	15.4
Oregon	11.5	9.2	10.7
Pennsylvania	9.8	11.0	8.9
Rhode Island	10.7	7.5	8.6
South Carolina	16.8	16.2	10.4
South Dakota	18.8	13.3	9.5
Tennessee	19.6	16.9	14.6
Texas	15.7	15.9	14.7
Utah	10.0	8.2	9.6
Vermont	12.0	10.9	10.6
Virginia	12.4	11.1	7.6
Washington	12.7	8.9	9.7
West Virginia	15.2	18.1	13.9
Wisconsin	8.5	9.3	9.2
Wyoming	10.4	11.0	10.9

Source: U.S. Bureau of the Census, *Poverty In The United States, 2000* (2001).

food stamps, Medicaid, and public housing. The poverty thresholds are updated every year to reflect changes in the Consumer Price Index.
Private domestic investment This consists of (1) non-residential fixed investment, i.e., firms' pur-chases of capital goods such as plants and equipment; (2) residential fixed investment (the building of single- and multi-family housing units); and (3) the change in business inventories, which are stocks on hand of raw materials and finished goods.

▶ECONOMIC INDICATORS

All market economies regularly go through cycles of recession—when output declines and unemployment rises—and expansion—when output and employment rise. These "business cycles" are one of the most important factors determining the socioeconomic conditions in any society. Although economists still have very little idea what actually causes recessions and what leads the economy to begin expanding again, they have had some success in predicting business cycles. Economic forecasting is the science of making these predictions. It is especially useful to be able to predict recessions sufficiently far in advance so that governments can take actions to stimulate the economy and reduce the severity of these downturns.

Economic indicators track developments in areas of the economy that are thought to be crucial to the future health of the economy, just as a barometer measures changes in air pressure that are crucial to changes in the weather. The development of economic indicators began around World War I but suffered a setback when the early forecasters failed to predict the Great Depression in 1929. During the depression the government asked a private research group, the National Bureau of Economic Research, to develop a set of measures that would help predict changes in business cycles. The group devised a list of measures based on analyses of previous business cycles. Since then, the list has been revised several times to reflect changes in the way the economy is structured.

Leading Indicators

There are currently 10 leading economic indicators, representing a broad spectrum of economic activity. These indicators are said to "lead" because their numbers change months in advance of a change in the general level of economic activity. They are as follows:

1. Average length of workweek of production workers in manufacturing.
2. Average weekly state unemployment insurance claims.
3. New orders for consumer goods and materials (in constant dollars).
4. Vendor performance (percent of companies receiving slower deliveries from suppliers).
5. Contracts and orders for plant and equipment (in constant dollars).
6. Index of new private housing units authorized by local building permits.

7. Index of stock prices, i.e., of 500 common stocks (Standard and Poor's 500).
8. Money supply-M2 in constant dollars. (See "Money and Banking" section.)
9. Interest rate spread.
10. Index of consumer expectations. (See "Note" below.)

This composite of leading economic indicators is published by the U.S. Department of Commerce, Bureau of Economic Analysis. The composite has a noteworthy record: since 1948 it has accurately predicted every downturn and upswing in the economy. One major reason for this success is that many of the indicators represent commitments to economic activity in the coming months. The average lead for the index is 9.5 months at business cycle peaks (indicating the end of a business cycle expansion and the beginning of a recession) and 4.5 months at business cycle troughs (indicating the end of a business cycle recession and the beginning of an expansion).

Coincident and Lagging Indicators

In addition to the leading economic indicators, two other sets of measures are used to track business cycles and the state of the economy. One set includes the coincident indicators, which measure how well the economy is doing at that moment (roughly, within three months of the business cycle turning points). These include the number of employees on nonagricultural payrolls; manufacturing and trade sales (in constant dollars); index of industrial production; and personal income less transfer payments (in constant dollars). The second set includes lagging economic indicators. These are the ratio of consumer installment credit outstanding to personal income; commercial and industrial loans outstanding (in constant dollars); the average prime interest rate charged by banks; the ratio of manufacturing and trade inventories to sales (in constant dollars); the average duration of unemployment in weeks (inverted); the change in

Composite Index of Economic Indicators, 1960–2001 (1996=100)

Year	Leading indicators	Coincident indicators	Lagging indicators
1960	72.7	37.2	82.2
1965	80.6	43.4	87.2
1970	83.1	53.1	96.9
1975	81.9	58.4	99.8
1980	88.0	70.8	100.4
1985	94.7	77.1	98.6
1990	97.8	88.1	101.7
1995	99.4	96.5	97.4
2000	106.4	114.2	103.4
2001	109.4	116.6	107.7

Note: As of January of each year.
Source: The Conference Board. www.tcb-indicators.org.

Purchasing Power of the Dollar, 1950–2000

| Year | Annual average as measured by: | |
	Producer prices	Consumer Prices
1950	$3.546	$4.151
1955	3.279	3.732
1960	2.994	3.373
1965	2.933	3.166
1970	2.545	2.574
1975	1.718	1.859
1980	1.136	1.215
1985	0.955	0.928
1990	0.839	0.766
1991	0.822	0.734
1992	0.812	0.713
1993	0.802	0.692
1994	0.797	0.675
1995	0.782	0.656
1996	0.762	0.638
1997	0.759	0.623
1998	0.766	0.614
1999	0.752	0.600
2000	0.725	0.581

Source: U.S. Bureau of Economic Analysis, *Survey of Current Business* (monthly).

Employment Cost Index (ECI) 1985–2001 (1989 = 100)

Group	Index				Percent Change		
	1985	1995	2000	2001	1984-85	1994-95	2000-01
Civilian workers	84.3	124.8	146.5	152.5	4.7%	2.9%	4.1%
White collar	83.0	125.5	148.4	154.4	5.3	3.0	4.0
Blue collar	86.5	123.6	142.7	148.2	3.8	2.7	3.9
Service occupations	84.5	125.0	146.0	152.0	4.7	2.8	4.1
Manufacturing	86.3	126.2	146.0	151.3	5.0	3.0	3.6
Non-manufacturing	83.5	124.4	146.6	152.6	4.6	2.9	4.1
Private Industry Workers	85.0	124.5	146.8	153.0	4.3	2.9	4.2
State & Local Government	81.0	126.4	145.5	150.3	6.3	3.1	3.3

Note: Figures are as of March of each year and are not seasonally adjusted. Excludes farm, household, and federal government workers.
Source: U.S. Bureau of Labor Statistics, *News, Employment Cost Index,* (quarterly)

index of labor cost per unit of output in manufacturing; and the change in the Consumer Price Index for services per unit labor costs. At business cycle peaks, the average lag of the index is 4.5 months, and at business cycle troughs 8.5 months. It seems reasonable to wonder what use there is for an indicator that tells you where you have already been. But in fact that is exactly their use: they provide another way of measuring whether turning points in the business cycle truly have occurred.

The government produces a wide variety of economic indicators in addition to those discussed here for use in tracking more specific aspects of the economy, such as labor or capital markets.

The Employment Cost Index (ECI)
The ECI measures the *rate of change* in total employee compensation (wages, salaries, employer cost for employee benefits) in nonfarm private industry and in state and local governments. Provided quarterly by the Bureau of Labor Statistics, the ECI has become one of the most closely watched indices because any significant rise could signal an inflationary trend. During the late 1980s, the ECI grew annually by 4 to 5 percent, but in the 1990s, it was 3 percent and less.

▶PRICES AND INFLATION
Inflation
Inflation is a sustained rise in the general price level in the economy. It affects the level and timing of spending in the economy since it indicates the extent to which income will cover the purchase of a consumer's basket of goods (food, clothes, entertainment, medical services, housing, gasoline, and so on). For example, if a consumer is considering purchasing a television and inflation is high (that is, prices are rising rapidly), he or she will buy the television as soon as possible since savings may not cover the cost a month or a year from now. Inflation is closely watched to determine wage contracts and Social Security benefits that contain cost-of-living adjustment clauses. If wage contracts cover a long period of time and inflation is rapid, consumers' standard of living will fall in the interim before new contracts can be negotiated. Savings will tend to fall as consumers store their wealth in the form of commodities.

The cause of inflation is often described as "too much money chasing too few goods," brought about by the money supply rising rapidly or pro-

Consumer Price Index (CPI–U) 1947–2000 (1982–84 100)

Year	CPI-U	Year	CPI-U
1947	22.3	1987	113.6
1950	24.1	1988	118.3
1955	26.8	1989	124.0
1960	29.6	1990	130.7
1965	31.5	1991	136.2
1970	38.8	1992	140.3
1975	53.8	1993	144.5
1980	82.4	1994	148.2
1981	90.9	1995	152.4
1982	96.5	1996	156.9
1983	99.6	1997	160.5
1984	103.9	1998	163.0
1985	107.6	1999	166.6
1986	109.6	2000	172.2

Source: U.S. Bureau of the Census, *Current Population Report*

duction of goods falling behind demand for them. Inflation may be due to (1) cost-push factors—that is, if the cost of inputs such as labor, raw materials, or other intermediate goods rises, the cost of the final product also rises; or (2) demand-pull factors—that is, if the demand for goods and services rises above the full employment level, wages rise as employers compete for labor, and the general price level of goods and services rises.

Consumer Price Index
Often referred to as the "cost of living index," the Consumer Price Index is the most commonly used measure of inflation. The index measures the average change in prices relative to an arbitrary base year of a common bundle of goods and services bought by the average consumer on a regular basis. The Bureau of Labor Statistics publishes two CPI's: (1) CPI-U for All Urban Consumers, which includes wage earners and clerical workers; professional, managerial, and technical workers; the self-employed; short-term workers; the unemployed; retirees and others not in the labor force—altogether covering 80 percent of the population—and (2) CPI-W for Urban Wage Earners and Clerical Workers, covering 32 percent of the population. Prices (including direct taxes) are collected from over 57,000 housing units and 19,000 establishments in 85 areas across the country. In calculating the index number, based on 100,000 price quotes a month, larger weights

Consumer Price Indexes for Selected Metropolitan Statistical Areas, 1999 (1982–84 = 100)

Area	All items	Food and beverages	Food	Housing	Apparel and upkeep	Transportation	Medical care	Fuel and Utilities
U.S. city average	166.6	164.6	164.1	163.9	131.3	144.4	250.6	128.8
Anchorage, Alaska	146.4	148.8	148.7	132.7	125.8	143.7	260.8	144.8
Atlanta, Ga.	164.8	167.6	172.1	165.1	132.4	130.3	254.0	143.1
Boston, Mass.	176.0	170.6	171.0	170.3	143.6	142.3	330.2	117.4
Chicago-Gary Ill.-Ind.	168.4	166.4	167.7	168.0	117.2	140.5	253.6	117.4
Cincinnati-Hamilton, Ohio-Ky.-Ind.	159.2	152.0	150.4	153.1	130.1	140.9	233.0	126.3
Cleveland-Akron-Lorain, Ohio	162.5	169.5	171.4	160.2	124.1	143.6	224.9	127.8
Dallas-Ft. Worth, Tex.	158.0	165.1	162.7	146.8	140.7	141.0	233.2	127.8
Denver-Boulder-Greely, Colo.	166.6	157.0	159.2	161.9	94.0	169.5	269.4	129.2
Detroit-Ann Arbor-Flint, Mich.	163.9	158.3	157.6	156.3	133.4	152.1	245.2	127.8
Honolulu, Hawaii	173.3	162.9	163.0	175.8	105.4	162.2	231.3	133.4
Houston-Galveston-Brazoria, Tex.	146.7	152.8	152.1	132.1	139.9	135.7	238.5	106.1
Kansas City, Mo.-Kans.	160.1	161.0	162.1	154.6	121.6	139.2	229.1	134.3
Los Angeles-Anaheim-Riverside, Calif.	166.1	169.9	168.0	164.5	118.2	146.8	244.5	145.4
Miami-Ft. Lauderdale, Fla.	162.4	171.0	171.3	155.2	138.2	148.8	231.3	115.8
Milwaukee, Wis.	163.7	163.7	164.6	162.6	116.8	142.5	251.5	112.4
Minneapolis-St. Paul, Minn.-Wis.	163.3	172.1	168.7	149.2	139.3	148.6	241.1	123.5
New York-Northern New Jersey-Long Island, N.Y.-N.J.-Conn.	177.0	170.5	169.6	179.6	125.5	152.3	265.3	116.1
Philadelphia-Wilmington-Trenton, Pa.-N.J.-Del.-Md.	171.9	159.4	158.6	172.5	107.5	152.2	264.8	130.4
Pittsburgh, Pa.	162.5	156.0	154.7	162.2	144.5	131.9	244.4	142.5
Portland, Oreg.	172.6	157.3	157.7	174.5	134.8	152.1	229.8	139.5
San Diego, Calif.	172.8	166.5	164.5	178.2	131.9	152.1	247.2	120.8
San Francisco-Oakland-San Jose, Calif.	172.5	170.8	171.5	185.6	114.2	135.8	232.6	145.3
Seattle-Tacoma, Wash.	172.8	169.6	170.0	177.3	125.5	149.9	240.3	123.6
St. Louis-East St. Louis, Mo.-Ill.	157.6	161.9	160.2	149.0	123.5	141.7	245.7	122.5
Tampa-St. Petersburg-Clearwater, Fla.[1]	140.6	137.7	136.8	135.3	148.2	126.3	191.9	120.1
Washington-Baltimore, D.C.-Md.-Va.-W.Va.[2]	104.2	103.1	103.1	105.5	98.3	100.3	106.9	106.1

1. 1987=100. 2. 1997=100, except for apparel and upkeep and Transportation, for which 1996=100.
Source: U.S. Bureau of Labor Statistics, *Monthly Labor Review* and *CPI Detailed Report* (Jan. issues).

are assigned to goods that represent larger proportions of consumer expenditure. The index costs $26 million a year to produce and requires 40 economists and analysts tracking price changes in 365 categories.

Producer Price Index

The Producer Price Index measures average changes in prices received by producers of all commodities, at all stages of processing, produced in the United States. Prices used in constructing the index are collected from sellers and generally apply to the first significant large-volume commercial transaction for each commodity—i.e., the manufacturer's or other producer's selling price or the selling price on an organized exchange or at a central market. The weights used in the index represent the total net selling value of commodities produced or processed in the country. Values are f.o.b. (free on board) at the production point and are exclusive of excise taxes.

Implicit Price Deflator

The implicit price deflator (also called the GDP deflator) is derived from the ratio of current-to-constant dollar GDP (multiplied by 100) and measures the value of current production in current prices relative to the value of the same goods and services in prices for the base year. For example, in 2000, GDP in current dollars was $9,963.1 billion and GDP in constant (1996) dollars was $9,318.5 billion. Therefore, the GDP deflator for 2000 was (9,963.1÷ 9,318.5) x 100, or 106.9, which is simply a comparison between 1996 and 2000 prices. It is a weighted average of the detailed price indexes used in the deflation of GDP, but the indexes are combined using weights that reflect the composition of GDP in each period. Thus changes in the implicit price deflator reflect not only changes in prices, but also changes in the composition of GDP.

▶ MONEY AND BANKING
Federal Reserve System

The government's interest in monitoring and controlling the banking industry and managing the money supply led to the Federal Reserve Act of 1913. The act created the Federal Reserve System (or the "Fed," as it is popularly known), the nation's central bank. There are 12 regional Fed

Producer Price Indexes for Selected Commodities, 1970–2000 (1982=100)

Commodity group	1970	1975	1980	1985	1990	1995	1999	2000
All commodities	**38.1**	**58.4**	**89.8**	**103.2**	**116.3**	**124.7**	**125.5**	**132.7**
Farm products & processed foods & feeds	**44.9**	**74.0**	**98.3**	**100.7**	**118.6**	**120.5**	**120.3**	**122.0**
Farm products	45.8	77.0	102.9	95.1	95.1	107.4	98.4	99.5
Processed foods and feeds	44.6	72.6	95.9	103.5	103.5	127.0	131.1	133.1
Industrial commodities	**35.2**	**54.9**	**88.0**	**103.7**	**115.8**	**125.5**	**126.5**	**134.8**
Textile products and apparel	52.4	67.4	89.7	102.9	114.9	120.8	121.1	121.4
Hides, skins, leather related products	42.0	56.5	94.7	108.9	141.7	153.7	146.0	151.5
Fuels, related products, power	15.3	35.4	82.8	91.4	82.2	78.0	80.5	103.5
Chemicals and allied products	35.0	62.0	89.0	103.7	123.6	142.5	144.2	151.0
Rubber and plastic products	44.9	62.2	90.1	101.9	113.6	124.3	122.5	125.5
Lumber and wood products	39.9	62.1	101.5	106.6	129.7	178.1	183.6	178.2
Pulp, paper, and allied products	37.5	59.0	86.3	113.3	141.3	172.2	174.1	183.7
Metals and metal products	38.7	61.5	95.0	104.4	123.0	134.5	124.6	128.1
Machinery and equipment	40.0	57.9	86.0	107.2	120.7	126.6	124.3	124.0
Furniture and household durables	51.9	67.5	90.7	107.1	119.1	128.2	131.7	132.6
Nonmetallic mineral products	35.3	54.4	88.4	108.6	114.7	129.0	138.9	142.5
Transportation equipment	41.9	56.7	82.9	107.9	121.5	139.7	141.8	143.8

Source: U.S. Bureau of Labor Statistics, *Producer Price Indexes*, monthly and annual.

banks located in major cities throughout the country (Boston, New York, Philadelphia, Cleveland, Richmond, Atlanta, Chicago, St. Louis, Minneapolis, Kansas City, Dallas, and San Francisco). Commercial banks within each region select a majority of the directors who run each regional Fed bank. The president of the United States appoints a board of governors for the whole system, and the board is responsible for coordinating policies across the system. But the regional Feds play an important role in shaping those policies by representing regional interests and decentralizing the decision-making process.

The Fed has three main policy tools for managing the overall economy. First, it controls the *reserve requirements* at all depository institutions. These requirements determine what percentage of a bank's deposits must be held in reserve in the form of either deposits with Federal Reserve banks or vault cash. Raising the reserve requirements reduces the amount of loans available to borrowers and helps slow down the economy.

A more frequently used instrument is *the discount rate*, the interest rate the Federal Reserve banks charge their commercial bank customers to borrow money. The Fed is known as the lender of last resort because of its responsibility to lend to banks in need, and it thus maintains the stability of the banking system. Raising the discount rate generally leads the commercial banks to raise the interest rates they charge their customers. This raises the costs of borrowing in the private sector and slows the economy. (Cutting the discount rate does the reverse and stimulates the economy.)

Most important, the Fed can also control the level of bank reserves through *open market operations*; that is, the direct sale on purchase of Treasury securities and other government debt instruments. When the Fed sells securities, it takes money from the buyer and holds it in its reserves, reducing the money supply; when it buys these instruments, it pays for them by taking money from its reserves, which then goes into circulation, increasing the money supply.

Federal Reserve Bank, Discount Rates, 1976–2001

Effective Date	Rate	Effective Date	Rate
Jan. 19, 1976	5.50%	March 7, 1986	7.00%
Nov. 22, 1976	5.25	April 21, 1986	6.50
Aug. 31, 1977	5.75	July 11, 1986	6.00
Oct. 26, 1977	6.00	Aug. 21, 1986	5.50
Jan. 9, 1978	6.50	Sept. 4, 1987	6.00
May 11, 1978	7.00	Aug. 9, 1988	6.50
July 3, 1978	7.25	Feb. 24, 1989	7.00
Aug. 21, 1978	7.75	Dec. 19, 1990	6.50
Sept., 22, 1978	8.00	Feb. 1, 1991	6.00
Oct. 16, 1978	8.50	April 30, 1991	5.50
Nov. 1, 1978	9.50	Sept. 13, 1991	5.00
July 20, 1979	10.00	Nov. 6, 1991	4.50
Aug. 17, 1979	10.50	Dec. 20, 1991	3.50
Sept. 19, 1979	11.00	July 2, 1992	3.00
Oct. 8, 1979	12.00	May 17, 1994	3.50
Feb. 15, 19801	13.00	Aug. 16, 1994	4.00
May 30, 1980	12.00	Nov. 15, 1994	4.75
June 13, 1980	11.00	Feb. 1, 1995	5.25
July 28, 1980	10.00	Jan. 31, 1996	5.00
Sept. 26, 1980	11.00	Oct. 15, 1998	4.75
Nov. 17, 1980	12.00	Nov. 17, 1998	4.50
Dec. 5, 1980	13.00	Aug. 24, 1999	4.75
May 5, 1981	14.00	Nov. 18, 1999	5.00
Nov. 2, 1981	13.00	Feb. 3, 2000	5.25
Dec. 4, 1981	12.00	Mar. 21, 2000	5.50
July 20, 1982	11.50	May 19, 2000	6.00
Aug. 2, 1982	11.00	Jan. 4, 2001	5.50
Aug. 16, 1982	10.50	Jan. 31, 2001	5.00
Aug. 27, 1982	10.00	Mar. 20, 2001	4.50
Oct. 12, 1982	9.50	Apr. 18, 2001	4.00
Nov. 22, 1982	9.00	May 15, 2001	3.50
Dec. 15, 1982	8.50	June 27, 2001	3.25
April 9, 1984	9.00	Aug. 21, 2001	3.00
Nov. 21, 1984	8.50	Sept. 17, 2001	2.50
Dec. 24, 1984	8.00	Oct. 1, 2001	2.00
May 20, 1985	7.50		

Note: The Discount Rate is for short term adjustment credit. Latest rate in effect as of Sept. 19, 2001. 1. The discount rates for 1980 and 1981 do not include the surcharge applied to frequent borrowings by large institutions. The surcharge reached 3% in 1980 and 4% in 1981, and was eliminated in November 1981.
Source: Board of Governors of the Federal Reserve System, *Federal Reserve Bulletin*, monthly, and *Annual Statistical Digest*.

Controlling the money supply through open market operations is certainly the most common and, many would argue, the most important function of the Fed. The money supply shapes interest rates, through the supply and demand of money. Because the Fed is constantly involved in these open market operations (in order to keep the size of the money supply in proportion with a growing economy, for example), adjustments can be made subtly.

In addition, the Federal Reserve regulates banks through the Federal Deposit Insurance Corporation, influences foreign-currency exchange rates through the sale or purchase of foreign currencies, and coordinates international financial policy.

The money supply   Money provides a medium of exchange as well as a way to store value. Traditionally, currency (paper money and coins) served that role exclusively. But over time, new financial instruments have developed that serve at least some of the functions of money. Checking accounts serve exactly the same role as currency, and to an extent, so do money market funds and other instruments.

The Fed uses four different measures of the money supply, which include different monetary instruments:

M1 is the original and most commonly reported measure of the money supply, which embraces currency and coins, demand deposits, traveler's checks, and other checkable deposits.

M2 is M1 plus money-market accounts, and savings and small time-deposits.

M3 is M2 plus money-market mutual-fund balances held by financial institutions, term repurchase agreements and term Eurodollars, and large time-deposits.

The U.S. Banking System

Commercial banks are the largest financial institutions in the country and are the principal vehicles for exchanging money. The nation's first commercial bank was the Bank of America (now First Pennsylvania Bank), established in Philadelphia in 1782. Commercial banks hold about two-thirds of the nation's money deposits. Savings and loans, the next-largest source of deposits, hold about half as much.

There are approximately 10,000 commercial banks in the country. They may be chartered either by the federal government or by individual states. While banks themselves may not operate across states, they may be owned by holding companies that can operate interstate, if state laws permit.

Commercial banks can make loans to individuals and to commercial operations, establish checking or demand deposits, maintain "trust" departments that make investments for customers, and perform a variety of other functions such as issuing credit cards. Until the deregulation of the 1980's, commercial banks were the

The Money Supply, 1970-2000 (billions of dollars)

Item	1970	1980	1990	1995	1998	1999	2000
M1, total	**$214**	**$408**	**$824**	**$1,126**	**$1,097**	**$1,124**	**$1,090**
Currency[1]	49	115	247	372	459	517	530
Travelers' checks[2]	1	3	7	8	8	8	8
Demand deposits[3]	165	261	277	389	379	356	313
Other checkable deposits[4]	(z)	28	294	357	250	244	239
M2, total	**$628**	**$1,600**	**$3,277**	**$3,642**	**$4,383**	**$4,650**	**$4,947**
M1	214	408	824	1,126	1,097	1,124	1,090
Non-M1 components in M2	414	1,192	2,453	2,515	3,286	3,528	3,857
Money market funds, retail	(z)	64	357	450	734	839	939
Savings deposits (including money market deposit accounts)	261	400	923	1,134	1,600	1,735	1,872
Commercial banks	99	186	581	775	1,186	1,287	1,420
Thrift institutions	162	215	342	359	414	449	452
Small time deposits[5]	151	729	1,173	931	952	956	1,046
Commercial banks	79	286	611	575	626	635	700
Thrift institutions	72	442	563	357	326	321	346
M3, total	**$677**	**$1,996**	**$4,150**	**$4,623**	**$6,027**	**$6,527**	**$7,093**
M2	628	1,600	3,277	3,642	4,383	4,650	4,947
Non-M1 components in M3	49	396	873	981	1,644	1,877	2,146
Large time deposits[6]	45	260	480	430	664	740	827
Commercial banks[7]	44	215	359	355	575	849	724
Thrift institutions	1	45	121	74	89	91	103
Repurchase agreements[8]	4	58	151	198	298	341	360
Eurodollars[8]	(z)	61	103	94	152	173	191
Money market funds, institution only	(z)	16	136	259	530	622	767

Note: As of December of year shown. Adjusted seasonally. Figures may not add up because of independent rounding. Z = less than $500 million. 1. Currency outside U.S. Treasury, Federal Reserve Banks, and the vaults of depository institutions. 2. Outstanding amount of nonbank issuers. 3. At commercial banks and foreign-related institutions. 4. Consists of negotiable order of withdrawal (NOW) and automatic transfer service (ATS) accounts at all depository institutions, credit union share draft balances and demand deposits at thrift institutions. 5. Issued in amounts of less than $100,000. Includes retail repurchase agreements. Excludes individual retirement accounts (IRAs) and Keogh accounts. 6. Issued in amounts of $100,000 or more. Excludes those booked at international banking facilities. 7. Excludes those held by money market mutual funds, depository institutions, U.S. Government, foreign banks, and official institutions. 8. Excludes those held by depository institutions and money market mutual funds. **Source:** Board of Governors of the Federal Reserve System, *Federal Reserve Bulletin*, monthly, and *Money Stock, Liquid Assets, and Debt Measures, Federal Reserve Statistical Release H.6*, weekly.

only ones permitted to issue checking accounts. Regulations that developed after bank failures in the Great Depression still keep these banks out of the investment business — largely to protect depositors and the solvency of banks from potential effects of bad investments. But deregulation of the banking industry in the 1980s is blurring many of these distinctions. In particular, investment companies are now permitted to issue demand deposits and to compete with banks in other areas as well. (As a result these companies are sometimes referred to as nonbanks.)

Bank failures are especially serious problems because of the domino effect they may have on other financial institutions and businesses. Banks, and indeed all depository institutions, ultimately fail when many of their loans go bad and cannot be repaid. But even before that happens, depositors may get nervous about the security of their accounts and withdraw them all at once—a "run on the bank." Because banks loan out deposits and hold in reserve only a small percentage of the value of those deposits, banks experiencing a run would have to call in some of their loans (mainly those already due), putting sudden pressure on many commercial borrowers and causing

some to fail. In addition the withdrawal of deposits and of loans reduces the money supply sharply. This process was an important cause of the Great Depression. Following the banking failures during the depression (2,293 banks failed in 1931, and 4,000 banks failed in 1933), the Federal Deposit Insurance Corporation (FDIC) was created in 1933 to protect the accounts of depositors and, more important, to help prevent bank failures. The FDIC charges banks a premium to pay for this coverage. The corporation is designed to prevent runs on banks by insuring deposits and lending to banks to prevent the need to call in loans.

But banks still fail because of bad loans. Between 1945 and 1980, U.S. banks failed at the rate of about six per year. Since then, hundreds of banks have failed each year. Most of these failures occurred in agricultural states where the failure of farms led to defaults on loans; more than half of all bank failures can be attributed to agriculture loans. Fraud also played an important role, especially in Tennessee, where more than 30 banks have failed since 1982. When a bank fails, the F.D.I.C. pays off each depositor and then sells the bank's assets. Sometimes the F.D.I.C. arranges for another bank's acquisition of the failed bank by subsidizing the sale.

Consumer Credit Outstanding, 1980-2000 (billions of dollars)

Type of Credit	1980	1985	1990	1995	1997	1998	1999	2000
Total	$349.4	$593.2	$789.3	$1,096.0	$1,234.5	$1,301.0	$1,393.7	$1,531.5
Revolving[1]	55.1	124.7	238.6	443.2	531.2	560.5	595.6	663.8
Other[2]	294.3	468.5	550.7	652.8	703.3	740.5	798.0	867.6

1. Consists mainly of outstanding balances on credit card accounts, but also includes borrowing under check credit and overdraft plans, and unsecured personal lines of credit. 2. Includes automobile loans and all other loans not included in revolving credit, such as loans for mobile homes, trailers or vacations. noninstallment credit.
Source: Board of Governors of the Federal Reserve System, Federal Reserve Bulletin (monthly).

Assets and Deposits of FDIC/BIF-Insured Banks, 1999-2000

Charter class	1999			2000		
	Banks	Assets (millions)	Deposits (millions)	Banks	Assets (millions)	Deposits (millions)
All banks	10,220	6,883,487	4,537,873	9,905	7,461,347	4,914,809
Commercial banks	8,580	5,734,761	3,830,776	8,315	6,238,713	4,176,575
National banks	2,365	3,271,469	2,154,437	2,230	3,414,489	2,250,464
State banks (Fed members)	1,010	1,423,360	899,256	991	1,644,645	1,032,110
State banks (Fed nonmembers)	5,205	1,040,014	777,083	5,094	1,179,578	894,000
Savings banks	1,640	1,148,726	707,097	1,590	1,222,635	738,234
Federal charter	928	829,700	487,404	913	905,531	516,583
State charter	712	319,026	219,693	677	317,103	221,651

Note: As of Dec. 31 of each year. **Source:** Federal Deposit Insurance Corp., Statistics on Banking, 2000(2001).

Assets and Deposits of Deposit-Taking Institutions, 2000

Type of institution	Number of institutions	Percent share	Assets (millions)	Percent share	Deposits (millions)	Percent share
Commercial banks	8,315	39.1%	$6,238,713	70.7%	4,176,575	71.7%
Savings banks[1]	1,590	7.5	1,222,635	13.8	738,234	12.7
Savings & Loans (thrifts) [2]	1,068	5.0	928,548	10.5	529,413	9.1
Credit unions[3]	10,316	48.5	438,200	5.0	379,200	6.5
Total	21,289	100.0%	$8,828,096	100.0%	$5,823,422	100.0%

1. Includes Federal and State-chartered Savings institutions. 2. Includes only thrifts regulated by the Office of Thrift Supervision. 3. Federally insured credit unions only. **Sources:** Federal Deposit Insurance Corp., Statistics on Banking, 2000 (2001); Office of Thrift Supervision. OTS Fact Book; National Credit Union Association, 2000 Year-End Statistics.

Top 100 U.S. Banking Companies, 2000

Rank, Bank, City	Assets (millions)
1. Citigroup Inc., New York	$902,210
2. J.P. Morgan Chase & Co., New York	715,348
3. Bank Of America Corp., Charlotte	642,191
4. Wells Fargo & Co., San Francisco	272,426
5. Bank One Corp., Chicago	269,300
6. First Union Corp., Charlotte	254,170
7. Taunus Corp., New York	197,815
8. Fleet Boston Financial Corp., Boston	179,519
9. Suntrust Banks, Inc., Atlanta	103,496
10. National City Corp., Cleveland	88,535
11. U.S. Bancorp, Minneapolis	87,336
12. Keycorp, Cleveland	87,165
13. Firstar Corp., Milwaukee	77,585
14. Bank Of New York Co., New York	77,114
15. Wachovia Corp., Winston-Salem, N.C.	74,032
16. PNC Financial Services Group, Pittsburgh	69,916
17. State Street Corp., Boston	69,298
18. BB&T Corp., Winston-Salem, N.C.	59,340
19. Mellon Financial Corp., Pittsburgh	50,564
20. Fifth Third Bancorp, Cincinnati	45,857
21. Southtrust Corp., Birmingham, Ala.	45,147
22. Regions Financial Corp., Birmingham, Ala.	43,910
23. Comerica Inc., Detroit	42,032
24. Summit Bancorp., Princeton, N.J.	39,668
25. Amsouth Bancorp., Birmingham, Ala.	38,968
26. MBNA Corp., Wilmington, Del.	38,666
27. Charles Schwab Corp., San Francisco	38,155
28. Northern Trust Corp., Chicago	36,022
29. Union Planters Corp., Memphis	34,721
30. Charter One Financial, Inc., Cleveland	33,034
31. M&T Bank Corp., Buffalo, N.Y.	28,949
32. Huntington Bancshares, Columbus, Ohio	28,599
33. Popular Inc., San Juan, P.R.	28,058
34. Marshall & Ilsley Corp., Milwaukee	26,078
35. Old Kent Financial Corp., Grand Rapids, Mich.	23,867
36. Zions Bancorp., Salt Lake City	21,938
37. Compass Bancshares, Birmingham, Ala.	20,023
38. First Tennessee Natl Corp., Memphis	18,556
39. Bancwest Corp., Honolulu	18,457
40. Banknorth Group, Inc., Portland, Maine	18,234
41. Hibernia Corp., New Orleans	16,698
42. National Commerce Bancorp., Memphis	16,637
43. Greenpoint Financial Corp., New York	15,765
44. TD Waterhouse Holdings, Inc., New York	15,330
45. North Fork Bancorp., Melville, NY	14,841
46. Pacific Century Financial Corp., Honolulu	14,027
47. Provident Financial Group, Cincinnati	13,978
48. Associated Banc-Corp, Green Bay, Wis.	13,128
49. Colonial BancGroup, Inc., Montgomery, Ala.	11,741
50. People's Mutual Holdings, Bridgeport, Conn.	11,608

Rank, Bank, City	Assets (millions)
51. Centura Banks, Inc., Rocky Mount, N.C.	$11,490
52. TCF Financial Corp., Wayzata, Minn.	11,289
53. Commerce Bancshares, Kansas City, Mo.	11,221
54. First Citizens Bancshares, Raleigh, N.C.	10,692
55. Firstmerit Corp., Akron, Ohio	10,215
56. BOK Financial Corp., Tulsa, Okla.	9,840
57. First Virginia Banks, Inc., Falls Church, Va.	9,516
58. Hudson City, MHC, Paramus, N.J.	9,380
59. First National of Nebraska, Omaha, Neb.	9,287
60. City National Corp., Beverly Hills, Calif.	9,097
61. Bancorpsouth, Inc., Tupelo, Miss.	9,064
62. Mercantile Bankshares Corp., Baltimore	8,938
63. Old National Bancorp, Evansville, Ind.	8,783
64. Citizens Banking Corp., Flint, Mich.	8,405
65. Sky Financial Group, Bowling Green, Ohio	8,387
66. Commerce Bancorp, Cherry Hill, N.J.	8,339
67. Emigrant Bancorp, New York	8,238
68. UMB Financial Corp., Kansas City, Mo.	7,867
69. Cullen/Frost Bankers, Inc., San Antonio	7,701
70. Imperial Bancorp, Inglewood, Calif.	7,562
71. Wilmington Trust Corp., Wilmington, Del.	7,371
72. Trustmark Corp., Jackson, Miss.	6,887
73. Hudson United Bancorp, Mahwah, N.J.	6,850
74. Fulton Financial Corp., Lancaster, Pa.	6,571
75. Valley National Bancorp, Wayne, N.J.	6,426
76. Whitney Holding Corp., New Orleans	6,243
77. Community First Bankshares, Fargo, N.D.	6,090
78. First Bancorp, San Juan, P.R.	5,920
79. First Midwest Bancorp., Itasca, Ill.	5,907
80. First Banks, Inc., St Louis	5,874
81. International Bncshrs Corp., Laredo, Tex.	5,861
82. Silicon Valley Bancshares, Santa Clara, Calif.	5,642
83. Riggs National Corp., Washington, D.C.	5,555
84. FBOP Corp., Oak Park, Ill.	5,515
85. Provident Bankshares, Baltimore	5,506
86. Doral Financial Corp., San Juan, P.R.	5,463
87. Central Bancompany, Jefferson City, Mo.	5,434
88. Bay View Capital Corp., San Mateo, Calif.	5,361
89. South Financial Group, Greenville, S.C.	5,221
90. Greater Bay Bancorp, Palo Alto, Calif.	5,130
91. Firstbank Holding Co., Lakewood, Colo.	4,915
92. United Bankshares, Charleston, W.Va.	4,905
93. BBVAPR Holding Corp., San Juan, P.R.	4,861
94. Investors Bancorp, MHC, Millburn, N.J.	4,833
95. Susquehanna Bancshares, Lititz, Pa.	4,793
96. New York Comm Bancorp, Westbury, N.Y.	4,715
97. Republic Bancorp, Owosso, Mich.	4,611
98. Arvest Bank Group, Bentonville, Ark.	4,464
99. First Commonwealth Financial Corp., Indiana, Pa.	4,383
100. W Holding Co., Mayaguez, P.R.	4,261

Source: *American Banker Bond Buyer* (2001).

Top 10 U.S. Thrift Holding Companies, 1999

Rank by assets/Name, city	Assets (millions)
1. Washington Mutual Inc., Seattle	$186,513.6
2. Golden State Bancorp, San Francisco	57,019.1
3. Golden West Financial Corp., Oakland, Calif.	42,142.2
4. Sovereign Bancorp, Philadelphia	26,587.3
5. Dime Bancorp, New York	23,921.0

Rank by assets/Name, city	Assets (millions)
6. Astoria Financial Corp., Lake Success, N.Y	$22,696.5
7. Bank United, Houston	17,352.2
8. Greenpoint Financial Corp., New York	15,395.4
9. Peoples Heritage Financial Group, Portland, Maine	13,919.1
10. Commercial Federal Corp., Omaha, Neb.	13,349.1

Source: *American Banker Bond Buyer* (2000).

Thrifts are depository institutions including savings and loans (S&Ls), savings banks, and credit unions. The largest and most important thrifts are the S&Ls, which were created to provide home mortgages for borrowers and long-term savings deposits for individual investors. Until recently, thrifts were prohibited from engaging in riskier loans—including most commercial loans—and issuing checking deposits, and a ceiling was placed on the rate of interest they could pay depositors. Congress lifted the ceiling on interest payments to depositors in 1980 and in 1982 allowed the S&Ls to issue commercial loans and to invest directly in real estate developments. Unwise investment in these areas by many thrifts was a major cause of the savings and loan debacle of the late 1980's and early 1990's.

The Federal Home Loan Bank System was established in 1932 to serve some of the same functions for S&Ls that the Federal Reserve provides for banks. It has now been succeeded by the Office of Thrift Supervision (O.T.S.), which identifies institutions that may be financially distressed or likely to fail. All federally chartered S&Ls are regulated by the system (and must have the word *Federal* in their name). Less than half the thrifts are federally chartered, however; the rest are chartered by states, although most of these have joined the system as well. The F.S.L.I.C. (Federal Savings and Loan Insurance Corporation) insured deposits at member S&Ls until 1989, when it became insolvent and was dismantled.

Savings and loan crisis The S&Ls came under enormous economic pressure during the 1970s, when interest rates paid by banks and other financial institutions rose well above the rate ceiling for thrifts, and they started losing depositors. Further, they were in a financial bind because their outstanding loans were all in mortgages—long-term, 30-year loans issued at low interest. In part because of this, the thrifts were deregulated, released from many of the restrictions on their activities and allowed to pursue a more diverse market for loans. With this new freedom, however, many S&Ls took on loans at a higher level of risk in order to earn a higher rate of return. Some argue that the insurance on deposits provided by the Federal Home Loan Bank encouraged the S&Ls to make loans that were too risky.

Lending institutions fail mainly if a large percentage of their loans go bad and cannot be collected. And mortgage loans fail, not just because buyers cannot make their payments, but also because the collateral (the buildings) may decline in price so that it is less than the value of the loan. Especially in the Southwest, many of the loans for real estate development failed when the oil industry declined in the 1980s, taking local economies with it. S&Ls started to collapse at an alarming rate—517 thrifts closed between 1980 and 1988. With liabilities of $100 billion in excess of assets, the F.S.L.I.C. ran out of money. Its insurance obligations passed to the F.D.I.C., and the Resolution Trust Corporation (R.T.C.) was formed to dispose of (sell) approximately $400 billion of insolvent thrifts' assets. The government dealt with 205 insolvent S&Ls in 1988 alone by subsidizing their sale to more secure institutions.

Credit unions are employer-sponsored cooperative organizations that provide consumer and mortgage credit to their members. Employers often arrange for payroll-deduction savings plans through the credit union. Perhaps in response to the high rates charged by commercial banks for maintaining checking accounts, the number of people joining credit unions has jumped dramatically in recent years, from 61.4 million members in 1992 to 75.4 million in 2000.

Mortgage loans Mortgages are loans backed by buildings—either private dwellings or commercial buildings. Until the 1970s, virtually all

Money Market Interest Rates and Mortgage Rates, 1970-2000

Type	1970	1980	1990	1995	1999	2000
Federal funds, effective rate	7.18%	13.35%	8.10%	5.83%	4.97%	6.24%
Prime rate charged by banks	7.91	15.26	10.01	6.83	8.00	6.58
Eurodollar deposits, 3-month	8.52	14.00	8.16	5.93	5.31	6.45
Finance paper, 3-month[2, 3]	7.18	11.49	7.87	N.A.	N.A.	N.A.
Bankers acceptances, 90-day[2, 4]	7.31	12.67	7.93	5.61	5.24	N.A.
Large negotiable certificates of deposit, 3-month, secondary market	7.56	13.07	8.15	5.92	5.19	6.35
Federal Reserve discount rate[5]	5.50-6.00	10.00-13.00	6.50-7.00	4.75-5.25	4.50-5.00	5.00-6.00
U.S. Government securities:[6]						
3-month Treasury bill	6.39	11.39	7.51	5.51	4.66	N.A.
6-month Treasury bill	6.51	11.32	7.47	5.59	4.75	N.A.
1-year Treasury bill	6.48	10.85	7.36	5.69	4.76	N.A.
Home mortgages (HUD series[7]):						
FHA insured, secondary market[8]	9.03	13.44	10.17	8.18	7.74	N.A.
Conventional, new-home[9, 10]	8.52	13.95	10.08	8.05	7.45	N.A.
Conventional, existing-home[9]	8.56	13.95	10.08	8.05	7.47	N.A.

N.A. = Not available. 1. Based on daily offering rates of dealers. 2. Yields are quoted on a bank-discount basis, rather than an investment yield basis (which would give a higher figure). 3. Placed directly; averages of daily offering rates quoted by finance companies. 4. Based on representative closing yields. From Jan. 1, 1981, rates of top-rated banks only. 5. Federal Reserve Bank of New York, low and high. The discount rates for 1980 and 1981 do not include the surcharge applied to frequent borrowings by large institutions. The surcharge reached 3% in 1980 and 4% in 1981. Surcharge was eliminated in November 1981. 6. Averages based on daily closing bid yields in secondary market, bank discount basis. 7. HUD = Housing and Urban Development. 8. Averages based on quotations for 1 day each month as compiled by FHA. 9. Primary market. 10. Average contract rates on new commitments. **Source:** Except as noted, Board of Governors of the Federal Reserve System, *Federal Reserve Bulletin,* monthly, and *Annual Statistical Digest.*

mortgages had fixed-interest payments and 30-year terms. With the escalation of interest rates beginning in the late 1970s, however, several alternative arrangements have developed. For example, in order to reduce the interest payments, many borrowers repay their loans in 15 years. Others use a *variable* or *adjustable rate mortgage* in which the interest rate varies with market rates. Some mortgages that hold payments down in the first few years and then increase them rapidly for the remaining term of the mortgage are known as balloon mortgages.

Money Instruments

Treasury bills, also called T-bills, are securities sold by the U.S. Treasury in denominations of $10,000 that mature at various dates, but all in less than one year. Treasury bills pay an interest rate that is adjusted by the Treasury according to supply and demand. The Treasury bill rate is thought to have the highest risk-free rate of return among all investments.

Federal funds are the reserves the Fed requires depository institutions such as commercial banks to hold on deposit at their regional Federal Reserve Bank as protection against withdrawals. Banks and other depository institutions can loan reserves in excess of those required by the Fed to each other. These Fed Fund loans can provide institutions with large amounts of liquid assets on very short notice, and most loans are for no more than one day.

Certificates of deposit (CDs) Customers who make these deposits at commercial banks or thrift institutions receive a certificate describing the maturity date of the deposit (e.g., a five-year CD). CDs guarantee a rate of return for as long as 10 years into the future. In addition, the fact that they can be purchased at local banks also makes them easy to secure. These factors make them appealing to the general public. The interest paid on CDs is set by the market and is generally the same across large institutions. Smaller institutions often offer higher rates to attract depositors.

Money-market accounts Customers pool their money into a fund that then purchases short-term debt such as Treasury bills and commercial paper in order to earn a high rate of return while maintaining liquidity (i.e., being able to convert assets quickly into cash). Customers typically can write checks on their money-market accounts, which are processed through cooperating banks, but checks generally have to be in large denominations—greater than $250—to prevent customers from using them as demand deposit accounts.

Capital Instruments

Stock, or equity, the most important source of capital for firms, represents a claim on the assets or equity of a business as well as on its earnings. See the chapter on U.S. Business later in this section.

Treasury bonds, or notes, have longer-term dates of maturity, from one to 10 years, than do Treasury bills. They are sold by the Treasury in denominations of $1,000 and are the principal means of funding government borrowing and the national debt. The interest on these bonds is paid out regularly. *Thirty-year Treasury Bonds,* commonly called the Long Bond, are also sold by the Treasury; their yield is watched closely because it forms the basis for all other interest rates, including mortgage-backed securities and fixed rates. Bond prices are determined by the relative number of investors willing to buy and sell them on the open market. Their decisions are in turn based on expectations about inflation. When the Federal Reserve announces that it will not change interest rates, indicating its belief that inflation will remain steady, more investors are willing to buy long-term investments, so bond prices rise, but result in a lower yield. When the economy heats up, however—that is, with increased business activity employing more workers—inflation is expected to rise, resulting in fewer investors willing to buy long-term instruments, and bond prices will fall as yields and other interest rates rise.

Other government securities Some agencies of the government that are involved in lend-

Bonds Yields, 1970-2000						
Type	1970	1980	1990	1995	1999	2000
U.S. Treasury, constant maturities:[1,2]						
3-year	7.29%	11.51%	8.26%	6.25%	5.49%	6.22%
5-year	7.38	11.45	8.37	6.38	5.55	6.16
10-year	7.35	11.43	8.55	6.57	5.65	6.03
U.S. Govt., long-term bonds [2,3]	6.58	10.81	8.74	6.93	6.14	6.41
State and local govt. bonds, Aaa[4]	6.12	7.86	6.96	5.80	5.29	5.58
State and local govt. bonds, Baa[4]	6.75	9.02	7.29	6.10	5.70	6.19
High-graded municipal bonds (Standard & Poor's)[5]	6.51	8.51	7.25	N.A.	N.A.	N.A.
Municipal (Bond Buyer, 20 bonds)	6.35	8.59	7.27	5.95	5.43	5.71
Corporate Aaa seasoned[4]	8.04	11.94	9.32	7.59	7.04	7.62
Corporate Baa seasoned[4]	9.11	13.67	10.36	8.20	7.87	8.36
Corporate (Moody's) [4,6]	8.51	12.75	9.77	7.83	6.87	7.44
Industrials (49 bonds)[7]	8.26	12.35	9.77	7.76	7.33	7.83
Public utilities (51 bonds)[8]	8.68	13.15	9.76	7.90	7.54	8.15

1. Yields on the more actively traded issues adjusted to constant maturities by the U.S. Treasury. 2. Yields are based on closing bid prices quoted by at least five dealers. 3. Averages (to maturity or call) for all outstanding bonds neither due nor callable in less than 10 years, including several very low yielding "flower" bonds. 4. **Source:** Moody's Investors Service, New York, NY. 5. **Source:** U.S. Bureau of Economic Analysis, Survey of Current Business, monthly. Annual averages of weekly figures. 6. For 1970-85, includes railroad bonds, which were discontinued as part of composite in 1989. 7. Covers 40 bonds for 1970-1980. 8. Covers 40 bonds for 1970-85.
Source: Except as noted, Board of Governors of the Federal Reserve System, *Federal Reserve Bulletin,* monthly.

ing are permitted to sell securities in order to raise funds. The most important of these is the Federal National Mortgage Association—FNMA, or "Fanny Mae." It buys and sells mortgages insured by the federal government and stabilizes the market for those mortgages in the process.

Municipal bonds are issued by state and local governments to raise funds, usually to provide public works and other facilities. The federal government is prohibited by the Constitution from interfering in the ability of state and local governments to raise revenue, so income from municipal bonds is not subject to federal taxes. So-called revenue bonds are paid for by user fees—for example, tolls collected on a parkway are used to pay for the bonds used to build it. General-obligation bonds are paid for through general taxes. Municipal bonds tend to be very safe, although there have been occasions on which some state and local governments have had to take extraordinary actions to avoid default—most notably, New York City in 1975, which received a federal loan and sold new bonds to its municipal employee unions in order to avoid default.

►GOVERNMENT DEBT

One of the most debated economic issues since the 1980's has been the importance of the government's budget deficit. The government raises most of its resources through taxes, but it can also raise money by borrowing. The government borrows by selling bonds (treasury bonds, savings bonds, for example) which have increasingly been purchased by investors outside the U.S. The bonds raise money now but must be repaid in the future through revenues from taxes. The *budget deficit* in any year indicates the difference between what the government takes in through taxes and other forms of revenues, and the expenditures it makes. The deficit therefore suggests how much the government needed to borrow to fill that gap. The total amount of present and past borrowing, plus interest, constitutes the total *national debt*.

Governments routinely borrow to pay for long-term projects that will give benefits to the community into the future. It can be argued that because much of the benefit from projects such as highways and other public works will be enjoyed by the next generation of taxpayers, they should also bear much of the cost. And they can do that by paying off the government debt (paying the premiums on the government bonds) through taxes in the future. Controversy arises when the government borrows to pay for its more routine expenditures. One justification for such borrowing is that it can be used to manage business cycles in the economy: in other words, during recessions, the government can borrow in order to increase expenditures and expand the economy without raising taxes, which would slow it down.

When the total amount of government debt becomes large, some economists believe that it damages the economy in the following ways. First the fact that the government is selling large amounts of debt means that it is competing for limited investor dollars with private borrowers, driving up the cost of borrowing, and making it harder for private sector businesses to make investments for future growth. Second, the future taxes needed to pay off large amounts of government debt may place a serious drain on the future economy, again diverting resources from investment in the private sector. Politicians are concerned because debt payments must be funded from tax revenues so they must either raise taxes or reduce government spending in other areas (e.g. in defense, or in entitlement programs).

The debate over debt really turns on how much is "too much." Between 1935 and 1981 the only two significant increases in the deficit occurred during World War II and certain years of the Vietnam War, when deficits were about $25 billion. Between 1981 an 1989, however, the Reagan Administration consistently ran annual deficits averaging $167 billion and increased the nation's total outstanding gross debt from just over $1 trillion to over $2.6 trillion.

Deficits and the Debt, 1940–2001 (billions of dollars)

Year	Total receipts	Total outlays	Surplus or Deficit	Gross Federal Debt	Debt held by the public	Net interest paid[1] Total	Net interest paid[1] As percent of federal outlays
1940	$ 6.5	$ 9.5	$ -2.9	$ 50.7	$ 42.7	$ 1.0	9.5%
1945	45.2	92.7	-47.6	260.1	235.2	3.1	3.4
1950	39.4	42.6	-3.1	256.9	219.0	4.8	11.4
1955	65.5	68.4	-3.0	274.4	226.6	4.9	7.6
1960	92.5	92.2	0.3	290.5	236.8	6.9	8.5
1965	116.8	118.2	-1.4	322.3	260.8	9.6	8.1
1970	192.8	195.6	-2.8	380.9	283.2	15.4	7.9
1975	279.1	332.3	-53.2	541.9	394.7	25.0	7.5
1980	517.1	590.9	-73.8	909.1	711.9	62.8	10.6
1985	734.1	946.5	-212.3	1,817.5	1,507.4	152.9	16.2
1990	1,032.0	1,253.2	-221.2	3,206.6	2,411.8	202.4	16.2
1995	1,351.8	1,515.8	-164.0	4,921.0	3,604.8	239.2	15.8
1996	1,453.1	1,560.6	-107.5	5,181.9	3,734.5	246.6	15.8
1997	1,579.3	1,601.3	-22.0	5,369.7	3,772.8	250.8	15.7
1998	1,721.8	1,652.6	69.2	5,478.7	3,721.6	250.0	15.1
1999	1,827.5	1,702.9	124.6	5,606.1	3,632.9	234.9	13.8
2000	2,025.2	1,788.8	236.3	5,629.0	3,410.1	233.1	13.0
2001[2]	2,136.9	1,856.2	280.7	5,625.0	3,174.2	215.3	11.6

Note: For fiscal years ending in year shown. Public debt excludes debt held by Federal Government accounts. 1. Net interest is interest paid on debt held by the public. 2. Estimate. Source: *Budget of the United States Government, Fiscal Year 2002* (2001).

The strong economy and prudent government accounting allowed the Clinton Administration to wipe out the annual deficit in 1998, posting a one-year surplus of $69.2 billion. Despite surpluses of $125 billion in 1999 and $236 billion in 2000, the total national debt did not begin to decrease until 2001. The interest alone on the huge debt created during the 1980s is still more than 10 percent of the entire federal budget, and until 2001, ate up the entire annual surplus.

▶ THE LABOR FORCE
Labor Force Participation Rate
The Labor Force Participation Rate (LFPR), often referred to simply as the labor force, is that proportion of the population that is either employed or actively seeking employment. It represents the supply of labor available to the economy. The LFPR is lower for young people because many are in school, and for older people because many have retired. It is highest for married men and for women who are heads of households.

Women in the work force
One of the most important developments in the labor force has been the sharp increase in the LFPR of women, which has virtually doubled since the early 1960s. With higher levels of education than ever before, most women now opt for careers in the labor force rather than homemaking. Women are having fewer children, and are having them later in life, after they have started to establish their careers, and are returning to work sooner after childbirth. Furthermore, women are continuing to make inroads into professions like law and medicine that have previously been dominated by men.

Women have joined the labor force at an astounding rate since 1960. In 2000, 60.2 percent of women were in the labor force, up from 37.7 percent in 1960. Over the same period, the percentage of men in the labor force has actually dropped, from 83.3 percent to 74.7 percent. Women constituted 52 percent of the entire civilian population in 2000, about the same as in 1960, but only 33 percent of the labor force was female in 1960; in 2000, it was 46 percent.

Unemployment rate
One of the most closely watched labor force statistics is the unemployment rate, which surged to 7.4 percent in 1992. But in early 1997, it fell below 5 percent for the first time in 30 years, and then dropped all the way to 4.0 percent in 2000. Contrary to popular opinion, the unemployment rate is only an indirect measure of the people without jobs, since it only measures the number of active (within the last four weeks) job seekers as a proportion of the total labor force. So the unemployment rate may rise as new job seekers enter the labor force. Every spring, for example, it rises slightly as school graduates enter the labor force and look for jobs. It may also fall as workers retire or otherwise leave the labor force. And when the economy is in a prolonged recession, the unemployment rate may actually drop slightly because some of the job seekers may give up trying to find a job and withdraw from the labor force.

Women, Blacks, and Hispanics in Selected Occupations, 1975–2000

| | As percent of total employed | | | | | | |
| Occupation | Women | | | Blacks | | Hispanics | |
	1975	1985	2000	1999	2000	1999	2000
Auto mechanic	0.5%	0.6%	1.2%	8.2%	7.3%	13.8%	15.6%
Bartender	35.2	47.9	51.8	4.1	2.0	12.9	13.2
Brickmasons and stonemasons	N.A.	N.A.	0.7	15.7	13.0	17.0	18.6
Bus driver	37.7	49.2	49.6	24.5	26.1	9.3	8.0
Butchers and meatcutters	N.A.	N.A.	27.3	16.8	14.5	34.5	38.3
Cab driver, chauffeur	8.7	10.9	10.8	23.9	26.0	16.2	14.0
Child care worker	98.4	96.1	97.5	10.2	11.6	21.5	19.9
Cleaners and servants	N.A.	N.A.	94.8	17.6	16.9	33.9	37.7
Computer programmer	25.6	34.3	26.5	6.4	8.1	3.8	3.5
Computer systems analyst	14.8	28.0	29.2	7.4	8.0	3.4	3.6
Data entry keyer	92.8	90.7	83.5	15.6	18.8	10.9	11.2
Data processing equipment repairer	1.8	10.4	15.4	9.4	9.8	6.3	4.8
Dentist	1.8	6.5	18.7	1.9	3.4	3.1	2.2
Drywall installers	N.A.	N.A.	5.6	6.0	6.1	32.2	39.2
Dental assistant	100.0	99.0	96.4	6.7	5.1	10.4	10.6
Dietitian	N.A.	N.A.	89.9	19.5	18.4	4.6	4.8
Economist	13.1	34.5	53.3	6.1	6.3	1.9	4.4
Editor, reporter	44.6	51.7	55.8	4.5	5.0	2.7	3.0
Firefighter	N.A.	N.A.	3.0	11.1	9.0	5.4	5.0
Lawyer, judge	7.1	18.2	29.7	5.1	5.7	4.0	4.1
Librarian	81.1	87.0	85.2	7.7	6.7	4.8	6.6
Mail carrier (Postal Service)	8.7	17.2	30.6	15.0	14.7	5.6	5.9
Physician	13.0	17.2	27.9	5.7	6.3	4.8	3.7
Police officer, detective (public service)	N.A.	N.A.	14.2	15.1	13.0	9.1	10.1
Registered nurse	97.0	95.1	92.8	9.6	9.5	3.1	2.8
Social worker	60.8	66.7	72.4	24.2	22.7	7.4	8.5
Teacher, elementary school	85.4	84.0	83.3	10.3	11.3	5.1	5.6
Telephone installer, repairer	4.8	12.8	13.1	13.2	11.3	6.9	9.5
Telephone operator	93.3	88.8	83.9	20.2	22.9	12.2	10.4
Waiter/waitress	91.1	84.0	76.7	5.1	4.4	10.2	11.0
Welder	4.4	4.8	4.9	9.5	10.2	14.9	15.3

N.A. = Not available.   **Source:** U.S. Department of Labor, Bureau of Labor Statistics, *Employment and Earnings* January issues.

Employment Status of the Population by Sex, Race, and Hispanic Origin 1960-2000 (numbers in thousands)

Year	Civilian noninstitutional population[1]	Civilian labor force				
		Total	Percent of population	Number employed	Employment/ population ratio[2]	Percent unemployed
			Total			
1960	117,245	69,628	59.4%	65,778	56.1%	5.5%
1970	137,085	82,771	60.4	78,678	57.4	4.9
1980	167,745	106,940	63.8	99,303	59.2	7.1
1990	188,049	124,787	66.4	117,914	62.7	5.5
1995[3]	198,584	132,304	66.6	124,900	62.9	5.6
1998[3]	205,220	137,673	67.1	131,463	64.1	4.5
1999[3]	207,753	139,368	67.1	133,488	64.3	4.2
2000[3]	209,699	140,863	67.2	135,208	64.5	4.0
			Male			
1960	55,662	46,388	83.3%	43,904	78.9%	5.4%
1970	64,304	51,228	79.7	48,990	76.2	4.4
1980	79,398	61,453	77.4	57,186	72.0	6.9
1990	89,650	68,234	76.1	64,435	71.9	5.6
1995[3]	95,178	71,360	75.0	67,377	70.8	5.6
1998[3]	98,758	73,959	74.9	70,693	71.6	4.4
1999[3]	99,722	74,512	74.7	71,446	71.6	4.1
2000[3]	100,731	75,247	74.7	72,293	71.8	3.9
			Female			
1960	61,582	23,240	37.7%	21,874	35.5%	5.9%
1970	72,782	31,543	43.3	29,688	40.8	5.9
1980	88,348	45,487	51.5	42,117	47.7	7.4
1990	98,399	56,554	57.5	53,479	54.3	5.4
1995[3]	103,406	60,944	58.9	57,523	55.6	5.6
1998[3]	106,462	63,715	59.8	60,771	57.1	4.6
1999[3]	108,031	64,855	60.0	62,042	57.4	4.3
2000[3]	108,968	65,166	60.2	62,915	57.7	4.1
			White			
1975	134,790	82,831	61.5%	76,411	56.7%	7.8%
1980	146,122	93,600	64.1	87,715	60.0	6.3
1990	160,415	107,177	66.8	102,087	63.6	4.7
1995[3]	166,914	111,950	67.1	106,490	63.8	4.9
1998[3]	171,478	115,415	67.3	110,931	64.7	3.9
1999[3]	173,085	116,509	67.3	112,235	64.8	3.7
2000[3]	174,428	117,574	67.4	113,475	65.1	3.5
			Black			
1975	15,751	9,263	58.8%	7,894	50.1%	14.8%
1980	17,824	10,865	61.0	9,313	52.2	14.3
1990	21,300	13,493	63.3	11,966	56.2	11.3
1995[3]	23,246	14,817	63.7	13,279	57.1	10.4
1998[3]	24,373	15,982	65.6	14,556	59.7	8.9
1999[3]	24,855	16,355	65.8	15,056	60.6	8.0
2000[3]	25,218	16,603	65.8	15,334	60.8	7.6
			Hispanic[4]			
1975	N.A.	N.A.	N.A.	N.A.	N.A.	N.A.
1980	9,598	6,146	64.0%	5,527	57.6%	10.1%
1990	14,297	9,576	67.0	8,808	61.6	8.0
1995[3]	18,629	12,267	65.8	11,127	59.7	9.3
1998[3]	21,070	14,317	67.9	13,291	63.1	7.2
1999[3]	21,650	14,665	67.7	13,720	63.4	6.4
2000[3]	22,393	15,368	68.6	14,492	64.7	5.7

Note: N.A.=Not Available. 1. Age 16 and over. 2. Civilians employed as a percent of the civilian noninstitutional population. 3. Data for 1995-2000 are not directly comparable with data for previous years because of a major redesign of the Current Population Survey questionnaire and collection methodology and the introduction of 1990 census-based population controls, adjusted for the estimated undercount. 4. Hispanic persons may be of any race. **Source:** U.S. Bureau of Labor Statistics, *Employment and Earnings,* January issues.

The unemployment rate over time for the United States is a measure associated with identifying periods of expansion and recession. It reached a peak of 9.6 percent during the 1982-83 recession. The relatively high periods of unemployment beginning in the mid-1970s are in part due to the expansion of the labor force as the Baby Boom generation left school and began looking for work. Unemployment rates for women have paralleled those for men since 1990.

Hispanics   People of Hispanic origin constitute the fastest-growing population group in the labor force, in large part due to immigration, with Mexicans making up the largest share. The pro-

portion of Hispanic women working—historically, these women were more likely to stay at home—has boosted Hispanic participation in the labor force. But a doubling of the Hispanic population in the U.S. since 1980 has been responsible for most of the growth. By the year 2000, the number of Hispanic workers in the labor force will account for 10 percent of the total labor force. Overall, however, Hispanic workers earn only 74 percent as much as the average for all workers. They also have a significantly higher unemployment rate.

Productivity   measures how much output an economy or organization can generate from a given amount of input. Higher levels of productiv-

Average Earnings of Year-Round Full-Time Workers by Age and Educational Attainment, 1999

Age and Sex	All workers	Less than 9th grade	Some high school	High school graduate	Some college	Associate degree	Bachelor's degree or more
Male, total	$40,257	$18,743	$18,908	$30,414	$33,614	$40,047	$66,810
18 - 24 years old	13,215	12,925	9,175	15,001	11,743	17,991	21,161
25 - 34 years old	35,282	18,128	19,895	29,162	32,803	34,392	50,164
35 - 44 years old	46,000	21,466	23,886	34,151	43,174	45,108	70,594
45 - 54 years old	53,411	21,159	26,479	36,484	46,916	47,041	80,024
55 - 64 years old	49,646	20,292	29,125	35,224	42,896	43,349	79,097
65 years and over	31,910	12,830	15,366	26,484	21,324	20,393	54,497
Female, total	$23,551	$12,392	$12,057	$18,092	$20,241	$25,079	$36,755
18 - 24 years old	10,590	10,051	6,851	10,729	9,345	13,279	19,007
25 - 34 years old	23,872	12,765	13,023	17,373	20,828	22,925	34,195
35 - 44 years old	26,632	13,223	13,145	19,573	25,099	26,802	40,012
45 - 54 years old	28,683	12,871	14,799	21,682	26,396	28,638	41,096
55 - 64 years old	25,876	13,975	20,006	20,502	25,517	28,088	37,801
65 years and over	13,739	6,778	10,751	10,766	16,359	15,168	21,506

Note: High school graduate category includes equivalency.   **Source:** U.S. Bureau of the Census, *Current Population Reports.*

Average Hourly and Weekly Earnings in Current and Constant (1982) Dollars, By Private Industry Group, 1970-2000

While average hourly and weekly wages (in current dollars) have more than quadrupled since 1970, the following table illustrates that when inflation is accounted for, real earnings (in constant dollars) have decreased steadily over the past two

decades. Hourly earnings have fallen 2.7% since 1970, while weekly earnings have dropped 8.8%. Thus, even though 2000 paychecks have more zeroes on the end, they don't go as far as a 1970 paycheck to cover living expenses.

Private industry group	Current dollars					Constant (1982)[1] dollars				
	1970	1980	1990	1995	2000	1970	1980	1990	1995	2000
Average hourly earnings	$3.23	$6.66	$10.01	$11.43	$13.74	$8.03	$7.78	$7.52	$7.39	$7.88
Mining	3.85	9.17	13.68	15.30	17.14	9.58	10.71	10.28	9.90	9.83
Construction	5.24	9.94	13.77	15.09	17.86	13.03	11.61	10.35	9.76	10.25
Manufacturing	3.35	7.27	10.83	12.37	14.38	8.33	8.49	8.14	8.00	8.25
Transportation, public utilities	3.85	8.87	12.92	14.13	16.22	9.58	10.36	9.71	9.14	9.31
Wholesale trade	3.43	6.95	10.79	12.43	15.18	8.53	8.12	8.11	8.04	8.71
Retail trade	2.44	4.88	6.75	7.69	9.45	6.07	5.70	5.07	4.97	5.42
Finance, insurance, real estate	3.07	5.79	9.97	12.32	15.07	7.64	6.76	7.49	7.97	8.65
Services	2.81	5.85	9.83	11.39	13.88	6.99	6.83	7.39	7.37	7.96
Average weekly earnings	$120	$235	$345	$394	$474	$296	$275	$259	$255	$272
Mining	164	397	603	684	770	409	464	453	442	442
Construction	195	368	526	587	702	486	430	395	380	403
Manufacturing	133	289	442	515	597	332	337	332	333	342
Transportation, public utilities	156	351	496	557	624	388	410	373	360	358
Wholesale trade	137	267	411	476	584	341	312	309	308	335
Retail trade	82	147	194	221	273	205	172	146	143	157
Finance, insurance, real estate	113	210	357	442	547	281	245	268	286	314
Services	97	191	319	369	454	240	223	240	239	260

Note: Constant dollar figures for 2000 are for June, and are not seasonally adjustted. 1. Earnings in current dollars divided by the Consumer Price Index on a 1982 base. **Source:** U.S. Bureau of Labor Statistics, *Employment and Earnings,* monthly.

ity suggest greater efficiency—doing more with the same amount of resources, just as an efficient or economical car goes farther on a gallon of gasoline. Increases in productivity, as the result of better tools or improved methods, provide the main mechanism for increasing output in an economy and ultimately for raising standards of living. Productivity is usually measured in terms of labor—output per worker or per hour of labor—not only because labor is the most important resource but also because it is one of the easiest to measure.

Wages vary not only among the different professions but also between sexes and regions of the country. For example, women in year-round, full-time executive, administrative, and managerial positions have a median yearly income of only 61 percent of the median income for men in the same occupation group. This percentage is higher in the field of laborers, precision production, craft, and repair; but for all major occupation groups reported by the U.S. Bureau of the Census, women receive only a fraction of that received by their male counterparts. This may be due, in part, to the fact that women enter and leave the work force more times throughout their lives than do men and spend a smaller percentage of their lives economically active.

Another factor influencing the discrepancy between men's and women's wages is the concentration of women in occupations that pay less. Women made up 98 percent of child care workers, 84 percent of telephone operators, and 84 percent of data entry keyers, three poorly paid positions.

Minimum wage in the nation was first enacted by the state of Massachusetts in 1912, covered only women, and was designed to shorten hours and raise pay in the covered industries. The nationwide minimum wage was established in 1938, and has grown in both dollar value and the types of employees it covers since then (see the accompanying table). Some states may establish minimum wages higher than the federal minimum.

Unions are organizations of workers who engage in collective bargaining with employers for higher wages, better working conditions, and increased benefits. In the United States, unions are organized at three levels: (1) labor federations or voluntary associations of national unions, which settle disputes between national unions, lobby for favorable labor legislation, and engage in public relations. There is only one labor foundation in the country—the American Federation of Labor and Congress of Industrial Organizations, or AFL-CIO—to which virtually all union members belong; (2) national unions, which coordinate agreements across local unions and conduct collective bargaining negotiations with industry employers; and (3) local unions, which administer labor contracts, serving individual members, employers, and in some cases, establishments di-

Federal Minimum Wage Rates, 1938–2001

The Fair Labor Standards Act of 1938 set a minimum wage of 25 cents per hour for employees engaged in interstate commerce or in the production of goods for interstate commerce. Over the years, the government has expanded the numbers of workers covered by the federal minimums (waiters and workers under age 20 in their first three months of work, for example, may be paid less than minimum wage) and has increased the minimum amount. But, as the following table shows, the increases have not always kept up with inflation.

Effective date	Hourly minimum (current dollars)	Purchasing power in constant (=1996) dollars
Oct. 24, 1938	$0.25	$2.78
Oct. 24, 1939	0.30	3.39
Oct. 24, 1945	0.40	3.49
Jan. 25, 1950	0.75	4.88
Mar. 1, 1956	1.00	5.77
Sept. 3, 1961	1.15[1]	6.03
Sept. 3, 1961	1.25	6.41
Feb. 1, 1967	1.40[2]	6.58
Feb. 1, 1968	1.60	7.21
May 1, 1974	2.00	6.37
Jan. 1, 1975	2.10	6.12
Jan. 1, 1976	2.30	6.34
Jan. 1, 1978	2.65	6.38
Jan. 1, 1979	2.90	6.27
Jan. 1, 1980	3.10	5.90
Jan. 1, 1981	3.35	5.78
Apr. 1, 1990	3.50	4.56
Apr. 1, 1991	4.25	4.90
Oct. 1, 1996	4.75	4.75
Sept. 1, 1997[3]	5.15	N.A.

Note: Purchasing power is based on the CPI-U Consumer Price Index. 1. A lower rate of $1.00 per hour was extended to employees in large retail and service enterprises as well as to local transit, construction, and gas service station employees. This rate was increased to $1.15 in 1964, and put on par with the higher rate on Sept. 3, 1965. 2. A lower rate of $1.00 was extended to state and local government employees of hospitals, nursing homes, and schools, and to laundries, dry cleaners, and large hotels, motels, restaurants, and farms. This rate continued to lag behind the rate guaranteed other workers until 1977 (1978 for farm workers). 3. Rate in effect as of Nov. 1, 2001
Source: U.S. Department of Labor.

Work Stoppages, 1947–2000

	Number of work stoppages[1]	Workers involved[2] ('000s)	Days idle	
			Number[3] ('000s)	Percent estimated working time[4]
1947	270	1,629	25,720	N.A.
1950	424	1,698	30,390	0.26%
1955	363	2,055	21,180	0.16
1960	222	896	13,260	0.09
1965	268	999	15,140	0.10
1970	381	2,468	52,761	0.29
1975	235	965	17,563	0.09
1980	187	795	20,844	0.09
1985	54	324	7,079	0.03
1990	44	185	5,926	0.02
1995	31	192	5,771	0.02
1996	37	273	4,887	0.02
1997	29	339	4,497	0.01
1998	34	387	5,116	0.02
1999	17	73	1,996	0.01
2000	39	394	20,419	0.06

Note: Excludes work stoppages involving fewer than 1,000 workers and lasting less than 1 day. 1. Beginning in year indicated. 2. Workers counted more than once if involved in more than one stoppage during the year. 3. Resulting from all stoppages in effect in a year, including those that began in an earlier year. 4. Agricultural and government employees are included in the total working time; private household, forestry and fishery employees are excluded. **Source:** U.S. Bureau of Labor Statistics, *Compensation and Conditions*, monthly.

rectly. Unions can be divided into two groups: (1) industrial unions, representing workers of a particular firm or industry, such as autoworkers and steelworkers, and (2) craft unions, representing employees with a specific skill, such as pilots and musicians.

Many workers choose not to unionize because of the potential costs involved in membership, such as dues, lost pay during strikes, and possible retribution by employers. Union membership in the nation has held steady at around 16 million since 1990 (13.9 percent of the workforce) but that's down significantly from 1954, when 25.4 percent of the total labor force was unionized. As

recently as 1983, more than 20 percent of the workforce was unionized. Notable examples of membership decline are among steelworkers, garment workers, and oil, chemical, and atomic workers, which each fell by about 50 percent during 1979-90. Virtually all of these losses are due to the loss of jobs in unionized firms. Several factors may have contributed to this decline, such as changes in technology that displace workers, increased factor costs and international competition, and "downsizing," in which firms lay off large numbers of employees to keep the company's stock prices high.

U.S. Membership in AFL-CIO Affiliated Unions, 1979-98

Labor organization	1979	1985	1995	1998
Total[1]	N.A.	N.A.	12,986,453	13,056,138
Actors and Artists	75,000	100,000	75,893	69,000
Automobile, Aerospace and Agriculture (UAW)	N.A.	974,000	760,038	741,706
Bakery, Confectionery and Tobacco	131,000	115,000	95,186	104,875
Boilermakers	129,000	110,000	42,802	39,728
Bricklayers	106,000	95,000	84,000	62,275
Carpenters and Joiners	626,000	609,000	354,306	323,929
Communications Workers (CWA)	485,000	524,000	490,482	510,631
Electrical Workers (IBEW)	825,000	791,000	673,117	658,647
Electronic, Electrical, and Salaried[2, 4]	243,000	198,000	136,502	115,336
Firefighters	150,000	142,000	151,000	171,500
Flight Attendants	N.A.	N.A.	31,776	38,757
Food and Commercial Workers (UFCW) [2]	1,123,000	989,000	1,009,523	1,122,521
Garment Workers (ILGWU)	314,000	210,000	N.A.	N.A.
Glass, Molders, Pottery, and Plastics[2]	50,000	72,000	69,000	60,667
Government Employees (AFGE)	236,000	199,000	157,100	181,317
Graphic Communications[2]	171,000	141,000	95,580	86,024
Hotel and Restaurant Employees	373,000	327,000	232,160	229,726
Ironworkers	146,000	140,000	80,485	83,054
Laborers	475,000	383,000	330,694	299,080
Letter Carriers (NALC)	151,000	186,000	210,000	210,000
Longshoreman's Association	63,000	65,000	60,595	61,849
Machinists and Aerospace (IAM) [2]	688,000	520,000	431,619	456,030
Mine Workers	N.A.	N.A.	75,021	75,250
Needletrades, Industrial and Textile Employees	308,000	228,000	244,783	205,000
Office and Professional Employees	83,000	90,000	82,987	80,635
Operating Engineers	313,000	330,000	295,833	289,083
Oil, Chemical, Atomic Workers (OCAW)	146,000	108,000	82,080	N.A.
Painters	160,000	133,000	90,000	97,103
Paper, Chemical and Energy Workers[2]	262,000	232,000	235,302	289,969
Plumbing and Pipefitting	228,000	226,000	219,800	219,800
Postal Workers	245,000	232,000	265,757	280,956
Retail, Wholesale, Department Store	122,000	106,000	73,133	N.A.
Rubber, Cork, Linoleum, Plastic	158,000	106,000	N.A.	N.A.
Seafarers	84,000	80,000	80,250	77,250
Service Employees (SEIU) [2, 5]	537,000	688,000	1,077,854	1,143,932
Sheet Metal Workers	120,000	108,000	103,042	93,000
Stage Employees, Moving Picture Machine Operators	50,000	50,000	50,900	49,100
State, County, Municipal (AFSCME) [5]	889,000	997,000	1,210,949	1,247,051
Steelworkers	964,000	572,000	516,880	468,313
Teachers (AFT)	423,000	470,000	631,529	786,921
Teamsters[6]	N.A.	N.A.	1,286,371	1,231,144
Transit Union	94,000	94,000	96,340	103,942
Transport Workers	85,000	85,000	75,000	75,000
Transportation Union, United	121,000	52,000	59,575	60,859

Note: Figures represent the labor organizations as constituted in 1989 and reflect past merger activity. Membership figures based on average per capita paid membership to the AFL-CIO for the 2-year period ending in June of the year shown and reflect only actively-employed members. Not all unions shown. 1. Includes other AFL-CIO affiliated unions, not shown separately. 2. Figures reflect mergers with one or more unions since 1979. 3. Includes Blacksmiths, Forgers and Helpers. 4. Includes Machine and Furniture Workers. 5. Excludes Hospital and Health Care Employees which merged into both unions on June 1, 1989 (membership of 23,000 in 1985, and 58,000 in 1989). 6. Includes Chauffeurs, Warehousemen and Helpers. **Source:** American Federation of Labor and Congress of Industrial Organizations, *Report of the AFL-CIO Executive Council* (annual).

Metropolitan Areas with Greatest Job Growth, 2000-25

Rank, Metropolitan statistical area	Number of jobs ('000s) 2000	2025	Jobs added 2000-25
1. Atlanta	2,715	4,892	2,177
2. Houston	2,639	4,370	1,731
3. Phoenix-Mesa, Ariz.	1,953	3,675	1,722
4. Dallas	2,461	4,101	1,641
5. Washington, D.C.-Md.-Va.-W.Va.	3,442	4,995	1,553
6. Los Angeles-Long Beach, Calif.	5,461	6,930	1,469
7. San Diego	1,720	3,035	1,316
8. Orange County, Calif.	1,885	3,140	1,255
9. Seattle-Bellevue-Everett, Wash.	1,788	3,005	1,218
10. Chicago	5,098	6,246	1,148
12. Denver	1,460	2,599	1,140
11. Tampa-St. Petersburg-Clearwater, Fla.	1,482	2,606	1,124
13. Orlando	1,098	2,207	1,109
14. Minneapolis-St. Paul	2,138	3,153	1,016
15. Boston[1]	3,920	4,903	983
16. Riverside-San Bernardino, Calif.	1,332	2,181	849
17. Las Vegas	882	1,675	793
18. Sacramento	955	1,724	769
20. Portland-Vancouver, Oreg.-Wash.	842	1,596	754
20. Austin-San Marcos, Texas	1,236	1,966	731
21. Salt Lake City-Ogden, Utah	912	1,634	721
22. Fort Worth-Arlington, Texas	1,318	2,031	713
23. San Jose, Calif.	1,001	1,702	701
24. Oakland	1,439	2,066	627
25. Raleigh-Durham-Chapel Hill, N.C.	858	1,479	621
26. San Antonio	946	1,537	591
27. Philadelphia	2,909	3,491	582
28. Fort Lauderdale	852	1,425	573
29. Charlotte-Gastonia-Rock Hill, N.C.	998	1,566	567
30. Miami	1,257	1,822	565
Total 30 MSA's	56,997	87,752	30,759

FASTEST JOB GROWTH Rank, Metropolitan statistical area	Number of jobs ('000s) 2000	2025	Annual percent increase, 2000-25
1. Punta Gorda, Fla.	55	117	3.08%
2. Orlando, Fla.	1,098	2,207	2.83
3. Naples, Fla.	139	278	2.83
4. Myrtle Beach, S.C.	133	256	2.64
5. Provo-Orem, Utah	196	374	2.62
6. Las Vegas	882	1,675	2.60
7. Austin-San Marcos, Texas	842	1,596	2.59
8. Phoenix-Mesa, Ariz.	1,953	3,675	2.56
9. Fort Pierce-Port St.Lucie, Fla.	144	268	2.50
10. Fort Collins-Loveland, Colo.	168	312	2.49
11. McAllen-Edinburg Mission, Texas	202	373	2.48
12. Laredo, Texas	83	153	2.48
13. Sarasota-Bradenton, Fla.	349	642	2.48
14. Bryan College Station, Texas	96	176	2.47
15. Fort Myers-Cape Coral, Fla.	223	411	2.47
16. Fort Walton Beach, Fla.	115	212	2.46
17. Olympia, Wash.	118	215	2.44
18. Ocala, Fla.	116	212	2.43
19. Santa Fe, N.Mex.	107	194	2.40
20. Sacramento	955	1,724	2.39
21. Tucson	444	800	2.39
22. Boulder-Longmont, Colo.	233	420	2.38
23. Atlanta	2,715	4,893	2.38
24. Fayetteville-Springdale-Rogers, Ark.	194	348	2.37
25. Vallejo-Fairfield-Napa, Calif.	290	521	2.37
26. Salt Lake City-Ogden, Utah	912	1,634	2.36
27. Yolo, Calif.	110	197	2.35
28. Tampa-St. Petersburg-Clearwater, Fla.	1,460	2,599	2.34
29. West Palm Beach-Boca Raton, Fla.	636	1,131	2.33
30. Boise City, Idaho	286	507	2.32

1. Includes Worcester, Lawrence, Lowell, Brockton, and portions of New Hampshire.
Source: NPA Data Services, Inc., *Regional Economic Growth in the U.S. Projections for 2000-2025* (2001).

U.S. BUSINESS

The Office of Management and Budget (O.M.B.) classifies the entire national economy into industries, based on principal product or activity. There are nine industrial divisions, which are further classified into groups and subgroups. For example, under "manufacturing" would fall "food and kindred products," and beneath that, "meat-packing plants." The nine industrial divisions listed in the O.M.B.'s Standard Industry Classification (SIC) are agriculture, forestry, and fishing; mining; construction; manufacturing; transportation and public utilities; finance, insurance and real estate; wholesale trade; retail trade; and services. In 1999, 7.0 million establishments employed 110 million workers with payrolls totaling $3.6 trillion.

Services and Manufacturing
Another way to view the economy is to divide it into manufacturing industries, producing tangible goods such as cars, shoes and furniture, and services industries, whose products are intangible, such as entertainment, tourism and banking. The manufacturing industries are further broken down into those that produce durable goods—that is, goods that are consumed over time, such as cars and houses—and nondurable goods that are consumed in the short run (food and soap). Services have played an increasingly important role in the economy, partly because companies in the manufacturing sector increasingly contract out services such as transportation, accounting, marketing and communications, previously performed in-house.

The service sector, which includes government, is responsible for approximately three-quarters of U.S. employment, and is expected to account for four of every five jobs by the year 2005. Seven of the 10 fastest-growing industries over the next 10 years are service industries. They include health services, computer and data processing services, and child day care services.

Financing Business
When an individual or a group of individuals decides to start a new company, they need money to rent or buy offfice space and equipment and to pay workers. Since there is a time lag between the day a business opens and the day a business sells its first good or service, funds must be borrowed from a bank or other financial institution or from individual investors to meet costs before revenues are generated. Additional funds may be needed throughout the life of the business to finance research and development of a new product or service or for the construction of new factories. Financing can take many forms, from short-term bank loans, commercial paper, or trade credit to long-term stocks and bonds.

Short-term Financing   *Trade credit*, the largest category of short-term financing, is an arrangement between a company and its suppliers, whereby materials and supplies are delivered to the company with a promise to pay the invoice, plus interest, usually within a specified number of weeks. Commercial bank lending may take the form of a single loan with repayment in a lump sum or in installments over the life of the loan, or it may be a line of credit up to a maximum the bank will allow the company to overdraw on its account. *Commercial paper* is a promissory note of a well-established firm sold primarily to other

Number of Business Establishments with Employees and Payroll, by Major Group, 1999

Major group	Number of establishments	Number of employees	Annual payroll ('000s)
Total	**7,008,444**	**110,705,661**	**$3,554,692 909**
Forestry, fishing, hunting, and agriculture support	26,926	192,155	4,812,649
Forestry and logging	13,694	83,833	2,256,428
Fishing, hunting & trapping	2,541	9,986	332,533
Agriculture & forestry support activities	10,691	98,336	2,223,668
Mining	23,699	456,645	20,975,962
Oil & gas extraction	7,556	90,012	5,377,469
Mining (except oil & gas)	7,280	215,949	9,625,175
Mining support activities	8,863	150,684	5,973,318
Utilities	16,578	667,062	39,354,990
Construction	698,541	6,201,626	219,087,088
Building, developing & general contracting	216,355	1,538,079	55,883,792
Heavy construction	39,556	848,373	35,807,866
Special trade contractors	442,630	3,815,174	127,395,430
Manufacturing	360,244	16,659,930	625,536,131
Food	26,734	1,464,354	41,857,959
Beverage & tobacco products	2,789	172,349	6,991,562
Textile mills	4,587	362,286	9,694,368
Textile product mills	7,152	221,971	5,313,455
Apparel	16,721	574,908	11,205,644
Leather & allied products	1,807	73,966	1,737,933
Wood products	17,473	595,176	16,372,899
Paper	5,883	559,020	23,226,723
Printing & related support activities	40,671	833,649	27,940,066
Petroleum & coal products	2,226	109,104	6,058,224
Chemical	13,534	886,354	44,738,273
Plastics & rubber products	16,646	1,046,935	33,350,608

Major group	Number of establishments	Number of employees	Annual payroll ('000s)
Nonmetallic mineral products	16,541	510,316	$18,272,582
Primary metals	5,900	597,623	24,765,637
Fabricated metal products	62,242	1,788,484	61,603,757
Machinery	30,177	1,398,226	55,874,118
Computer & electronic products	17,279	1,615,177	83,841,985
Electrical equipment, appliances & components	7,104	586,421	20,599,635
Transportation equipment	13,042	1,906,216	90,608,982
Furniture & related products	20,266	623,153	17,127,833
Miscellaneous	31,470	734,242	24,353,888
Wholesale trade	450,030	5,972,022	249,997,598
Wholesale trade, durable goods	290,053	3,527,913	158,783,498
Wholesale trade, nondurable goods	159,977	2,444,109	91,214,100
Retail trade	1,111,260	14,476,628	281,946,316
Motor vehicle & parts dealers	123,855	1,803,665	60,217,423
Building materials and garden supplies	92,293	1,183,696	12,179,769
Food & beverage stores	151,506	3,014,663	45,919,947
Health & personal care stores	82,392	938,245	17,760,222
Gasoline stations	121,095	930,034	12,825,358
Clothing & clothing accessories stores	151,674	1,293,439	19,134,168
Sporting goods, hobby, book & music stores	66,074	589,873	8,247,327
General merchandise stores	38,134	2,444,538	36,559,197
Miscellaneous store retailers	131,246	828,824	13,033,156
Nonstore retailers	43,566	540,045	16,089,022
Transportation & warehousing	187,339	3,627,057	116,682,214
Air transportation	5,285	582,838	24,414,357
Water transportation	1,950	71,844	3,039,510,
Truck transportation	108,749	1,384,178	43,626,168,
Transit & ground passenger transportation	16,254	370,022	6,729,332
Pipeline transportation	2,550	48,149	3,032,689
Scenic & sightseeing transportation	2,267	22,877	540,702
Transportation support activities	31,392	440,175	14,915,625
Couriers & messengers	11,938	578,368	16,725,960
Warehousing & storage	6,954	128,606	3,657,871
Information	126,510	3,234,530	170,282,356
Publishing industries	32,377	1,004,697	54,516,491
Motion picture & sound recording industries	23,102	293,369	10,531,411
Broadcasting & telecommunications	50,852	1,504,242	76,010,594
Information & data processing services	20,179	432,222	29,223,860
Finance & insurance	418,337	5,965,174	313,245,188
Credit intermediation & related activities	173,807	2,780,756	112,584,412
Security, commodity contracts & like activity	66,353	780,061	92,945,562
Insurance carriers & related activities	176,136	2,345,952	104,816,285
Real estate & rental & leasing	298,080	1,873,792	54,095,260
Real estate	231,337	1,225,995	36,593,436
Rental & leasing services	64,644	621,916	16,041,736
Professional, scientific & technical services	704,779	6,432,422	311,238,501
Management of companies & enterprises	46,528	2,788,276	192,378,035
Administrative, support, waste management, and remediation services	350,401	8,366,523	183,100,191
Administrative & support services	334,101	8,079,349	173,116,039
Waste management & remediation services	16,300	287,174	9,984,152
Educational services	66,492	2,431,718	56,871,035
Health care and social assistance	649,846	13,865,014	409,223,160
Ambulatory health care services	455,726	4,466,133	169,988,142
Hospitals	6,969	5,000,531	163,440,600
Nursing & residential care facilities	61,557	2,568,012	47,466,468
Social assistance	125,594	1,830,338	28,327,950
Arts, entertainment & recreation	102,786	1,640,030	39,415,855
Performing arts, spectator sports & related industries	32,906	330,381	17,380,510
Museums, historical sites & like institutions	5,714	104,607	2,321,151
Amusement, gambling & recreation industries	64,166	1,205,042	19,714,194
Accommodation & food services	539,576	9,638,007	116,924,965
Accommodation	59,278	1,737,734	32,200,402
Food services & drinking places	480,298	7,900,273	84,724,563
Other services (except public administration)	717,892	5,151,464	101,953,241
Repair & maintenance	234,555	1,318,467	34,369,540
Personal & laundry services	195,107	1,261,383	21,587,374
Religious, grantmaking, civic, professional & like organizations	288,230	2,571,614	45,996,327
Unclassified establishments	98,011	106,329	2,757,234

Note: Excludes most government employees, railroad employees, and self-employed persons. Totals include other categories not shown separately. **Source:** U.S. Bureau of the Census, *County Business Patterns 1999* (2001).

business firms, with repayments made in two to six months. The only problem with commercial paper is that its resources are limited to the liquidity that corporations have at any given time for lending to other firms.

Intermediate-term financing, with a time frame of one to 15 years, may take the form of *lease financing*, whereby a company rents, rather than buys, the assets it uses; conditional sales contracts, by which equpiment is bought over a period of time (the seller continues to have title of ownership until payment is completed); or term loans or business credit supplied by commercial banks and life insurance companies, repaid by amortization payments over the life of the loan (one to 15 years).

Long-term financing The issuance of stocks and bonds constitute the long-term source of finance for firms. *Bonds* are debt instruments (IOUs issued by a company to the bondholder) that obligate the firm to pay interest at specific times. Alternatively firms can raise money by issuing preferred and common stocks. Unlike bonds, *stocks* entitle the holder to share in ownership and profits made by the firm through dividends paid out for the entire period the investor owns the stock. However, if the business has low profits or limited funds, bondholders are paid first, preferred stockholders next, and common stockholders last.

▶ **WALL STREET**
The U.S. stock market, commonly known as Wall Street, began in the late 19th century as a merchant-organized public auction in stocks and government bonds for the purpose of financing the government and expanding business and trade. At that time, brokers handed over securities to auctioneers who sold securities to the highest bidder. Today, while the form of the stock exchange has changed dramatically, the purpose remains the same.

The most commonly cited index of Wall Street's performance is the Dow Jones Industrial average (see "Glossary of Financial Terms"). From the Dow's inception in 1896 until the early 1980s, the 1,000 mark was considered the benchmark of a bull market. During that period, the Dow passed

the 1,000 mark for the first time in 1972 and hovered around it in 1976 before eventually falling back below 1,000. In the 21st century, the 10,000 mark is a more likely measure of the health of the stock market. When the Dow fell below 10,000 in the spring of 2001, many economists were predicting the beginning of a bear market. And in the immediate aftermath of the World Trade Center tragedy, the Dow fell below 9,000 for the first time in more than three years.

The Dow's vicissitudes are of greater concern to larger numbers of people these days because many more people are invested in the stock market. The unprecedented growth of the 1990s, combined with easier access to trading due to on-line brokerages, has attracted hundreds of thousands of new investors to the stock market. In 1999, 48.2 percent of American households owned stocks, either directly or through pension plans or mutual funds. That was up from 31.7 percent in 1989 and 19 percent in 1983.

Even more startling is the percentage of the average American's wealth invested in the market. In 1999, stock investments made up a record 37 percent of Americans' household wealth, more even than the value of their homes. As recently as 1990, Americans had only 16 percent of their wealth invested in the stock market. Even during the bull market of the 1980's, the percentage of income invested in securities never topped 19 percent.

There are three major stock and bond markets in the U.S., all located in New York City. The growth of all three markets has been staggering. A total of 19.7 billion shares were traded on all three exchanges in 1980; by 2000, that number had soared to 717 billion shares.

New York Stock Exchange (NYSE) The oldest exchange in the country was formally founded in 1817, when fewer than 100 shares were traded each day. In 2000, more than 260 billion shares were traded on the New York Stock Exchange. The growth in the value of those stocks has been equally impressive. The market value of all stocks traded on the NYSE doubled between 1987 and 1993, and then more than doubled again between 1993 and 2000, when it reached a staggering $12.3 trillion.

NYSE: Daily Shares Traded, 1900–2000 (in thousands)

Year	Daily Average	Record High	Record Low
1900	505	1,627	89
1910	601	1,656	111
1920	828	2,008	227
1930	2,959	8,279	1,090
1940	751	3,940	130
1950	1,980	4,859	1,061
1960	2,578	7,717	1,230
1965	3,042	5,303	1,894
1970	6,176	11,434	3,028
1980	44,871	84,297	16,132
1985	109,169	181,027	62,055
1990	156,777	292,364	56,853
1995	346,101	652,829	117,723
1998	673,590	1,216,326	246,928
1999	809,183	1,349,711	312,093
2000	1,041,578	1,560,808	403,254

Source: New York Stock Exchange, *Fact Book, 2000*(2001).

NYSE Listed Stocks, 1924–2000 (in millions)

Year	Shares (millions)	Market value (millions)	Average price[1]
1924	43	$27,072	$62.45
1945	1,592	73,765	46.33
1950	2,353	93,807	39.86
1960	6,458	306,967	47.53
1970	16,065	636,380	39.61
1980	33,709	1,242,803	36.87
1985	52,427	1,950,332	37.20
1990	90,732	2,819,778	31.08
1995	154,719	6,012,971	38.86
1999	280,930	12,296,057	43.77
2000	313,937	12,372,304	42.14

1. This average cannot be used as an index of price trend owing to changes in shares listed caused by new listing, suspensions, stock splits, and stock dividends. **Source:** New York Stock Exchange, *Fact Book, 2000.*.

NASDAQ   The National Association of Securities Dealers Automated Quotations was founded in 1971 and was the first to use computers and high-technology telecommunications to trade—and to monitor the trading of—millions of securities daily. Today, all the major stock markets have followed suit. In terms of the number of shares traded, the NASDAQ is the largest stock exchange in the world, with a record 443 billion shares trading hands in 2000, many of them dot-coms that suffered tremendously in late 2000 and 2001. As a result, the NASDAQ's total market value plummeted from $5.2 trillion at the end of 1999 to $3.6 trillion a year later. That's still more double what it was at the end of 1997, but significantly lower than the New York Stock Exchange's total market value of $12.3 trillion at the end of 2000.

The American Stock Exchange (AMEX)
The American Stock Exchange, located a few blocks from the New York Stock Exchange in New York's financial district, is known as the stock market for the small investor and small companies. The stock issues of organizations that do not meet the listing and size requirements of the NYSE are typically traded there. For years, the Amex was known as the "New York Curb Exchange" because its trading was conducted on the street outside the office buildings of many brokers. The exchange moved indoors in 1921. In 1998, the NASDAQ stock market bought the American Stock Exchange bringing the NASDAQ's advanced technology to the Amex's trading floor, but the two exchanges continue to operate as separate entities.

Online trading
Internet, or online brokerages allow people to trade stocks directly without a broker for commissions as low as $5 per trade. The number of households with such accounts increased from 2.2 million in December, 1997, to more than 6.3 million in April, 1999, according to the most recent survey performed by NFO Worldwide. An estimated total of eight million accounts managed approximately $400 billion in assets in 1999. The popularity of online accounts has encouraged investors to make more trades, and to buy and sell more quickly to take advantage of short-term changes in market prices. Online trading has also sparked the creation of the day trader: an investor who buys and sells thousands of shares in hundreds of different stocks each day.

Mutual funds, in which investors pool their funds to purchase a variety of securities rather than investing in a single stock or bond, date back to 1924 in the U.S., but few Americans were aware of them until their popularity surged in the 1980s. In 2000, according to the Investment Company Institute, an estimated 88 million Americans in 51 million households owned some kind of mutual funds. Total assets of all mutual funds was $6.97

Milestones in the Dow Jones Industrial Average, 1906–2001

Date	Average	Date	Average
Jan. 12, 1906	100	Nov. 21, 1995	5,000
Sept. 1, 1929	381	Oct. 14, 1996	6,000
Mar. 12, 1956	500	Feb. 13, 1997	7,000
Nov. 14, 1972	1,000	July 16, 1997	8,000
Jan. 8, 1987	2,000	April 6, 1998	9,000
April 17, 1991	3,000	Mar. 16, 1999	10,000
Feb. 23, 1995	4,000	May 3, 1999	11,000

Source: Dow Jones.

Performances of the Three Major Stock Exchanges, 1986–2000

Year	NYSE	AMEX	NASDAQ
Companies listed			
1986	1,575	796	4,417
1990	1,771	859	4,132
1995	2,675	791	5,122
1999	3,025	769	4,829
2000	2,862	765	4,734
Shares traded (billions)			
1986	35,680	2,979	28,737
1990	39,665	3,329	33,380
1995	87,217	5,072	101,158
1999	203,914	8,230	272,604
2000	262,478	13,318	442,752
Dollar volume of shares traded (billions)			
1986	$1,388.8	$45.4	$378.2
1990	1,336.2	37.7	452.4
1995	3,110.2	72.7	2,398.2
1999	9,072.8	945.9	11,013.2
2000	11,204.8	N.A.	20,395.3

Source: New York Stock Exchange, *Fact Book*, 2001 , *NASDAQ Annual Report*, 2000.

Top U.S. Mutual Fund Managers, 2000–01, by Assets

Rank, Fund Manager	Assets (billions)	
	2000	2001
1. Fidelity Investments	$835.1	$818.8
2. Vanguard Group	547.3	574.3
3. Capital Research & Mgmt.	364.9	368.5
4. Putnam Funds	278.7	242.6
5. Merrill Lynch Asset Mgmt.	218.6	191.7
6. Federated Investors	142.7	177.0
7. Janus	228.3	176.6
8. AIM Group	160.2	172.2
9. Franklin Templeton Investments	168.6	171.7
10. Citigroup Asset Mgmt.	149.8	166.0
11. TIAA-CREF	175.8	155.1
12. Dreyfus Corporation	114.3	149.8
13. Schwab Funds	112.7	136.7
14. Morgan Stanley Dean Witter	130.6	131.2
15. Oppenheimer Funds/ MassMutual	126.6	130.3
16. Banc of America Advisors	89.9	120.4
17. MFS Investment Mgmt.	114.6	112.7
18. Zurich Scudder Investments	109.1	110.6
19. Alliance Capital Mgmt.	100.3	109.9
20. American Express Funds	121.3	107.1
21. T. Rowe Price	113.0	104.7
22. J.P. Morgan Chase & Co.	82.7	101.5
23. Prudential Mutual Funds	95.2	96.0
24. Goldman Sachs & Co.	68.1	94.7
25. SEI Investments	80.5	92.9

Note: As of May 31 of each year.
Source: Investment Company Institute.

trillion in 2000, up only slightly over the year before, but more than six times the amount invested in 1990 ($1.1 trillion). More money is invested in mutual funds today than in any other financial institution—more even than in commercial banks, which held a total of $6.2 trillion in assets in 2000, according to the Federal Deposit Insurance Corporation (FDIC).

There are four kinds of mutual funds: stock (or equity), bond, hybrid, and money market. Funds can consist of stocks, bonds, gold, government securities, or other assets. The share price of a mutual fund, called the *net asset value (NAV)*, is the market value of all the fund's securities, minus expenses, divided by the total number of shares outstanding, and rises or falls based on the performance of the securities in which

the fund is invested. Each fund employs a professional fund manager, who chooses a diverse range of securities, so that a drop in the value of one security will not cause a shock to the entire portfolio. As securities prices rise or fall, the fund manager may seek to change the composition of the fund's portfolio. Like securities, but unlike investments offered by banks, mutual funds are not insured by the FDIC or any other government agency.

There were 8,171 mutual funds in 2000, double the number in 1992, representing the full spectrum of investment objectives. Aggressive growth funds seek the maximum capital growth but also carry the greatest risk, because the stocks they invest in are very volatile. Income-equity funds forgo high growth rates in favor of a constant

Assets of IRA Plans by Type of Investment, 1990–2000

Year	Total (billions)	Bank and thrift deposits[1] Amount (billions)	Percent of total	Life insurance companies Amount (billions)	Percent of total	Mutual funds Amount (billions)	Percent of total	Securities[2] Amount (billions)	Percent of total
1990	$636	$266	41.8%	$53	8.3%	$140	22.0%	$177	27.8%
1995	1,288	261	20.2	94	7.3	479	37.2	454	35.2
1998	2,150	249	12.3	190	9.4	960	46.5	752	31.8
1999	2,663	244	9.9	245	8.9	1,243	49.4	931	31.8
2000	2,650	250	9.4	246	9.3	1,232	46.5	922	34.8

1. Includes Keogh deposits. 2. Stocks, bonds, CDs sold by brokers, and other investments held in brokerage accounts.
Source: Investment Company Institute, *Mutual Fund Fact Book* (2000).

Number of Funds, Accounts, and Total Assets of Mutual Funds, 1970–2000

Year	Type of Fund Total	Equity	Hybrid[1]	Bond & Income[1]	Money market Taxable	Tax exempt
Number of Funds						
1978	505	294	N.A.	150	61	—
1980	564	288	N.A.	170	96	10
1985	1,527	579	87	404	346	111
1990	3,081	1,100	194	1,046	506	235
1995	5,728	2,140	414	2,177	674	323
1998	7,314	3,513	525	2,250	685	341
1999	7,791	3,952	533	2,261	702	343
2000	8,171	4,395	525	2,210	704	337
Number of Accounts (millions)						
1978	8.7	6.8	N.A.	1.4	0.5	—
1980	12.1	5.8	N.A.	1.5	4.8	—
1985	34.8	11.5	1.5	6.9	14.4	0.5
1990	61.9	22.2	3.2	13.6	21.6	1.4
1995	131.2	69.3	10.9	20.8	23.3	2.0
1998	193.9	119.8	13.8	21.4	36.4	2.4
1999	226.9	148.3	14.3	20.7	41.2	2.4
2000	243.5	162.5	13.1	19.7	45.5	2.7
Total Net Assets (billions)						
1970	$47.6	$45.1	N.A.	$2.5	—	—
1975	45.9	37.5	N.A.	4.7	$3.7	—
1978	55.9	32.7	N.A.	12.3	10.9	—
1980	134.8	44.4	N.A.	14.0	74.5	$1.9
1985	495.4	116.9	12.0	122.6	207.5	36.3
1990	1,065.2	239.5	37.2	284.3	414.7	83.6
1995	2,811.5	1,249.1	210.5	598.9	630.0	123.0
1998	5,525.2	2,978.2	364.7	830.6	1,163.2	188.5
1999	6,846.3	4,041.9	383.2	808.1	1,408.7	204.4
2000	6,965.2	3,962.3	349.7	808.0	1,607.2	238.1

1. Bond and Income Funds were divided into Bond Funds and Hybrid Funds beginning in 1984. Data from before 1984 in all categories is not directly comparable to later years.   **Source:** Investment Company Institute, *Mutual Fund Fact Book* (2001).

stream of income from stocks with a history of steady dividends. Bond funds, which invest in corporate bonds and government-issued securities, are generally more conservative than stock funds. Hybrid funds invest in both stocks and bonds. Money market funds are called short-term funds because they invest in securities that mature in a year or less, such as Treasury bills, CDs, and commercial paper. Many money market funds offer tax-exempt income (though their rate of return is often lower than taxable money market funds). Special funds meet the needs of specific investors by investing only in certain segments of financial markets (e.g. biotechnology, telecommunications, small-companies) or by pegging the fund's net asset value to one of several economic indexes (hence the name index fund). Global equity funds invest in the stock markets of other countries (see "The International Economy") .

By far the largest segment of the mutual fund industry has been stock or equity funds. Assets of all equity funds in 2000 totaled $3.96 trillion, or 57 percent of all fund assets. The next biggest segment was taxable money market funds, which held $1.61 trillion in assets (23.1 percent of the total). Bond and income funds had assets of $808.0 billion, or 11.6 percent of the total).

Mergers and Acquisitions
Throughout the boom years of the 1980s, and then again in the '90s, an ever-increasing number of companies have sought to increase their power in the new global marketplace by buying rival companies or by merging with one. Because fierce competition tends to drive down prices, making profitability more difficult, and because one company needs fewer employees than two—not to mention the financial windfalls to the CEOs who broker the deals—the reasons for the current merger mania are very compelling.

More than 27,600 companies joined hands between 1995 and 1997, and the trend shows no sign of abating. In 1998, the Travelers' Group's $72.6 billion acquisition of Citicorp was the biggest merger ever; less than two years later, it ranked 6th all-time, and the top-ranked merger was worth nearly three times that amount (more than $200 billion). Meanwhile the 25th-largest deal was worth $18.3 billion in 1998; in 2001, it was worth double that amount. With more mergers announced every day, the accompanying table should be viewed only as a snapshot of this ever-burgeoning playing field.

▶ GLOSSARY OF FINANCIAL TERMS
Arbitrage   Simultaneous purchase and sale of a commodity or currency in at least two markets where price discrepancies exist. The arbitrageur makes a profit by buying an asset with a low price in one market and selling it in another market where the asset carries a higher price.
Bear/bull   A bear is a speculator who expects prices to fall and sells stocks or bonds in order to

Favorite Stocks

The following table lists (in alphabetical order) the stocks held by the largest number of accounts at Merrrill Lynch (as of Aug. 25, 2001)

AOL Time Warner	Lucent Technologies
AT&T	Merck & Co
Cisco Systems	Microsoft Corp
E M C Corporation	Oracle Corp
Exxon Mobil	Pfizer
General Electric	SBC Communications
Home Depot	Sun Microsystems
IBM	Verizon
Intel	Walmart
Johnson & Johnson	Walt Disney Co.

World's 25 Largest Mergers and Acquisitions

Acquiring Company	Acquired company	Date effective	Value (millions)
1. Vodafone AirTouch PLC.	Mannesmann	June 19, 2000	$202,785.1
2. America Online Inc.	Time Warner	Jan. 12, 2001	181,568.5
3. Pfizer Inc.	Warner-Lambert Co.	June 19, 2000	89,668.7
4. Exxon Corp.	Mobil Corp.	Nov. 30, 1999	86,398.8
5. GlaxoWellcome PLC.	SmithKline Beecham PLC.	Dec. 27, 2000	77,255.2
6. Travelers Group	Citicorp	Oct. 8, 1998	72,558.2
7. SBC Communications Inc.	Ameritech Corp.	Oct. 8, 1999	72,356.5
8. Bell Atlantic Corp.	GTE Corp.	June 30, 2000	71,323.6
9. AT&T Corp.	Tele-Communications Inc.	Mar. 9, 1999	69,896.5
10. Vodafone Group PLC.	AirTouch Communications	June 30, 1999	65,844.9
11. Shareholders	Nortel Networks Corp.	May 1, 2000	61,658.7
12. NationsBank Corp.	BankAmerica Corp	Sept. 30, 1998	61,633.4
13. Qwest Communications Intl.	US West Inc.	June 30, 1999	56,306.0
14. Total Fina SA	Elf Aquitaine	Mar. 27, 2000	55,339.8
15. British Petroleum Co. PLC.	Amoco Corp.	Dec. 31, 1998	55,040.1
16. AT&T Corp.	MediaOne Group Inc.	June 15, 2000	51,873.9
17. Sumitomo Bank	Sakura Bank Ltd.	Apr. 1, 2001	45,494.4
18. Vivendi SA	Seagram Co. Ltd.	Dec. 8, 2000	42,782.6
19. WorldCom Inc.	MCI Communications Corp.	Sept. 14, 1998	41,350.9
20. JDS Uniphase Corp.	SDL Inc.	Feb. 13, 2001	40,992.6
21. Viacom Inc.	CBS Corporation	May 4, 2000	40,882.2
22. Daimler-Benz-AG	Chrysler Corp.	Nov. 12, 1998	40,466.5
23. Fuji Bank Ltd.	Dai-Ichi Kangyo Bank	Aug. 20, 1999	40,096.6
24. France Telecom SA	Orange PLC (Mannesmann)	June 22, 2000	39,670.6
25. Royal Bank of Scotland	National Westminster Bank PLC	Mar. 13, 2000	39,524.6

Note: As of May 15, 2001   **Source:** Securities Data Company.

Securities Industry Revenues and Expenses, 1980–99 (millions)

Type	1980	1985	1990	1995	1998	1999
Revenues, total	**$19,829**	**$49,844**	**$71,356**	**$143,414**	**$234,964**	**$266,809**
Commissions	6,777	10,955	12,032	23,215	36,696	45,937
Trading/investment gains	5,091	14,549	15,746	28,963	32,754	55,464
Underwriting profits	1,571	4,987	3,728	8,865	16,237	17,782
Margin interest	2,151	2,746	3,179	6,470	12,732	15,246
Mutual fund sales	278	2,754	3,242	7,434	14,845	16,688
Other	3,960	13,854	33,428	68,468	121,700	115,692
Expenses, total	**$16,668**	**$43,342**	**$70,566**	**$132,089**	**$217,780**	**$237,693**
Interest expense	3,876	11,470	28,093	56,877	98,095	87,508
Compensation	7,619	18,112	22,931	41,541	65,027	81,738
Commissions/clearance paid	1,055	2,314	2,959	5,700	10,326	13,488
Other	4,119	11,446	16,583	27,970	44,332	54,960
Net income, pretax	**$3,160**	**$6,502**	**$790**	**$11,325**	**$17,184**	**$29,116**

Source: U.S. Securities and Exchange Commission, *2000 Annual Report* (2001).

buy them later at a lower price. A bull expects prices to rise and therefore buys now for resale later. Thus, a bearish (bullish) market is one in which prices are generally falling (rising).

Blue chip stock   A stock that is considered a safe investment, with a low yield and a high price per share, issued by companies that are well known and have a history of good management and increasing profit levels.

Bond   A debt obligation that requires the issuer to pay a fixed sum of money annually until maturity (interest payments) and then, at maturity, a fixed sum of money to repay the initial amount borrowed (principal). (See CORPORATE BONDS.)

Capital gain   An increase in the market value of an asset above the price originally paid for it, realized when the asset is sold.

Capital loss   A decrease in the market value of an asset below the price originally paid for it, realized when the asset is sold.

Common stock/equity   A piece of paper which entitles the owner to a share of the firm's profits and a share of the voting power in shareholder elections. In other words, a shareholder is part owner of the firm. If he owns 50 percent of the issued shares of common stock (when no preferred stock is issued), he owns 50 percent of the company, and will receive 50 percent of profits paid out in dividends. Over 40 million Americans invest in common stocks.

Convertible bond   A debt instrument which carries an option for the holder to convert it into a specified amount of company stock.

Corporate bonds   Debt obligations that require the corporation to pay a fixed sum of money annually until maturity (interest payments) and then, at maturity, a fixed sum of money to repay the initial amount borrowed (principal). Bonds carry no claim to ownership and therefore pay no dividends, but payments to bondholders take priority over payments to stockholders.

Debentures   Debt securities issued by a company that pay a fixed interest rate, in order to raise finance for commercial or industrial operations.

Divestiture   The sales by a company of a product line, subsidiary or division. The number of divestitures sold peaked in 1986, with a total of 1,316, for a record total price of $65.2 billion.

Top 25 Securities Firms by Capital, 2000–01

2001 Rank/Firm	2000	2001
1. Merrill Lynch & Co. Inc.[1]	$60,544	$88,527
2. Morgan Stanley Dean Witter[1,2]	39,699	61,322
3. Goldman Sachs Group[1,2]	31,097	47,925
4. Lehman Brothers Holdings[1,2]	37,600	43,014
5. Salomon Smith Barney[1]	28,147	32,114
6. Bear Stearns Companies[1,2]	22,218	26,250
7. Credit Suisse First Boston[1]	5,959	17,763
8. Deutsche Banc Alex Brown	6,188	7,472
9. J.P. Morgan Securities Inc.	1,883	5,059
10. Alliance Capital Management	553	4,916
11. Banc of America Securities	3,572	4,242
12. UBS PaineWebber Inc.	8,535	4,174
13. UBS Warburg LLC	3,109	3,334
14. Charles Schwab Corporation	2,727	2,866
15. Prudential Securities Inc.	2,219	2,693
16. Spear, Leeds & Kellogg	1,603	1,876
17. CIBC World Markets Corp.	1,321	1,798
18. A.G. Edwards, Inc.	1,721	1,634
19. First Union Securities, Inc.	1,356	1,586
20. TD Waterhouse Group, Inc.	621	1,560
21. D.E. Shaw & Co.	1,107	1,520
22. Nomura Securities Intl.	1,343	1,456
23. Robertson Stephens, Inc.	1,193	1,386
24. Fidelity Brokerage	1,193	1,305
25. Fleet Securities, Inc.	N.A.	1,010

Note: Data as of January 1 of year shown, except as noted.
1. Firm's capital is the sum of long-term borrowings and ownership equity. 2. Data as of Nov. 30 of previous year.
Source: Securities Industry Association.

Dividends   Payments made to common and preferred stockholders out of a firm's profits either in the form of cash or additional shares.

Dow Jones Industrial Average   Dating back to 1893, this index of 30 blue-chip stocks in industry traded on the New York Stock Exchange (and determined by the editors of the *Wall Street Journal*) is the most widely cited indicator of how the stock market is doing.

Establishment   A physical place of business activity such as a factory, assembly plant, retail store, warehouse, etc. where goods are made, stored or processed, or where services are performed.

Eurocurrency Currency of the major industrial and financial countries held in the banks of major financial and industrial countries for the purpose of lending and borrowing. Most loans are for up to one year and are used for payments of deficits. Eurodollars are U.S. dollars held in foreign banks.

Firm A business organization that owns and/or operates one or more establishments. Also called a company, enterprise or business venture. Firms can be of three types: 1) sole proprietorships—firms owned directly by one person; 2) partnerships—firms whose ownership is shared by a fixed number of proprietors; and 3) corporations—firms created by a government charter, granting them greater accessibility to financial capital through the selling of common or preferred stock, greater accessibility to debt capital through the selling of bonds, and limited liability in the event of bankruptcy.

Futures market/forward market A market in which commodities or securities are bought and sold at prices fixed now, for delivery at specified future date. Futures are traded on the American Stock Exchange; the Chicago Board of Trade; Chicago Board Options Exchange; Chicago Mercantile Exchange; Chicago Rice and Cotton Exchange; Commodity Exchange, New York (COMEX); Kansas City Board of Trade; MidAmerica Commodity Exchange, Chicago; Minneapolis Grain Exchange; New York Coffee, Sugar, and Coca Exchange (including the Citrus Associates); New York Cotton Exchange; New York Futures Exchange; and New York Mercantile Exchange; New York Stock Exchange; Pacific Stock Exchange, Los Angeles and San Francisco; and Philadelphia Stock Exchange.

Greenmail Analogous to blackmail, greenmail is the practice of purchasing enough shares in a firm or trading company to threaten a takeover, thereby forcing the owners to buy them back at a higher rate in order to retain control of the business.

Individual Retirement Account (IRA) An account set up by individual investors to hold and invest funds until retirement. Under a traditional IRA, which was established as an alternative for people not eligible for employee-sponsored pension plans, individuals may contribute up to $2,000 pre-tax per year to a tax-deferred retirement account. In 1997, Congress established the Roth IRA, which allows individuals to contribute $2,000 post-tax to a retirement account on which earnings are tax free forever in most cases.

Insider trading Trading in the stock market based on information that has not been made public, and which is intended to remain confidential—for example, information that a small company is about to become part of a national corporation. The penalties paid by individuals and corporations for such activities in recent years have reached into the hundreds of millions of dollars. Drexel Burnham Lambert, Inc., was fined $650 million to settle six charges of securities law violations; and investor Ivan Boesky was fined $100 million and imprisoned for his insider trading activities.

Junk bond/high-yield bond Bonds with a rating below investment grade (at or below Ba1 (Moody's Investors Service), at or below BB+ (Standard & Poor's), or unrated. Issuers of junk bonds are usually small companies who in the past have been limited to borrowing from banks to raise capital for corporate growth. Despite the fact that the major ratings services consider junk bonds risky (hence their name), they have a historically low default rate—only 1.5 percent between the mid 1970s and mid-1980s. The junk market grew considerably in the 1980s, and by 1987 accounted for over 25 percent of the value of all corporate bonds outstanding.

Leveraged buyout The purchase of a company by one of its employee groups (usually upper management) or a large shareholder with borrowed funds, usually using the company's assets as security for the loans. Leveraged buy-outs have been used to combat hostile takeover bids.

Mutual fund A pool of financial assets in which investors may buy shares and get the benefits (or share the losses) depending on the performance of the collective securities. Shares are sold publicly and can be redeemed at any time. Funds can consist of stocks, bonds, gold, government securities, or other assets, and their names are descriptive of their primary purpose; for example, bonds funds, equity-fund portfolios, income funds, money market-mutual funds, and municipal funds. (See the section on mutual funds earlier in this chapter; see also MONEY MARKET ACCOUNTS in "Money and Banking.")

Option A contract to buy or sell commodities or securities within a given time period at a fixed price. For stocks, this period is usually three months. A contract to sell is a *put option* (or put); to buy, a *call option* (or call) and one to buy or sell is a *double option*. A buyer (seller) will gain if the trading price rises (falls) by more than the cost of entering into the contract. Options are traded on the same exchanges as futures contracts (see FUTURES MARKET).

Over-the-counter (OTC) stock A security not listed on an exchange that is traded between two individuals. The name stems from the eighteenth century practice of merchants selling stocks over the counter in their own shops directly to investors without the use of stockbrokers or auctioneers.

Pension fund An arrangement whereby private or public-sector employers, unions, and—as in the case of individual retirement accounts (IRAs) and Keogh plans—individuals contribute to a fund from which money is paid out to the employees, union members, or contributors (or their dependents) upon death, disability or retirement. Contributions can be based on a percentage of salary or corporate profits; in some cases employees may make voluntary or mandatory contributions to the fund. Pension fund assets are usually held in the form of securities or property with a preference for long-term assets.

Preferred stock Similar to COMMON STOCK, except that owners of preferred stock have no voting rights, and preferred stock holders are paid their dividends at a fixed rate, before common stockholders receive any dividends.

Rating An agency evaluation of the quality of a debt instrument or a company issuing debt. Standard & Poor's and Moody's Investment Service are the two major credit ratings agencies in the U.S. The ratings measure the safety of interest and principal payments of bonds. S&P bond ratings are, from most to least secure: AAA, AA, A, BBB, BB, B, CCC, CC, C. Moody's ratings are: Aaa, Aa, A, Baa, Ba, B, Caa, Ca, C.

Russell Indexes These measure the performance of the largest U.S.-headquartered companies, based on total market capitalization. The Russell 3,000 Index measures the 3,000 largest U.S.-based companies (their total market capitalization represents approximately 98 percent of the investable U.S. equity market). The Russell 1,000 measures the largest 1,000 of these companies. The Russell 2,000 measures the smallest 2,000 companies in the Russell 3,000.

Securities Financial assets (usually long-term), such as equities/stocks and debentures/bonds; may also refer to shorter-term assets such as U.S. Treasury bills.

Securities and Exchange Commission (SEC) U.S. government agency that regulates the securities industry by requiring registration of brokers, dealers, and stock exchanges. The SEC also reviews the financial position of companies issuing securities for public sale, and investigates illegal activities such as insider trading.

Standard & Poor's 500 Composite Stock Price Index (S&P 500) A widely used measure of the movement of the U.S. stock market. The S&P 500 was introduced in 1957 and is one of 12 leading economic indicators used by the U.S. Commerce Department. The 500 issues include 400 industrial, 40 utility, 20 transportation and 40 financial companies—primarily those listed on the New York Stock Exchange (NYSE). The index is considered to be value-weighted because each stock is weighted according to its market value. As of December 31, 1987, the market value of issues tracked by the S&P 500 was equal to approximately 70 percent of the value of all publicly traded U.S. equities. Its value is calculated on a total return basis with dividends reinvested.

Stock exchange A market in which securities (other than bills and similar short-term instruments) issued by central and local government bodies, and public companies are traded (e.g., the New York Stock Exchange, the American Stock Exchange, the London Stock Exchange). Only members of a stock exchange may deal on it, and membership and arrangements for trading are strictly regulated. Stock exchanges in the United States are the American Stock Exchange (New York); Boston Stock Exchange; Cincinnati Stock Exchange; Intermountain Stock Exchange (Salt Lake City); Midwest Stock Exchange (Chicago); New York Stock Exchange; Pacific Exchange (Los Angeles, San Francisco); Philadelphia Stock Exchange; and Spokane Stock Exchange.

Stock market An institution where stocks and shares are traded, existing in all advanced Western countries. Stock markets enable companies to more easily raise equity or loan capital from the public since investors can quickly realize their holdings because of the stock exchange share quotation. In other words, there is a ready market. The principal overseas stock markets are located in Amsterdam, Brussels, Frankfurt, Hong Kong, Johannesburg, London, Milan, Paris, Singapore, Stockholm, Sydney, Tokyo, Toronto, and Zurich.

Stockbroker An individual who acts as an adviser and an agent (working on commission), to buy and sell stocks on behalf of a client on a particular stock exchange where the stockbroker is a member.

Wilshire 5000 Index The broadest measure of the U.S. stock market, containing some 5,000 issues including all publicly traded U.S. stocks for which daily pricing is available (i.e., includes all Amex, NYSE, and OTC stocks).

Yield The annual return on a security, as a percentage of its current market price. A stock's dividend yield is the annual dividend divided by its current stock price.

▶ BIG BUSINESS: THE *FORTUNE* 500

The ultimate measure of success in the business world is inclusion on *Fortune* magazine's annual list of the 500 biggest companies in America. In recent years, the global trend toward megamergers creating monolithic organizations have raised the bar for admission to this select circle. One such merger, between the oil giants Exxon and Mobil, resulted in the combined company leapfrogging to the number one position. Revenues for General Motors, which headed the list in 1999, declined from $189.1 billion to $184.6 billion, and fell to third place, behind Wal-Mart.

The accompanying tables list the top 100 companies of the *Fortune 500* by revenues, the top three companies in several performance categories, and the top companies by industry.

Fortune 500 Performance Leaders, 2000

Profits	(millions)
1. Exxon Mobil (1)	$17,720.0
2. Citigroup (6)	13,519.0
3. General Electric (5)	12,735.0

Market Value	(millions)
1. General Electric (5)	$407,054
2. Exxon Mobil (1)	288,350
3. Microsoft (79)	286,444

Fastest 1-year Revenue Growth	(percent)
1. Anadarko Petroleum (314)	711.0%
2. Qwest Communications (120)	322.9
3. Xcel Energy (166)	304.0

Return on Revenues	(percent)
1. Oracle (184)	62.2%
2. Cox Communications (466)	54.9
3. Science Applications Intl. (296)	46.6

Return to Investors, 1 year	(percent)
1. Quest Diagnostics (475)	364.6%
2. AmeriSource Health (165)	232.5
3. Dynegy (54)	219.9

Return to Investors (10 years)	(percent)
1. EMC (216)	82.0
2. Cisco Systems (107)	73.4
3. Oracle (184)	65.0

Note: Numbers in parentheses reflect overall *Fortune* 500 rank.

The Top U.S. Companies, by Industry and *Fortune* 500 Rank, 2000

Industry, Company, Rank	Revenues (millions)
Aerospace	
Boeing (15)	$51,321
United Technologies (64)	26,583
Lockheed Martin (69)	25,329
Airlines	
AMR (98)	20,245
UAL (104)	19,352
Delta Air Lines (123)	15,888
Apparel	
Nike (212)	8,995
VF (309)	5,748
Jones Apparel Group (404)	4,143
Beverages	
Coca-Cola (93)	20,458
PepsiCo (94)	20,438
Coca-Cola Enterprises (128)	14,750
Chemicals	
E.I. du Pont de Nemours (56)	29,202
Dow Chemical (78)	23,008
PPG Industries (220)	8,629
Commercial Banks	
J.P. Morgan Chase (12)	60,065
Bank of America Corp. (13)	57,747
Wells Fargo (62)	27,568
Computer Software	
Microsoft (79)	22,956
Oracle (184)	10,130
Computer Associates (295)	6,103
Computer/Data services	
Electronic Data Systems (106)	19,227
Computer Sciences (200)	9,371
America Online (271)	6,886
Computers, Office Equipment	
IBM (8)	88,396
Hewlett-Packard (19)	48,782
Compaq Computer (27)	42,383
Diversified Financials	
General Electric (5)	129,853
Citigroup (6)	111,826
Fannie Mae (26)	44,089
Electronics, Electrical Equipment	
Emerson Electric (126)	15,545
Whirlpool (181)	10,325
Eaton (213)	8,988
Energy	
Duke Energy (17)	49,318
Reliant Energy (55)	29,339
UtiliCorp United (60)	28,975
Engineering, Construction	
Halliburton (148)	13,344
Fluor (175)	11,056
Centex (302)	5,956
Entertainment	
Walt Disney (67)	25,402
Viacom (101)	20,044
Clear Channel Communications (331)	5,345
Food	
ConAgra (68)	25,386
Sara Lee (96)	20,414
H.J. Heinz (199)	9,408
Food Production	
IBP (117)	16,950
Archer Daniels Midland (152)	12,877
Farmland Industries (160)	12,239

Industry, Company, Rank	Revenues (millions)
Food Services	
McDonald's (138)	14,243
Tricon Global Restaurants (263)	7,093
Darden Restaurants (449)	3,701
Food & Drug Stores	
Kroger (18)	49,000
Albertson's (38)	36,762
Safeway (46)	31,977
Forest & Paper Products	
International Paper (61)	28,180
Georgia-Pacific (84)	22,218
Weyerhaeuser (122)	15,980
General Merchandisers	
Wal-Mart Stores (2)	193,295
Sears Roebuck (29)	40,937
Kmart (36)	37,028
Health Care	
Aetna (63)	26,819
UnitedHealth Group (91)	21,122
Cigna (102)	19,994
Hotels, Casinos & Resorts	
Marriott Intl. (186)	10,017
Park Place Entertainment (355)	4,896
Crestline Capital (359)	4,817
Industrial & Farm Equipment	
Caterpillar (99)	20,175
Deere (149)	13,137
Ingersoll-Rand (205)	9,220
Insurance	
State Farm Insurance (21)	47,863
American International Group (22)	45,972
TIAA-CREF (33)	38,064
Mail, Package, Freight Delivery	
United Parcel Service (52)	29,771
FedEx (112)	18,257
Pittston (397)	4,235
Metal Products	
Gillette (188)	9,986
Illinois Tool Works (189)	9,984
Crown Cork & Seal (250)	7,289
Metals	
Alcoa (77)	23,090
LTV (352)	4,934
AK Steel Holding (372)	4,612
Mining, Crude Oil Production	
Occidental Petroleum (133)	14,543
Unocal (207)	9,202
Plains Resources (281)	6,631
Network Communications	
Lucent Technologies (28)	41,420
Motorola (34)	37,580
Cisco Systems (107)	18,928
Petroleum Refining	
Exxon Mobil (1)	210,392
Texaco (16)	51,130
Chevron (20)	48,069
Pharmaceuticals	
Merck (30)	40,363
Pfizer (53)	29,574
Johnson & Johnson (57)	29,139
Pipelines	
Enron (7)	100,789
Dynegy (54)	29,445
El Paso Corp. (86)	21,950

Industry, Company, Rank	Revenues (millions)
Publishing & Printing	
Gannett (288)	6,244
R.R. Donnelley (307)	5,764
Tribune (344)	5,080
Railroads	
Union Pacific (162)	11,878
Burlington Northern Santa Fe (206)	9,205
CSX (225)	8,526
Savings Institutions	
Washington Mutual (124)	15,767
Golden State Bancorp (376)	4,547
Golden West Financial Corp. (421)	3,957
Scientific & Photo Equipment	
3M (118)	16,724
Eastman Kodak (141)	13,994
Applied Materials (196)	9,564
Securities	
Morgan Stanley Dean Witter Discover (24)	45,413
Merrill Lynch (25)	44,872
Goldman Sachs (42)	33,000
Semiconductors	
Intel (41)	33,726
Solectron (139)	14,138
Texas Instruments (163)	11,875
Soaps & Cosmetics	
Procter & Gamble (31)	39,951
Colgate-Palmolive (201)	9,358
Avon Products (310)	5,715
Specialty Retailers	
Home Depot (23)	45,738
Costco Wholesale (45)	32,164
Lowe's (108)	18,779
Telecommunications	
AT&T (9)	65,981
Verizon (10)	64,707
SBC Communications (14)	51,476
Temporary Help	
Manpower (177)	10,843
Kelly Services (381)	4,487
Spherion (443)	3,741
Tobacco	
Philip Morris (11)	63,276
R. J. Reynolds (235)	8,167
Universal (478)	3,402
Toys	
Mattel (319)	5,590
Hasbro (438)	3,787
Trucking	
CNF Transportation (289)	6,166
Ryder System (333)	5,337
Yellow (457)	3,588
Utilities	
Southern (76)	23,381
PG&E Corp. (82)	22,483
TXU (85)	22,009
Waste Management	
Waste Management (157)	12,492
Allied Waste Industries (312)	5,708
Republic Services (676)	2,103

Source: *Fortune* magazine, 2001. Reprinted by permission.

Fortune 100 Largest U.S. Corporations, 2000

Rank Company (1999 Rank)	Revenues (millions)	Rank Company (1999 Rank)	Revenues (millions)
1. Exxon Mobil (3)	$210,392.0	51. Cardinal Health (59)	$29,870.6
2. Wal-Mart Stores (2)	193,295.0	52. United Parcel Service (46)	29,771.0
3. General Motors (1)	184,632.0	53. Pfizer (N.A.)	29,574.0
4. Ford Motor Company (4)	180,598.0	54. Dynegy (N.A.)	29,444.9
5. General Electric (5)	129,853.0	55. Reliant Energy (N.A.)	29,339.0
6. Citigroup (7)	111,826.0	56. E.l. du Pont de Nemours (42)	29,202.0
7. Enron (18)	100,789.0	57. Delphi Automotive Systems (N.A.)	29,139.0
8. International Business Machines (6)	88,396.0	58. Johnson & Johnson (43)	29,139.0
9. AT&T (8)	65,981.0	59. Allstate (47)	29,134.0
10. Verizon Communications (N.A.)	64,707.0	60. UtiliCorp United (90)	28,974.9
11. Philip Morris (9)	63,276.0	61. International Paper (61)	28,180.0
12. J.P. Morgan Chase (92)	60,065.0	62. Wells Fargo (68)	27,568.0
13. Bank of America (11)	57,747.0	63. Aetna (49)	26,818.9
14. SBC Communications (12)	51,476.0	64. United Technologies (57)	26,583.0
15. Boeing (10)	51,321.0	65. Lehman Brothers Holdings (88)	26,447.0
16. Texaco (28)	51,130.0	66. BellSouth (58)	26,151.0
17. Duke Energy (69)	49,318.0	67. Walt Disney (66)	25,402.0
18. Kroger (14)	49,000.4	68. ConAgra (60)	25,385.8
19. Hewlett-Packard (13)	48,782.0	69. Lockheed Martin (52)	25,329.0
20. Chevron (35)	48,069.0	70. Bank One Corp. (50)	25,168.0
21. State Farm Insurance Cos. (15)	47,863.1	71. Honeywell International (65)	25,023.0
22. American International Group (17)	45,972.0	72. Tosco (N.A.)	24,545.0
23. Home Depot (21)	45,738.0	73. First Union Corp. (67)	24,246.0
24. Morgan Stanley Dean Witter Discover (30)	45,413.0	74. American Express (71)	23,675.0
25. Merrill Lynch (29)	44,872.0	75. Sprint (81)	23,613.0
26. Fannie Mae (26)	44,088.9	76. Southern (N.A.)	23,381.0
27. Compaq Computer (20)	42,383.0	77. Alcoa (N.A.)	23,090.0
28. Lucent Technologies (22)	41,420.0	78. Dow Chemical (89)	23,008.0
29. Sears Roebuck (16)	40,937.0	79. Microsoft (84)	22,956.0
30. Merck (34)	40,363.2	80. Prudential Insurance Company (48) of America	22,759.9
31. Procter & Gamble (23)	39,951.0	81. FleetBoston Financial (80)	22,608.0
32. WorldCom (N.A.)	39,090.0	82. PG&E Corp. (73)	22,483.0
33. TIAA-CREF (19)	38,063.5	83. AutoNation (63)	22,330.8
34. Motorola (37)	37,580.0	84. Georgia-Pacific (96)	22,218.0
35. McKesson HBOC (38)	37,100.5	85. TXU (N.A.)	22,009.0
36. Kmart (27)	37,028.0	86. El Paso Corp.	21,950.0
37. Target (32)	36,903.0	87. New York Life Insurance (70)	21,450.4
38. Albertson's (24)	36,762.0	88. Bristol-Myers Squibb (78)	21,331.0
39. USX (51)	35,570.0	89. Phillips Petroleum (N.A.)	21,227.0
40. Berkshire Hathaway (64)	33,976.0	90. Walgreen (95)	21,206.9
41. Intel (39)	33,726.0	91. UnitedHealth Group (N.A.)	21,122.0
42. Goldman Sachs Group (54)	33,000.0	92. Loews (72)	20,669.9
43. JCPenney (36)	32,965.0	93. Coca-Cola (83)	20,458.0
44. Conoco (74)	32,513.0	94. Pepsico (76)	20,438.0
45. Costco Wholesale (44)	32,164.3	95. Tech Data (N.A.)	20,427.7
46. Safeway (40)	31,976.9	96. Sara Lee (79)	20,414.0
47. MetLife (53)	31,947.0	97. Supervalu (99)	20,339.1
48. Dell Computer (56)	31,888.0	98. AMR (77)	20,245.0
49. Ingram Micro (41)	30,715.1	99. Caterpillar (85)	20,175.0
50. Freddie Mac (62)	30,000.0	100. CVS (93)	20,087.5

Source: *Fortune,* magazine, 2001. Reprinted by permission.

▶ SMALL BUSINESS

Small businesses account for 99 percent of the 24.8 million nonfarm businesses in the United States today, according to the Small Business Administration. Sole proprietorships (including artists, freelance writers, actors, and other self-employed people who are not technically businesses) make up the vast majority of these small businesses; the remainder are divided between partnerships and corporations. Small businesses employ 53 percent of the private workforce, make 47 of percent of all sales in America, and accounts for 51 percent of all private sector output. According to the Small Business Administration, two-thirds of small businesses survive at least two years, and just over half make it four years. In 1999, bankruptcies of small businesses declined dramatically to 37,639, or about half as many as in 1991. About three-quarters of new business owners are still employed in a salaried job when they start their own business; 60 percent of new businesses start at home.

Franchising, a century-old tradition, continues to grow in popularity. The Department of Commerce estimates that in the year 2000, franchising accounted for more than half of all sales. The benefits to the franchisor are enormous: expansion with little or no risk, royalties and licensing revenue from the franchisee, and an initial franchise fee (usually around $25,000). The benefits to the franchisee are less obvious, but may include name recognition, a national advertising campaign, and training and financial assistance from the parent company. Although tales of self-made millionaires abound in franchising circles, far greater numbers of franchisees go bankrupt. As the accompanying table demonsrates, opening a franchised business is no simple proposition, often requiring hundreds of thousands (or even millions) of dollars in startup costs.

Top 50 Franchises, by Number of Franchises, 2000

Rank Franchise	Business	Number of franchises	Startup costs ('000s)[1]	Franchise fees
1. Kumon Math & Reading Centers	Supplemental education	22,437	$2,600-7,900	$1,000
2. McDonald's	Hamburgers, chicken, salads	20,802	477,800-1.4 mil.	45,000
3. 7-Eleven Convenience Stores	Convenience stores	16,783	12,500+	(Varies)
4. Subway	Submarine sandwiches	14,531	63,400-175,000	10,000
5. Burger King	Hamburgers and fries	10,529	235,000-2 mil.	40,000
6. Jani-King	Commercial cleaning services	7,972	8,200-33,500	5,500-32,000
7. KFC	Chicken	7,233	1.1 mil-1.7mil.	25,000
8. Century 21 Real Estate	Real estate	6,532	35,900-546,200	12,500-25,000
9. Coverall Cleaning Concepts	Commercial cleaning	5,941	6,300-35,900	6,000-32,200
10. Dairy Queen	Soft-serve dairy products	5,913	170,800-622,300	20,000/35,000
11. Domino's Pizza Inc.[2]	Pizza	5,713	98,900-348,200	up to $3,300
12. Dunkin' Donuts	Donuts & baked goods	5,221	131,990-880,800	40,000
13. Jazzercise Inc.	Dance/exercise classes	5,124	1,800-20,600	325/650
14. Yogen Fruz Worldwide	Frozen yogurt & ice cream	4,879	25,000-250,000	25,000
15. Taco Bell Corp	Mexican fast-food restaurant	4,486	236,400-515,200	45,000
16. ServiceMaster	Contract cleaning	4,369	22,800-74,100	13,500-27,500
17. Snap-on Tools	Professional tools & equipment	4,335	166,400-232,400	5,000
18. Choice Hotels International	Hotels, inns, suites & resorts	4,303	4 mil. - 6 mil.	25,000-50,000
19. Pizza Hut Inc.[2]	Pizza	4,277	268,000-1.4 mil.	25,000
20. Mail Boxes Etc.	Postal/business/services	4,243	113,000-190,000	29,950
21. Baskin-Robbins USA	Ice cream & yogurt	4,220	179,300-429,400	up to 30,000
22. Wendy's Int'l. Inc.[3]	Quick-service restaurant	4,032	845,500-1.6 mil.	25,000
23. Chem-Dry	Carpet& upholstery cleaning	3,873	22,600-63,100	9,950
24. ServPro	Disaster restoration & cleaning	3,873	68,400-102,000	26,000
25. Re/Max Int'l. Inc.	Real estate services	3,536	20,000-200,000	10,000-25,000
26. Arby's Inc.	Roast beef sandwiches	3,263	212,900-2.3 mil.	25,000/375,000
27. Coldwell Banker Real Estate	Real estate	3,048	23,000-477,000	12,500-20,000
28. TCBY Treats[2]	Frozen yogurt, ice cream	3,033	113,000-330,200	5,000/20,000
29. Jackson Hewitt Tax Service	Computerized tax preparation	2,799	47,400-75,200	25,000
30. Midas International	Brake repair	2,716	302,400-418,000	20,000
31. Novus Windshield Repair	Windshield repair	2,494	26,100-195,950	10,000-17,500
32. Budget Rent A Car	Auto and truck rentals	2,179	166,100-449,200	20,000
33. RadioShack[2]	Consumer electronics	2,154	59,300	7,500
34. Blimpie Int'l. Inc.	Submarine sandwiches	2,122	85,300-285,700	18,000
35. CleanNet USA Inc.	Commercial office cleaning	2,042	3,900-35,500	2,950-32,000
36. Super 8 Motels Inc.	Economy motels	1,943	254,200-2.3 mil.	24,000+
37. Merle Norman Cosmetics	Cosmetics studios	1,922	33,500-109,700	0
38. Days Inn Worldwide	Hotels & inns	1,911	389,600-6.2 mil.	Varies
39. Sonic Drive In Restaurants	Drive-in restaurant	1,847	621,300-1.2 mil.	30,000
40. Tim Hortons[2]	Donuts & baked goods	1,732	434,700-775,100	35,000
41. GNC Franchising Inc.	Vitamin & nutrition stores	1,665	130,200-179,500	30,000
42. Jiffy Lube International Inc.	Fast oil change	1,660	174,000-194,000	35,000
43. Papa John's Pizza[2]	Pizza	1,553	156,800-431,700	20,000
44. Carlson Wagonlit Travel	Travel agency	1,460	3,000-164,000	1,500-29,900
45. Great Clips Inc	Family hair salons	1,371	87,200-161,500	17,500
46. Fantastic Sams	Hair salons	1,325	75,000-164,000	25,000
47. Popeyes Chicken & Biscuits	Fried chicken & biscuits	1,287	700,000-1.2 mil.	20,000
48. The Medicine Shoppe	Pharmacy	1,286	72,600-123,000	10,000-18,000
49. Thrifty Rent-A-Car System	Vehicle rentals and leasing	1,272	150,000+	17,500
50. Matco Tools	Automotive tools/ equipment	1,214	55,000-148,000	0

Note: Does not include franchises owned by the company. 1. Includes franchise fees. 2. Data shown is for 1999. 3. Data shown is for 1998. **Source:** *Entrepreneur* (Jan. 2001). Reprinted by permission.

ADVERTISING

Few facts and figures reveal the extraordinary growth of the mass-consumption society as vividly as those dealing with the advertising business. In 1950, as the postwar economy began to heat up, American business spent $5.7 billion to advertise its goods and services; by 1960 that figure would double, and then almost double again by 1970. Between 1970 and 1990, as the Baby Boom generation entered the marketplace and the economy expanded, advertising expenditures grew at a spiraling rate, topping $100 billion in 1986. That rate of growth has not been sustained, but advertising spending continues to reach new highs every year, nevertheless. Total expenditures on all forms of advertising in 2000 were more than $243 billion.

Nearly 60 percent of all advertising dollars are spent to place ads in newspapers or magazines or to run TV and radio commercials. The Internet continues to be the fastest-growing segment of the advertising market (expanding by more than 50 percent in 2000), but it still represents a tiny fraction of all advertising dollars spent. As the accompanying table shows, companies spent three times as much money to advertise in the Yellow Pages as they did on pop-up ads.

The biggest advertisers are the nation's largest manufacturers of automobiles, food, soft drinks, tobacco, and beer. Most advertising dollars are filtered through about 13,000 advertising agencies who mainly create the ads and buy the space or time from the media. The agency business has undergone a dramatic restructuring recently, as many of the largest agencies have merged to form enormous corporations. In May of 2000, the London-based WPP Group (which already owned J. Walter Thompson, Ogilvy & Mather, and the public relations firms Burson-Marsteller, Hill & Knowlton, and Cohn & Wolfe) purchased Young & Rubicam, one of the last remaining independent agencies. The takeover made WPP the world's largest advertising organization, with a worldwide gross income of $7.97 billion in 2000. That's a billion dollars more than the second-place organization, Omnicom, which was the number one company in 1999 with $5.7 billion in revenues.

Advertising Expenditures in the U.S., 1776–2000 (in millions)

Year	Amount[1]	Year	Amount[1]	Year	Amount[1]
1776	$0.2	1890	300	1980	54,780
1800	1	1900	450	1985	94,750
1820	3	1909	$1,000	1990	128,640
1840	7	1915	1,100	1995	160,930
1850	12	1940	2,110	1999	215,301
1860	22	1950	$5,700	2000	243,680
1867	40	1960	11,960		
1880	175	1970	19,550		

Source: *Advertising Age*. 1. These are estimated figures of the monies spent on placing advertising in all media; the costs of producing the advertising are not included.

Total U.S. Advertising Volume by Medium, 1999–2000

Medium	1999 Expenditures (millions)	1999 Percent share	2000 Expeditures (millions)	2000 Percent share	Percent change 1999–2000
Newspapers, total	$46,648	21.0%	$49,050	20.2%	+5.1%
National	6,358	2.9	7,229	3.0	+13.7
Local	40, 290	18.1	41,821	17.2	+3.8
Magazines, total	11,433	5.1	12,370	5.1	+8.2
Broadcast TV, total	40,011	18.0	44,802	18.4	+12.8
Four TV networks	13,961	6.3	15,888	6.5	+13.8
Syndication[1]	2,870	1.3	3,108	1.3	+8.3
Spot (national)	10,500	4.7	12,264	5.0	+16.8
Spot (local)	12,680	5.7	13,542	5.6	+6.8
Cable TV, total	12,570	5.6	14,429	5.9	+14.8
Cable networks	9,405	4.2	10,947	4.5	+16.4
Spot (local)	3,165	1.4	3,482	1.4	+10.0
Radio, total	17,215	7.8	19,295	7.9	+12.1
Network	684	0.3	780	0.3	+14.0
Spot (national)	3,275	1.5	3,668	1.5	+12.0
Spot (local)	13,256	6.0	14,847	6.1	+12.0
Yellow pages, total	12,652	5.7	13,228	5.4	+4.5
National	1,986	0.9	2,093	0.8	+5.4
Local	10,666	4.8	11,135	4.6	+4.4
Direct mail	41,403	18.6	44,591	18.3	+7.7
Business papers	4,274	1.9	4,915	2.0	+15.0
Out of home[2], total	4,780	2.2	5,176	2.1	+8.3
National	1,910	0.9	2,068	0.8	+8.3
Local	2,870	1.3	3,108	1.3	+8.3
Internet, total	2,832	1.3	4,333	1.8	+53.0
Miscellaneous, total	28,490	12.8	31,491	12.9	+10.5
National	21,279	9.6	23,844	9.8	+12.0
Local	7,211	3.2	7,647	3.1	+6.0
Total national	132,170	59.5	148,098	60.8	+12.0
Total local	90,138	40.5	95,582	39.2	+6.0
Grand total	$222,308	100.0%	$243,680	100.0%	+9.6%

1. Includes UPN and WB. **Source:** Prepared for *Advertising Age* by Robert J. Coen Universal McCann. www.adage.com

Top 25 U.S. Advertising Agencies, by Gross Domestic Income, 2000

Rank 2000/Agency (Rank 1999)	Headquarters	U.S. gross income, 2000 (millions)	Percent change, 1999-2000	U.S. billings, 2000 (millions)
1. Grey Worldwide (1)	New York	$610.0	13.8%	$4,068.7
2. J. Walter Thompson Co. (2)	New York	574.5	7.5	4,032.5
3. McCann-Erickson Worldwide (4)	New York	507.1	8.6	6,561.4
4. FCB Worldwide (3)	New York	502.2	7.5	5,712.1
5. Y&R Advertising (5)	New York	452.8	8.9	6,194.7
6. Leo Burnett Worldwide (6)	Chicago	428.1	7.9	3,140.0
7. Euro RSCG Worldwide1 (7)	New York	399.0	5.4	3,324.7
8. BBDO Worldwide (8)	New York	398.5	10.3	4,599.3
9. Ogilvy & Mather Worldwide (10)	New York	397.6	16.5	3,972.5
10. DDB Worldwide Communications (9)	New York	390.9	14.0	4,252.8
11. D'Arcy Masius Benton & Bowles (11)	New York	278.3	7.0	2,991.6
12. Saatchi & Saatchi (12)	New York	276.1	6.8	2,676.8
13. TBWA Worldwide (14)	New York	240.3	9.3	1,877.4
14. Lowe Lintas & Partners Worldwide (13)	New York	230.0	2.9	1,534.0
15. TMP Worldwide (15)	New York	217.1	9.0	2,382.5
16. Campbell-Ewald Co. (16)	Warren, Mich.	209.4	12.6	1,936.3
17. Bates USA (17)	New York	198.8	9.2	1,594.5
18. CommonHealth (18)	Parsippany, N.J.	168.8	19.2	1,118.8
19. Deutsch (20)	New York	165.0	24.0	1,515.0
20. Nelson Communications Worldwide (19)	New York	145.5	7.9	1,101.3
21. Arnold Worldwide (21)	Boston	145.3	13.7	1,300.2
22. Hill, Holliday, Connors, Cosmopolos (22)	Boston	145.1	17.0	967.0
23. Publicis USA (26)	New York	143.0	33.3	1,385.8
24. Lowe Healthcare Worldwide (23)	New York	137.6	15.5	917.8
25. Bozell Group (25)	New York	136.5	19.0	1,382.0

1. Estimate. **Source:** *Advertising Age* (April 23,2001); reprinted by permission of Crain Communications, Inc. www.adage.com

The 100 Leading U.S. Advertisers, 1991–99

1999 Rank, Company (1998 rank)	Total spending (millions)				
	1991	1995	1996	1998	1999
1. General Motors Corp. (1)	$1,056.5	$1,499.6	$1,712.1	$2,940.4	$4,040.4
2. Procter & Gamble Co. (2)	1,166.4	1,507.4	1,493.5	2,650.3	2,611.8
3. Philip Morris Cos. (3)	1,110.4	1,397.7	1,237.0	2,049.3	2,201.6
4. Pfizer (29)	N.A.	N.A.	144.8	678.9	2,142.4
5. AT&T Corp. (7)	391.7	675.2	659.8	1,428.0	1,950.9
6. DaimlerChrysler (4)	414.8	954.7	1,119.9	1,646.7	1,804.0
7. Ford Motor Co. (6)	517.7	891.8	897.7	1,520.7	1,639.8
8. Sears, Roebuck & Co. (5)	462.3	557.8	592.5	1,578.3	1,505.2
9. PepsiCo (9)	542.0	730.2	768.0	1,263.4	1,315.7
10. Verizon Communications (32)	N.A.	N.A.	134.6	652.9	1,312.7
11. Walt Disney Co. (8)	257.3	777.8	775.6	1,358.7	1,304.0
12. Time Warner (13)	311.3	543.0	747.3	1,077.3	1,202.9
13. Diageo (10)	N.A	N.A	N.A	1,205.7	1,198.4
14. McDonald's Corp. (14)	87.4	586.4	616.8	1,025.4	1,134.8
15. IBM Corp. (12)	387.4	490.6	599.1	1,079.3	1,128.5
16. Intel Corp. (30)	N.A.	N.A.	N.A.	678.8	1,119.3
17. WorldCom (17)	94.1	322.6	333.5	948.4	1,108.4
18. Viacom (21)	N.A.	N.A.	N.A.	825.9	1,064.5
19. Toyota Motor Corp. (18)	442.5	513.4	545.7	939.2	1,025.2
20. Johnson & Johnson (22)	371.1	601.3	840.5	816.4	1,004.5
21. U.S. Government (25)	123.4	219.9	365.9	792.0	998.0
22. J.C. Penney Co. (16)	105.2	273.9	305.7	991.9	995.9
23. SBC Communications (39)	N.A.	N.A.	165.3	586.7	926.1
24. Sony Corp. (20)	262.8	431.0	418.6	879.6	922.7
25. L'Oreal (23)	N.A.	N.A.	N.A.	806.3	899.8
26. Sprint Corp. (31)	N.A.	213.9	274.0	671.8	879.2
27. Hewlett-Packard Co. (57)	N.A.	N.A.	N.A.	466.0	877.5
28. Target Corp. (N.A..)	N.A.	N.A.	N.A.	N.A.	870.7
29. Coca-Cola Co. (28)	218.8	238.2	336.8	770.2	866.5
30. Bristol-Myers Squibb Co. (19)	184.0	219.4	315.4	923.6	859.2
31. Tricon Global Restaurants (27)	N.A.	N.A.	N.A.	773.3	858.8
32. Federated Department Stores (24)	111.4	407.6	407.4	794.2	854.8
33. Unilever (15)	371.4	442.7	593.8	1,015.0	794.0

1999 Rank, Company (1998 rank)	Total spending (milllions)				
	1991	1995	1996	1998	1999
34. News Corp. (56)	$358.6	$275.9	$573.5	$467.0	$786.5
35. Honda Motor Co. (33)	242.5	388.8	392.4	646.1	749.5
36. Sara Lee Corp. (36)	N.A.	N.A.	129.9	609.1	742.1
37. General Mills (38)	419.1	367.7	401.1	597.9	670.0
38. Bayer (37)	55.8	160.5	221.1	602.9	659.5
39. Nissan Motor Co. (40)	212.0	367.7	439.4	576.6	658.9
40. Anheuser-Busch Cos. (34)	327.9	320.5	317.1	630.6	654.4
41. Nestle (44)	307.6	490.1	477.5	534.4	642.8
42. Seagram Co. (59)	N.A.	333.1	261.3	461.3	619.9
43. General Electric Co. (71)	N.A.	N.A.	N.A.	373.1	613.0
44. American Home Products Corp. (41)	290.6	355.5	446.4	574.3	591.3
45. Nike (48)	109.5	146.3	196.0	521.4	591.2
46. Mars Inc. (43)	128.2	210.1	281.6	547.6	589.8
47. Microsoft Corp. (52)	N.A.	147.7	155.6	492.6	583.9
48. Cendant Corp. (42)	63.6	115.2	135.5	549.0	564.3
49. Novartis (49)	N.A.	N.A.	193.5	505.2	545.5
50. SmithKline Beecham (68)	83.3	173.2	252.2	398.2	534.3
51. Schering-Plough Corp. (35)	95.9	104.0	145.0	615.3	533.5
52. Home Depot (54)	N.A.	96.6	128.0	474.6	530.8
53. Gap Inc. (69)	N.A.	N.A.	N.A.	390.4	528.0
54. American Express Co. (60)	156.2	210.4	274.9	460.4	518.8
55. Wal-Mart Stores (67)	76.7	143.2	145.1	404.5	513.9
56. Estee Lauder Cos. (45)	N.A.	N.A.	N.A.	532.0	511.0
57. May Department Stores Co. (55)	194.0	339.4	384.5	470.0	508.5
58. Circuit City Stores (53)	128.2	291.6	390.2	491.4	504.2
59. Morgan Stanley Dean Witter & Co. (85)	93.1	122.6	200.7	300.1	494.7
60. Merck & Co. (51)	129.5	199.0	176.8	493.2	485.2
61. Volkswagen (80)	N.A.	N.A.	N.A.	233.3	483.1
62. Kmart Corp. (62)	186.5	241.2	242.9	442.2	482.3
63. Gateway (74)	N.A.	N.A.	137.3	358.6	454.4
64. Eastman Kodak Co. (65)	N.A.	N.A.	N.A.	431.7	441.8
65. Mattel (46)	63.8	184.5	278.3	530.0	438.5
66. Kroger Co. (63)	N.A.	N.A.	N.A.	440.2	428.3
67. Adolph Coors Co. (78)	N.A.	N.A.	N.A.	351.1	428.0
68. Glaxo Wellcome (83)	74.0	111.7	144.0	306.1	427.9
69. Reckitt Benckiser (N.A.)	N.A.	N.A.	N.A.	N.A.	422.0
70. ConAgra (50)	N.A.	N.A.	N.A.	493.8	417.3
71. Quaker Oats Co. (87)	N.A.	N.A.	N.A.	300.0	416.2
72. Kellogg Co. (61)	381.3	488.2	410.4	448.5	416.0
73. Gillette Co. (66)	37.1	132.7	138.2	409.2	413.6
74. Hershey Foods Corp. (64)	141.6	150.0	171.9	433.1	395.5
75. Dell Computer Corp. (96)	N.A.	N.A.	N.A.	227.1	384.6
76. Clorox Co. (70)	127.8	157.8	173.1	374.5	384.4
77. Visa International (N.A.)	N.A.	N.A.	N.A.	N.A.	368.6
78. U.S. dairy producers, processors (72)	N.A.	N.A.	N.A.	370.1	362.2
79. S.C. Johnson & Son (73)	93.1	115.6	133.3	361.7	358.5
80. Colgate-Palmolive Co. (75)	N.A.	N.A.	N.A.	358.2	354.0
81. Best Buy Co. (89)	N.A.	94.0	135.2	275.6	334.7
82. Ralston Purina Co. (58)	94.4	161.3	155.6	461.7	322.3
83. Revlon (81)	N.A.	N.A.	N.A.	320.8	311.2
84. Alltel Corp. (N.A.)	N.A.	N.A.	N.A.	N.A.	305.7
85. Sherwin-Williams Co. (90)	N.A.	N.A.	N.A.	256.4	303.7
86. Berkshire Hathaway (N.A.)	N.A.	N.A.	N.A.	N.A.	297.8
87. Charles Schwab & Co. (N.A.)	N.A.	N.A.	N.A.	N.A.	296.6
88. Pharmacia Corp. (N.A.)	N.A.	N.A.	N.A.	N.A.	294.4
89. Hyundai Motor Group (N.A.)	N.A.	N.A.	N.A.	N.A.	294.0
90. AutoNation (47)	N.A.	N.A.	N.A.	529.4	292.8
91. Office Depot (N.A.)	N.A.	N.A.	N.A.	N.A.	292.6
92. Kimberly-Clark Corp. (95)	111.7	133.1	184.7	228.1	291.8
93. BellSouth Corp. (76)	N.A.	N.A.	N.A.	353.4	284.8
94. Dillard's (84)	26.2	113.2	133.0	301.8	284.3
95. Wendy's International (91)	61.1	179.4	194.4	244.0	282.1
96. Campbell Soup Co. (79)	109.5	169.0	194.3	336.9	276.6
97. Compaq Computer Corp. (92)	N.A.	N.A.	N.A.	240.9	272.5
98. R.J. Reynolds Tobacco Holdings (86)	N.A.	N.A.	N.A.	300.0	271.1
99. Starwood Hotels & Resorts Worldwide (99)	N.A.	N.A.	N.A.	225.0	264.1
100. Nabisco Group Holdings Corp. (98)	N.A.	N.A.	N.A.	225.7	263.8
Total Top 100 companies	N.A.	N.A.	$33,746.2	$70,135.3	$73,457.6

Note: The top 100 companies in previous years are not the same as in 1999.
Source: Competitive Media Reporting *Top 100 Companies by 11-Media Advertising 1999* (2000).

Education

The American people's unwavering commitment to public education dates back more than 150 years. Fueled by a demand for literacy from two different creeds, one described in the Bible, the other in the Declaration of Independence, the American system of education grew to be an essential element in our faith that this nation was uniquely the land of opportunity.

Today that belief has evolved into what is called equality of opportunity, and this vital idea has helped to create a school system whose size, scope, and ambitions are unrivalled by any Western democracy. Over 68 million students and nearly 4 million teachers, administrators, and support staff are directly involved in education. The cost of this undertaking is, of course, staggering: more than half a trillion dollars annually—more than $7,000 per student—or 7 percent of the gross domestic product (G.D.P.), virtually all of it

for public education. The portion of G.D.P. spent on education rose rapidly between 1959 to 1969, declined in the 1970s as enrollment in elementary and secondary schools fell, and began rising steadily again in 1984. Since 1990, it has remained relatively stable. And while some complain bitterly about the quality of the results, or about overt waste, mismanagement, and even fraud, no one any longer questions the essential role of education in American life today.

▶ PUBLIC ELEMENTARY AND SECONDARY SCHOOLS

Expenditures on public elementary and secondary schools have been increasing faster than inflation in almost every year since figures were first kept in 1900. The exception was the period between 1978 and 1982, when inflation outpaced increases in expenditures. Total expenditures for public elementary and secondary schools topped $360 billion in 1999-2000; expenditures per student were $7,597. The accompanying table shows that even after adjusting for inflation, the amount spent to educate each student at public elementary and secondary schools continues to skyrocket.

In 1979, a historic shift occurred in the source of money to operate the American public school system. That was the year the state share of revenues rose above the local share for the first time. The federal share for elementary and secondary schools has always been relatively small.

Enrollment in public elementary schools declined dramatically from 1970 to 1985 (from 32.6 million to 27.0 million) as the number of young people decreased. That trend evidenced itself in secondary school populations between 1980 and 1990. Since 1990, however, populations of both elementary and secondary school populations are again on the rise, increasing slightly each year. In 2000, the public elementary school population reached a projected new high of 33.5 million, while public secondary school enrollment topped

Revenues for Public Elementary and Secondary Schools, 1920–98

School year	Total revenues (millions)	Percentage Federal	Percentage State	Percentage Local[1]
1919–20	$970	0.3%	16.5%	83.2%
1929–30	2,089	0.4	16.9	82.7
1939–40	2,261	1.8	30.3	68.0
1949–50	5,437	2.9	39.8	57.3
1959–60	14,747	4.4	39.1	56.5
1969–70	40,267	8.0	39.9	52.1
1979–80	96,881	9.8	46.8	43.4
1989–90	208,548	6.1	47.3	46.6
1994–95	273,149	6.8	46.8	46.4
1995–96	287,703	6.6	47.5	45.9
1996–97	305,065	6.6	48.0	45.4
1997–98	325,976	6.8	48.4	44.8

1. Includes a relatively small amount from nongovernmental sources (gifts and tuition and transportation fees from patrons). These sources accounted for 2.6 percent of total revenues in 1997–98. **Source:** U.S. Dept. of Education, National Center for Education Statistics, *Digest of Education Statistics, 2000.*

Education Expenditures, 1950–2000

School year	All educational institutions Total expenditures (millions)	All educational institutions As percentage of GDP	Elementary and Secondary schools Public Total (millions)	Elementary and Secondary schools Public Per pupil (constant dollars)[1]	Elementary and Secondary schools Private (millions)	Colleges and Universities Public (millions)	Colleges and Universities Private (millions)
1949–50	$ 8,911	N.A.	$ 5,838	$1,652	$ 411	$ 1,430	$ 1,233
1959-60	23,860	4.7%	15,613	2,535	1,100	3,904	3,244
1969-70	68,459	6.9	40,683	3,940	2,500	16,234	9,041
1979-80	165,627	6.5	95,962	4,993	7,200	41,434	21,031
1989-90	381,525	7.0	212,770	6,899	18,200	96,387	54,169
1994-95	503,925	7.1	279,000	6,988	23,400	127,594	73,930
1995-96	529,596	7.2	293,646	7,060	24,600	132,752	78,597
1996-97	562,251	7.2	313,151	7,206	25,800	139,600	83,600
1997-98[3]	596,222	7.2	334,322	7,475	27,100	146,700	88,100
1998-99[3]	623,200	7.1	349,200	7,608	27,700	152,400	93,900
1999-00[2]	646,800	7.0	360,600	7,597	28,400	159,700	98,100

1. Expenditure per pupil in fall enrollment, as measured in constant (1999-2000) dollars, based on the Consumer Price Index. 2. Estimated. 3. Preliminary. **Source:** U.S. Dept. of Education, National Center for Education Statistics, *Digest of Education Statistics, 2000* (2001).

Number of Schools and Teachers in the U.S., Fall, 1998

School type	Schools			Teachers		
	Total	Public	Private	Total	Public	Private
Elementary and secondary	**118,464[1]**	**91,062**	**27,402[1]**	**3,217,000**	**2,826,000**	**391,000[2]**
Elementary	80,197[1]	63,574	16,623[1]	1,978,000	1,701,000	277,000[2]
Secondary	24,590[1]	22,103	2,487[1]	1,239,000	1,125,000	114,000[2]
Combined	12,062[1]	3,770	8,292[1]	N.A.	N.A.	N.A.
Other schools	N.A.	1,615	N.A	N.A.	N.A.	N.A.
Colleges and universities	**4,070**	**1,688**	**2,382**	**677,736[3]**	**475,209[3]**	**202,527[3]**
4-year colleges	2,343	613	1,730	515,853[3]	321,664[3]	194,189[3]
2-year colleges	1,727	1,075	652	161,883[3]	153,545[3]	8,338[3]

1. Data on private elementary and secondary schools is from 1997, the latest year available. 2. Estimates. 3. Data is from Fall, 1995, the latest year available. **Source:** U.S. Dept. of Education, National Center for Education Statistics, *Digest of Education Statistics, 2000.*

School Enrollment, Kindergarten Through University Level, 1970-2000 (millions of students)

	Type of school						
	Elementary (K-8)		Secondary (9-12)		Higher education		
Year	Public	Private	Public	Private	Public	Private	Total
1970	32.6	4.1	13.3	1.3	6.4	2.2	**59.9**
1975	30.5	3.7	14.3	1.3	8.8	2.4	**61.0**
1980	27.6	4.0	13.2	1.3	9.5	2.6	**58.3**
1985	27.0	4.2	12.4	1.4	9.5	2.8	**57.2**
1990	29.9	4.1	11.3	1.1	10.8	3.0	**60.3**
1995	32.3	4.4[1]	12.5	1.3[1]	11.1	3.2	**64.8**
1997	33.1	4.6[1]	13.1	1.3[1]	11.2	3.3	**66.5**
1998	33.3	4.6[2]	13.2	1.3[2]	11.2	3.4	**67.0**
1999[2]	33.4	4.6	13.4	1.3	11.6	3.3	**67.6**
2000[2]	33.5	4.6	13.5	1.4	11.8	3.3	**68.1**

Note: Totals may not add up due to independent rounding. 1. Estimated. 2. Projected.
Source: U.S. Dept. of Education, National Center for Education Statistics, *Digest of Education Statistics, 2000.*

13.5 million. These numbers suggest that baby boomers started a baby boom of their own, the fruits of which are now starting to reach high school.

Teachers have more than kept pace with the growth in the number of students. There were 1.7 million elementary school teachers and 1.1 million secondary school teachers in 1999-2000, more than double the number in 1955. The number of secondary school teachers has remained at about one million since 1975, while the number of public elementary school teachers has risen consistently every year since 1982, when they numbered 1.2 million. A more telling statistic, though, is pupil-teacher ratios. Despite constant complaints about overcrowded inner-city classrooms, the average number of pupils supervised by each teacher has declined dramatically in the past 30 years. Each elementary school teacher was responsible for 17.6 students in 1999-2000, down from 24.3 in 1970, while secondary schools had a pupil-teacher ratio of 14.1 to 1, down from 19.8 to 1 in 1970.

According to a survey by the American Federation of Teachers, the average salary was $27,989 for first-year teachers in 1999-2000, and $41,820 for teachers with an average of 16 years of experience. That's 3.4 percent higher than the year before, but after adjusting for inflation, only slightly higher than 1972 levels ($39,733). Teachers, perhaps because their salaries come from tax revenues, earn significantly less than other college graduates. The survey found that teachers earn 53 percent as much as engineers, 63 percent of a computer analyst's paycheck, and 80 percent of what an accountant makes.

Nursery schools have increased dramatically in popularity since 1965, when 27.1 percent of 3-to-5-year-olds were enrolled in a kindergarten or pre-kindergarten program. That percentage has increased gradually ever since, reaching a high of 88.9 percent in 1994. (In 1999, it was 88.4 percent.) The percentage of youngsters attending full-time nursery school has also been on the rise. Only 17 percent of pre-primary students were in full-time programs in 1970; in 1999, 56.8 percent were full-time enrollees. Most nursery school students were in private schools, while most kindergarten students were enrolled in public schools.

School districts declined drastically between 1930, when there were 119,000 of them, and 1984, when there were a mere 15,747. Numbers since 1985 are not directly comparable with earlier years, but school districts have remained constant at about 15,000. There were 14,891 school districts in 1998-99. The greatest number of school districts had between 1,000 and 2,499 students in them, but school districts with 25,000 students or more were responsible for educating nearly one third of public school students.

How the States Rank in Public Education, 1999-2000

State	Enrollment	Rank	Expenditures per pupil	Rank	Average teacher salary	Rank
U.S.	46,540,114[1]	—	$6,627[1]	—	$41,724[1]	—
Alabama	730,037	23	4,946	47	36,689	31
Alaska	137,800	45	8,834	4	47,262[1]	7
Arizona	858,860[1]	20	4,505[1]	50	35,650[1]	37
Arkansas	447,352	34	5,540	42	33,386	43
California	5,946,421	1	5,967[1]	33	47,680	6
Colorado	708,109	24	5,282[1]	46	38,163	25
Connecticut	554,899	28	9,792	2	51,780	2
D.C.	77,194	51	8,277	8	47,076	8
Delaware	113,598	48	8,022[1]	9	44,435	12
Florida	2,378,882	4	5,872	35	36,722	30
Georgia	1,422,941	9	5,953[1]	34	41,023	17
Hawaii	185,036	42	6,257	24	40,578	20
Idaho	245,226	39	5,411	43	35,162	39
Illinois	2,027,600	5	6,149	26	46,486	10
Indiana	988,042	14	6,674[1]	19	41,850	14
Iowa	497,301	31	6,008	31	35,678	35
Kansas	469,377	33	6,386	23	38,453	24
Kentucky	632,573	26	6,425	22	36,380	32
Louisiana	750,982	22	5,701	39	33,109	45
Maine	209,254	40	7,619	12	35,561	38
Maryland	846,695	21	7,174	16	44,048	13
Massachusetts	967,336	15	8,750	5	46,250[1]	11
Michigan	1,700,885	8	7,451[1]	13	48,695[1]	4
Minnesota	861,488[1]	19	7,435[1]	14	39,802	21
Mississippi	499,387	30	4,605[1]	48	31,857	48
Missouri	894,466	17	5,846	37	35,656	36
Montana	157,556	43	6,131	28	32,121	47
Nebraska	286,970	38	6,000	32	33,284	44
Nevada	325,610	35	5,568	41	39,390	23
New Hampshire	206,783	41	6,202[1]	25	37,734	27
New Jersey	1,249,803[1]	10	9,775[1]	3	52,174[1]	1
New Mexico	324,253	36	5,861	36	32,554	46
New York	2,850,729[1]	3	9,797[1]	1	50,173[1]	3
North Carolina	1,248,548[1]	11	5,724[1]	38	39,419	22
North Dakota	115,315	47	4,512[1]	49	29,863	50
Ohio	1,821,276	6	6,479	21	41,436	15
Oklahoma	627,030	27	5,634	40	31,298	49
Oregon	545,033	29	8,605[1]	6	40,919	19
Pennsylvania	1,816,716	7	7,243[1]	15	48,321	5
Rhode Island	155,351	44	7,990[1]	10	47,041	9
South Carolina	653,779	25	6,113	29	36,081	34
South Dakota	129,093	46	5,369[1]	45	29,072	51
Tennessee	903,825	16	5,387	44	36,328	33
Texas	3,991,783	2	6,092	30	37,567	29
Utah	475,974	32	4,036[1]	51	34,946	41
Vermont	104,559	49	6,981[1]	17	37,714	28
Virginia	1,133,994	12	6,149	26	38,123[1]	26
Washington	1,003,714	13	6,528	20	41,013	18
West Virginia	290,944	37	8,488	7	35,008	40
Wisconsin	877,852	18	7,886	11	41,153	16
Wyoming	91,883	50	6,911[1]	18	34,140	42

1. Data estimated by NEA.   **Source:** National Education Association, *Rankings of the States*, 2000.

▶PRIVATE SCHOOLS

The U.S. Department of Education updates its data on private schools less frequently than it does for public institutions. The 1997–98 school year is the latest year for which data is available for private elementary and secondary schools. (Data for tuitions and teachers are from 1993–94, the latest year available).

Schools and enrollment There were 27,404 private schools engaged in educating 5,076,119 students. Of these schools, 16,623 were elementary schools (responsible for educating 2,824,844 students), 2,487 were secondary schools

(798,339 students), and 8,292 offered instruction in all 12 grades (1,452,937 students). Most private schools were religiously affiliated. One third, or 8,182 schools, were affiliated with the Catholic Church; 13,195 were affiliated with other religious groups. Only 6,025 private schools were nonsectarian.

Tuition Average tuition for private school students was $3,116 per year. But that average is kept low by the large number of parochial schools offering free or low-cost private education. The average cost of all nonsectarian private schools (elementary and secondary) was $6,631, and more

Catholic Schools, Pupils & Teachers, 1960–2001

Year	Schools	Pupils	Teachers Total	Religious	Lay
			Elementary schools		
1960	10,501	4,373,000	108,000	79,000	29,000
1970	9,362	3,355,000	112,000	52,000	60,000
1980	8,043	2,269,000	97,000	25,000	72,000
1990	7,291	1,883,906	91,039	10,837	80,202
1995	6,979	1,990,784	116,494	10,564	105,930
1999	6,990	2,013,112	105,943	7,609	98,334
2000	6,923	2,013,084	109,404	6,862	102,542
2001	6,920	2,004,037	112,402	6,390	105,548
			Secondary schools		
1960	2,392	880,000	44,000	33,000	11,000
1970	1,981	1,008,000	55,000	29,000	26,000
1980	1,516	837,000	49,000	14,000	35,000
1990	1,296	591,533	40,159	6,579	33,580
1995	1,238	614,571	46,599	6,193	40,406
1999	1,227	635,742	47,138	4,391	42,747
2000	1,221	639,954	47,730	4,149	43,581
2001	1,226	643,264	49,093	4,105	44,689

Source: National Catholic Educational Association.

Average SAT and ACT Scores by Group, 1987–2000

Group	Composite scores 1987	1990	1997	2000	Total test-takers, class of 2000
SAT Scores					
American Indian, Alaskan Native	934	934	963	963	7,658
Asian American, Pacific Islander	1,020	1,029	1,060	1,064	96,717
Black	839	847	860	860	119,591
Mexican-American	912	917	913	913	44,921
Puerto Rican	868	872	899	907	14,147
Other Hispanic	926	923	927	928	38,804
White	1,038	1,034	1,054	1,058	712,105
Men	1,035	1,026	1,040	1,040	583,331
Women	983	989	998	1,002	676,947
National average[1]	**1,008**	**1,001**	**1,017**	**1,019**	**1,260,278**
ACT Scores					
American Indian, Alaskan Native	17.5	18.0	19.0	19.0	10,976
Asian American, Pacific Islander	21.9	21.7	21.8	21.7	35,479
Black	16.6	17.0	17.1	17.0	110,617
Mexican-American	18.1	18.3	18.5	18.6	41,414
Other Hispanic	19.3	19.3	19.6	19.5	16,401
White	21.3	21.2	21.7	21.8	762,017
Men	21.2	21.0	21.2	21.2	455,817
Women	20.1	20.3	20.9	20.9	604,646
National average[1]	**20.6**	**20.6**	**21.0**	**21.0**	**1,065,138**

1. Includes students of other ethnicities and students who did not identify their gender or their ethnicity.
Source: The College Board, American College Testing Program.

than half of such schools charge at least $5,000 per year in tuition. Average tuition for nonsectarian secondary schools was over $9,000 per year.

Teachers   There were 378,365 full-time private school teachers; almost all of them were under the age of 50. The vast majority of these teachers (285,235) were women, and an even greater number (347,811) were white. The average teacher salary in private schools was $23,395, a fraction of the $35,924 earned by public school teachers. Male teachers earned substantially more than their female counterparts in both public and private schools, but the difference was most pronounced in private schools, where male compensation ($28,948) was 34 percent greater than female salaries ($21,657).

Race and ethnicity   Private schools remain almost entirely white enclaves.   More than half

(13,958) of all private schools had minority enrollments of under 9 percent, and another quarter (6,280) had minority populations below 29 percent, even though almost half of private school students came from central cities.

Student-teacher ratios   Students in private schools continue to get more teacher attention than do students in public schools. Pupil-teacher ratios were 16.6-1 in private elementary schools, compared with 18.6-1 in public elementary schools.   The difference was even more pronounced on the secondary school level, where private school teachers averaged 11.6 students, while each public school teacher was responsible for 14.2 pupils.

▶ COLLEGE ENTRANCE EXAMINATION SCORES

SATs (Scholastic Assessment Tests) purportedly measure verbal and mathematical reasoning abilities. These tests are developed and administered by the Educational Testing Service of Princeton, N.J., for the College Board, which is headquartered in New York City. The College Board is a nonprofit organization that provides tests and many other educational services for students, schools, and colleges. The test is scored on a range from 400 to 1600, with average scores usually around 900. Male students consistently outscore females on the SAT, and whites and Asians typically score at least 100 points higher than all other ethnic groups, and nearly 200 points higher than blacks. In response to criticisms of racial and gender bias, the College Board rewrote the SAT in 1994 to make it a test of aptitude, rather than of knowledge or test-taking techniques. The new test (called the SAT1) has fewer multiple choice questions and more open-ended questions, which the College Board claims makes the test uncoachable. But while scores for

---

Average Cost of 4-Year Colleges in Current and Constant Dollars, 1971–2001 (tuition and fees)

Despite low rates of inflation, the cost of a college education continues to skyrocket. Tuition in 2000-01 was more than three times what it was as recently as 1985-86. For years, the rule of thumb was that a year of college should cost about the same as a new Chevrolet. But in recent years, college costs have increased far faster than new car prices. In current dollars (not adjusted for inflation), the cost of a four-year college education increased 900 percent between 1971 and 2000.

In constant dollars (which negate the effect of inflation), the cost of college has more than doubled since 1981-82.   That's a departure from the trend during the 1970s, when the real cost of college actually decreased several times, and never rose above $7,200.

Parents of undergraduates bear most of this burden, but increasingly, students themselves are taking on heavy debt loads to finance their own educations.   Since 1993, the percentage of college graduates who owed more than $20,000 has more than doubled to 19 percent.   And since education debt is no longer tax-deductible, the impact is even more pronounced.

Year	Tuition and fees			
	Current dollars		Constant dollars	
	Private	Public	Private	Public
1971-72	$1,820	$376	$7,634	$1,577
1975-76	2,272	433	7,071	1,348
1980-81	3,617	804	7,207	1,602
1985-86	5,418	1,242	8,594	1,970
1990-91	9,391	1,809	12,104	2,332
1991-92	10,017	2,137	12,510	2,669
1992-93	10,498	2,315	12,713	2,804
1993-94	11,025	2,527	13,014	2,983
1994-95	11,709	2,686	13,437	3,082
1995-96	12,432	2,860	13,888	3,195
1996-97	12,823	2,966	13,928	3,222
1997-98	13,664	3,111	14,581	3,320
1998-99	14,709	3,247	15,443	3,409
1999-00	15,380	3,356	15,702	3,426
2000-01	16,332	3,510	16,332	3,510

Source: The College Board.

Most Popular Majors Among Incoming Freshmen, 1990–2000

Major	Percentage		
	1990	1999	2000
Elementary education	5.1%	6.2%	5.6%
Psychology	4.2	4.3	4.8
Premedicine, predental, preveterinary	3.2	4.3	4.4
Business administration	5.5	4.4	4.1
Computer science	1.7	3.8	3.7
General biology	1.8	3.0	3.6
Management	4.0	3.0	3.3
Political science	3.0	2.2	2.8
Communications	2.3	2.2	2.7
Marketing	2.5	2.3	2.7
Arts	2.0	2.6	2.5
Secondary education	1.9	2.1	2.5
Accounting	5.3	2.4	2.3
Nursing	4.2	2.9	2.1
Electrical engineering	2.5	1.9	2.0
Mechanical engineering	2.0	1.9	1.9
Therapy	2.3	2.5	1.9
English	1.0	1.5	1.7
Finance	N.A.	N.A.	1.7
Journalism	N.A.	N.A.	1.7

Source: Higher Education Research Institute, University of California, Los Angeles, *The American Freshman: National Norms for Fall, 2000.*

Number Of Degrees Conferred in U.S. by Type, 1950–2001

Year	All degrees[1]	Bachelor's	First professional[2]	Master's	Doctorate
1949–50	496,661		432,058[3]	58,183	6,420
1959–60	476,704		392,440[3]	74,435	9,829
1969-70	1,065,098	792,317	34,578	208,291	29,912
1979-80	1,330,244	929,417	70,131	298,081	32,615
1984-85	1,373,734	979,477	75,063	286,251	32,943
1989-90	1,485,004	1,051,344	70,988	324,301	38,371
1994-95	1,678,009	1,160,134	75,800	397,629	44,446
1995-96	1,692,479	1,164,792	76,734	406,301	44,652
1996-97	1,716,886	1,172,879	78,730	419,401	45,876
1997-98	1,739,178	1,184,406	78,598	430,164	46,010
1998-99[4]	1,709,200	1,178,000	80,300	405,000	45,900
1999-2000[4]	1,706,600	1,185,000	78,400	398,000	45,200
2000-01[4]	1,711,500	1,194,000	76,500	396,000	45,000

1. Does not include associate of arts (A.A.) or associate of science (A.S.) degrees; more than 500,000 of these have been given each year since 1992. 2. Degrees are: medical doctor, law, dentistry, optometry, podiatry, pharmacy, theology, chiropractic, and veterinary medicine. 3. Prior to 1961, bachelor's and first professional degrees were listed together. 4. Projected.
Source: U.S. Dept. of Education, National Center for Education Statistics, *Digest of Education Statistics, 2000.*

Educational Attainment of the Population 25+ Years, 1940–2000

Year	Completed 4 years of high school or more			Completed 4 years of college or more		
	Both Sexes	Male	Female	Both Sexes	Male	Female
1940	24.5%	22.7%	26.3%	4.6%	5.5%	3.8%
1950	34.3	32.6	36.0	6.2	7.3	5.2
1959	43.7	42.2	45.2	8.1	10.3	6.0
1970	55.2	55.0	55.4	11.0	14.1	8.2
1980	68.6	69.1	68.1	17.0	20.8	13.5
1991	78.4	78.5	78.3	21.4	24.3	18.8
1995	81.7	81.7	81.6	23.0	26.0	20.2
1998	82.8	82.8	82.9	24.4	26.5	22.4
1999	83.4	83.4	83.4	25.2	27.5	23.1
2000	84.1	84.2	84.0	25.6	27.8	23.6

Source: Bureau of the Census, *Current Population Survey: Educational Attainment in the United States, March, 2000 (2001).*

Educational Attainment of the Population, Ages 25 and Over, 2000

Characteristic	Number of people	4 years high school or more	Some college or more	4 years college or more
All persons	175,230,000	84.1%	50.9%	25.6%
Sex:				
Male	83,611,000	84.2	52.3	27.8
Female	91,620,000	84.0	49.7	23.6
Race:				
White	147,067,000	84.9	51.5	26.1
Black	20,036,000	78.5	43.3	16.5
Hispanic origin[1]	17,150,000	57.0	29.1	10.6
Age groups:				
25 to 29 years	18,268,000	88.1	58.3	29.1
30 to 34 years	19,518,000	88.2	56.9	29.5
35 to 39 years	22,320,000	88.5	54.8	27.4
40 to 44 years	22,485,000	88.8	55.0	26.7
45 to 49 years	19,748,000	89.5	58.3	30.3
50 to 54 years	16,882,000	88.3	57.4	30.2
55 to 59 years	12,868,000	84.0	48.7	25.0
60 to 64 years	10,519,000	78.8	42.6	21.6
65 to 69 years	9,352,000	75.4	37.2	18.5
70 to 74 years	8,444,000	71.6	35.2	16.4
75 years or older	14,825,000	64.6	30.5	13.4
Residence				
Metropolitan area	141,367,000	84.9	53.4	27.8
Non-metropolitan area	33,863,000	80.8	40.6	16.3

1. People of Hispanic origin may be of any race.
Source: Bureau of the Census, *Current Population Survey: Educational Attainment in the United States, March, 2000* (2001).

almost all ethnic and gender groups have gone up gradually every year since 1994, the gender and ethnicity gaps have not changed, suggesting that the new test may be just as biased as the old one.

ACTs are administered by the American College Testing Program, a nonprofit educational organization headquartered in Iowa City, Iowa. Its use is more popular than the SAT in states west of the Mississippi River. The ACT composite score is the average of four tests that measure academic abilities in English, mathematics, social studies, and natural sciences. Although similar numbers of students take each test, the ACT draws less criticism than the SAT, even though both tests evidence similar racial and gender biases.

▶HIGHER EDUCATION

The accompanying figures give a startling picture of just how the coming of age of the Baby Boom generation transformed U.S. higher education. In just one decade (the 1960s) the number of undergraduate degrees conferred more than doubled, while the number of doctorates actually tripled. These extraordinary changes were matched in kind by dramatic shifts in what students wanted to study: during the late 1960s, for example, the number of degrees in sociology and psychology jumped by more than 15,000 each in just a few years (1966-1970), while interest in business soared during the 1980s. That trend has begun to reverse in the 1990s, as the need for social workers and other health and human service professionals has expanded.

College enrollment Between 1980 and 1992, college enrollment increased about 20 percent, from just over 12 million to a record 14.5 million. Since then, enrollment has not fluctuated much, even though the traditional college age-population has dropped. Much of the growth in college enrollment was fueled by increases in older students, women, and minorities on campus. Women have outnumbered men on college campuses since 1979, when there were just under 6 million of each in institutions of higher education. Since then, male enrollment has increased only 13 percent, to 6.3 million, while female enrollment has leapt 34 percent to 8.0 million. Minorities, especially Hispanics and Asians, have increased from 15.7 percent of the campus population in 1976 to 26.8 percent in 1997, the latest year for which statistics are available. The percentage of blacks on campus fluctuated for many years, but began increasing again in 1990. Nearly 11 percent of college students were black in 1997, up from 9.3 percent in 1990.

▶EDUCATIONAL ATTAINMENT

Despite complaints about the state of education in America, there can be no doubt that the general population continues to grow more educated every year. In 2000, more than 84 percent of all adults over the age of 25 had completed high school, and more than a quarter of American adults had a bachelor's degree or more. It's not surprising that those numbers were both a lot lower in 1940, when only 24 percent of adults had graduated from high school and college degrees belonged to fewer than 5 percent of the population. But even as recently as 1980, only 69 percent of adults over 25 had a high school diploma and only 17 percent had graduated from college. (See the accompanying table.)

The greatest proof of the importance of education is the correlation between years of schooling and higher salaries. In 1998 (the latest year available), adults with bachelor's degrees earned an average of $43,782 per year, compared with $23,594 for those with only high school diplomas. Those with post-graduate educations made more than $63,000 while those who failed to graduate from high school averaged only $16,053.

Educational Attainment by State, 2000

State	Persons over 25 ('000s)	Completed 4 years high school or more (rank)	Completed 4 years college or more (rank)
U.S. Total	173,754	83.4% (–)	25.2% (–)
Alabama	2,790	77.5 (50)	20.4 (44)
Alaska	359	90.4 (5)	28.1 (13)
Arizona	2,996	85.1 (31)	24.6 (26)
Arkansas	1,635	81.7 (41)	18.4 (49)
California	20,983	81.2 (43)	27.5 (14)
Colorado	2,640	89.7 (9)	34.6 (2)
Connecticut	2,231	88.2 (13)	31.6 (6)
Delaware	490	86.1 (25)	24.0 (29)
Dist. of Columbia	346	83.2 (35)	38.3 (1)
Florida	10,156	84.0 (34)	22.8 (37)
Georgia	5,024	82.6 (38)	23.1 (35)
Hawaii	759	87.4 (17)	26.3 (20)
Idaho	759	86.2 (23)	20.0 (45)
Illinois	7,513	85.5 (29)	27.1 (17)
Indiana	3,893	84.6 (33)	17.1 (50)
Iowa	1,829	89.7 (10)	25.5 (23)
Kansas	1,624	88.1 (14)	27.3 (15)
Kentucky	2,543	78.7 (49)	20.5 (43)
Louisiana	2,641	80.8 (44)	22.5 (40)
Maine	847	89.3 (12)	24.1 (28)
Maryland	3,417	85.7 (27)	32.3 (4)
Massachusetts	4,075	85.1 (32)	32.7 (3)
Michigan	6,262	86.2 (24)	23.0 (36)
Minnesota	2,997	90.8 (3)	31.2 (7)
Mississippi	1,724	80.3 (45)	18.7 (48)
Missouri	3,500	86.6 (21)	26.2 (21)
Montana	563	89.6 (11)	23.8 (31)
Nebraska	1,019	90.4 (6)	24.6 (24)
Nevada	1,174	82.8 (37)	19.3 (46)
New Hampshire	796	88.1 (15)	30.1 (8)
New Jersey	5,380	87.3 (18)	30.1 (9)
New Mexico	1,098	82.2 (40)	23.6 (33)
New York	12,009	82.5 (39)	28.7 (11)
North Carolina	4,936	79.2 (47)	23.2 (34)
North Dakota	411	85.5 (30)	22.6 (38)
Ohio	7,240	87.0 (19)	24.6 (25)
Oklahoma	2,171	86.1 (26)	22.5 (39)
Oregon	2,201	88.1 (16)	27.2 (16)
Pennsylvania	7,788	85.7 (28)	24.3 (27)
Rhode Island	629	81.3 (42)	26.4 (19)
South Carolina	2,593	83.0 (36)	19.0 (47)
South Dakota	439	91.8 (1)	25.7 (22)
Tennessee	3,579	79.9 (46)	22.0 (41)
Texas	12,484	79.2 (48)	23.9 (30)
Utah	1,184	90.7 (4)	26.4 (18)
Vermont	390	90.0 (7)	28.8 (10)
Virginia	4,568	86.6 (22)	31.9 (5)
Washington	3,687	91.8 (2)	28.6 (12)
West Virginia	1,195	77.1 (51)	15.3 (51)
Wisconsin	3,352	86.7 (20)	23.8 (32)
Wyoming	311	90.0 (8)	20.6 (42)

Source: U.S. Bureau of the Census, *Current Population Survey, March 2000* (2001).

U.S. Energy

▶AN ENERGY CRISIS?

With gasoline prices surpassing $2 a gallon and California imposing rolling blackouts in the wake of a short-term electricity shortage in early 2001, President George Bush unveiled a national energy plan with more than 100 recommendations for increasing the supply of U.S. energy. The plan, which was long on easing restrictions on oil and gas development and short on policies that would reduce U.S. demand for energy, was immediately derided by conservationists as little more than a handout to the Administration's cronies in the oil industry. (*For additional information about the California energy crisis, see Part I: The Almanac of the Year."*)

▶ENERGY PRODUCTION AND CONSUMPTION

Energy is usually measured in millions or larger quantities of British thermal units (Btu). One Btu is approximately equal to the energy released in burning a wooden match. An engine burning eight gallons of gasoline releases one million (10^6) Btu. One quadrillion (10^{15}) Btu is the equivalent of the energy released from an engine burning eight billion gallons of gasoline.

Total U.S. energy production was 71.9 quadrillion Btu in 2000. Natural gas and coal each accounted for more than one-quarter of domestic energy production. Fossil fuels, which also include crude oil, accounted for 80 percent of all energy production, down from 95.3 percent as recently as 1970. Nuclear energy (11.1 percent) and renewable

energy forms like solar energy and wind power (9.1 percent) have made up the difference.

U.S. energy consumption hit an all-time high of 98.50 quadrillion Btu in 2000, down slightly from the year before. Even despite increasing prices for all forms of energy, American consumers continue to be lavish in their use, opting for convenience over energy efficiency at nearly every turn. The average home size increased by more than 500 square feet between 1973 and 1997 (bringing with it an attendant increase in heating costs), and is now packed with many more energy-sucking appliances than ever before, including whirlpool tubs, microwave ovens, toaster-ovens, washer-dryers, and central air-conditioning. In addition, Americans are driving bigger, less-efficient cars and trucks, and are driving them more total miles each year, thus consuming more gas than ever before. Between 1985 and 1999, every energy-efficient form of commuting to work (carpooling, public transportation, biking, walking, and working at home) declined in popularity; meanwhile, 78.2 percent of workers drove by themselves in 1999, up from 72.4 percent in 1985.

Petroleum continues to be the energy of choice among U.S. consumers. It accounted for 38 percent of all U.S. energy consumption in 2000, compared to 22.4 percent for coal and 23.3 percent for natural gas. Since the U.S. consumes more petroleum than it produces (and consumes more total energy than it produces), it must import the difference. Consumption of nuclear energy has grown steadily from nearly zero in 1960 to 8.01 quadrillion

U.S. Energy Overview, 1960–2000

Activity and energy source	(Quadrillion Btu)							As percent of total, 2000
	1960	1970	1980	1990	1995	1999	2000[1]	
Production, Total	**41.49**	**63.50**	**67.24**	**70.84**	**71.30**	**71.98**	**71.90**	**100.0%**
Coal	10.82	14.61	18.60	22.46	22.03	23.19	22.66	31.5
Natural gas (dry)	12.66	21.67	19.91	18.36	19.10	19.13	19.74	27.4
Crude oil[2]	14.93	20.40	18.25	15.57	13.89	12.45	12.38	17.2
Natural gas plant liquids	1.46	2.51	2.25	2.17	2.44	2.53	2.61	3.6
Nuclear electric power	0.01	0.24	2.74	6.16	7.18	7.74	8.01	11.1
Renewable energy[3]	1.61	4.08	5.49	6.14	6.69	7.02	6.56	9.1
Imports, Total	**4.23**	**8.39**	**15.97**	**18.95**	**22.57**	**27.55**	**28.52**	**100.0%**
Natural gas	0.16	0.85	1.01	1.55	2.90	3.66	3.81	13.4
Petroleum[4]	4.00	7.47	14.66	17.12	18.88	23.13	23.78	83.4
Other[5]	0.07	0.07	0.31	0.29	0.79	0.75	0.92	3.2
Exports, Total	**1.48**	**2.66**	**3.72**	**4.87**	**4.54**	**3.81**	**4.10**	**100.0%**
Coal	1.02	1.94	2.42	2.77	2.32	1.53	1.53	37.3
Petroleum	0.43	0.55	1.16	1.82	1.99	1.95	2.15	52.4
Other[6]	0.03	0.18	0.14	0.27	0.23	0.33	0.42	10.2
Consumption, Total	**43.80**	**67.86**	**78.44**	**84.34**	**90.94**	**96.87**	**98.50**	**100.0%**
Coal	9.84	12.26	15.42	19.25	20.02	21.69	22.41	22.75
Natural gas	12.39	21.79	20.39	19.30	22.16	22.29	23.32	23.68
Petroleum products[7]	19.92	29.52	34.20	33.55	34.55	37.96	37.96	38.54
Nuclear electric power	0.01	0.24	2.74	6.16	7.18	7.74	8.01	8.13
Renewable energy[3]	1.66	4.10	5.71	6.25	6.99	7.23	6.82	6.92

Note: Sum of components may not equal 100 percent due to independent rounding. 1. Preliminary. 2. Includes lease condensate. 3. Includes hydroelectric power, geothermal energy, solar energy, wind energy, and biofuels such as wood waste, landfill gases, fish oils, and other waste. 4. Includes imports of crude oil for the Strategic Petroleum Reserve, which began in 1977. 5. Includes coal, coal coke, and electricity. 6. Includes natural gas, coal coke, and petroleum products. 7. Petroleum products supplied include natural gas plant liquids and crude oil burned as fuel. **Source:** U.S. Dept. of Energy, *Annual Energy Review (2000)* 2001.

Btu in 2000. Renewable energy consumption has grown similarly, from 1.66 quadrillion Btu, in 1960, to 6.82 quadrillion Btu in 2000.

The relationship between total energy consumption and real gross domestic product (GDP) is a primary indicator of the energy intensity of the economy. In 1949, the country used 20,580 Btu of energy per dollar of GDP (measured in constant 1992 dollars). From 1949 to 1972, energy consumption more than doubled (from 30 quadrillion to 74 quadrillion Btu), increasing at approximately the same rate as GDP. Since then, consumption has continued to hit record levels every year, but increases in energy efficiency, conservation, and the expansion of the service sector of the economy have kept energy consumption to 13,100 Btu per dollar of GDP, or 32 percent less than in 1972. In other words, the country is using much more energy, but not paying much more for it.

A second indicator is per capita consumption, which rose from 215 million Btu per capita in 1949 to 361 million Btu in 1978. Efforts at conservation persuaded people to decrease their consumption to 321 million Btu in 1986, but per capita use has rebounded since then, to 350 million Btu in 2000. Alaska was the biggest per capita consumer of energy. New York and Hawaii used the least energy per capita—Hawaii because so few houses need to be heated, and New York because so many people live in apartments, which require much less energy to heat and insulate.

(For facts and figures about energy consumption and production worldwide, see the section on World Energy in Part III).

▶FOSSIL FUELS
Petroleum
Since 1958 the United States has consumed more energy than it produces; the difference has been met with energy imports. Net imports of energy (primarily petroleum) grew rapidly through 1973, when they totaled 13 quadrillion Btu, or 20 percent of consumption.

Despite the Arab oil embargo of 1973–74 and increases in the price of crude oil, petroleum net imports continued to grow, reaching a peak of nearly 19 quadrillion Btu in 1977. That year, U.S. dependence on petroleum net imports peaked at 47 percent of consumption. In 1985, petroleum

U.S. Energy Consumption, Total and Per Capita, 1950–2000

Year	Total energy consumption (million Btu)	Per capita consumption (million Btu)
1950	34,630,000,000	229
1955	40,240,000,000	244
1960	45,120,000,000	252
1965	54,020,000,000	279
1970	67,860,000,000	334
1980	78,440,000,000	346
1985	76,750,000,000	323
1990	84,340,000,000	339
1995	90,940,000,000	346
1998	94,610,000,000	350
1999	96,870,000,000	355
2000[1]	98,500,000,000	350

1. Preliminary.
Source: U.S. Dept. of Energy, *Annual Energy Review (2000)* 2001.

U.S. Fuel Consumption by Type and End-Use Sector, 1950–2000

Year	Residential and commercial	Industrial	Transportation	Electric utilities	Total
Petroleum (million barrels/day)					
1950	1.07	1.82	3.36	0.21	6.46
1960	1.71	2.71	5.14	0.24	9.80
1970	2.18	3.81	7.78	0.93	14.70
1980	1.52	4.84	9.55	1.15	17.06
1990	1.14	4.32	10.97	0.55	16.99
1995	1.11	4.60	11.73	0.29	17.43
1999	1.18	5.03	12.89	0.42	19.10
2000[1]	1.20	4.94	12.99	0.34	19.13
Natural gas (trillion cubic feet/year)					
1950	1.59	3.43	0.13	0.63	5.77
1960	4.12	5.77	0.35	1.72	11.97
1970	7.24	9.25	0.72	3.93	21.14
1980	7.36	8.20	0.63	3.68	19.88
1990	7.01	8.25	0.66	2.79	18.72
1995	7.88	9.80	0.70	18.38	21.58
1999	7.77	10.08	0.74	18.59	21.70
2000[1]	8.28	10.64	0.75	19.68	22.71
Coal (million short tons/year)					
1950	114.6	224.6	63.0	91.9	494.1
1960	40.9	177.4	3.0	176.7	398.1
1970	16.1	186.6	0.3	320.2	523.2
1980	6.5	127.0	(2)	569.3	702.7
1985	7.8	116.4	(2)	693.8	818.0
1990	6.7	115.2	(2)	773.5	902.9
1995	5.9	106.1	(2)	829.0	962.0
1999	4.9	93.6	(2)	894.1	1,045.3
2000[1]	4.9	94.9	(2)	857.6	1,079.7

1. Preliminary. 2. Small quantities consumed by transportation sector are included in industrial column.
Source: U.S. Dept. of Energy, *Annual Energy Review (2000)* 2001.

net imports dropped to 9 quadrillion Btu and U.S. dependence on foreign oil fell to 27 percent of consumption, its lowest level since 1972.

But a drop in the worldwide price of oil inhibited domestic production and caused U.S. reliance on imports to jump back up in the late 1980s. Oil prices rebounded briefly during the Gulf War, but by 1998, the price per barrel was down to $12.52, its lowest level in more than two decades. In 2000, the price per barrel jumped to $28.23, its highest price since 1984. But in constant dollars, the price per barrel was less than half of what it was in 1981, when the price (in 1996 dollars) was $56.50 . Dependence on imports in 2000 were a record high 51.6 percent of consumption, primarily because of the low price of foreign oil. Saudi Arabia, Venezuela, Canada and Mexico are the U.S.'s primary suppliers of foreign oil; each exports more than 1.3 million barrels of oil per day to the U.S.

Natural gas

Once considered a useless byproduct of oil well drilling (it was simply burned off at the site), natural gas is today the primary source of energy for space heating in 50 million U.S. households. U.S. natural gas trade was limited to the border countries of Mexico and Canada until shipping natural gas in liquefied form emerged as an alternative to pipelines. In 1969, the first shipments of liquefied natural gas (LNG) were sent to Japan, and U.S. imports from Algeria began the following year. In 2000, U.S. net imports of natural gas by all routes totaled 3.73 trillion cubic feet (the vast majority from Canada).

Coal

Since World War II coal has been the major U.S. energy export. Throughout most of the 1960s and 1970s, U.S. exports of coal increased, peaking at 113 million short tons in 1981. Exports dropped to just under 80 million short tons in 1987, but rebounded to 109 million in 1991. Since then, exports have dropped dramatically, to 58.5 million tons in 2000. Canada is the largest market for U.S. coal, importing close to 19 million tons in 2000. Japan and Italy, which each imported more than 11.9 million short tons as recently as 1990, imported less than 5 million tons in 2000.

Gasoline and Heating Oil Retail Prices per Gallon, 1950–2000

Year	Motor gasoline (including taxes)[1] Current dollars	Motor gasoline (including taxes)[1] Constant (1996) dollars[3]	Residential heating oil[2] Current dollars
1950	$0.27	$1.54	N.A.
1960	0.31	1.40	$0.15
1970	0.36	1.23	0.18
1975	0.57	1.42	0.37
1980	1.19	2.09	0.97
1985	1.12	1.51	1.05
1990	1.15	1.33	1.06
1995	1.21	1.23	0.87
1999	1.22	1.17	0.88
2000	1.56	1.46	1.41

1. Prices are calculated from a sample of stations providing all types of services. Prices are for leaded regular gasoline only from 1950-75, and for an average of all grades of gasoline after 1975.
2. Prices derived by dividing sum of estimated national retail sales for residential heating oil (No. 2 fuel oil) by the estimated volume of retail sales for residential heating.
Source: U.S. Dept. of Energy, *Annual Energy Review 2000* (2001).

Electric utilities are the primary domestic consumers of coal. Their consumption grew from a 17 percent share in 1949 to a 79 percent share in 2000. Over the same period, consumption in all other sectors declined, most dramatically in the transportation sector, due primarily to railroads switching from coal to petroleum-driven trains. Transportation sector consumption, which topped 70 million short tons in 1949, has totaled fewer than 50,000 short tons every year since 1975. Consumption by the residential and commercial sector has also declined steadily, from a high of 117 million short tons in 1949 to 4.9 million short tons in 2000.

▶THE STRATEGIC PETROLEUM RESERVE

In an attempt to minimize the wild fluctuations in prices caused by the Arab oil embargoes of the 1970s, the U.S. in 1977 created the Strategic Petroleum Reserve, which permitted the storage of 580 million barrels of oil. The reserve proved useful in preventing additional oil price hikes during the Iraqi invasion of Kuwait in 1990.

The reserve can also be used as an emergency supply of oil in case of a complete oil embargo. In 1985, the reserve held enough oil to provide a normal level of petroleum to the U.S. for 115 days in the absence of any other petroleum imports. With gasoline and heating oil prices skyrocketing in the summer of 2000, Pres. Clinton released 30 million barrels from the reserve, which will be returned (with interest) in 2001-02. The move temporarily reduced oil prices, but reduced the reserve to 53 days of oil.

▶ELECTRICITY

Net generation of electricity by electric utilities topped 3.7 trillion kilowatthours (kWh) in 2000. Coal continued to fuel most of the generation, accounting for 2.0 trillion kWh, while natural gas contributed 595.6 billion kWh. Higher petroleum prices contributed to an decrease in petroleum-fired generation, from 126.9 billion kWh in 1998 to 109 billion kWh in 2000. Nuclear-based generation helped make up the difference, increasing 674 billion kWh in 1998 to 754 billion kWh in 2000. Hydroelectric generation was 275 billion kWh, down from an all-time high of 359 billion kWh in 1997.

The weighted average real price (based on 1996 dollars) of electricity to all sectors in 2000 was 6.23 cents per kWh, 30 percent below the price in 1982, but about the same as in 1967. But although prices of other major energy sources increased significantly during the same period, electricity remained by far the most expensive source of energy on a Btu basis.

▶NUCLEAR POWER

The number of nuclear power plants in operation in the U.S. skyrocketed from 18 in 1970 to 112 in 1990, and net nuclear generation of electricity jumped from 21.8 to 753 kWh. Since 1990, two new plants have opened and 10 have closed, but generation nonetheless increased to 673 kWh. More than three-quarters of the 104 nuclear power plants in the U.S. are located east of the Mississippi River. The U.S. has the highest number of reactors of any country in the world, but far fewer than the 236 that were in the stages of planning, construction or operation as recently as 1975.

Several factors have contributed to the decline in the number of planned nuclear units. Growth in electricity demand has been slower than expected; longer lead times for licensing and construction coupled during the 1980s with higher financing expenses increased costs; and rising interest rates and an uncertain economic environment eroded electric utilities' willingness to commission new plants. Furthermore, nuclear plant operators have been able to increase their generation of electricity without increasing the number of reactors. Nuclear plants ran at 88.1 percent of capacity in 2000, up from 66.0 percent in 1990 and 56.3 percent in 1980.

A further deterrent has been the increased public opposition to nuclear power plants because of concerns about their safety and the disposal of spent nuclear fuel. These were heightened in the wake of the 1979 accident at Three Mile Island near Harrisburg, Pennsylvania, and the far more devastating one at Chernobyl in Ukraine in 1986.

U.S. Net Generation of Electricity by Energy Source, 1950–2000 (billion kilowatthours)

Year	Coal	Natural gas	Petroleum[1]	Nuclear Power	Hydroelectric power	Geothermal and other[2]	Total
1950	155	45	34	0	101	[3]	329
1955	301	95	37	0	116	[3]	547
1960	403	158	48	1	149	[3]	756
1965	571	222	65	4	197	0.2	1,055
1970	704	373	184	22	251	0.8	1,532
1975	853	300	289	173	303	3.4	1,918
1980	1,162	346	246	251	279	5.6	2,286
1985	1,402	292	100	384	285	10.6	2,470
1990	1,590	378	124	577	293	63.1	3,025
1995	1,710	498	75	673	311	75.0	3,558
1999	1,884	556	124	728	320	83.2	3,706
2000[4]	1,965	596	109	754	275	84.0	3,792

1. Includes distillate fuel oil, residual fuel oil (including crude oil burned as fuel), jet fuel and petroleum coke. 2. Other is wood, waste, photovoltaic and solar thermal energy used to generate electricity for distribution. 3. Less than 0.5 billion kilowatthours. 4. Preliminary.
Source: U.S. Dept. of Energy, *Annual Energy Review (2000)* 2001.

U.S. Commercial Nuclear Plants, 2000

There are 104 operable nuclear reactors in 31 states. The following table lists the states, with the total number of reactors in each, the names of the individual units and their location.

Alabama = 5
Browns Ferry 1, 2 & 3, Decatur
Joseph M. Farley 1 & 2, Dothan
Arizona = 3
Palo Verde 1, 2 & 3, Wintersburg
Arkansas = 2
Arkansas Nuclear 1 & 2,
Russellville
California = 4
Diablo Canyon 1 & 2, Avila Beach
San Onofre 2 & 3, San Clemente
Connecticticut = 2
Millstone 2 & 3, Waterford
Florida = 5
Crystal River 3, Red Level
St. Lucie 1 & 2, Ft. Pierce
Turkey Point 3 & 4, Florida City
Georgia = 4
Hatch 1 & 2, Baxley
Vogtle 1 & 2, Waynesboro
Illinois = 11
Braidwood 1 & 2, Braidwood
Byron 1 & 2, Byron
Clinton 1, Clinton
Dresden 2 & 3, Morris
La Salle 1 & 2, Seneca
Quad Cities 1 & 2, Cordova
Iowa = 1
Duane Arnold, Palo
Kansas = 1
Wolf Creek, Burlington
Louisiana = 2
River Bend 1, St. Francisville
Waterford 3, Taft

Maryland = 2
Calvert Cliffs 1 & 2, Lusby
Massachusetts = 1
Pilgrim 1, Plymouth
Michigan = 4
Donald C. Cook 1 & 2, Bridgman
Fermi 2, Newport
Palisades, South Haven
Minnesota = 3
Monticello, Monticello
Prairie Island 1 & 2, Red Wing
Mississippi = 1
Grand Gulf 1, Port Gibson
Missouri = 1
Callaway 1, Fulton
Nebraska = 2
Cooper, Brownville
Fort Calhoun 1, Fort Calhoun
New Hampshire = 1
Seabrook 1, Seabrook
New Jersey = 4
Hope Creek 1, Salem
Oyster Creek 1, Forked River
Salem 1 & 2, Salem
New York = 6
Indian Point 2 & 3, Buchanan
James Fitzpatrick 1, Scriba
Nine Mile Point 1 & 2,
Oswego
Robert E. Ginna, Rochester
North Carolina = 5
Brunswick 1 & 2, Southport
McGuire 1 & 2, Cowens Ford Dam
Shearon Harris 1, New Hill

Ohio = 2
Davis-Besse 1, Oak Harbor
Perry 1, North Perry
Pennsylvania = 9
Beaver Valley 1 & 2, Shippingport
Limerick 1 & 2, Pottstown
Peach Bottom 2 & 3, Lancaster
Susquehanna 1 & 2, Berwick
Three Mile Island 1, Middletown
South Carolina = 7
Catawba 1 & 2, Clover
H.B. Robinson 2, Hartsville
Oconee 1, 2 & 3, Seneca
Summer 1, Jenkinsville
Tennessee = 2
Sequoyah 1 & 2, Daisy
Watts Bar 1, Spring City
Texas = 4
Comanche Peak 1&2, Glen Rose
South Texas 1 & 2, Bay City
Vermont = 1
Vermont Yankee 1, Vernon
Virginia = 4
North Anna 1 & 2, Mineral
Surry 1 & 2, Surry
Washington = 1
Washington Nuclear 2, Richland
Wisconsin = 3
Kewaunee, Carlton
Point Beach 1 & 2, Two Creeks

Source: U.S. Dept. of Energy, *Nuclear Power Generation and Fuel Cycle Report,* annual.

U.S. Health and Medicine

►QUALITY OF HEALTH

Americans are living longer, healthier lives than ever before, yet many of the health problems they face could be avoided or alleviated with appropriate prevention or treatment. With this in mind, government health officials have three broad goals: increasing the span of healthy life, reducing health disparities, and achieving access to preventive services for everyone.

Health quality varies significantly by economic level, age group, and geographic region. Among the most persistent disparities are sickness and mortality rates for various racial and ethnic groups. These disparities are especially stark for white and black Americans. For example:

- A white baby can expect to live 77.3 years; a black baby, 71.4 years (1999 data).
- Whites can expect 63.8 years of healthy life; blacks, 55.6 years (1994).
- Whites experience 8.7 tuberculosis cases per 100,000 people; blacks, 23.9 (1995).
- Whites have 22.5 diabetes-related deaths per 100,000 people; blacks, 32.2 (1996).
- Blacks are 33 percent more likely to die of cancer than whites (1990-97).
- The age-adjusted death rate for stroke for blacks is 76 percent higher than for whites. (1997).
- Nearly half (45 percent) of reported AIDS cases are among blacks, though they represent only 12 percent of the population (1998).
- The age-adjusted homicide rate for black males is almost seven times the rate for white males (1998).
- The maternal mortality rate is 19.6 deaths per 100,000 for black pregnant women, 5.3 deaths for white pregnant women (1987-96).
- The infant mortality rate is 5.8 per 1,000 live births for whites, 14.6 for blacks (1999).
- The age-adjusted death rate for blacks is 32 percent higher than for whites (1999).

A growing body of evidence indicates that race, discrimination, and social and cultural factors influence the care that people receive and, consequently, their health.

►HEALTH CARE EXPENDITURES

National health care spending topped $1.2 trillion in 1999, up 5.8 percent from 1998. This was the sixth consecutive year in which spending growth remained below 6 percent. As a share of gross domestic product (GDP), health spending declined slightly in 1999 to 13.0 percent.

The United States spends more than any other developed nation on health care relative to its economy. The nation's 1999 health expenditures amounted to $4,358 per person, up from $2,737 in 1990—and only $143 in 1960. Close to 90 percent of these moneys were for personal health care; the remainder went to research, construction, program administration, the net cost of private health insurance, and public health activities.

A variety of factors contribute to the high costs of health care, including:

1. Use of sophisticated, expensive medical equipment.
2. New, higher priced prescription drugs and increased consumer demand induced by drug manufacturers' advertising.
3. Excessive and arguably unnecessary procedures, including duplication of tests and use of technologies that yield similar results.
4. Increasing elderly population, which use medical care more intensely than younger people.
5. Increasing number of accidents and other incidents that require emergency medical services.
6. Labor intensiveness and earnings growth for health care professionals and executives.
7. Malpractice insurance.
8. Administrative waste.
9. Fraud.

National Expenditures for Health Care, 1960–99

Category	1960	1970	1980	1990	1995	1997	1998	1999
Total expenditures (billions)	**$26.7**	**$73.1**	**$245.8**	**$695.6**	**$987.0**	**$1,093.9**	**$1,146.1**	**$1,210.7**
Private	20.1	45.5	141.0	413.2	528.8	588.0	623.2	662.1
Public	6.6	27.6	104.8	282.4	458.2	505.8	522.9	548.5
Federal	2.8	17.6	71.3	196.6	323.9	361.7	369.3	384.7
State and local	3.8	10.0	33.5	89.8	134.3	144.2	153.6	163.9
Per capita expenditures	**$143**	**$348**	**$1,067**	**$2,737**	**$3,686**	**$4,011**	**$4,164**	**$4,358**
Private	108	216	612	1,626	1,975	2,156	2,264	2,384
Public	35	131	455	1,111	1,711	1,855	1,900	1,975
Federal	15	84	309	758	1,210	1,326	1,342	1,385
State and local	20	48	146	353	502	529	558	590
Percent distribution	**100.0%**	**100.0%**	**100.0%**	**100.0%**	**100.0%**	**100.0%**	**100.0%**	**100.0%**
Private	75.2	62.3	57.4	59.4	53.6	53.8	54.4	54.7
Public	24.8	37.7	42.6	40.6	46.4	46.2	45.6	45.3
Federal	10.6	24.0	29.0	27.7	32.8	33.1	32.2	31.8
State and local	14.2	13.7	13.6	12.9	13.6	13.2	13.4	13.5
Health care expenditures as percent of GDP	**5.1%**	**7.0%**	**8.8%**	**12.0%**	**13.3%**	**13.2%**	**13.0%**	**13.0%**

Note: Figures may not add to totals because of rounding.
Source: U.S. Dept. of Health and Human Services, Health Care Financing Administration, Office of National Health Statistics.

Prescription Drugs

The fastest-growing health-care expenditure is prescription drugs. A study issued by the National Institute for Health Care Management Foundation found that spending on prescription drugs increased 18.8 percent in 2000, to $131.9 billion. Coupled with dramatic increases from 1998 to 1999, drug spending rose an estimated 40 percent from 1998 to 2000. Three main reasons were cited for the increase: doctors are writing more prescriptions; they are shifting from older, lower-cost drugs to newer, more costly ones; and drugs are becoming more expensive.

The study reported that the 50 top-selling drugs in 2000 accounted for 30 percent of all prescriptions and were almost twice as expensive as all other drugs. Retail pharmacies filled 2.9 billion prescriptions in 2000, an increase of 7.5 percent over 1999. But the number of prescriptions for the 50 best-selling drugs jumped 18.6 percent, to 866.6 million.

Hospital Care

Hospital care has long claimed the biggest share of health care dollars. In 1950 hospital care accounted for 30.4 percent of personal health care costs. By 1980, the percentage had zoomed to 47.3 percent. More recently it declined—to 37.5 percent in 1998—as hospitals contained costs with shorter hospital stays and increased treatment on an outpatient basis.

In 1999, the average adult stay in community hospitals (excluding federal hospitals, psychiatric institutions, and long-term hospitals) was 5.9 days. The average costs to the hospital were $1,103 per day and $6,512 per stay. In contrast, the average stay in 1980 was 7.6 days; average costs were $245 per day and $1,851 per stay.

People age 65 and older are major consumers of inpatient care. They represented less than 13 percent of the U.S. population in 1999, but accounted for 40 percent of the estimated 32.1 million patient discharges from community hospitals. Their average length of stay was also higher (6.1 days) than for other age groups.

Nursing-Home Care

In mid-1998 approximately 1.6 million elderly and disabled people were receiving care in some

---

Health Care Quality, by State, 1999

To measure the quality of health care across state lines, statisticians at Health Risk Management Inc. use a weighted average of 46 individual measures relating to population health, health care systems, and consumer health status, based on data contained in reports from various medical associations and U.S. government agencies. Examples of measures include drinking water quality, alcohol-related traffic deaths, public health expenditures, physician and dentist shortages, immunizations, infant mortality rate, and heart disease deaths. The average score is 100

Rank, State	Score	Rank, State	Score
1. Minnesota	118.2	25t. Montana	103.2
2. Hawaii	115.7	27. Illinois	102.8
3. Wisconsin	114.6	28. Michigan	101.9
4. New	113.9	29. Maryland	101.6
Hampshire		30. New York	100.6
5. Vermont	113.1	31. Indiana	99.8
6. Massachusetts	112.8	32. Delaware	98.8
7. Connecticut	111.9	33. Idaho	98.1
8. Washington	110.2	34. Missouri	98.0
9. Maine	110.0	35. Florida	96.6
10. Iowa	109.3	36. Georgia	95.8
11. Utah	108.8	37. No. Carolina	95.7
12. Colorado	108.4	38. Nevada	93.9
13. Alaska	108.3	39. Arizona	93.6
14. Nebraska	108.1	40. West Virginia	93.2
15. No. Dakota	107.7	41. Kentucky	92.5
16. Rhode Island	107.2	42. Texas	92.1
17. New Jersey	107.0	43. Alabama	91.0
18. Kansas	107.0	44. New Mexico	90.4
19. Virginia	106.7	45. So. Carolina	90.0
20. Wyoming	106.6	46. Oklahoma	88.9
21. So. Dakota	105.3	47. Tennessee	87.1
22. Oregon	105.0	48. Arkansas	86.6
23. Ohio	103.7	49t. Mississippi	83.1
24. Pennsylvania	104.5	49t. Louisiana	83.1
25t. California	103.2		

Source: Health Risk Management Inc., QualityFIRST Index, 1999.

Health Care Spending by Category, 1999

Category	Amount (billions)	Change 1998–99
Hospital care	$390.9	3.7%
Physicians' services	269.4	6.0
Dental services	56.0	5.6
Other professional services	33.2	5.6
Drugs, other non-durables	99.6	16.9
Vision products, other durables	47.6	5.7
Nursing-home care	90.0	2.3
Home health care	33.1	-1.4
Other personal health care	33.2	9.9
Administration and net cost of private health insurance	72.0	7.4
Government public health activities	41.1	6.6
Research	22.2	8.2
Construction	17.6	-0.6
Total	$1,210.7	5.6%

Source: U.S. Dept. of Health and Human Services, Health Care Financing Administration, Office of the Actuary.

Health Expenditures as a Percent of GNP for Selected Countries,1960–97

Nation	1960	1970	1980	1990	1997[1]
United States	5.1%	7.1%	8.9%	12.2%	13.4%
Germany	4.8	6.3	8.8	8.7	10.7
Switzerland	3.1	4.9	6.9	8.3	10.0
France	4.2	5.8	7.6	8.9	9.6
Canada	5.4	7.0	7.2	9.2	9.2
Sweden	4.7	7.1	9.4	8.8	8.6
Greece	3.1	5.7	6.6	7.6	8.6
Netherlands	3.8	5.9	7.9	8.3	8.5
Australia	4.9	5.7	7.3	8.2	8.4
New Zealand	4.3	5.2	6.0	7.0	7.6
Italy	3.6	5.2	7.0	8.1	7.6
Spain	1.5	3.7	5.6	6.9	7.4
Japan	3.0	4.6	6.5	6.1	7.2
United Kingdom	3.9	4.5	5.6	6.0	6.8

1. Preliminary.
Source: U.S. Dept. of Health and Human Services, National Center for Health Statistics, Health, United States, 2000 (2000).

16,800 nursing homes across the United States. The number of nursing home residents (of all ages) per 1,000 resident population 85 and older varied significantly, from lows in 1997 for Arizona (165.6), West Virginia (184.8), and Florida (200.8) to highs for Louisiana (573.9), Indiana (504.4), and Connecticut (498.2).

Because of the dramatic growth in the number of Americans over age 75, the nursing home population is frailer than ever before and requires more specialized care. Almost half of all nursing home residents have some form of dementia. In 1995 the average monthly charge in a nursing home was $3,135 per resident. This charge varied widely by geographic region from about $2,700 in the Midwest and South to $3,700 and $3,900 in the West and Northeast. Medicare payments to nursing facilities reached $9.1 billion in 1995; in addition, Medicare spent $1.9 billion on hospice care.

Americans spent $800 million on nursing-home care in 1960, $4.2 billion in 1970, $17.6 billion in 1980, and $50.9 billion in 1990. By 1999, the figure had reached $90 billion. Out-of-pocket payments, including personal savings and social security benefits, covered about one-third of this cost; Medicare and Medicaid covered most of the remaining costs.

Paying for Health Care

Medical care is usually paid for in one of three ways:

1. By patients; according to the U.S. Dept. of Health and Human Services, an estimated 17.6 percent of the nation's personal health care costs in 1999 were paid directly by patients.
2. By an insurance plan; employers, employees and individuals paid $355.3 billion for private health insurance premiums in 1999, funding one-third of all health care spending. Managed care plans enrolled 88.8 percent of employees in 1999—up from 48 percent in 1992.
3. As a public charge, which means that the government—and, ultimately, the taxpayer—pays the bill. In 1999, 43.3 percent of personal health care costs were paid for by federal, state, and local governments. In some instances, the percentage is even greater. For example, taxpayers pay 48 percent of the $2.3 billion spent each year to treat gunshot wounds according to a study published in the Journal of the American Medical Association in 1999, and 62 percent of nursing home care expenditures according to the Health Care Financing Administration.

Health insurance

There are five basic types of insurance:

1. Hospital expense insurance—pays costs of hospital room, X-rays, medicines, etc.
2. Surgical expense insurance—pays costs of an operation.
3. Medical expense insurance—pays for visits to a physician's office.
4. Major medical expense insurance—pays costs associated with extended sickness or injury.
5. Disability income insurance—pays a benefit when the person is unable to work because of illness or injury.

Federal insurance plans

Two government health programs, Medicare and Medicaid, financed $387.2 billion in health care services in 1998, one-third of the nation's total health care bill, and almost three-quarters of all public spending on health care. (The remaining federal health spending covers military and veterans' health care.)

Medicare is a federal health insurance plan for people age 65 and older, certain disabled people, and people with kidney failure. Medicaid is a health care program for poor people. It is funded jointly by federal and state agencies. (See also Part II: "Social Insurance Programs.")

Medicare reimburses about one-half of the health care goods and services used by the eligible population. About 80 percent of this population have supplementary insurance. In 2000, 83 percent of those covered by Medicare received their care in the fee-for-service sector and 17 percent were enrolled in managed care plans.

Population Over 65 in Nursing Homes, 1997

| Age | Residents in nursing homes per 1,000 population | | | |
| | Women | | Men | |
	White	Black	White	Black
65 and over	55.5	54.7	25.3	41.1
65-74 years	11.1	18.1	8.6	20.7
75-84 years	51.9	62.6	32.6	57.3
85 years and over	222.5	203.3	117.3	144.3

Source: Centers for Disease Control and Prevention, National Center for Health Statistics, National Nursing Home Survey. *Health, United States, 1999* (1999).

Hospital Facilities and Their Use, 1946–99

Year	Number of hospitals	Number of beds ('000s)	Admissions ('000s)	Average stay (days)	Outpatient visits ('000s)
1946	6,125	1,436	15,675	9.1	N.A.
1950	6,788	1,456	18,483	8.1	N.A.
1960	6,876	1,658	25,027	7.6	N.A.
1965	7,123	1,704	28,812	7.8	125,793
1970	7,123	1,616	31,759	8.2	181,370
1975	7,156	1,466	36,157	7.7	254,844
1980	6,965	1,365	38,892	7.6	262,951
1985	6,872	1,318	36,304	7.1	282,140
1990	6,649	1,213	33,774	7.3	368,184
1995	6,291	1,081	33,282	6.5	483,195
1999	5,890	994	34,181	5.9	573,461

Note: N.A.= Not Available.   Source: American Hospital Association, *Hospital Statistics* (annual).

Uninsured Americans, 1999

Category	Number('000s)	Percent uninsured
Total	**42,554**	**15.5%**
Sex		
Male	22,073	16.5
Female	20.481	14.6
Age		
Under 18	10,023	13.9
18-24	7,688	29.0
25-34	8,755	23.2
35-44	7,377	16.5
45-64	8,288	13.8
65 and older	422	1.3
Race/Ethnicity		
White[1]	21,363	11.0
Black[1]	7,536	21.2
Hispanic	10,951	33.4
Asian and Pacific Islands	2,272	20.8
Education level[2]		
No high school diploma	9,111	26.7
High school grad only	11,619	17.6
Some college	6,051	15.2
Associate degree	1,902	12.9
Bachelor's degree or higher	3,848	8.2
Citizenship		
Native-born	33,089	13.5
Foreign-born	9,465	33.4
Naturalized citizen	1,900	17.9
Non-citizen	7,565	42.6
Annual household income		
Under $25,000	15,577	24.1
$25,000-$49,999	13,996	18.2
$50,000-$74,999	6,706	11.8
$75,000 or more	6,275	8.3

1. Non-Hispanic. 2. Persons age 18 and older. **Source:** U.S. Bureau of the Census, *Current Population Survey,* March 2000.

People With and Without Health Insurance Coverage, by State, 1999

State	People with coverage ('000s)	People without coverage ('000s)	Percent of people without coverage
United States	**231,533**	**42,554**	**15.5%**
Alabama	3,801	633	14.3
Alaska	509	120	19.1
Arizona	3,838	1,036	21.2
Arkansas	2,183	377	14.7
California	27,057	6,901	20.3
Colorado	3,516	709	16.8
Connecticut	3,005	327	9.8
Delaware	679	88	11.4
District of Columbia	437	80	15.4
Florida	12,159	2,893	19.2
Georgia	6,550	1,260	16.1
Hawaii	1,080	135	11.1
Idaho	1,014	240	19.1
Illinois	10,448	1,718	14.1
Indiana	5,261	637	10.8
Iowa	2,599	235	8.3
Kansas	2,300	318	12.1
Kentucky	3,332	566	14.5
Louisiana	3,328	969	22.5
Maine	1,120	151	11.9
Maryland	4,457	598	11.8
Massachusetts	5,546	648	10.5
Michigan	8,996	1,131	11.2
Minnesota	4,417	387	8.0
Mississippi	2,304	459	16.6
Missouri	5,003	473	8.6
Montana	732	168	18.6
Nebraska	1,480	179	10.8
Nevada	1,532	400	20.7
New Hampshire	1,127	128	10.2
New Jersey	7,015	1,089	13.4
New Mexico	1,335	463	25.8
New York	15,464	3,044	16.4
North Carolina	6,355	1,155	15.4
North Dakota	543	73	11.8
Ohio	10,046	1,247	11.0
Oklahoma	2,698	571	17.5
Oregon	2,912	498	14.6
Pennsylvania	10,674	1,112	9.4
Rhode Island	915	68	6.9
South Carolina	3,145	673	17.6
South Dakota	621	83	11.8
Tennessee	4,900	637	11.5
Texas	15,380	4,664	23.3
Utah	1,846	305	14.2
Vermont	531	74	12.3
Virginia	5,875	967	14.1
Washington	4,799	898	15.8
West Virginia	1,456	301	17.1
Wisconsin	4,806	595	11.0
Wyoming	405	78	16.1

Source: U.S. Census Bureau, *Current Population Survey,* September 28, 2000.

Managed care (HMOs, PPOs)

A managed health care plan provides comprehensive health care coverage to enrolled members on a prepaid basis; that is, insurance and health care delivery are integrated within one system. The objective is to control costs, assure access to effective treatments, and eliminate inappropriate and duplicative services.

The oldest managed care providers are health maintenance organizations (HMOs), which started in the 1940s. They either employ physicians in clinics or hospital-like buildings, or contract with hundreds or even thousands of physicians who practice in their private offices.

HMO patients generally must use their HMO's physicians in order to be reimbursed. Preferred provider organizations (PPOs), a modified version of HMOs, permit enrollees to use non-plan providers (physicians and hospitals). However, patients who use services outside their PPO must pay a financial penalty.

Approximately 76.6 million people—28.6 percent of the population—were enrolled in HMOs in 1998. Percentages ranged from lows in Wyoming (0.7%), North Dakota (2.2%), and Mississippi (3.6%) to highs in Massachusetts (54.2%), Delaware (48.1%), and California (47.1%).

The Uninsured

After rising for 11 years, the number of Americans without health insurance declined in 1999, to 42.6 million, a reduction of 1.7 million from 1998. According to the Census Bureau, 15.5 percent of the population was without health insurance during all of 1999. The number of uninsured children under 18 was 15.5 million (13.9 percent).

The probability of being uninsured varied by the place of residence, earnings, and the size of the company for which a person worked. The Census Bureau, using three-year averages from 1997-99, found that uninsured rates ranged from 8.8 percent in Minnesota to 24.1 percent in Texas. High incomes and employment in large companies increase the likelihood that a person has health insurance.

Milestones in the History of Medicine

B.C.

c. 2700 Chinese emperor Shen Nung develops principles of herbal medicine and acupuncture.

c. 1700 The Code of Hammurabi, king of Babylon, comprises regulations concerning physicians, including what they may treat and what their fees should be.

c. 1500 The Ebers Papyrus describes many remedies used in Ancient Egypt to treat dental ailments.

c. 400 Hippocrates of Cos (Greek: c. 460–c. 377), teacher and medical practitioner known as Father of Medicine, writes Hippocratic Oath, which sets ethical standards still followed by physicians throughout the world.

c. 300 Herophilus (Greek: c. 355–280) pioneers dissection of human body and founds first school of anatomy.

A.D.

c. 20 Aulus Cornelius Celsus (Roman: first cent.) writes first-known medical textbook.

c. 100 Romans develop a public medical service and appoint physicians to provide medical help to poor.

c. 180 Galen (Greek: c. 130–c. 201) writes *Methodus Medando*, which summarizes medical knowledge of ancient times. Galen's views on human physiology and disease would influence medical thought for more than 1,500 years.

c. 450 Susruta (Indian) notes relationship of malaria to mosquitoes and of bubonic plague to rats.

c. 900 Rhazes (Persian: c. 865–923/35) is first to describe smallpox and establish criteria for diagnosing and treating it.

1030 Ibn Sina (Avicenna; Persian: 980–1037) publishes *Canon of Medicine*, which becomes leading medical encyclopedia for centuries.

c. 1270–80 Spectacles are introduced by Venetian glassmakers.

1403 Venice imposes world's first quarantine of infected areas as safeguard against Black Death (bubonic plague).

1543 Andreas Vesalius (Flemish: 1514–64) publishes first accurate anatomy text and establishes foundations of modern anatomy.

1597 Gaspare Tagliacozzi (Italian) publishes first textbook of plastic surgery and revives operation of rhinoplasty (nose surgery).

1601 Sir James Lancaster (English: c. 1554–1618) writes that lemon juice helps prevent scurvy.

1628 William Harvey (English: 1578–1657) describes functions of the heart and how blood circulates throughout the body.

1658 Jan Swammerdam (Dutch: 1637–80) discerns red blood cells.

1670 Thomas Willis (English: 1621–75) rediscovers connection between sugar in urine and diabetes (known in antiquity by Greeks, Chinese, and Indians).

1751 Pennsylvania Hospital, first general hospital in U.S., founded in Philadelphia by Quakers.

1761 Leopold Auenbrugger von Auenbrugg (Australian: 1722–1809) discovers that fluid in chest cavity and other health problems can be detected by tapping gently on the chest.

Giovanni B. Morgagni (Italian: 1682–1771) establishes modern pathological anatomy with publication of *On the Seats and Causes of Disease.*

1796 Edward Jenner (English: 1749–1823) develops smallpox vaccine from cowpox serum.

1816 René T.H. Laënnec (French: 1781–1826) invents stethoscope and introduces practice of auscultation (monitoring sounds made by internal organs).

1818 James Blundel (English) performs first successful human blood transfusion.

1831 Samuel Guthrie (American: 1782–1848) discovers chloroform.

1833 William Beaumont (American: 1785–1853) provides first clear insight into nature of gastric digestion.

1839 Horace Hayden (American: 1769–1844) and Chapin Harris (1806–60) found world's first dental school, Baltimore College of Dental Surgery.

1842 Crawford Long (American: 1815–78) removes tumor from patient inhaling ether—first known operation under general anesthesia; publishes his findings in 1849, three years after William Morton (American: 1819–68) demonstrates effectiveness of ether as anesthetic.

1850 Hermann Helmholtz (German: 1821–94) invents ophthalmoscope, instrument used to examine interior of the eye.

1855 Manuel Garcia (Spanish: 1805–1906) invents modern laryngoscope, device used to inspect the throat, especially the larynx and vocal cords.

1863 International Red Cross established at Geneva, Switzerland.

1865 Joseph Lister (English: 1827–1912) introduces use of disinfectants to reduce infection.

Louis Pasteur (French: 1822–95) shows that spoilage of wine can be prevented by partial heat-sterilization; process, called pasteurization, soon applied to milk and other foods.

1866 Sir Thomas C. Allbutt (English: 1836–1925) invents clinical thermometer.

1868 Carl Wunderlich (German: 1815–77) establishes that fever is a symptom, not a disease, and introduces use of thermometer for taking body temperature.

1881 Pasteur produces vaccine that successfully prevents anthrax.

1890 Emil von Behring (German: 1854–1917) and Shibasaburo Kitasato (Japanese: 1852–1931) independently discover antitoxins.

1892 Dmitri Ivanovski (Russian: 1864–1920) discovers filterable viruses (viruses tiny enough to pass through fine filters previously believed to trap all living organisms).

1893 Felix Hofmann (German) develops a process for production of acetylsalicylic acid, the form of aspirin used today.

1895 Wilhelm Röntgen (German: 1845–1923) discovers X rays.

1900 Sigmund Freud (Austrian: 1856–1955), founder of psychoanalysis, publishes *The Interpretations of Dreams.*

Karl Landsteiner (Austrian-American: 1868–1943) discovers three blood groups, later named A, B, and O; fourth group, to be named AB, discovered in 1902.

Walter Reed (American: 1851–1902) establishes that yellow fever virus is transmitted by mosquitoes.

1901 Jokichi Takamine (Japanese-American: 1854–1922) isolates adrenaline, first hormone to be isolated.

1902   Eugene Opie (American) establishes that diabetes results from destruction of specific portions of pancreatic tissue—the islets of Langerhans.

1905   Albert Einhorn (American) synthesizes procaine (novocaine), which becomes the most widely used dental anesthetic.

1906   August von Wassermann (German: 1866–1925) develops blood test for syphilis.

1910   Marie Curie (French: 1867–1934) isolates pure radium metal, which came to be used to treat cancer.

1913   Béla Schick (Hungarian-American: 1877–1967) perfects test for determining susceptibility to diphtheria.

1915   Death certificates come into general use in U.S.

Margaret Sanger (American: 1883–1966) founds the National Birth Control League, which in 1942 becomes Planned Parenthood.

1918   Francis Benedict (American: 1870–1957) devises basal metabolism test for measuring rate at which metabolism (total of all chemical reactions) occurs in the body.

1921   Sir Frederick G. Banting (Canadian: 1891–1941) and Charles H. Best (1899–1978) extract insulin from the pancreas.

1928   Sir Alexander Fleming (Scottish: 1881–1955) discovers penicillin, a substance in green mold *Penicillium notatum* that destroys certain bacteria.

1929   Hans Berger (German: 1873–1941) publishes his results of the first electroencephalograms (EEGs) of humans.

1935   Gerhard Domagk (German: 1895–1964) announces discovery of Prontosil (sulfonamidecrysoidin), the first useful sulfa drug.

1937   First blood bank is established, at Cook County Hospital in Chicago.

Alton Ochsner (American: 1896–1981) and Michael De Bakey (1908–) suggest that cigarette smoking is cause of lung cancer.

1944   Willem Kolff (Dutch-American: 1911–) develops first kidney dialysis machine.

Oswald Avery (Canadian: 1877–1955), Colin MacLeod, and Maclyn McCarty prove that DNA (deoxyribonucleic acid) is blueprint of heredity that determines how an organism develops.

First eye bank, Eye-Bank for Sight Restoration, founded in New York.

Albert Schatz (American: 1921–) and Selman Waksman (American: 1888–1973) isolate streptomycin, an antibiotic effective against bacterium that causes tuberculosis.

1945   Alfred Blalock (American: 1899–1964) introduces first operation to enable blue, or cyanotic, babies to survive (cyanosis, caused by poor circulatory flow or other problems, results in diminished oxygen in blood, causing bluish discoloration of the skin).

1947   Eugene Payne (American) uses chloromycetin, developed by Parke-Davis researchers, to treat typhus patients; first use of "broadspectrum" antibiotic.

1948   Philip S. Hench (American: 1896–1965) and Edward C. Kendall (1886–1972) synthesize cortisone and use it to treat arthritis victims.

1952   Jonas Salk (American: 1914–95) develops first vaccine against polio.

1953   John H. Gibbon, Jr. (American: 1903–73) uses heart-lung machine he invented in successful open-heart operation.

1954   Surgeons led by Joseph Murray (American: 1919–) perform first successful kidney transplant.

1957   Alick Isaacs (Scottish: 1921–67) and Jean Lindenmann (Swiss) discover interferon, a protein that interferes with viral reproduction.

1958   Wilson Greatbatch (American: 1919–) invents the implantable artificial pacemaker.

1961   Scientists at Bell Laboratories (Americans) announce first continuously operating laser, a tool having many surgical uses.

1963   Thomas Starzl (American: 1926–) performs first human liver transplant operation.

1964   James Hardy (American: 1918–) performs first human lung transplant.

1965   Medicare and Medicaid are established, guaranteeing medical insurance coverage for the aged and the poor.

1966   Paul Parkman and Harry Meyer (Americans) develop vaccine for rubella (German measles).

Insulin synthesized independently by U.S. and Chinese scientists—first hormone to be synthesized.

1967   Christiaan Barnard (South African: 1922–2001) performs world's first heart transplant.

Rene Favaloro (Argentinian: 1923–2000) performs first successful coronary bypass operation.

First modern hospice founded in London.

1969   Denton Cooley (American: 1920–) implants first temporary artificial heart in human being.

1972   Computerized axial tomography (CAT scan) is introduced in Great Britain.

1977   Scientists at Genentech Corporation (Americans) induce bacteria to make humanbrain hormone somatostatin—first human chemical produced by recombinant-DNA techniques.

The first known human cases of cyclospora infection are diagnosed.

1978   First "test tube baby" (person conceived outside human body) is born, in England.

1981   Scientists identify acquired immune deficiency syndrome (AIDS), a previously unknown disease.

Surgeons at University of California at San Francisco perform first successful operation on a fetus.

1982   William DeVries (American) performs first complete replacement of human heart with artificial heart at University of Utah.

1984   First baby produced from frozen embryo is born, in Melbourne, Australia.

Luc Montagnier (French) discovers virus believed to cause AIDS.

1990   R. Michael Blaese, W. French Anderson, and Kenneth W. Culver (Americans) develop procedure to infuse genetically engineered blood cells for treatment of immune system disorder—first gene therapy used in a human.

1993   The U.S. Environmental Protection Agency concludes that environmental tobacco smoke ("secondhand smoke") is a lung carcinogen and causes respiratory problems for infants and young children.

1996   British scientists announce the possibility that a new form of Creutzfeldt-Jakob disease is transmitted to humans through the meat of cattle infected with bovine spongiform encephalopathy ("mad cow disease").

1999   Surgeons at Vanderbilt University Medical Center perform first successful brain surgery on a fetus.

2000   Scientists announce they have deciphered most of the human genetic code, opening new frontiers in medicine.

U.S. surgeons perform first nonsurgical coronary bypass procedure.

2001   U.S. surgeons implant the first self-contained artificial heart.

▶SURGERY

Increases in the number of surgical operations during recent years have been accompanied by dramatic changes in the rates of some procedures. An example is the incidence of cesarean sections—surgical incisions through the abdomen and uterus for removal of a baby, performed when normal vaginal delivery is deemed hazardous for the mother or child. Cesareans accounted for 21.2 percent of all live births in 1998—a significant decline from a high of 24.4 percent in 1988, but almost four times the rate in 1970 (5.5 percent) and among the highest rates for developed nations.

The frequency of certain procedures varies according to age, but, surprisingly, there may also be variations from one geographical region to another. For example, the 1998 Cesarean rate ranged from 14.7 percent in Alaska to 27.0 percent in Mississippi. A survey by Dartmouth Medical Schools researchers released in 1996 also noted disparities in the treatment of choice. For example, they found that a person in Kingsport, Tennessee, with a herniated disk was seven times as likely to have back surgery as one in Provo, Utah.

Organ Transplantation

Transplant surgery is more successful than ever, thanks to improved surgical techniques, a better understanding of the body's immune system, and the development of drugs that combat rejection of implanted organs. Kidney transplants, for instance, enjoy a high rate of success and are much less expensive—and much more convenient—than maintaining a patient on dialysis. Unfortunately, a scarcity of donor organs keeps thousands of patients waiting, sometimes in vain. The number of donors has increased, but not as rapidly as the waiting list. On July 20, 2001, 77,569 patients were on the national patient waiting list for organ transplants. In 2000, 5,508 people died before they could receive the organs they needed.

In addition to organs, tissues—cornea, bone, and skin—can be transplanted. In fact, corneal transplants are the most frequently performed transplant surgery. According to the Eye Bank As-

Cardiovascular Operations in the U.S., 1998

Operation	Sex		Age			
	Male	Female	Under 15	15–44	45–64	65 plus
Total procedures	**3,364,000**	**2,427,000**	**171,000**	**547,000**	**2,033,000**	**3,040,000**
Cardiac catheterization	770,000	522,000	16,000	107,000	530,000	638,000
Angioplasty	594,000	332,000	—	60,000	410,000	456,000
Bypass	396,000	158,000	—	14,000	234,000	304,000
Endarterectomy	69,000	52,000	—	—	28,000	93,000
Pacemaker	82,000	88,000	—	—	21,000	145,000
Valve replacement	48,000	36,000	—	6,000	24,000	45,000
Defibrillator implants	19,000	7,000	—	—	9,000	13,000
Open heart surgery[1]	492,000	243,000	28,000	34,000	284,000	382,000

Note: Estimated figures. Breakdowns not available for some procedures, causing entries for some categories not to add up to the total. Does not include outpatient and other nonhospitalized procedures. 1. Includes valves, bypass, and "other" open heart procedures. **Source:** American Heart Association, *2001 Heart and Stroke Statistical Update.*

Common Operations and Procedures, 1999

Type of Operation	Total	Males	Females
All operations[1]	**41,500,000**	**16,188,000**	**25,312,000**
Endoscopy of large or small intestine	1,464,000	610,000	855,000
Cardiac catheterization	1,271,000	758,000	513,000
Diagnostic ultrasound	1,022,000	451,000	571,000
Respiratory therapy	1,117,000	560,000	557,000
Repair of lacerations due to giving birth	1,116,000	—	1,116,000
CAT scan	871,000	408,000	463,000
Coronary artery obstruction, removal	1,069,000	708,000	361,000
Cesarean section	841,000	—	841,000
Hysterectomy	616,000	—	616,000
Reduction of fracture	628,000	285,000	343,000
Coronary artery bypass	571,000	389,000	182,000
Removal of one or both ovaries	466,000	—	466,000
Hemodialysis	458,000	227,000	231,000
Gall bladder removal	428,000	137,000	292,000
Destruction or closing off of fallopian tubes	329,000	–	329,000
Pacemaker insertion, removal or replacement	336,000	159,000	176,000
Spinal tap	310,000	158,000	153,000
Spinal disc operation	313,000	167,000	146,000
Appendectomy	290,000	158,000	132,000
Nose, mouth, pharynx operations	284,000	175,000	109,000
Knee replacement (total)	267,000	105,000	162,000
Cancer chemotherapy	211,000	116,000	95,000
Prostatectomy	192,000	192,000	—

Note: Discharges of inpatients from non-Federal hospitals. Excludes newborn infants. 1. Includes operations not shown separately. **Source:** U.S. Dept. of Health and Human Services, National Center for Health Statistics, *1999 National Hospital Discharge Survey* (April 24, 2001).

sociation, there were 33,020 such operations in 1999, with a success rate averaging better than 90 percent. As with organs, the need for tissues frequently exceeds the supply.

There are 51 independent and 9 hospital organ procurement programs in the United States. Many have toll-free telephone numbers. The United Network for Organ Sharing (UNOS) operates the national waiting list (1-888-TX-INFO1).

To perform transplants, hospitals must be licensed. According to UNOS, 259 medical institutions operated organ transplant programs as of April, 2001. These can be separated into organ-specific programs, including:

245 kidney transplants
141 heart transplants
135 pancreas transplants
122 liver transplants
83 heart-lung transplants
76 lung transplants
39 intestine transplants

Number and Survival Rates of Transplant Operations, 2000

Organ	Year first performed	Number (2000)	Survival rates[1]
Heart	1967	2,197	77.4%
Heart-lung	1982	48	49.5
Intestine	1990	79	51.7
Kidney	1954	13,338	—
Cadaver	—	8,078	89.3
Living donor	—	5,260	94.8
Kidney-pancreas	1966	914	89.8
Liver	1963	4,934	78.1
Lung	1963	945	57.2
Pancreas	1966	436	85.8

1. Three-year patient survival rates for January 1994 through March 2000. **Source:** United Network for Organ Sharing.

Abortion

The deliberate termination of a pregnancy before the fetus is capable of living outside the womb has generally been legal in the United States since 1973, when the Supreme Court ruled (in *Roe v. Wade*) that abortion cannot be prohibited during the first three months of pregnancy. From 1973 through 1980, the ratio of abortions to live births increased significantly to 359 per 1,000 live births. Since then, the ratio has declined to 306 per 1,000 live births in 1997.

According to a report released by the Centers for Disease Control and Prevention (CDC) in 2000, women who obtained abortions in 1997 were predominantly 24 years of age or younger, white, unmarried, and had no live-born children. More than half of the abortions were performed during the first eight weeks of gestation; 88 percent were performed in the first 12 weeks. Curettage was the primary abortion procedure, accounting for 97 percent of all abortions.

▶ DISEASE

Five of the most common categories of disease are:

1. Hereditary diseases—transferred from parent to child by genes. Examples: hemophilia, Down's syndrome, cystic fibrosis, sickle cell anemia.
2. Deficiency diseases—caused by lack of vitamins or other essential nutrients. Examples: scurvy, pellagra.
3. Infectious diseases—caused by viruses, bacteria, fungi, and other organisms and transferred from person to person. Examples: common cold, influenza, chicken pox, measles, tuberculosis, AIDS.
4. Diseases caused by chemical and physical agents such as radiation, smoke, drugs, and poisons. Examples: allergies, asbestosis, bysinosis, lead poisoning.
5. Degenerative diseases—resulting from natural aging processes. In some cases, cancer and high blood pressure are degenerative diseases.

Reported Abortions, 1972–97

Category	1972	1980	1990	1995	1997
NUMBER OF ABORTIONS					
Reported Abortions	586,760	1,297,606	1,429,577	1,210,883	1,186,039
Number per 1,000 live births	180	359	345	311	306
PERCENT OF TOTAL					
Race					
White	77.0%	69.9%	64.8%	59.5%	58.5%
Black[1]	23.0	30.1	31.8	35.0	35.9
Other	—	—	3.3	5.4	5.7
Marital Status					
Married	29.7%	23.1%	21.7%	19.7%	19.0%
Unmarried	70.3	76.9	78.3	80.3	81.0
Age					
Under 20	32.6%	29.2%	22.4%	20.1%	20.1%
20-24	32.5	35.5	33.2	32.5	31.7
25 or older	34.9	35.3	44.4	47.4	48.2
Weeks of gestation					
Up to 8	34.0%	51.7%	51.6%	54.0%	55.4%
9-10	30.7	26.2	25.3	23.1	22.0
11-12	17.5	12.2	11.8	10.9	10.7
13-15	8.4	5.1	6.4	6.3	6.2
16-20	8.2	3.9	4.0	4.3	4.3
21 or more	1.2	0.9	1.0	1.4	1.4

1. Data for 1972 and 1980 include other nonwhite groups. **Source:** U.S. Dept of Health and Human Services, Centers for Disease Control and Prevention, *Morbidity and Mortality Weekly Report* (Dec. 8, 2000).

Heart Disease

Cardiovascular diseases (diseases of the heart and blood vessels) are America's number one killer, claiming more lives each year than the next seven leading causes of death combined. Almost one in four Americans—more than 60 million people—suffer some form of cardiovascular disease. During 1998 these diseases claimed 949,619 lives. This represented 40.6 percent of all deaths—an average of a death every 33 seconds.

Death rates vary according to age, sex, race, even geographical location. Rates increase with age and are higher among men than among women. For both sexes, death rates are significantly higher among blacks than among whites. In 1998, Hawaii had the lowest age-adjusted death rate from cardiovascular disease (295.7 per 100,000 population) followed by Utah, Colorado, Minnesota, and New Mexico. Mississippi had the

highest rate (474.8) followed by Tennessee, West Virginia, Oklahoma, and South Carolina.

The good news is that the death rates from cardiovascular disease have declined dramatically, falling 20.4 percent from 1988 to 1998. This is due in part to improved drug treatments and other medical advancements. Another factor has been improved personal health habits: people have stopped smoking, lowered the fat content of their diets, and taken other steps that reduce the risks of cardiovascular disease.

Evidence suggests that further significant reductions in deaths from heart disease could be achieved through aggressive treatment of high cholesterol. In 2001, a U.S. government panel recommended that some 36 million Americans are candidates for cholesterol-lowering drugs and about 65 million should be on cholesterol-lowering diets.

Reported Cases of Common Infectious Diseases, 1950–2000

Disease	1950	1960	1970	1980	1990	1995	2000[1]
Brucellosis (undulant fever)	3,510	751	213	183	85	98	63
Cholera	N.A.	N.A.	N.A.	9	6	23	2
Legionnellosis	N.A.	N.A.	N.A.	N.A.	1,370	1,241	969
Leprosy (Hansen's disease)	44	54	129	223	198	144	64
Malaria	2,184	72	3,051	2,062	1,292	1,419	1,288
Meningococcal infections	3,788	2,259	2,505	2,840	2,451	3,243	2,035
Mumps	N.A.	N.A.	104,953	8,576	5,292	906	323
Pertussis (whooping cough)	120,718	14,809	4,249	1,730	4,570	5,137	6,755
Plague[2]	N.A.	2	13	18	2	9	6
Poliomyelitis	33,300	3,190	33	9	6	7	0
Psittacosis	26	113	35	124	113	64	11
Rabies, in animals	7,901	3,567	3,224	6,421	4,826	7,811	5,834
Rabies, in humans	18	2	3	0	1	5	2
Rubella (German measles)	N.A.	N.A.	56,552	3,904	1,125	128	152
Tetanus	486	368	148	95	64	41	26
Toxic shock syndrome	N.A.	N.A.	N.A.	N.A.	322	191	125
Trichinosis	327	160	109	131	129	29	15
Tuberculosis[3]	121,742	55,494	37,137	27,749	25,701	22,860	12,942
Typhoid fever	2,484	816	346	510	552	369	317
Venereal disease							
Gonorrhea	286,746	258,933	600,072	1,004,029	690,042	392,651	335,098
Syphilis[4]	23,939	16,145	21,982	27,204	50,578	16,543	5,894

1. Incomplete due to late reporting. 2. Plague: disease caused by the bite of fleas infected with the bacterium *Yersinia pestis*. 3. Data after 1970 not comparable to prior years because of changes in reporting criteria effective in 1975. 4. Primary and secondary syphilis cases.
Sources: U.S. Dept. of Health and Human Services, Centers for Disease Control and Prevention, *Morbidity and Mortality Weekly Report,* Oct. 6, 1995, Dec. 31, 1999, and Jan. 5, 2001; *Health, United States,* 2000 (2000).

Heart Disease Death Rates, 1950–98 (per 100,000 population)

Age	1950[1]	1960[1]	1970	1980	1990	1995	1997	1998
All ages								
Age adjusted	307.2	286.2	253.6	202.2	152.0	138.3	130.5	126.6
Crude	355.5	369.0	362.0	336.0	289.5	280.7	271.6	268.2
Under 1 year	3.5	6.6	13.1	22.8	20.1	17.1	16.4	16.1
1-4 years	1.3	1.3	1.7	2.6	1.9	1.6	1.4	1.4
5-14 years	2.1	1.3	0.8	0.9	0.9	0.8	0.8	0.8
15-24 years	6.8	4.0	3.0	2.9	2.5	2.9	3.0	2.8
25-34 years	19.4	15.6	11.4	8.3	7.6	8.5	8.3	8.3
35-44 years	86.4	74.6	66.7	44.6	31.4	32.0	30.1	30.5
45-54 years	308.6	271.8	238.4	180.2	120.5	111.0	104.9	101.4
55-64 years	808.1	737.9	652.3	494.1	367.3	322.9	302.4	286.9
65-74 years	1,839.8	1,740.5	1,558.2	1,218.6	894.3	799.9	753.7	735.5
75-84 years	4,310.1	4,089.4	3,683.8	2,993.1	2,295.7	2,064.7	1,943.6	1,897.3
85 and older	9,150.6	9,317.8	7,891.3	7,777.1	6,739.9	6,484.1	6,198.9	6,009.6

1. Includes deaths of nonresidents of the U.S.   **Source:** U.S. Dept. of Health and Human Services, *Health, United States, 2000* (2000):

Heart attacks A heart attack occurs when the blood supply to the heart muscles is blocked. An uncomfortable pressure, fullness, squeezing, or pain in the center of the chest that lasts for two minutes or more may be a sign of a heart attack. Sweating, dizziness, nausea, fainting, or shortness of breath may also occur. Some 1.1 million people suffer heart attacks annually. One-third of these people do not survive. Of the survivors, 42 percent of the women and 24 percent of the men will die within one year. Many survivors develop congestive heart failure, which can leave the heart unable to pump blood effectively.

Strokes and bypass surgery Each year, approximately 600,000 Americans—72 percent of them age 65 or older—suffer a stroke; of these, more than 155,000 die. A stroke occurs when the

5-Year Survival Rates for Cancer, by Race and Site, 1960-96

Cancer Site	Whites				Blacks			
	1960-63	1970-73	1980-82	1989-96	1960-63	1970-73	1980-82	1989-96
All sites	39%	43%	52%	62%	27%	31%	40%	49%
Brain	18	20	25	30	19	19	31	38
Breast (females)	63	68	77	86	46	51	66	71
Cervix	58	64	68	72	47	61	61	59
Colon	43	49	56	63	34	37	49	52
Leukemia	14	22	40	45	N.C.	N.C.	33	34
Liver	N.C.	N.C.	4	6	N.C.	N.C.	2	3
Lung	8	10	14	14	5	7	12	11
Ovary	32	36	39	50	32	32	38	48
Pancreas	1	2	3	4	1	2	5	4
Prostate	50	63	75	94	25	55	65	87
Rectum	38	45	53	61	27	30	38	52
Stomach	11	13	16	20	8	13	19	22
Testis	63	72	92	96	N.C.	N.C.	90	88
Thyroid	83	86	94	96	N.C.	N.C.	95	91
Urinary bladder	53	61	79	82	24	36	59	64
Uterus	73	81	83	86	31	44	55	57

Note: Rates are an average of cases diagnosed in years shown. N.C.: valid rate could not be calculated. **Source:** U.S. Dept. of Health and Human Services, National Cancer Institute; published in American Cancer Society, *Cancer Facts and Figures.*

Estimated New Cancer Cases and Deaths by Site and Sex, 2001

Site	New cases			Deaths		
	Total	Male	Female	Total	Male	Female
All Sites	1,268,000	643,000	625,000	553,400	286,100	267,300
Skin[1]	56,400	31,700	24,700	9,800	6,300	3,500
Oral	30,100	20,200	9,900	7,800	5,100	2,700
Lung, bronchus, and other respiratory	184,600	102,400	82,200	162,500	93,900	68,600
Breast	193,700	1,500	192,200	40,600	400	40,200
Esophagus	13,200	9,900	3,300	12,500	9,500	3,000
Stomach	21,700	13,400	8,300	12,800	7,400	5,400
Small intestine	5,300	2,600	2,700	1,100	600	500
Colon, rectum, and anus	138,900	68,800	70,100	57,200	27,900	29,300
Liver and bile passages	23,100	13,900	9,200	17,400	10,100	7,300
Pancreas	29,200	14,200	15,000	28,900	14,100	14,800
Other digestive organs	4,300	1,200	3,100	1,400	500	900
Urinary (bladder, kidney, etc.)	87,500	59,400	28,100	25,000	16,100	8,900
Leukemia	31,500	17,700	13,800	21,500	12,000	9,500
Lymphoma	63,600	35,000	28,600	27,600	14,500	13,100
Multiple myeloma	14,400	7,500	6,900	11,200	5,800	5,400
Bone and joints	2,900	1,600	1,300	1,400	800	600
Endocrine system	21,400	5,600	15,800	2,300	1,000	1,300
Eye	2,100	1,100	1,000	200	100	100
Brain, other nervous system	17,200	9,800	7,400	13,100	7,200	5,900
Ovary	23,400	—	23,400	13,900	—	13,900
Uterus	51,200	—	51,200	11,000	—	11,000
Other genital, female	5,700	—	5,700	1,400	—	1,400
Prostate	198,100	198,100	—	31,500	31,500	—
Testis	7,200	7,200	—	400	400	—
Other genital, male	1,200	1,200	—	300	300	—
All other plus unspecified sites	40,100	19,000	21,100	40,600	20,600	20,000

Note: Except for bladder, figures for invasive cancer only. Carcinoma in situ of the breast accounts for about 46,400 new cases annually and melanoma carcinoma in situ accounts for about 31,400 cases annually. 1. Melanoma and other nonepithelial skin cancers only; highly curable basal cell and squamous cell skin cancers account for more than 1 million new cases annually
Source: American Cancer Society, *Cancer Facts & Figures 2001.*

blood supply to the brain is blocked, usually by a clot. The primary signal of a stroke is a sudden, temporary weakness or numbness of the face, arm, or leg on one side of the body. Other signals include temporary loss of speech, difficulty in speaking or understanding speech, temporary vision problems (particularly in one eye), unsteadiness, or unexplained dizziness.

The American Heart Association estimates that 553,000 bypass operations were performed on 336,000 patients in 1998; 49 percent of the procedures were performed on people under age 65. In this operation a blood vessel from elsewhere in the body is used to reroute blood around a blocked coronary artery. The purpose: to reduce the person's risk of a stroke. In 2001 it was announced that researchers from Massachusetts General Hospital had in 1999 successfully performed the first nonsurgical bypass, called percutaneous in-situ coronary venous arterialization. The procedure is considered safer and less painful than traditional bypass surgery.

Cancer

The nation's second leading cause of death is a group of diseases characterized by the unrestrained growth of cells. It afflicts people of all ages and races, although nearly 80 percent of all cancers are diagnosed at ages 55 and above. Cancers vary greatly in cause, symptoms, response to treatment, and possibility of cure.

A U.S. male has a 1 in 2 probability of developing invasive cancer at some time during his life; a female, 1 in 3. The incidence of cancer varies from state to state. Between 1993 and 1997, the highest cancer death rates occurred in the District of Columbia (278.5 cancer deaths per 100,000 males and 162.9 per 100,000 females). The lowest cancer death rates were in Utah (143.6 for males, 102.2 for females).

Cancer survival rates
The National Cancer Institute estimates that approximately 8.9 million Americans alive today have a history of cancer. Chances of surviving cancer have steadily improved. In the 1930s, about one in four American cancer patients survived at least five years after diagnosis. In contrast, six out of 10 who get cancer this year will be alive five years after diagnosis.

Survival depends on many factors. Two of the most important are the site of the tumor and how much the cancer has spread before treatment is begun. Lifestyle choices are also important. The American Cancer Society estimated that 172,000 lives would be lost in 2001 to cancer because of tobacco use, and evidence suggests that up to one-third of the cancer deaths each year are related to diet, including its effect on obesity.

Cancer death incidence and rates
After increasing steadily for most of the century, cancer incidence and death rates for all cancers combined and for most of the top ten cancer sites declined beginning in 1992. Overall incidence rates decreased an average of 1.1 percent per year between 1992 and 1998. During that same period, overall cancer death rates declined by 1.6 percent per year for men and 0.8 percent per year for women. The largest decrease, 2.5 percent per year, occurred in black men. Improved detection and treatment, coupled with healthier lifestyles, are believed to account for the declining rates.

The American Cancer Society estimated that about 553,400 Americans would die of cancer in 2001 — more than 1,500 people a day. Lung cancer is the leading cause of cancer deaths, killing an estimated 90,100 men and 67,300 women in 2001. Among women, breast cancer is the second most common killer, though if detected early and treated properly, it has a very high cure rate. Among men, prostate cancer causes the second greatest number of deaths. It, too, has a high survival rate if discovered while still localized within the general region of the prostate.

Cancer warning signs
Early detection is the key in fighting cancer. See your doctor if one of the following symptoms lasts longer than two weeks.
1. Unusual bleeding or discharge.
2. A sore that does not heal.
3. A change in a wart or mole.
4. A lump or thickening in the breast or elsewhere.
5. A change in bowel or bladder habits.
6. Nagging cough or hoarseness.
7. Indigestion or difficulty in swallowing.

AIDS

Following the discovery of acquired immune deficiency syndrome (AIDS) in 1981, the disease spread rapidly around the world. In the United States, sharp rises in new infections with human immunodeficiency virus (HIV), which causes AIDS, were recorded throughout the 1980s and into the early 1990s. The number of deaths also jumped annually, reaching almost 50,000 in 1995. The introduction of powerful AIDS drugs around that time showed significant success in controlling HIV before it progressed into AIDS. But the rate of HIV infection remained stubbornly high, leveling off at about 40,000 new cases a year. The Centers for Disease Control and Prevention reported that AIDS had been diagnosed in 774,467 people in the United States and its territories by the end of 2000; of these, more than 448,000 had died.

HIV is spread through contact with infected body fluids such as blood and semen. Infected people may harbor the virus within their bodies for several years or even longer before developing symptoms of AIDS. Though symptomless, they still can infect others. AIDS experts stressed that preventive measures, including sex education, condom distribution, and needle-exchange programs for drug addicts, need to be emphasized. They also feared that the new AIDS drugs were making people complacent and careless about their sexual behavior. Indeed, it was reported in 2000 that the rate of new HIV infections among gay and bisexual men in San Francisco nearly tripled from 1997 to 1999.

An encouraging change of the 1990s was the steep reduction in mother-to-fetus transmissions of HIV. This resulted from the use of zidovudine (ZDV), taken by the pregnant woman beginning as early as the 14th week of pregnancy and continuing until labor; at birth, the baby takes ZDV for six weeks. In 1999, there were 232 reported cases of AIDS transmission from mothers to newborns, bringing the total to 7,943 since the epidemic began.

No cure for AIDS is known. Many in the medical community are pinning hopes on preventative AIDS vaccines now being developed. The drug therapies that have been extremely effective in controlling AIDS progression for some patients are very expensive, putting them beyond the reach of the vast majority of the world's HIV-positive people. (See also "World Health" for information on AIDS worldwide.)

AIDS Cases and Deaths in the U.S., 1981–2000

Year	Cases diagnosed	Cases diagnosed to date	Known deaths	Known deaths to date
Pre-1981	100	100	30	30
1981	337	437	130	160
1982	1,199	1,636	465	625
1983	3,152	4,788	1,510	2,135
1984	6,364	11,152	3,522	5,657
1985	12,033	23,185	6,991	12,648
1986	19,379	42,564	12,155	24,803
1987	29,092	71,656	16,461	41,264
1988	36,099	107,755	21,204	62,468
1989	43,474	151,229	28,011	90,479
1990	49,511	200,740	31,782	122,261
1991	60,519	261,259	37,033	159,294
1992	79,595	340,854	41,623	200,917
1993	79,871	420,725	45,456	246,373
1994	72,988	493,713	50,134	296,507
1995	69,774	563,487	50,798	347,305
1996	60,716	624,203	37,475	384,780
1997	48,767	672,970	21,399	406,179
1998	40,784	713,754	17,304	423,483
1999	36,725	750,470	15,254	438,737
2000	23,988	774,467	8,911	447,648

Note: Delays in reporting cases and deaths substantially impact data, particularly for recent years. In addition, there were 412 people known to have died but whose dates of death are unknown. **Source:** U.S. Dept. of Health and Human Services, Centers for Disease Control and Prevention, *HIV/AIDS Surveillance Report*, Vol. 12, No. 2 (2001).

AIDS patients Homosexual and bisexual males make up almost 50 percent of all adult and adolescent AIDS cases reported in the United States since 1981. During the 1990s, however, the epidemic shifted steadily toward a growing proportion of AIDS cases in blacks and Hispanics, and in women. In absolute numbers, blacks outnumbered whites in new AIDS diagnoses and deaths beginning in 1996, and in the number of persons living with AIDS beginning in 1998. The proportion of women with AIDS increased steadily; they accounted for 32 percent of the cases reported in 1999. In the 13-to-24 age group, women accounted for 49 percent of reported cases.

Heterosexuals most at risk are those with venereal disease and multiple sex partners. Evidence suggests that sexually transmitted diseases that cause genital ulcers, such as herpes and syphilis, are especially dangerous because they cause breaks in the skin through which HIV can enter. People with these diseases are three to five times more likely than usual to get HIV if they have sex with an HIG-infected person.

The overwhelming majority of AIDS cases are found in large cities and metropolitan areas. Through mid-2000, metropolitan areas with 500,000 or more population accounted for 632,344 of the 753,907 reported AIDS cases (83.9 percent).

Sexually Transmitted Diseases

Sexually transmitted diseases (STDs) have been around since the beginning of recorded history, and while the prevalence of some have declined, rates for others have exploded. Today, millions of Americans suffer from STDs, in large part because they en-

Adults and Adolescents With AIDS, 1981–2000

Exposure category	Males Cases	Males Percent	Females Cases	Females Percent	Total Cases	Total Percent
Homosexual/Bisexual males	355,409	56%	—	—	355,409	46%
Intravenous (IV) drug abusers	140,536	22	52,991	41%	193,527	25
Homosexual male and IV drug abusers	48,989	8	—	—	48,989	6
Hemophilia/Coagulation disorder	4,907	1	283	0	5,190	1
Heterosexual contact	29,460	5	52,520	40	81,981	11
Blood transfusion, blood components, or tissue	4,971	1	3,806	3	8,777	1
Other/Undetermined[1]	51,179	8	20,504	16	71,686	9
Total[2]	635,451	100%	130,104	100%	765,559	100%

Note: Provisional data. Cases with more than one risk factor other than the combinations listed are tabulated only in the category listed first. 1. Includes patients whose mode of exposure to HIV is unknown; also includes 180 persons who acquired HIV infection perinatally but were diagnosed with AIDS after age 13. 2. Due to rounding, category totals may not total 100%. **Source:** U.S. Dept. of Health and Human Services, Centers for Disease Control and Prevention, *HIV/AIDS Surveillance Report*, Vol. 12, No. 2 (2001).

AIDS in the Cities, 2000

City	Number of cases	City	Number of cases	City	Number of cases
New York, N.Y.	117,792	Baltimore, Md.	13,904	Nassau–Suffolk, N.Y.	6,587
Los Angeles, Calif.	41,394	Ft. Lauderdale, Fla.	12,563	Seattle, Wash.	6,539
San Francisco, Calif.	27,567	Dallas, Texas	12,109	Jersey City, N.J.	6,491
Miami, Fla.	23,521	San Diego, Calif.	10,417	New Haven, Conn.	6,402
Washington, D.C.	22,321	Tampa–St. Petersburg, Fla.	8,225	Orlando, Fla.	5,853
Chicago, Ill.	21,173	Oakland, Calif.	7,932	Denver, Colo.	5,495
Houston, Texas	18,735	Detroit, Mich.	7,439	Orange County, Calif.	5,464
Philadelphia, Pa.	18,348	West Palm Beach, Fla.	7,415	Bergen-Passaic, N.J.	5,362
Newark, N.J.	16,739	New Orleans, La.	6,785	Phoenix, Ariz.	5,150
Atlanta, Ga.	15,524	Riverside–San Bernardino, Calif.	6,756		
Boston, Mass.	14,003				

Note: Provisional data. **Source:** U.S. Dept. of Health and Human Services, Centers for Disease Control and Prevention, *HIV/AIDS Surveillance Report*, Midyear edition, Vol. 12, No. 1. (2000).

gage in unprotected sex and have more than one sexual partner. According to a 1996 Institute of Medicine report, the United States has the highest rate of STDs of any developed country in the world.

An estimated 15.3 million new cases of STDs occur annually in the United States, and at least one in every three sexually active people will contract an STD by age 24, reported the American Social Health Association in 1998. The most prevalent STDs are the human papilloma virus, which causes warts and genital cancers (5.5 million new cases annually); trichomoniasis, caused by a protozoan (5.0 million); chlamydia, caused by a bacterium (3.0 million); genital herpes, caused by a virus (1.0 million), and gonorrhea, caused by a bacterium (650,000). Public health officials note that people with STDs have a significantly increased risk of becoming infected with HIV, in part because they may have open sores that provide the virus with an easy route of entry to the body.

Viral Hepatitis: A Major Cause of Liver Disease

Several viruses are responsible for viral hepatitis, a sometimes-fatal disease that attacks the liver. In the United States 97 percent of acute cases and 83 percent of chronic cases are accounted for by hepatitis viruses A, B, C, D, and E—particularly the first three.

Hepatitis A is spread primarily by fecal contamination of food and water and through person-to-person contact. The Centers for Disease Control and Prevention (CDC) estimates that the virus infects 150,000 Americans each year. In 1995, the United States licensed the first vaccine to prevent this disease.

Hepatitis B is generally transmitted via contact with the blood of an infected person during sex, during birth, or through contaminated needles and syringes. People at high risk are intravenous drug users who share needles, homosexual men, and heterosexuals with multiple partners.

According to the CDC, an estimated 200,000 new infections of hepatitis B are diagnosed annually. Some of those infected become chronic carriers. An estimated one million Americans are believed to be chronic carriers, capable of transmitting the virus to other people. Furthermore, chronic carriers are at high risk of developing cirrhosis or liver cancer; each year in the United States, about 4,000 to 5,000 hepatitis B patients die of these illnesses. The CDC and medical asso-

ciations recommend that all newborns be vaccinated against hepatitis B.

Hepatitis C is the leading reason for liver transplants in the United States and is believed to be responsible for much of the increase in liver cancer in recent years. An estimated 4 million Americans carry the virus, which is most commonly spread by needle sharing among intravenous blood users. Therapies often are ineffective or cause serious side effects, and no vaccine is available.

Alzheimer's disease

Alzheimer's disease is a progressive degenerative condition characterized by forgetfulness in early stages and, as the disease progresses, increasingly severe debilitating symptoms that create demanding care-giving needs. An estimated 4 million Americans, most of them elderly, have Alzheimer's disease. It caused 44,507 deaths in 1999, making it the eighth-leading cause of death. Many more women than men die from Alzheimer's, but this mainly reflects the larger number of women alive at older ages. Death rates are much higher for whites than blacks, but the risk of acquiring Alzheimer's is higher for blacks than whites.

Stem Cell Therapies and the Treatment of Disease

Among the most significant scientific developments of recent years has been the discovery of stem cells and the ability to isolate these cells and use them in research. Stem cells are immature cells that can give rise to other types of cells. Embryonic stem cells, isolated from very early embryos, can differentiate into all types of cells. Stem cells from adult tissue are less versatile, though not tissue-specific; for example, some stem cells produced in bone marrow can differentiate into muscle, bone, cartilage, and tendon cells.

Scientists believe that stem-cell therapies have the potential to revolutionize treatment of disease, particularly degenerative diseases like Parkinson's and Alzheimer's. Animal experiments show that stem-cell transplants create new cells and tissues that are assimilated into the animals' own organs. For example, stem cells injected into the damaged hearts of mice that suffered heart attacks helped repair the hearts by developing into new muscle and blood vessel cells. The study of human embryonic stem cells is controversial, however, and strongly opposed by abortion opponents.

Death Rates (per 100,000 population) by Sex and Race, 1940–99

Year	Total	All races		Whites		Black	
		Male	Female	Male	Female	Male	Female
1940	1,076.4	1,197.4	954.6	1,162.2	919.4	N.A.	N.A.
1950	963.8	1,106.1	823.5	1,089.5	803.3	N.A.	N.A.
1960	954.7	1,104.5	809.2	1,098.5	800.9	1,181.7	905.0
1970	945.3	1,090.3	807.8	1,086.7	812.6	1,186.6	829.2
1980	878.3	976.9	785.3	983.3	806.1	1,034.1	733.3
1985	876.9	948.6	809.1	963.6	840.1	989.3	734.2
1990	863.8	918.4	812.0	930.9	846.9	1,008.0	747.9
1995	880.0	914.1	847.3	932.1	891.3	980.7	759.0
1996	875.4	900.2	851.6	922.6	898.7	939.5	752.2
1997	864.9	880.8	849.6	908.0	900.0	882.6	733.1
1998	864.7	876.4	853.5	904.4	903.7	877.7	746.4
1999[1]	877.0	882.0	872.3	911.2	924.2	880.1	761.4

Note: Death rates are based on population estimates prepared by the U.S. Bureau of the Census.
Source: U.S. Dept. of Health and Human Services, National Center for Health Statistics. *National Vital Statistics Report* (June 26, 2001).

▶DEATH

In 1999, a record high total of 2.391,630 deaths were registered in the United States, an increase of 54,374 from the 1998 total. The age-adjusted death rate, which takes into account changes and variations in the age composition of the population, was 881.9 per 100,000 population, 1 percent higher than the 1998 rate of 875.8.

Males experience greater numbers of deaths and higher death rates than females, with black males having significantly higher numbers and rates than white males. Age-adjusted death rates for 1999 were: white females, 725.8 deaths per 100,000 population; black females, 955.0; white males, 1,035.8; and black males, 1,412.7.

Socioeconomic disparities in death rates also exist. A 1998 report from University of Michigan researchers said that adults in the lowest income group (less than $10,000 annual income) were 3.2 times more likely to die compared with those in the highest income bracket ($30,000 or more). Middle income adults ($10,000-$29,999) were 2.3 times as likely to die as those in the high-income

group. Possible factors for higher death rates among the poor include depression, social isolation, a lack of optimism, low self-esteem, and chronic stress.

Causes of Death

For the purposes of national mortality statistics, every death is attributed to one underlying condition. The 15 leading cases of death in 1998 accounted for 84.2 percent of all deaths in the United States. During the 20th century the leading causes of death changed significantly. In 1900, infectious diseases took may lives; indeed, the leading causes of death were (1) pneumonia and influenza and (2) tuberculosis. By century's end, heart disease and cancer headed the list.

Suicide

Each year, approximately 30,000 Americans kill themselves—about one person every 20 minutes. In addition, an estimated 500,000 people are treated in emergency rooms each year after attempting suicide. Although women make more

Leading Causes of Death, 1970–99

Cause of death	Deaths in 1999	Death rate per 100,000				
		1970	1980	1990	1998	1999
All causes	2,391,630	945.3	878.3	861.9	864.7	877.0
Heart diseases	724,915	362.0	336.0	289.0	268.2	265.8
Cancer	549,787	162.8	183.9	201.7	200.3	201.6
Cerebrovascular diseases	167,340	101.9	75.1	57.9	58.6	61.4
Pulmonary diseases	124,153	15.2	24.7	35.5	41.7	45.5
Accidents	97,298	56.4	46.7	37.3	36.2	35.7
Diabetes mellitus	68,379	18.9	15.4	19.5	24.0	25.1
Pneumonia and influenza	63,686	30.9	24.1	31.3	34.0	23.4
Alzheimer's disease	44,507	N.A.	N.A.	N.A.	8.4	16.3
Kidney diseases	35,524	4.4	7.4	8.3	9.7	13.0
Septicemia	30,670	1.7	4.2	7.9	8.8	11.2
Suicide	29,041	11.6	11.9	12.3	11.3	10.6
Liver disease and cirrhosis	26,225	15.5	13.5	10.2	9.3	9.6
Hypertension	16,964	N.A.	N.A.	N.A.	5.3	6.2
Homicide and legal intervention	16,831	8.3	10.7	10.2	6.8	6.2
Aortic aneurysm	15,806	N.A.	N.A.	N.A.	N.A.	5.8

Note: Causes of death are classified by the International Classification of Diseases, which has been revised periodically, resulting in new cause-of-death titles and breaks in comparability of cause-of-death statistics.
Source: U.S. Dept. of Health and Human Services, National Center for Health Statistics, *National Vital Statistics Reports.*

Deaths and Death Rates, 1999

Age	Total deaths	Rate per 100,000 population		
		Both sexes	Male	Female
All ages	2,391,630	877.0	882.0	872.3
Under 1 year	27,953	731.8	802.0	658.4
1-4 years	5,250	34.7	38.5	30.8
5-14 years	7,595	19.2	22.2	16.1
15-24 years	30,664	81.2	116.0	44.7
25-34 years	41,070	108.3	150.2	66.9
35-44 years	89,273	199.2	256.7	142.5
45-54 years	152,997	427.3	546.8	313.2
55-64 years	239,007	1,021.9	1,280.2	786.5
65-74 years	452,636	2,484.5	3,109.4	1,973.2
75-84 years	698,648	5,751.8	7,000.1	4,916.0
85 and older	646,181	15,477.1	16,931.0	14,862.7
Not stated	356	--	--	--

Note: Preliminary data.
Source: U.S. Dept. of Health and Human Services, National Center for Health Statistics. *National Vital Statistics Report* (June 26, 2001).

attempts at suicide, men are four times more likely to succeed at it. In 1998, 24,538 men, but only 6,037 women committed suicide.

Particularly troublesome is the suicide rate for teens and young adults, which has soared since 1950. Suicide is the eighth-leading cause of death for all Americans and the third-leading cause for young people age 15-24. The causes of youth suicide are not fully known, although some evidence suggests that suicide is not as frequently associated with depression in young people as it is in adults. Many young suicide victims had a history of impulsive, aggressive, or antisocial behavior, often complicated by drug abuse. Having a parent who committed suicide also seems to increase a person's vulnerability.

Significant differences in suicide rates exist among the states. For 1998, the highest rates were reported for Nevada (22.7 per 100,000 population), Alaska (21.0), Wyoming (18.1), Montana (17.9), and Arizona (17.2). The lowest were for New Jersey (7.2), New York (7.5), Connecticut (7.8), the District of Columbia (8.2), and Massachusetts (8.2).

Almost two-thirds of the Americans who commit suicide shoot themselves, usually with handguns. Other common methods, in decreasing order of frequency, include drug overdose (primarily drugs prescribed by physicians), cutting and stabbing, jumping from high places, inhaling poisonous gas, hanging, and drowning.

Many experts believe that suicide statistics are grimmer than reported. They contend that numerous suicides are categorized as accidents or other deaths to spare families.

Suicide in the U.S., 1950-98

Age	Total 1998	Rate per 100,000 population 1950	Rate per 100,000 population 1998
All ages	30,575[1]	11.4	11.3
0-4 years	--	--	--
5-14 years	324	0.2	0.8
15-24 years	4,135	4.5	11.1
25-34 years	5,365	9.1	13.8
35-44 years	6,837	14.3	15.4
45-54 years	5,131	20.9	14.8
55-64 years	2,963	27.0	13.1
65-74 years	2,597	29.3	14.1
75-84 years	2,355	31.1	19.7
85 and older	851	28.8	21.0

1. Includes 17 people of unknown age. **Source:** U.S. Dept. of Health and Human Services, National Center for Health Statistics, *National Vital Statistics Report*, July 24, 2000.

Changes in Leading Causes of Death, 1900-99

Cause of death	Death rate (per 100,000 population)
1900: All causes	**1,719.1**
Pneumonia and influenza	202.2
Tuberculosis	194.4
Diarrhea, enteritis, and ulceration of the intestines	142.7
1920: All causes	**1,298.9**
Pneumonia and influenza	207.3
Heart disease	159.6
Tuberculosis	113.1
1940: All causes	**1,074.1**
Heart disease	291.3
Cancer	120.0
Cerebrovascular disease	90.8
1960: All causes	**954.7**
Heart disease	369.0
Cancer	149.2
Cerebrovascular disease	108.0
1980: All causes	**878.3**
Heart disease	336.0
Cancer	183.9
Cerebrovascular disease	75.1
1990: All causes	**863.8**
Heart disease	289.5
Cancer	203.3
Cerebrovascular disease	57.9
1999: All causes	**877.0**
Heart disease	265.8
Cancer	201.6
Cerebrovascular disease	61.4

Source: U.S. Dept. of Health and Human Services, National Center for Health Statistics.

Estimated Number of Injuries in U.S. From Selected Products, 1999

Product group	Estimated injuries
Stairs, steps	1,048,257
Floors, flooring materials	1,033,938
Bicycles	627,164
Basketball	600,256
Beds	466,464
Knives	459,898
Football	399,501
Bathtubs, showers	201,465
Ladders, stools	197,309
Soccer	185,064
Nails, screws, tacks, bolts	158,982
Carpets, rugs	122,249
Fences, fence posts	118,603
Footwear	109,681
Trampolines	100,303
Drinking glasses	98,924
Wheelchairs	95,877
Power, hand saws	95,875
Skateboards	86,781
Lawn mowers	81,888
Bottles, jars	80,184
Swimming pools	80,110
Swings, swing sets	76,181
Fishing	72,751
Jewelry	72,300
Crutches, canes, walkers	69,349
Weightlifting	68,054
Snowboarding	67,979
Toilets	55,806
Golf, golf carts	54,137
Hot water	42,712
Hammers	40,707
Dancing	40,049
Razors, shavers	34,279
Scissors	31,512

Notes: These national estimates are based on injuries treated in hospital emergency rooms participating in the National Electronic Injury Surveillance System. Patients said their injuries were related to the products; this does not necessarily mean the injuries were caused by the products.
Source: Consumer Product Safety Commission, National Electronic Injury Surveillance System.

Types of Accidental Deaths in U.S., 1999

Type	Number of deaths	0–4	5–14	15–24	25–44	45–64	65–74	75+
				Age group (years)				
All accidents	96,900	2,500	3,100	13,100	25,700	19,500	8,200	24,800
Motor vehicle	41,300	900	1,900	9,800	12,300	8,400	3,300	4,700
Falls	17,100	60	40	300	1,100	1,900	1,800	11,900
Poisoning by solids and liquids[1]	10,500	20	20	350	6,300	2,900	260	350
Drowning	4,000	450	350	700	1,100	800	250	350
Suffocation	3,200	170	40	30	210	400	450	1,900
Fires and burns	3,100	350	200	200	600	700	350	700
Firearms	700	20	80	170	250	100	40	40
Poisoning by gases	500	30	20	50	190	100	50	60
All other[2]	16,500	500	450	1,200	3,650	4,200	1,700	4,800

1. Deaths from poisons, drugs, medicines, mushrooms, and shellfish. Excludes poisonings from spoiled foods, salmonella, etc., which are classified as disease deaths. 2. Medical complications, air and water transport, machinery, excessive cold, etc.
Source: National Safety Council, *Injury Facts* (2000).

Accidental Deaths in the U.S., 1910–99 (per 100,000 population)

Year	Death rate	Year	Death rate	Year	Death rate
1910	84.4	1950	60.3	1990	36.9
1920	71.2	1960	52.1	1995	35.5
1930	80.5	1970	56.2	1998	34.1
1940	73.4	1980	46.5	1999	35.5

Source: U.S. Dept. of Health and Human Services, National Center for Health Statistics.

▶ACCIDENTS

Every 10 minutes, two people are killed and about 370 suffer a disabling injury in accidents in the United States. Accidents are the nation's fifth most common cause of death. But for people between the ages of 1 and 44, accidents are the leading cause of death.

The accident death rate has declined significantly from the 1912 rate of 82.5 deaths per 100,000 population. In 1992 it reached a record low of 34.0. In 1999 the rate was 35.7, or a total of 97,298 accidental deaths, according to National Safety Council estimates. Accident rates vary significantly from one place to another. National Safety Council estimates indicate that the highest accidental death rates in 1999 were in New Mexico (59.4), Mississippi (57.5), and Wyoming (54.0); the lowest were in Massachusetts (20.8), Rhode Island (23.0), and New Jersey (23.8).

Approximately 20.8 million injuries disabled people for one or more days during 1999. The costs incurred from accidents totaled an estimated $469 billion in 1999—for medical care, wage loss, insurance administration, property damage, fire loss, and so on.

Motor Vehicle Deaths, 1999

Since the nation's first motor vehicle death (reportedly in New York City on September 13, 1899) some 2.9 million people have died in motor vehicle accidents. Over the years, however, the numbers of deaths per 100,000 population and per 100,000 registered vehicles have declined drastically. For example, noted the National Safety Council, there were 3,100 motor vehicle deaths in 1912, when the number of registered vehicles totaled only 950,000. In 1999, there were 41,300 fatalities, but registered vehicles had risen to more than 218 million. The

Life Expectancy in U.S., 1950–98

As the following table demonstrates, people who make it to the age of 65 are likely to live significantly longer than average. That's not because of any immunities they have built up over ther lives, but simply a function of statistics.

The average life expectancy for all people includes those who die at childbirth, in auto accidents in their teens, and of cancer, AIDS, and other diseases long before their 65th birthday, and thus drawing down the national average. On the other hand, the *minimum* life expectancy of the population 65 and over is 65, forcing the average higher.

Looked at another way, the average life expectancy at birth of three people, two of whom live to age 90, but one of whom dies at childbirth, is 60 years old. Meanwhile, the average life expectancy at age 65 of three people, even if all three of them died tomorrow, would be 65.

Year	All races Male	All races Female	Whites Male	Whites Female	Blacks Male	Blacks Female
At birth						
1950[1]	65.6	71.1	66.5	72.2	58.9	62.7
1960[1]	66.6	73.1	67.4	74.1	60.7	65.9
1970	67.1	74.7	68.0	75.6	60.0	68.3
1980	70.0	77.4	70.7	78.1	63.8	72.5
1990	71.8	78.8	72.7	79.4	64.5	73.6
1995	72.5	78.9	73.4	79.6	65.2	73.9
1997	73.6	79.2	74.3	79.8	67.3	74.7
1998	73.8	79.5	74.5	80.0	67.6	74.8
At age 65 (years remaining)						
1950[1]	12.8	15.0	12.8	15.1	12.9	14.9
1960[1]	12.8	15.8	12.9	15.9	12.7	15.1
1970	13.1	17.0	13.1	17.1	12.5	15.7
1980	14.1	18.3	14.2	18.4	13.0	16.8
1990	15.1	18.9	15.2	19.1	13.2	17.2
1995	15.6	18.9	15.7	19.1	13.6	17.1
1997	15.8	19.0	15.9	19.1	14.2	17.4
1998	16.0	19.2	16.1	19.3	14.3	17.4

1. Includes deaths of persons who were not residents of the 50 states and the District of Columbia.
Source: U.S. Dept. of Health and Human Services, National Center for Health Statistics, *Health United States 2000.*

motor vehicle death rate in 1999 was 1.5 deaths per 100 million vehicle miles. This ranged from a low of 0.8 deaths in Massachusetts to a high of 2.7 deaths in Mississippi. Here's how people died in motor vehicle accidents in 1999:

- 18,8500 died in collisions between two or more motor vehicles
- 11,100 died in collisions with guardrails and other fixed objects
- 5,800 pedestrians were struck by motor vehicles
- 4,300 died in non-collision accidents
- 900 died in collisions with cyclists
- 300 died in collisions with railroad trains
- 100 died in other types of collisions, usually involving animals or animal-drawn vehicles.

Data suggest that safety belts, air bags, bicycle and motorcycle helmets, child safety seats, strict drunk-driving laws, and speed limits save thousands of lives each year. In 1999, 63 percent of people killed in crashes were not wearing seatbelts.

▶ LIFE EXPECTANCY

Life expectancy figures represent the average number of years that infants are expected to live. Life expectancy has improved steadily over the years, due largely to a decline in deaths during childhood. The development of drugs to combat infectious diseases, plus improved nutrition and better environmental sanitation, have all played major roles in combating early deaths.

Average Remaining Life Expectancy in U.S. (in years)

Age in 1998	All races M	All races F	White M	White F	Black M	Black F	Age in 1998	All races M	All races F	White M	White F	Black M	Black F
At birth	73.8	79.5	74.5	80.0	67.6	74.8	50	27.6	31.8	27.9	32.0	23.9	28.8
1	73.4	79.0	74.0	79.4	67.7	74.8	51	26.8	30.9	27.0	31.1	23.2	28.0
2	72.5	78.0	73.0	78.5	66.8	73.8	52	25.9	30.0	26.2	30.2	22.5	27.2
3	71.5	77.1	72.1	77.5	65.8	72.9	53	25.1	29.1	25.3	29.3	21.8	26.4
4	70.5	76.1	71.1	76.5	64.9	71.9	54	24.3	28.2	24.5	28.4	21.1	25.6
5	69.5	75.1	70.1	75.5	63.9	70.9	55	23.5	27.4	23.7	27.6	20.4	24.8
6	68.5	74.1	69.1	74.5	62.9	69.9	56	22.7	26.5	22.9	26.7	19.7	24.0
7	67.6	73.1	68.1	73.5	61.9	69.0	57	21.9	25.7	22.0	25.8	19.0	23.2
8	66.6	72.1	67.1	72.5	60.9	68.0	58	21.1	24.8	21.3	25.0	18.4	22.5
9	65.6	71.1	66.2	71.6	60.0	67.0	59	20.3	24.0	20.5	24.1	17.8	21.7
10	64.6	70.2	65.2	70.6	59.0	66.0	60	19.6	23.2	19.7	23.3	17.1	21.0
11	63.6	69.2	64.2	69.6	58.0	65.0	61	18.8	22.3	18.9	22.5	16.5	20.2
12	62.6	68.2	63.2	68.6	57.0	64.0	62	18.1	21.5	18.2	21.6	16.0	19.5
13	61.6	67.2	62.2	67.6	56.0	63.0	63	17.4	20.8	17.5	20.8	15.4	18.8
14	60.6	66.2	61.2	66.6	55.0	62.1	64	16.7	20.0	16.8	20.1	14.9	18.1
15	59.7	65.2	60.2	65.6	54.1	61.1	65	16.0	19.2	16.1	19.3	14.3	17.4
16	58.7	64.2	59.3	64.6	53.1	60.1	66	15.3	18.4	15.4	18.5	13.7	16.8
17	57.8	63.3	58.3	63.7	52.2	59.1	67	14.7	17.7	14.7	17.8	13.2	16.1
18	56.8	62.3	57.4	62.7	51.3	58.1	68	14.0	17.0	14.1	17.0	12.6	15.4
19	55.9	61.3	56.4	61.7	50.4	57.2	69	13.4	16.2	13.4	16.3	12.0	14.8
20	55.0	60.3	55.5	60.8	49.5	56.2	70	12.8	15.5	12.8	15.6	11.5	14.1
21	54.0	59.4	54.6	59.8	48.6	55.2	71	12.2	14.8	12.2	14.9	11.0	13.5
22	53.1	58.4	53.6	58.8	47.7	54.3	72	11.6	14.2	11.7	14.2	10.5	13.0
23	52.2	57.4	52.7	57.8	46.8	53.3	73	11.1	13.5	11.1	13.5	10.1	12.4
24	51.3	56.4	51.8	56.8	45.9	52.4	74	10.5	12.8	10.5	12.8	9.6	11.9
25	50.3	55.5	50.8	55.9	45.1	51.4	75	10.0	12.2	10.0	12.2	9.2	11.3
26	49.4	54.5	49.9	54.9	44.2	50.5	76	9.5	11.6	9.5	11.5	8.8	10.8
27	48.5	53.5	49.0	53.9	43.3	49.5	77	9.0	10.9	8.9	10.9	8.4	10.2
28	47.5	52.6	48.0	52.9	42.4	48.6	78	8.5	10.3	8.4	10.3	7.9	9.7
29	46.6	51.6	47.1	52.0	41.5	47.6	79	8.0	9.8	7.9	9.7	7.5	9.2
30	45.7	50.6	46.1	51.0	40.6	46.7	80	7.5	9.2	7.5	9.1	7.1	8.7
31	44.7	49.7	45.2	50.0	39.7	45.7	81	7.0	8.6	7.0	8.6	6.7	8.2
32	43.8	48.7	44.3	49.1	38.8	44.8	82	6.6	8.1	6.6	8.1	6.4	7.8
33	42.9	47.7	43.3	48.1	38.0	43.9	83	6.2	7.6	6.2	7.6	6.1	7.4
34	41.9	46.8	42.4	47.1	37.1	42.9	84	5.9	7.2	5.8	7.1	5.8	7.0
35	41.0	45.8	41.5	46.2	36.2	42.0	85	5.5	6.7	5.4	6.6	5.5	6.6
36	40.1	44.9	40.5	45.2	35.3	41.1	86	5.2	6.3	5.1	6.2	5.2	6.2
37	39.2	43.9	39.6	44.2	34.4	40.2	87	4.9	5.9	4.8	5.8	5.0	5.9
38	38.3	43.0	38.7	43.3	33.6	39.3	88	4.6	5.6	4.5	5.4	4.7	5.5
39	37.3	42.0	37.7	42.3	32.7	38.4	89	4.3	5.2	4.2	5.1	4.5	5.2
40	36.4	41.1	36.8	41.4	31.9	37.5	90	4.1	4.9	4.0	4.7	4.3	4.9
41	35.5	40.1	35.9	40.4	31.0	36.6	91	3.8	4.6	3.7	4.4	4.1	4.6
42	34.6	39.2	35.0	39.5	30.2	35.7	92	3.6	4.3	3.5	4.1	3.9	4.4
43	33.7	38.2	34.1	38.5	29.4	34.8	93	3.4	4.1	3.3	3.9	3.7	4.1
44	32.8	37.3	33.2	37.6	28.5	33.9	94	3.2	3.8	3.1	3.6	3.6	3.9
45	31.9	36.4	32.3	36.7	27.7	33.1	95	3.0	3.6	2.9	3.4	3.4	3.7
46	31.1	35.5	31.4	35.7	26.9	32.2	96	2.9	3.4	2.7	3.2	3.3	3.5
47	30.2	34.5	30.5	34.8	26.2	31.4	97	2.7	3.2	2.6	3.0	3.1	3.3
48	29.3	33.6	29.6	33.9	25.4	30.5	98	2.6	3.0	2.4	2.8	3.0	3.1
49	28.5	32.7	28.8	32.9	24.7	29.7	99	2.5	2.9	2.3	2.6	2.9	2.9
							100+	2.3	2.7	2.2	2.4	2.7	2.8

Note: Based on an individual's age in 1998. For example, a white male age 27 in 1998 would be expected to live 49 more years, or to about 76 years old. A black female born in 1998 would be expected to live to almost 75 years of age. **Source:** U.S. Dept. Health and Human Services, National Center for Health Statistics, *National Vital Statistics Reports*, February 7, 2001.

In 1999, the average length of life in the U.S. was 76.7 years. Whites were expected to outlive blacks by almost 6 years: 77.3 years versus 71.4 years. Homicides, killings in police confrontations, auto accidents, AIDS, tuberculosis, and several other diseases have had a disproportionate impact on black people's life expectancy rates in recent years.

▶ INFANT MORTALITY

In 1999, there were 27,953 reported deaths of infants age one year or younger. The most commonly used index for measuring the risk of dying during the first year of life are infant mortality rates, which are calculated by dividing the number of infant deaths by the number of live births registered for the same period. The 1999 rate of 7.1 infant deaths per 1,000 live births was the lowest ever recorded for the United States.

The rate among white infants was less than half that of black infants: 6.0 infant deaths per 1,000 live births for whites in 1999, versus 14.6 per 1,000 for blacks. The reasons for this discrepancy are not clear, although an important factor is believed to be the quality of medical care received by people of different socioeconomic groups. For

U.S. Infant Mortality Rate, 1940–99 (per 1,000 live births)

Year	All races	White	Black
1940	47.0	43.2	72.9
1950	29.2	26.8	43.9
1960	26.0	22.9	44.3
1970	20.0	17.8	32.6
1980	12.6	11.0	21.4
1990	9.2	7.6	18.0
1995	7.6	6.3	15.1
1998	7.2	6.0	14.3
1999	7.1	6.0	14.6

Source: U.S. Dept. Health and Human Services, National Center for Health Statistics, *Monthly Vital Statistics Reports*, June 26, 2001

Childhood Vaccines: Recommended Immunization Schedule, 2001

Age	Vaccines
Birth	Hepatitis B
2 months	Hepatitis B; polio; diphtheria, tetanus, pertussis (DTaP); Haemophilus B (Hib), pneumonia and other pneumococcal bacteria (PVC)
4 months	Polio, DTaP, Hib, PVC
6 months	DTaP, Hib, PVC
6-18 months	Hepatitis B, Polio
12-15 months	Hib; measles, mumps, rubella (MMR); chicken pox, PVC
15-18 months	DTaP
4-6 years	Polio, DtaP, MMR
11-16 years	Tetanus

Note: It generally takes several doses of each vaccine for full protection. In some cases, there is a range of acceptable ages for vaccination. For example, the third dose of hepatitis B vaccine may be given between 6 and 18 months of age. Children who have not been vaccinated against Hepatitis B in infancy may begin the series during any childhood visit. For additional information, contact your physician.
Sources: American Academy of Pediatrics; American Academy of Family Physicians; and U.S. Dept. of Health and Human Services, Centers for Disease Control and Prevention.

example, several studies of infant deaths have shown that adequate prenatal care is strongly associated with higher infant birth weight and survival. Many black mothers, who are far more likely to be poor than white mothers, do not have access to proper prenatal care. Poor nutrition, alcohol and drug abuse, ant other social factors also play significant roles.

Disproportionate poverty among minority groups is not the whole story, however. Studies have shown that even black infants born to college-educated mothers had nearly twice the mortality rate of comparable white infants.

The leading cause of infant mortality, congenital malformations, accounted for 19.6 percent of all infant deaths in 1999. Low birth weight, the second leading cause of infant deaths, accounted for 15.7 percent.

(See also "World Health" for infant mortality rates in other nations.)

▶ SUBSTANCE ABUSE
Illicit Drugs

A significant portion of the American public uses illegal drugs. The 1999 National Household Survey on Drug Abuse estimated that 14.8 million Americans age 12 and older (6.7 percent of the population) were current users, meaning they had used an illicit drug in the month prior to interview. Although most illicit drug users were white, the percentage of blacks who use drugs (7.7 percent) was somewhat higher than for whites (6.6 percent) and Hispanics (6.8 percent), and significantly higher than Asians (3.2 percent). Rates of drug use generally decline with age. The highest rates were among young people age 19 (20.7 percent) and 20 (20.8 percent); only 0.6 percent of persons 65 and older reported current use.

A measure of the health consequences of drug use is the Drug Abuse Warning Network (DAWN), which collects information on patients seeking hospital emergency room treatment related to their abuse of legal and illicit drugs. An estimated 601,776 drug-related emergency-rom episodes occurred in 2000. The four drugs mentioned most frequently in emergency room reports were alcohol-in-combination (204,524 mentions), cocaine (174,896), heroin/morphine (97,287), and marijuana/hashish (96,446). Males (259 episodes per 100,000 population) and young adults age 18-25 (426) had the highest rates of emergency room drug episodes in 2000.

Marijuana is the most commonly used illegal drug, used by 75 percent of current U.S. drug users; approximately 57 percent of current illicit drug users consume no drugs other than marijuana. It is made from the leaves and flowering tops of the hemp plant, *Cannabis sativa*, which contains psychoactive substances called cannabinoids. The primary psychoactive ingredient in marijuana and hashish (a resin e xuded from the flowering tops) is tetrahydrocannabinol, or THC. The amount of each cannabinoid varies markedly from one plant to another depending on climate, soil, and other factors.

Marijuana is typically prepared as a tobacco-like mixture that is smoked in hand-rolled cigarettes or in pipes. It typically produces a "high"— a feeling of well-being, relaxation, and sleepiness. It also interferes with coordination and mental abilities. For instance, it distorts judgment and reaction time, which can be particularly dangerous when a user drives a car.

Possession or sale of marijuana has been illegal in the United States since 1937. Nonetheless, marijuana has legitimate medical uses. A significant body of evidence shows that marijuana combats nausea and weight loss in cancer and AIDS patients. It also helps reduce pressure within the eyes of glaucoma patients.

Lifetime Experience With Illicit Drugs, 1999

Age	Used in lifetime	Used in past year	Used in past month
Total[1]	39.7%	11.9%	6.7%
By Age			
12-17	27.6	20.3	10.9
18-25	52.6	29.6	17.1
26 and older	39.2	7.7	4.4
By Sex			
Male	43.6	14.3	8.7
Female	36.0	9.6	4.9
By Race/Ethnicity			
White[2]	42.0	11.8	6.6
Black[2]	37.7	13.4	7.7
Hispanic	31.2	11.4	6.8

Note: Includes marijuana, cocaine, heroin, hallucinogens, inhalants, or prescription-type psychotherapeutic drugs (stimulants, sedatives, tranquilizers, and analgesics) for nonmedical purposes. 1. Age 12 and older. 2. Non-Hispanic.
Source: U.S. Dept. of Health and Human Services, Substance Abuse and Mental Health Services Administration, *National Household Survey on Drug Abuse 1999* (August 2000).

A study commissioned by the federal government confirmed in 1999 that marijuana has medical uses and that there is no evidence that giving the drug to sick people would increase illicit use in the general population. But because the drug is illegal, most patients find it difficult or impossible to obtain. Voters in Alaska, California, Maine, Oregon, and Washington have approved initiatives to allow limited medical use of marijuana and in 2000 Hawaii became the first state to use legislation to approve medical use of the substance.

Cocaine is made from the leaves of the coca plant, a shrub native to South America. In the late 1800s and early 1900s, before its dangers were recognized, cocaine was used by doctors as an anesthetic because of its effectiveness in depressing nerve endings. It has since been replaced by less toxic, non-addictive anesthetics.

Cocaine causes a short-lived euphoria. It also suppresses appetite, interferes with sleep, and increases heart rate and blood pressure. Even small doses have been linked to heart attacks and cerebral hemorrhages. Repeated usage is required to maintain a "high." Abusers who try to abstain often experience a tremendous craving for the drug—a hallmark of addiction.

Crack is a highly addictive, smokable form of cocaine, sold in small beige chunks called pellets or rocks. Its effects on the brain are almost immediate, producing a brief but intense high. Within minutes, however, depression sets in, combined

Drug Use by U.S. High School Seniors, 1975–99

Drug	1975	1980	1985	1990	1995	1998	1999
Alcohol	68.2%	72.0%	65.9%	57.1%	51.3%	52.0%	51.0%
Cigarettes	36.7	30.5	30.1	29.4	33.5	35.1	34.6
Marijuana	27.1	33.7	25.7	14.0	21.2	22.8	23.1
LSD	2.3	2.3	1.6	1.9	4.0	3.2	2.7
Cocaine	1.9	5.2	6.7	1.9	1.8	2.4	2.6
Heroin	0.4	0.2	0.3	0.2	0.6	0.5	0.5

Note: Drug use during the 30 days preceding the survey.
Source: U.S. Dept. of Health and Human Services, National Institute on Drug Abuse, *Monitoring the Future Study*, 1999.

Commonly Abused Drugs

Drug	Primary Effect	Popular names
Alcohol	Depressant	Drink, booze
Amphetamines	Stimulant	Pep pills, uppers; *metamphetamines*: meth, speed, crystal, crank, ice
Amyl or butyl nitrites	Stimulant	Poppers, snappers rush, locker room
Barbiturates	Depressant	Sleeping pills, reds, yellowjackets
Cocaine	Stimulant	Coke, snow, lady; smokable form: crack
Ephedra	Stimulant	Ma huang; *brand names* Herbal Ecstasy, Euphoria, Buzz Tablets, Brain Wash
Heroin	Depressant	Snow, smack, horse, P-dope; *synthetic heroin*: China white, Persian heroin, gasoline dope; *combined heroin and cocaine*: speedball
D-lysergic acid diethylamide	Hallucinogen	LSD, acid, microdot, tabs, sugar cubes
Marijuana	Hallucinogen/depressant	Pot, grass, joint, dope, reefer, herb, weed, skunk
MDMA (combination of synthetic mescaline and an amphetamine	Stimulant/ hallucinogen	Ecstasy, E, Adam, love potion
Mescaline	Hallucinogen	Peyote, cactus
Morphine	Depressant	
PCP (phencyclidine)	Hallucinogen	Angel dust
Tranquilizers	Depressant	Downers

Alcohol Use in U.S. 1998

Characteristic	Total[1]	By Age		
		12-17	18-25	26 and older
Total	47.3%	18.6%	58.0%	49.4%
Race/Ethnicity				
White[2]	51.0	19.9	63.8	52.9
Black[2]	35.6	13.3	44.3	37.8
Hispanic	39.9	19.8	48.6	41.6
Asian	31.9	13.0	43.1	32.9
Sex				
Male	54.0	19.2	64.6	57.3
Female	41.1	18.1	51.5	42.4
Population Density				
Large Metro	50.4	18.5	57.3	53.7
Small Metro	46.2	18.7	60.9	47.4
Non-Metro	41.1	18.9	54.8	41.9
Region				
Northeast	51.6	20.1	62.9	53.8
Midwest	50.1	19.3	63.2	52.2
South	41.9	17.5	53.9	43.3
West	49.2	18.7	55.2	52.6
Adult Education				
Less than high school	N.A.	N.A.	46.1	32.6
High school graduate	N.A.	N.A.	53.8	45.9
Some college	N.A.	N.A.	64.7	54.4
College graduate	N.A.	N.A.	74.0	61.8
Current Employment				
Full-time	N.A.	N.A.	62.5	56.3
Part-time	N.A.	N.A.	57.8	51.8
Unemployed	N.A.	N.A.	52.1	54.4
Other[3]	N.A.	N.A.	47.5	35.0

Notes: Percentages reporting use of alcohol in the previous month. N.A.=Not Applicable. 1. Age 12 and older. 2. Non-Hispanic. 3. Includes retired, disabled, homemaker, student, etc.
Source: U.S. Dept. of Health and Human Services, Substance Abuse and Mental Health Services Administration, *National Household Survey on Drug Abuse, 1999* (August 2000).

U.S. Alcohol Consumption, 1940–98 (gallons of ethanol, per capita)

Year	Beer	Wine	Spirits	All beverages
1940	0.73	0.16	0.67	1.56
1950	1.04	0.23	0.77	2.04
1960	0.99	0.22	0.86	2.07
1970	1.14	0.27	1.11	2.52
1980	1.38	0.34	1.04	2.76
1990	1.34	0.33	0.78	2.46
1995	1.25	0.29	0.64	2.17
1997	1.24	0.31	0.63	2.18
1998	1.25	0.31	0.63	2.19

Note: Based on population age 15 and older prior to 1970 and on population age 14 and older thereafter.
Source: U.S. Dept. of Health and Human Services, National Institute on Alcohol Abuse and Alcoholism, www.niaa.nih.gov/databases/consum01.txt. (updated April 2001).

ing and dehydration, as well as stroke, heart attack, and neurological damage.

Alcohol

Consumption of alcohol constitutes the nation's most common drug abuse problem. Almost 20,000 deaths explicitly related to alcohol occur each year. In addition, alcohol is implicated in an additional 45,000 deaths. For example, in 1997, alcohol was involved in 12,870 traffic deaths (30.6 percent of all traffic deaths, a significant decline from 41.0 percent in 1990).

The 1999 National Household Survey on Drug Abuse reported that approximately 105 million people age 12 and older currently used alcohol (defined as any use in the previous month); 45 million engaged in binge drinking (defined as five or more drinks on at least one occasion in the past month), and 12 million were heavy drinkers (five or more drinks on the same occasion on at least five different days in the past month). About 10.4 million current drinkers were under age 21; of these, 5.1 million were binge drinkers, including 2.3 million heavy drinkers.

Consumption   According to the National Institute of Alcohol Abuse and Alcoholism (NIAAA), per capita consumption of beer, spirits, and wine grew slightly (1.0 percent) during the 1950s, rose rapidly (21.3 percent) during the 1960s, rose moderately (9.1 percent) in the 1970s, and decreased (12.0 percent) during the 1980s. The decline continued in the 1990s as annual per capita consumption from all alcoholic beverages dropped from 2.45 gallons in 1990 to a low of 2.15 gallons in 1995 before rising slightly to 2.1 gallons in 1999. Studies show that men are heavier drinkers than women, and much more likely to be binge drinkers. Younger people drink more than older people. Consumption was highest in New Hampshire (4.03 gallons of ethanol per capita), Nevada (3.90), and the District of Columbia (3.81). It was lowest in Utah (1.25), West Virginia (1.63), and Oklahoma (1.71).

Several factors have contributed to consumption declines, including the general aging of the population, increased state and federal taxes on alcoholic beverages, stricter penalties for drinking and driving, and the formation of minority advocacy groups to counter industry efforts to target minority populations.

with a craving for another "hit." People can become addicted to crack in weeks or even days.

Heroin is a synthetic compound derived from morphine, which is made from opium poppies (Papaver somniferum). Highly addictive, heroin fell out of favor in the United States during the 1970s but there has been an increasing trend in new use since 1992. A large portion of new users smoked, snorted, or sniffed heroin, and most were under age 26; an estimated 171,000 teenagers used heroin for the first time in 1996. Statistics from the Drug Abuse Warning Network show that heroin overdose deaths increased 25.7 percent between 1994 and 1998.

Ecstasy is a synthetic drug with both stimulant and hallucinogenic properties. Also known as MDMA, an acronym of its lengthy scientific name, it is available in pill form, with pills often embossed with smiley faces, shamrocks, and other enticing designs. Its popularity among young adults has grown dramatically in recent years. For example, according to the Monitoring the Future study, the proportion of 12th graders reporting use of ecstasy in the prior 12 months rose from 5.6 percent in 1999 to 8.2 percent in 2000.

Initially associated with dance venues such as raves, ecstasy now is being used in a variety of settings. However, a growing body of evidence indicates that its use can lead to severe overheat-

Tobacco

Smoking is the single most preventable cause of death in our society. Each year, an estimated 430,000 people die in the United States as a result of smoking. Government agencies and independent economists estimate that smoking costs the nation more than $100 billion a year — for lost productivity, medical bills, insurance premiums, heating and cooling expenses, maintenance, and cleaning costs. For medical care alone, smoking-attributable costs in 1993 totaled $72.7 billion.

The percentage of adults who smoke decreased dramatically after 1964, the year the U.S. surgeon general first warned about the link between smoking and health problems such as cancer and heart disease. At that time, 40 percent of the adult population were smokers; in 1998, less than 25 percent (47 million adults) smoked. The increased cost of cigarettes, a growing number of smoking restrictions in public places, and decreasing social acceptability of smoking also played roles in the decline. Cigarette smoking among adults was highest in Nevada, where 31.5 percent of the population age 18 and older were smokers in 1999. It was lowest in Utah (13.9 percent).

The adult smoking population has declined slightly since 1990, but teenage smoking has increased, and is a primary barrier to reducing smoking prevalence. Surveys indicate that more than 90 percent of adults who are regular smokers began smoking while they were teenagers and that 32 percent of young people who become regular smokers will die of a smoking-related disorder. Both sexes are equally likely to smoke, but male adolescents are significantly more likely than females to use smokeless tobacco.

Health effects The major effects of smoking include:

- Shortened life span. Each year, some 430,000 Americans—and about 4 million people worldwide—die prematurely as a result of smoking
- Cancer of the lungs, mouth, esophagus, stomach, bladder, kidney, pancreas, and cervix. Smoking accounts for at least 30 percent of all cancer deaths in the United States each year, including 87 percent of lung cancer deaths.
- Cardiovascular disease, including heart attack, stroke, aneurysm, and the peripheral vascular disease. Smoking weakens the heart's ability to pump blood, promotes clot formation, and damages the inner lining of blood vessels.
- Pulmonary illness, including emphysema, pneumonia, and chronic bronchitis. Annually, more than 80,000 Americans die from non-cancerous chronic lung diseases linked to smoking.
- Spontaneous abortions. Women who smoke during pregnancy are 10 times more likely to miscarry than are nonsmokers.
- Underweight, sickly babies. Each year, the deaths of more than 2,000 children under a year old are attributed to the mothers' smoking while pregnant. Infants of smokers have a 50 percent higher risk of developing Sudden Infant Death Syndrome (SIDS) and are 74 percent more likely to be of low birth weight than are infants born to mothers who do not smoke. An infant exposed to *any* cigarette smoke is 3.5 times more likely to die of SIDS than an infant not exposed to smoke.
- Environmental smoking risks. Nonsmokers who are exposed to the tobacco smoke of other people are at increased risk for various diseases. Exposure to secondhand smoke is responsible for approximately 3,000 lung cancer deaths annually among nonsmokers and 150,000 to 300,000 cases of lower respiratory tract infections such as bronchitis and pneumonia in children up to 18 months old. It also doubles a person's risk of heart attack.

U.S. Cigarette Consumption, 1900–2000

Year	Cigarettes (billions)	Per capita[1]	Year	Cigarettes (billions)	Per capita[1]
1900	2.5	54	1970	536.5	3,985
1910	8.6	151	1980	631.5	3,849
1920	44.6	665	1990	525.0	2,817
1930	119.3	1,485	1997	480.0	2,423
1940	181.9	1,976	1998	470.0	2,320
1950	369.8	3,552	1999	435.0	2,146
1960	484.4	4,171	2000	430.0	2,103

1. Among persons age 18 and older. **Source:** U.S. Dept. of Health and Human Services, Centers for Disease Control and Prevention; USDA, Economic Research Service.

Adult Cigarette Smokers in the U.S., 1998

Year	Men	Women	Total
Total	**26.4%**	**22.0%**	**24.1%**
Age			
18-24	31.3	24.5	27.9
25-44	29.4	25.6	27.5
45-64	27.7	22.5	25.0
65 and older	10.4	11.2	10.9
Race			
White[1]	26.5	23.6	25.0
Black[1]	29.0	21.3	24.7
Hispanic	24.7	13.3	19.1
Asian/Pacific Islander	17.9	9.9	13.7
Education[2]			
8 years or less	27.7	16.7	21.9
9-11 years	39.7	34.3	36.8
12 years	31.5	24.1	27.4
13-15 years	26.6	22.8	24.6
16 years or more	11.5	11.2	11.3

1. Non-Hispanic. 2. Among those age 25 and older. **Source:** U.S. Dept. of Health and Human Services, Centers for Disease Control and Prevention, *Morbidity and Mortality Weekly Report* (October 6, 2000).

Teenage Tobacco Users, 1999

Category	Cigarettes	Cigars	Smokeless Tobacco
Total	**34.8%**	**17.7%**	**7.8%**
Sex			
Male	34.7	25.4	14.2
Female	34.9	9.9	1.3
Race/Ethnicity			
White[1]	38.6	18.8	10.4
Black[1]	19.7	13.7	1.3
Hispanic	32.7	16.7	3.9
High school grade			
9	27.6	13.7	6.8
10	34.7	17.8	7.1
11	36.0	18.2	8.4
12	42.8	22.0	8.9

Note: Used at least once during the 30 days preceding the survey. 1. Non-Hispanic. **Source:** U.S. Dept. of Health and Human Services, Centers for Disease Control and Prevention, *Morbidity and Morality Weekly Report,* June 9, 2000.

The Media

THE PRINT MEDIA

▶NEWSPAPERS

The mutual distrust between government and the media dates back to the very first American newspaper in 1690, when a three-page publication called *Publick Occurrences, Both Foreign and Domestick* was suppressed by the government after one issue. A number of newspapers sprang up during the pre-Revolutionary period and by 1775, the colonies, with a population of 2.5 million people, were served by 48 weekly newspapers, small in both size and circulation.

The first daily, the *Pennsylvania Evening Post and Daily Advertiser*, was not published until 1783. By 1800 there were 20 daily newspapers and more than 1,000 small town and frontier weeklies. Most of the dailies, filled with political and business news, were expensive and aimed at educated, affluent readers. The first of the mass-circulation dailies, known as the penny press, was the *New York Sun*, started in 1833 and sold for the bargain price of one cent. The *Sun*, with its crime stories and soft features, marked a dramatic change in newspaper coverage.

The next major change in newspapers came in the era during and after the Civil War. Dramatic technological improvements like the transatlantic cable, the telephone, the electric light bulb, typewriters, web-fed, presses, and typesetting machine made possible cheap, mass circulation newspapers. By 1900 the number of daily newspapers had jumped to 2,326. Over the next half century, the number of newspapers steadily declined while readership increased, due in part to the popularity in Sunday editions.

Newspapers today

In 2000, there were 1,480 daily newspapers published in the United States. For the first time in history, morning papers outnumbered evening papers (766 to 727). As recently as 1985, there were twice as many evening newspapers as morning papers in the U.S. The total number of newspapers has been declining for decades, in part because of radio, television and the Internet, but also because in the fight for readers and advertising, competing papers have battled until a single winner emerged. Fewer than 50 cities have competing newspapers today, a major change from the turn of the century when most major cities had more than two newspapers. By contrast, 12 cities have competing newspapers only by virtue of a joint operating agreement that combines all of the two papers' operations except for their editorial staffs, which remain independent (in some cases fiercely) of each other.

Advertising expenditures on newspapers, however, continues to increase. A total of $48.67 billion was spent on newspaper advertising in 2000, up from $46.3 billion in 1999, and 32.3 billion in 1990.

The vast majority of newspapers have circulations of less than 50,000; 118 have circulations between 50,000 and 100,000; and 105 have a daily circulation of more than 100,000. The top six newspaper companies—Gannett, Knight-Ridder, Tribune Co., Advance Publications Inc., The New York Times Co., and Dow Jones & Co.—account for more than a third of all newspaper circulation. The newspapers with the greatest circulations in the world are all published in Japan and in Europe. The world's most widely read newspapers are Japan's *Yomiuri Shimbun*, with a circulation of over 14 million, and its rival, the *Asahi Shimbun*, read by more than 12 million people. By comparison, *The Wall Street Journal*, tops in the U.S. in circulation, reaches just 1.8 million people.

Daily circulation for all newspapers dropped for the 12th consecutive year in 2000, to 55.8 million, according to the American Newspaper Association. Evening newspapers were responsible for all of the drop-off, even counteracting a 775,130 increase in circulation by morning papers. Circulation of Sunday editions dropped slightly to 59.4 million. The percentage of people who read a newspaper continues to drop ever so slightly from year to year: 55.1 percent of people read a daily paper, down from 56.9 percent in 1999, and 62.4 in 1990. Sunday edition readership was 65.1 percent in 2000, down from 66.9 percent in 1999, and 72.6

Daily Newspapers, Number and Circulation, 1900–2000

Year	Total Number of Daily papers	Total Daily circulation ('000s)	Morning Number of papers	Morning Daily circulation ('000s)	Evening Number of papers	Evening Daily circulation ('000s)	Sunday Number of papers	Sunday Daily circulation ('000s)
1900	2,226	15,102	—		—		—	—
1920	2,042	27,791	437	—	1,605	—	522	17,084
1930	1,942	39,589	388	—	1,554	—	521	26,413
1940	1,878	41,132	380	16,114	1,498	25,008	525	32,371
1950	1,772	53,829	322	21,266	1,450	32,563	549	46,582
1960	1,763	58,882	312	24,029	1,459	34,853	563	47,699
1970	1,748	62,108	334	25,934	1,429	36,174	586	49,217
1980	1,745	62,202	387	29,414	1,388	32,787	735	54,672
1990	1,611	62,324	559	41,308	1,084	21,015	863	62,634
1995	1,533	58,193	656	44,310	891	13,883	888	61,529
1998	1,489	56,182	721	45,643	781	10,539	897	60,061
1999	1,483	55,979	736	45,997	760	9,981	905	59,894
2000[1]	1,480	55,773	766	46,772	727	9,000	917	59,421

Note: All-day newspapers are listed in both morning and evening columns, but are counted only once in the total. There were 12 such papers in 2000. 1. Preliminary.   **Source:** Newspaper Association of America, *Facts About Newspapers, 2001.*

Top 100 U.S. Daily Newspapers by Circulation, 2000

Rank Newspaper	Average daily paid circulation	Rank Newspaper	Average daily paid circulation
1. Wall Street Journal	1,762,751	51. Tampa Tribune	213,032
2. USA Today	1,692,666	52. St. Paul Pioneer Press	205,798
3. New York Times	1,097,180	53. Hartford Courant	202,509
4. Los Angeles Times	1,033,399	54. Los Angeles Daily News	200,387
5. Washington Post	762,009	55. Oklahoma City Daily Oklahoman	198,576
6. New York Daily News	704,463	56. Norfolk Virginian-Pilot	197,574
7. Chicago Tribune	661,699	57. Richmond Times-Dispatch	196,432
8. Long Island Newsday	576,345	58. Cincinnati Enquirer	195,360
9. Houston Chronicle	546,799	59. Austin American-Statesman	187,789
10. Dallas Morning News	495,597	60. Nashville Tennessean	186,793
11. Chicago Sun-Times	471,031	61. Contra Costa (Calif.) Times	182,682
12. Boston Globe	464,472	62. Seattle Post-Intelligencer	175,794
13. San Francisco Chronicle	457,028	63. Rochester Democrat and Chronicle	173,398
14. Phoenix Arizona Republic	445,322	64. Jacksonville Times-Union	172,734
15. New York Post	443,951	65. West Palm Beach Palm Beach Post	172,523
16. Denver Rocky Mountain News	426,465	66. Little Rock Democrat-Gazette	172,214
17. Denver Post	420,033	67. Riverside (Calif.) Press-Enterprise	166,935
18. Newark Star-Ledger	407,537	68. Providence Journal	162,358
19. Philadelphia Inquirer	400,385	69. Memphis Commercial Appeal	161,274
20. San Diego Union-Tribune	370,395	70. Raleigh News & Observer	161,175
21. Detroit Free Press	365,579	71. Asbury Park Press	160,069
22. Cleveland Plain Dealer	364,708	72. Las Vegas Review-Journal	158,970
23. Orange County Register	358,654	73. Fresno Bee	156,915
24. Portland Oregonian	348,468	74. Des Moines Register	155,698
25. Miami Herald	343,877	75. Philadelphia Daily News	154,145
26. Minneapolis Star Tribune	336,476	76. Birmingham News	148,851
27. St. Petersburg Times	325,633	77. Arlington Heights (Ill.) Daily Herald	145,902
28. Baltimore Sun	315,306	78. Tulsa World	145,697
29. Atlanta Constitution	311,342	79. Bergen County (N.J.) Record	145,595
30. Los Angeles Investor's Business Daily	303,596	80. White Plains (N.Y.) Journal News	143,685
31. St. Louis Post-Dispatch	294,434	81. Grand Rapids (Mich. Press	141,303
32. Sacramento Bee	289,751	82. Akron Beacon Journal	140,137
33. San Jose Mercury News	286,679	83. Toledo Blade	137,972
34. Milwaukee Journal Sentinel	278,377	84. Salt Lake City Tribune	134,542
35. Kansas City Star	267,664	85. Dayton Daily News	134,393
36. New Orleans Times-Picayune	264,001	86. Tacoma News Tribune	127,629
37. Orlando Sentinel	260,802	87. Allentown (Pa.) Morning Call	127,175
38. Boston Herald	257,761	88. Columbia (S.C.) State	118,783
39. Fort Lauderdale Sun-Sentinel	256,690	89. La Opinion (Los Angeles)	117,558
40. Indianapolis Star	248,144	90. Knoxville News-Sentinel	116,564
41. Columbus Dispatch	244,177	91. Albuquerque Journal	108,931
42. Charlotte Observer	240,594	92. Lexington (Ky.) Herald-Leader	108,550
43. Pittsburgh Post-Gazette	240,245	93. Honolulu Advertiser	106,590
44. Detroit News	237,518	94. Charleston (S.C.) Post & Courier	105,868
45. Louisville Courier-Journal	231,630	95. Sarasota Herald-Tribune	105,672
46. Buffalo News	226,342	96. Spokane Spokesman-Review	105,550
47. Seattle Times	225,687	97. Worcester (Mass.) Telegram & Gazette	103,565
48. San Antonio Express-News	221,246	98. Washington (D.C.) Times	102,957
49. Fort Worth Star-Telegram	220,096	99. Jackson (Miss.) Clarion-Ledger	101,886
50. Omaha World-Herald	214,651	100. Daytona Beach News-Journal	100,356

Source: *Editor and Publisher Yearbook, 2001.* Copyright © The Editor & Publisher Co. 2001. All Rights Reserved. www.mediainfo.com.

percent in 1995. Newspaper readership is highest among those with the most education, the highest income, and the greatest job responsibilities. And the audience for newspapers continues to grow older: 72 percent of people over 65 read a daily paper, compared with only 40 percent of 18-24-year-olds, a percentage that continues to decline.

Newspapers tomorrow

The future heralds even greater drops in readership, as more and more people turn to the Internet for their news, rather than wait for the paper to come out the next day. America Online currently has more than 20 million subscribers, or more than the readership of the top 20 newspapers in America combined. Newspapers have rushed to create a presence on the Web in an effort to capture this audience, with varying degrees of success. More than 1,200 newspapers in the U.S. (including the top 100 in circulation) have Web sites; most of them can be accessed from the Newspaper Association of America's site: www.newspaperlinks.com. According to the Newspaper Association, an online presence doesn't significantly cut into readership of the printed product. Some 82 percent of online readers say they read the printed paper with the same or increased frequency.

Weekly Newspapers in the U.S., 1960–2000

Year	Number of newspapers[1]	Average circulation	Total weekly circulation	Year	Number of newspapers[1]	Average circulation	Total weekly circulation
1960	8,174	2,566	20,974,338	1985	7,704	6,359	48,988,801
1965	8,061	3,106	25,036,031	1990	7,606	6,958	52,919,846
1970	7,612	3,660	27,857,332	1995[2]	8,453	9,425	79,668,266
1975	7,612	4,715	35,892,409	1999[3]	8,138	5,754	74,457,621
1980	7,954	5,324	42,347,512	2000[3]	7,689	5,857	70,949,633

1. Includes paid and free-circulation newspapers. 2. 1995 not comparable to prior years due to change in information collection procedures. 3. Preliminary. **Source:** Newspaper Association of America, *Facts About Newspapers, 2001.*

Top 100 U.S. Magazines by Circulation, 2000

Rank	Magazine	Average paid circulation per issue	Percent change 1999-2000	Rank	Magazine	Average paid circulation per issue	Percent change 1999-2000
1.	NRTA/AARP Bulletin	20,936,279	1.9%	52.	First For Women	1,511,395	-1.3%
2.	Modern Maturity	20,894,343	2.3	53.	Parenting Magazine	1,459,669	4.5
3.	Reader's Digest	12,589,919	-0.8	54.	Cooking Light	1,452,765	0.5
4.	TV Guide	10,388,083	-9.4	55.	American Rifleman	1,450,818	14.3
5.	National Geographic	7,892,852	-7.9	56.	Sunset	1,445,881	0.1
6.	Better Homes & Gardens	7,622,981	0.2	57.	Golf Magazine	1,403,074	0.0
7.	Family Circle	5,002,223	0.0	58.	Car And Driver	1,392,283	1.5
8.	Good Housekeeping	4,532,915	-1.2	59.	Health	1,382,005	20.3
9.	Woman's Day	4,195,200	0.4	60.	Outdoor Life	1,361,049	-0.2
10.	Ladies' Home Journal	4,137,423	-8.3	61.	Boys' Life	1,299,944	-0.6
11.	McCall's	4,104,990	-2.4	62.	Motor Trend	1,274,452	-1.1
12.	Time	4,064,815	-0.9	63.	PC World	1,266,730	3.8
13.	People Weekly	3,539,034	-1.7	64.	Bon Appetit	1,255,366	7.2
14.	Home & Away	3,250,983	0.6	65.	Rolling Stone	1,252,887	0.1
15.	Sports Illustrated	3,208,918	-1.8	66.	Self	1,242,399	1.6
16.	Newsweek	3,141,578	-0.7	67.	Familyfun	1,232,979	8.1
17.	Playboy	3,113,103	-2.8	68.	Popular Mechanics	1,231,821	-1.9
18.	Prevention	3,011,498	-1.9	69.	PC Magazine	1,227,460	-0.2
19.	Westways	2,676,605	0.4	70.	Scholastic Parent & Child	1,215,073	-1.3
20.	Cosmopolitan	2,651,192	-7.5	71.	Endless Vacation	1,207,106	3.0
21.	Via Magazine	2,612,806	2.4	72.	The Family Handyman	1,153,056	2.8
22.	The American Legion Magazine	2,612,135	-2.0	73.	Vogue	1,143,550	0.1
				74.	ESPN The Magazine	1,123,041	32.9
23.	Guideposts	2,546,565	N.A.	75.	Life	1,120,338	-30.2
24.	Southern Living	2,539,153	0.3	76.	The American Hunter	1,117,186	16.9
25.	Martha Stewart Living	2,373,557	2.8	77.	Sesame Street Magazine	1,115,526	-2.7
26.	Seventeen	2,372,269	-0.7	78.	The Elks Magazine	1,114,703	-2.7
27.	Maxim	2,307,737	63.9	79.	Soap Opera Digest	1,110,527	0.7
28.	Redbook	2,304,273	-8.8	80.	Mademoiselle	1,106,794	-3.1
29.	YM	2,202,797	-1.3	81.	Fitness	1,091,313	8.8
30.	Glamour	2,177,589	-1.2	82.	Vanity Fair	1,060,167	0.2
31.	U.S. News & World Report	2,100,014	-4.6	83.	Country Home	1,056,262	3.6
32.	National Enquirer	2,081,623	-4.0	84.	Kiplinger's Personal Finance	1,032,782	-1.8
33.	Teen	2,077,150	-0.8	85.	Michigan Living	1,028,858	0.4
34.	O, The Oprah Magazine	2,066,440	N.A.	86.	Smart Business For The New Economy	1,028,061	N.A.
35.	AAA Going Places	2,065,799	1.2				
36.	Smithsonian	2,053,466	0.9	87.	Discover	1,018,412	-12.0
37.	Parents	1,998,647	11.2	88.	Home	1,013,273	0.5
38.	Money	1,907,377	-2.3	89.	Essence	1,006,858	0.6
39.	V.F.W. Magazine	1,766,113	-1.6	90.	Vim & Vigor	1,004,165	N.A.
40.	Ebony	1,757,066	-0.6	91.	American Homestyle & Gardening	1,002,022	1.0
41.	Field & Stream	1,754,163	-1.6				
42.	Star	1,669,923	-5.6	92.	Sport	1,000,830	-7.0
43.	Country Living	1,662,499	0.2	93.	Consumers Digest	1,000,033	-16.7
44.	Men's Health	1,639,362	0.2	94.	Scouting	979,356	-5.1
45.	Teen People	1,635,921	2.0	95.	Victoria	967,410	0.2
46.	Woman's World	1,604,035	1.3	96.	Travel & Leisure	960,848	-3.7
47.	Shape	1,578,161	7.7	97.	Jet	955,074	0.8
48.	In Style	1,578,062	12.9	98.	Today's Homeowner	953,065	0.0
49.	Golf Digest	1,567,604	0.6	99.	Business Week	949,159	2.8
50.	Popular Science	1,560,758	0.3	100.	Yahoo! Internet Life	944,366	35.1
51.	Entertainment Weekly	1,518,689	1.4		**Total top 100**	**248,189,608**	**N.A.**

Note: Leading Audit Bureau of Circulation (ABC) magazines by average paid combined circulation per issue.
Source: Magazine Publishers of America, 2001.

Top 50 U.S. Magazines by Advertising Revenues, 2000

Rank Magazine	Advertising revenues ('000s)	Percent change 1999–2000	Rank Magazine	Advertising revenues ('000s)	Percent change 1999–2000
1. People Weekly	723,732,553	1.4%	26. Industry Standard	158,650,410	240.3%
2. Time	661,094,425	0.4	27. Parents	148,538,758	21.2
3. Sports Illustrated	649,551,743	5.8	28. Southern Living	142,631,692	3.7
4. Business Week	572,091,827	29.0	29. Vanity Fair	135,897,845	16.0
5. Fortune	476,848,553	46.6	30. Elle	133,183,197	9.7
6. Better Homes & Gardens	471,111,672	6.2	31. Bride's	128,437,896	32.6
7. TV Guide	450,406,442	-8.3	32. Redbook	125,280,820	5.5
8. Newsweek	439,551,603	0.4	33. Inc.	125,250,375	19.0
9. Forbes	434,344,335	35.4	34. Mccall's	122,570,717	-8.4
10. Good Housekeeping	288,484,416	11.5	35. Golf Magazine	121,046,769	7.8
11. Woman's Day	287,794,448	16.2	36. Car And Driver	117,721,032	0.9
12. Reader's Digest	274,995,892	20.0	37. Travel+Leisure	115,564,209	10.7
13. Cosmopolitan	260,492,715	14.2	38. Maxim	115,267,382	151.9
14. Family Circle	237,782,171	-0.2	39. W	113,692,247	21.8
15. In Style	231,820,743	52.7	40. ESPN Magazine	112,804,677	44.9
16. US News & World Report	224,890,757	-9.6	41. Seventeen	111,041,479	14.6
17. PC Magazine	222,005,942	-19.6	42. Parenting	108,319,271	12.0
18. Entertainment Weekly	213,292,537	3.7	43. GQ	106,699,111	15.4
19. Vogue	198,254,506	9.4	44. New Yorker	106,538,673	29.6
20. Martha Stewart Living	197,796,932	22.5	45. Modern Bride	104,822,280	10.2
21. Ladies' Home Journal	182,856,012	-5.1	46. Harper's Bazaar	102,788,003	20.3
22. Rolling Stone	171,977,469	7.5	47. Business 2.0	92,520,168	378.5
23. Glamour	164,522,632	6.8	48. House Beautiful	91,652,327	20.2
24. Money	164,071,428	5.5	49. Prevention	89,786,039	24.0
25. Golf Digest	160,988,239	4.1	50. Country Living	88,914,479	2.4

Source: Magazine Publishers of America, *Publishers Information Bureau Publications Ranked by Revenue, 2000* (2001).

►MAGAZINES

Consumer magazines range from the very specialized (*Fly Fisherman*) to the general interest (*People*) and are sold either by subscription or through retail outlets (supermarkets, newsstands, etc.) The Audit Bureau of Circulations (ABC) monitors the sales of about 500 of the most popular consumer magazines. Trade publications are magazines with a narrow focus in a particular area of business (e.g. trucking, restaurants, computers). There are about 2,700 trade publications; they are sold either by subscription or distributed free.

Almost all magazines make money through revenues from both circulation and advertising. The most financially successful magazines are not necessarily the largest sellers, the difference being in the advertising fees they are able to obtain. *Fortune*, for example, is among the top 10 of all magazines in revenues, but does not even make the top-100 list in circulation.

►BOOKS

Sales of books in the United States increased in 1999 for the ninth straight year, according to figures released by the Book Industry Study Group, which monitors the reading habits of American households. The dollar volume of book sales (6.1) increased faster than the number of books sold (2.6), indicating that the average price of books is also going up.

Ironically, it is the computer, predicted by many to be the book industry's death knell, which has been responsible for the increase in book production since 1990. Computers not only reduce publishers' production costs, enabling the publication of many more titles. Computers have also made possible the "superstore" in which computer indexes, rather than humans with encyclopedic knowledge, keep track of so many titles.

Steadily rising levels of educational attainment over two decades—nearly 83 percent of the population had finished high school in 1998, compared with 68.1 percent in 1980, while 24.4 percent had finished college, compared with 17.0 percent in 1980—has created a growing audience for the printed word. It has also fueled a corresponding increase in the number of libraries in the U.S. Since 1980, the number of libraries has increased by more than 8 percent.

Number of Libraries in U.S. and Canada by Type, 1980–2000

Type of Library	1980	1990	1999	2000
Public	8,717	9,060	9,837	9,480
Branches of public libraries	5,936	5,833	6,376	6,957
Special	7,649	9,051	9,691	9,948
Medical	1,674	1,861	1,906	1,955
Religious	913	946	1,001	767
Law	417	647	1,136	1,172
Academic	4,591	4,593	4,723	3,491
Junior college	1,191	1,233	1,274	1,148
Colleges, universities	3,400	3,360	3,449	2,251
Departmental	1,489	1,454	1,467	1,454
Law, medical, religious	269	501	493	418
Government	1,260	1,735	1,874	1,411
Armed forces	485	489	352	341
Total, U.S.	28,638	30,761	33,108	31,628
Total, U.S. and Canada	31,564	34,613	37,039	35,261

Source: R.R. Bowker Co., *The Bowker Annual: Library and Book Trade Almanac.* (2001). Used with the permission of R.R. Bowker ® a Unit of Cahners Business Information.

Number and Value of U.S. Books Sold, 1990-2000 (in millions)

Type of publication and market area	Publishers' units			Domestic consumer expenditures		
	1990	1999	2000	1990	1999	2000
TYPE OF PUBLICATION						
Trade	730.7	934.7	903.9	$6,497.8	$10,787.9	$11,514.4
Adult trade	420.4	529.0	457.1	4,776.8	8,141.5	8,690.7
Juvenile trade	310.3	405.7	446.8	1,721.0	2,646.4	2,823.7
Mass market paperback	488.8	485.1	471.3	1,775.4	2,456.7	2,622.2
Book clubs	110.6	145.7	143.1	704.7	1,233.1	1,316.2
Mail order publications	142.6	65.5	65.3	751.7	553.1	590.3
Religious	137.7	170.5	174.7	1,361.9	2,150.5	2,295.4
Professional	148.6	170.3	173.4	2,956.8	4,958.6	5,292.7
University press	15.8	32.0	31.0	284.1	474.1	506.1
Elementary and high school	218.7	305.4	333.6	1,947.9	3,294.4	3,516.3
College	149.7	183.8	186.3	2,319.0	3,483.1	3,717.8
Subscription reference	1.1	1.2	1.2	443.6	635.9	678.7
All books	**2,144.3**	**2,504.9**	**2,493.2**	**$19,042.9**	**$30,026.9**	**$32,050.1**
MARKET AREA						
Domestic (total)	2,005.0	2,348.3	2,338.5	$19,042.9	$30,026.9	$32,050.1
General retailers	1,009.8	1,198.8	1,180.6	8,465.4	13,813.0	14,556.8
Colleges	254.6	298.8	301.3	3,403.2	5,279.8	5,698.5
Libraries and institutions	88.4	104.8	105.9	1,591.8	2,496.3	2,663.8
Schools and school libraries	244.1	325.7	343.3	2,365.0	3,763.7	4,234.3
Direct to consumers	304.1	312.0	303.5	2,901.0	4,238.7	4,447.5
Other	104.1	108.2	103.9	316.5	435.4	449.2
Export	139.4	156.6	154.7	—	—	—
Total	**2,144.3**	**2,504.9**	**2,493.2**	**—**	**—**	**—**

Note: Includes all titles released by publishers in the United States, and imports that appear under the imprint of American publishers. Multi-volume sets such as encyclopedias are counted as one unit. School libraries included with school, not libraries. Does not include standardized tests. Source: Book Industry Study Group, Inc., *Book Industry Trends 2001*, reprinted by permission.

Best-Sellers in America, 1917-2000

Year	Fiction	Nonfiction
1917	*Mr. Britling Sees It Through*, H.G. Wells	*Rhymes of A Red Cross Man*, Robert W. Service
1918	*The U.P. Trail*, Zane Grey	*Rhymes of A Red Cross Man*, Robert W. Service
1919	*The Four Horsemen of the Apocalypse*, V. Blasco Ibañez	*The Education of Henry Adams*, Henry Adams
1920	*The Man of the Forest*, Zane Grey	*Now It Can Be Told*, Philip Gibbs
1921	*Main Street*, Sinclair Lewis	*The Outline of History*, H.G. Wells
1922	*If Winter Comes*, A.S.M. Hutchinson	*The Outline of History*, H.G. Wells
1923	*Black Oxen*, Gertrude Atherton	*Etiquette*, Emily Post
1924	*So Big*, Edna Ferber	*Diet and Health*, Lulu Hunt Peters
1925	*Soundings*, A. Hamilton Gibbs	*Diet and Health*, Lulu Hunt Peters
1926	*The Private Life of Helen of Troy*, John Erskine	*The Man Nobody Knows*, Bruce Barton
1927	*Elmer Gantry*, Sinclair Lewis	*The Story of Philosophy*, Will Durant
1928	*The Bridge of San Luis Rey*, Thornton Wilder	*Disraeli*, Andre Maurois
1929	*All Quiet on the Western Front*, Erich Maria Remarque	*The Art of Thinking*, Ernest Dimmet
1930	*Cimarron*, Edna Ferber	*The Story of San Michele*, Axel Munthe
1931	*The Good Earth*, Pearl S. Buck	*Education of a Princess*, Grand Duchess Marie
1932	*The Good Earth*, Pearl S. Buck	*The Epic of America*, James Truslow Adams
1933	*Anthony Adverse*, Hervey Allen	*Life Begins at Forty*, Walter Pitkin
1934	*Anthony Adverse*, Hervey Allen	*While Rome Burns*, Alexander Woollcott
1935	*Green Light*, Lloyd C. Douglas	*North to the Orient*, Anne Morrow Lindbergh
1936	*Gone With the Wind*, Margaret Mitchell	*Man the Unknown*, Alexis Carrel
1937	*Gone With the Wind*, Margaret Mitchell	*How to Win Friends and Influence People*, Dale Carnegie
1938	*The Yearling*, Marjorie Kinnan Rawlings	*The Importance of Living*, Lin Yutang
1939	*The Grapes of Wrath*, John Steinbeck	*Days of Our Years*, Piere von Paaseen
1940	*How Green Was My Valley*, Richard Llewellyn	*I Married Adventure*, Osa Johnson
1941	*The Keys of the Kingdom*, A.J. Cronin	*Berlin Diary*, William C. Shirer
1942	*The Song of Bernadette*, Franz Werfel	*See Here, Private Hargrove*, Marion Hargrove
1943	*The Robe*, Lloyd C. Douglas	*Under Cover*, John Roy Carlson
1944	*Strange Fruit*, Lillian Smith	*I Never Left Home*, Bob Hope
1945	*Forever Amber*, Kathleen Winsor	*Brave Men*, Ernie Pyle
1946	*The King's General*, Daphne du Maurier	*The Egg and I*, Betty MacDonald

Year	Fiction	Nonfiction
1947	*The Miracle of the Bells*, Russell Janney	*Peace of Mind*, Joshua L. Liebman
1948	*The Big Fisherman*, Lloyd C. Douglas	*Crusade in Europe*, Dwight D. Eisenhower
1949	*The Egyptian*, Mika Waltari	*White Collar Zoo*, Clare Barnes, Jr.
1950	*The Cardinal*, Henry Morton Robinson	*Betty Crocker's Picture Cookbook*
1951	*From Here to Eternity*, James Jones	*Look Younger, Live Longer*, Gayelord Hauser
1952	*The Silver Chalice*, Thomas B.Costain	*The Holy Bible: Revised Standard Version*
1953	*The Robe*, Lloyd C. Douglas	*The Holy Bible: Revised Standard Version*
1954	*Not As A Stranger*, Morton Thompson	*The Holy Bible: Revised Standard Version*
1955	*Marjorie Morningstar*, Herman Wouk	*Gift from the Sea*, Anne Morrow Lindbergh
1956	*Don't Go Near the Water*, William Brinkley	*Arthritis and Common Sense*, Dan Dale Alexander
1957	*By Love Possessed*, James Gould Cozzens	*Kids Say the Darndest Things!*, Art Linkletter
1958	*Doctor Zhivago*, Boris Pasternak	*Kids Say the Darndest Things!*, Art Linkletter
1959	*Exodus*, Leon Uris	*'Twixt Twelve and Twenty*, Pat Boone
1960	*Advise and Consent*, Allen Drury	*Folk Medicine*, D.C. Jarvis
1961	*The Agony and the Ecstasy*, Irving Stone	*The New English Bible: The New Testament*
1962	*Ship of Fools*, Katherine Anne Porter	*Calories Don't Count*, Dr. Herman Taller
1963	*The Shoes of the Fisherman*, Morris L. West	*Happiness Is a Warm Puppy*, Charles M. Schulz
1964	*The Spy Who Came in From the Cold*, John le Carré	*Four Days*, American Heritage
1965	*The Source*, James A. Michener	*How To Be a Jewish Mother*, Dan Greenburg
1966	*Valley of the Dolls*, Jacqueline Susann	*How to Avoid Probate*, Norman F. Dacey
1967	*The Arrangement*, Elia Kazan	*Death of a President*, William Manchester
1968	*Airport*, Arthur Hailey	*Better Homes & Gardens New Cook Book*
1969	*Portnoy's Complaint*, Philip Roth	*American Heritage Dictionary of the English Language*, ed. William Morris
1970	*Love Story*, Erich Segal	*Everything You Wanted to Know About Sex but Were Afraid to Ask*, David Reuben, M.D.
1971	*Wheels*, Arthur Hailey	*The Sensuous Man*, "M."
1972	*Jonathan Livingston Seagull*, Richard Bach	*The Living Bible*, Kenneth Taylor
1973	*Jonathan Livingston Seagull*, Richard Bach	*The Living Bible*, Kenneth Taylor
1974	*Centennial*, James A. Michener	*The Total Woman*, Marabel Morgan
1975	*Ragtime*, E. L. Doctorow	*Angels: God's Secret Agents*, Billy Graham
1976	*Trinity*, Leon Uris	*The Final Days*, Bob Woodward, Carl Bernstein
1977	*The Silmarillion*, J.R.R. Tolkien	*Roots*, Alex Haley
1978	*Chesapeake*, James A. Michener	*If Life is a Bowl of Cherries—What Am I Doing in the Pits?* Erma Bombeck
1979	*The Matarese Circle*, Robert Ludlum	*Aunt Erma's Cope Book*, Erma Bombeck
1980	*The Covenant*, James Michener	*Crisis Investing*, Douglas R. Casey
1981	*Noble House*, James Clavell	*The Beverly Hills Diet*, Judy Mazel
1982	*E.T. The Extra-Terrestrial Storybook*, William Kotzwinkle	*Jane Fonda's Workout Book*, Jane Fonda
1983	*Return of the Jedi Storybook*, Joan D. Vinge	*In Search of Excellence*, Thomas J. Peters, Robert H. Waterman Jr.
1984	*The Talisman*, Stephen King, Peter Straub	*Iacocca: An Autobiography*, Lee Iacocca with William Novak
1985	*The Mammoth Hunters*, Jean M.Auel	*Iacocca: An Autobiography*, Lee Iacocca with William Novak
1986	*It*, Stephen King	*Fatherhood*, Bill Cosby
1987	*The Tommyknockers*, Stephen King	*Time Flies*, Bill Cosby
1988	*The Cardinal of the Kremlin*, Tom Clancy	*The Eight-Week Cholesterol Diet*, Robert Kowalski
1989	*Clear and Present Danger*, Tom Clancy	*All I Really Need to Know I Learned in Kindergarten*, Robert Fulghum
1990	*The Plains of Passage*, Jean Auel	*A Life on the Road*, Charles Kuralt
1991	*Scarlett*, Alexandra Ripley	*Me: The Stories of My Life* , Katharine Hepburn
1992	*Dolores Claiborne*, Stephen King	*The Way Things Ought to Be*, Rush Limbaugh
1993	*The Bridges of Madison County*, Robert James Walker	*See, I Told You So*, Rush Limbaugh
1994	*The Chamber*, John Grisham	*In the Kitchen with Rosie*, Rosie Daley
1995	*The Rainmaker*, John Grisham	*Men are From Mars, Women are From Venus*, John Gray
1996	*The Runaway Jury*, John Grisham	*Make the Connection*, Oprah Winfrey & Bob Greene
1997	*The Partner*, John Grisham	*Angela's Ashes*, Frank McCourt
1998	*The Street Lawyer*, John Grisham	*The Nine Steps to Financial Freedom*, Suze Orman
1999	*The Testament*, John Grisham	*Tuesdays with Morrie*, Mitch Albom
2000	*The Brethren*, John Grisham	*Who Moved My Cheese?* Spencer Johnson

Sources: Alice Payne Hackett, *70 Years of Best Sellers; Publishers Weekly.*

New Books and Editions Published, by Subject, 1980-2000

Subject	1980	1990	1999	2000[1]	Subject	1980	1990	1999	2000[1]
Agriculture	461	514	1,037	881	Medicine	3,292	3,014	6,153	4,817
Art	1,691	1,262	4,795	3,896	Music	357	289	1,593	987
Biography	1,891	1,957	4,051	2,898	Philosophy,	1,429	1,688	5,861	4,317
Business	1,185	1,191	3,789	2,761	psychology				
Education	1,011	1,039	3,408	2,639	Poetry, drama	1,179	874	2,455	1,860
Fiction	2,835	5,764	12,371	11,808	Religion	2,055	2,285	6,044	5,086
General works	1,643	1,760	1,456	878	Science	3,109	2,742	7,862	7,140
History	2,220	2,248	7,486	6,948	Sociology,	7,152	7,042	14,579	12,039
Home economics	879	758	2,564	1,982	economics				
Juvenile	2,859	5,172	9,438	6,708	Sports, recreation	971	978	3,252	2,695
Language	529	649	2,565	2,132	Technology	2,337	2,092	8,896	6,449
Law	1,102	896	3,078	2,299	Travel	504	495	2,977	2,057
Literature	1,686	2,049	3,646	2,803	**Total**	**42,377**	**46,748**	**119,357**	**96,080**

Note: Comprises new books (published for the first time), and new editions (with changes in text or format). Includes mass-market paperbacks. Excludes government publications, books sold only by subscription, dissertations, periodicals, quarterlies, and pamphlets under 49 pages. 1. Preliminary. **Source:** R.R. Bowker Co., *The Bowker Annual Library and Book Trade Almanac,* copyright 2001 Reed Elsevier Inc. Used with the permission of R.R. Bowker ® a business unit of Reed Elsevier Inc.

The American Library Association's 75 Most Frequently Challenged Books of 1990-99

Rank, Title, Author

1. *Scary Stories* (Series), Alvin Schwartz
2. *Daddy's Roommate,* Michael Willhoite
3. *I Know Why the Caged Bird Sings,* Maya Angelou
4. *The Chocolate War,* Robert Cormier
5. *The Adventures of Huckleberry Finn,* Mark Twain
6. *Of Mice and Men,* John Steinbeck
7. *Forever,* Judy Blume
8. *Bridge to Terabithia,* Katherine Paterson
9. *Heather Has Two Mommies,* Leslea Newman
10. *The Catcher in the Rye,* J.D. Salinger
11. *The Giver,* Lois Lowry
12. *My Brother Sam is Dead,* James Lincoln Collier and Christopher Collier
13. *It's Perfectly Normal,* Robie Harris
14. *Alice* (Series), Phyllis Reynolds Naylor
15. *Goosebumps* (Series), R.L. Stine
16. *A Day No Pigs Would Die,* Robert Newton Peck
17. *The Color Purple,* Alice Walker
18. *Sex,* Madonna
19. *Earth's Children* (Series), Jean M. Auel
20. *The Great Gilly Hopkins,* Katherine Paterson
21. *In the Night Kitchen,* Maurice Sendak
22. *The Witches,* Roald Dahl
23. *A Wrinkle in Time,* Madeleine L'Engle
24. *The New Joy of Gay Sex,* Charles Silverstein
25. *Go Ask Alice,* Anonymous
26. *The Goats,* Brock Cole
27. *The Stupids* (Series), Harry Allard
28. *Anastasia Krupnik* (Series), Lois Lowry
29. *Final Exit,* Derek Humphry
30. *Blubber,* Judy Blume
31. *Halloween ABC,* Eve Merriam
32. *Julie of the Wolves,* Jean Craighead George
33. *Kaffir Boy,* Mark Mathabane
34. *The Bluest Eye,* Toni Morrison
35. *What's Happening to my Body? Book for Girls: A Growing-Up Guide,* Lynda Madaras
36. *Fallen Angels,* Walter Dean Myers
37. *The Handmaid's Tale,* Margaret Atwood
38. *The Outsiders,* S.E. Hinton

Rank, Title, Author

39. *The Pigman,* Paul Zindel
40. *To Kill a Mockingbird,* Harper Lee
41. *We All Fall Down,* Robert Cormier
42. *Deenie,* Judy Blume
43. *Flowers for Algernon,* Daniel Keyes
44. *Annie on my Mind,* Nancy Garden
45. *Beloved,* Toni Morrison
46. *The Boy Who Lost His Face,* Louis Sachar
47. *Cross Your Fingers, Spit in Your Hat,* Alvin Schwartz
48. *Harry Potter* (Series), J.K. Rowling
49. *Cujo,* Stephen King
50. *James and the Giant Peach,* Roald Dahl
51. *A Light in the Attic,* Shel Silverstein
52. *Ordinary People,* Judith Guest
53. *American Psycho,* Bret Easton Ellis
54. *Brave New World,* Aldous Huxley
55. *Sleeping Beauty Trilogy,* A.N. Roquelaure (Anne Rice)
56. *Bumps in the Night,* Harry Allard
57. *Asking About Sex and Growing Up,* Joanna Cole
58. *What's Happening to my Body? Book for Boys: A Growing-Up Guide,* Lynda Madaras
59. *The Anarchist Cookbook,* William Powell
60. *Are You There, God? It's Me, Margaret,* Judy Blume
61. *Boys and Sex,* Wardell Pomeroy
62. *Crazy Lady,* Jane Conly
63. *Athletic Shorts,* Chris Crutcher
64. *Killing Mr. Griffin,* Lois Duncan
65. *Fade,* Robert Cormier
66. *Guess What?,* Mem Fox
67. *Slaughterhouse-Five,* Kurt Vonnegut
68. *Lord of the Flies,* William Golding
69. *Native Son,* Richard Wright
70. *Women on Top: How Real Life Has Changed Women's Fantasies,* Nancy Friday
71. *Curses, Hexes and Spells,* Daniel Cohen
72. *On My Honor,* Marion Dane Bauer
73. *The House of Spirits,* Isabel Allende
74. *Jack,* A.M. Homes
75. *Arizona Kid,* Ron Koertge

Source: American Library Organization.

THE ELECTRONIC MEDIA

▶ **TELEVISION**

Few people today doubt the pervasiveness of television's influence on America. Once a symbol of luxury, the color television has found its way into almost every home in America, and a great majority of American households have two or more televisions. According to the A.C. Nielsen Company, which monitors television viewership, at least one of these televisions was on in each household for seven hours and 37 minutes during the 1998–99 television season. That's an hour and 18 minutes more than in 1971, when the average was just over 6 hours and 19 minutes, but three minutes less than in 1997–98. Average daily viewing per person is still much higher than 1970s levels, but down slightly from the year before. Women over the age of 18 watched longest: they averaged four hours and 51 minutes per day, (down two minutes from the year before), while men over 18 watched for four hours and 16 minutes (down from 4:16 in 1997–98). Children aged

Top 50 Single Shows in TV History, by Rating

Rank/Program	Date	Network	Rating	Share
1. M*A*S*H Special (Last episode)	2/28/83	CBS	60.2%	77%
2. Dallas (Who Shot J.R.?)	11/21/80	CBS	53.3	76
3. Roots, part 8	1/30/77	ABC	51.1	71
4. Super Bowl XVI (San Francisco/Cincinnati)	1/24/82	CBS	49.1	73
5. Super Bowl XVII (Washington/Miami)	1/30/83	NBC	48.6	69
6. XVII Winter Olympics (Figure skating round 1)	2/23/94	CBS	48.5	64
7. Super Bowl XX (Chicago/New England)	1/26/86	NBC	48.3	70
8. Gone With the Wind, part 1	11/7/76	NBC	47.7	65
9. Gone With the Wind, part 2	11/8/76	NBC	47.4	64
10. Super Bowl XII (Dallas/Denver)	1/15/78	CBS	47.2	67
11. Super Bowl XIII (Pittsburgh/Dallas)	1/21/79	NBC	47.1	74
12. Bob Hope Christmas Show	1/15/70	NBC	46.6	64
13. Super Bowl XVIII (L.A. Raiders/Washington)	1/22/84	CBS	46.4	71
14. Super Bowl XIX (San Francisco/Miami)	1/20/85	ABC	46.4	63
15. Super Bowl XIV (Pittsburgh/L.A. Rams)	1/20/80	CBS	46.3	67
16. Super Bowl XXX (Dallas/Pittsburgh)	1/28/96	NBC	46.0	68
17. ABC Theater "The Day After"	1/20/83	ABC	46.0	62
18. The Fugitive	8/29/67	ABC	45.9	72
19. Roots, part 6	1/28/77	ABC	45.9	66
20. Super Bowl XXI (N.Y. Giants/Denver)	1/25/87	CBS	45.8	66
21. Roots, part 5	1/27/77	ABC	45.7	71
22. Super Bowl XXVIII (Dallas/Buffalo)	1/30/94	NBC	45.5	66
23. Cheers (Last episode)	5/20/93	NBC	45.5	64
24. The Ed Sullivan Show	2/9/64	CBS	45.3	60
25. Super Bowl XXVII (Dallas/Buffalo)	1/31/93	NBC	45.1	66
26. Bob Hope Christmas Show	1/14/71	NBC	45.0	61
27. Roots, part 3	1/25/77	ABC	44.8	68
28. Super Bowl XXXII (Denver/Green Bay)	1/25/98	NBC	44.5	67
29. Super Bowl XI (Oakland/Minnesota)	1/9/77	NBC	44.4	73
30. Super Bowl XV (Oakland/Philadelphia)	1/25/81	NBC	44.4	63
31. Super Bowl VI (Dallas/Miami)	1/16/72	CBS	44.2	74
32. XVII Winter Olympics (Figure skating finals)	2/25/94	CBS	44.1	64
33. Roots, part 2	1/24/77	ABC	44.1	62
34. The Beverly Hillbillies	1/8/64	CBS	44.0	65
35. Roots, part 4	1/26/77	ABC	43.8	66
36. The Ed Sullivan Show (with the Beatles)	2/16/64	CBS	43.8	60
37. Super Bowl XXIII (San Francisco/Cincinnati)	1/22/89	NBC	43.5	68
38. Academy Awards	4/7/70	ABC	43.4	78
39. Super Bowl XXXI (Green Bay/New England)	1/26/97	FOX	43.3	65
40. Super Bowl XXXIV (St. Louis/Tennessee)	1/30/00	ABC	43.3	63
41. The Thorn Birds, part 3	3/29/83	ABC	43.2	62
42. The Thorn Birds, part 4	3/30/83	ABC	43.1	62
43. NFC Championship game (San Francisco/Dallas)	1/10/82	CBS	42.9	62
44. The Beverly Hillbillies	1/15/64	CBS	42.8	62
45. Super Bowl VII (Miami/Washington)	1/14/73	NBC	42.7	72
46. The Thorn Birds, part 2	3/28/83	ABC	42.5	59
47. Super Bowl IX (Pittsburgh/Minnesota)	1/12/75	NBC	42.4	72
48. The Beverly Hillbillies	2/26/64	CBS	42.4	60
49. Super Bowl X (Pittsburgh/Dallas)	1/18/76	CBS	42.3	78
50. Roots, part 7	1/29/77	ABC	42.3	65

Note: As of August 6, 2001. Does not include programs broadcast on more than one network, e.g. the Apollo moon landing or programs under 30 minutes scheduled duration. **Rating** is the number of people watching as a percentage of all television owners. **Share** is the number watching as a percentage of people with their TVs on at that particular time. **Source:** Nielsen Media Research.

12–17 watched an average of 2 hours and 54 minutes, down dramatically from 3:07 in 1997–98 and a half hour less than in 1984–85. Viewing by children 2–11 has dropped from 3 hours and 49 minutes in 1984–85 to three hours and 3 minutes in 1997–98. Primetime viewership is highest on Sunday nights (106 million people) and lowest on Friday and Saturday nights (89.7 million).

▶ CABLE TELEVISION

Cable television was originally designed as a means of improving TV reception in some rural areas. In the 1960s, operators realized that viewers were willing to pay for commercial-free pro-

gramming, but their efforts to capitalize on the idea were hampered by stringent Federal Communications Commission restrictions. Not until 1975, when RCA put its first communications satellite into operation, did the industry really

Longest Running National Network Series of All Time

Program	Seasons	Years[1]
Walt Disney	33	1954-90
60 Minutes	34	1968-
The Ed Sullivan Show	24	1948-71
Gunsmoke	20	1955-75
The Red Skelton Show	20	1951-71
Meet the Press	18	1947-65[2]
What's My Line	18	1950-67
I've Got a Secret	17	1952-76
Lassie	17	1954-71
The Lawrence Welk Show	17	1955-71

Note: Includes prime-time (6-11 p.m.) shows only; sports broadcasts and movie series are not included. 1. Dates reflect the first and last broadcasts of each show. Programs did not necessarily run continuously throughout this period. 2. Ceased broadcasting in prime-time in 1965, though still on the air.

Top 20 TV Shows of 2000-01

Rank, Program (Network)	Avg. rating	Avg. share
1. *Survivor II* (CBS)	17.4	27
2. *E.R.* (NBC)	15.2	25
3. *Who Wants to Be a Millionaire?* (ABC)[1]	13.7	22
4. *Who Wants to Be a Millionaire?* (ABC)[2]	13.0	21
5. *Friends* (NBC)	12.9	21
6. *NFL Monday Night Football* (ABC)	12.7	22
7. *Everybody Loves Raymond* (CBS)	12.6	19
8. *Who Wants to Be a Millionaire?* (ABC)[3]	12.6	18
9. *Law & Order* (NBC)	12.3	20
10. *The Practice* (ABC)	12.0	19
11. *CSI* (CBS)	11.7	19
12. *Who Wants to Be a Millionaire?* (ABC)[4]	11.6	18
13. *West Wing* (NBC)	11.6	18
14. *Will & Grace* (NBC)	11.4	17
15. *60 Minutes* (CBS)	11.1	19
16. *Cursed* (NBC)	10.9	17
17. *Becker* (CBS)	10.9	16
18. *Temptation Island* (FOX)	10.7	16
19. *Frasier* (NBC)	10.7	16
20. *Who Wants to Be a Millionaire?* (ABC)[5]	10.5	18

Note: For the 2000-2001 season through May 23, 2001. Does not include "movie of the week" programs or programs broadcast for fewer than 10 weeks. *Rating* is the percentage of all television owners watching that program. *Share* is the percentage of TVs that are on at the time of the program. For example, on a given Thursday night, 25 percent of the people watching TV at 10 P.M. were tuned to *E.R.*, but because not every TV owner was watching television that night, only 15.2 percent of all TV owners were tuned in to *E.R.* 1. Wednesday. 2.Tuesday. 3. Sunday. 4. Thursday. 5. Friday. **Source:** Nielsen Media Research.

Primetime Viewing Shares of Free and Cable TV Networks, 1995-2000

	'95-96	'96-97	'97-98	'98-99	'99-00
DAYTIME					
Pay Cable	5%	6%	7%	6%	5%
Basic Cable	30	33	35	36	41
Public	3	3	3	3	3
Independents	11	11	11	11	11
Network Affiliates	51	47	44	42	40
PRIMETIME					
Pay Cable	5%	5%	6%	6%	5%
Basic Cable	26	30	33	36	36
Public	3	3	4	3	3
Independents	10	10	10	11	11
Network Affiliates	56	51	48	45	45

Note: Due to multiset use and independent roundings, totals add up to more than 100. **Source:** Nielsen Media Research.

Top 15 Cable Television Networks, 2000-01

Rank/Network	Subscribers (millions)	Number of systems	Launch date	Content
1. TBS Superstation	82.0	11,668	1976	Movies, sports, original & syndicated shows
2. The Discovery Channel	81.7	N.A.	1985	Nonfiction, nature, science
3. TNT (Turner Network Television)	81.6	10,637	1988	Movies, sports, and original programming.
4. ESPN	81.0	N.A.	1979	Sports events and sports news
5. USA Network	81.0	N.A.	1980	Sports, family entertainment
6. Fox Family Channel	80.5	13,700	1998	Original and syndicated family programming.
7. A&E Television	80.4	12,000[1]	1984	Original programming, biographies, documentaries.
8. The National Network (TNN)	80.1	N.A.	1983	Original programming, syndicated shows
9. Lifetime Television	79.9	11,000[2]	1984	Programming aimed at women
10. Nickelodeon/Nick at Nite	79.8	11,788	1979	Programming for kids
11. Cable News Network (CNN)	79.7	11,528	1980	24-hour news, special interest reports
12. C-SPAN	79.4	7,047	1979	Public affairs, live Congressional coverage
13. The Weather Channel	78.9	12,763	1982	Weather updates
14. The Learning Channel (TLC)	78.0	N.A.	1980	Science, history, nonfiction
15. MTV (Music Television)	77.3	9,176	1981	Music videos

Notes: 1. US and Canada. 2. Estimate.
Source: National Cable & Telecommunications Association, *National Cable & Telecommunications Developments, 2001.*

bloom. Under the name Home Box Office, the company started to transmit programming that could be received by independent operators around the country and then relayed to subscribers at minimal cost. With the dismissal of most of the FCC's regulations by a federal court in 1977, the door was opened for the development of what is now a multibillion-dollar industry.

As the accompanying table demonstrates, cable has changed the television broadcasting landscape, drawing away more than one-third of the total television viewing audiences. As a result, the fractured total television audience means that no single program will likely ever reach the kind of viewership numbers achieved during the 1960s and 70s, when viewers had only three or four choices. A case in point: the final episode of Survivor II, broadcast in the summer of 2001, was one of the most talked-about programs in a decade, but it didn't attract as many viewers as regular episodes of The Beverly Hillbillies.

The number of cable subscribers is currently increasing by about a half million per year. But despite deregulation and increased competition from direct satellite providers, the average cable bill continues to increase. It was $7.69 in 1980; in 1999, it was $28.92, an increase of 276 percent over 19 years. The number of digital cable subscribers

Top 5 Pay-Cable Services, 2000

Rank/Network	Subscribers	Content
1. The Disney Channel[1]	67,000,000	Movies, cartoons
2. HBO/Cinemax	37,000,000	Movies, variety, sports, documentaries
3. Showtime/The Movie Channel	25,500,000	Movies, variety, comedy, sports
4. Encore	24,500,000	On-demand movies
5. Spice	11,000,000	Adult movies

1. Disney is a basic cable service on some cable systems.
Source: National Cable Television Association, Cable TV Developments (Spring, 2001).

Basic and Pay Cable TV Systems and Subscribers, 1952–2001

Year	Number of of systems	Basic cable Subscribers	Percent of U.S. TV households	Pay cable Subscribers	Percent of households with cable
1952	70	14,000	0.1%	N.A.	N.A.
1955	400	150,000	0.5	N.A.	N.A.
1960	640	650,000	1.4	N.A.	N.A.
1970	2,490	3,900,000	6.7	N.A.	N.A.
1975	3,506	9,196,690	13.2	469,000	23.6%
1980	4,225	17,671,490	22.6	9,144,000	50.6
1985	6,600	39,872,520	46.2	30,596,000	83.5
1990	9,575	54,871,330	59.0	39,900,000	77.1
1995	11,218	62,956,470	65.7	46,100,000	74.2
1998	10,845	67,011,180	67.4	47,700,000	72.2
1999	10,700	68,537,980	68.0	49,200,000	73.1
2000	11,197	69,368,920	67.9	48,300,000	71.5
2001	10,243	69,501,440	68.0	48,300,000	69.5

Sources: National Cable Television Association, Cable TV Developments (Spring, 2001) Nielsen Media Research.

Video and Audio: Sales & Penetration in U.S. Homes, 1990–2000

Product	Sales (thousands of units) 1990	1998	1999	2000[1]	Percent of U.S. homes 1990	1998	1999	2000
Video								
Analog color TV	20,384	22,204	23,218	23,776	96%	98%	98%	98%
Projection TV	351	1,070	1,232	1,460	6	13	14	15
Digital TV set	N.A.	14	121	625	N.A.	N.A.	N.A.	N.A.
TV/VCR combination	424	3,147	4,418	5,009	N.A.	13	17	20
VCR[2]	11,986	27,198	34,347	36,060	68	91	92	94
DVD player	N.A.	1,079	4,072	8,258	N.A.	0	3	7
Camcorder	2,962	4,006	4,790	5,702	10	32	35	38
Satellite dish	330	2,685	3,625	4,250	3	10	12	15
Audio								
Home Radio	21,585	18,734	19,899	21,654	99%	98%	98%	98%
Rack audio system	1,557	367	270	143	92	54	55	55
Compact disc player	9,155	40,507	45,225	56,531	19	49	52	55
Compact audio system	2,447	8,946	10,600	11,836	N.A.	36	38	40

N.A.= Not available. 1. Estimate. 2. Includes mono and stereo decks, but not machines that play but do not record. Does not include TV/VCR combinations. **Source:** Consumer Electronics U.S. Sales, © 2000 Electronic Industries Association. Reprinted by permission.

has increased from 1.5 million in 1998 to 12.2 million in August, 2001. Over the same time period, the number of cable modem subscribers (allowing cable connections to the Internet) has increased from 500,000 to 5.5 million.

The nation's two biggest cable providers are AT&T Broadband (14 million subscribers) and AOL Time Warner (12.7 million). In the wake of the government's decision to drop antitrust litigation against Microsoft, AOL announced a plan in the summer of 2001 to acquire AT&T's cable operations. The combined entity would have as many subscribers as the four next-largest cable companies combined.

Radio Stations by Primary Format, 1990–2001

Format	1990	1999	2001
Total commercial stations	9,444	10,444	10,516
Country	2,452	2,305	2,190
Adult contemporary	2,135	775	709
News, Talk, Business, Sports	405	1,159	1,139
Religion (teaching & music)	745	363	356
Oldies & Classic hits	659	766	786
Rock (Album, Modern, Classic)	419	730	760
Spanish & other ethnic	342	618	667
Adult standards	383	595	569
Top 40	824	401	468
R&B, Urban adult contemporary	N.A.	278	301
Jazz	N.A.	72	81
Variety	97	39	39
Classical, Fine arts	52	38	34
Easy listening	240	34	27
Pre-teen	3	51	55
Comedy	1	0	0
Off Air	210	96	113
Changing formats or not available	115	3	3
Total non-commercial stations	1,636	2,366	2,542
Total all stations	11,080	12,810	13,058

Note: As of November of each year. **Source:** M Street Corporation, 2001.

U.S. Radio Stations and Radio Sales, 1946–2000

Year	Radio stations on air[1]	Unit sales to dealers[2]
1946	961	N.A.
1950	2,773	N.A.
1955	3,211	7,327
1960	4,133	18,031
1965	5,249	31,689
1970	6,760	34,049
1975	7,744	25,276
1980	8,566	27,104
1985	10,359	21,575
1990	10,788	21,585
1995	11,834	17,051
1996	12,295	17,581
1997	12,482	17,664
1998	12,641	18,734
1999	12,641	19,899
2000	N.A.	21,654[3]

1. Includes AM and FM, commercial and noncommercial. 2. Includes table, clock, and portable—but not car—radios. 3. Estimate **Source:** M Street Corporation, 2001; Electronic Industries Association, *Consumer Electronics, U.S. Sales* (2000).

▶RADIO

According to statistics compiled by the Radio Advertising Bureau, 98 percent of all U.S. households own at least one radio. Of Americans over age 12, 95.3 percent listen to radio for an average of 3 hours and 20 minutes each workday. There are a total of 576.5 million radios in the U.S., 26 percent more than in 1980, distributed as follows: 367.4 million are in homes, 142.8 million in cars, 43.7 million in trucks, vans, and RVs, and 22.6 million in the workplace.

▶THE RECORDING INDUSTRY

In fewer than 10 years, the compact disc has gone from technological breakthrough to the music format of choice among most consumers. Along the way, it resuscitated an industry that many feared was sagging at the hands of video games, computers, and movies.

Fewer than 100,000 CDs were sold in 1983, the first year they were available, but the format quickly overtook LPs by 1988, and topped cassette sales in 1992. More than two-thirds of all music sold is now produced on CDs. The recording industry's willingness to support the new technology, by releasing a large amount of music on disc, has no doubt played a large part in the CD's growth. And why shouldn't it? Discs cost no more than albums or cassettes to produce, yet consumers are still willing to pay about twice as much for the digital format. The CD has also revived the entire music industry, which in the late 1970s and early 80s was worried about losing young consumers to movies and videogames. The industry was also concerned that home taping was cutting into sales of records. With the CD's superior sound quality, that's no longer a serious issue. The total U.S. dollar value of all music sold in 2000 was $14.3 billion, down from $14.6 billion in 1999, but more than double the amount as recently as 1989 ($6.6 billion).

Sales by Category

The sales of different types of music are in almost as constant a flux as the music types themselves. The category defined as rock accounted for nearly half of all music sales in 1987; in 1998, it was only a quarter. Country, Rhythm & Blues, and Rap have made up the difference. For many years, the single largest group of recorded music consumers (as a percentage of total dollar value) was teenagers (buyers aged 15-19). But the high price of music and Internet music sharing sites have cut into record sales among younger consumers. Since 1996, the percentage of music purchases by

Top-Selling Albums of 2000

Title	Artist	Copies sold (millions)
No Strings Attached	'N Sync	9.9
Marshall Mathers LP	Eminem	7.9
Oops!. . . I Did it Again	Britney Spears	7.9
Supernatural	Santana	5.8
Human Clay	Creed	6.6
One	The Beatles	5.0
Country Grammar	Nelly	5.0
Black and Blue	Backstreet Boys	4.3
Dr. Dre 2001	Dr. Dre	3.9
Writing's on the Wall	Destiny's Child	3.8

Source: *Soundscan*, 2001

Recorded Music Sales by Genre, Format, and Age Group, 1987–2000

Characteristic	1987	1990	1995	1996	1997	1998	1999	2000
Genre								
Rock	45.5%	36.1%	33.5%	32.6%	32.5%	25.7%	25.2%	24.8%
Country	10.6	9.6	16.7	14.7	14.4	14.1	10.8	10.7
R&B	9.0	11.6	11.3	12.1	11.2	12.8	10.5	9.7
Pop	13.5	13.7	10.1	9.3	9.4	10.0	10.3	11.0
Rap	3.8	8.5	6.7	8.9	10.1	9.7	10.8	12.9
Gospel	2.9	2.5	3.1	4.3	4.5	6.3	5.1	4.8
Classical	3.9	3.1	2.9	3.4	2.8	3.3	3.5	2.7
Jazz	3.8	4.8	3.0	3.3	2.8	1.9	3.0	2.9
Soundtracks	N.A.	0.8	0.9	0.8	1.2	1.7	0.8	0.7
Oldies	N.A.	0.8	1.0	0.8	0.8	0.7	0.7	0.9
New Age	N.A.	1.1	0.7	0.7	0.8	0.6	0.5	0.5
Children's	N.A.	0.5	0.5	0.7	0.9	0.4	0.4	0.6
Other[1]	6.2	8.8	10.1	8.2	9.4	11.3	9.1	8.3
Format								
CDs	11.5%	31.1%	65.0%	68.4%	70.2%	74.8%	83.2%	89.3%
Cassettes	62.5	54.7	25.1	19.3	18.2	14.8	8.0	4.9
LPs	20.1	4.7	0.5	0.6	0.7	0.7	0.5	0.5
Singles (all types)	5.7	8.7	7.5	9.3	9.3	6.8	5.4	2.5
Music videos	N.A.	N.A.	0.9	1.0	0.6	1.0	0.9	0.8
Age group								
10-14	7.3%	7.6%	8.0%	7.9%	8.9%	9.1%	8.5%	8.9%
15-19	24.2	18.3	17.1	17.2	16.8	15.8	12.6	12.9
20-24	19.1	16.5	15.3	15.0	13.8	12.2	12.6	12.5
25-29	14.5	14.6	12.3	12.5	11.7	11.4	10.5	10.6
30-34	10.8	13.2	12.1	11.4	11.0	11.4	10.1	9.8
35-39	8.2	10.2	10.8	11.1	11.6	12.6	10.4	10.6
40-44	4.8	7.8	7.5	9.1	8.8	8.3	9.3	9.6
45+	10.7	11.1	16.1	15.1	16.5	18.1	24.7	23.8

Note: Figures represent a percentage of that year's total U.S. dollar sales. 1. Includes Ethnic, Standards, Big Band, Swing, Latin, Electronic, Instrumental, Comedy, Humor, Spoken Word, Exercise, Language, Folk and Holiday Music. Totals may not add to 100 percent due to "Don't Know/No Answer" Responses. **Source:** Recording Industry Association of America, *2000 Consumer Profile.*

buyers over 40 has been increasing, while purchases by buyers under 25 have declined, compared with just 12.6 percent by 15-19-year-olds. Women made almost half of the music purchases in the U.S. in 2000, up from 45.9 percent in 1991.

A decision in 1996 by Wal-Mart stores to restrict music sales of albums with controversial lyrics caused understandable consternation among record executives because of discount stores' increasing influence on the industry's bottom line. In 1989, 71.7 percent of all recorded music was sold in record stores, while 15.6 percent was sold in "other stores," which includes discount and consumer electronic stores. In 2000, record stores accounted for less than half of all music purchases (42.4 percent), while the Wal-Marts, Kmarts, and Targets of America made up 40.8 percent of music sales. In many remote areas, the local Wal-Mart is the only place to buy recorded music of any kind, forcing many top musical acts to release special Wal-Mart versions of their albums, with bowdlerized lyrics. Music purchases via the Internet grew from 0.3 percent in 1997 to 3.2 percent in 2000.

Individual Record Sales
Up until 1958, the term **gold** album simply meant a hit album. But in that year, the Recording Industry Association of America codified the term to mean a record that had reached $1 million in sales. (Separate levels were established for singles, which have since been amended.) The cast album from *Oklahoma!* was the first gold album. By 1975, inflation had diluted the importance of the award, so the RIAA also required gold records to sell at

least 500,000 copies. The following year, it introduced the **platinum** record, awarded to albums that sell at least one million copies. The Eagles' *Their Greatest Hits 1971-1975* was the first platinum album, and is to date, the largest-selling album of all time, with 26 million copies sold. **Multi-platinum** awards go to albums selling more than two million copies. In 1999, the RIAA introduced the **diamond** award, for singles or records with U.S. sales of 10 million or more. As of August 2001, more than 80 titles had qualified for the award, in genres ranging from pop, R&B, and rock to rap, country, and instrumental. The Beatles have the most diamond records (five).

Napster, the online service that allowed users to find and copy music from other peoples' computers without paying for it, was forced to stop the process known as file sharing in 2000 because of a lawsuit brought by the music industry. Fearing that consumers would be able to share copies of DVDs, the movie industry joined the fight against file sharing in 2000. In the wake of the court decision against Napster, however, several other online services (most of them without central computer servers, thus making them more difficult to police) began facilitating file sharing among their users.

▶VIDEO
Video Cassette Recorders (VCRs)
In 20 years, the video cassette recorder (VCR) has gone from a curiosity to a luxury to an appliance found in more than 90 percent of American homes. The vast majority of people continue to use their VCRs simply to watch pre-recorded

videos from their local rental store. But a sizable number of owners have figured out how to program their VCRs and were responsible for the sale of 400 million blank cassettes in 2000.

DVD (Digital Video Discs)

DVD (Digital Video Discs) are the fastest-growing consumer electronics product in history, with 2001 sales of 12.5 million units, up 50 percent over the previous year. Industry analysts predict the DVD player will soon overtake the VCR. DVDs resemble CDs, but are capable of storing an entire feature-length film (and then some). The average wholesale price for a DVD is $15 to $20; they are more durable than VHS tapes and take up much less space. Although only about 15 percent of

American homes have a DVD player (compared with 94 percent number for a VCR), many video rental stores now carry movies in both VHS and DVD format. When DVD players are capable of recording, however, those numbers will change dramatically. Until then, most people are likely to continue to use their VCRs.

▶FILM

The motion picture industry does nearly $8 billion in business each year. A relatively small number of people are involved in this endeavor: only 631,000 in 2000. The various studios produce about 700 films per year; they submit about half of these films to the Motion Picture Association of America for ratings and wide release in theaters. Two-thirds of these movies (69 percent in 2000) receive an R rating. The rest receive a PG or PG-13 rating. Only 5 percent of 1999 movies were G-rated, and even fewer (less than 1 percent) received an NC-17 or X-rating. Because many theaters simply refuse to show NC-17 movies, producers are loath to release a film with an NC-17 label. The number of movie screens has more than doubled since 1985. Single-screen theaters made up 32 percent of all movie theaters; miniplexes accounted for 43 percent. There were 1,478 multiplexes (8-15 screens) and 405 megaplexes (16 or more screens) in 2000.

Movie Budgets

The cost of making movies has escalated dramatically in recent years. In 1988, the average price tag of a motion picture was $18.1 million. Today, that's less than the average marketing budget for a feature film. Rising actors' salaries, increased demand for special effects, and other spiraling costs drove the average cost of making a movie to a whopping $54.8 million in 2000, up a staggering 50.7 percent over 1995 ($36.4 million). The cost of making a movie has doubled just since 1991 ($26.1 million), when the special effects of *Terminator 2* were cutting edge. In addition to these production costs, studios spent an average of $27.3 million on advertising and publicity in 2000, or more than double what they spent in 1991 ($12.1 million).

Top Selling and Renting Videos, 2000

VHS	DVD
SALES	
1. Tarzan	1. The Matrix
2. Toy Story 2	2. The Sixth Sense
3. Stuart Little	3. The Green Mile
4. The Matrix	4. Gladiator (2000)
5. Star Wars Episode One: The Phantom Menace	5. American Pie
6. The Little Mermaid II: Return to Sea	6. End Of Days
7. Pokemon: The First Movie	7. Braveheart
8. The Sixth Sense	8. The Perfect Storm
9. Big Daddy	9. X-Men (Live Action)
10. Erin Brockovich	10. Erin Brockovich
RENTALS	
1. The Sixth Sense	1. The Matrix
2. The Green Mile	2. The Sixth Sense
3. The Matrix	3. The Green Mile
4. Double Jeopardy	4. American Pie
5. American Pie	5. Runaway Bride
6. Runaway Bride	6. Gladiator
7. American Beauty	7. Sleepy Hollow
8. Sleepy Hollow	8. Fight Club
9. The Bone Collector	9. The Bone Collector
10. The General's Daughter	10. The Patriot

Note: Rental figures are based on number of transactions; sales figures are based on number of purchases, not dollar value.
Source: Alexander & Associates/Video Flash.

U.S. Film Box-Office Receipts, Screens, Admission, and Admission Charges, 1926–2000 (in current dollars)

Year	Box office receipts (millions)	Movie Screens Indoor	Movie Screens Drive-in	Annual admissions Total (millions)	Annual admissions Per person	Average admission charge	Number of $20 million hits
1926	$ 720.0	N.A.	N.A.	2,600	N.A.	N.A.	N.A.
1930	732.0	N.A.	N.A.	4,680	N.A.	N.A.	N.A.
1935	566.0	N.A.	N.A.	3,900	N.A.	$0.24	N.A.
1940	735.0	N.A.	N.A.	4,160	N.A.	0.24	N.A.
1950	1,376.0	N.A.	N.A.	3,120	N.A.	0.53	N.A.
1960	951.0	N.A.	N.A.	2,080	N.A.	0.69	N.A.
1970[1]	1,162.0	10,335	3,720	920	N.A.	1.55	N.A.
1980	2,748.5	14,029	3,561	1,022	4.5	2.69	17
1990[2]	5,021.8	22,774	915	1,189	4.8	4.23	30
1995	5,493.5	26,958	847	1,263	4.8	4.35	36
1998	6,949.0	33,440	746	1,481	5.5	4.69	37
1999	7,448.0	36,448	737	1,465	5.4	5.08	42
2000	7,661.0	36,679	717	1,421	5.2	5.39	49

1. Theater figures are for 1971. 2. Beginning in 1990, admission totals and average prices are supplied by the National Association of Theater Owners and are not strictly comparable with data from previous years, which are based on the U.S. Department of Commerce's Consumer Price Index. **Source:** U.S. Dept. of Commerce; *Film Daily Yearbook; Motion Picture Association of America, 2000 U.S. Economic Review.*

20 Top-Grossing Feature Films, 2000

Rank, Film	Distributor	Director	Gross
1. *Dr. Seuss' How the Grinch Stole Christmas*	Universal	Ron Howard	$260,031,035
2. *Cast Away*	Fox	Robert Zemeckis	233,620,604
3. *Mission: Impossible 2*	Paramount	John Woo	215,409,889
4. *Gladiator*	Dreamworks	Ridley Scott	187,670,866
5. *What Women Want*	Paramount	Nancy Meyers	182,805,123
6. *The Perfect Storm*	Warner Bros.	Wolfgang Petersen	182,618,434
7. *Meet the Parents*	Universal	Jay Roach	166,225,040
8. *X-Men*	Fox	Bryan Singer	157,299,717
9. *Scary Movie*	Miramax/Dimension	Keenen Ivory Wayans	156,997,084
10. *What Lies Beneath*	Dreamworks	Robert Zemeckis	155,359,812
11. *Dinosaur*	Buena Vista	Eric Leighton/Ralph Zondag	137,748,063
12. *Crouching Tiger, Hidden Dragon*	SPC	Ang Lee	127,954,638
13. *Erin Brockovich*	Universal	Steven Soderbergh	125,548,685
14. *Charlie's Angels*	Sony	Joseph McGinty Nichol	125,305,545
15. *Traffic*	USA Films	Steven Soderbergh	124,107,476
16. *Nutty Professor II: The Klumps*	Universal	Peter Segal	123,307,945
17. *Big Momma's House*	Fox	Raja Gosnell	117,559,438
18. *Remember the Titans*	Buena Vista	Boaz Yakin	115,648,585
19. *The Patriot*	Sony	Roland Emmerich	113,330,342
20. *Chicken Run*	Dreamworks	Peter Lord/Nick Park	106,834,564

Note: As of July 2001. **Source:** Exhibitor Relations Co., Inc.

Most Popular Films, By Decade

Title (Year)	Director	Rental (millions)	Title (Year)	Director	Rental (millions)
Pre-1930			**1970–79**		
The Birth of a Nation (1915)	D.W. Griffith	$10.0	*Star Wars* (1977)	G. Lucas	$193.77
The Big Parade (1925)	K. Vidor	5.5	*Jaws* (1975)	S. Spielberg	129.55
The Singing Fool (1928)	L. Bacon	4.0	*Grease* (1978)	R. Kleiser	96.30
			The Exorcist (1973)	W. Friedkin	89.00
1930–39			*The Godfather* (1972)	F. F. Coppola	86.30
Gone With the Wind (1939)	V. Fleming	$77.6			
Snow White and the Seven Dwarfs (1937)	(Animated)	62.8	**1980–89**		
			E.T.—The Extra-Terrestrial (1982)	S. Spielberg	$228.17
King Kong (1933)	M. Cooper	5.0	*Return of the Jedi* (1983)	R. Marquand	168.19
The Wizard of Oz (1939)	V. Fleming	4.5	*Batman* (1989)	T. Burton	150.50
San Francisco (1936)	W.S. Van Dyke	4.0	*The Empire Strikes Back* (1980)	J. Kershner	141.67
			Ghostbusters (1984)	I. Reitman	132.72
1940–49[1]			*Raiders of the Lost Ark* (1981)	S. Spielberg	115.60
Cinderella (1949)	(Animated)	$38.5	*Indiana Jones and the Last Crusade* (1989)	S. Spielberg	115.50
Pinocchio (1940)	(Animated)	32.9			
Song of the South (1946)	H. Foster/ W. Jackson	29.2	*Indiana Jones and the Temple of Doom* (1984)	S. Spielberg	109.00
Fantasia (1940)	(Animated)	28.5	*Beverly Hills Cop* (1984)	M. Brest	108.00
Bambi (1942)	(Animated)	28.4	*Back to the Future* (1985)	R. Zemeckis	105.50
1950–59			**1990–99**		
The Ten Commandments (1956)	C.B. DeMille	$43.0	*Titanic* (1997)	J. Cameron	$600.8
Lady and the Tramp (1955)	(Animated)	40.2	*Star Wars: Episode One -The Phantom Menace* (1999)	G. Lucas	431.1
Ben-Hur (1959)	W. Wyler	36.7	*Jurassic Park* (1993)	S. Spielberg	357.1
Around the World in 80 Days (1956)	M. Anderson	23.1	*Forrest Gump* (1994)	R. Zemeckis	329.7
Sleeping Beauty (1959)	(Animated)	21.5	*The Lion King* (1993)	R. Allers/R. Minkoff	312.9
			Independence Day (1996)	R. Emmerich	306.2
1960–69			*The Sixth Sense* (1999)	M. Shyamalan	293.5
The Sound of Music (1965)	R. Wise	$79.98	*Home Alone* (1990)	C. Columbus	285.7
Doctor Zhivago (1965)	D. Lean	60.96	*Men in Black* (1997)	B. Sonnenfeld	250.7
Butch Cassidy and the Sundance Kid (1969)	G.R. Hill	45.95	*Toy Story 2* (1999)	A. Brannon	245.8
Mary Poppins (1964)	R. Stevenson	45.00			
The Graduate (1968)	M. Nichols	44.09			

Note: Films from the 1990s are ranked according to their gross box office receipts. Films for previous decades are ranked according to film rentals, the portion of a film's box-office receipts paid by theater owners to the film's distribution company for renting the film. Figures include the U.S. and Canada. 1. All films listed for this decade were made by Disney studios and have been rereleased on a regular basis ever since. Their dominance on this chart is partly due to the fact that they are continually generating revenue.
Sources: *Variety,* Exhibitor Relations Co., Inc.

Top-Grossing Movies of All-Time

Because of inflation and periodic re-releases, it is nearly impossible to compare the successes of films from different eras. What is simpler to compare is the number of people who went to see a film, regardless of when it was released, and regardless of how much they paid for their ticket. To arrive at this number, the Exhibitor Relations Co. divides domestic gross receipts by the average ticket prices for the year(s) in which the film was released. The estimated number of admissions is then multiplied by the average ticket price ($5.60 in 2001) to give an idea of what each film's domestic gross would be if it were released today. It is admittedly an imperfect measure, but it makes it quite clear that despite its $600 million gross, *Titanic* will have to be re-released several times to match the success of *Gone With the Wind*, which has made only $200 million over the years, but has been seen by 70 million more people.

Rank, Film, (Year of Release)	Estimated admissions	Inflation-adjusted domestic gross
1. *Gone With the Wind* (1939)[1]	202,044,569	$1,131,449,586
2. *Star Wars* (1977)[1]	178,119,595	997,469,732
3. *The Sound of Music* (1965)[1]	142,415,376	797,526,106
4. *E.T. The Extra-Terrestrial* (1982)[1]	135,987,938	761,532,455
5. *The Ten Commandments* (1956)	131,000,000	733,600,000
6. *Titanic* (1997)	129,201,761	723,529,861
7. *Jaws* (1975)[1]	128,078,818	717,241,379
8. *Snow White and the Seven Dwarfs* (1937)[1]	109,000,000	610,400,000
9. *101 Dalmatians* (1961)[1]	99,917,251	559,536,606
10. *The Empire Strikes Back* (1980)[1]	98,106,044	549,393,846

Note: As of July 10, 2001. 1. Includes re-issues. Grosses for all films prior to 1980 are estimated from the film rental, which is approximately 50 percent of the gross. **Source:** Exhibitor Relations Co., Inc.

▶COMPUTER AND VIDEO GAMES

Computer and video games have come a long way since Pong and Atari. The modern video game industry took root in the mid 1990s, as computers with CD-ROM players became standard equipment on PCs. The computer and video game industry showed dramatic growth in recent years, shooting from sales of $3.7 billion in 1996 to $6.1 billion in 1999. The industry remained relatively stable in 2000, with sales just over $6 billion.

Strictly speaking, computer games are played on personal computers, while video games require their own separate console. Video game sales totaled $4.1 billion in 1998, while computer game sales topped $1.55 billion. PC and video game unit sales increased from 215 million to 219 million in the U.S. alone; that's an average of nearly two games per household per year. PC owners also say they spend more time playing games than using any other application, including word processing and email.

The stereotypical computer and video game player is a young male, but in 2000 women constituted 43 percent of the game-playing population, while some 72 percent of PC game players were over the age of 18, compared to 58 percent of video game players. Overall, about 145 million Americans play these games on a regular basis, about double the number of people who attended Major League Baseball games in 1999 and three times the number of people who attended the top five amusement parks that year.

Top-Selling Computer & Video Games, 2000

Computer Games		Video Games	
Rank, Title	Publisher	Rank, Title (Platform)	Publisher
1. The Sims	Electronic Arts	1. Pokemon Silver (Game Boy)	Nintendo
2. Who Wants to be a Millionaire	Disney Interactive	2. Pokemon Gold (Game Boy)	Nintendo
		3. Pokemon Stadium (Nintendo 64)	Nintendo
3. Roller Coaster Tycoon	Hasbro Interactive	4. Pokemon Yellow	Nintendo
4. Diablo 2	Blizzard	5. Tony Hawk's Pro Skater 2 (PlayStation)	Activision
5. Who Wants to be a Millionaire 2	Disney Interactive		
		6. Legend of Zelda: Majora's Mask (Nintendo 64)	Nintendo
6. The Sims Livin' Large	Electronic Arts		
7. Sim Theme Park World	Electronic Arts	7. Tony Hawk's Pro Skater (Playstation)	Activision
8. Age of Empires II	Microsoft		
9. Roller Coaster Tycoon: Loopy Landscapes	Hasbro Interactive	8. Gran Turismo 2 (PlayStation)	Sony
		9. Pokemon Blue (Game Boy)	Nintendo
10. Roller Coaster Tycoon: Corkscrew Follies	Hasbro Interactive	10. Pokemon Red (Game Boy)	Nintendo

Note: Ranked by units sold. **Source:** Interactive Digital Software Association, *2001 State of the Industry Report.* www.idsa.com/pressroom.html.

Religion in America

►RELIGIOUS AFFILIATION

As of 1999, approximately 168 million Americans claimed affiliation with a religious group. The vast majority of these, 158 million, claimed membership in a Christian church. The rest were Jews (5.8 million), Muslims (3 million), Buddhists, or members of other religions.

Because the U.S. Census Bureau does not ask questions about religious affiliation, all of these numbers can be regarded as educated approximations at best. Each year, the *Yearbook of American and Canadian Churches* asks more than 200 Christian religious bodies "How many members does your organization have?" The answers to these questions, which necessarily vary from denomination to denomination, are reflected in the accompanying table, which arranges Christian churches by their size and family. Denominations listed in the same family nearly always share common historical roots and some principal doctrines, but they should not be assumed to be similar in belief or practice. Denominations with 80,000 or more members are shown separately within their families.

The following are brief descriptions of each of the Christian denominational families and of major non-Christian faiths in the U.S. *(For information about religion internationally, see Part III: World Religions.)*

►CHRISTIANITY
Roman Catholic Church

The Roman Catholic Church is the largest single Christian denomination in the United States. It claims nearly 37 percent of all religiously affiliated people—23 percent of the total population. Worldwide, there are nearly 900 million Roman Catholics (see "World Religions").

Many U.S. Catholics—descendants of immigrants from Ireland, Germany, Poland, Italy, and France—are concentrated in the Northeast and the industrial Midwest. Hispanic-Americans in Florida and the Southwest are also predominantly Catholic.

The church is hierarchically organized. Bishops, who administer church affairs in a given region, are appointed by higher authority. The world leader of the Roman church is the pope, who directs the church from Vatican City in Rome.

Priests are male and in most parts of the church must be and remain unmarried. Orders of nuns and monks provide many educational and charitable services. Many local churches operate parochial elementary schools. Regional bodies and religious orders operate high schools and help administer many seminaries and church-related colleges. In recent years the number of applicants for the priesthood and for religious orders has sharply decreased, even as membership in the church has continued to increase.

Catholic leaders have taken strong stands on many contemporary issues. The National Conference of Catholic Bishops has taken relatively liberal positions on efforts to bring about world peace and economic justice. In areas of personal conduct, the church is more conservative. It leads the campaign to outlaw abortion and opposes artificial means of birth control.

Baptist Churches

The Baptist family of churches is the largest Protestant family in the United States. Baptists trace their theological roots back to radical reformers in Europe in the 1500s, but the number of Baptists in the world was tiny until the 1800s, when Baptist faith and practice became predominant in the American South (both for whites and for blacks). Baptists are still most heavily represented in the southern and border states.

Local Baptist congregations have great independence, determining many of their own policies. At the same time, these churches share many practices. They agree that the rite of baptism should be administered only to those who have reached an age of independent judgment. Consequently, children are baptized no earlier than the age of six or seven, often by total immersion in the baptismal water. A Baptist child is not counted as a member until after baptism, which means that small children are not included in the membership totals reported above.

Most Baptists take a strong stand on the authority of the Bible, and many (though not all) believe that it should be interpreted literally. Baptists have traditionally been strong supporters of separation of church and state. Many Baptist denominations have mounted energetic missionary campaigns to bring the Christian message to people around the world.

The Southern Baptist Convention, a predominantly white church, is the largest Protestant denomination in the United States, but as of June 2000, the church was experiencing division within its membership. The split, involving a moderate minority, was sparked by reluctance to accept the increasingly conservative church leadership's insistence that the Bible be interpreted literally and that women submit to their husbands and be barred from serving as pastors.

The two National Baptist Conventions and the Progressive National Baptist Convention are predominantly black churches. Together they account for the religious affiliation of more blacks than any other family of churches.

Methodist Churches

Methodist churches trace their origins to John Wesley (1703-91), a minister in the Church of England who sought to bring a new sense of warmth and commitment to individuals' religious life. He urged his followers to set aside regular times to study the Bible and pray together. Wesley's opponents laughingly called his followers Methodists because of their discipline and seriousness. Wesley himself remained in the Church of England his whole life, but his followers began to develop independent organizations, both in England and the United States.

On the American frontier, Methodist "circuit riders" traveled from settlement to settlement, preaching and marrying, baptizing and burying members of pioneer families. Methodism grew with astonishing swiftness. By 1820 it was the largest religious family in the United States, and it remained the largest Protestant family until the 1920s.

The United Methodist Church accounts for nearly two-thirds of the Methodist family's total membership. This denomination is made up of not only traditional Methodists but also several churches of German origin whose beliefs and spirit accorded well with Methodism. The two "African" churches and the Christian Methodist Church are predominantly black churches, and they account for nearly all of the remaining third of the Methodist group.

Lutheran Churches

Lutherans trace their churches back to the German reformer Martin Luther (1483-1546). Luther sought to reform the doctrine and practice of the Roman Christian Church in Europe. He complained about corruption among the clergy and advocated worship in the language of the people rather than in Latin. He also came to favor a married, rather than a celibate, clergy. The Church of Rome considered Luther disloyal and eventually drove him out. He then helped establish independent churches in northern Germany.

Immigrants from Germany and Scandinavia brought the Lutheran faith to North America, concentrating first in Pennsylvania. Later immigrants settled in the upper Midwest. By 1900 scores of small Lutheran church bodies were divided from one another by language, theology, and degree of assimilation into American society. The Evangelical Lutheran Church in America represents a uniting of many of those earlier churches. The Lutheran Church-Missouri Synod, a national church despite its name, is more conservative theologically.

In July 2000, the Evangelical Lutheran Church announced a historic alliance with the Episcopal Church. The alliance, "Called to Common Mission," could play a significant role in helping both churches stem declines in membership.

Pentecostal Churches

The Pentecostal churches share a belief that God grants believers special spiritual gifts—especially the experience called "speaking in tongues," a common feature of Pentecostal services.

Pentecostal churches trace their origin to the day of Pentecost, described in the biblical book of Acts, when early Christians received ecstatic or mystical powers. Modern Pentecostalism began in the early 1900s, when members of some Holiness churches received the gift of tongues (see "Holiness Churches").

Pentecostal congregations tend to be small. They may meet in storefronts or in rented quarters on upper floors. Yet the Pentecostal faith, with its immediacy and emotional power, is perhaps the fastest-growing in the nation, attracting thousands of new adherents each year. In addition, Pentecostal beliefs have had an impact on Roman Catholic, Lutheran, Episcopal, and other denominations. These denominations report a growth among adherents of "charismatic renewal," a movement based on spiritual gifts.

The two Churches of God in Christ and the United Pentecostal Church are predominantly black denominations. The Assemblies of God is the largest predominantly white denomination. Many Pentecostal organizations are regional or purely local. Because of this loose organization, there are likely to be thousands of Pentecostal believers not counted here because their local congregations are not affiliated with a regional or national group.

Reformed Churches

The Reformed churches are those that trace their descent to the French-Swiss reformer John Calvin (1509-64). These churches were especially significant in the early settlement of the present-day United States. The Pilgrims and Puritans who settled in New England established the Congregational church, which is a main component of today's United Church of Christ. New York was settled by the Dutch, who established the present-day Reformed Church in America. Later, immigrants of Scottish and Scotch-Irish descent established a strong Presbyterian church. Presby-terians differed from Congregationalists in matters of church governance but shared many points of theology and practice.

Reformed church buildings are generally simple and sparsely adorned. Similarly, worship in these churches is austere and simple. Reformed churches generally value a well-educated clergy. In the past they helped found Harvard, Yale, and Princeton. Direct ties to these universities have ended, but Reformed organizations still support many colleges.

The Presbyterian Church (USA) is the result of several mergers between smaller Presbyterian churches that had been separated by regional and doctrinal differences. The United Church of Christ includes, in addition to Congregational churches, descendants of German Reformed churches and of the Evangelical and Reformed Church (also of German descent). The Reformed Church in America and the Christian Reformed Church are both of Dutch descent.

Orthodox Churches

The first great schism in the Christian church occurred in A.D.1054 between the Western church, centered at Rome, and the Eastern church, centered at Constantinople (present-day Istanbul). In 1054 Eastern Christianity was predominant in Greece and the Middle East, and missionaries had already introduced the faith in Russia. The Russian church celebrated its 1,000th anniversary in 1988. Immigrants from these countries brought Orthodox churches to the United States.

The two largest Orthodox churches in the U.S. today are Greek and Russian, respectively. The next largest represent Armenians and Syrians. Together these four churches have more than 80 percent of the Orthodox membership.

Orthodox churches are organized hierarchically. Archbishops and bishops possess special spiritual authority and administer church affairs. Religious observances tend to be solemn and elaborate. Ancient liturgies in the ancient languages have been carefully preserved. Orthodox clergy are male, and in most churches they are allowed to marry. Because of differences in calculating feast days, Easter and other movable feasts may occur on different dates in the Orthodox Church than in the Western churches.

In the U.S., many Orthodox churches have served as cultural centers for immigrants seeking to preserve their own ethnic heritage. At the same time, however, many denominations are active members of ecumenical groups such as the National Council of Churches.

Latter-day Saints (Mormons)

The Church of Jesus Christ of Latter-day Saints, known popularly as the Mormon church, was "established anew," according to Mormon doctrine, on Apr. 6, 1830, by a 19th-century American prophet named Joseph Smith (1805-44). Smith, who grew up in western New York State, reported direct revelations from God. The Book of Mormon, which Smith said he translated, tells of a visit by the resurrected Jesus Christ to pre-Columbian America.

Smith assembled a community of believers that settled first in western New York and later in Ohio, Missouri, and Illinois. Wherever they went, the Mormons aroused the antagonism of neighboring non-Mormons, in part because Mormons allowed men to take more than one wife. Persecution peaked with the murder of Smith himself in 1844.

The next great leader of the church was Brigham Young (1801-77), who led the majority of Mormons westward to settle in the then-uninhabited basin by the Great Salt Lake. There the church grew and prospered. To this day, the majority of religiously affiliated people in Utah are Mormons. There are also many adherents in surrounding states, especially Colorado and Idaho.

Most of the church's 10 million-plus members live in the United States, but the Mormons' legendary missionary work goes on around the globe. Since about 1900, the church has encouraged converts to stay in their own countries and organize congregations there.

The Reorganized Church is the largest of the groups that did not make the trek to the Great Salt Lake. Its headquarters are in Independence, Missouri, which Smith had designated as the site of a great future temple. Members of the Reorganized Church do not consider themselves Mormons.

Christian Churches and Churches of Christ

This family of churches traces its origins to a great religious awakening in 1800 on the Pennsylvania and Kentucky frontiers. Discouraged by sectarian competition among Methodists, Presbyterians, and others, leaders of the revival did not seek to form a denomination but to reestablish a single nondenominational Christian church. In time they became a denomination themselves.

In the 1870s the Churches of Christ and the Christian Church (Disciples) split over questions of using musical instruments in worship and over the issue of centralizing some church functions. The Churches of Christ opposed both instrumental music and national organization. The Disciples allowed instrumental music and established a central missionary board to coordinate mission work. They are ecumenically minded and have a long history of cooperation and discussion with other denominations.

The third group, the Christian churches and Churches of Christ, split from the Disciples in the 1920s–30s. They allow instrumental music but are theologically more conservative than the Disciples.

Episcopal Family of Churches

The Episcopal churches are descendants of the Church of England, which was established as a separate church by King Henry VIII in 1534. Churches descending from the English church make up the worldwide Anglican Communion. The American church takes its name from the word *bishop*, which suggests its hierarchical organization.

In colonial times the Church of England was established in the southern colonies and had some influence in the middle colonies, but was not welcome in New England, where Reformed churches were predominant. During the American Revolution, most Church of England members and clergy remained loyal to England. Thousands migrated to Canada. Those who remained were under suspicion, and some were persecuted. The church almost ceased to function.

After the Revolution, a small group of Anglicans loyal to the United States gradually revived the church. It never grew as rapidly as the Methodist and Baptist families, but it did gain considerable influence. Especially in eastern cities, many families of wealth and power were Episcopalian.

The Episcopal Church accommodates a wide spectrum of belief and practice. It is usually considered Protestant and shares much with other Protestant denominations, yet its worship services retain much of pre-Reformation Catholic tradition. One wing of the church retains a strong emphasis on the church's Catholic heritage. In July 2000, the Episcopal Church announced an alliance with the Evangelical Lutheran Church.

Holiness Churches

The Holiness churches grew from a religious revival in the late 1800s, primarily in Methodist congregations. The originators of the movement objected to the excessive bureaucracy of established denominations and sought to refocus attention on the need for deep personal change. They placed great emphasis on the teachings of Methodism's founder, John Wesley, that those who are saved may aspire to the gift of complete sanctification, or holiness.

Around 1900, groups of especially intense Holiness worshipers began experiencing further "gifts of the Spirit." From these experiences grew the first Pentecostal churches with their emphasis on speaking in tongues. Many who began as adherents of Holiness churches became Pentecostalists. The Holiness churches rejected Pentecostal worship as extremist.

Jehovah's Witnesses

Jehovah's Witnesses are a remarkably active and dynamic sect, visible to most from street-corner or door-to-door encounters. They were founded by Charles Taze Russell (1852–1916) in western Pennsylvania in the 1870s. The Witnesses preach a slightly unorthodox form of the Christian message and look intently for the end of the present world. They claim three million members worldwide, of whom about a quarter live in the U.S.

Church of Christ, Scientist

Christian Scientists, as adherents are often known, follow the teaching of Mary Baker Eddy (1821–1910), who founded the church in 1879 in Boston and wrote *Science and Health with a Key to the Scriptures*, which remains a major sourcebook for the church. Christian Science asserts that sickness and other adversities exist only in the mind and that disciplined spiritual thinking can correct them. Thus, Christian Scientists refuse most or all medical treatment. Christian Science practitioners help adherents deal with illness but do not serve as clergy. The church operates many reading rooms open to the public.

The Adventist Family of Churches

Adventist churches sprang up in the U.S. in the 1840s with a wave of concern about prophecies of the end of the world. Adventists anticipate and prepare for the world's end and the second coming of Jesus Christ. The largest Adventist group, the Seventh-day Adventists, is one of the most dynamic religious groups in the world today, claiming a worldwide membership of five million and a growth rate of more than 7 percent annually. As their name suggests, they worship on Saturday rather than Sunday. They operate parochial schools, colleges, medical schools, and hospitals.

The Salvation Army

The Salvation Army is familiar to outsiders through its work among the homeless and the poor and its fund-raising on the streets, especially before Christmas. The church, which originated in England in 1865, is organized in quasi-military style, and many of its members devote their lives to its service.

Roman Rite Churches

The Roman Rite churches are those that have split from the Roman Catholic Church in recent times but have maintained many of its rituals and doctrines. The Polish church was established in Scranton, Pennsylvania, in the 1890s by church leaders of Polish descent. The Old Catholic churches had their origin in Europe after 1870.

406 THE UNITED STATES

Mennonite Churches

Mennonites trace their roots to a small group of Christians after 1530 who sought a reformation even more radical than those advocated by Lutherans and Calvinists. They were called Mennonites after Menno Simons (1469-1561), one of their early leaders. Their most distinctive practice is adult baptism, offered only to those who have made a decision to follow Christ's teachings.

Because they would not swear oaths and would not bear arms in the service of their temporal leaders, Mennonites were severely persecuted. Small bands were scattered to many corners of the world. Some settled in Pennsylvania beginning in the late 1600s. In the 1870s other groups arrived from Russia. Today more that 40 percent of the world's Mennonites live in the U.S. The next-largest group (estimated to be 150,000) lives in the nations of the former Soviet Union. In recent times Mennonites have become well known for their world relief work.

The Amish are groups with Mennonite beliefs who seek to remain quite aloof from the surrounding culture. The Old Order Amish, centered in Pennsylvania, wear "plain" clothing and still drive horses and buggies rather than automobiles.

Christian Churches in the United States by Size and Family

Family/Denomination	Local congregations	Total clergy	Total membership
Total Christian Churches	**349,506**	**534,913**	**158,294,022**
Roman Catholic Church	**19,584**	**47,199**	**62,018,436**
Baptist Churches	**64,026**	**123,249**	**28,293,420**
Southern Baptist Convention	40,870	97,783	15,729,356
National Baptist Convention, USA Inc.	N.A.	N.A.	N.A.
National Baptist Convention of America	2,500	N.A.	3,500,000
Progressive National Baptist Convention Inc.	2,000	N.A.	2,500,000
National Missionary Baptist Convention of America	N.A.	N.A.	2,500,000
American Baptist Churches in the USA	3,800	7,846	1,507,400
Baptist Bible Fellowship International	4,500	7,500	1,200,000
Baptist Missionary Association of America	1,334	3,055	234,732
National Association of Free Will Baptists	2,297	2,900	210,461
Conservative Baptist Association of America	236	541	38,996
Baptist General Conference	876	N.A.	141,445
General Association of Regular Baptist Churches	1,415	N.A.	101,854
Other (7 denominations)	4,198	3,624	599,176
Methodist Churches	**50,840**	**15,809**	**13,090,542**
United Methodist Church	36,170	N.A.	8,400,000
African Methodist Episcopal Church	6,200	8,000	2,500,000
African Methodist Episcopal Zion Church	3,098	2,767	1,252,369
Christian Methodist Episcopal Church	2,340	N.A.	718,922
Wesleyan Church	1,590	3,144	119,914
Other (6 denominations)	1,442	1,898	99,337
Pentecostal Churches	**47,575**	**92,794**	**11,326,188**
Church of God in Christ	15,300	33,593	5,499,875
Assemblies of God	11,937	32,337	2,525,812
Pentecostal Assemblies of the World	1,750	4,500	1,500,000
Church of God (Cleveland, Tenn.)	6,060	5,556	753,230
International Church of the Foursquare Gospel	1,851	7,300	238,065
Full Gospel Fellowship of Churches and Ministers Intl.	896	2,424	275,200
International Pentecostal Holiness Church	1,716	1,936	176,846
Pentecostal Church of God	1,237	1,802	104,300
Other (11 denominations)	6,828	3,346	252,860
Lutheran Churches	**19,224**	**28,642**	**8,316,331**
Evangelical Lutheran Church in America	10,862	17,589	5,178,225
Lutheran Church-Missouri Synod	6,218	8,316	2,594,404
Wisconsin Evangelical Lutheran Synod	1,240	1,648	411,295
Other (9 denominations)	904	1,089	132,407
Latter-day Saints Churches	**12,110**	**55,999**	**5,066,052**
Church of Jesus Christ of Latter-day Saints	10,811	36,418	4,923,100
Reorganized Church of Jesus Christ of Latter-day Saints	1,236	19,319	140,245
Church of Jesus Christ (Bickertonites)	63	262	2,707
Orthodox (Eastern) Churches	**2,040**	**2,800**	**4,013,497**
Orthodox Church in America	625	785	1,000,000
Greek Orthodox Archdiocese of North & South America	532	806	1,954,500
Diocese of the Armenian Church of America	72	70	414,000
Coptic Orthodox Church	85	68	180,000
Armenian Apostolic Church of America	28	31	200,000
Other (11 denominations)	698	1,040	264,997
Churches of Christ	**24,397**	**23,616**	**3,451,052**
Churches of Christ	15,000	16,350	1,500,000
Christian Churches and Churches of Christ	5,579	N.A.	1,071,616
Christian Church (Disciples of Christ)	3,818	7,266	879,436
Presbyterian Churches	**14,444**	**26,265**	**4,114,350**
Presbyterian Church (USA)	11,260	20,940	3,574,959
Presbyterian Church in America	1,340	2,665	279,549
Cumberland Presbyterian Church	774	835	87,198
Other (6 denominations)	1,070	1,825	172,644

Family/Denomination	Local congregations	Total clergy	Total membership
Episcopal Church	**7,390**	**14,925**	**2,364,559**
Reformed Churches	**7,894**	**13,523**	**1,948,167**
United Church of Christ	6,017	10,303	1,421,088
Reformed Church in America	902	1,784	295,651
Christian Reformed Church in North America	733	1,148	199,290
Other (5 denominations)	242	288	32,138
Jehovah's Witnesses	**11,064**	**N.A.**	**1,040,283**
Adventist Churches	**4,720**	**5,475**	**866,081**
Seventh-Day Adventists	4,405	5,044	839,915
Other (2 denominations)	315	431	26,166
Church of the Nazarene	**5,101**	**9,998**	**627,054**
Salvation Army	**1,388**	**5,248**	**471,416**
Mennonite Churches	**2,763**	**7,636**	**316,267**
Mennonite Church	926	2,688	92,161
General Conference of Mennonite Brethren Churches	368	N.A.	82,130
Old Order Amish Church	898	3,617	80,820
Other (5 denominations)	571	1,331	61,156
Christian and Missionary Alliance	**1,964**	**2,535**	**345,664**
Churches of God	**2,900**	**5,985**	**277,255**
Church of God (Anderson, Ind.)	2,353	5,468	234,311
Other (3 denominations)	547	517	42,944
International Council of Community Churches	**150**	**263**	**250,000**
Evangelical Free Church of America	**1,224**	**2,436**	**242,619**
Brethren Churches	**2,421**	**4,311**	**280,411**
Church of the Brethren	1,095	1,945	141,400
Other (7 denominations)	1,326	2,366	139,011
Friends (Quaker) Churches	**2,413**	**552**	**186,280**
Religious Society of Friends (Conservative)	1,200	N.A.	104,000
Other (3 denominations)	1,213	552	82,280
Christian Congregation	**1,438**	**1,438**	**117,039**
Christian Brethren	**1,150**	**500**	**100,000**
Evangelical Covenant Church	**628**	**1,177**	**96,552**
Moravian Church in America	**94**	**177**	**26,641**
Church of Christ, Scientist	**2,200**	**N.A.**	**N.A.**
Other Christian Churches (39 denominations)	**5,297**	**8,152**	**480,479**

Note: Congregation, clergy and membership totals (in bold) do not include figures for denominations not reporting. **Source:** *2000 Yearbook of American and Canadian Churches.* Copyright ©National Council of the Churches of Christ in the U.S.A. Editor Eileen W. Lindner, www.nccusa.org. Reprinted by permission.

Christian Denominations in the U.S., 1999

The **30 largest churches** in the U.S. (by membership) comprise almost 90 percent of all Christian church membership. But because not all churches report membership figures to the Yearbook of American and Canadian Churches every year, these figures must be considered an approximation at best.

Denomination	Membership, 1999	Percent of total	Denomination	Membership, 1999	Percent of total
Roman Catholic Church	62,018,436	39.17%	**American Baptist Churches in the U.S.A.**	1,507,400	0.95%
Southern Baptist Convention	15,729,356	9.93	**Churches of Christ**	1,500,000	0.94
The United Methodist Church	8,400,000	5.30	**Pentecostal Assemblies of the World**	1,500,000	0.94
Church of God in Christ	5,499,875	3.47	**United Church of Christ**	1,421,088	0.89
Evangelical Lutheran Church in America	5,178,225	3.27	**African Methodist Episcopal Zion Church**	1,252,369	0.79
Church of Jesus Christ of Latter-day Saints	4,923,100	3.11	**Baptist Bible Fellowship International**	1,200,000	0.75
Presbyterian Church (U.S.A.)	3,574,959	2.25	**Christian Churches and Churches of Christ**	1,071,616	0.67
National Baptist Convention of America, Inc.	3,500,000	2.21	**Jehovah's Witnesses**	1,040,283	0.65
The Lutheran Church - Missouri Synod	2,594,404	1.63	**Orthodox Church in America**	1,000,000	0.63
Assemblies of God	2,525,812	1.59	**Christian Church (Disciples of Christ)**	879,436	0.55
African Methodist Episcopal Church	2,500,000	1.57	**Seventh-day Adventists**	839,915	0.53
National Missionary Baptist Convention of America	2,500,000	1.57	**Church of God (Cleveland, Tenn.)**	753,230	0.47
Progressive National Baptist Convention, Inc.	2,500,000	1.57	**Christian Methodist Episcopal Church**	718,922	0.45
Episcopal Church	2,364,559	1.49	**Church of the Nazarene**	627,054	0.39
Greek Orthodox Archdiocese of North and South America	1,954,500	1.23	**The Salvation Army**	471,416	0.29

Source: *2000 Yearbook of American and Canadian Churches.* Copyright ©National Council of the Churches of Christ in the U.S.A. Editor Eileen W. Lindner. www.nccusa.org. Reprinted by permission.

Churches of the Brethren

The Brethren, founded as a dissenting group in Germany in the early 1700s, immigrated to Pennsylvania in the 1720s to escape persecution. There they have remained. Brethren share many doctrinal points with their neighbors, the Mennonites. They practice adult baptism, refuse to swear oaths, and will not serve as combatants in war. The various Brethren denominations agree in basic theology but differ on less significant matters of interpretation.

Unitarian Universalist Association

Unitarianism was an outgrowth of New England Congregationalism in the late 1700s and early 1800s. Unitarians asserted God's unity and repudiated the doctrine of the Trinity. They also interpreted other Christian beliefs in a liberal, figurative manner. Universalism was a separate movement emphasizing the availability of God's care to all people, not only to a small chosen group. In 1961 Unitarian and Universalist organizations merged.

Friends (Quaker) Churches

Known popularly as Quakers, the Friends were established by the English religious mystic George Fox (1624–91) in the mid-1600s. They were persecuted in England for refusing to take oaths or to serve as combatants in war. Under the protection of William Penn (1644–1718), many settled in Pennsylvania. According to Fox, they were called Quakers because they were admonished to "tremble at the word of the Lord." In Pennsylvania the Quakers set themselves apart, dressing plainly and avoiding worldly amusements. In Philadelphia they became influential business people.

The most distinctive doctrine of the Friends is that of the Inner Light, the spark of God in each individual. Friends have avoided setting up formal church structures, and many groups have no clergy. Friends have organized remarkable world relief and peace organizations, by which they are perhaps best known to outsiders.

Other Christian Churches

Among the other denominations reported by the *Yearbook of American and Canadian Churches,* there is a wide variety of religious belief and practice. Many of the groups are radically congregational, making generalizations risky. Other groups are heterodox offshoots from the Pentecostal family. In many cases they depend on a single strong leader. The smallest denominations listed may actually be a single local congregation that reports as a separate church body.

Among the miscellaneous groups are spiritualist and other "New Age" groups. Some of these mix spiritualism with Christianity; others may not consider themselves Christian in any sense.

▶ JUDAISM

Judaism is the largest non-Christian religious family in the United States. Jewish organizations report that there are 5.8 million American Jews. Of these, perhaps 3.8 million are religiously affiliated or observant. The remaining two million consider their Judaism to be more ethnic or cultural than religious.

As descendants of the Jews of biblical times, Jews worship one God and follow the religious precepts in the Hebrew scriptures, the writings called the Old Testament by Christians. Jews recognize Jesus as a religious teacher but do not acknowledge him as the Messiah or Son of God. Jews still await the coming of the Messiah as foretold by the prophets.

A handful of Jews arrived in North America in the 1600s. In the 1800s, Jews from Germany arrived with other immigrants. Then between 1890 and 1920, several million Jews arrived from eastern Europe, fleeing persecution and hard times in Russia and Poland. In the 1930s and 1940s, Jews reached America as refugees from the Nazi extermination campaigns. The slaughter of some six million Jews by the Germans, called the Holocaust, is one of two central facts of modern Jewish experience. The second is the establishment of Israel as an independent state in 1948. Today more Jews live in Israel than in any other country except the U.S.

There are three main branches of religious Judaism in the U.S. today: Orthodox, Reform, and Conservative.

Orthodox Judaism is by far the most rigorous and by far the smallest of the three branches, with an estimated 400,000 adherents. Orthodox Jews may keep entirely separate kitchens for milk and meat, refuse to operate electric and mechanical devices on the Sabbath, and often attend temple services or hold prayer sessions every day. Orthodox services are conducted in Hebrew, and require men and women to pray separately, even when not in temple. Many orthodox communities, especially self-contained communities such as the Hasidic Jews (located mainly in New York), impose strict dress codes, dictating not only the clothes, but also the hairstyles of their members.

Reform Judaism is the least strict branch. It flowered in the U.S. in the late 1800s, especially among immigrants from Germany. Reform Jews do not generally wear yarmulkes, don't usually observe the kosher dietary laws, and conduct their religious services primarily in English (though most of the prayers are recited in Hebrew). About 1.4 million Jews are affiliated with Reform temples.

Conservative Judaism rose in response to the Reform movement. It sought to preserve more of the ancient observances of the old orthodoxy, but without losing touch with American culture and behavior. As a middle road between Reform and Orthodox Judaism, Conservative Judaism has gained many adherents. About two million Jews are affiliated with Conservative institutions.

▶ ISLAM

The Islamic faith, whose followers are called Muslims, is one of the three great theistic world religions, along with Judaism and Christianity. The first sizable group of Muslims arrived in the U.S. from Lebanon in the early 1900s. Later waves of immigration have brought Pakistanis, Indians, Arabs, and Iranians, among others.

There are about 600 Islamic centers in the U.S., many of which include a mosque for worship. An estimated 3,000,000 Muslims are in the U.S., most in cities in the Northeast and industrial Midwest. Observances may vary from one center to another, depending on the nationality of its adherents and their length of residence in the United States. In general, recent immigrants are more conservative and follow Islamic ritual and custom more closely.

▶ BUDDHIST CHURCHES OF AMERICA

The Buddhist Churches of America is the oldest and largest U.S. Buddhist group. It represents the Jodo Shinshu sect of Buddhism, and many of its members are of Japanese descent. There are many other Buddhist organizations in the U.S., and there may be as many as 500,000 additional Americans who subscribe to Buddhist tenets.

Transportation

Americans spend more than $900 billion annually on transportation products and services. Transportation expenditures (which include personal and governmental spending on motor vehicles and parts, gasoline and oil, airfares, and public transportation) accounted for 10.7 percent of gross domestic product in 1998, about the same as what the country spent on food, and much more than it spent on education. In 1998, the United States recorded 4.2 trillion passenger miles of travel and 3.7 trillion ton-miles of freight traffic. More than 200 million vehicles (most of them cars) were involved in domestic transportation, using more than 170 billion gallons of fuel, and causing 43,866 fatalities.

The government has traditionally played a leading role in the development of the nation's transportation infrastructure. Technological,

Passenger Miles and Ton-Miles of Freight, by Mode of Transportation, 1970–98 (numbers in millions)

Mode of transport	1970	1980	1990	1997	1998[1]
Passenger miles, total[2]	**2,042,002**	**2,653,510**	**3,561,209**	**4,132,709**	**4,243,637**
Air carrier[3]	108,442	204,368	345,873	450,612	463,262
General aviation, intercity	9,100	14,700	13,000	12,500	13,300
Highway:					
Passenger car and motorcycle	1,754,174	2,024,246	2,293,815	2,400,960	2,475,961
Truck	62,215	108,491	146,242	191,477	195,380
Transit	4,592	39,854	41,143	42,339	44,656
Amtrak	6,179	4,503	6,057	5,166	5,304
Ton-miles of freight, total	**2,207,000**	**2,989,000**	**3,196,000**	**3,682,000**	**3,710,000**
Air carrier[4]	2,709	4,528	9,064	13,601	13,756
Intercity trucks	412,000	555,000	735,000	996,000	1,027,000
Class I rail	764,809	918,958	1,033,969	1,348,926	1,376,802
Water transport	596,195	921,835	833,544	707,410	672,795
Oil pipeline	431,000	588,200	584,100	616,500	619,800

1. Preliminary. 2. Includes mileage not shown separately. 3. Domestic, all services. 4. Includes revenue ton-miles, U.S. and foreign mail, and express, as reported on AIM Form 41. **Source:** U.S. Dept. of Transportation, *National Transportation Statistics 2000* (2001).

Number of Vehicles in the U.S., 1970–98

Mode of Transport	1970	1980	1990	1997	1998[1]
Air, total	**134,422**	**205,305**	**202,883**	**200,016**	**212,821**
Air carrier, certificated, all services	2,679	3,808	6,083	7,616	8,111
General aviation	131,743	211,045	196,800	192,400	204,710
Highway, total[1]	**111,242,295**	**161,490,159**	**193,057,376**	**211,580,033**	**215,496,003**
Passenger car & motorcycle	92,067,655	127,294,783	137,959,958	133,575,077	135,717,988
Other 2-axle 4-tired vehicle	14,210,591	27,875,934	48,274,555	70,224,082	7,133,0205
Truck, total	4,586,487	5,790,473	6,195,876	7,083,326	773,2270
Intercity bus	377,562	528,789	626,987	697,548	71,5540
Local transit, total[2]	**61,298**	**75,388**	**92,961**	**126,360**	**129,260**
Motor bus	49,700	59,411	58,714	72,770	74,641
Light rail	1,262	1,013	913	1,229	1,505
Heavy rail	9,286	9,641	10,419	10,242	10,301
Trolley bus	1,050	823	832	859	880
Commuter rail	---	4,500	4,415	4,943	4,907
Demand response	---	---	16,471	32,509	32,889
Other	---	---	1,197	3,808	4,137
Rail, total[3]	**1,450,998**	**1,198,755**	**679,918**	**590,237**	**598,172**
Class I Freight cars	1,423,921	1,168,114	658,902	568,493	575,604
Class I Locomotives	27,077	28,094	18,835	19,684	20261
Amtrak[4]	---	2,547	2,181	2,060	2,307
Water transport, total	**7,427,371**	**8,639,652**	**11,036,334**	**12,354,878**	**12,608,432**
Non self-propelled vessels	19,337	31,662	31,209	33,011	33,509
Self-propelled vessels	6,455	7,126	8,236	8,408	8,523
Oceangoing ships5	1,579	864	636	477	470
Recreational boats	7,400,000	8,600,000	10,996,253	12,312,982	12,565,930

1. Registered vehicles. 2. Prior to 1984, excludes most rural and smaller transit systems. 3. Does not includes non-Class I freight cars or shippers' freight cars. 4. Includes passenger cars and locomotives. 5. Vessels 1,000 gross tons and over.
Source: U.S. Dept. of Transportation, *National Transportation Statistics 2000* (2001).

economic, and demographic changes all shape the government's priorities. In the 19th and early 20th centuries, for instance, the government made enormous direct and indirect contributions to the development of the nation's railroads. Today, the government spends vastly more on highways and aviation than on mass transit, railroad transportation, or water transportation.

▶ PASSENGER TRAVEL

In order to compare the costs of different modes of transportation, statisticians calculate the cost of carrying one passenger one mile. For modes of transportation that carry large numbers of passengers at once, these numbers are remarkably similar. In 1998, it cost 14.0 cents to carry a coach passenger one mile by plane, 14.6 cents by commuter rail, 17.5 cents by Amtrak, and 12.5 by intercity bus. By comparison, the average cost of operating a car in 1999 (including variable costs for gas and oil, maintenance and tires, and fixed

costs for insurance, registration, depreciation and finance charges) was 49 cents per mile. The average fare was $114 for an airline seat, $44 for a ride on Amtrak, $21 for an inter-city bus ticket, and $3.28 for a commuter rail trip. Fares are double what they were in 1980 for all modes of transportation except flying. Airfares have risen only 34 percent since 1980, a sure sign that despite all its flaws, airline deregulation has succeeded in making air travel more accessible to all Americans. The average trip was 813 miles by air (up from 791 in 1995), 22 miles on Amtrak, 144 miles by intercity bus, and 23 miles by commuter rail.

▶ TRANSPORTATION SAFETY

Because they kill large numbers of people at once, plane crashes attract much more attention than do automobile accidents. But over the course of a year, air travel accounts for only a tiny percentage of transportation fatalities; in a typical year, more people die in boating accidents than on the nation's major airlines. Between 1997 and 1999, the nation's major commerical carriers experienced a

World Motor Vehicle Production 2000

Country	Passenger cars	Commercial vehicles	Total vehicles
Argentina	238,921	100,711	339,632
Australia	323,649	24,621	348,270
Austria	115,979	25,047	141,026
Belgium	912,233	121,061	1,033,294
Brazil	1,347,923	323,170	1,671,093
Canada	1,550,500	1,411,136	2,961,636
China	620,000	1,388,500	2,008,500
Czech Republic	428,223	27,258	455,481
France	2,883,419	468,510	3,351,929
Germany	4,802,983	394,702	5,197,685
India	513,948	282,237	796,185
Italy	1,422,284	316,031	1,738,315
Japan	8,363,485	1,781,362	10,144,847
Korea, South	2,602,008	512,990	3,114,998
Malaysia	280,000	15,000	295,000
Mexico	1,130,488	792,401	1,922,889
Netherlands	215,085	52,234	267,319
Poland	532,845	23,520	556,365
Portugal	191,387	55,812	247,199
Romania	57,688	13,979	71,667
Spain	2,445,421	587,453	3,032,874
Sweden	260,000	35,800	295,800
Taiwan	265,000	100,000	365,000
United Kingdom	1,628,548	188,511	1,817,059
United States	5,542,217	7,228,497	12,770,714
Total[1]	40,731,620	16,796,464	57,528,084

1. Includes other countries not shown separately. **Source:** Ward's Communications, *Ward's Motor Vehicle Facts & Figures, 2000* (2001).

Traffic Deaths by Selected Country, 1995-99

Country	Deaths per 100,000 registered vehicles		
	1995	1997	1999
Austria	27.7	24.1	24.8
Belgium	30.5	26.9	29.3
Canada	20.1	18.2	16.0
China	N.A.	N.A.	609.0
Denmark	28.9	23.4	22.4
Finland	20.2	19.8	17.9
France	27.8	26.0	25.6
Germany	21.7	19.3	16.0
Hong Kong	52.0	28.1	N.A.
Italy	19.8	19.0	17.9
Japan	16.0	12.2	14.5
Korea, South	121.9	96.1	N.A.
Netherlands	21.2	17.1	15.8
Norway	14.8	14.8	14.2
Poland	175.3	66.4	74.0
Portugal	61.1	56.1	44.7
Romania	119.0	98.6	N.A.
Spain	N.A.	N.A.	25.8
Sweden	13.1	14.0	13.4
Switzerland	19.6	13.3	15.4
Turkey	148.6	154.0	84.1
United Kingdom	13.5	12.3	11.1
United States	21.5	20.7	19.4

Source: Ward's Communications, *Ward's Motor Vehicle Facts & Figures, 2000* (2001).

World Motor Vehicle Production, 1950-2000 (numbers in thousands)

Year	United States	Canada	Europe	Japan	Other	World total	U.S. share of total
1950	8,006	388	1,991	32	160	10,577	75.7%
1960	7,905	398	6,837	482	866	16,488	47.9
1970	8,284	1,160	13,049	5,289	1,637	29,419	28.2
1980	8,010	1,324	15,496	11,043	2,692	38,565	20.8
1985	11,653	1,933	16,113	12,271	2,939	44,909	25.9
1990	9,783	1,928	18,866	13,487	4,496	48,554	20.1
1995	11,985	2,408	17,045	10,196	8,349	49,983	23.0
1999	13,025	3,057	19,158	9,905	9,803	54,948	23.7
2000	12,771	2,962	17,161	10,145	14,490	57,528	22.2

Source: Ward's Communications, *Ward's Motor Vehicle Facts & Figures, 2000* (2001).

grand total of 21 fatalities; commuter airlines were responsible for 58 deaths over this period. More people than that are killed in automobile accidents every day.

More than 90 percent of transportation fatalities and 99 percent of transportation injuries are a result of automobile accidents. In 1999, the latest year available, there were 6,279,000 automobile accidents, resulting in 3,236,000 injuries and 41,611 fatalities. Despite safety improvements in the production of automobiles, wider highway lanes, better lighting, and lower speed limits, annual numbers of automobile accidents, injuries, and fatalities have not changed much since 1970. But over the same period, the number of miles traveled has more than doubled (from one trillion miles in 1970 to 2.7 trillion miles in 1998), indicating that Americans are driving more miles without more accidents.

What has changed, though, is the number of accidents involving light trucks, minivans, and sport-utility vehicles. Fewer than 4,000 crashes occurred between these vehicles and regular passenger cars in 1987; in 1995, there were 5,426. When someone is killed in such a crash, four out of five times it is the person in the car.

Another change is the number of accidents involving drunk drivers. In 1985, 22,716 people died in alcohol-related auto accidents (either because they were driving drunk or were killed by a drunk driver). In 1999, the total number of accidents had declined only slightly, but fatalities in alcohol-related accidents had dropped 30 percent, to 15,786. Ironically, the number of accidents involving sober drivers increased 22 percent over this same period.

▶MOTOR VEHICLES

Although the accompanying table would suggest that the average fuel efficiency of U.S. cars is on the rise, the statistics mask the explosion in the number of light trucks, minivans, and sport-utility vehicles. These vehicles get much poorer gas mileage than most cars, but because they are classified as trucks, they are not held to the same fuel efficiency standards as cars. In 1980, over 80 percent of all new vehicles were cars (9.1 million), with an average fuel efficiency of 23 miles per gallon. In comparison, there were only 2.2 million new trucks, which got 18 miles per gallon. But 1997 sales figures told a different story. The number of cars sold had dropped to 8.3 million, while the number of gas-guzzling pickups, minivans, and sport utility vehicles had tripled, to 6.5 million.

World Motor Vehicle Registrations, 1960–99

Year	Registrations ('000s)		Total vehicles	Population per car
	Cars	Trucks and buses		
1960	98,317	28,637	126,955	29
1970	193,516	52,852	246,368	18
1980	320,539	90,573	411,113	14
1985	374,727	112,816	487,544	13
1990	444,900	138,082	582,982	12
1995	477,010	169,749	646,759	12
1998	478,678	179,528	658,206	12
1999	491,597	190,201	681,799	11

Source: Ward's Communications, *Ward's Motor Vehicle Facts & Figures, 2000* (2001).

U.S. Retail Sales of Passenger Cars by Size and Country of Origin, 1983–2000

Category	1983	1990	1995	1999	2000
By size					
Small	38.8%	32.8%	27.1%	24.2%	28.1%
Middle	40.6	44.8	48.5	51.7	47.8
Large	10.7	9.4	10.8	7.6	7.0
Luxury	9.9	13.0	13.6	16.5	17.1
By origin					
U.S.	74.0%	74.2%	82.6%	80.2%	77.2%
Imports	26.0	25.8	17.4	19.8	22.8
Japan	20.9	18.5	11.4	8.7	9.8
Germany	3.0	2.9	2.4	5.4	5.8
Other	2.0	4.4	3.6	5.7	7.2

Source: Ward's Communications, *Ward's Motor Vehicle Facts & Figures, 2000* (2001).

U.S. Motor Vehicle Sales and Registrations, 1900–2000

Year	Factory sales			Motor vehicle registrations[1]
	Passenger cars	Trucks and buses	Total	
1900	4,192	—	4,192	8,000
1910	181,000	6,000	187,000	468,500
1920	1,905,560	321,789	2,227,349	9,239,161
1930	2,787,456	575,364	3,362,820	26,749,853
1940	3,717,385	754,901	4,472,286	32,453,233
1950	6,665,863	1,337,193	8,003,056	49,161,691
1960	6,674,796	1,194,475	7,869,271	73,857,768
1970	6,546,817	1,692,440	8,239,257	108,418,197
1980	6,400,026	1,667,283	8,067,309	155,796,219
1990	6,049,749	3,725,205	9,774,954	188,655,462
1995	6,309,836	5,713,469	12,023,305	201,530,021
1996	6,140,454	5,775,730	11,915,184	201,070,397
1997	6,069,886	6,152,817	12,222,703	205,042,639
1998	5,676,964	6,435,185	12,112,149	211,616,553
1999	5,427,746	6,699,113	12,126,859	216,308,623
2000	5,504,385	7,022,478	12,526,863	N.A.

1. Data exclude military vehicles as well as farm trucks registered at a nominal fee in certain states and restricted to use in the vicinity of owners' farms; in 1995, there were 60,490 such trucks. **Source:** Ward's Communications, *Ward's Motor Vehicle Facts & Figures, 2000* (2001).

Thus, despite government attempts to mandate improved fuel efficiency, the average new vehicle got worse mileage in 1999 (23.3 mpg) than it did in 1985 (26.3 mpg). As gas prices approached $2.00 per gallon in the summer of 2001, Congress began debating proposals to raise the fuel efficiency standards for SUVs and other light trucks.

The popularity of larger vehicles, which up until 1999 were allowed to produce up to three times as much pollution per mile as standard cars, has

U.S. Motor Vehicle Registrations and Insurance Costs by State, 1999

State	Automobiles[1]	Buses	Trucks	Total motor vehicles	Average expenditure per insured vehicle
Alabama	1,918,032	8,708	2,030,509	3,957,249	$632
Alaska	238,202	2,372	330,895	571,469	771
Arizona	2,037,370	4,551	1,564,306	3,606,227	818
Arkansas	945,871	6,468	865,486	1,817,825	589
California	16,657,441	47,017	9,658,010	26,362,468	718
Colorado	2,053,579	5,803	1,798,766	3,858,148	764
Connecticut	1,994,380	10,011	761,780	2,766,171	901
Delaware	401,917	1,986	211,708	615,611	845
District of Columbia	197,070	2,609	35,819	235,498	1,033
Florida	7,304,601	44,045	4,041,067	11,389,713	771
Georgia	4,011,725	17,520	2,943,465	6,972,710	672
Hawaii	454,341	4,184	259,582	718,107	797
Idaho	494,220	3,580	631,843	1,129,643	494
Illinois	6,307,479	17,691	3,030,090	9,355,260	607
Indiana	3,224,493	26,902	2,243,692	5,495,087	583
Iowa	1,723,848	8,115	1,318,004	3,049,967	459
Kansas	1,187,320	3,850	1,033,178	2,224,348	532
Kentucky	1,592,519	12,525	1,056,945	2,661,989	617
Louisiana	1,964,922	21,328	1,518,412	3,504,662	830
Maine	550,537	2,930	361,988	915,455	492
Maryland	2,665,572	11,476	1,219,249	3,896,297	789
Massachusetts	3,822,524	11,710	1,498,954	5,333,188	876
Michigan	5,069,808	25,536	3,194,300	8,289,644	737
Minnesota	2,265,392	14,664	1,729,661	4,009,717	680
Mississippi	1,299,441	10,544	1,006,787	2,316,772	653
Missouri	2,601,830	13,551	1,788,863	4,404,244	611
Montana	455,430	2,811	539,664	997,905	471
Nebraska	833,415	5,797	730,341	1,569,553	518
Nevada	620,131	1,771	540,474	1,162,376	843
New Hampshire	678,497	1,713	370,688	1,050,898	622
New Jersey	4,341,182	20,565	1,741,011	6,102,758	1,138
New Mexico	761,012	3,524	811,946	1,576,482	676
New York	7,892,118	50,731	2,813,177	10,756,026	960
North Carolina	3,423,588	29,987	2,236,865	5,690,440	564
North Dakota	342,786	2,289	359,337	704,412	452
Ohio	6,651,554	36,364	3,547,685	10,235,603	581
Oklahoma	1,524,424	16,169	1,390,893	2,931,486	575
Oregon	1,559,972	12,920	1,440,067	3,012,959	630
Pennsylvania	6,071,724	34,930	2,901,946	9,008,600	722
Rhode Island	535,034	1,900	210,076	747,010	852
South Carolina	1,872,502	15,816	1,137,929	3,026,247	655
South Dakota	379,168	2,721	400,072	781,961	479
Tennessee	2,621,508	17,380	1,787,631	4,426,519	587
Texas	7,738,292	82,589	6,247,839	14,068,720	731
Utah	856,699	1,242	719,239	1,577,180	619
Vermont	301,914	1,938	213,763	517,615	534
Virginia	3,769,276	17,854	2,084,027	5,871,157	584
Washington	2,741,257	9,137	2,111,756	4,862,150	710
West Virginia	759,648	3,211	616,272	1,379,131	725
Wisconsin	2,520,717	13,032	1,732,023	4,265,772	552
Wyoming	195,762	2,710	329,722	528,194	492
Total	132,432,044	728,777	83,147,802	216,308,623	$699

Note: Includes privately owned vehicles and federal, state, and municipal vehicles; does not include vehicles owned by the military services. Farm trucks, registered at a nominal fee and restricted to use on farms, are not included. 1. Includes taxicabs.
Sources: U.S. Dept. of Transportation, *Highway Statistics 1999* (2000); National Association of Insurance Commissioners, *State Average Expenditures and Premiums for Personal Automobile Insurance* (annual).

also had implications for the environment. To remedy that situation, the Clinton Administration in 1999 announced that minivans, pickup trucks, and sport utility vehicles would be subject to the same pollution standards as ordinary cars. The Administration also issued regulations requiring oil companies to reduce the amount of sulfur in gasoline sold in the U.S. by 90 percent, beginning in 2004.

Traffic

According to the Census Bureau, 90 percent of Americans have access to a motor vehicle, and half of the nation's households have two or more vehicles. In 1990 (the latest year available), approximately 87 percent of all U.S. workers drove to work: 74 percent drove alone; only 13 percent were in car pools. (Of the remaining 13 percent, only 5 percent used mass transportation, while 7 percent walked or worked at home and one percent used bicycles, motorcycles, boats, etc.) The average commute was 22.4 minutes in 1990, up from 21.7 minutes in 1980. The number of workers commuting more than 45 minutes each way increased from 10.9 million (11.6 percent of the total) to 13.9 million (12.5 percent) between 1980 and 1990.

It's no wonder, then, that traffic jams are routine. In 1982, roadways in the nation's 68 largest urban areas were congested for just over five hours per day, according to the Texas Transportation Institute's 2001 Mobility Study. In 1999, rush hours had expanded to seven hours per day. The average driver spent 36 hours per year stuck in traffic in 1999, up from 11 hours a year in 1982. Delays were highest in, not surprisingly, Los Angeles, where drivers lost 56 hours a year to congestion. Drivers in Atlanta (53 hours), Seattle (53), and Houston (50), also lost an hour a week sitting in traffic.

U.S. Roads and Streets, 1904–99

Year	State control[1]	County & local control	Total[2]	Percent paved
1904	—	—	2,351	N.A.
1921	203	2,957	3,160	N.A.
1930	324	2,935	3,259	N.A.
1940	551	2,666	3,287	N.A.
1950	609	2,623	3,313	23.5%
1960	694	2,725	3,546	34.7
1970	755	2,762	3,731	44.5
1980	848	2,764	3,860	53.7
1990	798	2,889	3,867	58.4
1995	803	2,937	3,912	60.8
1998	771	3,014	3,906	61.2
1999	774	3,039	3,932	62.4

Column headers: Mileage ('000s)

Note: Some years contain estimates by the Federal Highway Administration. 1. Reflects state highway agency roadways prior to 1980. Includes state park, state toll, and other state agency roadways beginning in 1980. 2. After 1930, includes mileage in federal parks, forests, and reservations not part of the state and local highway system and not shown separately. **Source:** U.S. Department of Transportation, *Highway Statistics Summary to 1995* and *Highway Statistics 1999*.

Fuel Efficiency of U.S. Passenger Cars and Trucks, 1955–99

Since 1980, the Federal Government has required car manufacturers to maintain a corporate average fuel efficiency (CAFE). Since 1985, the CAFE standard for cars has been 27.5 mpg, which automakers have exceeded by curtailing production of station wagons and full-size sedans. The CAFE standard for light trucks, minivans, and sport utility vehicles, however, is much lower (20.7 mpg), yet the average new light truck has never attained even this lower level of fuel efficiency.

Year	All passenger cars	Passenger cars	Light trucks	Average vehicle
1955	14.5 mpg	16.0 mpg	—	
1960	14.3	15.5	—	
1965	14.3	15.4	—	
1970	13.5	14.1	—	
1975	13.5	15.1	—	
1980	15.9	22.6	16.8 mpg	21.4 mpg
1985	17.4	26.3	19.6	24.0
1990	20.2	26.9	20.3	23.9
1995	21.1	27.7	20.3	23.8
1998	21.6	28.1	20.5	23.3
1999	21.4	28.2	20.4	23.3

Column headers: Average New Vehicle (model year)[1]

Note: Calculated on the basis of 55% city and 45% highway miles sales weighted average. 1. Domestic vehicles only. Imported vehicles average 2-3 mpg better fuel efficiency in most years shown. **Source:** U.S. Dept. of Transportation, *National Transportation Statistics 2000* (2001).

Top-Selling Passenger Cars and Trucks in the U.S., 1999–2000

CARS	Units sold, 1999	Units sold, 2000
1. Toyota Camry	448,162	422,961
2. Honda Accord	404,192	404,515
3. Ford Taurus	368,327	328,035
4. Honda Civic	318,308	324,528
5. Ford Focus	N.A.	286,166
6. Chevrolet Cavalier	272,122	236,803
7. Toyota Corolla	249,128	230,156
8. Pontiac Grand Am	234,936	214,923
9. Chevrolet Malibu	218,540	207,376
10. Saturn S	207,977	177,355
11. Chevrolet Impala	N.A.	174,358
12. Ford Mustang	166,915	173,676
13. Buick LeSabre	149,445	148,633
14. Pontiac Grand Prix	148,197	148,521
15. Volkswagen Jetta	130,054	144,853
16. Dodge Intrepid	144,355	143,840
17. Buick Century	157,035	143,085
18. Nissan Altima	153,525	136,971
19. Nissan Maxima	131,182	129,235
20. Oldsmobile Alero	N.A.	122,722

LIGHT TRUCKS	Units sold, 1999	Units sold, 2000
1. Ford F-Pickups	806,579	820,248
2. Chevrolet C/K	533,177	634,118
3. Ford Explorer	428,772	445,157
4. Dodge Ram Pickup	428,930	380,874
5. Ford Ranger	348,358	330,125
6. Dodge Caravan	293,100	285,739
7. Jeep Grand Cherokee	300,031	271,723
8. Chevrolet Blazer	232,140	225,948
9. Ford Windstar	N.A.	222,298
10. Ford Expedition	233,125	213,483

Source: Ward's Communications, *Ward's Motor Vehicle Facts & Figures, 2000* (2001).

▶ AVIATION

One obvious effect of deregulation in the airline industry has been the growth of the biggest airlines and the winnowing of smaller carriers from the market. The three largest airlines (Delta, United, and American) flew almost as many passengers as all other carriers combined in 2000, and threatened to become even bigger in 2001. American was poised to take over the financially troubled TWA, while United backed off a plan to acquire US Airways only after the Justice Department threatened to bring antitrust litigation against the deal. If the American/TWA takeover is approved, it will leave

Top Domestic Airline Routes, 2000

Rank	Cities		Passengers
1.	New York	Los Angeles	3,637,000
2.	New York	Chicago	3,067,000
3.	New York	Orlando	2,978,000
4.	New York	Boston	2,966,000
5.	New York	San Francisco	2,807,000
6.	New York	Atlanta	2,771,000
7.	New York	Fort Lauderdale	2,671,000
8.	Honolulu	Kahului, Maui	2,607,000
9.	New York	Miami	2,542,000
10.	New York	Washington, D.C.	2,534,000
11.	Los Angeles	Las Vegas	2,405,000
12.	Dallas/Fort Worth	Houston	2,289,000
13.	New York	San Juan, Puerto Rico	1,986,000
14.	Los Angeles	San Francisco	1,959,000
15.	Chicago	Los Angeles	1,817,000
16.	Honolulu	Lihue, Kauai	1,733,000
17.	New York	Las Vegas	1,602,000
18.	Los Angeles	Oakland	1,590,000
19.	New York	Dallas/Fort Worth	1,583,000
20.	New York	West Palm Beach, Fla.	1,563,000
21.	Chicago	Detroit	1,524,000
22.	Chicago	Atlanta	1,513,000
23.	Chicago	Dallas/Fort Worth	1,478,000
24.	Honolulu	Kona, Hawaii	1,466,000
25.	Chicago	Minneapolis/St. Paul	1,447,000
26.	Atlanta	Washington, D.C.	1,428,000
27.	Chicago	Las Vegas	1,410,000
28.	New York	Houston	1,382,000
29.	Boston	Washington, D.C.	1,381,000
30.	Los Angeles	Phoenix	1,376,000

Source: Air Transport Association of America, *Air Transport 2001: The Annual Report of the U.S. Scheduled Airline Industry* (2001).

On-time Performance and Mishandled Baggage by Major U.S. Airlines, 1987–2000

Airline	Percent of Flights Arriving On-Time 2000	Percent of Flights Arriving On-Time 1987-2000	Mishandled bags per 1,000 passengers, 2000
Alaska	68.1%	76.3%	3.48
America West	65.5	78.5	6.62
American	72.9	78.9	5.50
Continental	78.1	78.3	5.35
Delta	75.3	77.4	4.49
Northwest	77.4	79.7	5.24
Southwest	75.2	82.4	5.00
TWA	76.9	77.8	6.06
United	61.4	75.3	6.57
US Airways	72.3	78.1	4.76
Average	**72.6%**	**78.3%**	**5.29**

Source: Federal Aviation Administration, Office of Aviation Enforcement and Proceedings, *Air Travel Consumer Report*, February, 2001. www.dot.gov/airconsumer.

Top U.S. Airlines, 2000

Rank/Airline	Passengers ('000s)	Rank/Airline	Revenue Passenger Miles (millions)[1]	Rank/Airline	Cargo: Freight Ton Miles (millions)[2]
1. Delta	105,591	1. United	126,880	1. Federal Express	7,401.9
2. American	86,240	2. American	116,515	2. United Parcel Service	4,339.1
3. United	83,854	3. Delta	107,782	3. United	2,529.9
4. Southwest	72,568	4. Northwest	79,101	4. Northwest	2,205.1
5. US Airways	59,772	5. Continental	62,314	5. American	1,916.7
6. Northwest	56,835	6. US Airways	46,827	6. Delta	1,435.0
7. Continental	45,139	7. Southwest	42,230	7. Emery Worldwide	1,048.3
8. Trans World	26,365	8. Trans World	27,215	8. Polar Air Cargo	1,047.2
9. America West	19,942	9. America West	19,102	9. Atlas Air	995.1
10. Alaska	13,512	10. Alaska	11,979	10. Continental	887.0
11. American Eagle	12,176	11. America Trans Air	7,488	11. Evergreen International	792.0
12. Continental Express	7,770	12. Hawaiian	4,196	12. Airborne Express	648.2
13. AirTran	7,547	13. AirTran	4,111	13. DHL Airways	452.4
14. Atlantic Southeast	6,096	14. American Eagle	3,145	14. US Airways	277.7
15. Mesaba	6,068	15. Continental Micronesia	3,050	15. Gemini	223.5
16. American Trans Air	5,940	16. Continental Express	2,947	16. Arrow	154.1
17. Hawaiian	5,887	17. Spirit Air	2,741	17. Challenge	153.4
18. Comair	5,655	18. Sun Country	2,697	18. Trans World	129.6
19. Aloha	5,177	19. Frontier	2,596	19. Kitty Hawk International	74.6
20. Horizon Air	5,044	20. National	2,571	20. Southwest	69.1
21. Air Wisconsin	3,857	21. Comair	2,148	21. Alaska	57.4
22. Midway	2,937	22. Atlantic Southeast	2,116	22. Hawaiian	53.7
23. Frontier	2,893	23. Midwest Express	1,969	23. Kity Hawk	47.1
24. Spirit Air	2,836	24. Mesaba	1,692	24. Air Transport International	45.8
25. Sun Country	2,203	25. Horizon Air	1,429	25. Continental Micronesia	44.3

Note: Carriers certificated under section 401, Federal Aviation Act. 1. One paying passenger traveling one mile generates one revenue passenger mile. 2. One ton of freight traveling one mile generates one freight-ton mile.
Source: Air Transport Association of America, *Air Transport 2001: The Annual Report of the U.S. Scheduled Airline Industry* (2001).

only a small group of airlines (Southwest, Northwest, Continental, US Airways, America West, Alaska, and American Eagle) competing for passengers not well served by the bigger carriers. None of the rest of the top 25 airlines—primarily commuter and short hop companies—carried more than 8 million passengers in 2000.

On the other hand, deregulation has also resulted in significantly lower airfares. Fares kept pace with the Consumer Price Index from 1986-90, but since 1991, they have increased at a much slower rate. Using constant dollars to account for inflation, the average plane ticket cost $108 in 1998, more than 40 percent less than in 1990, when the average fare was $184.

The airline industry posted profits of $2.6 billion in 2000, down from its record high of $5.6 billion the year before.   More than 665 million

On-time Arrival and Departure Rates at Major U.S. Airports, 2000

City and Airport (Code)	On-Time Arrivals	On-Time Departures	City and Airport (Code)	On-Time Arrivals	On-Time Departures
Atlanta—Hartsfield Intl. (ATL)	56.9%	55.9%	Orlando Intl. (MCO)	60.5	69.4
Boston—Logan Intl. (BOS)	65.0	68.6	Miami Intl. (MIA)	63.1	71.9
Baltimore—Washington Intl. (BWI)	69.8	68.9	Minneapolis—St. Paul Intl. (MSP)	63.5	60.4
Charlotte—Douglas Intl. (CLT)	70.1	68.3	Chicago—O'Hare Intl. (ORD)	48.0	46.7
Cincinnati (CVG)	64.5	65.4	Portland (Oreg.) Intl. (PDX)	61.1	68.8
Washington National (DCA)	69.1	76.6	Philadelphia Intl. (PHL)	64.1	65.9
Denver Intl. (DEN)	64.1	65.8	Phoenix—Sky Harbor Intl. (PHX)	66.6	67.9
Dallas—Fort Worth Intl. (DFW)	67.1	67.9	Pittsburgh Intl. (PIT)	70.7	70.4
Detroit Metropolitan (DTW)	59.9	57.0	San Diego—Lindbergh Field (SAN)	62.2	68.0
Newark Intl. (EWR)	67.0	70.7	Seattle—Tacoma Intl. (SEA)	56.5	64.1
Houston Intercontinental (IAH)	73.7	79.4	San Francisco Intl. (SFO)	65.5	71.3
New York—Kennedy Intl. (JFK)	68.2	70.2	Salt Lake City Intl. (SLC)	60.3	65.0
Las Vegas— McCarran Intl. (LAS)	64.6	65.9	St.Louis—Lambert Intl. (STL)	60.2	59.7
Los Angeles Intl. (LAX)	61.4	67.9	Tampa Intl. (TPA)	60.1	71.2
New York—La Guardia Intl. (LGA)	46.6	57.0	**U.S. Average**	**62.3%**	**64.8%**

Source: Federal Aviation Administration, Office of Aviation Enforcement and Proceedings, *Air Travel Consumer Report, February, 2001.* www.dot.gov/airconsumer.

World's Busiest Airports, 2000

PASSENGERS		CARGO	
Rank, Airport (Code)	Passengers	Rank, Airport (Code)	Metric tons
1. Hartsfield Atlanta Intl. (ATL)	80,171,036	1. Memphis Intl., Tennessee (MEM)	2,489,070
2. Chicago O'Hare Intl. (ORD)	72,135,887	2. Hong Kong Intl. (HKG)	2,267,175
3. Los Angeles Intl. (LAX)	68,477,689	3. Los Angeles Intl. (LAX)	2,054,212
4. Heathrow Intl., London (LHR)	64,607,185	4. Tokyo Intl.—Narita (NRT)	1,932,694
5. Dallas—Fort Worth Intl. (DFW)	60,687,122	5. Anchorage Intl., Alaska (ANC)	1,883,825
6. Tokyo-Haneda Intl. (HND)	56,402,206	6. Kimpo Intl., Seoul (SEL)	1,874,228
7. Frankfurt—Main, Germany (FRA)	49,360,620	7. Kennedy Intl., New York (JFK)	1,825,906
8. Charles de Gaulle, Paris (CDG)	48,240,137	8. Frankfurt—Main, Germany (FRA)	1,710,144
9. San Francisco Intl. (SFO)	41,173,983	9. Changi, Singapore (SIN)	1,705,410
10. Schiphol, Amsterdam (AMS)	39,604,589	10. Miami Intl., Florida (MIA)	1,642,484
11. Denver Intl., Colo. (DEN)	38,748,781	11. Standiford, Louisville, Ky. (SDF)	1,519,558
12. McCarran Intl., Las Vegas (LAS)	36,856,186	12. Chicago O'Hare Intl. (ORD)	1,463,941
13. Kimpo Intl., Seoul (SEL)	36,727,124	13. Heathrow Intl., London (LHR)	1,402,088
14. Minneapolis-St. Paul Intl. (MSP)	36,688,159	14. Charles de Gaulle, Paris (CDG)	1,380,068
15. Sky Harbor Intl., Phoenix (PHX)	35,889,933	15. Schiphol, Amsterdam (AMS)	1,267,386
16. Detroit Metropolitan (DTW)	35,535,080	16. Chiang Kai Shek Intl., Taiwan (TPE)	1,208,838
17. Houston Intercontinental (IAH)	35,246,176	17. Indianapolis Intl., (IND)	1,173,967
18. Newark Intl., N.J. (EWR)	34,194,788	18. Newark Intl., N.J. (EWR)	1,082,668
19. Miami Intl. Florida (MIA)	33,569,625	19. Osaka Intl., Osaka (KIX)	1,000,693
20. Kennedy Intl., New York (JFK)	32,779,428	20. Dallas—Fort Worth Intl. (DFW)	904,994
21. Barajas, Madrid (MAD)	32,765,820	21. Hartsfield Atlanta Intl. (ATL)	871,602
22. Hong Kong Intl. (HKG)	32,746,737	22. Bangkok Intl. (BKK)	871,000
23. Gatwick Intl., London (LGW)	32,056,942	23. San Francisco Intl. (SFO)	870,113
24. Orlando Intl., Fla. (MCO)	30,822,580	24. Dayton Intl., Ohio (DAY)	832,205
25. Lambert—St. Louis Intl. (STL)	30,546,698	25. Tokyo-Haneda Intl. (HND)	769,733
26. Bangkok Intl. (BKK)	29,621,898	26. Oakland Intl., Calif. (OAK)	703,043
27. Pearson Intl., Toronto (YYZ)	28,820,326	27. Brussels Natl., Belgium (BRU)	634,342
28. Changi, Singapore (SIN)	28,618,200	28. Dubai Intl. (DXB)	581,997
29. Sea-Tac Intl., Seattle (SEA)	28,404,312	29. Kingsford Smith, Sydney (SYD)	564,616
30. Logan Intl., Boston (BOS)	27,412,926	30. Philadelphia Intl. (PHI)	562,752

Source: Airports Association Council International, *Worldwide Airport Traffic Report—Calendar Year 2000* (2001).

passengers flew on U.S. airlines in 2000, most of them on domestic flights. The average flight distance was 1,041 miles, a number that hasn't changed much over the years. Just under 9 million planes took off and landed in 2000, up from 6.9 million 10 years earlier. The average airplane was 72.4 percent full, up from 67.0 in 1995.

With more than 80 million people passing through its security detectors each year, Hartsfield Atlanta International Airport remained the world's busiest airport in 2000; Chicago's O'Hare International was second with 72 million. But the airport that handles the most cargo (2.4 million tons) each year is Tennessee's Memphis International, thanks to the fact that it is the primary hub for Federal Express, which logged more than 7 billion freight ton miles of cargo in 2000.

With increasing air traffic came traffic jams. Flight delays increased from 374,116 to a record-high 450,289 between 1999 and 2000; that's an increase of 76,173 delays, or 20.4 percent. Weather (309,482) was responsible for the majority of the delays and much of the increase. But excess volume played a large role, causing the delay of 63,048 flights in 2000, up from 44,317 the year before (a 42.3 percent increase). The worst offender was New York's La Guardia Airport, where only 46.6 of flights arrived on-time in 2000. La Guardia's 18,026 volume-related delays represented 28.6 percent of all delays in 2000. Chicago's O'Hare fared only slightly better: 48.0 percent of flights into O'Hare arrived on-time. O'Hare was even worse for departing flights; only 46.7 percent of flights left Chicago on time.

World's Top Tourist Destinations 2000

2000 Rank/ Destination	International Arrivals (millions) 1999	2000	1985 rank	1990 rank
1. France	73.0	74.5	1	1
2. United States	48.5	52.7	4	2
3. Spain	46.8	48.5	2	3
4. Italy	36.5	41.2	3	4
5. China	27.0	31.2	13	12
6. United Kingdom	25.4	24.9	6	7
7. Canada	19.5	20.4	7	10
8. Mexico	19.0	20.0	9	8
9. Germany	17.1	18.9	8	9
10. Russian Federation	18.5	N.A.	18	17
11. Poland	18.0	N.A.	22	27
12. Austria	17.5	17.8	5	6
13. Hungary	14.4	15.6	11	5
14. Hong Kong	11.3	13.1	19	19
15. Greece	12.2	12.5	14	13
World Total	650.0	698.3	N.A.	N.A.

Note: Preliminary. Excludes same-day visitors but includes people who pass through a country for one or more nights en route to another country.
Source: World Tourism Organization, *Tourism Highlights 2001.*

Top 20 Destinations for U.S. Tourists, 1987–97

1997 Rank/ Destination	U.S. tourist arrivals 1987	1995	1997
1. Mexico	13,044,000	19,220,523	18,193,715
2. Canada	12,719,800	13,005,200	13,401,300
3. United Kingdom	2,800,000	3,146,000	3,432,000
4. Italy	1,956,153	2,570,704	3,074,000
5. France	1,802,000	2,184,000	2,660,000
6. Puerto Rico	1,550,250	2,246,778	2,444,918
7. Germany	2,071,647	1,548,618	1,760,099
8. Bahamas	1,299,215	1,328,925	1,310,420
9. Spain	865,592	877,467	1,020,000
10. Jamaica	545,476	760,304	804,315
11. China[1]	793,341	748,911	800,539
12. Switzerland	N.A.	783,069	786,359
13. Japan	550,261	539,899	621,737
14. Colombia	N.A.	451,176	533,473
15. Philippines	N.A.	514,850	427,431
16. South Korea	326,330	358,872	424,258
17. Singapore	211,369	345,611	376,418
18. India	134,876	203,343	244,239
19. Egypt	102,603	154,851	176,346
20. South Africa	37,750	103,466	142,781

1. Includes Hong Kong.   Source: World Tourism Organization, *Tourism Market Trends, 1999 Edition.*

Tourists in the U.S., by Country of Origin, 1995–2000

2000 Rank/ Country	Arrivals in U.S. 1995	1999	2000
1. Canada	14,662,000	14,110,000	14,594,000
2. Mexico	8,018,000	9,915,000	10,322,000
3. Japan	4,598,000	4,826,000	5,061,000
4. United Kingdom	2,888,000	4,252,000	4,703,000
5. Germany	1,848,000	1,985,000	1,786,000
6. France	922,000	1,059,000	1,087,000
7. Brazil	838,000	665,000	737,000
8. South Korea	592,000	499,000	662,000
9. Italy	525,000	626,000	612,000
10. Venezuela	511,000	552,000	577,000
11. Netherlands	408,000	527,000	553,000
12. Australia	424,000	483,000	540,000
13. Argentina	382,000	502,000	534,000
14. Taiwan	413,000	453,000	457,000
15. Colombia	233,000	416,000	417,000
16. Switzerland	397,000	406,000	395,000
17. Spain	302,000	363,000	361,000
18. Israel	216,000	283,000	325,000
19. Sweden	219,000	314,000	322,000
20. Bahamas	281,000	282,000	294,000
21. Ireland	149,000	246,000	286,000
22. India	123,000	228,000	274,000
23. Belgium	206,000	249,000	250,000
24. China	167,000	191,000	249,000
25. Jamaica	196,000	234,000	243,000
26. Hong Kong	220,000	193,000	203,000
27. Dominican Republic	176,000	201,000	197,000
28. Chile	152,000	181,000	192,000
29. Peru	127,000	159,000	192,000
30. Guatemala	131,000	163,000	186,000
31. El Salvador	82,000	153,000	185,000
32. Costa Rica	118,000	161,000	176,000
33. Austria	173,000	194,000	176,000
34. Trinidad/Tobago	82,000	117,000	138,000
35. Ecuador	98,000	119,000	130,000
36. Panama	71,000	99,000	107,000
Other	2,368,000	3,085,000	3,367,000
World Total	43,317,000	48,491,000	50,891,000

Note: 2000 figures are preliminary. Source: World Tourism Organization, *Tourism Market Trends, 2001 Edition.*

Commuter and Rapid Rail Systems in the U.S., 1999

System	Passenger trips ('000s)	Passenger miles ('000s)	Stations	Route miles	Vehicles operated
Commuter Rail					
New York, Long Island RR	101,191.0	2,148,992.0	124	638.2	985
Chicago RTA-Metra	70,427.8	1,532,077.8	227	940.4	982
New York, Metro North	68,564.7	1,838,460.2	106	535.4	773
Newark, New Jersey Transit	58,249.6	1,190,410.4	162	975.2	686
Boston MBTA	35,873.1	697,193.2	119	710.2	379
Philadelphia SEPTA	29,492.0	411,703.8	177	443.4	285
Los Angeles, SCRRA	6,734.1	243,880.9	46	768.6	132
Indiana, NICTD	3,485.1	95,142.9	18	179.8	52
Rapid or Heavy Rail					
New York City TA	1,627,238.0	7,839,315.5	468	492.9	4,897
Washington Metro Area TA	212,621.0	1,044,703.5	76	187.7	626
Chicago RTA-CTA	166,477.1	925,035.3	142	206.3	928
Boston, MBTA	130,914.9	500,299.8	53	76.3	320
San Francisco, BART	86,299.5	1,056,714.9	39	190.1	523
Philadelphia, SEPTA	82,857.0	370,991.3	76	76.1	290
Atlanta, MARTA	80,398.1	476,175.4	36	92.1	178
New York, PATH	72,577.3	309,266.3	13	31.5	281
Miami/Dade Co. TA	13,604.5	107,591.6	21	42.2	68
Los Angeles MTA-Metro	13,287.1	28,717.8	13	19.6	36
Baltimore MTA	13,218.9	69,630.5	14	29.4	54
New Jersey/Philadelpia PA	10,918.9	96,446.1	13	31.5	96
Cleveland RTA	6,885.6	51,419.1	18	38.2	28
New York, Staten Island MTA	4,089.5	25,749.6	22	28.6	40

Note: Rapid rail includes subways, elevated trains, and metros. BART = Bay Area Rapid Transit Authority; MBTA = Metropolitan Boston Transit Authority; PATH = Port Authority Trans Hudson; SCRRA = Southern California Railroad Authority; SEPTA = Southeastern Pennsylvania Transit Authority.   **Source:** Federal Transit Administration, *1999 National Transit Database, Transit Summaries and Trends.*

U.S. Railroads: Mileage and Accident Rates, 1999-2000

Railroad	Train-miles operated (1999)	Accidents Total (1999)	Accidents Per million train miles (1999)	Train-miles operated (2000)	Accidents Total (2000)	Accidents Per million train miles (2000)
Amtrak (Natl. RR Passenger Corp.)	36,160,704	85	2.35	36,080,704	148	4.10
Burlington Northern Santa Fe	162,394,739	481	2.96	160,583,587	573	3.57
Consolidated Rail Corp. (Conrail)	19,616,230	104	5.30			
CSX Transportation	105,277,723	423	4.02	114,320,715	484	4.23
Grand Trunk Western Railroad Inc.	5,190,349	21	4.05	5,393,620	20	3.71
Illinois Central Railroad Co.	9,261,463	60	6.48	11,589,768	71	6.13
Kansas City Southern Railway Co.	8,478,654	79	9.32	7,936,611	94	11.84
Norfolk Southern Corp.	81,767,299	238	2.91	95,782,482	275	2.87
Soo Line Railroad Co.	8,059,333	46	5.71	8,199,680	23	2.80
Union Pacific Railroad Co.	176,431,457	719	4.08	180,750,917	758	4.19

Source: U.S. Dept. of Transportation, Federal Railroad Administration, Office of Safety, *Accident/Incident Bulletin Calendar Year 2000.* http://safetydata.fra.dot.gov/officeofsafety/

Amtrak Operating Statistics, 1985-2000

Category	1985	1990	1995	1999	2000
Ridership					
Passengers (millions)	20.8	22.2	20.7	21.5	22.5
Passenger miles (millions)	4,582	6,057	5,545	5,330	5,498
Passenger-Train Cars					
Operating fleet (active units)	1,854	1,863	1,722	1,992	1,894
Average age (years)	14.2	20.0	21.8	22.2	19.4
Train-miles operated (millions)	30	33	32	34	35
On-time performance	**81%**	**76%**	**76%**	**79%**	**78%**
Short Distance (<400 miles)	82	82	81	80%	81%
Long Distance (400+ miles)	78	53	57	61%	56%
Financial					
Revenues (millions)	$ 825	$1,308	$1,490	$2,011	$2,111
Expenses (millions)	1,600	2,012	2,257	2,660	2,876

Source: *Amtrak FY2000 Annual Report.*

►THE DAWN OF CIVILIZATION
(c. 3000–1500 B.C.)

The transition from pre-historic Neolithic culture to civilization seems to have involved in every case two things combined: the establishment of settled agricultural communities instead of nomadic food-gathering communities and, in those settled communities, the development of urban centers with literate religious and social hierarchies in control of irrigation projects. The first condition is found (independently, so far as is now known) in at least four centers: Mexico and Central America; the great bend of the Niger River in Africa; the Yellow River valley in China; and in Mesopotamia (the "land between the waters" of the Tigris and Euphrates Rivers). Priority in time belongs to Mesopotamia. And there also the second condition of civilization, the urban center, first emerged.

Mesopotamia

The 600-mile-long plain of the Tigris and Euphrates valleys stretching to the Persian Gulf is the site of earliest civilization. The city-state of Sumer gives its name to this first flowering which blossomed about 3000 B.C. Each of the cities was a sacred temple city, the realm of a god whose regent on earth was the priest-king. To the Sumerians we owe: the calendar, the invention of writing (cuneiform), the plow, the potter's wheel and wheeled carts, boats using sails, and a host of other "firsts."

The separate and frequently warring city-states such as Lagash, Nippur, and Ur fell under the control of the more northerly *Empire of Akkad* whose greatest king was Sargon (c. 2250 B.C.) which in turn fell under the sway of the *Babylonian Empire* whose king Hammurabi (c. 1750 B.C.) conquered all of Mesopotamia and who is credited with the first known Code of Laws. Shortly before 1500 B.C. this empire fell under the domination of the more barbarous *Kassites* whose advantage lay in the use of horse-and-chariot manned by bowmen.

Egypt

The great valley of the Nile, a thin stream traversing the eastern Sahara desert, had given birth by about 3000 B.C. to no urban centers but to a network of farming villages whose population was of urban density. The legendary founder of Egypt was Menes whose conquest of Lower (i.e., northern) Egypt established the *Old Kingdom* (c. 3000–2200 B.C.). Political unification, quite different from the pattern of Sumer, permitted a rapid assimilation of Sumerian technology while the desert meant relative freedom from invasion. The pharaohs did not rule by permission of the gods, but were divine beings themselves; the building of their colossal tombs, the pyramids, were great religious works directed by the unitary state. The most famous is the Great Pyramid of Cheops at Gizeh (c. 2500 B.C.).

The older diversity of the valley reasserted itself during a century of dissolution and division called the *First Intermediate Period*, after which the traditions of Menes asserted themselves in the *Middle Kingdom* (c. 2100–1800 B.C.). Architecture and sculpture were consciously restorationist, modeled after the Old Kingdom, though temple architecture testifies to the importance of various priesthoods. In literature, it was Egypt's "classical age."

But this age ended with the invasion from Syria-Palestine of the barbarian charioteers known as Hyksos who ruled during the *Second Intermediate Period* (c. 1800–1600 B.C.). But the Eighteenth Dynasty, with its capital at Thebes, at last managed to drive out the Hyksos and re-establish royal authority throughout the valley, thereby initiating the *New Kingdom* (c. 1600–1100 B.C.).

Other Significant Centers

The *Indus Valley*, stretching from Tibet to the Arabian Sea, had become by about 3000 B.C. another locus of settled agriculture with obvious Sumerian influence. Innumerable small villages but only two cities have been excavated and the ancient Indian script remains a mystery to scholars. This Indian civilization flourished from about 2500 to about 1500 B.C. until it was conquered by Aryan tribesmen also utilizing chariots and arrows.

About the year 2000 B.C. three centers of civilization influenced by Mesopotamia and Egypt began to develop: the *Canaanites* in Syria and Palestine, the *Hittites* in Asia Minor, and the *Minoan civilization* on the island of Crete. It is not clear whether Minos was a name or, like "pharaoh" a title, but it was his palace, the Labyrinth, which dominated the trading city of Knossos, center of an elegant "sea empire" whose ships were in contact with Italy, Egypt, Asia Minor and mainland Greece. Yet by about 1500 B.C. Minoan trade was in decline and not long after a Greek prince was ruling at Knossos.

In China around 1875 B.C., the millet-based agricultural villages of the North China Plain gave rise to the semi-legendary Xia Dynasty, which ushered in the Bronze Age in East Asia. The Xia were overthrown around 1550 B.C. by Tang the Victorious, who established the Shang Dynasty, which endured for five hundred years. The Shang Dynasty is noted for its sophisticated bronze vessels, used in worship of the royal ancestors, and for oracle bones inscribed with an early form of Chinese script asking questions of the gods. Shang culture was enriched after around 1350 B.C. by new technologies from western Eurasia, including the chariot, the cultivation of wheat, and sheep-raising.

►THE SPREAD OF CIVILIZATION
(c. 1500–500 B.C.)

The impact of the chariot warriors from the steppes of Eurasia, a huge stretch of grassland stretching from the Black Sea almost to the Pacific Ocean, altered the earliest civilizations in different ways and to different degrees—least in the Near East, most in India. In the millennium from about 1500 to about 500 B.C., the area of civilized life continued to spread as the civilizations took on their classic form in the "heroic age" of the ancient world.

Egypt

Almost immediately after the hated Hyksos had been expelled from Egypt proper, the pharaohs of the *New Kingdom* (1570–1065 B.C.)—preeminently Thutmose III (c. 1500–1447 B.C.) and his regent queen Hatshepsut (d. 1468 B.C.)—created an empire in Palestine and Syria in which local princes ruled their peoples while Egyptian bureaucrats and garrison commanders oversaw imperial interests, especially the tribute payments. Egyptian control southward along the Nile into the Sudan and Nubia was also reestablished. The empire functioned well until ruled by a pharaoh whose interests lay elsewhere.

The pharaoh Amenhotep IV (ruled c. 1372–1354 B.C.) changed his name to Akhenaton and led a movement after 1370 B.C. to obliterate the name and memory of all the Egyptian gods save for the sun-god Aton (and his incarnation on earth, the pharaoh). This almost-monotheistic revolution absorbed the attention of the monarchy to such an extent that it helped the empire to crumble and the dynasty to be overthrown. A rigid traditionalism accompanied the painful recovery of the empire. Tutankhamen (whose famous tomb was discovered in 1922) was Akhenaton's son-in-law; his name shows the return of the god Amon and the eclipse of Aton. But by 1200 B.C. a series of invasions brought the Egyptians to withdraw from the empire to defend the Nile Valley, a withdrawal complete by about 1100.

The *Post-Empire Period* (1065–525 B.C.) saw Egypt's survival in a cultural and religious sense; but the state grew disunified and finally fell victim to conquests by the Assyrians (671 B.C.) and the Persians (525 B.C.).

Mesopotamia and Persia

The Kassite conquest of the First Babylonian Empire led to no great revolution since the conquerors adopted the culture and political structure of the conquered. To the north, the Assyrians were left under native rulers, then took advantage of a series of barbarian incursions against the Kassites to gain their independence in the *First Assyrian Empire* (c. 1150–728 B.C.). The Assyrians were fierce warriors, and they fell upon the south of Mesopotamia, upon Syria and Palestine, and even, briefly, Egypt, and they established the *Second Assyrian Empire* (728–612 B.C.).

The destruction of the great Assyrian capital of Nineveh (612 B.C.) was the work of the mobile strike force of the cavalry of the Medes who proceeded to conquer the Assyrian territory east of the Tigris as well as Armenia and eastern Iran, forming the short-lived *Median Empire* (625–559 B.C.). Assyria's fall permitted the *Second Babylonian Empire* (625–538 B.C.) to arise in Mesopotamia.

Both fell victim to the *Persian Empire* (559–331 B.C.). Cyrus the Great (550–533 B.C.) overturned his Median overlord (559 B.C.), conquered King Croesus of Lydia in Asia Minor (546 B.C.) and overthrew King Nebuchadnezzar III of Babylon (538 B.C.). It was his son who conquered Egypt and his grandson Darius I (521–485 B.C.)who brought the empire to its greatest extent, expanding eastward beyond the Indus by 519 B.C. Dividing his empire into 20 "satrapies" (administrative offices), Darius improved communications by building good roads and was farsighted enough to commence the construction of a Mediterranean war fleet.

Under this Persian dynasty's patronage, the religious doctrines of Zoroaster (c. 628–c. 551 B.C.) spread through its immense empire. Zoroaster taught a dualist doctrine of a cosmic struggle between the god Ahuramazda, the good god of light, truth and peace, and Ahriman, the evil god of darkness, lies, and discord. It was to prove one of the most profoundly influential teachings in the history of the world.

Israel and Judah

Amidst the ebb and flow of empire emerged the people of Israel. Tracing their origin to the ancient city of Ur in Mesopotamia and the covenant between their patriarch Abraham and their god Yahweh, they migrated to Canaan sometime after 1900 B.C. Entering Egypt, probably in the Hyksos period, they dwelt in the Egyptian delta until about 1280 B.C. when, against strong resistance from the pharaoh, Moses led the Hebrews out of Egypt into the desert of Sinai where, according to the Old Testament, they became Yahweh's chosen people in the Sinai covenant. Shortly before 1200 B.C. they occupied Canaan during the decline of Egyptian power there.

The religious league of clans was transformed into the *Kingdom of Israel* (c. 1020–922 B.C.) which flourished under the kings Saul (1028–1013 B.C.), David (1013–973 B.C.), and Solomon (973–933 B.C.) in the interstices of the great powers. But after the death of Solomon, the kingdom divided into Israel in the north and Judah in the south. The northern kingdom fell to the Assyrians under Sargon II (722–705 B.C.) in 721 B.C. Judah held on until the Second Babylonian Empire under Nebuchadnezzar II (c. 605–562 B.C.)destroyed the capital Jerusalem in 587 B.C.

While ethnic Israel fell, the spiritual Israel was preserved through the work of *the prophets*, especially Isaiah (c. 700 B.C.), Jeremiah (c. 600 B.C.) and the second Isaiah (c. 540) who taught an uncompromising monotheism: Yahweh not the god of the Jews alone, but the one God of mankind. With the establishment of the Persian Empire, the Jews were permitted (538 B.C.) to return to Palestine and to build the second Temple, there to live under the great code of law, the *Torah*.

Greece

The Minoan culture of Crete had been in contact with the Greek mainland before 1650 B.C. The people of Greece (called Achaeans) had arranged themselves in small principalities of which Mycenae, located on the Greek mainland of the Peloponnesian peninsula, had pre-eminence. Adopting the courtly style of the life of Minoans and the war chariots of the Hyksos, the Achaeans expanded their settlements and with Cretan decline became heirs of Minoan trade with Egypt and Syria. This is the culture pictured for us in the epics of Homer's (c. 800 B.C.), *The Odyssey* and *The Iliad*.

About 1100 B.C., a second wave of Greek-speaking Dorians invaded from the north and the Achaeans were forced to migrate to the islands and the coast of Asia Minor. In defeat they performed their greatest work: the preservation of Mycenaean (and therefore also Minoan) traditions both socially and in the Homeric epics. Through these great poems the enterprise against Troy became the living symbol of the unity of the Greeks, the mythology of Mycenae provided a common religious background for local cults, and the language of the Achaeans became the norm for the whole Greek world.

By about 750 B.C. the Greek world had recovered. Colonies spread westward to Italy and Sicily and eastward to the northern Aegean and the Black Seas. The lyric poetry of Archilochus (c. 700 B.C.) and Sappho (c. 600 B.C.) flourished. The first philosophers (Thales, Heraclitus, Parmenides), later called the pre-Socratics, commenced their speculations on nature and the order of the universe; to this philosophy, the Pythagoreans added mathematical genius. And the characteristic unit of the city-state, the *polis* was created.

The greatest of these city-states were Athens and Sparta. *Sparta* emerged in 716 B.C. as conqueror of about 3,200 square miles of territory; by about 610 B.C. Sparta already had the formidable military organization based on strict education for citizenship to inculcate the "savage valor" that Spartans so esteemed. And by 540 B.C. Sparta had formed the Peloponnesian League, uniting all but two of the city-states of the peninsula.

The polis of *Athens* was, like other Greek cities, dominated by its aristocratic families. The grievous problem of increasing slavery for debt led the Athenian leaders to turn over power to Solon, a wealthy merchant and poet, descended from the old kings. Taking office in 594, he cancelled all debts, abolished debt-slavery, encouraged both agriculture and industry, and opened the assembly to all free men. But Athens remained divided among its landed wealth, its trading class and the poor peasants, the latter led by the nobleman Peisistratus who established a dictatorship in the name of the poor (546–528 B.C.). But its democratic constitution was not in place until it was imposed, in 508 B.C., by the aristocrat Cleisthenes.

India

The charioteers who invaded the civilization of the Indus valley called themselves Aryans, a word meaning "noble" in their Sanskrit language. Those they conquered were called Sudras, "slaves." The Aryans settled in villages along the Indus, organized in tribal principalities about which almost nothing is known. Over the half-millennium from about 800 B.C. to about 300 B.C. they moved south along the coast and east across the peninsula to the delta of the Ganges River. There, once the lush jungle vegetation was cleared (using the new tools of the iron age), rice could be cultivated in the rich soil, a food supply sufficient for a very dense and stable population.

Religiously, this is the classic age of Hinduism. The ancient *Vedas*, hymns to the gods, date back to about 1000 B.C.—though not written down until much later. The *Brahmanas* are a body of instructions for rituals, evidence of the rise of an important priestly body, composed over the years 800–600 B.C. Lastly, about 600 B.C. appeared the *Upanishads* with their stress on asceticism and mysticism.

Embodied in this classic religious literature are the germs of the later "caste" system, for they envision four *varnas* or castes: priests (brahmans), warriors (kshatriyas), peasants and artisans (vaisyas), and slaves (sudras).

China

The late Shang period, known for the extravagance of its royal burials, declined into misrule; the dynasty was overthrown around 1055 B.C. by the ruler of the state of Zhou, which controlled the Wei River Valley in northwestern China. The Duke of Zhou, regent for the third Zhou king, established a sort of feudal system in which the territory of China was parcelled out in small states governed by Zhou clansmen and supporters. These states gradually grew larger at the expense of the Zhou royal domain. The Zhou capital was forcibly moved eastwards from Chang'an (now Xi'an) to Luoyang around 770 B.C. but the Zhou kings continued to lose both territory and political authority. Zhou rule broke down altogether during the Warring States Period (c. 480–221 B.C.), when a handful of large feudal states swallowed up their smaller neighbors.

The principal states of northern China were known collectively as *zhongguo*, the "middle kingdoms"; the Chinese, isolated from the high cultures of western Eurasia and India, imagined their culture to be at the center of the world, surrounded by zones of ever-increasing barbarism. In this view, the Chinese ruler governed "all under heaven" by authority of the Mandate of Heaven (*tian ming*). This theory held that a dynastic founder, because of his own virtue, attracted the cosmic force of heaven itself in his support, bequeathing heaven's mandate to his descendants so long as they cherished the principle of virtuous rule. This poltical theory, which assumed that exhausted and corrupt dynasties would eventually be overthrown by righteous rebellions, was a force for renewal and long-term stability throughout Chinese history.

Confucius (c. 551–479 B.C.), China's first philosopher, sought a remedy for the political turmoil of his time in an attempted revival of the golden age of the Duke of Zhou. Thwarted in his search for a ruler who would put his ideas into practice, Confucius became a teacher whose disciples perpetuated his prescription for good government. Confucius looked to a natural aristocracy of virtue, rather than an hereditary elite, for social leadership; this led centuries later to the Chinese innovation of government by means of a professional civil service recruited through competitive examination. The Taoists, rivals of the Confucian school (and supposedly founded by Laozi, of whose life nothing is known) rejected government altogether in favor of individual self-cultivation.

The Warring States Period was an era of cultural brilliance in philosophy, technology, and the arts, a prelude to China's first great imperial age.

▶THE GROWTH OF WORLD EMPIRES (c. 500 B.C.–A.D. 500)

The millennium after 500 B.C. had as its most characteristic development the conquest of the earliest centers of civilization by certain small nations or tribes—Persians, Macedonians, Romans, Mauryans—on their peripheries. Territories of immense extent (the whole world as they knew it) were organized by these smaller nations, although without any attempt to integrate the conquered peoples into their own cultures. Rarely constructed according to any deliberate plan, these world empires grew up haphazardly.

Significant too was the extraordinary clustering in one generation (at about 500 B.C.) of Pythagoras and Heraclitus, the second Isaiah, Confucius, and the Buddha. And yet more so was the fourth century B.C. eruption of philosophic thought with Plato and Aristotle. Finally, at the middle of the millennium, appeared Jesus Christ.

The Persian Empire and the Greeks
The Persian Wars (499–479 B.C.) began with a failed revolt of the Greek cities of coastal Asia Minor against the Persian Empire (of which they had become a part in 546 B.C.). To punish the mainland Greek allies of the city-states of Athens and Eretria, the Persian Empire made war on Greece, but unsuccessfully. From a Persian point of view the Athenian and Spartan victories were only a border issue of minor import; but to the Greeks, the battles of Marathon, Salamis, Plataea and Mycale were inspiring symbols of the superiority of their ideals of liberty and free citizenship over the servitude of Eastern despotism, with the unity of Athens and Sparta embodying what had been prefigured in the united Greek enterprise against Troy. The historian Herodotus first told this story.

Under the leadership of Pericles' (d. 429 B.C.) Athens transformed its naval league into an Athenian Empire, thus allowing Sparta to appear the defender of Greek liberties. The former allies, with their leagues, entered their death-struggle, the *Peloponnesian War* (431–404 B.C.) in which the Spartans won a crushing victory. The saga was told by the second great Greek historian, Thucydides (c. 460–400 B.C.) Spartan hegemony in Greece lasted only until 387 B.C. when a league of Greek cities with Persian assistance imposed a settlement which made all Greek poleis autonomous (and therefore weak) except for those in Asia under Persian rule. It was all but the end of the golden age of Greece.

But in just over a century the Greeks had created tragedy (Aeschylus, Sophocles, Euripides), philosophy (Socrates, Plato, Aristotle), history (Herodotus, Thucydides), and the imperishable glory of their monumental architecture (the Parthenon, the Acropolis) and the sculpture of Myron and Phidias.

The Macedonian Empire
Brooding above the disunited Greek city-states lay the small but militarily powerful kingdom of Macedon, militaristic but greatly influenced by Greek civilization. King Philip (356–330 B.C.), having conquered Illyria and Thrace on the northern Aegean, intervened in Greece and forced the formation of a Hellenic League which with Macedon began war against Persia (336 B.C.). No sooner had war begun than Philip was assassinated, a death which occasioned the revolt of the Greek cities he dominated. But his son and successor, Alexander the Great (336–323 B.C.) ruthlessly crushed the revolt and plunged on into Asia; after his great victory in the battle of Issus (333 B.C.) over Darius III of Persia, Alexander declared himself successor to the last Persian emperor under the title King of Asia, continuing rule through the satrapies after the final defeat of the Persians in 330 B.C. In the meantime he added Egypt to his conquests (331 B.C.) and founded the great city of Alexandria. He pushed on into Bactria (modern Uzbekistan) and then to the Indus Valley beyond which his soldiers would not go. When he died of a fever in Babylon in 323 B.C. he had assembled in but a dozen years the largest empire the world had known; but his premature death meant the division of the empire among the *Diadochi* (Alexander's generals who claimed the succession) who battled for half a century before stabilizing into fragments, each a formidable military monarchy: descendants of Antigonus ruled Macedonia,

those of Ptolemy Egypt, those of Seleucus most of Asia. The fringes, the western Mediterranean and India, were left to their own development.

Rome: From Republic to Empire
About the midpoint of the western side of the 650-mile long peninsula of Italy the primitive, devout, peasant community of Rome overturned their Etruscan rulers and established a republic shortly before the year 500 B.C. as the Greek golden age was just beginning. A century of patient expansion against neighboring tribes in central Italy was undone in 390 B.C. when Celts (or Gauls) from the Po Valley plundered and burnt the city. But the Romans commenced anew and within three generations had brought under their sway all of the peninsula except the Greek cities (Magna Graecia) in the south; and these they added by 272 B.C., just at the time the Diodochi were stabilizing their sectors of Alexander's empire.

The move into southern Italy involved Rome in a struggle with Carthage. Originally a Canaanite colony, the city of Carthage in north Africa had established a necklace of commercial colonies along the Mediterranean coast from Sicily across North Africa and Spain to the mouth of the valley of the Rhone, commanding the western seas. In a prodigious struggle called the *Punic Wars* (264–146 B.C.), during which Rome itself was almost brought to ruin by Hannibal (247–183 B.C.), the Romans utterly vanquished Carthage.

After the Second Punic War (218–201 B.C.) Rome became embroiled in the east as Pergamum, Rhodes and Athens appealed for help against the Diodochi. With the war against Macedon (100–196 B.C.) Rome's eastward expansions began. One by one, Greece, Macedonia, Asia Minor, Syria, Palestine, Egypt, and the whole north African coast came under Roman rule by 62 B.C. making the Mediterranean Sea truly what the Romans called *mare nostrum:* our sea.

But Asia did not beckon; rather the Romans embarked on that extraordinary experiment in the west, the conquest of Gaul by Julius Caesar (100–44 B.C.) in which almost 100 small Celtic principalities were brought into the civilization of the Roman Mediterranean. In time Gaul would lead to Britain (A.D. 43–84), while eastern defense considerations would lead to the annexation of Armenia, Mesopotamia and Assyria (A.D. 114–16). At its greatest extent, the Roman Empire stretched from the North Sea to the Sahara Desert, from the highlands of Scotland to the Persian Gulf.

But in winning their empire, the Romans lost their republic, with its freely elected assemblies and magistrates and its famous "council of elders," the Senate. The tremendous population losses in the Second Punic War, the increase in the slave population with every conquest, the transformation from a peasant agriculture to huge *latifundia* (plantations), the rise of a class of financiers (the *equites*), the rivalry of military commanders, the involvement of the military in politics—all conspired to strangle the old republican institutions. In the century from 298 B.C. to 133 B.C., the rivalry for power among demagogues and generals—the Gracchi brothers, Marius, Sulla, the triumvirate of Pompey, Caesar and Crassus, the dictatorship of Caesar, the second triumvirate of Lepidus, Octavian, and Antony—meant endless civil war leading to the final victory of the revolutionary adventurer Octavian who, renamed Augustus, initiated imperial rule in Rome itself and the *Pax Romana*, 200 years of peace in the Roman imperial orbit (27 B.C.–A.D. 180).

Christianity and the Roman Empire

More impressive than the military aspect of the work of Rome was the spread of the Mediterranean civic tradition into continental Europe: colonies of veterans such as Cologne, legionary headquarters such as York, imitated the old Italian, Greek, Phoenician and Syrian cities as well as the numerous foundations of Alexander. The empire became a network of administrative departments centered on cities with central power at Rome; with the external forms of civic life came economic prosperity and the intellectual culture of the Hellenized Roman civilization.

It was in this world that Christ and Christianity were born. In the reign of Augustus Jesus of Nazareth was born (c. 4 B.C.) and in the reign of Tiberius he died, crucified as a criminal (c. A.D. 30). His closest followers affirmed to his resurrection from the dead and his ascent to the one he always called "My Father" and they eagerly preached the "good news" (gospel) that God himself had become man and died for man's sins. This preaching and their communion in their liturgies were the focal points of the early Christians, as the Romans called them. Considering themselves the "second Israel" they nonetheless broke with the synagogue and through missionaries like Paul, Barnabas, and Timothy preached to the Gentiles. While numerically few, they spread through the cities of the Roman world: from Palestine to Syria, Anatolia and Greece; to Africa and Italy; in the second century to Gaul, Germany, Yugoslavia and Spain.

Because they met in secret societies and because they reused to worship the Roman imperial gods, the Christians were persecuted by Roman magistrates; after A.D. 110, adherence to Christianity became a capital offense. Yet the church continued to spread, not only among the poor and outcast but among the nobles and the philosophers (like Justin the Martyr who perished in A.D. 165). These Christians viewed the Pax Romana as providential.

When after the death of the Stoic emperor Marcus Aurelius (A.D. 180) the empire fell into civil war, economic decline, the exhaustion of civic life through excessive taxation and centralized government control, the frontiers became unsafe as well: for after A.D. 226 a revived Persian Empire grew aggressive in the east while great confederations of tribes (Goths, Vandals, Allemani, Franks) arose on the Rhine and Danube Rivers. The emperor Diocletian (284–305) attempted to stem the decline with a political and military reorganization; but it was the emperor Constantine (312–37) who saw that much more was needed.

He attempted to provide a new internal principal of spiritual unity to the Roman Empire through Christianity. His "new Rome" of Constantinople was a Christian city from the start; from persecution to toleration to favored position to state religion—such was the changed estate of the Catholic Church in less than one century. But it had become the religion of a state far gone in decline. Visigothic troops sacked Rome in 410 (for the first time in 800 years) then carved out a realm in southern Gaul and Spain by 450. Vandals tore north Africa away from Rome (429–39). Franks reached the Loire by 486. Saxons, Angles and Jutes ended the Roman province of Britain. Disintegration in the west seemed complete, under the impact of the so-called *Barbarian Invasions*.

Meanwhile in the Roman east, imperial control remained intact but the subject peoples asserted their nationality in religious, not political, forms, adopting one or another of the heresies that flourished after the formal definition of Christian orthodoxy at the Council of Chalcedon (450); that Christ was truly God and truly man.

India and Southeast Asia

The India that the armies of Alexander entered was a complex welter of tribal principalities and republics, of which a certain primacy attached to the kingdom of Magadha in the Ganges valley ruled by the Nanda dynasty. Resistance to the Macedonians was strongest among the Brahman caste: the Kshatriya princes proved more practical and accommodating. After the last Macedonian satrap left India in 317 B.C. Chandragupta Maurya, who has met Alexander, attacked and conquered Magadha with the aid of northwestern tribes, exterminating the house of Nanda and commencing the *Mauryan Empire* (317–184 B.C.). Married to a Macedonian princess, Chandragupta subdued the Indus valley as well and gained recognition from the Diadochus, Seleucus Nicator. By the reign of his grandson Asoka (269–232 B.C.), central and most of southern India had been added to the empire which extended north to the foothills of the Himalayas and west to the eastern reaches of Afghanistan.

Asoka was known as *the Buddhist Emperor*, personally devout and publicly the protector and propagator of the religion of the *Buddha*. Like Asoka, prince Siddhartha Gautama (563–483 B.C.) was not Brahman but Kshatriya; enlightenment came when he realized that desire is the source of all suffering and that salvation therefore means escape from existence into *nirvana* (or nothingness) through rightful living. (Buddha, in Sanskrit, is a title meaning "the enlightened one.") He founded no church but disciples lived in communities following his "eightfold path" to holiness. It was these communities that Asoka fostered and patronized. The more sternly ascetical *Jainism*, founded by Mahavira (probably a contemporary of the Buddha) had spread without political support amongst an elite; its characteristic doctrines were the eternity of everything that is, even matter, and the attainment of nirvana after nine reincarnations.

After the death of Asoka (233 B.C.) the Mauryan Empire began to crumble into its constituent parts, the last emperor being assassinated by one of his generals in 184 B.C. One of the successor states was the Graeco-Indian kingdom in the north and north-west founded by a general of the Diodoch king of Bactria; another was the Kushan Empire of the first and second centuries A.D., which proved to be the route by which Buddhism expanded into central Asia.

A second Chandragupta was the founder of the last great Indian imperial regime, the *Gupta Empire* (320–535 A.D.) which at its greatest extent stretched across the subcontinent from the mouth of the Indus to the mouth of the Ganges. The source of its unity was a revived Hinduism whose brahmans provided advisors to the emperors and drew up the great codes of Hindu law which articulated the structures of the caste system. It was the age also of the revival of the Sanskrit language both in the drama of Kalidasa

(c. 400–55) and in the final composition of the epic poems Mahabharata and Ramayana. The Gupta period was the golden age of Indian science, especially astronomy, and mathematics, to which we owe the decimal system and the invention of the number zero. The sway of the classic Indian civilization was spread far beyond the political borders of the Gupta realm by traders and missionaries to Burma, Thailand, and Indo-China, to the Malay peninsula and beyond into Indonesia. The shores of the Bay of Bengal and of the South China Sea thus became a kind of "greater India", as the Diodoch kingdoms had become a "greater Greece."

The Chinese Empire

In 246 B.C. the cavalry troops of the far western state of Qin, hardened by years of warfare with the barbarian nomads of the steppe, hurtled eastward to conquer and subjugate, one by one, all of the other feudal principalities in a quarter century of war that brought the period of the "warring states" to an abrupt halt. On this territorial basis arose the first *Chinese Empire* under the *Qin Dynasty* (221–206 B.C.) Qin Shihuangdi ("The First Emperor of Qin") proved more than just a conqueror: he oversaw the completion of the Great Wall along the edge of Inner Mongolia and provided a structure of government for the empire by dividing the land into regions of administration and war, governed by deputies responsible to himself alone. The old nobility he destroyed by land confiscations; the Confucian schools he closed, executing many prominent scholars, cowing the rest into submission. And while a weakling successor proved unable to stem rebellion and met his death by assassination (206 B.C.) the structure of imperial rule inaugurated by the Qin would endure for over two thousand years.

A rebel leader named Liu Bang emerged victorious in the confused and bloody uprisings that brought the Qin Dynasty to an end. Liu proclaimed himself emperor of the Han Dynasty, which was to endure (with a brief interregnum under the usurper Wang Mang) for four centuries, from 206 B.C. to A.D. 220. The Han founder retained the imperial structure of Qin rule, while moderating its punitive harshness; he opened the way for renewed Confucian participation in government. The greatest Han ruler, Emperor Wu (r. 140–87 B.C.) instituted the practice of choosing officials on the basis of learning and merit. He brought the rich ricelands of the Yangtze River Valley firmly under imperial control, and also greatly extended the boundaries of the empire, conquering south to the South China Sea, southwest to the borders of Burma and Tibet, northeast to northern Korea, and westward to the deserts of Central Asia. He pacified the northern frontier, defeating the Xiongnu tribes whose descendants the Huns would later invade Europe. In an early arms race, the powerful laminated compound bow and cavalry tactics of the northern nomads were countered by Chinese infantry armed with mass-produced crossbows—a refinement of a weapon of Southeast Asian origin. At this time trade increased along the Silk Route, a network of caravan trails that, through many intermediaries, brought Chinese silk to the Roman Empire and warhorses from Central Asia to China.

The "dynastic cycle" completed its course in the last decades of the Han period, when court corruption, peasant uprisings, and military insurrec-

tions led to the overthrow of the last Han emperor in A.D. 220. There followed the Three Kingdoms Period (220–265), when rival states tries without success to reunite the empire, and the period of the Northern and Southern Dynasties (265–589), when northern China was frequently ruled by short-lived dynasties of invaders from the steppes, and southern China was fragmented into equally short-lived and ineffectual kingdoms. During this period of disunion Buddhism, which had entered China via Central Asia in late Han times, began to establish itself as one of China's major religions. Especially successful were sects of Mahayana ("Greater Vehicle") Buddhism, which promised salvation to the faithful through the mediation of saints called *bodhisattvas*.

Japan and Korea

Around 300 B.C., invaders from northeastern Asia had invaded Japan via the Korean Peninsula. These invaders, equipped with horses, bronze weapons, and the wealth produced by rice agriculture, displaced the ancient Jomon culture of the original inhabitants of Japan. This bronze-age Yayoi civilization, which also shows evidence of influence from Austronesian culture via Taiwan and Okinawa, laid the foundations for the subsequent Japanese empire. But for several centuries Japan was fragmented into small states ruled by military clans (uji), with those associated with the Shinto shrines at Izumo and Ise claiming some degree of primacy.

In Korea, the decline of the Chinese colony at Lolang led to the establishment of indigenous kingdoms; three of these—Silla, Paekche, and Koguryo—predominated during the period 313-668 A.D. Chinese cultural influence, via Korea, helped to transform the Japanese petty states into a centralized kingdom by the 5th century A.D.

▶ EUROPE'S "DARK AGE" AND THE IMPACT OF ISLAM (A.D. 500–1000)

The seventh-century eruption of Islam with its compact secular-religious civilization and its characteristic institution of the *jihad* (holy war), both rooted in the sacred writings of the Koran, created an empire stretching from the Iberian Peninsula to the Indus Valley but influencing events in far-off Ghana as well. It also provoked in response the formation of eastern and western Christendom.

Untouched by these developments, China underwent another dynastic cycle—one in which Chinese civilization spread to Korea and Japan. And in utter isolation, without iron or even the wheel, civilizations in Central America began.

The Roman Empire and Europe's "Dark Age"

The lapse of direct Roman rule in the west did not imply "the fall of the Roman Empire", for the Germanic barbarians lived in a "greater Rome" whose heir and representative was the Catholic Church while in the east Roman rule continued with enough vigor to experience a great revival under the emperor Justinian (527–65). Maintaining a rough alliance with the Christian Franks in Gaul under their *Merovingian* dynasty, Justinian's armies recovered the western provinces: Vandal Africa, Ostrogothic Italy and the Mediterranean sector of Visigothic Spain. Meanwhile his jurists codified and preserved the whole body of *Roman law* since the days of the republic. And under imperial patronage there grew up a magnificent cluster of churches whose pinnacle was the Hagia Sophia in Constantinople, constructed in 537.

But the cost was very great: the treasury was beggared and the eastern frontiers neglected so that the west might be rewon. After Justinian's death the empire had neither treasure nor troops enough to save Italy from new invaders, the Lombards. The city of Ravenna on its marshes kept its link with Constantinople and Rome itself was saved, principally through the work of the pope, Gregory the Great. In the 14 years of his papacy (590–604) he not only organized the defense of the city but oversaw the work of converting Visigothic Spain and began the restoration of Christianity in faraway Britain through the mission of St. Augustine to Kent. In this evangelizing effort Gregory relied upon the monks who followed the *Rule* of St. Benedict (480–547) who brought moderation and a Roman sense of order to the *monasticism* of the west. In a chaotic world, Benedict's *Rule* provided a uniform way of life for monks living as a community, including vows of poverty, chastity, and obedience, regular and frequent hours of prayer, study of the Bible, and manual work.

The empire, which barely held on in the east against Persia, met catastrophe at the hands of the armies of Islam (see next section). In half a dozen years (636–42) Syria, Egypt and Libya fell away; in a second wave of invasions (696–711) the rest of north Africa and Spain were lost as well; Frankish Gaul was only just saved by the cavalry of Charles Martel in the battle of Tours (732). The Mediterranean seemed on its way toward becoming a Moslem lake.

Two successor states to the old Roman empire emerged. In the east lay the empire proper, but now usually called the *Byzantine Empire* (610–1453). Its wealth and power were based in Asia Minor, its unity dependent upon three factors: Orthodox Christianity (slowly drifting away from Roman Catholicism until the final break with Rome in 1054); Hellenistic culture and the Greek language; and Roman law and administration. Missionary ventures carried Christianity and Byzantine influence to the Serbs and Croats in the Balkans, to the Moravians and Slovaks north of the Danube, and even as far as Kievian Rus, all in the ninth and tenth centuries.

In the west there arose the *Carolingian Empire* (751–888). The son of Charles Martel, Pepin III, cooperated with St. Boniface to reform the Frankish Church in close relation with Rome, deposed (with papal approval) the last Merovingian shadow-king, and was himself anointed king in 751. Before his death in 768 Pepin had made Frankish sovereignty felt southward to the Pyrenees and the Mediterranean. His son Charlemagne (768–814) conquered Lombardy, absorbed Bavaria, expanded into Saxony and beyond the Pyrenees, bringing under his sway an area equal in size to the old Roman Empire in the west. At the same time, to foster missionary endeavors, he ordered the creation of cathedral and monastic schools, drawing heavily for his scholars on Northumbria, the small English kingdom where Celtic and Roman monastic traditions had intermingled. The pinnacle of his work came on Christmas Day in the year 800 when in the city of Rome he was acclaimed and crowned as Roman Emperor, by the pope.

But with his death disintegration began. By 843 his grandsons divided his realm in three parts with a middle kingdom of the emperor Lothair separating the kingdoms of the East and West Franks (the nuclei of Germany and France yet to be). These realms faced deadly peril on all sides: Viking corsairs from the north (who also ravaged the British Isles and established commercial bases between the Baltic and Byzantium), Moslem pirates attacking from the south, and, just as these threats had abated, the fierce horsemen of the Hungarians, about the year 900. The family of the Carolingians proved unable to lead any effective resistance; that arose among the nobles of the empire who, inspired by the example of King Alfred the Great of Wessex (849–901) against the Danes in England, defended their people but demanded in return their obedience and support. This was the origin of that pattern of decentralized authority and allegiance known as *feudalism*. Not that monarchy died, but the medieval kings became "firsts amongst equals": Henry the Fowler (919–36) began the *Saxon Dynasty* of German kings while his son Otto I also assumed (962) the title of Emperor; and Hugh Capet in 987 began the *Capetian Dynasty* of France which ruled into the 19th century.

The aftermath of this terrible dark age was the creation of the new Christian monarchies on the fringe of the older Carolingian world: the restoration of the Empire in 962, replacing Charlemagne's empire, which barbarian tribes had destroyed; the consolidation and conversion of the Scandinavian monarchies about 990; the establishment of an independent and Catholic Poland (966) the already mentioned conversion of Kievian Rus (988) under St. Vladimir; and the founding in 1001 of a Catholic Hungarian kingdom under St. Stephen (997–1038).

The Islamic World

To the Roman Empire, the Arabs were a frontier annoyance, no menace as was Sassanid Persia; yet it was out of the Arabian Desert that the whirlwind of Islam arose. Its founder, Mohammed (or Muhammad) (570–632) was a religious prophet whose revelations came from God; these revelations form the heart of the Moslem sacred book, the *Koran*. Utter simplicity of doctrine (a stern monotheism and a focus on the world to come) and of moral code ("hard against the infidels, merciful among themselves") combine with an elaborate ceremonial (the strict fast of Ramadan, prayer five times daily, the Meccan pilgrimage). Driven out of Mecca to Yathrib (now Medina), Mohammed and his followers formed a religious and political community which, after eight years of desert warfare, returned to capture Mecca (630).

Within two years of Mohammed's death the armies of Islam were marching. From the Romans they wrested Syria, Mesopotamia, Egypt and Libya (636–46); the Persians they conquered outright (637–49). Not until 661 was the vexed question of the succession settled when the old tribal aristocracy triumphed over the family of the prophet and established *Umayyad Dynasty* (661–750) of caliphs ("successors") ruling not from Medina but from Damascus and utilizing the old Persian and Roman bureaucracies. For almost half a century Islam lay quiescent; then, with the conversion of the Berbers, Byzantine Africa was swept away (696) as was Visigothic Spain (711). In the same year a Moslem commander established himself in the lower Indus Valley.

A series of revolts protesting the purely Arabic dominance of the Umayyads led to the establishment of a new dynasty of caliphs, the *Abbasid Dynasty* (750–1258), descended from a cousin of Mohammed. Arab by descent, the Abbasids nonetheless moved the capital to the new city of Baghdad in Mesopotamia where Persian influence came to predominate in politics as in literature while the Islamic scientific and mathematical flowering owed as much to Gupta India and ancient Greece as to archaic Babylonian astral speculations, especially the decimal system of numeration and the use of the zero.

The Umayyads had not been totally overturned; Spain followed their rule when the rest of the empire turned to the house of Abbas; after about 800 there were independent Moslem states in Morocco, Tunis, and eastern Persia; and by about 875 in Egypt and Turkestan. Before the year 1000 the caliphs had lost almost all their political power, becoming largely a focus of religious unity, relying even then on the *ulema*, adepts of Islamic law and lore. To this day, ultimate authority in many Islamic states has remained with the religious leaders.

India and Africa on the Fringe of Islam

After the fall of the Gupta Dynasty in 535, India reverted to its older pattern of a large number of tribal principalities. The White Huns, whose incursion had overturned Gupta power, coexisted with the Hindu princes who knew them as *Rajputs* and established a feudal state across north India east of the Indus valley, the kingdom of Rajputana. The Sind (or lower Indus) was already in Moslem hands after 711. By the ninth century Buddhism had all but disappeared from India, absorbed into Hinduism; one exception was in the state of the Pala kings who ruled Bengal and Magadha into the 12th century. Buddhism remained influential in "greater India": in the small kingdoms of Burma, in the kingdom of Dvaravati in Siam, in Sri Lanka, and in the Sumatran state of Srivishaya under its Sailendra dynasty.

At the other extremity of the caliphate, Moslem traders from Morocco were in contact with the *Kingdom of Ancient Ghana* by about the year 800. Camel caravans crossed the Sahara to the grasslands between the upper Niger and Senegal rivers bearing salt and goods from the Mediterranean basin. There the king of Ghana supplied gold and ivory brought north from the southern reaches of the "shoulder" of Africa. Extracting import and export taxes and monopolizing the gold supply, the kings of Ghana exercised a kind of imperial control over the trading cities of the region, growing wealthy and powerful. Yet by 1076 the caliphs in Morocco were able to conquer the region.

At the opposite side of Africa, Moslem Arabs crossed the Red Sea and annexed the Somali coast (c. 1050) from the ancient Christian kingdom of Ethiopia.

China: Tang and Song Dynasties

Three centuries of disunion in China came to an end with the establishment of the *Sui Dynasty* in 589. Like the Qin, the Sui was a short-lived dynasty that paved the way for a long-enduring one. Extravagant expenditures on construction of the Grand Canal linking Hangzhou and Chang'an (a distance of over 1000 miles), a disastrous attempt to conquer Korea, and a Turkish invasion of northwestern China doomed the Sui. It was replaced in 618 by the *Tang Dynasty*, one of the most glorious eras in all of Chinese history. Buddhism flourished, as did poetry and the fine arts; Tang Chang'an was the largest and most cosmopolitan city in the world by around 700. But in 751 Chinese troops on the westernmost frontier were defeated by an Arab army in the Battle of Talas, and the Tang abandoned much of Central Asia; in 755, China's greatest general, An Lushan, rebelled against the throne. The rebellion was defeated, but the empire never recovered fully. An imperial persecution of Buddhism in the 840s, during which the wealth of many temples was confiscated, signaled the rise of Neo-Confucianism, reinvigorating China's oldest philosophical tradition. But with the imperial house in disarray, the Tang collapsed in 907.

After five decades of inconclusive attempts to restore central rule, the *Song Dynasty* was founded in 960, and endured until 1279. But the Song never had firm control of northern China. The northeast was controlled by the *Liao Dynasty* in the hands of the non-Chinese Khitan people (whose name gives us the world Cathay). They were replaced in the early 12th century by the *Jurchen Jin Dynasty*, which in 1127 conquered all of northern China, sending the Song emperors south to a new capital at Hangzhou. Although the Song were politically weak this was nevertheless a time of cultural brilliance, when Chinese landscape painting was perfected, poetry flourished, and urban life (rich with the wealth of overseas trade) attained new heights of sophistication. With the old northern aristocratic clans destroyed by the downfall of Tang and subsequent centuries of barbarian rule, the Song state was run by a surprisingly modern bureaucratic government recruited from a prosperous and well educated rural gentry.

Japan and Korea

In Korea, the state of Silla in 562 put an and to Japanese attempts to carve out colonial enclaves on the peninsula, and then, with Tang support, turned its attention to defeating its rivals Paekche and Koguryo. This process was completed by 670, and Silla grew prosperous with Tang support and cultural influence. But Silla in turn was defeated in 935 by the small western state of Koryo, which established a dynasty ruling all of Korea until 1392. Relatively isolated from Song influence by the intervening states of Liao, and later Jin, the Koryo state became culturally more independent of China.

In Japan, *the Yamato clan*, which had gradually pressed its claim to recognition as an imperial dynasty on the Chinese model, was firmly established on the throne by the fifth century A.D. Buddhism came to Japan in the following century, along with such continental innovations as the use of Chinese script to write (phonetically) the very different Japanese language. In 589 Prince Shotoku issued a 17-article "constitution" establishing imperial support for Buddhism and enjoining all aristocrats to respect the imperial throne. The throne thereupon came under the influence of the powerful *Soga clan* until 645; a restoration movement emphasized emulation of the Chinese model of government. But the principle of appointment to office on the basis of merit never caught on in Japan, which continued to be ruled by an hereditary aristocracy.

Japan's first permanent capital city was founded at Nara in 710; by 750 the city was wholly dominated by its rich and powerful Buddhist temples. In response the emperors moved the capital to the new city of Heian-kyo (now Kyoto) in 794; the emperors remained there for over a thousand years. Both Nara and Heian-kyo were built on a grid plan, modeled after Tang Chang'an; Heian-kyo especially boasted a glittering cultural life, supported by agrarian wealth from the provinces. The powerful *Fujiwara clan* gained control of the country's political life through the expedient of making sure that every emperor married a Fujiwara daughter, and abdicated the throne for a life of monastic retirement shortly after producing an heir; the head of the Fujiwara clan thus was always the father-in-law of one emperor and the legal guardian of the heir-apparent.

The Classic Age of Mayan Culture

Splendid archaeological remains wrapped in chronological obscurity give tantalizing hints of culture in central America before the year 1000. Sometime around 2500 B.C. (but perhaps a millennium earlier) the hybrid maize (or Indian corn) was developed on present-day Mexico's Gulf coast. Permanent agricultural settlements, stretching from Mexico's central plateau to the Guatemalan highlands, seem to date from about 1500 B.C. But it was not until the period A.D. 300–900 that Central America attained approximately to the cultural level of ancient Mesopotamia. From Guatemala to the Yucatan, the Mayans developed temples, ritual calendars and a system of writing as yet not deciphered. Similarly, in the Mexican Plateau, there grew up a culture associated with the great city of Teotihuacan. Both seem to have been "empires" of city-states, but except for Teotihuacan itself the sites were not really cities, rather religious centers surrounded by agricultural hamlets. The Mexican development seems to have been cut short by invasions about A.D. 900, probably by the Toltecs. The abandonment about the same time of the Mayan temple sites may have been the result of drought, deforestation, and other environmental factors.

▶THE MOSLEMS, THE TURKS, AND THE RISE OF THE CHRISTIAN WEST (A.D. 1000–1500)

The four major centers of civilization that had been established by the year 1000—European Christendom, the Islamic world, India and China—all underwent tremendous challenges from confederations of warlike Turkish and Mongol tribes in the next 500 years. Of all the developments the most significant for world history proved to be the maturation of western Christendom which had already commenced, before the period closed, its expansion to the Americas, to Africa and to southern Asia as well.

Expansion of the Moslem World: Asia and Africa

The *Abbasid* dynasty of caliphs of Baghdad had long employed Turkish auxiliaries (rather as the Romans had used German tribes) in their Near Eastern armies; one such army, under their chieftain Mohammed of Ghazni, moved out of Afghanistan into the Punjab about the year 1000

and by 1030 established a Moslem dynasty there. Over the next 200 years they spread their conquests over the Rajputs eastward into the plain of the Ganges, establishing their capital at Delhi about the year 1200. The rich Hindu temples were plundered and, as "heathen," destroyed by these Moslem Turks. Under the sultan (="ruler") Ala-ud-din (1296–1316) most of the subcontinent was brought under one rule for the first time since Asoka.

Unable to break the caste tradition, the ruling Turks became yet another caste, a minority of warrior-aristocrats extracting heavy taxes but relying upon the Hindu princes for administration. Though the Hindu temples had been destroyed, the Turks had to permit a practical tolerance for a now less sacerdotal Hinduism. After the death of Ala-ud-din his empire dissolved into a medley of warring kingdoms ruled by Moslem generals or Hindu princes over whom the sultans at Delhi exercised greater or lesser control.

In the "greater India" of Southeast Asia, Islamic influence expanded through trade and Chinese influence through trade and warfare. In Burma, the Buddhist kingdom founded by Anawrata in 1044 was destroyed by the Mongol armies of Kublai Khan in 1287 and the land was divided into a number of small principalities. Dvaravati Siam (briefly annexed to Cambodia in the 11th century) was overrun by Thai tribesmen from China in the 13th century; by 1350 a Thai kingdom of Siam had established its capital at Ayutthaya, which was to remain its capital until the end of the 18th century. Over the next century, Siam subdued the independent kingdom of Cambodia to the east and expanded against Burma as well. In the archipelago of Indonesia and curving north into the Philippines, Moslem traders and missionaries had established 20 Islamic states by the year 1500. The Hindu aristocracy of Java took refuge on the island of Bali, which still preserves elements of pre-Islamic Indonesian culture.

Moslem expansion occurred in western Africa as well. The conquest of ancient Ghana by Moslem Berbers in 1076 (who had conquered Morocco as well 20 years earlier) led to no new empire but a series of successor states. One of these, Kangaba, had by the 13th century established another trading state of immense size, the *Kingdom of Mali* which stretched, in the 14th century, from the Atlantic coast eastward beyond Gao on the Niger. Under king Mansa Musa (c. 1312–37) Islam spread through the western savanna, the king himself making a pilgrimage to Mecca in 1324. Further east, the king of the Songhay people on the great bend of the Niger had already converted to Islam in the 11th century; thus, when the dominance of Mali was replaced in the 15th century by the *Kingdom of Songhay*, Islam dominated not only the northern coast of Africa but almost the entire belt of savanna south of the Sahara as well.

It was also in this period, but obscurely and beyond the range of Islam, that African tribes (speaking various languages of the Bantu family) continued their long migrations. In the previous period (c. 600–900) they had moved out of the Cameroon highlands east to the Great Lakes; from there they migrated in two streams: southwest to the Congo basin, and south to the savanna of modern Zambia. Now in the period from about 1000 to about 1500, they occupied Kenya and Tanzania on the east and the lands south to the edge of the Kalahari desert.

Transformation of the Moslem World: The Turks

No sooner had Mohammed of Ghazni established Turkish rule in the Punjab than two brothers of the Seljuk clan revolted and took Afghanistan (1037), then expanded into Persia and Mesopotamia (by 1055). After the battle of Manzikert (1071) they took most of Asia Minor from Byzantium. When Syria was added (1084) the *Seljuk Empire* (1037–1243) stretched from Egypt to India. During the 12th century, in the aftermath of the First Crusade (1096–99), their empire became a jumble of small emirates ruled by Seljuk princes or their generals. What brought the Seljuks low was the sudden appearance in the 1240s of the Mongols in the Near East; though menacing to both Moslems and Christians, Mongols power proved ephemeral and the true heirs of the Seljuks proved to be another clan of Turks, the Ottomans. In 1326 they drove Byzantine forces entirely out of Asia Minor, thus beginning the *Ottoman Empire* (1326–1920). By century's end they controlled all of Asia Minor and the Balkans as far north as Bosnia. Half a century later (1453) they took Constantinople, turning Hagia Sophia into a mosque in their re-named capital of Istanbul.

Eastern Christendom Submerged: Mongols and Turks

The 11th century was the apogee of the *Eastern Roman Empire* (Byzantium) as it conquered the Christian kingdom of Bulgaria (1018) and made Serbia a client state in the west, while to the east Armenia and the Crimea were annexed (1022). But by mid-century the Normans, descendants of Vikings who settled in the French province of Normandy, were establishing themselves in Byzantine Italy (and Moslem Sicily), and the battle of Manzikert (1071) proved a catastrophe from which the Empire never recovered, losing both its granary and its military recruiting ground to the Turks in a single blow. Although the first three crusades (1096–1192) were initially successful in wresting the Holy Land from Islam, the subsequent organization of the territory in the French pattern of small squabbling and isolated feudal statelets rendered them impotent and hence of only marginal help to Byzantium. The Fourth Crusade (1202-1204) was a disaster, for the crusaders took Constantinople, establishing what is called the *Latin Empire* (1204–61). In 1261, Michael Palaeologus (1261–82) restored a rump Byzantium along the shores of the Aegean and it was against this state that the Ottoman Turks expanded. The doom of Constantinople brought Turkish power right to the borders of Hungary, with the Balkans absorbed into the Ottoman Empire for 450 years.

In the northeast it was not the Turks but the Mongols whose arrival transformed Christendom. Hungary, Poland and Kievian Rus were weakened by dynastic struggles from the 11th century on, yet maintained their independence of the Holy Roman Empire to the west and the Turkish Cumans in the east. But the uniting of the Mongol federation under Genghis Khan (1206-27) created a power great enough to strike at China, the Near East, and Europe at the same time; by his death his realm extended from Korea to the borders of Persia and Rus. A decade later Mongol armies under Genghis Khan's grandson Batu (d. 1255) fell upon Europe (1237–40) attacking beyond Russia into Poland and Hungary and the lands of the German knights on the Baltic; but with the death of the Khan, the Mongols retreated. Still the "Golden Horde," an independent Mongol Khanate organized by Batu on the lower Volga River, ruled all of south Russia and reduced the north Russian principalities to vassal status.

Not until the late 15th century was the prince of Moscow sufficiently established to refuse tribute money to the Empire. His marriage to the niece of the last Byzantine emperor established the claim of Ivan III to imperial succession as he took the title "czar" (= Caesar or emperor) and his conquest of the principality of Novgorod (1478) established a large Russian state northeast of Poland. Poland had attained its status as the largest state in Christendom with the marriage (1386) of its queen Jadwiga (1384–99) to the Grand Duke Jagiello of Lithuania; in the 15th century the Jagellon Dynasty (1386–1572) controlled the entire region between the Baltic and Black Seas. But thereby it was exposed to a four-fold danger: from Ottomans to the south, Germans to the west, Swedes to the north and Russians to the northeast.

The Rise of Western Christendom

For 600 years out of the ruins of the western Roman Empire and the anarchy of barbarian invasions, Western Christendom slowly emerged, the process essentially completed with the conversion to Christianity of the Scandinavians, the Poles and the Magyars (950–1050). It was not a society associated with a great empire (for the Carolingian Empire had fallen in the ninth century) but with the feudal states of France and the tribal duchies of Germany. Its unity, such as it was, was religious and cultural as well as political.

Whether the leadership of this society should fall to the Popes or the Holy Roman Emperors was settled in the 11th century in the *Investiture Struggle* in which the papacy emerged victorious. From Pope Gregory VII (1073–85) to Boniface VIII (1294–1303) the papacy gave the lead to western Christendom often in alliance with reforming monastic leaders. In the 12th and 13th centuries the characteristic architecture and sculpture of medieval Europe (*Romanesque* and *Gothic*) spread across Europe under Church patronage while the Leagues of the Peace and the Crusades attempted to limit and channel to constructive use the warrior ethos of the feudal nobles.

Beginning in 11th century Italy and 12th century Netherlands, the commune movement, in which all the inhabitants of a town bound themselves by oath to obey their magistrates, keep the peace, and defend their liberties, revived town life and created the medieval city as a confederation of self-governing guilds. *Guilds* were associations of craftsmen of one trade or merchants bound together for mutual aid. In the west the fairs of Champagne and Burgundy provided ground for the re-establishment of trade while in the Mediterranean, the Italian cities (especially Venice and Genoa) linked the west with Byzantium and the Moslem Near East.

In these towns arose the great universities (Paris, Bologna, Salerno, Oxford) where Greek and Arab learning met with the Christian traditions of the Carolingian schools; the insights of Aristotle re-thought in Christian terms issued into the legal, philosophic, theological and scientific work of *scholasticism*, the work of men like Albertus Magnus, Thomas Aquinas, Bonaventure, Roger Bacon, and Duns Scotus—all members also of the new religious orders, Franciscans (St. Francis, 1182–1226) and Dominicans (St. Dominic, 1170–1221), which arose in the towns of the 13th century. Committed to evangelical poverty and combating heresy, they played a role in university life as well.

Late in the 12th century in Spain and Italy, in the 13th in Germany, England and France, in the 14th and 15th in Hungary, Poland and Scandinavia, the custom arose for monarchs to call the elected representatives of the towns to meet with prelates and nobles to render advice; such was the origin of *parliaments*.

The development of these social and cultural and religious institutions was accompanied by the expansion of western Christendom. One aspect was internal with the clearing of forests and the cultivation of new farmland able to support an increased population. The other was external, not so much the ephemeral Kingdom of Jerusalem (1099-1162) or Latin Empire of Con-, stantinople (1204–61) as the reconquest of Spain from the Moslems (1085–1492), the conquest of Prussia and Livonia by the Teutonic Knights (1229–1466) and the conversion of Lithuania (1386 and after.)

The most significant check to population growth was the *Black Death*, an outbreak of bubonic plague that swept over Europe (1347–51), wiping out perhaps 25 million, a third of the population. The loose unity of western Christendom began to alter in the 14th century in significant ways. First of all, the universality of the papacy seemed compromised when seven popes in succession (1305–78) preferred to reside at Avignon rather than Rome, in too close an association with the kings of France; then, after the return to Rome arose that series of disputed elections to the papacy which is called the *Great Schism* (1378–1417); and third, with the end of the schism, the popes became more and more involved in the politics of Renaissance Italy.

Meanwhile, while theories of sovereignty derived from the study of Roman law exalted the authorities of kings, royal powers disastrously declined due to chronic feudal violence: the "age of princes" in Germany (1273-1493), the Hundred Years' War in England and France (1337–1453), and the dynastic Wars of the Roses in England (1455–85). Out of the turmoil arose the "new monarchies" of more unified states: the Tudors in England (1485), the Valois and in France (1328–1529), and in Spain the Spanish branch of the Habsburgs (1504–1700).

In the Italy of the 14th and 15th centuries, increasingly the plaything of the new monarchies, there began that great cultural transformation known as the *Renaissance*. Humanists like Petrarch (1304–74), and Boccaccio (1313–75) sought a revival of Latin antiquity, both pagan (Cicero, Virgil, Tacitus) and Christian (Augustine and the other Church fathers), in an educational movement that sought to unite the values of Hellenism with Christianity. At the same time artists, studying Roman architecture and Hellenistic sculpture on the one hand and the new sciences of anatomy and perspective on the other, created a new world of beauty. In painting, Botticelli and da Vinci, in architecture Brunelleschi (1377–1446), in sculpture Ghiberti (1378–1455) and Donatello (1386–1466)—these represent the output of the city of Florence alone.

Building on medieval foundations and new navigational discoveries (magnetic compasses, the astolabe, the quadrant), the Portuguese monarchy pioneered the exploration of the African coast; the Gulf of Guinea was reached by 1470, the Cape of Good Hope by 1487, and India itself by 1498. The Spanish monarchs sponsored the western route of Columbus whose four voyages (1492–1504) brought Europeans to the shores of the Caribbean (which he mistook for Japan and the Malay Peninsula). Finally, before the period closed, the new Tudor monarchy of England financed the more northerly westward explorations of the Cabots who reached Newfoundland and New England in 1497 and 1498. Like the humanists, by seeking a very old world, the explorers found something very new as well.

The Americas

The New World which Columbus discovered was dominated by two great empires. In Mexico, the Toltecs established an empire with its capital in the magnificent temple city of Tula; it included most of the old Mayan realm (c. 900–1200). But the 12th and 13th centuries saw a series of incursions of barbarian nomadic hunters from the south known collectively as Chichimecs whose armed might destroyed the Toltec civilization. In time, one of these tribes, the Aztecs, established a capital at Tenochtitlan and over the century from about 1360 to about 1470 conquered neighboring peoples and constructed the sanguinary *Aztec Empire* (c. 1360–1520). The king Montezuma I (died c. 1470) was a ruthless conqueror but a great builder as well, transforming the capital into a magnificent city of stone. By 1500 the Aztecs had reached Guatemala. For the subject peoples war and subjections were evil enough; worse was the Aztec worship of the sun god who required for his nourishment human blood.

Stretching thousands of miles along the west coast of South America lay the empire of the Incas with their capital at Cuzco. Unlike the military Aztec empire of subject states paying tribute including the blood tax, the *Inca Empire* was a centralized bureaucratic state which engaged in social engineering as well as road and bridge building and irrigation projects. Begun about 1200, the empire attained its greatest size under Huayna Capac (c. 1493–1527).

China and East Asia (1200–1500)

Genghis Khan (b. 1162–1227), leader of the Mongol federation, wished to unite all of the nomadic peoples of the Asian steppes under his rule. The Mongol conquest of northern China, ruled by Jurchen tribesmen from Manchuria, was completed by Genghis Khan's successors in 1234. The Mongols then turned their attention to Korea, which they conquered in 1231–36, and to the Chinese Song Dynasty in the Yangtze River Valley. The Song defended their territory vigorously, while the Mongols were slowed down as their horsemen learned to cope with wet ricefields and rivers defended by heavily armed ships; but in 1271 Kubilai Khan (b. 1215–94) proclaimed himself emperor of the *Yuan Dynasty* of China, and in 1279 the last Song emperor capitulated. During his reign Kubilai Khan tried twice to invade Japan; his fleets were stopped by *kamikaze*, "divine winds," i.e. typhoons. An attempt to conquer Java also met with only limited and temporary success.

In China the Mongols were seen as an alien occupying power; their habit of using foreign, Persian-speaking tax-collectors made them especially hated. The successors to Kubilai Khan were mediocre rulers; in 1368 a Chinese nativist rebellion led by a charismatic ex-Buddhist monk named Zhu Yuanzhang succeeded in overthrowing the Mongols and establishing the *Ming Dynasty* (1368–1644). The early Ming emperors were vigorous and forward-looking; they rebuilt the Great Wall, re-routed the Grand Canal to terminate near Beijing, built a new southern capital at Nanjing, and sent maritime expeditions on missions of exploration and diplomacy throughout the South China Sea and the Indian Ocean to the east coast of Africa. These expeditions, under Admiral Zheng He, were however abruptly terminated in 1433, criticized by the conservative Confucian bureaucracy as a waste of money and resources. Thus the Chinese missed by only three decades the chance to confront the Portuguese as rival maritime powers in the Indian Ocean.

In Korea, the *Koryo Dynasty* did not long outlast the rule of their Mongol patrons. The last Koryo king in 1388 sent his best general, Yi Songgye (famous for his victories over Japanese pirates), to invade China to try to overthrow the Ming Dynasty on behalf of the Mongols. General Yi instead turned back at the border, overthrew the Koryo king, and established his own dynasty, the *Kingdom of Choson*, which soon proclaimed its support for the Ming emperors. The third Choson (or Yi Dynasty) ruler, King Sejong (r. 1418–1450) was Korea's greatest sovereign, a patron of art, science and technology during whose reign Korean scholars and craftsmen perfected printing with moveable metal type, invented a syllabic script to write vernacular Korean, and equipped Seoul with what was, for a time, the best astronomical observatory in the world. The Choson monarchs tolerated Buddhism, promoted Confucianism, ruled through a very conservative aristocracy, and remained on the throne until 1910.

In Japan, the Fujiwara-dominated aristocrats of Heian-kyo ignored the rise of a provincial warrior aristocracy in the provinces until it was too late. The Fujiwaras were ousted by the western Taira clan in 1160; they in turn were defeated by Minamoto no Yoritomo at the naval battle of Dan-no-Ura in 1185. Yoritomo then took the hereditary title of *shogun* ("generalissimo"), and established a military capital at Kamakura, leaving the emperors to reign but not rule in Heian-kyo. The Minamoto were shunted aside by their own hereditary retainers, the *Hojo Clan*, in 1229. A crisis was precipitated in 1331 by Emperor Daigo II, who refused to abdicate on command of the shogun, and attempted to institute direct imperial rule. In 1333 another general, Ashikaga Takauji, helped Daigo II overthrow the Hojo, but Ashikaga then promptly proclaimed himself shogun, moved the military capital to the Muromachi district of Kyoto, and put the emperors firmly in their place once again. The *Muromachi* shogunate endured until 1568, though with little military power; the shoguns were better known as patrons of Zen Buddhism, Noh theater, and the tea ceremony. With the waning of central authority, Japanese merchants were more free to establish domestic and overseas trade routes (and to engage in piracy on the China coast), leading to economic prosperity amidst political instability.

▶ THE EXPANSION OF THE WEST AND THE ENDURANCE OF THE EAST (1500–1650)

During this period, the great empires of Asia—Ottoman Turkey, Safavid Persia, Mogul India and Ming China—remained intact and even expanded, but the dynamic power and movement of this extraordinary age were driven by the emerging nation-states of Europe. Despite severe internal divisions both religious (the Reformation) and national, which led to incessant warfare among all of them, the major powers managed to dominate the sea lanes of the globe and control the coasts and islands of Africa, southern Asia, and the Americas.

The Near East: Ottoman Empire and Safavid Persia

Under their sultans Selim I the Grim (1512–20) and Suleiman I the Magnificent (1520–66) the Ottoman Turks added Syria and Egypt to their domains, then from their fortress at Belgrade launched an invasion of Hungary which climaxed at the battle of Mohacs (1526), where over 20,000 Christian soldiers were slain and three-quarters of the realm fell under Turkish rule either directly or through Ottoman client princes of Transylvania. The Turks moved on to besiege Vienna (1529), halting the campaign because of troubles with Persia. On the seas Turkish fleets added Yemen and Aden on the Persian Gulf and Tripoli, Algeria, and Tunis on the southern shores of the Mediterranean.

But Suleiman's successor was Selim II (the Sot), the first in a series of weak sultans who came to the throne between 1566–1718 as a result of that perennial weakness of Moslem dynasties, harem intrigues of wives and eunuchs, and of the specifically Ottoman problem, the "praetorian guard" of Janissaries. In 1571, the Holy League (the Papacy, Venice, Tuscany and Spain) triumphed over the Turkish navy in the battle of Lepanto, though dissolution of the League after the victory meant that the Ottoman fleet could still raid almost at will through the Mediterranean.

Persia saw the revival of a native Iranian dynasty under the *Safavid Dynasty* (1501–1736). Its founder Shah Ismail seized power from the White Sheep Turks in 1501 and successfully defended Persia from Ottoman expansion into Mesopotamia, a work continued under his son and successor (1514–55). After the reign of the dynasty's greatest representative, Abbas I the Great (1587–1629), there began a period of harem intrigues which greatly weakened the dynasty. The Turks succeeded in taking Baghdad (1638).

Christian trading presence in Persia began with the Portuguese establishment at Hormuz in 1507; by 1622 the Portuguese were turned out by Abbas, English merchants supplanting them.

Mogul India and the Portuguese Spice Trade

In 1526, a descendent of Genghis Khan attacked the sultan at Delhi and established his dominance east of the Indus. Though a Turk, because of the long association of his family with the Mongols, his empire came to be called the *Mogul Empire* (1526–1857). Babur (b. 1483–1530), the founder then expanded east to the borders of Bengal. Although his son lost almost all Babur had conquered, his grandson Akbar (1556–1605), contemporary of Philip II of Spain and Elizabeth of England, restored Babur's realm and expanded it further until it included all of India north of the Deccan Plateau. Vigorous in warfare, gracious in victory, wise in administration, tolerant in religion, Akbar's empire knew peace and prosperity. Most of the Deccan was added in the reign of his grandson Shah Jahan (1628–58), who also built the Taj Mahal.

It seems almost miraculous that Portugal, a tiny state on the edge of the Atlantic, should create a seaborne empire dominating the Indian Ocean, but that is what Portugal did in the 16th century. In 1497, Vasco da Gama (c. 1469–1524) began a journey that took him around Africa's Cape of Good Hope and across the Indian Ocean to Calicut where he encountered the great riches of India's spice trade. After da Gama's second voyage (1502), the Moslem state of Gujerat, allied with Mameluke Egypt, declared a *jihad* against the Portuguese, but at Diu, the Portuguese won a complete victory (1508). The Portuguese viceroy organized the building of a "rosary" of over a dozen forts stretching from Hormuz on the Persian Gulf through Goa to Malacca on the Malay Peninsula. Thus the Portuguese could monopolize the carrying trade in the Indian Ocean as well as divert the spice trade around Africa. And from Malacca they established trading posts in the Spice Islands (Moluccas), China and Japan. This network provided the route for Christian missionaries as well.

But it proved all too much for Portugal. The English and the Dutch had established their East India Companies in 1600 and 1602 and in the 17th century the Dutch, piecemeal, took the place of the Portuguese by war and diplomacy. One portent for the future: by 1639 the English were at Madras.

East Asia: China, Korea, Japan

The late Ming emperors were great patrons of culture, but mediocre rulers. The former Chinese protectorate of Annam, while maintaining its mandarin culture, became independent, the first true monarchy of Vietnam. In 1557 the Portuguese established a trading colony at Macao (due to revert to Chinese rule in 1999). The danger to China from Mongolia, from where Altan Khan (1543–83) raided almost annually across the Great Wall, was kept in check by adroit Ming diplomacy, and further allayed by the Mongol acceptance of Tibetan religious authority; with the spread of Lamaism, monasteries absorbed surplus sons who might otherwise have become warriors. But danger lurked in the lands north of Korea, where descendants of the 12th-century Jurched rulers of the *Jin Dynasty* were forming a new tribal confederation of people who would become known as *Manchus*. Their chieftain Nurhachi took the title of emperor; his son brought all of Mongolia under his rule, overran Korea in 1627, and took the Ming northeastern outpost of Mukden in 1636.

Domestically in China, a combination of rising imperial expenditures and increasing land tax evasion by the rural gentry eventually destabilized even so rich an empire as the Ming. Factionalism and eunuch intrigues in the capital weakened the dynasty further; popular rebellions broke out and were not thoroughly suppressed. In desperation, the last Ming emperor invited a Manchu army to Beijing to expel a rebel band that had seized the city. Having expelled the rebels, the Manchus refused to leave. The Ming emperor hanged himself, and the Manchus proclaimed the founding of the Qing Dynasty

(1644–1911). Ming resistance in southern China was quashed by 1661; all Chinese men were required to braid their hair in a queue as a sign of submission.

During the last decades of the Ming, China began to feel the first effects of European influence. The Jesuit missionary Matteo Ricci reached Macao in 1582 and Beijing in 1601. Adapting himself to local custom, he became an accomplished Confucian scholar and used that guise as a means of introducing to China such things as the astrolabe, the weight-driven clock, prisms, and the Mercator map of the world. For a brief time Christianity became a vogue among some members of the mandarin class, but imperial disapproval (exacerbated by factional disputes among the Christian missionary orders) discouraged conversions. Under Qing rule the Jesuits were prohibited from preaching, but allowed to remain in China for their technical skills in astronomy, mathematics, painting, and cannon-founding.

In Korea, the *Choson Dynasty* was badly shaken by a destructive invasion (1592–98) from Japan under the leadership of the shogun Toyotomi Hideyoshi. The invasion was finally repelled with Chinese aid, but Korea suffered long-term economic and social damage. Conquered by the Manchus in 1627, the Koreans had no difficulty in transferring their loyalty from the Ming to the Qing; Choson remained a loyal vassal of China, and isolated from the rest of the world, until the late 19th century.

Japan borrowed the old Chinese term "Warring States Period" to describe the century from 1467 to 1568, when Muromachi rule dissolved in a welter of mutually hostile feudal domains. Order was gradually restored after 1568 by three remarkable generals: Oda Nobunaga, who was the first Japanese general to use firearms extensively in battle; Toyotomi Hideyoshi, a peasant who rose to rule Japan, only to squander his resources in a fruitless invasion of Korea; and Tokugawa Ieyasu, who defeated Hideyoshi's army at the Battle of Sekigahara in 1600 and established the Tokugawa shogunate, military rulers of Japan until 1868. The Tokugawa period is sometimes known as the *Edo Period*, after its capital (now Tokyo).

Japan readily absorbed European influence in the sixteenth century. The Portuguese arrived as traders in 1543; another Jesuit, Francis Xavier (1506–52) began his mission to the Japanese in 1549. Within three decades the number of Catholic converts, including some members of the high military aristocracy, reached 150,000. Thereafter Hideyoshi began to suppress Christianity as a foreign threat, banishing Portuguese missionaries in 1587. The Tokugawa shoguns persecuted Christianity even more fiercely, executing thousands after 1612 and driving the church underground after the Christian Shimbara Uprising of 1637–38 ended in an appalling slaughter. Thereafter no foreigners were allowed in Japan except for a small number of Dutch traders, who were rigorously confined to an island in Nagasaki harbor.

Africa's Time of Troubles 1500–1650

The Portuguese sea route to the east diverted attention from the earlier trading contacts with Africa where Portuguese traders brought cotton goods and metal manufactures to exchange for ivory and gold as far as the delta of the Niger river, and where, further south, at the mouth of the Congo, a Bantu-speaking Christian state developed after 1483. And the new world of the Americas, the Spanish Caribbean and Portuguese Brazil, provided a large market for traffic in human beings: the *slave trade* which the Portuguese monopolized until the Dutch drove them out of the Gold Coast in 1642. African slavery, once the result of tribal warfare, now became its cause. First the Portuguese, then the Dutch and, after 1562, the English encouraged tributary states along the west coast to provide them with workers for new world plantations.

The trading *Kingdom of Songhay* which had reached its greatest extent under Askia Mohammed and Askia Dawud in the 16th century was smashed by a Moroccan invasion in 1591. The fall of Songhay brought decline further east to the *Kingdom of Kanem (Bornu)* in the savanna surrounding Lake Chad after 1617. The paradoxical result was the decline of Islamic influence for with the destruction of the Moslem towns the old caravan routes across the Sahara dwindled to a trickle. Further south, the Portuguese established themselves on the west and east coasts in *Angola* (1574) and Mozambique (1508) and after 1628 reduced to vassal status the *Kingdom of the Makaranga* which stretched from the Zambesi to the Limpopo with its capital at Great Zimbabwe. At Africa's southern tip the Dutch established themselves, founding Capetown in 1652.

The Americas: Europe's New Provinces

The Treaty of Tordesillas (1494) between Spain and Portugal divided the world by a line 370 leagues west of the Azores, establishing monopolies for Spain westward and Portugal eastward of the line, approximately 45 degrees west longitude. Thus Brazil, not discovered until 1500, accidentally, by Pedro Cabral (c. 1467–c. 1520) on a voyage to India, became Portuguese territory. But the new world seemed a dead end: the shores of the Caribbean were clearly not the islands and coasts of Asia, the Spanish westward route to the Indies bumped up against an apparently interminable barrier, the Americas.

What altered the picture entirely were the events of 1519–22. In 1520, Ferdinand Magellan (c. 1480-1521) sailed around the southern tip of South America, bringing the Spanish to the Philippines and the Moluccas across the Pacific. Then in 1521, the *conquistador* (conqueror) Hernando Cortez's (1485–1547) brutally subdued the Aztec Empire in 1521. When Francisco Pizarro (1476–1541) toppled the Inca Empire in 1534, Spain acquired a stupendous world empire the wealth of whose silver mines dwarfed the riches of the Indies.

Organized into two vice-royalties, the *Spanish Empire* granted *encomiendas* or plantations to the conquerors; although enslavement of the Indians was forbidden, the Spanish reduced them to serf-like status and forced them to work for their new lords. Christian missions were immediately established with such success that over 20 bishoprics had been created by the mid-16th century. Five universities were flourishing by the middle of the 17th century.

France also sent exploratory ventures to America led by Giovanni da Verrazano (1524) and Jacques Cartier (1534); but it was not until the 17th century that a permanent settlement was established by Samuel de Champlain (1567–1635) who founded New France (1608) with a capital at Quebec. Missions began in 1615 but the process of christianizing the Indians met with no such success as did the Spanish endeavor although Jesuits were involved here. Jean de Brébeuf's conversion of the Huron tribe only exposed them the more to the Iroquois savagery who undid his work and that of Isaac Jogues among the Mohawks. The establishment of Montreal made that more westward site the focus of the fur trade on which the economy of New France was based. Earlier the French began colonizing the Lesser Antilles, right on the fringe of the Spanish Empire and by 1656 had colonized a dozen.

England's Queen Elizabeth (1558–1603) limited herself to encouraging courtiers like Sir Humphrey Gilbert and Sir Walter Raleigh in their ill-fated attempts at early settlement (Roanoke I., 1585) and pirates and slave traders like Sir Francis Drake and Sir John Hawkins in their plundering Spanish ships. Not until the Stuart Dynasty (1603–49) did English settlement begin in earnest. Through grants to commercial companies and individual proprietors, the English established colonies from the Chesapeake to Maine broken only by the Swedes on the lower Delaware River and the Dutch in the Hudson Valley. The Chesapeake became the center of a thriving agricultural region based upon tobacco, while New England flourished as a haven for the English Calvinists known as Puritans.

Europe in the Age of the Reformation

The Europe whose sea-borne enterprise established the first truly world-wide empires was a civilization menaced from without by the Ottoman Turks and divided within both by dynastic-national rivalries and the sundering of Christian unity by the *Reformation*. For many years, leading members of the church had cried out for reform of the clergy, who often led scandalous lives amidst great wealth and who sold God's forgiveness (indulgences) for cash. But not even the powerful voices of the Dutch humanist Desiderius Erasmus (1466–1536) or the English statesman Sir Thomas More (1478–1535) had any impact.

In 1517, the call of the Augustinian monk Martin Luther (1483-1546) for a cleansing of the Church on the basis of his doctrine of "salvation by faith alone" (with its implication of the worthlessness of the priesthood and the sacramental system) swept across northern Germany from the Rhine to the Memel; the adherence of the Scandinavian monarchies to the new faith made the Baltic almost a Lutheran lake. The English king Henry VIII (1509–47), while anti-Lutheran, severed his realm from the Catholic Church after 1532. But what secured Protestantism's hold in Europe was the work of John Calvin (1509–64) who, from 1541 until his death, made Geneva a theocratic state and directed the spread of Calvinism to France, the Low Countries and the British Isles.

The attempts of the Holy Roman Emperor Charles V (1519–56) to halt the spread of Lutheranism were hampered by his need to defend the West against the Ottoman Turks (and thus not offend the Lutheran princes) and to maintain his dynastic territories against the kings of France who allied with the Turks against him. For he ruled the Netherlands and Spain in addition to holding the office of Emperor. At his abdication he willed the Empire to his brother Ferdinand along with Habsburg holdings in central Europe; Spain with its empire, both in the new world and Europe (Netherlands, Burgundy, Milan and Naples), he willed to his son Philip II (1556–98).

Philip faced rebellion in the Netherlands where by the end of his reign the northern provinces had all but won their independence while the southern provinces were held. His Armada (1588) against England met disaster, thereby confirming Queen Elizabeth's rule and the triumph of Protestantism in both England and Scotland. France was given over to the Wars of Religion (1562–98) in which Philip ineffectively intervened on the Catholic side against the Calvinists; the upshot was victory for the Calvinist claimant Henry IV (1589–1610) who, however, turned Catholic but issued the Edict of Nantes (1598) granting French Calvinists ("Huguenots") equal rights, even to the extent of maintaining their own armies.

Philip II considered himself the Catholic champion and it was during his reign that the Catholic *Counter-Reformation* made its greatest strides, not politically but ecclesiastically. Spanish religious leadership came from the new Jesuit Order founded in 1540 by Ignatius Loyola (1491–1556), a fertile source of missionaries, preachers, scholars and schoolmasters, and from the great mystic theologians Theresa of Avila and John of the Cross. Institutionally the *Council of Trent* (1545–63), while not healing the breach with the Protestants, managed to reform the most gratuitous abuses in the Church and provide a clear and authoritative expression of Catholic belief that would last for four centuries.

The uneasy balance between the opposing forces at the start of the 17th century broke down, provoking a time of great crisis. Germany and the Empire were devastated by the Thirty Years' War (1618–48) in which the triumph of the Catholic Habsburgs was prevented by the interventions of Lutheran Sweden and Catholic France personified by King Gustavus Adolphus of Lutheran Sweden and Cardinal Richelieu of France. Britain was shaken by the struggle between Anglicans and Puritans religiously, between the Stuart kings and Parliament politically, the climax coming in the English Civil Wars (1642–49) where the Puritan victory entailed the beheading of King Charles I and the establishment of a military dictatorship under Oliver Cromwell (1649–58).

In eastern Europe there was instability as well. After the long reign of Ivan IV the Terrible (1533–84) in which the entire Volga came under Russian rule and expansion began beyond the Ural Mountains, Russia underwent its "time of troubles." The nobles ("boyars") whose power he thought he had broken rose again to prominence under his weaker son Theodore and confusion as to the succession permitted Polish penetration deep into Russia until the national assembly in 1613 elected Michael Romanov, founder of the *Romanov Dynasty* (1613–1917). In Poland, under Sigismund II (1548–72), the spread of the Reformation was checked and Lithuania was united with Poland into a single state (1569). But Sigismund was the last of the Jagellonian dynasty and at his death the monarchy became in fact what it had always been in theory, elective and thus increasingly the plaything of other great powers. From 1587 to 1648 two members of the Catholic branch of Sweden's royal family, the Vasas, ruled in Poland. Their interventions in Swedish affairs and in Russia during the time of trouble made significant enemies for Poland.

It was a Polish priest, Copernicus (1473–1543) who stands at the beginning of the *Scientific Revolution*, overturning the ancient cosmology of Ptolemy for the heliocentric theory. Expanded by the work of the Dane Tycho Brahe (1546–1601) and his scientific heir, the German Johannes Kepler (1571–1630), the movement reached its first climax in the system of the Italian Galileo (1564–1642), the greatest scientist of the age.

It was also the age of the great flowering of the vernacular literatures of Europe, especially in epic poetry and the drama: in England, Spenser and Shakespeare; in Italy, Ariosto and Tasso; in Spain, Cervantes, Lope de Vega, and Calderon; in Portugal, Camoens. Ironically, this turbulent age also saw the magnificent flowering of painting and sculpture from the universal genius of Michelangelo (1475–1564), the sculptor Bernini (1598–1680), and the painters Raphael, Titian (c. 1490–1576), El Greco (c. 1541–1614), Velasquez (1599–1660), Rubens (1577–1640), and Rembrandt (1606–69).

▶ EXPANSION OF THE EUROPEAN WORLD HEGEMONY (1650–1815)

The period in Europe was characterized by the predominance of France, absolutist at the start, revolutionary at the close—a dominance that was as much cultural as it was political. In the western hemisphere, the age saw the maturing of the colonial extensions of western civilization, with the British dominating the north and the Spanish the south. In Africa and the Middle East, western influence grew primarily through trade, principally British controlled. And in the great land mass of Eurasia, two huge empires grew, those of Russia and China.

Europe in Enlightenment and Revolution

The religious wars of the previous period had a double effect: the boundaries of religious division between Catholic and Protestant Europe solidified and there grew up, especially in northwest Europe, men whom the French called *politiques*, seeking peace beyond the reach of religious controversy and division. Parallel with the rise of the politique mentality there had arisen the philosophical movement known as *rationalism* which sought to reconstruct philosophy on the basis of "clear and distinct ideas" (Rene Descartes, 1596–1650). Then came the climax of the scientific revolution in the achievement of Isaac Newton (1642–1727), whose *Principia Mathematica* (1687) united the key ideas of inertia, gravitation, and centrifugal force.

These three streams flowed together in the movement known as the *Enlightenment* whose publicists, called "philosophes," skeptical of all things except reason (and reason understood as the application to all matters of the method of Newton), called all authority into question save their own and subjected all traditional institutions, including the Church, to the corrosive solvents of their argument and mockery.

The man who gave his name to the *Age of Louis XIV* (1661–1715) was no philosopher but an absolute monarch whose court at Versailles became the model for sovereigns across Europe, establishing a French cultural dominance more significant than her political power. Not that the latter was insignificant: in a series of four wars the "Sun King" expanded France's frontiers to the Rhine and his Bourbon dynasty to the throne of Spain. It took alliances of almost all Europe to limit him even to this, alliances organized principally by the Dutch stadtholder William of Orange who conspired as well with the Protestant English aristocracy to overturn their Catholic king James II, the second of the Stuarts restored after the Cromwellian dictatorship, and install him as William III of England. This event is known as the "Glorious Revolution" and it turned England essentially into an aristocratic republic dominated by Parliament.

Louis XIV's revocation of the Edict of Nantes (1685) forced the Protestant Huguenots to leave France for Holland, Britain, and Prussia where they became industrious businessmen and artisans; through their dominance of publishing, they laid the basis for the spread of the Enlightenment.

In eastern Europe the age of Louis XIV was principally the story of the decline of Polish and Ottoman power and the rise to dominance of Prussia and Russia in the Baltic region and the new *Habsburg Empire* in the southeast. With the Spanish Habsburgs sliding toward extinction and the Holy Roman Empire rendered ghostly by the Thirty Years' War, the Austrian Habsburgs drove the Ottomans out of Croatia and Hungary (1699) and added Galicia from helpless Poland (1772). Meanwhile, the War of the Spanish Succession (1702–13) which established the Bourbons on the throne of Spain also detached from Spain its holdings in the Netherlands (roughly modern Belgium) and Italy (Milan and Tuscany), awarding both to the Austrian Habsburgs. This unwieldy dynastic empire, so diverse as to lack even a name, is usually called the *Austrian Empire*, though that title was not taken until 1804. The heart of Catholic Baroque culture in art and architecture and music, Austria became in the reign of Joseph II (1765–80) the seat of an enlightened despotism as well.

More an army than a state, Brandenburg excelled in switching alliances: Frederick William the Great Elector gained sovereignty in the Duchy of Prussia from Poland (1660), and his son a royal title there from the Emperor (1701); thus the *Hohenzollern* dynasty's holdings are usually called *Prussia*. Under Frederick II the Great (1740–86), friend and patron of Voltaire, Prussia snatched Silesia from the Habsburgs (1748). Participating in the partitions of Poland (1772,1793,1795) the Hohenzollerns again doubled the size of their dynastic holdings.

Fought on three continents, the Seven Years' War (1756–63) was the first truly world war. In the European theater the alliances (Great Britain and Prussia against France, Austria and Russia) fought to a draw; the war was won overseas: in North America and in India the British drove out the French and established their hegemony. But in attempting to organize her new and gigantic North American holdings (the "new imperial system") Great Britain provoked into rebellion her old coastal colonies whose independence as the United States of America was recognized in the Peace of Paris (1783). (For North American developments afterward, see Part II: U.S. History.)

The French Revolution

A war for independence rather than, as its common name implies, a revolution, the American experience was an odd model for the tumultuous upheaval known as the *French Revolution*. France was the most prosperous state in Europe, but the long series of wars since 1660 combined with the clergy's and the aristocracy's exemption from taxation impoverished the monarchy. As a way out of the impasse, Louis XVI resurrected the old medieval Estates General (1789) but the representatives transformed themselves into a constitutional convention called the National Assembly. After abolishing serfdom, setting the peasants free, they remodeled the French state into a constitutional monarchy. But they also confiscated Church lands, dissolved the monasteries, and attempted to make the Church a department of the state, complete with elected bishops. This tore many devout Catholics away from the revolutionary cause.

The universal appeal of the French Revolution to so many people across Europe frightened the monarchs and encouraged the National Assembly to declare war on them all. The new mass armies of the French, fired by ideology and national pride, were a juggernaut against the old-fangled monarchical armies. At home, the war emergency and a revolt in a pro-royalist area (Vendee) against the newly declared republic were used to justify a Committee of Public Safety led by George Danton (1759–94) and Maximilien Robespierre (1758–94) and its *Reign of Terror* (1793–94); it's first victims were the royal family, including Louis XVI and his wife Marie Antoinette. The rule of the Directory (1795–99) that followed was overturned by its general, the Corsican adventurer and military genius Napoleon Bonaparte (1769–1821), who established a popular and military dictatorship (1799) first disguised as a republic, then under the name *French Empire* (1804–15).

Several coalitions of nations were formed to stop Napoleon, but he defeated all of them. Coalition after coalition broke up in defeat. At its peak, the Empire dominated all of Europe from the English Channel to the Ottoman Empire by incorporation into the Empire, or as satellites, or as allies. But a popular uprising in Spain, supported by Britain, and the failure of Napoleon's invasion of Russia (1812) began the breakup of his Empire. By 1814 the anti-French nationalisms that conquest had evoked and the recovery of the monarchs' courage brought Napoleon down and, when he returned in 1815, produced his final defeat at Waterloo (1815) at the hands of the first Duke of Wellington (1769–1852).

Scarcely noticed, another and perhaps more powerful revolution was already under way before the period ended. Enlightened British landowners were enclosing the commons (the village lands tenant farmers used to graze cattle) and developing new crops while inventors were creating the machinery (the spinning jenny, the waterframe, and the steam engine) which would provide the basis in the following period for the *Industrial Revolution*.

Europe Overseas: The Americas and Africa

Between the crises of the Cromwellian period (1643–60) and the Glorious Revolution (1688) the Stuart kings of England fostered new proprietary grants in the Hudson Valley, in Pennsylvania, and in the Carolinas. Thereafter the North American colonies became habituated to self-government under their elected assemblies in a period of "salutary neglect" by the home government. Legally colonies, they were in fact mature provinces of Britain overseas. When after the Seven Years' War the government attempted to limit settlement beyond the Appalachians, to tax the colonists for the costs of the enlarged British holdings, and to extend toleration to Catholics in Canada, the colonial resistance led to war and to independence.

The Spanish new world colonies, with new viceroyalties of New Granada (1717) (roughly modern Venezuela, Colombia, and Ecuador) and La Plata (1776) (Bolivia, Paraguay, Uruguay, and Argentina) remained essentially Indian states governed paternalistically by *Yo, el rey*—the king, in whose name all regulations were sent to the viceroys. After about 1650 Indian population grew rapidly. While rule remained in the hands of "peninsulares" from the home country and, to a lesser degree, in those of the "creoles," colonists of Spanish descent, in the towns, the Indians' chief contact with Spanish culture was in the Church whose missionaries and bishops provided a spiritual elite. Of special note were the Jesuit "reductions" on the upper Parana: self-governing, communistic Catholic Indian republics which fell victim to European politics and Brazilian incursions. Brazil by 1800 had a population larger than Portugal's.

To the viceroyalty of New Spain (Mexico) was attached the Philippines. No one was sure where in the Pacific lay the treaty line of 1494 so that while the Philippines were in fact on the Portuguese side, it was Spain which claimed them in 1565, founding Manila in 1571 which became the western terminus for the famous Manila galleons bearing Mexican silver. Through the whole period coasting voyages of English, Dutch and Spanish mariners discovered the islands of the South Pacific: the Carolines, the Marshalls, Tasmania, New Zealand and Australia; but no settlements disturbed the hunting and gathering culture of the Stone Age people who inhabited them.

It was otherwise in Africa where the slave trade continued until the end of the period, peaking in the 1780s but with demand dropping decade by decade thereafter. And in the early years of the 19th century Britain, Denmark and the United States abolished the trade, Britain actively but not always effectively blocking the trade along the African coast. In west Africa, there was an Islamic revival in the savanna as the *Fulbe people*, over the century after 1670, spread eastward toward Lake Chad in a series of *jihads* against *Hausa* cities. In south Africa, the *Zulu* nation, utilizing trained infantry units armed with spears established a small empire in the late 1700s over their neighbors who still relied on the hurling of javelins; while the Dutch at the southern tip, with its Mediterranean climate and its few Khoikhoi (Hottentots), built a Dutch-speaking, Calvinist, multi-racial colony which by 1815 had a population of about 80,000. The pioneering "trekboers" beyond the Cape found their expansion limited by the Xhosa people and when the colony passed from the Dutch to the British (1814), British governors attempted to halt the expansion in the name of peace. Finally, on the east coast trade reached inland as far as Lake Victoria, initiated by the Nyamwezi people of Tanzania but falling after 1800 into the hands of the trade network of Oman, an ally of Britain.

Two Eurasian Empires: Russian and Ottoman

In one aspect the development of the Russian Empire was an eastward expansion of Europe, in another it was the creation of a stupendous Oriental state menacing Europe. Russian pioneers had already reached the Pacific by 1637; expansion into Central Asia brought the Russians up against Chinese expansion westward into the same region, peace being established in 1689 by the Treaty of Nerchinsk which set the common boundary along the peaks of the Stanovoi Mountains, the Russians evacuating a fort they had constructed on the Amur. This shifted Russian interests to the northeast, leading eventually to Russian settlements in Canada and California (1805–1912).

A certain important but superficial "westernizing" of Russia took place under Peter the Great (1689–1725) who in a "revolution from above" autocratically imposed upon his land western modes in manufacturing, in political administration, in military techniques, in court manners and even in dress. Russia had already taken the eastern Ukraine including Kiev from Poland (1667), then the portion (1681) that their allies the Ottomans had won in that war. Peter's attempts to gain Azov—the warm-water port on the Black Sea that would provide access to the Mediterranean—from the Ottoman Empire proved ineffectual. But in the Great Northern War (1700-21) he proved more successful against Sweden, establishing Russia on the Baltic and founding a new capital at St. Petersburg.

Under Catherine II the Great (1762–96), another "enlightened despot" favored by Voltaire, Russia fought a war with the Ottoman Empire. The Treaty of Kuchuk Kainarji (1774) established Russia in the Crimea along the north of the Black Sea, granted navigation rights to Russia in Turkish waters, including the Straits into the Mediterranean, and provided a legal basis for Russia to intervene to protect Orthodox Christians in the provinces of Moldavia and Walachia—i.e. most of what Peter the Great wanted. Catherine also participated in the partitions of Poland (1772, 1793, 1795) which obliterated that ancient Christian state.

In a third stage of expansion Russia took Finland (1809) from Sweden and Bessarabia (1812) from the Ottomans during the Napoleonic Wars. After the invasion of Russia (1812) the czar Alexander I participated in the great coalition that at last brought Napoleon down. In 1815 Russian troops were participating in the occupation of Paris and the Polish Kingdom that emerged from the post-war settlement had Alexander as its king.

The Russian ascendancy was paralleled by Ottoman decline. Of the dozen sultans who ruled between 1648 and 1839 only Selim III (1789–1807) was a man of intelligence and vigor. The period began with misleading signs of strength, as the Turks took Podolia from Poland (1672) and advanced against the Habsburgs, climaxing in the siege of Vienna (1683). The failure of the siege proved a real turning point, the beginning of a long slow sag in Ottoman fortunes that made it by the 19th century "the sick man of Europe." Facing war after war against Austria and Russia (often in tandem) in the west and Persia in the east, the Empire yielded territory, strained its already chaotic finances, and developed a defensive mentality. Its domestic power waned as well as frontier garrisons meant for defense had to be used to suppress rebellions and endemic banditry.

The year after the siege of Vienna was lifted, the Austrians were victorious in the second Battle of Mohacs (1684) which reversed that of 1526, a victory confirmed by the Battle of Zenta (1697): Hungary and Croatia fell away. After the Treaty of Kuchuk Kainarji (1774), the Black Sea was no longer a Turkish lake and Russian ships sailed freely through Ottoman waters. Egypt, temporarily independent in 1769, gained its autonomy in 1805 while Serbia became the first Christian Balkan state to gain autonomy. Even Arabia, the original homeland of Islam, slipped from Ottoman rule as the Saud clan provided the political and economic support necessary for *Wahhabism* which sought a return to the primitive theocracy of the Prophet himself.

The Growth of British Influence in the Middle East and India

With the Portuguese control of the spice route in disarray and the Dutch diverted toward the Spice Islands, British commercial interests grew ascendant in India. Bombay became the headquarters of the *East Indian Company* (1661) from which Calcutta was founded (1690). But not uncontested: the French founded their East India Company in 1664 and established a trading post at Pondichery in 1674.

The Safavid Persian Empire with which the British East India Company had established trade in 1616 entered after 1664 a decline like that which had earlier begun in the Ottoman realm.

In the long reign of Mogul emperor Aurangzeb (1659–1707) the empire had reached its greatest territorial extent, principally through conquests in the Deccan plateau in south-central India. But within the empire his rule was weak as local governors grew increasingly independent. The Maratha people, under their raja Sivadi, established an independent Hindu state against which the emperor waged inconclusive war until his death, and the religious order of Sikhs (blending Hindu and Moslem beliefs) became under Govind Singh a military order.

After Aurangzeb's death Mogul decline became precipitous. Afghanistan became independent in 1709 then invaded Persia (1722) its leader, Mir Mohammed, becoming shah in 1725. With the death of the last Safavid in 1736 the general Nadir Shah reestablished rule over Afghanistan and even invaded India (1738). But all proved ephemeral. With his death Persia came under the rule of the *Zand Dynasty* (1750–94), then the *Kajar Dynasty* (1794-1925) under whom Great Britain gained the right by treaty (1814) to negate any Persian treaty contrary to her interests. The Afghans (1809) became British allies, bound to assist Britain were Persia or France to attack India.

In India during the 18th century the Maratha state became the dominant Indian body, collecting taxes (1720) in Southern India. Nadir Shah's invasion (1738) wrested the north and west from the Moguls. In the turmoil, the European companies began forming private armies of Indian troops ("sepoys") under European officers. After the War of the Austrian Succession (1746–48) French forces ruled virtually the entire south. But in the Indian theater of the Seven Years' War (1756–63) Robert Clive (1725–74) roundly defeated the French; the Treaty of Paris left but a few holdings to the French. In the aftermath, the East India Company gained from the *nawab* (viceroy) of Bengal landowner status over Calcutta, then pensioned off the *nawab* and ruled Bengal directly (1764).

During this struggle the Afghans invaded from the northeast establishing their rule over the Maratha and Sikhs (1761–62). Faced with the two foreign powers most Indian princes gravitated towards the British, a movement not halted by Parliament's India Act (1784) which brought the Company under government control and prohibited it from interfering in Indian affairs or from engaging in war. Still, between 1786 and 1813, the Company's governors-general began a judicial system, gained control over the foreign affairs of most southern principalities in return for British protection, and entered into the treaties with Persia and Afghanistan already mentioned.

In reality, there was no British empire. The Company ruled directly only certain territories whose princes could not secure peace and order and established treaty obligations with other princes. There were no missionaries, no conversions—not even British law: an odd combination of feelings of superiority with respect for Indian culture led to a hands-off policy. And to the Hindus, the British were but another caste.

Chinese Expansion, Japanese Isolation (1650–1800)

The Manchu emperors of China adapted themselves rapidly to the ancient system of empire government, maintaining the examination system for the bureaucracy (though sometimes doubling officials, one Manchu, one Chinese). So serene and sensible (and non-theological) did the Manchu state appear to the European mind that it almost rivaled England in their fantasies.

Taiwan was annexed in 1683, Tibet gradually brought under Chinese control (1705-51) with the emperor controlling succession of the Dalai Lamas. But the great expansion was into central Asia, settled diplomatically with the Russians in 1689 to China's advantage. All this was the work of Kang Xi, the contemporary of Louis XIV.

Under Qian Long, who ruled from 1736-95, Burma had to recognize Chinese overlordship (1769) as did Nepal (1792). Burma had only recently been re-united (1753) and that with British assistance to Alaungpaya, so the relationships became an avenue of British influence. At the same time Annam, largely Chinese in culture and recognizing its overlordship, nonetheless permitted Catholic missions which met with surprising success especially after Gia Long emerged as emperor in 1802.

The whole period was for China one of expansion, not only territorially. In agriculture new crops from the Americas (maize and yams) provided a larger and more diversified food supply, though by the end of the period population was pressing up against its limits. Trade with Europe and with Japan, carried in Portuguese ships, was based upon Chinese exports of tea, silk and porcelain, the latter increasingly produced on a mass basis in imperial and private kilns. But China showed little interest in the outside world. The late 19th-century mission of the British diplomat Lord George MacCartney was met with total indifference. China would soon suffer badly from this imperial self-satisfaction. The papacy's finding (1715) that reverence shown toward Confucius or toward one's ancestors was incompatible with Catholic belief led to the ban of Catholic missionaries in 1720.

In Japan the splendid isolation of the Tokugawa period continued. But the internal peace that they enforced left the samurai warriors functionless, increasingly dissolute and in debt to the thriving merchant class. The heyday of the latter in the *Genroku Period* (1688-1704) led to a flourishing of Japanese literature free of Chinese influence: the development of haiku poetry, especially under the master Matsui Basho (1644-94) and of the Kabuki drama. Late in the period there were signs of restiveness against the Tokugawa not only from the great clans excluded from power but from the imperial family as well, both merging patriotic feeling and imperial loyalty with the increasing vogue of the Shinto religion, both worried about the danger of the Westerners to Japan's isolated development.

▶ TRIUMPH AND TRAGEDY OF WESTERN CIVILIZATION (1815-1945)

With the defeat of Napoleon in 1815, Europe entered 100 years of peace, the ending of serfdom, the extraordinary development of industrial capitalism, the spread of liberal and democratic institutions, and the apogee of her world-wide imperial influence. But then ensued 30 years of tumultuous upheaval: two world wars, waged with new weapons of mass destruction, flanking the subjection of most of Europe to grim totalitarian domination. At the end Europe lay broken and prostrate, its fate and the fate of the world in the hands of the two atomic superpowers, liberal-democratic America and Communist Russia.

Europe: The Rise of Nationalism

After a quarter-century of exhausting warfare the conservative monarchs and statesmen of Britain, Austria, Prussia and Russia made a generous peace with France, restoring the Bourbon dynasty but hedging her borders with an enlarged Netherlands to the north, the Prussians on the Rhine and the Habsburgs in northern Italy. To maintain the peace they established the Concert of Europe, a series of international conferences (to which France was soon admitted) to regulate European affairs, initiating the longest sustained general European peace since Rome's Antonine emperors in the second century A.D. Fearing revolution as the source of war and so a threat to themselves, they suppressed liberal and nationalist organizations and sent troops into Italy and Spain to prop up their tottering monarchies; but Britain, supporting the "Monroe Doctrine," prevented any intervention against the revolts in Latin America. With the devolution of the Ottoman Empire in the Balkans, the powers supported an independent Greece (1829) and autonomy for Serbia, Moldavia and Walachia. Similarly, liberal revolts in Belgium and France (1830) led not to suppression but to independence for the first and a change of dynasty for the second; in the same year, however, Russia crushed a Polish revolt and absorbed that state into her empire. Britain herself, without revolution, carried out a liberal reform of her constitution (1832) abolishing "rotten" or underpopulated boroughs and expanding the electorate

by 50 percent, especially in the new manufacturing centers.

The year 1848 saw a remarkable series of liberal and nationalist revolts in virtually all the capitals of the German and Italian principalities and of the Habsburg realms. Yet all proved stillborn, and the armies remained loyal to their sovereigns. Still they had lasting effects, as serfdom was abolished throughout central Europe. The liberal route to national unity, which combined political goals (representative government) with nationalist ones seemed discredited; and the 1848 revolt in Paris led to the establishment of a brief Second Republic, then, in a revival of Bonapartism, a *Second Empire* (1852-70) under Napoleon III (Louis Napoleon Bonaparte, 1808-73).

His assistance was essential in aiding Piedmont's conquests of all the Italian states save Venice and Rome; the *Kingdom of Italy* was proclaimed in 1861 and by 1870 it included Venice and Rome as well. The latter two it gained as an ally of Otto von Bismarck's (1815-98) Prussia, which in a series of three brief wars incorporated all of non-Habsburg Germany into the *German Empire*, proclaimed in 1871. The third of those wars (the Franco-Prussian war), took Alsace and Lorraine from France, toppled Napoleon III, and led to the formation of France's *Third Republic* (1871–1940). The second, which had excluded Austria from German affairs, led that empire to its own reform, the establishment in 1867 of the "Dual Monarchy" of *Austria-Hungary*.

In one decade the map of Europe had been transformed, its most powerful state the new Germany which, with rapid industrialization, became stronger still in the years which led up to the World War I.

Europe: Two World Wars, 1914–45

Bismarck attempted to keep France isolated. He encouraged her colonial expansion to compensate for her diminished status in Europe and in the hope that imperial rivalry with Britain would keep those western states apart. He hoped for similar results from Russian and British rivalry in Persia and Afghanistan. And he formed the Triple Alliance of Germany, Austria-Hungary, and Italy.

But France and Russia allied in 1894 and a decade later, after settling colonial issues that had nearly brought them to war, France and Britain came too a "friendly understanding." The triangle was completed in 1907 when Britain and Russia established spheres of influence in Persia. Bismarck's diplomacy was undone by Kaiser Wilhelm II's (r. 1888–1918) aggressive foreign policy and a naval arms race with Britain.

Not in the colonies but in the Balkans events moved beyond any statesman's ability. In the disintegration of Ottoman power there, Serbia, Romania and Montenegro became independent in 1878 and Bulgaria in 1908. The powers consistently checked Russian advances there while the influence of Austria-Hungary grew. Struggling for territory from the Ottomans and from each other, the Balkan states fought a series of three wars in 1912, 1913 and 1914. It was the third one, which began with the assassination of the Archduke Francis Ferdinand in Sarajevo by a Serbian nationalist that expanded into the catastrophe of World War I.

Outside Europe fighting was slight: German holdings in the Pacific and Africa were taken by British and French imperial forces; Russian and British forces engaged the Ottomans in

Mesopotamia and Armenia; and western-backed Arab revolts further weakened Ottoman strength. But in Belgium and northern France developed the horror of four years of trench warfare and on the gigantic eastern front immense armies clashed but without resolution until 1917 when the Bolsheviks, led by Vladimir I. Lenin (1870–1924), took Russia out of the war after their revolution (Nov. 6, 1917) toppled the Provisional Government that had succeeded the czarist collapse. But Russia's withdrawal in the east was balanced in the west by the American entry that same year, provoked by Germany's resumption of unrestricted submarine warfare in a futile attempt to escape the noose of Britain's naval blockade. The fighting at last ended November 11, 1918.

Besides its immense cost to blood (over eight million died in battle and six million civilians perished) and treasure, the war overturned the old European state system as four empires collapsed and were partitioned. Germany, under the Versailles Treaty (1919) emerged as the Weimar Republic with small territorial losses to France and to a resurrected Poland but burdened with the war guilt clauses and the immense financial reparations they were meant to justify. Russia lost all her western gains since Peter the Great, retreating eastward into the cruel experiment of Communist Revolution. Austria-Hungary disappeared utterly, two little republics maintaining the names at least of those once great states. And by 1923 in Asia Minor a one-party Turkish Republic emerged under Mustafa Kemal Ataturk (1818–1938).

The successor states in eastern Europe, whether republican or monarchical inform, readily adopted the parliamentary government of the victorious western Allies which, in the years after 1848, had steadily democratized the franchise. But most contained substantial ethnic minorities whose rivalries poisoned parliamentary life; tariff barriers which arose everywhere fragmented the old common markets of the empires they replaced, protecting inefficient, penalizing efficient industry; in agriculture depression was chronic.

To the east brooded the reduced but still vast Soviet Union where with the death of Lenin in 1924 the dictatorship of the party turned increasingly into the dictatorship of Joseph Stalin (1879–1953)who oversaw the murderous collectivization of agriculture and the forced industrialization of the Five Year Plans, then purged the party and the army and the secret police of all but his own men. Millions died.

Western and central Europe seemed sheltered from these grim developments by the "cordon sanitaire" of the new states of east-central Europe. After a period of post-war adjustment, prosperity returned to the western democracies, especially in Germany whose adherence to the Locarno Treaties (1925) presaged enduring peace. Yet in Italy whose wartime sacrifices seemed unrewarded by territorial gains and whose economy did not recover but rather seemed to dissolve into the chaos of socialist and anarchist and capitalist violence there arose in 1922 the second (after Lenin) of the dictators, Benito Mussolini (1883-1945). His fascist movement promised a halfway house between liberal individualism and communist class war, stressing a belligerent nationalism with a corporative economy. In fact it was little more than bombast.

But with the collapse of the world economy after 1929, the social and ethnic divisions of the successor states, their boundary grievances, and the real or imagined fear of communist revolution, most of Europe outside the monarchies of the north and west turned to right-wing authoritarian regimes which, though often called "fascist," resembled Italy less than they did Latin America. The very different and very grievous case was Germany where after 1933 Adolf Hitler (1889-1945) established the Nazi dictatorship in the heart of Europe.

The western democracies dithered, deluded themselves, and sought peace through appeasement (not that they had much alternative, unprepared as they were for military action) as Hitler, bent on overturning the Versailles settlement, successfully re-militarized the Rhineland (1936) and absorbed Austria (the Anschluss) and the ethnically German parts of Czechoslovakia (1938) then turned the remainder of Czechoslovakia into a satellite, took the city of Memel from Lithuania, and began demands on Poland (1939). In August 1939, Germany and Russia agreed to partition Poland yet again and with Hitler's invasion in September began World War II.

It was, until 1941, a European war with nonstop totalitarian triumphs; by June of 1940, when France fell, all of Europe outside Britain was neutral or an ally or a satellite of Germany. But in June of 1941 Hitler invaded Russia and in December Hitler's ally, Japan, attacked the U.S. in Hawaii. Japanese dominion reached as far as Burma in 1942, while German armies penetrated as far east as Stalingrad. Nevertheless, the grand alliance of Britain and the U.S. with the USSR caused Nazi Germany to fight a two-front war, which ultimately spelled utter defeat in May of 1945—but not before Germany killed six million Jews during the Holocaust. Three months later, atomic bomb attacks on Hiroshima and Nagasaki, major Japanese cities, hastened Japan's surrender and World War II came to its end. The United States and the Soviet Union, with Great Britain a very junior partner, bestrode the globe. The European Age in world history was at an end.

The Troubled Independence of Latin America

The impact of the Napoleonic wars upon Europe's trans-Atlantic provinces (and the newly independent United States as well) was profound. For one thing, Haiti's success in maintaining its independence, gained in 1794, against Napoleon's attempt to reconquer it led to his abandonment of any scheme for a New World empire: Louisiana was therefore sold to the United States. For another, placing his brother Joseph on the throne of Spain (1808) threw Spanish America into confusion: which king to obey? Juntas loyal to the Bourbon king Ferdinand VII, led by creoles such as Simon Bolivar (1783–1830) and Jose San Martin (1778–1850), resisted French rule at first, then turned against the absolutism of the restored Ferdinand in whose name they had first risen up. In colony after colony the juntas' armies fought for and won their independence: La Plata (1810), Chile (1818), New Granada (1819), Peru (1821). In separate and more complicated developments, Mexico and Brazil followed in 1822.

The *Monroe Doctrine* (1823) of the United States, instigated and given force by Great Britain, shielded the new states from Spanish repression. But nothing could shield them from the effects of their own inexperience in politics (an effect of Spanish imperial centralization) or from boundary disputes (for New World boundaries too were purely Spanish creations) or from the internal struggles of local leader (*caudillos*) seeking autonomy within the new republics. Thus independence was followed by a long period of wars, civil wars, insurrections and coups.

When the trade links with Spain were cut, the new states found a welcome from Great Britain for their products. British investment fostered mining and industrial development; American investment entered late in the 19th century. The development in the 1880s of adequate methods of refrigeration on steamships meant that beef could join wheat and sugar and coffee as exports. The needs of the Allies in World War I for massive increases in raw materials brought a great increase in trade; large-scale post-war investment from the United States both in industry and in plantation agriculture helped continue economic growth but with serious decline after 1929 in the rate of growth.

This expansion brought social tension through the growth of both a middle class and agricultural and industrial working classes, adding new elements to the older political instability. In the 1930s governments in Mexico and Argentina respectively followed the "popular front" or "corporate state" models of Europe but these were usually but trappings for a new breed of *caudillo*. In the Caribbean, the interests of the United States predominated whether as "policeman" or, as after 1934, "good neighbor."

European Empires in Africa

For 60 years after the Napoleonic wars, Europeans evinced only small interest in Africa. Liberal economic thought supported free trade rather than empire. Trading forts dotted the west African coasts while steamboats penetrated only somewhat further inland and missionaries began evangelization on a small scale. "Cash crop" agriculture was no European imposition: the profits from nuts and palm products, especially oil for lighting and machine lubrication, were enough encouragement to African kings and chiefs, especially with the drying up of the trade in slaves. In the south, the expansion of the Zulu nation after 1818 led to disruptions lasting into the 1850s while amongst the Boers in the south, the British ban on slavery provoked the Great Trek of some 10,000 settlers into the high veld, (or grassy plateau) depopulating the old Cape Colony except for some new British settlers. On the east coast the sultan of Oman moved his capital to Zanzibar the better to control his network of trade in cloves and slaves; the latter brought increasing British estrangement from their protege. Along the Mediterranean coast, the Ottoman Empire was nominally sovereign though rule in fact was exercised by local beys and sultans who gladly countenanced piracy; this provoked the French in 1830 to occupy Algiers and a few coastal cities.

About 1880 a group of French projects—a railways scheme at Dakar, new trading posts on the Ivory Coast and north of the Congo river—alarmed the other powers into the witless "scramble for Africa" which brought Britain and Portugal and eventually even Germany into a contest to annex territory, principally to prevent the others from doing the same and gaining some unknown and unpredictable benefit. The Congress of Berlin (1885) sought to put some order into the competi-

tion and in 15 years the entire continent had been divided up, save for the colony of freed American slaves in Liberia and the ancient Christian empire of Ethiopia. Colonial theorists gained the ear of western governments for grand schemes of great belts of territory, the French to stretch from Dakar to the Red Sea, the British from Capetown to Cairo—all just after the construction of the Suez Canal (1859–69) had rendered such imaginings nugatory. One specific and concrete interest was the discovery of deposits of gold and diamonds in the republic of Transvaal which led to Britain's conquest of the Boer republics in the Boer War (1889-1901) and her formation (1910) of the Union of South Africa, which through elections Boers soon governed.

There was something illusory about it all: tiny armies setting up the national flag, treaties signed with hundreds of tribal chiefs who lacked authority, boundary lines drawn on maps in European capitals. But European administration did bring some measure of peace, some road and rail construction, some support for missionaries, some schools and hospitals, some westernizing of tribal leaders. The last would provide a certain leadership class in the independence movements after World War II which dismantled the empires even faster than they had been thrown together before World War I.

Europe's Asian Domination and the Rise of Japan

If Africa experienced European claims of sovereignty with only hints of the reality, Asia underwent the reverse as British rule was established in India, Burma and Malaya, Holland's in Indonesia, America's in the islands of the South Pacific (Hawaii, Samoa, and later the Philippines) and France's in Indochina. Two new provinces of western civilization grew in Australia and New Zealand. China underwent yet another cycle of imperial decline but with the new element of the presence of the "southern barbarians" (the Europeans) and the aggressive designs of a suddenly modernized Japan.

Three 19th century wars mark the decline of China's power and prestige. Her attempts to maintain Canton as the sole port for western trade and to end Britain's sale of opium led to the Opium War (1841–42) and a thorough British victory. The Treaty of Nanking opened four further cities to trade and ended the "tribute system," Westerners now accepted as China's equals, with a uniform tariff of 5 percent on trade; in addition Hong Kong was ceded to the United Kingdom. In the aftermath of the war, in 1844 and 1845, the United States gained the right of "extraterritoriality" (exemption from Chinese law) for its citizens, soon extended to all the western states, and the French gained toleration for Catholic Christianity, soon extended to Protestant Christians as well.

The social and economic dislocations caused by the Opium War in south China culminated in the *Taiping Rebellion* (1851-64), led by Hong Xiuquan, a failed examination candidate who, having read some Christian missionary pamphlets, imagined himself to be the younger brother of Jesus Christ. A charismatic figure, he raised a huge army and seized much of southern and central China, including the city of Nanjing. To put down the rebellion the Qing emperor resorted to the very dangerous expedient of allowing provincial governors-general to raise their own military units; these were effective but would prove destabilizing in the future. Some western military assistance helped keep the Taipings away from the trading port of Shanghai.

At the same time China experienced three other major rebellions: Moslem uprisings in the northwest and in Yunnan Province in the southwest, and the millenarian Nian Rebellion in the north-central plains. Total loss of life from these rebellions exceeded 20 million; the dynasty itself barely survived. In 1858, in the midst of this turmoil, the British provoked a small affray called the Arrow War, settled by the Treaty of Tientsin in 1860. The cost was the opening of yet another 11 ports, the legalization of the ōpium trade, and the collection of China's customs by Great Britain. Sir Robert Hart became, equivalently, China's finance minister through the years 1863–1908.

Japan's attempt to gain concessions like those of the western powers and to challenge Chinese control over the Manchu tributary state of Korea led to the Sino-Japanese War (1894-95): China had to cede Taiwan and certain mainland territories to Japan and recognize the independence of Korea, a prelude to that kingdom's incorporation into Japan in 1910.

Meanwhile in Indochina the French ignored Manchu protests and established protectorates over Annam (1883) and, right on China's border, Tonkin (1893).

After an unsuccessful attempt in 1898 to reform the imperial government, followed by the abortive, anti-western Boxer Rebellion (1900) discontent with the feebleness of the Manchu government led to the *Chinese Revolution* (1911). The new Chinese Republic's president, General Yuan Shih-k'ai, might have established yet another new dynasty but his death in 1916 permitted the republic to continue, at least in form. But in reality it was the return of feudal anarchy, this time with modern weapons and mass political organizations. Dr. Sun Yat-sen's party, the Kuo Min Tang (KMT), came after his death under the control of his brother-in-law, Chiang Kai-shek, the war lord who controlled south China and whose armies conquered the north in 1927. But the expelling of the Communists from the KMT in 1927 led to a failed series of Communist uprisings and their retreat in *The Long March* In their new stronghold in Yan'an, Mao Zedong (1893–1976) emerged as the party leader and Chiang's chief rival. Their struggle was submerged in the 1930s by the need to oppose Japanese dominance; Japan in 1931–32 occupied Manchuria as a protectorate and invaded China in 1937. The great powers, especially America, kept up the illusion that China was a great power with Chiang its ruler, an illusion blown to pieces within four years after the end of World War II.

Japan's rise to great power status was rooted in an extraordinary adaptability. After the American Commodore Matthew Perry forced the opening of Japan to western trade in 1853 and 1854 patriotic sentiment, anti-foreign and pro-imperial, grew until in 1867, young patriots at the court of the emperor Mutsuhito felt strong enough to end the shogunate and restore imperial control. From his reigning name, Meiji, we speak of the *Meiji Restoration*. During his long rule until 1912, Japan embarked on a course of furious imitation of western ways, as earlier they had imitated the

Chinese; western science, technology, industry and arms became the basis for attaining the goal of "wealthy land, strong army." The imitation reached the extent of inventing (1884) a Japanese peerage so that there might be an upper house on the British model when the Meiji Constitution (1889) established a Diet.

But it was the military (and industrial) aspects, not the political, that showed most rapid advance, providing the basis for triumphs over China (1895) and much more surprisingly Russia (1905), the take-over of some German holdings in the Pacific during World War I, and the incursions against China in the 1930s. The parliamentarianism of the west was repudiated in the reign of Mutsuhito's grandson Hirohito after 1926 as military cliques and gangs came to control government after government and political violence became the order of the day. The attack on Hawaii in December 1941 was designed to cripple the American Pacific fleet, protection for the invasion of southeast Asia which brought Japanese forces by mid-1942 to occupy the American Philippines, the Dutch East Indies, British Hong Kong, Malaya, Singapore and Burma while French Indochina and independent Thailand collaborated. By August 1945 however this whole proud bubble had burst and Japan itself was occupied by American forces.

In India the British kept up the fiction of Mogul rule but proceeded to act more and more like a sovereign power: commencing the repair of the Mogul system of canals (1818) and later building roads and irrigation projects; replacing Persian as the language of law courts with English in the higher courts and local tongues in local courts; founding schools whose curriculum was European and whose language of instruction was English; suppressing, in the 1830s, the funerary suicide of widows, banditry, and murder.

In the 1840s warfare in Afghanistan, in the Sind and against the Sikhs made Britain a true imperial power, the ruling authority in India, protecting Indian princes from subversion and aggression, annexing territory when princely families died out. After the *Great Mutiny* (1857–58) of the sepoys, Britain banished the last of the Moguls. Twenty years later came the symbolic climax, the proclamation (1877) of Queen Victoria as *Empress of India*.

But at the same time the British were establishing executive and legislative councils with Indians represented and courts with Indian justices sitting on the bench. And between the world wars, in which Indian troops fought loyally and with valor on the British side, the Indian National Congress, first established in 1885, came increasingly under the influence of Mahatma Gandhi. His campaigns of civil disobedience in 1921 and in 1930, which only a very liberal empire would have tolerated, presaged the post-war demands that would signal the end of British rule.

More enduring than British India or British rule in Singapore (1819) or Burma (1886) as vehicles of European influence were Australia, a convict colony founded in 1788 which was gradually transformed by generous land grants into the Commonwealth of Australia (1901) and New Zealand where assisted immigration after 1840 and land grants brought dominion status by 1907, both loyally supporting Britain in both of the world wars.

▶THE COLD WAR (1945–PRESENT)

The wartime alliance of Great Britain, France, the United States, and the Soviet Union was one of expediency rather than long-term mutual interest; suspicion and misunderstandings characterized the alliance even during the war. Soon after the war, hostility and divergent interests between the United States and its Western allies, on the one hand, and the Soviet Union, on the other, led to the Cold War, a period of international danger, distrust, and nuclear standoff, during which direct armed conflict was avoided, but wars fought indirectly by proxy nations and movements were endemic.

As the only major power to emerge from World War II with its population, infrastructure, and economy largely intact, the United States saw itself as the leader of the entire postwar world. Its goals, backed by a monopoly on nuclear weapons, included the rapid reconstruction of Western Europe, the fostering of independent and democratic countries in Eastern Europe, rendering Japan harmless in East Asia, encouraging democratic reform in Nationalist China, and promoting peaceful decolonization in Asia and Africa. The United Nations, organized under American leadership in 1945, was to be the vehicle for a postwar *pax Americana*.

The Soviet Union, devastated by the war, its industrial base and agricultural economy in a shambles, reeling from military and civilian casualties that probably exceeded 20 million persons dead, sought on the other hand to insulate itself behind a band of friendly and submissive neighbors, vowing never again to suffer the kind of invasion that Germany had mounted against the USSR during the war. The Soviet Union also determined to make a concerted effort to match the United States in production of nuclear weapons and delivery systems; the resulting arms race eventually resulted in the production of enough nuclear weapons by the two powers to obliterate the entire population of the world. (Beginning in the 1960s, a series of agreements between the US and the USSR succeeded in limiting the testing and production of nuclear weapons, and greatly reducing their numbers.)

Sharply differing visions of a desirable postwar world thus set the stage for a prolonged conflict between America and the Soviet Union.

In Europe, the Soviet Union's interpretation of the wartime Yalta agreements enabled it to move rapidly to depose fledgling democratic governments in the Eastern European countries under Soviet Occupation; as early as 1946 Winston Churchill warned that an "Iron Curtain" was being drawn around a Soviet zone in Eastern Europe. Soviet power was made credible with the rapid development of atomic weapons, using both Russian research and atomic secrets stolen from America during the war. Pro-USSR communist governments were in place in Poland, Czechoslovakia, Hungary, Yugoslavia, Bulgaria, and Romania by 1947. Austria and Finland accepted a neutral status highly deferential to the Soviet Union; communist movements in Italy, Greece and Turkey were defeated with American and British support.

The United States moved rapidly, especially after the development of the Marshall Plan aid program in 1948, to rebuild the economic and political stability of Western Europe in part to counter Soviet expansionism. A Soviet attempt to blockade the Western occupied zone of Berlin was met with the Berlin Airlift, which preserved a Western presence in the city; thereafter West and East Germany became for the balance of the Cold War in effect two separate and mutually hostile states. The Berlin Wall was built in 1961 to stem a tide of illegal migration from East to West Germany; its fall in 1989 marked the end of the Cold War. Meanwhile the North Atlantic Treaty Organization (NATO) was founded under American leadership in 1949 as a Soviet-containment strategy; it was countered by the organization of the Eastern-bloc Warsaw Pact in 1955. Later popular anti-Soviet uprisings in Hungary (1956), Czechoslovakia (1968), and Poland (1981) were ruthlessly suppressed.

Part of the European price for bowing to American leadership was American acquiescence in the postwar reconstitution of the old colonial empires of Britain, France, the Netherlands, and others. These colonial empires were gradually relinquished during the course of the Cold War, sometimes peacefully, as with the British African colonies, sometimes after bloody nationalist uprisings, as in Portuguese Africa and the French colonies of Algeria and Vietnam. The United States tended to step into the power-vacuum of the post-colonial world, in large part to forestall Soviet influence. The hysteria of McCarthyism in the early 1950s ushered in a long period of reflexive anti-communism that led America to support a series of corrupt, unpopular and repressive—but anti-communist—regimes in various parts of the Third World.

In *Asia*, the simmering conflict between Communist and Nationalist forces in China broke out into open civil war by 1946, despite American efforts at mediation. With only grudging material support from the USSR, Chinese Communists under the leadership of Mao Zedong (1893-1976) defeated the far larger and better equipped Nationalists, whose corruption, ineptitude, and bourgeois orientation proved no match for the simple Communist slogan, 'Land to the tiller.' The Nationalists retreated to Taiwan in 1948–49, and Mao proclaimed the founding of the People's Republic of China in Beijing on October 1, 1949. A break between the USSR and the People's Republic of China in the late 1950s, over both geopolitical and ideological issues, did not alter American policy assumptions of a monolithic international communism until the U.S.-Chinese rapprochement of 1973 under the leadership of Pres. Richard M. Nixon.

In Korea, divided after the war into separate occupation zones, a Soviet-backed government led by the veteran communist Kim Il-sung rapidly took control in the north, whereas in the south an inept and ill-prepared American occupation squandered the opportunity for democratic development, and eventually backed the corrupt right-wing movement of Singman Rhee. When North Korean troops invaded the south on June 25, 1950, the United States successfully obtained United Nations backing to rescue the south; the Korean War ensued, fought to a bloody standoff over the next three years.

The "loss" of China and the Korean war transformed American policy in Japan, which was suddenly seen as the anchor of a democratic and capitalist pro-American security zone surrounding communist Asia. India and Pakistan were similarly wooed by Britain and America. Elsewhere in Asia, communist-inspired uprisings in Malaysia and the Philippines were defeated, while an indigenous anti-communist backlash led to the slaughter of tens of thousands of people in Indonesia in 1965. But it was Vietnam that would prove to be the Asian battleground of the Cold War. After the French withdrawal in 1954, America felt impelled to step in to halt what seemed to be a clear case of international communist subversion of a friendly country; the results were devastating to all concerned, and in retrospect the Vietnamese communist movement seems certainly not to have been merely a cat's-paw for the Soviet Union and Communist China. The Soviet Union found its own "Vietnam" in Afghanistan, where its long attempt to install a communist government met with utter failure.

In *Latin America*, the 1959 triumph of Fidel Castro's Cuban revolution struck the American government as an unacceptable provocation on its own doorstep. The failed Bay of Pigs invasion of anti-Castro partisans trained by the CIA was a humiliation for American policy (1961). In 1954 the Russians had exploded a hydrogen bomb, and in 1957 Sputnik proclaimed the success of Soviet rocketry; the 1960 U.S. presidential election was held in an atmosphere of fear of Russian nuclear missiles. In 1962 the Cuban Missile Crisis was the most potentially deadly confrontation of the entire Cold War. Emboldened by success in that face-off, America intervened militarily to counter what it regarded as communist subversion in Guatemala, El Salvador, Nicaragua, Grenada, and elsewhere in Latin America.

In *Africa*, both the US and the USSR supported client states in the post-colonial period; America had some success in preserving the unity of the Congo (Zaire) and Nigeria, though at the cost of supporting kleptocratic regimes; the Soviet Union maintained an African presence in Angola and Mozambique (both garrisoned with Cuban troops), among other places.

The *Middle East* was an area of strong Soviet initiatives throughout the Cold War. With Israel seen as a creature of the United States, its Arab neighbors readily accepted Soviet aid and advice. Britain's inept and humiliating loss of the Suez Canal to Egypt in 1956 bolstered Nasser's socialist regime there, already friendly to Russia for aid in building the Aswan High Dam. Iraq, Syria, and Libya became anti-Israeli Soviet clients, while the U.S. sought support among the more conservative Arab monarchies. Further east, the CIA-sponsored overthrow of the democratic Mossadegh regime in 1953 led to the return to power of the shah; in 1979 his unpopular and autocratic government fell to a fundamentalist Islamic revolution. The subsequent Iran-Iraq war led the U.S. into the anomalous position of supporting the former Soviet client, Iraq's Saddam Hussein. America's strategy throughout the Cold War had been to use its economic power to intimidate the Soviet bloc militarily and tempt the uncommitted nations of the world commercially. In this sense, the dramatic images of Neil Armstrong walking on the moon on July 20, 1969 were a key element in American Cold War propaganda. Conversely, the image of Americans hastily evacuating Saigon at the end of the Vietnam War were devastating to American interests because it seemed to show American impotence in the face of communist-inspired nationalism, even if the reality of the situation was, of course, much more complicated.

The anti-Soviet rhetoric of Pres. Ronald Reagan in the 1980s seemed like a throwback to the Cold War paranoia of the 1950s, but it seems to have hastened the Cold War's end. With a restless population and a crumbling economy, Russia found itself unable to sustain the military expenditures needed to keep pace with the U.S. in Cold War competition around the world. With the domestic softening of policy of Mikahil Gorbachev's *glasnost* and *perestroika* in the mid-80s, people in Poland, East Germany, Czechoslovakia, and elsewhere in Eastern Europe, and also in the Baltic states, rapidly overthrew their governments and threw out Soviet troops. The fall of the Berlin Wall meant in effect the fall of international communism, and the end of the Cold War.

There was fallout, to be sure, in the Persian Gulf War (1990-91), in the turmoil of the ex-Soviet republics, in the struggle of Africa to emerge from the era of Cold War patronage and great-power rivalry. But in the end the Cold War did not seem to amount to much. For all its espionage and paranoia, all the arms races and space races, all the proxy wars in unhappy countries throughout the world, the Cold War passed away with only a whimper, an historical episode that had outlived its day. The U.S. emerged as the only superpower both militarily and economically. The challenges for the future were how to maintain peace around the world, helping poorer nations find prosperity, and still remaining faithful to its ideal of self-determination for all peoples of the world.

In the ensuing years, the U.S. response to these critical problems has centered on efforts to strengthen the world economy and to do so on its own terms by maintaining an overwhelming military dominance. Despite the absence of any serious threat from a large power or a coalition of smaller ones, American military budgets continued to exceed $250 billion a year, sufficient to maintain an advanced weaponry program and to keep 1.5 million men and women on active duty. Russia has nuclear weapons but its military is in disarray and its economy keeps hovering on the edge of collapse. Only China has a larger military force than the U.S., but it lacks anything like America's air and nuclear power.

Since 1990, China has been the focal point of U.S. foreign policy and economic strategy. Despite the Chinese government's overt acts of repression and manifest evidence of serious human rights abuses, Presidents Bush and Clinton have both aggressively pursued an economic alliance that has benefited both countries. Tens of billions of dollars have been invested in China in the last decade and, not surprisingly, China has become the chief supplier of low-cost consumer goods and other items to the U.S. In 1997, China sent exports worth $62 billion to the U.S. but imported only $13 billion.

During the 1990s, the U.S. and its allies have promulgated the idea that democracy and economic freedom are inseparable ideals that only market economy rules can bring to fruition. A central element in this creed is free trade, and the U.S. has led the fight to end tariffs and other barriers by helping to establish the 139-member World Trade Organization to develop international rules and policies for trade. In 1994, the North American Free Trade Agreement ended all trade barriers for Canada, Mexico, and the U.S. In Europe, the European Union moved nations closer to economic integration by regulating trade and establishing a single currency—the euro—that could rival the dollar in the not-too-distant future.

Rulers of the World

EMPERORS OF ROME 27 B.C.–A.D. 491

Augustus   27 B.C.–14 A.D.
Tiberius   14–37
Caligula   37–41
Claudius   41–54
Nero   54–68
Galba   68–69
Otho   69
Vitellius   69
Vespasian   69–79
Titus   79–81
Domitian   81–96
Nerva   96–98
Trajan   98–117
Hadrian   117–38
Antoninus Pius   138–61
Marcus Aurelius (co-emperor with Lucius Verus)   161–69
Marcus Aurelius alone   169–77
Marcus Aurelius (co-emperor with Commodus)   177–80
Commodus alone   180–92
Pertinax   193
Didius Julianus   193

Septimius Severus   193–98
Caracalla (co-emperor with Geta)   211–12
Caracalla alone   212–17
Macrinus   217–18
Heliogabalus   218–22
Severus Alexander   222–35
Maximinus   235–38
Gordian I (co-emperor with Gordian II)   238
Pupienus Maximus (co-emperor with Balbinus)   238
Gordian III   238–44
Philip ("The Arab")   244–49
Decius   249–51
Hostilianus   251
Gallus   251–53
Aemilianus   253
Valerian (co-emperor with Gallienus)   253–60
Gallienus alone   253–68
Claudius II ("Gothicus")   268–70
Aurelian   270–75
Tacitus   275–76
Florianus   276
Probus   276–82
Carus   282–83
Carinus (co-emperor with Numerianus)   283–84
Carinus alone   284–85

Between 270 and 283, there were seven emperors, all chosen by the army. Carus was killed in battle, and Numerianus died on the march. The other five were murdered by their soldiers. In an attempt to end the chaos of the "barracks emperors," Diocletian attempted to establish an orderly succession in the East and West halves of the Empire, the emperor in the East being the senior emperor. Dicocletian and Maximian both abdicated in 305, although Maximian was recalled in 306. Subsequently, the succession became disputed in both East and West, and between 305 and 474 there were 39 claimants to the imperial title, five of whom ruled both the East and the West, most notably Constantine (324–37). With the demise of the last emperor in the West (476), the eastern emperor, Zeno, reunited the imperial office in one person.

East		West
Diocletian 284–305		Maximian 286–308
Galerius 305–11		Constantius I 305–306
Licinius 311–24		Severus 306–307
		Maximin 307–13
	Constantine I 312–37	
Constantius II 337–61		Constantine II 337–40
		Constans 340–50
	Constantius II 350–61	
	Julian 361–63	
	Jovian 363–64	
Valens 364–78		Valentinian I 364–75
Theodosius I 378–92		Gratian 375–83
		Valentinian II 375–92
	Theodosius I 392–95	
Arcadius 395–408		Honorius[1] 395–423
Theodosius II 408–50		Valentinian III 425–55
Marcian 450–57		Petronius Maximus 455
Leo I 457–74		Avitus 455–56
Leo II 474		Marjorian 457–61
Zeno 474–91		Libius Severus 461–65
		Anthemius 467–72
		Olybrius 472–73
		Glycerius 473–74
		Julius Nepos 474–75
		Romulus Augustus 475–76

Note: Names in **bold italics** ruled in both the East and the West. These lists are designed to make history neater than it was, so they do not reflect the turmoil of the fourth and fifth centuries, when usurpers and pretenders were numerous.
1. Stilicho was regent until 408.

DYNASTIES OF EUROPE

▶THE CAROLINGIANS (751-887)

The first Carolingian king of the Franks was Pepin the Short who usurped the title from the Merovingian line in 751.Taking their dynastic name from Pepin's father, Charles (Carolus) Martel, the Carolingians divided their realm among surviving sons. It was in this family that the papacy revived the Roman imperial title in the year 800. The lists below cover only the major figures and ignore brief reigns and minor claimants.

Pepin the Short, King   751–68
Charlemagne and Carloman   768–71
Charlemagne, King   771–814
Charlemagne, Emperor   800–814
Louis the Pious, Emperor   814–40

West Franks

Charles the Bald   843–77 (Emperor 875–77)
Louis II, the Stammerer   877–879
Louis III   879–82
Carloman   879–84

Lotharingia

Lothair, Emperor   840–55
Louis II, Emperor   855–75
Charles, King of Provence   855–63
Lothair II, King of Lorraine   855–69

East Franks

Louis the German   843–76
Carloman   876–80
Louis   876–82
**Charles the Fat   882–887,
Emperor (881–87)**

▶HOLY ROMAN EMPIRE (962–1806)

The Holy Roman Empire refers to the second medieval "revival" of the Roman Empire in the West, in the year 962. Though drained of most of its power after 1250 and virtually all of its power after 1648, the Empire endured until 1806 when it was abolished by the Emperor Francis II (though he had no power to do so) who thereafter ruled as Francis I of the Austrian Empire which had been founded in 1804. Whatever the power of the Emperor, the title was the most prestigious in all of Europe. Normally the king of Germany was emperor once he was crowned by the pope; in 1356 the Golden Bull established a seven-member electoral college to choose the Emperor but from the fifteenth century on it was traditional for the electors to choose the Habsburg candidate.

Saxon Dynasty

The dukes of Saxony were most able in combatting the Hungarian menace in the 10th century and thus were chosen kings of Germany. The first was Henry the Fowler (919–936). His son Otto was the first Holy Roman Emperor.

Otto I, King   936, Emperor   962–73
Otto II   973–83
Otto III   983–1002
Henry II   1002–24

Franconian (or Salian) Dynasty

When Henry II died without heirs, Conrad of Franconia (a great-great grandson of Otto I) secured the succession. The dynasty intervened in

Rome to reform the papacy, perhaps too successfully, for the popes contended with the emperors for the leadership of the Christian world in the Investiture Controversy (1076–1122). Both the imperial office and the kingship of Germany were greatly weakened by the papal victory.

Conrad II   1024–39
Henry III   1039–56
Henry IV   1056–1106
Henry V   1106–25
Lothair II   1125–37

Hohenstaufen Dynasty

The Hohenstaufen of Swabia were nephews of Henry V but the Church tended to support candidates of the Guelph (also known as Welf) family of Saxony and Bavaria. The struggle of these families and the involvement of the papacy fatally weakened the empire ushering in the "Age of the Princes" in Germany and the "Great Interregnum" in the Empire.

Conrad III   1138–52
Frederick I "Barbarossa"   1152–90
Henry VI   1190–97
Philip of Swabia   1198–1208
Otto IV (Guelph) (anti-king)   1198–1208
Otto IV   1208–12
Frederick II   1212–50
Conrad IV   1250–54
Interregnum   1254–73

When kingship and the imperial office were restored in 1273 the princes refused to establish any one dynasty; for a century and a half candidates from four families were elected.

Rudolf I (Habsburg)   1273–91
Adolf (Nassau)   1292–98
Albert I (Habsburg)   1298–1308
Henry VII (Luxemburg)   1308–13
Louis IV (Wittelsbach)   1314–46
Charles IV (Luxemburg)   1346–78
Wenceslas (Luxemburg)   1378–1400
Rupert (Wittelsbach)   1400–1410
Sigismund (Luxemburg)   1410–37

The Habsburgs

The House of Habsburg (the name is a contraction of the name of their castle, Habichtsburg, in Switzerland) was the most illustrious of the European dynasties. From the 15th century they became hereditary rulers of the Empire and through a series of brilliant marriages gained, by inheritance, the Netherlands, the Spanish kingdoms and Spain's empire in the New World, and Hungary and Bohemia. (From the reign of Francis I, the official family name is Habsburg-Lorraine.)

Albert II   1440–93
Frederick III   1440–93
Maximilian I   1493–1519
Charles V   1519–56
Ferdinand I   1556–64
Maximilian II   1564–76
Rudolf II   1576–1612
Matthias   1612–19
Ferdinand II   1619–37
Ferdinand III   1637–57
Leopold I   1658–1705
Joseph I   1705–11
Charles VI   1711–40
Interregnum   1740–42
Charles VII   1742–45
Francis I   1745–65
Joseph II   1765–90
Leopold II   1790–92
Francis II   1792–1806

▶DYNASTIES OF FRANCE (987–1848)

In 987 the West Frankish nobles elected as their king Hugh Capet. His descendants ruled France continuously until the French Revolution and again from 1814 until 1848. The direct line died out in 1328, and the collateral *Valois* branch of the Capetian family succeeded. The Valois ruled with difficulty, as the Hundred Years' War (1337–1453) blighted the beginning and the Wars of Religion (1562–98) the end of their rule. The last three Valois produced no male heirs so the throne passed to the victor in the Wars of Religion, Henry of Navarre (a distant cousin in the male line of Louis IX), who began the reign of the *Bourbon* branch of the Capetians. (After 1700, the Bourbon family became, with many interruptions, kings of Spain.)

Direct Capetians

Hugh Capet	987–96
Robert II the Pious	996–1031
Henry I	1031–60
Philip I	1060–1108
Louis VI	1108–37
Louis VII	1137–80
Philip II Augustus	1180–1223
Louis VIII	1223–26
Louis IX	1226–70
Philip III	1270–85
Philip IV	1285–1314
Louis X	1314–16
John I the Posthumous	1316
Philip V	1316–22
Charles IV	1322–28

Valois Branch

Philip VI	1328–50
John	1350–64
Charles V	1364–80
Charles VI	1380–1422
Charles VII	1422–61
Louis XI	1461–83
Charles VIII	1483–98
Louis XII (Valois-Orléans)	1498–1515
Francis I (Valois-Angoulême)	1515–47
Henry II	1547–59
Francis II	1559–60
Charles IX	1560–74
Henry III	1574–89

Bourbon Branch

Henry IV	1589–1610
Louis XIII	1610–43
Louis XIV	1643–1715
Louis XV	1715–74
Louis XVI	1774–92

French Revolution and Napoleon 1792–1814

Restored Bourbons

Louis XVIII	1814–24
Charles X	1824–30
Louis Philippe (Bourbon-Orléans)	1830–48

▶DYNASTIES OF ENGLAND (871–PRESENT)

Saxons

With the end of Roman rule, seven Germanic kingdoms emerged in England. The leader of the resistance to the Vikings was Alfred the Great of Wessex (871–99) who began a reconquest of the island and is considered the first true king of England; his dynasty, with interruptions, continued until the Norman Conquest in 1066.

Alfred the Great	871–99
Edward the Elder	899–924
Aethelstan	924–39
Edmund	939–46
Eadred	946–55
Eadwig	955–59
Edgar	959–75
Edward	975–78
Aethelred "the Unready"	978–1016
Edmund Ironside	1016
Canute (of Denmark, by conquest)	1016–35
Harold Harefoot	1035–40
Hardicanute (of Denmark)	1040–42
Edward the Confessor	1042–66
Harold Godwinson	1066

Normans

Duke William of Normandy, a cousin of Edward the Confessor, made good his claim to the throne by conquest, bringing with him highly organized Continental feudalism and the French tongue which so enriched the English language.

William the Conqueror	1066–87
William II	1087–1100
Henry I	1100–1135
Stephen	1135–54

Angevins (Plantagenets)

The grandson of Henry I was Henry of Anjou who, by marrying the heiress Eleanor of Aquitaine, assembled for his family the greatest feudal state in 12th century Europe. In 1154 he established his family on the throne of England as well; the direct line continued until 1399 when Richard II was deposed and killed by his first cousin who then ruled as Henry IV and established the *Lancastrian Dynasty*. Another branch of the family, with a stronger claim than the usurping Lancastrians, contested the succession in the War of the Roses and after 1461 ruled briefly as the *Yorkist Dynasty*.

Henry II	1154–89
Richard I	1189–99
John I	1199–1216
Henry III	1216–72
Edward I	1272–1307
Edward II	1307–27
Edward III	1327–77
Richard II	1377–99

Lancastrian Kings

Henry IV	1399–1413
Henry V	1413–22
Henry VI	1422–61

Yorkist Kings

Edward IV	1461–83
Edward V	1483
Richard III	1483–85

Tudors

An obscure Welsh family and adherents of the Lancastrian line, the Tudors became champions of the faction supporting them. Richard III died in battle at Bosworth Field against Henry Tudor, who usurped the throne, ruling as Henry VII and founding the dynasty that brought the Reformation to England.

Henry VII 1485–1509
Henry VIII 1509–47
Edward VI 1547–53
Mary I 1553–58
Elizabeth I 1558–1603

Stuarts

Elizabeth never married and had no heirs, so the Tudor line died with her. Rule passed to Elizabeth's cousin, James VI of Scotland who ruled in England as James I. Serious troubles with the Puritans and Parliament twice turned the Stuarts from the throne: Charles I was beheaded and James II was betrayed by his daughters and the husband of one, William of Orange.

James I 1603–25
Charles I 1625–49
Interregnum—Oliver Cromwell 1649–58
Richard Cromwell 1658–59
Charles II 1660–85
James II 1685–88
William III and Mary II 1689–94
William III alone 1694–1702
Anne 1702–14

Hanoverians and Windsors

Queen Anne had 17 children but died without leaving an heir. Geneological and religious considerations (Anne's brother "James III," the Catholic pretender, was still alive) brought to the throne the German House of Hanover. After the reign of Victoria, the family is Saxe-Coburg-Gotha but in 1917, for political reasons, George V changed the name to Windsor.

George I 1714–27
George II 1727–60
George III 1760–1820
George IV 1820–30
William IV 1830–37
Victoria 1837–1901
Edward VII 1901–10
George V 1910–36
Edward VIII 1936
George VI 1936–52
Elizabeth II 1952–present

▶ DYNASTIES OF SPAIN (1506–PRESENT)

Until 1808 there was no kingdom called Spain but a number of separate kingdoms of which Castile and Aragon were only the principal ones. With the deaths of Isabella, then Ferdinand, the crowns passed to their grandson, the Habsburg Charles of Ghent; in the Empire he was Charles V, in the Spanish kingdoms Charles I. His *Habsburg Dynasty* ruled until 1700 when the line died out and was replaced by the *Bourbon Dynasty* which has ruled with numerous interruptions until the present day.

Habsburgs

Charles I (Holy Roman Emperor as
Charles V) 1506–56
Philip II 1556–98
Philip III 1598–1621
Philip IV 1621–65
Charles II 1665–1700

Bourbons

Philip V 1700–1746
Ferdinand VI 1746–59
Charles III 1759–88
Charles IV 1788–1808
Joseph Bonaparte 1808–13

Ferdinand VII 1814–33
Isabella II 1833–68
Interregnum 1868–70
Amadeo 1870–73
Republic 1873–75
Alphonso XII 1875–85
Alphonso XIII 1886–1931
Republic 1931–36
Civil War 1936–39
Franco regime 1939–75
Juan Carlos 1975–present

▶ AUSTRIAN HABSBURGS

When Charls V retired, his world-wide empire was divided into two parts, one Spanish, one Austrian. The Austrian branch always supplied the Holy Roman Emperors except during the reign of Maria Theresa (1740–80) when Charles Albert of Bavaria, then her husband and son held the imperial title. In 1804 Emperor Francis II proclaimed an Austrian Empire which he ruled as Francis I; two years later he abolished the Holy Roman Empire.

Francis II & I 1792–1835
Ferdinand I 1835–48
Francis Joseph 1848–1916
Charles I 1916–18

▶ HOHENZOLLERN DYNASTY

For centuries the Hohenzollern were electors of Brandenburg in northeastern Germany. In 1701, with permission of the emperor, they took the royal titles King in Prussia. (Prussia was a duchy of Poland which the family inherited in 1618.) In 1871 they added the title German Emperor. Both titles disappeared with Germany's loss in World War I.

Frederick William, the Great Elector
1640–88
Frederick III, Elector of Brandenburg
1688–1701
Frederick I, King of Prussia 1701–13
Frederick William I 1713–40
Frederick II 1740–86
Frederick William II 1786–97
Frederick William III 1797–1840
Frederick William IV 1840–61
William I (German Emperor after 1871)
1861–88
Frederick III 1888
William II 1888–1918

▶ ROMANOV DYNASTY (RUSSIA)

At the end of Russia's "time of troubles" early in the 17th century, the national assembly elected Michael Romanov as czar in 1613. The dynasty died out in 1762 when at the death of czarina Elizabeth, her nephew Peter III briefly succeeded. His family ruled until the Russian Revolution. Their name was Holstein-Gottorp but ruled under the name Romanov.

Michael 1613–45
Alexius 1645–76
Theodore III 1676–82
Ivan IV and Peter I 1682–89
Peter I, the Great, alone 1689–1725
Catherine I 1725–27
Peter II 1727–30
Anna 1730–40
Ivan VI 1740–41
Elizabeth 1741–62
Peter III 1762
Catherine II the Great 1762–96
Paul 1796–1801
Alexander I 1801–25

Nicholas I   1825–55
Alexander II   1855–81
Alexander III   1881–94
Nicholas II   1894–1917

►HOUSE OF SAVOY-CARIGNANO

The dukes of Savoy ruled in a personal union Piedmont, Nice, and Sardinia until 1831, when the line died out and a distant cousin, Charles Albert came to the throne. It was his son, Victor Emmanuel II of Savoy whose armies conquered the rest of Italy over the years 1858–71 and who was proclaimed King of Italy in 1861. The dynasty fell with the end of the Second World War.

Victor Emmanuel II   1861–78
Humbert I   1878–1900
Victor Emmanuel III   1900–46
Humbert II   1946

THE DYNASTIES AND EMPERORS OF CHINA

Dates for the Xia and Shang Dynasties, and for the beginning of the Zhou Dynasty, are uncertain. Rulers of these three dynasties were known as kings (*wang*); only a few notable individuals are listed below. The title "emperor" (*huangdi*) was instituted with the Qin Dynasty. As is customary, names of emperors prior to A.D. 1368 are given in the form of their posthumous "temple names" (*miaohao*); names of emperors for the Ming and Qing Dynasties are given as their reign-title names (*nianhao*).

Xia Dynasty   c. 1875–1550 B.C.
Yü the Great (legendary?)   c. 1875–1850 B.C.
King Jie   c. 1560–1550 B.C.

Shang Dynasty   c. 1550–1055 B.C.
Tang the Victorious   c. 1550–1500 B.C.
King Zhou   c. 1070–1055 B.C.

Zhou Dynasty   c. 1055–256 B.C.
Western Zhou Period   c. 1055–771 B.C.
King Wen (pre-conquest)   c. 1060–1055 B.C.
King Wu   c. 1055–1048 B.C.
Duke of Zhou, regent for
King Cheng   c. 1048–1011 B.C.
Era of the Spring and Autumn Annals 722–481 B.C.
Warring States Period   481–256 B.C.

Qin Dynasty   221–206 B.C.
Shihuangdi   221–209 B.C.
Erhuangdi   209–207 B.C.

Han Dynasty   206 B.C.–A.D. 220
Western or Former Han   206 B.C.–A.D. 9
Gaozu   206–195 B.C.
Huidi   195–188 B.C.
Gaohou (Empress Lü)   188–180 B.C.
Wendi   180–157 B.C.
Jingdi   157–141 B.C.
Wudi   141–87 B.C.
Zhaodi   87–74 B.C.
Xuandi   74–48 B.C.

Yuandi   48–33 B.C.
Chengdi   33–7 B.C.
Aidi   7–1 B.C.
Pingdi   1 B.C. –A.D. 6
Wang Mang (usurper)   A.D. 9–23
Eastern or Latter Han   A.D. 23–220
Guangwudi   25–57
Mingdi   57–75
Zhangdi   75–88
Hedi   88–105
Shangdi   105
Andi   106–25
Shaodi   125
Shundi   125–44
Chongdi   144–45
Zhidi   145–46
Huandi   146–68
Lingdi   168–89
Shaodi   189
Xiandi   189–220

Period of Disunion
The fall of the Han Dynasty ushered in a period of 369 years of disunion during which no dynasty succeeded in bringing all of China under its control This period is divided into the brief Three Kingdoms Period and the longer Period of Northern and Southern Dynasties, of which only the three most important dynasties are listed below.

Three Kingdoms   220–65
Kingdom of Shu Han   220–64
Kingdom of Wei   220–65
Kingdom of Wu   220–65

Period of Northern and Southern Dynasties   265–589
Western Jin Dynasty   265–317
Eastern Jin Dynasty   317–419
Northern Wei Dynasty   424–535

Sui Dynasty   589–618
Wendi   589–604
Yangdi   604–17
Gongdi   617–18

Tang Dynasty   618–907
Gaozu   618–26
Taizong   626–49
Gaozong   649–83
Zhongzong   683–84
Ruizong   684–90
Wuhou   690–705
Zhongzong   705–10
Ruizong   710–12
Xuanzong   712–56
Suzong   756–62
Taizong   762–79
Dezong   779–805
Shunzong   805
Xianzong   805–20
Muzong   820–24
Jingzong   824–26
Wenzong   826–40
Wuzong   840–46
Xuanzong   846–59
Yizong   859–73
Xizong   873–88
Zhaozong   888–904
Jingzong   904–7

Five Dynasties   907–60

Song Dynasty   960–1279
Northern Song   960–1127
Taizu   960–76
Taizong   976–97
Zhenzong   997–1022
Renzong   1022–63
Yingzong   1063–67
Shenzong   1067–85
Zhezong   1085–1100
Huizong   1100–1125
Qinzong   1125–27
Southern Song   1127–1279
Gaozong   1127–62
Xiaozong   1162–89
Guangzong   1189–94
Ningzong   1194–1224
Lizong   1224–64
Duzong   1264–74
Gongzong   1274–76
Duanzong   1276–79

Yuan (Mongol) Dynasty   1279–1368
Shizu (Kubilai Khan)   1260–94
Chengzong (Temür)   1294–1307
Wuzong (Khaishan)   1307–11
Renfeng (Buyantu)   1311–20
Yingzong (Sudhipela)   1320–23
Taiding (Yesen-Temür)   1323–28
Mingzong (Asikipa)   1328
Wenzong (Tog-Temür)   1328–33
Xunzong (Toghon-Temür)   1333–68

Ming Dynasty   1368–1644
Hongwu   1368–98
Jianwen   1398–1402
Yongle   1402–24
Hongxi   1424–25
Xuande   1425–35
Zhengtong   1435–49
Jingtai   1449–57
Tianshun   1457–64
Chenghua   1464–87
Hongzhi   1487–1505
Zhengde   1505–21
Jiaqing   1521–66
Wanli   1572–1620
Taichang   1620
Tianzhi   1620–27
Chongzhen   1627–44

Qing Dynasty   1644–1911
Shunzhi   1644–61
Kangxi   1661–1722
Yongzheng   1722–35
Qianlong   1735–96
Jiaqing   1796–1820
Daoguang   1820–50
Xianfeng   1850–61
Tongzhi   1861–75
Guangxu   1875–1908
Puyi   1908–11

CHRONOLOGICAL LISTING OF THE POPES

Peter, Apostle   d. c. 64
Linus   c.66–c.78
Anacletus   c.79–c.91
Clement I   c.91–c.101
Evaristus   c.100–c.109
Alexander I   c.109–c.116
Sixtus I   c.116–c.125
Telesphorus   c.125–c.136
Hyginus   c.138–c.142
Pius I   c.142–c.155
Anicetus   c.155–c.166
Soter   c.166–c.174
Eleutherius, or Eleutherus   c.174–89
Victor I   189–98
Zephyrinus   198/9–217
Callistus I (often Calixtus)   217–22
Hippolytus (antipope)   217–35
Urban I   222–30
Pontian   230–35
Anterus   235–36
Fabian   236–50
Cornelius   251–53
Novatian (antipope)   251–58
Lucius I   253–54
Stephen I   254–57
Sixtus II   257–58
Dionysius   260–68
Felix I   269–74
Eutychian   275–83
Gaius, or Caius   283–96
Marcellinus   296–304?
Marcellus I   306–8
Eusebius   310
Miltiades, or Melchiades   311–31
Silvester I   314–35
Mark   336

Julius I   337–52
Liberius   352–66
Felix II (antipope)[1]   355–65
Damasus I   366–84
Ursinus (antipope)   366–67
Siricius   384–99
Anastasius I   399–401
Innocent I   401–17
Zosimus   417–18
Eulalius (antipope)   418–19
Boniface I   418–22
Celestine I   422–32
Sixtus (Xystus) III   432–40
Leo I   440–61
Hilarus   461–68
Simplicius   468–83
Felix III[1]   483–92
Gelasius I   492–96
Anastasius II   496–98
Symmachus   498–514
Lawrence (antipope)   498–99, 501–6
Hormisdas   514–23
John I   523–26
Felix III[1]   526–30
Dioscorus (antipope)   530
Boniface II   530–32
John II   533–35
Agapitus I   535–36
Silverius   536–37
Vigilius   537–55
Pelagius I   556–61
John III   561–74
Benedict I   575–79
Pelagius II   579–90
Gregory I   590–604
Sabinian   604–6
Boniface III   607
Boniface IV   608–15

Deusdedit (later Adeodatus I)   615–18
Boniface V   619–25
Honorius I   625–38
Severinus   640
John IV   640–42
Theodore I   642–49
Martin I   649–53
Eugene I   654–57
Vitalian   657–72
Adeodatus II   672–76
Donus   676–78
Agatho   678–81
Leo II   682–83
Benedict II   684–85
John V   685–86
Conon   686–87
Theodore (antipope)   687
Paschal (antipope)   687
Sergius I   687–701
John VI   701–5
John VII   705–7
Sisinnius   708
Gregory II   715–31
Gregory III   731–41
Zacharias   741–52
Stephen (II)[2]   752
Stephen II (III)[2]   752–57
Paul I   757–67
Constantine (antipope)   767–68
Philip (antipope)   768
Stephen III (IV)[2]   768–72
Hadrian I   772–95
Leo III   795–816
Stephen IV (V)[2]   816–17
Paschal I   817–24
Eugene II   824–27
Valentine   827
Gregory IV   827–44

John (antipope)   844
Sergius II   844–47
Leo IV   847–55
Benedict III   855–58
Anastasius Bibliothecarius
  (antipope)   855
Nicholas I   858–67
Hadrian II   867–72
John VIII   872–82
Marinus I   882–84
Hadrian III   884–85
Stephen V (VI)[2]   885–91
Formosus   891–96
Boniface VI   896
Stephen VI (VII)[2]   896–97
Romanus   897
Theodore II   897
John IX   898–900
Benedict IV   900–903
Leo V   903
Christopher (antipope)   903–4
Sergius III   904–11
Anastasius III   911–13
Lando   913–14
John X   914–28
Leo VI   928
Stephen VII (VIII)[2]   928–31
John XI   931–36?
Leo VII   936–39
Stephen VIII (IX)[2]   939–42
Marinus II   942–46
Agapitus II   946–55
John XII   955–64
Leo VIII   963–65
Benedict V   964
John XIII   965–72
Benedict VI   973–74
Boniface VII (antipope)   974,
  984–85
Benedict VII   974–83
John XIV   983–84
John XV   985–96
Gregory V   996–99
John XVI (antipope)   997–98
Silvester II   999–1003
John XVII   1003
John XVIII   1003–1009
Sergius IV   1009–12
Benedict VIII   1012–24
Gregory (VI) (antipope)   1012
John XIX   1024–32
Benedict IX   1032–44, 1045,
  1047–48
Silvester III   1045
Gregory VI   1045–46
Clement II   1046–47
Damasus II   1048
Leo IX   1049–54
Victor II   1055–57
Stephen IX (X)[2]   1057–58
Benedict X (antipope)
  1058–59
Nicholas II   1058–61
Alexander II   1061–73
Honorius (II) (antipope)
  1061–64
Gregory VII   1073–85
Clement III (antipope)   1080,
  1084–1100
Victor III   1086–87

Urban II   1088–99
Paschal II   1099–1118
Theoderic (antipope)
  1100–1101
Albert or Adalbert (antipope)
  1101
Silvester IV (antipope)
  1105–11
Gelasius II   1118–19
Gregory (VIII) (antipope)
  1118–21
Callistus II   1119–24
Celestine (II)   1124
Honorius II   1124–30
Innocent II   1130–43
Anacletus II (antipope)
  1130–38
Victor IV (antipope)   1138
Celestine II   1143–44
Lucius II   1144–45
Eugene III   1145–53
Anastasius IV   1153–54
Hadrian IV   1154–59
Alexander III   1159–81
Victor IV (antipope)[3]   1159–64
Paschal III (antipope)   1164–68
Callistus (III) (antipope)
  1168–78
Innocent (III) (antipope)
  1179–80
Lucius III   1181–85
Urban III   1185–87
Gregory VIII   1187
Clement III   1187–91
Celestine III   1191–98
Innocent III   1198–1216
Honorius III   1216–27
Gregory IX   1227–41
Celestine IV   1241
Innocent IV   1243–54
Alexander IV   1254–61
Urban IV   1261–64
Clement IV   1265–68
Gregory X   1271–76
Innocent V   1276
Hadrian V   1276
John XXI   1276–77
Nicholas III   1277–80
Martin IV   1281–85
Honorius IV   1285–87
Nicholas IV   1288–92
Celestine V   1294
Boniface VIII   1294–1303
Benecict XI   1303–4
Clement V   1305–14
John XXII   1316–34
Nicholas (V) (antipope)
  1328–30
Benedict XII   1334–42
Clement VI   1342–52
Innocent VI   1352–62
Urban V   1362–70
Gregory XI   1370–78
Urban VI   1378–89
Clement (VII) (antipope)
  1378–94
Boniface IX   1389–1404
Benedict (XIII) (antipope)
  1394–1417
Innocent VII   1404–6

Gregory XII   1406–15
Alexander V (antipope)
  1409–10
John (XXIII) (antipope)
  1410–15
Martin V   1417–31
Clement (VIII) (antipope)
  1423–29
Benedict (XIV) (antipope)
  1425–?
Eugene IV   1431–47
Felix V (antipope)   1439–49
Nicholas V   1447–55
Callistus III   1455–58
Pius II   1458–64
Paul II   1464–71
Sixtus IV   1471–84
Innocent VIII   1484–92
Alexander VI   1492–1503
Pius III   1503
Julius II   1503–13
Leo X   1513–21
Hadrian VI   1522–23
Clement VII   1523–34
Paul III   1534–49
Julius III   1550–55
Marcellus II   1555
Paul IV   1555–59
Pius IV   1559–65
Pius V   1566–72
Gregory XIII   1572–85
Sixtus V   1585–90
Urban VII   1590
Gregory XIV   1590–91
Innocent IX   1591
Clement VIII   1592–1605
Leo XI   1605
Paul V   1605–21
Gregory XV   1621–23
Urban VIII   1623–44
Innocent X   1644–55
Alexander VII   1655–67
Clement IX   1667–69
Clement X   1670–76
Innocent XI   1676–89
Alexander VIII   1689–91
Innocent XII   1691–1700
Clement XI   1700–21
Innocent XIII   1721–24
Benedict XIII   1724–30
Clement XII   1730–40
Benedict XIV   1740–58
Clement XIII   1758–69
Clement XIV   1769–74
Pius VI   1775–99
Pius VII   1800–23
Leo XII   1823–29
Pius VIII   1829–30
Gregory XVI   1831–46
Pius IX   1846–78
Leo XIII   1878–1903
Pius X   1903–14
Benedict XV   1914–22
Pius XI   1922–39
Pius XII   1939–58
John XXIII   1958–63
Paul VI   1963–78
John Paul I   1978
John Paul II   1978–

Note: Antipopes, *listed in italics*, were appointed in opposition to the one canonically chosen by the college of cardinals, usually by a prince, king, or emperor. 1. Because Felix II was an antipope, subsequent Felixes were sometime misnumbered. 2. Although elected and installed as Pope, Stephen (II) died before his consecration. Though the Vatican's *Annuario Pontifico* has excluded him from the official list of Popes since 1961, subsequent Stephens have a dual numbering. 3. He should have been Victor V, but he used Victor IV because the previous Victor IV's tenure (1138) as antipope was largely ignored.

World Geography

▶GLOSSARY OF GEOGRAPHICAL WORDS AND TERMS

(Note: See also Part IV: Science and Technology, Composition of the Earth)

Altitude   How high a place or a thing is, usually measured from sea level or the surface of the land.

Archipelago   A cluster of islands.

Arctic Circle   An imaginary line drawn along approximately latitude 66° 30'N. The climate north of the Arctic Circle is very cold, and relatively few people live there.

Atmosphere   The mass of air that extends outward from the surface of the earth into space. The atmosphere is divided into four layers: the troposphere, in which temperature decreases as altitude increases; the stratosphere, in which temperature is constant, then increases; the mesosphere, in which it decreases; and the thermosphere, in which it increases again.

Atoll   A coral reef that partially or completely surrounds a lagoon.

Basin   A portion of land that is lower than the surrounding area. Basins are created when vertical movement causes the earth's crust to warp. Also, the area drained by a river and its tributaries.

Bay   Part of an ocean, sea, or other body of water which extends inland. Bays are generally smaller than gulfs.

Bight   A bay formed by a bend in the coastline.

Caldera   A huge crater formed when the top of a volcano collapses or is exploded away.

Canyon   A narrow, deep valley with steep sides. Many canyons have a river on their floor.

Climate   General weather conditions over a long period. (See "Climates of the World.")

Continent   A large unbroken land mass, distinguished from an island or peninsula. The seven continents are North America, South America, Europe, Asia, Africa, Australia, and Antarctica, though Europe and Asia are a continuous land mass divided along the spine of the Ural Mountains running south from the Arctic Ocean.

Continental drift theory   The theory, proposed in 1915 by Alfred Wegener, that all of the continents used to be joined in one supercontinent, Pangaea. Some 200 million years ago Pangaea began to break up, and the continents "drifted" through the oceans to their present locations. The continental drift theory has now largely been replaced by the *plate tectonics theory*. (See the section "Earth Sciences.")

Continental shelf   The edge of a continent covered by shallow ocean water, up to about 100 fathoms (600 feet), beyond which is the continental slope, which decends to the deep-sea plain, about 13,000-20,000 feet (4,000-6,000 m).

Cove   A small and sheltered bay or inlet. Also, a small valley in a mountain.

Crater   The bowl-shaped depression at the top of a volcano. Also, the depression made when a meteorite hits the earth. (See also *caldera*.)

Delta   A triangular-shaped piece of land formed by sediment at the mouth of a river.

Desert   (See "The Great Deserts" later in this section).

Dune   A hill or ridge of sand that has been deposited by wind.

Equator   An imaginary line circling earth halfway between the Poles. The equator is at latitude 0°.

Equinox   The two times during the year (on or about March 21 and September 23) when the sun's rays strike the equator vertically. At equinox, day and night are the same length everywhere in the world. (See also *Solstice*.)

Erosion   The gradual wearing away of the surface of the land. For example, soil is eroded by wind and water; rock is eroded by freezing and thawing.

Estuary   A valley at the mouth of a river where fresh water and sea water mix. Estuaries are created either when the land sinks or when the sea level rises, and are generally shaped like a funnel.

Fjord   A long, narrow inlet of the ocean with steeply sloping sides.

Floodplain   Flat, low-lying land along either side of a river that is subject to flooding.

Geyser   A jet of hot water or steam periodically thrown up by a hot spring.

Glacier   A large mass of slowly moving ice. Glaciers are formed on land when snow is compacted and recrystallizes.

Gorge   An especially narrow and steep-walled canyon.

Gulf   Part of an ocean or sea that extends inland. Gulfs are generally larger than bays.

Hemisphere   One half of the earth's surface, however it is divided. For example, the northern hemisphere lies north of the equator; the southern hemisphere, south of the equator. By convention, the eastern hemisphere consists of the continents of Europe, Asia, and Africa; the western hemisphere, of North America and South America.

Inlet   An indentation in the shore of a sea or an ocean or in the bank of a river. Also, a narrow waterway which connects a lagoon to a larger body of water or which passes between two peninsulas.

Island   A land mass completely surrounded by water.

Isthmus   A narrow strip of land that connects two larger land masses.

Lagoon   A shallow pool or pond completely or almost completely separated from the sea.

Lake   A body of water, often of considerable size, surrounded by land.

Latitude and Longitude   Latitude is the angle (measured in degrees, minutes, and seconds) between a point on the earth's surface north or south of the equator, the center of the earth, and the equator (0°0'0" latitude). Longitude is the angle between a point on the earth's surface, the center of the earth, and the prime meridian (0°0'0" longitude). There are 90° of latitude between the equator and each of the poles (shown on a globe as parallel horizontal lines). There are 360° of longitude (shown as vertical lines) divided into 180° east and west of the prime meridian (180°E and 180°W are thus the same). Since 1884, Greenwich, England (near London), has been universally recognized as the point through which the prime meridien passes. A degree (°) is 1/360 of a circle, a minute (') 1/60 of a degree, and a second (") 1/60 of a minute.

Lava   Magma which reaches the surface of the earth and from which most of the gases have escaped. (See *Magma, Volcano*.)

Leeward   The direction or side sheltered from the wind. (See *Windward*.)

Magma   Molten rock that lies deep within the earth. In a volcanic eruption, magma bursts through the outer surface of the earth's crust. (See *Lava, Volcano.*)

Mountain Land that rises above its surroundings. Mountains are higher than hills. Older mountain ranges, like the Appalachians, are rounded because they are old and worn down; younger ranges, like the Andes or the Himalayas, have jagged peaks because they are still rising.

North Pole The northernmost point of the Earth's axis, at latitude 90°N. From this point, the only direction is south. It is entirely surrounded by water, and usually covered by ice. The first successful expedition to the North Pole—there is some doubt as to whether they actually reached the pole—was led by by Adm. Robert E. Peary, Apr. 6, 1909.

Ocean (See "Oceans of the World," later in this section).

Peninsula A portion of land surrounded by water on three sides.

Plain A large portion of level or rolling land which is treeless.

Plate tectonics theory The theory, first proposed in 1968, that Earth's crust is made up of 20 sections or "plates," each of which consists of continental and ocean crust. The plates shift, moving continents, changing the size and shape of oceans, causing earthquakes, and creating volcanos and mountains. The plate tectonics theory has largely replaced the *continental drift theory*.

Plateau A portion of land, generally large and with a level surface, which is sharply elevated above the surrounding land. Plateaus are created when vertical movement causes the earth's crust to warp.

Pond A small body of water surrounded by land.

Prairie Level or rolling land generally covered with grasses, with few trees.

Rain shadow An area on the leeward side of a mountain range which receives little rainfall.

River A large stream.

Sahel The Arabic word for "shore," the Sahel is a dry region separating the Sahara desert from tropical and West Central Africa running from Senegal to Sudan. The meager rainfall (4-8 inches per year) supports limited crops and grazing.

Savanna A portion of land in the tropics or subtropics with only scattered trees but whose grasses can survive with scant rainfall.

Sea A large body of saltwater, generally considered smaller than an ocean.

Solstice The time when the sun's rays strike vertically the Tropic of Cancer or the Tropic of Capricorn. At solstice, the daylight hours reach their maximum or minimum. In the Northern Hemi-

sphere, for example, summer solstice occurs on or about June 22; that is the "longest day of the year" and signals the beginning of summer. The winter solstice occurs on or about December 22; that is the "shortest day of the year" and signals the beginning of winter. In the southern hemisphere, the longest and shortest days of the year occur on December 22 and June 22, respectively. (See also *Equinox.*)

Sound A body of water which separates an island from the mainland; or which connects two oceans, seas, or other bodies of water. Sounds are generally long and narrow.

South Pole The southernmost point of the Earth's axis, at 90°S. First reached by Norwegian explorer Roald Admundsen in 1911, the South Pole lies in the South Polar region.

Steppe A portion of land with little rainfall, extreme temperature variations, and drought-resistant vegetation.

Strait A narrow body of water that connects two large bodies of water.

Stream Any body of running water that flows on or under the surface of the earth. Brooks and creeks are small streams; rivers are large streams.

Swamp A portion of wet, waterlogged, or flooded land.

Tide The rise and fall of the surface of the ocean and of bays, gulfs, and other bodies of water connected to the ocean. Tides are caused by the gravitational pull of the moon, which passes over the same meridian of the Earth about once every 24 hours and 50 minutes. The length of time between successive high (or low) tides is about 12 hours and 25 minutes.

Tributary A stream or river that flows into a larger stream or river.

Tropic of Cancer Latitude 23½°N, which marks the northernmost limit of the sun's vertical rays. The area between the Tropic of Cancer and the Tropic of Capricorn is known as the "tropics."

Tropic of Capricorn Latitude 23½°S, the southernmost limit of the sun's vertical rays.

Tundra An area of treeless plain near or above the Arctic Circle. Tundra subsoil is permanently frozen, but the soil thaws enough to support the growth of mosses, lichens, and some small flowering shrubs.

Valley A long and sometimes narrow depression on the surface of the earth, usually between two mountain ridges or ranges.

Volcano A mountain formed by lava and/or other materials which have burst forth from deep within the earth. (See *Caldera, Lava, Magma.*)

Windward The direction or side facing the wind.

World Land Area and Population by Selected Region

Region	Land Area			Population			
	Square miles	Square kilometers	Percent of world total	Total ('000s)	Percent of total	Per square mile	Per square kilometer
World total[1]	57,308,738	148,429,000	100.0%	6,068,511	100.0%	99.5	38.4
Africa	11,608,156	30,065,000	20.3	805,243	13.3	69.4	40.9
Antarctica	5,404,000	14,000,000	9.4	(2)	(2)	(2)	(2)
Asia	17,212,041	44,579,000	30.0	3,688,072	60.8	214.3	82.7
Australia	2,967,966	7,687,000	5.2	19,164	0.3	6.5	2.5
Europe	3,837,082	9,938,000	6.7	728,981	12.0	190.0	73.4
North America	9,365,290	24,256,000	16.3	480,545	8.0	51.3	19.8
South America	6,879,952	17,819,000	8.9	346,504	5.7	50.4	19.4

1. Land only. Includes small islands not shown separately. 2. Antarctica has no indigenous population.
Source: *National Geographic Atlas of the World* (1995); U.S. Census Bureau, midyear 2000 population estimates.

The Continents: Highest and Lowest Elevations

Continent	Highest point	Location	Feet above sea level	Meters above sea level
Africa	Mt. Kilimanjaro	Tanzania	19,340	5,895
Antarctica	Vinson Massif	Ellsworth Mts.	16,066	4,897
Asia	Mt. Everest	Nepal-China	29,028	8,848
Australia	Mt. Kosciusko	New South Wales	7,310	2,228
Europe	Mt. Elbrus	Russia	18,510	5,642
North America	Mt. McKinley	U.S. (Alaska)	20,320	6,194
South America	Mt. Aconcagua	Argentina	22,834	6,960

Continent	Lowest point	Location	Feet below sea level	Meters below sea level
Africa	Lake Assal	Djibouti	512	156
Antarctica	ice covered	—	8,327	2,538
Asia	Dead Sea	Israel-Jordan	1,339	408
Australia	Lake Eyre	South Australia	52	16
Europe	Caspian Sea	Russia, Kazakhstan	92	28
North America	Death Valley	U.S. (California)	282	86
South America	Valdes Peninsula	Argentina	131	40

Source: *National Geographic Atlas of the World* (1995).

The Oceans of the World

Name	Area ('000s) Sq. km.	Area ('000s) Sq. mi.	Average depth Meters	Average depth Feet	Maximum depth Meters	Maximum depth Feet
Arctic ocean	**14,090**	**5,440**	**1,205**	**3,950**	**5,450**	**17,881**
Greenland Sea	1,205	465	1,450	4,750	4,846	15,899
Hudson Bay	1,230	470	128	420	259	850
Atlantic ocean	**82,440**	**31,830**	**3,926**	**12,877**	**9,219**	**30,246**
w/ marginal seas	106,450	41,100	3,332	10,932	—	—
Caribbean Sea	2,754	1,063	—	—	7,680	25,197
Mediterranean Sea	2,505	967	—	—	5,020	16,470
Norwegian Sea	1,547	597	—	—	4,020	13,189
Gulf of Mexico	1,544	596	—	—	4,380	14,370
North Sea	575	222	94	310	659	2,170
Black Sea	461	178	—	—	2,237	7,360
Baltic Sea	422	163	55	180	437	1,440
Indian ocean	**73,440**	**28,360**	**3,890**	**12,760**	**7,450**	**24,442**
w/marginal seas	74,920	28,930	—	—	—	—
Arabian Sea	3,863	1,492	2,734	8,970	5,800	19,029
Bay of Bengal	2,172	839	2,600	8,500	5,258	17,251
Red Sea	438	169	—	—	2,240	7,370
Pacific Ocean	**165,250**	**63,800**	**4,270**	**14,000**	**11,034**	**36,200**
w/marginal seas	179,680	69,370	—	—	—	—
South China Sea	3,447	1,331	1,060	3,478	5,560	18,241
Bering Sea	2,270	876	1,440	4,720	4,191	13,750
Sea of Okhotsk	1,580	610	838	2,750	3,372	11,063
East China Sea	1,248	482	349	1,145	2,717	8,912
Yellow Sea	1,243	480	40	131	91	300
Sea of Japan	1,007	389	1,752	5,748	3,733	12,280

Sources: International Hydrographic Organization; U.S. Navy Oceanographer (6/23/00), **oceanographer.navy.mil**; Central Intelligence Agency, *World Factbook 1999*, **www.cia.gov/cia/publications/factbook/index.html.**

▶**THE OCEANS OF THE WORLD**

The water of the world's oceans covers more than 70 percent of the world's surface. While for many years the so-called World Ocean was divided into five parts—the Pacific, Atlantic, Indian, Arctic and Antarctic—scientists today commonly recognize only the first three as separate and distinct oceans. The Arctic and Antarctic, as well as other large bodies of water such as the Caribbean Sea, the Gulf of Mexico, Hudson Bay, the Mediterranean and Black Seas, and the South China Sea are termed marginal seas. The International Hydrographic Organization identifies 66 seas, gulfs, bays, bights, straits, channels, and passages, many of which are further subdivided. For instance, the Mediterranean Sea is divided into western and eastern basins, and the western basin is subdivided into the Strait of Gibraltar, Aboran Sea, Balearic Sea, Ligurian Sea, Tyrrhenian Sea, Ionian Sea, Adriatic Sea, and Aegean Sea. The table (above) gives the area and maximum depths of the world's three major oceans and selected marginal seas.

Great Deserts of the World

Desert	Location	Approximate size	
		Sq. mi.	Sq. km.
An Nafud[1]	N Saudi Arabia	40,000	103,600
Arabian	Arabian Peninsula	900,000	2,330,000
Atacama	N Chile	70,000	181,300
Australian	Australia	600,000	1,554,000
Black Rock	NW Nevada	1,000	2,600
Chihuahuan	Texas, New Mexico, Arizona; Mexico	140,000	362,600
Dasht-e-Kavir	Central Iran	30,000	77,600
Dasht-e-Lut	E Iran	20,000	51,800
Death Valley	E California, SW Nevada	3,000	7,800
Gibson[2]	W Australia	120,000	310,800
Gobi	Mongolia; China	500,000	1,295,000
Great Sandy[2]	NW Australia	150,000	338,500
Great Victoria[2]	SW Australia	150,000	338,500
Kalahari	S Africa	225,000	582,800
Kara Kum (Turkestan)	Turkmenistan	120,000	310,800
Kyzyl Kum	Uzbekistan	100,000	259,000
Libyan[3]	Libya; SW Egypt; Sudan	450,000	1,165,500
Mojave	S California, W Arizona	15,000	38,900
Namib	Namibia	52,000	135,000
Negev	S Israel	4,700	12,200
Nubian[3]	NE Sudan	100,000	259,000
Painted Desert	N Arizona	5,000	12,950
Rub al-Khali ("Empty Quarter")[1]	S Saudi Arabia	250,000	647,500
Sahara	N Africa	3,500,000	9,065,000
Simpson[2]	Central Australia	40,000	103,600
Sonoran	SW Arizona; SE California; NW Mexico	70,000	181,300
Syrian[1]	N Saudi Arabia; E Jordan; S Syria; W Iraq	100,000	259,000
Taklimakan	Xinjiang Uygur Autonomous Region, China	140,000	362,600
Thar (Great Indian)	NW India; Pakistan	100,000	259,000

1. Part of Great Arabian Desert. 2. Part of Great Australian Desert. 3. Part of Sahara Desert. 4. Length; width varies from 30-100 mi. (48-160 km). 5. Length; width varies from 15-30 mi. (24-48 km).

▶THE GREAT DESERTS OF THE WORLD

To many people, the word *desert* brings to mind images of shifting sand dunes, scorching sun, and occasional lush oases. But there are actually many kinds of deserts, because a desert is simply an area that receives little precipitation and has little plant cover. Thus polar areas can be considered deserts, for their precipitation is locked into ice and snow. So are places like the Taklimakan in China, which lies in a rain shadow on the leeward side of mountain ranges, and the Atacama, which is near cold ocean currents that cool the air and prevent the formation of rain clouds. But most deserts are found in the tropics, where giant high-pressure cells keep rain from forming. Some deserts are indeed flat and sandy, but others are solid rock, loose pebbles, or even mountain plateaus. One of the many fascinating characteristics of deserts is their strangely shaped rock formations, created by wind-whipped sand.

Altogether, arid lands cover about a fifth of the Earth's total land surface—a third if semi-arid areas are also included. About a billion people live in arid and semiarid areas, and more than 100 countries are facing problems associated with expanding deserts.

Uses of the desert   Even the hot, sandy tropical deserts are not necessarily, as their name implies, deserted. Traders, herders, and farmers have called the desert home for thousands of years. Settlements have grown up around oases or in irrigated areas, from ancient times to the pre-

sent. Deserts are important to historians, archaeologists, paleontologists, and other scientists, for the relics of the past that are preserved there. Dinosaur eggs have been found in the Gobi Desert, for instance, and whole cities are said to lie buried beneath the Taklimakan Desert.

Deserts are also important for extractive industries. The Negev was the site of the fabled King Solomon's mines. In the 19th century, borax was mined in Death Valley. Petroleum is found in the Sahara and in the deserts of the Arabian Peninsula. The Atacama is famed for its deposits of nitrate and copper. The Rub al-Khali, or "Empty Quarter" of Saudi Arabia, is thought to contain deposits of limestone and gravel—but no one is certain because it has never been fully explored.

Desert extremes

- The Sahara is the largest desert, with an area greater than the continental United States.
- The driest place on earth is in the Atacama Desert of Chile, where no rainfall at all was recorded between 1570 and 1971.
- The highest temperature ever recorded—136° F (58° C)—was at Al-Aziziya, in the Libyan Desert, but the Dalol, Denakil Depression in Ethiopia is consistently the hottest place on earth, with an annual average temperature of 93°F (34 °C)
- The lowest point in the world—1,312 feet (400m) below sea level—is on the shores of the Dead Sea in the Negev Desert.
- The lowest point in the Western Hemisphere—282 feet (86 meters) below sea level—is in Death Valley, California.

The World's Highest Mountain Peaks

Mountain peak	Range	Location	Height Feet	Meters
Everest	Himalayas	Nepal-China	29,028	8,848
K2 (Godwin Austen)	Karakoram	Kashmir	28,250	8,611
Kanchenjunga	Himalayas	Nepal-India	28,208	8,598
Lhotse I	Himalayas	Nepal-China	27,923	8,511
Makalu I	Himalayas	Nepal-China	27,824	8,481
Lhotse II	Himalayas	Nepal-China	27,560	8,400
Dhaulagiri	Himalayas	Nepal	26,810	8,172
Manaslu I	Himalayas	Nepal	26,760	8,156
Cho Oyu	Himalayas	Nepal-China	26,750	8,153
Nanga Parbat	Himalayas	Kashmir	26,660	8,126
Annapurna	Himalayas	Nepal	26,504	8,078
Gasherbrum	Karakoram	Kashmir	26,470	8,068
Broad	Karakoram	Kashmir	26,400	8,047
Gosainthan	Himalayas	China	26,287	8,012
Annapurna II	Himalayas	Nepal	26,041	7,937
Gyachung Kang	Himalayas	Nepal-China	25,910	7,897
Disteghil Sar	Himalayas	Kashmir	25,858	7,882
Himalchuli	Himalayas	Nepal	25,801	7,864
Nuptse	Himalayas	Nepal-China	25,726	7,841
Masherbrum	Karakoram	Kashmir	25,660	7,821
Nanda Devi	Himalayas	India	25,645	7,817
Rakaposhi	Karakoram	Kashmir	25,550	7,788
Kanjut Sar	Karakoram	Kashmir	25,461	7,761
Kamet	Himalayas	India-China	25,447	7,756
Namcha Barwa	Himalayas	China	25,445	7,756
Kua-la-man-ta-t`a (Gurla Mandhata)	Himalayas	China	25,355	7,728
Wu-lu-k'o-mu-shih (Ulugh Muztagh)	Kunlun	China	25,340	7,724
Kung-ko-erh (Kungur)	Mu-ssu-t'a-ko-a-t'e (Muztagh Ata)	China	25,325	7,719
Tirich Mir	Hindu Kush	Pakistan	25,230	7,690
Saser Kangri	Karakoram	Kashmir	25,172	7,672
Makalu II	Himalayas	Nepal-China	25,120	7,657
Minya Konka (Gonggashan)	Daxue Shan	China	24,900	7,590
Kula Kangri	Himalayas	Bhutan-China	24,784	7,554
Chang-tzu	Himalayas	Nepal-China	24,780	7,553
Mu-ssu-t'a-ko-a-t'e (Muztagh Ata)	Mu-ssu-t'a-ko-a-t'e (Muztagh Ata)	China	24,757	7,546
Skyang Kangri	Himalayas	Kashmir	24,750	7,544
Communism Peak	Pamirs	Tajikistan	24,590	7,495
Jongsong Peak	Himalayas	Nepal-India	24,472	7,459
Pobeda Peak	Tien Shan	Kyrgyzstan-China	24,406	7,439
Sia Kangri	Himalayas	Kashmir	24,350	7,422
Haramosh Peak	Karakoram	Kashmir	24,270	7,397
Istoro Nal	Hindu Kush	Pakistan	24,240	7,388
Tent Peak	Himalayas	Nepal-India	24,165	7,365
Chomo Lhari	Himalayas	Bhutan-China	24,040	7,327
Chamlang	Himalayas	Nepal	24,012	7,319
Kabru	Himalayas	Nepal-India	24,002	7,316
Alung Gangri	Himalayas	China	24,000	7,315
Baltoro Kangri	Himalayas	Kashmir	23,990	7,312
Muztagh Ata	Kunlun	China	23,890	7,282
Mana	Himalayas	India	23,860	7,273
Baruntse	Himalayas	Nepal	23,688	7,220
Nepal Peak	Himalayas	Nepal-India	23,500	7,163
Amne Machin	Kunlun	China	23,490	7,160
Gauri Sankar	Himalayas	Nepal-China	23,440	7,145
Badrinath	Himalayas	India	23,420	7,138
Nunkun	Himalayas	Kashmir	23,410	7,135
Lenin Peak	Pamirs	Tajikistan	23,405	7,134
Pyramid	Himalayas	Nepal-India	23,400	7,132

Mountain peak	Range	Location	Height	
			Feet	Meters
Api	Himalayas	Nepal	23,399	7,132
Pauhunri	Himalayas	India-China	23,385	7,128
Trisul	Himalayas	India	23,360	7,120
Korzhenevski Peak	Pamirs	Tajikistan	23,310	7,105
Kangto	Himalayas	India-China	23,260	7,090
Nyainqentanglha	Nyainqentanglha Shan	China	23,255	7,088
Trisuli	Himalayas	India	23,210	7,074
Dunagiri	Himalayas	India	23,184	7,066
Revolution Peak	Pamirs	Tajikistan	22,880	6,974
Aconcagua	Andes	Argentina	22,834	6,960
Ojos del Salado	Andes	Argentina-Chile	22,572	6,880
Bonete	Andes	Argentina	22,546	6,872
Tupungato	Andes	Argentina-Chile	22,310	6,800
Moscow Peak	Pamirs	Tajikistan	22,260	6,785
Pissis	Andes	Argentina	22,241	6,779
Mercedario	Andes	Argentina	22,211	6,770
Huascaran	Andes	Peru	22,205	6,768
Llullaillaco	Andes	Argentina-Chile	22,057	6,723
El Libertador	Andes	Argentina	22,047	6,720
Cachi	Andes	Argentina	22,047	6,720
Kailas	Himalayas	China	22,027	6,714
Incahuasi	Andes	Argentina-Chile	21,720	6,620
Yerupaja	Andes	Peru	21,709	6,617
Kurumda	Pamirs	Tajikistan	21,686	6,610
Galan	Andes	Argentina	21,654	6,600
El Muerto	Andes	Argentina-Chile	21,457	6,540
Sajama	Andes	Bolivia	21,391	6,520
Nacimiento	Andes	Argentina	21,302	6,493
Illimani	Andes	Bolivia	21,201	6,462
Coropuna	Andes	Peru	21,083	6,426
Laudo	Andes	Argentina	20,997	6,400
Ancohuma	Andes	Bolivia	20,958	6,388
Ausangate	Andes	Peru	20,945	6,384
Toro	Andes	Argentina-Chile	20,932	6,380
Illampu	Andes	Bolivia	20,873	6,362
Tres Cruces	Andes	Argentina-Chile	20,853	6,356
Huandoy	Andes	Peru	20,852	6,356
Parinacota	Andes	Bolivia-Chile	20,768	6,330
Tortolas	Andes	Argentina-Chile	20,745	6,323
Ampato	Andes	Peru	20,702	6,310
El Condor	Andes	Argentina	20,669	6,300
Salcantay	Andes	Peru	20,574	6,271
Chimborazo	Andes	Ecuador	20,561	6,267
Huancarhuas	Andes	Peru	20,531	6,258
Famatina[1]	Andes	Argentina	20,505	6,250
Pumasillo	Andes	Peru	20,492	6,246
Solo	Andes	Argentina	20,492	6,246
Polleras	Andes	Argentina	20,456	6,235
Pular	Andes	Chile	20,423	6,225
Chani	Andes	Argentina	20,341	6,200
McKinley	Alaska	U.S. (Alaska)	20,320	6,194
Aucanquilcha	Andes	Chile	20,295	6,186
Juncal	Andes	Argentina-Chile	20,276	6,180
Negro	Andes	Argentina	20,184	6,152
Quela	Andes	Argentina	20,128	6,135
Condoriri	Andes	Bolivia	20,095	6,125
Palermo	Andes	Argentina	20,079	6,120
Solimana	Andes	Peru	20,068	6,117
San Juan	Andes	Argentina-Chile	20,049	6,111
(Sierra) Nevada	Andes	Argentina-Chile	20,023	6,103
Antofalla	Andes	Argentina	20,013	6,100
Marmolejo	Andes	Argentina-Chile	20,013	6,100

1. Formerly General Manuel Belgrano.

Major Natural Lakes of the World

Lake	Surface area		Location	Maximum depth		Elevation	
	Sq. mi.	Sq. km.		Feet	Meters	Feet	Meters
Caspian Sea[1]	143,240	370,992	Russia, Kazakhstan, Azerbaijan, Turkmenistan, Iran	3,363	1,025	-92	-28
Superior	31,700	82,103	Ontario, Canada; Mich., Wis., Minn.	1,333	406	600	183
Victoria	26,820	69,464	Uganda, Kenya, Tanzania	279	85	3,720	1,134
Aral Sea[1]	24,904	64,501	Uzbekistan, Kazakhstan	220	67	174	53
Huron	23,000	59,570	Ontario, Can.; Mich.	750	229	576	176
Michigan	22,300	57,757	Mich., Ind., Ill., Wis.	923	281	579	176
Tanganyika	12,350	31,987	Burundi, Tanzania, Zambia, Zaire	4,800	1,463	2,543	775
Baikal	12,160	31,494	Russia	5,315	1,620	1,493	455
Great Bear	12,028	31,153	Northwest Terr., Canada	1,356	413	512	156
Nyasa (Malawi)	11,150	28,879	Tanzania, Mozambique, Malawi	2,280	695	1,550	472
Great Slave	11,030	28,568	Northwest Terr., Canada	2,015	614	513	156
Erie	9,910	25,667	Ontario, Canada; N.Y., Pa., Ohio, Mich.	210	64	570	174
Winnipeg	9,417	24,390	Manitoba, Canada	92	28	713	217
Ontario	7,540	19,529	Ontario, Canada; N.Y.	802	244	245	75
Balkhash[1]	7,115[2]	18,428[2]	Kazakhstan	87	27	1,115	340
Ladoga	6,835	17,703	Russia	755	230	13	4
Chad	6,300	16,317	Chad, Nigeria, Niger	24	7	787	240
Maracaibo[3]	5,200	13,468	Venezuela	197	60	sea level	
Patos[3]	3,920	10,153	Brazil	15	5	[4]	[4]
Onega	3,720	9,635	Russia	394	120	108	33
Titicaca	3,200	8,288	Bolivia, Peru	990	302	12,500	3,810
Nicaragua	3,150	8,159	Nicaragua	230	70	102	31
Mai-Ndombe	3,100	8,029[2]	Zaire	36	11	1,116	340
Athabasca	3,064	7,936	Saskatchewan, Alberta, Canada	407	124	700	213
Eyre[r]	2,970[2]	7,692[2]	Australia	4	1	-52	-16
Reindeer	2,568	6,651	Saskatchewan, Manitoba, Canada	720	219	1,106	337
Tonle Sap	2,500[2]	6,475[2]	Cambodia	39	12	[4]	[4]
Rudolf[1]	2,473	6,405	Kenya, Ethiopia	720	219	1,230	375
Issyk-Kul[1]	2,355	6,099	Kyrghyzstan	2,303	702	5,279	1,609
Torrens[1]	2,230[2]	5,776[2]	Australia	0.5	0.2	92	28
Albert	2,160	5,594	Uganda, Zaire	168	51	2,030	619
Vanern	2,156	5,54	Sweden	325	99	144	44
Nettilling	2,140	5,543	Baffin Island, Canada	[4]	[4]	95	29
Winnipegosis	2,075	5,374	Manitoba, Canada	39	12	830	253
Bangweulu	1,930	4,999	Zambia	5	2	3,500	1,067
Nipigon	1,872	4,848	Ontario, Canada	541	165	1,050	320
Gairdner[1]	1,840[2]	4,763[2]	Australia	0.5	0.2	112	34
Urmia[1]	1,815[2]	4,701[2]	Iran	49	15	4,180	1,274
Manitoba	1,800	4,662	Manitoba, Canada	92	28	813	248
Kyoga	1,710	4,429	Uganda	26	8	4	4
Khanka	1,700	4,403	China, Russia	33	10	4	4
Lake of the Woods	1,695	4,390	Ontario, Manitoba, Canada; Minn.	55	17	1,060	323
Great Salt[1]	1,680	4,351	Utah	48	15	4,200	1,280
Mweru	1,680	4,351	Zambia, Zaire	10	3	3,008	917
Peipus	1,660	4,299	Estonia, Russia	41	12	98	30
Koko Nor (Tsing Hai)	1,650	4,274	China	125	38	10,515	3,205
Dubawnt	1,600	4,144	Northwest Terr., Canada	[4]	[4]	774	236
Tung-t'ing Hu	1,430[2]	3,704[2]	China	[4]	[4]	36	11
Van Golu[1]	1,420	3,678	Turkey	82	25	5,643	1,720
Tana	1,390	3,600	Ethiopia	30	9	6,003	1,830

1. Saltwater. A lake is a body of water surrounded by land. The Caspian Sea is thus a lake. It was called a "sea" by the Romans because of its salty water. 2. Subject to large seasonal variation in surface area. 3. Lagoon. 4. No information available. **Source:** U.S. Department of Commerce, National Oceanic and Atmospheric Administration, *Principal Rivers and Lakes of the World* (1982).

Major Rivers of the World, by Length

River	Length Miles	km	Source	Outflow
Nile	4,145	6,673	Tributaries of LakeVictoria, E. Africa	Mediterranean Sea
Amazon	4,000	6,440	Andes Mts., Peru	Atlantic Ocean
Mississippi-Missouri	3,740[1]	6,021[1]	Confluence of Jefferson, Madison, and Galatin R., Montana	Gulf of Mexico
Changjiang (Yangtze)	3,720	5,989	Kunlun Mts., China	China Sea
Yenisei-Angara	3,650[2]	5,877[2]	Lake Baikal, Russia	Kara Sea (Arctic Ocean)
Amur-Argun	3,590[2]	5,780[2]	Khingan Mts., China	Tatar Strait
Ob-Irtysh	3,360[2]	5,410[2]	Altai Mts., China	Gulf of Ob (Arctic Ocean)
Plata-Parana	3,030[2]	4,878[2]	Confluence of the Paranaiba and Grande rivers, Brazil	Atlantic Ocean
Huang He (Yellow)	2,903	4,674	Kunlun Mts., China	Gulf of Chihli (Yellow Sea)
Congo (Zaire)	2,900	4,669	Confluence of the Luapula and Lualaba rivers, Zaire	Atlantic Ocean
Lena	2,730	4,395	Baikal Mts., Russia	Laptev Sea (Arctic Ocean)
MacKenzie	2,635[2]	4,242[2]	Headwaters of Finlay Rivers, British Columbia, Canada	Beaufort Sea (Arctic Ocean)
Mekong	2,600	4,186	T'ang-ku-la Mts., Tibet	South China Sea
Niger	2,600	4,186	Guinea	Gulf of Guinea
Missouri	2,315	3,725	Confluence of Jefferson, Madison, and Montana Galatin rivers, Montana	Mississippi River
Mississippi	2,348[3]	3,780[3]	Lake Itasca, northwestern Minnesota	Gulf of Mexico
Murray-Darling	2,330	3,751	Great Dividing Range, Australia	Indian Ocean
Volga	2,290	3,687	Valdai Hills, Russia	Caspian Sea
Madeira	2,013	3,241	Confluence of the Mamore and Beni rivers, Bolivia/Brazil	Amazon River
Sao Francisco	1,988	3,201	Minas Gerais State, Brazil	Atlantic Ocean
Yukon	1,979	3,186	Confluence of Lewes and Pelly rivers, Yukon Territory, Canada	Bering Sea
Rio Grande	1,885	3,035	San Juan Mts., southwestern Colorado	Gulf of Mexico
Purus	1,860	2,995	Andes Mts., Peru	Amazon River
Tunguska, Lower	1,860	2,995	North of Lake Baikal, Russia	Yenesei River
Indus	1,800	2,898	Himalayas, Tibet	Arabian Sea
Danube	1,776	2,859	Confluence of Breg and Brigach rivers, Germany	Black Sea
Brahmaputra	1,770	2,850	Himalayas, Tibet	Ganges River
Salween	1,750	2,818	Tibetan Plateau, Tibet	Bay of Bengal
Para-Tocantins	1,710[2]	2,753[2]	Goias State, Brazil	Atlantic Ocean
Zambezi	1,700	2,737	Northwestern Zambia	Mozambique Channel
Paraguay	1,610	2,592	Mato Grosso State, Brazil	Parana River
Kolyma	1,320	2,130	Kolyma Mts., Russia	Arctic Ocean
Nelson-Saskatchewan	1,600	2,576	Rocky Mts., Canada	Hudson Bay
Orinoco	1,600	2,576	Sierra Parima Mts., Venezuela	Atlantic Ocean
Amu Darya	1,578	2,541	Pamir Mts., Uzbekistan/ Turkmenistan	Aral Sea
Ural	1,575	2,536	Ural Mountains, Russia	Caspian Sea
Ganges	1,560	2,512	Himalayas, India	Bay of Bengal
Euphrates	1,510	2,431	Confluence of the Murat Nehri and Kara Su rivers, Turkey	Shatt-al-Arab
Arkansas	1,450	2,335	Central Colorado	Mississippi River
Colorado	1,450	2,335	Northern Colorado	Gulf of California
Dneiper	1,420	2,286	Valdai Hills, Russia	Black Sea
Atchafalaya-Red	1,400	2,254	Eastern New Mexico	Gulf of Mexico
Syr Darya	1,370	2,206	Tien Shan, China/Kyrghyzstan	Aral Sea
Kasai	1,338	2,154	Central Angola	Congo (Zaire) River
Irrawaddy	1,300	2,093	Confluence of Mali and Nmai rivers, Myanmar	Bay of Bengal
Ohio-Allegheny	1,300	2,093	Pennsylvania	Mississippi River
Orange	1,300	2,093	Lesotho	Atlantic Ocean
Columbia	1,243	2,001	Columbia Lake, British Columbia, Canada	Pacific Ocean
Tigris	1,180	1,900	Eastern Turkey	Shatt-al-Arab
Rhine	820	1,320	Confluence of Hinterrhein and Vorderrhein rivers, Switzerland	North Sea
St. Lawrence	800	1,288	Lake Ontario	Gulf of St. Lawrence

1. From the mouth of the Mississippi, up the Missouri to the Red Rock River in Montana. 2. Includes the length of tributaries that are part of the main trunk stream. 3. From the mouth of the Mississippi, up to its source in Minnesota. **Source:** U.S. Dept. of Commerce, National Oceanic and Atmospheric Administration, *Principal Rivers and Lakes of the World* (1982).

The World's Largest Islands

Island	Location	Flags	Area Sq. mi.	Area Sq. km.
Greenland	N. Atlantic Ocean	Denmark	840,000	2,175,600
New Guinea	S. Pacific Ocean	Indonesia, Papua New Guinea	306,000	792,540
Borneo	Pacific Ocean	Indonesia, Malaysia, Brunei	280,100	725,459
Madagascar	Indian Ocean	Madagascar	226,658	587,044
Baffin	Arctic Ocean	Canada	195,928	507,454
Sumatra	Indian Ocean	Indonesia	165,000	427,350
Honshu	N. Pacific Ocean	Japan	87,805	227,415
Great Britain	N. Atlantic Ocean	United Kingdom	84,200	218,078
Victoria	Arctic Ocean	Canada	83,896	217,291
Ellesmere	Arctic Ocean	Canada	75,767	196,237
Celebes	Pacific Ocean	Indonesia	69,000	178,710
South Island	S. Pacific Ocean	New Zealand	58,305	151,010
Java	S. Pacific Ocean	Indonesia	48,900	126,651
Cuba	Caribbean Sea	Cuba	44,218	114,525
North Island	S. Pacific Ocean	New Zealand	44,035	114,051
Newfoundland	N. Atlantic Ocean	Canada	42,030	108,858
Luzon	N. Pacific Ocean	Philippines	40,880	105,879
Iceland	N. Atlantic Ocean	Iceland	39,769	103,002
Mindanao	N. Pacific Ocean	Philippines	36,775	95,247
Novaya Zemlya	Arctic Ocean	Russia	35,000	90,650
Ireland	N. Atlantic Ocean	Irish Republic, United Kingdom	32,599	84,431
Hokkaido	N. Pacific Ocean	Japan	30,144	78,073
Hispaniola	Caribbean Sea	Haiti, Dominican Republic	29,530	76,483
Sakhalin	N. Pacific Ocean	Russia	29,500	76,405
Banks	Arctic Ocean	Canada	27,033	70,015
Tasmania	S. Pacific Ocean	Australia	26,178	67,801
Sri Lanka	Indian Ocean	Sri Lanka	25,332	65,610
Devon	Arctic Ocean	Canada	21,331	55,247

▶THE POLAR REGIONS

Antarctica

• **GEOGRAPHY   Location:** continent mostly south of Antarctic Circle at 90°S. **Boundaries:** None. Bordered by South Atlantic, Indian and South Pacific oceans. **Total land area:** about 5,404,000 sq. mi. (14,000,000 sq. km.). **Coastline:** 11,165 mi. (17,968 km). **Comparative area:** twice the size of Australia. **Land use:** 98% continental ice sheet; 2% barren rock. **Natural Resources:** None presently exploited. Iron ore, chromium, copper, gold, nickel, platinum, and other minerals, as well as coal and hydrocarbons have been found in small uncommercial qualities. **Temperature:** Varies with location and altitude. East Antarctica is coldest; Antarctic Peninsula in the west is mildest; mean annual temperature of the interior regions is -57°C (-71°F); mean temperatures at the coastal McMurdo station range from -28°C (-18°F) in August to -3°C (27°F) in January. **Major cities:** none.

• **THE LAND**   Some 200 million years ago Antarctica was joined to South America, Africa, India and Australia as one large continent. Geological changes caused the breakup into separate continents. Studies indicate that Antarctica once had a tropical environment, but that its present ice form is at least 20 million years old. Approximately 98 percent of the continent is covered by ice; contains about 90 percent of the world's ice and 70 percent of the fresh water. Elevations average from 6,600 ft. to 13,200 ft. (2,000-4,000 m); mountain ranges up to 16,500 ft. (5,500 m) high. Ice-free coastal areas include parts of southern Victoria Land, Wilkes Land and Ross Island. The Antarctic ice sheet averages 7,090 ft. (2,160 m) in depth and is 15,670 ft. (4,776 m) deep at its thickest point. Altitude at the South Pole is about 9,800 ft. (3,000 m)

• **LAND/SEA LIFE:**   Land life includes bacteria, lichens, mosses, two kinds of flowering plants in the ice-free areas, penguins and some flying birds. Sea life includes several types of seals and whales many of which were hunted to near extinction but are now protected by international conventions.

• **EXPLORATION:**   British Captain James Cook circumnavigated the continent without sighting land in 1772-75. U.S. Capt. John Davis made the first known landing on the continent on Feb. 7, 1821. In 1908 the U.K. became the first nation to claim a "slice" of the continent, subsequently followed by claims from New Zealand (1923), France (1924), Australia (1933), Norway (1939), Chile (1940) and Argentina (1943). The U.S. and Russia have never claimed any Antarctica territory. Claims made by other nations are not recognized by other countries nor by the U.N.

In 1911 Capt. Robert F. Scott and Roald Amundsen of Norway began a "race to the pole." Amundsen's party arrived at the South Pole on 14 December 1911 while Scott located the pole on 18 January 1912.

• **SCIENTIFIC RESEARCH:**   The greatest scientific study ever conducted in Antarctica occurred in 1957-58 when 67 nations participated in the International Geophysical Year (IGY). Twelve countries established more than 50 stations to study the effects of the continent's huge ice mass on global weather, the oceans, the aurora australis and the ionosphere. During the late 1980s research was focused on the study of the ozone depletion in the

World's 25 Largest Capacity Reservoirs

Reservoir	Capacity (mil.) Cubic yards[1]	Capacity (mil.) Cubic meters[1]	River or basin and location	Year completed
1. Owen Falls[2]	3,537,000	2,700,000	Lake Victoria/Nile, Uganda	1954
2. Kakhovskaya	238,420	182,000	Dnieper, Ukraine	1955
3. Kariba	236,586	180,600	Zambezi, Zimbabwe/Zambia	1959
4. Bratsk	221,744	169,270	Angara, Russia	1964
5. Aswan High	221,259	168,900	Nile, Egypt	1970
6. Akosombo	200,430	153,000	Volta, Ghana	1965
7. Daniel Johnson	185,826	141,852	Manicouagan, Quebec	1968
8. Guri	180,780	138,000	Caroni, Venezuela	1986
9. Krasnoyarsk	96,023	73,300	Yenesei, Russia	1967
10. W.A.C. Bennett	92,105	70,309	Peace, British Columbia	1967
11. Zeya	89,604	68,400	Zeya, Russia	1978
12. Cabora Bassa	82,530	63,000	Zambezi, Mozambique	1974
13. La Grande 2	80,847	61,715	La Grande, Quebec	1978
14. La Grande 3	78,626	60,020	La Grande, Quebec	1981
15. Ust-Ilim	77,683	59,300	Angara, Russia	1977
16. Boguchany	76,242	58,200	Russia	1989
17. Volga-V.I. Lenin (Kuibyshev)	75,980	58,000	Volga, Russia	1955
18. Caniapiscau	70,478	53,800	Caniapiscau, Quebec, Canada	1981
19. Bukhtarma	65,238	49,800	Irtysh, Russia	1960
20. Atatürk	63,797	48,700	Euphrates, Turkey	1990
21. Irkutsk	60,260	46,000	Angara, Russia	1956
22. Tucurui	56,330	45,800	Tocantins, Brazil	1984
23. Lower Kama	58,858	45,000	Kama, Russia	1987
24. Vilyui	47,029	35,900	Vilyui, Russia	1967
25. Sanmenxia	46,374	35,400	Huanghe (Yellow), China	1960

Note: Uncompleted reservoirs are not officially ranked. 1. One cubic yard equals 0.765 cubic meters. 2. Includes a natural lake.
Source: *International Water Power & Dam Construction Handbook 1993.*

World's 25 Largest Volume Dams

Reservoir	Volume ('000s) Cubic yards[1]	Volume ('000s) Cubic meters[1]	River or basin and location	Year completed
1. New Cornelia Tailings	274,445	209,500	Ten Mile Wash, Arizona	1973
2. Tarbela	138,297	106,000	Indus, Pakistan	1976
3. Fort Peck	125,825	96,050	Missouri, Montana	1937
4. Lower Usuma	121,830	93,000	Usuma, Nigeria	1990
5. Tucurui	111,612	85,200	Tocantins, Brazil	1984
6. Atatürk	111,350	84,500	Euphrates, Turkey	1990
7. Guri (Raul Leoni)	102,142	77,971	Caroni, Venezuela	1986
8. Oahe	87,137	66,517	Missouri, South Dakota	1958
9. Gardiner	85,726	65,400	South Saskatchewan, Saskatchewan	1968
10. Mangla	85,646	65,379	Jhelum, Pakistan	1967
11. Afsluitdijk	83,093	63,430	Zuider Zee, Netherlands	1932
12. Oroville	80,125	61,164	Feather, California	1968
13. San Luis	78,022	59,559	San Luis, California	1967
14. Nurek	75,980	58,000	Vakhsh, Tajikistan	1980
15. Garrison	66,607	50,845	Missouri, North Dakota	1956
16. Cochiti	65,801	50,230	Grande, New Mexico	1975
17. Oosterschelde	65,500	50,000	Vense Gat Oosterschelde, Netherlands	1986
18. Tabqua (Thawra)	60,260	46,000	Euphrates, Syria	1976
19. Aswan, High	58,033	44,300	Nile, Egypt	1970
20. W.A.C. Bennett	57,290	43,733	Peace, Canada	1967
21. Kiev	55,544	42,400	Dnieper, Ukraine	1964
22. Dantiwada	53,762	41,040	Banas, India	1965
23. Saratov	52,924	40,400	Volga, Russia	1967
24. Earthquake Lake	50,079	38,228	Madison, Montana	1959
25. Fort Randall	50,042	38,200	Missouri, South Dakota	1952

Note: Volume refers to amount of material (earth, concrete, etc.) used in construction of dam. UC=Under Construction. Tailings dams are formed from waste ore (tailings) from mining. Uncompleted reservoirs are not officially ranked. 1. One cubic meter equals 1.31 cubic yards. **Source:** *International Water Power & Dam Construction Handbook 1993.*

stratosphere—called the "ozone hole"—which allows high levels of potentially harmful ultraviolet radiation to reach the earth's surface.

In 1998, 18 different countries maintained 42 research stations year-round. Argentina and the former Soviet Union each had six, the U.K. maintained five, Australia, Chile, South Africa and the U.S. kept three, China and Japan each had two, and Brazil, Finland, France, Germany, India, South Korea, New Zealand, Poland, and Uruguay each had one.

● **PEOPLE** **Population:** No indigenous inhabitants. Staffing of research stations varies seasonally; Summer (January) popuation: approximately 4,415; Winter (July) population: approximately 1,046

● **GOVERNMENT** **Antarctica Treaty:** Signed in 1959 by the 12 IGY nations (in force as of June 23, 1961), it establishes a legal framework for the management of Antarctica. The treaty was renewed in 1991 in Madrid, where 24 countries, including the United States, signed a protocol to ban mineral-and oil exploration for 50 years and to provide wildlife protection. The treaty states that the area is to be used for peaceful purposes only and military activity such as weapons testing is prohibited; calls for freedom of scientific investigation and cooperation and a free exchange of information and personnel; nuclear explosions or disposal of radioactive wastes is forbidden; and, treaty-state observers have free access, including aerial observation, to any area and may inspect all stations, installations and equipment.

At the Treaty's 17th meeting in November, 1992, there were 26 consultative (voting) members and 15 acceding (non-voting) members. The 26 consultative members include the seven countries that claim part of Antarctica as national territory (Argentina, Australia, Chile, France, New Zealand, Norway, and the U.K.) as well as 15 nonclaimant nations. The claimant nations all signed the Antarctica Treaty in 1959; the 15 non-claimant nations (followed by the year they signed the treaty) are Belgium (1959), Brazil (1983), China (1985), Ecuador (1990), Finland (1989), Germany (1981), India (1983), Italy (1987), Japan (1959), South Korea (1989), Netherlands (1990), Peru (1989), Poland (1977), South Africa (1959), Spain (1988), Sweden (1988), Uruguay (1985), the U.S. (1959), and Russia (1959). The nonvoting members (and their year of accession) are Austria (1987), Bulgaria (1978), Canada (1988), Colombia (1988), Cuba (1984), Czechoslovakia (1962), Denmark (1965), Greece (1987), Guatemala (1991), Hungary (1984), North Korea (1987), Papua New Guinea (1981), Romania (1971), Slovakia (1993), Switzerland (1990), and Ukraine (1992).

The Arctic

● **GEOGRAPHY** **Location:** The Arctic Regions comprise all the lands north of the Arctic Circle—66°30'N—including the northern reaches of Asia, Europe, and North America, the Arctic Ocean, and its islands. In terms of climate, geography, and culture this demarcation is relatively insignificant, but within the Arctic Circle there is at least one 24-hour period during which the sun never sets (summer solstice), and one in which it never rises (winter solstice). The Arctic Ocean is the fourth largest after the Pacific, Atlantic and Indian; its primary marginal seas are Baffin Bay, the Barents Sea, the Beaufort Sea, the Chukchi Sea, the East Siberian Sea, the Greenland Sea, Hudson Bay, Hudson Strait, the Kara Sea, and the Laptev Sea. Some oceanographers consider the Arctic Ocean to be a marginal sea of the Atlantic Ocean.

Boundaries: None. **Total area:** The Arctic Ocean is 5,440,000 sq. mi. (14,090,000 sq km). The main island groups are the Canadian Arctic Archipelago (550,000 sq. mi.; 1,424,483 sq km), Greenland (840,000 sq. mi.; 2,175,590 sq km), Novaya Zemlya (31,000 sq. mi.; 80,290 sq km), and Svalbard (24,000 sq. mi.; 62,160 sq km). **Coastline:** 17,525 sq. mi. (45,389 km). **Comparative area:** The Arctic Ocean is about 1.5 times the size of the United States. **Land use:** The central surface is covered by a perennial drifting polar ice cap which averages about 3 meters thick, although pressure ridges may be three times that size. It drifts in a clockwise pattern in the Beaufort Gyral Stream, but exhibits nearly straight-line movement from the New Siberian Islands (Russia) to the Denmark Strait (between Greenland and Iceland). The ice pack is surrounded by open seas during the summer, but more than doubles in size during the winter and extends to the encircling land masses; the ocean floor is about 50 percent continental shelf (the highest percentage of any ocean) with the remainder a central basin interrupted by three submarine ridges (the Alpha Cordillera, Nansen Cordillera, and Lomonsov Ridge). The maximum depth is 17,881 ft. (5,450 m) in the Fram Basin. **Natural resources:** In the Arctic Ocean there are sand and gravel aggregates, placer deposits, polymetallic nodules, oil and gas fields, fish, and marine mammals (seals and whales). **Climate:** The dominant fact of life is the frigid conditions: persistent cold and relatively modest annual temperature ranges; winters characterized by continuous darkness, cold and stable weather conditions and clear skies; summers characterized by continuous daylight, damp and foggy weather, and weak cyclones with rain or snow. Between 60°N and 75°N there is seasonal freezing, while north of 75°N there is permanent ice. In North America, temperatures during the colder months average -25°F (-31°C), while Siberia is somewhat colder at -35°F (-37°C). **Environment:** Endangered marine species include walruses and whales; ice islands occasionally break away from northern Ellesmere Island; icebergs calved from western Greenland and extreme northeastern Canada; maximum snow cover in March or April is about 20-50 cm over the frozen ocean and lasts about 10 months; permafrost in islands; virtually ice-locked from October to June; fragile ecosystem slow to change and slow to recover from disruptions or damage.

● **PEOPLE** **Population** Ethnologists distinguish three native cultural areas—the Western Arctic, including Eskimo peoples (from the east coast of Greenland to Alaska), and Aleuts; Paleo-Siberian, including the Chukchi and Eskimos of Eastern Asia; and Eurasian Arctic, including some Chukchi, Yakut, Nenets, and Lapps. Today, however, the vast majority of the people living and working within the Arctic Circle are non-native peoples in industry or scientific enterprises.

● **GOVERNMENT** Governments with territory north of the Arctic Circle are Canada, the United States, Russia, Finland, Sweden, Norway, and Denmark (Greenland). Svalbard is the focus of a maritime boundary dispute between Norway and Russia.

● **ECONOMY** While there is a fair amount of economic activity in the continental portions of the Arctic—principally extractive industries in Siberia, northern Canada, and Alaska's North Slope—conditions in the numerous Arctic islands all but prevent significant development there. Norwegian and Russian miners extract about 1 million tons of coal per year from mines on Svalbard, and in Greenland there are large deposits of cryolite, lead, and other minerals, but only lead can be mined economically. Economic activity in the Arctic Ocean is limited to the exploitation of natural resources including crude oil, natural gas, fishing and sealing.

• **COMMUNICATIONS Ports:** Churchill (Canada), Murmansk (Russia), Prudhoe Bay (U.S.). **Telecommunications:** No submarine cables. **Transportation:** There is a sparse network of air, ocean, river, and land routes. The Arctic provides the shortest marine link between the extremes of east-

ern and western Russia. The two major waterways are the Northwest Passage, in North America, and the Northern Sea Route, in Asia, but ships are subject to superstructure icing from October to May. The U.S. and Russia operate floating research stations. Access to the Arctic Ocean from the Pacific Ocean is through the Bering Strait; from the Atlantic, through the Davis Strait (between Canada and Greenland), the Denmark Strait (between Greenland and Iceland), or the Norwegian Sea (between Iceland and Norway).

The 50 Tallest Buildings in the World

The two towers of New York City's World Trade Center were, until their destruction by a terrorist plane attack on Sept. 11, 2001, the fifth- and sixth-tallest buildings in the world, at 1,368 and 1,362 feet.

Rank/Building	City, Country	Year	Stories	Height Meters	Feet
1. Petronas Tower 1	Kuala Lumpur, Malaysia	1998	88	452	1,483
2. Petronas Tower 2	Kuala Lumpur, Malaysia	1998	88	452	1,483
3. Sears Tower	Chicago	1974	110	442	1,450
4. Jin Mao Building	Shanghai, China	1999	88	421	1,380
5. Citic Plaza	Guangzhou, China	1996	80	391	1,283
6. Shun Hing Square	Shenzhen, China	1996	69	384	1,260
7. Empire State Building	New York	1931	102	381	1,250
8. Central Plaza	Hong Kong	1992	78	374	1,227
9. Bank of China Tower	Hong Kong	1989	70	369	1,209
10. Emirates Tower One	Dubai, U.A.E.	2000	55	355	1,165
11. The Center	Hong Kong	1998	79	350	1,148
12. T&C Tower	Kaohsiung, Taiwan	1997	85	348	1,140
13. Amoco	Chicago	1973	80	346	1,136
14. Kingdom Centre	Riyadh, Saudi Arabia	2000	30	345	1,132
15. John Hancock Center	Chicago	1969	100	344	1,127
16. Burj al Arab Hotel	Dubai, U.A.E.	2000	60	321	1,053
17. Baiyoke Tower II	Bangkok, Thailand	1997	90	320	1,050
18. Chrysler Building	New York	1930	77	319	1,046
19. Bank of America Plaza	Atlanta	1993	55	312	1,023
20. Library Tower	Los Angeles	1990	75	310	1,018
21. Telekom Malaysia Headquarters	Kuala Lumpur, Malaysia	1999	55	310	1,017
22. Emirates Tower Two	Dubai, U.A.E.	2000	54	309	1,014
23. AT&T Corporate Center	Chicago	1989	60	307	1,007
24. Chase Tower	Houston	1982	75	305	1,000
25. Two Prudential Plaza	Chicago	1990	64	303	995
26. Ryugyong Hotel	Pyongyang, North Korea	1995	105	300	984
27. Commerzbank Tower	Frankfurt, Germany	1997	56	299	981
28. Wells Fargo Plaza	Houston	1983	71	296	972
29. Landmark Tower	Yokohama, Japan	1993	70	296	971
30. South Wacker Drive	Chicago	1990	65	293	961
31. American International Building	New York	1932	67	290	952
32. Cheung Kong Center	Hong Kong	1999	70	290	951
33. First Canadian Place	Toronto, Canada	1975	72	290	951
34. Key Tower	Cleveland	1991	57	290	950
35. One Liberty Place	Philadelphia	1987	61	287	945
36. Plaza	Shanghai, China	2000	66	288	945
37. Columbia Seafirst Center	Seattle	1984	76	287	943
38. Sunjoy Tomorrow Square	Shanghai, China	1999	59	285	934
39. The Trump Building	New York	1930	72	283	927
40. NationsBank Plaza	Dallas	1985	72	281	921
41. Overseas Union Bank Plaza	Singapore	1986	66	280	919
42. United Overseas Bank Plaza	Singapore	1992	66	280	919
43. Republic Plaza	Singapore	1995	66	280	919
44. Citicorp Center	New York	1977	59	279	915
45. Scotia Plaza	Toronto	1989	68	275	902
46. Williams Tower	Houston	1983	64	275	901
47. Faisaliah Complex	Riyadh, Saudi Arabia	2000	30	274	899
48. Renaissance Tower	Dallas	1975	56	270	886
49. 900 North Michigan	Chicago	1989	66	265	871
50. SunTrust Plaza	Atlanta	1992	60	265	871

Note: Height is measured from sidewalk level of main entrance to structural top of building. Television and radio antennas and flag poles are not included. **Source:** Council on High Buildings and Urban Habitat, Lehigh University (2001).

Time Zones and Area Codes for Selected Nations and Territories

Country	Hours from EST	Country Code	City Codes
Afghanistan	+9.5	93	Not required
Albania	+6	355	Durres 52, Elbassan 545, Tirana 42
Algeria	+6	213	Adrar 7, Ain Defla 3, Bejala 5, Guerrar 9
American Samoa	-6	684	Not required
Andorra	+6	376	Not required
Angola	+6	244	Not required
Argentina	+2	54	Buenos Aires 11, Cordoba 51, Rosario 41, Santa Fe 42
Armenia	+8	374	Not required
Aruba	+1	297	All points 8
Ascension Island	+5	247	Not required
Australia[1]	+15	61	Brisbane 07, Canberra 02, Melbourne 03, Perth 08, Sydney 02
Austria	+6	43	Graz 316, Innsbruck 5122, Linz 70, Salzburg 662, Vienna 1
Azerbaijan	+8	994	Baku 12, Dashkasan 216, Sumgayit 264
Bahrain	+8	973	Not required
Bangladesh	+11	880	Chittagong 31, Dhaka 2, Khulna 41
Belarus	+8	375	Loev 2347, Minsk 172, Mogilev 22
Belgium	+6	32	Antwerp 3, Brussels 2, Ghent 9, Liege 4
Belize	-1	501	Belize City 2, Belmopan 8, Orange Walk 3
Benin	+6	229	Not required
Bhutan	+10.5	975	Not required
Bolivia	+1	591	Cochabamba 42, La Paz 2, Santa Cruz 33, Sucre 64
Bosnia/ Herzegovina	+6	387	Mostar 88, Sarajevo 71, Zenica 72
Botswana	+7	267	Jwaneng 380, Molepolole 320, Serowe 430
Brazil[2]	+2	55	Belo Horizonte 31, Brasília 61, Porto Alegre 512, Recife 81, Rio de Janeiro 21, Salvador 71, São Paulo 11
Brunei	+13	673	Bandar Seri Begawan 2, Kuala Belait 3, Tutong 4
Bulgaria	+7	359	Plovdiv 32, Sofia 2, Varna 52
Burkina Faso	+5	226	Not required
Burundi	+7	257	Bujumbura 2, Gitega 40, Muyinga 30
Cambodia	+12	855	Phnom Penh 23
Cameroon	+6	237	Not required
Canada	Similar to U.S. (See "Area Codes of the U.S., Canada, and the Caribbean")		
Cape Verde Islands	+4	238	Not required
Central African Rep.	+6	236	Not required
Chad	+6	235	Not required
Chile	+1	56	Concepcion 41, La Serena 51, Santiago 2, Valparaíso 32
China (PRC)	+12	86	Beijing 10, Fuzhou 591, Ghuangzhou (Canton) 20, Shanghai 21
Colombia	0	57	Barranquilla 5, Bogotá 1, Cali 2, Cartagena 5, Medellín 4
Comoros	+9	269	Not required
Congo, Dem. Rep.[3]	+6	243	Kinshasa 12, Lubumbashi 2
Congo Republic	+6	242	Not required
Cook Islands	-5	682	Not required
Costa Rica	-1	506	Not required
Croatia	+6	385	Dubrovnik 20, Rijeka 51, Split 21 Zagreb 41
Cuba	0	53	Havana 7, Santiago de Cuba 226
Cyprus	+7	357	Kyrenia 357, Larnaca 4, Limassol 5, Nicosia 2
Czech Republic	+6	420	Brno 5, Ostrava 69, Prague 2
Denmark	+6	45	Not required
Djibouti	+8	253	Not required
Ecuador	0	593	Cuenca 7, Guayaquil 4, Machala 7, Quito 2
Egypt	+7	20	Alexandria 3, Aswan 97, Cairo 2, Port Said 66
El Salvador	-1	503	Not required
Equatorial Guinea	+6	240	Bata 8, Malabo 9
Eritrea	+8	291	All locations 1
Estonia	+7	372	Rakvere 32, Tallinn 2, Tartu 7
Ethiopia	+8	251	Addis Ababa 1, Dire Dawa 5, Nazareth 2
Faeroe Islands	+5	298	Not required
Fiji	+17	679	Not required
Finland	+7	358	Espoo 9, Helsinki 9, Tampere 3, Turku 2
France[4]	+6	33	Bordeaux 56, Marseille 91, Nice 493, Paris 1, Toulouse 5
French Antilles	+1	596	Not required
French Guiana	+2	594	Not required
French Polynesia[5]	-5	689	Not required
Gabon	+6	241	Not required
Gambia	+5	220	Not required
Georgia	+8	995	Sukhumi 881, Tblisi 32
Germany	+6	49	Berlin 30, Cologne 221, Frankfurt (west) 69, Frankfurt (east) 335, Hamburg 40, Leipzig 341, Munich 89
Ghana	+5	233	Accra 21, Koforidua 81, Kumasi 51, Takoradi 31

Country	Hours from EST	Country Code	City Codes
Gibraltar	+6	350	Not required
Greece	+7	30	Athens 01, Patras 061, Thessaloniki 031
Greenland	+2	299	Not required
Guadeloupe	+1	590	Base Terre 81, Jarry 26, Point a Pitre 8 or 9
Guam	+15	671	Not required
Guatemala	-1	502	Guatemala City 2, Quezaltenango 9
Guinea	+5	224	Conakry 4, Faranah 81, Kindia 61, Labe 51, Mamou 68
Guinea-Bissau	+5	245	Not required
Guyana	+2	592	Georgetown 2, New Amsterdam 3
Haiti	0	509	Not required
Honduras	-1	504	Not required
Hong Kong	+13	852	Not required
Hungary	+6	36	Budapest 1, Miskole 46
Iceland	+5	354	Not required
India	+10.5	91	Bombay 22, Calcutta 33, Hyderabad 40, Madras 44, New Delhi 11
Indonesia[6]	+12	62	Bandung 22, Jakarta 21, Medan 61, Surabaya 31
Iran	+8.5	98	Isfahan 31, Mashad 51, Tehran 21
Iraq	+8	964	Baghdad 1, Basra 40, Kirkuk 50, Mosul 60
Ireland	+5	353	Cork 21, Dublin 1, Galway 91, Limerick 61, Waterford 51
Israel	+7	972	Haifa 4, Jerusalem 2, Tel Aviv 3
Italy	+6	39	Florence 055, Milan 02, Naples 081, Rome 06, Venice 041
Ivory Coast	+5	225	Not required
Japan	+14	81	Kyoto 75, Nagoya 52, Osaka 6, Sapporo 11, Tokyo 3, Yokohama 45
Jordan	+7	962	Amman 6, Irbid 2, Zarqa 9
Kazakhstan	+11	7	Chimkent 325, Guryev 312, Petropavlovsk 3152
Kenya	+8	254	Mombasa 11, Kisumu 35, Nairobi 2, Nakuru 37, Thika 151
Kiribati	+17	686	Not required
Korea, North	+14	850	Pyongyang 2
Korea, South	+14	82	Inchon 32, Kwangju 62, Pusan 51, Seoul 2, Taegu 53
Kuwait	+8	965	Not required
Kyrgyzstan	+11	7	Osh 332
Laos	+12	856	Not required
Latvia	+7	371	Daugav'pils 54, Jelgava 30, Liepaja 34, Riga 34
Lebanon	+7	961	Beirut 1, Tripoli 6, Zahleh 8
Lesotho	+7	266	Not required
Liberia	+5	231	Not required
Libya	+6	218	Benghazi 61, Misurata 51, Tripoli 21
Liechtenstein	+6	423	Not required
Lithuania	+7	370	Kaunas 7, Klaipeda 6, Siauliai 1, Panavezys 5, Vilnius 2
Luxembourg	+6	352	Not required
Macau	+13	853	Not required
Macedonia	+6	389	Bitola 97, Skopje 91
Madagascar	+8	261	Antananarivo 2, Finanrantsoa 7, Moramanga 4
Malawi	+7	265	Domasi 531, Likuni 766, Thornwood 486
Malaysia[7]	+13	60	Ipoh 5, Johor Bahru 7, Kuala Lumpur 3
Maldives	+10	90	Not required
Mali Republic	+5	223	Not required
Malta	+6	356	Not required
Marshall Islands	+17	692	Ebeye 329, Majuro 625
Mauritania	+5	222	Not required
Mauritius	+9	230	Not required
Mayotte Island	+8	269	Not required
Mexico[8]	-1	52	Acapulco 74, Cancun 98, Guadalajara 3, Mexico City 5, Monterrey 8, Puebla 22, Tampico 12, Tijuana 66
Micronesia	+16	691	Kosrae 370, Truk 330, Yap 350
Moldova	+8	373	Benderi 32, Kishinev 2
Monaco	+6	377	Not required
Mongolia	+13	976	Ulan Bator 1
Morocco	+4	212	Casablanca 2, Fes 5, Marrakech 4, Rabat 7, Tangiers 9
Mozambique	+7	258	Maputo 1 Matola 4, Nampula 6
Myanmar	+11.5	95	Bassein 42, Mandalay 2, Yangon (Rangoon) 1
Namibia	+7	264	Swakopmund 64, Windhoek 61
Nauru	+17	674	Not required
Nepal	+10.5	977	Gorkha 64, Kathmandu 1
Netherlands	+6	31	Amsterdam 20, Rotterdam 10, The Hague 70, Utrecht 30
Netherlands Antilles	+1	599	Bonaire 7, Curaçao 9, St. Maarten 5
New Caledonia	+16	687	Not required
New Zealand	+17	64	Auckland 9, Christchurch 3, Hamilton 7, Wellington 4
Nicaragua	-1	505	Granada 552, León 311, Managua 2, Masaya 522
Niger Republic	+6	227	Not required
Nigeria	+6	234	Abuja 9, Kaduna 62, Lagos 1, Port Harcourt 84
Niue	-6	683	Not required

Country	Hours from EST	Country Code	City Codes
Norfolk Island	+16.5	672	Not required
Norway	+6	47	Not required
Oman	+9	968	Not required
Pakistan	+10	92	Faisalabad 41, Islamabad 51, Karachi 21, Lahore 42
Palau	+14	680	Not required
Panama	0	507	Not required
Papua New Guinea	+15	675	Not required
Paraguay	+2	595	Asunción 21, Encarnacion 71, Pedro Juan Caballero 36
Peru	0	51	Arequipa 54, Callao 14, Cuzco 84, Lima 14, Trujillo 44
Philippines	+13	63	Cebu 32, Davao 82, Iloilo 33, Manila 2
Poland	+6	48	Gdansk 58, Krakow 12, Lodz 42, Warsaw 22
Portugal	+5	351	Coimbra 39, Lisbon 1, Porto 2, Setubal 65
Qatar	+8	974	Not required
Reunion Island	+9	262	Not required
Romania	+7	40	Bucharest 1, Constanta 16, Iasi 81, Timisoara 61
Russia[9]	+8	7	Magadan 413, Moscow 095, St. Petersburg 812
Rwanda	+7	250	Not required
St. Helena	+5	290	Not required
St. Pierre/ Miquelon	+2	508	Not required
San Marino	+6	378	All points 549
São Tomé	+5	239	Not required
Saudi Arabia	+8	966	Jeddah 2, Mecca 2, Medina 4, Riyadh 3
Senegal	+5	221	Not required
Seychelles	+9	248	Not required
Sierra Leone	+5	232	Not required
Singapore	+13	65	Not required
Slovakia	+6	421	Bratislava 7, Presov 91
Slovenia	+6	386	Llubljana 61, Maribor 62
Solomon Islands	+16	677	Not required
Somalia	+8	252	Not required
South Africa	+7	27	Cape Town 21, Durban 31, Johannesburg 11, Pretoria 12
Spain	+6	34	Barcelona 3, Bilbao 94, Madrid 91, Seville 95, Valencia 96
Sri Lanka	+10.5	94	Colombo 1, Kandy 8
Sudan	+7	249	Not required
Suriname	+2	597	Not required
Swaziland	+7	268	Not required
Sweden	+6	46	Göteburg 31, Malmö 40, Stockholm 8, Uppsala 18
Switzerland	+6	41	Basel 61, Berne 31, Geneva 22, St. Moritz 82, Zurich 1
Syria	+8	963	Aleppo 21, Damascus 11, Hama 33, Homs 31, Latakia 41
Taiwan	+13	886	Kaohsiung 7, Taichung 4, Tainan 6, Taipei 2
Tajikistan	+11	7	Dushanbe 3772
Tanzania	+8	255	Dar Es Salaam 51, Mwanza 68, Tanga 53
Thailand	+12	66	Bangkok 2, Chiang Mai 53, Chon Buri 39
Togo	+5	228	Not required
Tonga	+18	676	Not required
Tunisia	+6	216	Bizeria 2, Kef 8, Tunis 1, Sousse 3
Turkey	+7	90	Adana 322, Ankara 312, Istanbul 216 (Asia) or 212 (Europe), Izmir 232
Turkmenistan	+10	993	Chardzou 422
Tuvalu	+17	688	Not required
Uganda	+8	256	Entebbe 42, Jinja 43, Kampala 41
Ukraine	+8	380	Kharkov 57, Kiev 44
UnitedArab Emir.	+9	971	Abu Dhabi 2, Dubai 4, Sharjah 6
United Kingdom	+5	44	Belfast 2890, Birmingham 121, Glasgow 141, Leeds 1532 London: inner 207, outer 208, Manchester 161, Sheffield 114
Uruguay	+2	598	Montevideo 2, Paysandu 722, Punta del Este 42
Uzbekistan	+11	998	Not required
Vanuatu	+16	678	Not required
Vatican City	+6	39	All points 6
Venezuela	+1	58	Caracas 2, Maracaibo 61, Maracay 243, Valencia 41
Vietnam	+12	84	Da Nang 51, Hai Phong 31, Hanoi 4, Ho Chi Minh City 8
Wallis & Futuna Isl.	+17	681	Not required
Western Samoa	-6	685	Not required
Yemen	+8	967	Aden 2, San'a 1, Taiz 4
Yugoslavia	+6	381	Belgrade 11, Novi Sad 21, Titograd 81
Zambia	+7	260	Kitwe 2, Lusaka 1, Ndola 2
Zimbabwe	+7	263	Bulawayo 9, Harare 4, Mutare 20

1. More than one time zone; difference based on Sydney. 2. More than one time zone; difference based on Rio de Janeiro. 3. Formerly known as Zaire. 4. All codes in Paris are 1 + 8 digits beginning with 3, 4, or 6. 5. More than one time zone; difference based on Tahiti. 6. More than one time zone; difference based on Jakarta. 7. More than one time zone; difference based on Kuala Lumpur. 8. More than one time zone; difference based on Mexico City9. More than one time zone; difference based on Moscow.
Source: *The AT&T Guide to Calling the World* (2001). www.att.com/traveler/tools/codes.html

Climate and Weather

▶CLIMATES OF THE WORLD

Knowing the similarities and differences between climates in various parts of the world helps us understand many things about our planet: why people live where they do; how they make their living; the problems and potentials of their land. Climates are very complex, however, and no climatic classification is ideal. The most commonly used classification was developed more than 50 years ago by a German climatologist, Wladimir Koppen. The Koppen system uses temperature and precipitation as the major criteria for grouping climates. Boundaries between climatic zones are determined by the limits of where certain plants grow. The five major climatic zones are known by the capital letters **A**, **B**, **C**, **D**, and **E**; each major zone has subzones. High-altitude areas are sometimes shown with the letter **H** because their climates are so complex that small maps cannot show all the detail.

(Note: In the following chart, **R** stands for the annual rainfall in centimeters; **T** is the average annual temperature in degrees Celsius.)

A Humid tropical climates.   The average temperature of every month is 64° F (18° C) or higher. There is no winter.
Af *Rain forest.*   The driest month has at least 2.4 inches (6 cm) of rain. The Amazon Basin is an example of an **Af** climate.
Am *Monsoon.*   Similar to **Af** but with a short dry season. The amount of rainfall in the driest month is less than 2.4 inches (6 cm) but equal to or greater than 10 - (R/25). The southwestern coast of India is an example of an **Am** climate.
Aw *Savanna.*   There is a well-defined dry season in the winter. The amount of rainfall in the driest month is less than 10 - (R/25). The Brazilian Highlands are a large area with an **Aw** climate.
As (Rare)   There is a well-defined dry season in the summer.

B Dry climates.   Annual rainfall is less than annual potential evaporation. The boundary between dry areas and humid areas is R < 2T + 28 when at least 70% of the rainfall occurs in the warmer six months; R < 2T when at least 70 percent of the rainfall occurs in the cooler six months; or R < 2T + 14 when neither half of the year receives at least 70 percent of the total annual rainfall.
BS *Steppe.*   The boundary between steppe and desert is half of the dry/humid boundary. Steppes border many of the world's large deserts.
BSh *Low-latitude steppe.*   The average annual temperature is at least 64° F (18° C).
BSk *Mid-latitude steppe.*   The average annual temperature is less than 64° F (18° C).
BW *Desert.*   The boundary between desert and steppe is half of the dry/humid boundary. The Sahara Desert is the largest area with a **BW** climate.
BWh *Low-latitude desert.*   The average annual temperature is at least 64° F (18° C).
BWk *Mid-latitude desert.*   The average annual temperature is less than 64° F (18° C).

C Subtropical climates.   The average temperature of the coldest month is between 64° F (18° C) and 27° F (-3° C). These are mainly humid mid-latitude areas with mild winters. The principal natural vegetation is broad-leafed forest.
Cw (Rare)   The wettest month occurs in summer and has at least ten times as much rainfall as the driest month in winter. **Cw** zones are mainly areas of evergreen forest in mountainous **Aw** zones.
Cs *Dry summer.*   The wettest month occurs in winter and has at least three times as much rainfall as the driest month in summer. Less than 1.5 inches (4 cm) of rain falls during the driest summer month.
Csa *Warm, dry summer.*   The average temperature of the warmest month is more than 72° F (22° C), and for at least four months the average temperature is more than 50° F (10° C). Italy and other Mediterranean countries have a **Csa** climate.
Csb *Cool, dry summer.*   In no month is the average temperature more than 72° F (22° C), but for at least four months the average temperature is more than 50° F (10° C). **Csb** climates are found near San Francisco, California; on the coast near Santiago, Chile; and in Portugal.
Cf *Humid summer.*   Areas that cannot meet the criteria for **Cw** and **Cs**.
Cfa *Humid, warm summer.*   The average temperature of the warmest month is more than 72° F (22° C), and for at least four months the average temperature is more than 50° F (10° C). Much of the eastern United States is in a **Cfa** zone.
Cfb *Marine west coast.*   In no month is the average temperature more than 72° F (22° C), but for at least four months the average temperature is more than 50° F (10° C). Great Britain, New Zealand, and the west coast of Alaska are all examples of **Cfb** climates.

D Continental climates.   The average temperature of the warmest month is more than 50° F (10° C), and the average temperature of the coldest month is 27° F (-3° C) or below. Forests are the principal natural vegetation.
Dfa *Humid, warm summer.*   All seasons have some precipitation. The average temperature of the warmest month is more than 72° F (22° C), and for at least four months the average temperature is more than 50° F (10° C). The northern Great Plains of the United States have a **Dfa** climate.
Dwa *Humid, warm summer.*   The wettest month occurs in summer and has at least ten times as much rainfall as the driest month in winter. The average temperature of the warmest month is more than 72° F (22° C), and for at least four months the average temperature is more than 50° F (10° C). The land around the northern part of the Yellow Sea has a **Dwa** climate.
Dfb *Humid, cool summer.*   All seasons have some precipitation. In no month is the average temperature more than 72° F (22° C), but for at least four months the average temperature is more than 50° F (10° C). A large **Dfb** area stretches from eastern Europe into Asia.
Dwb *Humid, cool summer.*   The wettest month occurs in summer and has at least ten times as much rainfall as the driest month in winter. In no month is the average temperature more than 72° F (22° C), but for at least four months the average temperature is more than 50° F (10° C). Much of the area between Manchuria and the Sea of Okhotsk has a **Dwb** climate.
Dfc *Subpolar.*   All seasons have some precipitation. For one to three months, the average temperature is 50° (10° C) or more. A huge **Dfc** area is in Siberia and adjacent parts of the Soviet Union.

E Polar climates.   The average temperature of the warmest month is less than 50° F (10° C). There is no summer, and no trees grow.

ET *Tundra.* The average temperature of the warmest month is less than 50° F (10° C) but more than 32° F (0° C). Vast areas of northern North America, Europe, and Asia lie in the **ET** climate zone.
EF *Ice cap.* The average temperature of the warmest 8 month is 32° F (0° C) or less. The **EF** climate is found at the North and South Poles and in interior Greenland.

▶ WEATHER EXTREMES
Hottest: Dalol Danakil Depression, Ethiopia. Average annual temperature: 35°C/95°F.
Coldest: Plateau Station, Antarctica. Average annual temperature: -56.7°C/-71.7°F.
Wettest: Mawsynram, Assam, India. Average annual rainfall: 11.873 m/38.925 ft.
Driest: Atacama Desert, Chile. Average annual rainfall: too small to measure.

▶ EL NIÑO AND LA NIÑA
The two ends of a natural, very complex climatic balancing act, caused by the interaction between the surface layers of the tropical Pacific Ocean and the atmosphere above it, with winds and planetary-scale ocean waves shipping the changing conditions from one side of the ocean to the other.

The sheer size and breadth of the Pacific allow El Niños and La Niñas time to develop and to have widespread effects. During La Niñas, tropical ocean temperatures become colder in the eastern and central Pacific regions and warmer in the west; tradewinds are stronger and normally wet regions become drier. During El Niños the shift is exactly the opposite: weaker tradewinds, colder tropical water in the west and warmer water in the east off the coast of South America, and much

Worst Hurricanes in U.S. History

Measuring the cost of hurricanes is an imperfect science, primarily because of the difficulty in determining whether different kinds of damages are directly attributable to a particular storm. The following table ranks hurricanes by the amount of insured losses they cause (in constant 1996 dollars, to discount the effects of inflation). Insured losses are the amount claimed by property owners against their insurance policies. It is impossible to calculate the costs incurred by those without insurance. Note that even after discounting inflation,

most of the costliest hurricanes have come within the past 30 years, as more and more people have built homes closer to shore, and harm's way. Improved meteorology, however, has insured that while the financial cost of hurricanes has increased, the loss of human life has declined. The 25 deadliest hurricanes in U.S. history all occurred before 1975.

The most intense hurricane (as measured by atmospheric pressure) was an unnamed storm that hit the Florida Keys in 1935 with winds greater than 155 mph.

COSTLIEST HURRICANES

Rank, Hurricane (year)	Location of primary damage	Insured losses (billions)[1]	Deaths
1. Andrew (1992)	Florida, Louisiana	$26.5	26
2. Hugo (1989)	South Carolina	7.0	<30
3. Fran (1996)	North Carolina	3.2	34
4. Opal (1995)	Florida, Alabama	3.0	59
5. Frederic (1979)	Alabama, Mississippi	2.3	31
6. Agnes (1972)	Northeast states	2.1	122
7. Alicia (1983)	Texas	2.0	<30
8. Bob (1991)	North Carolina, Northeast states	1.5	600
9. Juan (1985)	Louisiana	1.5	<30
10. Camille (1969)	Mississippi, Alabama	1.4	256

DEADLIEST HURRICANES

Rank, Hurricane (year)	Deaths
1. Galveston, Texas (1900)	8,000[2]
2. Lake Okeechobee, Fla. (1928)	1,836
3. Florida Keys /S. Texas (1919)	600[3]
4. New England (1938)	600
5. Florida Keys (1935)	408
6. Audrey, SW La., N. Texas (1957)	390
7. Northeast states (1944)	390[4]
8. Grand Isle, La. (1909)	350
9. New Orleans, La. (1915)	275
10. Galveston, Texas (1915)	275

1. In constant (1996) dollars. 2. Estimate. 3. Includes 500 lost at sea. 4. Includes 344 lost at sea.
Source: National Oceanic and Atmospheric Administration, National Hurricane Center/ www.nhc.noaa.gov.

Worst Tornadoes in the U.S., 1890-1999

COSTLIEST TORNADOES

Rank, Location	Date	Damages (millions)[1]
1. Oklahoma City, Okla.	May 3, 1999	$963
2. Wichita Falls, Texas	April 10, 1979	884
3. Omaha, Neb.	May 6, 1975	745
4. Lubbock, Texas	May 11, 1970	558
5. Topeka, Kansas	June 8, 1966	494
6. Windsor Locks, Conn.	Oct. 3, 1979	442
7. St. Louis, Mo.- East St. Louis, Ill.	May 27, 1896	380
8. Xenia, Ohio	April 3, 1974	325
9. Conyers, Ga	Mar. 31, 1973	321
10. Worcester, Mass.	June 9, 1953	311

DEADLIEST TORNADOES

Rank, Location	Date	Deaths
1. Missouri-Illinois-Indiana	Mar. 18, 1925	695
2. St. Louis, Mo.- E. St. Louis, Ill.	May 27, 1896	255
3. Tupelo, Miss.	April 5, 1936	216
4. Gainesville, Ga.	April 6, 1936	203
5. Woodward, Okla.	April 9, 1947	181
6. Louisiana-Mississippi	April 24, 1908	143
7. New Richmond, Wisc.	June 12, 1899	117
8. Flint, Mich.	June 8, 1953	115
9. Goliad, Texas	May 18, 1902	114
10. Waco, Texas	May 11, 1953	114

1. In constant (1997) dollars. **Source:** NOAA/National Severe Storms Laboratory, *Normalized Damage from Major Tornadoes in the United States: 1890-1999.* www.nssl.noaa.gov/~brooks/damage/tdam1.html

more rain in dry areas—and more frequent and more intense hurricanes in the eastern Pacific. These systemic changes also noticeably affect winters in the continental U.S.: La Niñas bring warmer than normal winters to the Southeast and colder than normal to the Northwest, while El Niños generally cause warmer winters in the North Central states and colder winters in the Southeast and Southwest.

Fishermen off the coasts of Peru, Ecuador and Colombia first noticed and named El Niño for the tendency of its very warm waters to arrive around Christmastime. Before the 1982-83 El Niño, scientists had no ability to forecast these massive weather changes, and, despite great advances in the field, still missed the rapid onset, the great magnitude and sudden demise of the 1997-98 El Niño. Yet once forecasters had some of the data, they were able to predict six months in advance the unusual 1997-98 winter in the U.S. season and government, business and individuals were better prepared for disaster. La Niñas often (but not always) occur after El Niños. Typically, La Niñas occur less frequently than El Niños, which occur irregularly every 2-7 years (1976-77, 1982-83, 1986-87, 1991-94, 1997-98) and last 12-18 months. In between these extremes is "normal" weather.

So far, researchers have been unable to link El Niños-La Niñas to sunspots or volcanic eruptions. Scientists are studying the compelling question of whether there is a relationship between El Niños-La Niñas and the greenhouse effect. And there is still considerable disagreement and contending theories about exactly what constitutes these phenomena, what their effects are and what role they play in Earth's complex climate and ecology.

Source: National Oceanic and Atmospheric Administration (2000), www.noaa.gov.

▶GLOSSARY OF WEATHER WORDS

Air mass   A large body of air that, at a given elevation, has about the same temperature and humidity throughout.

Barometric pressure   The weight of a column of air at a particular place is determined by measuring the height of a column of mercury under a vacuum. The instrument for making such a measurement is called a barometer. At sea level, the standard barometric pressure is 29.92 inches (76 cm). In the International System, air pressure is measured in bars or in kiloPascals. A bar is slightly less than the standard air pressure at sea level, and a kiloPascal is one-hundredth of a bar. At any location, however, barometric pressure is affected by changes in temperature, humidity, or elevation. When the barometric pressure is falling, the air pressure is decreasing, usually a sign of a storm. When the barometer is rising, fairer weather is on its way.

Climate   General weather conditions over a long period of time.

Cold front   The place where cold air that is advancing meets warm air that is retreating before it. This kind of weather not only lowers temperature as it passes but also causes high winds and may cause thunderstorms.

Cyclone   A region of low atmospheric pressure (see "Depression"). Severe cyclones are known as hurricanes, tropical cyclones, and typhoons.

Degree-days   A degree-day is one degree of deviation of the daily mean temperature from a given norm, usually 65°F. Cooling degree-days are the number of degrees Fahrenheit by which the mean temperature exceeds 65°F, while heating degree-days are the number of degrees the mean temperature is below 65°F. During a year, keeping track of the total number of degree days for each day is used to keep track of cooling or heating needs. For example, oil companies use heating degree-days

Determining the Wind-Chill Factor

Sometimes called a wind-chill index, this is a measure of the cooling power of air movement and low temperature on the human body. Because heat passes directly from a warm body to the cooler air surrounding it—a process known as convection—wind produces a continuing source of cooler air and a chilling effect that is equivalent to a lower temperature. The effect on a warm day is pleasant, but as temperatures approach freezing, wind chill is not only unpleasant, but can be dangerous. As the table below shows, a temperature of 5°F combined with a breeze of 10 mph produces a wind-chill temperature of -15°F—a temperature at which frostbite occurs much sooner than at 5°F. Wind speeds above 45 mph have little additional cooling effect.

Actual Temperature	Wind speed								
	5 mph	10 mph	15 mph	20 mph	25 mph	30 mph	35 mph	40 mph	45 mph
35°F	33°F	22°F	16°F	12°F	8°F	6°F	4°F	3°F	2°F
30°F	27	16	9	4	1	-2	-4	-5	-6
25°F	21	10	2	-3	-4	-10	-12	-13	-14
20°F	16	3	-5	-10	-15	-18	-20	-21	-22
15°F	12	-3	-11	-17	-22	-25	-27	-29	-30
10°F	7	-9	-18	-24	-29	-33	-35	-37	-38
5°F	0	-15	-25	-31	-36	-41	-43	-45	-46
0°F	-5	-22	-31	-39	-44	-49	-52	-53	-54
-5°F	-10	-27	-38	-46	-51	-56	-58	-60	-62
-10°F	-15	-34	-45	-53	-59	-64	-67	-69	-70
-15°F	-21	-40	-51	-60	-66	-71	-74	-76	-78
-20°F	-26	-46	-58	-67	-74	-79	-82	-84	-85
-25°F	-31	-52	-65	-74	-81	-86	-89	-92	-93
-30°F	-36	-58	-72	-81	-88	-93	-97	-100	-102
-35°F	-42	-64	-78	-88	-96	-101	-105	-107	-109
-40°F	-47	-71	-85	-95	-103	-109	-113	-115	-117
-45°F	-52	-77	-92	-102	-110	-116	-120	-123	-125

to estimate how much oil their customers have used and when they might need a refill.

Depression Any period of low air pressure. In temperate regions over land, the typical depression is a *low*. The often more powerful depression occurring over tropical waters is called a *tropical depression*. If the air pressure in a tropical depression continues to fall, it becomes a tropical storm, or, lower still, a *hurricane*.

Dew point The temperature at which dew (drops of water) begins to form as air cools. Air can hold only a certain amount of water vapor at a given temperature. When the temperature falls, excess water vapor must turn into a liquid.

El Niño (see above)

Front The boundary between two different air masses.

High An air mass characterized by higher-than-normal air pressure; usually this is a fair-weather system. Some highs are typically found in the same place each year, such as the one that occurs over Bermuda in most summers.

Hurricane A huge tropical rainstorm with winds that swirl rapidly around a calm, dry central "eye." To be classified a hurricane, a tropical storm must have wind speeds of more than 74 mph (119 km/hr). The average hurricane is 375 miles (600 km) in diameter and extends up 40,000 feet (12,000 m) above the surface of the ocean. The eye averages 12.5 miles (20 km) in diameter. When a hurricane hits land, its fierce winds and floods can do great damage. On average five hurricanes each year threaten the eastern and southern United States.

Jet stream A strong river or two of high winds in the upper atmosphere (but below the stratosphere) that travels from west to east at between 75 and 150 mph (120-240 km/hr), most often in the middle latitudes. Discovered by American bomber pilots in World War II, it is now known to have significant effects on weather.

La Niña (see above)

Low An air mass characterized by lower-than-normal air pressure; usually this is the heart of a storm system. Some lows are found in the same region most of the year, such as the low in the Pacific just off the coast of Alaska.

Mean temperature Technically, this should be the average of all temperatures during the day. Sometimes it is the average of 24 temperatures taken once each hour, but most often the mean temperature is simply the average of the high and low for the day.

Monsoon A wind system in which the prevailing direction of the wind reverses itself from season to season. Southeast Asia is the most typical monsoon region. The summer (southwest) monsoon, characterized by hot, moist air and heavy rains lasts from April to September. The winter (northeast) monsoon lasts from October to March and is characterized by cool, dry air.

Occluded front When a cold front overtakes a warm front, the denser cold air flows under the less dense warm air.

Prevailing winds Throughout the world, winds follow regular patterns. In some places winds are so light and infrequent as to scarcely exist, such as in the doldrums along the equator and in the horse latitudes near latitude 30° north and south. In other places the winds tend to come from a particular direction and are called prevailing winds.

Rain shadow An area on the leeward side of a mountain range that receives little rainfall.

Relative humidity The amount of moisture (water vapor) in the air compared with the total amount it can hold expressed as a percent. Warm air can hold more water vapor than cold air, so a relative humidity of 75 percent on a warm summer day is moister than a relative humidity of 75 percent on a cool winter day. However, because evaporation is greater on warm days, the relative humidity is generally higher in summer than in winter.

Secondary cold front A cold front that sometimes forms behind another cold front and that is often even colder than the first front.

Secondary depression A low that forms to the south or east of a low that is a storm center.

Squall line A line of instability that often precedes a cold front, marked by wind gusts and often by heavy rain.

Stationary front A front that stays in the same place.

Storm surge The rise in water levels in the ocean or a large lake that comes from a combination of wind and low pressure during a storm, especially pronounced during a hurricane.

Temperature-humidity index A number derived from a formula relating temperature and humidity to discomfort. When it is 75, many are uncomfortable, while at 80 or above, almost everybody is uncomfortable. Temperatures are less comfortable at high humidities because cooling by sweating is less efficient (see also "The Heat Index," later in this section).

Temperature inversion A layer of warm air on top a layer of cooler surface air. Such layering, usually occurring at night, can prevent air pollutants near the surface from rising into the upper air. A long-lasting inversion, especially in industrial areas, can cause an excessive concentration of pollutants to accumulate in the surrounding air.

Tornado A small and short-lived but very severe windstorm. Tornadoes are whirling columns of air that reach down from a cloud, and they often accompany thunderstorms, rain, and hail. With wind speeds up to 300 mph (480 km/hr), tornadoes can do tremendous damage. The diameter of the average tornado is between 500 and 2,000 feet (150-600 m). The average tornado moves along the ground at 28 mph (45 km/hr) and has a "path" that is 16 miles (26 km) long. In the United States, some 750 tornadoes are reported every year, most frequently between April and June.

Tropical storm A storm that forms over the ocean in the tropics and often moves onto land, where it loses strength. Technically, a storm is designated a tropical storm only when winds are between 39 and 73 miles per hour. If winds become greater, a tropical storm becomes a hurricane.

Trough A low that is long, rather than nearly circular.

Typhoon A hurricane formed in the western Pacific Ocean.

Warm front The boundary of a moving warm air mass.

Weather The condition of the atmosphere—temperature, rain, and wind, for example—in a particular place. A climate is defined by weather conditions over a long period of time.

Wind Any current of air, measured on land in miles per hour, and at sea in knots. The direction of a given wind is determined from the point of the compass from which it blows (e.g., northeast, south). In various regions of the world, names are given to seasonal winds of particular quality. Among these are the *bora,* a cold usually dry north/northeast wind along the eastern Adriatic; *brickfielder,* a hot north wind of southeastern Australia; *buran,* a cold, violent north/northeast wind of Siberia and Central Asia, common in winter; *chinook,* a dry winter or spring wind which blows down the eastern slopes of the Rocky Mountains often warm enough to melt the snow; *harmattan,* a hot, dry north wind in West Africa which cools as it evaporates the moist air of the coast; *mistral,* a cold, strong north/northwest wind of the western Mediterranean with a surface strength of 60 km/hour, frequent in winter; *pampero,* a sudden, cold south or west wind in Argentina and Uruguay frequent in summer; *Santa Ana* a hot, dry wind that blows from the north or east in Southern California; *sirocco,* a hot south wind of North Africa and southern Italy; *southerly burster,* a cold, violent south wind of southeastern Australia; *williwaw,* a violent squall that blows in the Strait of Magellan (South America); and *zonda,* a hot, dry north wind of Argentina and Uruguay.

Beaufort Wind Scale

In 1806 Adm. Francis Beaufort devised a scale for recording wind force at sea based on the effect of the wind on a full-rigged ship. In 1838, this scale was adopted by the British Admiralty, and in 1874 it was adopted for international use. It is now the chief scale for specifying the force of the wind and is used in all parts of the world, both on land and at sea. Originally, there were no specific wind speeds corresponding to various force numbers on the Beaufort Wind Scale. Since 1946, wind speed has been determined according to measurements made by an anemometer (a device for measuring wind) at 10m (30 ft) above the ground.

Force	Description of wind	Mean wind speed in knots[1]	Specification for use on land and at sea
Force 0	Calm	Less than 1	Calm, smoke rises vertically. Sea like a mirror.
Force 1	Light air	1-3	Direction of wind shown by smoke drift, but not by wind vanes. Ripples with appearance of scales are formed, but without foam crests.
Force 2	Light breeze	4-6	Wind felt on face; leaves rustle; ordinary vane moved by wind. Small wavelets, still short but more pronounced; crests have a glassy appearance and do not break.
Force 3	Gentle breeze	7-10	Leaves and small twigs in constant motion; wind extends light flag. Large wavelets; crests begin to break; foam of glassy appearance; perhaps scattered white horses.
Force 4	Moderate breeze	11-16	Raises dust and loose paper; small branches are moved. Small waves becoming longer; fairly frequent white horses.
Force 5	Fresh breeze	17-21	Small trees in leaf begin to sway; crested wavelets form on inland waters. Moderate waves, taking a more pronounced long form; many white horses are formed (chance of some spray).
Force 6	Strong breeze	22-27	Large branches in motion; whistling heard in telegraph wires; umbrellas used with difficulty. Large waves begin to form; the white foam crests are more extensive everywhere (probably some spray).
Force 7	Moderate gale, near gale	28-33	Whole trees in motion; inconvenience felt when walking against wind. Sea heaps up and white foam from breaking waves begins to be blown in streaks along the direction of the wind.
Force 8	Fresh gale, gale	34-40	Breaks twigs off trees; generally impedes progress. Moderately high waves of greater length; edges of crests begin to break into spindrift; foam is blown in well-marked streaks.
Force 9	Strong gale	41-47	Slight structural damage occurs (chimney pots and slate removed). High waves; dense streaks of foam; crests of waves begin to topple, tumble and roll over.
Force 10	Whole gale, storm	48-55	Seldom experienced inland; trees uprooted; considerable structural damage occurs. Very high waves with long overhanging crests; the resulting foam, in great patches, is blown in dense white streaks; the sea takes a white appearance; the tumbling of the sea becomes heavy and shock like; visibility affected.
Force 11	Storm, violent storm	56-63	Very rarely experienced; accompanied by widespread damage. Exceptionally high waves at sea (medium-sized ships might be lost to view behind the waves); the sea is completely covered with white patches of foam; visibility affected.
Force 12+	Hurricane[2]	64 and above	The air is filled with foam and spray; sea completely white with driving spray; visibility very seriously affected.

1. Nautical miles-per-hour; 1 nautical mile = 1.151 statute miles. 2. Force 13: 72-80 knots; force 14: 81-89; force 15: 90-99; force 16: 100-108; force 17: 109-118.   **Source:** Smithsonian Institution, *Smithsonian Meteorological Tables* (1966); Hydrographer of the Navy (U.K.), *Ocean Passages for the World* (1977).

Climate of Selected U.S. Cities

The first line following each city lists the normal daily high temperatures for each month (in degrees Fahrenheit); the second line lists the normal monthly precipitation (rain, snow, and melted ice).

	Jan.	Feb.	Mar.	Apr.	May	June	July	Aug.	Sept.	Oct.	Nov.	Dec.
Atlanta,	50°	55°	64°	73°	80°	86°	88°	87°	82°	73°	63°	54°
Georgia	4.8"	4.8"	5.8"	4.3"	4.3"	3.6"	5.0"	3.7"	3.4"	3.1"	3.9"	4.3
Baltimore,	40°	44°	54°	64°	74°	83°	87°	85°	79°	67°	57°	45°
Maryland	3.1"	3.1"	3.4"	3.1"	3.7"	3.7"	3.7"	3.9"	3.4"	3.0"	3.3"	3.4"
Boston,	36°	38°	46°	56°	67°	76°	82°	80°	73°	63°	52°	40°
Massachusetts	3.6"	3.6"	3.7"	3.6"	3.3"	3.1"	2.8"	3.2"	3.1"	3.3"	4.2"	4.0"
Cincinnati,	37°	41°	53°	64°	74°	82°	86°	84°	78°	66°	53°	42°
Ohio	2.6"	2.7"	4.2"	3.8"	4.3"	3.8"	4.2"	3.4"	2.9"	2.9"	3.5"	3.2"
Charlotte,	49°	53°	62°	71°	78°	86°	89°	88°	82°	72°	63°	52°
North Carolina	3.7"	3.8"	4.4"	2.7"	3.8"	3.4"	3.9"	3.7"	3.5"	3.4"	3.2"	3.5"
Chicago,	29°	34°	46°	59°	70°	80°	84°	82°	75°	63°	48°	34°
Illinois	1.5"	1.4"	2.7"	3.6"	3.3"	3.8"	3.7"	4.2"	3.9"	2.4"	2.9"	2.5"
Cleveland,	32°	35°	46°	58°	69°	78°	82°	81°	74°	62°	50°	37°
Ohio	2.0"	2.2"	2.9"	3.1"	3.5"	3.7"	3.5"	3.4"	3.4"	2.5"	3.2"	3.1"
Columbus,	34°	38°	51°	62°	72°	80°	84°	82°	76°	65°	51°	39°
Ohio	2.2"	2.2"	3.3"	3.2"	3.9"	4.0"	4.3"	3.7"	3.0"	2.2"	3.2"	2.9"
Dallas-Fort Worth,	54°	59°	68°	76°	83°	92°	97°	96°	88°	79°	67°	58°
Texas	1.8"	2.2"	2.8"	3.5"	4.9"	2.9"	2.3"	2.2"	3.4"	3.5"	2.3"	1.8"
Denver,	43°	47°	52°	62°	71°	81°	88°	86°	77°	66°	53°	45°
Colorado	0.5"	0.6"	1.3"	1.7"	2.4"	1.8"	1.9"	1.5"	1.2"	0.9"	0.9"	0.6"
Detroit,	30°	33°	44°	58°	70°	79°	83°	81°	74°	62°	48°	35°
Michigan	1.8"	1.7"	2.6"	3.0"	2.9"	3.6"	3.2"	3.4"	2.9"	2.1"	2.7"	2.8"
El Paso,	56°	62°	70°	79°	87°	97°	96°	94°	87°	78°	66°	58°
Texas	0.4"	0.4"	0.3"	0.2"	0.3"	0.7"	1.5"	1.6"	1.7"	0.8"	0.4"	0.6"
Honolulu,	80°	81°	82°	83°	85°	87°	88°	89°	89°	87°	84°	81°
Hawaii	3.6"	2.2"	2.2"	1.5"	1.1"	0.5"	0.6"	0.4"	0.8"	2.3"	3.0"	3.8"
Houston,	61°	65°	71°	78°	85°	90°	93°	93°	88°	82°	72°	65°
Texas	3.3"	3.0"	2.9"	3.2"	5.2"	5.0"	3.6"	3.5"	4.9"	4.3"	3.8"	3.5"
Indianapolis,	34°	38°	51°	63°	74°	83°	86°	84°	78°	66°	52°	39°
Indiana	2.3"	2.5"	3.8"	3.7"	4.0"	3.5"	4.5"	3.6"	2.9"	2.6"	3.2"	3.3"
Jacksonville,	64°	67°	73°	79°	85°	89°	91°	91°	87°	80°	74°	67°
Florida	3.3"	4.0"	3.7"	2.8"	3.6"	5.7"	5.6"	7.9"	7.1"	2.9"	2.2"	2.7"
Kansas City,	35°	41°	53°	65°	74°	83°	89°	86°	78°	68°	53°	39°
Missouri	1.1"	1.1"	2.5"	3.1"	5.0"	4.7"	4.4"	4.0"	4.9"	3.3"	1.9"	1.6"
Las Vegas,	57°	63°	69°	78°	88°	100°	106°	103°	95°	82°	67°	58°
Nevada	0.5"	0.5"	0.4"	0.2"	0.3"	0.1"	0.4"	0.5"	0.3"	0.2"	0.4"	0.4"
Los Angeles,	68°	69°	69°	72°	74°	78°	84°	84°	83°	79°	72°	68°
California	2.9"	3.1"	2.6"	1.0"	0.2"	0.0"	0.0"	0.1"	0.5"	0.3"	2.0"	2.0"
Memphis,	49°	54°	63°	73°	81°	89°	92°	91°	84°	74°	62°	53°
Tennessee	3.7"	4.4"	5.4"	5.5"	4.9"	3.6"	3.8"	3.4"	3.5"	3.0"	5.1"	5.7"
Miami,	75°	77°	79°	82°	85°	88°	89°	89°	88°	85°	80°	77°
Florida	2.0"	2.1"	2.4"	2.9"	6.2"	9.3"	5.7"	7.6"	7.6"	5.6"	2.7"	1.8"
Milwaukee,	26°	30°	40°	53°	64°	75°	80°	78°	71°	59°	45°	31°
Wisconsin	1.6"	1.5"	2.7"	3.5"	2.8"	3.2"	3.5"	3.5"	3.4"	2.4"	2.5"	2.3"
Minneapolis-St. Paul,	21°	27°	39°	57°	69°	79°	84°	81°	71°	59°	41°	26°
Wisconsin	1.0"	0.9"	1.9"	2.4"	3.4"	4.1"	3.5"	3.6"	2.7"	2.2"	1.6"	1.1"
New Orleans,	61°	64°	72°	79°	84°	89°	91°	91°	87°	79°	71°	64°
Louisiana	5.1"	6.0"	5.0"	4.5"	4.6"	5.9"	6.1"	6.2"	5.5"	3.1"	4.4"	5.8"
New York City,	38°	40°	50°	61°	72°	80°	85°	84°	76°	65°	54°	43°
New York	3.4"	3.3"	4.1"	4.2"	4.4"	3.7"	4.4"	4.0"	3.9"	3.6"	4.5"	3.9"
Oklahoma City,	47°	52°	62°	72°	79°	87°	93°	93°	84°	74°	60°	50°
Oklahoma	1.1"	1.6"	2.7"	2.8"	5.2"	4.3"	2.6"	2.6"	3.8"	3.2"	1.9"	1.4"
Philadelphia,	38°	41°	52°	63°	73°	82°	86°	85°	78°	66°	55°	43°
Pennsylvania	3.2"	2.8"	3.5"	3.6"	3.8"	3.7"	4.3"	3.8"	3.4"	2.7"	3.3"	3.4"
Phoenix,	66°	71°	76°	84°	94°	104°	106°	104°	98°	88°	75°	66°
Arizona	0.7"	0.7"	0.9"	0.2"	0.1"	0.1"	0.8"	1.0"	0.9"	0.7"	0.7"	1.0"
Pittsburgh,	34°	37°	49°	60°	71°	79°	83°	81°	74°	63°	50°	39°
Pennsylvania	2.5"	2.4"	3.4"	3.1"	3.6"	3.7"	3.8"	3.2"	3.0"	2.4"	2.9"	2.9"
Portland,	45°	51°	56°	61°	67°	74°	80°	80°	75°	64°	53°	46°
Oregon	5.4"	3.9"	3.6"	2.4"	2.1"	1.5"	0.7"	1.1"	1.8"	2.7"	5.3"	6.1"
St. Louis,	38°	43°	55°	67°	76°	85°	89°	87°	80°	69°	55°	42°
Missouri	1.8"	2.1"	3.6"	3.5"	4.0"	3.7"	3.9"	2.9"	3.1"	2.7"	3.3"	3.0"
Salt Lake City,	36°	44°	52°	61°	72°	83°	92°	89°	79°	66°	51°	38°
Utah	1.1"	1.2"	1.9"	2.1"	1.8"	0.9"	0.8"	0.9"	1.3"	1.4"	1.3"	1.4"
San Antonio,	61°	66°	74°	80°	85°	92°	95°	95°	89°	82°	72°	64°
Texas	1.7"	1.8"	1.5"	2.5"	4.2"	3.8"	2.2"	2.5"	3.4"	3.2"	2.6"	1.5"
San Diego,	66°	67°	66°	68°	69°	72°	76°	78°	77°	75°	70°	66°
California	1.8"	1.5"	1.8"	0.8"	0.2"	0.1"	0.0"	0.1"	0.2"	0.4"	1.5"	1.6"
San Francisco,	56°	60°	61°	62°	63°	64°	65°	66°	69°	69°	63°	56°
California	4.1"	3.1"	3.1"	1.3"	0.3"	0.2"	0.0"	0.1"	0.3"	1.3"	3.2"	3.1"
Seattle,	46°	51°	54°	58°	64°	70°	74°	74°	69°	60°	52°	46°
Washington	5.4"	4.0"	3.8"	2.5"	1.8"	1.6"	0.9"	1.2"	1.9"	3.3"	5.7"	6.0"
Washington,	42°	46°	57°	67°	76°	85°	89°	87°	80°	69°	58°	47°
D.C.	2.7"	2.7"	3.2"	2.7"	3.7"	3.4"	3.8"	3.9"	3.3"	3.0"	3.1"	3.1"

Note:— = no precipitation; T = trace.   **Source** U.S. Department of Commerce, National Oceanic and Atmospheric Administration, *Climatic Averages and Extremes for U.S. Cities* (June, 1995).

Climate of Selected World Cities

Average low and high temperatures for selected months in degrees Fahrenheit. Precipitation is the average monthly amount in inches of rainfall equivalent.

City	January Temp. Max.	Min.	Avg. precip.	April Temp. Max.	Min.	Avg. precip.	July Temp. Max.	Min.	Avg. precip.	October Temp. Max.	Min.	Avg. precip.
Accra, Ghana	87°	73°	0.6″	88°	76°	3.2″	81°	73°	1.8″	85°	74°	2.5″
Amsterdam, Netherlands	40	34	2.0	52	43	4.6	69	59	2.6	56	48	2.8
Athens, Greece	54	42	2.2	67	52	0.8	90	72	0.2	74	60	1.7
Auckland, New Zealand	73	60	3.1	67	56	3.8	56	46	5.7	63	52	4.0
Baghdad, Iraq	60	39	0.9	85	57	0.5	110	76	t	92	61	0.1
Bangkok, Thailand	89	67	0.2	95	78	2.3	90	76	6.9	88	76	9.9
Beirut, Lebanon	62	51	7.5	72	58	2.2	87	73	t	81	69	2.0
Berlin, Germany	35	26	1.9	55	38	1.7	74	55	3.1	55	41	1.7
Bogotá, Colombia	67	48	2.3	67	51	5.8	64	50	2.0	66	50	6.3
Bombay, India	88	62	0.1	93	74	t	88	75	24.3	93	73	2.5
Budapest, Hungary	35	26	1.5	62	44	2.0	82	61	2.0	61	45	2.1
Buenos Aires, Argentina	85	63	3.1	72	53	3.5	57	42	2.2	69	50	3.4
Cairo, Egypt	65	47	0.2	83	57	0.1	96	70	0.0	86	65	t
Calcutta, India	80	55	0.4	97	76	1.7	90	79	12.8	89	74	4.5
Cape Town, South Africa	78	60	0.6	72	53	1.9	63	45	3.5	70	52	1.2
Caracas, Venezuela	75	56	0.9	81	60	1.3	78	61	4.3	79	61	4.3
Casablanca, Morocco	63	45	2.1	69	52	1.4	79	65	0.0	76	58	1.5
Copenhagen, Denmark	36	29	1.6	50	37	1.7	72	55	2.2	53	42	2.1
Dakha, Bangladesh	77	56	0.3	92	74	5.4	89	79	13.0	88	75	5.3
Dakar, Senegal	79	64	t	81	65	t	88	76	3.5	89	76	1.5
Dublin, Ireland	47	35	2.7	54	38	1.9	67	51	2.8	57	43	2.7
Geneva, Switzerland	39	29	1.9	58	41	2.5	77	58	2.9	58	44	3.8
Hanoi, Vietnam	68	58	0.8	80	70	3.6	92	79	11.9	84	72	3.5
Hong Kong	64	56	1.3	75	67	5.4	87	78	15.0	81	73	4.5
Istanbul, Turkey	45	36	3.7	61	45	1.9	81	65	1.7	67	54	3.8
Jakarta, Indonesia	84	74	11.8	87	75	5.8	87	73	2.5	87	74	4.4
Jerusalem, Israel	55	41	5.1	73	50	0.9	87	63	0.0	81	59	0.3
Kabul, Afghanistan	36	18	1.3	66	43	3.3	92	61	0.1	73	42	0.4
Karachi, Pakistan	77	55	0.5	90	73	0.1	91	81	3.2	91	72	0.1
Kinshasa, Congo, Dem. Rep.	87	70	5.3	89	71	7.7	81	64	0.1	88	70	4.7
Lagos, Nigeria	88	74	1.1	89	77	5.9	83	74	11.0	85	74	8.1
Lima, Peru	82	66	0.1	80	63	t	67	57	0.3	71	58	0.1
Lisbon, Portugal	56	46	3.3	64	52	2.4	79	63	0.2	69	57	3.1
London, United Kingdom	44	35	2.0	56	40	1.8	73	55	2.0	58	44	2.3
Madrid, Spain	47	33	1.1	64	44	1.7	87	62	0.4	66	48	1.9
Manila, Philippines	86	69	0.9	93	73	1.3	88	75	17.0	88	74	7.6
Melbourne, Australia	78	57	1.9	68	51	2.3	56	42	1.9	67	48	2.6
Mexico City, Mexico	66	42	0.2	78	52	0.7	74	54	4.5	70	50	1.6
Montreal, Canada	21	6	3.8	50	33	2.6	78	61	3.7	54	40	3.4
Moscow, Russia	21	9	1.5	47	31	1.9	76	55	3.0	46	34	2.7
Nairobi, Kenya	77	54	1.5	75	58	8.3	69	51	0.6	76	55	2.1
New Delhi, India	71	43	0.9	97	68	0.3	95	80	7.1	93	64	0.4
Osaka, Japan	47	32	1.7	65	47	5.2	87	73	5.9	72	55	5.1
Oslo, Norway	30	20	1.7	50	34	1.6	73	56	2.9	49	37	2.9
Paris, France	42	32	1.5	60	41	1.7	76	55	2.1	59	44	2.2
Prague, Czechoslovakia	34	25	0.9	55	40	1.5	74	58	2.6	54	44	1.2
Rio de Janeiro, Brazil	84	73	4.9	80	69	4.2	75	63	1.6	77	66	3.1
Riyadh, Saudi Arabia	70	46	0.1	89	64	0.1	107	78	0.0	94	61	0.0
Rome, Italy	54	39	3.3	68	46	2.0	88	64	0.4	73	53	4.3
Santiago, Chile	85	53	0.1	74	45	0.5	59	37	3.0	72	45	0.6
São Paulo, Brazil	77	63	8.8	73	59	2.2	66	53	1.5	68	57	4.6
Seoul, South Korea	32	15	1.2	62	41	3.0	84	70	14.8	67	45	1.6
Shanghai, China	47	32	1.9	67	49	3.6	91	75	5.8	75	56	2.9
Singapore	86	73	9.9	88	75	7.4	88	75	6.7	87	74	8.2
Stockholm, Sweden	31	23	1.5	45	32	1.5	70	55	2.8	48	39	2.1
St. Petersburg, Russia	23	12	1.0	45	31	1.0	71	57	2.5	45	37	1.8
Sydney, Australia	78	65	3.5	71	58	5.3	60	46	4.6	71	56	2.8
Tahiti, French Polynesia	89	72	13.2	89	72	6.8	86	68	2.6	87	70	3.4
Taipei, Taiwan	66	53	3.8	77	64	5.3	92	76	8.8	80	68	5.5
Tehran, Iran	45	27	1.8	71	49	1.4	99	72	0.1	76	53	0.3
Tokyo, Japan	47	29	1.9	63	46	5.3	83	70	5.6	69	55	8.2
Toronto, Canada	30	16	2.7	50	34	2.5	79	59	3.0	56	40	2.4
Vienna, Austria	34	26	1.5	57	41	2.0	75	59	3.0	55	44	2.0
Warsaw, Poland	30	21	1.2	54	38	1.5	75	56	3.0	54	41	1.7

t= trace.   **Source:** U.S. Department of Commerce, National Oceanic and Atmospheric Administration, *Climates of the World (1991).*

World Population

In 2001, the world's population reached 6.134 billion people. Of those, 1.92 billion were in developed countries and 4.94 billion were in the less developed regions. The United Nations Population Fund estimates that world population will reach seven billion in 2013 and eight billion in 2028.

World population growth rate has fallen from its peak of 2 percent per year to around 1.2 percent today. Even so, global fertility is still above replacement level (i.e. the number of children needed to replace people who die) despite an increasing number of countries with below-average fertility rates. Of the 77 million people added to the world in 2001, 95 percent were in less developed regions of Africa, Asia and Latin America. Six countries contributed half of the annual increase: India (21 percent), China (12 percent), Pakistan (5 percent), Nigeria (4 percent), Bangladesh (4 percent), and Indonesia (3 percent).

China and India each have more than a billion people (China has 1.285 billion; India is close behind with 1.025 billion). The United States has the third largest population, with 285.9 million people, followed by Indonesia with 214.8 million. Brazil is fifth with 172.6 million.

By 2016, the UN estimates that India will have a population of 1.22 billion, making it larger than all the more developed countries (Australia, New Zealand, Japan, Canada, the U.S., and all of Europe) combined. The UN also predicts that India will surpass China in population by 2045, when it will have a total of 1.501 billion, compared to 1.496 billion for China.

During the coming 25 years, crude birth rates and death rates will continue to decrease in the less developed countries. However, in these years 131 to 136 million babies will be born each year, even though women will be having fewer children over their reproductive lifetime. Despite falling fertility in every major region, the number of births has remained roughly the same because the number of women of childbearing age (15 to 49) has been growing.

▶ WORLD POPULATION TRENDS

Four factors are now impacting future world population: birth and death rates, aging of the population, AIDS, and migration. While birth rates continue to decline and couples in developing regions have three children on average, the total population continues to increase with 77 million persons added in 2001.

A century ago, most people died before the age of 50. Today, life expectancy averages 66 years. By 2050, the United Nations Population Division estimates that the average person will live to the age

Distribution of the World's Population, 1950–2050

Area	1950	2000	2050[1]
More developed regions	32.3%	19.7%	12.7%
Less developed regions	67.7	80.3	87.3
Africa	8.8%	13.1%	21.5%
Asia	55.5	60.6	58.2
Latin America and the Caribbean	6.6	8.6	8.6
Europe	21.8	12.0	6.5
Northern America	6.8	5.2	4.7
Oceania	0.5	0.5	0.5
Total world population (millions)	2,519	6,057	9,322

1. Based on the U.N.'s medium population projections.
Source: U. S. Bureau of the Census, *World Population Prospects: The 2000 Revision Highlights* (2001).

Countries with Declining Population Estimates, 2000–25

Country	2000	2025	Decrease
Russia	146,900,000	137,900,000	9,000,000
Italy	57,300,000	51,300,000	6,000,000
Japan	126,700,000	121,200,000	5,500,000
Ukraine	50,500,000	47,700,000	2,800,000
Spain	39,900,000	36,700,000	2,900,000
Romania	22,300,000	19,900,000	2,400,000
Germany	82,200,000	80,200,000	2,000,000
Hungary	10,000,000	8,900,000	1,100,000
Bulgaria	8,200,000	7,000,000	1,200,000
Belarus	10,200,000	9,500,000	700,000
Czech Republic	10,200,000	9,500,000	700,000
Greece	10,600,000	9,900,000	700,000
Portugal	9,900,000	9,300,000	600,000
Estonia	1,600,000	1,100,000	500,000
Latvia	2,400,000	1,900,000	500,000
Croatia	4,500,000	4,200,000	300,000
Lithuania	3,700,000	3,400,000	300,000
Slovenia	2,000,000	1,800,000	200,000
Belgium	10,200,000	9,900,000	100,000
Denmark	5,300,000	5,200,000	100,000

Source: United Nations Population Fund (UNFPA), *The State of World Population 1998* (1998).

World Births, Deaths, and Population Growth, 2001

Characteristic	World	More Developed	Less Developed
Population	6,157,400,560	1,188,748,457	4,968,652,103
Births	131,389,622	13,216,000	119,563,000
Deaths	54,409,824	12,248,000	41,898,000
Natural increase	76,979,798	968,000	77,665,000
Births per 1,000 population	21.4	11.2	23.8
Deaths per 1,000 population	8.9	10.2	8.6
Growth rate (percent)	1.25%	0.27%	1.49%

Source: U.S. Bureau of the Census, *International Data Base* (2001), and *World Population Profile*, 1998 (1998).

of 76. Life expectancy is already 75.9 years in developed nations, but in less-developed countries, it is only 56.8 years. Longer life expectancy and the ravages of AIDS are having a dramatic impact on median ages and the traditional ratio of old to young worldwide. The median age increased from 23.5 years in 1950 to 26.5 years in 2000 and is estimated to reach 36.2 years in 2050. Those younger than 15 years of age comprised 34 percent of total population in 1950, 30 percent in 2000, and will drop to only 21 percent in 2050. The proportion of people over the age of 60 was 8 percent in 1950, 10 percent in 1999 and is expected to reach 22 percent in 2050. In numbers, there were 593 million persons over 60 years of age in 1999, and by 2050, this figure will triple to nearly two billion. Among the oldest old—those over 80 years of age —65 percent are women.

In 2000, Japan had the oldest median age population, 41.2 years, followed by Italy and Switzerland with an average age of 40.2. Germany had an average of 40.1 years, and Sweden had a popula-

Years to Reach Population Milestones

Milestone	Year Reached	Years to Reach	Milestone	Year Reached	Years to Reach
1 billion	1804	N.A.	6 billion	1999	12
2 billion	1927	123	7 billion	2012	13
3 billion	1960	33	8 billion	2026	14
4 billion	1974	14	9 billion	2043	17
5 billion	1987	13			

Source: U.S. Census Bureau, *World Population Profile: 1998* (1999).

World Vital Events per Time Unit, 2001

Time unit	Births	Deaths	Natural Increase
Year	131,571,719	55,001,289	76,570,430
Month	10,964,310	4,583,441	6,380,869
Day	360,470	150,688	209,782
Hour	15,020	6,279	8,741
Minute	250	105	146
Second	4.2	1.7	2.4

Source: U.S Bureau of the Census, *International Data Base* (2001).

Countries with Oldest and Youngest Populations, 2000 and 2050

Country Median age, 2000		Country Median age, 2050	
Oldest Population			
1. Japan	41.2	1. Spain	55.2
2. Italy	40.2	2. Slovenia	54.1
3. Switzerland	40.2	3. Italy	54.1
4. Germany	40.1	4. Austria	53.7
5. Sweden	39.7	5. Armenia	53.4
6. Finland	39.4	6. Japan	53.1
7. Bulgaria	39.1	7. Czech Republic	52.4
8. Belgium	39.1	8. Greece	52.3
9. Greece	39.1	9. Switzerland	52.0
10. Denmark	38.7	10. China	51.9
Youngest Population			
1. Yemen	15.0	1. Niger	20.4
2. Niger	15.1	2. Yemen	21.1
3. Uganda	15.4	3. Angola	21.2
4. Burkina Faso	15.6	4. Somalia	21.5
5. Dem. Republic of the Congo	15.6	5. Uganda	22.1
6. Angola	15.9	6. Burkina Faso	22.8
7. Somalia	16.0	7. Liberia	22.9
8. Burundi	16.0	8. Mali	22.9
9. Zambia	16.5	9. Burundi	23.2
10. Benin	16.1	10. Malawi	23.7
World average	**26.5**	**World average**	**36.2**

Source:United Nations Population Division, *World Population Prospects The 2000 Revision: Highlights* (2001).

World's Largest Countries, by Population, 2001, 2025, and 2050

2001		2025		2050	
Rank, Country	Population	Rank	Population	Rank	Population
1. China	1,285,000,000	1	1,480,400,000	2	1,462,100,000
2. India	1,025,100,000	2	1,330,400,000	1	1,572,100,000
3. United States	285,900,000	3	332,500,000	4	397,100,000
4. Indonesia	214,800,000	4	273,400,000	6	311,300,000
5. Brazil	172,600,000	6	217,900,000	7	247,200,000
6. Pakistan	145,000,000	5	263,000,000	3	344,200,000
7. Russia	144,700,000	9	137,900,000	16	104,300,000
8. Bangladesh	140,400,000	8	178,800,000	8	265,400,000
9. Japan	127,300,000	10	121,200,000	17	109,200,000
10. Nigeria	116,900,000	7	183,000,000	5	278,800,000
11. Mexico	110,400,000	11	130,200,000	12	146,700,000
12. Germany	82,000,000	18	80,200,000	N.A.	70,800,000
13. Vietnam	79,200,000	14	108,000,000	14	123,800,000
14. Philippines	77,100,000	13	108,300,000	13	128,400,000
15. Iran	71,400,000	16	94,500,000	10	121,400,000
16. Egypt	69,100,000	15	95,600,000	15	113,800,000
17. Turkey	67,600,000	17	87,900,000	18	98,800,000
18. Ethiopia	64,500,000	12	115,400,000	9	186,500,000
19. Thailand	63,600,000	19	72,700,000	N.A.	82,500,000
20. France	59,500,000	20	61,700,000	N.A.	61,800,000

Source: United Nations Population Fund, *The State of World Population 2001* (2001), United Nation Population Division, *World Population Prospects:* The 1996 Revision (Draft) January (1998).

tion average age of 39.7 years. In contrast, Yemen had the youngest median age population: 15 years. The average age was 15.1 years in Niger, 15.4 in Uganda, and 15.6 in both Burkina Faso and the Democratic Republic of the Congo.

According to UN estimates, net migration to more developed regions from developing nations was 10.9 million during 1990-1995; another 9.9 million people migrated between 1995 and 2000. Migration accounted for 46 percent of population growth in developed countries between 1990 and 1995; between 1995 and 2000, migrants were responsible for 60.7 percent of population growth in developed nations. By contrast, net migration slowed population growth in developing countries by 2.9 percent in 1990-95 and by 2.6 percent in 1995-2000.

Africa has been and will continue to be the fastest-growing region. In 1950 Africa had 222 million people, 8.8 percent of the world total. In 1990, the population reached 642 million (12.1 percent) and in 2000, it topped 821 million (13.3 percent). The UN projects Africa's population at 1.582 billion in 2025, and 2.265 billion in 2050. By 2050 Africa will contain 23 percent of the world's people.

▶ URBANIZATION

According to the United Nations, 47 percent of the world's population resided in urban areas in 2000. Seventy-six percent of the people in developed countries lived in urban areas, and 39.9 percent of the people in developing regions lived in cities. Worldwide, 2.9 billion of the world's 6.1 billion people (or 47.5 percent) lived in urban areas. Urbanites are expected to make up half the world's population by 2007, and by 2030, they are expected to increase to about 60 percent (4.9 bil-

lion out of a world population of 8.1 billion). Eighty-four percent of people in developed areas will live in urban areas, and 56 percent of people in developing countries will be urbanized in 2030. The urban population of developing nations will nearly double by 2030, when developing countries reach a level of urbanization similar to that exhibited by the more developed regions in 1950.

Latin America and the Caribbean is one of the most highly urbanized developing regions in the world, with 75 percent of the people living in cities in 2000. By contrast, Asia was 37 percent urbanized and Africa 38 percent in 2000. The UN projects that by 2030, Africa and Asia will be 55 and 53 percent urban respectively; Latin America and the Caribbean will be 83 percent urban.

As the accompanying table demonstrates, the world's largest cities have changed dramatically over the last 50 years. In 1950 New York was the only city with a population over 10 million, and London was the world's second-largest city with 8.7 million people. Eleven of the 15 largest cities were in developed regions. Berlin, the 15th largest city, had a population of 3.3 million.

In 2000, 19 cities had populations over 10 million, and five of them had more than 15 million people. Four cities have surpassed New York in population: Tokyo, Mexico City, Bombay, and São Paulo, each with more than 17 million people.

By 2015, at least five cities will exceed 20 million people and 23 cities will have more than 10 million people. With 26.4 million people, Tokyo will still be the world's largest city, followed by Bombay, Lagos, Dhaka, and São Paulo. New York will fall to eighth, while London, Paris, Moscow, and Chicago will all fall off the list of the top 20 cities.

The World's Largest Urban Areas, 1950-2015

2000 Rank, Urban area	Population (millions)					Rank	
	1950	1970	1990	2000	2015[1]	1950	2015
1. Tokyo, Japan	6.9	16.5	25.0	26.4	26.4	3	1
2. Mexico City, Mexico	3.1	9.1	15.1	18.1	19.2	13	7
3. Bombay, India	2.9	5.8	12.2	18.1	26.1	15	2
4. São Paulo, Brazil	2.4	8.1	14.8	17.8	20.4	18	5
5. New York, U.S.	12.3	16.2	16.1	16.6	17.4	1	8
6. Los Angeles, U.S.	4.0	8.4	11.5	13.1	14.1	11	14
7. Shanghai, China	5.3	11.2	13.5	12.9	14.6	6	13
8. Lagos, Nigeria	N.A.	N.A.	7.7	13.4	23.2	N.A.	3
9. Calcutta, India	4.4	6.9	10.7	12.9	17.3	9	9
10. Buenos Aires, Argentina	5.0	8.4	10.6	12.6	14.1	7	15
11. Dhaka, Bangladesh	N.A.	N.A.	5.9	12.3	21.1	N.A.	4
12. Karachi, Pakistan	N.A.	N.A.	8.0	11.8	19.2	N.A.	6
13. Delhi, India	N.A.	3.5	8.2	11.7	16.8	N.A.	11
14. Osaka, Japan	4.1	9.4	10.5	11.0	11.0	10	20
15. Beijing, China	3.9	8.1	10.9	10.8	12.3	12	18
16. Jakarta, Indonesia	N.A.	3.9	9.3	11.0	17.3	N.A.	10
17. Metro Manila, Philippines	N.A.	3.5	8.0	10.9	14.8	N.A.	12
18. Rio de Janeiro, Brazil	2.9	7.0	9.5	10.6	11.9	14	19
19. Cairo, Egypt	2.4	5.3	8.6	10.6	13.8	16	16
20. Istanbul, Turkey	N.A.	N.A.	6.5	9.3	12.5	N.A.	17
21. Tianjin, China	2.4	5.2	9.3	N.A.	10.7	17	21
22. Hyderabad, India	N.A.	N.A.	N.A.	N.A.	10.5	N.A.	22
23. Bangkok, Thailand	N.A.	N.A.	5.9	N.A.	10.1	N.A.	23
24. Paris, France	5.4	8.5	9.3	9.6	N.A.	5	N.A.
25. Moscow, Russia	5.4	7.1	9.0	9.3	N.A.	4	N.A.
26. London, U.K.	8.7	8.6	7.3	7.3	N.A.	2	N.A.
27. Chicago, U.S.	4.9	6.7	6.8	7.0	N.A.	8	N.A.

Note: An urban area is a central city or central cities, and the surrounding urbanized areas, also called a metropolitan area. 1. Projected.
Source: United Nations Population Division, *World Urbanization Prospects: The 1999 Revision* (2000).

▶FERTILITY

Across the world, women are having fewer children now than 20 years ago. The United Nations estimates world fertility per woman at 2.79 births from 1995-2000. In developed regions fertility rates dropped from an average of 2.6 per woman in 1970 to 1.59 births in 1995-2000. Births in less developed regions dropped to an average of 3.08 births per woman and to 5.25 in the least developed countries in this same time period.

Replacement level fertility represents the point at which each couple has only the number of births required to replace themselves in the population. The replacement level fertility rate is usually 2.1 births per woman. Most countries in Europe and North America have fertility rates at or below that level. For the period 1995-2000, some 22 countries will have average fertility levels of 1.5 or less children per woman, with Italy (1.2) and Spain (1.2) having the lowest rates. Hong Kong and Japan are the only non-European countries with fertility levels of 1.5 or less.

The United Nations reports that fertility rates are declining in Sub-Saharan Africa and South-central Asia, where fertility levels have been very high for decades. From 1980-85 to 1995-2000 Tanzania's fertility rate dropped from 6.7 to 5.48 births per woman and Namibia's declined from 5.8 to 4.9. Bangladesh dropped from 6.2 births per woman to 3.1, India from 4.5 to 3.1, and Nepal from 6.3 to 5.

China, Thailand and Mexico made the greatest fertility rate reductions from 1970 to 1995-2000. China's fertility rate went from 6.0 to 1.8, Thailand's from 6.1 to 1.7, and Mexico's from 6.7 to 2.8.

These reductions in family size are largely due to contraceptive use. The U.N. estimates that 18 million couples reached their childbearing years each year during the 1990s. Almost all research indicates that couples the world over want fewer children. Thirty years ago, less than 10 percent of couples in the developing world had access to family planning. Today 60 percent of those couples have access, causing family size to drop from an average of six children during the 1960s to less than three today.

Nevertheless, there are still close to 150 million women who want to limit or space their pregnancies, but cannot do so effectively. Some 350 million couples continue to lack information about contraception and access to a range of contraceptive services.

▶GLOSSARY OF DEMOGRAPHIC TERMS

Birth rate   The average annual number of births during a year per 1,000 population at midyear; also known as the crude birth rate.

Contraception   Deliberate use of methods to prevent conception or pregnancy. Contraception is an important portion of family planning.

Death rate   The average annual number of deaths during a year per 1,000 population at midyear; also known as the crude death rate.

Growth rate   The average annual percent change in the population, resulting from a surplus (or deficit) of births over deaths and the balance of migrants entering and leaving a country. The rate may be positive or negative; also known as population growth rate or average annual rate of growth.

Infant mortality rate   The number of deaths to infants under one year of age in a given year per 1,000 live births occurring in the same year.

Least developed countries   Defined by the United Nations as the countries with the poorest living standards. In 1995, the U.N. counted 48 countries, most of them landlocked, among the least developed.

Less developed countries   Defined by the U.N. as countries with poorer people than in a more developed country, with economies based on agricultural production, with low GNPs, and lacking in advanced technologies. Approximately 77 countries, including those in Africa, Latin America, and the Caribbean, Asia (except Japan), and regions of Melanesia, Micronesia, and Polynesia, are considered less developed.

More developed countries   The U.N. defines developed countries as industrialized nations with a high gross national product (GNP), high per capita GNP, and advanced science and technology. Approximately 45 countries including those in Europe, North America, Japan, Australia, and New Zealand, are considered developed.

Projections   Data on population and vital rates derived for future years based on statistics from population censuses, vital registration system or sample surveys pertaining to the recent past, and on assumptions about future trends.

Vital events   Births and deaths.

Vital rates   Birth rates and death rates.

Nations with Highest and Lowest Fertility Rates, 2000-05

HIGHEST FERTILITY RATES

Country	Fertility rate per woman
Niger	8.00
Yemen	7.60
Somalia	7.30
Angola	7.20
Uganda	7.10
Mali	7.00
Afghanistan	6.80
Burkina Faso	6.80
Burundi	6.80
Liberia	6.80
Ethiopia	6.75
Congo, Democratic Republic of	6.70
Chad	6.65

LOWEST FERTILITY RATES

Country	Fertility rate per woman
Armenia	1.10
Latvia	1.10
Bulgaria	1.10
Ukraine	1.10
Spain	1.13
Slovenia	1.14
Russian Federation	1.14
Czech Republic	1.16
China, Hong Kong	1.17
Belarus	1.20
Estonia	1.20
Hungary	1.20
Italy	1.20

Source: United Nations Population Fund (UNFPA), *The State of World Population 2001.* (2001)

Population Indicators by Region and Nation

Region/Country	Population estimate ('000s) 2000	2050	Birth rate per 1,000, 1998	Death rate per 1,000, 1998	Life expectancy, 2000 -2005	Percent urban, 2000	Fertility rate per woman 2000 -2005
World Total	6,134,100	9,322,300	24	9	65%	47%	2.7%
More Developed Regions	1,193,900	1,181,100	12	10	74	76	1.5
Less Developed Regions	4,940,300	8,141,100	27	9	68	40	2.9
Least Developed Countries	675,000	1,829,500	40	15	50	26	5.2
Africa	812,600	2,000,400	41	14	52	38	5.0
Asia	3,720,700	5,428,200	24	8	65	37	2.5
Europe	726,300	603,300	11	11	73	75	1.3
Latin America and the Caribbean	526,500	805,600	25	7	68	75	2.5
North America	317,100	437,600	15	9	76	77	1.9
Oceania	30,900	47,200	19	8	73	70	2.4
Afghanistan	22,500	72,300	50	22	43	22	6.8
Albania	3,100	3,900	24	6	74	42	2.3
Algeria	30,800	51,200	31	6	70	60	2.8
Angola	13,500	53,300	51	19	46	34	7.2
Argentina	37,500	54,500	21	8	74	90	2.4
Armenia	3,800	3,200	18	7	74	70	1.1
Australia	19,300	26,500	15	7	79	85	1.8
Austria	8,100	6,500	11	11	79	65	1.2
Azerbaijan	8,100	8,900	23	6	72	57	1.5
Bahrain	652	1,008	26	4	73	92	2.3
Bangladesh	140,400	265,400	27	11	61	25	3.6
Belarus	10,100	8,300	12	12	69	71	1.2
Belgium	10,300	9,600	12	11	79	97	1.5
Belize	200	400	34	5	74	54	2.9
Benin	6,400	18,100	45	14	54	42	5.7
Bhutan	2,100	5,600	42	15	63	7	5.1
Bolivia	8,500	17,000	36	10	64	63	3.9
Bosnia and Herzegovina	4,100	3,500	13	7	74	43	1.3
Botswana	1,600	2,100	37	11	36	50	3.9
Brazil	172,600	247,200	22	7	68	81	2.2
Brunei Darussalam	335	565	26	3	76	72	2.5
Bulgaria	7,900	4,500	11	13	71	70	1.1
Burkina Faso	11,900	46,300	48	18	48	19	6.8
Burundi	6,500	20,200	46	20	41	9	5.9
Cambodia	13,400	29,900	38	14	56	16	4.8
Cameroon	15,200	32,300	41	13	50	49	4.7
Canada	31,000	40,400	14	7	79	77	1.6
Central African Republic	3,800	8,200	39	17	44	41	4.9
Chad	8,100	27,700	44	18	46	24	6.7
Chile	15,400	22,200	22	6	76	86	2.4
China	1,285,000	1,462,100	18	7	71	32	1.8
Colombia	42,800	70,900	26	6	72	74	2.6
Congo, Dem. Rep. of	52,500	203,500	48	15	52	30	6.7
Congo, Republic of	3,100	10,700	45	15	52	63	6.3
Costa Rica	4,100	7,200	26	4	77	48	2.7
Croatia	4,700	4,200	11	12	74	58	1.7
Cuba	11,200	10,800	15	7	76	75	1.6
Czech Republic	10,300	8,400	12	13	78	75	1.2
Denmark	5,300	5,100	13	12	78	85	1.7
Djibouti	644	1,068	39	16	38	83	5.8
Dominican Republic	8,500	12,000	27	6	66	65	2.7
Ecuador	12,900	21,200	28	6	72	65	2.8
Egypt	69,100	113,800	29	8	68	45	2.9
El Salvador	6,400	10,900	30	6	70	47	2.9
Eritrea	3,800	10,000	43	16	52	19	5.3
Estonia	1,400	0,800	11	13	71	69	1.2
Ethiopia	64,500	186,500	49	18	43	18	6.8
Fiji	823	916			70	49	3.0
Finland	5,200	4,700	13	10	78	67	1.6
France	59,500	61,800	13	9	79	76	1.8
Gabon	1,300	3,200	35	15	53	81	5.4
Gambia	1,337	2,605	43	19	47	33	4.8
Georgia	5,200	3,200	16	9	74	61	1.4
Germany	82,000	70,800	10	12	78	88	1.3
Ghana	19,700	40,100	40	12	57	38	4.2

Region/Country	Population estimate ('000s) 2000	Population estimate ('000s) 2050	Birth rate per 1,000, 1998	Death rate per 1,000, 1998	Life expectancy, 2000-2005	Percent urban, 2000	Fertility rate per woman 2000-2005
Greece	10,600	9,000	10	10	79	60	1.2
Guatemala	11,700	26,600	39	8	66	40	4.4
Guinea	8,300	20,700	51	20	49	33	5.8
Guinea-Bissau	1,200	3,300	42	22	45	24	6.0
Guyana	763	504	58	—	62	38	2.3
Haiti	8,300	14,000	35	13	53	36	4.0
Honduras	6,600	12,800	37	6	66	53	3.7
Hong Kong	7,000	9,600	12	6	80	100	1.2
Hungary	9,900	7,500	11	15	72	64	1.2
Iceland	281	333	17	7	79	93	1.9
India	1,025,100	1,572,100	27	10	64	28	3.0
Indonesia	214,800	311,300	25	8	67	41	2.3
Iran	71,400	121,400	38	7	70	62	2.8
Iraq	23,600	53,600	38	10	65	77	4.8
Ireland	3,800	5,400	14	9	77	59	2.0
Israel	6,200	10,100	21	7	79	91	2.7
Italy	57,500	43,000	10	10	79	67	1.2
Ivory Coast	16,300	32,200	39	13	48	46	4.6
Jamaica	2,600	3,800	24	6	76	56	2.4
Japan	127,300	109,200	10	7	82	78	1.3
Jordan	5,100	11,700	39	5	71	74	4.3
Kazakhstan	16,100	15,300	20	8	65	56	2.0
Kenya	31,300	55,400	38	12	49	33	4.2
Korea, North	22,400	28,000	22	5	65	60	2.1
Korea, South	47,100	51,600	16	6	76	82	1.5
Kuwait	2,000	4,000	24	2	77	98	2.7
Kyrgyzstan	5,000	7,500	28	7	69	33	2.3
Laos	5,400	11,400	45	15	55	24	4.8
Latvia	2,400	1,700	11	14	71	69	1.1
Lebanon	3,600	5,000	27	7	74	90	2.2
Lesotho	2,100	2,500	37	11	40	28	4.5
Liberia	3,100	14,400	49	28	56	45	6.8
Libya	5,400	10,000	42	8	71	88	3.3
Lithuania	3,700	3,000	13	11	73	68	1.2
Luxembourg	442	715	13	11	78	91	1.8
Macedonia	2,000	1,900	16	7	75	62	1.5
Madagascar	16,400	47,000	44	11	54	30	5.7
Malawi	11,600	31,100	51	22	39	25	6.3
Malaysia	22,600	37,800	29	5	73	57	2.9
Maldives	300	868	54	—	68	26	5.4
Mali	11,700	41,700	51	19	52	30	7.0
Malta	392	400	15	8	78	90	1.8
Mauritania	2,700	8,500	40	14	53	58	6.0
Mauritius	1,200	1,400	21	7	72	41	1.9
Melanesia	6,600	14,200	32	9	59	24	4.1
Mexico	100,400	146,700	27	5	73	74	2.5
Moldova	4,300	3,600	16	10	67	46	1.4
Mongolia	2,600	4,100	29	8	64	64	2.3
Morocco	30,400	50,400	29	8	69	56	3.0
Mozambique	18,600	38,800	45	19	38	40	5.9
Myanmar	48,400	68,500	29	11	56	28	2.8
Namibia	1,800	3,700	38	12	44	31	4.9
Nepal	23,600	52,400	40	13	60	12	4.5
Netherlands	15,900	15,800	13	9	78	89	1.5
New Zealand	3,800	4,400	17	8	78	86	2.0
Nicaragua	5,200	11,500	36	6	69	56	3.8
Niger	11,200	51,900	53	19	46	21	8.0
Nigeria	116,900	278,800	45	15	52	44	5.4
Norway	4,500	4,900	14	11	79	76	1.7
Oman	2,600	8,800	44	5	72	84	5.5
Pakistan	145,000	344,200	39	9	61	37	5.1
Panama	2,900	4,300	25	5	74	56	2.4
Papua New Guinea	4,900	11,000	33	11	58	17	4.3
Paraguay	5,600	12,600	34	6	71	56	3.8
Peru	26,100	42,100	27	7	70	73	2.6
Philippines	77,100	128,400	31	6	70	59	3.2
Poland	38,600	33,400	13	10	74	66	1.3
Portugal	10,000	9,000	11	11	76	64	1.5

Region/Country	Population estimate ('000s)		Birth rate per 1,000, 1998	Death rate per 1,000, 1998	Life expec- tancy, 2000 -2005	Percent urban, 2000	Fertility rate per woman 2000 -2005
	2000	2050					
Puerto Rico	4,000	4,800	18	7	76	75	1.9
Qatar	575	831	20	3	70	92	3.3
Romania	22,400	18,100	11	11	70	56	1.3
Russian Federation	144,700	104,300	11	13	66	78	1.1
Rwanda	7,900	18,500	44	45	40	6	5.8
Saudi Arabia	21,000	59,700	35	5	72	86	5.5
Senegal	9,700	22,700	43	16	54	47	5.1
Sierra Leone	4,600	14,400	49	30	41	37	6.5
Singapore	4,100	4,600	18	5	78	100	1.5
Slovakia	5,400	4,700	14	11	74	57	1.3
Slovenia	2,000	1,500	10	11	76	50	1.1
Somalia	9,200	40,900	50	18	49	28	7.3
South Africa	43,800	47,300	31	9	47	50	2.9
Spain	39,900	31,300	10	9	79	78	1.1
Sri Lanka	19,100	23,100	19	6	73	24	2.1
Sudan	31,800	63,500	35	14	57	36	4.5
Suriname	419	418	25	6	71	74	2.1
Swaziland	938	1,391	39	11	38	26	4.4
Sweden	8,800	7,800	14	11	80	83	1.3
Switzerland	7,200	5,600	12	9	79	68	1.4
Syria	16,600	36,300	33	6	72	55	3.7
Tajikistan	6,100	9,800	33	7	68	28	2.9
Tanzania	36,000	82,700	43	14	51	33	5.0
Thailand	63,600	82,500	18	6	74	22	2.0
Togo	4,700	11,800	44	15	51	33	5.4
Trinidad and Tobago	1,300	1,400	18	6	75	74	1.5
Tunisia	9,600	14,100	26	6	71	66	2.1
Turkey	67,600	98,800	23	7	71	75	2.3
Turkmenistan	4,800	8,400	32	8	67	45	3.2
Uganda	24,000	101,500	51	22	46	14	7.1
Ukraine	49,100	30,000	11	13	68	68	1.1
United Arab Emirates	2,700	3,700	21	3	75	86	2.9
United Kingdom	59,500	58,900	13	11	78	90	1.6
United States	285,900	397,100	16	9	78	77	1.9
Uruguay	3,400	4,200	17	10	75	91	2.3
Uzbekistan	25,300	40,500	31	7	70	37	2.3
Vanuatu	200	500	—	—	69	20	4.3
Venezuela	24,600	42,200	27	5	74	87	2.7
Vietnam	79,200	123,800	29	8	69	20	2.3
Yemen	19,100	102,400	49	12	62	25	7.6
Yugoslavia	10,500	9,000	14	10	73	52	1.6
Zambia	10,600	29,300	44	18	42	40	5.7
Zimbabwe	12,900	23,500	40	14	43	35	4.5

Note: Totals may not add because of independent rounding.
Source: United Nations Population Fund (UNFPA), *The State of World Population 2001* (2001); UN Population Division, *World Population Prospects The 2000 Revision;* and *World Population Prospects: The 2000 Revision Highlights* (2001).

World Health

The World Health Organization (WHO), a specialized agency of the United Nations, is the global intergovernmental directing and coordinating authority for international health work. Headquartered in Geneva, Switzerland, WHO gathers health statistics, sets international health standards, provides assistance to individual countries when invited, and issues publications. Most of the information here is from the World Health Organization (WHO). (For information on the United States, see the section "Health and Medicine" in Part II.)

In 2000, WHO conducted the first-ever analysis of the world's health care systems and ranked them based on, among other indicators, their responsiveness to their patient's needs, inequities

in care, and who pays the costs of the care. France ranks as the country providing the best overall health care, followed by Italy, San Marino, Andorra, and Singapore. The United States ranks 37th of the 191 WHO member countries. The countries with the worst overall health care are Sierra Leone, Myanmar, the Central African Republic, and the Democratic Republic of the Congo.

Health care in developing countries is expected to improve due to the new infusion of information and resources. In June 2001, thousands of chemical safety documents became available for free at one site on the Internet. In July 2001, the leaders of the G-8 industrialized nations summit launched a global fund to fight HIV/AIDS, malaria and tuberculosis. Leading drug companies announced reductions of up to 94 percent on tuberculosis drug prices. And, the world's six biggest medical journal publishers will provide 1,000 of the top 1,240 biomedical journals to medical schools and research institutes in 100 developing countries over the internet beginning in January 2002.

(For information on the United States, see the section "Health and Medicine" in Part II.)

▶ THE GLOBAL SITUATION

The World Health Organization estimates that of the 56 million deaths that occurred in 1999, over 30 percent, or 16.97 million were due to cardiovascular diseases (heart attacks and strokes), 18 percent, or 9.99 million were due to infectious and parasitic diseases (tuberculosis, sexually transmitted diseases, childhood diseases, etc.), 12.6 percent, or 7.07 million were due to cancers, and 9.1 percent or 5.10 million were due to injuries. Acute lower respiratory infections caused 3.96 million deaths, or 7.1 percent of world total deaths; respiratory diseases (including chronic obstructive pulmonary disease and asthma) accounted for 3.58 million deaths, or 6.4 percent; and HIV/AIDS caused 2.67 million deaths, or 4.8 percent the total deaths.

Communicable diseases, maternal and perinatal conditions and nutritional deficiencies caused 17.38 million deaths in 1999, or 31.1 percent of total deaths. Noncommunicable conditions caused 33.48 million deaths, or 59.8 percent of the total. WHO estimates that noncommunicable diseases will rise to 73 percent by 2020.

Aging Populations Globally

WHO estimates that the number of people over 65 will rise from 606 million in 2000 to 800 million by 2025 and almost two billion in 2050. In 2000, 69 million people were aged 80 or over; this population will increase to 379 million by 2050.

In 1996, life expectancy worldwide reached 65 for the first time in human history. As people live longer, noncommunicable diseases become more common. Most deaths among the elderly will be due to cancers, and lung and heart diseases. Cancer and heart disease are found in people 70 to 75 more than in any other age group; people over 75 are more likely to experience impairments of hearing, vision, mobility, and mental function. Over 80 percent of circulatory diseases occur in people over 65. Worldwide, circulatory disease is the leading cause of death and disability in people over 65.

Resurgence of Old Diseases

Worldwide, infectious and parasitic diseases kill nearly 18 million people a year, or 17.8 percent of all deaths. Most of the victims of parasitic diseases are young children. In recent years, there have been widespread outbreaks of infectious diseases once thought to be under control.

Tuberculosis   By the late 1970s, public health experts were predicting that this chronic bacterial disease would be almost completely eliminated in the United States by the end of the century. Beginning in 1988, however, the number of cases increased annually, reaching 26,673 new cases in 1992. According to WHO, tuberculosis is the "world's most neglected health crisis." An estimated 2 billion people are infected with tuberculosis worldwide, and the disease kills 1.5 million people annually. A tuberculosis vaccine, known as BCG, has been injected in an estimated 3 billion

Nations with Highest and Lowest Infant Mortality Rates, 2000–05

Country	Highest Infant Mortality Rate[1]	Country	Lowest Infant Mortality Rate[1]
Afghanistan	161	Japan	3
Sierra Leone	146	Sweden	3
Malawi	130	Belgium	4
Mozambique	128	Hong Kong	4
Niger	126	Finland	4
Mali	121	Australia	5
Guinea Bissau	121	Austria	5
Rwanda	119	Belgium	5
Angola	118	Canada	5
Djibouti	117	Czech Republic	5
Gambia	115	Denmark	5
Guinea	114	France	5
Somalia	113	Germany	5
Lesotho	112	Iceland	5
Liberia	111	Italy	5
Ethiopia	106	Netherlands	5
		Norway	5
		Singapore	5
		Spain	5
		Switzerland	5

Note: Estimates. Rate is number of deaths per 1,000 live births. **Source:** United Nations Department of Economic and Social Affairs, Population Division, *World Population Prospects – The 2000 Revision Highlights* (2000).

Infant Mortality Rates by Region, 2000–05

Region	Infant mortality rate (per 1,000 live births)
World	**55**
More developed regions	8
Less developed regions	59
Least developed countries	92
Africa	83
Asia	53
Arab States	39
Europe	9
Latin America and Caribbean	32
North America	7
Oceania	24
Former USSR	20

Note: Estimates. **Source:** United Nations Population Fund (UNFPA), *The State of World Population 2001* (2001).

people worldwide but is used infrequently in the United States.

Malaria   is caused by a parasite transmitted by the anopheles mosquito. The number of infected people has risen steadily during the 1980s and 1990s, in part because developing equatorial countries have encouraged development in swampy, anopheles-infected regions. Worldwide, an estimated 300 to 500 million cases occur annually, and 1.1 million people — mostly in sub-Saharan Africa — die from the disease. Almost all of the approximately 1,000 Americans who contract malaria each year get the disease while traveling abroad.

Cholera   is caused by a bacterium that is spread principally through food and drinking water contaminated with human feces. The disease is associated with poverty and is most prevalent in places that lack clean water supplies and hygienic sewage-disposal systems. In 1991 a cholera epidemic broke

Killer Diseases, 1999

Cause	Estimated deaths	Percent of total
Cardiovascular disease	16,970,000	30.3%
Ischaemic heart disease	7,089,000	12.7
Cerebrovascular disease	5,544,000	9.9
Cancer	7,065,000	12.6
Trachea, bronchus, lung	1,193,000	2.1
Stomach	801,000	1.4
Liver	589,000	1.1
Colon and rectum	509,000	0.9
Esophagus	381,000	0.7
Breast	467,000	0.8
Mouth/oropharynx	282,000	0.5
Acute lower respiratory infections	3,963,000	7.1
Respiratory diseases[1]	3,575,000	6.4
HIV/AIDS	2,673,000	4.8
Diarrhea (including dysentery)	2,213,000	4.0
Perinatal conditions	2,356,000	4.2
Childhood diseases	1,554,000	2.8
Tuberculosis	1,669,000	3.0
Malaria	1,086,000	1.9

1. Includes chronic obstructive pulmonary disease, asthma, and other respiratory diseases.
Source: World Health Organization, *The World Health Report 2000 - Health Systems: Improving Performance* (2000).

Leading Worldwide Causes of Death, 1999

Cause	Estimated deaths (millions)	Percent of total
World total deaths	**56.0**	**100.0%**
Communicable diseases, maternal and perinatal conditions, and nutritional deficiencies	17.4	33.1
Infectious and parasitic diseases	9.9	17.8
Respiratory infections	4.0	7.2
Noncommunicable conditions	33.5	59.8
Cardiovascular diseases	16.9	30.3
Cancers	7.1	12.6
Injuries	5.1	9.1
Respiratory diseases	3.6	6.4
Digestive diseases	2.5	3.7

Source: World Health Organization, *The World Health Report 2000: Health Systems: Improving Performance* (2000).

out in Peru —the first major outbreak of cholera in the Western Hemisphere in the 20th century. By September 1994 a total of 1,041,422 cases and 9,643 deaths had been reported throughout Central and South America. Meanwhile, a new strain of cholera was spreading across south Asia; attacks from older strains do not produce lasting immunity to this new strain. Cholera epidemics also occur regularly in crowded refugee camps. In 1994, for example, an estimated 20,000 to 30,000 Rwandan refugees in Zaire died from cholera.

Dengue fever another disease once thought to be nearly eliminated in the Western Hemisphere, has also made a comeback, reaching epidemic proportions in Latin America. There were 86 confirmed cases in the United States in 1995, almost twice the average number reported annually between 1987 and 1994. According to the World Health Organization, there are some 20 million cases a year worldwide. Caused by a virus, dengue fever is transmitted by mosquitoes. Though painful, recovery usually is complete within 10 days of the onset of symptoms. However, people who have been exposed to one strain of the virus and then infected with a second strain may develop hemorrhagic dengue, which is fatal about 10 percent of the time.

▶TOBACCO USE: A GLOBAL HEALTH PROBLEM

The World Health Organization estimates that in 1998 about 30 percent of the world's population smoked. The highest prevalence was in the Western Pacific (where 34 percent of the population smoked); the lowest was in the Eastern Mediterranean (22 percent). Globally, 48 percent of men and 12 percent of women smoked. In Europe and the Americas, 23 percent of women smoked. A WHO survey showed that about 20 percent of schoolchildren in developing countries were already regular smokers, that 25 percent of them started before the age of 10, and two-thirds wanted to quit.

Today about 1.1 billion people smoke worldwide and the number is expected to rise to 1.6 billion by 2025. Smoking is declining in the high-income countries but increasing in the poorer regions. WHO estimates that tobacco killed three million people worldwide in 1990 and four million in 1998. WHO predicts that tobacco will likely cause 10 million deaths by 2030, making smoking the largest single cause of death in the world. the situation is even worse in poorer nations, where by 2020, smoking is expected to cause seven of every ten deaths.

In the Western Pacific, tobacco consumption increased by 7.8 percent from 1992 to 1997. China is the largest cigarette market in the world, accounting for 30 percent of estimated global consumption. But Japan has the second-highest cigarette consumption per captia: 2,270 cigarettes per person per year (or 6.2 cigarettes per person per day).

WHO reports that second-hand smoke contains at least 40 substances shown to cause cancer and that tobacco smoke contains large amounts of carbon monoxide, a gas that inhibits the blood's ability to carry oxygen throughout the body including to the heart and brain, and other substances that contribute to heart disease and stroke.

Smoking is such a serious global health problem that in 2000 the World Health Programme launched political negotiations to implement a "Framework Convention on Tobacco Control" to help countries educate their people on the deadly affects of smoking.

▶CIRCULATORY DISEASES

According to the World Health Organization, diseases of the heart and circulation—cardiovascular and cerebrovascular—such as heart attacks and stroke—kill over 13 million people worldwide and account for 23.2 percent of the total number of deaths each year. Additional millions are disabled, frequently in their prime years. Worldwide, heart disease accounts for 7.4 million deaths and strokes kill another 5.1 million, but in developing countries, strokes kill twice as many people as heart disease

Coronary heart disease became an epidemic in North America, Europe, and Australasia in the early 1900s, peaked in the 1960s and early 1970s, and has since declined dramatically—by over 50 percent in some countries. The world's highest rates are now in eastern and central Europe.

In developed countries, almost half of all deaths—5 out of 12 million each year—are due to circulatory diseases. As the developing nations adopt Western lifestyles, these diseases are increasing rapidly; they now account for about 25 percent of all deaths.

Decades of research show that lifestyle, beginning in childhood, is the main cause of coronary heart disease. The major risk factors are high blood pressure, cigarette-smoking, poor dietary habits, especially the intake of saturated fat, elevated blood cholesterol, lack of physical activity, obesity, and diabetes. Lack of physical activity is the most common risk factor in industrialized countries than can be changed.

► CANCER

The World Health Organization estimates that in 1998 more than 10 million people developed cancer and another 7.2 million died from it. Eight types of cancer caused 60 percent of all cancer deaths: lung, stomach, breast, colon/rectum, mouth, liver, cervix and esophagus. Several risk factors are linked to cancer: diet, tobacco, infections, alcohol and hormones.

In 1996 there were an estimated 17.9 million people with cancer surviving up to five years after diagnosis. Of these, 10.5 million women, 5.3 million of whom had cancer of the breast, cervix or colon-rectum. Among men, prostate, colorectal and lung cancers were the most prevalent.

Lung cancer is the biggest cancer killer, causing almost one million deaths a year and over 1.3 million new cases. Globally, about 85 percent of lung cancers in men and 46 percent in women are tobacco-related. In developed countries, the ratios are 91 percent for men and 62 percent in women. While there is no effective treatment for lung cancer, most cases can be prevented through diet and exercise. Only 7-12 percent of patients survive five years after diagnosis. Rates of lung cancer are increasing in most countries; however, in countries where smoking is declining—Finland, United Kingdom and the United States—lung cancer is also now declining.

► MATERNAL DEATHS WORLDWIDE

Approximately 585,000 women—one every minute—die around the world each year from pregnancy-related causes, according to the World Health Organization. In parts of some developing countries, the chance of a woman dying this way is 100 times greater than in the industrialized countries.

The five major causes of maternal death are: hemorrhage (25 percent), indirect causes (19 percent), sepsis or postpartum infection (15 percent), hypertensive disorders of pregnancy and eclampsia (13 percent), and unsafe abortion (13 percent). About 70,000 women die each year from unsafe abortion—600 in developed countries and 69,000 in less developed countries—and an unknown but much larger number suffer infection, injury and trauma. There are an estimated 20 million unsafe abortions each year, 90 percent of them in developing countries.

Women who do not have adequate family planning materials and services have unwanted pregnancies and bear too many children, or they have children when they are too young or too old, or have children too close together. Virtually all studies report that most women would prefer using contraceptives and resort to abortion as a last resort.

► DEATHS OF CHILDREN

In 1991 UNICEF and the World Health Organization certified that 80 percent of all the world's one-year-olds were immunized against the six deadly childhood diseases: diphtheria, whooping cough, measles, tuberculosis, polio and tetanus, thereby effectively stopping the spread of these diseases. An estimated 3.2 million infants in the developing world are now saved from measles, neonatal tetanus and pertussis, and 445,000 infants will not be paralyzed by polio. WHO announced the eradication of smallpox from all peoples on Earth in 1980 and expect to have polio eradicated from all countries by the year 2005.

In recent years UNICEF and WHO have turned their attention to promoting 80 percent ORT (oral rehydration therapy) use, as part of controlling diarrheal disease, eliminating vitamin A deficiency, promoting universal iodization of salt in countries with iodine deficiency disorders, and eliminating guinea worm disease (also called river blindness).

Recent conflicts and wars have had tragic effects on children. It is estimated that in the past decade, wars have killed 2 million children, disabled at least 1 million, left 12 million homeless, and separated another million from their parents. That's not counting the thousands of children under the age of 16 who have fought in wars in more than 25 countries.

► GLOBAL SEX FACTS

According to the World Health Organization, sexual intercourse occurs more than 100 million times a day around the world. As a result, approximately 910,000 conceptions take place, as well as 350,000 cases of sexually transmitted diseases.

WHO estimates that 1,440 women die each day (an average of one a minute) because of complications during pregnancy or childbirth. About 150,000 unwanted pregnancies end each day in abortion.

The number of people using contraception in Third World countries has increased sharply in recent years, rising from 31 million in the 1960–65 period to 381 million during 1985–90. Women in developing countries had, on average, 6.1 children in the years 1965–70, but the figure declined to 3.9 in 1985–90.

Source: World Health Organization, *The World Health Report* (1998).

► SEXUALLY TRANSMITTED DISEASES (STDs)

One million people die each year from reproductive tract infections, including sexually transmitted diseases other than HIV/AIDS. There are an estimated 333 million new cases of STDs each year. STDs are most frequent in young people aged 15 to 24. Women contract STDs five times more often than men. Almost two-thirds of all cases of infertility are due to STDs. WHO estimates that in 1995, there were 150 million cases of STDs in adults in southern/southeastern Asia, 65 million cases in sub-Saharan Africa, 36 million in Latin America and the Caribbean, and 14 million in North America.

Current World Health Indicators, by Nation

Country	Life expectancy at birth (years) 1970	Life expectancy at birth (years) 2000-05	Daily calorie supply, 1997	Infant mortality per 1,000 births[1] 2000-05	Population with access to: Sanitation, 1999	Population with access to: Safe water, 1999	Population with access to: Essential drugs, 1999
Afghanistan	37	43	1,523	161	29%	12%	—
Albania	67	74	2,523	25	—	—	60%
Algeria	53	70	3,020	42	73	94	95
Angola	37	46	1,983	118	44	38	20
Argentina	67	74	3,136	20	85	79	70
Armenia	—	73	2,147	15	67	84	40
Antigua & Barbuda	—	75	2,365	17	—	—	—
Australia	71	79	3,001	5	100	100	100
Austria	70	79	3,343	5	100	100	100
Azerbaijan	—	72	2,139	29	—	—	66
Bahamas	65	69	2,443	17	93	96	80
Bahrain	62	74	—	14	—	—	100
Bangladesh	45	61	2,105	67	53	97	65
Barbados	69	77	3,207	11	100	100	100
Belarus	—	69	3,101	13	—	100	70
Belgium	71	79	3,543	5	—	—	99
Belize	—	74	2,862	30	42	76	80
Benin	44	54	2,415	81	23	63	77
Bhutan	42	63	—	54	69	62	85
Bolivia	46	64	2,170	56	66	79	70
Bosnia & Herzegovina	—	74	—	14	—	—	—
Botswana	50	36	2,272	67	—	—	90
Brazil	59	68	2,938	38	72	83	40
Brunei Darussalam	—	76	2,331	9	—	—	99
Bulgaria	70	71	2,756	15	100	100	88
Burkina Faso	40	48	2,137	87	29	—	60
Burundi	45	42	1,708	112	—	—	20
Cambodia	42	56	1,974	73	18	30	30
Cameroon	49	50	2,175	79	92	62	66
Canada	73	79	3,056	5	100	100	100
Cape Verde	56	71	3,135	50	71	74	80
Central African Republic	42	44	1,938	93	31	60	50
Chad	38	46	1,972	116	29	27	46
Chile	62	76	2,810	12	97	94	88
China	59	71	2,844	37	38	75	85
Colombia	59	80	2,800	26	85	91	88
Comoros	48	61	1,824	67	98	96	90
Congo	51	52	2,107	66	—	51	61
Congo, Democratic Republic	—	52	1,815	77	20	45	—
Costa Rica	67	77	2,822	11	96	98	100
Croatia	—	74	2,458	8	100	95	100
Cuba	70	76	2,357	7	100	89	92
Cyprus	71	78	3,102	8	95	100	100
Czech Republic	69	75	3,177	5	—	—	88
Denmark	73	77	3,808	5	—	100	99
Djibouti	40	41	1,920	117	91	100	80
Dominica	—	74	3,093	17	—	—	—
Dominican Republic	59	67	2,316	36	71	79	66
Ecuador	58	71	2,592	42	59	71	40
Egypt	51	68	3,289	41	94	95	88
El Salvador	58	70	2,515	26	83	74	80
Equatorial Guinea	40	52	—	99	53	43	44
Eritrea	—	52	1,585	82	13	46	57
Estonia	—	71	3,004	10	—	—	100
Ethiopia	43	43	1,845	106	15	24	66
Fiji	64	70	3,038	18	43	47	100
Finland	70	78	2,916	4	100	100	99
France	72	79	3,551	5	—	—	99
Gabon	44	53	2,517	80	21	70	30
Gambia	36	47	2,332	115	37	62	90
Georgia	—	74	2,184	18	99	76	30
Germany	71	78	3,330	5	—	—	100
Ghana	49	57	2,560	62	63	64	44
Greece	72	79	3,575	6	—	—	100
Guatemala	53	66	2,191	41	85	92	50
Guinea	36	49	2,099	114	58	48	93

Country	Life expectancy at birth (years) 1970	Life expectancy at birth (years) 2000-05	Daily calorie supply, 1997	Infant mortality per 1,000 births[1] 2000-05	Population with access to: Sanitation, 1999	Population with access to: Safe water, 1999	Population with access to: Essential drugs, 1999
Guinea-Bissau	36	45	2,381	121	47	49	44
Guyana	65	62	2,392	53	87	94	44
Haiti	48	53	1,855	61	28	46	30
Honduras	53	69	2,368	33	77	90	40
Hong Kong	—	80	3,282	4	—	—	—
Hungary	70	72	3,402	9	99	99	100
Iceland	74	79	3,104	5	—	—	100
India	48	64	2,415	65	31	88	35
Indonesia	47	67	2,930	40	66	76	80
Iran	55	70	2,824	36	81	95	85
Iraq	55	65	2,252	64	93	78	70
Ireland	71	77	3,636	6	—	—	99
Israel	71	79	3,272	6	—	—	99
Italy	72	79	3,504	5	—	—	99
Ivory Coast	—	48	2,421	81	—	77	80
Jamaica	67	76	2,575	20	84	71	95
Japan	72	82	2,905	3	—	—	100
Jordan	55	71	2,681	23	99	96	100
Kazakhstan	—	65	3,007	42	99	99	66
Kenya	50	49	1,971	59	86	49	36
Kiribati	—	56	—	60	—	—	—
Korea, South	60	75	3,336	7	63	92	99
Korea, North	—	71	2,834	39	—	—	—
Kuwait	66	77	3,075	11	—	—	99
Kyrgzstan	—	69	2,489	37	100	77	66
Laos	40	55	2,143	88	46	90	66
Latvia	—	71	2,861	14	—	—	90
Lebanon	—	74	3,279	17	99	100	88
Lesotho	49	40	2,209	111	92	91	80
Liberia	47	56	1,640	79	39	46	30
Libya	52	71	3,132	25	97	72	100
Lithuania	—	73	2,805	9	—	—	88
Luxembourg	70	78	—	6	—	—	99
Macedonia	—	74	2,336	16	93	99	66
Madagascar	45	54	2,001	92	42	47	65
Malawi	40	39	2,097	130	77	57	44
Malaysia	62	73	2,899	10	98	95	70
Maldives	—	68	2,495	37	56	100	50
Mali	40	52	2,027	121	69	65	60
Malta	70	79	3,417	7	—	100	100
Mauritania	39	54	2,653	97	33	37	66
Mauritius	62	72	2,952	16	99	100	100
Mexico	62	73	3,137	28	73	86	92
Micronesia	—	71	—	25	—	—	—
Moldova	—	67	2,562	21	—	100	66
Monaco	—	63	2,985	58	70	55	41
Mongolia	60	64	2,098	58	30	60	60
Morocco	52	69	3,244	42	75	82	66
Mozambique	41	38	1,799	128	43	60	50
Myanmar	51	56	2,752	87	46	68	60
Namibia	48	44	2,168	65	41	77	80
Nepal	42	60	2,339	71	27	81	20
Netherlands	74	78	3,259	5	100	100	100
New Zealand	72	78	3,405	6	—	—	100
Nicaragua	54	69	2,328	36	84	79	46
Niger	38	46	2,116	126	20	59	66
Nigeria	44	52	2,609	79	63	57	10
Norway	74	79	3,350	5	—	100	100
Oman	45	72	—	23	92	32	90
Pakistan	48	61	2,408	87	61	88	65
Panama	66	75	2,556	19	94	87	80
Papua New Guinea	47	58	2,253	62	82	42	90
Paraguay	65	71	2,485	37	95	79	44
Peru	54	70	2,310	37	76	77	60
Philippines	57	70	2,356	29	83	87	66
Poland	70	74	3,344	9	—	—	88
Portugal	—	76	3,658	6	—	—	100
Qatar	61	70	—	11	—	—	99

Country	Life expectancy at birth (years) 1970	Life expectancy at birth (years) 2000-05	Daily calorie supply, 1997	Infant mortality per 1,000 births[1] 2000-05	Population with access to: Sanitation, 1999	Population with access to: Safe water, 1999	Population with access to: Essential drugs, 1999
Romania	69	70	2,943	22	53	58	85
Russian Federation	—	66	2,704	16	—	99	66
Rwanda	48	41	2,142	119	8	41	44
Samoa	—	70	—	26	99	99	100
São Tomé & Principe	—	64	2,156	61	—	—	—
Saudi Arabia	52	72	2,735	21	100	95	99
Senegal	43	54	2,394	57	70	78	66
Seychelles	—	71	2,424	14	—	—	—
Sierra Leone	34	41	2,002	146	28	28	44
Singapore	68	78	—	5	100	100	100
Slovakia	—	74	3,030	8	100	100	100
Slovenia	—	76	3,117	6	—	100	100
Solomon Islands	40	69	2,103	21	—	—	—
Somalia	—	49	1,505	113	27	37	18
South Africa	53	47	2,933	59	86	86	80
Spain	72	79	3,295	5	—	—	100
Sri Lanka	64	73	2,240	20	83	83	95
St. Kitts & Nevis	—	70	2,263	30	—	—	—
St. Lucia	62	70	2,822	24	—	—	—
St. Vincent and The Grenadines	63	73	2,434	18	—	—	—
Sudan	—	57	2,391	78	62	75	15
Suriname	64	71	2,578	26	83	95	100
Swaziland	46	38	2,529	92	—	—	100
Sweden	75	80	3,160	4	100	100	99
Switzerland	73	79	3,280	5	100	100	100
Syria	56	72	3,339	22	90	80	80
Tajikistan	—	67	2,129	53	—	—	44
Tanzania	45	51	2,028	72	90	54	66
Thailand	58	71	2,334	21	96	80	95
Togo	45	52	2,155	75	34	54	70
Tonga	—	68	—	21	—	—	—
Trinidad and Tobago	66	75	2,751	13	88	86	77
Tunisia	54	71	3,250	26	—	—	51
Turkey	57	71	3,568	39	91	83	99
Turkmenistan	—	67	2,563	49	100	58	66
Uganda	47	46	2,110	94	75	50	70
Ukraine	—	68	2,753	15	—	—	66
United Arab Emirates	61	75	3,366	11	—	—	99
United Kingdom	72	78	3,237	5	100	100	99
United States	71	78	3,642	7	100	100	99
Uruguay	—	75	2,830	13	95	98	66
Uzbekistan	—	70	2,550	37	100	85	66
Vanuatu	—	69	2,624	29	—	—	—
Venezuela	65	73	2,398	19	74	84	90
Vietnam	—	69	2,502	34	73	56	85
Yemen	42	62	2,041	63	45	69	50
Yugoslavia	68	73	3,634	13	—	83	63
Zambia	47	42	1,939	80	78	64	66
Zimbabwe	51	43	2,083	55	68	85	70

Note: Not every nation reports in all categories, and some do not report any information at all. Nonreporting nations do not appear in the table. 1. Rate for children under 5 per 1,000 live births. **Source:** United Nations Department for Economic and Social Affairs, Population Division, *World Population Prospects – The 2000 Revision Highlights (2000),* UN Department for Economic and Social Information and Policy Analysis, chart: *World Population 1996;* United Nations Development Programme, *Human Development Report 2001* (2001).

▶ **AIDS WORLDWIDE**

In mid-2001, the Joint United Nations Programme on HIV/AIDS (UNAIDS) estimated that 36.1 million people worldwide were living with HIV/AIDS, the vast majority of them in sub-Saharan Africa. June 5, 2001 marked 20 years since the first official report on AIDS was published by the U.S. Centers for Disease Control, which catalogued five cases. Over these 20 years, 58 million people have been infected with HIV, with 22 million having died. The AIDS epidemic was recognized in Africa by 1983 and by 1985 at least one case of HIV/AIDS was reported from each region of the world. The first drug to treat AIDS was approved by the Fed-

eral Drug Administration in the U.S. in 1987 and triple antiretroviral therapy began in 1996.

Sub-Saharan Africa has been the region hardest hit by the HIV/AIDS pandemic. More than two-thirds of all people with HIV/AIDS (24.5 million people) are in this region. Another 5.6 million are in South and South-East Asia. South Africa, with 4.2 million infected people, has the most cases in the world. But South Africa's HIV infection rate of 19.9 percent pales in comparison with Botswana, where 35.8 percent of adults have the disease. In all, there are 16 countries where 10 percent or more of the adult population (aged 15-49) suffers from HIV.

Ethiopia has an estimated 3 million people living with HIV/AIDS, Nigeria has 2.7 million, Kenya has 2.1 million, Zimbabwe has 1.5 million, and Tanzania, Mozambique, and the Democratic Republic of the Congo all have more than a million. While infections are rising in most areas, Uganda has lowered its rate from a high of nearly 14 percent in the early 1990s to about 8 percent today. Zambia seems to be following Uganda's strong prevention campaign and is also reducing its rate of infection.

Since the global HIV/AIDS pandemic began in the late 1970s, 18.8 million people have died of HIV/AIDS. Again, sub-Saharan Africa has been the most devastated region. Close to 15 million (78 percent of all AIDS-related deaths) have come in this part of the world. Another 2.6 million AIDS deaths occurred in South and South-East Asia; by comparison, there have been fewer than a half million deaths from AIDS in all of North America (and only 210,000 in Western Europe).

AIDS is having a devastating impact on children around the world but especially in Africa. According to UNAIDS, 3.8 million children under the age of 15 have died from HIV/AIDS since the pandemic began, 3.3 million of them in sub-Saharan Africa. A total of 13.2 million children under 14 have been orphaned by HIV/AIDS. Some 1,700 children were newly infected with HIV each day in 1999, resulting in a total of 620,000 new infections

for the year. At the end of 1999, 1.3 million children worldwide were living with HIV, 1 million of them in sub-Saharan Africa.

Sixteen million children in sub-Saharan Africa have lost at least one parent to AIDS. By 2010, it is estimated that 28 million children in Africa who will have lost at least one parent to AIDS. Most children born with AIDS will die before the age of five. In Botswana, no less than two-thirds of to-day's 15-year-old boys will die prematurely from AIDS. In South Africa and Zimbabwe, where nearly 25 percent of the adults are infected, AIDS is expected to take the lives of around half of to-day's 15 year olds.

The HIV/AIDS crisis is so severe across sub-Saharan Africa that United Nations experts now say that this health crisis is affecting the economic and social structures of many countries. The challenge of losing so many people in their most productive years and the costs of care is now threatening the very security of these nations.

Compared to Africa, HIV infection rates in Asia are low. Only three countries— Cambodia, Myanmar, and Thailand—have infection rates above 1 percent among adults 15 to 49: However, China and India have 36 percent of the world's population and even low rates in those countries translate into large raw numbers. India's infection rate is only 7 per 1,000 population, but that's still 3.7 million people living with HIV/AIDS at the beginning of the millennium.

In Latin America and the Caribbean, most HIV/AIDS transmission occurs between heterosexual partners. Haiti has the highest rate of infection: 8 percent of adults in urban areas and 4 percent in rural areas, or a total of 210,000 people. Brazil has the highest number of infected people, 540,000. Honduras, Guatemala and Belize have

Nations with the Greatest Number of People with HIV/AIDS, 1999

Country	Adults and children with HIV/AIDS	Country	Adults and children with HIV/AIDS
South Africa	4,200,000	Uganda	820,000
India	3,700,000	Ivory Coast	760,000
Ethiopia	3,000,000	Thailand	755,000
Nigeria	2,700,000	Brazil	540,000
Kenya	2,100,000	Cameroon	540,000
Zimbabwe	1,500,000	Myanmar	530,000
Tanzania	1,300,000	China	500,000
Mozambique	1,200,000	Rwanda	400,000
Democratic Republic of Congo	1,100,000	Burundi	360,000
		Burkina Faso	350,000
Zambia	870,000	Ghana	340,000
USA	850,000	World Total	34,300,000

Source: United Nations AIDS and World Health Organization, *Epidemic Update Report* (June 2000).

HIV/AIDS Worldwide: 1999 (numbers in millions)

	Total	Adult males	Adult females	Children under 15
New infections in 1999	5.4	2.4	2.3	0.6
People living with HIV/AIDS	24.3	17.3	15.7	1.3
AIDS deaths in 1999	2.8	1.1	1.2	0.5
Cumulative AIDS deaths	18.8	7.3	7.7	3.8

Source: United Nations AIDS and World Health Organization, *Report on the Global HIV/AIDS Epidemic* (June 2000).

HIV/AIDS Estimates By Region, 1999

Region	Epidemic started	Adults and children living with HIV/AIDS Number	Percent	Percent women	New infections
Sub-Saharan Africa	late 1970s/ early 1980s	24,500,000	8.57%	55%	4,000,000
North Africa and Middle East	late 1980s	220,000	0.12	20	20,000
South and Southeast Asia	late 1980s	5,600,000	0.54	35	800,000
East Asia and the Pacific	late 1980s	530,000	0.06	13	120,000
Latin America	late 1970s/ early 1980s	1,300,000	0.49	25	150,000
Caribbean	late 1970s/ early 1980s	360,000	2.11	35	60,000
Eastern Europe and Central Asia	early 1990s	420,000	0.21	25	130,000
Western Europe	late 1970s	520,000	0.23	25	30,000
North America	late 1970s/ early 1980s	900,000	0.58	20	45,000
Australia/New Zealand	late 1970s/ early 1980s	15,000	0.13	10	500
WORLD TOTAL		34,300,000	1.07	47	5,400,000

Source: United Nations AIDS and World Health Organization, *Report on the Global HIV/AIDS Epidemic* (June 2000).

the fastest-growing heterosexual epidemics with one to two percent of the adults infected.

In the countries of the former Soviet Union, the HIV epidemic continues to be concentrated in injecting drug users. The Ukraine has 240,000 infected people, most of whom are injecting drug users. About 130,000 Russians have HIV/AIDS, most of whom are injecting drug users.

In high-income countries, HIV infections are concentrated mainly among injecting drug users and gay men. The United States has 850,000 people living with HIV/AIDS. France has 130,000 cases, Spain has 120,000, and Italy has 95,000.

(For more detailed information on AIDS in the United States, see "Health and Medicine" in Part II. See also Part I, "Major News Stories.")

World Religions

In 1996, 4.7 billion, or an estimated 80 percent of the world's population, identified themselves as adherents of one religion or another. Four religions—Christianity, Islam, Hinduism and Buddhism—claim 4.2 billion adherents, or 72 percent of the world's population, Approximately 19 percent of the world's people are atheist or nonreligious.

This section describes the major religions of the world, their basic tenets, scriptures, schools and sects, and their history. (Additional details may be found in the section "Religion in America.")

▶ JUDAISM

Origins Judaism is the oldest of the world's three major monotheistic religions and a forerunner of Christianity and Islam. The Hebrew Bible recounts the story of the world and mankind from the creation, through the flood, and the work of the patriarch Abraham who brought his people from Mesopotamia to Canaan—the Promised Land. His descendants were enslaved in Egypt until Moses led them out of captivity. During the exodus, Moses received from God the Ten Commandments that form the bedrock of Jewish law. Jewish custom and law further evolved from the 10th century B.C. and the conquest of Canaan to the destruction of Jerusalem by the Romans in 70 A.D.

Scripture The sacred scripture of the Hebrew Bible, or Masorah, consists of 24 books. (The Christian Old Testament divides the same text into 39 books.) The *Torah*, or Law, was composed between the 10th and 5th centuries B.C. These five books—Genesis, Exodus, Leviticus, Numbers, and Deuteronomy—are also known by their Greek name, *Pentateuch*. The later history of Israel and the divided kingdom is told in two separate but overlapping traditions known as the Prophets (13th-6th centuries B.C.) and the Writings (11th-2nd centuries B.C.). The Hebrew Bible is also known by the Greek name *Septuagint* ("seventy"), a reference to the number of authors engaged in its translation from Hebrew to Greek in the 3rd century B.C. In addition to scripture, there is a rich ancient tradition of rabbinical commentary called the *Talmud*, a huge compilation of the Oral Law and the accepted authority for Orthodox Jews. First codified around 200 A.D., the Talmudic tradition continued through the centuries and constitutes not only commentary on the law (*Halakah*), but also stories from the Bible and parables, legends, etc. (*Haggadah*) illustrating religious principles.

Beliefs Central to Jewish belief is the idea of a single God—Yahweh—who made a covenant (i.e. an agreement or contract) with His chosen people that He would protect them and provide for them if they swore Him love and obedience. Yahweh shapes history (the end of which is the kingdom of God) and imposes His will upon mankind; He saves, and He judges. The people of *Israel* have a unique relationship with God affirmed on the one hand by His covenant, and on the other, by His law. While Yahweh the creator guides human destiny, the humanity of mankind is defined by the ability of individuals to make ethical choices in keeping with His law. The failure to act according to His law—that is, to know God—is sin, and a basic tenet of Jewish faith is that sin is a willful act; so, too, is turning, or returning, to God.

The book of Isaiah (8th century B.C.) brings to the fore a messianic tradition identifying a future Israel under a divine ruler descended from the house of David as a restoration of paradise and the attainment of salvation.

Practice Jews worship in synagogues in congregations led by a rabbi—a teacher or master. The Sabbath is observed from sunset Friday to sunset Saturday; worship consists of readings from scripture, prayer, and singing. The most important holidays in the Jewish calendar are Rosh Hashanah (New Year), Yom Kippur (Day of Atonement), Hanukah (Festival of Lights), and Pesach (Passover). (See Part I: " Holidays and Holy Days").

Schools and sects There are three main branches of modern Judaism. Orthodox Jews rigorously observe Jewish law, ritual and custom. Reform Judaism professes a more liberal interpretation of Jewish doctrine and ritual, and is especially prevalent in the United States. Conservative Judaism combines elements of doctrinal reform with more traditional observance. Hasidism is today a branch of Orthodox Judaism with origins in a mystical movement in 18th-century Poland that stressed prayer over studying the Torah. Hasidim are very strict observers of the Jewish religious laws.

History The Bible recounts the history of the Jewish people from the creation, through the flood and the covenant of the rainbow, the patriarchs Abraham, Isaac and Jacob, and the story of the tribe of Israel in Egypt. The foundation of Jewish faith began with the exodus from Egypt, and the transmission of the Ten Commandments (the Decalogue) from God to his people through Moses, probably sometime between 1450 and 1290 B.C. The people of Israel conquered and settled in Canaan—the promised land—and were ruled by a succession of judges. The monarchical period under Samuel and David dates to the 11th and 10th centuries B.C. Israel and Judah continued under separate rulers until the fall of Israel in 722 B.C. Judah was conquered by Babylonians, and the Temple of David in Jerusalem was destroyed in 586 B.C. at the start of the Babylonian captivity, which also marks the start of the Jewish Diaspora, or dispersal. Exile lasted until 538 b.c., and the Second Temple was dedicated in 516 B.C. Under Seleucid rule the Maccabees successfully resisted efforts to suppress Judaism (168-142 B.C.). Under Roman rule (63 B.C.-135 A.D.), there were several revolts, the first of which resulted in the destruction of the Second Temple (70 A.D.). It was at around this time that Christianity began to diverge sharply from its Jewish sectarian origins.

The early Middle Ages saw the rise of the Talmudic tradition. Following the rise of Islam, Judaism evolved into two distinct strains, the Sephardim, centered in Spain, and the Ashkenazim, found mainly in France and Germany. Organized persecution of European Jewry began with their expulsion from France (1306) and Spain (1492), and culminated in the Nazi regime in Germany's attempt to eradicate all Jews during the Holocaust (1933-45). The Jewish enlightenment (*Haskala*) in 18th-century Germany gave rise to Reform Judaism and Conservative Judaism (1845). The nationalistic Zionist movement, a reaction to extreme anti-Semitism, led eventually to the birth of the State of Israel in 1948. Though Israel is a secular republic, religious parties play an active role in politics.

Geography and numbers There are an estimated 15 million Jews in 134 countries, the overwhelming majority of whom live in the United States (5.8 million) and Israel (4.3 million). There are an estimated 2.4 million Jews in Europe.

▶ CHRISTIANITY

Origins Christianity is based on the acts and sayings of Jesus of Nazareth as related by his followers and apostles. Jesus was born a Jew in Bethlehem in about 4 B.C., but details of his life before about 26-28 A.D. are obscure. In his early 30s, Jesus was baptized by John the Baptist, whose ministry prophesied the coming judgment of God, and who recognized Jesus as the Messiah (Greek for the Christ, or anointed one). Jesus' ministry, chiefly among the poor and dispossessed, lasted only a few years before he was crucified by Roman authorities. According to Christian belief, Jesus rose from the dead three days after his crucifixion, and 40 days later he ascended to heaven to sit at the right hand of God.

Scripture The Bible consists of the Old Testament (the Hebrew Bible), originally written in Hebrew and Aramaic, and the New Testament (first written in Greek in the first century), which relates the life and teachings of Jesus and his early followers. A 3rd-century translation of the Bible into Latin is called the Vulgate. The central portion of the New Testament consists of the Four Gospels (each attributed to one of Christ's earliest followers: Matthew, Mark, Luke, and John). While each tells the story of Jesus' life and death, they differ in details, with Luke and John providing more stories and greater emphasis on Christ's divinity. The story of the spread of Christianity in the first century is told in the Acts of the Apostles and the epistles (letters) of St. Paul. The Roman Catholic canon also includes 15 books found in the Greek Septuagint but not in the Hebrew Bible. The Orthodox Church accepts four of these Apocryphal books; Protestants accept none.

Beliefs Christian belief is rooted in three basic ideas: incarnation—Christ was the human embodiment of God; atonement—mankind was reconciled to God through the agency of Christ; and the Trinity—the belief that the one God has three natures, God the Father, God the Son (Jesus), and God the Holy Spirit.

Practice Central to the practice of most Christians are the seven sacraments: baptism, confirmation, holy matrimony, holy orders, sacrament of the sick, reconciliation (confession), and the Eucharist, (or communion), the sacramental offering and consumption of bread and wine representing the body and blood of Christ. Christians are organized into congregations and worship in churches led by priests or ministers who administer the sacraments. Most denominations designate Sunday as the sabbath and the day for special observance and worship.

Schools and sects Christianity has three major branches: Eastern Orthodoxy, Roman Catholicism, and Protestantism. The division between Eastern Orthodoxy and Roman Catholicism came in 1054. In the sixteenth century, reform-minded priests broke with Rome and there emerged a number of distinct denominations known collectively as Protestantism.

The hierarchical authority of the Catholic Church starts with the Pope, and includes cardinals, bishops, and priests, all celibate men. In addition there are a number of Catholic lay and priestly orders for men and/or women.

The Eastern Orthodox Church embraces a number of national or regional churches. The laity are invested with more authority than are Catholics, and the bishop of Constantinople, titular head of the eastern church, is regarded as "first among equals."

Protestant denominations number in the hundreds. There is no single governing authority for all of them. (See Part II: "Religion in America" for a summary of the major sects).

History At the time of his death, Jesus had a small handful of followers among Jews. His teachings were not widely accepted among the larger Jewish community, however, and his disciples preached to non-Jewish gentiles throughout the Roman Empire. Jesus' teachings were gathered in a collection of books known as the Gospel, or New Testament. Christians were widely persecuted until the Emperor Constantine legalized the religion in 313; in 380 Christianity became the official religion of the Roman Empire. Christianity also reached northern Ethiopia.

Disputes over theological issues such as the nature of the Trinity and the person of Christ were resolved at a series of ecumenical councils. In 1054 the Eastern and Western churches split over differences of theology, politics, geography and language. The papacy in Rome acquired the nature of a civil authority and within the Western church ascetic, spiritual traditions competed with secular ones. In the sixteenth century, papal authority was challenged by such reform-minded priests as Martin Luther and John Calvin, abetted by England's King Henry VIII, who transferred authority over the church in England from the Pope to himself. Sectarian wars engulfed Europe for more than a century as Catholics and Protestants vied for temporal and spiritual power.

European explorers and colonists spread Christianity to the Americas, Asia and Africa. The Spanish and Portuguese brought Catholicism to Latin America, while North America became a haven for Protestant denominations from northern Europe. Since the mid-1800s, Protestant and Catholic evangelists have carried out energetic missionary programs to Africa and East Asia.

Geography and numbers Christianity is the most populous and most widespread religion in the world, with almost 2 billion adherents in 260 countries. Europe is home to more than 555 million Christians (76 percent of the region's population), but Latin America has proportionally the highest number of Christian adherents—93 percent of the population. There are more Christians in Africa (360 million, or 48 percent of the population) and Asia (303 million) than in North America (255 million).

▶ ISLAM

Origins The precepts of Islam were revealed through Mohammed, the last of a line of prophets including Abraham, Moses and Jesus. Mohammed was born about 570 at Mecca (in western Saudi Arabia) and died in 632 in the nearby city of Medina.

Scripture The Koran ("recitation") consists of 114 chapters. The text is the infallible word of God as revealed to Mohammed and transcribed by his followers over the course of 23 years.

Beliefs Islam is a monotheistic religion with explicit links to Judaism and Christianity. The Koran's narrative includes stories of Abraham and Isaac, and Moses and the Ten Commandments. Unlike Jews, who trace their descent from Abraham through Isaac, the son of Sarah, Muslims trace their descent through Ishmael, Abraham's son by Hagar. The Koran recounts the virgin birth of Jesus, but does not accept his divinity.

The word Islam comes from the Arabic root *s-l-m*, meaning "peace" and "submission," and a hallmark of Islam is obedience to God.

Practice A Muslim's relations with God are regulated by the Five Pillars of Islam: the Shahadah, or profession of faith—"There is no God but God, and Mohammed is his prophet;" public and collective prayer five times daily; charity to the poor; fasting during the holy month of Ramadan; and pilgrimage to Mecca, the most holy place in the Muslim world, at least once in one's lifetime.

Islam has strict dietary laws and prohibitions against promiscuity, theft, gambling and lying. Muslims worship in mosques led by imams. The principal weekly worship is on Friday at midday.

Schools and sects The overwhelming majority of Muslims are Sunnites, or "traditionalists" (83 percent, or 934 million people). Shi'ites, or "partisans," represent another 16 percent (180 million) and smaller sects make up the rest. The Shi'ite/Sunnite schism reflects differences about who should have succeeded Mohammed. Shi'ites follow somewhat different rites than Sunnites, and recognize additional holy days and places.

History Mohammed was born in Arabia in about 570 A.D. Raised by his uncle, at the age of 25 he became a trader, and later married his employer, the widow Khadija. In 610, an angel descended on Mohammed and ordered him to proclaim the word of God. Rebuked in Mecca, in 622 he was invited to Medina to help bring order to the city. He accepted on the condition that the citizens worship Allah—the one God—and accept the precepts of Islam. This move—the *hegira*—is the year from which the Muslim calendar dates. Eight years later Mohammed returned to Mecca, and by the time of his death in 632, most Arabs were Muslims.

Under a succession of secular and theocratic caliphates, Islam swept east and west from Arabia. Muslims reached the Indus River in 713, and their advance in France was only stopped in 733 at the Battle of Tours; Muslims remained in Spain until 1492. Islamic armies captured the Byzantine capital of Constantinople in 1453, and controlled much of southeastern Europe until the 19th century. In the east, Muslims swept through India at the end of the 10th century and reached the East Indies in the 15th century.

The arts, architecture and technology flourished in the golden age of Islam and Islamic learning and culture was responsible for the transmission of much of classical philosophy and science to the West.

From the 18th to 20th centuries, traditionally Islamic countries came under Western cultural and political influence. In the 20th century, some traditionally Islamic countries like Turkey opted for a secular state; others such as Saudi Arabia and Iran came under strict fundamentalist rule.

Geography and numbers With 1.3 billion adherents in 184 countries, Islam is the second largest religion in the world. It is the dominant religion throughout the Middle East, North Africa, Central Asia, Afghanistan, Pakistan, and Indonesia, the country with the largest number of adherents (172 million people). There are 104 million Muslims in India—11 percent of that country's population.

▶ HINDUISM

Origins Hinduism is a complex of polytheistic religion and philosophy that evolved from Vedism, an ancient Indian religion of Indo-European origin dating from the second millennium B.C.

Scripture Different Hindu sects rely on different holy texts, but common to the majority are the Vedic texts called the *Upanishads*. The *Svetasvatara Upanishad* describes Siva, the creator, preserver and destroyer of the universe. Sources for Hindu mythology include the *Mahabharata*, *Ramayana* (concerning Rama, the incarnation of the great god Vishnu), and the *Puaranas*. The *Bhagavad Gita* ("Lord's song," a part of the *Mahabharata*), is a dialogue between Krishna (another incarnation of the god Vishnu) and Prince Arjuna in which are described the three paths to union with God.

Beliefs Hinduism is rooted in the belief that individuals should connect their selves (Atman) with Brahman, or Godhead, the spiritual source of the tangible universe. Hindus also believe in reincarnation—*samsara*—one's subsequent status being dependent on one's actions (*karma*) and duties (*dharma*) in this life. The cycle of reincarnation is broken when one attains liberation (moksha) from the finite world through self-discovery—the union of self with the Godhead, or *Atman-Brahman*. There are four paths to union with Brahman: *jnana yoga*, based on knowledge; *bhakti yoga*, based on service to God; *karma yoga*, based on work for God (as opposed to oneself); and *raja yoga*, based on psychophysical exercise.

Hinduism has three primary theistic traditions revolving around the cults of anthropomorphic gods. Vishnu is a loving god incarnated as Krishna; Siva is a god at once protective and destructive; and Brahma is creator. Saktism is a form of worship dedicated to the female consorts of Vishnu and Siva.

Hindus have a deep respect for all living things; the most revered animal is the cow.

Practice Hindu worship is largely an individual and family matter. Hindu temples are devoted to a particular god or group of gods. Worship in temples or before domestic shrines includes prayers and offerings to an image of the god. Such rituals are intended to bring the worshipper and the god closer together.

Hindu pilgrimage sites include seven sacred cities, among others, where thousands or even millions of Hindus worship at annual festivals. Some of the most famous temples are on the banks of the Ganges River, which is sacred to Hindus, in northern India. Important festival days include Dipavali, "festival of lights," sacred to Lakshmi, goddess of prosperity; holi, a spring festival; and Dashara, a harvest festival.

Individuals follow a code of moral and religious conduct called *dharma*. Traditional Hinduism observes complex societal divisions into four primary (and thousands of subsidiary) castes defined by occupation and social standing: *brahmins:* leaders, philosophers, artists and their families; *kshatriyas:* princes, soldiers and administrators; *vaishyas:* merchants and landowners; and *shudras,* or laborers. Beyond the caste system are untouchables, or outcasts. India's modern constitution outlawed the caste system.

Schools and sects Hinduism comprises myriad religious cults and various schools of philosophy. The principle of religious toleration is reflected in the Hindu belief that Christianity, Islam and other religions offer alternative paths to the same goal. Among the more prominent modes of belief are *yoga* and *tantrism*, both of which evolved in both Hinduism and Buddhism, and *bhakti*. Tantrism emphasizes meditation and ritual involving mystical diagrams (mandalas) and chants (mantras) as a means to enlightenment. *Yoga* emphasizes an eightfold path to enlightenment through physical and mental training. *Bhakti* focuses on the primacy of love for a deity.

History Hinduism is the oldest of the world's great religions. Originating in India, it spread to Nepal and southeast Asia. The oldest Hindu writings are actually Vedic texts brought by Aryan invaders in the second millennium B.C. To the Vedic concept of future life, Hinduism attached the ideas of karma, reincarnation and ultimately release from the cycle of life, death and rebirth. Following the rise of rival religions such as Buddhism and Jainism in the 6th century B.C., ritual sacrifice to Vedic deities overseen by priests gave way to polytheistic worship intended to unite the worshipper with the god worshipped.

The classical period of Hinduism dates from the 6th century B.C. to the 10th century A.D., when the major theistic sects emerged and many of the classic works of Hinduism were composed, including the epic *Mahabharata* and *Ramayana* and a variety of works that discuss the duties of caste, advice to rulers, the attainment of pleasure and the attainment of liberation, or moksha. Hindu princes successfully resisted Muslim encroachment from the West until the 10th century. The Muslim ascendancy was coupled with the rise of *bhakti*, a devotional Hinduism that stresses love for the deity, and the adoption of vernacular languages for worship rather than Sanskrit.

Since the 18th century there have been several movements to strip Hinduism of its polytheistic practices, and in this century, great emphasis has been laid on Hindu prescriptions for non-violence and social equality, especially as practiced by the founder of modern India, Mahatma Gandhi.

Geography and numbers Hinduism has an estimated 793 million adherents worldwide. With deep roots in India, and lacking a missionary tradition, it is found almost nowhere outside of India and neighboring countries except in expatriate Indian communities.

▶**BUDDHISM**

Origins Buddhism was established by the followers of Siddhartha Gautama (ca. 563-483 B.C.), who was born into a kshatriya caste Hindu family in present-day Nepal. At the age of 29, he left his wife and young son in search of enlightenment. This he attained, according to tradition, while sitting under a bodhi tree near Patna. After 49 days of rapture, and withstanding the temptations of the devil Mara, Buddha—the enlightened one—inspired an order of monks and went forth to preach his philosophy of enlightenment for 45 years before passing into nirvana, in which "ideas and consciousness cease to be."

Scripture Of primary importance to all Buddhists is the *Tipitaka* ("Three baskets"), a record of the Buddha's teachings set down set down by Buddha's early followers after his death. These tell the story of his life (Buddha), his laws (Dharma) for personal conduct, and the guidelines for the monastic order (Sangha). There is a large body of other writings peculiar to individual sects and schools. The Buddhist canon continued to evolve over many centuries.

Beliefs Buddhists share with Hinduism a belief in the cycle of reincarnation and that this cycle could be broken. Buddha's teachings are predicated on the Four Noble Truths. Life is impermanent and fundamentally produces suffering, or *dukkha*, perpetuated due to the endless cycle of life, death, and rebirth. This suffering results from the pursuit of mortal desires. Desire can be overcome by attaining *nirvana. Nirvana* can be reached by adhering to the Eightfold Path. This path, or Middle Way, consists of right belief, thought, speech, action, livelihood, effort, mindfulness and concentration. These are the backbone of Buddhist ethics.

Practice A hallmark of Buddhist practice is the monastic order, to which monks withdraw from the everyday world and live austere lives of meditation either for a few years or for a lifetime. Mendicants also live on alms contributed by lay Buddhists. In certain sects, adolescents spend time in a monastery as part of a rite of passage into adulthood.

Buddhist temples are primarily for individual meditation, and collective rituals play a smaller part in the life of a Buddhist than in the lives of Jews, Christians and Muslims, or even of Hindus.

Schools and sects There are three main sects in Buddhism. Theravada (or Hinayana) Buddhism, which predominates today in Sri Lanka, Myanmar and Thailand, adheres most closely to the tenets of the early Buddhist sects. In this tradition, attainment of nirvana for oneself is the goal. Mahayana Buddhism, which became the larger sect, spread along the Silk Road from India to China and East Asia. This includes the worship of Buddha and Buddhist saints (*bodhisattvas*). Stressing compassion for others, *boddhisatvas*—literally "wisdom beings"—withhold themselves from attaining nirvana in order to help others attain enlightenment. In Zen Buddhism, a sect of Mahayana, adherents strive for enlightenment through mental conditioning and meditation. The third sect of Tantric Buddhism (Vajrayana), most common in Tibet and Mongolia, attempts to identify the initiate with a visualized deity. The Tantric canon includes esoteric texts, and meditation engages both the mind and the senses with the use of *mantras* (chants), *mudras* (hand gestures) and *mandalas* (visible icons of the universe). The spiritual and temporal leader of Tibetan Buddhists is the Dalai Lama.

History Following Buddha's death, his *sutras* (sermons) and *vinaya* (regulations) were written down by his disciples. Originally, Buddhist mendicants taught for nine months and held retreats during the monsoon. These retreats led to the establishment of monasteries and the rise of differing interpretations of Buddha's teaching. The Mahayana school more easily absorbs (and is absorbed by) different cultures. It received its greatest impetus in India from the Buddhist emperor Ashoka (272-232 B.C.), who sent missionaries to Ceylon, Southeast Asia and China, from where it was carried to Korea and Japan in the 6th century A.D.

The 7th century saw the rise of Zen Buddhism in China and Japan, and of Tantric Buddhism in Tibet. Chinese Buddhism reached its height in the 9th century during the T'ang Dynasty, when it was partially suppressed. Buddhism flourished in Japan until the 19th century, when Shintoism gained imperial favor.

Buddhism lost its influence in India beginning in the 8th century, partly through absorption of its ideas into Hinduism, and partly because of the rise of Islam. By the 13th century, Buddhism was all but extinct there.

Geography and numbers There are an estimated 350 million people in 92 countries who adhere to Buddhist beliefs and practices. Mahayana Buddhists account for about 53 percent (185 million) of all Buddhists, mostly in Japan, Korea and China; Theravada Buddhists account for 35 percent (124 million), in Southeast Asia and Sri Lanka. Lamaist Buddhists account for about 6 percent (21 million) in Tibet and Mongolia. Buddhist practice in Tibet is under threat from the Chinese government.

▶ OTHER ORGANIZED RELIGIONS

Baha'i Founded by Baha'Ullah ("glory of God") in Iran in 1844, Baha'i teaches that the revealed religions of the world are in agreement and that the respective prophet-founders of each revealed the will of God for a particular time and place in history. There are approximately 6 million members of the Baha'i faith; the center of the Baha'i faith is in Haifa, Israel. A major temple in Wilmette, Illinois, attracts many visitors.

Chinese folk religions Chinese folk religions consist of a blend of ancient ancestor worship with elements of Buddhism, Confucianism, and Taoism. Taoism is a philosophy or religion based on the teachings of Lao-tzu, another great teacher of Confucian times. The vast majority of the world's 215 to 220 million adherents of Chinese folk religions live in China; the remainder live in scattered Chinese settlements around the world.

Confucianism As much a code of ethical conduct as a religion, Confucianism takes its name from the 6th-century B.C. scholar and civil servant Kung Fu-Tzu (Confucius), whose *Analects* prescribe the proper conduct for life. His impact on China has been enormous, and at times his cult has attained the status of a quasi-official religion. There are about 5 million Confucianists in the world; most of them live in South Korea.

Jainism Jainism is a polytheistic religion established in India by Vardhamana in the 6th century B.C. Its primary features are a belief in the perfection of the soul and in non-injury to living creatures. Almost all of the world's 5 million Jainists live in India.

New Religion This term applies to a variety of more or less organized religious systems that have grown up, primarily in East Asia, since the turn of the century. These religions are characterized by a synthesis of indigenous folk religion with various major Asian traditions (Hinduism, Buddhism, Confucianism and/or Taoism) overlaid with modern Western philosophy. There are more than 100 million people professing adherence to these religions, the majority of them in the Philippines, Indonesia, and Japan.

Parsiism This religion has its roots in Zoroastrianism, an ancient Iranian religion whose central focus is the struggle between good and evil. Its monotheistic tendencies are thought to have influenced the development of Judaism and Christianity. Parsis emigrated to India between the 10th and 15th centuries, and prospered as merchants, especially in Bombay.

Shintoism Evolved from ancient Japanese religious traditions, Shintoism became a state religion under the Meijis in the 19th century. Although some sacred Shinto (literally "way of the gods") texts date from the 8th century, none is considered authoritative. There are three strains of Shinto practice: State Shinto, Shrine Shinto, and Folk Shinto.

Sikhism The Sikh religion was founded by Guru Nanak in the early 16th century. A hybrid of Hindu and Islamic beliefs, it advocates a search for eternal truth and, while believing in reincarnation, rejects the notion of divine incarnation. It was led by a succession of ten gurus, the last of whom declared himself the last human guru. Sikhs now follow the sacred text known as Guru Granth Singh, or Collection of Sacred Wisdom. There are almost 19 million Sikhs in the world; almost all of them live in the Punjab region of India.

▶ NONRELIGIOUS AND ATHEISTS

An estimated 887 million people (15 percent of the world's population) profess no religion, are agnostic or are indifferent to religion. Another 222 million people (4 percent) are declared atheists who do not believe in God. More than three-quarters (852 million) of these nonreligious and atheists live in China, where religious observance is sharply curtailed by the government. An estimated 12 percent of people in Europe are nonreligious, compared with 9.8 percent in Oceania, 7.2 percent in North America, and 3.3 percent in Latin America.

▶ CHRONOLOGY OF WORLD RELIGION
B.C.
3000 Earliest elements of Hinduism develop in India.
c. 2500 Egyptian pyramids at Giza completed.
c. 1500 Aryan peoples invade India; bring additional elements of Hinduism.
c. 1290 Moses leads Israelites out of Egypt.
1010-922 Reigns of Hebrew kings David and Solomon. A great temple built at Jerusalem.
740 Hebrew prophet Isaiah flourishes.
628 Traditional birth date of Zoroaster, religious teacher in Persia. Followers today are Parsees in India.
587 Babylonians destroy Hebrew temple at Jerusalem and take many Hebrews as slaves. Fifty years later, Hebrews are freed and begin to rebuild temple.
560 Birth of Siddartha Gautama in northern India; later known as Buddha. Dies c. 480. His teachings, on which Buddhism is based, gain many followers in India, later spread to Southeast Asia.
551 Birth of Chinese teacher Confucius. Dies c. 479.
200 Mahayana Buddhism begins to spread in China and Japan.
4 Birth of Jesus Christ. The Western calendar dates from the supposed year of his birth.
A.D. 30 Death and resurrection of Jesus Christ.
66-70 Jewish revolt against Romans ends in destruction of second temple and scattering of Jews (a.k.a. The First Diaspora).
175 Apostles' Creed, a brief statement of Christian beliefs, formulated.
303-12 In final organized program of persecution, Romans kill estimated 500,000 Christians.

313   The emperor Constantine decrees toleration for Christianity in Roman Empire. In 325, he calls synod of Nicaea, which formulates Nicene Creed. By end of 300s, Christianity is official religion of empire.
354   Birth of St. Augustine, influential Christian teacher, in North Africa. Dies 430.
451   Council of Chalcedon (fourth ecumenical council) formulates long-held Christian understanding of Christ, the union in one person of two distinct natures, human and divine.
570   Muhammad, founder of Islam, born in Mecca (now in Saudi Arabia). Dies in 632 in nearby city of Medina.
600+   Tantrism, a Hindu school, grows up, emphasizing special rituals as means of enlightenment; uses mystical diagrams (mandalas) and chants (mantras).
650+   Islam enters India, gains many converts.
700+   Development in China of Zen, a school of Buddhism, which later attracted particular attention in the modern Western world.
711-715   Muslim Arabs settle in Spain.
800   Roman Empire revived in the West with the coronation of Charlemagne as emperor on Christmas Day, in St. Peter's in Rome.
988   Christianity reaches Russia through missionaries from eastern churches.
1054   Eastern (or Orthodox) and Western (or Roman) churches go separate ways after disputes about doctrine and authority.
1096   Christians in Europe go on first Crusade to take Holy Land from Muslims. Seven other major Crusades pursued between 1100 and 1300. Christian warriors temporarily occupy Jerusalem and other cities, but soon lose them again to Muslims.
1216   Pope Innocent III approves formation of Franciscans and Dominicans.
1227   Thomas Aquinas, great Christian theologian, born in Italy.
1300+   Bhakti, a Hindu sect, develops emphasizing primacy of love for a deity and using love between humans as illustration; rejects caste, ritual, and creeds, and emphasizes need for sincerity.
1309   The papacy moves from Rome to Avignon, France, where it remains until 1377 ("The Babylonian Captivity of the Church").
1377   English theologian and religious reformer John Wycliffe accused of heresy by Pope Gregory XI for attacks on worldliness of the church.
1378-1417   The Great Western Schism, during which first two, then three, claimants sought recognition as pope.
1415   Excommunication and execution of Czech religious leader Jan Hus, who protested sale of indulgences and other papal excesses, sets off Hussite Wars, which end with Compactata of Prague.
1453   Ottoman Turks (Muslims) conquer capital of Eastern Roman Empire, Constantinople. Turks push westward into Europe.
1454   Johannes Gutenberg prints first Bible with moveable type.
1469   Birth of Nanak, founder of Sikhism, in Punjab region of India.
1492   Muslims overthrown in Spain; Spanish Inquisition begins.
1517   Martin Luther, a German priest, posts 95 theses on cathedral door, questioning church teachings. Luther refuses to recant; is excommunicated from Catholic church. With cooperation of north German princes, he forms new Protestant churches. This begins Reformation, which ultimately divides European Christianity into two warring camps.

1534   King Henry VIII of England denies power of pope over church in England and establishes Church of England responsible to monarch. New church gradually adopts Protestant beliefs but maintains many practices of earlier Catholic era.
1536   John Calvin, a young French scholar, publishes *Institutes of the Christian Religion*, and becomes second major leader of Protestant Christianity; helping to create Presbyterian and other Reformed churches.
1540   Ignatius Loyola, a Spaniard, establishes the Jesuits (Society of Jesus) with papal approval. This order becomes powerful instrument of Catholic church in disputes with Protestants, in missionary efforts around world, and in education.
1545-63   Council of Trent makes major reforms in Catholic church and defines disagreements with Protestants. Its work begins Catholic Reformation, or Counter-Reformation.
1598   In the Edict of Nantes, Henry IV proclaims "peaceful coexistence" of Catholics and Calvinists in France. Revoked in 1685 by Louis XIV.
1618-48   Thirty Years War, caused in part by Protestant-Catholic hatreds, decimates central Europe. Calvinist leaders in England overthrow monarchy and execute king in civil war (1642-49). Monarchy is restored in 1660.
1620   Pilgrims, a small group of English Calvinists, establish colony at Plymouth in North America to escape persecution in England.
1683   Muslim Turks defeated near Vienna, Austria, in their last attempt to establish foothold in western Europe.
1734   The Great Awakening, a religious revival, sweeps New England, begun by prominent Massachusetts preacher Jonathan Edwards. English evangelist George Whitefield tours American colonies beginning in 1738, preaching to outdoor gatherings.
1738   Christian conversion experienced by brothers John and Charles Wesley in England. They begin evangelical activities, leading to development of independent Methodist church.
1789   U.S. Constitution guarantees separation of church and state.
1792   Second Awakening sweeps new United States, lasting more than 20 years. Revivals in Kentucky in 1800 result in formation of new denominations, ancestors of Disciples of Christ, Churches of Christ, and Christian churches.
1830   American Joseph Smith has religious visions that lead him to organize the Church of Jesus Christ of the Latter-Day Saints (Mormons).
1844   Baha'i established in Iran.
1869-79   Vatican Council I, convened by Pope Pius IX, declares that teachings of pope in matters of faith and morals are infallible.
1875   Mary Baker Eddy publishes *Science and Health with Key to the Scriptures* in Boston; it becomes basis of Church of Christ, Scientist.
1900   First documented modern Pentecostal experience—worshipers speak in unknown tongues during prayer meeting in Kansas. Within 20 years, Pentecostal churches form major new Christian denomination.
1935-45   Nazi government in Germany carries out destruction of estimated six million European Jews. This event known as the Holocaust.
1945-46   Compulsory adherence to Shintoism ended in Japan; Emperor Hirohito disavows his divinity to Japanese people.
1947   U.N. approves creation of the new state of Israel in Middle East for settlement by Jews.
1948   World Council of Churches established at huge assembly in Amsterdam. This ecumenical

organization supported by many Protestant, Anglican, and Orthodox denominations. Headquarters are in Geneva, Switzerland.
1962-65   Vatican Council II, convened by Pope John XXIII, announces many liberalizing changes in Roman Catholic liturgy and practice; supports cautious involvement in ecumenical discussions with other Christians.

1978   Karol Josef Wojtyla, archbishop of Krakow, Poland, elected to papacy as John Paul II, the first non-Italian pope since Hadrian VI in 1523.
1988   For the first time, a woman is elected to a bishopric in U.S. Episcopal church.
1991   Religious freedom granted in U.S.S.R.

The Books of the Bible

The first five books of the Bible are known as the Torah ("to teach" in Hebrew) in the Jewish faith. Roman Catholic canon recognizes additional "deuterocanonical" books, as well as additional parts of other books. Together, they are known as the Apocrypha. They are listed in *italics* following the Old Testament.

Old Testament	Job	Zephaniah	*Second Maccabees*	Philippians
Genesis	Psalms	Haggai	*First Esdras*	Colossians
Exodus	Proverbs	Zechariah	*The Prayer of Manasseh*	First Thessalonians
Leviticus	Ecclesiastes	Malachi	*Psalm 151*	Second
Numbers	Song of Solomon	***The Apocrypha***	*Third Maccabees*	Thessalonians
Deuteronomy	Isaiah	*Tobit*	*Second Esdras*	First Timothy
Joshua	Jeremiah	*Judith*	*Fourth Maccabees*	Second Timothy
Judges	Lamentations	*Additions to Esther*	**New Testament**	Titus
Ruth	Ezekiel	*Wisdom of Solomon*	Matthew	Philemon
First Samuel	Daniel	*Ecclesisasticus (Sirach)*	Mark	Hebrews
Second Samuel	Hosea	*Baruch*	Luke	James
First Kings	Joel	*The Letter of Jeremiah*	John	First Peter
Second Kings	Amos	*The Prayer of Azariah*	Acts	Second Peter
First Chronicles	Obadiah	*and the Song of the*	Romans	First John
Second Chronicles	Jonah	*Three Young Men*	First Corinthians	Second John
Ezra	Micah	*Susanna*	Second Corinthians	Third John
Nehemiah	Nahum	*Bel and the Dragon*	Galatians	Jude
Esther	Habakuk	*First Maccabees*	Ephesians	Revelation

The Ten Commandments

Significant differences exist among the Protestant, Catholic, and Jewish versions of the Ten Commandments, both in wording and in numbering. Even within the King James Bible, the Commandments are presented twice, first in Exodus and later in Deuteronomy. The Exodus version (Exodus 20: 2-17) is the most familiar, and is reprinted here. Numbers refer to commandment numbers, not Biblical verses.

1 I am the Lord thy God, which have brought thee out of the land of Egypt, out of the house of bondage.

2 Thou shalt have no other gods before me.
Thou shalt not make unto thee any graven image, or any likeness of any thing that is in heaven above, or that is in the earth beneath, or that is in the water under the earth:
Thou shalt not bow down thyself to them, nor serve them: for I the Lord thy God am a jealous God, visiting the iniquity of the fathers upon the children unto the third and fourth generation of them that hate me;
And showing mercy unto thousands of them that love me and keep my commandments.

3 Thou shalt not take the name of the Lord thy God in vain; for the Lord will not hold him guiltless that taketh his name in vain.

4 Remember the sabbath day, to keep it holy.
Six days shalt thou labor, and do all thy work:
But the seventh day is the sabbath of the Lord thy God: in it thou shalt not do any work, thou, nor thy son, nor thy daughter, thy manservant, nor thy maidservant, nor thy cattle, nor thy stranger that is within thy gates:
For in six days the Lord made heaven and earth, the sea, and all that in them is, and rested the seventh day: wherefore the Lord blessed the sabbath day, and hallowed it.

5 Honor thy father and thy mother: that thy days may be long upon the land which the Lord thy God giveth thee.

6 Thou shalt not kill.

7 Thou shalt not commit adultery.

8 Thou shalt not steal.

9 Thou shalt not bear false witness against thy neighbor.

10 Thou shalt not covet thy neighbor's house, thou shalt not covet thy neighbor's wife, nor his manservant, nor his maidservant, nor his ox, nor his ass, nor any thing that is thy neighbor's.

The Koran

The sacred book of Islam was revealed by God to the prophet Mohammed over his life at Mecca and Medina. Its various versions were reconciled in the 7th century by Uthman, the third Caliph. It is divided into 114 chapters of verses, with chapters appearing in size order from longest to shortest, rather than in chronological order.

The Seven Deadly Sins

1 Pride
2 Envy
3 Anger
4 Sloth
5 Greed
6 Gluttony
7 Lust

Major Languages of the World

There are approximately 100 languages designated as "official" by national governments around the world. These run the gamut from Chinese and English—with hundreds of millions of speakers worldwide—to local languages whose speakers may number only in the tens of thousands.

Chinese   This is the mother tongue of more than one billion people. Although spoken dialects of Chinese are not mutually intelligible, they share the same writing system—Chinese characters, or *hanzi*—and two people can speak different dialects and still be able to read each other's writing. This is possible because *hanzi* characters represent words independently of their pronunciation (just as Arabic numerals can represent the words for numbers in any language), and also because written Chinese has diverged less from a common standard than have the various spoken dialects.

Based on the dialect spoken in northern China around Beijing, Mandarin is an official language in China, Taiwan, and Singapore, where it is the primary language of more than 800 million people. The other principal dialects are Cantonese (or *Yue*), spoken in southern China and Hong Kong; *Wu*, spoken in Shanghai and nearby provinces in eastern China; *Min*, found in southeastern China, Taiwan and Malaysia; and *Xiang*, *Kan*, and *Hakka*, all spoken in southeastern China and Taiwan. Chinese is also an official language of the U.N.

English   Although there are fewer native speakers of English than of Chinese, English is by far the most commonly found language outside of China. Some estimates suggest that as many as one-third of the world's people can speak English—which means four billion people can't. From the island kingdom in northwest Europe, the language spread throughout the British Empire to the Americas, Africa, India and Oceania. Today, 58 countries and the U.N. designate English as an official language, and these countries account for more than 460 million speakers. The main concentrations of English speakers are the United States (258 million), United Kingdom (57 million), Philippines (37 million), India (31 million), Canada (18 million), Australia (17 million) and Nigeria (16 million).

Hindi   Spoken by an estimated 430 million people in India alone, Hindi is one of that country's two official languages, the other being English. There are significant numbers (relative to the local population) of Hindi speakers in Trinidad, Guyana, South Africa, Mauritius and other countries with large Indian expatriate communities.

Spanish   Carried by Spanish conquistadors from Europe to the Americas and Asia, Spanish is now an official language of 21 nations, territories and colonies in which it is the mother tongue of more than 300 million people. By far the greatest number of Spanish speakers live in Mexico (85 million), followed by Colombia (35 million), Argentina (34 million), Spain (29 million) and Venezuela (21 million). Although the United States does not recognize an official language per se, the U.S. ranks sixth in the number of people who consider Spanish a first language with 20 million. Spanish is also an official language of the U.N.

Arabic   Twenty-five countries around the world have adopted Arabic as an official language, more than any other language but English and French. These 25 countries alone represent nearly 200 million Arabic speakers. Arabic is also the language of the Koran—and thus, for many Muslims, of God. For this reason, it is the second language of many Indians, Indonesians, Iranians and other inhabitants of largely Muslim countries. Arabic is also an official language of the U.N.

Portuguese   The transmission of Portuguese paralleled that of Spanish, but today it is used as an official language in only seven countries outside of Portugal (where there are a scant 10 million speakers): five in Africa, one in Latin America, and one in Macau, a special administrative region of China. Of the 168 million native Portuguese speakers worldwide, the vast majority of them live in Brazil (154 million). In Angola, there are just over 4 million.

Russian   There are an estimated 130 million people who claim Russian as their mother tongue in the two countries where it is an official language, Russia (127 million) and Belarus (3 million). There are still significant numbers of people claiming Russian as a first language in the former republics of the Soviet Union, especially Ukraine (17 million) and Kazakhstan (8 million), Uzbekistan (2.5 million), and Kyrgyzstan and Moldova (1 million each). Russian is an official language of the U.N.

Japanese   The official language of only one country, Japanese is spoken by more than 125 million. The most significant Japanese-speaking minorities outside of Japan are found in Brazil (600,000 people) and the United States (490,000). Modern Japanese employs four writing systems: *kanji* (adapted from the Chinese *hanzi*), *hiragana*, *katakana* and *romaji*.

Bengali   The official language of Bangladesh, where it is the mother tongue of more than 120 million people, Bengali is also the first language of an estimated 72 million Indians, chiefly the state of West Bengal.

German   An official language of six European countries (Germany, Austria, Switzerland, Luxembourg, Liechtenstein, and Belgium), German is spoken by more than 117 million in those countries. There are also significant German-speaking minorities in Eastern Europe (500,000 in Poland and 350,000 in Russia), Brazil (870,000) and the United States (1.8 million).

French   Although there are fewer speakers of French than of other languages—fewer than 100 million people claim it is as a first language worldwide—its significance stems from the fact that it is an official language of 32 countries—more than any other language except English—and of the U.N. (These countries account for 88 million native speakers of French.) The most important in terms of numbers are France (55 million), Canada (7 million), Ivory Coast (Côte d'Ivoire) (5 million). Democratic Republic of the Congo, Belgium, Cameroon, Niger, Madagascar and Switzerland also have more than 1 million each claiming French as a first language.

Malay   Variants and dialects of Malay are used as an official language in Indonesia (where it is known as *Bahasa Indonesia*), Malaysia (*Bahasa Nalaysia*), and Singapore and Brunei (*Bahasa Melayu*). Although these four countries have a combined population of more than 220 million people, Malay is not the mother tongue of the majority in any of them. A mere 33 million people claim Malay as their first language. In Indonesia, Malay runs a distant third to Javanese (78 million speakers) and Sundanese (31 million).

World Energy

The world's primary energy sources in 1999 were crude oil and natural gas liquids, natural gas, coal, and electricity from hydroelectric and nuclear power. In order to compare the energy produced by different sources, energy is measured in British thermal units (Btu) . Energy production and consumption worldwide increased drastically during the 1980s, but their growth has slowed somewhat in the 1990s. Petroleum production and consumption continues to increase, but whereas petroleum once constituted almost half the world's energy, it now accounts for less than 40 percent. Natural gas and nuclear power have made up most of the difference.

Petroleum World production of petroleum (which includes crude oil and natural gas plant liquids) was 72.7 million barrels per day in 1999, down slightly from 73.6 million in 1998. The United States, Russia, and Saudi Arabia are the world's largest producers of petroleum; the three countries together account for nearly one-third of the world's petroleum production.

Consumption of petroleum has kept pace with the increase in production. But the United States is by far the biggest consumer. The U.S. consumed 19.5 million barrels of petroleum per day, more than one-fourth the world's total. That's more than double the 7.7 million barrels the U.S. produces each day, forcing America to import 11.8 million barrels of petroleum each day. No other country consumes even half as much oil as the United States. Japan was second in world consumption with 5.5 million barrels (most of which it imported), followed by China (4.3 million barrels), Germany (2.8 million), and Russia (2.4 million). Saudi Arabia, the world's largest petroleum producer, consumed a mere 1.3 million barrels per day, or 1.7 percent of the world total.

World Energy Production by Region, 1980–99

Region	1980	1985	1990	1995	1998	1999
Crude oil (thousand barrels/day)	**59,599**	**53,981**	**60,566**	**62,335**	**66,921**	**65,870**
North America	11,968	13,187	11,461	10,982	11,303	10,694
Central & South America	3,647	3,602	4,318	5,481	6,435	6,293
Western Europe	2,531	3,847	4,125	5,878	6,275	6,349
Eastern Europe & Former USSR	12,038	11,909	11,216	7,017	7,066	7,416
Middle East	18,442	10,307	16,545	18,979	21,178	20,502
Africa	6,125	5,371	6,432	6,954	7,340	7,296
Far East & Oceania	4,848	5,758	6,468	7,043	7,324	7,319
Dry Natural Gas (trillon cubic ft)	**53.19**	**62.17**	**73.57**	**77.96**	**82.79**	**84.69**
North America	23.17	20.45	22.56	25.16	26.02	26.17
Central & South America	1.20	1.76	2.01	2.58	3.12	3.32
Western Europe	7.32	7.22	7.24	8.80	9.64	9.90
Eastern Europe & Former USSR	17.04	24.50	30.13	25.93	25.16	25.41
Middle East	1.33	2.38	3.72	4.99	6.60	6.81
Africa	0.69	1.86	2.46	3.01	3.70	4.10
Far East & Oceania	2.44	4.00	5.44	7.50	8.55	8.98
Coal (million short tons)	**4,196.13**	**4,869.40**	**5,386.18**	**5,161.04**	**5,006.20**	**4,736.62**
North America	877.37	955.77	1,113.01	1,125.80	1,213.00	1,190.01
Central & South America	16.66	21.31	32.86	39.07	50.75	50.25
Western Europe	845.33	928.34	872.60	555.04	522.18	494.87
Eastern Europe & Former USSR	1,282.36	1,331.37	1,339.45	892.80	774.07	765.29
Middle East	0.99	1.38	1.21	1.25	1.02	1.07
Africa	137.91	197.48	201.77	236.06	254.83	255.81
Far East & Oceania	1,035.51	1,433.75	1,825.27	2,311.03	2,190.35	1,979.32
Hydroelectric power (bil. kWh)	**1,735.2**	**1,973.1**	**2,167.4**	**2,474.7**	**2,566.9**	**2,607.2**
North America	546.9	611.1	606.6	667.6	671.8	678.3
Central & South America	199.3	285.7	364.8	471.5	521.4	528.5
Western Europe	431.7	453.2	453.4	503.7	519.8	523.1
Eastern Europe & Former USSR	211.3	230.7	253.6	271.8	261.3	261.7
Middle East	9.6	9.5	12.5	15.4	15.8	16.0
Africa	60.2	46.7	55.5	57.3	63.1	65.6
Far East & Oceania	276.2	336.4	420.9	487.3	513.7	534.1
Nuclear power (billion kWh)	**684.4**	**1,425.7**	**1,905.1**	**2,206.0**	**2,315.3**	**2,395.9**
North America	287.0	440.8	649.0	774.4	750.2	807.5
Central & South America	2.2	8.4	9.0	9.5	10.3	10.5
Western Europe	219.2	572.5	707.5	793.0	841.0	850.2
Eastern Europe & Former USSR	83.2	200.3	251.3	224.3	239.3	245.7
Middle East	0.0	0.0	0.0	0.0	0.0	0.0
Africa	0.0	5.5	8.4	11.3	13.6	12.8
Far East & Oceania	92.7	198.2	279.9	393.6	460.8	469.1

1. Preliminary. **Source:** Energy Information Administration, *International Energy Annual, 1999* (2001).

Dry natural gas World production of dry natural gas increased 15 percent between 1990 and 1999, when it reached an all-time high of 85 trillion cubic feet. Russia is the world's largest producer of natural gas (20.83 trillion cubic feet, or 25 percent of the world total in 1999), followed by the United States (18.62 trillion cubic feet, or 22 percent of world production in 1999. The United States was responsible for 26 percent of world consumption, while Russia accounted for 17 percent.

Coal World coal production decreased in 1999 to 4.7 billion short tons, its lowest level in more than a decade. China continues to lead the world in production, with more than 1.1 billion short tons per year. The United States, which had been the world leader until 1987, produced just under 1.1 billion short tons. Together, the U.S. and China account for close to half the world's coal production. They also accounted for the bulk of coal consumption in 1999. China consumed 1.1 billion short tons (23 percent of world consumption) and the U.S. consumed 1.0 million short tons (22 percent).

Hydroelectric power Generation of hydroelectric power worldwide rose 20 percent between

Top 10 Producers of Primary Energy, by Source, 1999

Crude oil[1]	(thousand barrels per day)	Natural gas plant liquids[2]	(thousand barrels per day)	Dry natural gas	(trillion cubic feet)
1. Saudi Arabia	7,833	1. United States	1,850	1. Russia	20.83
2. Russia	6,079	2. Saudi Arabia	666	2. United States	18.62
3. United States	5,881	3. Canada	653	3. Canada	6.26
4. Iran	3,557	4. Mexico	439	4. United Kingdom	3.49
5. China	3,195	5. United Kingdom	238	5. Algeria	2.90
6. Norway	3,018	6. Russia	231	6. Netherlands	2.65
7. Mexico	2,906	7. Algeria	190	7. Indonesia	2.34
8. Venezuela	2,826	8. Venezuela	170	8. Uzbekistan	1.96
9. United Kingdom	2,684	9. United Arab Emirates	160	9. Iran	1.87
10. Iraq	2,508	10. Norway	121	10. Norway	1.76

Coal[3]	(million short tons)	Hydroelectric power[4,5]	(billion kWh)	Nuclear electric power[5]	(billion kWh)
1. China	1,118.11	1. Canada	340.3	1. United States	728.2
2. United States	1,099.12	2. Brazil	305.9	2. France	375.1
3. India	327.98	3. United States	305.6	3. Japan	308.7
4. Australia	320.59	4. China	222.8	4. Germany	161.0
5. Russia	276.31	5. Russia	157.9	5. Russia	110.9
6. South Africa	248.13	6. Norway	120.0	6. South Korea	97.9
7. Germany	226.12	7. Japan	85.0	7. United Kingdom	91.5
8. Poland	190.40	8. India	80.8	8. Canada	69.8
9. Ukraine	90.77	9. France	71.6	9. Ukraine	67.4
10. North Korea	85.45	10. Sweden	69.3	10. Sweden	66.6

Note: Preliminary. 1. Includes lease condensate. 2. Does not include China, for which data are unavailable. 3. Includes anthracite, subanthracite, bituminous, subbituminous, lignite, and brown coal. 4. Net generation; data consist of both utility and non-utility sources. Excludes generation from pumped storage. 5. Net generation; excludes energy consumed by the generating unit.
Source: U.S. Dept. of Energy, *International Energy Annual, 1999* (2001).

World Crude Oil Production, 1960–99 (million barrels per day)

Country	1960	1970	1980	1990	1995	1998	1999
Organization of Petroleum Exporting Countries (OPEC)[1]	8.70	23.30	26.61	23.20	26.00	28.77	27.58
Iran	1.07	3.83	1.66	3.09	3.64	3.63	3.56
Iraq	0.97	1.55	2.51	2.04	0.56	2.15	2.51
Kuwait[2]	1.69	2.99	1.66	1.18	2.06	2.08	1.90
Nigeria	0.02	1.08	2.06	1.81	1.99	2.15	2.13
Saudi Arabia	1.31	3.80	9.90	6.41	8.23	8.39	7.83
United Arab Emirates	0.00	0.78	1.71	2.12	2.23	2.34	2.17
Venezuela	2.85	3.71	2.17	2.14	2.75	3.17	2.83
Non-OPEC countries[2]	12.29	22.59	32.99	37.37	36.33	38.15	38.29
Canada	0.52	1.26	1.44	1.55	1.80	1.98	1.91
China	0.10	0.60	2.11	2.77	2.99	3.20	3.20
Mexico	0.27	0.49	1.94	2.55	2.62	3.07	2.91
Norway	0.00	0.00	0.53	1.70	2.77	3.02	3.02
Russia[3]	2.91	6.99	11.71	10.98	6.00	5.85	6.08
United Kingdom	(4)	(4)	1.62	1.82	2.49	2.62	2.68
United States	7.04	9.64	8.60	7.36	6.56	6.25	5.88
Total world	20.99	45.89	59.60	60.57	62.34	66.92	65.87

1. Includes other countries not shown separately. In addition to those listed separately, current OPEC members are: Algeria, Indonesia, Libya, and Qatar. 2. Includes about one-half of the production in the Neutral Zone between Kuwait and Saudi Arabia. 3. Figures for Russia before 1995 refer to the former Soviet Union. 4. Fewer than 5,000 barrels per day.
Source: U.S. Dept. of Energy, *International Energy Annual, 1999* (2001).

Leading Suppliers of U.S. Oil

The United States imports about half of the oil it consumes, or more than 10 million barrels a day. Since 1993, the U.S. has imported more of its oil from non-OPEC countries than from OPEC countries.

Country	U.S. imports, (barrels/day) 1990	2000[1]
Canada	934,000	1,686,000
Saudi Arabia	1,339,000	1,566,000
Venezuela	1,025,000	1,519,000
Mexico	755,000	1,359,000
Nigeria	800,000	887,000
Iraq	518,000	613,000
United Kingdom	189,000	330,000
Total OPEC countries	4,296,000	5,136,000
Non-OPEC countries	3,721,000	5,957,000
Total, all imports	**8,018,000**	**11,093,000**

1. Preliminary figures. **Source:** Energy Information Administration, *Annual Energy Review, 1999* (2001).

1990 and 1999 to a high of 2.6 trillion kilowatthours (kWh). Canada (340 billion kWh), the U.S. (306 billion kWh), and Brazil (306 billion kWh) together produced 37 percent of the worldwide total. They were also the three biggest users of hydroelectric power, together making up 37 percent of world consumption.

Nuclear electric power World generation of nuclear electric power nearly quadrupled between 1980 and 1999, from 684.4 billion to 2,395.9 billion kWh. In 1999, the U.S. alone produced more nuclear power (728.2 billion kWh) than the entire world total in 1980. France (375.1 billion kWh) and Japan (308.7 billion kWh) followed the U.S. in total nuclear production in 1999, as well as in the total number of reactors .

The Strategic Petroleum Reserve In an attempt to minimize the wild fluctuations in prices caused by the Arab oil embargoes of the 1970s, the U.S. in 1977 created the Strategic Petroleum Reserve, which permitted the storage of 580 million barrels of oil. The Reserve proved useful in preventing additional oil price hikes during the Iraqi invasion of Kuwait in 1990.

World Energy Consumption by Type and Region, 1986–99

Energy Type and Region	Consumption (quadrillion Btu)					
	1986	1990	1995	1997	1998	1999
Petroleum	**126.70**	**134.87**	**142.30**	**148.34**	**149.84**	**152.20**
North America	38.35	40.39	41.49	43.63	44.57	45.80
Central & South America	7.02	7.34	8.66	9.47	9.97	10.15
Western Europe	26.54	27.42	29.61	30.38	30.92	30.54
Eastern Europe & Former USSR	21.99	20.32	11.93	10.57	10.39	10.27
Middle East	6.25	7.08	8.55	8.81	9.09	9.27
Africa	3.67	4.17	4.77	5.04	5.08	5.20
Far East & Oceania	22.88	28.15	37.30	40.45	39.81	40.96
Dry Natural Gas	**62.37**	**74.51**	**80.23**	**83.82**	**84.50**	**86.89**
North America	19.80	22.73	26.17	26.84	26.23	26.77
Central & South America	1.86	2.20	2.80	3.17	3.39	3.53
Western Europe	9.08	10.12	12.88	13.84	14.28	14.99
Eastern Europe & Former USSR	23.22	28.51	23.31	22.49	22.47	22.66
Middle East	2.65	3.77	4.96	6.13	6.53	6.64
Africa	1.21	1.52	1.87	1.94	1.99	2.13
Far East & Oceania	4.55	5.67	8.24	9.42	9.61	10.16
Coal	**86.39**	**89.96**	**89.40**	**92.12**	**89.26**	**84.77**
North America	18.57	20.52	21.61	23.23	23.46	23.45
Central & South America	0.63	0.60	0.65	0.80	0.95	0.91
Western Europe	14.40	13.95	10.11	10.32	10.26	9.72
Eastern Europe & Former USSR	20.74	19.85	12.73	11.96	10.83	10.70
Middle East	0.13	0.15	0.23	0.28	0.29	0.29
Africa	4.01	2.98	3.41	3.81	3.72	3.62
Far East & Oceania	27.91	31.92	40.67	41.73	39.74	36.09
Hydroelectric power	**21.34**	**22.66**	**25.98**	**26.96**	**26.88**	**27.29**
North America	6.85	6.40	7.18	7.78	7.18	7.23
Central & South America	3.21	3.79	4.90	5.31	5.42	5.50
Western Europe	4.57	4.74	5.24	5.23	5.41	5.44
Eastern Europe & Former USSR	2.47	2.64	2.83	2.61	2.72	2.72
Middle East	0.09	0.13	0.16	0.16	0.16	0.17
Africa	0.51	0.58	0.60	0.67	0.66	0.68
Far East & Oceania	3.63	4.38	5.07	5.19	5.34	5.55
Nuclear electric power	**16.34**	**20.37**	**23.31**	**23.90**	**24.41**	**25.25**
North America	5.25	6.99	8.31	7.66	8.01	8.62
Central & South America	0.06	0.10	0.11	0.12	0.12	0.12
Western Europe	6.47	7.43	8.30	8.80	8.82	8.91
Eastern Europe & Former USSR	2.17	2.89	2.46	2.75	2.63	2.70
Middle East	N.A.	N.A.	N.A.	N.A.	N.A.	N.A.
Africa	0.09	0.09	0.11	0.13	0.14	0.13
Far East & Oceania	2.29	2.87	4.02	4.45	4.69	4.78
Geothermal, solar, and wind electric power	**0.37**	**1.72**	**2.24**	**2.47**	**2.63**	**2.83**
Total energy consumption	**313.48**	**346.18**	**365.60**	**379.77**	**379.69**	**381.88**

Source: Energy Information Administration, *International Energy Annual, 1999* (2001).

The reserve can also be used as an emergency supply of oil in case of a complete oil embargo. In 1985, the reserve held enough oil to provide a normal level of petroleum to the U.S. for 115 days in the absence of any other petroleum imports. With gasoline prices skyrocketing in the summer of 2000, Pres. Clinton released 30 million barrels from the reserve, which will be returned (and then some) in 2001-02. The move temporarily reduced oil prices, but reduced the reserve to 53 days of oil.

World Primary Energy Production By Source, 1980-99 (quadrillion Btu)

Source	1980	1985	1990	1995	1998	1999
Petroleum[1]	133.22	121.21	136.35	141.46	151.89	149.71
Natural gas	52.65	61.38	75.91	80.23	85.39	87.31
Coal	74.48	85.77	91.87	89.24	89.36	84.90
Hydroelectric power	18.05	20.56	22.57	25.71	26.68	27.10
Nuclear electric power	7.58	15.37	20.37	23.31	24.41	25.25
Geothermal, solar, and wind electric power	0.40	0.60	1.72	2.24	2.63	2.83
Total, all sources	286.38	304.89	351.04	364.70	382.85	380.05

Note: Totals may not add up due to independent rounding. 1. Includes natural gas plant liquids.
Source: Energy Information Administration, *International Energy Annual, 1999* (2001).

World Nuclear Power Generation, by Region and Country, 1980-99

Region and country	Generation (billion killowatthours)						Operable reactors 2000
	1980	1985	1990	1995	1998	1999	
North America	287.0	440.8	649.0	774.4	750.2	807.5	120
Canada	35.9	57.1	69.2	93.0	67.7	69.8	14
Mexico	0.0	0.0	2.8	8.0	8.8	9.5	2
United States	251.1	383.7	577.0	673.4	673.7	728.2	104
Central and South America	2.2	8.4	9.0	9.5	10.3	10.5	4
Argentina	2.2	5.4	7.0	7.1	7.1	6.7	2
Brazil	0.0	2.9	1.9	2.4	3.1	3.8	2
Western Europe	207.4	572.5	707.5	793.0	841.0	850.2	151
Belgium	11.9	32.7	40.6	39.3	43.9	46.6	7
Finland	6.6	18.0	18.3	18.3	20.8	21.8	4
France	63.4	211.2	298.4	358.4	368.6	375.1	59
Germany[1]	55.0	138.6	145.1	145.4	153.6	161.0	19
Italy	2.1	6.6	0.0	0.0	0.0	0.0	0
Netherlands	4.0	3.7	3.3	3.8	3.6	3.6	1
Slovenia[2]	0.0	4.0	4.4	4.5	5.0	4.5	1
Spain	5.2	28.0	51.6	52.7	56.0	55.9	9
Sweden	25.3	55.8	64.8	66.4	69.9	66.6	11
Switzerland	12.9	20.1	22.4	23.7	24.5	23.7	5
United Kingdom	32.3	53.8	58.7	80.6	95.1	91.5	35
Eastern Europe	90.7	200.3	251.3	224.3	239.3	245.7	68
Bulgaria	5.9	12.4	13.5	16.4	15.5	14.5	6
Former Czechoslovakia	4.3	11.9	23.4	N.A.	N.A.	N.A.	N.A.
Czech Republic	N.A.	N.A.	N.A.	11.6	12.5	12.7	5
Slovakia	N.A.	N.A.	N.A.	10.9	9.8	10.0	6
Hungary	0.0	6.1	13.0	13.3	13.3	13.4	4
Romania	N.A.	N.A.	N.A.	N.A.	4.9	4.8	1
Former USSR	69.3	170.0	201.3	N.A.	N.A.	N.A.	N.A.
Armenia	N.A.	N.A.	N.A.	0.0	1.4	2.1	1
Kazakhstan	N.A.	N.A.	N.A.	0.1	0.1	0.1	1
Lithuania	N.A.	N.A.	N.A.	10.6	12.9	9.9	2
Russia	N.A.	N.A.	N.A.	94.3	98.3	110.9	29
Ukraine	N.A.	N.A.	N.A.	67.0	70.6	67.4	13
Middle East	0.0	0.0	0.0	0.0	0.0	0.0	0
Africa	0.0	5.5	8.4	11.3	13.6	12.8	2
South Africa	0.0	5.5	8.4	11.3	13.6	12.8	2
Far East and Oceania	92.6	198.2	279.9	393.6	460.8	469.1	94
China	N.A.	N.A.	N.A.	12.4	13.5	14.1	3
India	2.7	4.7	5.6	6.5	10.6	11.5	14
Japan	78.7	149.7	192.2	276.7	315.7	308.7	53
Korea, South	3.3	15.8	50.2	63.7	85.2	97.9	16
Pakistan	0.1	0.3	0.4	0.5	0.4	0.1	2
Taiwan	7.8	27.8	31.6	33.9	35.4	36.9	6
World total[3]	684.4	1,425.7	1,905.1	2,206.0	2,315.3	2,395.9	437

Note: Net generation; does not include energy consumed by the generating unit. 1. Data before 1995 includes both the former East Germany and West Germany. 2. Data before 1995 refers to the former Yugoslavia. 3. Totals include other countries not shown separately.
Source: Energy Information Administration, *International Energy Annual, 1999* (2001) and International Atomic Energy Agency, *Nuclear Power Reactors in the World* (2001).

The Global Military Situation

As the 20th century drew to a close and the Cold War receded into history, the world continued on a course of demilitarization. According to the London-based International Institute for Strategic Studies (IISS), global defense spending fell to $808.5 billion in 1999—a tiny fraction lower than in 1998 but a full 35 percent lower than the $1.2 trillion spent in 1985.

The ranks of the world's armed forces also declined precipitously from mid-1980s levels. At the end of 1999, according to the IISS, active-duty military personnel totaled approximately 21.9 million worldwide, down more than 200,000 from the year before and more than 6 million (22 percent) from 1985 levels.

The worldwide totals, however, conceal notable regional differences and shifts in military priorities on the part of major powers. Strategic interventions on the part of the United States and NATO allies, concern over the spread of chemical, biological, and nuclear weapons development, anti-terrorist initiatives, and local conflicts all have yielded a redistribution of military resources.

After several consecutive years of decline, U.S. defense spending rose 1.2 percent in 1999 to $283.1 billion—still about $100 billion and 25 percent less than in 1985. The ranks of active-duty U.S. military personnel shrank by another 30,000 (2.1 percent) to 1.37 million in 1999—780,000 (36 percent) fewer than in 1985. Underlying these trends has been a shift away from expensive nuclear weapons systems and toward the so-called "Bottom Up Review" study of 1993, which said that the nation should maintain the capacity to fight conventional wars in two major theaters simultaneously. President George W. Bush, who advocated a modernization of defense forces, higher wages for military personnel, and a higher standard of readiness, called for larger increases in defense spending as a budget priority in the years to come.

Nuclear weapons aside, naval strength remains a cornerstone of U.S. military superiority. The nation's 370,700 Navy personnel and fleet of 126 "principal surface combatants" (surface ships with 1,000 tonnes of displacement and non-defensive weapon systems) far exceed those of any other nation. The largest area of new military investment, however, remains aviation, with airpower procurements expected to reach $62 billion in 2001.

Combat readiness was a contentious issue in the 2000 presidential campaign, after a government report in November 1999 rated two of the army's 10 divisions as unprepared for battle. Some experts doubted that the nation's armed forces could meet the objective of fighting two wars simultaneously, and candidate Bush blamed the Clinton-Gore administration for inadequate funding and lax command.

The European NATO nations, meanwhile, have made even deeper cuts in military spending. Despite the intervention in Kosovo, total NATO defense spending in 1999 (including new members Czech Republic, Hungary, and Poland) was down $10 billion (5.3 percent) from the year before. In the longer term, the European nations that now make up NATO cut their combined defense spending by 23 percent from 1985 ($226 billion) to 1999 ($174 billion).

Corresponding figures for the same period are difficult to estimate for Russia and the former Soviet Union, but the cutbacks are certainly even more drastic. In November 2000, Russian President Vladimir Putin announced that the nation would reduce its military personnel by another 600,000, or about 20%, over the next five years. At the same time, he appealed to the United States for a mutual reduction in active nuclear warheads to between 1,000 and 1,500 each.

In other regions of the world, political developments and ongoing security issues have held military commitments steady or given rise to expansion. In the Middle East and North Africa, where the Arab-Israeli peace process has proceeded in fits and starts, and where local conflicts have contributed to ongoing instability, total defense spending totaled $60.0 billion in 1999, on par with the previous year. The regional picture is somewhat brighter in the longer term, as slowdowns in arms purchasing have reduced aggregate military spending by some 28 percent ($24 billion) from 1985 to 1999. Active military personnel in the region was 450,000 less in 1999 than in 1985.

In Central and South Asia, nuclear testing by India and Pakistan have altered the strategic landscape, while insurgencies in Sri Lanka, Bangladesh, and and elsewhere have forced heavy militarization. In 1999, total defense spending in the region rose slightly to $21.7 billion. Active-duty personnel climbed to 2.65 million, up 37 percent from 1985.

In East Asia and Australasia, where regional strategic and defense policies are defined by the ongoing tensions between North and South Korea and between China and Taiwan, estimated military expenditures jumped 21 percent from 1985 ($112 billion) to 1999 ($135.2 billion). The latter figure represented a $7.7 billion increase from 1998.

Strategic Missile Forces and Nuclear Stockpiles in the Major Nuclear Powers, 2000

Country	ICBMs[1]	SLBMs/ SSBNs[2]	Estimated Total Deployed Strategic Nuclear Warheads
United States	550	432/18	7,200
Russia	756	324/19	5,900
China	20+	12/1	400
France	---	64/4	470
Great Britain	---	58/4	190
Total	1,326+	890/46	14,160

1. Intercontinental Ballistic Missiles. 2. Submarine-Launched Ballistic Missiles and nuclear-fueled ballistic-missile submarines.
Source: The Military Balance, 2000/2001, The International Institute for Strategic Studies; Center for Strategic and International Studies; Natural Resources Defense Council. 1998 Natural Resources Defense Council (Washington, D.C.). Reprinted by permission.

Defense Expenditures and Military Personnel, by Country, 1999

Country	Defense Expenditures			Military Personnel ('000s)	
	Total (millions)[1]	Per Capita[1]	Percent of GDP	Active	Reserve
North America					
Canada	$7,504	$257	1.2%	60.6	43.3
Mexico	4,289	42	0.9	178.8	300.0
United States	283,096	1,036	3.1	1,371.5	1,303.3
NATO Europe					
Belgium	3,445	341	1.4	41.8	152.1
Czech Republic	1,164	113	2.3	58.2	240.0
Denmark	2,682	510	1.6	24.3	81.2
France	37,893	640	2.7	317.3	419.0
Germany	31,117	379	1.6	332.8	344.7
Greece	5,206	489	5.0	165.6	291.0
Hungary	745	74	1.6	43.4	90.3
Italy	22,046	381	2.0	265.5	72.0
Netherlands	6,964	442	1.8	56.4	75.0
Norway	3,149	712	2.2	30.7	234.0
Poland	3,242	84	2.1	240.7	406.0
Portugal	2,280	231	2.2	49.7	210.9
Spain	7,263	185	1.3	186.5	447.9
Turkey	10,183	156	5.5	639.0	378.7
United Kingdom	36,876	628	2.6	212.4	254.3
Non-NATO Europe					
Albania	140	37	3.6	54.0	155.0
Armenia	159	42	8.6	53.4	300.0
Austria	1,664	205	0.8	40.5	100.7
Azerbaijan	203	28	4.4	69.9	575.7
Belarus	466	44	5.0	80.9	289.5
Bosnia	366	82	8.4	40.0	150.0
Bulgaria	392	47	3.3	80.8	303.0
Croatia	776	172	4.1	61.0	220.0
Cyprus	530	609	6.1	10.0	88.0
Finland	1,695	328	1.4	31.7	540.0
Ireland	745	202	0.9	11.5	14.8
Romania	607	27	1.8	207.0	470.0
Russia	56,800	380	5.1	1,004.1	2,400.0
Serbia-Montenegro	1,654	149	12.4	108.7	400.0
Slovakia	329	61	1.9	44.9	20.0
Slovenia	337	167	1.8	9.6	61.0
Sweden	5,245	588	2.3	53.1	570.0
Switzerland	3,108	439	1.3	27.7	384.9
Ukraine	1,437	29	2.9	311.4	1,000.0
Middle East and North Africa					
Algeria	3,086	104	6.6	122.0	150.0
Bahrain	411	706	7.7	11.0	N.A.
Egypt	2,988	48	3.4	450.0	254.0
Iran	5,711	91	6.2	545.6	350.0
Iraq	1,500	68	7.6	429.0	650.0
Israel	8,846	1,465	8.9	173.5	425.0
Jordan	588	117	7.7	104.0	35.0
Kuwait	3,275	1,440	11.1	15.3	23.7
Lebanon	563	132	3.4	67.9	N.A.
Libya	1,311	211	4.7	65.0	40.0
Morocco	1,761	59	5.0	196.3	150.0
Oman	1,631	737	10.9	43.5	N.A.
Qatar	1,468	2,156	15.4	11.8	N.A.
Saudi Arabia	21,876	1,099	15.5	162.5	20.0
Syria	989	60	5.6	316.0	396.0
Tunisia	348	37	1.7	35.0	N.A.
United Arab Emirates	3,187	1,203	6.2	64.5	N.A.
Yemen	429	24	6.7	66.3	40.0
Central and Southern Asia					
Afghanistan	265	11	14.9	400.0	N.A.
Bangladesh	667	5	1.9	137.0	N.A.

| Country | Defense Expenditures | | | Military Personnel ('000s) | |
	Total (millions)[1]	Per Capita[1]	Percent of GDP	Active	Reserve
India	14,991	15	3.4	1,173.0	528.4
Kazakhstan	504	34	3.5	65.8	N.A.
Pakistan	3,523	24	5.7	587.0	513.0
Sri Lanka	807	43	5.1	115.0	4.2
Uzbekistan	615	26	3.9	74.0	N.A.
East Asia and Australasia					
Australia	7,775	407	1.9	55.2	27.7
Brunei	402	1,240	6.7	5.0	0.7
Cambodia	176	17	5.1	139.0	N.A.
China	39,889	32	5.4	2,820.0	1,200.0
Indonesia	1,502	7	1.1	299.0	400.0
Japan	40,383	319	0.9	242.6	48.6
Korea, North	2,100	98	14.3	1,055.0	4,700.0
Korea, South	12,088	257	3.0	672.0	4,500.0
Malaysia	3,158	146	4.0	105.0	40.6
Myanmar	1,995	42	5.0	343.8	N.A.
New Zealand	824	215	1.6	9.5	6.3
Philippines	1,627	22	2.1	110.0	131.0
Singapore	4,696	1,174	5.6	73.0	275.0
Taiwan	14,964	687	5.2	376.0	1,657.5
Thailand	2,638	43	1.9	306.0	200.0
Vietnam	890	11	3.1	484.0	3,000.0
Caribbean and Central America					
Cuba	750	67	4.8	65.0	39.0
El Salvador	171	28	1.1	24.6	15.0
Guatemala	149	13	1.1	31.4	35.0
Haiti	50	7	1.3	N.A.	N.A.
Honduras	95	14	1.8	8.3	60.0
Panama	128	45	1.3	N.A.	N.A.
South America					
Argentina	5,418	148	1.9	70.5	375.0
Bolivia	149	18	1.7	32.5	N.A.
Brazil	15,978	98	2.7	291.0	1,115.0
Chile	2,694	181	4.0	93.0	50.0
Colombia	2,164	52	2.8	144.0	60.7
Ecuador	339	27	2.3	57.1	100.0
Paraguay	128	23	1.4	20.2	164.5
Peru	888	35	1.6	115.0	188.0
Uruguay	317	98	2.3	25.6	N.A.
Venezuela	1,329	56	1.5	56.0	8.0
Sub-Saharan Africa					
Angola	1,005	83	16.5	112.5	N.A.
Botswana	259	157	5.2	9.0	N.A.
Cameroon	154	10	1.5	13.1	N.A.
Congo	73	24	3.4	10.0	N.A.
Congo, Deomcratic Republic	411	9	7.8	55.9	N.A.
Eritrea	309	77	44.4	200.0	120.0
Ethiopia	444	8	7.1	325.5	N.A.
Gabon	135	92	2.1	4.7	N.A.
Ghana	121	6	1.2	7.0	N.A.
Kenya	327	11	3.1	24.2	N.A.
Nigeria	2,237	20	4.4	94.0	N.A.
Rwanda	135	20	6.2	47.0	N.A.
South Africa	1,755	44	1.3	70.0	88.0
Sudan	424	14	4.9	94.7	N.A.
Tanzania	141	4	1.7	34.0	80.0
Uganda	199	9	2.5	40.0	N.A.
Zimbabwe	418	35	6.1	39.0	N.A.
Total, World	**$808,546**	**$221**	**4.1%**	**21,875.9**	**36,342.6**

1. In constant (1999) U.S. dollars.
Source: *The Military Balance, 2000/2001,* The International Institute for Strategic Studies. Reprinted by permission.

In Central America, South America, and the Caribbean, several countries—notably Colombia and Mexico—faced a proliferation of armed opposition and organized crime during the 1990s. Overall defense spending for the region fell by $3.5 billion in 1999, but the total of $35.4 billion was still 54 percent more than in 1985.

►NUCLEAR WEAPONS AND DISARMAMENT

The demise of the Soviet Union and compliance with disarmament agreements have resulted in large-scale reductions in the global nuclear arsenal. Although the precise size of national nuclear stockpiles and number of deployment vehicles remain official secrets, treaty compliance protocols and estimates from a variety of sources provide some reliable figures for the major nuclear powers. The arsenals of more recent members of the nuclear-weapons "community," such as Israel, India, and Pakistan, are less known. By common estimates, the total number of nuclear warheads in the world declined by 100 percent in about 15 years—from approximately 70,000 in the mid-1980s to fewer than 35,000 in 2000.

Moreover, less than half of the world's warhead-stockpile is operational. The five major nuclear powers—the United States, Russia, China, France, and Great Britain—had a combined 14,100 deployed nuclear warheads in 2000. The U.S. accounted for a reported 7,200 of these, and Russia accounted for an estimated 5,900, down 4,300 from two years earlier.

The first years of the new century brought some progress and notable changes in the course of global nuclear disarmament. The destruction of stockpiles in Ukraine, Belarus, and Kazakhstan, mandated by treaty, was on target for completion by December 2001. The United States and Russia, meanwhile, began SALT III talks in 2000, shortly after approval by the Duma (Russian parliament) of SALT II. But the U.S. still had not approved SALT II, which would reduce the deployed missile stockpiles of both nations to 3,500 by 2007, and had rejected the Comprehensive Test Ban Treaty (CTBT), which would prohibit nuclear testing.

The direction of nuclear disarmament took a new turn in 2001 with the installation of the Bush administration. To protect against future attack by outlaw nuclear nations, Bush called for the development of a space-based national missile defense (NMD) system. China, Russia, and even European NATO allies expressed grave misgivings at the prospect, fearing that such an initiative could undermine international stability and risk starting a new arms race. Building NMD would violate the 1972 ABM treaty, the cornerstone of cold-war arms control, and Bush's outspoken support for it raised questions about his commitment to the spirit and goals of strategic disarmament talks.

Those fears were confirmed at the NATO summit in June 2001, at which Bush said that the U.S. was ready to move forward on NMD with or without the backing of allies and dismissed the ABM Treaty as a relic of the cold war. The U.S. position implied an abandonment of arms control negotiation with nonthreatening allies and called for a forward-looking approach to new dangers. NATO leaders urged him not to dismiss 30 years of progress for the sake of unproven technology, and to work with allies in seeking multilateral solutions.

►ARMS SALES SURGE

According to a report by the Congressional Research Service, international arms sales for the year 1999 rose to nearly $30.3 billion, the highest level since1996—but still well below the peaks reached after the Persian Gulf War in 1991-93.. The United States solidified its position as the largest arms dealer with more than a third of the world total. U.S. sales of $11.8 billion, up from $10.3 billion in 1998, were greater than those of all European nations combined.

Russia, the second-biggest dealer with $4.8 billion, almost doubled its 1998 total of $2.6 billion; nearly half of its 1999 sales came from a deal with China for fighter jets. China itself emerged as a major supplier, more than doubling its sales to $1.9 billion.

Developing nations remained the largest market for new weapons, accounting for about two thirds of the total. The countries of the Middle East—Saudi Arabia, the United Arab Emirates, Egypt, and Israel—were major consumers, but South Africa was the year's leading purchaser among developing nations, signing agreements for $3.3 billion in warships, submarines, and other goods.

CHILDREN AT WAR

A 2001 report by the London-based Coalition to Stop the Use of Child Soldiers found that more than half a million children under 18 are in government armies or guerrilla groups in more than 40 countries around the world, with 300,000 of them in actual combat. It said that children—small, agile, and relatively powerless—are "widely perceived to be a cheap and expendable commodity," and that lighter-weight weapons make it easier to arm them.

The dangers to children in war go beyond the battlefield. "While many children fight in the frontline, others are used as spies, messengers, sentries, porters, servants and sexual slaves," the report said. "Children are often used to lay and clear land mines or conditioned to commit atrocities even against their own families and communities."

At a news conference Ishmael Beah, 19, of Sierra Leone, told how he became a soldier. "I lost both my parents in the war," he said. "I had to kill or get killed."

In the last year, 80 countries including the United States have signed an international agreement barring children in armed conflict. But only five—Andorra, Bangladesh, Canada, Congo and Sri Lanka—have ratified the treaty.

Excerpted from the *New York Times*, June 14, 2001.

The Global Economy

(Note: for definitions of G.D.P., G.N.P., etc. see Part II, "The U.S. Economy")

The 1990s were a time of strong economic growth around much of the world. The efficient and rapid movement of capital around the globe and a surging increase in world trade led many economists to believe that an integrated global economy would be a reality in the near future.

From 1983 to 1995, world output grew steadily at about 3 percent. In 1996, however, it rose to 4.0 percent, driven in large part by rapid growth in developing nations such as China (10 percent

growth), Singapore and Malaysia (7-8 percent), and Chile (6 percent). The advanced economies (U.S., Japan, and Germany) grew at only 2 to 3 percent, but it was capital from these wealthy nations that fueled the rapid growth of the poorer ones, especially in Asia. The 1997 Asian financial crisis resulted when growth in these countries returned to normal rates, and investors and currency speculators withdrew rapidly. The growth rate for world output fell from 4.2 percent in 1997 to 2.8 percent in 1998, and the International Monetary Fund was forced to make enormous loans to keep these economies from collapse.

Since then, output has rebounded to a staggering 4.8 percent in 2000. The IMF projects more regular growth of 3.2 percent for 2001, and an optimistic 3.9 percent in 2002.

G.N.P. per Capita, by World Regions, 1999

Region	G.N.P. per Capita
South Asia	$440
Sub-Saharan Africa	490
East Asia and the Pacific	1,010
Middle East and North Africa	2,060
Eastern Europe and Central Asia	2,160
Latin America and the Caribbean	3,800
Western Europe, U.S. Japan, and other high-income areas	26,440

Source: The World Bank, *The World Bank Atlas 2001*.

Countries With Highest and Lowest G.N.P. per Capita, 1999 (in U.S. dollars)

Highest Country	G.N.P. per capita	Lowest Country	G.N.P. per capita
Luxembourg	$42,930	Ethiopia	$100
Switzerland	38,380	Burundi	120
Norway	33,470	Sierra Leone	130
Denmark	32,050	Guinea-Bissau	160
Japan	32,030	Malawi	180
United States	31,910	Niger	190
Iceland	29,540	Eritrea	200
Sweden	26,750	Chad	210
Germany	25,620	Nepal	220
Austria	25,430	Mozambique	220
Netherlands	25,140	Mali	240
Finland	24,730	Burkina Faso	240
Belgium	24,650	Rwanda	250
Hong Kong	24,570	Madagascar	250
France	24,170	Tanzania[1]	260
Singapore	24,150	Nigeria	260
United Kingdom	23,590	Cambodia	260
Ireland	21,470	São Tomé and Principe	270
Australia	20,950	Angola	270
Italy	20,170	Tajikistan	280
Canada	20,140	Laos	290
Israel	16,310	Central African Republic	290
Spain	14,800	Kyrgyzstan	300
New Zealand	13,990	Togo	310
Greece	12,110	Uganda	320

Note: Rankings based on countries reporting G.N.P. per capita to The World Bank. Does not include countries for which G.N.P. per capita has been estimated. 1. Mainland only.
Source: The World Bank, *The World Bank Atlas 2001*.

World G.N.P. per Capita, by Type of Economy, 1999

Nearly 75 percent of the world's 6 billion people live in areas where per capita GNP is less than $2,995 according to these World Bank statistics, while only 15 percent live in economies whose GNP per capita is over $9,266.

Type of Economy (Number of Economies)	Population	G.N.P. per Capita
High-income (50)	896,000,000	$26,440
Upper-middle (38)	571,000,000	4,870
Lower-middle (55)	2,093,000,000	1,200
Low-income (64)	2,417,000,000	420
Total (207)	5,978,000,000	5,020

Source: The World Bank, *The World Bank Atlas 2001*.

Change in World Economic Output, 1983-2001

Category	Annual percent change 1983-92	1995	2000	2001[1]
World Total	**3.4%**	**3.6%**	**4.8%**	**3.2%**
Advanced economies	3.3	2.7	4.1	1.9
United States	3.4	2.7	5.0	1.5
European Union	2.6	2.4	3.4	2.4
Japan	3.9	1.6	1.7	0.6
Other economies	4.7	5.0	5.9	2.9
Developing countries	4.7	6.1	5.8	5.0
Africa	2.0	2.9	3.0	4.2
Developing Asia	7.3	9.0	6.9	5.9
Middle East, Malta, and Turkey	3.4	4.3	5.4	2.9
Western Hemisphere	2.3	1.7	4.1	3.7
Countries in transition	-0.4	-1.5	5.8	4.0
Central & Eastern Europe	—	5.5	3.8	3.9
Commonwealth of Independent States and Mongolia	—	-5.5	7.1	4.1
Russia	—	-4.2	7.5	4.0

Note: Output is the value of production minus the cost of inputs by all businesses. 1. Projection. Source: International Monetary Fund, *World Economic Outlook*, May, 2001.

▶ **THE HIERARCHY OF NATIONS**

Most contemporary analyses of the global economy begin with the assumption that the nations of the world are divided into two basic categories, developed and developing. The developed ones are those with the highest G.N.P. figures, and are characterized by high per capita income, low rates of population growth and illiteracy, as well as having a low proportion of their labor force in agriculture and/or mining.

The wealthiest nations are at the center of the global economy and are responsible for promot-

ing international trade, for helping to finance development in the poorer countries, and for maintaining a stable economic world. They attempt to do this through several organizations including:

Group of Seven (G-7): a loosely knit group of the largest economic powers who meet once a year to discuss policy in what has become a well-publicized media event. In 1997 Russia was invited to join despite its serious economic problems, so the G-7 is now the G-8. **Members:** Canada, France, Germany, Italy, Japan, Russia, U.K., U.S.

Net Foreign Direct Investment in Developing Countries, 1990-99

| Region and country | Billions of U.S. dollars | | | | | |
	1990	1992	1995	1997	1998	1999
All developing countries	**$24.5**	**$46.1**	**$105.4**	**$163.4**	**$155.0**	**$185.4**
By region						
East Asia and the Pacific	$11.1	$22.2	$52.0	$64.3	$61.0	$56.0
Latin America and the Caribbean	8.2	14.6	30.7	61.6	57.9	90.4
Europe and Central Asia	1.1	4.6	17.0	22.3	20.9	26.5
Sub-Saharan Africa	0.8	1.5	3.5	5.2	4.8	8.0
South Asia	0.5	0.8	2.9	4.7	4.4	3.1
Middle East and North Africa	2.8	2.4	-0.7	5.4	5.9	1.5
Top 10 recipients						
China	$3.5	$11.2	$35.8	$44.2	$45.0	$38.8
Brazil	1.0	2.1	4.9	19.7	24.0	32.7
Argentina	1.8	4.0	4.8	6.6	5.7	23.9
Mexico	2.6	4.4	9.5	12.5	10.2	11.8
Korea	N.A	N.A	N.A	N.A	5.1	9.3
Chile	0.6	0.9	3.0	5.4	4.8	9.2
Poland	0.1	0.7	3.7	4.9	5.5	7.3
Thailand	2.4	2.1	2.1	3.7	6.8	6.2
Czech Republic	N.A	N.A	N.A	N.A	N.A	5.1
Russian Federation	N.A	N.A	N.A	N.A	N.A	3.3

Note: Developing countries includes countries in transition. Not every country shown was among the top 12 for each year shown.
Source: The World Bank, *Global Development Finance* (2001) and unpublished data.

Net Private Capital Flows to Developing Nations by Region and Nation, 1990-99 (billions of U.S. dollars)

Region and country	1990	1992	1994	1996	1998	1999
All developing countries	**$43.9**	**$98.3**	**$178.1**	**$275.9**	**$267.9**	**$293.4**
by Region						
East Asia and the Pacific	$19.4	$45.0	$87.4	$121.5	$67.2	$108.0
Latin America and the Caribbean	12.6	30.9	59.8	100.9	126.9	98.6
Europe and Central Asia	7.7	17.2	10.8	38.0	53.5	45.3
Sub-Saharan Africa	1.3	1.0	4.9	4.5	3.5	20.4
South Asia	2.2	3.3	9.2	9.0	7.6	13.0
Middle East and North Africa	0.7	0.7	6.1	1.9	9.2	8.3
12 Leading nations						
China	$8.1	$21.3	$44.4	$50.1	$42.6	$42.7
Argentina	-0.2	5.6	10.1	16.1	18.8	33.0
Mexico	8.3	9.2	20.7	25.2	23.1	25.1
Brazil	0.6	9.7	12.3	29.7	54.3	23.5
Chile	2.1	1.8	5.1	7.4	9.2	11.8
Poland	N.A	N.A	N.A	N.A	N.A	10.5
Korea, South	1.1	7.5	17.7	21.1	7.6	9.8
Turkey	1.8	4.4	1.6	8.0	1.6	8.1
Hungary	N.A	N.A	N.A	N.A	N.A	5.2
Russia	5.6	9.3	0.4	7.5	19.3	5.1
Philippines	N.A	N.A	N.A	N.A	N.A	5.0
Czech Republic	N.A	N.A	N.A	N.A	N.A	4.9
Top 12 countries as percentage of total	**85.3%**	**87.4%**	**78.7%**	**77.7%**	**72.7%**	**63.0%**

Note: Developing countries includes countries in transtition. Not every country shown was among the top 12 for each year shown.
Source: The World Bank, *World Bank Atlas (2001)* and unpublished data.

U.S. Merchandise Trade Partners, 2000 (millions of dollars)

Country	U.S. exports to	U.S. imports from	U.S. net balance of trade
TOTAL[1]	$772,210	$1,224,417	$-452,207
Belgium and Luxembourg	14,266	10,258	4,008
France	20,200	29,773	-9,573
Germany	28,923	58,501	-29,578
Italy	10,951	25,031	-14,080
Netherlands	21,717	9,624	12,093
United Kingdom	40,727	43,388	-2,661
Canada	178,987	233,678	-54,691
Japan	63,576	146,497	-82,921
Australia	12,189	6,422	5,767
Brazil	15,257	13,853	1,404
Mexico	111,171	136,811	-25,640
Venezuela	5,508	18,623	-13,115
China	16,138	100,021	-83,883
Hong Kong	14,510	11,455	3,055
South Korea	27,150	40,297	-13,147
Singapore	17,621	19,201	-1,580
Taiwan	23,833	40,507	-16,674

1. Includes other countries not shown separately. **Source:** U.S. Dept. of Commerce, *Survey of Current Business,* July, 2001.

Organization of Economic Cooperation and Development (OECD) HQ: 2 rue André Pascal, F-75775 Paris Cedex 16, France. OECD Washington Center, 2001 L St. NW, Washington D.C. 20036. **www.oecdwash.org.** Estab. 1961, ". . . to help member countries promote economic growth, employment, and improved standards of living through the coordination of policy (and) . . . to help promote the sound and harmonious development of the world economy and improve the lot of the developing countries, particularly the poorest." **Members (29):** Australia, Austria, Belgium, Canada, Czech Republic, Denmark, Finland, France, Germany, Greece, Hungary, Iceland, Ireland, Italy, Japan, Luxembourg, Mexico, Netherlands, New Zealand, Norway, Poland, Portugal, South Korea, Spain, Sweden, Switzerland, Turkey, UK, U.S.

The International Monetary Fund (I.M.F.) and The World Bank

Both of these organizations are specialized agencies of the United Nations (see the separate section on the UN below) charged with making loans to nations having trouble with debt (I.M.F.) or for long-term growth and development among poorer nations (World Bank).

I.M.F. Classification of Countries

Advanced economies (28): These include the seven largest countries by G.D.P., all the other

World's Leading Exporters and Importers in Merchandise Trade, 1999

Rank and country	Value (billions)	Share of world trade	Change in value, 1998-99	Rank and country	Value (billions)	Share of world trade	Change in value, 1998-99
EXPORTERS				**IMPORTERS**			
1. United States	$695.2	12.4%	2%	1. United States	$1,059.1	18.0%	12%
2. Germany	541.5	9.6	0	2. Germany	472.5	8.0	0
3. Japan	419.4	7.5	8	3. United Kingdom	320.3	5.4	2
4. France	300.4	5.3	-2	4. Japan	311.3	5.3	11
5. United Kingdom	269.0	4.8	-1	5. France	290.1	4.9	0
6. Canada	238.4	4.2	11	6. Canada	220.2	3.7	7
7. Italy	230.6	4.1	-6	7. Italy	216.9	3.7	-1
8. Netherlands	200.4	3.6	0	8. Netherlands	187.6	3.2	0
9. China	195.2	3.5	6	9. Hong Kong	180.7	3.1	-3
10. Belgium	176.3	3.1	-	10. China	165.8	2.8	18
11. Hong Kong	174.4	3.1	0	11. Belgium	160.9	2.7	-
12. South Korea	144.7	2.6	9	12. Mexico	148.7	2.5	14
13. Mexico	136.7	2.4	16	13. Spain	144.8	2.5	9
14. Taiwan	121.6	2.2	10	14. South Korea	119.8	2.0	28
15. Singapore	114.7	2.0	4	15. Singapore	111.1	1.9	9
16. Spain	110.1	2.0	1	16. Taiwan	110.7	1.9	5
17. Sweden	84.9	1.5	0	17. Switzerland	79.9	1.4	0
18. Malaysia	84.5	1.5	15	18. Australia	69.1	1.2	7
19. Switzerland	80.4	1.4	2	19. Austria	68.8	1.2	1
20. Russian Federation	74.3	1.3	0	20. Sweden	68.5	1.2	0
21. Ireland	70.4	1.3	9	21. Malaysia	65.0	1.1	11
22. Austria	63.5	1.1	1	22. Brazil	51.7	0.9	-15
23. Thailand	58.4	1.0	7	23. Thailand	50.3	0.9	17
24. Australia	56.1	1.0	0	24. Ireland	46.4	0.8	4
25. Saudi Arabia1	50.5	0.9	27	25. Poland	45.9	0.8	-2
26. Denmark	49.0	0.9	2	26. India	44.6	0.8	4
27. Indonesia	48.7	0.9	0	27. Denmark	44.3	0.8	-4
28. Brazil	48.0	0.9	-6	28. Russian Federation	41.1	0.7	-30
29. Norway	44.9	0.8	13	29. Turkey	40.4	0.7	-12
30. Finland	41.7	0.7	-3	30. Portugal	38.6	0.7	1
World Total[2]	**$5,625.0**	**100.0%**	**3%**	**World Total[2]**	**$5,881.0**	**100.0%**	**4%**

1. Estimate. 2. Includes significant re-exports or imports for re-export and other countries not shown separately.
Source: World Trade Organization, International Trade Statistics 2000 (2001). www.wto.org

members of the E.U., the four "tigers" of Asia (Singapore, South Korea, Hong Kong, and Taiwan), and Australia, New Zealand and Israel.

Countries in transition (28): These are almost all industrialized countries that are moving from a centrally planned economy to one based on free market principles. All of the former republics of the Soviet Union (Kazakhstan, Ukraine) the nations of central and eastern Europe (including Poland, the Czech Republic, and Estonia) and Mongolia are included.

Developing countries (127): These include the burgeoning economies of China, India, Brazil and Chile as well as the poorest nations of sub-Saharan Africa (Mozambique, Ethiopia, Niger, for example) and Asia (Bangladesh, Cambodia, Vietnam).

10 Largest U.S. Merchandise Imports and Exports, 1987-2000

Product Group	Volume (millions)			
	1987	1990	1999	2000
TOTAL TOP TEN EXPORTS	**$130,940**	**$213,249**	**$422,690**	**$473,256**
1. Electrical machinery and appliances	16,670	31,554	88,655	110,095
2. Motor vehicles	21,370	30,524	56,640	59,992
3. Office and ADP machines	19,945	27,766	48,604	57,595
4. Transportation equipment	17,917	32,346	52,742	43,399
5. Miscellaneous manufactured articles	10,303	20,903	32,206	35,538
6. General industrial machinery	8,573	16,032	30,729	34,455
7. Power generating machinery	10,311	15,885	32,380	34,345
8. Telecommunications equipment	5,656	9,901	27,709	32,980
9. Specialized machinery	9,676	15,737	26,120	32,529
10. Professional scientific instruments	8,381	12,601	26,905	32,326
TOTAL TOP TEN IMPORTS	**$217,548**	**$258,293**	**$585,212**	**$676,962**
1. Motor vehicles	72,585	73,017	146,202	161,682
2. Electrical machinery and appliances	23,747	33,601	88,592	108,813
3. Office and ADP machines	18,318	26,917	84,443	92,165
4. Telecommunications equipment	20,797	22,288	50,959	70,487
5. Apparel and clothing	20,495	25,533	56,413	64,296
6. Miscellaneous manufactured articles	19,467	25,028	51,313	56,718
7. General industrial machinery	11,403	14,484	31,447	34,709
8. Power generating machinery	10,650	14,591	31,533	33,815
9. Organic Chemicals	N.A.	N.A.	21,860	28,563
10. Nonmetallic minerals	N.A.	9,890	22,450	25,714

Note: In current U.S. dollars.   **Source:** U.S. Dept. of Commerce, International Trade Administration, *U.S. Foreign Trade Highlights 2000* (2001). www.ita.doc.gov/td/industry/otea/usfth/aggregate/HL00t22.txt

U.S. Exports and Imports in Services, by Type, 1986-99 (millions)

Category	1986	1990	1995	1998	1999
EXPORTS, TOTAL	**$77,545**	**$137,232**	**$203,768**	**$244,099**	**$254,665**
Travel	20,385	43,007	63,395	71,286	74,881
Passenger fares	5,582	15,298	18,909	20,098	19,776
Other transportation	15,438	22,042	26,081	25,604	27,033
Royalties and license fees	8,113	16,634	30,289	36,197	36,467
Other private services[1]	28,027	40,251	65,094	90,914	96,508
Education	3,495	5,126	7,515	9,037	9,572
Financial services	3,301	4,417	7,029	11,273	13,925
Insurance, net	1,385	230	1,296	2,189	2,295
Telecommunications	1,827	2,735	3,228	5,538	4,460
Business, professional, and technical services	4,813	7,752	16,078	22,175	24,368
IMPORTS, TOTAL	**$64,731**	**$98,210**	**$128,781**	**$167,607**	**$174,825**
Travel	25,913	37,349	44,916	56,509	59,351
Passenger fares	6,505	10,531	14,663	19,971	21,405
Other transportation	17,766	24,966	27,034	30,363	34,137
Royalties and license fees	1,401	3,135	6,919	11,713	13,275
Other private services[1]	13,146	22,229	35,249	49,051	46,657
Education	433	658	1,125	1,591	1,840
Financial services	1,769	2,475	2,472	3,561	3,574
Insurance, net	2,200	1,910	5,360	9,080	4,078
Telecommunications	3,253	5,583	7,305	7,687	6,766
Business, professional, and technical services	1,303	2,093	4,822	6,869	7,430

1. Includes other services not shown separately.   **Source:** U.S. Bureau of Economic Analysis. *Survey of Current Business*, October, 2000.

Hourly Compensation Costs in U.S. Dollars For Production Workers, Selected Countries, 1975-2000

Country	1975	1980	1985	1990	1995	1999	2000
Australia	$5.62	$8.47	$8.20	$13.07	$15.27	$15.66	$14.15
Austria	4.51	8.88	7.58	17.75	25.32	21.85	19.46
Belgium	6.41	13.11	8.97	19.17	27.62	23.92	21.11
Canada	5.96	8.67	10.95	15.95	16.10	15.65	16.16
Denmark	6.28	10.83	8.13	18.04	24.07	22.96	20.44
Finland	4.61	8.24	8.16	21.03	24.10	21.33	19.50
France	4.52	8.94	7.52	15.49	20.01	17.98	16.38
Germany[1]	6.29	12.21	9.50	21.81	30.26	25.64	22.99
Greece	1.69	3.73	3.66	6.76	9.17	—	—
Hong Kong	1.76	1.51	1.73	3.20	4.82	5.44	5.53
Ireland	3.05	6.03	5.99	11.81	13.78	13.61	12.50
Israel	2.25	3.79	4.06	8.55	10.54	11.91	12.88
Italy	4.67	8.15	7.63	17.45	16.22	16.60	14.66
Japan	3.00	5.52	6.34	12.80	23.82	20.89	22.00
Korea, South	0.32	0.96	1.23	3.71	7.29	7.05	8.13
Luxembourg	6.50	12.03	7.81	16.74	22.62	18.65	16.69
Mexico	1.47	2.21	1.59	1.58	1.51	2.09	2.46
Netherlands	6.58	12.06	8.75	18.06	24.12	21.30	19.08
New Zealand	3.15	5.22	4.38	8.17	9.91	9.14	8.13
Norway	6.77	11.59	10.37	21.47	24.38	23.91	22.05
Portugal	1.58	2.06	1.53	3.77	5.37	5.35	4.75
Singapore	.84	1.49	2.47	3.78	7.33	7.13	7.42
Spain	2.53	5.89	4.66	11.38	12.88	12.11	10.85
Sri Lanka	0.28	0.22	0.28	0.35	0.48	0.46	—
Sweden	7.18	12.51	9.66	20.93	21.44	21.60	20.14
Switzerland	6.09	11.09	9.66	20.86	29.30	23.56	21.24
Taiwan	0.40	1.00	1.50	3.93	5.94	5.62	5.98
United Kingdom	3.37	7.56	6.27	12.70	13.67	16.48	15.88
United States	$6.36	$9.87	$13.01	$14.91	$17.19	$19.11	$19.86

Note: Hourly compensation includes wages, premiums, bonuses, vacation, holidays and other leave, insurance, and benefit plans. 1. Prior to 1991, data for Germany were for West Germany. Source: U.S. Bureau of Labor Statistics, *International Comparisons of Hourly Compensation Costs for Production Workers in Manufacturing*, September, 2001. http://www.bls.gov/news.release/ichcc.t02.htm.

▶ INTERNATIONAL FINANCE–BASIC CONCEPTS

Exchange rates Because countries have their own currencies, trade between them also involves exchanging or trading currencies. The *exchange rate* between currencies represents the ratio at which they can be exchanged or the price of one currency in terms of the other. For example, if the exchange rate between the British pound and the U.S. dollar is $1.50, then one British pound can be purchased at that price.

The exchange rate for almost all world currencies is now determined by the market. The exchange rate of a currency rises or appreciates when the demand for it rises and/or the supply falls. This may happen because foreign buyers want to buy more of a nation's goods or because consumers within the country decide to buy fewer imports. It may also happen because the country reduces its money supply. Finally, the central banks of countries can manipulate their exchange rates slightly by buying and selling their own and other currencies (see also Part II: "The Federal Reserve").

The gold standard Before World War I, exchange rates for world currencies were fixed, artificially, by tying them to a certain amount of gold—$32, for example, might equal one ounce of gold. Central banks would then buy and sell gold in order to equalize supply and demand for the currencies and maintain the fixed exchange rates. For this reason, the central banks maintained enormous gold stockpiles, like the one the U.S.

had at Fort Knox. People therefore referred to currencies as being "backed by gold." Long-term changes in trading relationships and in the demand for various currencies eventually made the fixed exchange rates of the gold standard impossible to support. In 1944, the Bretton Woods agreement established the U.S. dollar as the world standard, but the U.S. still backed its dollars with gold and used gold to settle its debts. After 1973, the U.S. abandoned that role, and most of the world's exchange rates were set by the market.

Balance of payments The balance of payments account is the list of transactions between a country and the rest of the world. This account has three parts: *the current account:* a record of exports and imports of goods (e.g. oil, clothing) and services (e.g. tourism); *the capital account:* a record of exports and imports of assets such as bank loans and corporate stock purchases; and *the official-reserves account:* a record of a country's sales and purchases of official reserve assets at the central bank.

Balance of trade When a country imports goods from another country worth more than the value of its exports to it, there is said to be a deficit in the balance of trade between the countries. Changes in exchange rates tend to equalize the supply and demand for currencies and the balance of trade; in the above case, the exchange rate for the first country's currency should fall relative to the second country's, reducing imports by making them more expensive and encouraging

U.S. International Trade Balance (millions of U.S. dollars) 1965–2000

Year	Exports		Imports		Balance		Total
	Goods[1]	Services[2]	Goods[1]	Services[2]	Goods[1]	Services[2]	
1965	$ 26,461	$ 8,824	$ 21,510	$ 9,111	$ 4,951	$ -287	$ 4,664
1970	42,469	14,171	39,866	14,520	2,603	-349	2,254
1975	107,088	25,497	98,185	21,996	8,903	3,501	12,404
1980	224,250	47,584	249,750	41,491	-25,500	6,093	-19,407
1985	215,915	73,155	338,088	72,862	-122,173	294	-121,880
1990	389,307	147,922	498,337	120,021	-109,030	27,901	-81,129
1995	575,845	219,802	749,574	145,964	-173,729	73,838	-99,891
1999	684,553	272,800	1,029,987	189,204	-345,434	83,596	-261,838
2000	772,210	293,492	1,224,417	217,024	-452,207	76,468	-375,739

Note: The balance is equal to exports minus imports. 1. Adjusted, excluding military. 2. Includes some military goods.
Source: U.S. Bureau of Economic Analysis, Foreign Trade Division, *U.S. International Transactions, 2000*. www.bea.doc.gov.

exports by making them cheaper. But this equalization may take a long time to occur since consumers and producers in the two countries must change their behavior. And central banks may want to slow the pace at which exchange rates adjust to slow the effects on trading sectors within their economies.

The balance of trade is an important issue because it indicates something about how a nation's economy is changing and, ultimately, about its competitiveness vis-à-vis other countries. A rising balance of trade deficit indicates that an economy is not able to sell its goods abroad and that consumers are favoring imports over domestically produced goods.

Over the last five years, as the economy has grown increasingly robust, the U.S. *trade deficit* has continued to widen, climbing from $19.4 billion in 1990 to $164 billion in 1998. The entire U.S. trade deficit is in the manufactured goods sector; the U.S. runs a small surplus in the services sector. U.S. exports of goods have not kept up with imports in part because the strength of the dollar makes American goods more expensive for foreign nations to buy, while people in the U.S. have more money to spend on cheaper imports.

▶ GLOBAL CAPITAL MOVEMENT

The current dynamic interaction among these very disparate economies—aided greatly by the technological revolution—has set in motion an unprecedented global movement of capital from the wealthiest nations to developing ones. Because holders of capital always seek greater returns on their investments, they will put their money in economies that show potential growth; if they own or run corporations, they will look for ways to reduce the costs of manufacturing, especially labor costs, so they realize a greater profit. By investing in foreign companies or by establishing their businesses in foreign nations, the power of capital can rapidly transform the economies of poorer nations while rearranging the patterns of daily life for millions.

The increase in the total amount of private capital going overseas (*net private capital flows*) from the U.S., Japan, and the E.U. nations to developing countries has exploded from $43.9 billion in 1990 to $201.5 billion in 1995, and an estimated $299 billion in 1997. Over 80 percent of it came in two categories: foreign direct investment and portfolio investment.

Foreign Direct Investment (FDI) is simply investment by private companies of one nation in the territory of another nation. The investment can be in an existing enterprise of the host nation or the building of new facilities for the investing foreign company (which would then be known as a *multinational enterprise*). The amount of money flowing from the wealthy nations to the developing ones in this way increased from $24.5 billion in 1990 to $155 billion in 1998. East Asian nations received almost half of the total ($61 billion). China alone received $45 billion.

According to the World Bank, foreign direct investment "provides an important channel for global integration" while bringing technological knowledge and equipment to the host countries, and infrastructure that has been sorely lacking.

Portfolio Investment is investing in the stocks and bonds of foreign nations. In 1990 only $5.5 billion was invested in the markets of developing nations, about 12 percent of total private capital flows. By 1996, $91.8 billion (38 percent) was so invested. In the U.S. alone the number of mutual funds investing in stocks and bonds of emerging nations grew from 3 in 1990 to over 70 in 1997. The Asian financial collapse of 1997-98 curtailed this growth quickly, as stock markets in Asia plunged by as much as 50 percent, followed by strong declines in Latin American markets.

▶ INTERNATIONAL TRADE

After rising by more than 10 percent in 1997, global trade fell back to 3.5 percent growth in 1998, according to the World Trade Organization. The continuing economic slump in Asia was responsible for most of the contraction. Exports of merchandise and commercial services amounted to $6.5 trillion in 1998, down about 2 percent from 1997 levels, but still up from the numbers recorded in 1996.

The U.S. is by far the world's leading importer and exporter, accounting for over 12 percent in each category. Trade has become a crucial factor in the U.S. economy. The U.S. Dept. of Commerce estimates that trade as a percentage of G.D.P. has grown to 23 percent and should rise to about 30 percent by the year 2000, up from 11 percent in 1990. By then, over 16 million jobs in the U.S. will be based on exports.

International trade takes place because some nations have an advantage in producing certain kinds of products either because they have a comparative wealth of resources (capital, labor, natural resources) or more efficient production techniques. Even an economy with the most efficient technology has a limit on its resources, and rather than using them to produce all variety of products, it concentrates its resources on what it makes most efficiently. It then trades that good for other commodities, importing those that it produces least efficiently. As a result, all countries are better off because specialization results in the expansion of the total supply of goods, and the cost of acquiring them falls.

Just which commodities a country will export and import depends on the relative prices of the factors used in production. A country like India has abundant labor and low wages. It therefore exports labor-intensive products such as garments. A country like Canada, which has abundant natural resources, specializes in agriculture and raw materials. Countries such as Canada and India then import goods for which the factors of production are in relatively short supply.

Of course, there are political reasons why countries do not completely specialize their production. No country, for example, wants to import all of its military equipment for fear that supplies would be cut off in the event of international conflict. Similarly, even inefficient producers, such as farmers in Japan, where land is scarce and expensive, may have political power that forces their governments to subsidize them.

Tariffs and Quotas

One way to protect a country's own producers, especially where they are inefficient compared with the international competition, is with import tariffs—taxes on goods that are produced abroad. Import tariffs raise the price of imports relative to domestic alternatives and discourage demand for the former. If one country is the sole importer or even the main importer of another's exports, it is possible that an import tariff will simply force the exporter to cut its selling price (in order to keep the price to consumers—including the tariff—from rising sharply and cutting off demand). In this case, the exporter pays virtually the whole cost of the tariff. If, on the other hand, the importer badly needs the import and there are few substitutes, raising the tariff simply raises the costs to one's own consumers. Critics of U.S. trade policy have pointed out that because Japan has become virtually the sole supplier of many consumer electronic products in the U.S., any tariffs against those products would simply raise their prices and fuel U.S. inflation.

Import quotas attempt to achieve a restriction on imports without the price rises associated with tariffs by setting direct limits on the number of items imported. So-called trade wars start when one country imposes a tariff on imports from a second country, and the latter responds with tariffs of its own against the first country. The arguments presented above about the benefits of trade have led to efforts to restrict the use of tariffs and maintain free trade, i.e. trade without any restrictions. Economists argue that unrestricted trade will always promote economic growth by forcing domestic prices to reflect world prices, thereby encouraging the efficient allocation of resources. Over the last 50 years, i.e. since the end of World War II, many of the leading nations have made a strong and continuous effort to lower or eliminate tariffs, first regionally, then around the world. The most successful regional organization has been the European Union, which encouraged the formation of many other such alliances in all parts of the world.

Global trade has grown rapidly over the last decade, in large part because of the General Agreement on Tariffs and Trade (GATT) and its successor organization, the World Trade Organization (WTO).

GATT The General Agreement on Tariffs and Trade was first established in 1948. In an attempt to regulate the world's trade, the representatives of 23 leading nations agreed to find ways to lower tariffs, lower quotas, and to make free trade, i.e. trade without restrictions of any kind, their final goal. The United Nations provided headquarters for the group in Geneva, Switzerland. Over a period of almost 50 years the most important trading nations met regularly to discuss specific trade matters and to continue to remove restrictions from trade. Each series of negotiations called "rounds" lasted several years. By 1975 tariffs on manufactured goods had been reduced from 40 percent to 10 percent and world trade more than tripled. By the 1980s, however, the nature of world trade had changed. In 1986 the so-called Uruguay Round of GATT (now with 92 nations represented) addressed these and other issues over a period of eight years. The results—lowering of tariffs of all kind, banning quotas, and protecting copyrights and patents—have been projected to add $500 billion annually to the global economy; the E.U. nations were projected to receive $164 billion of this total, the U.S. $122 billion, Japan $275 billion. Nations at the next level of development including the former Communist-ruled ones in Eastern Europe should realize $116 billion.

World Trade Organization Potentially the most important accomplishment of the 1994 GATT Agreement, the World Trade Organization (W.T.O.), was the establishment of a permanent institution with real power to oversee trade agreements, enforce trade rules, and settle disputes. When it was approved by the U.S. Congress (Jan. 1, 1995), the organization became a reality, with 110 members. The basic principles of the W.T.O., derived from the GATT negotiations are the encouragement of fair competition and increased access to markets as well as the development of trade without discrimination (MFN, "most favored nation" status, i.e. no nation will be given preferential trading terms). **HQ:** Centre William Rappard, 154 rue de Lausanne, CH-1211 Geneva 21, Switzerland. **Internet Address: www.wto.org Membership:** (142) Albania, Angola, Antigua and Barbuda, Argentina, Australia, Austria, Bahrain, Bangladesh, Barbados, Belgium, Belize, Benin, Bolivia, Botswana, Brazil, Brunei Darussalam, Bulgaria, Burkina Faso, Burundi, Cameroon, Canada, Central African Republic, Chad, Chile, Colombia, Congo, Congo (Democratic Rep.), Costa Rica, Croatia, Cuba, Cyprus, Czech Republic, Denmark, Djibouti, Dominica, Dominican Republic, Ecuador, Egypt, El Salvador, Estonia, E.U., Fiji, Finland, France, Gabon, The Gambia, Georgia, Germany, Ghana, Greece, Grenada, Guatemala, Guinea, Guinea Bissau, Guyana, Haiti, Honduras, Hong Kong, Hungary, Iceland, India, Indonesia, Ireland, Israel, Italy, Ivory Coast, Jamaica, Japan, Jordan, Kenya, Kuwait, Kyrgyzstan, Latvia, Lesotho, Liechtenstein, Lithuania, Luxembourg, Macao, Madagascar, Malawi, Malaysia, Maldives, Mali, Malta, Mauritania, Mauritius, Mexico, Moldova, Mongolia, Morocco, Mozambique, Myanmar, Namibia, Netherlands , New Zealand, Nicaragua, Niger, Nigeria, Norway,

Oman, Pakistan, Panama, Papua New Guinea, Paraguay, Peru, Philippines, Poland, Portugal, Qatar, Romania, Rwanda, Saint Kitts & Nevis, Saint Lucia, Saint Vincent & the Grenadines, Senegal, Sierra Leone, Singapore, Slovak Republic, Slovenia, Solomon Islands, South Africa, South Korea, Spain, Sri Lanka, Suriname, Swaziland, Sweden, Switzerland, Tanzania, Thailand, Togo, Trinidad & Tobago, Tunisia, Turkey, Uganda, United Arab Emirates, United Kingdom, United States , Uruguay, Venezuela, Zambia, Zimbabwe. **Observers and applicants:** (32): Algeria, Andorra, Armenia, Azerbaijan, Bahamas, Belarus, Bhutan, Bosnia & Herzegovina, Cambodia, Cape Verde, China, Ethiopia, Macedonia, Holy See, Kazakhstan, Laos, Lebanon, Nepal, Russian Federation, Samoa, São Tome & Principe, Saudi Arabia, Seychelles, Sudan, Taiwan, Tonga, Ukraine, Uzbekistan, Vanuatu, Vietnam, Yemen, Yugoslavia. *(With the exception of the Holy See, observers must start accession negotiations within five years of becoming observers.)*

▶EUROPEAN UNION

In 1997, the 40th year since its founding, the European Union appeared successful beyond the dreams of its founders: the world's largest economic superpower, a gigantic market of over 370 million people in 15 nations with ever more countries aspiring to join, Yet, at the same time, it faced two daunting major projects: the introduction of a common currency and the inclusion of many of the countries of post-Communist east-central Europe.

Many people in government have expressed great caution, if not skepticism, about both ideas. The very notion of replacing the traditional drachma, escudo, franc, guilder, krone, lire, mark, peseta, pound, and schilling with a new single currency (the "euro") has aroused emotional opposition; and more serious difficulties surround the schedule of its introduction, agreed to in the 1991 Maastricht Treaty. And while enthusiasm for membership seems high in east-central Europe, the task of integrating their relatively backward economies with those of the highly developed West still appears almost Herculean.

Origins   Out of the wreckage of World War II, with generous American Marshall Plan aid after 1948, western Europe commenced reconstruction; by 1954, several "economic miracles" occurred. Yet without economic integration, the recoveries of the separate nations involved duplications, inefficiencies, diminished competition, and the threats of local gluts and shortages. A small sign of what might be achieved was Benelux, the customs union between Belgium, the Netherlands, and Luxembourg, constructed even before war's end in 1944 and a going concern by 1948 despite the very unequal status of the three economies.

On May 9, 1950, France's foreign minister, Robert Schuman, proposed that German and French coal and steel production (the sinews of war) be placed under a supra-national, not intergovernmental, "high authority"; the West German chancellor, Konrad Adenauer, responded positively that very evening. By May 1952, ratification of the six-nation European Coal and Steel Community was complete, with Italy and the Benelux countries joining the French and Germans. The dramatic successes of the ECSC led the six toward broader integration, with negotiations culminating in the March 1957 Treaties of Rome which es-

tablished the European Economic Community (EEC) and the European Atomic Energy Commission (Euratom).

The EEC was designed to reduce and eventually abolish all tariffs among the six; to establish a single external tariff for the Community; and to foster the free movement of not only goods but of labor and capital as well. Euratom was intended for the common peaceful development of nuclear power, though common action proved subsequently difficult to agree on. In 1958 the United Kingdom, which had refused to join the original negotiations, proposed that the EEC be expanded into an Atlantic free-trade area, but France, under her new president, Charles de Gaulle, exercised the veto. The rebuff led Britain with Portugal, Austria, Switzerland and the Scandinavian kingdoms to form in 1959 the European Free Trade Association. The EFTA's successes were real but no match for the burgeoning EEC. So in 1961 Britain sought EEC membership. But de Gaulle, fearing American influence and objecting to the special terms that Britain sought for Commonwealth countries, again exercised the veto.

At the same time, de Gaulle was pushing for agricultural integration to match the EEC's industrial unity: the huge German market beckoned for France's chronic farm surpluses, yet Germany hesitated to sacrifice her own farmers in return for cheaper food. In fact, a serious crisis impended since each of the Six had its own system of protectionist duties, farm subsidies, and crop controls. But the Dutch ("Mansholt") proposals met with relatively easy and rapid agreement. The Common Agricultural Policy of 1962 eventually established a highly bureaucratized, centrally financed common market with managed prices, common duties upon imports, and subsidies for exports.

The European Community (EC)   With agricultural integration, the stage was set for the Brussels treaty of 1965 (often called the "The Second Treaty of Rome") which founded the European Community. The earlier three communities (ECSC, EEC and Euratom) were merged into one and were provided with a four-part structure of Commission, Council, Parliament, and Court.

It was this "refounded" EC that the United Kingdom was at last permitted to join in 1973 (after another Gaullist veto in 1967). As in its earlier attempts, it was accompanied by Ireland, Denmark and Norway (though Norwegian voters subsequently rejected admission in a referendum). The Nine subsequently became the Twelve with the admission of Greece (1981), Spain, and Portugal (1986).

Twenty years after the Brussels Treaty, with the accession of Jacques Delors as president of the European Commission, the EC received new impetus toward what the Treaty of Rome had envisioned: a single market free of all barriers to the free movement of goods, services, capital, and labor. The first result was the Single European Act of 1987, an unwieldy compendium of almost 300 rules and directives to bring about by 1992 a "Europe without frontiers." Even a decade later, its full meaning remains unclear, although both families and giant corporations have been able to hunt for bargains across national borders, tax and interest rates have been leveled, and trans-national regional ties have developed. The abolition of capital controls in 1990 has proven decisive in the movement toward monetary union, the second result of the Delors presidency (and of the strong support given by Helmut Kohl's Germany).

The European Union	
Year admitted	Member countries
1957	Belgium, France, Germany, Italy, Luxembourg, Netherlands
1973	Denmark, Ireland, United Kingdom
1981	Greece
1986	Portugal, Spain
1995	Austria, Finland, Sweden
Current Applicants	Bulgaria, Cyprus, Czech Republic, Estonia, Hungary, Latvia, Lithuania, Malta, Poland, Romania, Slovakia, Slovenia, Turkey

The European Union (E.U.) In December 1991, the EC approved its third foundational treaty, the Treaty of Maastricht. Its three "pillars" were: monetary union, common foreign and security policies, and cooperation in justice and "home affairs." The latter two "pillars" are intergovernmental, not supranational affairs, and have not been dealt with since 1991, as the E.U.'s clumsy responses to the Bosnian and Albanian crises attest.

Following the simple idea that a single market requires a single currency, the Maastricht Treaty established a three-stage (1991, 1994, 1997) creation of the *European Monetary Union* (EMU). During the first two stages, the E.U. members were to converge according to five criteria: inflation rates, interest rates, currency exchange, rate stability (variation within 2.25 percent), budget deficits (less than 3 percent of G.D.P.), and public indebtedness (a debt-to-G.D.P. ratio of less than 60 percent). During the second stage would occur the transition from central bank financing of government spending to creation of the European Central Bank. With the third stage, the European Central Bank would propose and carry out the E.U.'s monetary policies and the "euro" would circulate as "bank money"—all preparatory to the actual introduction of the monetary union.

A tone of unreality attended attempts to establish the EMU. When Danish voters rejected Maastricht in a June 1992 referendum (unanimous approval being required for the treaty to take force), the E.U., at the time still called the EC, permitted Denmark a sort of *à la carte* membership: Denmark could ratify while opting out of the single currency (and other treaty matters). Danish voters in May 1993 thereupon reversed themselves and approved the treaty. German ratification in November 1993 brought the treaty into effect. But between those two votes, the exchange

rate variation was altered from 2.25 percent to 15 percent lest the French withdraw from the pact.

It was this oddly flexible E.U. that Austria, Finland, and Sweden joined on January 1, 1995. The Norwegian government had sought membership and been approved, but Norwegian voters, as they had in 1973, said no.

The European Monetary Union The EMU had a strong domestic political impact in the member states. The European Commission forecast, April 23, 1997, of 1997 member deficits, claimed that only Italy and Greece would top the permitted 3 percent; but the very same day, the I.M.F. predicted that four others would as well: Spain, Britain, France, and (embarrassingly) Germany.

What permitted the E.U. finance ministers to insist (in September, 1997) that they would hold to the Maastricht timetable was an informal agreement to scrap four of the five criteria and retain only the 3 percent deficit-to-GDP ratio. On this score, Greece was the only applicant of 12 to fall short. In March 1998, the European Commission recommended, and in May the Brussels summit formally endorsed, participation in the EMU by the following countries: Austria, Belgium, Finland, France, Germany, Ireland, Italy, Luxembourg, Netherlands, Portugal, and Spain. (Of the 11, only Finland, France, and Luxembourg can meet the 60 percent indebtedness-to-GDP limit; Belgium and Italy had ratios in excess of 120 percent. Despite failing the debt criterion, Greece was permitted to join the common currency on January 1, 2001, bringing the number of member states back to 12.

On January 1, 1999, the E.U. introduced the euro. Initially well received in world financial markets, the euro sagged over the next six months, losing almost 20 percent of its value against the dollar. One reason for the flop seems to have been the E.U.'s decision to permit Italy's budget deficit to substantially exceed the target 2 percent of GDP; one member's excessive spending was dragging the whole currency down. By September, it had lost about 27 percent of its value against the dollar. In late Sept. 2000, the U.S., Japan, and European central banks undertook a surprise rescue attempt, buying up billions of euros. The move did little to shore up the currency: it initially rose to 90 cents, but declined to 88 cents by the end of the day. On Sept. 28, the people of Denmark voted not to give up their krone and accept the euro. In June 2001, the euro was trading at about 85 cents.

On January 1, 2002, 50 billion new euro coins and 14.5 billion euro notes will begin circulating

Unemployment Rates in Leading Developed Nations, 1975-2001								
Year	1975	1980	1985	1990	1995	1999	2000	2001[1]
Australia	4.9%	6.1%	8.3%	6.7%	8.2%	7.0%	6.3%	6.5%
Canada	6.9	7.5	10.5	7.7	8.5	6.8	5.8	5.9
France	4.2	6.5	10.5	9.1	11.8	11.2	9.7[2]	8.8
Germany	3.4	2.8	7.2	5.0	8.2	8.7	8.3[2]	8.1
Italy	3.4	4.4	6.0	7.0	12.0	11.5	10.7[2]	9.9
Japan	1.9	2.0	2.6	2.1	3.2	4.7	4.8	4.8
Sweden	1.6	2.0	2.8	1.8	9.1	7.1	5.8	5.1
United Kingdom	4.6	7.0	11.2	6.9	8.7	6.1[2]	5.8[2]	5.1
United States	8.5	7.1	7.2	5.6	5.6	4.2	4.0	4.2

Note: Seasonally adjusted. 1. First quarter only. 2. Estimate.
Source: U.S. Bureau of Labor Statistics. ftp://ftp.bls.gov/pub/special.requests/ForeignLabor/flsjec.txt

in the 12 member countries. For the next two months, those countries will accept both euros and their own national currencies. All national notes and coins must be withdrawn from circulation by February 28, 2002.

In the matter of the E.U.'s expansion eastward, the December 1997 Luxembourg summit extended formal invitations to six of 12 applicants: Cyprus, the Czech Republic, Estonia, Hungary, Poland, and Slovenia. Five other countries (known as the "second wave")—Bulgaria, Latvia, Lithuania, Romania, and Slovakia—were encouraged to continue to apply. The formal invitations came in Dec. 1999, with Malta added as well. Even Turkey, explicitly turned down only two years earlier, was extended a "tentative" invitation, conditional upon an improved human rights record and upon reaching an accord with Greece over Cyprus.

In light of its proposed expansion from 15 to 27 members (in two waves of six) the E.U., at its December 2000 summit, hammered out the Treaty of Nice. It settled three broad issues: a revision of the European Commission's structure, a reweighing of power in the Council of Ministers, and the end of member vetos in 29 legislative areas. Ireland's June 2001 veto of the treaty (by 54-to-46 percent in a referendum) exploded the whole scheme and put the issue of eastward expansion on hold.

Additional information about the European Union (in 11 languages) can be found at the E.U. Web server. The address is **http://europa.eu.int.**

Structure of the E.U.
The Commission   is composed of 20 commissioners appointed by member governments. The five largest countries, France, Germany, Italy, Spain, and the United Kingdom, appoint two commissioners each. The remaining ten countries each appoint one commissioner. The treaties direct Commission members to act independently of their governments and represent the entire community's interests. The Commission supervises implementation of E.U. treaties, initiates and implements E.U. policy, transacts negotiations with non-member states, and manages E.U. funds. The Commission can be forced to resign by two-thirds majority vote of the European Parliament. The Commission headquarters are in Brussels. The president, who is appointed by the Council, serves a two-year term.

The Council of Ministers   consists of the foreign ministers of the 15 member governments and is the chief decision-making body of the E.U., passing legislation on the major issues affecting all members. Each country takes the presidency for six months, and votes are by majority, though each country's vote is weighted differently. Germany, France, Italy, and the United Kingdom each have 10 votes; Spain has 8; Belgium, Greece, the Netherlands and Portugal have five votes; Austria

Foreign Exchange Rates: Currency Units Per Dollar, 1975–2001

Country/currency	1975	1985	1990	1995	1999	2000	2001[1]
Australia/dollar	0.77	1.43	1.28	1.35	1.55	1.72	1.93
Austria/schilling	17.44	20.68	11.33	10.08	12.80	14.86	16.10
Belgium/franc	36.80	59.34	33.42	29.47	37.52	43.57	47.20
Canada/dollar	1.02	1.37	1.17	1.37	1.49	1.49	1.52
China/yuan	N.A.	2.94	4.79	8.37	8.28	8.28	8.23
Denmark/krone	5.75	10.60	6.19	5.60	6.99	8.10	8.74
European Community/ecu	N.A.	N.A.	N.A.	0.78	0.93	1.08	1.17
Finland/markka	3.67	6.20	3.83	4.38	5.53	6.42	6.96
France/franc	4.29	8.98	5.45	4.99	6.10	7.08	7.67
Germany/deutsche mark	2.46	2.94	1.62	1.43	1.82	2.11	2.29
Greece/drachma	32.30	138.41	158.59	231.68	306.30	365.92	398.68
Hong Kong/dollar	4.94	7.79	7.79	7.74	7.76	7.79	7.80
India/rupee	8.40	12.33	17.49	32.412	43.13	45.00	47.04
Ireland/pound	0.45	0.94	0.60	0.62	0.73	0.95	0.92
Italy/lira	653.10	1,908.88	1,198.27	1,629.45	1,800.73	2,091.17	2,265.44
Japan/yen	296.79	238.47	145.00	93.96	113.73	107.80	122.35
Malaysia/ringgit	2.40	2.48	2.70	2.51	3.80	3.80	3.80
Mexico/peso	12.64	256.90	2,813.00	6.45	9.55	9.46	9.09
Netherlands/guilder	2.53	3.32	1.82	1.60	2.05	2.38	2.58
New Zealand/dollar	0.82	2.01	1.68	1.52	1.89	2.19	2.41
Norway/krone	5.23	8.59	6.26	6.34	7.81	8.81	9.30
Portugal/escudo	25.51	172.07	142.70	149.88	186.45	216.52	234.56
Singapore/dollar	2.37	2.20	1.81	1.42	1.70	1.72	1.82
South Africa/rand	0.74	2.23	2.59	3.63	6.12	6.95	8.06
South Korea/won	484.00	872.45	710.64	772.69	1,189.84	1,130.90	1,295.05
Spain/peseta	57.43	170.09	101.96	124.64	154.74	179.70	194.67
Sri Lanka/rupee	6.98	27.19	40.08	51.05	70.87	76.96	90.37
Sweden/krona	4.15	8.60	5.92	7.14	8.27	9.17	10.79
Switzerland/franc	2.58	2.46	1.39	1.18	1.50	1.69	1.79
Taiwan/dollar	38.00	39.89	26.92	26.50	32.32	31.26	34.83
United Kingdom/pound	0.45	0.77	0.56	0.64	0.62	0.66	0.71
Venezuela/bolivar	N.A.	N.A.	N.A.	174.85	606.82	680.52	717.27

Note: Averages of certified noon buying rates in New York for cable transfers. 1. Figures are for June, 2001.
Source: *Federal Reserve Bulletin*, monthly.

and Sweden have four votes; Ireland, Denmark, and Finland have three votes; and Luxembourg has two. The Council meets in Brussels.

The European Parliament   The 626 deputies of the European Parliament are elected directly by the citizens of the individual countries. The Parliament oversees the E.U. budget and passes on Commission proposals to the Council of Ministers. The Parliament also passes on new applications to the E.U.. Deputies are elected to five-year terms and meet monthly in Strasbourg.

The Court of Justice   is the court of last resort for the E.U., interpreting E.U. treaties and legislation and hearing complaints about member-government violations. The Court also resolves differences between E.U. legislation and national laws. The 13 justices are appointed by the member governments and serve six-year terms.

The Economic and Social Committee   is composed of 222 members representing labor, farmers, and consumer groups. Through consultation, the Committee presents its views to the Council of Ministers and the E.U. Commission.

▶**MAJOR REGIONAL TRADING GROUPS**

Africa

Common Market for Eastern and Southern Africa (COMESA) HQ: Lotti Hous, Cairo Rd. Box 30051, 10101 Lusaka, Zambia. **Founded:** 1994. **Purpose:** To create an environment for foreign and domestic investment by developing rational production and marketing structures. Help to maintain peace and stability among member states. **Members:** (20) Angola, Burundi, Comoros,

Democratic Republic of the Congo, Eritrea, Ethiopia, Kenya, Lesotho, Madagascar, Malawi, Mauritius, Mozambique, Namibia, Rwanda, Sudan, Swaziland, Tanzania, Uganda, Zambia, Zimbabwe.

Economic Community of West African States (ECOWAS) HQ: 6 King George V Rd. PMB 12745, Lagos, Nigeria. **Founded:** 1975. **Purpose:** to promote the regional economic cooperation; in recent years it has also created joint military force to deal with the civil war in Liberia. **Members:** (16) Benin, Burkina Faso, Cape Verde, The Gambia, Ghana, Guinea, Guinea-Bissau, Ivory Coast, Liberia, Mali, Mauritania, Niger, Nigeria, Senegal, Sierra Leone, Togo.

Southern African Development Community (SADC) HQ: Private Bag 0095, Gaborone, Botswana. **Founded:** 1992. **Purpose:** To promote regional economic development and integration. **Members:** (12) Angola, Botswana, Lesotho, Malawi, Mauritius, Mozambique, Namibia, South Africa, Swaziland, Tanzania, Zambia, Zimbabwe.

Asia

Asia Pacific Economic Cooperation (APEC) HQ: 438 Alexandra Rd., Alexandra Point Building, Singapore 119958, Singapore. **Founded:** 1989. **Purpose:** an alliance of nations from east and west seeking to promote trade and investment in the Pacific Basin. **Members:** (19) Australia, Brunei, Canada, Indonesia, Chile, China, Hong Kong, Japan, Malaysia, Mexico, New Guinea, New Zealand, Philippines, Singapore, South Korea, Taiwan, Thailand, Vietnam.

World's 50 Largest Banking Companies by Assets, 2000

Rank, Company, Country	Assets (millions)	Rank, Company, Country	Assets (millions)
1. Citigroup Inc., New York	$902,210	26. Fortis Bank, Brussels	$412,897
2. Deutsche Bank AG, Frankfurt	872,627	27. Industrial Bank of Japan Ltd., Tokyo	408,787
3. Bank of Tokyo-Mitsubishi Ltd., Tokyo	720,809	28. Westdeutsche Landesbank	377,042
4. J.P. Morgan Chase & Co., New York	715,348	Girozentrale, Duesseldorf	
5. UBS, Zurich	673,706	29. Lloyds TSBGroup, London	325,305
6. Hsbc Holdings, London	673,475	30. Rabobank, Utrecht, Netherlands	323,226
7. Bayerische Hypo-und	653,862	31. Banco Santander, Santander, Spain	321,204
Vereinsbank AG, Munich		32. Intesabci Spa, Milan	313,195
8. BNP Paribas, Paris	652,411	33. Abbey National, London	305,018
9. Bank of America Corp., Charlotte, N.C.	642,191	34. Tokai Bank Ltd., Nagoya Japan	293,689
10. ING NV, Amsterdam	612,833	35. Bayerische Landesbank	284,130
11. Credit Suisse Group, Zurich	612,098	Girozentrale, Munich	
12. Fuji Bank Ltd., Tokyo	548,720	36. Asahi Bank Ltd., Tokyo	276,584
13. Sumitomo Banking Corp., Chuo-Ku, Japan	515,238	37. Banco Bilbao Vizcaya Argentaria, Bilbao, Spain	275,921
14. ABN AMRO Holding NV, Amsterdam	509,733	38. Wells Fargo & Co., San Francisco	272,426
15. Caisse Nationale de Credit Agricole, Paris	503,814	39. Halifax Group, West Yorkshire. U.K.	272,418
		40. Bank One Corp., Chicago	269,300
16. Dai-Ichi Kangyo Bank Ltd., Tokyo	499,408	41. First Union Corp., Charlotte, N.C.	254,170
17. Norinchukin Bank, Tokyo	498,438	42. Dexia, Brussels	242,458
18. Royal Bank of Scotland Group, London	477,619	43. Nordea AB, Stockholm	210,719
19. Barclays, London	471,919	44. Zenshinren Bank, Osaka, Japan	208,948
20. Sakura Bank Ltd., Tokyo	464,953	45. Almanij NV, Antwerpen	205,029
21. Dresdner Bank, Frankfurt	454,803	46. Washington Mutual Inc., Seattle	194,716
22. Sanwa Bank Ltd., Chuo-Ku, Japan	450,034	47. Unicredito Italiano, Genoa	190,973
23. Axa SA, Paris	447,253	48. Royal Bank of Canada, Toronto	189,677
24. Societe Generale, Paris	429,042	49. National Australia Bank Ltd., Melbourne	186,476
25. Commerzbank, Frankfurt	428,751	50. FleetBoston Financial Corp., Boston	179,519

Note: Consolidated data, including affiliates in which ownership exceeds 50 percent, are used whenever possible.
Source: *American Banker,* August 7, 2001.

Association of South East Asian Nations (ASEAN) HQ: P.O. Box 2072, 70 A Jalan Sisingamangaraja, Jakarta, Indonesia. **Founded:** 1967. **Purpose:** to promote political and economic cooperation among states in region by coordinating policies in trade, transportation, communications, agriculture, science, finance, and culture. **Members:** (9) Brunei, Indonesia, Laos, Malaysia, Myanmar, Philippines, Singapore, Thailand, Vietnam.

Latin America
Mercado Comun del Cono Sur (MERCOSUR) HQ: Rincon 575 P12, 11000 Montivideo, Uruguay. **Founded:** 1991 (established 1995). **Purpose:** to establish a free trade area and a customs union, and to negotiate free trade agreements with other Latin American countries that will eventually produce a Latin American Free Trade Area (LAFTA). **Members:** (4) Argentina, Brazil, Paraguay, Uruguay. **Associate Member:** Chile

The *Fortune* 100 World's Largest Industrial Corporations, 2000

2000 Rank	Company, Country (1999 rank)	Sales (millions)	2000 Rank	Company, Country (1999 rank)	Sales (millions)
1.	Exxon Mobil, U.S. (3)	$210,392.0	51.	Texaco, U.S. (86)	51,130.0
2.	Wal-Mart Stores, U.S. (2)	193,295.0	52.	Fujitsu, Japan (45)	49,603.5
3.	General Motors, U.S. (1)	184,632.0	53.	Duke Energy, U.S. (N.A.)	49,318.0
4.	Ford Motor Company, U.S. (4)	180,598.0	54.	Kroger, U.S. (49)	49,000.4
5.	DaimlerChrysler, Germany (5)	150,069.7	55.	NEC, Japan (51)	48,928.0
6.	Royal Dutch/Shell Group, Netherlands (11)	149,146.0	56.	Hewlett-Packard, U.S. (41(44)	48,782.0
			57.	HSBC Holdings, U.K. (68)	48,632.8
7.	BP Amoco, Britain (17)	148,062.0	58.	Koninklijke Ahold, Netherlands (85)	48,491.7
8.	General Electric, U.S. (9)	129,853.0	59.	Nestlé, Switzerland (41)	48,225.0
9.	Mitsubishi, Japan (7)	126,579.4	60.	Chevron, U.S. (N.A.)	48,069.0
10.	Toyota Motor, Japan (8)	121,416.2	61.	State Farm Group, U.S. (52)	47,863.1
11.	Mitsui, Japan (6)	118,013.7	62.	Tokyo Electric Power, Japan (48)	47,555.7
12.	Citigroup, U.S. (18)	111,826.0	63.	UBS, Switzerland (N.A.)	47,315.8
13.	Itochu, Japan (10)	109,756.5	64.	Dai-Ichi Mutual Life Insurance, Japan (33)	46,435.6
14.	Total Fina Elf, France (50)	105,869.6			
15.	Nippon Telegraph & Telephone, Japan (13)	103,234.7	65.	American International Group, U.S. (60)	45,972.0
			66.	Home Depot, U.S. (71)	45,738.0
16.	Enron, U.S. (62)	100,789.0	67.	Morgan Stanley Dean Witter, U.S. (91)	45,413.0
17.	AXA, France (15)	92,781.6	68.	Sinopec, China (58)	45,346.0
18.	Sumitomo, Japan (12)	91,168.4	69.	ENI, Italy (89)[1]	45,139.0
19.	IBM, U.S. (16)	88,396.0	70.	Merrill Lynch & Co., Inc., U.S. (87)	44,872.0
20.	Marubeni, Japan (14)	85,351.0	71.	Fannie Mae, U.S. (81)	44,088.9
21.	Volkswagen, Germany (19)	78,851.9	72.	Unilever, Britain/Netherlands (54)	43,973.6
22.	Hitachi, Japan (23)	76,126.8	73.	Fortis, U.S. (55)	43,830.9
23.	Siemens, Germany (21)	74,858.3	74.	ABN-AMRO Holding, Netherlands (69)	43,389.6
24.	ING Group, Netherlands (27)	71,195.9	75.	Metro Holding, Switzerland (46)	43,371.1
25.	Allianz Holding, Germany (22)	71,022.3	76.	Prudential Insurance, U.S. (56)	43,125.5
26.	Matsushita Electric Industrial, Japan (24)	69,475.3	77.	State Power Corporation, U.S. (83)	42,548.7
27.	E.ON, Germany (37)	68,432.6	78.	RWE Group, Germany (73)	42,513.7
28.	Nippon Life Insurance, Japan (20)	68,054.8	79.	Compaq Computer, U.S. (70)	42,383.0
29.	Deutsche Bank, Germany (31)	67,133.2	80.	Repsol YPF, Mexico (N.A.)	42,273.2
30.	Sony, Japan (30)	66,158.4	81.	Pemex, Mexico (N.A.)	42,166.8
31.	AT&T, U.S. (28)	65,981.0	82.	McKesson HBOC, U.S. (80)	42,010.0
32.	Verizon Communications, U.S. (97)	64,707.0	83.	China Petroleum, China (N.A.)	41,683.7
33.	U.S. Postal Service (26)[1]	64,540.0	84.	Lucent Technologies, U.S. (74)	41,420.0
34.	Philip Morris, U.S. (29)	63,276.0	85.	Sears Roebuck, U.S. (59)	40,937.0
35.	CGNU, U.K. (57)	61,498.7	86.	Peugeot, France (61)	40,830.6
36.	J.P. Morgan Chase, U.S. (N.A.)	60,065.0	87.	Munich Re Group, Germany (72)	40,671.6
37.	Carrefour, France (66)	59,887.8	88.	Merck, U.S. (100)	40,363.2
38.	Credit Suisse Group, Switzerland (43)	59,315.5	89.	Procter & Gamble, U.S. (75)	39,951.0
39.	Nissho Iwai, Japan (25)	58,557.3	90.	WorldCom, U.S. (79)	39,090.0
40.	Honda Motor, Japan (34)	58,461.6	91.	Vivendi Universal, France (53)	38,628.3
41.	Bank of America (39)	57,747.0	92.	Samsung Electronics, South Korea (N.A.)	38,490.7
42.	BNP Paribas, France (64)	57,611.6	93.	TIAA-CREF, U.S. (67)	38,063.5
43.	Nissan Motor, Japan (36)	55,077.1	94.	Deutsche Telekom, Germany (77)	37,834.4
44.	Toshiba, Japan (38)	53,826.6	95.	Motorola, U.S. (N.A.)	37,580.0
45.	PDVSA, Venezuela (N.A.)	53,680.0	96.	Sumitomo Life Insurance, Japan (47)	37,535.8
46.	Assicurazioni Generali, Italy (35)	53,333.1	97.	Zurich Financial Services, Switzerland (65)	37,431.0
47.	Fiat, Italy (40)	53,190.4			
48.	Mizuho Holdings, Japan (N.A.)	52,068.5	98.	Mitsubishi Electric, Japan (92)	37,348.9
49.	SBC Communications, U.S. (42)	51,476.0	99.	Renault, France (63)[1]	37,128.4
50.	Boeing, U.S. (32)	51,321.0	100.	KMart, U.S. (84)	37,028.0

Note: 1. Government-owned.   **Source:** *Fortune*, July, 2001. Reprinted by permission.

Central American Common Market (CACM) HQ: c/o SIECA, Apart Postal 1237, 4a Avenida 10-25, Zona 14, Guatemala 01901, Guatemala. **Founded:** 1961. **Purpose:** to promote the establishment of a Central American Common Market and to liberalize trade with other nations including the U.S. **Members:** Costa Rica, El Salvador, Guatemala, Honduras, Nicaragua.

Caribbean Community and Common Market (CARICOM) HQ: Bank of Guyana Building, P.O. Box 10827, 1 Avenue of the Republic, Georgetown, Guyana. **Founded:** 1973. **Purpose:** to create greater unity in Caribbean, and to formulate policies and cooperation in services such as education, health, labor matters, and foreign policy. **Members:** (14) Antigua and Barbuda, Bahamas, Barbados, Belize, Dominica, Granada,

World Economic Indicators, 1999

Country	G.N.P. (millions of U.S. dollars) 1999	G.N.P. per capita (in U.S. dollars) 1999	Real growth rate 1980-91	Real growth rate 1990-99	Average inflation rate 1990-99	Agriculture's share in G.D.P. 1970	Agriculture's share in G.D.P. 1999	Net private capital flows (millions) 1999[1]	Foreign direct investment as percent of G.D.P. 1999
Albania	$3,146	$930	—	2.8%	44.7%	—	53%	$37	1.1%
Algeria	46,548	1,550	-0.8%	-0.5	19.1	10%	11	-1,486	1.5
Angola	3,276	270	—	-2.8	813.7	45	7	2,373	28.9
Antigua and Barbuda	606	8,990	3.8	2.7	2.5	—	4	—	—
Argentina	276,097	7,550	-1.5	3.6	6.2	13	5	32,296	8.5
Armenia	1878	490	2.1	-3.9	269.2	N.A.	29	122	6.6
Australia	397,345	20,950	1.2	2.9	1.3	6	—	—	1.4
Austria	205,743	25,430	2.1	1.4	2.2	7	2	—	1.4
Azerbaijan	3,705	460	0.4	-10.7	250.0	N.A.	23	596	12.7
Bahamas	—	—	1.3	-0.1	2.6	—	—	—	—
Bahrain	—	—	-3.8	0.8	-0.2	—	—	—	—
Bangladesh	47,071	370	1.9	3.1	4.1	55	25	198	0.4
Barbados	2,294	8,600	1.3	1.5	3.1	11	6	-13	0.7
Belarus	26,299	2,620	3.3	-2.9	393.5	N.A.	13	394	0.8
Belgium	252,051	24,650	2.1	1.4	2.2	4	1	—	15.5
Belize	673	2,730	2.5	0.7	2.9	—	19	16	0.5
Benin	2,320	380	-1.1	1.8	9.3	49	38	31	1.3
Bhutan	399	510	6.8	3.4	9.6	—	38	0	0
Bolivia	8,092	990	-2.0	1.8	9.1	17	18	1,016	12.2
Bosnia & Herzegovina	4,706	1,210	N.A.	32.7	-1.0	N.A.	15	N.A.	0
Botswana	5,139	3,240	5.8	1.8	10.0	33	4	36	0.6
Brazil	730,424	4,350	0.4	1.5	263.9	12	9	2,279	4.3
Brunei	—	—	—	-0.5	1.1	—	—	—	—
Bulgaria	11,572	1,410	1.7	-2.1	112.0	—	15	1,112	6.5
Burkina Faso	2,602	240	1.3	1.4	6.0	44	31	10	0.4
Burundi	823	120	1.4	-5.0	11.8	71	52	0	2.8
Cambodia	3,023	260	—	1.9	28.7	—	—	122	4.0
Cameroon	8,798	600	-0.9	-1.5	5.5	31	44	-13	0.4
Canada	614,003	20,140	2.1	1.7	1.4	—	—	—	4.0
Cape Verde	569	1,330	2.2	3.2	5.1	—	12	16	2.6
Central African Rep.	1,035	290	-1.5	-0.3	4.9	35	55	13	1.2
Chad	1,555	210	3.8	-0.9	7.6	43	36	14	1.0
Chile	69,602	4,630	1.7	5.6	8.0	7	8	11,851	13.7
China	979,894	780	7.8	9.5	8.2	35	18	40,632	3.9
Colombia	90,007	2,170	1.2	1.4	22.7	25	13	3,635	1.3
Comoros	189	350	-1.0	-3.1	3.8	—	39	1	0.5
Congo, Dem. Republic	—	—	-0.2	-8.1	1,423.1	18	—	1	—
Congo Republic	1,571	550	-1.6	-3.3	8.6	16	10	5	0.2
Costa Rica	12,828	3,570	1.0	3.0	16.7	23	11	924	4.4
Croatia	20,222	4,530	N.A.	1.0	104.9	N.A.	9	2,392	6.9
Cyprus	9,086	11,950	4.9	2.8	3.5	—	—	—	0.7
Czech Republic[2]	51,623	5,020	0.4	0.9	12.4	—	4	4,837	9.6
Denmark	170,685	32,050	2.1	2.0	2.0	—	2	—	4.9
Djibouti	511	790	—	-5.1	4.4	—	—	5	—
Dominica	238	3,260	4.7	1.8	3.2	—	19	13	4.9
Dominican Republic	16,130	1,920	-0.2	3.9	9.9	20	11	1,404	7.7
Ecuador	16,841	1,360	-0.3	0.0	33.8	24	12	943	3.6
Egypt	86,544	1,380	2.0	2.4	8.8	29	17	1,558	1.2
El Salvador	11,806	1,920	-0.3	2.8	8.1	28	10	360	1.9
Equatorial Guinea	516	1,170	3.4	16.3	13.1	—	16	120	17.2
Eritrea	779	200	—	2.2	9.4	—	17	—	0
Estonia	4,906	3,400	2.1	-0.3	62.7	N.A.	6	569	5.8
Ethiopia	6,524	100	-1.6	2.4	7.6	56	52	78	1.4
Fiji	1,848	2,310	0.0	1.2	3.5	29	18	-41	-1.9

Country	G.N.P. (millions of U.S. dollars) 1999	G.N.P. per capita			Average inflation rate 1990-99	Agriculture's share in G.D.P.		Net private capital flows (millions) 1999[1]	Foreign direct investment as percent of G.D.P. 1999
		(in U.S. dollars) 1999	Real growth rate 1980-91	Real growth rate 1990-99		1970	1999		
Finland	$127,764	$24,730	2.5%	2.0%	2.0%	—	3%	—	3.7%
France[3]	1,453,211	24,170	1.8	1.1	1.6	—	—	—	2.7
Gabon	3,987	3,300	-4.2	0.6	5.8	17%	8	$207	4.6
Gambia	415	330	-0.1	-0.6	3.7	33	31	14	3.6
Georgia	3362	620	2.2	—	—	N.A.	36	86	3.0
Germany[4]	2,103,804	25,620	2.2	1.0	1.9	3	1	—	2.5
Ghana	7,451	400	-0.3	1.6	27.4	47	36	-16	0.2
Greece	127,648	12,110	1.2	1.8	9.5	18	—	—	2.7
Grenada	334	3,440	5.3	2.2	2.6	—	8	42	11.7
Guatemala	18,625	1,680	-1.8	1.5	10.9	—	23	98	0.8
Guinea	3,556	490	—	1.5	5.6	—	24	63	1.8
Guinea-Bissau	194	160	1.3	-1.9	37.6	47	62	3	1.4
Guyana	651	760	-4.2	5.2	14.3	19	35	43	7.1
Haiti	3,584	460	-2.4	-3.4	22.2	—	29	30	0.7
Honduras	4,829	760	-0.7	0.3	19.7	32	16	251	4.3
Hong Kong	165,122	24,570	—	0.7	4.7	0	—	—	—
Hungary	46,751	4,640	0.7	1.4	20.6	18	—	4,961	4.0
Iceland	8,197	29,540	1.3	1.8	3.3	—	—	—	1.0
India	441,834	440	3.3	4.1	8.5	47	28	1,813	0.5
Indonesia	125,043	600	3.9	3.0	14.7	45	19	-8,416	-1.9
Iran	113,729	1,810	-1.1	1.9	27.0	19	21	-1,385	7.7
Iraq	—	—	—	—	—	17	—	—	—
Ireland	80,559	21,470	2.2	6.1	3.4	—	—	—	20.4
Israel	99,574	16,310	1.8	2.3	10.7	—	—	—	2.3
Italy	1,162,910	20,170	2.1	1.2	4.0	8	3	—	0.6
Ivory Coast	10,387	670	-3.4	0.6	8.2	40	26	74	3.1
Jamaica	6,311	2,430	-0.3	-0.6	27.6	7	7	425	7.6
Japan	4,054,545	32,030	3.7	1.1	0.1	6	—	—	0.3
Jordan	7,717	1,630	-3.3	1.1	3.5	10	2	112	2.0
Kazakhstan	18,732	1,250	0.9	-4.9	255.9	N.A.	11	1,477	10.0
Kenya	10,696	360	0.3	-0.3	14.9	33	23	-51	0.1
Kiribati	81	910	0.5	1.0	3.9	—	—	—	—
Korea, South	397,910	8,490	8.8	4.7	5.8	26	5	6,409	2.3
Kuwait	—	—	—	—	—	0	—	—	0.2
Kyrgyzstan	1,465	300	2.1	-6.4	129.7	N.A.	38	-16	2.8
Laos	1,476	290	1.2	3.8	22.9	—	—	79	5.5
Latvia	5,913	2,430	2.8	-3.7	57.9	N.A.	4	303	5.6
Lebanon	15,796	3,700	—	5.7	24.0	9	—	1,771	—
Lesotho	1,158	550	0.0	2.1	9.6	35	—	168	18.7
Liberia	—	—	—	—	—	24	—	10	—
Libya	—	—	—	—	—	2	—	—	—
Lithuania	9,751	2,640	2.5	-3.9	90.7	N.A.	9	1,148	4.6
Luxembourg	18,545	42,930	3.8	3.8	2.4	-4	1	—	—
Macedonia	3,348	1,660	N.A.	-1.5	94.2	N.A.	12	51	0.9
Madagascar	3,712	250	-2.4	-1.2	20.6	30	30	52	1.6
Malawi	1,961	180	0.1	0.9	34.3	44	38	60	3.3
Malaysia	76,944	3,390	2.9	4.7	3.9	29	11	3,247	2.0
Maldives	322	1,200	6.7	3.9	8.2	—	—	14	—
Mali	2,577	240	0.1	1.1	8.1	61	47	19	0.7
Malta	3,492	9,210	3.8	4.2	2.9	7	—	-213	—
Marshall Islands	99	1,950	—	—	6.3	N.A.	—	—	—
Mauritania	1,001	390	-1.8	1.3	6.0	29	25	-0	0.2
Mauritius	4,157	3,540	6.1	3.9	6.3	16	6	102	1.2
Mexico	428,877	4,440	-0.5	1.0	19.5	12	5	26,780	2.4
Micronesia	212	1,830	N.A.	-1.8	3.5	N.A.	—	—	—
Moldova	1,481	410	1.8	-10.8	142.1	N.A.	25	112	2.9
Mongolia	927	390	—	-0.6	66.6	—	32	28	3.3
Morocco	33,715	1,190	1.6	0.4	3.2	20	15	-118	7.7
Mozambique	3,804	220	-3.6	3.8	36.4	—	33	374	9.7
Myanmar	—	—	—	5.1	26.1	38	60	203	—
Namibia	3,211	1,890	-1.5	0.8	9.8	—	13	—	—
Nepal	5,173	220	2.1	2.3	8.6	67	42	-8	8.8
Netherlands	397,384	25,140	1.5	2.1	1.9	6	3	—	8.7
New Zealand	53,299	13,990	0.2	1.8	1.4	—	—	—	—
Nicaragua	2,012	410	-4.6	0.4	38.6	25	32	382	13.2
Niger	1,974	190	-4.1	-1.0	6.4	65	41	-8	0.7
Nigeria	31,600	260	-1.7	-0.5	31.6	40	—	860	2.9

Country	G.N.P. (millions of U.S. dollars) 1999	G.N.P. per capita (in U.S. dollars) 1999	Real growth rate 1980-91	Real growth rate 1990-99	Average inflation rate 1990-99	Agriculture's share in G.D.P. 1970	Agriculture's share in G.D.P. 1999	Net private capital flows (millions) 1999[1]	Foreign direct investment as percent of G.D.P. 1999
Norway	$149,280	$33,470	2.2%	3.2%	2.1%	6%	2%	—	—
Oman			4.5	0.3	-2.9	16	—	$-413	—
Pakistan	62,915	470	3.2	1.3	10.6	37	27	53	0.9%
Palau	—	—	—	—	6.4	—	—	—	—
Panama	8,657	3,080	-1.8	2.4	2.1	15	7	620	0.2
Papua New Guinea	3,834	810	-0.7	2.3	7.1	37	30	499	8.3
Paraguay	8,374	1,560	-0.8	-0.2	13.4	32	29	109	0.9
Peru	53,705	2,130	-2.6	3.2	31.0	19	7	3,140	3.8
Philippines	77,967	1,050	-1.2	0.9	8.6	30	18	4,915	0.7
Poland	157,429	4,070	0.5	4.4	25.0	—	3	10,452	4.7
Portugal	110,175	11,030	2.7	2.3	5.6	—	—	—	1.0
Qatar	—	—	-10.9	—	—	—	—	—	—
Romania	33,034	1,470	-0.1	-0.5	105.6	—	16	714	3.1
Russian Federation	328,995	2,250	1.3	-5.9	190.4	N.A.	7	3,780	0.8
Rwanda	2,041	250	-2.6	-3.0	16.3	62	46	2	8.7
Saint Kitts and Nevis	259	6,330	5.8	4.9	3.1	—	4	83	25.6
Saint Lucia	590	3,820	2.9	0.9	2.7	—	8	94	13.3
Saint Vincent and the Grenadines	301	2,640	5.2	2.6	2.3	—	10	83	7.6
Samoa	181	1,070	5.1	1.4	4.5	—	—	2	1.1
São Tomé and Principe	40	270	-3.5	-0.9	54.1	37	21	—	0
Saudi Arabia	139,365	6,900	-4.2	-1.1	1.2	6	—	—	—
Senegal	4,685	500	0.0	0.6	5.0	24	18	54	1.3
Seychelles	520	6,500	2.5	1.3	1.5	—	4	55	11.0
Sierra Leone	653	130	-1.3	-7.0	31.1	28	43	1	0.1
Singapore	95,429	24,150	4.9	4.7	1.6	2	0	—	8.2
Slovak Republic	20,318	3,770	N.A.	1.6	11.4	N.A.	4	281	1.8
Slovenia	19,862	10,000	N.A.	2.5	23.3	N.A.	4	—	0.9
Solomon Islands	320	750	3.5	0.3	8.5	—	—	-6	3.3
Somalia	—	—	—	—	—	59	—	—	—
South Africa	133,569	3,170	0.9	-0.2	10.2	8	4	4,533	1.0
Spain	583,082	14,800	2.9	2.0	4.1	—	4	—	1.6
Sri Lanka	15,578	820	2.5	4.0	9.4	28	21	109	1.1
Sudan	9,435	330	-2.4	—	—	—	43	371	3.8
Suriname	..		-4.5	3.3	90.0	7	—	—	—
Swaziland	1,379	1,350	3.1	-0.2	12.1	33	16	33	2.7
Sweden	236,940	26,750	1.7	1.2	2.2	—	—	—	24.9
Switzerland	273,856	38,380	1.6	-0.1	1.4	—	—	—	3.8
Syria	15,172	970	-2.1	2.7	8.7	20	—	87	0.5
Tajikistan	1,749	280	-0.1	—	—	N.A.	19	10	1.3
Tanzania[5]	8,515	260	-1.1	-0.1	23.1	41	45	171	2.1
Thailand	121,051	2,010	5.9	3.8	4.6	26	10	2,471	5.0
Togo	1,398	310	-1.7	-0.5	7.6	34	41	30	2.1
Tonga	172	1,730	1.5	0.7	4.1	—	—	1	1.3
Trinidad and Tobago	6,142	4,750	-5.2	2.0	5.8	5	2	713	9.2
Tunisia	19,757	2,090	1.2	2.9	4.6	20	13	739	1.7
Turkey	186,490	2,900	2.9	2.2	78.3	30	16	8,667	0.4
Turkmenistan	3,205	670	0.7	-9.6	516.9	N.A.	27	-54	2.5
Uganda	6,794	320	3.3	4.0	13.8	54	44	221	3.5
Ukraine	41,991	840	2.3	-10.3	339.1	—	13	371	1.3
United Arab Emirates	..		-5.8	-1.6	2.4	—	—	—	—
United Kingdom	1,403,844	23,590	2.6	2.1	3.0	—	1	—	5.9
United States	8,879,500	31,910	2.1	2.0	2.1	3	—	—	3.0
Uruguay	20,604	6,220	-0.4	3.0	35.2	13	6	65	1.1
Uzbekistan	17,613	720	0.8	-3.1	293.0	N.A.	33	658	0.6
Vanuatu	227	1,180	-0.2	-0.8	3.9	—	—	20	8.1
Venezuela	87,313	3,680	-1.5	-0.5	47.5	6	5	3,130	3.1
Vietnam	28,733	370	—	6.2	16.8	—	25	828	5.6
Yemen	6,088	360	—	-0.4	26.1	52	17	-150	-2.2
Yugoslavia[6]	—	—	-1.4	—	—	18	—	0	—
Zambia	3,222	330	-2.9	-2.4	57.4	11	25	151	5.2
Zimbabwe	6,302	530	0.2	0.6	23.6	15	20	70	1.1

Note: The World Bank reports data on Gross National Income (GNI) rather than Gross National Product (GNP). Figures in italics are for years other than those specified. 1. Data are shown for low and middle income countries only. 2. Data for years before 1990 refer to Czechoslovakia. 3. Data includes French Guiana, Guadeloupe, Martinique, and Réunion. 4. Data for years before 1990 refer to West Germany. 5. Data refers to mainland Tanzania only. 6. Former Yugoslav Republics of Serbia and Montenegro.
Source: The World Bank, The 2001 World Bank Atlas.

NATIONS OF THE WORLD

The following section presents major facts about all the nations of the world, including statistics on each nation's geography, people, government, economy, and written text describing highlights of the country's history.

The commonly used name for each country is listed first, followed by the formal name. A list of colonial and other former names is found in the following section, "Territories of the World." Geographical descriptions are listed in both miles and kilometers, and the latitude and longitude of most islands are given.

Sources of information include the Central Intelligence Agency of the United States, the United Nations, the U.S. Bureau of the Census, and the U.S. Department of State. Names of heads of government are from the United Nations official protocol office and are valid as of Sept. 2001.

▶AFGHANISTAN
Islamic State of Afghanistan
• **GEOGRAPHY Location:** landlocked country in southwestern Asia. **Boundaries:** Turkmenistan to NW, Tajikistan to N, China to NE, Pakistan to E and S, Iran to W. **Total area:** 250,000 sq. mi. (647,500 sq km). **Coastline:** none. **Comparative area:** slightly smaller than Texas. **Land use:** 12% arable land; negl. % permanent crops; 46% meadows and pastures; 3% forest and woodland; 39% other; includes negl. % irrigated. **Major cities:** (1982 est.) Kabul (capital) 1,036,407; Qandahar 191,345; Herat 150,497; Mazar-i-Sharif 110,367; Jalalabad 57,824.
• **PEOPLE Population:** 26,813,057 (July 2000 est.). **Nationality:** noun—Afghan(s); adjective—Afghan. **Ethnic groups:** 38% Pashtun, 25% Tajik, 19% Hazara, 6% Uzbek. **Languages:** 50% Afghan Persian (Dari), 35% Pashtu, 11% Turkic langs. (primarily Uzbek and Turkmen), 4% minor langs. (30, primarily Balochi and Pashai); much bilingualism. **Religions:** 84% Sunni Muslim, 15% Shi'a Muslim, 1% other.
• **GOVERNMENT Type:** transitional government. **Independence:** Aug. 19, 1919 (from U.K.). **Constitution:** none. **National holiday:** Victory of the Muslim Nation, Apr. 28. **Heads of government:** Since 1995 country ruled by Taliban military leaders; a civil war was ongoing as of September 1999.
• **ECONOMY Monetary unit:** afghani. **Budget: income:** N.A.; **expend.:** N.A. **GDP:** (2000 est.) $21 bil., $800 per capita. **Chief crops:** wheat, fruits, nuts, karakul pelts; wool, mutton. **Natural resources:** natural gas, crude oil, coal, copper, talc. **Major industries:** small-scale production of textiles, soap, furniture, shoes, fertilizer, and cement; hand-woven carpets; natural gas, oil, coal, and copper. **Labor force:** 10 mil.; 70% agriculture and animal husbandry, 15% services and other, 15% industry (1990 est.). **Exports:** $80 mil. (1996); opium, fruits and nuts, hand-woven carpets, wool, and cotton. **Imports:** $150 mil. (1996); food supplies, petroleum products. **Major trading partners:** former U.S.S.R., Pakistan, Iran.

Mountainous and landlocked, Afghanistan has been a crossroads of trans-Asian trade and conquest since antiquity. A part of the Persian Empire, Bactria was conquered by Alexander the Great, and became independent in the third century B.C. before falling to the Parthians in the next century. In the seventh century A.D., a flourishing Buddhist civilization there fell. to Islamic conquests. Genghis Khan overthrew the 11th-century empire of Mahmud of Gazni in the early 13th century, and Afghanistan was the center of Tamerlane's empire in the late 14th century. Thereafter, the region was divided among various tribes and petty kingdoms.

Modern Afghan history began with the establishment of a united emirate by Ahmed Shah Durrani in 1747. In the 19th century, Russia and Great Britain contested domination of Afghanistan. The British Afghan Wars of 1838-42 and 1878-80 left Afghanistan unconquered but within Britain's sphere of influence. Afghanistan achieved full independence from Britain in 1919 under Amanullah Khan, who proclaimed himself king in 1926. Modern reforms were instituted by Amanullah and his successors Mohammed Nadir Shah (1929-33) and Mohammed Zahir Shah (1933-73).

The monarchy fell to a military coup in 1973, and Mohammed Daud Khan established a republic. In 1978 pro-Soviet leftists took power in a coup, and, ostensibly at the government's invitation, Soviet troops invaded Afghanistan in December 1979 to put down widespread popular revolts against Communist rule. In the ensuing civil war, the government's forces and their Soviet allies (with an eventual troop strength of more than 100,000) controlled the cities and main transportation routes, but guerrilla forces contested the countryside. In 1988 the Soviet Union began a withdrawal of its troops, completed by February 1989. The rebel factions failed to achieve a united front and the pro-Soviet government confounded predictions that it would fall soon after the Soviet departure.

The government finally fell on Apr. 15, 1992, and rebel troops entered Kabul. A respected religious leader, Sibghatullah Mujaddidi, was named interim president, with the backing of a coalition of forces dominated by rebel commanders Abdul Rashid Dostam and Ahmad Shah Masoud. However, Gulbaddin Hekmatyar, leader of the fundamentalist Hizbe Islami faction, declined to join the ruling coalition. Fighting broke out in and around Kabul between coalition forces and Hekmatyar's troops.

On June 28 Mujaddidi turned over his power to the Leadership Council, which then elected Burhanuddin Rabbani as president. Fighting for control of Kabul continued between forces loyal to the Rabbani government and those backing Hekmatyar. Other factions later joined the fighting, and Kabul was subjected to continual rocket attacks in late 1992 and into the spring of 1993. Hekmatyar was named prime minister in an attempt to make peace. Fighting broke out again in early 1994 with Rabbani's followers getting the upper hand after fierce battles in Kabul.

By early 1995, the U.N. had brokered a scheme uniting the nine major factions in a council to which Rabbani would turn over power. But it was no sooner arranged than it was undone by the emergence of a new force: a fundamentalist Islamic militia called the Taliban, 20,000 strong and composed of students from the Islamic schools. Since 1995 Taliban forces have overrun most of the country and established a fundamentalist regime based on Islamic law. In Oct. 1996, three remaining groups of opposition factions formed a loose Northern Alliance and kept up sporadic fighting; but by 1999 the Taliban controlled over 90 percent of Afghanistan's territory.

The Taliban then consolidated its power and began to enforce a strict Muslim code of behavior. In

2001, the U.N. reported a precipitate drop in opium poppies grown in Afghanistan (producer of 75 percent of the world's opium), though whether it was attributable to the previous year's ban by the government, or to drought, is indeterminable. A second ban, in Feb. 2001, on all statues in the country led to the destruction in March of 1,400-year-old Buddhist cliff carvings in the region of Bamiyan, despite a wave of world protest. In Sept. 2001 Afghanistan became the focus of world attention when the U.S. demanded the Taliban turn over the terrorist leaders suspected of plotting the attack on the World Trade Center. (See "Major News Stories.")

▶ ALBANIA
Republic of Albania
● **GEOGRAPHY   Location:** southeastern Europe. **Boundaries:** Yugoslavia to N, Macedonia to E, Greece to S, and Adriatic and Ionian Seas (parts of Mediterranean Sea) to W. **Total area:** 11,100 sq. mi. (28,750 sq km). **Coastline:** 225 mi. (362 km). **Comparative area:** slightly smaller than Maryland. **Land use:** 21% arable land; 5% permanent crops; 15% meadows and pastures; 38% forest and woodland; 21% other; includes 1% irrigated. **Major cities:** (1990 est.) Tiranë (Tirana; capital) 244,200; Durrës (Durazzo) 85,400; Elbasan 83,300; Shkodër (Scutari) 81,900; Vlorë (Vlonë or Valona) 73,800.
● **PEOPLE   Population:** 3,510,484 (July 2001 est.). **Nationality:** noun—Albanian(s); adjective—Albanian. **Ethnic groups:** 95% Albanian, 3% Greek, 2% Vlach, Gypsy, Serb, and Bulgarian (1989 est.). **Languages:** Albanian (Tosk is official dialect), Greek. **Religions:** 70% Muslim, 20% Albanian Orthodox, 10% Roman Catholic (all churches and mosques were closed in 1967 and religious observances prohibited; in November 1990, Albania began allowing private religious practice).
● **GOVERNMENT   Type:** emerging democracy. **Independence:** Nov. 28, 1912 (from Ottoman Empire). **Constitution:** Nov. 28, 1998. **National holiday:** Independence Day, Nov. 28. **Heads of Government:** Rexhep Mejdani, president (since July 1997); Pandeli Majko, prime minister (since Oct. 1998). **Structure:** executive—president, prime minister, Council of Ministers; legislative—unicameral People's Assembly; judicial—Supreme Court.
● **ECONOMY   Monetary unit:** lek. **Budget:** (1997 est.) *income:* $393 mil.; *expend.:* $676 mil. **GDP:** (2000 est.) $10.5 bil., $3,000 per capita. **Chief crops:** vegetables, wheat, potatoes, fruits, sugar beets, corn. **Natural resources:** crude oil, natural gas, coal, chromium, copper. **Major industries:** food processing, textiles and clothing, lumber. **Labor force:** 1.7 mil. (1994 est.); 50% agriculture, 50% industry and services. **Exports:** $310 mil. (f.o.b., 2000 est.); textiles, footwear, asphalt, metals and ores, electricity, crude oil, vegetables, fruits, tobacco. **Imports:** $1 bil. (f.o.b., 2000 est.); machinery, consumer goods, grains. **Major trading partners:** Italy, Greece, Germany, Turkey.

The city of Epidamnus (Durrës) was colonized by Greeks from Corinth and Corcyra in 625 B.C. Later the Roman province of Illyricum, Albania was a much-coveted area after the fall of Rome and was in turn ruled by Byzantines, Normans, Venetians, Slavs, and the kings of Naples. Under the leadership of Skanderbeg (1405-68), Albania repelled repeated Turkish invasions. But Albania was part of the Ottoman Empire from 1478 until 1912. Ottoman rule succeeded in converting most of the populace to Islam (with Catholic minorities in the north and Greek Orthodox in the south) but did not destroy the Albanian sense of national identity, based on ties of tribe, clan, and family.

Independence came in 1912 as a result of the First Balkan War, when Austria-Hungary and Italy fostered the creation of an Albanian state. Occupied by its sponsors during World War I, Albania emerged from the war in a state of near-anarchy. With Yugoslav support, a tribal chief, Ahmed Zogu, became president of the republic in 1924; he proclaimed himself King Zog I in 1928.

In 1939 Italy invaded and annexed Albania. During World War II, partisan resistance was dominated by Communist forces under the leadership of Enver Hoxha. In 1944 Hoxha seized control of the government. A socialist republic was established in 1946: foreigners were expelled and their assets nationalized; churches were closed; agriculture and industry were collectivized. Albania under Hoxha became one of the world's most thoroughly totalitarian states.

A doctrinaire Stalinist, Hoxha broke with Nikita Khruschev's Soviet Union in 1961 and became a client state of China. But with liberalization in China after 1977, Hoxha broke that link as well. Albania became almost totally isolated from world affairs.

Hoxha died in April 1985 and was succeeded as president and first secretary of the Albanian Communist party by Ramiz Alia. In 1990, Alia eased restrictions on religion, tourism, and foreign investment, expanded trade, and allowed the formation of an opposition Democratic party. But he scheduled elections to the National Assembly for 1991, before awareness had spread of the old regime's faltering power. The Communists carried the rural districts and formed a coalition government with the Democrats, who carried the cities.

A year later, the Democrats completed the rout of the Communists, winning 92 of the 140 seats in the Assembly, and replacing Alia with Sali Berisha, a heart surgeon. But by the end of the year, factions within the Democratic party were already complaining about Pres. Berisha's "autocratic rule." Meanwhile, anarchy plagued much of the country, with food riots in the cities and armed brigandage in the countryside. EC and U.N. grants helped pay for needed imports and Italy provided invaluable assistance to the Albanian police forces. By 1993, zones of law and order were being established, churches were reopening, and 90 percent of farming had been privatized. But in November 1994, voters rejected (54-42) a new constitution proposed by Pres. Berisha.

In 1996 Berisha's Democratic Party won a major electoral victory amidst widespread complaints of fraud, but he and his followers were driven from office in 1997 after a series of pryamid schemes collapsed ruining the finances of tens of thousands of families who had participated in them. Violence and looting occured in many areas and a multi-national force of 7,000 was sent in to help restore order. The Socialists (formerly Communists) returned to power under Fatos Nana. In the spring of 1998 NATO advisors began to train Albania's tiny army as ethnic Albanians in the Kosovo province of Yugoslavia began a violent rebellion. Yugoslavia's suppression of the rebellion drove thousands of ethnic Albanians out of Kosovo into Albania. Amidst this further tumult, internal struggles continued between supporters of the Democratic Party and the Socialists, erupting into serious violence in September 1998. At the end of the month, prime minister Nano resigned and was replaced by Pandeli Majko. When, in October 1999, the Socialists chose Nano as their chairman, Majko resigned and was replaced by Deputy Premier, Ilir Meta.

▶ALGERIA
People's Democratic Republic of Algeria

● GEOGRAPHY **Location:** northern coast of Africa. **Boundaries:** Mediterranean Sea to N, Tunisia and Libya to E, Mali and Niger to S, Morocco, Western Sahara, Mauritania to W. **Total area:** 919,591 sq. mi. (2,381,740 sq km). **Coastline:** 620 mi. (998 km). **Comparative area:** slightly less than 3.5 times size of Texas. **Land use:** 3% arable land; negl. % permanent crops; 13% meadows and pastures; 2% forest and woodland; 82% other; includes negl. % irrigated. **Major cities:** (1984 est.) Algiers (capital) 1,721,607; Oran 663,504; Constantine 448,578; Annaba 348,322; Blida 191,314.
● PEOPLE **Population:** 31,736,053 (July 2001 est.). **Nationality:** noun—Algerian(s); adjective—Algerian. **Ethnic groups:** 99% Arab-Berber, less than 1% European. **Languages:** Arabic (official), French, Berber dialects. **Religions:** 99% Sunni Muslim (state religion), 1% Christian and Jewish.
● GOVERNMENT **Type:** republic. **Independence:** July 5, 1962 (from France). **Constitution:** Nov. 19, 1976, effective Nov. 22, 1976. **National holiday:** Anniversary of the Revolution, Nov. 1. **Heads of Government:** Abdelaziz Bouteflika, head of state (since Apr. 1999), Ali Benflis, prime minister (since Aug. 2000). **Structure:** executive; bicameral legislature; judicial—Supreme Court.
● ECONOMY **Monetary unit:** Algerian dinar. **Budget:** (2000 est.) *income:* $15.8 bil.; *expend.:* $16 bil. **GDP:** $171 bil., $5,500 per capita. **Chief crops:** wheat, barley, oats, grapes, olives. **Natural resources:** crude oil, natural gas, iron ore, phosphates, uranium. **Major industries:** petroleum, light industries, natural gas, mining. **Labor force:** 9.1 mil. (2000 est.); 29% government, 25% agriculture, 15% construction and public works, 11% industry, 20% other (1996 est.). **Exports:** $19.6 bil. (f.o.b., 2000 est.); petroleum and natural gas. **Imports:** $9.2 bil. (f.o.b., 2000 est.); capital goods, food, beverages, consumer goods. **Major trading partners:** *exports:* 22% Italy, 15% U.S., 12% France. *imports:* 30% France, 9% Italy, 7%Germany.

From around 3000 B.C. nomadic ancestors of the Berbers inhabited Algeria, as the expanding Sahara desert displaced prehistoric grasslands and forests. The Phoenicians established trading centers in the Mediterranean coastal plain around 1200 B.C. Those centers were taken over by the Romans beginning around 200 B.C. With Roman support the Berber chief Masinissa formed the kingdom of Numidia in what is now northern Algeria. From 46 B.C. to about A.D. 640, the area was controlled successively by the Romans, Germanic Vandal tribes, and the Byzantine Empire.

In the eighth century A.D., the Islamic conquests spread Arab culture to Numidia. Most of the Berbers converted to Islam. The blend of Berber and Arab culture in Algeria gave rise to a flourishing and rich Islamic civilization in the coastal plain, while Tuareg and other nomadic peoples controlled the sparsely inhabited interior.

Around 1500 the Christian kingdom of Spain captured Algiers and other coastal cities. In 1518 Barbarossa, a Turkish sea captain, captured Algiers and drove the Spanish out. In so doing, he joined Algeria to the expanding Turkish Ottoman Empire. Piracy became a key source of income for the Ottoman cities of Algeria. In the early 1800's,

France, along with England and the United States, began military operations to suppress piracy in the Mediterranean. In 1830 France invaded Algeria, putting an end to Ottoman rule and establishing their own administration. Algeria was ruled as part of France itself. Many French settlers (colons) migrated to Algeria. Both they and the native Algerians were considered citizens of France, but the colons were granted substantial political and economic advantages over the indigenous population.

In 1847 a rebellion led by Abd-al-Qadir, a powerful Muslim leader, was suppressed by the French. In 1848, in the wake of the rebellion, all of Algeria was conquered by the French and legally confirmed as an integral part of France. During World War II, many Algerians joined the Free French, hoping that their display of loyalty would be rewarded with greater self-rule after the war. Those hopes were disappointed, as French administration was resumed in 1945.

In 1954 the Front de Liberation Nationale (FLN) began a guerrilla war against the French in Algeria. They were opposed by French police and military forces and by the Secret Army Organization (OAS), an underground movement of colons who favored continued French rule. As the FLN gained strength, by 1958 French premier Charles de Gaulle established a policy designed to prepare Algeria for self-rule.

Algerian independence was proclaimed on July 3, 1962; a million colons fled to France. A power struggle within the new Algerian government was resolved when Ahmed Ben Bella became the country's first premier in 1963. In 1965 Ben Bella was deposed by Col. Houari Boumidienne, who ruled as the head of a military government. In 1967 Algeria declared war on Israel, broke with the West, and established close relations with the U.S.S.R. Since the early 1970's, relations with the West, and particularly with France, have improved (mainly because of oil).

The first free, multiparty elections were held on June 12, 1990. The Islamic Salvation Front, which advocates turning Algeria into an Islamic Republic, won overwhelming control of local assemblies. In 1991 it won 188 seats in Parliament out of 231 up for election and seemed poised to win control of the government when the army interceded to keep the old power structure in place. On June 19, 1992, Pres. Mohammed Boudiaf was assassinated, presumably by Islamic fundamentalists.

The military's High Security Council, knowing the Islamic parties would win any free election, repeatedly postponed a return to democracy. In January 1994 the High Security Council replaced the collective presidency of the High State Council with Gen. Liamine Zeroual. November 1995 saw the first contested presidential election since 1962, with Gen. Zeroual winning over 60 percent of the vote as major opposition groups boycotted the election. Elections in June 1997 produced Algeria's first mutli-party parliament since 1962, but the ruling military council still remained in control and in August Islamic fundamentalists killed over 300 in one night of terror. These vicious assasinations continued into 1998 with hundreds more having their throats cut in over several nights. Civil strife and assassinations have claimed the lives of over 40,000 since 1992. In Sept. 1998 Gen. Zeroual announced that elections would be held in Feb. 1999 and he would not be a candidate.

By the time the elections were held in April, all candidates had withdrawn from the race save one, the army-backed Abdelaziz Bouteflika. His new government reached an accord with the rebel Islamic Salvation Front: in return for the end of the uprising, Pres. Bouteflika pledged to release thousands of militant Islamic prisoners on July 5, Algeria's national holiday, and to submit the peace agreement to a referendum. In Sept. 98 percent of voters favored the agreement that gave amnesty to militants who surrendered. When the amnesty period ended (January 2000), the government claimed that 80 percent of the rebels had surrendered—probably an exaggeration—then commenced a major army offensive against remaining rebels, now organized as the "Armed Islamic Group" (GIA).

▶ ANDORRA
Principality of Andorra
● **GEOGRAPHY Location:** Pyrenees Mountains, southwestern Europe. **Boundaries:** France to N and E, Spain to S and W. **Total area:** 174 sq. mi. (450 sq km). **Coastline:** none. **Comparative area:** 2.5 times size of Washington, D.C. **Land use:** 4% arable land; 0% permanent crops; 45% meadows and pastures; 35% forest and woodland; 16% other. **Major cities:** (1989) Andorra la Vella (capital) 19,566.
● **PEOPLE Population:** 67,627 (July 2001 est.). **Nationality:** noun—Andorran(s); adjective—Andorran. **Ethnic groups:** 43% Spanish, 33% Andorran, 11% Portuguese, 7% French, 6% other. **Languages:** Catalan (official); many also speak some French and Castilian. **Religions:** virtually all Roman Catholic.
● **GOVERNMENT Type:** parliamentary democracy (since March 1993) that retains as head of state a co-principality; the two princes are the president of France and Spanish bishop of Seo de Urgel, who are represented locally by officials called veguers. **Independence:** 1278. **Constitution:** March 1993. **National holiday:** Mare de Deu de Meritxell, Sept. 8. **Heads of Government:** French co-prince Jacques Chirac, president of France (since 1995) and Spanish co-prince Episcopal Msgr. Joan Marti Alanís, bishop of Seo de Urgel, Spain (since 1971); Don Marc Forne Molne, prime minister (since Dec. 1994). **Structure:** executive—co-princes, executive council; unicameral legislature; judiciary—Supreme Court at Perpignan, France.
● **ECONOMY Monetary unit:** French franc and Spanish peseta. **Budget:** (1997) *income:* $385 mil.; *expend.:* $342 mil. **GDP:** $1.2 bil., $18,000 per capita (1996 est.). **Chief crops:** sheep raising; small quantities of tobacco, rye, wheat, barley, oats, and vegetables. **Natural resources:** hydropower, mineral water, timber, iron ore, lead. **Major industries:** tourism (particularly skiing), sheep, timber, tobacco, banking. **Labor force:** 30,787 salaried employees. **Exports:** $58 mil. (f.o.b., 1998); tobacco products, furniture. **Imports:** $1.077 bil. (c.i.f., 1998). **Major trading partners:** *exports:* 34% France, 58% Spain; *imports:* France, Spain, 4.2% U.S.

Set high in the Pyrenees, the tiny state of Andorra has been both a medieval relic and a modern capitalist land. Since 1278 Andorra has owed feudal allegiance to two co-rulers, the bishop of Seo de Urgel in Spain and, now, the president of France. Until 1993, Andorra had no constitution, so the exact rights of the corulers remained vague. Foreign affairs were handled by France.

Andorra's traditional economic mainstay had been the "transshipment of goods" (i.e., smuggling) between France and Spain. Andorra attracts tourists drawn by bargain shopping, and it is a banking center. Spain's 1986 entry into the E.U. led Andorra to seek a customs union with the EU. The March 1990 treaty was Andorra's first in over 700 years. In the same year, the co-princes introduced Andorra's first penal code and a sales tax, soon followed by the adoption of the EU's external tariff. In March 1993 voters—of whom there are only 9,123—adopted a modern constitution that will reduce the power of the co-princes and establish a government of three branches that will have authority to tax and to make foreign policy. In 1997 Premier Molne's party won a majority of seats in the General Council ending the coalition government.

▶ ANGOLA
Republic of Angola
● **GEOGRAPHY Location:** southwestern Africa. **Boundaries:** Zaire to N and NE, Zambia to E, Namibia to S, South Atlantic Ocean to W; Cabinda district separated from rest of country by Congo to N, Zaire to S. **Total area:** 481,352 sq. mi. (1,246,700 sq km). **Coastline:** 994 mi. (1,600 km). **Comparative area:** slightly less than twice size of Texas. **Land use:** 2% arable land; negl. % permanent crops; 23% meadows and pastures; 43% forest and woodland; 32% other. **Major cities:** Luanda (capital) 1,200,000 (1982 est.); Huambo (Nova Lisboa) 61,885; Lobito 59,258; Benguela 40,996; Lubango (São da Bandeira) 31,674 (1970 census).
● **PEOPLE Population:** 10,366,031 (July 2000 est.). **Nationality:** noun—Angolan(s); adjective—Angolan. **Ethnic groups:** 37% Ovimbundu, 25% Kimbundu, 13% Bakongo, 2% Mestiço, 1% European, 22% other. **Languages:** Portuguese (official), Bantu and other African languages. **Religions:** 47% indigenous beliefs, 38% Roman Catholic, 15% Protestant.
● **GOVERNMENT Type:** multiparty democracy (transitional). **Independence:** Nov. 11, 1975 (from Portugal). **Constitution:** Nov. 11, 1975 (last revised Aug. 26, 1992). **National holiday:** Independence Day, Nov. 11. **Heads of Government:** José Eduardo dos Santos, president (since Sept. 1979); Fernando van Dunem, prime minister (since June 1996). **Structure:** executive; unicameral legislature; judiciary.
● **ECONOMY Monetary unit:** new kwanza. **Budget:** (1992 est.) *income:* $928 mil.; *expend.:* $2.5 bil. **GDP:** $10.1 bil. (2000 est.), $1,000 per capita. **Chief crops:** bananas, sugarcane, coffee, sisal, corn, cotton, manioc (tapioca), vegetables. **Natural resources:** petroleum, diamonds, iron ore, phosphates, copper. **Major industries:** petroleum, mining (diamonds, iron ore, phosphates), food processing. **Labor force:** 5 mil. (1997 est.); 85% agriculture, 15% industry. **Exports:** $7.8 bil. (f.o.b., 2000 est.); 90% oil, diamonds, petroleum products, gas, coffee. **Imports:** $2.5 bil. (f.o.b., 2000 est.); machinery, electrical equipment, vehicles and spare parts, medicines, food, textiles and clothing; substantial military deliveries. **Major trading partners:** *exports:* 54% U.S., 14% South Korea; *imports:* 16% South Korea, 15% Portugal.

Bantu peoples have occupied Angola for at least 2,000 years. Portuguese explorers searching for a sea route to India founded Luanda (1575) and Benguela (1617). Portugal, at first in alliance with the north Angolan kingdom of Bakongo, engaged in an extensive trade of slaves to Brazil—3 million in 300 years.

In the late 19th century, Angola was organized as a Portuguese colony, sometimes called Portuguese West Africa. Portuguese settlers dominated local government, and trade, organized plantation-style cultivation of cotton, palm oil, bananas, and coffee. A railroad was built to transport exports of metal from the Katanga region of the Belgian Congo (now Zaire) to the coast.

By the 1950's non-Portuguese Angolans began to agitate for independence. The National Front spearheaded the liberation movement. Guerrilla warfare began in 1961, with several feuding factions fighting the Portuguese. Following the Portuguese revolution of 1974, factional warfare intensified and most Portuguese settlers fled the country. Independence came on Nov. 11, 1975.

Civil war between the National Front, the Popular Movement for the Liberation of Angola (MPLA), and the National Union for the Total Independence of Angola (UNITA) led, in 1976, to the victory of the MPLA, which organized a Marxist state with Soviet backing and Cuban technical support including 37,000 soldiers. Large portions of the country remained in the hands of UNITA, which continued the civil war with Chinese and American support through the 1980's.

Direct clashes between Angolan and South African troops occurred during the 1980's, as Angola gave shelter to SWAPO guerrilla forces seeking independence for Namibia. Cuban troops withdrew from Angola between January 1989 and May 1991, and a cease-fire between the government and UNITA was also concluded in May 1991. While agreeing to recognize the dos Santos government in the interim, UNITA called for elections to be held by September 1992, Angola's first since 1975.

In the elections, MPLA's candidate, José Eduardo dos Santos, decisively defeated UNITA's leader, Jonas Savimbi, but Savimbi's refusal to honor the results led to renewed fighting. The presence of thousands of U.N. peacekeepers from Feb. 1994 until Feb. 1999 made little dent in the continuing struggle which has claimed perhaps 100,000 lives. The government succeeded, in 2000, in taking two diamond-mining provinces as well as the town of Cazombo from UNITA, capping the year with an offer of amnesty, in a gesture of reconciliation.

▶ANTIGUA AND BARBUDA
• **GEOGRAPHY Location:** eastern Caribbean Sea approximately 300 mi. (480 km) SE of Puerto Rico. Antigua 17°06'N, 61°50'W; Barbuda 17°38'N, 61°48'W. **Boundaries:** Atlantic Ocean to N and E, Caribbean Sea to S and W. **Total area:** 170 sq. mi. (440 sq km). **Coastline:** 95 mi. (153 km). **Comparative area:** 2.5 times size of Washington, D.C. **Land use:** 18% arable land; 0% permanent crops; 9% meadows and pastures; 11% forest and woodland; 62% other. **Major cities:** (1986 est.) St. John's (capital) 36,000.
• **PEOPLE Population:** 66,970 (July 2001 est.). **Nationality:** noun—Antiguan(s), Barbudan(s); adjective—Antiguan, Barbudan. **Ethnic groups:** almost entirely of black African origin; some of British, Portuguese, Lebanese, and Syrian origin. **Languages:** English (official), local dialects. **Religions:** Anglican (predominant), other Protestant sects, some Roman Catholic.
• **GOVERNMENT Type:** parliamentary democracy. **Independence:** Nov. 1, 1981 (from U.K.). **Constitution:** Nov. 1, 1981. **National holiday:** Independence Day, Nov. 1. **Heads of Government:** Dr. James B. Carlisle, governor-general (since June 1993); Lester B. Bird, prime minister (since Mar. 1994). **Structure:** executive—governor general, prime minister, and cabinet; bicameral legislature; judiciary—East Caribbean Supreme Court.

• **ECONOMY Monetary unit:** East Caribbean (EC) dollar. **Budget:** (1997) *income:* $122.6 mil.; *expend.:* $141.2 mil. **GDP:** $533 mil., $8,200 per capita (1999 est.). **Chief crops:** cotton, fruits and vegetables, sugar. **Natural resources:** negl.; pleasant climate fosters tourism. **Major industries:** tourism, construction, light manufacturing (clothing, alcohol, household appliances). **Labor force:** 30,000 (1983); 82% commerce and services, 11% agriculture, 7% industry; 7% unemployment (1995 est.). **Exports:** $38 mil. (1998); 48% petroleum products, 23% manufactures, 17% machinery and transportation equipment, 4% food and live animals. **Imports:** $330 mil. (1998); food and live animals, machinery and transport equipment, manufactures, chemicals, oil. **Major trading partners:** *exports:* 26% OECS, 15% Barbados, 4% Guyana, 2% Trinidad and Tobago; *imports:* 27% U.S., 16% U.K., 4% Canada.

Columbus visited and claimed Antigua for Spain in 1493. It was settled by the British in 1632, who grew tobacco, and later sugar. The island's economy was hobbled by abolition of slavery in 1834, a succession of natural disasters in the 1840's, and the closing of the Royal Dockyard in 1854. Today, tourism is a mainstay of the economy, fostered by the ruling Antigua Labor Party, which won its sixth consecutive parliamentary victory in March 1999. But its second economic mainstay, offshore banking, has been shaken by a U.S. Treasury warning in April 1999 that lax standards make it susceptible to money-laundering.

▶ARGENTINA
Argentine Republic
• **GEOGRAPHY Location:** southern South America. **Boundaries:** Bolivia, Paraguay, Brazil to N.; Uruguay, South Atlantic Ocean to E.; Chile to W. **Total area:** 1,068,298 sq. mi. (2,766,890 sq km) (figures exclude Falkland Islands and Antarctic territory claimed by Argentina). **Coastline:** 3,099 mi. (4,989 km). **Comparative area:** slightly less than three-tenths the size of the United States. **Land use:** 9% arable land; 1% permanent crops; 52% meadows and pastures; 19% forest and woodland; 19% other. **Major cities:** (1991 census) Buenos Aires (capital) 12,960,976; Córdoba 1,148,305; La Matanza 1,111,811; Rosario 894,645; Morón 641,541.
• **PEOPLE Population:** 37,384,816 (July 2001 est.). **Nationality:** noun—Argentine(s); adjective—Argentine. **Ethnic groups:** 97% white, 3% mestizo, Indian, and other nonwhite groups. **Languages:** Spanish (official), English, Italian, German, French. **Religions:** 92% Roman Catholic (less than 20% practicing), 2% Protestant, 2% Jewish, 4% other.
• **GOVERNMENT Type:** republic. **Independence:** July 9, 1816 (from Spain). **Constitution:** May 1, 1853 (revised Aug. 1994). **National holiday:** Revolution Day, May 25. **Head of Government:** Fernando de la Rúa, president (since Dec. 1999). **Structure:** executive; bicameral legislature; judiciary.
• **ECONOMY Monetary unit:** nuevo peso argentino. **Budget:** (2000 est.) *income:* $44 bil.; *expend.:* $48 bil. **GDP:** (2000 est.) $476 bil., $12,900 per capita. **Chief crops:** wheat, corn, sorghum, soybeans, sugar beets. **Natural resources:** fertile plains of the pampas, lead, zinc, tin, copper, iron ore, petroleum. **Major industries:** food processing (especially meat packing), motor vehicles, consumer durables. **Labor force:** 15 mil. (1999 est.); 57% services, 31% industry, 12% agriculture; 12% unemployment (1998 est.). **Exports:** $26.5 bil. (f.o.b., 2000 est.); edible oils, cereals, feed, mo-

tor vehicles, crude petroleum, steel manufactures. **Imports:** $25.2 bil. (f.o.b., 2000 est.); motor vehicles and parts, chemicals, telecommunications equipment, plastics. **Major trading partners:** *exports:* 24% Brazil, 21% EU, 11% U.S.; *imports:* 28% EU, 21% Brazil, 22% U.S.

The indigenous nomads of the area around the river La Plata resisted Spanish intrusion, which began with the first founding of Buenos Aires by Pedro de Mendoza in 1536. Argentina was part of Spain's Viceroyalty of Peru until reforms in the Bourbon dynasty and a need to defend against Portuguese encroachment from Brazil led to the formation of the Viceroyalty of La Plata, including Argentina, Bolivia, Paraguay, and Uruguay, in 1776. Following the relaxation of trade restrictions two years later, Buenos Aires grew from a small town to a city of 50,000 by 1800. A provisional junta of the Provinces of Río de la Plata was established in 1810 after the Napoleonic occupation of Spain, and in 1816 the United Provinces of the Río de la Plata declared their independence.

After independence the question of political relations among the United Provinces was settled by a federalist solution in which the provinces dissolved into a number of practically independent republics. In 1824, a constituent assembly created the office of president, first held by Bernardino Rivadavia. However, the failure to ratify a workable constitution caused Rivadavia to resign.

Juan Manuel de Rosas became governor of Buenos Aires in 1829 and presided over the construction of a federal agreement between the provinces in 1831. Rosas governed Buenos Aires with an iron hand until his expulsion in 1852. The other provinces formed the Argentine Federation, based on a federal constitution of 1853, but Buenos Aires refused to join. Buenos Aires and the Argentine Federation entered into war between 1859 and 1861; they reached an agreement on the inclusion of Buenos Aires in the Argentine Republic in 1862.

Argentina joined Brazil and Uruguay in a war (1865-70) against Paraguay. During the latter part of the 1870's, the government took the initiative against the indigenous populations of Patagonia and Tierra del Fuego, which were partitioned with Chile. Immigration from Europe, especially Spain and Italy, resulted in enormous growth from the mid-19th century. In 1869, there were 2 million inhabitants; by 1914, 8 million; by 1955, 19 million; and by 1990, 32 million. Prior to World War II, Argentina was acutely Eurocentric, with an eye to British finance and French culture; this has changed since.

The Argentine military, led by Lt. Gen. José F. Uriburu, ousted the civilian government of the Radical party in 1930 with the intention of following the European model of politics. In 1946 Juan Domingo Perón won the presidential election and constructed a populist political alliance that included workers, industrialists, and the armed forces. The Perón-inspired populist ideology of justicialismo included extension of the franchise to women and redistribution of income to workers and the poor. The activities of Perón's charismatic wife, Eva, bolstered justicialismo through her effort to distribute goods to the poor through the Social Aid Foundation.

Tied in with Perón's populist strategy was his policy of nationalist economic development, whereby state-led development was financed through extraction of capital from the old export-agricultural elite and politically supported through populism. The Perón government incurred great expense to gain control over foreign-owned economic infrastructure, including railway systems, telephone companies, and dock facilities. A number of events led to Perón's downfall in 1955. The market for Argentine goods deteriorated after World War II. As Perón shifted his strategy to encourage foreign investment and impose economic austerity, repression against the political opposition grew. The death of Eva Perón in 1952 robbed Perón of an important political resource, and when the government challenged the Catholic church on a number of issues, the military ousted Perón.

After a brief period of military rule, in which an attempt was made to roll back "Perónismo," Arturo Frondizi of the "Intransigent" faction of the Radical party won the presidency and assumed office in 1958. In the following years, the military repeatedly attempted to keep the Perónistas from returning to power. In 1962 the military forced Frondizi to annul Perónist victories in provincial elections and removed him from office. Pres. Arturo Illia was ousted from office in 1966 for the same reason: his failure to tame Perón's followers.

A military bureaucratic authoritarian regime led by a series of Argentine officers was established during 1966-73. Extreme violence by factions on the Left and Right led the military to accept Perón's return to the presidency in 1973. Perón died the following year, and his third wife, Isabel, replaced him in office; she was unable to retain power, and the military removed her in 1976 in the midst of economic and political upheaval.

Determined to deal with what they saw as a leftist threat, the military again opted for a bureaucratic authoritarian solution. As part of this "solution," the armed forces launched what was later called the "dirty war" against leftists, during which up to 20,000 people disappeared and were never heard from again. The authoritarian government collapsed after the ill-starred 1982 Falkland/Malvinas Islands War against Britain led to the resignation of the junta and the holding of elections. Raúl Alfonsín, of the Radical Union party, was elected president in the wake of these events in 1983. In 1989, he was succeeded by Carlos Saúl Menem, who agreed to take office early, in the midst of a severe economic crisis during which inflation reached 3,000 percent and foreign debt $58 billion.

Menem encouraged free enterprise and good relations with the U.S. Government controls on foreign investment and trade were relaxed, and the government sold off many state enterprises. In 1993 Argentina's 11-year debt crisis officially ended, and by 1995 inflation was down to 4 percent.

In 1995 the government introduced an austerity plan to fight the budget deficit and to cushion the shocks of Mexico's devaluation. As Argentina's economy began to flourish, Menem was reelected, and his party won majorities in both houses of the legislature and control of more than half of Argentina's provincial governments. But in May 1997, violent protests erupted in several major cities, as unemployment rose to nearly 20 percent. In October, the Peronistas lost control of the Chamber of Deputies, for the first time since 1983, to a left-wing coalition known as The Alliance. Presidential elections in October 1999 brought the first-ever Peronista defeat, as Alliance's Fernando de la Rúa defeated Eduardo Duhalde, while further Alliance legislative victories brought them within five seats of an absolute majority in the House of Deputies.

Throughout 2000, the rather fragile Alliance managed to move gingerly to fight corruption, to reform certain privileges of organized labor, and to balance the federal and state budgets. This was sufficient to gain a pledge from the I.M.F. and other international lenders for a $40 billion bailout, but by the middle of 2001 the recession had grown worse and the government put a severe austerity plan in place.

▶ARMENIA
Republic of Armenia

• **GEOGRAPHY Location:** southwest Transcaucasia between Europe and Asia. **Boundaries:** Georgia to N, Azerbaijan to E, Iran to S, Turkey to W. Nakhichevan Autonomous Republic, an Azerbaijan territory, is an enclave within Armenian territory. **Total area:** 11,506 sq. mi. (29,800 sq km). **Coastline:** none. **Comparative area:** slightly smaller than Maryland. **Land use:** 17% arable land; 3% permanent crops; 24% meadows and pastures; 15% forest and woodlands; 41% other. **Major cities:** (1990 est.) Yerevan (capital) 1,202,000; Kumayri (formerly Leninakan) 123,000; Kirovakan 76,000.

• **PEOPLE Population:** 3,336,100 (July 2001 est.). **Nationality:** noun—Armenian(s); adjective—Armenian. **Ethnic groups:** 93% Armenian, 3% Azeri, 2% Russian. **Languages:** 96% Armenian, 2% Russian, 2% other. **Religions:** 94% Armenian Orthodox.

• **GOVERNMENT Type:** republic. **Independence:** Sept. 23, 1991 (from U.S.S.R.). **Constitution:** July 5, 1995. **National holiday:** Referendum Day, Sept. 21. **Heads of Government:** Robert Kocharian, president (since April 1998); Andranik Markaryan, prime minister (since May 2000). **Structure:** executive; unicameral legislatiure; judiciary.

• **ECONOMY Monetary unit:** dram. **Budget:** (1999 est.) *income:* $360 mil.; *expend.:* $566 mil. **GDP:** $10 bil., $3,000 per capita (2000 est.). **Chief crops:** fruit (especially wine grapes), vegetables, livestock. **Natural resources:** small deposits of gold and copper. **Major industries:** Industrial machinery, electrical equipment, tires, textiles (much of industry). **Labor force:** 1.5 mil. (1999). **Exports:** $284 mil. (f.o.b, 2000 est.); diamonds, scrap metal, machinery. **Imports:** $913 mil. (f.o.b., 2000 est.); natural gas, petroleum, tobacco products, foodstuffs. **Major trading partners:** Iran, Russia, Belgium.

Armenia, a small landlocked country just south of the great Caucasus mountain range, is but a fragment of ancient Armenia, one of the world's oldest civilizations dating back to the sixth century B.C. In about A.D. 300, Armenia adopted Christianity, which today is still an important component of Armenian national identity. Because Armenia forms part of a land bridge between the Black and the Caspian Seas, and between Turks and Slavs, it has long been overrun and controlled by the Byzantine, Arab, Ottoman, Mongol, and Russian Empires. In 1236 the Tatar and Mongol invasion spelled the end of Armenia as a separate state. In 1639, after the conclusion of a major war between Turkey and Iran, the territory of Armenia was partitioned. By the end of the 17th century, czarist Russia was also involved in Armenia, and in 1828 eastern Armenia was ceded to the Russian empire by the Treaty of Turkmenchai.

During the First World War, those Armenians living in the western part of the country under Ottoman rule were increasingly subjected to persecution by the Turks. In April 1915, the Turks forcibly removed the Armenians from the border area, during which more than a million of them either starved or were killed. In 1918, an Armenian republic emerged as the Russian empire collapsed, but this entity was short-lived, as Turkey, Russia, and later Britain fought for control. Finally, the Soviet Red Army moved into the territory and on Nov. 29, 1920, declared it a Soviet republic. Armenia was made part of the Transcaucasian Soviet Federal Socialist Republic of the U.S.S.R. in 1922, and in 1936, it became one of the Soviet Union's constituent union republics.

Armenian Christians have been subjected to many years of persecution by various invaders, causing a great diaspora of Armenians, especially to the United States and Europe. This large expatriate community has helped Armenia from abroad through difficult times.

Since 1988, Armenia's most pressing issue has been the war over Nagorno-Karabakh, the Armenian Christian enclave of Muslim Azerbaijan. Fighting broke out when 180,000 ethnic Armenians in Azerbaijan demanded that their homeland become part of Armenia. The war continued even as both nations declared their independence from the Soviet Union (Armenia on Sept. 23, 1991; Azerbaijan a month later). In October 1991, Levon Ter-Petrossian was elected president of independent Armenia, and in December, Armenia was one of 11 former Soviet republics to sign the Alma-Ata Declaration, creating the Commonwealth of Independent States. Since independence, Armenia has remained committed to the war over Nagorno-Karabakh, even though it has hindered the functioning of the stagnant Armenian economy.

In 1995, a new "strong president" constitution was approved by 68 percent in a referendum and Pres. Ter-Petrossian's six-party Republic Coalition carried a majority of seats in the first elections for the 190-seat National Assembly. He was reelected in 1996 but resigned in February 1998 in a dispute over policy toward Nagorno-Karabakh with his hard-line premier Robert Kocharian. In March, Kocharian easily won the presidential election over Soviet-era ruler Karen Demirchyan. In October 1999, gunmen entered Parliament, murdering premier Vazgen Sargissian and seven others. President Kocharian named Sargissian's brother, Aram, a political neophyte, as new premier. Talks with Azerbaijan over the status of Nagorno-Karabakh were reopened in 2001.

▶AUSTRALIA
Commonwealth of Australia

• **GEOGRAPHY Location:** continent of Australia, between Indian and Pacific Oceans. **Boundaries:** nearest neighbor is Papua New Guinea, to N. **Total area:** 2,967,897 sq. mi. (7,686,850 sq km). **Coastline:** 16,010 mi. (25,760 km). **Comparative area:** slightly smaller than U.S. **Land use:** 6% arable land; negl. % permanent crops; 54% meadows and pastures; 19% forest and woodland; 21% other; includes negl. % irrigated. **Major cities:** (1993 est.) Canberra (capital) 325,400; Sydney 3,719,000; Melbourne 3,187,500; Brisbane 1,421,700; Perth 1,221,300.

• **PEOPLE Population:** 19,357,594 (July 2001 est.). **Nationality:** noun—Australian(s); adjective—Australian. **Ethnic groups:** 92% Caucasian, 7% Asian, 1% aboriginal and other. **Languages:** English, native langs. **Religions:** 26.1% Anglican, 26% Roman Catholic, 24.3% other Christian, 11% non-Christian.

• **GOVERNMENT Type:** democratic, federal-state system. **Independence:** Jan. 1, 1901 (from federation of U.K. colonies). **Constitution:** July 9, 1900; effective Jan. 1, 1901. **National holiday:** Australia Day, Jan. 26. **Heads of Government:** Sir William Deane, governor general (since Feb. 1996); John Howard, prime minister (since Mar. 1996). **Structure:** executive—governor general (appointed by the Queen), prime minister, and cabinet; bicameral legislature; independent judiciary.

●**ECONOMY Monetary unit:** Australian dollar. **Budget:** (1999 est.) *income:* $94 bil.; *expend.:* $103 bil. **GDP:** (2000 est.) $445.8 bil.; $23,200 per capita. **Chief crops:** wheat, barley, sugarcane, fruits; poultry. **Natural resources:** bauxite, coal, iron ore, copper, tin. **Major industries:** mining, industrial and transportation equipment, food processing. **Labor force:** 9.5 mil. (1999); 73% services, 22% industry, 5% agriculture, 6.4% unemployment (2000). **Exports:** $69 bil. (f.o.b., 2000 est.); coal, gold, meat, wool. **Imports:** $77 bil. (f.o.b., 2000 est.); machinery and transport equipment, computers and office machines, telecommunication equipment and parts. **Major trading partners:** *exports:* 19% Japan, 12% ASEAN, 14% EU; *imports:* 24% EU, 22% U.S., 14% Japan.

The continent-nation of Australia is distinguished by its geographical isolation and by the unique flora and fauna which that isolation has fostered. The ancestors of today's aborigines arrived from Southeast Asia as much as 40,000 years ago. Thereafter, aborigine culture evolved in isolation except for some contact between the peoples of the northern coast and New Guinea. Australia was first sighted by Europeans at the beginning of the 17th century. In the 18th century, it was visited by the Dutch, who named it New Holland. The eastern coast was systematically explored in 1770 by Capt. James Cook, who claimed it for Great Britain.

British settlement began in 1788, with the landing of about 700 convicts near Sydney. Australia remained a penal colony during the first half of the 19th century, during which time the continent was explored and separate colonies were established. Aboriginal populations were displaced and in some areas (most notably the island Tasmania) totally exterminated. Discovery of gold in Victoria in 1851 created a gold rush that greatly accelerated immigration. By the end of the 19th century, the three mainstays of the Australian economy—livestock (beef and sheep), mining, and wheat growing—were firmly established.

In 1901, a commonwealth was established consisting of a confederation of the various states except for the Northern Territory, which was added in 1911. The British Crown is represented by an appointed governor-general; the national government is a parliamentary system, but much local authority resides in the separate states. Comprehensive social welfare legislation was passed by the state and national governments soon after the commonwealth's formation. The population is highly educated and enjoys a generally high standard of living, but most aborigines are detribalized and live in considerable poverty.

Australian troops fought with distinction in both world wars. A Japanese threat to Australia in 1942 was averted by Allied victory in the Battle of the Coral Sea. Australia and the United States are firm allies, and Australian troops joined U.S. forces in Korea, Vietnam, and the Persian Gulf War. Australia administers several external island groups and claims territory in Antarctica. (See "Territories of the World.")

The abandonment of discriminatory immigration practices in 1973 led to a new wave of immigration, particularly from Asia. In the process Australian economic ties to Asia and the Pacific Rim have expanded considerably. New exploitation of mineral resources has in many cases been accomplished with Japanese investment or with long-term export contracts to Japan. Australia has undergone considerable industrial development in the past two decades.

After 10 years in office, Prime Minister Bob Hawke was ousted by his own Labour party in 1991 and replaced by Paul Keating. Keating's government was convincingly reelected in 1993 elections, despite a persistent economic slump. But continued high spending and taxes took their toll, and in 1996, 13 years of Labour rule ended. A coalition of the more conservative Liberal and Nationalist parties captured 94 of 148 seats in the House of Representatives, with Labour falling to 47. The popular Liberal party leader John Howard became the new prime minister.

In Oct. 1998 elections, the Liberal-Nationalist coalition maintained its control of the House of Representatives, though by a diminished margin, with 79 of the 148 seats. In the interim, Australia's Constitutional Convention voted (in Feb. 1998) to proclaim Australia a republic, severing its residual ties to the British Crown. But in a November 1999 referendum, voters rejected the republic by 55 percent to 45 percent. With respect to aboriginal claims to Australian land, the government carried a Native Title Bill in July 1998, giving Australia's state governments authority to rule on the issue, and requiring claimants to prove an actual connection to the land claimed.

▶ **AUSTRIA**
Republic of Austria
●**GEOGRAPHY Location:** landlocked country in central Europe. **Boundaries:** Germany and Czech Republic to N, Hungary and Slovak Republic to E, Slovenia and Italy to S, Switzerland and Liechtenstein to W. **Total area:** 32,377 sq. mi. (83,858 sq km). **Coastline:** none. **Comparative area:** slightly smaller than Maine. **Land use:** 17% arable land; 1% permanent crops; 23% meadows and pastures; 39% forest and woodland; 20% other; includes negl. % irrigated. **Major cities:** (1991 census) Vienna (capital) 1,533,176; Graz 232,155; Linz 202,855; Salzburg 143,971; Innsbruck 114,996.
●**PEOPLE Population:** 8,150,835 (July 2001 est.). **Nationality:** noun—Austrian(s); adjective—Austrian. **Ethnic groups:** 98% German, Croatian, Slovene, other. **Languages:** German. **Religions:** 78% Roman Catholic, 5% Protestant, 17% none or other.
●**GOVERNMENT Type:** federal republic. **Constitution:** 1920; revised 1929; reinstated May 1945. **National holiday:** National Day, Oct. 26. **Heads of Government:** Thomas Klestil, president (since July 1992); Dr. Wolfgang Schüssel, chancellor (since Feb. 2000). **Structure:** executive; bicameral legislature; directly elected president whose functions are largely representational; independent federal judiciary.
●**ECONOMY Monetary unit:** Austrian schilling. **Budget:** (2000 est.) *income:* $56.3 bil.; *expend.:* $60.5 bil. **GDP:** (2000 est.) $203 bil., $25,000 per capita. **Chief crops:** grain, fruits, potatoes, sugar beets. **Natural resources:** iron ore, crude oil, timber, magnesite, lead. **Major industries:** construction machinery, vehicles and parts, food. **Labor force:** 3.7 mil. (1999); foreign laborers number 298,000; 68% services, 29% industry and crafts, 0.7% agriculture and forestry; 5.4% unemploy-

ment (2000 est.); estimated 150,000 Austrians are employed in other European countries. **Exports:** (2000 est.) $63.2 bil.; machinery and equipment, paper and cardboard, metal goods.. **Imports:** (2000 est.) $65.6 bil.; vehicles, machinery and equipment, apparel, metal goods. **Major trading partners:** (1999) *exports:* 64.2% EU, 4.5% U.S.; *imports:* 70.3% EU, 5.4% U.S., 2.8% Hungary.

The Celtic tribes in what is now Austria were conquered by Rome under Emperor Augustus. After the fall of Rome, it was overrun by Huns, Lombards, Ostrogoths, and Bavarians. In 788 it was incorporated into the empire of Charlemagne. From the 9th to the 13th century, its territory was divided among a variety of feudal domains. In the late 13th century, Austria was reunited under Rudolph I of Habsburg, whose dynasty became synonymous with Austrian history for the next seven centuries. Rudolph's successors steadily enlarged their domain by conquest and marital diplomacy until, by the reign of Charles V (1500-58), they ruled not only the Holy Roman Empire (encompassing most of central Europe) but also the Netherlands, Spain, and all of its colonies.

After the reign of Charles V, the Habsburg Empire was split into two branches, one governing Spain, the other the Holy Roman Empire. Habsburg power in Germany declined after the Thirty Years' War (1618-48) but was affirmed in the Danube valley after the defeat of the Turkish siege of Vienna in 1683 and the subsequent reconquest of Hungary from the Turks. The marriage of Maria Teresa to Francis of Lorraine gave rise to the House of Habsburg-Lorraine in 1745. In 1804 the Austrian empire was founded, and two years later, the defunct Holy Roman Empire was abolished. The Ausgleich ("compromise") of 1867 transformed the empire into the Dual Monarchy of Austria-Hungary.

In 1914 the assassination of Archduke Franz Ferdinand, the heir to the Austrian throne, led to the outbreak of World War I, which resulted in a wholesale redrawing of national boundaries in Central Europe. Austria emerged as a small Alpine republic, with about 12 percent of the territory of the old Dual Monarchy. The new republic faced a severe postwar economic crisis, as well as a political stalemate between the Christian Social party and the Social Democratic party, each with the support of about half of the electorate, and each with its own paramilitary organization.

In 1933, as Hitler's National Socialists rose to power in Germany, Austrian Chancellor Engelbert Dollfuss, leader of the Christian Social party, instituted rule by decree and began building a corporate state modeled on Italian fascism. His attempt to disarm the Social Democratic militia led to civil war. The government triumphed, but Dollfuss was assassinated in an attempted coup by Austrian Nazis in July 1934. Hitler finally forced Austrian union with Germany (the Anschluss) in 1938, after which Austria was considered a part of Greater Germany.

Conquered by American and Soviet troops early in 1945, Austria was divided into French, British, American, and Russian zones of occupation after World War II. But the occupying powers permitted the formation of a unified national government, formed in November 1945 and recognized by the Western powers in 1946. The occupation ended in 1955 with the signing of the Austrian State Treaty. The four powers withdrew their forces, and Austria pledged itself to a policy of permanent neutrality, with no foreign military alliances or military bases on Austrian territory.

The coalition government continued to 1966, when the People's party under Josef Klaus gained a parliamentary majority. In 1970 the Socialist party under Bruno Kreisky came to power. Socialist dominance continued until 1983, when the Socialists had to form a coalition with the right-wing Freedom party in order to stay in power. Kreisky resigned and was succeeded by Fred Sinowatz.

From 1986 to 1997, a "Grand Coalition" of the Socialist and People's Parties governed Austria under Socialist Chancellor Franz Vranitzky. In ten years, the government cautiously privatized state-owned enterprises of the mild Austrian form of socialism, while tourism, a highly developed maunfacturing sector, and substantial petroleum reserves contributed to the country's prosperity. The government dramatically cut taxes and began promoting regional trade with the newly-independent states of East-Central Europe. On Jan. 1, 1995, Austria entered the European Union.

Tensions arising from increasing unemployment and growing immigration of "economic refugees" from Asia and Africa as well as from Eastern Europe led to some worrisome results: amending Austria's asylum law, consideration of immigration quotas, and the growing strength of the right-wing Freedom Party. The desire to meet the EU's single currency standards led to welfare spending cuts which provoked further voter dissatisfaction. In Oct. 1996 Austrian voters (participating for the first time in European Parliament elections), gave Freedom Party candidates, who are opposed to Austria's participation in EMU, 27.6% of their votes, while Socialists garnered only 29.1% and the People's Party took 29.6%.

Denying any connection with these voting results, Chancellor Vranitzky resigned in January 1997 and was succeeded by Socialist Finance Minister Viktor Klima. In the October 1999 elections to the National Council, the Social Democrats received only one-third of the votes, while the People's Party and the Freedom Party each took 27 percent. When it proved impossible to reconstruct the "Grand Coalition," the latter two parties, together controlling 104 of 183 seats, formed their own coalition government, taking office on February 4, 2000 with Wolfgang Schuessel of the People's Party as chancellor.

With the Freedom Party (but not its now-resigned party leader Joerg Haider) entering the Austrian government, the other 14 E.U. governments cut off bilateral diplomatic contacts, as did Israel and the U.S. The E.U. lifted the sanctions in September after their blue-ribbon investigative panel reported the superiority of Austria's treatment of immigrants to that of many other E.U. members; subsequently, in some state and local elections, the Freedom Party's share of the vote has shown slippage.

▶ AZERBAIJAN
Azerbaijani Republic

● GEOGRAPHY **Location:** southern Transcaucasia between Europe and Asia. **Boundaries:** Georgia to NW, Russian Federation to N, Caspian Sea to E, Iran to S, Armenia to SW. Nakhichevan Autonomous Republic (ASSR) is part of Azerbaijan although it is inside Armenian territory. **Total land area:** 33,436 sq. mi. (86,600 sq km). **Coastline:** Caspian Sea. **Comparative area:** about the size of Maine. **Land use:** 18% arable land, 5% permanent crops, 25% meadows and pastures, 11% forests and woodland, 41% other. **Major cities:** (1990 est.) Baku (capital) 1,149,000; Gyanja (formerly Kirovabad) 281,000; Sumgait 235,000.

●**PEOPLE   Population:** 7,771,092 (July 2001 est.). **Nationality:** noun—Azerbaijani(s) or Azeri(s); adjective—Azerbaijani. **Ethnic groups:** 90% Azeri, 3.2% Dagestani Peoples, 2.5% Russian. **Languages:** 89% Azeri, 3% Russian, 2% Armenian, 6% other (1995 est.). **Religions:** 93.4% Muslim, 2.5% Russian Orthodox, 2.3% Armenian Orthodox, 1.8% other (1995 est.).

●**GOVERNMENT   Type:** republic. **Independence:** Aug. 30, 1991 (from U.S.S.R.). **Constitution:** Nov. 12, 1995. **National holiday:** May 28. **Heads of Government:** Heydar Aliyev, president (since Oct. 1993); Artur Rasizade, prime minister (since Nov. 1996). **Structure:** executive; unicameral legislatiure; judiciary.

●**ECONOMY   Monetary unit:** manat. **Budget:** (1999 est.) *income*: $777 mil.; *expend.:* $995 mil. **GDP:** $23.5 bil., $3,000 per capita (2000 est.). **Chief crops:** cotton, tea, tobacco, grain, fruit. **Natural resources:** petroleum, natural gas, iron ore. **Major industries:** petroleum and natural gas, construction materials, chemicals. **Labor force:** 2.9 mil. (1997). **Exports:** $1.9 bil. (f.o.b., 2000 est.); oil, gas, oil field equipment, textiles, cotton. **Imports**: $1.4 bil. (f.o.b., 2000 est.); machinery and parts, foodstuffs, metals. **Major trading partners:** Turkey, Russia, Iran.

The territory of present-day Azerbaijan has been inhabited since Paleolithic times. The name Azerbaijan is derived (via Arabic and Turkish) from Atropates (a vassal of Alexander III of Macedonia), who founded an independent state here in the fourth century B.C. The population of Azerbaijan is approximately seven million, but nearly seven million additional Azeris with the same language and faith live across the border in Iran.

For much of its history, the territory of Azerbaijan, home to an indigenous nomadic people, has been occupied by Persians, Muslim Arabs, Turkic tribes from Mongolia, Ottoman Turks, Mongols, and in the 18th century, Russians. The capital city of Baku was an important outlet on the Volga River-Caspian Sea route; under Peter the Great, the Russians occupied Baku and Derbent, and for a while controlled the Caspian Sea. Command of this territory shifted between Ottomans, Persians, and Russians in the 18th and 19th centuries, with the Russians ultimately establishing military rule by 1828 with the Treaty of Turkmenchai. This treaty ceded the southern half of the country to Persia and the northern half to Russia.

Under the Russians, Azerbaijan became an industrial center and eventually a major oil producer. In 1883 the Russians finished building the Transcaucasian Railway, which linked Baku with the Black Sea coast and central Russia and made Baku one of the most important industrial hubs in the Russian empire. Baku became a revolutionary center around the turn of the century. In 1918 an independent republic was formed, but in 1920 it was overthrown by the Soviet Red Army, and in April 1920 the Azerbaijan Soviet Socialist Republic (SSR) was proclaimed. Two years later, it was joined with the Armenian and Georgian SSRs to form the Transcaucasian Soviet Federal Socialist Republic; in 1936, however, the three again became separate union republics.

While a Soviet republic, Azerbaijan was industrialized, its agriculture collectivized, and religious persecution was severe. It also entered into a war in 1988 with neighboring Armenia over the Nagorno-Karabakh region, which is largely populated with ethnic Armenians but lies within Azerbaijani territory. The local council of Nagorno-Karabakh petitioned the Armenian and Azerbaijani Supreme Soviets to transfer the region to Armenia in February 1988, but Azerbaijan refused, spurring a war that lasts to this day and has resulted in thousands of casualties on both sides.

In January 1990, a series of attacks on Communist party buildings and against Armenians in Azerbaijan precipitated a brutal Soviet Army intervention to restore order. A state of emergency was declared, and the first secretary of the Communist party was fired and replaced by Ayaz Mutalibov. He was elected president in Sept. 1991, and on Oct. 18, 1991, Azerbaijan's Supreme Soviet declared the country's independence. On Dec. 21, 1991, Azerbaijan joined 10 other former Soviet republics in forming the Commonwealth of Independent States.

After the dissolution of the U.S.S.R., Soviet power was diminished, but Azerbaijan had problems consolidating its own political future. In early 1992, Pres. Mutalibov was forced from office. His successor, Abulfaz Elchibey, was in turn driven out of office by armed rebels after the fighting in Nagorno-Karabakh turned decisively in Armenia's favor. He was replaced by Heydar Aliyev, a former Communist party boss, in 1993. Aliyev survived two coup attempts and the country's flagging fortunes in Nagorno-Karabakh to complete a $7.4 billion deal with western companies to develop oil fields in the Caspian Sea in Sept. 1994. In parliamentary elections in 1995, Aliyev's New Azerbaijan party won 70 percent of the vote, despite charges of vote-rigging. And in Jan. 1996, Aliyev negotiated an agreement to transport oil from the Caspian Sea via pipeline (through Chechnya) to the Russian port of Novorossiysk for export to the world market. The pipeline opened Nov. 12, 1997 only three months after Aliyev met with Pres. Clinton in Washington to sign a treaty allowing unrestricted transfer of profits and capital between U.S. and Azerbaijan.

In Oct. 1998, Aliyev held presidential elections which were boycotted by opposition parties and which European monitors declared to be seriously irregular. Aliyev took 76 percent of the vote. In parliamentary elections in Nov. 2000, his New Azerbaijan Party carried 70 percent of the vote, to no one's surprise.

▶**BAHAMAS**
Commonwealth of The Bahamas

●**GEOGRAPHY   Location:** nearly 700 islands in an archipelago that extends 590 mi. (950 km) SE-NW between Florida and Haiti. Nassau 25°05'N, 77°20'W. **Boundaries:** western Atlantic Ocean to N, E, S, and W. **Total land area:** 5,382 sq. mi. (13,940 sq km). **Coastline:** 2,200 mi. (3,542 km). **Comparative area**: slightly larger than Connecticut. **Land use:** 1% arable land; negl. % permanent crops; negl. % meadows and pastures; 32% forest and woodland; 67% other. **Major cities:** (1990) Nassau (capital) 191,542.

●**PEOPLE   Population:** 297,852 (July 2001 est.). **Nationality:** noun—Bahamian(s); adjective—Bahamian. **Ethnic groups:** 85% black, 12% white. **Languages:** English, some Creole among Haitian immigrants. **Religions:** 32% Baptist, 20% Anglican, 19% Roman Catholic; smaller groups of other Protestants, Greek Orthodox, and Jews.

●**GOVERNMENT   Type:** constituional parliamentary democracy. **Independence:** July 10, 1973 (from U.K.). **Constitution:** July 10, 1973. **National holiday:** National Day, July 10. **Heads of Government:** Sir Orville Turnquest, governor-general (since Jan. 1995); Hubert A. Ingraham, prime minister (since Aug. 1992). **Structure:** executive—governor general (appointed by queen); bicameral legislature; judiciary.

• **ECONOMY Monetary unit:** Bahamian dollar. **Budget:** (FY97/98) *income:* $766 mil.; *expend.:* $845 mil. **GDP:** (2000 est.) $4.5 bil., $15,000 per capita. **Chief crops:** citrus fruits, vegetables; poultry. **Natural resources:** salt, aragonite, timber. **Major industries:** tourism, banking, cement. **Labor force:** 156,000 (1999); 40% tourism, 50% other services; 9% unemployment (1998 est.). **Exports:** $376.8 mil. (2000 est.); pharmaceuticals, cement, rum, crawfish. **Imports:** $1.73 bil. (2000 est.); foodstuffs, manufactured goods, crude oil. **Major trading partners:** *exports:* 22.3% U.S., 15.6% Switzerland, 15% U.K. *imports:* 27.3% U.S., 26.5% Italy, 10% Japan, 4.2% Denmark.

Christopher Columbus made his first landfall in the Americas in the Bahamas Oct. 12, 1492. Though the Spanish never settled the islands, they enslaved and removed to Hispaniola 40,000 of the indigenous Arawaks by 1508. Their shallow seas (baja mar) made the islands a haven for pirates in the 17th century—as well as during the Civil War, Prohibition, and for drug smugglers today. British colonization of the Bahamas began in 1629 and continued slowly over the next two centuries.

Tourism has been the mainstay of the economy in this century, but high unemployment is a continuing problem. Parliament relaxed restrictions on offshore banking to stem the flight of international capital prompted by allegations of government corruption and involvement in drug trafficking. In 1992 the government of Prime Minister Lynden Pindling was defeated after 25 years in office, largely because of corruption charges. In recent years the economy has grown and diversified but rising crime related to gangs of unemployed young men worries the electorate.

▶ **BAHRAIN**
State of Bahrain
• **GEOGRAPHY Location:** group of 35 islands in western Persian Gulf. Manama 26°17′N, 50°33′E. **Boundaries:** Saudi Arabia about 15 mi. (24 km) to W and Qatar about 17 mi. (28 km) to SE. **Total land area:** 239 sq. mi. (620 sq km). **Coastline:** 161 mi. (259 km). **Comparative area:** slightly less than 3.5 times size of Washington, D.C. **Land use:** 1% arable land; 1% permanent crops; 6% meadows and pastures; 0% forest and woodland; 92% other; includes negl. % irrigated. **Major cities:** (1990 est.) Manama (capital) 138,784; Muharraq Town 75,906.
• **PEOPLE Population:** 645,361 (July 2001 est.). **Nationality:** noun—Bahraini(s); adjective—Bahraini. **Ethnic groups:** 63% Bahraini, 19% Asian, 10% other Arab, 8% Iranian. **Languages:** Arabic, English, Farsi, Urdu. **Religions:** 70% Sh'ia Muslim, 30% Sunni Muslim.
• **GOVERNMENT Type:** constitutional monarchy. **Independence:** Aug. 15, 1971 (from U.K.). **Constitution:** adopted late Dec. 2000. **National holiday:** Dec. 16. **Heads of Government:** Hamad Bin Isa Al-Khalifa, amir (since March 1999); Khalifa bin Sulman al-Khalifa, prime minister (since Jan. 1970). **Structure:** executive—amir is traditional arab monarch, appoints cabinet led by prime minister; legislative—amir dissolved National Assembly (Aug. 1975), appointed Advisory Council Dec. 1992; independent judiciary.
• **ECONOMY Monetary unit:** Bahraini dinar. **Budget:** (2001 est.) *income:* $1.8 bil.; *expend.:* $2.2 bil. **GDP:** (2000 est.) $10.1 bil., $15,900 per capita. **Chief crops:** not self-sufficient in food production; produces some fruits and vegetables;

engages in shrimping and fishing. **Natural resources:** oil, associated and nonassociated natural gas, fish. **Major industries:** petroleum processing and refining, aluminum smelting, offshore banking. **Labor force:** 295,000 (1998 est.); 79% industry, commerce and service (note: 44% of 15-64 age group is non-national). **Exports:** $5.8 bil. (f.o.b. 2000); 61% petroleum, 7% aluminum. **Imports:** $4.2 bil. (f.o.b., 2000); 59% nonoil, 41% crude oil. **Major trading partners:** (1997) *exports:* India, Japan, Saudi Arabia; *imports:* Saudi Arabia, U.S., U.K.

Bahrain has been an entrepôt of trade between Arabia and India since the second millenium B.C. The Portuguese fortified Bahrain in the 16th century but were driven out by the Persian shah Abbas I early in the 17th century. At the end of the 18th century, it became an Arab sheikhdom within the Ottoman Empire. Bahrain entered into treaty relations with Great Britain in 1820 and became a British protectorate in 1861. After British forces withdrew from the gulf, the nation became an independent emirate, in August 1971, under Amir Isa bin Sulman al-Khalifa, who came to the throne in 1961. Today the U.S. maintains a large military base here that served as naval headquarters during the Persian Gulf War.

Oil reserves—first discovered in 1932—were depleted by the mid-1970's. The economy diversified to include oil refining, aluminum smelting, international banking, and shipping. Bahrain has close relations with Saudi Arabia; a causeway permits communication between them.

In June 1995 social and political unrest caused by uneven distribution of wealth, high unemployment, and a repressive government erupted into serious rioting. Protests by the Shiite majority began again in early 1996; a government crackdown led to the arrest of over 600 dissidents. Bahrain's family-run, Sunni Moslem government continued with the March 1999 death of its founding emir and his replacement with his son, Hamad bin Isa al-Khalifa. The new emir, in Feb. 2001, fostered a trio of reform measures: extending amnesty to 400 political prisoners and repatriation to 100 exiles; repealing the State Security Law and abolishing the State Security Court, both of which had been designed to quash Shiite unrest; and sponsoring a referendum which approved (by 98 percent) the restoration of a parliament, the founding of an independent judiciary, and the extension of the right to vote to women.

▶ **BANGLADESH**
People's Republic of Bangladesh
• **GEOGRAPHY Location:** southern Asia. **Boundaries:** India to N, E, and W; Myanmar to E, Bay of Bengal to S. **Total land area:** 55,598 sq. mi. (144,000 sq km). **Coastline:** 360 mi. (580 km). **Comparative area:** between Arkansas and Wisconsin. **Land use:** 73% arable land; 2% permanent crops; 5% meadows and pastures; 15% forest and woodland; 5% other; includes 14% irrigated. **Major cities:** (1991 census) Dhaka (formerly Dacca) (capital) 3,637,892; Chittagong 1,566,070; Khulna 601,051; Rajshahi 324,532; Barisal 180,014.
• **PEOPLE Population:** 131,269,860 (July 2001 est.). **Nationality:** noun—Bangladeshi(s); adjective—Bangladesh. **Ethnic groups:** 98% Bengali, 250,000 Biharis, less than 1 mil. tribals. **Languages:** Bangla (official); English widely used. **Religions:** 83% Muslim, 16% Hindu, 1% Buddhist, Christian, and other.
• **GOVERNMENT Type:** republic. **Independence:** Dec. 16, 1971 (from Pakistan). **Constitution:** Nov.

4, 1972, effective Dec. 16, 1972, suspended following coup of Mar. 24, 1982, restored Nov. 10, 1986; amended many times. **National holiday:** March 26, Independence Day. **Heads of Government:** Shahabuddin Ahmed, president (since Oct. 1996); Latifur Rahman, prime minister (since July 2001). **Structure:** executive—president appoints prime minister and Advisory Council; unicameral legislature dissolved by president following elections on Feb. 15, 1996 and named caretaker prime minister; judiciary.

● ECONOMY **Monetary unit:** taka. **Budget:** (FY99/00 est.) *income:* $4.9 bil.; *expend.:* $6.8 bil. **GDP:** (2000 est.) $203 bil., $1,570 per capita. **Chief crops:** large-scale subsistence farming, heavily dependent on monsoon rain; main crops are jute, rice, wheat, tea, sugarcane, and potatoes. **Natural resources:** natural gas, arable land, timber. **Major industries:** jute manufactures, cotton textiles, food processing. **Labor force:** 64.1 mil. (1998); extensive export of labor to Saudi Arabia, UAE, and Oman; 63% agriculture, 26% services, 11% industry and mining. **Exports:** $5.9 bil. (2000); garments, jute, leather, seafood. **Imports:** $8.1 bil. (2000); machinery, chemicals, iron and steel, textiles. **Major trading partners:** (1999) *exports:* 31.2% U.S., 9.95% Germany, 8.1% U.K.; *imports:* 12% India, 7.8% Singapore, 6.7% Japan.

Located on the alluvial plain of the Ganges River northeast of India, Bengal was ruled by Buddhist kings from the eighth to 12th centuries. Conquered by Muslim invaders around 1200, many inhabitants converted to Islam and Bengal became part of the Moghul Empire in the 16th century. The British East India Company established a settlement in 1642, and by 1750 all of Bengal was under British rule. The formerly diverse agricultural economy became dominated by export crops of opium and jute, while rice continued to be grown in the fertile delta. The region's trade flowed through the British-built city of Calcutta.

With Indian independence in 1947, Bengal was partitioned along religious lines, Hindu West Bengal (including Calcutta) remaining with India and Muslim East Bengal becoming the eastern province of Pakistan. In the elections of 1971, the Bengali Awami League gained control of Pakistan's National Assembly. Seating of the new National Assembly was postponed, and riots broke out in East Pakistan. Troops from West Pakistan were sent to quell the riots on May 25; the following day East Pakistan declared its independence as Bangladesh. Civil war followed; 10 million refugees fled to India. Following Indian intervention, Pakistan acknowledged Bangladesh's independence on Dec. 15.

Since independence, Bangladesh has consistently been one of the world's poorest countries, plagued by violent political instability, military coups, overpopulation, a flagging economy, and frequent catastrophic floods (including one in 1975 that killed half a million people). The first president, Sheik Mujibur Rahman, was assassinated in 1975. Lt. Gen. Hossain Mohammad Ershad, who seized power in a coup in March 1982, was elected president in 1986, but resigned in 1990 in the face of opposition unrest.

In 1991, the Bangladesh Nationalist party (BNP) of Begum Khaleda Zia (widow of former president Ziaur Rahman, who was assassinated in 1981) won 138 of 330 parliamentary seats running on a platform of free enterprise, privatization, and an Islamic state. In September 1991, the constitution was amended to put the prime minister in charge of the government and make the presidency a largely ceremonial post.

In 1994, nearly 150 opposition members of Parliament resigned en masse, eliciting a promise from Prime Minister Zia to hold general elections in June 1996. In those elections, the Awami League, led by Sheik Hasina Wazed, returned to power for the first time since 1975, when the military massacred most of her family, including her father, Pres. Sheik Mujibur Rahman. In 1998, fifteen were convicted and sentenced to death for their role in the assassinations. Zia's call for nation-wide protest strike went unanswered, but her BNP (in Jan. 1999) was one of three parties, with General Ershad's Jatiya and the Moslem Jamaat-e-Islami, to form a bloc seeking to force early elections upon prime minister Wazed.

▶ BARBADOS

● GEOGRAPHY **Location:** easternmost of Caribbean islands, about 200 mi. (320 km) NE of Trinidad. Bridgetown 13°06′N, 59°36′W. **Boundaries:** Atlantic Ocean. **Total land area:** 166 sq. mi. (430 sq km). **Coastline:** 60 mi. (97 km). **Comparative area:** slightly less than 2.5 times size of Washington, D.C. **Land use:** 37% arable land; 5% meadows and pastures; 46% other. **Major cities:** (1990 census) Bridgetown (capital) 6,070.

● PEOPLE **Population:** 275,330 (July 2001 est.). **Nationality:** noun—Barbadian(s); adjective—Barbadian. **Ethnic groups:** 80% black, 16% other, 4% white. **Languages:** English. **Religions:** 67% Protestant, 4% Roman Catholic, 29% none or other.

● GOVERNMENT **Type:** parliamentary democracy recognizing Queen Elizabeth II as chief of state. **Independence:** Nov. 30, 1966 (from U.K.). **Constitution:** Nov. 30, 1966. **National holiday:** Independence Day, Nov. 30. **Heads of Government:** Sir Clifford Husbands, governor general (since June 1996); Owen Arthur, prime minister (since Sept. 1994). **Structure:** executive—governor general (appointed by the queen) prime minister; bicameral legislature; judiciary.

● ECONOMY **Monetary unit:** Barbadian dollar. **Budget:** (FY97/98 est.) *income:* $725.5 mil.; *expend.:* $750.6 mil. **GDP:** (2000 est.) $4 bil., $14,500 per capita. **Chief crops:** sugarcane, vegetables, cotton. **Natural resources:** crude oil, fish, natural gas. **Major industries:** tourism, sugar, light manufacturing. **Labor force:** 136,000 (1998 est.); 75% services, 15% industry, 10% agriculture (1996 est.). **Exports:** $260 mil. (2000 est.); sugar and molasses, rum, other foods and beverages, chemicals. **Imports:** $800.3 mil. (2000 est.); consumer goods, machinery, foodstuffs. **Major trading partners:** *exports:* 14.8% U.K., 11.6% U.S. *imports:* 30.7% U.S., 10.2% Trinidad and Tobago, 7.7% U.K., 2.2% Canada.

Barbados is the only Caribbean island not to have changed hands prior to independence. Although the Spanish removed virtually all the indigenous Arawaks of Barbados by the mid1500's, the island was not claimed until the British arrived in the 1620's. Tobacco, cotton, and sugarcane—harvested with slave labor until 1833—were mainstays of the economy. The 1966 constitution mandates the promotion of economic equality among Barbadians, and the country was fairly prosperous relative to other Caribbean states until recently, when declining tourism and record-low sugar production have had serious adverse effects. Still, the Barbados Labor Party retains its popularity, winning 26 of the parliament's 28 seats in Jan. 1999 elections.

▶ BELARUS
Republic of Belarus

● **GEOGRAPHY Location:** northeastern Europe. **Boundaries:** Lithuania and Latvia to N, Russian Federation to NE and E, Ukraine to S, Poland to W, Lithuania and Latvia to NW. **Total land area:** 80,154 sq. mi. (207,600 sq km). **Coastline:** none. **Comparative area:** slightly smaller than Kansas. **Land use:** 29% arable land; 1% permanent crops; 15% meadows and pastures; 34% forest and woodland; 21% other. **Major cities:** (1990 est.) Minsk (capital) 1,613,000; Gomel (Homel) 506,000; Mahilou (Mogilev) 363,000; Vitebsk 356,000; Grodno 277,000.

● **PEOPLE Population:** 10,350,194 (July 2001 est.). **Nationality:** noun—Belarusian(s); adjective—Belarusian. **Ethnic groups:** 81.2% Byelorussian, 11.4% Russian, 7.4% Polish, Ukrainian and other. **Languages:** Byelorusian (official), Russian. **Religions:** 80% Eastern Orthodox.

● **GOVERNMENT Type:** republic. **Independence:** Aug. 25, 1991 (from U.S.S.R.). **Constitution:** Adopted Nov. 1996. **National holiday:** Independence Day, July 3. **Heads of Government:** Aleksander Lukashenko, president (since July 1994); Vladimir Yermoshin, prime minister (since Mar. 2000). **Structure:** executive—president, prime minister, Council of Ministers; bicameral legislature—most members apointed by the president; judiciary.

● **ECONOMY Monetary unit:** Belarusian rubel. **Budget:** (1997 est.) *income:* 4 bil.; *expend.:* 4.1 bil. **GDP:** (2000 est.) $78.8 bil., $7,500 per capita. **Chief crops:** grain, potatoes, vegetables. **Natural resources:** forest, peat, oil, and natural gas. **Major industries:** tractors, metalworking, heavy-duty vehicles. **Labor force:** 4.8 mil. (2000). **Exports:** $7.4 bil. (f.o.b., 2000); machinery, transport equipment, chemicals, metals. **Imports:** $8.3 bil. (f.o.b., 2000); mineral products, machinery and equipment, metals, chemicals. **Major trading partners:** Russia, Ukraine, Poland, Germany.

Belarus, also known as White Russia or Byelorussia, has been inhabited since the seventh century. In the 13th and 14th centuries, present-day Belarus became part of the Grand Duchy of Lithuania, which then became part of Poland in the 16th century. Between 1772 and 1795, Poland was partitioned, which resulted in Belarus becoming part of the Russian empire. After the Bolshevik revolution in 1917, Soviet troops came to Minsk, but they were forced to withdraw in the face of approaching German troops. The Treaty of Brest-Litovsk in March 1918 ceded to Germany most of the territory of Belarus. The same year, an independent Belarusian Democratic Republic was founded, but it had little real power. Once the Germans left, the Soviets easily retook Belarus, and on Jan. 1, 1919, the Belarusian Soviet Socialist Republic (SSR) was proclaimed.

This did not end the divisions of the traditional Belarusian lands. In February 1919 they were merged within the Soviet Union with Lithuania, but the Poles launched an attack in April of the same year and took both Lithuania and Belarus. In 1920 the Belarusian SSR was re-formed, but it included only the eastern portion of historical Belarusian lands. The Treaty of Riga in March 1921 granted the western territories of Belarus to Poland and the eastern portion to the Russian Federation. In 1924 and 1925 the eastern regions were returned to the Belarusian SSR.

After the Soviets invaded Poland in 1939, the lands that Belarus had lost in 1921 were returned to it. Between 1941 and 1945, the Germans occupied the Belarusian lands, and more than a million lost their lives, including most of the large Jewish population. After the war, the Belarusian SSR was restored with all of its historic lands, and Belarus was finally unified. However, when Stalin redrew the Soviet Union's borders, he included Belarus's capital of Vilnius in Lithuania.

Under Soviet rule, Belarus turned from a mainly agricultural to an industrial land. Large numbers of Belarusians fiercely fought Stalin's collectivization plan in the 1930's, and thousands were killed or deported. Both Stalin's purges of the 1930's and World War II, which devastated both its agriculture and industry, inflicted great losses on Belarus. After the war, Soviet policy in Belarus concentrated on rebuilding its economy and encouraging Russian immigration (Russian replaced Belarusian as the official language).

The Belarusian SSR was one of the more prosperous and stable of the union republics, so Mikhail Gorbachev's policy of glasnost, or openness, in the 1980's was relatively slow to have an impact. In 1987, however, two issues had come to the fore in the Belarusian SSR: the status of the Belarusian language and the ecological dangers of Chernobyl, the famous nuclear reactor that had exploded in nearby Ukraine in 1986, but which dropped almost three-quarters of its fallout on Belarus. In voicing these concerns, the Belarusians formed several new, non-Communist parties that challenged the authority of the ruling Communist party. On July 27, 1990, Belarus declared its sovereignty from the U.S.S.R.

After the fall of the Soviet government, Belarus was one of the strongest supporters of maintaining a union of republics. On Dec. 8, 1991, Belarus, Ukraine, and Russia hosted the talks leading to the Minsk Agreement, which created the Commonwealth of Independent States (CIS). On Dec. 21, 11 former Soviet republics joined the commonwealth by signing the Alma-Ata Declaration.

While Belarus at first seemed to view the CIS as a temporary expedient, Pres. Aleaksander Lukashenko fostered closer ties with Russia. A 1995 customs union was expanded by the 1996 Union Treaty to include a common currency, joint tax and legal systems, shared energy and transport networks, and common defense and foreign policies. Lukashenko tightened his dictatorial hold on Belarus with a new constitution (Nov. 1996) which permits presidential rule by decree and gives Lukashenko power to appoint half the members of the Constitutional Court and 20 of the 64 members of the Council of the Republic, the newly-created upper house of the legislature. In 1997, the U.S. announced it was cutting off $4 mil. in aid to protest the new authoritarian government.

In July 1999, 35 members of the disbanded parliament designated its former speaker, Semyon Sharetsky, as president. Sharetsky promptly fled to Lithuania for safety but claimed the presidency. October saw large demonstrations in Minsk protesting the disappearance of opposition leaders and the proposed reunion with Russia. That reunion was forestalled by a wary Pres. Yeltsin in Dec. 1999, but Pres. Lukashenko was gratified by his party's sweep of all the seats in Oct. 2000 elections for the Chamber of Representatives in what he described as an "absolutely democratic" vote, a stance he took in the presidential election he won overwhelmingly in Sept. 2001. Protests were vigorous but without effect.

▶**BELGIUM**
Kingdom of Belgium
●**GEOGRAPHY Location:** northwestern Europe. **Boundaries:** Netherlands to N, Luxembourg and Germany to E, France to S, and North Sea to W. **Total land area:** 11,780 sq. mi. (30,510 sq km). **Coastline:** 40 mi. (64 km). **Comparative area:** slightly larger than Maryland. **Land use:** 24% arable land; 1% permanent crops; 20% meadows and pastures; 21% forest and woodland; 34% other; includes negl. % irrigated. **Major cities:** (1993) Bruxelles (Brussels—capital) 949,070; Antwerpen (Anvers, Antwerp) 462,880; Gent (Gand, Ghent) 228,490; Charleroi 206,898; Liège (Luik) 195,389.
●**PEOPLE Population:** 10,258,762 (July 2001 est.). **Nationality:** noun—Belgian(s); adjective—Belgian. **Ethnic groups:** 58% Fleming, 31% Walloon, 11% mixed or other. **Languages:** 58% Flemish (Dutch), 32% French, 1% German; 10% legally bilingual (divided along ethnic lines). **Religions:** 75% Roman Catholic, remainder Protestant or other.
●**GOVERNMENT Type:** federal parliamentary democracy under a constitutional monarch. **Independence:** Oct. 4, 1830 (from Netherlands). **Constitution:** Feb. 7, 1831; last revised July 14, 1993. **National holiday:** National Day, July 21. **Heads of Government:** Albert II, king (since Aug. 1993); Guy Verhofstadt, prime minister (since July 1999). **Structure:** executive—king, prime minister, and cabinet; bicameral legislature; independent judiciary.
●**ECONOMY Monetary unit:** Belgian franc. **Budget:** (1999 est.) *income:* $114.8 bil.; *expend.:* $117 bil.. **GDP:** (2000 est.) $259.2 bil., $25,300 per capita. **Chief crops:** sugar beets, vegetables, fruit, grain. **Natural resources:** coal, natural gas. **Major industries:** engineering, metal products, motor vehicle assembly, processed food, beverages, chemicals. **Labor force:** 4.34 mil. (1999); 73% services, 25% industry; 2% agriculture (1999 est.). **Exports:** (Belgium-Luxembourg Economic Union) $181.4 bil. (f.o.b., 2000); machinery and equipment, chemicals, diamonds. **Imports:** (Belgium-Luxembourg Economic Union) $166 bil. (c.i.f., 2000); machinery and equipment, chemicals, metals. **Major trading partners:** (Belgium-Luxembourg Economic Union, 1994) *exports:* 76% EU, U.S.; *imports:* 71% EU, U.S.
The country now known as Belgium was, during the Middle Ages, part of the powerful duchy of Burgundy. By marriage and diplomacy, the "Low Countries" became part of the Habsburg Empire in 1482 (see "Austria"). In a struggle lasting from the late 16th century to the Treaty of Westphalia in 1648, the northern part of that region (Netherlands) became independent, but the southern portion remained part of the Habsburg Empire—under the Spanish branch until 1715, then under the Austrian branch until the French Revolution. The Congress of Vienna attached the lands to an enlarged Kingdom of the Netherlands in 1815.
In 1830 the Belgians revolted against the Dutch, and in 1831 the Treaty of London recognized an independent Kingdom of Belgium. Throughout the 19th century, its unity was precarious, as the country was bitterly divided politically between Catholic and Liberal parties, and ethnically between Dutch-speaking Flemings and French-speaking Walloons. In 1885 Belgium became a colonial power in Africa with Leopold II's establishment of the Congo Free State (later the Belgian Congo), which gained independence in 1960 as Zaire.

Belgium was a major battleground during World War I, but its boundaries were reestablished in 1919 by the Treaty of Versailles. When German troops of Hitler's Third Reich overran Belgium in May 1940, King Leopold III quickly signed an armistice, hoping to placate Hitler and avert further fighting. But the Belgian government fled to England, repudiated the armistice, and joined the Allies. The Germans controlled Belgium until the liberation of Brussels in September 1944.
Belgium made a swift postwar recovery. But the political atmosphere was poisoned by the issue of what to do about wartime collaborators up to and including the king. A referendum in 1950 narrowly approved Leopold III's return to the throne, but he was persuaded to abdicate in 1951 in favor of his son, Baudouin I.
Belgium has a flourishing economy with a modernized industrial sector complemented by tourism and agriculture. The issue of language dominates politics; since the 1960's, Belgium has devolved into a de facto confederation of Flemish-, French-, and German-speaking regions, with Brussels a multilingual region unto itself.
In the May 1995 election, the first under the new decentralized constitution of 1993, the Christian Democrat-Socialist coalition government retained a majority in the Chamber of Representatives. Since August 1996, the government has been shaken by massive demonstrations against inept police and legal handling of a widespread child prostitution and pornography ring with possible links to prominent politicians. But it was the additional "poultry scandal" of early 1999 (the government's tardy reaction to the discovery of dioxin in certain Belgian meat, eggs and dairy products) that toppled the coalition of Prime Minister Jean-Luc Dehaene. June 1999 elections to the Chamber of Deputies resulted in a coalition government of Liberals, Socialists and Greens controlling a 19-seat majority under Flemish Liberal premier Guy Verhofstadt. The Greens were participants in government for the first time.

▶**BELIZE**
●**GEOGRAPHY Location:** northeastern coast of Central America. **Boundaries:** Mexico to N, Caribbean Sea to E, Guatemala to S and W. **Total land area:** 8,865 sq. mi. (22,960 sq km). **Coastline:** 240 mi. (386 km). **Comparative area:** between Massachusetts and New Hampshire. **Land use:** 2% arable land; 2% meadows and pastures; 92% forest and woodland; 3% other; includes negl. % irrigated. **Major cities:** (1993 est.) Belmopan (capital) 3,852; Belize City 47,723; Orange Walk 11,922; San Ignacio 9,702; Corozal 7,644.
●**PEOPLE Population:** 256,062 (July 2001 est.). **Nationality:** noun—Belizean(s); adjective—Belizean. **Ethnic groups:** 44% mestizo, 30% Creole, 10% Maya, 6.2% Garifuna. **Languages:** English (official), Spanish, Mayan, Garifuna (Carib). **Religions:** 62% Roman Catholic, 30% Protestant.
●**GOVERNMENT Type:** parliamentary democracy. **Independence:** Sept. 21, 1981 (from U.K.). **Constitution:** Sept. 21, 1981. **National holiday:** Independence Day, Sept. 21. **Heads of Government:** Sir Colville Norbert Young, governor general (since Nov. 1993); Said Musa, prime minister (since Aug. 1998). **Structure:** executive—governor general (appointed by Queen Elizabeth II, who is recognized as the head of state), prime minister, cabinet; bicameral legislature; judiciary.
●**ECONOMY Monetary unit:** Belizean dollar. **Budget:** (1999 est.) *income:* $157 mil.; *expend.:*

$279 mil. **GDP:** $790 mil., $3,200 per capita (2000 est.). **Chief crops:** bananas, coca, citrus, sugarcane; cultured shrimp; illegal producer of cannabis for international drug trade. **Natural resources:** arable land potential, timber, fish. **Major industries:** garments, food processing, tourism. **Labor force:** 71,000 (1997 est.); 38% agriculture, 32% industry, 30% services; shortage of skilled labor and all types of technical personnel; 12.8% unemployment (1999 est.). **Exports:** $235.7 mil. (f.o.b., 2000 est.); sugar, citrus, bananas, clothing. **Imports:** $413 mil. (c.i.f., 2000 est.); machinery and transportation equipment, manufactured goods, food, fuels, chemicals. **Major trading partners:** (1997) *exports:* 42% U.S., 33% U.K., 12% EU; *imports:* 58% U.S., 12% Mexico, 5% U.K.

During the 1700's, Spain held sovereignty over Belize but never attempted to settle it. The British gradually did settle there, however, and in 1862, British Honduras, as it was called, became a Crown colony. Although Britain granted Belize independence in 1981, Guatemala claimed sovereignty over the area until 1992, when it finally recognized Belize's independence. But as British defense forces withdrew in 1994, Guatemala reasserted its old claims but without consequence.

▶**BENIN**
Republic of Benin
• **GEOGRAPHY Location:** western coast of Africa. **Boundaries:** Burkina Faso and Niger to N, Nigeria to E, Gulf of Guinea to S, Togo to W. **Total land area:** 43,483 sq. mi. (112,620 sq km). **Coastline:** 75 mi. (121 km). **Comparative area:** between Tennessee and Pennsylvania. **Land use:** 13% arable land; 4% permanent crops; 4% meadows and pastures; 31% forest and woodland; 48% other; includes negl. % irrigated. **Major cities:** (1985 est.) Porto-Novo (capital) 208,258; Cotonou 402,290.
• **PEOPLE Population:** 6,590,782 (July 2000 est.). **Nationality:** noun—Beninese (sing., pl.); adjective—Beninese. **Ethnic groups:** 99% African (predominantly Fon, Adja, Yoruba, Bariba); 5,500 Europeans. **Languages:** French (official); Fon and Yoruba in south; at least six major tribal languages in north. **Religions:** 50% indigenous beliefs, 20% Muslim, 30% Christian.
• **GOVERNMENT Type:** Multiparty democratic republic since Apr. 4, 1991. **Independence:** Aug. 1, 1960 (from France). **Constitution:** Dec. 2, 1990. **National holiday:** National Day, Aug. 1. **Head of Government:** Mathieu Kérékou, head of state (since Apr. 2001). **Structure:** executive—president, executive council; unicameral legislature; judiciary.
• **ECONOMY Monetary unit:** Communauté Financiere Africaine franc. **Budget:** (1995 est.) *income:* $299 mil.; *expend.:* $445 mil. **GDP:** (2000 est.) $6.6 bil., $1,030 per capita. **Chief crops:** corn, sorghum, cassava, yams. **Natural resources:** small offshore oil deposits, limestone, marble, timber. **Major industries:** textiles, cigarettes, beverages. **Labor force:** 1.9 mil. (1987); 60% agriculture, 2% industrial sector, remainder employed in transport, commerce, and public services. **Exports:** $396 mil. (f.o.b., 1999); cotton, crude oil, palm products, cocoa. **Imports:** $566 mil. (f.o.b., 1999); foodstuffs, beverages, tobacco, petroleum products. **Major trading partners:** *exports:* Brazil, Indonesia, Spain; *imports:* France, China, U.K.

Although the early history of Benin is sketchy, a number of kingdoms had appeared in the region by the 11th century, and it was a center of wealth and power by the 1300's. In the 16th century, the Allada kingdom was founded in the south. In 1625, three brothers divided their power between Allada, Adjatché (Porto Novo), and Abomey. Under Ouegbadja (r. 1645-85) the latter, known as Dahomey, predominated. Much of its wealth derived from contact with Europeans, and especially the slave trade, which continued until 1885.

European contact began with the arrival of the Portuguese in 1485. Although traders and missionaries were established at Ouidah and Porto Novo in the 1500's, European influence remained slight. Dahomey expansion continued well into the 19th century. A commercial treaty with the French was signed in 1842, but relations between Dahomeyans and Europeans soon worsened. Outright hostilities began under Behanzin (r. 1858-89), who was defeated by the French, and in 1893 the French assimilated Abomey, Allada, and Porto Novo into the colony of Dahomey.

Independence from French rule came in 1960, followed by several coups until Mathieu Kerekou came to power in 1972. Kerekou established a Marxist regime, nationalizing large private businesses and abolishing opposition parties.

By December 1989, with the economy in a shambles and most trade conducted on the black market, there were demonstrations calling for Kerekou's resignation. A new constitution was approved in a Nov. 1990 referendum, and Nicéphore Soglo, a former World Bank official, was named prime minister. Soglo defeated the Marxist Kerekou in the 1991 presidential election, and appealed to western nations for a "Marshall Plan" for Africa. But in a rematch four years later, Kerekou regained the presidency with 53 percent of the vote. Yet, only three years later, in April elections for the National Assembly, it was Soglo's Renaissance of Benin Party that carried the majority. In March 2001 Kerekou won again over Soglo, this time with 84 percent of the vote.

▶**BHUTAN**
Kingdom of Bhutan
• **GEOGRAPHY Location:** Himalaya Mountains in southern Asia. **Boundaries:** China to N and W, India to S and E. **Total land area:** 18,147 sq. mi. (47,000 sq km). **Coastline:** none. **Comparative area:** between Maryland and West Virginia. **Land use:** 2% arable land, 6% meadows and pastures, 66% forest and woodland, 23% other. **Major cities:** (1990 est.) Timphu (capital) 27,000.
• **PEOPLE Population:** 2,049,412 (July 2000 est.). **Nationality:** noun—Bhutanese (sing., pl.); adjective—Bhutanese. **Ethnic groups:** 50% Bhote, 35% ethnic Nepalese, 15% indigenous or migrant tribes. **Languages:** Dzongkha (official), various Tibetan dialects, various Nepalese dialects. **Religions:** 75% Lamaistic Buddhism, 25% Indian- and Nepalese-influenced Hinduism.
• **GOVERNMENT Type:** monarchy; special treaty relationship with India. **Independence:** Aug. 8, 1949 (from India). **Constitution:** no written constitution or bill of rights. **National holiday:** Dec. 17. **Head of Government:** Jigme Singye Wangchuk, king (since July 1972); Khandu Wangchuk, prime minister (since Aug. 2001). **Structure:** executive—king, Royal Advisory Council, Council of Ministers; indirectly elected unicameral National Assembly consisting of 105 village elders, 10 monastic representatives, and 35 designated by the king; judicial—Supreme Court is the king.
• **ECONOMY Monetary unit:** ngultrums and Indian rupees are legal tender. **Budget:** (FY95/96) *income:* $146 mil.; *expend.:* $152 mil. **GDP:** (2000 est.) $2.3 bil., $1,100 per capita. **Chief crops:** rice, corn, barley, wheat, potatoes. **Livestock:** cattle,

poultry, pigs, sheep, yaks. **Natural resources:** timber, hydropower, gypsum, calcium carbide. **Major industries:** cement, wood products, fruits. **Labor force:** N.A.; (1983) 93% agriculture, 5% services, 2% industry and commerce. **Exports:** $154 mil. (f.o.b., 2000 est.); cardamom, gypsum, timber, handicrafts. **Imports:** $269 mil. (c.i.f., 2000 est.); fuels and lubricants, grain, machinery and parts, vehicles. **Major trading partner:** India (94% of exports, 77% of imports).

A Tibetan-style Lamaistic Buddhist theocracy was established in this Himalayan enclave in the 16th century. The region came under the domination of the British raj in India in 1865, and Britain established a protectorate in 1910. A 1949 treaty with India granted independence to Bhutan. The present Druk Gyalpo, or Precious Ruler of the Dragon People, is the fourth in a dynasty dating from 1907. During the early years of his reign, he introduced reforms into this feudal, medieval country by broadening educational opportunities and compelling Buddhist monks to take up social work outside their monasteries.

From 1998 to 1999, King Wangchuk ruled through a rubber-stamp National Assembly, passing a series of laws aimed at driving out Nepalese and Indian settlers even if their families have resided in Bhutan for decades. More than 70,000 refugees have been registered by the U.N. high commissioner for refugees since 1991, and the numbers continue to grow. A "Gorkha Liberation Movement" has carried out raids in Bhutan from sanctuaries in India and Nepal.

In 1998 King Wangchuk began a second wave of reform, permitting the National Assembly to elect members of the Council of Ministers and even, by two-thirds vote, to call for the King's abdication. 1999 saw a mass amnesty of political prisoners.

▶ **BOLIVIA**
Republic of Bolivia
● **GEOGRAPHY   Location:** landlocked country in central South America. **Boundaries:** Brazil to N and E, Paraguay and Argentina to S, Chile and Peru to W. **Total land area:** 424,162 sq. mi. (1,098,580 sq km). **Coastline:** none. **Comparative area:** between Texas and Alaska. **Land use:** 2% arable land; negl. % permanent crops; 24% meadows and pastures; 53% forest and woodland; 21% other; includes negl. % irrigated. **Major cities:** (1992 est.) La Paz (administrative capital) 1,115,403; Sucre (legal capital and seat of judiciary) 130,952; Santa Cruz de la Sierra 694,616; Cochabamba 404,102; Oruro 183,194.
● **PEOPLE   Population:** 8,300,463 (July 2001 est.). **Nationality:** noun—Bolivian(s); adjective—Bolivian. **Ethnic groups:** 30% Quechua, 25% Aymara, 30% mixed, 15% white. **Languages:** Spanish, Quechua, and Aymara (all official). **Religions:** 95% Roman Catholic; active Protestant minority, especially Methodist.
● **GOVERNMENT   Type:** republic. **Independence:** Aug, 6, 1825 (from Spain). **Constitution:** Feb. 2, 1967. **National holiday:** Independence Day, Aug. 6. **Head of Government:** Jorge Quiroga Ramírez, president (since Aug. 2001). **Structure:** executive; bicameral legislature; judiciary.
● **ECONOMY   Monetary unit:** boliviano. **Budget:** (1998 est.) *income:* $2.7 bil.; *expend.:* $2.7 bil. **GDP:** (2000 est.) $20.9 bil., $2,600 per capita. **Chief crops:** soybeans, coffee, coca, cotton, corn, sugarcane, rice, potatoes. **Natural resources:** tin, natural gas, crude oil, zinc, tungsten. **Major industries:** mining, smelting, petroleum. **Labor force:** 2.5 mil.; NA% agriculture, NA% services and

utilities. **Exports:** $1.26 bil. (f.o.b., 2000 est.); soybeans, natural gas, zinc, gold. **Imports:** $1.86 bil. (f.o.b., 2000 est.); capital goods, chemicals, petroleum. **Major trading partners:** (1998 est.) *exports:* U.S., U.K., Colombia, Peru, Argentina. *imports:* U.S., Japan, Brazil, Chile.

The Incan Empire conquered the region that is now Bolivia in the 13th century. The Spanish discovered the fabulous silver deposits of the region and established their presence in the area in the cities of Sucre (1538) and Potosí (1545). From the early colonial period on, Bolivia—then called Upper Peru and part of the Viceroyalty of Peru—depended heavily on the export of minerals. The exploitation of tin and later oil and natural gas has had an important economic and political impact on the country's development.

In 1776, Upper Peru was transferred to the new Viceroyalty of La Plata centered in Buenos Aires. Upper Peru began agitating for independence in 1809, but it was not until liberation by Símon Bolívar (for whom the country was renamed) in 1825 that Bolivia became the last Spanish possession in South America to achieve independence. During 1836-39, Peru formed a brief union with Bolivia, until Chile broke up the confederation.

Bolivia has lost much of its original territory to its neighbors. The dictator Mariano Melgarejo sold large chunks of territory from 1865 to 1871. After the War of the Pacific (1879-84), Bolivia lost its access to the sea. And in the 1932-35 Chaco War with Paraguay, Bolivia lost more territory in the east.

Bolivia has suffered from Indian/non-Indian racial and cultural divisions, and political rivalry between the elites from the Potosí region and those from La Paz and Santa Cruz. Conservatives of the silver-mining southern region of Potosí controlled the government until their ouster in 1898 by the Liberal tin interests of the La Paz region, who presided over a period of stable republican politics that lasted until the Great Depression and the Chaco War.

One of the results of the Chaco War was the fragmentation of the Bolivian military into competing factions in the struggle for power between conservative landowners and middle-class reformers. In 1941 the National Revolutionary Movement (MNR) was formed with the aim of transferring control of the country from conservative landowning elites to the middle sectors. The leadership of the movement found itself outpaced by revolts sponsored by workers and peasants; the MNR incorporated these elements into its program. When the 1952 revolution brought the MNR to power, its leadership, which included the future four-time president Victor Paz Estenssoro, embarked on a reformist political program. The military overthrew the MNR in 1964, and civilian rule was not restored until 1982. Paz Estenssoro was again elected to the presidency in 1985. Jaime Paz Zamora, leader of the Movement of the Revolutionary Left, gained the presidency in 1989.

In June 1993, MNR candidate Gonzalo Sanchez de Lozada won the presidential election. An advocate of free-market economic reform, as planning minister (1986-88) he reduced the country's hyperinflation rate from 25,000 percent to 15 percent. In January 1995, Bolivia sought membership in the newly-formed Southern Common Market (of Argentina, Brazil, Paraguay, and Uruguay). But opposition to free-market reforms brought a general strike by the leftist Bolivian Workers' Confederation. The government declared a state of siege in April 1995, and suspended civil liberties. Further privatization plans led to another general strike in 1996, with 50,000 demonstrators in the streets of La Paz. Faced with widespread rioting and looting, the government granted large raises to government employees.

Presidential elections in 1997 led to a run-off (settled in Congress) in which retired general Hugo Banzer Suarez, military dictator from 1971 to 1978, was elected president, pledging to continue economic reforms while ensuring that the poor benefit from the reforms. His government was confronted in April 2000 with nationwide riots over a planned increase in water rates and a general strike by the Workers Confederation. Timely retreats ended the protests and ensured survival for the present.

▶ BOSNIA AND HERZEGOVINA
Republic of Bosnia and Herzegovina
• **GEOGRAPHY Location:** southeastern Europe. **Boundaries:** Croatia to N, W, Yugoslavia to S, E, and SE, Adriatic Sea to SW. **Total land area:** 19,776 sq. mi. (51,233 sq km). **Coastline:** 13 mi. (20 km). **Comparative area:** Slightly larger than Tennessee. **Land use:** 39% forest and woodland, 20% meadows and pastures, 14% arable land, 5% permanent crops, 22% other. **Major cities:** Bosnia: (1991) Sarajevo (capital) 525,980, Banja Luka 195,139. Herzegovina: (1991) Mostar 126,067.
• **PEOPLE Population:** 3,922,205 (July 2001 est.) Note: all population data is subject to considerable error due to dislocations caused by military actions and ethnic cleansing. **Nationality:** noun—Bosnian(s); adjective—Bosnian; noun—Herzegovine(s) or Herzegovinian(s); adjective—Herzegovine or Herzegovinian. **Ethnic groups:** 31% Serb, 44% Bozniak, 17% Croat. **Languages:** Croatian, Serbian, Bosnian. **Religions:** 40% Muslim, 31% Orthodox, 15% Catholic, 4% Protestant, 10% other.
• **GOVERNMENT Type:** emerging democracy. **Independence:** Apr. 1, 1992. **Constitution:** Dayton agreement, signed Dec. 1995, included a new constitution now in force. **National holiday:** National Day, Nov. 25 **Heads of Government:** Zivko Radisic (since Oct. 2000); Bosidar Matic, prime minister (since Feb. 2001). **Structure:** executive—3-member rotating presidency, prime minister, cabinet; bicameral legislature; judiciary.
• **ECONOMY Monetary unit:** convertible marka. **Budget:** (1999 est.) *income:* $1.9 bil.; *expend.:* $2.2 bil. **GDP:** (2000 est.) $6.5 bil.; $1,700 per capita. **Chief crops:** corn, wheat, fruits, vegetables; livestock. **Natural resources:** coal, iron, bauxite, manganese, timber. **Major industries:** steel production, mining, manufacturing, armaments. **Labor force:** 1,026,254 (1991 est.). **Exports:** $950 mil. (f.o.b., 2000 est.). **Imports:** $2.45 bil. (f.o.b., 2000 est.). **Major trading partners:** Croatia, Switzerland, Slovenia, Germany, Italy.

Bosnia-Herzegovina has been in the middle of European power struggles since the 14th century. Its constantly changing boundaries have meant that its population has always been a hodgepodge of races and ethnicities. The name Bosnia comes from the region's geographic location on the Bosna River; Herzegovina was originally an Austrian border duchy (Herzog means "duke" in German). The two lands were conquered by the Ottoman Empire in the 15th century, Bosnia in 1463, Herzegovina 20 years later. The conquered peoples, united into one administrative district by the Turks, were Roman Catholic Croatians and Orthodox Serbs. Over the centuries, a number of Slavic families, Croatians more than Serbs, gave

up their Christianity and adopted the religion of their conquerors: Islam.

A peasant uprising (1875) over Turkish refusal to institute reforms ultimately led to the Russo-Turkish War of 1877-78. In 1878, the Congress of Berlin put Bosnia-Herzegovina under the control of Austria-Hungary. Sarajevo, the capital city, was the birthplace of World War I, where a Serbian nationalist assassinated the Austro-Hungarian archduke Francis Ferdinand in 1914. By 1918, Serbia had annexed Bosnia-Herzegovina and held it until World War II, when Germany incorporated it into the state of Croatia. In 1946, Bosnia-Herzegovina was made one of Yugoslavia's six constituent republics, along with Serbia, Croatia, Slovenia, Montenegro, and Macedonia.

The constant redrawing of Bosnia-Herzegovina's borders has also meant that ethnicity in the region came to be based on religion, rather than a national origin. Thus a Serb who converted to Roman Catholic Christianity was considered a Croatian, while a Croatian who converted to Eastern Orthodoxy was considered a Serb. And to both groups, converts to Islam appeared to be collaborators with the Ottoman Turks.

Nevertheless, the three ethnic groups coexisted peacefully under the iron hand of president-for-life Marshall Tito (Josip Broz). And even after Tito's death in 1980, his rotating presidency scheme, in which the leaders of each republic took turns serving as "president of the presidency," worked smoothly, as long as Yugoslavia was dominated by communism. At times, the president was a Muslim, the prime minister was a Croatian, and the president of the Assembly was a Serb. But when communism fell in 1989, only Serbia and Montenegro returned Communist governments to power; the other four republics established non- and even anti-Communist governments, and quickly sought to establish political independence from the ultra-Marxist regime of Serbian president Slobodan Milosevic.

Milosevic rigged elections in the provinces of Kosovo and Vojvodina to keep them under Serbian control, but he was unsuccessful in ethnically Serbian areas of Slovenia, Croatia, and Bosnia-Herzegovina. Croatia and Slovenia declared their independence in 1991, forcing Bosnia to choose between independence or a diminished role in a Serb-dominated Yugoslavia.

Bosnia-Herzegovina voted for independence in March 1992. But the mostly Serbian military of the former Yugoslavian army refused to go along with the vote. Led by Radovan Karadzic, they gained control of the region's artillery and proclaimed the existence of the "Serbian Republic of Bosnia-Herzegovina." The siege of Sarajevo began a month after the vote for independence, with Serbia waging a ferocious war of "ethnic cleansing," in which they sought to rid Bosnia of Muslims and Croats. By July 1993, the Serbs surrounded the city, cutting off delivery of arms and supplies to Bosnian forces. Despite evidence that the Serbs were raping and torturing Muslims, the Bosnian Parliament in Sept. 1993 rejected a U.N.-sponsored peace plan that would have ended the war.

Several other cease-fire agreements were brokered throughout 1993 and 1994, but none led to a lasting peace in the Balkans until a 1995 pact brokered by U.S. negotiator Richard Holbrooke, in which the Bosnian Serbs agreed to follow the decisions of Yugoslavia's president Slobodan Milosevic in all peace talks. And on Nov. 21, 1995, the presidents of Bosnia-Herzegovina, Croatia, and Serbia met in Dayton, Ohio, to sign a peace accord ending the civil war and dividing Bosnia-Herzegovina into two entities: a Serb republic and a Muslim-Croat federation. The two statelets would be governed by the same legislature and president.

The U.N. sent 60,000 peacekeeping troops (20,000 Americans) in Dec. 1995 to supervise the transition. Elections in Sept. 1996 selected a three-member collective presidency, chaired by Muslim Alijia Izetbegovic, and a legislature whose 42 members were selected in two separate elections, 28 from the Federation and 14 from the Srpska Republic. In Jan. 1997, parliament approved a cabinet with joint (Serb and Muslim) premiers.

Yugoslavia and Bosnia established diplomatic relation in Oct. 1996, with Yugoslavia agreeing to respect Bosnia's boundaries while Bosnia dropped charges of genocide. A new crisis arose when on the same day (March 5, 1999), the West's "high authority" (under the Dayton Accords) deposed the President of the Serb Republic, who had just been elected, while a Western arbitrator awarded the strategic Sava River town of Brcko to the Moslem-Croat Federation, resulting in the Serb republic's effective withdrawal from Bosnia-Herzegovnia. NATO planned to reduce its troops from 30,000 to 21,000 after the April 2000 municipal elections. But with voters largely returning national parties to power in the towns, the troop reduction grew less likely.

Through 2000 and 2001 incidents of friction continued, provoking further interventions by the High Authority and NATO troops, which themselves became further sources of tension and even riots.

▶ **BOTSWANA**
Republic of Botswana
● **GEOGRAPHY   Location:** landlocked country in southern Africa. **Boundaries:** Namibia to N and W, Zimbabwe to NE, South Africa to SE and S. **Total land area:** 231,803 sq. mi. (600,370 sq km). **Coastline:** none. **Comparative area:** about size of Texas. **Land use:** 2% arable land; 75% meadows and pastures; 2% forest and woodland; 21% other. **Major cities:** (1989 est.) Gaborone (capital) 110,973; Francistown 49,396; Selebi-Phikwe 46,490; Molepolole 29,212; Serowe 28,267.
● **PEOPLE   Population:** 1,586,119 (July 2001 est.). **Nationality:** noun and adjective—Motswana (sing.), Batswana (pl.). **Ethnic groups:** 79% Tswana, 11% Kalanga, 3% Basarwa, 7% other. **Languages:** English (official), Setswana. **Religions:** 50% Christian, 50% indigenous beliefs.
● **GOVERNMENT   Type:** parliamentary republic. **Independence:** Sept. 30, 1966 (from U.K.). **Constitution:** Mar. 1965, effective Sept. 30, 1966. **National holiday:** Independence Day, Sept. 30. **Head of Government:** Festus G. Mogae, MP, head of state (since April 1998). **Structure:** executive; bicameral legislature; judiciary.
● **ECONOMY   Monetary unit:** pula. **Budget:** (FY96) *income:* $1.6 bil.; *expend.:* $1.8 bil. **GDP:** $10.4 bil., $6,600 per capita (2000 est.). **Chief crops:** sorghum, maize, millet, pulses, peanuts. **Natural resources:** diamonds, copper, nickel, coal, salt, soda ash. **Major industries:** diamonds, copper, nickel, coal, salt, soda ash, potash. **Labor force:** (1992) 428,000; 235,000 formal-sector employees; 14,300 employed in mines in South Africa; most others engaged in cattle raising and subsistence agriculture; 40% unemployment (2000 est.). **Exports:** $2.6 bil. (f.o.b., 2000 est.); 72% diamonds, copper and nickel, meat. **Imports:** $2.2 bil. (f.o.b., 2000 est.); foodstuffs, vehicles, textiles, petroleum products. **Major trading partners:** (1998) *exports:* 77% EU, 18% South African Customs Union (SACU), 3% Zimbabwe; *imports:* 76% SACU, 10% Europe, 5% South Korea.

Botswana, occupying a high and relatively arid tableland in southern Africa, was traditionally occupied by diverse groups of farmers, pastoralists, and hunter-gatherers. European missionaries arrived from South Africa in the early 19th century. In the late 19th century, native peoples resisted the encroachment of Afrikaners from the Transvaal; in response the British government established a protectorate in what was then called Bechuanaland in 1886. The southern part of the protectorate was organized as a Crown Colony and ultimately passed under the control of South Africa. During the 20th century, the territory remaining in the protectorate saw a steady evolution of local rule.

In 1920 two advisory councils were established to represent the interests of native and European inhabitants. In 1934 British authorities promulgated regulations establishing the powers and jurisdictions of native chiefs and the functions of native councils and courts. Local fiscal powers were established soon thereafter. In 1951 a joint (native-European) advisory council was set up, and 10 years later an elected legislature met under the provisions of a new constitution.

In 1963-64 the British government accepted Botswanan proposals for self-government. A new capital was established at Gaborone in February 1965; a new constitution came into effect in the following month, and Botswana became fully independent on Sept. 30, 1966. Since independence, Botswana has been a multiparty, multiracial democracy that has remained untouched by the political turmoil affecting most of its neighbors. In Oct. 1999 National Assembly elections, voters gave the Botswana Democratic Party, the ruling party since 1966, 33 of the 40 seats, ensuring President Mogae of five more years.

Botswana is one of the most prosperous countries in Africa. It is the world's largest producer of diamonds; revenues from diamond exports have been wisely managed, leading to significant budgetary surpluses in recent years. Gold and soda ash are also mined. Tourism, bolstered by Botswana's large herds of big game, is the country's major nonmining industry. Botswana is one of Africa's largest exporters of meat and animal products.

▶ **BRAZIL**
Federative Republic of Brazil
● **GEOGRAPHY   Location:** central and northeastern South America. **Boundaries:** Colombia, Venezuela, Guyana, Suriname, French Guiana to N; Atlantic Ocean to E; Uruguay, Argentina, Paraguay to S; Peru, Bolivia to W. **Total land area:** 3,286,475 sq. mi. (8,511,965 sq km). **Coastline:** 4,652 mi. (7,491 km). **Comparative area:** slightly smaller than U.S. **Land use:** 5% arable land; 1% permanent crops; 22% meadows and pastures; 58% forest and woodland; 14% other. **Major cities:** (1991 est.) Brasília (capital) 1,841,028; São Paulo 9,700,111; Rio de Janeiro 6,011,181; Belo Horizonte 2,339,039; Salvador 2,075,392.
● **PEOPLE   Population:** 174,468,575 (July 2001 est.). **Nationality:** noun—Brazilian(s); adjective—Brazilian. **Ethnic groups:** Portuguese, Italian, German, Japanese, black, Amerindian; 55% white, 38% mixed, 6% black, 1% other. **Languages:** Portuguese (official), Spanish, English, French. **Religions:** 80% Roman Catholic.
● **GOVERNMENT   Type:** federative republic. **Inde-**

pendence: Sept. 7, 1822 (from Portugal). **Constitution:** Oct. 5, 1988. **National holiday:** Independence Day, Sept. 7. **Head of Government:** Fernando Henrique Cardoso, president (since Jan. 1995). **Structure:** strong executive with broad powers; bicameral legislature with growing powers; judiciary.

● **ECONOMY Monetary unit:** real. **Budget:** (1998) *income:* $151 bil.; *expend.:* $149 bil. **GDP:** $1.13 tril., $6,500 per capita (2000 est.). **Chief crops:** coffee, soybeans, wheat, rice; beef. **Natural resources:** bauxite, gold, iron ore, manganese, nickel. **Major industries:** textiles and other consumer goods, shoes, chemicals. **Labor force:** 79 mil. (1999 est.); 53.2% services, 23.1% agriculture, 23.7% industry; 7.1% unemployment (2000 est.). **Exports:** $55.1 bil. (f.o.b., 2000); iron ore, soybean bran, orange juice, footwear. **Imports:** $55.8 bil. (f.o.b., 2000); capital goods, chemical products, oil, electricity. **Major trading partners:** (1999) *exports:* 23% U.S., 11% Argentina, 5% Germany; *imports:* 24% U.S., 12% Argentina, 10% Germany.

The Portuguese arrived on the coast of what would become Brazil with the expedition of Pedro Alvares Cabral in 1500 and found an indigenous population of semisedentary and nonsedentary cultures. Many of the semisedentary Indians spoke the Tupian language and shared similar cultural features. The Tupians quickly formed economic relationships with the first Europeans, who were interested in the valuable dyewood that was so abundant in Brazil.

The transition from Indian-European economic relations from barter to slavery was given momentum by the introduction of sugar export agriculture, a trend that began in the region in the 1540's. The 1560's saw epidemics of smallpox and measles in the coastal areas, which greatly reduced the indigenous population. Although the European sugar growers initially favored the use of indigenous peoples over imported African slave labor (owing to the lower price of Indian slaves), the shortage of labor resulting from the epidemics led to increasing use of African slave labor by the Portuguese.

The Portuguese vied with other European powers for control of Brazilian territory, and in 1630 the Dutch briefly seized the northeastern sugar-growing area. Brazil's southern regions were underpopulated during the early colonial period, and Portuguese activity was largely limited to cattle raising. With the discovery of gold (1690's) and diamonds (1729), European interest in and settlement of the Minas Gerais area in the southeast quickened.

In 1808, the Portuguese royal court escaped Napoleon's armies with the help of the British fleet, and the prince regent, Dom João VI, sought refuge in Brazil and made it the seat of the Portuguese empire. Dom João returned to a Portugal liberated from Napoleonic occupation in 1821, leaving his son Dom Pedro behind as prince regent. In 1822, defying orders to return to Portugal and opposed to the imminent reversion of Brazil to colonial status, Dom Pedro declared Brazil's independence and was crowned emperor. In 1825 an agreement mediated by the British led to Portuguese recognition of Brazil as a separate kingdom.

The early years of independence were rocky. Dom Pedro became increasingly estranged from his people and began losing control of the Brazilian political situation owing to a continuing series of landowner revolts and to the loss of a war with the United Provinces of Rio de la Plata over what

would become Uruguay. In 1831 Dom Pedro abdicated in favor of his five-year-old son, Dom Pedro II; a regency governed Brazil until his accession to the throne in 1840.

The Brazilian empire found itself continually involved in the wars and internal politics of Uruguay, Argentina, and Paraguay in the 1850's and 1860's. The bloody five-year war with Paraguay that began in 1865 resulted in Paraguay's eventual defeat, but the process of the war had important consequences for the future of Brazil: the expansion of military power, the fragmentation of the political party system, and the undermining of the legitimacy of slavery. Slavery was abolished in 1888, and the following year, a military coup overthrew the emperor.

The "Old Republic," which lasted from 1889 to 1930, was a federal system in which much of the political control in Brazilian society was relegated to state-based political networks with local bosses. The presidency was assigned in a de facto rotation system called the "politics of the governors," in which the president's office was controlled by the most important state power networks. The world depression of 1929 hit the Brazilian agricultural export economy hard, and in 1930 the military overthrew the elected president; Getúlio Vargas, a politician from the state of Rio Grande do Sul, took over the presidency.

Vargas proceeded to centralize power in the presidency, diminishing states' rights dramatically. Civil unrest allowed Vargas to declare a state of siege with military backing, and in 1937 he declared the establishment of the Estado Novo, a state wherein Vargas had absolute power, in imitation of Portuguese and Italian regimes of the period. The military ousted Vargas in 1945, ushering in the period of the "Second Republic." Vargas again won re-election in 1950 but committed suicide in 1954. Juscelino Kubitschek, elected president in 1955, sought to develop the country and led the way for construction of the new capital of Brasília in the previously undeveloped interior.

His successor, Jânio da Silva Quadros, resigned in 1961 after only seven months in office, and the presidency passed to populist Vice Pres. João Goulart. The populist mobilization of peasants and workers endorsed by the Goulart government led to his overthrow by the military in 1964.

The Brazilian military governed the country until 1985. Military rule was not maintained in the form of a dictatorship; rather, the military ruled as a more or less cohesive institution. The succession of generals and their technocratic allies attempted to develop the country through a pattern of state-led growth from which civilian politics were excluded. In 1985, Tancredo Neves was elected president, but he died before taking office. José Sarney, the vice presidential candidate, became Brazil's first civilian president since 1964.

Promising to revitalize the economy with a free-market revolution, less government, and more growth, conservative Fernando Collor de Mello became president in 1990. The military's share of the budget was reduced from 6 to 2.2 percent, and some companies were privatized, but inflation and debt still strained the economy. The 1988 murder of environmental activist Chico Mendes focused world attention on the rapidly accelerating deforestation of the Amazon River basin. Pres. Collor campaigned actively to halt the destruction in Amazonia—including protecting the Stone Age Yanomami Indians—and in June 1992 Rio De Janeiro was the site of a U.N.-sponsored conference on development and the environment.

Pres. Collor lost the confidence of the legislature and the people as evidence mounted that he stole or misappropriated over $20 million, and he resigned in December 1992 (after a two-year investigation he was cleared of all charges). His successor, Vice Pres. Itamar Franco, worked to privatize government industries and halt rampant inflation, but a new corruption scandal involving at least 18 members of the legislature halted most government activity in 1994.

In presidential elections held in Oct. 1994, former finance minister Fernando Henrique Cardoso ran on an anti-inflation platform and won a landslide victory. The Cardoso government focused on establishing federal control over state banks and supporting land reform for peasants. The rewards were a dramatic drop in both inflation and unemployment and great popularity for Cardoso. In 1997 Congress passed a Constitutional Amendment permitting Cardoso to run for a second term.

In October 1998 Cardoso easily won re-election for a four-year term over his nearest opponent by a convincing margin and pro-Cardoso governors were elected in 21 of the 27 states. Despite an unexpected January 1999 devaluation of the *real*, the I.M.F. released the remainder of its 1998 aid package in March. In April, Brazil was able to sell $2 billion in bonds—a sign of continuing confidence by the world money markets. But Cardoso's popularity plummeted during the summer to record lows causing new fears.

▶ BRUNEI
Negara Brunei Darussalam
● GEOGRAPHY Location: southeastern Asia, Kalimantan (Borneo) island. Bandar Seri Begawan 4°56'N, 114°58'E. Boundaries: surrounded on landward side by Sarawak, state, of Malaysia; South China Sea to N. Total land area: 2,228 sq. mi. (5,770 sq km). Coastline: 100 mi. (161 km). Comparative area: slightly larger than Delaware. Land use: 1% arable land; 1% permanent crops; 1% meadows and pastures; 85% forest and woodland; 12% other. Major cities: Bandar Seri Begawan (formerly Brunei Town) (capital) 50,500 (1986 est.); Seria, Kuala Belait, Tutong.
● PEOPLE Population: 343,653 (July 2001 est.). Nationality: noun—Bruneian(s); adjective—Bruneian. Ethnic groups: 67% Malay, 15% Chinese, 12% other. Languages: Malay (official), English, Chinese. Religions: 67% Muslim (official), 13% Buddhist, 10% Christian, 10% indigenous and other.
● GOVERNMENT Type: constitutional sultanate. Independence: Jan. 1, 1984 (from U.K.). Constitution: Sept. 29, 1959 (some provisions suspended since Dec. 1962, others since independence). National holiday: National Day, Feb. 23. Head of Government: Sir Hassanal Bolkiah Mu'izzaddin Waddaulah, sultan and prime minister (since Aug. 1968). Structure: chief of state is sultan; unicameral legislature; judiciary.
● ECONOMY Monetary unit: bruneian dollar. Budget: (1997) income: $2.5 bil.; expend.: $2.6 bil. GDP: $5.9 bil., $17,600 per capita (2000 est.). Chief crops: rice, cassava, bananas. Natural resources: petroleum, natural gas, timber. Major industries: petroleum, petroleum refining, liquefied natural gas, construction. Labor force: 144,000 (1995 est.); 48% government, 42% oil, natural gas, services, and construction. Exports: $2.55 bil. (f.o.b., 1999 est.); crude oil, liquefied natural gas, petroleum products. Imports: $1.3 bil. (c.i.f., 1999 est.); machinery and transport equip-

ment, manufactured goods, foodstuffs, chemicals. Major trading partners: (1999 est.) *exports:* 42% Japan, 17% U.S., 14% South Korea; *imports:* 34% Singapore, 15% U.K., 15% Malaysia, 5% U.S.

The Islamic sultanate of Brunei became dominant in northern Borneo in the 16th century but declined in power after the 17th century under pressure from the Dutch and other foreign powers. An Anglo-Dutch agreement of 1824 assigned North Borneo to Great Britain's sphere of influence in Asia. In 1841 a British adventurer, James Brooke, aided the sultan of Brunei in putting down a rebellion and was rewarded by being given the province of Sarawak, comprising more than half of the sultanate's area. Britain established a protectorate over Sabah, the eastern portion of Brunei, in 1881. That left the sultan with a tiny realm on the Brunei River, which was ultimately placed under British protection in 1888. The discovery of Southeast Asia's richest oilfield in Brunei and its offshore waters made the sultanate an enclave of tremendous wealth from the late 1920's onward.

Following Japanese occupation during World War II, British rule resumed in North Borneo. Sarawak and Sabah became part of Malaysia in 1963. Brunei was granted independence from Great Britain on Dec. 1, 1984. The sultan of Brunei, an absolute monarch, rules from the world's largest royal palace in Bandar Seri Begawan, the nation's capital. The economy is centered almost entirely on petroleum and international banking and investments.

▶ BULGARIA
Republic of Bulgaria
● GEOGRAPHY Location: southeastern Europe. Boundaries: Romania to N, Black Sea to E, Turkey and Greece to S, Macedonia and Yugoslavia to W. Total land area: 42,822 sq. mi. (110,910 sq km). Coastline: 220 mi. (354 km). Comparative area: between Tennessee and Pennsylvania. Land use: 43% arable land; 2% permanent crops; 14% meadows and pastures; 38% forest and woodland; 3% other. Major cities: (1992 est.) Sofia (capital) 1,114,476; Plovdiv 341,374; Varna 308,601; Burges 195,986; Ruse 170,203.
● PEOPLE Population: 7,707,495 (July 2001 est.). Nationality: noun—Bulgarian(s); adjective—Bulgarian. Ethnic groups: 83% Bulgarian, 8.5% Turk. Languages: Bulgarian; secondary languages closely correspond to ethnic breakdown. Religions: 83.5% Bulgarian Orthodox, 13% Muslim, 0.8% Jewish, 1.5% Roman Catholic, 1% Protestant, Gregorian-Armenian, and other.
● GOVERNMENT Type: parliamentary democracy. Independence: March 3, 1878 (from Ottoman Empire). Constitution: July 12, 1991. National holiday: Independence Day, Mar. 3. Heads of Government: Petar Stoyanov, president (since Nov. 1996); Simeon Saxe-Coburg-Gotha, prime minister (since July 2001). Structure: executive; unicameral legislature; judiciary.
● ECONOMY Monetary unit: lev. Budget: (2000 est.) income: $4.85 bil.; expend: $4.92 bil. GDP: $48 bil., $6,200 per capita (2000 est.). Chief crops: vegetables, fruits, tobacco; livestock. Natural resources: bauxite, copper, lead, zinc, coal. Major industries: machine building and metal working, food processing, chemicals. Labor force: 3.83 mil. (2000); 31% industry, 26% agriculture; 17.7% unemployment (2000 est.). Exports: $4.8 bil. (f.o.b., 2000 est.); machinery and equipment, metals and ores, chemicals and plastics, food, textiles. Imports: $5.9 bil. (f.o.b., 2000 est.); fuels, minerals,

and raw materials; machinery and equipment; food; textiles and apparel. **Major trading partners:** *exports:* 14% Italy, 10% Turkey, Germany, Greece, Russia; *imports:* 24% Russia, 14% Germany, Italy, Greece, U.S.

Turkic Bulgars arrived at the west shore of the Black Sea in the seventh century, mingling with the indigenous Slavic population. The Bulgars accepted Eastern Orthodox Christianity in the ninth century and were conquered and inccrporated into the Byzantine Empire by Basil II in the late 10th century. With the decline of Byzantium, Bulgaria became an independent kingdom, but it was conquered by the Ottoman Turks in 1396 and remained part of the Ottoman Empire for the next 500 years.

In the Treaty of San Stefano, ending the Russo-Turkish War in 1878, a Bulgarian state was promised that was to stretch from the Adriatic to the Black Sea. But the Great Powers would not permit so large a Russian client state, and instead the Berlin Conference of 1878 sanctioned a much smaller Bulgarian state, under a German dynasty with the Ottoman sultan as nominal overlord. Bulgaria gained full independence in 1908.

The Balkan Wars of 1912 and 1913 led to a reduction of Bulgarian territory, and after World War I, Bulgaria, which had been allied with the Central Powers, lost its Aegean Coastline to Greece. A series of weak parliamentary governments under King Boris III (r. 1918-43) ended when the king established a personal dictatorship in 1935. Bulgaria joined the Axis powers in 1941 and declared war against the Western powers but not against Russia.

Russian troops entered Bulgaria in 1944 and organized a Communist government. The boy-king Simeon II remained on the throne until 1946, when the monarchy was abolished by a popular referendum. The People's Republic of Bulgaria was established in 1947.

Until the end of World War II, Bulgaria was a peasant society, with 80 percent of the population engaged in agriculture; industrial development was rudimentary. The People's Republic established a planned economy on the Soviet model; Russian credits and trade agreements permitted a rapid industrialization focused on machinery and equipment for export.

In 1954 Todor Zhivkov became first secretary of the Bulgarian Communist party. He served as premier in the 1960's and president from 1971 to 1990. In the 1960's Zhivkov promoted decentralization and responsiveness to market forces, but with the 1968 Russian invasion of Czechoslovakia, he returned the economy to central planning, collective farming, and giant state-industrial enterprises. In October 1985 Zhivkov met with Gorbachev and reforms based on Gorbachev's "self-management" policies were instituted.

Democratic reform began with Zhivkov's resignation in Nov. 1989. There followed a year of popular unrest and political turmoil with a succession of changes in the ruling hierarchy, culminating in the election of Zheliu Zhelev of the reform Union of Democratic Forces as president (Bulgaria's first non-Communist leader in 40 years), and the appointment in 1990 of political independent, Dimitar Popov, as premier of a coalition government dominated by the Socialist (formerly Communist) party.

Elections in October 1991 ended the Socialist grip on power, as the Union of Democratic Forces formed a government under Philip Dimitrov. But within a year the government was bankrupt, infla-

tion at 30 percent and unemployment 40 percent, and Dimitrov's government was ousted by Parliament. Lyuben Berov, an economic adviser to Zhelev, came to power for two years and then he was ousted in elections (Dec. 1994) by the Socialists, led by Zhan Videnov.

Under the Videnov-Zhelev "gridlock," matters only grew worse, with a food crisis developing atop growing unemployment and 300 percent inflation in 1996. Protests and riots marked the latter half of 1996, and in the Nov. presidential elections, the UDF candidate, Peter Stoyanov (who defeated Zhelev in a party primary) won easily. And in the April 1997 elections to parliament, the UDF coalition took 137 seats to the Socialists 58. With the promise of economic reform, the I.M.F. and the E.U. provided large new grants.

The new prime minister, Ivan Kostov, commenced some serious reforms of the all-but-insolvent economy, reforms that were on the one hand painful and on the other not radical enough to rid the economy of state control. In April 2001 Bulgaria's last king, Simeon II, founded a political movement which in the June parliamentary elections won half the seats and transformed the one-time king into the Republic's new prime minister.

▶ BURKINA FASO

● **GEOGRAPHY   Location:** landlocked country in western Africa. **Boundaries:** Mali to N and W, Niger to E, Benin, Togo, Ghana, Ivory Coast to S. **Total land area:** 105,869 sq. mi. (274,200 sq km). **Coastline:** none. **Comparative area:** between Colorado and Nevada. **Land use:** 13% arable land; 22% meadows and pastures; 50% forest and woodland; 15% other. **Major cities:** (1985 census) Ouagadougou (capital) 441,514; Bobo-Dioulasso 228,668; Koudougou 51,926; Ouahigouya 38,902; Banfora 35,319.

● **PEOPLE   Population:**   12,272,289 (July 2001 est.). **Nationality:** noun—Burkinabe (sing., pl.); adjective—Burkinabe. **Ethnic groups:** over 40% Mossi, Gurunsi, Senufo, Lobi, Bobo, Mande, Fulani. **Languages:** French (official); tribal languages spoken by 90% of population. **Religions:** 50% Muslim, 40% indigenous beliefs, 10% Christian (mainly Roman Catholic).

● **GOVERNMENT   Type:** parliamentary. **Independence:** Aug. 5, 1960 (from France). **Constitution:** June 2, 1991. **National holiday:** Republic Day, Dec. 11. **Heads of Government:** Blaise Compaore, president (since Dec. 1991); Paramanga Ernest Yonly, prime minister (since Nov. 2000). **Structure:** executive; bicameral legislature; judiciary.

● **ECONOMY   Monetary unit:** Communauté Financière Africaine (CFA) franc. **Budget:** (1995) *income:* $277 mil.; *expend.:* $492 mil. **GDP:** $12 bil., $1,000 per capita (2000 est.). **Chief crops:** peanuts, shea nuts, sesame, cotton. **Natural resources:** manganese, limestone, marble; small deposits of gold, antimony, copper, nickel, bauxite. **Major industries:** cotton, beverages, agricultural processing. **Labor force:** 5 mil. (1999); 90% agriculture, industry, commerce, services, government; a large part of male labor force migrates to neighboring countries for seasonal employment. **Exports:** $220 mil. (f.o.b., 2000 est.); cotton, gold, animal products. **Imports:** $610 mil. (f.o.b., 2000 est.); machinery, food products, petroleum. **Major trading partners:** (1985) *exports:* France, Italy, Indonesia, Thailand; *imports:* Ivory Coast, France, Spain, Benelux.

The Mossi empire dominated the area of what is now Burkina Faso, a landlocked nation in western Africa with few natural resources and poor agricultural conditions, from as early as the 11th century. They ruled the region, often resisting Muslim invaders, until modern times.

The region was hardly visited by Europeans before the 1880's, but by 1896 the French had captured the Mossi capital city of Ouagadougou and established a protectorate over the area. The French created Upper Volta in 1919, naming it for the upper basin of the Volta River. Upper Volta became a self-governing state with the French Overseas Community in 1958 and gained independence Aug. 5, 1960.

After a brief period of military rule, the nation ratified a new constitution on June 14, 1970, and made a peaceful transition to civilian rule based on the French model. In 1980 the constitution was overthrown and a military government was set up. There was another coup on Aug. 4, 1983, and a government was established patterned after the Libyan government of Muammar al-Qaddafi. On Aug. 14, 1984, Upper Volta officially changed its name to Burkina Faso.

Two attempted coups against the government of Capt. Blaise Compaore, in September and December 1989, were put down and the leaders executed. In 1992, as president, Compaore convened a National Reconciliation Forum followed by legislative elections that resulted in a new prime minister. In 1994 the World Bank reported significant economic progress in this desperately poor country.

▶ **BURUNDI**
Republic of Burundi
• **GEOGRAPHY Location:** landlocked country on northeastern shore of Lake Tanganyika in central Africa. **Boundaries:** Rwanda to N, Tanzania to E and S, Zaire to W. **Total land area:** 10,745 sq. mi. (27,830 sq km). **Coastline:** none. **Comparative area:** slightly larger than Maryland. **Land use:** 44% arable land; 9% permanent crops; 36% meadows and pastures; 3% forest and woodland; 8% other. **Major cities:** Bujumbura (capital) 215,243 (1987 est.); Gitega 15,943 (1978).
• **PEOPLE Population:** 6,223,897 (July 2001 est.). **Nationality:** noun—Burundian(s); adjective—Burundi. **Ethnic groups:** 85% Hutu (Bantu), 14% Tutsi (Hamitic), 1% Twa (Pygmy), 3,000 Europeans, 2,000 South Asians. **Languages:** Kirundi and French (both official), Swahili (along Lake Tanganyika and in Bujumbura area). **Religions:** 67% Christian (62% Roman Catholic, 5% Protestant), 32% indigenous beliefs, 1% Muslim.
• **GOVERNMENT Type:** republic. **Independence:** July 1, 1962 (from U.N. trusteeship under Belgian administration). **Constitution:** Mar. 13, 1992. **National holiday:** Independence Day, July 1. **Heads of Government:** Pierre Buyoya, president (since Sept. 1996); **Structure:** executive; unicameral legislature; judiciary. (Note: a miltary government took office during a 1996 coup, but the new leadership has not been officially recognized.)
• **ECONOMY Monetary unit:** Burundi franc. **Budget:** (2000 est.) *income:* $125 mil; *expend.:* $176 mil. **GDP:** $4.4 bil., $720 per capita (2000 est.). **Chief crops:** coffee, cotton, tea, corn, sorghum. **Natural resources:** nickel, uranium, rare earth oxide, peat, cobalt. **Major industries:** light consumer goods such as blankets, shoes, soap; assembly of imported components; public works construction. **Labor force:** (1983 est.) 1.9 mil.; 93% agriculture, 7% other. **Exports:** $32 mil. (f.o.b., 2000); coffee, tea, cotton, hides. **Imports:** $110 mil. (f.o.b., 2000); capital goods, petroleum

products, foodstuffs. **Major trading partners:** *exports:* Germany, Belgium, U.S.; *imports:* Belgium, Zambia, Kenya, South Africa.

Burundi's population is divided between two ethnic groups, the majority Hutu and the minority, but politically powerful, Tutsi. The Hutu were the original settlers of the country and practiced agriculture; the cattle-herding Tutsi arrived several hundred years ago and established a form of feudal overlordship over the Hutu. The traditional government was monarchical, with a king (mwami) chosen from among a group of aristocratic families (ganwa).

European exploration of Burundi began in 1858, and the territory was incorporated into German East Africa in 1899. Following World War I, the League of Nations (1923) awarded Burundi, along with neighboring Rwanda, to Belgium as a mandated territory. Belgian rule over the Territory of Ruanda-Urundi, as it was then called, continued under a U.N. trusteeship after World War II.

Burundi became independent on July 1, 1962, as a constitutional monarchy under the traditional mwami. The country rapidly lapsed into political chaos. In 1966, with the backing of the army, Capt. Michel Micombero overthrew the monarchy and proclaimed a republic. A Hutu rebellion in 1972 against Tutsi political domination left 10,000 Tutsi dead; Tutsi reprisals in 1972-73 resulted in the slaughter of 150,000 Hutu. The Micombero government was overthrown in a bloodless coup, and on Nov. 1, 1976, Lt. Col. Jean-Baptiste Bagaza took control of the government.

Bagaza was overthrown in Sept. 1987, and his successor, Maj. Pierre Buyoya, proclaimed a policy of nonalignment, seeking closer links with the West, while maintaining relations with Libya and the eastern bloc. Domestically, the government pledged to eradicate Bagaza's record of persecution of the Catholic church (62 percent of Burundians are Catholic) and to seek ethnic reconciliation between Hutu and Tutsi, but renewed outbreaks of ethnic violence occurred in 1988. Buyoya led the country to its first free presidential elections in June 1993. Melchior Ndadaye, a Hutu, defeated Buyoya by a wide margin.

But in Oct. 1993 Ndadaye was assassinated, as was his Hutu successor (April 1994). The succeeding regime of Hutu president Ntibantunganya, unsuccesful in forming a stable, ethically balanced goverment, was overturned in a military coup (July 1996) which dissolved parliament, outlawed all political parties, and named Pierre Buyoya to return as president. Vowing yet another return to democracy after the end of civil war, Buyoya faced economic sanctions by the Organization of African Unity. Meanwhile, the complicated civil war was only worsened by Zaire's attempt to expel almost half a million Tutsi (the Banyamulenge people, settled south on Lake Kivi since the 18th century) in October 1996. The Tutsi succesful self defense had the paradoxical effect of driving yet more Hutu (50,000) into Burundi—and almost half a million more into neighboring Rwanda.

The civil war continued into 2000, with at least 200,000 dead, with 350,000 Hutu rebels "regrouped" into 50 camps, and with Burundian army involvement (unadmitted) in the Congo conflict. A promising peace accord, brokered by Nelson Mandela in Aug. 2000, collapsed in Feb. 2001 as the capital of Bujumbura fell to Hutu rebels. Government forces re-took it on March 1, and another accord again forged by Mandela was signed by all parties in July 2001. Based on a power-sharing arrangement for three years, observers believed it would last.

▶ CAMBODIA
Kingdom of Cambodia

● GEOGRAPHY   Location: on Indochinese peninsula in Southeast Asia. Boundaries: Thailand to W and N, Laos to N, Gulf of Thailand to S, Vietnam to E. Total land area: 69,900 sq. mi. (181,040 sq km). Coastline: 275 mi. (443 km). Comparative area: between Missouri and Oklahoma. Land use: 13% arable land; negl % permanent crops; 11% meadows and pastures; 66% forest and woodland; 10% other; includes 1% irrigated. Major cities: (1991 est.) Phnom Penh (capital) 900,000.

● PEOPLE Population: 12,491,501 (July 2001 est.). Nationality: noun—Cambodian(s); adjective—Cambodian. Ethnic groups: 90% Khmer (Cambodian), 5% Vietnamese, 1% Chinese, 5% other minorities. Languages: Khmer (official), French. Religions: 95% Theravada Buddhism.

● GOVERNMENT Type: multiparty liberal democracy under a constitutional monarchy. Independence: November 9, 1953 (from France). Constitution: promulgated Sept. 21, 1993. National holiday: Independence Day, November 9. Heads of Government: Norodom Sihanouk, king (reinstated Sept. 1993); Hun Sen, prime minister (since Nov. 1998). Structure: executive; bicameral legislature; judiciary.

● ECONOMY Monetary unit: new riel. Budget: (2000 est.) income: $363 mil.; expend.: $532 mil. GDP: $16.1 bil., $1,300 per capita (2000 est.). Chief crops: rice, rubber, corn, vegetables. Natural resources: timber, gemstones, some iron ore, manganese, phosphates, hydropower potential. Major industries: garments, rice milling, fishing, wood and wood products. Labor force: 6 mil.; 80% agriculture (1999 est.). Exports: $942 mil. (f.o.b., 2000 est.); timber, garments, rubber, soybeans, sesame. Imports: $1.3 bil. (f.o.b., 2000 est.); cigarettes, gold, construction materials, petroleum products. Major trading partners: Vietnam, Thailand.

The dominant power in Indochina from the Eighth through the 13th centuries, the Khmer Empire encompassed present-day Cambodia and much of western Thailand, southern Laos, and central and southern Vietnam. It built magnificent Buddhist temple cities at Angkor Wat and Angkor Thon. From the 14th century onward, the Khmer Empire came under increasing pressure from the expansionist Vietnamese state of Annam, which absorbed the territories east of the Mekong River. In the 18th century, the kingdom of Siam (Thailand) annexed three western provinces of the Khmer Empire. The remaining Khmer territory became the French protectorate of Cambodia in 1863, and a French colony as part of the Union of Indochina in 1887. In 1907 France forced Siam to return some territory to Cambodia.

During World War II, Cambodia was occupied by Japan from 1942 to 1945, when French control was restored. After the French defeat in Indochina, Cambodia became independent in 1953 under Prince Norodom Sihanouk, who had ascended the throne in 1941. In 1960 Sihanouk was named head of state under a constitutional monarchy. Shaken by the Vietnam War in the 1960's, Cambodia broke relations with the United States in 1965 because of South Vietnamese incursions across the border. In 1969 relations were restored when Sihanouk charged North Vietnam with arming the Khmer Rouge Cambodian Communist rebels. In the same year, American planes began secret bombing raids in Cambodia. In 1970 Sihanouk was ousted by a coup led by pro-U.S. Gen. Lon Nol; the monarchy was abolished, and Prince Sihanouk went into exile.

In April 1975 the Khmer Rouge, led by Pol Pot, captured the capital, Phnom Penh, and established a new government, the Kampuchean People's Republic. In an ensuing reign of terror, an estimated 3 million people died and hundreds of thousands more fled to refugee camps in Thailand. In 1978, Vietnamese troops invaded, capturing Phnom Penh on Jan. 7, 1979, and installing a new government led by Heng Samrin. The Kampuchean People's Republic continued to be recognized as the legal government of Cambodia in the United Nations and by most non-Soviet-bloc nations. A coalition dominated by the Khmer Rouge resisted the Vietnamese takeover, but by 1985 almost all of the country was under Vietnamese control with the Communist Party's Hun Sen as Prime Minister.

Most Vietnamese troops withdrew in 1989, and Prince Sihanouk emerged as the leader of a coalition of antigovernment forces. Starting in late 1988 conferences including representatives from all Cambodian factions were held to forge a political settlement to end the 20-year-old civil war. A peace agreement was signed on Oct. 23, 1991, providing for a cease-fire under U.N. supervision, the disarmament of all military factions, the formation of a coalition government, and the scheduling of a national election.

Despite bloody efforts by Khmer Rouge forces to disrupt the planned election, Cambodians went to the polls in large numbers on May 23, 1993. The Royalist party emerged with about 42 percent of the vote, ousting Hun Sen's Cambodian People's party. Hun Sen agreed to take part in a coalition cabinet as "second premier," with Sihanouk's son, Prince Ranariddh, as "first premier." Sihanouk took the title "king." In Jan. 1994, the united government went on the offensive and captured the Khmer Rouge stronghold of Pailin, driving 3,000 troops and 20,000 civilians into Thailand. Sihanouk succesfully negotiated international loans for rebuilding the country.

The coaltion government proved ineffective due to the inherent rivalry between the prince and Hun Sen, both of whom built up their security forces. When the Khmer Rouge leadership split in mid-1997, with Pol Pot either assasinated or imprisoned, Hun Sen seized the moment and his forces attacked those of his co-ruler's and drove the prince into exile. New elections were held in July 1998 and Hun Sen emerged victorious but agreed to form a coalition government. Hun Sen became "sole premier" with 12 cabinet posts while Ranariddh became President of the Assembly with 11 cabinet posts. In December, the last Khmer Rouge troops surrendered, and by March 1999, all of the remaining Khmer Rouge leaders had surrendered or were captured. In Jan. 2001 the Senate and National Assembly approved Hun Sen's agreement with the U.N. for an international tribunal to try the mass murderers.

▶ CAMEROON
Republic of Cameroon

● GEOGRAPHY Location: western coast of central Africa. Boundaries: Nigeria to NW, Chad to NE, Central African Republic to E, Congo to SE, Gabon, Equatorial Guinea to S, Gulf of Guinea to W. Total land area: 183,568 sq. mi. (475,440 sq km). Coastline: 250 mi. (402 km). Comparative area: slightly larger than California. Land use: 3%

arable land; 2% permanent crops; 4% meadows and pastures; 78% forest and woodland; 13% other. **Major cities:** (1986 est.) Yaoundé (capital) 653,670; Douala 1,029,731; Nkongsamba (and environs) 123,149; Maroua (and environs) 103,653.
• **PEOPLE Population:** 15,803,220 (July 2001 est.). **Nationality:** noun—Cameroonian(s); adjective— Cameroonian. **Ethnic groups:** 31% Cameroon Highlanders, 19% Equatorial Bantu, 11% Kirdi, 10% Fulani, 8% Northwestern Bantu, 7% Eastern Nigritic, 13% other African; less than 1% non-African. **Languages:** English and French (both official); 24 major African language groups. **Religions:** 40% indigenous beliefs, 40% Christian, 20% Muslim.
• **GOVERNMENT Type:** unitary republic; multiparty presidential regime. **Independence:** Jan. 1, 1960 (from U.N. trusteeship under French administration). **Constitution:** May 20, 1972. **National holiday:** Republic Day, May 20. **Heads of Government:** Paul Biya, president (since Nov. 1982); Peter Mafany Musonga, prime minister (since Sept. 1996). **Structure:** executive; unicameral legislature; judiciary.
• **ECONOMY Monetary unit:** Communauté Financière Africaine franc. **Budget:** (FY00/01 est.) *income:* $2.1 bil.; *expend.:* $2.1 bil. **GDP:** $26 bil., $1,700 per capita (2000 est.). **Chief crops:** coffee, cocoa, cotton, rubber. **Natural resources:** crude oil, bauxite, iron ore, timber, hydropower potential. **Major industries:** crude oil production and refining, food processing. **Labor force:** (1983) 74.4% agriculture, 11.4% industry and transport, 14.2% other services. **Exports:** $2.1 bil. (f.o.b., 2000 est.); crude oil and petroleum products, lumber, cocoa beans, aluminum. **Imports:** $1.6 bil. (f.o.b., 2000 est.); machines and electrical equipment, transport equipment, fuel, food. **Major trading partners:** *exports:* 24% Italy, 18% France, 10% Netherlands; *imports:* 29% France, 6% U.S., 7% Germany.

Cameroon was settled by the Sao people about 1,000 years ago. In later times others, including the Bamileke, Bassa, Douala, and Fulani, migrated into the region. Portuguese trading stations were established along the coast beginning in the 15th century, and between 1500 and the early 19th century, the population was severely depleted by the slave trade in the hands of various European nations. European rivalries for domination in Cameroon were settled temporarily in 1884 when Germany established a protectorate.

British and French troops invaded German Cameroon during World War I, and following the war the League of Nations divided the protectorate into two mandated territories—French in the eastern sector and British in the west. French Cameroon rejected the Vichy government in World War II and became an important African base for Charles de Gaulle's Free French. In 1946 British and French rule in Cameroon was reaffirmed under U.N. trusteeships.

In 1958 the French trusteeship was abolished, and the Republic of Cameroon became independent on Jan. 1, 1960. In February 1961 a U.N.-supervised plebiscite was held in British Cameroon, allowing the people of that region to choose between union with Nigeria and union with the Republic of Cameroon. The northern two-thirds of the British territory elected union with Nigeria; the southern portion joined the Republic of Cameroon on Oct. 1, 1961, to form the Federal Republic of Cameroon. In 1972 the federal structure was abolished by a national referendum, and the United Republic of Cameroon was established. In 1984 the nation's name reverted to the Republic of Cameroon.

During the federal period, Cameroon had a multiparty political system, with party divisions coinciding with the old distinctions between west and east Cameroon. In 1966 all political parties were amalgamated to form the Cameroon National Union, which, with various changes in name, has dominated the political life of Cameroon ever since. In 1980 Pres. Ahidjo, the long-time political leader of Cameroon, was elected without opposition to a fifth five-year term in office. He resigned in 1982 and was replaced by Prime Minister Paul Biya, who was re-elected in his own right in 1984. He instituted political reforms whereby multiple candidates ran for office within the structure of the country's single-party system. In 1992 he was elected president in the nation's first multiparty elections. His closest rival was put under house arrest.

The economy of Cameroon is based primarily on agriculture. The country is self-sufficient in food and exports coffee, cocoa, rubber, cotton, palm oil, and timber. Oil is the principal export, however, accounting for 60 percent of export earnings.

▶ CANADA

• **GEOGRAPHY Location:** northern North America (excluding Alaska and Greenland); second largest country in the world. **Boundaries:** Arctic Ocean to N, Greenland to NE across Baffin Bay, Atlantic Ocean to E, United States to S, Pacific Ocean and Alaska to W. **Total land area:** 3,851,794 sq. mi. (9,976,140 sq km). **Coastline:** 151,492 mi. (243,791 km). **Comparative area:** slightly larger than U.S. **Land use:** 5% arable land, 3% meadows and pastures, 54% forest and woodland, 38% other. **Major cities:** (1991 census) Ottawa (capital) 912,100; Toronto 3,863,105; Montréal 3,091,115; Vancouver 1,584,115; Edmonton 832,155.
• **PEOPLE Population:** 31,592,805 (July 2001 est.). **Nationality:** noun—Canadian(s); adjective—Canadian. **Ethnic groups:** 28% British Isles origin, 23% French origin, 15% other European, 2% Amerindian, 6% other, mostly Asian. **Languages:** 59.3% English, 23.2% French (both official). **Religions:** 42% Roman Catholic, 12% United Church, 8% Anglican.
• **GOVERNMENT Type:** confederation with parliamentary democracy. **Independence:** July 1, 1867 (from U.K.). **Constitution:** amended British North America Act of 1867 transferred power and rights to Canada, Apr. 17, 1982; charter of rights and unwritten customs. **National holiday:** Canada Day, July 1. **Heads of Government:** Jean Chrétien, prime minister (since Nov. 1993); Adrienne Clarkson, governor-general (since Oct. 1999). **Structure:** executive—cabinet collectively responsible to House of Commons and headed by prime minister; legislative—bicameral Parliament with queen represented by governor general, Senate, and House of Commons; judiciary—judges appointed by governor general with Supreme Court as highest tribunal.
• **ECONOMY Monetary unit:** Canadian dollar. **Budget:** (2000 est.) *income:* $126.1 bil.; *expend.:* $125.3 bil. **GDP:** $774.7 bil., $24,800 per capita (2000 est.). **Chief crops:** grain (principally wheat), oilseeds, tobacco. **Natural resources:** iron ore, nickel, zinc, copper, gold, lead. **Major industries:** processed and unprocessed minerals, food products, wood and paper products. **Labor force:** 16.1 mil.; 74% services, 15% manufacturing; 6.8% unemployment (2000 est.). **Exports:** $272.3 bil.

(f.o.b., 2000 est.); motor vehicles and parts, newsprint, wood pulp, timber, petroleum. **Imports:** $238.2 bil. (f.o.b., 2000 est.); machinery and equipment, petroleum, chemicals, motor vehicles. **Major trading partners:** U.S., Japan, U.K., Germany.

Canada is geographically the second-largest country in the world, but most of its territory is very sparsely settled. The vast majority of the country's 26 million people live in a narrow band along the border with the U.S. Despite a long tradition of national independence, Canada's history has been dominated by relations with Great Britain, the U.S., and, to a lesser extent, France.

Canada's earliest inhabitants arrived via the Bering land bridge from Asia around 15,000 years ago and diversified to form the various Inuit (Eskimo), Northwest Indian, Plains Indian, and forest Indian cultures that still contribute significantly to Canada's national identity. The earliest-known European settlers of Canada were Vikings, who established a short-lived colony in Newfoundland around A.D. 1000. Other European explorers made numerous voyages to Canada during the 16th century, stimulated by Canada's rich resources of fish, forest products, and furs.

The first permanent European settlement in Canada was the French trading station at Quebec, founded by Samuel de Champlain in 1608. Fur traders rapidly spread into the interior along the St. Lawrence River and the Great Lakes; European diseases, particularly smallpox, decimated Native American populations as the explorers advanced. In 1663 New France was organized as a French Crown Colony, and royal governors replaced private commercial interests in governing Quebec.

The Hudson Bay Company was chartered by the British Crown in 1670, inaugurating a long period of commercial and territorial rivalry in Canada between Britain and France. In general, France sought to expand New France northward and westward, while Britain sought to expand its domination southward and westward from Hudson Bay. French and British interests clashed directly along the Atlantic coast, where both British and French settlements were established. Local and regional wars between the French and the British were endemic in Canada throughout the 17th and 18th centuries; each side enlisted Native American allies. These wars were often inconclusive, but in Queen Anne's War (1702-13), Britain gained a significant advantage by winning control of Acadia and Newfoundland, and by driving the French from Hudson Bay.

The French and Indian Wars of 1756-63, a North American extension of Europe's Seven Years' War, proved to be the decisive turning point in the Anglo-French rivalry in Canada. Prior to the outbreak of full-scale war, in 1755 the British deported some 7,000-10,000 French settlers from Acadia, in Nova Scotia, to the West Indies; many later settled in Louisiana. When war broke out in Europe in 1756, Britain employed its superior sea power to cut New France off from Europe and captured Quebec in the Battle of the Plains of Abraham in 1759. Montreal capitulated in 1760, leaving Britain in control of New France.

Faced with the problem of governing New France's large and rapidly growing French population (which far outnumbered Canada's English-speaking population), the British in 1774 passed the Quebec Act, which recognized the territory's legal code and manorial system of land tenure, and granted legal status to the Roman Catholic church. The act also extended Canadian territory south to the Ohio River, enraging the inhabitants of the 13 American colonies and helping to fuel the American Revolution.

During the American Revolution, nearly 40,000 loyalists fled to Canada from the rebellious colonies, establishing English-speaking settlements in New Brunswick and western Quebec. Friction between English- and French-speaking Canadians led the British in 1791 to divide Canada (west of the Atlantic maritime provinces) into two provinces, Upper Canada and Lower Canada. Each was granted a legislature; Upper Canada's was based on British institutions, Lower Canada's retained the French forms established by the Quebec Act of 1774.

During the War of 1812 between Great Britain and the U.S., Canada became a battleground; Toronto was captured and pillaged by the Americans in 1813. Many Americans hoped to expand the territory of the U.S. at the expense of Canada, or even to entice Canada into a continental American union, but Canadians, whether English- or French-speaking, showed no enthusiasm for joining the U.S. A small British garrison, with the support of Native American irregular forces, kept the Americans at bay. The Convention of 1818 established the border between Canada and the U.S. at latitude 49° north, as far west as the Rocky Mountains, and provided for joint U.S.-British control of Oregon (i.e., the entire Columbia River basin).

Following the War of 1812, British authorities encouraged British immigration to Canada, and between 1815 and 1855, one million Britons answered the call. This immigration radically altered Canada's ethnic balance, making French-speaking Canadians a minority population for the first time. The francophones of Lower Canada, hemmed in on all sides by English speakers, rose in rebellion under the leadership of the Parti Patriote in 1837-38. Lord Durham recommended in 1839 that Canada be united under a single government, and the Union of Canada was enacted in 1841. This move did not, however, quell the growing nationalism of French Canadians.

War with the U.S. threatened in 1844, as the U.S. claimed the entire Columbia River basin north to 54°40′ ("fifty-four forty or fight"). But diplomacy triumphed in the end: In 1846 the boundary at 49° was extended westward to the Pacific Ocean. Meanwhile, gold was discovered in British Columbia in 1856, leading to a gold rush and a substantial increase in the population of western Canada.

Growing trade between Canada and the U.S. from the 1840's onward, and the development of a continental system of railroads in both Canada and the U.S. in the 1850's, led to a relative decline in British influence in Canada. The American Civil War had the indirect effect of prompting Canadians to seek self-government in a federal union. Previously, there had been little contact between the Canadas (Upper and Lower) and the maritime provinces, while the vast territories of the west were still privately administered by the Hudson Bay Company. A federal union was forged in a series of conferences beginning in 1864, and the federation of Quebec, Ontario, Nova Scotia, and New Brunswick was recognized by the British North America Act of July 1, 1867.

The Dominion of Canada thus established in 1867 became a self-governing entity within the British Empire; Sir J.A. Macdonald became Canada's first prime minister (1867-73). The dominion rapidly expanded. In 1869 it purchased the western territories of the Hudson Bay Company, and in 1870, in response to a rebellion of

French-speaking Métis in Manitoba, Manitoba was granted provincial status within the federation. In 1871 the union of British Columbia with Canada was secured with the promise of a transcontinental railway; the Canadian Pacific Railway was completed in 1885. Prince Edward Island joined the federation in 1873, but neighboring Newfoundland remained a British colony outside the Canadian federation until 1949.

A second francophone rebellion broke out in Saskatchewan in 1885. Its leader, Louis Riel, was executed and became a symbol of French Canadian grievances against the English-speaking majority. Wilfred Laurier became Canada's first francophone prime minister in 1896, but he was unable to solve the problem of the rights of Catholics and French-speakers outside Quebec. Legislation restricting those rights had already been enacted in Manitoba in 1890.

The Klondike Gold Rush of 1897-98 brought Canada to worldwide attention and indirectly helped promote the settlement of rich agricultural lands in the Canadian west. Immigrants to the prairie region came not only from eastern Canada, but also from Europe, notably Germany, Scandinavia, and the Ukraine. Japanese farmers and Chinese railroad and mining workers settled west of the Rockies, further increasing Canada's ethnic diversity, though Asian immigrants were denied citizenship through discriminatory legislation. Alberta and Saskatchewan were granted provincial status in 1905; the Yukon Territory and the Northwest Territories continued to be governed by controllers appointed by the federal government and patrolled by the famous Royal Canadian Mounted Police.

Urbanization and industrialization were stimulated in the early 20th century by the exploitation of extensive mineral resources in western Canada and in northern Quebec, and by the development of hydroelectric projects and transportation facilities throughout the country. The long-lived Laurier government fell in 1911, when his proposal for free trade with the U.S. evoked widespread fears that Canada's nascent industries would suffer without protective tariffs.

Laurier's Conservative successor, Robert Borden, sent Canadian troops to fight in World War I in 1914 and, over the objections of most French Canadian leaders, bolstered Canada's war efforts in Europe through national conscription in 1917. The distinguished performance of Canada's armed forces in the war bought the country renewed international respect.

Borden's wartime English-speaking Conservative-Liberal coalition collapsed in 1921. He was succeeded by the Liberal leader William L. Mackenzie King, who was to be Canada's prime minister for over 20 years (1921-30, 1935-48). He skillfully managed the economic prosperity of the 1920's, which saw the establishment in Canada of branch plants of many American industrial firms.

The Statute of Westminster, which created the British Commonwealth in 1931, had the effect of granting full self-government to Canada within the Commonwealth.

Canada's federal structure was ill-equipped to manage the economic collapse of the 1930's, which brought both industrial depression and a drought-induced agricultural crisis. Efforts to deal with unemployment, land foreclosures, and other economic ills fell to the provincial governments, which were not up to the task.

Canada's recovery from the Great Depression was stimulated by the advent of World War II, which Canada entered in 1939. Although the war brought price controls, rationing, and other emergency measures, the overall effect of the war was to strengthen all sectors of Canada's economy and to enhance Canada's international status as a leading military and industrial power. A Liberal electoral victory of 1945 gave Mackenzie King a renewed mandate for the postwar era.

The two decades following the war saw the gradual expansion of federal financial responsibility for national welfare measures, including pensions, unemployment insurance, and comprehensive medical care, though the administration of such programs remained a provincial matter. These developments coincided with an increase in urbanization and industrialization in the major centers of Vancouver, Toronto, and Montreal. Formal "equalization payments" were enacted in the 1950's to reduce economic disparities between rich and poor provinces. The early stages of these developments played a part in persuading Newfoundland to join the federation as Canada's 10th province in 1949.

A landslide Conservative victory in 1958 brought John Diefenbaker to the prime ministership, but the Conservatives proved unable to offer a coherent political program and were ousted in the elections of 1963, which returned the Liberals to power. Canadian politics since the 1960's have been marked by increasing regionalization; the Liberal party is based largely in the east, while the New Democratic party, organized in 1961, has little support east of Ontario. The Conservatives offer a broad but insecure national alternative.

The language issue continues to divide Canada politically and ideologically. The rise of an aggressive Quebecois nationalism in the 1960's led directly to the Liberal prime ministership of Pierre Trudeau, a Quebecois known as a supporter of a strong federal constitution. Trudeau's efforts toward conciliation and for constitutional guarantees for Quebec within a strong federal structure proved unavailing, however. In 1970 he invoked the War Measures Act to send troops to Quebec to put down a wave of separatist terrorism, leaving the province subdued but sullen.

The 1976 electoral victory in Quebec of the Parti Québécois under René Lévesque provoked fears that Quebec would secede from Canada. Lévesque's plan for a separate "sovereignty-association" status for Quebec was rejected by a popular referendum in 1980, but only because of Trudeau's pledge to seek full autonomy for Canada in order to secure constitutional protection for Quebec's special interests.

In November 1981, Canada's provincial governments reached agreement on proposals for constitutional change. The result was the passage by the British Parliament of the Canada Act, which came into effect on Apr. 17, 1982, granting full independence and constitutional autonomy to Canada and severing its last colonial ties to the British government. Canada's new 1982 Constitution more clearly delineated the powers of the federal and provincial governments, provided for Supreme Court review of legislation, and included a Charter of Rights to protect civil liberties.

A nationwide recession led to the fall of Trudeau's Liberal government and to the election of the Conservative party leader Brian Mulroney (also a native of Quebec) as prime minister in 1984. The Mulroney government encouraged foreign investment and privatization as a means of revitalizing Canada's economy. But its most significant achievement was the negotiation and passage, in 1988-89, of a free-trade agreement with the U.S. (that also came to include Mexico).

The Meech Lake Agreement, containing a number of articles clarifying the 1982 Constitution, was worked out between Mulroney and Quebec's Liberal premier Robert Bourassa, along with the leaders of Canada's nine other provinces, and signed on June 23, 1987. Its provisions enhanced the power of the provinces; a key provision gave constitutional protection to Quebec's efforts to remain a "distinct society," linguistically and culturally French. But the aggressive measures of the Quebec government to eradicate the use of English in the public affairs of the province provoked a backlash against bilingualism. The Meech Lake Agreement failed to become law when the legislatures of Newfoundland and Manitoba declined to ratify it by the June 23, 1990, deadline. Canada plunged into the most serious constitutional crisis in its history.

An alternative agreement to restructure the federal government and give more power to the 10 provincial governments met initial opposition in Quebec, and was decisively defeated in a national referendum, leaving the nation to deal once again with the awkward status quo.

Faced with a drastic decline in his popularity, Mulroney resigned in Feb. 1991. In June the Progressive Conservative party convention chose Kim Campbell to lead the government, the first woman to do so in the country's history. In the 1993 general election, however, the Conservatives were routed by Jean Chrétien and the Liberals, who gained nearly 100 additional seats in the House of Commons. The new government announced plans in early 1995 to cut the budget deficit through higher taxes and spending cuts on health care and social programs. Although they accomplished this goal, many Canadians were disconcerted because of high unemployment (9 percent in 1996) and a decrease in benefits. Chretien was also vulnerable on the problem of Quebec because he and the Liberal Party seemed to favor giving special status to the French province, where in 1995 a separatist referendum was only narrowly defeated. In July 1997 elections, the Liberals lost 19 seats, but still held a slim majority. Since the other major parties (Reform, Bloc Quebecois) are not united in any meaningful way, the Liberals have been able to govern. The issue of separatism rose to prominence again in Aug. 1998 when the Supreme Court ruled that a referendum on Quebec secession would be invalid without negotiations on the terms with both the provinces and the federation as a whole.

On April 1, 1999 the government officially created a new Arctic territory called Nunavut which is governed solely by the Inuit tribe (called Eskimos in Alaska and Greenland). In Nov. 2000 Chretien's Liberals won their third consecutive victory by a very large margin.

▶ **CAPE VERDE**
Republic of Cape Verde
• **GEOGRAPHY** **Location:** archipelago of 15 islands in Atlantic Ocean, off northern Africa. **Boundaries:** Senegal about 300 mi. (500 km) to E. **Total land area:** 1,556 sq. mi. (4,030 sq km). **Coastline:** 600 mi. (965 km). **Comparative area:** slightly larger than Rhode Island. **Land use:** 11% arable land; negl. % permanent crops; 6% meadows and pastures; negl. % forest and woodland; 83% other; includes 1% irrigated. **Major cities:** (1990 census) Cidade de Praia (capital) 62,000.
• **PEOPLE** **Population:** 405,163 (July 2001 est.).

Nationality: noun—Cape Verdean(s); adjective—Cape Verdean. **Ethnic groups:** 71% Creole (mulatto), 28% African, 1% European. **Languages:** Portuguese and Crioulo (blend of Portuguese and West African). **Religions:** Roman Catholicism fused with indigenous beliefs.
• **GOVERNMENT** **Type:** republic. **Independence:** July 5, 1975 (from Portugal). **Constitution:** Sept. 25, 1992. **National holiday:** Independence Day, July 5. **Heads of Government:** Pedro Verona Rodrigues Pires, president (since Mar. 2001); José Maria Neves, prime minister (since Feb. 2001). **Structure:** executive; unicameral legislature; judiciary.
• **ECONOMY** **Monetary unit:** Cape Verdean escudo. **Budget:** (1996 est.) *income:* $188 mil.; *expend.:* $228 mil. **GDP:** $670 mil., $1,700 per capita (2000 est.). **Chief crops:** bananas, corn, beans. **Natural resources:** salt, basalt rock, pozzolana, limestone, kaolin, fish. **Major industries:** food and beverages, fish processing, salt mining. **Labor force:** 102,000 (1985 est); 57% agriculture, 29% services, 14% industry (1981); 24% unemployment (1999 est.). **Exports:** $40 mil. (f.o.b., 2000 est.); shoes, garments, fish, bananas. **Imports:** $250 mil. (f.o.b., 2000 est.); foodstuffs, consumer goods, industrial products. **Major trading partners:** *exports:* Portugal, U.K., Germany; *imports:* Portugal, Netherlands, France, U.K.

In 1462 the Portuguese founded the first European city in the tropics at Ribeira Grande on Santiago, one of the 15 islands that compose the Republic of Cape Verde. Located 385 miles off the west coast of Africa, the Cape Verde Islands prospered during the slave trade in the 16th century and later served as supply stations on sea routes and trading lanes. The rise of whaling in the 19th century led to contact with the U.S., as American ships recruited crews from the islands. The United States set up an American consulate, headquarters for the U.S. Navy African Squadron, and a transatlantic cable station in the islands.

Portugal changed the status of the archipelago from colony to overseas province in 1951; five years later, citizens of Cape Verde and Portuguese Guinea organized the African Party for the Independence of Guinea-Bissau and Cape Verde (PAIGC) to petition Portugal to improve living conditions. Beginning as a clandestine organization, the PAIGC became an overt political movement on the islands after the 1974 revolution in Portugal. An agreement between the PAIGC and Portugal, providing for a transitional government in Cape Verde, paved the way for full independence in 1975.

In 1980 the PAIGC became the PAICV, which remained the "supreme expression" of Cape Verdeans' political will until the opposition party, Movement for Democracy, won a parliamentary majority in the nation's first multiparty elections in Jan. 1991. The new government instituted free market reforms, including privatization of industries. Voters approved of the reforms, giving the Movement for Democracy 50 of the 72 seats in Parliament in Dec. 1995 elections.

▶ **CENTRAL AFRICAN REPUBLIC**
• **GEOGRAPHY** **Location:** landlocked country in central Africa. **Boundaries:** Chad to N, Sudan to E, Zaire, Congo to S, Cameroon to W. **Total land area:** 240,533 sq. mi. (622,980 sq km). **Coastline:** none. **Comparative area:** slightly smaller than Texas. **Land use:** 3% arable land; 5% meadows and pastures; 75% forest and woodland; 17% other. **Major cities:** (1988) Bangui (capital) 451,690; Berbérati 41,891; Bouar 39,676.

• **PEOPLE Population:** 3,576,884 (July 2001 est.). **Nationality:** noun—Central African(s); adjective— Central African. **Ethnic groups:** 34% Baya, 27% Banda, 21% Mandija, 10% Sara, 4% Mboum, 4% M'Baka; 6,500 Europeans, of which 3,600 are French. **Languages:** French (official), Sangho (lingua franca and national language), Arabic, Hunsa, Swahili. **Religions:** 25% Protestant, 25% Roman Catholic, 24% indigenous beliefs, 15% Muslim, 11% other; indigenous beliefs and practices strongly influence Christian majority.

• **GOVERNMENT Type:** republic. **Independence:** Aug. 13, 1960 (from France). **Constitution:** Adopted Jan. 7, 1995. **National holiday:** Republic Day, Dec. 1. **Heads of Government:** Ange-Félix Patassé, head of state (since Oct. 1993); Martin Ziguele, prime minister (since Apr. 2001). **Structure:** executive; unicameral legislature; judiciary.

• **ECONOMY Monetary unit:** Communauté Financière Africaine (CFA) franc. **Budget:** (1994 est.) *income:* $638 mil.; *expend.:* $1.9 bil. **GDP:** $6.1 bil., $1,700 per capita (2000 est.). **Chief crops:** cotton, coffee, tobacco. **Natural resources:** diamonds, uranium, timber, gold, oil. **Major industries:** sawmills, breweries, diamond mining. **Labor force:** 775,413 (1986 est.); 85% agriculture, 9% commerce and services. **Exports:** $166 mil. (f.o.b., 2000 est.); diamonds, timber, cotton, coffee, tobacco. **Imports:** $154 mil. (f.o.b., 2000); food, textiles, petroleum products, machinery, electrical equipment, motor vehicles. **Major trading partners:** *exports:* 64% Belgium-Luxembourg, Ivory Coast, Spain; *imports:* 35% France, Ivory Coast, Cameroon, Germany.

A landlocked country in Africa's central region, the Central African Republic is one of the least-developed countries in the world. Most of its people are farmers, and the nation has little manufacturing, few reliable roads, and no railroad. Europeans first came to the area in the early 1800's in their search for slaves, but it was not until 1889 that the French established an outpost as the current capital city of Bangui. The region was organized as the territory of Ubangi-Shari five years later. In 1910, it was incorporated into French Equitorial Africa along with what are now the countries of Chad, the Congo, and Gabon.

The country was granted internal selfgovernment by the French under its present name in 1958 and became a member of the French Overseas Community. Independence was achieved on Aug. 13, 1960. The first prime minister, Barthelemy Boganda, was killed in an airplane crash in 1959 and was succeeded by his nephew, David Dacko. Dacko was elected to a seven-year term in January 1964, but an army coup in 1966 overthrew his government. The head of the army, Jean-Bedel Bokassa, was installed as president. Named president for life in 1972, in 1976 Bokassa declared himself emperor and changed the name of the country to the Central African Empire.

Dacko returned to power in 1979, however, and Bokassa went into exile in France. The name of the country was changed back to the Central African Republic. A multiparty political system was reinstated in March 1981, but army officers threw Dacko out of office once again six months later and banned all political parties. Opposition parties were legalized in 1991, and Bokassa was released shortly before elections in 1993, elections that made Ange Félix Patassé president. He tried to reduce the army's power but has been met with several rebellions requiring the intervention of peacekeepers from neighboring states. France intervened on his behalf twice in 1996. In Dec.

2000 riots and a civil service strike disrupted the government but Patisse stayed in power, even surviving a coup attempt in May 2001.

►CHAD
Republic of Chad

• **GEOGRAPHY Location:** landlocked country in north central Africa. **Boundaries:** Libya to N, Sudan to E, Central African Republic to S, Cameroon, Nigeria to SE, Niger to W. **Total land area:** 495,753 sq. mi. (1,284,000 sq km). **Coastline:** none. **Comparative area:** between Texas and Alaska. **Land use:** 3% arable land; negl. % permanent crops; 36% meadows and pastures; 26% forest and woodland; 35% other; includes negl. % irrigated. **Major cities:** (1988 est.) N'Djamena (capital) 594,000; Sarh 113,400; Moundou 102,000; Abéché 83,000.

• **PEOPLE Population:** 8,707,078 (July 2001 est.). **Nationality:** noun—Chadian(s); adjective— Chadian. **Ethnic groups:** 200 distinct ethnic groups, most of whom are Muslims (Arabs, Toubou, Fulbe, Kotoko, Hausa, Kanembou, Baguirmi, Boulala, and Maba) in north and center and non-Muslims (Sara, Ngambaye, Mbake, Goulaye, Moudang, Moussei, Massa) in south. **Languages:** French and Arabic (both official); Sara and Sango in south; more than 100 different languages and dialects. **Religions:** 50% Muslim, 25% Christian, 25% indigenous beliefs (mostly animism).

• **GOVERNMENT Type:** republic. **Independence:** Aug. 11, 1960 (from France). **Constitution:** Mar. 31, 1995. **National holiday:** Independence Day, Aug. 11. **Heads of Government:** Idriss Deby, president (since Dec. 1990); Nagoum Yamassoum, prime minister (since Dec. 1999). **Structure:** executive; unicameral legislature; judiciary.

• **ECONOMY Monetary unit:** Communauté Financière Africaine (CFA) franc. **Budget:** (1998 est.) *income:* $198 mil.; *expend.:* $218 mil., **GDP:** $8.1 bil., $1,000 per capita (2000 est.). **Chief crops:** cotton, sorghum, millet, peanuts. **Natural resources:** small quantities of crude oil (unexploited but exploitation beginning), uranium, natron (sodium carbonate), kaolin, fish (Lake Chad). **Major industries:** cotton textile mills, slaughterhouses, brewery, natron. **Labor force:** 85% agriculture— unpaid subsistence farming, herding and fishing, 15% other. **Exports:** $172 mil. (f.o.b., 2000 est.); cotton, cattle, textiles. **Imports:** $223 mil. (f.o.b., 2000 est.); machinery and transport equipment, industrial goods, petroleum products, foodstuffs. **Major trading partners:** *exports:* 38% Portugal, 12% Germany, Thailand; *imports:* 40% France, 12% Nigeria, 13% Cameroon, 5% India.

The Sao and other ancient peoples built centers of civilization near Lake Chad that flourished for many centuries until they were displaced by the medieval kingdoms of Kanem-Bornu, Baguirmi, and Ouaddai. From about 1400 onward, Chad became a meeting ground between the Muslim cultures of the Sahara and the Sahel and the black African societies of the tropics. Between 1500 and 1800, Arab slave raiders were active around Lake Chad, supplying slaves for European traders on Africa's west coast.

French military forces reached Chad from West Africa in 1891 and fought a series of battles over the next two decades with the Arab rulers of the region. A French governorship of Chad was established in 1905 (based in Brazzaville, the Congo), but the country was not brought entirely under French control until 1914. Chad was incorporated into the federation of French Equatorial Africa in

1910 and was organized as a colony within the federation in 1920.

French Equatorial Africa was dissolved in 1959, and Chad became an autonomous member of the French Community. Full independence followed on Aug. 11, 1960; François Tombalbage became Chad's first president. In 1965 the Muslim northern and eastern parts of the country rebelled against the southern-led government; despite the aid of French troops, the government was unable to suppress the rebellion, and a long civil war ensued.

Tombalbage was overthrown in 1975 in a military coup led by Gen. Felix Malloum. Efforts to broaden the composition of the national government broke down, and in 1979 Prime Minister Hissein Habre broke with the government and led northern forces against the national army. A cease-fire was negotiated under international auspices, and a National Unity Transitional Government (GUNT) was installed in 1979, but civil war broke out again in 1980. Pres. Goukouni Oueddei sought Libyan aid in restoring order; a contingent of 7,000 Libyan troops occupied the country until 1981. They were replaced by an international peacekeeping force organized by the Organization of African Unity.

Civil war broke out again in 1982, and northern forces occupied the capital. A new republican government under the presidency of Hissein Habre was proclaimed on June 7. OAU forces withdrew, and Habre's government soon controlled all of the country except for a few northern areas held by GUNT. In 1983 GUNT launched a counterattack and regained some territory with the aid of Libyan forces. French and Zairian troops were sent to aid Habre's forces. In Sept. 1984 France and Libya agreed to the withdrawal of all foreign forces from Chad, but Libyan forces remained. GUNT forces controlled the country north of the 16th parallel; Libyan forces occupied the Aozou Strip, along the border, with the apparent intention of annexing it to Libya.

Between 1984 and 1986 Habre persuaded most Chadean dissident forces to rejoin the national government, and in Nov. 1986 he launched a campaign to recapture the north. The Chadean forces won a series of victories, and in May 1988 Libya's Col. Qaddafi declared an end to the 20-year war with Chad.

In Nov. 1990, forces led by renegade Gen. Idriss Deby launched attacks from Sudan and ousted Pres. Habre. Deby, who favors multiparty democracy, proclaimed a provisional government and suspended the constitution. A national charter calling for a new constitution and elections to be held within 30 months came into force in March 1991. Deby functioned as president after that, suppressing two attempted coups in 1992, and legalizing opposition parties. Deby's "Higher Transitional Council" remained in command until presidential elections were held in June 1996, which Deby won. He was re-elected in May 2001.

▶ **CHILE**
Republic of Chile
● GEOGRAPHY **Location:** South Pacific coast of South America. **Boundaries**: Peru, Bolivia to N, Argentina to E, Pacific Ocean to W. **Total land area**: 292,259 sq. mi. (756,950 sq km). **Coastline**: 3,999 mi. (6,435 km). **Comparative area**: slightly larger than Texas. **Land use:** 5% arable land; negl. % permanent crops; 18% meadows and pastures; 22% forest and woodland; 55% other; includes 2% irrigated. **Major cities**: (1995) Gran Santiago (cap-

ital) 5,076,808; Viña del Mar 322,220; Concepción 350,268; Valparaíso 282,168; Temuco 239,340.
● PEOPLE **Population:** 15,328,467 (July 2001 est.). **Nationality:** noun—Chilean(s); adjective—Chilean. **Ethnic groups:** 95% white and white Amerindian, 3% Amerindian, 2% other. **Languages:** Spanish. **Religions:** 89% Roman Catholic, 11% Protestant, small Jewish population.
● GOVERNMENT **Type:** republic. **Independence:** Sept. 18, 1810 (from Spain). **Constitution:** Sept. 11, 1980, effective Mar. 11, 1981; modified by public referendum on July 31, 1989. **National holiday:** Independence Day, Sept. 18. **Head of Government:** Ricardo Lagos Escobar, president (since Mar. 2000). **Structure:** executive; bicameral legislature; judiciary.
● ECONOMY **Monetary unit:** Chilean peso. **Budget:** (2000 est.) *income:* $16 bil.; *expend.:* $17 bil. **GDP:** $153.1 bil., $10,100 per capita (2000 est.). **Chief crops:** wheat, corn, grapes, beans, sugar beets. **Natural resources:** copper, timber, iron ore, nitrates, precious metals. **Major industries:** copper, other minerals, foodstuffs, fish processing. **Labor force:** 5.8 mil. (1999); 59% services, 27% industry and commerce, 14% agriculture, forestry, fishing; 9% unemployment (2000 est.). **Exports:** $18 bil. (f.o.b., 2000); copper, fish and fishmeal, other metals and minerals. **Imports:** $17 bil. (c.i.f., 2000); consumer goods, chemicals, motor vehicles, fuels. **Major trading partners:** *exports:* 27% EU, 16% U.S., 14% Japan; *imports:* 23% EU, 24% U.S., 6% Japan, 6% Brazil.

Before the arrival of Europeans in the mid 1530's, indigenous habitation of the territory that would become Chile included the Araucanian population in the south and peoples under the influence of the Inca Empire in the north.

The Spanish founded the cities of Valparaíso in 1536, Santiago in 1541, and Concepción in 1550. Chile was under the authority of the Viceroyalty of Peru, established in 1544. Between 1810 and 1818, fortunes of the Chilean independence movement ebbed and flowed, culminating in the victory of Bernardo O'Higgins and the separatist forces in 1817. Independence was finally achieved in 1818.

From 1818 to 1833, Chile underwent a period of political instability due to power struggles among elite Chilean families. In 1833 a strong presidential-dominant constitution was written under the influence of leading political figure Diego Portales that set the form of government in Chile until 1891. Chile expanded its territory at the expense of Peru and Bolivia, first in a war with the Peruvian-Bolivian Confederation (1836-39) and later as a result of the War of the Pacific (1879-83).

A civil war was fought in 1890-91 between forces of the president, José Balmaceda, and the Chilean Congress over the issue of the limits of presidential authority. The defeat of the presidential forces led to the establishment of a congressional-dominant parliamentary system. The checks on policy initiative resulting from the parliamentary system left government deadlocked in the face of mounting social and political problems arising at the turn of the century. The occurrence of a number of bloody strike actions crystallized political debate around social issues such as better wages and working conditions. The immobilized parliamentary system was unable to respond to these problems. In 1925, when Congress failed to allocate funds for military pay, the forces overthrew the parliamentary government.

A new constitution was drawn up that same year that moved governmental structure toward presidential dominance. Nevertheless, political instability continued until 1933, when the new constitution was implemented. The Chilean balance of political power from 1958 until 1973 remained almost equally divided among parties representing the right, the center, and the left of the political spectrum. In order to prevent an electoral victory for the leftist parties, forces on the right allied themselves with the centrist Christian Democrats in the 1964 election, and this resulted in the victory of Christian Democratic presidential candidate Eduardo Frei Montalva.

The program of the Christian Democrats included ambitious agrarian reform and attempts to organize Chile's urban poor. It was believed that these stances would benefit the Christian Democrats at the polls in the 1970 presidential election. As in 1958, the 1970 election fielded three presidential candidates who represented the political right, center, and left. The leftist Popular Unity coalition candidate, Dr. Salvador Allende Gossens, won with 36.3 percent of the vote, but only after bitter debate did Congress recognize Allende's victory.

The Allende government nationalized the foreign-owned copper industry, but an international boycott of Chilean copper imposed in retaliation for this action seriously hurt the country's economy. The government also nationalized the coal and steel industries as well as 60 percent of private banking. The Popular Unity government found itself unable to control peasant seizures of land and factory takeovers by workers. The copper embargo, land and factory seizures, government subsidies to the poor for basic goods, and runaway inflation resulted in a deterioration of the national economy that particularly affected the middle classes. Members of congress from the center and right had hoped to gain enough seats in the 1973 elections to impeach Allende, but instead the Popular Unity made impressive electoral gains. In order to bolster the legitimacy of the Popular Unity administration in the eyes of political opponents, Allende resorted to inclusion of military officers in the government.

On Sept. 11, 1973, segments of the military led by commanders of three of Chile's four armed forces took control of the government, killing Allende in the process. Gen. Augusto Pinochet Ugarte emerged from the junta as the new president. The junta announced the arrest of some 13,000 persons, many of whom then lost their lives in a wave of brutal repression. (Mass graves were discovered in the desert in 1990, and in 1991 a commission reported that between 1973 and 1990, more than 2,000 people were killed by the government.) In March 1974 the dictatorship published its Declaration of Principles, which included a laissez-faire economic orientation, anti-Marxism, and nationalism.

A new constitution was approved by plebiscite in 1980. The two-phase evolution of Chile's political structure included an authoritarian "transitional period" between 1980 and 1989 and implementation of a new political structure thereafter. The constitution created a presidential system with very extensive executive powers and a "guardian" role for the military.

In an Oct. 1988 plebiscite, Chileans rejected continuation of Pinochet rule and called for an end to the dictatorship. On Dec. 14, 1989, Patricio Aylwin Azocar of the Christian Democratic party (one of a 17-party alliance) was elected president with over 55 percent of the vote; he took office in March 1990, ending 17 years of military dictatorship. He was succeeded by Eduardo Frei Ruiz-Tagle in March 1994.

In recent years, Chile's economy has expanded, exports have increased, and it has succeeded in lowering its large external debt. Although exports are still dominated by copper, other minerals and manufactures have gained in importance. In 1996, Chile joined Mercosur, a free trade agreement among six of the largest South American nations. In 1997 the U.S. agreed to sell Chile advanced fighter jets, ending a 20-year ban.

In March 1998 Gen. Pinochet resigned as head of the armed forces after 25 years and was sworn in as senator-for-life. In Oct., while in Britain, Pinochet was arrested after Spain sought his extradition for the murder of Spanish citizens. A long legal minuet ended in Jan. 2000 when Britain's Home Secretary declared Pinochet unfit to stand trial. Only days later, in a run-off presidential election, the candidate of the center-left Concertacion Coalition, Ricardo Lagos Escobar, took 51.3 percent of the vote. Though Lagos was the first Socialist president since Allende, he supports a market economy.

▶ CHINA
People's Republic of China

● **GEOGRAPHY Location:** covers vast area of eastern Asia. **Boundaries:** Russia, Mongolia to N; N. Korea to NE; Pacific Ocean to E; India, Nepal, Bhutan, Myanmar, Laos, and Vietnam to S; Afghanistan and Pakistan to W., Kazakhstan, Kyrgyzstan, and Tajikistan to NW. **Total land area:** 3,705,392 sq. mi. (9,596,960 sq km). **Coastline:** 9,112 mi. (14,500 km). **Comparative area:** between U.S. and Canada. **Land use:** 10% arable land; 43% meadows and pastures; 14% forest and woodland; 33% other; includes 5% irrigated. **Major cities:** (1994 est.) Beijing (capital) 11,250,000; Shanghai 13,560,000; Tianjin 9,350,000; (1990 est.) Shenyang 4,540,000; Wuhan 3,750,000. ● **PEOPLE Population:** 1,273,111,290 (July 2001 est.). **Nationality:** noun—Chinese (sing., pl.); adjective—Chinese. **Ethnic groups:** 91.9% Han Chinese; 8.1% Zhuang, Uygur, Hui, Yi, Tibetan, Miao, Manchu, Mongol, Buyi, Korean, and numerous others. **Languages:** Standard Chinese or Mandarin (Putonghua based on the Beijing dialect); Yue (Cantonese), Wu (Shanghainese), Minbei (Fuzhou), Minnan (Hokkien-Taiwanese), Xiang, Gan, Hakka dialects, and minority langs. (see "Ethnic groups" above). **Religions:** officially atheist, but traditionally pragmatic and eclectic; Taoism, Buddhism, 2-3% Muslim, 1% Christian. ● **GOVERNMENT Type:** Communist state. **Constitution:** Dec. 4, 1982. **National holiday:** National Day, Oct. 1, (1949) **Heads of Government:** Jiang Zemin, president (since Mar. 1993); Zhu Rongji, prime minister (since 1988). **Structure:** executive; unicameral legislature; judiciary. ● **ECONOMY Monetary unit:** yuan. **Budget:** $NA. **GDP:** $4.5 trillion, $3,600 per capita (2000 est.). **Chief crops:** rice, potatoes, sorghum, peanuts. **Natural resources:** coal, iron ore, crude oil, mercury, tin; world's largest hydropower potential. **Major industries:** iron, steel, coal. **Labor force:** 700 mil. (1998 est.); 50% agriculture and forestry, 24% industry and commerce. **Exports:** $232 bil. (f.o.b. 2000); machinery and equipment, textiles, clothing. **Imports:** $197 bil. (f.o.b. 2000); machinery and equipment, chemicals, plastics, iron and steel. **Major trading partners:** (1999) *exports:* Hong Kong, U.S., Japan, Germany, South Korea; *imports:* Japan, U.S., Taiwan, South Korea.

China is one of the world's oldest civilizations. Dynastic rule in the North China Plain began around 2000 B.C. The unifying Qin (221 B.C.) and Han (206 B.C.) dynasties greatly expanded the territory of the empire and established the basic pattern of imperial bureaucratic government that would endure until the beginning of the 20th century. Major dynasties during that period include the Han (206 B.C.—A.D. 220), Tang (618-907), Song (960-1279), Yuan or Mongol (1279-1368), Ming (1368- 1644), and Qing (1644-1911).

By the late 18th century, the Qing dynasty faced increasingly dangerous problems of explosive population growth, bureaucratic stagnation, and trade pressure from the West. Opium— introduced by Great Britain to balance its trade in tea, silk, porcelain, and other goods—created severe social problems. Western demands for free trade resulted in the Opium War (1839-42), in which China was humiliatingly defeated by the British. The treaties of Nanjing (1842) and Tianjin (1858) opened China to Western merchants and missionaries and created foreign-ruled enclaves on Chinese soil. At the same time, the Taiping Rebellion and other popular uprisings led to the deaths of at least 20 million Chinese between 1850 and 1870.

Such reform efforts as the Self-Strengthening Movement (1870's) and the 1898 Reform Movement proved inadequate to the task of strengthening and modernizing China's dynastic government. Japan, modernizing rapidly after the Meiji Restoration of 1868, joined the race for commercial access to China, decisively winning the Sino-Japanese War of 1894-95. The antiforeign Boxer Uprising of 1900 was put down by a joint foreign military force, dealing a mortal blow to Qing rule. On Oct. 10, 1911, the dynasty fell to a coalition of forces led by the veteran revolutionary nationalist Sun Yat-sen.

China's first attempt at republican government, under Pres. Yuan Shikai and subsequent presidents, quickly degenerated into factionalism and warlord control in the provinces. In 1915 Japan successfully demanded further concessions, provoking public outcries. When news reached China on May 4, 1919, that the Treaty of Versailles granted Japan all of Germany's former concessions in China, students rioted throughout the country, demanding reforms and modernization (the May Fourth Movement). Sun Yat-sen's Nationalist party (Kuomintang, or KMT) and the Chinese Communist party (CCP, founded in 1921 by Mao Zedong) joined forces in 1922 in an attempt to create a second republican revolution.

Sun Yat-sen died in 1925. His successor, Chiang Kai-shek, consolidated KMT forces in Guangzhou and mounted the Northern Expedition (1927-29) to defeat or co-opt the various provincial warlords and reunify the country. In the course of this successful effort, Chiang turned on his Communist allies. A series of failed Communist uprisings and KMT anti-Communist extermination campaigns between 1927 and 1934 nearly wiped out the CCP. Remnants of the party broke out of encirclement in Jiangxi Province in 1934 and undertook the 6,000-mile Long March to a secure base in Yan'an, Shanxi Province. There, under Mao, Zhou Enlai, and Zhu De, the CCP recovered its strength. In the Xi'an Incident of December 1936, Chiang was kidnapped by mutinous KMT allies and forced at gunpoint to agree to forming a United Front with the CCP against Japan.

Meanwhile Japan continued its penetration of China, with the assassination of Manchurian warlord and KMT ally Jiang Zuolin in 1928, the invasion of Manchuria on Sept. 18, 1931, and the establishment of the puppet state of Manchuguo in 1934. On July 7, 1937, fighting erupted between Japanese and Chinese troops near Beijing. The Japanese rapidly moved south to the Yangtse Valley, bombing and capturing Shanghai. The Nationalist capital at Nanjing fell in November 1937, amid widespread atrocities against civilians. The KMT army and government retreated to a wartime capital at Chongqing. The remainder of World War II in China was largely a stalemate, with Japan occupying most of the country. KMT-held areas opposed the Japanese with conventional forces (supported, after 1941, by the Americans), while the Communists harassed the Japanese with guerrilla tactics.

At the end of World War II, American forces ensured that the KMT would receive Japan's surrender throughout most of China, giving the Nationalists a commanding position while U.S. general George Marshall attempted to mediate the creation of a KMT-CCP coalition government. That effort failed, and civil war broke out. The KMT advantage was dissipated by ruinous inflation, corruption, mismanagement, and military ineffectiveness. At the end of 1947, with the Communist forces making continual advances, the United States pulled out of China. After losing several major battles throughout 1948-49, KMT forces retreated to Taiwan; in Beijing, Mao Zedong proclaimed the establishment of the People's Republic of China (PRC) on Oct. 1, 1949.

With American backing, the Republic of China established a temporary capital at Taipei (see "Taiwan") and continued to claim sovereignty over all of China, retaining China's seat in the United Nations. The PRC was quickly granted diplomatic recognition by Soviet bloc nations and some Western nations, notably Great Britain, but was effectively isolated in most international affairs by American support for Nationalist China. Chinese troops entered the Korean War in November 1950, as U.N. forces approached the Sino-Korean border at the Yalu River. This direct confrontation between China and the United States forestalled any possibility of normal contacts for more than two decades thereafter, as U.S.-Chinese relations were held in the grip of the Cold War.

Within China the CCP rapidly consolidated its control of the country and began the task of rebuilding the nation after decades of internal and external warfare. Priority was given to land reform. Land was confiscated from landlords and returned to peasant ownership; landlords and other "class enemies" were tried and condemned by People's Courts set up under party auspices. Under the first five-year plan, announced in 1953, peasants were urged to set up rural cooperatives, while industrial recovery began with Soviet assistance. Artists, writers, and intellectuals were ordered to devote themselves to the service of the party and the nation. In 1956 Mao announced a policy of "let a hundred flowers bloom, let a hundred schools of thought contend," inviting criticism of the party and government. He was shocked by the vigor of the criticism thus produced; many critics were sent to labor camps in the ensuing Anti-Rightist Campaign of 1957.

Angered by the arrogance of Soviet advisers and by Soviet refusal to share nuclear weapons technology with China, Mao broke with the Soviet Union and expelled all Soviet personnel in 1958. At the same time, he announced the policy of the Great Leap Forward, under which China was to make rapid progress on all fronts without outside aid. Huge rural communes took the place of peasant smallholdings and cooperatives, and agriculture was placed under the direction of centralized planning. In industry, labor and enthusiasm were expected to make up for a shortage of capital and technical expertise. The Great Leap was a catastrophic failure, causing widespread famine and social dislocation, as Mao admitted in a forced self-criticism in 1960. Mao temporarily withdrew into the background as a group of party pragmatists led by Liu Shaoqi assumed power in the early 1960's.

In foreign affairs Chinese shelling of the Nationalist-held offshore islands of Quemoy and Matsu in 1958 led to a crisis in the Taiwan Straits, patrolled by the U.S. Seventh Fleet to prevent a recurrence of China's civil war. A rebellion in Tibet in 1959 was suppressed with much bloodshed, and the dalai lama fled to India. Chinese troop movements into Tibet contributed to the outbreak in 1960 of a border war with India. Throughout the 1960's China worried about being drawn into the Vietnam War.

In late 1965 Mao made a bid to return to full power. His vehicle was the Great Proletarian Cultural Revolution, formally launched in 1966. Shock troops of teenage Red Guards were used to attack the entrenched party bureaucracy; Liu Shaoqi was placed under house arrest, and other prominent officials, including Deng Xiaoping, were exiled to rural areas. By 1968 internal disorder was so great that the military intervened to restore control in many areas. Most established organs of power were replaced under the Cultural Revolution by Revolutionary Committees; intellectuals, technical workers, and bureaucrats were severely persecuted. In 1971 Mao's second-in-command, Marshal Lin Biao, staged an abortive coup and died while attempting to flee the country. With Mao increasingly old and ill, most of his power was exercised by his wife, Jiang Qing, and her associates. Her rival, Premier Zhou Enlai, attempted to maintain orderly government functions in the face of this turmoil.

The 1968 Soviet invasion of Czechoslovakia convinced Mao that the U.S.S.R. was a greater threat to China than America, and he quietly encouraged the growth of better relations with the U.S. With tacit American approval, the PRC replaced the Republic of China (Taiwan) in the U.N. on Oct. 25, 1971. During Feb. 21-28, 1972, U.S. president Richard Nixon visited China. The Shanghai Communiqué, issued at the end of that visit, clarified the positions of both sides and paved the way for the resumption of U.S.-China relations short of formal diplomatic recognition.

Zhou Enlai died in January 1976, and Deng Xiaoping became acting premier. In April 1976 a rally in Beijing commemorating Zhou's birthday was dispersed by police on orders from Jiang Qing, and a riot ensued. Deng was dismissed from office. But when Mao died on Sept. 9, 1976, Deng reemerged as China's paramount leader, behind the new acting premier and acting party chairman, figurehead Hua Guofeng. Jiang Qing and three associates were arrested along with many of their allies. Labeled the Gang of Four, Jiang Qing's clique was blamed for all the ills of the Cultural Revolution; they were tried and convicted for crimes against the state in 1981.

China's post-Mao transformation took a decisive turn in 1978, with the announcement of the policy of the Four Modernizations (agriculture, industry, science and technology, and defense). Foreign investment and technology transfer were encouraged, and thousands of students were sent to study abroad. In the winter of 1978-79, the authorities tolerated the public posting of written critiques of the government ("Democracy Wall"). Deng consolidated power in his own hands, still acting behind the scenes; Hua Guofeng was dismissed from office, while Deng's allies Hu Yaobang and Zhao Ziyang were promoted to leadership of the party and government in 1982.

On Jan. 1, 1979, China and the United States entered into formal diplomatic relations; the United States rescinded its recognition of the Republic of China as China's legal government but maintained separate nongovernmental relations with the ROC under the Taiwan Relations Act. China's relations with Vietnam deteriorated in 1978 following Vietnam's invasion of Cambodia. In February 1979, China attempted, with little success, to "teach Vietnam a lesson" in a brief but violent border war. A conflict with Great Britain was resolved in 1984 as both sides agreed that Hong Kong would be returned to Chinese sovereignty, but with considerable local autonomy, in 1997. Relations with the Soviet Union remained strained, China insisting that no improvement could come before the U.S.S.R. reduced its troop concentrations on the Sino-Soviet border, withdrew from Afghanistan, and pressured Vietnam into withdrawing from Cambodia. China's overall foreign-policy stance in the post-Mao era has been low-key and nonconfrontational.

In the 1980's, China achieved spectacular improvements in agricultural production through dismantling rural communes and returning land to individual peasant holdings under long-term leases. Small-scale private enterprise has been encouraged in both rural and urban areas. Reform in industry and in the centrally controlled price structure has been harder to achieve and has led to such side effects as inflation and increased corruption. Within the overall context of reform, factions of relatively more conservative and reformist leaders have coexisted uneasily. A conservative drive against "spiritual pollution" in 1986 was quickly blunted by Deng, but in January 1987, the reformist party-secretary Hu Yaobang was ousted after student demonstrations calling for more democracy. The CCP 12th Party Congress in October 1987 forced the retirement of some older conservatives, named the reformist Zhao Ziyang as party secretary, and elevated the conservative pragmatist Li Peng as premier.

In April 1989 student demonstrators in Beijing mourning the death of Hu Yaobang launched a general movement for greater democracy. Demonstrators began a hunger strike and disrupted a summit visit by Soviet president Gorbachev. Martial law was proclaimed in May as demonstrations spread to other cities. Troops opened fire in Tienanmen Square on June 3-4, killing hundreds of demonstrators. In the aftermath, Zhao Ziyang was replaced as party secretary by Jiang Zemin, thousands of protesters and suspected dissidents were arrested (and an unknown number executed), and hard-liners in the government took firm control of the country.

World opinion was outraged by the Tienanmen incident; the United States and many other countries instituted sanctions against China, tourism plummeted, and the economy went into general decline. International trade resumed during 1989-90, and the U.S. renewed China's most-favored-nation status in June 1990 after several hundred dissidents were released from prison.

China strove to put Tienanmen Square behind it by holding speedy trials of those charged in connection with demonstrations. The government also made overtures to the former U.S.S.R., and from its permanent seat on the U.N. Security Council supported coalition efforts against Iraq in the Persian Gulf conflict.

Economic sanctions were lifted by Western governments in 1991. China continued to pursue its economic reform policies while repressing all signs of political dissent. While national politics, dominated by an aging leadership, seemed torpid and adrift, the private-sector economy continued to grow vigorously.

In 1992-93 runaway growth made China's economy the world's fourth-largest by some standards of measurement. This resulted in higher wages and increased consumer spending, but also widening income disparities, increased corruption, smuggling, theft, etc. Official government figures put 1994 growth at 12 percent, inflation at 24 percent.

Deng's long-expected death, in 1997, produced little immediate effect on the Chinese leadership, except for a new crackdown as leaders competed to seem tough on dissent. But the transition of power to Jiang Zemin, 71, went smoothly.

Domestic affairs in general were overshadowed by national jubilation over the return of Hong Kong to Chinese sovreignty on July 1. Macao would follow, in December 1999, after 442 years as a Portuguese colony. In June 1997, America's Congress voted to renew China's most-favored-nation trade status despite misgivings about its dismal human-rights record. Pres. Clinton made a long state visit in 1998 and appeared on Chinese TV criticizing China for human rights abuses and urged Mr. Jiang to open Chinese society. Undismayed, the Chinese government proceeded to crush the fledgling China Democracy Party, sentencing three of its leaders to long prison terms for subversion. In Feb. 1999, new missiles menaced Taiwan; tensions grew worse in July when Taiwan's president said publicly that his country was a separate Chinese state. When the U.S. accused China of nuclear spying in the U.S., China's response was: "typical racial prejudice".

In the face of not only these issues but also the newer "human rights" issue of China's ban on and persecution of the Falun Gong religious movement, the U.S. reached a trade agreement with China at the end of 1999 (as had Japan in July) and the Senate approved it in Sept. 2000. (See "Major News Stories" for developments in 2001.)

▶ **COLOMBIA**
Republic of Colombia
● **GEOGRAPHY** **Location:** northwestern coast of South America. **Boundaries:** Caribbean Sea to N, Venezuela, Brazil to E, Peru, Ecuador to S, Panama, Pacific Ocean to W. **Total land area:** 439,734 sq. mi. (1,138,910 sq km). **Coastline:** 1,992 mi. (3,208 km). **Comparative area:** between Texas and Alaska. **Land use:** 4% arable land; 1% permanent crops; 39% meadows and pastures; 48% forest and woodland; 8% other; includes negl. % irrigated. **Major cities:** (1995 est.) Bogotá (capital) 5,237,635; Cali 1,718,871; Medellín 1,621,356; Cartagena 745,689.
● **PEOPLE** **Population:** 40,349,388 (July 2001 est.). **Nationality:** noun—Colombian(s); adjective—Colombian. **Ethnic groups:** 58% mestizo, 20% white, 14% mulatto, 4% black, 4% other. **Languages:** Spanish. **Religions:** 90% Roman Catholic.
● **GOVERNMENT** **Type:** republic; executive branch

dominates government structure. **Independence:** July 20, 1810 (from Spain). **Constitution:** July 5, 1991. **National holiday:** Independence Day, July 20. **Head of Government:** Andrés Pastrana Arango, president (since Aug. 1998). **Structure:** executive; bicameral legislature; judiciary.
● **ECONOMY** **Monetary unit:** Colombian peso. **Budget:** (2000 est.) *income:* $22 bil.; *expend.:* $24 bil. **GDP:** $250 bil., $6,200 per capita (2000 est.). **Chief crops:** coffee, flowers, bananas, rice; illegal producer of coca and cannabis for international drug trade. **Natural resources:** crude oil, natural gas, coal, iron ore, nickel. **Major industries:** textiles, food processing, oil. **Labor force:** 18.3 mil. (1999 est.); 46% services, 30% agriculture, 24% industry (1990); 20% unemployment (2000 est.). **Exports:** $14.5 bil. (f.o.b., 2000 est.); petroleum, coffee, coal, bananas, flowers. **Imports:** $12.4 bil. (f.o.b., 2000 est.); industrial equipment, transportation equipment, consumer goods, chemicals. **Major trading partners:** *exports:* 50% U.S., 14% EU; *imports:* 35% U.S., 16% EU.

The territory that is now Colombia was home to various sedentary and semisedentary cultures prior to the arrival of Europeans. The Chibcha population of the Andean region might have numbered about one million prior to European contact. Portions of the area that make up modern Colombia fell under the authority of the Inca Empire.

In 1538 the colony of New Granada was established with its capital at Bogotá, and for most of the period up until 1740, the area was within the jurisdiction of the Viceroyalty of Peru. In that year a new viceroyalty was established that included modern-day Colombia, Ecuador, Panama, and Venezuela. During the wars of independence against Spain, forces under Simón Bolívar were victorious over the royalists at the Battle of Boyacá in 1819, and the region gained its independence in 1821.

Colombian territory was a part of the federation of Gran Colombia until the collapse of the federal arrangement in 1830. Thereafter, the country—called New Granada—remained a separate political entity (which included the area of Panama). By the 1850's a federal system had been adopted for the country. But this arrangement rapidly disintegrated, and the practically semisovereign states were involved in a constant struggle with the central government for autonomy. The effort to define the political structure was largely resolved with the constitution of 1886, which ended federalist regional autonomy and made Colombia a unitary republic.

Colombian political struggle since the 1850's had been characterized by a rivalry between two groups that coalesced into the Liberal and Conservative parties. During much of the 19th century, the Liberal-Conservative ideological battle was influenced to a great extent by the definition of the role of the Roman Catholic church in political and social life. The 1887-88 Concordat gave the church "official protection," while the state was given authority over public education. The settlement left a central position for the church in Colombian society that was not substantially altered by the Concordat of 1942.

The Liberal-Conservative struggle led to at least six civil wars, which often ended in interparty compromise. A struggle in 1854 involved the issue of the future direction of the country's economic development and was followed by a settlement among elites. The Liberal-Conservative war of 1860-63 led to a Liberal victory and a period of

Liberal political hegemony that lasted until 1886. The period of Conservative rule from 1886 until 1930 was punctuated by the "War of a Thousand Days" (1899-1902), in which the Conservatives defeated the Liberals. In 1903 the Colombian government rejected a U.S. offer for construction of a canal in Panama. Panama (backed by the U.S.) revolted against the Colombian government, ending in the separation of Panama from Colombia.

The world depression of 1929 seriously disrupted both the economy and the politics of Colombia. The loss of popularity of the ruling Conservatives due to both the overall economic collapse and their increasingly brutal repression of the labor movement led to a Liberal victory in 1930. A new civil war between peasants loyal to the two parties also broke out that year. By 1934 Liberal president Alfonso López Pumarejo had inaugurated his "Revolution on the March" program of socioeconomic reform.

During the 1946 presidential election, Conservatives won the presidency with a minority of the overall vote, defeating a split Liberal party. Armed conflict originally instigated by the two party elites erupted. This marked the beginning of La Violencia (1948-57) during which more than 200,000 people died. In the summer of 1957, leaders of the Liberal and Conservative parties reached an agreement on constitutional reform in an attempt to end the violence. The agreement, known as the National Front, was to be in force for 16 years and included provisions for regular alternation of the presidency between the parties, as well as an accord on equal staffing of all political positions by both parties. The Liberal and Conservative parties agreed they alone would monopolize the arena of legitimate political competition for the 16-year period. The agreement held up until 1968 constitutional revisions allowed for other political groups to be officially recognized.

The emergence of terrorist and paramilitary groups on both the right and left—some with ties to the drug trade—in the 1960's and 1970's weakened the two-party power-sharing monopoly. In March 1990, one of the most notorious left-wing groups, M-19, elected to lay down its arms and enter the political mainstream and immediately captured 19 of 70 seats in a constitutional convention called to rewrite the constitution. Other groups followed suit in 1991.

Colombia has also had to cope with a burgeoning narcotics trade. Throughout the 1980's, narco-terrorists murdered government officials, journalists, and innocent bystanders with impunity. Despite the assassination of four presidential candidates prior to the May 1990 election, the Liberal party's César Gaviria Trujillo won the election campaigning vigorously against the drug traffickers. In 1994 another Liberal party president (Ernesto Samper Pizano) took office pledging to continue the fight against drug traffickers. Samper also promised to invest billions of dollars to improve the infrastructure with money from the newly discovered Cusiana oil field scheduled to be operational in 1996.

In the summer of 1995, the Samper government arrested three of the top seven members of the Cali drug cartel; by Sept. 1996, all seven had been apprehended. Meanwhile, Samper faced accusations that he knew of $6 million contributed by the Cali cartel. Formal charges instituted by Prosecutor General Valdivieso in Feb. 1996 were found groundless in May by the legislature's Accusations Committee. Still, the United States, which had decertified Colombia as a drug-war partner in March, revoked Samper's visa in May even as Colombian farmers protested government anti-coca and -poppy programs. In 1997 radical leftist terrorist groups began a wave of murders, kidnappings, and other violence against local government officials, and in 1998 attacked and defeated an army battalion. The election of Conservative Andres Pastrana in June 1998 held out promise of victory in the drug war despite violent outbursts during the remainder of 1998 and early 1999. Government meetings with FARC, the principal rebel group, and National Peace Council meetings with ELN, the second major insurgent group, continued into mid-1999. On Dec. 20, FARC announced a cease-fire (the first since 1984) until January 10. When, on Jan. 11, 2000, FARC forces attacked four towns, the Clinton administration approved a two-year aid package to Colombia of $1.4 billion.

▶COMOROS
Federal Islamic Republic of the Comoros

● **GEOGRAPHY Location:** part of archipelago in Mozambique Channel; three main islands, Njazidja, Nzwami, and Mwali (formerly Grande-Comore, Anjouan, and Mohéli). Moroni, Njazidja Is., 11°40'S, 43°16'E. **Boundaries:** between Madagascar and southeast Africa. **Total land area:** 838 sq. mi. (2,170 sq km). **Coastline:** 211 mi. (340 km). **Comparative area:** slightly more than 12 times size of Washington, D.C. **Land use:** 35% arable land; 10% permanent crops; 7% meadows and pastures; 18% forest and woodland; 30% other. **Major cities:** (1980 census) Moroni (capital) 17,267; Mutsamudu 13,000; Fomboni 5,400.
● **PEOPLE Population:** 596,202 (July 2001 est.). **Nationality:** noun—Comoran(s); adjective—Comoran. **Ethnic groups:** Antalote, Cafre, Makoa, Oimatsaha, Sakalava. **Languages:** Arabic and French (both official), Comoran (a blend of Swahili and Arabic). **Religions:** 98% Sunni Muslim, 2% Roman Catholic.
● **GOVERNMENT Type:** independent republic. **Independence:** July 6, 1975 (from France). **Constitution:** June 1992. **National holiday:** Independence Day, July 6. **Heads of Government:** Colonel Azali Assoumani, head of state (since Apr. 1999). **Structure:** executive; bicameral legislature; judiciary.
● **ECONOMY Monetary unit:** Comoran franc. **Budget:** (1997) *income:* $48 mil.; *expend.:* $53 mil. **GDP:** $419 mil., $720 per capita (2000 est.). **Chief crops:** vanilla, cloves, perfume essences. **Natural resources:** negligible. **Major industries:** tourism, perfume distillation. **Labor force:** 144,500 (1996); 80% agriculture; 20% unemployment (1996). **Exports:** $7.9 mil. (f.o.b., 1999 est.); vanilla, ylang-ylang, cloves, perfume oils. **Imports:** $55.1 mil. (f.o.b., 1999 est.); rice and other foodstuffs, consumer goods, petroleum products, cement. **Major trading partners:** *exports:* 50% France, 25% Germany; *imports:* 38% France, 13% Pakistan, 8% South Africa.

The Federal Islamic Republic of Comoros is part of an archipelago composed of four prominent islands (the fourth, Mayotte, is a French dependency) and several smaller islands. Numerous groups from Africa, Europe, and Asia invaded the islands over the centuries. Shirazi Arabs introduced Islam to Comoros around the turn of the 16th century, and the French established colonial rule over the archipelago between 1841 and 1912 and developed a plantation-based economy. The islands remained a French territory until 1961 when political autonomy was granted. Comoros gained independence in 1975. Overthrown by foreign mercenaries in 1975, Pres. Ahmed Abdallah Abderemane returned to power in 1978 and helped establish the country's first constitution. In Nov. 1989 he was assassinated by a small group of rebels who quickly dispersed under pressure from the French government. A new constitution was approved in 1992, and the country's first democratic elections were held in Nov. 1992. An attempt, begun in 1997, by the islands of Anjouan and Moheli to gain independence or at least autonomy led to an army coup in April 1999 and Anjouan's claim of independence in Jan. 2000, a claim he renounced in September.

Much of the nation's soil is laden with lava, making it unsuitable for farming, especially on the island of Njazidja (Grand Comore), which is dominated by Mount Kartala, an active volcano. This obstacle to agriculture hinders the growth of Comoros, one of the poorest and least developed nations in the world. Poor transportation links between the islands and a harsh cyclone season add further to the country's problems. But Comoros has invested heavily in its tourism industry.

▶ CONGO
Democratic Republic of the Congo (formerly Zaire)

• **GEOGRAPHY Location:** equatorial country in central Africa. **Boundaries:** Central African Republic, Sudan to N, Uganda, Rwanda, Burundi, Tanzania to E, Zambia to S, Angola to SW, Atlantic Ocean, Cabinda district of Angola, Congo to W. **Total land area:** 905,564 sq. mi. (2,345,410 sq km). **Coastline:** 23 mi. (37 km). **Comparative area:** about 1.5 times size of Alaska. **Land use:** 3% arable land; negl. % permanent crops; 7% meadows and pastures; 77% forest and woodland; 13% other; includes negl. % irrigated. **Major cities:** (1984 census) Kinshasa (capital) 2,653,558; Lubumbashi (Elizabethville) 543,268; Mbuji-Mayi (Bakwanga) 423,363; Kananga (Luluabourg) 290,898; Kisangani (Stanleyville) 282,650.
• **PEOPLE Population:** 53,624,718 (July 2001 est.). **Nationality:** noun—Zairian(s); adjective—Zairian. **Ethnic groups:** 45% of the people belong to one of four largest groups—Mongo, Luba, Kongo (all Bantu), and Mangbetu-Azande; over 200 other ethnic groups. **Languages:** French (official), Lingala, Kingwana, Kikongo, Tshiluba. **Religions:** 50% Roman Catholic, 20% Protestant, 10% Kimbanguist, 10% Muslim, 10% other syncretic sects and traditional beliefs.
• **GOVERNMENT Type:** dictatorship; presumably undergoing a transition to representative government. **Independence:** June 30, 1960 (from Belgium). **Constitution:** Transitional constitution promulgated Apr. 1994; draft constitution approved by former president Laurent Kabila in Nov. 1998, but not yet ratified by national referendum. **National holiday:** Independence Day, Nov. 24. **Heads of Government:** Joseph Kabila, president (since Jan. 2001). **Structure:** executive—president elected originally for seven-year term; legislative—300-member Transitional Constitutional Assembly est. Aug. 2000; judiciary.
• **ECONOMY Monetary unit:** zaire. **Budget:** (1996 est.) *income*: $269 mil. *expend.*: $244 mil. **GDP:** $31 bil., $600 per capita (2000 est.). **Chief crops:** coffee, sugar, palm oil, rubber, tea. **Natural resources:** cobalt, copper, cadmium, crude oil, industrial and gem diamonds. **Major industries:** mining, mineral processing, consumer products (incl. textiles, footwear, cigarettes). **Labor force:** 14.5 mil (1993 est.); 65% agriculture, 16% industry,

19% services. **Exports:** $960 mil. (f.o.b., 2000 est.); diamonds, copper, coffee, cobalt, crude oil. **Imports:** $660 mil. (c.i.f., 2000 est.); foodstuffs, mining and other machinery, transport equipment, fuels. **Major trading partners:** *exports:* 62% Benelux, 18% U.S., South Africa; *imports:* 28% South Africa, 14% Benelux, 9% Nigeria.

Pygmies were probably the earliest inhabitants of the Congo region, followed much later by Bantu and Nilotic peoples. By the eighth century A.D., a number of well-established kingdoms and empires occupied the lower reaches of the Congo (now Zaire) River and the coastal plain; these included Kongo (Bakongo), Kuba, Luba, and Lunda.

Portuguese explorers and merchants arrived along the coast in the 1480's and initially traded with these kingdoms on a basis of relative equality; an indigenous Catholic church became established. Soon, however, the Portuguese established a slave trade that brought turmoil and decline to the native states. Europeans did not penetrate the interior of Zaire until the 19th century, but the slave trade (partly in Arab hands, in inland regions) had repercussions everywhere.

Henry Stanley descended the Congo River from east to west in 1876, opening the area for further exploration. In 1878 Stanley was engaged by King Leopold II of Belgium to establish Belgian trading stations along the river. King Leopold established the Congo Free State in 1885, not as a Belgian colony but as a personal possession of which he was king as well as chief stockholder.

The management corporation that ran the Free State abolished slavery but instituted a harsh and exploitative regime that reduced native peoples to a condition of involuntary servitude. Forced labor and harsh suppression of rebellion resulted in the deaths of unnumbered thousands of people. Protests against these conditions, led by Great Britain and the United States, led to the transformation of the Free State into the colony of the Belgian Congo in 1908 with promises of reforms.

By the 1920's the Belgian Congo had become a major world producer of copper, diamonds, gold, rubber, palm oil, and other commodities. Railroads were developed to bring these goods to market, notably the line from Elizabethville (now Lubumbashi) in the Katanga region through Angola to the Atlantic coast. River navigation on the Congo was also developed. All mining, plantation agriculture, industry, and administration was in Belgian hands with no native participation in government except at the most local level.

In the 1950's agitation for increased native participation in government led, in 1957, to elections for local councils. In 1959 rioting against Belgian rule broke out. Elections were held on May 31 in anticipation of independence. Joseph Kasavubu became president, and Patrice Lumumba, head of the Congolese National Movement, became prime minister. On June 30, 1960, Belgium granted independence to the Congo; many Europeans fled the country. On July 4 the army mutinied, and on July 11 the southern province of Katanga (now Shaba), under the leadership of Moise Tshombe, seceded from the Congo and declared its independence. Belgium sent troops to quell the disorder.

On Aug. 9 the United Nations called on Belgium to withdraw its troops. Kasavubu removed Lumumba as prime minister. Lumumba, with the backing of Ghana, fought for control. He fled to Stanleyville (now Kisangani) but was kidnapped in January 1961 and taken to Katanga, where he was murdered, apparently with American and Belgian complicity. Fighting continued in Katanga, where Tshombe's regime was supported by European mercenaries and opposed by U.N. peacekeeping forces. The Katangan rebellion ended in late 1963; rebels fled to Angola, and U.N. forces were withdrawn in June 1964. In a surprising political settlement, Tshombe became president of the Congo on June 30. On Sept. 7 leftist rebels attempted to establish a "people's republic" based in Stanleyville. Tshombe again resorted to the use of mercenaries to put down the rebellion. Many white settlers, as well as Congolese, were killed in fighting and terrorist atrocities. The rebellion ended in July 1965. In Nov. 1965 Tshombe was deposed in a military coup led by Joseph Mobutu, whose government took immediate steps to reduce European influence.

In 1971 Mobutu changed the country's name to Zaire and also changed the name of Leopoldville to Kinshasa. In 1972 he ordered all Zairians with European names to change them to African names; he became Mobutu Sese Seko. Attempts in 1974 to force foreign investors to sell their holdings to Zairians brought economic disruption, and foreign investors were invited back in 1977.

In 1977 another rebellion broke out in Katanga (now Shaba) Province; the government put down the rebellion with the aid of France, Egypt, and Morocco. The rebels fled to Angola, but the province's rich mining economy was again disrupted; many European technical workers fled, and production plummeted.

Although Congo is rich with minerals, forest products, hydroelectric potential, and agriculture, most of these natural resources remain undeveloped and the country was impoverished by the nearly unprecedented corruption of the Mobutu regime. The president is estimated to have amassed a fortune of $3 billion. Rival leaders attempted to organize opposition to the Mobutu government in late 1987 and 1988, but most were arrested or driven into exile.

In June 1991, Mobutu agreed to draft a new constitution and end a 20-year ban on multiparty elections. Étiene Tshisekedi was elected prime minister by a national conference in 1992, but Mobutu fired him in 1993. France and Belgium dispatched troops to protect their nationals and together with the United States demanded that Mobutu transfer power to Tshisekedi. Mobutu did not comply, and as his nation's economy sank, he continued to live in luxury, protected by the army and police. In May, 1997, Mobutu was driven from office by the army of Laurent Kabila, who immediately changed the name of the country to Congo and began the huge task of rebuilding the nation. But in the summer of 1998 a new military rebellion began—a rebellion joined by Uganda and Rwanda. By June 1999, a cease-fire seemed near, one that would involve the U.N. and the Organization of African Unity as peacemakers with a mandate to disarm the rebels. The cease-fire, when it came in July 1999, was not signed by the rebels but by the six outside states. And an August split in the rebel group brought Rwanda and Uganda to war with each other, each supporting its "own" rebel faction. In 2000 Rwanda proved victorious over Uganda; and by June, the U.N. security council decided that peacekeepers would not be sent.

In Jan.2001, Pres. Kabila was shot to death by a bodyguard; the (appointed) parliament chose his son, Joseph, as new president. Unexpectedly, the cabinet that he appointed in April excluded numerous cronies of his father. February saw another U.N.-brokered withdrawal accord, which seemed in tatters by May.

▶ CONGO, REPUBLIC OF THE

● **GEOGRAPHY Location:** equatorial country on western coast of Africa. **Boundaries:** Cameroon to NW, Central African Republic to NE, Zaire to E and S, Angolan district of Cabinda to S, Gulf of Guinea to SW, Gabon to W. **Total land area:** 132,046 sq. mi. (342,000 sq km). **Coastline:** 105 mi. (169 km). **Comparative area:** between New Mexico and Montana. **Land use:** negl % arable land; 29% meadows and pastures; 62% forest and woodland; 9% other. **Major cities:** (1984 census) Brazzaville (capital) 596,200; Pointe-Noire 298,014; Pool 219,329; (1974) Bouenza 135,999; Cuvette 127,558.

● **PEOPLE Population:** 2,894,336 (July 2001 est.). **Nationality:** noun—Congolese (sing., pl.); adjective—Congolese or Congo. **Ethnic groups:** 48% Kongo, 20% Sangha, 17% Teke, 12% M'Bochi; about 8,500 Europeans (may be half that number following 1997 civil war). **Languages:** French (official); many African languages with Lingala and Kikongo most widely used. **Religions:** 50% Christian, 48% indigenous beliefs, 2% Muslim.

● **GOVERNMENT Type:** republic. **Independence:** Aug. 15, 1960 (from France). **Constitution:** Draft approved by transitional parliament Sept. 2000. **National holiday:** National Day, Aug. 15. **Heads of Government:** Denis Sassou Nguesso, president (since 1997). **Structure:** executive; bicameral legislature; judiciary.

● **ECONOMY Monetary unit:** Communauté Financière Africaine (CFA) franc. **Budget:** (1997 est.) *income:* $870 mil.; *expend.:* $970 mil. **GDP:** $3.1 bil., $1,100 per capita (2000 est.). **Chief crops:** cassava, sugar, rice. **Natural resources:** petroleum, timber, potash, lead, zinc. **Major industries:** crude oil, cement, sawmills. **Labor force:** 79,100 (1985); 75% agriculture, 25% commerce, industry, government. **Exports:** $2.6 bil. (f.o.b., 2000); petroleum, lumber, plywood. **Imports:** $870 mil. (f.o.b., 2000); petroleum products, capital equipment, construction materials. **Major trading partners:** *exports:* 23% U.S., 14% Belgium-Luxembourg, Taiwan, China; *imports:* 23% France, 9% U.S., 8% Belgium, 7% U.K.

About 1,500 years ago, the lower reaches of the Congo River formed the focus of a number of well-organized states. The Kongo and Ndonga flourished south of the river; north of the river, in what is now the Congo, the Loango, Teke, and Bobangi were dominant. Some of these states were weakened beginning in the 16th century by the Portuguese slave trade, although the Loango benefited from it through the 19th century.

With the weakening of Portuguese power, the French became the dominant European power in western Africa. In 1883 they established a protectorate over the Teke kingdom, which they renamed Middle Congo. The treaty with the Teke king was concluded by Pierre Savorgnan de Brazza, for whom the capital was—and is—named.

In 1910 the French confederated their protectorates of Gabon, Middle Congo, Ubangi-Shari (later the Central African Republic), and Chad to form French Equatorial Africa. The territory became an important base of Free French activity during World War II, in acknowledgment of which Gen. Charles de Gaulle granted French citizenship to the territory's inhabitants in 1946, and local power was devolved upon advisory assemblies. The Republic of the Congo attained full autonomy upon the dissolution of the confederation of French Equatorial Africa in 1959, and the nation gained full independence on Apr. 15, 1960.

In 1963 Pres. Fulbert Youlou was driven from office by violent labor unrest; the military took control and then installed a provisional civilian government led by Alphonse Massamba-Debat, who was subsequently elected president for a five-year term.

In 1968 Massamba-Debat was overthrown in a military coup and replaced by Capt. Marien Ngouabi, who in 1969 reorganized the Congo as a People's Republic. Despite its Marxist-Leninist stance, Congo remained strongly linked to France, its main source of trade, aid, and foreign investment. Ngouabi was assassinated in 1977 and replaced by a military committee of the Congolese Labor party led by Gen. Joachim Yhomby-Opango, who resigned and was arrested for treason in 1979. He was succeeded by Denis Sassou-Nguesso, who was reelected to a third five-year term in 1989.

In 1990, Congo began a relatively smooth transition to multiparty democracy. Following mounting calls for liberalization and labor strikes, opposition parties were legalized as of Jan. 1, 1991. Pascal Lissouba was elected president in Aug. 1992. In June 1997, however, heavy fighting erupted in Brazzaville when Lissouba tried to have his rival, Sassou-Nguesso, arrested just weeks before a new election on the grounds that Sassou-Nguesso was planning a coup.

▶ COSTA RICA
Republic of Costa Rica
● **GEOGRAPHY Location:** Central American isthmus. **Boundaries:** Nicaragua to N, Caribbean Sea to E, Panama to S, and Pacific Ocean to W. **Total land area:** 19,730 sq. mi. (51,100 sq km). **Coastline:** 801 mi. (1,290 km). **Comparative area:** slightly smaller than West Virginia. **Land use:** 6% arable land; 5% permanent crops; 46% meadows and pastures; 31% forest and woodland; 12% other; includes 1% irrigated. **Major cities:** (1995 est.) San José (capital) 318,765; Alajuela 171,840; Cartago 118,205; Puntarenas 100,266; Heredia 73,268.
● **PEOPLE Population:** 3,773,057 (July 2001 est.). **Nationality:** noun—Costa Rican(s); adjective—Costa Rican. **Ethnic groups:** 94% white, 3% black, 1% Indian, 1% Chinese. **Languages:** Spanish (official), Jamaican dialect of English spoken around Puerto Limón. **Religions:** 76.3% Roman Catholic, 13.7% Evangelical Protestant, other Protestant, Jehovah's Witness.
● **GOVERNMENT Type:** democratic republic. **Independence:** Sept. 15, 1821 (from Spain). **Constitution:** Nov. 7, 1949. **National holiday:** Independence Day, Sept. 15. **Head of Government:** Miguel Ángel Rodríguez Echeverría, president (since May 1998). **Structure:** executive; unicameral legislature; judiciary.
● **ECONOMY Monetary unit:** Costa Rican colón. **Budget:** (2000 est.) *income:* $1.95 bil.; *expend.:* $2.4 bil. **GDP:** $25 bil., $6,700 per capita (2000 est.). **Chief crops:** coffee, bananas, sugarcane, corn, rice, cocoa. **Natural resources:** hydropower potential. **Major industries:** microprocessors, food processing, textiles, clothing, construction materials. **Labor force:** 1.9 mil. (1999 est.); 22% industry and commerce, 20% agriculture; 5.2% unemployment (1998 est.). **Exports:** $6.1 bil. (f.o.b.

2000 est.); manufactured products, coffee, bananas, textiles, sugar. **Imports:** $5.9 bil. (f.o.b. 2000 est.); raw materials, consumer goods, capital equipment. **Major trading partners:** *exports:* U.S., E.U., Central America; *imports:* U.S., E.U., Japan, Mexico, Venezuela.

Costa Rica was under the jurisdiction of the Spanish colonial kingdom of Guatemala until it broke with Spain in 1821, along with other parts of Central America. With the collapse of the United Provinces of Central America in 1838, Costa Rica became an independent republic, and the country held its first democratic elections in 1889.

An attempt at electoral fraud in 1948 led to a brief civil war, which was won by the National Liberation forces under "Don Pepé" Jose Figueres Ferrer. The Costa Rican army was subsequently abolished.

In the 1980's, under Pres. Oscar Arias Sánchez, Costa Rica vigorously promoted the settlement of civil strife in Nicaragua and El Salvador and he was awarded the 1987 Nobel Peace Prize for his Central American peace plan.

Subsequent governments focused on economic matters. In February 1994 Jose Maria Figueres Olsen, son of the legendary "Don Pepé," was elected president of Costa Rica, besting free-market and austerity-minded Miguel Angel Rodriguez. But out-of-control public spending brought gigantic new debt and consumer-goods price inflation. In Feb. 1998 not only did Rodriguez capture the presidency, but his Social Christian Unity party carried an absolute majority in the Legislative Assembly.

▶ COTE D'IVOIRE
(see Ivory Coast)

▶ CROATIA
Republic of Croatia
● **GEOGRAPHY Location:** southeastern Europe. **Boundaries:** Slovenia and Hungary to N, Yugoslavia and Bosnia and Herzegovina to E, Adriatic Sea to S, Slovenia to W. **Total land area:** 21,824 sq. mi. (56,538 sq km). **Coastline:** 1,105 mi. (1,778 km). **Comparative area:** Slightly smaller than West Virginia. **Land use:** 21% arable land, 2% permanent crops, 20% meadows and pastures, 38% forest and woodland, 19% other. **Major cities:** (1991 census) Zagreb (capital) 708,770; Split 189,388; Rijeka 167,064; Osijek 104,761; Zadar 76,343.
● **PEOPLE Population:** 4,334,142 (July 2001 est.). **Nationality:** noun—Croat(s); adjective—Croatian. **Ethnic groups:** 78% Croat, 12% Serb, 0.9% Muslim. **Languages:** 96% Serbo-Croatian. **Religions:** 76.5% Catholic, 11.1% Orthodox, 1.2% Slavic Muslim.
● **GOVERNMENT Type:** presidential/parliamentary democracy. **Independence:** June 25, 1991. **Constitution:** Dec. 22, 1990. **National holiday:** Statehood Day, May 30. **Heads of Government:** Stjepan Mesić, president (since Feb. 2000); Ivica Račan, prime minister (since Jan. 2000). **Structure:** executive; bicameral legislature; judiciary.
● **ECONOMY Monetary unit:** Croatian kuna. **Budget:** (1999 est.) *income:* $6 bil. *expend.:* $4.7 bil. **GDP:** $24.9 bil.; $5,800 per capita (2000 est.). **Chief crops:** wheat, corn, sugar beets, sunflowers, alfalfa. **Natural resources:** oil, coal, bauxite, low-grade iron ore, calcium. **Major industries:** chemicals and plastics, machine tools, fabricated metal, electronics, pig iron and rolled steel products. **Labor force:** 1.68 mil. (2000 est.); industry and mining, government, agriculture. **Exports:** $4.3 bil.

(f.o.b., 1999); textiles, foodstuffs, fuels, chemicals. **Imports:** $7.9 bil. (c.i.f., 1999); machinery and transport equipment, chemicals, food and live animals, fuels and lubricants. **Major trading partners:** Germany, Italy, Slovenia.

Croatia is one of Europe's most ancient states, King Tomaslav having created an independent Catholic realm in 924. In the sixth century the Croats, led by their eponymous chieftain Chrovatos, had migrated to the old Roman province of Illyricum, south of the Danube, where they dwelt in practical independence of the Byzantine Empire. Pope Gregory VII sent a papal crown, and therewith international recognition, to King Zvonimir (1076-89), but the king's death spelt the demise of the native dynasty. In 1102 Hungary's king Kalman was recognized as king of Croatia as well, in a dynastic union in which Croatia retained its own nobility and institutions. From the 14th century, Croatia (along with Hungary and Serbia) formed Europe's bulwark against the Ottoman Empire. After the Turkish victory at Mohacs (1526), the Hungarian and Croatian crowns were added to the Habsburg dynasty. Escaping Turkish sway, Croatia became controlled by Austrian military authorities as the frontier district against the Ottomans.

With the proclamation of the Austrian Empire in 1804, amalgamating the Habsburg possessions into one unified state, the estates of Croatia resisted the royal absolutism, stressing their autonomous status and ties to the Hungarian kingdom, but to slight avail, even after the Croat army of Baron Josip Jellacid proved essential in suppressing the Hungarian revolt of 1848. However, after the 1867 Ausleich ("compromise"), which established a practically independent Hungary within the Dual Monarchy, a further compromise (Nagoda) in the following year recognized Croatian autonomy within the Hungarian realm.

When the Habsburg monarchy collapsed during World War I, Croatia joined the new Yugoslavia, but since that state proved to be no federation but rather a greater Serbia, Croatia resisted Serbian dominance. And after the ferocious ethnic hostility provoked a royal dictatorship in 1929, Ante Pavelic formed the Ustase, a terrorist organization similar to and having ties with the Macedonian IMRO, with the aim of attaining Croatian independence. Just a week before the outbreak of World War II, Croatia was again granted autonomy, but with Hitler's 1941 conquest and dismemberment of Yugoslavia, an "Independent Croat State" was established under Italian protection. While Aimone, Duke of Spoleto was proclaimed king of Croatia under the preposterous name of Tomaslov II, he had the good sense never to enter "his" kingdom, whose governance was left to Pavelic and the Ustase. An "ethnic cleansing" of Croatia commenced, in which perhaps 100,000 Serbs and Jews lost their lives. Since the "chetniks" of Gen. Mihajlovic were Serbs and royalists, anti-Ustase Croats had nowhere to turn but to the Communist "partisans" of Tito (himself a Croat). Postwar vengeance against Tito's enemies, especially the Ustase, was severe but short-lived and Croatia in 1946 became one of the "republics" of the reconstituted Yugoslavia.

With Croatia's June 1991 secession from Yugoslavia, Serbian militias backed by the Yugoslavian army seized about one-third of Croatian territory, but by mid-1995 Croat forces had regained almost all of its land. President Franjo Tudjman also fostered the Muslim-Croat Federation in Bosnia to preserve a sort of Bosnian independence. The Yugoslav-Croat war came to an end in September 1996 with the establishment of diplomatic relations in which Yugoslavia recognized Croatia's boundaries, leaving ethnic Serbs in the lurch. And in Jan. 1998, a U.N. decision returned eastern Slavonia, part of historic Croatia captured by Serb militias in 1991, to Croatia.

Having won a third presidential term in January 1997, despite a stagnant economy, widespread corruption and complaints of autocracy, Tudjman succumbed to stomach cancer in Dec. 1999. Within a month, a six-party opposition coalition had captured 94 of 152 parliamentary seats, with Social Democrat Ivica Racan named premier. In a February 2000 presidential run-off, Stipe Mesic took over 56 percent of the votes.

▶ CUBA
Republic of Cuba
• **GEOGRAPHY Location:** largest island in Caribbean Sea, about 100 mi. (160 km) S of Florida. **Boundaries:** North Atlantic Ocean to N, Windward Passage to E, Caribbean Sea to S, Yucatan Channel to W. **Total land area:** 42,803 sq. mi. (110,860 sq km). **Coastline:** 2,319 mi. (3,735 km). **Comparative area:** between Tennessee and Pennsylvania. **Land use:** 24% arable land; 7% permanent crops; 27% meadows and pastures; 24% forest and woodland; 18% other; includes 10% irrigated. **Major cities:** (1993 est.) Havana (capital) 2,175,995; Santiago de Cuba 440,084; Camagüey 293,961; Holguín 242,085; Guantánamo 207,796.

• **PEOPLE Population:** 11,184,023 (July 2001 est.). **Nationality:** noun—Cuban(s); adjective—Cuban. **Ethnic groups:** 51% mulatto, 37% white, 11% black, 1% Chinese. **Languages:** Spanish. **Religions:** at least 85% Roman Catholic before Castro assumed power.

• **GOVERNMENT Type:** Communist state. **Independence:** May 20, 1902 (from Spain). **Constitution:** Feb. 24, 1976. **National holiday:** Independence Day, Oct 10. **Head of Government:** Fidel Castro Ruz, prime minister from February 1959, president (since Dec. 1976). **Structure:** executive; unicameral legislature; controlled judiciary.

• **ECONOMY Monetary unit:** Cuban peso. **Budget:** (2000 est.) *income:* $13.5 bil.; *expend.:* $14.3 bil. **GDP:** $19.2 bil., $2000 per capita (1999 est.). **Chief crops:** sugar cane, tobacco, citrus, coffee, rice. **Natural resources:** cobalt, nickel, iron ore, copper, manganese. **Major industries:** sugar, petroleum, food and tobacco processing. **Labor force:** 4.3 mil. (2000); 51% services and government, 24% industry, 25% agriculture. **Exports:** $1.8 bil. (f.o.b., 2000 est.); sugar, nickel, shellfish, tobacco. **Imports:** $3.4 bil. (f.o.b., 2000 est.); petroleum, food, machinery, chemicals. **Major trading partners:** *exports:* 23% Russia, 23% Netherlands, 13% Canada; *imports:* 18% Spain, 13% Venezuela, 8% Canada.

At the time of Christopher Columbus's arrival in 1492, Cuba was home to Arawak, Ciboney, and Guanahatabey Indian people. Cuba served as a launching point for Spanish imperial conquests in the Americas, and the early- 19th-century wars of independence that swept the rest of Spanish America did not overthrow the imposing Spanish garrison there. Slavery was abolished in 1886, but Spanish colonialism lingered in Cuba until the 1890's.

Spanish control of the island began to deteriorate in the late 1860's with the beginning of the "Ten Years War" (1868-78). Under the terms of the 1898 Treaty of Paris, which ended the Cuban-U.S.-

Spanish War, Cuba became a U.S. protectorate. The U.S.-sponsored Platt Amendment (1901) to the new Cuban constitution gave the United States the right to intervene in Cuban affairs.

Corruption and political repression plagued Cuban politics during the first half of the 20th century. Gerardo Machado won election to the presidency in 1925, but quickly turned his administration into a dictatorship that lasted until his ouster by a progressive coalition of students and labor in 1933. The "revolution" of 1933 installed Ramón Grau San Martín as the new head of the government, but the U.S. supported Grau's ouster, and army sergeant Fulgencio Batista replaced him. Batista ruled the country either directly or indirectly for the next quarter century.

In 1953 Fidel Castro Ruz led a failed attack on the Moncada army barracks in Santiago. In Dec. 1956 Fidel and Raúl Castro, Argentine physician Ernesto "Che" Guevara, and 79 others returned to Cuba and waged a guerrilla campaign against the government. Batista's military failed to defeat the guerrillas, and in the wake of increasing demonstrations of public antipathy for his government, the dictator fled the country. The Communist Fidelistas took control Jan. 1, 1959.

By mid-1959, revolutionary tribunals had tried and executed more than 500 political "enemies." The leaders announced an agrarian reform, and by 1960 the nationalization of the economy was in full swing. In 1961 U.S.-Cuban diplomatic relations were severed, and the U.S.-sponsored Bay of Pigs invasion by Cuban exiles failed. In 1962 the Cuban missile crisis brought the world to the brink of nuclear war when U.S. spy planes uncovered Soviet intentions to place nuclear weapons on the island. The Soviets agreed to the withdrawal of missiles in exchange for a U.S. pledge not to invade Cuba.

In its active foreign policy, Cuba provided assistance to a number of left-wing regimes in Africa and Latin America, most notably its military presence in Angola from 1975 to 1991. With the collapse of the Soviet Union in 1991, Cuba lost huge subsidies, forcing its economy into a downward spiral. In 1994, the worsening economy and a growing dissatisfaction with the Castro government fueled migration of Cubans to U.S. shores. With thousands of refugees arriving in Florida each day—aboard boats, homemade rafts, ferries—the U.S. and Cuba negotiated an agreement in which the United States would increase annual acceptance levels of Cuban immigrants to 20,000 in return for Cuba's promise to curb illegal migration.

Tensions flared between the U.S. and Cuba on Feb. 24, 1996, when Cuban MiGs shot down two private jets operating out of Miami. The U.S. responded by tightening economic sanctions, with penalties for foreigners investing in Cuba (the Helms-Burton Act). Castro and his party called for a renewed commitment to Marxism and shortly thereafter Castro met with Pope John Paul II who Visited Cuba in 1999 and publicly confronted Castro on issues of freedom and religious liberty.

▶ **CYPRUS**
Republic of Cyprus
● **GEOGRAPHY Location:** eastern Mediterranean Sea. Nicosia 35°11'N, 33°23'E. **Boundaries:** 62 mi. (100 km) S of Turkey, Syria to E. **Total land area:** 3,571 sq. mi. (9,250 sq. km). **Coastline:** 403 mi. (648 km). **Comparative area:** between Delaware and Connecticut. **Land use:** 12% arable land; 5% permanent crops; negl% meadows and pastures; 13% forest and woodland; 70% other; includes 10%

irrigated. **Major cities:** Nicosia (capital) 149,100 (excludes Turkish-occupied portion); Limassol 107,200; Larnaca 48,300 (1982); Famagusta (Gazi Magusa) 39,500 (mid-1974); Phaphos 20,800 (1982).
● **PEOPLE Population:** 762,887 (July 2001 est.). **Nationality:** noun—Cypriot(s); adjective—Cypriot. **Ethnic groups:** 78% Greek, 18% Turkish. **Languages:** Greek, Turkish, English. **Religions:** 78% Greek Orthodox, 18% Muslim.
● **GOVERNMENT Type:** republic. **Independence:** Aug. 16, 1960 (from U.K.). **Constitution:** Aug. 16, 1960; negotiations have been held intermittently to create basis for new or revised constitution to govern the island and relations between Greek and Turkish Cypriots. **National holiday:** Independence Day, Oct. 1. **Heads of Government:** Glafcos Clerides, president (since Feb. 1993); Turkish sector—Rauf Denktash, president (since 1975). **Structure:** currently, government of Cyprus has effective authority over only Greek Cypriot community; headed by president of republic and comprising Council of Ministers, House of Representatives, and Supreme Court; Turkish Cypriots declared their own constitution and governing bodies within Turkish Federated State of Cyprus in 1975; state renamed Turkish Republic of Northern Cyprus in 1983.
● **ECONOMY Monetary unit:** Cypriot pound; Turkish lira. **Budget:** (2000 est.) *income:* $2.9 bil., Greek area; $294 mil., Turkish area; *expend.:* $3.2 bil., Greek area; $495 mil., Turkish area. **GDP:** (2000 est.) $9.7 bil., $16,000 per capita Greek area; $830 mil., $5,300 per capita Turkish area. **Chief crops:** potatoes, citrus, vegetables, barley, grapes. **Natural resources:** copper, pyrites, asbestos, gypsum, timber. **Major industries:** food, beverages, textiles, chemicals. **Labor force:** (2000) Greek area—291,000; 73% services, 22% industry, 5% agriculture; 3.6% unemployment; Turkish area—86,300; 56.4% services, 22.8% industry, 20.8% agriculture. **Exports:** Greek area (f.o.b., 1999 est.)—$1 bil.; citrus, potatoes, grapes; Turkish area (f.o.b., 1999)—$51.1 mil.; citrus, potatoes, textiles. **Imports:** Greek area (f.o.b., 1999 est.)—$3.6 bil.; consumer goods, petroleum and lubricants, foodstuffs; Turkish area (f.o.b., 1999)—$402 mil.; food, minerals, chemicals. **Major trading partners:** *exports:* Greek area—Russia, U.K., Greece; Turkish area—Turkey, U.K., other EU; *imports:* Greek area—U.S., U.K., Italy; Turkish area—Turkey, U.K., other EU.

Recent excavations on Cyprus indicate a human presence at least 10,000 years ago. Mycenean (Greek) culture flourished in the second millenium B.C. Phoenicians colonized the island in the 10th century B.C., and it remained a major entrepôt for eastern Mediterranean trade. Annexed to Rome in 58 B.C. it was later part of the Byzantine Empire until the English Richard I (Lion Hearted) established a crusader state in A.D. 1191. The Lusignan dynasty ruled until 1489, when Cyprus was annexed by Venice. It was subsequently conquered by the Ottoman Empire in 1571.

In 1878 the Congress of Berlin placed Cyprus under British administration. In 1914 it was annexed outright by Great Britain and was made a British colony in 1925. From 1945 to 1948, the British used Cyprus as a detention area for "illegal" Jewish immigrants to Palestine.

After 1947 the Greek Cypriot community continued its long-standing agitation for union (enosis) with Greece, a policy strongly opposed by the Turkish Cypriot community. Communal violence broke out in 1954-55. In 1960 Cyprus was granted full independence under an agreement that forbade either enosis or partition and included guarantees of the rights of both Greeks and Turks. Attempts by the president, Archbishop Makarios, to alter the constitution to favor the Greek majority provoked further communal clashes in 1964, when a U.N. peacekeeping force was sent to the island. On July 15, 1974, a military coup by officers favoring union with Greece deposed the Makarios government. On July 20 Turkey invaded Cyprus and, after the collapse of cease-fire talks in August, occupied the northern two-fifths of the island. In 1975 the Turkish government announced a de facto partition of Cyprus; the northern territory was proclaimed the Turkish Federated State of Cyprus, under Pres. Rauf Denktash.

Makarios returned as president of the Republic of Cyprus, which was thus reduced in size, and remained in office until his death in 1977. He was succeeded by Spyros Kyprianou. Some 200,000 Greek Cypriots were expelled from the Turkish sector to the Republic; many Turks fled from the Republic to the Turkish sector. With a return of political stability, renewed foreign investment, and a customs union negotiated with the EEC, the Republic's economy has prospered, led by agriculture, light manufacturing, and tourism.

In the Turkish sector, the economy remains stagnant, hampered by the loss of population, wartime damage, and stringent economic controls. The Turkish sector proclaimed its independence as the Turkish Republic of Northern Cyprus in 1983, but the new republic has not gained international recognition.

The decision of the E.U. to invite Cyprus to apply for membership and to deny Turkey's application (July and December, 1998) heightened tensions. In June 1998, both Greece and Turkey sent aircraft to Cyprus and the newly-reelected government of President Clerides sought anti-aircraft missiles from Russia. But by December Cyprus had cancelled plans for deployment, at the urging of Greek Premier Simitis. With the peaceful resolution of so serious a crisis, it became possible for Greek-Turkish relations (the key to reunification of Cyprus) to improve, as they did in 1999, climaxing in the January 2000 accords on the Aegean environment, immigration, tourism and the like.

▶ CZECH REPUBLIC
● GEOGRAPHY Location: Central Europe. Boundaries: Poland to N, Slovakia to E, Austria to S, Germany to W. Total land area: 30,387 sq. mi. (78,703 sq km). Coastline: none. Comparative area: about the size of South Carolina. Land use: 41% arable land; 2% permanent crops; 11% meadows and pastures; 34% forest and woodland; 12% other. Major cities: (1994 est.) Prague (capital) 1,213,299; Brno 389,576; Ostrava 325,827; Pilsen (Plzen) 171,908; Olomouc 106,278.
● PEOPLE Population: 10,264,212 (July 2000 est.). Nationality: noun—Czech; adjective—Czech. Ethnic groups: 81.2% Czech, 13.2% Moravian, 3.1% Slovak. Languages: Czech. Religions: 39.8% atheist, 39.2% Roman Catholic, 4.6% Protestant.
● GOVERNMENT Type: parliamentary democracy. Independence: Oct. 29, 1918 (from Austro-Hungarian Empire); Jan. 2, 1993 (from Czechoslovakia). Constitution: Jan. 1, 1993. National holiday: Founding of the Republic, Oct. 28. Heads of Government: Václav Havel, president (since Jan. 1993), Miloš Zeman, prime minister (since July 1998). Structure: executive; bicameral legislature; judiciary.

● ECONOMY Monetary unit: koruna. Budget: (2001 est.) income: $16.7 bil.; expend.: $18 bil. GDP: $132.4 bil., $12,900 per capita (2000 est.). Chief crops: wheat, rye, barley, oats, corn, potatoes. Natural resources: coal, kaolin, clay, graphite. Major industries: fuels, metallurgy, machines. Labor force: (1999) 5.203 mil.; 40% industry, 55% services, 5% agriculture. Exports: $28.3 bil., (f.o.b., 2000); manufactured goods, machinery and equipment, chemicals, raw materials and fuels. Imports: $31.4 bil. (f.o.b., 2000); machinery and equipment, manufactured goods, chemicals. Major trading partners: (1997) Germany, Slovakia, Austria, Poland.

A Moravian empire, Christianized by Cyril and Methodius, existed in the ninth century until destroyed by the Magyars. From the 10th through the 14th century, Bohemia and Moravia, "lands of the crown of St. Vaclav," formed an independent kingdom within the Holy Roman Empire under the Czech Premsylid dynasty. In 1526 the crown lands came under Habsburg rule, a rule that lasted until World War I.

They were the richest crown lands of the Austro-Hungarian Empire. Prosperous agriculture in the central plains and mineral wealth in the hill country were supplemented in the 19th century by industrial development led by urban middle classes, who were largely German and Jewish.

With the crumbling of the Habsburg monarchy during the war, a new multinational state of Czechoslovakia emerged, founded by Eduard Beneš and Thomas Masaryk, in which the Czechs (only 45% of the population) ruled over Germans, Slovaks, Magyars, Poles, and Ukranians. Yet it was the most democratic state in Central Europe between the wars.

Following the Munich Pact of September 1938, Hitler annexed the German-speaking regions of the "Sudetenland," and in 1939 he established a "protectorate" over the Czech lands, while Slovakia became a self-governing satellite republic. With the collapse of Hitler's Reich, Czechoslovakia was reestablished (except for the Carpatho-Ukraine, which it was compelled to cede to the U.S.S.R.) with Beneš again as president and a socialist government, independent but pro-Soviet. Three million Germans were expelled, with tens of thousands killed either in mob violence or after hasty trials before "Special People's Courts." In 1948 a Communist coup forced Beneš to resign; he was replaced by the Communist leader Klement Gottwald. Jan Masaryk, the foreign minister, committed suicide or was murdered. Purges and persecutions followed.

With Stalin's death in 1953, Gottwald was replaced as party first secretary by Stalinist hardliner Antonin Novotny, who also became president in 1957. In 1968 Novotny was replaced as first secretary by a Slovak liberal, Alexander Dubcek. Czechoslovakia suddenly was in the vanguard of communist reform. The new regime abolished censorship, denounced Stalin, decentralized economic decision-making, and granted real power to the National Assembly.

The brief "Prague Spring" ended in August 1968, when Warsaw Pact troops invaded. In 1969 Dubcek was replaced by Gustáv Husak. The party was purged, censorship restored, dissent repressed, and the centralized economy restored.

The 1970's brought inflation and economic stagnation but produced no change in policy. The rise of the Solidarity movement in Poland in the early 1980's provoked a backlash of preventive repression in Czechoslovakia, aimed especially at

Charter 77, a human-rights organization, and at the Catholic church.

The pro-democracy movement began in earnest in October 1989, inspired by a lack of confidence in Communist rule and by reform movements throughout Eastern Europe. The resignation of Communist leaders throughout December culminated in the parliamentary election of Václav Havel, a dissident playwright and head of a loose coalition of opposition groups called Civic Forum, as president, and the vindicated Alexander Dubcek as chairman of Parliament.

Despite severe economic difficulties, revelations of state security abuses, environmental pollution, and other problems inherited from the Communist era, Czechoslovakia's "Velvet Revolution" seemed a resounding political and popular success. Soviet troops left by March; and in June Civic Forum and its Slovakian ally, Public Against Violence, won 47% of the vote in parliamentary elections, against 14% for the Communists and 12% for the Christian Democrats. Vaclav Havel was elected president, and Marian Calfa became prime minister.

But Slovak-Czech resentments and Slovakia's economic distress led to a separation of the two republics, effective Jan. 1, 1993. In June 1996, the first elections in the new Czech Republic gave 99 (out of 200) seats to the three-party center-right coalition (led by Prime Minister Vaclav Klaus and President Vaclav Havel) which had guided the Czech Republic's successful transition to a market economy. After several years of prosperity, the Czech Republic suddenly fell on hard times in 1997, and Klaus was forced to introduce austerity measures. Revelations of campaign finance irregularities brought Klaus' resignation in Nov. 1997. In the subsequent June 1998 elections, the Social Democrats won a plurality of seats and, with the Civic Democrats' agreement, formed not a coalition but a minority government for the next four years. (In return, the CDs were to appoint the speakers of both houses and to chair the budget and secret service committees of the legislature.) The budget adopted in Jan. 1999 included the republic's first planned deficit as the nagging recession continued, with little economic growth forecast and unemployment rising to 9.5 percent.

▶ DENMARK
Kingdom of Denmark
● GEOGRAPHY Location: northern Europe. Boundaries: Skagerrak channel to N, Baltic Sea to E, Germany to S, North Sea to W. Total land area: 16,629 sq. mi. (43,070 sq km). Coastline: 2,100 mi. (3,379 km). Comparative area: between Maryland and West Virginia. Land use: 60% arable land; negl. % permanent crops; 5% meadows and pastures; 10% forest and woodland; 25% other; includes 9% irrigated. Major cities: (1995) København (Copenhagen—capital) 1,353,333; Århus (Aarhus) 277,477; Odense 182,617; Alborg (Aalborg) 159,056; Esbjerg 82,579.
● PEOPLE Population: 5,352,815 (July 2001 est.). Nationality: noun—Dane(s); adjective—Danish. Ethnic groups: Scandinavian, Eskimo, Faeroese, German. Languages: Danish, Faroese, Greenlandic (Eskimo dialect); small German-speaking minority. Religions: 95% Evangelical Lutheran, Protestant and Roman Catholic, other.
● GOVERNMENT Type: constitutional monarchy. Constitution: June 5, 1953. National holiday: Constitution Day, Apr. 16. Heads of Government: Margrethe II, queen (since Jan. 1972); Poul Nyrup Rasmussen, prime minister (since Jan. 1993).

Structure: executive power vested in Crown, exercised by cabinet responsible to Parliament; unicameral legislature; Supreme Court.
● ECONOMY Monetary unit: Danish krone. Budget: (2001 est.) income: $52.9 bil.; expend.: $51.3 bil. GDP: $136.2 bil., $25,500 per capita (2000 est.). Chief crops: grain, potatoes; meat, dairy; fish. Natural resources: crude oil, natural gas, fish, salt, limestone. Major industries: food processing, machinery and equipment, textiles, clothing. Labor force: 2.856 mil.; 79% services, 17% industry; 5.3% unemployment (2000). Exports: $50.8 bil. (f.o.b., 2000); machinery and instruments, meat and meat products, fuels, dairy products. Imports: $43.6 bil. (f.o.b., 2000); machinery and equipment, petroleum, chemicals, grain and foodstuffs. Major trading partners: (1999) exports: 66.5% E.U., 5.8% Norway; imports: 72.1% E.U., 4.2% Norway, 4.5% U.S.

Scandinavian by history, not geography, Denmark in the 11th century, under its second Christian king, Canute, ruled a great northern empire including Greenland, Iceland, the Faeroe Islands, Great Britain, and Norway. By 1387 Britain was long independent, but Denmark added Sweden and Finland to its domain. Yet it was never a great power. Its kings never really controlled the nobility, while in foreign affairs it was dominated by the Hansa, the league of German trading cities.

In the 16th century Denmark had to recognize the independence of Sweden and Finland. In the 19th century it lost Norway (to Sweden in 1814) and Schleswig-Holstein (to Prussia in 1864). In the 20th century Denmark sold the Virgin Islands to the United States in 1914 and had to recognize Iceland's independence in 1944.

In the 19th century, Denmark was transformed from a poor peasant society to one of Europe's richest agricultural nations by means of reforms that established agricultural cooperatives and emphasized intensive specialization in the production of dairy products and pork. These products remain a mainstay of the Danish economy.

Denmark remained neutral during World War I. In 1939 Denmark signed a 10-year nonaggression pact with Germany, but Germany nevertheless invaded Denmark in April 1940; the country surrendered without a fight. In 1941 Denmark's ambassador in Washington transferred defense of Greenland to the United States, and much of Denmark's merchant fleet joined the Allied war effort. Denmark was placed under German martial law in August 1943 and was treated as an enemy nation. Danish resistance succeeded in evacuating 7,000 Jews to neutral Sweden. Denmark was liberated by British troops in May 1945.

Although Denmark was not technically a participant on the Allied side in World War II, it became a U.N. member in 1946 and a founding member of NATO in 1949. By the latter year, the postwar recovery was complete, with industrial levels exceeding those of the prewar period. High taxes, unemployment, and inflation remained problems, but the economy was aided by the growth of trade with West Germany.

In 1953 the king assented to a constitutional reform that abolished the upper house of the legislature, leaving the Folketing as the sole legislative body. Proportional representation meant that it was virtually impossible for any political party to gain a parliamentary majority; Denmark is always governed by coalition regimes. In the postwar period, these normally have been led by the Social Democrats.

In the 1950's Denmark adopted a characteristically Scandinavian program of free enterprise, high taxes, and extensive social welfare systems. A high rate of economic growth, spurred by agricultural exports, continued throughout the 1960's. Denmark joined the EC in 1972. The 1970's brought economic difficulties, as Danish oil exploration in the North Sea yielded disappointing results, and inflation reached double digits.

The elections of 1982 installed Denmark's first Conservative government since 1905. A Conservative four-party coalition formed in 1984 remained in office until January 1993 when Prime Minister Schlüter resigned over charges of misleading the Folketing about restrictions on the immigration of Tamil refugees. Social Democrat Poul Nyrup Rasmussen formed a coalition government with only a one-seat majority.

The general revival of the world economy in the 1980's coupled with government austerity measures has led to renewed growth and lowered inflation. Although as recently as 1986 Danish voters renewed their commitment to the EC, in the June 1992 referendum on the Maastricht Treaty—providing for common defense and foreign policy as well as a common currency and central bank—Denmark said "no." The E.U. quickly made concessions that guaranteed Denmark's right to opt out of any common E.U. citizenship, police force, defense policy, or judicial arrangement. In May 1993 Danish voters approved this radically different version of the treaty. In Sept. 2000 a referendum on the euro was defeated and later the Danes said they would not be part of the E.U.'s army.

▶ DJIBOUTI
Republic of Djibouti
● **GEOGRAPHY Location:** northeastern Africa. **Boundaries:** Red Sea to N, Gulf of Aden to E, Somalia to SE, Ethiopia to S, W, and NW. **Total land area:** 8,494 sq. mi. (22,000 sq km). **Coastline:** 195 mi. (314 km). **Comparative area:** between Massachusetts and New Hampshire. **Land use:** 9% meadows and pastures; 91% other. **Major cities:** Djibouti (capital) 200,000 (1981); Dikhil, Ali-Sabieh, Tadjourah, Obock.
● **PEOPLE Population:** 460,700 (July 2001 est.). **Nationality:** noun—Djiboutian(s); adjective—Djiboutian. **Ethnic groups:** 60% Somali, 35% Afar, 5% French, Arab, Ethiopian, and Italian. **Languages:** French and Arabic (official); Somali and Afar widely used. **Religions:** 94% Muslim, 6% Christian.
● **GOVERNMENT Type:** republic. **Independence:** June 27, 1977 (from France). **Constitution:** Sep. 4, 1992. **National holiday:** Independence Day, June 27. **Heads of Government:** Ismail Omar Guelleh, president (since May 1999); Mohamed Dilleita, prime minister (since Mar. 2001). **Structure:** executive; unicameral legislature; judiciary.
● **ECONOMY Monetary unit:** Djiboutian franc. **Budget:** (1999 est.) **income:** $133 mil., **expend.:** $187 mil. **GDP:** $574 mil., $1,300 per capita (2000 est.). **Chief crops:** limited fruits and vegetables; goats, sheep, camels. **Natural resources:** geothermal areas. **Major industries:** limited to a few small-scale enterprises, such as dairy products and mineral-water boiling. **Labor force:** 282,000 (1991 est.); 75% agriculture, 14% services, 11% industry; over 30% unemployment (1994 est.). **Exports:** $260 mil. (f.o.b., 1999 est.); hides and skins and transit of coffee. **Imports:** $440 mil. (f.o.b., 1999 est.); foods, beverages, transport equipment, chemicals, petroleum. **Major trading partners:** **exports:** 53% Somalia, 23% Yemen, 5% Ethiopia;

imports: 13% France, 12% Ethiopia, 9% Italy, 6% Saudi Arabia.

This small, arid region on the Horn of Africa near the southern mouth of the Red Sea became the object of British-French rivalry with the opening of the Suez Canal in 1869. The French sphere of influence, called French Somaliland, was affirmed by agreements with Ethiopia in 1897, 1945, and 1954. In the early 20th century, the French constructed a railroad from Addis Ababa to Djibouti, adding to the colony's strategic value.

French and Italian forces clashed at the border of Ethiopia and French Somaliland with the Italian invasion of Ethiopia in the 1930's. During World War II, the territorial administration at first sided with the Vichy government but in December 1942 established ties with the Free French and the Allies.

The colony was reorganized in 1957 and in 1958 became, by referendum, a French Overseas Territory. In July 1967 its name was changed to the Territory of the Afars and Issas. Growing nationalist sentiment led to a referendum in favor of complete independence. The Republic of Djibouti became independent on June 27, 1977. A new constitution was approved in 1992 and multiparty elections in December resulted in a clean sweep for Popular Rally for Democracy.

▶ DOMINICA
Commonwealth of Dominica
● **GEOGRAPHY Location:** eastern Caribbean Sea, between Guadeloupe to N and Martinique to S. Roseau 15°18'N, 61°23'W. **Boundaries:** Dominica Passage to N, Atlantic Ocean to E, Martinique Passage to S, Caribbean Sea to W. **Total land area:** 290 sq. mi. (750 sq km). **Coastline:** 92 mi. (148 km). **Comparative area:** slightly more than four times size of Washington, D.C. **Land use:** 9% arable land; 13% permanent crops; 3% meadows and pastures; 67% forest and woodland; 8% other. **Major cities:** (1991 census) Roseau (capital) 20,755.
● **PEOPLE Population:** 70,786 (July 2001 est.). **Nationality:** noun—Dominican(s); adjective—Dominican. **Ethnic groups:** black, Carib Amerindians. **Languages:** English (official), French patois. **Religions:** 77% Roman Catholic, 15% Protestant.
● **GOVERNMENT Type:** parliamentary democracy. **Independence:** Nov. 3, 1978 (from U.K.). **Constitution:** Nov. 3, 1978. **National holiday:** Independence Day, Nov. 3. **Heads of Government:** Vernon Lorden Shaw, president (since Oct. 1998); Pierre Charles, acting prime minister (since Oct. 2000). **Structure:** executive; unicameral legislature; judiciary—East Caribbean Supreme Court.
● **ECONOMY Monetary unit:** East Caribbean (EC) dollar. **Budget:** (FY97/98 est.). **income:** $72 mil.; **expend.:** $79.9 mil. **GDP:** $290 mil., $4,000 per capita (2000 est.). **Chief crops:** bananas, citrus, mangoes; forestry and fisheries. **Natural resources:** timber, hydropower, arable land. **Major industries:** soap, coconut oil, tourism. **Labor force:** 25,000 (1984); 40% agriculture, 32% industry and commerce, 28% services; 20% unemployment (1999 est.). **Exports:** $60.7 mil. (2000 est.); bananas, soap, bay oil. **Imports:** $126 mil. (2000 est.); manufactured goods, machinery and equipment, foodstuffs. **Major trading partners:** **exports:** 47% Caricom countries, 36% U.K., 7% U.S.; **imports:** 41% U.S., 25% Caricom, 13% U.K.

Pre-Columbian Dominica was a stronghold of Carib Indians, who had expelled the Arawaks in the 14th century, and today it is the only island in the Caribbean with a native Carib population.

Dominica was visited by Columbus on his second American voyage; but though frequented by Spanish ships, it was not settled until French missionaries arrived in the 1630's. Carib resistance was so strong that the French and British agreed to consider the island neutral territory, until it passed under British control in 1763.

Later it was administratively joined to the Leeward and then the Windward Islands, and then became part of the West Indies Federation. It entered into political association with the United Kingdom in 1967. In 1978 Dominica gained independence from Britain. Prime Minister Mary Eugenia Charles's Freedom party has held power since 1980 on a program of economic reconstruction. Hurricanes in 1979-80 largely destroyed the island's agriculture. The government of Prime Minister Mary Eugenia Charles's Freedom party implemented a program of economic reconstruction and diversification after the disaster. In 1992 it began a controversial policy of granting citizenship to businessmen, Asians in particular, in exchange for investment in Dominica's economy. In 1995, Charles resigned after 15 years in office. The United Workers party took 11 of 21 seats in parliamentary elections and named its leader, Edison James, the new prime minister. But Jan. 2000 Assembly elections produced a coalition of the Labor and Freedom Parties, as the United Workers went again into opposition. Labor Party leader Roosevelt "Rosie" Douglas was named prime minister, but he died unexpectedly on Oct. 2, leaving former Communications and Works minister Pierre Charles to serve as acting prime minister.

▶DOMINICAN REPUBLIC

• **GEOGRAPHY   Location:** eastern Hispaniola, in Caribbean Sea. Santo Domingo 19°30′N, 70°42′W. **Boundaries:** North Atlantic to N, Mona Passage to E, Caribbean Sea to S, Haiti to W. **Total land area:** 18,815 sq. mi. (48,730 sq km). **Coastline:** 800 mi. (1,288 km). **Comparative area:** slightly more than four times size of Washington, D.C. **Land use:** 21% arable land; 9% permanent crops; 43% meadows and pastures; 12% forest and woodland; 15% other; includes 4% irrigated. **Major cities:** (1981) Santo Domingo (capital) 1,313,172; Santiago de los Caballeros 278,638; La Romana 91,571; San Pedro de Macorís 78,562; San Francisco de Macorís 64,906.
• **PEOPLE   Population:** 8,581,477 (July 2001 est.). **Nationality:** noun—Dominican(s); adjective—Dominican. **Ethnic groups:** 73% mixed, 16% white, 11% black. **Languages:** Spanish. **Religions:** 95% Roman Catholic.
• **GOVERNMENT   Type:** representative democracy. **Independence:** Feb. 27, 1844 (from Haiti). **Constitution:** Nov. 28, 1966. **National holiday:** Independence Day, Feb. 27. **Head of Government:** Hipólito Mejía Domínguez, president (since Aug. 2000). **Structure:** executive; bicameral legislature; judiciary.
• **ECONOMY   Monetary unit:** Dominican peso. **Budget:** (1999 est.) *income:* $2.3 bil.; *expend.:* $2.9 bil. **GDP:** $48.3 bil., $5,700 per capita (2000 est.). **Chief crops:** sugarcane, coffee, cotton, cocoa, tobacco; cattle, pigs. **Natural resources:** nickel, bauxite, gold, silver. **Major industries:** tourism, sugar processing, ferronickel and gold mining. **Labor force:** 2.3–2.6 mil. (1998 est.); 58.7% services and government, 24.3% industry, 17% agriculture. **Exports:** $5.8 bil. (f.o.b, 2000); ferronickel, sugar, gold, coffee. **Imports:** $9.6 bil. (f.o.b, 2000); foodstuffs, petroleum, cotton and fabrics, chemicals and pharmaceuticals. **Major trading part-** ners: *exports:* 66.1% U.S., 7.8% Netherlands (1999); *imports:* 25.7% U.S., 9.2% Venezuela, 4% Mexico (1999).

The Dominican Republic takes up the eastern two-thirds of the island of Hispaniola, which it shares with Haiti. Christopher Columbus visited the island in 1492, and Santo Domingo is the oldest continually inhabited European settlement in the Americas, with the oldest cathedral, hospital, and monastery in the Western Hemisphere.

Western Hispaniola (Haiti) was ceded to France in 1697, and the eastern part of the island in 1795. Liberated with the Haitian slave revolts of 1801, it fell under Haitian rule from 1804 to 1808 (when it reverted to Spanish rule), and again from 1822 to 1844. It was again occupied by Spain from 1861 to 1865. Under Ulises Heureux (1882-99), the Dominican Republic enjoyed a period of independence and prosperity. The U.S. occupied the Dominican Republic between 1916 and 1924. In 1930 Rafael Trujillo set up a dictatorship lasting 31 years. Dominican political strife triggered another U.S. invasion (1965-66) to end the revolution. Reformist party candidate Joaquín Balaguer, president from 1966 to 1978, regained the presidency in 1986, was reelected in 1990, and again (at age 87) in 1994, but only for two years, a compromise arranged in the face of charges of election fraud.

The 1996 elections resulted in a runoff between Haitian-born Jose Pena Gomez and Leonel Fernandez—both center-left in politics, both committed to economic privatization. Fernandez was the winner. But even the small and halting steps towards economic reform provoked strikes by labor unions and students over low wages, chronic water and electric outages. The death in May 1998 of Pena one week before legislative elections added a sentimental boost to real opposition. His Dominican Revolutionary Party captured large majorities in both the Senate and Chamber of Deputies. And in May 2000, for the first time, the party's candidate for president won, Hipolito Mejia. (At 93, Balaguer tried one more time but finished third.)

▶ECUADOR
Republic of Ecuador

• **GEOGRAPHY   Location:** northwestern South America. **Boundaries:** Colombia to N, Peru to E and S, Pacific Ocean to W. **Total land area:** 109,483 sq. mi. (283,560 sq km); incl. Galapagos Islands, 0°45′S, 90°19′W. **Coastline:** 1,389 mi. (2,237 km). **Comparative area:** between Colorado and Nevada. **Land use:** 6% arable land; 5% permanent crops; 18% meadows and pastures; 56% forest and woodland; 15% other; includes 2% irrigated. **Major cities:** (1990 census) Quito (capital) 1,401,389; Guayaquil 1,877,031; Cuenca 239,896; Machala 184,588; Portoviejo 159,566.
• **PEOPLE   Population:** 13,183,978 (July 2001 est.). **Nationality:** noun—Ecuadorian(s); adjective—Ecuadorian. **Ethnic groups:** 65% mestizo, 25% Indian, 7% Spanish, 13% black. **Languages:** Spanish (official), Amerindian languages, especially Quechua. **Religions:** 95% Roman Catholic.
• **GOVERNMENT   Type:** republic. **Independence:** May 24, 1822 (from Spain). **Constitution:** Aug. 10, 1979. **National holiday:** Independence Day, Aug. 10. **Head of Government:** Gustavo Noboa Bejarano, president (since Jan. 2000). **Structure:** executive; unicameral legislature; independent judiciary.
• **ECONOMY   Monetary unit:** sucre. **Budget:** (1999) *income:* planned 5.1 bil.; *expend.:* $5.1 bil. **GDP:** $37.2 bil., $2,900 per capita (2000 est.).

Chief crops: bananas, coffee, cocoa, rice; cattle, sheep, pigs. **Natural resources:** petroleum, fish, timber. **Major industries:** petroleum, food processing, textiles. **Labor force:** 4.2 mil. (1999); 30% agriculture, 45% services and other activities, 25% industry; 13% unemployment (2000 est.). **Exports:** $5.6 bil. (f.o.b., 2000 est.); petroleum, bananas, shrimp. **Imports:** $3.4 bil. (f.o.b., 2000 est.); transport equipment, consumer goods, vehicles, machinery. **Major trading partners:** *exports:* 37% U.S., 5% Colombia, 5% Italy; *imports:* 30% U.S., 13% Colombia, 6% Venezuela.

The Inca Empire maintained control over the territory that is now Ecuador until the arrival of Spanish conqueror Francisco Pizarro in 1532. The Spanish conquistadores quickly dismantled the indigenous political structure, which had been weakened by a series of wars between the Inca chief Atahualpa and his half brother Huáscar. The Spaniards arrived in the Quito region in 1533 and established the city of Guayaquil shortly thereafter. The administrative center of Spanish rule was originally established through the viceroyalty of Peru in 1544, and an audiencia (a regional high court under the nominal authority of the viceroy) was established at Quito in 1563. Administrative control of the region was transferred to Bogotá and the viceroyalty of New Granada in 1718.

The local junta in Quito ousted the audiencia in 1809, but they did not achieve independence for the region until after the military victory of the rebel forces over the royalists at the battle of Pichincha in 1822. Ecuador formed a part of the Confederation of Gran Colombia until the confederation's collapse in 1830. The leader of the forces for independence, Gen. Juan José Flores, removed the country from the Gran Colombian confederation and ruled as dictator until his ouster in 1845. A political rivalry existed between the Liberals of Guayaquil and the Conservatives of Quito, but Conservative dominance of the government lasted until 1895.

During the rule of Conservative president Gabriel García Moreno (1861-75), the Roman Catholic church gained a central place in the political and cultural life of the country. García Moreno tied citizenship requirements to Catholic religious affiliation, brought in the Jesuits to "purify" the country through education, and dedicated the country to the Sacred Heart of Jesus. He was assassinated in 1875.

In 1895 the Radical Liberal (anticlerical) party seized power and held it until 1944. José María Velasco Ibarra, in and out of power until 1972, dominated the political scene. Political stability within the country had much to do with the state of the economy. The traditional reliance on cacao production was superseded in the 1950's by a "banana boom," and the discovery of large oil deposits by U.S. corporations in the 1960's led to a shift toward reliance on oil revenues by the 70's.

In 1988 Rodrigo Borja, of the Democratic Left party (ID), was elected to the presidency. In 1992 conservative Sixto Durán Ballén, an advocate of free market reforms, won the presidency and immediately moved to eliminate government subsidies and encourage foreign investment.

Duran's successor in 1996 was the bizarre Abdala Bucaram Ortiz, who was removed by Congress in Feb. 1997 for "mental incapacity." Not until July of 1998 was normality restored with the election of Quito mayor Jamil Mahuad Witt. While his austerity measures provoked widespread discontent, Congress passed most of the measures and the 50-year-long border dispute with Peru

was peaceably settled in October 1998. Still, in Sept. 1999, Equador defaulted on part of its international debt. But Witt was overturned in a brief army coup (with Indian support) in January 2000; his vice-president, Gustavo Noboa, was installed as president, a change ratified by Congress the next day. In March, Witt's plan to replace the sucre with the American dollar as the national currency was adopted (though it had been the occasion of his overthrow).

▶ EGYPT
Arab Republic of Egypt

● **GEOGRAPHY Location:** northeastern Africa and Asia (Sinai peninsula). **Boundaries:** Mediterranean Sea to N, Israel to NE, Red Sea to E, Sudan to S, and Libya to W. **Total land area:** 386,660 sq. mi. (1,001,450 sq km). **Coastline:** 1,523 mi. (2,450 km). **Comparative area:** slightly more than three times the size of New Mexico. **Land use:** 2% arable land; 98% other. **Major cities:** (1992 est.) Cairo (capital) 6,800,000; El-Iskandriyah (Alexandria) 3,380,000; Giza 3,700,100; Shoubra el-kheima 834,000; Port Said 460,000.

● **PEOPLE Population:** 69,536,644 (July 2001 est.). **Nationality:** noun—Egyptian(s); adjective—Egyptian. **Ethnic groups:** 99% Eastern Hamitic stock. **Languages:** Arabic (official), English and French widely understood by educated classes. **Religions:** 94% Muslim (mostly Sunni), 6% Coptic Christian and other.

● **GOVERNMENT Type:** republic. **Independence:** Feb. 28, 1922 (from U.K.). **Constitution:** Sept. 11, 1971. **National holiday:** Anniversary of the Revolution, July 23. **Heads of Government:** Mohammed Hosni Mubarak, president (since 1981); Dr. Atef Muhammad Muhammad Ebeid, prime minister (since Oct. 1999). **Structure:** executive—president nominated by parliament which is validated by popular referendum; bicameral legislature; judiciary.

● **ECONOMY Monetary unit:** Egyptian pound. **Budget:** (FY99) *income:* $22.6 bil.; *expend.:* $26.2 bil. **GDP:** $247 bil., $3,600 per capita (2000 est.). **Chief crops:** cotton, rice, corn, wheat, beans, fruit, vegetables; cattle, water buffalo, sheep, goats; fish. **Natural resources:** crude oil, natural gas, iron ore, phosphates, manganese. **Major industries:** textiles, food processing, tourism. **Labor force:** 19.9 mil. (2000 est.); 29% agriculture, 49% services, including government, 22% industry (FY99); 11.5% unemployment (2000 est.). **Exports:** $7.3 bil. (f.o.b., 2000 est.); crude oil and petroleum products, cotton yarn, raw cotton, textiles, metal products, chemicals. **Imports:** $17 bil. (f.o.b., 2000 est.); machinery and equipment, foods, fertilizers, wood products, durable consumer goods, capital goods. **Major trading partners:** EU, U.S., Afro-Asian countries.

Civilization began in the fertile valley of the Nile River around 5000 B.C. In about 3200 B.C., King Menes established the first of many dynasties of pharaohs that unified the country from the Nile Delta to Upper Egypt, creating a distinctive ancient civilization of great wealth and cultural brilliance.

The last pharaonic dynasty was overthrown by the Persians in 341 B.C. The Persians in turn were replaced by the Alexandrian and Ptolemaic Greek dynasties and then by the rule of the Roman Empire. Egypt was part of the Byzantine Empire from the third to the seventh centuries A.D., when it was conquered by the Arab Islamic expansion. Arab rule was ended around 1250 when the Mameluke dynasty, of Caucasian origin, established control.

The Mamelukes were defeated by the Turks in 1517, and Egypt was incorporated into the Ottoman Empire.

The Suez Canal was built by a French corporation during 1859-69 but was taken over by the British in 1875. This, together with the expansion of the British Empire in East Africa and the Sudan, led to the establishment of de facto British rule in Egypt in 1882, although Egypt remained nominally part of the Ottoman Empire until 1914. A British protectorate in Egypt was established in that year, replaced by a League of Nations Mandate in 1922. The autonomy of the Egyptian monarchy was strengthened in an Anglo-Egyptian treaty of 1936, but Great Britain continued to maintain military forces in Egypt and controlled the Sudan as an Anglo-Egyptian condominium.

Egypt saw heavy fighting between British and Axis forces during World War II. After the war, a nationalist movement gained strength. The 1936 treaty was abrogated by Egypt in 1951. An uprising of the Society of Free Officers on July 23, 1952, forced King Farouk to abdicate. A republic was proclaimed on June 18, 1953. Lt. Col. Gamal Abdel Nasser became premier in 1954 and president in 1956.

British troops were withdrawn from the Suez Canal zone in June 1956. On July 26, 1956, Egypt announced the nationalization of the canal. Israel invaded the Sinai Peninsula at the end of October 1956. France and Great Britain landed forces and bombed Egyptian positions; a cease-fire went into effect under U.N. supervision on Nov. 17. A U.N. peacekeeping force patrolled the border between Egypt and Israel from 1957 to 1967.

Increasing Soviet involvement in Egypt was confirmed with its aid to Egypt in the construction of the Aswan High Dam. The dam, completed in 1971, provides both irrigation and hydropower but at the cost of extensive environmental damage.

Egypt and Syria joined together as the United Arab Republic in 1958. Later joined by Yemen, the union was dissolved in 1961.

Egyptian incursions into the Gaza Strip and the Sharm el Sheikh in early June 1967 led to the outbreak of full-scale war with Israel on June 5. The Six-Day War ended on June 10 with Israel in full control of Gaza and the Sinai peninsula to the banks of the Suez Canal. Sporadic fighting between Egyptian and Israeli forces continued throughout 1969-70. The Suez Canal remained closed to shipping until 1975.

Nasser died in 1970 and was succeeded by Vice Pres. Anwar Sadat, who concluded a treaty of friendship with the U.S.S.R., but expelled all Soviet troops and advisers in 1972.

On Oct. 6, 1973, Egyptian forces crossed the Suez Canal and attacked Israeli positions in the Sinai (Syrian forces also attacked Israeli positions in the Golan Heights). Israel drove back the attackers, and the Yom Kippur War ended in a cease-fire on Oct. 24.

In 1974 Sadat's government became increasingly friendly to the West, welcoming foreign investment and American aid. In 1974 and 1975 disengagement accords were signed with Israel, providing for the return of the Sinai to Egypt in stages. In November 1977 Sadat visited Jerusalem as a gesture of peace, and a peace treaty between Israel and Egypt was signed (after a series of talks mediated by Pres. Jimmy Carter at Camp David, Maryland) on Mar. 26, 1979. Formal diplomatic relations were established in 1982. As a result of the peace treaty with Israel, Egypt was suspended

from the Arab League—it was readmitted in 1989—and attacked by Libyan forces on several occasions along the Egyptian-Libyan border.

Popular unrest fomented by the Muslim Brotherhood in September 1981 led to a military crackdown. Pres. Sadat was assassinated by members of a military conspiracy on Oct. 6, 1981, and was succeeded by Vice Pres. Mohammed Hosni Mubarak. The government has remained on friendly terms with Israel and the United States and has gradually improved relations with the rest of the Arab world. During the Persian Gulf War, it was a staunch member of the anti-Iraq coalition, in return for which the United States forgave $7 billion in debt.

Through the 1990's Egypt has been troubled by bombings and assassinations by Moslem extremist groups such as Islamic Group and Islamic Jihad (the latter claiming to have killed Sadat). But late in the decade, government crackdowns seem to have been effective; Islamic Group, for instance, in March 1999 announced a permanent cease-fire. In Sept. 1999 President Murabak ran virtually unopposed, winning a fourth six-year term.

▶ EL SALVADOR
Republic of El Salvador

● **GEOGRAPHY   Location:** Pacific coast of Central America. **Boundaries:** Honduras to N and E, Pacific Ocean to S, Guatemala to W. **Total land area:** 8,124 sq. mi. (21,040 sq km). **Coastline:** 191 mi. (307 km). **Comparative area:** about size of Massachusetts. **Land use:** 27% arable land; 8% permanent crops; 29% meadows and pastures; 5% forest and woodland; 31% other; includes 5% irrigated. **Major cities:** (1992 census) San Salvador (capital) 422,570; Soyapango 251,811; Santa Ana 202,337; San Miguel 182,817; Mejicanos 145,000.

● **PEOPLE   Population:** 6,237,662 (July 2001 est.). **Nationality:** noun—Salvadoran(s); adjective—Salvadoran. **Ethnic groups:** 90% mestizo, 1% Amerindian, 9% white. **Languages:** Spanish, Nahua (among some Amerindians). **Religions:** 86% Roman Catholic; extensive activity by Protestant groups throughout country.

● **GOVERNMENT   Type:** republic. **Independence:** Sept. 15, 1821 (from Spain). **Constitution:** Dec. 23, 1983. **National holiday:** Independence Day, Sept. 15. **Head of Government:** Francisco Guillermo Flores Pérez (since June 1999). **Structure:** executive; unicameral legislature; judiciary.

● **ECONOMY   Monetary unit:** Salvadoran colón. **Budget:** (1999 est.) *income:* $1.8 bil.; *expend.:* $2.2 bil. **GDP:** $24 bil., $4,000 per capita (2000 est.). **Chief crops:** coffee, sugarcane, corn; beef, dairy; shrimp. **Natural resources:** hydropower and geothermal power, crude oil. **Major industries:** food processing, beverages, petroleum. **Labor force:** 2.35 mil. (1999); 30% agriculture, 55% services, 15% manufacturing. **Exports:** $2.8 bil. (f.o.b., 2000); offshore assembly exports, coffee, sugarcane, shrimp. **Imports:** $4.6 bil. (f.o.b., 2000); raw materials, consumer goods, foodstuffs, capital goods. **Major trading partners:** *exports:* 63% U.S., 11% Guatemala, 7% Honduras, 4% Costa Rica; *imports:* 52% U.S., 9% Guatemala, 6% Mexico.

A number of Indian tribes, of which the Pipil were dominant, originally inhabited the area now called El Salvador. The native population resisted the first attempt at Spanish colonization, begun in 1524, for almost 15 years. In 1821 El Salvador gained its independence from Spain, first as a jurisdiction under the Mexican empire and two years later as a member of the United Provinces of

Central America. The Central American Federation collapsed in 1838, and in 1840 El Salvador emerged from a bloody two-year struggle as an independent republic.

The Salvadoran economy was dominated by coffee production from the 1860's onward, and a series of laws in the 1880's allowed for concentration of both land ownership and political power in the hands of a coffee oligarchy. In 1931 a reformist president won election, but the military subsequently dismissed him. A revolt ensued (1932) in which 10,000 to 20,000 Salvadorans—mostly peasants—were killed. The result of the massacre, which was called La Matanza, was a period of relative political stability that lasted until the 1970's.

In 1979 a political coup led by a group of junior military officers overthrew Pres. Gen. Carlos Humberto Romero. Owing to the polarization between conservative and reformist political groups, the first two civilian-military juntas resigned as a result of their failure to have their programs implemented by the military. A third government, which included Christian Democrat José Napoleón Duarte, took over on Mar. 5, 1980, on the basis of an armed forces' pledge to carry out an agrarian reform program. In 1980 the coalition of opposition political organizations became the Democratic Revolutionary Front (FDR), and five revolutionary military organizations consolidated under the banner of the Farabundo Marti Front for National Liberation (FMLN). Six social-democratic political leaders were assassinated in November 1980, further cementing the political opposition around the FMLN-FDR coalition.

A three-part agrarian reform program was initiated in 1980 in El Salvador, but the central part of the program—to redistribute most of the land involved in export agriculture—was dropped as a result of opposition from the agricultural elite.

In March 1982 elections for a constituent assembly, a majority of seats went to the rightist ARENA coalition. In December 1983 a new constitution went into effect, and in 1984 Christian Democrat José Napoleón Duarte assumed the presidency.

In 1989, Alfredo Cristiani of the conservative Alliance for National Renovation was elected president. On Nov. 11, 1989, FMLN guerrillas launched a new offensive that lasted for several weeks before fading away. The government's failure to prosecute military officers implicated in the murder of six Jesuit priests shortly thereafter jeopardized U.S. military aid, which totaled $6 billion between 1979 and 1992.

In January 1992, the government signed a peace treaty with the FMLN and the 12-year civil war, in which 70,000 people died, officially ended on December 15. The treaty called for the military to cut its forces by almost half (to 31,000 soldiers), and for the FMLN to lay down its arms and become a political party. A U.N.-sponsored Truth Commission found that 85 percent of all human-rights violations during the war were attributable to the Salvadoran army, security forces, or intelligence-unit death squads. Although the legislature narrowly passed a general amnesty for public officials, military officers, and political party leaders linked to human rights violations in March of 1993, the United States tried to link further military aid to the dismissal of the worst offenders in the military.

In the March 1994 elections, ARENA's candidate Armando Calderon Sol was elected president. ARENA also carried half the seats in the National Assembly. In the 1997 mid-term election, FMLN made a vary strong showing running virtually even with ARENA on the national level. In the March 1999 elections, ARENA and the FMLN carried almost the same number of seats in the National Assembly, but in the presidential election, ARENA easily won for the third straight time, their candidate (Francisco Flores Perez) gaining 51 percent of the vote, with the FMLN candidate winning only 29 percent.

▶ EQUATORIAL GUINEA
Republic of Equatorial Guinea

● GEOGRAPHY Location: mainland territory of Río Muni in western Africa and five inhabited islands: Bioko (3°45'N, 8°50'E), Corisco, Great Elobey, Small Elobey, and Pagalu (Annaban). Boundaries: Cameroon to N, Gabon to E and S, Gulf of Guinea to W. Total land area: 10,830 sq. mi. (28,050 sq km). Coastline: 184 mi. (296 km). Comparative area: slightly larger than Maryland. Land use: 5% arable land; 4% permanent crops; 4% meadows and pastures; 46% forest and woodland; 41% other. Major cities: (1983 census) Malabo (capital) 15,323; Bata 24,100.

● PEOPLE Population: 486,060 (July 2001 est.). Nationality: noun—Equatorial Guinean(s); adjective— Equatorial Guinean. Ethnic groups: Bioko (primarily Bubi, some Fernandinos); Río Muni (primarily Fang), less than 1,000 Europeans, mostly Spanish. Languages: Spanish (official), pidgin English, Fang. Religions: Christian, predominantly Roman Catholic; indigenous practices.

● GOVERNMENT Type: republic. Independence: Oct. 12, 1968 (from Spain). Constitution: Nov. 17, 1991. National holiday: Independence Day, Oct. 12. Heads of Government: Col. Teodoro Obiang Nguema Mbasogo, president (since Aug. 1979); Cándido Muatetema Rivas, prime minister (since Feb. 2001). Structure: executive; unicameral legislature; judiciary.

● ECONOMY Monetary unit: Communauté Financière Africaine (CFA) franc. Budget: (1996 est.) income: $47 mil.; expend.: $43 mil. GDP: $960 mil., $2,000 per capita (2000 est.). Chief crops: coffee, cocoa, rice, yams; livestock; timber. Natural resources: timber, crude oil, small unexploited deposits of gold, manganese, uranium. Major industries: petroleum, fishing, sawmilling. Labor force: NA. Exports: $860 mil. (f.o.b., 2000 est.); petroleum, timber, cocoa. Imports: $300 mil. (f.o.b., 1999); petroleum, foodstuffs, beverages, clothing, machinery. Major trading partners: exports: 62% U.S., 17% Spain, 9% China; imports: 10% Cameroon, 10% Spain, 15% France, 35% U.S.

Equatorial Guinea consists of the Mbini River basin on the West African coast, and a number of offshore islands, chiefly Bioko and Pagalu (Annobón). Indigenous Pygmies were displaced beginning in the 17th century by migrations of various peoples that now inhabit the coastal region and by the Fang, who comprise 80 percent of the present population.

Bioko was discovered in 1473 by the Portuguese explorer Fernando Po, and until modern times the island bore his name. Portugal controlled the islands and adjacent mainland, exploiting them for the slave trade, until 1778 when the territory was ceded to Spain. Equatorial Guinea remained underdeveloped because of conflicting territorial claims and a lack of Spanish investment. Eventually, however, a plantation system was developed for the cultivation of cocoa, particularly on Bioko, using workers imported from Nigeria.

In 1959 the Spanish territories in the Gulf of Guinea were given status equivalent to a province of Spain. Investment in education, health care facilities, and other social programs, combined with the flourishing plantation economy, made the territory one of the most prosperous and best educated in West Africa. Local autonomy came in 1963, full independence in 1968.

Francisco Macias Nguema was elected Equatorial Guinea's first president in 1968. In 1970 he dissolved all opposition parties and declared a one-party state, and in 1972 proclaimed himself president for life and commenced rule by decree. During the next seven years, a reign of terror resulted in the death or exile of one-third of the country's people. Nigerian workers, along with other foreigners, were expelled from the country in 1976; without their labor and technical skills, the economy was quickly ruined.

Macias Nguema was overthrown in August 1979 in a military coup led by his nephew, Lt. Col. Teodoro Obiang Nguema Mbasogo. Macias Nguema was tried and executed a month later. The Spanish-educated Obiang moved to reduce Soviet influence and to improve relations with Spain. A new constitution was approved in a referendum in August 1982 and again in 1991, the latter calling for a multiparty political system. Obiang, however, retains firm control. Economic prospects have improved with the discovery of oil reserves estimated at over 65 million barrels a year.

▶ **ERITREA**
State of Eritrea
● **GEOGRAPHY** **Location:** Horn of Africa (central-eastern Africa). **Boundaries:** Sudan to N and W, Red Sea to E, Djibouti and Ethiopia to S. **Total land area:** 46,842 sq. mi. (121,320 sq km). **Coastline:** 680 mi. (1,094 km) on Red Sea. **Comparative area:** about the size of New York. **Land use:** 12% arable land, 1% permanent crops (coffee), 19% meadows and pastures, 6% forest and woodland, 32% other. **Major cities:** (1993 est.) Asmara (capital) 400,000; Asseb, Massawa, Keren.
● **PEOPLE** **Population:** 4,298,269 (July 2001 est.). **Nationality:** noun—Eritrean(s); adjective—Eritrean. **Ethnic groups:** 50% Tigrinya, 40% Tigre and Kunama, 4% Afar, 3% Saho. **Languages:** Afar, Amharic, Arabic, Tigre and Kunama, Tigrinya, minor ethnic group languages. **Religions:** Muslim, Coptic Christian, Roman Catholic, Protestant.
● **GOVERNMENT** **Type:** transitional government. **Independence:** May 27, 1993 (from Ethiopia). **Constitution:** promulgated May 1997. **National holiday:** Independence Day, May 24. **Head of Government:** Isaias Afwerki, president (since May 1993). **Structure:** executive; unicameral legislature; judiciary.
● **ECONOMY** **Monetary unit:** birr. **Budget:** (1997 est.) **income:** $283.9 mil.; **expend.:** $351.6 mil. **GDP:** $2.9 bil; $710 per capita (2000 est.). **Chief crops:** sorghum, lentils, vegetables; livestock; fish. **Natural resources:** gold, potash, zinc, copper. **Major industries:** food processing, beverages, clothing and textiles. **Labor force:** N.A. **Exports:** $26 mil. (f.o.b., 1999); livestock; sorghum, textiles. **Imports:** $560 mil. (c.i.f., 1999); processed goods, machinery, petroleum products. **Major trading partners:** Ethiopia, Italy, Saudi Arabia.

In May 1993, after 30 years of fighting, leaders of the Eritrean People's Liberation Front (EPLF) formally declared this small area of north and northeast Ethiopia to be an independent state. Ethiopia, along with the U.S., the Sudan, and several other states, quickly recognized the authority of the new transitional government led by Issaias Afwerki, former head of the liberation movement.

During the early 20th century, the region of Eritrea was an outpost of the Italian empire, but it came under British rule during World War II. The British made Eritrea part of Ethiopia when independence was granted in 1952. The secessionist movement began immediately, first against Haile Selassie, then in the 1970's and '80's against the Marxist Mengistu Haile Mariam, who was finally driven from office by other forces in 1991. The new government quickly made peace with the Eritrean rebels, who promised continued access to the sea after independence became a fact. Late in 1995 Eritrea began to contest with Yemen control of Greater Hanish Island at the mouth of the Red Sea, a struggle serious enough to elicit U.N. mediation. Further troubles broke out in May 1998 when a small skirmish over the border with Ethiopia escalated into major military clashes in June. The U.S. was attempting to mediate. The bloody and incomprehensible border war continued, with much loss of life on both sides, into 2000 until June 18 when Eritrean and Ethiopian foreign ministers signed a cease-fire restoring the borders of May 1998.

▶ **ESTONIA**
Republic of Estonia
● **GEOGRAPHY** **Location:** northeastern Europe. **Boundaries:** Gulf of Finland to N and NE, Russian Federation to SE, Latvia to SW, Baltic Sea to NW. **Total land area:** 17,413 sq. mi. (45,100 sq km). **Coastline:** Gulf of Finland. **Comparative area:** about twice the size of New Hampshire. **Land use:** 25% arable land; 11% meadows and pastures; 44% forest and woodland; 20% other (mostly urban and swampland). **Major cities:** (1994 est.) Tallinn (capital) 442,700; Tartu 105,800; Narva 79,100; Kohtla-Järve 56,600; Pärnu 52,000.
● **PEOPLE** **Population:** 1,423,316 (July 2001 est.). **Nationality:** noun—Estonian(s); adjective—Estonian. **Ethnic groups:** 65.1% Estonian, 28.1% Russian, 2.5% Ukrainian. **Languages:** Estonian (official), Russian, Ukrainian, English, Finnish, other. **Religions:** Lutheran, Orthodox Christian, others.
● **GOVERNMENT** **Type:** parliamentary democracy. **Independence:** Sep. 6, 1991. **Constitution:** June 28, 1992. **National holiday:** Independence Day, Feb. 24. **Heads of Government:** Lennart Meri, president (since Oct. 1992); Mart Laar, prime minister (since March 1999). **Structure:** executive; unicameral legislature; judiciary.
● **ECONOMY** **Monetary unit:** Estonian kroon. **Budget:** (1997) **income:** $1.37 bil.; **expend.:** $1.37 bil. **GDP:** $14.7 bil., $10,000 per capita (2000 est.). **Chief crops:** potatoes, vegetables, fruit; livestock and dairy products; fish. **Natural resources:** oil shale (world's number two producer), peat, phosphorites. **Major industries:** oil shale processing, shipbuilding, phosphates. **Labor force:** 785,500 (1999 est.). **Exports:** $3.1 bil. (f.o.b., 2000); 24% machinery and equipment, 17% textiles, 9% food products. **Imports:** $4 bil. (f.o.b., 2000); 31% machinery and equipment, 13% chemical products. **Major trading partners:** Finland, Russia, Germany, Sweden.

Ethnic and linguistic "cousins" of the Finns, the Ests acquired their own independent state only in the 20th century. Previously they had been "colonized" by the Danes (who founded the capital, Tallinn), then in the 13th century by the Teutonic Knights, in the 16th century by the Swedes (who brought the Lutheran Reformation), in the 17th century by the Poles, and in the 18th century by the Russians. Through all these regimes the German element predominated, the "Baltic barons" forming a territorial aristocracy with German burghers ruling the towns. The Ests were restricted to farming, normally as serfs, with serfdom not abolished until 1819.

With that abolition there began a cultural revival with the study of folklore, the collecting of folk songs, the compilation of the national epic, Kalevipoeg, published between 1857 and 1861, and the circulation of newspapers in the Estonian language. Political expression of this revived national spirit came with the 1918 Treaty of Brest-Litovsk in which the new Soviet Union recognized the independence of Estonia. By 1920 Estonia was fully independent, under its own constitution adopted on June 15 of that year.

A radical land reform dispossessed German landowners of large estates, which were distributed to peasant owners and tenants. Dangers from extremists of Left (Communists) and Right ("liberators") were averted by the strong presidency of Constantice Päts, but the Hitler-Stalin Pact of 1939 spelled the end of Estonian independence. Allotted to Stalin's sphere of influence, Estonia was forced to accept Soviet garrisons larger than its national army in 1939, and 65,000 Germans were "repatriated" (after 700 years) to the Third Reich. Rigged elections in 1940 led to a government that "requested" incorporation into the U.S.S.R., an annexation never recognized by the United States.

There followed nationalization of private property, amalgamation of Estonia's national forces into the Red Army, and a reign of terror against former political leaders and religious and cultural organizations. During and after the war the Estonian people suffered enormous losses through death in battle, murder, flight, and deportation.

Estonia's return to freedom began Mar. 30, 1990, when a freely elected government declared its intention to secede after an unspecified transition period. Violence provoked by Russian "black berets," mass demonstrations, defiance of Gorbachev's economic sanctions and his January 1991 military crackdown, all marked stages toward the Kremlin's recognition in September 1991 of Estonian independence. Estonia, like the other Baltic states, declined to sign the December 1991 Alma-Ata Declaration that created the Commonwealth of Independent States.

Elections in Sept. 1992 produced a divided Parliament, with the majority a center-right coalition led by the Fatherland Alliance. Parliament in October chose as president Lennart Meri, a nationalist and devotee of free markets. The effective disenfranchisement of 40% of the population, mostly Russians, through laws requiring citizenship since 1940, provoked Russian ire. But by July 1994 the law was modified and Russian troops left by the end of August.

In March 1995, parliamentary elections brought into power a far-left alliance of parties led by the Coalition Party (the Communists' new name). Still, in 1998 the E.U. invited Estonia to apply for membership. In the March 1999 parliamentary elections, a coalition of three center-right parties regained control of the legislature, winning 53 of its 101 seats. Free-marketeer Mart Laar became Prime Minister for the second time.

► **ETHIOPIA**
Federal Democratic Republic of Ethiopia
● **GEOGRAPHY   Location:** Horn of Africa (central eastern Africa). **Boundaries:** Eritrea to N, Djibouti and Somalia to E, Kenya to S, Sudan to W. **Total land area:** 435,184 sq. mi. (1,127,127 sq km). **Coastline:** none. **Comparative area:** somewhat smaller than Alaska. **Land use:** 12% arable land; 1% permanent crops; 40% meadows and pastures; 25% forest and woodland; 22% other; includes negl. % irrigated. **Major cities:** (1993 est.) Addis Ababa (New Flower) 2,200,186; Dire Dawa 173,588; Harar 162,645; Gondar 146,777; Nazret 131,585.
● **PEOPLE   Population:** 65,891,874 (July 2001 est.). **Nationality:** noun—Ethiopian(s); adjective—Ethiopian. **Ethnic groups:** 40% Oromo, 32% Amhara and Tigrean, 9% Sidamo, 6% Shankella. **Languages:** Amharic, Tigrinya, Orominga, Guaraginga, Somali, Arabic, English (major foreign language taught in schools). **Religions:** 45-50% Muslim, 35-40% Ethiopian Orthodox, 12% animist.
● **GOVERNMENT   Type:** federal republic. **Independence:** oldest independent country in Africa and one of oldest in the world—at least 2,000 years. **Constitution:** Dec. 1994. **National holiday:** May 28. **Heads of Government:** Negasso Gidada, president (since Aug. 1995); Meles Zenawi, prime minister (since Aug. 1995). **Structure:** executive; bicameral legislature; judiciary.
● **ECONOMY   Monetary unit:** birr. **Budget:** (FY96/97 est.) **income:** $1 bil.; **expend.:** $1.48 bil. **GDP:** $39.2 bil., $600 per capita (2000 est.). **Chief crops:** cereals, pulses, coffee, oilseed; hides, cattle. **Natural resources:** small reserves of gold, platinum, copper, potash. **Major industries:** food processing, beverages, textiles. **Labor force:** 80% agriculture and animal husbandry, 12% government and services. **Exports:** $460 mil. (f.o.b., 1999 est.); coffee, leather products, gold, oilseeds. **Imports:** $1.25 bil. (f.o.b., 1999); food and live animals, petroleum, chemicals, machinery (1994). **Major trading partners:** **exports:** 16% Germany, 13% Japan, 10% Djibouti; **imports:** 28% Saudi Arabia, 10% Italy, 6% U.S.

Ethiopia played an important role in the Red Sea trade of the classical world and was mentioned by the Greek historian Herodotus in the fifth century B.C. According to legend, the Ethiopian monarchy was founded by Melelik I, son of Israel's King Solomon and the Queen of Sheba (Sab'a, i.e., North Yemen). Coptic Christianity became Ethiopia's dominant religion in the fourth century A.D. Ethiopia successfully resisted Islamic invasions in the seventh century except in areas along the Red Sea coast but was cut off from the rest of the Christian world by the Islamic states of North Africa and the Middle East.

Portugal established forts and trading stations on the Red Sea coast beginning in 1493, strengthening their domination of trade in the Indian Ocean. The Portuguese also sponsored Roman Catholic missionaries but with little success. A century of religious strife ended with the expulsion of all foreign missionaries in the 1630's. Ethiopia successfully resisted an attempted Italian invasion in 1880.

Ethiopia began to emerge into the modern world under Melelik II (r. 1889-1913). A period of instability after his death ended with the accession in 1930 of Haile Selassie. Italy invaded again in 1936 and soon conquered the entire country. Protests by the League of Nations had no effect; Haile Selassie fled to exile in England. The Italians were driven out during World War II by British and Ethiopian forces, and Haile Selassie returned to his throne.

Civil unrest broke out in February 1974, and Haile Selassie was deposed on Sept. 13, 1974. A coalition of urban elites and the armed forces took over, abolishing the monarchy in 1975 and curbing the power of the Coptic church. Land reform was instituted, and a socialist state proclaimed. In 1977-78 a period of "red terror" resulted in the arrest and execution of thousands of the regime's opponents. A provisional military council, the Dergue, was confirmed in power under Col. Mengistu Haile-Mariam's leadership.

A military assistance agreement in 1976 between Ethiopia and the U.S.S.R. ended an earlier military relationship with the United States; American military advisers were expelled. In 1977 Somalia, taking advantage of Ethiopia's shifting military situation, attacked across the Ogaden desert, aiming to restore certain disputed areas of Ethiopia to Somalia. A massive infusion of Soviet arms and Cuban troops expelled the Somalis in March 1978, but border clashes continued thereafter.

After the expulsion of the Italians during World War II, the province of Eritrea, under a U.N. plan, was to have become autonomous in a federation with Ethiopia. Instead, Eritrea was made a province of the Ethiopian Empire in 1962. A coalition of Marxist and non-Marxist liberation forces—most prominent among them the Eritrean People's Liberation Front (EPLF)— resisted the annexation from the beginning. By the spring of 1991, Eritrean forces had gained control of all of Eritrea, including Ethiopia's outlets to the sea.

Another rebel group, the Ethiopian People's Revolutionary Democratic Front (EPRDF), sought autonomy for Tigre, a northern region between Ethiopia and Eritrea. In February 1991, the EPRDF launched a major offensive, forcing Mengistu Haile Mariam's flight, a week before scheduled cease-fire talks were to start in London. The talks proceeded quickly under the auspices of the United States, and rebel forces under the leadership of the EPRDF entered Addis Ababa virtually unopposed at the end of May.

Nevertheless, years of civil war and devastating famines have left Ethiopia in shambles. A transition government was installed to draft a constitution in July 1991, and acknowledged Eritrean independence without incident. But the country's first multiparty elections in June 1992 were so badly handled that the powerful OLF withdrew from the government.

In June 1994, the EPRDF won 484 of the 547 seats in the Constituent Assembly, which by November had drawn up a constitution for a parliamentary government over nine partially autonomous regions. But most opposition parties boycotted the country's first multiparty elections under the new constitution, resulting in decisive victories by the EPRDF, and its leader Meles Zenawi, who became premier. A small border war with Eritrea in May-June 1998 threatened the fragile political structure. By early 1999, the small war had ballooned into a major conflict with thousands of soldiers on each side struggling for control of some barren borderland near the outpost of Badme. It ended with a cease-fire, signed by the Ethiopian and Eritrean foreign ministers in June 2000, restoring the May 1998 borders.

▶ **FIJI**
Republic of Fiji

● **GEOGRAPHY Location:** more than 300 islands (100 inhabited), in South Pacific Ocean. Suva 18°08'S, 178°25'E. **Boundaries:** South Pacific Ocean to N, S, and W; Koro Sea to E; nearest neighbor is Vanuatu, about 600 mi. (1,000 km) to W. **Total area:** 7,054 sq. mi. (18,270 sq km). **Coastline:** 702 mi. (1,129 km). **Comparative area:** slightly smaller than New Jersey. **Land use:** 10% arable land; 4% permanent crops; 10% meadows and pastures; 65% forest and woodland; 11% other; includes negl. % irrigated. **Major cities:** (1986 census) Suva (capital) 69,665; Lautoka, 29,000.

● **PEOPLE Population:** 844,330 (July 2001 est.). **Nationality:** noun—Fijian(s); adjective—Fijian. **Ethnic groups:** 51% Fijian, 44% Indian. **Languages:** English (official), Fijian, Hindustani. **Religions:** 52% Christian, 38% Hindu, 8% Muslim; Fijians are mainly Christian, Indians are Hindu with Muslim minority.

● **GOVERNMENT Type:** republic. **Independence:** Oct. 10, 1970 (from U.K.). **Constitution:** new constitution to allow a non-ethnic Fijian to become prime minister was signed by the president on July 25, 1997 and came into force July 28, 1998. **National holiday:** Independence Day, Oct. 10. **Heads of Government:** Ratu Josefa Holio, head of state (since July 2000); Laisenia Qarase, prime minister (since July 2000). **Structure:** executive; bicameral legislature; judiciary.

● **ECONOMY Monetary unit:** Fijian dollar. **Budget:** (1999 est.) *income:* $610 mil.; *expend.:* $501 mil. **GDP:** $5.9 bil., $7,300 per capita (1999 est.). **Chief crops:** sugar cane, coconuts, cassava; cattle, pigs, horses; fish. **Natural resources:** timber, fish, gold, copper, offshore oil potential. **Major industries:** sugar, tourism, copra. **Labor force:** 235,000 (1987); 33% paid employees; remainder involved in subsistence agriculture. **Exports:** $537 mil. (f.o.b., 1999); sugar, clothing, gold, processed fish. **Imports:** $653 mil. (f.o.b., 1999); machinery and transport equipment, petroleum products, food, chemicals. **Major trading partners:** *exports:* 33.1% Australia, 14.8% U.S., 13.8% U.K.; *imports:* 41.9% Australia, 14% U.S., 13.3% New Zealand, 4.8% Japan.

First reported to the West by the Dutch navigator Abel Tasman in 1643, the Fiji Islands were annexed as a British Crown Colony in 1874. Between 1879 and 1916, large numbers of Indian indentured laborers were imported to work on sugar plantations; eventually the original Melanesian inhabitants were outnumbered by persons of Indian descent. Fiji became an independent parliamentary democracy on Oct. 10, 1970, with most land ownership and political power vested in the Fijian minority. A parliamentary election in 1987 brought the Indian party to power; the elected government was ousted in a military coup, and Lt. Col. Sitiveni Rabuka assumed control of the government on May 21, 1987. On June 2, 1992, he was sworn in as prime minister under a new constitution that guarantees a majority of seats for ethnic Fijians in the national legislature. He was reelected as the head of a coalition government in Feb. 1994.

Yet another constitution (1997) restored Indian political rights, and elections in May 1999 led to formation of a government with Fiji's first Indian prime minister, Mahendra Chaudhry. But in May 2000 a hostage crisis/coup led to the formation in July of an all-new, all-Fijian government which satisfied no one.

Fiji's economy is based largely on agriculture. Rice, vegetables, and livestock are produced for local consumption; sugar, copra, and ginger are important export crops. Gold and silver mining and limestone quarrying are economically important, as is tourism.

▶ FINLAND
Republic of Finland
● GEOGRAPHY Location: northern Europe. Boundaries: Norway to N, Russian Federation to E, Baltic Sea to S, Gulf of Bothnia, Sweden to W. Total area: 130,127 sq. mi. (337,030 sq km). Coastline: 700 mi. (1,126 km) excluding islands and coastal indentations. Comparative area: slightly smaller than Montana. Land use: 8% arable land; 76% forest and woodland; 16% other; includes negl. % irrigated. Major cities: (1995) Helsinki (capital) 525,031; Espoo 191,247; Tampere 182,742; Vantaa 166,480; Turku 164,370.
● PEOPLE Population: 5,175,783 (July 2001 est.). Nationality: noun—Finn(s); adjective—Finnish. Ethnic groups: 93% Finn, 6% Swede, Lapp, Gypsy. Languages: 93.5% Finnish, 6.3% Swedish (both official); small Lapp- and Russian-speaking minorities. Religions: 89% Evangelical Lutheran, 1% Greek Orthodox.
● GOVERNMENT Type: republic. Independence: Dec. 6, 1917 (from Russia). Constitution: July 17, 1919. National holiday: Independence Day, Dec. 6. Heads of Government: Tarja Halonen, president (since Mar. 2000); Paavo Tapio Lipponen, prime minister (since Mar. 1995). Structure: executive; unicameral legislature; judiciary.
● ECONOMY Monetary unit: markka. Budget: (2000 est.) income: $36.1 bil.; expend.: $31 bil. GDP: $118.3 bil., $22,900 per capita (2000 est.). Chief crops: cereals, sugar beets, potatoes; dairy, cattle; fish. Natural resources: timber, copper, zinc, iron ore, silver. Major industries: metal manufacturing, shipbuilding, forestry and wood processing (pulp, paper), copper refining. Labor force: 2.6 mil. (2000 est.); 32% public services, 22% industry, 14% commerce; 9.8% unemployment (2000). Exports: $44.4 bil. (f.o.b., 2000); machinery, chemicals, paper and pulp. Imports: $30.7 bil. (f.o.b., 1998); foodstuffs, petroleum and petroleum products, chemicals, transport equipment. Major trading partners: exports: 58% E.U., 8% U.S.; imports: 60% E.U., 8% U.S.

The Finns originated in the Ural Mountains, and their language is akin to Hungarian and closely similar to Estonian. Migrating from western Siberia to what is now Finland in the eighth century, they drove the indigenous Lapps to northernmost Scandinavia. Finland was conquered and Christianized by the Swedes in the 12th century and in the 16th century became a Swedish grand duchy. Ethnic Swedes make up about 7 percent of the present population. Finland was frequently a battleground in wars between Sweden and Russia; about one-third of the population perished in a war-induced famine in 1696. In 1721 Sweden ceded the province of Viborg to Russia, and all of Finland was taken over by Russia in 1809.

Under the Russians the czars became simultaneously grand dukes of Finland and ruled it as a semiautonomous province. Attempts to "Russify" Finland in the later 19th century provoked great popular resistance. When the Russian empire and then the Russian Republic fell in the 1917 Revolution, Finland lapsed into a fierce civil war between Communists and non-Communists. The "whites" under Baron Gustaf Mannerheim were the victors, and Finland became an independent country for the first time in its history.

In 1939 the U.S.S.R. attacked the Finnish Republic; Finland's resistance in the "Winter War" was heroic but unavailing. Defeated, it was forced to cede Western Keralia to the U.S.S.R. After the German invasion of Russia in 1941, fighting between Finland and Russia resumed; England, but not America, declared war on Finland as a cocombatant with Germany. Russia again defeated Finland in 1944 and obliged the Finns to wage war against the German occupying army in northern Finland; much of the country was devastated.

The terms of the 1944 armistice between Finland and the U.S.S.R. were very harsh: Finland ceded the Petsamo region to the Soviet Union, and thus was cut off from the Barents Sea; the Porkkala peninsula was leased to the Soviets for 50 years, and reparations amounting to 80 percent of Finland's exports were paid in kind. Soviet pressure forced Finland to reject Marshall Plan aid after World War II, but Finland benefited indirectly from the rapid postwar recovery of the Scandinavian region. The gross national product returned to prewar levels by 1947.

Finland's economy had traditionally been centered on timber and other forest products, including pulp and paper, and on small-scale, highly productive agriculture. In the postwar period, industrial development was emphasized; the production of heavy machinery became the country's leading industry.

In 1948 the Finns signed a mutual defense pact with the U.S.S.R., renewed in 1955, 1970, and 1983. Finland's presidents, Juho Paasikivi (1946-56), Urho Kekkonen (1956-81), and Mauno Koivisto (1982-94), although conservative and nationalistic, realized that the country's independence required the avoidance of any appearance of anti-Soviet moves in foreign policy.

With the establishment of good Soviet-Finnish relations, the Porkkala peninsula was returned to Finland in 1956. Finland joined the Nordic Council and the United Nations in 1955. It became an associate member of the European Free Trade Association in 1961 and a full member in 1985.

With a strong presidency providing stability despite revolving-door coalition governments in the Eduskunta (parliament), and a prudent foreign policy in the shadow of the U.S.S.R., Finland preserved its free economy and civil liberties.

The U.S.S.R.'s collapse struck a heavy blow to Finland's economy; through the 1980's 15-25 percent of Finland's exports had gone to the Soviet Union. Unemployment, recession and currency devaluation were constant reminders of these changes.

In politics the U.S.S.R.'s demise brought a rightward shift, with the first nonsocialist coalition government in 25 years being elected in April 1991 under Esko Aho of the Center party as prime minister. 1994 saw Finland's first direct election of a president with Social Democrat Martti Ahtisaari carrying 54 percent of the vote. In March, the E.U. voted to accept Finland as a member in 1995. Prime Minister Aho announced that Finland would join NATO's "partnership for peace" but not as a step to full membership, preferring to maintain Finland's neutrality.

The Finnish electorate and Parliament approved membership in the E.U. by plebiscite and ratification in late 1994. But years of recession and high unemployment led to the toppling of the Center party government in March 1995 as the Social Democrats emerged as Finland's largest party, with Paavo Lipponen as prime minister. Presidential elections in February 2000 gave victory to Social Democrat Tarja Halonen (Finland's first woman president) over ex-premier and Center Party candidate, Esko Aho.

▶ FRANCE
French Republic

• **GEOGRAPHY** **Location:** western Europe. **Boundaries:** English Channel to N, Belgium, Luxembourg, Germany, Switzerland, Italy to E, Mediterranean Sea, Spain to S, Atlantic Ocean to W. **Total area:** 211,209 sq. mi. (547,030 sq km). **Coastline:** 2,130 mi. (3,427 km). **Comparative area:** slightly less than twice the size of Colorado. **Land use:** 33% arable land; 2% permanent crops; 20% meadows and pastures; 27% forest and woodland; 18% other; includes 2% irrigated. **Major cities:** (1990 census) Paris (capital) 2,152,423; Marseille (Marseilles) 800,000; Lyon (Lyons) 415,487; Toulouse 358,688; Nice 342,439.
• **PEOPLE** **Population:** 59,551,227 (July 2001 est.). **Nationality:** noun—Frenchman (men), Frenchwoman (women); adjective—French. **Ethnic groups:** Celtic and Latin with Teutonic, Slavic, North African, Indochinese, and Basque minorities. **Languages:** French (100% of population); rapidly declining regional dialects (Provençal, Breton, Alsatian, Corsican, Catalan, Basque, Flemish). **Religions:** 90% Roman Catholic, 2% Protestant, 1% Jewish, 3% Muslim (North African workers), 4% unaffiliated.
• **GOVERNMENT** **Type:** republic. **Constitution:** Sept. 28, 1958, amended concerning election of president in 1962. **National holiday:** Bastille Day, July 14. **Heads of Government:** Jacques Chirac, president (since May 1995); Lionel Jospin, prime minister (since June 1997). **Structure:** executive; bicameral legislature; judiciary.
• **ECONOMY** Monetary unit: French franc. **Budget:** (2000) *income:* $210 bil.; *expend.:* $240 bil. **GDP:** $1.448 trillion, $24,400 per capita (2000 est.). **Chief crops:** cereals, sugarbeets, potatoes, wine grapes (western Europe's foremost producer); beef, dairy products; fish. **Natural resources:** coal, iron ore, bauxite, fish, timber. **Major industries:** steel, machinery, chemicals, automobiles. **Labor force:** 25 mil. (2000); 71% services, 25% industry, 4% agriculture; 9.7% unemployment (2000 est.). **Exports:** $325 bil. (f.o.b., 2000 est.); machinery and transport equipment, chemicals, foodstuffs, agricultural products, iron and steel products. **Imports:** $320 bil. (f.o.b., 2000 est.); crude petroleum, machinery and equipment, vehicles, aircraft, chemicals, iron and steel products. **Major trading partners:** *exports:* 63% E.U., 8% U.S.; *imports:* 62% E.U., 7% U.S.

Pre-Roman France, known as Gaul, was populated by Celtic tribes. The Mediterranean coast, colonized by Phoenician and Greek traders, was conquered by Rome in the second century B.C. The Roman conquest of all of Gaul was carried out by Julius Caesar between 58 and 51 B.C. Gaul became a prosperous and thoroughly Latinized province of the Roman Empire and Christianity was introduced in the first century A.D.

Barbarian invaders including Visigoths, Franks, and Burgundii swept through France in the fifth century. In 486 Clovis, chief of the Franks, unified the country, accepted Christianity, and established the Merovingian dynasty. France was invaded by Muslim Saracens in the seventh century, but in 732 Charles Martel defeated the Saracens. His son, Pepin the Short, overthrew the last Merovingian ruler in 751 and proclaimed himself king. Pepin's son, Charlemagne, greatly expanded his kingdom and was crowned emperor of the West by the pope in 800.

Ninth-century Viking invasions greatly weakened the power of the Carolingians and France broke up into estates, some of them effectively independent countries, ruled by great aristocrats. Among the most important were the duke-doms of Aquitaine and Burgundy and the counties of Flanders, Blois, and Anjou. In 911 the Vikings, who had repeatedly raided the Atlantic coast of France, established the duchy of Normandy.

In 987 the Carolingian dynasty died out in France (although it survived in the Holy Roman Empire) and was replaced by a new line, the Capetians. Steadily expanding in both territory and power from their base in Paris, the Capetians solidified the foundations of the French monarchy. Paris became a great monastic and university city as well as a center of trade and manufacturing. Under the crusader-king Louis IX (St. Louis), France also became an international power.

During the 14th century, the Black Death, peasant rebellions, and the beginning of the Hundred Years' War (1337-1453) with England further weakened the French monarchy. The Norman conquest of England in 1066 had entwined the fortunes of the French and English monarchies, and with the Capetian line in decline, England pursued its claims in France. Henry V of England defeated the French at Agincourt in 1415, and in 1420 Charles IV made Henry heir to the throne of France. Henry's forces were defeated by French armies inspired by Joan of Arc, and in 1429 his claim to the French throne was overturned. In 1435 Burgundy allied itself with France, and in 1453 the English were driven out of France, except for an enclave at Calais.

Louis XI completed the consolidation of France under the French monarchy. France prospered as a center of commerce, industry, agriculture, learning, and culture throughout the 16th century but was disrupted by religious civil wars stemming from the Reformation. The Protestant Henry of Navarre, heir to the throne, was obliged to accept Catholicism before being crowned in 1594; he became founder of the Bourbon monarchy.

The consolidation of power under a highly centralized monarchy continued under Henry's heirs. With a foreign policy shaped by the powerful prime ministers Cardinal Richelieu and Cardinal Mazarin, France under Louis XIII and Louis XIV enhanced its stature in Europe by defeating the Habsburgs in the Thirty Years' War (1618-48). Louis XIV—the Sun King—moved the court from Paris to his new palace at Versailles and presided over the wealthiest and most powerful monarchy in Europe.

Louis XIV's persecution of the Huguenots resulted in a great emigration of Protestants from France. A grand alliance of European states thwarted France's expansionist aims on the continent, but France became a major colonial power in North America, controlling Canada and Louisiana (including most of the Mississippi-Missouri valley), and pursued overseas ventures in Africa and Asia as well.

In the mid-18th century, France was weakened internationally by the expensive and fruitless Wars of the Austrian Succession and the Seven Years' War. Under the Treaty of Paris (1763), France ceded control of Canada to Great Britain. The Enlightenment made France a world center of intellectual activity but also led to the questioning of the political and social bases of the French monarchy. An increasingly wealthy but powerless bourgeoisie chafed under the restrictions of an archaic socioeconomic order.

France under Louis XVI supported the American colonies in the Revolutionary War, incurring a large public debt in the process. Combined with unrestrained extravagance on the part of the court and the aristocracy, poverty increased among the rural peasantry and the urban working class, while the bourgeoisie demanded a greater voice in government. These trends came to a head with the storming of the Bastille on July 14, 1789; soon thereafter, the Estates-General took control of the country, and France was in the throes of revolution.

Revolutionary leaders at first allowed Louis XVI to remain on the throne in a limited monarchy, but the king and Marie Antoinette were subsequently tried for treason and executed in 1793. Thousands died during the Reign of Terror which continued until July 1794, ending with the execution of its primary architects, Augustin Robespierre and Georges Danton. The Directory, with five heads of each division of government (1795-99), failed to maintain public order and suffered military reverses in foreign wars in which successive revolutionary governments had been embroiled since 1792. On Nov. 9, 1799, the Directory was overthrown by the Consulate, with Napoleon Bonaparte named first consul.

Napoleon proclaimed himself emperor of France in 1804. He transformed French law through the Code Napoleon and initially expanded the French empire in Europe and the Middle East. Suffering repeated reverses against British naval forces and disastrous losses in his 1812 invasion of Russia, Napoleon was defeated by the British under Wellington at Waterloo in 1815, and the French empire collapsed.

France restored its monarchy in 1815 but not its monarchical absolutism. Charles X, successor to Louis XVIII, was ousted in a coup d'état in 1830 and replaced by the liberal Louis Philippe. The monarchy came to an end in the wave of popular revolt that swept France, along with most of Europe, in 1848; Louis Napoleon (nephew of Bonaparte) became president of the Second Republic. In 1852 he created the Second Empire, ruling as Napoleon III and presiding over a court that set the standards of fashion for the wealthy bourgeois society of 19th-century Europe.

During the 19th century, France again became a major colonial power, acquiring important possessions in North and West Africa and Indochina. It also became a world leader in art, science, and literature and began its slow transformation into a major industrial power. Politically, however, France suffered from endemic weakness. The Second Empire ended disastrously with defeat in the Franco-Prussian War of 1870-71; the Paris Commune, formed during that war, was overthrown with great bloodshed. The Third Republic (1871-1914), despite the glittering pleasures of the Belle Epoque and France's considerable prestige as a world power, was shaken by the Dreyfus Affair of 1894-1906.

France joined with Great Britain and Russia in forming the Triple Entente of 1907, a defensive agreement against the Triple Alliance of Germany, Italy, and the Austro-Hungarian empire. During World War I—in effect a war between these two alliances—France suffered millions of casualties and severe damage in the north. Although its role as a leader of the victorious alliance was confirmed at the Versailles Conference of 1919,

France was seriously weakened by the war and played a diminished role as a world power.

France suffered badly in the world depression of the 1930's and could muster neither political nor military energy to offer effective opposition to the rise of Nazi Germany and fascist Italy. France was a participant in the Munich Agreement of 1938, which sealed the fate of central Europe. When World War II broke out in 1939, Hitler initially held off his attack on France, but when it came in May-June 1940, France was swiftly and ignominiously defeated.

During World War II, northern France was under German occupation, while in the south a collaborationist, semifascistic state was organized, with its capital at Vichy. Meanwhile, in London, Gen. Charles de Gaulle rallied the Free French forces, which fought on the Allied side in various campaigns. After the liberation of Paris a "provisional government" of various Resistance groups combined with de Gaulle's supporters drew up a constitution for the Fourth French Republic.

Although it suffered from inherent political weaknesses and often failed to provide stable cabinets, the Fourth Republic presided over postwar recovery, aided by the Marshall Plan; it promoted a mixed socialist-free enterprise economy and instituted social reforms such as women's suffrage and social security. It also led the way toward a united Europe, playing a leading role in the organization of the EEC in 1957. France became a founding member of NATO in 1949.

The Fourth Republic was unable, however, to withstand the strains of the dismantling of France's empire during the postwar wave of decolonization. France's recovery of Indochina in 1945 set off a war of national liberation there that lasted until France withdrew from the colony in 1954. Morocco and Tunisia won their independence in 1956; in Algeria, regarded as part of France itself, France fought on against Front de Liberation Nationale (FLN) rebels.

The Algerian War seriously polarized French public opinion, and, threatened with an army coup, the National Assembly voted in 1958 to grant Pres. Charles de Gaulle emergency powers for six months. De Gaulle outmaneuvered his army backers and negotiated to turn Algeria over to the FLN, a process completed in 1962. Meanwhile he also restored order at home and presided over the drafting of a new constitution that created the Fifth Republic in 1958.

The new constitution created a strong presidency, with powers to name the premier and the Council of Ministers and to preside over their meetings. The legislature was required to give priority to government initiatives and lacked authority over national defense, education, labor, and local government. Under the governments of premiers Michel Debré and Georges Pompidou, the Gaullist regime further advanced modernization of French industry and greatly benefited French agriculture by expanding the Common Market to include agricultural goods.

De Gaulle followed an independent foreign policy, pursuing European integration as well as closer relations with the Communist bloc and the Third World. He blocked British entry into the Common Market; developed an independent nuclear force, refusing to sign nuclear test-ban and nonproliferation treaties; pursued a historic rapprochement with Germany; recognized the People's Republic of China; established a leading French role in the former French colonies of

Africa; and withdrew French forces from the NATO military command.

Reelected president in 1965, after a runoff election against the Socialist-Communist alliance candidate François Mitterrand, de Gaulle continued his independent policy until student riots in early 1968 provoked police repression, which led to further popular support for the students, especially in Paris. De Gaulle dissolved the National Assembly and, in an emotional campaign on behalf of national stability, won a large electoral majority. In 1969, however, following minor political reverses, de Gaulle resigned as president.

The elections of June 1969 gave the presidency to former premier Georges Pompidou, who died in office in April 1974. He was succeeded by the Independent Republican Valery Giscard d'Estaing, who served until May 1981. During these years the Gaullist heritage was developed and consolidated. In foreign policy the movement toward European unity continued with the development of the European Parliament and, in a reversal of policy in 1973, French support for British membership in the EEC. The economic shock of the OPEC price rises of 1973-74 led to a decision to stress new industrial ventures in high-technology fields, symbolized by the Anglo-French Concorde supersonic transport.

The 1970's were years of social ferment, with a relaxation of divorce laws and the legalization of contraception advertisements and abortion, and a decline in church membership and attendance. In 1978 disillusionment stemming from inflation and social difficulties under Giscard d'Estaing brought about a leftist electoral victory for the first time under the Fifth Republic.

The Gaullist era came to an end in 1981, when Socialist François Mitterrand defeated Giscard in a presidential election. He dissolved the National Assembly and led his party to an absolute majority. Socialist premier Pierre Mauroy formed a government which pursued an aggressive program of nationalization of banks and major industries and reform of local government. Continued economic difficulties led to a loss of popular support for Mitterrand's policies. In the elections of 1986, Jacques Chirac's coalition of Gaullists and Giscardists won an almost absolute majority in the National Assembly, and Chirac became premier—the first time since 1958 that the president and the premier were of opposing parties. An accommodation was worked out in which Mitterrand concentrated on foreign affairs, and Chirac on domestic matters. Mitterrand oversaw a restoration of French military cooperation with NATO and a continuation of Franco-German cooperation.

At home Chirac and his party reversed Mitterrand's policy of nationalization of banking and industry, cut taxes, and brought about a significant reduction in the inflation rate. Chirac ran for president against Mitterrand in 1988 but was defeated. Mitterrand's reelection with over 54 percent of the vote carried his Socialist party to a near majority in the assembly, where they constructed a coalition government of the non-Communist Left under Premier Michel Rocard, whose policies were difficult to distinguish from those of the Chirac government. Persistent 9 percent unemployment and the growing appeal of Jean-Marie Le Pen's anti-immigrant National Front brought a cabinet shake-up in May 1991 and the designation of France's first female premier, Edith Cresson.

But the shake-up did nothing to stem voter dissatisfaction with the governing Socialists. Elections to regional councils in 1992 saw the Socialist vote drop to 18 percent, but not to the benefit of the center-right coalition Union for France, which gained only one-third of the vote. The National Front and the two rival "green" parties together gained 28 percent of the vote.

Mitterand strongly supported U.N. intervention in the Balkans and France's participation in the Maastricht Treaty (which voters approved by a very narrow margin). But not even the formidable Mitterand could prevent the Socialist rout in the March 1993 assembly elections. The Rally for France won the most lopsided victory in the republic's history, carrying 460 (of 577) seats while the left took only 93. Rejecting calls for his resignation, Mitterand reasserted his constitutional prerogatives in defense and foreign policy, vowing to stay on until 1995, when his unprecedented 14-year presidency ended as Jacques Chirac won the second round of voting over Lionel Jospin.

Pledged to tax and spending cuts and continued dismantling of state enterprises, Chirac and his followers met with surprisingly limited success as unemployment reached its highest level ever. A giant truckers' strike blocked French highways without government action, and cutting social welfare spending (to meet the EU's Euro conditions) proved elusive. So, seeking a public mandate for France's participation in the Euro, President Chirac dissolved the Assembly a year early. But the result was yet another French "cohabitation:" the left coalition took 319 seats and Lionel Jospin became prime minister. In May 1999 the Jospin government narrowly survived a censure motion over its handling of separatist unrest on Corsica and in December entered negotiations with all Corsican parties. In a referendum in Sept. 2000, voters—only 30 percent of the electorate—gave their approval to reducing the term of the president from seven to five years.

▶ GABON
Gabonese Republic

• **GEOGRAPHY   Location:** western coast of Africa. **Boundaries:** Equatorial Guinea to NW, Cameroon to N, Congo to E and S, Atlantic Ocean to W. **Total area:** 103,348 sq. mi. (267,670 sq km). **Coastline:** 550 mi. (885 km). **Comparative area:** slightly smaller than Colorado. **Land use:** 1% arable land; 1% permanent crops; 18% meadows and pastures; 77% forest and woodland; 3% other. **Major cities:** (1993 census) Libreville (capital) 419,596; Port-Gentil 78,225; Masuku 75,000 (1988).

• **PEOPLE   Population:** 1,221,175 (July 2001 est.). **Nationality:** noun—Gabonese (sing., pl.); adjective—Gabonese. **Ethnic groups:** Bantu tribes, including four major tribal groupings (Fang, Eshira, Bapounou, Bateke); 154,000 other Africans and Europeans, including 6,000 French and 11,000 of dual nationality. **Languages:** French (official), Fang, Myene, Bateke, Bapounou/Eschira, Bandjabi. **Religions:** 55-75% Christian, less than 1% Muslim, remainder indigenous beliefs.

• **GOVERNMENT   Type:** republic; multi-party presidential regime since 1990. **Independence:** Aug. 17, 1960 (from France). **Constitution:** Mar. 14, 1991 **National holidays:** Independence Day, Aug. 17. **Heads of Government:** El Hadj Omar Bongo, president (since Dec. 1967); Jean-François Ntoutoume-Emane, prime minister (since Jan. 1999). **Structure:** executive; bicameral legislature; independent judiciary.

• **ECONOMY   Monetary unit:** Communauté Financière Africaine (CFA) franc. **Budget:** (1996 est.) *income:* $1.5 bil.; *expend.:* $1.3 bil. **GDP:** $7.7 bil.,

$6,300 per capita (2000 est.). **Chief crops:** coffee, cocoa, sugar; rubber; wood; cattle; fishing. **Natural resources:** crude oil, manganese, uranium, gold, timber, iron ore. **Major industries:** food, beverages; textiles, wood. **Labor force:** 600,000; 60% agriculture, industry and commerce, services; 21% unemployment (1997). **Exports:** $3.4 bil. (f.o.b., 2000 est.); 75% crude oil, wood, manganese. **Imports:** $1 bil. (f.o.b., 2000 est.); machinery and equipment, foodstuffs, chemicals, petroleum products, construction materials. **Major trading partners:** *exports:* 47% U.S., 8% China, 19% France; *imports:* 64% France, 4% U.S., 2% U.K.

Gabon, an equatorial nation largely covered by dense rain forest, is inhabited by a highly diverse mixture of people who migrated into the region over the course of the past 700 years; the now-dominant Fang arrived during the 19th century. The first Europeans to reach the area were the Portuguese in the 15th century; they were followed by Dutch, French, and British traders in the 16th century. All engaged in the slave trade.

France established an informal protectorate in 1839-41 and set about suppressing the slave trade. In 1849 a group of freed slaves settled near the American mission station at Baraka and renamed the town Libreville. France established a colonial administration in 1903 and in 1910 made it part of French Equatorial Africa. The territory became an important base of Free French activity during World War II, and in 1946 Gen. Charles de Gaulle granted French citizenship to the territory's inhabitants, and local power was devolved upon advisory assemblies. Gabon became fully independent on Aug. 17, 1960.

Gabon has remained politically stable under its 1961 constitution. Gabon's first president, Leon M'Ba, was briefly deposed by a military coup in 1964 but quickly reinstated with the aid of French troops. He died in 1967 and was succeeded by the vice president, Omar Bongo, who combined all political parties into the Gabonese Democratic party in 1968; he was elected president in his own right in 1975, was reelected in each subsequent election through 1998 (which he won with a highly dubious 67 percent). Despite initial resistance from the government, Gabon has recently made the transition to multiparty democracy, thereby attracting more foreign investment. Bongo's Gabonese Democratic party remains in power.

Although its per capita income is much higher than almost every African nation, there is substantial income inequality and a good deal of poverty in Gabon.

▶THE GAMBIA
Republic of The Gambia
● GEOGRAPHY **Location:** narrow territory around Gambia River on northwestern coast of Africa. **Boundaries:** Senegal to N, E, and S, Atlantic Ocean to W. **Total area:** 4,363 sq. mi. (11,300 sq km). **Coastline:** 50 mi. (80 km). **Comparative area:** slightly less than twice the size of Delaware. **Land use:** 18% arable land; 0% permanent crops; 9% meadows and pastures; 28% forest and woodland; 45% other; includes 3% irrigated. **Major cities:** (1993 census) Banjul (capital) 43,326; Kombo St. Mary (surrounding urban area) 228,214.
● PEOPLE **Population:** 1,411,205 (July 2001 est.). **Nationality:** noun—Gambian(s); adjective—Gambian. **Ethnic groups:** 42% Mandinka, 18% Fula, 16% Wolof, 10% Jola, 9% Serahuli, 1% non-

African. **Languages:** English (official), Mandinka, Wolof, Fula, and others. **Religions:** 90% Muslim, 9% Christian, 1% indigenous beliefs.
● GOVERNMENT **Type:** republic under multiparty democratic rule. **Independence:** Feb. 18, 1965 (from U.K.). **Constitution:** Apr. 24, 1970, (suspended July 1994); rewritten, approved and reestablished in Jan. 1997. **National holiday:** Independence Day, Feb. 18. **Head of Government:** Colonel Yahya Jammeh, president (since July 1994). **Structure:** following the coup on July 22, 1994 all elective officers were dissolved; military leaders have promised to return control to a democratically-elected government.
● ECONOMY **Monetary unit:** dalasi. **Budget:** (2001 est.) *income:* $90.5 mil.; *expend.:* $80.9 mil. **GDP:** $1.5 bil., $1,100 per capita (2000 est.). **Chief crops:** peanuts, millet, sorghum, rice, maize; cattle, goats, sheep. **Natural resources:** fish. **Major industries:** agricultural processing, tourism, beverages. **Labor force:** 400,000; 75% agriculture, 19% industry, commerce, and services, 6.1% government. **Exports:** $125.8 mil. (f.o.b., 1999); peanuts and peanut products, fish, cotton. **Imports:** $202.5 mil. (f.o.b., 1999 est.); foodstuffs, manufacturing, raw materials. **Major trading partners:** *exports:* Benelux, Japan, U.K., Spain; *imports:* China, U.K., Netherlands.

Thirty miles across at its widest point, and 295 miles long, the serpentine republic of The Gambia was gerrymandered into being out of competing French and British colonial interests. Once the westernmost part of the kingdom of Mali, The Gambia was visited by the Portuguese in 1455. In 1588, they sold British traders exclusive rights to the Gambia River, and in 1660 British merchants established a trading fort. England and France struggled for 200 years to gain political and economic control over the territory, but in 1783 the French ceded to Great Britain possession of The Gambia. Its present boundaries were established in 1889 when it became a British Crown Colony. Between 1901 and 1906, legislative councils were established to encourage self-government, and slavery was abolished.

After World War II the country moved quickly toward constitutional government, achieving independence as a constitutional monarchy within the British Commonwealth of Nations in 1965. The Gambia became a republic on Apr. 24, 1970, and it had the same president, Sir Dawda K. Jawara, until 1994.

In 1994, Yahya Jammeh, a 29-year-old lieutenant fresh from a military police training course in the United States, led a bloodless coup deposing the government of Pres. Jawara. Jammeh pledged to restore civilian government "as soon as we have set things right." Later that year the United Kingdom, the United States, and the European Union cut off all economic and military aid pending a return to democracy.

▶GEORGIA
● GEOGRAPHY **Location:** west and central Transcaucasia between Asia and Europe. **Boundaries:** Russian Federation to N and E, Azerbaijan, Armenia to S, Turkey to SW, Black Sea to W. **Total area:** 26,911 sq. mi. (69,700 sq km). **Coastline:** Black Sea. **Comparative area:** slightly smaller than South Carolina. **Land use:** 9% arable land; 4% permanent crops; 25% meadows and pastures; 34% forest and woodland; 28% other. **Major cities:** (1994 est.) Tbilisi (capital) 1.3 mil.; Kutaisi 235,000; Rustavi 159,000; Batumi 136,000; Sukhumi 121,000.

● **PEOPLE** **Population:** 4,989,285 (July 2001 est.). **Nationality:** noun—Georgian(s); adjective—Georgian. **Ethnic groups:** 70.1% Georgian, 8.1% Armenian, 6.3% Russian, 5.7% Azeri, 3% Ossetian, 1.8% Abkhazian. **Languages:** 71% Georgian (official), 9% Russian, 7% Armenian, 6% Azeri. **Religions:** 75% Christian Orthodox, 11% Muslim, 8% Armenian Apostolic.

● **GOVERNMENT** **Type:** republic. **Independence:** Apr. 9, 1991 (from Soviet Union). **Constitution:** Oct. 17, 1995. **National holiday:** Independence Day, May 26. **Heads of Government:** Eduard A. Shevardnadze, president (since 1992); Otar Patsatsia, prime minister. **Structure:** executive; unicameral legislature; judiciary.

● **ECONOMY** **Monetary unit:** lari. **Budget:** (1999 est.) *income:* $437 mil; *expend.:* $626 mil. **GDP:** $22.8 bil., $4,600 per capita (2000 est.). **Chief crops:** citrus, grapes, tea, vegetables. **Natural resources:** forests, hydropower, manganese. **Major industries:** steel, aircraft, machine tools. **Labor force:** 3.08 mil. (1997); 20% industry and construction, 40% agriculture and forestry, 40% other; 14.9% unemployment (1999 est.). **Exports:** $372 mil. (2000); citrus fruits, tea, wine. **Imports:** $898 mil. (2000); fuel, grain and other foods, machinery and parts. **Major trading partners:** Russia, Turkey, E.U., Azerbaijan.

Georgia is a land of rugged natural beauty, renowned for its famous war heroes and its hospitality. Georgia's most famous son, Iosif Djugashvili, known as Josef Stalin, was born in the mountain village of Gori in 1879. The name of Georgia derives from the Persian name for the native people, Gorj.

Georgian culture is ancient. An independent state was founded in the fourth century B.C. following the conquest of the Persian Empire by Alexander III. Christianity became the state religion in the 4th century A.D. Both the Georgian language and the capital city of Tbilisi date from the fifth century A.D. The Georgian people, whose main occupation was cattle raising and agriculture, began to develop feudal states in the sixth century.

Georgia's subsequent history, however, is one of almost continuous foreign domination. In the 12th century, Georgia gained independence from the Persian Empire, but this was short-lived, as it came under the Mongol yoke in 1236. For centuries Georgia was a battleground between Turks and Persians, and the territory was ultimately divided into principalities, some under the control of Persia and some under Turkey. In 1801, the Persian principalities were absorbed into the Russian empire, and by the end of the century the remaining Georgian state under Turkish domination was also annexed to Russia.

Once the Russian Empire collapsed in 1917 with the Bolshevik revolution, independent Georgia was once again proclaimed in May 1918. It was dominated by Mensheviks (from the Russian word "minority," as opposed to Bolshevik, meaning "majority"), whose hold on power was short-lived. Although the Soviet Union and Georgia signed a treaty in May 1920 agreeing on their respective borders, the Soviet Red Army came into Georgia and forcibly incorporated it into the Soviet Union as a Socialist republic in early 1921. In 1922 it was made part of the Transcaucasian Soviet Federal Socialist Republic with Armenia and Azerbaijan, and in 1936 it became one of the U.S.S.R.'s union republics.

The Georgians have always been fiercely nationalistic, even in the face of the U.S.S.R.'s "one

Soviet people" policy. Georgian pride was evident from the first demonstrations against "russification" in 1956, and again in 1978 when the rewritten U.S.S.R. constitution attempted to weaken the status of Georgian language. In November 1988, during Mikhail Gorbachev's policy of "glasnost," or openness, great numbers of Georgians began to call for Georgian sovereignty.

Even as Georgia fought for its independence from the U.S.S.R., the autonomous provinces of Abkhazia, Adzharia, and South Ossetia began fighting for independence from Georgia. Tensions continue to run high in Adzharia, where allegiances to Islam frighten many in Christian Georgia, and in South Ossetia, which is struggling to end its association with Georgia and to unite with North Ossetia in the Russian Federation.

But the greatest conflict raged in Abkhazia, the home region of Zviad Gamsakhurdia, who was elected the country's first president in May 1991, but ousted from office seven months later. Fighting between the Georgian army and troops loyal to Gamsakhurdia continued from 1991 to 1993, resulting in more than 2,000 casualties, including Gamsakhurdia, until Pres. Eduard Shevardnadze persuaded Parliament to give him emergency powers to quell the insurgency.

His political power consolidated, Shevardnadze began to renew ties to Russia. In 1994 he agreed to a cooperation pact to increase Russia's military influence in his country and, over the objections of the opposition National Radical party, Parliament ratified Georgia's membership in the Commonwealth of Independent States.

In Aug. 1995 Parliament overwhelmingly approved a new "strong president" constitution. And in November 1995 Shevardnadze easily won election to a new five-year term, while his two-party coalition captured close to 80 percent of the seats in Parliament. But continued instability in Abkhazia, the presence of Russian troops, and several assasination attempts on Shevardnadze leave future development in doubt. Still, Shevardnadze easily won reelection in April 2000 and in June, Georgia became the WTO's 137th member.

▶ **GERMANY**
Federal Republic of Germany

● **GEOGRAPHY** **Location:** central Europe. **Boundaries:** Denmark, Baltic Sea to N, Poland, Czech Republic to E, Austria, Switzerland to S, France, Luxembourg, Belgium, Netherlands to W, North Sea to NW. **Total area:** 137,803 sq. mi. (356,910 sq km). **Coastline:** 1,385 mi. (2,389 km). **Comparative area:** slightly smaller than Montana. **Land use:** 33% arable land; 1% permanent crops; 15% meadows and pastures; 31% forest and woodland; 20% other; includes 1% irrigated. **Major cities:** (1994) Berlin (capital) 3,477,900, Hamburg 1,703,800; München (Munich) 1,251,100; Köln (Cologne) 963,300; Frankfurt 656,200.

● **PEOPLE** **Population:** 83,029,536 (July 2001 est.). **Nationality:** noun—German(s); adjective—German. **Ethnic groups:** 91.5% German, 2.4% Turkish. **Languages:** German. **Religions:** 38% Protestant, 34% Roman Catholic, 1.7% Muslim, 26.3% unaffiliated or other.

● **GOVERNMENT** **Type:** federal republic. **Constitution:** May 23, 1949; provisional constitution known as Basic Law became constitution of reunited German state Oct. 3, 1990. **National holiday:** German Unity Day, Oct. 3. **Heads of Government:** Johannes Rau, president (since July 1999); Gerhard Schröder, chancellor (since Oct. 1988). **Structure:** president (titular head of state);

bicameral parliament—Bundesrat (Federal Council, upper house), Bundestag (National Assembly, lower house); independent judiciary.
● **ECONOMY Monetary unit:** deutsche mark. **Budget:** (1999 est.) *income:* $996 bil.; *expend.:* $1.036 tril. **GDP:** $1.936 trillion, $23,400 per capita (2000 est.). **Chief crops:** wheat, barley, rye, potatoes, sugar beets, fruit; cattle, pigs, poultry. **Natural resources:** iron ore, coal, potash, timber. **Major industries:** among world's largest producers of iron, steel, coal, cement, chemicals, machinery, vehicles, machine tools, electronics, food and beverages; shipbuilding; textiles. **Labor force:** 40.5 mil. (1999 est.); 33.4% industry, 2.8% agriculture, 63.8% services. **Exports:** $578 bil. (f.o.b., 2000 est.); machinery, vehicles, chemicals. **Imports:** $505 bil. (f.o.b., 2000 est.); machinery, vehicles, chemicals, foodstuffs. **Major trading partners:** *exports:* 56.4% EU, 9.4% U.S., 1.9% Japan; *imports:* 53.7% EU, 8.3% U.S., 5.0% Japan.

The ancient tribes of Germany resisted Roman conquest with mixed success. German federated troops served in the Roman legions, and Germanic invasions contributed to the fall of Rome. Most of Germany was united within the empire of Charlemagne. Divided among his three sons in 843, the empire's eastern regions became the heart of the Germanies. The Holy Roman Empire, founded in 962, gave some unity to the politically fragmented German territories, but its boundaries included more than Germany, and some Germans remained outside it. But that unity was fragile; the Holy Roman emperor was a feudal overlord rather than a ruler, and hundreds of separate political bodies coexisted within the imperial domain. Along the North Sea and Baltic coasts, the Hanseatic League controlled much of the commerce of northern Europe.

With the Reformation in the 16th century, religious divisions added to Germany's existing political fragmentation and local allegiances. The Thirty Years War (1618-48) resulted in the virtual extinction of the Holy Roman Empire and left Germany without even a shadow of unity.

After the Napoleonic Wars, in which much of Germany was conquered by France, the Congress of Vienna (1814-15) sanctioned the creation of a German League to succeed the Holy Roman Empire. The league consisted of 39 states, including five substantial kingdoms and the German parts of the Austrian empire. Prussia, one of the five kingdoms, had already risen to prominence under Frederick the Great in the 18th century. In a series of wars in the mid-19th century, Prussia conquered the other German states; after defeating France in the Franco-Prussian War of 1870-71, Prussia declared the establishment of the German empire. Under its chancellor, Otto von Bismarck, Germany became a major European power in the late 19th century, with a booming industrial economy, flourishing agriculture, a small colonial empire, and growing military might.

The German Empire reached its height under Kaiser Wilhelm II on the eve of World War I. Germany's disastrous defeat in that war was compounded by the harsh terms of the Treaty of Versailles (1919), which stripped Germany of its colonial empire, and returned part of Schleswig to Denmark, Alsace-Lorraine to France, and part of Prussia to Poland.

The Weimar Republic, established in 1919, gradually overcame economic difficulties, including ruinous inflation, to achieve a measure of recovery in the 1920's. The republic was disrupted by labor strife, political fragmentation, and the rise of armed extremist political movements on both left and right. After the onset of the world economic depression in 1929, Adolf Hitler's National Socialist movement gained increasing power, both at the polls and through open thuggery against its opponents. Hitler's appointment as chancellor in 1933 effectively put an end to the Weimar Republic as a functioning democracy.

The onset of World War II in Europe was presaged by Hitler's annexation of Austria and Czechoslovakia in 1938 and precipitated by the German invasion of Poland in 1939. Early military successes gave Germany control of most of Europe, but the eventual victory of the Allied powers in 1945 left the country exhausted and in ruins. Much of the Jewish population of Germany, and of other territories under German control, had been killed during the Holocaust. German cities were reduced to rubble, and a quarter of the country's homes were uninhabitable. Famine and fuel shortages added to the general misery.

Politically, Germany had essentially ceased to exist in 1945. The Allies divided the country into four zones of occupation, with a similar four-part division of Berlin. As the Cold War rift between the Western powers and the U.S.S.R. intensified during the late 1940's, so too the division of Germany hardened. In 1948 the U.S.S.R. imposed a blockade on West Berlin; the city was supplied by a massive airlift from the West for several months. In 1949 two Germanies were created: the German Democratic Republic in the Russian zone in the east, and the Federal Republic of Germany in the Allied zone in the west.

The Federal Republic was largely the creation of one man, Konrad Adenauer. A veteran pre-Hitler politician, he founded the Federation of Christian Democratic Parties (CDU-CSU) in 1945, and as president of the Parliamentary Council formed during the occupation, he virtually wrote the new constitution for West Germany. In the first elections held in the Federal Republic (August 1949), the "bourgeois coalition" led by the CDU-CSU won a parliamentary majority in the Bundestag, and Adenauer became chancellor, a post he held for 14 years. In 1951 the Western powers granted the new state autonomy in foreign affairs, and recognized its full sovereignty in 1954.

Even before the fighting in Germany subsided in 1945, the Soviet Air Force brought Walter Ulbricht, the exiled leader of the German Communist party, back to the U.S.S.R.'s zone of occupation in Germany. Backed by 20 Soviet divisions, Ulbricht and the party commenced the communization of the eastern zone. After local and state elections embarrassed the Communists, Stalin and Ulbricht forced all other parties into the National Front. With no other electoral lists permitted, voters gave a 99.7 percent approval to the National Front in the first elections to East Germany's "People's Chamber" in 1950.

While Ulbricht attempted to collectivize agriculture and plan industrial development in the eastern zone, the Soviet Union extracted heavy reparations payments, bringing on an acute economic crisis. In June 1953, shortly after Stalin's death, strikes and riots erupted. The U.S.S.R. renounced further reparation payments and declared East Germany a sovereign state.

In foreign affairs Adenauer relied heavily on friendship with the United States and reconciliation with France. He also supported European integration. In 1951 West Germany joined both the Council of Europe and the Coal and Steel Community. West Germany was admitted to NATO in

1955 and in 1957 became one of the six founding members of the EEC.

In domestic affairs the political alliance between Adenauer and Ludwig Erhard led to political stability and the creation of a marketdriven economy. With a currency reform program and Marshall Plan aid in place by 1948 under occupation administration, the stage was set for Germany's "economic miracle" of the 1950's. Between 1949 and 1964, industrial production increased by 60 percent and gross national product tripled, while unemployment fell to 1 percent, even as millions of refugees from East Germany were integrated into the West German economy. In the same period, over 8 million houses and apartments were constructed.

In 1963 Erhard succeeded Adenauer as chancellor. Economic growth slowed to an annual 3 percent rate, but West Germany was already one of Europe's strongest economic powers, even providing jobs for hundreds of thousands of "guest workers" from southern Europe and Turkey.

By 1963 East Germany had become the second-largest industrial power in Eastern Europe, and in 1968 it surpassed Czechoslovakia in output. A significant shift of labor to industry reduced the farm population to under 20 percent of total population by 1960. Though farming became mechanized, it remained relatively inefficient.

Although East Germany enjoyed prestige within the Eastern bloc as an industrial power, the steady stream of emigrants to West Germany told a different story. After a renewed collectivization policy was implemented in 1960, the stream became a flood, and East Germany responded by building the Berlin Wall. The wall was a visible sign of political failure, but it did slow the stream of emigration to a trickle.

Erhard resigned in 1966 when his coalition fell apart over the issue of a planned tax increase. He was succeeded by Kurt Kiesinger, who presided over a historic "great coalition" of Christian Democrats and Social Democrats. Under Willi Brandt (who served as deputy chancellor and foreign minister), the Social Democrats had shifted their orientation from a Marxist party to a reformist, market-oriented stance.

Elections in 1969 produced a majority for the coalition headed by the Social Democrats who governed until 1982. Brandt succeeded Kiesinger and pursued an Ostpolitik ("opening to the east"), regularizing relations with East Germany, signing a nonaggression pact with the U.S.S.R., and recognizing the border between East Germany and Poland. But domestically, West Germany suffered serious dislocations from the OPEC oil price increases of the early 1970's; inflation reached almost 8 percent. Revelations that a Brandt aide was an East German spy led to his replacement as chancellor by Helmut Schmidt in 1974.

Schmidt continued Brandt's eastern policy but also pursued improved relations with the West. Economic difficulties persisted, however, and Schmidt's government fell in 1982. The Christian Democrats returned to power under chancellor Helmut Kohl. The improvement of the world economy in the 1980's led to economic recovery in Germany, boosting Kohl's popularity. Meanwhile, in East Germany an aging Ulbricht was replaced in May 1971 as party first secretary by Erich Honecker, who also became head of state in 1976. Honecker completed state ownership of all industry in 1972.

After Brandt's Ostpolitik, the two Germanies grew closer, at least economically. East Germany's trade with West Germany gave it access to the EC. However, East Germany resisted Mikhail Gorbachev's reform policies in the 1980's, trying to establish itself as a model of old-style communism in Eastern Europe.

In the fall of 1989 tens of thousands of East Germans fled to West Germany through Hungary and Czechoslovakia, triggering a series of dramatic demonstrations and the dismantling of the Berlin Wall in October. Honecker's government collapsed, as did that of his successor, as the momentum for unification became unstoppable. In March 1990 Christian Democrat Lothar de Maizière was elected prime minister on a unification platform.

In July an economic and fiscal union of the Germanies was completed, and in September the victorious wartime allies (the U.S., U.S.S.R., U.K., and France) agreed to a peace treaty that paved the way for political unification. On October 3, six regions of the former East Germany entered the Federal Republic as member states; eleven days later the Christian Democrats won elections in five of them, the Social Democrats winning one.

In December 1990, all-German elections to the Bundestag were held for the first time in 58 years. The CDU-CSU and the Free Democrats won 398 seats, the Social Democrats 239. Helmut Kohl was sworn in as chancellor Jan. 17, 1991. In June Parliament voted to move the capital back to Berlin.

In the years following unification, euphoria gave way to sober realism; economic restructuring would take many years, since the economy of East Germany proved to be in even worse shape than anyone imagined, West Germans have had to pay a higher sales tax and an income tax surcharge as the cost of unification.

Related to these economic woes was the wave of violent attacks by radical nationalists and neo-Nazi gangs upon immigrants and asylum seekers (who numbered over 2 million). In 1993 the government banned several violent groups and amended Germany's liberal asylum law to prevent refugees seeking economic betterment from entering the country.

In the Bundestag elections of October 1994, the Kohl coalition (CDU, CSU, and FD) took 341 seats, maintaining its majority over the opposition, led by the Social Democrats. Kohl was reelected chancellor, for a fourth time, as the economy remained strong (3 percent growth in 1994). By 1996, however, unemployment was at an all-time postwar high and the Kohl government announced that the budget deficit required sweeping spending cuts, especially in social welfare programs. The economy worsened in 1997 and rebounded in 1998 but not enough to give Kohl another electoral victory as he lost to the Social Democrats and their leader, Gerhard Schröder.

On Oct. 27, the Bundestag approved new Chancellor Schröder's "red-green" cabinet whose personnel and program appeared further left than Schröder. By March 1999, finance minister LaFontaine, an old-style SD, had been replaced by "moderate" Hans Eichel, financial markets responding positively. Already, in the previous month, the government coalition lost control of the state government of Hesse, thereby losing its majority in the Bundesrat, the upper house whose members are elected by the states, apparently dooming the government's plan to loosen citizenship restrictions (a major and controversial plank in the "red-green" platform). Schröder's attempts to introduce an austerity budget led to further electoral setbacks in state elections in Sep. 1999.

The series of large Christian Democratic advances in state and municipal elections were brought to a halt with the shocking revelations, at the end of 1999, of massive illegal contributions to the CDs over the years 1982–1998, leading to heavy fines upon the CDU and the ruin of the reputations of numerous CD politicians, preeminently of former chancellor Helmut Kohl.

▶ **GHANA**
Republic of Ghana
● **GEOGRAPHY** **Location:** western Africa. **Boundaries:** Burkina Faso to N, Togo to E, Gulf of Guinea to S, Ivory Coast to W. **Total area:** 92,100 sq. mi. (238,540 sq km). **Coastline:** 335 mi. (539 km). **Comparative area:** slightly smaller than Oregon. **Land use:** 12% arable land; 7% permanent crops; 22% meadows and pastures; 35% forest and woodland; 24% other; includes negl. % irrigated. **Major cities:** (1988 est.) Accra (capital) 949,113; Kumasi 385,192; Tamale 151,069; Tema 109,975; Sekondi-Takoradi 103,653.
● **PEOPLE** **Population:** 19,894,014 (July 2001 est.). **Nationality:** noun—Ghanaian(s); adjective—Ghanaian. **Ethnic groups:** 99.8% black African (major groups—44% Akan, 16% Moshi-Dagomba, 13% Ewe, 8% Ga), 0.2% European and other. **Languages:** English (official), Akan, Moshi-Dagomba, Ewe, Ga. **Religions:** 38% indigenous beliefs, 30% Muslim, 24% Christian, 8% other.
● **GOVERNMENT** **Type:** constitutional democracy. **Independence:** Mar. 6, 1957 (from U.K.). **Constitution:** Apr. 28, 1992. **National holiday:** Independence Day, Mar. 6. **Head of Government:** John Agyekum Kufuor (since Jan. 2001). **Structure:** executive; unicameral legislature; judiciary.
● **ECONOMY** **Monetary unit:** new cedi. **Budget:** (1996 est.) *income:* $1.39 bil.; *expend.:* $1.47 bil. **GDP:** $37.4 bil., $1,900 per capita (2000 est.). **Chief crops:** cocoa, rice, coffee, timber. **Natural resources:** gold, timber, industrial diamonds, bauxite, manganese. **Major industries:** mining, lumbering, light manufacturing. **Labor force:** 9 million; 60% agriculture and fishing, 15% industry, 25% services; 20% unemployed (1997). **Exports:** $1.6 bil. (f.o.b., 2000); gold, cocoa, timber, tuna. **Imports:** $2.2 bil. (f.o.b., 2000); capital equipment, petroleum, consumer goods, food. **Major trading partners:** *exports:* Togo, U.K., Italy; *imports:* U.K., Nigeria, U.S.
The connection between modern Ghana and the 10th century Ghana empire of southern Mali is obscure. In the 13th century, the Akan around the city of Kumasi were trading gold and other commodities with the Mande to the north. The number of competing states in the region grew rapidly after European contact. The Asante empire began in the early 17th century under Osei Tutu. By 1750 it controlled the northern part of Ghana, and by 1820 it had brought the coastal Fante empire, with its access to the European trade, under its control.
The Portuguese first explored the area, on Africa's west coast, in 1471, naming it the Gold Coast because of its gold deposits and its reserves of "black gold"—slaves. In the 16th and 17th centuries, the British, Danes, and Dutch established slave trading posts there, which is where most American slaves came from. The slave trade ended in the 1850's, and the British gained control of the Gold Coast, making it a protectorate in 1871 and a colony in 1886. Great Britain gave the colony a new constitution in 1946 under which Africans held a majority of seats in the legislature. Kwame Nkrumah became prime minister of the

colony in 1952 and the first prime minister of the nation when it became independent in 1960.
At independence, Ghana boasted Africa's largest man-made deep-water port and the most productive gold mine in the world, and it was the second largest producer of industrial diamonds. Nkrumah began to court Communist bloc nations and exert absolute authority. In January 1964 all opposition parties were outlawed. A military council seized power in February 1966 and ousted Nkrumah.
Civilian governments ran the country briefly, but in 1981, Flt. Lt. Jerry Rawlings took power in a coup and ruled until 2000. Ghana suffered severe economic problems throughout the 1970's and 1980's, and many of Ghana's people left for Nigeria to find work. In 1983 Nigeria returned more than one million of these migrant workers, increasing Ghana's economic woes.
After five years of stagnation, Ghana achieved a 6 percent economic growth rate in 1989 under a World Bank restructuring program. But political unrest remained. A new constitution was approved in an April 1992 referendum, and in November Rawlings received 58 percent of the vote. His National Democratic Congress all but swept the legislative elections due to an opposition boycott. Under the constitution, Rawlings was not permitted to run for a third term and in Dec. 2000 John Kufuor of the opposition New Patriotic Party won the presidency in a run-off election.

▶ **GREAT BRITAIN (see United Kingdom)**

▶ **GREECE**
Hellenic Republic
● **GEOGRAPHY** **Location:** southeastern Europe. **Boundaries:** Albania, Macedonia, Bulgaria to N, Turkey to NE, Aegean Sea to E, Mediterranean Sea to S, Ionian Sea to W, Albania to NW; numerous islands surround mainland. **Total area:** 50,942 sq. mi. (131,940 sq km). **Coastline:** 8,500 mi. (13,676 km). **Comparative area:** slightly smaller than Alabama. **Land use:** 19% arable land; 8% permanent crops; 41% meadows and pastures; 20% forest and woodland; 12% other; includes 7% irrigated. **Major cities:** (1991 census) Athinai (Athens, capital) 772,072; Thessaloniki 383,967; Piraeus 196,389; Patras 153,344; Iraklion 116,178.
● **PEOPLE** **Population:** 10,623,835 (July 2001 est.). **Nationality:** noun—Greek(s); adjective—Greek. **Ethnic groups:** 98% Greek, 2% other (note: Greek government states there are no ethnic divisions in Greece). **Languages:** Greek (official); English and French widely understood. **Religions:** 98% Greek Orthodox, 1.3% Muslim, 0.7% other.
● **GOVERNMENT** **Type:** parliamentary republic; monarchy rejected by referendum Dec. 8, 1974. **Constitution:** June 11, 1975. **National holiday:** Independence Day, Mar. 25. **Heads of Government:** Constantinos Stephanopoulos, president (since Mar. 1995); Konstandinos Simitas, prime minister (since Jan. 1996). **Structure:** executive—president elected by unicameral legislature; judiciary.
● **ECONOMY** **Monetary unit:** drachma. **Budget:** (1998 est.) *income:* $45 bil.; *expend.:* $47.6 bil. **GDP:** $181.9 bil., $17,200 per capita (2000 est.). **Chief crops:** wheat, corn, barley, sugar beets, olives; meat, dairy products. **Natural resources:** bauxite, lignite, magnesite, crude oil, marble. **Major industries:** tourism, food and tobacco processing, textiles, chemicals. **Labor force:** 4.32 mil. (1999); 59% services, 20% agriculture, 21% industry; 9.9% unemployment (1999 est.). **Exports:**

$15.8 bil. (f.o.b., 2000); manufactured goods, foodstuffs, fuels. **Imports**: $33.9 bil. (c.i.f., 2000); manufactured goods, foodstuffs, fuels. **Major trading partners:** *exports:* 49% EU, 6% U.S.; *imports:* 66% EU.

The Bronze Age and Iron Age cultures of Greece evolved to create the most glorious civilization of the ancient world. During their high point, from the fifth to the third century B.C., the city-states of Greece led the world in art, philosophy, political culture, and science. Greece vied with the Persian Empire for control of Asia Minor and competed with the Phoenicians in maritime commerce in the Mediterranean. Alexander the Great, king of Macedonia, spread Greek civilization widely by conquering much of the Middle East and western Asia, but his empire did not long outlast his death in 323 B.C.

Greece was absorbed into the Roman Empire during the second and first centuries B.C. In the fourth century A.D., with the division of the Roman Empire, Greece became part of the Byzantine (Eastern Roman) Empire. Seven years after the Ottoman Turks captured Constantinople in 1453, they overran Greece and ruled it as part of the Ottoman Empire for 350 years.

Under Ottoman rule, much of the administration of Greece was left in local hands, keeping alive a sense of Greek nationhood and a tradition of Greek leadership, particularly through the clergy of the Greek Orthodox church. Inspired by the French Revolution, a romanticized ideal of the classical past, and the tradition of Greek orthodoxy, in 1821 Greece rebelled against Turkish rule. With the support of England, France, and Russia, Greek independence was won in 1827, although the country included only about half of its present territory.

The Western powers sponsored a monarchical government in Greece, ruled by a German prince. Deposed in a revolt, he was succeeded by King George I, a Danish prince who ruled from 1863 until his assassination in 1913. In the three Balkan Wars of 1912, 1913, and 1914, Greece expanded its borders to reach approximately its present size.

In 1923 a Greek Republic was established, but in 1935 King George II returned to his throne, placing government control in the hands of the patriotic but authoritarian Gen. Ioannis Metaxas. In 1940 Metaxas resisted Italy's attempt to conquer Greece, defeating Mussolini's armies so badly that Hitler sent crack troops to his ally's assistance. The German occupation of Greece was complete by June 1941. The Germans pillaged the country and massacred Jews; their Bulgarian allies colonized Macedonia.

During World War II, resistance grew among both Communist and anti-Communist groups. With the German withdrawal in October 1944, resistance groups battled each other; this led to full-scale civil war by 1946. British, and then American assistance (under the Truman Doctrine), enabled the Greek government to defeat the Communist forces when Stalin refused to intervene. King George II died in 1947, succeeded by his brother, King Paul I. Political instability—16 governments during 1946-52—prevailed until, under American pressure, the Greeks adopted a new constitution.

Until the postwar period, Greece's economy had been dominated by agriculture and livestock raising. Industry was limited largely to textiles and food processing; shipping was the major service industry. Under policies instituted in 1952 by the government of Marshall Alexandros Papagos, the industrial sector led a period of vigorous economic growth lasting into the 1960's. A market-oriented economy, tariff protection for Greek industry, tight internal security, and close ties with the West formed the mainstays of Greek policy.

Greece joined NATO in 1951, as did Turkey. Conflict over Cyprus divided the two nominal allies, however. The failure of the government of Constantine Karamanlis to resolve the Cyprus situation eroded his popularity, and he was replaced in 1964 by George Papandreou, who governed at the head of a left-center coalition. King Constantine, who succeeded his father in 1963, forced Papandreou to resign in 1964, after he and members of his government were accused of various improprieties. A military coup, led by Col. George Papadopoulos, toppled the government in 1967. A countercoup by King Constantine failed, and the king fled the country.

A military dictatorship ruled from 1967 to 1974. Its failed attempt to intervene in Cyprus in 1974 provoked a Turkish invasion of the island and led to the military regime's collapse. Karamanlis headed the government once again and a republic was established with the promulgation of a new constitution in 1975. Karamanlis's New Democracy party again received a majority in parliamentary elections in 1977.

Greece, an associate member of the EC since 1961, became a full member in 1981. Full military membership in NATO was restored in 1980. In 1981 the Panhellenic Socialist Movement under Andreas Papandreou won a parliamentary majority, renewed in 1984. The left-wing Papandreou government was outspokenly anti-NATO, anti-EC, and anti-American, but its policy was more moderate than its rhetoric, extending even to modest cooperation with Turkey in the Aegean. The Papandreou government was shaken by several pro-Palestinian terrorist incidents in Greece, and by a scandal involving the married Papandreou's relationship with a younger woman.

During 1989-90 Greece struggled through three parliamentary elections in less than a year. In the first two, no major party won a clear victory, leading to weak, short-lived coalition governments. The third, in the spring of 1990, resulted in a slim majority for the New Democracy party (headed by Prime Minister Constantine Mitsotakis) and the apparent decline of Papandreou's stature.

But Papandreou strengthened his grip on power in October 1993, leading his PASOK party to a landslide (47%) victory over the New Democrats (39%), as Greek voters expressed their displeasure with Mitsotakis's deficit-cutting "austerity" policies. Papandreou returned to office promising salary and pension increases and a halt to privatization. But serious illness forced him to resign in January 1996. His successor, Costas Simitas, promised to speed up the stalled privatization program, and his new cabinet removed most Papandreou loyalists. Elections later that year gave PASOK a smaller majority.

Greece's economy failed to meet the E.U.'s criteria for participating in the European Monetary Union in 1998, but the door was kept open for 2002. New tensions with Turkey over Cyprus, however, threatened to erupt into serious conflict during mid-year. Domestic discontent at what appeared to be Greek assistance in the Turks's capture of Kurdish rebel leader Ocalan in Nairobi led to a shakeup in the Simitis cabinet in Feb. 1999 but in March, government investigators were recommending trials for 18 Greek officials accused of assisting Ocalan's flight from the Turks.

In 1999 and 2000 a series of improvements occurred in Greek-Turkish relations: reciprocal earthquake assistance, agreements on sales of electricity (to Turkey) and water (to Cyprus, both Greek and Turkish, from Turkey) and foreign ministers' accords on crime, immigration, commerce, tourism and the Aegean environment. Greece even agreed to support Turkey's admission to the E.U. In April 2000, in Greece's closest parliamentary elections, PASOK became the first Greek party to win three consecutive elections.

The success of the government's austerity program led the E.U. to approve Greece's joining the E.M.U. in early 2001.

▶ **GRENADA**
• **GEOGRAPHY   Location:** southeastern Caribbean Sea, about 100 mi. (160 km) N of Trinidad. St. George's 12°03'N, 61°45'W. **Boundaries:** Atlantic Ocean to NE, E, and SE.; Caribbean Sea to SW, W, and NW. **Total area:** 131 sq. mi. (340 sq km). **Coastline:** 75 mi. (121 km). **Comparative area:** twice size of Washington, D.C. **Land use:** 15% arable land; 18% permanent crops; 3% meadows and pastures; 9% forest and woodland; 55% other. **Major cities:** (1991 census) St. George's (capital) 4,439.
• **PEOPLE   Population:** 89,227 (July 2001 est.). **Nationality:** noun—Grenadian(s); adjective—Grenadian. **Ethnic groups:** mainly of black African descent. **Languages:** English (official), some French patois. **Religions:** 53% Roman Catholic, 13.8% Anglican, 33.2% other Protestant sects.
• **GOVERNMENT   Type:** constitutional monarchy with Westminster-style parliament. **Independence:** Feb. 7, 1974 (from U.K.). **Constitution:** Dec. 19, 1973. **National holiday:** Independence Day, Feb. 7. **Heads of Government:** Sir Daniel C. Williams, governor-general (since Aug. 1996); Dr. Keith C. Mitchell, prime minister (since Jan. 1999). **Structure:** executive (cabinet led by prime minister); bicameral legislature; judiciary (West Indies Associate States Supreme Court).
• **ECONOMY   Monetary unit:** East Caribbean (EC) dollar. **Budget:** (1997 est.) *income:* $85.8 mil.; *expend.:* $102.1 mil. **GDP:** $394 mil., $4,400 per capita (2000 est.). **Chief crops:** bananas, cocoa, nutmeg, mace. **Natural resources:** timber, tropical fruit, deep-water harbors. **Major industries:** food and beverages, textiles, light assembly operations. **Labor force:** 42,300 (1996); 62% services, 24% agriculture, 8% construction, 5% manufacturing, 32% other. **Exports:** $63.3 mil. (2000 est.); bananas, cocoa beans, nutmeg. **Imports:** $217.5 mil. (2000 est.); food, manufactured goods, machinery, chemicals, fuel (1989). **Major trading partners:** U.S., U.K., Caricom countries.

Dominated in the early 1600's by the warlike Carib Indians, Grenada alternated between French and British possession between 1650 and 1783, when British rule was established.

Independence came in 1974. The leftist New Jewel Movement seized power in a 1979 coup, but its leader, Maurice Bishop, was assassinated during a military coup in 1983. Shortly thereafter, the United States invaded and returned power to the governor-general until 1984. Prime Minister Nicholas Braithwaite of the National Democratic Congress party presided over a coalition government from 1990-95, when he was succeeded by George Brizan. In June 1995 the opposition New National party gained an absolute majority in Parliament and designated its leader, Keith Mitchell, as Prime Minister. It won all 18 seats in 1999.

▶ **GUATEMALA**
Republic of Guatemala
• **GEOGRAPHY   Location:** northern part of Central American isthmus. **Boundaries:** Mexico to N and W, Honduras and Belize to E, El Salvador to S. **Total area:** 42,042 sq. mi. (108,890 sq km). **Coastline:** 248 mi. (400 km). **Comparative area:** slightly smaller than Tennessee. **Land use:** 12% arable land; 5% permanent crops; 24% meadows and pastures; 54% forest and woodland; 5% other; includes 1% irrigated. **Major cities:** (1994 est.) Guatemala City (capital) 1,150,452; Quezaltenango 100,983; Escuintla 67,958; Mazatenango 42,328; Puerto Barrios 39,267.
• **PEOPLE   Population:** 12,974,361 (July 2001 est.). **Nationality:** noun—Guatemalan(s); adjective—Guatemalan. **Ethnic groups:** 55% Ladino (mixed Spanish and Amerindian), 43% Amerindian. **Languages:** 60% Spanish, 40% Amerindian languages (23 Amerindian dialects, including Quiche, Cakchiquel, Kekchi). **Religions:** predominantly Roman Catholic, some Protestant and traditional Mayan.
• **GOVERNMENT   Type:** constitutional democratic republic. **Independence:** Sept. 15, 1821 (from Spain). **Constitution:** May 31, 1985, effective Jan. 1986. **National holiday:** Independence Day, Sept. 15. **Head of Government:** Alfonso Portillo Cabrera, president (since Jan. 2000). **Structure:** executive; unicameral legislature (113 seats, elected by popular vote to four-year terms); judiciary.
• **ECONOMY   Monetary unit:** quetzal. **Budget:** (2001 est.) *income:* $2.2 bil.; *expend.:* $1.8 bil. **GDP:** $46.2 bil., $3,700 per capita (2000 est.). **Chief crops:** sugarcane, corn, bananas; cattle, sheep, pigs. **Natural resources:** crude oil, nickel, rare woods, fish, chicle. **Major industries:** sugar, textiles and clothing, furniture. **Labor force:** 4.2 mil. (1999 est.); 50% agriculture, 15% industry, 35% services; 7.5% unemployment (1999 est.). **Exports:** $2.9 bil. (f.o.b., 2000); coffee, sugar, bananas. **Imports:** $4.4 bil. (f.o.b., 2000); fuel and petroleum products, machinery, grain, fertilizers, motor vehicles. **Major trading partners:** *exports:* 57.4% U.S., 8.7% El Salvador, 5% Honduras; *imports:* 42.8% U.S., 9.9% Mexico, 4.8% Japan.

Modern Guatemala was the heart of the Maya civilization that began early in the Christian era and flourished from the fourth to the 10th centuries. From the 11th century on there were two major powers, the Cakchiquel and the Quiché. They were overthrown by the Spanish who invaded from the north in 1524.

The captaincy general of Guatemala was the seat of Spanish military authority in Central America until the 19th century. After an earthquake destroyed Antiqua in 1773, the capital was moved to Guatemala City. Guatemala was the center of the United Provinces of Central America after independence was gained from Spain (1821) and Mexico (1823). The United Provinces collapsed after an uprising by Rafael Carrera, and Guatemala became a separate country in 1838.

The Liberal party held power from 1851 to 1944. There was considerable economic development under the repressive regimes of Manuel Estrada Cabrera (1898-1920) and Jorge Ubico (1931-44). Juan José Arévalo was elected president in 1945. He was succeeded, with strong Communist support, by Jacobo Arbenz, who was deposed in 1954 by a U.S.-backed coup led by Col. Carlos Castillo Armas. The military has ruled either directly or indirectly since then, although democratic rule resumed officially in 1986.

A civil war involving the army, right-wing death squads, and the antigovernment guerrilla group known as the Guatemalan National Revolutionary Union (URNG) began in 1960 and intensified through the 1980's, resulting in the deaths of more than 100,000 civilians.

In May 1993, Pres. Jorge Serrano Elias, backed by the military, suspended the constitution in an effort to crack down on labor and student strikes. Eight days later, in the face of overwhelming popular discontent and international protest, the military replaced Serrano with Atty. Gen. for Human Rights Ramiro de Leon Carpio. In March 1994, the URNG and the government reached an agreement to end the 30-year-old civil war, but talks stalled for a year until the two sides could agree on a pact amending the constitution to defend Indian rights. Meanwhile, the United States cut off military aid to Guatemala for its failure to prosecute security officers for crimes committed during the civil war.

In January 1996, URNG called a cease-fire during elections, in which Álvaro Arzú Irigoyen won a narrow but clear victory over a candidate considered a puppet of the military. The new government immediately purged the military of its most corrupt members, and made plans to privatize all aspects of the economy. The 36-year civil war seemed to end when the last 200 rebels turned in their arms in May 1997.

The April 1998 slaying of a Catholic bishop, a human rights advocate who had authored a report blaming 80 percent of the killings and kidnappings upon the military and right-wing paramilitary forces, remained unsolved a year later, as the lead prosecutor and two successive judges resigned in an atmosphere of threats. In Feb. 1999, an independent report, more comprehensive than Bishop Gerardi's, accused the army and paramilitaries of over 90 percent of the civil war abuses.

In May 1999, as the first prosecutions of military and security forces were beginning, Guatemalan voters rejected all the constitutional changes proposed in the 1996 peace. In November elections for Congress, they gave a majority to the Guatemalan Republican front; then, in December, they overwhelmingly elected its candidate as president.

▶ GUINEA
Republic of Guinea
● **GEOGRAPHY Location:** western Africa. **Boundaries:** Guinea-Bissau to NW, Senegal to N, Mali to NE, Ivory Coast to SE, Liberia, Sierra Leone to S, Atlantic Ocean to W. **Total area:** 94,927 sq. mi. (245,860 sq km). **Coastline:** 199 mi. (320 km). **Comparative area:** slightly smaller than Oregon. **Land use:** 2% arable land; 22% meadows and pastures; 59% forest and woodland; 17% other; includes negl. % irrigated. **Major cities:** (1983 est.) Conakry (capital) 656,000.
● **PEOPLE Population:** 7,613,870 (July 2001 est.). **Nationality:** noun—Guinean(s); adjective—Guinean. **Ethnic groups:** 40% Peuhl, 30% Malinke, 20% Soussou, 10% smaller tribes. **Languages:** French (official), tribal languages. **Religions:** 85% Muslim, 8% Christian, 7% indigenous beliefs.
● **GOVERNMENT Type:** republic. **Independence:** Oct. 2, 1958 (from France). **Constitution:** Dec. 23, 1990. **National holiday:** Independence Day, Oct. 2. **Head of Government:** Lamine Sidimé, prime minister (since Mar. 1999). **Structure:** executive; unicameral legislature; judiciary.
● **ECONOMY Monetary unit:** Guinean franc.

Budget: (2000 est.) *income:* N.A.; *expend.:* $417.7 mil. **GDP:** $10 bil., $1,300 per capita (2000 est.). **Chief crops:** rice, coffee, pineapples; cattle, sheep, goats; timber. **Natural resources:** bauxite, iron ore, diamonds, gold, uranium. **Major industries:** bauxite mining, alumina, diamond mining. **Labor force:** 3 mil. (1999); 80% agriculture, 11% industry and commerce. **Exports:** $820 mil. (f.o.b., 2000 est.); bauxite (the world's second largest producer), alumina, diamonds, coffee, fish. **Imports:** $634 mil. (f.o.b., 2000 est.); petroleum products, metals, machinery and transport equipment, foodstuffs, textiles. **Major trading partners:** *exports:* U.S., Benelux, Ukraine; *imports:* France, Ivory Coast, U.S., Benelux.

Guinea was formed out of the remains of a series of empires that flourished in West Africa between the 10th and 15th centuries. Situated to the southwest of the Sahara desert on the west coast of Africa, Guinea was a crossroads of West African trade long before Europeans arrived.

French merchants began trading in what is now Guinea in the early 17th century. France began acquiring land in the area in the mid19th century, and in 1845 the territories were organized as a separate colony. The colony received the name French Guinea in 1893.

Most high political posts were held by Europeans until after World War II. In 1946 French Guinea became a territory in the federation of French West Africa. In September 1958 Guinea became the only French colony to reject membership in the Fifth French Republic, resulting in the severance of political ties with France. The territorial assembly proclaimed Guinean independence on Oct. 2, 1958, and a new government headed by Sékou Touré was formed on the same day.

Touré was adamant in his rejection of French colonialism, severing ties with France (1960-63) and soliciting economic and other assistance from the U.S.S.R., China, and the United States. Touré remained in power until his death in April 1984. Within a week, a military government headed by Gen. Lansana Conti took power and by 1987 had improved relations with France while introducing market mechanisms into the command economy. Conti was elected president in 1993 and in June 1995, in Guinea's first-ever multiparty election, his Unity Progress party took 71 of the 114 legislative seats. He was succeeded by Sidia Toure a year later.

▶ GUINEA-BISSAU
Republic of Guinea-Bissau
● **GEOGRAPHY Location:** northwestern coast of Africa. **Boundaries:** Senegal to E and S, Atlantic Ocean to W. **Total area:** 13,946 sq. mi. (36,120 sq km). **Coastline:** 217 mi. (350 km). **Comparative area:** slightly less than three times the size of Connecticut. **Land use:** 11% arable land; 1% permanent crops; 38% meadows and pastures; 38% forest and woodland; 12% other. **Major cities:** (1979 census) Bissau (capital) 109,214; Bafatá 13,429; Gabú 7,803; Mansoa 5,390; Catió 5,170.
● **PEOPLE Population:** 1,315,822 (July 2001 est.). **Nationality:** noun—Guinean(s); adjective—Guinean. **Ethnic groups:** about 99% African (30% Balanta, 20% Fula, 14% Manjaca, 13% Mandinga, 7% Papel); less than 1% European and mulatto. **Languages:** Portuguese (official), Criolo, numerous African languages. **Religions:** 50% indigenous beliefs, 45% Muslim, 5% Christian.
● **GOVERNMENT Type:** republic; multi-party since mid-1991. **Independence:** Sept. 24, 1973 (unilat-

erally declared by Guinea-Bissau); Sept. 10, 1974 (recognized by Portugal). **Constitution:** May 16, 1984, amended May 4, 1991, Dec. 4, 1991, Feb. 26, 1993, June 9, 1993, and 1996. **National holiday:** Independence Day, Sept. 24. **Heads of Government:** Kumba Yalá, president (since Feb. 2000); Faustino Fdut Imbali, prime minister (since Mar. 2001). **Structure:** executive; unicameral legislature; no judiciary (Ministry of Justice).

● **ECONOMY Monetary unit:** Communauté Financière Africaine (CFA) franc. **Budget:** N.A. **GDP:** $1.1 bil., $950 per capita (2000 est.). **Chief crops:** rice, corn, beans; fishing, forestry. **Natural resources:** fish, timber, phosphates, bauxite, unexploited deposits of petroleum. **Major industries:** agricultural processing, beer, soft drinks. **Labor force:** 480,000. **Exports:** $80 mil. (f.o.b., 2000 est.); 70% cashews, fish, peanuts. **Imports:** $55.2 mil. (f.o.b., 2000 est.); foodstuffs, transport equipment, petroleum products. **Major trading partners:** *exports:* 59% India, 12% Singapore, 10% Italy; *imports:* 26% Portugal, 8% France, 8% Senegal, 7% Netherlands.

The Portuguese began exploring and trading in what is now Guinea-Bissau in the 15th century and in 1630 began to exert administrative control over the territory. The area became the center of the Portuguese slave trade. When the slave trade declined in the 19th century, the coastal port of Bissau became a major commercial center. Later in the 19th century, the Portuguese began to conquer the interior of the territory and in 1879 consolidated the region into a territory called Portuguese Guinea, which in 1952 became an overseas province of Portugal.

A nationalist movement began in 1956 under the leadership of Amilcar Cabral and the African Party for the Independence of Guinea and Cape Verde (PAIGC). Armed insurrection broke out in 1961. By 1972 the PAIGC exerted influence over much of the country. Civilian rule was established in the territory that it controlled, and elections were held for a national assembly. Cabral was assassinated in 1973, but soon after the PAIGC National Assembly declared the independence of Guinea-Bissau from Portugal. Portugal acknowledged the country's new status on Sept. 24, 1973.

The civilian government was overthrown by a military coup in 1980, and the country was run by a Revolutionary Council headed by Brig. Gen. João Bernardo Vieira until a new constitution was adopted in May 1984. Under the new constitution, a new national assembly was selected, and Vieira was elected president in 1984 and 1989. In 1991 the government legalized opposition parties, but presidential elections were postponed.

In June 1998 a former army chief of staff, Ansumane Mane, launched a coup attempt against Vieira who was supported by loyalist troops and the Senegalese army. Hundreds of thousands fled the capital and the surrounding areas as the Senegalese shelled the city. By May 1999, General Mane had driven President-General Vieira to seek asylum with the Portuguese and had installed the leader of the National Popular Assembly, Malan Sanha, as interim president until he was defeated in Jan. 2000 by Kumba Yala.

▶ **GUYANA**
Co-operative Republic of Guyana
● **GEOGRAPHY Location:** northeastern South America. **Boundaries:** North Atlantic Ocean to N, Suriname to E, Brazil to S, Venezuela to W. **Total area:** 83,000 sq. mi. (214,970 sq km). **Coastline:** 285 mi. (459 km). **Comparative area:** slightly smaller than Idaho. **Land use:** 2% arable land; 6% meadows and pastures; 84% forest and woodland; 8% other; includes 1% irrigated. **Major cities:** (1976 est.) Georgetown (capital) 72,049.

● **PEOPLE Population:** 697,181 (July 2000 est.). **Nationality:** noun—Guyanese (sing., pl.); adjective—Guyanese. **Ethnic groups:** 49% East Indian, 32% black, 12% mixed, 6% Amerindian, 1% European and Chinese. **Languages:** English, Amerindian dialects. **Religions:** 50% Christian, 33% Hindu, 9% Muslim, 8% other.

● **GOVERNMENT Type:** republic within Commonwealth. **Independence:** May 26, 1966 (from U.K.). **Constitution:** Oct. 6. 1980. **National holiday:** Republic Day, Feb. 23. **Heads of Government:** Bharrat Jagdeo, executive president (since Aug. 2000); Samuel Hinds, prime minister (since Feb. 1998). **Structure:** executive—president, who appoints and heads cabinet; unicameral legislature; judiciary.

● **ECONOMY Monetary unit:** Guyanese dollar. **Budget:** (1997 est.) *income:* $220.1 mil.; *expend.:* $286.4 mil. **GDP:** $3.4 bil., $4,800 per capita (2000 est.). **Chief crops:** sugarcane, rice, wheat; beef, pork, poultry. **Natural resources:** bauxite, gold, diamonds, hardwood timber, shrimp, fish. **Major industries:** bauxite mining, sugar, rice milling. **Labor force:** 245,492 (1992). **Exports:** $570 mil. (f.o.b., 2000); sugar, gold, bauxite/alumina, rice, shrimp, molasses. **Imports:** $660 mil. (c.i.f., 2000); manufactures, machinery, food, petroleum. **Major trading partners:** (1994 est.); *exports:* 22% Canada, 22% U.S., 18% U.K.; *imports:* 28% U.S., 21% Trinidad and Tobago, 14% Netherlands Antilles.

Although the region was visited by Europeans in the 15th century, Guyana was only colonized in the early 1600's by the Dutch. Rule in the area was contested by the French and the British, and it became the colony of British Guiana in 1831. After slavery was abolished, indentured servants from the East Indies were brought to work the land, and their descendants are in the majority today.

The People's National Congress was in power from 1964 to 1992, and socialist policies dominated the political landscape. Most of the country's large companies were nationalized, so despite its having the purest bauxite in the world, some gold, and conditions favorable to agriculture, it remains poor, dependent on foreign aid and remittances from overseas workers for much of its revenue.

In 1992 Cheddi Jagan of the People's Progressive party won the presidency, but attempts to privatize the sugar and bauxite industries have failed. In March 1997 Jagan died and Samuel Hinds, the prime minister became president while Jagan's widow took over as prime minister. In the presidential elections in Dec. 1997, Mrs. Jagan won election in her own right, with 56 percent of the vote, but her appointment of Hinds to be Prime Minister did nothing to stop the rioting and demonstrations by followers of the opposition People's National Congress. The PNC represents, principally, black, while the PPP does the same for East Indians. In Aug. 1999, Jagan resigned for health reasons and was succeeded by Bharrat Jagdeo, a 35-year-old Moscow-educated economist.

▶ **HAITI**
Republic of Haiti
● **GEOGRAPHY Location:** western part of Hispaniola in northern Caribbean Sea. Port-au-Prince 18°33'N, 72°20'W. **Boundaries:** North Atlantic Ocean to N, Dominican Republic to E, Caribbean

Sea to S, Windward Passage to W. **Total area:** 10,714 sq. mi. (27,750 sq km). **Coastline:** 1,100 mi. (1,771 km). **Comparative area:** slightly smaller than Maryland. **Land use:** 20% arable land; 13% permanent crops; 18% meadows and pastures; 5% forest and woodland; 44% other; includes 3% irrigated. **Major cities:** (1984 est.) Port-au-Prince (capital) 738,342.

● **PEOPLE Population:** 6,964,549 (July 2001 est.). **Nationality:** noun—Haitian(s); adjective—Haitian. **Ethnic groups:** 95% black, 5% mulatto and European. **Languages:** French (official, but spoken by only 20% of population); all speak Creole. **Religions:** 80% Roman Catholic—of which majority also practice voodoo (called vodun), 16% Protestant.

● **GOVERNMENT Type:** republic. **Independence:** Jan. 1, 1804 (from France). **Constitution:** Mar. 1987, suspended June 1988; return to constitutional rule Oct. 1994. **National Holiday:** Independence Day, Jan. 1. **Heads of Government:** Jean-Bertrand Aristide, president (since Feb. 2001); Jean-Marie Chérestal, prime minister (since Mar. 2001). **Structure:** executive; bicameral legislature; judiciary.

● **ECONOMY Monetary unit:** gourde. **Budget:** (FY 97/98) *income:* $317 mil.; *expend.:* $362 mil. **GDP:** $12.7 bil., $1,800 per capita (2000 est.). **Chief crops:** coffee, mangoes, sugarcane, rice, corn, sorghum. **Natural resources:** bauxite, copper, calcium carbonate, gold, marble, hydropower. **Major industries:** sugar refining, textiles, flour milling. **Labor force:** 3.6 mil. (1995); 66% agriculture, 25% services, 9% industry; shortage of skilled labor, unskilled labor abundant; 66% unemployment (1999 est.). **Exports:** $185 mil. (f.o.b., 1999); light manufactures, coffee, other agriculture. **Imports:** $1.2 bil. (c.i.f., 1999); machines and manufactures, food and beverages, petroleum products. **Major trading partners:** *exports:* 89% U.S., 8% EU; *imports:* 60% U.S., 13% EU.

The Arawak island of Haiti was discovered by Christopher Columbus, who renamed it Hispaniola, in 1492. In the next century the Arawaks were worked to death, murdered, or killed by disease. The western third of the island was harassed by French pirates and was ceded to France in 1697. With a diverse slave-based agricultural economy, the colony accounted for two-thirds of French overseas investment.

A slave revolt in 1791 led to abolition in 1794, and the island came under French rule the same year. Toussaint Louverture, an ex-slave, became governor-general in 1801, but he was deposed by the French. In 1803 a black army under Jean-Jacques Dessalines (Emperor Jacques I, 1804-6) and Henry Christophe (Henry I, 1806-20) defeated the French in 1803. Independence was declared in 1804. Under Jean-Pierre Boyer (1820-43), Haiti occupied Santo Domingo (which had been restored to Spain in 1808) from 1822 to 1844.

The next century was marked by political instability and an increased U.S. business and military presence in Haitian affairs. From 1905 to 1947, the United States had direct or indirect control of Haitian finances, and from 1915 to 1934 the country was under U.S. military occupation.

François "Papa Doc" Duvalier took power in 1957 and ruled Haiti with a stern hand. In 1971, he transferred power to his son, Jean-Claude (aka "Baby Doc"), whose regime was just as authoritarian. Most of Haiti's wealthy and educated population fled the country, leaving it the poorest and most illiterate nation in the Western Hemisphere.

In 1986, the military ousted Baby Doc, and imposed a succession of short-lived but brutal and incompetent governments. In 1989, Supreme Court Justice Ertha-Pascal Troillot was named interim president, and in 1990, Haiti held its first democratic national elections ever. The winner of those elections was the Rev. Jean-Bertrand Aristide, a 37-year-old Roman Catholic priest. But seven months into his five-year term, Aristide was overthrown in yet another military coup. Aristide fled to the U.S., which refused to recognize the junta and suspended $650 million worth of aid to Haiti. But succesive trade embargoes by the United States, Canada, and most of Western Europe only served to increase hardship among the poorest segments of the population. The junta leaders, propped up by Haiti's wealthy elite and by money from drug trafficking, began a campaign of violence against Aristide supporters, killing more than 3,000 of them.

After many months of threats, the U.S. finally invaded on Oct. 15, 1994, forcing the junta's resignation and reinstating Aristide as president. Aristide disbanded the army altogether, replacing it with a civilian police force. In mid-1995, Aristide's three-party coalition, Lavalas Political Organization, won overwhelming victories; in December, the Lavalas candidate, René Préval, took 88 percent in Haiti's first peaceful presidential election since independence.

By 1997 Lavalas and Pres. Préval had split. From June of that year, Haiti was without a government until Jan. 1999 when Préval announced he would rule by decree, and appointed his own prime minister. The U.S. and the U.N. ended their military mission in early 2000. Senate elections were held in May, giving 16 of 17 contested seats to Lavalas candidates. But in run-off elections held in July, opposition candidates and international observers refused to participate because of irregularities in the earlier election. In November, with the opposition and international monitors boycotting, the presidential election returned Aristide with 92 percent, while in remaining run-offs, Lavalas won all 9 Senate races and took 80 percent of the Assembly votes. When in March 2001 Jean-Marie Cherestal was sworn in as premier, his cabinet included some opposition members, though the opposition Democratic Convergence coalition had named its own "parallel" president a month earlier.

▶ **HOLY SEE**
The Holy See (State of the Vatican City)

● **GEOGRAPHY Location:** entirely within city of Rome, Italy; outside Vatican City, 13 buildings in Rome and Castel Gandolfo (the pope's summer residence) enjoy extraterritorial rights. **Boundaries:** surrounded by Italian territory. **Total area:** 0.17 sq. mi. (0.44 sq km). **Coastline:** none. **Comparative area:** about seven-tenths size of the Mall in Washington, D.C. **Land use:** 0% arable land; 0% permanent crops; 0% meadows and pastures; 0% forest and woodland; 100% other. **Major cities:** Vatican City (capital).

● **PEOPLE Population:** 890 (July 2001 est.). **Nationality:** N.A. **Ethnic groups:** Italians, Swiss, other. **Languages:** Italian, Latin, various other languages. **Religion:** Roman Catholic.

● **GOVERNMENT Type:** monarchical-sacerdotal state. **Independence:** Feb. 11, 1929 (from Italy). **Constitution:** Apostolic Constitution of 1967 (effective Mar. 1, 1968). **National holiday:** Installation Day of Pope John Paul II, Oct. 22. **Heads of**

Government: John Paul II, supreme pontiff (Karol Wojtylla, elected pope Oct. 16, 1978); Archbishop Angelo Sodano, Pro-Secretary of State of the Holy See. **Structure:** pope possesses full executive, legislative, and judicial powers; he delegates these powers to president of Pontifical Commission, who is subject to pontifical appointment and recall; Secretariat of State and Council of Public Affairs (which handles Vatican diplomacy) and Prefecture of Economic Affairs; College of Cardinals acts as chief papal adviser.

● **ECONOMY Monetary unit:** Vatican issues its own coinage called Vatican lira, which is interchangeable with Italian lira. **Budget:** (1997 est.) *income:* $209.6 mil.; *expend.:* $198.6 mil., supported financially by contributions (known as Peter's Pence) from Roman Catholics throughout world; some income derived from sale of Vatican postage stamps and tourist mementos, fees for admission to museums, and sale of publications. **GDP:** N.A. **Chief crops:** N.A. **Natural resources:** N.A. **Major industries:** consists of printing and production of small amount of mosaics and staff uniforms; worldwide banking and financial activities. **Labor force:** N.A.; dignitaries, priests, nuns, guards, and 3,000 lay workers who live outside the Vatican; Vatican City employees are divided into three categories—executives, office workers, and salaried employees. **Exports:** N.A. **Imports:** N.A. **Major trading partners:** N.A.

The Holy See is the smallest sovereign state in the world both in size and in population. It is a remnant of the "Patrimony of St. Peter," the secular state donated to the popes in the eighth century by Pepin the Short, father of Charlemagne. One of the major political powers on the Italian peninsula throughout the Middle Ages and into modern times, the States of the Church were conquered in 1870 by the new kingdom of Italy, which made Rome its capital.

In 1929 Mussolini's government made peace with the papacy in the Lateran Treaty, which recognized the Holy See as an independent state. The treaty was incorporated into the Italian Constitution of 1947. Under the terms of the treaty, the pope is pledged to perpetual neutrality and may intervene in international affairs as a mediator only upon request.

The pope is the sovereign of the Holy See in his capacity as bishop of Rome, and in that capacity, he accepts the credentials of foreign ambassadors assigned to the Holy See. The United States opened diplomatic relations with the Holy See in 1984, following the repeal of an 1867 law forbidding such relations. Pope John Paul II, a native of Poland, has been a source of spiritual leadership especially for Catholics in Eastern Europe. Since the collapse of communism in Eastern Europe, many countries there have renewed diplomatic relations with the Holy See. In a historic breakthrough the Holy See established diplomatic relations with Israel on Dec. 30, 1993.

As sovereign of the Holy See, the pope is an elected absolute monarch who appoints a Pontifical Council to govern the city on his behalf. The council meets only a few times each year. The economy is based on service industries, including printing; its revenues come from museum fees, philatelic sales, and sales of publications.

▶ HONDURAS
Republic of Honduras
● **GEOGRAPHY Location:** Central America. **Boundaries:** Caribbean Sea to N, Nicaragua to E, El Salvador, Nicaragua to S, Guatemala, El Salvador to W. **Total area:** 43,278 sq. mi. (112,090 sq km). **Coastline:** 509 mi. (820 km). **Comparative area:** slightly larger than Tennessee. **Land use:** 15% arable land; 3% permanent crops; 14% meadows and pastures; 54% forest and woodland; 14% other; includes 1% irrigated. **Major cities:** (1994 est.) Tegucigalpa (capital) 775,300; San Pedro Sula 368,500; El Progreso 81,200; Danli 43,300; Choluteca 72,800.

● **PEOPLE Population:** 6,406,052 (July 2001 est.). **Nationality:** noun—Honduran(s); adjective—Honduran. **Ethnic groups:** 90% mestizo, 7% Amerindian, 2% black, 1% white. **Languages:** Spanish, Amerindian dialects. **Religions:** 97% Roman Catholic, small Protestant minority.

● **GOVERNMENT Type:** democratic constitutional republic. **Independence:** Sept. 15, 1821 (from Spain). **Constitution:** Jan. 11, 1982 (effective Jan. 20, 1982). **National holiday:** Independence Day, Sept. 15. **Head of Government:** Carlos Roberto Flores Facussé, president (since Jan. 1998). **Structure:** executive—elected president; unicameral legislature (128-seat National Congress); elected judicial branch.

● **ECONOMY Monetary unit:** lempira. **Budget:** (1999 est.) *income:* $607 mil.; *expend.:* $411.9 mil. **GDP:** $17 bil., $2,700 per capita (2000 est.). **Chief crops:** bananas, coffee, citrus; beef; timber; shrimp. **Natural resources:** timber, gold, silver, copper, lead. **Major industries:** agricultural processing (sugar and coffee), textiles, clothing. **Labor force:** 2.3 mil. (1997); 29% agriculture, 60% services, 21% industry; 30% underemployment (1997). **Exports:** $2 bil. (f.o.b., 2000 est.); bananas, coffee, shrimp, lobster. **Imports:** $2.8 bil. (f.o.b., 2000 est.); machinery and transport equipment, chemicals, basic manufactures. **Major trading partners:** *exports:* 35.4% U.S., 7.5% Germany, Belgium; *imports:* 47.1% U.S., 7.4% Guatemala, 5.9% El Salvador.

Early in the Christian era, the Mayan civilization extended south to the pre-Columbian city of Copán in what is now northwestern Honduras. The territory was also home to the Lenca Indians and the indigenous people of the Moskitia area.

A silver strike in the 1570's prompted the first major influx of Spanish. The region was also celebrated for its tropical hardwood forests. Although the British controlled the Caribbean coast in the late 1700's, Honduras was a province of the Spanish captaincy of Guatemala. It became a member of the United Provinces of Central America after independence from Spain and Mexico, and an independent republic after the 1838 collapse of the Central American Federation.

Conservatives dominated Honduran politics until the 1870's, when the Liberals came to power and adopted a new constitution that reduced the influence of the church, among other things. Economic development came especially from a number of U.S. firms whose efforts were regarded as exploitative rather than beneficial; in 1912, U.S. president William Howard Taft sent marines to protect U.S. interests.

Political unrest continued until the presidency of Gen. Tiburcio Carías Andino (1932-49), who was followed by a succession of pro-labor presidents. In 1963, a coup led by Col. Osvaldo López Arellano deposed the civilian president, and the military ruled almost uninterrupted until 1982. In 1969, the expulsion of thousands of Salvadoran peasants who had immigrated during the 1950's and 1960's led to the Soccer War with El Salvador. An armistice was negotiated by the OAS.

During the 1980's, Honduras was threatened by civil wars in El Salvador and Nicaragua. Honduran territory was used by Nicaraguan Contras, for which Honduras received substantial U.S. military and other aid. Demobilization of the Contras alleviated tensions between Left and Right, and in Jan. 1994 the new president, Carlos Roberto Reina Idiaquez, took office with the promise of controlling and reducing the power of the military which was more easily accomplished when the U.S. made severe cuts in military aid. In late 1997 the same Liberal Party easily won reelection, maintaining their control of the National Congress, while their candidate, Carlos Roberto Flores, won election as president.

In Oct. 1999, Honduras was devastated by Hurricane Mitch: 7,000 were dead, 600,000 homeless, and 70 percent of its crops destroyed — losses which were somewhat mitigated by international aid and debt reductions. Significantly, in Jan. 1999, the legislature unanimously voted to place the previously all-but-autonomous military under civilian control, control that the military has thus far given every sign of accepting.

▶ **HUNGARY**
Republic of Hungary
● **GEOGRAPHY   Location:** landlocked country in eastern Europe. **Boundaries:** Slovakia to N, Ukraine to NE, Romania to E, Yugoslavia to SE, Croatia to SW, Slovenia to W, Austria to NW. **Total area:** 35,919 sq. mi. (93,030 sq km). **Coastline:** none. **Comparative area:** slightly smaller than Indiana. **Land use:** 51% arable land; 3.6% permanent crops; 12.4% meadows and pastures; 19% forest and woodland; 14% other; includes 2% irrigated. **Major cities:** (1994) Budapest (capital) 1,995,696; Debrecen 217,706; Miskole 189,655; Szeged 178,878; Pécs 172,177.
● **PEOPLE   Population:** 10,106,017 (July 2001 est.). **Nationality:** noun—Hungarian(s); adjective—Hungarian. **Ethnic groups:** 89.9% Hungarian, 4% Gypsy, 2.6% German, 2% Serb, 0.8% Slovak, 0.7% Romanian. **Languages:** 98.2% Hungarian, 1.8% other. **Religions:** 67.5% Roman Catholic, 20.0% Calvinist, 5.0% Lutheran, 7.5% atheist and other.
● **GOVERNMENT   Type:** parliamentary democracy. **Constitution:** Aug. 18, 1949; effective Aug. 20, 1949; revised Oct. 18, 1989; 1997 amendment streamlined judicial system. **National holiday:** St. Stephen's Day, Aug. 20. **Heads of Government:** Ferenc Mádl, president (since Aug 2000); Viktor Orbán, prime minister (since July 1998). **Structure:** executive—president elected by National Assembly; unicameral legislature—National Assembly (elected by direct suffrage); judicial—elected by Parliament.
● **ECONOMY   Monetary unit:** forint. **Budget:** (2000 est.) *income:* $13 bil.; *expend.:* $14.4 bil. **GDP:** $113.9 bil., $11,200 per capita (2000 est.). **Chief crops:** corn, wheat, sunflower seeds, potatoes, sugar beets; chickens, pigs, cattle. **Natural resources:** bauxite, coal, natural gas, fertile soils. **Major industries:** mining, metallurgy, construction materials. **Labor force:** 4.2 mil. (1997); 65% services; 27% industry; 8% agriculture; 10% unemployment (1999). **Exports:** $25.2 bil. (f.o.b., 2000); 59.5% machinery and equipment, 29.4% other manufactures, 6.9% agriculture and food products. **Imports:** $27.6 bil. (f.o.b., 2000); 57.1% machinery and equipment, 35.9% other manufactures, 8.1% fuels and electricity, 2.8% agricul-

tural and food products, 3.0% raw materials. **Major trading partners:** *exports:* Germany, Austria, Italy.

The Magyars, a tribe of Central Asian horsemen, terrorized Europe in the ninth century A.D. and settled in the Hungarian plain where, under their chieftain Arpad, they displaced earlier Germanic and Slavic settlers and organized a kingdom in 896. The Hungarians converted to Christianity late in the 10th century, and King Stephen (later St. Stephen) received a royal crown from Pope Sylvester II in 1001.

After the Battle of Mohacs in 1526, most of Hungary fell under Ottoman rule. The Turks were driven out in a series of battles with the Habsburg Holy Roman emperors at the end of the 17th century. Thereafter Hungary was part of the Habsburg Empire until 1867, when the Dual Monarchy of Austria-Hungary was organized, making Hungary independent of Austria in all but finance, the military, and foreign affairs.

During the 18th and 19th centuries, Hungary experienced extensive immigration of Romanians from the east and Slovaks from the north; by 1900 Magyars formed only a bare majority of the population. The pre-World War I economy was largely agricultural. Agriculture-related industry (beet sugar factories, breweries, tanneries, textile mills) developed in the late 19th century, along with some heavy industry.

In the dismemberment of Austria-Hungary following the defeat of the Central Powers in World War I, Hungary surrendered extensive territories to Romania, Yugoslavia, and Czechoslovakia. With the Treaty of Trianon ("Bloody Trianon") in 1920, the country lost 70 percent of its territory and 60 percent of its population; one-third of the Magyar people lived on foreign soil.

Short-lived governments—a republic under Michael Karolyi, and a Bolshevist state under Bela Kun—were replaced in 1920 by a new regime, with Adm. Miklós Horthy serving as regent. The Horthy regime was authoritarian but not fascist; its main objective was the recovery of Hungary's lost territories. Hungary established common cause with Germany in 1938 and 1940, recovering some territory from Czechoslovakia and Romania in the bargain, but at the price of participating in Hitler's war with the Soviet Union. Germany occupied Hungary in 1944 and set up a Hungarian Nazi regime. Late in 1944 the Russian army drove out the Germans and set up their own occupation.

The establishment of a full-scale Soviet-satellite regime was relatively slow. A republic was declared in February 1946, and the non-Communist Zoltan Tildy was elected president. Tildy was forced out in 1947, however, and replaced by the Stalinist dictator, Matias Rakosi. After the death of Stalin in 1953, the moderate Imre Nagy became premier and introduced some economic reforms. Nagy was forced out of office in 1955.

Nikita Khrushchev's denunciation of Stalin in 1956, combined with rising expectations for reforms in Hungary, led to a popular uprising in October 1956. Nagy, backed by the army, formed a coalition government on Oct. 23, proclaimed Hungary's neutrality, ended censorship, opened the borders, and withdrew from the Warsaw Pact. On Nov. 4, Soviet troops launched a massive invasion that crushed the rebellion. The Soviet army installed János Kádár as premier; Nagy was executed. About 200,000 Hungarians fled the country, and many more were imprisoned.

After several years of repressive rule, the Kádár regime announced, in 1963, amnesty for participants in the 1956 rebellion. Stalinists were gradually removed from the government, economic reforms emphasizing profit and productivity were introduced, and trade with the West was expanded. Hungary reluctantly took part in the suppression of Czechoslovakia's "Prague Spring" in 1968. In the same year, it announced the New Economic Mechanism (NEM) policy, ending central economic planning and introducing semifree enterprise under bureaucratic control.

After a brief return to central planning in the 1970's, the NEM was reintroduced in 1979 and expanded in 1982, when Hungary joined the World Bank and the I.M.F. Private ownership of subsidiaries of state-owned enterprises was permitted. In 1987 a pro-Gorbachev premier, Karoly Grosz, took office and in 1988 became head of the Communist party as well.

In 1989 the boundary with Austria was opened, making Hungary a key escape point for refugees from East Germany and Czechoslovakia. Nagy's reburial was attended by 300,000. Free elections were held in 1990, and the Democratic Forum, led by Jozsef Antall, won a plurality and formed a coalition government with the Smallholders and Christian Democratic parties. Having already achieved substantial perestroika-style economic reforms under communism, Hungary was well-placed to make a rapid transition to free enterprise and was seeking admission to the E.U. Sluggish production reduced tax revenues, resulting in serious deficits and an austerity budget.

Hungarian voters signaled just how painful they found the transition in the May 1994 parliamentary elections by giving the Communists (now renamed Socialists) an absolute majority in Parliament. Privatization moved at a snail's pace, though the new government did appoint a committee to arrange the selling off of about 1,000 state-owned enterprises and soon foreign investment increased faster than anywhere in Central Europe. In 1997 Hungary was one of three eastern European nations invited to apply for admission to NATO and it was admitted in 1999.

Elections in May 1998 gave the Socialists only 134 seats (of 386) in Parliament; the new government was formed by Civic Party which won 148 seats of its own, in coalition with the Smallholders and other parties of the right. Hungary now aims for admission to the E.U.

▶ **ICELAND**
Republic of Iceland
● **GEOGRAPHY Location:** near Arctic Circle in North Atlantic Ocean. Reykjavík 64°09'N, 21°58'W. **Boundaries:** Greenland about 190 mi. (300 km) to NW, Norway about 620 mi. (1,000 km) to E, U.K. 500 mi. (800 km) to S. **Total area:** 39,768 sq. mi. (103,000 sq km). **Coastline:** 3,100 mi. (4,988 km). **Comparative area:** slightly smaller than Kentucky. **Land use:** 0% arable land; 0% permanent crops; 23% meadows and pastures; 1% forest and woodland; 76% other. **Major cities:** (1994 est.) Reykjavík (capital) 103,020.
● **PEOPLE Population:** 277,906 (July 2001 est.). **Nationality:** noun—Icelander(s); adjective—Icelandic. **Ethnic groups:** homogeneous mixture of descendants of Norwegians and Celts. **Languages:** Icelandic (official). **Religions:** 91% Evangelical Lutheran, other Protestant and Roman Catholic, no affiliation.
● **GOVERNMENT Type:** constitutional republic. **Independence:** June 17, 1944 (from Denmark).

Constitution: June 16, 1944; effective June 17, 1944. **National holiday:** Anniversary of the Establishment of the Republic, June 17. **Heads of Government:** Ólafur Ragnar Grímsson, president (since Aug. 1996); David Oddsson, prime minister (since Apr. 1991). **Structure:** executive power vested in president but exercised by cabinet responsible to Parliament; unicameral legislature; judiciary (Supreme Court justices appointed for life by president).
● **ECONOMY Monetary unit:** Icelandic króna. **Budget:** (1999 est.) *income:* $3.5 bil.; *expend.:* $3.3 bil. **GDP:** $6.85 bil., $24,800 per capita (2000 est.). **Chief crops:** potatoes, turnips; cattle, sheep; fish. **Natural resources:** fish, hydroelectric and geothermal power, diatomite. **Major industries:** fish processing, aluminum smelting, ferrosilicon production. **Labor force:** 159,000 (2000); 12.9% manufacturing; 11.8% fishing and fish processing; 10.7% construction, 5.1% agriculture, 59.5% other services; 2.4% unemployment (1999). **Exports:** $2 bil. (f.o.b. 2000); 70% fish and fish products, animal products, aluminum, ferrosilicon, diatomite. **Imports:** $2.2 bil. (f.o.b., 2000); machinery and equipment, petroleum products, foodstuffs, textiles. **Major trading partners:** *exports:* 64% EU, 15% U.S.; *imports:* 56% EU, 11% U.S.

The volcanic island of Iceland was settled in the ninth century A.D. by Vikings, who established Europe's oldest body of representative government, the Althing, in 930. Christianity was introduced around 1000. In the 13th century, Iceland acknowledged Norwegian rule. In 1380 Denmark, by then in control of all of Scandinavia, conquered Iceland as well. Iceland gained its independence in 1918 but shared a common king, Christian X, with the Danes. During World War II, first British, and then American, troops garrisoned the island; in 1944, with Denmark occupied by the Nazis, Iceland deposed its king and proclaimed itself a republic.

Iceland became a U.N. member in 1946 and a member of NATO in 1949. Lacking its own armed forces, it grudgingly tolerated the presence of an American air base at Keflavik. The republic developed a Scandinavian-style welfare state, with comprehensive social benefits that have produced one of the world's healthiest and best-educated peoples.

Less than 1 percent of Iceland's territory is arable; the island imports grain and vegetables but is self-sufficient in meat and dairy products. Fishing is the principal industry, accounting for 75 percent of exports, 20 percent of GDP, and engaging one-seventh of the work force.

Multiparty representation in the Althing has created a trend of government by coalitions or minority cabinets. Politically stable, the republic recently faced economic problems brought on by high taxes, chronic inflation, and a huge national debt. In 1997 and 1998, however, the economy made a strong recovery with GDP growing by 5 percent a year.

Iceland maintains close ties with Scandinavia and actively participates in the Nordic Council, but not the EU, membership in which the government views as harmful to Iceland's all-important fishing industry.

▶ **INDIA**
Republic of India
● **GEOGRAPHY Location:** Asian subcontinent, with Himalayan mountain range to N. **Boundaries:** Pakistan to NW; China, Bhutan, Nepal to N; Myanmar to NE; Bangladesh to E (surrounded by Indian territory except for short frontier with

Myanmar); Bay of Bengal to E; Sri Lanka to SE across Palk Strait; Arabian Sea to W. **Total area:** 1,269,340 sq. mi. (3,287,590 sq km). **Coastline:** 4,350 mi. (7,000 km). **Comparative area:** slightly more than one-third the size of U.S. **Land use:** 56% arable land; 1% permanent crops; 4% meadows and pastures; 23% forest and woodland; 16% other; includes 13% irrigated. **Major cities:** (1991 census) New Delhi (capital) · 7,174,755; Greater Bombay 9,909,547; Calcutta 4,388,262; Madras 3,795,208; Hyderabad 3,005,496.

• **People   Population:** 1,029,991,145 (July 2001 est.). **Nationality:** noun—Indian(s); adjective—Indian. **Ethnic groups:** 72% Indo-Aryan, 25% Dravidian, 3% Mongoloid and other. **Languages:** Hindi, English, and 14 other official languages; 24 languages spoken by a million or more persons each; numerous other languages and dialects; Hindi is national language and primary tongue of 30% of the people; English enjoys associate status but is the most important language for national, political, and commercial communication; Hindustani, a variant of Hindi/Urdu, is spoken throughout northern India. **Religions:** 80% Hindu, 14% Muslim, 2.4% Christian, 2% Sikh.

• **Government   Type:** federal republic. **Independence:** Aug. 15, 1947 (from U.K.). **Constitution:** Jan. 26, 1950. **National holiday:** Anniversary of the Proclamation of the Republic, Jan. 26. **Heads of Government:** K.R. Narayanan, president (since July 1997); A. B. Vajpayee, prime minister (since March 1998). **Structure:** executive; bicameral parliament—Council of States, 250 members, up to 12 appointed by pres., remainder chosen by regionally elected officials; judiciary.

• **Economy   Monetary unit:** Indian rupee. **Budget:** (FY 00/01 est.) *income:* $44.3 bil.; *expend.:* $73.6 bil. **GDP:** $2.2 trillion, $2,200 per capita (2000 est.). **Chief crops:** rice, wheat, oilseed, cotton; cattle, water, buffalo, sheep; fish. **Natural resources:** coal (4th largest reserves in world), iron ore, manganese, mica, bauxite. **Major industries:** textiles, chemicals, food processing, steel. **Labor force:** NA; 67% agriculture, 18% services, 15% industry. **Exports:** $43.1 bil. (f.o.b., 2000 est.); clothing, gems and jewelry, engineering goods, chemicals. **Imports:** $60.8 bil. (f.o.b., 2000 est.); petroleum, machinery, gems, fertilizer. **Major trading partners:** *exports:* 22% U.S., 6% U.K., 5% Germany, 5% Hong Kong; *imports:* 9% U.S., 8% Benelux, 6% U.K., 6% Saudi Arabia.

Indian civilization is one of the oldest in the world. Neolithic agricultural communities had appeared in the Indus River valley by 3000 B.C. and cities at Harappa and Mohenjo-Daro were founded around 2500 B.C. Around 1500 B.C. Indo-Europeans (Aryans) from Central Asia imposed their religion and political system on the indigenous population and generated population movements toward southern India.

Indo-European civilization was characterized by caste; everyone was a member of one of four fundamental divisions of society: Brahmins, hereditary priests responsible for higher learning and rituals; Ksatrias, warriors and administrators; Vaisas, merchants; and Sudras, farmers and subjugated peoples. At the bottom were casteless people, known later as untouchables.

By the mid-first millennium B.C., Brahminism had declined into a state of religious formalism. That situation prompted two reformations around 600 B.C., the first of which produced the Jain religion; the second, Buddhism. Jainism remained confined largely to India, while Buddhism eventually influenced most of the cultures of Asia, though it died out in India itself. Buddhism was adopted as a state religion by Asoka, third and greatest emperor of the Mauryan empire (325-184 b.c) under which much of India was united for the first time. Following the collapse of the Mauryan empire, Hinduism evolved out of Buddism, Brahminism, and other local cults and became the dominant religion of India.

South India in the post-Mauryan period was divided into numerous states, the most prominent of which was Chola, a Tamil kingdom in the southeast that had extensive trade connections throughout the Indian Ocean.

The Gupta dynasty (c. A.D. 320-544), based in the Ganges River valley, established its rule over most of northern India and created what is generally regarded as a golden age of north Indian culture, with flourishing cities and significant achievements in art, literature, and science.

In the seventh century, King Sri Harsha created a short-lived feudal empire that united most of the petty states in the upper Ganges valley, while the Chalyuka dynasty dominated southern India. In the early eighth century, the Indus River valley was invaded by Arabs who introduced Islam to the region. The empire of Sri Harsha fell apart, replaced by the petty kingdoms of the Rajputs.

The 11th century saw the ascendency of Islam throughout northern India, which came under the shadow of the empire of Mamud of Ghazni, based in Afghanistan. In 1192 the Ghaznavid general Kutb ud-din Aibak defeated a coalition of Rajput states; in 1206 he founded the Sultanate of Delhi, which in the 13th century held off Mongol invasions in northwestern India and brought all of the subcontinent, except for the southernmost states, under its control. While the rulers of the sultanate were Muslims, most of their subjects remained Hindu.

Internal rebellions combined with the sacking of Delhi by Timur Leng (Tamerlane) in 1398 weakened the Sultanate of Delhi. In 1526 Babur, a descendant of Timur Leng, conquered all of northern India and established the Moghul empire. Under Akbar the Great, the empire flourished; Moghul culture gave rise to new styles of architecture, painting, and music.

In the 17th century, the Moghul emperors were threatened by the Hindu Marathas, whose kingdom on the west-central coast rapidly encompassed most of south India. By the late 18th century, Maratha power had spread to the north, and most of the petty kingdoms of the Moghul empire became part of a Maratha confederacy, owing only nominal allegiance to Delhi. By that time all of India was threatened by the expansion of the European powers.

Vasco da Gama had landed at Calicut in 1498, and in 1510 the Portuguese founded a colony at Goa. Dutch traders competed with the Portuguese during the 16th century, and British and French merchants followed in the 17th century. British trading stations were established at Surat (1612), Bombay (1661), and Calcutta (1690). In the mid-18th century, war broke out between British and French forces in India, and the French were confined to a few small enclaves. The growing instability of the Moghul empire in the face of Marathan and Rajput revolts and the expansion of the southern kingdom of Mysore encouraged the British to seek further control of Indian territory. Robert Clive's victory at Plassey in 1757 brought Orissa, Bihar, and Bengal under British control; British rule was extended to the upper Ganges in

1775. Victory over the maharaja of Mysore in 1792 paved the way for British control over the south.

British parliamentary acts of 1773 and 1784 placed these acquisitions firmly under government control, and in 1803 the Moghul emperor accepted the offer of a protectorate, and British suzerainty in India was assured. After a protracted war, 1812-23, Marathan resistance to British control was broken. The first Anglo-Afghan War, 1838-42, was inconclusive in Afghanistan but led to consolidation of British control of the Punjab.

In 1833 Parliament assumed political control of British interests in South Asia, while private merchants had unrestricted access to the economy. Plantation crops, such as opium and cotton, began to displace agriculture, which made India more dependent on imported goods.

In 1857 Indian troops in the British colonial forces staged a mutiny in north-central India that lasted 14 months. In 1858 the Moghul empire was dissolved, as was the East India Company. The government of India was made directly subject to the British Crown, which exercised control through a viceroy and through the British Colonial Office. Queen Victoria was crowned empress of India in 1877.

British sovereignty in India—the raj—was a patchwork of direct and indirect rule. In general, coastal areas, river valleys, and strategic frontier regions were ruled by British authorities, while interior states continued as British protectorates controlled by British advisers to native princes. In 1861 Indians were appointed to advisory councils of the viceroy and provincial governors.

The Indian National Congress was organized in 1885. In the wake of popular demonstrations in 1905, elections were instituted to choose Indian members of the viceroy's legislative council. Separate electorates were created for the Muslim and Hindu communities, formalizing a divisive force in Indian politics and weakening opposition to British rule. In 1914, with Chinese loss of control in Tibet, India's northern boundary was pushed forward to the McMahon Line, following the highest peaks in the Himalayas. This set the stage for numerous later boundary disputes between China and India, Pakistan, and Burma.

The Government of India Act of 1919 transferred some political power to elected provincial officials but left the appointed British governors firmly in control. In that year Mohandas K. Gandhi organized the first passive-resistance campaigns and was imprisoned. In 1935 the Government of India Act created elected provincial legislatures. In the first elections (1937) the Congress party under Jawaharlal Nehru won control of seven of the 11 provinces. Nehru's goal of a united Indian opposition to British rule was thwarted by Mohammed Ali Jinnah's Muslim League, which demanded the creation of a separate Muslim state.

During World War II, the British military position in South Asia was complicated by calls for Indian independence. An offer of local autonomy, with independence to follow, was spurned by Nehru, and an Indian National army under Subhas Bose fought with the Japanese. Jinnah's call for an independent Pakistan was greatly enhanced by his support of the British.

In 1947, the British raj became two independent nations, predominantly Hindu India and predominantly Muslim Pakistan. Despite its considerable stature in the international community at large, India has been troubled by a number of disputes with its neighbors and separatist movements within its own borders. Following independence hundreds of semiautonomous princely states were brought under control of the central government. The French ceded their remaining trading colonies in the 1950's, and Portugal gave up Goa in 1961. In 1962, India warred with China in a still unresolved dispute over their border along Kashmir and Assam. The state of Bhutan was granted independence in 1971, and in 1974 Sikkim was annexed and its monarchy abolished.

India's most intractable disputes have been with Pakistan. Immediately after independence, Hindus in Pakistan and Muslims in India were set upon by the majority populations; hundreds of thousands were killed, and at least 12 million refugees fled over the border in both directions. On Jan. 30, 1948, Gandhi was assassinated by a Hindu extremist who blamed him for partition.

In granting independence, Britain had divided states of Bengal and Punjab between the two countries, but fighting erupted over the status of Jammu and Kashmir, and a cease-fire line negotiated by the U.N. in 1949 has never been ratified as a formal national boundary. In 1989, separatists in the Indian part of Kashmir began calling for an end to Indian rule, and relations with Pakistan have worsened as India accused its neighbor of providing support for the guerrillas. In 1971, after 10 million refugees poured across its border, India intervened in the Pakistani civil war in an action that prompted an almost immediate cease-fire and the creation of an independent Bangladesh.

India's main separatist movement involves Sikh separatists in the Punjab who seek the formation of an independent state of Khalistan, but who are thought to be supported by Pakistan. The government is also contending with separatist movements in the northeastern states of Assam and its neighbor Nagaland.

The British legacy in India included a sizable national elite, well educated and committed to principles of parliamentary democracy. The English language linked the elites of India's linguistically diverse regions, easing minorities' fears of domination by a Hindi-speaking majority. India's economy had seen some industrial development under the British, but its infrastructure was geared to integration in a colonial empire rather than to independence. Port cities, heavy industry, and plantation agriculture coexisted with widespread rural poverty and the years following independence saw a massive migration of the rural poor into overburdened cities.

Under Prime Minister Jawaharlal Nehru, India assumed a leadership role in the world movement of nonaligned nations and followed a policy of neutrality in international affairs. The development of good relations between the United States and Pakistan led to correspondingly difficult U.S.-India relations. In August 1971 India signed a 20-year friendship treaty with the Soviet Union.

Nehru died on May 27, 1964, and was succeeded by Lal Bahadur Shastri. Nehru's daughter, Mrs. Indira Gandhi, was named prime minister on Jan. 19, 1966. In 1967 the dominant Congress party faced electoral setbacks; in 1969 it split into "Old" and "New" wings. Mrs. Gandhi's New Congress party won control of the legislature.

Faced with protests and strikes after the New Congress party was convicted of voting irregularities in 1975, Mrs. Gandhi declared a state of emergency in June; censorship was imposed, thousands were arrested for political offenses, and various economic-control measures were adopted. An opposition coalition led by the Janata

Dal party won a massive victory in parliamentary elections in 1977. Mrs. Gandhi was driven from office, and the state of emergency was annulled. Mrs. Gandhi's party was returned to power in 1980, and she resumed the prime ministership. After an army attack on the Sikhs' Golden Temple in Amritsar, Gandhi was assassinated by Sikh bodyguards in October 1984. She was succeeded in office by her son, Rajiv, who placed the Punjab under direct control of the federal government.

On Dec. 3, 1984, methyl isocyanate gas leaked from a Union Carbide plant in Bhopal, killing over 2,500 people. The accident prompted a broad inquiry into industrial safety standards in India.

Indian troops, in July 1987, intervened in the growing civil war in Sri Lanka between the government and Tamil separatists. A negotiated truce under Indian auspices broke down, and Indian troops were involved in the conflict until their withdrawal in late 1989.

In November 1989, Rajiv Gandhi's Congress party was voted out of office in general elections after people close to the government were accused of taking kickbacks in a government arms purchase scandal. Gandhi was succeeded by V.P. Singh of the Janata Dal party, whose government collapsed after 11 months over a dispute involving Hindu plans to build a temple on the site of a mosque in Ayodhya. (Hindus contend the mosque was built on the site of Rama's birthplace.) Middle-class Hindus also protested an affirmative action policy to set aside federal government jobs for members of lower castes.

Singh was followed by Chandra Shekhar, whose minority government served only with the backing of the Congress party. After a parliamentary boycott by the Congress party instigated by Rajiv Gandhi, Shekhar quit the government in March 1991, agreeing to stay on as a caretaker until the May election. The election, postponed two weeks following the assassination of Gandhi, was won by the Congress party, and P.V. Narasimha Rao became prime minister.

During 1992 the Rao government attempted to foster economic growth by relaxing the centralized planning and controls on international trade and investment that had long stifled the nation's potential. This policy produced impressive economic gains despite a concurrent rise in corruption-related scandals.

A rise in Hindu extremist feeling, however, strengthened the hand of the opposition Bharatiya Janata party. On Dec. 6, 1992, a Hindu mob demolished a mosque built several hundred years earlier on a Hindu sacred site in the city of Ayodhya; in the ensuing turmoil, riots broke out in dozens of cities, most notably Bombay, leading to the deaths of hundreds of Muslims at the hands of Hindu attackers. A series of bomb explosions killed hundreds in Bombay on Mar.12, 1993, while dozens more were killed by an explosion in Calcutta four days later. Further riots followed, amid unsubstantiated accusations that Muslims, aided by Pakistan, were responsible for the explosions.

In 1993 separatist movements in Punjab and Assam waned, but violence in Kashmir and Jammu increased dramatically; despite several attempts by India and Pakistan to institute effective talks on the issue, violence continued unabated with loss of life in the hundreds if not thousands.

The Rao government's economic policies produced good results, but as India's economy strengthened its political stability weakened. The Congress Party continued to lose power to the Hindu Baratiya Janata Party. Congress was defeated in parliamentary elections in May 1996, ushering in an era of short-lived, weak coalition governments under Pres. K. R. Narayanan. Inder Kumer Gurjal formed a government in April, 1997 that fell in November. The BJP won a plurality of seats in March 1998 elections, but, to govern (under Prime Minister Vajapyee) required a 19-party coalition. Fragile authority need not exclude vigorous policy: it was the BJP coalition that carried out underground tests of five nuclear devices in May, vigorously asserted India's claims in Kashmir, and cut food subsidies as a means of reducing the deficit. It was the latter that dislodged the coalition and in April 1999, Pres. Narayanan dissolved the Lok Sabha, preparatory to India's third election campaign in three years. Perhaps sensing weakness, Muslim insurgents launched attacks against Indian forces in Kashmir. But India retaliated forcefully and peace was restored in July, although India continued to blame Pakistan for the violence. In the election results, the National Democratic Alliance, a 24-party coalition led by the Bharatiya Janata Party, won an absolute majority; so, for the first time in 27 years, an incumbent prime minister won re-election.

Despite this recent instability, India has enjoyed significant domestic and international achievements in the first 50 years after independence. The nation's territory was consolidated, and separatist movements in various provinces successfully resisted. The federal parliamentary system has proved workable, and the federal government has established its constitutional right to intervene in state affairs under some conditions. India's armed forces are large, well trained, and well equipped, with some nuclear capability. India has maintained watchful, but generally peaceful, relations with two unfriendly neighbors, Pakistan and China. The Green Revolution of the 1970's made the country self-sufficient in food for the first time since the 19th century. India has a large, well-educated middle class and a growing industrial economy.

▶ INDONESIA
Republic of Indonesia

• **GEOGRAPHY Location:** archipelago of about 13,700 islands stretching from Malay peninsula to New Guinea between mainland of Southeast Asia and Australia. Jakarta 6°08'S, 106°45'E. **Boundaries:** land borders with Papua New Guinea, to E of Irian Jaya, and with Malaysian states of Sarawak and Sabah in northern Borneo. **Total area:** 741,097 sq. mi. (1,919,440 sq km). **Coastline:** 34,006 mi. (54,716 km). **Comparative area:** slightly less than three times the size of Texas. **Land use:** 10% arable land; 7% permanent crops; 7% meadows and pastures; 62% forest and woodland; 14% other; includes 3% irrigated. **Major cities:** (1990 census) Jakarta (capital) 8,222,515; Surabaya 2,473,272; Bandung 2,056,915; Medan 1,730,052; Semarang 1,249,230.

• **PEOPLE Population:** 228,437,870 (July 2000 est.). **Nationality:** noun—Indonesian(s); adjective—Indonesian. **Ethnic groups:** 45% Javanese, 14% Sudanese, 7.5% Madurese, 7.5% coastal Malays. **Languages:** Bahasa Indonesia (modified form of Malay; official); English and Dutch, leading foreign languages; local dialects, most widely spoken of which is Javanese. **Religions:** 88% Muslim, 5% Protestant, 3% Roman Catholic, 2% Hindu, 1% Buddhist.

• **GOVERNMENT Type:** republic. **Independence:** Aug. 17, 1945 (from Netherlands). **Constitution:** Aug. 1945, abrogated by Federal Constitution of

1949 and Provisional Constitution of 1950, restored July 5, 1959. **National holiday:** Independence Day, Aug. 17. **Head of Government:** Ms. Megawati Soekarnoputri, president. (since July 2001). **Structure:** executive—headed by president who is chief of state and head of cabinet; cabinet selected by president; unicameral legislature (DPR, or House of Representatives) of 500 members (100 appointed, 400 elected); second body (MPR, or People's Consultative Assembly) of 1,000 members includes legislature and 500 other members (chosen by several processes but not directly elected); MPR meets every five years and elects president and vice president and theoretically determines national policy; judicial—Supreme Court Judges appointed by president.

● ECONOMY   **Monetary unit:** Indonesian rupiah. **Budget:** (2000 est.) *income:* $26 bil.; *expend.:* $30 bil. **GDP:** $654 bil., $2,900 per capita (2000 est.). **Chief crops:** rice, cassava, peanuts, rubber, cocoa; poultry, pork, beef. **Natural resources:** crude oil, tin, natural gas, nickel, timber. **Major industries:** petroleum and natural gas, textiles, mining. **Labor force:** 99 mil. (1999 est.); 45% agriculture, 16% industry, 39% services; 15%-20% unemployment (1998 est.). **Exports:** $64.7 bil. (f.o.b., 2000); textiles/garments, gas, plywood, rubber. **Imports:** $40.4 bil. (c.i.f., 2000 est.); manufactures, chemicals, foodstuffs, fuels. **Major trading partners:** *exports:* 21% Japan, 14% U.S., Singapore; *imports:* 12% Japan, 12% U.S., 10% Singapore.

The precolonial East Indies consisted of several Islamic and Hindu kingdoms in the western islands and tribal societies in the easterly ones. The Portuguese established trading posts in the 16th century; by the 17th century, control had largely passed to the Dutch East India Company. With the company's bankruptcy in 1799, the Dutch established direct colonial rule. Several 19th-century anticolonial uprisings, though costly to the Dutch, failed to dislodge them. Nationalist sentiment grew in the early 20th century, organized around Islamic groups, the Indonesian Communist party (PKI, founded 1920), and the Indonesian Nationalist party (PNI, founded 1927). Sukarno, founder of the PNI, achieved prominence as a nationalist leader and was jailed by the Dutch.

The Dutch East Indies fell quickly to the Japanese early in 1942. Some nationalists at first hailed the Japanese as liberators but quickly turned against their harsh occupation. On Aug. 17, 1945, Sukarno proclaimed Indonesia's independence. With British aid, the Dutch returned and tried to reestablish colonial rule; in 1949, threatened with a cutoff of American Marshall Plan aid, they withdrew and acknowledged Indonesia's independent status. Under Sukarno Indonesia took a leading role in international affairs among the nonaligned nations of the Third World.

In 1963 Indonesia gained control of the last Dutch outpost in the Indies, Irian Jaya (western New Guinea). Sukarno's politics moved steadily to the left, and Indonesia became hostile to the West and friendly with China. The influence of the PKI grew steadily. On Sept. 30, 1965, the army crushed an attempted coup by the PKI, setting off a popular reaction in which several hundred thousand people were killed as suspected Communists. Sukarno was shunted aside, and power devolved to Gen. Suharto, who became president in 1968. The PKI was banned, and Indonesian policy swung sharply in favor of the West.

The economy grew rapidly, aided by oil revenue, timber exports to Japan, and the Green Revolution in rice agriculture. Foreign investment aided industrial development, which was hampered, however, by domestic content laws and other trade restrictions. A policy of "transmigration" attempted, with mixed success, to move farmers from overcrowded Java and Bali to underdeveloped areas in Sumatra, Borneo, Sulawesi, and Irian Jaya. In 1975 Indonesia invaded the former Portuguese colony of East Timor, which was annexed in 1976. More than 100,000 East Timorese have been killed and the annexation was never recognized internationally.

In recent years declining oil revenues have been partly offset by the growth of industry and tourism. Pres. Suharto remained in power, at the head of the Golkar united-front party, and was reelected president for a fifth term in 1993. Despite the most violent campaign in Indonesia's history, the ruling Golkar Party was returned to power with nearly 75 percent of the vote in the 1997 parliamentary elections. But Suharto's regime faced serious problems, including continuing unrest in East Timor and rising public dissatisfaction with the alleged corruption of Suharto's family and close associates. The economy boomed in recent years and per capita income steadily grew but in 1998 the financial crisis that swept through Asia revealed the hollowness of the Indonesian approach. Strikes, protests, and riots forced Suharto to resign in May and his trusted aide, Vice-Pres. Habibie took power promising reforms and new elections in 1999. Habibie dropped half of Suharto's cabinet, began reforming the banking system, initiated inquiries into Suharto family wealth, and agreed with Portugal to hold a referendum on the status of East Timor. Elections were held in June 1999 with Golkar taking about 25 percent of the votes and seats; an anti-Golkar coalition headed by Sukarno's daughter, Megawati Sukarnoputri, held a plurality. Megawati was expected to be elected president in October. The people of East Timor voted overwhelmingly for independence from Indonesia, leading to violent attacks by militia groups and the sending of U.N. troops to stop the violence.

On Oct. 20, the Assembly approved the East Timor referendum and elected, not Megawati, but ailing Moslem cleric Abdurrahman Wahid as president, with Megawati as vice president. Under attack for his bumbling governance in a time of crisis, Wahid turned over day-to-day management to Megawati in mid-2000. On July 23, 2001 Mahid was formally impeached and replaced by Megawati, as the military refused to act in his behalf. (See "Major News Stories.")

▶ IRAN
Islamic Republic of Iran
● GEOGRAPHY   **Location:** western Asia. **Boundaries:** Armenia and Azerbaijan to N, Caspian Sea and Turkmenistan to NE, Pakistan and Afghanistan to E, Persian (Arabian) Gulf and Gulf of Oman to S, and Turkey and Iraq to W. **Total area:** 636,294 sq. mi. (1,648,000 sq km). **Coastline:** 1,516 mi. (2,440 km); Iran also borders the Caspian Sea (740 km). **Comparative area:** slightly larger than Alaska. **Land use:** 10% arable land; 1% permanent crops; 27% meadows and pastures; 7% forest and woodland; 55% other; includes 2% irrigated. **Major cities:** (1991 census) Tehran (Teheran, capital) 6,475,527; Mashad (Meshed) 1,759,155; Isfahan (Esfahan) 1,127,050; Tabriz 1,088,985; Shiraz 965,117.

● PEOPLE   **Population:** 66,128,965 (July 2001 est.). **Nationality:** noun—Iranian(s); adjective—Iranian. **Ethnic groups:** 51% Persian, 24% Azer-

baijani, 8% Gilaki and Mazandarani, 7% Kurd. **Languages:** 58% Persian, 26% Turkic, 9% Kurdish. **Religions:** 89% Shi'a Muslim; 10% Sunni Muslim; 1% Zoroastrian, Jewish, Christian, and Baha'i.
• **GOVERNMENT Type:** theocratic republic. **Constitution:** Dec. 2-3, 1979; revised 1989 to expand powers of the presidency and eliminate the prime minister. **National holiday:** Islamic Republic Day, April 1. **Head of Government:** Seyed Mohammed Khatami, president (since Aug. 1997). **Structure:** executive; unicameral legislature (Islamic Consultative Assembly); judicial.
• **ECONOMY Monetary unit:** Iranian rial. **Budget:** *income:* $27 bil.; *expend.:* $27 bil. **GDP:** $413 bil., $6,300 per capita (2000 est.). **Chief crops:** wheat, rice, sugar beets; dairy, wool; caviar. **Natural resources:** petroleum, natural gas, coal, chromium. **Major industries:** petroleum, petrochemicals, textiles. **Labor force:** 17.3 mil. (1998 est.); 33% agriculture, 25% manufacturing; shortage of skilled labor; 25% unemployment. **Exports:** $25 bil. (f.o.b., 2000 est.); 85% petroleum; carpets, fruits, nuts, hides. **Imports:** $15 bil. (f.o.b., 2000 est.); machinery, military supplies, metal works, foodstuffs, pharmaceuticals. **Major trading partners:** *exports:* Japan, Italy, UAE; *imports:* Germany, Italy, South Korea.

In 549 B.C. Cyrus the Great established the Persian empire by uniting Persia and conquered Babylonia. Alexander the Great conquered Persia in 333 B.C., but the Persians regained their independence after his death. The Persian Sassanian empire, established in A.D. 226, was the principal eastern rival of the Roman Empire. In 641 the Sassanians were defeated by invading Arabs, and Islam replaced the indigenous Zoroastrian religion. Persia reasserted its national identity—though not its political independence—under Islam and became a major center of Shia Muslim culture. In the early 13th century, Persia was conquered by the Mongols, who ruled the country until 1502.

The brilliant Safavid dynasty (1499-1736) was followed by two centuries of decline. During the 19th century, Persia lost control over Afghanistan and the Caucasus, while internal affairs came increasingly under British and Russian control. In 1907 an Anglo-Russian agreement formally divided Persia into spheres of influence. Following World War I, Persia was recognized as an independent nation, but was virtually a British protectorate. The Soviet Union renounced all claims to Persia in 1921.

In 1921 Reza Khan established a military dictatorship and had himself declared a hereditary monarch, Reza Shah Pahlavi, in 1925. In March 1935, the country's name was formally changed to Iran. In 1941 Great Britain, anxious over access to Iran's rich oil fields, charged Iran with pro-Axis activity, occupied Iran, and forced the abdication of Reza Shah in favor of his son, Mohammad Reza Shah Pahlavi. In 1945 Iran became a charter member of the United Nations.

Under Mohammed Mossadegh the National Front gained power in 1951. Parliament nationalized the oil industry; Britain responded with an economic blockade. The shah was briefly driven from power, but in August 1953, monarchist elements with clandestine British and American support ousted Mossadegh and restored the shah to the throne. The shah pursued a pro-Western policy of modernization and anticommunism and was rewarded with massive military and economic aid. His combination of secular, authoritarian rule and economic and social modernization was popular with the urban business

sector but deeply resented by the rural and urban poor. Unrestrained use of the secret police to suppress dissent led to widespread disaffection.

Religiously inspired protests resulted in widespread violence in late 1978. A military government was installed by the shah on Nov. 6, with Prime Minister Shahpur Bakhtiar given sweeping powers. The shah went into exile on Jan. 16, 1979. On Jan. 31 Iran's dominant religious leader, Ayatollah Ruhollah Khomeini, returned to Iran from his exile in France. Government forces were routed by Khomeini's supporters, and Bakhtiar's government fell on Feb. 11. In 1979 clashes took place between rival religious factions, between religious parties and secular leftists, and between the urban middle class and the disenfranchised poor. Thousands were arrested and executed by the religious militia forces.

On Nov. 4, 1979, militants seized the U.S. embassy in Tehran and held 62 Americans hostage, provoking a long international crisis. An American military raid in April 1980 failed in an attempt to free the hostages. The hostages were finally freed on Jan. 21, 1981, minutes after Ronald Reagan's inauguration. The following day Iran's president, Abolhassan Bani-Sadr, was dismissed and the Ayatollah Khomeini took over executive power. A new wave of executions followed, with political moderates and non-Islamic religious believers among the principal victims.

On Sept. 22, 1980, a dispute between Iran and Iraq over the Shatt al-Arab waterway flared into open warfare. The war severely crippled Iran. Estimates on casualties range from 450,000 to over a million dead on both sides, and the war absorbed nearly all Iran's revenue from oil exports, leaving it nearly bankrupt. The U.S. was also drawn into the conflict. In 1986, Reagan administration officials attempted to secure the release of hostages in Lebanon by trading arms to the Iranians; and on July 3, 1988, an American ship patrolling in the Persian Gulf accidently shot down an Iranian civilian airliner, killing all aboard.

In Sept. 1988, a U.N. initiative led to a cease-fire between Iran and Iraq and to the opening of negotiations to find a permanent settlement to the war. Largely isolated from the world community, Iran's domestic priority was rebuilding the nation's economy. On June 3, 1989, Ayatollah Khomeini died, but the dire predictions that his death would cause turmoil within the Iranian political hierarchy proved wrong. Ali-Akbar Rafsanjani assumed the presidency.

In elections held Apr. 10, 1992, supporters of Rafsanjani's moderate policies wrested a parliamentary majority from the radical fundamentalist Islamic factions that had controlled the Iranian Parliament for 13 years. But "moderation" proved elusive, as Rafsanjani's party was subjected to pressure from religious extremists.

Although Iran had condemned the presence of Western troops in the Middle East during the Persian Gulf conflict, it abided by U.N. sanctions against Iraq and grounded Iraqi planes that sought refuge from Allied bombing raids. In 1995 the U.S. accused Iran of beginning a strategic military buildup and forbade all trade with Iran.

Iran has remained mired in economic and political stagnation with evidence of popular discontent for several years. In the 1997 elections the religious authorities gave the voters a genuine choice of presidential candidates and they shockingly chose (in a landslide) a moderate reformist, Mohammed Khatami. Since May 1997 Khatami has carefully maneuvered for moderate reforms in the face of Islamic clerical opposition, opening non-governmental dialogue with the American "great Satan", quietly replacing provincial governors with reformers, reining in secret police agents and the like. In Feb. 1999, the religious leaders permitted the first local elections in twenty years: Khatami's new party, formed only in December, swept all 15 seats in the Tehran city council, winning large victories nationwide.

In July 1999, a militant Islamic group attacked pro-democracy students in Tehran, killing several. Student demonstrations against the government erupted in many cities across the country and in Tehran the police dispersed the crowd with severe violence after students attacked buildings and burned cars. Pres. Khatami condemned the riots, leaving many questions about the future of democratic reform.

In Feb. 2000 parliamentary elections, voters gave about two-thirds of the seats in the 290-seat Majlis to reformers. But authorities closed most reform newspapers and a Revolutionary Court in Shiraz tried 17 Iranians (13 Jews and four Moslems) for "spying for Israel,"finding 10 of the Jews and two of the Moslems guilty—convictions denounced by the E.U., the U.S., and Israel. In June 2001, Khatami won a landslide victory for re-election.

▶ IRAQ
Republic of Iraq
● **Geography** **Location**: western Asia with narrow outlet to Persian (Arabian) Gulf. **Boundaries**: Turkey to N, Iran to E, Saudi Arabia and Kuwait to S, Syria and Jordan to W. **Total area**: 168,754 sq. mi. (437,072 sq km). **Coastline**: 36 mi. (58 km). **Comparative area**: slightly more than twice the size of Idaho. **Land use**: 12% arable land; 0% permanent crops; 9% meadows and pastures; 0% forest and woodland; 79% other; includes 4% irrigated. **Major cities**: Baghdad (capital) 3,236,000 (1987 census); Basra (Basia) 1,540,000; Mosul 1,220,000; Kirkuk 535,000 (1977 census).
● **People** **Population**: 22,331,985 (July 2001 est.). **Nationality**: noun—Iraqi(s); adjective—Iraqi. **Ethnic groups**: 75-80% Arab, 15-20% Kurdish, 5% Turkoman, Assyrian, and other. **Languages**: Arabic (official), Kurdish (official in Kurdish areas), Assyrian, Armenian. **Religions**: 97% Muslim (60-65% Shi'a, 32-37% Sunni), 3% Christian and other.
● **Government** **Type**: republic. **Independence**: Oct. 3, 1932 (from League of Nations mandate under British administration). **Constitution**: Sept. 22, 1968, effective July 16, 1970 (provisional constitution); new constitution drafted in 1990 but not adopted. **National holiday**: Anniversary of the Revolution, July 17. **Heads of Government**: Saddam Hussein, president (since July 1979); Ahmed Hussein Khudair, prime minister (since 1994). **Structure**: executive; unicameral legislature (National Assembly)—Kurdish assembly elected in Kurdish areas, but unrecognized by Baghdad.
● **Economy** **Monetary unit**: Iraqi dinar. **Budget**: N.A. **GDP**: $57 bil., $2,500 per capita (2000 est.). **Chief crops**: wheat, barley, rice, cotton; cattle, sheep. **Natural resources**: crude oil, natural gas, phosphates, sulphur. **Major industries**: petroleum, chemicals, textiles, construction materials. **Labor force**: 4.4 mil. (1989); 48% services, 30% agriculture, 22% industry. **Exports**: $21.8 bil. (2000 est.); crude oil. **Imports**: $13.8 bil. (2000 est.); food, medicine, manufactures. **Major trading partners**: Russia, France, Switzerland, Egypt.

The fertile lands of Mesopotamia, between the Tigris and Euphrates rivers, were the site of one of the world's oldest civilizations. The city-states of Sumer were founded before 3000 B.C. and later became the heart of the Babylonian empire. Babylon became subject to the Assyrian empire after 1350 B.C. and was conquered by the Persians under Cyrus and Darius in the mid-sixth century B.C. Mesopotamia remained under the control of various Persian dynasties for the next 1,000 years.

In the seventh century A.D., the region was rapidly incorporated into the expanding Islamic world. The battle of Basra in 656 decisively established Arab control. In 762 the Caliphate, the center of Islamic rule, was moved from Damascus to the newly founded city of Baghdad, near the ruins of ancient Babylon. Mongol invaders sacked Baghdad in 1258 and destroyed its irrigation works; thereafter the region entered a period of long-term decline. Baghdad fell to the Ottoman Turks in 1534, and Iraq remained a province of the Ottoman Empire until the 20th century.

British troops occupied Iraq in 1915, and Great Britain governed the country under a League of Nations mandate after World War I. A Hashemite monarchy was organized under British protection in 1921. The kingdom of Iraq was granted independence in 1932 but remained closely tied to Great Britain by treaties guaranteeing British interests in petroleum and regional defense. Iraqi oil flowed through British-controlled pipelines traversing Jordan to Haifa (in Israel) and through a French-controlled pipeline traversing Syria.

After 1932 several attempted coups by anti-British factions were put down with the aid of British troops. One such coup in April 1941 sought aid from Italy and Germany; British troops landed at Basra in May and restored the pro-British monarchy. Iraq declared war against the Axis powers in 1943. In 1948 Iraq joined the Arab League and participated in the first Arab-Israeli War. Most of Iraq's 85,000 Jews emigrated to Israel after the war ended.

In 1952 a new agreement with Great Britain gave the Iraq Petroleum Company greater control over the country's oil, and a greater share of oil revenues. While remaining part of the Arab League, Iraq in 1955 broke ties with Egypt and also expelled the Soviet ambassador. Iraq signed a mutual defense treaty with Turkey.

A leftist pan-Arab revolutionary coup overthrew the monarchy in 1958 and established a republic, reversing Iraq's former pro-Western stance in international affairs. Oil resources and other industries were nationalized, and large landholdings were broken up. In 1968 a local branch of the international Ba'ath Socialist party came to power and established rule by decree within the republican framework of government. In 1972 the Soviet Union sent arms and advisers to Iraq. In the 1973 Arab-Israeli War, Iraq sent troops to aid Syrian forces on the front lines.

Iranian aid to a long-standing Kurdish rebellion in Iraq's northern mountains strained relations between the two countries. The Kurds were defeated in a bloody campaign in 1975, though the rebellion continued, leading to Iraq's bombing of Kurdish villages in 1979 and other incidents.

The execution of 21 alleged Communist conspirators in 1978 disrupted relations between Iraq and the U.S.S.R. Trade relations with the West were resumed. On July 16, 1979, Gen. Saddam Hussein at-Takriti assumed control of the government and purged leftist elements in the Ba'ath movement.

Several months of fighting in 1980 between Iraq and Iran for control of the Shatt al-Arab waterway in southern Iraq led to the outbreak of open warfare on Sept. 22, when each country launched bombing attacks on the other's cities. Warfare quickly spread along the entire Iraq-Iran border. The Iran-Iraq War produced eight years of fierce but generally stalemated fighting, with reports of the use of poison gas by both sides. On June 7, 1981, Israeli war planes destroyed a nuclear reactor near Baghdad, claiming it was capable of producing nuclear weapons. The war spread to the gulf in 1984, as both Iran and Iraq attacked tankers using each other's ports.

On May 17, 1987, the USS Stark, an American frigate on station in the gulf, was struck by missiles fired by an Iraqi fighter; 37 American sailors were killed. Iraq claimed that the attack was inadvertent and apologized to the United States.

In September 1988, a U.N. conference led to a cease-fire in the Iran-Iraq War. In the autumn of 1988, refugees in Turkey reported that poison gas had been used against Kurdish villages in northeastern Iraq as the Kurdish rebellion there continued. During 1989-90 Iraq's repressive internal policies and arms buildup provoked international criticism. Iraqi agents were caught attempting to smuggle components of nuclear weapons from the U.S. and Great Britain.

On Aug. 2, 1990, 120,000 Iraqi troops invaded and later annexed neighboring Kuwait. The invasion was met with almost universal disapproval, led by the U.N. Security Council, and U.S. troops were deployed to Saudi Arabia to defend it against a possible invasion. Coalition forces eventually totaled 500,000 troops from 13 countries.

After a six-week air war that destroyed most of Iraq's military capabilities and much of the country's infrastructure, Allied ground forces liberated Kuwait and occupied much of southern Iraq in only four days. Emboldened by the proximity of such overwhelming force, Kurdish and Sunni minorities in Iraq began a civil war that was put down with surprising speed and resulted in the displacement of hundreds of thousands of refugees to Turkey and Iran.

During 1992, while the Iraqi people continued to suffer from the war's devastation, Saddam Hussein solidified his hold on the military and remained in total control of the nation. However, U.N. inspectors discovered his secret plans to build nuclear weapons, and he was forced to destroy the program.

Throughout 1992-93 American warplanes provided protection for Kurdish areas in the north and Sunni Muslim areas in the southern marshlands. U.N. arms inspectors continued to press for access to Iraqi weapons plants and military research centers. On June 19, 1993, American missiles destroyed the Baghdad headquarters of Iraq's military intelligence service, in retaliation for a 1992 Iraq-backed plot to assassinate Pres. George Bush.

In Nov. 1994 Iraq formally recognized the sovereignty and territorial integrity of Kuwait. Nonetheless, the U.N. retained sanctions against Iraq until two conditions were met: destroying its stockpiles of weapons of mass destruction and improving its treatment of minorities. Sanctions were renewed in January 1995.

In Oct. 1995 Hussein received a triumphant 99.96 percent approval in a referendum on a second seven-year term as president. In May 1996 the U.N. agreed to ease sanctions on Iraq, permitting the sale of $2 billion worth of oil to purchase food and medical supplies. In late 1997 Iraq reneged on its agreement to allow U.N. weapons inspectors free access to all sites causing new tension in the region. Hussein's on-again, off-again cooperation with international inspection teams climaxed in the Dec. 1998 U.S./U.K. air strikes against Iraq. Since then, with a few brief halts, U.S. and U.K. patrols in the "no fly" zones have regularly clashed with Iraqi MIGs. After the Security Council decision to review all aspects of U.N.-Iraqi relations in Jan. 1999, U.S. influence was further diminished by revelations that its intelligence agents had infiltrated the U.N. Special Commission and used UNSCOM to spy on Iraq. Three compromise recommendations by U.N. panels now met Iraqi rejection in April; nonetheless, the Security Council in May extended "oil-for-food" sales for six more months.

Iraw continuously rejected U.N. arms-monitoring schemes unless sanctions were lifted first. Yet, "oil-for-food" sales were renewed. British and U.S. airstrikes continued sporadically through 2001.

▶ IRELAND

- **GEOGRAPHY   Location:** 26 of 32 counties comprising island of Ireland, in North Atlantic Ocean. Dublin 53°20'N, 6°15'W. **Boundaries:** Northern Ireland (U.K.) to N, Great Britain 50 mi (80 km) to E. **Total area:** 27,135 sq. mi. (70,280 sq km). **Coastline:** 900 mi. (1,448 km). **Comparative area:** slightly larger than W. Virginia. **Land use:** 13% arable land; negl. % permanent crops; 68% meadows and pastures; 5% forest and woodland; 14% other. **Major cities:** (1991 census) Dublin (capital) 915,516; Cork 173,694; Limerick 75,436; Galway 50,853; Waterford 41,853.
- **PEOPLE   Population:** 3,840,838 (July 2001 est.). **Nationality:** noun—Irishman (men), Irishwoman (women), Irish (collective pl.); adjective—Irish. **Ethnic groups:** Celtic, with English minority. **Languages:** Irish (Gaelic) and English (official); English widely spoken. **Religions:** 91.6% Roman Catholic, 2.5% Church of Ireland, 5.9% other.
- **GOVERNMENT   Type:** republic. **Independence:** Dec. 6, 1921 (from U.K.). **Constitution:** Dec. 29, 1937. **National holiday:** St. Patrick's Day, Mar. 17. **Heads of Government:** Mary McAleese, president (since Oct. 1997); Bertie Ahern, prime minister (since June 1997). **Structure:** executive; bicameral parliament (Seanad, Dail); judiciary appointed by president on advice of government.
- **ECONOMY   Monetary unit:** Irish pound. **Budget:** (2000) *income:* $25.7 bil.; *expend.:* $19.2 bil. **GDP:** $81.9 bil., $21,600 per capita (2000 est.). **Chief crops:** turnips, barley, potatoes, sugar beets, wheat; meat, dairy. **Natural resources:** zinc, lead, natural gas, barite, copper. **Major industries:** food products, brewing, textiles, clothing. **Labor force:** 1.82 mil. (2000 est.); 64% services, 28% manufacturing and construction, 9% agriculture, forestry, fishing; 4.1% unemployment (2000). **Exports:** $73.5 bil. (f.o.b., 2000); chemicals, computers, industrial machinery. **Imports:** $45.7 bil. (c.i.f., 2000 est.); data processing equipment, chemicals, petroleum and petroleum products. **Major trading partners:** *exports:* 59% E.U. (29% U.K., 6% Germany, 5% France), 18% U.S.; *imports:* 54% E.U. (29% U.K., 6% Germany, 5% France), 18% U.S.

Ireland, a collection of warring Celtic chieftainships, was converted to Christianity by St. Patrick in the fifth century. Over the next two centuries, Ireland became a great center of monastic Christianity, sending missionaries to Scotland, England, and the Continent. While the Roman Empire decayed, Ireland was a center of peace, culture, and learning. Viking invasions in the ninth and 10th centuries caused substantial damage and overturned the rule of the great monasteries and their secular allies. By the time an Irish monarchy was reestablished by Brian Boru in 1014 and the surviving invaders were integrated into Irish society, Ireland had become an isolated, poor backwater on the periphery of Europe.

Trade gave rise to English commercial interests in Ireland and to Henry II's claim to overlordship of Ireland in the 12th century. Henry VIII declared himself king of Ireland and introduced the Reformation there. Large-scale Scottish immigration to Ulster began during the reign of Elizabeth I. Penal laws were applied, banning Catholics from public life and making the Mass an act of treason. A rebellion in 1641 was crushed by Oliver Cromwell over the course of a decade, ending with a massacre of thousands of Irish at Drogheda. After William of Orange's "Glorious Revolution" of 1688, the Irish supported James II, who was defeated at the Battle of the Boyne in 1690.

Following these events, British economic sanctions destroyed Ireland's flourishing export trade in wool. "Plantations" were established by British and Scottish Presbyterian landlords and farmers on lands seized from Irish Catholics. Much of the native aristocracy fled into exile, and the Gaelic language declined to near extinction.

A separate Irish Parliament, dominated by the Anglo-Irish establishment, was instituted in 1782, but it had little power. In 1798 a popular uprising led by Wolfe Tone, with inspiration and aid from revolutionary France, was put down with great loss of life.

In 1800 Ireland and England were joined by the Act of Union, whereby Ireland was ineffectively represented in the British Parliament. After popular agitation led by Daniel O'Connell, the Catholic Emancipation Act was enacted by Parliament in 1829, though mandatory tithes continued to support the established Anglican church until 1869.

Under absentee landlords, the Irish population was reduced to a subsistence diet based largely on potatoes. When a potato blight struck the country in the 1840's, disaster ensued. Between 1846 and 1851, one million people starved to death, and 1.6 million emigrated, most to America.

In the late 19th century, a home-rule movement under Charles Stewart Parnell won wide popular support. A Home Rule Act finally was passed by Parliament in 1914, but its effect was postponed for the duration of World War I. The Land Purchase Acts of the early 20th century enabled dispossessed peasants to buy land from absentee landlords, creating a rural economic basis for an independent Ireland. The country's economy, based largely on agriculture and pasturage, began to recover. (Industry, principally shipbuilding and textiles, was largely confined to Northern Ireland.)

The postponement of home rule led to the Easter Rebellion of 1916; brutally suppressed, it was followed by the "Troubles," a period of guerrilla warfare lasting to 1920. In that year the Government of Ireland Act established six of Ulster's nine counties as Northern Ireland, an integral part of the United Kingdom but with its own home-rule Parliament. The south's refusal of similar status led to the passage on Dec. 11, 1922, of the Irish Free State Act, by which Ireland became an independent dominion within the British Commonwealth.

The Fine Gael (People of Ireland) party governed until 1932, when Eamon De Valera, as the head of the Fianna Fail (Soldiers of Destiny) party, was elected president, holding that office until 1948. In 1938 the Constitution was revised to sever all connections with the British government except for an "external association" with the British monarchy. The outlawed Irish Republican Army (IRA) pressed for forcible reunification of Ireland and carried out attacks on British interests in both Ireland and Northern Ireland.

Ireland remained neutral during World War II, and its government objected to British military activities in Northern Ireland. But it was generally sympathetic to the Allied war effort, especially after the United States entered the war in 1941.

In 1949 Ireland severed all ties to the British Crown, becoming a fully independent republic. The Fianna Fail won a majority in the republic's first elections, and De Valera became prime minister. In 1954 a coalition government under John Costello took power. De Valera was elected president of the republic in 1959.

During the 1950's, Ireland developed a moderate welfare state with the support of both the Fianna Fail and Fine Gael. In the 1960's attention turned to industrial development: zinc and lead mining, and export-oriented production of textiles, ceramics, and machinery. Ireland was admitted to the E.C. in 1973.

Beginning in the late 1960's, civil rights demonstrations led frequently to civil disorders and an increase in I.R.A. guerrilla activity in the north. While the 1970's were a boom period for the Irish Republic, sectarian violence and terrorism in the north left over 2,500 dead. The 1980's saw the establishment of an Anglo-Irish Intergovernmental Council (1981) and the Hillsborough accords (1985) between the Thatcher government and the Fine Gael-Labour coalition, which gave Ireland a consultative role in Northern Ireland disputes.

The government of Charles Haughey, leader of Fianna Fail, elected in 1987, faced economic problems, including high inflation and unemployment, forcing Haughey to form a coalition government in the spring of 1989. After serious losses in June 1991 local elections, and amid charges of corruption, Haughey resigned in 1992. His successor, Albert Reynolds, faced a deep recession with unemployment rates of about 20 percent. In June 1992, a national vote strongly supported the E.C.'s Maastricht Treaty. Reynolds' coalition fell in Nov. 1992, but he created a new coalition between Fianna Fail and Labour.

In 1993, Reynolds and U.K. prime minister John Major announced the "Downing Street Declaration" that Sinn Fein, the political arm of the IRA, would be invited to participate in negotiations on Northern Ireland in return for the IRA's promise to halt terrorism and violence. In 1994, the IRA announced a cease-fire in its 25-year-old effort to expel British troops from Northern Ireland.

Preliminary talks began optimistically, but bogged down over the British demand that the IRA disarm and the IRA demand that Britain withdraw its forces from Ulster. In 1996, the IRA announced an end to the 17-month-old cease-fire less than an hour before setting off a powerful bomb in East London, injuring 100 people. And in June, an even stronger bomb exploded in Manchester, injuring 200 and casting serious doubt on Sinn Fein leader Gerry Adams's ability to control the more militant members of his party.

Meanwhile, Ireland's governing coalition fell in Nov. 1995, and was replaced by an odd coalition with John Bruton of Fine Gael as prime minister. The new government passed legislation permitting Irish doctors to provide information about foreign abortion providers and sponsored a referendum that overturned the consitutional ban on divorce with remarriage. The Dail elections of June 1997 turned Bruton's coalition out of office, replaced by a new coalition of Fianna Fail and the Progressive Democrats with Fianna Fail's Bertie Ahern as prime minister.

In April 1998 came the breakthrough agreement (overwhelmingly approved in referendums in Northern Ireland and the Republic in May): extensive home rule in a Northern Ireland remaining part of the U.K. with some Republic of Ireland participation and with all paramilitary groups disarmed. When the deadline of Feb. 1, 2000 came and went without the IRA or any other armed group disarming, Great Britain suspended the government that had been functioning for only 10 weeks (since Dec. 2). But when the IRA in May pledged to put its arms "beyond use" and permit inspections, the Ulster Unionist Party accepted and the new government was functioning again by May 29. On July 26, the inspectors reported to Tony Blair that inspections had begun and that arms dumps were secure against use. Yet the refusal of the I.R.A. and other paramilitary groups to disarm led (on July 1, 2001) to the resignation of Protestant leader David Trimble as first minister, once again jeopardizing the peace accord. (See Part I, "Major News Stories of the Year.")

▶ **ISRAEL**
State of Israel
• **GEOGRAPHY   Location:** western Asia, on eastern shore of Mediterranean Sea; has outlet to Red Sea via Gulf of Aqaba. **Boundaries:** Lebanon to N, Syria to NE, Jordan to E, Egypt to SW, Mediterranean Sea to W. **Total area:** 8,019 sq. mi. (20,770 sq km). **Coastline:** 170 mi. (273 km). **Comparative area:** slightly smaller than New Jersey. **Land use:** 17% arable land; 4% permanent crops; 7% meadows and pastures; 6% forest and woodland; 66% other; includes 11% irrigated. **Major cities:** (1993 est.) Jerusalem (capital) 567,100; Tel Aviv-Jaffa 357,400; Haifa 246,500; Holon 162,800; Petach-Tikva 151,100.
• **PEOPLE   Population:** 5,938,093 (July 2001 est.). **Nationality:** noun—Israeli(s); adjective—Israeli. **Ethnic groups:** 80.1% Jewish, 19.9% non-Jewish (mostly Arab). **Languages:** Hebrew (official), Arab (official for Arab minority); English most widely used foreign language. **Religions:** 80.1% Judaism, 14.6% Islam (mostly Sunni Muslim), 2.1% Christian, 3.2% other.
• **GOVERNMENT   Type:** parliamentary democracy. **Independence:** May 14, 1948 (from League of Nations Mandate under British administration). **Constitution:** no formal constitution; some functions of constitution are filled by Declaration of Establishment (1948), the basic laws of the Knesset (legislature)— relating to the Knesset, Israeli lands, the president, government—and Israeli citizenship law. **National holiday:** Israel declared independence on May 14, 1948; because Jewish calendar is lunar, however, holiday varies from year to year; all major Jewish religious holidays are also observed as national holidays. **Heads of Government:** Moshe Katsav, president (since Aug. 2000); Ariel Sharon, prime minister (since Mar. 2001). **Structure:** executive-president has largely ceremonial functions, except for authority to decide which political leader should try to form ruling coalition following election or fall of previous government, power vested in cabinet; unicameral legislature (Knesset); judiciary-legal system based on combination of English common law, British Mandate regulations, and religious law.
• **ECONOMY   Monetary unit:** new Israeli shekel. **Budget:** (2000 est.) *income:* $40 bil.; *expend.:* $42.4 bil. **GDP:** $110.2 bil., $18,900 per capita

(2000 est.). **Chief crops:** citrus and other fruits, vegetables, cotton; beef, poultry, dairy products. **Natural resources:** copper, phosphates, bromide, potash, clay. **Major industries:** food processing, diamond cutting and polishing, textiles and clothing. **Labor force:** 2.4 mil. (2000 est.); 31.2% public services; 20.2% manufacturing; 13.1% finance and business, 12.8% commerce, 7.5% construction, 6.4% personal and other services, 6.2% transport, storage, and communications, 2.6% agriculture, forestry, and fishing; 9.1% unemployment (1999 est.). **Exports:** $31.5 bil. (f.o.b., 2000); machinery, software, cut diamonds, chemicals, textiles and clothing. **Imports:** $35.1 bil. (f.o.b., 2000); raw materials, military equipment, investment goods, rough diamonds, oil. **Major trading partners:** U.S., EU, Japan.

In ancient times called the Land of Canaan, the region between the Jordan River and the Mediterranean Sea was one of the earliest sites of agricultural civilization in the Middle East. Hebrew exiles from Egypt arrived c. 1200 B.C.; their kingdom, Eretz Israel, was well established by 1000 B.C., with its capital at Jerusalem. The kingdom expanded under Kings Saul and David, who extended domination over the Philistines, a local seafaring people, and established the norms of Jewish religious worship at the great temple of Jerusalem.

After the reign of King Solomon, the kingdom split into two parts, Israel and Judah. Israel was conquered by the Assyrians in 722 B.C., and Judah by the Babylonians in 586 B.C. A locally autonomous state was reestablished under the Persian empire in the fifth century B.C. And in the fourth century B.C., Alexander the Great conquered the region, beginning a period of Hellenizing influence.

A new Jewish state was established in 141 B.C. after the revolt of the Maccabees against hellenic rule, the state falling to the Roman Empire around 70 B.C. Roman rule was exerted through the puppet kings of the Herodian dynasty. Christianity, a messianic religion centering on the teachings of Jesus of Nazareth, was suppressed in Israel by both the Herodian kings and the Jewish priesthood but spread widely in the eastern Mediterranean in the early first century A.D.

A Jewish rebellion against Rome in A.D. 66 was forcibly suppressed, and the temple at Jerusalem was destroyed by the Romans in A.D. 70. Large numbers of Jews were expelled from Judea, beginning the Jewish Diaspora throughout the Roman world and beyond. A second rebellion of Jews in Israel was quelled in A.D. 132.

The territory of the kingdoms of Israel and Judah became generally known as Palestine, after the name of its ancient inhabitants, the Philistines. With the official toleration of Christianity in the Roman Empire under Constantine I (early 4th century), Palestine became a major center of Christian pilgrimage. Politically, Palestine was administered as part of the Byzantine Empire.

Expansion of Islam from Arabia brought Palestine under Islamic rule in 636. Thereafter the region was ruled by the Caliphates of Damascus (661-750) and Baghdad (762-1258). Part of Palestine was captured in 1099 by European Crusaders, who established the short-lived Latin Kingdom of Jerusalem. The region was conquered by the Mongols in 1258; defeat of the Mongols in 1260 at the battle of Ain Jalyut, near Nazareth, prevented a Mongol invasion of Egypt.

Palestine next became part of the Mamluk empire and was incorporated into the Ottoman Empire in 1516. The Ottoman period was one of administrative decline, although the holy places of Judaism, Christianity, and Islam were maintained by local religious authorities.

The emigration of Jews from Europe to the homeland of Israel began around 1870, under the influence of the Zionist movement. Zionism, traceable in part to the thought of Moses Mendelssohn (1729-86), originally emphasized the need to maintain Jewish identity and religious consciousness as well as to promote Jewish assimilation into European culture. By the time of the First World Zionist Congress, convened in Basel by Theodor Herzl in 1897, emphasis had shifted to the need for a specific Jewish homeland. After 1905, under the leadership of Chaim Weizmann, Jewish emigration to Palestine increased as Weizmann attempted to win Turkish approval for a new state of Israel.

With the collapse of the Ottoman Empire during World War I, Palestine came under British rule in 1917. In that year the British government issued the Balfour Declaration, committing Britain to aiding the establishment of a Jewish homeland in Palestine. After Britain received a League of Nations Mandate to govern Palestine (as well as Transjordan) in 1923, Jewish immigration into Palestine increased significantly. Faced with rising Palestinian Arab opposition to a further increase in Jewish immigration, Britain reinterpreted the Balfour Declaration in restricted terms and attempted to limit the number of Jewish arrivals.

The crisis lasted until the outbreak of World War II. During the war the Palestinian Jewish community (then about 500,000) generally supported the British war effort, while some Palestinian Arab leaders translated anti-Zionist sentiments into sympathy for the Axis. Despite the horrible revelations about the Holocaust—the systematic killing of six million Jews during the War—in 1946 British authorities refused a recommendation of the Anglo-American Committee of Inquiry that they permit resettlement of 100,000 European Jews in Palestine and they limited further immigration to 2,000 per month. Jewish leaders pressed their cause at the United Nations, while in Palestine, Zionist terrorist organizations waged covert war against the British authorities.

In 1947 a U.N. Special Committee on Palestine, boycotted by Palestinian Arabs, recommended the partition of Palestine into Jewish and Arab sectors, with Jerusalem to be administered under international control. The U.N. adopted the recommendations on Nov. 29, 1947, and the British began to withdraw their forces, while Palestinian Jews and Arabs prepared for war.

On May 14, 1948, the independent state of Israel was established, with its capital at Tel Aviv. On the same day, troops from the Arab League nations attacked Israel. Fighting and cease-fires alternated throughout 1948; Israel lost control of the Old City of Jerusalem but retained the New City, and elsewhere consolidated its territorial control. Separate armistices between Israel and the Arab nations were concluded in 1949; Jordan retained control of the West Bank, and Egypt occupied Gaza. Large numbers of Palestinian Arab refugees departed for camps in Jordan, Lebanon, and Syria, while equally large numbers of Jews from Arab countries resettled in Israel.

Elections to the Knesset (Parliament) were held in Jan. 1949 and resulted in a coalition government. Chaim Weizmann was elected president, and David Ben-Gurion became prime minister. Laws were enacted to ensure religious control of education and civil law and to affirm the "Right of Return" of all Jews to Israel. The role of labor was protected by law, as was the establishment of agricultural collectives (kibbutzim).

Taking advantage of the Suez Crisis involving Great Britain, France, and Egypt, Israel invaded Egypt's Sinai Peninsula on Oct. 29, 1956. Israeli forces withdrew under the terms of a U.N. cease-fire on Nov. 6 but retained control of Gaza.

Throughout this period Israel's population continued to swell with immigrants from Europe, the U.S. and also from the dwindling Jewish communities of the Arab world. Israel's economy, aided by foreign aid and private remittances, grew rapidly, while foreign military aid and the growth of a substantial domestic armaments industry increased its military preparedness.

On May 19, 1967, U.N. peacekeeping forces withdrew from the Egypt-Israel border on the insistence of Egypt's president Gamal Abdel Nasser. Egyptian forces then reoccupied Gaza and closed the Gulf of Aqaba to Israeli shipping. In the Six-Day War, June 5-10, Israel recaptured Gaza, occupied the Sinai Peninsula to the Suez Canal, and captured the West Bank and the Old City of Jerusalem from Jordan and the Golan Heights from Syria. Another U.N.-supervised cease-fire went into effect.

Egypt and Syria, backed by Soviet airlifts, invaded Israel on Yom Kippur, Oct. 6, 1973. Israel, with strong U.S. support, counterattacked, driving back the Syrian forces and crossing the Suez Canal from the Sinai into Egypt. Fighting ceased on Oct. 24, and a disengagement agreement was signed on Jan. 18, 1974. Israeli forces withdrew from the west bank of the Suez Canal and, in stages, from the Sinai Peninsula, completing the withdrawal in 1982.

The government of Prime Minister Golda Meir fell after the Yom Kippur War, and a new coalition took power. A period of domestic and international difficulties followed, with severe inflation in the economy and a marked rise in Palestinian and other terrorist attacks against Israeli targets. Israeli forces repeatedly attacked Palestinian bases in southern Lebanon and aided the Christian militia forces in the Lebanese civil war of 1975-76. On July 3, 1976, Israeli commandos raided the airport at Entebbe, Uganda, to rescue 103 hostages held by Arab and German hijackers.

The 1977 parliamentary elections brought a conservative coalition to power, with Menachem Begin elected prime minister. Egypt's president Anwar Sadat visited Jerusalem in November 1977, and Begin and Sadat met at a conference with U.S. president Jimmy Carter at Camp David in 1979. On Mar. 26, 1979, Egypt and Israel signed a formal peace treaty ending 30 years of war and establishing diplomatic relations between the two nations.

In July 1980 Israel affirmed the transfer of its national capital from Tel Aviv to Jerusalem and the incorporation of the (formerly Jordanian) Old City into Israeli territory. The Israeli government decided in 1980 to promote increased Jewish settlement in the West Bank, provoking protest from Palestinian leaders.

Israeli forces invaded southern Lebanon in March 1978. After a brief occupation, most Israeli forces withdrew and were replaced by a U.N. peacekeeping force, but Israel continued to cooperate with Lebanese Christian militia forces in anti-Palestinian operations.

Israeli and Syrian forces clashed briefly in April 1981. On June 7, 1981, Israeli jets destroyed a nuclear reactor near Baghdad, Iraq, that Israel claimed could have been used to manufacture materials for nuclear weapons. Prime Minister Begin was returned to office in a close election in 1981, and he retired in 1983.

Attacking Palestine Liberation Organization strongholds in Lebanon in May, 1982, Israel mounted a full-scale invasion of Lebanon in June. Israeli and Syrian forces fought in Lebanon's Bekaa Valley but disengaged after a few days. On June 14 Israeli forces surrounded and shelled Beirut, forcing the PLO to evacuate the city. On Sept. 14 Israeli forces occupied West Beirut, following the assassination of the newly elected Lebanese president, Bashir Gemayel. Lebanese Christian militia, with tacit Israeli permission, entered two Palestinian refugee camps at Sabra and Shatila on Sept. 16 and massacred hundreds of civilians, provoking an international outcry against Israel's occupation of Lebanon. Israeli forces withdrew from Lebanon in June 1985, except for a narrow "security zone" along the border.

Parliamentary elections in 1984 resulted in a coalition government, with power shared by Likud leader Yitzhak Shamir and Labor leader Shimon Peres.

In December 1987, Palestinian residents of Gaza and the West Bank launched a series of violent demonstrations against Israeli authorities. The *intifada*, or uprising, continued into 1991 in a cycle of protest and police reaction that led to the deaths of hundreds of demonstrators and a crisis of Israeli control in the occupied territories. Tensions were exacerbated by the immigration of hundreds of thousands of Soviet Jews to Israel.

Parliamentary elections in Nov. 1988 continued the Likud-Labor stalemate and brought increased power to the minor religious parties. A new grand-coalition government announced in Jan. 1989, with Yitzhak Shamir as prime minister and Shimon Peres as minister of finance, collapsed in mid-March because of disagreements over an American-backed plan for peace talks with the Palestinians. This plunged the country into a crisis, resolved in June 1990 with the formation of a coalition government of Likud and several right-wing religious parties. Shamir managed to survive several no-confidence votes, and his alliance with religious party Agudat Israel in Nov. solidified his party's power as the Persian Gulf crisis unfolded.

After months of diplomacy spearheaded by the U.S., direct talks between Israel and a (non-PLO) Jordanian-Palestinian joint delegation opened in Washington in December 1991. The talks broke down in stalemate as Israel refused to compromise over the key issue of new Jewish settlements on the West Bank. In the election of June 1992, the Labor party led by Rabin scored an upset victory over Shamir's Likud coalition government. Rabin disclosed that the Shamir government had pursued a deliberate policy of intransigence in the peace talks in order to allow the accelerated West Bank settlement program to continue.

The Palestinian *intifada* gained renewed momentum in Dec. 1992 when Israel deported 400 Palestinians to Lebanon on the grounds that they were responsible for acts of violence. Both the U.S. and the U.N. opposed the move, which impeded the peace talks. Israel launched a series of air and land attacks on suspected terrorist bases in Lebanon, resulting in many casualties.

The world was stunned only a few weeks later, when on Sept. 13, 1993, Prime Minister Yitzhak Rabin and PLO leader Yasir Arafat signed an agreement in principle for a peace settlement based on Palestinian recognition of Israel's right to exist, and Israel's acceptance of partial self-rule for the Palestinians. Soon, areas in Gaza and the West Bank were under Palestinian control.

By fall of 1995, Israeli troops had begun withdrawing from Palestinian settlements on the West Bank, but a month later an Israeli extremist assassinated Rabin. His successor, Shimon Peres, vowed to continue moves toward peace and moved elections forward from October to May. In early 1996 Israel faced the worst suicide bomber attacks in 20 years: in five days 60 people were dead. Hamas, the Palestinian resistance group, took responsibility for the attacks.

In Israel's first direct election of a prime minister, Likud's hard-line Benjamin Netanyahu narrowly defeated Peres as Israelis chose "security" over "peace." By 1997 the peace process came to a virtual standstill as the Netanyahu government pushed ahead with new settlements in the West Bank and in East Jerusalem. The first sign of a break in the impasse came in June 1998 when Pres. Weizman declared that Netanyahu was undermining peace talks. Negotiations with the Palestinians began anew in July and on Oct. 23, in Washington, Netanyahu and Arafat agreed to the Wye Memorandum by which Israel agreed to surrender about 13 percent of her West Bank holdings. But the Knesset toppled Netanyahu's government and rejected the agreement. Elections in May 1999 brought Ehud Barak, former army chief of staff, to the office of prime minister and his One Israel party to dominance.

The roller-coaster peace talks between the Barak government and the Palestinians lasted for a year but broke off bitterly (July 25, 2000); what was seen in the Knesset as excessive concessions, especially on Jerusalem, led to the unravelling of Barak's coalition and a call for new elections. In the interim, Israel completed (on May 24) a withdrawal from the security zone it had established in 1978 in Lebanon. In late Sept. renewed violence between Israeli troops and Palestinians cast serious doubts on the whole peace process. Barak was forced to resign in December and in Feb. 2001 hard-liner Ariel Sharon won 63 percent of the vote to become prime minister. Nearly 400 people, mainly Palestinians, had died since September and in March began a series of suicide bombings by Palestinians in Israel. (See "Part I, "Major News Stories of the Year.")

▶ ITALY
Italian Republic

● GEOGRAPHY Location: peninsula, extending from southern Europe into Mediterranean Sea, with a number of adjacent islands, principally Sicily to SW, and Sardinia to W. Boundaries: Switzerland and Austria to N, Slovenia to NE, Adriatic Sea to E, Ionian Sea to SE, Mediterranean Sea to W, France to NW. Total area: 116,305 sq. mi. (301,230 sq km). Coastline: 4,723 mi. (7,600 km). Comparative area: slightly larger than Arizona. Land use: 31% arable land; 10% permanent crops; 15% meadows and pastures; 23% forest and woodland; 21% other; includes 10% irrigated. Major cities: (1993) Roma (Rome; capital) 2,687,881; Milano (Milan) 1,334,171; Napoli (Naples) 1,061,583; Torino (Turin) 945,551; Palermo 694,749.

● PEOPLE Population: 57,679,825 (July 2001 est.). Nationality: noun—Italian(s); adjective—Italian. Ethnic groups: primarily Italian, but includes small clusters of German-, French-, and Slovene-Italians in north and Albanian-Italians in south; Sicilians. Languages: Italian; parts of

Trentino-Alto Adige region (e.g., Bolzano) are predominantly German-speaking; significant French-speaking minority in Valle d'Aosta region; Slovene-speaking minority in Trieste-Gorizia area. **Religions:** 98% Roman Catholic.

● **GOVERNMENT Type:** republic. **Constitution:** Jan. 1, 1948. **National holiday:** Anniversary of the Republic, June 2. **Heads of Government:** Carlo Azeglio Ciampi, president (since May 1999); Silvio Berlusconi, prime minister (since June 2001). **Structure:** executive—president empowered to dissolve Parliament and call national election; commander of armed forces presides over Supreme Defense Council; otherwise, authority to govern invested in Council of Ministers; bicameral legislature—popularly elected Parliament (315-member Senate, 630-member Chamber of Deputies); judiciary—independent.

● **ECONOMY Monetary unit:** Italian lira. **Budget:** (2000 est.) *income:* $488 bil.; *expend.:* $501 bil. **GDP:** $1.273 tril., $22,100 per capita (2000 est.). **Chief crops:** fruits, vegetables, grapes, potatoes, sugar beets, soybeans, grain, olives; meat and dairy products. **Natural resources:** mercury, potash, marble, sulfur, dwindling natural gas and crude oil reserves. **Major industries:** tourism, machinery and transport equipment, iron, steel, chemicals. **Labor force:** 23.4 mil.; 61% services, 32% industry, 7% agriculture (1996); 10.4% unemployment (2000 est.). **Exports:** $241.1 bil. (f.o.b., 2000); engineering products, textiles and clothing, production machinery, motor vehicles. **Imports:** $231.4 bil. (f.o.b. 2000); engineering products, chemicals, transport equipment, energy products. **Major trading partners:** *exports:* 56.8% EU, 9.5% U.S.; *imports:* 61% EU, 5% U.S.

Rome became the major power in Italy around 500 B.C., dominating the Etruscans in the north and Greek settlements in the south. The Roman Republic already dominated most of the Mediterranean and western Europe by the time imperial rule was established under Julius Caesar. The empire was divided between Rome and Byzantium in the fourth century A.D. The Roman Empire in the west was severely weakened by Germanic invasions in the fifth century and gradually dissolved, so that Italy became a disunited collection of aristocratic holdings and independent cities.

By the 10th century, the city-states, especially in the north, emerged as major powers, rivaling the Papal States of the central peninsula. Venice and Genoa emerged as major maritime powers during the medieval period, while Florence, Siena, and other cities developed into centers of agricultural and commercial wealth, impelling the successive renaissances of the 12th and 15th centuries. With the rise of the Habsburg empire, the monarchical powers of northern Europe vied for power in Italy, and the peninsula's small states became pawns of France, Spain, and Austria.

At the turn of the 19th century, Napoleon created the short-lived Kingdom of Italy as a French satellite, but after his fall, there was a general return to the old pattern, with Austria dominating the north. Metternich in 1815 called Italy a "geographic expression."

The 19th century saw a growing sense of nationalism in both politics and culture. The revolutionary military leader, Giuseppe Garibaldi, and the statesman, Conte Camillo di Cavour, brought about the establishment of the Kingdom of Italy in 1861. The kingdom wrested Venice away from Austria (1866) and absorbed the Papal States in 1870. Although united territorially, the kingdom was divided by conflict between church and state,

north and south, modern urban industry versus semifeudal rural poverty. Parliamentary politics under the constitutional monarchy created a regime that was weak and venal, inspiring little popular support.

Italy joined the Allied powers in World War I, but its minor gains in the Peace of Paris scarcely seemed to justify its wartime suffering and one million dead. Postwar economic dislocation, fear of communism, and political disillusionment abetted the rise of fascism. Benito Mussolini took over the Italian government at the invitation of the king in 1922 and soon acquired dictatorial powers. Papal secular authority in Vatican City was reestablished by the Lateran Agreement of 1929. In the late 1920's and early 1930's, Italy appeared to be a major power, defending Austria from Germany, colonizing Ethiopia, supporting Francisco Franco in the Spanish civil war, and joining in an "axis" with Hitler's Germany.

Mussolini, the senior partner in the fascist axis, soon was eclipsed by Hitler, and Italy was drawn into the disaster of World War II in 1939. Italy annexed Albania and invaded Greece, but that campaign turned into a fiasco from which German troops had to save the Italian army. In 1943 Allied attacks on Italy began; the fascist Grand Council deposed Mussolini, and the king, Victor Emmanuel III, had him arrested. Hitler intervened in September 1943 and began the war in Italy anew, rescuing Mussolini who established another fascist regime in northern Italy, while the legal Italian government in the south switched sides and welcomed Italy's liberation.

The head of the first postwar government was a Christian Democrat, Alcide de Gasperi. The monarchy was abolished by plebiscite in 1946, and the Republic of Italy was established. The north supported the republic, while monarchism retained significant support in the south.

This division reflected a roughly accurate generalization that sees Italy as a progressive commercial and industrial north and a backward agricultural/pastoral south. Despite such industrial giants of the north as Fiat and Pirelli, however, Italy's manufacturing is primarily carried on by medium-size and small firms, while agriculture is characteristic of the whole country. As late as 1956, there were more Italian workers in agriculture than in industry.

In the first elections under the republic, in 1948, the Christian Democrats benefited from American patronage and a split in the ranks of the Left to win a clear parliamentary majority. Italy accepted Marshall Plan aid and membership in NATO; reintegration into the European mainstream found expression in membership in the Council of Europe and the Coal and Steel Community.

Domestically, reconstruction was the major task, with both industrial and agricultural output severely hampered by social and physical damage from the war; inflation was rampant and basic social services impaired. The Christian Democrats, normally in Center-Right coalitions in the 1950's and Center-Left coalitions in the 1960's, adopted a policy directed at creating a stable currency, a free market, comprehensive social welfare programs, and occasional state intervention in the economy. This created an Italian "economic miracle," with industrial production doubling between 1953 and 1961 and increasing an additional 40 percent by 1966, led by steel, automobiles, machinery, and electrical equipment.

In1970's the Christian Democrats gradually declined in political influence, normally gaining less than 40 percent of the popular vote while continuing to provide premiers in often short-lived coalition cabinets. Left-wing terrorism became a major national problem. The Christian Democratic leader and former prime minister Aldo Moro was kidnapped and murdered in 1978, and U.S. Brig. Gen./NATO officer James Dozier was kidnapped (and subsequently rescued) in 1981. The government of Bettino Craxi, Italy's first Socialist premier, was severely shaken after it refused to cooperate with the United States in apprehending and trying the hijackers of the Achille Lauro in 1985. Craxi resigned in 1987.

Lacking effective political unity, Italy's coalition governments—there have been 60 since the war—tended to muddle along in the face of slow economic growth, inflation, and high unemployment. But awareness of Mafia assassinations and revelations of government corruption far beyond even this tolerant people's expectations led to demands for dramatic changes. In April 1993 the electorate overwhelmingly approved reforms that changed the basic elements of Italian political life. The first elections under the reformed system were held in March 1994, and ended half a century of Christian Democrat-led coalition governments. The Christian Democrats, hastily renamed the Italian Popular Party, won only 11 percent of the vote, while the Socialists, normally the second largest party, fell to 2 percent. What replaced the old guard was not the early favorite Progressive Alliance, but rather the right-wing Alliance for Freedom which captured 43 percent of the popular vote. In May, wealthy publishing executive Silvio Berlusconi was sworn in as prime minister, but his government lasted only into December. Political disputes, union opposition to his austerity budget, and the announcement that magistrates were investigating charges he had bribed tax officials diminished his authority.

Rather than call new elections, Italy's president asked Lamberto Dini to form a new "nonparty" cabinet of businessmen, judges, and professors, a cabinet that won the requisite votes of confidence in the two chambers by Feb.1, 1995. The new government showed surprising staying power, successfully passing its budget (combining tax hikes and spending cuts) and negotiating reform of Italy's bloated pension system with leading trade unions. It even began the politically touchy process of investigating the anticrime magistrates for possible violations of civil rights.

As corruption trials continued, the Dini government survived successive votes of confidence, the last on condition that he resign with the new year, which he did. New elections were not held until April 1996. The left-wing "Olive Tree Coalition," led by the once-Communist "Democratic Party of the Left," trounced the right-wing "Freedom Alliance." Its new prime minister was Professor Romano Prodi of the Popular party. Prodi concentrated on bringing the economy into line so Italy would be eligible for participation in the EMU which, with much manevering, including a stringent austerity budget, and a sudden economic upswing, he did – formal endorsement coming in May 1998. Yet, in October, the Prodi government lost a vote of confidence over budget's cuts in social spending, unacceptable to the "Reconstructed Communists". Prodi endorsed Massimo D'Alema of the Democratic Party of the Left (the old Communist Party).

The "Olive Tree" government muddled along under various ministers until the May 2001 elections,

convincingly won by the right-wing House of Freedom coalition, spearheaded by Forza Italia, and bringing back Silvio Berlusconi as prime minister.

▶ IVORY COAST
Republic of Côte d'Ivoire

● **GEOGRAPHY** **Location:** western coast of Africa. **Boundaries:** Mali and Burkina Faso to N, Ghana to E, Gulf of Guinea to S, Liberia and Guinea to W. **Total area:** 124,502 sq. mi. (322,460 sq km). **Coastline:** 320 mi. (515 km). **Comparative area:** slightly larger than New Mexico. **Land use:** 8% arable land; 4% permanent crops; 41% meadows and pastures; 22% forest and woodland; 25% other; includes negl. % irrigated. **Major cities:** (1988) Yamoussoukro (capital—not recognized by U.S., which recognizes Abidjan) 106,786; Abidjan 1,929,079; Bouaké 329,850.

● **PEOPLE** **Population:** 16,393,221 (July 2001 est.). **Nationality:** noun—Ivorian(s); adjective—Ivorian. **Ethnic groups:** 23% Baoule, 18% Bete, 15% Senoufou, 11% Malinke and Agni; over 60 ethnic groups; 3 million foreign Africans, mostly Burkinabe and Malians. **Languages:** French (official); over 60 African languages and dialects with Dioula most widely spoken. **Religions:** 60% Muslim, 22% Christian, 18% indigenous beliefs.

● **GOVERNMENT** **Type:** republic; multiparty presidential regime established 1960. **Independence:** Aug. 7, 1960 (from France). **Constitution:** Nov. 3, 1960. **National holiday:** National Day, Dec. 7. **Heads of Government:** Laurent Gbagbo, president (since Oct. 2000); Affi N'Guessan, prime minister (since Oct. 2000). **Structure:** executive—president has broad powers; unicameral legislature—175-member National Assembly; judiciary.

● **ECONOMY** **Monetary unit:** Communauté Financière Africaine franc. **Budget:** (2000) *income:* $1.5 bil.; *expend.:* $2.1 bil. **GDP:** $26.2 bil., $1,600 per capita (2000 est.). **Chief crops:** coffee, cocoa, bananas, palm oil; cotton, rubber; timber. **Natural resources:** crude oil, diamonds, manganese, iron ore, cobalt. **Major industries:** foodstuffs, wood processing, oil refinery. **Labor force:** N.A. **Exports:** $3.8 bil. (f.o.b, 2000 est.); 37% cocoa, coffee, tropical woods. **Imports:** $2.5 bil. (f.o.b, 2000 est.); food, consumer goods, capital goods, fuel. **Major trading partners:** *exports:* 7% Netherlands, 15% France, 8% U.S.; *imports:* 26% France, 10% Nigeria, 7% China.

The peoples of the Ivory Coast belong to various tribes that had established small and mutually hostile kingdoms prior to the 18th century. The dominant Baulé migrated to the Ivory Coast from Ghana about 200 years ago. European contact began with the Portuguese, who established coastal trading stations in the 15th century. They were followed in rapid succession by the Dutch, British, and finally the French, who landed at Assinie in 1637. Dense tropical forests and a lack of good harbors retarded European exploration.

France established a protectorate over the coastal zone in 1842 and during the remainder of the 19th century expanded its control, by conquest and diplomacy, into the interior. In 1893 the Ivory Coast was organized as a French colony, and in 1904 it was made part of French West Africa.

France's Vichy government controlled French West Africa during World War II and harshly suppressed the region's growing nationalist movements. In 1946 a group of West African leaders, inspired by Félix Houphouet-Boigny, formed the African Democratic Assembly, which later cooperated with the French in the implementation of reforms, including, by 1956, universal suffrage and the formation of locally autonomous assemblies. Complete independence for the Ivory Coast came on Aug. 4, 1960.

Félix Houphouet-Boigny was unanimously elected the first president of the Ivory Coast. Until 1990, when his Democratic party was the only political party allowed in the country, Houphouet-Boigny easily won reelection. But even after he liberalized the political process, Houphouet-Boigny retained control, winning a new five-year term in multiparty elections held in 1990. Under his presidency, the Ivory Coast enjoyed both political stability and economic prosperity.

Houphouet-Boigny died in 1993, and was succeeded by his fellow Democrat Henri Konan Bedie, who was president of the National Assembly. Bedie won reelection in 1995, and continued the policies of his predecessor. In Sept. 1999, however, hidden political tensions surfaced when Pres. Bedie ordered the arrest of several hundred members of an opposition party, Rally of the Republicans. On Christmas Eve 1999, a military coup led by General Robert Gueï (pronounced "gay") overturned the Bedie government and suspended the constitution. But Gueï's attempt to rig the 2000 elections provoked demonstrations that forced him to flee. Laurent Gbagbo became president.

▶JAMAICA
● **GEOGRAPHY Location:** northern Caribbean Sea. Kingston 17°58'N, 76°48'W. **Boundaries:** Cuba 87 mi. (145 km) to N. **Total area:** 4,243 sq. mi. (10,990 sq km). **Coastline:** 635 mi. (1,022 km). **Comparative area:** slightly smaller than Connecticut. **Land use:** 14% arable land; 6% permanent crops; 24% meadows and pastures; 17% forest and woodland; 39% other; includes 3% irrigated. **Major cities:** (1982 census) Kingston (capital) 524,638; Spanish Town 89,097; Montego Bay 70,265.
● **PEOPLE Population:** 2,665,636 (July 2001 est.). **Nationality:** noun—Jamaican(s); adjective—Jamaican. **Ethnic groups:** 90.9% black, 1.3% East Indian, 0.2% white, 0.2% Chinese, 7.3% mixed, 0.1% other. **Languages:** English, Creole. **Religions:** 61.3% Protestant, 4% Roman Catholic, some spiritualist cults.
● **GOVERNMENT Type:** constitutional parliamentary democracy. **Independence:** Aug. 6, 1962 (from U.K.). **Constitution:** Aug. 6, 1962. **National holiday:** Independence Day, first Monday in August. **Heads of Government:** Gov. Gen. Howard F.H. Cooke, governor-general (since Aug. 1991); Percival James Patterson, prime minister (since Apr. 1993). **Structure:** cabinet headed by prime minister; bicameral legislature; judiciary follows British tradition under chief justice.
● **ECONOMY Monetary unit:** Jamaican dollar. **Budget:** (FY99/00 est.) *income:* $2.23 bil.; *expend.:* $2.56 bil. **GDP:** $9.7 bil., $3,700 per capita (2000 est.). **Chief crops:** sugarcane, bananas, coffee, citrus, potatoes, vegetables; poultry, goats, milk. **Natural resources:** bauxite, gypsum, limestone. **Major industries:** tourism, bauxite mining, textiles. **Labor force:** 1.13 bil. (1998); 60% services, 21% agriculture, 19% industry and commerce; 15.5% unemployment. **Exports:** $1.7 bil. (f.o.b., 2000 est.); alumina, bauxite, sugar, bananas, rum. **Imports:** $3 bil. (f.o.b., 2000 est.); machinery and transport equipment, construction materials, fuel, food; chemicals. **Major trading partners:** *exports:* 35.7% U.S., 15.8% E.U. (excluding U.K.), 11.5% Canada; *imports:* 47.8% U.S., 4.7% E.U. (excluding U.K.), 12.4% Caricom.

Christopher Columbus visited Jamaica in 1494, and the Spanish ruled the island—exterminating the native Arawaks in the process—until it fell to British control in 1655. A haven for buccaneers, by the 18th century Jamaica was a major sugar producer and the site of one of the busiest slave markets in the world. Emancipation of the slaves in 1833 and abolition of tariff protection in 1846 contributed strongly to the subsequent downfall of the plantation economy.

In 1962 the island gained its independence. The country has been plagued by racial and class division set within the context of an underdeveloped economy. Michael Manley of the People's National party became prime minister in 1972. He nationalized some industry and established closer ties with Cuba. Edward Seaga's Jamaica Labour party came to power in 1980 and encouraged more private-sector involvement in developing the economy. Though Manley was reelected to office in 1989, he did not reverse this general trend; in 1992 he was succeeded by Percival James Patterson, who led the People's National party to a landslide victory in violence-marred elections in March 1993. He was reelected in 1997 despite continuing economic problems.

▶JAPAN
● **GEOGRAPHY Location:** chain of more than 3,000 islands extending 1,300 mi. (2,200 km) NE to SW between Sea of Japan and western Pacific Ocean; southern Japan about 93 mi. (150 km) E of S. Korea; islands of Hokkaido, Honshu, Shikoku, and Kyushu account for 98% of land area. Tokyo 35°40'N, 139°45'E. **Boundaries:** Sea of Okhotsk to N, Pacific Ocean to E, East China Sea to SW, and Sea of Japan to W. **Total area:** 145,882 sq. mi. (377,835 sq km). **Coastline:** 18,487 mi. (29,751 km). **Comparative area:** slightly smaller than California. **Land use:** 11% arable land; 1% permanent crops; 2% meadows and pastures; 67% forest and woodland; 19% other; includes 9% irrigated. **Major cities:** (1995 est.) Tokyo (capital) 7,836,665; Yokohama 3,273,609; Osaka 2,478,628; Nagoya 2,086,745; Sapporo 1,733,133.
● **PEOPLE Population:** 126,771,662 (July 2001 est.). **Nationality:** noun—Japanese (sing., pl.); adjective—Japanese. **Ethnic groups:** 99.4% Japanese, 0.6% other (mostly Korean). **Languages:** Japanese. **Religions:** most Japanese observe both Shinto and Buddhist rites; about 16% belong to other faiths, including 0.7% Christian.
● **GOVERNMENT Type:** constitutional monarchy. **Constitution:** May 3, 1947. **National holiday:** Birthday of the Emperor, Dec. 23. **Heads of Government:** Akihito, emperor (since Jan. 1989); Junichiro Koizumi, prime minister (since Apr. 2001). **Structure:** executive—emperor is symbolic head of state; power is vested in cabinet appointed by prime minister; bicameral legislature; judiciary.
● **ECONOMY Monetary unit:** yen. **Budget:** (FY01/02 est.) *income:* $441 bil.; *expend.:* $718 bil. **GDP:** $3.15 trillion, $24,900 per capita (2000 est.). **Chief crops:** rice, sugar beets, vegetables, fruits; chickens, pigs, cattle; world's largest fish catch. **Natural resources:** negl. mineral resources, fish. **Major industries:** metallurgical and engineering industries, electrical and electronic industries, motor vehicles. **Labor force:** 67.7 mil. (2000); 65% trade and services, 30% manufacturing, mining, and construction. **Exports:** $450 bil. (f.o.b., 2000 est.); semiconductors, office machinery, chemicals, motor vehicles. **Imports:** $355 bil. (c.i.f., 2000); fuels, foodstuffs, chemicals, textiles, office machinery. **Major trading partners:** U.S., EU, Southeast Asia.

Japan's ancient Jomon civilization was displaced by proto-Japanese Yayoi migrants from mainland northeast Asia beginning in the fourth century B.C. In the early Yayoi period, a mounted military aristocracy dominated rice-growing commoners. The shamanic religion of the time was ancestral to Japan's later indigenous religion, Shinto. Yayoi society evolved into the Yamato protostate, c. A.D. 250-500. The Yamato kings were buried in large, elaborate tomb mounds together with haniwa clay sculptures. From the third century A.D., contact with the mainland increased. Korean missionaries introduced Buddhism and Chinese writing in the mid-sixth century. A centralized monarchy developed in the Yamato Plain, central Honshu Island; Prince Shotoku, a great patron of Buddhism, founded the Horyuji and other great temples in the early seventh century.

In 710 the Yamato kings established a permanent capital for the first time, at Nara; the city was modeled on the Chinese capital. In 785 the court, split by factionalism and dominated by Nara's large and wealthy Buddhist temples, abandoned the capital; in 794 the new capital at Heian (Kyoto) was completed. The ensuing Heian period was one of the most brilliant in Japanese history. A small civil aristocracy, dominated by the Fujiwara family, drew great wealth from provincial estates and created a metropolitan culture of extreme refinement. From the ninth through the 11th centuries, strong Chinese influences were incorporated into Japanese culture.

In the 12th century the power of the Heian court waned as the influence of the provincial military aristocracy (samurai) grew stronger. In 1156 the capital was seized by the Taira family; in 1185 the Taira were overthrown by their rivals, the Minamoto. The Minamoto established a military government under a shogun (generalissimo) at Kamakura; the emperor remained at Kyoto, stripped of all governmental authority. In Kamakura the Minamoto were soon displaced by their former vassals, the Hojo. During the Kamakura period, the Japanese drew away from Chinese influence in art, architecture, literature, and religion in the process of creating a more distinctively Japanese culture. In 1274 and again in 1281, Mongol invasions were repulsed with the aid of timely typhoons (*kamikaze*, "divine winds").

In the course of a failed attempt at imperial restoration, the Kamakura shogunate was overthrown, in the 1330's, by the Ashikaga family, which in 1338 established a new shogunal government at Muromachi, a precinct of Kyoto. The Muromachi period saw the flowering of a new warrior culture, marked by such military virtues as bravery, loyalty, personal honor, and skill with weapons and by adherence to Zen Buddhism and its associated arts (tea ceremony, flower arranging, calligraphy, etc.). With the Onin Wars of the mid-15th century, the Muromachi shogunate lost most of its power, and the country fell into a century of civil war.

The civil wars were brought to an end during the second half of the 16th century by three successive unifiers, Oda Nobunaga, Hideyoshi, and Tokugawa Ieyasu. At the same time, the Jesuit Francis Xavier and his successors established a short-lived Japanese Christian community. Hideyoshi made several attempts (1592-98) to conquer and annex Korea. In 1601 Tokugawa Ieyasu defeated his rivals in the Battle of Sekigahara. He established a shogunal government at Edo (later Tokyo) in 1603; he and his successors formalized the structure of Japanese feudalism, created a rigid class structure, suppressed Christianity, and enforced the isolation of Japan from virtually all outside influence. Some trade with the mainland and a small Dutch trading station at Nagasaki provided Japan's only windows to the outside world for the next 250 years. The Edo period was marked by urbanization and the development of urban culture (Kabuki theater, wood-block prints, etc.) as the merchant class prospered from internal trade.

The Tokugawa shogun's inability to repel the 1854 visit of American commodore Matthew Perry and subsequently to avoid establishing commercial and diplomatic relations with Western nations deeply shocked the samurai class. Patriotic young samurai from Choshu, Satsuma, and other outlying feudal domains began to call for the abolition of the shogunate and the restoration of imperial rule in order to confront the threat of contact with the West. Quickly realizing that isolationism was doomed, the young radicals' program changed from "respect the emperor, expel the barbarians" to "enrich the state, strengthen the military." With the accession of the Meiji emperor in 1868, shogunal government ended.

Under direct imperial rule, feudalism was abolished and a wide-ranging program of military, industrial, commercial, and social modernization was implemented. The Meiji Constitution of 1889 created a constitutional monarchy and a parliamentary system of government. Having avoided domination by Western nations, Japan itself became an imperialist power. Defeating China in the Sino-Japanese War of 1894-95 and Russia in the Russo-Japanese War of 1904-05, Japan gained a dominant position in Manchuria and in Korea, which became a Japanese colony in 1910.

Under the ineffectual Taisho emperor (reigned 1912-26), parliamentary government flourished. Japan sided with the Allied Powers in World War I, and the Treaty of Versailles advanced Japan's international interests, particularly in China. The general prosperity of the 1920's was threatened by the Tokyo earthquake of 1923, by labor strife, and by a stagnant agricultural economy. Militant right-wing nationalism began to play an important role in domestic politics.

During the international economic depression of the early 1930's, right-wing militants gained the upper hand; they assassinated many moderate political figures. Japan invaded Manchuria in 1931 and established the puppet state of Manchuguo in 1934. An attempted military coup in 1936 failed in its immediate objectives but led to the establishment of martial law, under which the Showa emperor (Hirohito; reigned 1926-89) became a pawn of the ultranationalists. An invasion and military takeover of eastern China in 1937 was seen as the first step in the creation of a "Greater East Asian Co-prosperity Sphere," designed to unite Asia under Japanese control.

In 1940 Japan entered the Tripartite Alliance with Italy and Nazi Germany. Japan occupied French Indochina in June 1941, provoking increased Allied resistance to Japanese imperial ambitions. Gen. Hideki Tojo became prime minister in Oct. 1941 and ordered simultaneous preemptive strikes against Pearl Harbor, the Philippines, and Malaya on Dec. 7-8. By mid 1942, Japan controlled most of Southeast Asia and the western Pacific, but American victories at the Battle of the Coral Sea in May 1942 and the Battle of Midway in June 1942 halted Japanese expansion. Thereafter, Japanese forces were steadily pushed back in "island-hopping" campaigns in the central Pacific and along the western Pacific rim, and by Allied counterattacks in Burma. Air attacks on Japan itself culminated in the atomic bombing of Hiroshima and Nagasaki in August 1945.

Following Japan's formal surrender on Sept. 2, 1945, an American army in Japan under Gen. Douglas MacArthur took control of the country. A new constitution was promulgated, relegating the emperor to purely symbolic status, renouncing the use of military force, and guaranteeing the civil rights of citizens. The industrial combines that had lent strength to Japan's empire were partially dismantled. An international tribunal tried many wartime leaders as war criminals in 1948. In 1949 considerable authority was returned to the conservative government of Premier Shigeru Yoshida. Japan served as a base for American forces during the Korean War, 1950-53, greatly accelerating Japan's postwar economic recovery. On Apr. 28, 1952, a peace treaty between Japan and the United States went into effect, ending the Occupation. On Mar. 8, 1954, the two nations signed a mutual defense assistance pact.

Japan was admitted to the United Nations in 1956. The success of Japan's postwar recovery was symbolized by the Tokyo Olympic Games of 1964 and Expo '70 at Osaka. Violent student-protest movements in 1968-69 had no clear political goals and no lasting effect. Politically stable under an unbroken succession of Liberal Democratic party governments, Japan emerged as a major and steadily expanding world industrial power.

In general, Japan has been reluctant to play an international political role consistent with its vast economic power. From the mid-1970's onward, the balance of trade between Japan and the U.S. has weighed heavily in Japan's favor, leading to strains in U.S.-Japan relations and American charges that Japan engages in unfair trade practices. Several times during the 1980's and 1990's, especially when the yen was appreciating rapidly against the dollar, Japan pledged to take measures to even the trade balance by improving foreign access to Japan's domestic economy.

Domestically, Japan in the 1980's enjoyed a very high standard of living, marred by the extremely high cost and relatively low quality of housing, and by underinvestment in the public infrastructure. A real estate boom led prices of commercial property in downtown Tokyo to increase as much as 200-fold in the span of a decade. This boom extended to the United States, where the rapidly declining dollar made Japanese investment in the United States especially attractive.

For most of its postwar history, Japan has been essentially a one-party state, run by political professionals of the Liberal Democratic party (LDP) according to a system of consensus. But by the end of the 1980's, the system started to crumble as the regime's widespread corruption was revealed. Prime Minister Noburu Takeshita was force to resign in May 1989 after a bribery scandal. His successor, Sousuke Uno, lasted only two months before resigning in a scandal over his sexual conduct. Public opinion turned sharply against the LDP, which lost control of the upper house of the Diet in July 1989 elections; the Socialist party, led by Takako Doi, posted significant gains.

Uno's successor, Toshiki Kaifu, emerged as an unexpectedly skillful leader who enhanced Japan's international reputation by offering aid to Eastern Europe and the former Soviet Union, and by pledging billions of dollars to support the Persian Gulf War. In Oct. 1991, Kaifu was replaced as LDP chairman by Kiichi Miyazawa, who succeeded in passing legislation authorizing the

posting abroad of Japanese troops—for the first time since World War II—for peacekeeping missions in noncombat areas.

An economic slump and political scandals continued to buffet the LDP throughout 1992 and 1993. LDP kingmaker Shin Kanemaru and other party officials resigned after admitting ties to gangsters. The LDP was forced from office in 1993 for the first time in 38 years, and formed successive coalition governments with the Socialist Party and other parties. The weak coalition governments paved the way for a LDP return to power in 1994; the years since have brought continued economic stagnation, bank failures, scandals involving government and business ties to organized crime, and general malaise.

The city of Kobe was hit by a severe earthquake in January, 1995; the government was criticized for inneffective rescue and relief efforts. The country's confidence was further shaken in March, 1995, by a bizarre attack with poison gas in the Tokyo subway, perpetrated by a religious cult, Aum Shinrikyo. Its leader, Shoko Asahara, was eventually arrested and convicted of murder.

Several instances of violent crime involving U.S. servicemen in Okinawa led Pres. Clinton and Prime Minister Hashimoto to sign an agreement in April, 1996, reducing the number of American bases in Okinawa.

Prime Minister Ryutaro Hashimoto, first elected in Jan. 1996, was re-elected leader of the LDP in Sept., 1997. But the Asian economic crisis took a toll on Japan, still in the midst of a long-term recession. In the spring of 1998 a plunge in the value of the yen doomed the Hashimoto government; he resigned and was replaced by party stalwart, Keizo Obuchi.

In 1999 Japan's economy rebounded slightly as the Obuchi government tried desperately to raise the levels of spending throughout the economy. In April 2000, Premier Obuchi suffered a stroke. His successor Yoshiro Mori led the Liberal Democrats to a near majority in parliamentary elections June 25, forming a coalition government with New Komeito and the Conservatives (a new party, composed of former Liberals). With Mori's resignation in April 2001, the Liberal Democrats (operating under new party rules) selected as their leader, and the lower house named as Prime Minister, Junichiro Koizumi, a man outside the old party "factions" and promising modernizing liberal economic reforms. But Japan's economy grew worse during 2001.

▶ JORDAN
Hashemite Kingdom of Jordan

● **GEOGRAPHY** Location: western Asia. **Boundaries:** Syria to N, Iraq to NE, Saudi Arabia to SE, Israel to W. **Total area:** 34,445 sq. mi. (89,213 sq km). **Coastline:** 16 mi. (26 km). **Comparative area:** slightly smaller than Indiana. **Land use:** 4% arable land; 1% permanent crops; 9% meadows and pastures; 1% forest and woodland; 85% other; includes 0.5% irrigated. **Major cities:** (1991) Amman (capital) 965,000; Zarqa 359,000; Irbid 216,000; Russeita 115,500.

● **PEOPLE** Population: 5,153,378 (July 2001 est.). **Nationality:** noun—Jordanian(s); adjective—Jordanian. **Ethnic groups:** 98% Arab, 1% Circassian, 1% Armenian. **Languages:** Arabic (official); English widely understood among upper and middle classes. **Religions:** 96% Sunni Muslim, 4% Christian.

● **GOVERNMENT** Type: constitutional monarchy. **Independence:** May 25, 1946 (from League of

Nations Mandate under British administration). **Constitution:** Jan. 8, 1952. **National holiday:** Independence Day, May 25. **Heads of Government:** Abdullah Bin Al Hussein, king (since Feb. 1999); Ali Abul Ragheb, prime minister (since June 2000). **Structure:** executive—king is chief of state, prime minister and cabinet are appointed by king; bicameral legislature—House of Representatives has been dissolved by the king several times since 1974; House of Notables appointed by the king; judiciary.

● ECONOMY **Monetary unit:** Jordanian dinar. **Budget:** (2000 est.) *income:* $2.8 bil.; *expend.:* $3.1 bil. **GDP:** $17.3 bil., $3,500 per capita (2000 est.). **Chief crops:** wheat, barley, citrus, tomatoes, melons, olives; poultry, goats, sheep. **Natural resources:** phosphates, potash, shale oil. **Major industries:** phosphate mining, petroleum refining, cement. **Labor force:** 1.15 mil plus 300,000 foreign workers (1997); 11.4% industry, 10.5% commerce, 10% construction, 8.7% transport and communications, 7.4% agriculture, 52% other services; unemployment 25-30% (1999). **Exports:** $2 bil. (f.o.b., 2000 est.); phosphates, fertilizers, potash, agricultural products, manufactures. **Imports:** $4 bil. (f.o.b., 2000 est.); crude oil, machinery, transport equipment, food, live animals, manufactured goods. **Major trading partners:** *exports:* Iraq, India, Saudi Arabia; *imports:* EU, Iraq, U.S.

The present territory of the Kingdom of Jordan corresponds to the biblical lands of Edom, Gilead, and Moab. The ancient rock city of Petra was the capital of the Edomite and Nabataean kingdoms. The region was incorporated into the Roman Empire, and later the Latin Kingdom of Jerusalem; it was an important early center of Christianity.

In the 630's Jordan became one of the first areas outside Arabia to fall to the expansion of Islam. It became subject to the Caliphate, located at Damascus and later at Baghdad, and in the 11th century became part of the empire of the Seljuk Turks. The Crusades brought European invaders, but with little lasting impact. The Mongols conquered Jordan in the mid-13th century, and it later passed into the control of the Mamluk sultanate. In 1517 Jordan was incorporated into the Ottoman Empire.

Following the post-World War I breakup of the Ottoman Empire, Jordan came under British control as part of a League of Nations Mandate of Palestine. In 1921 Great Britain sponsored the establishment of a monarchy by Abdullah, son of Hussein ibn Ali, ruler of the Hejaz in Arabia. Britain recognized the independence of the Hashemite Kingdom of Transjordan in 1923; a 1928 treaty gave Britain the unrestricted right to station troops in the kingdom.

Transjordan supported the Allies in World War II and was rewarded with full independence in 1946, although strong military ties to Great Britain were maintained. In 1948 the kingdom joined the Arab League, changed its name to Jordan, and joined other Arab states in the first Arab-Israeli War. The war resulted in the occupation by Jordanian troops of the West Bank and the Old City of Jerusalem, which were annexed in 1950. King Hussein I came to the throne on Aug. 11, 1952. All British military forces were withdrawn from the kingdom in 1957.

Israel recaptured the West Bank and the Old City of Jerusalem in the Six-Day War of 1967, and large numbers of Palestinian refugees fled to Jordan. Jordan played no substantial role in the 1974 Arab-Israeli War. In 1974 Jordan accepted the decision of an Arab summit conference designating the Palestine Liberation Organization the sole representative of Palestinians in the West Bank. Jordan's role as a front-line opponent of Israel won it a large annual subvention from Arab oil states; King Hussein's reputation as an Arab moderate led to significant American economic and military support.

King Hussein strongly opposed the 1979 Camp David Accords and the Egypt-Israeli peace treaty; Jordan broke off diplomatic relations with Egypt in March 1979 but resumed full relations in 1984.

In July 1981 King Hussein, charging the Palestine Liberation Organization with subversion, forced the withdrawal of PLO troops and political headquarters from Jordan. While some hoped that Hussein would represent the Palestinians in talks with Israel, in 1988 the king flatly rejected any such role, implied that the PLO should declare an independent state on the West Bank and in the Gaza Strip, and declared that a settlement would require talks between Israel and the PLO.

The Persian Gulf War had a drastic impact on Jordan's economy. King Hussein actively backed Iraq, thus jeopardizing direct aid from Kuwait and Saudi Arabia. But the historic peace treaty signed with Israel in October 1994 restored Hussein's standing while returning some territory taken in the 1967 war. In August 1998, while in the U.S. for medical care, King Hussein made a dramatic visit to the PLO-Israeli talks to appeal for a settlement. Back in Jordan, Hussein deposed his brother Hassan as Crown Prince, swearing in his eldest son Abdullah instead. Twelve days later (Feb. 7), the king died. The new king, Abdullah, pledged to continue his father's policies, asking the current cabinet to stay on. King Abdullah moved cautiously against radical Moslem groups (winning Israeli praise) and restructured the army command in 1999. His first cabinet change came in June 2000, as he appointed reformer Ali Abu Ragher as prime minister.

▶ **KAZAKHSTAN**
Republic of Kazakhstan

● GEOGRAPHY **Location:** central Asia. **Boundaries:** Russian Federation to N and NE, China to SE, Kyrgystan, Uzbekistan, and Turkmenistan to S, Caspian Sea to W. **Total area:** 1,049,151 sq. mi. (2,717,300 sq km). **Coastline:** 1,441 mi. (2,320 km) on Caspian Sea. **Comparative area:** slightly less than four times the size of Texas. **Land use:** 12% arable cropland; 11% permanent crops; 57% meadows and pastures; 4% forest and woodland; 16% other (mainly mountain and desert). **Major cities:** (1993 est.) Astana (capital) 300,000; Almaty (formerly Alma-Ata) 1,176,000; Karaganda 596,000.

● PEOPLE **Population:** 16,731,303 (July 2001 est.). **Nationality:** noun—Kazakhstani(s); adjective—Kazakhstani. **Ethnic groups:** 53.4% Kazakh, 30% Russian, 3.7% Ukrainian, 2.5% Uzbek. **Languages:** over 40% Kazakh (state language); 66% Russian (official, used in everyday business). **Religions:** 47% Muslim, 44% Russian Orthodox, 2% Protestant.

● GOVERNMENT **Type:** republic. **Independence:** Dec. 16, 1991 (from the Soviet Union). **Constitution:** Jan 28, 1993. **National holiday:** Day of the Republic, Oct. 25. **Heads of Government:** Nursultan A. Nazarbaev, president (since Dec. 1991); Kassymzhomart K. Tokaev, prime minister (since Oct. 1999). **Structure:** executive—president, prime minister, Council of Ministers; bicameral legislature; judicial.

● **ECONOMY Monetary unit:** tenge. **Budget:** (1999 est.) *income:* $3.1 bil.; *expend.:* $3.6 bil. **GDP:** $85.6 bil., $5,000 per capita (2000 est.). **Chief crops:** grains, cotton; wool, meat. **Natural resources:** major deposits of petroleum, natural gas, coal, iron ore, manganese. **Major industries:** oil, coal, iron ore, manganese. **Labor force:** 8.8 mil. (1997); 27% industry, 23% agriculture; 13.7% unemployment (1997). **Exports:** $8.8 bil. (f.o.b., 2000 est.); oil, ferrous and nonferrous metals, chemicals, grain, wool. **Imports:** $6.9 bil. (f.o.b., 2000 est.); machinery and parts, industrial materials, oil and gas. **Major trading partners:** *exports:* 23% EU, 8% China, 20% Russia; *imports:* 37% Russia, Ukraine, U.S., Uzbekistan.

Kazakhstan, the largest nation in central Asia, is a land of deserts and plateaus stretching across the rolling tablelands of the Eurasian landmass; approximately 20 percent is mountainous. The Kazakhs are descended from Mongol and Turkic tribes who settled in the area known as Kazakhstan about the 1st century B.C. In the sixth century A.D. the area formed part of the Turkish Khaganate, a loose federation of nomadic tribes, and in the seventh to ninth centuries Islam became established among the settled population. Although the Mongols ruled the area from 1219 to 1447, the Turkish subjects of the Mongol Horde were to play a decisive role in the future of the region.

In the 15th century, the Kazakhs emerged as a distinct people, but by the 17th century, due to internecine fighting, the Kazakhs split into three nomadic federations, known as the Larger, the Middle, and the Lesser Hordes. In the mid-17th century, the Mongols began to invade the region, and the Kazakhs, not being unified enough to repel them, sought protection from the Russians. By the mid-18th century, the Kazakh lands were completely under Russian control. With the freeing of serfs in 1861 in Russia, Kazakhstan experienced its first major influx of Russian and Ukrainian peasants, who were given Kazakh lands. Resentment over this grew until the Kazakhs rebelled against Russian rule in 1916. The Russians brutally repressed the uprising, but not before thousands of Kazakhs and many Russians were killed.

After the 1917 Communist revolution in Russia, a civil war ensued in Kazakhstan, from which the Bolsheviks emerged victorious. The Kazakh territory was incorporated into Russia in 1920, granted "autonomous" status in 1925, and in 1936 it formally became one of the U.S.S.R.'s union republics. Kazakhstan was industrialized, but it suffered enormously from the U.S.S.R.'s policies. In the 1930's, the traditionally nomadic Kazakh people were forcibly settled on collectivized farms, and more than a million died of starvation. In the 1950's, Khrushchev's failed "Virgin Lands" scheme and the Soviet government's repeated nuclear tests wreaked environmental havoc on Kazakhstan. As a result of years of Soviet economic development programs, the rate of Russian and Ukrainian immigration into Kazakhstan greatly increased. By 1979, 41 percent of Kazakhstan's population was Russian; 36 percent were native Kazakhs.

Under Mikhail Gorbachev's policy of glasnost, or openness, in the 1980's, the corrupt Communist party leader of Kazakhstan and Brezhnev crony Dinmukhamed Kunayev was deposed. He was ultimately replaced by Nursultan Nazarbayev, an ethnic Kazakh, who was elected in April 1990 to the new post of president.

Kazakhstan declared its independence in March 1991 and joined the Commonwealth of Independent States in December. It has pursued closer economic but not political ties with Russia and Belarus. The May 1995 customs union among the three was expanded in March 1996 to include coordination of agricultural and industrial policies and the establishment of joint transport, energy and information systems, with Kyrgystan added as a fourth member. Kazakhstan took part (April 1996) in a five-power non-agression treaty with Russia, China, Kyrgyzstan, and Tajikistan which was extended a year later to include reduction of military forces in border areas. The last remaining Soviet-era nuclear missle was detonated underground in May 1995 and the last ballistic missle silo was torn down in September 1996. In Feb. 1997 the supposedly tame legislature refused to ratify a Russian lease of four nuclear test sites in Kazakhstan.

Independent Kazakhstan's first presidential election was held in December 1991 with Nazarbayev the only candidate. An April 1995 referendum cancelled the 1996 election and extended Nazarbayev's term to 2000 with a gratifying 95 percent "yes" vote; and in August of the year 89 percent approved a new "strong president" constitution, making the president head of the Supreme Court and permitting him to dissolve parliament at will. Nazarbayev had already dissolved parliament in March 1995, a parliament in which his supporters held two-thirds of the seats, but whose pace of economic reform displeased him. He ruled by decree until new elections late in 1995 and early in 1996.

Kazakhstan's economic future looks bright because of its enormous untapped gas and oil reserves, perhaps 25 billion barrels. Several global corporations have negotiated development rights. In April 1996, Kazakhstan, Russia and Oman established a consortium with eight oil companies to build a 900-mile pipeline linking the Tengiz fields with Russia's Black Sea port of Novorossiyak. And in July of that year, the I.M.F. chipped in with a loan of $446 million.

In 1998 the capital was moved— ostensibly for security reasons—from Almaty to remote Akmola, which was renamed Astana, a word meaning "capital" in Kazakh. In July, Navarbayev signed a pact with Russia, settling the thorny question of dividing the northern Caspian Sea (with its petroleum riches). But with falling world oil prices, the Kazakh economy stalled, bringing Nazarbayev to call for presidential elections 18 months early, elections he not surprisingly won handily, this time with 80 percent of the votes, in January 1999.

▶ **KENYA**
Republic of Kenya
● **GEOGRAPHY Location:** eastern Africa. **Boundaries:** Sudan to NW, Ethiopia to N, Somalia to E, Indian Ocean to SE, Tanzania to SW, Lake Victoria, Uganda to W. **Total area:** 224,962 sq. mi. (582,650 sq km). **Coastline:** 333 mi. (536 km). **Comparative area:** slightly more than twice the size of Nevada. **Land use:** 7% arable land; 1% permanent crops; 37% meadows and pastures; 30% forest and woodland; 25% other; includes negl. % irrigated. **Major cities:** (1989 est.) Nairobi (capital) 1,346,000; Mombasa 465,000; Nakuru 162,800; Kisumu 185,100; Thika 57,100.
● **PEOPLE Population:** 30,765,916 (July 2001 est.). **Nationality:** noun—Kenyan(s); adjective—Kenyan. **Ethnic groups:** 22% Kikuyu, 14% Luhya, 13% Luo, 12% Kalenjin, 11% Kamba, 6% Kisii, 6%

Meru, 15% other African, 1% non-African (Asian, European, and Arab). **Languages:** English and Kiswahili (both official), indigenous languages. **Religions:** 38% Protestant, 28% Roman Catholic, 26% indigenous beliefs, 7% Muslim, 2% other.

• **GOVERNMENT Type:** republic. **Independence:** Dec. 12, 1963 (from U.K.). **Constitution:** Dec. 12, 1963. **National holiday:** Independence Day, Dec. 12. **Head of Government:** Daniel T. arap Moi, president (since Oct. 1978). **Structure:** executive—president and cabinet; unicameral legislature—first multiparty election since repeal of one-party state law in 1991; judiciary.

• **ECONOMY Monetary unit:** Kenyan shilling. **Budget:** (2000 est.) *income:* $2.9 bil.; *expend.:* $2.97 bil. **GDP:** $45.6 bil., $1,500 per capita (2000 est.). **Chief crops:** coffee, tea, corn, wheat, sugarcane; cattle, pork, poultry. **Natural resources:** gold, limestone, soda ash, salt barites. **Major industries:** small-scale consumer goods (plastic, furniture, batteries, textiles, soap, cigarettes, flour), agricultural processing, oil refining. **Labor force:** 9.2 mil. (1998); 75-80% agriculture, 20-25% non-agriculture; 50% unemployment (1997). **Exports:** $1.7 bil. (f.o.b., 2000 est.); tea, coffee, petroleum products (1995). **Imports:** $3 bil. (f.o.b., 2000 est.); machinery and transport equipment, consumer goods, petroleum and petroleum products **Major trading partners:** *exports:* 18% Uganda, 12% Tanzania, 15% U.K.; *imports:* 12% U.K., 8% UAE, 8% Japan.

Kenya formed part of an ancient network of trade between the Red Sea and the coast of East Africa as early as the fourth century B.C. Persian and Arab trading posts were established on the coast by the eighth century A.D. At about the same time, the indigenous Cushitic people of Kenya had been joined by Bantu and Nilotic immigrants. Swahili, a mixture of Bantu and Arabic, developed as a language of trade throughout the region.

Portuguese explorers reached Kenya in 1498. Portuguese control of the coastal area ended in 1729, when the region came under the control of the sultans of Oman. British adventurers explored Kenya in the late 19th century. In 1885 the Berlin Conference divided East Africa into European spheres of influence. The British East Africa Company established a protectorate over the coastal region in 1890 and extended its control into the interior in 1895. British settlers established farms, mission stations, and towns, and Kenya was given colonial status in 1920.

During World War II, northern Kenya was briefly occupied by troops from the Italian colony of Ethiopia. After the British reasserted control, Africans were granted the right to participate in local government in 1944.

From 1952 to 1959, a state of emergency was declared in Kenya because of the "Mau Mau" rebellion against British colonial rule. In response to local unrest, British authorities widened African participation in government and Africans were elected to the Legislative Council in 1957.

Kenya became independent on Dec. 12, 1963, and in 1964 assumed the status of a republic within the British Commonwealth. Jomo Kenyatta, a member of the dominant Kikuyu population and leader of the main political party, the Kenya African National Union (KANU), was elected Kenya's first president. A leftist party, the Kenya People's Union (KPU) was organized in 1966, led by Oginga Odinga. In 1969 it was implicated in the assassination of Tom Mboya, a prominent political leader; its leaders were im-

prisoned and the party dissolved. From 1969 to 1992 KANU was Kenya's sole political party.

Kenyatta died on Aug. 22, 1978, and Vice Pres. Daniel arap Moi succeeded him. In 1982 the constitution was amended to make Kenya a one-party state. Moi was reelected president in 1983 and again in 1988, the latter being the first election conducted without secret ballots. Foreign observers accused the Moi government of widespread human rights abuses. Riots broke out in several cities in 1991, and sporadic ethnic violence cost thousands of lives.

In 1991, Odinga formed the opposition Forum for the Restoration of Democracy (FORD), in direct defiance of the government. With Western aid conditioned on economic reform, political pluralism, and improved human rights, Moi allowed presidential elections to be held in Dec. of 1992. The three opposition parties split, and Moi was returned to office for a fourth time.

Kenya has traditionally been viewed as the success story of postcolonial Africa, but by the 1990's, widespread government corruption, and economic inefficiency had taken a heavy toll. Tourism has fallen due to the rise in violence, and the economy was further strained by the presence of refugees from Ethiopia, Somalia, and Sudan.

Early in 1994 the government announced reforms aimed at restoring confidence in the economy, including lifting the restrictions on foreign investment. But Pres. Moi's (April 1995) arrest of two leading opposition figures (bringing the total arrested since 1993 to more than 50) led to increased frustrations among his many political enemies. In mid-1997, large demonstrations demanding Moi reform the electoral system in time for Dec. presidential elections were broken up by police with a great amount of violence. In the face of international condemnation Moi agreed to the proposed reforms (July 15), but little progress was made in subsequent meetings between the government and the opposition leaders. In the Jan. 1998 Moi won reelection but with only 40 percent of the ballots. His KANU party won 107 of the 210 legislative seats. (In an unrelated story, the U.S. embassy was attacked by a terrorist truck-bomb August 7, with 250 deaths.)

▶ **KIRIBATI**
Republic of Kiribati

• **GEOGRAPHY Location:** 33 atolls, in three main groups (E to W: Line Is., Phoenix Is., Gilbert Is.) in mid-Pacific Ocean; about 2,400 mi. (3,870 km) E to W and 1,275 mi. (2,050 km) N to S. Tarawa (Gilberts) 1°30'N, 173°00'E. **Boundaries:** surrounded by Pacific Ocean; nearest neighbors are Nauru to W, and Tuvalu and Tokelau to S. **Total area:** 277 sq. mi. (717 sq km). **Coastline:** 710 mi. (1,143 km). **Comparative area:** four times the size of Washington, D.C. **Land use:** 0% arable land; 51% permanent crops; 0% meadows and pastures; 3% forest and woodland; 46% other. **Major cities:** (1990 census) Tarawa (capital) 25,154.

• **PEOPLE Population:** 94,149 (July 2001 est.). **Nationality:** noun—I-Kiribati (sing., pl.); adjective—I-Kiribati. **Ethnic groups:** Micronesian. **Languages:** English (official), Gilbertese. **Religions:** 54% Roman Catholic, 30% Protestant (Congregational), some Seventh-Day Adventist, Church of God, Mormon and Baha'i.

• **GOVERNMENT Type:** republic. **Independence:** July 12, 1979 (from U.K.). **Constitution:** July 12, 1979. **National holiday:** Independence Day, July 12. **Head of Government:** Teburoro Tito, president (since Oct. 1994). **Structure:** executive; unicameral legislature; judiciary—all judges appointed by the president.

• **ECONOMY Monetary unit:** Australian dollar. **Budget:** (1996 est.) *income:* $33.3 mil.; *expend.:* $47.7 mil. **GDP:** $76 mil., $850 per capita (2000 est.). **Chief crops:** copra; taro, bread fruit, vegetables; fish. **Natural resources:** phosphate (production discontinued in 1979). **Major industries:** fishing and handicrafts. **Labor force:** 7,870 economically active (1985 est.). **Exports:** $6 mil. (f.o.b., 1998 est.); 62% copra, seaweed, fish. **Imports:** $44 mil. (c.i.f., 1999 est.); foodstuffs, machinery and quipment. **Major trading partners:** *exports:* U.S., Australia, Bangladesh; *imports:* Australia, Fiji, Japan.

In 1892 the British established a protectorate over the Gilbert Islands, inhabited principally by Micronesians. In 1915 Britain joined the islands administratively with the Polynesian-speaking Ellice Islands to the south to form a British colony, the Gilbert and Ellice Islands (later expanded to include other islands). The Japanese occupied the Gilberts in 1942; in 1943 the Allied forces recaptured them, and Tarawa was the scene of some of the fiercest combat in the Pacific.

In 1971 Britain granted the colony self-rule. The Ellice Islands broke away in 1975, becoming the independent nation of Tuvalu in 1978. On July 12, 1979, the Gilbert Islands became independent as Kiribati. United States claims to portions of the Line and Phoenix islands were settled by a friendship treaty in 1979.

Kiribati's economy is based on subsistence farming and on fishing. Copra exports and the sale of fishing rights (principally to Japan) are the main earners of hard currency. The islands were expected to join the United Nations in late 1999.

▶ KOREA, NORTH
Democratic People's Republic of Korea

• **GEOGRAPHY Location:** northern part of Korean peninsula in eastern Asia. **Boundaries:** China to NW, Sea of Japan to E, Republic of Korea to S, Yellow Sea to SW. **Total area:** 46,541 sq. mi. (120,540 sq km). **Coastline:** 1,551 mi. (2,495 km). **Comparative area:** slightly smaller than Mississippi. **Land use:** 14% arable land; 2% permanent crops; negl. % meadows and pastures; 61% forest and woodland; 23% other; includes 9% irrigated. **Major cities:** (1986 est.) Pyongyang (capital) 2,000,000; Hamhung 670,000; Chongjin 530,000; Sinuju 330,000; Kaesong 310,000.

• **PEOPLE Population:** 21,968,228 (July 2001 est.). **Nationality:** noun—Korean(s); adjective—Korean. **Ethnic groups:** racially homogeneous. **Languages:** Korean. **Religions:** Buddhism and Confucianism; autonomous religious activities now almost nonexistent.

• **GOVERNMENT Type:** authoritarian socialist; one-man dictatorship. **Constitution:** adopted 1948, revised Apr. 1992 and Sept. 1998. **National holiday:** Foundation Day, Sept. 9. **Heads of Government:** Kim Jong Il, president (since Oct. 1994); Hong Song San, prime minister (since Dec. 1992). **Structure:** executive—president is dominant figure in government; Supreme People's Assembly theoretically supervises legislative and judicial functions; State Administration Council (cabinet) oversees ministerial operations.

• **ECONOMY Monetary unit:** North Korean won. **Budget:** N.A.; **GDP:** $22 bil., $1,000 per capita (2000 est.). **Chief crops:** corn, rice, vegetables; pigs, cattle. **Natural resources:** coal, lead, tungsten, zinc, graphite. **Major industries:** machine building, military products, electric power, chem-

icals. **Labor force:** 9.6 mil.; 36% agricultural, 64% nonagricultural. **Exports:** $520 mil. (f.o.b., 1999 est.); minerals, metallurgical products, agricultural and fishery products, manufactures. **Imports:** $960 mil. (c.i.f., 1999 est.); petroleum, machinery and equipment, coking coal, grain. **Major trading partners:** *exports:* 5% China, 28% Japan, 21% South Korea; *imports:* 33% China, 17% Japan, 5% Russia.

(For pre-1945 history, see "Republic of Korea.")

The Soviet Union's declaration of war against Japan in the waning days of World War II strengthened its position in northeast Asia, and particularly in Korea. After Japan's surrender, Korea was arbitrarily divided into zones of Soviet and American occupation, north and south of latitude 38° north. The Korean Communist party (KCP), founded in 1922, had functioned in exile in the U.S.S.R. during the Japanese occupation, and KCP workers were quickly moved into the Soviet zone in 1945.

U.S.-Soviet talks aimed at Korean reunification broke down, and in 1948 the establishment of separate regimes in North and South Korea formalized the postwar occupation zones. The Korean Democratic People's Republic was proclaimed on May 1, 1948, It inherited most of the industrial and hydroelectric power infrastructure built during the Japanese colonial period and enjoyed strong Soviet backing.

On June 25, 1950, North Korean troops crossed the 38th parallel in an effort to force the reunification of Korea under a communist regime. U.N. troops under American leadership came to the defense of the South. (For the Korean War, see "South Korea.") The war was fought to a stalemate, and a truce was signed on July 27, 1953.

Until 1994 North Korea had a single leader throughout its national history: Kim Il Sung, chairman of the KCP from 1945 and president of the DPRK from 1972. Under Kim Il Sung, North Korea was a typically Stalinist Soviet nation, concentrating its economic energies on heavy industry and imposing a strictly regimented political and social life on its citizens. Economic development was supported by aid from the Soviet Union and China. After an impressive program of postwar reconstruction in the 1950's and 1960's, the country fell into economic stagnation.

Relations between North and South Korea were implacably hostile; the North has made numerous attempts to infiltrate and sabotage the South. In 1983, 17 people, including four South Korean cabinet ministers, were killed in Rangoon, Burma, by a bomb planted by North Korean agents. In 1990 the leaders of both countries held three cordial but unproductive meetings. Much of the goodwill accumulated by these gestures was greatly harmed by the continuous assertions of the U.S. and others that North Korea was planning to build nuclear weapons.

In August 1992, China, North Korea's long-term ally established diplomatic relations with South Korea, leaving North Korea completely isolated. High-level contacts between North and South Korea continued, but reconciliation talks stalled in 1993 as the issue of North Korean nuclear weapons came to the fore. North Korean leaders refused to allow international arms inspectors access to some facilities and withdrew from the Nuclear Non-Proliferation Treaty. In June 1994 former U.S. president Jimmy Carter met with Kim Il Sung and arranged for a summit meeting with South Korea and for another with Pres. Clinton to resolve the nuclear weapons issue. Kim Il Sung's sudden death in July prevented immediate progress, but in 1995 an agreement was reached that called for North Korea to dismantle its nuclear facilities in exchange for two new reactors from which weapons-grade plutonium is hard to extract. In 1996 severe floods destroyed most of the rice crop, left half a million homeless, and forced North Korea to accept emergency grants of rice from Japan and South Korea.

Continued severe famine spurred North Korea to pursue reconciliation talks with the South, but those talks were repeatedly disrupted by strife over North Korean nuclear-weapons development programs, several incidents of clandestine landing of northern commandos in the south, and the defection of several senior communist officials. In the fall of 1997 Kim Jung II assumed his father's old position as general secretary of the Worker's Party. U.S. suspicions, voiced in 1998, of a new underground nuclear plant were proven baseless in May of 1999, the Great Leader permitting an inspection in return for food aid. (Estimates of 2.3 million deaths from the famine must have influenced the decision). Talks with South Korea in Beijing were broken off in June 1999 after South Korea sank a North Korean torpedo boat in the Yellow Sea. But talks in Geneva continued with South Korea, China and the U.S., supplemented in March 2000 with secret talks with South Korea, as diplomatic relations were opened with Italy and Australia. The secret talks led, in June, to a Pyongyang visit by South Korea's president Kim. The two pledged themselves to peace and reunification. Family visits across the border ensued. (See part I, "Major News Stories of the Year.")

▶ **KOREA, SOUTH**
Republic of Korea
● **GEOGRAPHY Location:** southern part of Korean peninsula in eastern Asia. **Boundaries:** North Korea to N, separated by frontier roughly following 38th parallel; Sea of Japan to E, East China Sea to S, and Yellow Sea to W. **Total area:** 38,023 sq. mi. (98,480 sq km). **Coastline:** 1,500 mi. (2,413 km). **Comparative area:** slightly larger than Indiana. **Land use:** 19% arable land; 2% permanent crops; 1% meadows and pastures; 65% forest and woodland; 13% other; includes 12% irrigated. **Major cities:** (1995 est.) Seoul (capital) 10,776,201; Pusan 3,802,319; Taegu 2,228,843; Inchon 1,818,293; Kwangju 1,144,695.
● **PEOPLE Population:** 47,904,370 (July 2001 est.). **Nationality:** noun—Korean(s); adjective—Korean. **Ethnic groups:** homogeneous; small Chinese minority (about 20,000). **Languages:** Korean; English widely taught in high school. **Religions:** 49% Christianity, 47% Buddhism, 3% Confucianism; pervasive folk religion.
● **GOVERNMENT Type:** republic. **Constitution:** Feb. 25, 1988. **National holiday:** Liberation Day, Aug. 15. **Heads of Government:** Kim Dae Jung, president (since Feb. 1998); Lee Han Dong, premier (since May 2000). **Structure:** executive; unicameral legislature (National Assembly); judiciary.
● **ECONOMY Monetary unit:** South Korean won. **Budget:** (1999 est.) *income:* $81.8 bil.; *expend.:* $94.9 bil. **GDP:** $764.6 bil., $16,100 per capita (2000 est.). **Chief crops:** rice, root crops, barley, vegetables, fruit; cattle, pigs, chickens, milk, eggs; fish catch of 2.9 mil. metric tons, seventh largest in the world. **Natural resources:** coal, tungsten, graphite, molybdenum. **Major industries:** electronics, automobiles, chemicals, shipbuilding. **Labor force:** 22 mil. (1998); 68% services and

other, 20% mining and manufacturing; 12% agriculture, fishing, and forestry; 6.3% unemployment (1999). **Exports:** $172.6 bil. (f.o.b., 2000); electronic and electrical equipment, electrical machinery, steel, automobiles. **Imports:** $160.5 bil. (f.o.b., 2000); machinery, electronics and electronic equipment, oil, steel, transport equipment, textiles. **Major trading partners:** U.S., Japan, China.

From ancient times Korea has struggled successfully to preserve its national independence. To the native culture—marked by a warrior aristocracy, shamanic religion, and a subject class of rice cultivators—was added, under continuous Chinese influence, a strong adherence to Buddhism and a system of government modeled on Chinese Confucian bureaucratism. The three rival kingdoms of Silla, Paekche, and Koguryo were united, through Chinese intervention, in the seventh century A.D.; unified dynastic rule was maintained thereafter.

The Yi dynasty (1392-1910), under which Korea was known as the Kingdom of Choson, was a staunch tributary ally of China under both the Ming (1368-1644) and Qing (1644-1911) dynasties. A Japanese invasion of Korea in 1592 conquered most of the country but was finally repelled by combined Chinese and Korean forces. From the late 17th century to the 1870's, all non-Chinese foreign influence was rigorously excluded from the country.

Korea's isolation, and its status as a Chinese tributary, ended in 1874, when Japan imposed on it the Treaty of Kangwha, guaranteeing Japanese commercial access and other interests. The Sino-Japanese War of 1894-95 was fought primarily over the status of Korea; following Japan's victory in that war, Korea was made a Japanese protectorate and was annexed as a Japanese colony in 1910. A harsh regime was established with the aim of eradicating Korean culture and incorporating Korea entirely into the Japanese empire.

During the colonial period, Korean resistance to the Japanese regime was violently suppressed, but resistance movements survived in exile—notably the Korean Communist party in the Soviet Union and a republican movement in China. During World War II, tens of thousands of Koreans were conscripted as forced laborers to work in Japan and in Japanese-occupied territories.

Following Japan's surrender, Korea was arbitrarily divided into zones of Soviet and American occupation, north and south of 38° north latitude. The dividing line split Korea economically as well as geographically and politically; Korea's industry and hydroelectric power was concentrated in the north, while the south was primarily agricultural. In contrast to well-laid Soviet plans for installing a Communist government in the north (see "North Korea"), American attempts to reunify the country under a republican regime were inept. By 1948 it had become clear that plans for reunification were hopeless. In May of that year, the Republic of Korea was organized in the south, with Dr. Syngman Rhee as president. The United States withdrew its occupation forces in June 1949.

On June 25, 1950, North Korean troops invaded the south in an apparent attempt to unify the country forcibly under the communist regime. An emergency session of the U.N. Security Council voted to send troops to Korea; the U.S.S.R., having boycotted the session, was unable to exercise its veto on North Korea's behalf. U.N. troops, dominated by American forces and commanded by Gen. Douglas MacArthur, launched a counterattack in September with a landing at Inchon and swept north, reaching the Chinese border by Nov. 20. On Nov. 26 the tide turned again when Chinese troops entered the war, ostensibly to defend the Chinese border but also to aid their North Korean allies in driving the U.N. forces south again. Seoul fell once more on Jan. 4, 1951. In February and March another U.N. counteroffensive drove the combined Chinese and North Korean forces back to the 38th parallel again. Thereafter, the battle lines remained generally stable, although fierce fighting continued at intervals for another two years. On Apr. 11, 1951, Gen. MacArthur was relieved of the Korean command for making unauthorized policy statements and was replaced by Gen. Matthew Ridgway.

Armistice talks began in July 1951 but broke down repeatedly. A truce was signed on July 27, 1953, creating a demilitarized zone along the 38th parallel and establishing a framework for talks on a permanent settlement of the war. Negotiations have continued fruitlessly at the Panmunjom armistice conference headquarters ever since.

Postwar reconstruction, with significant U.S. aid, was overseen by the government of Syngman Rhee. Pres. Rhee resigned in 1960 after a wave of student demonstrations charging him with corruption and undemocratic practices. On May 16, 1961, Gen. Park Chung Hee seized power in a military coup. The military government was given democratic trappings when in 1972 a referendum was passed allowing Gen. Park to run for an unlimited series of six-year presidential terms. Gen. Park was assassinated on Oct. 26, 1979, by the government's chief of intelligence. Gen. Chun Doo Hwan rose to power, continuing the military rule of Gen. Park. Gen. Chun's regime was marked by widespread violent political protests.

South Korea's economy made great strides during Gen. Chun's regime. The traditionally agrarian country was transformed into a modernized, urban, industrial nation. In 1986 South Korea for the first time achieved a favorable balance-of-payments ratio in foreign trade, and the favorable balance has increased rapidly, led by exports of automobiles, textiles and clothing, and consumer electronic goods.

After weeks of widespread demonstrations in mid-1987, Gen. Chun agreed to allow direct presidential elections to choose his successor. In the elections, the government candidate, Roh Tae Woo, achieved a plurality over the sharply divided opposition parties. Under Pres. Roh, the political situation calmed, although student demonstrations continued, calling for greater efforts for Korean reunification and protesting the presence of large numbers of American troops.

High-level talks between North and South began in 1990, and an agreement in principle was reached that reunification would take place in the near future. South Korea has grown more cautious about reunification, however, after witnessing the tremendous costs West Germany continues to bear in helping East Germany. But South Korea remains one of the strongest economic powers in Asia, and the establishment of diplomatic relations with China in 1992 was a clear signal that it would remain so.

In 1992, longtime political opposition leader Kim Young Sam won election as South Korea's first postwar civilian president. Although he was initially able to liberalize some aspects of civil rights in South Korea, the renewed threat of war with North Korea became the overriding preoccupation of the government until late 1994, when an agreement was reached calling for North Korea to dismantle its nuclear facilities in exchange for new reactors.

The ruling Democratic Labor Party was plagued by scandals and political embarrassments that hampered its effectiveness. Pres. Kim's predecessor, Pres. Roh, was arrested for bribe-taking, as was his predecessor, Gen. Chun. Several key businessmen, including Kim's own son, were jailed for corruption. In legislative elections in April 1996 the party lost its parliamentary majority but continued to govern as part of a coalition.

South Korea's economy was battered by the Asian economic crisis of 1997-98, leading to severe hardship for many workers. On Dec. 18, 1997, long-time democracy advocate and dissident Kim Dae Jung was elected. In May 1999 (after promising economic figures suggested a rising GDP and falling unemployment) he was able to reshuffle the cabinet to more closely accord with his "sunshine policy" of reforming the great conglomerate business empires and of improving relations with North Korea. In June talks with the North, held in Beijing, were abbreviated after South Korea sank a North Korean torpedo boat in a fishing grounds dispute in the Yellow Sea. Yet talks in Geneva continued and secret talks began in March 2000, leading to a "summit" in Pyongyang in June between President Kim and Kim Jong Il which promised peace and reunification.

▶ KUWAIT
State of Kuwait

● **GEOGRAPHY Location:** northeastern Arabian peninsula. **Boundaries:** Iraq to N, Saudi Arabia to S, Persian Gulf to E. **Total area:** 6,880 sq. mi. (17,820 sq km). **Coastline:** 310 mi. (499 km). **Comparative area:** slightly smaller than New Jersey. **Land use:** negl. % arable land; negl. % permanent crops; 8% meadows and pastures; negl. % forest and woodland; 92% other; includes negl. % irrigated. **Major cities:** (1995 census): Kuwait City (capital) 28,859; Salmiya 130,215; Hawalli 82,238; Faranawiya 53,100; Abraq Kheetan 45,120.
● **PEOPLE Population:** 2,041,961 (July 2000 est.). **Nationality:** noun—Kuwaiti(s); adjective— Kuwaiti. **Ethnic groups:** 45% Kuwaiti, 35% other Arab, 9% South Asian, 4% Iranian, 7% other. **Languages:** Arabic (official), English widely spoken. **Religions:** 85% Muslim (40% Shi'a, 45% Sunni), 15% Christian, Hindu, Parsi, and other.
● **GOVERNMENT Type:** nominal constitutional monarchy. **Independence:** June 19, 1961 (from U.K.). **Constitution:** Nov. 11, 1962 (some provisions suspended since Aug. 29, 1962). **National holiday:** National Day, Feb. 25. **Head of Government:** Jaber al-Ahmad al-Jaber al Sabah, amir (since Dec. 1977); Saad Al-Abdulla Al-Salem Al-Sabah, prime minister (since Oct. 1992). **Structure:** executive; unicameral legislature; judiciary.
● **ECONOMY Monetary unit:** Kuwaiti dinar. **Budget:** (FY01/02) *income:* $11.5 bil.; *expend.:* $17.2 bil. **GDP:** $29.3 bil., $15,000 per capita (2000 est.). **Chief crops:** virtually none; extensive fishing; about 75% of potable water must be distilled or imported. **Natural resources:** petroleum, fish, shrimp, natural gas. **Major industries:** petroleum, petrochemicals, desalination. **Labor force:** 1.3 mil. (1998 est.); 50% government and social services, 40% services, 10% industry and agriculture; 68% of population in 15-64 age group is non-Kuwaiti. **Exports:** $23.2 bil. (f.o.b., 2000 est.); oil and refined products, fertilizers. **Imports:** $7.6 bil. (f.o.b., 2000 est.); food, construction materials, vehicles and parts, clothing. **Major trading part-**

ners: *exports:* 23% Japan, 12% U.S.; *imports:* 15% U.S., 10% Japan, 7% U.K.

Kuwait, at the head of the Persian Gulf, was part of the Abbasid empire from the eighth century and was absorbed into the Ottoman Empire in the late 16th century. It was organized as a principality under the al-Sabah dynasty in 1756, but the Ottomans continued to assert sovereignty. Increasing British influence during the 19th century was formalized in 1899, when Kuwait became a British protectorate.

The discovery of oil, first exported from Kuwait after World War II, rapidly made the principality one of the wealthiest in the Middle East. The British protectorate ended in 1961, when Kuwait gained full independence. The great majority of oil field workers in Kuwait are non-Kuwaiti Arabs, including many Palestinians. Oil revenues have made possible a total welfare state for Kuwaiti citizens, who pay no taxes and enjoy a wide range of free social services.

Kuwait allied itself with Iraq in the Iran-Iraq War of 1980-88; Kuwaiti tankers came under heavy attack from Iranian warships in the gulf. In July 1987, Kuwaiti tankers were reflagged with the U.S. flag and placed under escort of American warships in an operation that continued into 1989. Most of Kuwait's territory is barren and sparsely inhabited but with proven crude oil reserves of 94 bil. barrels—10 percent of the world's reserves—other economic endeavors are not needed.

On Aug. 2, 1990, Kuwait was invaded, and later annexed, by Iraq. In February 1991 it was liberated by a coalition of Arab, non-Arab Muslim, and Western nations led by the United States. Much of the country was destroyed or looted by the Iraqis. After its return to power, the ruling al-Sabah family came under strong pressure to institute democratic reforms. Parliamentary elections were held in 1992, and opposition candidates won 30 of 50 seats. The sultan then announced a new cabinet with more nonroyal members than ever before.

A brief war-scare flared up in October 1994 as 20,000 Iraqi Republican Guards were moved to the Kuwaiti border, only to retreat in the face of U.S. military opposition. In November, Iraq formally recognized Kuwait's sovereignty.

▶ **KYRGYZSTAN**
Kyrgyz Republic
● **GEOGRAPHY Location:** eastern central Asia. **Boundaries:** Kazakhstan to N and NE, China to SE and S, Tajikistan to SW, Uzbekistan to W. **Total area:** 76,641 sq. mi. (198,500 sq km). **Coastline:** none. **Comparative area:** slightly smaller than South Dakota. **Land use:** 7% arable land; 44% permanent pasture; 4% forest and woodland; 45% other (mostly urban and mountain). **Major cities:** (1990) Bishkek (known as Frunze 1926-91) (capital) 626,900.
● **PEOPLE Population:** 4,753,003 (July 2001 est.). **Nationality:** noun—Kyrgyzstani(s); adjective—Kyrgyzstani. **Ethnic groups:** 52.4% Kirghiz, 18% Russian, 12.9% Uzbek, 2.5% Ukrainian, 2.4% German, 11.8% other. **Languages:** Kirghiz and Russian (both official), Kirghiz is a member of south Turkic language group written in Cyrillic since 1940. **Religions:** 75% Muslim; 20% Russian Orthodox.
● **GOVERNMENT Type:** republic. **Independence:** Aug. 31, 1991 (from Soviet Union). **Constitution:** adopted May 5, 1993. **National holiday:** National Day, Dec. 2; Independence Day, Aug. 31. **Heads of Government:** Askar A. Akayev, president (since

Oct. 1991); Amangeldy Muraliev, prime minister (since April 1999). **Structure:** executive—president, prime ministers, Cabinet of Ministers; bicameral legislature; judiciary.
● **ECONOMY Monetary unit:** som. **Budget:** (1999 est.) *income:* $207.4 mil.; *expend.:* $238.7 mil. **GDP:** $12.6 bil., $2,700 per capita (2000 est.). **Chief crops:** wool, tobacco, cotton; sheep, goats, cattle. **Natural resources:** hydroelectric potential; gold; coal, natural gas, petroleum, lead, zinc. **Major industries:** small machinery, textiles, food processing, cement. **Labor force:** 1.7 mil. (1999); 55% agriculture and forest, 15% industry and construction. **Exports:** $482 mil. (f.o.b., 2000 est.); cotton, wool, meat, tobacco; ferrous and nonferrous metals. **Imports:** $579 mil. (f.o.b., 2000 est.); foodstuffs, fuel, machinery. **Major trading partners:** Germany, Kazakhstan, Russia.

Kyrgyzstan is largely mountainous, dominated by the massive Tien Shan range in the northeast and the Pamir-Alay range in the southwest. Most of the population lives in one of three major valleys, the Fergana, the Chu, and the Talas, since much of the country is permanently ice-capped and covered with glaciers. The Kyrgyz people are mentioned in early Turkic inscriptions that date back at least to the eighth century A.D.

They were one of the great nomadic tribes of central Asia, who until the 10th century settled around the Upper Yenisei River. With the Mongol invasions of the 13th century, they migrated to the areas of the Tien Shan range in present-day Kyrgyzstan, a territory that has been controlled variously by Mongols, Kalmyks, Manchus, the large tribal empire of the Kokand khanate (or state), and the Russians. In the mid-17th century, the Kyrgyz began to be converted to Islam, but at nearly the same time, the Manchus defeated the Mongols and the Kyrgyz people became Chinese subjects. The Chinese did not interfere with their nomadic life, but in the 19th century they were attacked and came under the control of the khanate of Kokand, during which time Islam was strengthened. In 1868 the khanate became a Russian protectorate and in 1876, the area was merged into the Russian empire as Fergana region. A large Russian influx followed, and many Kyrgyz migrated to China and Afghanistan.

The period immediately following the 1917 Bolshevik revolution was one of great confusion and fighting between the Kyrgyz, the Reds, the Whites, and foreign interventionists. Soviet power was established in 1919, although fighting continued in some parts until 1922. In 1918, Kyrgyzstan was included in the Russian republic's Turkestan Autonomous Soviet Socialist Republic; then, with the National Delimitation of Central Asian Republics in 1924, its name changed to Kara-Kirghiz Autonomous Province (also within the Russian republic). On Dec. 5, 1936, it became a full Soviet Socialist Republic (SSR) of the U.S.S.R.

As a Soviet republic, advances were made in literacy, education, and public health, although repression of nationalist Kyrgyz was also evident. In the 1920's and 1930's, land reform and collectivization ended the traditional nomadic way of life. Kyrgyz nationalists strongly opposed the changes that Soviet rule brought, but the central government won in the end, and the nationalists were repressed. From the 1930's, ethnic Russians held most of the leading Communist party and government positions in the Kyrgyz SSR.

Mikhail Gorbachev's policy of glasnost, or openness, was responsible for the first public discussion of corruption in government, the emergence of a more liberal Kyrgyz press by 1988, and the emergence of opposition parties and ethnic conflicts. In 1990 disputes over housing and land in the Osh region of the crowded Fergana Valley led to violent confrontations between the Kyrgyz and the republic's Uzbeks. Osh had been incorporated into Kyrgyzstan in 1924, even though the majority population was Uzbek, and at various times the Uzbeks had lobbied for the establishment of an autonomous Uzbek region in Osh.

In Feb. 1990 traditional Soviet-style elections brought into office many Communist party officials, and in April the Supreme Soviet elected Absamat Masaliyev, who had been the Kyrgyz republic's Communist party First Secretary. In Oct. 1990, however, largely due to the violence in Osh, Masaliyev did not receive enough Supreme Soviet votes, and the reformer Askar Akayev was elected as president. After the failed coup in Moscow in August 1991, Communist party activities were suspended, although most leaders were still party members. In Dec. 1991 Kyrgyzstan signed the Alma-Ata Declaration that founded the Commonwealth of Independent States.

Beginning in 1992, with the help of the International Monetary Fund, Akayev embarked on a radical economic program that included lowering wages, raising prices, and abolishing customs duties and tariffs with Central Asian neighbors Kazakhstan and Uzbekistan. Although the program initially caused hardship, it proved successful. In 1995, elections, Akayev was elected to a second term with 60 percent of the vote. This came six months after international lenders, led by the World Bank, agreed in June to $680 million in aid.

In 1996 Kyrgyzstan joined the common market among Russia, Belarus, and Kazakhstan as it expanded to include development of common energy, transport and information systems. The government signed a non-aggression pact with Russia, China, Kazakhstan and Tajikistan, a pact extended a year later. In Oct. 2000 Akayev won a third term with 75 percent of the vote.

▶ LAOS
Lao People's Democratic Republic
● GEOGRAPHY Location: landlocked country in Southeast Asia. Boundaries: Myanmar to NW, China to N, Vietnam to E, Cambodia to S, and Thailand to W. Total area: 91,429 sq. mi. (236,800 sq km). Coastline: none. Comparative area: slightly larger than Utah. Land use: 3% arable land; negl. % permanent crops; 3% meadows and pastures; 54% forest and woodland; 40% other; includes 1% irrigated. Major cities: (1985 census) Vientiane (capital) 377,409; (1973) Savannaket 50,690; Pakse 44,860; Luang Prabang 44,244; Saya Bury 13,775.
● PEOPLE Population: 5,635,967 (July 2001 est.). Nationality: noun—Lao or Laotian (sing. and pl.); adjective—Lao or Laotian. Ethnic groups: 68% Lao Loum, 22% Lao Theung, 9% Lao Soung including Hmong and Yao. Languages: Lao (official), French, English, ethnic languages. Religions: 60% Buddhist, 40% animist and other.
● GOVERNMENT Type: communist state. Independence: July 19, 1949 (from France). Constitution: Aug. 14, 1991. National holiday: National Day, Dec. 2. Heads of Government: Khamtai Siphandone, president (since Feb. 1998); Sisavath Keobounphanh, prime minister (since Feb. 1998). Structure: executive; unicameral legislature; independent judiciary.

● ECONOMY Monetary unit: new kip. Budget: (FY98/99) income: $211 mil.; expend.: $462 mil. GDP: $9 bil., $1,700 per capita (2000 est.). Chief crops: sweet potatoes, vegetables, coffee, sugarcane, cotton; water buffalo, pigs, cattle, poultry; tobacco. Natural resources: tin, timber, gypsum, hydropower potential. Major industries: timber, hydropower, tin and gypsum. Labor force: about 1-1.5 mil.; 80% agriculture; 5.7% unemployment (1997). Exports: $323 mil. (f.o.b., 2000 est.); electricity, wood products, coffee, tin. Imports: $540 mil. (f.o.b., 2000 est.); machinery and equipment, vehicles, fuel. Major trading partners: exports: Vietnam, Thailand, Germany; imports: Thailand, Japan, Vietnam.

Inhabited by the Thai-speaking Lao people in the river valleys and by Hmong and other tribal people in the highlands, Laos historically had little national cohesion and was dominated by its more powerful neighbors, Siam (Thailand) to the west and Vietnam to the east. In 1893 France forced Siam to recognize Laos as a French protectorate; the country was thereafter incorporated into the French Union of Indochina. Laos was occupied by Japan during World War II but saw little major fighting.

In 1946 Laos was united under the Luang Prabang dynasty and was granted local autonomy as a constitutional monarchy in 1949. During the final phases of the Indochina War against French colonialism in 1953-54, Vietnamese Communist (Vietminh) incursions reinforced the position of the Laotian Communist party (Pathet Lao) in Laotian politics. Following the French withdrawal in December 1954, Laos became an independent nation and was admitted to the United Nations in 1955.

The creation of a coalition government under Prince Souvana Phouma in 1962 temporarily resolved a turbulent political situation; an international agreement signed in Geneva that year guaranteed Laos's neutrality. The Pathet Lao withdrew from the coalition in 1964 and renewed its armed uprising against the government, with North Vietnamese support. American planes bombed Vietnamese supply lines along the Ho Chi Minh trail, and American agents recruited Hmong tribesmen as irregular troops to attack Pathet Lao positions. The Pathet Lao nevertheless made steady gains, especially after 1970. In 1973, Prince Souvana Phouma ordered a ceasefire, and in 1975 the Pathet Lao took control of the capital, Vientiane. The Lao People's Democratic Republic was proclaimed on Dec. 3, 1975. Large numbers of Hmong and other tribal people fled to Thailand.

Subsequently, Laos was strongly dominated by Vietnam, which stationed significant numbers of troops in the country. In 1989, in Laos's first election since the communist takeover, a Supreme People's Assembly was elected specifically to approve a new constitution, which it did in 1991; the constitution confirmed the Lao People's Revolutionary party as the sole legal political party. Single-party elections in 1992 did little to alter the country's political climate, though observers predicted changes as the Communists began to pass from the scene. In 1995 Laos signed a treaty with Cambodia, Thailand, and Vietnam to establish a Mekong Commission to regulate water use among the four nations. In 1997 Laos was admitted to the Association of Southeast Asian Nations.

►LATVIA
Republic of Latvia
● GEOGRAPHY Location: eastern coast of Baltic Sea in northeastern Europe. Boundaries: Baltic Sea to N, Estonia to NE, Russian Federation, Belarus to S, Lithuania to W. Total area: 24,749 sq. mi. (64,100 sq km). Coastline: Baltic Sea. Comparative area: slightly larger than West Virginia. Land use: 27% cropland; 13% permanent pasture; 46% forest and woodland; 14% other. Major cities: (1994 est.) Riga (capital) 856,281; Daugav'pils 121,974; Liepāja 104,628; Jelgava 71,332; Jurmala 59,581.
● PEOPLE Population: 2,385,231 (July 2001 est.). Nationality: noun—Latvian(s); adjective—Latvian. Ethnic groups: 56.5% Latvian, 30.4% Russian, 4.3% Belarussian, 2.8% Ukrainian, 2.6% Polish. Languages: Lettish (official), Lithuanian, Russian, other. Religions: Lutheran, Roman Catholic, Russian Orthodox.
● GOVERNMENT Type: parliamentary democracy. Independence: Sep. 6, 1991 (from Soviet Union). Constitution: the 1991 Constitutional Law which supplements the 1922 constitution, provides for basic rights and freedoms. National holiday: Independence Day, Nov. 18. Heads of Government: Vaira Viķe-Freiberga, president (since July 1999); Andris Šķéle, prime minister (since July 1999). Structure: executive; unicameral legislature; judiciary.
● ECONOMY Monetary unit: lat. Budget: income: $1.33 bil.; expend: $1.27 bil. (1998 est.) GDP: $17.3 bil., $7,200 per capita (2000 est.). Chief crops: grain, potatoes, sugar beets, vegetables; meat, milk, eggs; fish. Natural resources: minimal; amber, peat, limestone, dolomite. Major industries: machine building, metalworking, chemical processing. Labor force: 1.4 mil. (1997); 25% industry, 10% agriculture, 65% services (2000); 7.8% unemployment (2000). Exports: $2.1 bil. (f.o.b., 2000 est.); timber, textiles, foodstuffs. Imports: $3.2 bil. (f.o.b., 2000 est.); fuels, machinery and equipment, chemicals. Major trading partners: exports: 16% Germany, 11% U.K., 11% Sweden; imports: 15% Russia, 10% Germany, 9% Finland.

Though the Letts ethnically and linguistically are quite distinct from their northern neighbors the Ests, Latvia's history parallels that of Estonia. German merchants, knights, and missionaries made Latvia a semi-ecclesiastical German colony in the 13th century; in the 16th century Latvia passed under first Swedish, then Lithuanian rule; in the 18th century Peter the Great's Russian empire absorbed the land.

A 19th-century cultural revival, inspired in part by Johann von Herder, a native of Riga, found expression in folkloric societies, archaeological research and the compilation of the epic poem, Lacplesis. Brest-Litovsk, the Soviet Union's 1918 peace treaty with Germany, granted Latvia's political independence for the first time in its history.

The constitution of 1922 established a one-house legislature in whose system of proportional representation about 20 different political parties participated. To avoid violence between left and right armed extremists, Prime Minister Karlis Umanlis dissolved the Parliament in May 1934 and ruled as dictator until a new constitution that provided for expanded presidential powers and a second house of the legislature, based on the conception of a corporate state, came into existence in 1938 just before the Hitler-Stalin Pact awarded Latvia to the Russian sphere of interest. Stalin garrisoned troops in Latvia, rigged elections, and in-

corporated the country as a new union republic of the U.S.S.R. in 1940.

For 50 years, harsh Soviet rule continued. The larger cities were Russianized and the highly educated middle and upper-middle classes were deported throughout Russia. Industrialization brought relative prosperity, but the national consciousness was never eradicated.

Mikhail Gorbachev's policy of glasnost, or openness, led to the creation of dissident groups who staged public demonstrations on the anniversaries of the Stalin-Hitler Pact and of the establishment of Latvian independence. After the head of the Latvian Communist party, Boris Pugo was transferred to Moscow, Latvia's Communist party came under the influence of the newly created Latvian Popular Front. With the new political influence of non-Communists, on Sept. 29, 1988, Latvia replaced Russian as the official language.

In March 1990, following Lithuania's example, Latvia announced its intention to secede, survived Gorbachev's January 1991 military crackdown, and after the failed August 1991 coup in Moscow, declared independence.

In June 1995 Latvia gained associate status with the E.U. and made formal application for membership. Summer elections revealed deep political divisions as the three major political parties took barely half the seats. It was not until December that Andris Skele was able to become premier, heading a cabinet containing members of six of Latvia's nine parties. Skele was forced to resign in July 1997 because of corruption charges and over disappointment that the E.U. would not consider Latvia's application until the "second wave." Parliamentary elections in Oct. 1998 resulted in the same degree of part splintering, with no party taking even 25 percent of the seats; but Vilis Kristopans was able to form a government. More significantly, in a referendum voters, by 53 percent to 45 percent, eased the citizenship laws, making it simpler for ethnic Russians (one-third of the population) to become citizens. In June 1999 Pres. Ulmanis' second term ended; his successor, Vaira Vike Freiberga, became the first female president of an ex-Soviet republic. Coalition discord brought the end of the Kristopanis government in July 1999; the successor government, under Andris Skele collapsed in April 2000, and the mayor of Riga, Andris Berzins, nominated as his successor.

►LEBANON
Lebanese Republic
● GEOGRAPHY Location: western Asia. Boundaries: Syria to N and E, Israel to S, Mediterranean Sea to W. Total area: 4,015 sq. mi. (10,400 sq km). Coastline: 140 mi. (225 km). Comparative area: about 0.7 times the size of Connecticut. Land use: 21% arable land; 9% permanent crops; 1% meadows and pastures; 8% forest and woodland; 61% other; includes 7% irrigated. Major cities: (1975 est.) Beirut (capital) 1,500,000; Tarabulus (Tripoli) 160,000; Zahleh 45,000; Saida (Sidon) 38,000; Sur (Tyre) 14,000.
● PEOPLE Population: 3,627,774 (July 2001 est.). Nationality: noun—Lebanese (sing., pl.); adjective— Lebanese. Ethnic groups: 95% Arab, 4% Armenian, 1% other. Languages: Arabic (official), French, Armenian, English. Religions: 70% Islam, 30% Christian, negl. Judaism.
● GOVERNMENT Type: republic. Independence: Nov. 22, 1943 (from League of Nations Mandate under French administration). Constitution: May 23, 1926 (amended). National holiday: Indepen-

dence Day, Nov. 22. **Heads of Government:** Emile Lahoud, president (since Nov. 1998); Rafic Hariri, prime minister (since Oct. 2000). **Structure:** executive—by custom, president is Maronite Christian, prime minister is Sunni Muslim, and president of legislature is Shia Muslim; unicameral. legislature; judiciary—three courts for civil and commercial cases, one court for civil cases.

• ECONOMY **Monetary unit:** Lebanese pound. **Budget:** (2000 est.) *income:* $3.31 bil.; *expend.:* $5.55 bil. **GDP:** $18.2 bil., $5,000 per capita (2000 est.). **Chief crops:** citrus, vegetables, potatoes, olives, tobacco, hemp (hashish); sheep, goats. **Natural resources:** limestone, iron ore, salt; water-surplus state in water-deficit region. **Major industries:** banking, food processing, textiles. **Labor force:** 1.3 mil. plus as many as 1 mil. foreign workers (1996 est.); 62% services, 31% industry, 7% agriculture; 18% unemployment (1997 est.). **Exports:** $700 mil. (f.o.b., 2000 est.); foodstuffs and tobacco, textiles, chemicals, metals. **Imports:** $6.2 bil. (f.o.b., 2000 est.); foodstuffs, machinery & transport equipment, consumer goods. **Major trading partners:** *exports:* 8% Saudi Arabia, 9% UAE, 6% Syria; *imports:* 13% Italy, 7% U.S., 11% France, 8% Germany.

The ancient history of Lebanon is essentially coextensive with that of Syria, of which it was long a part. The port cities of Tripoli, Tyre, and Sidon were important centers of the Phoenician empire. The parallel ranges of the Lebanon and Anti-Lebanon mountains, crowned with the country's famous cedar trees, enclose the fertile Bekaa Valley. The coastal cities became strongholds of early Christianity, later fragmented into numerous sects, including Maronites (Syrian Catholic), Roman Catholic, Greek Orthodox, Syrian Orthodox, and others. The mountains of the south became the center of the Druze sect of Islam, while orthodox Sunni Islam dominated in the Bekaa Valley.

Lebanon came under French influence in the late 18th century, as France claimed the role of protector of Syria's Christian community. France intervened in Lebanon in 1841 and again in 1860 when fighting between Maronite and Druze communities led to the massacre of many Christians. Under pressure from France, the Ottoman Empire granted some local autonomy to the Maronites of greater Lebanon.

In the dismemberment of the Ottoman Empire after World War I, France was granted a League of Nations Mandate over the Levant States (Lebanon and Syria), ensuring French control of the Iraq Petroleum Company pipeline from Iraq to Tripoli. In 1926 Lebanon became a selfgoverning republic under the mandate, but internal unrest and anti-French sentiment continued.

In June 1940 the French administration in Lebanon declared its allegiance to the Vichy government. British and Free French forces occupied Lebanon in June 1941 and declared it an independent republic; but France retained control, and full independence did not come until Jan. 1, 1944.

Under a National Covenant in 1943, political power in the Lebanese parliament was apportioned among the nation's various communities. The president was always to be a Maronite Christian, the prime minister a Sunni Muslim. This provided a workable formula for power sharing but also ensured that the national government would always be hostage to the considerable power of separate communities and clans.

The years from the end of World War II to the early 1970's were a brief golden age for Lebanon. Beirut developed into a wealthy, cosmopolitan city, the center of Middle Eastern banking and trade, while agriculture and small-scale industry flourished in the rest of the country. A Syrian-backed Muslim uprising in 1958 had no significant impact; U.S. Marines landed in May 1958 to protect American interests and remained until October. By the late 1960's, however, Lebanon's stability was threatened by PLO attacks on Israel from refugee camps in southern Lebanon and by a shift in the country's demographic balance. Muslims had become a majority in Lebanon by the late 1960's and demanded a revision of the National Covenant, while Maronite Christians continued to cling to their position of political dominance.

Throughout the 1970's, Palestinian raids from Lebanon into Israel brought Israeli retaliatory strikes in southern Lebanon. Israeli troops occupied southern Lebanon in 1978 and again in 1980. The Palestinian-Israeli conflict polarized opinion within Lebanon, inflaming anti-Western feelings among Lebanon's Sunni Muslims.

Civil war broke out in 1975, with Palestinian and leftist Muslim militias battling militias of the Maronite community, the Christian Phalange party, and other groups. More than 60,000 died, and damage ranged into the billions of dollars. Syrian troops intervened in 1976, battling Palestinian forces in an attempt to restore the status quo. Arab League efforts to negotiate a cease-fire produced an unstable peace at the end of 1976, though Syrian troops remained in Lebanon.

Fighting broke out between Syrian forces and Christian militiamen near Zahle on Apr. 1, 1981. Other groups joined the fighting in a general war of each against all. Israel staged commando raids against Palestinian positions in Tyre and Tulin. Israeli air raids on Beirut caused extensive loss of life and property damage.

Israel invaded Lebanon in a full-scale air and sea assault on June 6, 1982, in an attempt to drive out the PLO. Israeli forces surrounded Beirut and began a heavy bombardment of the city. On Aug. 1, Palestinian forces withdrew from Beirut under international supervision. On Sept. 14 newly elected Pres. Bashir Gemayel, a Maronite Christian, was assassinated; Israeli troops occupied the Muslim quarters of West Beirut in response. With tacit Israeli approval, Christian militiamen invaded two refugee camps and slaughtered hundreds of Palestinian civilians.

Beirut remained a battle zone in 1983, divided by the "Green Line" into Christian and Muslim sectors. Terrorist bombings were common. The U.S., France, Italy, and other Western nations stationed troops in Beirut in an attempt to enforce a cease-fire. Fifty people were killed when a bomb partly destroyed the U.S. embassy on Apr. 18; separate attacks on military installations on Oct. 23 killed 241 U.S. Marines and 58 French soldiers.

Rashid Karami became premier with Syrian support on Apr. 26, 1984. The civil war continued, with fighting among various groups of Christian, Druze, Sunni, Shiite, and Palestinian militias. Kidnappings of foreign nationals at the hands of various terrorist factions became commonplace. War between Shiite and Palestinian forces broke out in May 1985. Israeli forces withdrew from most of Lebanon in June, but maintained a "security zone" in the southern part of the country. Premier Karami was assassinated on June 1, 1987, when a bomb destroyed his helicopter.

At an October 1989 Arab League-sponsored meeting, Christian and Muslim leaders agreed on a new national charter. The Taif accord was condemned by Christian militants, led by Gen. Michel Aoun, and Muslim militia leaders. Newly elected Pres. René Mowad, a Syrian-backed Christian, was assassinated on Nov. 22 and succeeded by Elias Hraoui.

In November 1990, rival Shiite militias—the Syrian-backed Amal and Iranian-backed Party of God—signed an agreement ending three years of fighting. In February 1991 Lebanese troops moved to defend the area for the first time in 13 years and called for Israel to abandon its "security zone" in southern Lebanon. In addition to leaving 150,000 dead, the civil war severely disrupted the economy, virtually wiping out the international sector and causing significant damage to the domestic sector.

The government of Christian prime minister Omar Karami collapsed in May 1992, after riots protesting widespread economic hardship. New elections were held under Syrian supervision with Hizbollah and other Islamic fundamentalist parties gaining the most seats in the new parliament, in part because the Christian parties called for an electoral boycott.

In early 1994, as Israeli-Hizbollah skirmishes continued in southern Lebanon, the government banned the Christian political party Lebanese Forces, arrested some of its leaders, and stopped all "political" broadcasts not government-controlled. In 1995, Syria-backed premier Rafik Hariri won a second term together with a 2-1 backing in Parliament. Although he sought to address economic reconstruction, he was hindered by repeated skirmishes between Israel and Hizbollah Shiite guerrillas in Israel's "security zone" in southern Lebanon. In April 1996 the fighting escalated as Israel launched 600 airraids and 24,000 artillery shells some of which hit a U.N. refugee camp near Tyre, killing over 100 and wounding 100 more. The U.N. voted 64-2 (with 65 abstaining) to condemn the attack.

By the following year order had been essentially restored but no peace agreement reached with Israel. With $3 bil. in U.S. and E.U. aid the government set about to rebuild this ravaged land. The U.S. officially lifted its ban on travel to Lebanon in July 1997. Deadly skirmishes still occured in the "security zone." In 1998 Lebanon held its first municipal elections in 35 years; no clear pattern emerged. In Oct., the (pro-Syrian) National Assembly unanimously elected General Emile Lahoud as president. He nominated Selim al-Hoss as prime minister after Hariri declined a fourth consecutive government. In 1999 the Israeli-Hizbollah warfare in south Lebanon intensified until, suddenly, Israel withdrew completely (May 24, 2000), accompanied by about 3,000 Christian militiamen of the South Lebanese Army to whom Israel offered haven. Apparently at Syria's behest, only a token force of Lebanese troops and police entered the border area, effectively under Hizbollah control. In early Sept. Hariri won a decisive victory in parliamentary elections.

▶ LESOTHO
Kingdom of Lesotho

● **GEOGRAPHY   Location:** landlocked country in southern Africa. **Boundaries:** entirely surrounded by South African territory. **Total area:** 11,718 sq. mi. (30,350 sq km). **Coastline:** none. **Comparative area:** slightly smaller than Maryland. **Land use:** 11% arable land; 0% permanent crops; 66% meadows and pastures; 0% forest and woodland; 23% other. **Major cities:** (1976) Maseru (capital) 45,000.

● **PEOPLE   Population:** 2,177,062 (July 2001 est.). **Nationality:** noun—Mosotho (sing.), Basotho (pl.); adjective—Basotho. **Ethnic groups:** 99.7% Sotho; 1,600 Europeans, 800 Asians. **Languages:** Sesotho (southern Sotho), English (official), Zulu, Xhosa. **Religions:** 80% Christian, 20% indigenous beliefs.

● **GOVERNMENT   Type:** parliamentary constitutional monarchy. **Independence:** Oct. 4, 1966 (from U.K.). **Constitution:** Apr. 2, 1993. **National holiday:** Independence Day, Oct. 4. **Heads of Government:** Letsie III, king (since Feb. 1996); Pakalitha Bethuel Mosisili, prime minister (since May 1998). **Structure:** executive—king is chief of state but has no power and can be deposed by College of Chiefs; legislature—bicameral legislature; judiciary.

● **ECONOMY   Monetary unit:** loti. **Budget:** (FY99/00 est.) *income:* $76 mil.; *expend.:* $80 mil. **GDP:** $5.1 bil., $2,400 per capita (2000 est.). **Chief crops:** corn, wheat, pulses, sorghum, barley; livestock. **Natural resources:** some diamonds and other minerals, water, agricultural and grazing land. **Major industries:** tourism, food, beverages. **Labor force:** 700,000 economically active; 86% subsistence agriculture; 35% work in South Africa. **Exports:** $175 mil. (f.o.b., 2000 est.); 75% manufactures, wool and mohair, food and live animals. **Imports:** $700 mil. (f.o.b., 2000 est.); food, building materials, vehicles, machinery. **Major trading partners:** *exports:* 65% South African Customs Union, 34% North America; *imports:* 90% South African Customs Union, 7% Asia.

Lesotho, formerly Basutoland, is an independent kingdom surrounded entirely by the Republic of South Africa. The area was sparsely populated by Bushmen until the 16th century when refugees from tribal wars in surrounding areas began to move in, an influx that continued through the 19th century. These immigrants coalesced into a homogenous cultural group, the Basothos.

Under King Moshoeshoe (1823-70), several Basotho groups were consolidated, but much land was lost in a series of wars with South Africa. Moshoeshoe appealed to Queen Victoria for aid, and in 1868 the nation became a British protectorate. Between 1884 and 1959 all executive and legislative authority was in the hands of a British high commissioner. In 1903 a Basotho consultative body was established, and in 1959 a new constitution gave the council power to legislate on internal affairs.

On Oct. 4, 1966, Basutoland achieved full independence as the Kingdom of Lesotho. The first elections after independence, in 1970, were nullified by the ruling Basutoland National party (BNP) when early returns indicated that the party might lose. A state of emergency was declared, the constitution was suspended, and parliament dissolved.

Elections in 1985 were boycotted by opposition parties, and in 1986 the BNP government was ousted in a coup. The nation was run by a military council, which in February 1990 stripped King Moshoeshoe II of his remaining powers. Military rule ended finally in April 1993 when Ntsu Mokhehle was elected prime minister and his Basotholand Congress party (BCP) gained all 243 seats in the legislature. King Moshoeshoe II was restored in January 1995 but ruled for barely a year before dying in an auto accident. The Traditional College of Chiefs named his son Letsie III as his successor.

Elections in May 1998 kept the ruling party in

power with a new Prime Minister, Pakalitha Mosisili, but the opposition and some outside observers said the elections were not entirely honest. In September, pro-opposition army officers mutinied and only with the assistance of troops from South Africa was the government able to quell the uprising. The government pledged new and free elections within 18 months.

▶ LIBERIA
Republic of Liberia
● **GEOGRAPHY   Location:** western Africa. **Boundaries:** Sierra Leone, Guinea to N, Ivory Coast to E, Atlantic Ocean to S and W. **Total area:** 43,000 sq. mi. (111,370 sq km). **Coastline:** 360 mi. (579 km). **Comparative area:** slightly larger than Tennessee. **Land use:** 1% arable land; 3% permanent crops; 59% meadows and pastures; 18% forest and woodland; 19% other; includes negl. % irrigated. **Major cities:** (1984) Monrovia (capital) 421,058.
● **PEOPLE   Population:** 3,225,837 (July 2001 est.). **Nationality:** noun—Liberian(s); adjective—Liberian. **Ethnic groups:** 95% indigenous peoples, including Kpelle, Bassa, Gio, Kru, Grebo, Mano, Krahn, Gola, Gbandi, Loma, Kissi, Vai, Bella; 2.5% descendants of repatriated slaves known as Americo-Liberians. **Languages:** 20% English (official); more than 20 languages of Niger-Congo language group. **Religions:** 40% indigenous beliefs, 20% Muslim, 40% Christian.
● **GOVERNMENT   Type:** republic. **Independence:** July 26, 1847. **Constitution:** Jan. 6, 1986. **National holiday:** Independence Day, July 26. **Head of Government:** Charles Taylor, president (since July 1997). **Structure:** executive—president, appointed cabinet; bicameral legislature; judiciary.
● **ECONOMY   Monetary unit:** Liberian dollar. **Budget:** N.A. **GDP:** $3.35 bil., $1,100 per capita (2000 est.). **Chief crops:** rubber, coffee, cocoa, rice, cassava, palm oil, sugarcane; sheep, goats; timber. **Natural resources:** iron ore, timber, diamonds, gold. **Major industries:** rubber processing, palm oil processing, diamonds. **Labor force:** 70% agriculture. **Exports:** $55 mil. (f.o.b., 2000 est.); diamonds, iron ore, rubber, timber, coffee. **Imports:** $170 mil. (f.o.b., 2000 est.); fuels, chemicals, machinery, transportation equipment. **Major trading partners:** *exports:* 53% Belgium, 9% Switzerland, 6% U.S.; *imports:* 30% South Korea, 15% Japan, 24% Italy, Singapore.

Liberia was populated by migrants from the north and east beginning in the 12th century, but it remained relatively isolated from the remainder of West Africa and was not incorporated into any of the region's premodern kingdoms and empires. Portuguese explorers first reached the Liberian coast in 1461 to be followed by other European traders. Until the 19th century, Liberia was largely ignored by the world except for a small-scale coastal trade in slaves and forest products.

In 1816 the U.S. Congress granted a charter to the American Colonization Society, ACS, a private organization dedicated to the African repatriation of freed slaves. The first settlers landed in 1822 at the town that was later to become Monrovia. In 1838 the settlers organized the Commonwealth of Liberia under a governor appointed by the ACS. The commonwealth declared its independence as the Republic of Liberia in 1847 and adopted a constitution modeled after that of the United States. The new government, Africa's first independent republic, was granted diplomatic recognition by Great Britain in 1848, France in 1852, and the United States in 1862.

Bolstered by the moral backing of the United States, Liberia in its first 100 years of independence succeeded, with difficulty, in fending off British and French attempts to encroach on its territory from their neighboring colonies. Although descendants of freed American slaves are a minority in Liberia's ethnically diverse population, they have consistently dominated the country's political life.

William V.S. Tubman was elected president in 1944 and served until his death in 1971, successfully steering Liberia through the post-World War II age of African nationalism and decolonization. He was succeeded by William R. Tolbert, Jr. On Apr. 12, 1980, Tolbert was deposed in a military coup led by Master Sgt. Samuel K. Doe. Doe suspended the constitution and imposed martial law but pledged a new constitution by 1985.

Presidential elections were held on Oct. 15, 1985, under the terms of a provisional constitution that for the first time enacted universal suffrage. Doe was elected and his party won 80 percent of the seats in the legislature. Despite allegations of fraud that led to a violent but unsuccessful coup attempt in November 1985, the Second Republic, under the new constitution, was inaugurated on Jan. 6, 1986.

On Dec. 24, 1989, about 150 antigovernment guerrillas of the National Patriotic Forces of Liberia (NPFL), led by Charles Taylor, crossed the border from the Ivory Coast. The fighting degenerated into ethnic warfare between the Krahn and Mandingo, in support of the government, and the Gio and Mano, who supported the rebels. Prince Johnson split from Taylor's forces and took up fighting both government troops and Taylor. A peacekeeping force of the Economic Community of West African States (ECOWAS) landed at Monrovia on Aug. 24 to mediate a cease-fire and prepare for free elections. On Sept. 10 Pres. Doe was killed by Prince Johnson, but a cease-fire was not agreed upon until Nov. 28, 1990.

From 1990 to 1992 Charles Taylor solidified his hold on the country despite the establishment of a government (under Amos Sawyer) in Monrovia by the West African States. By 1993 the government and ECOWAS forces succeeded in containing Taylor's forces. In 1994 an interim coalition government representing the country's three major factions came into power as peace talks began. Elections were scheduled for November 1995 but extensive fighting broke out continually until in April 1996, Monrovia experienced its worst fighting of the war. Yet another cease-fire was signed April 18. Over 150,000 had died up to then.

In early 1997 some positive signs could be seen as ECOWAS, led by a Nigerian peacekeeping force, helped to restore order, disarm many of the militias, and arrange for elections in July. Charles Taylor won a landslide victory. The nation's economy has been devastated by the war and the government faces a daunting task as rebuilding begins.

Doubts arose about domestic peace when Pres. Taylor attempted to arrest opposition militia leader Roosevelt Johnson in September: 50 died in the fighting as Johnson fled to the U.S. Embassy for safety. In early 1999, Taylor faced broad international condemnation for Liberia's aid to rebels in Sierra Leone. But the U.N. agreed to Taylor's proposal to place international monitors along Liberia's border with Sierra Leone. In return for Pres. Taylor's support for the RUF rebels in Sierra Leone, he controls their illegal diamond trade, skimming as much as 90 percent of the profit.

▶LIBYA
Socialist People's Libyan Arab Jamahiriya

● **GEOGRAPHY   Location:** along Mediterranean coast of North Africa. **Boundaries:** Mediterranean Sea to N, Egypt to E, Sudan to SE, Niger, Chad to S, Tunisia, Algeria to W. **Total area:** 679,359 sq. mi. (1,759,540 sq km). **Coastline:** 1,100 mi. (1,770 km). **Comparative area:** slightly larger than Alaska. **Land use:** 1% arable land; 0% permanent crops; 8% meadows and pastures; 0% forest and woodland; 91% other. **Major cities:** in Jan. 1987, Col. Qaddafi designated Hun, a town 404 mi. (650 km) SE of Tripoli, as administrative capital of country (population N.A.); (1985) Tripoli 858,000; Benghazi 368,000; Misurata 117,000.
● **PEOPLE   Population:** 5,240,599 (July 2001 est.). **Nationality:** noun—Libyan(s); adjective—Libyan. **Ethnic groups:** 97% Berber and Arab; some Greeks, Maltese, Italians, Egyptians, Pakistanis, Turks, Indians, Tunisians. **Languages:** Arabic, Italian, and English widely understood in major cities. **Religions:** 97% Sunni Muslim.
● **GOVERNMENT   Type:** Jamahiriya (a state of the masses) in theory, governed by populace through local councils; in fact, a military dictatorship. **Independence:** Dec. 24, 1951 (from Italy). **Constitution:** Dec. 11, 1969, amended Mar. 2, 1977. **National holiday:** Revolution Day, Sept. 1. **Head of Government:** Col. Muammar al-Qaddafi (no official title; runs country and is treated as chief of state) (since Sept. 1969); Imbarak Abdullah Al-Shamekh, prime minister (since March 2000). **Structure:** officially, paramount political power and authority rests with General People's Congress, which theoretically functions as a parliament with a cabinet called General People's Committee; elections are indirect.
● **ECONOMY   Monetary unit:** Libyan dinar. **Budget:** (2000 est.) **income:** $6.85 bil.; **expend.:** $4.4 bil. **GDP:** $45.4 bil., $8,900 per capita (2000 est.). **Chief crops:** wheat, barley, olives, dates, citrus fruits; meat, eggs. **Natural resources:** crude oil, natural gas, gypsum. **Major industries:** petroleum, food processing, textiles. **Labor force:** 1.5 mil.; 29% industry, 54% services and government, 17% agriculture. **Exports:** $13.9 bil. (f.o.b., 2000 est.); petroleum. **Imports:** $7.6 bil. (f.o.b., 2000 est.) machinery and transport equipment, food. **Major trading partners:** *exports:* 33% Italy, 24% Germany, 10% Spain; *imports:* 24% Italy, 12% Germany, 7% U.K.

The coastal cities of Libya played an important cultural and commercial role in the Mediterranean in antiquity and were prized possessions of numerous empires. The Libyan coast was successively ruled by Phoenicians, Carthaginians, Berbers, Romans, and Vandals before being incorporated into the Byzantine Empire in the fourth century A.D.; nomadic tribes in the interior were beyond the reach of any government. The Islamic conquests of the seventh and eighth centuries brought Libya into the Muslim world.

Libya was incorporated into the Ottoman Empire shortly after the Ottoman conquest of Egypt in 1517 and was ruled by local Ottoman vassals until 1835 when direct Ottoman government was established. In 1911 Libya was invaded and conquered by Italy. After World WarI, local resistance to Italian colonial rule was led by King Idris I, Emir of Cyrenaica. British troops drove Italian and German forces from Libya in 1943. King Idris returned from exile in 1944. Following World War II, most of Libya was ruled as a British protectorate with a smaller portion under French administration.

Libya became an independent constitutional monarchy on Dec. 24, 1951. In 1959 significant oil reserves were discovered, rapidly transforming Libya from one of the poorest states in North Africa to one of the wealthiest.

A military coup on Sept. 1, 1969, led by Col. Muammar al-Qaddafi, deposed the monarchy and declared the establishment of the Libyan Arab Republic. Qaddafi moved rapidly to nationalize foreign assets, expel foreign troops, and close foreign libraries and cultural centers. He also assumed full dictatorial powers under a political system that gives equal weight to Islamic law and his own political philosophy. Popular participation in elections is mandatory, although no government organization outside Qaddafi and his circle of advisers exerts any real authority.

Libya has given strong political and financial aid to various radical Palestinian groups and other enemies of Israel, sponsoring terrorist activities throughout Europe and the Middle East in support of the Palestinian cause. Numerous anti-Qaddafi Libyan exiles were assassinated in Europe. Libya also engaged in sporadic military campaigns against Egypt and the Sudan.

Relations between Libya and the United States were very hostile in the 1980's. On May 6, 1981, the U.S. closed the Libyan "People's Bureau" (embassy) in Washington, D.C. On Aug. 2, 1981, American jets shot down two attacking Libyan warplanes during U.S. naval exercises in the Gulf of Sidra, which Libya claims as national waters. In 1986 the United States imposed economic sanctions on Libya, ordered all Americans to leave the country, and froze Libyan assets in the U.S. Another clash in March 1986 ended with the loss of two Libyan ships.

On Apr. 5, 1986, Libyan-sponsored terrorists bombed a nightclub in West Berlin, killing two U.S. soldiers; in response, American bombers attacked Tripoli and Benghazi on Apr. 14 in an apparent attempt to kill Col. Qaddafi himself. In 1990, investigators announced they had linked Libyan agents to the bombing of a Pan Am Jet over Lockerbie, Scotland, in 1988.

In January 1989 an international outcry arose when a West German company admitted selling equipment to Libya for a chemical weapons plant. Qaddafi's difficulties with the Western powers continued in 1992, as they demanded he release the suspected terrorists in the Lockerbie bombing. The U.N. imposed sanctions on Libya, including a prohibition on sales of military equipment and a ban on all flights in and out of the country. U.S. attempts to gain a worldwide embargo on Libyan oil failed in 1995. In Sept. 1995 Qaddafi began the expulsion of the 30,000 Palestinians in Libya, provoking fighting between Libyan security forces and Islamic militants. In 1997 as the Vatican announced that it would establish diplomatic relations, the U.S. listed Libya as one of several nations sponsoring terrorism.

Elaborate diplomatic maneuvers in 1998 and 1999 led finally in April to President Qaddafi's handing over two Libyans for trial in the 1988 bombing of Pan Am flight 103. U.N. sanctions were suspended but the U.S. announced that its anti-terrorism sanctions would continue. The U.S. later eased food and medicine sanctions. In Jan. 2001 the Pan Am 103 trial ended with one conviction (with life imprisonment) and one acquittal. Qaddafi denounced the conviction.

▶LIECHTENSTEIN
Principality of Liechtenstein

● **GEOGRAPHY   Location:** landlocked country in central Europe. **Boundaries:** Austria to N and E, Switzerland to S and W. **Total area:** 62 sq. mi. (160 sq km). **Coastline:** none. **Comparative area:** about 0.9 times the size of Washington, D.C. **Land use:** 24% arable land; 0% permanent crops; 16% meadows and pastures; 35% forest and woodland; 25% other. **Major cities:** (1994) Väduz (capital) 5,067; Schaan 5,143; Balzers 3,917; Triesen 3,789; Eschen 3,443.
● **PEOPLE   Population:** 32,528 (July 2001 est.). **Nationality:** noun—Liechtensteiner(s); adjective—Liechtenstein. **Ethnic groups:** 87.5% Alemannic, 12.5% Italian, Turkish and other. **Languages:** German (official), Alemannic dialect. **Religions:** 80% Roman Catholic, 7.4% Protestant.
● **GOVERNMENT   Type:** hereditary constitutional monarchy. **Independence:** Jan 23, 1719. **Constitution:** Oct. 5, 1921. **National holiday:** Assumption Day, Aug. 15. **Heads of Government:** Hans-Adam II, prince (since Nov. 1989); Otmar Hasler, prime minister (since Apr. 2001). **Structure:** executive—hereditary prince; unicameral legislature; judiciary—independent.
● **ECONOMY   Monetary unit:** Swiss franc. **Budget:** (1998); *income:* $424.2 mil.; *expend.:* $414.1 mil. **GDP:** $730 mil., $23,000 per capita (1998 est.). **Chief Crops:** wheat, barley, maize, potatoes; livestock, dairy products. **Natural resources:** hydroelectric potential. **Major industries:** electronics, metal manufacturing, textiles. **Labor force:** 22,891 of which 13,847 are foreign workers (mostly from Switzerland and Austria); 53% services; 45% industry, trade, and building; 2% agriculture, fishing, forestry, and horticulture; 1.8% unemployment (1999). **Exports:** $2.47 bil. (f.o.b., 1996 est.); small specialty machinery, dental products, stamps, hardware, pottery. **Imports:** $917.3 mil. (c.i.f., 1996 est.); machinery, metal goods, textiles, foodstuffs, motor vehicles. **Major trading partners:** *exports:* 60.57% E.U. and EFTA countries, Switzerland; *imports:* E.U. countries, Switzerland.

The alpine principality of Liechtenstein, bordered by Austria and Switzerland, is a remnant of the Holy Roman Empire, an ancient constitutional monarchy with a modern industrial economy. The current dynasty was established in 1699; Prince Franz Josef II came to the throne in 1938, yielding his executive powers to his heir apparent, Hans Adam, in 1984.

Liechtenstein was tied to the Austro-Hungarian monarchy until 1918. Since then it has remained in a customs union with Switzerland, which also handles its foreign affairs. The single-chamber diet, the Landtag is elected by universal suffrage, women having won the right to vote in 1984. For almost 60 years the government was a coalition of the conservcative Progressive Citizens Party and the liberal Fatherland Union. Since April, 1997 Premier Mario Frick has governed with a cabinet of his own Fatherland Union with the PCP in opposition. Liechtenstein joined the United Nations in 1990.

The economy, dominated by dairy farming before 1945, has since been radically transformed by industrialization and the development of service industries. Liechtenstein is a corporate haven, with some 25,000 corporations maintaining nominal headquarters there. Foreign workers constitute about 40 percent of the work force.

▶LITHUANIA
Republic of Lithuania

● **GEOGRAPHY   Location:** eastern coast of Baltic Sea in northeastern Europe. **Boundaries:** Latvia to N, Belarus to E and SE, Poland to SW, Russian Federation (Kaliningrad) to W, Baltic Sea to NW. **Total area:** 25,174 sq. mi. (65,200 sq km). **Coastline:** Baltic Sea. **Comparative area:** slightly larger than West Virginia. **Land use:** 35% arable land; 12% permanent crops; 7% meadows and pastures; 31% forest and woodland; 15% other. **Major cities:** (1995 est.) Vilnius (capital) 575,700; Kaunas 415,300; Klaipeda 202,800; Siauliai 147,200; Panevezys 132,000.
● **PEOPLE   Population:** 3,610,535 (July 2000 est.). **Nationality:** noun—Lithuanian(s); adjective—Lithuanian. **Ethnic groups:** 80.6% Lithuanian, 8.7% Russian, 7% Polish, 1.6% Belarussian. **Languages:** Lithuanian (official), Russian, Polish, ethnic languages. **Religions:** primarily Roman Catholic, also Lutheran, Russian Orthodox, Protestant, evangelical Christian Baptist, Islam, Judaism.
● **GOVERNMENT   Type:** parliamentary democracy. **Independence:** Sept. 6, 1991 (from Soviet Union). **Constitution:** Oct. 25, 1992. **National holiday:** Statehood Day, Feb. 16. **Heads of Government:** Valdas Adamkus, president (since Feb. 1998); Algirdas Mykolas Brazauskas, premier (since July 2001). **Structure:** executive; unicameral legislature; judiciary.
● **ECONOMY   Monetary unit:** litas. **Budget:** (1997 est.). *income:* $1.5 bil.; *expend.:* $1.7 bil. **GDP:** $26.4 bil., $7,300 per capita (2000 est.). **Chief crops:** grain, potatoes, sugar beets, vegetables; meat, milk, eggs; fish; flax fiber. **Natural resources:** peat. **Major industries:** machine building, metalworking, food processing. **Labor force:** 2 mil. (2000 est.); 30% industry, 20% agriculture and forestry. **Exports:** $3.7 bil. (f.o.b., 2000); 22% machinery and equipment, 15% mineral products, 12% chemicals. **Imports:** $4.9 bil. (f.o.b., 2000); 18% machinery and equipment, 16% mineral products, 10% chemicals. **Major trading partners:** *exports:* 6.9% Russia, 15.8% Germany, 12.6% Latvia; *imports:* 20.4% Russia, 16.5% Germany.

Lithuanians and Latvians are closely related peoples whose languages, the only two in the Baltic family of languages, are quite similar. But their histories, at least until 1795, were radically different. Fierce warriors able to stem the German tide during the Middle Ages, the Lithuanians repeatedly defeated the Teutonic knights, defending their independence and retaining their own religion.

In the 14th century, under Grand Duke Gediminas and his sons, Lithuania conquered White Russia (Belarus) and Ukraine and extended the dynasty from the Baltic almost to the Black Sea. The completion of Gediminas's policies came in 1386 when his grandson Jogaila was baptized, married the Polish heiress Jadwiga, and was crowned king of Poland under the title Wladislaw II, thereby creating the Poland-Lithuania Commonwealth. A condition of the union was that Lithuania had to adopt Christianity, which it did in 1387.

With the Third Partition of Poland in 1795, Lithuania was absorbed into Russia. The upper and educated classes took part in Poland's anti-Russian rebellions in 1830 and 1863. After the latter, the Russians required Lithuanians to use the Russian alphabet instead of the Latin as a move to stop any national renaissance; but after

1883 literature smuggled into the czarist empire from Prussia and secret Lithuanian schools and societies kept alive a national identity based on ethnic, religious, and linguistic grounds rather than on the medieval and Renaissance traditions of political independence.

In Jan. 1921 the victorious allies of World War I acknowledged a new Lithuanian republic in the Soviet-German Treaty of Brest-Litovsk of March 1918. Formal recognition came in 1922. The territory of Memel (Klaipeda in Lithuanian), separated from Germany in the Treaty of Versailles, was seized in Jan. 1923 and organized as an autonomous unit of the new republic. The city itself was largely German, but its countryside was Lithuanian and it was Lithuania's only possible outlet to the sea. With the historic capital Vilnius annexed by the new Polish state, the de facto capital became the university city of Kaunas.

Danger from communists and fascists led the army to dispense with Parliament in Dec. 1926; an authoritarian regime under Pres. Antana Smetona followed. In 1939 Lithuania was doomed by the "secret protocols" of the 1939 Nazi-Soviet Pact. In June 1940 the Soviet Army invaded Lithuania and a Soviet-approved "people's government" was formed. After an election in which only pro-Soviet candidates were permitted to run, the Lithuanian Soviet Socialist Republic was proclaimed on July 21, 1940.

Thousands of Lithuanians fled westward, while other thousands disappeared into Siberia. Stalin returned Vilnius (from Poland) and Klaipeda (which Hitler had taken) to Lithuania and fostered industrialization, which elevated living standards above most of the U.S.S.R. A high Lithuanian birth rate enabled the country to resist "Russification" more easily than Latvia or Estonia.

Mikhail Gorbachev's policy of glasnost, and openness, spurred the already strong Lithuanian nationalist and dissident movement into action. It began with a public discussion of the "secret protocols" of the 1939 Nazi-Soviet Pact, which had permitted the U.S.S.R. to annex Lithuania and which the Soviet government long had denied existed. In 1987 the Soviet government tolerated demonstrations in Vilnius, but by February 1988, Soviet troops prevented the Lithuanians from celebrating their 70th year of independence. The Soviet stance resulted in the founding of the new Lithuanian Movement for Reconstruction (Sajudis), which became the main political vehicle for Lithuanian independence from the U.S.S.R.

On Mar. 11, 1990, Lithuania declared its independence, and in response the Soviets began a 72-day-long economic blockade. On Jan. 13, 1991, the world watched as Soviet paratroopers and tanks attacked the radio and television centers, beginning a standoff between the Soviets and the Lithuanians that lasted until Sept. 6, 1991, when the U.S.S.R. recognized Lithuanian independence.

After independence, Lithuania struggled to break a political deadlock caused by its lack of a constitution. In November 1992 free elections were held. The Democratic Labor party (the renamed Communists) gained 47 percent of the vote and 77 seats in Parliament, while Sajudis gained only 22 percent of the vote and 28 seats. In February 1993 the Democratic Labor candidate, Algirdas Brazauskas, handily won the presidential election with 61 percent of the vote.

The last Soviet troops left Lithuanian soil Aug. 31, 1993 and the government moved on a path to

a free economy and worked for good relations with Russia and the other former Soviet states to the east. In 1996, however the Communists were routed and the Homeland Union party took control of the government. Over the next few years Lithuania followed strict fiscal and monetary policies thereby attracting over $1 bil. in foreign investment and strong GDP growth of 6 to 7 percent. In 1997-1998 presidential elections, Brazauskas-backed Valdas Adamkus, after being trounced in the first round, won a close victory. Brazauskas returned as president in 2001.

▶ LUXEMBOURG
Grand Duchy of Luxembourg

• **GEOGRAPHY   Location:** landlocked country in western Europe. **Boundaries:** Belgium to N and W, Germany to E, France to S. **Total area:** 998 sq. mi. (2,586 sq km). **Coastline:** none. **Comparative area:** slightly smaller than Rhode Island. **Land use:** 24% arable land; 1% permanent crops; 20% meadows and pastures; 21% forest and woodland; 34% other. **Major cities:** (1995 est.) Luxembourg-Ville (capital) 76,446; Esch-sur-Alzette 24,255; Differdange 16,196; Dudelange 15,833.

• **PEOPLE   Population:** 442,972 (July 2001 est.). **Nationality:** noun—Luxembourger(s); adjective—Luxembourg. **Ethnic groups:** Celtic base, with French and German blend; also, guest and worker residents from Portugal, Italy, and other European countries. **Languages:** Luxembourgian, German, French, English. **Religions:** 97% Roman Catholic, 3% Protestant and Jewish.

• **GOVERNMENT   Type:** constitutional monarchy. **Independence:** 1839 **Constitution:** Oct. 17, 1868, occasional revisions. **National holiday:** Grand Duke's birthday, National Day, June 23. **Heads of Government:** Henri de Luxembourg, grand duke (since Oct. 2000); Jean-Claude Juncker, prime minister (since Aug. 1999). **Structure:** executive—prime minister appointed by Grand Duke but responsible to parliament; unicameral legislature—Chamber of Deputies, appointed for approximately for five-year term; judiciary.

• **ECONOMY   Monetary unit:** Luxembourg franc. **Budget:** (2000 est.) *income:* $5.6 bil.; *expend.:* $5.6 bil. **GDP:** $15.9 bil., $36,400 per capita (2000 est.). **Chief crops:** barley, oats, potatoes, wheat, fruits, wine grapes; livestock products. **Natural resources:** iron ore (no longer exploited). **Major industries:** banking, iron and steel, food processing. **Labor force:** 248,000, of whom 70,200 are foreign (2000); 83.2% services, 14.3% industry, 2.5% agriculture. **Exports:** $7.6 bil. (f.o.b., 2000); finished steel products, chemicals, rubber products, glass, aluminum. **Imports:** $10 bil. (c.i.f., 2000); minerals, metals, foodstuffs, machinery, quality consumer goods. **Major trading partners:** *exports:* 75% EU, 4% U.S.; *imports:* 81% EU, 9% U.S.

One of hundreds of small principalities in the Holy Roman Empire, Luxembourg joined the German league when the empire was abolished in 1806. It shared a monarchy with the Netherlands, but the two countries remained distinct under a single sovereign. In 1831 Luxembourg lost its French-speaking territory to Belgium. The Treaty of London granted sovereignty to Luxembourg in 1867. When King William III died in 1890, different rules of succession severed the dual monarchy; Queen Wilhelmina succeeded him in the Netherlands, while Adolf of Nassau became grand duke of Luxembourg. The nation's full independence dates from that event.

During the 19th century, Luxembourg developed a balanced modern economy, with prosperous small farms being complemented by industry, particularly mining and steel production. As late as 1970, steel accounted for over 25 percent of the nation's GDP and five-eighths of export earnings, although rising international competition has led to a decline since then.

Luxembourg was overrun by Germany during World War I and again in May 1940, in the early stages of World War II. Archduchess Charlotte fled to London and returned with the Allied armed forces in 1944. The constitutional monarchy has enjoyed political stability since the war, with the Christian Social party normally the senior partner in a three-way coalition.

Luxembourg formed a customs union with Belgium in 1921 and joined the Benelux (Belgium, Netherlands, Luxembourg) union even before World War II had ended. A founding member of the United Nations in 1945, Luxembourg abandoned its traditional neutrality in 1948 and joined NATO in 1949. It was a founding member of the EEC under the 1956 Treaty of Rome and is now home to numerous European Union institutions. International banking accounts for over half of its gross national product. The country's chief problem is a shrinking and aging citizenry. After 35 years Grand Duke John abdicated in 2000, succeeded by his son Henri.

▶ MACEDONIA
The Former Yugoslav Republic of Macedonia

• **GEOGRAPHY Location:** southern part of the Balkan Peninsula. **Boundaries:** Serbia to N, Bulgaria to E, Greece to S, Albania to W, Yugoslavia to NE and N. **Total area:** 9,781 sq. mi. (25,333 sq. km.). **Coastline:** none. **Comparative area:** slightly larger than Vermont. **Land use:** 39% forest and woodland, 25% meadows and pastures, 24% arable land, 10% other. **Major cities:** (1994 census) Skopje (Skoplje or, in Turkish, Uskub) 440,577; Bitola 75,386; Kumanovo 66,237; Tetovo 50,376.
• **PEOPLE Population:** 2,046,209 (July 2001 est.). **Nationality:** noun—Macedonian(s); adj.—Macedonian. **Ethnic groups:** 66% Macedonian, 23% Albanian, 4% Turkish, 2% Serb, 7% other (includes gypsies). **Languages:** 70% Macedonian (official), 21% Albanian, 3% Turkish, 3% Serbo-Croatian, 3% other. **Religions:** 67% Macedonian Orthodox, 30% Muslim, 3% other.
• **GOVERNMENT Type:** emerging democracy. **Independence:** Sept. 17, 1991 (from Yugoslavia). **Constitution:** Nov. 17, 1991. **National holiday:** Independence Day, Sept. 8. **Heads of Government:** Boris Trajovski, president (since Dec. 1999); Ljubco Georgievski, prime minister (since May 2001). **Structure:** executive; unicameral legislature; judiciary.
• **ECONOMY Monetary unit:** denar. **Budget:** (1996 est.) *income:* $1.06 bil.; *expend.:* $1 bil. **GDP:** $9 bil.; $4,400 per capita (2000 est.). **Chief crops:** rice, tobacco, wheat, corn, millet; beef, pork, poultry, mutton. **Natural resources:** chrome, lead, marble, zinc. **Major industries:** metallurgy and metal processing, chemicals, textiles, timber. **Labor force:** 1 mil. (1999 est.); 40% industry and mining; 35% unemployed (1999 est.). **Exports:** $1.4 bil. (f.o.b., 2000 est.); food, beverage, tobacco, machinery and transport equipment, other manufactured goods. **Imports:** $2 bil. (f.o.b., 2000 est.); machinery and transport equipment, chemicals, fuels. **Major trading partners:** Germany, Yugoslavia, Ukraine.

Located at the geographic center of the Balkan peninsula, Macedonia is an epitome of the entire region in its history and ethnic complexity as well. While there is a Macedonian language (a Slavic tongue more akin to Bulgarian than to Serbo-Croatian and codified in grammar and orthography only after World War II), the question of whether or not there is a Macedonian nation is contested: to Serbians, Macedonians are "south Serbs"; to Greeks, they are "Slavophone Greeks"; to Bulgars, they are kindred people, ethnic "cousins."

In any case, Macedonians are not related to the classical people of King Philip and Alexander the Great. Their realm had become a Roman province by 146 B.C. and remained part of the Byzantine Empire even after being invaded and settled by Slavic peoples in the sixth and seventh centuries. Contested in the Middle Ages by the Byzantine, Bulgarian, and Serbian empires, Macedonia fell at last to the Ottoman Turks in 1371. Well into the 19th century its population called itself "Christian" or "Slav," while Greek served as the language of culture and business until a literary awakening associated with scholarly collections of folk songs and heroic poetry brought a Macedonian consciousness. This found significant political expression with the formation in 1893 of the IMRO (Internal Macedonian Revolutionary Organization) that sought to unify all non-Turks—Bulgars, Greeks, Albanians, Vlacha—in an autonomous or independent state and which did not shrink from terrorism and revolution.

The peace treaties of Paris concluding World War I divided Macedonia among three states: Greece, Bulgaria, and the newly created Yugoslavia. IMRO turned against Serbian dominance in Yugoslavia and filled the 1930's with violent struggles against "denationalization." It was Bulgarian claims to Macedonia that led that state to ally with Hitler's Germany and to occupy Macedonia in 1941. With the victory of Tito's partisans and the reconstruction of the Yugoslav state as a federation of Communist "republics," a Macedonian People's Republic was established in 1946.

After the dictator's death in 1980, Macedonia took part in the "collegial rule" whereby the presidency of Yugoslavia and the chairmanship of the Communist party Presidium rotated annually among the republics. But as the separate republics declared independence in 1991 and civil war began, Macedonia declared its own independence in January 1992. Greece's opposition to the new nation's name and flag—as menaces to the northern Greek province of the same name—prevented international recognition until a 1995 agreement between the two countries. Under the pact, Macedonia removed an ancient Greek symbol from its flag and changed its constitution so as to remove any suggestion of a claim on Greek Macedonia. With U.N. recognition came both U.N. "peacekeeping forces" (including 300 American troops) to patrol the frontier with rump Yugoslavia and the painful need to comply with the U.N. embargo against Serbia, to whose economy Macedonia has been closely tied. An April 1996 treaty with Yugoslavia resolved border questions and renounced territorial claims.

Elections in 1998 saw the ruling Social Democrats ousted by the right-wing Coalition for Changes which organized a government under Ljuplo Georgievski. In April, NATO pledged to defend Macedonia from Yugoslav incursions in the latter's struggle again Albanian separatists in Kosovo. Refugees from Kosovo flooded Macedonia, straining its humanitarian capacities. The decision of "founding" president Gligorov not to seek a second term brought presidential elections (Oct.–Dec. 1999) won by Boris Trajkovski of the governing coalition. (See Part I, "Major News Stories.")

▶MADAGASCAR
Republic of Madagascar
• **GEOGRAPHY Location:** off southeast Africa in western Indian Ocean. Antananarivo: 18°52'S, 47°30'E. **Boundaries:** about 300 mi. (500 km) E of Mozambique. **Total area:** 226,656 sq. mi. (587,040 sq km). **Coastline:** 3,000 mi. (4,828 km). **Comparative area:** slightly less than twice the size of Arizona. **Land use:** 4% arable land; 1% permanent crops; 41% meadows and pastures; 40% forest and woodland; 14% other; includes 1% irrigated. **Major cities:** Antananarivo (capital) 662,585 (1985 est.); Antsirabé 78,941; Toamasina (Tamatave) 77,395; Fianarantsoa 68,054; Mahajanga (Majunga) 65,864 (1975 census).
• **PEOPLE Population:** 15,982,560 (July 2001 est.). **Nationality:** noun—Malagasy (sing., pl.); adjective— Malagasy. **Ethnic groups:** highlanders of predominantly Malayo-Indonesian origin (Merina and related Betsileo); coastal peoples collectively termed Cotiers, with mixed African, Malayo-Indonesian, and Arab ancestry (Betsimisaraka, Tsimihety, Antaisaka, Sakalava); French, Indian, Creole, Comoran. **Languages:** French and Malagasy (both official). **Religions:** 52% indigenous beliefs, 41% Christian, 7% Muslim.
• **GOVERNMENT Type:** republic. **Independence:** June 26, 1960 (from France). **Constitution:** Aug. 19, 1992. **National holiday:** Independence Day, June 26. **Heads of Government:** Didier Ratsiraka, president (since Feb. 1997); Tantely René Gabrio Andrianarivo, premier (since May 1996). **Structure:** executive; unicameral legislature, scheduled to become bicameral —two-thirds of upper house will be filled from directly elected regional assemblies, rest by presidential appointment; judiciary.
• **ECONOMY Monetary unit:** Malagasy franc. **Budget:** (1998) *income:* $553 mil; *expend.:* $735 mil. **GDP:** $12.3 bil., $800 per capita (2000 est.). **Chief crops:** coffee, vanilla, cloves, sugar; livestock. **Natural resources:** graphite, chromite, coal, bauxite, salt. **Major industries:** agricultural processing (meat canneries, soap factories, brewery, tanneries, sugar refining), light consumer goods industries (textiles, glassware), cement. **Labor force:** (1999) 7 mil. **Exports:** $538 mil. (f.o.b, 1998 est.); 45% coffee, 20% vanilla, cloves, shellfish, sugar, petroleum products. **Imports:** $693 mil. (f.o.b, 1998); 30% intermediate manufactures, 28% capital goods, 15% petroleum, 14% consumer goods, 13% food. **Major trading partners:** *exports:* 41% France, 19% U.S., 13% Germany; *imports:* 34% France, 6% Hong Kong, 6% China.

The largest island nation, and fourth largest island, in the world, Madagascar was settled by Malayo-Indonesian migrants some 2,000 years ago. Although later waves of African and Arab migrants were absorbed into the population, to a large extent it is still ethnically and culturally Asian. A Portuguese attempt to colonize the island in the 16th century failed, and during the 18th and 19th centuries, a unified kingdom backed by the British ruled the country. Foreign interests—largely British and French—developed extensive coffee plantations, and the French made Madagascar a protectorate in 1885 and a colony in 1896.

During World War II Madagascar sided with the Free French, and French colonial rule was reestablished after the war. The Malagasy Republic was founded as an independent nation on June 26, 1960. A coup in 1972 brought a repressive anti-French government to power.

A new federal constitution was approved in 1992, and in 1993 elections, Albert Zafy defeated the 17-year incumbent Didier Ratsiraka for the presidency, but the results were reversed in 1997 and Ratsiraka immediately set out to cut inflation, and renegotiate the nation's many foreign loans.

Madagascar's wildlife (a mixture of African species and others of domestic evolution) and its isolation make it of unique scientific interest. (In 1990, scientists discovered the smallest mammal known to science: the dwarf lemur.) But some 75 percent of the population live in poverty. Conditions greatly worsened in 2000 with severe cyclone damage.

▶MALAWI
Republic of Malawi
• **GEOGRAPHY Location:** landlocked country in southern central Africa. **Boundaries:** Tanzania to N, Mozambique to E, S, and SW, Zambia to W; Lake Malawi forms much of eastern boundary. **Total area:** 45,745 sq. mi. (118,480 sq km). **Coastline:** none. **Comparative area:** slightly smaller than Pennsylvania. **Land use:** 34% arable land; negl. % permanent crops; 20% meadows and pastures; 39% forest and woodland; 7% other; includes negl. % irrigated. **Major cities:** (1994 est.) Lilongwe (capital) 395,500; Blantyre 446,800.
• **PEOPLE Population:** 10,548,250 (July 2001 est.). **Nationality:** noun—Malawian(s); adjective—Malawian. **Ethnic groups:** Chewa, Nyanja, Tumbuko, Yao, Lomwe, Sena, Tonga, Ngoni, Asian, European. **Languages:** English and Chichewa (both official); Tombuka and other regional languages. **Religions:** 55% Protestant, 20% Roman Catholic, 20% Muslim, indigenous beliefs.
• **GOVERNMENT Type:** multiparty democracy. **Independence:** July 6, 1964 (from U.K.). **Constitution:** May 18, 1995. **National holiday:** Republic Day, July 6. **Head of Government:** Elson Bakili Muluzi, president (since May 1994). **Structure:** executive; legislature—National Assembly of 193 members elected to five-year terms; judiciary.
• **ECONOMY Monetary unit:** Malawian kwacha. **Budget:** (FY99/00 est.) *income:* $490 mil.; *expend.:* $523 mil. **GDP:** $9.4 bil., $900 per capita (2000 est.). **Chief crops:** tobacco, tea, sugar, cotton; cattle, goats. **Natural resources:** limestone; hydropower; unexploited deposits of uranium, coal, bauxite. **Major industries:** agricultural processing (tea, tobacco, sugar), sawmilling, cement. **Labor force:** 3.5 mil. (1990 est.); 86% agriculture. **Exports:** $416 mil. (f.o.b, 2000); tobacco, tea, sugar, coffee, wood products. **Imports:** $435 mil. (f.o.b, 2000); food, petroleum products, semimanufactures, consumer goods. **Major trading partners:** *exports:* 15% U.S., 16% South Africa, 16% Germany; *imports:* 43% South Africa, 14% Zimbabwe, 5% U.K.

Malawi derives its name from the Maravi, a Bantu people who settled in the region in the 13th century and whose descendants, the Chewas, make up a significant segment of the current population. In the 1830's, the Ngoni, driven from what is now South Africa by the Zulus, arrived in the area around Lake Nyasa. The arrival of the Scottish missionary David Livingstone in 1859 led to the establishment of the British-controlled

Nyasaland Protectorate in 1891. In 1953 Nyasaland formed a federation with Northern and Southern Rhodesia (Zambia and Zimbabwe) and began to organize an independence movement. The fight for independence was led by Dr. H. Kamuzu Banda, an expatriate who assumed the presidency of the Nyasaland African Congress, later the Malawi Congress party, upon his return in 1958. The British granted Nyasaland self-governing status in 1962, and Banda was elected prime minister the following year. Malawi achieved full independence under its present name in 1964.

Banda soon introduced one-party rule and had himself declared president for life in 1971. All dissent was crushed while corruption and nepotism strangled the economy, leaving Malawi's citizens among the poorest in the world.

By 1990 internal unrest and the decline of Banda's popularity (he was now in his 90's) rapidly led to change. In 1992 a series of violent strikes by workers in the two largest cities resulted in more than 35 deaths. The United States, Great Britain, and Germany, hoping to push the Banda government to institute democratic reforms, cut off most of the $500 million they had been giving annually in aid. In June 1993 Malawians voted 2 to 1 to institute a multiparty system and in May 1994 Banda lost his nation's only free election in 30 years to Bakili Muluzi's United Democratic Front (UDF). In December 1995, Banda was acquitted of conspiring to murder four of his political rivals in 1983.

▶ MALAYSIA

● **GEOGRAPHY Location:** 13 states in Southeast Asia; 11 are in Peninsular Malaysia and two, Sabah and Sarawak, lie about 400 mi. (640 km) across South China Sea on northern coast of island of Borneo (Kalimantan). **Boundaries:** Peninsular Malaysia—Thailand to N, South China Sea to E, Island of Singapore to S across Johor Strait, and Indonesian island of Sumatra to W across Strait of Malacca; Sabah and Sarawak—South China Sea to NW, Sulu Sea to NE, Celebes Sea to E, Indonesia to S; Brunei is enclosed within Sarawak on coast of South China Sea. **Total area:** 127,317 sq. mi. (329,750 sq km). **Coastline:** 2,905 mi. (4,675 km). **Comparative area:** slightly larger than New Mexico. **Land use:** 3% arable land; 12% permanent crops; negl. % meadows and pastures; 68% forest and woodland; 17% other; includes 1% irrigated. **Major cities:** (1991 census) Kuala Lumpur (capital) 1,145,075; Ipoh 382,633; Johor Baharu 328,646; Melaka (Malacca) 295,999; Petaling Jaya 254,849.

● **PEOPLE Population:** 22,229,040 (July 2001 est.). **Nationality:** noun—Malaysian(s); adjective—Malaysian. **Ethnic groups:** 58% Malay and other indigenous, 26% Chinese, 7% Indian. **Languages:** Bahasa Melayu (official); English, Chinese dialects, Tamil, Telugu, Malalalam, Panjabi, Thai; note – in addition, in East Malaysia several indigenous languages are spoken, the largest of which are Iban and Kadazan. **Religions:** Islam, Buddhism, Daoism, Hinduism, Christianity, Sikhism; note – in addition, Shamanism is practiced on East Malaysia.

● **GOVERNMENT Type:** constitutional monarchy; Peninsular Malaysian states—hereditary rulers in all but Melaka and Penang, where governors are appointed by Malaysian government, with powers of state governments limited by federal constitution; Sabah—self-governing state, holding 20 seats in House of Representatives, with foreign af-

fairs, defense, internal security, and other powers delegated to federal government; Sarawak—self-governing state, which holds 24 seats in House of Representatives, with foreign affairs, defense, internal security, and other powers delegated to federal government. **Independence:** Aug. 31, 1957 (from U.K.). **Constitution:** Aug. 31, 1957, amended Sept. 16, 1963, when Federation of Malaya became Federation of Malaysia. **National holiday:** National Day, Aug. 31. **Heads of Government:** Sultan Salahuddin Abdul Aziz Shah, king; Dr. Mahathir Mohamad, prime minister (since July 1981). **Structure:** executive—paramount ruler chosen by and from the nine state rulers for five-year term; bicameral legislature; judiciary.

● **ECONOMY Monetary unit:** Malaysian ringgit. **Budget:** (2000 est.) *income:* $16.4 bil. *expend.:* $17.8 bil. **GDP:** $223.7 bil., $10,300 per capita (2000 est.). **Chief crops:** Peninsular Malaysia—natural rubber, palm oil, rice; Sabah—mainly subsistence, main crops are rubber, timber, coconut, rice; Sarawak—rubber, timber, pepper. **Natural resources:** tin, crude oil, timber, copper, iron ore. **Major industries:** Peninsular Malaysia—rubber and oil-palm processing and manufacturing, light manufacturing industry, electronics; Sabah—logging, petroleum production; Sarawak—agriculture processing, petroleum production and refining, logging. **Labor force:** 9.6 mil. (2000 est.); 27% manufacturing, 16% agriculture, forestry, and fisheries; 17% local trade and tourism. **Exports:** $97.9 bil. (2000 est.); electronic equipment, petroleum products, palm oil, wood products, rubber, textiles. **Imports:** $82.6 bil. (2000 est.); machinery and equipment, chemicals, food. **Major trading partners:** *exports:* 21% U.S., 18% Singapore, 13% Japan; *imports:* 21% Japan, 17% U.S., 14% Singapore.

From ancient times a group of petty principalities in the southern part of the Malay Peninsula, bordering the Strait of Malacca, maintained extensive ties of maritime commerce throughout Southeast Asia. The early Malay states were Hindu, under Indian influence; with the rise of the Kingdom of Malacca in the 15th century, conversion to Islam was widespread. European influence in the Spice Islands began in the 16th century; the Portuguese, initially dominant, gave way to the Dutch, who seized Malacca in 1641.

British influence grew during the 18th century, with the founding of a trading settlement at Penang in 1789. Singapore was founded in 1819, and the Dutch ceded Malacca to Britain in 1824. By a series of treaties in the late 19th century, the various Malay states became British protectorates; Britain controlled the entire southern peninsula after 1909. Under British rule, commercial tin mining and the establishment of extensive rubber plantations led to the importation of many Indian and Chinese laborers; eventually ethnic Chinese dominated Malaya's domestic economy.

In the 19th century, Great Britain also gained a dominant position in northern Borneo. (Borneo is divided among Brunei, Indonesia and Malaysia.) Japan overran Malaya by February 1942. Following World War II, the various Malay states (except Singapore) organized into a federation, which replaced the confusing prewar regime of federated and unfederated protectorates. A Communist rebellion disrupted the country throughout the early 1950's. Following the suppression of the Communist movement, elections were held in mid-1955 for a home-rule government. The elections brought the Alliance party of Tungku Abdul

Rahman to power, and the Federation of Malaya became independent in 1957.

The nation expanded on Sept. 16, 1963, with the creation of Malaysia, incorporating the Federation of Malaya as well as Singapore and the former British colonies of North Borneo (thereafter called Sabah) and Sarawak. Singapore seceded from Malaysia in 1965 and became an independent nation. Malaysia is a constitutional monarchy with a parliamentary system; monarchs are chosen for five-year terms from among the hereditary rulers of the nine Malay states.

Malaysia has been ruled since 1981 by the coalition government of Mahathir Mohamad, who has transformed the country from an agriculture-based economy to one of the fastest-growing economies in Asia. The country sustained annual growth rates of 8 percent through the 1980's. In 1995 Malaysia received $5.8 bil. in foreign direct investment, the most in East Asia. The Asian financial crisis of 1997-98 hit Malaysia very hard as the currency and stockmarkets declined steeply.

Facing Malaysia's first recession in 13 years, Mahathir announced that the free market system had proven a failure and dismissed his finance minister, Anwar Ibrahim in Sept. 1998. Arrested and beaten by police, Anwar faced charges of sodomy and corruption in a nightmare trial. In April 1999 he was found guilty and sentenced to six years in prison. His wife, Azizah Ismail announced a new opposition National Justice Party. But when elections were suddenly called in November, her new party took only five of the 193 seats, as Mahathir's National Front carried 148.

▶ MALDIVES
Republic of Maldives

● GEOGRAPHY Location: chain of more than 1,200 small coral islands (about 220 inhabited), 475 mi. (764 km) from N to S and 80 mi. (207 km) from W to E in Indian Ocean; northernmost atoll about 370 mi. (960 km) southwest of India. Malé 4°00'N, 73°28'E. Boundaries: Laccadive Sea to NE, Arabian Sea to N, Indian Ocean to S and W. Total area: 116 sq. mi. (300 sq km). Coastline: 400 mi. (644 km). Comparative area: about 1.7 times size of Washington, D.C. Land use: 10% arable land; 0% permanent crops; 3% meadows and pastures; 3% forest and woodland; 84% other. Major cities: (1995) Malé (capital) 62,973.

● PEOPLE Population: 310,764 (July 2001 est.). Nationality: noun—Maldivian(s); adjective—Maldivian. Ethnic groups: Sinhalese, Dravidian, Arab, and African. Languages: Maldivian Divehi (dialect of Sinhala; script derived from Arabic); English spoken by most government officials. Religions: Sunni Muslim.

● GOVERNMENT Type: republic. Independence: July 26, 1965 (from U.K.). Constitution: Adopted Jan. 1998. National holiday: Independence Day, July 26. Head of Government: Maumoon Abdul Gayoom, president (since Nov. 1978). Structure: executive; unicameral legislature; judiciary.

● ECONOMY Monetary unit: rufiyaa. Budget: (1999 est.) income: $166 mil.; expend.: $192 mil. GDP: $594 mil., $2,000 per capita (2000 est.). Chief crops: coconut, corn, sweet potatoes; fishing. Natural resources: fish. Major industries: fishing, tourism, shipbuilding, some coconut processing. Labor force: about 67,000 (1995 est.); 22% fishing industry and agriculture, 18% services,60% industry. Exports: $88 mil. (f.o.b., 2000 est.); fish, clothing. Imports: $372 mil. (f.o.b., 2000 est.); intermediate and capital goods, consumer goods, petroleum products. Major trading partners: exports: Sri Lanka, U.S., U.K.; imports: Singapore, India, Sri Lanka.

The small sultanate of the Maldive Islands, with an Islamic population of Sinhalese descent, was made a British protectorate in 1887. The islands' tiny area and poor soil limited development; fishing and fish processing are the main industries, and copra (dried coconut meat for coconut oil) is the only significant crop. The Maldives became an independent nation on July 26, 1965. In 1968 the sultanate was abolished and replaced by a republic. Since independence, tourism has become economically important and now accounts for 18 percent of the GDP. Protests over the concentration of development on the island of Malé in recent years have led to political unrest in the other islands, while attempts to address the basic needs of those islands have strained the nation's tiny economic base.

The current president, Maumoon Abdul Gayoom, was elected to office in 1978 and subsequently reelected twice. The elections of September 1988 were marked by considerable unrest and demonstrations. An attempted coup against the Gayoom government on Nov. 4, 1988, was put down with the intervention of Indian troops.

▶ MALI
Republic of Mali

● GEOGRAPHY Location: northwestern Africa. Boundaries: Algeria to N, Niger to E, Burkina Faso, Ivory Coast, Guinea to S, Senegal and Mauritania to W. Total area: 478,765 sq. mi. (1,240,000 sq km). Coastline: none. Comparative area: slightly less than twice the size of Texas. Land use: 2% arable land; negl. % permanent crops; 25% meadows and pastures; 6% forest and woodland; 67% other; includes negl. % irrigated. Major cities: (1976 census) Bamako (capital) 404,000; Ségou 65,000; Mopti 54,000; Sikasso 47,000; Kayes 45,000.

● PEOPLE Population: 11,008,518 (July 2001 est.). Nationality: noun—Malian(s); adjective—Malian. Ethnic groups: 50% Mande (Bambara, Malinke, Sarakole), 17% Peul, 12% Voltaic, 6% Songhai, 10% Tuareg and Moor. Languages: French (official); Bambara spoken by 80% of population. Religions: 90% Muslim, 9% indigenous beliefs, 1% Christian.

● GOVERNMENT Type: republic. Independence: Sept. 22, 1960 (from France). Constitution: Jan. 12, 1992. National holiday: Anniversary of the Proclamation of the Republic, Sept. 22. Heads of Government: Alpha Oumar Konaré, president (since June 1992); Mande Sidibé, prime minister (since May 2000). Structure: executive; unicameral legislature; judiciary.

● ECONOMY Monetary unit: Communauté Financière Africaine (CFA) franc. Budget: (1997 est.) income: $730 mil.; expend.: $770 mil. GDP: $9.1 bil., $850 per capita (2000 est.). Chief crops: cotton, millet, rice, corn; goats, sheep, cattle. Natural resources: gold, phosphates, kaolin, salt, limestone, uranium; bauxite, iron ore, manganese, tin, and copper deposits are known but not exploited. Major industries: small local consumer goods and food processing, construction, phosphate, gold. Labor force: N.A.; 80% agriculture, 19% services. Exports: $480 mil. (f.o.b., 2000 est.); cotton, livestock, gold. Imports: $575 mil. (f.o.b., 2000 est.); machinery and equipment, foodstuffs, construction materials, petroleum. Major trading partners: exports: 20% Thailand, 20% Italy, 9%

China; *imports:* 19% Ivory Coast, 17% France, other franc zone and E.U. countries.

Mali has been a center of West African civilization for over 4,000 years. Iron Age civilizations flourished on the middle reaches of the Niger River from about 200 B.C. The kingdom of Ghana arose about A.D. 750 on the strength of the gold trade with North African Berbers. Ghana was overthrown by the Muslim Almoravids, who ruled only 11 years, though Islam remained a major influence from that time. From 1200 to 1400, the Kingdom of Mali was dominant in the region and was renowned throughout Islam and even in Christian Europe for its wealth and power; when Mansa Musa's retinue stopped in Cairo en route to Mecca, it carried so much gold that the price of gold fell 20 percent. By the end of the 14th century, the Mali empire had been eclipsed by the Songhai (Soyinka) empire, centered on the Niger River cities of Gao and Timbuktu.

The Songhai empire collapsed after Timbuktu was sacked by Moroccans in 1591. It fragmented into a series of smaller states, and power shifted from the desert fringe back to the Niger valley, bringing with it a further spread of Islam.

French exploration of Mali led to conquest in 1896 and the creation of the colony of French Sudan in 1898, governed from Dakar, Senegal. Timbuktu declined in importance, and Bamako became the country's principal urban center.

Malians were granted French citizenship and limited self-rule in 1946. In 1958 the territory became autonomous within the French Overseas Community. In 1959, with French support, the French Sudan and Senegal formed the Federation of Mali, which became independent on June 20, 1960. Senegal seceded from the federation almost immediately, and Mali became an independent republic on Sept. 22, 1960. Modibo Keita was elected the country's first president.

Keita's program of radical control of society and the economy by the central government provoked discontent, and he was overthrown in 1968 by military officers led by Lt. Moussa Traore. Traore's Military Committee of National Liberation ruled until 1979 when it was reorganized under a new constitution as the Malian People's Democratic Union. Traore, an autocratic military order, was ousted in a 1991 coup and a transitional government under a civilian prime minister, Soumana Sacko, set up multiparty elections for June 1992. Alpha Konaré was elected president and his Alliance for Democracy in Mali party won 76 of 116 legislative seats. In 1995, the government reached an agreement in its longstanding dispute with the ethnic Tuareg nomads in the northern part of the country.

Pres. Konaré's government has succeeded in reviving the economy (cotton and gold production rank among the top in Africa) and winning praise from the World Bank. Political opposition, though small, turned violent in 1997 and caused a cancellation of the results of elections in April. Opposition parties claimed the Government had fixed the elections and boycotted new ones held in May that gave Konare victory. He governs unopposed in the National Assembly and many fear political instability is possible.

▶ MALTA
Republic of Malta
● **GEOGRAPHY   Location:** archipelago (largest islands are Malta, Gozo, and Comino) in central Mediterranean. Valletta 35°54′N, 14°32′E. **Bound-** aries: Sicily 58 mi. (93 km) to N, Libya 180 mi. (290 km) to S, Tunisia to W. **Total area:** 124 sq. mi. (320 sq km). **Coastline:** 87 mi. (140 km). **Comparative area:** slightly less than twice the size of Washington, D.C. **Land use:** 38% arable land; 3% permanent crops; 0% meadows and pastures; 0% forest and woodland; 59% other; includes 3% irrigated. **Major cities:** (1994 est.) Valletta (capital) 7,953, Birkirkara 21,551, Qormi 17,928, Sliema 13,823.

● **PEOPLE   Population:** 394,583 (July 2001 est.). **Nationality:** noun—Maltese (sing., pl.); adjective—Maltese. **Ethnic groups:** Maltese (descendants of ancient Carthaginians and Phoenicians, with strong elements of Italian and other Mediterranean stock) **Languages:** Maltese and English (both official). **Religions:** 91% Roman Catholic.

● **GOVERNMENT   Type:** parliamentary democracy. **Independence:** Sept. 21, 1964 (from U.K.). **Constitution:** Dec. 13, 1974. **National holiday:** Independence Day, Sept. 21. **Heads of Government:** Prof. Guido de Marco, president (since Apr. 1999); Dr. Edward Fenech Adami, prime minister (since Sept. 1998). **Structure:** executive; unicameral legislature—seats are given to largest popular party to ensure a majority, usually 65; judiciary.

● **ECONOMY   Monetary unit:** Maltese lira. **Budget:** (1999 est.) *income:* $1.6 bil.; *expend.:* $1.73 bil. **GDP:** $5.6 bil., $14,300 per capita (2000 est.). **Chief crops:** potatoes, cauliflower, grapes, wheat, barley; milk, pork, poultry. **Natural resources:** limestone, salt. **Major industries:** tourism, electronics, ship repair yard, construction. **Labor force:** 145,901 (1999); 24% industry, 71% services, 5% agriculture; 5% unemployment (1997). **Exports:** $2 bil. (f.o.b., 1999); machinery and transport equipment, manufactures. **Imports:** $2.6 bil. (f.o.b., 1999); machinery and transport equipment, manufactured goods; food, drink and tobacco. **Major trading partners:** *exports:* 15.2% France, 21.4% U.S., 12.6% Germany; *imports:* 16.7% Italy, 19.1% France, 10.9% U.K.

Malta, an ancient crossroads of Mediterranean trade, was ruled successively by Phoenicians, Carthaginians, Greeks, Romans, and Byzantines before being conquered by Islamic Saracens from North Africa in the ninth century. In 1090 the Norman kings of Sicily conquered it and made it a way station for the First Crusade. In 1530 Charles V gave the island to the Knights Hospitalers (the Knights of Malta). The island withstood a siege by the Ottoman Turks in 1565 and fell only to Napoleon in 1798.

The Maltese came under British rule in 1800, and it was annexed in 1814. Limited self-rule was granted under the constitutions of 1921 and 1939. During World War II, Malta suffered devastating air raids by German and Italian forces; the entire population was awarded the George Cross for bravery.

In 1964 Malta was granted independence within the British Commonwealth, with Elizabeth II as its sovereign. Abrogating its mutual defense treaty with Great Britain in 1971, the Maltese government severed all ties to the British Crown, becoming a fully independent republic. British forces withdrew from the island in 1979.

Malta was governed by the leftist, anticlerical, and neutralist Labour party from 1971 to 1987, whose leader, the ardent nationalist Dominic Mintoff, was prime minister from 1971 to 1984, succeeded by Mifsud Bonnici. In 1997 the Catholic and pro-Western Nationalist party won a popular electoral majority but not a majority in Parliament. Under a 1987 constitutional amendment, it was granted sufficient extra seats in Parliament to allow it to organize a government under Prime Minister Eddie Fenech Adami.

The Nationalist party ruled for nine years until in 1996 elections the Labour party won a slim majority, but returned to power in Sept. 1998 with Adami returning as prime minister.

▶ **MARSHALL ISLANDS**
Republic of the Marshall Islands

• **GEOGRAPHY Location:** two groups of islands, the Ratak and Ralik chains, comprising 31 atolls in western Pacific. Majuro 7°09'N, 171°12'E. **Boundaries:** Guam about 1,300 mi. (2,100 km) to NW, Hawaii about 2,000 mi. (3,200 km) to NE, Kiribati to S, Federated States of Micronesia to W. **Total area:** 70 sq. mi. (181 sq km). **Coastline:** 230 (370 km). **Comparative area:** about the size of Washington, D.C. **Land use:** negl. % arable land; 60% permanent crops; negl. % meadows and pastures; negl. % forest and woodland; 40% other. **Major cities:** Majuro (capital—pop. N.A.).

• **PEOPLE Population:** 70,822 (July 2001 est.). **Nationality:** noun—Marshallese; adjective—Marshallese. **Ethnic groups:** Micronesian. **Languages:** English (official), two major Marshallese dialects from Malayo-Polynesian family, Japanese. **Religions:** Christian, mostly Protestant.

• **GOVERNMENT Type:** constitutional government in free association with U.S.; Compact of Free Association entered into force Oct. 21, 1986. **Independence:** Oct. 21, 1986 (from U.S.-administered U.N. trusteeship). **Constitution:** May 1, 1979. **National holiday:** Proclamation of the Republic of the Marshall Islands, May 1. **Head of Government:** Kessai Note, president (since Jan. 2000). **Structure:** executive; unicameral legislature; judiciary.

• **ECONOMY Monetary unit:** U.S. dollar. **Budget:** (FY95/96) *income:* $80.1 mil.; *expend:* $77.4 mil. **GDP:** $105 mil., $1,670 per capita (1998 est.). **Chief crops:** coconuts, cacao, taro, breadfruit, fruits; pigs, chickens. **Natural resources:** phosphate deposits, marine products, deep seabed minerals. **Major industries:** copra, fish, tourism. **Labor force:** NA. **Exports:** $28 mil. (f.o.b., 1997 est.); coconut oil, fish, trochus shells. **Imports:** $58 mil. (c.i.f., 1997 est.); foodstuffs, machinery and equipment, fuels, beverages and tobacco. **Major trading partners:** U.S., Japan, Australia.

The Marshall Islands, part of the geographic region known as Micronesia, are made up of 31 atolls of the Ratak (Sunrise) and Ralik (Sunset) chains located between 4° and 14°N and 160° and 173°E. Although claimed by Spain in 1592, the islands were left undisturbed by the Spanish empire for 300 years. In 1885, Germany took over the administration on the islands of Jaluit and Ebon. At that time copra (dried coconut meat) trade was the primary industry. Japan assumed control of the Marshalls at the beginning of World War I and held them until 1944, when Allied forces occupied the islands. In 1947 the islands were included in the U.N. Trust Territory of the Pacific and placed under U.S. administration. In 1946 the U.S. government resettled the inhabitants of Bikini and Enewetak in order to begin nuclear tests, which continued through 1958. Residents began returning to Enewetak in 1980; but the estimated cost of a complete clean-up of Bikini is $100 million.

▶ **MAURITANIA**
Islamic Republic of Mauritania

• **GEOGRAPHY Location:** northwestern Africa. **Boundaries:** territory of Western Sahara to N, Algeria to NE, Mali to E and S, Senegal to S, Atlantic Ocean to W. **Total area:** 397,954 sq. mi. (1,030,700 sq km). **Coastline:** 469 mi. (754 km). **Comparative area:** slightly larger than three times the size of New Mexico. **Land use:** negl. % arable land; negl. % permanent crops; 38% meadows and pastures; 4% forest and woodland; 58% other; includes negl. % irrigated. **Major cities:** Nouakchott (capital) 350,000 (1984 est.); Nouadhibou (Port Etienne) 21,961; Kaédi 20,848; Zouérate 17,474; Rosso 16,466 (1977 census).

• **PEOPLE Population:** 2,747,312 (July 2001 est.). **Nationality:** noun—Mauritanian(s); adjective—Mauritanian. **Ethnic groups:** 40% mixed Maur/black, 30% Maur, 30% black. **Languages:** Hasaniya Arabic (official), Wolof (official), Pular, Soninke, French. **Religions:** 100% Muslim.

• **GOVERNMENT Type:** republic. **Independence:** Nov. 28, 1960 (from France). **Constitution:** July 12, 1991. **National holiday:** Independence Day, Nov. 28. **Heads of Government:** Col. Maaouya Ould Sid' Ahmed Taya, president (since Dec. 1984); Cheikh El Avia Ould Mohamed Khouna, prime minister (since Nov. 1998). **Structure:** executive; bicameral legislature; judiciary.

• **ECONOMY Monetary unit:** ouguiya. **Budget:** (1996 est.) *income:* $329 mil.; *expend.:* $265 mil. **GDP:** $5.4 bil., $2,000 per capita (2000 est.). **Chief crops:** dates, millet, sorghum; cattle, sheep; fish. **Natural resources:** iron ore, gypsum, fish, copper, phosphate. **Major industries:** fish processing, mining of iron ore and gypsum. **Labor force:** 750,000 (1999 est.); 47% agriculture, 29% services, 14% industry and commerce, 10% government; 45,000 wage earners (1980); 23% unemployment (1995). **Exports:** $333 mil. (f.o.b., 1999); fish and fish products, iron ore, gold. **Imports:** $305 mil. (f.o.b., 1999); machinery and equipment, foodstuffs, consumer goods, petroleum products, capital goods. **Major trading partners: *exports:*** 18% Japan, 16% Italy, 17% France; *imports:* 27% France, 9% Benelux.

The population of Mauritania is divided between an Arab and Berber majority in the north and various black African peoples in the south and southwest. From the ninth through the 15th centuries, southern Mauritania was part of the kingdoms of, successively, Ghana, Mali, and Sanghay. In the 1050's, a puritanical Muslim sect, the Almoravids, arose in the Tidra Islands, Between 1054 and 1086 they conquered Ghana, Morocco, Western Algeria, and Spain; they were eclipsed in the next century.

Portuguese trade on the Mauritanian coast began in the early 15th century; the Portuguese remained dominant until about 1600 when their control was contested by the British, French, and Dutch. France established a protectorate in 1903, and the area was made a French colony in 1920.

In 1958 Mauritania became a self-governing republic within the French Overseas Community. In 1959 Mokhtar Ould Daddah was elected prime minister, and the country became fully independent on Nov. 28, 1960. A new constitution was adopted in 1961, establishing a presidential form of government. The four major political parties were combined into a single party in 1965.

Morocco claimed Mauritania as part of its sphere of influence; after talks about unifying the two countries broke down, Morocco recognized Mauritanian independence in 1970.

Spain relinquished its claim to the Spanish Sahara in 1976. The southern part of that territory was annexed by Mauritania, while the larger

International Time Zones

GREENLAND
EUROPE
ALASKA
−9
−3
0
ICELAND
−4
0
+7 +9
+3
+11 +12
−8 −7 −6
+4
−1
+5
RUSSIA
+10
NORTH
−2
AMERICA
+2
+6
−5
AZORES
−3½
+1
ASIA
+8
ALEUTIAN IS.
−10
+5¾
+3½
+6½
CAPE
+5½
HAWAII
VERDE
+4½
MARSHALL IS.
CENTRAL
AFRICA
KIRIBATI
AMERICA
MIDDLE EAST
MARQUESAS IS.
−4
−9½ −8½
SOUTH
EASTER I.
AMERICA
−12
PITCAIRN I.
−6
AUSTRALIA
+13
+9½
−3

Date Line

−11

Greenwich Mean Time

| −10 | −9 | −8 | −7 | −6 | −5 | −4 | −3 | −2 | −1 | 0 | +1 | +2 | +3 | +4 | +5 | +6 | +7 | +8 | +9 | +10 | +11 | +12− |

160° West   140°   120°   100°

Arctic Ocean

Canada

0   Miles   500

GREENLAND
(DENMARK)

ICELAND

ALASKA

QUEEN
ELIZABETH
IS.

Beaufort
Sea

BANKS I.

Baffin Bay

Inuvik
Mackenzie R.
Great
Bear Lake

VICTORIA I.

70°
North

Dawson

Cambridge Bay

BAFFIN I.

Davis
Strait

YUKON
TERRITORY
Whitehorse

NORTHWEST
TERRITORIES
Yellowknife

NUNAVUT

Iqaluit

Labrador Sea
60°

QUEEN
CHARLOTTE
IS.

Great
Slave Lake

Prince
Rupert

Lake
Athabasca

NEWFOUNDLAND

Prince
George

ALBERTA

Churchill

Hudson
Bay

LABRADOR

50°

BRITISH
COLUMBIA
Vancouver

Edmonton

SASKATCH-
EWAN

MANITOBA

CANADA

St. John's

Calgary

Saskatoon

ONTARIO

NEW
BRUNSWICK

PRINCE EDWARD I.

VANCOUVER I.

Regina

Lake
Winnipeg

QUEBEC
St. Lawrence R.

Sydney

Victoria

Winnipeg

Quebec

Fredericton
Halifax

Pacific
Ocean

Thunder
Bay

Montreal
Ottawa

NOVA SCOTIA

Lake Superior

Lake Huron

Lake Michigan

Toronto   Lake Ontario

UNITED STATES

Atlantic
Ocean

CANADA

• Bellingham

Port
Angeles
Olympia • **Seattle**
WASHINGTON • **Tacoma**   Sandpoint
Spokane

Astoria   • **Yakima**   Coeur d'Alene   • Kalispell   • Havre
Portland   • Great Falls
• Salem   Pendleton   • **Helena**   **MONTANA**
Eugene   **84**   **82**
Bend   **90**   **Butte**   • **Billings**   Sheridan

OREGON   **IDAHO**   Gillette
Medford   • **Boise**   Jackson   **WYOMING**   Casper
• Klamath Falls   Idaho Falls   **25**
Twin Falls   Pocatello   Evanston   **Cheyenne**
Eureka   Winnemucca   **Ogden**   Rock Springs
Redding   Elko   **Salt Lake City**   **Provo**   Boulder
Ukiah   **80**   **UTAH**   **70**   **Denver**
Sacramento   **Reno**   Ely   Richfield   Grand Junction   Aspen   **Colorado Springs**
Oakland   **Carson City**   **NEVADA**   Moab   Cedar City   **Pueblo**
San Francisco   **COLORADO**
San Jose   Tonopah   Las Vegas   Grand Canyon   Farmington
Monterey   Fresno
5   Bakersfield   Boulder City   **ARIZONA**
Santa Barbara   **CALIFORNIA**   San Bernadino   **Flagstaff**   **Santa Fe**   Las Vegas
Los Angeles   Prescott   **Winslow**   Tucumcari
Long Beach   **10**   **Phoenix** • Mesa   **Albuquerque**
San Diego   **8**   Yuma   **NEW MEXICO**   Roswell
120° West   **Tucson**   **25**
19   Deming   Las Cruces
El Paso   Odessa   Midland

Pacific Ocean   **MEXICO**   San Angelo   **TEXAS**

110°   Del Rio   **San Antonio**
Rio Grande

NORTH DAKOTA   • Minot   Grand Forks
Bismarck   **Fargo**
• Bowman   Fergus Falls
SOUTH DAKOTA   Aberdeen
29
• **Pierre**
Rapid City   **90**   Sioux Falls
Valentine   **Sioux City**
NEBRASKA
Sidney   North Platte   Omaha
Grand Island   **Lincoln**
Goodland   **70**   Topeka
KANSAS   Salina
Hutchinson   **35**   **Wichita**
Dodge City
OKLAHOMA   Enid   **Tulsa**
Clinton   **44**
Lawton   **Oklahoma City**
Wichita Falls   **Dallas**   **30**
Abilene   **20**   **Ft. Worth**
Waco   **45**
Lubbock   **35**
Amarillo   **27**   **10**
Austin   **Houston**
Laredo   Corpus Christi
Brownsville

0   Miles   300   110°

HAWAII   *Pacific Ocean*
KAUAI   *OAHU*   *MOLOKAI*
NIHAU   *MAUI*   • Hana
Honolulu   *LANAI*
KAHOOLAWE   • Hilo
0   Miles   100   *HAWAII*

Barrow
Prudhoe Bay   Miles
0   400
Fairbanks
Nome   **ALASKA**   **CANADA**
Anchorage   • Valdez
Homer   **Juneau**
Kodiak   Sitka
Pacific Ocean

CANADA

*Gulf of
St. Lawrence*

Houlton

International
Falls
MINN.
Grand
Rapids   *Lake
Superior*
Duluth   Marquette   Sault
Ste. Marie   *Lake
Huron*   MAINE   Bangor

Montpelier   Augusta
Burlington   Brunswick

WISCONSIN   MICHIGAN   VT. N.H.
Minneapolis   Green
Bay   *Lake
Michigan*   L. Ontario
Syracuse   N.Y.   MASS.   *CAPE
COD*
Eau Claire   Rochester   CONN.
St. Paul   94   R.I.   40° North
Rochester   La Crosse   Grand Flint   L. Erie   Buffalo
Milwaukee   Rapids   Erie   *Atlantic
Ocean*
Madison   Lansing   Detroit
Waterloo   Rockford   PENNSYLVANIA
Des   Dubuque   Chicago   Kalamazoo   Cleveland   Harrisburg   N.J.
Moines   Cedar   Gary   Fort   OHIO   Akron   Pittsburgh
IOWA   Rapids   South   Wayne   Columbus   Wheeling   Hagerstown   DEL.
Burlington   Peoria   Bend   Muncie   Dayton   Washington   MD.   *Area of
detail*
35   Springfield   Decatur   70   Cincinnati   D.C.
Kansas   Quincy   INDIANA   77   Clarksburg
City   Columbia   Indianapolis   Charleston   Richmond
Joplin   St. Louis   ILLINOIS   Frankfort   Huntington   VIRGINIA   Newport News
Jefferson   Evansville   Louisville   Lexington   W.VA.   Lynchburg   Norfolk
City   44   Roanoke   NORTH
MISSOURI   KENTUCKY   95   CAROLINA
Springfield   Paducah   Bowling   81   Greensboro
Green   Durham
24   Winston-   Raleigh
Fayetteville   Nashville   Knoxville   Salem   Charlotte   40
ARKANSAS   TENNESSEE   Asheville   Fayetteville
Fort   Memphis   Chattanooga   Spartanburg   Wilmington   70°
Smith   Huntsville   Greenville
Little   Decatur   Columbia
Hot   Rock   Atlanta   SOUTH
Springs   Pine   Oxford   Birmingham   CAROLINA   30°
Bluff   Augusta   Charleston
Texarkana   MISSISSIPPI   Tuscaloosa   Macon   20
Monroe   Vicksburg   Montgomery   GEORGIA   Savannah
Shreveport   ALABAMA   Brunswick
Jackson   Meridian   Albany   United States:
LOUISIANA   Hattiesburg   Dothan   Political
Baton   Mobile   Tallahassee   Jacksonville
Lake   Rouge   Biloxi   Pensacola   Panama   Gainesville   Daytona
Charles   City   FLORIDA   Beach
Lafayette   New   Orlando
Beaumont   Orleans   75   80°
Tampa   West Palm
St. Petersburg   Sarasota   Beach
Gulf of Mexico   Fort Myers   Fort Lauderdale
Miami
90° West   Key West

20°

CUBA

MEXICO

VERMONT   N.H.   Portland
Rutland   Portsmouth
87   Glens Falls   Concord
Manchester   Lowell
Schenectady   Brattleboro   Boston
90   Albany   Pittsfield   MASS.
NEW YORK   Springfield   Worcester
90   Providence
Kingston   CONN.
Binghamton   Hartford   R.I.
84   New
81   Newburgh   London   Newport
New   95
Scranton   Paterson   Haven
80   Newark   New York City
Allentown   78
Princeton
Trenton
Philadelphia   NEW JERSEY
PA.   76
Camden   Atlantic City
95   Wilmington
Baltimore   Dover
Annapolis   DELAWARE
Salisbury
MARYLAND

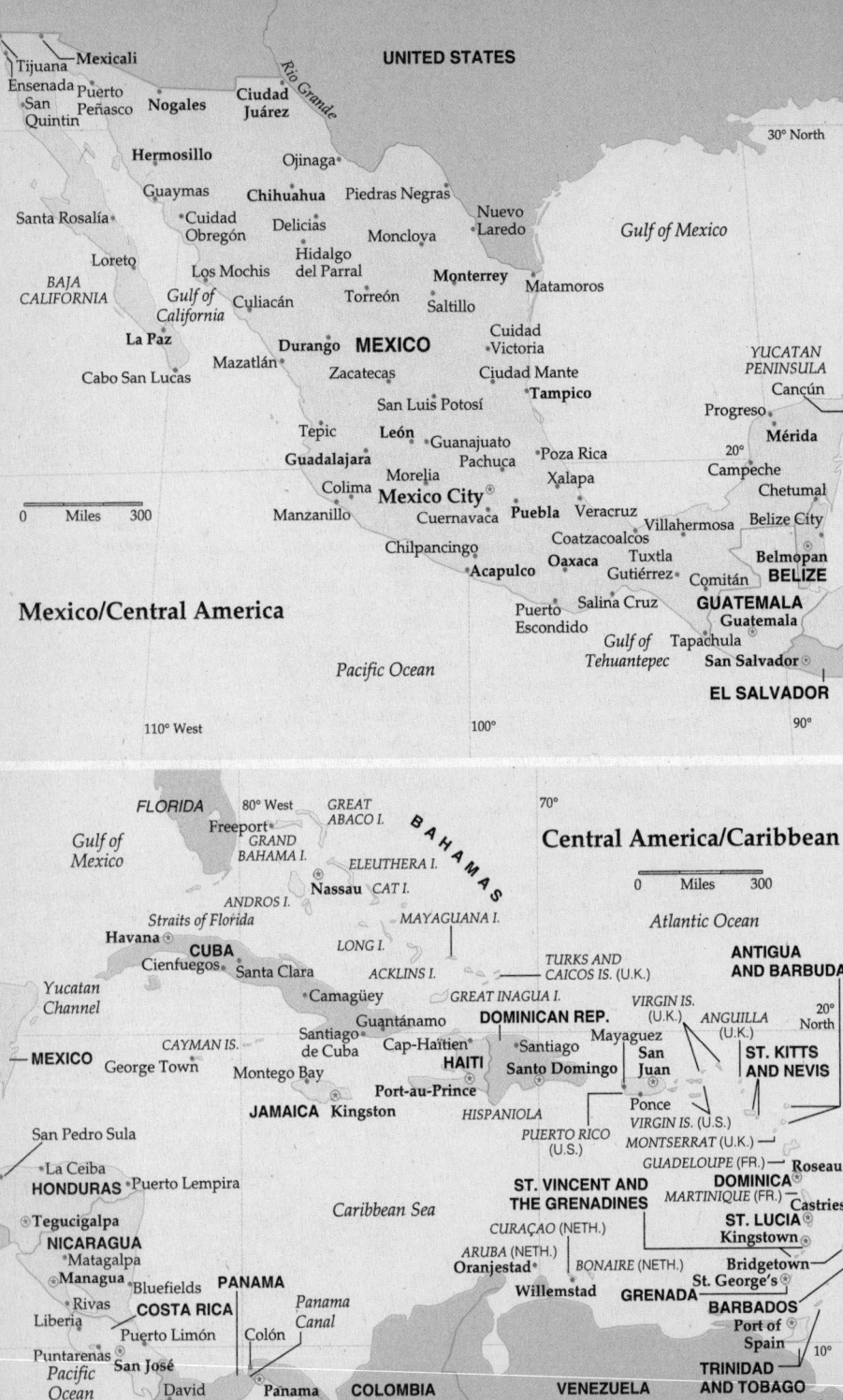

Mexico/Central America

UNITED STATES

Tijuana Mexicali
Ensenada Puerto Nogales Ciudad
San Peñasco Juárez
Quintin

Rio Grande

30° North

Hermosillo Ojinaga

Guaymas Chihuahua Piedras Negras

Santa Rosalía Cuidad Delicias Moncloya Nuevo *Gulf of Mexico*
Obregón Laredo

Loreto Hidalgo
BAJA Los Mochis del Parral Monterrey Matamoros
CALIFORNIA *Gulf of* Culiacán Torreón Saltillo YUCATAN
California PENINSULA

La Paz Durango MEXICO Cuidad Cancún
Mazatlán Victoria Progreso
Cabo San Lucas Zacatecas Ciudad Mante Mérida
San Luis Potosí Tampico 20° Campeche

Tepic León Guanajuato Chetumal
Guadalajara Pachuca Poza Rica
Morelia Xalapa Campeche
Colima Mexico City Veracruz Belize City
0 Miles 300 Manzanillo Cuernavaca Puebla Villahermosa
Chilpancingo Coatzacoalcos Belmopan
Acapulco Oaxaca Tuxtla BELIZE
Gutiérrez Comitán

Mexico/Central America Puerto Salina Cruz GUATEMALA
Escondido Guatemala
Gulf of Tapachula
Pacific Ocean *Tehuantepec* San Salvador

EL SALVADOR

110° West 100° 90°

Central America/Caribbean

FLORIDA 80° West GREAT 70°
ABACO I. BAHAMAS
Gulf of Freeport GRAND
Mexico BAHAMA I. ELEUTHERA I.
0 Miles 300
Nassau CAT I.
ANDROS I. MAYAGUANA I. *Atlantic Ocean*
Straits of Florida LONG I. TURKS AND ANTIGUA
Havana CUBA ACKLINS I. CAICOS IS. (U.K.) AND BARBUDA
Cienfuegos Santa Clara GREAT INAGUA I.
Yucatan Camagüey VIRGIN IS. ANGUILLA
Channel Guantánamo DOMINICAN REP. (U.K.) (U.K.)
Santiago Santiago
MEXICO CAYMAN IS. de Cuba Cap-Haïtien Santo Domingo San ST. KITTS
George Town HAITI Juan AND NEVIS
Montego Bay Port-au-Prince Ponce
JAMAICA Kingston HISPANIOLA VIRGIN IS. (U.S.) MONTSERRAT (U.K.) Roseau
San Pedro Sula PUERTO RICO GUADELOUPE (FR.) DOMINICA
(U.S.) MARTINIQUE (FR.) Castries
La Ceiba *Caribbean Sea* ST. VINCENT AND ST. LUCIA
HONDURAS Puerto Lempira THE GRENADINES Kingstown
CURAÇAO (NETH.) Bridgetown
Tegucigalpa ARUBA (NETH.) BONAIRE (NETH.) St. George's
NICARAGUA Oranjestad GRENADA BARBADOS
Matagalpa Willemstad Port of
Managua PANAMA Spain
Bluefields Panama
Rivas COSTA RICA Canal TRINIDAD
Liberia Colón AND TOBAGO
Puerto Limón
Puntarenas San José
Pacific David Panama COLOMBIA VENEZUELA
Ocean

20° North

10°

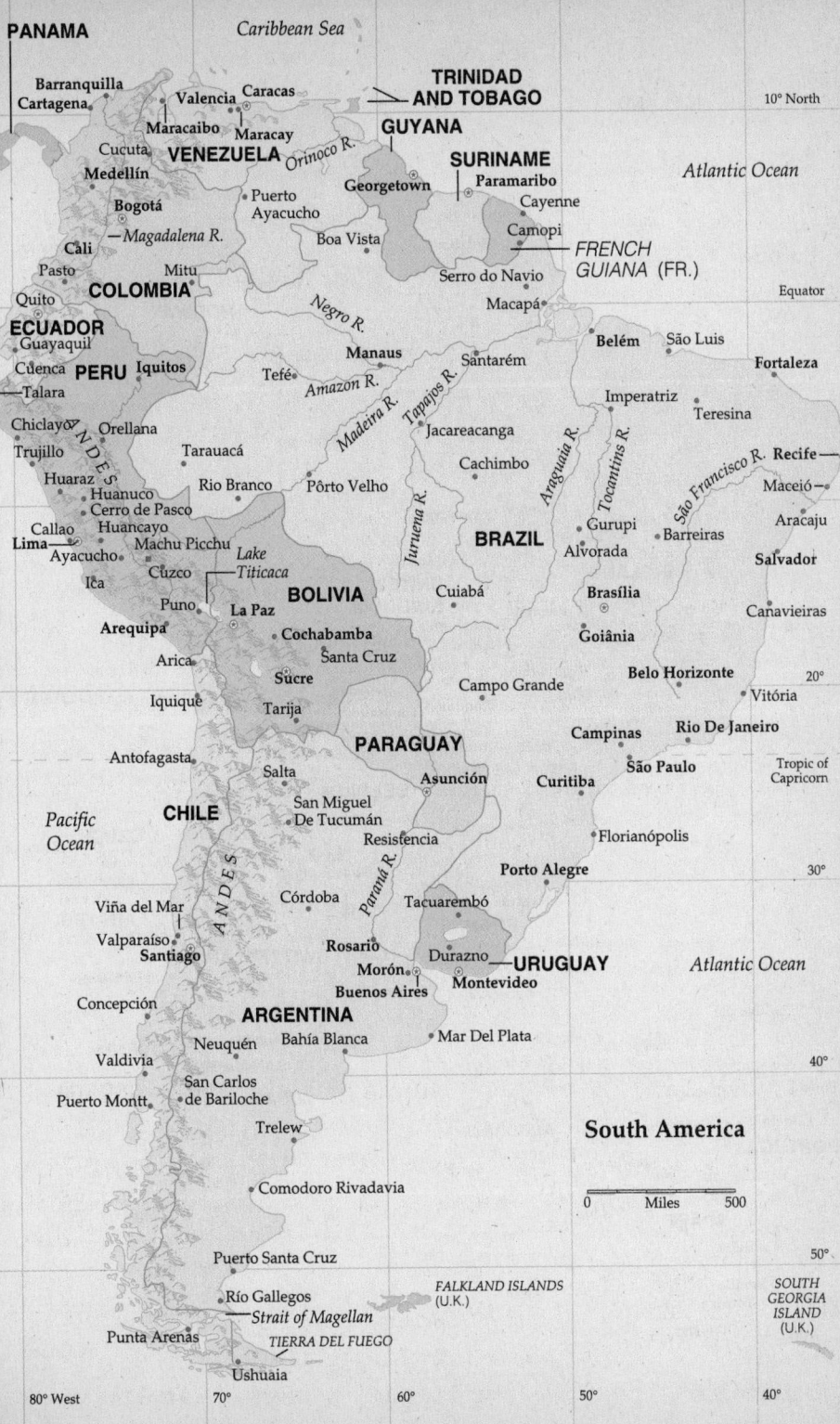

Europe

0 Miles 200

ICELAND
Reykjavik

Norwegian Sea

60° North

FAROE IS.
(DENMARK)
Torshavn

SHETLAND IS.
Lerwick

ORKNEY IS.

HEBRIDES
Inverness
SCOTLAND

N. IRELAND
Donegal
Glasgow • Edinburgh
Belfast
Sunderland
IRELAND
Limerick Dublin
Cork Waterford Leeds UNITED
Liverpool KINGDOM
WALES Manchester ENGLAND
Birmingham • Leicester
Ouse R.
Cardiff
London
Plymouth Thames R.
Portsmouth
English Channel
CHANNEL IS. (U.K.) < Le Havre
Brest
Seine R.

15° West

Atlantic
Ocean

Bodo

SWEDEN
Trondheim

Alesund
NORWAY
Sundsvall

Bergen Oslo Gavle
Stavanger Uppsala
Stockholm

North Sea Alborg Göteborg
Viborg
Arhus
DENMARK Copenhagen
Vejle

Hamburg
NETHERLANDS
POLAND
Amsterdam GERMANY Berlin
The Hague Poznan
Rotterdam
Brussels Essen Elbe R.
BELGIUM Cologne Leipzig
Bonn Prague
Luxembourg Rhine R. CZECH
LUX. Frankfurt REP. Brno
Paris Nürnberg
Strasbourg Stuttgart Bratislava
Danube R. Munich Vienna
Nantes Salzburg AUSTRIA
FRANCE Dijon Bern Zurich Vaduz (LIECH.) Graz
Clermont-Ferrand Geneva SWITZERLAND Ljubljana
Bay of Biscay Lyons ALPS SLOVENIA
Bordeaux Milan Po R. Venice Zagreb
La Coruña Bayonne Rhône R. Genoa CROATIA
Bilbao Garonne R. SAN MARINO
Toulouse Nice Florence Adriatic
Porto PYRENEES Marseilles MONACO Sea
Valladolid Duero R. ANDORRA APENNINES ITALY
Coimbra Salamanca Zaragoza Rome
Ebro R. Madrid CORSICA (FR.) Bari
PORTUGAL Barcelona
Lisbon Tagus R. Toledo MALLORCA Naples
SPAIN Valencia (SPAIN) SARDINIA
Córdoba Palma (ITALY) Tyrrhenian Sea
Seville Guadalquivir R. BALEARIC IS.
Málaga (SPAIN) Palermo
Strait of IBIZA SICILY
Gibraltar Gibraltar 0° Mediterranean Sea Catania
(U.K.)

45°

MOROCCO ALGERIA TUNISIA MALTA Valletta

15°

Nations of Former Soviet Union

0   500
Miles

— Arctic Circle

RUSSIA

SIBERIA

U.K.

GER.

NORWAY

SWEDEN

DEN.

FINLAND

POL.

ESTONIA

LATVIA

LITHUANIA

RUSSIA

MOLDOVA

BELARUS

UKRAINE

GEORGIA

ARMENIA

AZERBAIJAN

TURKEY

IRAQ

IRAN

TURKMENISTAN

UZBEKISTAN

KAZAKHSTAN

KYRGYZSTAN

TAJIKISTAN

MONGOLIA

CHINA

NORTH KOREA

SOUTH KOREA

JAPAN

North Sea

Baltic Sea

Barents Sea

Arctic Ocean

Kara Sea

Laptev Sea

East Siberian Sea

Bering Sea

Sea of Okhotsk

Sea of Japan

Yellow Sea

Black Sea

Caspian Sea

Aral Sea

Lake Balkhash

Lake Baikal

NOVAYA ZEMLYA

FRANZ JOSEF LAND

NORTH LAND

NEW SIBERIAN IS

SAKHALIN I.

KURILE IS.

KAMCHATKA PENINSULA

180° East
160°
140°
120°
100°
80°
60°
40°
20°
50°
60°
70°
80° North
North

Kaliningrad
Tallinn
Riga
Vilnius
Minsk
Pskov
Novgorod
St. Petersburg
Petrozavodsk
Murmansk
Archangel
Vologda
Yaroslavl
Kostroma
Ivanovo
Vladimir
Syktyvkar
Perm
Kirov
Nizhniy Novgorod
Moscow
Tver
Smolensk
Kaluga
Tula
Ryazan
Orel
Bryansk
Kursk
Belgorod
Lipetsk
Tambov
Penza
Voronezh
Simbirsk
Kazan
Saratov
Samarkand
Yekaterinburg
Chelyabinsk
Orenburg
Tyumen
Kurgan
Omsk
Novosibirsk
Tomsk
Barnaul
Kemerovo
Abakan
Kyzyl
Krasnoyarsk
Norilsk
Dudinka
Salekhard
Khanty-Mansiysk
Yakutsk
Irkutsk
Ulan Ude
Chita
Blagoveshchensk
Khabarovsk
Vladivostok
Magadan
Anadyr
Palana
Petropavlovsk Kamchatskiy
Yuzhno-Sakhalinsk
Volgograd
Rostov
Astrakhan
Stavropol
Sevastopol
Odessa
Chisinau
Dnepropetrovsk
Kiev
Lviv
Khmelnitskiy
Sokhumi
Tbilisi
Yerevan
Ganca
Baku
Ashgabat
Charjew
Bukhoro
Urganch
Chimbay
Tashkent
Dzhambul
Bishkek
Osh
Dushanbe
Samarkand
Almaty
Astana
Karaganda
Semipalatinsk
Oskemen
Pavlodar
Petropavlovsk
Aktyubinsk
Guryev
Aral
Kzyl-Orda

Volga R.
Ob R.
Ob R.
Irtysh R.
Yenisei R.
Lena R.
Kolyma R.
Amur R.
Syr Darya R.

Amur R.

North Sea

Middle East

0   Miles   200

Mediterranean Sea

Caspian Sea

TURKMENISTAN

AFGHAN.

PAK.

20° North

Arabian Sea

60° East

Mashhad

IRAN

Teheran

Qom

Isfahan

Yazd

Kerman

Shiraz

Rasht

Tabriz

Lake Urmia

Hamadan

Bakhtaran

Kirkuk

Arbil

Mosul

Baghdad

Al Hillah

Karbala

An Najaf

Basra

Abadan

Tigris R.

Euphrates R.

SYRIAN DESERT

TURKEY

Aleppo

Hamah

SYRIA

LEBANON

Al Ladhiqiyah

ISRAEL

JORDAN

Area of detail

Tabuk

Suez Canal

EGYPT

Red Sea

Jeddah

Mecca

At Taif

Medina

SAUDI ARABIA

SUDAN

ERITREA

ETHIOPIA

YEMEN

Sana

Al-Hudaydah

Aden

Al-Mukalla

ARABIAN PENINSULA

OMAN

Muscat

Al-Jawarah

SOCOTRA (YEMEN)

Gulf of Oman

Strait of Hormuz

Bandar-e Abbas

Dubai

Abu Dhabi

UNITED ARAB EMIRATES

QATAR

Ad Dawhah

BAHRAIN

Manama

Al-Hufuf

Dhahran

Riyadh

Persian Gulf

KUWAIT

Kuwait

IRAQ

50°

Israel detail map

Mediterranean Sea

0   Miles   30

Tripoli

LEBANON

Baalbek

Beirut

Sidon

Tyre

BEKAA

Damascus

SYRIA

GOLAN HEIGHTS

As-Suwayda

Jordan R.

Az-Zarqa

Amman

JORDAN

Madaba

Dead Sea

Ma'an

Nahariya

Haifa

Sea of Galilee

Nablus

WEST BANK

Jericho

Jerusalem

Bethlehem

Hebron

Tel Aviv

Gaza

GAZA STRIP

Beersheba

Dimona

Masada

NEGEV

ISRAEL

Elat

Aqaba

EGYPT

SINAI PENINSULA

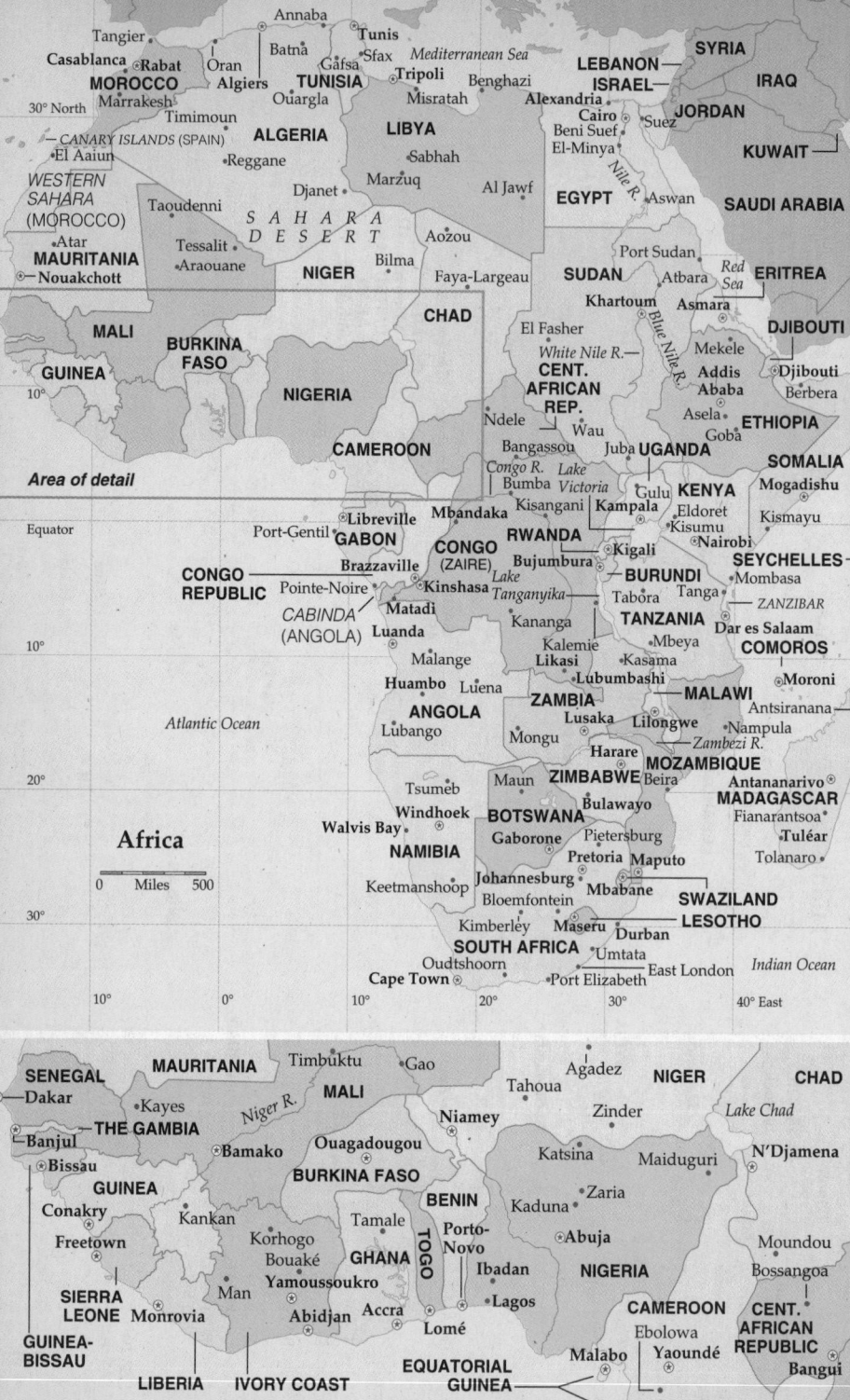

Tangier · Casablanca · Rabat · MOROCCO · Marrakesh · Timimoun · Oran · Algiers · Batna · Annaba · Tunis · TUNISIA · Gafsa · Sfax · Tripoli · Misratah · Benghazi · Mediterranean Sea · LEBANON · ISRAEL · SYRIA · IRAQ · JORDAN · KUWAIT

30° North · CANARY ISLANDS (SPAIN) · El Aaiun · WESTERN SAHARA (MOROCCO) · ALGERIA · LIBYA · Sabhah · Alexandria · Cairo · Beni Suef · El-Minya · Suez · Nile R. · SAUDI ARABIA

Reggane · Marzuq · Al Jawf · EGYPT · Aswan

Taoudenni · Djanet · Atar · MAURITANIA · Nouakchott · Tessalit · Araouane · SAHARA DESERT · NIGER · Bilma · Aozou · Faya-Largeau · CHAD · SUDAN · Port Sudan · Atbara · Red Sea · ERITREA · DJIBOUTI · Khartoum · Asmara · Djibouti · Berbera

10° · MALI · BURKINA FASO · GUINEA · NIGERIA · CAMEROON · El Fasher · CENT. AFRICAN REP. · Ndele · Bangassou · Wau · Juba · UGANDA · White Nile R. · Blue Nile R. · Mekele · Addis Ababa · Asela · Goba · ETHIOPIA · SOMALIA · Mogadishu

Area of detail · Congo R. · Bumba · Lake Victoria · Kisangani · Gulu · Kampala · KENYA · Kismayu · Equator · Libreville · Port-Gentil · GABON · Mbandaka · RWANDA · Kigali · Eldoret · Kisumu · Nairobi · Mombasa · SEYCHELLES

CONGO REPUBLIC · Brazzaville · Pointe-Noire · Kinshasa · Matadi · CONGO (ZAIRE) · Bujumbura · BURUNDI · Lake Tanganyika · Tabora · Tanga · ZANZIBAR · TANZANIA · Dar es Salaam · COMOROS · Moroni

10° · CABINDA (ANGOLA) · Luanda · Malange · Kananga · Kalemie · Likasi · Lubumbashi · Mbeya · Kasama · MALAWI · Antsiranana

Atlantic Ocean · Huambo · Luena · ZAMBIA · Lusaka · Lilongwe · Lubango · ANGOLA · Mongu · Harare · Zambezi R. · Nampula · MOZAMBIQUE · Beira · Antananarivo · MADAGASCAR

20° · Tsumeb · Maun · ZIMBABWE · Bulawayo · Fianarantsoa · Tuléar · Tolanaro · Windhoek · BOTSWANA · Gaborone · Pietersburg · Maputo · Walvis Bay · NAMIBIA · Pretoria · Johannesburg · Mbabane · SWAZILAND · LESOTHO

Africa · Keetmanshoop · Bloemfontein · Kimberley · Maseru · Durban · 0 Miles 500 · SOUTH AFRICA · Umtata · East London · Indian Ocean · Oudtshoorn · Cape Town · Port Elizabeth

30° · 10° · 0° · 10° · 20° · 30° · 40° East

SENEGAL · Dakar · MAURITANIA · Timbuktu · Gao · Tahoua · Agadez · NIGER · CHAD · Kayes · MALI · Niger R. · Niamey · Zinder · Lake Chad · Banjul · THE GAMBIA · Bamako · Ouagadougou · Katsina · Maiduguri · N'Djamena · Bissau · GUINEA · BURKINA FASO · Zaria · Conakry · Kankan · BENIN · Kaduna · Freetown · Tamale · Porto-Novo · Abuja · Moundou · Korhogo · GHANA · TOGO · Ibadan · NIGERIA · Bossangoa · SIERRA LEONE · Bouaké · Yamoussoukro · Lagos · Man · Abidjan · Accra · Lomé · CAMEROON · CENT. AFRICAN REPUBLIC · Monrovia · Ebolowa · Yaoundé · Bangui · GUINEA-BISSAU · LIBERIA · IVORY COAST · EQUATORIAL GUINEA · Malabo

Pacific Islands/Australia

RUSSIA

KAZAKHSTAN

•Hovd   Ulaanbaatar•

Altay•   MONGOLIA

Aral
Sea   *L. Balkhash*   •Karamay   •Dalandzadagad

•Urumqi   *G O B I*
KYRGYZSTAN   •Korla   *D E S E R T*

UZBEKISTAN   Kashi *Yarkant R.*   *Tarim R.*   •Yumen

TAJIKISTAN   *TAKLIMAKAN*   CHINA   •Yinchuǎn
DESERT   •Qiemo
TURKMEN.   •Lǎnzhou
•Herat   **Kabul**   •Hotan   —Area claimed by India   •Xining   Xian—
•Mazar-i-Sharif   *JAMMU AND*   •Golmǔd
Islamabad• Peshawar• **Srinagar** *KASHMIR*   Chongqing•
Kandahar •Rawalpindi•   *T I B E T*   Mianyang•
AFGHANISTAN •Amritsar•   Chengdǔ•
Faisalabad• Lahore•   **MOUNT**   Zigong•
Multan•   **EVEREST** *Brahmaputra R.*
Yamuna R.   •Katmandu *HIMALAYAS*   •Guiyang
PAKISTAN *Indus R.* New Delhi• **NEPAL**   •Kunming
IRAN   •Jaipur Agra• Kanpur• •Patna **BHUTAN**   Nanning•
Hyderabad• *GREAT INDIAN* Allahabad• *Ganges R.*   **VIETNAM**
•Karachi   *DESERT*   Dhaka• **MYANMAR**   **LAOS** Hanoi•
•Ahmadabad   **INDIA** Calcutta• Chitta- •Mandalay Luang Prabang•
Arabian Sea   •Surat •Nagpur   gong Chang Mai• Vinh•
Bombay• *Godavari R.*   **BANGLADESH** Vientiane• *HAINAN*
•Pune •Hyderabad   *Bay of Bengal* •Yangon **THAILAND** Da Nang•
15° North   •Bangkok
•Bangalore •Madras   *ANDAMAN IS.* Dawei• **CAMBODIA**
•Mangalore   *(INDIA)* *Andaman* Phnom Penh•
•Madurai   *Sea*   *Gulf of* **Ho Chi**
•Jaffna   *Thailand* **Minh**
SRI LANKA *NICOBAR IS.*   **City**
Colombo• •Kotte *(INDIA)* Hat Yai• **(Saigon)**
Kota Baharu•
⊛ **Male**   Medan• **Kuala Lumpur** **MALAYSIA**
MALDIVES   **SINGAPORE**
SUMATRA
Equator   Padang• Pontianak•
Jambi•
Indian Ocean   Palembang•
INDONESIA
Asia/Pacific   Bandar Lampung•
Bandung• Jakarta•
0   Miles   500   *JAVA*

70° East   90°

RUSSIA

Manzhouli

Nen R.

RUSSIA

SAKHALIN I.

Sea of Okhotsk

MONGOLIA

Qiqihar

Songhua R.

Baicheng

KURILE IS.
(RUSSIA)

45° North

Harbin

Jixi

Changchun

Jilin

Sapporo

HOKKAIDO I.

Fuxin

Shenyang

Chongjin

Kimchaek

Benxi

NORTH KOREA

Beijing

Tianjin

Dalian

Pyongyang

Sea of Japan

Sendai

Taiyuan

Inchon

SOUTH
KOREA

Seoul

JAPAN

HONSHU I.

Tokyo

*Huang
(Yellow R.)*

Qingdao

Yellow Sea

Pusan

Kyoto

Nagoya

Kaifeng

Hiroshima

Kwangju

Osaka

Xuzhou

Fukuoka

SHIKOKU I.

CHINA

Hefei

Nagasaki

KYUSHU I.

Wuhan

Shanghai

30°

*Chang Jiang
(Yangtze R.)*

Ningbo

*East China
Sea*

Huangshi

Wenzhou

*RYUKYU IS.
(JAPAN)*

Pacific Ocean

Yueyang

Xi R.

Fuzhou

OKINAWA I.

Guangzhou
(Canton)

Taipei

Xiamen

TAIWAN

Shantou

Kaohsiung

Hong Kong

LUZON I.

*MACAO
(PORTUGAL)*

*South
China
Sea*

Baguio

Philippine Sea

*NORTHERN
MARIANA IS. (U.S.)*

15°

Manila

PHILIPPINES

MINDORO I.

SAMAR I.

Iloilo

CEBU I.

GUAM (U.S.)

PALAWAN I.

Cebu

PANAY I.

Davao

CAROLINE IS.

BRUNEI

MINDANAO I.

PALAU

FEDERATED STATES
OF MICRONESIA

Bandar Seri
Begawan

MALAYSIA

Manado

Equator

I N D O N E S I A

BORNEO

SOLOMON IS.

Banjarmasin

*SULAWESI I.
(CELEBES)*

*IRIAN
JAYA*

Madang

Rabaul

Java Sea

Ujungpandang

Banda Sea

PAPUA
NEW
GUINEA

*NEW
BRITAIN*

Surabaya

FLORES

Arafura Sea

Honiara

JAVA

BALI

TIMOR

Port Moresby

BOUGAINVILLE

Kupang

130°

Torres Strait

GUADALCANAL

Timor Sea

*Gulf of
Carpentaria*

Coral Sea

AUSTRALIA

150° East

Arctic Ocean

75° North

Beaufort Sea

Baffin Bay

GREENLAND
(DENMARK)

Norwegian
Sea

Reykjavik

ICELAND

60°

ALASKA

Hudson
Bay

Labrador Sea

UNITED KINGDOM

Bering Sea

Gulf of
Alaska

CANADA

Dublin

IRELAND

45°

Ottawa

Atlantic Ocean

Bay of Biscay

SPAIN

UNITED
STATES

PORTUGAL
Lisbon

Washington, D.C.

Madrid

Rabat

30°

MOROCCO

Gulf of
Mexico

BAHAMAS

Canary Islands

ALG

MEXICO

Havana

CUBA

HAITI

W. SAHARA
(MOROCCO)

15°

HAWAII

Mexico City

BELIZE

DOM. REP.

MAURITANIA

Nouakchott

MALI

HONDURAS

SENEGAL

Bamako

GUATEMALA

Caribbean Sea

GUYANA

GAMBIA

Dakar

EL SALVADOR

Caracas

SURINAME

GUINEA-BISSAU

Equator

NICARAGUA

VENEZUELA

GUINEA

KIRIBATI

COSTA RICA

Bogotá

SIERRA LEONE

PANAMA

COL.

FRENCH GUIANA (FR.)

Monrovia

Quito

Pacific Ocean

ECUADOR

LIBERIA

PERU

BRAZIL

IVORY
COAST

15°

Lima

BURKINA FASO

La Paz

Brasília

BOLIVIA

Sucre

30°

CHILE

PARAGUAY

Asunción

Atlantic Ocean

Santiago

Buenos
Aires

URUGUAY

Montevideo

45°

ARGENTINA

FALKLAND IS. (U.K.)

SOUTH GEORGIA I. (U.K.)

165°
West

150°

135°

120°

105°

90°

75°

CAPE
HORN

60°

45°

30°

15°

60°

75° South

ANTARCTICA

Arctic Ocean   75° North

Barents Sea

NORWAY
SWEDEN
FIN.
Helsinki   ESTONIA
Stockholm   LATVIA
DENMARK   LITHUANIA
    Moscow
Berlin   BELA.   RUSSIA   Sea of Okhotsk   60°
1.   POL.   Kiev
2. GER.   UKRAINE   KAZAKHSTAN
Paris   3
.5   6   7   GEORGIA   Astana   Ulaanbaatar   45°
R.   8   9   ARMENIA   MONGOLIA
London   10   UZBEKISTAN   AZERBAIJAN   NORTH
    11 12 13   KYRGYZSTAN   KOREA   Sea of
Rome   14   15 16   Black Sea   CHINA   Beijing   Japan   Tokyo
ITALY   17   Ankara   TURKMEN.   TAJIKISTAN   Seoul   JAPAN   30°
Algiers   Athens   TURKEY   Teheran   Kabul   BHUTAN   SOUTH
TUNISIA   SYRIA IRAQ   IRAN   AFGH.   Islamabad   BANGLADESH   KOREA
Tripoli   LEBANON   Baghdad   NEPAL   TAIWAN
    ISRAEL   QATAR   PAK.   New   THAILAND
LIBYA   Cairo   JORDAN   KUWAIT   Delhi   MYANMAR   LAOS   Pacific Ocean
GERIA   EGYPT   Riyadh   UNITED   Yangon   South   15°
    Red   SAUDI   ARAB   INDIA   Bay of   China Sea   Philippine Sea
NIGER   Sea   ARABIA   EMIRATES   Bengal   Bangkok   VIETNAM   PHILIPPINES
    CHAD   ERITREA   OMAN   Arabian   SRI LANKA   CAMBODIA   MARSHALL
NIGERIA   Khartoum   YEMEN   Sea   MALDIVES   MALAYSIA   PALAU   IS.
    CENT.   SUDAN   DJIBOUTI   MICRONESIA
    AF. REP.   Addis Ababa   Equator
CAMEROON   ETHIOPIA   SOMALIA   INDONESIA
Equator   UGANDA   KENYA   PAPUA
GABON   CONGO   Nairobi   RWANDA   SINGAPORE   Java Sea   NEW GUINEA   TUVALU
CONGO   Kinshasa   BURUNDI   Jakarta   Port Moresby   15°
REP.   Luanda   TANZANIA   Dar es Salaam   SEYCHELLES   Timor Sea   VANUATU   FIJI
BENIN   ANGOLA   COMOROS   Indian Ocean   Coral Sea
GO   ZAMBIA   MADAGASCAR   MAURITIUS   AUSTRALIA   30°
    ZIMBABWE   MALAWI   Canberra
NAMIBIA   MOZAMBIQUE   Tasman Sea
BOTSWANA   Pretoria   SWAZILAND   Wellington
    LESOTHO   1. NETHERLANDS   10. SLOVENIA   NEW ZEALAND   45°
SOUTH AFRICA   2. BELGIUM   11. CROATIA
CAPE OF   3. CZECH REPUBLIC   12. BOSNIA AND
GOOD HOPE   4. SLOVAKIA   HERZEGOVINA
    5. SWITZERLAND   13. YUGOSLAVIA
    6. AUSTRIA   14. ALBANIA
    7. HUNGARY   15. MACEDONIA
    8. ROMANIA   16. BULGARIA
    9. MOLDOVA   17. GREECE

15°   30°   45°   60°   75°   90°   105°   120°   135°   150°   165° East   60°

75° South

ANTARCTICA

United States: Physical

WHITE MOUNTAINS
GREEN MOUNTAINS
Mount Washington
CAPE COD
LONG I.
Connecticut R.
CAPE MAY
Susquehanna R.
Potomac R.
James R.
Roanoke R.
Atlantic Ocean
ADIRONDACK MOUNTAINS
Mount Marcy
Hudson R.
Chesapeake Bay
CAPE HATTERAS
OUTER BANKS
UPPER PENINSULA
Lake Ontario
Niagara Falls
Lake Erie
APPALACHIAN MOUNTAINS
Cape Fear R.
Pee Dee R.
Santee R.
Savannah R.
COASTAL PLAIN
Mount Mitchell
Okefenokee Swamp
Lake Okeechobee
The Everglades
Straits of Florida
FLORIDA KEYS
Lake Huron
Grand R.
Oconee R.
Chattahoochee R.
Alabama R.
Suwannee R.
Lake Superior
Ohio R.
Wabash R.
Cumberland R.
Tennessee R.
Mobile Bay
Tombigbee R.
Gulf of Mexico
Lake Michigan
CENTRAL LOWLAND
Illinois R.
Mississippi R.
Lake of the Woods
Red R. of the North
Mississippi R.
Minnesota R.
Des Moines R.
Missouri R.
James R.
OZARK PLATEAU
Red R.
Sabine R.
Brazos R.
Colorado R.
COASTAL PLAIN
Sheyenne R.
Platte R.
Republican R.
Canadian R.
Pecos R.
Missouri R.
BLACK HILLS
Cheyenne R.
Lake Oahe
North Platte R.
GREAT PLAINS
Fort Peck Lake
Yellowstone R.
Bighorn R.
BIGHORN MTS.
FRONT RANGE
Longs Peak
South Platte R.
Pikes Peak
Arkansas R.
SACRAMENTO MTS.
Rio Grande
ROCKY MOUNTAINS
Gannett Peak
Grand Teton
Kings Peak
Mount Elbert
San Juan R.
Colorado R.
Mount Baker
BITTERROOT RANGE
Snake R.
Green R.
Lake Powell
Grand Canyon
SONORAN DESERT
Salt R.
Gila R.
SALMON RIVER MTS.
St. Joe R.
Great Salt Lake
GREAT BASIN
Lake Mead
Mount Olympus
CASCADE RANGE
Mount Rainier
Mount St. Helens
Mount Hood
Columbia R.
Willamette R.
Humboldt R.
Mount Shasta
Pyramid Lake
Lake Tahoe
Boundary Peak
Mount Whitney
SIERRA NEVADA
San Joaquin Valley
MOJAVE DESERT
Salton Sea
Sacramento R.
Pacific Ocean
CHANNEL IS.

HAWAII

Haleakala
Mauna Kea
Mauna Loa
Kauai Channel
Pacific Ocean
Miles
0   100

ALASKA

Point Barrow
BROOKS RANGE
Yukon R.
ALASKA RANGE
Mount McKinley
ALEXANDER ARCHIPELAGO
Gulf of Alaska
Bristol Bay
ALASKA PEN.
Bering Sea
Miles
0   200

northern section was annexed by Morocco. Rebels of the Polisario Front proclaimed the independent state of Western Sahara, and in 1980 Mauritania relinquished its claims to its portion of the Western Sahara, signed a treaty with Polisario, and resumed relations with Algeria, Polisario's chief backer.

In 1978 Ould Daddah was removed from office in a military coup and was replaced as president by Lt. Col. Haidalla. He in turn was overthrown on Dec. 12, 1984, by Chief of Staff Maaouya Ould Sid' Ahmed Taya. Taya normalized relations with Morocco and held regional and local elections in 1986 and 1987 in a first step toward the restoration of democracy.

Border incidents erupted between Mauritania and Senegal in 1989 and Mauritania expelled 40,000 black Senegalese workers. Racial and religious strife has severely hampered the country's economy. Taya introduced multiparty elections in 1991 and a new constitution was approved; Taya and his Democratic and Social Republican party won the presidency and control of the legislature in 1992 and again in 1997

▶MAURITIUS
Republic of Mauritius
●GEOGRAPHY Location: southwestern Indian Ocean. Port Louis 20°09′S, 57°29′E. Boundaries: nearest neighbor is Réunion to SW. Total area: 718 sq. mi. (1,860 sq km). Coastline: 110 mi. (177 km). Comparative area: almost 11 times the size of Washington D.C.. Land use: 49% arable land; 3% permanent crops; 3% meadows and pastures; 22% forest and woodland; 23% other; includes 9% irrigated. Major cities: (1994 est.) Port Louis (capital) 144,776; Beau Bassin/Rose Hill 96,621; Vacoas-Phoenix 94,042; Curepipe 76,610; Quatre Bornes 73,501.
●PEOPLE Population: 1,189,825 (July 2001 est.). Nationality: noun—Mauritian(s); adjective—Mauritian. Ethnic groups: 68% Indo-Mauritian, 27% Creole, 3% Sino-Mauritian, 2% Franco-Mauritian. Languages: English (official), Creole, French, Hindi, Urdu, Hakka, Bojpoori. Religions: 52% Hindu, 28.3% Christian (mostly Roman Catholic with a few Anglicans), 16.6% Muslim.
●GOVERNMENT Type: parliamentary democracy. Independence: Mar. 12, 1968 (from U.K.). Constitution: Mar. 12, 1968, amended Mar. 12, 1992. National holiday: Independence Day, Mar. 12. Heads of Government: Cassam Uteem, president (since July 1992); Sir Aneerood Jugnauth, prime minister (since Sept. 2000). Structure: executive; unicameral legislature; judiciary.
●ECONOMY Monetary unit: Mauritian rupee. Budget: (1999 est.) income: $1.1 bil.; expend.: $1.2 bil. GDP: $12.3 bil., $10,400 per capita (1999 est.). Chief crops: sugarcane, tea, corn, potatoes; cattle, goats; fish. Natural resources: arable land, fish. Major industries: food processing (largely sugar milling), textiles, and wearing apparel. Labor force: 514,000 (1995); 36% construction and industry, 24% services, 14% agriculture and fishing, 16% trade, restaurants, hotels, 7% transportation and communication, 3% finance. Exports: $1.6 bil. (f.o.b., 1999); clothing and textiles, sugar. Imports: $2.3 bil. (f.o.b., 1999); manufactured goods, capital equipment, foodstuffs, petroleum products, chemicals. Major trading partners: exports: 32% U.K., 19% France, 14% U.S.; imports: 12% South Africa, 19% France, 9% India.

The volcanic island of Mauritius and its seven smaller neighbors lie about 500 miles east of

Madagascar and 2,400 miles southwest of India. They were uninhabited when discovered by the Dutch in 1507. Following sporadic Dutch settlement in the 17th century, the French took over in 1721, establishing sugarcane plantations worked by slaves imported from Africa. Mauritius was captured by the British in 1810. Following the abolition of slavery in the British Empire (1834), Indian workers were imported to labor in the cane fields. A majority of the population is of Indian descent. On Mar. 12, 1968, Mauritius became an independent parliamentary democracy within the British Commonwealth. In 1992 it became a republic and the National Assembly elected Cassam Uteem as the country's first president.

In December 1995 the opposition party of Navinchandra Ramgoolam won 65.2 percent of the votes, and captured all 60 seats in Parliament defeating Aneerood Jugnauth, PM for 13 years. These results were reversed in Sept. 2000.

Although sugar remains an important element in the economy, textile manufacturing and tourism have helped to make Mauritius one of the strongest economies in Africa.

▶MEXICO
United Mexican States
●GEOGRAPHY Location: southernmost state in North America. Boundaries: U.S. to N, Gulf of Mexico to E, Belize and Guatemala to S, Pacific Ocean to W. Total area: 761,603 sq. mi. (1,972,550 sq km). Coastline: 5,798 mi. (9,329 km). Comparative area: slightly less than three times the size of Texas. Land use: 12% arable land; 1% permanent crops; 39% meadows and pastures; 26% forest and woodland; 22% other; includes 3% irrigated. Major cities: (1990 census) Ciudad de México (Mexico City) (capital) 8,236,960; Guadalajara 1,628,617; Netzahualcóyotl 1,259,543; Monterrey 1,064,197; Heróica Puebla de Zaragoza (Puebla) 1,054,921.
●PEOPLE Population: 101,879,171 (July 2001 est.). Nationality: noun—Mexican(s); adjective—Mexican. Ethnic groups: 60% mestizo, 30% Amerindian or predominantly Amerindian, 9% white or predominantly white, 1% other. Languages: Spanish, various Mayan, Nahuatl, and other regional indigenous languages. Religions: 89% Roman Catholic, 6% Protestant.
●GOVERNMENT Type: federal republic. Independence: Sept. 16, 1810 (from Spain). Constitution: Feb. 5, 1917. National holiday: Independence Day, Sept. 16. Head of Government: Vincente Fox, president (since Dec. 2000). Structure: dominant executive; bicameral legislature (National Congress—Senate, Federal Chamber of Deputies); Supreme Court.
●ECONOMY Monetary unit: peso. Budget: (2000 est.) income: $125 bil.; expend.: $130 bil. GDP: $915 bil., $9,100 per capita (2000 est.). Chief crops: corn, wheat, soybeans, rice, beans, cotton, coffee, fruit, tomatoes; beef, poultry, dairy products; wood products. Natural resources: crude oil, silver, copper, gold, lead. Major industries: food and beverages, tobacco, chemicals. Labor force: 39.8 mil. (2000); 56% services; 20% agriculture, forestry, hunting, fishing; 24% industry; 2.2% unemployment (2000), plus considerable underemployment. Exports: $168 bil. (f.o.b., 2000); crude oil, oil products, coffee, silver, engines, cotton. Imports: $176 bil. (f.o.b., 2000); metal manufactures, agricultural machinery, electrical equipment. Major trading partners: (1999) exports: 88.6% U.S., 2% Canada, Japan, Spain, Chile,

Brazil; *imports:* 73.6% U.S., 3.7% Japan, 3.3% Germany.

The pre-Columbian history of indigenous Mexican cultures is very rich and includes the high civilizations of the Olmecs, Mayas, Toltecs, and Aztecs, in addition to numerous nomadic cultures. In 1519 Hernán Cortés and several hundred Spanish soldiers entered Tenochtitlán (now Mexico City). A two-year campaign against the Aztecs under Montezuma II ended with the Spanish capture of the city. The Viceroyalty of New Spain—with its center at Mexico City—was proclaimed in 1535. At its height it encompassed the lands from California to Panama, Florida, Spain's Caribbean holdings, and the Philippines.

As was the case with the rest of Spanish America, the movement for independence in New Spain coincided with the weakening of the authority of the Spanish Crown as a result of the Napoleonic takeover of Spain in 1808. In 1810 Miguel Hidalgo led a failed uprising and was executed. Following in Hidalgo's footsteps, José María Morelos led another uprising in the south, and he in turn was captured and put to death. Agustín de Iturbide, leader of the royalist forces, defected to the side of those struggling for independence in 1821. Envisioning independent Mexico as a monarchy, military groups proclaimed Iturbide emperor of Mexico in 1822.

The Mexican empire did not last long, and the Central American counties seceded after Iturbide's ouster by Antonio de Santa Anna in 1823. A republic was declared and Guadalupe Victoria was the first president (1824-29). In 1836, Texas seceded from Mexico in a revolution that cost Santa Anna the presidency. Between 1845 and 1848, Mexico fought the United States over U.S. annexation of Texas, and in 1847 U.S. troops occupied Mexico City. Under the Treaty of Guadalupe Hidalgo (1848), Mexico sold about half its territory—including California, Nevada, Utah, most of Arizona, and parts of New Mexico, Colorado, and Wyoming to the United States—for $15 million.

Santa Anna ruled again, as dictator, from 1853 to 1855, before being toppled by the liberal movement, La Reforma. A new constitution was proclaimed in 1857, but Conservatives declared it void. Following the War of Reform (1858-61), France, Britain, and Spain all claimed compensation for destruction of their nations' property, and in 1862 they landed troops at Veracruz. Britain and Spain withdrew, but Napoleon III attempted to establish a dependent empire in Mexico and installed Archduke Ferdinand Maximilian of Austria on the Mexican throne in 1864. In the face of Mexican resistance and U.S. threats, France ended its Mexican adventure, and in 1867 Maximilian was captured and executed by Liberal forces.

Benito Juárez, who served as provisional president during the War of Reform, was a major force behind the liberal movement called La Reforma, which stressed the promotion of capitalism and the destruction of what were seen as vestiges of feudalism in Mexico. Juárez won a third presidential term in 1871 but died in office and was succeeded in office by Sebastián Lerdo de Tejada, who was in turn overthrown by Gen. Porfirio Díaz. During the stable dictatorship known as the Porfiriato (1876-1911), Mexico experienced economic growth, though wealthy landowners and the church benefited at the expense of the poor.

The Mexican Revolution began in 1910 after Porfirio Díaz had his electoral opponent, Francisco I. Madero, jailed. Madero formulated his Plan of San Luis Potosí, calling for armed resistance. Rebellions broke out in the northern state of Chihuahua under the leadership of Pancho Villa and in the southern state of Morelos led by Emiliano Zapata. The two states soon came under rebel control, and in 1911 Díaz left Mexico. Madero was elected president, but his failure to carry through promised reforms resulted in the continuation of the rebellion.

Backed by the U.S., Gen. Victoriano Huerta overthrew Madero in 1913. But the fighting continued, and Huerta lost the support of the U.S. and was forced from office by Zapata, Villa, and Venustiano Carranza, who became president (1914-20). Zapata and Villa continued their resistance, but by 1916 Gen. Alvaro Obregón had driven Villa back to Chihuahua and Zapata's armies had been contained. Carranza called for the election of delegates to a constitutional convention in 1916, and by the following year, the progressive Mexican Constitution of 1917 was in place.

Obregón deposed Carranza in 1920 and served as president until 1924. He was reelected to succeed Plutarco Elías Calles in 1928 but was assassinated before he could take office. In 1929 Calles founded the National Revolutionary party, which became the Institutional Revolutionary party (PRI) in 1946.

Lázaro Cárdenas won the presidency in 1934, sending Calles, the long-time power behind the scene, into exile. This, coupled with Cárdenas's decision to remove himself from politics at the end of his term, greatly stabilized the institutional structure created by the Mexican Revolution. Cárdenas was the last of the "revolutionary" leaders to make good on the promises to labor and the peasantry. He presided over extensive redistribution of land and in 1938 reorganized the ruling party into four constituencies: peasants, labor, the military, and the popular sector (middle class, professionals). Cárdenas also used the national ownership of subsoil rights enshrined in the Mexican constitution to nationalize U.S. oil companies, thus assuring his credentials as a hero of Mexican nationalism.

The political movement of Mexican presidents since Cárdenas has been away from its peasant and labor constituencies toward business and the popular sector, beginning with Miguel Alemán's election in 1946.

The PRI's stability was seriously challenged in the 1980's as a result of the economic crisis stemming from the severe decline in the price of oil. Mexico borrowed heavily from foreign creditors during the 1970's on the expectation that oil prices would remain high. The debt problem led to cutbacks in government spending, a catastrophic drop in the value of the currency, and capital and human flight out of the country. It also nearly caused the PRI's downfall. Carlos Salinas de Gortari, the PRI's candidate in the 1988 presidential election, won by one of the narrowest margins ever in a contest that was widely believed to have been rigged.

Pres. Salinas vigorously pursued economic reform and lobbied for passage of the North American Free Trade Agreement with the United States and Canada, which promised to bring more jobs and much-needed increases in capital investment. But the very day NAFTA went into effect, Jan. 2, 1994, a guerrilla group of poor Indians calling itself the Zapata Army of National Liberation declared war against the government and began fighting government troops in the southern state of Chiapas under the leadership of "Subcomandante Marcos."

The (unrelated) assassination of the PRI presidential candidate at a campaign stop in Tiajuana led Salinas to appoint the campaign manager Ernesto Zedillo, a member of the PRI's reform-minded wing, as the PRI's presidential candidate (over the objections of the "old guard").

With just over 50 percent of the vote (the lowest majority ever for the PRI), Zedillo won an election unusually free from fraud. The immediate crisis he faced was the collapse of the peso, which declined by 40 percent in less than two months. In 1995, in exchange for austere economic measures by the Zedillo government, the I.M.F. and U.S. offered an enormous bail-out aid package with Mexican oil revenues as collateral. By June 1996 Mexico managed the early repayment of $4.7 billion to the U.S. by privately refinancing the debt.

Zedillo was equally successful with the situation in Chiapas, arranging 1996 peace talks with the rebels to end fighting and increase Indian autonomy. The appearance of a similar group (the Popular Revolutionary army) in the state of Guerrero began troubles which continued into 1997.

The July 1997 elections, almost entirely free of fraud, saw the PRI lose its majority in the Chamber of Deputies, as it carried only 39 percent of the vote, with PAN second at 27 percent, and PRD third at 26 percent. In March 1999, Pres. Zedillo broke with tradition by not nominating a successor. Democracy entered the PRI itself with primary elections won by Francisco Labastida. But in the July 2000 presidential elections, it was the National Action Party (PAN) candidate, Vincente Fox, who triumphed with about 43 percent in a three-way race. (See Part I, "Major News Stories of the Year.")

▶ MICRONESIA
Federated States of Micronesia

• **GEOGRAPHY Location:** forms (with Palau) archipelago of Caroline Islands, Ponape (6°52'N, 158°15'E), Yap (9°32'N, 138°08'E), Kosrae (5°19'N, 162°59'E), and Truk (7°22'N, 151°54'E), in western Pacific Ocean. **Boundaries:** Guam to NW, Marshall Islands to E, Papua New Guinea to S, Philippines about 497 mi. (800 km) to W. **Total area:** 271 sq. mi. (702 sq km). **Coastline:** 3,798 (6,112 km). **Comparative area:** about four times size of Washington, D.C. **Land use:** N.A. **Major cities:** Palikir (capital—population N.A.).

• **PEOPLE Population:** 134,597 (July 2001 est.). **Nationality:** noun—Micronesian(s); adjective—Micronesian, Kosrae(s), Pohnpeian(s), Trukese, Yapese. **Ethnic groups:** nine ethnic Micronesian and Polynesian groups. **Languages:** English (official and common language), Trukese, Pohnpeian, Yapese, Kosrean. **Religions:** 50% Roman Catholic, 47% Protestant.

• **GOVERNMENT Type:** constitutional government in free association with U.S.; the Compact of Free Association entered into force Nov. 3, 1986. **Independence:** Nov. 3, 1986 (from U.S.-administered U.N. Trusteeship). **Constitution:** May 10, 1979. **National holiday:** Proclamation of the Federated States of Micronesia, May 10. **Head of Government:** Leo A. Falcam, president (since May 1999). **Structure:** executive; unicameral legislature; judiciary.

• **ECONOMY Monetary unit:** U.S. dollar. **Budget:** (1998 est.) **income:** $161 mil.; **expend.:** $160 mil. **GDP:** $263 mil., $2,000 per capita (1999 est.). **Chief crops:** black pepper, tropical fruits and veg-

etables, coconuts, cassava, sweet potatoes; pigs, chickens. **Natural resources:** forests, marine products, deep seabed minerals. **Major industries:** tourism, construction, fish processing. **Labor force:** two-thirds are government employees. **Exports:** $73 mil. (f.o.b., 1996 est.); fish, garments, bananas, black pepper. **Imports:** $168 mil. (c.i.f., 1996 est.); food, manufactured goods, machinery and equipment, beverages. **Major trading partners:** U.S., Japan, Guam, Australia.

The Federated States of Micronesia extend 1,800 miles across an archipelago of the Caroline Islands in the larger island group of Micronesia. Ethnically diverse (there are eight primary languages, not including dialects), the islands are thought to be the first in the Pacific settled by argonauts from the Philippines and Indonesia, about 1500 B.C. Ferdinand Magellan landed in the Marianas in 1521, and Spain claimed sovereignty from 1565 to 1899, when the Caroline Islands were sold to Germany. After World War I, the League of Nations mandated the islands to Japan, which developed agriculture (especially sugarcane), mining, and fishing. After World War II, the islands were included in the U.N. Trust Territory of the Pacific and placed under U.S. administration. A compact of free association between Micronesia and the United States was signed in 1986, and Micronesia's trust territory status with the U.N. trusteeship council was dissolved in December 1990.

▶ MOLDOVA
Republic of Moldova

• **GEOGRAPHY Location:** southeastern Europe. **Boundaries:** Ukraine to N, E, S, Romania to W. **Total area:** 13,012 sq. mi. (33,700 sq km). **Coastline:** none. **Comparative area:** slightly more than twice the size of Hawaii. **Land use:** 53% arable land; 14% permanent crops; 13% meadows and pastures; 13% forest and woodland; 7% other. **Major cities:** (1992 est.) Kishinev (Chisinău) (capital) 667,100; Tiraspol 186,200; Beltsy (Balti) 159,000.

• **PEOPLE Population:** 4,431,570 (July 2001 est.). **Nationality:** noun—Moldovan(s); adjective—Moldovan. **Ethnic groups:** 64.5% Moldovan, 13.8% Ukrainian, 13% Russian, 3.5% Gagauz, 1.5% Jewish, 2% Bulgarian. **Languages:** Moldovan (official), based on Romanian, but using a Cyrillic alphabet; Russian, Gagauz. **Religions:** 98.5% Eastern Orthodox, 1.5% Jewish.

• **GOVERNMENT Type:** republic. **Independence:** Aug. 27, 1991 (from Soviet Union). **Constitution:** July 28, 1994. **National holiday:** Independence Day, Aug. 27. **Heads of Government:** Vladimir Voronin, president (since Apr. 2001); Vasile Tarlev prime minister (since Apr. 2001). **Structure:** executive; unicameral legislature; judiciary.

• **ECONOMY Monetary unit:** leu. **Budget:** (1998 est.) **income:** $536 mil.; **expend.:** $594 mil. **GDP:** $11.3 bil., $2,500 per capita (2000 est.). **Chief crops:** sugar beets, grain, vegetables, wine grapes, other fruit. **Natural resources:** lignites, phosporites, gypsum. **Major industries:** food processing, agricultural machinery, foundry equipment, textiles, chemicals. **Labor force:** 1.7 mil. (1998); 40.2% agriculture, 14.3% industry. **Exports:** $500 mil. (f.o.b., 2000); foodstuffs, wine, tobacco, textiles, footwear. **Imports:** $761 mil. (f.o.b., 2000); oil, gas, coal, steel, machinery. **Major trading partners:** Russia, Ukraine, Romania.

Historical Moldavia, of which present-day Moldova is only a small portion, encompassed territories that are now in Romania and Ukraine (including southern Bessarabia and northern

Bukovina). Moldova is a hilly, fertile land, bounded by two great rivers, the Dniester and the Prut, that flow into the Black Sea. Its climate is very favorable to agriculture.

Moldavia was part of Scythia in the first millennium B.C. and later came under the Roman Empire. Lying on the gateway to Europe, it was invaded successively, but came under the control of Kievan Rus between the 10th and 12th centuries A.D., and in the 13th century it was invaded by the Mongolian empire. In the 16th century, eastern Moldavia, or Bessarabia, came under Turkish control but in 1812 was ceded to the Russian empire. Southern Bessarabia (now in Ukraine) was controlled variously by the Russian empire and by Romania, and in 1878 it again became part of Russia. After the Bolsheviks came to power in 1917 and created the U.S.S.R., a Moldavian Autonomous Soviet Socialist Republic (ASSR) was formed on the eastern side of the Dniester River, a territory claimed by Romania but populated by Ukrainians. In June 1940, as a result of the Nazi-Soviet Pact of 1939, Romania was forced to cede Bessarabia and northern Bukovina to the Soviet Union. These lands were made part of the Ukrainian Soviet Socialist Republic (SSR), and the remaining Bessarabian sections were merged with the old Moldavian ASSR to create on Aug. 2, 1940, the Moldavian SSR. Between 1941 and 1944, while Romania and the U.S.S.R. were at war, Bessarabia again became part of Romania, but in 1944 the Soviets retook the territory and reestablished it as a union republic.

While under Soviet control, Moldavians in the new republic were officially differentiated from their counterparts across the border in Romania. In 1940, the Cyrillic alphabet was imposed on the Romanian language; this official language was called "Moldavian." Contacts between the two countries were discouraged, and the U.S.S.R. encouraged Russian and Ukrainian immigration to the Moldavian SSR. While a part of the U.S.S.R., Moldavia created a diversified economy, which is based on agriculture and food processing, with a small industrial base.

Mikhail Gorbachev's policy of glasnost, or openness, in the late 1980's gave vent to Moldavian complaints about "Russification" and immigration of non-Moldavians. In September 1989, Romanian, now in a Latin script, was restored as the official language. Glasnost also gave birth to new political parties, the largest of which was the Popular Front of Moldavia, which organized protest demonstrations against Soviet power. Disturbances during the 1989 celebration of Soviet Revolution Day in the capital city of Kishinev led to the dismissal of the Slavic Communist party First Secretary, and his replacement by an ethnic Romanian.

The Communist party was banned in Moldova in 1990, and laws to develop the basics of a multiparty system were adopted in September 1991. Moldova officially declared its independence from the U.S.S.R. on Aug. 27, 1991, and in December, United Front-supported Mircea Snegur was elected president with 98.2% of the votes cast in the elections.

At the time Moldova declared its independence, sentiment was strong for reunification with Romania. So strong, in fact, that ethnic Russians and Ukrainians living in the Trans-Dniester region in eastern Moldova, fearing reunification with Romania, declared an independent Trans-Dniester republic, sparking ethnic violence there. But since then, most activity has focused on reestablishing ties with countries from the former U.S.S.R. In 1991, Moldova singed the Alma-Ata Declaration, joining the other former Soviet republics in the Commonwealth of Independent States. And in the country's first parlimantary elections, held in February of 1994, two nationalist parties captured a combined 15 percent of the vote, while the pro-Russian Socialist party won 25 percent, and the Agrarian Democratic Party, led by former Communists, took 45 percent. Then, in a plebiscite held Mar. 6, 1994, an overwhelming majority (90 percent) of voters rejected reunification with Romania in favor of an independent Moldova. Two-thirds of Moldova's 2.3 million eligible voters cast ballots on the plebiscite. Snegur intended to use the referendum result to entice Trans-Dniester to rejoin Moldova.

In late 1996 Snegur lost the presidency to Petro Lucinschi who quickly recognized Trans-Dniester as autonomous within a single state and began a reform program to stimulate the weak economy. A strong Communist showing in 1998 legislative elections made this agenda more difficult to establish. The slow pace of reform led Prime Minister Ion Ciubuc to resign in Feb. 1999 (replaced by Ion Sturza) and Pres. Lucinschi to propose a referendum to increase the constitutional powers of the president, a model more in accord with the other ex-Soviet states.

▶ MONACO
Principality of Monaco

● **GEOGRAPHY Location:** tiny enclave on Mediterranean coast of France. **Boundaries:** France to N, E, and W; Mediterranean Sea to S. **Total area:** 1.21 sq. mi. (1.95 sq km). **Coastline:** 2.6 mi. (4.1 km). **Comparative area:** about three times size of the Mall in Washington, D.C. **Land use:** 0% arable land; 0% permanent crops; 0% meadows and pastures; 0% forest and woodland; 100% other. **Major cities:** Monaco (capital).

● **PEOPLE Population:** 31,842 (2001 est.). **Nationality:** noun—Monacan(s) or Monegasque(s); adjective—Monacan or Monegasque. **Ethnic groups:** 47% French, 16% Monegasque, 16% Italian, 21% other. **Languages:** French (official), English, Italian, Monegasque. **Religions:** 90% Roman Catholic.

● **GOVERNMENT Type:** constitutional monarchy. **Independence:** 1419. **Constitution:** Dec. 17, 1962. **National holiday:** National Day, Nov. 19. **Head of Government:** Prince Ranier III, chief of state (since Nov. 1949); Patrick Leclercq, prime minister (since Jan. 2000). **Structure:** executive—prince, minister of state (senior French civil servant appointed by prince), and Council of Government as cabinet; unicameral legislature—prince and National Council of 18 members; judiciary—authority delegated by prince to Supreme Tribunal.

● **ECONOMY Monetary unit:** French franc. **Budget:** (1995 est.) *income:* $518 mil.; *expend:* $531 mil. **GDP:** $870 mil., $27,000 per capita (1999 est.). **Chief crops:** N.A. **Natural resources:** none. **Major industries:** Tourism, construction, small-scale industry and consumer products. **Labor force:** (1994 est.) 30,540. **Exports:** N.A. **Imports:** N.A. **Major trading partners:** full customs integration with France, which collects and rebates Monacan trade duties; also participates in E.U. market system through customs union with France.

Known to Phoenicians and Greeks from the beginning of the first millenium B.C., the history of the port of Monaco is coextensive with that of southeastern France for much of its history. A western colony of the great trading city-state of

Genoa in the 13th century, Monaco in 1368 became an independent principality under the rule of the Matignon-Grimaldi family. At various times a protectorate of Spain, France, and Sardinia, it was restored to independence in 1861 by the Franco-Monegasque treaty.

In 1911 Monaco became a constitutional monarchy under the Matignon-Grimaldi dynasty. In 1918 France required the principality to conform to its national interests in all respects; by an agreement of 1919, should the dynasty fail to produce a male heir, Monaco would be absorbed into France. However, the family is allowed to adopt an heir if they so choose. The marriage of Prince Ranier III to the U.S film star Grace Kelly produced an heir apparent for this generation. The constitutional monarchy under its "Most Serene Prince" is essentially a one-party state in which the National and Democratic Union won all 18 seats in the National Council in 1968, 1978, 1983, and 1988, though in competition with the Socialist party. In 1993 Monaco became the smallest member nation of the U.N..

Despite the fame of the Monte Carlo casino, gambling accounts for only 4 percent of the principality's revenues. The principal industry is tourism, followed by light manufacturing. Monaco also supports a prominent institute of oceanography. Land reclamation projects, impelled by a real estate boom, have added about 20 percent to the nation's territory since World War II.

▶**MONGOLIA**
● **GEOGRAPHY Location:** landlocked country in central Asia. **Boundaries:** Russia to N, China to E, S, and W. **Total area:** 604,247 sq. mi. (1,565,000 sq km). **Coastline:** none. **Comparative area:** slightly larger than Alaska. **Land use:** 1% arable land; 0% permanent crops; 80% meadows and pastures; 9% forest and woodland; 10% other; includes negl. % irrigated. **Major cities:** (1994 est.) Ulan Bator (capital) 680,000; Darhan 85,800; Erdenet 63,000.
● **PEOPLE Population:** 2,654,999 (2001 est.). **Nationality:** noun—Mongolian(s) adjective—Mongolian. **Ethnic groups:** 85% Mongol, 7% Kazakh, 4.6% Tungusic, 3.4% other. **Languages:** Khalkha Mongol used by over 90% of population; Turkic, Russian, Chinese. **Religions:** predominantly Tibetan Buddhist, about 4% Muslim.
● **GOVERNMENT Type:** republic. **Independence:** Mar. 13, 1921 (from China). **Constitution:** Feb. 12, 1992. **National holiday:** National Day, July 11. **Heads of Government:** Natsagiin Bagabandi, president (since June 1997); Nambar Enkhbayar, prime minister (since July 2000). **Structure:** executive; unicameral legislature; judiciary.
● **ECONOMY Monetary unit:** tughrik. **Budget:** (2000) *income:* $262 mil.; *expend.:* $328 mil. **GDP:** $4.7 bil., $1,780 per capita (2000 est.). **Chief crops:** livestock raising predominates; wheat, barley. **Natural resources:** oil, coal, copper, molybdenum, tungsten, phosphates. **Major industries:** copper, processing of animal products, building materials, foods and beverages. **Labor force:** 1.3 mil. (1999); primarily herding agricultural; over half adult population is in labor force, including large percentage of women; shortage of skilled labor. **Exports:** $454.3 mil. (f.o.b., 1999); copper, livestock, animal products, wool, hides, fluorospar, nonferrous metals. **Imports:** $510.7 mil. (c.i.f., 1999); machinery and equipment, fuels, food products, industrial consumer goods, chemicals. **Major trading partners:** *exports:* 60% China, 20% U.S., 9% Russia; *imports:* 33% Russia, 21% China, 12% Japan.

Mongols under Genghis Khan conquered most of Eurasia in the early 13th century. The Mongol empire broke up in the mid-14th century, and Mongolia lapsed into tribal disunion and political insignificance. Chinese rule was established thereafter in Inner Mongolia (ruled directly) and, in 1691, in Outer Mongolia (a province under local rule). With the 1911 Chinese Revolution, Outer Mongolia unsuccessfully proclaimed its independence from China. The nationalist religious leader, the Bogdo Lama, sought Russian support in 1920. Under the revolutionary leaders Sukhe Bataar and Khorloin Choibalsan, a "provisional people's government" again declared independence in 1921. Sukhe Bataar died in 1923; on Nov. 26, 1924, the Mongolian People's Republic (MPR) was established with Soviet sponsorship. The early years of the republic were marked by repeated Stalinist purges of Mongol revolutionary leaders and by disastrous attempts at centralized planning.

Choibalsan emerged as party leader and was confirmed as premier in 1940. In 1939 Soviet and Mongolian armies prevented a Japanese conquest of Mongolia. In 1945 the Republic of China recognized the MPR; recognition was reaffirmed by the People's Republic of China in 1949. In 1948 the first of a series of five-year plans began to bring industrial and agricultural development to Mongolia, with extensive Soviet aid and support. Choibalsan died in 1952 and was succeeded as premier by Yumjaagiyn Tsedenbal. Following the Sino-Soviet split of 1958, heavy concentrations of Soviet troops and missiles were stationed along the Chinese-Mongolian border. On Oct. 27, 1961, the MPR was admitted to the United Nations and diplomatic relations with various other non-Soviet bloc nations developed gradually. Tsedenbal was ousted in 1984 and replaced by Zhambyn Batmonh as party chairman and by Dumaagiin Sodnom as premier. The MPR established diplomatic relations with the United States in 1987.

Following widespread demonstrations calling for human rights, religious freedom, and an end to special privileges for Communist officials, the Communist party voted to give up its constitutional power in March 1990. After the resignation of Pres. Zhambyn Batmonh, Parliament elected Punsalmaagiin Ochirbat as president. That same year, in an attempt to strengthen economic ties with China, Ochirbat became the first Mongolian head of state to visit Beijing since 1962. But the Communists returned to power in 1992, when the ex-Communist Mongolian People's Revolutionary party, running on a platform of more moderate reform, won an overwhelming majority in Parliament. Nevertheless, the more reform-minded Ochirbat put together a coalition of opposing parties in 1993 to win reelection as president. He held office until 1997 when he was defeated by Natsagiin Bagabandi who won again in 2000

With a young and rapidly growing population, an obsolete industrial base, and a shrinking economy, Mongolia has endured a painful transition to democracy and free markets. Aided by international loans, the government is pursuing a program of privatization, currency and banking reform. Trading on Mongolia's first stock exchange began in Aug. 1995. Since 1991 over 10,000 private businesses have been created, many of them small trading companies dealing with Russia and China. In Apr. 1997 parliament approved a decision to abolish all taxes on trade. U.S. Secretary of State Madeleine Albright visited in 1998 and pledged continued support and friendship.

▶MONTENEGRO
See "Yugoslavia"

▶MOROCCO
Kingdom of Morocco
• **GEOGRAPHY Location:** northwestern Africa. **Boundaries**: North Atlantic Ocean to W and NW, Strait of Gibraltar to N, Mediterranean Sea to NE, Algeria to E and SE, Western Sahara to SW. **Total area**: 172,413 sq. mi. (446,550 sq km). **Coastline**: 1,140 mi. (1,835 km). **Comparative area:** slightly larger than California. **Land use:** 21% arable land; 1% permanent crops; 47% meadows and pastures; 20% forest and woodland; 11% other; includes 1% irrigated. **Major cities:** (1990 census) Rabat (including Sale; capital) 1,385,872; Casablanca 2,940,623; Marrakech (Marrakesh) 745,541; Fès (Fez) 774,754; Oujda 678,778.

• **PEOPLE Population:** 30,645,305 (2001 est.). **Nationality:** noun—Moroccan(s); adjective—Moroccan. **Ethnic groups:** 99.1% Arab-Berber, 0.7% non-Moroccan, 0.2% Jewish. **Languages:** Arabic (official), several Berber dialects; French is language of business, government, diplomacy, and postprimary education. **Religions:** 98.7% Muslim, 1.1% Christian, 0.2% Jewish.

• **GOVERNMENT Type:** constitutional monarchy. **Independence:** Mar. 2, 1956 (from France). **Constitution:** Mar. 10, 1972, revised Sept. 4, 1992, amended to create bicameral legislature Sept. 1996. **National holiday:** National Day, July 30. **Heads of Government:** Mohammed IV, king (since July 1999); Abderrahman El-Youssoufi, prime minister (since Feb. 1998). **Structure:** executive—king has paramount powers; bicameral legislature—two-thirds of members are directly elected and one-third are indirectly elected; judiciary—independent of other branches.

• **ECONOMY Monetary unit:** dirham. **Budget:** (2001 est.) *income:* $9.6 bil.; *expend.:* $8.6 bil. **GDP:** $105 bil., $3,500 per capita (2000 est.). **Chief crops:** cereal farming and livestock raising predominant; barley, wheat, citrus fruit, wine, vegetables; livestock. **Natural resources:** phosphates, iron ore, manganese, lead, zinc, fish, salt. **Major industries:** phosphate rock mining and processing, food processing, leather goods. **Labor force:** 11 mil. (1997); 50% agriculture, 26% services, 15% industry; 19% unemployment (1998 est.). **Exports:** $7.6 bil. (f.o.b., 2000 est.); food and beverages, semiprocessed goods, consumer goods. **Imports:** $12.2 bil. (f.o.b., 1999 est.); semiprocessed goods, capital goods, food and beverages, fuel and lubricants. **Major trading partners:** France, Spain, U.K., Italy.

Neolithic inhabitants of Morocco were displaced by Berbers around 1000 B.C. Phoenician and Carthaginian settlements were established along the Mediterranean coast. Morocco came under Roman rule around 40 A.D. and was invaded via Spain by Germanic Vandals in the fifth century. The Islamic invasions of the mid-seventh century established Arab rule in Morocco, and most of the indigenous Berbers converted to Islam. Ethnic tension between Berbers and Arabs has been a basic element of Moroccan politics and society ever since.

In the late eighth century, King Idris ibn Adballah united Berbers and Arabs in a monarchy that lasted for 200 years and made the capital city of Fez one of the major religious and cultural centers of the Islamic world. In the 11th century, the Almoravid dynasty from Mauritania conquered Morocco, western Algeria, and Spain. It was ousted by another Muslin sect, the Almohads, led by Ibn Tumart. After about 1200 the tide of Moorish expansion in the Iberian Peninsula turned; in 1492 Ferdinand and Isabella expelled the last Moors from Grenada.

Naval conflict between Morocco, Spain, and Portugal continued in the western Mediterranean and along the Atlantic coast of northwestern Africa for several centuries more. In the mid-17th century, Morocco was reunited under the present Alawid dynasty. In the early 19th century, American and British forces combatted Moroccan piracy in the Mediterranean, and Spain established colonies in Tangier in the north and along the Atlantic coast between Morocco and Mauritania.

The attempts of Sultan Hassan I (r. 1873-94) to implement reforms to strengthen Morocco's independence were thwarted by European interests. By the early 20th century, France, securely established in Algeria, began exerting increasing control in Morocco. A multipower conference at Algeciras in 1906 affirmed Moroccan independence but upheld the special rights claimed by Spain and France. The Treaty of Fez, signed in 1912 between France and Sultan Abd-al-Hafidn, ended Moroccan independence by granting the country to France and reaffirming a Spanish sphere of influence in the southwest.

Nationalist unrest and tribal uprisings disrupted French administration in Morocco throughout the 1920's and 1930's. Morocco became a battleground during World War II between the Axis-supported Vichy French government and the Free French and their Allied backers. In 1943 Churchill and Roosevelt met at Casablanca to discuss wartime strategy; in the same year, the Istiqlal (Independence) party was founded to fight for independence from the French in the postwar era.

In 1947 Moroccan liberation forces began open warfare against the French. The exiled Sultan Mohammad V was allowed to return, and France promised independence by 1955.

With the withdrawal of French forces, Morocco became independent on Mar. 2, 1956. Tangier (under international administration since 1923) was incorporated into the newly independent state in October 1956, and the Spanish enclave of Ifni was ceded to Morocco in 1969.

A period of instability ensued after 1957 as newly formed political parties vied for power. King Mohammad I died in 1961 and was succeeded by his son, Hassan II. In 1962 an elected parliamentary government took power under the constitutional monarchy. Political unrest and economic difficulties led to the declaration of states of emergency in 1965 and 1970 and a new constitution in 1977.

Spain withdrew from its former territory of Spanish (now Western) Sahara, a phosphate-rich desert territory on Morocco's southern border, in Feb. 1976. On Apr. 14, 1976, Morocco annexed the northern two-thirds of the territory, while Mauritania claimed the remainder. The Polisario Spanish Saharan liberation movement, backed by Algeria and Libya, conducted guerrilla operations against Moroccan and Mauritanian forces. In 1979 Mauritania gave up its claims, and Morocco claimed the entire region.

In April 1987, Morocco completed construction of a 2,000-mile sand wall completely enclosing Western Sahara. Polisario forces, partly cut off from Algerian aid, nevertheless control much of the Western Saharan countryside, while Morocco holds the cities and towns. In May 1987 a Moroccan-Algerian summit was held under the sponsorship of Saudi Arabia, which offered King Hassan $260 million to rebuild Morocco's war-torn economy in return for allowing a self-determination referendum in the Western Sahara. The king refused. By mid-1992 the situation was in effect resolved as Polisario's top leaders accepted an offer of anmesty, leaving the Moroccan government in possession of the territory although U.N. sponsored negotiations have failed to produce a settlement in almost a decade.

The Persian Gulf crisis made an already weak economy weaker, and riots during a general strike protesting low wages, economic hardship, and poor job prospects in Fez left 100 dead and hundreds more injured in 1991. Although Morocco was an active member of the Allied coalition against Iraq, Moroccans also staged huge demonstrations in support of Saddam Hussein in Feb. at the height of the war.

In 1992, demands of Muslim fundamentalist factions for greater political power threatened the stability of King Hassan II's government. In a gesture toward political reform, parliamentary elections were held in June 1993, but the results never posed any immediate challenge to the monarchy.

In March 1998 the king appointed Morocco's first opposition-led government, a coalition of seven political parties. Hassan died in July 1999 and was succeeded by his son Mohammed IV. A government trial balloon on women's rights produced a protest rally of 500,000 in March 2000; a compromise will be sought from a body of Islamic scholars and reformers.

▶ **MOZAMBIQUE**
Republic of Mozambique
● **GEOGRAPHY   Location:** eastern coast of Africa. **Boundaries:** Zambia and Malawi to NW, Tanzania to N, Indian Ocean to E and SE, South Africa and Swaziland to SW, Zimbabwe to W. **Total area:** 309,494 sq. mi. (801,590 sq km). **Coastline:** 1,535 mi. (2,470 km). **Comparative area:** slightly less than twice size of California. **Land use:** 4% arable land; negl. % permanent crops; 56% meadows and pastures; 18% forest and woodland; 22% other; includes negl. % irrigated. **Major cities:** (1987 est.) Maputo (capital) 1,006,765.
● **PEOPLE   Population:** 19,371,057 (2001 est.). **Nationality:** noun—Mozambican(s); adjective—Mozambican. **Ethnic groups:** 99.66% indigenous tribal groups (Shangaan, Chokwe, Manyika, Sena, Makua, and others). **Languages:** Portuguese (official), indigenous languages. **Religions:** 50% indigenous beliefs, 30% Christian, 20% Muslim.
● **GOVERNMENT   Type:** republic. **Independence:** June 25, 1975 (from Portugal). **Constitution:** Nov. 30, 1990. **National holiday:** Independence Day, June 25. **Heads of Government:** Joachím Alberto Chissanó, president (since Nov. 1986); Dr. Pascoal Manuel Mocumbi, prime minister (since Nov. 1994.). **Structure:** executive; unicameral legislature; judiciary.
● **ECONOMY   Monetary unit:** metical. **Budget:** (2000 est.) *income:* $466.9 mil.; *expend:* $1.004 bil. **GDP:** $19.1 bil., $1,000 per capita (2000 est.). **Chief crops:** cotton, cashew nuts, sugar, tea; beef, poultry. **Natural resources:** coal, natural gas, titanium. **Major industries:** food and beverages, chemicals (fertilizer, soap, paints), petroleum. **Labor force:** 7.4 mil. (1997 est.); 81% agriculture. **Exports:** $390 mil. (f.o.b, 2000 est.); 40% shrimp; cashews, cotton, sugar. **Imports:** $1.4 bil. (c.i.f,

2000 est.); food, clothing, farm equipment, petroleum. **Major trading partners:** *exports:* 27% E.U.% South Africa, 15% Zimbabwe; *imports:* 44% South Africa, 16% E.U., 6.5% U.S.

Mozambique has been inhabited since prehistoric times by a variety of Bantu peoples. Portuguese trading stations were established starting in 1505, and Portugal developed an extensive coastal trade in gold and ivory. Mozambique also served as a way station for Portuguese trade to East Asia.

Despite competition from other European nations, Portugal maintained control of the Mozambique coast. Settlement by sizable numbers of Portuguese immigrants began in the late 19th century. Mozambique was organized as a colony, sometimes called Portuguese East Africa, in 1885; boundaries in the interior were defined in 1891.

Economic development of Mozambique in the 20th century remained almost entirely in Portuguese hands. By the 1950's native peoples began to protest Portuguese rule; a rebellion of the Frelimo (Front for the Liberation of Mozambique) guerrilla movement began in 1961. Rebels controlled most of the northern part of the country by 1964. Fighting continued for another decade.

Following the Portuguese revolution of 1974, Portugal agreed to independence for Mozambique, and many Portuguese settlers returned to Portugal, leaving the country bereft of administrative personnel and infrastructure support. Mozambique became fully independent on June 25, 1975. A Marxist Frelimo government took office, with Samora Michel as the country's first president. The new government formed agricultural collectives and nationalized most private land and industry as well as all social services.

In the late 1970's, fighting broke out between Mozambique and Rhodesia. When Rhodesia achieved independence (and changed its name to Zimbabwe) in 1980, relations between the two governments improved. But a rebel movement, Renamo (Mozambique National Resistance), dedicated to overthrowing the Frelimo government grew stronger during the 1980's.

In 1986, following the death of Samora Michel, Joachím Chissanó became president. The Chissano government reintroduced some private agriculture, loosened ties to the Eastern bloc, and appealed to the West for economic assistance. In 1987 a U.N.-led relief effort began. In 1989 Mozambique signed a cooperation agreement with South Africa, which cut off its aid to the Renamo insurgents. But fighting continued into 1990.

In Nov. 1990, Mozambique adopted a new constitution widening individual rights and freedoms, including abolition of the death penalty, freedom of the press and speech, and an independent judiciary, as well as establishing multiparty democracy, a presidential regime, and free-market economy. On Oct. 4, 1992, Pres. Chissanó and Renamo leader Afonso Dhlakama signed a ceasefire; the U.N. dispatched 7,500 military and civilian personnel to oversee the disarmament and organize elections.

Mozambique's first-ever multiparty elections were held in October 1994. Pres. Chissanó was elected with 53 percent of the vote while his Frelimo party took 129 of the Parliament's 250 seats. (Renamo carried all but nine of the remaining seats.) Chissano was re-elected in Dec. 1999 with Frelimo garnering 133 seats.

Mozambique is rich in agricultural land and mineral resources. Nevertheless, years of communism, drought, and civil war have left the country poor and dependent on foreign aid. In 1992 the worst drought in memory brought the nation to a virtual standstill, as an estimated 1.8 million people became dependent on donations of food from outsiders for survival. In recent years the I.M.F. has helped enormously with loans and planning advice but Mozambique remains one of the poorest nations. Devastating floods in March 2000 set back much of the progress that had been made.

▶ MYANMAR
Union of Burma

● **GEOGRAPHY** **Location:** NW region of Southeast Asia. **Boundaries:** China and Laos to NE, Bangladesh, India to NW, Thailand to SE, Andaman Sea to S, and Bay of Bengal to SW. **Total area:** 261,969 sq. mi. (678,500 sq km). **Coastline:** 1,200 mi. (1,930 km). **Comparative area:** slightly smaller than Texas. **Land use:** 15% arable land; 1% permanent crops; 1% meadows and pastures; 49% forest and woodland; 34% other; includes 2% irrigated. **Major cities:** (1983 census) Yangon (formerly Rangoon) (capital) 2,458,712; Mandalay 532,895; Bassein 335,000; Moulmein 219,991; Akyab 143,000.

● **PEOPLE** **Population:** 41,984,678 (2001 est.). **Nationality:** noun—Burmese (sing., pl.); adjective—Burmese. **Ethnic groups:** 68% Burman, 9% Shan, 7% Karen, 4% Rakhine, 3% Chinese, 2% Mon, 2% Indian, 5% other. **Languages:** Burmese, minority ethnic languages. **Religions:** 89% Buddhist, 4% Muslim, 4% Christian, 1% animist beliefs.

● **GOVERNMENT** **Type:** military regime. **Independence:** Jan. 4, 1948 (from U.K.). **Constitution:** Jan. 3, 1974; new constitution being drafted. **National holiday:** Independence Day, Jan.4. **Head of Government:** Gen. Than Shwe, chairman State Law and Order Restoration Council (SLORC) (since Apr. 1992). **Structure:** executive—military junta controls legislature—last election held in 1990, but never convened; judiciary—not independent, no guarantees.

● **ECONOMY** **Monetary unit:** kyat. **Budget:** (FY96/97) *income:* $7.9 bil.; *expend.:* $12.2 bil. **GDP:** $63.7 bil., $1,500 per capita (2000 est.). **Chief crops:** paddy rice, corn, oilseeds; hardwood. **Natural resources:** crude oil, timber, tin, copper, tungsten. **Major industries:** agricultural processing, textiles and footwear, wood and wood products. **Labor force:** 19.7 mil. (FY98/99 est.); 65% agriculture, 10% industry, 25% services (1999 est.); **Exports:** $1.3 bil. (f.o.b., 1999); teak, rice, pulses, beans. **Imports:** $2.5 bil. (f.o.b., 1999); machinery, transport equipment, chemicals, food products. **Major trading partners:** *exports:* India, China, Singapore; *imports:* Singapore, Thailand, China.

(Until the summer of 1989 this country was known as Burma.)

Burma, an independent Buddhist monarchy from the 11th century, fell to the Mongol empire in the 13th century, and after the 14th century was a satellite state of China. Anglo-French rivalry over trade left Burma under French influence in the early 19th century, but in a series of three wars (1824-26, 1852, 1885), Great Britain succeeded in bringing all of Burma into the British raj of India. The country became self-governing under a British protectorate in 1937.

Japanese occupation of Burma in early 1942 made the country a major theater of fighting during World War II. The Burma Road, built by the Allies to connect northeastern India with southwestern China, was a key link in bringing supplies to the Chinese Nationalist army during the war.

Burma achieved independence as the Union of Burma on Jan. 4, 1948. Promises of autonomy for ethnic minority regions such as the Shan and Karen States have not been fulfilled, leading to armed separatist movements in those areas ever since. In 1962 a coup led by Gen. Ne Win overthrew the democratic government and established a one-party state under the Burmese Socialist Program party. The party's "Burmese Path to Socialism" resulted in self-imposed international isolation and economic stagnation at home despite the country's potential wealth in agriculture, timber, minerals, and gems.

In July 1988 Ne Win resigned from office in the face of mounting popular demonstrations. A series of short-lived successor governments were unable to restore public order and normal governmental functions; direct military rule was announced in September 1988 as demonstrations continued.

In the general election held on May 27, 1990 (the first multiparty free elections in three decades), the opposition National League for Democracy, led by Aung San Suu Kyi, won a decisive victory, but the results of the election were nullified by the State Law and Order Restoration Council (SLORC), and leaders of the elected government were placed under house arrest. In 1991 the continued political repression in Myanmar was brought to international attention when Aung San Suu Kyi was awarded the Nobel Peace Prize. This helped usher in a period of diminishing repression. A new leader of the ruling military junta, Gen. Than Shwe, began peace talks with the Karen rebels in early 1994, and released Aung San Suu Kyi in July 1995. In 1998, renewed pressure by NLD upon the junta (since Nov. 1997 renamed the State Peace and Development Council) to convene the 1990 parliament brought renewed repression and mass arrests; a committee of NLD delcared itself to be the legal parliament of Myanmar in September, asserting that all the junta legislation since 1990 was null and void.

▶ NAMIBIA
Republic of Namibia

● **GEOGRAPHY** **Location:** southwest Africa. **Boundaries:** Angola to N, Botswana to E, South Africa to S, Atlantic Ocean to W. **Total area:** 318,259 sq. mi. (824,290 sq km). **Coastline:** 976 mi. (1,572 km). **Comparative area:** slightly more than half the size of Alaska. **Land use:** 1% arable land; negl. % permanent crops; 46% meadows and pastures; 22% forest and woodland; 31% other; includes negl. % irrigated. **Major cities:** (1990) Windhoek (capital) 125,000.

● **PEOPLE** **Population:** 1,797,677 (2001 est.). **Nationality:** noun—Namibian(s); adjective—Namibian. **Ethnic groups:** 87.5% black, 6% white, 6.5% mixed; 50% of the population belongs to the Ovambo tribe. **Languages:** Afrikaans common language, 32% German, and 7% English (official); several indigenous languages. **Religions:** 80%-90% Christian, 10%-20% indigenous religions.

● **GOVERNMENT** **Type:** republic. **Independence:** Mar. 21, 1990 (from South Africa). **Constitution:** Feb. 9, 1990. **National holiday:** Independence Day, Mar. 21. **Heads of Government:** Sam Nujoma, president (since Mar. 1990); Hage G. Geingob, prime minister (since Mar. 1990). **Structure:** executive; bicameral legislature; judiciary.

● **ECONOMY** **Monetary unit:** Namibian dollar. **Budget:** (1998) *income:* $883 mil.; *expend.:* $950 mil. **GDP:** $7.6 bil., $4,300 per capita (2000 est.). **Chief crops:** millet, sorghum, peanuts; livestock;

fish. **Natural resources:** diamonds, copper, uranium, gold, lead. **Major industries:** meat packing, fish processing, dairy products, mining (copper, lead, zinc, diamonds, and uranium). **Labor force:** about 500,000; 47% agriculture, 25% industry and commerce, 28% services; 30-40% unemployment (1997 est.). **Exports:** $1.4 bil. (f.o.b., 2000 est.); diamonds, copper, gold, zinc, lead, uranium; meat, processed fish. **Imports:** $1.6 bil. (f.o.b., 2000 est.); foodstuffs, petroleum products, machinery and equipment, chemicals. **Major trading partners:** *exports:* 43% U.K., 26% South Africa, 14% Spain; *imports:* 81% South Africa, Germany, U.S.

The Kalahari desert, on the Namibian plateau, has been inhabited since ancient times by San hunter-gatherers. Various Nama and Bantu peoples migrated into the area more recently. British and Dutch explorers and traders began to penetrate Namibia in the 18th century.

In 1872 Great Britain occupied the area around Walvis Bay and in 1884 annexed it to the Cape Colony. Also in 1884 Germany claimed most of South-West Africa; negotiations between the two powers resulted in German acceptance of Britain's claim of Walvis Bay and British acceptance of Germany's claim to the rest of the coastal region with a sphere of influence in the interior.

During World War I, British troops from South Africa occupied South-West Africa in 1915. In 1920 South Africa received a League of Nations mandate to administer the area. In 1946 when the United Nations succeeded the League, the United Nations proposed that South Africa continue its administration under a U.N. trusteeship. South Africa refused and annexed South-West Africa.

The proposed U.N. trusteeship was revoked by the United Nations in 1966. At the same time, the South-West Africa People's Organization (SWAPO), operating from bases in Zambia and Angola, began guerrilla actions against South African troops in the region. In 1968 the United Nations formally renamed the territory Namibia and appointed an 11-nation council to supervise its affairs and devise a plan leading to independence.

In 1971 the International Court of Justice upheld the U.N.'s authority over Namibia and ruled that South Africa's continued occupation of the territory was illegal. In 1975 South Africa convened the Turnhalle Conference, which proposed a plan for Namibian independence based on the racial-separation principles of apartheid. This was rejected by the United Nations, and in 1978 the U.N. Security Council approved Resolution 435, which called for a general cease-fire to be followed by U.N.-supervised elections.

In response, South Africa unilaterally held elections in Namibia, which were boycotted by SWAPO and other African organizations and rejected by the United Nations. In 1982 South Africa declared that it would enter into talks about the future of Namibia only after Cuban troops were withdrawn from Angola. In 1983 South Africa launched a major military operation against SWAPO forces in Angola.

In October 1984 Angolan president dos Santos agreed to work out a plan for withdrawal of Cuban troops as part of a settlement in Namibia. In June 1985 South Africa granted limited local authority to a Namibian government made up of a coalition of parties, excluding SWAPO. In 1987 South African troops occupied southern Angola (to aid Angolan rebels), and in early 1988, fighting between South African troops and Namibian rebels in northern Namibia and southern Angola intensified.

A new round of talks on the future of Namibia between South Africa, Cuba, and Angola, mediated by the United States, began in May 1988, and on Dec. 13, 1988, the three parties agreed on a plan for Namibian independence and a pullout of Cuban troops from Angola.

In January 1989 the Cuban withdrawal from Angola began. On Apr. 1 U.N. Resolution 435 went into effect in Namibia, and a U.N. peacekeeping force arrived to supervise the transition to independence. Elections were held in November 1989: SWAPO leader Sam Nujoma won an overwhelming victory, and opposition leaders pledged their support. A Western-style democratic constitution was adopted Feb. 16, 1990, and full independence came on Mar. 21. The first elections under the new constitution were held in December 1994 with SWAPO gaining even stronger control of Parliament. In November 1999 elections, Sam Nujoma won a third term as president with 77% percent of the vote while SWAPO took 76% of the votes for the National Assembly.

▶ **NAURU**
Republic of Nauru

● **GEOGRAPHY Location:** central Pacific Ocean (0°32'S, 166°56'E), about 2,800 mi. (4,500 km) southwest of Hawaii. **Boundaries:** nearest neighbor is Banaba (Ocean Island), in Kiribati, about 185 mi. (300 km) to E. **Total area:** 8 sq. mi. (21 sq km). **Coastline:** 19 mi. (30 km). **Comparative area:** about one-tenth size of Washington, D.C. **Land use:** 0% arable land; 0% permanent crops; 0% meadows and pastures; 0% forest and woodland; 100% other. **Major cities:** none as such; government offices in Yaren district.

● **PEOPLE Population:** 12,088 (2001 est.). **Nationality:** noun—Nauruan(s) adjective—Nauruan. **Ethnic groups:** 58% Nauruan, 26% other Pacific Islander, 8% Chinese, 8% European. **Languages:** Nauruan, a distinct Pacific Island language (official); English widely understood and spoken and used for most government and commercial purposes. **Religions:** Christian (two-thirds Protestant, one-third Catholic).

● **GOVERNMENT Type:** republic. **Independence:** Jan. 31, 1968 (from U.N. trusteeship under Australia, New Zealand, and U.K.). **Constitution:** Jan. 29, 1968. **National holiday:** Independence Day, Jan. 31. **Head of Government:** Rene R. Harris, president (since Mar. 2001). **Structure:** executive—president elected from and by Parliament for unfixed term; unicameral legislature; judiciary.

● **ECONOMY Monetary unit:** Australian dollar. **Budget:** (FY95/96) *income:* $23.4 mil.; *expend.:* $64.8 mil. **GDP:** $59 mil., $5,000 per capita (2000 est.). **Chief crops:** coconuts. **Natural resources:** phosphates. **Major industries:** phosphate mining (about 2 mil. tons per year), financial services, coconuts. **Labor force:** N.A. **Exports:** $25.3 mil. (f.o.b., 1991); phosphates. **Imports:** $21.1 mil. (c.i.f., 1991); food, fuel, manufactures, building materials, machinery. **Major trading partners:** Australia, New Zealand, U.K.

Nauru, formerly known as Pleasant Island, is an isolated island lying west of the Gilbert Islands. It became a German protectorate in 1888. After World War I, Nauru was administered by Australia under a League of Nations mandate. It was occupied by Japan throughout World War II. In 1947 it became a U.N. Trust Territory administered by Australia, and on Jan. 31, 1968, an independent republic. Nauru has a parliament of 18 members, who elect a prime minister and a cabinet.

Most of the island's assets are owned by the state-controlled Nauru Phosphate Corporation and by the Nauru Cooperative Society.

Much of the island is covered by phosphate deposits. Phosphate mining and exports, under leases largely controlled by Australian interests, have given Nauru one of the world's highest per-capita incomes. In 1999 Nauru was expected to join the U.N.

▶**NEPAL**
Kingdom of Nepal
• **GEOGRAPHY   Location:** central Asia, in Himalayan mountain range. **Boundaries:** China to N, India to E, S, and W. **Total area:** 54,363 sq. mi. (140,800 sq km). **Coastline:** none. **Comparative area:** slightly larger than Arkansas. **Land use:** 17% arable land; negl. % permanent crops; 15% meadows and pastures; 42% forest and woodland; 26% other; includes 2% irrigated. **Major cities:** (1991 census) Kathmandu (capital) 419,073.
• **PEOPLE   Population:** 25,284,463 (2001 est.). **Nationality:** noun—Nepalese (sing. and pl.); adjective—Nepalese. **Ethnic groups:** Newars, Indians, Tibetans, Gurungs, Magars, Tamangs, Bhotias, Rais, Limbus, Sherpas. **Languages:** Nepali (official); 20 other languages divided into numerous dialects. **Religions:** 90% Hindu, 5% Buddhist, 3% Muslim; only official Hindu kingdom in world, although no sharp distinction between many Hindu and Buddhist groups.
• **GOVERNMENT   Type:** parliamentary democracy. **Constitution:** Nov. 9, 1990. **National holiday:** Birthday of His Majesty the King, Dec. 28. **Heads of Government:** Gyanendra Bir Bikram Shah Dev, king (since June 2001), Sher Bahadur Deuba, prime minister (since July 2001). **Structure:** executive—prime minister appointed by king from leading party in parliament; bicameral legislature—upper house (National Assembly) consists of 60 members, 50 appointed by lower house, 10 by the king; judiciary.
• **ECONOMY   Monetary unit:** Nepalese rupee. **Budget:** (FY96/97 est.) *income:* $536 mil.; *expend.:* $818 mil. **GDP:** $33.7 bil., $1,360 per capita (2000 est.). **Chief crops:** rice, corn, wheat, sugarcane; milk, water buffalo meat. **Natural resources:** quartz, water, timber, hydroelectric potential, scenic beauty. **Major industries:** carpet and textiles, small rice, jute, sugar, and oilseed mills; cigarette and brick factories; tourism. **Labor force:** 10 mil. (1996 est.); 81% agriculture, 16% services, 3% industry; severe lack of skilled labor. **Exports:** $485 mil. (f.o.b., 1998) (does not include unrecorded border trade with India); clothing, carpets, leather goods, jute goods, grain. **Imports:** $1.2 bil. (f.o.b., 1998); gold, petroleum products, fertilizer, machinery. **Major trading partners:** *exports:* 33% India, 26% U.S., 25% Germany; *imports:* 31% India, 14% Singapore, 16% China.

The birthplace of Gautama Buddha (c. 600 B.C.), Nepal was for many centuries a collection of petty principalities, inhabited by various Tibeto-Burman peoples who mostly practiced Lamaistic Buddhism. In 1769 the country's three geographical zones—floodplain, foothills, and high mountains—were united under the Gurkhas, who made Hinduism the country's official religion. Nepal established treaty relations with Great Britain in 1792 and fought a border war with British India in 1814-16, but it was never incorporated into the British Empire.

A revolution in 1950 overthrew a government of heriditary rulers that had overthrown the Shah dynasty in the 19th century. King Tribuhavan (a Shah) was restored and tried to introduce democratic reforms, but his son Mahendra dissolved Parliament and introduced a tiered system of town, district, and national councils. Road and air links to India, Pakistan, and Tibet were improved, and Nepal began to emerge from its customary isolation. The successful climb of Mt. Everest by Sir Edmund Hillary and Tenzing Norgay in 1953 focused international attention on Nepal.

Mahendra was succeeded in 1972 by his son, Birendra. Antigovernment demonstrations in 1990 led to the shooting deaths of 63 civilians, so Birendra lifted a 30-year-old ban on political parties and ordered the constitution rewritten to establish multiparty democracy and human rights as essentials of the political system. The king retains control of the military and is still head of state.

The Nepali Congress Party formed the first government in 1991, but after 1994 a series of brief coalitions, often including the Communist Party, governed Nepal until the May 1999 elections permitted the Nepali Congress Party to again govern without coalition partners as they again carried 110 seats. But prime minister Krishna Prasad Bhattarai proved too ill to deal with Nepal's depressed economy and with the Maoist guerrilla force ("People's War") afflicting Nepal since 1996; he resigned in March 2000 to be replaced by (three times ex-premier) Giriji Prasad Koirala.

In recent years tourism, especially mountaineering and trekking, increased the country's prosperity but also created new ecological problems. The economy remains largely in the stage of small-scale agriculture and craft industries.

On June 1, 2001 Crown Prince Dipendra murdered his parents and eight other members of the royal family, after which he shot himself. His uncle became King Gyanendra. In the turmoil, the Maoist rebels increased their depredations. (See Part I, "Major News Stories of the Year.")

▶**NETHERLANDS**
Kingdom of The Netherlands
• **GEOGRAPHY   Location:**   western Europe. **Boundaries:** North Sea to N and W, Germany to E, Belgium to S. **Total area:** 14,413 sq. mi. (37,330 sq km). **Coastline:** 280 mi. (451 km). **Comparative area:** slightly less than twice the size of New Jersey. **Land use:** 25% arable land; 3% permanent crops; 25% meadows and pastures; 8% forest and woodland; 39% other; includes 15% irrigated. **Major cities:** (1994) Amsterdam (capital) 724,096; Rotterdam 598,521; The Hague 445,271; Utrecht 234,106; Eindhoven 196,130. The Hague is the seat of government.
• **PEOPLE   Population:** 15,981,472 (2001 est.). **Nationality:** noun—Dutchman (men), Dutchwoman (women); adjective—Dutch. **Ethnic groups:** 91% Dutch, 9% Moroccans, Turks, and other. **Languages:** Dutch (official). **Religions:** 34% Roman Catholic, 25% Protestant, 36% unaffiliated, 3% Muslim.
• **GOVERNMENT   Type:** constitutional monarchy. **Independence:** 1579 (from Spain). **Constitution:** 1814; last amended Feb. 17, 1983. **National holiday:** Queen's Day, Apr. 30. **Heads of Government:** Beatrix Wilhelmina Armgard, queen (since Apr. 1980); Wim Kok, prime minister (since Aug. 1994). **Structure:** executive—queen is constitutional monarch, prime minister is head of government; bicameral parliament; independent judiciary.
• **ECONOMY   Monetary unit:** guilder, gulden, or

florin. **Budget:** (2001 est.) *income:* $134 bil.; *expend.:* $134 bil. **GDP:** $388.4 bil., $24,400 per capita (1999 est.). **Chief crops:** grains, potatoes, sugar beets; livestock. **Natural resources:** natural gas, crude oil, fertile soil. **Major industries:** agroindustries, metal and engineering products, electrical machinery and equipment. **Labor force:** 7.2 mil. (2000 est.); 73% services, 23% manufacturing and construction, 4% agriculture; 3.5% unemployment (1998). **Exports:** $210.3 bil. (f.o.b. 2000); machinery and equipment, chemicals, fuels, food and tobacco. **Imports:** $201.2 bil. (c.i.f., 2000 est.); machinery and transport equipment, chemicals, foodstuffs, fuels, clothing. **Major trading partners:** (2000) *exports:* 78% EU, Central and Eastern Europe, U.S.; *imports:* 56% EU, 9% U.S., Central and Eastern Europe.

Historically, the name Netherlands referred to the low-lying areas of the Holy Roman Empire near the mouths of the Rhine, Meuse, and Scheldt rivers. The Habsburg emperor Charles V willed these territories to his son Philip II of Spain in 1555, but by the end of the 16th century, the northern provinces—the Union of Utrecht, formed in 1579 by William the Silent, of the House of Orange—won their independence in a war that was both religious (Calvinist vs. Catholic) and constitutional (aristocratic/patrician vs. foreign monarchy). The independence of the Netherlands was recognized in the Treaty of Westphalia, which ended the Thirty Years' War in 1648.

Dutch prosperity, founded on the woolen trade with England, grew tremendously through trade and seafaring under the 17th-century republic. The Netherlands amassed a world empire, including the Indonesian archipelago, the island of Sri Lanka (then Ceylon), South Africa, Surinam, parts of the West Indies, and the Hudson valley in New Amsterdam (later New York); in addition it monopolized Western trade with Japan after 1637.

The Netherlands were incorporated into the Napoleonic empire. At the Congress of Vienna in 1815, a Dutch monarchy was established, which included Belgium until 1830. Land drainage and reclamation programs maintained the prosperity of the country's small-scale agriculture, while trade and colonial revenues were increasingly supplemented by industrial development in the 19th century. Dutch prosperity and the country's strategic position gave the Netherlands extraordinary influence and prestige in European affairs into the 20th century, despite the country's small size. It remained neutral in World War I.

Germany invaded the Netherlands in May 1940, taking control of the country after five days of fighting. Preparing to incorporate Holland into the Third Reich, Hitler installed a Nazi civilian government that ruled through totalitarian exploitation and cooperated in the persecution of Jews. But Queen Wilhelmina and the Dutch government escaped to England and maintained a government-in-exile throughout the war.

The final stages of fighting on the western front inflicted severe damage on the country, while in Asia the recovery of Indonesia from Japan led immediately to a declaration of independence under Sukarno. Marshall Plan aid was intended to support a domestic postwar recovery; an equal amount was spent by the Dutch government in an attempt to recapture control of Indonesia before that country's independence was recognized in 1949.

Devastated by World War II and the loss of its empire, the country faced a bleak future in the postwar years. Forced to turn its attention to recovery at home, the Netherlands worked through the Benelux (Belgium, Netherlands, Luxembourg) union (founded in 1944) and the Common Market to create another European "economic miracle" between the early 1950's and the 1970's. The older bases of the economy—commerce, maritime industry, dairy farming, and flower farming—were expanded and modernized; Rotterdam was rebuilt to become Europe's most important port. Newer industries, such as chemicals and oil refining, electronics, and steel, relied on the country's highly skilled and productive labor force to turn imported raw materials into finished high-value exports. A huge impoundment project turned the Zuider Zee into a new province, increasing the country's land area by 10 percent.

This postwar prosperity has been based in large part on political stability. A coalition of the Catholic State party and the Labor (formerly Social Democratic) party governed for 10 years under Premier Willem Drees. After 1958 cabinets normally were formed from coalitions headed by three Christian parties (merged in 1980 to form the United Christian Appeal) or by the Liberal party; all pursued essentially the same policies of free enterprise, comprehensive social welfare programs, high taxation, and social liberalism.

Queen Juliana was succeeded in 1980 by Queen Beatrix. From 1982 to 1989 a coalition of Christian Democrats and Liberals provided a cabinet headed by Prime Minister Ruud Lubbers; since 1989 the coalition has been of Christian Democrats and Labor. In 1994 Wim Kok, head of Labor, became prime minister, the first government to exclude the Christian Democrats since 1945.

▶ NEW ZEALAND

● **GEOGRAPHY Location:** South Pacific Ocean about 1,100 mi. (1,750 km) SE of Australia. **Boundaries:** South Pacific Ocean to N, E, and S; Tasman Sea to W. **Total area:** 103,738 sq. mi. (268,680 sq km). **Coastline:** 9,406 mi. (15,134 km). **Comparative area:** about size of Colorado. **Land use:** 9% arable land; 5% permanent crops; 50% meadows and pastures; 28% forest and woodland; 8% other; includes 1% irrigated. **Major cities:** (1993 est.) Wellington (capital) 326,900; Auckland 910,200; Christchurch 312,600; Hamilton 151,800; Napier-Hastings 111,200.

● **PEOPLE Population:** 3,864,129 (July 2001 est.). **Nationality:** noun—New Zealander(s); adjective— New Zealand. **Ethnic groups:** 74.5% New Zealand European, 9.7% Maori, 4.6% other European, 3.8% Pacific Islander, 7.4% Asian and other. **Languages:** English (official) and Maori. **Religions:** 24% Anglican, 18% Presbyterian, 15% Roman Catholic, 5% Methodist, 2% Baptist, 3% other Protestant, 33% none or unspecified.

● **GOVERNMENT Type:** parliamentary democracy. **Independence:** Sept. 26, 1907 (from U.K.). **Constitution:** no formal, written constitution; consists of various documents, including certain acts of U.K. and New Zealand Parliaments. Constitution Act 1986 was to have come into force Jan. 1, 1987, but has not been enacted. **National holiday:** Waitangi Day, Feb. 6. **Heads of Government:** Sir Michael Hardie Boys, governor-general (since March 1996); Helen Clark, prime minister (since Dec. 1999). **Structure:** executive—governor-general represents queen, prime minister is head of government; unicameral legislature; judiciary.

● **ECONOMY Monetary unit:** New Zealand dollar. **Budget:** (1999 est.) *income:* $19.2 bil.; *expend.:*

$19.2 bil. **GDP:** $67.6 bil., $17,700 per capita (2000 est.). **Chief crops:** wheat, barley, potatoes, fruits; wool, meat, dairy. **Natural resources:** natural gas, iron ore, sand, coal, timber. **Major industries:** food processing, wood and paper products, textiles, aluminum smelting, tourism. **Labor force:** 1.88 mil. (2000); 65% services, 25% industry, 10% agriculture; 7% unemployment (1999). **Exports:** $14.6 bil. (f.o.b., 2000 est.); wool, lamb, mutton, beef, fruit, fish. **Imports:** $14.3 bil. (f.o.b., 2000 est.); machinery and equipment, vehicles and aircraft, petroleum, consumer goods, plastics. **Major trading partners:** *exports:* 22% Australia, 13% Japan, 14% U.S.; *imports:* 24% Australia, 17% U.S., 12% Japan.

New Zealand was settled by Maori voyagers from Polynesia from about the ninth century A.D. The first European to sight it was the Dutch explorer Abel Tasman, in 1642; he named it, but did not take possession. In 1769, Capt. James Cook visited and claimed it for Britain. The first British missionaries arrived in 1814, and New Zealand became a full-fledged British colony in 1841. By the Treaty of Waitangi in 1840, the Maoris recognized Queen Victoria's protection and agreed to admit British settlers; in return, they were guaranteed possession of their lands. But in a series of bloody wars lasting until 1870, the Maoris were displaced from lands devoted to the expanding British settlements.

As a result of their defeat and of introduced diseases, the Maori population dwindled to about 40,000 by the 1890's. Their numbers have since recovered to over 400,000, and in recent decades, the Maoris have become a cohesive culture and significant political force, directly electing several members of Parliament. In 1985, the Waitangi Tribunal was given wide power to hear Maori claims for repayment for land taken without compensation since the 1840 treaty. Large financial settlements are now being negotiated by the government.

New Zealand was one of the first nations to introduce universal adult suffrage (1893) and to establish a comprehensive welfare state. Legislation beginning in 1898 regulates labor practices, and mandates universal old-age pensions, public sector medical care, and other social services. Since 1907, the country has been an independent member of the British Commonwealth. The crown is represented by a governor-general; government is drawn from a parliament and headed by a prime minister. Since the 1930's, government has alternated between the National and Labour parties.

New Zealand troops fought on the side of the Allies in both world wars, with U.N. forces in Korea, and with the United States in Vietnam. In 1951, New Zealand joined Australia and the United States in the ANZUS mutual-defense treaty, but was excluded from it in 1986 after denying port facilities to ships carrying nuclear weapons. New Zealand has also objected strenuously to French testing of nuclear weapons in the South Pacific and pressed for a comprehensive international nuclear test ban treaty.

Upon its election in 1984, the Labour government launched a profound economic restructuring program to transform the country from a protected agrarian economy to an open free-market economy. This program, continued by the National Party, which regained power in 1990, eliminated government subsidies, cut government spending, liberalized imports, deregulated financial markets, reduced tax rates, and deregulated the labor market, largely disempowering the unions. The reforms resulted in an expanding and competitive economy with low inflation, and, in 1993-94, the first budget surplus in 18 years. The government responded in 1995 by cutting taxes again, this time by a total of $1.4 billion, the largest tax cut ever in New Zealand's history. October 1996 election results, however, forced the Nationalist Party into coalition with the new populist/zenophobic New Zealand First Party. The terms commit the new government to defer tax cuts, halt sales of state-owned businesses, freeze immigration levels, and increase spending on health and education. The coalition lasted 19 months until New Zealand First left the cabinet over government plans to privatize Wellington International Airport. Yet the government did not fall as votes of confidence in September 1998 and February 1999 permitted continuance of a minority government headed by New Zealand's first female prime minister, Jenny Shipley. Nine years of National Party rule ended in November 1999 as a coalition government of Labor and Alliance established Helen Clark as prime minister.

▶ NICARAGUA
Republic of Nicaragua

• **GEOGRAPHY Location:** Central American isthmus. **Boundaries:** Honduras to N, Caribbean Sea to E, Costa Rica to S, Pacific Ocean to W. **Total area:** 49,998 sq. mi. (129,494 sq km). **Coastline:** 565 mi. (910 km). **Comparative area:** slightly smaller than New York State. **Land use:** 9% arable land; 1% permanent crops; 46% meadows and pastures; 27% forest and woodland; 17% other; includes 1% irrigated. **Major cities:** (1983) Managua (capital) 682,111; (1985 est.) León 100,982; Granada 88,636; Masaya 74,946; Chinandega 67,792.

• **PEOPLE Population:** 4,918,393 (2001 est.). **Nationality:** noun—Nicaraguan(s); adjective—Nicaraguan. **Ethnic groups:** 69% mestizo, 17% white, 9% black, 5% Amerindian. **Languages:** Spanish (official); English- and Amerindian-speaking minorities on Atlantic coast. **Religions:** 85% Roman Catholic, Protestant.

• **GOVERNMENT Type:** republic. **Independence:** Sept. 15, 1821 (from Spain). **Constitution:** Jan. 9, 1987 with reforms in 1995 and 2000. **National holiday:** Independence Day, Sept. 15. **Head of Government:** Arnoldo Alemán Lacayo, president (since Jan. 1997). **Structure:** executive branch; unicameral legislature; judiciary.

• **ECONOMY Monetary unit:** córdoba. **Budget:** (1999 est.) *income:* $734 mil.; *expend.:* $836 mil. **GDP:** $13.1 bil., $2,700 per capita (2000 est.). **Chief crops:** cotton, bananas, coffee, sugarcane, rice, corn, beans. **Natural resources:** gold, silver, copper, tungsten, lead. **Major industries:** food processing, chemicals, metal products. **Labor force:** 1.7 mil. (1999); 43% services, 42% agriculture, 15% industry; 10.5% unemployment (1999). **Exports:** $631 mil. (f.o.b., 2000 est.); coffee, seafood, cotton, tobacco, sugar, gold, bananas. **Imports:** $1.6 bil. (c.i.f., 2000 est.); consumer goods, machinery and equipment, petroleum products. **Major trading partners:** *exports:* U.S., Central America, Germany; *imports:* Central America, U.S.

Nicaragua gained independence from Spain in 1821 and formed a constituent part of the United Provinces of Central America in 1823. With the dissolution of the federation in 1838, Nicaragua became an independent republic. Throughout the United Provinces, an intra-elite struggle between Liberal and Conservative factions defined the political arena during the early 19th century. Nicaraguan Liberals invited the adventurer William Walker of Tennessee to take their part against their Conservative rivals in 1855. Walker took control of the country in 1856 but was driven out by a combined Central American force the following year.

The Conservatives held power in Nicaragua until 1893, when a planters' revolt brought Liberal José Santos Zelaya to the presidency. Because of Zelaya's intention to pursue an isthmian canal project, the U.S. government intervened in support of a Conservative uprising. The United States sent marines to Nicaragua in 1909, and Zelaya resigned in 1910. The marines occupied the country during 1909-25 and 1926-33.

Refusing to abide by a political settlement between the U.S. government and Nicaraguan Liberal forces in 1927, Augusto César Sandino, led a guerrilla war against U.S. occupation forces. In 1934, Anastasio Somoza García, head of the Nicaraguan National Guard, had Sandino assassinated and took over the presidency in 1937. Somoza and his sons Luis and Anastasio Somoza Debayle controlled Nicaragua until 1979.

A broad coalition of groups led by the Sandinista National Liberation Front (FSLN) overthrew the Somoza dictatorship in 1979. Elections were held in 1984 for the presidency, vice presidency, and a constituent assembly. The Sandinistas won the election for the presidency, captured a working majority in the National Assembly, and wrote a new constitution in 1987.

Between 1981 and 1990, the United States actively, but covertly supported Contra rebels fighting the Sandinista regime in a civil war that cost the country dearly. In 1989, Pres. Daniel Ortega announced elections for early 1990, which he lost in a stunning upset to Violeta Barrios de Chamorro, who headed a 17-party coalition, the United Nicaragua Opposition. Since then, the transition has been relatively peaceful, highlighted by Gen. Humberto Ortega's uneventful transfer of command of the army in 1995, the first peaceful transfer in Nicaragua's history. In late 1996 presidential elections the Liberal Alliance candidate, Arnoldo Alemán, won a decisive victory over former president Daniel Ortega and voters opted for a return to free enterprise and closer ties with the U.S. Even as the Sandinistas were further weakened by Ortega's invoking of immunity (as a member of the National Assembly) against 1998 charges by his step-daughter of sexual abuse, limitations on the Aleman government's free enterprising policies were shown by student protests and transport workers' strikes which forced the government to boost university spending and abandon bus line deregulation while cutting back fuel taxes.

▶ **NIGER**
Republic of Niger
● **GEOGRAPHY** **Location:** landlocked country in western Africa. **Boundaries:** Algeria and Libya to N, Chad to E, Nigeria to S, Benin, Burkina Faso to SW, Mali to W. **Total area:** 489,189 sq. mi. (1,267,000 sq km). **Coastline:** none. **Comparative area:** slighlty less than twice the size of Texas. **Land use:** 3% arable land; 0% permanent crops; 7% meadows and pastures; 2% forest and woodland; 88% other; includes negl. % irrigated. **Major cities:** (1988 census) Niamey (capital) 392,169;

Zinder 119,838; Maradi 109,386; Tahoua 49,941; Agadez 49,361.
● **PEOPLE** **Population:** 10,355,156 (2001 est.). **Nationality:** noun—Nigerien(s); adjective—Nigerien. **Ethnic groups:** 56% Hausa, 22% Djerma, 8.5% Fula, 8% Tuareg, 4.3% Beri Beri (Kanouri); 1.2% Arab, Toubou, and Gourmantche; about 1,200 French expatriates. **Languages:** French (official), Hausa, Djerma. **Religions:** 80% Muslim, 20% indigenous beliefs and Christians.
● **GOVERNMENT** **Type:** republic. **Independence:** Aug. 3, 1960 (from France). **Constitution:** revised May 12, 1996 and July 18, 1999. **National holiday:** Republic Day, Dec. 18. **Heads of Government:** Tandja Mamadou, president (since Dec. 1999); Amadou Hama, prime minister (since Dec. 1999). **Structure:** executive; unicameral legislature; judiciary.
● **ECONOMY** **Monetary unit:** Communauté Financière Africaine (CFA) franc. **Budget:** (1999 est.) *income:* $377 mil.; *expend.:* $377 mil. **GDP:** $10 bil., $1,000 per capita (2000 est.). **Chief crops:** cowpeas, cotton, peanuts, millet, sorghum, cassava, rice; goats, sheep, cattle. **Natural resources:** uranium, coal, iron ore, tin, phosphates. **Major industries:** uranium mining, cement, brick, textiles. **Labor force:** 70,000 receive regular wages or salaries; 90% agriculture; 6% industry and commerce, 4% government. **Exports:** $385 mil. (f.o.b., 1999 est.); 65% uranium ore, livestock, cowpeas, onions. **Imports:** $317 mil. (f.o.b., 1999); consumer goods, primary materials, machinery, vehicles and parts, petroleum, cereals. **Major trading partners:** *exports:* U.S., France, Nigeria, U.K.; *imports:* France, Ivory Coast, Nigeria.

Most of Niger's territory is dominated by the Sahara and the Sahel (the "shore" of the desert), which have spread southward since prehistoric times. Much of the population lives in the narrow fertile belt south of the Niger River. Much of Niger was incorporated during medieval times in large empires centered in neighboring Mali, Chad, and Nigeria.

In the 18th century, Tuaregs migrating from the northern desert began to form tribal confederations in Niger. They united with local Hausa peoples to wage war against the Fulani empire. In the 19th century, British and German explorers explored the region. In the European rivalry that followed, the French, from bases in Mali and Chad, began to dominate Niger by 1900; Niger became a French colony in 1922, administered from Dakar, Senegal.

In 1946 the people of Niger, in common with other peoples in French Africa, were granted French citizenship, and limited self-rule began. This local autonomy was expanded in 1956, and in 1958 Niger became an autonomous state within the French Overseas Community. Full independence followed on Aug. 3, 1960; Niger maintained close ties to France.

Hamani Diori was elected Niger's first president in 1960, reelected in 1965 and 1970. He was overthrown in 1974 in a military coup led by Lt. Col. Seyni Kountche. In 1987, Pres. Kountche died and was succeeded by Col. Ali Saibou, who was elected president by the Supreme Military Council. The country began moving toward democracy again in 1989, and a new constitution was approved in 1992. Mahame Ousmane was elected president in 1993, but he and prime minister Hama Amadou were ousted in a violent military coup in Jan. 1996. The leader of the coup, Lt. Col. Ibrahim Barré, who criticized Ousmane's handling of the Taureg Liberation Front, became the new president. He survived an assasination attempt in Jan. 1998, but fell to another in April 1999. Junior army officers formed a junta, supported by all the civilian opposition parties,maintaining Ibrahim Mayaki in his post as prime minister. The junta promised a "nine-month transition", and presidential elections were held in Nov. 1999 in which Tandja Mamadou defeated former premier Mohamadou Issoufou.

▶ NIGERIA
Federal Republic of Nigeria
• GEOGRAPHY Location: western coast of Africa. Boundaries: Niger to N, Cameroon to E, Gulf of Guinea to S, Benin to W. Total area: 356,668 sq. mi. (923,770 sq km). Coastline: 530 mi. (853 km). Comparative area: slightly more than twice the size of California. Land use: 33% arable land; 3% permanent crops; 44% meadows and pastures; 12% forest and woodland; 8% other; includes negl. % irrigated. Major cities: (1992) Abuja (capital) 305,900; Lagos 13,470,000; Ibadan 1,295,000; Kano 699,900; Ogbomosho 660,600.
• PEOPLE Population: 123,337,822 (2000 est.). Nationality: noun—Nigerian(s); adjective— Nigerian. Ethnic groups: 20% Hausa and Fulani, 21% Yoruba, 18% Ibo, 10% Ijaw, Kanuri, Ibibio, Tiv. Languages: English (official); Hausa, Yoruba, Ibo, Fulani. Religions: 50% Muslim, 40% Christian, 10% indigenous beliefs.
• GOVERNMENT Type: republic in transition from military rule. Independence: Oct. 1, 1960 (from U.K.). Constitution: New constitution adopted in 1999. National holiday: Independence Day, Oct. 1. Head of Government: Olusegun Obasanjo, president (since May 1999). Structure: executive; bicameral legislature; judiciary.
• ECONOMY Monetary unit: naira. Budget: (1998 est.) income: $13.9 bil.; expend: $13.9 bil. GDP: $110.5 bil., $970 per capita (1999 est.). Chief crops: peanuts, cocoa, palm oil, rubber, corn; goats, sheep, cattle, pigs; fish. Natural resources: crude oil, tin, columbite, iron ore, coal. Major industries: crude oil, coal, tin, columbite; palm oil, peanuts, cotton, rubber; textiles, cement, building materials. Labor force: 42.8 mil. (1985); 54% agriculture; 19% industry, commerce, and services; 15% government; 28% unemployment (1999 est.). Exports: $13.1 bil. (f.o.b., 1999); 95% petroleum and petroleum products, cocoa, rubber. Imports: $10 bil. (f.o.b., 1999); machinery, chemicals, transportation equipment, manufactured goods, food and animals. Major trading partners: exports: 35% U.S., 11% Spain, 9% India; imports: 12% U.S., 13% U.K., 10% Germany, 9% France.

The Nok culture of central Nigeria (500-200 B.C.) was one of the richest and most advanced ancient civilizations in western Africa. Around A.D. 1000, the Muslim Kanem civilization expanded into northern Nigeria; by the 14th century, the amalgamated kingdom of Kanem-Bornu took northern Nigeria as its political center, from which it dominated the Sahel and developed trade routes stretching throughout northern Africa and as far as Europe and the Middle East. During the 15th and 16th centuries, the Hausa Songhai empire rose to power. It was overthrown by the Fulani Muslim leader Uthman Dan Fodio, who created the Sokoto caliphate.

Southern Nigeria is dominated by the Yoruba, whose Oyo kingdom, centered at Ife, became a major power by A.D. 1000. Oyo gave rise to the Benin civilization, which flourished from the 15th to the 18th centuries and is famous for its brass, bronze, and ivory sculpture.

The Portuguese established trading stations on the Benin coast in the 15th century; initially, trade relations were cordial, and Benin became wellknown in Europe as a powerful and advanced kingdom. With the rise of the slave trade (which began with the cooperation of the Benin kings, who brought slaves from the interior), relations became hostile, and Benin declined under European pressure. The Dutch, British, and other Europeans competed strenuously with Portugal for control of the slave trade, and by the 18th century, most of the coastal region of Nigeria was under British control. By the turn of the 19th century, Britain suppressed the slave trade; slaves captured aboard European ships were transported by the British to Freetown in Sierra Leone.

The British traded with Nigerians for agricultural and forest products and commenced exploration of the Niger River. Lagos came under British control in 1851, and in 1861 Nigeria was made a British colony. Despite native resistance the colony was expanded in 1906 to include territory east of the Niger River, which was called the Protectorate of Southern Nigeria, The two areas were administratively joined in 1914.

During the 1920's Britain began to respond to Nigerian demands for self-rule. In 1946 the colony was divided into three regions, each with an advisory assembly. In 1954 the colony was reorganized as the Nigerian Federation, and the assemblies were given more authority. Sir Akubar Tafawa Balewa became Nigeria's first prime minister.

The 1960's were marked by a struggle for political dominance among the major ethnic groups of Nigeria, including the Ibo (or Igbo), Yoruba, Hausa, and Fulani. Attempts to partition the country on tribal lines for administrative purposes provoked controversy, and charges of corruption and fraud in elections held in 1964 and 1965 led to violence and rioting.

In January 1966 civil war broke out when a group of Ibo army officers overthrew the central government and several of the regional governments. Prime Minister Balewa was killed, along with many other political leaders in the northern and western parts of the country. Gen. Johnson Aguiyi-Ironsi, leader of the Ibo forces, took control of the government.

Aguiyi-Ironsi abolished the country's federal structure and set up a strong central government, dominated by the Ibo. Anti-Ibo riots broke out in the north, and many Ibo were massacred. In July 1966 Aguiyi-Ironsi was assassinated by a group of northern army officers. Army Chief of Staff Yakubu Gowon became head of a new military government.

In 1967 Gowon reapportioned Nigeria into 12 states. The Eastern Region rejected this plan and seceded from Nigeria to form the independent state of Biafra, provoking a civil war that lasted until January 1970, when Biafra was rejoined with Nigeria. An estimated one million Biafrans, mostly Ibos, died in the war.

Gowon tried to rebuild the Eastern Region and create a harmonious multitribal government, but he was overthrown in a coup in 1975. His successor was assassinated in 1976 and succeeded by Lt. Gen. Olusegun Obasanjo who increased the number of states from 12 to 19 and promised a return to civilian rule. Shehu Shagari was elected president in 1979 and reelected in 1983, but in Dec. 1983 the military again intervened.

Nigeria's crude oil resources fueled the economy and made it attractive for foreign investment. During the 1970's, petroleum exports helped Nigeria recover from the Biafran War. But corruption and overspending of projected petroleum revenues led to an economic crisis in the early 1980's as oil prices collapsed worldwide. Inflation, unemployment, and food shortages led to rioting in major population centers in 1986. And in 1987, religious violence broke out between the Christian south and the Muslim north.

The government of Maj. Gen. Ibrahim Babangida responded by announcing plans for a new constitution, various economic austerity measures, and the restoration of civilian rule by 1992. He also limited the number of political parties and dictated both party platforms in National Assembly elections held in 1992, and in 1993, he annulled the results of the presidential election, which international monitors said would have been won by opposition leader Moshood K. Abiola, who was taken prisoner for the "treason" of declaring himself the election winner. Babangida resigned in Aug. 1993, but his self-appointed successor was ousted in a November 1993 coup by Defense Minister Sani Abacha.

Abacha's tyranny survived until his death (of a heart attack) in June 1998. A "transitional" military government led by army chief of staff, Abdusalem Abubakar, freed political prisoners (Abiola dying just before his release), held local, state, and national elections (Dec.– Feb.), and turned over power, May 29, 1999 to the first popularly-elected president in 16 years, former general and once military ruler, Olusegun Obasanjo. The new government faced formidable problems: increased Moslem-Christian violence as northern states attempted to impose Sharia (Koranic law); civil disorder and rioting in the face of increased fuel prices.

In July 2000, violence and bloodshed over the imposition of Sharia increased. Attempts to meet I.M.F. loan conditions, such as ending subsidies which kept oil prices low or reducing government payrolls, provoked riots and strikes. Hausa-Yoruba tribal conflict in Lagos left over 100 dead.

▶ NORWAY
Kingdom of Norway
• GEOGRAPHY Location: western Scandinavian peninsula, northern Europe. Boundaries: Norwegian Sea to N and W, Russian Federation, Finland to NE, Sweden to E, North Sea to S and W. Total area: 125,182 sq. mi. (324,220 sq km). Coastline: 13,626 mi. (21,925 km)—2,125 mi. (3,419 km) mainland; 1,500 mi. (2,413 km) large islands; 10,002 mi. (16,093 km) long fjords, numerous small islands, and minor indentations. Comparative area: slightly larger than New Mexico. Land use: 3% arable land; negl.% permanent crops; negl. % meadows and pastures; 27% forest and woodland; 70% other; includes negl. % irrigated. Major cities: (1995) Oslo (capital) 483,401; Bergen 221,717; Trondheim 142,927; Stavanger 103,590; Kristiansand 68,609.
• PEOPLE Population: 4,503,440 (2001 est.). Nationality: noun—Norwegian(s); adjective—Norwegian. Ethnic groups: Norwegian (Nordic, Alpine, Baltic), 20,000 Lapps (Sami). Languages: Norwegian (official), Lapp- and Finnish-speaking minorities. Religions: 86% Evangelical Lutheran (state church), 3% other Protestant and Roman Catholic, 1% other, 10% none and unknown.
• GOVERNMENT Type: constitutional monarchy. Independence: Oct. 26, 1905 (from Sweden). Constitution: May 17, 1814, and modified in

1884. National holiday: Constitution Day, May 17. Heads of Government: Harald V, king (since Jan. 1991); Jens Stoltenberg, prime minister (since March 2000). Structure: executive—prime minister heads government; unicameral legislature—for certain purposes, Storting divides itself into two chambers and elects 25 percent of its members to an upper house; judiciary.
• ECONOMY Monetary unit: Norwegian kroner. Budget: (2000 est.) income: $71.7 bil.; expend.: $57.6 bil. GDP: $124.1 bil., $27,700 per capita (2000 est.). Chief crops: oats, feed grains; beef, milk; fish (among worlds top ten fishing nations). Natural resources: crude oil, copper, natural gas, pyrites, nickel. Major industries: petroleum and gas, food processing, shipbuilding. Labor force: 2.4 mil.; 74% services, 22% industry, 4% agriculture, forestry and fishing; 2.9% unemployment (1999). Exports: $59.2 bil. (f.o.b., 2000 est.): petroleum and petroleum products, metals, chemicals, ships, fish. Imports: $35.2 bil. (f.o.b., 2000 est.); machinery and equipment, chemicals, metals, foodstuffs. Major trading partners: exports: 73% EU, 5% U.S.; imports: 66% EU, 10% U.S.

The Viking age began in 793 with the sack of Lindisfarne in Ireland. By the 10th century, Norse and Danish Vikings had touched in almost every navigable river of Western Europe from Germany to Spain. In addition to coastal raiding, the Norse were beginning the first open-ocean voyages from Europe, sailing direct to Iceland (800 miles) and even to Greenland (2,200 miles), which they colonized in the 10th century.

At the beginning of the 10th century, Harold I united the petty kingdoms of western Scandinavia and extended his realm as far as the Orkney and Shetland islands. Viking nobles fleeing from his conquests consolided the Norse duchy of Normandy in France. Christianity was established under Olaf II at the beginning of the 11th century.

Under Magnus VI (1263-80), medieval Norway reached the height of its power and prosperity. Norwegian independence ended with the accession in 1319 of Magnus VII, who was king of Sweden as well. Under the Kalmár Union of 1397, the three kingdoms of Scandinavia were merged under Danish control; Norway ceased to exist as a nation-state and was governed by the Danes for the following four centuries.

In 1814 Denmark, which had sided with France in the Napoleonic wars, was forced by the victorious powers to cede Norway to Sweden. Under Sweden's military control Norway attempted to establish its own monarchy. The attempt failed, but in 1815 Sweden acknowledged the independence of Norway in perpetual union with the Swedish Crown.

Relations between Norway and Sweden remained strained throughout the 19th century. In 1905 the Norwegian legislature, the Storting, declared the union void and deposed Swedish King Oscar II as king of Norway. Sweden acquiesced, and Prince Charles of Denmark was enthroned as king of Norway, ruling as Haakon VII for 52 years.

During the 19th century, large numbers of Norwegians emigrated to North America. A rising tide of cultural nationalism was expressed in the flourishing Norwegian literature and art, as well as in a tradition of Arctic exploration. In the 20th century, industrialization, aided by the development of hydroelectric power, began to supplement Norway's traditional economic mainstays of fishing and seafaring.

Norway remained neutral during World War I and was relatively unaffected by the postwar upheavals. Norway attempted to remain neutral in World War II as well but was invaded by German troops in April 1940; the country fell after a brief resistance aided by a Franco-British expeditionary force. The king and government fled to London and established a government-in-exile there. The Norwegian merchant marine fleet was also largely transferred to Great Britain and contributed to the Allied cause in the North Atlantic. At home, resistance grew to the collaborationist government of the Fascist leader Vidkun Quisling. As the Nazis retreated in 1945, King Haakon and his government returned home in triumph.

Elections in 1945 returned a majority Labor government in the Storting. Labor set about establishing a characteristic Scandinavian welfare state, emphasizing privately owned, free-market industry, publicly owned utilities, state planning to ensure ample housing as well as full employment through export-oriented industries, a comprehensive social welfare system, and—to pay for the latter—high taxes.

Norway was a founding member of the United Nations and provided that body with its first secretary-general, Trygve Lie. With the hardening of the Cold War, Norway joined the NATO alliance in 1949. In 1959 Norway became one of the original members of the European Free Trade Association. Through the 1960's industrial development and exports continued to fuel an economic boom that led to great national prosperity and stability.

The 1970's were the decade of oil and gas, with extensive development of North Sea fields at the beginning of the decade. As international energy prices rose, the government's petroleum monopoly, Statoil, seemed to provide an endless source of funds. Because Norway's hydroelectric plants made the country self-sufficient in electric power, almost all of the oil and gas was available for export; by 1981 energy exports amounted to one-third, and by 1985 one-half, of Norway's total exports. The government expanded the welfare state and encouraged large wage increases. Public spending swelled and government debt mounted; meanwhile Norway became an economic hostage to OPEC oil prices.

In the 1981 elections, the Conservative party formed a government for the first time since 1928; its austerity policy of holding down government spending while increasing taxes on consumer goods aroused popular opposition, and the government fell in 1986. The new Socialist coalition government faced even greater drops in oil revenues, combined with labor unrest and continued inflation. But in 1987 Norway negotiated the sale of gas to E.U. countries, and the recovery of energy prices brought a partial return to economic stability and prosperity. King Olav died in Jan. 1991; his son Harald V succeeded him in June.

In 1993 the government of Prime Minister Brundtland sought admission to the EU. On Mar. 29, 1994, the E.U. agreed to admit Norway to membership after long and intricate negotiations limiting Spanish and Portuguese fishing rights in Norwegian waters. But Norweigian voters in a Nov. 1994 referendum rejected E.U. membership. Brundtland resigned in Oct. 1996 and was replaced by Thorbjoern Jagland, but he remained prime minister less than a year. After 1997 elections to the Storting, a right-wing three-party coalition, which controlled only 24 of the 165 seats, formed a government under Christian Democrat Kjell Magne Bondevik. Even Bondevik's three-week leave of absence (to treat depression) in Sept. 1998 failed to shake the stability of Nor-

way's politics. But a March 2000 no-confidence vote toppled the government, replacing it with a Labor-Conservative coalition under Labor's Jens Stoltenberg as prime minister.

▶ OMAN
Sultanate of Oman

● **GEOGRAPHY   Location:** southeastern Arabian peninsula. **Boundaries:** Gulf of Oman to N, Arabian Sea to E and S, Yemen to SW, Saudi Arabia to W, United Arab Emirates to NW; detached portion of Oman lies at tip of Musandam peninsula, on Strait of Hormuz. **Total area:** 82,031 sq. mi. (212,460 sq km). **Coastline:** 1,299 mi. (2,092 km). **Comparative area:** slightly smaller than Kansas. **Land use:** 0% arable land; negl. % permanent crops; 5% meadows and pastures; negl. % forest and woodland; 95% other; includes negl. % irrigated. **Major cities:** (1993 census) Muscat (capital) 549,150; Al-Batinah 564,677; Al-Sharquia 258,344.

● **PEOPLE   Population:** 2,622,198 (2001 est.). **Nationality:** noun—Omani(s); adjective—Omani. **Ethnic groups:** Arab, Baluchi, South Asian, African. **Languages:** Arabic (official), English, Baluchi, Urdu, Indian dialects. **Religions:** 75% Ibadhi Muslim, Sunni Muslim, Shi'a Muslim, Hindu.

● **GOVERNMENT   Type:** monarchy. **Constitution:** none. **National holiday:** National Day, Nov. 18. **Head of Government:** Qaboos bin Said, sultan and prime minister (since July 1970). **Structure:** executive—sultan is hereditary monarch; bicameral legislature-advisory powers only; judiciary—traditional Islamic judges in nascent civil court system; supreme court with non-Islamic judges.

● **ECONOMY   Monetary unit:** Omani rial. **Budget:** (1999 est.) *income:* $4.7 bil.; *expend.:* $5.9 bil. **GDP:** $19.6 bil., $7,700 per capita (2000 est.). **Chief crops:** dates, limes, bananas, alfalfa, vegetables, cattle, camels; annual fish catch averages 100,000 metric tons. **Natural resources:** crude oil, copper, asbestos, some marble, limestone. **Major industries:** crude oil production and refining, natural gas production, construction. **Labor force:** 850,000 (1997 est.). **Exports:** $11.1 bil. (f.o.b., 2000 est.); petroleum, reexports, fish, metals, textiles. **Imports:** $4.5 bil. (f.o.b., 2000 est.); machinery, transportation equipment, manufactured goods, food, livestock, lubricants. **Major trading partners:** *exports:* 27% Japan, 12% China, 18% Thailand; *imports:* 26% UAE, 16% Japan, 9% U.K.

Oman occupies the southeastern corner of Arabia. From ancient times an important center of trade in the Persian Gulf and the Indian Ocean, Oman was frequently dominated by Persia prior to the mid-18th century. The principal port, Muscat, was captured by the Portuguese in 1508 and held by them until 1659, when the Ottoman Turks took possession. They were driven out in 1741 by Ahmed ibn Said of Yemen, who consolidated the sultanate of Oman in 1744 and founded the present royal line.

In the early 19th century, Oman was the most powerful state in Arabia, controlling Zanzibar, the southern coast of Iran, and much of Baluchistan (between Pakistan and Iran). Zanzibar was separated from Oman in 1856, and the Persian coast and much of Baluchistan was detached from Oman during the latter half of the 19th century. In 1958 Oman's sole remaining Baluchi possession, the city-state of Gwadar, was ceded to Pakistan in return for a monetary settlement.

Growing British influence was consolidated by the formation of a British protectorate in 1891, reconfirmed in 1951. In the 1950's Britain aided the sultanate in putting down rebellions in the desert interior. The British protectorate ended with Britain's withdrawal from the gulf in 1971. On July 23, 1970, Sultan Said ibn Taimur was overthrown by his son, Sultan Qaboos bin Said, who instituted a national development program and in 1975 defeated a leftist uprising in the western desert.

Petroleum makes up 95 percent of exports. Banking and shipping services are also important. The country is generally barren, with scattered flocks of sheep and camels. In April 1996 Oman joined with Russia and Kazakhstan to establish a consortium with eight oil companies to build a 900 mile pipeline to move oil to Russia's port in the Black Sea.

▶ PAKISTAN
Islamic Republic of Pakistan

● **GEOGRAPHY   Location:** southern Asia. **Boundaries:** Afghanistan to N, China to far NE, India to E, Arabian Sea to S, and Iran to W. **Total area:** 310,402 sq. mi. (803,940 sq km). **Coastline:** 650 mi. (1,046 km). **Comparative area:** slightly less than twice the size of California. **Land use:** 27% arable land; 1% permanent crops; 6% meadows and pastures; 5% forest and woodland; 61% other; includes 19% irrigated. **Major cities:** (1991 est.) Islamabad (capital) 400,000; Karachi 7,000,000; Lahore 3,500,000; Faisalabad (Lyallpur) 2,000,000; Rawalpindi 800,000.

● **PEOPLE   Population:** 144,616,639 (2001 est.). **Nationality:** noun—Pakistani(s); adjective—Pakistani. **Ethnic groups:** Punjabi, Sindhi, Pashtun (Pathan), Baloch, Muhajir (immigrants from India and their descendants). **Languages:** 48% Punjabi, 12% Sindhi, 10% Siraiki, 8% Pashtu, 8% Urdu (official), 3% Balochi, 2% Hindko, 1% Brahui, English (official and lingua franca of Pakistani elite and most government ministries), 8% Burushaski and other. **Religions:** 97% Muslim (77% Sunni, 20% Shi'a); 3% Christian, Hindu, and other.

● **GOVERNMENT   Type:** federal republic. **Independence:** Aug. 14, 1947 (from U.K.). **Constitution:** Apr. 10, 1973; suspended July 5, 1977; restored Dec. 30, 1985; suspended Oct. 15, 1999. **National holiday:** Pakistan Day, Mar. 23. **Heads of Government:** General Pervez Musharraf, president (since June 2001). **Structure:** executive—prime minister is head of government; bicameral legislature—dissolved after military takeover; judiciary.

● **ECONOMY   Monetary unit:** Pakistani rupee. **Budget:** (FY00/01 est.) *income:* $8.9 bil.; *expend.:* $11.6 bil. **GDP:** $282 bil., $2,000 per capita (2000 est.). **Chief crops:** wheat, rice, sugarcane, cotton; beef, milk, mutton, eggs. **Natural resources:** land, extensive natural gas reserves, limited petroleum, poor quality coal, iron ore. **Major industries:** cotton textiles, food processing. **Labor force:** 40 mil.; 44% agriculture, 17% mining and manufacturing, 39% services; extensive export of labor, mostly to the Middle East, and use of child labor. **Exports:** $8.6 bil. (f.o.b., FY99/00); cotton, textiles, clothing, rice, leather, carpets. **Imports:** $9.6 bil. (f.o.b., FY99/00); petroleum, petroleum products, machinery, transportation equipment, cooking oils. **Major trading partners:** *exports:* 24% U.S., 7% Hong Kong; *imports:* 8% Saudi Arabia, 8% UAE.

Pakistan occupies the heartland of ancient South Asian civilization, in the Indus River valley. Agricultural settlements in that area arose by 3000 B.C., and the great cities at Harappa and Mohenjo-Daro were founded some 500 years later. Indo-European (Aryan) invaders from Central Asia overthrew the ancient civilization around 1500 B.C. and established a new culture that spread throughout Pakistan and northern India. Brahmanism, the religious culture of the early Indo-European invaders, gave rise to Buddhism and Jainism around the sixth century B.C., and evolved into Hinduism in the early centuries A.D. The Indus valley was incorporated into the empire of Alexander the Great, c. 350 B.C., and then into the Mauryan empire of Asoka, which by the third century B.C. controlled all of South Asia except for the southernmost portion of India.

Under various rulers the Indus Valley and the areas to its northwest were a great center of Buddhist culture until the beginning of the eighth century, when the area fell to Muslim Arab invaders. Thereafter, Islam was firmly established throughout the region. But Baluchistan and the Northwest Frontier region became culturally allied to the Persian civilization of Iran and Afghanistan, while Sind and the Punjab were more closely akin to the culture of northern India.

Northern Pakistan was incorporated into the empire of Mahmud of Gazni in the 11th century, and fell to the Mongols in the 13th century. The Indus River became the boundary between the Mongol Inkhanate of Persia and the sultanate of Delhi. The region was conquered by Timur Leng at the end of the 14th century, and after the fall of the Timurid empire was divided between the kingdoms of Sind and Multan, in southern and central Pakistan, and the sultanate of Delhi, in the Punjab. All of Pakistan and northern India was reunited after 1526, when the conquests of Babur established the Mogul empire.

The expansion of British power in India during the 18th century left Pakistan largely untouched; the area was divided among various states, including Sind, the Punjab, Kashmir, and the western reaches of Rajputana. In the first half of the 19th century, British rule extended to the northwest; after the defeat of the Indian Mutiny of 1857, the entire Indus valley came under British rule. Sind and the Punjab were ruled directly by the British, while the native states were ruled as British protectorates.

From the beginning of the 20th century, various nationalist movements arose throughout British India. The Muslim League, under the leadership of Mohammad Ali Jinnah after 1916, advocated greater popular political participation, dominion status for India, and a strong Muslim voice in Indian administration. Muslims and Hindus were allied in the Non-Cooperation movement of the 1920's, but the alliance soon broke down and degenerated into communal frictions. With growing power of the Congress party in Hindu areas and Gandhi's civil disobedience movement in the 1930's, Jinnah's Muslim League charted an increasingly separate course and called for the creation of a separate Muslim state in 1940.

With the British withdrawal from India in 1947, Hindus in the Muslim majority areas of the Indus valley and in East Bengal fled to Hindu northern India, while Muslims in Hindu areas fled in the opposite direction. These massive population movements were accompanied by widespread violence leading to the loss of hundreds of thousands of lives. Jinnah, the father of modern Pakistan, died in 1948. Pakistan, encompassing Sind, the Punjab, Baluchistan, the Northwest Frontier Territories, part of Jammu and Kashmir, and adjacent areas in the west and East Bengal in the east, was granted dominion status within the British Commonwealth in 1947, becoming an independent republic in 1956.

Pakistan joined the Central Treaty Organization and became allied with the West, in contrast to the Soviet-leaning nonalignment of India. In 1958 Gen. Mohammad Ayub Khan seized power in a coup; he was elected president in 1960 and re-elected in 1965. Following border clashes with India in 1962, Pakistan entered into friendly relations with China, which also had engaged in border warfare with India. Ayub Khan resigned as president in early 1969 after failing to put down widespread demonstrations in East Pakistan. A new government was formed under Gen. Yahya Khan, and martial law was declared. A parliamentary victory by the East Pakistani Awami League in December 1970 led to civil war and the secession of East Pakistan in 1971 (see "Bangladesh").

India's intervention on behalf of East Bengal had led to war on a western front with Pakistan. On July 3, 1972, India and Pakistan agreed to a mutual withdrawal of troops and entered into negotiations designed to settle border disputes and other problems. Diplomatic relations between India and Pakistan were resumed in 1976.

The elections of 1970 that had precipitated the civil war also brought Zulfikar Ali Bhutto to the presidency. He remained in office until July 1977, when he was overthrown in a military coup led by Gen. Mohammad Zia ul-Haq. He was convicted of complicity in a 1974 political murder and hanged in April 1979. Under Pres. Zia, Pakistan moved toward the implementation of Islamic law in parallel with the constitutional law of Pakistan's parliamentary system. In 1986 Bhutto's daughter, Benazir Bhutto, returned to Pakistan from exile in Europe to organize opposition parties against Pres. Zia, leading to widespread rioting.

On Aug. 17, 1988, Pres. Zia, several senior government officials, and the American ambassador were killed in an airplane crash. From 1988 to 1999 the position of prime minister has alternated between Benazir Bhutto as head of the Pakistan People's Party and Nawaz Sharif as leader of the Muslim League, each accusing the other in turn of tyranny and corruption, amidst endless tension with India over Jammu-Kashmir. The latter struggle lay at the root of the nuclear-test rivalry in May 1998, after which the prime ministers, Vajpayee and Sharif, attempted to lower the political temperature while not appearing to "cave in" to the other. Sharif's July 1999 agreement in Washington D.C. to withdraw support for Moslems in Kashmir made it appear that he was the one to blink first.

Sharif's dismissal of General Musharraf over the army's support of Kashmir rebels led to a military coup and Sharif's trial on corruption (and other) charges which ended April 6, 2000 with a guilty verdict and a sentence of life imprisonment. Musharraf pledged a return to civilian rule within three years, but in June 2001 he appointed himself president.

▶ **PALAU**
Republic of Palau
● **GEOGRAPHY   Location:** more than 200 islands, in a chain about 400 mi. (650 km) long, in western central Pacific Ocean; Koror 71°21′N, 134°31′E. **Boundaries:** Guam 720 mi. (1,160 km) to NE, Federated States of Micronesia to E, island of New Guinea to S, Philippines 530 mi. (850 km) to NW. **Total area:** 177 sq. mi. (458 sq km). **Coastline:** 944 mi. (1,519 km). **Comparative area:** slightly more than 2.5 times size of Washington, D.C. **Land use:** N.A.% arable land; N.A.% permanent crops; N.A.% meadows and pastures; N.A.% forest and woodland; N.A.% other. **Major cities:** (1990 census) Koror state 10,501; Koror is the current capital; a new capital is being built at Babelthuap, 20 km northeast.

● **PEOPLE   Population:** 19,092 (2001 est.). **Nationality:** noun—Palauan(s); adjective—Palauan. **Ethnic groups:** composite of Polynesian, Malayan, and Melanesian races. **Languages:** English (official) in all 16 states; Palauan (official) in 13 states; Sonsoralese, Angaur, Japanese, Tobi in one state each. **Religions:** Christian (Catholic, Seventh-Day Adventist, Jehovah's Witness, the Assembly of God, the Liebenzell Mission, and Latter-Day Saints), 33% Modekngei (indigenous faith).

● **GOVERNMENT   Type:** constitutional government in free association with the U.S.; the Compact of Free Association entered into force Oct. 1, 1994. **Independence:** Oct. 1, 1994 (from U.S.-administered U.N. Trusteeship). **Constitution:** Jan. 1, 1981. **National holiday:** Constitution Day, July 9. **Heads of Government:** Tommy E. Remengesau, Jr., president (since Jan. 2001). **Structure:** executive—president and vice president popularly elected; legislative—bicameral legislature; judicial—Supreme Court headed by chief justice.

● **ECONOMY   Monetary unit:** U.S. dollar. **Budget:** (FY98/99 est.) *income:* $57.7 mil.; *expend.:* $80.8 mil. **GDP:** $129 mil., $7,100 per capita (1998 est.). **Chief crops:** coconuts, copra, cassava, sweet potatoes. **Livestock:** N.A. **Natural resources:** forests, minerals (especially gold), marine products, deep-seabed minerals. **Major industries:** tourism, craft items (shell, wood, pearl), some commercial fishing and agriculture. **Labor force:** 8,300 (1999). **Exports:** $14.3 mil. (f.o.b., 1996); trochus, tuna, copra, handicrafts. **Imports:** $126 mil. (f.o.b., FY99/00). **Major trading partners:** U.S., Japan.

The first inhabitants of Palau (or Belau) probably arrived from Indonesia and the Philippines about 1500 B.C. The first European to visit the area was Ferdinand Magellan, in 1521. However, it was the British who dominated trade to Palau until 1885, when Pope Leo XIII acknowledged Spain's claims to the Carolines. Spain controlled Palau from 1885 to 1899, when it sold the territory to Germany. The Germans introduced coconut planting and phosphate mining, and introduced sanitary measures that arrested the deadly epidemics of dysentery and influenza, which over 120 years had reduced the population from 40,000 to 4,000.

Japan occupied Palau in 1914, and over the next 30 years increased the mining, agriculture, and fishing industries. In 1938, Palau became a closed military area, and it was the site of heavy fighting during World War II. On July 18, 1947, the United Nations Trusteeship Council placed the Trust Territory of the Pacific Islands, including Palau, under U.S. authority. This trusteeship ended on Oct. 1, 1994, when the Compact of Free Association with the United States (approved by the voters of Palau) went into effect, making Palau an independent country in association with the United States. The United States continues to provide for Palau's defense and to provide aid. In return, the United States has the right to dock military vessels (including nuclear-powered vessels) in the islands for 50 years, and will consult closely on economic and environmental matters.

▶ **PANAMA**
Republic of Panama
● **GEOGRAPHY   Location:** southern Central America. **Boundaries:** Caribbean Sea to N, Colombia to E, Pacific Ocean to S, Costa Rica to W. **Total area:**

30,193 sq. mi. (78,200 sq km). **Coastline:** 1,546 mi. (2,490 km). **Comparative area:** slightly smaller than South Carolina. **Land use:** 7% arable land; 2% permanent crops; 20% meadows and pastures; 44% forest and woodland; 27% other; includes negl. % irrigated. **Major cities:** (1992 est.) Panamá (Panama City—capital) 625,150; Colón 137,825; David 99,811.

● **PEOPLE Population:** 2,845,647 (2001 est.). **Nationality:** noun—Panamanian(s); adjective—Panamanian. **Ethnic groups:** 70% mestizo, 14% Amerindian and mixed (West Indian), 10% white, 6% Amerindian. **Languages:** Spanish (official), 14% speak English as native tongue; many Panamanians are bilingual. **Religions:** 85% Roman Catholic, 15% Protestant.

● **GOVERNMENT Type:** constitutional democracy. **Independence:** Nov. 3, 1903 (from Colombia); became independent from Spain Nov. 28, 1821. **Constitution:** Oct. 11, 1972, with major reforms ∙adopted in Apr. 1983 and in 1994. **National holiday:** Independence Day, Nov. 3. **Head of Government:** Mireya Elisa Moscoso Rodríguez, president (since Sept. 1999). **Structure:** executive—president, two vice presidents, cabinet; unicameral legislature; judiciary.

● **ECONOMY Monetary unit:** balboa. **Budget:** (2000) *income:* $2.8 bil.; *expend.:* $2.9 bil. **GDP:** $16.6 bil., $6,000 per capita (2000 est.). **Chief crops:** bananas, rice, sugarcane, coffee, corn; livestock, fishing. **Natural resources:** copper, mahogany forests, shrimp. **Major industries:** manufacturing and construction, petroleum refining, brewing, cement and other construction material. **Labor force:** 1.1 mil. (2000 est.); 18% agriculture, 18% industry, 64% services. **Exports:** $5.7 bil. (f.o.b., 2000 est.); bananas, shrimp, clothing, sugar, coffee. **Imports:** $6.9 bil. (f.o.b., 2000 est.); capital goods, crude oil, foodstuffs. **Major trading partners:** *exports:* 42% U.S., EU, Central America; *imports:* 39% U.S., EU, Central America and Caribbean.

The Spanish first arrived in what is now Panama in 1501. Vasco Nuñez de Balboa returned in 1510, and Pedro Arias Dávila founded the City of Panama in 1519. Panama became attached to the viceroyalty of New Granada after 1739 and left the Spanish empire with the rest of New Granada in 1821, becoming a part of Gran Colombia. The first canal company proposing the construction of a transisthmian passageway was formed in 1825-26. The completion of a U.S.-financed railway from Colón to Panama City by 1855 enhanced Panama's importance as a transoceanic passage.

Panamanian nationalists waged a "War of a Thousand Days" against the Bogotá government between 1899 and 1902. In 1903 Panama gained independence from Colombia with U.S. complicity. Within a month Panamanian officials accepted an agreement with the United States that created a canal zone under the control of the U.S. government "in perpetuity," and the Panama Canal was completed and opened in 1914.

Panama experienced protectorate status under U.S. control after independence insofar as the United States "guaranteed the independence" of Panama. The United States explicitly upheld its right of unilateral military intervention in Panama when in 1918 it sent troops there without the permission of the Panamanian government. The 1936 Hull-Alvaro Treaty eliminated protectorate status, and the U.S. dropped its claim to a right of intervention in the cities of Panama and Colón.

In 1968 a power struggle between Pres. Arnulfo Arias and the Panamanian National Guard led to the ouster of the president. A National Guard junta took control of the government, and Col. (later Gen.) Omar Torrijos Herrera became the ruler of the country the following year. In 1972 a new assembly under Torrijos's control offered him the title of Jefe Maximo (chief executive) in addition to drafting a new constitution for the country. Torrijos constructed a populist following through the creation of housing projects, a new labor code, an agrarian reform, and an increase in tax rates imposed on foreign banana-interests.

The Panamanian government and the U.S. concluded a new canal treaty in 1977, the key provisions of which included integration of the Canal Zone with the rest of Panamanian territory and full Panamanian control of the canal in 2000. In 1981 Omar Torrijos died in an air accident.

In 1988 the head of the military and de facto ruler of the country, Gen. Mañuel Noriega, was indicted in the U.S. on narcotics charges. But Noriega refused to submit to demands by the U.S. and by Panamanian president Eric Arturo Delvalle for his resignation. Delvalle was forced to go into hiding, and Manuel Solis Palma replaced him in the presidency. The United States responded by freezing Panamanian assets in the United States.

In May 1989 Gen. Noriega annulled election results that showed him losing to Guillermo Endara and assumed the role of dictator. After an unsuccessful coup attempt, the United States invaded Panama on December 20, captured Noriega, and brought him to Miami, where he was convicted on narcotics charges. Endara was restored to the presidency and in December 1990 U.S. forces helped put down a rebellion led by Noriega's former chief of the national police.

Endara's government was often accused of corruption but he left power peacefully in 1994. He helped to arrange honest elections that saw U.S.-educated businessman Ernesto Perez Balladares come to power with promises of improving the economy as Panama prepared to take over control of the canal. His free market reforms and a loosening of trade barriers (Panama joined WTO in 1998) have brought strong growth in GDP. An August 1998 referendum turned down (by 64 percent) Perez' seeking a second term. Voters in May 1999 chose Mireya Moscoso de Grubar, widow of three-time president Arnulfo Arias, over Martin Torrijos, son of the dictator who negotiated the 1977 Canal Treaty with the U.S., as Panama's new president.

▶ **PAPUA NEW GUINEA**
Independent State of Papua New Guinea

● **GEOGRAPHY Location:** eastern section of island of New Guinea and about 600 smaller islands in Bismarck Archipelago (New Britain, New Ireland, and Manus) and northern part of Solomon Islands. Port Moresby 9°30'S, 147°07'E. **Boundaries:** Bismarck Sea to N, Solomon Sea to E, Australia to S, and Indonesia to W. **Total area:** 178,259 sq. mi. (461,690 sq km). **Coastline:** 3,202 mi. (5,152 km). **Comparative area:** slightly larger than California. **Land use:** 0.1% arable land; 1% permanent crops; 0% meadows and pastures; 92.9% forest and woodland; 6% other. **Major cities:** (1990 est.) Port Moresby (administrative capital) 173,500.

● **PEOPLE Population:** 5,049,055 (2001 est.). **Nationality:** noun—Papua New Guinean(s); adjective—Papua New Guinean. **Ethnic groups:** predominantly Melanesian and Papuan; some Negrito, Micronesian, and Polynesian. **Languages:** 715 indigenous languages; English spoken by 1%-2%, pidgin English widespread, Motu spoken in Papua region. **Religions:** 22% Roman Catholic, 16% Lutheran, 28% other Christian, 34% indigenous beliefs.

• **GOVERNMENT   Type:** parliamentary democracy. **Independence:** Sept. 16, 1975 (from U.N. trusteeship under Australian administration). **Constitution:** Sept. 16, 1975. **National holiday:** Independence Day, Sept. 16. **Heads of Government:** Silas Atopare, governor-general (since Nov. 1997); Sir Mekere Morauta, prime minister (since July 1999). **Structure:** executive—British monarch (represented by governor general), chief of state, prime minister; unicameral legislature; judiciary.

• **ECONOMY   Monetary unit:** kina. **Budget:** (1998 est.) *income:* $1.6 bil.; *expend.:* $1.9 bil. **GDP:** $12.2 bil., $2,500 per capita (2000 est.). **Chief crops:** cocoa, coffee, coconuts, rubber, palm kernels; pigs, chickens. **Natural resources:** gold, copper, silver, natural gas, timber. **Major industries:** copra crushing, palmoil processing, plywood processing. **Labor force:** 1.941 mil., 85% agriculture. **Exports:** $2.1 bil. (f.o.b., 2000 est.); gold, copper ore, oil, logs, coffee, palm oil, cocoa, lobster. **Imports:** $1 bil. (f.o.b, 2000 est.); machinery and transport equipment, manufactured goods, food, fuels, chemicals. **Major trading partners:** *exports:* 30% Australia, 12% Japan, 7% Germany; *imports:* 53% Australia, 13% Singapore, 6% Japan.

The island of New Guinea, the world's second-largest, was settled many thousands of years ago by waves of Papuan and Melanesian migrants who developed large numbers of linguistically diverse and mutually hostile tribes of hunters and small cultivators. In the 19th century, the island was divided between the Dutch (to the west, in what is now the Indonesian province of Irian Jaya), Germany, and the British. The German sector was occupied by Australia in 1914 and administered under a League of Nations mandate after World War I.

Japanese attempts to occupy New Guinea in 1942 met with only partial success. In a series of counteroffensives, the Allies regained control over the entire island by mid-1944.

Beginning in 1949 the former German and British colonies were administered by Australia under a U.N. mandate. The territories were made self-governing in 1973 and achieved full independence as Papua New Guinea on Sept. 16, 1975. The nation maintains close ties with Australia.

Most of the population is still engaged in small-scale agriculture. Mining is a major source of foreign investment and export earnings. An ongoing rebellion on the island of Bougainville since 1989 has closed a large Australian-run copper mine, led to the deaths of many people (including, in 1996, Bougainville's chief minister, Theodore Miriung), and frightened away many potential foreign investors. An inexplicable decision to recognize Taiwan rather than mainland China, made July 5, 1999 by prime minister Bill Skate, brought domestic (as well as Chinese) opposition, Skate's resignation, and the designation of Sir Mekere Morauta as the new prime minister. He immediately reversed the Taiwan agreement. In February 2000 the government began a program of privatizing all state-owned enterprise within three years. In March, an agreement was reached with secessionists on the island of Bouganville: a referendum will be held on independence with an "interim provincial assembly" governing the island's internal affairs until then.

▶**PARAGUAY**
Republic of Paraguay

• **GEOGRAPHY   Location:** landlocked country in central South America. **Boundaries:** Bolivia to N, Brazil to E, Argentina to S and W. **Total area:** 157,046 sq. mi. (406,750 sq km). **Coastline:** none. **Comparative area:** slightly smaller than California. **Land use:** 6% arable land; 0% permanent crops; 55% meadows and pastures; 32% forest and woodland; 7% other; includes negl. % irrigated. **Major cities:** (1992 census) Asunción (capital) 637,737; Ciudad del Este (formerly Presidente Stroessner) 133,893; Pedro Juan Caballero (1982) 37,331; Encarnación (1982) 27,632; Villarrica (1982) 21,203.

• **PEOPLE   Population:** 5,734,139 (July 2001 est.). **Nationality:** noun—Paraguayan(s); adjective—Paraguayan. **Ethnic groups:** 95% mestizo, 5% white and Amerindian. **Languages:** Spanish (official), Guaraní. **Religions:** 90% Roman Catholic, Mennonite and other Protestant denominations.

• **GOVERNMENT   Type:** constitutional republic. **Independence:** May 14, 1811 (from Spain). **Constitution:** June 20, 1992. **National holiday:** Independence Days, May 14-15. **Head of Government:** Luis Ángel González Macchi, president (since Mar. 1999). **Structure:** president heads executive; bicameral legislature (Senate, Chamber of Deputies); judiciary.

• **ECONOMY   Monetary unit:** guarani. **Budget:** (1999 est.) *income:* $1.3 bil.; *expend.:* $2 bil. **GDP:** $26.2 bil., $4,750 per capita (2000 est.). **Chief crops:** sugarcane, soybeans, cotton, wheat; beef, pork; timber. **Natural resources:** iron ore, manganese, limestone, hydropower, timber. **Major industries:** sugar, cement, textiles, beverages. **Labor force:** 2 mil. (2000 est.); 45% agriculture; 12% unemployment (1998 est.). **Exports:** $3.5 bil. (f.o.b., 2000 est.); cotton, soybeans, timber, vegetable oils, feed, tung oil. **Imports:** $3.3 bil. (f.o.b., 2000 est.); consumer goods, tobacco, raw materials, fuels. **Major trading partners:** *exports:* Brazil, Argentina; *imports:* Brazil, U.S., Argentina.

When Europeans arrived in what is now Paraguay in the early 16th century, they encountered various groups of indigenous peoples. The Spanish entered into alliances with the Tupian semisedentary Guaraní against the nomadic Guaycuru Indians in the west of the region. Asunción, founded in 1537, was little more than a Spanish defense outpost against the Portuguese and a trading stopover between the silver mines of Potosí and Buenos Aires.

From early in the 17th century, the Jesuits established an extensive network of missions in the southern portion of the colony, and a rivalry grew between the Jesuits and the elites of Asunción over who would determine the colony's social and economic structure. The isolation of the settlers from the mainstream of Spanish colonial society combined with the lack of valuable resources led to the evolution of a relatively egalitarian social structure. The political elite of Asunción deposed Spanish authority in 1811, and Paraguayan independence was declared in 1813.

Authoritarian rule marked the period from independence until 1870. José Gaspar Rodríguez de Francia was declared ruler for life in 1816 and remained in power until his death in 1840. A period of political turmoil followed but was resolved in the election of Carlos Antonio López in 1844; in 1857 he was named president for life. López chose his son Francisco Solano López to succeed him in office in 1862. He intervened in a Brazilian attempt to control the fate of Uruguay, beginning the Paraguayan War, or the War of the Triple Alliance (Brazil, Argentina, Uruguay) from 1865 to 1870. The war was catastrophic for Paraguay, reducing the population from 450,000 to 220,000; and Paraguay lost 60,000 square miles of territory while being saddled with a war debt of 19 million gold pesos ($200,000,000), later dropped as unrealistic.

After the war the Colorado and Liberal parties developed, although the real political distinctions were dependent more on individuals and families than political ideology. Colorado-party general Bernardino Caballero, backed by Brazil, was the power behind the scenes of frequent changes in government personnel between 1874 and 1904. The Liberals, backed by Argentina, were in power from 1904 until 1936.

After 18 years of authoritarian military rule, Gen. Alfredo Stroessner, with the backing of Colorado party factions, began his rule in 1954. Stroessner held power until 1989, when Gen. Andrés Rodríguez overthrew him. Nevertheless, the Colorados maintained their hold on the presidency in hotly contested elections in 1993, when Juan Carlos Wasmosy gained 40 percent of the vote. However, a strong showing by the opposition Authentic Radical Liberal Party (PLRA) and National Encounter prevented a Colorado majority in Congress. A complex political struggle between Pres. Wasmosy and Lino Oviedo, one of the generals who overthrew Stroessner, led to Oviedo's imprisonment. His ally, Raul Cubas Grau, won the 1998 election by vowing to have Oviedo share power even from prison. Three days after taking office in August, however, Cubas released the popular general, causing an outburst of hostility among Congressional leaders.

In the extraordinary last week of March 1999, the vice president was assassinated, Congress accusing Cubas and Oviedo. Impeached the next day, Cubas remanded Oviedo to state custody but refused to appear at his own trial in the Senate. Oviedo fled to Argentina, Cubas to Brazil. Congress named the president of the Senate, Luis Gonzalez Macchi, as president of Paraguay. No coup ensuing, Gonzalez appointed a cabinet with four opposition members among the 10, the first coalition since 1946. A coup attempt by Oviedo allies was foiled in May 2000. Three weeks later, Oviedo was arrested in Brazil, with Paraguay seeking his extradition.

▶ **PERU**
Republic of Peru
● **GEOGRAPHY Location:** western coast of South America. **Boundaries:** Ecuador, Colombia to N, Brazil, Bolivia to E, Chile to S, Pacific Ocean to W. **Total area:** 496,224 sq. mi. (1,285,220 sq km). **Coastline:** 1,546 mi. (2,414 km). **Comparative area:** slightly smaller than Alaska. **Land use:** 3% arable land; negl. % permanent crops; 21% meadows and pastures; 66% forest and woodland; 10% other; includes 1% irrigated. **Major cities:** (1993 est.) Lima (capital) 5,706,127; Arequipa 619,156; Trujillo 509,312; Chiclayo 411,536; Callao 3699,768.
● **PEOPLE Population:** 27,483,864 (2001 est.). **Nationality:** noun—Peruvian(s); adjective—Peruvian. **Ethnic groups:** 45% Amerindian, 37% mestizo, 15% white, 3% black, Japanese, Chinese, and other. **Languages:** Spanish and Quechua (official), Aymara. **Religions:** predominantly Roman Catholic.
● **GOVERNMENT Type:** constitutional republic. **Independence:** July 28, 1821 (from Spain). **Constitution:** Dec. 31, 1993. **National holiday:** Independence Day, July 28. **Heads of Government:** Alejandro Toledo Manrique, president (since July 2001); Robert Daniño, prime minister (since July 2001). **Structure:** executive; unicameral legislature; judiciary.
● **ECONOMY Monetary unit:** nuevo sol. **Budget:** (1996 est.) *income:* $8.5 bil.; *expend.:* $9.3 bil. **GDP:** $123 bil., $4,550 per capita (2000 est.). **Chief crops:** coffee, cotton, sugarcane, rice, poultry, meat, wool; fish. **Natural resources:** copper, silver, gold, petroleum, timber. **Major industries:** mining of metals, petroleum, fishing. **Labor force:** 7.6 mil. (1996); agriculture, mining and quarrying, manufacturing, construction, transport, services; 7.7% unemployment (1997 est.). **Exports:** $7 bil. (f.o.b., 2000 est.); copper, zinc, gold, petroleum. **Imports:** $7.4 bil. (f.o.b., 2000 est.); machinery, transport equipment, foodstuffs, petroleum. **Major trading partners:** *exports:* 29% U.S., 25% EU; *imports:* 32% U.S., 21% EU.

Peru was the site of the civilization of the Inca empire before the arrival of Europeans. The Incas had extended their control over most of the Andean region by the late 15th century. The civilization was advanced in terms of its ability to provide for the welfare of its subjects and was in possession of sophisticated knowledge in a number of fields, including medicine. By the time of the arrival of the Spanish conqueror Francisco Pizarro in 1532, the empire was already in decline, and a combination of plague and civil war in the decade prior to the appearance of Europeans no doubt made the empire more vulnerable to Spanish conquest. Inca resistance to Spanish domination was not quelled until the execution of Tupac Amarú in 1571. European-borne diseases such as smallpox and measles devastated the Indian population of the region.

Because of the great wealth of precious metals discovered by the Spanish and the adaptability of a sedentary indigenous civilization to the imposition of Spanish imperial control, Peru quickly became a major focal point of Spanish colonialism; they founded Lima in 1535. The viceroyalty of Peru, established in 1544, originally served as the political and administrative nerve center of Spanish colonization of South America. For nearly two centuries, Lima was the seat of power and wealth for the whole region. Peru was "liberated" by Simón Bolívar and José de San Martín in 1821 when Bolívar's army defeated the royalist forces at the battles of Junín and Ayacucho.

In the 40 years after independence, the presidency changed hands 35 times, and the country generated at least 15 different constitutions. Only four of the presidents of the period were constitutionally chosen, and the vast majority were military figures. In 1829 Peru tried and failed to annex Ecuador; in the 1830's an attempt at political federation between Peru and Bolivia collapsed with the Chilean invasion of 1839.

A political movement in favor of civilian rule, the Civilistas, began to organize by the 1860's. Chile defeated Peru in the War of the Pacific (1879-83), and Chileans occupied Lima and its port city of Callao for two years. The Peruvian government was deeply in debt after the war, resulting in the loss of ownership of much of Peru's infrastructure and natural resources to foreigners.

Peru experienced a period of civilian leadership between 1895 and 1930. Pres. Augusto B. Leguía (1908-12, 1919-30) extended his rule in an extraconstitutional manner until 1930, when Col. Luis Sánchez Cerro seized power; he ruled until his assassination in 1933. Gen. Oscar Benavides succeeded Cerro and managed to restore confidence in the economy. In 1939 civilian banker Manuel Prado was elected to the presidency, and the military allowed him to complete his term in office, which expired in 1945. During Prado's administration, Peru went to war with Ecuador and was victorious, seizing a great deal of territory.

Víctor Raúl Haya de la Torre founded Peru's most prominent political party, the American Popular Revolutionary Alliance (APRA), in 1924. As initiated, the party put forward an "anti-imperialist" platform aiming at nationalization of land and reconstruction of society in favor of oppressed people. Haya de la Torre was apparently fraudulently deprived of a presidential electoral victory in 1931. The following year Apristas (APRA supporters) seized Trujillo and killed some military personnel. By way of revenge, the army massacred 6,000 Apristas. The result was a continuing enmity between the Peruvian armed forces and the APRA party lasting until the 1980's. Although APRA clearly had majority support from the Peruvian electorate, the party was not allowed to take power directly until 1985.

The Peruvian military, led by Gen. Juan Velasco Alvarado, seized power in 1968 and embarked upon a course of reform that included the nationalization of Standard Oil's International Petroleum Company holdings. The Peruvian military took steps to restructure economic and political power in the country by joining the Andean Pact and undermining the power of the traditional agricultural elite in the country by sponsoring an agrarian reform that mobilized peasant sectors of the population and changed the relations between landlord and peasant.

The presidency of Peru returned to civilian leadership under Fernando Belaúnde Terry (1980-85). In 1985, the military allowed the APRA presidential candidate, Alan García Pérez, to take office. García promised to spend no more than 10 percent of the country's export earnings on payment of Peru's huge outstanding foreign debt and he was popular during his first years in office. But his public support was undermined by a growing insurgency sponsored by the Sendero Luminoso ("Shining Path") Maoist guerrillas and by runaway inflation.

On June 10, 1990, political novice Alberto Fujimori, the son of Japanese immigrants, defeated the well-known writer Mario Vargas Llosa for the presidency. Throughout 1991 and 1992, Shining Path's influence spread, demoralizing and almost paralyzing the government, and at a cost of 25,000 lives. But in April 1992, Fujimoro implemented a "zero tolerance" policy toward terrorism, dissolving the legislature and proclaiming martial law. The capture in September of Abimael Guzmán Reynoso, Path's founder-leader, broke the back of the insurgency. The movement lived on, but diminished in numbers, and its last commander was captured in July 1999.

Meanwhile, economically, Fujimori pursued free-market reforms, taming runaway inflation and privatizing state-run dinosaurs, so that by 1994 the Peruvian economy was growing at a rate of 12 percent, fastest in the world. In April of that year, Fujimoro was elected to a second term with 64 percent of the vote.

The dramatic liberation in April 1997 of 600 prisoners held for ransom in the Japanese ambassador's compound by another radical terrorist group maintained the president's repute. In Nov. 1997, Peru completed negotiations with Ecuador (the treaty being signed in Oct. of 1998) ending a 50-year old border conflict. But all these achievements were accompanied by a rather ham-handed authoritarian streak which cost Fujimori much esteem. In elections for Congress, held in April 2000, his Peru 2000 party carried a plurality of seats but he himself just failed of a majority in the presidential race. A week before the May 28 run-off, his remaining opponent withdrew, claiming the election was a fraud; the final tally brought Fujimori only 51 percent. His July 28 inauguration was marred by serious rioting, with six dead and many public buildings in Lima burnt. While in Japan, Fujimori resigned, but Congress refused to accept, so it could remove him for abandoning office and dereliction of duty. In June 2001, in a close run-off against former president Alan García, Alejandro Toledo was elected president, the first Indian elected president in Peru's history. (See Part I, "Major News Stories of the Year.")

▶ **PHILIPPINES**
Republic of the Philippines

● **GEOGRAPHY Location:** archipelago of some 7,100 islands about 500 mi. (800 km) off southeastern Asia; about 1,100 mi. (2,800 km) from N to S and 650 mi. (1,684 km) from W to E; Luzon in N and Mindanao in S account for 66% of land area. Manila 14°36'N, 120°59'E. **Boundaries:** Luzon Strait to N, Philippine Sea to E, Celebes Sea to S, Sulu Sea to SW, and South China Sea to W. **Total area:** 115,830 sq. mi. (300,000 sq km). **Coastline:** 22,554 mi. (36,289 km). **Comparative area:** slightly larger than Arizona. **Land use:** 19% arable land; 12% permanent crops; 4% meadows and pastures; 46% forest and woodland; 19% other; includes 5% irrigated. **Major cities:** (1990 census) Manila (capital) 1,598,918; Quezon City 1,666,766; Davao City 849,947; Caloocan City 761,011; Cebu City 610,417.

● **PEOPLE Population:** 82,841,518 (2001 est.). **Nationality:** noun—Filipino(s); adjective—Philippine. **Ethnic groups:** 91.5% Christian Malay, 4% Muslim Malay, 1.5% Chinese, 3% other. **Languages:** Pilipino (based on Tagalog) and English (both official). **Religions:** 83% Roman Catholic, 9% Protestant, 5% Muslim, 3% Buddhist and other.

● **GOVERNMENT Type:** republic. **Independence:** July 4, 1946 (from U.S.). **Constitution:** Feb. 2, 1987, effective Feb. 11, 1987. **National holiday:** Independence Day, June 12. **Head of Government:** Gloria Macapagal-Arroyo, president (since Jan. 2001). **Structure:** executive; bicameral legislature; judiciary.

● **ECONOMY Monetary unit:** Philippine peso. **Budget:** (1998) *income:* $14.5 bil.; *expend.:* $12.6 bil. **GDP:** $310 bil., $3,800 per capita (2000 est.). **Chief crops:** rice, corn, coconut, sugarcane, bananas; pork, eggs, beef; fish. **Natural resources:** timber, crude oil, nickel, cobalt, silver. **Major industries:** textiles, pharmaceuticals, chemicals. **Labor force:** 48.1 mil. (2000 est.); 39.8% agriculture, 19.4% government services, 17.7% services; 10% unemployment (2000). **Exports:** $38 bil. (f.o.b., 2000 est.); electronics and telecommunications, machinery and transport, garments. **Imports:** $35 bil. (f.o.b., 2000 est.); raw materials and intermediate goods, capital goods, consumer goods, fuels. **Major trading partners:** *exports:* 34% U.S., 14% Japan, 20% EU; *imports:* 20% Japan, 22% U.S.

The Philippines were anciently settled by various Malayan peoples in several waves of migration from Southeast Asia. Tribal societies coexisted with petty principalities that had trade links to China, the East Indies, and countries in the Indian Ocean. The Philippines were visited by Magellan (who was killed there) in 1521, and Spanish conquest of the islands began in 1564. The Spanish colonial capital at Manila was founded in 1571 and became a key transit point for trade between Mexico and the Far East. Under Spanish rule a majority of Filipinos became Christian except in the southwestern islands, which remained Muslim. The Spanish period was marked by a torpid colonial administration and a rise in the power and wealth of the Catholic church.

In the late 19th century, a nationalist movement led by José Rizal gained a wide following. In 1896 an armed uprising began, led by Emilio Aguinaldo. The 1898 victory of Adm. George Dewey at the Battle of Manila Bay during the Spanish-American War led Spain to cede the Philippines to the U.S. in return for a payment of $20 million. Expecting immediate independence with U.S. support, Aguinaldo declared the islands a republic. When this was not recognized by the U.S., Aguinaldo led a new war for independence, which was bloodily suppressed by American troops in a six-year campaign, 1899-1905.

American policy in the Philippines combined military control with a desire to encourage home rule leading to independence. In 1935 the Commonwealth of the Philippines was established, with Manuel Quezon as its first president, beginning what was conceived of as a 10-year period of controlled autonomy leading to full independence on July 4, 1946. In November 1941, Quezon was reelected to the presidency. On Dec.8, 1941, Japan attacked Manila and destroyed the American bases there. American and Filipino troops, after weeks of fierce fighting, evacuated the islands in March 1942. The battle to recapture the Philippines began with the Battle of Leyte Gulf in October 1944 and was completed by July 1945.

In April 1946, Manuel Roxas was elected president of the Commonwealth. Independence came as scheduled on July 4 of that year, with the United States retaining military bases by treaty and establishing a special economic relationship with the Philippines. The leftist Hukbalahap Rebellion, originally a partisan campaign against the Japanese, caused severe difficulties for the new nation until it was finally defeated in military campaigns led by Ramon Magsaysay who was elected to the presidency in November 1953.

The early years of independence were marked by some economic development, but also great economic inequality. Most land was held by huge estates, and the economy depended primarily on plantation crops (sugar, copra), mining, and timber. Villagers fleeing the rural subsistence economy poured into the cities, leading to huge slums and a climate of urban poverty and violence. Many Filipinos emigrated to America.

In 1966 Ferdinand Marcos was elected president on a reform platform. Overwhelmed in the early 1970's by demonstrations, a new leftist guerrilla movement, and a separatist rebellion by Islamic Moros in Mindinao, Marcos declared martial law on Sept. 21, 1972. On Jan. 17, 1973, Marcos promulgated a new constitution giving unprecedented power to the presidency. His wife, Imelda, began to wield considerable influence, and the climate of unrest, poverty, and corruption worsened throughout the 1970's. Martial law was lifted, however, on Jan. 17, 1981, and Marcos was reelected to a new six-year term as president.

The airport assassination of opposition leader Benigno Aquino on his return to the Philippines on Aug. 21, 1983, led to a new phase in opposition to Marcos's rule. Marcos retained a majority in elections to the National Assembly in 1984, amid widespread reports of electoral fraud. In a bitterly contested presidential election in February 1986, Marcos was officially declared the winner over Aquino's widow, Corazon. Mrs. Aquino also declared herself the winner, and her supporters took to the streets in massive anti-Marcos demonstrations. Deserted by key supporters in the military, church, and middle class, Marcos fled the country on Feb. 25, 1986. Mrs. Aquino took office pledging land reform, a new constitution, and a commission to recover the wealth Marcos had plundered.

Under Pres. Aquino the Philippines remained unsettled. Her former ally, Vice Pres. Salvadore Laurel, formed an opposition party. Military and political measures aimed at putting down the Communist insurrection yielded mixed results. The economy of the Philippines continued to be dependent on U.S. and international assistance, and sentiment against the continued presence of U.S. military bases (Clark Air Base, Subic Bay Naval Base, and four smaller installations) was strong. Ironically, an eruption of Mount Pinatubo in June 1991 caused massive devastations in central Luzon and destroyed Clark Air Base. In September, the national legislature voted not to renew the leases on American military bases; the United States moved to close Subic Bay Naval Base.

Aquino declined to run for re-election in 1992. Fidel Ramos won the presidency in a field of strong contenders, including Imelda Marcos. Lifted by a coalition that gave him a controlling majority in both houses of Congress after the 1994 legislative elections, Ramos made "national reconciliation" his highest domestic priority. In 1994 he proclaimed a cease-fire and amnesty for various insurgencies, though the Moro rebellion on Mindinao flared up again.

The Philippines' robust economic growth was slowed but not crippled by the Asian economic crisis of 1997-98. After some hesitation, Pres. Ramos decided not to seek re-election in 1998; in a crowded field of candidates, Joseph Estrada, a popular actor, won the presidential election of May 11, 1998, but the ruling LAKAS party elected the vice-president and took control of the lower house. In 1998 the long-running dispute with China over the Spratly Islands heated up, the Philippine Navy sequestering Chinese fishing boats. A series of hostage crises with Muslim rebels on Mindanao punctuated the year 2000 but became overshadowed by serious bribery charges against Pres. Estrada. As the House of Representatives moved toward impeachment, gigantic demonstrations for and against Estrada brought reminders of the fall of Pres. Marcos. When the Senate in Jan. 2001 suspended the president's trial, the protests expanded to a general strike; and when the heads of the armed forces joined the protests, Estrada's days were through. Vice-president Gloria Macapagal Arroyo was sworn in as Estrada resigned. By May the anti-Estrada coalition controlled the Congress and Estrada was under arrest.

▶ POLAND
Republic of Poland
● **GEOGRAPHY Location:** eastern Europe. **Boundaries:** Baltic Sea to N, Russia and Lithuania to NE, Belarus and Ukraine to E, Czech Republic and Slovakia to S, Germany to W. **Total area:** 120,726 sq. mi. (312,680 sq km). **Coastline:** 305 mi. (491 km). **Comparative area:** slightly smaller than

New Mexico. **Land use:** 47% arable land; 1% permanent crops; 13% meadows and pastures; 29% forest and woodland; 10% other; includes negl. % irrigated. **Major cities:** (1994 est.) Warszawa (Warsaw, capital) 1,640,700; Lodz 828,500; Krakow (Cracow) 746,000; Wroclaw 642,900; Poznan 582,300.

● **PEOPLE   Population:** 38,633,912 (2001 est.). **Nationality:** noun—Pole(s); adjective—Polish. **Ethnic groups:** 97.6% Polish, 1.3% German, 0.6% Ukrainian, 0.5% Byelorussian. **Languages:** Polish. **Religions:** 95% Roman Catholic (about 75% practicing), 5% Eastern Orthodox, Protestant, and other.

● **GOVERNMENT   Type:** republic. **Independence:** Nov. 11, 1918 (independent republic proclaimed). **Constitution:** Oct. 16, 1997; adopted by the National Assembly on Apr. 2, 1997; passed by national referendum May 23, 1997. **National holiday:** Constitution Day, May 3. **Heads of Government:** Aleksander Kwasniewski, president (since Dec. 1995); Jerzy Buzek, prime minister (since Oct. 1997). **Structure:** executive—prime minister is head of government; bicameral legislature—2 seats in lower house are constitutionally assigned to ethnic German parties; judiciary.

● **ECONOMY   Monetary unit:** zloty. **Budget:** (1999 est.) *income:* $49.6 bil.; *expend.:* $52.3 bil. **GDP:** $327.5 bil., $8,500 per capita (2000 est.). **Chief crops:** potatoes, milk, cheese, fruits, vegetables, wheat; poultry and eggs; pork, beef. **Natural resources:** coal, sulfur, copper, natural gas, silver. **Major industries:** machine building, iron and steel, extractive industries. **Labor force:** 17.2 mil. (1999 est.); 22.1% industry and construction, 27.5% agriculture, 50.4% services. **Exports:** $28.4 bil. (f.o.b., 2000); manufactured goods, chemicals; machinery and equipment; food and live animals. **Imports:** $42.7 bil. (f.o.b., 2000); manufactured goods, chemicals; machinery and equipment; mineral fuels. **Major trading partners:** *exports:* 36% Germany, 6.5% Italy; *imports:* 25.2% Germany, 9.4% Italy, 6.8% France.

The Slavic people known as Polonians accepted Christianity in the second half of the 10th century, during the reign of Duke Mieszko, whose close relationship with the papacy prevented the Holy Roman Empire from absorbing Poland. A strong and united Polish kingdom existed under the Piast dynasty until 1370. With that dynasty's extinction, the Anjou king of Hungary succeeded to the throne, followed by his daughter Jadwiga, who in 1386 married the grand duke of Lithuania. Thus was formed the great Commonwealth of Poland-Lithuania.

With the extinction of the Jagellonian line in 1572, the monarchy became elective. With a large nobility, equaling about 10 percent of the population, the monarchy grew weak, and Poland increasingly was subject to foreign intervention. The rise of the expansionist powers of Sweden, Prussia, Russia, and Austria came in part at the expense of the Poles. Jan Sobieski (1624-96), who ruled Poland as John III, saved Vienna from the Turks and briefly revived the Polish monarchy, but Polish royal power ended with his death. In a series of partitions in 1772, 1793, and 1795, Poland was dismembered and finally obliterated as a state.

Napoleon revived a Polish national entity with the Grand Duchy of Warsaw; with Napoleon's fall, the Congress of Vienna re-created a Kingdom of Poland in 1815, under the rule of the czar of Russia. After 1830 Poland was subjected to systematic Russification.

The fall of Russia in World War I led to Poland's revival. The Lithuanian Socialist Jósef Pilsudski led Poland in war against the new Bolshevik government of Russia until, in the 1921 Treaty of Riga, Poland emerged with its boundaries restored to approximately those after the partition of 1793. It was ethnically about 70 percent Polish, a triumph for Polish nationalism but the end of Pilsudski's dream of a federation of northeastern Europe. Poland also had the largest Jewish population of any country in Europe.

With a strong legislature and a weak president, the new state seemed to Pilsudski too weak for its own defense. He became a virtual dictator in 1926 and ruled until his death in 1935. After his death a weak parliamentary government was controlled by military officers; the tentative revival of republicanism was halted by Hitler's and Stalin's aggression in 1939, yet another partition of Poland.

Like other countries of east-central Europe, Poland was primarily an agricultural country, with grains, sugar beets, and potatoes its principal crops. The postwar republic attempted land reform, with some success; about 750,000 new private farm holdings were created by 1938. Mining—of coal and copper—was the principal traditional industrial activity in the 20th century, supplemented by extraction of natural gas. In the mid-1930's shipbuilding and railroad construction led the way toward a modern economy.

World War II commenced in September 1939, with attacks on Poland by Germany and the Soviet Union. The war brought severe destruction to Poland and the extermination of virtually its entire Jewish population. A government-in-exile was established in London, but the Soviet Union broke relations with it in 1943 when it requested a Red Cross investigation into the murder of 14,000 Polish officers whose bodies were discovered in Katyn Forest. (The Soviet government acknowledged responsibility for the massacre in 1990.) The Soviets established a puppet government in Lublin in 1944. In August the Red Army paused in its western advance on the outskirts of Warsaw, permitting the Nazis to obliterate the Polish Home Army. On Jan. 1, 1945, the U.S.S.R. recognized the Lublin regime as Poland's government.

By the time of the Allied Powers Conference in Yalta in February 1945, the Red Army was only 40 miles from Berlin and had total control of Poland. The Allies agreed to Stalin's proposal concerning the eastern boundary of Poland (allowing Russia to incorporate the eastern half of the country) and agreed that the government should be constituted from an enlargement of the Lublin regime. At Potsdam in August 1945, it was further agreed that Poland should absorb the eastern portion of Germany. Poland's borders were shifted approximately 200 miles westward from the prewar configuration, becoming once again those of the 10th century. The German population was expelled remorselessly.

The free elections promised in the Yalta Agreement were postponed until 1947, by which time a Communist victory could be assured. In 1948 the Socialists were forcibly merged into the Communist party; in 1949 Premier Boleslaw Bierut requested that Soviet general Konstantin Rokossovski be appointed minister of defense and commander in chief of the Polish army. All cultural periodicals and all writers' and artists' associations were taken over by the Communist party.

But there was little collectivization of Polish agriculture or forced industrialization on the Stalinist model. Intellectuals, bolstered by the

Catholic church (which deeply resented a 1953 law requiring government approval for appointment of bishops), questioned the regime with some boldness. In 1956 both Bierut and Party Secretary Minc died, and Wladislaw Gomulka was elected party chairman in Oct. 1956. As Soviet warships sailed through the Baltic toward Poland, Nikita Khrushchev flew to Poland with a delegation of Soviet generals, where Gomulka assured them that Poland would follow the Soviet lead in foreign policy. Distracted by the crisis in Hungary, the Russians left Gomulka in power and even canceled Poland's debt and allowed the dismantling of agricultural collectives.

For a short time Gomulka permitted cultural and educational freedom, but by 1958 he had reverted to Stalinist form, imposing controls and pursuing a somewhat anti-Semitic Polish nationalism. Gomulka ruled until 1971, when he was replaced as party secretary by Edward Gierek. But moral leadership within Poland had clearly passed to Stefan Cardinal Wyszynski, leader of the increasingly vocal Catholic church; Gierek was forced to improve relations with the church in order to maintain his own credibility as a national leader.

Gierek presided over a decade of increasing unrest and growing discontent. Polish exports of ham and furniture to the West earned some hard currency but could not curb the rising national debt. The most significant event in Poland in the 1970's was the election of Karol Wojtyla, bishop of Krakow, as Pope John Paul II in October 1978. His visit to Poland in 1979 set the stage for the extraordinary events of the 1980's.

Gierek's austerity program of February 1980 sent meat prices soaring. Strikes for wage adjustments, especially at the Lenin Shipyards in Gdansk, thrust Lech Walesa, a shipyard worker, into a position of national leadership. Walesa was elected chairman of the national coordinating committee of independent labor unions, Solidarity. Solidarity's demands went far beyond lower prices and higher wages; they included independent labor unions with the right to strike, freedom for political prisoners, and an end to censorship. In Sept. 1980 Gierek resigned as party secretary and was replaced by Stanislaw Kania.

By December, 40 independent trade unions had been formed, and a "rural Solidarity" movement was growing. In Feb. 1981 Soviet Army general Wojciech Jaruzelski was named prime minister. When in December Solidarity announced plans to hold a referendum on the Jaruzelski regime, martial law was declared; Solidarity leaders were arrested, all its activities banned, and the right to strike was abolished.

But the government was never able to suppress Solidarity as a popular force, and it was legalized in 1989. In 1989 elections Solidarity won 99 of 100 Senate seats and 299 of 460 seats in the lower house, although 65 percent had been reserved for the Communist party. Jaruzelski was elected president by Parliament and Solidarity leader Tadeusz Mazowiecki became prime minister.

The Communist party voted to disband on Jan. 28, 1990, and the Mazowiecki government announced a program of radical economic reform, winning promises of foreign aid and increased investment from Western governments. In June 1990, a commission was appointed to draft a new constitution. Jaruzelski resigned in September, and in presidential elections, Walesa, at the head of Solidarity's labor/Catholic faction, defeated Mazowiecki, representing Solidarity's political/technocrat faction.

The new prime minister, Krzysztof Bielecki, continued the reformist policies of curbing inflation and government spending, fostering foreign investment, and privatizing state enterprises. But the shock therapy, with its higher prices and unemployment (even while creating more than a million new jobs), led to disillusionment.

In the first fully free parliamentary elections, held in October 1991, only 42 percent of the voters participated, electing a fragmented 29-party Parliament. Reluctantly, Pres. Walesa named Jan Olszewski as prime minister of a coalition government. The Olszewski coalition collapsed in June 1992, replaced by an equally fragile seven-party coalition led by Hanna Suchocka, Poland's first female prime minister.

Despite high inflation (40 percent) and high official unemployment (13 percent), under Poland's "iron lady" the private sector expanded and even the remaining state-owned enterprises responded to market demand, pushing exports from $8 billion in 1988 to $14 billion in 1992. And in May 1993, Parliament passed a bill privatizing 600 companies.

Still, at the end of May 1993, the Suchocka government fell, by one vote, to a Solidarity-sponsored no-confidence measure, in protest against her austerity budget. In new elections held in Oct. 1993, the Communist party (now called the Democratic Left Alliance) formed a coalition with the Peasants party to forge a surprising return to power. The Communist prime minister, Josef Oleksy, was joined by his party-mate Aleksander Kwasniewski, who defeated Walesa in presidential elections held in November 1995. Kwasniewski ran especially strong with younger voters, who regarded communism as an antiquated system that posed no threat of returning to Poland. A month after the presidential election, though, Oleksy was accused of spying for Russia, and although he protested his innocence, he resigned as premier.

Poland's economy was among the fastest growing in Europe (a 7 percent rise in GDP in recent years and billions in direct foreign investment) although inflation ran high through 1997. In 1997, a new constitution and invitations to join NATO and eventually the E.U. gave the Poles a reason to believe the future looked very positive. The first elections under the new constitution produced a center-right coalition government. In 1999 Poland joined NATO, finally achieving security against the Russian expansion it always feared, but the economy slowed considerably.

▶ PORTUGAL
Portuguese Republic

• **GEOGRAPHY** **Location:** Iberian Peninsula in southwest Europe; also two archipelagos in Atlantic Ocean: Azores (37°29'N, 25°40'W) and Madeira Islands (32°40'N, 16°55'W). **Boundaries:** Spain to N and E, Atlantic Ocean to S and W. **Total area:** 35,552 sq. mi. (92,080 sq km). **Coastline:** 1,114 mi. (1,793 km). **Comparative area:** slightly smaller than Indiana. **Land use:** 26% arable land; 9% permanent crops; 9% meadows and pastures; 36% forest and woodland; 20% other; includes 7% irrigated. **Major cities:** (1991 census) Lisboa (Lisbon, capital) 681,063; Porto (Oporto) 309,485; Amadora 176,137; Setubal 103,241; Coimbra 147,722.

• **PEOPLE** **Population:** 10,066,253 (2001 est.). **Nationality:** noun—Portuguese (sing., pl.); adjective—Portuguese. **Ethnic groups:** homogeneous Mediterranean stock on mainland, in Azores, and on Madeira Islands; citizens of African descent who immigrated during decolonization number less than 100,000. **Languages:** Portuguese. **Religions:** 94% Roman Catholic, Protestant, other.

● **GOVERNMENT Type:** parliamentary democracy. **Independence:** Oct. 5, 1910. **Constitution:** Apr. 25, 1976, revised Oct. 1982 and June 1989, Nov. 1992, Sept. 1997. **National holiday:** Day of Portugal, June 10. **Heads of Government:** Jorge Sampaio, president (since Feb. 1996); Antonio Guterres, prime minister (since Oct. 1995). **Structure:** executive—president and prime minister; unicameral legislature-(popularly elected 230-seat Assembly of the Republic); judiciary.

● **ECONOMY Monetary unit:** escudo. **Budget:** (2000) *income:* $48.6 bil.; *expend.:* $50.7 bil. **GDP:** $159 bil., $15,800 per capita (2000 est.). **Chief crops:** grains, potatoes, olives, grapes for wine; livestock. **Natural resources:** fish, forests (cork), tungsten, iron ore, uranium ore. **Major industries:** textiles, footwear, wood pulp, paper, cork. **Labor force:** 5 mil. (1999); 60% services, 30% industry, 10% agriculture, forestry, fisheries, 4.6% unemployment (1999 est.). **Exports:** $26.1 bil. (f.o.b., 2000 est.); clothing and footwear, machinery, chemicals, cork and paper products, hides. **Imports:** $41 bil. (f.o.b., 2000 est.); machinery and transport equipment, chemicals, petroleum, textiles, agricultural products. **Major trading partners:** *exports:* 83% EU, 5% U.S.; *imports:* 78% EU, U.S., Japan.

Portugal traces its origins back to the warlike Lusitanian tribes of Roman times. The nation-state originated as a county of the kingdom of Leon-Castile, reconquered from the Moors in the 11th century. Portugal won recognition as an independent kingdom in 1143, and conquered Lisbon four years later. In 1267 the Algarve was conquered, and by then Portugal had expanded to its modern boundaries. Except for the period 1580-1640, when it was ruled by the Spanish Habsburgs, the Portuguese dynasty maintained its independence into the 20th century.

Portuguese fishermen had probably frequented the Grand Banks from before the time of Columbus, and the nation's tradition of seafaring gave rise to a world empire in the 15th and 16th centuries. Prince Henry the Navigator (1394-1460) colonized the Azores and the Madeiras and sponsored voyages of exploration along the west coast of Africa. Under his successors, Portugal controlled the west African coast, the shores of the Indian Ocean, and large stretches of southern Asia, as well as, in the Western Hemisphere, Brazil. Yet the rise of the empires of Spain and the Netherlands quickly reduced the Portuguese to second-rank status, leaving only Macao, Goa, and Timor in Asia; Portuguese Guinea (Guinea Bissau), Mozambique, and Angola in Africa; and the great territory of Brazil in Latin America.

In the 19th century, a series of dynastic civil wars weakened the monarchy, allowing Britain to gain control of the country's foreign policy (in addition to the wine trade of Oporto, long in British hands). Brazil declared its independence in 1822.

In 1910 Portugal became the first kingdom in the 20th century to be transformed into a republic. But in the next 15 years, chaos ensued: eight presidents, 44 governments, and a nearcollapse of the economy. Finally, the military established a dictatorship, lasting until recent times. In 1928 the military installed a civilian dictator, a professor of economics, Antonio Salazar. A firm believer in law and order, he managed to control the turbulence of political life and made the escudo one of Eu-

rope's most stable currencies, yet he could do nothing to alter Portugal's fundamental poverty. Although he ruled through civilian governments, his essential support always came from the army.

Portugal has long been Western Europe's poorest country. As late as 1960, almost half of the country's work force was engaged in agriculture, forestry, and fishing. In the north, agriculture was traditionally carried on in smallholdings; the south was characterized by large estates, remnants of feudal fiefs. Exports were traditionally cork, olive oil, port wine, and fish. Industrialization came late to Portugal, and today manufacturing is mostly carried on by small firms engaged in textile and clothing production and other labor-intensive production.

World War II affected Portugal very little. Salazar deftly managed to remain Britain's ally while keeping his country out of the war as a neutral state. In the postwar period, Portugal accepted Marshall Plan aid and became a member of NATO in 1949. Portugal was a founding member of the European Free Trade Association in 1959 and negotiated a special relationship with the EC in 1972 (when its trading partner and ally, Great Britain, joined that body).

Portugal joined the United Nations in 1955, just in time to become embroiled in the worldwide movement for decolonization. Protesting that Portugal had, not colonies, but "overseas provinces," Salazar refused to bow to the pressure of world opinion. In 1961 India forcibly annexed Goa and other Portuguese enclaves on the subcontinent. In the same year, nationalist revolts broke out in Angola, Guinea and Mozambique.

The colonial wars of the 1960's placed a terrible strain on Portugal's economy and resulted in severe military losses. And in the end, the colonies gained their independence. Salazar, gravely ill, retired in 1968 and was replaced by Marcelo Caetano. In 1974 Caetano was deposed in a bloodless coup staged by the secret Armed Forces movement. The coup's leader, Antonio de Spinola, after reaching agreements on the independence of most of Portugal's old colonies, resigned as head of government in September 1974. Costa Gomes replaced Spinola, as a Revolutionary Council was instituted. The council survived two coup attempts, one by right-wing soldiers, the other by Communists, and it promulgated a Socialist constitution in 1976. Through a series of unstable governments (16 between 1974 and 1987), the old agrarian estates were expropriated, and banking, insurance, and large industrial concerns were nationalized. The shock of this economic transformation, along with the OPEC price rises, created an economic recession in the 1970's. In addition Portugal had to absorb a million Portuguese refugees from the former colonies.

Attempts by center-right coalitions in the 1980's to undo the nationalizations of the 1970's were thwarted by vetoes of the Constitutional Tribunal (successor to the Revolutionary Council), even when the free-market Social Democratic party held an absolute majority in the assembly. Portugal entered the EC on Jan. 1, 1986, pledging to reduce tariffs and end agricultural subsidies over a 10-year transitional period.

In 1987 the Social Democrats, running on a platform of spending cuts, privatization of state-owned firms, reversal of agricultural collectivism, and reliance on free enterprise, became the first party since 1974 to win an absolute majority in the legislative assembly. Per capita income tripled over the years 1985-92, so that Portugal was no longer the poorest country in the EU. The 1992 sale of the huge state-owned Petrogal oil company was a harbinger of a return to free enterprise. In October 1995, Antonio Guterres of the Socialist party displaced the Social Democrats. And in January 1996, Jorge Sampaio won the presidential election, giving Portugal both a Socialist president and prime minister for the first time since democracy was restored.

Portugal's economic stability was ratified in 1998 by the E.U. when the latter approved Portugal's membership in the Monetary Union. GDP growth averaged 3.5 percent through the late 1990's. Portugals' international standing was affirmed by her central role in negotiating the East Timor referendum with Indonesia. In Dec. 1999 the colony of Macao was returned to Chinese rule after 442 years. In 2001 Sampaio was easily reelected.

▶ **QATAR**
State of Qatar
● **GEOGRAPHY Location:** occupies a peninsula projecting northward from Arabian mainland into western part of Persian (Arabian) Gulf. **Boundaries:** Persian Gulf to N, E, and W; Saudi Arabia and United Arab Emirates to S. **Total area:** 4,247 sq. mi. (11,000 sq km). **Coastline:** 350 mi. (563 km). **Comparative area:** slightly smaller than Connecticut. **Land use:** 1% arable land; 0% permanent crops; 5% meadows and pastures; 0% forest and woodland; 94% other. **Major cities:** (1993) Doha (capital) 339,471; Al Rayyan 143,046; Al Wakrah 30,976.
● **PEOPLE Population:** 769,152 (2001 est.). **Nationality:** noun—Qatari(s); adjective—Qatari. **Ethnic groups:** 40% Arab, 18% Pakistani, 18% Indian, 10% Iranian, 14% other. **Languages:** Arabic (official), English commonly used as second language. **Religions:** 95% Muslim.
● **GOVERNMENT Type:** traditional monarchy. **Independence:** Sept. 3, 1971 (from U.K.). **Constitution:** provisional constitution enacted Apr. 19, 1972. **National holiday:** Independence Day, Sept. 3. **Head of Government:** Hamad bin Khalifa al-Thani (since June 1995). **Structure:** executive—amir is head of government and chief of state; unicameral legislature—consultative, no elections since 1970, members terms extended every four years; judiciary.
● **ECONOMY Monetary unit:** Qatari riyal. **Budget:** (1999 est.) *income:* $3.9 bil.; *expend.:* $4 bil. **GDP:** $15.1 bil., $20,300 per capita (2000 est.). **Chief crops:** fruits, vegetables; poultry, dairy products, beef; fish. **Natural resources:** crude oil, natural gas, fish. **Major industries:** crude oil production and refining, fertilizers, petrochemicals. **Labor force:** 233,000 (1993 est.). **Exports:** $9.8 bil. (f.o.b., 2000 est.); 80% petroleum products, steel, fertilizers. **Imports:** $3.8 bil. (f.o.b., 2000 est.); machinery, consumer goods, food, chemicals. **Major trading partners:** *exports:* 52% Japan, 9% Singapore, 8% South Korea; *imports:* 10% U.K., 8% France, 6% Germany.

The Qatar peninsula was ruled as part of the sheikhdom of Bahrain from the late 18th century until the mid-19th century. An informal British protectorate was established in 1868; the Ottoman Empire also asserted authority over the sheikhs of Qatar from 1872 to 1916. The Ottomans ceded authority to the British in that year, and a formal British protectorate was organized. When British forces withdrew from the Persian Gulf region in 1971, Qatar entered into negotiations with the emirates of the Trucial Coast to join the federation of the United Arab Emirates. When those negotiations broke down, Qatar declared its independence on Sept. 3, 1971. For over 30 years it has been politically stable under one ruler, Sheik Hamad bin Khalifa al-Thani, although he was deposed by his son in a bloodless coup in June 1995. He has claimed he wants to move the country toward democracy and has called for a free press, limited elections, and allowing women to vote.

Qatar's economy is dominated by oil, natural gas (Qatar has the world's third largest supply) banking, and shipping services in the port of Doha.

▶ **ROMANIA**
● **GEOGRAPHY Location:** southeastern Europe. **Boundaries:** Ukraine to N, Moldova to NE, Black Sea to E, Bulgaria to S, Yugoslavia (Serbia) to SW, Hungary to NW. **Total area:** 91,699 sq. mi. (237,500 sq km). **Coastline:** 140 mi. (225 km). **Comparative area:** slightly smaller than Oregon. **Land use:** 41% arable land; 3% permanent crops; 21% meadows and pastures; 29% forest and woodland; 6% other; includes 11% irrigated. **Major cities:** (1993 est.) Bucharesti (Bucharest, capital) 2,066,723; Constanta 348,985; Iasi 337,643; Timisoara 325,359; Cluj-Napoca 321,850.
● **PEOPLE Population:** 22,364,022 (July 20001 est.). **Nationality:** noun—Romanian(s); adjective—Romanian. **Ethnic groups:** 89.5% Romanian, 7.1% Hungarian, 1.8% Roma, German, Ukrainian, Serb, Croat, Russian, Turk, and Gypsy. **Languages:** Romanian, Hungarian, German. **Religions:** 70% Romanian Orthodox, 6% Roman Catholic, 6% Protestant.
● **GOVERNMENT Type:** republic. **Independence:** 1881 (from Turkey). **Constitution:** Dec. 8, 1991; republic proclaimed Dec. 30, 1947. **National holiday:** National Day, Dec. 1. **Heads of Government:** Ion Iliescu, president (since Dec. 2000); Adrian Nastase, prime minister (since Dec. 2000). **Structure:** executive; bicameral legislature; judiciary.
● **ECONOMY Monetary unit:** leu. **Budget:** (1999 est.): *income:* $11.7 bil.; *expend.:* $12.4 bil. **GDP:** $132.5 bil., $5,900 per capita (2000 est.). **Chief crops:** corn, wheat; milk, eggs, meat. **Natural resources:** crude oil (reserves declining), timber, natural gas, coal, iron ore. **Major industries:** mining, timber, construction materials. **Labor force:** 9.9 mil. (1999 est.). **Exports:** $11.2 bil. (f.o.b., 2000 est.); 26% textiles and footwear, 15% metals and metal products, 11% machinery and equipment. **Imports:** $11.9 bil. (f.o.b., 2000 est.); 23% machinery and equipment, 12% fuels and minerals, 9% chemicals. **Major trading partners:** (1999) *exports:* 23% Italy, 18% Germany, 6% France; *imports:* 19% Germany, 20% Italy, 7% France.

The Roman province of Dacia was sufficiently Latinized to retain the name of Rome long after the legions withdrew in A.D. 27. Overrun by invading Bulgars in the eighth century, the Romanians retained their Latinate language and orthodox Christianity; Romania remained beyond the borders of the Byzantine Empire but was in close contact with it. The area was conquered by the Mongols in the 13th century and formed the independent principalities of Moldavia and Walachia after the Mongols withdrew.

By the 15th century, Moldavia and Walachia had become vassal states of the Ottoman Empire, though with some local autonomy that permitted retention of orthodox Christianity and the creation of a rich local culture. Attempts at national unity against Ottoman rule in 1601 and 1711 failed; in 1861 the provinces united as an autonomous state under the name Romania, within the Ottoman Empire, under Greek administration. Independence came in 1878.

Romania was for centuries the poorest country in Europe. Thoroughly agricultural, it was a land of unfree peasants working the great estates of landowners who were generally wealthy, usually absentee, and often Greek. The peasants not only paid taxes but also were required to perform feudal labor services for the estate owners.

After enlarging itself at Bulgaria's expense in the Second Balkan War (1913), Romania switched sides three times in World War I, joining the Allies just before the war's end. Its reward was a huge expansion, doubling its territory with lands taken from Austria, Hungary, Russia, and Bulgaria.

The interwar period was one of political turbulence, marked by violence and assassinations. Twice King Carol II went into exile, leaving his throne to his son Prince Michael; the second time was in 1940, when Russia (in accordance with the Hitler-Stalin pact) reclaimed the territories of Bessarabia and northern Bukovina it had lost to Romania in 1920; Hitler required Romania to return about half of Transylvania to Hungary.

During World War II, the pro-Hitler dictator Marshall Ion Antonescu took power, supported by a semifascist "Iron Guard," but when the latter attempted a coup, the military crushed the uprising. Romanian troops participated in Hitler's invasion of Russia in 1941, and the country paid the price in 1944 when Russian troops "liberated" the country, with devastating results.

The country was quickly transformed into a Soviet satellite through rigged elections in which the communist National Democratic Front replaced the Peasant Alliance in power; a People's Republic was proclaimed on Dec. 30, 1947, and King Michael was forced to abdicate. A peace treaty in 1947 confirmed the loss of Bessarabia to Russia but returned Transylvania to Romania.

Under Russian occupation Romania was a virtual Soviet colony. The occupying armies did not leave until after reparation payments were completed in 1958, leaving the dictator Gheorghe Gheorghiu-Dej in power. Despite Council of Mutual Economic Assistance (COMECON) plans for Romania to become a major food supplier to the Soviet bloc, Gheorghiu-Dej pursued industrialization on the Stalinist model, in the process ruining Romanian agriculture while creating large, labor-intensive, and highly inefficient factories. The result was an economic depression; politically, however, it produced a de facto independence for Romania within the Soviet bloc. Russian troops were forbidden on Romanian soil, and Romania declined to participate in COMECON policies.

With the death of Gheorghiu-Dej in 1965, power passed to Nicolae Ceaușescu. He promulgated a new constitution and instituted a series of purges; he became party leader in 1965, prime minister in 1967, and president of the republic in 1974. Ceaușescu continued his predecessor's economic policy, deepening the country's misery; he also pursued a policy of "independence" from the U.S.S.R., refusing to go along with Soviet policies of de-Stalinization and liberalization.

Romania's "national communism" was expressed in militant nationalism, coupled with severe repression of ethnic minorities, especially Germans and Magyars in Transylvania. Hundreds of Hungarian villages were bulldozed into oblivion in the name of agricultural collectivization.

Ceaușescu's ambitions included the creation of a family dynasty in the Romanian leadership. In 1979 his wife Elena was named first deputy premier and elevated to the Council of Ministers. Her brothers were given important government positions; Ceaușescu's son, despite his reputation as a playboy, was groomed to replace his father.

Romania's transition from Communist rule was sudden and violent. On Dec. 16-18, 1989, demonstrations in Timisoara calling for Ceaușescu's ouster were put down with brute force by the Securitate (secret police), but they spread and citizens and regular army troops fought pitched battles with Securitate forces in Bucharest. Ceaușescu and his wife fled Bucharest but were captured, tried, and executed. The newly organized Council of National Salvation established a provisional government, consisting primarily of anti-Ceaușescu Communists in league with the Romanian army, with former Communist party official Ion Iliescu as president.

The Communist party was outlawed on Jan. 12, 1990. Despite the Council's domination by former Communists, no effective opposition movement emerged, and in hastily called and rigged elections on May 20, Iliescu was elected president in a landslide and the Council won 233 of 296 seats in the lower house.

In June 1990, many anti-Communist demonstrators were beaten and several killed by troops and armed miners brought to Bucharest by the government. Calls for Iliescu's resignation and a purge of Communists from government continued into the fall. Tensions were aggravated when the government's abrupt move to a market economy resulted in food shortages and sharp price increases.

Continued rioting in 1991 led to the replacement of ex-Communist prime minister Petre Roman by the non-Communist Theodor Stolojan at the head of a "caretaker" coalition. More or less free elections in 1992 gave the National Salvation Front 28 percent of the seats in Parliament while the opposition Democratic Convention gained 20 percent; Iliescu defeated the Democratic Convention candidate in the presidential election with 61 percent of the vote. Both Iliescu and the prime minister he named (Nicolae Vacaroiu) were pledged to slowing the transition to a market economy but by 1994 with inflation at over 250 percent (leading to a massive workers' strike in Feb.) the government agreed to I.M.F.'s demand for increased privatization and fiscal austerity in order to receive a $700 mil. loan. Iliescu's presidency ended in Nov. 1996 with a coalition government headed by Emil Constantinescu immediately forging public links to the Romanian Orthodox Church ending decades of official atheism and taking action against corrupt banking officials, businessmen, and politicians. The economy remained in dire straits but in early 1997 loans were secured from the I.M.F. and the World Bank.

Elections in Nov. 1997 were won by Emil Constantinescu of the Democratic Convention party who became president and Victor Ciorbea the prime minister. Inflation and unemployment were falling but GDP growth was lagging and, with a patchwork tax system, international default looked likely. I.M.F. demands for restructuring as a condition of further loans produced government plans which included the closing of mines whose operation had lost $4 billion since 1990.

But that in turn produced, in early 1999, widespread protest marches and violence by mine workers whose role in 1990 was not forgotten.

Parliamentary elections in Nov. 2000 gave a preponderance to the parties of the left, but the presidential election drew greater interest: Ion Iliescu, claiming now to be a reformer and a prowesterner, carried two-thirds of the vote in the December run-off.

▶ RUSSIA
Russian Federation

• **GEOGRAPHY Location:** northeastern Europe and northern Asia. **Boundaries:** Baltic Sea, Barents Sea, Kara Sea, East Siberian Sea to N, Bering Sea, Sea of Okhotsk, Sea of Japan to E, China, North Korea, Mongolia, Kazakhstan, Caspian Sea, Azerbaijan, Georgia, Black Sea to S, Ukraine, Belarus to W, Latvia, Estonia, Finland, Norway to NW. **Total area:** 6,592,745 sq. mi. (17,075,200 sq. km). **Coastline:** 23,402 mi. (37,653 km). **Comparative area:** slightly less than 1.8 times the size of the United States. **Land use:** 8% arable land, 4% meadows and pastures, 46% forest and woodland, 42% other. **Major cities:** (1995) Moscow (capital) 8,717,000; St. Petersburg 4,838,000; Nizhnyi Novgorod 1,383,000; Novosibirsk 1,369,000.

• **PEOPLE Population:** 145,470,197 (2001 est.). **Nationality:** noun—Russian(s); adjective—Russian. **Ethnic groups:** 81.5% Russian, 3.8% Tatar, 3% Ukrainian, 1.2% Chuvash. **Languages:** Russian, other. **Religions:** Russian Orthodox, Muslim, other.

• **GOVERNMENT Type:** federation. **Independence:** Aug. 24, 1991 (from Soviet Union). **Constitution:** Dec. 12, 1993. **National holiday:** Independence Day, June 12, celebrating first presidential election. **Heads of Government:** Vladimir V. Putin, president (since May 2000); Mikhail M. Kasyanov, prime minister (since May 2000). **Structure:** executive—president, premier, various advisory bodies; bicameral legislature; judiciary.

• **ECONOMY Monetary unit:** ruble. **Budget:** (2000 est.) *income:* $40 bil..; *expend.:* $33.7 bil. **GDP:** $1.12 tril., $7,700 per capita (2000 est.). **Chief crops:** grain, sugar beets, vegetables, sunflower seed; meat, milk. **Natural resources:** oil, natural gas, coal, timber. **Major industries:** extraction and processing raw materials, machine building from rolling mills to high-performance aircraft. **Labor force:** 66 mil. (1997). **Exports:** $105.1 bil. (2000 est.); petroleum and petroleum products, natural gas, wood and wood products, coal, metals, chemicals. **Imports:** $44.2 bil. (2000 est.); machinery and equipment, consumer goods, medicines, meat, grain, sugar, semifinished metal products. **Major trading partners:** Ukraine, Germany, U.S.

Russia is the largest and most powerful of the states to emerge from the former Soviet Union. As the seat of the Soviet empire that existed for over 70 years, the Russians wielded tremendous power both within the U.S.S.R. and in the international sphere. Almost from their emergence as a separate people, the Russians have extended the boundaries of their country to include a wide variety of non-Russian people. Both the Russian Czars and the Bolsheviks who came to power in 1917 have a long history of expansionist policies, which explains why, even today, an important part of the Russian national identity is that of leader of a large empire.

In the ninth century A.D., Viking traders organized a state, which they called Rus, in the river valleys between the Baltic and the Black Seas, centered on the cities of Kiev and Novgorod. In time the Vikings were absorbed into the native Slavic population; in 998 a Ruthenian prince of Kiev accepted Christianity from Constantinople. In the 13th century, Mongols under Genghis Khan and his descendants conquered most of Russia, and the Mongol Golden Horde maintained its power through the 14th century, exercising loose control over Novgorod and Moscow.

From the mid-19th century, Moscow grew to become the center of a new state that gathered in other cities and territories as Mongol power waned. Ivan III (Ivan the Great, 1440-1505) consolidated the power of Moscow; his marriage to a Byzantine princess led him to regard his empire as a third Rome, heir to the religious tradition of Constantinople. His grandson, Ivan IV (Ivan the Terrible, 1530-84), adopted the title czar (from the Latin caesar) when he came to power. He broke the power of the aristocratic boyar class and greatly extended the power of Moscow through military conquest.

Over the next two centuries, Russia carried out a steady program of expansion eastward into Siberia and across the Bering Strait to Alaska, until the empire covered one-sixth of the land surface of the globe. Peter the Great (1672-1725) made Russia a Baltic and Black Sea naval power, brought Russia into the European state system, and instituted a sweeping, if superficial, Westernization of his realm. His new capital at St. Petersburg became one of the most splendid cities in Europe. At the end of the 18th century, Catherine the Great (1729-96) participated with Prussia and Austria in the partitions of Poland, and Russia thereby became a major power in central Europe.

Catherine's grandson Alexander I (1777-1825), member of the grand coalition that defeated Napoleon, was not only czar of Russia but also king of Poland and grand duke of Finland. His troops occupied Paris in 1815. The Russian aristocracy became ardent Francophiles in the 19th century, ignoring growing problems at home. After losing the Crimean War in 1856, Russia began to develop Siberia and the southern territories near the border of Persia. Alaska was sold to the United States in 1867. In a major reform of the agricultural system, serfdom was abolished under Alexander II in 1861, though the newly independent peasantry, organized into agricultural cooperatives, only slowly derived benefits from its freedom. The late 19th century also marked the beginning of modern industrialization in Russia and of extensive development in Siberia, aided by state investment in railroads and mining.

Under the last czar, Nicholas II (1868-1918), Russia was defeated by Japan in a war over Manchuria in 1905. The defeat sparked a naval mutiny and an abortive revolution, which led to the establishment of a constitutional monarchy and other limited political reforms. Further military losses in World War I set the stage for the monarchy's downfall in the revolution of 1917.

The initial revolution of March 1917 brought a relatively moderate socialist (Menshevik) group to power. Its principal leader, Aleksandr Kerensky, organized a republican government and tried to maintain the Russian war effort but failed to gain control of the many contending revolutionary factions of the time. The Germans allowed the radical Bolshevik leader, Vladimir I. Lenin, to return to Russia, where he and his followers organized workers' soviets (councils) hostile to the Menshevik republic. Bolshevik forces occupied

Petrograd (St. Petersburg was renamed in 1914) on Nov. 7, 1917 (October in the old Byzantine calendar, hence the name October Revolution), arrested the cabinet, and put in place a Council of People's Commissars, under Lenin's chairmanship. There followed four years of civil war between Bolshevik, Menshevik, and czarist forces, in the course of which Nicholas II and his family were executed by the Bolsheviks in 1918.

Decreeing land to the peasants, worker management in industry, and repudiation of czarist debts, the Bolsheviks won the survival of their regime by withdrawing from World War I. The 1918 Treaty of Brest-Litovsk, which gained peace with Germany, granted freedom to Finland, the Baltic republics, Poland, Ukraine, and Bessarabia. At the conclusion of the civil war in 1921, the Soviet state was established, with Ukraine reabsorbed into the Soviet Union. The Bolshevik victory also resulted in the creation in 1921 of the Mongolian People's Republic as a close Soviet ally.

The early 1920's are now remembered as a "golden age" of Soviet history. Lenin's New Economic Policy (NEP) allowed some role for market forces and private ownership and led to a brief burst of economic growth. Art, literature, and science flourished in an atmosphere of revolutionary enthusiasm and little censorship.

Lenin died on Jan. 21, 1924, and after a power struggle, was succeeded by Josef Stalin. Stalin supported Communist revolutions in China and elsewhere through the Communist International (Comintern) but generally withdrew from foreign engagements in order to concentrate on domestic affairs. Under Lenin, and even more under Stalin, the Communist party established a police state, condemning millions of people to internal exile in the 1920's and consolidating all power in the hands of the state. In 1929 agriculture was forcibly collectivized, leading to the starvation or execution of millions of peasants, while forced industrialization was carried out under a series of five-year plans.

Under the guise of socialist revolution, the Russians continued in much the same manner as their czarist heirs. The Bolsheviks forcibly incorporated most of the territories of the old empire, and once in charge, insisted that Russian be the state language and that Russian Communist party officials run the republics.

On the national level, Stalin's chief rival, Leon Trotsky, was expelled from the U.S.S.R. in 1929 (and assassinated by Stalinist agents in Mexico in 1940). Stalin's obsession with eliminating all possible rivals for power led to a series of purges which saw the summary execution of an estimated seven million of presumed "enemies of the state" and the imprisonment in concentration camps of an estimated 12 million more.

Russia's reemergence as a world power was signaled by the signing in August 1939 of the Hitler-Stalin Pact, a nonaggression treaty through which Stalin aimed to recover territories lost to Russia in 1918. Poland was again partitioned, Bessarabia annexed (as the Moldavian republic), Finland conquered and partitioned, and the Baltic republics absorbed.

When in June 1941 Hitler turned against his ally and invaded Russia, unprepared Russian armies retreated. But Stalin emerged as a national leader in the "Great Patriotic War," restructuring the army and enlisting the support of the Orthodox church and relying on calls to Russian patriotism in rallying the population. In the early winter of 1942, the war changed course as Russia broke the

German siege of Stalingrad, and Russian armies began their westward push that would carry them to the Elbe River by April 1945.

By the end of World War II, Stalin had reestablished the old czarist boundaries of Russia, and he had a ring of occupied states along his western boundary and a divided Germany beyond. Over the years 1945-48, he engineered a thorough communization of those occupied states, turning them into Russian satellites.

Stalin died in March 1953. He was succeeded by a collegial form of party and government leadership, from which Nikita Khrushchev, the party chairman, emerged as the paramount figure. In a secret speech to the party leadership in 1956, Khrushchev denounced Stalin for crimes against the party. He announced a set of new policies designed to bring about rapid modernization and consolidated his power when he became premier in 1958. The Khrushchev years brought a small but steady rise in living standards and a "thaw" in police state methods, the KGB (state security police) being brought under party control.

In foreign policy there was a thaw as well. In 1953 the Soviets agreed to an armistice in Korea and tolerated the formation of a more liberal government in Hungary. In 1955 Russia returned the Porkkala peninsula to Finland and agreed to the Austrian State Treaty, which created an independent and neutral Austria. But the limits of disengagement became clear in 1956 with the ruthless Soviet suppression of the Hungarian uprising. A summit conference between Khrushchev and Eisenhower in 1960 led to a propaganda victory for Russia when an American U-2 spy plane was shot down over Russian territory on May 1. And in 1962 Khrushchev tried to install Soviet missiles in Cuba, a reckless adventure from which he had to back down during the Cuban missile crisis.

While on vacation in 1964, Khrushchev was removed from office and replaced as party secretary by Leonid Brezhnev and as premier by Aleksei Kosygin. His failure to deliver on promises for domestic economic growth and his recklessness in foreign affairs seem to have been responsible for his downfall. The new leaders embarked on an ambitious program of military (especially naval) expansion and pressed ahead vigorously with a space program that had begun with the triumphant launching of Sputnik I in 1957.

Under Brezhnev and Kosygin the U.S.S.R. became more aggressive in foreign policy. The severe suppression of Czechoslovakia's "Prague Spring" in 1968 occasioned development of the Brezhnev Doctrine, whereby Russia claimed the right to intervene militarily in any socialist state. Soviet involvement in the Third World grew, with Russia supporting Vietnam against China; Syria and the PLO against Israel; leftist regimes in Angola, Ethiopia, and elsewhere in Africa; and the Sandinistas in Nicaragua. Cuba emerged as the principal Soviet proxy in supplying troops for leftist causes in the Third World. In 1979 Soviet troops moved into Afghanistan, allegedly at the invitation of its Marxist government, and remained bogged down there for a decade. Under American pressure, Brezhnev permitted the emigration of about 130,000 Jews and 40,000 ethnic Germans.

Domestically, the regime grew more oppressive; censorship was tightened and dissidents sentenced to terms in penal mental institutions. Elitism and nepotism created a self-perpetuating and interlocking network of power at the top, while the nation as a whole stagnated.

Brezhnev's death in 1982 brought about a rapid

series of leadership transfers. Yuri Andropov, head of the KGB, succeeded Brezhnev as party secretary but died after only 15 months. He was succeeded by Konstantin Chernenko, who died 13 months later. In March 1985 Mikhail Gorbachev became party secretary, ushering in a new era.

Gorbachev first instituted a cautious shake-up of state and party bureaucrats, promoting younger men who were technocrats rather than party professionals. Under the slogan *glasnost* (openness, candor), censorship was relaxed, and policy was openly debated in the press. Jamming of broadcasts from the West was ended. By the end of 1990, freedom of the press and of religion had been approved, and private citizens were given limited rights to own small businesses.

Gorbachev's other slogan, *perestroika* (restructuring), addressed his aim to boost morale and increase economic efficiency by devolving responsibility for economic decisions away from the party and government and toward industrial and agricultural managers. Perestroika raised expectations but not output; the system remained sluggish, inefficient, and burdened with the vested interests of state planners. The nuclear power plant disaster of Chernobyl in April 1986 and a gas pipeline fire that killed hundreds of passengers in passing railroad trains in June 1989 exemplified the industrial mismanagement against which Gorbachev's policies were aimed. During 1989-91 there were strikes by coal miners, and shortages of food and consumer goods worsened.

In foreign policy Gorbachev pursued arms reduction agreements with the United States and withdrew Soviet forces from Afghanistan. His international stature exceeded that of any previous Soviet leader; but his problems at home made him increasingly unpopular. Foremost among his problems at home concerned the U.S.S.R.'s various ethnic nationalities. The southern Muslim regions of the U.S.S.R. were the scene of turmoil since the anti-Russian riots in Kazakhstan in 1986; in 1988 riots broke out in the Christian republic of Armenia over the status of ethnic Armenians in the neighboring Muslim republic of Azerbaijan. Fighting in Armenia and Azerbaijan worsened in 1989-90, leading to a breakdown of government control in some areas. Ethnic warfare between Uzbeks and Turks in Uzbekistan led to numerous deaths, and sporadic violence in other central Asian republics broke out in 1990.

The Baltic republics of Estonia, Latvia, and Lithuania raised their old national flags, enacted laws giving their native languages priority over Russian, and proclaimed the superiority of local republican law over the laws of the Soviet Union. Lithuania proclaimed its independence from the U.S.S.R. in Dec. 1989, provoking a confrontation with international ramifications; Lithuania finally agreed to postpone its independence in 1990 pending negotiations with the Soviet government. Within the U.S.S.R. itself, the Russian republic elected maverick Boris Yeltsin as president and pressed for greater autonomy; Yeltsin resigned from the Communist party in July 1990.

The total collapse of communist governments in Eastern Europe in 1989-90 added to Gorbachev's problems and led to the dissolution of the Warsaw Pact; the Berlin Wall fell in Nov. 1989; and the Council of Mutual Economic Assistance (COMECON) was dissolved in July 1990. Gorbachev responded by assuming the presidency of the U.S.S.R. and increasing the powers of that office, and he held off challenges to his leadership in 1990-91. Yet defections from the party by both

right- and left-wing groups threw the party's future role in the U.S.S.R. itself in doubt. Demonstrations against Gorbachev and the Communist party took place in Moscow and elsewhere as the economy worsened and food supplies dwindled.

In June of 1991, Boris Yeltsin was elected president of the Russian republic in the first direct elections for the post. His stature soared when he rallied opposition to an unsuccessful coup to topple Gorbachev in August. In December 1991 Gorbachev and Yeltsin agreed that the U.S.S.R. would cease to exist as of Jan. 1, 1992.

In early December 1991, Ukraine, Belarus, and the Russian Federation signed the Minsk Agreement that created the Commonwealth of Independent States, and on Dec. 21, Ukraine and 11 other former union republics officially committed themselves to the union by signing the Alma-Ata Declaration. In Feb. 1992 Russian president Yeltsin agreed to begin dismantling the vast arsenal of Russian nuclear weapons, 80 percent of which were on Russia's territory, the rest being scattered across Ukraine, Belarus, and Kazkhstan. While Belarus agreed to allow Russia to control the weapons, Kazakhstan and Ukraine used their weapons as bargaining chips.

Throughout 1992, Pres. Yeltsin took center stage, first signing the historic second Strategic Arms Reduction Treaty (START II) with the U.S. in January, then in April rallying the people to support a referendum on government elections and to approve his policies, and finally in June calling together a Constitutional Assembly to write a new constitution. As the Russian economy continued to founder, however, Yeltsin became the target of attacks by former Communists. In Dec. 1992, Yeltsin barely survived a series of votes in Parliament that would have severely limited his control.

This struggle came to a violent head on Sept. 21, 1993, when Yeltsin and Parliament effectively threw each other out of office: Yeltsin declared Parliament dissolved and called for new elections to be held in December; Parliament voted to impeach Yeltsin and appointed Vice Pres. Aleksandr V. Rutskoi to replace him. Anti-Yeltsin forces called for a national strike and barricaded themselves inside the Parliament building for two weeks. Anti-Yeltsin rallies escalated into serious violence when 10,000 protesters overwhelmed riot police and broke through government barricades, causing Yeltsin to summon military police. The leaders of the revolt surrendered after tanks fired directly on the Parliament building, and were immediately sent to prison. At least 100 people were killed in the exchange.

In the aftermath, Yeltsin moved quickly to parlay his victory into even greater political power, by banning several opposition parties, firing powerful opponents, and calling for new parliamentary elections. He announced he would stay in office until his term expired in 1996, and in Nov. 1993 he unveiled the country's first post-Soviet constitution, which centralized power in the executive presidency and limited the powers of the constituent regions. One of these regions, Chechnya, had long threatened secession from Russia and in 1994 its leaders took that action. In Dec. Yeltsin ordered the army to restore government control, but it took months of fighting before Grozny, the rebel capital, fell to Russian troops.

In 1996, unrest by Russia's nationalist faction eroded much of Yeltsin's support, forcing him into a runoff election against the Communist candidate Gennadi Zyuganov in May 1996. But in the runoff, Yeltsin decisively beat back the Communist challenger. In August, Yeltsin formed a cabinet of pro-business technocrats; in the Fall he chucked National Security advisor (and future rival) Lebed, and he agreed to the final withdrawl of Russia's Chechnya brigades.

Yeltsin met Pres. Clinton in Helsinki in March 1997 subsequently agreeing to NATO's eastward expansion in return for NATO's agreement neither to deploy nor to store nuclear weapons there. Economic difficulties reached serious proportions in 1998 and the I.M.F. and the U.S. pledged huge amounts to keep the economy from crumbling. In the spring, Yeltsin replaced many of his ministers with reform-minded bureaucrats. But in the summer, the economy turned down again, and Yeltsin was forced to devalue the ruble. As the economy worsened day-by-day and international lenders refused aid, Russia stood on the brink of collapse.

Even with Mr. Yeltsin's physical illnesses, personal volatility, and political capriciousness (the August 1999 appointment of Vladimir Putin as prime minister made him the fifth in 18 months, the third in a row drawn from the secret police), Russia was able in 1999 to play a significant role in the diplomacy concerning and the occupation of Yugoslavia's Kosovo province. And the I.M.F. and various western investment "Clubs" managed to keep rescheduling Russian debt, so Russia was able to stumble on despite essentially defaulting on loan repayments. One day after Putin's appointment, insurgents in the Federal Republic of Dagestan, operating out of Chechnya, proclaimed an independent Islamic state; hence, Putin's determination to have it out with Chechnya. Vigorously pursued and (unlike the 1994-96 debacle) very popular, the war went well for Russia and Putin's popularity soared; Grozny fell, again (Feb. 6). Putin triumphed in the March presidential election occasioned by Yeltsin's December resignation. But in 2000, the war was still dragging on and would until 2001. Putin consolidated his power and took a leading role in opposing U.S. plans to build a missile shield but cooperating with U.S. determination to end terrorism. (See Part I, "Major News Stories of the Year.")

▶ **RWANDA**
Rwandese Republic
• **GEOGRAPHY Location:** landlocked country in central Africa. **Boundaries:** Uganda to N, Tanzania to E, Burundi to S, Zaire to W. **Total area:** 10,170 sq. mi. (26,340 sq km). **Coastline:** none. **Comparative area:** slightly smaller than Maryland. **Land use:** 35% arable land; 13% permanent crops; 18% meadows and pastures; 22% forest and woodland; 12% other; includes negl. % irrigated. **Major cities:** (1993) Kigali (capital) 234,500; Butare (1978) 21,691; Ruhengeri (1978) 16,025; Gisenyi (1978) 12,436.
• **PEOPLE Population:** 7,312,756 (2001 est.). **Nationality:** noun—Rwandan(s); adjective—Rwandan. **Ethnic groups:** 84% Hutu, 15% Tutsi, 1% Twa (Pygmoid). **Languages:** Kinyarwanda (official) universal Bantu vernacular, French and English (both official), Kiswahili (Swahili) used in commercial centers. **Religions:** 65% Catholic, 9% Protestant, 1% Muslim; 25% indigenous beliefs and others.
• **GOVERNMENT Type:** republic; presidential system; multiparty system. **Independence:** July 1, 1962 (from U.N. trusteeship under Belgian administration). **Constitution:** May 5, 1995, the Transitional National Assembly adopted a new constitution. **National holiday:** Independence Day, July 1. **Heads of Government:** Paul Kagame, president (since April 2000); Bernard Makuza, prime minister (since March 2000). **Structure:** executive—president; unicameral legislature; judiciary.
• **ECONOMY Monetary unit:** Rwandan franc. **Budget:** (2000 est.) *income:* $198 mil.; *expend.:* $411 mil. **GDP:** $6.4 bil., $900 per capita (2000 est.). **Chief crops:** coffee, tea, pyrethrum, bananas, beans, sorghum, potatoes; livestock. **Natural resources:** gold, cassiterite (tin ore), wolframite (tungsten ore), natural gas, hydropower. **Major industries:** agricultural products, small-scale beverage, soap, furniture industries, cement. **Labor force:** 3.6 mil. (1985); 90% agriculture, government and services, commerce. **Exports:** $68.4 mil. (f.o.b., 2000 est.); coffee, tea, hides, tin ore. **Imports:** $245.9 mil. (f.o.b., 2000 est.); foodstuffs, machines and equipment, petroleum products, cement and construction material. **Major trading partners:** *exports:* Brazil, Germany; *imports:* Italy, Kenya, Tanzania.

Tutsi cattle-breeders came to Rwanda, in the late 15th century and slowly conquered the native Hutu farmers. The Tutsi established a monarchy, forcing the Hutus into serfdom. Germans were the first Europeans to arrive in Rwanda and declared it a protectorate in 1899. After World War I Belgium was given a League of Nations mandate over the territory, which became a U.N. trusteeship after World War II.

Tutsi traditionalists resisted Belgian attempts in the 1950's to institute democratic political institutions. In 1959 the Hutus revolted against the monarchy in a bloody conflict which led to a mass exodus of Tutsis. Two years later the Hutus won a U.N.-supervised referendum and were granted internal autonomy by Belgium on Jan. 1, 1962. Full independence came on July 1, 1962. Political unrest led to the overthrow of the government in 1973. Maj. Gen. Juvénal Habyarimana dissolved the National Assembly and banned all political activity.

Tutsi refugees in Uganda fought with the army from Oct. 1990, and by 1993 as many as one million people were displaced. A cease-fire and amnesty paved the way for political reform, and a new constitution allowing for multi-party democracy, separation of powers, and presidential term limits went into effect in June 1992. Proposals to merge the armies of the government (Hutu) and the Tutsi Rwandan Patriotic Front were signed in 1993.

But in April 1994, the Hutu presidents of Rwanda and Burundi were both killed when rocket fire (perhaps launched by Hutu dissidents) shot down their plane as it returned from a peace conference in Tanzania. In renewed civil war, the Hutu dominated army of Rwanda and the Hutu militias were driven by the Tutsi-led Patriotic Front into Zaire, Tanzania, Uganda and Burundi; the Hutus reportedly slaughtered over 500,000 Tutsi and countless Hutu moderates as they went. The result was threefold: a million dead, three million refugees, and a Tutsi-dominated but multi-ethnic "government of national unity".

As the Mobutu regime collapsed in neighboring Zaire, the Zaire military attempted to expel a Tutsi community of 400,000 (the Banyamulenge people) who had been settled south of Lake Kivu since the 18th century. The Tutsi resistance gained support from the Rwandan government (Oct. 1996); thus commenced a de facto war between Rwanda and Zaire. The 500,000 Hutu militiamen and other refugees who, as a result, fled Zaire back to Rwanda joined another half million driven from Tanzania by the Tanzanian army. Yet another wave of killings by Hutu militants had begun in Rwanda. By 1999 the Hutu rebellion was petering out in small but vicious skirmishes and the government of Rwanda was continuing its military aid to insurgents in Congo while attacking Hutu bases in the eastern parts of that country, despite the July cease-fire. In April 2000, Paul Kagame was elected the first Tutsi president of Rwanda.

▶SAINT KITTS AND NEVIS
Federation of Saint Kitts and Nevis
• **GEOGRAPHY   Location:** two islands in eastern Caribbean Sea, about 45 mi. (72 km) NW of Antigua. Nevis 17°08′N, 62°37′W; St. Kitts 17°17′N, 62°43′W. **Boundaries:** Caribbean Sea to N, E, S, and W. **Total area:** 104 sq. mi. (269 sq km). **Coastline:** 84 mi. (135 km). **Comparative area:** 1.5 times the size of Washington, D.C. **Land use:** 22% arable land; 17% permanent crops; 3% meadows and pastures; 17% forest and woodland; 41% other; includes N.A. % irrigated. **Major cities:** (1994 est.) Basseterre (capital) 12,605.
• **PEOPLE   Population:** 38,756 (2001 est.). **Nationality:** noun—Kittitian(s), Nevisian(s); adjective—Kittitian, Nevisian. **Ethnic groups:** mainly of black African descent. **Languages:** English. **Religions:** Anglican, other Protestant sects, Roman Catholic.
• **GOVERNMENT   Type:** constitutional monarchy. **Independence:** Sept. 19, 1983 (from U.K.). **Constitution:** Sept. 19, 1983. **National holiday:** Independence Day, Sept 19. **Heads of Government:** Cuthbert Sebastian, governor-general (since Jan. 1996); Denzil Douglas, prime minister (since July 1995). **Structure:** executive—cabinet headed by prime minister; unicameral legislature; judiciary—East Caribbean Supreme Court, based on Saint Lucia.
• **ECONOMY   Monetary unit:** East Caribbean (EC) dollar. **Budget:** (1997 est.) *income:* $64.1 mil.; *expend.:* $73.3 mil. **GDP:** $274 mil., $7,000 per capita (2000 est.). **Chief crops:** sugarcane, rice, yams, vegetables, bananas. **Natural resources:** negl. **Major industries:** sugar processing, tourism, cotton. **Labor force:** 18,172 (1995); 69% services, 31% manufacturing. **Exports:** $53.2 mil. (2000 est.); machinery, food, electronics, beverages, tobacco. **Imports:** $151.5 mil. (2000 est.); machinery, manufactures, food, fuel. **Major trading partners:** (1995) *exports:* 68.5% U.S., 22.3% U.K., 5.5% Caricom nations; *imports:* 42.4% U.S., 17.2% Caricom nations, 11.3% U.K.

The French settled St. Kitts in 1627; the English settled Nevis in 1628. In 1783 both became British possessions, and the two islands were united in 1882. Britain granted them independence in 1983. The country's economy is almost entirely based on sugar exports, so when Hurricane Hugo devastated sugar yields in 1990, the welfare of the entire population was affected. The reign of Kennedy Alphonse Simmonds, the only prime minister St. Kitts and Nevis had ever known, ended in July 1995, when Denzil Douglas's opposition Labour party defeated Kennedy's increasingly unpopular People's Action Movement. March 2000 elections confirmed the change: Labour took eight of the 11 seats, PAN took none. The continued fall of world sugar prices has hurt the economy and in 1997 some leaders in Nevis started a movement to separate from St. Kitts because of high taxes. In 1998 a referendum on separation resulted in a majority yes-vote but not the two-thirds necessary.

▶SAINT LUCIA
• **GEOGRAPHY   Location:** southeastern Caribbean Sea, between Martinique to N and St. Vincent to SW. Castries 14°01′N, 60°59′W. **Boundaries:** St. Lucia Channel to N, Atlantic Ocean to E, St. Vincent Passage to S, Caribbean Sea to W. **Total area:** 239 sq. mi. (620 sq km). **Coastline:** 98 mi. (158 km). **Comparative area:** 3.5 times size of Washington, D.C. **Land use:** 8% arable land; 21% permanent crops; 5% meadows and pastures; 13% forest and woodland; 53% other; includes 2% irrigated. **Major cities:** (1992 est.) Castries (capital) 53,883.
• **PEOPLE   Population:** 158,178 (2001 est.). **Nationality:** noun—St. Lucian(s); adjective—St. Lucian. **Ethnic groups:** 90% black African descent, 6% mixed, 3% East Indian, 1% Caucasian. **Languages:** English (official), French patois. **Religions:** 90% Roman Catholic, 7% Protestant, 3% Anglican.
• **GOVERNMENT   Type:** parliamentary democracy. **Independence:** Feb. 22, 1979 (from U.K.). **Constitution:** Feb. 22, 1979. **National holiday:** Independence Day, Feb. 22. **Heads of Government:** Perlette Louisy, governor-general (since Sept. 1997); Kenny D. Anthony, prime minister (since May 1997). **Structure:** executive—cabinet headed by prime minister; bicameral legislature—Senate, House of Representatives; judiciary—East Caribbean Supreme Court.
• **ECONOMY   Monetary unit:** East Caribbean (EC) dollar. **Budget:** (FY97/98 est.) *income:* $141.2 mil.; *expend.:* $146.7 mil. **GDP:** $700 mil., $4,500 per capita (2000 est.). **Chief crops:** bananas, coconuts, vegetables, root crops, citrus, cocoa. **Natural resources:** forests, sandy beaches, minerals (pumice), mineral springs, geothermal potential. **Major industries:** clothing, assembly of electronic components, beverages. **Labor force:** 43,800 (1983 est.); 43.4% agriculture, 38.9% services, 17.7% industry and commerce; 15% unemployment (1996). **Exports:** $68.3 mil. (2000 est.); 41% bananas, clothing, cocoa, vegetables, fruits, coconut oil. **Imports:** $319.4 mil. (2000 est.); 23% food, 21% manufactured goods, 19% machinery and transport equipment, chemicals, fuels. **Major trading partners:** *exports:* 50% U.K., 24% U.S., 16% Caricom countries; *imports:* 36% U.S., 22% Caricom countries, 11% U.K.

In 1650 the French settled St. Lucia, which was ceded to Britain in 4. A member of the Federation of the West Indies from 1958 to 1962, St. Lucia became internally self-governing in 1967 but was still under Great Britain's protection. In 1979 St. Lucia gained full independence and now enjoys stable competitive politics. Hurricane Allen destroyed many of the country's banana plantations in 1980, and the economy took years to recover from the disaster. The government of Prime Minister John Compton of the United Workers party worked for agrarian reform and proposed legalizing gambling to stimulate tourism but after 15 years in power lost the 1997 elections to the Labour Party led by Kenny B. Anthony.

▶SAINT VINCENT AND THE GRENADINES
• **GEOGRAPHY   Location:** large island of St. Vincent (13°12′N, 61°14′W) and about 50 smaller islands in southeastern Caribbean Sea about 21 mi. (34 km) SW of St. Lucia and 100 mi. (160 km) W of Barbados. **Boundaries:** St. Vincent Passage to N, Atlantic Ocean to E and SE, Caribbean Sea to SW and W. **Total area:** 131 sq. mi. (340 sq km). **Coast-

line: 52 mi. (84 km). **Comparative area**: twice size of Washington, D.C. **Land use**: 10% arable land; 18% permanent crops; 5% meadows and pastures; 36% forest and woodland; 31% other; includes 3% irrigated. **Major cities**: (1991 census) Kingstown (capital) 15,670.

● **PEOPLE Population**: 115,942 (2001 est.). **Nationality**: noun—St. Vincentian(s) or Vincentian(s); adjective—St. Vincentian or Vincentian. **Ethnic groups**: mainly of black African descent, remainder mixed, with some white, East Indian, and Carib Amerindian. **Languages**: English, French patois. **Religions**: Anglican, Methodist, Roman Catholic, Seventh-Day Adventist.

● **GOVERNMENT Type**: parliamentary monarchy. **Independence**: Oct. 27, 1979 (from U.K.). **Constitution**: Oct. 27, 1979. **National holiday**: Independence Day, Oct. 27. **Heads of Government**: Charles Antrobus, governor-general (since June 1997); Ralph E. Gonsalves, prime minister (since Mar. 2001). **Structure**: executive—prime minister is head of government; bicameral legislature—15-member elected House of Representatives and 6-member appointed Senate; judiciary—East Caribbean Supreme Court.

● **ECONOMY Monetary unit**: East Caribbean (EC) dollar. **Budget**: (1997 est.) *income*: $85.7 mil.; *expend.*: $98.6 mil. **GDP**: $322 mil., $2,800 per capita (2000 est.). **Chief crops**: bananas, coconuts, sweet potatoes, spices; small numbers of cattle, sheep, pigs, goats; small fish catch used locally. **Natural resources**: negl. **Major industries**: food processing (sugar, flour), cement, furniture. **Labor force**: 67,000 (1984 est.); 26% agriculture, 17% industry, 57% services; 22% unemployed (1997). **Exports**: $53.7 mil. (2000 est.); 39% bananas, eddoes and dasheen (taro), arrowroot starch, tennis racquets. **Imports**: $185.6 mil. (2000 est.); foodstuffs, machinery and equipment, chemicals and fertilizers, minerals and fuels. **Major trading partners**: *exports:* 49% Caricom countries, 16% U.K., 10% U.S.; *imports:* 36% U.S., 28% Caricom countries, 13% U.K.

Although ceded to Britain in 1763, St. Vincent was inhabited by the fierce Carib Indians, who continued fighting for control of the island until 1796, when they had all been either killed or deported. Just prior to its independence in 1979, St. Vincent and the Grenadines was a self-governing state in association with Great Britain. It is one of the poorest countries in the West Indies. Several natural disasters have plagued the economy, including a 1979 volcanic eruption and two destructive hurricanes in 1980 and 1986. Prime Minister James Mitchell of the New Democratic party currently governs the country, winning his fourth term after June 1997 elections gave his New Democratic Party a slender one-vote majority in the 15-seat legislature.

▶ SAMOA
Formerly Western Samoa
Independent State of Samoa
● **GEOGRAPHY Location**: two large and seven small islands (five inhabited) in South Pacific Ocean, about 1,500 mi. (2,400 km) NE of New Zealand. Apia 13°49′S, 171°45′W. **Boundaries**: surrounded by Pacific Ocean; nearest neighbor is American Samoa to E. **Total area**: 1,104 sq. mi. (2,860 sq km). **Coastline**: 250 mi. (403 km). **Comparative area**: slightly smaller than Rhode Island. **Land use**: 19% arable land; 24% permanent crops; negl. % meadows and pastures; 47% forest and woodland; 10% other. **Major cities**: (1991 census) Apia (capital) 34,260.

● **PEOPLE Population**: 179,058 (2001 est.). **Nationality**: noun—Samoan(s); adjective—Samoan. **Ethnic groups**: 92.6% Samoan; about 7% Euronesians (persons of European and Polynesian blood), 0.4% Europeans. **Languages**: Samoan (Polynesian), English. **Religions**: 99.7% Christian (about half of population associated with London Missionary Society; includes Congregational, Roman Catholic, Methodist, Latter-Day Saints, Seventh-Day Adventist).

● **GOVERNMENT Type**: constitutional monarchy under native chief. **Independence**: Jan. 1, 1962 (from U.N. trusteeship administered by New Zealand). **Constitution**: Jan. 1, 1962. **National holiday**: National Day, Jan. 1. **Heads of Government**: Malietoa Tanumafili II, head of state (since 1962); Tuilaepa Sailele Malielegaoi, prime minister (since Nov. 1998). **Structure**: executive—chief of state appoints prime minister; unicameral legislature (47-member Legislative Assembly); judiciary.

● **ECONOMY Monetary unit**: tala. **Budget**: (1999 est.) *income*: $74.8 mil.; *expend.*: $81.4 mil. **GDP**: $571 mil., $3,200 per capita (2000 est.). **Chief crops**: coconuts, bananas, taro, yams. **Natural resources**: hardwood forests, fish. **Major industries**: timber, tourism, food processing. **Labor force**: 90,000 (2000 est.); 65% agriculture, 30% services. **Exports**: $17 mil. (f.o.b., 2000); coconut oil and cream, copra, fish, beer. **Imports**: $96.6 mil. (f.o.b., 1998); intermediate goods, food, capital goods. **Major trading partners**: *exports:* Australia, New Zealand; *imports:* Australia, New Zealand, Japan, Fiji.

The Polynesian island group of Samoa (Navigator's Islands) was partitioned in 1899 between the United States, which had established a naval base at Pago Pago on Tutuila in 1878, and Germany, which organized the westerly islands into a colony in 1894. In 1914 New Zealand troops occupied the German-held islands. New Zealand administered Western Samoa under a League of Nations mandate beginning in 1920 and continued to control the islands as a U.N. Trust Territory after 1945. In 1959 home rule was established under an elected local government. Western Samoa became an independent nation on Jan. 1, 1962. The constitution blends Western parliamentary government and traditional Samoan forms of rule. The parliamentary electorate is limited to the malai, heads of extended families; the malai are wholly responsible for local affairs. The local culture is similarly a blend of Samoan tradition with Christianity.

The economy is based on subsistence agriculture, forestry, fishing, and tourism.

In November 1998, after 16 years of stable and peaceful rule, Prime Minister Tofilau Eti Alesana resigned for health reasons and was replaced by his deputy, Tuilaepa Sailele Malielegaoi.

▶ SAN MARINO
Republic of San Marino
● **GEOGRAPHY Location**: on slopes of Mt. Titano, in the Apennines, within central Italian region of Emilia-Romagna. **Boundaries**: surrounded by Italian territory. **Total area**: 23 sq. mi. (60 sq km). **Coastline**: none. **Comparative area**: about three-tenths the size of Washington, D.C. **Land use**: 17% arable land; 0% permanent crops; 0% meadows and pastures; 0% forest and woodland; 83% other. **Major cities**: (1995 est.) San Marino (capital) 4,498.

● **PEOPLE Population**: 27,336 (2001 est.). **Nationality**: noun—Sammarinese (sing., pl.); adjective—

Sammarinese. **Ethnic groups:** Sammarinese, Italian. **Languages:** Italian. **Religions:** Roman Catholic.

•**GOVERNMENT Type:** republic. **Independence:** 301 A.D. **Constitution:** Oct. 8, 1600; electoral law of 1926 serves some of functions of constitution. **National holiday:** Anniversary of the Foundation of the Republic, Sept. 3. **Heads of Government:** Maria Domenica Michelotti (Apr.-Sept. 2000) and Gian Marco Marcucci (since Sept. 2000), minister of foreign affairs. **Structure:** executive—two captain-regents with six-month terms elected by and from the legislature, actual power wielded by secretary of state for foreign affairs; unicameral legislature—Great and General Council elected by popular vote for five-year terms; judicial—Council of Twelve is supreme judicial body.

•**ECONOMY Monetary unit:** Italian lira. **Budget:** (2000 est.) *income:* $400 mil.; *expend:* $400 mil. **GDP:** $860 mil., $32,000 per capita (2000 est.). **Chief crops:** wheat, grapes, maize, olives; cattle, pigs, horses, meat, cheese, hides. **Natural resources:** building stones. **Major industries:** tourism, textiles, electronics. **Labor force:** 18,500 (1999); 60% services, 38% industry, 2% agriculture. **Exports:** trade data included with Italian statistics; commodity trade consisting primarily of exchanging building stone, lime, wood, chestnuts, wheat, and wine for a wide variety of consumer manufactures. **Imports:** see exports. **Major trading partners:** N.A.

The "Most Serene Republic" of San Marino, entirely surrounded by Italy near the city of Rimini, is the oldest republic in the world, with communitarian roots dating to the fourth century A.D. While Piedmont-Sardinia was conquering all of the rest of the Italian peninsula during the period 1860-70, it left San Marino independent; the new kingdom of Italy signed a treaty of friendship and cooperation with the republic in 1862.

Leftist coalitions governed from 1978 through 1986, giving San Marino the only Communist government west of the Soviet bloc. Since 1986 the government has been controlled by a coalition of Communists and Christian Democrats. In 1992 San Marino joined the United Nations.

The economy is balanced between small-scale agriculture (primarily wine grapes and livestock) and industry, including textiles, ceramics, and furniture. Philatelic sales and tourism are important sources of revenue. Lacking extremes of wealth and poverty and with low unemployment, the republic enjoys general prosperity.

▶ **SÃO TOMÉ AND PRÍNCIPE**
Democratic Republic of Saõ Tomé and Príncipe
•**GEOGRAPHY Location:** two main islands, São Tomé (0°19′N, 6°43′E) and Príncipe, and Caroço, Pedras, Tinhosas (off Príncipe), and Rolas (off São Tomé), off west coast of Africa. **Boundaries:** west of Gabon in Gulf of Guinea. **Total area:** 371 sq. mi. (960 sq km). **Coastline:** 130 mi. (209 km). **Comparative area:** more than 5.5 times size of Washington, D.C. **Land use:** 2% arable land; 36% permanent crops; 1% meadows and pastures; 0% forest and woodland; 61% other. **Major cities:** (1991) São Tomé (capital) 43,420.

•**PEOPLE Population:** 165,034 (2001 est.). **Nationality:** noun—São Toméan(s); adjective—São Toméan. **Ethnic groups:** mestiço, angolares (descendants of Angolan slaves), forros (descendents of freed slaves), servicais (contract laborers from Angola, Mozambique, and Cape Verde), tongas (children of servicais born on the islands), and

Europeans (primarily Portuguese). **Languages:** Portuguese (official). **Religions:** Roman Catholic, Evangelical Protestant, Seventh-Day Adventist.

•**ECONOMY Type:** republic. **Independence:** July 12, 1975 (from Portugal). **Constitution:** Sept. 10, 1990. **National holiday:** Independence Day, July 12. **Heads of Government:** Fradique Bandeira Melo de Menezes, president (since Sept. 2001); Guilherme Posser Da Costa, prime minister (since July 1999). **Structure:** executive—president assisted by cabinet of ministers; unicameral legislature; judiciary.

•**ECONOMY Monetary unit:** dobra. **Budget:** (1993 est.) *income:* $58 mil.; *expend.:* $114 mil. **GDP:** $178 mil., $1,100 per capita (2000 est.). **Chief crops:** cocoa, copra, coconuts, coffee, palm kernels, bananas, cinnamon, pepper, papaya, beans; poultry, fish. **Natural resources:** fish. **Major industries:** small processing factories producing shirts, soap, beer; fish and shrimp processing. **Labor force:** most of population engaged in subsistence agriculture and fishing; labor shortages of skilled workers. **Exports:** $3.2 mil. (f.o.b., 2000 est.); 90% cocoa, copra, coffee, palm oil. **Imports:** $40 mil. (f.o.b., 2000 est.); machinery and electrical equipment, food products, fuels. **Major trading partners:** *exports:* 18% Netherlands, 9% Germany, 9% Portugal; *imports:* 42% Portugal, 20% U.S.

The islands of São Tomé and Príncipe, located in the Atlantic Ocean 275 and 125 miles, respectively, off the northern coast of Gabon, make up one of Africa's smallest nations. They were uninhabited when first discovered by the Portuguese in 1470 but by the mid-1500's became Africa's foremost exporter of sugar. As the sugar market declined, the islands became a major slave-trading center and producer of coffee and cocoa. By 1908 São Tomé was the world's largest cocoa producer.

Portugal did not abolish slavery until 1876, and abusive labor practices continued until well into the 20th century. In 1953 hundreds of workers were killed in clashes with the Portuguese. Soon after, a small number of São Toméans formed the Movement for the Liberation of São Tomé and Príncipe (MLSTP) with its base in Gabon. But the islands did not gain independence until July 12, 1975.

The MLSTP took over after independence and became the country's only official party. By 1986 the country relied on foreign aid for approximately 41 percent of its gross national product. Although in the past it received military advisers from the former Soviet Union and economic advisers from Cuba, São Tomé and Príncipe has announced a foreign policy based upon nonalignment. Multi-party democracy was introduced in 1991.

▶ **SAUDI ARABIA**
Kingdom of Saudi Arabia
•**GEOGRAPHY Location:** occupies four-fifths of Arabian peninsula in southwestern Asia. **Boundaries:** Jordan, Iraq, and Kuwait to N, Persian Gulf, Qatar, and United Arab Emirates to E, Oman to SE, Yemen to S and SE, Red Sea to W. **Total area:** 756,982 sq. mi. (1,960,582 sq km). **Coastline:** 1,641 mi. (2,640 km). **Comparative area:** slightly more than one-fifth the size of the U.S. **Land use:** 2% arable land; negl. % permanent crops; 56% meadows and pastures; 1% forest and woodland; 41% other. **Major cities:** (1991 est.) Riyadh (capital) 1,800,000; Jid'dah 1,500,000; Mecca 630,000; Taif 410,000; Medina 400,000.

● **PEOPLE   Population:** 22,757,092 (2001 est.). **Nationality:** noun—Saudi(s); adjective—Saudi or Saudi Arabian. **Ethnic groups:** 90% Arab, 10% Afro-Asian. **Languages:** Arabic. **Religions:** 100% Muslim.

● **GOVERNMENT   Type:** monarchy. **Constitution:** none; governed according to Shari'a or Islamic law. **National holiday:** Unification of the Kingdom, Sept. 23. **Head of Government:** Fahd bin Abdul-Aziz al-Saud, king (since June 1982). **Structure:** king rules in consultation with royal family and Council of Ministers; no elected legislature; Supreme Council of Justice.

● **ECONOMY   Monetary unit:** Saudi riyal. **Budget:** (2000 est.) *income:* $66 bil.; *expend.:* $66 bil. **GDP:** $232 bil., $10,500 per capita (2000 est.). **Chief crops:** wheat, barley, tomatoes, melons, dates, citrus; mutton, chickens, eggs, milk. **Natural resources:** crude oil, natural gas, iron ore, gold, copper. **Major industries:** crude oil production, petroleum refining, basic petrochemicals. **Labor force:** 7 mil.; 25% industry, 63% services, 12% agriculture. **Exports:** $48 bil. (f.o.b., 1999); 90% petroleum and petroleum products. **Imports:** $28 bil. (f.o.b., 1999); machinery and equipment, foodstuffs, chemicals, motor vehicles, textiles. **Major trading partners:** 17% Japan, 15% U.S., 11% South Korea; *imports:* 21% U.S., 9% U.K., 9% Japan.

In ancient times various cultures flourished in parts of the Arabian peninsula, particularly along the western rim, in cities devoted to trade between the Gulf of Aden and the eastern Mediterranean, and in such agricultural and trading centers as Yemen and Oman. Cultural and political unity was lacking, however, until the rise of Mohammed, the prophet of Islam. In A.D. 622 Mohammed fled from Mecca, the holy city of Arabian paganism, to the nearby city of Medina; the Islamic era dates from that year. Preaching from Medina, Mohammed soon gained converts to Islam throughout Arabia. His army captured Mecca in 630, converting its sacred shrine, the Kaaba, to an Islamic place of worship. By 632, when Mohammed died, all of Arabia was unified under Islamic rule.

In 661 the Caliphate, the ruling body of early Islam, moved from Medina to Damascus. Thereafter Arabia was nominally unified under Islamic rule—but in practice was usually divided among various principalities in the arable areas and trading centers, and under tribal rule in the arid interior. Mecca fell to the Ottoman Empire in 1517, but Ottoman control of Arabia was never complete. The rise of the Wahabi sect of Islam in the 18th century posed a challenge to Ottoman rule. In the 19th century, the Saud family rose to leadership in the Wahabi movement and established a kingdom in Nejd, the central region of Arabia, with a capital at Riyadh.

In 1902 Ibn Saud (1880-1953) consolidated his family's control at Riyadh and in 1912-13 led a new Wahabi revolt against the Ottoman Turks. During World War I, the British aided Ibn Saud's rebellion in the Nejd, along with that of Ibn Saud's rival Hussein ibn Ali in the Hejaz, in the mountains of western Arabia along the coast of the Red Sea. A British protectorate was established in both regions in 1915, and Great Britain maintained a dominant position in Arabia immediately after World War I.

In 1924 Ibn Saud captured Hussein ibn Ali's capital at Mecca, and he proclaimed himself king of Hejaz in 1926 and of Nejd in 1927. Ibn Saud consolidated his control over the following two years, and his kingdom was formally recognized by Great Britain in 1927. The country was renamed Saudi Arabia in 1932.

Saudi Arabia is an absolute monarchy based on Islamic law; it has no written constitution and no parliament. The king exercises sole authority and rules in consultation with a Council of Ministers. Islamic law is enforced; alcohol is prohibited and the public activities of women severely restricted. The Saudi kings have great power within the Islamic world through their control over the holy cities of Mecca and Medina and their administration of the annual Muslim pilgrimages to those cities.

The discovery of oil in eastern Arabia in the early 1930's rapidly transformed Saudi Arabia from an impoverished nation to a center of great wealth. In 1933 an exclusive concession for the exploitation of Saudi Arabian oil was granted to an American-chartered corporation, the Arabian-American Oil Company (Aramco). For many years wealth remained concentrated in the hands of the Saudi clan, and little change was felt in the desert interior, where Bedouin nomads continued to raise sheep and camels. Large numbers of Yemenis, Palestinians, Pakistanis, and other foreign workers are employed in the oil fields.

Saudi Arabia remained neutral during most of World War II but declared war on the Axis powers in March 1945; in the same year, it became a founding member of both the United Nations and the Arab League.

Ibn Saud became a leader of Arab anti-Zionism and contributed a small contingent of troops to the 1948 Arab-Israeli War. That policy was maintained by Ibn Saud's second son and successor, King Faisal, who instituted a policy of providing large annual subsidies to Egypt and other Arab League states following the 1967 Arab-Israeli War. In 1973 King Faisal sent Saudi units to fight in the Arab-Israeli War of that year. He played a leading role in organizing the 1973-74 Arab oil embargo in an effort to force the United States and its allies to take a harder line with Israel.

King Faisal was assassinated by his nephew, Prince Faisal, on Mar. 25, 1975, and was succeeded by King Khalid. Little change in policy resulted. In 1979 Saudi Arabia denounced the Camp David talks and the Egyptian-Israeli peace treaty and led the Arab League effort to ostracize Egypt within the Arab world.

Saudi Arabia has consistently opposed leftist and radical movements in the Arab world, sending troops to help put down leftist rebellions in North Yemen and Oman in the 1970's. Saudi kings have taken a moderate approach toward relations with the West. Following the transfer of Aramco assets to full Saudi Arabian ownership during 1973-76, Saudi Arabia used its leading position within the Organization of Petroleum Exporting Countries (OPEC) to argue for a policy of stable production and prices.

This moderate policy has been rewarded by the willingness of the United States, Great Britain, France, and other Western nations to sell arms—including jet fighters, tanks, and other sophisticated weapons—to Saudi Arabia despite Israeli protests. The multibillion-dollar arms trade has helped to offset the Western oil trade deficit with Saudi Arabia.

Saudi Arabia experienced repeated disturbances in the 1980's. Muslim fundamentalist terrorists seized the Grand Mosque at Mecca on Nov. 20, 1979, provoking a crisis for the Saudi monarchy. On July 31, 1987, Iranian pilgrims rioted in Mecca and were fired upon by Saudi security forces; 402 persons died, including 275 Iranians. Iran's Ayatollah Khomeini denounced the Saudi government and said it was unworthy of being the guardian of Islam's sacred shrines.

A longtime supporter of the Palestine Liberation Organization, the Saudi government gave the PLO $850 million during the 1980's, but ceased when the PLO backed Saddam Hussein's invasion of Kuwait in 1990.

During the Persian Gulf War, King Fahd granted permission to station U.S. troops in Saudi Arabia to guard against a possible Iraqi attack. The Saudis promised the United States $16.8 billion and Egypt $1.5 billion to defray the costs of the war. Little ground fighting took place on Saudi soil, but massive oil spills threatened the operation of crucial desalination plants in the Persian Gulf.

Since the war, Saudi Arabia has played a prominent and pivotal role in the diplomatic efforts of the United States and its allies to reach a permanent accord in the Middle East.

Two events in 1996 raised concerns about Saudi Arabia's future stability. The first was in January, when King Fahd, ailing from a 1995 stroke, temporarily ceded power to his legal successor, Crown Prince Abdullah. The second came in June, when terrorists bombed an apartment complex in Dhahran, killing 19 American soldiers stationed there and wounding more than 300 people.

▶ SENEGAL
Republic of Senegal

● **GEOGRAPHY   Location:** northwestern coast of Africa. **Boundaries:** Mauritania to N, Mali to E, Guinea and Guinea-Bissau to S, Atlantic Ocean to W; The Gambia forms narrow enclave extending 200 mi. (320 km) inland from Atlantic coast. **Total area:** 75,749 sq. mi. (196,190 sq km). **Coastline:** 330 mi. (531 km). **Comparative area:** slightly smaller than South Dakota. **Land use:** 12% arable land; 0% permanent crops; 16% meadows and pastures; 54% forest and woodland; 18% other. **Major cities:** (1992 census) Dakar (capital) 1,729,823; Thies 201,350; Kaolack 179,894.
● **PEOPLE   Population:** 9,987,494 (1999 est.). **Nationality:** noun—Senegalese (sing., pl.); adjective—Senegalese. **Ethnic groups:** 43.3% Wolof, 23.8% Pular, 14.7% Serer, 3.7% Diola, 3% Mandink, 1.1% Soninke, 1% European and Lebanese. **Languages:** French (official), Wolof, Pulaar, Diola, Mandingo. **Religions:** 92% Muslim, 6% indigenous beliefs, 2% Christian (mostly Roman Catholic).
● **GOVERNMENT   Type:** republic under multi-party democratic rule. **Independence:** Apr. 4, 1960 (from France). **Constitution:** Mar. 3, 1963, revised 1991. **National holiday:** Independence Day, Apr. 4. **Heads of Government:** Abdoulaye Wade, president (since Apr. 2000); Mame Madior Boye, prime minister (since May 2001). **Structure:** executive—president; unicameral legislature; judiciary—Constitutional Court, Council of State, Court of Final Appeals, Court of Appeals.
● **ECONOMY   Monetary unit:** Communauté Financière Africaine (CFA) franc. **Budget:** (1996 est.) *income:* $885 mil.; *expend.:* $885 mil. **GDP:** $16.6 bil., $1,650 per capita (1999 est.). **Chief crops:** peanuts, millet, corn, sorghum, rice, cotton, tomotoes, green vegetables; cattle, poultry, pigs; fish. **Natural resources:** fish, phosphates, iron ore. **Major industries:** fishing, agricultural pro-

cessing, phosphate mining. **Labor force:** 60% agriculture. **Exports:** $925 mil. (f.o.b. 1998); fish, peanuts, petroleum products, phosphates, cotton. **Imports:** $1.2 bil. (f.o.b., 1998); foods and beverages, consumer goods, capital goods, petroleum products. **Major trading partners:** *exports:* 22% France, other E.U. countries, India, Ivory Coast; *imports:* 36% France, other E.U. countries, Nigeria.

Inhabited since ancient times, Senegal was dominated in the 13th and 14th centuries by the Mandingo and Jolof empires. Portuguese traders and explorers arrived in Senegal in the early 15th century and later competed with the British, Dutch, and French for domination in Senegal. The French established a trading station at Saint-Louis in 1659 and maintained possession thereafter, except for the British enclave along the Gambia River.

In the early 19th century, the French began a series of campaigns to bring the entire country under their control; the last independent sultanate surrendered in 1893. Senegal became a French colony in 1920, and Dakar became the capital of French West Africa. Senegal became a major contributor of African troops to the French armed forces.

In 1946 a territorial assembly was established, with a limited electorate and advisory powers, which were gradually expanded in subsequent years. With the creation of the French Community of Nations in 1958, Senegal achieved local self-rule within the community.

In 1959, with the encouragement of France, Senegal and French Sudan (now Mali) formed the Federation of Mali, which became fully independent on June 20, 1960. Senegal seceded from the federation on Aug. 20 and declared itself the Republic of Senegal. Leopold Sedar Senghor became Senegal's first president.

In 1962 Prime Minister Mamdou Dia attempted a coup against the Senghor government; it failed, and Dia was imprisoned. A new constitution was subsequently adopted, strengthening the power of the presidency. Senghor retired from office in 1981 and was succeeded by Abdou Diouf. He encouraged political pluralism and has presided over a generally stable government. Diouf was elected in his own right in 1983 and reelected in 1988. Following the 1988 elections, riots broke out over charges of electoral fraud, and a state of emergency was declared.

Diouf, who has taken a lead in African affairs, was reelected for the third time in 1993, but his Socialist party's legislative majority was diminished. At home, Diouf consolidated his power so well that in 1998 Parliament passed a law allowing him to become President for life. His involvement in the civil war in Guinea-Bissau, however, has caused dissension in the army. His January 1999 creation of a Senate as "upper house" to the National Assembly meant little for democracy since, with all opposition parties boycotting the election, his Socialist Party carried all 45 seats up for election. So the March 2000 presidential election was a surprise: Abdoulaye Wade of the Democratic Party (who had run four times since 1978) took 60 percent of the vote to become Senegal's third, and first non-Socialist, president.

Senegal remains closely tied to France commercially, culturally, and in foreign affairs. Senegal's economy is primarily agricultural. Industries include fishing and fish processing (the principal source of export earnings), food processing, light manufacturing, and phosphate mining. Senegalese merchants are active in commercial networks throughout West Africa.

▶ SERBIA AND MONTENEGRO
See "Yugoslavia"

▶ SEYCHELLES
Republic of Seychelles
• **GEOGRAPHY Location:** more than 90 widely scattered islands in western Indian Ocean about 1,000 mi. (1,600 km) E of Kenya and Tanzania. Victoria (Mahé Is.) 4°37'S, 55°28'E. **Boundaries:** surrounded by Indian Ocean; nearest neighbor is Madagascar about 130 mi. (210 km) S of southernmost island group. **Total area:** 176 sq. mi. (455 sq km). **Coastline:** 305 mi. (491 km). **Comparative area:** 2.5 times the size of Washington, D.C. **Land use:** 2% arable land; 13% permanent crops; 0% meadows and pastures; 11% forest and woodland; 74% other. **Major cities:** (1987) Victoria (capital) 24,325 (includes suburbs).
• **PEOPLE Population:** 79,326 (2000 est.). **Nationality:** noun—Seychellois (sing., pl.); adjective—Seychelles. **Ethnic groups:** Seychellois (mixture of Asians, Africans, Europeans). **Languages:** English, French (both official); Creole. **Religions:** 90% Roman Catholic, 8% Anglican, 2% other.
• **GOVERNMENT Type:** republic. **Independence:** June 29, 1976 (from U.K.). **Constitution:** June 18, 1993. **National holiday:** National Day, June 18. **Head of Government:** France Albert René, president (since June 1977). **Structure:** executive—president; unicameral legislature; judiciary.
• **ECONOMY Monetary unit:** Seychelles rupee. **Budget:** (1994 est.) *income:* $220 mil.; *expend.:* $241 mil. **GDP:** $590 mil., $7,500 per capita (1999 est.). **Chief crops:** coconuts, cinnamon, vanilla, sweet potatoes, cassava, bananas; broiler chickens; tuna fishing (expansion under way). **Natural resources:** fish, copra, cinnamon trees. **Major industries:** tourism is largest industry; processing of coconut and vanilla; fishing. **Labor force:** 26,000 (1996); 19% industry, 57% services, 14% government, 10% agriculture, forestry, and fishing. **Exports:** $91 mil. (f.o.b., 1998); fish, cinnamon bark, copra, petroleum products (reexports). **Imports:** $403 mil. (c.i.f., 1998); food, petroleum products, machinery, transportation equipment. **Major trading partners:** *exports:* France, U.K., Netherlands; *imports:* South Africa, U.S., China.

The Seychelles Islands were occupied by France in the 18th century and seized by Great Britain in 1794. They were administered along with Mauritius until 1903, when the Seychelles became a separate British colony. African and Indian workers were brought in to work in coconut and spice plantations and in guano mining. The present population is of mixed African, Indian, and European descent.

In the post-World War II period, a home-rule government rejected independence as impracticable. At the urging of the Organization of African Unity and the United Nations, the Seychelles declared independence on June 29, 1976. Its first president was ousted in a socialist coup in 1977 led by Prime Minister France Albert René. A new constitution, promulgated in March 1979, formalized one-party Socialist rule. In July 1992 a commission was elected to rewrite the constitution before the end of the year, but the delegates defeated the first results.

Since independence, the economy of the Seychelles has become heavily dependent on the tourist industry, which accounts for 90 percent of the country's foreign exchange earnings. Fishing accounts for 40 percent of exports.

▶ SIERRA LEONE
Republic of Sierra Leone
• **GEOGRAPHY Location:** west central Africa. **Boundaries:** Guinea to N and E, Liberia to S, Atlantic Ocean to W. **Total area:** 27,699 sq. mi. (71,740 sq km). **Coastline:** 250 mi. (402 km). **Comparative area:** slightly smaller than South Carolina. **Land use:** 7% arable land; 1% permanent crops; 31% meadows and pastures; 28% forest and woodland; 33% other.; **Major cities:** Freetown (capital) 384,499 (1985 census); Koindu 82,474; Bo 59,768; Kenema 52,473; Makeni 49,474.
• **PEOPLE Population:** 5,232,624 (2000 est.). **Nationality:** noun—Sierra Leonean(s); adjective—Sierra Leonean. **Ethnic groups:** over 90% African (30% Temne, 30% Mende), rest European, Creole, and Asian. **Languages:** English (official); regular use limited to literate minority; principal languages are Mende in south and Temne in north; Krio is language of resettled ex-slave population of Freetown area and is lingua franca. **Religions:** 60% Muslim, 30% indigenous beliefs, 10% Christian.
• **GOVERNMENT Type:** constitutional democracy. **Independence:** Apr. 27, 1961 (from U.K.). **Constitution:** Oct. 1, 1991. **National holiday:** Republic Day, Apr. 27. **Heads of Government:** Alhaj Ahmad Tejan Kabbah, president (since Mar. 1996). **Structure:** executive—president; unicameral legislature-68 elected seats, 12 filled by paramount chiefs; judiciary.
• **ECONOMY Monetary unit:** leone. **Budget:** (1996 est.) *income:* $96 mil.; *expend.:* $150 mil. **GDP:** $2.5 bil., $500 per capita (1999 est.). **Chief crops:** palm kernels, coffee, cocoa, rice, palm oil, peanuts; poultry, cattle, sheep, pigs; fish. **Natural resources:** diamonds, titanium ore, bauxite, iron ore, gold. **Major industries:** mining (diamonds, iron ore, bauxite, rutile), small-scale manufacturing (beverages, textiles, cigarettes, footwear), petroleum refinery. **Labor force:** 1.369 mil. (1981); 65% agriculture, 19% industry, 16% services; only small minority, some 65,000, earn wages. **Exports:** $41 mil. (f.o.b., 1998); diamonds, rutile, cocoa, coffee, fish. **Imports:** $166 mil. (c.i.f., 1998); foodstuffs, machinery and equipment, fuels and lubricants. **Major trading partners:** *exports:* 49% Belgium, 10% Spain, 8% U.S.; *imports:* 24% U.K., 14% Ivory Coast, 10% Benelux.

Portuguese domination of the Sierra Leone coast began in 1462. English explorers, including Francis Drake, arrived in the late 16th century. Europeans traded for slaves in Sierra Leone, but in 1787 Freetown was founded by the British Sierra Leone Co. as a haven for freed slaves. The settlement was populated by former slaves from Great Britain, North America, and the Caribbean, and later by slaves liberated from slave trading ships by the British navy.

Sierra Leone was reorganized as a British colony in 1808. The ex-slave population, from diverse tribal and national backgrounds, developed an English-speaking Creole culture unique in Africa. Freetown became the center of British colonial administration and trade in West Africa and was the focus of missionary-supported projects in health care and economic development.

The native peoples of Sierra Leone staged numerous rebellions against the British and the Creole elite; resentment focused on the tax system and on the privileges of the English-speaking descendents of ex-slaves. During the 20th century, home rule developed through an elected advisory legislature. In 1951 a constitutional framework had been developed as the basis of decolonization. Sir Milton Margei became chief minister in 1953, and prime minister in 1961. The last ties with the British Crown were cut on Apr. 27, 1961, when Sierra Leone became a republic. A referendum in 1978 created a one-party state. In 1984 and 1985 student and public employee protests against the government led to riots and the restoration of multi-party elections.

In April 1992, Momoh was ousted in a coup by Capt. Valentine Strasser. Despite the country's wealth of natural resources, Strasser's corruption and mismanagement threatened to derail the economy. Strasser was overthrown in Jan. 1996 by army officers who pledged to continue his plan for multi-party elections the following month. Those elections proceeded smoothly, with Ahmad Tejan Kabbah of the People's party capturing close to 60 percent of the votes.

Since 1991 Sierra Leone has been afflicted by a murderous gang led by "rebel" Fodaj Sankoh, calling itself the Revolutionary United Front. By July 1999 it controlled perhaps half of the country's territory, including invaluable diamond mines which they loot, then market through Liberia's president, Charles Taylor. In May 1997 regular army troops loyal to Major Johnny Paul Koroma briefly overthrew President Kabbah's government until Nigerian-led west African troops restored Kabbah and assisted against the RUF gang. A July 1999 cease-fire brought four RUF killers into the government and an amnesty for Sankoh. But the RUF did not disarm, and continued the struggle into 2000. Sankoh was captured late in May. In 2001 Parliament, with U.N. and British approval, postponed the scheduled March elections and extended President Kabbah's term for six months. With Sankoh captured, more U.N. troops in the country, and, most importantly, diminished support from Pres. Taylor, RUF began in May to disarm and to release hundreds of its boy-soldiers. But fighting continued in the diamond-rich east.

▶ **SINGAPORE**
Republic of Singapore
● **GEOGRAPHY Location:** Singapore Island and some 57 islets off southern Malay peninsula (linked by a causeway). **Boundaries**: Johor Strait to N; Pacific Ocean to E; Strait of Malacca to SW, separating Singapore from Indonesian island of Sumatra; and Indian Ocean to W. **Total area**: 244 sq. mi. (633 sq km). **Coastline**: 120 mi. (193 km). **Comparative area**: slightly more than 3.5 times size of Washington, D.C. **Land use:** 2% arable land; 6% permanent crops; 0% meadows and pastures; 5% forest and woodland; 87% other. **Major cities:** Singapore (capital).
● **PEOPLE Population:** 4,151,264 (2000 est.). **Nationality:** noun—Singaporean(s); adjective—Singapore. **Ethnic groups:** 77% Chinese, 14% Malay, 7.6% Indian, 1.4% other. **Languages:** Chinese, Malay, Tamil, and English (all official); Malay (national). **Religions:** majority of Chinese are Buddhists or atheists; Malays nearly all Muslim; minorities include Christians, Hindus, Sikhs, Taoists, Confucianists.
● **GOVERNMENT Type:** parliamentary republic. **Independence:** Aug. 9, 1965 (from Malaysia). **Constitution:** June 3, 1959, amended 1965; based on preindependence State of Singapore constitution. **National holiday:** Aug. 9. **Heads of Govern-**

ment: S.R. Nathan, president (since Sept. 1999); Goh Chok Tong, prime minister (since Nov. 1990). **Structure:** executive—ceremonial president, power exercised by prime minister and cabinet; unicameral legislature; judiciary.
● **ECONOMY Monetary unit:** Singapore dollar. **Budget:** (FY98/99 est.) *income:* $13.9 bil.; *expend.:* $16.9 bil. **GDP:** $98 bil., $27,800 per capita (1999 est.). **Chief crops:** rubber, copra, fruits, vegetables; poultry. **Natural resources:** fish, deepwater ports. **Major industries:** financial services, petroleum refining, electronics, oil drilling equipment. **Labor force:** 1.932 mil. (1998 est.); 38% financial, business, and other services, 21.6% manufacturing, 21.4% commerce, 7% construction. **Exports:** $114 bil. (1999 est.); computer equipment, petroleum products, telecommunications equipment. **Imports:** $111 bil. (1999 est.); machinery and equipment, petroleum, chemicals, foodstuffs. **Major trading partners:** *exports:* 17% Malaysia, 19% U.S., 8% Hong Kong; *imports:* 17% Japan, 16% Malaysia, 17% U.S.

Singapore was founded in 1819 by Sir Thomas Stamford Raffles on land ceded to the East India Company by the sultanate of Johore (see "Malaysia"). An Anglo-Dutch treaty turned Singapore over to the British Crown in 1824, and eventually it was administered as part of the Straits Settlements. With its excellent harbor, Singapore eclipsed Penang and Malacca as the dominant port for trade through the Straits of Malacca.

Fortified as a bastion of British defense in Southeast Asia, Singapore was overrun by Japanese troops in Feb. 1942. The British reoccupied the city in Sept. 1945 and reorganized it as a British colony in 1946. On June 5, 1959, Singapore became a self-governing parliamentary democracy within the British Commonwealth. Lee Kwan Yew became prime minister. On Sept. 16, 1963, Singapore, along with Malaya, Sarawak, and Sabah, formed the Malaysian Federation. Singapore, ethnically Chinese, was uncomfortable within the Malay-dominated federation and seceded after two years, becoming an independent nation on Aug. 9, 1965.

Independent Singapore has enjoyed orderly, if authoritarian, government, economic growth, and a high standard of living. Still a major port, its economy now encompasses international banking, finance, communications, high-technology manufacturing, and tourism. On Nov. 26, 1990, Lee Kuan Yew, Singapore's only prime minister since independence and the longest serving prime minister in the world, resigned. He was succeeded by Goh Chok Tong, but he remains a force in Singapore's political life.

Measures in 2000 opened up segments of the economy to foreign firms, especially telecommunications and law, while the government ended its monopoly on broadcasting and newspapers. In 2001 Lee Kwan Yew's son, Lee Hsien Loong, currently chairman of the central bank and deputy prime minister, became prime minister.

▶ **SLOVAKIA**
Slovak Republic
● **GEOGRAPHY Location:** Central Europe. **Boundaries**: Czech Republic and Poland to N, Ukraine to E, Hungary to S, Austria to W. **Total area:** 18,859 sq. mi. (48,845 sq km). **Coastline:** none. **Comparative area**: about twice the size of New Hampshire. **Land use:** 31% arable, 3% permanent crops, 17% pastures, 41% forests, 8%

other. **Major cities:** (1994 est.) Bratislava (capital) 450,776; Kosice 239,927; Nitra 87,127; Presov 92,013; Banská Bystrica 84,741.

● **PEOPLE Population:** 5,407,956 (2000 est.). **Nationality:** noun—Slovak(s); adjective—Slovak. **Ethnic groups:** 85.7% Slovak, 10.7% Hungarian, 1.5% Gypsy. **Languages:** Slovak (official), Hungarian. **Religions:** 60.3% Roman Catholic, 9.7% atheist, 8.4% Protestant, 4.1% Orthodox.

● **GOVERNMENT Type:** parliamentary democracy. **Independence:** Jan. 1, 1993 (from Czechoslovakia). **Constitution:** Jan. 1, 1993; changed Sept. 1996 to allow direct election of president. **National holiday:** Slovak Constitution Day, Sept. 1. **Heads of Government:** Rudolf Schuster, president (since Jun. 1999); Mikuláš (Dzurinda, prime minister (since Oct. 1998). **Structure:** executive—president, prime minister, Council of Ministers; legislative—unicameral (National Council); judicial—Supreme Court.

● **ECONOMY Monetary unit:** koruna. **Budget:** (1999 est.) *income:* $5.4 bil.; *expend.:* $5.8 bil. **GDP:** $45.9 bil., $8,500 per capita (1999 est.). **Chief crops:** grains, potatoes, sugar beets, hops, fruit; hogs, cattle, poultry; forest products. **Natural resources:** brown coal and lignite; small amounts of iron ore, copper and manganese ore, salt. **Major industries:** metal working, food, beverages, fuels, chemicals. **Labor force:** 3.32 mil.; 29.3% industry, 8.9% agriculture, 8.0% construction, 8.2% transport and communication, 45.6% services. **Exports:** $10.1 bil. (f.o.b., 1999 est.); 37% machinery and transport equipment; 30% intermediate manufactured goods, 13% miscellaneous manufactured goods. **Imports:** $11.2 bil. (f.o.b., 1999 est.); 40% machinery and transport equipment; 18% intermediate manufactured goods, 11% fuels. **Major trading partners:** *exports:* 56% EU, 20% Czech Republic, 7% Austria; *imports:* 50% EU, 18% Czech Republic, 10% Russia.

Though the Czech and Slovak languages are similar, the two peoples have always been far apart culturally and historically (much like the Letts and Lithuanians). The ninth-century Moravian Empire has been claimed as heritage by both peoples; but with the Magyar invasion of the Pannonian Plain in the 10th century, the Slovaks passed under Hungarian rule for 1,000 years. When in the 19th century a romantic-nationalist revival occurred, the Slovaks, under the leadership of Ludovit Štúr, decided to use their own language in literature (though some of the most prominent writers in the Czech tongue were of Slovak origin, such as the poet Jan Kollár and the historian P.J. Šafarík). Unlike the Czechs, the Slovaks took no part in the revolutions of 1848. They lacked a native aristocracy; their national leadership came from wealthy peasants, small-town shopkeepers and, above all, their priests.

In the peacemaking at the end of World War I, as the Austro-Hungarian Empire collapsed, the Czech politicians Beneš and Masaryk claimed to speak for the (nonexistent) Czechoslovak nation. They carried the day despite apparent Slovak loyalty to Hungary and even the opposition of Fr. Hlinka's Slovak Populist party to union with the Czechs. The synthetic "nation" of Czechoslovakia was created, governed by a sort of benevolent democratic dictatorship of the Czechs over the other nations. With the Munich crisis of October 1939, Hitler imposed a federal structure giving Slovakia almost complete autonomy in the renamed Czecho-Slovakia; in the following March, when Hitler obliterated Czech independence, an "independent" Slovakia was formed with Hlinka's successor, Magr Tiso, as president.

But under the circumstances independence was illusory. German protection (against Hungarian revisionism) required complete Slovak accord with Reich foreign policy, including declarations of war on Poland (1939) and on the U.S.S.R., the United States, and Great Britain (1941). Domestically, Msgr. Tiso organized a one-party state with anti-Jewish legislation, half unwilling and half unable to resist the expulsion (and eventual extermination) of 60,000 Jews.

The cement for a restored Czechoslovakia after the war was the Communist tyranny imposed in 1948. But the "Velvet Revolution" in 1989 overturned not only Yalta but also St. Germain and Trianon. While the victory over the Communists was won by an alliance of the Czech Civic Forum and the Slovak Public against Violence, the allies soon fell out. As the Czech premier Václav Klaus pushed for free-market "shock therapy," the Slovak premier Vladimír Meciar defended a slower "Slovak way" to capitalism. Economic differences inflamed by ancient Slovak resentment of the Czech majority led to a much-diminished federal government by the spring of 1992. In the summer the split became the "Velvet Divorce."

In July 1992 Slovak deputies to the federal Parliament blocked the reelection of Václav Havel to the presidency, and the Slovak National Council approved, by a vote of 113 to 24, a declaration of sovereignty. In September the two parliaments agreed to the terms. In accord with a two-to-one ratio of the republics' populations, the military and financial assets of Czechoslovakia were divided. By February even plans for a common currency had gone by the board, with only a customs union linking the two parts of the old state.

On Feb. 15, 1993, the Slovak Parliament elected its first president, Michal Kovác, with Meciar, architect of the divorce, remaining as prime minister. Spiraling inflation and high unemployment coupled with a corruption scandal toppled the Meciar government early in 1994, but a coalition government including many former Communists restored him as prime minister later that year. In Sept. 1998, a four-party opposition coalition toppled Meciar's regime. Mikuláš Dzurinda became Prime Minister, heading a government whose principal focus was NATO and E.U. membership, more of a possibility now that Meciar was gone. On May 29, 1999, in Slovakia's first popular rather than parliamentary election of a president, Rudolf Schuster defeated Meciar in a run-off; but in July 2000, the cabinet, with Schuster incapacitated by illness, transferred presidential powers to the prime minister and parliament's speaker. Meciar was arrested in April on charges of fraud and abuse of power.

▶ SLOVENIA
Republic of Slovenia

● **GEOGRAPHY Location:** southeastern Europe. **Boundaries:** Austria to N, Hungary to NE, Croatia to E and S, Adriatic Sea and Italy to W. **Total area:** 7,836 sq. mi. (20,296 sq km). **Coastline:** 20 mi. (32 km). **Comparative area:** Slightly smaller than New Jersey. **Land use:** 54% forest and woodland, 24% meadows and pastures, 12% arable land, 3% permanent crops, 7% other. **Major cities:** (1994 est.) Ljubljana (capital) 269,972; Maribor 103,113; Celje 39,782; Kranj 36,770.

● **PEOPLE Population:** 1,930,132 (2001 est.). **Nationality:** noun—Slovene(s); adjective—Slovenian. **Ethnic groups:** 88% Slovene, 3% Croat, 2% Serb, 1% Bosniak. **Languages:** 91% Slovenian, 6% Serbo-Croatian. **Religions:** 70.8% Catholic, 1% Lutheran, 1% Muslim, 27.2% other.

● GOVERNMENT **Type:** parliamentary democratic republic. **Independence:** June 25, 1991 (from Yugoslavia). **Constitution:** Dec. 23, 1991. **National holiday:** National Statehood Day, June 25. **Heads of Government:** Milan Kŭcan, president of the presidency (four other members) (since Apr. 1990); Janez Drnovsek, prime minister (since Nov. 2000). **Structure:** executive—president, prime minister, cabinet; legislative—unicameral parliament-second chamber has only advisory powers; judicial—Supreme Court, Constitutional Court.

● ECONOMY **Monetary unit:** tolar (SIT). **Budget:** (1997 est.) *income:* $8.11 bil.; *expend.:* $8.32 bil. **GDP:** $22.9 bil., $12,000 per capita (2000 est.). **Chief crops:** potatoes, hops, wheat, sugar beets, corn, grapes; cattle, sheep, poultry. **Natural resources:** lignite coal, lead, zinc, mercury, uranium. **Major industries:** ferrous metallurgy and rolling mill products, aluminum reduction and rolled products, lead and zinc smelting, electronics, trucks, electric power equipment, wood products, textiles. **Labor force:** 857,400. **Exports:** $8.9 bil. (f.o.b., 2000); 45% manufactured goods, 30% machinery and transport equipment, 10% chemicals. **Imports:** $9.9 bil. (f.o.b., 2000); 31% machinery and transport equipment, 31% other manufactured goods, 11% chemicals. **Major trading partners:** *exports:* 31% Germany, 14% Italy, 8% Croatia; *imports:* 21% Germany, 17% Italy, 11% France.

In the sixth century, as part of the great Slavic migrations out of the Vistula and Oder basins, the Slovene people crossed the Carpathians into the Danube plain, penetrating as far as the eastern Alps. In the eighth and ninth centuries the lands they inhabited were subject to Bavarian colonization as part of the Ostmark (Eastern March) of the Carolingian Empire. It is probable, although contested, that most current Austrians are German-speaking Slovenes while the Slovenes are Slavophone Austrians. In any case, for 1,000 years, Slovene history was Austrian history. Thus, like the Croats, Christianity came in its western (Roman Catholic) form.

Lacking their own nobility and even a burgher class for most of their history, the Slovenes tended to look to their priests for leadership, regularly electing them as their representatives to the Reichstag in Vienna (as they did later to the Skupstina in Belgrade after Slovenia became part of Yugoslavia). The 19th-century rise of a national consciousness, associated with literary collections of legend and folklore, took a special turn in the Slovene case because of Napoleon's conquests. His "province of Illyria" was the first association of the Slovenes with Croats and Serbs and his minister of education there was the Slovene Franciscan Valentin Vodnik, so that Slovene "nationalism" had from a start a "Yugoslav" tinge.

In 1815 the Slovenes were again part of the Austrian Empire and were confirmed in the Ausgleich of 1867 as part of the Austrian, not Hungarian, part of the dual Monarchy. As that monarchy collapsed in World War I, it was the Slovene monsignor Anton Korosec who served as president of "The National Council of the Serbs, Croats, and Slovenes" out of which the new state of Yugoslavia emerged. Though the new Yugoslavia was a highly centralized, unitary state with no provision for Slovene autonomy, certain circumstances

brought a kind of privileged position to Slovenia. Their distinct language made Serbian administration a practical impossibility and Serbian struggles against Croat separatism led them to favor the Slovenes to Croatia's north, forestalling any additional separatism there. Moreoover, as a part of the long Austrian connection, the Slovenes were better educated and more industrially advanced than any other part of Yugoslavia.

After the interlude of Hitler's break-up of Yugoslavia (in which Slovenia itself was partitioned between Germany and Italy) Slovenia became a constituent "republic" in Tito's reconstructed Yugoslavia and, despite the enduring enmity provoked by the Communist slaughter of the Slovene Domobranci (Home Guard), again assumed a kind of privileged status in Yugoslavia. After the dictator's death in 1980, the Slovene Socialist Republic took part in the "collegial rule" of Yugoslavia, but with the end of Communist rule in 1990, Slovenia became the first of the republics to secede, in June 1991. After the Slovene militia inflicted a humiliating defeat on the Yugoslav army in July and with E.U. recognition in December, Slovenia became independent for the first time in its history. Forging economic ties with Austria, Hungary, and Italy, it has remained prosperously apart from the debacle to its south.

In Nov. 1996 elections, the center-right coalition calling itself Slovenian Spring captured 45 (of 90) seats in the Parliament with the Liberal Democrats and its allies controlling the other 45. After months of deadlock LD leader Janos Drnovsek was confirmed as prime minister. In 1998 the E.U. invited Slovenia to apply for membership, its per capita GDP already more than 90 percent that of Portugal (the E.U.'s poorest member).

▶ **SOLOMON ISLANDS**
● GEOGRAPHY **Location:** archipelago in South Pacific E of Papua New Guinea. Honiara (Guadalcanal Is.) 9°28′S, 159°57′E. **Boundaries:** South Pacific Ocean to N, E, and S, Solomon Sea to W; nearest neighbor is Santa Cruz Islands to SE. **Total area:** 10,985 sq. mi. (28,450 sq km). **Coastline:** 3,302 mi. (5,313 km). **Comparative area:** slightly smaller than Maryland. **Land use:** 1% arable land; 1% permanent crops; 1% meadows and pastures; 88% forest and woodland; 9% other. **Major cities:** (1990 est.) Honiara (capital) 35,288.

● PEOPLE **Population:** 480,442 (2001 est.). **Nationality:** noun—Solomon Islander(s); adjective—Solomon Islander. **Ethnic groups:** 93% Melanesian, 4% Polynesian, 1.5% Micronesian, 0.8% European, 0.3% Chinese. **Languages:** 120 indigenous languages; Melanesian pidgin in much of country is lingua franca; English spoken by 1-2% of population. **Religions:** 34% Anglican, 19% Roman Catholic, 17% Baptist, 11% United (Methodist/Presbyterian), 11% Seventh-Day Adventist, 5% other Protestant, 4% traditional beliefs.

● GOVERNMENT **Type:** parliamentary democracy. **Independence:** July 7, 1978 (from U.K.). **Constitution:** July 7, 1978. **National holiday:** Independence Day, July 7. **Heads of Government:** Rev. John Inni Lapli, governor-general (since July 1999); Manasseh Sogavare, prime minister (since July 2000). **Structure:** executive—authority in governor-general; unicameral legislature; judiciary.

● ECONOMY **Monetary unit:** Solomon Islands dollar. **Budget:** (1997 est.) *income:* $147 mil.; *expend.:* $168 mil. **GDP:** $900 mil., $2,080 per capita (2000 est.). **Chief crops:** cocoa, beans, coconuts, palm kernels, rice, potatoes, vegetables, fruits; cattle, pigs; timber; fish. **Natural resources:** fish, forests, gold, bauxite, phosphates. **Major industries:** fish (tuna), mining, timber. **Labor force:** 26,842 (1992 est.); 41.5% services, 23.7% agriculture, forestry, and fishing, 21.7% commerce, transport, and finance, 13.1% construction, manufacturing, and mining. **Exports:** $165 mil. (f.o.b., 1999 est.); timber, fish, palm oil, cocoa, copra. **Imports:** $152 mil. (c.i.f., 1998 est.); plant and equipment, manufactured goods, food and live animals, fuel. **Major trading partners:** (1996) *exports:* 35.5% Japan, 47.3% other Asian countries; *imports:* 38.5% Australia, 10.6% Japan, 15% Singapore.

In 1893 Britain established a protectorate over the South Solomon Islands, including the large islands of Guadalcanal, San Cristobal, and Malata; the protectorate was extended to the smaller easterly islands of the chain in 1898. In 1900 Germany relinquished to Great Britain its claim to the North Solomons, including Choiseul and Santa Isabel; Bougainville Island was retained by Germany (see "Papua New Guinea"). The major islands were occupied by Japan in 1942 and retaken by the Allies in a series of battles in 1943.

The Solomon Islands were made self-governing in January 1976 and became an independent nation on July 7, 1978. The economy is based on subsistence agriculture and fishing. Some light manufacturing and craft industries have been established in recent years. Copra, cocoa, palm oil, and lumber are the principal exports. The sale of tuna fishing rights in the surrounding waters has given the nation a favorable balance of payments.

In June 1999 ethnic violence erupted on Guadalcanal against settlers from the island of Malaita, with perhaps 2,000 fleeing over the next year. Then, in June 2000, gunmen from the Malaita Eagle Force (MEF) placed the prime minister under house arrest and captured Honiara airport. On the eve of a parliamentary no-confidence vote, prime minister Ulufa'alu resigned June 14. On July 1 parliament elected opposition leader Mannasseh Sogavare to be prime minister.

▶ **SOMALIA**
● GEOGRAPHY   **Location:** eastern coast of Africa. **Boundaries:** short frontier with Djibouti to NW, Gulf of Aden to N, long coastline on Indian Ocean to E, Kenya to SW, Ethiopia to W. **Total area:** 246,201 sq. mi. (637,660 sq km). **Coastline:** 1,880 mi. (3,025 km). **Comparative area:** slightly smaller than Texas. **Land use:** 2% arable land; negl. % permanent crops; 69% meadows and pastures; 26% forest and woodland; 3% other. **Major cities:** (1987 est.) Mogadishu (capital) 1,000,000; Hargeysa 400,000; Kismayo 200,000; Merca 100,000.
● PEOPLE   **Population:** 7,488,773 (2001 est.). **Nationality:** adjective—Somali. **Ethnic groups:** 85% Somali, rest mainly Bantu; 30,000 Arabs. **Languages:** Somali (official), Arabic, Italian, English. **Religions:** almost entirely Sunni Muslim.
● GOVERNMENT   **Type:** none. **Independence:** July 1, 1960 (from a merger of British Somaliland, which became independent from U.K. June 26, 1960, and Italian Somaliland, which became independent from Italian-administered U.N. trusteeship July 1, 1960, to form the Somali Republic). **Constitution:** Aug. 25, 1979, presidential approval Sept. 23, 1979. **National holiday:** N.A. **Heads of Government:** Abdikassim Salad Hassan, president (since Aug. 2000); Ali Khalif Galaydh, prime minister (since Aug. 2000).
● ECONOMY   **Monetary unit:** Somali shilling.

Budget: N.A. **GDP:** $4.3 bil., $600 per capita (2000 est.). **Chief crops:** bananas, sorghum, corn, mangoes, sugarcane, sesame seeds, beans; cattle, sheep, goats; fishing potential largely unexploited. **Natural resources:** uranium, largely unexploited reserves of iron ore, tin, gypsum, bauxite. **Major industries:** a few small industries, including sugar refining, textiles, petroleum refining. **Labor force:** about 3.7 mil. (1993 est.); very few are skilled laborers; 71% agriculture (pastoral nomadism), 29% industry and services. **Exports:** $106 mil. (f.o.b., 1999 est.); livestock, bananas, hides, fish. **Imports:** $314 mil. (f.o.b., 1999 est.); manufactures, petroleum products, foodstuffs, construction materials. **Major trading partners:** (1996 est.) *exports:* 53% Saudi Arabia, 19% Yemen, 14% UAE; *imports:* 14% Kenya, 24% Djibouti.

Arab trading settlements in Somalia were established in the seventh century and gradually evolved into independent sultanates. Portuguese traders established settlements and forts along the coast during the 15th and 16th centuries.

In the early 19th century, Great Britain arranged through local treaties to use harbors along the Somali coast and gained control over the northern part of the country by 1840. The border between Somalia and Ethiopia was demarcated by a treaty between Great Britain and Ethiopia in 1897. In 1885 the sultan of Zanzibar granted commercial advantages to Italy, and in 1897 and 1908 Italy gained control over southern Somalia.

During the early 20th century, an uprising against British rule was led by Mohamed Abdullah. Abdullah was defeated by the British with help from his local rivals but is now regarded as the father of Somali nationalism.

The Italian invasion of Ethiopia in 1936 gave Italy a dominant position in the Horn of Africa. In the early phases of World War II, Italian troops drove the British from British Somaliland, but a 1940 counterattack led to British occupation of all of Somalia by 1941. After World War II, as discussions of Somalia's future continued, Britain handed over the Ogaden and neighboring territories to Ethiopia.

A U.N. pact of 1949 created an Italian trusteeship in the former Italian Somaliland. Italy terminated its trusteeship and British Somaliland, a U.K. protectorate, achieved independence on June 26, 1960. On July 1 the two entities joined to become Somalia.

The new country was plagued by clan-based rivalries, with the Somali Youth League emerging as a unifying national force. In 1969 Maj. Gen. Mohamed Siad Barre took control, established a ruling Supreme Revolutionary Council, a socialist regime, and relations with the U.S.S.R.

In 1972 Somali forces began border raids into Ethiopia's Ogaden region, peopled largely by ethnic Somalis. The Somali army invaded the Ogaden in 1977. The Soviet Union switched its support to Ethiopia, and with Soviet aid and Cuban troops, Ethiopia drove back the Somali invasion. Over a million refugees fled from Ethiopia into Somalia. The United States was Somalia's principal source of military and economic aid after 1978.

In May 1988, the Somali National Movement captured a number of cities in the northwest and held them against the army. In the summer of 1990, the United Somali Congress began a peaceful antigovernment movement around Mogadishu. In Dec. 1990, this flared into a brief but bloody civil war that resulted in the ouster of Pres. Barre on Jan. 26. The Somali National Congress proclaimed a provisional government, but it was not recognized either by the United Somali Movement, which threatened secession, or the Somali Patriotic Movement, which controlled much of central and southern Somalia.

The continued unrest made it difficult to deliver humanitarian aid despite the efforts of Western governments and nongovernment organizations to do so. An estimated 50,000 people were killed between 1988-90.

Despite U.N. attempts to initiate peace talks, widespread clan and tribal warfare led to a complete breakdown of government authority in 1991-92. A severe drought helped to create over two million refugees, and widespread starvation gripped the nation. Relief workers were prevented by warring armed factions from distributing emergency food supplies. An estimated 300,000 people died in 1991-92.

In Dec. 1992, the United States began Operation Restore Hope, sending 28,000 troops to secure distribution of food and humanitarian aid. But while the U.S. presence deterred the factions from further open hostilities and brought warring leaders to the peace table, once the United States transferred control of the operation to UN peacekeeping forces the fighting resumed. Led by the followers of Gen. Mohammed Farah Aidid, Somali renegades ambushed UN troops and shot down UN helicopters. The U. S. withdrew in March 1994. The last UN troops left Mogadishu a year later.

Clan warfare reignited in March 1995, and in June, Aidid declared himself president for life. However, no other country recognized any Somali government and in Aug. 1996 Aidid was shot and killed. His son, a former U.S. Marine, replaced him but brutal clan violence continued. In Dec. 1997 a tentative peace agreement was reached among the major factions. Peace settled in during 1998, helped by the worst flooding in 40 years that killed 2,000 and made 200,000 homeless. Increased inter-clan fighting in Sept. 1999 threatened to cause crop shortfalls and famine yet again. During the summer of 2000, however, a group of leaders met in Djibouti and formed a new government with Abdikassim Salad Hassan as president. But by March 2001 many warlords met in Ethiopia to form an opposition group and by May new clan warfare erupted.

▶ SOUTH AFRICA
Republic of South Africa
● **GEOGRAPHY Location:** southern Africa. **Boundaries**: Namibia to NW, Botswana, Zimbabwe to N, Mozambique to NE, Swaziland, Indian Ocean to E, Atlantic Ocean to W; Lesotho entirely surrounded by South African territory. **Total area**: 471,444 sq. mi. (1,221,040 sq km). **Coastline**: 1,739 mi. (2,798 km). **Comparative area**: slighlty less than twice the size of Texas. **Land use:** 10% arable land; 1% permanent crops; 67% meadows and pastures; 7% forest and woodland; 15% other; includes 1% irrigated. **Major cities**: (1991 census) Note: Figures are for metropolitan areas: Cape Town (legislative capital) 2,350,157; Pretoria (administrative capital) 1,080,187; Johannesburg 1,916,061; Durban 1,137,378; Port Elizabeth 853,205.
● **PEOPLE   Population:** 43,586,097 (2001 est.). **Nationality:** noun—South African(s); adjective— South African. **Ethnic groups:** 75.2% black, 13.6% white, 2.6% Indian; 8.6% other. **Languages:** Afrikaans, English, Zulu, Xhosa, Sotho, Ndebele, Pedi, Swazi, Tsonga, Venda, Tswana (all official).

Religions: 68% Christian (most whites and about 60% of blacks), 2% Muslim, 1.5% Hindu (60% of Indians), 28.5% traditional and animistic beliefs.
● **GOVERNMENT   Type:** republic. **Independence:** May 31, 1910 (from U.K.). **Constitution:** signed Dec. 10, 1996 by then-President Mandela—being implemented in phases. **National holiday:** Freedom Day, Apr. 27. **Head of Government:** Thabo Mbeki, president (since June 1999). **Structure:** executive—president is head of government and chairman of cabinet; bicameral legislature—National Assembly, National Council of Provinces; judiciary—courts maintain substantial independence from government influence.
● **ECONOMY   Monetary unit:** South African rand. **Budget:** (FY01/02 est.) *income:* $31.1 bil.; *expend.:* $34.4 bil. **GDP:** $369 bil., $8,500 per capita (2000 est.). **Chief crops:** corn, wheat, sugarcane, fruits, vegetables; beef, poultry, mutton, wool, dairy products. **Natural resources:** gold, chromium, antimony, coal, iron ore. **Major industries:** mining (world's largest producer of platinum, gold, chromium), automobile assembly, metalworking. **Labor force:** 17 mil. economically active (1997); 45% services, 30% agriculture, 25% industry and commerce; 30% unemployment (2000 est.). **Exports:** $30.8 bil. (f.o.b, 2000 est.); gold, minerals and metals, food, chemicals. **Imports:** $27.6 bil. (f.o.b, 2000 est.); machinery, chemicals, transport equipment. **Major trading partners:** *exports:* U.K., Italy, Japan, U.S.; *imports:* Germany, U.S., U.K., Japan.

South Africa was originally inhabited by San and related peoples. Bantu peoples, including the Zulu and Xhosa, migrated to the region beginning around the 15th century and established large native kingdoms.

The Portuguese explorer Bartholomew Diaz discovered and named the Cape of Good Hope in 1488. The Dutch East India Company established a permanent settlement at Cape Town in 1652, which served as a supply and transshipment point for Dutch trade to the East Indies. It attracted Protestant settlers from throughout Western Europe. In a series of wars, the Xhosa people were expelled from the area under Dutch rule.

Great Britain began to dispute Dutch control of the Cape of Good Hope region in the late 18th century. To escape increasing British hegemony, in 1836 many Dutch farmers undertook the Great Trek, a northward migration to lands not under the control of any European power. These Afrikaner pioneers later became known as Boers (farmers). They came into conflict with the Zulu kingdom that, under King Shaka, had recently widened its dominion in the South African interior. The Zulus were defeated at the Battle of Blood River in 1838, but they retained substantial power and territory for another 40 years.

Great Britain formally took control of the Cape Colony in 1841 and annexed Natal in 1843. The other two Afrikaner provinces, the Orange Free State and the Transvaal, remained free of British control. But when diamonds were discovered in the Orange Free State in 1867 and gold in the Transvaal in 1886, an influx of British miners and entrepreneurs provoked Boer rebellions.

In 1878 the Zulu Kingdom under its last great king, Cetewayo, rebelled against British rule in Natal. British troops attacked Zululand in 1878 and crushed the rebellion in 1879.

The first Anglo-Boer War of 1881-82 led to total British victory. A renewed uprising led to the Boer War of 1899-1902, which was fought with great ferocity between British regular troops and Afrikaner guerrilla forces. The eventual British victory led to the establishment of British rule in all of South Africa and to the formation of the Union of South Africa in 1910. The union became a self-governing state within the British Empire in 1934.

South African politics became dominated by friction between British and Afrikaner whites; no effective black participation in government was permitted. The United South African party, led by Jan C. Smuts, advocated cooperation between the two groups and led South Africa to join World War II on the Allied side, over the opposition of the pro-Afrikaner Nationalist party.

After the war the Nationalists prevailed and won control of the government in 1948. Racial politics became the country's paramount concern, and the Nationalists introduced the policy of "apartheid" (separateness), under which racial groups were rigidly defined as white, black, Asian (primarily Indian), and colored (mixed ancestry). Each group was to be kept physically separate and develop its own political institutions within defined areas of residence; mixed neighborhoods, intermarriage, and other relations were prohibited. Blacks, in particular, were restricted to "pass laws" that allowed them only temporary access to white areas for employment.

International condemnation of these policies began almost immediately, as India broke relations with South Africa in 1946 over discrimination against Asians, and South Africa became the focus of mounting protest, U.N. resolutions, and international sanctions beginning in the 1960's. On May 31, 1961, South Africa gave up its dominion status and became a republic; its application for membership in the British Commonwealth was withdrawn in the face of strong opposition. The African National Congress (ANC), organized in 1912, was banned by South African authorities. The imprisonment of its leader, Nelson Mandela, provided a focus for black political protest and nationalist aspirations.

Homelands were established under the Promotion of Bantu Self-Government Act of 1959 to further the policy of apartheid by creating separate, but dependent, states for South Africa's blacks. Their form of government was set up in the Black Constitution Act of 1971. The South African government intended that the homelands be regarded as separate nations, but none was ever internationally recognized. The scattered homeland territories comprised only a tiny portion of the total area of South Africa, and tended to include marginal and underdeveloped lands. Residents of the homelands were not considered citizens of South Africa, but rather citizens only of their homeland. As such, they could be considered temporary migrant workers and were therefore ineligible for unemployment and other benefits.

An uprising in Soweto in 1976 was put down by South African police and armed forces with the loss of hundreds of lives, providing a further focus of black protest. Pieter Willem Botha was elected president in 1978, pledging to uphold apartheid while seeking solutions to racial problems. In 1983, a majority of white voters approved a new constitution that provided for limited power sharing by coloreds and Asians. Blacks, however, continued to be excluded.

In the early 1980's, South African troops intervened in civil wars in Angola and Mozambique and were deployed to counteract growing proindependence rebellions in Namibia. Within South Africa, terrorism and uprisings led by the African National Union grew in intensity in 1983-84. A state of emergency was declared in 1985, accompanied by renewed political and economic pressure from abroad. In 1986, Bishop Desmond Tutu, a leading black nationalist, addressed the United Nations and called for renewed sanctions. The Botha government announced an end to the pass laws and promised limited black participation in government. Fighting among black groups in 1986-87 further increased domestic tension.

On May 19, 1986, South African troops conducted raids against ANC bases in Zambia, Zimbabwe, and Botswana. A new national state of emergency was declared as strikes and riots marked the 10th anniversary of the Soweto uprising. The U.S. announced measures designed to end American investment in South Africa.

In early 1989, in anticipation of elections to be held in September, various proposals were put forward for constitutional reform. Most called for expanded power sharing but still within the context of defined racial groups. In July 1989 Pres. Botha had an unprecedented meeting with Nelson Mandela, amid strong suggestions that the white government was seeking an accommodation with the antiapartheid leadership. Botha's successor, F.W. de Klerk, continued that policy.

A series of measures in 1989-90 resulted in the partial dismantling of apartheid, against the vehement opposition of the white right wing, but violence between supporters of the ANC and the Zulu Inkatha movement in Natal led to the declaration of a state of emergency in the province.

Mandela was released from prison in the spring of 1990 and received a rapturous welcome from South Africa's blacks, and later made a triumphant tour of Western Europe and North America. His glory was short-lived, however, as the struggle for supremacy again erupted in murder and violence between Mandela's ANC and Mangosuthu Buthelezi's Inkatha Freedom party throughout the latter part of 1990 and 1991.

At the same time, Pres. de Klerk and Parliament continued to move the nation toward the ending of apartheid by repealing 60 years of segregation in hospitals, libraries, schools, and other public institutions. The government also released other political prisoners and completely repealed the legal foundations of apartheid: the Land Acts of 1913 and 1936, the Group Areas Act, and the Population Registration Act. The United States and other countries began lifting trade sanctions against South Africa in the summer of 1991.

In September 1991, de Klerk, Mandela, and Buthelezi, together with 20 smaller antiapartheid groups, signed an accord to end factional violence. De Klerk proposed a new constitution that would provide universal suffrage and create a two-chamber parliament open to all races. The new constitution abolished the black homelands, consolidating them into one large, multiracial South Africa. In March 1992 a referendum of white voters overwhelmingly approved a government proposal to dismantle all forms of apartheid and to conduct talks with black leaders designed to end white-only rule.

The new constitution was approved on Nov. 17, 1993, by all of the country's major political parties, except for Chief Mangosuthu Buthelezi's Zulu-based Inkatha Freedom party, which withheld its support until a week before the country's first-ever multiracial elections in April. More than 22 million voters cast ballots. An overwhelming majority chose the 75-year-old Mandela to lead a coalition government that included de Klerk's National party and Buthelezi's Inkatha Freedom party.

In May 1996 South Africa completed the transition to democracy when it approved a permanent constitution to replace the transitional one implemented three years earlier. It created a strong central government, an independent judiciary, and a bill of rights with one of the broadest guarantees of liberty in the world. In addition to freedom of speech, movement, and political activity, the South African Bill of Rights protects rights to adequate food, housing, water, education, and health care. The day after the new constitution was approved, de Klerk and his colleagues in the National party quit their cabinet posts, saying that the government was strong enough to handle "robust opposition."

In 1997 there were reminders that troubles remain: in February, riots in Johannesburg suburbs by coloreds against discrimination in favor of blacks and in March, a mass rally (which turned violent) in Johannesburg by still-unsatisfied Zulus. Bitter feelings between the Inkatha Freedom Party and Mandela's ANC surfaced again when the Truth and Reconciliation Committee reported testimony linking Inkatha leaders to assassination squads during the apartheid era.

On June 2, 1999, South Africa held its second post-apartheid elections: the ANC won a gigantic victory, taking 266 seats in the 400-seat Assembly. An "alliance" with the one member of the (Indian) Minority Front gave ANC the 2/3 majority that permits it to amend the Constitution. Thabo Mbeki, who replaced Nelson Mandela as party chief in December, was elected unopposed to be his successor as South Africa's president as well. There has been subsequent slippage in ANC popularity. As inflation heats up strikes grow more frequent. In Dec. 2000 local elections the ANC took only 59 percent and a serious bribery scandal is developing over a 1999 $3.5 billion arms deal. And the government's own report of March 2001 highlighted the gravity of South Africa's AIDS crisis.

South Africa has the continent's most highly developed economy; it is a fully-developed, capitalist industrial-commercial society with manufacturing, mining, agricultural, service, and other sectors. It remains the world's largest producer of gold, a key source of chromium and other strategic metals, and of gem-quality diamonds.

▶ **SPAIN**
Kingdom of Spain
● **GEOGRAPHY Location:** Iberian Peninsula in southwest Europe; Canary Is. off West Africa (28°07'N, 15°26'W). **Boundaries:** Bay of Biscay and France to N; Mediterranean Sea to E; Morocco 19 mi. (30 km) to S, across Strait of Gibraltar; Portugal to W. **Total area:** 194,884 sq. mi. (504,750 sq km). **Coastline:** 3,085 mi. (4,964 km). **Comparative area**: slightly more than twice the size of Oregon. **Land use:** 30% arable land; 9% permanent crops; 21% meadows and pastures; 32% forest and woodland; 8% other; includes 6% irrigated. **Major cities:** (1991 est.) Madrid (capital) 2,984,576; Barcelona 1,653,175; Valencia 777,427; Sevilla (Seville) 683,487; Zaragoza (Saragossa) 614,401.
● **PEOPLE Population:** 40,037,995 (2001 est.). **Nationality:** noun—Spaniard(s); adjective—Spanish. **Ethnic groups:** composite of Mediterranean

and Nordic types. **Languages:** 74% Castilian Spanish; 17% Catalán, 7% Galician, 2% Basque. **Religions:** 99% Roman Catholic.
● **GOVERNMENT Type:** parliamentary monarchy. **Independence:** 1492 (expulsion of Moors and unification). **Constitution:** Dec. 6, 1978, effective Dec. 29, 1978. **National holiday:** Oct. 12. **Heads of Government:** Juan Carlos I, king (since Nov. 1975); José María Aznar, prime minister (since May 1996). **Structure:** executive—king is chief of state, prime minister is head of government; bicameral legislature; judiciary— independent.
● **ECONOMY Monetary unit:** peseta. **Budget:** (2000 est.) *income:* $105 bil.; *expend.:* $109 bil. **GDP:** $720.8 bil., $18,000 per capita (2000 est). **Chief crops:** grains, vegetables, olives, wine grapes, sugar beets, citrus; beef, pork, poultry, dairy prodcts; fish. **Natural resources:** coal, lignite, iron ore, uranium, mercury. **Major industries:** textiles, apparel (including footwear), food and beverages, metals and metal manufacturing. **Labor force:** 17 mil. (2000); 64% services, 28% manufacturing, mining and construction, 8% agriculture. **Exports:** $120.5 bil. (f.o.b., 2000 est.); cars and trucks, manufactured goods, foodstuffs, other consumer goods. **Imports:** $153.9 bil. (f.o.b., 2000 est.); machinery, transport equipment, fuels, semifinished goods, foodstuffs, consumer goods, chemicals. **Major trading partners:** *exports:* 71% EU, 5% U.S.; *imports:* 68% EU, 8% U.S., 5% OPEC.

Prehistoric Spain was populated by Iberians, Basques, and Celts. Its Mediterranean ports were frequented by Phoenician traders, and part of the country was incorporated into the empire of Carthage. Spain fell under the Roman Empire around 200 B.C.; Roman rule ended when the Visigoths invaded and took control of the Iberian Peninsula in the fifth century. The Visigoths adopted Christianity but were in turn conquered by Moors from northwest Africa in A.D. 711. The Berber/Arab civilization of the Moors produced the most elegant and cultivated culture in medieval Europe, and was an important conduit for the reintroduction of Greek science into Europe in the 12th century.

The Christian reconquest of the Iberian Peninsula began almost immediately after the Moors had established themselves and proceeded slowly but steadily over a period of 750 years. The consolidation of the region's small, contentious Christian kingdoms came with the marital alliance of Ferdinand of Aragon and Isabella of Castile in 1469. Granada, the last Moorish outpost in Spain, fell to the forces of Ferdinand and Isabella in 1492, just as Columbus, with Isabella's sponsorship, was discovering the lands that were to become Spain's New World empire. Under the Inquisition, begun in 1478, Jews were expelled from Spain in 1492, and Muslims in 1502.

Under the Habsburg dynasty (1516-1700), Spain reached the zenith of its power and prestige around the year 1600 (despite the 1588 defeat of the Spanish Armada by England), controlling an empire that embraced nearly all of South America (except Brazil), Central America, Mexico, western North America, the Philippines, and smaller territories in Africa and Asia. But Spain's loss of the Netherlands, endless struggles with the French in Europe and the Turks in the Mediterranean, and relentless inflation caused by imports of New World silver—all took their toll. During the 18th century, the Bourbons ruled a declining but still powerful Spain, until Napoleon installed his brother as king in 1808.

After Napoleon's defeat, the Bourbons returned in 1814, but in the 19th century, the loss of the South American colonies, three dynastic wars, and a brief republican interlude after 1868 were all signs of progressive weakness. The crowning blow to Spanish power and prestige was the loss of the Spanish-American War to the United States in 1898, leading to the independence of Cuba and the American takeover of Puerto Rico and the Philippines.

Spain remained neutral in World War I. In 1923 Primo de Rivera established a dictatorship; he was forced out of office by King Alfonso XIII in 1930, but in 1931 the king himself was forced to abdicate. A republic replaced the monarchy. Its volatile mixture of socialism, anticlericalism, and decentralization provoked a right-wing reaction. The government moved to the Right, and in 1934 a miner's strike in Asturia was put down with great bloodshed. A left-wing government was elected in 1936 and deposed in a coup, which led to the terrible Civil War of 1936-39, in which Spain became a battleground for competing world ideologies. The Nationalists, aided by Hitler and Mussolini, defeated the Republicans, aided by Stalin and by leftist volunteers from many countries. Out of the wreckage emerged the dictatorship of the intensely patriotic and Catholic general Francisco Franco.

At the time of the Civil War, Spain was still an agricultural country, with small holdings in the north and great estates in the south. In the Basque country, the mining of iron, copper, and lead provided both exports and a domestic iron and steel industry, which had been the case since the 19th century. In the 20th century, shipbuilding and chemicals were added to the traditional textile industries of the Mediterranean coastal cities. The war largely destroyed this industrial base, which was not rebuilt until the 1950's.

Except for a contingent of troops sent to fight with the German invaders of the Soviet Union, Spain remained precariously neutral during World War II; Franco declined to repay Hitler for his support in the Civil War. But wartime Spain, despite its neutrality, could not muster the resources to undertake national reconstruction.

In postwar Europe, the Franco regime seemed like a remnant of the fascism of the 1930's; Stalin's active hostility led the United Nations to treat Spain as an international pariah. At home Franco represented peace and stability; few Spaniards were willing to risk a return to civil strife by opposing him. Over time the military and Catholic aspects of the regime grew more pronounced, while fascist elements were downplayed. In 1947 the Law of Succession made Spain a monarchy without a king, awaiting the restoration of the throne in the post-Franco era.

The Cold War led to friendlier American relations with Spain and the establishment of American military bases in 1953. U.N. membership followed in 1955. Despite some resultant growth in international trade, Spain's economy lagged, with industrialization barely beginning.

In 1958 Franco turned the direction of the economy over to a group of technocrats, mostly neoliberal members of the Opus Dei lay Catholic order. With U.S. economic and military aid, a growing tourist industry, increased foreign investment, and, especially, freer markets, the economy revived. Older industries like iron, steel, and textiles were rejuvenated, while newer ones, such as chemicals, plastics, automobile assembly, and power plants, were created. Agriculture was increasingly mechanized, and it shifted to export-oriented ranching and horticulture.

In 1967 Franco proclaimed the Organic Law, which, while confirming him as head of state, granted some independence to the Cortes (legislature) and permitted heads of families to vote for some of its delegates. This, along with a relaxation of censorship, softened the growing opposition to the regime among students, labor unions, and regional separatists. In 1969 Prince Juan Carlos was named heir apparent to the Spanish throne.

Franco died in 1975 and was duly succeeded by Juan Carlos. With the new prime minister, Adolfo Suarez, the king worked to liberalize the Franco inheritance: Political parties were legalized; the Cortes was transformed into a bicameral legislature, with both houses elected by universal suffrage; the first elections since 1936 were held; and a new constitution was promulgated—all by 1978.

In 1980, Catalonia and the Basque country were granted home rule, following overwhelming plebiscite victories. In the Basque lands, however, violent terrorist agitation for complete independence continues to this day.

Under the new monarchy, Spain became a full participant in the affairs of Europe. It joined the Council of Europe in 1977, NATO in 1982, and the E.U. in 1986. The Socialist Workers' party controlled both houses of the Cortes from 1982 to 1996, but the party abandoned both Marxism and the traditional labor radicalism of prewar Spain. Instead, it resembled the mainstream Social Democratic parties of Western Europe.

Under Prime Minister Felipe Gonzalez Marquéz, Spain was for a time the economic darling of Europe. GDP grew by an average of almost 5 percent between 1986 and 1990, and business investment jumped by over 10 percent a year. In 1992, the Summer Olympics in Barcelona and the Universal Exposition in Seville focused world attention on two very different parts of Spain.

But the economic growth slowed in 1992, unemployment reached 22 percent, and the conservative Popular party made strong gains in the Cortes in 1993. In 1994, Gonzalez's power eroded when several members of his government were indicted for their involvement with an antiterrorist death squad accused of assassinating 27 Basque separatists during the 1980's. After 10 years of Gonzalez and the Socialists, the May 1996 elections brought the Popular Party and its leader Jose Maria Aznar to governmental power (the Popular Party being supported by, though without a formal coalition with, Basque and Catalan nationalists). In July 1998, 12 officials of the Gonzalez government were sentenced to jail for crimes in the anti-Basque "dirty war," although Gonzalez himself was not implicated.

Spain's economy has quickly reversed itself and annual growth is projected at three percent, so that Spain was able to meet the criteria for membership in the European Monetary Union.

Somewhat unexpectedly the E.T.A., the Basque terrorist organization, declared on September 16, 1998, a "total and indefinite" cease-fire. But despite talks with the Aznar government and the release of "political prisoners," the E.T.A., in late 1999, resumed its war with car-bombings and assassinations. In March 2000, the Popular Party won an unexpected majority (183 of 350 seats) in the Congreso (lower house).

▶ SRI LANKA
Democratic Socialist Republic of Sri Lanka

● **GEOGRAPHY   Location:** Indian Ocean about 50 mi. (80 km) SE of India. Colombo 6°55'N, 79°52'E. **Boundaries:** Palk Strait to N, Bay of Bengal to E, Indian Ocean to S and SW, and Gulf of Mannar to NW. **Total area:** 25,332 sq. mi. (65,610 sq km). **Coastline:** 833 mi. (1,340 km). **Comparative area:** slightly larger than West Virginia. **Land use:** 14% arable land; 15% permanent crops; 7% meadows and pastures; 32% forest and woodland; 32% other. **Major cities:** (1990 est.) Colombo (capital) 615,000; Dehiwala-Mount Lavinia 196,000; Moratuwa 170,000.

● **PEOPLE   Population:** 19,408,635 (2001 est.). **Nationality:** noun—Sri Lankan(s); adjective—Sri Lankan. **Ethnic groups:** 74% Sinhalese; 18% Tamil; 7% Moor; 1% Burgher, Malay, and Veddah. **Languages:** Sinhala (official); Sinhala and Tamil listed as national languages; Sinhala spoken by about 74% of population, Tamil spoken by about 18%; English commonly used in government and spoken by about 10% of population. **Religions:** 70% Buddhist, 15% Hindu, 8% Christian, 7% Muslim.

● **GOVERNMENT   Type:** republic. **Independence:** Feb. 4, 1948 (from U.K.). **Constitution:** Aug. 16, 1978. **National holiday:** Independence Day, Feb. 4. **Heads of Government:** Chandrika Bandaranaike Kumaratunga, president (since Nov. 1994); Ratnasiri Wickremanayake, prime minister (since Aug. 2000). **Structure:** executive—president is head of government and chief of state; unicameral legislature; judiciary—Supreme Court, Court of Appeals.

● **ECONOMY   Monetary unit:** Sri Lankan rupee. **Budget:** (1998) *income:* $2.7 bil.; *expend.:* $4.2 bil. **GDP:** $50.5 bil., $2,600 per capita (1999 est.). **Chief crops:** rice, sugarcane, grains, pulses, oilseed, roots, spices, coconuts, tea, rubber; milk, eggs, hides, meat. **Natural resources:** limestone, graphite, mineral sands, gems, phosphates. **Major industries:** processing of rubber, tea, coconuts, and other agricultural commodities; cement, petroleum refining. **Labor force:** 6.6 mil. (1998 est.); 45% services, 38% agriculture, 17% industry. **Exports:** $4.7 bil. (f.o.b., 1998); tea, textiles and garments, petroleum products, gems, rubber. **Imports:** $5.3 bil. (f.o.b., 1998 est.); machinery and equipment, textiles, petroleum. **Major trading partners:** *exports:* 40% U.S., 11% U.K., 9% Middle East; *imports:* 10% India, 10% Japan, 8% South Korea.

The ancient Veddah inhabitants of Sri Lanka were conquered by Sinhalese migrants from northern India in the sixth century B.C. The island's spices and precious stones and its position on the trans-Indian Ocean trade routes made it well known in ancient times. Sri Lanka was known to the Greeks as Tabrobane and to the Arabs as Serendip. From the third century A.D., Sri Lanka became a major center of Buddhist culture. Despite numerous invasions from India, the island was usually ruled by native kingdoms, but the invasions added a Tamil community to the premodern population.

The Portuguese conquered the coastal areas after 1505 and also introduced Roman Catholicism. The Dutch displaced the Portugese in 1648; the British expelled the Dutch in 1795. Great Britain was the first foreign power to extend its rule over the entire island, with the defeat of the central kingdom of Kandy in 1833. In that year all of Sri Lanka was incorporated into the British Crown colony of Ceylon. Under British rule, tea and rub-

ber plantations were established in the island's interior, and coconut plantations in coastal areas were consolidated under foreign control.

Ceylon became an independent member of the British Commonwealth on Feb. 4, 1948; the Republic of Sri Lanka was proclaimed on May 22, 1972.

Prime Minister W.R.D. Bandaranaike was assassinated on Sept. 25, 1959. His widow, Sirimavo Bandaranaike, leader of the Freedom party, was elected as his successor. In 1962 her government expropriated the property of foreign oil companies. The conservative United National party won a majority in Parliament in 1965 and agreed to pay compensation for the expropriated assets. In May 1970 Mrs. Bandaranaike was again elected prime minister. Leftists secured the nationalization of foreign plantations in the mid-1970's. Mrs. Bandaranaike's party was ousted by the United National party in 1977. Constitutional reform in 1978 aimed at increasing stability by establishing a presidential form of government. Pres. J.R. Jayawardene was elected on Feb. 4, 1978.

But stability has eluded Sri Lanka because of the long struggle between Tamils and the Sinhalese. The political power acquired by the Tamil (mostly Hindu) middle class under the British was deeply resented by the Sinhalese (Buddhist) majority, which after independence slowly eroded Tamil rights. In 1957 the government proposed a Tamil state in a federal union and gave Tamil the status of a national (but not official) language. The pact was not fully implemented, and in the 1970's extremists began agitating for an independent Tamil state. The Tamils' minority status was reaffirmed in the constitution of 1972, the year the oldest insurgent group, the Liberation Tigers or Tamil Tigers, was founded.

In July 1987 Pres. Jayawardene accepted an offer from India's Prime Minister Rajiv Gandhi to supervise a truce in the Jaffna region under which the government pledged to hold a referendum aimed at granting self-rule to Tamil majority areas in the north. The plan failed, however; Indian troops became bogged down in battling the rebels, while the planned referendum was disrupted by fighting between separatists who demanded total independence for Tamil areas.

At the Sri Lankan government's request, India withdrew its forces in March 1989, and the Tamil Tigers agreed to a cease-fire as the government prepared its plan for Tamil-area autonomy. But this cease-fire soon broke down. The assassination of both the opposition political leader in April 1993 and Pres. Ranasinghe Premadasa a month later left the nation in shock, although peaceful legislative elections were held later in May. In parliamentary elections held in 1994, the People's Alliance ended the United National party's 17-year rule. Three months later, Prime Minister Chandrika Bandaranaike Kumaratunga won a landslide (62%) victory in presidential elections, and appointed her 78-year-old mother, Sirimavo Bandaranaike, as prime minister for a third time.

Hours after the new president's inauguration, the Tamil Tigers announced a cease-fire. The truce was formalized in Jan. 1995, but when the government offered a peace plan to divide Sri Lanka into autonomous regions, the Tamil rebels renewed the civil war which by 2000 had cost at least 60,000 lives and displaced at least a million people. Pres. Kumaratunga handily won re-election in Dec. 1999 but on the battlefield the Tamils grew more successful in 2000. A series of failed offensives against the Tigers in 2001 brought a defection from the governing coalition in June and the loss of its majority; to avert a no confidence vote, Pres. Kumaratunga on July 10 suspended parliament for two months and called for a referendum on a new constitution to include greater Tamil autonomy.

▶ SUDAN
Republic of the Sudan

• GEOGRAPHY Location: northeastern Africa. Boundaries: Egypt to N, Red Sea, Eritrea, and Ethiopia to E, Kenya, Uganda, and Zaire to S, Central African Republic, Chad and Libya to W. Total area: 967,495 sq. mi. (2,505,810 sq km). Coastline: 530 mi. (853 km). Comparative area: slightly more than one-quarter the size of the U.S. Land use: 5% arable land; negl. % permanent crops; 46% meadows and pastures; 19% forest and woodland; 30% other; includes 1% irrigated. - Major cities: (1993 census) Khartoum (capital) 924,505; Nyala 1,267,077; Shargen-Nil 879,105; Port Sudan 305,385; Omdurman 228, 778.

• PEOPLE Population: 36,080,373 (2001 est.). Nationality: noun—Sudanese (sing., pl.); adjective—Sudanese. Ethnic groups: 52% black, 39% Arab, 6% Beja, 2% foreigners. Languages: Arabic (official), Nubian, Ta Bedawie, diverse dialects of Nilotic, Nilo-Hamitic, and Sudanic languages, English; program of Arabization in progress. Religions: 70% Sunni Muslim in north, 25% indigenous beliefs, 5% Christian (mostly in south).

• GOVERNMENT Type: transitional, previously military junta. Independence: Jan. 1, 1956 (from Egypt and U.K.). Constitution: Apr. 12, 1973, suspended following coup of Apr. 6, 1985; new constitution implemented June 1998, partially suspended Dec. 12 1999 by President Bashir. National holiday: Independence Day, Jan. 1. Head of Government: Lt. Gen. Omer Hassan Ahmed Al Bashir, president (since Jan. 1993). Structure: executive—president is head of government and chief of state; unicameral legislature; judiciary.

• ECONOMY Monetary unit: Sudanese pound. Budget: (2000 est.) income: $1.2 bil.; expend.: $1.3 bil. GDP: $35.7 bil., $1,000 per capita (2000 est.). Chief crops: cotton, peanuts,sorghum, millet, wheat, gum arabic, sesame; sheep. Natural resources: petroleum, reserves of iron oil, copper, chromium ore, zinc. Major industries: cotton ginning, textiles, cement. Labor force: 11 mil. (1996 est.); 80% agriculture, 10% industry and commerce, 6% government; labor shortages for almost all categories of skilled employment. Exports: $1.7 bil. (f.o.b., 2000 est.); cotton, sesame, livestock/meat. Imports: $1.2 bil. (f.o.b., 2000 est.); foodstuffs, petroleum products, manufactured goods, machinery and equipment, medicines and chemicals, textiles. Major trading partners: exports: 16% Saudi Arabia, 10% Italy, 5% Germany; imports: 14.7% China, 14.7% Libya, 8.9% Saudi Arabia.

The northern Sudan, the ancient land of Nubia, was loosely controlled by Egypt in antiquity and incorporated into the Arab world by the Islamic expansion of the seventh century. The southern Sudan was part of tribal black Africa, under no external control but subject to continual raids by slave traders from the north.

Ottoman Egypt conquered the northern Sudan in 1820-21; British influence in Egypt in the 19th century extended into the Sudan as well. In 1881 Muhammed Ahmed ibn Abdalla, a religious leader known as the Mahdi, united northern and north-central Sudan and led a resistance movement against Anglo-Egyptian control. Khartoum, defended by British general Charles George Gordon, fell in 1885, but the Mahdi died soon thereafter, and his revolt came to an end. An Anglo-Egyptian force under Kitchener regained control in 1898; Anglo-Egyptian joint rule was established in the Sudan in 1899.

Great Britain and Egypt granted self-government and self-determination to the Sudan in 1953, and a Sudanese parliament was seated in 1954. Full independence came in 1956. Gen. Ibrahim Abboud took power in a bloodless coup in 1958 but was forced to resign after riots in 1964. In 1969 a new military coup installed a ruling Revolutionary Command Council and instituted a socialist regime. The council's leader, Gen. Muhammed Nimeiri, became prime minister. Disputes between Marxists and non-Marxists, and between arabized northerners and black southerners, led to continual difficulties. In 1972 Sudan's three black southern provinces were granted local autonomy. Another attempted coup in 1976 was put down by the Nimeiri government, and hundreds of prominent citizens were arrested and executed.

In 1983 attempts by the Nimeiri government to institute Islamic law throughout the Sudan led to riots in the south and the imposition of a nationwide state of emergency in 1984. Popular unrest was exacerbated by drought and famine in 1985. On Apr. 6, 1985, Nimeiri was overthrown in a coup by Gen. Suwar El Dahab. After a brief period of rule by a transitional military council, a civilian cabinet was installed, and free parliamentary elections were held in 1986.

In June 1989 the government was overthrown in a coup led by Lt. Gen. Omar Ahmed al-Bashir. The Bashir government renewed the fight against the southern rebels, and supported the imposition of Islamic law throughout the nation. Within three years the civil service, the military, the judiciary, and the educational system were under the control of Muslims and their political organization, the National Islamic Front headed by Hassan al-Turabi who was also the leader of parliament and the most powerful figure in Sudan. All opposition parties, newspapers, and unions were banned and a stepped up military campaign against christians in the South was launched.

In Oct. 1990, the U.S. government stopped aid to the Sudan, which openly supported Iraq during the Persian Gulf War. In 1991, the U.N. suspended relief efforts to help the estimated 7.1 million Sudanese threatened by famine. In 1993, the U.S. added Sudan to its list of states that sponsor terrorism, and in 1995, the U.N. endorsed an accusation that Sudan was sheltering the Islamic militants who attempted to assassinate Egyptian Pres. Hosni Mubarak. The government in 1995 announced plans to free all political prisoners and to hold national elections in 1996 but an increase in violence against the government by rebels in the south delayed them. In 1997 the government made peace with some rebel factions, promising a referendum on self determination. The main force of the Sudan People's Liberation Army (SPLA), led by John Garang, continued to fight.

Another famine in 1998 brought a ceasefire as aid workers transported huge amounts of food to over 300,000 in the south. In Aug. 1998 the U.S. launched cruise missiles at Khartoum to retaliate for the bombing of its embassies in Kenya and Tanzania and to destroy a chemical weapons plant. Since July 1998, both the SPLA and the Sudanese government have declared a series of cease-fires to permit international food relief, though no settlement seems in sight. The rebels have lost some international support as Uganda, Ethiopia and Eritrea became embroiled in wars of their own. The Sudanese government's "restoration" of a multi-party system at the start of 1999 has thus far been met principally with skepticism by the opposition. Throughout 1999 Pres. Bashir sought some sort of reconciliation with opposition parties and with the southern rebels. In December he struck against Turabi, declaring a state of emergency and dissolving parliament; in Jan. 2000 he dismissed the entire government, replacing it with his supporters.

▶ **SURINAME**
Republic of Suriname
● **GEOGRAPHY   Location:** northeastern coast of South America. **Boundaries:** North Atlantic Ocean to N, French Guiana to E, Brazil to S, Guyana to W. **Total area:** 63,039 sq. mi. (163,270 sq km). **Coastline:** 240 mi. (386 km). **Comparative area:** slightly larger than Georgia. **Land use:** negl. % arable land; negl. % permanent crops; negl. % meadows and pastures; 96% forest and woodland; 4% other; includes negl. % irrigated. **Major cities:** (1993 est.) Paramaribo (capital) 200,970.
● **PEOPLE   Population:** 433,998 (2001 est.). **Nationality:** noun—Surinamer(s); adjective—Surinamese. **Ethnic groups:** 37% Hindustani (East Indian), 31% Creole (black and mixed), 15.3% Javanese, 10.3% Bush black. **Languages:** Dutch (official), English widely spoken, Sranang Tongo (Surinamese, sometimes called Taki-Taki, the native language of Creoles and much of younger population and lingua franca among others), Hindustani, Javanese. **Religions:** 27.4% Hindu, 25.2% Protestant (predominantly Moravian), 22.8% Roman Catholic, 19.6% Muslim.
● **GOVERNMENT   Type:** constitutional democracy. **Constitution:** Sept. 30, 1987. **Independence:** Nov. 25, 1975 (from Netherlands). **National holiday:** Independence Day, Nov. 25. **Heads of Government:** Runaldo Ronald Venetiaan, president (since Aug. 2000); **Structure:** executive—president is chief of state and head of government, Commander in Chief of the National Army maintains significant power; unicameral legislature; judiciary.
● **ECONOMY   Monetary unit:** Surinamese guilder. **Budget:** (1997 est.) *income:* $393 mil.; *expend.:* $403 mil. **GDP:** $1.48 bil., $3,400 per capita (1999 est.). **Chief crops:** rice, bananas, palm oil, timber. **Natural resources:** timber, hydropower potential, fish, shrimp, bauxite. **Major industries:** bauxite mining, alumina and aluminum production, lumbering. **Labor force:** 100,000; agriculture, industry, services; 20% unemployment (1997). **Exports:** $443 mil. (f.o.b., 1999); alumina, aluminum, crude oil, lumber, shrimp and fish, rice, bananas. **Imports:** $525 mil. (f.o.b., 1999); capital equipment, petroleum, foodstuffs, cotton, consumer goods. **Major trading partners:** (1997) *exports:* 19% Norway, 11% Netherlands, 23% U.S.; *imports:* 35% U.S., 15% Netherlands, 12% Trinidad and Tobago.

In the early 17th century, the Dutch and English settled Suriname, which became a Dutch colony in 1667. Except for brief episodes of British rule, Suriname remained under Dutch control until its independence in 1975, shifting toward authoritarian military rule in 1980. The military created its own political party (the February 25 movement)

and banned opposition organizations. The 1988 National Assembly election of Pres. Ramsewak Shankar ended direct military rule, but the restriction of civil liberties continued.

The Shankar government was overthrown in a bloodless coup led by Cmdr. Ivan Graanoogst in 1990, and civilian rule was restored in 1991 although the former military ruler, Col. Desi Bouterse, who led the coup and remains "Advisor of the State," is apparently still the defacto ruler. The current President, Jules Wijdenbosch, agreed in June 1999, after the National Assembly voted "no confidence," to resign—but to remain in office until after the May 2000 National Assembly elections, elections in which the four-party, labor-backed coalition, New Front, carried 33 of the 52 seats, one shy of the 2/3 needed to elect a president alone.

▶ **SWAZILAND**
Kingdom of Swaziland
● **GEOGRAPHY   Location:** landlocked country in southern Africa. **Boundaries:** South Africa to N, SE, S, and W; Mozambique to E. **Total area:** 6,703 sq. mi. (17,360 sq km). **Coastline:** none. **Comparative area:** slightly smaller than New Jersey. **Land use:** 11% arable land; negl. % permanent crops; 62% meadows and pastures; 7% forest and woodland; 20% other. **Major cities:** (1996 census) Mbabane (capital) 38,290; Manzini 18,084.
● **PEOPLE   Population:** 1,104,343 (2001 est.). **Nationality:** noun—Swazi(s); adjective—Swazi. **Ethnic groups:** 97% African, 3% European. **Languages:** English and siSwati (both official); government business conducted in English. **Religions:** 60% Christian, 30% indigenous beliefs.
● **GOVERNMENT   Type:** monarchy; independent member of Commonwealth. **Independence:** Sept. 6, 1968 (from U.K.). **Constitution:** suspended Apr. 12, 1973; new constitution promulgated Oct. 13, 1978, but not yet formally presented to people. **National holiday:** Somhlolo (Independence) Day, Sept. 6. **Heads of Government:** Mswati III, king (since Apr. 1986); Sibusiso Barnabas Dlamini, prime minister (since Aug. 1996). **Structure:** executive—king is hereditary monarch, appoints prime minister; bicameral legislature (lower house-10 members appointed by king, 55 elected; upper house-20 members appointed by king, 10 elected by lower house); judiciary—judges appointed by king.
● **ECONOMY   Monetary unit:** lilangeni. **Budget:** (FY96/97) *income:* $400 mil.; *expend.:* $450 mil. **GDP:** $4.4 bil., $4,000 per capita (2000 est.). **Chief crops:** sugarcane, maize, cotton, maize, tobacco, rice, citrus fruits; cattle, goats, sheep. **Natural resources:** asbestos, coal, clay, cassiterite, hydropower. **Major industries:** mining (coal and asbestos), wood pulp, sugar. **Labor force:** 70% private sector, 30% public sector. **Exports:** $881 mil. (f.o.b., 2000); soft drink concentrates, sugar, wood pulp, cotton yarn. **Imports:** $9.28 mil. (f.o.b., 2000); motor vehicles, machinery, transport equipment, foodstuffs, chemicals, petroleum products. **Major trading partners:** (1998) *exports:* 65% South Africa, 12% EU, Mozambique; *imports:* 84% South Africa, 5% EU, Japan, U.K.

The Kingdom of Swaziland, a landlocked African country, is surrounded on three sides by South Africa and on the fourth by Mozambique. The Swazi are of Bantu origin. They are believed to have migrated in the late 1700's, under their chief Ngwane II, into what is now southeastern Swaziland, finding several different peoples there.

Ngwane II and his successors united these tribal clans by the beginning of the 19th century.

Although British and Boer traders began exploring the area in the 1830's, it was not until gold was discovered in the 1880's that settlers began coming in large numbers. They hoodwinked the illiterate Swazi leadership into signing away their rights to the land. The British and Boer governments agreed in 1894 that the Boers would control Swaziland, but power reverted to Great Britain after they defeated the Boers in the Boer War, which ended in 1902. Not until the 1967 did they give Swaziland authority over its internal affairs. Under the Britishauthored constitution, Swaziland gained its independence in September 1968 as a constitutional monarchy led by King Sobhuza II. He set aside the constitution in 1973 and disbanded the legislature. He ruled the country with the aid of a council of conservative ministers and named a committee to write a new constitution that was supposed to be more in keeping with Swazi traditions. A new legislature was created in 1979. The king died in 1982 and was replaced by his 18-year-old son, who took the name King Mswati III, in 1986.

In 1986 South African forces conducted raids into Swaziland, allegedly in pursuit of African National Congress activists. Swaziland maintains cooperative but cool relations with South Africa and Mozambique.

▶SWEDEN
Kingdom of Sweden
● **GEOGRAPHY Location:** Scandinavian peninsula, northwest Europe. **Boundaries:** Norway to NE and W, Finland to NE, Gulf of Bothnia to E, Baltic Sea to E and S, Skagerrak channel to SW. **Total area:** 173,731 sq. mi. (449,964 sq km). **Coastline:** 2,000 mi. (3,218 km). **Comparative area:** slightly larger than California. **Land use:** 7% arable land; 0% permanent crops; 1% meadows and pastures; 68% forest and woodland; 24% other; includes negl. % irrigated. **Major cities:** (1994 est.) Stockholm (capital) 703,627; Göteburg (Gothenburg) 444,553; Malmö 242,706; Uppsala 181,191; Linköping 130,489.
● **PEOPLE Population:** 8,875,053 (2001 est.). **Nationality:** noun—Swede(s); adjective—Swedish. **Ethnic groups:** homogeneous white population; small Lappish minority; about 12% foreign-born or first-generation immigrants (Finns, Yugoslavs, Danes, Norwegians, Greeks, Turks). **Languages:** Swedish, small Lapp- and Finnish-speaking minorities. **Religions:** 87% Lutheran, Roman Catholic, Orthodox, Baptist, other.
● **GOVERNMENT Type:** constitutional monarchy. **Constitution:** Jan. 1, 1975. **National holiday:** Day of the Swedish Flag, June 6. **Head of Government:** Carl XVI Gustaf, king (since Nov. 1973); Göran Persson, prime minister (since Mar. 1996). **Structure:** executive—prime minister is head of government; unicameral legislature; judiciary.
● **ECONOMY Monetary unit:** Swedish krona. **Budget:** (2000 est.) *income:* $133 bil.; *expend.:* $125.2 bil. **GDP:** $197 bil., $22,200 per capita (2000 est.). **Chief crops:** grain, sugar beets, potatoes; meat, milk. **Natural resources:** zinc, iron ore, lead, copper, silver. **Major industries:** iron and steel, precision equipment (bearings, radio and telephone parts, armaments), wood pulp. **Labor force:** 4.4 mil. (2000); 74% services, 24% industry, 2% agriculture. **Exports:** $95.5 bil. (f.o.b., 2000); 35% machinery, motor vehicles, paper products, pulp and wood, iron and steel products. **Imports:** $80 bil. (f.o.b., 2000); machinery, petroleum and petroleum products, chemicals, motor vehicles, foodstuffs. **Major trading partners:** *exports:* 55% EU, 8% Norway; 9% U.S.; *imports:* 67% EU, 8% Norway, 6% U.S.

The earliest Swedes, the Svear, conquered and merged with their southern neighbors, the Gotar, by the sixth century. Organized into petty kingdoms, Swedes joined with other Norsemen in the Viking raids of the seventh through 11th centuries; in the 10th century, they began to dominate a trading empire that stretched through Russia to the Black Sea. Christianity was introduced by St. Ansgar in 829 but became fully established only in the 12th century, during the reign of Eric IX, who also conquered Finland. For centuries Sweden warred with its neighbors, Norway and Denmark, for control in the north, and it competed with the German Hanseatic League for control of the Baltic trade.

The Swedish and Norwegian monarchies were merged in 1319 by Magnus VII, and in 1397 Queen Margaret effected the Kalmar Union, which united Sweden, Denmark, and Norway under a single monarchy. Sweden resisted Danish rule, and in 1520 King Christian II responded with the massacre of the Swedish nobility at Stockholm. Sweden then rose against the Danish throne and in 1523 enthroned Gustavus Wasa as Gustavus I, founder of the Swedish monarchy. The Wasa dynasty slowly introduced Lutheran Christianity and in 1604 banned Catholicism.

Sweden became a European champion of Protestantism in the 17th century, intervening against the Habsburgs in the Thirty Years' War. Emerging among the victors after 1648, Sweden successfully waged wars with Denmark and Poland, built a great northern empire, and made the Baltic Sea virtually a Swedish lake. But in the late 17th century and into the 18th, the Russians deprived Sweden of the Baltic's eastern shore and, in 1808, of Finland, while the Prussians drove Sweden from the southern Baltic coast.

The kings of Sweden during the 18th century pursued a pointless despotism that weakened the country politically and socially. Sweden joined the European powers against Napoleon in 1813 and was rewarded with Norway in 1814. In 1905 Norway gained its independence, and in Sweden took on its modern boundaries.

Sweden's greatest natural resources are timber, iron ore, and hydroelectric power. The first two were exploited by traditional industries, which supplemented other economic activities (fishing, maritime trade). All provided the basis for industrialization in the 19th and 20th centuries, leading to an economic prosperity that was enhanced by political neutrality.

Sweden's neutrality was largely respected by Hitler during World War II. Through the war Sweden continued to be ruled, under King Gustavus V, by a national coalition government lasting until 1945. Sweden's gross national product (GNP) rose by 20 percent during the war years.

The Social Democratic party dominated the Swedish government after 1936, and again after 1945, lasting until 1976 under the leadership of Tage Erlander. Sweden, like its Scandinavian neighbors, constructed an economy based on free enterprise, public ownership of utilities, exports, social welfare, and high taxes.

A U.N. charter member, Sweden accepted Marshall Plan aid and joined the Council of Europe in 1948. Sweden's plan for a Nordic Defense Alliance failed when Norway and Denmark joined NATO (Sweden refused to join the North Atlantic pact), but the political and economic Nordic Council (Sweden, Norway, Denmark, Iceland, and, after 1956, Finland) was formed in 1952-53. This consultative body backed the establishment of SAS as the joint national airline of the first three members; coordination of the welfare programs of member states; and abolition of passport controls and controls on the migration of labor within Scandinavia.

Erlander retired as prime minister in 1969 and was succeeded by Olaf Palme, who pursued a more rigid socialist program than his predecessor. He advocated legislation to make incomes more equal, provoking some labor unrest. When King Gustav VI Adolf died in 1973 the Palme government passed the 1974 Instrument of Government Act, divesting the king of his role as commander in chief of the armed forces and of his right to appoint prime ministers.

Economic growth came to a virtual halt in the 1970's; lacking petroleum and gas resources, Sweden's oil import costs rose 700 percent between 1972 and 1979. Consumer prices rose sharply, and labor unrest grew. The Social Democrats were turned out of office by a conservative coalition in 1976 but returned with a minority cabinet in 1982.

Palme was assassinated in 1986, and he was succeeded by Ingvar Carlsson, whose Social Democratic program focused on a scheme whereby business profits are taxed to fund labor union purchases of sufficient stock to gain labor ownership of private enterprise.

September 1991 elections unseated Carlsson and the Social Democrats, who had ruled Sweden for 53 of the last 59 years. A coalition government of four conservative parties pledged to cut taxes and phase out some welfare programs.

But in elections held in Sept. 1994, Carlsson returned to power as voters expressed dissatisfaction with inflation, unemployment, and an enormous public debt, all of which spiraled under the conservative coalition. The Social Democrats fell 13 votes short of a majority in Parliament, however, forcing them to seek the support of the right-centrist Liberal party in a coalition government. On Jan. 1, 1995, Sweden entered the European Union. In March 1996, Finance Minister Göran Persson succeeded Carlsson, who resigned as prime minister for personal reasons. In 1998 Sweden announced it would not join the European Monetary Union, and in Sept. elections Persson's Government won enough votes to keep power by pledging more money for social welfare services. More significant for Sweden's future was the 1999 completion of the 10-mile, $2.6 billion bridge over (and under) the Baltic, linking Copenhagen with Malmoe (Sweden's third largest city). After almost 500 years, the Lutheran Church was disestablished on Dec. 17, 1999.

▶ **SWITZERLAND**
Swiss Confederation
● **GEOGRAPHY   Location:** landlocked country in central Europe. **Boundaries:** Germany to N, Austria to E, Italy to S, and France to W. **Total area:** 15,942 sq. mi. (41,290 sq km). **Coastline:** none. **Comparative area:** slightly less than twice the size of New Jersey. **Land use:** 10% arable land; 2% permanent crops; 28% meadows and pastures; 32%

forest and woodland; 28% other. **Major cities:** (1994 est.) Berne (Bern, capital) 128,422; Zürich 342,872; Basel 175,561; Genève (Geneva or Genf) 172,737; Lausanne 116,795.
● **PEOPLE   Population:** 7,283,274 (2001 est.). **Nationality:** noun—Swiss (sing., pl.); adjective—Swiss. **Ethnic groups:** 65% German, 18% French, 10% Italian, 1% Romansch, 6% other. **Languages:** 63.7% German, 19.2% French, 7.6% Italian (all official); 0.6% Romansch, 8.9% other. **Religions:** 46.1% Catholic, 40% Protestant.
● **GOVERNMENT   Type:** federal republic. **Independence:** Aug. 1, 1291. **Constitution:** May 29, 1874. **National holiday:** Anniversary of the Founding of the Swiss Confederation, Aug. 1. **Head of Government:** Moritz Leuenberger, president (since Jan. 2001). **Structure:** executive—president is head of government and chief of state; bicameral legislature—National Council, Council of States; judiciary left chiefly to cantons.
● **ECONOMY   Monetary unit:** Swiss franc. **Budget:** (1998 est.) *income:* $32.66 bil.; *expend.:* $34.89 bil. **GDP:** $207 bil., $28,600 per capita (2000 est.). **Chief crops:** grains, fruits, vegetables; meat, eggs. **Natural resources:** hydropower potential, timber, salt. **Major industries:** machinery, chemicals, watches. **Labor force:** 3.9 mil.; 964,000 foreign workers, mostly Italian; 69.1% services, 26.3% industry, 4.6% agriculture. **Exports:** $91.3 bil. (f.o.b., 2000); machinery, chemicals, metals, watches, agricultural products. **Imports:** $91.6 bil. (f.o.b., 2000); machinery, chemicals, vehicles, metals, agricultural products. **Major trading partners:** (1998 est.) *exports:* 65.8% EU, 12.4% U.S., 4% Japan; *imports:* 77.7% EU, 7.1% U.S. 2.9% Japan.

Switzerland, the Roman province of Helvetia, began to assume its modern form in A.D. 1291, when three independent cantons formed a defensive league against the expansion of Habsburg power. The Swiss League grew to eight cantons in 1353, 13 in 1513, 22 in 1815. The league continues to evolve; it reached its present size of 20 cantons and six half-cantons with the creation of the Canton of Jura in 1979.

The Treaty of Westphalia, which ended the Thirty Years' War in 1648, gave international recognition to the independence of Switzerland from the Holy Roman Empire. Switzerland became a client state of France in the Napoleonic period; the European powers guaranteed Swiss independence and neutrality at the Congress of Vienna in 1815. Constitutional changes in 1848 and 1874 somewhat increased the power of the central government, but the individual cantons cling stubbornly to their independence within the confederation. This policy has helped ensure stability within a multilingual nation.

The Swiss government consists of an upper house, representing the cantons, and a lower house that is directly elected. No executive can veto, nor court disallow, a bill of the Swiss legislature. Executive power is vested in a seven-member committee chosen by the legislature, with a rotating presidency.

Swiss neutrality is defended by more than simply international guarantees. Switzerland is a highly militarized society; every male is required to serve in the citizen's militia until age 47, keeping an assault rifle and other equipment ready at home. The armed forces are equipped with modern weapons, and military spending amounts to 30 percent of the Swiss federal budget.

Landlocked, with little fertile farmland and lacking both natural resources and a colonial empire, Switzerland was traditionally one of Europe's poorest countries. Until the 19th century, its principal export was mercenaries who supplied military services to any European sovereign who could pay for them. (The pope's Swiss Guard is a remnant of this tradition.) With the spread in the late 18th century of the Romantic movement, Europeans learned to appreciate the Alpine scenery, and a tourist industry was born. It was expanded in the 20th century with the development of Alpine skiing. Tourism remains a conspicuous, though minor, part of the Swiss economy.

Swiss prosperity came in the 20th century with specialized manufacturing and free trade within the world economy. By 1940 half of the population was engaged in manufacturing, producing products requiring high degrees of skill: processed foods, watches, electrical machinery, engines, fine textiles, and the like.

Neutral in both world wars, Switzerland required no postwar recovery in the 1940's. It capitalized on the restructuring of European politics and economics to expand into the service sector, which now employs half of the work force (while manufacturing has declined to about 40 percent). Tourism, banking, insurance, and clerical/bureaucratic services to the many international organizations with headquarters in Switzerland help give the nation one of Europe's highest standards of living. Under pressure from the EC and the United States, Switzerland agreed to phase out its famous "Form B" (i.e., secret bank accounts).

In the postwar period, Switzerland has enjoyed both political and economic stability. A cautious approach to economic development led to annual growth rates of over 6 percent in the 1950's and early 1960's, declining to 2 percent in the 1970's; the world economic boom of the 1980's produced higher growth rates. In general the economy has avoided inflation, and the stability of the Swiss franc has been maintained.

Referenda at this time brought overwhelming rejection of U.N. membership (it currently has observer status), and support for restrictive immigration legislation. The most significant political changes were the gradual extension of women's right to vote and the 1993 approval of casino gambling to fund social security.

In 1996 and 1997 the Swiss government, responding to international pressures, appointed a panel to examine what funds in Swiss banks the Nazis might have stolen or that Holocaust victims (or their families) might have deposited and were unable to retrieve. A less than rigorous accounting, however, resulted in several lawsuits which were settled in Aug. 1998 with the Swiss banks reluctantly agreeing to pay $1.2 bil. On Dec. 9, 1998, Social Democrat Ruth Dreifuss became Switzerland's first female and first Jewish president. A June 1999 referendum (carried 70 percent–30 percent) to restrict refugee asylum prefigured a very strong showing in the October National Council elections by the nativist Swiss People's Party which had the largest total vote and won the second largest number of seats.

Recent referenda reflect divisions in Swiss minds over the country's identity and her role in the new Europe. In 2000, 64 percent refused to set a limit (18%) on the number of foreigners residing in Switzerland, and 74 percent refused to begin negotiations for E.U. membership. Yet in July, by a slender margin (50.9 percent), voters approved the arming of Swiss troops serving under international auspices as well as joint training of Swiss soldiers with foreign armies.

▶ SYRIA
Syrian Arab Republic

● **GEOGRAPHY   Location:** western Asia. **Boundaries:** Turkey to N, Iraq to E, Jordan to S, Lebanon and Israel to SW, Mediterranean Sea to W. **Total area:** 71,498 sq. mi. (185,180 sq km). **Coastline:** 193 mi. (193 km). **Comparative area:** slightly larger than North Dakota. **Land use:** 28% arable land; 4% permanent crops; 43% meadows and pastures; 3% forest and woodland; 22% other. - **Major cities:** (1994 est.) Damascus (capital) 1,444,138; Aleppo 1,542,000; Homs 558,000; Latakia 303,000; Hama 273,000.

● **PEOPLE   Population:** 16,728,808 (2001 est.). **Nationality:** noun—Syrian(s); adjective—Syrian. **Ethnic groups:** 90.3% Arab, 9.7% Kurds, Armenians, and other. **Languages:** Arabic (official), Kurdish, Armenian, Aramaic, Circassian, French. **Religions:** 74% Sunni Muslim; 16% Alawite, Druze, and other Muslim sects; 10% Christian.

● **GOVERNMENT   Type:** republic under military regime since Mar. 1963. **Independence:** Apr. 17, 1946 (from League of Nations Mandate under French administration). **Constitution:** Mar. 13, 1973. **National holiday:** National Day, Apr. 17. **Heads of Government:** Dr. Bashar Al-Assad, president (since July 2000); Dr. Mohammad Mostafa Miro, prime minister (since Mar. 2000). **Structure:** executive powers vested in president and Council of Ministers; unicameral legislature (People's Council); judiciary.

● **ECONOMY   Monetary unit:** Syrian pound. **Budget:** (2000 est.) *income:* $2.25 bil.; *expend.:* $5.4 bil. **GDP:** $50.9 bil., $3,100 per capita (2000 est.). **Chief crops:** cotton, wheat, barley, lentils; beef, lamb, eggs, poultry, milk. **Natural resources:** crude oil, phosphates, chrome and manganese ores, asphalt, iron ore. **Major industries:** petroleum, textiles, food processing, beverages. **Labor force:** 4.7 mil. (1998 est.); 40% services, 40% agriculture, 20% industry. **Exports:** $4.8 bil. (f.o.b., 2000 est.); 65% petroleum, 10% textiles, 9% food and live animals. **Imports:** $3.5 bil. (f.o.b., 2000 est.); 23% machinery, 20% foodstuffs/animals, 15% metal and metal products, 10% textiles, 10% chemicals. **Major trading partners:** (1998 est.) *exports:* 12% Italy, 21% Germany, 10% France, 8% Turkey; *imports:* 11% France, 8% Italy, 7% Germany, 5% Turkey.

The home of some of the world's most ancient centers of civilization, Syria was successively part of the Hittite, Assyrian, and Persian empires. At various times it was conquered by the Babylonians and the Egyptians. From about 1250 B.C., the coastal cities came under Phoenician rule. Alexander the Great brought Syria into the Hellenic world with his conquests in 332 B.C. After the fall of the Alexandrian empire, Syria came under the domain of the Seleucid empire but was constantly threatened by the Hellenic kingdom of Egypt, based in Alexandria.

In the classical period, Syria embraced a much larger territory than that of the present Syrian nation; it included the entire Levant and parts of present-day Turkey, Iraq, Iran, and Jordan. Greater Syria was conquered by Rome in 63 B.C. Under Roman rule the oasis region of Palmyra grew into a powerful semiautonomous kingdom. With the division of the Roman Empire in the fourth century A.D., Syria became part of the Eastern Roman (Byzantine) Empire. Throughout the Roman and Byzantine periods, the country was an important center of Christianity.

Syria was one of the first areas conquered when Islam began expansion from Arabia; Islamic rule was established by 636. From 661 to 751, Damascus was the center of the Caliphate, the ruling body of the Islamic world. By the late 11th century, the Seljuk Turks had conquered Syria. The large Syrian Christian population welcomed the European Crusaders as liberators from the Turks, but both Christians and Turks were defeated by the Arab general Saladin in the late 12th century. Saladin's rule was followed by that of the Mamluk empire of Egypt. During the Mamluk period, Mongol armies twice invaded Syria, in the mid-13th century and at the turn of the 15th century.

An Ottoman army defeated the Mamluks in Syria in 1516, making Syria part of the Ottoman Empire. In the 18th century, France declared itself the protector of Syria's Christian community against Ottoman abuses. Napoleon invaded Syria in 1799 but withdrew after a brief occupation. In the 1830's Egyptian troops occupied Syria but were forced to withdraw under pressure from the European powers.

Syrian nationalist aspirations emerged as the Ottoman Empire began to crumble before World War I. During the war the British encouraged Syrians to rebel against Turkish rule. After World War I, France governed both Syria and Lebanon under a League of Nations mandate. Under French rule, the region was divided into small territorial states along communal lines; Lebanon became independent in 1926. After prolonged negotiations much of Syria was organized into a semi-autonomous state in 1930-32.

In June 1940 the French administration in Syria declared its loyalty to the Vichy government. British and Free French forces invaded in June 1941, and an independent Syrian republic was established in September 1941. Separately administered territories were consolidated with the republic over the next two years, and full independence was declared on Jan. 1, 1944; foreign troops did not withdraw, however, until April 1946.

Syria became a founding member of the Arab League and participated in the first Arab-Israeli War in 1948. An armistice with Israel was signed in July 1949. Severe political instability marked the early years of Syrian independence; the government was overthrown by military coups three times in 1949 alone.

Most of Syria's Jews emigrated to Israel before or during 1948, and much of its once-substantial Christian population has emigrated also. Syrian politics remain dominated by communal concerns, however; the Arab majority is divided into Sunni, Shiite, Alawite, and Druze communities.

Syria and Egypt merged as the United Arab Republic in February 1958; Syria seceded from the federation on Sept. 30, 1961. In Mar. 1963 a military coup established the pan-Arab Socialist Baath party in power; all other political parties were abolished. The Baath party leadership is dominated by the minority Alawite community. Pres. Hafez al-Assad took power on Feb. 22, 1971.

In the 1967 Arab-Israeli War (the Six Day War), Israel seized and held the Golan Heights region of Syria, from which Syria had long shelled Israeli communities and military installations. The Golan Heights have since been incorporated into Israeli territory.

Syrian troops aided Palestinian forces fighting government troops in Jordan in September 1970. After the expulsion of Palestinian forces from Jordan in July 1971, Syria broke off relations with Jordan; relations were restored in 1975.

On Oct. 6, 1973, Syrian and Egyptian forces attacked Israel, touching off the third Arab-Israeli War, the Yom Kippur War. A cease-fire took effect on Oct. 24; Syria failed to regain territory lost to Israel in 1967. Following the 1973 war, Syria became a major recipient of economic aid from the Arab oil states and of military equipment from the Soviet Union.

In 1976 Syrian troops entered Lebanon in an attempt to mediate a civil war there and became enmeshed in that conflict. Major fighting between Syrian troops and Lebanese Christian militiamen broke out in April 1981. On June 6, 1982, Israeli troops invaded Lebanon and engaged Syrian troops in a five-day war in the Bekaa Valley. Following serious losses of aircraft and troops, Syria agreed to a cease-fire with Israel on June 11. Syrian troops continue to occupy parts of Lebanon.

An attempted coup, in February 1982, by the Muslim Brotherhood, led to serious fighting within Syria, but the rebellion was put down; casualties topped 5,000 on both sides.

From the time of the 1973 Arab-Israeli War (the Yom Kippur War), Syria consistently adopted a radical stance in Middle Eastern politics, rejecting the 1979 Egyptian-Israeli accord and all other attempts at Arab-Israeli reconciliation. Supporting radical movements within the Palestine Liberation Organization, Syria aided Palestinian militants in driving Yasir Arafat's centrist faction of the PLO from its headquarters in Tripoli in 1983. The government was implicated in various acts of international terrorism in support of Palestinian, Libyan, and Iranian causes.

Syria played a major role in the Lebanese peace process and accommodating a peace settlement between rival Shiite militias. Syria also took part in the anti-Iraq coalition in 1990-91, sending 20,000 troops to Saudi Arabia, as well as mobilizing forces on its common border with Iraq. Syria in 1994 made serious efforts toward achieving peace in the Middle East, including an offer to normalize relations in exchange for a return of the Golan Heights. But talks between the two countries were suspended after several bombings by the militant Islamic group Hamas.

In Oct. 1998, Syria reached an accord with Turkey; with 10,000 Turkish troops massed on Syria's border, Syria agreed to cease supporting Kurdish rebels. The legislative elections in Dec. 1998 contained no surprises: Assad's National Progressive Front won all 167 seats that they chose to contest. Then, in Feb. 1999, Assad himself won, with 99.95 percent approval in his sole candidacy, election to a fifth seven-year term as president. A cabinet shake-up in March 2000 produced 22 new members among the 36 under new premier Mohammed Mustafa Zubi just three months before the death of Assad. After his 30 years of rule, the government backed his son (and armed forces commander) Bashar al-Assad, 34.

▶ **TAIWAN**
● **GEOGRAPHY   Location:** one large and several smaller islands about 100 mi. (160 km) off SE coast of mainland China. Taipei 25°03′N, 121°30′E. **Boundaries:** East China Sea to N, Pacific Ocean to E, Bashi Channel to S, and Formosa Strait to W; separated from mainland by Formosa Strait. **Total area:** 13,892 sq. mi. (35,980 sq km).

Coastline: 900 mi. (1,448 km). **Comparative area:** slightly smaller than Maryland. **Land use:** 24% arable land; 1% permanent crops; 5% meadows and pastures; 55% forest and woodland; 15% other; includes 14% irrigated. **Major cities:** (1992 est.) Taipei (capital) 2,696,073; Kaohsiung 1,405,909; Taichung 794,960; Tainan 694,630; Panchiao 543,982.

● **PEOPLE   Population:** 22,370,461 (2001 est.). **Nationality:** noun—Chinese (sing., pl.); adjective—Chinese. **Ethnic groups:** 84% Taiwanese, 14% mainland Chinese, 2% aborigine. **Languages:** Mandarin Chinese (official); Taiwanese and Hakka dialects also used. **Religions:** 93% mixture of Buddhist, Confucian, and Taoist; 4.5% Christian, 2.5% other.

● **GOVERNMENT   Type:** multi-party democratic regime headed by popularly elected president. **Constitution:** Jan. 1, 1947, amended 1992, 1994, and 1997. **National holiday:** National Day, Oct. 10. **Heads of Government:** Chen Shui-bian, president (since March 2000); Chang Chunsiung, premier (since Oct. 2000). **Structure:** executive—president appoints premier; two-chamber legislature—Legislative Yuan, National Assembly; judiciary—Judicial Yuan.

● **ECONOMY   Monetary unit:** New Taiwan dollar. **Budget:** (2001 est.) *income:* $42.74 bil.; *expend.:* $48.8 bil. **GDP:** $386 bil., $17,400 per capita (2000 est.). **Chief crops:** rice, wheat, corn, soybeans, vegetables, fruit, tea; pigs, poultry, beef, milk; fish. **Natural resources:** small deposits of coal, natural gas, limestone, marble, and asbestos. **Major industries:** electronics, petroleum refining, textiles, clothing, chemicals. **Labor force:** 9.8 mil. (2000 est.); 37% industry and commerce, 55% services, 8% agriculture. **Exports:** $148.38 bil. (f.o.b., 2000); 52% electrical equipment and machinery, metals, textiles, plastics, chemicals, electronic products. **Imports:** $140.01 bil. (c.i.f., 2000); 51% machinery and electrical equipment, electronic products, minerals, precision instruments. **Major trading partners:** (2000) *exports:* 23.5% U.S., 21.1% Hong Kong, 16% Europe; *imports:* 27% Japan, 18% U.S., 13.6% Europe.

Nominally part of the Chinese empire since the Song dynasty (960-1279), Taiwan was inhabited only by non-Chinese aboriginals before the 17th century. Around 1600 the Portuguese established a trading station on Taiwan; they named the island Ilha Formosa. In 1620 the Dutch built Fort Zeelandia near present-day Tainan, controlling the island until they were driven out by the Chinese pirate-patriot Koxinga (Zheng Chenggong). Remnants of the overthrown Ming dynasty (1368-1644) held out on the island until 1683, when it came under the sway of the Qing dynasty (1644-1911). Thereafter, substantial numbers of farmers from Fujian Province migrated to the fertile western lowlands of the island, driving the aboriginals into the central mountains. The Qing dynasty administered Taiwan as a semiautonomous subprovince of Fujian Province.

Following China's defeat by Japan in the Sino-Japanese War of 1894-95, Taiwan was ceded to Japan as a colony. The Japanese built roads and railroads to exploit Taiwan's resources of rice, timber, and minerals. In 1945, after Japan's defeat in World War II, Taiwan was returned to China.

As the Chinese civil war turned against the Nationalist party of Chiang Kai-shek (see "China"), Nationalist troops began to prepare Taiwan as a base for a retreat from the mainland.

In 1947 Nationalist agents executed several thousand students and others suspected of favoring Taiwan's independence from China. In 1949 approximately two million Nationalist soldiers, government officials, and civilian sympathizers retreated to Taiwan. The relocated Republic of China (ROC) continued to claim to be the legitimate government of all of China, now under Communist control. In addition to Taiwan proper, the Nationalists occupied the P'eng-hu Islands in the Taiwan Straits and the small islands of Quemoy and Matsu just off the coast of Fujian. Recovery of the mainland became a cornerstone of ROC policy, but no serious attempt was made to do so. U.S. policy in the Taiwan Straits was to defend Taiwan against Communist attack but also to keep the two rival governments of China separated.

A successful program of land reform in the early 1950's led to the creation of surplus capital, which fueled the development of an industrial base on the island. Foreign investment from Japan and the United States, and American military and economic aid, also enhanced economic development. By the early 1970's, the island had developed an export-oriented economy, producing textiles, cement, plastics, assembled electronic appliances, and other manufactured goods.

Chiang Kai-shek, president of the Republic of China since 1928, died in 1975 and was succeeded by his son, Chiang Ching-kuo. Under both father and son, the Nationalist party (Kuomintang, or KMT) controlled both the ROC and the Taiwan Provincial governments; mainland refugees and their descendants (15% of the population) dominated senior government posts and the military officer corps. Native Taiwanese played the leading role in agriculture, industry, and in local and county governments.

In 1971 China's seat in the United Nations was taken away from the ROC and awarded to the People's Republic of China, leaving Taiwan in international diplomatic limbo. On Jan. 1, 1979, the United States withdrew its recognition of the ROC and inaugurated mutual diplomatic relations with the People's Republic. Under the Taiwan Relations Act of 1979, nominally nongovernmental relations were maintained between the U.S. and Taiwan through the American Institute in Taipei and Taiwan's Coordination Council for North American Affairs in Washington, D.C. Taiwan's economy has continued to be one of the world's most vigorous; Taiwan enjoys a substantial favorable balance of trade with the U.S.

In 1986 Pres. Chiang Ching-kuo began a policy of liberalization; in 1987, he abolished martial law and allowed non-KMT political parties to function legally. Some barriers to travel and communication with the mainland by ROC citizens were eased, but Taiwan's government continued to rebuff all calls from the mainland for direct contacts and discussions of reunification. Chiang Ching-kuo died in Jan. 1988 and was succeeded by his vice president, Lee Teng-hui. In March 1990, Lee was overwhelmingly reelected by the National Assembly in the first election for the office.

The ruling KMT maintained its hold on power in legislative elections on Dec. 19, 1992, but the opposition Democratic Progressive party scored a stunning success, tripling its number of legislative seats and bringing the issue of Taiwanese independence to the forefront. Factional rivalry deepened in the KMT, with Pres. Lee's Wisdom Coalition challenged by the New Kuomintang Alliance of Prime Minister (and former general) Hau Pei-tsun. Hau reluctantly resigned on Feb. 3, 1993, to take responsibility for the electoral fiasco, but his faction, with military backing, continued to pose a threat to Pres. Lee's power.

During the campaign for Taiwan's presidential election in March, 1996, China held aggressive military exercises off the coast of Taiwan in an effort to influence the voting; the United States sent two aircraft carriers to the area. In a rebuke to Beijing, President Lee, who had campaigned for a more visible international role for Taiwan, was resoundingly re-elected; he was also re-elected as the head of the KMT in August, 1997. Since then, talks for cross-straits cooperation between Taiwan and the PRC have been inconclusive, and the ruling KMT saw its power eroded in local elections as voters protest against corruption and economic stagnation related to the Asia-wide economic crises of 1997-98. The KMT rebounded strongly in 1998 elections but tensions rose in 1999 with mainland China, when President Lee's expressed interest in Taiwan's being included in a proposed anti-missile defense of its Asian allies (the "last straw" to Beijing). Later, Lee announced that Taiwan would conduct its relations with China on a "state-to-state" basis, meaning Taiwan was an independent state—to Beijing, an "extremely dangerous step". In March 2000, the KMT was peacefully voted out of power after 50 years. Chen Shui-Bian of the Democratic-Progressive Party was elected president.

▶ **TAJIKISTAN**
Republic of Tajikistan
● **GEOGRAPHY   Location:** southeast central Asia. **Boundaries:** Kyrgyzstan to NE, China to E, Afghanistan to S and SW, Uzbekistan to NW and N. **Total area:** 55,251 sq. mi. (143,100 sq km). **Coastline:** none. **Comparative area:** slightly smaller than Wisconsin. **Land use:** 6% arable land; 25% permanent pasture; 4% forest and woodland; 65% other. **Major cities:** (1990 est.) Dushanbe (Stalinabad 1929-61) (capital) 602,000; Khodzhent (formerly Leninabad), 163,000 (1989). ● **PEOPLE   Population:** 6,578,681 (2001 est.). **Nationality:** noun—Tajikstani(s); adjective—Tajikstani. **Ethnic groups:** 64.9% Tajik, 25% Uzbek, 3.5% Russian, 6.6% other. **Languages:** Tajik (official) is closely related to Farsi (Persian) and was written in Cyrillic script since 1940; Russian widely used in government and business. **Religions:** 80% Sunni Muslim, 5% Shi'a Muslim. ● **GOVERNMENT   Type:** republic. **Independence:** Sept. 9, 1991 (from Soviet Union). **Constitution:** Nov. 6, 1994. **National holiday:** National Day, Sept. 9. **Heads of Government:** Emomali Rakhmonov; head of state (since Nov. 1994); Akil Akilov, prime minister (since Dec. 1999). **Structure:** executive—popularly-elected president appoints prime minister and cabinet; bicameral legislature; judiciary. ● **ECONOMY   Monetary unit:** Tajikistani ruble. **Budget:** (2000 est.) *income:* $146 mil.; *expend.:* $196 mil. **GDP:** $7.3 bil., $1,140 per capita (2000 est.). **Chief crops:** cotton, vegetables, fruit, grain, grapes; cattle, sheep, goats. **Natural resources:** significant hydropower potential, some petroleum, uranium, mercury, brown coal. **Major industries:** mineral processing, chemicals, fertilizers, cement. **Labor force:** 1.9 mil. (1996); 50% agriculture and forestry, 20% industry, 30% services. **Exports:** $761 mil. (f.o.b, 2000 est.); cotton, aluminum, electricity, fruits, vegetable oil, textiles. **Imports:** $782 mil. (f.o.b, 2000 est.); fuel, electricity, chemicals, machinery and transport equipment, foodstuffs. **Major trading partners:**

exports: Liechtenstein, Russia; *imports:* Europe, Uzbekistan, Russia.

Tajikistan is a mountainous country, with over half of its territory above 10,000 feet. Its mountain ranges are the northern and southern Tian Shan and the Pamirs, where the former Soviet Union's highest points of Lenin Peak and Communism Peak are found. The dense river system and the many fertile valleys make habitation possible in such a mountainous country, although the entire territory is prone to earthquakes.

Tajikistan exemplifies the complexities of central Asia, since, unlike other ethnic groups on the region, the Tajiks were not nomadic but sedentary, and their language was Persian, not Turkic. They are a population that somehow escaped the waves of Turkish influence that swept through central Asia. As early as the eighth century A.D., the Tajiks probably formed a distinctive ethnic group, although they have never been a completely independent people. Despite the formation of several semi-independent states in their history, they have always been a small part of the larger Uzbek lands. In the mid-19th century, the Russian empire expanded southward, and the northern Tajik territories came under Russian rule. At the same time, the tribal state known as the Khanate of Bukhara controlled the southern Tajik territories.

In April 1918 northern Tajikistan came under Soviet control and was included in the Turkestan Autonomous Soviet Socialist Republic (ASSR). Three years later, the Red Army took the other regions that had been ruled by Bukhara. There was local opposition to Soviet rule, and the fighting meant that full Soviet authority over all of the area was not established until 1925. When the U.S.S.R. created the National Delimitation of the Central Asian Republics in 1924, it founded the Tajik ASSR as part of the Uzbek Soviet Socialist Republic (SSR); on Oct. 16, 1929, it became the Tajik SSR.

The Tajiks were fiercely opposed to the policies of land reform and collectivization, and during the ensuing Soviet repression of the 1930's, almost all native Tajiks were replaced by Russians in leading government and party positions. There have been reports of rising Islamic influence and increasing anti-Russian sentiment and even riots during the 1970's, evidence that the animosity toward the Russians that stemmed with its forced incorporation into the U.S.S.R. had not abated since the 1920's. Under Soviet rule, there was some economic and social progress.

However, living standards in Tajikistan are still among the lowest in the former union. Most people continue to live in rural qishlaqs, or settlements, consisting of 200-700 one-family houses built along an irrigation ditch or a river. The country is a major producer of cotton, and its industries are nonferrous metallurgy, cotton processing, fruit canning, and wine making.

Mikhail Gorbachev's glasnost, or openness, policy resulted in a campaign against corruption, a relaxation of censorship in the press, and increased ethnic tensions over alleged discrimination against Tajiks living in Uzbekistan. In June 1989 there were violent clashes between the two groups on the border between the two republics. There were also riots in February 1990 in Dushanbe, when the suggestion that Armenian refugees would be resettled there spurred the local Tajiks into action. Increased freedom of the press has given rise to a growing interest in Iran and Iranian culture, for even though they are closely related, contact between Iran and the Tajiks was severely limited during the Soviet period.

In large part due to the riots, opposition candidates were barred from the March 1990 elections and the Communist party won 94 percent of the seats. After the failed Aug. 1991 coup in Moscow, the Communist party was banned, and the president was forced to resign over his support of the coup. Since then, there have been several Communist party coups, and the party has been banned and reinstated several times. In the presidential elections, former Communist party leader Rakhmon Nabiyev won with 58 percent of the vote. But after a relatively tranquil six months, Islamic fundamentalists, armed allegedly by Iran and Afghanistan, rose up against the Nabiyev regime. Vicious fighting for almost four months led to Nabiyev's resignation at gunpoint and the launching of a fundamentalist government.

In 1992 the pro-Communist forces launched a successful counterattack in which thousands were killed and perhaps 300,000 displaced. Voters in Nov. 1994 approved by referendum a new (highly presidential) constitution with 90 percent of the vote, and elected as president Emomali Rakhmonov with 60 percent. But the civil war of the current, ex-Communist and Russian-backed government against Islamic rebels continues, despite U.N.-mediated cease-fires signed in Sept. 1994 and May 1995. Two renegade military commanders mutinied in Feb. 1996, but called off the coup when Rakhmonov dismissed several senior officials. Sporadic fighting between government troops and several rebel groups continued throughout 1997, and while the government appeared to be taking control, flareups continued into 2000. In Sept. 1999 voters amended the constitution to allow opposition Moslem parties and to extend the presidential term from 5 to 7 years. In November President Rakhmanov won a new term with 96 percent of the vote.

▶ TANZANIA
United Republic of Tanzania

● **GEOGRAPHY   Location:** Tanganyika, on eastern coast of Africa, and islands of Zanzibar and Pemba, about 25 mi. (40 km) off Tanganyika coast in Indian Ocean. **Boundaries:** Burundi, Rwanda to NW, Uganda, Kenya to N, Indian Ocean to E, Mozambique, Malawi to S, Zambia to SW, Zaire to W. **Total area:** 364,900 sq. mi. (945,090 sq km). **Coastline:** 885 mi. (1,424 km). **Comparative area:** slightly larger than twice size of California. **Land use:** 3% arable land; 1% permanent crops; 40% meadows and pastures; 38% forest and woodland; 18% other; includes negl. 1% irrigated. **Major cities:** (1985 est.) Dar es Salaam (capital) 1,096,000; Mwanza 252,000; Tabora 214,000; Mbeya 194,000; Tanga 172,000.

● **PEOPLE   Population:** 36,232,074 (2001 est.). **Nationality:** noun—Tanzanian(s); adjective—Tanzanian. **Ethnic groups:** mainland—99% native Africans of over 130 groups; 1% Asian, European, and Arab; Zanzibar—Arab, native African, mixed Arab and native African. **Languages:** Kiswahili and Swahili and English (all official); English primary language of commerce, administration, higher education; Swahili widely understood, generally used for communication between ethnic groups; first language of most people is one of local languages; primary education generally in Swahili. **Religions:** mainland—45% Christian, 35% Muslim, 20% indigenous beliefs; Zanzibar—almost all Muslim.

● **GOVERNMENT   Type:** republic. **Independence:** Tanganyika became independent Dec. 9, 1961 (from U.N. trusteeship under British administration); Zanzibar became independent Dec. 19, 1963 (from U.K.); Tanganyika united with Zanzibar Apr. 26, 1964. **Constitution:** Apr. 25, 1977, revised Oct. 1984 (Zanzibar has own constitution but remains subject to provisions of union constitution). **National holiday:** Union Day, Apr. 26. **Heads of Government:** Benjamin William Mkapa, president (since Nov. 1995); **Structure:** executive—president is head of government and chief of state; unicameral legislature (Zanzibar has its own House of Representatives to make laws especially for Zanzibar; judiciary.

● **ECONOMY   Monetary unit:** Tanzanian shilling. **Budget:** (1999 est.) *income:* $1.21 bil.; *expend.:* $1.36 bil. **GDP:** $25.1 bil., $710 per capita (2000 est.). **Chief crops:** cotton, coffee, sisal, vegetables, fruits, grain on mainland; cloves and coconuts on Zanzibar; cattle, sheep, goats. **Natural resources:** hydropower potential, tin, phosphates, iron ore and coal, gemstones. **Major industries:** agricultural processing (sugar, beer, cigarettes, sisal twine), diamond mining, oil refining. **Labor force:** 13.5 mil. (2000 est.); 80% agriculture, 20% industry and commerce. **Exports:** $937 mil. (f.o.b., 2000 est.); coffee, manufactured goods, cotton, sisal, cashew nuts, tobacco, cloves. **Imports:** $1.57 bil. (f.o.b., 2000 est.); consumer goods, machinery and transport equipment, crude oil. **Major trading partners:** *exports:* 20% India, 8% Germany, 8% Japan; *imports:* 7% South Africa, 7% Kenya.

Formerly known as Tanganyika, Tanzania's indigenous population includes people of diverse ethnic background, including San, Bantu, and Nilotic peoples. It has been the site of a number of relatively advanced and well-organized societies.

Zanzibar and the neighboring island of Pemba have been a crossroads of trade in East Africa since ancient times. Trade via Zanzibar between the Tanganyika coast and the Middle East, primarily ivory, gold, and iron, dates to the late Roman Empire. The coast was dominated by various Arab and Persian powers, usually based in Zanzibar, from about the eighth century. Zanzibar and Tanganyika were visited by Vasco da Gama in 1498, and Portugal claimed Zanzibar in 1503 and the entire Tanganyika coast in 1506. The Portuguese established coastal trading stations but did not colonize the interior.

The Portuguese were driven from Zanzibar in 1652 by the sultanate of Oman, which soon expelled them from the mainland as well. Under Omani rule, trade in gold, ivory, and gems was supplemented by a sizable slave trade, and the clove plantations of Zanzibar became commercially important. Under Sultan Seyyid Said, the capital of the sultanate of Oman was transferred to Zanzibar in 1824, and Zanzibar became independent of Oman upon his death in 1856.

Both Germany and Great Britain became active in the region in the 19th century. Tanganyika was organized as the colony of German East Africa in 1884, while Zanzibar became a British protectorate in 1890. Tanganyika became a secondary battlefield of World War I, with frequent clashes between German and British troops.

Britain assumed control of Tanganyika in 1920 under a League of Nations Mandate and maintained control under a U.N. trusteeship after 1946. The temperate southern highlands were extensively colonized by British immigrants, and railroads and mines were developed by the British administration.

Elections for a local legislature were held in Zanzibar in July 1957. The island's politics were dominated by a split between Arab and African residents. Zanzibar became independent on Dec. 19, 1963. In January 1964 an African revolt overthrew the sultan of Zanzibar and resulted in the deaths of thousands of Arab residents and the emigration of many more. Political control shifted to the African party and Abeid Karume became president.

Tanganyika became independent in 1961. Julius K. Nyerere was Tanganyika's dominant political figure. Tanzania was formed from the union of Tanganyika and Zanzibar on April 26, 1964, with Zanzibar retaining local autonomy.

Nyerere advocated an "African socialist" form of development and formed close ties with China. Some British settlers left the country, but relations with Great Britain remained important. The Tan-Zan Railroad between Dar es Salaam and Lusaka, Zambia was built with Chinese aid between 1970 and 1975. The ruling parties of Tanganyika and Zanzibar were united in 1977 under Nyerere's leadership.

Political tensions eased and Tanzania adopted a more open political structure in the 1980's. Pres. Ali Hassan Mwinyi encouraged free-market economic reforms, including encouragement of foreign investment and strengthened ties with Kenya and Uganda (Tanzania invaded the latter in 1979 in an effort to depose Idi Amin). Tanzania's economy has great potential because of the country's extensive natural resources and one of Africa's best educational systems; literacy in both English and Swahili is relatively high.

Although only an estimated 20 percent of the population was found to be in favor of political pluralism, in 1992 the Revolutionary party of Tanzania voted in favor of a secular multiparty system, that is one based on neither ethnic nor regional lines. It won the country's first-ever multiparty elections in 1995. Benjamin Mkapa succeeded Mwinyi, who was barred by law from seeking a third term as president.

The elections of Oct. 2000 returned Mkapa to the presidency with 72 percent of the vote while the ruling party carried 167 of the National Assembly's 181 seats; similar results were reported from semiautonomous Zanzibar. The obviously rigged elections provoked demands for new elections from the opposition's Civic United Front and demonstrations in which over 40 were killed. In 2001, Tanzania formed, with Uganda and Kenya, the East African Community, a common market with stated but vague aspirations toward political unity.

▶ **THAILAND**
Kingdom of Thailand
● **GEOGRAPHY Location:** extends southward, along isthmus of Kra, to Malay peninsula, in Southeast Asia. **Boundaries**: Myanmar to W and N, Laos to NE, Cambodia and Gulf of Thailand to E, Malaysia to S, Andaman Sea to SW. **Total area:** 198,456 sq. mi. (514,000 sq km). **Coastline:** 2,001 mi. (3,219 km). **Comparative area**: slightly more than twice the size of Wyoming. **Land use:** 34% arable land; 6% permanent crops; 2% meadows and pastures; 26% forest and woodland; 32% other; includes 7% irrigated. **Major cities:** (1990 census), Bangkok metropolis (capital) 5,876,000; Songkhla 172,604; Chon Buri 115,350; Nakhon Si Thammarat 102,123; Chiang Mai 101,594.
● **PEOPLE Population:** 61,797,751 (2001 est.). **Nationality:** noun—Thai (sing., pl.); adjective—Thai. **Ethnic groups:** 75% Thai, 14% Chinese, 11%

other. **Languages:** Thai; English is secondary language of elite; ethnic and regional dialects. **Religions:** 95% Buddhist, 3.8% Muslim, 0.5% Christianity, 0.1% Hinduism.
● **GOVERNMENT Type:** constitutional monarchy. **Constitution:** new constitution signed by King Phumiphon Oct. 11, 1997. **National holiday:** Birthday of His Majesty the King, Dec. 5. **Heads of Government:** Bhumibol Adulyadej, king (since June 1946); Thaksin Shinawatra, prime minister (since Feb. 2001). **Structure:** executive—king is head of state with nominal powers, prime minister is head of government; bicameral legislature (National Assembly—Senate appointed by king, to be phased into an elected body starting in 2000; elected House of Representatives); judiciary relatively independent except in important political subversion cases.
● **ECONOMY Monetary unit:** baht. **Budget:** (2000 est.) *income:* $19 bil. *expend.:* $21 bil. **GDP:** $413 bil., $6,700 per capita (2000 est.). **Chief crops:** rice, cassava, sugar, corn, rubber, manioc, coconuts, soybean. **Natural resources:** tin, rubber, natural gas, tungsten, tantalum. **Major industries:** tourism, textiles and garments, agricultural processing, beverages; world's second-largest tungsten producer and third-largest tin producer. **Labor force:** 32.6 mil. (1997 est.); 54% agriculture, 15% industry, 31% services including government; 45% unemployment (1998). **Exports:** $68.2 bil. (f.o.b, 2000 est.); computers and parts, textiles, rice. **Imports:** $61.8 bil. (f.o.b,. 2000 est.); capital goods, intermediate goods, consumer goods, fuels. **Major trading partners:** (1997) *exports:* 22% U.S., 14% Japan, 9% Singapore; *imports:* 26% Japan, 14% U.S., 6% Singapore.

Ethnic Thai migrating south from China after about A.D. 1000 created a number of petty states in the region, most notably the kingdom of Sukhothai. These came under the influence of Indian civilization from the adjacent states of Burma and the Khmer empire, and Buddhism became established as the dominant religion of the Thai. A unified kingdom of Siam was established c. 1350, with its capital at Ayutthaya. Portuguese and other European traders and missionaries were active in Siam after 1511.

In 1767 Ayutthaya was destroyed in a war with Burma. In 1782 the Chakkri dynasty was established at Bangkok and restored the power of the Thai monarchy. By skillfully playing off the European powers against one another, Kings Mongkut (r. 1851-68) and Chulalongkorn (r. 1868-1910) enabled Siam to be the only Southeast Asian nation to escape European colonization or political domination. In a series of treaties with Great Britain and France, however, King Chulalongkorn was forced to renounce Siam's claims to portions of Malaya, Laos, and Cambodia.

Absolute monarchy ended in 1932, when a military coup forced the granting of a constitution. Japanese troops occupied Siam in Dec. 1941. Siam concluded a nominal alliance with Japan in 1942 and declared war on Great Britain and the U.S, while the monarchy secretly supported a strong anti-Japanese resistance movement. A period of postwar political turmoil ended with the accession in 1950 of King Phumiphon, who instituted a reformist and pro-Western policy. Thai politics since World War II have been democratic but dominated by an oligarchy of military officers and civilians with strong military ties.

During the Vietnam War, Thailand was an important staging area for American forces. Since then, U.S. and other foreign investment contributed to significant industrialization and economic growth, making Thailand one of Asia's fastest-growing economies. Its prosperity has attracted a large number of refugees from Laos, Vietnam, and Cambodia.

On Dec. 8, 1990, Prime Minister Chatichai Choonhavan resigned amid charges of corruption. Reappointed by the king the next day, Chatichai was overthrown on Feb. 23 by military forces, who invited former diplomat Anand Panyarachun to serve as interim prime minister.

After parliamentary elections in March 1992, Gen. Suchinda Kraprayoon, who held no parliamentary seat, was named prime minister in a government dominated by the military. Mass demonstrations against the Suchinda government, led by former Bangkok governor Chamlong Srimuang, culminated on May 17-18, when troops fired on demonstrators, causing hundreds of fatalities. The king intervened and Suchinda resigned.Chamlong agreed to call off the demonstrations and Anand Panyarachun was invited to head another transitional government, and Parliament agreed in principle to a new constitution with a provision that the prime minister must be an elected member of Parliament.

Parliamentary elections in 1992 gained a majority for a five-party coalition headed by Chuan Leekpai that managed to govern for almost three years, liberalizing financial arrangements, spending heavily on infrastructure, and bringing Thailand to an 8 percent growth rate in 1994. In elections held in 1995, the Thai Nation party captured the largest number of seats; its leader, Banharn Silpa-Archa, became prime minister but the party lost the 1996 elections and a coalition government led by General Chavalit took over. Only six months later the Thai economy began a steep decline and the currency was devalued in June 1997. The U.S. and the I.M.F. agreed to provide loans of $4 bil. to stabalize the economy with more promised if the government took appropriate action. Chuan Leekpai returned as prime minister in Nov. 1997 but economic recovery was only slowly under way by mid-1998. Still the government survived a Dec. 1999 no confidence vote just before the Bank of Thailand announced a 4 percent rise in G.D.P. for the year.

Elections in Jan. 2001 brought a near majority to the Thai Rak Thai party of computer and telecommunications billionaire Thaksin Shinawatra, who was named prime minister but who faced serious legal charges of tax evasion.

▶ TOGO
Togolese Republic
● GEOGRAPHY Location: western coast of Africa. Boundaries: Burkina Faso to N, Benin to E, Gulf of Guinea to S, Ghana to W. Total area: 21,927 sq. mi. (56,790 sq km). Coastline: 35 mi. (56 km). Comparative area: slightly smaller than West Virginia. Land use: 38% arable land; 7% permanent crops; 4% meadows and pastures; 17% forest and woodland; 34% other. Major cities: (1990 est.) Lomé (capital) 450,000; Sokodé 55,000; Kpalimé 31,000; Atakpamé 30,000; Tsevie 26,000.
● PEOPLE Population: 5,153,088 (2001 est.). Nationality: noun—Togolese (sing., pl.); adjective—Togolese. Ethnic groups: 37 groups; largest are Ewe, Mina, and Kabre; under 1% European and Syrian-Lebanese. Languages: French (both official and language of commerce); Ewe and Mina in south, Dagomba and Kabyè in north. Religions:

about 70% indigenous beliefs, 20% Christian, 10% Muslim.
● GOVERNMENT Type: republic under transition to multiparty democratic rule; Independence: Apr. 27, 1960 (from U.N. trusteeship under French administration). Constitution: Sept. 27, 1992. National holiday: Independence Day, Apr. 27. Heads of Government: Gen. Gnassingbé Eyadema, president (since 1992); Agbéyomé Messan Kodjo, prime minister (since Oct. 2000). Structure: executive—president appoints prime minister; unicameral legislature—National Assembly; judiciary.
● ECONOMY Monetary unit: Communauté Financière Africaine (CFA) franc. Budget: (1997 est.) income: $232 mil.; expend.: $252 mil. GDP: $7.3 bil., $1,500 per capita (2000 est.). Chief crops: coffee, cocoa, cotton, yams, cassava, corn, beans, rice; meat, fish. Natural resources: phosphates, limestone, marble. Major industries: phosphate mining, agricultural processing, cement, handicrafts, textiles, beverages. Labor force: 1.74 mil. (1996 est.); 65% agriculture, 30% services, 5% industry. Exports: $336 mil. (f.o.b., 2000); cotton, phosphates, coffee, cocoa. Imports: $452 mil. (f.o.b., 2000); machinery and equipment, consumer goods, petroleum products. Major trading partners: (1999) exports: Nigeria, Brazil, Canada; imports: Ghana, France, Ivory Coast, China.

Ewe-speaking peoples began to migrate into what is now Togo, located on Africa's west coast, early in the 14th century. Portuguese explorers arrived in the late 15th century, turning the coast into a point of departure for slaves captured from nearby villages, and between the 1600's and 1800's, the region became known as the "Slave Coast." Germans started to explore and trade in the region in the mid-19th century and declared a protectorate over the area in 1884. After World War I, however, Britain and France divided the nation between them, Britain receiving the western third, France the eastern two-thirds. The League of Nations confirmed this arrangement, giving mandates to British Togoland (later a part of Ghana) and French Togoland.

In 1956 France made French Togo an autonomous republic but retained control of its foreign affairs, defense, and currency; Nicholas Grunitzky was prime minister. The United Nations rejected this plan and in elections in 1958 advocates of complete independence won control of the legislature. On Apr. 27, 1960, French Togo cut its ties with France and became the fully independent Republic of Togo. Sylvanus Olympio became the new nation's first prime minister. Grunitzsky went into exile but returned when Olympio was assassinated in January 1963. He led the new government and oversaw the writing of a new constitution allowing more political freedoms.

In 1967 army officers led by Lt. Col. Gnassingbé Eyadema overthrew Grunitzsky, suspended the constitution, and named Eyadema president.

In 1990, Eyadema was forced out by democratic reformers, and Kokou J. Koffigoh was elected prime minister by a national conference in 1991. Eyadema resumed the presidency in 1992, but his refusal to embrace multiparty democracy and Koffigoh's weak leadership led to violence and public calls for the ouster of both men. A new constitution was ratified in September 1992, and in elections held in March 1994, Edem Kodjo took over as prime minister, he was succeeded by Kwassi Klutse in 1996, and Eugène Koffi Adoboli in 1999.

▶TONGA
Kingdom of Tonga
● **GEOGRAPHY Location:** 172 islands in South Pacific Ocean, 36 permanently inhabited. Nuku'alofa 21°09'S, 175°14'W. **Boundaries:** surrounded by South Pacific Ocean; Fiji is about 400 mi. (650 km) to NW and Western Samoa lies N. **Total area:** 289 sq. mi. (748 sq km). **Coastline:** 260 mi. (419 km). **Comparative area:** four times the size of Washington, D.C. **Land use:** 24% arable land; 43% permanent crops; 6% meadows and pastures; 11% forest and woodland; 16% other. **Major cities:** (1986 census) Nuku'alofa (capital) 28,899; Tongatapu 63,614; Vava'u 15,170; Ha'apai 8,979; Eua 4,393.
● **PEOPLE Population:** 104,227 (2001 est.). **Nationality:** noun—Tongan(s); adjective—Tongan. **Ethnic groups:** Polynesian; about 300 Europeans. **Languages:** Tongan, English. **Religions:** Christian (Free Wesleyan Church claims over 30,000 adherents).
● **GOVERNMENT Type:** hereditary constitutional monarchy. **Independence:** June 4, 1970 (from U.K.). **Constitution:** Nov. 4, 1875; revised Jan. 1, 1967. **National holiday:** Emancipation Day, June 4. **Heads of Government:** Taufa'ahau Tupou IV, king (since Dec. 1965); Prince 'Ulukalala Lavaka Ata, premier (since Jan. 2000). **Structure:** executive—king, prime minister, cabinet; unicameral legislature—30-seat Legislative Assembly, 9 elected by popular vote, 12 are for cabinet ministers, 9 reserved for nobles; judiciary—appointed by king.
● **ECONOMY Monetary unit:** pa'anga. **Budget:** (FY96/97) *income:* $49 mil.; *expend.:* $120 mil. **GDP:** $225 mil., $2,700 per capita (2000 est.). **Chief crops:** squash, coconut, copra, bananas, vanilla beans, cocoa, coffee, ginger, black pepper, fish. **Natural resources:** fish, fertile soil. **Major industries:** tourism, fishing. **Labor force:** 34,000 (FY96/97 est.); 65% engaged in agriculture. **Exports:** $8 mil. (f.o.b., 1998); squash, fish, vanilla. **Imports:** $69 mil. (f.o.b., 1998); food products, machinery and transport equipment, fuels, chemicals. **Major trading partners:** (1996) *exports:* 53% Japan, 18% U.S., 6% New Zealand; *imports:* 30% New Zealand, 19% Australia, 11% U.S.

The Polynesian islands that now compose Tonga were settled some 3,000 years ago. A highly stratified society evolved; the kings of Tonga dominated much of Polynesia by the 13th century. The islands were visited in 1643 by Abel Tasman, and in 1773 by Capt. James Cook, who named them the Friendly Islands. English missionaries arrived in 1797, and the islands came under British political influence. A code of laws was promulgated in 1862, and a constitutional monarchy established in 1875. A series of treaties with Western powers recognized Tonga's independence, but the kingdom became a British protectorate in 1900.

The islands were outside the Japanese perimeter in the Pacific theater of World War II. On June 4, 1970, the British dissolved their protectorate and the Kingdom of Tonga became independent as a member of the British Commonwealth. The present king, Taufa'ahau Tupou IV, came to the throne in 1965.

The Tongan economy is based on subsistence farming and fishing, with some handicraft industries and light manufacturing. The tourist industry is developing rapidly. Tonga was expected to join the U.N. in late 1999.

▶TRINIDAD AND TOBAGO
Republic of Trinidad and Tobago
● **GEOGRAPHY Location:** two islands (Port of Spain, Trinidad Is., 10°38'N, 61°31'W; Tobago Is., 11°11'N, 60°45'W) in southeastern Caribbean Sea, off northeastern South America. **Boundaries:** Caribbean Sea to N and W, Atlantic Ocean to E and S. **Total area:** 1,981 sq. mi. (5,130 sq km). **Coastline:** 225 mi. (362 km). **Comparative area:** slightly smaller than Delaware. **Land use:** 15% arable land; 9% permanent crops; 2% meadows and pastures; 46% forest and woodland; 28% other; includes 4% irrigated. **Major cities:** (1991) Port of Spain (capital) 51,076; San Fernando 30,115; Arima (borough) 29,483.
● **PEOPLE Population:** 1,169,682 (2001 est.). **Nationality:** noun—Trinidadian(s), Tobagonian(s); adjective—Trinidadian, Tobagonian. **Ethnic groups:** 40% black, 40.3% East Indian, 14% mixed, 1% white, 1% Chinese. **Languages:** English (official), Hindi, French, Spanish. **Religions:** 29.4% Roman Catholic, 23.8% Hindu, 10.9% Anglican, 14% other Protestant, 5.8% Muslim.
● **GOVERNMENT Type:** parliamentary democracy. **Independence:** Aug. 31, 1962 (from U.K.). **Constitution:** Aug. 1, 1976. **National holiday:** Independence Day, Aug. 31. **Heads of Government:** Arthur Napoleon Robinson, president (since Mar. 1997); Basdeo Panday, prime minister (since Nov. 1995). **Structure:** executive—is cabinet led by prime minister; bicameral legislature (elected House of Representatives and appointed Senate); judiciary headed by chief justice and includes court of appeal, high court, and lower courts.
● **ECONOMY Monetary unit:** Trinidad and Tobago dollar. **Budget:** (1998 est.) *income:* $1.54 bil.; *expend.:* $1.6 bil. **GDP:** $11.2 bil., $9,500 per capita (2000 est.). **Chief crops:** sugar, cocoa, coffee, rice, citrus, bananas; poultry. **Natural resources:** crude oil, natural gas, asphalt. **Major industries:** petroleum, chemicals, tourism. **Labor force:** 558,700 (1998 est.); 64.1% services, 14% manufacturing, mining, and quarrying, 12.4% construction and utilities, 9.5% agriculture. **Exports:** $3.2 bil. (f.o.b., 2000); petroleum and petroleum products, chemicals, steel products, fertilizer, sugar, cocoa, coffee, citrus, flowers. **Imports:** $3 bil. (f.o.b., 2000 est.); machinery, transport equipment, manufactured goods, food, live animals. **Major trading partners:** *exports:* 36.9% U.S., 29.4% CARICOM countries, 9.7% Latin America; *imports:* 44.7% U.S., 18.9% Latin American, 13.7% EU.

Trinidad was a possession of Spain from 1498 to 1797, when it was surrendered to the British. England took control of Tobago in 1802. Together the two islands achieved independence from the U.K. in 1962. Prime Minister Arthur Robinson's National Alliance for Reconstruction currently governs the country. Civil and political rights are well respected, and political party competition tends to divide along ethnic (black, East Indian) lines. Agrarian reform designed to create tenable landholdings is a central political issue.

In 1990, militant Muslims seized Prime Minister A.N.R. Robinson and dozens of others in Parliament, paralyzing the government for five days. Peace was restored when the government promised reforms. People's National Movement candidate Carson Charles was elected prime minister in 1991, and in the interest of preserving the peace, he granted the Muslim militants amnesty in 1992. Robinson won the presidential election in 1997 in a landslide.

▶ TUNISIA
Republic of Tunisia

● **GEOGRAPHY** **Location:** northern coast of Africa. **Boundaries**: Mediterranean to N and E, Libya to SE, Algeria to W. **Total area**: 63,170 sq. mi. (163,610 sq km); includes land and inland waters. **Coastline:** 714 mi. (1,148 km). **Comparative area**: slightly larger than Georgia. **Land use:** 19% arable land; 13% permanent crops; 20% meadows and pastures; 4% forest and woodland; 44% other; includes 1% irrigated. **Major cities:** (1994 census) Tunis (capital) 674,100; Sfax (Safaqis) 230,900; Ariana 152,700; Ehadhamen 149,200; Sousse 125,000.

● **PEOPLE** **Population:** 9,705,102 (2001 est.). **Nationality:** noun—Tunisian(s); adjective—Tunisian. **Ethnic groups:** 98% Arab, 1% European, 1% Jewish and other . **Languages:** Arabic (official), Arabic and French (commerce). **Religions:** 98% Muslim, 1% Christian, 1% Jewish and other.

● **GOVERNMENT** **Type:** republic. **Independence:** Mar. 20, 1956 (from France). **Constitution:** June 1, 1959, amended July 12, 1988. **National holiday:** National Day, Mar. 20. **Heads of Government:** Zine el-Abidine Ben Ali, president (since Nov. 1987); Mohamed Ghannouchi, prime minister (since Nov. 1999). **Structure:** executive dominant; unicameral legislature (Chamber of Deputies) largely advisory; judiciary patterned on French and Koranic systems.

● **ECONOMY** **Monetary unit:** Tunisian dinar. **Budget:** (2000 est.) *income:* $7.5 bil.; *expend.:* $8.1 bil. **GDP:** $62.8 bil., $6,500 per capita (2000 est.). **Chief crops:** olives, dates, oranges, almonds, grain, sugar beets, grapes; poultry, beef, dairy products. **Natural resources:** crude oil, phosphates, iron ore, lead, zinc. **Major industries:** petroleum, mining (particularly phosphates and iron ore), tourism, textiles. **Labor force:** 2.65 mil.; 55% services, 23% industry, 22% agriculture; 16.5% unemployment (1999 est.); shortage of skilled labor. **Exports:** $6.1 bil. (f.o.b., 2000 est.); hydrocarbons, textiles, agricultural products, phosphates and chemicals. **Imports:** $8.4 bil. (f.o.b., 2000 est.); industrial goods, hydrocarbons, food. **Major trading partners:** *exports:* 22% France, 17% Italy, 28% Germany; *imports:* 23% France, 15% Italy, 23% Germany.

The Phoenicians, an ancient seafaring people from the eastern Mediterranean, founded settlements in Tunisia dating back to 1000 B.C. The most important trade in these was Carthage, which dominated trade in the central Mediterranean until it was conquered and destroyed by Rome in 146 B.C. Tunisia remained part of the Roman Empire until it was conquered by the Vandals in the mid-fifth century A.D. The Byzantine Empire reconquered Tunisia in the sixth century.

Tunisia became part of the Arab world with the expansion of Islam in the seventh century and soon emerged as a principal center of Islamic culture in North Africa. Tunisia was incorporated into the Ottoman Empire in 1574 and was ruled from Constantinople by Turkish governors, or beys.

With the waning of Ottoman power in the 19th century, Tunisia became a French protectorate in 1881. Nationalist movements began in the early 20th century. During World War II Tunisia was under Vichy French rule and was the scene of fighting between the Axis and Allies in 1942-43. Nationalist unrest resumed when France reestablished its rule in the postwar period. Widespread popular unrest in the early 1950's led to a French grant of self-rule in 1954. Full independence was proclaimed on Mar. 20, 1956; large numbers of French settlers returned to France. The French-sponsored monarchy was abolished in 1957, and the Neo-Destour (New Constitution) party under the leadership of Habib Bourguiba took power. Bourguiba was elected president in 1959 without opposition and was named president for life. Under his rule, political parties ranging from Communist to monarchist flourished, leading to both democratic politics and political confusion.

Relations with France were strained in 1964 when Tunisia nationalized foreign assets but have since improved. The basic thrust of Tunisian government was socialist, with state ownership of principal industries and heavy subsidies of basic commodities. In foreign affairs Tunisia has been closely tied to France and has been a moderate voice within the Arab League.

Popular unrest and labor strife characterized Tunisia's internal situation in the 1980's, as political maneuvering began in anticipation of the end of the Bourguiba era, which came in 1987 when the aged leader was overthrown by Ben Ali. In 1989 new elections were planned as part of a political and economic restructuring. Ben Ali was elected president, twice winning 99 percent of the vote, while his party won virtually all the seats in the National Assembly. In 1994 and 1995, however, the political stability was threatened by radical Muslim groups both from within and from Algeria. Rumors of brutal repression were rife. In Oct. 1999, in Tunisia's first "multiparty" elections, Ben Ali was re-elected president, again with 99.42 percent of the vote while his Constitutional Union Party carried 148 of the 182 parliamentary seats.

Tunisia's economy, though plagued by labor difficulties, has developed rapidly, led by textiles, food processing and other light industry, tourism, phosphate mining, and other mineral processing. The large agricultural sector includes grain, olives, dates, and winter fruits and vegetables for export to Europe. In 1998 the government reached an accord with the E.U. to lower trade barriers.

▶ TURKEY
Republic of Turkey

● **GEOGRAPHY** **Location:** partly in southeastern Europe and partly in western Asia. **Boundaries**: Black Sea to N; Georgia and Armenia to NE; Iran to E; Iraq, Syria, Mediterranean Sea to S; Aegean Sea, Greece to W; and Bulgaria to NW. **Total area**: 301,382 sq. mi. (780,580 sq km). **Coastline:** 4,471 mi. (7,200 km). **Comparative area:** slightly larger than Texas. **Land use:** 32% arable land; 4% permanent crops; 16% meadows and pastures; 26% forest and woodland; 22% other; includes 3% irrigated. **Major cities:** (1993 est.) Ankara (capital) 2,719,981; Istanbul 7,331,927; Izmir 1,920,807; Adana 1,010,363; Bursa 949,810.

● **PEOPLE** **Population:** 66,493,970 (July 2001 est.). **Nationality:** noun—Turk(s); adjective—Turkish. **Ethnic groups:** 80% Turkish, 20% Kurdish. **Languages:** Turkish (official), Kurdish, Arabic. **Religions:** 99.8% Muslim (mostly Sunni), 0.2% other (mostly Christian and Jewish).

● **GOVERNMENT** **Type:** republican parliamentary democracy. **Independence:** Oct. 29, 1923 (from Ottoman Empire). **Constitution:** Nov. 7, 1982. **National holiday:** Anniversary of the Declaration of the Republic, Oct. 29. **Heads of Government:** Ahmet Necdet Sezer, president (since May 2000); Bülent Ecevit, prime minister (since Jan. 1999). **Structure:** executive—president empowered to call new elections, promulgate laws (elected for seven-year term); unicameral legislature; independent judiciary.

• **ECONOMY   Monetary unit:** Turkish lira. **Budget:** (2000) *income:* $54.5 bil.; *expend.:* $75.2 bil. **GDP:** $444 bil., $6,800 per capita (2000 est.). **Chief crops:** cotton, tobacco, grain, olives, sugar beets, pulses, citrus; livestock. **Natural resources:** antimony, coal, chromium, mercury, copper. **Major industries:** textiles, food processing, mining (coal, chromite, copper, boron minerals). **Labor force:** 23 mil.; 38% agriculture, 38% services, 24% industry; about 1.5 million Turks work abroad; 5.6% unemployment (2000 est.). **Exports:** $26 bil. (f.o.b., 1999 est.); 28% textiles and apparel, 17% foodstuffs, 9% iron and steel products. **Imports:** $55.7 bil. (c.i.f., 2000 est.); 29% machinery, fuels, minerals, foodstuffs. **Major trading partners:** *exports:* 19% Germany, 11% U.S., 7% U.K.; *imports:* 13% Germany, 7% U.S., 8% Italy.

The Hittites, an Indo-European people, created an empire in Anatolia before 2000 B.C. and controlled most of what is modern-day Turkey for nearly 1,000 years. The rise of Troy and other Hellenic city-states on the coast of Asia Minor and the expansion of the Assyrian empire led to the collapse of Hittite power by around 900 B.C. Except for some Hellenic enclaves on the Aegean Coast (Ionia), all of Turkey was incorporated into the Persian empire of Cyrus and Darius in the sixth century B.C. Alexander the Great conquered Turkey, but it returned to Persian rule following the collapse of his empire, c. 300 B.C.

All of Turkey, comprising Thracia, Galatia, Cappadocia, Cilicia, and other provinces, was incorporated into the Roman Empire by the end of the first century A.D. Constantine the Great founded the city of Constantinople on the site of ancient Byzantium in 330 as the empire's eastern capital. Following the decline of the western Roman Empire in the seventh century, Constantinople became the capital of the independent Eastern Roman (Byzantine) Empire. The Byzantine Empire fought off repeated attacks by Arab Islamic forces in the seventh and eighth centuries but lost control of central Anatolia to the Seljuk Turkish rulers of Persia after 1038.

The 13th-century Mongol invasions left Turkey largely untouched but weakened both Byzantine and Seljuk power. At the end of the 13th century, the Ottomans, a small Turkish tribe, expanded from their stronghold in western Anatolia and within a century captured most of Turkey, Bulgaria, and Serbia. Constantinople fell to the Ottomans in 1453. By the middle of the 16th century, the Ottoman Empire extended from southeastern Europe into the Crimea and Iran and included most of the Middle East, Egypt, and Arabia.

At its height the Ottoman Empire was a great world power and a substantial participant in European international relations. But in the 18th century, the empire lost much of its autonomy through unequal treaties with European powers, and throughout the 19th century, parts of the empire were detached and either granted independence or placed under European protection. The Ottoman Empire became the "Sick Man of Europe." A liberal constitution was adopted in 1876 but largely ignored until the Young Turk Rebellion of 1908 forced the sultan to accept its provisions.

Siding with the Central Powers in World War I, the Ottoman Empire lost most of its non-Turkish possessions to the Allies. The Treaty of Sèvres (1920) reduced the Ottoman state to a small part of northern Anatolia. Before the treaty was ratified, however, Kemal Ataturk seized power and regained much territory in a series of campaigns with Soviet assistance. The Treaty of Lausanne (1923) established the present boundaries of Turkey, and Turkey was proclaimed a republic in October 1923. The Caliphate was renounced in 1924, ending the Ottoman claim of spiritual leadership in the Islamic world.

The Turkish Republic became officially a secular and multiethnic state. Large numbers of Armenians had been killed or driven from the country in widespread campaigns of persecution in the late 19th and early 20th centuries; after 1923 most Greek and Bulgarian residents were forcibly repatriated. The large minority of Kurds in southeastern Turkey were pressured to abandon their ethnic identity. Today more than 85 percent of the population is Turkish, ultimately of Central Asian origin. Islam is widely practiced, but the veil and other Islamic dress are prohibited, as are religious political parties. In 1928 the Latin alphabet was adopted in place of Arabic script for writing Turkish. In 1930 Constantinople was officially renamed Istanbul.

Turkey joined the League of Nations in 1932. A series of treaties in the 1930's made small adjustments to Turkey's borders and confirmed Turkey's status as a European nation. Under Ismet Inonu, who became president upon Ataturk's death in 1938, Turkey remained neutral throughout most of World War II but declared war against Germany in Jan. 1945 and became a founding member of the United Nations at the end of the war.

Following World War II, Turkish relations with the Soviet Union cooled; Turkey became a major recipient of American aid under the Truman Doctrine. Turkish troops joined U.N. forces in the Korean War. Continuing the Europe-oriented policy, Turkey joined both NATO and the OECD and sought membership in the European Union.

In 1974, long-standing discord with Greece erupted over the status of Cyprus, an independent nation with strong ties to Greece. On July 20, 1974, Turkish troops invaded Cyprus, occupying the northeastern 40 percent of the island. The United States cut off military aid to Turkey in 1975. Turkey forced resettlement of Greek and Turkish Cypriot residents; the Turkish sector seceded from Cyprus and became a Turkish federated state on July 8, 1975. American aid was restored in 1978.

Politically, postwar Turkey has alternated between civil and military governments. In the wake of mounting violence, martial law was imposed in 1978, and a military takeover of the government occurred on Sept. 12, 1980. Civil government was restored in 1983, and martial law lifted in 1984.

Turkey tried to remain aloof from the political turmoil of the Middle East, but it was a crucial member of the anti-Iraq coalition in the Persian Gulf War. It supported the U.N. trade embargo and allowed the Allies to use Turkish bases. The Kurdish problem was aggravated after the war as Turkey tried to offer humanitarian assistance to Kurdish refugees from Iraq without encouraging Kurdish nationalists at home. A continuing insurgency in the southeast led to sporadic but serious violence in 1992-93. Muslim fundamentalists became more active and several violent episodes resulted in deaths and destruction.

Pres. Turgut Özal died in Apr. 1993. He was succeeded as president by Prime Minister Suleyman Demirel. On June 14 the ruling True Path party elected as the new prime minister, Mrs. Tansu Ciller, Turkey's first-ever woman prime minister, and the first since 1923 to be born on the European side of the Bosporous. While the economy was her first concern (inflation hit 70 percent in 1994), military operations against the Kurdish rebels intensified with the launching of an attack into Iraq by 50,000 Turkish troops who aimed to end guerrilla raids by the Kurds.

The Ciller government collapsed in a corruption scandal, and elections held in Dec. 1995 gave Refah (Welfare), a pro-Islamic political party, its first national victory. The other parties, committed to the long tradition of secularism, refused to form a government with the Welfare party. After months of successive coalition governments, in June 1996 the Welfare party leader, Necmettim Erbakan, became prime minister of Turkey's first openly pro-Islamic government. A year later, he was forced from office by pressure from Turkey's military, a blow for secularism but against democratic government. In the wake of this de facto military coup, the new prime minister, Mesut Yilmaz, put together a seemingly fragile coalition government in July 1997. The new government closed some Islamic schools and banned traditional Moslem garb while the Supreme Court ruled that Erbakan could not be in politics for five years.

Violence in Cyprus flared up in 1998 but the E.U.'s rejection of Turkey's application was the most serious event of the year. In 1999 Turkey finally wrung an accord from Syria not to aid Kurd rebels (with 10,000 Turkish troops poised on Syria's border), but the Yilmaz government still lost a vote of confidence, not on foreign policy issues but corruption charges. Pres. Demirel asked Bulent Ecevit to form a minority, interim government until the April elections. The results were splintered, the Democratic Left gaining the plurality of 136 seats (of 550), and the president asked Ecevit to stay on as head of a coalition government. Meanwhile, Kurdish leader Ocalan was apprehended in Nairobi and, after trial, sentenced to death by hanging. From his cell, Ocalan renounced Kurdish independence and called upon his band to stop fighting, and to disarm.

In Aug. 1999 an earthquake brought great devastation and the loss of thousands of lives. It also brought aid from both the E.U. and Greece; Turkey reciprocated in the September earthquake in Greece—the two events initiating greatly improved relations summed up in six accords signed in Jan. 2000. In February the Kurd leadership renounced all violence. In May, Parliament elected chief justice Ahmet Necdet Sezer president to succeed Demirel, constitutionally prohibited from a second term.

Faced with a mass hunger strike by political prisoners in December, Pres. Sezer announced an amnesty plan to release 72,000. A largely personal but acrimonious argument between Sezer and Premier Ecevitin, in early 2001, provoked great fears of government instability which led to a serious economic crisis as foreign investors pulled their capital out of Turkey and the currency lost one-third of its value.

▶ **TURKMENISTAN**

● **GEOGRAPHY Location:** southwestern central Asia. **Boundaries:** Kazakhstan to N, Uzbekistan to N and E, Iran to S, Afghanistan to SE, Caspian Sea to W. **Total area:** 188,456 sq. mi. (488,100 sq km). **Coastline**: Caspian Sea. **Comparative area:** slightly larger than California. **Land use:** 3% arable land; 63% permanent pasture; 8% forest and woodland; 26% other (mostly urban and mountain). **Major cities:** (1994 est.) Ashkhabad (capital) 517,200; Chardzou (Carzou) 164,000.

● **PEOPLE Population:** 4,603,244 (2001 est.). **Nationality:** noun—Turkmen; adjective—Turkmen. **Ethnic groups:** 77% Turkmen, 9.2% Uzbek, 6.7% Russian, 2% Kazakh. **Languages:** 72% Turkmen (official), member of southern Turkic language group written in Cyrillic script since 1940; 12% Russian, 9% Uzbek, ethnic languages. **Religions:** 89% Muslim, 9% Eastern Orthodox, 2% unknown.

● **GOVERNMENT Type:** republic. **Independence:** Oct. 27, 1991 (from Soviet Union). **Constitution:** May 18, 1992. **National holiday:** Independence Day, Oct. 27. **Head of Government:** Saparmurat A. Niyazov, president (since Dec. 1991). **Structure:** executive—president, Council of Ministers; bicameral legislature; judicial—Supreme Court.

● **ECONOMY Monetary unit:** Turkmen manat. **Budget:** (1999 est.) *income:* $588.6 mil; *expend.:* $658.2 mil. **GDP:** $19.6 bil., $4,300 per capita (2000 est.). **Chief crops:** cotton, grain; livestock. **Natural resources:** petroleum, natural gas, coal, sulfur, sodium chloride. **Major industries:** natural gas, oil, petroleum products, textiles. **Labor force:** 2.34 mil. (1996). **Exports:** $2.4 bil. (f.o.b., 2000 est.); 63% oil and gas, 18% cotton. **Imports:** $1.65 bil. (c.i.f., 2000 est.); chemicals, foodstuffs, machinery and parts. **Major trading partners:** FSU, Turkey.

Turkmenistan, long a battleground for warring Asian empires, is bordered on the north by Uzbekistan and Kazakhstan, and on the west by the Caspian Sea. It also has a long international border with Iran and Afghanistan. About 90 percent of Turkmenistan is covered by the Kara Kum (Black Sand) desert, one of the largest in the world, and the southern areas are mountainous and prone to serious earthquakes.

A very remote and sparsely populated country, Turkmenistan has been inhabited since prehistoric times, first by Iranian-speaking people, then by Turkic tribes. In the 10th century A.D., Oghuz tribes (from Mongolia) arrived, bringing Islam with them. Although the Turkmen had emerged as a distinct ethnic group by the 15th century, they were ruled by the Persians in the south and the Uzbek khanates in the north for about 200 years. In the 19th century, Russian expansionism into Turkmen territory had begun, culminating in the Russian victory in the famous 1881 battle of Gok Tepe that killed an estimated 150,000 Turkmen.

In 1917 the Bolsheviks unsuccessfully attempted to seize power in Turkmen territory. By Apr. 30, 1918, the Soviets succeeded in creating the Turkestan Autonomous Soviet Socialist Republic (ASSR) as part of the Russian republic, but in July the ASSR was overthrown by nationalist elements with the help of the British. Once the British withdrew, however, the territory of Turkmen fell to the Soviets, and in 1924 the National Delimitation of Central Asian Republics took place. This created several central Asian republics, including the Turkmen Soviet Socialist Republic, which came into being on Oct. 27, 1924.

During the Soviet period, there were advances in medicine and public health, but the nomadic Turkmen people suffered enormously under forced collectivization and the many bloody antireligious campaigns. The purges of Turkmen intelligentsia in the 1930's were widespread. The Soviets undertook a small-scale industrialization campaign in Turkmenistan, but aside from the extraction of natural gas and petroleum, the majority of the population continued to work in agriculture, mainly growing cotton and fruits.

Under Gorbachev, the main issue for Turkmenistan became the environment. Large-scale cotton planting had led to serious environmental and health hazards. The Kara Kum Canal, which carries water from the Amu-Dar'ya to Turkmenistan's arid regions, is one of the main factors leading to the desiccation of the Aral Sea. Turkmenistan's main cultural issue was the status of the Turkmen language, for until May 1990 the official language had been listed as Russian (although only 25% of Turkmen people claimed to speak Russian). Due to its remoteness, Turkmenistan did not become involved in the democratic changes that engaged the other former union republics. Its Communist party dominated and still dominates Turkmen politics, although the Turkmen president, Saparmurat A. Niyazov, stood for popular election and was elected by direct ballot in Oct. 1990 by 98.3 percent of the population. However, the Turkmen government has banned demonstrations, picketing, and strikes, and it censors its media.

Turkmenistan was one of the early supporters of Gorbachev's proposal to form a new Union Treaty. When that led to the August 1991 coup in Moscow, the Turkmen Supreme Soviet claimed independence on Oct. 27, 1991. Turkmenistan was one of the signatories of the Alma-Ata Declaration that created the Commonwealth of Independent States in December 1991. Since then, Turkmenistan has begun to develop political and economic relations with its neighbor Iran and is working on improving its relations with Turkey. With vast oil and gas reserves Turkmenistan faces a brighter future than it ever expected.

Niyazov was overwhelmingly endorsed in a referendum, held Jan. 15, 1994 extending his mandate until 2002, bypassing a constitutional requirement for the reelection of a president every five years. In 1998 Niyazov visited the U.S., conferring with Pres. Clinton and concluding agreements with several U.S. energy firms to study the possibility of a cross-Caucasian gas pipeline to Turkey and the west (bypassing Iran). In Dec. 1999 the 50-member parliament elected (unanimously) Niyazov president-for-life (as recommended by the People's Council, headed by Niyazov).

▶ **TUVALU**
● **GEOGRAPHY   Location:** group of nine small atolls, about 350 mi. (560 km) from N to S, in South Pacific Ocean. Funafuti 8°30'S, 179°12'E. **Boundaries:** surrounded by South Pacific Ocean; Kiribati to N, Fiji to S, Solomon Islands to W. **Total area:** 10 sq. mi. (26 sq km). **Coastline:** 15 mi. (24 km). **Comparative area:** one-tenth size of Washington, D.C. **Land use:** 0% arable land; 0% permanent crops; 0% meadows and pastures; 0% forest and woodland; 100% other. **Major cities:** (by atoll; 1985 census) Funafuti (capital) 2,810; Vaitupu 1,231; Niutao 904; Nanumea 879; Nukufetau 694.
● **PEOPLE   Population:** 10,991 (2001 est.). **Nationality:** noun—Tuvaluan(s); adjective—Tuvaluan. **Ethnic groups:** 96% Polynesian. **Languages:** Tuvaluan, English. **Religions:** 97% Church of Tuvalu (Congregationalist), 1.4% Seventh-Day Adventists, 1% Baha'i.
● **GOVERNMENT   Type:** constitutional monarchy with a parliamentary democracy; began debating

republic status in 1992. **Independence:** Oct. 1, 1978 (from U.K.). **Constitution:** Oct. 1, 1978. **National holiday:** Independence Day, Oct. 1. **Heads of Government:** Manuella Tulaga, governor-general (since June 1994); Bikenibeu Paeniu, prime minister (since Dec. 1996). **Structure:** executive—prime minister and cabinet; unicameral legislature—12-member House of Assembly; judicial—high court, chief justice presides over sessions twice a year.
● **ECONOMY   Monetary unit:** Tuvaluan dollar or Australian dollar. **Budget:** (1998) *income:* $6.2 mil.; *expend.:* $6.1 mil. **GDP:** $11.6 mil., $1,100 per capita (1995 est.). **Chief crops:** coconuts; fish. **Natural resources:** fish. **Major industries:** fishing, tourism, copra. **Labor force:** N.A. **Exports:** $165,000 (f.o.b., 1989); copra. **Imports:** $4.4 mil. (c.i.f., 1989); food, animals, mineral fuels, machinery, manufactured goods. **Major trading partners:** Fiji, Australia, New Zealand.

A British protectorate was established in 1892, and the islands were incorporated into the British colony of the Gilbert and Ellice Islands in 1915. The nine principal islands that make up the Ellice group escaped Japanese occupation in World War II and were used as Allied bases in the campaign to recapture the Pacific.

The Gilbert and Ellice Islands colony was granted self-rule in 1971. In 1975 the Ellice Islands, inhabited mainly by Polynesians, seceded from the other (mainly Micronesian) islands of the colony and became independent as Tuvalu on Oct. 1, 1978. (See also "Kiribati.") In a 1979 U.S.-Tuvalu friendship treaty, the United States relinquished claims, based on 19th-century guano mining, to the four southernmost islands, in return for access to World War II military airfields and veto power over other nations' use of the islands for military purposes.

The economy is based on subsistence farming and fishing. Exports include copra and woven palm-leaf products, and hydroponic agriculture and offshore fisheries are being developed. Tuvalu remains heavily dependent on foreign aid, principally from Australia, New Zealand, and the United Kingdom. In 2000, Tuvalu was admitted to the U.N.

▶ **UGANDA**
Republic of Uganda
● **GEOGRAPHY   Location:** landlocked equatorial country in eastern Africa. **Boundaries:** Sudan to N, Kenya to E, Tanzania to S, Rwanda to SW, Zaire to W. **Total area:** 91,135 sq. mi. (236,040 sq km). **Coastline:** none. **Comparative area:** slightly smaller than Oregon. **Land use:** 25% arable land; 9% permanent crops; 9% meadows and pastures; 28% forest and woodland; 29% other; includes negl. % irrigated. **Major cities:** (1991 census) Kampala (capital) 773,463; Jinja 60,979; Mbale 53,634; Masaka 49,070; Gulu 42,841.
● **PEOPLE   Population:** 23,985,712 (2001 est.). **Nationality:** noun—Ugandan(s); adjective—Ugandan. **Ethnic groups:** 17% Baganda, 12% Karamojong, 8% Basogo, 8% Iteso, 6% Langi, 6% Rwanda, 5% Bagisu, 4% Acholi, 4% Lugbara, 3% Bunyoro. **Languages:** English (official), Luganda, Swahili, Arabic and other Niger-Congo languages. **Religions:** 33% Roman Catholic, 33% Protestant, 16% Muslim, 18% indigenous beliefs.
● **GOVERNMENT   Type:** republic. **Independence:** Oct. 9, 1962 (from UK). **Constitution:** Oct. 8, 1995. **National holiday:** Independence Day, Oct. 9.

Heads of Government: Yoweri Kaguta Museveni, president (since Jan. 1986); Prof. Apolo Nsibambi, prime minister (since Apr. 1999). **Structure:** executive—president is head of government and state; unicameral legislature; judiciary.
• ECONOMY   **Monetary unit:** Ugandan shilling. **Budget:** (FY98/99) *income:* $959 mil.; *expend.:* $1.04 bil. **GDP:** $26.2 bil., $1,100 per capita (2000 est.). **Chief crops:** coffee, cotton, tobacco; beef, milk, poultry. **Natural resources:** copper, cobalt, limestone, salt. **Major industries:** sugar, brewing, tobacco. **Labor force:** 8.361 mil. (1993 est.); 82% agriculture, 13% services, 5% industry. **Exports:** $500.1 mil. (f.o.b., 1999); coffee, gold, fish. **Imports:** $1.1 bil. (f.o.b., 1999); transportation equipment, petroleum, medical supplies, cereals. **Major trading partners:** *exports:* EU, Kenya; *imports:* Kenya, U.K., U.S., India.

Prior to 1800 Uganda was the site of several important kingdoms, notably Buganda, centered on Kampala on the northern shore of Lake Victoria. After 1830, Arabs from the sultanate of Oman, based in Zanzibar, asserted loose control over the region and dominated its trade. British explorers, seeking the source of the Nile, reached the Lake Victoria region in the mid-19th century. Mission stations were established in 1877; a Muslim rebellion destroyed the missions and occupied Kampala in 1888.

Buganda was brought under the control of the British East Africa Company in 1890, and Britain established a protectorate in 1894 that was expanded to include neighboring territories in 1896. In 1902 some of the protectorate's territory was transferred to Kenya. British immigrants extensively developed the agricultural potential of Uganda's fertile and temperate highlands, establishing large and prosperous farms. Lake Victoria was the scene of naval battles between Great Britain and Germany (established in neighboring Tanganyika) during World War I.

In 1955 the British administration created a local parliamentary government in which both whites and Africans held ministerial office. Talks on the terms for independence began in 1961 and after some difficulty arrived at a formula for a national structure in which Buganda and other traditional kingdoms would retain local autonomy. Several political parties competed for power; the Uganda People's Congress led by Milton Obote became dominant. Uganda became independent within the British Commonwealth on Oct. 9, 1962. Several constitutional changes in the early 1960's led to an end to the autonomy of the kingdoms and the effective concentration of all power in Obote's presidency. In 1967 a new constitution proclaimed Uganda an independent republic.

Obote was overthrown on Jan. 25, 1971, by Idi Amin Dada, commander of Uganda's armed forces. Amin declared himself president, dissolved the Parliament, and assumed absolute powers. In 1972 he expelled Uganda's Asians (primarily people of Indian and Pakistani descent), who controlled most of the country's small-scale commerce. The U.S. broke off diplomatic relations in 1973. In 1976 Amin declared himself president for life. His eight-year reign was marked by extreme violence and persecution of political and tribal opponents; as many as 300,000 may have been killed between 1971 and 1979. The country's prosperous agricultural, mining, and commercial economy was devastated, and its infrastructure, including a good road and rail network and Makerere University, fell into ruins.

On July 3, 1976, Israeli airborne troops landed at Entebbe and rescued 103 hostages who had been captured in a skyjacking carried out by Palestinian and German terrorists.

In 1978 Amin, with the aid of Libyan troops, invaded Tanzania. In the following year, Tanzanian troops countered by invading Uganda; they captured Kampala on Apr. 11, 1979, and drove Amin into exile. Diplomatic relations with the United States resumed. After a series of interim governments, elections in 1981 returned Obote to power. Obote's new regime was marked by repression of opponents and by rebellion in the northern part of the country by the National Resistance Army (NRA) under Yoweri Museveni.

Obote fled into exile in 1985 and was succeeded by Lt. Gen. Basilio Olara-Okello, but the NRA rebellion continued. Kenyan president Daniel arap Moi mediated peace talks between Olara-Okello and the NRA in late 1985; in Jan. 1986 Olara-Okello fled, and Museveni organized a new government. Despite continued insurgencies by rival military factions and a rebellion led by the charismatic religious leader Alice Lakwena, the Museveni government restored order and, with aid from the World Bank and the I.M.F., began to rebuild Uganda's shattered society.

A constituent assembly was elected in 1994. In 1995, it enacted a new constitution, which extended for five years a ban on political parties, and scheduled presidential elections for 1996, elections Museveni won with 74 percent of the vote. By 1997 Uganda had the fastest growing economy in Africa and in 1998 Pres. Clinton's visit helped to create interst among foreign investors. In a June 2000 referendum voters extended the "no party" system Museveni advocates. Museveni won re-election as president in March 2001 with 69 percent of the vote and announced in April that although Uganda was withdrawing from the Congo peace accord, its troops were withdrawing also, since they had accomplished their aim of defeating the Hutu extremists who threatened Uganda's borders

▶ UKRAINE

• GEOGRAPHY   **Location:** east-central Europe. **Boundaries:** Belarus to N, Russian Federation to NE and E, Sea of Azov and Black Sea to S, Moldova and Romania to SW, Hungary, Slovakia, Poland to W. **Total area:** 233,089 sq. mi. (603,700 sq km). **Coastline:** Black Sea. **Comparative area:** slightly smaller than Texas. **Land use:** 58% arable land; 2% permanent crops, 13% meadows and pastures; 18% forest and woodland; 9% other (mostly urban). **Major cities:** (1995 est.) Kiev (capital) 2,635,000; Kharkov (Kharkiv) 1,576,000; Dnepropetrovsk 1,162,000; Donetsk (Donetske) 1,102,000; Odessa (Odesa) 1,060,000.
• PEOPLE   **Population:** 48,760,474 (2000 est.). **Nationality:** noun—Ukrainian(s); adjective—Ukrainian. **Ethnic groups:** 73% Ukrainian, 22% Russian, 1% Jewish. **Languages:** Ukrainian, Russian, Romanian, Polish, Hungarian. **Religions:** Ukrainian Orthodox—Moscow Patriarchate, Ukrainian Orthodox—Kiev Patriarchate, Ukrainian Autocephalous Orthodox, Ukrainian Catholic, Protestant; Jewish.
• GOVERNMENT   **Type:** republic. **Independence:** Dec. 1, 1991 (from Soviet Union). **Constitution:** June 28, 1996. **National holiday:** Independence Day, Aug. 24. **Heads of Government:** Leonid Kuchma, president (since Dec. 1991); Anatoly Kinakh, prime minister (since May 2001). **Structure:**

executive—president, Cabinet of Ministers; legislative—Supreme Council (450 deputies); judicial—Supreme Court.

● **ECONOMY** **Monetary unit:** hryvnia. **Budget:** (1999) *income:* $8.3 bil.; *expend.:*$8.8 bil. **GDP:** $189.4 bil., $3,850 per capita (2000 est.). **Chief crops:** grain, sugar beets, sunflower seeds, vegetables; meat, milk. **Natural resources:** coal, iron ore, manganese, natural gas, oil. **Major industries:** coal, electric power, metals, machinery and transport, chemicals. **Labor force:** 22.8 mil. (1997); 32% industry and construction, 24% agriculture and forestry, 17% health, education and culture, 8% trade and distribution, 7% transport and communication. **Exports:** $14.6 bil. (2000 est.); energy, chemicals, machinery and transport equipment. **Imports:** $15 bil. (2000 est.); energy, machinery and parts, transportation equipment, chemicals. **Major trading partners:** Russia, Europe, U.S.

Ukraine is the center of the original Russian state, known as Kievan Rus, which came into existence in the ninth century A.D. In the 13th and 14th centuries, during the Mongol invasion, Ukraine was controlled by Lithuania and Poland, and in 1654 it first entered the Russian empire. In the latter half of the 17th century, Ukraine was divided, with the eastern regions becoming part of Russia and the western part annexed by Poland; when Poland was subsequently partitioned, the western sections were ceded to Austria.

Until 1917 eastern Ukraine was a province of Russia called "Little Russia," and for two centuries the dominant country tried to Russianize the Ukrainian clergy and upper classes, and ban the Ukrainian language. Nevertheless, secret societies for the study of Ukrainian history, language, and culture formed, and when in the 19th century the Russians exiled Ukrainians to Siberia, modern Ukrainian nationalism was born.

In 1917, when the Russian empire collapsed, Ukrainian nationalists demanded Ukraine's autonomy by establishing a Ukrainian People's Republic, but within a few months, Red Army troops had occupied Ukraine. For the next few years, however, Ukraine was in the middle of the civil war and was even ceded to Germany under the Brest-Litovsk treaty of 1918, but in December 1920 a Ukrainian Soviet Socialist Republic (SSR) was established. Ukraine again was divided under the 1921 Treaty of Riga, which gave western Ukraine to Poland, Czechoslovakia, and Romania, while eastern Ukraine formed the Ukrainian SSR. Ukraine became one of the original members of the U.S.S.R. in December 1922.

The Ukrainians strongly opposed Stalin's policy of forced collectivization of agriculture in the 1930's, and the resulting chaos, famine, and deportation resulted in the deaths of millions of Ukrainians. Likewise, Stalin's great terror of the 1930's hit Ukraine hard, with the first victims being Ukrainian nationalists. World War II largely devastated Ukraine and killed millions of Ukrainians, but as a result of the war, Ukraine regained its old territories from Romania and Poland and was enlarged by the addition of historical Tatar lands in 1954. (The native Tatar inhabitants were forcibly deported to central Asia in the mid-1940's.)

Mikhail Gorbachev's policy of glasnost was slow to take root in Ukraine, largely because the head of the Communist party in Ukraine was a loyal Brezhnev crony, Vladimir Shcherbitsky. Outwardly, he appeared to agree with Gorbachev's policies, but Ukraine dissidents were still being arrested and cultural groups harassed by secret police. In 1986 a deadly nuclear power explosion at Chernobyl—and Soviet attempts at covering it up—turned international attention to Ukraine and gave rise to a number of new, powerful opposition movements. Rukh (the Ukrainian People's Movement for Restructuring), the most important of these, was founded in Kiev by a prominent group of intellectuals. By 1989 branches of Rukh had been organized in most parts of Ukraine. At the same time, Ukrainian miners became active in strikes, and the Ukrainian Catholic church and the Ukrainian Orthodox church became politically active. Shcherbitsky's failure to contain these groups led to his dismissal in 1989.

On July 16, 1990, the Ukrainian Supreme Soviet adopted a declaration of sovereignty, and Communist party Second Secretary Leonid Kravchuk became chairman of the Supreme Soviet. In March 1991 Ukraine participated in the negotiations to form a new union treaty, despite more radical demands by Rukh for complete independence. The Ukrainian Communist party's failure to denounce the attempted coup in Moscow in August 1991 led to significant changes in Ukraine's political situation. After the coup collapsed, the Communist party was banned, and on Aug. 24, 1991, Ukraine adopted a declaration of total independence. In December, Kravchuk was elected president.

That same month, Ukraine, Belarus, and the Russian Federation signed the Minsk Agreement that created the Commonwealth of Independent States, and on Dec. 21, Ukraine and 10 other former union republics officially committed themselves to the union by signing the Alma-Ata Declaration.

Potentially dangerous conflicts with Russia remained, however, including control of the powerful Black Sea fleet. Soon after the fall of the Soviet government armed conflict erupted in April 1994, when Russia removed a ship from Odessa laden with marine-research and navigational equipment valued at more than $10 million. A compromise was reached in 1995 that divided the 635-vessel fleet equally, with Russia then buying 32 percent of the ships from the Ukraine and paying rent for use of the naval base at Sevastopol.

The other conflict involved 2,000 nuclear warheads present in Ukraine. In Jan. 1994, Kravchuk, Boris Yeltsin, and Bill Clinton negotiated an agreement to dismantle Ukraine's 175 long-range missiles and more than 1,800 warheads. But Ukraine's Parliament refused to approve the agreement, even after Clinton made a $350 million U.S. aid package conditional on total disarmament. Parliament's intransigence was seen as an embarrassment to Kravchuk, and in July 1994 he lost the presidential election to reformer Leonid Kuchma. In Nov. Parliament overwhelmingly approved the Nuclear Nonproliferation Treaty and loans from the U.S. and the I.M.F. ensued. The U.S. also pledged $400 million to help dismantle the missiles.

In July 1996 the Rada approved a new "strong president" Constitution which guaranteed rights to own property and to engage in business, which abolished local councils ("soviets"), and which made Ukrainian the only legal language (although Russian is the language of about one-fifth of the population). The May 1997 Friendship Treaty with Russia settled the Black Sea fleet division, guaranteed Russia's right to rent part of the port facilities of Sevastopol to service the fleet, and confirmed Ukrainian sovereignty over all of Crimea.

In Aug. 1998 the I.M.F. agreed to loans totalling $2.2 bil. to assist the government despite its inability to make necessary reforms. Kuchma easily won re-election in a Nov. 1999 run-off against the Communist candidate. In April 2000 his referendum to expand presidential power was approved.

Soon after this triumph, Kuchma's authority began to unravel: in November, charges, backed by tape recordings, surfaced that he had connived in the murder of an opposition journalist; the tapes also held evidence of election tampering and bribery. An odd alliance of the Communists with the business parties in Parliament toppled Prime Minister Yushchenko's government in April 2001; his replacement was the business coalition's Anatoly Kinakh. But Kuchma's future seemed in doubt.

▶ UNITED ARAB EMIRATES

● **GEOGRAPHY Location:** eastern Arabian peninsula. **Boundaries:** Persian Gulf to N, Gulf of Oman to NE, Oman to E, Saudi Arabia to S and W, short frontier with Qatar to NW. **Total area:** 31,969 sq. mi. (82,880 sq km). **Coastline:** 819 mi. (1,318 km). **Comparative area:** slightly smaller than Maine. **Land use:** 2% meadows and pastures; 98% other. **Major cities:** (1995 est.) Abu Dhabi (capital) 928,360; Dubai 674,100; Sharjah 400,400.
● **PEOPLE Population:** 2,407,460 (2001 est.). **Nationality:** noun—Emirian(s); adjective—Emirian. **Ethnic groups:** 19% Emirian, 23% other Arab and Iranian, 50% South Asian, 8% other expatriates (includes Westerners and East Asians); less than 20% of population are UAE citizens (1982). **Languages:** Arabic (official), Persian, English, Hindi, Urdu. **Religions:** 96% Muslim (16% Shia), 4% Christian, Hindu, and other.
● **GOVERNMENT Type:** federation with specified powers delegated to UAE central government and other powers reserved to member emirates. **Independence:** Dec. 2, 1971 (from UK). **Constitution::** Dec. 2, 1971; made permanent 1996. **National holiday:** National Day, Dec. 2. **Heads of Government:** Sheikh Zayed bin Sultan al-Nahyan of Abu Dhabi, president (since Dec. 1971); Maktoum al-Maktoum, prime minister (since Oct.1990). **Structure:** executive—Supreme Council of Rulers (seven members), from which president and vice president are elected; prime minister and Council of Ministers; unicameral legislature—Federal National Council; judicial—Union Supreme Court.
● **ECONOMY Monetary unit:** Emirian dirham. **Budget:** (2000 est.) *income:* $6.5 bil.; *expend.:* $7.3 bil. **GDP:** $54 bil., $22,800 per capita (2000 est.). **Chief crops:** dates, vegetables, watermelons; poultry, eggs, dairy products; fish. **Natural resources:** crude oil, natural gas. **Major industries:** petroleum, petrochemicals. **Labor force:** 1.38 mil. (1998 est.); 60% services, 32% industry and commerce, 8% agriculture; 75% of the labor force is foreign. **Exports:** $46 bil. (f.o.b., 2000 est.); 45% crude oil, natural gas, re-exports, dried fish, dates. **Imports:** $34 bil. (f.o.b., 2000 est.); manufactured goods, machinery and transport equipment, chemicals, food. **Major trading partners:** *exports:* 30% Japan, 7% India; *imports:* 8% U.S., 9% Japan, 8% U.K.

In the 1820's Great Britain established protectorates over seven small sheikhdoms along the gulf coast between Qatar and Oman—Abu Dhabi, Dubai, Sharjah, Ajmar, Fujairah, and Umm al-Qaiwain. The region, which had been known as the Pirate Coast, then was generally referred to as the Trucial Coast or Trucial Oman. Under terms of a treaty in 1892, the sheikhdoms agreed not to enter into relations with any other country.

After Great Britain announced that it would withdraw its forces from the gulf in 1971, the seven sheikhdoms formed a federation and became independent as the United Arab Emirates on Dec. 2, 1971.

Just prior to his invasion of Kuwait in August 1990, Saddam Hussein threatened both the UAE and Kuwait for overproduction of petroleum, and the UAE was an integral part of the Allied coalition against Iraq. In 1995 the government signed a defensive alliance with France, who supplies the army with most of its weapons.

The economy is almost entirely dominated by petroleum. Citizens of the UAE receive extensive social services and enjoy one of the world's highest per capita incomes.

▶ UNITED KINGDOM
United Kingdom of Great Britain and Northern Ireland

● **GEOGRAPHY Location:** northwestern Europe, occupying major portion of British Isles. **Boundaries:** Atlantic Ocean to NW and W, North Sea to E; separated from France by English Channel to S; Republic of Ireland to W. **Total area:** 94,525 sq. mi. (244,820 sq km). **Coastline:** 7,723 mi. (12,429 km). **Comparative area:** slightly smaller than Oregon. **Land use:** 25% arable land; negl. % permanent crops; 46% meadows and pastures; 10% forest and woodland; 19% other; includes 1% irrigated. **Major cities:** (1994 est.) London (capital) 6,976,500; Birmingham 1,008,400; Leeds 724,400; Glasgow 680,000; Sheffield 530,100.
● **PEOPLE Population:** 59,647,790 (2001 est.). **Nationality:** noun—Briton(s), British (collective pl.); adjective—British. **Ethnic groups:** 81.5% English, 9.6% Scottish, 2.4% Irish, 1.9% Welsh, 1.8% Ulster, 2.8% West Indian, Indian, Pakistani, and other. **Languages:** English, Welsh (about 26% of population of Wales), Scottish form of Gaelic (about 60,000 in Scotland). **Religions:** 27 mil. Anglican, 9 mil. Roman Catholic, 1 mil. Muslim, 800,000 Presbyterian, 760,000 Methodist, 400,000 Sikh, 350,000 Hindu, 300,000 Jewish.
● **GOVERNMENT Type:** constitutional monarchy. **Independence:** N.A. **Constitution:** unwritten; partly statutes, partly common law and practice. **National holiday:** Celebration of the Birthday of the Queen, second Saturday in June. **Heads of Government:** Elizabeth II, queen (since Feb. 1952); Tony Blair, prime minister (since May 1997). **Structure:** executive authority lies with collectively responsible cabinet led by prime minister; legislative authority rests with Parliament (House of Lords, House of Commons); House of Lords is supreme judicial authority and highest court of appeals.
● **ECONOMY Monetary unit:** British pound. **Budget:** (FY00) *income:* $555.2 bil.; *expend.:* $510.8 bil. **GDP:** $1.36 trillion, $22,800 per capita (2000 est.). **Chief crops:** cereals, oilseed, potatoes, vegetables; cattle, sheep, poultry; fish. **Natural resources:** coal, crude oil, natural gas, tin, limestone. **Major industries:** machinery and transportation equipment, metals, food processing. **Labor force:** 29.2 mil. (1999); 80% services, 19% industry, 1% agriculture, 5.5% unemployment (2000 est.). **Exports:** $282 bil. (f.o.b., 2000); manufactured goods, machinery, fuels, chemicals. **Imports:** $324 bil. (f.o.b., 2000); manufactured goods, machinery, fuels, foodstuffs. **Major**

trading partners: *exports:* 58% E.U. (12% Germany, 10% France, 8% Netherlands), 13% U.S.; *imports:* 53% E.U. (14% Germany, 9% France, 7% Netherlands, 5% Ireland), 13% U.S.

Early megalithic and Iron Age peoples of Britain, primarily Celtic, developed tribal states that were conquered by Roman invaders in A.D. 43. After Roman legions withdrew from Britain in 410, invasions of Jutes, Angles, and Saxons conquered much of England, while Celtic peoples flourished in Wales, Scotland, and especially Ireland. Viking invaders established settlements in the eighth century. A united Saxon kingdom fell to the Norman invasion of William the Conquerer in 1066.

An aristocratic rebellion against the royal absolutism of King John in 1215 led to the royal acceptance of the Magna Carta, guaranteeing legal rights and laying the foundations of parliamentary government. From the 12th to the 15th century, the Plantagenet dynasty ruled England and claimed overlordship over Ireland; Wales was conquered in 1283. The Plantagenets also controlled sizable territories in France.

The Hundred Years' War (1337-1453) cost England its French possessions; the War of the Roses, (1455-85) ended the Plantagenet dynasty and brought Henry Tudor (Henry VII) to the throne. The Tudors gradually centralized royal control by bringing pressure against both the church and the nobility. Henry VIII broke with Rome in 1534 and established the Church of England. Under Elizabeth I, the last of the Tudors, England defeated Spain at sea and laid the foundations of later worldwide English sea power. The English Renaissance began under Elizabeth I (1533-1603) with the works of Shakespeare and continued into the 17th century with Milton and Newton.

The Stuart dynasty was founded by James I (1566-1625), uniting the crowns of England and Scotland in 1603. The English Civil War (1642-49) culminated in the execution of Charles I and the proclamation of the Commonwealth (later the Protectorate) under Oliver Cromwell. The monarchy was restored with Charles II in 1660. In the bloodless Glorious Revolution (1688), James II fled before a Protestant army under the Dutch William of Orange, who married and ruled jointly with James's daughter Mary II. The English Bill of Rights established the supremacy of Parliament and made the government a model of constitutional monarchy.

In the last gasp of the Stuart claimants to the throne, Irish supporters of James II were defeated at the Battle of the Boyne (1690), which temporarily crushed Irish resistance to annexation by England. The United Kingdom was created when Scotland was joined with England in a common Parliament by the Act of Union in 1707. A Scottish uprising led by the Young Pretender, Charles Edward Stuart, was crushed at Culloden Moor in 1745. Ireland was made part of the United Kingdom in 1801.

In the 1700's the United Kingdom became the greatest sea power in the world, controlling an empire that included much of North America and India. Agrarian "enclosures" of the 18th century ruined the peasantry but created an entrepreneurial revolution in agriculture that ultimately led to greatly increased agricultural productivity. The capital created in the process contributed to the success of the Industrial Revolution, which over the next century made England the wealthiest land on earth.

Despite the loss of the 13 colonies after the American Revolution (1775-83), England consolidated its holdings in the Indian subcontinent, Australia and New Zealand, Malaya, Hong Kong, much of eastern Africa from "Cape to Cairo," and elsewhere. Britain's prosperity and moral purpose were embodied in the person of Victoria, Queen of Great Britain and Ireland (1836-1901) and Empress of India (from 1836).

The repeal of the protectionist Corn Laws in 1846 led to an agricultural depression and hastened the migration of labor from the countryside to the industrial cities. The rise of labor activism led in 1906 to laws granting privileged status to trade unions, which organized the Labour party to promote their interests.

Britain's involvement in the Triple Entente with France and Russia ensured its participation in World War I (1914-18) against Germany, Italy, and Austria-Hungary. Victory came at the cost of an entire generation of British youth, but Britain emerged from the war with its empire at a high point, adding Tanganyika, Jordan, Palestine, and Iraq as part of the postwar division of spoils. Most of Ireland became independent in 1921, however, leaving only Northern Ireland as part of the United Kingdom.

Between the two world wars, Britain's navy and air force were the largest in the world, its army the third largest. Yet its industry was aging, the Great Depression hit especially hard in the British Isles, strikes and labor unrest weakened the social fabric, and colonial ties began to weaken in the 1930's. Economic retrenchment led to a failure to rearm in the face of the rising threat of Hitler's Germany and Mussolini's Italy.

The Munich Pact of 1938 gave Hitler a license for war; his invasion of Poland in 1939 forced Britain into the conflict. When Winston Churchill became prime minister in 1940, Britain was under daily air attack and in danger of an invasion by sea, and the country was dependent on American friendship and lend-lease war materials. But 1941 brought alliance with the United States and the Soviet Union, and a slowly turning tide of war leading to victory in 1945. Still, postwar Britain dropped to the second rank of superpowers.

The coalition between the Conservative and Labour parties that had governed Great Britain during the war seemed no longer necessary in 1945 as the war wound down. Labour won a landslide victory in the 1945 elections; Churchill was recalled in the midst of the Potsdam Conference, and Clement Atlee became prime minister. A brief Labour flirtation with the U.S.S.R. quickly ended in the postwar 1940's; England became a founding member of the United Nations and also, in 1949, of NATO. As the Cold War took shape, Britain developed its own nuclear arsenal.

The Labour party nationalized the Bank of England along with railroads, public utilities, and heavy industry. A comprehensive welfare state apparatus was created, including a national health service, unemployment and retirement benefits, and free education at all levels. But Britain was in many respects too poor to afford such changes; in order to cut expenditures, the government hastened the process of withdrawal from colonies and military bases around the world. India was granted independence in 1947, and Palestine, Burma, and Ceylon in 1948-49.

The elections of 1951 brought Churchill back to the prime ministership at the head of a Conservative majority that would last for 13 years. The Conservatives returned steel and trucking to the private sector but in general refrained from undoing the social policies of their Labour predecessors. Economic growth began in the 1950's and held steady at about 2.5 percent per year, a significantly lower rate than in continental Europe; obsolescence, excessive wage and benefit settlements, and a low savings rate all took their toll. The coronation of Elizabeth II in 1953 added a much-needed element of national celebration.

Churchill retired in 1955 and was succeeded by Anthony Eden. Eden's government fell in 1956 over the failed Anglo-French invasion of Suez. Eden's fall in 1957 brought to power Harold Macmillan, who pursued close relations with the United States. Most important, he presided over the transformation of an empire to a commonwealth; in the early 1960's, Ghana, Nigeria, Malaya, Singapore, and numerous other colonies were granted independence and Commonwealth status. Immigrants from the Commonwealth promptly flocked to England, straining housing, social services, and the labor market and creating problems of assimilation that remain unsolved.

Britain under Macmillan was the moving force behind the European Free Trade Association in 1960. In 1961 Britain applied for membership in the EEC, but that application was humiliatingly vetoed by France's Charles de Gaulle in 1963. Macmillan's government fell with the Profumo Scandal of 1963, and Douglas Home became a caretaker prime minister pending new elections.

The 1964 elections brought the Labour party to power under Harold Wilson, whose moderate positions made him unpopular with his own party, especially when he sponsored legislation to ban wildcat strikes. Strikes, wage inflation, the steady growth of the public sector (including renationalization of the steel industry), and the rise of turmoil in Northern Ireland in 1968-69 combined to make public support for Labour evaporate.

The Conservative victory in the 1970 elections brought Edward Heath to the office of prime minister. Promising to cut expenditures and taxes, reward initiative, and curb union power, the Conservatives were able to accomplish none of those aims. Heath's government imposed ineffective wage controls in an attempt to slow inflation and passed the 1971 Industrial Relations Act to regulate unions. When unions defied that act, the government fell. Heath's major achievement was the United Kingdom's admission to the EC in 1973. Continued turmoil in Northern Ireland was met with the abolition of Ulster's Stormount Parliament in 1972 and the imposition of direct British rule—a policy that did nothing to stem the growing sectarian violence.

Wilson returned to the prime ministership in 1974 and retired in 1976, passing on the office to James Callaghan, who governed until 1979 at the head of a Labour-Liberal coalition. The continued power of trade unions was seen in the repeal of the Industrial Relations Act and the extension of union privileges. The left wing of the Labour party brought increasing pressure against defense spending, membership in NATO, and also loudly criticized American involvement in Vietnam.

The OPEC oil price rises of 1972-74 hurt Great Britain in the short run but also encouraged development of oil and gas fields in the North Sea, which made the nation a major petroleum exporter and helped revitalize its economy. Oil exploration in the North Sea also encouraged

Scottish nationalism, with some damage to national unity, although in both Scotland and Wales, proposals in 1979 for separate parliaments were soundly defeated by plebiscites.

The 1979 elections brought the Conservatives to power again, behind Margaret Thatcher, Great Britain's (and Europe's) first female prime minister. She proved to be the only British prime minister in modern times to lead her party successfully in three elections. Thatcher took office with an agenda that involved undoing much of the course of postwar British history.

The first target was inflation, attacked through a freeze on expenditures and reduction of government borrowing. The policy was a success; inflation fell from 18 percent in 1980 to 3 percent in 1989. But the austerity program had a high cost in unemployment, which remained at 14 percent in the mid-1980's.

In 1982 national attention turned abruptly to overseas concerns, as Argentina invaded the Falkland ("Malvinas") Islands (only 300 miles east of Argentina), which it had long claimed as Argentine national territory, on Apr. 2. On May 21 British forces launched a counteroffensive, and the invading Argentine forces surrendered on June 14. The nation's success in mounting an amphibious operation 6,500 miles away provoked an upsurge of patriotism that swept Thatcher's party into a second term in 1983.

After the election the government turned to denationalization of industry. Over $30 billion in state property—from industrial giants, such as Britoil and British Gas, to individual apartments in municipal housing projects—was sold to private interests. This program was followed in 1986 by tax cuts, in which the top income-tax rate dropped from 98 percent to 40 percent. In foreign affairs, Britain agreed in 1985 to return Hong Kong to Chinese sovereignty in 1997.

The 1987 elections pitted the Conservatives against a weak Labour party that opposed NATO missile deployment in Great Britain, advocating unilateral disarmament and calling for renationalization of industry and a return to higher taxes for the wealthy. The Conservatives easily won their third straight election. By 1989 the "Thatcher Revolution" had produced a decisive long-term economic recovery, but one that was unevenly distributed: the southern part of the country enjoyed an economic boom, while the older industrial cities of the north remained stagnant. In 1990 an economic slowdown and rising inflation led to a strong decline in support for Mrs. Thatcher and her government. She resigned in November 1990.

Thatcher was replaced by Chancellor of the Exchequer John Major, whose greatest challenge has been Britain's role in a united Europe, to which Britain now has a land link (for the first time in 9,000 years) via the 31-mile Channel Tunnel (Chunnel), completed in 1994.

In the April 1992 elections, the Conservatives, led by Major, won a comfortable 21-seat margin in Parliament despite a recession. Not since the Napoleonic Wars has a British political party been able to form four consecutive governments. Yet only 13 months later Major's ratings in the polls had fallen to 21 percent as the economy stalled and the Conservatives themselves split badly over some elements in the EC's Maastricht Treaty. The Conservatives were further beset in 1994 with a series of tabloid scandals and allegations of political corruption concerning arms sales to Iraq and Malaysia. Tories only 25 percent. Conservative chances in parliamentary elections, due in the spring of 1997, were looking very slim, and they looked worse in March after the government clumsily handled the news that scientists had concluded that eating English beef could cause the fatal "mad-cow" disease. After insisting that there was no cause for alarm the government was forced to deal with an E.U. boycott.

The parliamentary election of May 1997 ended 18 years of Tory government with Labour winning its largest majority since 1935, 419 seats to the Conservatives 165. The new Prime Minister Tony Blair appointed a cabinet of political moderates. In 1997 Hong Kong was returned to China without incident and in April 1998 the Blair government succeeded in negotiating a settlement in Northern Ireland although problems still remain.

In the January 1999 speech from the throne opening Parliament, Queen Elizabeth read the Blair government proposal to strip hereditary peers of their votes in the House of Lords, to create 50 new Labour life-peers (giving Labour a majority in that House) and to establish a commission to study a replacement body for the Lords. In May the first elections to the Scottish Parliament and the Welsh Assembly were held. Labour won a plurality in both (over nationalist parties). The two bodies have authority over education, environment, health care, housing, and law enforcement. The Scottish Parliament also possesses authority to tax. On Oct. 26 the House of Lords voted, 221-81, to abolish the right of hereditary peers to sit and vote in that House.

In the 2001 elections Blair's Labour Party won a huge victory, taking 413 of 659 seats, the first time Labour had won two consecutive victories.

▶ UNITED STATES OF AMERICA

● **Geography   Location:** 48 conterminous states in North America, between Atlantic and Pacific Oceans; Alaska in northwest North America; Hawaiian Islands in Pacific Ocean about 3,000 miles W of California. **Boundaries:** Canada to N; Atlantic Ocean to E; Gulf of Mexico, Mexico to S; Pacific Ocean to W. Alaska bounded on E by Canada, on S and W by Pacific Ocean, on W and N by Arctic Ocean. **Total area:** 3,717,797 sq. mi. (9,629,091 sq km). **Coastline:** 11,954 mi. (19,924 km). **Comparative area:** slightly larger than Brazil; fourth-largest country. **Land use:** 19% arable land; negl. % permanent crops; 25% meadows and pastures; 30% forest and woodland; 26% other; includes 2% irrigated. **Major cities:** (1994 est.) Washington, D.C. (capital) 567,094; New York 7,333,253; Los Angeles 3,448,613; Chicago 2,731,743; Houston 1,702,086; Philadelphia 1,524,249.

● **People   Population:** 278,058,881 (July 2001 est.). **Nationality:** noun—American(s); adjective—American. **Ethnic groups:** 83.5% white, 12.4% black, 3.3% Asian, 0.8% Amerindian. **Languages:** predominantly English; sizable Spanish-speaking minority. **Religions:** 56% Protestant, 28% Roman Catholic, 10% none, 2% Jewish, 4% other.

● **Government   Type:** federal republic; strong democratic tradition. **Independence:** July 4, 1776 (from U.K.). **Constitution:** Sept. 17, 1787, effective March 4,1789. **National holiday:** Independence Day, July 4. **Heads of Government:** George W. Bush, president (since Jan. 2001); Richard Cheney, vice president (since Jan. 2001). **Structure:** executive—president, vice president, cabinet; legislative—bicameral Congress (House of Representatives and Senate); judicial—Supreme Court;

branches, in principle, independent and maintain balance of power.

● **Economy   Monetary unit:** United States dollar **Budget:** (1999) *income:* $1.828 trillion; *expend:* $1.703 tril. **GDP:** $9.963 tril., $36,200 per capita (2000). **Chief crops:** wheat, other grains, corn, fruits, vegetables, cotton; beef, pork, poultry, dairy products; forest products; fish. **Natural resources:** coal, copper, lead, molybdenum, phosphates. **Major industries:** leading industrial power in the world, highly diversified; petroleum, steel, motor vehicles, aerospace, telecommunications, chemicals, electronics, food processing, consumer goods, fishing, lumber, mining. **Labor force:** 140.9 mil., includes unemployed (2000); 30.2% managerial and professional, 29.2% sales and administrative support, 13.5% services, 24.6% manufacturing, mining, transportation, and crafts, 2.5% farming, forestry, and fishing; 4% unemployment (2000). **Exports:** $776 bil. (f.o.b., 2000 est.); capital goods, automobiles, industrial supplies and raw materials, consumer goods, agricultural products. **Imports:** $1.223 tril. (f.o.b., 2000 est.); crude oil and refined petroleum, machinery, automobiles, consumer goods, industrial raw materials, food and beverages. **Major trading partners:** (2000) *exports:* 23% Canada, 14% Mexico, 10% Japan; *imports:* 19% Canada, 11% Mexico, 11% Japan.

(For current events and history see Part I: "Major News Stories of the Year," and Part II: "Chronology of American History.")

▶ URUGUAY
Oriental Republic of Uruguay

● **Geography   Location:** southeastern coast of South America. **Boundaries:** Brazil to N, Atlantic Ocean to E and S, Argentina to W. **Total area:** 68,039 sq. mi. (176,220 sq km). **Coastline:** 410 mi. (660 km). **Comparative area:** slightly smaller than Washington State. **Land use:** 7% arable land; negl. % permanent crops; 77% meadows and pastures; 6% forest and woodland; 10% other; includes 1% irrigated. **Major cities:** (1992 census) Montevideo (capital) 1,383,660; Salto 77,400; Paysandú 75,200; Las Piedras 61,300; Rivera 55,400.

● **People   Population:** 3,360,105 (2001 est.). **Nationality:** noun—Uruguayan(s); adjective—Uruguayan. **Ethnic groups:** 88% white, 8% mestizo, 4% black. **Languages:** Spanish, Portunol, or Brazilero; Portuguese-Spanish mix on the Brazilian frontier. **Religions:** 66% Roman Catholic, 2% Protestant, 2% Jewish, 30% nonprofessing or other (less than half adult population attends church regularly).

● **Government   Type:** republic. **Independence:** Aug. 25, 1825 (from Brazil). **Constitution:** Nov. 27, 1966; effective Feb. 1967; suspended June 27, 1973; constitutional reforms approved Jan. 7, 1997. **National holiday:** Independence Day, Aug. 25. **Head of Government:** Jorge Batlle Ibanez, president (since Mar. 2000). **Structure:** executive—headed by president; bicameral legislature (Senate and House of Deputies); national judiciary headed by Supreme Court.

● **Economy   Monetary unit:** Uruguayan peso. **Budget:** (2000 est.) *income:* $4 bil.; *expend.:* $4.6 bil. **GDP:** $31 bil., $9,300 per capita (2000 est.). **Chief crops:** wheat, rice, corn, sorghum; livestock; fishing. **Natural resources:** fertile soil, hydropower potential, minor minerals, fisheries. **Major industries:** meat processing, wool and hides, sugar. **Labor force:** 1.5 mil. (1999 est.); 25% government; 19% manufacturing; 12% commerce; 12% utilities, construction, transport, and communications; 11% agriculture; 14% unemployment (2000). **Exports:** $2.6 bil. (f.o.b., 2000 est.); wool and textile manufactures, beef and other animal products, rice, fish. **Imports:** $3.4 bil. (f.o.b., 2000 est.); machinery and equipment, vehicles, chemicals, minerals, plastics, oil. **Major trading partners:** Brazil, Argentina, U.S.

Uruguay was known as the Banda Oriental del Uruguay (Eastern Shore of the Uruguay River) during the colonial period. Although the Spanish first explored the area in 1516, they did not immediately settle there. Instead, the Portuguese founded the Colonia de Sacramento, near Buenos Aires, in 1680. They did not permanently establish the settlement of Montevideo until 1726. Under the leadership of José Gervasio Artigas, Uruguayans fought against both the Portuguese and the junta of Buenos Aires between 1811 and 1814 in an effort to establish their independence; in 1815 they proclaimed the Autonomous Government of the Eastern Provinces.

In 1817 the Portuguese again took control of the region, but Uruguay nationals ousted them in 1828. A new constitution for the country was promulgated in 1830; however, domestic rivalry among elites soon led to civil war. The two contending factions, Liberals (Colorados) and Conservatives (Blancos), wore red and white armbands, respectively. Civil war continued through the 1840's and 1850's, until the victory of the Colorados in 1865. In the War of the Triple Alliance (1865-70), Uruguay allied itself with Argentina and Brazil against Paraguay. The consequence of the war for Uruguay was independence from the other regional powers.

The Colorado party dominated Uruguayan government from 1865 until 1958. Waves of European immigrants transformed Uruguayan society during the latter half of the 19th century, and by 1880 immigrants made up almost half of the population. The last civil war between the Blancos and the Colorados took place in 1904; the Colorados won victory under Pres. José Batlle y Ordóñez, one of Uruguay's political legends.

Batlle inaugurated a labor and social-welfare reform program that created Latin America's first eight-hour working day as well as progressive legislation on women's rights. Impressed with the Swiss plural executive Federal Council during his stay in Switzerland, Batlle believed such a structure could help Uruguay avoid the Latin American hazard of caudillismo (authoritarian rule). Batlle proposed the idea of a plural executive, and a version of the idea became part of the constitution in 1919. The new constitution provided for both a president and a collegial National Council, both of which would make up the executive structure of the government.

In 1933 a military coup by Pres. Gabriel Terra sought to dissolve both the legislature and the National Council and to reestablish the single executive presidential system. He managed this by sponsoring a constituent assembly that drew up a new constitution in 1934. In a 1951 plebiscite, Uruguayan voters approved a return to the plural executive system, and a new constitutional order reflecting this went into effect the following year. The debate over the form of the executive was not over, however; in 1966 the public voted for yet another constitution, which once again established the single president as the executive power.

Uruguay's economy began to falter during the 1950's. This, combined with the expansion of governmental bureaucracy tied to the country's social welfare programs, led to increasing popular discontent. In 1958 the Blancos won two successive victories at the polls. A candidate from the conservative wing of the Colorado party, Jorge Pacheco Areco, regained the presidency for the traditional ruling party in 1967, but neither the Blancos nor the Colorados were able to deal with Uruguay's deteriorating economy or with its growing political unrest.

Uruguay's politics became increasingly polarized during the 1960's and into the 1970's. The leftist National Liberation Movement (MLN or Tupamaros), formed in 1967, began urban guerrilla activity that included robbery and kidnapping. The Tupamaros, many of whom were young and middle class, embarrassed government officials and were largely successful in eroding the public image of the civilian government. Tupamaro activity generated violence from the military and police, and as the political situation deteriorated in the early seventies, the government granted the military increasing authority.

By 1973 the military was in control of the country, and they dissolved the Congress. The military allowed Pres. Juan María Bordaberry to remain in office until 1976, at which time they installed Aparicio Méndez in the presidency. It was Bordaberry, however, who proposed the dismantling of the political parties in 1976. Uruguayan military rule was brutally repressive, and the armed forces perpetrated many human rights abuses. By some estimates, the Uruguayan military regime had the world's largest number of political prisoners in proportion to the population.

In 1980, Uruguayans rejected in a plebiscite the army's constitution, which would have amounted to continued de facto military control. So began a slow process in which the military tried to bargain with civilian political elites while promising to restore civilian rule. Finally, in 1984, Colorado party candidate Julio María Sanguinetti won a civilian presidential election.

Sanguinetti approved a general amnesty for the leaders of the military regime, but also had success in attracting foreign investment and righting the Uruguayan economy. He was unseated five years later by National party candidate Luis Alberto Lacalle, who further liberalized trade. But his austerity on social problems led voters to overturn some of his reforms by referendum. In 1994 elections, Sanguinetti won back the presidency. In Nov. 1999 the Colorado candidate, Jorge Batlle, pledged to continue the pro-market reforms of Sanguinetti, defeated in a run-off the (left-wing) Broad Front candidate, Tabare Vazquez, who had led in the first round.

▶ UZBEKISTAN
Republic of Uzbekistan

● **GEOGRAPHY Location:** central Asia. **Boundaries:** Kazakhstan to N, NE, and NW, Kyrgyzstan to E, Tajikistan to SE, Afghanistan to S, Turkmenistan to SW and W. **Total area:** 172,741 sq. mi. (447,400 sq km). **Coastline:** Aral Sea. **Comparative area:** slightly larger than California. **Land use:** 9% arable land; 1% permanent crops; 46% permanent pasture; 3% forest and woodland; 41% other (mostly urban and mountain). **Major cities:** (1994 est.) Tashkent (capital) 2,100,000; Samarkand 370,000; Namangan 312,000; Andizhan 297,000; Bukhara 228,000.

● **PEOPLE Population:** 25,155,064 (2001 est.). **Nationality:** noun—Uzbekistani(s); adjective—

Uzbekistani. **Ethnic groups:** 80% Uzbek, 5.5% Russian, 5% Tajik, 3% Kazakh, 2.5% Karakalpak, 1.5% Tatar. **Languages:** 74.3% Uzbek (official), member of Eastern Turk language group written in Cyrillic script since 1940; 14.2% Russian, 4.4% Tajik, 7.1% other languages. **Religions:** 88% Muslim (mostly Sunnis), 9% Eastern Orthodox, 3% other.

• **GOVERNMENT   Type:** republic. **Independence:** Aug. 31, 1991 (from Soviet Union). **Constitution:** Dec. 8, 1992. **National holiday:** Independence Day, Sept. 1. **Heads of Government:** Islam A. Karimov, president (since Dec. 1991); Utkir T. Sultanov, prime minister (since Dec. 1995). **Structure:** executive—president, Cabinet of Ministers; legislative—Supreme Assembly; judicial—Supreme Court.

• **ECONOMY   Monetary unit:** som. **Budget:** (1999 est.) *income:* $4 bil.; *expend:* $4.1 bil. **GDP:** $60 bil., $2,400 per capita (2000 est.). **Chief crops:** cotton, vegetables, fruits, grain; livestock. **Natural resources:** natural gas, coal, petroleum, gold, uranium. **Major industries:** textiles, food processing, machine building, metallurgy, natural gas. **Labor force:** 11.9 mil. (1998). **Exports:** $2.9 bil. (2000); cotton, gold, natural gas, mineral fertilizers, ferrous metals, textiles, food products, autos. **Imports:** $2.6 bil. (2000); machinery and parts, foodstuffs, chemicals, metals. **Major trading partners:** other former Soviet republics.

Uzbekistan, a land of deserts and steppe, lies in the heart of central Asia. Although the territory has been inhabited since prehistoric times, today's Uzbeks are actually descendants of nomadic Mongol, Iranian, and Turkic tribes who mixed with the populations there beginning in the 13th century A.D. The Uzbeks take their name from Khan Uzbek (1282-1342), the ruler responsible for converting the Mongol Golden Horde (the westernmost part of the Mongolian empire) to Islam. In the 18th and 19th centuries, the tribal states known as the Uzbek khanates of Bukhara, Samarkand, and Kokand were formed. Russian conquest of the Uzbek lands began in the 18th century and was completed in 1876 with the conquering of the khanate of Kokand. The Russian empire quickly built the Transcaucasian Railway to connect it with the region's major cities, thus sealing its hold on the area.

As with Kazakhstan, there was a large influx of Russians into Uzbekistan, mainly to its cities. Uzbek resentment of Russian immigrants precipitated a riot in 1898 in Andidzhan and again in 1916, when a decree that drafted central Asians into the Army was promulgated. At the time of the revolution, Soviet power was established in 1917 in the largely Russian city of Tashkent, and after some fighting, the region of Uzbekistan was incorporated into the Russian republic as the Turkestan Autonomous Soviet Socialist Republic (ASSR) in April 1918. In October 1924, the Uzbek Soviet Socialist Republic (SSR) came into being.

During 1924-25, the Soviet government initiated the National Delimitation of the Central Asian Republics to create Uzbek national symbols, to develop a new literary language, and to increase literacy among Uzbeks. It also conducted a brutal campaign against Islam and its believers. The Soviets modernized agriculture and industrialized the territory, although the native Uzbek population for the most part continued to live in rural areas and worked harvesting cotton, while the Russian population worked in industry. During World War II, Uzbekistan's industrial base expanded as many major factories and plants were moved there from the Russian areas to keep them safe from enemy attack.

Mikhail Gorbachev's policy of glasnost, or openness, did not immediately result in political changes in Uzbekistan. In time, Uzbeks became politically active over many of the same issues that affected their Kazakh neighbors, such as the environmental problems causing the drying up of its rivers, the desiccation of the Aral Sea, and the salinization of the soil. They also demanded that Uzbek (and not Russian) be the official language of Uzbekistan.

In March 1990 the Supreme Soviet elected Islam Karimov as president, and in April 1991 Uzbekistan agreed to sign a new union treaty, which was derailed by the failed August 1991 coup in Moscow. On Aug. 31, 1991, Uzbekistan declared its independence, and in December signed the Alma-Ata Declaration and joined the Commonwealth of Independent States (CIS).

In December 1991 Islam Karimov won the presidential election, and he moved to reduce Uzbekistan's dependence on Russia. In 1994 he signed an economic free-trade agreement with Kazakhstan and Kyrgyzstan and he banned use of the ruble in order to strengthen the som, Uzbekistan's monetary unit. In December 1994 Karimov's supporters (calling themselves the Democratic party) won an overwhelming majority in Uzbekistan's first parliamentary elections. Since then the country has made a slow but steady economic recovery. In Feb. 1999, Uzbekistan refused to renew its collective security treaty with the CIS.

▶ **VANUATU**
Republic of Vanuatu

• **GEOGRAPHY   Location:** chain of 12 principal and some 60 smaller islands in Pacific Ocean, about 500 mi. (800 km) W of Fiji and 1,100 mi. (2,800 km) E of Australia. Port Vila 17°45'S, 168°18'E. **Boundaries:** surrounded by South Pacific Ocean; nearest neighbor is Santa Cruz Islands to N. **Total area:** 5,699 sq. mi. (14,760 sq km). **Coastline:** 1,571 mi. (2,528 km). **Comparative area:** slightly larger than Connecticut. **Land use:** 2% arable land; 10% permanent crops; 2% meadows and pastures; 75% forest and woodland; 11% other. **Major cities:** (1989 census) Port Vila (capital) 19,311.

• **PEOPLE   Population:** 192,910 (2001 est.). **Nationality:** noun—Ni-Vanuatu (sing. and pl.); adjective—Ni-Vanuatu. **Ethnic groups:** 94% indigenous Melanesian, 4% French; remainder Vietnamese, Chinese, and Pacific Islanders. **Languages:** English and French (official); pidgin (known as Bislama or Bichelama). **Religions:** 36.7% Presbyterian, 15% Anglican, 15% Catholic, 7.6% indigenous beliefs, 6.2% Seventh-Day Adventist, 3.8% Church of Christ, 15.7% other.

• **GOVERNMENT   Type:** republic. **Independence:** July 30, 1980 (from France and U.K.). **Constitution:** July 30, 1980. **National holiday:** Independence Day, July 30. **Heads of Government:** John Bani, president (since Mar. 1999); Barak Edward Natapei, prime minister (since Apr. 2001). **Structure:** executive—president, prime minister, council of ministers; unicameral legislature; judiciary.

• **ECONOMY   Monetary unit:** vatu. **Budget:** (1996 est.) *income:* $94.4 mil. *expend.:* $99.8 mil. **GDP:** $245 mil., $1,300 per capita (1999 est.). **Chief crops:** copra, coconuts, cocoa, coffee, taro, yams, fruits, vegetables; fish, beef. **Natural resources:**

manganese, hardwood forests, fish. **Major industries:** food and fish freezing, forestry processing, meat canning. **Labor force:** 65% agriculture, 32% services, 3% industry (1995 est.) **Exports:** $33.8 mil. (f.o.b., 1998); copra, beef, cocoa, timber, coffee. **Imports:** $76.2 mil. (f.o.b., 1999); machines and vehicles, food and beverages, fuels. **Major trading partners:** *exports:* 32% Japan, 8% Spain,14% Germany; *imports:* 52% Japan, 20% Australia, 8% Singapore.

Formerly known as the New Hebrides, Vanuatu is a rugged, volcanic island chain with heavily forested mountains; peaks rise to over 6,000 feet (on Espiritu Santo, the largest island). The people are Melanesians. In 1887 the islands were placed under the administration of an Anglo-French naval commission, becoming a joint Anglo-French colony (condominium) in 1906. The islands escaped Japanese occupation during World War II; they sided with the Free French and were used as bases for Allied campaigns in the Pacific. The New Hebrides were granted independence as Vanuatu on July 30, 1980, with membership in the British Commonwealth. The government is a parliamentary system, complemented by a National Council of Chiefs to decide matters of tradition and customary law.

The economy is based on subsistence agriculture, cattle raising, and fishing. Tourism is developing rapidly, and the sale of long-term tuna-fishing rights, principally to Japan, Australia, and the United States, is an important earner of foreign exchange.

▶ **VENEZUELA**
Republic of Venezuela
● **GEOGRAPHY Location:** northern coast of South America. **Boundaries:** Caribbean Sea to N, Guyana to E, Brazil to S, Colombia to W. **Total area:** 352,144 sq. mi. (912,050 sq km). **Coastline:** 1,739 mi. (2,800 km). **Comparative area:** slightly more than twice the size of California. **Land use:** 4% arable land; 1% permanent crops; 20% meadows and pastures; 34% forest and woodland; 41% other; includes negl. % irrigated. **Major cities:** (1990 est.) Caracas (capital) 3,435,795; Maracaibo 1,400,643; Valencia 1,274,354; Maracay 956,656; Barquisimeto 787,359.
● **PEOPLE Population:** 23,916,810 (2001 est.). **Nationality:** noun—Venezuelan(s); adjective—Venezuelan. **Ethnic groups:** Spanish, Italian, Portuguese, Arab, German, African, indigenous people. **Languages:** Spanish (official), native dialects (spoken by about 200,000 Amerindians in remote interior). **Religions:** 96% Roman Catholic, 2% Protestant.
● **GOVERNMENT Type:** federal republic. **Independence:** July 5, 1811 (from Spain). **Constitution:** Jan. 23, 1961. **National holiday:** Independence Day, July 5. **Head of Government:** Hugo Chávez Frías, president (since Feb. 1999). **Structure:** executive (president); bicameral legislature (National Congress—Senate, Chamber of Deputies); judiciary.
● **ECONOMY Monetary unit:** bolívar. **Budget:** (2000 est.) *income:* $26.4 bil.; *expend.:* $27 bil. **GDP:** $146.2 bil., $6,200 per capita (2000 est.). **Chief crops:** corn, sorghum, sugarcane, rice, bananas, vegetables, coffee; beef, pork, milk, eggs; fish. **Natural resources:** crude oil, natural gas, iron ore, gold, bauxite. **Major industries:** petroleum, iron ore mining, construction materials. **Labor force:** 9.9 mil. (1999); 64% services, 23% industry, 13% agriculture; 18% unemployment (1997). **Exports:** $32.8 bil. (f.o.b., 2000 est.); petroleum, bauxite, aluminum, steel, chemicals, agricultural products, basic manufactures. **Imports:** $14.7 bil. (f.o.b., 2000 est.); raw materials, construction materials, machinery and transport equipment. **Major trading partners:** (1989) *exports:* 57% U.S. and Puerto Rico, Colombia, Brazil; *imports:* 53% U.S., Japan, Colombia.

At the time of European contact in the early 16th century, coastal Venezuela was home to nearly 50,000 semisedentary Indians. Although the region was "discovered" by Christopher Columbus in 1498, European settlement of the area was slow in comparison with the neighboring region of New Granada. The Spaniards explored and exploited Venezuela in the 1520's, searching for gold and pearls.

Early attempts at agriculture by the Spaniards failed until they discovered that the area around Caracas (founded in 1567) could sustain the production of both wheat and cocoa. African slave labor was an important part of the economic structure, and as markets for cocoa expanded, Caracas grew in importance. Venezuela became a captaincy general (an administrative region below the level of viceroyalty) with an audiencia (high court) established at Caracas in 1777-78.

As early as 1797, Venezuelan society was in rebellion against the Spanish empire. A major hindrance to the revolutionary leadership of Simón Bolívar was the need to accommodate both conservative landowners and the pardos, lower class citizens of mixed African and European ancestry.

The wars of independence were particularly destructive in Venezuela, but in 1821 the region achieved independence and became part of the federation of Gran Colombia, which also included New Granada and Ecuador. By 1830 Gran Colombia was in a state of political collapse, and Venezuela became an independent republic.

The military caudillo (leader) José Antonio Páez controlled the country for three decades. With the demise of Páez and his conservative allies in the 1860's, the forces of liberalism under Antonio Guzmán Blanco took over. The Guzmán Blanco era ended during a brief civil war in 1889, won by Gen. Cipriano Castro, who proceeded to establish his own rule. In 1908 Gen. Juan Vicente Gómez occupied the presidency, and he controlled the politics of Venezuela until his death in 1935.

The shift from dictatorship to democracy began with the Generation of 28, a student movement that organized urban workers and peasants into a viable political opposition. The Generation of 28 later became the modern Democratic Action party. In 1945 a group of young military officers overthrew the conservative dictatorship and supported the Democratic Action group in writing a new democratic constitution. Democratic Action won the elections of 1947, but military elements overthrew the new government the following year. The coup brought Col. Marcos Pérez Jiménez to power until his ouster in 1958.

The election of Democratic Action candidate Romulo Betancourt as president marked the beginning of multiparty democratic politics in Venezuela. The stability of the system owed much to political possibilities provided by the country's petroleum revenues.

Venezuela nationalized foreign-owned oil and iron firms in 1975 and 1976, but dependence on petroleum revenues still precipitated economic and political problems for the country in the 1980's. The downturn of the global oil market caused Venezuela's economic base to shrink, and the country's massive foreign debt hindered the expansion of populist political strategies.

The Christian Democrats defeated Democratic Action in 1968 and again in 1978. Pres. Luis Herrera Cámpíns's administration (1979-84) took the country in a more conservative direction but Democratic Action regained the presidency in 1983 under Jaime Lusinchi.

Venezuela's huge foreign debt in the 1980's led to tight economic controls and a reduction in social spending. The administration of Pres. Carlos Andrés Perez, elected in 1989, began with antigovernment riots in which hundreds died. In Feb. 1992, Latin America's oldest civilian government thwarted an attempted coup by soldiers angered over connections between high-ranking officers and drug traffickers; a second coup in November also failed. But in early 1993, Pres. Perez was suspended after the Senate ordered impeachment proceedings against him on charges he embezzled $17 million from the government; the Congress overwhelmingly elected Sen. Ramon Jose Valasquez Mujica to serve as interim president.

In early 1994 Rafael Caldera became president and immediately faced severe economic problems as the currency depreciated by more than 80 percent in only a few months. In June Caldera imposed price and currency controls and suspended several constitutional guarantees, including the guarantee against search and arrest without a warrant. In July 1995, he restored those rights, except along Venezuela's borders with Colombia and Brazil, where crime and economic crises were most severe. Violent anti-government demonstrations continued into 1996 but Caldera persisted in austerity plans that resulted in a $1.4 bil. loan from I.M.F. By early 1997 inflation seemed to be in check and the economy stabilizing although the continuing fall in worldwide oil prices added more pressure for budget cuts. By the summer of 1998 Venezuela's economy was caught in the worldwide financial crisis and spinning toward chaos as the presidential election approached.

In the December elections, the two old parties (Christian Democrats and Democratic Action) which had dominated for 40 years all but disappeared. The Patriotic Pole Coalition candidate, Hugo Chavez Frias (who had led the unsuccessful coup in 1992 against President Perez) easily triumphed over Henrique Salas Romer. Two days later stock shares rose 22 percent despite Chavez' calls for redistribution of wealth, privatization of the government oil company and abolition of Congress. Chavez called for a Constitutional Assembly to rewrite the constitution (88 percent voted their approval in April 1999). In elections for the Assembly Chavez's supporters won all but seven of 128 seats. In December the Assembly adopted a new constitution (Venezuela's 26th) whose major features are a unicameral National Assembly and a six-year renewable presidential term. Elections in Aug. 2000 confirmed Chavez for a new term and "Chavista" dominance of the Assembly. Chavez demanded OPEC cut production and travelled to major oil producers (including Iraq) to make his point. In October he agreed to sell oil to Castro's Cuba at bargain prices. In Nov. the new National Assembly gave him authority to rule by decree in 37 legislative areas.

►VIETNAM
Socialist Republic of Viet Nam

● GEOGRAPHY Location: Southeast Asia. Boundaries: China to N, Gulf of Tonkin to NE, South China Sea to E, Laos and Cambodia to W. Total area: 127,243 sq. mi. (329,560 sq km). Coastline: 2,140 mi. (3,444 km) excluding islands. Comparative area: slightly larger than New Mexico. Land use: 17% arable land; 4% permanent crops; 1% meadows and pastures; 30% forest and woodland; 48% other; includes 5% irrigated. Major cities: (1989) Hanoi (capital) 1,088,862; Ho Chi Minh City (formerly Saigon) 3,169,135; Haiphong 456,049; Da Nang 370,670; Long Xuyen 217,171.

● PEOPLE Population: 79,939,014 (2000 est.). Nationality: noun—Vietnamese (sing., pl.); adjective—Vietnamese. Ethnic groups: 85-90% Vietnamese, 3% Chinese; ethnic minorities include Muong, Thai, Meo, Khmer, Man, Cham. Languages: Vietnamese (official); French, Chinese, English, Khmer, ethnic langs. (Mon-Khmer and Malayo-Polynesian). Religions: Buddhist, Taoist, Roman Catholic, indigenous beliefs, Islam, Protestant, Cao Dai, Hoa Hao.

● GOVERNMENT Type: Communist state. Independence: Sept. 2, 1945 (from France). Constitution: Apr. 15, 1992. National holiday: Independence Day, Sept. 2. Heads of Government: Tran Duc Luong, president, (since Sept. 1997); Phan Van Khai, prime minister (since Sept. 1997). Structure: executive—president, prime minister, cabinet; unicameral legislature; judiciary—elected by legislature.

● ECONOMY Monetary unit: new dong. Budget: (1996 est.) income: $5.6 bil.; expend.: $6 bil. GDP: $143.1 bil., $1,850 per capita (1999 est.). Chief crops: paddy rice, corn, potatoes, rubber, soybeans, coffee, tea, bananas; poultry, pigs; fish. Natural resources: phosphates, coal, manganese, bauxite, chromate. Major industries: food processing, textiles, machine building. Labor force: 38.2 mil. (1998 est.); 67% agriculture, 33% industry and services, 25% unemployment (1995 est.). Exports: $11.5 bil. (f.o.b., 1999 est.); crude oil, marine products, rice, coffee, rubber, tea, garments, shoes. Imports: $11.6 bil. (f.o.b., 1999 est.); machinery and equipment, petroleum products, fertilizer, steel products, raw cotton, grain, cement, motorcycles. Major trading partners: exports: Japan, Germany, Singapore; imports: Singapore, South Korea, Japan.

The southward expansion of the Chinese empire in the first millennium B.C. drove the Vietnamese peoples southward into northern Vietnam (Tonkin). The area came under direct Chinese rule in 111 B.C. Chinese rule endured, with some interruptions, until A.D. 948; thereafter, Vietnam was independent under strong Chinese influence.

The Hindu-Buddhist kingdom of Annam, in central Vietnam, gradually increased in size and power at the expense of Tonkin and the Khmer empire and Champa, to the west and south. In 1558 the kingdom of Annam split, with independent courts established at Hanoi, controlling Tonkin and the Red River valley, and Hue, in central Vietnam. A remnant of the old Champa state remained independent in the Mekong delta in the south. In 1802 the monarchy was reunited, with the court at Hue controlling all of Vietnam and exercising hegemony over Cambodia.

European penetration of the region began in the 16th century; by the early 19th century, France was the dominant foreign power in Indochina. Efforts to establish French military control began in 1858-59 with the establishment of a colony in Cochin China, in southern Vietnam. Campaigns in the Red River valley in 1873 and 1882 were complicated by Chinese intervention and the determined resistance of the Vietnamese court. In 1884 separate protectorates were established in Tonkin and Annam; in 1887 those, along with Cochin China and Cambodia, were combined into the Union of Indochina under French colonial rule. Rubber plantations were established, and rice and timber exports were under French control. A nationalist rebellion under Phan Boi Chau was suppressed in the early 20th century.

Nationalist resistance to French colonialism continued, resulting in the creation in 1939 of the Vietminh, or Independence League. In 1940 Japanese troops occupied French Indochina, with the collaboration of colonial administrators loyal to the Vichy regime. The Vietminh spearheaded anti-Japanese guerrilla resistance and in 1945 forced the abdication of King Bao Dai, head of a pro-Japanese puppet state. In 1945 France reoccupied Indochina; in 1946 the leader of the Vietminh, Ho Chi Minh, became president of a separatist government at Hanoi. France ceded local autonomy to Tonkin and Annam but sought to retain Cochin China as a colony. Fighting between the French and the Vietminh resumed. On July 1, 1949, the French reinstalled Bao Dai as king of Vietnam, and in February 1950 recognized the independence of Vietnam within the French Union. Ho Chi Minh's republican government also claimed control of all of Vietnam.

Fighting between the two rivals culminated in the French defeat at Dienbienphu on May 7, 1954. An armistice was concluded according to which the country was partitioned at a demilitarized zone at latitude 17° north, the northern part going to the Communist-controlled Vietminh government, the southern to Bao Dai. Nearly one million refugees, including many ethnic Chinese, fled from the north to the south. An international conference in Geneva agreed that elections would be held throughout Vietnam in 1956. In June 1954 Ngo Dinh Diem became premier of South Vietnam; full sovereignty in the south was transferred by France to the Vietnamese government in December 1954. In October 1955 Diem held elections in the south that resulted in the dismissal of Bao Dai as king and the proclamation of an independent Republic of Vietnam.

The scheduled elections of 1956 were never held. French troops withdrew from South Vietnam in that year. Fighting continued in the south, as the Vietminh-backed National Liberation Front (Vietcong) sought to overthrow the Diem government. On Dec. 31, 1959, the Democratic Republic of Vietnam in the north adopted a new constitution calling for the reunification of the country; northern aid to the Vietcong increased significantly, as did American aid to the south. After 1962 American military advisers increased in number and combat exposure.

In 1963 widespead demonstrations, under Buddhist leadership, led to a coup on Nov. 1-2 in which Diem was deposed and assassinated. A series of short-lived military regimes followed until Sept. 1967, when Nguyen Van Thieu was elected president. U.S. air strikes against North Vietnam began in 1964. In the same year, the flow of troops and supplies from north to south increased. American combat troops entered the war in 1965.

Despite U.S.-South Vietnamese superiority in arms and troops, and total control of the air, Vietcong control over the countryside increased. Both Operation Phoenix, in which antigovernment rural leaders were assassinated, and the establishment of fortified strategic hamlets to control the rural population, failed to reverse the tide.

The combined Vietcong-North Vietnamese Tet Offensive in early 1968 resulted in serious losses for South Vietnamese and American forces. The war spread to Laos and to Cambodia, the latter bombed in 1969. American air strikes in North Vietnam were stepped up, and U.S. troop strength reached a maximum of 543,000 in 1969. In July 1969 a series of U.S. troop withdrawals began, and secret talks were initiated in search of a negotiated settlement of the war. Following heavy U.S. bombardment of the north in 1972, a cease-fire agreement was signed in Paris by South Vietnam, North Vietnam, the Vietcong, and the United States on Jan. 27, 1973. It was never implemented, but the American withdrawal continued. In early 1975 South Vietnamese forces collapsed in the face of a series of North Vietnamese-Vietcong offensives. Remaining U.S. personnel were evacuated, and Saigon fell on Apr. 30, 1975. Hundreds of thousands of refugees ("boat people") fled the country over the next decade.

Following the fall of Saigon, the country was occupied by northern troops and administrators. Businesses were nationalized, agriculture collectivized, and tens of thousands of people sent to labor camps for "reeducation." A unified National Assembly met in 1976, and the country was officially reunified on July 2, 1976, under the existing government of the north. Saigon was renamed Ho Chi Minh City. A Soviet naval base was established at the former U.S. base at Cam Ranh Bay.

In 1978 Vietnamese troops occupied Cambodia ousting the government of Pol Pot and installing Heng Samrin as premier. In February 1979 China launched an unsuccessful attack over its border with Vietnam to display displeasure with the invasion of Cambodia and with the treatment of ethnic Chinese in Vietnam. In 1988 Vietnam pledged to withdraw its troops from Cambodia and completed the withdrawal in September 1989.

Vietnam's communist government ruled through the party's powerful Central Committee; no strong personalities emerged to replace the leaders of the wartime generation. The economy was functioning only at a basic level, with the infrastructure in disrepair and agriculture hampered by excessive collectivization. The collapse of the Soviet Union brought about a drastic reduction of the Soviet aid that had kept the Vietnamese economy afloat. Facing economic ruin, Vietnam's leadership eventually turned a blind eye to individual private enterprise. By 1992 the government was encouraging foreign investment.

Resumption of contacts with the U.S. had been precluded by American insistence that Vietnam account more fully for American prisoners of war and troops missing in action. But high-level talks on the normalization of relations and the Cambodian question opened in 1990, and the success of those negotiations helped to open diplomatic channels between Vietnam and the U.S.

In 1994, Pres. Clinton, satisfied with Vietnam's efforts to account for POWs and MIAs, ended the 19-year U.S. trade embargo against Vietnam; the following day, American firms were operating in Ho Chi Minh City. In July 1995, full diplomatic relations were established.

In October 1995, Vietnam's National Assembly adopted its first-ever national civil code under the Communist government. The document spelled out rights to land, personal property, inheritances, and raising capital. Close to 90 percent of the Assembly members voted in favor of the code, which went into effect in July 1996.

In recent years the Government has encouraged many Western companies to build factories and open businesses but poverty and the Asian financial crisis slowed progress. In March 1998 Pres. Clinton waived the Jackson-Vanik amendment in order to permit U.S. firms in Vietnam to borrow from the Import-Export Bank. In the same month Pope John Paul II was able to name a new Catholic archbishop of Ho Chi Minh City (though the government in July announced that it was stepping up control of religion). In July 2000 the U.S. and Vietnam signed a far-reaching trade agreement. In April 2001, the Central Committee of the Communist Party appointed a new Secretary General, Nong Duc Manh, with the aim of modernizing the economy (especially the industrial side) and ending corruption. By rumor, Nong is an illegitimate son of Ho Chi Minh.

▶ WESTERN SAMOA
see "Samoa"

▶ YEMEN
Republic of Yemen

● GEOGRAPHY   Location: southern shore of Arabian peninsula and southwest corner of Arabian peninsula. Boundaries: Saudi Arabia to N, Oman to E, Gulf of Aden to S, Red Sea to W. Total area: 203,850 sq. mi. (527,970 sq km). Coastline: 1,184 mi. (1,906 km). Comparative area: slightly larger than twice the size of Wyoming. Land use: 3% arable land; negl. % permanent crops; 30% meadows and pastures; 4% forest and woodland; 63% other; includes 1% irrigated. Major cities: (1995 est.) Sana'a (capital) 972,000; Aden 562,000; Hodeida 155,110; Mukalla 154,360; Taiz 178,043.
● PEOPLE   Population: 17,479,206 (2000 est.). Nationality: noun—Yemini(s); adjective—Yemeni. Ethnic groups: predominantly Arab; Afro-Arab concentrations in western coastal locations; South Asians in southern regions; small European communities in major metropolitan areas. Languages: Arabic. Religions: Muslim including Shaf'i (Sunni) and Zaydi (Shia), small numbers of Jewish, Christian, and Hindu.
● GOVERNMENT   Type: republic. Independence: May 22, 1990 (merger of North and South Yemen). Constitution: May 16, 1991: amended Sept. 29, 1994. National holiday: Proclamation of the Republic, May 22. Heads of Government: Ali Abdullah Saleh, president (since May 1994); Abdulqader Bajammal, prime minister (since Apr. 2001). Structure: executive—president and cabinet; unicameral legislature; judicial—Supreme Court and lesser courts.
● ECONOMY   Monetary unit: Yemeni rial. Budget: (1999 est.) income: $1.8 bil.; expend: $1.95 bil. GDP: $12.7 bil., $750 per capita (1999 est.). Chief crops: grain, fruits, vegetables, qat, coffee, cotton; dairy products, poultry, meat; fish. Natural resources: petroleum, fish, rocksalt, marble, small deposits of coal. Major industries: crude oil, petroleum refining, cotton textiles and leather goods, food processing, handicrafts, aluminum products, cement. Labor force: mostly agriculture and herding; also services, construction, industry, commerce. Exports: $2 bil. (f.o.b., 1999 est.);

crude oil, cotton, coffee, dried and salted fish. Imports: $2.3 bil., (f.o.b., 1999 est.); food and live animals, machinery and equipment, manufactured goods. Major trading partners: exports: 31% China, 25% S. Korea, 22% Thailand; imports: 8% UAE, 7% Saudi Arabia, 9% U.S., 8% France.

Yemen—in ancient times Sheba or Saba—is strategically located in the southwestern corner of the Arabian peninsula, near the southern end of the Red Sea. In biblical times and for many centuries thereafter, Yemen dominated the caravan trade in spices, gold, and other luxury goods from India and Africa to the Middle East.

The Islamic unification of Arabia in 628 resulted in the incorporation of Yemen into Arabia as a whole, but many local uprisings broke out over the course of the following three centuries. In the 10th century, control passed to a line of Yemeni kings who were simultaneously imams of the Zaidi sect of Islam; the Zaidi imams ruled until 1962.

Aden was the most important port of the ancient kingdom of Sheba and retained that status under the Zaidi imams of Yemen. Portuguese activity around Aden began in the 15th century; from the mid-16th century, control of the port was disputed by the Portuguese, the Yemeni kings, the Ottoman Turks, and, later, the British.

In 1839, Aden was made a British Crown Colony; the Hadramaut region of southern Arabia, north and east of Aden, became the British Protectorate of Aden. The colony and protectorate were both administered as part of British India.

Yemen came under the control of the Ottoman Empire from the mid-16th to the mid-17th centuries, and again from 1849 to 1918. The Turks were expelled at the end of World War I, and Yemen became an independent kingdom in 1918. The kingdom's independence was threatened by a Saudi invasion in 1934 and by a 1954 dispute with Great Britain over the status of Aden, which was the key to British military power in the western Indian Ocean and Persian Gulf after India's independence in 1947.

Imam Ahmed came to the throne of Yemen in 1948, following the assassination of his predecessor. Most of Yemen's large Jewish population was evacuated to Israel in 1949-50. A palace coup against the imam in 1955 failed, but after his death in 1962, his successor was quickly ousted and the country was proclaimed the Yemen Arab Republic (North Yemen) under the leadership of Brig. Gen. Abdullah al-Salal.

A struggle for independence began in Aden and the protectorate in 1963, with two rival groups competing for power. The National Liberation Front (NLF) gained the upper hand over the Egyptian-backed Front for the Liberation of Occupied South Yemen, as both groups waged guerrilla war against the British. British forces withdrew in 1967, and South Yemen became independent. The nation's territory included Socotra and adjacent islands off the Horn of Africa, which had been British possessions since 1876.

In 1969 a leftist faction of the NLF seized power, nationalized key industries, and instituted a socialist regime. In the mid-1970's, South Yemeni troops aided leftist guerrillas in Oman, and fought in Ethiopia against Eritrean rebels. Subsequently Pres. Salem Robaye Ali took a more moderate stance and improved relations with Oman and Saudi Arabia. He was overthrown in a coup in June 1978 and executed. The succeeding government was overthrown on Jan. 13, 1986; on Feb. 8, Hasin Said Numan became prime minister.

In North Yemen, civil war between royalist and republican factions lasted until April 1970, when a coalition republican government was formed with the aid of Saudi mediation. Col. Ibrahim al-Hamidi came to power in a military coup in 1974; he was assassinated in 1977. Pres. Ali Abdullah Saleh assumed office in 1978, after the assassination of Pres. al-Gashmi.

Border skirmishes between North Yemen and South Yemen broke out during 1972-73. After several years of uneasy peace, South Yemen launched a full-scale war against the north on Feb. 24, 1979. Arab League pressure quickly led to a truce. Relations improved during the 1980's and North Yemen and South Yemen merged as the Republic of Yemen on May 22, 1990. Ali Abdullah Saleh, president of North Yemen, became the new country's president. San'a was proclaimed the capital of the United Yemen, though Aden remained its most important economic center.

The Gulf War forced the repatriation of tens of thousands of Yemeni workers from Kuwait and other Gulf states; later Saudi Arabia expelled 850,000 more to express its displeasure with Yemen's unenthusiastic stance toward the Gulf War. These repatriations deprived Yemen of a most important source of foreign exchange, and severely damaged the economy.

Yemen held its first general election since unification on Apr. 27, 1993, and a coalition government was formed. In Feb. 1994, fighting began and a full-scale civil war broke out in May. But in July the capture of Aden by government troops ended the conflict and Pres. Saleh has ruled in relative peace since. The first direct presidential electrion was held in Sept. 1999 but the Socialist Party was not allowed to field a candidate so Saleh won easily.

On Oct. 10, 2000, over 50,000 protested in Aden against U.S. support for Israel; two days later, the U.S. destroyer Cole, refueling in Aden, was attacked, leaving 17 dead and 39 wounded. The Saleh government permitted F.B.I. attendance at the questioning of witnesses; but the F.B.I. (and Navy) investigators became a new object of attack, by the terrorist "Islamic Army of Aden," in June. However, the F.B.I.'s response, attempts to arm its investigators with rifles and heavy weapons, provoked the U.S. ambassador's banning the F.B.I. team leader from Yemen.

▶ YUGOSLAVIA
Socialist Federal Republic of Yugoslavia

(Note: The U.S. does not formally recognize the union of Serbia and Montenegro as Yugoslavia.)

● **GEOGRAPHY Location:** Southern central Europe. **Boundaries:** Hungary to N, Romania to NE, Bulgaria to E, Macedonia and Albania to S, Adriatic Sea, Bosnia and Herzegovina to W., Croatia to NW. **Total area:** 39,517 sq. mi. (102,350 sq km). **Coastline:** 124 mi. (199 km). **Comparative area:** Slightly smaller than Kentucky. **Land use:** N.A. **Major cities:** (mid-1992 est.) Belgrade (capital) 1,500,000; Nis 300,000; Kragujevac 250,000; Novi Sad 250,000; Podoricj 80,000.
● **PEOPLE Population:** 10,662,087 (2000 est.). **Nationality:** noun—Serb(s) and Montenegrin(s); adjective—Serbian and Montenegrin. **Ethnic groups:** 62.6% Serbian, 10.5% Albanian, 5% Montenegrin, 3.3% Hungarian, 9.2% other. **Languages:** 95% Serbian, 5% Albanian. **Religions:** 65% Orthodox, 19% Muslim, 4% Roman Catholic, 1% Protestant, 11% other.

● **GOVERNMENT Type:** republic. **Independence:** Proclaimed itself successor to former Socialist Federal Republic of Yugoslavia Apr. 11, 1992. **Constitution:** Apr. 27, 1992. **National holiday:** St. Vitus Day, June 28. **Heads of Government:** Vojislav Kostunica, president (since Oct. 2000); Dragisa Pesic, prime minister (since July 2001); **Structure:** executive—president; bicameral legislature; judiciary—judges elected by legislature.
● **ECONOMY Monetary unit:** Yugoslav new dinar. **Budget:** N.A. **GDP:** $20.6 bil., $1,800 per capita (1999 est.). **Chief crops:** cereal, fruits, vegetables, tobacco, olives; cattle, sheep, goats. **Natural resources:** oil, gas, coal, antimony, copper. **Major industries:** machine building, metallurgy, mining, consumer goods, electronics, petroleum products, chemicals, pharmaceuticals. **Labor force:** 1.6 mil. (1999). **Exports:** $1.5 billion (1999); manufactured goods, food and live animals, raw materials. **Imports:** $3.3 bil. (1999); machinery and transport equipment, fuels and lubricants, manufactured goods, chemicals, food and live animals, raw materials. **Major trading partners:** Bosnia and Herzegovnia, Italy, Germany.

The lands that composed Yugoslavia until 1991 were incorporated into the Roman Empire as the province of Illyricum in the first century A.D. Christianity became dominant by A.D. 600. Its nucleus was Serbia, settled in the seventh century by South Slav migrants from the Over and Vistula, and converted to Christianity, in its Eastern Orthodox form, in the ninth century. Twice (in 1077 and again in 1202), the Vatican sent royal crowns to Serbian kings, emphasizing their independence, despite the religious differences. Serbia's medieval zenith came during the reign of Stephen Dushan (1331-55), who subjected Albania, Macedonia, Thessaly, and Epirus to his rule, and who gained the vassalage of Bulgaria in addition. But within 30 years of his death, the Ottoman Turks had overrun his realm, a dominance sealed by the Serbian catastrophe at the Battle of Kosovo (1389). Not until 1878 did Serbia regain independence.

The complexities of Balkan politics occupied European statesmen throughout the late 19th century, and the Balkan Wars of 1912 and 1913 led directly to the outbreak of World War I. After the collapse of the Austro-Hungarian Empire during the war, the multiethnic and multinational state of Yugoslavia was patched together in 1918-19. To Serbia were annexed the old Austro-Hungarian lands of Slovenia and Croatia, as well as the ethnically Croatian and Serbian lands of Bosnia and Herzegovina, Macedonia and Kosovo. The last three were Serbian, Bulgarian, and Albanian in nationality, respectively.

The nationalities coexisted in a state of mutual hostility, provoking a royal dictatorship, instituted by King Alexander in 1929 and enduring after his assassination in 1934. Hitler invaded Yugoslavia in 1941; German troops were welcomed in Croatia as liberators from the Serbs. Resistance began almost immediately, split into two mutually hostile groups: Draza Mihajlovic's Serbian royalist Chetniks, and the Partisans, a group of pan-Yugoslav Communists and non-Serbian anti-German forces led by Tito (a.k.a. Josip Broz). By the end of the war, over 2 million Yugoslavs had died, and 3.5 million were homeless. As marshal, backed by both Churchill and Stalin, Tito ruled over a ruined land: the newly created Federal People's Republic of Yugoslavia.

Tito imposed agricultural collectivization on the Stalinist model, and pushed for the development of industry under state ownership. Politically, harsh repression fell on members of the Chetnik resistance as well as on the Slovene Home Guard and the Croatian Ustasa. But the postwar period of tyranny was short-lived.

Tito refused to permit Yugoslavia to become a Soviet satellite; in 1948 he expelled Russian military advisers, and was himself expelled from the Comintern.

In the face of economic pressure and military threats, Tito turned westward. Stalinism yielded to decentralized communism. The 1953 Agrarian Reform Law permitted private agricultural small-holdings, and over 80 percent of the land returned to private ownership; in the rest, "self-management" rather than central control was encouraged. Self-management was instituted in the industrial sector as well. Economic growth averaged over 7 percent per year for three decades, lifting Yugoslavia into the ranks of the semideveloped countries.

Despite a reconciliation with Khruschev's Soviet Union in 1955-56, Tito continued to chart an independent course, taking a leading role in the Third World Non-Aligned Movement and providing a political and economic alternative model for Eastern Europe. But Yugoslavian nationalism masked the development of separate nationalisms within the Yugoslavian federation.

The country's three major ethnic groups (Serbs, Croats, and Muslims) coexisted peacefully under Tito's iron hand, and even after Tito's death in 1980, his rotating presidency scheme, in which the leaders of each republic took turns serving as "president of the presidency," worked smoothly, as long as Yugoslavia was dominated by communism. But when communism fell in 1989, only Serbia and Montenegro voted for Communist governments, while the republics of Croatia, Slovenia, Macedonia, and Bosnia-Herzegovina sought independence.

A vicious civil war ensued in which Yugoslavia's Serbian president Slobodan Milosevic sought to keep all ethnically Serbian areas under Serbian control. While Serb militias captured about one-third of Croatia in 1991, the Croatian army won back most of the region in 1995. And Yugoslavia's attempt to keep Bosnia-Herzegovina within a "greater Serbia" failed as well, the failure ratified in the November 1995 "Dayton Accords," which brought NATO peacekeepers to the region. The year 1996 saw the formal end of the civil wars, as Milosevic endorsed treaties guaranteeing the boundaries of Macedonia, Croatia and Bosnia; additionally, a pact with the Albanians of Serbia's Kosovo province permitted Albanian as the language of instruction in Kosovo's schools.

Though Milosevic and his political allies won 84 of 138 seats in Yugoslavia's parliament in Nov. 1996, the political opposition, called Zajedno ("Together"), won control of 14 large cities. The annulments of these results by Yugoslav courts and electoral commissions provoked 11 weeks of popular protests until Milosevic conceded in Feb. 1997. In July, however, Milosevic maneuvered to take back the presidency by receiving a majority of votes in Parliament.

In 1998 ethnic Albanians in the Kosovo province of Serbia launched a terrorist campaign to secede from Serbia and join Albania. The Serbs put down the rebellion with unexpected ferocity. In the winter of 1999 Serbia launched a full-scale attack against Kosovo that drove 700,000 ethnic Albanians from their homes. Despite NATO warn-

ings, Pres. Milosevic continued his ethnic cleansing of Serbia's province and at the end of March NATO began a bombing campaign that lasted 72 days. In June Serbia surrendered and Milosevic agreed to 50,000 NATO troops in Kosovo and the withdrawal of all Yugoslav troops. The U.N. supervised peace was slow to form and soon Serbs were being driven from Kosovo. In 2000 Milosevic managed to maintain his power but his attempt to rig elections in the summer led to mass protests.

In 2000, as NATO troops attempted to defend Serbia proper against Albanian incursions from Kosovo, opposition in Serbia to continuance of the Milosevic regime faced police-state measures. A coalition of 15 parties backed Vojislav Kostunica against Milosevic in the September presidential elections. Hundreds of thousands protested the Milosevic attempts to force a run-off and Kostunica was sworn in Oct. 7. Milosevic was turned over to the U.N. for trial on war-crimes charges. (See Part I, "Major News Stories of the Year.")

▶ ZAIRE (SEE CONGO, DEMOCRATIC REPUBLIC)

▶ ZAMBIA
Republic of Zambia
• **GEOGRAPHY Location:** landlocked country in southern central Africa. **Boundaries:** Zaire to N, Tanzania to NE, Malawi to E, Mozambique to SE, Zimbabwe to S, Namibia to SW, Angola to W. **Total area:** 290,583 sq. mi. (752,610 sq km). **Coastline:** none. **Comparative area:** slightly larger than Texas. **Land use:** 7% arable land; negl. % permanent crops; 40% meadows and pastures; 39% forest and woodland; 14% other. **Major cities:** (1990 census) Lusaka (capital) 982,362; Kitwe 338,207; Ndola 376,311; Kabwe 166,519.
• **PEOPLE Population:** 9,582,418 (2000 est.). **Nationality:** noun—Zambian(s); adjective—Zambian. **Ethnic groups:** 98.7% African, 1.1% European, 0.2% other. **Languages:** English (official), major vernaculars—Bemba, Kaonda, Lozi, Lunda, Luvale, Nyanja, Tonga, and about 70 indigenous languages. **Religions:** 50-75% Christian, 24-49% Muslim and Hindu, 1% indigenous beliefs.
• **GOVERNMENT Type:** republic. **Independence:** Oct. 24, 1964 (from U.K.). **Constitution:** Aug. 2, 1991. **National holiday:** Independence Day, Oct. 24. **Heads of Government:** Frederick Chiluba, president (since Nov. 1991). **Structure:** executive—modified presidential system; legislative—unicameral National Assembly; judiciary.
• **ECONOMY Monetary unit:** kwacha. **Budget:** (1998 est.) *income:* $606 mil.; *expend.:* $547 mil. **GDP:** $8.5 bil., $880 per capita (1999 est.). **Chief crops:** corn, sorghum, rice, peanuts, sunflower seed, tobacco, cotton, sugarcane, cassava; cattle, goats, pigs, poultry, beef, pork, milk, eggs, hides. **Natural resources:** copper, cobalt, zinc, lead, coal. **Major industries:** copper mining and processing, foodstuffs, construction. **Labor force:** 3.4 mil.; 85% agriculture, 9% transport and services, 6% mining, manufacturing, and construction. **Exports:** $900 mil. (f.o.b., 1999 est.); copper, cobalt, zinc, lead, tobacco. **Imports:** $1.15 bil. (f.o.b., 1999 est.); machinery, transport equipment, foodstuffs, fuels, petroleum products, electricity. **Major trading partners:** Saudi Arabia, Japan, South Africa.

Bantu peoples—including Luba, Lunda, Ngoni, and others—moved into what is now Zambia between the 15th and the 19th centuries, displacing or absorbing aboriginal populations. Occasional Portuguese explorers from Angola and Mozambique entered the region, and Angolan slave-raiders were active in the late 18th and early 19th centuries, but serious European influence did not begin until the mid-19th century. At that time British missionaries and merchants arrived, most notably David Livingstone and Cecil Rhodes.

Local rulers granted mineral concessions to Rhodes in both Northern and Southern Rhodesia (now Zambia and Zimbabwe). Rhodesia was declared a British sphere of influence in 1888; a British protectorate was established in 1891 and enlarged in 1894-95. The borders of Northern Rhodesia were established in 1911. The country was administered by the British South Africa Co. until 1924, when direct colonial rule began. Large numbers of British settlers arrived and developed farms and ranches and mined the region's substantial copper deposits. A railroad was built linking Northern Rhodesia with Elizabethville in the Belgian Congo (now Lubumbashi, Zaire).

In 1953 Northern and Southern Rhodesia (Zimbabwe) were joined with Nyasaland (now Malawi) to form the Federation of Rhodesia and Nyasaland. The country entered a period of unrest with native peoples demanding greater participation in government, while white settlers clung to their privileged positions.

As the result of an election in 1962, the federation was dissolved in 1963. A National Assembly was created on the basis of a broader, multiracial electorate. Northern Rhodesia became independent as the Republic of Zambia on Oct. 24, 1964. Relations between Zambia and white-ruled Rhodesia (formerly Southern Rhodesia) became strained in 1965 in a dispute over ownership and administration of the railway that spanned both countries. A new constitution was promulgated in 1973, creating a stronger presidency and a unicameral legislature; the United National Independence party was made the sole legal political party. Opposition parties were allowed to form again starting in December 1990.

Pres. Kenneth Kaunda, in office after Zambia's independence, led a generally moderate government that won the support of both whites and blacks. Zambia's economy, however, did not fare well under independence. Although the country has diverse mineral resources, copper is overwhelmingly the nation's main earner of foreign exchange. A steep decline in the world price of copper led to massive foreign debt and labor unrest at home. The I.M.F. demanded reforms as a condition for future aid, and in 1987 Pres. Kaunda announced a program of economic restructuring. In 1990 his government survived an attempted coup precipitated by a doubling in the price of the staple food, maize meal.

At the end of 1991, Kaunda was defeated by Frederick Chiluba, head of the new Labor party. Chiluba's economic reforms helped Zambia repay more than $1.2 billion in outstanding debt, prompting the I.M.F. to restore its eligibility for international loans. But political problems resurfaced when Chiluba's government found a way to block Kaunda from winning in the 1996 presidential election. Kaunda was shot and wounded by a sniper in Aug. 1997 as he continued to criticize the government. In Oct. 1997 a failed coup attempt by junior army officers was blamed on Kaunda who was arrested in Dec. and put on trial in Jan. He was freed in June and all charges dropped probably on condition that he leave politics for good. In March 1999 Zambia's High Court declared him not a citizen.

▶ ZIMBABWE
Republic of Zimbabwe

● GEOGRAPHY   **Location:** landlocked country in southern Africa. **Boundaries:** Zambia to NW, Mozambique to E, South Africa to S, Botswana to SW. **Total area:** 150,803 sq. mi. (390,580 sq km). **Coastline:** none. **Comparative area:** slightly larger than Montana. **Land use:** 7% arable land; negl. % permanent crops; 13% meadows and pastures; 23% forest and woodland; 57% other; includes negl. % irrigated. **Major cities:** (1992) Harare (capital) 1,184,169; Bulawayo 620,936; Chitungwiza 274,035; Mutare 131,808; Gweru 124,735.

● PEOPLE   **Population:** 11,342,521 (2000 est.). **Nationality:** noun—Zimbabwean(s); adjective—Zimbabwean. **Ethnic groups:** 98% African (71% Shona, 16% Ndebele, 11% other), 1% white, 1% mixed and Asian. **Languages:** English (official), Shona, Sindebele. **Religions:** 50% syncretic (part Christian, part indigenous beliefs), 25% Christian, 24% indigenous beliefs, 1% Muslim.

● GOVERNMENT   **Type:** parliamentary democracy. **Independence:** Apr. 18, 1980 (from U.K.). **Constitution:** Dec. 21, 1979. **National holiday:** Independence Day, Apr. 18. **Head of Government:** Robert Gabriel Mugabe, president (since Dec. 1987). **Structure:** executive—cabinet led by president; unicameral legislature—120 of 150 members are popularly elected, others appointed; judiciary.

● ECONOMY   **Monetary unit:** Zimbabwean dollar. **Budget:** (FY96/97 est.) *income:* $2.5 bil.; *expend.:* $2.9 bil. **GDP:** $26.5 bil., $2,400 per capita (1999 est.). **Chief crops:** tobacco, corn, tea, sugarcane, cotton, wheat, coffee, peanuts; cattle, sheep, goats, pigs. **Natural resources:** coal, chromium ore, asbestos, gold, nickel. **Major industries:** mining, steel, clothing and footwear. **Labor force:** 5 mil. (1997 est.). **Exports:** $2 bil. (f.o.b., 1999 est.); 23% tobacco, 14% gold, ferroalloys, cotton. **Imports:** $2 bil. (f.o.b., 1998 est.); 39% machinery and transport equipment, 18% manufactures, 15% chemicals, 10% fuels. **Major trading partners:** *exports:* 12% South Africa, 11% U.K., 8% Germany; *imports:* 37% S. Africa, 7% U.K., 6% U.S.

Massive stone structures at Great Zimbabwe give evidence of a sizable urban society that flourished from the ninth to the 13th centuries and dominated Iron Age trade in southeastern Africa. Bantu peoples migrated into the region beginning in the 15th century; the Mashona dominated until the early 19th century, when they were displaced by the Matebele.

Portuguese slave traders from Mozambique were active in Zimbabwe from the 16th to the mid-19th centuries. Mineral concessions were granted to Cecil Rhodes by local rulers in the late 19th century, and the region became a British protectorate in 1888. Salisbury (now Harare) was founded in 1890, and the territory comprising Zimbabwe and Zambia was named Rhodesia in 1895. Rhodesia was governed by the British South Africa Co. until 1923, when it was partitioned into Northern and Southern Rhodesia. Northern Rhodesia became a British colony; Southern Rhodesia, rejecting union with South Africa, became a self-governing (and whiteruled) state within the British Empire.

Southern Rhodesia had been heavily settled by whites from Great Britain, South Africa, and elsewhere, who developed extensive farms and ranches, forest products industries, and the country's rich mines. The country prospered but with little native participation in government except at the most local level.

In 1953 Northern Rhodesia, Southern Rhodesia, and Nyasaland were joined in the Federation of Rhodesia and Nyasaland. Increasing agitation for black participation in government, especially in the north and in Nyasaland, led to the dissolution of the federation in 1963; Northern Rhodesia subsequently became independent as Zambia, Nyasaland as Malawi. In 1961 Southern Rhodesia adopted a constitution that guaranteed the continuation of white rule. White resistance to black political demands led to the rise of the Rhodesian Front party, whose leader, Ian D. Smith, became prime minister of Rhodesia (formerly Southern Rhodesia). After British-led negotiations for a biracial political compromise broke down, the Smith government on Nov. 11, 1965, issued a unilateral declaration of independence, which was declared illegal and invalid by the British government.

The U.N. condemned the Smith government and imposed economic sanctions. In May 1968 the U.N. voted to impose a trade embargo on Rhodesia.

A constitution adopted in 1970 effectively barred black participation in national politics. By 1974 mounting pressure from other African countries led the Smith government to enter into more serious negotiations. Guerrilla warfare pitting black nationalist groups against white settlers and mercenaries raged sporadically throughout the country, and many white settlers emigrated. A 1977 British-American proposal for majority rule provided the basis for a settlement of the crisis. An "internal settlement" was announced in April 1978 by Smith and three major nationalist leaders: Bishop Abel Muzorewa, leader of the United African National Congress, the Rev. Ndabaningi Sithole, former leader of the Zimbabwe African National Union (ZANU), and Chief Jeremiah Chirau. The settlement was rejected by the Patriotic Front that united ZANU (now led by Robert Mugabe) and Joshua Nkomo's Zimbabwe African People's Union (ZAPU).

Elections were held in April 1979 and Bishop Muzorewa assumed office on June 1 as prime minister of "Zimbabwe-Rhodesia," but the Patriotic Front continued to oppose the government. On Dec. 10 the "Zimbabwe-Rhodesia" Parliament dissolved itself, and the country reverted briefly to British colonial rule. On Dec. 21 all parties agreed to a cease-fire and to a period of transitional British rule leading to independence. International economic sanctions were lifted.

Elections held in 1980 resulted in a clear majority for Mugabe's ZANU party. Zimbabwe became independent, with Mugabe as prime minister, on April 18. As Mugabe embarked on an ambitious program of national reconstruction, Nkomo became leader of the opposition. Guerrillas linked to ZAPU, with Nkomo's tacit leadership and with alleged support from South Africa, continued to engage in sporadic warfare against Mugabe's government, and banditry disrupted the countryside.

The elections of 1985 increased ZANU's majority in Parliament. In 1987 the constitution was amended to strengthen the presidency and to end the separate role of blacks and whites in government; new elections were held for black members of Parliament to fill seats formerly reserved for whites. Guerrillas renewed attacks on white-owned farms.

In Dec. 1987 Mugabe and Nkomo agreed to merge ZANU and ZAPU (ZANU-PF), creating a de facto one-party state under Mugabe. A presidential election was scheduled for 1996, but in 1995, the Rev. Ndonga Sithole, leader of the opposition Zimbabwe African National Union, was arrested and charged with plotting to kill Mugabe.

Amidst a fuel crisis, 60 percent inflation and 50 percent unemployment, Zimbabwe voters in Feb. 2000 rejected a new constitution granting Mugabe 12 more years and power to seize white farmlands without compensation. But, with government approval, squatters began seizing white farms and preventing the tobacco harvest (30 percent of Zimbabwe's export earnings). June elections gave 57 of 120 seats contested to the opposition, sufficient to block any plan for a new constitution. But throughout 2001 Mugabe continued his plan to seize white-owned farms and began to arrest his political opponents.

Selected Territories Of The World

NON-SELF-GOVERNING STATES

The community of nations has long recognized the existence of territories that do not have the status of independent states and that are subordinate in some degree to another power. The United Nations refers to these as "non-self-governing territories." Except for mandates and trusteeships specified by the League of Nations and the U.N., the relationships between more and less powerful states have tended to evolve outside any rigid legal framework, and none of the following terms has an absolutely fixed meaning.

Colonies are dependent possessions whose inhabitants are not constitutionally under the dominant state's system of government but whose inhabitants are nationals of that state.

Commonwealths are autonomous states equal in status, united in their allegiance to a central power but not subordinate either to it or to one another in internal or external affairs.

Dependencies are states, provinces, or other places subject to the control of another power of which they do not form an integral part. The best known is Hong Kong, which China ceded to the United Kingdom in perpetuity in 1842, but which reverted to Chinese rule in 1997. The governor is appointed by the British monarch and foreign relations and defense are the responsibility of the U.K., but Hong Kong has substantial autonomy in commercial relations.

Mandates were territories surrendered by Turkey and Germany after World War I and, according to the League of Nations, "inhabited by peoples not yet able to stand by themselves" and therefore placed under the "tutelage" of different members of the League as "mandatories on behalf of the League." The last mandate to gain independence was South West Africa, now Namibia.

Protectorates *(associated states)* are states or territories partly under the control of another state but autonomous in domestic and certain external affairs. Protectorates are established by treaties.

Territories are regions (especially of Australia, Canada, and the United States) administered by a federal government and having some degree of self-government but not organized as a province or a state.

AUSTRALIA

▶ CHRISTMAS ISLAND
Territory of Christmas Island
● GEOGRAPHY Location: eastern Indian Ocean; 10°25'S, 105°39'E. Boundaries: Java Head, Indonesia, 224 mi. (360 km) to N, North West Cape, Australia, 875 mi. (1,408 km) to SE. Total area: 52 sq. mi. (135 sq km). Coastline: 86 mi. (138.9 km). Comparative area: about seven-tenths size of Washington, D.C. Land use: 0% arable land; 0% permanent crops; 0% meadows and pastures; 0% forest and woodland; 100% other. City: The Settlement (capital).
● PEOPLE Population: 2,564 (2000 est.). Nationality: noun—Christmas Islander(s); adjective—Christmas Island. Ethnic groups: 61% Chinese, 25% Malay, 11% European, 3% other; no indigenous population. Language: English. Religions: 55% Buddhist, 15% Christian, 10% Muslim.
● GOVERNMENT Type: territory of Australia. Constitution: Christmas Island Act of 1958. National Holiday: N.A. Head of government: Administrator (acting) Graham Nicholls (since N.A.). Structure: administrator appointed by the governor general of Australia; unicameral Christmas Island Shire Council; Supreme Court.
● ECONOMY Monetary unit: Australian dollar. Budget: N.A. GDP: N.A. Chief Crops: N.A. Natural resources: phosphate. Major industries: phosphate extraction (near depletion). Labor force: N.A.; 400 people in tourism, 100 people in mining. Exports: phosphate. Imports: consumer goods. Major trading partners; Australia, NZ.

▶ COCOS (KEELING) ISLANDS
Territory of Cocos (Keeling) Islands
● GEOGRAPHY Location: 27 islands in eastern Indian Ocean. West Island 12°05'S, 96°53'E. Boundaries: island of Sumatra (part of Indonesia) about 932 mi. (1,500 km) to NE; Perth, Australia 1,720 mi. (2,768 km) to SE. Total area: 5.4 sq. mi. (14.0 sq km). Coastline: 1.6 mi. (2.6 km). Comparative area: about 24 times size of the Mall in Washington, D.C. Land use: 0% arable land; 0% permanent crops; 0% meadows and pastures; 0% forest and woodland; 100% other. City: West Island (capital).
● PEOPLE Population: 635 (2000 est.). Nationality: noun—Cocos Islander(s); adjective—Cocos Islander. Ethnic groups: mostly Europeans on West Island and Cocos Malays on Home Island. Languages: English, Malay. Religions: 57% Sunni Muslim, 22% Christian.
● GOVERNMENT Type: territory of Australia. Constitution: Cocos (Keeling) Islands Act of 1995. National Holiday: N.A. Head of government:

Administrator (acting) Maureen Ellis (since N.A.). Structure: administrator appointed by the governor general of Australia; unicameral Cocos (Keeling) Islands Shire Council; Supreme Court.
● ECONOMY Monetary unit: Australian dollar. Budget: N.A. GDP: N.A. Chief crops: vegetables, bananas, pawpaws, coconuts. Natural resources: vegetables, bananas, pawpaws, coconuts. Major industries: copra products. Labor force: N.A.; the Cocos Island Cooperative Society Ltd. employs construction workers, stevedores, and lighterage worker operations; tourism employs others. Exports: copra. Imports: foodstuffs. Major trading partners: Australia.

▶ NORFOLK ISLAND
Territory of Norfolk Island
● GEOGRAPHY Location: island in western Pacific Ocean; 29°04'S, 167°57'E. Boundaries: Vanuatu to N, New Zealand to SE, Brisbane, Australia 870 mi. (1,400 km) to W. Total area: 13.3 sq. mi. (34.6 sq km). Coastline: 20 mi. (32 km). Comparative area: about one-fifth size of Washington, D.C. Land use: 0% arable land; 0% permanent crops; 25% meadows and pastures; 0% forest and woodland; 75% other. City: Kingston (capital).
● PEOPLE Population: 1,892 (2000 est.). Nationality: noun—Norfolk Islander(s); adjective—Norfolk Islander. Ethnic groups: descendants of Bounty mutineers; Australian, New Zealander, Polynesians. Languages: English (official), Norfolk (a mixture of 18th-century English and ancient Tahitian). Religions: 39% Anglican, 11.7% Roman Catholic, 16.4% Uniting Church in Australia, 4.4% Seventh-Day Adventist.
● GOVERNMENT Type: territory of Australia. Constitution: Norfolk Island Act of 1979. National holiday: Pitcairners Arrival Day Anniversary, June 8. Head of government: Assembly President and Chief Minister George Charles Smith, (since 1997). Structure: administrator appointed by the governor general of Australia; unicameral nine-member elected Legislative Assembly; Supreme Court.
● ECONOMY Monetary unit: Australian dollar. Budget: (FY92/93) *income:* $4.6 mil.; *expend.:* $4.8 mil. GDP: N.A. Chief crops: Norfolk Island pine seed, Kentia palm seed, cereals, vegetables, fruit; cattle, poultry. Natural resources: fish. Major industries: tourism. Labor force: 1,395 (1991 est.) Exports: $1.5 mil. (f.o.b., FY91/92); postage stamps, seeds of Norfolk Island pine and Kentia Palm, small quantities of avocados. Imports: $17.9 mil. (c.i.f., FY91/92). Major trading partners: Australia, Pacific Islands, New Zealand, Asia, Europe.

▶ UNINHABITED TERRITORIES OF AUSTRALIA
Ashmore Is. (12°15'S, 123°05'E); Cartier Is. (12°30'S, 123°30'E); Coral Sea Is. (18°00'S, 158°00'E); Heard Is. (53°00'S, 73°35'E); McDonald Is. (52°29'S, 72°50'E).

DENMARK

▶ FAEROE ISLANDS
● GEOGRAPHY Location: group of 18 islands (17 inhabited) in Atlantic Ocean SE of Iceland. Tórshavn 62°02'N, 6°47'W. Boundaries: Iceland to NW, Norwegian Sea to N, Norway to E, Shetland

Islands to SE, U.K. to S. **Total area:** 541 sq. mi. (1,399 sq km). **Coastline:** 694 mi. (1,117 km). **Comparative area:** eight times size of Washington, D.C. **Land use:** 6% arable land; 0% permanent crops; 0% meadows and pastures; 0% forest and woodland; 94% other. **City:** (1991 est.) Tórshavn (capital) 16,223.

• **PEOPLE   Population:** 45,296 (2000 est.). **Nationality:** noun—Faroese (sing., pl.); adjective—Faroese. **Ethnic groups:** homogeneous Scandinavian population. **Languages:** Faroese (derived from Old Norse), Danish. **Religions:** Evangelical Lutheran.

• **GOVERNMENT   Type:** self-governing (since 1979) overseas administrative division of Denmark. **Constitution:** June 5, 1953 (Danish constitution). **National Holiday:** Birthday of the Queen, April 16. **Head of government:** Anfinn Kallsberg, prime minister (since Apr. 1998). **Structure:** executive—High Commissioner, Prime Minister; legislative—32-member Parliament (Lagting) islands elect 2 representatives to Danish parliament; no separate judiciary.

• **ECONOMY   Monetary unit:** Danish krone. **Budget:** (1996 est.) *income:* $467 mil.; *expend.:* $468 mil. **GDP:** $700 mil., $16,000 per capita (1996 est.). **Chief crops:** milk, potatoes, vegetables, sheep; salmon farming; fish. **Natural resources:** fish, whales. **Major industries:** fishing. **Labor force:** 20,345 (1995 est.); fishing, manufacturing, transportation, commerce. **Exports:** $362 mil. (f.o.b., 1995 est.); 92% fish and fish products, animal feedstuffs, transport equipment. **Imports:** $315.6 mil. (c.i.f., 1995 est.); 17% machinery and transport equipment, 33% consumer goods, 26.9% raw materials and semi-manufactures, 11.4% fuels, 6.7% fish and salt. **Major trading partners:** *exports:* 31% Denmark, 25% U.K., 9% Germany; *imports:* 33% Denmark, 18% Norway, 8% U.K.

▶ **GREENLAND**

• **GEOGRAPHY   Location:** North Atlantic Ocean, largely within Arctic Circle. Godthåb 64°11′N, 51°44′W. **Boundaries:** Iceland about 190 mi. (300 km) to E across Denmark Strait, Canada to SW and W across Baffin Bay and Davis Strait. **Total area:** 840,000 sq. mi. (2,175,600 sq km); land area 131,931 sq. mi. (341,700 sq km) ice free. **Coastline:** 27,400 mi. (44,087 km). **Comparative area:** slightly more than three times size of Texas. **Land use:** 0% arable land; 0% permanent crops; 1% meadows and pastures; negl. % forest and woodland; 99% other. **City:** (1992) Godthåb (Nuuk, capital), 12,233.

• **PEOPLE   Population:** 56,309 (2000 est.). **Nationality:** noun—Greenlander(s); adjective—Greenlandic. **Ethnic groups:** 87% Greenlander (Eskimos and Greenland-born whites), 13% Danish and others. **Languages:** Eskimo dialects, Danish, Greenlandic (an Inuit dialect). **Religions:** Evangelical Lutheran.

• **GOVERNMENT   Type:** parliamentary democracy with constitutional monarch. **Constitution:** June 5, 1953 (Danish constitution). **National Holiday:** Birthday of the Queen, April 16. **Head of government:** Prime Minister Jonathan Motzfeldt (since Sept. 1997); named to post to replace Gunnar Martens, who retired ahead of scheduled election. **Structure:** prime minister is elected by the Parliament; unicameral Parliament or Landsting (31 seats); High Court or Landsrete.

• **ECONOMY   Monetary unit:** Danish krone. **Budget:** (1995 est.) *income:* $706 mil.; *expend:* $697 mil. **GDP:** $945 mil., $16,100 per capita (1997 est.). **Chief crops:** forage crops, small garden vegetables; sheep; fish. **Natural resources:** zinc, lead,

iron ore, coal, molybdenum. **Major industries:** mining, fishing. **Labor force:** 24,500 (1995 est.). **Exports:** $363.4 mil. (f.o.b., 1995 est.); fish and fish products. **Imports:** $421 mil. (c.i.f., 1995 est.); 25% machinery and transport equipment, 18% manufactured goods, 11% food and live animals, 6% petroleum products. **Major trading partners:** *exports:* 89% Denmark, 5% Japan, 5% U.K.; *imports:* 7.5% Denmark, 3.8% Iceland, 3.3% Japan.

FRANCE

▶ **FRENCH GUIANA**
Department of Guiana

• **GEOGRAPHY   Location:** NE coast of South America. **Boundaries:** North Atlantic Ocean to N, Brazil to E and S across Oyapock River, Suriname to W across Maroni River. **Total area:** 35,135 sq. mi. (91,000 sq km). **Coastline:** 235 mi. (378 km). **Comparative area:** slightly smaller than Indiana. **Land use:** negl. % arable land; negl. % permanent crops; negl. % meadows and pastures; 83% forest and woodland; 17% other. **City:** (1990) Cayenne (capital) 41,637.

• **PEOPLE   Population:** 172,605 (2000 est.). **Nationality:** noun—French Guianese (sing., pl.); adjective—French Guianese. **Ethnic groups:** 66% black or mulatto, 12% Caucasian, 12% East Indian, Chinese or Amerindian, 10% other. **Language:** French. **Religion:** predominantly Roman Catholic.

• **GOVERNMENT   Type:** overseas department of France. **Constitution:** Sept. 28, 1958 (French constitution). **National Holiday:** National Day, Taking of the Bastille, July 14. **Head of government:** President of the General Council Stephan Phinera (since March 1994); President of the Regional Council Antoine Karam (since March 1992). **Structure:** presidents of the General and Regional Councils are appointed by the members of those councils, who vote on party lines; unicameral 19-member General Council, 31-member Regional Council—both elected by popular vote to serve 6-year terms.; Court of Appeals.

• **ECONOMY   Monetary unit:** French franc. **Budget:** (1996 est.) *income:* $225 mil.; *expend.:* $390 mil. **GDP:** $1 bil., $6,000 per capita (1998 est.). **Chief crops:** rice, corn, manioc, cocoa, vegetables, bananas, sugar; cattle, pigs, poultry. **Natural resources:** bauxite, timber, gold, cinnabar, kaolin. **Major industries:** construction, shrimp processing, forestry products. **Labor force:** 58,800 (1997); 60.6% services, government and commerce, 21.2% industry, 18.2% agriculture; 25.7% unemployment (1997). **Exports:** $158 mil. (f.o.b., 1997); shrimp, timber, gold, rum, rosewood essence, clothing. **Imports:** $625 mil. (c.i.f., 1997); food (grains, processed meat), machinery and transport equipment, fuels and chemicals. **Major trading partners:** *exports:* 62% France, 7% EU; *imports:* 52% France, 14% U.S., 6% Trinidad and Tobago.

▶ **FRENCH POLYNESIA**
Territory of French Polynesia

• **GEOGRAPHY   Location:** five island groups or archipelagoes—Gambier, Marquesas, Society (includes Tahiti and Bora Bora), Tuamotu, and Tubuai (Austral Islands)—in South Pacific Ocean about halfway between South America and Australia. Papeete (Society Is.) 17°32'S, 149°34'W. **Boundaries:** Kiribati to NW, Cook Islands to W. **Total area:** 2,589 sq. mi. (4,167 sq km). **Coastline:** 1,569 mi. (2,525 km). **Comparative area:** slightly less than one-third size of Connecticut. **Land use:** 1% arable land; 6% permanent crops; 5% meadows and pastures; 31% forest and woodland; 57% other. **Cities:** (1996) Papeete (capital) 25,553; Faa'a 25,888.

• **PEOPLE Population:** 249,110 (2000 est.). **Nationality:** noun—French Polynesian(s); adjective—French Polynesian. **Ethnic groups:** 78% Polynesian, 12% Chinese, 6% local French, 4% metropolitan French. **Languages:** French, Tahitian (both official). **Religions:** 54% Protestant, 30% Roman Catholic, 16% other.

• **GOVERNMENT Type:** overseas territory of France. **Constitution:** Sept. 28, 1958 (French constitution). **National Holiday:** National Day, Taking of the Bastille, July 14. **Heads of government:** President of the Territorial Government of French Polynesia Gaston Flosse (since April 4, 1991), President of the Territorial Assembly Justin Arapari (since May 13, 1996). **Structure:** presidents of the Territorial Government and Assembly are elected by the members of the assembly; unicameral Territorial Assembly (41-seats; members are elected by popular vote to serve five-year terms); Court of Appeal.

• **ECONOMY Monetary unit:** Colonial Francs Pacifique (CFP). **Budget:** (1999) *income:* $1 bil.; *expend.:* $900 mil. **GDP:** $2.6 bil., $10,800 per capita (1997 est.). **Chief crops:** coconuts, vanilla, vegetables, fruits; poultry, beef, dairy products. **Natural resources:** timber, fish, cobalt. **Major industries:** tourism, pearls, agricultural processing. **Labor force:** 118,744 employed (1988); 13% agriculture, 19% industry, 68% services. **Exports:** $212 mil. (f.o.b., 1996); 53.8% cultured pearls, coconut products, mother-of-pearl, vanilla, shark meat. **Imports:** $860 mil. (c.i.f., 1996); fuels, foodstuffs, equipment. **Major trading partners:** *exports:* 6% France, 11% U.S.; *imports:* 44.7% France, 13.9% U.S.

▶ GUADELOUPE
Department of Guadeloupe
• **GEOGRAPHY Location:** eastern Caribbean Sea: Guadeloupe 16°00'N, 61°42'W; St. Barthélemy 17°55'N, 63°50'W; Marie Galante 15°57'N, 61°20'W. **Boundaries:** Antigua to N, Dominica to S. **Total area:** 687 sq. mi. (1,780 sq km). **Coastline:** 190 mi. (306 km). **Comparative area:** 10 times size of Washington, D.C. **Land use:** 14% arable land; 4% permanent crops; 14% meadows and pastures; 39% forest and woodland; 29% other; includes 1% irrigated. **Cities:** (1990 census) Basse-Terre (capital) 14,107; Les Abymes 62,809; Pointe à Pitre 26,083.

• **PEOPLE Population:** 426,493 (2000 est.). **Nationality:** noun—Guadeloupian(s); adjective—Guadeloupe. **Ethnic groups:** 90% black or mulatto, 5% white, 5% East Indian, Lebanese, Chinese. **Languages:** 99% French (official), Creole patois. **Religions:** 95% Roman Catholic, 4% Hindu and pagan African, 1% Protestant sects.

• **GOVERNMENT Type:** overseas department of France. **Constitution:** Sept. 28, 1958 (French constitution). **National Holiday:** National Day, Taking of the Bastille, July 14. **Head of government:** President of the General Council Marcellin Lubeth (since 1998), President of the Regional Council Lucette Michaux-Chevry (since March 1992). **Structure:** presidents of the General and Regional

Councils are elected by the members of those councils; unicameral General Council with 42 seats, members are elected by popular vote to serve 6-year terms; unicameral Regional Council with 41 seats, members are elected by popular vote by to serve 6-year terms; Court of Appeal.

• **ECONOMY Monetary unit:** French franc. **Budget:** (1997) *income:* $200 mil.; *expend:* $350 mil. **GDP:** $3.7 bil., $9,000 per capita (1996 est.). **Chief crops:** sugarcane, bananas, tropical fruits and vegetables; cattle, pigs, goats. **Natural resources:** cultivable land, beaches and climate that foster tourism. **Major industries:** construction, cement, rum. **Labor force:** 125,900; 68% services, 17% industry, 15% agriculture; 27.8% unemployment. **Exports:** $140 mil. (f.o.b., 1997); bananas, sugar, rum. **Imports:** $1.7 bil. (c.i.f., 1997); foodstuffs, fuels, vehicles, clothing and consumer goods, construction materials. **Major trading partners:** (1997) *exports:* 60% France, 18% Martinique; *imports:* 63% France, 13% EU, 4% Martinique.

▶ MARTINIQUE
Department of Martinique
• **GEOGRAPHY Location:** eastern Caribbean Sea (14°36'N, 61°05'W). **Boundaries:** Dominica to N, St. Lucia to S. **Total area:** 425 sq. mi. (1,100 sq km). **Coastline:** 218 mi. (350 km). **Comparative area:** slightly more than six times size of Washington, D.C. **Land use:** 8% arable land; 8% permanent crops; 17% meadows and pastures; 44% forest and woodland; 23% other; includes 5% irrigated. **City:** (1990 census) Fort-de-France (capital) 101,540.

• **PEOPLE Population:** 414,516 (2000 est.). **Nationality:** noun—Martiniquais (sing., pl.); adjective—Martiniquais. **Ethnic groups:** 90% African and African-Caucasian-Indian mixture, 5% Caucasian, 5% East Indian, Lebanese, Chinese. **Languages:** French, Creole patois. **Religions:** 95% Roman Catholic, 5% Hindu and pagan African beliefs.

• **GOVERNMENT Type:** overseas department of France. **Constitution:** Sept. 28, 1958. **National Holiday:** National Day, Taking of the Bastille, July 14. **Head of government:** President of the General Council Claude Lise (since March 1992), President of the Regional Council Alfred Marie-Jeanne (since March 1998). **Structure:** presidents of the General and Regional Councils are elected by the members of those councils; unicameral 45-seat General Council and unicameral 41-seat Regional Assembly members are elected by popular vote to serve 6-year terms. .

• **ECONOMY Monetary unit:** French franc. **Budget:** (1996 est.) *income:* $900 mil.; *expend.:* $2.5 bil. **GDP:** $4.24 bil., $10,700 per capita (1996). **Chief crops:** bananas, pineapples, vegetables, avocados, flowers, sugarcane for rum. **Natural resources:** coastal scenery and beaches, cultivable land. **Major industries:** construction, rum, cement. **Labor force:** 170,000 (1997); 73% services, 17% industry, 10% agriculture (1997). **Exports:** $250 mil. (f.o.b., 1997); refined petroleum products, bananas, rum, pineapples. **Imports:** $2 bil. (c.i.f., 1997); petroleum products, crude oil, foodstuffs, construction materials, vehicles, clothing and other consumer goods. **Major trading partners:** (1991) *exports:* 57% France, 31% Guadeloupe, French Guiana; *imports:* 62% France, U.K., Italy.

▶ MAYOTTE
Territorial Collectivity of Mayotte
• **GEOGRAPHY Location:** Comoros archipelago in eastern Indian Ocean (12°47'S, 45°12'E).

Boundaries: Indian Ocean to N, Madagascar 300 mi. (480 km) to SE, Mozambique Channel to S, Mozambique to W. **Total area:** 145 sq. mi. (375 sq km). **Coastline:** 115 mi. (185.2 km). **Comparative area:** slightly more than twice size of Washington, D.C. **Land use:** N.A. **Cities:** (1985 census) Dzaoudzi (capital) 5,865; Mamoudzou 12,026; Pamanzi-Labattoir 4,106.

• **PEOPLE Population:** 155,911 (2000 est.). **Nationality:** noun—Mahorais (sing., pl.); adjective—Mahoran. **Ethnic groups:** N.A. **Languages:** Mahorian (a Swahili dialect), French. **Religions:** 99% Muslim, 1% Christian (mostly Roman Catholic).

• **GOVERNMENT Type:** territorial collectivity of France. **Constitution:** Sept. 28, 1958 (French constitution). **National Holiday:** National Day, Taking of the Bastille, July 14. **Heads of government:** President of General Council Younoussa Bamana (since 1977). **Structure:** president of the General Council elected by the members of the General Council for a six-year term; unicameral 16-seat General Council members elected by popular vote to serve 3-year terms; Supreme Court.

• **ECONOMY Monetary unit:** French franc. **Budget:** (1991). *income:* N.A.; *expend.:* $73 mil. **GDP:** $85 mil., $600 per capita (1998 est.). **Chief crops:** vanilla, ylang-ylang, coffee, copra. **Natural resources:** negl. **Major industries:** newly created lobster and shrimp industry. **Labor force:** N.A. **Exports:** $3.44 mil. (f.o.b. 1997); ylang-ylang, vanilla, copra. **Imports:** $141.3 mil. (f.o.b. 1997); building materials, machinery and transportation equipment, metals, chemicals, rice, clothing, flour. **Major trading partners:** *exports:* 80% France, 15% Comoros, Reunion; *imports:* 66% France, 14% Africa, 20% Southeast Asia.

▶ **NEW CALEDONIA**
Territory of New Caledonia and Dependencies

• **GEOGRAPHY Location:** one large and several smaller islands in western South Pacific. Nouméa 22°16'S, 166°26'E. **Boundaries:** Vanuatu to N, Australia about 930 mi. (1,500 km) to W. **Total area:** 7,359 sq. mi. (19,060 sq km). **Coastline:** 1,401 mi. (2,254 km). **Comparative area:** slightly smaller than New Jersey. **Land use:** negl. % arable land; negl. % permanent crops; 12% meadows and pastures; 39% forest and woodland; 49% other. **City:** (1989) Nouméa (capital) 65,110.

• **PEOPLE Population:** 201,816 (2000 est.). **Nationality:** noun—New Caledonian(s); adjective—New Caledonian. **Ethnic groups:** 42.5% Melanesian, 37.1% European, 8.4% Wallisian, 3.8% Polynesian, 3.6% Indonesian, 1.6% Vietnamese, 3.0% other. **Languages:** French, Melanesian-Polynesian dialects. **Religions:** 60% Roman Catholic, 30% Protestant, 10% other.

• **GOVERNMENT Type:** overseas territory of France. **Constitution:** Sept. 28, 1958 (French Constitution). **National Holiday:** National Day, Taking of the Bastille, July 14. **Heads of government:** President of the Territorial Congress Simon Loueckhote (since 1998). **Structure:** president of the Territorial Congress elected by the members of the congress; unicameral 54-seat Territorial Congress members are elected by popular vote to serve 6-year terms; Court of Appeal.

• **ECONOMY Monetary unit:** Colonial Francs Pacifique (CFP). **Budget:** (1996 est.) *income:* $861.3 mil.; *expend.:* $735.3 mil. **GDP:** $2.1 bil., $11,400 per capita (1996 est.). **Chief crops:** vegetables; beef, other livestock products. **Natural resources:** nickel, chrome, iron, cobalt, man-

ganese. **Major industries:** nickel mining. **Labor force:** 79,395 (1996 est.); 40% services, 32% agriculture, 20% industry, 8% mining. **Exports:** $381 mil. (f.o.b. 1998); ferronickels, nickel ore. **Imports:** $922 mil. (c.i.f. 1998); food, transport equipment, machinery and electrical equipment, fuels and minerals. **Major trading partners:** *exports:* 31% Japan, 29% France, 12% U.S.; *imports:* 45% France, 18% Australia, 7% Singapore.

▶ **RÉUNION**
Department of Réunion

• **GEOGRAPHY Location:** southwestern Indian Ocean (20°15'S, 55°27'E). **Boundaries:** 500 mi. (800 km) E of Madagascar. **Total area:** 969 sq. mi. (2,510 sq km). **Coastline:** 125 mi. (201 km). **Comparative area:** slightly smaller than Rhode Island. **Land use:** 17% arable land; 2% permanent crops; 5% meadows and pastures; 35% forest and woodland; 41% other; includes 2% irrigated. **Cities:** (1990 census) Saint-Denis (capital) 121,999; Saint-Paul 71,669; Saint-Pierre 58,846.

• **PEOPLE Population:** 720,934 (2000 est.). **Nationality:** noun—Reunionese (sing., pl.); adjective—Reunionese. **Ethnic groups:** mostly intermixed French, African, Malagasy, Chinese, Pakistani, Indian ancestry. **Languages:** French (official), Creole. **Religions:** 94% Roman Catholic, Hindu, Islam, Buddhist.

• **GOVERNMENT Type:** overseas department of France. **Constitution:** Sept. 28, 1958, (French constitution). **National Holiday:** National Day, Taking of the Bastille, July 14. **Head of government:** President of the General Council Christophe Payet (since April 1994), President of the Regional Council Margarite Sudre (since June 25, 1993). **Structure:** presidents of the General and Regional Councils are elected by the members of those councils who vote on party lines; unicameral 47-seat General Council and unicameral 45-seat Regional Council members are elected by direct popular vote to serve 6-year terms.; judiciary

• **ECONOMY Monetary unit:** French franc. **Budget:** (1995) *income:* $1.2 bil.; *expend.:* $2.6 bil. **GDP:** $3.4 bil., $4,800 per capita (1998 est.). **Chief crops:** sugarcane, vanilla, tobacco, tropical fruits and vegetables. **Natural resources:** fish, arable land. **Major industries:** sugar, rum, cigarettes, handicraft items. **Labor force:** 261,000 (1995); 73% services, 19% industry, 8% agriculture; 35% unemployment (1994). **Exports:** $214.162 mil. (f.o.b. 1997); 63% sugar, 4% rum and molasses, 3% lobster, 2% perfume essences. **Imports:** $2.5 bil. (c.i.f. 1997); manufactured goods, food, beverages, tobacco, machinery and transportation equipment, raw materials, petroleum products. **Major trading partners:** *exports:* 74% France, 6% Japan, 4% Comoros; *imports:* 67% France, 4% Bahrain, 3% Italy.

▶ **ST. PIERRE AND MIQUELON**
Territorial Collectivity of St. Pierre and Miquelon

• **GEOGRAPHY Location:** North Atlantic off east coast of Canada. St. Pierre 46°46'N, 56°12'W. **Boundaries:** Newfoundland, Canada 16 mi. (25 km) to N, North Atlantic Ocean to E and S. **Total area:** 93 sq. mi. (242 sq km). **Coastline:** 75 mi. (120 km). **Comparative area:** 1.5 times size of Washington, D.C. **Land use:** 13% arable land; 0% permanent crops; 0% meadows and pastures; 4% forest and woodland; 83% other. **Cities:** (1990 census) St. Pierre (capital) 5,683; Miquelon 709.

• **PEOPLE Population:** 6,896 (2000 est.). **Na-**

tionality: noun—Frenchmen; adjective—French. **Ethnic groups:** Basques and Bretons (French fishermen). **Languages:** French. **Religions:** 99% Roman Catholic.

• **GOVERNMENT Type:** territorial collectivity of France. **Constitution:** Sept. 28, 1958 (French constitution). **National Holiday:** National Day, Taking of the Bastille, July 14. **Heads of government:** Bernard Le Soavec, president of the General Council. **Structure:** president of the General Council is elected by members of the General Council; unicameral 19-seat General Council members are elected by popular vote to serve six-year terms; Superior Tribunal of Appeals.

• **ECONOMY Monetary unit:** French franc. **Budget:** (1996 est.) *income:* $70 mil.; *expend.:* $60 mil. **GDP:** $74 mil., $11,000 per capita (1996 est.). **Chief crops:** vegetables; cattle, sheep, pigs; fish. **Natural resources:** fish, deep-water ports. **Major industries:** fishing, supply base for fishing fleets, tourism. **Labor force:** 3,000 (1996). **Exports:** $5 mil. (f.o.b., 1997); fish and fish products, fox and mink pelts. **Imports:** $66 mil. (c.i.f., 1997); meat, clothing, fuel, electrical equipment, machinery, building materials. **Major trading partners:** *exports:* 58% U.S., 17% France, 11% Canada; *imports:* Canada, France, U.S.

▶ **WALLIS AND FUTUNA**
Territory of the Wallis and Futuna Islands

• **GEOGRAPHY Location:** two island groups (Wallis to NE, Hooru, incl. Futuna Is., to SW) in South Pacific. Mata-Utu (Wallis group) 13°22'S, 176°12'W. **Boundaries:** Western Samoa to E, Fiji to SW. **Total area:** 106 sq. mi. (274 sq km). **Coastline:** 80 mi. (129 km). **Comparative area:** 1.5 times the size of Washington, D.C. **Land use:** 5% arable land; 20% permanent crops; 0% meadows and pastures; 0% forest and woodland; 75% other. **City:** Mata-Utu (capital) (1983 census) 815.

• **PEOPLE Population:** 15,283 (2000 est.). **Nationality:** noun—Wallisian(s), Futunan(s), or Wallis and Futuna Islander(s); adjective—Wallisian, Futunan, or Wallis and Futuna Islander. **Ethnic groups:** almost entirely Polynesian. **Languages:** French (official) Wallisian (indigenous Polynesian language). **Religions:** largely Roman Catholic.

• **GOVERNMENT Type:** overseas territory of France. **Constitution:** Sept. 28, 1958 (French constitution). **National Holiday:** N.A. **Head of government:** President of the Territorial Assembly Victor Brial (since June 1, 1997). **Structure:** presidents of the Territorial Assembly and Government are elected by the members of the assembly; unicameral 20-seat Territorial Assembly members are elected by popular vote to serve 5-year terms; three traditional kings administer customary law and there is a magistrate in Mata-Utu.

• **ECONOMY Monetary unit:** Colonial Francs Pacifique (CFP). **Budget:** (1998 est.) *income:* $20 mil.; *expend.:* $17 mil. **GDP:** $28.7 mil., $2,000 per capita (1995 est.). **Chief crops:** breadfruit, yams, taro, bananas; pigs, goats. **Natural resources:** negl. **Major industries:** copra, handicrafts. **Labor force:** N.A.; 80% agriculture, livestock, and fishing, 4% government. **Exports:** $370,000. (f.o.b., 1995 est.); copra, handicrafts. **Imports:** $13.5 mil. (c.i.f., 1995 est.); foodstuffs, manufactured goods, transportation equipment, fuel, clothing. **Major trading partners:** *exports:* N.A.; *imports:* France, Australia, New Zealand.

▶ **UNINHABITED TERRITORIES OF FRANCE**

Bassas da India (21°25'S, 39°42'E); Clipperton Is. (10°21'N, 109°13'W); Europa Is. (22°20'S, 40°22'E); French Southern and Antarctic Lands (Kerguelen Is. 49°20'S, 69°30'E); Glorioso Is. (11°30'S, 47°20'E); Tromelin Is. (15°52'S, 54°25'E).

MOROCCO

▶ **WESTERN SAHARA**

• **GEOGRAPHY Location:** northwestern coast of Africa. **Boundaries:** Morocco to N, Algeria, Mauritania to E, Atlantic Ocean to W. **Total area:** 102,703 sq. mi. (266,000 sq km). **Coastline:** 690 mi. (1,110 km). **Comparative area:** about the size of Colorado. **Land use:** 19% arable land; 24% permanent crops; 0% meadows and pastures; 47% forest and woodland; 10% other. **City:** (1982) El Aaiun (capital) 93,785.

• **PEOPLE Population:** 244,943 (2000 est.). **Nationality:** noun—Sahrawi(s), Sahraoui; adjective—Sahrawian, Sahraouian. **Ethnic groups:** Arab, Berber. **Languages:** Hassaniya Arabic, Moroccan Arabic. **Religion:** Muslim.

• **GOVERNMENT Type:** legal status and sovereignty still unresolved. Morocco and Polisario Front have fought over this since 1976. A U.N.-sponsored ceasefire has been in effect since Sept., 1991. A vote is scheduled for July 2000. **Constitution:** N.A. **National Holiday:** N.A. **Head of government:** N.A. **Structure:** N.A.

• **ECONOMY Monetary unit:** Moroccan dirham. **Budget:** N.A. **GDP:** N.A. **Chief crops:** fruits and vegetables in the few oases; camels, sheep, goats. **Natural resources:** phosphates, iron ore. **Major industries:** phosphate, fishing, handicrafts. **Labor force:** 12,000; 50% animal husbandry and subsistence farming. **Exports:** N.A.; 62% phosphates. **Imports:** N.A.; fuel for fishing fleet, foodstuffs. **Major trading partners:** Morocco claims administrative control over Western Sahara and controls all trade with country; trade figures are included in overall Moroccan accounts.

NETHERLANDS

▶ **ARUBA**

• **GEOGRAPHY Location:** southern Caribbean Sea (12°32'N, 70°02'W), off NW Venezuela. **Boundaries:** Curaçao, Netherlands Antilles 42 mi. (68 km) to E, Venezuela 16 mi. (25 km) to S. **Total area:** 75 sq. mi. (193 sq km). **Coastline:** about 45 mi. (about 72 km). **Comparative area:** slightly larger than Washington, D.C. **Land use:** 11% arable land; 0% permanent crops; 0% meadows and pastures; 0% forest and woodland; 89% other. **City:** Oranjestad (capital).

• **PEOPLE Population:** 69,539 (2000 est.). **Nationality:** noun—Aruban(s); adjective—Aruban. **Ethnic groups:** 80% mixed European/Caribbean Indian. **Languages:** Dutch (official), Papiamento (a Spanish-Portuguese-Dutch-English dialect); English widely spoken, Spanish. **Religions:** 82%

Roman Catholic, 8% Protestant; also Hindu, Muslim, Confucian, Jewish minorities.

● **Government**   Part of the Netherlands, but full autonomy in internal affairs obtained in 1986 upon separation from Netherlands Antilles. **Type:** parliamentary democracy. **Constitution:** Jan. 1, 1986. **National Holiday:** Flag Day, Mar. 18. **Head of government:** Prime Minister Jan. H. Eman (since July 29, 1994). **Structure:** prime minister elected by the Staten for a four-year term; unicameral 21-seat Legislature members elected by direct popular vote and serve 4-year terms; Joint High Court of Justice.

● **Economy**   **Monetary unit:** Aruban florin. **Budget:** (1997) *income:* $N.A. mil.; *expend.:* $541 mil. **GDP:** $1.6 bil., $22,800 per capita (1998 est.). **Chief crops:** aloes; livestock; fishing. **Natural resources:** negl.; white sandy beaches. **Major industries:** tourism, transshipment, oil refining. **Labor force:** 41,501 (1997 est.); mostly tourism. **Exports:** $1.17 bil. (1998); including oil re-exports; mostly petroleum products. **Imports:** $1.52 bil. (1998); including oil for processing and re-export, foodstuffs, consumer goods. **Major trading partners:** U.S., EU.

▶ NETHERLANDS ANTILLES

● **Geography**   **Location:** two island groups in Caribbean Sea, about 500 mi. (800 km) apart. Curaçao Is. 12°12′N, 68°56′W; St. Maarten Is. 18°03′N, 63°05′W. **Boundaries:** southern group (Curaçao and Bonaire)— Venezuela to S; northern group (St. Eustatius, Saba, and St. Maarten)— Antigua to E, Virgin Islands to W. **Total area:** 371 sq. mi. (960 sq km). **Coastline:** 226 mi. (364 km). **Comparative area:** more than 5 times size of Washington, D.C. **Land use:** 10% arable land; 0% permanent crops; 0% meadows and pastures; 0% forest and woodland; 90% other. **City:** Willemstad (capital).

● **People**   **Population:** 210,134 (2000 est.). **Nationality:** noun—Netherlands Antillean(s); adjective—Netherlands Antillean. **Ethnic groups:** 85% mixed African; remainder Carib Amerindian, European, East Asian. **Languages:** Dutch (official), Papiamento (a Spanish-Portuguese-Dutch-English dialect) predominates; English widely spoken; Spanish. **Religions:** predominantly Roman Catholic; Protestant, Jewish, Seventh-Day Adventist.

● **Government**   **Type:** autonomous part of Netherlands; parliamentary. **Constitution:** Dec. 29, 1954. **National holiday:** Queen's Day, April 30. **Head of government:** Miguel Pourier, prime minister (since Feb. 1994). **Structure:** leader of the majority party is usually elected prime minister by the Staten; unicameral 22-seat Staten members are elected by popular vote to serve 4-year terms; Joint High court of Jusice, appointed by the Netherlands monarch.

● **Economy**   **Monetary unit:** Netherlands Antillean guilder. **Budget:** (1997 est.) *income:* $710.8 mil.; *expend.:* $741.6 mil. **GDP:** $2.4 bil., $11,800 per capita (1998 est.). **Chief crops:** aloes, sorghum, peanuts. **Natural resources:** phosphates (Curaçao only), salt (Bonaire only). **Major industries:** tourism on Curaçao and St. Maarten; petroleum refining on Curaçao; petroleum transshipment facilities on Curaçao and Bonaire; light manufacturing on Curaçao. **Labor force:** 89,000 (1983); 86% services, 13% industry, 1% agriculture (1994 est.). **Exports:** $268.2 mil. (f.o.b, 1997); 98% petroleum products. **Imports:** $1.4 bil. (c.i.f., 1997); 64% crude petroleum, food, manufactures. **Major trading partners:** *exports:* 28.6% U.S.,

6.4% Honduras, 6% Belgium-Luxembourg; *imports:* 34% Venezuela, 16.4% U.S., 15.5% Mexico.

NEW ZEALAND

▶ COOK ISLANDS

● **Geography**   **Location:** 15 islands (13 inhabited) in South Pacific. Avarua 21°12′S, 159° 46′W. **Boundaries:** French Polynesia to E, American Samoa to W. **Total area:** 93 sq. mi. (240 sq km). **Coastline:** 75 mi. (120 km). **Comparative area:** 1.3 times size of Washington, D.C. **Land use:** 9% arable land; 13% permanent crops; 0% meadows and pastures; 0% forest and woodland; 78% other. **City:** Avarua (capital).

● **People**   **Population:** 20,407 (2000 est.). **Nationality:** noun—Cook Islander(s); adjective—Cook Islander. **Ethnic groups:** 81.3% Polynesian (full blood), 7.7% Polynesian and European, 7.7% Polynesian and other, 2.4% European, 0.9% other. **Languages:** English (official), Maori. **Religions:** Christian; majority of populace members of Cook Islands Christian church.

● **Government**   **Type:** self-governing parliamentary democracy in free association with New Zealand; Cook Islands government is fully responsible for internal affairs and has right at any time to move to full independence by unilateral action; New Zealand responsible for external affairs, in consultation with Cook Islands government. **Constitution:** Aug. 4, 1965. **National holiday:** Constitution Day, Aug. 4. **Head of government:** Terepai Maoake, prime minister (since Nov. 1999). **Structure:** leader of the party that wins the most seats usually becomes prime minister; unicameral 25-seat Parliament members elected by popular vote to serve 5-year terms; High Court.

● **Economy**   **Monetary unit:** New Zealand dollar. **Budget:** N.A. **GDP:** $112 mil., $5,600 per capita (1998 est.). **Chief crops:** copra, citrus fruits, pineapples, tomatoes, beans, pawpaws, bananas, yams, taro, coffee. **Labor force:** (1993) 6,601; 29% agriculture, 27% government, 25% services, 15% industry. **Natural resources:** negl. **Major industries:** fruit processing, tourism. **Exports:** $4.2 mil. (f.o.b., 1994); copra, fresh and canned citrus fruit, coffee; fish; pearls and pearl shells; clothing. **Imports:** $85 mil. (c.i.f., 1994); foodstuffs, textiles, fuels, timber, capital goods. **Major trading partners:** *exports:* 80% New Zealand, Japan, Hong Kong; *imports:* 49% New Zealand, Italy, Australia.

▶ NIUE

● **Geography**   **Location:** coral island in western South Pacific (19°02′S, 169°55′W). **Boundaries:** Tonga 300 mi. (480 km) to W, southern Cook Islands 580 mi. (930 km) to E. **Total area:** 100 sq. mi. (260 sq km). **Coastline:** 40 mi. (64 km). **Comparative area:** 1.5 times size of Washington, D.C. **Land use:** 19% arable land; 8% permanent crops; 4% meadows and pastures; 19% forest and woodland; 50% other. **City:** Alofi (capital).

● **People**   **Population:** 2,113 (2000 est.). **Nationality:** noun—Niuean(s); adjective—Niuean. **Ethnic groups:** Polynesian, with about 200 Europeans, Samoans, Tongans. **Languages:** Polynesian dialect closely related to Tongan and

Samoan; English. **Religions:** 75% Ekalesia Niue (Niuean Church)—a Christian Protestant church closely related to London Missionary Society, 10% Latter-Day Saints, 15% Roman Catholic, Jehovah's Witnesses, Seventh-Day Adventist.

• **GOVERNMENT Type:** self-governing parliamentary democracy territory in free association with New Zealand. **Constitution:** Oct. 19, 1974. **National holiday:** Waitangi Day, Feb. 6. **Heads of government:** Sani Lakatani, premier (since Apr. 1999). **Structure:** executive—premier (elected by assembly); Legislative Assembly consists of 20 members (14 village representatives and six elected on a common roll); Supreme Court of New Zealand.

• **ECONOMY Monetary unit:** New Zealand dollar. **Budget:** N.A. **GDP:** $4.5 mil., $2,250 per capita (1994 est.). **Chief crops:** coconuts, passion fruit, honey, limes, taro, yams, cassava (tapioca), sweet potatoes; pigs, poultry, beef cattle. **Natural resources:** fish, arable land. **Major industries:** tourism, handicrafts. **Labor force:** 450 (1992 est.); most Niueans work on family plantations; paid work exists only in government service, small industry, and Niue Development Board. **Exports:** $117,500 (f.o.b., 1989); canned coconut cream, copra, honey, passion fruit products, pawpaw. **Imports:** $4.1 mil. (c.i.f., 1989); food, live animals, manufactured goods, machinery, fuels, lubricants, chemicals, drugs. **Major trading partners:** *exports:* 89% New Zealand, Fiji, Cook Islands; *imports:* 59% New Zealand, 20% Fiji, 13% Japan.

▶ TOKELAU

• **GEOGRAPHY Location:** three atolls (Atafu, Nukunonu, Fakaofo) in South Pacific. Atafu 8°33'S, 172°30'W. **Boundaries:** northern Cook Islands to E, Western Samoa 300 mi. (480 km) to S, Tuvalu to W. **Total area:** 4 sq. mi. (10 sq km). **Coastline:** 62 mi. (101 km). **Comparative area:** about 17 times size of the Mall in Washington, D.C. **Land use:** 0% arable land; 0% permanent crops; 0% meadows and pastures; 0% forest and woodland; 100% other. **City:** none; each atoll has own administrative center.

• **PEOPLE Population:** 1,458 (2000 est.). **Nationality:** noun—Tokelauan(s); adjective—Tokelauan. **Ethnic groups:** Polynesian. **Languages:** Tokelauan (a Polynesian language), English. **Religions:** 70% Congregational Christian church, 28% Roman Catholic; on Atafu, all Congregational Christian Church of Samoa; on Nukunonu, all Roman Catholic; on Fakaofo, both denominations.

• **GOVERNMENT Type:** territory of New Zealand. **Constitution:** administered under the Tokelau Islands Act of 1948, as amended in 1970. **National holiday:** Waitangi Day, Feb. 6. **Head of government:** Aliki Faipule Falimateao (since 1997). **Structure:** head of government is chosen from the Council of Faipule and serves a one-year term; unicameral 15-seat General Fono members chosen by each atoll's Council of Elders or Taupulega to serve 3-year terms; Supreme Court.

• **ECONOMY Monetary unit:** New Zealand dollar. **Budget:** (1987) *income:* $430,830; *expend.:* $2.8 mil. **GDP:** $1.5 mil., $1,000 per capita (1993 est.). **Chief crops:** coconuts, copra, breadfruit, papaya, bananas; pigs, poultry, goats. **Natural resources:** negl. **Major industries:** small-scale enterprises for copra production, woodwork, plaited craft goods, stamps, coins. **Labor force:** N.A. **Exports:** $98,000 (f.o.b., 1983); stamps, copra, handicrafts.

Imports: $323,400 (c.i.f., 1983); foodstuffs, building materials, fuel. **Major trading partners:** New Zealand.

NORWAY

▶ SVALBARD

• **GEOGRAPHY Location:** nine large and numerous smaller islands in Arctic Ocean. **Boundaries:** Longyearbyen (Spitsbergen Is.) 78° 13'N, 15°38'W; Bear Is. 74°30'N, 19°00'E. Norway to S, Greenland to W. **Total area:** 38,557 sq. mi. (62,049 sq km). **Coastline:** 2,229 mi. (3,587 km). **Comparative area:** slightly smaller than West Virginia. **Land use:** 0% arable land; 0% permanent crops; 0% meadows and pastures; 0% forest and woodland; 100% other; no trees; only bushes are crowberry and cloudberry. **City:** Longyearbyen (capital).

• **PEOPLE Population:** 2,416 (2000 est.). **Nationality:** N.A. **Ethnic groups:** 62% Russian and Ukrainian, 38% Norwegian. **Languages:** Russian, Norwegian. **Religions:** N.A.

• **GOVERNMENT Type:** territory of Norway. **Constitution:** N.A. **National holiday:** N.A. **Head of government:** Morten Ruud, governor (since Nov. 1998). **Structure:** governor responsible to the Polar Department of the Ministry of Justice

• **ECONOMY Monetary unit:** Norwegian krone. **Budget:** (1997 est.) *income:* $11.7 mil.; *expend.:* $11.7 mil. **GDP:** N.A. **Chief Crops:** N.A. **Natural resources:** coal, copper, iron ore, phosphate, zinc. **Major industries:** coal mining; trapping of seal, polar bear, fox, walrus. **Labor force:** N.A. **Exports:** N.A. **Imports:** N.A. **Major trading partners:** N.A.

▶ UNINHABITED TERRITORIES OF NORWAY

Bouvet Is. (54°26'S, 3°24'E); Jan Mayen Is. (71°00'N, 8°30'W).

UNITED KINGDOM

▶ ANGUILLA

• **GEOGRAPHY Location:** island in northeastern Caribbean (18°03'N, 63°04'W). **Boundaries:** St. Martin 5 mi. (8 km) to S, St. Kitts 70 mi. (113 km) to SE. **Total area:** 35 sq. mi. (91 sq km). **Coastline:** 38 mi. (61 km). **Comparative area:** about one-half size of Washington, D.C. **Land use:** N.A.; mostly rock with sparse scrub oak, few trees, some commercial salt ponds. **City:** The Valley (capital).

• **PEOPLE Population:** 11,797 (2000 est.). **Nationality:** noun—Anguillan(s); adjective—Anguillan. **Ethnic groups:** mainly of black African descent. **Languages:** English. **Religions:** 40% Anglican, 33% Methodist, 7% Seventh-Day Adventist, 5% Baptist, 3% Roman Catholic.

• **GOVERNMENT Type:** dependent territory of U.K. **Constitution:** Apr. 1, 1982. **National holiday:** Anguilla Day, May 30. **Heads of government:** Chief Minister Hubert Hughes (since Mar. 16,

1994). **Structure:** chief minister appointed by the governor from among the members of the House of Assembly; unicameral 11-seat House of Assembly members elected by direct popular vote to serve 5-year terms; High Court.

• **ECONOMY Monetary unit:** East Caribbean dollar. **Budget:** (1997) *income:* $20.4 mil.; *expend.:* $23.3 mil. **GDP:** $88 mil., $7,900 per capita (1998 est.). **Chief crops:** pigeon peas, corn, sweet potatoes; sheep, goats, cattle, poultry; fishing (including lobster). **Natural resources:** salt, fish, lobster. **Major industries:** tourism, boat building, off shore financial services. **Labor force:** 4,400 (1992); 7% unemployment (1992). **Exports:** $4.5 mil. (1998); lobsters, fish, livestock, salt. **Imports:** $57.6 mil. (1998). **Major trading partners:** N.A.

▶ **BERMUDA**
• **GEOGRAPHY Location:** archipelago of about 150 islands, in southern North Atlantic Ocean (32° 18'N, 64°47'W). **Boundaries:** Cape Hatteras 580 mi. (933 km) to W. **Total area:** 19 sq. mi. (50 sq km). **Coastline:** 64 mi. (103 km). **Comparative area:** about three-tenths size of Washington, D.C. **Land use:** 6% arable land; N.A.% permanent crops; N.A.% meadows and pastures; N.A.% forest and woodland; 55% developed and 39% rural and open space comprise 94% of Bermudian land area. **Cities:** (1990 est.) Hamilton (capital) 6,000; St. George's 3,000.
• **PEOPLE Population:** 62,997 (2000 est.). **Nationality:** noun—Bermudian(s); adjective— Bermudian. **Ethnic groups:** 61% black, 39% white and other. **Languages:** English (official), Portuguese. **Religions:** 28% Anglican, 15% Roman Catholic, 12% African Methodist Episcopal (Zion), 6% Seventh-day Adventist, 5% Methodist, 34% other.
• **GOVERNMENT Type:** British dependent territory. **Constitution:** June 8, 1968. **National holiday:** Bermuda Day, May 24. **Heads of government:** Jennifer Smith, premier (since Nov. 1998). **Structure:** premier appointed by the governor; bicameral 11-seat Parliament members appointed by the governor, 40-seat House of Assembly members are elected by popular vote to serve 5-year terms; Supreme Court.
• **ECONOMY Monetary unit:** Bermudian dollar. **Budget:** (FY97/98) *income:* $504.6 mil.; *expend.:* $537 mil. **GDP:** $2.0 bil., $31,500 per capita (1999 est.). **Chief crops:** bananas, vegetables, flowers, dairy products, citrus fruits. **Natural resources:** limestone, pleasant climate fostering tourism. **Major industries:** tourism, finance, structural concrete products. **Labor force:** 35,296 (1997); 23% clerical, 22% services, 17% laborers, 17% professional and technical, 12% administrative and managerial, 7% sales, 2% agriculture and fishing. **Exports:** $32 mil. (1998); reexports of pharmaceuticals. **Imports:** $624 mil. (1998); miscellaneous manufactured articles, machinery and transport equipment, food and live animals, chemicals. **Major trading partners:** *exports:* 29.5% U.K., 9.8% U.S., *imports:* 34% U.S., 9% U.K.

▶ **BRITISH VIRGIN ISLANDS**
• **GEOGRAPHY Location:** more than 40 mountainous islands (15 inhabited) in northeastern Caribbean. City of Road Town (on Tortola Is.), 18°26'N, 64°32'W. **Boundaries:** Puerto Rico about 100 mi. (161 km) to W. **Total area:** 58 sq. mi. (150 sq km). **Coastline:** 50 mi. (80 km). **Comparative area:** 0.9 times the size of Washington, D.C. **Land use:** 20% arable land; 7% permanent crops; 33% meadows and pastures; 7% forest and woodland; 33% other. **City:** (1987 est.) Road Town (capital), 2,500.
• **PEOPLE Population:** 19,615 (2000 est.). **Nationality:** noun—Virgin Islander(s); adjective— British Virgin Islander. **Ethnic groups:** over 90% black, remainder of white and Asian origin. **Languages:** English. **Religions:** 86% Protestant (45% Methodist, 21% Anglican, 7% Church of God, 5% Seventh-Day Adventist, 4% Baptist, 2% Jehovah's Witness, 2% other), 6% Roman Catholic, 2% none.
• **GOVERNMENT Type:** dependent territory of U.K. **Constitution:** June 1, 1977. **National holiday:** Territory Day, July 1. **Heads of government:** Ralph T. O'Neal, chief minister (since May 1995). **Structure:** chief minister appointed by the governor from among the members of the Legislative Council; unicameral 13-seat Legislative Council members are elected by direct popular vote to serve 5-year terms; Eastern Caribbean Supreme Court.
• **ECONOMY Monetary unit:** U.S. dollar. **Budget:** (1997) *income:* $121.5 mil.; *expend.:* $115.5 mil. **GDP:** $287 mil., $15,000 per capita (1999). **Chief crops:** fruit, vegetables; livestock, poultry, fish. **Natural resources:** negl. **Major industries:** tourism, construction, rum. **Labor force:** 4,911 (1980). **Exports:** $6.0 mil. (1998); rum, fresh fish, gravel, sand, fruits, vegetables. **Imports:** $175 mil. (1998); building materials, automobiles, foodstuffs, machinery. **Major trading partners:** Virgin Islands (U.S.), Puerto Rico, U.S.

▶ **CAYMAN ISLANDS**
• **GEOGRAPHY Location:** three main and numerous smaller islands in western Caribbean. George Town (Grand Cayman Is.) 19°20'N, 81°23'W. **Boundaries:** Cuba to N, Jamaica 180 mi. (290 km) to SE. **Total area:** 100 sq. mi. (260 sq km). **Coastline:** 100 mi. (160 km). **Comparative area:** 1.5 times size of Washington, D.C. **Land use:** 0% arable land; 0% permanent crops; 8% meadows and pastures; 23% forest and woodland; 69% other. **Cities:** (1989 census) Georgetown (capital) 12,921; West Bay 5,632.
• **PEOPLE Population:** 34,763 (2000 est.). **Nationality:** noun—Caymanian(s); adjective—Caymanian. **Ethnic groups:** 40% mixed, 20% white, 20% black, 20% expatriates of various ethnic groups. **Languages:** English. **Religions:** United Church (Presbyterian and Congregational), Anglican, Baptist, Roman Catholic, Church of God, other Protestant denominations.
• **GOVERNMENT Type:** British dependent territory. **Constitution:** 1959, revised 1972 and 1992. **National holiday:** Constitution Day, first Monday in July. **Head of government:** Peter Smith, governor and president of Executive Council (since May 1999). **Structure:** governor is appointed by the queen; unicameral 18-seat Legislative Assembly members elected by popular vote and serve 4-year terms; Grand Court, Cayman Islands Court of Appeals.
• **ECONOMY Monetary unit:** Caymanian dollar. **Budget:** (1997) *income:* $265.2 mil.; *expend.:* $248.9 mil. **GDP:** $930 mil., $24,500 per capita (1997 est.). **Chief crops:** fruits and vegetables; livestock, turtle farming. **Natural resources:** fish, climate and beaches that foster tourism. **Major industries:** tourism, banking, insurance, finance. **Labor force:** 19,820 (1995); 86% services, 12.6% industry, 1.4% agriculture. **Exports:** $2.17 mil.

(1997); turtle products, manufactured consumer goods. **Imports:** $432 mil. (1997); foodstuffs, manufactured goods. **Major trading partners:** *exports:* mostly U.S.; *imports:* U.S., Trinidad and Tobago, U.K.

▶FALKLAND ISLANDS
Colony of the Falkland Islands
• GEOGRAPHY **Location:** two large and about 2,000 smaller islands in southwestern Atlantic Ocean. Stanley (East Falkland) 51°45'S, 57° 56'W. **Boundaries:** Cape Horn, South America, about 480 mi. (770 km) to SW. **Total area:** 4,699 sq. mi. (12,173 sq km). **Coastline:** 800 mi. (1,288 km). **Comparative area:** slightly smaller than Connecticut. **Land use:** 0% arable land; 0% permanent crops; 99% meadows and pastures; 0% forest and woodland; 1% other. **City:** (1991 census) Stanley (capital) 1,557.
• PEOPLE **Population:** 2,826 (2000 est.). **Nationality:** noun—Falkland Islander(s); adjective—Falkland Island. **Ethnic groups:** mostly British. **Languages:** English. **Religions:** predominantly Anglican, Roman Catholic, United Free Church, Evangelist Church, Jehovah's Witnesses, Lutheran, Seventh-Day Adventist.
• GOVERNMENT **Type:** colony of U.K. **Constitution:** Oct. 3, 1985. **National holiday:** Liberation Day, June 14. **Head of government:** Donald Lamont, governor (since May 1999). **Structure:** governor appointed by the queen; unicameral 10-seat Legislative Council members are elected by popular vote to serve 5-year terms; Supreme Court.
• ECONOMY **Monetary unit:** Falkland Island pound. **Budget:** (1997/98) *income:* $66.1 mil.; *expend.:* $66.8 mil. **GDP:** N.A. **Natural resources:** fish, wildlife. **Major industries:** wool processing. **Labor force:** 1,100 (est.); 95% agriculture, mostly sheepherding. **Exports:** $7.6 mil. (1995); wool, hides, meat. **Imports:** $24.7 mil. (1995); food and drink, clothing, fuels, building materials. **Major trading partners:** U.K., Netherlands, Japan.

▶GIBRALTAR
• GEOGRAPHY **Location:** narrow peninsula running southward from southwest coast of Spain, to which it is connected by an isthmus. **Boundaries:** Spain to W and N, Mediterranean Sea to E, Morocco to S across Strait of Gibraltar. **Total area:** 3 sq. mi. (6.5 sq km). **Coastline:** 7.5 mi. (12 km). **Comparative area:** about 11 times size of the Mall in Washington, D.C. **Land use:** 0% arable land; 0% permanent crops; 0% meadows and pastures; 0% forest and woodland; 100% other. **City:** Gibraltar (capital).
• PEOPLE **Population:** 29,481 (2000 est.). **Nationality:** noun—Gibraltarian(s); adjective—Gibraltar. **Ethnic groups:** Italian, English, Maltese, Portuguese, and Spanish descent. **Languages:** English and Spanish are primary languages; Italian, Portuguese, Russian also spoken; English used in schools and for official purposes. **Religions:** 76.9% Roman Catholic, 6.9% Church of England, 6.9% Muslim.
• GOVERNMENT **Type:** colony of UK. **Constitution:** May 30, 1969. **National holiday:** Commonwealth Day, second Monday of March. **Heads of government:** Peter Caruana, chief minister (since May 1996). **Structure:** chief minister appointed by the governor; unicameral 18-seat House of Assembly members elected by popular votes to serve 4-year terms; Supreme Court, Court of Appeals.
• ECONOMY **Monetary unit:** Gibraltar pound.

Budget: (FY96/97) *income:* $119.3 mil.; *expend.:* $122.1 mil. **GDP:** $500 mil., $17,500 per capita (1997 est.). **Chief crops:** N.A. **Natural resources:** negl. **Major industries:** tourism, banking and finance, construction; support to large U.K. naval and air bases. **Labor force:** about 14,800 (including non-Gibraltar laborers); 60% services, 40% industry. **Exports:** $81.1 mil. (f.o.b., 1997); principally re-exports—51% petroleum, 41% manufactured goods, 8% other. **Imports:** $492 mil. (c.i.f, 1997); manufactured goods, fuels, foodstuffs. **Major trading partners:** *exports:* U.K., Morocco, Portugal; *imports:* U.K., Spain, Japan.

▶MONTSERRAT
(Two years of volcanic eruptions have left the southern half of this small island covered with ash and rock. More than half of its population had fled by mid-1997)
• GEOGRAPHY **Location:** eastern Caribbean Sea (16°44'N, 62°14'W). **Boundaries:** Guadeloupe 35 mi. (55 km) to S, Antigua 27 mi. (47 km) to NE. **Total area:** 39 sq. mi. (100 sq km). **Coastline:** 25 mi. (40 km). **Comparative area:** about three-fifths size of Washington, D.C. **Land use:** 20% arable land; 0% permanent crops; 10% meadows and pastures; 40% forest and woodland; 30% other. **City:** (1980) Plymouth (capital) 3,500.
• PEOPLE **Population:** 6,409 (2000 est.); an estimated 8,000 refugees left the island following volcanic activity in 1995; some have returned. **Nationality:** noun—Montserratian(s); adjective—Montserratian. **Ethnic groups:** mostly black, with a few Europeans. **Languages:** English. **Religions:** Anglican, Methodist, Roman Catholic, Pentecostal, Seventh-Day Adventist, other Christian denominations.
• GOVERNMENT **Type:** colony of U.K. **Constitution:** present constitution came into force Dec. 19, 1989. **National holiday:** Celebration of the Birthday of the Queen, second Saturday of June. **Heads of government:** Chief Minister David Brandt (since Aug. 1997). **Structure:** the leader of the majority party ususally becomes chief minister; unicameral 11-seat Legislative Council members popularly elected to serve 5-year terms; Eastern Caribbean Supreme Court.
• ECONOMY **Monetary unit:** East Caribbean dollar. **Budget:** (1997 est.) *income:* $31.4 mil.; *expend.:* $31.6 mil. **Chief crops:** cabbages, carrots, cucumbers, tomatoes, onions, peppers; livestock products. **Natural resources:** negl. **Major industries:** tourism, rum, textiles, electronic appliances. **Labor force:** 4,521 (1992 est.); 40.5% community, social, and personal services, 13.5% construction, 12.3% trade, restaurants, and hotels, 10.5% manufacturing. **Exports:** $1.5 mil. (1998); electronic components, plastic bags, apparel, hot peppers, live plants, cattle. **Imports:** $26.0 mil. (1998); machinery and transportation equipment, foodstuffs, manufactured goods, fuels, lubricants, related materials. **Major trading partners:** U.S., Ireland.

▶PITCAIRN ISLANDS
Pitcairn, Henderson, Ducie, and Oeno Islands
• GEOGRAPHY **Location:** group of islands (one inhabited) in South Pacific. Pitcairn 25°04'S 130°04'W. **Boundaries:** about halfway between Panama and New Zealand; French Polynesia to NW. **Total area:** 18 sq. mi. (47 sq km). **Coastline:**

32 mi. (51 km). **Comparative area:** three-tenths size of Washington, D.C. **Land use:** N.A. **City:** Adamstown (capital).

• **PEOPLE Population:** 54 (2000 est.). **Nationality:** noun—Pitcairn Islander(s); adjective—Pitcairn Islander. **Ethnic groups:** descendants of Bounty mutineers and their Tahitian wives. **Languages:** English (official), also a Tahitian/English dialect. **Religion:** 100% Seventh-Day Adventist.

• **GOVERNMENT Type:** colony of U.K. **Constitution:** Local Government Ordinance of 1964. **National holiday:** Celebration of the Birthday of the Queen, second Saturday in June. **Head of government:** Island Magistrate and Chairman of the Island Council Jay Warren. **Structure:** magistrate elected by popular vote for a 3-year term; unicameral 10-seat Island Council members (6 popularly elected, 2 appointed) serve 1-year terms; Island Court.

• **ECONOMY Monetary unit:** New Zealand dollar. **Budget:** (FY94/95) *income:* $729,884; *expend.:* $878,119. **GDP:** N.A. **Chief crops:** wide variety of fruits and vegetables. **Natural resources:** miro trees (used for handicrafts), fish. **Major industries:** postage stamps, handicrafts. **Labor force:** 12 able-bodied men; no business community in usual sense; some public works; subsistence farming and fishing. **Exports:** fruits, vegetables, curios. **Imports:** fuel oil, machinery, building materials, flour, sugar, other foodstuffs. **Major trading partners:** N.A.

▶ **ST. HELENA**

• **GEOGRAPHY Location:** eastern South Atlantic (15°56'S, 5°43'W). Dependencies are Ascension Is. (7°56'S, 14°25'W) 700 mi. to NW, and Tristan da Cunha (37°05'S, 12°17'W) 1,500 mi to SSW. **Boundaries:** Angola about 1,200 mi. (1,930 km) to E. **Total area:** 158 sq. mi. (410 sq km). **Coastline:** 37 mi. (60 km). **Comparative area:** slightly more than two times size of Washington, D.C. **Land use:** 6% arable land; N.A.% permanent crops; 6% meadows and pastures; 6% forest and woodland; 82% other. **Cities:** (1987) Jamestown (capital) 1,413; Ascencion 1,152 (1996).

• **PEOPLE Population:** 7,212 (2000 est.). **Nationality:** noun—St. Helenian(s); adjective—St. Helenian. **Ethnic groups:** African descent, white. **Languages:** English. **Religions:** Anglican majority; also Baptist, Seventh-Day Adventist, Roman Catholic.

• **GOVERNMENT Type:** dependent territory of U.K. **Constitution:** Jan. 1, 1989. **National holiday:** Celebration of the Birthday of the Queen, second Saturday in June. **Head of government:** David Hollanby, governor and commander-in-chief. **Structure:** governor is appointed by the queen; unicameral 16-seat Legislative Council members elected by popular vote to serve 4-year terms; Supreme Court.

• **ECONOMY Monetary unit:** Saint Helenian pound. **Budget:** (FY92/93) *income:* $11.2 mil.; *ex-*

pend.: $11 mil. **GDP:** $13.9 mil.; $2,000 per capita (FY94/95 est.) **Chief crops:** maize, potatoes, vegetables; timber production being developed; crawfishing on Tristan de Cunha. **Natural resources:** fish. **Major industries:** crafts (furniture, lacework, fancy woodwork), fish. **Labor force:** 2,416 (1991 est.); 8.7% professional, technical, and related; 12.8% managerial, administrative, and clerical; 8.1% sales; 5.4% farmers and fishermen; 14.7% production process workers; 50.3% other (1987). **Exports:** $704,000 (f.o.b., 1995); fish (frozen, canned, and salt-dried skipjack, tuna), handicrafts. **Imports:** $14.434 mil. (c.i.f., 1995); food, drink, tobacco, fuel oils, animal feed, building materials. **Major trading partners:** U.K., South Africa.

▶ **TURKS AND CAICOS ISLANDS**

• **GEOGRAPHY Location:** more than 30 islands forming southeastern end of Bahamas Islands in Caribbean Sea. **Boundaries:** Haiti 90 mi (145 km) to S. **Total area:** 166 sq. mi. (430 sq km). **Coastline:** about 186 mi. (about 389 km). **Comparative area:** 2.5 times size of Washington, D.C. **Land use:** 2% arable land; 0% permanent crops; 0% meadows and pastures; 0% forest and woodland; 98% other. **Cities:** Jamestown (capital).

• **PEOPLE Population:** 17,502 (2000 est.). **Nationality:** none. **Ethnic groups:** mostly African descent. **Languages:** English. **Religions:** 41.2% Baptist, 18.9% Methodist, 18.3% Anglican, 1.7% Seventh-Day Adventist.

• **GOVERNMENT Type:** colony of U.K. **Constitution:** introduced on Aug. 30, 1976, suspended in 1986, restored and revised March 5, 1988. **National holiday:** Constitution Day, Aug. 30. **Head of government:** Derek Taylor, chief minister (since Jan. 1995). **Structure:** chief minister appointed by governor; unicameral 19-seat Legislative Council members (13 of which are popularly elected) serve 4-year terms; Supreme Court.

• **ECONOMY Monetary unit:** U.S. dollar. **Budget:** (1997/98 est.) *income:* $47 mil.; *expend.:* $33.6 mil. **GDP:** $117 mil., $7,700 per capita (1997 est.). **Chief crops:** corn, beans, cassava, citrus fruis, fish. **Natural resources:** spiny lobster, conch. **Major industries:** fishing, tourism, offshore financial services. **Labor force:** 4,848 (1990 est.); 33% government, 20% agriculture and fishing; majority engaged in fishing and tourist industries. **Exports:** $4.7 mil. (1993); lobster, dried and fresh conch, conch shells. **Imports:** $46.6 mil. (1993); food and beverages, tobacco, clothing, manufactures, construction materials. **Major trading partners:** U.S., U.K.

▶ **UNINHABITED TERRITORIES OF THE UNITED KINGDOM**

British Indian Ocean Territory (Diego Garcia 6°34'S, 72°24'E); South Georgia Is. (54°15'S, 36°45'W); South Orkney Is. (60°35'S, 45°30'W); South Sandwich Is. (56°00'S, 26°30'W); South Shetland Is. (62°00'S, 58°00'W).

The United Nations

▶STRUCTURE

Establishment Pres. Franklin D. Roosevelt coined the name "United Nations," which was first used in the "Declaration by United Nations" of Jan. 1, 1942, during World War II, when representatives of 26 countries pledged their governments to continue fighting together against the Axis Powers. From August to October 1944, representatives of China, the Soviet Union, the United Kingdom and the United States met at Dumbarton Oaks, a mansion in Washington, D.C., to discuss creating an international peacekeeping organization. Out of these meetings came a general outline for the United Nations.

At the United Nations Conference on International Organization, which met at San Francisco from Apr. 25 to June 26, 1945, representatives from 50 countries drew up the United Nations Charter and signed it on June 26, 1945. Poland, not present at the Conference, signed on October 15, 1945, and is considered one of the founding member states.

The United Nations officially came into existence on Oct. 24, 1945, when the charter was ratified by China, France, the Soviet Union, the United Kingdom, and the United States and by a majority of the other signatories.

U.N. Charter Full text of the Charter may be purchased for $3.00 from the United Nations, Sales Section, New York, NY 10017 U.S. The Preamble to the Charter sets forth the hopes for the United Nations:

WE THE PEOPLES OF THE UNITED NATIONS DETERMINED

- to save succeeding generations from the scourge of war . . .
- to reaffirm faith in fundamental human rights, in the dignity and worth of the human person, in the equal rights of men and women and of nations large and small . . .
- to establish conditions under which justice and respect for the obligations arising from treaties and other sources of international law can be maintained . . .
- to promote social progress and better standards of life in larger freedom.

AND FOR THESE ENDS

- to practice tolerance and live together in peace with one another as good neighbors
- to unite our strength to maintain international peace and security
- to ensure, by the acceptance of principles and the institution of methods, that armed force shall not be used, save in the common interest
- to employ international machinery for the promotion of the economic and social advancement of all peoples.

HAVE RESOLVED TO COMBINE OUR EFFORTS TO ACCOMPLISH THESE AIMS. Accordingly, our respective Governments, through representatives assembled in the city of San Francisco, who have exhibited their full powers found to be in good and due form, have agreed to the present Charter of the United Nations and do hereby establish an international organization to be known as the United Nations.

Purposes The purposes of the United Nations are set forth in Article 1 of the Charter. They are: 1. To maintain international peace and security. 2. To develop friendly relations among nations based on respect for the principle of equal rights and self-determination of peoples. 3. To cooperate in solving international problems of an economic, social, cultural or humanitarian character, and in promoting respect for human rights and fundamental freedoms for all. 4. To be a center for harmonizing the actions of nations in the attainment of these common ends.

Official languages Originally, there were five official languages of the United Nations: Chinese, English, French, Russian and Spanish. Arabic was added to the General Assembly in 1973, to the Security Council in 1982 and to the Economic and Social Council in 1983. Major United Nations documents and all meetings of the General Assembly, the Security Council and the Economic and Social Council are translated into the six working languages.

United Nations headquarters United Nations, New York, NY 10017 U.S. U.N. headquarters covers a 16-acre site in New York City along the East River from 42nd to 48th Streets. It consists of the interconnected General Assembly, Secretariat and Dag Hammarskjöld Library buildings. Acquisition of the site was made possible by a gift of $8.5 million from John D. Rockefeller, Jr., and one-third of that amount from New York City. In 1951, the 39-story Secretariat building was completed and began functioning as the official home of the United Nations.

Permanent observers to the U.N. at New York headquarters cannot vote and do not have diplomatic privileges or immunities unless connected to the member nation's consulate. They do have free access to the public meetings and distribution of relevant documentation.

Non-member observers are the Holy See and Switzerland.

Intergovernmental and other observer organizations: More than 25 organizations have observer status at the U.N. Following is a representative sample: Caribbean Community, Commonwealth of Independent States; Council of Europe; International Federation of Red Cross and Red Crescent Societies; League of Arab States; Organization of African Unity; Organization of American States; Organization of Islamic Conference; Palestine.

PRINCIPAL ORGANS

General Assembly

The Assembly is the world's forum for discussing major issues facing the international community including world peace and security, human rights, global environment, disarmament, health issues including AIDS, and the rights of women and children.

The Assembly consists of all 188 member states, each having one vote. On important issues a two-thirds majority of those present and voting is required; other questions require a simple majority vote. It holds its annual session from September to December, and may call for extra sessions as needed. Its agenda of more than 150 matters for discussion is first dealt with in six main commit-tees: Its agenda of more than 150 matters for discussion is first dealt with in six main committees: First Committee: Disarmament and International Security; Second Committee: Economic and Financial; Third Committee: Social, Humanitarian and Cultural; Fourth Committee: Special Political and De-colonization; Fifth Committee: Administrative and Budgetary; Sixth Committee: Legal. After discussing issues facing the world, it adopts recommendations (called resolutions) but has no power to enforce its decisions (resolutions), except the power of world opinion.

The Assembly considers and approves U.N. budget and assesses member states according to their ability to pay.

Security Council

The Council may investigate any dispute or situation that might lead to international friction, and may recommend methods for adjusting such disputes or terms for their settlement. While other organs of the U.N. make recommendations to governments, the Security Council alone has the power to take decisions that member states are obligated under the Charter to carry out.

The Security Council has 15 members: five permanent members, and the General Assembly elects 10 other members for two-year terms. They are not eligible for immediate re-election. The Council may be called into session at any time, and a representative of each member state must be present at U.N. headquarters at all times.

The five permanent members are China, France, Russia, the United Kingdom, and the United States.

The terms of office of each non-permanent member ends on December 31 of the year indicated in parentheses: Bangladesh (2001), Colombia (2002), Ireland (2002), Jamaica (2001), Mali (2001), Mauritius (2002), Norway (2002), Singapore (2002), Tunisia (2001), Ukraine (2001).

Decisions on matters of procedure require the approval of at least nine of the 15 members. Decisions on all other matters also require nine votes, including the concurring votes of all five permanent members. A negative vote by any permanent member on a non-procedural matter is often referred to as the "veto," which results in the rejection of the proposal. A state that is involved in a dispute may not vote.

Economic and Social Council (ECOSOC)

The Council is the principal organ to co-ordinate the economic and social work of the U.N. and its specialized agencies. It makes recommendations and initiates activities relating to world trade, industrialization, natural resources, human rights, the status of women, population, social welfare, education, health and related matters, science and technology and many other economic and social questions.

ECOSOC has 54 members elected for three-year terms by the General Assembly.

International Court of Justice (World Court)

The Court is the judicial organ of the U.N. and sits in The Hague, Netherlands. All U.N. member states are automatically members of the Court. One country that is not a member of the U.N. is party to the Court–Switzerland. The Court is not open to individuals. It issues judgments on all questions that states refer to it and all matters provided for in the U.N. Charter or in treaties or conventions in force. Both the General Assembly and the Security Council can ask the Court for an advisory opinion on any legal question as can other organs of the U.N. or specialized agencies, when authorized to do so by the Assembly.

The Court has dealt with a wide variety of subjects, including territorial rights, the delimitation of territorial waters and continental shelves, fishing jurisdiction, questions of nationality and the right of individuals to asylum, territorial sovereignty, and the right of passage through foreign territory.

The judgment of the Court is final and without appeal. However, a revision may be applied for within ten years from the date of the judgment on the ground of a new decisive factor. If a party rejects the judgment, the other party may take the issue to the Security Council.

Judges: The ICJ has 15 independent judges, of different nationalities, elected by both the General Assembly and the Security Council. Judges hold 9-year terms and may be re-elected. All questions are decided by a majority of the judges present; the president votes only in case of a tie.

Secretariat

The Secretariat services the other organs of the U.N. and administers the programs and policies they develop. Headed by the Secretary-General, it consists of an international staff of more than 25,000 men and women from over 150 countries.

Secretaries-General: The General Assembly elects the Secretary-General to terms of office of five years (they may be re-elected). The Secretary-General, by tradition, does not come from one of the permanent member States of the Security Council–China, France, Russia, UK or the U.S. Those who have served in this post are: **Trygve Lie**, Norway, Feb. 1, 1946, to Nov. 10, 1952; **Dag Hammarskjöld**, Sweden, Apr. 11, 1953, to Sept. 17, 1961;

U Thant, Burma, Nov. 3, 1961, to Dec. 31, 1971; **Kurt Waldheim**, Austria, Jan. 1, 1972, to Dec. 31, 1981;

Javier Perez de Cuellar, Peru Jan. 1, 1982 to Dec. 31,1991

Boutros Boutros-Ghali, Egypt, Jan 1, 1992, to Dec. 31, 1996;

Kofi Annan, Ghana, Jan. 1, 1997 to present.

▶UNITED NATIONS PROGRAMS

Each U.N. program was created by the General Assembly and reports to it through the Economic and Social Council (ECOSOC). Each member of the U.N. is a member of each Program.

International Research and Training Institute for the Advancement of Women (INSTRAW) Estab.: 1979. (made U.N. program in 1985); **HQ:** Calle Cesar Nicolas Penson, 102-A, Santo Domingo, Dominican Republic. Carries out research, training and information activities worldwide to show and increase women's key role in development.

U.S. Representatives to the UN

The U.S. representative to the UN holds the title of Ambassador Extraordinary and Plenipotentiary Permanent Representative and heads the U.S. Mission to the UN.

Year	Ambassador
1946	Edward R. Stettinius, Jr.
1946–47	Herschel V. Johnson (acting)
1947–53	Warren R. Austin
1953–60	Henry Cabot Lodge, Jr.
1960–61	James J. Wadsworth
1961–65	Adlai E. Stevenson
1965–68	Arthur J. Goldberg
1968	George W. Ball
1968–69	James Russell Wiggins
1969–71	Charles W. Yost
1971–73	George Bush
1973–75	John A. Scali
1975–76	Daniel P. Moynihan
1976–77	William W. Scranton
1977–79	Andrew Young
1979–81	Donald McHenry
1981–85	Jeane J. Kirkpatrick
1985–89	Vernon A. Walters
1989–92	Thomas J. Pickering
1992–93	Edward J. Perkins
1993–96	Madeleine K. Albright
1997–98	Bill Richardson
1999–2001	Richard C. Holbrooke
2001–	John D. Negroponte

United Nations Centre for Human Settlements (Habitat) Estab.: 1978; **HQ:** P.O. Box 30030, Nairobi, Kenya. Works to provide models and tools so people can improve their housing. Major concerns are planning, financing, and management of human settlements– especially in developing countries.

United Nations Children's Fund (UNICEF) Estab.: 1946; **HQ:** UNICEF House, Three United Nations Plaza, New York, NY 10017, U.S. Provides care for children in developing countries by providing low-cost community-based services in maternal and child health, immunization, breastfeeding, growth monitoring, nutrition, clean water and sanitation, and education.

United Nations Conference on Trade and Development (UNCTAD) Estab.: 1964; **HQ:** Place des Nations, 1211 Geneva 10, Switzerland. Works to bring developing countries into global trade by formulating international trade policies, mediating multilateral trade agreements and providing assistance to governments.

United Nations Development Programme (UNDP) Estab.: 1965; **HQ:** One United Nations Plaza, New York, NY 10017, U.S. Coordinates development activities within the U.N. Operates over 5,000 projects in 150 countries and territories to facilitate development in economic and social sectors, including: farming, fishing, forestry, mining, manufacturing, power, transport, communications, housing, trade, health and environmental sanitation, economic planning and public administration.

United Nations Environment Programme (UNEP) Estab.: 1972; **HQ:** P.O. Box 30552, Nairobi, Kenya. Coordinates international environment issues, including international environment conventions, monitors significant changes in environment and coordinates sound environmental practices.

United Nations Fund for Population Activities (UNFPA) Estab.: 1969; **HQ:** 220 E. 42nd Street, New York, NY 10017, U.S. Provides assistance to population programs in developing countries; promotes understanding of key population factors: population growth, fertility, mortality, spatial distribution and migration.

Office of the United Nations High Commissioner for Refugees (UNHCR) Estab.: 1950; **HQ:** Palais des Nations, CH1211 Geneva 10, Switzerland. Provides food, clothing and shelter for refugees and works with governments to establish safe conditions whereby refugees may return home and, when that is not possible, seeks to ensure that refugees receive asylum.

United Nations Institute for Training and Research (UNITAR) Estab: 1965; **HQ:** Palais des Nations, CH1211 Geneva 10, Switzerland. Provides training for members of U.N.'s permanent missions, including courses on international economics, workshops on drafting and negotiating international legal instruments, dispute settlement, and training on peace, security, human rights and humanitarian assistance.

United Nations University (UNU) Estab.: 1973; **HQ:** 53-70 Jingumae 5-chome, Shibuya-ku, Tokyo 150, Japan. UNU has no students of its own, no campus and no faculty. It is an international community of scholars engaged in research operating through worldwide networks of academic research institutions.

World Food Council (WFC) Estab.: 1974; **HQ:** Via delle Terme di Caracalla, 00100 Rome, Italy. Encourages developing countries to adopt a national food strategy whereby they assess their food situation needs, supply, potential for increasing production, storage, processing, transportation and distribution.

World Food Programme (WFP) (Joint program operated by U.N. and Food and Agriculture Organization (FAO) **Estab.:** 1963; **HQ:** Via Cristoforo Colombo, 426, 00145 Rome, Italy. Provides food to support development activities and in times of emergencies. Operates projects in forestry, soil erosion control, irrigation, land rehabilitation and rural settlements.

▶SPECIALIZED AGENCIES OF THE U.N.

The specialized agencies associated with the United Nations are self-governing, independent organizations that work with the U.N. system and each other through the coordination machinery of the Economic and Social Council (ECOSOC). Each country affiliates with each agency on an individual basis. Membership in an agency is separate from U.N. membership. Nongovernmental organizations (NGOs) having expertise in the area may affiliate with each agency on a separate basis.

Food and Agriculture Organization of the United Nations (FAO) Member States: 174; **Estab.:** Oct. 16, 1945; **HQ:** Via delle Terme di Caracalla, 00100 Rome, Italy. Works to increase output of farmlands, forests and fisheries and to raise nutritional levels. Co-sponsors World Food Programme, which uses food, cash and services donated by member states for emergency situations.

International Atomic Energy Agency (IAEA) Member States: 127; **Estab.**: July 29, 1957; **HQ:** Vienna International Centre, P.O. Box 100, A-1400 Vienna, Austria. (Not regular specialized agency in that it does not report through ECOSOC but directly to General Assembly.) Fosters and guides development of peaceful uses of atomic energy, establishes standards for nuclear safety and environmental protection, aids member countries through technical cooperation, and fosters exchange of information on nuclear energy.

International Civil Aviation Organization (ICAO) Member States: 183; **Estab.**: Apr. 4, 1947; **HQ:** 1000 Sherbrooke Street West, Suite 400, Montreal, Quebec H3A 2R2, Canada. Works for safer air travel conditions worldwide. Establishes visual and instrument flight rules for pilots and crews; develops aeronautical charts for navigation; coordinates aircraft radio frequencies and works with customs procedures.

International Fund for Agricultural Development (IFAD) Member States: 160; **Estab.**: Nov. 30, 1977; **HQ:** Via del Serafico 10, 00142 Rome, Italy. Lends money to peoples in developing countries for agricultural development projects, including livestock, fisheries, processing and storage, irrigation, research and training.

International Labor Organization (ILO) Member States: 173; **Estab.**: 1919, under the Treaty of Versailles; (became U.N. specialized agency Dec. 14, 1946);. **HQ:** 4, route des Morillons, CH-1211 Geneva 22, Switzerland. Promotes social justice for working people everywhere by formulating international policies and programs to help improve working and living conditions; creates international labor standards as guidelines for governments and assists in vocational training, management techniques, occupational safety and health.

International Maritime Organization (IMO) Member States: 152; **Estab.**: Mar. 17, 1958; **HQ:** 4 Albert Embankment, London SE1 SR, England. Works to improve international shipping procedures and encourages highest standards in maritime safety; seeks to prevent and control marine pollution from ships and sets standards for training and certification of seafarers.

International Telecommunication Union (ITU) Member States: 184; **Estab.**: 1865, it became a U.N. specialized agency in Jan. 1949; **HQ:** Place des Nations, 1211 Geneva 20, Switzerland. Coordinates use of radio frequencies, tracks positions assigned by countries to geostationary satellites; coordinates modem and Internet standards.

United Nations Educational, Scientific and Cultural Organization (UNESCO) Member States: 186; **Estab.**: Nov. 4, 1946; **HQ:** 7, Place de Fontenoy, 75007 Paris, France. Promotes literacy through teacher training, building schools, and developing textbooks. Natural science programs include Man and the Biosphere and Intergovernmental Oceanographic Commission. Undertakes study and development of cultures, and conservation of world's inheritance of books, art and monuments.

United Nations Industrial Development Organization (UNIDO) Member States: 166; **Estab.**: 1966 (became U.N. specialized agency Jan. 1, 1986); **HQ:** Wagramerstrasse 5, Vienna XXII, Austria. Promotes and accelerates industrialization of developing countries by providing technical assistance, training programs and advisory services.

Universal Postal Union (UPU) Member States: 189; **Estab.**: July 1, 1875 (became U.N. specialized agency July 1, 1948); **HQ:** Weltpoststrasse 4, Berne, Switzerland. Establishes regulations for smooth exchange of mail worldwide.

World Bank Group Group of five closely related institutions. **HQ:** 1818 H Street, N.W., Washington, D.C. 20433 *International Bank for Reconstruction and Development (IBRD)* **Member States**: 178; **Estab.**: Dec. 27, 1945, to provide loans and technical assistance to developing countries to assist in their reconstruction and development. *International Finance Corporation (IFC)* **Member States**: 165 (Membership is open only to World Bank members.); **Estab.**: July 20, 1956, to stimulate flow of private capital into productive investment in member countries. While closely associated with Bank, IFC is separate legal entity and its funds are distinct from those of Bank. *International Development Association (IDA)* **Member States**: 158; **Estab.**: Sept. 24, 1960. (Affiliate of the Bank, IDA has same directors and staff as Bank.) Lends money to poor countries with interest-free credits. Financial resources are from contributions by donor governments. *International Monetary Fund (IMF)* **Member States**: 181; **Estab.**: Dec. 27, 1945; **HQ:** 700 19th Street, N.W., Washington, D.C. 20431. Makes financing available to members in balance-of-payments difficulties and provides technical assistance to improve their economic management. *Multilateral Investment Guarantee Agency (MIGA)* **Member States**: 128; **Estab.**: 1988. Augments capacity of other insurers through coinsurance or reinsurance, thereby insuring investment in countries restricted or excluded by policies of other insurers.

World Health Organization (WHO) Member States: 190; **Estab.**: April 7, 1948; **HQ:** 20, avenue Appia, 1211 Geneva 27, Switzerland. Coordinates programs aimed at solving health problems by working with governments, other U.N. agencies and non-governmental organizations. See "World Health" section.

World Intellectual Property Organization (WIPO) Member States: 161; **Estab.**: 1883, (became U.N. specialized agency Dec. 17, 1974); **HQ:** 34, chemin des Colombettes, 121 Geneva 20, Switzerland. Promotes protection of intellectual property and cooperation in enforcement of agreements on matters such as copyrights, trademarks, industrial designs and patents.

World Meteorological Organization (WMO) Member States: 179; **Estab.**: 1873. (became U.N. specialized agency Mar. 23, 1950); **HQ:** 41, avenue Giuseppe-Motta, 1211 Geneva 20, Switzerland. Facilitates exchange of weather reports among countries; "World Weather Watch" tracks global weather conditions.

▶PEACEKEEPING OPERATIONS

United Nations peacekeeping is the use of multinational forces, under U.N. command, to keep disputing countries or communities from fighting while efforts are made to help them negotiate a solution. It is undertaken only with the agreement of both hostile parties. United Nations Peacekeeping Forces received the Nobel Peace Prize in 1988. As of June 2001, the U.N. had 15 peacekeeping operations, comprising 43,871 military personnel and civilian police from 89 countries. The total number of fatalities in peacekeeping operations from 1948 to June 2001 is 1,674. There were 26 fatalities from January to August, 2001. The majority of soldiers come from developing nations with large armies (India, Nigeria and Jordan, for example). Fewer than 1,000 U.S. soldiers serve under the U.N.

United Nations Truce Supervision Organization (UNTSO) Estab.: 1948. Mandate has evolved. Currently U.N. observers (166) assist peacekeeping operations in Middle East.

United Nations Military Observer Group in India and Pakistan (UNMOGIP) Estab.: 1948. U.N. observers (44) are stationed on both sides of Line of Control agreed upon by India and Pakistan under Simla agreement of July 1972 to observe cease-fire.

United Nations Peacekeeping Force in Cyprus (UNFICYP) Estab.: 1964. U.N. uniformed personnel (1,215) control 112-mile (180-km) buffer zone between cease-fire lines agreed on by Cyprus National Guard and Turkish forces.

United Nations Disengagement Observer Force (UNDOF) Estab.: 1974. U.N. troops and observers (1,133) maintain an "area of separation" on Golan Heights between Israel and Syria and verify arms limitation on both sides.

United Nations Interim Force in Lebanon (UNIFIL) Estab.: 1978. U.N. troops (4,488) are in Southern Lebanon to confirm withdrawal of Israeli forces, restore international peace and security, and assist Lebanese government in ensuring return of its authority in area.

United Nations Iraq-Kuwait Observation Mission (UNIKOM) Estab.: 1991. U.N. troops (1,099) monitor demilitarized zone set up by Security Council along Khor Abdullah waterway. First-time observers from five permanent members of Security Council serve together.

UN Mission for the Referendum in Western Sahara (MINURSO) Estab.: Sept. 1991. Military observers (200) monitor and verify crease-fire, pending agreement between parties on criteria for eligibility to vote in referendum.

U.N. Mission in Bosnia and Herzegovina (UN-MIBH) Estab.: Dec. 1995. Civil police (1,902) monitor, observe, impart law enforcement activities, maintain peace. Work with NATO-led multinational Force (IFOR) to ensure compliance with Dayton Peace Agreement.

U.N. Mission of Observers in Prevlaka (UNMOP) Estab.: Jan. 1996. Military observers (27) monitor demilitarization of Prevlaka peninsula in Croatia.

United Nations Interim Administration Mission in Kosovo (UNMIK) Estab.: June 1999. First U.N. peacekeeping mission to involve other multilateral organizations as full partners under U.N. leadership.

United Nations Organization Mission in the Democratic Republic of the Congo (MONUC) Estab.: Nov. 1999. Some 5,537 military personnel and up to 500 observers including civilians to monitor the implementation of the Cease-fire Agreement.

United Nations Mission in Sierra Leone (UNAMSIL) Estab.: Oct. 1999. Consists of 12,474 total uniformed personnel and 500 international and local civilian staff to cooperate with the Government and the other parties in implementing the Lome Peace Agreement and to assist in the implementation of the disarmament, demobilization and reintegration plan.

United Nations Transitional Administration in East Timor (UNTAET) Estab.: Aug. 1999 Comprises 9,390 uniformed personnel observers; supported by 716 international civilian personnel and 1,879 local civilian staff to administer the territory and exercise legislative and executive authority during the transition period towards independence that the people of East Timor voted for in a free election.

UN Mission in Ethiopia and Eritrea (UNMEE) Estab.: July 2001. July 2000. Mission is to maintain liaison with the parties and establish mechanism for verifying ceasefire. Up to 4,200 troops.

UN Observer Mission in Georgia (UNOMIG) Estab.: July 2001. Mission consists of 101 military observers, 87 international civil personnel and 188 local civilian staff to verify compliance with ceasefire agreement between Georgia and Abkhaz authorities in Georgia.

▶FURTHER U.N. INFORMATION

United Nations Bookstore Room GA-32, New York, NY, 10017; 212-963-7680; 1-800-553-3210; Fax: 212-963-4910. International publications issued by U.N. bodies and independent publishers.

▶U.N. INFORMATION ON-LINE

Official Web site for U.N. System: http://www.unsystem.org
U.N. Headquarters: http://www.un.org

▶KEY EVENTS IN U.N. HISTORY

1946 (Jan. 10)   First session of General Assembly begins at London with delegates of 51 member states.

1947 (Nov. 29)   General Assembly passes Plan of Partition with Economic Union concerning future government of Palestine, thereby paving way for government of Tel Aviv to declare State of Israel on May 14, 1948.

1948 (Dec. 10)   Universal Declaration of Human Rights adopted by General Assembly.
U.N. pioneers concept of peacekeeping observer missions and peacekeeping forces (1956).

1949   Mediates cease-fire between India and Pakistan, ending two years of fighting over Kashmir.

1950   Security Council calls members states to help South Korea repel invasion by North Korea.
Economic and Social Council adopts Standard International Trade Classification as basis for gathering world trade statistics.

1953   U.N. coordinates first global-census effort to establish earth's population for first time in history–2.4 billion people.

1955   First of ongoing congresses of criminologists and police officials draws up international principles and standards of criminal justice.

1959   U.N. General Assembly adopts Declaration on the Rights of the Child.

1960   Under de-colonization program, 17 territories become newly independent states; 16 in Africa join U.N.

1962 Secretary-General plays key role in resolving U.S.-Soviet confrontation over issue of nuclear missiles in Cuba.
1963 Security Council calls for arms embargo against South Africa. (Made mandatory in 1972.)
1967 After war erupts in Middle East, Security Council adopts Resolution 242, calling for withdrawal of forces from occupied territories, and recognizes right of all states in area to security.

Mediates settlement of Six-Day Arab-Israeli War.
1970 General Assembly adopts first international agreed-upon set of principles on seabed and ocean floor beyond national jurisdiction. Declares area "common heritage" of humanity.
1972 Security Council orders cease-fire in 17-day-old Middle East War and sends peacekeeping force to prevent further fighting between Israel and Arab states.
1975 U.N. conference at Mexico City launches Decade for Women to begin major effort toward women's equality worldwide.
1979 World Health Organization announces smallpox eradicated from all peoples on earth.
1987 First International Conference on Drug Abuse and Illicit Trafficking develops program on international coordination of illicit-drug issues.
1988 Mediates ending of Iran-Iraq War. Mediates Soviet withdrawal from Afghanistan.
1989 Mediates withdrawal of Cuban troops from Angola and South African troops from Namibia. U.N. sends peacekeeping troops and advisers to Namibia to supervise elections aimed at setting up self-government.
1990 Upon invitation, U.N. monitors demobilization of Nicaraguan rebel forces, and for first time monitors a presidential campaign and election in an independent nation.

Security Council Resolution 678 calls upon member states to restore peace and security in Kuwait by "all necessary means."

Responding to request by Haiti, U.N. supervises election of Haiti's first freely elected president.
1991 (Apr. 3) Security Council Resolution 687 sets terms of cease-fire in Gulf War and gives U.N. variety of duties to ensure peace.

Secretary-General negotiates cease-fire in 16-year-old civil war in Angola.

(Dec. 4) Secretary-General negotiates release of last six hostages held in Lebanon.

General Assembly rescinds Resolution 3379 of Nov. 10, 1975, equating Zionism with racism.
1992 Secretary-General completes peace negotiations between government of El Salvador and rebel Farabundo Marti National Liberation Front.
1993 145 nations co–sponsor Convention on Prohibition of the Development, Production, Stockpiling and Use of Chemical Weapons.

(Feb. 23) Human Rights Commission adopts Resolution 1993/8, which states that "abhorrent practice of rape and abuse of women and children in the former Yugoslavia. . . . constitutes a war crime. This is first formal statement that declares rape, conducted during war, an international war crime under Geneva Convention.

(Dec. 13) General Assembly creates post of High Commissioner for Human Rights with power to intervene wherever basic freedom are suppressed.

1994 Security Council removes South Africa from its agenda, declaring end of apartheid.

Security Council establishes International Tribunal for Rwanda to prosecute persons responsible for genocide and other violations of international humanitarian law.
1995 Secretary-General launches 50th anniversary commemoration. International Tribunal for Former Yugoslavia, established in 1993 to prosecute persons responsible for serious violations of international humanitarian law in former Yugoslavia since 1991, schedules first trials for September with 15 judges from 15 countries.

(June) Upon request of government of Haiti, U.N. supervises free elections in the country.
1996 (Feb.-Mar.) Upon request of the government, U.N. supervises free and fair elections in Sierra Leone that changes rule from military regime to democracy.

(May) Hague-based International Criminal Tribunal for the former Yugoslavia begins trial for first war crimes in 50 years. Dusan Tadic, Bosnian Serb charged with torturing and murdering Bosnian Muslims and Croats at Omarska prison camp in Prijedor, Bosnia, in 1992. He is convicted in 1997 and sentenced to 20 years in prison.
1997 U.N. launches CyberSchoolBus to reach tens of thousands of students worldwide; provides lesson plans, global trends, quizzes; on-line Model U.N. discussion is first of its kind to reach 60,000 high schools and college students.

Thirteen nations ask for and receive U.N. assistance in holding their elections, including Algeria, Cambodia, Gambia, Guyana, Haiti, Honduras, Liberia, Mali, and Yemen.
1998 (July) U.N. establishes Permanent International Criminal Court to try individuals for genocide, war crimes, and crimes against humanity.

(July) U.N. conference in Rome adopts statute to create Permanent International Criminal Court to try individuals for genocide, war crimes and crimes against humanity.
1999 (Mar.) Secretary-General issues Global Compact—enlisting businesses to advance universally agreed principles on human rights, labor, and environment.

(June) Security Council invests U.N. peacekeeping mission authority over Kosovo territory and people, including all legislative, executive, and judicial administration. First ever cooperation with non-U.N. organizations, including the EU and the Organization for Security in Europe.

(July) Economic and Social Council holds first live broadcast of its high-level meeting over the Internet allowing global viewing.
2000 Millennium Summit, the largest single gathering of Heads of State and/or Government, brings 180 presidents, prime ministers, and monarchs to the UN. They issue the Millennium Declaration which intends to solve humanity's most pressing problems, send every child to school, and deliver millions from poverty by 2015.
2001 World Health Organization reports that in 2000 there were less than 3,500 polio cases worldwide.

"This organization is created to prevent you from going to hell. It isn't created to take you to heaven." **—Henry Cabot Lodge, Jr.**

United Nations Member States (189)

Country	Joined U.N.	Country	Joined U.N.	Country	Joined U.N.
Afghanistan	1946	Ghana	1957	Pakistan	1947
Albania	1955	Greece	1945	Palau	1994
Algeria	1962	Grenada	1974	Panama	1945
Andorra	1993	Guatemala	1945	Papua New Guinea	1975
Angola	1976	Guinea	1958	Paraguay	1945
Antigua and Barbuda	1981	Guinea-Bissau	1974	Peru	1945
Argentina	1945	Guyana	1966	Philippines	1945
Armenia	1992	Haiti	1945	Poland	1945
Australia	1945	Honduras	1945	Portugal	1955
Austria	1955	Hungary	1955	Qatar	1971
Azerbaijan	1992	Iceland	1946	Moldova	1992
Bahamas	1973	India	1945	Romania	1955
Bahrain	1971	Indonesia	1950	Russian Federation	1945
Bangladesh	1974	Iran	1945	Rwanda	1962
Barbados	1966	Iraq	1945	Saint Kitts and Nevis	1983
Belarus	1945	Ireland	1955	Saint Lucia	1979
Belgium	1945	Israel	1949	Saint Vincent and the	1980
Belize	1981	Italy	1955	Grenadines	
Benin	1960	Ivory Coast	1960	Samoa	1976
Bhutan	1971	Jamaica	1962	San Marino	1992
Bolivia	1945	Japan	1956	São Tome and Principe	1975
Bosnia and Herzegovina	1992	Jordan	1955	Saudi Arabia	1945
Botswana	1966	Kazakhstan	1992	Senegal	1960
Brazil	1945	Kenya	1963	Seychelles	1976
Brunei Darussalam	1984	Kiribati	1999	Sierra Leone	1961
Bulgaria	1955	Kuwait	1963	Singapore	1965
Burkina Faso	1960	Kyrgyzstan	1992	Slovakia[2]	1993
Burundi	1962	Laos	1955	Slovenia	1992
Cambodia	1955	Latvia	1991	Solomon Islands	1978
Cameroon	1960	Lebanon	1945	Somalia	1960
Canada	1945	Lesotho	1966	South Africa	1945
Cape Verde	1975	Liberia	1945	South Korea	1991
Central African Republic	1960	Libya	1955	Spain	1955
Chad	1960	Liechtenstein	1990	Sri Lanka	1955
Chile	1945	Lithuania	1991	Sudan	1956
China	1945	Luxembourg	1945	Suriname	1975
Colombia	1945	Macedonia[3]	1993	Swaziland	1968
Comoros	1975	Madagascar	1960	Sweden	1946
Congo	1960	Malawi	1964	Syria	1945
Congo, Democratic Republic of[1]	1960	Malaysia	1957	Tanzania	1961
		Maldives	1965	Tajikistan	1992
Costa Rica	1945	Mali	1960	Thailand	1946
Croatia	1992	Malta	1964	Togo	1960
Cuba	1945	Marshall Islands	1991	Tonga	1999
Cyprus	1960	Mauritania	1961	Trinidad and Tobago	1962
Czech Republic[2]	1993	Mauritius	1968	Tunisia	1956
Denmark	1945	Mexico	1945	Turkey	1945
Djibouti	1977	Micronesia	1991	Turkmenistan	1992
Dominica	1978	Monaco	1993	Tuvalu	2000
Dominican Republic	1945	Mongolia	1961	Uganda	1962
Ecuador	1945	Morocco	1956	Ukraine	1945
Egypt	1945	Mozambique	1975	United Arab Emirates	1971
El Salvador	1945	Myanmar	1948	United Kingdom	1945
Equatorial Guinea	1968	Namibia	1990	United States	1945
Eritrea	1993	Nauru	1999	Uruguay	1945
Estonia	1991	Nepal	1955	Uzbekistan	1992
Ethiopia	1945	Netherlands	1945	Vanuatu	1981
Fiji	1970	New Zealand	1945	Venezuela	1945
Finland	1955	Nicaragua	1945	Viet Nam	1977
France	1945	Niger	1960	Yemen[4]	1947
Gabon	1960	Nigeria	1960	Yugoslavia	1945
Gambia	1965	North Korea	1991	Zambia	1964
Georgia	1992	Norway	1945	Zimbabwe	1980
Germany	1973	Oman	1971		

Source: United Nations. 1. Formerly Zaire. 2. Czechoslovakia was an original member of the UN; when the nation split into separate Czech and Slovak Republics, both new republics were admitted as member states on Jan. 19, 1993. 3. Provisionally referred to for all purposes within the UN as "The former Yugoslav Republic of Macedonia" pending settlement of a difference with Greek Macedonia over the name. 4. Includes the former Democratic Yemen (admitted as a separate member in 1967), which merged with Yemen in 1990.

Major Political International Organizations

Commonwealth HQ: Marlborough House, Pall Mall, London, SW1Y 5HX, UK. **Estab.:** By some members of British Empire through evolutionary process formalized by Statute of Westminster on Dec. 31, 1931. As voluntary association of independent states, Commonwealth has no written constitution and no rigid contractual obligations. Emphasis is on consultation and exchange of views for cooperation, especially in economic affairs, drug trafficking, international terrorism and technical assistance to less developed states. Some countries that were part of British Empire are not part of Commonwealth. **Members** (54): Antigua and Barbuda, Australia, Bahamas, Bangladesh, Barbados, Belize, Botswana, Brunei, Cameroon, Canada, Cyprus, Dominica, Fiji, Gambia, Ghana, Grenada, Guyana, India, Jamaica, Kenya, Kiribati, Lesotho, Malawi, Malaysia, Maldives, Malta, Mauritius, Mozambique, Namibia, Nauru, New Zealand, Nigeria, Papua New Guinea, Saint Kitts and Nevis, Saint Lucia, Saint Vincent and the Grenadines, Samoa, Seychelles, Sierra Leone, Singapore, Solomon Islands, South Africa, Sri Lanka, Swaziland, Tanzania, Tong, Trinidad and Tobago, Tuvalu, Uganda, United Kingdom, Vanuatu, Western Samoa, Zambia, Zimbabwe.
Commonwealth of Independent States (CIS) HQ: Uliza Kirowa 17, Minsk 220000. **Estab.:** Dec. 8, 1991, by Byelorussia (Belarus), Russia, and Ukraine, which dissolved USSR and created CIS. Members agree to broad cooperation, including to cooperate in political, economic, ecological, humanitarian, and cultural fields. **Members** (12): Armenia, Azerbaijan, Belarus, Georgia, Kazakhstan, Kyrgyzstan, Moldova, Russia, Tajikistan, Turkmenistan, Ukraine, Uzbekistan.
European Union (EU, the Common Market), See Part III: "The Global Economy."
League of Arab States (LAS, the Arab League) HQ: Tahrir Square, Cairo, Egypt. **Estab.:** By treaty signed on Mar. 22, 1945 at Cairo, Egypt, to strengthen relations among members in financial, communications, cultural, health, social, nationality and social areas. **Members** (22): Algeria, Bahrain, Comoros, Djibouti, Egypt, Iraq, Jordan, Kuwait, Lebanon, Libya, Mauritania, Morocco, Oman, Palestine Liberation Organization, Qatar, Saudi Arabia, Somalia, Sudan, Syria, Tunisia, United Arab Emirates, Yemen.
North Atlantic Treaty Organization (NATO) HQ: B-1110 Brussels, Belgium. **Estab.:** By North Atlantic Treaty on Aug. 24, 1949, to maintain security among member states. NATO attempted to maintain military balance with countries of the Warsaw Pact: Bulgaria, Czechoslovakia, East Germany, Hungary, Poland, Romania, USSR. Since 1989 security challenges have shifted to possible adverse consequences from serious economic, social, and political difficulties, including ethnic rivalries and territorial disputes, arms proliferation, and terrorism. In 1997, leaders of NATO voted to admit Czech Republic, Hungary and Poland, and their official membership received final approval in 1999. **Members** (19): Belgium, Canada, Czech Republic, Denmark, France, Germany, Greece, Hungary, Iceland, Italy, Luxembourg, Netherlands, Norway, Poland, Portugal, Spain, Turkey, United Kingdom, U.S.

Organization of African Unity (OAU) HQ: African Unity Hall, POB 3243, Addis Ababa, Ethiopia. **Estab.:** By charter on May 25, 1963 at Addis Ababa, to promote unity and solidarity among African states. OAU works to eradicate all forms of colonialism from Africa and to defend their sovereignty and independence. **Members** (53): Algeria, Angola, Benin, Botswana, Burkina Faso, Burundi, Cameroon, Cape Verde, Central African Republic, Chad, Comoros, Congo, Democratic Republic of Congo, Djibouti, Egypt, Equatorial Guinea, Eritrea, Ethiopia, Gabon, Gambia, Ghana, Guinea, Guinea-Bissau, Ivory Coast, Kenya, Lesotho, Liberia, Libya, Madagascar, Malawi, Mali, Mauritania, Mauritius, Mozambique, Namibia, Niger, Nigeria, Rwanda, São Tomé and Principé, Senegal, Seychelles, Sierra Leone, Somalia, South Africa, Sudan, Swaziland, Tanzania, Togo, Tunisia, Uganda, Western Sahara, Zambia, Zimbabwe.
Organization of American States (OAS) HQ: 1889 F St., NW, Washington, DC 20006-4499, U.S. **Estab.:** By charter signed at Bogotá, Columbia, effective Dec. 13, 1951, to strengthen peace and security on continent, promote cooperation in human rights, education, economic and social development and scientific exchanges, and to seek solutions to political, juridical and economic problems. **Members** (35): Antigua and Barbuda, Argentina, Bahamas, Barbados, Belize, Bolivia, Brazil, Canada, Chile, Colombia, Costa Rica, Cuba (suspended from OAS activities but not membership in 1962), Dominica, Dominican Republic, Ecuador, El Salvador, Grenada, Guatemala, Guyana, Haiti, Honduras, Jamaica, Mexico, Nicaragua, Panama, Paraguay, Peru, Saint Kitts and Nevis, Saint Lucia, Saint Vincent and the Grenadines, Suriname, Trinidad and Tobago, U.S., Uruguay, Venezuela.
Organization of the Petroleum Exporting Countries (OPEC) HQ: Obere Donaustrasse 93, A-1020 Vienna, Austria. **Estab.:** Nov. 14, 1960 by resolution adopted at Baghdad Conference, to coordinate and unify petroleum policies and to stabilize international oil prices to prevent harmful fluctuations. **Members** (11): Algeria, Indonesia, Iran, Iraq, Kuwait, Libya, Nigeria, Qatar, Saudi Arabia, United Arab Emirates, Venezuela.
Organization for Security and Cooperation in Europe (OSCE) HQ: Kärtnerring 5-7, A-1010 Vienna, Austria. **Estab.:** by Final Act of Conference on Security and Cooperation in Europe in 1975. In 1990, CSCE members declared end of "era of confrontation and division of Europe" and beginning of "a new era of democracy, peace and unity." Serves as forum for dialogue, negotiation, cooperation, and direction in shaping new Europe. **Members** (55): Albania, Andorra, Armenia, Austria, Azerbaijan, Belarus, Belgium, Bosnia and Herzegovina, Bulgaria, Canada, Croatia, Cyprus, Czech Republic, Denmark, Estonia, Finland, France, Georgia, Germany, Greece, Holy See, Hungary, Iceland, Ireland, Italy, Kazakhstan, Kyrgyzstan, Latvia, Liechtenstein, Lithuania, Luxembourg, Macedonia, Malta, Moldova, Monaco, Netherlands, Norway, Poland, Portugal, Romania, Russia, San Marino, Slovakia, Slovenia, Spain, Sweden, Switzerland, Tajikistan, Turkmenistan, Ukraine, UK, U.S., Uzbekistan, Yugoslavia (suspended).

ASTRONOMY

Astronomy is the oldest science, but it continues to be at the forefront of scientific thought. The ancients of the Northern Hemisphere knew the skies, probably better than most of us do. They recognized that most stars appear to rise in the east at night and travel in circular paths across the sky, and that a few are wanderers—planets—that move among the other stars. They named the groups of stars that we call constellations and recognized that constellations visible in winter are

different from those visible in summer (although some are visible all year). They learned how to find the extremities of the sunrise and built giant stone structures, such as Stonehenge, probably to locate certain of the positions of the Sun or other stars.

In 1609 Galileo introduced the first artificial device for exploring the universe—the astronomical telescope. Even in that first year, he saw wonders the ancients never knew. Since then, we have built larger and better telescopes, devices for detecting radio waves, microwaves, X rays, infrared waves, and gamma rays from space, and have even traveled to our own Moon. We have sent space probes to eight of the nine planets of the solar system and to comets and asteroids.

Major Events in Astronomy and Space

B.C.
585 Thales of Miletus (Greek: c. 625–c. 547) predicts solar eclipse in Asia Minor.
c. 480 Astronomer Oenopides of Chios (Greek: 5th cent.) discovers that Earth is tilted with respect to Sun.
352 Chinese report "guest star," or supernova, the earliest known sighting.
c. 340 Astronomer Kidinnu (Kidenas; Babylon: c. 379) discovers precession of equinoxes, the apparent change in position of stars caused by Earth's wobbling on its orbit.
c. 300 Chinese astronomers compile star maps.
c. 240 Chinese astronomers observe Halley's comet.
Eratosthenes of Cyrene (Greek: c.276–c.194) correctly calculates Earth's size.
165 Chinese astronomers notice sunspots.
c. 130 Astronomer Hipparchus of Nicea (Greek: 147–127) correctly determines distance to Moon and rediscovers precession of equinoxes (see 340 B.C.).

A.D.
c. 140 *Almagest* of Ptolemy (Greek: c. 90–168) develops astronomy of solar system in form based on Sun and planets revolving about Earth.
1543 *De Revolutionibus* by Nicholas Copernicus (Polish: 1473–1543) presents convincing arguments that Earth and other planets orbit Sun.
1577 Tycho Brahe (Danish: 1546–1601) proves that comets are visitors from space, not weather phenomena as previously believed.
1592 David Fabricius (German: 1564–1617) discovers star, later named Mira, that gradually disappears; in studying it in 1638, Phocyclides Holawarda recognizes that it appears and reappears on regular basis—the first-known variable star.
1609 Johannes Kepler (German: 1571–1630) discovers that the planets move in elliptical orbits.
1610 Galileo observes Jupiter's moons, phases of Venus, and (although he does not recognize what they are) rings of Saturn.
1611 Several astronomers simultaneously discover sunspots for first time in West.
1671 Giovanni Domenico Cassini (Italian-French: 1625-1712) correctly determines distances of the planets from Sun.

1682 Edmond Halley (English: 1656–1742) describes comet now known by his name and in 1705 correctly predicts its return in 1758.
1718 Halley discovers that stars move with respect to each other.
1755 Immanuel Kant (German: 1724–1804) proposes that many nebulas are actually composed of millions of stars and that solar system formed when giant cloud of dust condensed.
1781 William Herschel (German-English: 1738–1822) discovers planet Uranus.
1785 Herschel demonstrates that Milky Way is disk- or lens-shaped group of many stars, one of which is the Sun.
1801 Guiseppe Piazzi (Italian: 1746–1826) discovers first-known asteroid, Ceres.
1838 Friedrich W. Bessel (German: 1784–1846) determines distance to star other than the Sun.
1846 Johann G. Galle (German: 1812–1910) discovers planet Neptune using predictions of Urbain J.J. Leverrier (French: 1811–77) and John Couch Adams (English: 1819–92).
1924 Edwin Hubble (American: 1889–1953) shows that galaxies are "island universes"—giant aggregations of stars as large as Milky Way.
1929 Hubble finds that universe is expanding.
1930 Clyde Tombaugh (American: 1906–97) discovers planet Pluto.
1931 Karl Jansky (American: 1905–50) discovers that radio waves are coming from space, leading to founding of radio astronomy.
1948 George Gamow (Russian-American: 1904–68), Ralph Alpher (American: 1921–), and Robert Herman (American: 1914–97) develop Big Bang theory of origin of universe.
Jan Hendrik Oort (Dutch: 1900–1992) proposes that comets come from a vast cloud of material orbiting far beyond Pluto; the material is now known as the Oort Cloud.
1957 USSR launches *Sputnik 1*, the first manmade satellite.
1961 Soviet cosmonaut Yuri A. Gagarin (Russian: 1934-68) is first human to orbit Earth.
1962 U.S. space probe *Mariner 2* is first to reach neighborhood of another planet, Venus.
1963 Maarten Schmidt (Dutch-American: 1929–) is first astronomer to recognize a quasar.

1964 Arno Penzias (German-American: 1933–) and Robert Wilson (American: 1936–) find radio waves pervading space, proving to most astronomers that Big Bang actually occurred.
1967 Jocelyn Bell-Burnell (English: 1943–) discovers first-known pulsar while working for Antony Hewish (English: 1924–); Hewish later gets Nobel Prize for discovery.
1969 Neil Armstrong (American: 1930–) and Edwin E. ("Buzz") Aldrin (American: 1930–) walk on Moon.
1971 American spacecraft, *Mariner 9*, is first to orbit another planet, Mars.
1975 Soviet space probe transmits pictures from surface of Venus.
1976 U.S. Viking space probes begin transmitting pictures of surface of Mars—unsuccessful in detecting life on planet.
1977 Rings of Uranus are discovered.
1979 U.S. space probe *Voyager 1* discovers that, like Saturn and Uranus, Jupiter has rings.
1980 Alan Guth (American: 1947–) develops theory of inflationary universe, an explanation of how Big Bang occurred.
1981 U.S. introduces reusable spacecraft, the space shuttle.
1987 The explosion of Supernova 1987A, the nearest supernova that has been visible from Earth since 1604, is observed.
1989 U.S. space probe *Voyager 2* flies by Neptune, farthest planet from the Sun at that time, imaging the planet, its rings, and its moons.
1990 The Hubble Space Telescope is launched.
1991 Aleksander Wolszczan (American 1946-) discovers planets orbiting pulsar PSR 1257+12, the first planets confirmed to orbit a body other than the Sun.
1992 The Magellan Venus orbiter completes mapping 95 percent of the planet's surface with radar.
Observations from the *Cosmic Background Explorer Satellite (COBE)* confirm the Big Bang theory.
1993 Members of the crew of the Space Shuttle *Endeavour* successfully repair the main lens of the Hubble Space Telescope.
1994 Comet Shoemaker-Levy 9, broken into 21 fragments, some nearly half a kilometer in diameter, slams into the far side of Jupiter in July.
1995 Astronomers Michel Mayor (Swiss:) and Didier Queloz (Swiss: 1966–) announce the first planet to orbit an ordinary star other than the Sun.
The Hubble Space Telescope focuses on a single patch of the northern sky long enough to reveal previously unknown objects at great distances from Earth. The experiment, called the Hubble Deep Field, is repeated for the sky's southern hemisphere in 1998.
1996 Andrea Dupree (American: 1952–) and Ronald Gilliland (American: 1939-) use the Hubble Space Telescope to make images of Betelgeuse, the first to show a star's disc.
Firm evidence is found for a massive black hole at the center of the Milky Way galaxy.
1997 Jupiter's moon Europa is found to have a sea of liquid water beneath a surface of ice crossed by giant fissures; astronomers conclude that it is possible that living organisms could exist in Europa's ocean.
The space probe *Pathfinder* lands safely on Mars on July 4. Pathfinder's rover, Sojourner, leaves the craft and sends to Earth reports of its close-up observation of Martian rocks in what appears to be an ancient flood plain.
1998 Astronomers conclude that there isn't enough matter in the universe to stop expansion; expansion may be accelerated by a small antigravity force.
The largest known explosion since the Big Bang is observed--a burst of gamma rays as luminous for a second or two as the rest of the universe; the cause is unknown.
1999 Two independent teams of astronomers determine that a system of at least three planets orbits the star Upsilon Andromedae.
The Sloan Digital Sky Survey, based in Apache Point, New Mexico, begins. The project maps millions of galaxies and other objects visible from the northern hemisphere using the largest electronic camera ever built.
2000 Studies using the Chandra X-Ray Observatory, a satellite launched in 1999, reveal that the pervasive X-ray background of the universe is caused by black holes that lurk in the hearts of most galaxies.
Permanent occupation of the International Space Station begins on May 19.
Calculations based on the US BOOMERANG (Balloon Observations of Millimetric Extragalactic Radiation and Geophysics) experiment, a balloon-borne study of the cosmic background radiation conducted in 1998, reveal that the universe is flat, not curved.
Michael C. Malin (American: 1950–) and Kenneth S. Edgett (American: 1965–), using images from *Mars Global Surveyor*, detect places where liquid water appears to have burst out of Mars' surface and run down a hillside before evaporating into the thin Martian atmosphere; later studies show that the cause of the erosion could have been dry ice, not liquid water.
2001 Timothy Beers (American: 1957–) of Michigan State University and coworkers use uranium-238 to date the oldest stars in the universe at 12.5 billion years (with an uncertainty of 3 billion years), giving the minimum age for the universe.
In February the space probe *NEAR-Shoemaker* lands softly on asteroid 433 Eros, after orbiting it for a year.
Astronomers from the Space Telescope Institute in Baltimore, MD, confirm that the universe is expanding more rapidly as it ages, apparently because of a small force that eventually overwhelms gravity.
The orbit of comet 200 CR-105 is calculated to be distorted as if by the presence of a planet larger than Pluto orbiting far beyond Neptune, now or at some time in the distant past—although the planet could have been Neptune itself if Neptune once occupied an orbit much farther from the Sun.

▶ GLOSSARY OF PLANETARY TERMS

Escape velocity The speed needed for an object to be propelled from the surface of a planet and not fall back. The escape velocity for Earth is 6.96 miles (11.2 km) per second, thus an object must travel at least that fast, or approximately 7 miles per second, to leave Earth's gravitational influence.

Inclination of axis The angle that the axis about which a planet rotates makes with the plane defined by its path around the Sun.
Orbital period The time it takes for a planet to orbit the Sun.
Orbital velocity The speed of a planet in its path around the Sun.
Rotation period The time it takes for a planet to rotate once about itself.

Basic Facts About the Planets

Characteristic	Terrestrial Planets				Gas Giants				
	Mercury	Venus	Earth	Mars	Jupiter	Saturn	Uranus	Neptune	Pluto
Distance from Sun									
miles (millions)	36.0	67.2	93.0	141.6	483.78	890.75	1,784.86	2,793.0	3,647.23
km (millions)	57.9	108.2	149.6	227.9	778.57	1,433.53	2,872.46	4,495.1	5,869.66
Rotation period	59 days	243 days[1]	23.9 hrs	24.6 hrs	9.925 hrs	10.656 hrs	17.24 hrs	16.1 hrs	6.4 days
Orbital period (days)	88	224.7	365.256	686.98	4,331	10,747	30,589	59,800	90,588
Orbital velocity									
(miles/second)	29.74	21.76	18.51	14.99	8.12	6.02	4.23	3.37	2.93
Inclination of axis	0.01	3.39	23.45	25.19	3.13	26.73	97.77	28.32	122.53
Equatorial diameter									
miles	3,032	7,521	7,926	4,222	88,846	74,897	31,763	30,775	1,485
km	4,879	12,104	12,756	6,794	142,984	120,536	51,118	49,528	2,930
In relation to Earth:									
Diameter	38.3%	94.9%	100%	53.3%	1,121%	945%	401%	388%	18.7%
Mass	5.53%	81.5%	100%	10.7%	31,783%	9,516.2%	1,453.6%	1,714.7%	0.21%
Gravity	37.8%	90.7%	100%	37.7%	236.4%	91.6%	88.90%	112%	5.9%
Escape velocity									
miles/second	2.7	6.4	7.0	3.1	37.0	22.1	13.2	14.6	0.7
km/second	4.3	10.36	11.186	5.03	59.5	35.5	21.3	23.5	1.1
Average surface	332.4°F	867.0°F	59°F	-85°F	-166°F	-220°F	-320°F	-330°F	-375°F
temperature	166.9°C	463.9°C	15°C	-65°C	-110°C	-140°C	-195°C	-200°C	-225°C
Planetary satellites	0	0	1	2	28	30	20/21[2]	8	1

1. Venus's rotation is retrograde, or opposite the direction of other planets. 2. One observed satellite awaiting official confirmation by International Astronomical Union. **Source:** NASA: National Space Science Data Center (NSSDC) http://nssdc.gsfc.nasa.gov.

▶THE SOLAR SYSTEM

Earth is a planet. A planet is a large, fairly cool body traveling in a path, called its orbit, around a star. All of the bodies under the gravitational influence of our local star, the Sun, together with the Sun, form the solar system. There are nine known planets in the solar system, as well as other planets around other stars, which are discussed below. Six of the nine solar-system planets were known to the ancients, and astronomers found the remaining three by early in the 20th century. Often smaller, cool bodies orbit planets. These are called satellites or moons.

Cool rocky or metallic bodies smaller than planets that orbit the Sun are called asteroids. Small icy bodies are called comets. Comets often have orbits that take them from the edge of the system to locations near the Sun (some actually hit the Sun and burn up). Very small objects in space are called meteoroids. A meteoroid that burns up in Earth's atmosphere is called a meteor. One that reaches Earth's surface without burning completely is a meteorite.

It is currently believed that the solar system formed when a cloud of gas condensed to form the Sun. Parts of the cloud formed small bodies similar to today's asteroids, comets, and meteoroids. Collectively, these small bodies are called planetesimals or planetoids. Early in the history of the solar system, about 4.6 billion years ago or even before, the planetoids frequently crashed into one another. While this sometimes resulted in one or more of the planetoids breaking up, often a small planetoid would stick to a larger one, making it larger still. The end products of this process, it is proposed, are the nine solar-system planets and their moons, along with the existing asteroids, comets, and meteoroids.

The solar system is located in a large system of stars called the Milky Way galaxy. The solar system is 28,000 light-years (defined below) from the center of the Milky Way and 67 light-years from the plane defined by the galactic spiral.

The Terrestrial Planets

In terms of distance from the Sun, these are the first four planets of the solar system— Mercury, Venus, Earth, and Mars. Terrestrial planets all have a comparatively high density, a concentration of metallic elements, and hard, rocky surfaces. Earth is the largest of the terrestrial planets but is dwarfed by the enormous sizes of the outer "gas giant" planets (Jupiter, Saturn, Uranus, and Neptune). Mercury, Earth, and Mars have magnetic fields; Venus does not have a detectable magnetic field. Earth and Venus have thick atmospheres, Mars has a thin atmosphere, and Mercury's atmosphere is almost nonexistent.

Mercury

Main components of atmosphere: 98% helium, 2% hydrogen. Mercury is the planet closest to the Sun and in keeping with its namesake—Mercury, the winged messenger—moves the fastest in its orbit. Usually obscured from view from Earth by the Sun's glare, it is sometimes visible on Earth's horizon just after sunset, when it is called the Evening Star, or just before dawn, when it is called the Morning Star. About 14 times in each 100 years, Mercury can also be seen crossing directly in front of the Sun's disk.

Mercury was long thought to be the smallest planet, but better measurements of Pluto's size have shown that Pluto is even smaller. The U.S. *Mariner 10* space probe provided the first detailed pictures of Mercury's surface during flybys in 1974 and 1975. *Mariner 10* mapped about 35 percent of the planet's heavily cratered, moonlike surface. No space probe has visited the planet since.

Mercury is a waterless, airless world that alternately bakes and freezes as it orbits the Sun. Its tenuous atmosphere is thought to be one-trillionth the density of Earth's atmosphere and largely composed of helium. On Mercury's sunlit side temperatures reach 850°F (450°C) and plummet to -300°F (-180°C) on the dark side. These extremes are largely due to Mercury's slow rate of rotation: one single rotation is two-thirds of a Mercury year, or 59 days for a rotation compared to 88 days for a revolution. Mercury's axis is almost perpendicular to its plane of rotation, so any single place on the planet sees dawn only once every 176 days—the planet must rotate three times and go through two of its "years" before a new day dawns.

Mercury's surface is scarred with hundreds of thousands of meteor craters. Many such craters were probably formed during the planetoid showers believed to have occurred soon after the formation of the solar system. Many areas have had the craters smoothed over by ancient lava flows, however. This indicates extensive volcanic activity on Mercury during and after the time of the planetoid showers. The surface is also crisscrossed by huge cliffs, or scarps. These probably formed as Mercury's surface cooled and shrank. Some of the scarps are up to 1.2 miles (1.9 km) high and 932 miles (1,500 km) long.

Mercury is so dense for its size that astronomers think that its rocky outer crust is very thin and that the planet is mostly iron. It probably was once larger. During the early bombardment, it is conjectured that one of the larger planetoids (about a sixth of the size of the early planet) hit Mercury so hard that it blasted most of the rocky crust away.

Venus

Main components of atmosphere: 96.5% carbon dioxide, 3.5% nitrogen. As seen in the night sky from Earth, Venus is second only to the Moon in brightness. Venus, named for the Roman goddess of love, is the planet that passes closest to Earth (24,000,000 mi., or 39,000,000 km). Since it is between Earth and the Sun, Venus, like Mercury, is seen either as the Morning Star or the Evening Star.

Because of its proximity to Earth and its position between Earth and the Sun, Venus became (in 1962) the first planet beyond Earth to be scanned by a space probe in its neighborhood (*Mariner 2*). The pull of the Sun's gravity makes Venus and Mercury "downhill" from the Earth; one must travel against the Sun's gravity to reach other planets. Since 1962 Venus has been visited by numerous U.S. and Soviet spacecraft. Soviet space probes *Venera 13* and *Venera 14* were the first to make a soft landing and send back pictures from the Venusian surface.

The Venusian atmosphere is thick with clouds that have shrouded the planet's surface from view, making the planet somewhat mysterious. The Venusian clouds range from about 28 to 37 miles (45 to 60 km) above the planet's surface and are differentiated into three layers. Droplets of sulfuric acid and water have been identified in the clouds.

The clouds and high level of carbon dioxide in the atmosphere have combined to trap heat in the lower atmosphere of Venus. This is an extreme form of the greenhouse effect and is responsible for high temperatures in the lower atmosphere, 870°F (460°C)—hot enough to melt lead. The atmospheric pressure at the surface is 92 times that of Earth. Radiation of heat from the lower atmosphere is so inefficient that there is little variation of temperature between night and day.

One feature of the Venusian upper atmosphere is markedly different from that of Earth. The atmosphere superrotates on Venus—that is, the atmosphere above the clouds moves 60 times faster than the planet rotates—whereas the Earth and its atmosphere rotate at the same speed. So, high winds and steady upper-atmosphere winds—100 mph (160 km/hr) or faster—are a dominant factor in Venusian weather. But at ground level, winds are calmer, with an average closer to 2 mph (3.6 km/hr).

Soviet space probes that soft-landed on Venus have provided photographs of the planet's surface. Radar maps of 99 percent of the Venusian surface, completed by the U.S. Pioneer spacecraft (from 1978 to 1993), and *Magellan* (from 1989 to 1994), now give a detailed picture of features as small as 350 ft. (100 m) in diameter. More than a thousand Venusian mountains, volcanoes, rifts, basins, impact craters, and other features have been identified.

About 10 percent of the surface is highland terrain, 70 percent rolling uplands, and 20 percent lowland plains. There are two major highland areas: one about half the size of Africa and located in the equatorial region and the other, about the size of Australia, located to the north. The highest mountain on Venus—Maxwell Montes—is in the northern highlands and is higher than Earth's Mt. Everest. Volcanic activity dominates Venus; the planet is covered with volcanic domes and lava channels.

Like Earth, Venus is thought to have an internal structure. The crust, however, is much thicker than that of Earth, perhaps twice as deep on the average, making the crust of Venus about 60 mi. (100 km) thick. Below the crust is a large layer called the mantle; below the mantle is a core thought to be molten nickel-iron, similar to Earth's outer core.

Earth

Main components of atmosphere: 78% nitrogen, 21% oxygen, 1% water, 0.93% argon. Earth is the third planet from the Sun and the only one in the solar system known to harbor life. From space, our planet appears as a bright, blue-and-white sphere—blue because some 70 percent of the surface is covered by water, and white because clouds cover about half the planet's surface.

Earth's atmosphere and composition are discussed in **Earth Science** below. Earth's mass is 6.583×10^{21} tons. (5.972×10^{21} metric tons).

The Moon is Earth's only natural satellite. It is over one-quarter the size of Earth in diameter (2,160 mi. or 3,476 km). At an average distance of 238,000 mi. (380,000 km), it is the brightest object in Earth's nighttime sky. The Moon regularly changes in appearance as seen from Earth. See the discussion of these changes, called "Phases of the Moon," in Part I.

The Moon is slightly egg-shaped, and the same side of the satellite always faces Earth—this side being the elongated small end. As a result, the Moon rotates once during each revolution. The side we do not see is called the far side (not the dark side—all parts of the moon undergo 14 Earth days of light, followed by 14 days of darkness).

Over a decade of exploration of the Moon by space probes was capped by the landing of two U.S. astronauts on the Moon on July 20, 1969. A total of six two-man crews of American astronauts eventually landed on the Moon between 1969 and 1972, and they brought back some 842 pounds (382 kg) of samples of Moon rocks. The world these astronauts found was airless and devoid of life. Temperatures on the Moon range from up to 273°F (134°C) on the bright side to -274°F (-170°C) on the unlighted side.

A mixture of fine powder and broken rock blankets the Moon's surface. The near side also has large regions (called maria, or seas) of solidified lava. The lunar surface is pockmarked with craters up to 56 miles (90 km) across and is broken by huge mountain ranges. Some craters at the poles may contain frozen water in their depths.

Mars

Main components of atmosphere: 95% carbon dioxide, 3% nitrogen, 2% argon. Mars is the outermost of the four terrestrial planets and has a distinctive reddish coloring, coming from iron oxide in the Martian soil. The Romans named the planet after their god of war, and the two irregularly shaped satellites of Mars have been named after the horses—Deimos (terror) and Phobos (fear)—that pulled the war god's chariot. Mars is usually visible in Earth's nighttime sky and is lined up with Earth between it and the Sun once every 780 days, though its closest approach to Earth (33,800,000 mi., or 54,500,000 km) comes at 15- or 17-year intervals; 2003 will be the closest approach since 1986.

The so-called canals on Mars—later found to be optical illusions—were first observed by 19th-century astronomers and led to the widespread belief that there was life on Mars. (In 1900 the French Academy offered a prize to the first person to find life on any planet except Mars, presumably because everyone knew that there was life on that planet.) The planet thus became the target of numerous space probes, both U.S. and Soviet, from the early years of interplanetary exploration.

The first successful flyby of Mars was achieved by the U.S. spacecraft *Mariner 4* in 1965. The Soviets became the first to land a probe successfully on the surface of Mars in 1971, but the probe malfunctioned and stopped transmitting after only 20 seconds. It was not until 1976, when the U.S. *Viking 1* and *Viking 2* landers touched down on Mars, that extensive study of the planet from its surface became possible. The *Viking 1* lander continued to function until 1983. *Pathfinder* landed on Mars on July 4, 1997. Using a remote-controlled robot called *Sojourner*, whose travels to Martian rocks were televised, the *Pathfinder* mission reported the details of the weather and geology of Mars.

The big question of whether there is (or was) life on Mars has yet to be answered with certainty. The *Viking* landers conducted three experiments on Martian soil to check for biological processes. Some of the tests yielded positive results, but these could also be explained by the soil chemistry. The lack of other evidence of organic molecules adds to the case against life on Mars.

Orbiting satellites have mapped the entire planet down to a resolution of 500-1,000 ft. (150–300 m). The planet's surface is heavily cratered, and there is extensive evidence of once-active volcanoes. There are also such spectacular features as Olympus Mons (an extinct volcano three times as high as Earth's Mt. Everest); mammoth canyons, one of which is four times deeper than the Grand Canyon; and a gigantic basin (larger than Alaska) in the southern hemisphere that was probably created by a single, huge asteroid. The planet has ice caps at both poles (water ice with some frozen carbon dioxide), and the ice caps advance and recede with changes in the seasons.

But the most intriguing aspect of the Martian surface is that water once flowed there in great quantities. Parts of the terrain apparently have sedimentary origins, and there are many long channels, complete with smaller tributary channels and islands, that extend for hundreds of kilometers. Scientists speculate that Mars once had a much thicker atmosphere, made up of gases vented during volcanic eruptions, which would have made it possible for water in its liquid state to exist on the surface. Martian atmospheric pressure is now so low, however, that surface water would immediately vaporize. It is conjectured that in the past, water flowed through the channels to lowland areas and then sank into the Martian regolith, or upper soil layer, since there is no geologic evidence that standing bodies of water ever existed. Astronomers believe that at least some of the primordial water may still be trapped as ice in the regolith.

Mars is too small to sustain continual volcanic activity. Its atmosphere apparently thinned out after volcanic activity ceased. Atmospheric pressure is now just seven one-thousandths of that on Earth at sea level, and the predominant gas is carbon dioxide, which is relatively heavy. A small amount of water vapor in the atmosphere is enough to form some clouds, small patches of fog in some valleys, and occasionally even patches of frost. Surface temperatures vary from a high of about 70°F (20°C) during summer at the equator to a low of about -220°F (-140°C) during winter at the poles.

By far the most pronounced feature of Martian weather is dust storms, which regularly engulf the entire planet for a period of several months.

The asteroids

Also called minor planets, the asteroids are very small bodies ranging from less than 1 to 600 miles in diameter. The name asteroid means "starlike" and was given to asteroids because they are so small they appear as points of light (as do stars) even in powerful telescopes. Otherwise, asteroids are not like stars at all.

The first four asteroids were discovered between 1801 and 1807. Today several hundred thousand asteroids are known and a million may exist in all. But the total mass of all known asteroids is less than that of Earth's Moon; only 26 asteroids are more than 130 miles (200 km) in diameter. Many asteroids occur in pairs that orbit each other. Some are thought to be solid bodies, while others may be collections of rocks held together by slight gravitational interactions.

Asteroids are found in several locations. The main belt is between Mars and Jupiter, but many inside the orbit of Mars are known as near-Earth asteroids. Asteroids that are thought to be larger than about 500 feet (150 m) in diameter that may travel as close as about 5 million miles (7.5 million km) to Earth are called potentially hazardous objects (PHOs). There are about 300 known PHOs, but none are expected to impact Earth in the foreseeable future. Two groups in the same orbit as Jupiter are called the Trojans because the larger ones are named for characters from Homer's *Iliad*.

The Outer Planets

Beyond Mars and the asteroid belt lie the five known outer planets of our solar system. Four of these planets—Jupiter, Saturn, Uranus, and Neptune—are the so-called gas giants. Many times larger than the terrestrial planets, these planets are huge, dense balls of hydrogen and other gases. Orbiting beyond them (most of the time) lies the solar system's outermost and smallest known planet, Pluto, which may be nothing more than a tiny ball of ice.

Jupiter

Main components of atmosphere: 90% hydrogen, 10% helium. Jupiter is the largest planet in the solar system. It has 2.5 times more mass than all the other planets of the solar system together and is 11 times as large as Earth in diameter. Jupiter is so large that scientists believe it almost became a star: as the gases and dust contracted to form the planet, gravitational forces created tremendous pressure and temperature inside the core—perhaps as high as tens of thousands of degrees. But there was not enough mass available to create the temperatures needed to start a fusion reaction such as that of the Sun (above 27,000,000°F, or 15,000,000°C, at the Sun's core); thus Jupiter has been slowly cooling down ever since. Even so, Jupiter still radiates about 2.5 times as much heat as it receives from the Sun.

The first object to reach Jupiter from Earth was *Pioneer 10*. It returned the first close-up pictures of the giant planet in 1973. Subsequently, the more sophisticated space probes *Voyager 1* and *Voyager 2* passed by Jupiter in 1979 and sent back images and more data on the planet. One of the most exciting discoveries by *Voyager 1* was that Jupiter has a faint but extensive ring system that extends almost 186,000 miles (300,000 km) out from the planet's surface. *Galileo* found another faint ring at 1 million miles (1.6 million km) in 1998. A probe from *Galileo* arrived at Jupiter on December 7, 1995, finding winds of 435 mph (700 km/hr) and much less water vapor than expected. Scientists later determined that the probe had arrived in what amounts to a Jovian desert.

Jupiter's thick atmosphere, which may extend above the planetary surface as much as 600 miles (1,000 km), is primarily made up of hydrogen, with some helium and traces of other gases. Because the planet spins so fast (one rotation in just under 10 hours), its clouds tend to form bands that give the planet a striped appearance. Darker bands are called belts, while light ones are zones. Clouds at higher altitudes are carried eastward by jet streams, while those at lower levels are blown westward.

There are numerous eddies and swirls in Jupiter's atmosphere, but none can compare with the Great Red Spot, apparently a massive hurricane (rotating counterclockwise) located in the southern hemisphere near the equator. The Great Red Spot was first observed some 300 years ago, and this storm continues unabated today. Since 1938 three smaller white ovals have been observed to the south of the Great Red Spot.

Jupiter's cloud tops are extremely cold (about -202°F, or -130°C), but temperatures increase deeper inside the atmosphere. Pressure also increases, and at about 600 miles (1,000 km) below the outermost atmospheric layers, great oceans of liquid hydrogen form Jupiter's surface. These may be some 12,000 miles (20,000 km) deep. Beneath them the hydrogen is so densely compacted it is thought to be in a metallic state. Within this is the core, thought to be an iron and silicate rock ball about the size of Earth.

Jupiter is now known to have 28 moons, the four largest being the Galilean moons, so called because they were first observed by Galileo. The Galilean moons are Ganymede, Callisto, Europa, and Io—after the Roman god Jupiter's cupbearer (Ganymede) and three of Jupiter's inamorata. Ganymede is the largest moon in the solar system and is larger even than the planets Pluto and Mercury. It is a huge, cratered ball of ice and may have a core of solid silicate rock with liquid water between the thick ice covering and the core. Callisto, with an orbit outside that of Ganymede, is also covered with ice and is riddled with thousands of craters. Europa, which orbits inside Ganymede, is about the size of our Moon and has a smooth surface marked by networks of cracks. The most interesting of Jupiter's moons are Io, which orbits closest to Jupiter, and Europa, which may have liquid water oceans beneath an icy surface. The *Voyagers* and *Galileo* photographed volcanoes erupting on Io. Orange-red patches on Io's mottled surface are apparently molten sulfur beds, but most other parts of Io's surface are apparently very cold (about -229°F or -145°C).

Io undergoes the most intense volcanic activity known, heated, it is thought, by tidal energy from orbiting near Jupiter. One giant volcano may have been erupting for the past 19 years. Europa, on the other hand, is covered in ice, but some have speculated that a liquid ocean beneath the ice could contain life. The liquid, which probably contains salts like oceans on Earth, could be heated by the same tidal forces that propel Io's volcanoes.

One small moon was discovered in 1999 and ten more in 2000.

Saturn

Main components of atmosphere: 90% hydrogen, 3% helium. Saturn is the sixth planet of the solar system and the second largest, after Jupiter. The outermost of the planets that can be identified easily in Earth's nighttime sky with the unaided eye, Saturn has a pale yellowish color and is not nearly so bright as Mars. Saturn's spectacular ring system, which makes it one of the most interesting of the planets, is visible only through a telescope. Its rings are more extensive than those of any other planet.

Like Jupiter, Saturn is composed of densely compacted hydrogen, helium, and other gases. Liquid or metallic hydrogen probably exists underneath the planet's thick atmosphere, and scientists believe there is a solid core of rock about two times the size of Earth at its center. Saturn's high rotational speed (once every 10 hours, 12 minutes) makes it the most oblate (flattened) of all the planets; it is almost 6,800 miles (11,000 km) wider at the equator than on a line through the poles.

Exploration of Saturn began in 1979 with the first fly-by (*Pioneer 11*), but the *Voyager 1* (1980) and *Voyager 2* (1981) missions provided the first detailed look at the planet. Scientists have spent years sifting through the data gathered. Though there were important new findings, many questions about Saturn remain unanswered. The *Cassini-Hygens* probe, due to arrive in 2004, should provide many answers.

The *Voyagers* found a huge storm thousands of miles across on Saturn, along with a wide band of extremely high winds—up to 1,000 miles (1,600 km) per hour—at the equator. Winds in this band all travel in the direction of the planet's rotation (unlike bands of wind on Jupiter). The *Voyagers* also discovered a vast hydrogen cloud circling the planet above the equator.

The *Voyagers'* most exciting discoveries concern the planetary rings. Previously, about six different rings had been identified within the ring system, but *Voyager 1* pictures show as many as 1,000 separate rings. Narrow rings can even be seen within the Cassini Division, once thought to be an empty gap between the two major parts of the ring system. Some rings are not circular, and at least two rings are intertwined, or "braided." A strange new phenomenon was also discovered in the rings. *Voyager 1* pictures clearly show dark, radial fingers—"spokes"—moving inside the rings in the direction of rotation. Scientists speculate that they are made of ice crystals.

Voyager 2 pictures show that Saturn has far more than 1,000 rings—perhaps as many as a hundred thousand or more. One of the brightest rings is under 152 meters (500 ft.) thick. *Voyager 2* also found seasonal differences between the planet's two hemispheres and photographed a storm 4,000 miles (6,500 km) wide.

Twelve of Saturn's moons were known before the arrival of the *Voyagers*, and instruments aboard the space probe helped locate five new ones in the 1980s. In 1990 an 18th moon, later named Pan, was located in images made by *Voyager 2*. The discovery of 12 small moons of Saturn, found with ground-based telescopes, was reported in 2001, bringing the total number of moons to 30. Most of Saturn's moons are relatively small and composed of rock and ice. All but one of the small moons are pock-marked by meteor craters, and in some cases the moons appear to have been cracked by collisions with especially large meteors. But *Voyager* pictures show that one moon, Enceladus, is smooth in large regions apparently unmarked by collisions with meteors. Scientists believe that Enceladus is being pulled and stretched by the combined gravities of a nearby moon and Saturn itself. Tidal forces have apparently heated the core of Enceladus and made its surface soft enough to smooth over any craters formed by meteor impacts.

Titan, Saturn's largest moon (3,000 mi., or 4,800 km in diameter) is one of the few moons in the solar system known to have an atmosphere of any substance. Scientists suspect that at least some precursors of life may have formed there. For this reason *Voyager 1* was guided to within about 2,500 miles (4,000 km) of Titan during the Saturn flyby. Though Titan's surface was obscured by dense clouds, Voyager's sensors nevertheless returned a considerable amount of information about the moon and its atmosphere. Titan's atmosphere is composed mostly of nitrogen, like that of Earth, with only a small percentage of methane and carbon monoxide. Atmospheric pressure is at least 1.5 times that on Earth and temperatures range around -294°F (-181°C). Titan in fact appears to be a frozen version of Earth before life evolved.

The possibility of oceans of liquid methane (or of nitrogen or methane rain) on Titan was a matter of considerable controversy for some time after *Voyager 1* investigated the moon. But Titan is "dry," at least in the regions investigated. Pools of liquid methane might still exist in other low-lying regions, but it is unlikely that either methane or nitrogen condenses to liquid form on Titan.

Uranus

Main components of atmosphere: 82% hydrogen, 15% helium, 2% methane. Uranus is the seventh planet in the solar system and the third of the gas giants. The planet is barely visible in Earth's night-time sky (it looks like a faint star) and for that reason, it went undiscovered until 1781.

Nearly the same size as Neptune and only about 5 percent of Jupiter's mass, Uranus is a faintly greenish color, perhaps because its atmosphere contains methane. The planet's axis of rotation is tipped over on its side. Astronomers discovered a system of nine faint rings in 1977, and *Voyager* found two more rings in 1986. There are thought to be 21 moons of Uranus. Among these, Caliban and Sycorax were found in 1997; a still-unnamed moon was noticed in 1999 by a researcher studying a 1986 photograph taken by *Voyager 2*. Three

more discovered later in 1999 are provisionally named Prospero, Setebos, and Stephano.

Uranus's atmosphere is very cold (-355°F, or -215°C). No clouds have been observed. Scientists speculate that, as on Jupiter and Saturn, temperatures and pressures increase dramatically down through the outer layer of atmosphere. At some point the hydrogen and helium would be sufficiently compressed to form a liquid or slushy surface "crust." Underneath this crust they believe is a mantle of solidified methane, ammonia, and water; and inside this mantle, a rocky core of silicon and iron about 15 times as massive as Earth. The core is thought to be hot, probably about 12,000°F (7,000°C).

Neptune

Main components of atmosphere: 80% hydrogen, 19% helium, 1% methane. The last of the gas giants, Neptune is the eighth planet in the solar system. It was discovered in 1846 after mathematical calculations based on irregularities in the orbit of Uranus provided astronomers with the correct location of the planet. Neptune, like Uranus, has been surrounded by considerable uncertainty because of its enormous distance from Earth. The 1989 visit by *Voyager 2* contributed greatly to improved understanding of the planet.

Neptune is a pale bluish color, but it has a clear atmosphere, and is very cold at the cloud tops (about -365°F or -220°C).

Scientists believe Neptune has a three-layered structure similar to that of Uranus: a crust of solidified or liquid hydrogen and helium that gradually thins outward into an atmosphere; a mantle of solidified gases and water; and a hot, rocky core (about 12,000°F or 7,000°C) some 15 times as massive as Earth. But one aspect of Neptune remains a mystery. Despite similarities with Uranus, Neptune has been found to radiate 2.7 times as much heat as it receives from the Sun (at a rate of 0.03 microwatts per ton of mass). Uranus, on the other hand, does not emit as much excess heat.

Neptune has eight known moons, Triton and Nereid, discovered from Earth, and six others discovered by *Voyager 2*, and a ring system containing two bright rings and three dim ones. Triton is the largest moon and has an atmosphere. Triton is unusual in that it travels in a direction opposite that of Neptune's rotation, suggesting that it has a different origin from the planet. Triton also has volcanic activity: geysers of nitrogen rising as high as five miles (8 km).

Pluto

Main components of atmosphere: Methane and nitrogen (quantities unknown) The ninth and outermost (most of the time) known planet of the solar system is a ball of frozen gases probably only about the size of Earth's Moon. Pluto was discovered in 1930 as a result of an extensive search by Clyde Tombaugh. Because of its relatively small size and chaotic orbit (which at times crosses inside Neptune's orbit), some scientists think that Pluto is not really a planet at all. Instead, they theorize that Pluto is only one of the large comets in the Kuiper belt, discovered outside the orbit of Neptune over several years beginning in 1992.

Frozen methane and a thin atmosphere of methane and some other gases have been detected on Pluto. Pluto has one known moon, Charon, discovered in 1978. Charon is about half the size of Pluto. Pluto and Charon rotate and revolve synchronously like a double planet system.

The Sun

Virtually all of the energy used by living things comes from the Sun. The Sun's light causes photosynthesis in green plants, and its heat causes winds. Fossil fuels, such as coal, oil, and natural gas, got their energy originally from photosynthesis, as does wood. Animals derive their energy from plants that photosynthesize, either directly or indirectly. The only natural nonsolar energy sources are nuclear reactions (which also produce geothermal energy), some bacteria that metabolize sulfur, and the tides, which on Earth are produced largely by the Moon, but in part by the Sun.

Because the Sun is a ball of gases, it does not rotate as a whole. The equator rotates in about 25 days, while gas near the poles rotates in about 30 days. The period of rotation at each latitude can be found by observing sunspots, which are magnetic storms. Sunspots appear and disappear in a mysterious 11-year cycle that many think influences weather on Earth, although convincing proof is lacking. Sometimes sunspots disappear for tens of years at a time, as during the period from 1645 to 1715. It may or may not be a coincidence that those years coincided with the "Little Ice Age" in Europe, when temperatures were far below average.

Like Earth, the Sun is composed of various layers. The part we see is called the photosphere. In the Sun's interior, energy is generated when hydrogen in the core fuses to become helium. Above the photosphere is a region of pinkish gases, the chromosphere. Above that is a large halo, visible only in eclipses, called the corona. Particles from the Sun, the solar wind, stream through the solar system, creating among other things auroras on Earth. Strong increases in solar wind during solar flares can interfere with radio communication.

▶PLANETS OUTSIDE THE SOLAR SYSTEM

A detectable wobble, observed in more than 70 nearby stars, indicates that each such star is orbited by one or more planets, known as "extrasolar planets." The star Upsilon Andromedae is known to have at least three extrasolar planets, and six other stars show evidence of two. At least two pulsars have planets, and several stars are surrounded by dusty regions that may indicate planet formation.

In 1995 the first planet that orbits an ordinary star other than the Sun was established on the basis of regular changes in the position of the Sun-like star 51 Pegasi, which is nearly 50 light-years from the solar system. This discovery by Michel Mayor (Swiss:) and Didier Queloz (Swiss: 1966–) was soon followed by detection of many other ordinary stars that move back and forth in space. Such small movements indicate one or more large planets in orbit about the each star. This method works for relatively nearby stars orbited by very large planets—planets about half the size of Saturn to eleven times the size of Jupiter. The planets found generally orbit closer to their stars than the orbit of Mercury about the Sun, although one system discovered in 2001 has two planets in orbits about as far from the star as Mars and Jupiter are from the Sun. Some planets have also been detected as they reduce visible light from their stars by passing between the stars and Earth. In the next few years new equipment for existing telescopes and several newly built telescopes are expected to make it possible to observe smaller extrasolar planets than any found so far.

Changes in the pulses from a pulsar are easier to observe than the exact position of an ordinary star, so the first known extrasolar planet was found at a pulsar. In 1991, Aleksander Wolszczan (American: 1946–) observed that the pulsar PSR 1257+12 regularly changed the timing of its pulses as if being pulled back and forth in space by several bodies in orbit. Calculations since then show that two of the bodies, each about the size of Earth, move in small, swift orbits about the pulsar. A third planet is about the size of Earth's Moon and orbits inside the other two.

As early as 1983, infrared studies from space revealed dust clouds that might be the seeds of planets around such nearby stars as Vega and Fomalhaut. In 2001, astronomers studying a young star in the Orion nebula observed what appear to be larger clumps of dust, the predicted next step in planet building. In 2001 even larger clumps about the star Zeta Leopris—perhaps forming an asteroid belt—were proposed to explain its higher-temperature dust halo

▶STARS AND THE UNIVERSE

Astronomical Distances

The very large distances between stars and the even larger ones between the vast groups of stars called galaxies are usually expressed in terms of units of length that are peculiar to astronomy. The most familiar is the **light-year,** defined as the distance light travels through a vacuum in a year (approximately 365¼ days). Light travels through a vacuum at the rate of about 186,250 miles per second (exactly 299,792,458 m/s—exact because the meter is defined in terms of the speed of light in a vacuum). A light-year is approximately 5,880 billion miles (9,460 billion km).

Astronomers also use a measure even larger than the light-year, the parsec, equal to about 3.26

Characteristics of the Sun	
Position in solar system	Center
Mean distance from Earth	92,960,000 mi. (149,600,000 km)
Distance from center of Milky Way galaxy	27,710 light-years
Period of rotation	25.45 days at 16° longitude
Inclination (relative to Earth's orbit)	7.25°
Equatorial diameter	865,000 mi. (1,392,000 km)
Diameter relative to Earth	109.2 times
Mass	2.192×10^{27} tons (1.9891×10^{30} kg)
Mass converted to energy each second	9,500 pounds (4,300 kg)
Surface gravity relative to Earth's	28 times
Temperature at core	28,280,000°F (15,710,000°C)
Temperature at bottom of photosphere	12,400°F (6,900°C)
Main components	Hydrogen and helium
Present age	4.6 billion years
Expected future life of hydrogen fuel supply	6.4 billion years

The Constellations

Name	Genitive	Abbr.	Translation	Remarks
Andromeda	Andromedae	And	Andromeda	Character in Greek myth
Antlia	Antliae	Ant	Air pump	Named by Nicolas Lacaille in 1750
Apus	Apodis	Aps	Swift, or Bird of Paradise	Named by Johann Bayer in 1603
Aquarius	Aquarii	Aqr	Water Bearer	In zodiac
Aquila	Aquilae	Aql	Eagle	Contains Altair
Ara	Arae	Ara	Altar	Part of the Centaurus group
Aries	Arietis	Ari	Ram	In zodiac
Auriga	Aurigae	Aur	Charioteer	Contains Capella
Boötes	Boötis	Boo	Herdsman	Contains Arcturus
Caelum	Caeli	Cae	Chisel, or graving tool	Lacaille, 1750
Camelopardalis	Camelopardalis	Cam	Giraffe	Named by Johannes Bartsch in 1661
Cancer	Cancri	Cnc	Crab	In zodiac
Canes Venatici	Canum Venaticorum	CVn	Hunting dogs	Named by Johannes Hevelius in 1687
Canis Major	Canis Majoris	CMa	Big Dog	Contains Sirius and Adhara
Canis Minor	Canis Minoris	CMi	Little Dog	Contains Procyon
Capricornus	Capricorni	Cap	Goat	In zodiac
Carina	Carinae	Car	Ship's Keel[1]	Lacaille, 1750; contains Canopus
Cassiopeia	Cassiopeiae	Cas	Cassiopeia	Character in Greek myth
Centaurus	Centauri	Cen	Centaur	Character in Greek myth; contains Rigil Kentaurus and Hadar/Agena
Cepheus	Cephei	Cep	Cepheus	Character in Greek myth
Cetus	Ceti	Cet	Whale	Sea monster slain by Perseus
Chamaeleon	Chamaeleontis	Cha	Chameleon	Bayer, 1603
Circinus	Circini	Cir	Compass	Lacaille, 1750
Columba	Columbae	Col	Dove	Bayer, 1603
Coma Berenices	Comae Berenices	Com	Berenice's Hair	Third Century B.C. Egyptian Queen
Corona Australis	Coronae Australis	CrA	Southern Crown	Also Sagittarius' crown
Corona Borealis	Coronae Borealis	CrB	Northern Crown	Also Ariadne's crown
Corvus	Corvi	Crv	Crow	Companion of Orpheus
Crater	Crateris	Crt	Cup	—
Crux[2]	Crucis	Cru	Southern Cross	Named by Augustine Royer in 1679; Contains Beta Crucis and Acrux
Cygnus	Cygni	Cyg	Swan	Contains Deneb
Delphinus	Delphini	Del	Dolphin	—
Dorado	Doradus	Dor	Goldfish	Bayer, 1603
Draco	Draconis	Dra	Dragon	Dragon slain by Hercules
Equuleus	Equulei	Equ	Little Horse	—
Eridanus	Eridani	Eri	River Eridanus	Contains Achernar
Fornax	Fornacis	For	Furnace	Lacaille, 1750.
Gemini	Geminorum	Gem	Twins	In zodiac; contains Pollux
Grus	Gruis	Gru	Crane	Bayer, 1603
Hercules	Herculis	Her	Hercules	Character from Greek myth
Horologium	Horologii	Hor	Clock	Lacaille, 1750.
Hydra[3]	Hydrae	Hya	Hydra	Monster from Greek myth
Hydrus	Hydri	Hyi	Sea serpent	Bayer, 1603
Indus	Indi	Ind	Indian	Bayer, 1603
Lacerta	Lacertae	Lac	Lizard	Hevelius, 1687
Leo	Leonis	Leo	Lion	In zodiac; contains Regulus
Leo Minor	Leonis Minoris	LMi	Little Lion	Hevelius, 1687
Lepus	Leporis	Lep	Hare	Prey of Orion
Libra	Librae	Lib	Scales	In zodiac
Lupus	Lupi	Lup	Wolf	Part of Centaurus group
Lynx	Lyncis	Lyn	Lynx	Hevelius, 1687
Lyra	Lyrae	Lyr	Harp	Contains Vega
Mensa	Mensae	Men	Table (mountain)	Lacaille, 1750
Microscopium	Microscopii	Mic	Microscope	Lacaille, 1750
Monoceros	Monocerotis	Mon	Unicorn	Royer, 1679
Musca	Muscae	Mus	Fly	Bayer, 1603
Norma	Normae	Nor	Carpenter's Square	Lacaille, 1750
Octans	Octanis	Oct	Octant	Lacaille, 1750
Ophiuchus	Ophiuchi	Oph	Serpent Bearer	Character in Greek myth
Orion	Orionis	Ori	The Hunter	Character in Greek myth; contains Rigel, Betelgeuse, and Bellatrix
Pavo	Pavonis	Pav	Peacock	Bayer, 1603.
Pegasus	Pegasi	Peg	Pegasus	Winged horse in Greek myth

Name	Genitive	Abbr.	Translation	Remarks
Perseus	Persei	Per	Perseus	Character in Greek myth
Phoenix	Phoenicis	Phe	Phoenix	Bayer, 1603
Pictor	Pictoris	Pic	Easel	Lacaille, 1750
Pisces	Piscium	Psc	Fish	In zodiac
Piscis Austrinus	Piscis Austrin	PsA	Southern Fish	Contains Fomalhaut
Puppis	Puppis	Pup	Ship's Stern[1]	Lacaille, 1750
Pyxis	Pyxidis	Pyx	Ship's Compass[1]	Lacaille, 1750
Reticulum	Reticuli	Ret	Net	Lacaille, 1750
Sagitta	Sagittae	Sge	Arrow	—
Sagittarius	Sagittarii	Sgr	Archer	In zodiac
Scorpius	Scorpii	Sco	Scorpion	In zodiac; contains Antares and Shaula
Sculptor	Sculptoris	Scl	Sculptor	Lacaille, 1750
Scutum	Scuti	Sct	Shield	Hevelius, 1687
Serpens	Serpentis	Ser	Serpent	Snake held by giant Ophiuchus
Sextans	Sextantis	Sex	Sextant	Hevelius, 1687
Taurus	Tauri	Tau	Bull	In zodiac; contains Aldebran and Elnath
Telescopium	Telescopii	Tel	Telescope	Lacaille, 1750
Triangulum	Trianguli	Tri	Triangle	Contains spiral galaxy M33
Triangulum Australe	Trianguli Australis	TrA	Southern Triangle	Bayer, 1603
Tucana	Tucanae	Tuc	Toucan	Bayer, 1603
Ursa Major	Ursae Majoria	UMa	Big Bear	Big Dipper
Ursa Minor	Ursae Minoris	UMi	Little Bear	Little Dipper
Vela	Velorum	Vel	Ship's Sails[1]	Lacaille, 1750
Virgo	Virginis	Vir	Virgin	In zodiac; contains Spica
Volans	Volantis	Vol	Flying Fish	Bayer, 1603
Vulpecula	Vulpeculae	Vul	Little Fox	Hevelius, 1687

1. Formerly part of the constellation Argo Navis, the Argonauts' ship. 2. Smallest constellation. 3. Largest constellation.

light-years, or about 19,170 billion miles (30,840 billion km).

A smaller unit, for measurements within the solar system, is the astronomical unit, which is the average distance between the Earth and the Sun, or about 93 million miles (150 million km).

The Constellations

Constellations consist of several bright stars that are treated as a group. Long ago, before recorded history, people began naming these groups. By Sumerian times (3000-2500 B.C.), stories were already being told about how particular constellations were formed. Most of our present knowledge of such stories, however, comes from the ancient Greeks.

One group of constellations has exerted a special influence on human thought, at least since 1500 B.C. As the Sun, Moon, and planets move through the sky, they pass through a group of 12 constellations, called the constellations of the zodiac. The ancient belief that the presence of the Sun in one of these constellations at a person's birth influences happenings on Earth is called astrology.

Today astronomers use constellations for mapping the sky. Each part of the sky is named by a particular constellation. These constellations, especially in the southern hemisphere, may not be traditional ones, but rather, groups of stars astronomers have named so that for reference purposes all of the sky is labeled.

Star Names

While astronomers often use the traditional names of stars, most of which come to us from Latin or Arabic sources, they also use another system for naming objects in the sky that is based on constellations. Generally, the brightest star in a particular astronomical constellation is called alpha (α), the next brightest beta (ß), and so on through several letters of the Greek alphabet; then numbers are used. All astronomers' constellations are named in Latin. When astronomers refer to a star within its constellation, they use the genitive case, meaning "of the thing." Thus the constellation Big Dog is officially Canis Major, and Sirius is alpha Canis Majoris, or "alpha of Big Dog," usually abbreviated to αCMa. This means it is the brightest star in the constellation Big Dog (Sirius has long been known as the dog star). Since Sirius is a binary star (see "Binary stars," below), the much brighter main star is officially αCMa A. Further along, numbers are used instead of Greek letters. Numbered stars in the news in the 1990s included 51 Pegasi and 71 Virginis.

Magnitude

The brightness of a star is designated by a number called its magnitude, although the relationship between size and brightness is complicated. When the magnitude system was first developed, by the early Greek astronomers Hipparchus (c. 190–c. 120 B.C.) and Ptolemy (c. 100–c. 170), astronomers did not know the actual distances to stars, so magnitude always referred to brightness as seen from Earth. They classed the brightest stars as the first magnitude and the dimmest they could see as the sixth. These numbers were somewhat arbitrary until 1856, when George Phillips Bond (American: 1825–65) determined that photographs of stars show magnitude in a way that is directly measurable—bright stars appear as larger spots than dim stars in photographs even though all stars appear as points to the naked eye. Astronomers could use accurate measures to compare two stars and thus measure magnitude with mathematical precision.

Under Bond's system, stars with a magnitude of 1.00 are exactly 100 times as bright as those with a magnitude of 6.00. On this scale, the very brightest stars have negative magnitudes.

Roughly, each whole number difference in magnitude corresponds to 2.5 times the brightness.

25 Brightest Stars: Magnitudes and Distances From Earth

The stars we see in the evening sky differ in how bright they appear because of a combination of two factors: 1) their total energy output, or **luminosity** (directly related to their absolute magnitude) and 2) their distance from Earth. Astronomers refer to this combination of effects as the **apparent magnitude** of a star, a measure of how bright the star appears in the nighttime sky. To separate the two effects, astronomers define **absolute magnitude** as the brightness of a star as measured from a fixed distance. Most of the stars we see in the sky have a large absolute magnitude but are relatively far away. If all the stars were placed the same distance from Earth, Deneb would be the brightest and the Sun would be the faintest (about 250,000 times fainter than Deneb). Note that negative magnitudes are higher than positive magnitudes.

Rank/ Common name	Star name	Apparent magnitude	Absolute magnitude	Distance from Earth (light-years)
1. Sirius	α CMa	-1.44	1.45	8.6
2. Canopus[1]	α Car	-0.62	-5.53	312.6
3. Rigil Kentaurus[2]	α Cen A	-0.28	4.07	4.4
4. Arcturus	α Boo	-0.05	-0.31	36.7
5. Vega	α Lyr	0.03	0.58	25.3
6. Capella	α Aur A	0.08	-0.48	42.2
7. Rigel[1]	β Ori	0.18	-6.69	772.5
8. Procyon	β CMi	0.40	2.68	11.4
9. Achernar	α Eri	0.45	-2.77	143.7
10. Betelgeuse[1]	α Ori	0.45	-5.14	427.3
11. Hadar[1]	β Cen	0.61	-5.42	525.0
12. Altair	α Aql	0.76	2.20	16.8
13. Acrux[1,3]	α Cru	0.77	(3)	320.6
14. Aldebaran	α Tau	0.87	-0.63	65.1
15. Spica	α Vir	0.98	-3.55	262.1
16. Antares[1]	α Sco	1.06	-5.28	603.7
17. Pollux	β Gem	1.16	1.09	33.7
18. Fomalhaut	α PsA	1.17	1.74	25.1
19. Mimosa	β Cru	1.25	-3.92	352.4
20. Deneb[1]	α Cyg	1.25	-8.73	3,227.7
21. Regulus	α Leo	1.36	-0.52	77.5
22. Adhara[1]	ε CMa	1.5	-4.10	430.6
23. Castor[1]	α Gem	1.58	0.59	51.5
24. Gacrux	γ Cru	1.59	-0.56	87.9
25. Shaula[1]	λ Sco	1.62	-5.05	702.6

Note: The magnitudes of many stars on this list vary slightly over time, although for most stars, the variation is quite small. Betelgeuse and Antares have the largest variations (about 1 magnitude). For consistency, median magnitudes are shown for all stars. 1. Stars more than 300 light-years away have an uncertainty of about 20 percent or more in their distances (and therefore in their absolute magnitudes as well). The distance of Deneb, in particular, may be wrong by half (i.e. only 1,600 light-years away). That would reduce Deneb's absolute magnitude to -7.22, still higher than any other star on this list. 2. A binary star, with both stars orbiting around each other. They appear to the naked eye to be the same star, with a combined apparent and absolute magnitude. 3. Acrux appears to the naked eye to be a single star, but in fact, it is the combined light of two stars, each at different distances from Earth. Its absolute magnitude, therefore, is impossible to define.
Source: NASA.

By the time this system was introduced, astronomers already were able to determine the distances of some stars from Earth. Friedrich Wilhelm Bessel was the first to make such a measurement, which he announced in 1838. A closer star appears brighter than a similar star that is farther away. To better understand the relative brightness of stars as they actually are, astronomers imagine viewing all stars from the same distance away. A star's brightness from this distance, which is 10 parsecs or 32.6 light-years, is called its absolute magnitude.

If we could see it clearly, the star Cygnus OB2 #12 would be the brightest star in the Milky Way galaxy (absolute magnitude -9.9), but it is not only far from Earth but also is obscured by dust. The brightest single object known is not a star, but a quasar (see "The Universe," below), BR 1202-07, with an absolute magnitude of about -33. The Sun has the brightest apparent magnitude of any star, -26.8, but its absolute magnitude is only 4.75.

The Universe

Most of the universe was greatly misunderstood until the 20th century. The most common notion from the time of the ancient Greek philosophers until the end of the Middle Ages was that a number of crystal spheres revolved about Earth, and that each of the planets, the Sun, and Earth's Moon occupied one of these spheres. All the stars occupied the farthest sphere. There were only about 6,000 stars known, those visible to the naked eye (and about half of these were south of the equator, so few Europeans had ever seen them).

In 1609 Galileo of Italy turned the first astronomical telescope on the heavens. Galileo's early telescopes were good enough to show that the Milky Way was not merely a whitish band across the sky but consisted of a vast number of stars, far more than the few thousand visible with the naked eye. His observations also disproved the old idea of crystal spheres. People began to speculate about astronomical entities beyond a simple sphere of stars. Not until 1924 were telescopes sufficiently powerful to show that many cloudy patches in the sky consisted of millions of stars far away from the Milky Way. This discovery led to the recognition of the enormous complexity and diversity of the universe.

Big Bang   The accepted theory of how the universe began is known as the Big Bang theory, since it proposes that the universe began as something like an explosion, which has caused all parts of the universe to rush away from one another (the expansion of the universe). Evidence for the Big Bang theory includes the discovery of cosmic background radiation, a radiation that seems to come equally from all directions. Cosmic background radiation has the characteristics expected if the universe resulted from a small, dense region exploding.

Binary stars   Almost half the stars in the visible universe are actually pairs of stars that orbit each other. Astronomers can sometimes see both stars, but more commonly they recognize that a star is part of a binary because of the influence of the dimmer star's gravitational pull on the other star.

Black holes   When a body becomes so dense for its size that not even light can escape the powerful gravitational pull it exerts, it is called a black hole. Black holes were predicted as early as 1784 (by John Michell) and invoked later by various astronomers and physicists to explain many strange astronomical phenomena. Black holes have been observed at the center of many galaxies, including our own Milky Way. Several smaller black holes, thought to be remains of supernova explosions, have also been located.

Brown dwarfs   are bodies too small to be stars, but too large to be planets. They glow dimly as a result of energy released by gravitational contraction. A brown dwarf must be between 10 and 80 times the size of Jupiter. The first brown dwarf to be definitely established orbits the star Gliese 229. Although about 50 times Jupiter's mass, its diameter is about the same as Jupiter's. Since then, a number of brown dwarfs have been located, including some not in orbit about other stars.

Clusters of stars   Stars often form together, forming associations of hundreds or thousands or clusters of millions of stars. Open clusters, such as the Pleiades (Seven Sisters), contain several hundred to a thousand stars gathered in an irregular region perhaps tens of light years across. There are about a thousand open clusters in the Milky Way Galaxy. Globular clusters contain millions of stars, most very old, that have formed into a sphere a 100 to 200 light-years in diameter. There are about 125 known globular clusters associated with the Milky Way.

Dwarfs   Dwarfs are small stars—the brightest are blue dwarfs, the dimmest red dwarfs. The Sun is a yellow dwarf; there are also white and brown dwarfs.

Expanding universe   When Albert Einstein developed his general theory of relativity, he found it predicted that the universe would either expand as if it were exploding, or else collapse. He tried to correct this prediction by inserting a term in his equations to counteract the prediction, but in the 1920s, Edwin Hubble discovered that the universe actually is expanding. It is easier to measure the speed of recession than the distance, so astronomers commonly use the speed at which something is moving away as the measure of its distance from us. Of course, it is not just moving away from us. In the expanding universe, everything is moving away from everything else.

Galaxies   are systems of very many stars separated from one another by largely empty space (sometimes galaxies are called island universes). In the 18th century, William Herschel concluded that many cloudy patches of light seen among the stars were actually giant systems of billions of stars, but so far away from Earth as to look like clouds. Better telescopes proved him right in the early 20th century, and these far-off, great masses of stars became known as galaxies, after our own Milky Way, the galaxy that includes the Sun. Observation with large telescopes in the 20th century has revealed two main types of galaxies—spiral and elliptical—although some galaxies are neither (irregular).

Milky Way   This is the galaxy to which the Sun and Earth belong; it contains about 100 billion stars. If you are in a place unafflicted with much light pollution, when you look at the night sky, you can see a faint band crossing it. The ancient

Greeks named this the Milky Way (galaxy in Greek). Early in the 19th century, William Herschel determined that our Sun was a star in a vast lens-shaped star system, and that the Milky Way was the part of the star system we see from our vantage point inside it. Today, recognizing there are very many other such star systems, scientists often call it the Milky Way galaxy.

Missing mass   is matter that is apparently in the universe but that has not been observed. Astronomers note that galaxies are rotating as if they were embedded in larger, invisible bodies. Furthermore, there are theoretical reasons to believe there is even more matter in the universe than can be accounted for by the invisible matter surrounding galaxies. Ideas as to what this "missing mass" might be include everything from brown dwarfs to undiscovered subatomic particles.

Nebulae   are patches of gas and dust observable in telescopes. Before Herschel discovered that some cloudy patches seen through telescopes were vast collections of stars, all such patches were called nebulae (meaning clouds). Some "clouds" turned out to be galaxies, but many did not. The patches of gas emit light, often by the same mechanism that a fluorescent light does; energy from stars ionizes the gas, which gives off visible light. Some patches of dust also glow, usually reflecting the light of nearby stars. Other patches of dust are opaque or nearly so, blocking out part of the sky. Some of the most striking nebulae consist of glowing gas surrounded by opaque dust or vice versa, which gives the nebula a definite shape, such as the North America Nebula (shaped like the continent of North America) or the Horsehead Nebula (which looks like a black horse's head against a glowing background). Herschel also studied a class of nebulae that looked to be giant spheres. He correctly concluded that these planetary nebulae were balls of gas produced when a star exploded.

Neutron stars   are stars that have collapsed in a violent explosion, such as a supernova, so that the force keeping electrons apart is overcome. All the neutrons and protons can touch, forming the equivalent of a giant atomic nucleus. The star is electrically neutral because of the charge of the collapsed electrons. Such a star may be only a dozen miles in diameter but may have a mass twice that of the Sun.

Novae   are stars that seem to appear out of nowhere. Later, they disappear. Early peoples were surprised from time to time by the appearance of a new (nova) star in the sky. Ancient Chinese astronomers called them guest stars. It is now clear that a truly new star does not appear; instead, a dim, existing star suddenly brightens. In early days, before the telescope, the dim stars could not be seen at all, so it looked as if a star came from nowhere. Today we know that there are two different types of "guest stars," and we reserve the name nova for one type and call the other a supernova (see below). The type referred to today as novae are less bright than supernovae and may appear more than once. It is thought that they occur when material from one star in a binary pair falls on the other star, causing it suddenly to flare up.

Pulsars   are neutron stars that emit electromagnetic signals from their magnetic poles in a direction that reaches Earth. All neutron stars emit signals and rotate very rapidly (at least when they are first formed; they gradually slow down). These signals form a tight beam. If the beam intersects Earth, a radio telescope observes a fast pulsing on and off. The pulses are so regular that when they were first discovered, they were thought to be the work of extraterrestrial beings.

Quasars   are distant sources of great energy. The name quasar is short for Quasi-Stellar Object, and the objects are so called because they seem to be about the size and general appearance of stars, but produce far too much energy to be stars. No one knows for sure what they are, but there is some evidence that quasars are caused by black holes in the central part of distant galaxies. The stars in the galaxies cannot be seen because of the great distance, so we see only the central part, which is the quasar.

Red giants   are stars that have used their hydrogen fuel and expanded as a result. Young stars "burn" hydrogen in a nuclear fusion process that leads to helium. When a star has consumed the hydrogen in its core, new fusion reactions that start with helium begin, leading to carbon. The new reactions are hotter than the fusion of hydrogen to helium. This added energy causes the hydrogen and helium outside the core to expand. The star is red because the outer layers are relatively cool. When the Sun becomes a red giant in

the distant future, it will expand almost to the orbit of Earth, completely engulfing Mercury and Venus, and charring Earth to a cinder.

Stars   are bodies of gas large enough to undergo fusion reactions in their core. As a result of the energy produced by fusion, stars emit visible light, as well as electromagnetic radiation at other wavelengths. The Sun is a star. The hotter or larger a star is, the brighter it is.

Superclusters and clusters of galaxies are groups of galaxies associated in space. There may be just a few members of a cluster or as many as thousands. About two dozen galaxies near us form, with the Milky Way, our Local Group. The members of the Local Group also include the Andromeda galaxy and the Large and Small Magellanic Clouds. All are traveling through the universe together. The Local Group is a member of a supercluster of galaxies, called the Local Supercluster, that contains about 100 clusters. Clusters and superclusters are recognized because the average distance within a cluster or a supercluster from one galaxy or cluster to another is much less than the distance to other galaxies or clusters.

Supernovae   are explosions of large stars. A supernova explosion is much more dramatic than the brightening of a nova. A supernova reported by Chinese astronomers from A.D. 1054 was visible in the daytime. The remnants of this explosion are known today as the Crab Nebula. At its heart

Optical Telescopes

Telescopes were first developed in Holland about 400 years ago. The first telescopes used lenses to gather light and focus it. Later in the 17th century, scientists realized that curved mirrors could also gather and focus light. Since the light did not need to pass through the mirror (as light passes through a lens), mirrors proved to be more efficient than lenses for large telescopes.

Year	Type	Importance
1608	Lens	Hans Lippershey (Dutch: d. ca. 1916) applies for first patent on a telescope
1609	Lens	Galileo builds first astronomical telescopes, eventually reaching 30 power (or 30X enlargement)
1611	Lens	Johannes Kepler introduces convex eyepiece, producing greater power
1663	Mirror	James Gregory (Scottish: 1638-1676) is first to think that reflecting telescope can be made
1668	Mirror	Isaac Newton builds first telescope to use mirror to collect light, rather than lens
1723	Mirror	John Hadley (English: 1682-1744) invents reflecting telescope based on parabola, which concentrates light at a point
1789	Mirror	William Herschel builds telescope with 48-in. (122-cm) mirror, largest for many years
1895	Lens	Alvan Clark (American: 1832-1897) builds what is still world's largest telescope to use lens instead of mirror, 40 in. (102 cm)
1917	Mirror	Hooker Telescope at Mount Wilson in California is put into operation; at the time, it was world's largest (100 in., or 2.5 m)
1930	Combination	Bernard Schmidt (Estonian–German: 1879-1935) makes first telescopes combining lenses and mirrors; they become workhorse of astronomy
1948	Mirror	Hale Telescope (200 in., or 5 m) on Mt. Palomar, Calif., becomes largest and best on Earth
1962	Mirror	Largest telescope devoted to observing the Sun is erected at Kitt Peak in Arizona
1990	Mirror	Hubble Space Telescope (94 in., or 2.4 m) becomes first optical telescope in space
1993	Mirrors	Keck I Telescope in Hawaii uses world's largest mirror, 394 in. (10-m) in diameter; joined on May 8, 1996, with identical Keck II Telescope, both on Mauna Kea volcano
1999	Mirror	Japan's Subaru telescope begins operations on Mauna Kea; its 338-in (8.3m) mirror is the world's largest made from a single piece of glass
1999	Mirror	Gemini North is a 319-in (8.0 m) telescope on Mauna Kea, built by a seven-member consortium including the U.S. It was joined by its twin, Gemini South, in Chile, in 2000.
1999	Mirror	The Hobby-Eberly Telescope, dedicated primarily to spectroscopy, begins operation in October. It has the world's largest primary mirror—433 inches (11 m)—but is considered the world's third largest telescope (after the two Kecks), because only 362 inches (9.2 m) of its surface is available for use at any one time
2000	Mirror	All four 323 in. (8.2m) mirrors of the The Very Large Telescope (VLT) of the European Southern Observatory (ESO) in Chile are in operation

the Crab Nebula has a pulsar, all that is left of the star that exploded.

Variable stars Any star that periodically changes brightness is called a variable (a nova changes brightness but not at regular intervals). The period varies with the cause of the change and the individual star. Some variables are part of a binary system in which one star periodically passes in front of the other. Other kinds of variables are called Mira variables and Cepheid vari-

ables, after the first stars known of each type. It is not clear what causes the brightness to vary.

White dwarfs are stars whose cores have collapsed until all the atoms are pressed very close together. A single teaspoonful of the matter in a white dwarf weighs about five tons. The core collapses because a red giant has used all its helium for fuel, but the star is too small to start burning carbon.

Radio Telescopes

Before 1931, all telescopes were optical, i.e. they gathered and focused electromagnetic radiation in the range people can sense with their eyes. Stars, planets, and other objects in the universe also produce other wavelengths of radiation, however. A radio telescope gathers and focuses radiation at long wavelengths, the same kind of electromagnetic radiation used for transmission of radio signals. Several radio telescopes working together produce sharper images.

Year	Type	Importance
1931	Ordinary antenna	Karl Jansky accidentally discovers, in trying to track down sources of static, that radio waves are coming from space
1937	Parabolic dish	Grote Reber (American: 1911–) builds first intentional radio telescope dish, Wheaton Ill.
1957	Steerable dish	Parabolic dish (250 ft. or 75 m) at Jodrell Bank in England is first major radio telescope
1962	Steerable dish	Dish (300 ft., or 90 m) at Green Bank, W.Va., first used to search for extraterrestrial life; it collapsed on Nov. 15, 1988
1963	Fixed dish	Largest fixed-dish radio telescope, 1,000 ft. (305 m) across, is built in valley at Arecibo, Puerto Rico
1970	Steerable dish	World's largest steerable dish, at Effelsberg, Germany, is 328 ft. (100 m) in diameter
1977	Several antennae	First Very Long Baseline Interferometry telescope begins operating at Cal Tech's Owens Valley Radio Observatory
1980	27 antennae	Very Large Array (VLA) is built in 13-mi. (21 km) Y shape near Socorro, New Mexico
1993	10 antennae	Very Long Baseline Array (VLBA) uses techniques that produce a resolution 500 times better than the best optical telescopes
1995	30 antennae	The Giant Meterwave Radio Telescope north of Pune, India, contains 30 parabolic 45-m (148-ft) antennae arranged in a 25-km (15-mi.) Y
2000	Steerable dish	The rebuilt Green Bank Telescope, often called "the 100-meter GBT" is, at 328 feet (100 m) by 361 feet (110 m), the worlds' largest fully steerable dish

Major Accomplishments of Satellites and Space Probes, 1957–2001

While much attention is focused on human beings in space, most of the serious scientific progress has been made by satellites or probes—the general name for space vehicles that neither carry humans nor orbit Earth—that are directed internally or from Earth.

10/4/57 *Sputnik 1* First satellite to orbit Earth (USSR).
11/3/57 *Sputnik 2* Carries Laika, first dog in space; burns in atmosphere 4/14/58.
1/31/58 *Explorer 1* First satellite to detect Van Allen radiation belts; first U.S. satellite.
3/17/58 *Vanguard* Demonstrates Earth is pear-shaped with a bulge in Southern Hemisphere (U.S.).
1/2/59 *Mechta* First space probe to go into orbit around Sun, passing 5,000 mi. from Moon (at which it was aimed) (USSR).
3/3/59 *Pioneer 4* First American probe aimed at Moon; like Mechta it misses and goes into orbit about Sun.
9/12/59 *Lunik 2* First space probe to reach Moon, where it crash-lands (USSR).
10/4/59 *Lunik 3* First space probe to return photographs of far side of Moon (USSR).
4/1/60 *Tiros 1* First weather satellite (U.S.).

6/22/60 *Transit 1-B* First navigational satellite (U.S.).
8/12/60 *Echo 1* First communications satellite—actually a large balloon off which radio signals could be bounced (U.S.).
8/18/60 *Corona* First U.S. spy satellite.
8/19/60 *Sputnik 5* Carries dogs Belka and Streika. Successfully returns them to Earth; 18 orbits.
12/12/61 *Venera 1* First space probe intended to reach another planet—Venus (USSR).
3/7/62 *OSO 1* Orbiting Solar Observatory—first major astronomical satellite (U.S.).
4/23/62 *Ranger 4* First U.S. space probe to reach Moon.
4/26/62 *Cosmos 4* First Soviet spy satellite.
7/10/62 *Telstar* First active communications satellite, allowing direct television between Europe and U.S. (U.S.).
8/27/62 *Mariner 2* First space probe to reach vicinity of another planet (Venus) and return scientific information (U.S.).

11/1/62 *Mars 1* First space probe aimed at Mars; contact lost about 66 million mi. from Earth (USSR).

6/26/63 *Syncom 2* First communications satellite to go into synchronous orbit with Earth (U.S.).

7/28/64 *Ranger 7* Returns close-up photographs of Moon, then crashes into it (U.S.).

8/28/64 *Nimbus 1* First weather satellite to be stabilized so that its cameras always point toward Earth (U.S.).

11/28/64 *Mariner 4* Flies by Mars and takes 21 pictures of its surface, successfully transmitting them back to Earth; its closest approach is 6,118 mi. (U.S.).

4/6/65 *Early Bird* First commercial satellite (U.S.).

7/16/65 *Proton 1* At 26,896 lbs., it is largest Earth satellite to this date (USSR).

11/16/65 *Venera 3* Crash-lands on Venus; first space probe to make physical contact with another planet; radio contact lost before it reaches immediate vicinity of planet (USSR).

11/26/65 *A-1* First satellite to be launched by nation other than the USSR or U.S. (France).

12/16/65 *Pioneer 6* Launched into solar orbit; still partially functions today (U.S.).

1/31/66 *Luna 9* Although main vehicle crash-lands, ejected capsule lands safely on Moon and transmits photographs to Earth (USSR).

5/30/66 *Surveyor 1* First soft landing of complete vehicle on Moon (U.S.).

3/31/66 *Luna 10* First space vehicle to go into orbit about Moon (USSR).

8/10/66 *Lunar Orbiter 1* First American space vehicle to go into orbit about Moon.

9/15/68 *Zond 5* First Soviet satellite to return to Earth from vicinity of Moon.

2/11/70 *Ohsumi* First satellite launched by Japan.

4/24/70 *Mao 1* First Chinese satellite; it broadcasts song "The East Is Red" once a minute, pausing at the end for other signals.

8/17/70 *Venera 7* First Venus probe to return signals from planet's surface (USSR).

9/12/70 *Luna 16* First space probe to land on Moon without humans aboard, scoop up samples, and return them to Earth (USSR).

11/10/70 *Luna 17* Carries roving vehicle to Moon's surface; vehicle roams for 2 weeks at a time (during daylight), then "sleeps"; as it roams, it returns photos and other data to Earth (USSR).

12/12/70 *Uhuru* First X-ray satellite telescope (U.S.).

5/28/71 *Mars 3* First space probe to soft-land on Mars; it quickly ceases functioning (USSR).

5/30/71 *Mariner 9* First space probe to orbit another planet (Mars); returns 7,329 photographs of planet (U.S.).

3/2/72 *Pioneer 10* First space probe to study Jupiter and, on June 13, 1983, first to leave solar system (U.S.); contact still maintained as of April 28, 2001.

7/23/72 *Landsat 1* First Earth resources satellite (U.S.).

3/6/73 *Pioneer 11* First space probe to reach vicinity of Saturn (U.S.).

11/3/73 *Mariner 10* First space probe to observe 2 planets, Venus and Mercury, and only probe ever to observe Mercury (U.S.).

12/10/74 *Helios* First W. German space probe.

6/8/75 *Venera 9* Returns first photographs from surface of Venus (USSR).

8/20/75 *Viking 1* First American space probe to soft-land on Mars; returns data until Nov., 1982.

9/20/75 *Viking 2* Successfully soft-lands on Mars (U.S.).

8/20/77 *Voyager 2* After studying Jupiter and Saturn, it becomes first space probe to reach vicinities of Uranus and Neptune (U.S.).

9/5/77 *Voyager 1* After studying Jupiter, it becomes first space probe to reach vicinity of Saturn. Becomes furthest space probe from Sun on Feb. 17, 1998; by 2001 is more than 7 billion miles (12 billion km) from Earth (U.S.).

1/26/78 *IUE* International Ultraviolet Explorer— the first astronomical satellite to be placed in geosynchronous orbit; it sends back data until 1996 (European Space Agency, or ESA, U.S., and Britain).

5/20/78 *Pioneer 12 (Venus 1)* First space probe to go into orbit about Venus. (U.S.).

6/26/78 *Seasat* Analyzes ocean currents and ice flow (U.S.).

8/12/78 *ISEE-3* Originally the third International Sun-Earth Explorer. Renamed International Cometary Explorer when it is redirected to study tail of comet Giacobini-Zinner in 1983 (U.S.).

12/13/78 *HEAO-2* High-Energy Astronomy Observatory, also known as the Einstein Observatory— it makes high-resolution X-ray images of the universe (U.S.).

2/24/79 *P78-1* Studies solar radiation until purposely shot down by U.S. Air Force 9/13/85.

2/14/80 *Solar Max* Studies solar radiation; after failure in Nov. 1980, it is repaired and relaunched from space shuttle in April 1984; finally plunged to its destruction by massive solar flare, 12/2/89 (U.S.).

1/25/83 *IRAS* Infrared Astronomical Satellite studies galactic and extragalactic infrared sources and discovers new planets forming (U.S.).

12/15/84 *Vega 1* First Soviet mission to study Halley's comet; along the way it drops balloon probe into atmosphere of Venus.

12/21/84 *Vega 2* Second Soviet mission to Halley's comet; releases a balloon probe at Venus.

1/7/85 *Sakigake* First Japanese mission to study Halley's comet (this one from far away).

7/2/85 *Giotto* Joint European mission to Halley's comet; passes closest to the comet—375 mi. (600 km)—and later is redirected to comet Grigg-Skjellerup, which it passes 7/10/92 at a distance of 125 mi. (200 km).

8/18/85 *Suisei* Japanese mission to Halley's comet.

2/21/86 *SPOT* French satellite; photographs surface details of Earth as small as 30 ft. across.

5/4/89 *Magellan* American probe orbits Venus and maps it in detail with radar.

10/18/89 *Galileo* After passing near Venus and Earth (twice), it is now in orbit around Jupiter, reporting on Jupiter's moons; dropped probe into Jupiter's atmosphere on 12/7/95 (U.S.).

11/18/89 *Cosmic Background Explorer (COBE)* Studied cosmic background radiation in hopes of learning cause of galaxy formation.

4/24/90 *Hubble Space Telescope* Flawed optical telescope placed in orbit about Earth by U.S.; successfully repaired 12/10/93.

10/6/90 *Ulysses* Studying previously unobserved north and south poles of the Sun (U.S.-ESA).

4/5/91 *Compton Gamma Ray Observatory* A 17-ton telescope that observed the universe at very short wavelengths until June 4, 2000.

8/31/91 *Yohkoh* Japanese satellite that reports on X-rays and gamma rays from the Sun.

6/7/92 *Extreme Ultraviolet Explorer (EUVA)* American satellite studies high range of ultraviolet radiation in universe.

7/3/92 *Solar Anomalous and Magnetospheric Particle Explorer (SAMPEX)* American satellite that reports on particles in space, including space dust and the solar wind.

7/24/92 *Geotail* Japanese satellite launched by NASA to study Earth's magnetosphere.

10/6/92 *Freja* A Swedish satellite launched by a Chinese rocket from the Gobi Desert, Freja carries experiments from the U.S., Sweden, Canada, France, and Germany; The U.S. experiment measures Earth's magnetosphere.

2/9/93 *Pegasus 3* Brazilian satellite to monitor environment in Amazonia, launched by Orbital Sciences Corp. of Fairfax, Va.

2/20/93 *ASCA* Japanese X-ray telescope.

1/25/94 *Clementine* Joint U.S. military-science mission; maps the moon from lunar orbit and later visits the asteroid Geographos.

11/1/94 *WIND* Goes into a figure-8 orbit around the Earth and Moon at first, studying the solar wind; in 1996, moved to a point in Earth's orbit and orbits the Sun itself, staying in the same relation to the Earth as it revolves, a million miles from Earth.

3/18/95 *Infrared Telescope in Space (IRTS)* Japan's infrared space telescope surveyed 7 percent of the sky over a period of 28 days.

11/17/95 *Infrared Space Observatory (ISO)* A European Space Agency satellite that extends the work of the earlier IRAS. Nicknamed "Europe's Hubble" (ESA).

12/2/95 *Solar and Heliospheric Observatory (SOHO)* Studies the sun from an orbit of about 930,000 miles (1.5 million km) from Earth (ESA/U.S.).

12/30/95 *Rossi X-Ray Timing Explorer (XTE)* First U.S. X-ray telescope since 1978; studies X-ray sources in Milky Way including stars, pulsars, and possible black holes.

2/17/96 *Shoemaker Near Earth Asteroid Rendezvous (NEAR-Shoemaker)* First of the new, less-expensive Discovery series of space probes. It passes close to asteroid 253 Mathilde in June 1999. *NEAR* orbits asteroid 433 Eros starting in February 2000, and lands on asteroid on February 12, 2001 (U.S.).

2/24/96 *Polar* Like WIND, Polar is reporting on the interaction of the solar wind and Earth's magnetic field, concentrating especially on the poles. It can take UV images of Earth's auroras and X-ray images of high-speed electrons in the solar wind (U.S.).

4/30/96 *BeppoSAX (Satellite per Astronimica a Raggi X)* This small orbiting observatory studies X-ray-emitting events from outer space. It scores a major triumph when it pinpoints the location of a gamma-ray burster for the first time, showing that these events are the most powerful explosions known (Italy/Netherlands/ESA).

8/21/96 *FAST (Fast Auroral Snapshot)* Smaller, cheaper satellite of the Small-Class Explorer series studies auroras from low-Earth orbit (U.S.).

11/7/96 *Mars Global Surveyor* A probe to Mars orbits the planet and surveys it from space for one Mars year (687 Earth days) starting in March, 1999, after delays caused by a defective solar panel. (U.S.).

12/4/96 *Mars Pathfinder* This probe bounces to the surface of Mars in the Ares Vallis region on 7/4/97, where it releases a rover named *Sojourner* to travel the surface during the day and report on Martian geology. (U.S.).

12/24/96 *Bion 11* Life sciences study involving two monkeys that orbit Earth and then are returned; one monkey dies after successful return (Russia).

2/12/97 *HALKA (VSOP)* A radio observatory that adds a space component to radio telescopes on Earth, creating the Very Long Baseline Space Observatory for high-resolution astronomy (Japan).

4/21/97 *Celestis 1* Burials in space; small satellite contains some ashes of 24 individuals, notably Gene Roddenberry, creator of *Star Trek;* Gerard K. O'Neill, advocate of living in space; and Timothy Leary, LSD guru of the 1960s (U.S.).

8/25/97 *Advanced Composition Explorer (ACE)* Studies solar wind and particles from interstellar space (cosmic rays) as it orbits a stable point where the gravity from the Earth and Sun are in balance (U.S.).

10/15/97 *Cassini-Huygens* Mission to orbit Saturn and study its satellites; *Cassini* is the orbiter that will reach Saturn in July 2004 while *Huygens* is a probe into Saturn's atmosphere (U.S./ESA).

11/27/97 *TRMM (Tropical Rainfall Measuring Mission)* An Earth-observing satellite that uses microwave radar, visible light, and infrared light to investigate how El Niño is affecting precipitation in tropical and subtropical latitudes (U.S./Japan).

12/2/97 *Equator-S* A satellite orbiting the equatorial plane that studies Earth's magnetic field (Germany).

1/6/98 *Lunar Prospector* Confirms presence of water at the Moon's poles (U.S.).

2/26/98 *Student Nitric Oxide Explorer (SNOE)* Measures the effects of solar energy and Earth's magnetic field on nitric oxide in the upper atmosphere. (U.S.).

4/2/98 *Transition Regions and Coronal Explorer (TRACE)* Uses ultraviolet telescope to study magnetism in the Sun's corona from a polar orbit about Earth. (U.S.).

7/4/98 *Nozomi/Planet B Neutral Mass Spectrometer (NMS)* Planned orbit about Mars begins October 1999; the satellite will study the Martian atmosphere and its interaction with the solar wind.

10/24/98 *Deep Space 1* Tests new technologies for space use including ion-propulsion system. (U.S.).

12/4/98 *SAC-A* Experiments in space with digital global positioning, a space camera, magnetosphere measurements, and whale tracking. (Argentina).

12/5/98 *Submillimeter Wave Astronomy Satellite (SWAS)* Space-based radio telescopes analyze microwaves to study chemical composition of interstellar gas clouds, the homes of new star formation. (U.S.).

2/7/99 *Stardust* The first mission to return materials from a comet, Stardust is due to reach comet Wild 2 in January 2004, gather samples there (as well as interstellar dust samples along the way), and parachute them back to Earth in 2006. (U.S.).

2/23/99 *Ørsted* Making a high-precision map of Earth's magnetic field (Denmark).

6/24/99 *Far Ultraviolet Spectroscopic Explorer (FUSE)* Exploring the universe at wavelengths slightly longer than X-rays, FUSE fills a significant gap in coverage of the electromagnetic spectrum (U.S./Canada/France).

7/23/99 *Chandra X-Ray Observatory* Its X-ray telescopes reveal previously unknown details of black holes, white dwarfs, neutron stars, and the X-ray background radiation. (U.S.).

12/10/99 *X-Ray Multi-Mirror Telescope (XXM-Newton)* The most powerful X-ray detector ever, XXM-Newton has 3 X-ray telescopes using 58 mirrors each as well as 2 X-ray spectrographs and an optical telescope. Its orbit takes it 1/3 the way to the Moon, giving it long periods for observation of active stars, galaxies, and black holes (ESA).

3/25/2000 *Imager for Magnetopause-to-Aurora Global Exploration (IMAGE)* The first satellite mission dedicated to imaging the Earth's magnetosphere, the region of space controlled by the Earth's magnetic field and containing extremely tenuous plasmas of both solar and terrestrial origin. (U.S.).

7/12/00 and **8/9/00** *Cluster II* Four spacecraft that maintain positions as the vertices of a pyramid as they orbit Earth in formation and study the interactions of Earth with the solar wind. (ESA).

10/9/00 *High Energy Transient Explorer (HETE II)* Observes, reports, and locates gamma-ray bursts for follow up by astronomers and surveys X-ray sources across the universe. (U.S., France, Japan, Italy).

4/7/01 *Mars Odyssey* Expected to enter Mars orbit on October 24, 2001; it will search for water using instruments that recognize certain minerals and that detect hydrogen and also study the amount of radiation present; it will also be a communication relay for other Mars probes. (U.S.)

6/30/01 *Microwave Anisotropy Probe (MAP)* Mission to measure temperature fluctuations in the cosmic microwave background; will go into solar orbit at the L2 Lagrange point, keeping 1 million miles (1.6 million km) from Earth. Data will help us understand how and when galaxies formed. (U.S.)

8/8/01 *Genesis* A mission designed to spend three years in solar orbit, collecting particles from the solar wind, and then returning the material to Earth. (U.S.)

Spaceflights Carrying People, 1961–2001

The space programs of the former Soviet Union and the United States both had dramatic flights by human pilots as an important component, although many scientists felt that most goals of the space program could be achieved without risking lives. The *Vostok, Voskhod,* and *Soyuz* missions were part of the Soviet program; *Mercury, Gemini, Apollo, Skylab,* and the shuttle are part of the U.S. program.

Proving that People Can Venture into Space

4/12/61 *Vostok 1* (1 hr. 48 min.) Yuri A. Gagarin, First spaceflight by human.

5/5/61 *Mercury 3* (15 min.) Alan B. Shepard Jr. Suborbital.

7/21/61 *Mercury 4* (16 min.) Virgil "Gus" Grissom. Suborbital.

8/6/61 *Vostok 2* (25 hrs. 18 min.) Gherman S. Titov. First multiorbit flight; 17 orbits.

2/20/62 *Mercury 6* (5 hrs. 55 min.) John H. Glenn. First orbital flight by American; 3 orbits.

5/24/62 *Mercury 7* (4 hrs. 56 min.) M. Scott Carpenter. 3 orbits.

8/11/62 *Vostok 3* (94 hrs. 24 min.) Andrian G. Nikolayev. 64 orbits; landing by parachute.

8/12/62 *Vostok 4* (70 hrs. 57 min.) Pavel R. Popovitch. Dual launch with *Vostok 3;* 48 orbits.

10/3/62 *Mercury 8* (9 hrs. 13 min.) Walter Schirra. 6 orbits.

5/15/63 *Mercury 9* (34 hrs. 20 min.) Gordon Cooper. 22 orbits.

6/14/63 *Vostok 5* (119 hrs. 6 min.) V. Bikovsky. 81 orbits.

6/16/63 *Vostok 6* (70 hrs. 50 min.) Valentina V. Tereshkova. First woman cosmonaut; 48 orbits; dual launch with *Vostok 5.*

10/12/64 *Voskhod 1* (24 hrs. 17 min.) Vladimir M. Komarov, Konstantin P. Feoktistov, Boris B. Yegorov. First multihuman crew; 3 cosmonauts make 16 orbits.

Planning for Operations in Space

3/18/65 *Voskhod 2* (26 hrs.) A. Leonov, P. Belyayev. First extravehicular activity (EVA) by Leonov (20 min.); 17 orbits.

3/23/65 *Gemini 3* (4 hrs. 53 min.) Virgil "Gus" Grissom, John Young. First American multi-person crew; 3 orbits.

6/3/65 *Gemini 4* (97 hrs. 56 min.) James McDivitt, Edward White II. 62 orbits; first American EVA; first use of personal propulsion unit.

8/21/65 *Gemini 5* (190 hrs. 56 min.) Gordon Cooper, Charles Conrad 120 orbits; demonstrates feasibility of lunar mission; simulated rendezvous.

12/4/65 *Gemini 7* (330 hrs. 35 min.) Frank Borman, James Lovell. 206 orbits; extensions of testing and performance; target for first rendezvous.

12/16/65 *Gemini 6A* (25 hrs. 51 min.) Walter Schirra, Thomas Stafford. 15 orbits; rendezvous with *Gemini 7.*

3/16/66 *Gemini 8* (10 hrs. 42 min.) Neil Armstrong, David Scott. 6.5 orbits; first dual launch and docking; first Pacific landing.

6/3/66 *Gemini 9A* (72 hrs. 21 min. Thomas Stafford, Eugene Cernan. 44 orbits; unable to dock with target vehicle; 2 hrs. 7 min. of EVA.

7/18/66 *Gemini 10* (70 hrs. 47 min.) John Young, Michael Collins. 43 orbits; first dual rendezvous; docking maneuvers, umbilical EVA.

9/12/66 *Gemini 11* (71 hrs. 17 min.) Charles Conrad Jr., Richard Gordon Jr. 44 orbits; rendezvous and docking.

11/11/66 *Gemini 12* (94 hrs. 34 min.) James Lovell, Edwin "Buzz" Aldrin Jr. 59 orbits; final *Gemini* mission; 5 hours of EVA.

To the Moon and Beyond

4/23/67 *Soyuz 1* (26 hrs. 48 min.) Vladimir M. Komarov, 18 orbits; Komarov is killed when parachute fails; first fatality of space program.

10/11/68 *Apollo 7* (260 hrs. 8 min.) Walter Schirra, Donn Eisele, Walter Cunningham. 8 service propulsion firings; 7 live TV sessions with crew; rendezvous with S-IVB stage performed.

10/26/68 *Soyuz 3* (94 hrs. 51 min.) G. Beregovoi. 64 orbits; approaches unpiloted *Soyuz 2* to distance of 650 ft. (198 m).

12/21/68 *Apollo 8* (147 hrs.) Frank Borman, James Lovell, William Anders. First *Saturn-V* propelled flight; first lunar orbital mission (10 orbits); returns lunar photography.

1/14/69 *Soyuz 4* (71 hrs. 14 min.) V. Shatalov, 48 orbits; docks with *Soyuz 5* in first linkup of 2 space vehicles both carrying people.

1/15/69 *Soyuz 5* (72 hrs. 46 min.) B. Volynov, A. Yeliseyev, Y. Khrunov. 3 cosmonauts perform EVA, transferred to *Soyuz 4* in rescue rehearsal.

3/3/69 *Apollo 9* (241 hrs. 1 min.) James McDivitt, David Scott, Russell Schweickart. First flight of all lunar hardware in Earth orbit, incl. lunar module.

5/18/69 *Apollo 10* (192 hrs. 3 min.) Eugene Cernan, John Young, Thomas Stafford. Lunar mission development flight to evaluate lunar module performance in lunar environment; descent to within 50,000 ft. of Moon.

7/16/69 *Apollo 11* (165 hrs. 18 min.) Neil Armstrong, Michael Collins, Edwin "Buzz" Aldrin Jr. First lunar landing (July 20); limited inspection, photography, evaluation, and sampling of lunar soil.

10/11/69 *Soyuz 6* (118 hrs. 42 min.) G. Shonin, V. Kubasov. First triple launch (with *Soyuz 7* and *8*).

10/12/69 *Soyuz 7* (118 hrs. 41 min.) A. Filipchenko, V. Volkov, V. Gorbatko. With *Soyuz 6* and *8*, conducts experiments in navigation and photography.

10/13/69 *Soyuz 8* (118 hrs. 59 min.) V. Shatalov, A. Yeliseyev. 80 orbits.

11/14/69 *Apollo 12* (244 hrs. 36 min.) Charles Conrad Jr., Richard Gordon Jr., Alan Bean. Second lunar landing; demonstrates point landing capability; samples more area.

4/11/70 *Apollo 13* (142 hrs. 55 min.) James Lovell Fred Haise Jr., John Swigert Jr. Third lunar landing attempt aborted owing to loss of pressure in liquid oxygen in service module and fuel cell failure.

6/2/70 *Soyuz 9* (424 hrs. 59 min. [17 days 16 hrs.]) A. Nikolayev, V. Sevastianov. Longest spaceflight to this time.

1/31/71 *Soyuz 10* (9 days 42 min.) Alan Shepard Stuart Roosa, Edgar Mitchell. Third lunar landing, returns 98 lbs. of material.

4/23/71 *Soyuz 10* (47 hrs. 46 min.) V. Shatalov, A. Yeleseyev, N. Rukavishnikov. Docks with *Salyut 1*, the first space station.

6/6/71 *Soyuz 11* (23 days 18 hrs. 22 min.) G. Dobrovolsky, V. Patsayev, V. Volkov. All 3 cosmonauts killed during reentry.

7/26/71 *Apollo 15* (12 days 7 hrs. 12 min.) David Scott, Alfred Worden, James Irwin. Fourth lunar landing; first to carry Lunar Roving Vehicle (LRV).

4/16/72 *Apollo 16* (11 days 14 hrs. 51 min.) John Young, Ken Mattingly, Charles Duke Jr. Fifth lunar landing; second to carry LRV. Returns 213 lbs. of material.

12/7/72 *Apollo 17* (12 days 13 hrs. 52 min.) Eugene Cernan, Ronald Evans, Harrison Schmitt. Last manned lunar landing; third with LRV; total EVA time: 44 hrs. 8 min.; returns 243 lbs. of material.

First Stations in Space

5/25/73 *Skylab 2* (28 days 49 min.) Charles. Conrad Jr., Joseph Kerwin, Paul Weitz. First *Skylab* launch; establishes *Skylab Orbital Assembly* in earth orbit; conducts medical and other experiments.

7/29/73 *Skylab 3* (59 days 11 hrs. 9 min.) Alan Bean, Owen Garriott, Jack Lousma. Second *Skylab*; crew performs systems and operational tests and thermal shield deployment.

9/27/73 *Soyuz 12* (47 hrs. 16 min.) V. Lazarev, O. Makarov. First Soviet spaceflight to carry humans since *Soyuz 11* tragedy.

11/16/73 *Skylab 4* (84 days 1 hr. 7 min.) Gerald P. Carr, Edward G. Gibson, William R. Pogue. Services unmanned Saturn workshop; obtains medical data for extending spaceflights.

12/18/73 *Soyuz 13* (7 days 20 hrs. 55 min.) P. Klimuk, V. Lebedev. Performs astrophysical and biological experiments.

7/3/74 *Soyuz 14* (15 days 17 hrs. 30 min.) P. Popovich, Y. Artyukhin. Crew occupies *Salyut 3* space station; studies Earth resources.

8/26/74 *Soyuz 15* (48 hrs. 12 min.) G. Sarafanov, L. Demin. Makes unsuccessful attempt to dock with *Salyut 3*.

12/2/74 *Soyuz 16* (5 days 22 hrs. 24 min.) A. Filipchenko, N. Rukavishnikov. Taken to check modifications to *Salyut* system.

1/10/75 *Soyuz 17* (29 days 13 hrs. 20 min.) A. Gubarev, G. Grechko. Docks with *Salyut 4*; sets Soviet endurance record.

4/5/75 *Soyuz · 18A* (22 min.) V. Lazarev, O. Makarov. Separation from booster fails, and craft fails to reach orbit, but crew successfully lands in western Siberia.

5/24/75 *Soyuz 18B* (63 days) P. Klimuk, V. Sevastyanov. Docks with *Salyut 4*.

7/15/75 *ASTP* (9 days 1 hr. 30 min.) Thomas Stafford, Vance Brand, Donald Slayton. *Apollo-Soyuz* Test Project, cooperative U.S.-Soviet mission.

7/15/75 *Soyuz 19* (5 days 23 hrs. 31 min.) A. Leonov, V. Kubasov. Docks with *ASTP*, the U.S. *Apollo* capsule.

The Soviet Study of Human Biology in Space

11/17/75 *Soyuz 20* (90 days) No crew. Biological mission; docks with *Salyut 4*.

7/6/76 *Soyuz 21* (49 days) B. Volynov, V. Zholobov. Docks with *Salyut 5* and performs Earth resource work.

9/15/76 *Soyuz 22* (8 days) V. Bykovsky, V. Aksenov. Takes Earth-resources photo-graphs.

10/14/76 *Soyuz 23* (2 days) V. Zudov, V. Rozhdestvensky. Unsuccessful attempt to dock with *Salyut 5*; first landing in water (unplanned) for Soviet program (crew survives).

2/7/77 *Soyuz 24* (7 days) V. Gorbatko, Y. Glazkov. Docks with *Salyut 5* for 18 days of experiments.

10/9/77 *Soyuz 25* (2 days) V. Kovalyonok, V. Ryumin. Unsuccessful attempt to dock with *Salyut 6*.

12/10/77 *Soyuz 26* (96 days) Y. Romanenko, G. Grechko. Docks with *Salyut 6*; crew sets endurance record.

1/10/78 *Soyuz 27* (6 days) V. Dzhanibekov, O. Makarov. Carries second crew to dock with *Salyut 6* space station.

3/2/78 *Soyuz 28* (8 days) V. Remek, A. Gubarev. Carries third crew to board *Salyut 6*; Remek first non-Russian, non-American in space (Czech).

6/15/78 *Soyuz 29* (140 days) V. Kovalyonok, A. Ivanchenkov. Docks with *Salyut 6*; crew sets new endurance record.

6/27/78 *Soyuz 30* (8 days) P. Klimuk, M. Hermaszewski. Carries second international crew to *Salyut 6*; first Polish cosmonaut, Hermaszewski.

8/25/78 *Soyuz 31* (8 days) V. Bykovsky, S. Jahn. Carries third international crew to *Salyut 6*; first East German, Jahn.

2/25/79 *Soyuz 32* (175 days) V. Lyakhov, V. Ryumin. Carries crew to *Salyut 6*; sets new endurance record.

4/10/79 *Soyuz 33* (2 days) N. Rukavishnikov, Georgi Ivanov. Engine failure prior to docking forces early termination; first Bulgarian, Ivanov.

6/6/79 *Soyuz 34* (74 days) No crew. Launches no crew; returns with crew from *Salyut 6*.

4/9/80 *Soyuz 35* (185 days) V. Ryumin, L. Popov. Carries 2 crew members to *Salyut 6*.

5/26/80 *Soyuz 36* (8 days) V. Kubasov, B. Farkas. Carries 2 crew members to *Salyut 6*; crew returns in *Soyuz 35*; first Hungarian, Farkas.

6/5/80 *Soyuz T-2* (4 days) Y. Malyshev, V. Aksenov. Test of modified *Soyuz* craft; docks with *Salyut 6*.

7/23/80 *Soyuz 37* (8 days) V. Gorbatko, P. Tuan. Exchanges cosmonauts in *Salyut 6*; returns *Soyuz 35* crew after 185 days in orbit; first Vietnamese in space, Tuan.

9/18/80 *Soyuz 38* (8 days) Y. Romanenko, A. Tamayo-Mendez. Ferries to *Salyut 6*; first Cuban in space, Tamayo-Mendez.

11/27/80 *Soyuz T-3* (13 days) L. Kizim, O. Makarov, G. Strekalov. Ferries to *Salyut 6*; first 3-person crew since *Soyuz 11*.

3/12/81 *Soyuz T-4* (75 days) V. Kovalyonok, V. Savinykh. Mission to *Salyut 6*.

3/22/81 *Soyuz 39* (8 days) V. Dzhanibekov, J. Gurragcha. Docks with *Salyut 6*; first Mongolian, Gurragcha.

The Space Shuttle: U.S. Reentry in Space

4/12/81 *Columbia* (2 days 6 hrs.) John Young, Robert Crippen. First flight of reusable space shuttle; first landing of U.S. spacecraft on land.

5/14/81 *Soyuz 40* (8 days) L. Popov, D. Prunariu. First Romanian (Prunariu), in space.

11/12/81 *Columbia* (2 days 6 hrs.) Joe Engle, Richard Truly. First reuse of space shuttle; ends early due to loss of fuel cell.

3/22/82 *Columbia* (8 days) Jack Lousma, Gordon Fullerton. Third shuttle flight; payload includes space science experiments.

5/13/82 *Soyuz T-5* (211 days) A. Berezovoy, V. Lebedev. First flight in *Salyut 7*; space station equipped to measure body functions.

6/24/82 *Soyuz T-6* (8 days) V. Dzhanibekov, J. Chrètien, A. Ivanchenkov. Mission to *Salyut 7*; Soviet/French team; first French cosmonaut, Chrétien.

6/27/82 *Columbia* (7 days 1 hr.) Ken. Mattingly Henry Hartsfield Jr. Fourth shuttle mission; first landing on hard surface.

8/16/82 *Soyuz T-7* (8 days) L. Popov, S. Savitskaya, A. Serebrov. Mission to *Salyut 7*; Svetlana Savitskaya, second Soviet woman in space.

11/11/82 *Columbia* (5 days 2 hrs.) Vance Brand, Robert Overmyer, Joseph Allen, William Lenoir. First operational mission; first 4-man crew; first deployment of satellites from shuttle.

4/4/83 *Challenger* (5 days) Paul Weitz, Karol Bobko, Donald Peterson, Story Musgrave. Second shuttle joins fleet; deploys TDRS tracking satellite; first shuttle EVA.

4/20/83 *Soyuz T-8* (48 hrs.) V. Titov, G. Strekalov, A. Serebrov. Planned rendezvous with *Salyut 7* fails.

6/18/83 *Challenger* (6 days) Robert Crippen, Frederick Hauck, John Fabian, Sally Ride, Norman Thagard. First 5-person crew; Ride is first U.S. woman in space; first use of Remote Manipulator Structure ("Arm") to deploy and retrieve satellite.

6/27/83 *Soyuz T-9* (150 days) V. Lyakhov, A. Aleksandrov. Crew spends 149 days in *Salyut 7* after *Soyuz 10* fails in relief mission.

8/30/83 *Challenger* (6 days) Richard Truly, Daniel Brandenstein, William Thornton, Guion Bluford, Dale Gardner. First night launch. Bluford is first black American in space. Launches weather/communications satellite for India.

11/28/83 *Columbia* (10 days) John Young, Brewster Shaw Robert Parker, Owen Garriott, Byron Lichtenberg, Ulf Merbold. Launches *Spacelab*; crew performs experiments in astronomy and medicine.

2/3/84 *Challenger* (8 days) Vance Brand, Bruce McCandless, Robert Stewart, Ronald McNair, Robert Gibson. Jet-propelled backpacks carry 2 astronauts on first untethered space walks; 2 satellites lost; first landing at Kennedy Space Center.

2/8/84 *Soyuz T-10B* (237 days) L. Kizim, O. Atkov, V. Solovyev. Mission to *Salyut 7* to repair propulsion system; sets new duration-in-space record for crew.

4/2/84 *Soyuz T-11* (8 days) Y. Malyshev, G. Strekalov, R. Sharma. Docks with *Salyut 7*; first Indian cosmonaut, Sharma.

4/6/84 *Challenger* (7 days) Robert Crippen, Richard Scobee, Terry Hart, George Nelson, James van Hoften. Deploys Long Duration Exposure Facility for experiments in space durability; snares Solar Max satellite; repairs altitude-control system.

7/18/84 *Soyuz T-12* (12 days) S. Savitskaya, V. Dzhanibekov, I. Volk. Savitskaya becomes first woman to walk in space.

8/30/84 *Discovery* (7 days) Henry Hartsfield Jr., Michael Coats, Steven Hawley, Judith Resnik, Richard Mullane, Charles Walker. Third shuttle in fleet; deploys 3 satellites and tests a solar sail.

10/5/84 *Challenger* (8 days) Robert Crippen, Jon McBride, Kathryn Sullivan, Sally Ride, Marc Garneau, David Leestma, Paul Scully-Power. First Canadian astronaut, Garneau; deploys Earth Radiation Budget Satellite and uses Sir-B radar system to see beneath surface of sand.

11/8/84 *Discovery* (8 days) Frederick Hauck, David Walker, Anna Fisher, Joseph Allen, Dale Gardner. Salvages two inoperative satellites.

1/24/85 *Discovery* (4 days) Ken Mattingly, Loren Schriver, James Buchli, Ellison Onizuka, Gary Payton. Secret military mission.

4/12/85 *Discovery* (7 days) Karol Bobko, Donald Williams, Jake Garn, Charles Walker, Jeffrey Hoffman, David Griggs, Margaret Rhea Seddon. First U.S. senator in space, Garn.

4/29/85 *Challenger* (7 days) Robert Overmyer, Frederick Gregory, Don Lind, Taylor Wang, Lodewijk van den Berg, Norman Thagard, William Thornton. Carries European Spacelab module.

6/6/85 *Soyuz T-13* (112 days) V. Dzhanibekov, V. Savinykh. Successful mission to repair damage to *Salyut 7*, which had suffered power failure.

6/17/85 *Discovery* (7 days) John Creighton, Shannon Lucid, Steven Nagel, Daniel Brandenstein, John Fabian, Prince Salman al-Saud, Patrick Baudry. First Arabian in space, al-Saud; successfully launches 4 satellites.

7/29/85 *Challenger* (8 days) Roy Bridges, Anthony England, Karl Henize, Story Musgrave, Gordon Fullerton, Loren Acton, John-David Bartoe. Carries *Spacelab* 2, a group of scientific experiments.

8/27/85 *Discovery* (7 days) John Lounge, James van Hoften, William Fisher, Joe Engle, Richard Covey. Repairs satellite Syncom 3.

9/17/85 *Soyuz T-14* (65 days) V. Vasyutin, A. Volkov, G. Grechko. Takes supplies to *Salyut 7*.

10/3/85 *Atlantis* (4 days) Karol Bobko, Ronald Grabe, David Hilmers, William Pailes, Robert Stewart. Fourth shuttle.

10/30/85 *Challenger* (7 days) Henry Hartsfield Jr., Steven Nagel, Bonnie Dunbar, Guion Bluford, Ernst Messerschmid, Reinhard Furrer, Wubbo Ockels. Carries Spacelab 1-D; scientific experiments conducted by Germans.

11/26/85 *Atlantis* (7 days) Brewster Shaw, Bryan O'Conner, Charles Walker, Rudolfo Neri Vela, Jerry L. Ross, Sherwood C. Spring, Mary Cleave. First Mexican in space, Vela.

1/12/86 *Columbia* (5 days) Robert Gibson, Charles Bolden Jr., George Nelson, Franklin Chang-Diaz, Steven Hawley, Robert Cenker. First U.S. congressman in space, Nelson.

1/28/86 *Challenger* (73 seconds) Richard Scobee, Michael Smith, Robert McNair, Ellison Onizuka, Judith Resnik, Gregory Jarvis, Christa McAuliffe. O-rings in solid-fuel boosters wear through, and fuel supply explodes, killing all 6 regular astronauts and schoolteacher McAuliffe.

The First Space Station (Soyuz flight durations N.A.)

2/20/86 *Mir* Soviet space station. No crew.

3/13/86 *Soyuz T-15* V. Solovyev, L. Kizim. First cosmonauts to board *Mir* space station.

2/6/87 *Soyuz TM-2* Y. Romanenko, A. Laveykin. Romanenko and Laveykin begin marathon tours in space.

7/21/87 *Soyuz TM-3* A. Alexandrov, A. Viktorenko, M. Faris. First Syrian in space, Faris.

12/21/87 *Soyuz TM-4* V. Titov, M. Manarov, A. Levchenko. Cosmonauts set new record of a year in space, mostly in *Mir* space station: 366 days.

6/7/88 *Soyuz TM-5* A. Alexandrov, V. Savinykh, A. Solovyev. First Bulgarian in space, Alexandrov.

8/29/88 *Soyuz TM-6* V. Lyakhov, V. Polyakov, A. Ahad. Ahad first Afghan in space; on 9/6/88 Lyakhov and Ahad are stranded as they attempt to return in *Soyuz TM-5*, but land safely on 9/7/88.

9/29/88 *Discovery* (4 days) John Lounge, David Hilmers, Frederick Hauck, George Nelson, Richard Covey. Redesigned shuttle makes first flight since the Challenger disaster.

11/26/88 *Soyuz TM-7* A. Volkov, S. Krikalev, J. Chrétien. *Mir* temporarily abandoned for first time.

12/2/88 *Atlantis* (4 days) Robert Gibson, Jerry Ross, William Shepherd, Guy Gardner, Richard Mullane. Secret military mission known to have deployed radar spy satellite.

3/13/89 *Discovery* (5 days) Michael Coats, John Blaha, James Buchli, James Bagian, Robert Springer. Deploys NASA's third relay satellite and tests thermal control system for proposed U.S. space station.

5/4/89 *Atlantis* (4 days) David Walker, Ronald Grabe, Mary Cleave, Norman Thagard, Mark Lee. Launches space probe *Magellan* on its way to map Venus with radar.

8/9/89 *Columbia* (5 days) Brewster Shaw, Richard Richards, David Leestma, James Adamson, Mark Brown. Secret military mission to launch spy satellite.

9/5/89 *Soyuz TM-8* A. Viktorenko, A. Serebrov. Reoccupies *Mir*.

10/18/89 *Atlantis* (5 days) Donald Williams, Michael McCulley, Shannon Lucid, Franklin Chang-Diaz, Ellen Baker. Launches *Galileo* probe.

11/22/89 *Discovery* (5 days) Frederick Gregory, John Blaha, Story Musgrave, Kathryn Thornton, Manley Lanier Carter Jr. Secret military mission.

1/9/90 *Columbia* (11 days) Daniel Brandenstein, Bonnie Dunbar, Marsha Ivens, David Low, James Wetherbee. Launches communication satellite Syncom IV and retrieves the *Long Duration Exposure Facility* (see 4/6/84).

2/11/90 *Soyuz TM-9* A. Solovyev, A. Balandin. Relieves Viktorenko and Serebrov. Solovyev and Balandin briefly locked out of *Mir* via faulty hatch.

2/28/90 *Atlantis* (4 days) John Creighton, John Caspar, David Hilmers, Richard Mullane, Pierre Thuot. Secret military mission.

4/24/90 *Discovery* (5 days) Loren Shriver, Charles Bolden Jr., Bruce McCandless, Steven Hawley, Kathryn Sullivan. Launches Hubble Space Telescope.

8/1/90 *Soyuz TM-10* G. Manakov, G. Strekalov. Replace Solovyev and Balandin.

10/6/90 *Discovery* (4 days) Richard Richards, Robert Cabana, Bruce Melnick, William Shepherd, Thomas Akers. Launches *Ulysses* space probe into solar orbit.

11/15/90 *Atlantis* (5 days) Richard Covey, Frank Culbertson Jr., Charles Gemar, Carl Meade, Robert Springer. NASA announces this as last secret military mission.

12/2/90 *Columbia* (9 days) Vance Brand, Guy Gardner, Jeffrey Hoffman, John Lounge, Robert Parker, Samuel Durrance, Ronald Parise. Carries 3 UV and 1 X-ray telescope.

12/2/90 *Soyuz TM-11* V. Afansev, M. Manarov, T. Akiyama. Journalist Akiyama, sponsored by Japanese corporations; others replace Manakov and Strekalov on *Mir*.

4/5/91 *Atlantis* (6 days) Steven Nagel, Kenneth Cameron, Linda Godwin, Jerry Ross, Jerome East. Launches 17-ton *Gamma Ray Observatory*; unscheduled spacewalk required to open satellite's antenna properly.

4/28/91 *Discovery* (8 days) Michael Coats, Blaine Hammond Jr., Gregory Harbaugh, Charles Lacy Veach, Guion Bluford Jr., Richard Hieb, Donald McMonagle. Tests detection devices and recovers Star Wars satellite.

5/18/91 *Soyuz TM-12* S. Krikalev, A. Artsebarsky, H. Sharman. Political problems in Soviet Union result in Krikalev's spending an unexpected 313 days in space; Sharman is first Briton in space; returns with Manarov and Afansev.

6/5/91 *Columbia* (9 days) Bryan D. O'Connor, Sidney M. Gutierrez, James P. Bagian, Margaret Rhea Seddon, Francis A. Gaffney, Millie Hughes-Fulford, Tamara E. Jernigan. Performs human and animal space-adaptation experiments.

8/21/91 *Atlantis* (9 days) John Blaha, Michael Baker, Shannon Lucid, David Low, James Adamson. Performs 22 experiments and launches communications satellite.

9/12/91 *Discovery* (5 days) John Creighton, Kenneth Reightler Jr., Mark Brown, James Buchlim, Charles Gemar. Launches upper-atmosphere research satellite.

10/2/91 *Soyuz TM-13* A. Volkov, F. Viehboeck, T. Aubakirov. Viehboeck, first Austrian in space, returns with Artsebarsky and Aubakirov.

11/24/91 *Atlantis* (7 days) Frederick Gregory, Tom Henricks, James Voss, Mario Runco Jr., Story Musgrave, Thomas Hennen. First completely nonsecret military flight; studies how well military installations can be seen from space.

1/22/92 *Discovery* (8 days) Ronald Grabe, Stephen Oswald, Norman Thagard, William Readdy, David Hilmers, Roberta Bondar, Ulf Merbold. Performs experiments as the First International Microgravity Lab.

3/17/92 *Soyuz TM-14* K. Flade, A. Viktorenko, A. Kaleri. On March 25, Flade, a German, returns with Sergei Krikalev and Aleksandr Volkov.

3/24/92 *Atlantis* (9 days) Charles Bolden Jr., Brian Duffy, Kathryn Sullivan, David Leestma, Michael Foale, Byron Lichtenberg, Dirk Frimout. Inaugural flight of Mission to Planet Earth studies Earth's atmosphere and auroras.

5/7/92 *Endeavour* (9 days) Daniel Brandenstein, Kevin Chilton, Thomas Akers, Richard Hieb, Bruce Melnick, Kathryn Thornton, Pierre Thout. The first flight of the replacement for *Challenger* succeeds relaunching an erring communications satellite; first ever 3-person EVA.

6/25/92 *Columbia* (14 days) Richard Richards, Kenneth Bowersox, Bonnie Dunbar, Lawrence DeLucas, Ellen Baker, Eugene Trinh, Carl Meade. Sets record for duration of shuttle mission; carries U.S. Microgravity Laboratory.

7/27/92 *Soyuz TM-15* A. Solovyev, S. Avdeyev, M. Tognini. The third trip by a French astronaut, Tognini, to *Mir*.

7/31/92 *Atlantis* (8 days) Loren Schriver, Andrew Allen, Marsha Ivins, Jeffrey Hoffman, Franklin Chang-Diaz, Claude Nicollier, Franco Mallerba. Launches European Retrievable Carrier (Eureca) satellite. First Swiss astronaut (Nicollier); first Italian (Mallerba).

9/12/92 *Endeavour* (8 days) Robert Gibson, Curtis Brown Jr., Jay Apt, Jan Davis, Mae Carol Jemison, Mark Lee, Mamoru Mohri. First professional Japanese astronaut in space (Mohri); first married couple in space (Lee and Davis); first black female astronaut (Jemison). Japanese-sponsored mission to study biology in space.

10/22/92 *Columbia* (10 days) James Wetherbee, Michael Baker, Glenwood MacLean, Tamara Jernigan, William Shepherd, Charles Lacy Veach. Launches the Italian-made satellite *LAGEOS-2*, designed to provide information about Earth's gravitational field.

12/2/92 *Discovery* (7 days) Daniel Walker, Robert Cabana, Guion Bluford Jr., James Voss,

Michael Clifford. Last scheduled military flight for the space shuttle; future military flights to use disposable rockets. Launches secret military satellite.

1/13/93 *Endeavour* (6 days) John Caspar, Gregory Harbaugh, Donald McMonagle, Susan Helms, Mario Runco Jr.. Observes X-rays and launches a TDRS (Tracking and Data Relay Satellite).

1/24/93 *Soyuz TM-16* A. Polishchuk, G. Manakov. Docks with *Mir* on Kristall module, using U.S.-compatible port first developed for the joint Soviet-U.S. mission in 1975; A. Solovyev and S. Avdeyev return after six months aboard *Mir*.

4/8/93 *Discovery* (9 days) Kenneth Cameron, Stephen Oswald, Kenneth Cockrell, Michael Foale, Ellen Ochoa. Launches and retrieves the *Spartan* Sun probe, used to study the solar corona, and observes Earth's ozone layer.

4/26/93 *Columbia* (10 days) Steven Nagel, Tom Henricks, Jerry Ross, Charles Precourt, Bernard Harris Jr., Ulrich Walter, Hans Schlegel. The European Spacelab with two German scientists (Walter and Schlegel) aboard conducts experiments on weightlessness.

6/21/93 *Endeavour* (10 days) Ronald Grabe, Brian Duffy, Donald Low, Peter Wisoff, Nancy Jane Sherlock, Janice Voss. Recovers Europe's *Eureca* satellite; and conducts experiments using a pressurized laboratory called Spacehab.

7/1/93 *Soyuz TM-17* V. Tsiblyev, A. Serebrov, J. Haignere. Haignere is French astronaut who returns with A. Solovyev and S. Andreyev on July 29.

9/12/93 *Discovery* (10 days) Frank Culbertson Jr., William Readdy, James Newman, Daniel Bursch, Carl Walz. Tests equipment and procedures to be used in repairing Hubble Space Telescope; first night landing at Kennedy.

10/18/93 *Columbia* (14 days) John Blaha, Richard Searfoss, William McArthur Jr., Shannon Lucid, Martin Fettman, Margaret Rhea Seddon, David Wolf. Conducts biological experiments on humans and rats; first dissection of animal in space.

12/2/93 *Endeavour* (11 days) Richard Covey, Kenneth Bowersox, Claude Nicollier, Story Musgrave, Thomas Akers, Kathryn Thornton, Jeffrey Hoffman. Installs corrective lenses on defective Hubble Space Telescope.

1/8/94 *Soyuz TM-18* V. Afanasyev, Y. Usachyov, V. Polyakov. Trip planned to last 14 months for Polyakov, but Afanasyev and Usachyov return after six months. Previous *Mir* crew returns to Earth.

The U.S. and Russia Work Together in Space

2/3/94 *Discovery* (8 days) Charles Bolden Jr., Sergei Krikalev, Kenneth Reightler Jr., Jan Davis, Franklin Chang-Diaz, Ronald Sega. Krikalev first Russian on U.S. space shuttle mission.

3/4/94 *Columbia* (14 days) John Caspar, Andrew Allen, Charles Gemar, Marsha Ivins, Pierre Thuot. Develops techniques for use in space-station construction.

4/9/94 *Endeavour* (11 days) Sidney Gutierrez, Kevin Chilton, Michael Clifford, Linda Godwin, Jay Apt, Thomas Jones. Uses radar to map details of Earth in 3-D.

7/1/94 *Soyuz TM-19* Y. Malenchenko, T. Musabayev. Mission to relieve Afanasyev and Usachyov on *Mir*.

7/8/94 *Columbia* (15 days) Robert Cabana, Leroy Chiao, James Halsell Jr., Richard Hieb, Chiaki Naito-Mukai, Donald Thomas, Carl Walz. Orbits Earth 236 times, a new record. First Japanese woman in space (heart surgeon Naito-Mukai).

9/9/94 *Discovery* (11 days) Richard Richards, Blaine Hammond Jr., Susan Helms, Mark Lee, J.M. Lineger, Carl Meade. Conducts laser experiments to mea-

sure pollution in atmosphere. Releases and recaptures satellite that collects data on solar wind; Meade and Lee use jet pack for untethered spacewalk.

9/30/94 *Endeavour* (11 days) Michael Baker, Daniel Bursch, Thomas Jones, Steven Smith, Jeff Wisoff, Terrence Wukcytt. The *Space Radar Laboratory* 2 mission is follow-up of nearly identical mission flown in the spring to detect seasonal changes.

10/4/94 *Soyuz TM-20* A. Viktorenko, Y. Kondakova, U. Merbold. Merbold, from the European Space Agency, studies space biology aboard *Mir* and returns to Earth on 11/4/94. Viktorenko and Kondakova relieve Malenchenko and Musabaye on *Mir*.

11/3/94 *Atlantis* (11 days) Curtis Brown, Donald McMonagle, Jean-François Clervoy (from ESA), Scott Parazynski, Joseph Tanner. Third shuttle flight since 1992 to carry the *Atlas* lab (Atmospheric Laboratory for Applications and Science).

2/3/95 *Discovery* (8 days) James Wetherbee, Eileen Collins, Michael Foale, Bernard Harris Jr., Vladimir Titov, Janice Voss. Carries Russian Titov to within 11 m (37 ft.) of Mir.

3/2/95 *Endeavour* (17 days) Stephen Oswald, Samuel Durrance, Tamara Jernigan, William Gregory, John Grunsfeld, Wendy Lawrence, Ronald Parise. Carries the lab *Astro 2*, used to study volcanic eruptions on Jupiter's moon Io.

3/14/95 *Soyuz TM-21* N. Thagard, V. Dezhurov, G. Strekalov. Thagard becomes the first U.S. astronaut to live aboard *Mir*; he studies the body's reaction to weightlessness; Polyakov, who returns on 3/22/95, with Kondakova and Viktorenko, sets new endurance record of 14.5 straight months in space.

6/27/95 *Atlantis* (10 days) Robert Gibson, Charles Precourt, Ellen Baker, Gregory Harbaugh, Bonnie Dunbar, Anatoly Solovyev, Nikolai Budarin. Docks with *Mir* for 5 days. Spacelab on Atlantis and Spekter module of Mir used for biomedical research. Solovyev and Budarin relieve Thagard, Dezhurov, and Strekalov as crew of *Mir*.

7/13/95 *Discovery* (9 days) Tom Henricks, Kevin Kregel, Nancy Currie, Donald Thomas, Mary Ellen Weber. Launches Tracking and Data Relay Satellite (TDRS) to replace one lost when *Challenger* blew up.

9/3/95 *Soyuz TM-22* T. Reiter (Germany), Y. Gidzenko, S. Avdeyev. Replaces Solovyev and Budarin, who return to Earth 9/11/88.

9/7/95 *Endeavour* (11 days) Michael Gernhart, David Walker, Kenneth Cockrell, James Newman, James Voss. Uses an orbiting shield to produce a vacuum in its wake 10,000 times greater than any found on Earth.

10/20/95 *Columbia* (16 days) Kenneth Bowersox, Kent Rominger, Kathryn Thornton, Cady Coleman, Michael Lopez-Alegria, Fred Leslie, Albert Sacco Conducts microgravity experiments in Spacelab and other medical and commercial experiments.

11/12/95 *Atlantis* (8 days) Kenneth Cameron, James Halsell Jr., Jerry Ross, William McArthur Jr., Chris Hadfield (Canada). Changes configuration of *Mir* to make docking easier in future missions.

1/11/96 *Endeavour* (9 days) Brian Duffy, Brent Jett Jr., Leroy Chiao, Winston Scott, Daniel Barry, Koichi Wakata (Japan). Recovers Japanese science-experiment orbiting platform, which had been launched by a Japanese H-2 rocket in March 1995.

2/21/96 *Soyuz TM-23* Y. Onufrienko, Y. Usachev. Relieves *Mir* crew.

2/22/96 *Columbia* (15 days) Nobie Stone, Jeffrey Hoffman, Andrew Allen, Doc Horowitz, Franklin Chang-Diaz, Claude Nicollier (ESA), Maurizio Cheli (ESA), Umberto Guidoni (Italian Space Agency).. Tethered satellite experiment partly successful, but satellite is mysteriously lost from end of tether.

3/22/96 *Atlantis* (9 days) Kevin Childon, Richard Seafoss, Ronald Sega, Michael Clifford, Shannon Lucid, Linda Godwin. Docks with *Mir*. Lucid stays behind on the space station.

5/19/96 *Endeavour* (10 days) John Caspar, Curtis Brown Jr., Daniel Bursch, Mario Runco Jr., Marc Garneau (Canadian), Andrew Thomas. Deploys first inflatable antenna from Spartan satellite. Conducts rendezvous studies of the *PAMS* satellite, a test of a system in which a satellite stabilizes itself without expending rocket fuel.

6/20/96 *Columbia* (17 days) Tom Henricks, Kevin Kregel, Rick Linnehan, Susan Helms, Charles Brady, Jean-Jacques Favier (Canada), Robert Thirsk. Carries the Life/Microgravity Spacelab, to study the effects of space flight on the human body, on rats, and on fish embryos; and SAREX-II.

8/17/96 *Soyuz TM-24* V. Korzun, A. Kaleri, C. Andre-Deshays (France). Korzun and Kaleri relieve Onufrienko and Usachev on *Mir*.

9/16/96 *Atlantis* (10 days) William Readdy, Terrence Wilcutt, Tom Akers, Jay Apt, Carl Walz, John Blaha, Shannon Lucid. Blaha relieves Lucid on *Mir*.

11/19/96 *Columbia* (18 days) Kenneth Cockrell, Kent Rominger, Story Musgrave, Thomas Jones, Tamara Jernigan. Deploys and retrieves *ORFEUS-SPAS*, a satellite gathering data about matter in space between the stars and the WSF-3/Wake Shield Facility, a satellite used in testing a method of producing a high vacuum to be used in manufacturing ultra pure semiconductor devices.

1/12/97 *Atlantis* (10 days) Mike Baker, Brent Jett, Jeff Wisoff, John Grunsfeld, Marsha Ivins, J.M. Linenger, John Blaha. Linenger relieves Blaha on *Mir*.

2/10/97 *Soyuz TM-25* V. Tsbliyev, A. Lazutkin, R. Ewald (Germany), V. Korzun, A. Kaleri. Tsbliyev and Lazutkin relieve Korzun and Kaleri on *Mir*.

2/11/97 *Discovery* (10 days) Ken Bowersox, Scott Horowitz, Joe Tanner, Steve Hawley, Greg Harbaugh, Mark Lee, Steve Smith. Replaces eight instruments in the Hubble Space Telescope and adds two new ones, greatly improving its abilities.

4/4/97 *Columbia* (4 days) Jim Halsell, Susan Still, Janice Voss, Mike Gernhardt, Don Thomas, Roger Crouch, Greg Linteris. Carries the Microgravity Science Lab, but 85 percent of the experiments are canceled because of a problem with the fuel cells.

5/15/97 *Atlantis* (9 days) Charlie Precourt, Eileen Collins, Jean-François Clervoy, Carlos Noriega, Ed Lu, Elena Kondakova (Russia), Mike Foale, Jerry Linenger. Docks with Mir, taking Linenger back to Earth and leaving Foale. Brings needed supplies and replacement equipment to aging *Mir*, which has had problems with fires and failures.

7/1/97 *Columbia* (16 days) James Halsell, Susan Still, Janice Voss, Michael Gernhardt, Donald Thomas, Roger Crouch, Gregory Linteris. Replacement for flight of 4/4/97.

8/7/97 *Discovery* (11 days) Curt Brown, Kent Rominger, Jan Davis, Robert Curbeam, Steve Robinson, Bjarni Tryggvason. In the fourth cooperative German-American scientific mission, various experiments using infrared imagining, lasers, and cryogenic devices are conducted.

9/25/97 *Atlantis* (11 days) James Wetherbee, Mike Bloomfield, Vladimir Titov, Scott Parazynski, Jean-Loup Chrétien, Wendy Lawrence, David Wolf, Michael Foale. Takes Wolf to *Mir*, returns with Foale.

11/19/97 *Columbia* (16 days) Kevin Kregel, Steve Lindsey, Kalpana Chawla, Winston Scott, Takao Doi, Leonid Kadenyuk (first Ukranian to fly aboard a shuttle). Conducts microgravity experiments and attempts to launch *SPARTAN* solar research satellite;

when *SPARTAN* malfunctions, astronauts retrieve it for a future attempt on a later flight.

1/22/98 *Endeavour* (9 days) Terrence Wilcutt, Joe Edwards, James Reilly, Michael Anderson, Bonnie Dunbar, Salizhan Sharipov, Andrew Thomas, David Wolf. Thomas relieves Wolf on *Mir*. Performs microgravity experiments with plants and crystals.

4/17/98 *Columbia* (16 days) Richard Searfoss, Scott Altman, Kathryn Hire, Richard Linnehan, Dave Williams, Jay Buckey, James Pawelczyk. Carries the *Neurolab* into space where the effects of space flight on the brains and reproduction of various species of animals and plants are studied.

6/2/98 *Discovery* (10 days) Charles Precourt, Dominic Gorie, Wendy Lawrence, Franklin Chang-Diaz, Janet Kavandi, Andrew Thomas, Valery Victorovitch Ryumin. Final U.S. astronaut mission on *Mir* completed as Thomas is returned to Earth.

11/20/98 *Discovery* (9 days) Curtis Brown Jr., Steven Lindsey, Scott Parazynski, Stephen Robinson, Pedro Duque, Chiaki Mukai, John Glenn. Glenn, first American to orbit the Earth in 1962, becomes oldest astronaut for study of how weightlessness affects older humans.

Era of the International Space Station (ISS)

12/04/98 *Endeavour* (12 days) Robert Cabana, Frederick Sturckow, James Newman, Nancy Currie, Jerry Ross, Sergei Konstantinovich Krikalev (Russia). Crew docks with the Russian-built Functional Energy Block Zarya and adds Node-1 (Unity) to begin assembly of the International Space Station.

5/27/99 *Discovery* (10 days) Kent Rominger, Rick Husband, Tamara Jernigan, Ellen Ochoa, Daniel Barry, Julie Payette (Canada), Valery Ivanovich Tokarev (Russia). Brings cargo for outfitting International Space Station (ISS) including Russian cargo crane to be mounted on exterior of Functional Energy Block.

7/22/99 *Columbia* (5 days) Eileen Collins, Jeffrey Ashby, Steven Hawley, Catherine Coleman, Michael Tognini (France). Collins first female commander. Launches Chandra X-ray Observatory.

12/19/99 *Discovery* (8 days) Curtis Brown Jr., Scott Kelly, John Grunsfeld, Michael Foales, Steven Smith, Jean-François Clervoy (France), Claude Nicollier (Switzerland). Captures, services, and relaunches the Hubble Space Telescope.

2/11/00 *Endeavour* (11 days) Kevin Kregel, Dominic Gorie, Janet Kavandi, Janice Voss, Gerhard Thiele (German-ESA), Mamoru Mohri (Japan). The Shuttle Radar Topography Mission obtain the most detailed topographical map of the Earth to this date.

5/19/00 *Atlantis* (10 days) James Halsell Jr., Scott Horowitz, Susan Helms, Mary Ellen Weber, Jeffrey Williams, James Voss, Yury Usachev (Russian). Carries supplies to ISS. Helms and Usachev remain on ISS as part of first crew.

9/8/00 *Atlantis* (12 days) Terry Wilcutt, Scott Altman, Dan Burbank, Ed Lu, Rick Mastracchio, Yuri Malenchenko (Russia), and Boris Morukov (Russia). Brings supplies to ISS and conducts space walk to perform station maintenance.

10/11/00 *Discovery* (13 days) Brian Duffy, Pamela Melroy, Leroy Chiao, Peter "Jeff" Wisoff, Michael Lopez-Alegria, William McArthur, Jr., Koichi Wakata (Japan). Brings and installs parts needed for solar arrays, communications, and attitude control for ISS.

10/31/00 *Soyuz* (139 days) Bill Shepherd, Yuri Gidzenko, Sergei Krikalev. This was Expedition One to begin permanent occupation of ISS.

11/30/00 *Endeavour* (12 days) Brent Jett, Michael Bloomfield, Joseph Tanner, Carlos Noriega,

Marc Garneau (Canada). Adds the photovoltaic modules to the solar arrays to the ISS and brings radiators for cooling the photovoltaic cells; activates the S-band communications system.
2/7/01 *Atlantis* (13 days) Kenneth Cockrell, Mark Polansky, Robert Curbeam, Thomas Jones, Marsha Ivins. Installs the "Destiny" laboratory module on the ISS.
3/8/01 *Discovery* (13 days) Jim Wetherbee, Jim Kelly, Andy Thomas, Paul Richards, bring Yury Usachev, (Russia) James Voss, and Susan Helms to become the Expedition Two resident crew of the ISS and returns Expedition One crew (Bill Shepherd, Sergei Krikalev, and Yuri Gidzenco) to Earth; brings additional laboratory equipment as well.
4/19/01 *Endeavour* (12 days) Kent Rominger , Jeffrey Ashby, Scott Umberto Guidoni (ESA), Scott Parazynski, Chris Hadfield (Canada), Yuri Lonchakov (Russia), John Phillips.. Delivers the Italian "Raffaello" module and the Canadian mechanical arm to the ISS.
7/12/01 *Atlantis* (11 days) Steven Lindsey, Charles Hobaugh, Michael Gernhardt, Janet Kavandi, James Reilly. Delivers the Joint Airlock to the ISS and resolves problems with the Canadian robotic arm.
8/10/01 *Discovery* (12 days) Scott Horowitz, Rick Sturckow, Daniel Barry, PAtrick Forrester. Installs the Leonardo Multi-Purpose Module and launches *Simplesat*, a demonstration satellite built with "off-the-shelf" commercial hardware. Bring Expedition Three Crew (Frank Culberston, Vladimir Dezhurov, and Mikhail Tyurin) to relieve Expedition Two crew (Yury Usachev, Jim Voss, and Susan Helms) on the ISS.

The International Space Station

The International Space Station began at the end of the Cold War era with separate plans by the United States and Soviet Union. The Soviet Union had operated the successful space station *Mir* since 1986 and the United States was working with several other countries to launch its own space station, tentatively named Freedom. With the collapse of the Soviet Union in 1989-90 and the creation of the Russian Republic in 1991, plans were altered and Russia joined the American-led effort, which was redesigned to replace *Mir*. Today there are 16 nations supporting the International Space Station (ISS)--the United States, Russia, Japan, Canada, Italy, Belgium, the Netherlands, Denmark, Norway, France, Spain, Germany, Sweden, Switzerland, the United Kingdom, and Brazil.

Construction of ISS is in modules, requiring some 45 different space flights to put all the parts in place. The first module, known as Zarya, was launched by Russia on November 20, 1998. Other modules have included the U.S. Unity passageway and docking port (launched December 4, 1998); Russia's Zvezda (installed September 10, 2000), early living quarters for station crews; the U.S. Destiny workstation module (installed February 10, 2001), and the Italian Raffaello multipurpose logistic module (MPLM). Other important components are trusses, the Canadian robot arm, and an airlock. Still to come are two more Italian MPLMs as well as modules from the European Space Agency, Japan, and Russia. The completed space station will weight about a million pounds (453 metric tons) and be 361 feet (110 m) from end to end. The interior working space will be somewhat larger than the volume of a Boeing 747 airliner, but there will be only four windows. ISS is powered by solar arrays that cover more than half an acre of space. Fifty-two separate computers will control operations.

EARTH SCIENCES

Earth sciences include geology (the study of Earth's rocks and interior), oceanography (the study of ocean water, currents, and the ocean floor), paleontology (the study of fossils and ancient lifeforms), parts of astronomy, and meteorology (the study of the atmosphere, including weather). Except for astronomy and weather, which are covered elsewhere, this section deals with all of these studies.

▶ THE EARTH'S COMPOSITION

In their study of the Earth, scientists distinguish a number of distinct layers from the inner core—the center of which is about 6,400 km (roughly 4,000 mi.) below the surface—to the farthest limit of the atmosphere, about 1,000 km (600 mi.) above the surface. This section describes these layers, from the innermost to the outermost.

Core The core consists of two parts—one solid, the other liquid—both thought to be a mixture of iron and a lighter element, probably sulfur or oxygen. The solid inner core begins about 4,650 km (2,890 mi.) from the surface, and the liquid outer core at about 2,900 km (1,800 mi.) from the surface.

Mantle The bulk of the Earth—roughly two-thirds of its mass—is composed of the mantle, which extends from the outer core to within about 90 km (55 mi.) of the Earth's surface below the higher mountains, and to within only 5 to 8 km (3 to 5 mi.) of the Earth's surface below some areas of the oceans. Silicon dioxide constitutes almost half of the mantle, and there is an abundance of magnesium oxide, some iron oxide, and smaller amounts of oxides of other metals. (Although silicon dioxide is known as quartz when found in the Earth's crust, under the heat and pressure of the mantle it may have very different properties from the form we know.) Part of the upper mantle is somewhat fluid and is known as the asthenosphere.

Crust The crust is the outermost solid layer of the Earth. Under the continents, the crust varies from 30 to 90 km (19 to 55 mi.) in thickness, while under the oceans it is generally only 5 to 8 km (3 to 5 mi.) thick. Continental and oceanic crust differ from each other in thickness and composition. Continental crust consists of granite and other relatively light rocks, while oceanic crust is made up chiefly of basalt. The crust is separated from the mantle by the Mohorovičić discontinuity, or Moho. The crust that is accessible to accurate measurements contains the following principal elements:

Element	Percent	Element	Percent
Oxygen	45.6%	Magnesium	2.8%
Silicon	27.3	Sodium	2.3
Aluminum	8.4	Potassium	1.8
Iron	6.2	Hydrogen	1.5
Calcium	4.7	Titanium	0.6

Note: Adds to more than 100% due to independent rounding.

Hydrosphere   Water—virtually all of it sea water—covers about 71 percent of the Earth's surface and thereby constitutes a distinct layer of the Earth. Sea water varies in composition from place to place, but on average it is about 3.5 percent salts—that is, evaporating 100 lb. of sea water would yield 3.5 lb. of salt. Sodium chloride (ordinary table salt) constitutes 2.7 percent of sea water, or 77.8 percent of total solids in sea water. The typical composition of solids in sea water is as follows:

Compound	Percent
Sodium chloride	77.8%
Magnesium chloride	10.9
Magnesium sulfide	4.7
Calcium sulfate	3.6
Potassium sulfate	2.5
Calcium carbonate	0.3
Magnesium bromide	0.2
Other compounds	trace

Atmosphere   The atmosphere is the gaseous layer that envelopes the Earth. The lower atmosphere consists of the troposphere and the stratosphere. The *troposphere* has an average thickness of about 11 km (7 mi.), although it is only 8 km (5 mi.) at the poles and as much as 16 km (10 mi.) around the equator. Most clouds and weather phenomena occur in this region. The composition of dry air at

Geologic Time Scale

The history of the planet has been divided by geologists and other earth scientists into periods of varying length based on the fossils found in rock strata. Geologists often speak of the period before 545 million years ago as Precambrian Time. The eras after 545 million years ago are grouped into the Phanerozoic Eon.

Mass extinctions—brief periods when large numbers of species become extinct—often mark the boundaries between geologic time periods. In the greatest such extinction, known as the Final Permian (250 million years ago), perhaps as many

as 80 to 90 percent of all species became extinct in less than a million years. No one knows what causes most mass extinctions, but the Final Cretaceous of 65 million years ago (also called the K-T extinction) and the Final Permian were almost certainly caused by impacts of asteroids. The most recent extinction, at the end of the last ice age (11,000 years ago), may have been caused by human hunting. Some biologists believe that human activities are causing a new mass extinction today as well.

Era or Eon, Period, Epoch	Organisms	Beginning of Interval (millions of years ago)
ARCHEAN EON	Monerans: bacteria and blue-green algae	4,600
PROTEROZOIC EON	Protists, algae, and soft-bodied creatures similar to jellyfish and worms	2,500
PHANEROZOIC EON		
PALEOZOIC ERA		
Cambrian period	Tiny fossils with skeletons followed by animals with shells, notably trilobites	545
Ordovician period	Brachiopods (shellfish similar to clams), corals, starfish, and some organisms that have no modern counterparts, called sea scorpions and conodonts	500
Silurian period	Snails, clams, land mussels, ammonoids (similar to the nautilus), jawless fish, sea scorpions, land plants and animals (club mosses, land scorpions); modern groups of algae and fungi	425
Devonian period	Spiders, amphibians, jawed fish, lobe-finned fish, sharks, lungfish, and ferns	395
Carboniferous period	Insects, land snails, amphibians, early reptiles, sea lilies, giant club mosses, and seed ferns	350
Permian period	Mammal-like reptiles and fin-backed reptiles, cycads, ginkgoes, and conifers	290
MEZOZOIC ERA		
Triassic period	Marine reptiles (plesiosaurs and ichthyosaurs), crocodiles, frogs, turtles, early mammals, and early dinosaurs	235
Jurassic period	Dinosaurs (such as stegosaurs), pterosaurs (such as pterodactyl), early birds, dinoflagellates, diatoms, early flowering plants	190
Cretaceous period	Dinosaurs (such as tyrannosaurs, triceratops, and apatosaurs), salamanders, modern bony fishes, mosasaurs (marine lizards), flowering plants, placental and marsupial mammals	130
CENOZOIC ERA		
Tertiary period		
Paleocene epoch	Early primates, early horses, rodents, sycamores	66.5
Eocene epoch	Whales, penguins, roses, bats, camels, early elephants, dogs, cats, weasels	57.8
Oligocene epoch	Deer, pigs, saber-toothed cats, monkeys	36.6
Miocene epoch	Seals, dolphins, grasses, daisies, asters, sunflowers, lettuce, giraffes, bears, hyenas, early apes	23.5
Pliocene epoch	Apes, australopithecines (early hominids) *Homo habilis* (first human species), mammoths, giant sloths, and armadillos	5.2
Quaternary period		
Pleistocene epoch	*Homo erectus* and related human species, modern humans, and Neandertal humans; large mammals such as giant bison and beavers; many kinds of hoofed animals	1.6
Holocene epoch	Modern humans and flora and fauna of today	0.01 (11,000 years)

sea level is: nitrogen, 78.08%; oxygen, 20.05%; argon, 0.93%; and carbon dioxide, 0.03%. There are also lesser amounts of neon, helium, krypton, and xenon. These proportions change with altitude, lighter gases being more common at higher altitudes, but they are approximately the same everywhere on Earth at the same altitude. There are also variable quantities of water vapor, dust particles, and other compounds whose proportions change from place to place at the same altitude—fewer dust particles being found over oceans, and less

water vapor over deserts. Temperature decreases with altitude in the troposphere.

The *stratosphere* is found between 11 km and 50 km (7-30 mi.) out from the Earth's surface. Temperatures in this region rise slightly as altitude increases, to a maximum of about 0°C (32°F). Virtually coextensive with the stratosphere is the *ozonosphere*, or ozone layer, the region in which most of the atmosphere's ozone is found. Because ozone absorbs most of the sun's ultraviolet radiation, it is vital to the continued existence of life on the planet.

Major Discoveries in Earth Sciences

B.C.
c.300   Dicaearchus (Greek: c. 320) develops map of Earth on a sphere using lines of latitude.

A.D.
132   Zhang Heng (Chinese: 78–139) develops first crude seismograph.
1600   William Gilbert (English: 1544–1603) suggests that Earth is giant magnet, which is why magnetic compasses indicate north.
1669   Nicolaus Steno (Niels Stensen; Danish: 1638–86) correctly explains origin of fossils.
1777   Nicolas Desmarest (French: 1725–1815) proposes that the rock basalt starts as lava.
1785   James Hutton (Scottish: 1726–97) explains features of Earth on basis of tiny changes taking place over long periods of time (uniformitarianism).
1795   Baron Georges Cuvier (French: 1769–1832) shows that giant bones found in Meuse River are remains of extinct giant reptile.
1797   Sir James Hall (Scottish: 1761–1832) shows that melted rocks form crystals upon cooling.
1822   Gideon A. Mantell (English: 1790–1852) and his wife, Mary Ann, discover and recognize dinosaur bones as those of a giant, extinct reptile.
1830   Sir Charles Lyell (Scottish: 1797–1875) begins to publish *Principles of Geology,* the work that convinced geologists that Earth is at least several hundred million years old.
1880   John Milne (English: 1850–1913) invents modern seismograph.
1896   Svante A. Arrhenius (Swedish: 1859–1927) calculates that global temperatures will rise with higher levels of carbon dioxide in atmosphere (greenhouse effect).
1902   Léon-Philippe Teisserenc de Bort (French: 1855–1913) discovers the stratosphere.
1906   Richard D. Oldham (English: 1858–1936) establishes existence of Earth's core.
1907   Bertram B. Boltwood (American: 1870–1927) shows that age of rocks containing uranium can be determined by measuring ratio of uranium to lead.
1909   Andrija Mohorovičić (Croatia: 1857–1936) discovers boundary between Earth's crust and mantle, now known as Mohorovičić discontinuity, or "Moho."
1912   Alfred L. Wegener (German: 1880–1930) proposes theory of continental drift, idea that a single continent—Pangaea—split into present-day continents, which have drifted away from each other.
1925   The German *Meteor* expedition discovers Mid-Atlantic Ridge, a giant mountain range in middle of the Atlantic Ocean.
1929   Motonori Matuyama (Japanese: 1884–1958) shows that Earth's magnetic field reverses every few hundred million years.

1958   James A. Van Allen (American: 1914–) discovers belts of radiation that surround Earth in space, now known as Van Allen belts.
1960   Harry H. Hess (American: 1906–69) develops theory of seafloor spreading—oceans become wider as new seafloor is formed at midocean ridges.
1979   American oceanographers discover hot vents in oceans, surrounded by exotic forms of life based on sulfur, not oxygen.
1980   Walter Alvarez (American: 1940–) and coworkers discover geologic layer of iridium in region identified with the demise of the dinosaurs; attributes both iridium and extinction to a large comet or meteorite striking Earth.
1993   Ice cores from Greenland and Antarctica reveal the record of Earth's climate for the past 250,000 years.

Weather scientists discover unexpected displays of electromagnetism in Earth's upper atmosphere; the displays are named Sprites, ELVES, and blue jets.
1996   A farmer in Liaoning Province in China discovers a dinosaur whose skin is covered with a feathery down, the first major find at what proves to be an important fossil site that also includes dinosaurs with more highly developed feathers.

Scientists from the Scripps Institution of Oceanography at San Diego find evidence that life has existed on Earth for at least 3.85 billion years.
1998   Frank T. Kyte (American: 1949–) of the University of California finds in ocean sediments near Hawaii fragments of the object that 65 million years ago crashed into Yucatán. thereby causing the mass extinction that finished off the dinosaurs.

Paul F. Hoffman (Canadian: 1941–) of Harvard University proposes that some 200 million years ago the surface of Earth was completely frozen from the poles to the equator, a condition that becomes known as "snowball Earth;" computer studies in 2000, however, indicate that a narrow band at the equator remained unfrozen.
2000   Michael Hammer (American: 1944–), a professional fossil collector, discovers the fossilized heart of a Thescelosaurus, a dinosaur from about 65 million years ago.

Michael R. Rampino of New York University and co-workers find evidence that Earth's largest mass extinction, known as the Late Permian, occurred during a period of less than 8,000 years some 250 million years ago, killing 95 percent of all species in the oceans; analysis of sediments at the Permian-Triassic boundary by Luann Becker of the University of Washington in Seattle demonstrates that these had an extraterrestrial source, implying that the extinction was caused by the impact of a comet or asteroid.

Beyond the stratosphere is the upper atmosphere, or *ionosphere*, so called because it is the layer in which atmospheric gases have been ionized by solar radiation. The ionosphere reflects certain wavelengths back to the surface, making it possible to transmit radio waves around the curve of the Earth. The ionosphere is further divided into the *mesosphere*, between 50 km and 80 km (30-50 mi.), in which the temperature decreases with altitude to -90°C (-130°F); and the *thermosphere*, from about 80 km to 450 km (50-280 mi.), in which the molecular temperature increases to as much as 1475°C (2690°F). To spacecraft traveling in the atmosphere, as the space shuttle does, however, the temperature seems cold because the molecules are so widely spaced. Beyond the thermosphere is the *exosphere*, extending to about 1,000 km (600 mi.). In this layer, temperature no longer has its customary meaning. (See also "Global Warming" and "The Ozone Layer.")

▶ THE CHANGING EARTH

Despite its apparent solidity, the crust and interior of the Earth are constantly changing.

Plate tectonics   The earth's outer crust is composed of about 20 lithospheric (or tectonic) plates that move from a few millimeters to several centimeters per year. Hundreds of millions of years ago, these plates formed a continuous landmass known as Pangaea, surrounded by ocean. Eventually the plates separated, until they reached the positions they occupy today.

As plates move away from each other, molten rock emerges from the mantle to form oceanic crust. Where they come together, one plate is usually forced under the other, forming either oceanic trenches or mountain ranges (such as the Himalayas) or both. In a few places, one plate slips by the other along a giant crack called a fault, such as the San Andreas Fault in California. These areas are also the site of greatest volcanic and earthquake activity.

Earthquakes and tsunamis   Most earthquakes are caused when rock on one side of a fault (or crack) in the Earth's crust moves with respect to the rock on the other side of the fault. The motion causes vibrations in the crust that travel through the rock as shock waves. When these reach the surface, they cause it to move in various ways, which is called seismic motion. Small earthquakes that accompany volcanic eruptions are caused by the motion of liquid rock, or magma.

More than 800,000 earthquakes are registered by seismographs each year, but the overwhelming majority go unnoticed. However, large earthquakes are of great concern to many people living in regions of significant seismic activity. Although research on earthquake prediction has yielded no breakthroughs, death and destruction have been reduced somewhat by improvements in construction codes and techniques.

One common side effect of undersea earthquakes is tsunamis—or (incorrectly) tidal waves—against which there is little protection. Tsunamis are caused when an earthquake raises or lowers a section of seabed, thereby producing a wave that, while not generally noticeable at sea, can reach great heights as it approaches land. Similar to and as destructive as tsunamis, harbor waves are generated when a landslide falls into a bay, strait, or other confined body of water causing almost immediate flooding. High waves are also caused by volcanic explosions or collapses, such as the explosion and collapse of Krakatau in 1883.

Volcanoes   are openings in the Earth's crust that emit molten or partially molten rock (lava), various hot gases, and ash. (A volcano is also the mountain formed by solidified lava or ash ejected from the opening.) If the opening is like a crack, it is called a vent. If it is larger and fairly circular, it is called a crater. A caldera is a basin formed by the settling of the top of a volcanic mountain, and it may have several vents or craters on its floor.

Richter Scale and Effects Near the Epicenter

Note: The epicenter is the point on Earth's surface above the center of the quake

Below 2.5   Not felt except by a very few under specially favorable circumstances.
2.5 to 3.5   Felt only by a few persons at rest, especially on upper floors of buildings.
3.5 to 4.5   At lower levels or further from the quake, it is felt by many people, sometimes quite noticeably indoors, especially on upper floors of buildings, but many people do not recognize it as an earthquake. At somewhat higher levels or nearer to the epicenter, during the day the quake is felt indoors by many; outdoors by few. Sensation is like heavy truck striking building. At the highest level, the earth movement is felt by nearly everyone; with many awakened if during the night. Disturbances of trees, telephone poles, and other tall objects sometimes can be noticed.
4.5 to 6.0   Felt by all; many frightened and run outdoors. Some heavy furniture moved; there will be a few instances of fallen plaster or damaged chimneys. Other slight local damage may occur. At higher level, however, everybody runs outdoors. At the upper level, while damage is still negligible in buildings of good design and construction, there can be moderate damage even to well-built ordinary

structures; there will be considerable damage to poorly built or badly designed structures.
6.0 to 7.0   A destructive earthquake. Damage may still be slight in specially designed structures, but will be considerable in ordinary substantial buildings, often with partial collapse. Damage will be great in poorly built structures, including collapse of chimneys, factory stacks, columns, monuments, and walls. At the upper level, damage is likely to be considerable even in specially designed structures. Most ordinary buildings will be shifted off foundations. Even the ground will be cracked conspicuously.
7.0 to 8.0   A major earthquake. Worldwide, about 10 of these occur each year. Some well-built wooden structures will be destroyed. Most masonry and frame structures will be destroyed along with their foundations. Ground becomes badly cracked.
8.0 and above   Great earthquakes. These occur once every five to 10 years. Few, if any masonry structures remain standing. Bridges are destroyed. Broad fissures appear in ground. At the highest levels and near the epicenter, damage total. Waves seen on solid ground. Heavy objects thrown upward into air.

Most volcanoes are found where two tectonic plates meet, such as along the famous "Ring of Fire" around the Pacific Ocean. A few, such as the volcanoes of the Hawaiian Islands, appear to be over "hot spots" in the Earth's crust where liquid rock flows upward with sufficient force to burn through the crust.

Although volcanoes are associated with destruction, they have many positive effects. Minerals from deep within the Earth make the land around many volcanoes extremely fertile; volcanoes can create new landforms in the sea; and the study of volcanoes contributes enormously to our understanding of the Earth's interior.

Although geologists consider a volcano active if it has shown signs of activity in historic times, it is not usually clear whether a volcano is extinct or only dormant and could be active again. (Thus Tambora, which has not erupted since 1815, is considered active.) Some volcanoes once thought to be extinct have become active, and there are now about 600 volcanoes that are considered active. The accompanying list contains about a fourth of all volcanoes known to have been active in recent years, with special emphasis on volcanoes in the United States and volcanoes that have had famous eruptions.

The destruction caused by volcanoes is usually localized, but their effects can be felt around the world and take many forms. At their worst, volcanoes can blow themselves to pieces, as the island of Thera did about 1650 B.C. More often, volcanic ash blankets an area (as Mt. Vesuvius did at Pom-

peii), or clouds of hot gases and dust sweep down the side of the volcano poisoning the air. Lava generally moves too slowly to be a menace to people. Even more unpredictable, heat from a volcano can melt glaciers or snowcaps, triggering massive mud slides (as happened in Colombia in 1985) or releasing lakes of boiling water.

▶MEASURING EARTHQUAKES

The size of an earthquake is generally reported in the United States using the Richter scale, a system developed by seismologist Charles Richter (American: 1900-85) in 1935. The Richter scale measures the magnitude of an earthquake, that is, the size of ground waves generated by an earthquake as shown on a measuring device called a seismograph. Each whole number on the scale represents a tenfold increase (or decrease) in magnitude: a magnitude 6 earthquake produces a ground wave 10 times greater than a magnitude 5.

This does not mean, however, that a magnitude 6 earthquake has 10 times the energy as one of magnitude 5. Measuring the actual energy requires instruments placed at the site of the earthquake. Various methods have been developed for inferring energy from magnitude and these suggest that one change in magnitude corresponds to a thirty- to sixtyfold change in energy. Using these proportions, the energy of a magnitude 8 earthquake, a very serious event, can be as much as 1 million to 10 million times as much as that of a magnitude 4 earthquake, one that can be felt but causes almost no damage.

Major Earthquakes, 856–2001

Date	Location and remarks	Estimated deaths	Richter magnitude	Date	Location and remarks	Estimated deaths	Richter magnitude
856	Corinth, Greece	45,000	--	Dec. 24, 1854	Tokai, Japan	3,000	8.4
Dec. 22, 856	Iran	200,000	--	Oct. 1855	Tokyo, Japan	2,000+	--
Mar. 23, 893	Iran	150,000	--	Jan. 9, 1857	Fort Tejon, California	1	7.9
1036	Shansi	23,000	--	1857	East of Naples, Italy	10,000+	--
1057	Chihli (Hopeh), China	25,000	--	Aug. 13-15, 1868	Peru and Ecuador	40,000	--
Aug. 9, 1138	Aleppo, Syria	230,000	--	May 16, 1875	Venezuela and Colombia	16,000	--
1170	Sicily	15,000	--	Aug. 31, 1886	Charleston, South Carolina	60	7.6
1268	Silicia (Turkey)	60,000	--	Oct. 28, 1891	Central Japan	7,300	--
Sept. 1290	Chihli, China	100,000	--	June 15, 1896	Sanriku and Kamaishi, Japan (tsunami)	26,000	--
May 20, 1293	Kamakura, Japan	30,000	--	Apr. 4, 1905	Kangra, India	19,000	8.6
Jan. 26, 1531	Lisbon, Portugal	30,000	--	Apr. 18, 1906	San Francisco, California	3,000	7.7
Jan. 23, 1556	Shansi, China	830,000	--	Aug. 17, 1906	Santiago, Chile	20,000	8.6
Nov. 1667	Shemakha, Azerbaijan	80,000	--	1907	Tajikistan	40,000	--
June 7, 1692	Port Royal, Jamaica	30,000	--	Dec. 28, 1908	Messina, Sicily	75,000	7.5
Jan. 11, 1693	Catania province, Sicily	60,000	--	Jan. 13, 1916	Avezzano, Italy	29,980	7.5
1693	Naples, Italy	93,000	--	Dec. 16, 1920	Gansu, China	200,000	8.5
1707	Tsunami hits Japan	30,000	--	Sept. 1, 1923	Tokyo/Yokohama, Japan	143,000	8.3
Nov. 18, 1727	Tabriz, Iran	77,000	--	Mar. 7, 1927	Tango, Japan	3,020	7.9
Dec. 30, 1730	Hokkaido Island, Japan	137,000	--	May 22, 1927	Nan-Shan, China	200,000	8.3
1731	Beijing, China	100,000	--	Dec. 25, 1932	Gansu, China	70,000	7.6
Oct. 11, 1737	Calcutta, India	300,000	--	Mar. 2, 1933	Sanriku, Japan (tsunami)	2,990	8.9
June 7, 1755	Northern Iran	40,000	--	Mar. 11, 1933	Long Beach, California	115	6.3
Nov. 1, 1755	Lisbon, Portugal (earthquake, tsunami)	60,000	8.6	Jan. 15, 1934	Bihar, India and Nepal	10,700	8.4
Feb. 4, 1783	Calabria, Italy	50,000	--	May 30, 1935	Quetta, India (Pakistan)	50,000	7.5
Feb. 4, 1797	Quito, Ecuador and Cuzco, Peru	41,000	--	Jan. 25, 1939	Chillan, Chile	30,000	8.3
Dec. 16, 1811	New Madrid, Missouri	<10	7.7	Dec. 27, 1939	Erzincan, Turkey	30,000	8.0
Feb. 7, 1812	New Madrid, Missouri	0	7.9	Apr. 1, 1946	Earthquake at Unimak Island, Alaska, causes tsunami striking Hilo, Hawaii	165	7.3
Sept. 5, 1822	Aleppo (Syria)	22,000	--				
Dec. 28, 1828	Echigo, Japan	30,000	--				

Date	Location and remarks	Estimated deaths	Richter magnitude
Dec. 20, 1946	Tonankai, Japan	1,330	8.4
June 28, 1948	Fukui, Japan	5,390	7.3
Oct. 5, 1948	Ashkabad, Turkmenistan	110,000	7.3
Aug. 5, 1949	Pelileo, Ecuador	6,000	6.8
Aug. 15, 1950	Assam State, India	1,530	8.7
July 21, 1952	Bakersfield, California	12	7.5
June 10-17, 1956	Northern Afghanistan	2,000	7.7
July 2, 1957	Northern Iran	1,200	7.4
Dec. 13, 1957	Western Iran	1,130	7.3
Aug. 17, 1959	Hebgen Lake, Montana	28	7.3
Feb. 29, 1960	Agadir, Morocco	12,000	5.9
May 21-30, 1960	Southern Chile; tsunami strikes various Pacific islands, killing 61 in Hawaii; greatest earthquake ever recorded	5,700	9.5
Sept. 1, 1962	Northwestern Iran	12,230	7.3
Mar. 28, 1964	Southern Alaska	125	9.2
Aug. 19, 1966	Eastern Turkey	2,520	7.1
Aug. 31, 1968	Khurasan, Iran	12,000	7.3
July 25, 1969	Eastern China	3,000	5.9
Jan. 5, 1970	Yunnan Province, China	10,000	7.5
May 31, 1970	Yungay, Ranrahirca, and Huarás, Peru	66,000	7.8
Feb. 9, 1971	San Fernando Valley, California	65	6.6
Apr. 10, 1972	Ghir, Iran	5,054	7.1
Dec. 23, 1972	Managua, Nicaragua	5,000	6.2
Dec. 28, 1974	North Pakistan	5,300	6.2
Feb. 4, 1975	Liaoning Province, China (predicted)	10,000	7.4
Sept. 6, 1975	Lice, Turkey	2,300	6.7
Feb. 4, 1976	Guatemala City,	23,000	7.5
June 25, 1976	New Guinea and Irian Jaya	8,000+	7.1
July 27, 1976	Tangshan, China	655,000	8.0
Aug. 16, 1976	Mindanao, Philippines (earthquake and tsunami)	8,000	7.9
Nov. 24, 1976	Eastern Turkey	5,000	7.3
Sept. 16, 1978	Northeast Iran	15,000	7.8
Oct. 10, 1980	Northwestern Algeria	3,500	7.7
Nov. 23, 1980	Southern Italy	3,000	7.2
July 28, 1981	Kerman province, Iran	2,500	7.3
Dec. 13, 1982	Yemen	2,800	6.0
Sept. 19, 1985	Mexico City	9,500	8.1
Oct. 10, 1986	San Salvador, El Salvador	1,000+	5.5
Mar. 6, 1987	Ecuador	1,000+	7.0
Dec. 7, 1988	Armenia	25,000	7.0

Date	Location and remarks	Estimated deaths	Richter magnitude
Oct. 18, 1989	Loma Prieta, California (Santa Cruz Mountains), destructive in San Francisco and Oakland	63	7.2
June 20, 1990	Caspian Sea, Iran	50,000	7.7
July 16, 1990	Cabanatuan (Luzon I.), Philippines	1,621	7.8
Oct. 21, 1991	India and Nepal	2,000	7.0
Dec. 12, 1992	Flores Island, Indonesia (tsunami)	2,500	7.5
Sept. 29, 1993	Bombay, India	9,748	6.3
Jan. 17, 1994	Northridge, California	61	6.8
Oct. 4, 1994	Kuril Islands of Japan and Russia	190	8.3
Jan. 16, 1995	Near Kobe, Japan	5,502	6.9
May 27, 1995	Sakhalin Island, Russia	1,989	7.5
Feb. 17, 1996	Tsunamis in Irían Jaya, Indonesia	108	8.2
Feb. 27, 1997	Western Pakistan	100+	7.3
Feb. 28, 1997	Northwestern Iran	1,000+	6.1
May 10, 1997	Northeastern Iran	1,560	7.5
Feb. 4, 1998	Afghanistan	2,323	6.1
May 22, 1998	Central Bolivia	105	6.6
May 30, 1998	Afghanistan and Tajikistan	4,000	6.9
June 27, 1998	Adana, Turkey	136	6.3
July 17, 1998	Tsunamis strike Papua, New Guinea	2,183	7.1
Jan. 25, 1999	Armenia, Colombia	1,885	6.4
Aug. 17, 1999	Northwestern Turkey	17,118	7.4
Sept. 7, 1999	Athens, Greece	143	5.8
Sept. 20, 1999	Nantou, Taiwan	2,101	7.6
Oct. 5, 1999	Dodecanese Islands, Greece	103	4.6
Nov. 12, 1999	Turkey	843	7.5
Jan. 14, 2000	Yunnan, China	7	5.9
May 4, 2000	Sulawesi, Indonesia	46	7.5
May 17, 2000	Taiwan	3	5.3
June 4, 2000	Southern Sumatera, Indonesia	103	8.0
July 7, 2000	Nicaragua	7	5.1
Sept. 3, 2000	Napa Valley, Northern Calif.	0	4.9
Nov. 25, 2000	Turkmenistan and Azerbaijan	31	5.8
Dec. 6, 2000	Turkmenistan	11	7.5
Jan. 10, 2001	Kodiak Island region, Alaska	0	6.8
Jan 13, 2001	El Salvador	844	7.7
Jan. 26, 2001	Southern India	20,085	7.7
Feb. 13, 2001	El Salvador	315	6.6
Feb. 23, 2001	Sichuan, China	10	5.4
Feb. 28, 2001	Washington State	1	6.8
June 23, 2001	Coast of Peru	95	8.4

Volcano Eruptions and Landslides, 1628 B.C.–2001 A.D

Date	Event	Deaths
B.C.		
1628 or 1645	Mediterranean volcanic island of Thera (Santorini) explodes.	N.A.
A.D.		
Aug. 24–26, 79	Mt. Vesuvius, near Naples, Italy, erupts, destroying towns of Pompeii and Herculaneum.	2,000 +
260	Mt. Ilopango in El Salvador erupts, apparently destroying the early Maya civilization.	N.A.
Sept. 4, 1618	Landslides hit Chiavenna Valley, Italy.	2,420
Dec. 16, 1631	Mt. Vesuvius erupts.	4,000 +
Mar. 25, 1669	Mt. Etna at Catania, Sicily, erupts.	20,000

Date	Event	Deaths
Jan. 11, 1683	Mt. Etna erupts, accompanied by earthquakes.	60,000
Aug. 11–12, 1772	Mt. Papandayan on Java explodes.	3,000 +
1782	Eruption of Mt. Unzen in Japan causes tidal wave.	15,000
June 1783– Feb. 1784	Laki fissure on Mt. Skaptar, Iceland erupts; poisonous gases kill crops and livestock, and thick haze interrupts fishing on oceans.	9,800
Sept. 2, 1806	Rossberg Peak collapses, causing landslides in Goldau Valley, Switzerland.	500
Apr. 5, 1815	Mt. Tambora on Sumbawa in East Indies begins series of eruptions that kill about 10,000 people; another 80,000 die of famine and disease locally	162,000

Date	Event	Deaths
Oct. 8 and 12, 1822	Mt. Galunggung on Java erupts, causing slides of mud and boiling water.	4,000
1845	Eruption of Nevada del Ruiz in northern Colombia causes mud slides from melting snow.	1,000
July 28, 1883	Epomeo volcano on Italian Isle of Ischia erupts, causing destructive earthquakes.	2,000 +
Aug. 26, 1883	Krakatau volcano in East Indies erupts, producing giant waves that strike nearby islands.	36,000
May 7, 1902	La Soufriére on St. Vincent in West Indies erupts.	1,500–2,000
May 8, 1902	Pelée on neighboring Martinique erupts, pouring cloud of flaming gas on city of St. Pierre.	29,000
Aug. 30, 1902	Mt. Pelée erupts.	2,000
Apr. 18, 1906	Mt. Vesuvius near Naples erupts.	150 +
1911	Taal volcano, near Manila, Philippines, erupts.	1,300
May 1919	Crater lake of Mt. Kelut in Indonesia, boiling from volcanic activity, breaks through side of the mountain.	5,000 +
1937	Eruption of Rabaul caldera on New Britain, Papua New Guinea.	500 +
Jan. 15, 1951	Mt. Lamington on New Guinea produces cloud of hot gas and dust, similar to that at Mt. Pelée in 1902 and Mt. St. Helens in 1980.	3,000–5,000
Dec. 4, 1951	Mt. Catarman (Hibokhibok) in Philippines releases cloud of hot gas.	500
Sept. 24, 1952	Japanese research ship investigating undersea volcano is destroyed in eruptive event.	29
Dec. 25, 1953	Dam, created by 1945 eruption of Ruapehu volcano on New Zealand, gives way; avalanche of mud and snow strikes passenger train.	150
Jan. 10, 1962	Landslide on Mt. Huascarán, Peru.	3,000
Mar. 14, 1962	Two landslides near Paucartambno Hydroelectric Station in Peru.	204
Mar. 17-21, 1963	Mt. Agung volcano in Bali, Indonesia, erupts.	1,584
Aug. 10, 1963	Landslide in Nepal sweeps villages into Trisuli River.	200
Oct. 9, 1963	Flood occurs when Valont Dam near Langarone, Italy, overflows as result of landslide into its reservoir.	2,200
1965	Taal volcano near Manila in the Philippines erupts.	150
Aug. 30, 1965	Avalanche near Saas-Fee, Switzerland, from Allalin glacier strikes workers building dam.	40-100
1968	Eruption of Arenal in Costa Rica.	78
July 22, 1970	Landslide diverts Alaknanda River in India, causing sudden flood.	600
Mar. 18, 1971	Landslide into Lake Yanahuani, creates 60-foot wave that sweeps over Chungar, Peru.	200
July 29, 1971	Landslide into high lake in Hindu Kush mountains of Afghanistan causes instant flood.	1,000 +
June 28, 1974	Landslides along Quebrada Blanca Canyon in Eastern Colombia.	200
Jan. 10, 1977	Fast-moving stream of lava from volcano near Goma, Zaire, overtakes fleeing residents.	70
Feb. 21, 1979	Sinila volcano in Java, Indonesia	175 +
Apr. 30, 1979	Landslide covers side of Marapi volcano in Sumatra, Indonesia.	82 +
July 18, 1979	Landslide on Mt. Werung causes wave to strike beach areas on Lomblen Island, Indonesia.	539
May 18, 1980	Mt. St. Helens volcano erupts in Washington.	61
May 20, 1981	Landslides caused by eruption of Semeru in Java, Indonesia.	252
Mar. 28 and Apr. 3-4, 1982	El Chichón in Chiapas, Mexico, erupts, sending cloud of volcanic ash around world.	2,000
Aug. 16, 1984	Carbon dioxide emitted by Lake Monoun, Cameroon, spreads in region around lake.	37
Nov. 13, 1985	Eruption of Nevada del Ruiz in northern Colombia causes massive mud slide covering town of Armero.	25,000
Aug. 21, 1986	Carbon dioxide from Lake Nyos, Cameroon, spreads through region.	1,700 +
Feb. 10, 1990	Eruption of Mt. Kelut on Java, Indonesia.	32
July 13, 1990	Earthquake triggers landslide in Pamir Mts., Tajikistan, USSR.	40+
Oct. 13, 1990	Geyserlike explosion in the Ahuachapán Geothermal Field, El Salvador, releases wave of carbon dioxide and water.	26
Jan. 5, 1991	Landslide at Zuñil Geothermal Field, Guatemala.	33
June 3, 1991	Eruption of Mt. Unzen, Kyushu, Japan.	43
June 9, 1991	Mount Pinatubo erupts, as predicted, in Luzon, Philippines; 358 killed by disease in evacuation camps.	754
Jan. 14, 1993	Galeras in Colombia unexpectedly erupts during a scientific workshop, killing six volcanologists who had been on the rim studying the volcano.	9
Feb. 2, 1993	An unexpected eruption of Mayon on Luzon, Philippines produces a cloud of hot gas and dust that rolls down the slope.	70
June 6, 1994	An earthquake at the Volcano Nevada de Huila in Colombia causes mud slides that destroy a dozen villages on its slopes.	650 +
Nov. 22, 1994	Various flows of hot ash and gases down the slope of Merapi volcano on Java in Indonesia kill workers at a water-treatment plant and sweep through villages where superstitious villagers ignored a call to evacuate.	64
Nov. 3, 1995	Mud landslide set off by eruption of Rinjani on Lombok Island, Indonesia.	30 +
Feb. 18, 1997	Mudslide caused by heavy rains destroys two Peruvian villages	300
May 5-6, 1998	Mudslides caused by heavy rains pour down Mount Sarno, east of Naples, Italy.	135
Oct. 30, 1998	Hurricane Mitch causes landslide on San Cristobal volcano in Nicaragua.	1600
Apr. 22, 1999	Rain triggers landslides of mountains denuded of trees on Mindanao in the Philippines.	19
Dec., 1999	Heavy rains cause floods and landslides in northern Venezuela.	20,000
Jan. 13, 2001	Landslides triggered by an earthquake near Santa Tecla, El Salvador, bury villages.	585

Major Active Volcanoes

Volcano	Location	Height (feet above sea level)	Last reported eruption
Africa and the Indian Ocean			
Cameroon Mt.	Cameroon	13,435	2000
Karthala	Comoros	8,000	1991
Ol Donyo Lengai	Tanzania	9,482	1998
Nyamuragira	Zaire	10,033	2001
Nyirangongo	Zaire	12,381	1995
Asia			
Agung	Bali, Indonesia	10,308	1964
Alaid	Kuril Islands, Russia	7,674	1996
Asama	Honshu, Japan	8,339	1983
Aso	Kyushu, Japan	5,223	1995
Azuma	Honshu, Japan	6,640	1977
Batur	Bali, Indonesia	5,631	1994
Bezymianny	Russia	9,455	2000
Bulusan	Philippines	5,135	1995
Chokai	Honshu, Japan	7,300	1974
Dukono	Indonesia	3,566	1995
Fuji	Honshu, Japan	12,388	1707
Galunggung	Java, Indonesia	7,113	1982
Gamalama	Indonesia	5,625	1994
Karagetang	Indonesia	5,850	2001
Karymsky	Russia	4,785	2000
Kelut	Java, Indonesia	5,679	1990
Kerinci	Sumatra, Indonesia	12,467	1999
Kliuchevskoi	Russia	15,584	2001
Komaga-take	Japan	5,449	2000
Koryasky	Russia	11,339	1957
Krakatau	Indonesia	2,667	2000
Lewotobi	Indonesia	5,587	1999
Lokon-Empung	Indonesia	5,187	2001
Mayon	Philippines	8,077	2001
Me-akan	Japan	4,918	1996
Merapi	Java, Indonesia	9,550	2001
Nasu	Japan	6,289	1977
Nigata Yakeyama	Japan	8,064	1987
On-Take	Kyushu, Japan	10,049	1979
Oyama	Japan	2,686	2001
Peuet Sague	Indonesia	9,154	1998
Pinatubo	Luzon, Philippines	5,250	1991
Raung	Java, Indonesia	10,131	1997
Rinjani	Lombok Island, Indonesia	12,224	1995
Sakura-jima	Kyushu, Japan	3,665	2000
Sangeang Api	Indonesia	6,351	1988
Sarychev	Kuril Isl. Russia	5,115	1986
Semeru	Java, Indonesia	12,057	2000
Shiveluch	Russia	10,779	2001
Sinila	Indonesia	7,000	1979
Slamet	Java, Indonesia	11,260	1989
Soputan	Indonesia	5,853	1996
Suwanose-jima	Ryukyu Islands, Japan	2,621	1997
Taal	Luzon, Philippines	1,015	1977
Tambora	Sumbawa, Indonesia	9,348	1815
Tengger Caldea	Java, Indonesia	7,641	1995
Tiatia	Kuril Isl., Russia	6,013	1973
Unzen	Kyushu, Japan	4,921	1996
Usu	Japan	2,398	2000
Europe and the Atlantic Ocean			
Askja	Iceland	4,594	1961
Beerenberg	Jan Mayen Island, Norway	7,470	4,921
Etna	Italy	10,991	2001
Fogo	Cape Verde Islands	9,281	1995
Grimsvotn	Iceland	5,658	1998
Helka	Iceland	4,892	2000
Krafla	Iceland	2,145	1984
Leirhnukur	Iceland	2,145	1975
Stromboli	Italy	3,038	1998
Tristan de Cunha	St. Helena	6,760	1961
Vesuvius	Italy	3,888	1944
North America			
Akutan	Alaska	4,275	1996
Amukta	Alaska	3,490	1996
Augustine	Alaska	3,995	1986
Carlisle	Alaska	5,315	1838
Cerberus	Alaska	2,560	1873
Cinder Cone	California	7,985	1851
Cleveland	Alaska	5,675	2001
Colima	Mexico	13,448	2001
El Chichón	Mexico	3,478	1983
Fisher	Alaska	3,545	1826
Gareloi	Alaska	5,370	1982
Great Sitkin	Alaska	5,775	1974
Iliamna	Alaska	10,140	1978
Kagamil	Alaska	2,945	1929
Kanaga	Alaska	4,288	1994
Katmai	Alaska	7,540	1974
Kiska	Alaska	4,025	1990
Korovin	Alaska	4,885	1998
Lassen Peak	California	10,453	1921
Little Sitkin	Alaska	3,945	1828
Mageik	Alaska	7,295	1946
Makushin	Alaska	6,680	1987
Martin	Alaska	6,102	1960
Mt. Baker	Washington	10,778	1870
Mt. Hood	Oregon	11,245	1801
Mt. Rainier	Washington	14,410	1882
Mt. St. Helens	Washington	8,368	1998
Mt. Shasta	California	14,160	1855
Novarupta	Alaska	2,759	1912
Okmok	Alaska	3,540	1997
Parícutin	Mexico	1,500	1953
Pavlof	Alaska	8,960	1997
Pavlof Sister	Alaska	7,050	1786
Pogromni	Alaska	7,545	1964
Popocatépetl	Mexico	17,930	2001
Redoubt	Alaska	10,265	1990
Sarichef	Alaska	2,015	1812
Seguam	Alaska	3,465	1993
Shishaldin	Alaska	9,430	2000
Spurr	Alaska	11,070	1992
Tanaga	Alaska	7,015	1914
Tobert	Alaska	11,413	1953
Trident	Alaska	6,830	1974
Veniaminof	Alaska	8,225	1995
Westdahl	Alaska	5,055	1992
Yunaska	Alaska	1,980	1937
Central America and the Caribbean			
Acatenango	Guatemala	12,992	1972
Arenal	Costa Rica	5,436	2001
Concepción	Ometepe Island, Nicaragua	5,577	2000
Fuego	Guatemala	12,346	2000
Irazu	Costa Rica	11,260	1965
Izalco	El Salvador	6,396	1966
Cerro Negro	Nicaragua	2,214	1999

Volcano	Location	Height (feet above sea level)	Last reported eruption
Masaya	Nicaragua	2,083	2001
Pacaya	Guatemala	8,346	2000
Pelée	Martinique	4,500	1930
Póas	Costa Rica	8,885	1994
Rincón de la Vieja	Costa Rica	6,286	1998
San Cristóbal	Nicaragua	5,725	2000
San Miguel	El Salvador	6,988	1987
Santa Maria	Guatemala	12,375	1999
Soufriére	St. Vincent and the Grenadines	4,048	1979
Soufriére Hills	Montserrat, West Indies	3,090	2000
Tacaná	Guatemala	12,400	1988
Telica	Nicaragua	3,314	1999
South America			
Alcedo	Galapagos Islands, Ecuador	3,707	1993
Cerro Azul	Galapagos Islands, Ecuador	5,543	1998
Copahue	Argentina/Chile	9,800	1992
Cotachachi	Ecuador	16,204	1955
Galeras	Colombia	14,025	1993
Guagua Pichincha	Ecuador	15,696	2000
Guallatiri	Chile	19,918	1960
Hudson	Chile	8,580	1991
Láscar	Chile	18,346	1995
Llaima	Chile	10,250	1995
Lonquimay	Chile	9,400	1990
Puracé	Colombia	15,604	1977
Reventador	Ecuador	11,434	1976
Ruiz	Colombia	17,457	1991
Sangay	Ecuador	17,020	1988
Tungurahua	Ecuador	16,480	2001
Villarica	Chile	9,338	2000
Oceania—Australia, New Zealand, and the Pacific Islands			
Ambrym	Vanuatu	4,376	2000
Bagana	Bougainville Island, Papua New Guinea	5,742	1991
Haleakala	Hawaii	10,025	1790
Hualalai	Hawaii	8,251	1801
Karkar	Papua New Guinea	4,920	1979
Kilauea	Hawaii	4,009	2000
Langila	New Britain, Papua New Guinea	4,364	1999
Lopevi	New Hebrides, Vanuatu	4,636	2001
Manam	Papua New Guinea	5,928	1999
Mauna Loa	Hawaii	13,678	1984
Ngauruhoe	North Island, New Zealand	7,515	1977
Pagan	Mariana Islands	1,870	1993
Piton de la Fournaise	Réunion Island	8,631	2001
Rabaul	New Britain, Papua New Guinea	2,257	2000
Ruapehu	New Zealand	9,177	1996
Ulawun	New Britain, Papua New Guinea	7,657	2001
White Island	New Zealand	1,053	2000
Antarctica			
Big Ben	Heard Island	9,007	1993
Mount Erebus	Ross Island	13,444	2001

CHEMISTRY

Chemistry is concerned with the way substances interact with one another. These interactions are chiefly the result of outer electrons of an atom interacting with the outer electrons of another atom. It has increasingly become clear that the shapes of the various combinations of atoms (called molecules) also affect chemical reactions, and physical chemistry is one of the most vital parts of chemistry today. Another vital branch is biochemistry, the study of the chemistry of molecules in living organisms. Organic chemistry generally deals with chemicals formed by living organisms and other chemicals containing carbon, but it treats them as chemicals outside the organism. Inorganic chemistry is concerned with chemicals that do not contain carbon.

▶ THE PERIODIC TABLE

In the 19th century, chemists began to determine how much one atom of an element weighed with respect to another—the atomic weight (also known as the atomic mass and measured in atomic mass units, or amu; one amu is a mass equal to one-twelfth the mass of the most common form of carbon atom). The first comprehensive list of atomic weights was prepared by Jöns Jakob Berzelius in 1828. When chemists made lists of elements in the order of atomic weights, they noticed that every seven or eight elements in the list had similar properties. In 1869 Dmitri Mendeleyev boldly interchanged some elements in the list and left blanks for others to make sure the properties matched for every "period" of eight elements. This was the first periodic table. Mendeleyev had only 63 elements to work with, but he correctly predicted three more that would make his list more complete. Today there are 114 elements in the periodic table.

Early in the 20th century, atoms were discovered to consist of protons and electrons (in 1932 it was discovered that neutrons also are found in atoms). The number of protons is the atomic number, which is a different counting number for every element from hydrogen (atomic number 1) to the unnamed element numbered 116 (elements 113 and 115 have yet to be synthesized). The periodic table was improved by arranging the elements in order of atomic number instead of atomic weight. This clearly showed where the blanks were.

Each column of the periodic table includes elements with similar properties, although hydrogen in the first column is less typical in this respect. But the other elements in the first column are all soft metals that are highly reactive. Similarly, the last column of the table contains the gases that react only minimally. In general, elements are met-

Major Discoveries in Chemistry

B.C.

c. 450   Leucippus of Miletus (Greek: 5th cent.) introduces concept of atom, later expanded upon by his pupil Democritus of Abdera (c. 460–c. 370).

A.D.

1662   Robert Boyle (Anglo-Irish: 1627–91) announces what becomes known as Boyle's law: For gas kept at constant temperature, pressure and volume vary inversely.

1755   Joseph Black (Scottish: 1728–99) discovers carbon dioxide.

1766   Henry Cavendish (English: 1731–1810) discovers hydrogen.

1772   Joseph Priestley (English-American: 1733–1804) notes that burning hydrogen produces water.

Daniel Rutherford (Scottish: 1749–1819) and several other chemists discover nitrogen. Karl Wilhelm Scheele (Swedish: 174286) discovers oxygen but does not announce discovery until after independent discovery by Joseph Priestley in 1774.

1778   Antoine-Laurent Lavoisier (French: 1743–94) discovers that air is mostly mixture of nitrogen and oxygen.

1784   Cavendish announces water is compound of hydrogen and oxygen.

1789   Lavoisier explicitly states law of conservation of matter: In chemical change, matter is neither created nor destroyed.

1791   Jeremias Benjamin Richter (German: 1762–1807) shows that acids and bases always neutralize each other in same proportion.

1803   John Dalton (English: 1766–1844) establishes atomic theory of matter.

1811   Amedeo Avogadro (Italian: 1776–1856) proposes that equal volumes of gas at same temperature and pressure contain same number of molecules (Avogadro's law).

1824   Joseph-Louis Gay-Lussac (French: 1778–1850) discovers chemical isomers, chemicals with same formula but different structures.

1828   Friedrich Wöhler (German: 1800–1882) prepares organic compound from inorganic chemicals, showing that life is basically same as other matter.

1859   Gustav Robert Kirchhoff (German: 1824–87) and Robert Wilhelm Bunsen (German: 1811–99) introduce use of spectroscope to identify elements from light they give off when heated.

1868   Pierre-Jules-César Janssen (French: 1824–1907) and Sir Joseph Norman Lockyer (English: 1836–1920) discover helium by observing Sun's spectrum.

1869   Dmitry Ivanovich Mendeleyev (Russian: 1834–1907) publishes his first version of periodic table of elements.

1875   Paul-Emile Lecoq de Boisbaudran (French: 1838–1912) discovers gallium, the first discovery of an element predicted by Mendeleyev.

1906   Mikhail Tsvett (Russian: 1872–1919) develops paper chromatography, the beginning of modern methods of chemical analysis.

1908   Fritz Haber (German: 1868–1934) develops cheap process for making ammonia from nitrogen in the air.

1962   Neil Bartlett (English: 1932–) creates a compound of xenon, platinum, and fluorine, showing that the noble gases can form compounds.

1984   Dany Schechtman (American) and coworkers discover first quasicrystal, a "crystal" that violates the symmetry rules of all other crystals.

1985   Richard E. Smalley (American: 1943–) and Harry Kroto (English: 1939–) discover buckminsterfullerene, a carbon molecule containing 60 carbon atoms arranged in a geodesic sphere (nicknamed "the bucky ball").

1991   Sumio Iijima of NEC Corp. discovers that carbon forms tiny hollow cylinders called nanotubes.

1998   Research on carbon nanotubes shows that they conduct electricity with almost no resistance at room temperature (although they are not superconductors), emit light when carrying an electric current, and can behave either as semiconductors or metals depending on the alignment of atoms in the tube.

2000   Chemists from the University of Helsinki in Finland create argon fluorohydride (HArF), the first compound of argon, leaving only neon and helium as elements that have never formed compounds.

Scientists at the Institute for Nuclear Research in Dubna, Russia, extend the periodic table to include element 116, created by bombarding curium with calcium ions.

2001   Lionel Goodman and Vojislava Pophristic of Rutgers University in New Jersey discover that quantum effects determine the structure of organic molecules, not simple crowding of atoms together as was previously believed.

---

als on the left side of the table (hydrogen is a metal only under great pressure), becoming mostly nonmetals in the last six columns. These last columns include some elements that are metals, such as aluminum. (A broken, heavy line separates the metals from the nonmetals.)

The row of rare-earth elements beginning with lanthanum and the row of actinide elements beginning with actinium do not fit neatly into the rest of the table. Elements from atomic number 57 to 71 are all similar to lanthanum, while elements from atomic number 89 to 103 are similar to actinium. The rare earths are not generally rare, nor do they resemble soil. They are moderately common metals that, because of atomic structure, are very similar chemically. The actinide elements are radioactive metals.

The periodic table as shown here also includes the atomic mass as well as the atomic number. The atomic mass is essentially the sum of the protons and neutrons in an atom of an element. As protons and neutrons join to form an atomic nucleus, a little of their energy becomes mass,

the amount of which depends on how many protons and neutrons there are. Consequently, a particular atom is chosen upon which to base the amu. Today the atomic mass is adjusted to make the most common form of carbon have an atomic mass of exactly 12 (6 protons and 6 neutrons). Most elements occur with several different atomic masses (in addition to carbon-12, for example, there are both carbon-13 and carbon-14; carbon-14 has 6 protons and 8 neutrons and is radioactive). These different forms are called isotopes. Therefore, in the periodic table, the atomic mass given for most elements is the one that would be found by averaging the different isotopes in the amounts they naturally occur. Carbon is given an atomic mass of 12.01 because there is so much more carbon-12 than there is carbon-13 or carbon-14 in an ordinary sample of carbon. For some radioactive elements, natural abundance is meaningless, since there is no stable form. For these, the atomic mass of the most stable form is given, indicated by putting the atomic mass in parentheses.

THE PERIODIC TABLE OF THE ELEMENTS

Legend:
- 6 — atomic number
- C — chemical number
- 12.01 — atomic mass
- Carbon — name of element

	IA	IIA	IIIB	IVB	VB	VIB	VIIB	VIII	VIII	VIII	IB	IIB	IIIA	IVA	VA	VIA	VIIA	O (noble gases)
Period 1	1 **H** 1.01 Hydrogen																	2 **He** 4.00 Helium
Period 2	3 **Li** 6.94 Lithium	4 **Be** 9.01 Beryllium											5 **B** 10.81 Boron	6 **C** 12.01 Carbon	7 **N** 14.01 Nitrogen	8 **O** 16.00 Oxygen	9 **F** 19.00 Fluorine	10 **Ne** 20.18 Neon
Period 3	11 **Na** 22.99 Sodium	12 **Mg** 24.31 Magnesium											13 **Al** 26.98 Aluminium	14 **Si** 28.09 Silicon	15 **P** 30.97 Phosphorus	16 **S** 32.07 Sulfur	17 **Cl** 35.45 Chlorine	18 **Ar** 39.95 Argon
Period 4	19 **K** 39.10 Potassium	20 **Ca** 40.08 Calcium	21 **Sc** 44.96 Scandium	22 **Ti** 47.88 Titanium	23 **V** 50.94 Vanadium	24 **Cr** 52.00 Chromium	25 **Mn** 54.95 Manganese	26 **Fe** 55.85 Iron	27 **Co** 58.93 Cobalt	28 **Ni** 58.70 Nickel	29 **Cu** 63.55 Copper	30 **Zn** 65.39 Zinc	31 **Ga** 69.72 Gallium	32 **Ge** 72.61 Germanium	33 **As** 74.92 Arsenic	34 **Se** 78.96 Selenium	35 **Br** 79.90 Bromine	36 **Kr** 83.80 Krypton
Period 5	37 **Rb** 85.47 Rubidium	38 **Sr** 87.62 Strontium	39 **Y** 88.91 Yttrium	40 **Zr** 91.22 Zirconium	41 **Nb** 92.91 Niobium	42 **Mo** 95.94 Molybdenum	43 **Tc** (98) Technetium	44 **Ru** 101.07 Ruthenium	45 **Rh** 102.91 Rhodium	46 **Pd** 106.4 Palladium	47 **Ag** 107.87 Silver	48 **Cd** 112.41 Cadmium	49 **In** 114.82 Indium	50 **Sn** 118.71 Tin	51 **Sb** 121.74 Antimony	52 **Te** 127.60 Tellurium	53 **I** 126.90 Iodine	54 **Xe** 131.29 Xenon
Period 6	55 **Cs** 132.91 Cesium	56 **Ba** 137.33 Barium	Lanthanide series (see below)	72 **Hf** 178.49 Hafnium	73 **Ta** 180.94 Tantalum	74 **W** 183.85 Tungsten	75 **Re** 186.21 Rhenium	76 **Os** 190.23 Osmium	77 **Ir** 192.22 Iridium	78 **Pt** 195.08 Platinum	79 **Au** 196.97 Gold	80 **Hg** 200.59 Mercury	81 **Tl** 204.38 Thallium	82 **Pb** 207.2 Lead	83 **Bi** 208.98 Bismuth	84 **Po** (209) Polonium	85 **At** (210) Astatine	86 **Rn** (222) Radon
Period 7	87 **Fr** (223) Francium	88 **Ra** 226.03 Radium	Actinide series (see below)	104 **Rf** (261) Rutherfordium	105 **Db** (262) Dubnium	106 **Sg** (263) Seaborgium	107 **Bh** (262) Behrium	108 **Hs** (265) Hassium	109 **Mt** (266) Meitnerium	110 (269)	111 (272)	112 (277)		114 (281)		116 (292)		

Group labels: alkali metals (IA), alkaline earth metals (IIA), transition metals, nonmetals, noble gases (O).

rare earth elements — Lanthanide series

57 **La** 138.91 Lanthanum	58 **Ce** 140.12 Cerium	59 **Pr** 140.91 Praseodymium	60 **Nd** 144.24 Neodymium	61 **Pm** (145) Promethium	62 **Sm** 150.4 Samarium	63 **Eu** 151.96 Europium	64 **Gd** 157.25 Gadolinium	65 **Tb** 158.93 Terbium	66 **Dy** 162.50 Dysprosium	67 **Ho** 164.93 Holmium	68 **Er** 167.26 Erbium	69 **Tm** 168.93 Thulium	70 **Yb** 173.04 Ytterbium	71 **Lu** 174.97 Lutetium

Actinide series

89 **Ac** 227.03 Actinium	90 **Th** 232.04 Thorium	91 **Pa** 231.04 Protactinium	92 **U** 238.03 Uranium	93 **Np** 237.05 Neptunium	94 **Pu** (244) Plutonium	95 **Am** (243) Americium	96 **Cm** (247) Curium	97 **Bk** (247) Berkelium	98 **Cf** (251) Californium	99 **Es** (252) Einsteinium	100 **Fm** (257) Fermium	101 **Md** (258) Mendelevium	102 **No** (259) Nobelium	103 **Lr** (260) Lawrencium

Properties and Discovery of the Elements

All ordinary matter is made from one or more substances called elements (because they cannot be changed by chemical means). Ninety elements are found in nature, and people have created others, for a current total of 114. In this table each of the elements is listed in alphabetical order. The chemical symbol and the atomic number can be used to locate other information about the elements in the periodic table reprinted below. Many elements, known from ancient times, are labeled "prehistoric." Others are given with their first discovery—many elements having been independently rediscovered by others. In the following table, elements 110–12, 114, and 118, as yet unnamed, are listed as "Element 110" and so forth.

Element/Type[1]	Symbol/Atomic number	Melting point[1]	Boiling point[1]	Derivation of name (Discoverer, Year)
Actinium	Ac	1924°F	5788°F	Greek *aktis*, a ray. (André-Louis Debierne, 1899)
Radioactive metal	89	1051°C	3198°C	
Aluminum	Al	1220°F	4566°F	Latin *alumen*, a substance with astringent taste (Hans
Metal	13	660°C	2519°C	Christian Oersted, 1825)
Americium	Am	2149°F	3652°F	Named for America (Glenn T. Seaborg & coworkers,1944)
Radioactive metal	95	1176°C	2011°C	
Antimony	Sb	1168°F	2889°F	Greek *antimonos*, opposed to solitude; symbol Sb from
Metal	51	631°C	1587°C	Latin *stibium*. (Rhazes, c. 900)
Argon	Ar	-308°F	-303°F	Greek *argus*, neutral inactive. (Sir William Ramsay, 1894)
Gas	18	-189°C	-186°C	
Arsenic[2]	As	N.A.	1117°F	Latin *arsenicum*; folk etymology connects with yellow
Nonmetal	33		603°C	and maleness. (Albertus Magnus, 1250)
Astatine	At	576°F	unk.	Greek *astatos*, unstable. (Emilio Segrè, D.R. Corson, &
Radioactive nonmetal	85		302°C	K.R. MacKenzie, 1940)
Barium	Ba	1341°F	3447°F	Greek *baros*, heavy, because of its dense compounds.
Metal	56	727°C	1897°C	(Humphry Davy, 1808)
Berkelium	Bk	1922°F	unk.	First made at Univ. of California. (Glenn T. Seaborg &
Radioactive metal	97	1050°C		coworkers,1949)
Beryllium	Be	2349°F	4480°F	Latin *beryllus*, Greek beryllos, gem. (Louis-Nicolas
Metal	4	1287°C	2471°C	Vauquelin,1798)
Bismuth	Bi	520°F	2847°F	German *weisse masse*, white mass; changed to *bismat*.
Metal	83	271°C	1564°C	(Claude J. Geoffrey, 1753
Bohrium	Bh	unk.	unk.	Named for Danish physicist Niels Bohr. (Russian
Radioactive metal	107			scientists at Dubna, 1977)
Boron	B	3767°F	7232°F	Arabic *borak* (borax); BORax + carbON. (Joseph-Louis
Nonmetal	5	2075°C	4000°C	Gay-Lussac & Louis-Jacques Thénard, 1808)
Bromine	Br	19°F	138°F	Greek *bromos*, a stench; because of odor of its vapors.
Liquid nonmetal	35	-7°C	59°C	(Antoine-Jérôme Balard, 1826)
Cadmium	Cd	610°F	1413°F	Greek *cadmia*, earthy. (Friedrich Strohmeyer, 1817)
Metal	48	321°C	767°C	
Calcium	Ca	1548°F	2703°F	Latin *calx, calcis*, lime. (Humphry Davy, 1808)
Metal	20	842°C	1484°C	
Californium	Cf	1652°F	unk.	First made at Univ. of California. (Glenn T. Seaborg &
Radioactive metal	98	900°C		coworkers, 1949)
Carbon[2]	C	N.A.	6917°F	Latin *carbo*, coal. (Prehistoric)
Nonmetal	6	N.A.	3825°C	
Cerium	Ce	1468°F	6229°F	Named for asteroid Ceres, discovered in 1801. (Martin
Rare earth	58	798°C	3443°C	Klaproth, 1803)
Cesium	Cs	84°F	1240°F	Latin *caesius*, bluish gray. (Gustav Kirchhoff & Robert
Metal	55	29°C	671°C	Bunsen, 1860)
Chlorine	Cl	-152°F	-29°F	Greek *chloros*, grass-green; from color of gas. (Humphry
Gas	17	-102°C	-34°C	Davy, 1810)
Chromium	Cr	3465°F	4840°F	Greek *chroma*, color; because many of its compounds
Metal	24	1907°C	2671°C	are colored. (Louis-Nicolas Vauquelin, 1797)
Cobalt	Co	2723°F	5301°F	German *Kobalt*, a goblin. (Georg Brandt, 1735)
Metal	27	1495°C	2927°C	
Copper	Cu	1985°F	4644°F	Latin *cuprum*; for island of Cyprus. (Prehistoric)
Metal	29	1085°C	2562°C	
Curium	Cm	2453°F	5612°F	Named after Pierre and Marie Curie. (Glenn T. Seaborg &
Radioactive metal	96	1345°C	3100°C	coworkers, 1944)
Dubnium	Db	unk.	unk.	Named for the Joint Institute for Nuclear Research at
Radioactive metal	105			Dubna,Russia. (Russian scientists at Dubna, 1967)
Dysprosium	Dy	2574°F	4653°F	Greek *dysprositos*, difficult of access. (Paul-Emile Lecoq
Rare earth	66	1412°C	2567°C	deBoisbaudran, 1886)
Einsteinium	Es	1580°F	unk.	Named after Albert Einstein. (Albert Ghiorso &
Radioactive metal	99	860°C		coworkers, 1952)

Element/Type[1]	Symbol/ Atomic number	Melting point[1]	Boiling point[1]	Derivation of name (Discoverer, Year)
Element 110 Radioactive metal	N.A. 110	unk.	unk.	(Society for Heavy Ion Research, Darmstadt, Germany, 1994)
Element 111 Radioactive metal	N.A. 111	unk.	unk.	(Society for Heavy Ion Research, Darmstadt, Germany, 1994)
Element 112 Radioactive metal	N.A. 112	unk.	unk.	(Society for Heavy Ion Research, Darmstadt, Germany, 1996)
Element 114 Radioactive metal	N.A. 114	unk.	unk.	(Dubna and Lawrence Livermore, 1998)
Element 116 Radioactive metal	N.A. 116	unk.	unk.	(Scientists at Dubna, 2000)
Erbium Rare earth	Er 68	2784°F 1529°C	5194°F 2868°C	Named for Ytterby, village in Sweden. (Carl Gustav Mosander, 1843)
Europium Rare earth	Eu 63	1512°F 822°C	2784°F 1529°C	Named for Europe. (Eugène-Anatole Demarçay, 1896)
Fermium Radioactive metal	Fm 100	2781°F 1527°C	unk.	Named after Italian physicist Enrico Fermi. (Albert Ghiorso & coworkers, 1952)
Fluorine Gas	F 9	-364°F -220°C	-306°F -188°C	Latin *fluere*, to flow. (Ferdinand-Frédéric-Henri Moissan, 1886)
Francium Radioactive metal	Fr 87	81°F 27°C	unk.	Named for France. (Marguerite Perey, 1939)
Gadolinium Rare earth	Gd 64	2395°F 1313°C	5923°F 3273°C	Named after gadolinite, mineral named for Johan Gadolin, Finnish chemist. (Jean-Charles Marignac, 1880)
Gallium Metal	Ga 31	86°F 30°C	3999°F 2204°C	Latin *Gallia*, France; also Latin *gallus*, a cock—a pun on Lecoq. (Paul-Emile Lecoq de Boisbaudran, 1875)
Germanium Metal	Ge 32	1721°F 938°C	5131°F 2833°C	Named for Germany. (Clemens Winkler, 1886)
Gold Metal	Au 79	1948°F 1064°C	5173°F 2856°C	Anglo-Saxon *gold*; Sanskrit *juel*, to shine; symbol from Latin *aurum*, shining down. (Prehistoric)
Hafnium Metal	Hf 72	4051°F 2233°C	8317°F 4603°C	From *Hafnia*, ancient name of Copenhagen. (Dirk Coster & György Hevesy, 1923)
Hassium Radioactive metal	Hs 108	unk.	unk.	Named for the German province of Hesse, where Darmstadt is located. (Society for Heavy Ion Research, Darmstadt, Germany, 1984)
Helium Gas	He 2	N.A. N.A.	-452°F -269°C	Greek *helios*, the Sun; first observed in Sun's atmosphere. (Pierre-Jules-César Janssen & Sir Joseph Norman Lockyer, 1868)
Holmium Rare earth	Ho 67	2685°F 1474°C	4892°F 2700°C	From *Holmia*, Latinized form of Stockholm. (Per Teodor Cleve, 1879)
Hydrogen Gas	H 1	-435°F -259°C	-423°F -253°C	Greek *hydor*, water, plus *gen*, forming. (Henry Cavendish, 1766)
Indium Metal	In 49	314°F 157°C	3762°F 2072°C	Latin *indicum*, indigo. (Ferdinand Reich & Hieronymus Theodor Richter, 1863)
Iodine[2] Nonmetal	I 53	237°F 114°C	364°F 184°C	Greek *iodes*, violet; from color of its vapor. (Bernard Courtois, 1811)
Iridium Metal	Ir 77	4435°F 2446°C	8002°F 4428°C	Greek *iris*, a rainbow, from changing color of its salts. (Smithson Tennant , 1803)
Iron Metal	Fe 26	2800°F 1538°C	5182°F 2861°C	Anglo-Saxon *iren*; symbol from Latin *ferrum*. (Prehistoric)
Krypton[3] Gas	Kr 36	-251°F -157°C	-244°F -153°C	Greek *kryptos*, hidden. (Alexander Ramsay & Morris William Travers, 1898)
Lanthanum Rare earth	La 57	1684°F 918°C	6267°F 3464°C	Greek *lanthanein*, to be concealed. (Carl Gustav Mosander, 1839)
Lawrencium Radioactive metal	Lr 103	2961°F 1627°C	unk.	Named after American physicist Ernest Lawrence. (Albert Ghiorso & coworkers, 1961)
Lead Metal	Pb 82	621°F 327°C	3180°F 1749°C	Anglo-Saxon *lead*; symbol from Latin *plumbum*. (Prehistoric)
Lithium Metal	Li 3	351°F 181°C	2448°F 1342°C	Greek *lithos*, stony. (Johann A. Arfvedson, 1817)
Lutetium Rare earth	Lu 71	3025°F 1663°C	6159°F 3404°C	Latin *Lutetia*, ancient name for Paris. (Georges Urbain, 1907)
Magnesium Metal	Mg 12	1202°F 650°C	1994°F 1090°C	Latin *Magnesia*, a district in Asia Minor. (Humphry Davy, 1808)
Manganese Metal	Mn 25	2275°F 1246°C	3742°F 2061°C	Latin *magnes*, magnet; because of confusion with magnetic iron ores. (Johann Gottlieb Gahn, 1774)
Meitnerium Radioactive metal	Mt 109	unk.	unk.	Named for the Austrian-Swedish physicist Lise Meitner. (Society for Heavy Ion Research, Darmstadt, Germany, 1982)
Mendelevium Radioactive metal	Md 101	1521°F 827°C	unk.	Named after Russian chemist Dmitri Mendeléev. (Albert Ghiorso & coworkers, 1955)

Element/Type[1]	Symbol/ Atomic number	Melting point[1]	Boiling point[1]	Derivation of name (Discoverer, Year)
Mercury	Hg	-38°F	674°F	Named for Roman god Mercurius; symbol from Latin
Liquid metal	80	-39°C	357°C	*hydrargyrum*. (Prehistoric)
Molybdenum	Mo	4753°F	8382°F	Greek *molybdos*, lead. (Karl Wilhelm Scheele, 1778)
Metal	42	2623°C	4639°C	
Neodymium	Nd	1870°F	5565°F	Greek *neo*, new, plus *didymon*, twin (with the element
Rare earth	60	1021°C	3074°C	praseodymium). (Karl Auer (Baron von Welsbach), 1885)
Neon	Ne	-415°F	-411°F	Greek *neo*, new. (Alexander Ramsay & Morris William
Gas	10	-249°C	-246°C	Travers, 1898)
Neptunium	Np	1191°F	unk.	Named for planet Neptune. (Edwin McMillan & Philip
Radioactive metal	93	644°C		Abelson,1940)
Nickel	Ni	2651°F	5308°F	German *Nickel*, Satan (Old Nick). (Axel Cronstedt, 1751)
Metal	28	1455°C	2931°C	
Niobium	Nb	4491°F	8571°F	Latin *Niobe*, daughter of Tantalus. (Charles Hachett,
Metal	41	2477°C	4744°C	1801)
Nitrogen	N	-346°F	-320°F	Latin, forming *niter*, a compound of nitrogen. (Daniel
Gas	7	-210°C	-196°C	Rutherford, 1772)
Nobelium	No	1521°F	unk.	Named after Alfred Nobel; made at Nobel Institute.
Radioactive metal	102	827°C		(Albert Ghiorso & coworkers, 1958)
Osmium	Os	5491°F	9054°F	Greek *osme*, smell; for malodorousness. (Smithson
Metal	76	3033°C	5012°C	Tennant, 1803)
Oxygen	O	-362°F	-297°F	Greek *oxys*, sharp, plus *gen*, forming; from incorrect
Gas	8	-219°C	-183°C	belief that oxygen forms acids. (Joseph Priestley, 1774)
Palladium	Pd	2831°F	5365°F	Named for Greek goddess Pallas; from asteroid Pallas.
Metal	46	1555°C	2963°C	(William Hyde Wollaston, 1803)
Phosphorus	P	111°F	537°F	Greek *phosphoros*, light-bringer; glows because of rapid .
Nonmetal	15	44°C	281°C	oxidation(Hennig Brand, 1669)
Platinum	Pt	3215°F	6917°F	Diminutive of Spanish *plata*, silver, *platina*. (Antonio de
Metal	78	1768°C	3825°C	Ulloa, 1735)
Plutonium	Pu	1184°F	5842°F	Named for planet Pluto. (Glenn T. Seaborg & coworkers,
Radioactive metal	94	640°C	3228°C	1940)
Polonium	Po	489°F	1764°F	Named by Marie Curie for her native Poland. (Marie &
Radioactive metal	84	254°C	962°C	Pierre Curie, 1898)
Potassium	K	146°F	1398°F	Named for potash, a compound of potassium; symbol
Metal	19	64°C	759°C	from Latin *kalium*. (Humphry Davy, 1807)
Praseodymium	Pr	1708°F	6368°F	Greek *prasios*, green, plus *didymos*, twin (with
Rare earth	59	931°C	3520°C	neodymium). (Karl Auer (Baron von Welsbach), 1885)
Promethium	Pm	1908°F	5432°F	Named for Greek god Prometheus, who stole fire from
Radioactive rare earth	61	1042°C	3000°C	heaven. (J.A. Marinsky, L.E. Glendenin, & C.D.Coryell, 1945)
Protactinium	Pa	2862°F	unk.	Latin *proto*, first, plus actinium, one of the elements.
Radioactive metal	91	1572°C		(Otto Hahn & Lise Meitner, 1918)
Radium	Ra	1292°F	unk.	Latin *radius*, ray. (Marie Curie & Pierre Curie, 1898)
Radioactive metal	88	700°C		
Radon	Rn	-96°F	-79°F	*Radium* plus *on*, as in *neon*. (Friedrich Ernst Dorn, 1900)
Radioactive gas	86	-71°C	-62°C	
Rhenium	Re	5767°F	10105°F	Latin *Rhenus*, Rhine. (Walter Noddack, Ida Tacke, & Otto
Metal	75	3186°C	5596°C	Berg, 1925)
Rhodium	Rh	3567°F	6683°F	Greek *rhodon*, rose; for red color of its salts. (William
Metal	45	1964°C	3695°C	Hyde Wollaston, 1803)
Rubidium	Rb	103°F	1270°F	Latin *rubidus*, red; from red lines in its spectrum. (Gustav
Metal	37	39°C	688°C	Kirchhoff & Robert Bunsen, 1861)
Ruthenium	Ru	4233°F	7502°F	Named for Ruthenia in Urals, where ore was first found.
Metal	44	2334°C	4150°C	(Carl Claus, 1844)
Rutherfordium	Rf	unk.	unk.	Named for the New Zealand-born English physicist Ernest
Radioactive metal	104			Rutherford. (Russian scientists at Dubna, 1964)
Samarium	Sm	1965°F	3261°F	Named for Scandinavian mineral samarskite. (Paul-Emile
Rare earth	62	1074°C	1794°C	Lecoq de Boisbaudran, 1879)
Scandium	Sc	2806°F	5137°F	Named for Scandinavia. (Lars Fredrik Nilson, 1879)
Metal	21	1541°C	2836°C	
Seaborgium	Sg	unk.	unk.	Named for American physicist Glenn T. Seaborg. (Russian
Radioactive metal	106			scientists at Dubna and U.S. team from Berkeley and Lawrence Livermore Laboratories, 1974)
Selenium	Se	429°F	1265°F	Greek *selene*, the Moon. (Jöns Jakob Berzelius, 1818)
Nonmetal	34	221°C	685°C	
Silicon	Si	2577°F	5909°F	Latin *silex*, flint. (Jöns Jakob Berzelius, 1824)
Nonmetal	14	1414°C	3265°C	
Silver	Ag	1763°F	3924°F	Anglo-Saxon *sealfor*; symbol is from Latin *argentum*.
Metal	47	962°C	2162°C	(Prehistoric)

Element/Type[1]	Symbol/ Atomic number	Melting point[1]	Boiling point[1]	Derivation of name (Discoverer, Year)
Sodium	Na	208°F	1621°F	English *soda*, a sodium compound; symbol from Latin
Metal	11	98°C	883°C	*natrium* (Humphry Davy, 1807)
Strontium	Sr	1431°F	2520°F	For Strontian, a town in Scotland. (Humphry Davy, 1808)
Metal	38	777°C	1382°C	
Sulfur	S	247°F	832°F	Sanskrit *solvere*, Latin *sulphur*. (Prehistoric)
Nonmetal	16	120°C	445°C	
Tantalum	Ta	5463°F	9856°F	For mythical king Tantalus, condemned to thirst; because
Metal	73	3017°C	5458°C	of its insolubility. (Anders Ekeberg, 1802)
Technetium	Tc	3915°F	7709°F	Greek *technetos*, artificial; first artificial element. (Emilio
Radioactive metal	43	2157°C	4265°C	Segrè,1937)
Tellurium	Te	841°F	1810°F	Latin *tellus*, the Earth. (Franz Joseph Müller, 1782)
Metal	52	450°C	988°C	
Terbium	Tb	2473°F	5846°F	For Ytterby, village in Sweden. (Carl Gustav Mosander,
Rare earth	65	1356°C	3230°C	1843)
Thallium	Tl	579°F	2683°F	Greek *thallos*, a green twig; after color of its spectrum.
Metal	81	304°C	1473°C	(William Crookes, 1861)
Thorium	Th	3182°F	8650°F	For Norse god Thor. (Jöns Jakob Berzelius, 1829)
Radioactive metal	90	1750°C	4788°C	
Thulium	Tm	2813°F	3542°F	Greek *Thule*, Greek name for land north of Britain. (Per.
Rare earth	69	1545°C	1950°C	Teodor Cleve, 1879)
Tin	Sn	449°F	4716°F	Anglo-Saxon *tin*; symbol from Latin *stannum*. (Prehistoric)
Metal	50	232°C	2602°C	
Titanium	Ti	3034°F	5949°F	For Titans of classical mythology. (William Gregor, 1791)
Metal	22	1668°C	3287°C	
Tungsten	W	6192°F	10,031°F	Swedish *tung sten*, heavy stone; symbol from German
Metal	74	3422°C	5555°C	*Wolfram*. (Fausto and Juan José d'Elhuyar, 1783)
Uranium	U	2075°F	7468°F	For planet Uranus. (Martin Klaproth, 1789)
Radioactive metal	92	1135°C	4131°C	
Vanadium	V	3470°F	6165°F	For Scandinavian goddess Vanadis. (Andrès del Rio,
Metal	23	1910°C	3407°C	1801)
Xenon[3]	Xe	-169°F	-163°F	Greek *xenon*, stranger. (Alexander Ramsay & Morris
Gas	54	-112°C	-108°C	William Travers, 1898)
Ytterbium	Yb	1506°F	2185°F	For Ytterby, a village in Sweden. (George Urbain, 1907)
Rare earth	70	819°C	1196°C	
Yttrium	Y	2772°F	6053°F	For Ytterby, a village in Sweden. (Carl Gustav Mosander,
Rare earth	39	1522°C	3345°C	1843)
Zinc	Zn	787°F	1665°F	German *zink*. (Prehistoric)
Metal	30	420°C	907°C	
Zirconium	Zr	3371°F	7968°F	Arabic *zargun*, gold color. (Martin Klaproth, 1789)
Metal	40	1855°C	4409°C	

1. At a pressure of one atmosphere and, for type, at room temperature. 2. This element sublimes (goes directly from a solid to a gas). 3. Liquefaction also requires great pressure.

PHYSICS

Physics is the basis of the other sciences because it is concerned with the fundamental interactions of matter and energy. The first physicists studied how ordinary objects and very large objects (Moon, planets, and stars) moved in response to forces. Their study was extremely successful. Near the end of the 19th century, physicists began to investigate radiation in detail, leading to the discovery of various forms of electromagnetic radiation (of which only forms of light, including infrared and ultraviolet, were known previously) and particles smaller than the atom (subatomic

particles, such as the electron and proton). In the 20th century, the study of subatomic particles, called particle physics, became a major branch of the science. Many particle physicists limit their work to the particles in the nucleus of atoms and to the behavior of nuclei. Another major branch, condensed-matter physics, is concerned with the physical behavior of materials—for example, their electrical and magnetic properties. Major successes in condensed-matter physics include development of the transistor and related devices (chips) and superconductivity, a state in which electric currents can be transmitted with no resistance. Today many physicists are also cosmologists, who study how the universe began and is constructed, or astrophysicists, who study processes in stars.

Major Discoveries in Physics

1586 Simon Stevinus (Belgian-Dutch: 1548–1620) shows that two different weights dropped at same time from same height will reach ground at same time.

1604 Galileo (Italian: 1564–1642) announces his discovery that a body falling freely will increase its distance as the square of time.

1663 Blaise Pascal (French: 1623–62) proposes what becomes known as Pascal's law: pressure in fluid is transmitted equally in all directions

1675 Ole Rømer (Danish: 1644–1710) becomes first to measure speed of light, although his value is somewhat too slow by today's standards.

1676 Robert Hooke (English: 1635–1703) discovers what becomes known as Hooke's law: The amount a spring stretches varies directly with its tension.

1678 Christiaan Huygens (Dutch: 1629–95) introduces wave theory of light.

1687 Sir Isaac Newton's (English: 1642–1727) *Principia* is published, containing his laws of motion and theory of gravity.

1746 At least two experimenters in Leyden, the Netherlands, invent method for storing static electricity, which becomes known as Leyden jar.

1752 Benjamin Franklin (American: 1706–90) performs kite experiment, demonstrating that lightning is form of electricity.

1787 Jacques A.C. Charles (French: 1746–1823) discovers what is later known as Charles's law: All gases expand same amount with given rise in temperature; e.g., same rise in temperature that will cause hydrogen to double in volume will also cause air to double in volume.

1791 Luigi Galvani (Italian: 1737–98) announces his discovery that when two different metals touch in frog's muscle, they produce electric current.

1798 Benjamin Thompson, Count von Rumford (American-German: 1753–1814) shows that heat is form of motion.

Henry Cavendish (English: 1731–1810) determines gravitational constant and mass of Earth.

1800 William Herschel (German-English: 1738–1822) announces his discovery of infrared light.

1801 Johann W. Ritter (German: 1776–1810) discovers ultraviolet light.

1802 Thomas Young (English: 1773–1829) develops his wave theory of light.

1820 Hans Christian Oersted (Danish: 1777–1851) discovers that magnetism and electricity are two different manifestations of same force.

André-Marie Ampère (French: 1775–1836) formulates first laws of electromagnetism.

1831 Michael Faraday (English: 1791–1867) in England and Joseph Henry (American: 1797–1878) in U.S. (in 1830) independently discover principle of dynamo.

1842 Julius Robert von Mayer (German: 1814–78) is first scientist to state law of conservation of energy.

1848 William Thompson, Baron Kelvin (Scottish: 1824–1907), proposes concept of absolute zero, the lowest possible temperature (-460°F, or -273°C).

1850 Rudolf J.E. Clausius (German: 1822–88) makes first clear statement of second law of thermodynamics: Energy in closed system tends to degrade into heat.

1873 James Clerk Maxwell (Scottish: 1831–79) publishes complete theory of electromagnetism.

1888 Heinrich P. Hertz (German: 1857–94) produces and detects radio waves.

1895 Wilhelm Konrad Röntgen (German: 1845–1923) discovers X rays.

1896 Henri Becquerel (French: 1852–1908) discovers natural radioactivity.

1897 Sir Joseph John Thomson (English: 1856–1940) discovers electron.

1900 Max K.E.L. Planck (German: 1858–1947) explains behavior of electromagnetic radiation by proposing that there is smallest step a physical process can take, which he names quantum.

1905 Albert Einstein (German-American: 1879–1955) shows that photoelectric effect—ejection of electrons from metal by action of light—can be explained if light has particle nature as well as wave nature.

Einstein shows that motion of small particles in liquid ("Brownian motion") can be explained by assuming that the liquid is made of molecules.

Einstein develops his special theory of relativity and the law $E = mc^2$ (energy equals mass times square of speed of light).

1911 Heike Kamerlingh Onnes (Dutch: 1853–1926) discovers superconductivity.

Ernest Rutherford (British: 1871–1937) discovers the proton.

1915 Einstein completes his general theory of relativity, a theory of gravity more accurate than that of Sir Isaac Newton, and publishes it the following year.

1924 Louis-Victor de Broglie (French: 1892–1987) publishes his theory that particles, such as electrons, also have wave nature.

1925 Wolfgang Pauli (Austrian-American: 1900–1958) discovers exclusion principal: Two electrons or protons described by same numbers (called quantum numbers) cannot exist in same atom.

Werner Karl Heisenberg (German: 1901–76) develops matrix version of quantum mechanics, a mathematical treatment that explains behavior of electrons and protons.

1926 Erwin Schrödinger (Austrian: 1887–1961) develops wave version of quantum mechanics, a different mathematical treatment producing same results as Heisenberg's matrix mechanics.

1927 Heisenberg develops his uncertainty principle: It is impossible to measure accurately position and momentum of electron or proton at same time.

1932 Sir James Chadwick (British: 1891–1974) discovers neutron, a neutral particle about same mass as proton.

Carl D. Anderson (American: 1905–91) discovers positron, a positively charged analog of electron.

Sir John G. Cockcroft (English: 1897–1967) and Ernest Walton (Irish: 1903–95) develop first particle accelerator, a device for speeding subatomic particles, which causes them to react more intensely with atoms or other particles (often still known as "atom smasher").

1937 Carl Anderson, with other physicists, performs the work that culminates in the discovery of the muon.

1938 Otto Hahn (German: 1870-1968), in experiments interpreted by Lise Meitner (Austrian-Swedish: 1878-1968), splits uranium atom, opening way for nuclear bombs and nuclear power.

1945 Scientists funded by U.S. government and led by J. Robert Oppenheimer (American: 1904–67) detonate first nuclear-fission explosion (atomic bomb).

1947 Cecil Frank Powell (English: 1903–69) and coworkers discover pion, first-known meson, a subatomic particle involved in holding nucleus of atom together.

1955   Owen Chamberlain (American: 1920–) and Emilio Segrè (Italian-American: 1905–89) produce antiprotons, negatively charged analogs of proton.

1956   Clyde Cowan Jr. (American: 1919-74) and Frederick Reines (American: 1918-98) are first to observe neutrino, a subatomic particle with no mass or charge produced in certain forms of radioactive decay.

1957   Experiments by group led by Chien-Shiung Wu (Chinese-American: 1912–97) and quickly confirmed by others show that right and left are distinguished by behavior of electrons emitted in certain forms of radioactivity.

John Bardeen (American: 1908–91), Leon Cooper (American: 1930–), and Bob Schrieffer (American: 1931–) develop a theory explaining superconductivity.

1961   Murray Gell-Mann (American: 1929–) and, independently, Yu'val Ne'eman (Israeli: 1925–) and others develop method of classifying heavy sub-atomic particles that comes to be known as "eight-fold way."

1964   Murray Gell-Mann introduces concept of quarks as components of heavy subatomic particles, such as protons and mesons.

1967   Steven Weinberg (American: 1933–), Abdus Salam (Pakistani-British: 1926–96), and Sheldon Lee Glashow (American: 1932–) independently develop theory that combines electromagnetic force with weak force.

1980   Heinrich Rohrer (Swiss: 1933–) and Gerd Binnig (German: 1947–) invent the scanning tunneling microscope, with which it is possible to produce images of individual atoms on crystal surfaces.

1986   Karl Alexander Müller (Swiss: 1927–) and Johannes Georg Bednorz (German: 1950–) discover first "high-temperature" superconductor.

1995   Physicists at Fermilab in Batavia, Ill., announce the first observations of the sixth and last expected quark, known as top.

Eric Cornell of the U.S. National Institute of Standards and Technology and coworkers produce the first sample of the fifth state of matter, known as a Bose-Einstein Condensate (BEC), in which atoms huddle together in essentially the same place and condition.

Physicists at CERN (the European Laboratory for Particle Physics) produce the first few atoms of anti-hydrogen, with a positron orbiting an antiproton.

1997   Two groups of physicists, one in Austria and one in Rome, show that it is possible to entangle two particles so that measuring an exact quantum state of one of them will instantly determine the corresponding state of the other across any distance, a phenomenon known as "quantum teleportation."

1998   Scientists working with the Super-Kamiokande neutrino telescope in Japan establish indirectly that the neutrinos must have a nonzero, although small, mass.

1999   Scientists at the U.S. National Institutes of Standards and Technology create the first directional atom laser.

2000   Experimenters at the European Laboratory for Particle Physics (CERN) produce short-lived clouds of free quarks and gluons.

An experiment at Fermilab creates and detects the tau neutrino, predicted in 1975 and associated with tauons the way that ordinary neutrinos are with electrons.

Humphrey Maris reports experiments that appear to split individual electrons into two parts, each inside a different bubble floating in liquid helium.

2001   Jun Akimitsu of Aoyama Gakuin University in Tokyo and coworkers discover that the common compound magnesium diboride is a superconductor at temperatures as high as -389°F (-234°C, or 39K), considerably higher than other simple materials (although not as high as some of the complex ceramics).

Physicists at Harvard University and the Harvard-Smithsonian Center for Astrophysics, both in Cambridge, MA, independently stop light completely for brief intervals as it travels through ultracold gases; a laser nudge starts the light wave on its way again.

Experiments at Brookhaven National Laboratory in Upton, NY, that measure the magnetic strength of the muon suggested that the Standard Model that is the basis of particle physics may need modification.

▶ THE BASIC LAWS OF PHYSICS

Key Terms

Mass   is a measure of the amount of matter; it is proportional to weight. Near the surface of Earth it is roughly equivalent to weight.

Velocity   measures how an object changes position with time.

Acceleration   is how an object changes velocity with time.

Momentum   is the product of mass and velocity.

Energy   is the ability to do work.

Law of Gravity

The gravitational force between any two objects is proportional to the product of their masses and inversely proportional to the square of the distance between them. If F is the force, G is the number that represents the ratio (the gravitational constant), m and M are the two masses, and r is the distance between the objects:

$$F = \frac{GmM}{r^2}$$

In metric measure, the gravitational constant is 0.0000000000667390 (6.67390 x 10⁻¹¹) newton m^2/kg^2, so another way of writing the basic law of gravity is

$$F = \frac{0.0000000000667390\, mM}{r^2}$$

This law implies that objects falling near the surface of Earth will fall with the same rate of acceleration (ignoring drag caused by air). This rate is 32.174 feet per second per second (ft./sec²), or 9.8 m/sec², and is conventionally labeled g. Applying this rate to falling objects gives the velocity, v, and distance, d, after any amount of time, t, in seconds. If the object starts at rest and 32 ft./sec² is used as an approximation for g,

$$v = 32t$$
$$d = 16t^2$$

For example, after 3 seconds, a dropped object that is still falling will have a velocity of 32 x 3 = 96 feet per second and will have fallen a distance of 16 x 3² = 144 feet.

If the object has an initial velocity v_0 and an initial height above the ground of a, the equations describing the velocity and the distance, d, above the ground (a positive velocity is up and a negative velocity is down) become

$$v = v_0 - 32t$$

and

$$d = -16t^2 + v_0 t + a.$$

After 3 seconds, an object tossed in the air from a height of 6 feet with a velocity of 88 feet per second will reach a speed of $88 - 96 = -8$ feet per second, meaning that it has begun to descend, and will have a height of $(-16 \times 9) + (88 \times 3) + 6 = -144 + 264 + 6 = 126$ feet above the ground.

The maximum height, H, reached by the object with an initial velocity v_0 and initial height a is

$$H = a + \frac{v_0^2}{64}$$

For the object tossed upward at 88 feet per second from a height of 6 feet, the maximum height reached would be $6 + 88^2/64 = 6 + 121 = 127$ feet. Therefore, after 3 seconds, the object has just reached its peak and has fallen back only 1 foot.

Albert Einstein's general theory of relativity introduced laws of gravity more accurate than those just given, which were discovered by Sir Isaac Newton. Newton's gravitational theory is extremely accurate for most practical situations, however. For example, Newton's theory is used to determine how to launch satellites into proper orbits.

Newton's Laws of Motion

Newton's Laws of Motion apply to objects in a vacuum and are not easily observed in the real world, where forces such as friction tend to overwhelm the natural motion of objects. To obtain realistic solutions to problems, however, physicists and engineers begin with Newton's laws and then add in the various forces that also affect motion.

1. *Any object at rest tends to stay at rest. A body in motion moves at the same velocity in a straight line unless acted upon by a force.* This is also known as the law of inertia. Note that this law implies that an object will travel in a curved path only so long as a force is acting on it. When the force is released, the object will travel in a straight line. A weight on a string swung in a circle will travel in a straight line when the string is released, for the string was supplying the force that caused circular motion.

2. *The acceleration of an object is directly proportional to the force acting on it and inversely proportional to the mass of the object.* This law, for an acceleration a, a force F, and a mass m, is more commonly expressed in terms of finding the force when you know the mass and the acceleration. In this form it is written as

$$F = ma.$$

The implication of this law is that a constant force will produce acceleration, which is an increase in velocity. Thus, a rocket, which is propelled by a constant force as long as its fuel is burning, constantly increases in velocity. Even with an infinite supply of fuel, the rocket would eventually cease to increase in velocity, however, because Einstein's other relativity theory, the special theory of relativity, states that no object can exceed the speed of light in a vacuum (see "Conservation of mass-energy" below). Nevertheless, even a small force, constantly applied, can cause a

large mass to reach velocities near the speed of light if enough time is allowed.

3. *For every action there is an equal and opposite reaction.*

Conservation Laws

Many results in physics come from various conservation laws. A conservation law is a rule that a certain entity must not change in amount during a certain class of operations. All such conservation laws treat closed systems. Anything added from outside the system could affect the amount of the entity being conserved.

Conservation of momentum   In a closed system, momentum stays the same. This law is equivalent to Newton's third law. Since momentum is the product of mass and velocity, if the mass of a system changes, then the velocity must change. For example, consider a person holding a heavy anchor in a stationary rowboat in the water. The momentum of the system is 0, since the masses have no velocity. Now the person in the rowboat tosses the anchor toward the shore. The momentum of the anchor is now a positive number if velocity toward the shore is measured as positive. To conserve momentum, the rowboat is accelerated in the opposite direction, away from the shore. The positive momentum of the anchor is balanced by the negative momentum of the rowboat and its cargo. In terms of two masses, m and M, and matching velocities v and V,

$$mv = MV$$

Conservation of angular momentum

An object moving in a circle has a special kind of momentum, called angular momentum. As noted above, motion in a circle requires some force. Angular momentum combines mass, velocity, and acceleration (produced by the force). For a body moving in a circle, the acceleration depends on both the speed of the body in its path and the square of the radius of the circle. The product of this speed, the mass, and the square of the radius is the angular momentum of the mass.

In a closed system, angular momentum is conserved. This effect is used by skaters to change their velocity of spinning. Angular momentum is partly determined by the masses of a skater's arms combined with the rate of rotation and the square of the radius to the center of mass of each arm (the point that can represent the total mass of the arm). When skaters bring their arms close to their body, this would tend to reduce the angular momentum, because the center of mass is closer to the body. But, since angular momentum is conserved, the rate of rotation has to increase to compensate for the decreased radius. Because the rate depends on the square of the radius, the rate increases dramatically.

Conservation of mass   *In a closed system, the total amount of mass appears to be conserved in all but nuclear reactions and other extreme conditions.*

Conservation of energy   *In a closed system, energy appears to be conserved in all but nuclear reactions and other extreme conditions.* Energy comes in very many forms: mechanical, chemical, electrical, heat, and so forth. As one form is changed into another (excepting nuclear reactions and extreme conditions), this law guarantees that the total amount remains the same. Thus, when you change the chemical energy of a dry cell into electrical energy and use that to turn a motor, the total amount does not change (although some becomes heat energy—see "Laws of Thermodynamics" below).

Conservation of mass-energy

Einstein discovered that his special theory of relativity implies that energy and mass are related. Consequently, mass and energy by themselves are not conserved, since one can be converted into the other. Mass and energy appear to be conserved in ordinary situations because the effect of Einstein's discovery is very small most of the time. The more general law, then, is the law of conservation of mass-energy: *The total amount of mass and energy must be conserved.* Einstein found the following equation that links mass and energy:

$$E = mc^2$$

In this equation, E is the amount of energy, m is the mass, and c is the speed of light in a vacuum.

One instance of energy changing to mass occurs in Einstein's equation for how the mass increases with velocity. If m_0 is the mass of the object when it is not moving, v is the velocity of the object in relation to an observer who is considered to be at rest, and c is the speed of light in a vacuum, then the mass, m, is given by the equation

$$m = \frac{m_0}{\sqrt{1 - \dfrac{v^2}{c^2}}}$$

This accounts for the rule that no object can exceed the speed of light in a vacuum. As the object approaches this speed, so much of the energy is converted to mass that it cannot continue to accelerate.

In both nuclear fission (splitting of the atomic nucleus) and nuclear fusion (the joining of atomic nuclei, producing the energy of a hydrogen bomb), mass is converted into energy.

Conservation for particles

Many properties associated with atoms and subatomic particles are also conserved. Among them are charge, spin, isospin, and a combination known as CPT for *charge conjugation, parity*, and *time*.

First and Second Laws of Thermodynamics

First law This is the same as the law of conservation of energy. It is a law of thermodynamics, or the movement of heat, because heat must be treated as a form of energy to keep the total amount of energy constant. All bodies contain heat as energy no matter how cold they are, although there is not much heat at temperatures close to absolute zero.

Second law *Heat in a closed system can never travel from a low temperature region to one of higher temperature in a self-sustaining process.* Self-sustaining in this case means a process that does not need energy from outside the system to keep it going. In a refrigerator, heat from the cold inside of the refrigerator is transferred to a warmer room, but energy from outside is required to make the transfer happen, so the process is not self-sustaining.

The second law has many implications. One of them is that no perpetual motion machine can be constructed. Another is that all energy in a closed system eventually becomes heat that is diffused equally throughout the system, so that one can no longer obtain work from the system.

The equations that describe the behavior of heat also can be applied to order and therefore to information. The word *entropy* refers to diffuse heat, disorder, or lack of information. Another form of the second law of thermodynamics is that in a closed system, entropy always increases.

Laws of Current Electricity

Key terms When electrons flow in a conductor, the result is electric current. The amount of current is based on an amount of electric charge called the *coulomb*, which is the charge of about 6.25 quintillion (6.25 x 10^{18}) electrons. When 1 coulomb of charge moves past a point in 1 second, it creates a current of 1 ampere. Just as a stream can carry the same amount of water swiftly through a narrow channel or slowly through a broad channel, the energy of an electric current varies depending on the difference in charge between places along the conductor. This is called *potential difference* and is measured in volts. The voltage is affected by the nature of the conductors. Some substances conduct an electric current much more easily than others. This resistance to the current is measured in ohms. *Electric power* is the rate at which electricity is used.

Ohm's law *Electric current is directly proportional to the potential difference and inversely proportional to resistance.* If you measure current, I, in amperes, potential difference, V, in volts, and resistance, R, in ohms, then the current is equal to the potential difference divided by the resistance.

$$I = \frac{V}{R}$$

Law of electric power If electric power, P, is measured in watts, then the power is equal to the product of the current measured in amperes and the potential difference measured in volts.

$$P = IV$$

Laws of Light and Electromagnetic Radiation

Key terms Light is a part of a general form of radiation known as *electromagnetic waves*, or, when thought of as particles, *photons*. Here, electromagnetic radiation is considered as a wave phenomenon for the most part. The velocity of a wave is how fast the wave travels as a whole. The *wavelength* is the distance between one crest of the wave and the next crest. The *frequency* is how many crests pass a particular location in a unit of time. One crest passing each second is called a hertz.

Law of electromagnetic energy The energy of an electromagnetic wave depends on a small number known as Planck's constant. Measured in joules per hertz (energy per frequency), Planck's constant is 6.67259 x 10^{-34}. *The energy is equal to the product of Planck's constant and the* *frequency*. Using *E* for energy, *h* for Planck's constant, and *f* for frequency,

$$E = hf$$

When thought of in terms of the particles called photons, the energy of a photon obeys the same law. The law of wave motion and the law of electromagnetic energy can be combined with the speed of light in a vacuum *(c)* to give

$$E = \frac{hc}{l}$$

The energy of a photon is the product of Planck's constant and the speed of light, divided by the wavelength *(l)* of the photon.

Inverse-square law All radiation obeys an inverse-square law, which is similar to the law of gravity. *The intensity of the radiation decreases as the inverse of the square of the distance from a point source of radiation.*

Two Basic Laws of Quantum Physics

When one considers effects on very small masses and at very small distances, it is necessary to recognize that objects behave differently from their action at sizes and distances one can observe directly. Since these effects occur in discrete steps based upon Planck's constant times the frequency, called the quantum—which is the size by which energy changes in steps (instead of continuously)—the science of such effects is called quantum physics. Small masses act sometimes like particles and sometimes like waves. Two laws in particular that describe the behavior of small masses are basic and easily stated.

Heisenberg's uncertainty principle *It is impossible to specify completely the position and momentum of a particle, such as an electron.*

Pauli's exclusion principle *Two particles of matter cannot be in the same exact state.* Particles of matter include the electron, neutron, and proton. Bosons, particles of force, do not obey Pauli's exclusion principle. (See "Subatomic Particles.")

▶ SUBATOMIC PARTICLES

The idea of an atom goes back to the ancient Greek philosophers, who thought that matter was composed of tiny indivisible particles. The concept was put on a scientific basis by John Dalton (English: 1766–1844) in 1803 and became the foundation of chemistry. Nearly a hundred years later, experiments by J.J. Thomson (English: 1856–1940) in 1899 were the first to show that atoms are not indivisible after all. In the past hundred years, physics at almost all levels has been completely revolutionized by the study of the particles that make up atoms or that are smaller than atoms. In the last decades of the 20th century physicists developed the standard model of elementary particles. This model incorporates three of the four fundamental forces in nature, the strong and weak nuclear forces and electromagnetic forces (the other force is gravity). In the model, bosons mediate the forces: gluons, for the strong nuclear force; the photon for electromagnetism, and W and Z particles for the weak nuclear force. Within this model, the weak and electromagnetic forces have been combined into electroweak theory. The standard model has thus far met all experimental challenges, but it has some gaps in addition to the omission of gravity: in particular, the strong and electroweak forces

are not completely unified. Theories that attempt to unify the strong and electroweak forces are called Grand Unified Theories (GUTs). Beyond Grand Unified Theories, a great challenge for physicists is a Theory of Everything (TOE) that would account for all of the fundamental forces in nature. Below is a list of all the most important subatomic particles given in the chronological order of their discovery.

1897 Electron The first subatomic particle to be identified, also by J.J. Thomson, was the electron, a low-mass particle that can be found in the outer reaches of the atom. One property of the electron is charge, the response to electric or magnetic fields. The charge of a single electron is always the same, which is identified as –1 (negative one). Each atom consists of a cloud of electrons around a center of positive charge, which is called the nucleus.

1905 Photon The photon is the particle that carries the electromagnetic force. This concept began with Albert Einstein (German-American: 1879–1955) in 1905, when he established that light acts sometimes as a particle instead of as waves. Although we usually think of the photon as the particle of light, it is also the particle form of radio waves, X-rays, or gamma rays. The mass of the photon is 0.

1911 Proton At least one proton is always found in the nucleus of every atom. The proton has a charge that is the same in size as that of the electron, but responds in the opposite direction to an electric or magnetic field. This charge is +1 (positive one). Each proton is almost 2,000 times as heavy as an electron, or about the same as the mass of a single hydrogen atom.

1924 Bosons While matter is made from subatomic particles, the forces that act on matter are also produced by subatomic particles. The particles that create these forces are collectively called bosons because the mathematics of the behavior of this type of particle was worked out originally by Satyendranath Bose (Indian: 1894–1974) in 1924, although put into final form by Einstein. The observed bosons are the photon, pions, gluons, W particles, and Z particles. Bosons that are predicted, but that have not been observed, include the Higgs particle and the graviton.

1925–26 Quantum Mechanics The basic theory of subatomic particles, called quantum mechanics, was developed in two different forms, in 1925 by Werner Heisenberg (German: 1901–76) and in 1926 by Erwin Schrödinger (Austrian: 1887–1961). Although the two forms appear very different, they produce the same results.

1926 Fermions All the particles that make up matter are called fermions, as opposed to the bosons that create forces. The fermions include all the leptons and quarks as well as the particles made from quarks (see below). Fermions are named for Enrico Fermi (Italian-American: 1901–54), who first worked out the mathematics of their interactions in 1926. Fermions all obey the *Pauli exclusion principle* (see the section on *Basic Laws of Physics*, earlier in this chapter), which means that they occupy a definite space. Two fermions cannot be in the same place at the same time.

1930 Antiparticles When Paul A.M. Dirac (English-American: 1902–84) completed his mathematical version of the theory of the electron in 1930, he observed that one solution to his equations predicted a particle that would be a mirror image of the electron, exactly the same as the electron but with a positive charge instead of negative. The particle, discovered two years later in 1932, was named the positron. The same equations predicted mirror images for all subatomic particles. These particles are called the antiparticles, so another name for positron is antielectron.

1932 Neutron The neutron is very much like a neutral proton, with just slightly more mass. Neutrons are stable when they are found in atoms, but decay into other particles when left to themselves.

1935 Muon The muon is now recognized as a high energy analog to the electron with a mass about 200 times that of the electron.

1947 Pion A pion carries the strong force that holds the nucleus of atoms together, but since each pion appears and disappears almost instantly, the pions are not usually counted as part of the nucleus. (Predicted in 1935.) In the same year that the pion was found, theoreticians were able to work out a comprehensive theory of the electron, called quantum electrodynamics (QED).

1950 Strange particles Starting in 1950 experimenters observed a number of previously undetected particles that did not behave as particles were expected to do. Because these particles have masses greater than that of the proton and neutron, they were called hyperons. Other unexpected particles, about the size of the pion, were classed as mesons. A classification scheme for the hyperons developed in 1961 helped physicists understand them better, but their essential difference was already labeled "strangeness."

1955 Neutrinos Neutrinos are thought to be among the most common particles in the universe, but they interact with ordinary matter so weakly that they are very difficult to observe. Predicted in 1930, neutrinos were thought to have no rest mass, but Canadian experiments in 2001 indicate that they have a very small mass equal to less than about 10^{-7} of the mass of an electron. Different neutrinos are associated with electrons, muons, and tauons.

1964–95 Quarks Murray Gell-Mann (American: 1928–) and several other physicists determined that a way to explain the properties of protons, neutrons, mesons, and hyperons, is to think of the heavy particles as made from combinations of light ones, just as the atom is made from combinations of electrons, protons, and neutrons. The smaller particles are quarks; there are six of them in all. Two quarks, known as up and down, form protons and neutrons. The top quark is the most massive—about as heavy as an atom of gold—and the last to be detected. (First version of theory in 1964, evidence for top quark in 1995.)

1965–73 Gluons The eight different bosons that produce a force between quarks known as the color force are called gluons. The color force is also the basis of the strong force that holds the nucleus together. Because of the color force, the study of quarks and gluons is today called quantum chromodynamics (QCD).

1974 J/psi particle Like the strange hyperons, the J/psi particle is a heavy particle that appears at high energies. It also is produced by a different kind of quark, the charm quark. The odd name J/psi comes from the particle having been discovered independently by two investigators, one of whom called it J and the other of whom named it psi.

1983 W and Z particles The particles that produce the weak force are called W and Z. At high energies, however, the weak force merges with the electromagnetic force, so the W and Z are to some extent analogs to the photon, although they could not be more different, since the photon has a 0 rest mass and both W particles and the single Z particle are very massive.

1995 Antiatoms Since antiparticles have all the properties of ordinary particles except for being mirror images, it is possible to create an antiatom by combining subatomic antiparticles. This was accomplished in 1995 with the production of a few antiatoms of antihydrogen made by causing an antielectron (positron) to orbit an antiproton.

(Not yet observed) Graviton and Higgs particle A particle that produces gravitational force by its exchange between all kinds of particles is known as the graviton, but so far it is only known in theory. The Laser Interferometer Gravitational Wave Observatory (LIGO) that began operations in 2000 seeks to observe gravity waves, the wave version of the graviton. The Higgs particle is the main undetected particle of the standard model of subatomic particles. Physicists believe that the Higgs, named after Peter Higgs (English (1919–) who predicted it in 1964, confers mass to all other particles.

LIFE SCIENCES

While the scientific study of living creatures seems to have begun with Aristotle, there was considerable practical experimentation with living things much earlier, going back to the domestication of a species, the dog, perhaps as early as 14,000 B.C. In the years that followed the Scientific Revolution of the 17th century, the science of biology came to include most of the then-known life sciences: zoology (the study of animals), botany (the study of plants), and taxonomy (the classification of living things). In the 19th century, biology began to fragment into other studies: microbiology (the study of creatures visible only through the microscope), genetics (the study of how traits are inherited), biochemistry (the study of molecules in living things), and so forth. At the same time, different ways of studying living organisms were developed, among them anthropology (the study of human beings), ecology (the study of interactions between different living things and their environment), and ethology (the study of animal behavior).

▶ MAJOR GROUPS OF LIVING ORGANISMS

Biologists classify all living things (organisms) according to a system first introduced by Carolus Linnaeus in 1735. At that time Linnaeus and other scientists divided all life forms into two kingdoms: plants and animals. Since then, biologists have learned that there are fundamental differences among organisms that go beyond the differences between plants and animals and have added four kingdoms. The six kingdoms commonly recognized today are: Monera, Archaea, Protists, Fungi, Plants, and Animals.

Following Linnaeus, all classification terms are usually given in Latin. In the following list, English terms are substituted when they are an exact translation—for example, animals instead of Animalia and birds instead of Aves. If there is no exact translation, the Latin form is kept.

Each kingdom is divided into two or more phyla (singular: phylum). Organisms within one phylum are more closely related to one another than to members of other phyla.

The phyla are also divided into parts, which are then further divided, each time on the basis of closer and closer relationships. In descending order of size, the main divisions are as follows:

Kingdom
  Phylum
    Class
      Order
        Family
          Genus
            Species

Many biologists add to this list by classifying groups of species with sub- or super-, as in subphylum or superfamily.

By convention, Latin names except for genus and species are given in Roman type; genus and species are italicized.

Kingdom: Monera One-celled organisms with simple cells that lack a membrane around the genetic material. Bacteria do not produce their own food; blue-green algae do.
Phylum: Bacteria (also called Eubacteria)
Phylum: Blue-green algae, also called blue-green bacteria or cyanobacteria

Kingdom: Archaea One-celled organisms, sometimes called Archaeobacteria, that are genetically more like the other kingdoms than they are like the Monera. The Archaea were first discovered as creatures living in hot springs and other high-temperature situations. They were later observed among the one-celled creatures that metabolize chemicals such as methane or sulfur instead of using oxygen. They also have been found in great abundance in the oceans and deep in the Earth's crust.

Kingdom: Protists One-celled or colonial; complex cells that have a membrane around their genetic material; protozoans and slime molds do not produce their own food; all other phyla in this kingdom can.
Phylum: Ciliated protozoans, such as Paramecium
Phylum: Protozoans with flagella, such as the trypanosome that causes African sleeping sickness.
Phylum: Amoebas and similar protozoans
Phylum: Protozoans that have no means of motion during most of their life, such as the plasmodia that cause malaria.
Phylum: Euglenas
Phylum: Golden algae and diatoms
Phylum: Fire or golden brown algae
Phylum: Green algae
Phylum: Brown algae
Phylum: Red algae
Phylum: Slime molds

Kingdom: Fungi One-celled or multicelled; cells have nuclei, which stream between cells, giving the appearance that cells have many nuclei; fungi do not produce their own food.
Phylum: Zygomycetes (e.g., black bread mold)
Phylum: Ascomycetes (includes Penicillium, truffles, yeasts)
Phylum: Basidiomycetes (includes mushrooms)

Kingdom: Plants Multicellular organisms that carry out photosynthesis; cells have nuclei and cell walls.
Phylum: Mosses and liverworts
Phylum: Club mosses
Phylum: Horsetails
Phylum: Ferns
Phylum: Conifers
Phylum: Cone-bearing desert plants
Phylum: Cycads
Phylum: The ginkgo
Phylum: Flowering plants
  Subphylum: Dicots (plants with two seed leaves—e.g., most fruits and vegetables, common flowers, and trees)
  Subphylum: Monocots (plants with a single seed leaf—e.g., onions, lilies, and grasses)

Kingdom: Animals Multicellular organisms that get their food by ingestion; most are able to move from place to place; cells have nuclei but not cell walls.
Phylum: Porifera (sponges)
Phylum: Cnidaria (jellyfish, anemones, corals)
Phylum: Platyhelminthes (flatworms)
Phylum: Nematodes (roundworms)
Phylum: Rotifers (microscopic wormlike or spherical animals)
Phylum: Bryozoa (moss animals)
Phylum: Brachiopods (lampshells)
Phylum: Phoronida (tube worms)
Phylum: Annelids (segmented worms, such as earthworms, leeches)
Phylum: Mollusks (soft-bodied animals with a mantle and foot)
  Class: Chitons
  Class: Bivalves (clams, oysters, mussels)
  Class: Scaphopoda (tooth or tusk shells)
  Class: Gastropods (slugs and snails)
  Class: Cephalopods (octopus, squid)
Phylum: Arthropods (segmented animals with an external skeleton)
  Class: Horseshoe crabs
  Class: Crustaceans (lobsters, crabs, shrimp)
  Class: Arachnids (scorpions, spiders, mites, ticks)
  Class: Insects
  Class: Millipedes and centipedes
Phylum: Cycliophora (known only as a tiny species growing in the mouths of lobsters)
Phylum: Echinoderms (starfish, brittle stars)
Phylum: Hemichordata (acorn worms)
Phylum: Chordates
  Subphylum: Tunicates
  Subphylum: Lancelets
  Subphylum: Vertebrates (animals with backbones)
    Class: Agnatha (lampreys, hagfish)
    Class: Sharks and rays
    Class: Bony fish
    Class: Amphibians
    Class: Reptiles
    Class: Birds
    Class: Mammals
      Subclass: Monotremes (egg-laying mammals)
      Subclass: Marsupials
      Subclass: Placentals
      Order: Insectivores (shrews, moles, hedgehogs)
      Order: Flying lemurs
      Order: Bats
      Order: Primates (lemurs, monkeys, apes, humans)
      Order: Edentates (anteaters, sloths, armadillos)
      Order: Pangolins

Order: Lagomorphs (rabbits, hares)
Order: Rodents (squirrels, rats, mice, porcu-
pines)
Order: Cetaceans (whales, dolphins)
Order: Carnivores (wolves, cats, bears, rac-
coons, weasels, badgers, skunks, ot-
ters, hyenas)
Order: Seals
Order: The aardvark
Order: Elephants
Order: Hyraxes
Order: Sirenians (dugongs, manatees)
Order: Odd-toed ungulates (horses, tapirs,
rhinoceroses)
Order: Even-toed ungulates (pigs, hippo-
potamuses, camels, deer, giraffes,
pronghorns, cattle, goats, sheep)

▶ CLASSIFYING HUMANS

KINGDOM: Animals Organisms that use other
organisms for food and that sometimes move
rapidly.

PHYLUM: Chordates Animals that are partially
supported by a rod of cartilage or bone vertebrae
and an internal skeleton.

SUBPHYLUM: Vertebrates Chordates that have
vertebrae, such as fish, amphibians, reptiles,
birds, and mammals.

CLASS: Mammals Vertebrates that have hair
and suckle their young.

ORDER: Primates Mammals that use sight
more than scent, have nails instead of claws on
grasping hands and feet, are mostly active in daylight, and have relatively large brains.

SUPERFAMILY: Hominoids Primates that are
tailless, generally large in size, can climb trees,
and have relatively flat faces; specifically, the
great apes, *Ardipithecus, Kenyapithecus*, australopithecines, and human beings.

FAMILY: Hominids Hominoids that walk upright,
have small canines, and large brains; specifically,
the australopithecines and human beings.

GENUS: Homo Hominids, with especially large
brains, that speak and show other signs of culture;
specifically, *Homo habilis, Homo erectus* and related species, and *Homo sapiens*.

SPECIES: Homo sapiens Modern human beings.

▶ THE HUMAN GENOME PROJECT

On June 25, 2000, President Clinton, British Prime
Minister Tony Blair, and Craig Venter of Celera Genomics jointly announced the completion (on
June 23) of decoding all the bases that make up
the genes in a human. Many assumed it meant
that the Human Genome Project had succeeded
in deciphering all human genes. But while the announcement marked a major milestone in biology, decoding the bases was actually just a step
along the way. It was not until February 15-16,
2001, that scientists from the International Human Genome Sequencing Consortium and from
Celera completed the original goal of the Human
Genome Project: releasing lists of all the bases in
order. And even then, the lists were still slightly incomplete. Yet to come is the recognition of which
bases are identified with which genes, and what
the function of each gene is. Also, scientists increasingly recognize that knowledge of genes
alone is not the whole story.

Every organism is almost completely described
by its own genes, combinations of triplets of four
chemical building blocks, called bases, carried on
long molecules of a chemical named deoxyribonucleic acid (DNA). Several different DNA molecules are found in every cell. Most human cells
have 46 such molecules as the working parts of
the chromosomes. The total group of all the genes
for an organism is called its genome. The Human
Genome Project has been a step-by-step process
to determine the complete sequence of the more
than 3 billion bases in human DNA, to identify the
genes in that sequence, and to determine what
the immediate purpose of each gene is. The DNA
bases are usually known by their abbreviations, T,
G, C, and A; thus, the goal of the project reached in
February 2001 was to determine a giant string of
the letters T, G, C, and A.

One of the surprises of the list so far has been
that there are only about 30,000-40,000 human
genes—less than half of what had been expected
before the sequencing was accomplished. Ultimately other questions will need to be resolved,
such as how genes interact with each other and
with other molecules in the body. It appears the
number of proteins encoded in the genes is much
greater than the number of genes, so a new goal
for researchers is to determine all the proteins--
known as the proteome. Another task will be identification of variations from human to human
called single-nucleotide polymorphisms (SNPs).
Such variations are though to be behind susceptibility to such complex diseases as cancer, diabetes, cardiovascular syndromes, and some types
of mental illnesses.

The National Center for Human Genome Research was instituted on January 3, 1989. The
name changed to the Human Genome Project
when both the U.S. Department of Energy and
National Institutes for Health became involved in
1990. Scientists from the European Union, Japan,
and China also participate, forming together the
International Human Genome Sequencing Consortium.

Along the way, the project has sequenced
genomes of organisms other than human. Celera
achieved the first—the small bacterium
Haemophilus influenzae, in 1995. Since then, bacteria that cause syphilis, chlamydia, tuberculosis,
cholera, and staph infections, among some 60 different bacteria, have all had their genomes sequenced. In 1996 the gene of yeast, a more
complex organism, was added to the list. Another
one-celled organism, the malaria parasite, is also
being sequenced.

The project then targeted commonly used experimental organisms. Teams from the U.S. and
Great Britain completed the genome of the first
animal, *Caenorhabditis elegans*, a nematode
worm, at the end of 1998. Expected to have 6,000
genes, *C. elegans* was found to have 20,000, suggesting that the human genome might also be
more complicated than expected. Celera concentrated on the fruit fly, *Drosophila melanogaster*,
and established its sequence of 1.8 billion bases
by September 9, 1999. The first success in plants
came at the end of 2000 with the mustard *Arabidopsis thaliana*, the common laboratory plant
for botanists. The next focus is on food crops, especially rice, with some efforts on barley and
tomatoes. Celera is also developing the rough sequence for the laboratory mouse genome, which,
like the human genome, contains about 30,000
genes. Other laboratory animals like the rat and
the zebrafish will follow. Among farm animals, the
pig is in progress. The chimpanzee, thought to be
genetically nearly identical to humans, is also under
discussion for a genome project that might identify
the exact differences at the genetic level. An international group may convene to discuss priorities so
that dilution of effort can be minimized.

Major Discoveries in Life Sciences

B.C.

c.9000 Agricultural Revolution starts in Near East with domestication of sheep and goats in Persia (Iran) and Afghanistan and of pigs in Anatolia (Turkey); and cultivation of wheat in Canaan (Israel and Jordan).

c.8000 Agricultural Revolution starts independently in what are now Peru, Central America, and Indochina.

c.350 Aristotle (Greek: 384–322 B.C.) classifies known animals in system that will continue to be used until 1735.

A.D.

1648 Jan Baptista van Helmont (Flemish: 1580–1644) shows that plants do not obtain large amounts of material for their growth from soil.

1665 Robert Hooke (English: 1635–1703) observes and names the cell.

1668 Francesco Redi (Italian: 1626–97) shows that maggots in meat do not arise spontaneously but are hatched from flies' eggs.

1669 Anton van Leeuwenhoek (Dutch: 1632–1723) discovers microorganisms—creatures too small to see with naked eye—and recognizes that sperm are part of reproduction.

1683 Leeuwenhoek is first to observe bacteria.

1735 Carolus Linnaeus (Carl Linné; Swedish: 1707–78) introduces system in use today for classifying plants and animals.

1779 Jan Ingenhousz (Dutch: 1730–99) discovers that plants release oxygen when exposed to sunlight and they consume carbon dioxide; this is first step in understanding photosynthesis.

1839 Theodor A.H. Schwann (German: 1810–82), building on work of Matthias Jakob Schleiden (German: 1804–81) in 1838, develops cell theory of life.

1856 First skeleton of what we now call Neandertals is found in cave in Neander Valley, near Düsseldorf (Germany).

Louis Pasteur (French: 1822–95) discovers that fermentation is caused by microorganisms.

1858 Charles R. Darwin (English: 1809–82) and Alfred R. Wallace (English: 1823–1913) announce their theory of evolution by natural selection to the Linnean Society.

1859 Darwin publishes *On the Origin of Species.*

1865 Gregor Johann Mendel's (Austrian: 1822–84) theory of dominant and recessive genes is published in obscure local journal.

1868 Workers building road in France discover skeletons of first-known Cro-Magnons in cave.

1894 Eugène Dubois (Dutch: 1858–1940) announces discovery of "Java ape-man," now known to be first specimen of *Homo erectus.*

1898 Mosaic disease of tobacco plants is recognized as being caused by virus, the first identification of a virus.

1900 Three different biologists rediscover laws of genetics originally found by Mendel.

1924 Raymond A. Dart (Australian-South African: 1893–1988) identifies first fossil of an australopithecine, a close relative of early humans.

1953 James D. Watson (American: 1928–) and Francis Crick (English: 1916–) determine structure of DNA, the basis of heredity.

1961 Louis S.B. Leakey (English: 1903–72) and Mary D. Leakey (English: 1913–96) discover a previously unknown ancestor of humans, *Homo habilis,* in the Olduvai Gorge of northern Tanzania.

Marshall W. Nirenberg (American: 1927–) learns to read one of the "letters" of genetic code.

1973 Stanley Cohen (American: 1922–) and Herbert Boyer (American: 1936–) put specific gene into bacterium, the first instance of true genetic engineering.

1974 Donald C. Johanson (American: 1943–) and coworkers discover Lucy in Afar region of Ethiopia, the nearly complete skeleton—but not the skull—of *Australopithecus afarensis,* an early relative of humans (more than 3 million years old).

1995 César Milstein (Argentine-English: 1927–) announces discovery of how to produce monoclonal antibodies, highly specific chemicals that can be made to react with particular proteins or other chemicals in the body.

1980 Martin Cline (American: 1934–) and coworkers succeed in transferring functioning gene from one mouse to another.

1983 Kary B. Mullis (American: 1945–) invents the use of the polymerase chain reaction to make copies of DNA sequences, a vital tool in finding specific genes.

1988 The complete developmental history of every cell in the nematode *Caenorhabditis elegans* published.

1994 Gen Suwa (Japanese), discovers the first fossil of *Ardipithecus ramidus,* the oldest known hominid, in Ethiopia.

1995 Craig Venter (American: 1946–) of the Institute for Genomic Research publishes the complete base sequences for all the genes of a free-living organism, the bacterium *Haemophilus influenzae.*

1997 Ian Wilmut (English: 1944–) succeeds in cloning a sheep from a cell from an adult ewe, the first mammalian clone using a differentiated cell as the source of the chromosomes; in 1998, the cloned ewe, named Dolly, bears a lamb the natural way.

Geneticists at the Case Western Reserve School of Medicine in Cleveland create the first artificial human chromosome.

Svante Pääbo of the University of Munich, Germany, and coworkers clone DNA from the first discovered Neandertal fossil and compare the DNA to that of modern humans. They conclude that the Neandertal is a different species from our own.

1998 Elizabeth Gould and co-workers at Princeton University demonstrate that adult monkeys continue to grow new brain cells, a feat previously thought impossible for adult primates.

1999 A 24,500-year-old fossil excavated from a shallow grave in Portugal appears to be a hybrid of Neandertals and modern humans.

Researchers find active colonies of bacteria live in the ice at the bottom of glaciers.

Berhane Asfaw (Ethiopian: 1954-) and co-workers announce the discovery in Ethiopia of fossils of a new hominid species, *Australopithecus garhi* ("surprising southern ape").

Studies in mice show that a process in cell division called "telomere shortening" produces the effects of aging.

2000 Tools are found at a Cactus Hill site in Virginia from 15,000 years ago, tending to disprove the theory that early Americans reached the continent through Alaska about 12,000 years ago.

The Human Genome Project and Celera Genomics announce jointly that they have developed a rough draft of the entire human genetic sequence.

An international team of biologists sequences the genome of a flowering plant, *Arabidopsis thaliana,* the first flowering plant all of whose genes have been found.

In October, biologists who had searched forests of West Africa in vain, declare Miss Waldron's red colobus monkey extinct. It is the first large primate to become extinct since 1800.

Jack Horner of the Museum of the Rockies in Bozeman, Montana, and co-workers discover the fossilized parts of five separate *Tyrannosaurus rex* dinosaurs, a 35 percent increase in the number of individuals collected of this famous species.

2001 Meave G. Leakey (English-Kenyan: 1942-) of the National Museums of Kenya in Nairobi discovers the skull of a 3.5-million-year-old human ancestor, which she names *Kenyanthropus platyops* ("flat-faced man from Kenya").

The Human Family Tree

EVOLUTION OF THE HUMAN FAMILY

The understanding of the various relatives of modern human beings and how they are related is undergoing great changes. Currently there is little consensus among paleoanthropologists, the people who study early humans and their relatives, about the details of who is related to whom.

Purgatorius *c. 60 million years ago. Africa.* The earliest known primate, a toothy creature somewhat like a lemur of today.

Catopithecus *c. 40 million years ago, Egypt.* The earliest known representative of the higher primates, which include the Old World Monkeys, apes, and humans.

Aegyptopithecus *c. 30 million years ago. Egypt.* Monkey-like creature, size of a large house cat. May be the earliest known ancestor of the hominoids. First fossils found in 1965.

Morotopithecus *c. 20 million years ago. Uganda.* Thought to be the first ape that could swing through trees as modern apes do.

Proconsul: *three known species. c. 20 million years ago. East Africa.* Named after Consul, a chimpanzee at the London Zoo, these apes are generally recognized as ancestors of all hominoids.

Afropithecus *c. 17 million years ago. Kenya.* Discovered in the mid-1980s. Like *Proconsul,* a candidate for ancestor of all hominoids.

Kenyapithecus *14 to 11 million years ago. Kenya.* A large ape that was somewhat more "advanced" than either *Afropithecus* or *Proconsul.*

Dryopithecus *c. 12 to 10 million years ago. France, Spain, and Hungary.* A small ape identified in 1992 as the common ancestor of the great apes, australopithecines, and modern humans.

Ardipithecus ramidus *c. 4.4 million years ago. Ethiopia.* Discovered in 1994 at Aramis, Ethiopia, this woodland-dweller is one candidate for the direct ancestor of the australopithecines and very close to the common ancestor great apes and humans.

Australopithecus anamensis *c. 4.2 to 3.9 million years ago. Northern Kenya (Lake Turkana region).* This group is represented by 21 fossils found by Meave G. Leakey and Alan Walker in 1994 and announced late in 1995. *A. anamensis* seems to have walked on two legs like later hominids.

Kenyapithecus platyops *c. 3.5 million years ago. Kenya.* Named for a skull found in 2001 by Meave G. Leakey and coworkers, who declare that it represents a new genus; Leakey suggests that the skull listed below as *Homo rudolfensis* may also be in the *Kenyapithecus* genus.

Australopithecus afarensis *"Lucy" and "The First Family." c. 4 million years ago to 3 million years ago. Ethiopia and East Africa.* A. afarensis is thought to be on the direct line to humans. In addition to the famous skeleton of "Lucy" and the collection known as The First Family, all from Ethiopia and dating from about 3.3 million years ago, the trail of footprints, left in volcanic ash at Laetoli, Tanzania, discovered in 1978, demonstrated that *A. afarensis* walked upright, unlike any of the great apes.

Australopithecus bahrelghazali *c. 3 to 3.5 million years ago, Chad.* Known only from a single mandible, the fossil nevertheless extends the early hominid range to West Africa.

Paranthropus aethiopicus *c. 2.5 million years ago. East Africa.* Known mainly from "The Black Skull" discovered in Kenya in 1985 by Alan Walker and Richard Leakey, *P. aethiopicus* is thought to be the link between *A. africanus* and the other two *Paranthropus* species.

Australopithecus garhi *c. 2.5 million years ago. Ethiopia.* Another candidate for the ancestor of the *Homo* line, its fossils are found at the same sites as tools and butchered animal bones, although it is not clear who did the butchering.

Homo habilis *c. 2.5 to 1.5 million years ago. Tanzania and South Africa.* Earliest known member of our own genus, *H. habilis* ("Handy Man") is named for tools found at sites that are physically and chronologically close to where *H. habilis* fossils have been found. It seems likely that there were several species of *Homo* in Africa at this time, however, and it is not clear who made the tools; they could be australopithecine in origin.

Homo rudolfensis *c. 2.5 to 1.5 million years ago. Kenya.* Recently a skull originally thought to have been *H. habilis* has been assigned to a contemporaneous species of *Homo* known as *rudolfensis* and alternatively to a different genus from *Homo* entirely, *Kenyapithecus.*

Paranthropus robustus and P. boisei *c. 2.3 to 1.2 million years ago. Eastern and Southern Africa.* These australopithecines represent a branch of the human family that has become extinct without issue.

Homo ergaster *c. 1.8 to 1.6 million years ago. Africa and Central Asia (Georgia).* Current thinking is that a larger species of *Homo* that evolved from one of small earlier species, such as *H. habilis* or *H. rudolfensis,* was the ancestor of both *H. erectus* and modern humans. This species is called *Homo ergaster,* or "Work Man."

Homo erectus *c. 1.6 million to perhaps 50,000 years ago. Africa, Europe, and Asia—notably known from Indonesia and China.* Many of the most famous fossils, including the "Java Ape Man" of 1891 and the "Peking Man" of 1927, are now classified as *H. erectus,* "Upright Man." Originally thought to have been the ancestor of modern humans, it is now believed that this long-existing species became extinct without issue on Java so recently that the last members of *H. erectus* were contemporary with the first modern humans.

Homo heidelbergensis *c. 700,000 years ago to 120,000 years ago. Europe and northern Africa.* This species, whose type specimen is the Mauer Mandible from Germany, was the transition between *Homo ergaster* in Africa and the Neanderthal in Europe. Some anthropologists group the earlier fossils, most from Spain or northwest Africa, as *Homo antecessor.*

Homo neanderthalensis *c. 200,000 years ago to 30,000 years ago. Europe and the Near East.* Neandertals were a species of hominid who in some places lived side by side with *H. sapiens* but became extinct shortly after modern humans occupied Europe. Several studies of DNA from Neandertal fossils have shown that *H. neanderthalensis* was a different species from *H. sapiens,* but some recent fossil discoveries have suggested that the two species were able to breed with each other.

Homo sapiens *c. 150,000 years ago to present. Worldwide.* Very early humans from Africa and the Near East as well as some early humans from Asia and Australia are termed "archaic" or "anatomically modern," since they appear physically to be *H. sapiens* but do not show the toolmaking ability of modern humans. Fully modern humans, known also as Cro-Magnons from an early fossil site, are first observed in Europe about 36,000 years ago.

Elements in a 150-Pound Person

Element/Weight	Use by the body	Element/Weight	Use by the body
Oxygen 97.5 lbs	Part of all major nutrients, which make up tissues of the body, but also vital to production of energy in the form of elemental oxygen obtained from air.	Chlorine 0.3 lbs	Used in form of chloride ions to transport messages from the body to cells; helps regulate electrical activity.
Carbon 27.0 lbs	Essential element for life—most compounds based on carbon are called organic, meaning "from life." An essential part of proteins, carbohydrates, and fats, the building blocks of human cells	Sodium 0.165 lbs	Required by vertebrates to control fluid pressure in cells.
		Magnesium 0.06 lbs	Required by both plants (it is in chlorophyll) and animals. In humans, works with enzymes to speed chemical reactions, is involved in transmission of messages between nerves, and has a role in bone structure.
Hydrogen 15.0 lbs	Part of each of major nutrients, and thus a building block of every cell. Unlike oxygen, has no part in respiration.		
Nitrogen 4.5 lbs	Essential part of proteins, DNA, and RNA, the compounds most active in controlling cells; most of the body's functions depend on nitrogen compounds at one stage or another.	Iron 0.006 lbs	Essential for carrying oxygen to cells and carbon dioxide waste away. Lack of iron causes anemia.
		Cobalt 0.00024 lbs	Part of vitamin B12, found in meats and dairy products; its exact role in the body is not well understood.
Calcium 3.0 lbs	Mostly locked into hard compounds that form nonliving parts of bone. One of principal messengers between cells, telling them when to act and when to stay quiet.	Copper 0.00023 lbs	Helps form red blood cells, maintain nervous system, and regulate cholesterol levels.
		Manganese 0.00020 lbs	Aids in bone formation, helps regulate nervous system, and is part of sex hormones.
Phosphorus 1.8 lbs	Important element in bone building, but, like calcium, has another role: it is essential in producing energy in cell.	Iodine 0.00006 lbs	Part of thyroid hormone that controls rate at which food is burned for energy.
Potassium 0.3 lbs	Regulates contraction of muscle cells (and some other cell functions) along with sodium. Potassium is involved with muscle contractions and general maintenance of pressure a cell exerts on its covering membrane.	Zinc trace	Needed for some enzymes, for proper sex development, in healing wounds, for sense of taste, and for normal sperm count.
		Fluorine trace	Strengthens teeth and bones.
		Chromium trace	Used in metabolism of sugar and the regulation of fats.
Sulfur 0.3 lbs	Essential to most forms of life. An important constituent of proteins.	Selenium trace	In small amounts, may reduce cell damage and promote growth.

Note: In addition, the body contains trace amounts of boron, aluminum, vanadium, molybdenum, and silicon. Their roles, however, are not fully understood.

MATHEMATICS

Strictly speaking, mathematics is not considered a science but a separate branch of learning on its own. Because the use of mathematics has been so important to science, however, it is generally treated along with sciences.

Mathematics consists of a set of abstract symbols and of rules for manipulating them, along with the results of that manipulation. Because of this, some have classified mathematics as a kind of language, while others view it as a kind of game. Many mathematicians believe there is a much deeper reality than those classifications, but it is one that is very difficult to explain. Even when mathematics is treated as a game, the results seem to be strongly connected to the real world.

The 20th century was an era of impressive progress in many fields of mathematics and statistics (see the discoveries listed in Milestones), and this progress continues today. Applied methods of statistical inference ("confidence intervals" and other techniques) based on the work of Sir

R.A. Fisher (British, 1890-1962) and others have been highly developed and widely applied, through computer programs, in the sciences, engineering, and social sciences. There have also been dramatic advances in the ancient science of geometry, such as the development of fractal geometry (Benoit Mandelbrot, French-American, b. Poland, 1924-), in which patterns of smaller parts (such as a coastline seen very close up) relate in complex ways to the same coastline seen from a distance. Encryption methods have developed rapidly, spurred by the need to protect information sent by the internet. An important class of such methods is based on the use of prime numbers (numbers divisible only by 1 and themselves). (The largest prime currently identified (6/99) is $(2\exp6972593)-1$, a number with over 2 million digits.) Another area in which important advances have been made is in computerizing numerical techniques for solving the equations in weather forecasting models, a use of mathematics that affects everyone's life. These and many other modern developments in mathematics and statistics mean that, while students today study some math that is thousands of years old--Greek geometry; and some that is hundreds of years old--the calculus of Leibniz and Newton; they also study, and their lives are affected by, up-to-date mathematical techniques embodied in powerful computational packages.

▶COMMONLY USED MATHEMATICAL FORMULAS

Most formulas needed in solving everyday problems are collected below, with special emphasis on formulas relating to measurements, as these are used in everything from sewing to building a house. However, some important formulas from algebra, graphing, and trigonometry are at the end. Additional formulas can also be found in "Basic Laws of Physics."

General

The **distance** d, given the rate r and the time t:

$$d = rt.$$

Length

The **perimeter (distance around)** p **of any polygon** (closed plane figure with straight sides that do not cross), given the lengths of the sides a, b, c, and so forth:

$$p = a + b + c + \ldots$$

Perimeter p **of a rectangle,** given the length l and the width w:

$$p = 2l + 2w.$$

Perimeter p **of a square**, given the length of a side s:

$$p = 4s.$$

Circumference (distance around) C **of a circle**, given the diameter d (distance across) or the radius r (distance from the center to the circle):

$$C = \pi d$$
$$\text{or } C = 2\pi r.$$

The number π is an infinite decimal that begins $3.14159\ldots$, which is often approximated as either 3.14 or as $\frac{22}{7}$.

Area

In each of the following, the area (amount of surface) is A. For three-dimensional figures, A is the total surface area.

Rectangle, given the length l and the width w:

$$A = lw.$$

Square, given the length of a side s:

$$A = s^2$$

Circle, given the radius r:

$$A = \pi r^2$$

Triangle, given the base b and the height h:

$$A = \tfrac{1}{2} bh$$

Right triangle, given the lengths a and b of the two sides (legs) that form the right angle:

$$A = \tfrac{1}{2} ab$$

Parallelogram, given the base b and the height h:

$$A = bh$$

Trapezoid, given the two bases B and b and the height h:

$$A = \tfrac{1}{2} h(B + b)$$

Kite, given the lengths of the two diagonals D and d:

$$A = \tfrac{1}{2} Dd$$

Regular polygon (polygon with all sides of equal length and all angles of equal measure), given the perimeter p and the apothem a (the distance from the center of the regular polygon to one of its sides):

$$A = \tfrac{1}{2} ap$$

Equilateral triangle (all sides the same length), given the length of a side s:

$$A = \frac{s^2\sqrt{3}}{4}$$

Heron's formula Any **triangle**, given half the length of the perimeter (the semiperimeter) s and the lengths of the sides a, b, and c:

$$A = \sqrt{s(s-a)(s-b)(s-c)}.$$

Right circular cylinder (a cylinder with a circular region as its base whose sides make a right angle with the base), given the radius r of the base and the height h of the cylinder:

$$A = 2\pi r(h + r)$$

Right circular cone (a cone with a circular region as its base and whose altitude makes a right angle with the base), given the radius r of the base and the slant height l of the cone (the shortest distance from the tip of the cone to the circle of the base):

$$A = \pi r(l + r).$$

Sphere, given the radius r:

$$A = 4\pi r^2$$

Volume

In each of the following, the volume (space enclosed) is V.

Cube, given the length of an edge e:

$$V = e^3$$

Right rectangular prism (box), given the length l, the width w, and the height h:

$$V = lwh$$

Prism, given the area of the base B and the height h:

$$V = Bh$$

Right circular cylinder, given the radius r of the base and the height h:

$$V = \pi r^2 h$$

Right circular cone, given the radius r of the base and the height h:

$$V = \tfrac{1}{3} \pi r^2 h$$

Pyramid, given the area of the base B and the height h:

$$V = \tfrac{1}{3} Bh$$

Sphere, given the radius r:

$$V = \tfrac{4}{3} \pi r^3$$

Milestones in the History of Mathematics

B.C.

c. 30,000   People in Europe begin using scratches or notches to record numbers.

c. 3500   Egyptians develop numeration system that can record very large numbers, with different symbols for ones, tens, hundreds, etc.

c. 2400   A numeration system based on place value (similar to Hindu-Arabic system) is introduced in Mesopotamia.

c. 2000   Mesopotamian mathematicians learn how to solve quadratic equations.

c. 1900   Mesopotamian mathematicians discover what we now call the Pythagorean theorem: The sum of the squares of the legs of a right triangle equals the square of the hypotenuse.

c. 470   Mathematician Hippasus of Metapontum (Greek: c. 500) discovers dodecahedron, a regular solid with 12 faces.

c. 450   Pythagoreans show that some lengths, such as the diagonal of a 1×1 square ($\sqrt{2}$), cannot be measured exactly using a side as a unit.

c. 300   Euclid's (Greek: c. 300) *Elements* shows that virtually all parts of mathematics known at the time can be proved from short list of assumptions.

c. 260   In Central America, Maya develop numeration system based on place value.

c. 250   Archimedes (Greek: c. 287–212) establishes important theorems about volumes of solids, calculates an excellent approximation of π, and develops a system for representing very large whole numbers.

c. 230   Apollonius of Perga (Greek: c. 262–190) writes *Conics*, an analysis of such curves as parabola, ellipse, and hyperbola.

A.D.

876   The first-known use of a symbol for zero as a number occurs in India.

c. 1100   Poet, mathematician, and astronomer Omar Khayyám (Persian: 1048-c. 1131) develops geometric methods for solving cubic equations.

1321   Levi ben Gershom (Gersonides; French: 1288–1344) is first to use mathematical induction.

c.1515   Scipione del Ferro (Italian: 1465–1526) discovers algebraic method for solving one form of cubic equations.

1536   Niccolò Tartaglia (Italian: 1499–1557) solves two types of cubic equations.

1545   Girolamo Cardano's (Italian: 1501–76) *Ars Magna* contains Lodovico Ferrari's (Italian: 1522–65) complete solution of the quartic, and a complete solution of the cubic based on Tartaglia's work.

1572   Rafael Bombelli (Italian: 1526–c. 1573) uses complex numbers to solve equations.

1614   John Napier (Scottish: 1550–1617) describes logarithms.

1637   René Descartes (French: 1596–1650) publishes first account of analytic geometry; also discovered by Pierre de Fermat (French: 1601–65).

1639   Gérard Desargues (French: 1591–1661) introduces projective geometry.

1654   Blaise Pascal (French: 1623–62) and Pierre de Fermat develop basic laws of probability.

1666   Sir Isaac Newton (English: 1642–1727) describes his invention of the calculus but does not have it published at this time.

1684   Gottfried Wilhelm Leibniz (German: 1646–1716) publishes first account of his independent discovery of the calculus.

1763   Gaspard Monge (French: 1746–1818) invents descriptive geometry, the mathematical techniques that are basis of mechanical drawing.

1799   Karl Friedrich Gauss (German: 1777–1855) proves fundamental theorem of algebra, which is that every polynomial equation has solution.

Paolo Ruffini (Italian: 1765–1822) offers first proof that not all polynomial equations of fifth degree can be solved by algebraic methods.

1826   Nikolai Ivanovich Lobachevski (Russian: 1793–1856) gives first public address concerning non-Euclidean geometry.

1854   Bernhard Riemann (German: 1826–66) shows that several non-Euclidean geometries are possible.

1877   Georg F.L.P. Cantor (German: 1845–1918) shows that number of points in a line segment is same as number in interior of a square.

1881   Josiah Willard Gibbs (American: 1839–1903) introduces vector analysis.

1882   Ferdinand von Lindemann (German: 1852–1939) proves that the circle cannot be squared with straightedge and compass.

1892   Cantor proves there are at least two types of infinities—specifically, that infinity of real numbers (including all infinite decimals) is bigger than infinity of counting numbers (1, 2, 3, . . .).

1900   David Hilbert (German: 1862–1943) proposes his famous list of 23 unsolved problems.

1931   Kurt Gödel (Austrian-American: ·1906–78) shows that mathematical systems are either incomplete or inconsistent: *incomplete* if not all true theorems can be proved from within the system, and *inconsistent* if two contradictory theorems can be proved.

1936   Independently, Alan M. Turing (English: 1912–54) and Alonzo Church (American: 1903–95) discover there is no single infallible method for proving whether a mathematical statement in mathematics is true or false.

1949   Claude E. Shannon (American: 1916–2001) publishes his work on information theory, a general approach to handling communications.

1976   In first major computer-assisted proof, it is shown that any map can be colored with four colors in such a way that no two regions of the same color share common border.

1980   Classification of all finite simple groups, started in 1830, is completed, perhaps longest proof in history of mathematics.

1995   Andrew Wiles (American: 1953-) publishes a corrected version of his 1993 proof that the equation $x^n + y^n = z^n$ has no solution for n greater than 2 when x, y, and z are counting numbers—known as Fermat's last theorem.

1998   Thomas C. Hales of the University of Michigan uses a computer to establish that Johannes Kepler's 1611 conjecture that stacking spheres in a face-centered cubic pattern results in the densest concentration of spheres.

1999   Hales proves that, of all possible ways to cover a plane completely, a tiling of regular hexagons uses the least total amount of edge--known as the honeycomb conjecture since honeybees use hexagonal cells to store honey and have long been thought to do so in the way that requires the least wax.

2000   A computer at the University of Giessen in Germany verifies to 400 trillion the 1742 conjecture of Christian Goldbach (Russian: 1690-1764) that every even number greater than 2 is the sum of two primes.

Mathematicians from AT&T Laboratories develop formulas that identify the centers of all small circles packed into a large one provided that the curvature of each is an integral multiple of the smallest circle (curvature is the radius divided into 1).

Algebra

If a, b, and x are any numbers or variables ("unknowns"):

$$(a + b)^2 = a^2 + 2ab + b^2$$
$$(a - b)^2 = a^2 - 2ab + b^2$$
$$x^2 - a^2 = (x + a)(x - a)$$
$$x^3 - a^3 = (x - a)(x^2 + ax + a^2)$$
$$x^3 + a^3 = (x + a)(x^2 - ax + a^2)$$

If a, b, c, and d are any numbers or variables except that neither b nor d can be zero:

$$a/b + c/d = (ad + bc)/bd$$
$$a/b - c/d = (ad - bc)/bd$$
$$a/b \times c/d = ac/bd$$
$$a/b \div c/d = ad/bc \ (c \neq 0)$$

Quadratic formula for the solutions of a second degree polynomial equation in one variable of the form $ax^2 + bx + c = 0$:

$$x = \frac{-b \pm \sqrt{b^2 - 4ac}}{2a}$$

Laws of exponents, given that a, b, x, and y are numbers or variables:

$$a^x a^y = a^{x+y}$$
$$(a^x)^y = a^{xy}$$
$$(ab)^x = a^x b^x$$
$$(a/b)^x = a^x/b^x$$
$$a^x/a^y = a^{x-y}$$
$$a^{-x} = \frac{1}{a^x}$$
$$a^0 = 1$$
$$a^1 = a.$$

Laws of logarithms, given that a, b, x, and y are positive numbers, c is any real number, and $a \neq 1$, $b \neq 1$.

$$\log_a (xy) = \log_a x + \log_a y$$
$$\log_a 1/x = - \log_a x$$
$$\log_a (x/y) = \log_a x - \log_a y$$
$$\log_a (x^c) = c \log_a x$$
$$\log_b x = (\log_a x)/(\log_a b)$$
$$\log_a 1 = 0$$
$$\log_a a = 1$$
$$a^{\log_a x} = x$$
$$\log_a (a^c) = c$$

Graphs

In a rectangular (Cartesian) coordinate plane, where the horizontal axis is x and the vertical axis is y:

Slope of a line, m, given two particular points (x_1, y_1) and (x_2, y_2) where $x_1 \neq x_2$:

$$m = (y_2 - y_1)/(x_2 - x_1).$$

Point-slope equation of a line, given the slope m and a point on the nonvertical line (x_1, y_1):

$$y - y_1 = m(x - x_1).$$

Slope-intercept equation of a line, given the slope m and the y-intercept b (the number on the y axis where the line crosses the y axis):

$$y = mx + b.$$

Distance d between any two points, (x_1, y_1) and (x_2, y_2):

$$d = \sqrt{(x_2 - x_1)^2 + (y_2 - y_1)^2}.$$

Trigonometry

In a **right triangle** whose two shorter sides (or legs) are a and b, opposite angles A and B respectively, and whose longest side (or hypotenuse, always the side opposite the right angle, C) is c:

Pythagorean theorem:

$$c^2 = a^2 + b^2.$$

Trigonometric functions:

sine: $\sin A = a/c$
cosine: $\cos A = b/c$
tangent: $\tan A = a/b$
cotangent: $\cot A = b/a$
secant: $\sec A = c/b$
cosecant: $\csc A = c/a$.

Fractions, Decimals, and Percents

To find the equivalent of a fraction in decimal form, divide the numerator (top number) by the denominator (bottom number). To change from a decimal to a percent, multiply by 100. To change from a percent to a decimal, divide by 100.

Fraction	Decimal	Percent
1/16	0.0625	6.25%
1/8 (= 2/16)	0.125	12.5
3/16	0.1875	18.75
1/4 (= 2/8; = 4/16)	0.25	25.0
5/16	0.3125	31.25
1/3	0.3 . . .	33 1/3
3/8 (= 6/16)	0.375	37.5
7/16	0.4375	43.75
1/2 (= 2/4; = 4/8; = 8/16)	0.5	50.0
9/16	0.5625	56.25
5/8 (= 10/16)	0.625	62.5
2/3	0.6 . . .	66 2/3
11/16	0.6875	68.75
3/4 (= 6/8; = 12/16)	0.75	75.0
13/16	0.8125	81.25
7/8 (= 14/16)	0.875	87.5
15/16	0.9375	93.75
1 (=2/2;=4/4;=8/8;=16/16)	1.0	100.0

Large Numbers

There are two primary naming systems for large numbers. The United States and France (among others) use one system, while Germany and Great Britain use the other. (Googol and googolplex, invented by the nephew of mathematician and author Edward Kasner, are rarely used outside the United States.) (See also "Standard Weights and Measures.")

Number of zeroes after 1	American name	British name
6	million	million
9	billion	milliard
12	trillion	billion
15	quadrillion	1,000 billion
18	quintillion	trillion
21	sextillion	1,000 trillion
24	septillion	quadrillion
27	octillion	1,000 quadrillion
30	nonillion	quintillion
33	decillion	1,000 quintillion
100	googol	googol
googol	googolplex	googolplex

In any triangle labeled such that side a is opposite angle A, side b is opposite angle B, and side c is opposite angle C:

Angle sum:

$$A + B + C = 180°$$

Law of sines:

$$(\sin A)/a = (\sin B)/b = (\sin C)/c$$

Law of cosines:

$$c^2 = a^2 + b^2 - 2ab \cos C$$

If x is any real number or a measure of an angle in degrees, the following statements are true:

Defining trigonometric identities:

$$\tan x = \sin x/\cos x \qquad \csc x = 1/\sin x$$
$$\cot x = \cos x/\sin x \qquad \cot x = 1/\tan x$$
$$\sec x = 1/\cos x$$

Trigonometric identities of symmetry:

$$\sin(-x) = -\sin x \qquad \cos(-x) = \cos x$$
$$\tan(-x) = -\tan x \qquad \cot(-x) = -\cot x$$
$$\sec(-x) = \sec x \qquad \csc(-x) = -\csc x.$$

Pythagorean identities:

$$\sin^2 x + \cos^2 x = 1$$
$$\tan^2 x + 1 = \sec^2 x$$
$$\cot^2 x + 1 = \csc^2 x$$

Sum and difference formulas: If x and y are any two real numbers or measures of angles:

$$\sin(x + y) = \sin x \cos y + \cos x \sin y$$
$$\cos(x + y) = \cos x \cos y - \sin x \sin y$$
$$\tan(x + y) = (\tan x + \tan y)/(1 - \tan x \tan y)$$
$$\sin(x - y) = \sin x \cos y - \cos x \sin y$$
$$\cos(x - y) = \cos x \cos y + \sin x \sin y$$
$$\tan(x - y) = (\tan x - \tan y)/(1 + \tan x \tan y).$$

Prefixes Used in the International System of Units (SI)

Prefix	Abbre-viation	Factor by which unit is multipled	Scientific Notation
Exa-	E	1,000,000,000,000,000,000	10^{18}
Peta-	P	1,000,000,000,000,000	10^{15}
Tera-	T	1,000,000,000,000	10^{12}
Giga-	G	1,000,000,000	10^{9}
Mega-	M	1,000,000	10^{6}
Kilo-	k	1,000	10^{3}
Hecto-	h	100	10^{2}
Deka-	da	10	10^{1}
Deci-	d	0.1	10^{-1}
Centi-	c	0.01	10^{-2}
Milli-	m	0.001	10^{-3}
Micro-	μ	0.000 001	10^{-6}
Nano-	n	0.000 000 001	10^{-9}
Pico-	p	0.000 000 000 001	10^{-12}
Femto-	f	0.000 000 000 000 001	10^{-15}
Atto-	a	0.000 000 000 000 000 001	10^{-18}

STANDARD WEIGHTS & MEASURES

▶SYSTEMS OF MEASUREMENT

There are two widely used measurement systems. Most of the world uses a system known as the metric system, or the International System, abbreviated SI from *Système Internationale*, its name in French. The United States continues to use a system called U.S. customary measure, which derives from (and differs from) the British imperial series of weights and measures. From time to time, our government has taken steps to change from the customary system to the International System, but these efforts have had limited success. Metric measure is legal in the United States, but nearly everyone continues to use the customary system in everyday use. The International System is generally used in scientific pursuits and increasingly in international trade.

The following tables show first the U.S. customary system, then the International System, and finally some important conversion factors between the two.

Length or Distance
U.S. customary system

1 foot (ft.)	=	12 inches		
1 yard (yd.)	=	3 feet	=	36 inches
1 rod (rd.)	=	5.5 yards	=	16.5 feet
1 furlong (fur.)	=	40 rods	=	220 yards
	=	660 feet		
1 mile (mi.)	=	8 furlongs		
	=	1,760 yards	=	5,280 feet

An international nautical mile has been defined as 6,076.1155 feet.

International System

The basic unit for length is the meter, which is slightly longer than the customary yard. Other units of length are decimal subdivisions or multiples of the meter.

1 decimeter (dm)	=	10 centimeters
	=	0.1 meter
1 centimeter (cm)	=	0.01 meter
1 millimeter (mm)	=	0.1 centimeter
	=	0.001 meter
1 micrometer (μm)	=	0.001 millimeter
	=	0.0001 centimeter
	=	0.000001 meter
1 angstrom (Å)	=	0.0001 micrometers
	=	0.0000001 milimeter

1 dekameter (dam) = 10 meters
1 hectometer (hm) = 10 dekameters
                   = 100 meters
   1 kilometer   = 10 hectometers
                   = 100 dekameters
                   = 1,000 meters

Conversions

In 1959 the relationship between between customary and international measures of length was officially defined as follows:

0.0254 meter (exactly) = 1 inch
0.0245 meter x 12   = 0.3048 meter
                        = 1 international foot

This definition, which makes many conversions simple, defines a foot that is shorter (by about 6 parts in 10 million) than the survey foot, which had earlier been defined as exactly 1200/3937, or 0.3048006, meter.

Following the international foot standard, the major equivalents are as listed below:

1 in. = 2.54 cm = 0.0254 m
1 ft. = 30.48 cm = .3048 m
1 yd. = 91.44 cm = 0.9144 m
1 mi. = 1,609.344 m = 1.609344 km
1 cm   = 0.3937 in.
1 m   = 1.093613 yd. = 3.28084 ft.
1 km   = 0.62137 mi.

Area
U.S. customary system

Areas are derived from lengths as follows:

1 square foot   = 144 square inches
1 square yard   = 9 sq. ft.
1 square rod (rd.^{2}) = 30.25 square yards
                     = 272.25 square feet
   1 acre   = 160 square rods
                     = 4,840 square yards
                     = 43,560 sq. ft.
1 square mile   = 640 acres
   1 section   = 1 mile square
   1 township   = 6 miles square
                     = 36 square miles

Simplified Conversion Table (alphabetical order)

To convert	to	multiply by:
centimeters	feet	0.0328
centimeters	inches	0.3937
cubic cm	cubic in.	0.061
cubic feet	cubic m	0.0283
degrees	radians	0.0175
feet	cm	30.5
feet	meters	0.305
gallons	liters	3.785
galon of water	pound of water	8.3
grams	ounces	0.035
inches	cm	2.54
kilograms	pounds	2.2
kilometers	feet	3,281
kilometers	miles	0.62
knots	mi./hr.	1.15
liters	gallons	0.264
liters	pints	2.1
meters	feet	3.28
miles	km	1.61
ounces	grams	28.35
pounds	kg	0.454

International System

1 sq. millimeter (mm^2) = 1,000,000 sq. micrometers
1 sq. centimeter (cm^2) = 100 mm^2
1 sq. decimeter (dm^2)   = 100 cm^2
   1 sq. meter (m^2)   = 10,000 cm^2
      1 are (a)   = 100 m^2
   1 hectare (ha)   = 100 ares
                           = 10,000 m^2
1 sq kilometer (km^2)   = 100 hectares
                           = 1,000,000 m^2

Conversions

1 square inch = 6.4516 cm^2
1 square foot = 929.0304 cm^2
               = 0.09290304 m^2
1 square yard = 8,361.2736 cm^2
               = 0.83612736 m^2
   1 acre   = 4,046.8564 m^2
               = 0.40468564 hectares
1 square mile = 2,589,988.11 m^2
               = 258.998811 hectares
               = 2.58998811 km^2
   1 cm^2 = 0.1550003 sq. in.
   1 m^2 = 1,550.003 sq. in.
               = 10.76391 sq. ft.
               = 1.195990 sq. yds.
1 hectare   = 107,639.1 sq. ft.
               = 11,959.90 sq. yds.
               = 2.4710538 acres
   1 km^2 = 247.10538 acres
               = 0.3861006 sq. miles

Cubic Measure
U.S. customary system

1 cu foot (ft.^{3}) = 1,728 cubic inches (in.^{3})
1 cubic yard (yd.^{3}) = 27 cubic feet (ft.^{3})

International System

1 cubic centimeter (cm^3) = 1,000 cubic millimeters (mm^3)
1 cubic decimeter (dm^3) = 1,000 cubic centimeters (cm^3)
   1 cubic meter (m^3)   = 1,000 cubic decimeters (dm^3)
                           = 1,000,000 cubic centimeters (cm^3)

Cubic centimeter is sometimes abbreviated cc and is used in fluid measure interchangeably with milliliter (ml).

Conversions

1 in.^{3} = 16.387064 cm^3
1 ft.^{3} = 28.316846592 cm^3
           = 0.028316847 cm^3
1 yd.^{3} = 764,554.857984 cm^3
           = 0.764554858 m^3
1 cm^3 = 0.06102374 in.^{3}
1 m^3 = 61,023.74 in.^{3}
           = 35.31467 ft.^{3}
           = 1.307951 yd.^{3}

Fluid Volume
U.S. customary system

A gallon is equal to 231 cubic inches of liquid or capacity.

1 tablespoon (tbs.) = 3 teaspoons (tsp.)
                     = 0.5 fluid ounce (fl. oz.)
      1 cup   = 8 fl. oz.
   1 pint (pt.)   = 2 cups = 16 fl. oz.
   1 quart (qt.)   = 2 pt. = 4 cups
                     = 32 fl. oz.
   1 gallon (gal.)   = 4 qt. = 8 pt. = 16 cups
   1 bushel (bu.)   = 8 gal. = 32 qt.

International System

Fluid-volume measurements are directly tied to cubic measure. One milliliter of fluid occupies a volume of 1 cubic centimeter. A liter of fluid (slightly more than the customary quart) occupies a volume of 1 cubic decimeter, or 1,000 cubic centimeters.

1 centiliter (cL)	=	10 mililiters (mL)		
1 deciliter	=	10 cl	=	100 mL
1 liter (L)	=	10 dl	=	1,000 mL
1 dekaliter (daL)	=	10 L		
1 hectoliter (hL)	=	10 daL	=	100 L
1 kiloliter (kL)	=	10 hl	=	1,000 L

Conversions

1 fluid ounce	=	29.573528 mL	=	0.02957 L
1 cup	=	236.588 mL	=	0.236588 L
1 pint	=	473.176 mL	=	0.473176 L
1 quart	=	946.3529 mL	=	0.9463529 L
1 gallon	=	3,785.41 mL	=	3.78541 L
1 milliliter	=	0.0338 fluid ounce		
1 liter	=	33.814 fluid ounces		
	=	4.2268 cups	=	2.113 pints
	=	1.0567 quarts	=	0.264 gallon

Dry Volume
Conversions

1 pint, dry	=	33.600 cu. in.	=	0.551 L
1 quart, dry	=	67.201 cu. in.	=	1.101 L

Mass & Weight

Mass and weight are often confused. Mass is a measure of the quantity of matter in an object and does not vary with changes in altitude or in gravitational force (as on the Moon or another planet). Weight, on the other hand, is a measure of the force of gravity on an object and so does change with altitude or gravitational force.

U.S. customary system

In customary measure it is more common to measure weight than mass. The most common customary system of weight is avoirdupois:

1 pound (lb.)	=	16 ounces (oz.)
1 (short) hundred-	=	100 lb.
weight (cwt.)		
1 (short) ton	=	20 hundredweights
	=	2,000 lb.
1 long hundred-	=	112 lb.
weight		
1 long ton	=	20 long hundredweights
	=	2,240 lb.

A different system called troy weight is used to weigh precious metals. In troy weight the ounce is slightly larger than in avoirdupois, but there are only 12 ounces to the troy pound.

International System

Instead of weight, the International System generally is used to measure mass. The International System's basic unit for measurement of mass is the gram, which was originally defined as the mass of 1 milliliter (= 1 cm³) of water at 4 degrees Celsius (about 39°F). Today the official standard of measure is the kilogram (1,000 g).

1 centigram (cg)	=	10 milligrams (mg)				
1 decigram (dg)	=	10 cg	=	100 mg		
1 gram (g)	=	10 dg	=	100 cg	=	1000 mg
1 kilogram (kg)	=	10 hectograms (hg)				
	=	100 dekagrams (dag)				
	=	1,000 g				
1 metric ton (t)	=	1000 kg				

Conversions

Since mass and weight are identical at standard conditions (sea level on Earth), grams and other International System units of mass are often used as measures of weight or converted into customary units of weight. Under standard conditions:

1 ounce	=	28.3495 grams
1 pound	=	453.59 grams
	=	0.45359 kilogram
1 short ton	=	907.18 kilograms
	=	0.907 metric ton
1 milligram	=	0.000035 ounce
1 gram	=	0.03527 ounce
1 kilogram	=	35.27 ounces
	=	2.2046 pounds
1 metric ton	=	2,204.6 pounds
	=	1.1023 short tons

Time
Customary and International System

The International System in 1967 adopted a second that is based on the microwaves emitted by the vibrations of hot cesium atoms. A second (abbreviated sec. in customary usage, s in SI usage) is the time it takes the atoms to vibrate exactly 9,192,631,770 times. In the customary measure of time, the day is divided into 24 hours, the hour into 60 minutes, and the minute into 60 seconds. Since the Earth's rotation is gradually slowing, scientists must periodically add a second to a day to keep the year in sequence with their clocks. The change is so small that for almost all practical purposes an International System second and a customary second are the same.

Decimal fractions of time are used to measure smaller time intervals:

millisecond (ms)	=	0.001 second (10^{-3})
microsecond (µs)	=	0.000001 second (10^{-6})
nanosecond (ns)	=	0.000000001 second (10^{-9})
picosecond (ps)	=	0.000000000001 second (10^{-12})

Temperature
U.S. customary system

In the U.S., temperature is usually measured in degrees Fahrenheit: water freezes at 32°F and boils at 212°F. The basis of the Fahrenheit scale was 0°F, the coldest temperature that its originator, G.D. Fahrenheit (1686–1736), could obtain under laboratory conditions.

International System

The Swedish astronomer Anders Celsius (1701–44) devised the temperature scale that bears his name in 1742. On the Celsius scale, water freezes at 0°C and boils at 100°C. Very low temperatures are measured on the Kelvin scale, named for William Thomson, Baron Kelvin (1824–1907). It is also called the absolute scale because absolute zero— 0°K (-273.15° C)—is the temperature at which no body can give up heat. The interval of a degree Kelvin equals the interval of a degree Celsius. At very high temperatures, differences between the Kelvin and Celsius scales are insignificant.

Conversions

Fahrenheit to Celsius: Subtract 32 from the temperature and multiply the difference by 5; then divide the product by 9. The formula is: $C = \frac{5}{9}(F-32)$

Fahrenheit and Celsius Temperature Conversions

You can roughly convert a Celsius temperature to Fahrenheit by doubling the number and adding 30. For example, 20°C Celsius is approximately 70°F. (Conversely, subtract 30 from Fahrenheit temperature and divide by two for a Celsius temperature.) For a closer equivalent, consult the table below.

Celsius		Fahrenheit	Fahrenheit		Celsius
-45°	=	-49°	-45°	=	-42.8°
-40°	=	-40°	-40°	=	-40.0°
-35°	=	-31°	-35°	=	-37.2°
-30°	=	-22°	-30°	=	-34.4°
-25°	=	-13°	-25°	=	-31.7°
-20°	=	-4°	-20°	=	-28.9°
-15°	=	5°	-15°	=	-26.1°
-10°	=	14°	-10°	=	-23.3°
-5°	=	23°	-5°	=	-20.6°
0°	=	32°	0°	=	-17.8°
5°	=	41°	5°	=	-15.0°
10°	=	50°	10°	=	-12.2°
15°	=	59°	15°	=	-9.4°
20°	=	68°	20°	=	-6.7°
25°	=	77°	25°	=	-3.9°
30°	=	86°	30°	=	-1.1°
35°	=	95°	32°	=	0.0°
40°	=	104°	35°	=	1.7°
45°	=	113°	40°	=	4.4°
50°	=	122°	45°	=	7.2°
55°	=	131°	50°	=	10.0°
60°	=	140°	55°	=	12.8°
65°	=	149°	60°	=	15.6°
70°	=	158°	65°	=	18.3°
75°	=	167°	70°	=	21.1°
80°	=	176°	75°	=	23.9°
85°	=	185°	80°	=	26.7°
90°	=	194°	85°	=	29.4°
95°	=	203°	90°	=	32.2°
100°	=	212°	95°	=	35.0°
125°	=	257°	100°	=	37.8°
150°	=	302°	105°	=	40.6°
175°	=	347°	110°	=	43.3°
200°	=	392°	212°	=	100.0°
225°	=	437°	225°	=	107.2°
250°	=	482°	250°	=	121.1°
275°	=	527°	275°	=	135.0°
300°	=	572°	300°	=	148.9°
325°	=	617°	325°	=	162.8°
350°	=	662°	350°	=	176.7°
375°	=	707°	375°	=	190.6°
400°	=	752°	400°	=	204.4°
425°	=	797°	425°	=	218.3°
450°	=	842°	450°	=	232.2°
475°	=	887°	475°	=	246.1°

Celsius to Fahrenheit: Multiply the temperature by 1.8 (or $\frac{9}{5}$), then add 32. The formula is: $F = \frac{9}{5} C + 32$
Celsius to Kelvin: Add 273.15 to the temperature. The formula is: $K = C + 273.15$

Force, Work/Energy, Power
U.S. customary system

The foot/pound/second system of reckoning includes the following units:

Kelvin, Celsius, and Fahrenheit Equivalents

Characteristic	K	C°	F°
Absolute zero	0	-273.15°	-459.7°
Freezing point, water	273.15	0°	32°
Traditional human body temperature	310.15	37°	98.6°
Boiling point, water	373.15	100°	212°

slug = the mass to which a force of 1 poundal will give an acceleration of 1 foot per second per second (= approximately 32.17 lbs.)
poundal = fundamental unit of force
foot-pound = the work done when a force of 1 poundal produces a movement of 1 foot
foot-pound/second = the unit of power equal to 1 foot/pound per second

Another common unit of power is horsepower, which is equal to 550 foot-pounds per second.

Thermal work or energy is often measured in British thermal units (Btu), One Btu is defined as the energy required to increase the temperature of 1 pound of water by 1 degree Fahrenheit. The Btu is equal to about 0.778 foot-pound.

International System

In physics, compound measurements of force, work or energy, and power are essential. There are two parallel systems using International System units: the centimeter/gram/second system (cgs) is used for small measurements, and the meter/kilogram/second system (mks) is used for larger measurements. The mks system is the official one for SI. They are described below.

Measurement of force

cgs unit   dyne (dy)   The force required to accelerate a mass of 1 g 1 cm/s² (cm/s² means "centimeter per second per second")

mks unit   newton (N)   The force required to accelerate a mass of 1 kg 1 m/s²

Measurement of work or energy

cgs unit   erg   The dyne-centimeter, i.e., the work done when a force of 1 dy produces a movement of 1 cm

mks unit   joule (j)   The newton-meter, i.e., the work done when a force of 1 N produces a movement of 1 m (=10,000,000 ergs)

Heat energy is also measured using the calorie (cal), which is defined as the energy required to increase the temperature of 1 cubic centimeter (1 ml) of water by 1 degree C. One calorie is equal to about 4.184 joules. The kilocalorie (Kcal or Cal) is equal to 1,000 calories and is the unit in which the energy values of food are measured. This more familiar unit, also commonly referred to as a Calorie, is equal to about 4,184 joules.

Measurement of power

cgs unit   erg/second   A rate of 1 erg per second

mks unit   watt (W)   The joule/second, i.e., a rate of 1 joule per second

Conversions
Measurement of force

1 poundal	=	13,889 dynes
	=	0.13889 newtons
1 dyne	=	0.000072 poundals
1 newton	=	7.2 poundals

Measurement of work or energy

1 foot-pound	=	1,356 joules
British thermal unit	=	1,055 joules
	=	252 calories
1 joule	=	0.0007374 ft.-lbs.
1 calorie	=	0.003968 Btu
1 Kilocalorie	=	3.968 Btu

Measurement of power

1 foot-pound/second	=	1.3564 watts
1 horsepower	=	746 watts
	=	0.746 kilowatts
1 watt	=	0.73725 ft.-lb/sec.
	=	0.00134 horsepower
1 kilowatt	=	737.25 ft.-lb./sec.
	=	1.34 horsepower

Electrical Measure

Originally, the basic unit of quantity in electricity was the coulomb. A coulomb is equal to the passage of 6.25×10^{18} electrons past a given point in an electrical system.

The unit of electrical flow is the ampere, which is equal to a coulomb/second, i.e., the flow of 1 coulomb per second. The ampere is analogous in electrical measure to a unit of flow such as gallons-per-minute in physical measure. In SI, the ampere is taken as the basic unit.

The unit for measuring electrical potential energy is the volt, which is defined as 1 joule/coulomb, i.e., 1 joule of energy per coulomb of electricity. The volt is analogous to a measure of pressure in a water system.

The unit for measuring electrical power is the watt as defined in the previous section. Power in watts (P) is the product of the electrical flow in amperes (I) and the potential electrical energy in volts (E):

$$P = IE.$$

Since the watt is such a small unit for practical applications, the kilowatt (= 1,000 watts) is often used. A kilowatt-hour is the power of 1,000 watts over an hour's time.

The unit for measuring electrical resistance is the ohm, which is the resistance offered by a circuit to the flow of 1 ampere being driven by the force of 1 volt. It is derived from Ohm's law, which defines the relationship between flow or current (amperes), potential energy (volts), and resistance (ohms). It states that the current in amperes (I) is proportional to potential energy in volts (E) and inversely proportional to resistance in ohms (R). Thus, when voltage and resistance are known, amperage can be calculated by the simple formula

$$I = \frac{E}{R}$$

Measure of Angles and Arcs

Angles are measured by systems based on arcs (portions) of circles. Arcs of a circle can be measured by length, but they are also often measured by angles. In the latter case, the measure of the arc is the same as the measure of an angle whose vertex is at the center of the circle and whose sides pass through the ends of the arc. Such an angle is said to be subtended by the arc.

The most commonly used angle measure is degree measure. One degree is the angle subtended by an arc that is 1/360 of a circle. This is an ancient system of measurement probably originally developed by Sumerian astronomers. These astronomers used a numeration system based on 60 ($60 \times 6 = 360$), as well as a 360-day year. They divided the day into 12 equal periods of 30 smaller periods each ($12 \times 30 = 360$) and used roughly the same system for dividing the circle. Even when different years and numeration systems were adopted by later societies, astronomers continued to use a variation of the Sumerian system for angles.

1 degree (1°)	=	60 minutes (60')
	=	3,600 seconds (3,600")
1 minute	=	60 seconds

When two lines are perpendicular to each other, they form four angles of the same size, which are called right angles. Two right angles make up a line, which in this context is considered a straight angle.

1 right angle = 90°
1 straight angle = 180°

While this system is workable for most purposes, it is artificial. Mathematicians discovered that using a natural system of angle measurement produces results that make better sense in mathematical and many scientific applications. This system is called radian measure. Radian measure is considered a supplement to SI. One radian is the measure of the angle subtended by an arc of a circle that is exactly as long as the radius of the circle.

1 radian = about 57° 17' 45"

The circumference, C, of a circle is given by the formula $C = 2\pi r$, where π is a number (approximately 3.14159) and r is the radius. Therefore, a semicircle whose radius is 1 is π units long, which implies that there are π radians in a straight angle. Many of the angles commonly encountered are measured in multiples of π radians:

0° = 0 radians	90° = $\pi/2$ radians
30° = $\pi/6$ radians	180° = π radians
45° = $\pi/4$ radians	270° = $3\pi/2$ radians
60° = $\pi/3$ radians	360° = 2π radians

To convert from radians to degrees, use the formula $t\ radians = (180/\pi)\ t°$. To convert from degrees to radians, use the formula

$$w° = (\pi/180)w \text{ radians.}$$

The U.S. artillery uses the mil to measure angles. A mil is the angle subtended by an arc that is 1/6400 of a circle.

1 mil = 0.05625° = 3' 22.5"
1 mil = almost 0.001 radian

The Environment

The modern environmental movement in the United States dates from Earth Day 1970 (April 22), when the American public first began to take stock of the ecological devastation going on around them. Then there were no pollution controls on cars; people and municipalities dumped untreated sewage into the nation's rivers, some of which were so saturated with chemical waste that they actually caught fire; and industrial cities were routinely shrouded with thick acrid smoke.

Many of these problems have been effectively addressed and dramatically diminished. Today the Environmental Protection Agency (EPA), established in 1970, routinely monitors air quality at thousands of sites around the country. Toxic emissions from smokestacks at smelters, factories, and garbage incinerators have been sharply reduced. Mandatory pollution control standards on automobiles have led to an overwhelming drop in lead emissions. Recycling as a way of reducing solid waste has taken hold in cities and towns throughout the country. Many people, however, oppose strong environmental safeguards on economic and other grounds, making it difficult to improve and enforce regulations. Growing population pressures also create environmental threats, particularly to natural habitats, arable soil, and drinking water supplies.

▶ GLOBAL WARMING

Most climatologists are convinced that over the past century the Earth has begun to warm significantly—about 1°F (0.5°C)—and that at its current rate, it is likely to warm as much as 2.5° to 10°F (1.4° to 5.8°C) by the year 2100. A 1998 study based on tree rings, ice cores, growth of corals, and historical records shows that the 1990s have been the warmest decade in the past 600 years. The Earth's average surface temperature in 1998 was the highest since thermometer records were first kept in the mid-19th century, as the effects of El Niño heightened the underlying warming trend. If global temperatures continue to increase, the potential devastation is staggering. Worldwide temperatures have risen only 9°F (5°C) since the end of the last ice age 12,000 years ago. Additional warming could cause melting of polar ice caps, setting off a chain of events that begins with a rise in sea level worldwide and could end with the destruction of water supplies, forests, and agriculture in many parts of the world.

Global warming occurs when certain gases in the atmosphere prevent sunlight from being reflected from the Earth. Ordinarily, sunlight that reaches the surface of the Earth is partly absorbed and partly reflected. The absorbed light heats the surface and is later emitted from the surface as infrared radiation. Gases that are not transparent to infrared radiation (carbon dioxide is one) collect this heat and keep it in the atmosphere, hence their name, greenhouse gases. The Earth's atmosphere is only 0.03 percent carbon dioxide, but combined with other gases, this is enough to trap 30 percent of the reflected heat (the rest is radiated out to space), and maintain the Earth's average temperature at about 59°F (15°C).

In a 1996 report, the Intergovernmental Panel on Climate Change (IPCC), a group of 2,500 scientists commissioned by the U.N., concluded that "the balance of evidence suggests that there is a discernible human influence on global climate." The most recent (2001) IPCC report adds considerable strength to this conclusion. Since the Industrial Revolution, human activities have released an unprecedented amount of greenhouse gases into the atmosphere, particularly carbon dioxide, chlorofluorocarbons (CFCs), methane, and nitrogen oxides.

The increased presence of carbon dioxide is due primarily to the burning of carbon fuels including oil, coal, and natural gas, as well as burning trees for deforestation. CFCs, now being phased out by many countries, are used as aerosols, in air-conditioning units, and in various industrial processes. Methane is emitted by decomposing organic wastes, natural-gas leaks, and fermenting rice paddies. The primary sources of nitrogen oxides are automobile exhaust and industrial smoke stacks. At a December 1997 conference in Kyoto, Japan, representatives of more than 150 countries reached tentative agreement to reduce greenhouse gases an average of 5 percent worldwide (from 1990 levels) by the year 2010. In the United States, which accounts for nearly a quarter of global emissions, the target is a 7 percent reduction.

In the ensuing time, the U.S. has done little to meet that goal, even though emissions in America are projected to *increase* by 30 percent by 2008 if the status quo is not altered. Meanwhile, a team of NASA scientists reported in early 1999 that two cubic miles of ice per year have been melting away from Greenland since 1993 due to increased global temperatures. They warned that if the trend continued, the results could ultimately be catastrophic.

Global warming produces complex and interrelated effects that could under some scenarios spell environmental disaster. Some of the elements of global warming are:

Weather patterns Climatologists think that higher global temperatures and changing precipitation patterns are already disrupting local weather in places around the world. For example, the IPCC (2001) reports that more intense precipitation events (storms) have likely increased in the Northern hemisphere, including the United States, and are very likely to increase in most areas of the world in this century. The U.S. National Climatic Data Center in Asheville, NC reports that Northern Hemisphere snow cover has been below normal since 1987, and that extreme extratropical cyclone activity over the North Atlantic has increased since 1988.

Changed weather patterns can have a severe impact on crops and other forms of vegetation, as well as on the animals that depend on them. Rising temperatures also enable insects and fungal pests to migrate to previously unaffected regions. Long-lived plants, however, such as trees, spread much more slowly in the face of climate change.

Warming patterns Although global warming will cause an increase in average world temperatures, this increase is not expected to be uniform. In general, climatologists expect greater warming during winter months and at high latitudes (closer to the poles than to the equator). Some places will experience more severe effects than others. For example, the number of +95°F days in

Major Events in the History of the Environment

1775   Percival Pott observes that chimney sweeps develop cancer as a result of their contact with soot, the first recognition of environmental factors on cancer.

1864   George Perkins Marsh (American: 1801-81) publishes *Man and Nature*, the first textbook on conservation and the first detailed study of human influence on the environment.

1872   Robert Angus Smith (Scottish: 1817-84) describes acid rain.

1885   Yellowstone, world's first national park, opens.

1892   Canada establishes first national park at Banff, Alberta.

1895   Svante Arrhenius (Swedish, 1859-1927) is the first person to investigate effect of increasing carbon dioxide in the atmosphere on global climate.

1903   John Muir (Scottish-American: 1838-1914) founds the Sierra Club.

1905   U.S. president Theodore Roosevelt opens the first national refuge, Pelican Island in Florida, to protect nesting sites of brown pelicans.

U.S. Forest Service established.

National Audubon Society founded.

1911   Canada, Japan, Russia, and the United States sign treaty to limit the harvest of northern fur seals.

1916   National Park Service established.

1928   Boulder Canyon project (Hoover Dam) authorized to bring irrigation, electric power, and flood control system to western United States.

1933   Tennessee Valley Authority created to develop the Tennessee River for flood control, navigation, electric power, agriculture, and forestry.

1939   Paul Müller (Swiss: 1899-1965) discovers insecticidal properties of DDT.

1952   Smog blamed for 4,000 deaths in London.

1955   Link between exposure to asbestos and lung cancer established.

1957   Nuclear wastes stored by the Soviet Union in a remote mountain region of the Urals explode; radioactive contamination affects thousands of square miles; several villages permanently evacuated.

1961   Investigations in Scandinavia and the U.S. Adirondacks confirm that acid rain kills some species living in lakes.

1962   *Silent Spring* by Rachel Carson (American: 1907-64) attacks pesticide use and stimulates major environmental movement.

1963   Congress passes first Clean Air Act, allocating $95 million to local, state, and national air pollution control efforts.

1964   Congress passes Wilderness Act, setting up the National Wilderness Preservation System.

1965   Congress passes Highway Beautification Act, banning many highway billboards.

Congress passes Water Quality Act, giving federal government power to set water standards.

Congress passes the Solid Waste Disposal Act, its first major solid waste legislation.

1966   Congress passes Rare and Endangered Species Act.

1967   S. Manabe and R.T. Wetherald predict that increased amounts of carbon dioxide in the atmosphere will lead to global warming.

1968   Congress passes Wild and Scenic Rivers Act, identifying areas of scenic beauty for preservation and recreation.

1970   First Earth Day celebrated on April 22.

Environmental Protection Agency created.

1972   Congress passes Clean Water Act, forbidding discharges of pollutants into navigable waters.

Oregon passes the nation's first bottle recycling law.

The EPA bars registration and interstate sales of DDT because of its persistence in the environment and accumulation in the food chain.

1973   Representatives of 80 nations sign the Convention of International Trade in Endangered Species of Wild Fauna and Flora, which prohibits commercial trade in 375 endangered species of wild animals.

1974   F. Sherwood Rowland and Mario Molinas warn that chlorofluorocarbons (CFCs) produced by spray cans and air conditioners are destroying ozone layer.

1976   Congress passes Toxic Substances Control Act to control hazardous industrial chemicals.

1978   Community of Love Canal, near Niagara, N.Y., evacuated after hazardous waste dumps are uncovered. EPA declares site safe in 1990.

1979   Nuclear reactor at Three Mile Island, near Harrisburg, Pa., suffers partial meltdown; radiation confined to reactor dome.

1980   Congress passes Comprehensive Environmental Response, Compensation and Liability Act (the "Superfund") to clean up hazardous waste sites.

1984   More than 2,000 die and thousands more are injured by toxic gas from an accident at the U.S.-owned Union Carbide plant in Bhopal, India.

1985   British scientists discover that a "hole" in the ozone layer develops over Antarctica each winter.

The U.S. sets up a Conservation Reserve Program to remove environmentally sensitive farmland from agricultural use.

1986   A worldwide ban on whaling begins.

Chernobyl nuclear reactor number 4 explodes and burns, causing 31 deaths within days, shortening the lives of thousands, and forcing the evacuation of hundreds of square miles in Soviet Ukraine for an unknown length of time.

1987   The worst forest fire in history burns more than 3 million acres of China's timber reserve and up to 15 million acres in the Soviet Union.

1988   The U.S. Ocean Dumping Ban Act mandates an end to ocean dumping of industrial waste and sewage sludge.

1989   Exxon *Valdez* grounds, leaking 35,000 tons of oil into Prince William Sound, Alaska.

Thirteen industrial nations agree to halt production of CFCs by the year 2000.

1991   Iraq dumps over a million tons of oil from occupied Kuwait into Persian Gulf.

1992   Representatives from 178 countries attend the first-ever Earth Summit in Rio de Janeiro, where they sign treaties pledging to increase the diversity of animal and plant species and to halt global warming.

1994   U.S. Fish and Wildlife Service recommends that status of American bald eagle be reduced from "endangered" to "threatened" in most of the U.S..

1995   The United Nations Working Group I of the Intergovernmental Panel on Climate Change endorses global warming, reporting that "the balance of evidence suggests that there is a discernible human influence on global climate."

1996   The U.S. National Oceanic and Atmospheric Administration reports that measurements show that a global campaign to lower production of chemicals that damage the ozone layer has succeeded and that by 2010 the ozone layer will have begun to recover and by 2050 the Antarctic ozone "hole" will have closed.

1997   Representatives from more than 150 countries meet in Kyoto, Japan, where they agree to reduce emissions of greenhouse gases 5.2 percent worldwide by 2010.

2001   The Intergovernmental Panel on Climate Change (IPCC) reports that there is new and stronger evidence that most of the warming in the last half century is due to human activities.

Rio de Janeiro would increase tenfold, from 5 to 52 days. Rome would go from 6 to 55 days and Tokyo from 5 to 41.

Higher temperatures have an even more dire effect than increased numbers of hot days. Increased heat expands the volume of ocean water, and also increases flows to the oceans through melting of glaciers and ice caps. These two effects cause:

Sea level rise Climatologists generally expect the sea level to rise between 3.4 inches and almost three feet (.09 to .88 meters) by the end of this century. Generally speaking, a rise in sea level would be uniform, both geographically and seasonally, because sea level is a global phenomenon. The impact of such a rise, however, would vary greatly from place to place. A three-foot (1 m) rise would inundate 7,000 square miles (18,000 km^2) of dry land—an area the size of Massachusetts—in the United States, mostly in the southeast. It would also destroy a comparable area of coastal wetlands, erode recreational beaches 100 to 200 meters, exacerbate coastal flooding, and increase the salinity of aquifers and estuaries. It is likely that the people of an industrialized continental nation such as the United States could sustain the population shifts caused by such climatic changes. However, an estimated one-third of the world's population—about 1.75 billion people, today—lives within 40 miles of the sea, mostly along low-lying floodplains and estuaries. How the low-lying Bangladesh or the island nations of the Pacific can or will respond to such forces is impossible to see.

Changing temperatures and precipitation patterns may also lead to basic changes in the deep circulation patterns of the oceans, the so-called thermohaline ("heat and salt") circulation, which brings heat to the North Atlantic region and keeps it considerably warmer than places at equal latitudes in the Pacific. Increased freshwater inflow to the oceans through more precipitation and glacier and ice cap melting could alter the balance that produces these patterns and shut them down, which is believed to have happened in the geologic past. If a shutdown occurs, extremely rapid temperature changes (cooling) would result. According to the 2001 IPCC report current climate models mostly show a weakening of the thermohaline circulation, but not a complete shutdown, over the course of this century.

▶ THE OZONE LAYER

There are two distinct problems associated with the chemical ozone (O_3): ground-level ozone, the main component of smog (discussed under "Air Pollution," below), and stratospheric ozone. The primary difference between the two problems is that at ground level there is too much ozone, while in the stratosphere there is not enough.

The problem of stratospheric ozone depletion is closely related to global warming in that the chlorofluorocarbons (see below) that are its principal cause are greenhouse gases, but the science is different. Stratospheric ozone (sometimes referred to as upper-atmosphere or atmospheric ozone) absorbs most of the Sun's ultraviolet radiation. A significant reduction of the ozone layer would lead to sharp increases in the incidence of skin cancer and cataracts in humans. It is also thought that there would be serious losses of small ocean algae, which produce oxygen and break down carbon dioxide, and of bacteria important to crop production.

Complex natural forces are continually at work creating and destroying ozone in the atmosphere. This involves first the breakdown of individual molecules of oxygen (O_2) into atomic oxygen (O), through the absorption of ultraviolet radiation. In turn, each atomic oxygen normally combines with an additional molecule of O_2 to form ozone (O_3). Destruction of ozone can be caused by the occasional recombination of ozone with atomic oxygen to form two molecules of O_2. As long as the Earth's sunlit atmosphere contains molecular oxygen, as it has for more than one billion years, ozone will be maintained in this dynamic balance.

In 1974, scientists saw the first suggestion that a group of chemicals known as chlorofluorocarbons (CFCs) was destroying the ozone balance by adding chlorine to the atmosphere. Chemically inert, nontoxic, and easily liquefied, CFCs were developed in the 1930s as an ammonia substitute for use in refrigeration, but their use became widespread in air conditioning, packaging and insulation, as a solvent for cleaning electronic circuit boards, and as an aerosol propellant.

It is this very absence of chemical reactivity that makes CFCs so dangerous to the ozone layer. Unlike less inert compounds, CFCs are not destroyed or removed in the lower atmosphere by rain, oxidation, or sunlight, where their lifetimes have been estimated to be between 75 and 110 years. Instead they drift into the upper atmosphere, where their chlorine components are released into the atmosphere under the effects of ultraviolet radiation. Almost all of these freed chlorine atoms find and react with the ozone, creating chlorine monoxide and molecular oxygen. In a subsequent reaction, the chlorine monoxide releases its oxygen atom to form a second molecule of oxygen, and the chlorine atom is freed once again to repeat the process. Through this continuing cycle of reactions, each chlorine atom can destroy about 100,000 molecules of ozone before the chain reaction ends. In the Antarctic, ice crystals in the air speed up reactions, producing an "ozone hole," a region of extremely low levels of atmospheric ozone, over the south polar region during the Antarctic winter. A system of cold winds called the Antarctic Vortex amplifies this effect. NASA reported that the ozone hole on September 9, 2000, was the largest on record.

To combat ozone depletion, there have been stringent reductions in CFC use. The United States, Russia, Japan, and the nations of the European Union have agreed to eliminate CFC use and production 100 percent by 2000. Even so, adverse effects on the ozone layer from human-produced CFCs will likely continue until at least 2020.

▶ AIR POLLUTION

Although we tend to think of air pollution as a local problem, studies reported in 1995 demonstrate that there are widespread effects. Air pollution, they report, is so pervasive in industrial regions of northeastern North America, central Europe, and eastern Asia that it partly blocks sunlight, counteracting global warming with regional cooling.

The U.S. Environmental Protection Agency (EPA) monitors air quality at about 3,000 sites for six pollutants: particulate matter (soot and dust), sulfur dioxide, carbon monoxide (mostly from automobiles), nitrogen oxides, lead, and ozone. In addition to health concerns, the effects of air pollution on vegetation, materials, and visibility are monitored.

The basic federal law dealing with air pollution is the Clean Air Act of 1990, which directs the EPA to set standards for air quality. The main pollutants are discussed here.

Particulate matter (PM₁₀) The EPA measures particulate matter with an aerodynamic diameter smaller than 10 micrometers down to 2.5 micrometers. This includes dust, dirt, soot, smoke, and liquid droplets directly emitted into the air from factories, power plants, cars, construction sites, fires, and natural erosion, as well as particles formed in the atmosphere by condensation or transformation of emitted gases such as sulfur dioxide and volatile organic compounds.

Particulate matter is responsible for most adverse health effects in the lower regions of the respiratory tract. People with chronic obstructive pulmonary or cardiovascular disease, individuals with influenza, asthmatics, the elderly, and children are especially sensitive.

Sulfur dioxide (SO₂) Ambient sulfur dioxide comes mostly from stationary-source coal and oil combustion, refineries, pulp and paper mills, and nonferrous smelters. The health hazards associated with exposure to SO₂ include impaired breathing, respiratory illness, alterations in the lungs' defenses, and aggravation of existing respiratory and cardiovascular disease. Those most sensitive to SO₂ include asthmatics and people with chronic lung disease or cardiovascular disease, children, and the elderly. Sulfur dioxide also damages leaves on trees and crops and it is an agent of acid rain.

Carbon monoxide (CO) Carbon monoxide is a colorless, odorless, and poisonous gas produced by incomplete burning of carbon in fuels. Carbon monoxide enters the bloodstream and disrupts delivery of oxygen to the body's organs and tissues. The health threat from carbon monoxide is serious for those who suffer from car-

Unhealthy Days in Selected Metropolitan Areas, 1980-99

To measure air quality in urban areas, the Environmental Protection Agency has developed an indicator called the Air Quality Index (AQI, formerly the Pollutant Standard Index, PSI). The AQI integrates into a single number emission levels of five major pollutants: particulate matter (PM₁₀). Sulfur Dioxide (SO₂), carbon monoxide (CO), ground level ozone (O₃) and nitrogen dioxide (NO₂). An AQI of 0-50 reflects good air, 51-100 denotes moderate air, and an AQI of over 100 is classified as unhealthy (201-300 signifies very unhealthy air; 301-500 is hazardous). The following chart lists the number of days in which the AQI exceeded 100 in metropolitan areas.

Metropolitan area	1980	1985	1990	1995	1996	1997	1998	1999
Atlanta	7	9	42	35	25	31	50	61
Bakersfield, Calif.	N.A.	29	99	105	109	55	76	88
Baltimore	N.A.	221	29	36	28	30	51	40
Boston	8	3	7	8	2	8	7	5
Chicago	34	8	4	21	6	9	7	12
Cincinnati	N.A.	N.A.	12	19	10	11	14	12
Cleveland	N.A.	1	10	24	18	11	20	18
Dallas	19	15	24	36	12	20	28	23
Denver	35	38	9	2	0	0	5	1
Detroit	N.A.	2	11	14	13	12	17	15
El Paso	N.A.	24	19	8	7	4	6	6
Fresno, Calif.	N.A.	21	62	61	70	75	67	81
Houston	10	48	51	66	26	47	38	50
Indianapolis	N.A.	N.A.	9	19	13	12	19	21
Las Vegas	N.A.	55	4	0	2	0	0	0
Los Angeles	220	194	173	113	94	60	56	27
Miami	N.A.	5	1	2	1	3	8	5
Milwaukee	N.A.	N.A.	8	14	5	4	10	13
Minneapolis-St. Paul	N.A.	21	4	5	0	0	1	0
New York	119	61	36	19	15	23	17	24
Oakland, Calif.	N.A.	N.A.	4	12	11	0	11	5
Orange County, Calif.	N.A.	69	45	9	9	3	6	1
Philadelphia	52	25	39	30	22	32	37	32
Phoenix	N.A.	84	12	22	17	12	17	12
Pittsburgh	20	9	19	25	11	21	39	23
Riverside-San Bernardino, Calif.	N.A.	142	159	124	119	105	95	93
Sacramento, Calif.	N.A.	67	61	41	42	15	27	38
St. Louis	N.A.	10	23	34	20	15	23	29
San Diego	N.A.	54	96	48	31	14	33	16
San Francisco	2	5	0	2	0	0	0	0
Seattle	33	24	9	0	6	1	3	1
Ventura, Calif.	N.A.	19	70	66	62	45	29	22
Washington, D.C.	38	15	25	29	18	29	47	39

Note: Figures reflect data from selected EPA trend sites. Number of unhealthy days recorded by all active EPA monitoring sites may be slightly higher in some cities.
Source: Environmental Protection Agency, *National Air Quality and Emissions Trends Report 1999* (2001). www.epa.gov/airtrends.

diovascular diseases. Healthy individuals are also affected, and exposure to elevated carbon monoxide levels is associated with impairment of visual perception and manual dexterity.

Federal regulations have succeeded in cleaning up much of the carbon monoxide pollution that plagued the U.S. in the 1980s. In 1990, 26 metropolitan areas exceeded the National Ambient Air Quality Standards for carbon monoxide at least once. Los Angeles exceeded the standard a whopping 47 times, while Las Vegas exceeded it 17 times. But in 1998, only six metropolitan areas exceeded the standard more than once. In 1999, only three cities exceeded it the standard: Calexico, Calif. (13 times), Los Angeles-Long Beach, Calif (8 times), and Fairbanks, Alaska (2 times).

Nitrogen oxides (NO$_x$) These highly reactive gases play a major role, together with volatile organic compounds, in the formation of ozone. Nitrogen oxides form when fuel is burned at high temperatures. When released into the atmosphere, they are one of the major causes of smog. The two major emissions sources are cars and trucks, and stationary fuel-combustion sources such as electric-utility and industrial boilers.

Nitrogen oxides can irritate the lungs and lower resistance to respiratory infections such as influenza. Prolonged exposure to higher than normal concentrations can cause pulmonary angina. Nitrogen dioxide (NO$_2$) is also an agent of acid rain and plays a key role in nitrogen loading of forests and ecosystems. Over the past decade, Los Angeles is the only urban area that has consistently recorded violations of the EPA's annual NO$_2$ standards. Many other urban areas violate the EPA's standards on occasional hot summer days, when the Sun cooks hydrocarbons and nitrogen oxides, thus producing smog.

Ozone (O$_3$) Ground-level ozone is a colorless gas and the main component of smog. Unlike most other air pollutants, ozone is not emitted by factories or automobiles, but is formed by the interaction of volatile organic compounds (VOCs) and nitrous oxide. These reactions are stimulated by sunlight and temperature so that peak ozone levels occur typically during the warmer times of year. The severity of a smog problem in a given locale is directly related to the temperature and ultraviolet radiation intensity in that area. While the problems associated with ozone depletion

Emissions Estimates for EPA-Monitored Pollutants, 1940-99 (thousand short tons)

Year	Carbon monoxide (CO)	Nitrogen oxides (NO$_x$)	Volatile organic compounds	Sulfur dioxide (SO$_2$)	Particulate matter (PM$_{10}$)	Lead (Pb)
1940	93,615	7,374	17,161	19,953	15,956	N.A.
1950	102,609	10,093	20,936	22,358	17,133	N.A.
1960	109,745	14,140	24,459	22,227	15,558	N.A.
1970	128,079	20,625	30,646	31,161	13,044[1]	219,471
1980	115,625	23,281	25,893	25,905	7,050[1]	74,956
1990	95,794	23,436	20,935	23,678	29,845	4,975
1996	90,611	23,391	18,736	19,121	30,143	3,910
1997	94,410	24,824	18,876	19,622	31,396	3,915
1998	89,454	24,454	17,917	19,647	31,916	3,973
1999	97,441	25,393	18,145	18,867	23,679	4,199

1.Particulate matter totals before 1990 do not include estimates for fugitive dust, which arises from construction activities, mining and quarrying and paved road resuspension. It is the leading source of PM$_{10}$ emissions.
Source: Environmental Protection Agency, *National Air Quality and Emissions Trends Report, 1999* (2001); www.epa.gov/airtrends.

Emissions Estimates for EPA-Monitored Pollutants By Source, 1999 (thousand short tons)

Source	Carbon monoxide (CO)	Nitrogen oxides (NO$_x$)	Volatile organic compounds	Sulfur dioxide (SO$_2$)	Particulate matter (PM$_{10}$)
Fuel combustion, Electric utility	445	5,715	56	12,698	225
Fuel combustion, Industrial	1,178	3,136	178	2,805	236
Fuel combustion, Other	3,699	1,170	670	588	568
Chemical & Allied Processing	1,081	131	395	262	66
Metals Processing	1,678	88	77	401	147
Petroleum & Related Industries	366	143	424	341	29
Other Industrial Processes	599	470	449	418	343
Solvent Utilization	2	3	4,825	1	6
Storage and Transport	72	16	1,240	5	88
Waste Disposal and Recycling	3,792	91	586	37	587
On-Road Vehicles	49,989	8,590	5,297	363	295
Non-Road Sources	25,162	5,515	3,232	936	458
Miscellaneous[1]	9,378	320	716	12	20,634
Total	**97,441**	**25,393**	**18,145**	**18,867**	**23,679**

Note: Some columns may not sum due to independent rounding. 1. Miscellaneous includes PM$_{10}$ natural sources like fugitive dust, which arises from construction activities, mining and quarrying and paved road resuspension. It is the leading source of PM$_{10}$ emissions.
Source: Environmental Protection Agency, *National Air Quality and Emissions Trends Report, 1999* (2001). www.epa.gov/airtrends.

(see "The Ozone Layer," above) and ground-level ozone are usually viewed separately, it is worth noting that as upper-atmosphere ozone is depleted, more ultraviolet radiation reaches the Earth and stimulates the production of ozone/smog.

Both VOCs and nitrous oxide are emitted by transportation and industrial sources as diverse as autos, chemical manufacturing, dry cleaners, paint shops, and other solvent-using industries. High levels of ozone affect people with impaired respiratory systems, such as asthmatics, and exposure to relatively low concentrations of ozone for only a few hours has been found to significantly reduce lung function in normal, healthy people during exercise. This is generally accompanied by symptoms including chest pain, coughing, sneezing, and pulmonary congestion. Ozone is also responsible each year for several billion dollars worth of domestic crop yield losses, and it causes noticeable damage to leaves in many crops and species of trees.

Lead (Pb) People can be exposed to lead via air, diet, and ingestion of lead in soil and dust. Lead accumulates in the body in blood, bone, and soft tissue, and because it is not readily excreted, it also affects the kidneys, nervous system, and blood-forming organs. Excessive exposure to lead may cause seizures, mental retardation, and/or behavioral disorders. Even at low doses, lead exposure is harmful; infants and children are especially susceptible to low doses of lead and often suffer central nervous system damage.

Lead gasoline additives, nonferrous smelters, and battery plants are the most significant contributors to atmospheric lead emissions. The decline in the share of lead emissions from internal-combustion engines of all kinds is due primarily to the introduction of unleaded gasoline in 1975, for use in automobiles equipped with catalytic control devices, which reduce emissions of carbon monoxide, VOCs, and nitrogen oxides. Today more than 99.8 percent of the lead once added to gasoline in the United States has been removed.

Air pollution worldwide The worst air pollution is undoubtedly in Asia, where wildfires burned unchecked throughout the summer of 1998, choking the air with thick toxic smoke and a haze across all of Southeast Asia that only went away with the onset of monsoon season. According to the World Health Organization, more than 1.5 million Asians die each year from the effects of air pollution alone, and another half million die from water pollution.

Anything over 100 micrograms of particles per cubic meter of air is considered dangerous, yet in cities like Taiyuan, China, and Delhi, India, the levels routinely top 500 micrograms. The threat is compounded by the fact that so many people in these areas cook indoors with coal briquettes. Particles in the air are a major cause of respiratory ailments in Asia; such ailments are a leading cause of death in China.

▶ **ACID RAIN**

Acid rain refers to acidic precipitation of all kinds, including rain, snow, and fog, as well as acidic dust particles. The main component of acid rain is sulfuric acid, a product of reactions of sulfur dioxide released by industrial and power plants fueled by coal or oil. Another major agent of acid rain is nitrogen oxides, which form nitric acid and which are found in motor vehicle exhaust and in emissions from industrial plants that burn any fuel at high temperatures. Burning vegetation also produces nitric acid, as well as formic acid and acetic acid. Acid rain can travel great distances from its source: 10 percent to 80 percent increases in acidity have been detected as far away as 2,500 miles from a source.

Acid rain has been implicated in the destruction of lakes, the weathering of man-made structures, and the death of trees, crops, and animals. When acid rain ends up in lakes, it can increase the level of acidity to such an extent that the lake loses its ability to buffer the acidity with alkaline chemicals from the surrounding soil and rocks. How quickly this occurs is to some extent determined by the nature of the surrounding soil, which means that lakes in some regions are more vulnerable to the effects of acid rain than others. As lakes become more acidic, small invertebrates

Ozone in Metropolitan Areas, 1992-99

The following metropolitan areas are the most serious violators of ozone standards set by the Clean Air Act of 1990. They are ranked by the number of days they exceeded standards in 1997-99.

Metropolitan area	Average number of days exceeding standards		
	1992–94	1995–97	1997–99
Los Angeles South Coast Air Basin, Calif.	103.3	56.7	39.3
Southeast Desert, Calif.	47.5	24.3	24.1
San Joaquin Valley, Calif.	N.A.	N.A.	13.5
Houston-Galveston-Brazoria, Tex.	6.5	14.9	11.7
Atlanta, Ga.	N.A.	N.A.	10.2
Dallas-Fort Worth, Tex.	N.A.	N.A.	9.9
Sacramento Metro Area, Calif.	6.9	7.4	5.2
Baltimore, Md.	3.8	5.7	4.5
Philadelphia, Pa-Wilmington, Del.-Trenton, N.J.	4.0	4.2	4.4
Washington, D.C.	N.A.	N.A.	4.2

Note: The National ambient air quality standard for ozone is 0.12 parts per million (ppm) daily maximum one-hour average.
Source: Environmental Protection Agency Office of Air and Radiation, *Ozone and Carbon Monoxide 1997-99 Air Quality Data Update.* www.epa.gov/oar/aqtrnd99/carboz99.html

World Carbon Dioxide Emissions from Consumption and Flaring of Fossil Fuels, 1999

Rank, Country	Millions of metric tons[1]	Rank, Country	Millions of metric tons[1]
1. U.S.	1,519.89	6. Germany	229.93
2. China	668.73	7. United Kingdom	152.39
3. Russia	400.09	8. Canada	150.90
4. Japan	306.65	9. Italy	121.28
5. India	243.28	10. France	108.59

Note: 1 metric ton is equal to 2,204.62 pounds. 1. Preliminary figures. **Source:** U.S. Dept. of Energy, Energy Information Administration, *International Energy Annual, 1999.*

die off. This begins a reaction up the food chain: as the smallest organisms disappear, the food supply for larger vertebrates such as fish and frogs is depleted. Because lakes are not closed ecosystems, the demise of these organisms also affects land dwellers that depend on them, directly or indirectly, for survival.

A 1999 federal study revealed that regulation has succeeded in reducing harmful levels of sulfur dioxide in the air, but that the problem remains serious. At current rates, more than half of the 2,800 lakes in the Adirondacks will be too acidic to support life by the year 2040. The study also concludes that the San Gabriel Mountains near Los Angeles are already "saturated" with nitrogen, meaning that excess nitrogen is seeping into the surrounding waters.

▶ WATER POLLUTION

Although the bad effect of air pollution on health was suspected even earlier, the first proven environmental cause of illness was water pollution. In England, a famous demonstration by physician John Snow in 1854 showed that removing the handle of a pump could reduce the incidence of cholera by depriving people living near a contaminated well from using the water. Chlorine used for water purification was already known at that time, and by the 20th century most major cities in the United States provided treated water.

Problems not directly connected to health also were recognized in the 19th century. Mining in California was, in some locations, polluting the water supply so greatly that crops could not be grown; a law against using water in extracting ores was instituted in the state in 1884. Industrial water pollution was also recognized, although not stopped. Five years after Dr. Snow's famous demonstration, a new source of water pollution was introduced when the first oil well was drilled.

The 20th century brought with it additional forms of water pollution. A series of revolutions in agriculture included use of artificial fertilizers, introduction of long-lasting pesticides, and concentration of animal wastes. Each change also introduced new forms of water pollution from runoff—water from rain or snow that fails to sink into the soil. "Point sources," such as sewage pipes and factory waste ponds, were now supplemented with the "nonpoint sources" of farming.

In 1999, the EPA released its first ever national index on the quality of the nation's 2,111 watersheds. The index asserts that 21 percent of the watersheds have serious problems, including fish-consumption advisories, pollution, and loss of wetlands. Another 36 percent are of only moderate quality.

The 1972 Clean Water Act was intended to solve many of the nation's water pollution problems, but it has been only partially effective in doing so. In 1972, only about a third of the nation's rivers were safe for fishing and swimming. That number improved to more than 50 percent during the 1970s and 1980s, but by 1998, the levels of pollution had crept back up again. The primary cause was no longer industrial pollution, residue from mining, and untreated sewage; instead, nonpoint sources from runoff, both agricultural and municipal, had taken over as the older point sources were eliminated.

Drinking Water

Americans have for many years taken their drinking water for granted. But despite this compla-

cency, there are many threats to the water supply. These include biological threats to health from contamination, dangerous chemicals in the water supply from a variety of sources, and toxic elements introduced by water treatment or defects in plumbing. A related problem is that high water levels during storms overwhelm both industrial and municipal water treatment. This last source is somewhat more easily controlled than other nonpoint pollution, and revisions of the Clean Water Act in 1987, which went into effect in 1992, attack this problem for urban runoff at the city and county levels.

The Safe Drinking Water Act Amendments of 1996 further strengthened and expanded drinking water protections. They increased standards for microbial contamination such as cryptosporidium, which has been the source of several disease outbreaks, including a 1993 instance in Milwaukee, in which more than 100 people died.

Many municipal water supply systems regularly are found to contain levels of bacterial contamination that exceed EPA standards. Most, but not all bacterial contamination stems from the use of surface waters—rivers, lakes, and reservoirs. The other major source of water is groundwater—subsurface water contained for the most part in small cavities, or pores, in rock or soil. One common way to obtain unpolluted groundwater is to dig deep wells that find "fossil" water that has been at those levels for thousands of years. This source, however, is not renewable. Most shallow wells obtain their water from groundwater that recently was surface water and therefore subject to greater contamination.

Groundwater pollution is especially difficult to remedy. Almost all solutions are expensive and, in many cases, not feasible at any price. Such remedies include pumping detoxification agents into the ground or treating the water before use.

Groundwater can be contaminated by industrial pollutants stored or released in ways that put them in contact with the water supply; by leakage from underground storage of volatile chemicals, such as gasoline, cleaning fluid, or petroleum; and by seepage into the soil of agricultural pesticides. A privately funded review of federal and state water tests by the Environmental Working Group reported in 1994 that the water supplies used by 14.1 million Americans contain agricultural pesticides in amounts that would be banned if these levels were found in food.

Formerly one of the main sources of ground water contamination had been municipal landfills, but most of these are now sealed with clay liners to prevent seepage; and truly hazardous chemicals, such as mercury or lead from batteries or volatile organic compounds, are banned from landfills.

Some drinking water pollution takes place between the time the water comes from the well or from a surface source and the time it leaves faucets. For example, even though water from municipal plants is tested for lead and kept lead-free, service pipes, home plumbing, and some brass fixtures can leach lead into water, especially hot water. People who depend on private wells can have additional problems, as most of the pumps sold in recent years contain lead in brass or bronze parts that seeps into water contained in or surrounding the pump. Lead from plumbing or from pumps can be flushed from drinking or cooking water by letting the water run before use, but for water supplied by submerged pumps in

Major Ship Oil Spills

Date	Ship Name	Location	Oil Lost (metric tons)
1979	Atlantic Empress	off Tobago, West Indies	287,000
1991	ABT Summer	700 nautical miles off Angola	260,000
1983	Castillo de Bellver	off Saldanha Bay, South Africa	252,000
1978	Amoco Cadiz	off Brittany, France	223,000
1991	Haven	Genoa, Italy	144,000
1988	Odyssey	700 nautical miles off Nova Scotia	132,000
1967	Torrey Canyon	Scilly Isles, UK	119,000
1976	Urquiola	La Coruna, Spain	100,000
1977	Hawaiian Patriot	300 nautical miles off Honolulu	95,000
1979	Independenta	Bosphorus, Turkey	95,000

Note: One metric ton = 1.1 U.S. tons. Some spills did not impact coastlines, which is why some ship names are unfamiliar to the general public. The Exxon Valdez (1989) spill is estimated to be number 34 in the list of large spills.
Source: International Tanker Owners Pollution Federation.

deep wells, it may be necessary to run water for as long as 10 minutes to get to the lead-free supply.

Even municipal treatment of drinking water is suspected of potentially dangerous side effects. About 70 percent of all Americans drink water that has been disinfected by chlorination. But chlorine can react with organic material in water to form compounds such as chloroform that have been implicated in causing cancer in rats and mice. Except possibly for persons who have some reason for extra caution, however, the benefits of chlorination far outweigh any known danger.

Ocean Pollution

Pollution of the oceans disturbs marine ecosystems. It is thought to be the trigger for the algal growth that has all but eliminated the scallop fishery in Long Island Sound, for example. Other ocean fisheries in protected bays and sounds have also been damaged by pollution.

Ocean pollution from oil is primarily noted by the public when an oil well at sea is damaged or when an oil-carrying ship leaks large amounts of oil into the sea as a result of an accident like the 1989 Exxon *Valdez* disaster. Despite this perception, most oil pollution in the ocean actually comes from municipal and industrial runoff, cleaning of ships' bilges or tanks, and other routine events.

Ocean pollution is often in evidence on beaches. Tar balls from oil spills, plastic, and sometimes sewage wash up on beaches. Occasionally beaches have to be closed because of high bacteria counts in the water, making swimming hazardous.

Plastic, which generally does not break down in the ocean, is a hazard to larger organisms, such as endangered sea turtles. An international treaty prohibits disposal of plastic wastes that can kill or maim creatures that become entangled, but the treaty is very difficult to enforce.

▶ SOLID WASTE

Many areas of the United States continue to face serious problems in safely and effectively managing the garbage they generate. As a nation, we are generating more trash than ever before, and as the generation of municipal solid waste (MSW) increases, the capacity to handle it is decreasing. Municipal solid waste is distinct from industrial wastes produced by factories, tailings from mines, construction and demolition waste, sludge from sewage treatment, and junked machinery.

Disposing of Solid Waste
The average person disposes of more than 4 pounds of solid waste each day, up significantly from 1960, when per person disposal was 2.7 pounds. This waste consists of paper (38 percent), yard trimmings (18 percent), metals (8 percent), plastic (8 percent), glass (7 percent), food waste (7 percent), and other materials (14 percent). There are four primary methods of dealing with this waste: putting it in landfills, incinerating it, recycling it, and composting. But a fifth option, source reduction, may be the most effective way of reducing the nation's volume of MSW, which totals more than 200 million tons per year.

Landfills
By far the greatest amount of MSW is sent to MSW landfills, of which there were 3,581 in 1995, a drop from 5,345 in 1992. Landfills are the cheapest method of disposing of MSW but they pose a number of environmental problems. Because most landfills are dry, they preserve garbage by cutting it off from the rotting influences of air and moisture. Even biodegradable materials do not decay; newspapers 40 years old can still be read and hot dogs thrown out years before look more or less unchanged.

EPA regulations favor dry landfills for two reasons. As biodegradation in wet landfills occurs there is a buildup of hazardous methane gas, and contaminated water leaching out of landfills (leachate) can pollute the surrounding groundwater. But wet landfills have their supporters, who argue that by enhancing decay, a landfill's biological life can be compressed from 40-to-50 years to 5-to-10 years. Since landfills can contain hundreds of hazardous chemicals, they require continuous monitoring anyway; so shortening their active biological life can yield significant savings. Moreover, by decreasing the volume of trash through biodegradation, landfills can be kept open longer. This is important because some estimates indicate that 80 percent of the nation's landfills will be closed within 20 years, and people are increasingly adamant about not having landfills in their communities, which makes it harder to site new landfills.

Incineration/combustion
One popular method of disposing of municipal waste used to be simply to burn it. In the 1940s there were approximately 700 municipal incinerators in the United States. Despite the efficiency with which they reduced the volume of waste, they stank,

their stacks emitted sizable particles of ash, and they produced noxious gases. For these aesthetic rather than environmental reasons, their numbers declined dramatically in the 1950s. By the time of the Clean Air Act of 1970, there were only 67 incinerators still in operation—most with no energy recovery and no air pollution controls.

Incinerator use increased in the 1980s and early 1990s as space for landfills became scarce, and as the energy produced by incineration became a valuable commodity. But in May, 1994, the U.S. Supreme Court ruled that waste from incinerators had to be treated as toxic on the same basis as any other waste. This was a blow because most incinerator ash contains dioxins that are produced by combustion and heavy metals such as lead, cadmium, and mercury, which do not burn.

In that same month, the Court ruled that localities could not prevent landfills from taking waste away from incinerators if the landfills offered better bargains. Because landfill was usually cheaper, few chose to incinerate their waste, and few municipalities could afford to subsidize the cost of incinerators. Within six months of the Court's decision, plans for 77 proposed incinerators were canceled.

Recycling/composting In 1995, Americans generated 208 million tons of MSW—4.3 pounds per person per day. Recycling and composting recovered 27 percent of these wastes. Recovery of paper and paperboard reached 40 percent (32.6 million tons), accounting for half of the total MSW recovered. Metal recovery reached 38.9 percent (6.2 million tons), yard trimmings 30.3 percent (9 million tons), glass 24.5 percent (3.1 million tons), and plastics 5.1 percent (1 million tons). There were more than 7,000 curbside recycling programs as well as nearly 9,000 drop-off centers for recyclables.

In addition to significantly reducing the volume of wastes that winds up in landfills and incinerators, recycling and composting limit pollution and unnecessary depletion of natural resources. They also have the potential to generate revenues from the sale of secondary materials. According to the EPA, the 56 million tons of materials recovered in the United States in 1995 through recycling (including composting) had a total market value of more than $3.6 billion. Costs of recycling are still high, but these are expected to decline as recycling programs mature and become fully integrated with the total MSW management system. The EPA has set a nationwide recycling goal of 35 percent by the year 2005.

Source reduction Many experts believe that the key to solving the municipal waste problem is source reduction—minimizing the volume of products used and the toxins they contain, and extending their lives in use. Removal of toxins enhances the safety of recycling, landfilling, and combustion, while volume reduction helps to extend the capacity of existing waste systems.

A broad variety of products and packaging that reduce waste and save money have been developed. By reducing the textured design on napkins, for example, the McDonald's Corporation found that it could fit 23 percent more napkins into a shipping container, saving 294,000 pounds of corrugated cardboard and 150 truckload shipments annually.

▶HAZARDOUS WASTE

Superfund In 1980, Congress enacted the Comprehensive Environmental Response, Compensation, and Liability Act (CERCLA), better known as the Superfund, a $1.6 billion, five-year program to clean up thousands of hazardous waste sites. The fund was renewed in 1986 by the Superfund Amendments and Reauthorization Act (SARA). The EPA, which administers the Superfund, estimated in 1996 that 70 million Americans lived within 4 miles of a toxic waste site.

The EPA evaluates hazardous waste sites for their levels of soil and water contamination, the mobility of toxins, and their proximity to human food supplies. (Contamination of petroleum, however, is excluded from this evaluation.) It then ranks the sites on a numerically based system that factors in risks to groundwater, surface water, and air. The highest ranking sites are placed on the EPA's National Priorities List (NPL). CERCLA also allows states and territories to designate one top-priority site regardless of its score; there are several such sites that would not make the NPL on the basis of their numerical score alone.

Once the EPA deems a site a national priority, it can take two types of action. It can remove the hazard in an emergency action limited to one year and/or $2 million. Or it can try to compel the individual or company responsible for the problem to provide a long-term solution.

But the second option is rarely exercised. Many of the original polluters are bankrupt or cannot be found when bills for the cleanup (which averages $25–$30 million, according to the EPA) are presented. And the EPA continues to add sites to the National Priorities List faster than it cleans them up. In 23 states, a site from the first list (issued in September, 1983) was still the state's top cleanup priority in 1998.

Nuclear Waste Nuclear waste in the United States comes from nuclear weapons production facilities, nuclear power plants, medical equipment (primarily used in radiation treatments), industrial sources of radioactivity used as a more powerful alternative to X rays, and residues from uranium mining. Nuclear waste is often grouped into two categories, labeled "low-level" and "high-level." Low-level waste is slightly radioactive, often from exposure to a high-level source. High-level waste is often grouped as either civilian, mainly spent fuel from nuclear reactors, or military, wastes produced in the manufacture of nuclear weapons.

The problem with nuclear waste is that it is radioactive and can remain that way for years—in some cases, thousands of years. Early methods of disposal included dumping the wastes at sea and suspending them in a liquid or in cement and injecting the radioactive combination into wells. The United States was among the signatories of a 1976 international convention banning ocean dumping and stopped deep-well injection in 1984.

Current plans call for consortiums of states to develop sites for storage of low-level wastes. One such "temporary" site is in Barnwell County, S.C., which has handled low-level waste for 37 states since 1970. Meanwhile, the federal government continues to search for suitable sites for storage of high-level wastes from nuclear power plants and for very long-lived radioactive materials from weapons production. For the time being, these wastes remain on the sites where they were generated.

In 1998, the EPA certified the Department of Energy's Waste Isolation Pilot Plan in Carlsbad, N.M., the nation's first deep-underground facility for disposal of transuranic waste generated from defense activities. (Transuranic wastes consist primarily of sludges, tools, rags, glassware, and protective clothing that has been contaminated with radioactive elements from weapons production.) The facility is approximately 2,100 feet (640 meters) underground in excavated, natural salt formations. The first shipment of transuranic waste was delivered to the facility in March of 1999. By 2010, shipments from 23 military waste sites from across the nation to this site will reduce the number of Americans living within 50 miles of nuclear waste from 61 million to 4 million. Of course, the 113,000 people living within 50 miles of Carlsbad (as well as many New Mexicans beyond that radius) were understandably opposed, and fought its operation since the site was first proposed in 1974.

The Nuclear Regulatory Commission is the agency charged with monitoring the disposal of waste generated by civilian-operated nuclear reactors. However, most of the nuclear waste in the United States is the by-product of the federal government's nuclear weapons programs. Disposal and monitoring of this waste—which includes millions of cubic yards of contaminated soil and other debris at more than 100 sites in 32 states and the Marshall Islands—is the responsibility of the Department of Energy, the Department of Defense, the Nuclear Waste Technical Review Board, and the Office of the Nuclear Waste Negotiator. Total cost of the cleanup could be about $300–$400 billion over 30 years.

The difficulty of resolving nuclear waste disposal issues is illustrated by the saga of Yucca Mountain, Nevada. This site, about 100 miles northwest of Las Vegas, Nevada, is the Department of Energy's potential geologic repository for storage and disposal of spent nuclear fuel and high-level radioactive waste. Under review for years, since 1987 it has been the only site studied, by Congressional directive. It has been the subject of scientific disputes and fierce opposition in Nevada, and the earliest it could open, if approved, is 2010. The recent (2001) changes in Senate control have been accompanied by statements that Yucca Mountain will not be approved; if not, the DOE will be back to square one after decades of effort.

▶ HABITATS

The place where a species lives and its surroundings, both living and non-living, is called a habitat. Broadly speaking, habitats include forests, grasslands, deserts, tundra, and wetlands. But there are many specific types of habitats within each of these categories. The habitat of a giant panda, for example, is a bamboo forest in China, not a pine forest in Canada; that of a tuna is the open ocean, not a Florida lake.

When a species' habitat is destroyed or altered, the species may suffer dramatic population declines. For example, because so much of North America's native grasslands have been replaced by farms and other developments, many songbirds have been left without homes and food, and their populations have decreased. Similarly, destruction of China's bamboo forests threaten the giant panda with extinction.

When a species becomes extinct, the Earth's biodiversity is diminished. Biodiversity is all the organisms in the world or in a particular habitat, including all their individual variations. Loss of biodiversity affects humans as well as the threatened species. For example, all major food crops depend on new genetic material from the wild to remain healthy and productive. Noted the 1992 U.N. Earth Summit report, "Our planet's essential goods and services depend on the variety and variability of genes, species, populations and ecosystems."

The major reasons for loss of biological diversity are habitat destruction and modification, overhunting and overfishing, climate change, pollution, and the introduction of so-called alien species (non-native species, such as African tulip trees in Hawaii and Amazon water hyacinths in Africa's Lake Victoria; native species often are unable to compete with the introduced species).

▶ RAIN FORESTS

Rain forests are defined as forests that grow in regions that receive more than 70 inches (1.8 meters) of rain each year. Some rain forests occur in temperate places, such as southern Chile or the northwest coast of North America, but the majority are found in the tropics. Tropical rain forests cover more than 2 billion acres (0.8 billion hectares) or about 7 percent of the Earth's land surface. They are found in Central and South

---

Superfund Hazardous Waste Sites, 1981–2001

Date	Number of sites	Date	Number of sites
Oct. 23, 1981[1]	115	May 10, 1993	1,201
Dec. 30, 1982[1]	418	Feb. 23, 1994	1,190
Sept. 8, 1983	406	Sept. 29, 1995	1,232
Oct. 15, 1984	538	June 17, 1996	1,227
June 10, 1986	703	April, 1997	1,208
July 22, 1987	802	Feb. 1998	1,197
Oct. 4, 1989	981	July 22, 1999	1,226
Feb. 21, 1990	1,081	July 31, 2000	1,236
Feb. 11, 1991	1,189	June 14, 2001	1,236
Feb., 1992	1,183		

1. Proposed sites only. Final sites not calculated until release of first National Priorities list in 1983. **Source:** Environmental Protection Agency, National Priorities List, Supplementary Materials. (June, 2001). **www.epa.gov/superfund/sites**

States with the Most NPL Hazardous Waste Sites, 2001

State	Nonfederal	Federal	Total
New Jersey	103	8	111
California	72	24	96
Pennsylvania	89	6	95
New York	84	4	88
Michigan	67	0	67
Florida	46	6	52
Washington	33	14	47
Wisconsin	39	0	39
Illinois	35	4	39
Texas	34	4	38

Source: Environmental Protection Agency, National Priorities List, Supplementary Materials, (June, 2001). **www.epa.gov/superfund/sites**

America, equatorial Africa, Southeast Asia, and northeastern Australia.

It is estimated that the world may be losing more than 49 million acres (20 million hectares) of tropical forest each year. As the 1990s began, Brazil was losing 12.5-22.5 million acres (5-9 million hectares) of rain forest annually; India was losing 3.7 million acres (1.5 million hectares); and Indonesia was losing 2.2 million acres (0.9 million hectares). Other countries experiencing rapid losses included Myanmar, Costa Rica, Sri Lanka, Vietnam, Thailand, the Philippines, and Ghana.

Tropical rain forests are lush habitats, filled with a greater variety of organisms than any other type of habitat. According to a U.S. National Academy of Sciences report, a typical patch of rain forest covering four square miles (10.4 km^2) contains 750 species of trees, 750 species of other plants, 125 species of mammals, 400 species of birds, 100 species of reptiles, and 60 species of amphibians.

The dominant plants in a tropical rain forest are broad-leaved evergreens, while northern-hemisphere temperate rain forests are filled with needle-leaved conifers. In both, the tallest trees form a dense canopy high above the forest floor. Vines climb up the trees in search of sunlight. In a tropical rain forest, nonparasitic plants grow high in the canopy, using the large trees as perches. In both types of forest, the floor is in deep shade; comparatively few shrubs and grasses grow there.

The rich plant life supports food chains that include many of the world's most spectacular animals: brightly colored frogs, fierce harpy eagles, agile monkeys, powerful tigers, slow-moving sloths, and huge columns of army ants, among many others.

While the diversity of plant life in rain forests is rich, the soil generally is not. The lush plants take up so much of the nutrients in rain forests that little is left for the soil below. A study of a rain forest in Venezuela found that 75 percent of the nutrients were in living organisms like plants and trees, 17 percent were in debris, and only 8 percent were in the soil. When an organism dies and decomposes in a rain forest, the nutrients in its cells are quickly absorbed by nearby plants.

Deforestation has many sources. Individuals often cut down rain forest trees for firewood and to clear land on which to raise crops, build ranches, and raise cattle. But erosion and poor soil fertility soon make these farms and ranches worthless. Large commercial operations deforest vast areas for lumber, paper, and other products, much of which are exported to pay debts owed to foreign governments and banks. Development projects such as roads, hydroelectric dams, and mines also destroy large areas of rain forest.

▶ **WETLANDS**

A wetland is a location other than a river, lake, or open ocean in which the soil for at least part of the year contains as much water as it will hold (the soil is saturated with water). Saturated soil often slows decomposition of organic matter, resulting in a thin mud or muck, or in the decayed plant remains known as peat. Common names for wetlands include: **Potholes**, which are dry land most of the year, but seasonally become shallow ponds; **Tidal flats**, which are underwater at high tide but become muddy land at low tide; **Permafrost**, which is saturated soil that is frozen most of the year at the surface, and year-round below the surface; **Bogs**, which contain saturated soil and organic material all year, but have little or no standing water; **Marshes**, which contain standing shallow water and low vegetation; and **Swamps**, where trees grow on small hillocks surrounded by standing water. Often these informal categories overlap in a given wetland.

Wetlands produce numerous invaluable benefits. They provide a natural means of flood control, absorbing water from nearby rivers and lakes during periods of high runoff. This buffers the impact of storms and reduces shoreline erosion, thereby protecting against the loss of life and property. And by filtering out pollutants and trapping sediment, wetlands help maintain water quality.

Wetlands are the nurseries for many fish, almost all amphibians, and various birds and mammals. For instance, coastal wetlands are spawning grounds and nurseries for more than two-thirds of U.S. commercial fisheries, a $10 billion a year industry.

Despite all the benefits associated with wetlands, the definition of what is and is not a wetland is still a bone of contention among environmentalists (who would like to preserve the swampy areas), developers (who would like to drain them and erect housing complexes), and farmers (who would like to divert the water to their crops). In 1987, the U.S. Army Corp. of Engineers defined a wetland as "any ground that has mucky or peat-based soils, nourishes specific plant life, and is saturated with water at least seven days a year." Partisans on all sides of the issue have sought since then to modify that definition. Since colonial days, the contiguous United States has lost 53 percent of its wetlands, and now retains just under 104 million acres (42 million hectares). The rate of decline has slowed in recent years, but it is still significant: A 1997 report by the U.S. Fish and Wildlife Service estimated that the U.S. lost an average of 117,000 acres (47,000 hectares) of wetlands every year between 1985 and 1995.

The majority of the nation's wetlands are located in Alaska (170 to 200 million acres). Ohio, Indiana, Iowa, and California have lost the greatest percentage of their wetlands, but the wet states of Florida and Louisiana have lost the greatest total number of acres of wetlands.

ENDANGERED SPECIES

A species is a specific kind of organism, such as the common earthworm, the daffodil, the American opossum, or the human. There are about 1.75 million known species of all kinds, including plants, microorganisms, mammals, and fish. This is thought to represent no more than about 10 percent of all species. (And if the results of some surveys of rain forest canopies in Panama are correct, there may be as many as 30 million insect species alone.) Since life developed more than 600 million years ago, innumerable species have appeared and become extinct. Today, biological diversity faces a rate of species destruction greater than any since the mass extinctions of the dinosaurs 65 million years ago.

Animal and plant species are threatened on a number of fronts. Their natural habitats face destruction through deforestation, wetlands loss, and urban sprawl, and are also affected by processes that derive from global warming such as shifting climate and vegetation zones. Another problem is the shift to "monocultures" in agriculture, producing only one strain of crop for food. Some types of environments present special vulnerabilities. As an example, islands have small populations, limited habitats, and allow the introduction of new (alien) species easily

International controls

The U.S. Endangered Species Act of 1966 is the chief bulwark protecting species in the United States. The United States is also a signatory to international treaties that protect species. The Convention on International Trade in Endangered Species of Wild Fauna and Flora (CITES) has been in force since 1975. Signed by more than 120 nations, it lists species for which international trade in the live organisms, meat, lumber, or other parts of species is banned or restricted. While smugglers are thought to violate CITES restrictions regularly in what is believed to be a $5 billion annual illegal trade, CITES continues to be one of the main forces in species preservation.

Supplementing the CITES bans on international acts against species is the Convention on Biodiversity, agreed to at the 1992 Earth Summit in Rio de Janeiro. Ratified by 161 countries (though not the U.S.), this treaty commits nations to protect and preserve species and habitats within their own borders.

Other international treaties affect more limited interests. The International Whaling Commission, with 40 members currently, has been in business since 1949. The commission has probably saved whales from extinction with its near-total ban on whaling since the late 1980s. (Despite this moratorium, however, Norway and Japan have each killed hundreds of whales annually since the early 1990s; Norway, for example, authorized the killing of 425 minke whales in 1996.) Other groups, such as the 10-nation Inter-American Tropical Tuna Commission, are modeled on the whaling group.

To reverse the trend toward species extinction, governments around the world have set aside a total of about 425 million hectares (about 16.4 million square miles) of protected lands in about 3,500 parks and preserves. In addition, many countries try to identify and improve the status of species threatened with extinction.

The efforts come none too soon In 2000, the World Conservation Union issued its updated list of threatened species of animals and plants worldwide, the "Red List" (www.redlist.org). Species judged as Critically Endangered, Endangered, or Vulnerable are regarded as threatened with extinction: the Red List contains 11,046 species of threatened plants and animals. These include 24% (one in four) of mammalian species, and 12% (1 in 8) of bird species. Indonesia, India, Brzil and China are among the countries with the most threatened mammals and birds; plant species are declining rapidly in South and Central America, Central and West Africa, and Southeast Asia. The list includes 5,611 threatened plants, but because only a small percentage (about 4%) of plant species have been evaluated for threat the number actually endangered is believed to be much larger. Among the most gravely affected types of animals and birds are primates: the number of critically endangered species went from 13 to 19 from 1996 to 2000. The number of threatened albatross species has increased from 3 to 16 over the same period because of long-line fisheries, and the number of Critically Endangered freshwater turtle species, used for food and medicines in Asia, went from 10 to 24.

► SELECTED ENDANGERED MAMMALS OF THE WORLD

Although the list of endangered species includes plants and animals of every type, it is the growing group of endangered mammals that have been of special interest and concern to both conservationists and the general public. The World Conservation Union Red List of Endangered Animals indicated in 2000 that 1,130 mammals are considered threatened: 610 are listed as vulnerable, 340 as endangered, and 180 as critically endangered. The "critically endangered," a term indicating that a species' numbers have declined by at least 80 percent, include:

Endangered and Threatened Species, 2001

Group	Endangered U.S.	Endangered Foreign	Threatened U.S.	Threatened Foreign	Total Listed
Mammals	63	251	9	17	340
Birds	78	175	14	6	273
Reptiles	14	64	22	15	115
Amphibians	10	8	8	1	27
Fishes	70	11	44	0	125
Snails	20	1	11	0	32
Clams	61	2	8	0	71
Crustaceans	18	0	3	0	21
Insects	33	4	9	0	46
Arachnids	12	0	0	0	12
Total Animals	**379**	**516**	**128**	**39**	**1,062**
Flowering Plants	565	1	141	0	707
Conifers	2	0	1	2	5
Ferns and others	26	0	2	0	28
Total Plants	**593**	**1**	**144**	**2**	**740**
Total Species	**972**	**517**	**272**	**41**	**1,802**

Note: Separate populations of a species, listed both as endangered and threatened, are with few exeptions, tallied only once, for the endangered population only. (For details, see source.) Figures are as of May 31, 2001.
Source: U.S. Fish and Wildlife Service, Box Score of U.S. List of Endangered and Threatened Species, http:ecos.fws.gov

Endangered and Threatened Species in the U.S., 1980-2001

Year	Endangered Animals	Endangered Plants	Endangered Total	Threatened Animals	Threatened Plants	Threatened Total	Total species listed
1980	174	50	224	48	9	57	281
1985	207	93	300	59	25	84	384
1990	263	179	442	93	61	154	596
1995	324	432	756	113	93	206	962
1996	324	513	837	115	101	216	1,053
1997	343	553	896	121	115	236	1,132
1998	357	567	924	135	135	270	1,194
1999	358	581	939	126	140	266	1,205
2000	368	593	961	129	142	271	1,232
2001[1]	379	593	972	128	144	272	1,244

1. As of May 31, 2001. Source: U.S. Fish and Wildlife Service, U.S. Species listed per Calendar Year, 1980-present. http://endangered.fws.gov/stats/count.

Bandicoot, eastern barred *(Perameles gunnii nova)* Range: Australia
Bat, Bulmer's fruit *(Aproteles bulmerae)* Range: Papua New Guinea
Bat, Pemba flying-fox *(Pteropus voeltzkowi)* Range: Tanzania
Bear, Baluchistan *(Ursus thibetanus gedrosianus)* Range: Iran, Pakistan
Chinchilla, short-tailed *(Chinchilla brevicaudata)* Range: Andes of South America
Cougar, Eastern *(puma concolor couguar)* Range: Canada, U.S.
Deer, Pere David's *(Elaphurus davidianus)* Range: China
Gazelle, acacia *(Gazella gazella acaciae)* Range: Israel
Gazelle, Przewalski's *(Procapra przewalskii)* Range: China
Gibbon, silvery *(Hylobates moloch)* Range: Indonesia
Goat, Chiltan *(Capra aegagrus chialtanensis)* Range: Pakistan
Hog, pygmy *(Sus salvanius)* Range: Himalayas of Asia
Hutia, large-eared *(Mesocapromys auritus)* Range: Cuba
Lemur, golden bamboo *(Hapalemur aureus)* Range: Madagascar
Leopard, North African *(Panthera pardus panthera)* Range: North Africa
Mole, Juliana's golden *(Amblysomus julianae)* Range: South Africa
Monkey, Northern brown howling *(Alouata guariba guariba)* Range: Brazil
Pika, Helan Shan *(Ochotona helanshanensis)* Range: China
Potoroo, Gilbert's *(Potorous gilbertii)* Range: Australia
Pronghorn, Baja California *(Antilocapra americana peninsularis)* Range: Mexico
Rabbit, Omiltemi *(Sylvilagus insonus)* Range: Mexico
Rhinoceros, black *(Diceros bicornis)* Range: Subsaharan Africa
Rhinoceros, Javan *(Rhinoceros sondaicus)* Range: Southeast Asia
Seal, Mediterranean monk *(Monachus monachus)* Range: Mediterranean and Black Sea
Shrew, Gansu *(Sorex cansulus)* Range: China
Sika, Ryukyu *(Cervus nippon keramae)* Range: China, Japan
Tamarin, black-faced lion *(Leontopithecus caissara)* Range: Brazil
Tamarin, golden lion *(Leontopithecus rosalia)* Range: Brazil
Tiger, Amur *(Panthera tigris altaica)* Range: Northeast Asia
Tiger, South China *(Panthera tigris amoyensis)* Range:China
Titi, northern Bahian blond *(Callicebus barbarabrownae)* Brazil
Vaquita *(Phocoena sinus)* Range: eastern central Pacific
Wombat, northern bairy-nosed *(Lasiorhinus krefftii)* Range: Australia

▶ENDANGERED ANIMALS IN THE UNITED STATES

Although the world's attention is often on large endangered mammals from Africa or the oceans, the United States is home to hundreds of endangered species and subspecies. A subspecies, sometimes called a race, is a local population of a given animal that has some distinctive trait, such as size or color, that sets it apart from the main species.

In the United States, species are classified as threatened or endangered by the U.S. Fish and Wildlife service in accordance with the 1973 Endangered Species Act. The list of endangered species maintained by the Department of the Interior goes back to the original Endangered Species Act of 1966. The first list of endangered species, in March 1967, included 78 species. Today's list contains more than 375 endangered animals and close to 600 endangered plants. Species listed are protected in various ways, most specifically by a prohibition against killing them. Also, a critical habitat can be protected against change if the change would contribute to species extinction. The animals and plants listed (www.endangered.fws.gov) range from the large and well-known, such as the Whooping Crane (Grus americana) and the Florida Panther (Felis concolor coryi), to the small and little-known plants and animals that are nonetheless important for the maintenance of the environment.

Since the Endangered and Threatened Wildlife and Plants listing was started in 1967, several listed species have become extinct, including the Tecopa pupfish (Cyprinodon nevadensis calidae, 1982), the blue pike (Stizostedion vitreum glaucum, 1983), the Santa Barbara song sparrow (Melospiza melodia graminea, 1983), Sampson's pearly mussel (Epioblasma (=Dysnomia) sampsoni, 1984), and the dusky seaside sparrow (Ammodramus (=Ammospiza) maritimus nigrescens, 1990).

There have also been success stories: several species listed as either threatened or endangered have recovered sufficiently to be removed from the list, including the Brown Pelican (Pelecanus occidentalis, 1985), the American Alligator (Alligator mississippiensis, 1987), and the American peregrine Falcon (Falco peregrinus anatum, 1999). Perhaps the most visible success has been the recovery of bald eagle populations, which had been severely threatened by the effects of the pesticide DDT in the food chain. (DDT is now banned in the United States.) Other causes included loss of habitat and lead in shot in waterfowl carcasses on which eagles and other birds of prey feed (the use of lead shot has been phased out in the U.S.) The bald eagle has not yet been delisted, but this step has been proposed. Even if it is removed from the Endangered Species List; it will remain protected under various other statues.

Animals in the U.S. Officially Listed as Endangered

MAMMALS
Bat, gray
Bat, Hawaiian hoary
Bat, Indiana
Bat, lesser long-nosed
Bat, little Mariana fruit
Bat, Mariana fruit
Bat, Mexican long-nosed
Bat, Ozark big-eared
Bat, Virginia big-eared
Caribou, woodland
Deer, Columbian white-tailed
Deer, Key
Ferret, black-footed
Fox, San Joaquin kit
Jaguar
Jaguarundi, Gulf Coast
Jaguarundi, Sinaloan
Kangaroo rat, Fresno
Kangaroo rat, giant
Kangaroo rat, Morro Bay
Kangaroo rat, San Bernardino
    Merriam's
Kangaroo rat, Stephens'
Kangaroo rat, Tipton
Manatee, West Indian
Mountain beaver, Point Arena
Mouse, Alabama beach
Mouse, Anastasia Island beach
Mouse, Choctawhatchee beach
Mouse, Key Largo cotton
Mouse, Pacific pocket
Mouse, Perdido Key beach
Mouse, salt marsh harvest
Mouse, St. Andrew beach
Ocelot
Panther, Florida
Pronghorn, Sonoran
Puma, eastern
Rabbit, Lower Keys marsh
Rabbit, riparian brush
Rice rat
Seal, Caribbean monk
Seal, Hawaiian monk
Sea-lion, Steller
Sheep, bighorn
Sheep, bighorn
Squirrel, Carolina northern flying
Squirrel, Delmarva Peninsula fox
Squirrel, Mount Graham red
Squirrel, Virginia northern flying
Vole, Amargosa
Vole, Florida salt marsh
Vole, Hualapai Mexican
Whale, blue
Whale, bowhead
Whale, finback
Whale, humpback
Whale, right
Whale, Sei
Whale, sperm
Wolf, gray
Wolf, red
Woodrat, Key Largo
Woodrat, riparian

BIRDS
`O`o, Kauai
`O`u
Akepa, Hawaii
Akepa, Maui
Akialoa, Kauai
Akiapola`au
Albatross, short-tailed
Blackbird, yellow-shouldered
Bobwhite, masked
Broadbill, Guam
Cahow
Condor, California
Coot, Hawaiian
Crane, Mississippi sandhill
Crane, whooping
Creeper, Hawaii
Creeper, Molokai
Creeper, Oahu
Crow, Hawaiian
Crow, Mariana
Crow, white-necked
Curlew, Eskimo
Duck, Hawaiian
Duck, Laysan
Elepaio, Oahu
Falcon, northern aplomado
Finch, Laysan
Finch, Nihoa
Flycatcher, southwestern willow
Goose, Hawaiian
Hawk, Hawaiian
Hawk, Puerto Rican broad-
    winged
Hawk, Puerto Rican sharp-
    shinned
Honeycreeper, crested
Kingfisher, Guam Micronesian
Kite, Everglade snail
Mallard, Mariana
Megapode, Micronesian
Millerbird, Nihoa
Moorhen, Hawaiian common
Moorhen, Mariana common
Nightjar, Puerto Rican
Nukupu`u
Palila
Parrot, Puerto Rican
Parrotbill, Maui
Pelican, brown
Petrel, Hawaiian dark-rumped
Pigeon, Puerto Rican plain
Plover, piping
Po`ouli
Prairie-chicken, Attwater's greater
Pygmy-owl, cactus ferruginous
Rail, California clapper
Rail, Guam
Rail, light-footed clapper
Rail, Yuma clapper
Shrike, San Clemente loggerhead
Sparrow, Cape Sable seaside
Sparrow, Florida grasshopper
Stilt, Hawaiian
Stork, wood
Swiftlet, Mariana gray
Tern, California least
Tern, least
Tern, roseate
Thrush, large Kauai
Thrush, Molokai
Thrush, small Kauai
Vireo, black-capped
Vireo, least Bell's
Warbler, Bachman's
Warbler, golden-cheeked
Warbler, Kirtland's
Warbler, nightingale reed
White-eye, bridled
Woodpecker, ivory-billed
Woodpecker, red-cockaded

REPTILES
Anole, Culebra Island giant
Boa, Puerto Rican
Boa, Virgin Islands tree
Crocodile, American
Gecko, Monito
Lizard, blunt-nosed leopard
Lizard, St. Croix ground
Sea turtle, green
Sea turtle, hawksbill
Sea turtle, Kemp's ridley
Sea turtle, leatherback
Snake, San Francisco garter
Turtle, Alabama red-belly
Turtle, Plymouth redbelly

AMPHIBIANS
Salamander, Barton Springs
Salamander, California tiger
Salamander, desert slender
Salamander, Santa Cruz long-toed
Salamander, Shenandoah
Salamander, Sonoran tiger
Salamander, Texas blind
Toad, arroyo
Toad, Houston
Toad, Wyoming
FISHES
Cavefish, Alabama
Chub, bonytail
Chub, Borax Lake
Chub, humpback
Chub, Mohave tui
Chub, Oregon
Chub, Owens tui
Chub, Pahranagat roundtail
Chub, Virgin River
Chub, Yaqui
Cui-ui
Dace, Ash Meadows speckled
Dace, Clover Valley speckled
Dace, Independence Valley
    speckled
Dace, Kendall Warm Springs
Dace, Moapa
Darter, amber
Darter, bluemask
Darter, boulder
Darter, duskytail
Darter, Etowah
Darter, fountain
Darter, Maryland
Darter, Okaloosa
Darter, relict
Darter, watercress
Gambusia, Big Bend
Gambusia, Clear Creek
Gambusia, Pecos
Gambusia, San Marcos
Goby, tidewater
Logperch, Conasauga
Logperch, Roanoke

Madtom, pygmy
Madtom, Scioto
Madtom, smoky
Minnow, Rio Grande silvery
Pikeminnow, Colorado
Poolfish, Pahrump
Pupfish, Ash Meadows Amargosa
Pupfish, Comanche Springs
Pupfish, desert
Pupfish, Devils Hole
Pupfish, Leon Springs
Pupfish, Owens
Pupfish, Warm Springs
Salmon, Atlantic
Salmon, chinook
Salmon, sockeye
Shiner, Cahaba
Shiner, Cape Fear
Shiner, palezone
Shiner, Topeka
Spinedace, White River
Springfish, Hiko White River
Springfish, White River
Steelhead
Stickleback, unarmored
    threespine
Sturgeon, Alabama
Sturgeon, pallid
Sturgeon, shortnose
Sturgeon, white
Sucker, June
Sucker, Lost River
Sucker, Modoc
Sucker, razorback
Sucker, shortnose
Topminnow, Gila
Trout, Gila
Woundfin

CLAMS

Acornshell, southern
Bean, Cumberland
Bean, purple
Blossom, green
Blossom, tubercled
Blossom, turgid
Blossom, yellow
Catspaw
Catspaw, white
Clubshell
Clubshell, black
Clubshell, ovate
Clubshell, southern
Combshell, Cumberlandian
Combshell, southern
Combshell, upland
Elktoe, Appalachian
Elktoe, Cumberland
Fanshell
Heelsplitter, Carolina
Higgins eye
Kidneyshell, triangular
Lampmussel, Alabama
Lilliput, pale
Mapleleaf, winged
Moccasinshell, Coosa

Moccasinshell, Gulf
Moccasinshell, Ochlockonee
Monkeyface, Appalachian
Monkeyface, Cumberland
Mucket, pink
Mussel, oyster
Pearlymussel, birdwing
Pearlymussel, cracking
Pearlymussel, Curtis
Pearlymussel, dromedary
Pearlymussel, littlewing
Pigtoe, Cumberland
Pigtoe, dark
Pigtoe, finerayed
Pigtoe, flat
Pigtoe, heavy
Pigtoe, oval
Pigtoe, rough
Pigtoe, shiny
Pigtoe, southern
Pimpleback, orangefoot
Pocketbook, fat
Pocketbook, Ouachita rock
Pocketbook, shinyrayed
Pocketbook, speckled
Rabbitsfoot, rough
Riffleshell, northern
Riffleshell, tan
Ring pink
Spinymussel, James
Spinymussel, Tar River
Stirrupshell
Three-ridge, fat
Wartyback, white
Wedgemussel, dwarf

SNAILS

Ambersnail, Kanab
Campeloma, slender
Limpet, Banbury Springs
Lioplax, cylindrical
Marstonia, royal
Pebblesnail, flat
Riversnail, Anthony's
Rocksnail, plicate
Snail, armored
Snail, Iowa Pleistocene
Snail, Morro shoulderband
Snail, Snake River physa
Snail, tulotoma
Snail, Utah valvata
Snail, Virginia fringed mountain
Snails, Oahu tree
Springsnail, Alamosa
Springsnail, Bruneau Hot
Springsnail, Idaho
Springsnail, Socorro

INSECTS

Beetle, American burying
Beetle, Coffin Cave mold
Beetle, Comal Springs dryopid
Beetle, Comal Springs riffle
Beetle, Hungerford's crawling
    water
Beetle, Kretschmarr Cave mold

Beetle, Mount Hermon June
Beetle, Tooth Cave ground
Butterfly, Behren's silverspot
Butterfly, callippe silverspot
Butterfly, El Segundo blue
Butterfly, Fender's blue
Butterfly, Karner blue
Butterfly, Lange's metalmark
Butterfly, lotis blue
Butterfly, mission blue
Butterfly, Mitchell's satyr
Butterfly, Myrtle's silverspot
Butterfly, Palos Verdes blue
Butterfly, Quino checkerspot
Butterfly, Saint Francis' satyr
Butterfly, San Bruno elfin
Butterfly, Schaus swallowtail
Butterfly, Smith's blue
Butterfly, Uncompahgre fritillary
Dragonfly, Hine's emerald
Fly, Delhi Sands flower-loving
Grasshopper, Zayante band-
    winged
Ground beetle, [unnamed]
Ground beetle, [unnamed]
Mold beetle, Helotes
Moth, Blackburn's sphinx
Skipper, Laguna Mountains

ARACHNIDS

Harvestman, Bee Creek Cave
Harvestman, Bone Cave
Harvestman, Robber Baron Cave
Pseudoscorpion, Tooth Cave
Spider, [unnamed]
Spider, Government Canyon
    cave
Spider, Kauai cave wolf or pe'e
    pe'e maka 'ole
Spider, Madla's cave
Spider, Robber Baron cave
Spider, spruce-fir moss
Spider, Tooth Cave
Spider, Vesper cave

CRUSTACEANS

Amphipod, Hay's Spring
Amphipod, Illinois cave
Amphipod, Kauai cave
Amphipod, Peck's cave
Crayfish, cave
Crayfish, cave
Crayfish, Nashville
Crayfish, Shasta
Fairy shrimp, Conservancy
Fairy shrimp, longhorn
Fairy shrimp, Riverside
Fairy shrimp, San Diego
Isopod, Lee County cave
Isopod, Socorro
Shrimp, Alabama cave
Shrimp, California freshwater
Shrimp, Kentucky cave
Tadpole shrimp, vernal pool

Note: As of July 9, 2001.
Source: U.S. Fish and Wildlife Service, Threatened and Endangered Species System (TESS), *U.S. Listed Animal Species Reports*, 2001.

Times in FΩcus

►ENDING LOGJAM, U.S. REACHES ACCORD ON ENDANGERED SPECIES

Breaking a logjam that had all but stopped the Fish and Wildlife Service from listing new endangered species, the Bush administration in late August promised quick action to protect 29 vanishing plant and animal species, including some that are on the verge of extinction.

In exchange, a coalition of environmental groups agreed not to demand the government's immediate compliance with court orders affecting a few other species.

The arrangement meant that the government, which had been directed to designate habitats for newly listed endangered species at the center of lawsuits, could divert the money it was spending to the more urgent task of saving these 29 plant and animal species from disease, predators and bulldozers.

"Things will start moving through the system very quickly," said Gary Frazer, assistant director for endangered species at the wildlife service. "This will allow us to do the things that are the most beneficial for those species that need protection under the act."

In November of 2000, the agency said it had lost control of the protection process because it was overwhelmed by court orders. Once a plant or animal species is listed as endangered, government agencies and private companies are blocked from doing anything that harms it or disrupts its habitat.

The animals that the wildlife service agreed to protect include the Chiricahua leopard frog and the Mississippi gopher frog, which once ranged across the Deep South but now exists in just one pond in Harrison County, Miss., where it is threatened by a housing development and highways.

Another animal on the list is the pygmy rabbit, the smallest in the United States. Once common in Washington State, the pygmy rabbit has been ravaged by development, disease and predators and now numbers just 50.

Declining too is the island fox, which inhabits six islands off Southern California. The plunge in the fox population — to less than 2,000 from 6,000 — has been attributed to canine distemper and attacks by golden eagles.

Kieran Suckling, executive director of the Center for Biological Diversity, who helped negotiate the agreement, said the island fox was the top predator on the islands, influencing the distribution of smaller mammals and birds. This in turn controls the distribution of seeds, which then affects the presence of plants, which ultimately affects the course of wildfires.

"That whole Channel Island system is imperiled by the loss of the fox species," Mr. Suckling said. "When you're talking about species that are this close to extinction, it is desperate, and it is time to pull out the stops and do whatever you can and worry about the politics later on."

While extinction occurs naturally, he said, the current rate of extinction rivals the very high rates during earlier geological epochs when meteors crashed into Earth and tidal waves swept over vast land masses.

"The difference is that this is caused by humans and can be turned around by humans," he said.

The federal government had listed 1,244 endangered species as of the end of last year. From 1996 to 2000, the list grew by about 50 species a year. The last time the wildlife service added a species without a court order was on Dec. 26, 2000, listing nine species of invertebrates in Bexar County, Tex.

Since the beginning of the Bush administration, only one species, the milky vetch plant, has been listed, and that was under a court order. But it was in November 2000, in the waning days of the Clinton administration, that the service announced that it would be unable to consider any new species for listing, except for emergencies, saying all of its time and money were being sapped by compliance with legal actions.

While those involved in the negotiations have come to an agreement, the wildlife service said a formal settlement document must still be written and approved by the Departments of Interior and Justice before it is presented to courts with jurisdiction over the cases.

The agreement diverts $588,000, an almost negligible sum in the federal government's $1.9 trillion budget. But Mr. Frazer of the wildlife service said it was a significant part of the $6.3 million that the wildlife service had for species protection. "There is a disconnect between what we need to do under the act and the funds we have to do it," he said.

The Interior Department has requested an additional $1.3 million for species protection for the 2002 fiscal year, which began on Oct. 1, although the service has said it needs $120 million to cover its endangered species backlog and comply with court orders.

Chris Tollefson, a spokesman for the wildlife service, said, "Our entire fiscal 2001 listing budget was consumed with complying with settlement agreements and court orders relating to critical habitats."

Mr. Suckling of the Center for Biological Diversity said that the new agreement highlighted how Congress had shucked its responsibility to provide money for the mandates of the Endangered Species Act.

"Making money available should be the responsibility of Congress," he said. "Instead, citizen groups are by necessity having to step in and figure out creative ways to funnel money to the agency so the agency can do its job. That's not how it should work."

The agreement also gives the government some breathing room on court-imposed deadlines to designate habitats for other imperiled species. The other groups involved in the settlement, apart from the Center for Biological Diversity, were the Southern Appalachian Biodiversity Project and the California Native Plant Society, which were involved in the original legal actions.

They have agreed to a six-month delay in the mapping of critical habitats for four Hawaiian invertebrates and a nine-month delay in a critical habitat for the California plants and a freshwater clam from the Appalachians.

In exchange for those delays, the wildlife service agreed to various levels of action on 29 other plant and animal species.

(This article is excerpted from the New York Times, Aug. 30, 2001)

--Katharine Q. Seelye

Technology

Major Discoveries in the History of Technology

(See also "Chronology of Information Processing" in "Computers" and "Satellites and Space Probes" and "Spaceflights Carrying People" in "Astronomy")

B.C.

2,400,000 Ancestors of human beings begin to manufacture stone tools.

1,000,000 Ancestors of human beings learn to control fire.

90,000 People from the Katranda culture in what is now Congo make barbed bone points, probably for use in harpoons.

25,000 People in what is now the Czech Republic begin weaving cloth.

23,000 Bow and arrow developed in Mediterranean regions of Europe and Africa.

10,000 The Jomon culture of Japan makes the first known pottery.

5000 Egyptians start mining and smelting copper ore.

3500 Potter's wheel and (shortly after) wheeled vehicles appear in Mesopotamia.

2900 Great Pyramid of Giza and first form of Stonehenge (a ditch and bank) are built.

2000 Interior bathrooms are built in palaces in Crete.

1500 Earliest glass vessels used in Egypt.

522 Eupalinus of Megara (Greek: 6th cent.) constructs 3,600-ft. tunnel on Samos to supply water from one side of Mt. Castro to other.

290 Pharos lighthouse at Alexandria is built.

260 Archimedes (Greek: c. 287–212 b.c.) develops mathematical descriptions of the lever and other simple machines.

200 Romans develop concrete.

140 Chinese start making paper but do not use it for writing.

100 In Illyria (now Yugoslavia and Albania), water-powered mills are introduced.

A.D.

c. 1 Chinese invent centerline rudder for ships and magnetic compass; neither found in West for 1,000 years.

190 Chinese develop porcelain.

600 First windmills are built in what is now Iran.

704 Between 704 and 751, Chinese start printing with woodblocks.

1040 Chinese develop gunpowder.

1041 Between 1041 and 1048, Chinese inventor Bi Sheng develops movable type.

1190 First-known reference to a compass in Europe.

1267 Book written by Roger Bacon (English: c. 1220–92) in 1267 mentions eyeglasses to correct farsightedness.

1288 First-known gun, a small cannon, made in China.

1310 Mechanical clocks driven by weights begin to appear in Europe.

c. 1440 Johannes Gutenberg (German: c. 1398–1468) reinvents printing with movable type.

1450 Nicholas of Cusa (German: 1401–64) develops eyeglasses for the nearsighted.

1555 Georg Bauer (Georgius Agricola; German: 1494-1555) writes *De re metallica*, a handbook of mining techniques.

c. 1590 Compound microscope (using two lenses) developed in Holland.

1608 Telescope developed in Holland, probably by Hans Lippershey (German-Dutch: c. 1570–1619).

1620 Cornelis Jacobszoon Drebbel (Dutch: 1572–1633) builds first navigable submarine.

1643 Evangelista Torricelli (Italian: 1608–47) makes first barometer, thereby producing first vacuum known to science.

1654 Christiaan Huygens (Dutch: 1629–95) develops pendulum clock.

1658 Robert Hooke (English: 1635–1703) invents balance spring for watches.

1698 Thomas Savery (English: c. 1650–1715) patents the "Miner's Friend," first practical steam engine.

1701 Jethro Tull (English: 1674–1741), possibly inspired by Chinese devices, invents device for planting seeds called a seed drill.

1709 Daniel Gabriel Fahrenheit (German-Dutch: 1686–1736) invents alcohol thermometer; 1714, mercury thermometer.

1733 John Kay (English: 1704–64) invents flying-shuttle loom, which, along with the steam engine and improvements in making iron, is a key to the start of Industrial Revolution.

1751 Benjamin Huntsman (English: 1704–76) invents crucible process for casting steel.

1762 John Harrison (English: 1693–1776) designs a marine chronometer (clock) accurate enough to enable navigators to calculate longitude at sea.

1764 James Hargreaves (English: 1720–78) introduces spinning jenny, a machine that spins from 8 to 120 threads at once.

1765 James Watt (Scottish: 1736–1819) builds model of his improved steam engine.

1769 Sir Richard Arkwright (English: 1732–92) patents the water frame, a spinning machine that complements spinning jenny.

1783 Joseph-Michel and Jacques-Etienne Montgolfier (French: 1740-1810; 1745–99) develop first hot air balloon. Jacques A.C. Charles (French: 1746–1823) builds first hydrogen balloon.

1785 Edmund Cartwright (English: 1743–1823) invents first form of the power loom.

1792 William Murdock (Scottish: 1754–1839) is first to use coal gas for lighting.

1793 Eli Whitney (American: 1765–1825) invents cotton gin, a machine for separating cotton fibers from seeds.

1800 Alessandro G.A.A. Volta (Italian: 1745–1827) invents first form of chemical battery for producing electric current.

1804 Nicolas-François Appert (French: c.1750–1841) develops canning as means of preserving food.

1807 Robert Fulton (American: 1765–1815) introduces first commercially successful steamboat.

1816 Sir David Brewster (Scottish: 1781–1868) invents kaleidoscope.

1822 Joseph N. Niepce (French: 1765–1833) produces earliest form of the photograph.

1823 Charles Macintosh (Scottish: 1766–1843) patents a waterproof fabric.

1825 George Stephenson (English: 1781–1848) develops first steam-powered locomotive to carry both passengers and freight.

1835 William Henry Fox Talbot (English: 1800–77) invents photographic negative using silver chloride, essentially how black-and-white pictures are made today.

1837 Samuel Finley Breese Morse (American: 1791–1872) patents first commercially successful version of the telegraph.

1839 Louis J.M. Daguerre (French: 1789–1851) announces his process for making photographs, which come to be called daguerreotypes.

Charles Goodyear (American: 1800–60) discovers how to make rubber resistant to heat and cold, a process called vulcanization.

1842 Sir John Bennet Lawes (English: 1814–99) patents manufacture of superphosphate, the first manufactured fertilizer.

1843 Isambard Kingdom Brunel's (English: 1806–59) *Great Britain* is first iron-hulled screw-propellor ship to cross the Atlantic.

1846 Elias Howe (American: 1819–67) patents lock-stitch sewing machine.

Richard March Hoe (American: 1812–96) invents rotary printing press.

1851 Isaac Merritt Singer (American: 1811–75) patents continuous-stitch sewing machine.

1852 Elisha Graves Otis (American: 1811–61) installs first elevator incorporating safety device that prevents cage from falling if the cable breaks.

1856 Henry Bessemer (English: 1813–98) develops method of making inexpensive steel (Bessemer process).

1859 Edwin L. Drake (American: 1819–80) drills first oil well, in Titusville, Pa.

1862 Richard Jordan Gatling (American: 1818–1903) invents first form of machine gun.

1866 Robert Whitehead (English: 1823–1905) invents naval torpedo. Georges Leclanché (French: 1839–82) develops first form of dry cell for producing electricity.

1867 Latham Sholes (American: 1819–90) and two others invent first practical typewriter.

1869 Hippolyte Mège Mouriés (French: 1817–80) patents margarine.

1866 Cyrus W. Field (U.S.: 1819–92) succeeds in laying the Trans-Atlantic Cable under the Atlantic Ocean, connecting Europe to America by telegraph wire.

1874 Joseph Farwell Glidden (American: 1813–1906) invents the kind of barbed wire used today.

1876 Alexander Graham Bell (Scottish-American: 1847–1922) invents telephone.

Karl von Linde (German: 1842–1934) invents first practical refrigerator.

1877 Nikolaus A. Otto (German: 1832–91) invents type of internal combustion engine still used in most automobiles.

Thomas Alva Edison (U.S.: 1847–1931) invents phonograph, which uses a tinfoil-covered cylinder.

1878 Louis-Marie-Hilaire Bernigaud (French: 1839–1924) develops rayon.

Carl Gustaf Patrik de Laval (Swedish: 1845–1913) invents turbine operated centrifugal cream separator.

1879 Edison and Sir Joseph W. Swan (English: 1828–1914) independently discover how to make practical electric lights.

1885 Karl Benz (German: 1844–1929) builds precursor of modern automobile.

Rover Safety Bicycle, built in England, is first bicycle with essentially modern features.

1886 George Westinghouse (American: 1846–1914) invents air brake for railroad cars.

1888 Emile Berliner (German: 1851–1929) invents phonograph disk.

John B. Dunlop (Scottish: 1840–1921) patents air-filled tire.

George Eastman (American: 1854–1932) develops first camera using roll film.

1889 Gustave Eiffel (French: 1832–1923) builds his famous tower in Paris; at 993 ft., it is tallest freestanding structure of the time.

Guglielmo Marconi (Italian: 1874–1937) transmits signals for a mile with his wireless telegraph (a precursor of radio) near Bologna, Italy.

1893 Rudolf Diesel (German: 1858–1913) describes diesel engine.

1895 First public showing of a motion picture, "Workers Leaving the Lumière Factory" by Auguste and Louis Lumière (French: 1862–1954; 1864–1948), in Paris.

1897 Karl Ferdinand Braun (German: 1850–1918) invents cathode-ray tube oscilloscope.

1898 Valdemar Poulsen (Danish: 1869–1942) invents magnetic wire recorder, the precursor to the modern tape recorder.

1902 Willis H. Carrier (American: 1876–1950) invents air conditioning.

1903 Orville and Wilbur Wright (American: 1871–1948; 1867–1912) fly the first successful airplane at Kitty Hawk, N.C.

1904 John Fleming (English: 1849–1945) develops first vacuum tube, a device for changing alternating current to direct.

1907 Lee De Forest (American: 1873–1961) patents Audion vacuum tube, a device for magnifying weak electronic signals.

1908 Henry Ford (American: 1863–1947) introduces Model T, the first affordable automobile.

1909 Leo Baekeland (Belgian-American: 1863–1944) patents Bakelite, the first truly successful plastic.

1912 Reginald Aubrey Fessenden (CanadianAmerican: 1866-1932) develops heterodyne circuit, an important improvement in radio reception.

1917 Clarence Birdseye (American: 1886–1956) develops freezing as a means of preserving food.

1919 Sir Arthur W. Brown (British: 1886–1948) and Sir John W. Alcock (British: 1892–1919) make first transatlantic flight, Newfoundland to Ireland.

1924 Vladimir Kosma Zworykin (Russian-American: 1889–1982) develops iconoscope, the beginning of modern television.

1929 Robert H. Goddard (American: 1882–1945) launches first instrumented, liquid-fueled rocket.

1930 Sir Frank Whittle (British: 1907–96) patents jet engine.

1931 Ernst A.F. Ruska (German: 1906–88) builds first electron microscope.

1934 Wallace Hume Carothers (American: 1896–1937) invents nylon, first marketed in 1938.

1935 Sir Robert Alexander Watson-Watt (Scottish: 1892-1973) begins work on radio detection and ranging (radar).

1937 Chester F. Carlson (American: 1906–68) invents xerography, the first method of photocopying.

1939 Paul H. Müller (Swiss: 1899–1965) discovers that DDT is potent and long-lasting insecticide.

Igor I. Sikorsky (Russian-American: 1889–1972) designs and flies first helicopter developed for mass production.

1940 Peter Carl Goldmark (Hungarian-American: 1906–77) demonstrates first successful color television system.

1941 John Rex Whinfield (British: 1901–66) invents Dacron.

1942 Enrico Fermi (Italian-American: 1901–54) builds first nuclear reactor.

1947 Dennis Gabor (Hungarian-British: 1900–79) develops holography, a method of recording and displaying a three-dimensional object.

1948 Goldmark develops the 33⅓ rpm long-playing phonograph record.

Georges de Mestral (Swiss: 1908–90) invents Velcro, patented in 1955.

John Bardeen (American: 1908–91), Walter H. Brattain (American: 1902–87), and William B. Shockley (English-American: 1910-89) invent the transistor.

1957 Gordon Gould (American: 1920–) develops basic idea for the laser, which he succeeds in patenting in 1986 after long struggle.

The Soviet spacecraft *Sputnik 1* becomes the first satellite to orbit Earth.

1958 United States opens first experimental nuclear power plant.

1959 First industrial robot is marketed.

1962 First active communications satellite, Telstar, goes into orbit.

1963 Audiocassettes introduced.

1964 Touch-tone telephones introduced.

1966 Engineers at ITT demonstrate fiber optics as a method of transmitting data.

1968   The first supersonic airliner, the Soviet Tupolev TU-144, is demonstrated on Dec. 31.
1969   ATMs and bar-code scanners introduced.
1970   Boeing 747 jets go into service.
1975   IBM introduces first laser printer.
1982   Compact disc players introduced.
1984   Motorola introduces first commercial version of cellular phone in U.S.
1989   The U.S. Defense Department launches the first satellite in the Global Positioning System.
1990   Leigh T. Canham (British) develops a method for producing light from stimulated silicon.
1991   Woo Paik and coworkers produce the first prototype of digital high-definition television.
1994   Channel Tunnel, also known as the Chunnel, connecting England and France beneath the English Channel, is officially opened.

Charles K. Rhodes of the University of Chicago develops an X-ray-emitting laser.
1995   Scientists at Los Alamos National Laboratory in New Mexico develop a flexible tape that is superconducting at the temperature of liquid nitrogen (about −325°F).

A group led by Junji Kido of Yamagata Univ. in Japan combines three different diode layers, including a blue-emitting diode that is a major advance of its own, to make white light.

Competing groups agree on standards for the Digital Video Disc (DVD), an improved compact disc that can store a complete motion picture on a disc the size of a CD.

1998   John A. Turner and Oscar Khaselev of the U.S. National Renewable Energy Laboratory in Golden, Colo. develop a solar cell that can split water into hydrogen and oxygen.

Utility Patents Issued for Inventions, 1790–2000

Period	Patents issued	Period	Patents issued
1790-1800	309	1901-10	315,193
1801-10	1,093	1911-20	383,117
1811-20	1,930	1921-30	423,089
1821-30	3,086	1931-40	439,863
1831-40	5,519	1941-50	308,436
1841-50	5,933	1951-60	430,120
1851-60	23,065	1961-70	585,115
1861-70	79,459	1971-80	687,800[1]
1871-80	125,438	1981-90	737,017
1881-90	207,514	1991-2000	1,175,523
1891-1900	220,608		

Note: Excludes patents granted for designs and botanical plants. 1. Numbers rounded in source. Sources: U.S. Bureau of the Census, *The Statistical History of the United States* (1976) and U.S. Patent Office, *All Technologies Report* (March, 2001).

Utility Patents Granted, 1901–2000

Utility patents, also known as patents for inventions, are issued for the invention of or improvement to a new and useful process, machine, manufacture, or composition of matter. They allow their owners to prohibit others from making, using, or selling the invention for up to 17 years from the date of the grant.

Utility patents represent about 90 percent of all patents. The other 10 percent are divided among plant patents, for a new and distinct, invented, or discovered asexually reproduced plant; and design patents, for a new, original, and ornamental design for an article of manufacture. Design patents last only 14 years.

Year	Total patents granted	U.S. ownership			Foreign ownership		
		Corporations	Government[1]	Individuals	Corporations	Government	Individuals
1901	25,546	4,370	N.A.	20,896[2]	280	N.A.	(2)
1921	37,798	9,860	N.A.	27,098[2]	840	N.A.	(2)
1930	45,226	19,700	N.A.	23,726[2]	1,800	N.A.	(2)
1940	42,238	22,165	40	17,627[2]	2,406	N.A.	(2)
1950	43,040	21,782	622	18,960[2]	1,660	N.A.	(2)
1960	47,170	28,187	1,244	13,069[2]	4,670	N.A.	(2)
1970	64,427	36,896	1,726	13,511[2]	12,294	N.A.	(2)
1980	61,819	27,640	1,237	9,956	18,874	254	3,858
1990	90,364	36,093	983	12,542	35,548	423	4,775
1995	101,419	44,035	1,028	12,885	38,688	245	4,538
1996	109,646	48,741	923	13,729	41,477	259	4,516
1997	111,983	50,220	944	12,914	42,907	273	4,725
1998	147,519	66,053	1,027	16,407	57,668	256	6,108
1999	153,492	69,390	983	16,698	60,168	162	6,084
2000	157,497	70,894	921	6,129	63,182	104	6,267

1. Excludes patents issued to Alien Property Custodian until 1942. 2. Patents issued to foreign individuals before 1980 are included with U.S. individuals. **Source:** Department of Commerce, Patent and Trademark Office, *All Technologies Report*, March, 2001.

National Inventors Hall of Fame

In 1973 the U.S. National Council of Patent Law Associations (now the National Council of Intellectual Property Law) began the practice of naming inventors who hold U.S. patents to the National Inventors Hall of Fame. Although many of those honored have many patents, the committee selects one patent for each inventor (or group

of inventors) as the occasion for the award, which they identify by the title of the original patent application. When an invention is the work of more than one person, the description of the invention is given only for one inventor. The date at the end of each of the following entries denotes the year of induction. The Hall is located in Akron, Ohio.

Edward Acheson (American: 1856–1931) CARBORUNDUM The hardest man-made surface, carborundum was integral to the development of interchangeable metal parts. It was cited by the Patent and Trademark Office as one of the inventions most responsible for the industrial age. (1997)

Ernst Alexanderson (Swedish-American: 1878–1975) HIGH FREQUENCY ALTERNATOR This device makes it possible for radio (and television) to transmit voices and music, not just dots and dashes. (1983)

Andrew Alford (Russian-American: 1904–92) LOCALIZER ANTENNA SYSTEM Alford developed the radio system for navigation as well as instrument landing systems for airplanes. (1983)

Luis Walter Alvarez (American: 1911–88) RADIO DISTANCE AND DIRECTION INDICATOR Alvarez is better known for developing methods of studying subatomic particles, which brought him a Nobel Prize for Physics in 1968. (1978)

Edwin Howard Armstrong (American: 1890–1954) METHOD OF RECEIVING HIGH FREQUENCY OSCILLATIONS Armstrong's several inventions connected with radio broadcasting and reception made possible the "radio days" of the 1920s. In 1939 he invented FM broadcasting and reception, which helped lead to another revolution in radio. (1980)

George H. Babcock (American: 1832–93) WATER TUBE STEAM BOILER The boilers designed by Babcock and Stephen Wilcox Jr. were much less likely to explode than the fire tube boilers that preceded them. To this day, nearly half the electricity produced in the U.S. comes from boilers based on Babcock and Wilcox's original design. (1997)

Leo Hendrik Baekeland (Belgian-American: 1863–1944) SYNTHETIC RESINS Baekeland's plastic (synthetic resin), which he named Bakelite, made people realize the potential of plastics. (1978)

Robert L. Banks (American: 1921-89) POLYMERS Banks and Paul Hogan created high-density polyethylene (HDPE), which did not require the extremely high pressures used to manufacture low-density polyethylene. Products that use HDPE include milk jugs, laundry baskets, and artificial turf. (2001)

John Bardeen (American: 1908–91) TRANSISTOR The transistor is the essential semiconductor device used on microprocessors and other chips. (1974)

Arnold O. Beckman (American: 1900–) APPARATUS FOR TESTING ACIDITY Beckman developed a precise instrument to measure how acidic a substance is as well as other precision instruments. (1987)

S. Joseph Begun (Polish-American: 1905–95) MAGNETIC RECORDING. He built the first tape recorder used for broadcasting. (1998)

Alexander Graham Bell (Scottish-American: 1874–1922) TELEGRAPHY Bell's most famous of many inventions was the telephone. (1974)

Willard H. Bennett (American: 1903–87) RADIO FREQUENCY MASS SPECTROMETER This device measures the chemical composition of elements. (1991)

Emile Berliner (German-American: 1851–1929) MICROPHONE AND GRAMOPHONE. Berliner's microphone made it possible to use the telephone over long distances. Berliner also developed the gramophone, the forerunner of the record-player. (1994)

Gerd Karl Binnig (German: 1947–) SCANNING TUNNELING MICROSCOPE, which can trace details as small as 0.1 angstrom, or one-tenth the size of an atom. It opened entirely new views of the study of the structure of atoms and won Binnig and his partner Heinrich Rohrer the Nobel Prize for Physics in 1986. (1994)

Forrest Bird (American: 1921–) MEDICAL RESPIRATORS The little green box known as "The Bird" prevented thousands from dying from cardiopulmonary failure. Bird also developed the Babybird respirator for low birthweight babies, reducing mortality rates for infants with respiratory problems. (1995)

Harold Stephen Black (American: 1898–) NEGATIVE FEEDBACK AMPLIFIER The basic principle of the negative feedback amplifier has become fundamental to many other devices since Black first used it to control distortion. (1981)

Baruch S. Blumberg (American: 1925–) HEPATITIS B VACCINE This vaccine (invented with Irving Millman) has protected hundreds of millions of people worldwide against the hepatitis B virus, still one of the leading causes of death worldwide. (1993)

Robert A. Bower (American: 1936–) FIELD EFFECT DEVICE WITH INSULATED GATE, which gave semiconductors the speed necessary for modern microelectronic applications. It became the primary device used in almost all modern integrated circuits. (1997)

Herbert W. Boyer (American: 1936-) PROCESS FOR PRODUCING BIOLOGICALLY FUNCTIONAL MOLECULAR CHIMERAS When Boyer and Stan Cohen added genes from an organism to a simple cell, they discovered that the genes replicated themselves in the cell. Known as recombinant DNA, these experiments launched the biotechnology industry; Boyer and Cohen founded the biotechnology firm Genentech, Inc., which created the first genetically engineered human insulin. (2001)

Walter H. Brattain (American: 1902–87) TRANSISTOR (see John Bardeen) (1974)

Rachel Fuller Brown (American: 1898–1980) NYSTATIN (See Elizabeth Lee Hazen) (1994)

Luther Burbank (American: 1849–1926) PEACH Burbank's work in developing more than 800 new varieties of plants contributed to the development of the Plant Patent program in 1930. Burbank holds 16 plant patents, all issued posthumously. (1986)

Joseph H. Burckhalter (American: 1912–) FITC This yellow-green compound, known to doctors as fluorescein isothiocyanate, has proved invaluable in identifying different antibodies. In addition to helping identify the causes of AIDS, FITC has been used to speed the diagnosis of leukemia and lymphoma. (1995)

William Seward Burroughs (American: 1857–98) CALCULATING MACHINE Although the calculating machine dates from the 17th century, Burroughs's was the first that could be mass produced and easily used. (1987)

William Meriam Burton (American: 1865–1954) MANUFACTURE OF GASOLINE Burton developed the first commercially successful cracking process, which yielded twice the amount of gasoline from crude oil than the previous methods. (1984)

Donald L. Campbell (American: 1904–) FLUID CATALYTIC CRACKING This process revolutionized the petroleum industry by more efficiently transforming higher boiling oils into lighter, usable products. It is used to produce over half of the world's gasoline. (1999)

Marvin Camras (American: 1916–95) METHOD AND MEANS OF MAGNETIC RECORDING Before the tapes currently used to record sound and pictures, sound was recorded on the wire recorder that Camras invented in the 1930s. (1985)

Chester F. Carlson (American: 1906–68) ELECTROPHOTOGRAPHY Carlson invented the dry copying method called xerography. Although patented in 1940, the dry copier was not marketed until 1958, by which time Carlson had patented many improvements. (1981)

Wallace Hume Carothers (American: 1896–1937) DIAMINE-DICARBOXYLIC ACID SALTS AND PROCESS OF PREPARING SAME AND SYNTHETIC FIBER This is better known as nylon. Carothers also developed the first successful synthetic rubber. (1984)

Willis Haviland Carrier (American: 1876–1950) APPARATUS FOR TREATING AIR Carrier invented the first successful air-conditioning system, and many of the techniques used in modern refrigerators. (1985)

George Washington Carver (American: c. 1864–1943) PRODUCTS USING PEANUTS AND SWEET POTATOES A successful scientist in Iowa who later taught at the Tuskégee Institute, Carver developed over 300 uses for the peanut and 118 sweet-potato by-products as an incentive for farmers to plant regenerative crops rather than the traditional soil-destroying cotton and tobacco. (1990)

Stanley N. Cohen (American: 1935-) PROCESS FOR PRODUCING BIOLOGICALLY FUNCTIONAL MOLECULAR CHIMERAS (see Herbert W. Boyer) (2001)

Frank B. Colton (Polish-American: 1923–) ORAL CONTRACEPTIVES Colton not only developed the first "pill" in 1960, but he also pioneered the development of anabolic steroids. (1988)

Lloyd H. Conover (American: 1923–) TETRACYCLINE Before Conover created tetracycline, no one thought that a natural drug could be chemically modified to improve its action; tetracycline remains the drug of choice for tick-spread disease such as Rocky Mountain spotted fever and Lyme disease. (1992)

William D. Coolidge (American: 1873–1974) VACUUM TUBE The "Coolidge tube" is actually an X-ray generator. Among his many other inventions was the modern tungsten-filament electric light. (1975)

Frederick G. Cottrell (American 1877–1948) ELECTROSTATIC PRECIPITATOR Cóttrell's invention uses high-voltage electricity to capture the particulates, including fly ash, dust, and droplets of acid or other chemicals, found in smoke from the burning of fossil fuels and many industrial processes; the tons of waste can then be removed from smoke instead of being spread around the countryside. (1992)

Seymour Cray (American: 1925–96) SUPERCOMPUTER Cray's supercomputer processed information much faster than other computers because of its extraordinarily high number of integrated circuits. (1997)

Raymond V. Damadian (American: 1936–) APPARATUS AND METHOD FOR DETECTING CANCER IN TISSUE Damadian was the first to realize that the nuclear magnetic resonance technique could be used on living creatures and could detect cancer cells. (1989)

Mark Dean (American: 1957–) MICROCOMPUTER WITH BUS CONTROL MEANS FOR PERIPHERAL DEVICES Dean and Dennis Moeller, two IBM scientists, developed improvements in computer architecture that permitted rapid communication between internal and external components of IBM-compatible computers. (1997)

John Deere (American: 1804–86) PLOW Deere's vastly improved plow launched his commercial success,. (1989)

Lee De Forest (American: 1873–1961) AUDION AMPLIFIER De Forest's invention of the triode was the key to modern radio and later developments in the amplification of signals. (1977)

Robert H. Dennard (American: 1932–) DYNAMIC RANDOM ACCESS MEMORY (RAM) Dennard's dense, cost-effective memory system allowed computers to shrink dramatically from warehouse size to desktop size. RAM has been used as the memory system in all computers since the 1970s. (1997)

Rudolf Diesel (German: 1858–1913) INTERNAL COMBUSTION ENGINE The pressure-ignited heat engine is still called the diesel engine. (1976)

Walt Disney (American: 1901-66) MULTIPLANE CAMERA Years after he brought Mickey Mouse to the screen, his multiplane camera brought about richer animation. It was first used for a full-length feature in 1937's "Snow White and the Seven Dwarfs." (2000)

Carl Djerassi (Austrian-American: 1923–) ORAL CONTRACEPTIVES Djerassi's research into the chemistry of steroids and his synthesis of antihistamines are two of his many contributions to modern organic chemistry. (1978)

Herbert Henry Dow (Canadian-American: 1866–1930) BROMINE Besides new methods of extracting bromine and chlorine from naturally occurring salt deposits, Dow patented over 90 inventions and founded Dow Chemical. (1983)

Charles Stark Draper (American: 1901–87) GYROSCOPIC EQUIPMENT Draper's gyroscopic stabilizer helped antiaircraft guns and falling bombs hit their targets during World War II. Later he developed gyro-

scopic systems for air and marine navigation and for guided missiles. (1983)

Graham J. Durant (British-American: 1934–) CIMETIDINE (TAGAMET) With John C. Emmet and C. Robin Ganellin, Durant developed the major drug used to suppress acid in stomach and intestinal ulcers. (1990)

George Eastman (American: 1854–1932) METHOD AND APPARATUS FOR COATING PLATES FOR USE IN PHOTOGRAPHY Eastman developed the dry plate negative and transparent roll film for still cameras, and a motion picture film for use in the newly invented cinema. (1977)

Harold E. Edgerton (American: 1903–90) STROBOSCOPE This device produced flashes that stopped action in a photograph at regular intervals. (His photograph of the crown produced by a drop of milk falling into a bowl of milk dates from the 1930s.) (1986)

Thomas Alva Edison (American: 1847–1931) ELECTRIC LAMP In addition to the carbon-filament electric lamp, Edison patented a phonograph, the mimeograph, the fluoroscope, and motion picture cameras and projectors. (1973)

Gertrude B. Elion (American: 1918–99) DNA-BLOCKING DRUGS Elion was the first woman elected to the Hall of Fame, for her discovery of drugs crucial to cancer treatment and anti-viral research. (1991)

John C. Emmet (British: 1938–) CIMETIDINE (TAGAMET®) (See Graham J. Durant). (1990)

Douglas Engelbart (American: 1925–) COMPUTER MOUSE Officially known as the X-Y Position Indicator for a Display System, this was the only patentable part of his pioneering work in computer design. (1998)

John Ericsson (American: 1803–89) PROPELLOR Ericsson's invention offered a highly efficient, difficult to damage, and easily maintained means of propulsion that sped the transition from wind to steam power (1993)

Oliver Evans (American: 1755-1819) HIGH PRESSURE STEAM ENGINE Although James Watt had already invented a low-pressure steam engine, Evans placed the cylinder and the crankshaft at the same end instead of at opposite ends, greatly reducing the overall weight (2001)

Federico Faggin (Italian-American 1941–) MICROPROCESSOR Faggin and Stanley Mazor refined Ted Hoff's microprocessor concept to produce the first single-chip central processing unit in 1971. All three men helped persuade Intel to make the new computers available to the general public. (1996)

Philo Taylor Farnsworth (American: 1906–71) TELEVISION SYSTEM Farnsworth patented many components of all-electronic television. He also worked on the electronic microscope, the use of ultraviolet light for seeing in the dark, and nuclear fusion. (1984)

James L. Fergason (American: 1934–) LIQUID CRYSTAL DISPLAY This invention is used annually in more than five billion products, including computers, medical devices, and consumer electronics. (1998)

Enrico Fermi (Italian-American: 1901–54) NEUTRONIC REACTOR Fermi's nuclear reactor is the basis of nuclear power today. His many contributions to modern physics include basic theoretical work and experimental physics. (1976)

Reginald Aubrey Fessenden (American: 1866-1932) WIRELESS RADIO COMMUNICATION A disciple of both Alexander Graham Bell and Thomas Edison, he discovered the means for radio waves, which previously had carried only Morse Code, to transmit voice and other sounds directly. (2000)

Thomas J. Fogarty (American: 1934-) EMBOLECTOMY CATHETER This device, which utilizes a thin balloon to withdraw vascular occlusions, is still the most widely used technique for blood clot removal, and has encouraged advances for other minimally invasive surgeries, including angioplasty. (2001)

Henry Ford (American: 1863–1947) TRANSMISSION MECHANISM Best remembered for his innovative business practices, Ford also invented and patented numerous mechanisms used in automobiles. (1982)

Jay W. Forrester (American: 1918–) MULTICOORDI-NATED DIGITAL INFORMATION STORAGE DEVICE Forrester's main invention was the magnetic storage of information. Most computers today, from giant mainframes to lightweight laptops, still use magnetic storage to store data. (1979)

Alfred Free (American: 1913–2000) and **Helen Murray Free** (American: 1923–) DIP-AND-READ TESTS FOR URINALYSIS These tests, developed by the husband and wife team of scientists, was the first to allow diabetics to easily and accurately monitor their blood glucose levels on their own. (2000)

C. Robin Ganellin (British: 1934–) CIMETIDINE (TAGAMET®) (See Graham J. Durant). (1990)

Edmund Germer (German-American: 1901–87) FLU-ORESCENT LIGHT Germer's high-pressure mercury-vapor lamp vastly increased the efficiency and safety of lighting while producing less heat. (1996)

Charles P. Ginsburg (American: 1920–) VIDEOTAPE RECORDER The VCR was originally developed by an engineering team led by Ginsburg. (1990)

Robert Hutchings Goddard (American: 1882–1945) CONTROL MECHANISM FOR ROCKET APPARATUS The father of American rocketry, Goddard devised successful rocket weapons and rocket-assisted take-off mechanisms for carrier-based airplanes for the military. (1979)

Charles Goodyear (American: 1800–60) IMPROVE-MENT IN INDIA-RUBBER FABRICS In 1844 Goodyear discovered vulcanization, a process to make rubber resistant to heat and cold. (1976)

Gordon Gould (American: 1920–) OPTICALLY PUMPED LASER AMPLIFIERS Gould envisioned the basic idea for the laser in 1957, but did not win his first patent until 1977. (1991)

Wilson Greatbatch (American: 1919–) MEDICAL CAR-DIAC PACEMAKER Greatbatch's pacemaker has helped millions of people with heart disease. He also invented batteries to keep the pacemaker running without adverse effects from the battery chemicals. (1986)

Leonard M. Greene (American: 1918–) AIRPLANE STALL WARNING DEVICE Patented in 1949. (1991)

Charles Martin Hall (American: 1863–1914) MANU-FACTURE OF ALUMINUM In 1886, Hall developed a cheap method to make aluminum (then selling at $5 a pound). (1976)

Robert N. Hall (American: 1919–) HIGH VOLTAGE HIGH POWER SEMICONDUCTOR PIN RECTIFIER This invention greatly reduced the waste of power and dangerous heat build-up that accompanies large-scale power transmission. Hall also invented the first semi-conductor laser, which is now commonly found in CD players. (1994)

W.E. "Butch" Hanford (American: 1908–) POLYURETHANE This 1942 patent (won with Donald F. Holmes) remains the basis for chemistry used in manufacture of all polyurethanes. (1991)

Elizabeth Lee Hazen (American: 1885–1975) NYSTATIN, the world's first non-toxic anti-fungal antibiotic. This medicine cures many disfiguring and disabling skin, mouth, and throat infections. Nystatin has also been used to treat Dutch elm disease and to rescue water-damaged artworks from mold. (1994)

William R. Hewlett (American: 1913–) VARIABLE FREQUENCY OSCILLATION GENERATOR Hewlett's first invention was the audio oscillator in 1939, a device for generating high-quality audio frequencies that could be used for many different purposes; among the first uses was production of special sounds for the Disney movie *Fantasia*. (1992)

René Alphonse Higonnet (French: 1902–83) PHOTO COMPOSING MACHINE Along with Louis Marius Moyroud, Higonnet developed (in 1946) the first machine to set type by recording the images of letters on film. Film composition became the standard way of setting type, replacing type set from metal. (1985)

James Hillier (Canadian-American: 1915–) ELEC-TRON LENS CORRECTION DEVICE Although Hillier was not the first to make a microscope using electrons, his microscopes became the standard in the field. Electron microscopes can enlarge much smaller details than light microscopes because the wavelength of an electron is much smaller than the wavelength of a photon of visible light.

Marcian Edward "Ted" Hoff, Jr. (American: 1937–) MICROPROCESSOR CONCEPT AND ARCHITEC-TURE Hoff was the first to recognize the possibility of a single-chip CPU, thus helping to transform the computer from a machine that occupied an entire room to one that could fit onto a desk. (1996)

Paul Hogan (American: 1919–) POLYMERS (see Robert L. Banks) (2001)

Herman Hollerith (American: 1869–1929) STORAGE AND PROCESSING OF NUMERICAL DATA Hollerith's punched cards and readers, developed for the 1890 U.S. Census, became the basis of modern data processing. (1990)

Donald Fletcher Holmes (American: 1910–80) POLYURETHANE (see W.E.Hanford). (1991)

Eugene J. Houdry (French: 1892–1962) CATALYTIC CRACKING OF PETROLEUM Houdry developed a process to make high-grade gasoline and airplane fuel from crude oil, as well as other catalytic processes and devices, including the basic catalytic converter used in mufflers. (1990)

J. Franklin Hyde (American: 1903–99) FUSED SILICA AND SILICONES Hyde discovered first new way of making glass in more than 3,000 years. His ultra-pure glass has many uses, including spacecraft windows, telescopes, and precision lenses for manufacturing equipment. It also provided the bases for the semiconductor and fiber optics industries. (2000)

Percy F. Julian (American: 1899–1975) SYNTHESIS OF CORTISONE AND OTHER HORMONES Julian discovered that soybeans could be used as the basis for synthesizing cortisone, an important hormone with many medical applications. (1990)

Donald B. Keck (American 1941–) FUSED SILICA OP-TICAL WAVEGUIDE (See Robert D. Maurer). (1993)

Charles Franklin Kettering (American: 1875–1958) ENGINE STARTING DEVICES AND IGNITION SYS-TEM Kettering's Delco company produced the self-starter for automobiles and a small generator for use in isolated farms. (1980)

Jack S. Kilby (American: 1923–) MINIATURIIZED ELECTRONIC CIRCUITS The monolithic integrated circuit that Kilby developed for Texas Instruments in 1959 was the beginning of the modern integrated circuit. (1982)

Willem J. Kolff (Dutch-American: 1911–) SOFT-SHELL MUSHROOM-SHAPED HEART The patent cited is for an early version of an artificial heart, but Kolff's most important work was the development of the artificial kidney dialysis machine. (1985)

William Justin Kroll (Luxembourgian 1889–1973) TI-TANIUM AND ZIRCONIUM PROCESSING Kroll discovered a process to produce metallic titanium, an abundant element that had previously proved difficult to obtain from its natural state, and when heated, had yielded a useless substance. He later applied the same process to zirconium. (2000)

Stephanie Kwolek (American: 1923–) KEVLAR This substance is five times as strong as steel and weighs 40% less than glass, making it ideal for use in aircraft construction, golf clubs and tennis racquets, fiber optic cables, and perhaps most important, bullet-proof vests. (1995)

Edwin Herbert Land (American: 1909–91) PHOTO-GRAPHIC PRODUCT COMPRISING A RUPTURABLE CONTAINER CARRYING PHOTOGRAPHIC PROCESS-ING LIQUID Land's first success was the development and application of substances that polarize light. He also invented the instant Polaroid camera. (1977)

Irving Langmuir (American: 1881–1957) INCANDESCENT ELECTRIC LAMP In 1913, Langmuir realized that filling the original Edison-Swan lightbulb with a nonburning gas would result in a longer-lasting light. He later won a Nobel Prize (1932) for his work on the chemistry of surfaces. (1989)

Ernest Orlando Lawrence (American: 1901–58) METHOD AND APPARATUS FOR THE ACCELERA-TION OF IONS Although Lawrence did not develop the very first particle accelerator (known as an "atom smasher"), his 1930 cyclotron has been the basic pattern for the most successful and powerful machines of its kind ever since. (1982)

William P. Lear (American: 1902–78) AUTOMOBILE RADIO Though he was better known for inventing the Learjet, Lear's first claim to fame was in radio technology, with a company that went on to become Motorola. (1993)

Robert S. Ledley (American: 1926–) WHOLE-BODY C.A.T. SCANNER Ledley's device for making three-dimensional images of living tissues quickly became an established medical technique for looking inside the human body. (1990)

Theodore Harold Maiman (American: 1927–) RUBY LASER SYSTEMS Although there has been much dispute about the invention of the laser, Maiman's ruby laser was the first to be recognized worldwide and to be commercially successful. (1984)

Guglielmo Marconi (Italian: 1874–1937) TRANSMIT-TING ELECTRICAL SIGNALS Marconi's patent for using radio waves to carry coded messages is best known as wireless telegraphy. (1975)

Homer Z. Martin (American: 1910–1993) FLUID CAT-ALYTIC CRACKING (See Donald L. Campbell) (1999)

Robert D. Maurer (American: 1924–) FUSED SILICA OPTICAL WAVEGUIDE (With Donald B. Keck and Peter C. Schultz). This optical fiber helped launch the information age: it carries 65,000 times more information than copper wire 30-50 times farther without boosting the signal. (1993)

Stanley Mazor (American: 1941–) MICROPROCES-SOR (See Federico Faggin) (1996)

Cyrus McCormick (American: 809–94) REAPER McCormick's machine for harvesting grain (patented in 1834) and other inventions revolutionized American agriculture. (1976)

Elijah J. McCoy (Canadian-American: 1844–1929) IM-PROVEMENT IN LUBRICATORS FOR STEAM-EN-GINES Until McCoy's invention, engines had to be stopped before they could be lubricated. McCoy's automatic lubricator, which saved time and therefore money, became known among heavy equipment users as "the real McCoy." (1975)

Ottmar Mergenthaler (German-American: 1854–99) MACHINE FOR PRODUCING PRINTING BARS Mergenthaler's invention, known as the Linotype, was the first major improvement in printing since Gutenberg's movable type in the 15th century. This machine, which is controlled by a keyboard, casts individual lines of type from melted lead. (1982)

George de Mestral (Swiss: 1907–1990) VELCRO® The success of his "hook and loop fastener" can be measured by the fact that the trademarked name is more commonly known than the generic name.

Irving Millman (American: 1923–) HEPATITIS B VACCINE (See Baruch S. Blumberg). (1993)

Dennis Moeller (American: 1950–) MICROCOM-PUTER WITH BUS CONTROL MEANS FOR PERIPH-ERAL DEVICES (See Mark Dean). (1997)

Bryan B. Molloy (American: 1939–) PROZAC Unlike other antidepressants, Prozac (fluoxetine hydrochloride) does not have undesirable side effects like grogginess and gastrointestinal problems. (1999)

Samuel F.B. Morse (American: 1791–1872) TELEGRAPH SIGNALS Morse developed the first commercially successful telegraph, with a dot-dash-dot code that made instantaneous long-distance communications possible. (1975)

Andrew J. Moyer (American: 1899–1959) METHOD FOR PRODUCTION OF PENICILLIN Moyer, a microbiologist for the U.S. Department of Agriculture, developed a way of producing penicillin in bulk during World War II. The basic method is still used in manufacture of antibiotics and other substances produced by micro-organisms. (1987)

Louis Marius Moyroud (French: 1914–) PHOTO COMPOSING MACHINE (see René Alphonse Higonet). (1985)

Eger V. Murphree (American: 1898–1962) FLUID CAT-ALYTIC CRACKING (See Donald L. Campbell) (1999)

Kary Banks Mullis (American: 1944–) POLYMERASE CHAIN REACTION (PCR) This method has revolutionized the fields of microbiology, medical diagnostics, and forensics, by allowing scientists to identify a fragment of DNA genetic code and reproducing it infinitely. (1998)

Julius A. Nieuwland (Belgian-American : 1878–1936) SYNTHETIC RUBBER Known as Neoprene, Nieuwland's invention is superior to rubber because of its resistance to sunlight, abrasion, fluctuations in temperature, and corrosion by oil. (1996)

Alfred Nobel (Swedish: 1833–96) DYNAMITE Nobel's Improved Explosive Compound made explosives far safer to handle for use in mining and construction. (1998)

Robert N. Noyce (American: 1927–90) SEMICON-DUCTOR DEVICE-AND-LEAD STRUCTURE Noyce was at the center of development for two important semiconductor producers, the Fairchild and Intel corporations. (1983)

Kenneth H. Olsen (American: 1926–) IMPROVED MAGNETIC CORE MEMORY Olsen founded Digital Equipment Corp. to manufacture computers based on his new memory devices. He has also contributed extensively to the development of the minicomputer. (1990)

Elisha Graves Otis (American: 1811–61) IMPROVE-MENT IN HOISTING APPARATUS Otis devised the safety elevator in 1853, when his employer asked him to build a hoist to lift heavy equipment. Eight years later Otis installed the first passenger elevators. (1988)

Nikolaus August Otto (German: 1832–91) GAS MOTOR ENGINE Otto's four-stroke engine of 1876 is the basis of the modern internal combustion engine. (1981)

Louis W. Parker (Hungarian-American: 1906–) TELEVISION RECEIVER Parker invented the basic television receiver in common use today, and the type of color television transmission and reception that is most commonly used. (1988)

John T. Parsons (American: 1913–) NUMERICAL CONTROL OF MACHINE TOOLS This 1958 patent introduced automation to manufacturing and design and provided machines that can mill steel with an accuracy of one tenth the thickness of newsprint. (1993)

Louis Pasteur (French: 1822–95) BREWING OF BEER AND ALE Pasteur's work on beer and ale is generally considered unsuccessful, but his development of pasteurization, the heating process that protects food and beverages from microbe contamination, was a landmark contribution. (1978)

Charles J. Plank (American: 1915–89) CATALYTIC CRACKING OF HYDROCARBONS WITH A CRYS-TALLINE ZEOLITE CATALYST COMPOSITE Along with Edward J. Rosinski, Plank discovered in the early 1960s that zeolites (various aluminum silicates, a fairly common kind of mineral) could be used to improve the production of gasoline and other petroleum products. (1979)

Roy J. Plunkett (American: 1910–94) TETRAFLUO-ROETHYLENE POLYMERS In 1938 Plunkett discovered the substance known as Teflon. He later developed many of the hydrofluorocarbons (freons) since found to be eroding the ozone layer. (1985)

Robert H. Rines (American: 1922–) CONTRIBU-TIONS TO HIGH RESOLUTION IMAGE-SCANNING RADAR Rines's patents were the basis for almost all the high-definition radar used to provide the armed forces with early warning radar during the Persian Gulf War. (1994)

Heinrich Rohrer (Swiss: 1933–) SCANNING TUN-NELING MICROSCOPE (See Gerd Karl Binnig) (1994)

Edward J. Rosinski (American: 1921–) CATALYTIC CRACKING OF HYDROCARBONS WITH A CRYSTALLINE ZEOLITE CATALYST COMPOSITE (see Charles J. Plank) (1979)

Benjamin A. Rubin (American: 1917–) BIFURCATED VACCINATION NEEDLE Rubin's needle enabled easy use of small amounts of smallpox vaccine, making it possible to stretch vaccine supplies and helping eliminate smallpox entirely as a disease by 1980. (1992)

Lewis Hastings Sarett (American: 1917–99) TREATING PREGENE COMPOUNDS In 1944, Sarett found a way to produce cortisones as an artificial steroid. By 1949, he and his collaborators had learned to make cortisone from simple inorganic chemicals. Cortisone and related steroids are used for treatment of conditions ranging from psoriasis to arthritis. (1980)

Arthur Schawlow (American: 1921–99) MASER Schawlow's work on masers dates back to 1954, continued through his invention of the laser (patented in 1960 with Charles Townes), and culminated with a 1981 Nobel Prize in physics. (1996)

Klaus K. Schmiegel (German-American: 1939–) PROZAC (See Bryan B. Molloy). (1999)

Peter C. Schultz (American: 1942–) FUSED SILICA OPTICAL WAVEGUIDE (See Robert D. Maurer). (1993)

Robert J. Seiwald (American: 1925–) RITC (See Joseph H. Burckhalter). (1995)

Waldo Semon (American 1898–1999) PVC PLASTISOLS Semon accidentally discovered the first synthetic rubber that bounces. It went on to become a $30 billion industry. (1995)

Gerhard M. Sessler (German: 1931–) FOIL ELECTRET MICROPHONE. This small, lightweight microphone combines high performance, accuracy, and reliability at a low cost. Nearly 90% of all microphones are based on the Foil Electret principle. (1999)

John C. Sheehan (American: 1915–92) SEMI-SYNTHETIC PENICILLIN Sheehan's research developed a synthetic penicillin that could be produced more cheaply and quickly than the natural way of producing it. (1995)

Patsy O. Sherman (American: 1930–) SCOTCHGARD™ The generic name for this trademarked stain repellent is "block and graft copolymers containing water solvatable polar groups and fluoroaliphatic groups." (2001)

William Bradford Shockley (English-American: 1910–89) TRANSISTOR (See John Bardeen). (1974)

Christopher L. Sholes (American: 1819-90) TYPEWRITER Sholes's typewriter was the first to arrange the keys in the QWERTY pattern (rather than alphabetically), so the levers wouldn't jam when frequently used letters were struck in quick succession. (2001)

Igor I. Sikorsky (Russian-American: 1889–1972) HELICOPTER CONTROLS Sikorsky in 1931 made a critical breakthrough in helicopter design. His continued developments led to the helicopter of today. (1987)

Samuel Smith (American: 1927–) SCOTCHGARD™ (See Patsy O. Sherman) (2001)

Percy L. Spencer (American: 1894–1970) RADAR His contributions to radar research during World War II earned him the Distinguished Public Service Award. He also designed the first microwave oven. (1999)

Elmer A. Sperry (American: 1860–1930) SHIP'S GYROSCOPIC COMPASS Patented in 1917. (1991)

William Stanley (American: 1858–1916) ELECTRIC TRANSFORMER This invention allowed for the long-distance transmission of Alternating Current (AC), which was far less dangerous than transmitting Direct Current (DC) at very high voltages. (1995)

Charles Proteus Steinmetz (German-American: 1865–1923) SYSTEM OF ELECTRICAL DISTRIBUTION Steinmetz's most significant work was in developing the theory of alternating current that made power grids possible. Among his inventions was a machine that produced "lightning in the laboratory." (1977)

George R. Stibitz (American: 1904–95) COMPLEX COMPUTER Stibitz was one of several scientists who developed electromechanical computers in the late 1930s and during World War II. (1983)

Leo Szilard (Hungarian-American: 1898–1964) NUCLEAR REACTOR As chief physicist at the Manhattan Project in 1942, Szilard actively campaigned for the opportunity to set off the first controlled nuclear reaction. (1996)

Donalee L. Tabern (American: 1900–74) THIOBARBITURIC ACID DERIVATIVE This 1936 invention is better known as Pentothal, anesthetic of choice for short surgical procedures. He later introduced therapeutic use of radioactive chemicals. (1986)

Nikola Tesla (Croatian-American: 1857–1943) ELECTRO-MAGNETIC MOTOR Tesla's induction motor was simpler than previous electric motors and was powered by alternating current (AC), which can be distributed more easily over a long distance than direct current (DC). (1975)

Henry Timken (American: 1831–1909) TAPERED ROLLER BEARING This invention, now used on nearly every mode of transportation, releases the strong side pressures exerted on wheels and their bearings when a vehicle turns. (1998)

Max Tishler (American: 1906–) RIBOFLAVIN AND SULFAQUINOXALINE In the late 1930s, Tishler developed an economical method for synthesizing riboflavin (vitamin B2). Later he and his co-workers developed a commercial way to produce sulfaquinoxaline, an antibiotic that prevents common poultry diseases. (1982)

Charles Hard Townes (American: 1915–) MASERS The maser, which preceded the better-known laser, is essentially a laser that works at microwave wavelengths instead of at the shorter wavelength of visible light. (1976)

Charles W. Tyson (American: 1900–1977) FLUID CATALYTIC CRACKING (See Donald L. Campbell) (1999)

Ernest H. Volwiler (American: 1893–1992) THIOBARBITURIC ACID DERIVATIVES (see Donalee L. Tabern) (1986)

An Wang (Chinese-American: 1920–90) MAGNETIC PULSE CONTROLLING DEVICE Although best known for his state-of-the-art word processor of the 1960s, Wang contributed many ideas to the development of electronic computers, including the principle on which magnetic core memory is built. (1988)

James Edward West (American: 1931–) FOIL ELECTRET MICROPHONE (See Gerhard M. Sessler). (1999)

George Westinghouse (American: 1846–1914) STEAM-POWERED BRAKE DEVICES In 1869 Westinghouse patented an air brake for locomotives, his most important contribution to railroad safety. (1989)

Eli Whitney (American: 1765–1825) COTTON GIN By making it possible to remove seeds from cotton mechanically, the gin made large-scale cotton farming possible. Whitney also introduced interchangeable parts, the beginning of mass production. (1974)

Stephen Wilcox Jr. (American: 1830–93) WATER TUBE STEAM BOILER (See George H. Babcock). (1997)

Robert R. Williams (American: 1886–1965) ISOLATION OF VITAMIN B (THIAMINE) In 1935, Williams also synthesized thiamine for commercial production. (1991)

Steve Wozniak (American: 1950–) PERSONAL COMPUTER Apple Computer, the company he and Steve Jobs started from Wozniak's garage in 1976, helped to created the personal computer industry and shrink computers from room-size to desktop size. (2000)

Orville Wright (American: 1871–1948) & **Wilbur Wright** (American: 1867–1912) FLYING MACHINE The Wright brothers not only invented the first airplane in 1903, they also popularized, manufactured, and sold the new machines. (1975)

Vladimir Kosma Zworykin (Russian-American: 1889–1982) CATHODE RAY TUBE The cathode ray tube that Zworykin invented in 1928 is the kinescope, the basic picture tube used in modern television. Ten years later he developed the iconoscope, the first practical television camera. (1977)

COMPUTERS

A computer is a machine for storing and processing information. It converts any information that it receives into a binary code—a string of signals, in which each signal is either 1 or 0. The basic working component of a computer is a series of switches, each of which can be set either "off" or "on" and thus represent 1 or 0 in the binary system. The history of computers is, to some extent, a history of the switching devices that have been used to represent 1 and 0. Early computers were based on mechanical switches; computers based on electronic switches proved much faster. These fall into three main categories: vacuum tubes, transistors, and integrated circuits.

The relative size and power of these three types are so disparate that it is almost impossible to compare them; there is no single scale against which they can be measured. In 1946 the ENIAC (Electronic Numerical Integrator and Calculator)—which occupied 2,000 square feet, weighed 50 tons, and used 18,000 vacuum tubes—could perform about 10,000 multiplications per second and had an internal memory capacity of 200 decimal digits, or about 20 words. The fastest computer in 1997 was about 4 billion times as fast as the ENIAC. A silicon chip measuring a quarter inch across has been developed that is capable of storing 200 million words in memory. The newest magnetic disk drives for personal computers in 2001 can store up to 40 billion bits of information. Experimental disk drives store several billion bits per square inch, as compared with the 2,000 bits per square inch when disk drives were introduced some 40 years earlier.

▶ A GLOSSARY OF COMPUTER TERMS

Application   A computer *program* designed for a specific task or use, like word procesing, accounting, or missile guidance.

Artificial intelligence (AI)   The underlying assumption of artificial intelligence is that machines can be programmed to perform human functions. The primary AI functions are *expert systems*, programs that contain a body of knowledge (contributed by experts) that the machine can draw on to solve specific types of problems; *natural language interfaces* that make it possible for users to access a computer's database with commands entered in ordinary written or spoken language (for example, "Give me a list of countries bordering the Atlantic Ocean"); *speech recognition, speech synthesis, and optical recognition systems* that enable computers to understand spoken commands, make speech, and interpret visible images (such as bar codes on retail goods); and *robotics*, machines whose design and systems enable them to imitate complex "eye-hand" coordination of humans.

ASCII (American Standard Code for Information Interchange)   Computers work with numbers, not letters. ASCII is the numerical code used by personal computers (*microcomputers*). While many programs also use special codes of their own, data from one computer to another are best transmitted in "pure ASCII."

Baud rate   A transmission rate used in sending data from one computer to another, with a baud approximately equal to one *bit* per second. Rates must be the same between *modems* for data to be transmitted.

Buffer   Any memory location where data can be stored temporarily while the computer is doing something else; specifically, a memory location in the computer, in a printer, or in a separate storage device (*peripheral*) that stores a file being printed so that the computer is not tied up waiting for the printing to finish.

Bug   An error in a *software* program or the *hardware*.

Cache   A region of memory where frequently used data is stored for rapid access.

Cathode ray tube (CRT)   The display device, or *monitor*, similar to a television screen, used with most desktop computers.

CD-ROM   A Compact Disc ("CD") used as a Read-Only-Memory ("ROM"). The CD, essentially the same as an audio CD, stores data in a form readable by a laser, resulting in a storage device of great capacity and quick accessibility.

Central processing unit (CPU)   The group of circuits that directs the entire computer system by (1) interpreting and executing *program* instruction and (2) coordinating the interaction of input, output, and storage devices.

Complex Instruction Set chip   See "Reduced Instruction Set Computer chip."

Computer-aided design (CAD), engineering (CAE) and manufacturing (CAM)   Systems that automate many complex tasks such as drafting, computation, or repetitive actions. CAM is closely related to *robotics* (see "Artificial intelligence").

Cursor   A marker on the computer display that shows which region of the screen is active.

Database   Either a *program* for arranging facts in the computer and retrieving them (the computer equivalent of a filing system) or a *file* set up by such a system. Often databases are central files that can be accessed by a *modem* for a fee.

Directory   An area or data structure in which information is stored regarding the location and contents of files or file structures.

Disk drive   A mechanism for retrieving information stored on a magnetic disk. The drive rotates the disk at high speed and "reads" the data with a magnetic head similar to those used in tape recorders.

DVD   Digital Versatile Disc, an improvement on the CD-ROM that is capable of storing an entire motion picture.

DOS   Acronym for Disk Operating System and shorthand for MS-DOS, the standard operating system for 16-bit and most 32-bit IBM and IBM-compatible PCs.

File   Any group of data treated as a single entity by the computer, such as a word processor document, a *program*, or a *database*.

Floppy disk   A thin, flexible magnetic disk encased in a protective jacket. On the disk's surface are a number of "tracks" on which data may be recorded in the form of magnetic spots.

Graphical user interface (GUI)   A system that uses icons (symbols) seen on the screen to represent available functions. These icons are generally manipulated by a mouse and/or a keyboard. This approach contrasts with the more traditional method of using typed commands.

Groupware   Network programming that enables groups of users to work together by providing communication, workflow and task-sharing functions.

Hard disk   A sealed cartridge containing magnetic storage disk(s) that holds much more memory—typically 40 *megabytes* to 2 *gigabytes*—than *floppy disks*. Usually a hard disk is built into the computer, but it can be a peripheral.

Hardware   The physical equipment, as opposed to the programs and procedures, used in data processing. It covers not only computers themselves but also *peripherals* (see "Software").

Host   The computer used to run programs and store files for remote users or in a LAN.

Icon   A graphic symbol on the display screen that represents a file, peripheral, or some other object or function; for example, scissors are generally used to indicate cut-and-paste editing.

Integrated circuit An entire electronic circuit contained on one piece of material. Originally, electronic components (transistors, capacitors, etc.) were placed on a metal chassis and wired together. The first integrated circuit began with a single board (originally plastic), onto which strips of conducting material were sprayed. Electronic components could then be inserted directly onto the board (see "Silicon chip").

Laptop A portable *microcomputer* small enough to operate in one's lap. Generally a laptop weighs less than 15 pounds and uses a *liquid crystal display* monitor rather than a *cathode ray tube*.

Liquid crystal display (LCD) A type of flat-panel display monitor used in *portable computers*.

Local area networks (LANs) Systems that allow users to connect PCs to one another or to *minicomputers* or *mainframes*.

Mainframe computer Generally the largest, fastest, and most expensive kind of computer, usually costing millions of dollars and requiring special cooling. Mainframe computers can accommodate hundreds of simultaneous users and normally are run around the clock; typically they are owned by large companies (see "Microcomputer"; "Minicomputer"; "Supercomputer").

Massively parallel A form of computer architecture that uses hundreds or thousands of inexpensive *microprocessors* to perform many operations simultaneously.

Menu-driven A *program* that uses a number of "menus," or lists of possible activities from which the operator chooses in order to activate the appropriate commands. This is the alternative to a command-driven program, for which the operator must remember a number of commands in order to tell the computer what to do.

MHz Megahertz, the measure of speed used for a microprocessor, typically from 50 to 300 MHz.

Microcomputer Generally the least expensive kind of computer, and small enough to fit on a desktop. The heart of the microcomputer is the *microprocessor* (see "Mainframe computer"; "Minicomputer").

Microprocessor A complete central processing unit assembled on one single silicon chip.

Minicomputer A small computer, usually used by medium-size or smaller businesses. Minicomputers often perform scientific or industrial tasks, cost tens or hundreds of thousands of dollars, and are housed in large cabinets (see "Mainframe computer"; "Microcomputer").

MIPS (million instructions per second) A measure of computer processing speed.

Modem (modulator-demodulator) A device capable of converting a digital (computer-compatible) signal to an analog signal, which can be transmitted via a telephone line, reconverted, and then "read" by another computer.

Monitor The display device on a computer, similar to a television screen.

Mouse A small box connected by cable to a computer and featuring one or more button-style switches. When moved around a desk, the mouse causes a symbol on the computer screen to make corresponding movements. By selecting items on the screen and pressing a button on the mouse, the user can perform certain functions much more quickly than by typing commands on the keyboard.

Network An interconnected group of computers that can exchange information or work together on different parts of the same problem.

Notebook A type of full-function *portable computer* that uses miniaturized components, weighs about 4-6 pounds, and can be carried in a briefcase.

Operating system A sequence of programming codes that instructs a computer about its various parts and how to operate them. Operating systems deal only with the workings of the *hardware* and are separate from *software* programs.

Peripheral A device connected to the computer that provides communication or auxiliary functions. There are three types of peripherals: input devices, such as keyboards; output devices, such as *monitors* and printers; and storage devices, such as magnetic discs.

Personal computer A *microcomputer* used by an individual at home or in the office.

Platform A fundamental layer of software required to make other systems run—used interchangeably with operating system, the most common type of platform. The Internet, local networks, Web browsers, and Java are all frequently viewed as platforms.

Program As a noun, a prepared set of instructions for the computer, often with provisions for the operator to choose among various options. As a verb, to create such a set of instructions.

Random-access memory (RAM) A temporary storage space in which data may be held on a chip rather than being stored on disk or tape. The contents of RAM may be accessed or altered at any time during a session, but will be lost when the computer is turned off (see "Read-only memory").

Read-only memory (ROM) A type of *chip* memory, the contents of which have been permanently recorded in a computer by the manufacturer and cannot be altered by the user (see "Random access memory").

RISC chip Reduced Instruction Set Computer chip, such as the Apple-IBM Power PC chip, which gains speed by using fewer instructions than the more familiar Complex Instruction Set chip.

Server The central computer in a network, providing a service or data access to client computers on the network.

Silicon chip A special kind of *integrated circuit* in which traditional electronic components have been replaced by chemicals. Tiny wafers (chips) of silicon are covered with layers of chemicals, each of which acts as an electrical component (a *transistor*, capacitor, etc.). The first chips, made in the early 1960s, contained two transistors. By 1992 chips existed that contained 64 million transistors.

Software The *programs* and procedures, as opposed to the physical equipment, used in data processing (see "Hardware").

Spreadsheet A *program* that performs mathematical operations on numbers arranged in large arrays; used mainly for accounting and other record keeping.

Supercomputer The fastest of the *mainframe* class of computers, usually used for complex scientific calculations.

Transistor A small piece of semiconducting material (material that conducts electricity better than, say, wood but not as well as metal). Flows of electrons within the transistor can be controlled, enabling it to act as an electronic "switching" device. In other words, it can record information in the form of an "on" or an "off" signal. Early transistors were about one-hundredth the size of *vacuum tubes*, required very little energy, and generated no heat.

UNIX A multi-user, multitasking operating system designed to run on a wide variety of computers, from microcomputers to mainframes.

Virus A computer program segment or string of code that can attach itself to another program or file, reproduce itself, and spread from one computer to another. Viruses can destroy or change data and in other ways sabotage computer systems.

Window A portion of the screen display used to view simultaneously a different part of the file in use or a part of a different file than the one in use.

Workstation High-performance *microcomputers* with advanced graphics capabilities designed for use by scientists and engineers.

Bits and Bytes: Quantifying Data

Bit   In the binary system, a bit (for *bi*nary dig*it*) is either of the digits 0 or 1. It is the basic unit for storing data, with "off" representing 0 and "on" representing 1.

Byte   A group of eight *bits* that together represent one character, whether alphabetic, numeric, or other. A byte is the smallest accessible unit in a computer's memory.

Kilobyte (K)   A unit of measure for data storage or transmission equivalent to 1,024 *bytes*, but often rounded to 1,000.

Megabyte (M)   One million *bytes*.

Gigabyte (G)   One billion *bytes*.

Terabyte (TB)   One trillion *bytes*.

Personal Computer Sales, 1985–2001

Year	Unit sales[1] (thousands)	Dollar sales[1] (millions)	Average unit price
1985	3,200	2,175	700
1990	4,000	4,187	1,050
1995	8,400	12,600	1,500
1996	9,400	15,040	1,600
1998	12,800	16,640	1,300
1999	14,900	16,390	1,100
2000	16,800	16,800	1,000
2001[2]	17,500	16,600	949

1. Sales to dealers. 2. Estimate.
Source: Consumer Electronics Manufacturers Association.

Personal Computer Households, 1995–2000

Year	Total U.S. households (millions)	Households with PCs (millions)	Percent of households with computers
1995	99.0	31.36	31.7%
1996	99.6	35.39	35.5
1997	101.0	39.56	39.2
1998	102.5	43.67	42.6
1999	103.6	50.00	48.2
2000[1]	104.8	55.49	53.0

1. Estimate.
Sources: U.S. Department of Commerce; Media Metrix

Chronology of Information Processing

B.C.
500   Bead-and-wire abacus in use in Egypt.

A.D.
200   Computing trays in use in China and Japan.
1340   Double-entry bookkeeping originates in Lombardy.
c. 1621   Mathematician William Oughtred (English: 1574–1660) invents slide rule.
1642   Blaise Pascal (French: 1623–62) invents "pascaline"—the first calculating machine, capable of addition and subtraction.
1679   Gottfried Wilhelm Leibniz (German: 1646–1716) perfects binary system of notation that eventually will be used by all computers; also develops improved version of pascaline, capable of multiplication and division.
1801   Joseph-Marie Jacquard (French: 1752–1834) uses punched cards to control operation of his mechanical loom—precursor of cards used in early data-storage systems.
1822   Charles Babbage (English: 1792–1871) designs and builds prototype of "Difference Engine" for calculating logarithms.
1833   Babbage designs "Analytical Engine," a computing machine featuring printed card input, memory, and printed output, and capable of being programmed to perform different tasks. Forerunner of modern computer, it never goes beyond design stage.
1847   George Boole (English: 1815–64) publishes *Mathematical Analysis of Logic*, which treats logic as a branch of mathematics (Boolean Algebra).
1853   Pehr Georg Scheutz and his son Edvard G.R. Scheutz (Swedish: 1785–1873; 1821–81) complete version of Babbage's Difference Engine.
1886   William S. Burroughs (American: 1855–98) develops first commercially successful mechanical adding machine.
1887   U.S. Census Bureau holds competition for device to speed up computation of census information; Herman Hollerith (American: 1860-1929) designs winning tabulating machine. His Tabulating Machine Co. (founded 1911) becomes IBM in 1924.
1890   Hollerith's electromechanical machine processes U.S. Census results in six weeks—one-third the time taken in 1880.

1894   Otto Steiger develops "Millionaire," the first commercially successful machine capable of direct multiplication, as opposed to multiplication by repeated addition.
1931   Vannevar Bush (American: 1890–1974) completes "differential analyser," first computing machine to use electronic components (vacuum tubes in which values could be stored as voltages).
1936   Mathematician Alan M. Turing (English: 1912–54) publishes "On Computable Numbers," which describes hypothetical computer with infinite storage capacity, capable of performing any conceivable calculation.
1937   John V. Atanasoff (American: 1903–) starts work on first electronic computer.
1938   Konrad Zuse (German: 1910–95) builds "Z1," the first computing machine to use binary, instead of decimal, method of operation. Other features include keyboard to input information and system of electric bulbs to signal results of calculations.
1939   Atanasoff and Clifford Berry complete ABC device, first digital computer.
1940   Zuse's Z2 machine introduces electromagnetic relays (as used in telephone switching gear) to store numbers.

First Generation: Vacuum Tubes
1943   British government uses first fully electronic computer to crack German military codes. Designed by Turing, "Colossus" uses 2,000 vacuum tubes to perform calculations and digest information at rate of 5,000 characters per second.
1944   Completion of "Harvard Mark I," designed by Howard H. Aiken (American: 1900–1973) and built by IBM. Vast, over 50 ft. long, it was obsolete almost immediately because it used electromagnetic relays rather than vacuum tubes.
1946   At the University of Pennsylvania, the ENIAC (Electronic Numerical Integrator and Calculator) multiplies five-digit number by itself 5,000 times in half a second. Designed by J. Presper Eckert, Jr. (American: 1919–) and John W. Mauchly (American: 1907–80) to calculate ballistic trajectories, ENIAC occupies 2,000 sq. ft., weighs 50 tons, uses 18,000 vacuum tubes, and can store about 20 words in its memory.

John von Neumann (Hungarian-American: 1903–57) publishes paper suggesting that instructions given to computer—"programs"—can themselves be stored by computer in numerical form.

First use of term *bit* to mean binary digit.

1948 "Mark I," designed by Tom Kilburn (English: 1921–) and Sir Frederic C. Williams (English: 1911–77) at Manchester University, England, is first computer to utilize von Neumann's concept of stored programs.

John Bardeen (American: 1908–91), Walter H. Brattain (American: 1902–87), and William B. Shockley (English-American: 1910–89) invent the transistor, which will eventually replace vacuum tube and make computers faster.

IBM, Bell Telephone, and Sperry-Rand each begin production of commercial computers.

First chess-playing computer built at M.I.T.

1950 Eckert and Mauchly's EDVAC (Electronic Discrete Variable Automatic Computer) is first to use magnetic disks for storage.

1951 Lyons Tea Shop Co. in England uses specially designed computer ("LEO") to perform routine administrative functions.

Eckert and Mauchly's UNIVAC (Universal Automatic Computer) is installed at U.S. Bureau of Census. UNIVAC uses magnetic tape for input and becomes first commercially successful machine, selling over 50 models.

1952 One hour after polls close, CBS television network uses UNIVAC to predict Eisenhower's landslide victory in U.S. presidential election. Prediction was based on less than 10 percent of the votes.

1953 First high-speed printer linked to a computer.

IBM introduces its first stored-program computer, the vacuum-tube-based "701."

1956 First use of term artificial intelligence.

Second Generation: Transistors

1958 Control Data Corp. introduces first fully transistorized computer, the CDC 1604, designed by Seymour Cray (American: 1925–).

Jack St.C. Kilby (American: 1923–) of Texas Instruments and Robert Noyce (American: 1927–90) of Intel Corp. independently produce first integrated circuits.

1959 First commercially marketed program.

IBM markets its first transistorized computers, the 1620 and 1790.

1960 The PDP-1, developed by Digital Equipment Corp., is the first commercial computer to use a keyboard and monitor instead of punched cards.

Introduction of removable magnetic disks for data storage.

Third Generation: Integrated Circuits

1965 IBM markets its first integrated-circuit based computer, the 360.

Digital Equipment Corp. markets the first minicomputer, the PDP-8.

1969 Graduate student Alan Kay, later to become top designer with Apple Computer Co., writes doctoral thesis describing hypothetical "personal computer."

First international conference on artificial intelligence.

ARPANET, the first part of the Internet, is set up to link Defense Department contractors.

1970 Lexitron introduces first word processor, a computer designed specifically to handle written text. It features a cathode ray tube (CRT) terminal, as used in television sets, to display information.

Floppy disk is introduced for data storage.

1971 Intel Corp. announces first microprocessor, several integrated circuits contained on one silicon chip.

First electronic pocket calculator produced by Texas Instruments; it weighs about 2½ lbs. and costs about $150.

1973 IBM introduces "Winchester" disc drive, a sealed storage module containing several rotating magnetic discs.

Introduction of "bit-mapped" monitor capable of high-resolution graphics display.

Xerox markets first hand-held "mouse," a time-saving device for giving commands to computer.

Intel introduces 8080 microprocessor, which will become the central processing unit (CPU) of several microcomputers.

1975 First personal computer, the MITS Altair 8800, is marketed in kit form, with memory of 256 bytes.

Cray Research (founded 1972) announces the Cray-1 supercomputer, capable of 100 million operations per second.

1976 Apple Computer Co. founded by Stephen Wozniak and Steven Jobs (American: 1955–) in the Jobs family garage; first Apple "boards" (self-assembly personal computer kits) go on sale.

1977 Apple markets Apple II—the first widely accepted personal computer. Commodore and Tandy also begin to sell personal computers.

Microsoft Corp. founded by Bill Gates and Paul Allen.

1978 Hayes Microcomputer Products introduces Micromodem 100, the first microcomputer-compatible modem.

1979 Micropro International releases WordStar word processing program for personal computers.

1980 Microsoft adapts the UNIX operating system for use with microcomputers; paves way for personal computers to begin performing tasks associated with larger machines.

1981 IBM introduces its first personal computer, the IBM PC. Using operating system called PC-DOS, developed by Microsoft, it almost immediately becomes the industry standard.

First fully portable computer, the Osborne 1, is introduced.

Ashton-Tate introduces dBASE II, the first popular database program for microcomputers.

1982 Microsoft introduces MS-DOS, a version of the PC-DOS operating system designed for IBM PC; allows other manufacturers to produce copies ("clones") of the IBM machine.

Compaq announces its first portable computer (IBM-compatible).

1983 Apple introduces Apple IIe and "Lisa."

First IBM-compatible "laptop" computer introduced by Gavilan Corp.

Lotus Development Corp. introduces 1-2-3, a best-selling program for managing business spreadsheets.

Introduction of optical (laser-readable) disks.

1984 Apple introduces Macintosh. With list price of $2,495, it includes Apple's first "Mac" software programs, MacWrite (for text) and MacPaint (for graphics). Fifty thousand are sold within three months. IBM markets the PC AT (Advanced Technology) model.

1985 Apple's LaserWriter printer and Aldus Corp.'s PageMaker program usher in age of desktop publishing.

Introduction of erasable optical storage disks.

Toshiba markets first widely used laptop computer.

Cray 2 supercomputer is capable of 1.2 billion operations per second.

1986 IBM announces OS/2, a new operating system that allows personal computers to run several programs simultaneously (called multitasking).

1987 Apple introduces Macintosh SE and Macintosh II. IBM introduces Personal System/2 (PS/2), features of which include high-resolution VGA (Video Graphics Array) display.

1988 Computer security becomes an urgent issue when a "worm" program penetrates thousands of systems on Internet information network.

Motorola announces new microprocessor, the 88000, a 32-bit RISC (Reduced Instruction Set Computer) chip.

First IBM PS/2 "clones" announced.

IBM and Sears launch Prodigy, an on-line service enabling subscribers with a computer and modem to access a central information bank.

Parallel processing technique introduced that utilizes many inexpensive microprocessors to perform a large number of operations simultaneously.

1989 Intel announces the iPSC/860 chip, containing one million transistors; designed to give a microcomputer the power and speed normally associated with supercomputers.

IBM announces production of commercial quantities of four-megabyte chips.

First portable computers with color liquid crystal displays (LCDs) announced.

1990 Software writer Tim Berners-Lee writes the program for the World Wide Web to make the Internet easier to use for physicists at CERN in Geneva.

1991 The Thinking Machines Inc. CM-200 massively parallel supercomputer can perform 9.03 billion calculations per second.

1993 Intel begins shipping the Pentium chip with 3.1 million transistors on it; it operates twice as fast as the best previous Intel chip for personal computers.

Electrical engineers from the Univ. of Colorado claim the first fully optical computer that can store, transmit, and process data entirely in the form of light, with no electron intermediaries.

1994 Apple introduces the first personal computers to use the Power PC RISC Chip.

1995 Microsoft introduces its Windows 95 operating system software, featuring an improved interface and better multimedia support.

1997 In a six-game match, the IBM RS/6000 SP supercomputer (known as Deep Blue) defeats world chess champion Garry Kasparov, the first time a computer has beaten a player of this caliber.

Called the world's fastest computer, Intel's Janus supercomputer is installed at the Sandia National Laboratories in Albuquerque, N.Mex. It is the first tetraflop machine, meaning it can perform trillions of operations per second.

Intel introduces a Pentium chip with MMX technology, enhancing multimedia capabilities on a PC.

1999 The total number of Internet users in the U.S. reaches an estimated 90 million at year's end.

2000 The century begins with minimal disruption from the much-feared Y2K programming bug.

Household penetration of personal computers in the United States surpasses 50 percent.

A federal circuit court judge finds the software giant Microsoft in violation of antitrust laws and orders the company broken up into two parts. Microsoft appeals.

2001 The U.S. high-tech industry faces hard times. The investment "bubble" in dot.com companies bursts, forcing numerous Web ventures to shut down. PC sales slow, leading to major stock devaluations and layoffs. Still, the number of Internet users continues to climb, exceeding 104 million—or 56% of the adult population—early in the year.

In a widely followed case, a federal district judge issues an injunction against Napster, Inc., to curb the free exchange of copyright-protected music on the company's popular Internet site.

TELECOMMUNICATIONS

Over the course of barely two decades, innovations in information processing and data transfer technologies have combined with increased satellite access, the spread of fiber optic cable, and the explosive growth of the Internet to fuel a communications revolution in North America, Europe, and the industrialized nations of Asia. The proliferation of cellular phones, mobile radio phones, paging services, and personal communication systems (PCS) has supplemented conventional telephone service and brought accelerated growth to the entire telecommunications industry. The ongoing expansion of these segments, with the rise of wireless Internet service and local multipoint distribution systems, promises continued industry growth—and enhanced communication capabilities for consumers and businesses—for the foreseeable future.

In 2000, according to the Telecommunications Industry Association (TIA), the U.S. marketplace generated revenues of an estimated $609.2 billion, a 12.5 percent increase over 1999 (after 12.1 percent growth that year). Of the total 2000 revenues, $287.5 billion (up 8.9 percent) went for so-called transport services—local exchange access, toll calling, and wireless services. Another $179.8 billion went for equipment and software, and $168.2 billion for network and wireless infrastructure and other support.

The TIA is projecting more than 11 percent annual growth for the U.S. telecommunications industry every year through 2004. Revenues for service, however, are expected to lag by several percentage points as increased competition keeps prices down—to the advantage of consumers.

Continued expansion of the Internet user base (still dominated by dial-up service) and competitive pricing in the long-distance market have steadily increased consumer demand for conventional phone service. By the beginning of 2000, the total number of U.S. home and business access lines reached 228 million, up from 130 million at the start of the 1990s. This does not even include the new, rapid-growth wireless segments. In 1999, Americans placed 554 billion local calls, generating an estimated $58 billion in revenues for the industry. America's drive to get onto the Internet has been heavily responsible for the increase in usage, as both residences and small businesses have added lines. (Larger businesses and some home users have taken greater advantage of broadband access options.) Deregulation of local phone service has long been discussed, but consumers cannot expect lower prices until it becomes a reality.

Largest U.S. Telephone Companies, 2000

Rank, Company	Access lines ('000s)	Operating revenues (millions)
1. AT&T	—	$65,981
2. Verizon	63,000	64,707
3. SBC Communications	61,250	51,476
4. MCI WorldCom	—	39,090
5. BellSouth	54,200[1]	26,151
6. Sprint	—	23,613
7. Qwest	17,000	16,610
8. Alltel	2,433[2]	7,067

1. Includes switched access lines and access-line equivalents. 2. As of Dec. 31, 1999.
Source: U.S. Federal Communications Commission, *Statistics of Communications Common Carriers* (annual); annual reports.

The long-distance market remained the largest segment of the phone service industry, even as rates have declined dramatically. Americans placed an estimated 102 billion toll calls in 1999, spending $98 billion. The effects of deregulation in the long-distance market are clear. The average price of a domestic long-distance call fell from about 30 cents per minute in 1988 to less than 15 cents per minute by the end of the 1990s. Long-distance service has been deregulated for some 20 years, and the number of providers continues to increase while AT&T's market share continues to shrink.

Wireless Communications By far the most rapid growth in the telecommunications industry has come in the wireless segment. From 1996 to 2000, the overall wireless market more than doubled in size, from $26.8 billion to $57.6 billion, with another 30 percent increase (to $75.0 billion) expected in 2001 and 17 percent (to $88.0 billion) in 2002. Cellular telephones accounted for the majority share in 2000 (51 percent), but pagers, handheld devices with fax capability and Internet access, and other equipment are expected to gain an increasing share of the wireless market. Many experts expected wireless usage to account for half of all U.S. telecom service revenues within the next few years.

From 1990 to 2000, the number of subscribers to a cellular phone system jumped from 5.3 million to more than 109 million. Some 23 million subscribers were added in 2000 alone, an increase of 27 percent. Service revenues skyrocketed from $4.5 billion at the start of the 1990s to $52.5 billion in 2000. The one-year increase in 2000 was over 31 percent, from $40.1 billion to $52.5 billion, and the explosion was expected to continue in the new decade.

The growth of the paging and messaging market was also impressive throughout the 1990s, as the number of new subscribers rose from 9.9 million in 1990 to 53.5 million in 2000; total spending jumped from $1.7 billion to $5.7 billion. The rate of increase began to slow in the latter years of the decade, however, as cellular telephones began serving the purposes of many pager users.

New forms of wireless communication promise even greater versatility and broader usage. Personal communication service (PCS), which transmits cellular calls digitally, brings superior reception. It will also allow users to download information from the Internet or a corporate data network right to wireless, handheld phone screens. Pagers, too, are becoming more versatile; recent versions can collect news headlines, stock prices, street guides, and even voice mail.

Satellites Despite the rapid growth of wireless telecommunications in the U.S., much of the technology is being developed in Europe. Still, the U.S. is expected to exert the greatest influence on future development on the strength of its superior space technology. By 2000, American companies had launched well over 125 communications satellites into low Earth orbit, with about 350 more scheduled for deployment by the year 2002.

U.S. Telecommunications Marketplace, 1998–2002 (millions of dollars)

Service	1998	1999	2000	2001[1]	2002[2]
Total Transport Services	$245,640	$264,035	$287, 552	$317,928	$344,867
Local Exchange Services	100,320	109,016	117,000	125,000	133,400
Toll Service	105,055	108,268	113,000	117,950	123,500
Wireless Services	40,265	46,751	57,552	74,978	87,967
Specialized Services	2,559	3,570	5,790	8,771	10,815
Support Svcs./Infrastructure	118,728	142,784	168,210	200,646	239,868
Equipment and Software	122,782	141,348	179,773	178,358	194,619
Industry Total[3]	**$482,939**	**$541,600**	**$609,214**	**$689,801**	**$770,541**

1. Estimated. 2. Projected. 3. Installation charges included in both support services and equipment but only once in industry total.
Source: Telecommunications Industry Association (Arlington, Va.), *MultiMedia Telecommunications Market Review and Forecast (2001)*. Reprinted by permission.

U.S. Telephone Systems, 1985–99

Year	1985	1990	1995	1997	1998	1999
Local Exchange Carriers						
Carriers	55	51	53	51	52	52
Access lines (millions)	112	130	166	193	205	228
Business (millions)	31	36	46	53	57	57
Residential (millions)	79	89	101	108	110	115
Other (millions)	2	6	19	32	39	53
Local calls (billions)	365	402	484	522	544	554
Local service revenues (billions)	N.A.	$32	$46	$52	N.A.	$58
Long-Distance Carriers						
Carriers	N.A.	325	583	621[1]	N.A.	N.A.
Presubscribed lines	N.A.	132	153	159[1]	N.A.	N.A.
Toll calls (billions)	N.A.	63	94	101	N.A.	102
Toll service revenues (billions)	$43	$52	$74	$90	$94	N.A.
International Service						
U.S.-billed calls (millions)	411	984	2,821	4,229	4,547	N.A.
U.S.-billed minutes (billions)	3.4	8.0	15.9	22.6	24.4	N.A.
U.S.-billed revenues (billions)	$3.5	$8.0	$14.0	$15.1	$15.4	N.A.

1. 1996 figures. **Source:** U.S. Federal Communications Commission, *Statistics of Communications Common Carriers* (annual).

Meanwhile, global satellite telecommunications continued to make advances. Globalstar, a 48-satellite low-altitude system for worldwide mobile telephone and paging service was launched in late 1999. In 2000, the selective availability limitation was removed from the global positioning system (GPS), increasing the accuracy of locating a position from 100 yards to 10 feet. And the early months of 2001 saw the initiation of satellite radio broadcasting and nationwide two-way satellite Internet access.

Telecom Industry Competition for the burgeoning wireless market, declining prices for long-distance service, turbulence in the investment market, and the bursting of the dot.com bubble made for a difficult year 2000 in the U.S. telecommunications industry. Several major companies, facing a squeeze on profits, announced cutbacks.

The scramble for market share and general turmoil was further reflected in a rush of merger activity and corporate realignment. The year 2000 saw the merger of Bell Atlantic and GTE—giving birth to Verizon—and of Qwest and US West. MCI WorldCom's merger with Sprint was called off in July 2000, but the former company announced its acquisition of Intermedia Communications late in the year. AT&T, meanwhile, announced a four-way breakup—into wireless, cable, consumer, and business units—in October 2000, soon after its acquisition of MediaOne Group.

The end results were increased consolidation and a shift in rank among the largest U.S. telecom companies in 2000. AT&T remained at the top of the list; Verizon jumped ahead of SBC into the second position, and MCI WorldCom fell to fourth.

Wireless Communication Services Spending in U.S.,1996-2002 (in millions)

Year	Cellular	Personal Communication Systems	Paging	Specialized Mobile Radio	Local Multipoint Distribution Systems	Total
1996	$21,526	$280	$4,404	$610	----	$26,820
1997	25,004	2,560	4,811	1,440	5	33,819
1998	26,575	5,738	5,304	2,646	2	40,265
1999	26,575	10,658	5,429	4,084	6	46,751
2000	29,624	16,202	5,650	6,017	59	57,552
2001[1]	36,684	24,813	6,005	7,232	243	74,978
2002[2]	39,993	32,345	6,360	8,585	685	87,967

1. Estimated. 2. Projected. **Source:** The Strategis Group; Donaldson, Lufkin & Jenrette; Cellular Telecommunications Industry Association; Telecommunications Industry Association.

Cellular Telephone Industry Growth in the U.S., 1990-2000

Year	Systems	Subscriber	Cell sites[1]	Employees	Service revenue (millions)	Average monthly bill
1990	751	5,283,000	5,616	21,382	$4,548	$80.90
1995	1,827	33,786,000	22,683	68,165	19,081	51.00
1996	1,740	44,043,000	30,045	84,161	23,635	47.70
1997	2,228	55,312,293	51,600	109,387	27,486	42.78
1998	3,073	69,209,321	65,887	134,754	33,133	39.43
1999	3,518	86,047,003	81,698	155,817	40,018	41.24
2000	N.A.	109,478,031	104,288	188,449	52,466	45.27

1. A cell site is the basic geographic unit of a cellular system. A city or county is divided into smaller cells, each of which is equipped with a low-powered radio transmitter/receiver. The cells can vary in size depending on terrain, capacity demands, etc. By controlling the transmission power, the radio frequencies assigned to one cell can be limited to the boundaries of that cell. When a cellular phone moves from one cell to another, a computer at the switching office monitors the movement and transfers the phone call to the new cell and another radio frequency. **Source:** Cellular Telecommunications Industry Association, *State of the Cellular Industry*, (annual).

U.S. Paging and Messaging Market, 1990-2001

Year	Subscribers	Annual Percent Increase	Total Spending (millions)	Annual Percent Increase	Average Monthly Spending	Annual Percent Change
1990	9.9	22.2%	$1,744	17.8%	$14.68	-3.7%
1995	34.5	31.2	3,841	18.8	9.28	-9.4
1996	42.1	22.0	4,404	14.7	8.59	-7.4
1997	48.3	14.7	4,811	9.2	8.30	-3.4
1998	52.0	7.7	5,307	10.3	8.50	2.4
1999	52.3	0.6	5,429	2.4	8.65	1.8
2000	53.5	2.3	5,650	4.1	8.80	1.7
2001[1]	55.6	3.9	6,005	6.3	9.00	2.3

1. Estimated. **Source:** The Strategis Group; Donaldson, Lufkin & Jenrette; Telecommunications Industry Association.

Radios, Televisions, Telephones, and Computers per Capita, by Selected Nation, (number per 1,000 people), 1999

Nation	Radio receivers[1]	Television receivers[1]	Telephone main lines	Mobile telephones	Personal computers
Algeria	242	105	52	2	6
Argentina	681	223	201	121	49
Australia	1,391	554	521	344	471
Austria	751	525	472	519	257
Belgium	797	466	500[2]	315	315
Brazil	434	223	149	90	36
Bulgaria	537	394	342	42	27
Canada	1,067	710	635[2]	230	361
Chile	354	215	207	151	67
China	335	321	86	34	12
Colombia	524	115	160	75	34
Cuba	352	239	39	1	7
Czech Republic	803	531	371	190	107
Denmark	1,145	594	683	499	414
Dominican Republic	178	95	93[2]	31[2]	N.A.
Ecuador	348	130	91	31	20
Egypt	317	119	60[2]	7	11
Finland	1,498	622	553	667	360
France	946	595	579	364	221
Germany	948	567	588	286	297
Ghana	236	93	8	4	3
Greece	475	240	528	311	60
Guatemala	79	61	55	32	10
Honduras	410	95	44	12	10
Hungary	690	435	402	160	74
India	120	65	22[2]	1[2]	3
Indonesia	155	68	29	11	9
Iran	263	71	125	7	52
Iraq	229	83	31[2]	—[2]	N.A.
Ireland	697	402	478	378	324
Israel	524	288	459	459	246
Italy	880	528	462	528	192
Jamaica	483	183	199	56	43
Japan	956	686	494	449	287
Korea, South	1,039	348	441	504	183
Kuwait	678	505	240	158	121
Lebanon	907	375	194[2]	196	46
Malaysia	434	172	203	101	69
Mexico	329	272	112	78	44
Morocco	247	115	66	4	11
Netherlands	980	519	606	435	360
New Zealand	997	512	490	230	327
Norway	917	462	712	618	450
Pakistan	94	22	22	2	4
Panama	299	187	165	86	32
Peru	273	126	67	39	20
Philippines	161	52	34[2]	24[2]	17
Poland	522	337	260	102	62
Portugal	306	336	424	468	93
Puerto Rico	714	270	327[2]	150[2]	N.A.
Romania	319	233	167	63	27
Russia	417	410	197[2]	9	37
Saudi Arabia	321	262	143[2]	31[2]	57
Singapore	744	388	577	475	527
South Africa	355	134	138	132	60
Spain	331	409	418	312	122
Sweden	932	519	665	578	451
Switzerland	979	457	699	420	462
Syria	278	70	102	—	15
Taiwan	N.A.	N.A.	544	521	181
Thailand	234	254	84	33[2]	23
Turkey	178	330	265	117	32
United Kingdom	1,443	521	557[2]	408	306
United States	2,116	806	661[2]	312	511
Uruguay	603	239	271	95	100
Venezuela	472	180	109	143	42

1. 1996 figures. 2.1998 figures. **Source:** International Telecommunications Union, *World Telecommunication Indicators*; U.S. Census Bureau, *Statistical Abstract of the United States* (annual).

Area Codes of the United States and Canada, by State and Province

The continuing proliferation of fax machines, modems, pagers, and cellular phones has played havoc with the number of area codes in the U.S, Canada, and the Caribbean. In 1990, there were 120 area codes, a number that increased only to 146 by 1996. But in 2001, there were more than 300. Several cities had two or more area codes in the exact same area (known as an overlay), requiring customers to dial 11 digits just to make a local call. At current growth rates, the North American area code system will run out of three-digit codes some time between 2007 and 2012. (For International Dialing codes, see Part III: "The World.")

201 New Jersey (Hoboken, Jersey City)
202 Washington, D.C.
203 Connecticut (Greenwich, New Haven)
204 Manitoba, Canada
205 Alabama (Birmingham, Tuscaloosa)
206 Washington (Seattle)
207 Maine
208 Idaho
209 California (Modesto, Stockton)
210 Texas (San Antonio)
212 New York City (Manhattan)[1]
213 California (dowtown Los Angeles)
214 Texas (Dallas)[1]
215 Pennsylvania (Philadelphia)[1]
216 Ohio (Cleveland)
217 Illinois (Decatur, Springfield)
218 Minnesota (Duluth)
219 Indiana (Gary, South Bend)
225 Louisiana (Baton Rouge)
228 Mississippi (Biloxi, Gulfport)
229 Georgia (Albany, Americus)
231 Michigan (Muskegon)
234 Ohio (Akron, Canton, Youngstown)[1]
240 Maryland (Rockville, Bethesda)[1]
242 Bahamas
246 Barbados
248 Michigan (Pontiac)
250 British Columbia (Vancouver, Victoria)
251 Alabama (Mobile, Montgomery)[1]
252 North Carolina (Rocky Mount)
253 Washington (Tacoma)
254 Texas (Waco)
256 Alabama (Huntsville)
262 Wisconsin (Racine, Kenosha)
264 Anguilla
267 Pennsylvania (Philadelphia)[1]
268 Antigua/Barbuda
270 Kentucky (Bowling Green, Hopkinsville)
281 Texas (Houston)[1]
283 Ohio (Cincinnati)[1]
284 British Virgin Islands
289 Ontario (Hamilton, Niagara Falls)[1]
301 Maryland (Rockville, Bethesda)[1]
302 Delaware
303 Colorado (Denver, Englewood)[1]
304 West Virginia
305 Florida (Miami)[1]
306 Saskatchewan (Regina, Saskatoon)
307 Wyoming
308 Nebraska (North Platte)
309 Illinois (Moline, Peoria)

310 California (Santa Monica, Malibu)
312 Illinois (Chicago Loop)
313 Michigan (Detroit)
314 Missouri (downtown St. Louis)
315 New York (Syracuse, Utica)
316 Kansas (Wichita)
317 Indiana (Indianapolis)
318 Louisiana (Shreveport)
319 Iowa (Cedar Rapids, Iowa City)
320 Minnesota (St. Cloud)
321 Florida (Melbourne, Orlando)[2]
323 California (Los Angeles, except downown)
330 Ohio (Akron, Canton, Youngstown)[1]
334 Alabama (Mobile, Montgomery)[1]
336 North Carolina (Greensboro)
337 Louisiana (Lafayette, Lake Charles)
339 Massachusetts (Arlington, Revere, Woburn)[1]
340 U.S. Virgin Islands
345 Cayman Islands
347 New York (Bronx, Brooklyn, Queens, Staten Island)[1]
351 Massachusetts (Andover, Salem)[1]
352 Florida (Gainesville, Ocala)
360 Washington (Bellingham, Vancouver)
361 Texas (Corpus Christi)
386 Florida (Lake City)
401 Rhode Island
402 Nebraska (Lincoln, Omaha)
403 Alberta (Calgary)
404 Georgia (Atlanta)
405 Oklahoma (Oklahoma City)
406 Montana
407 Florida (Orlando, Kissimmee)[2]
408 California (San Jose)
409 Texas (Galveston)
410 Maryland (Baltimore, Annapolis)[1]
412 Pennsylvania (Pittsburgh, New Castle)[1]
413 Massachusetts (Pittsfield, Springfield)
414 Wisconsin (Milwaukee)
415 California (San Francisco)
416 Ontario (Toronto)[1]
417 Missouri (Joplin, Springfield)
418 Quebec (Quebec City)
419 Ohio (Sandusky, Toledo)
423 Tennessee (Chattanooga, Bristol)
425 Washington (Bellevue, Redmond)
434 Virginia (Lynchburg, Danville)
435 Utah (Ogden)
440 Ohio (Cleveland suburbs)

441 Bermuda
443 Maryland (Baltimore, Annapolis)[1]
445 Pennsylvania (Philadelphia)[1]
450 Quebec (Montreal suburbs)
469 Texas (Dallas)[1]
473 Grenada
478 Georgia (Macon)
480 Arizona (Mesa, Scottsdale)
484 Pennsylvania (Allentown, Reading)[1]
501 Arkansas (Little Rock, Hot Springs)
502 Kentucky (Louisville)
503 Oregon (Portland, Salem)[1]
504 Louisiana (New Orleans)
505 New Mexico
506 New Brunswick, Canada
507 Minnesota (Rochester, Winona)
508 Massachusetts (Cape Cod, Plymouth, Worcester)[1]
509 Washington (Spokane, Yakima)
510 California (Berkeley, Oakland)
512 Texas (Austin)
513 Ohio (Cincinnati)[1]
514 Quebec (downtown Montreal)
515 Iowa (Ames, Des Moines)
516 New York (Western Long Island: Nassau County)
517 Michigan (Lansing, Saginaw)
518 New York (Albany, Schenectady)
519 Ontario, Canada (London)
520 Arizona (Tucson)
530 California (Chico, Redding)
540 Virginia (Roanoke, Winchester)
541 Oregon (Eugene, Medford)
559 California (Fresno)
561 Florida (Boca Raton, West Palm Beach)
562 California (Long Beach)
563 Iowa (Davenport, Dubuque)
570 Pennsylvania (Scranton)
571 Virginia (Alexandria, Arlington)[1]
573 Missouri (Columbia, Jefferson City)
580 Oklahoma (Lawton, Stillwater)
601 Mississippi (Jackson, Natchez)
602 Arizona (Phoenix, Tempe)
603 New Hampshire
604 British Columbia (Whistler)
605 South Dakota
606 Kentucky (Ashland, Middlesborough)
607 New York (Binghampton, Elmira)
608 Wisconsin (La Crosse, Madison)

609 New Jersey (Atlantic City, Long Branch)
610 Pennsylvania (Allentown, Reading)[1]
612 Minnesota (Minneapolis)
613 Ontario (Ottawa)
614 Ohio (Columbus)
615 Tennessee (Nashville)
616 Michigan (Grand Rapids, Kalamazoo)
617 Massachusetts (Boston)[1]
618 Illinois (Centralia, E. St. Louis)
619 California (downtown San Diego)
620 Kansas (Dodge City, Parsons)
623 Arizona (Glendale, Peoria)
626 California (Pasadena)
630 Illinois (Oak Brook)
631 New York (Eastern Long Island, Suffolk County)
636 Missouri (St. Louis suburbs)
641 Iowa (Mason City, Oskaloosa)
646 New York (Manhattan)[1]
647 Ontario (Toronto)[1]
649 Turks & Caicos Islands
650 California (Palo Alto, San Mateo)
651 Minnesota (St. Paul)
660 Missouri (Sedalia)
661 California (Bakersfield)
662 Mississippi (Yazoo City, Tupelo)
664 Montserrat
670 Northern Mariana Islands
671 Guam
678 Georgia (Marietta, Smyrna)[1]
682 Texas (Arlington, Fort Worth)[1]
701 North Dakota
702 Nevada (Las Vegas)
703 Virginia (Alexandria, Arlington)[1]
704 North Carolina (Charlotte, Gastonia)[1]
705 Ontario (North Bay)
706 Georgia (Augusta)
707 California (Eureka, Napa)
708 Illinois (Cicero, Oak Lawn)
709 Newfoundland
712 Iowa (Council Bluffs, Sioux City)
713 Texas (Houston)[1]
714 California (Huntington Beach, Santa Ana)
715 Wisconsin (Eau Claire, Wausau)
716 New York (Buffalo, Rochester)
717 Pennsylvania (Harrisburg, Scranton)
718 New York City outside Manhattan
719 Colorado (Colorado Springs, Pueblo)
720 Colorado (Denver, Englewood)[1]
724 Pennsylvania (Pittsburgh, New Castle)[1]
727 Florida (St. Petersburg)
731 Tennessee (Jackson, Union City)
732 New Jersey (Middlesex)
734 Michigan (Ann Arbor, Ypsilanti)

740 Ohio (Cambridge, Marietta)
754 Florida (Ft. Lauderdale, Hollywood)[1]
757 Virginia (Virginia Beach)
758 St. Lucia
760 California (Palm Springs)
763 Minnesota (Brooklyn Center, Fridley)
765 Indiana (Kokomo, Muncie)
767 Dominica
770 Georgia (Marietta, Smyrna)[1]
773 Illinois (Chicago except the Loop)
774 Massachusetts (Cape Cod, Plymouth, Worcester)[1]
775 Nevada (Carson City, Reno)
780 Alberta (Edmonton)
781 Massachusetts (Arlington, Revere, Woburn)[1]
784 St. Vincent and the Grenadines
785 Kansas (Topeka, Manhattan)
786 Florida (Miami)[1]
787 Puerto Rico
801 Utah (Salt Lake City, Alta)
802 Vermont
803 South Carolina (Augusta, Columbia)
804 Virginia (Richmond)
805 California (Santa Barbara Lompoc,)
806 Texas (Amarillo)
807 Ontario (Fort William, Thunder Bay)
808 Hawaii
809 Dominican Republic
810 Michigan (Flint)
812 Indiana (Evansville, Terre Haute)
813 Florida (Tampa)
814 Pennsylvania (Altoona, Erie)
815 Illinois (Joliet, Rockford)
816 Missouri (Kansas City, St. Joseph)
817 Texas (Arlington, Fort Worth)[1]
818 California (Burbank, San Fernando)
819 Quebec (Sherbrooke)
828 North Carolina (Asheville, Morganton)
830 Texas (Fredericksburg)
831 California (Monterey, Salinas)
832 Texas (Houston)[1]
835 Pennsylvania (Allentown, Reading)[1]
843 South Carolina (Charleston)
845 New York (Kingston, Poughkeepsie)
847 Illinois (Des Plaines, Evanston)
850 Florida (Pensacola, Tallahassee)
856 New Jersey (Camden, Trenton)[1]
857 Massachusetts (Boston)[1]
858 California (Northern San Diego, La Jolla)
859 Kentucky (Covington, Lexington)
860 Connecticut (Hartford)

863 Florida (Lakeland, Winter Haven)
864 South Carolina (Greenville-Spartanburg)
865 Tennessee (Knoxville)
867 Yukon and Northwest Territories
868 Trinidad & Tobago
869 St. Kitt's & Nevis
870 Arkansas (Jonesboro, Arkadelphia)
876 Jamaica
878 Pennsylvania (Pittsburgh, New Castle)[1]
901 Tennessee (Memphis)
902 Nova Scotia, Prince Edward Island
903 Texas (Sherman, Tyler)
904 Florida (Jacksonville, St. Augustine)
905 Ontario (Hamilton, Niagara Falls)[1]
906 Michigan (Upper Peninsula)
907 Alaska
908 New Jersey (Elizabeth)
909 California (Pomona, San Bernardino)
910 North Carolina (Fayetteville, Wilmington)
912 Georgia (Savannah)
913 Kansas (Kansas City)
914 New York (White Plains, Yonkers)
915 Texas (Abilene, El Paso)
916 California (Sacramento)
917 New York (New York City: cell phones and pagers)
918 Oklahoma (Muskogee, Tulsa)
919 North Carolina (Raleigh, Durham)
920 Wisconsin (Appleton, Green Bay)
925 California (Concord, Pleasanton)
928 Arizona (Flagstaff, Yuma)
931 Tennessee (Clarksville, Columbia)
936 Texas (Crocket, Nacogdoches)
937 Ohio (Dayton)
940 Texas (Wichita Falls)
941 Florida (Fort Myers, Sarasota)
949 California (Irvine)
952 Minnesota (Bloomington, Minnetonka)
954 Florida (Ft. Lauderdale, Hollywood)[1]
956 Texas (Laredo, McAllen)
970 Colorado (Aspen, Grand Junction)
971 Oregon (Portland, Salem)[1]
972 Texas (Dallas)[1]
973 New Jersey (Newark)
978 Massachusetts (Andover, Salem)[1]
979 Texas (Bryan, College Station)
980 North Carolina (Charlotte, Gastonia)[1]
985 Louisiana (Bogalusa, Houma)
989 Michigan (Alpena)

Note: When no cities are listed, area code is for entire state or province. 1. Area in which there is an overlay, or more than one area code for the area. 2. The 321 area code is an overlay on the 407 area code in the Orlando area only. Area codes in this area may be either 321 or 407, but all area codes in the Melbourne area are 321.
Source: Lockheed Martin, North American Numbering Plan Relief Letters, 2001. www.nanpa.com.

U.S. Consumer Telecommunications Market, 1990–2002

Product	1990	1995	1999	2000	2001[1]	2002[2]
Total Unit Shipments (millions)	**47.2**	**65.6**	**99.3**	**106.2**	**110.9**	**115.6**
Corded telephone	22.0	25.8	35.8	37.7	39.2	40.5
Cordless telephone	10.1	19.5	40.1	43.3	45.3	47.4
Answering machine	13.6	17.5	20.4	22.2	23.5	24.8
Home fax machine	1.5	2.8	3.0	3.0	2.9	2.9
Total Dollar Sales (millions)	**$3,988**	**$4,923**	**$4,633**	**$4,812**	**$4,826**	**$4,846**
Corded telephone	765	668	688	678	666	660
Cordless telephone	1,170	1,913	2,204	2,384	2,400	2,418
Answering machine	953	1,242	1,195	1,222	1,242	1,262
Home fax machine	1,100	1,100	546	528	518	506

1. Estimated. 2. Projected. **Source:** MultiMedia Telecommunications Association (Arlington, Va.), *MultiMedia Telecommunications Market Review and Forecast* (2001). Reprinted by permission.

Sales & Penetration of Telecommunications Products in U.S. Homes, 1990–2001

Product	Sales (thousands of units)				Percent of U.S. homes			
	1990	1995	2000[1]	2001[2]	1990	1997	2000	2001[1]
Telephone answering device	13,560	17,498	23010	24,552	31%	65%	74%	77%
Cordless telephone	10,148	19,510	43,352	45,705	25	66	78	81
Home computer	5,500	8,400	16,400	17,500	23	40	54	58
Fax and/or fax modems	350	7,497	14,200	15,065	N.A.	19	51	55
Wireless telephone	1,888	10,295	18,876	22,274	N.A.	34	51	59

Note: As of January of year shown. 1. Estimate. 2. Projected. **Source:** Consumer Electronics Manufacturers Association.

THE INTERNET

The Internet, an intricate global web of hundreds of thousands of computer networks linked by conventional telephone lines (and now such high-speed alternatives as cable modem and *DSL*), was created by the U.S. Defense Department in 1969 as a faster way for agencies to share information and as an emergency means of communications in case more traditional means were cut off. But the potential for consumer Internet use didn't occur until the 1980s, when the National Science Foundation created equipment that would allow other computer networks to connect to the government's larger network. From there, commercial services such as CompuServe, Prodigy, and America Online tapped into the ever-growing network and brought a wealth of information to anybody with a computer, a modem, and the monthly fee. In 1993 some three million people worldwide were connected to the Internet. By the end of 2000, according to one estimate, the total number of users exceeded 400 million.

Today, the Internet is the world's largest communications network. The number of names registered in the *domain name system*—Web sites of commercial enterprises, public institutions, and private individuals—reached 30 million by 2001. The networks and switches that make up the Internet carry data around the world in seconds, and link even the most remote user to a vast wealth of resources. The most popular network on the Internet is the *World Wide Web* (WWW, or simply, "the Web"), created in 1989 by CERN, the European Particle Physics Lab in Geneva and made available on the Internet in Aug. 1991. In 1993, the creation of software (Mosaic) that displayed the Internet in a format that resembled a magazine with text and graphics dramatically increased Net usage. In 1994, the Netscape browser came on the market, and since then, the Internet has become hugely popular, as computer users found they could navigate the Web quickly and easily.

In just a few short years, the Internet and the Web have quite literally transformed the way millions of people go about their daily lives. Everything from mundane tasks like banking or ordering tickets to more eventful activities like searching for a job or a date, planning a vacation, or buying a house, can all be done sitting in front of a computer. The Internet also directly affects the work life of people in hundreds of occupations. Physicians, lawyers, real estate agents, and marketing specialists, among others, can all get vital public documents and statistics over the Internet. Meanwhile businesses can market products, purchase materials and services, and carry out other essential activities. There are thousands of sites on the Web where you can order almost any kind of consumer product. If sometimes overhyped and overinvested, the Internet is accurately described as the fastest-growing and most versatile resource in media history.

Who Uses the Internet?

Almost unheard of before 1990, the Internet has entered the vocabulary of most Americans and the homes of a large number of them. Because Internet use is decentralized and almost completely unregulated, statistics on the number of users are difficult to verify and vary significantly among reporting services. By most accounts, however, the number of regular Internet users in the United

States reached 50 million in 1998, about five years after the medium became viable for ordinary consumers. That narrow time frame easily eclipsed the 10 years for cable TV, 13 for television, and 38 for radio. And the rate of growth has remained unprecedented. A 19% increase from April 2000 to April 2001 put the number of U.S Internet users at more than 125 million. Frequency of use has also risen; at the end of 2000, a reported 58 million Americans were logging onto the Net daily—9 million more than at the middle of the year

As the user base has expanded, the demographic profile of the average user has changed. According to several surveys, disparities in gender, age, income, education level, and race between Net users and non-users have shrunk. The median age of the average user in 2000 was 33, compared with 36 for all Americans; 51% of users were male (down from 59% in 1999), while 49% of the general population were male; whites made up 76% of the Internet user base and 74% of the overall population. Disparities remained in online access by income and age: 82% of those with a

household income of $75,000 or more had Internet access, while only 38% of those living in households earning less than $30,000 had access; 75% of Americans aged 18-29 had a Net connection, compared with only 15% of those 65 and over. But a user survey in mid-2001 suggested a closing of the income and age gaps. The most rapid increases in Internet access over the previous 12 months were found among those aged 55 or over (33%) and among nonprofessional laborers.

In addition to the increases in user base, frequency of use, and duration of use—and partly responsible for those increases—have come changes in the means of access for many users. As high-speed alternatives to standard phone lines, some 3.4 million U.S. Internet users at year-end 2000 had access through broadband cable modems, and another 1.2 million were linked by DSL (Digital Subscription Line). By 2005, according to industry monitor Jupiter Communications, those figures were expected to reach 13.8 million and 11.2 million, respectively.

Internet Users Worldwide, 2000

Region	Users[1] (millions)
Canada and United States	167.12
Europe	113.14
Asia/Pacific	104.88
Latin America	16.45
Africa	3.11
Middle East	2.40
World Total	**407.10**

1. Estimated as of November 2000.
Source: NUA Internet Surveys.

25 Most Visited .com Web sites, 2001

Rank, Site	Visitors[1] (000s)
1. AOL Time Warner Network	70,701
2. Microsoft sites	61,350
3. Yahoo!	57,559
4. Lycos	32,853
5. X10.com	28,603
6. Excite Network	28,186
7. About the Human Internet	25,661
8. Infospace Infrastructure Services	20,236
9. Amazon	20,016
10. Walt Disney Internet Group	19,876
11. NBC Internet sites	19,363
12. eBay	19,236
13. CNET Networks	18,581
14. AltaVista Network	15,145
15. Ask Jeeves	13,899
16. eUniverse Network	13,835
17. Viacom Online	12,839
18. GOOGLE.com	12,579
19. Flipside sites	12,281
20. Real.com Network	12,124
21. Ticketmaster	11,156
22. AT&T Web sites	11,151
23. Napster Digital	10,909
24. The Weather Channel	10,585
25. GoTo	10,539

Note: As measured during the period May 1-31, 2001. Includes aggregations of commonly owned or branded domain names. 1. Unique visitors, combined at home and at work. **Source:** Media Metrix (2001).

►THE WORLD WIDE WEB

The World Wide Web is a vast network of information within the Internet, which uses a hypertext system for quickly transmitting graphics, sound, and video over phone lines. To read the information, users must have a *browser* (such as Netscape Navigator or Microsoft Internet Explorer). Because the hypertext system arranges information based on its relationship to other information rather than in linear or alphabetical order, the Web allows users to find information quickly, especially if they don't know exactly what they're looking for. Each piece of information, or *Web page*, can be connected to one or more other pages via a *link*. For example, the U.S. Census Bureau's Web site (www.census.gov) provides thousands of data tables produced by the Department of Commerce, and is also linked to data from 70 other government agencies.

The Web is divided into zones, which organize pages according to the type of information generally contained within them. There is of course some overlap, but generally, Web pages of educational institutions end in .edu; government Web pages end in .gov; Web pages of Internet-related institutions end in .net; commercial entities end with .com; and other organizations end with .org. In an attempt to relieve overcrowding in the .com and .net areas, the ICANN (Internet Corporation for Assigned Names and Numbers), the official governing body for domain names, created seven new suffixes (or TLDs, "Top-Level Domains") for use beginning in 2001: .aero, .biz, .coop, .info, .museum, .name, and .pro.

Growth of the Web   It is becoming increasingly easy for companies, organizations, and even individuals to create their own Web sites. Millions of institutions, groups, and individuals have done so, resulting in such dramatic growth that the Web's 30 million sites in 2001 contained an estimated 3-4 billion pages (up to double the previous year's total) with 10K-20K of data per page. With so many sites throughout cyberspace, surfers would find it close to impossible to find what they were looking for without a *search engine*. Like a librarian who knows where in the library to find valuable information, search engines look through countless Web pages and create an index of what appears on each one. If you're looking for the rules of badminton, you can ask the search engine to sift

Guide to Domain Name Suffixes

Suffix	Used by
.aero	Air transport industry (*Reserved*)
.biz	Businesses (*alternative to .com*)
.com	Commercial entities
.coop	Business cooperatives (*Reserved*)
.edu	Educational institutions
.gov	Government bodies (*at any level*)
.info	General use (*alternative to .com*)
.museum	Museums (*Reserved*)
.name	Private individuals for personal sites
.net	Internet-related institutions
.org	Nonprofit organizations
.pro	Professionals

Note: "Reserved for" domains are sponsored by an organization that represents the specific domain community and is responsible for policies concerning those sites. Unsponsored domains operate under policies established by the global Internet community through ICANN.

U.S. Online Households and Internet Users, 1996–2002

Year	Total U.S. households (millions)	Online households Number (millions)	Percent	Total Internet users (millions)
1996	99.6	8.5	8.5%	37
1997	101.0	14.5	14.3	60
1998	102.5	24.8	24.2	83
1999	103.7	29.7	28.6	104
2000	104.8	35.0	33.4	122
2001[1]	105.8	41.7	39.4	138
2002[2]	107.0	48.0	44.9	153

1. Estimate. 2. Projection.
Source: U.S. Department of Commerce; Jupiter Media Metrix.

hundreds of thousands of Web pages for the word badminton and it will return a list of Web pages that mention badminton. Yahoo!, AltaVista, Excite, Infoseek, WebCrawler, and Lycos are some of the most popular *search engines*.

As the Internet has emerged as a mass medium, the major online service providers, search services, and other Web companies have competed ever more vigorously for user "audience." To attract the greatest number of visitors on a regular basis, many Web sites have expanded from their core services and established broad-based *portals*—whole arrays of services (such as E-mail, search, special-interest forums and bulletin boards, and chat rooms), information (news, weather, stock reports, reference resources), and links to other useful sites, all accessible from a single home page.

Business on the Web   The increasing sophistication of both technology and users have made the World Wide Web a major and rapidly expanding business medium. No longer just a vehicle for publishing brochures and annual reports, the Web has emerged as a low-cost sales channel for producers of goods and services and as a highly convenient purchasing vehicle for end users.

The second half of 2000 and the early months of 2001 brought a measure of reality to the Internet industry, as the sky-high valuations of online ventures were brought down to earth, investors began demanding profitability, and a number of sites simply shut down. Yet, while estimates of e-commerce growth were scaled back, industry analysts reported strong increases. According to Forrester Research, worldwide online business nearly doubled in 2001 to $1.2 trillion; U.S. e-commerce rose from $488.7 billion to $864.1 billion. By 2004, e-commerce was predicted to reach $6.8 trillion worldwide and $3.2 trillion in the U.S.

A vast majority of all e-commerce is conducted between businesses, as the Internet has helped cut transaction costs, locate surplus or low-cost goods, and otherwise increase efficiencies. According to Forrester, total business-to-business net purchases in the U.S. will increase from $176 billion in 1999 to $2.7 trillion by 2004.

Retail online purchasing, more familiar to the average consumer, suffered more severe setbacks in the dot-com shakeout, as numerous Net vendors were forced out of business. But reports of the death of online business-to-consumer merchandising were also premature. Retailers would

be forced to show profits, but consumers continued to increase online spending. According to Jupiter Media Metrix, online retail revenues in the U.S. doubled in 2000 to $24 billion, would increase another 42% in 2001 to $34 billion, and were projected to reach $104 billion by 2005. One survey reported that 40% of the online population made retail purchases in 2000, and that the figure would rise to 52% by 2002. Travel (air, hotel, car rental), personal computers and consumer electronics, and books and music are the leading online retail categories.

One of the innovative and increasingly popular forms of e-commerce is online auctioning, which enables consumers to bid from their home computers on product offerings from private owners or original manufacturers and service providers. E-bay, the largest person-to-person online trading community, claimed 19 million registered users and over $5 billion in annualized gross merchandise sales by the end of 2000.

Few industries have undergone more radical and rapid change as a consequence of online commerce than stock brokerage and financial services. Round-the-clock access, lower service fees, and push-button immediacy have made it easier, cheaper, and faster for ordinary consumers to buy stock or apply for a loan directly online.

Advertising on the Web   Much as it has evolved as a communications and information medium, the World Wide Web, like television and and radio, has also emerged as a major vehicle of commercial advertising. The ads come in the form of banners, pop-up windows, and other Web-page design elements. E-mail has also proven to be viable as an advertising medium, giving birth to the next generation of direct-mail marketing.

The U.S. economic slowdown and shakeout in the dot-com industry in 2000-2001 slowed the growth of Internet advertising, but the rate of increase over the short life of the medium still far exceeded that of any other. And robust increases were expected in the years to come. Jupiter Media Metrix put global online ad spending in 2000 at $7 billion (a 63% increase over 1999) and $10 billion in 2001 (up 43%). The projected increase to $16.5 billion by 2004 would put the Web ahead of several major traditional advertising media.

Privacy and Intellectual Property Rights   As the popularity and purchasing power of the Internet have grown, and as monitoring tools have improved, many people have perceived a growing threat to their personal privacy. Software that tracks usage habits, network database technology, and the ability to transmit vast amounts of data have made it possible to collect and share detailed information about the browsing habits, interests and hobbies, buying patterns, financial history, and contact information of ordinary Internet-using citizens. The U.S. Congress in 2000 conducted in-depth hearings to consider protections and remedies in the online environment.

In a similar vein, the data-sharing power of the Internet has undermined traditional protections for proprietary information and copyright materials. The issue came to the fore in 2000-2001, as the music industry filed suit against Napster.com, which enabled tens of millions of visitors to swap MP3 music files of popular commercial recordings for free. A federal judge in early 2001 issued an injunction against Napster, thereby halting the practice, but copyright protection and intellectual property rights on the Internet loomed as major long-term issues.

▶ A GLOSSARY OF COMMONLY USED INTERNET TERMS

Account Permission to use a computer on a network, or an access agreement with an Internet provider

Address The location of an Internet host. An e-mail address might take the form johndoe@xyz.com; a web address might look like www.xyztech.com. See also URL.

Applet A small program, typically embedded in an Web page, that a user can quickly download and launch, thus enhancing the Web page's content.

Bandwidth The amount of data, graphics, sound, and other information that can be transmitted through cyberspace at a certain time. Bandwidth is measured in kilobits per second (kbps). Most modems have a bandwidth of 28.8 kbps (or simply 28k), though modems offering 56k bandwidth are becoming more common

Bookmark A browser feature (called "Favorites" in Microsoft Explorer) that stores a pointer to a Web site for easy access.

Browser A program that translates the hypertext markup language of the World Wide Web into languages ordinary people can understand. Netscape and Microsoft Internet Explorer are the two most common Web browsers.

Cable Modem A high-speed, broadband Internet connection via cable TV; services often include a selection of localized content.

Cache (Pronounced "cash") The place on a hard drive where a Web browser stores images a user has downloaded off the Internet. If the user wants to see the same Web page again, the browser loads it from the cache rather than retrieve it again from the Internet.

Chat line "talk" An electronic forum in which Internet users can communicate with each other online.

Cookie A small piece of information that a Web browser picks up from another site and stores. Such bits of information can be read and altered by another site, thereby making it possible to identify users who have been to the site before. Cookies allow you to add items to your "shopping cart" as you browse several pages in a virtual shopping mall.

Cyberspace An all-encompassing term for the digital world of computer networks.

Domain The identifying portion of an Internet address (which follows the @ in an E-mail address. Domain names are followed by a period and a three-letter zone that indicates the type of organization. Commercial entities end with .com; Educational institutions end with .edu; government bodies end with .gov; and other organizations end with .org.

Download A way to transfer files, graphics, or other information from the Internet to your computer. HTTP and FTP are the most common downloading methods.

DSL Digital Subscription Line, a high-speed Internet connection that uses the ultra-high frequency portion of ordinary telephone lines, allowing users to send and receive voice and data on the same line at the same time.

Encryption A method of encoding files so only the recipient can read the information. Encryption is necessary for transmitting secure data like credit card numbers over computer networks.

FAQs Frequently Asked Questions. This is generally the first place to stop on a newsgroup or a Web site. It has the answers to the most common questions and indicators of where to go to find the answers to less frequently asked questions.

FTP File Transfer Protocol, the easiest way to download files not on the World Wide Web.

Freeware Free software available over the Internet. This is in contrast with *shareware*, which is available freely, but usually asks the user to send payment for using the software.

GIF Graphic Interchange Format (pronounced "jif"), a common file format for image files; best-suited for nonphotographic material.

Home page The first or main page of a Web site.

HTML HyperText Markup Language, the high-speed computer language used to create documents on the World Wide Web (WWW). To read documents written in HTML, one must have a browser.

HTTP HyperText Transport Protocol, the easiest way to transfer World Wide Web pages from one computer to another.

Hyperlink A connection between two tagged elements in a Web page, or separate sites, that makes it possible to click from one to the other.

Hypertext A system of organizing information based on its relationship to other information, rather than linear or alphabetical orders. Hypertext allows users to *link* related Web pages and to store information in more than one place. For example, in a hypertext almanac, the winners of the National Book Awards could be accessed either through the section on books or on awards.

Intranet A smaller network of computers accessible only by members of the network, often members of one firm. Also known as an internal network.

ISDN Integrated Services Digital Network, a digital type of phone service that permits higher speed transmission of data than conventional phone lines. ISDN lines operate as fast as 128 kilobytes per second (kbps), compared with 28.8 or 56 kbps for the fastest modems.

ISP Internet Service Provider, a company that provides end-user access to the Internet via its central computers and local access lines. American Online (AOL), Earthlink, and Erols are some popular ISPs.

Java A computer language developed by Sun Microsystems that produces programs that run on almost any computer or operating system. Its compatibility and ease of use make it popular for for developing *applets*, tiny applications that can be sent quickly over the World Wide Web.

JPEG Joint Photographic Experts Group, a common file format for photographic images.

Link A hypertext connection that allows a user to jump from one Internet site to another by pointing and clicking. On the World Wide Web, links are underlined or highlighted.

MIDI Musical Instrument Digital Interface, a file format for high-quality sound.

Mirror site An identical backup site that serves as an alternative for a busy web host.

MPEG Motion Picture Experts Group, a file format for high-quality video in small file sizes.

Newsgroups Discussion forums on the Internet, arranged by category of special interest. To read, respond to, or post information on a newsgroup, you must have a program known as a Newsreader.

Push technology Technology that pushes information onto a user's computer rather than requiring the user to navigate the Internet and "pull" the information from another computer network. E-mail and newsgroups are simple examples of push technology.

Search engine A tool used to look up Web pages. Also known as an index or a directory. Yahoo!, Excite, Lycos, and AltaVista are some of the most popular search engines.

Server The central computer in a network, providing a service or data access to client computers on that network. Frequently, a Web server is dedicated to a specific function, such as E-mail.

Shareware An honor system in which providers make their programs freely accessible over the Internet, with the understanding that those who use them will send payment to the provider after using them. See also *freeware*.

Spam Junk E-mail: As a verb, it means to send thousands of copies of a junk E-mail message.

Thumbnail A tiny picture on a Web page which, when clicked, is replaced by a larger version of the same image.

URL Uniform Resource Locator, the address that identifies a Web page to a browser. Also known as a Web address.

Usenet A system of thousands of newsgroups.

Web page An HTML file, containing text, graphics, and/or mini-applications, viewed with a Web *browser*.

Web site An organized, linked collection of *Web pages* stored on an Internet *server* and read using a Web *browser*. The opening page of a site is called a *home page*.

WebTV A commercial service that accesses the World Wide Web through a television and cable TV wires rather than through a computer and phone wires.

WWW The World Wide Web, or simply the Web, a vast network of information, particularly business, commercial, and government resources, that uses a hypertext system for quickly transmitting graphics, sound, and video over phone, cable TV, and fiber optic lines, allowing easy navigation among related subjects.

Zip file A file that has been compressed for simpler transmission over the Internet. To read a ZIP file, you need a program to decompress the file, such as PKUNZIP or WinZip.

▶A FIELD GUIDE TO SEARCHING THE WEB

To search the Web successfully, you need to pick the right engine and learn how to use it. Few people understand the fundamental difference between search engines and Web directories. The former use software agents called "spiders" or "crawlers" to index contents of individual Web pages, then follow links to other pages. Web directories such as Yahoo are compiled by humans who classify sites under topical headings. Most search sites now offer both options, along with information and other services, but topical directories that accompany powerful search engines may be weak, and vice-versa. Moreover, the various search engines themselves operate differently.

The first step in conducting an effective search is to pick an appropriate search site for the job. For a general search, a strong Web directory such as Yahoo or Look Smart is a good place to start. A directory-style search provides two ways to research broad topics: dive through a list of broad topics by clicking on the appropriate links or fill out a search box to find listings.

But directory searches are less effective when looking for specific information—things like the author of a book, the complete text of the Declaration of Independence or research on drug treatments for a medical condition. For this kind of information, search engines like Hotbot and Alta Vista are the way to go. Because they search an index of keywords drawn by spiders from millions of Web pages, the chances are greater that they will find obscure terms in obscure Web pages.

There's a third kind of search site, one that includes popular sites like Metacrawler, Ask Jeeves and Dogpile. These sites—also called *metasearch* tools—issue search requests to fistfuls of other Web search sites. When Google, Excite, Alta Vista and the like return their results, the metasearch site collects them onto a single Web page for display.

Because no two search sites index exactly the same set of Web pages, metasearch tools give you a wider scope of results—but it's worth remembering that more does not necessarily equal better. What really counts is relevant results that are sorted in a relevant order. And that's the rub.

Simply picking one of two or three types of sites to search from is no guarantee of good results. Brad Hill, the author of *World Wide Web Searching for Dummies* (IDG), says most search sites deliver too much information. "Search engines do a good job on indexing," he said. "But because of that, they deliver more than you want."

So when you're faced with several hundred thousand results over dozens of pages, what should you do? "Don't go past the first page of results," Hill said. "If it doesn't have something of interest, you've probably entered the wrong search string."

Most people could get much more relevant results with a few simple tricks for constructing a search "string"—the words you enter in the search box. The most obvious is to type in several relevant words instead of just one or two. In general, the fewer words you enter, the more general your results will be.

Alta Vista (www.altavista.net) A powerful general search engine with accurate hit data and a standard topical directory. Also a rich portal with lots of links, services, and tools.

Ask Jeeves (www.askjeeves.com) An excellent beginner's metasearch site. Ask Jeeves leads you through simple questions to help narrow your search and simultaneously queries several other search engines for relevant Web pages. Highly user friendly, Ask Jeeves organizes results by topic, source, and relevancy. "Personal Jeeves" tailors news and other data to your interests.

Dogpile (www.dogpile.com) Another metasearch site, Dogpile can go through 20+ Web search engines, dozens of online news services, or other types of sources and sort the results by the engine that found them. While this may not be the most useful presentation if all you want is the facts, it's a good way to check which engine works best for you.

Excite (www.excite.com) Especially good for searches on broad general topics, Excite adds extras like a simultaneous search of the Web, news headlines, sports scores, and company information—and groups relevant results on a single page. Also offers a personalized Start Page.

Google (www.google.com) Fast and reliable, Google is a superior search engine for over 1.3 billion Web pages and has a strong topical index. Known for yielding high-relevance results and few broken links.

Hotbot (www.hotbot.com) Now part of the Lycos network, this search site—powered byInktomi—is an excellent choice for finding specific information. In addition to a thoroughand up-to-date index, it provides an easy interface for constructing precise queries.

Lycos (www.lycos.com) Offers a strong selection of advanced search capabilities, including the ability to find specific media types. Search results, however, are listed first by popularity rather than relevancy, which can be frustrating. The site is a major portal with extensive data and service options which can be personalized in your own home page.

Metacrawler (www.metacrawler.com) Perhaps the leading metasearch site, Metacrawler simultaneously queries Lycos, Excite, Google, and over a dozen other engines, then aggregating the results. It's excellent for getting a quick list of everything that's out there, but its limited search options make it difficult to issue really precise queries.

Northern Light (www.nlsearch.com) In addition to its index of Web pages, Northern Light searches full-text databases—from pay-per-view articles to books and other materials—not available elsewhere. Large indexes, extensive search options, and topical list organization increase the chances of search success and enhance usability.

Yahoo (www.yahoo.com) The world's most popular portal and by many accounts the best directory index for broad general topics, Yahoo is a comprehensive directory of selected Web sites with limited ability to search the contents of individual Web pages. Reliable and easy to use, Yahoo remains an excellent choice for basic research while offering a full slate of customizable services.

▶ **Steps to Smart Searching**

Pick Your Site No one site is good for every search. Search directories like Yahoo and Lycos are good for researching general topics. Search engines like Hotbot and Alta Vista are better for very specific information. Metasearch sites like Dogpile and Metacrawler use more than one search engine.

Use The Phrase That Pays Enter the two words Strawberry Fields in a search box, and you could get results as diverse as W. C. Fields and strawberry shortcake. Yahoo, Alta Vista, Hotbot and others recognize words in quotes—"Strawberry Fields"—as a phrase. Metacrawler and others provide phrase searching as an option.

Use Browser Click Tricks When checking out results, view them in a new browser window so you can quickly return to the results page without clicking the browser's Back button. In most browsers, you can open a link in a new browser window by holding down the Shift key while clicking on the link. And if a page fails to load the first time you click on a link, try clicking again.

Check Your Spelling Many Web sites are riddled with spelling errors, but for the ones that are worth finding, correct spelling helps. Ask Jeeves and Infoseek provide spelling help for the orthographically challenged. Also, vary the styling of terms, so that a search for CD-ROM, for example, will also turn up CDROM or CD ROM.

Cover All the Bases If you're looking for gardening tips, for example, you may need to account for several different words—garden, gardens, gardening, gardener and so on. Infoseek and Lycos handle plurals and word stems automatically. Alta Vista uses a different approach, the wildcard character. Enter garden* and you'll get results on all the different options. Search sites that don't recognize word stems or wildcards need you to think up variants by yourself and search for them all (e.g., garden OR gardening OR gardens).

Ask for Directions Not every search site works the same way, but all of them provide a help section and tips. A couple of minutes spent checking the help pages can pay dividends later.

Don't Stick Around If you don't find what you're looking for in the first couple of results screens, either go back and enter a different set of search terms or move on to another search site.

Take Advantage of the Operators Most search sites use code words or symbols called operators to make searches more precise. The operators vary from site to site, but the common ones are AND, OR, NOT, quotation marks and the plus and minus signs.

How Operators Work "" (quotation marks) enclose words to search for a phrase: *"Strawberry Fields Forever"*

AND connects two or more words, all of which must appear in the results: *Strawberry AND Fields AND Forever*

OR connects two or more search words, any of which may appear in the results: Strawberry Fields OR Strawberryfields

NOT excludes the word after it from the results: *Strawberry Fields NOT W.C.*

- (minus sign), like NOT, excludes the word that follows it: *Strawberry Fields -W.C.*

+ (plus sign) precedes a word that must appear: *+Strawberry +Fields*

Note that it's possible to string together several operators to construct a very precise query. To exclude certain cover versions of a certain song, for example, you could try: *"Strawberry Fields" AND "The Beatles" NOT "Sandy Farina" NOT "Nashville Superpickers"*

Source: Excerpted from *Desperately Seeking Susan OR Suzie NOT Sushi*, by Matt Lake. Reprinted from *The New York Times*, Sept. 3, 1998.

▶ **A WEBSITE DIRECTORY**

The Internet provides users with an ever-expanding world of information and online services in virtually every field of interest. Along with the popular *search engines* and portals described above, the sites listed below may provide the beginnings of your personal index. Explore the sites yourself and add the ones you like to the "Bookmarks" or "Favorites" list in your *browser*.

Computer/Communication Services

CNET (www.cnet.com) An informative and well-designed technology portal. Product reviews, industry news, usage trends. Extensive selection of downloads.

eFax (www.efax.com) A free service that provides private fax numbers. Receive faxes by E-mail; send or forward them for a fee.

ICQ (www.icq.com) Free downloads for private chat anywhere in the world. Leave messages, alert friends to when you're online. Tens of millions of subscribers.

TalkCity (www.talkcity.com) Chat, scheduled chat events, forums, member home pages, celebrity events—a Web community.

ZD Net (www.zdnet.com) Sponsored by Ziff-Davis Interactive, connects to a dozen online computer magazines; also has links, search, shareware.

Entertainment and Learning

Broadcast.com (broadcast.com) Live TV and radio broadcasts, CD jukebox of over 1,000 albums, movie trailers, audio books, and more. RealPlayer plug-in available. Now part of the Yahoo network.

Discovery.com (www.discovery.com) Fun, adventure, and learning for children and adults, from the producers of The Discovery Channel.

Disney.com (www.disney.com) Features games and activities for kids, content for parents, shopping for Disney merchandise.

Electronic Zoo (netvet.wustl.edu/e-zoo.htm) A virtual zoological garden, with extensive animal information, online magazines, links, user groups, and multimedia galore.

How Stuff Works (www.howstuffworks.com) Engaging, clear, informative explanations of common devices and instruments, digital technologies, the human body, natural phenomena.

The Internet Movie Database (www.imbd.com) The biggest and best film resource on the Web, covering more than 200,000 movies, extensive filmographies, and hundreds of thousands of biographical profiles.

Learn2.com (www.learn2.com) Dubbed the "ability utility," this award-winning site provides practical tutorials on everything from knot tying to computer software to academics.

NASA (www.nasa.gov) The largest repository of space-related information on the Net. Rich in photos and the latest scoop on current and future missions, astronauts, etc.

National Geographic (www.nationalgeographic.com) Magazine articles, virtual museum exhibits, lectures, a mini-encyclopedia, and more—for kids and adults.

PBS Online (www.pbs.org) Educational and entertaining media presentations, transcripts, quizzes, learning guides, and more, based on public television programs and documentaries.

Spinner (www.spinner.com) Self-proclaimed "First and Largest Internet Music Service." Offers a RealAudio-based player, 150+ music channels, and 375,000 songs.

Family and Health

America's Doctor (www.americasdoctor.com) A leader in the hot new category of expert sites. Chat online with a real doctor or consult the site's extensive collection of medical reference content.

Genealogy.com (www.genealogy.com) Type in a name, begin your search. Take classes, post queries, find links to other sites. A great place to start a family tree. Subscription.

Healthfinder (www.healthfinder.gov) U.S. government site with thousands of documents, well-organized interface, medical news, databases, and links. A useful gateway.

Health Risk Assessment (www.youfirst.com) Tools and information for in-depth personal health assessment; create a confidential personal profile.

SeniorNet (www.seniornet.com) Online services and information for people over 50. Classes, chat, and more.

SuperFamily (www.superfamily.com) Set up a private Web site that makes it easy for the extended family to stay in touch: share photos, post news, keep birthday and anniversary lists, etc. Subscription.

Finance and Investment

E*Trade (www.etrade.com) The first and leading Internet trading/investment firm. Includes personalized portfolio management and news.

The Motley Fool (www.fool.com) Free, easy-to-understand financial information, including timely stock updates, portfolio tracker, and investor chat boards.

MSN MoneyCentral (moneycentral.msn.com) Portfolio management, stock screening, investment tracking and advice, financial headlines, real-time stock tracker, 401(k) planner, and more.

Quicken.com (quicken.com) Personal finance site, featuring interactive tools to help with insurance, home-loan, tax-preparation, investment, and retirement-planning needs.

TheStreet.com (thestreet.com) Extensive online financial information, including daily market analysis and real-time stock ticker.

General Information/Reference

Britannica.com (www.britannica.com) The entire encyclopedia free, with links to related magazine articles and 125,000 Web sites.

FreeTranslation.com (www.freetranslation.com) Uses the Transparent Language translation engine for free translation of documents or Web pages—English, French, German, Italian, Portuguese, and Spanish.

InfoSpace.com (infospace.com) A rich general reference portal site: white and yellow pages, classifieds, financial information, TV listings, shopping, mapping, and many other directories.

OneLookDictionaries (www.onelook.com) Access to over 600 general and specialized dictionaries.

Virtual Reference Desk (refdesk.com) Vast collection of links to general and topical information sites.

Government

FedStats (www.fedstats.gov) A full range of statistics and information from more than 100 U.S. federal agencies.

Internal Revenue Service (www.irs.gov) Tax forms and instructions, advice, online filing.

The Library of Congress (www.loc.gov) Photos, documents, online exhibits, legislation text, and other resources make this site valuable for serious research or casual enjoyment.

Stamps.com (www.stamps.com) Users download software that allows them to print metered postage stickers from their desktop printers and pay for the cost of postage with a credit card account.

Thomas (thomas.loc.gov) Authoritative, in-depth information on federal legislation, a service of the Library of Congress.

U.S. Census Bureau (www.census.gov) Authoritative, extensive information on U.S. population, demographics, economy, industry and agriculture, education, law enforcement, etc.

The White House (www.whitehouse.gov) Write to the president, read documents and policy statements, take a tour, browse the archives, etc.

Jobs/Career Development

Career Builder (www.careerbuilder.com) Leading career management site for job seekers and employers.

HotJobs (www.hotjobs.com) 3,000 registered recruiters and over 300,000 resumes; no headhunters allowed.

Jobs.com (www.jobs.com) Local job search, resume posting. Extensive listings.

Monster.com (www.monster.com) Online employment services, including job searches by location, a resume database available to recruiters, and online job application. Includes resources for freelancers.

News

ABCNews.com (www.abcnews.com) Headlines, online-only features, videos, instant polls, abundant links. Deep coverage with frequent updates.

BBC Online (www.bbc.co.uk) The vast international resources of BBC's news organization. World news with a unique perspective.

CNN Interactive (cnn.com) Late-breaking news and background: multimedia galleries, in-depth analysis, polls, searchable background material, links. Includes the CNNfn financial news network, and CNNSI, sports coverage with Sports Illustrated.

MSNBC (www.msnbc.com) The most interactive of all the news sites. Includes a personalized news page and compelling polls, chats, and discussions.

The New York Times (www.nytimes.com) Most of the daily paper is available online, as are extensive archives (now for a small fee).

Shopping/Auctions

Alibris (www.alibris.com) Locate use, rare, and hard-to-find books. Millions of titles from a worldwide network of dealers.

Amazon.com (www.amazon.com) The "granddaddy"of consumer online shopping sites, it began with books, then moved into music, video, consumer electronics, and toys. Deep discounts.

Autoweb.com (www.autoweb.com) Online car shopping, with thousands of participating dealers. No-haggle price quotes in 24 hours.

Bibliofind (www.bibliofind.com) Millions of used and rare books, periodicals, and ephemera offered by thousands of booksellers around the world. Search for out-of-print titles. Owned by Amazon.com

eBay (www.ebay.com) The largest online auction site, with millions of items at all times.

Internet Shopping Network (www.isn.com) Find reliable, objective product information and prices for a myriad of items. Search by brand, manufacturer, model number, etc. Specializes in computer products.

MSN CarPoint (www.carpoint.msn.com) Online car shopping service, with 2,000 affiliated dealers and 100,000 used car listings. Personal Auto Pages for tracking your car's service schedule.

Fashion Mall (www.fashionmall.com) Browse the offerings of dozens of top apparel retailers and buy with a single shopping cart.

myGeek.com (www.mygeek.com) Post the item you're looking for and wait for sellers to answer.

MySimon (www.mysimon.com) The largest comparison shopping site on the web, with over 2,000 consumer-goods merchants; includes product information, price comparison, availability.

Priceline.com (www.priceline.com) A popular buying service that asks you what you're willing to pay and seeks providers. Great for airline tickets, car rentals, hotel rooms, and other products.

uBid (www.ubid.com) A central (not person-to-person) online auction house. Great deals on discontinued consumer electronics and computing equipment and more typical auction items.

Sports and Games

CBS SportsLine (cbs.sportsline.com) In-depth, comprehensive, up-to-the-minute coverage. News, multimedia features, personalized information, live celebrity chats, forums, calendars, and numerous links.

ESPNET SportsZone (espn.go.com) Scores, stories, stats, schedules, standings, video, sound. Up-to-the minute analyses and features. Game-Cast lets you follow games on your screen as they happen.

Games Domain (www.gamesdomain.com) One of the Net's largest shareware directory sites, plus reviews, tips, contests, walkthroughs, industry news, and more.

Mplayer.com (www.mplayer.com) A free multiplayer gaming service, with over 11 million monthly visitors and 200 games.

The Sporting News (www.sportingnews.com) Hardcore, in-depth coverage. Analysis by 30 well-known columnists. Abundant stats and links, with customizable team/score reporting.

Sportspages.com (www.sportspages.com) Fresh links to the world's best sports pages.

Travel and Weather

BizTravel.com (www.biztravel.com) A multiple-service site for the busy business traveler, including a detailed personal profile, award-program tracking, rate-finder, booking, etc.

City.net (www.travelexcite.com) Gateway site to Web-based information from and about cities around the world—travel, culture, education, etc. Valuable for trip-planning. Part of the Excite network.

Expedia.com (expedia.com) Makes travel planning easy, from research to booking. Find special deals and unique vacations ideas on the Travel Network. Includes mapping features and a staff of travel agents.

Intellicast (www.intellicast.com) Instant access to local, regional, and worldwide weather; current conditions and forecasts.

National Park Service: ParkNet (www.nps.gov) Click on "Visit Your Parks" link for detailed maps and general information on the U.S. national parks.

National Weather Service (www.nws.noaa.gov) World, national, and regional forecasts—daily and long-term. Includes maps, satellite imagery, specialized data, and abundant links..

Travelocity.com (www.travelocity.com) Owned by Sabre Group, which mainatins the largest worldwide reservation system. Best current fares and packages, E-mail and pager bulletins.

Mapquest.com (www.mapquest.com) Interactive maps and driving directions, customized mapping, and travel information for businesses and consumers.

Part V

AWARDS AND PRIZES
Awards in the Arts and Entertainment

Academy Awards 1928–2000

The "Oscars" are officially known as the Academy of Motion Picture Arts and Sciences Awards. They were inaugurated in 1928 as part of Hollywood's drive to improve its less-than-respectable image. Academy librarian and eventual executive director Margaret Herrick remarked that the statuette looked like her uncle Oscar, and the nickname has stuck ever since. Membership in the Academy (currently over 3,000) is by invitation only, with members divided into 13 branches. Each branch selects up to five nominees for awards in its area of expertise; the entire membership makes "Best Film" nominations and then votes on all the categories. Major awards are shown in the chart. Awards for Best Cinematography and for Best Foreign Language Film are shown in a separate table. Best Directors are named for films winning Best Picture except where otherwise indicated.

Year	Best picture	Best director	Best actor	Best actress	Best supporting actor	Best supporting actress
1928	Wings	Frank Borzage, Seventh Heaven Lewis Milestone, Two Arabian Knights	Emil Jannings, The Way of All Flesh, The Last Command	Janet Gaynor, Seventh Heaven, Sunrise, Street Angel	No Awards Given	No Awards Given
1929	Broadway Melody	Frank Lloyd, The Divine Lady	Warner Baxter, In Old Arizona	Mary Pickford, Coquette	No Awards Given	No Awards Given
1930	All Quiet on the Western Front	Lewis Milestone	George Arliss, Disraeli	Norma Shearer, The Divorcee	No Awards Given	No Awards Given
1931	Cimarron	Norman Taurog, Skippy	Lionel Barrymore, A Free Soul	Marie Dressler, Min and Bill	No Awards Given	No Awards Given
1932	Grand Hotel	Frank Borzage, Bad Girl	Wallace Beery, The Champ Fredric March, Dr. Jekyll and Mr. Hyde	Helen Hayes, The Sin of Madelon Claudet	No Awards Given	No Awards Given
1933	Cavalcade	Frank Lloyd	Charles Laughton, The Private Life of Henry VIII	Katharine Hepburn, Morning Glory	No Awards Given	No Awards Given
1934	It Happened One Night	Frank Capra	Clark Gable, It Happened One Night	Claudette Colbert, It Happened One Night	No Awards Given	No Awards Given
1935	Mutiny on the Bounty	John Ford, The Informer	Victor McLaglen, The Informer	Bette Davis, Dangerous	No Awards Given	No Awards Given
1936	The Great Ziegfeld	Frank Capra, Mr. Deeds Goes to Town	Paul Muni, The Story of Louis Pasteur	Luise Rainer, The Great Ziegfeld	Walter Brennan, Come and Get It	Gale Sondergaard, Anthony Adverse
1937	The Life of Emile Zola	Leo McCarey, The Awful Truth	Spencer Tracy, Captains Courageous	Luise Rainer, The Good Earth	Joseph Schildkraut, The Life of Emile Zola	Alice Brady, In Old Chicago
1938	You Can't Take It With You	Frank Capra	Spencer Tracy, Boys Town	Bette Davis, Jezebel	Walter Brennan, Kentucky	Fay Bainter, Jezebel
1939	Gone With the Wind	Victor Fleming	Robert Donat, Goodbye, Mr. Chips	Vivien Leigh, Gone With the Wind	Thomas Mitchell, Stagecoach	Hattie McDaniel, Gone With the Wind
1940	Rebecca	John Ford, The Grapes of Wrath	James Stewart, The Philadelphia Story	Ginger Rogers, Kitty Foyle	Walter Brennan, The Westerner	Jane Darwell, The Grapes of Wrath
1941	How Green Was My Valley	John Ford	Gary Cooper, Sergeant York	Joan Fontaine, Suspicion	Donald Crisp, How Green Was My Valley	Mary Astor, The Great Lie

Year	Best picture	Best director	Best actor	Best actress	Best supporting actor	Best supporting actress
1942	Mrs. Miniver	William Wyler	James Cagney, Yankee Doodle Dandy	Greer Garson, Mrs. Miniver	Van Heflin, Johnny Eager	Teresa Wright, Mrs. Miniver
1943	Casablanca	Michael Curtiz	Paul Lukas, Watch On The Rhine	Jennifer Jones, The Song of Bernadette	Charles Coburn, The More the Merrier	Katina Paxinou, For Whom the Bell Tolls
1944	Going My Way	Leo McCarey	Bing Crosby, Going My Way	Ingrid Bergman, Gaslight	Barry Fitzgerald, Going My Way	Ethel Barrymore, None But the Lonely Heart
1945	The Lost Weekend	Billy Wilder	Ray Milland, The Lost Weekend	Joan Crawford, Mildred Pierce	James Dunn, A Tree Grows in Brooklyn	Anne Revere, National Velvet
1946	The Best Years of Our Lives	William Wyler	Fredric March, The Best Years of Our Lives	Olivia De Havilland, To Each His Own	Harold Russell, The Best Years of Our Lives	Anne Baxter, The Razor's Edge
1947	Gentleman's Agreement	Elia Kazan	Ronald Colman, A Double Life	Loretta Young, The Farmer's Daughter	Edmund Gwenn, Miracle on 34th Street	Celeste Holm, Gentleman's Agreement
1948	Hamlet	John Huston, The Treasure of the Sierra Madre	Laurence Olivier, Hamlet	Jane Wyman, Johnny Belinda	Walter Huston, The Treasure of the Sierra Madre	Claire Trevor, Key Largo
1949	All the King's Men	Joseph L. Mankiewicz, A Letter to Three Wives	Broderick Crawford, All the King's Men	Olivia De Havilland, The Heiress	Dean Jagger, Twelve O'Clock High	Mercedes McCambridge, All the King's Men
1950	All About Eve	Joseph L. Mankiewicz	José Ferrer, Cyrano de Bergerac	Judy Holliday, Born Yesterday	George Sanders, All About Eve	Josephine Hull, Harvey
1951	An American in Paris	George Stevens, A Place in the Sun	Humphrey Bogart, The African Queen	Vivien Leigh, A Streetcar Named Desire	Karl Malden, A Streetcar Named Desire	Kim Hunter, A Streetcar Named Desire
1952	The Greatest Show on Earth	John Ford, The Quiet Man	Gary Cooper, High Noon	Shirley Booth, Come Back, Little Sheba	Anthony Quinn, Viva Zapata!	Gloria Grahame, The Bad and the Beautiful
1953	From Here to Eternity	Fred Zinnemann	William Holden, Stalag 17	Audrey Hepburn, Roman Holiday	Frank Sinatra, From Here to Eternity	Donna Reed, From Here to Eternity
1954	On the Waterfront	Elia Kazan	Marlon Brando, On the Waterfront	Grace Kelly, The Country Girl	Edmond O'Brien, The Barefoot Contessa	Eva Marie Saint, On the Waterfront
1955	Marty	Delbert Mann	Ernest Borgnine, Marty	Anna Magnani, The Rose Tattoo	Jack Lemmon, Mister Roberts	Jo Van Fleet, East of Eden
1956	Around the World in 80 Days	George Stevens, Giant	Yul Brynner, The King And I	Ingrid Bergman, Anastasia	Anthony Quinn, Lust for Life	Dorothy Malone, Written on the Wind
1957	The Bridge on the River Kwai	David Lean	Alec Guinness, The Bridge on the River Kwai	Joanne Woodward, The Three Faces of Eve	Red Buttons, Sayonara	Miyoshi Umeki, Sayonara
1958	Gigi	Vincente Minnelli	David Niven, Separate Tables	Susan Hayward, I Want to Live!	Burl Ives, The Big Country	Wendy Hiller, Separate Tables
1959	Ben-Hur	William Wyler	Charlton Heston, Ben-Hur	Simone Signoret, Room at the Top	Hugh Griffith, Ben-Hur	Shelley Winters, The Diary of Anne Frank
1960	The Apartment	Billy Wilder	Burt Lancaster, Elmer Gantry	Elizabeth Taylor, Butterfield 8	Peter Ustinov, Spartacus	Shirley Jones, Elmer Gantry
1961	West Side Story	Jerome Robbins, Robert Wise	Maximilian Schell, Judgment At Nuremberg	Sophia Loren, Two Women	George Chakiris, West Side Story	Rita Moreno, West Side Story
1962	Lawrence of Arabia	David Lean	Gregory Peck, To Kill a Mockingbird	Anne Bancroft, The Miracle Worker	Ed Begley, Sweet Bird of Youth	Patty Duke, The Miracle Worker
1963	Tom Jones	Tony Richardson	Sidney Poitier, Lilies of the Field	Patricia Neal, Hud	Melvyn Douglas, Hud	Margaret Rutherford, The V.I.P.s

Year	Best picture	Best director	Best actor	Best actress	Best supporting actor	Best supporting actress
1964	My Fair Lady	George Cukor	Rex Harrison, My Fair Lady	Julie Andrews, Mary Poppins	Peter Ustinov, Topkapi	Lila Kedrova, Zorba the Greek
1965	The Sound of Music	Robert Wise	Lee Marvin, Cat Ballou	Julie Christie, Darling	Martin Balsam, A Thousand Clowns	Shelley Winters, A Patch of Blue
1966	A Man for All Seasons	Fred Zinnemann	Paul Scofield, A Man for All Seasons	Elizabeth Taylor, Who's Afraid of Virginia Woolf?	Walter Matthau, The Fortune Cookie	Sandy Dennis, Who's Afraid of Virginia Woolf?
1967	In the Heat of the Night	Mike Nichols, The Graduate	Rod Steiger, In the Heat of the Night	Katharine Hepburn, Guess Who's Coming to Dinner	George Kennedy, Cool Hand Luke	Estelle Parsons, Bonnie and Clyde
1968	Oliver!	Carol Reed	Cliff Robertson, Charly	Katharine Hepburn, The Lion in Winter, Barbra Streisand, Funny Girl	Jack Albertson, The Subject Was Roses	Ruth Gordon, Rosemary's Baby
1969	Midnight Cowboy	John Schlesinger	John Wayne, True Grit	Maggie Smith, The Prime of Miss Jean Brodie	Gig Young, They Shoot Horses, Don't They?	Goldie Hawn, Cactus Flower
1970	Patton	Franklin J. Schaffner	George C. Scott, Patton	Glenda Jackson, Women in Love	John Mills, Ryan's Daughter	Helen Hayes, Airport
1971	The French Connection	William Friedkin	Gene Hackman, The French Connection	Jane Fonda, Klute	Ben Johnson, The Last Picture Show	Cloris Leachman, The Last Picture Show
1972	The Godfather	Bob Fosse, Cabaret	Marlon Brando, The Godfather	Liza Minnelli, Cabaret	Joel Grey, Cabaret	Eileen Heckart, Butterflies Are Free
1973	The Sting	George Roy Hill	Jack Lemmon, Save the Tiger	Glenda Jackson, A Touch of Class	John Houseman, The Paper Chase	Tatum O'Neal, Paper Moon
1974	The Godfather, Part II	Francis Ford Coppola	Art Carney, Harry And Tonto	Ellen Burstyn, Alice Doesn't Live Here Anymore	Robert De Niro, The Godfather, Part II	Ingrid Bergman, Murder on the Orient Express
1975	One Flew Over the Cuckoo's Nest	Milos Forman	Jack Nicholson, One Flew Over the Cuckoo's Nest	Louise Fletcher, One Flew Over the Cuckoo's Nest	George Burns, The Sunshine Boys	Lee Grant, Shampoo
1976	Rocky	John G. Avildsen	Peter Finch, Network	Faye Dunaway, Network	Jason Robards, All the President's Men	Beatrice Straight, Network
1977	Annie Hall	Woody Allen	Richard Dreyfuss, The Goodbye Girl	Diane Keaton, Annie Hall	Jason Robards, Julia	Vanessa Redgrave, Julia
1978	The Deer Hunter	Michael Cimino	Jon Voight, Coming Home	Jane Fonda, Coming Home	Christopher Walken, The Deer Hunter	Maggie Smith, California Suite
1979	Kramer vs. Kramer	Robert Benton	Dustin Hoffman, Kramer vs. Kramer	Sally Field, Norma Rae	Melvyn Douglas, Being There	Meryl Streep, Kramer vs. Kramer
1980	Ordinary People	Robert Redford	Robert De Niro, Raging Bull	Sissy Spacek, Coal Miner's Daughter	Timothy Hutton, Ordinary People	Mary Steenburgen, Melvin and Howard
1981	Chariots of Fire	Warren Beatty, Reds	Henry Fonda, On Golden Pond	Katharine Hepburn, On Golden Pond	John Gielgud, Arthur	Maureen Stapleton, Reds
1982	Gandhi	Richard Attenborough	Ben Kingsley, Gandhi	Meryl Streep, Sophie's Choice	Louis Gossett Jr., An Officer and a Gentleman	Jessica Lange, Tootsie
1983	Terms of Endearment	James L. Brooks	Robert Duvall, Tender Mercies	Shirley MacLaine, Terms of Endearment	Jack Nicholson, Terms of Endearment	Linda Hunt, The Year of Living Dangerously

Year	Best picture	Best director	Best actor	Best actress	Best supporting actor	Best supporting actress
1984	Amadeus	Milos Forman	F. Murray Abraham, Amadeus	Sally Field, Places in the Heart	Haing S. Ngor, The Killing Fields	Peggy Ashcroft, A Passage to India
1985	Out of Africa	Sydney Pollack	William Hurt, Kiss of the Spider Woman	Geraldine Page, The Trip to Bountiful	Don Ameche, Cocoon	Anjelica Huston, Prizzi's Honor
1986	Platoon	Oliver Stone	Paul Newman, The Color of Money	Marlee Matlin, Children of a Lesser God	Michael Caine, Hannah and Her Sisters	Dianne Wiest, Hannah and Her Sisters
1987	The Last Emperor	Bernardo Bertolucci	Michael Douglas, Wall Street	Cher, Moonstruck	Sean Connery, The Untouchables	Olympia Dukakis, Moonstruck
1988	Rain Man	Barry Levinson	Dustin Hoffman, Rain Man	Jodie Foster, The Accused	Kevin Kline, A Fish Called Wanda	Geena Davis, The Accidental Tourist
1989	Driving Miss Daisy	Oliver Stone, Born on the Fourth of July	Daniel Day-Lewis, My Left Foot	Jessica Tandy, Driving Miss Daisy	Denzel Washington, Glory	Brenda Fricker, My Left Foot
1990	Dances with Wolves	Kevin Costner	Jeremy Irons, Reversal of Fortune	Kathy Bates, Misery	Joe Pesci, Goodfellas	Whoopi Goldberg, Ghost
1991	The Silence of the Lambs	Jonathan Demme	Anthony Hopkins, The Silence of the Lambs	Jodie Foster, The Silence of the Lambs	Jack Palance, City Slickers	Mercedes Ruehl, The Fisher King
1992	Unforgiven	Clint Eastwood	Al Pacino, Scent of a Woman	Emma Thompson, Howard's End	Gene Hackman, Unforgiven	Marisa Tomei, My Cousin Vinny
1993	Schindler's List	Steven Spielberg	Tom Hanks, Philadelphia	Holly Hunter, The Piano	Tommy Lee Jones, The Fugitive	Anna Paquin, The Piano
1994	Forrest Gump	Robert Zemeckis	Tom Hanks, Forrest Gump	Jessica Lange, Blue Sky	Martin Landau, Ed Wood	Dianne Wiest, Bullets Over Broadway
1995	Braveheart	Mel Gibson	Nicolas Cage Leaving Las Vegas	Susan Sarandon, Dead Man Walking	Kevin Spacey, The Usual Suspects	Mira Sorvino, Mighty Aphrodite
1996	The English Patient	Anthony Minghella	Geoffrey Rush, Shine	Frances McDormand, Fargo	Cuba Gooding Jr., Jerry Maguire	Juliette Binoche, The English Patient
1997	Titanic	James Cameron	Jack Nicholson, As Good as it Gets	Helen Hunt, As Good as it Gets	Robin Williams Good Will Hunting	Kim Basinger, L.A. Confidential
1998	Shakespeare in Love	Steven Spielberg, Saving Private Ryan	Roberto Benigni Life is Beautiful	Gwyneth Paltrow, Shakespeare in Love	James Coburn, Affliction	Judi Dench, Shakespeare in Love
1999	American Beauty	Sam Mendes	Kevin Spacey, American Beauty	Hilary Swank Boys Don't Cry	Michael Caine, The Cider House Rules	Angelina Jolie, Girl, Interrupted
2000	Gladiator	Steven Soderbergh, Traffic	Russell Crowe, Gladiator	Julia Roberts, Erin Brockovich	Benicio Del Toro, Traffic	Marcia Gay Harden, Pollock

Source: Academy of Motion Picture Arts & Sciences. www. oscar.org

Academy Awards for Cinematography, 1928–2000

Year	Cinematographer, Film	Year	Cinematographer, Film
1928	Charles Rosher, Karl Struss, Sunrise	1935	Hal Mohr, A Midsummer Night's Dream
1929	Clyde DeVinna, White Shadows, In the South Seas	1936	Gaetano Gaudio, Anthony Adverse
		1937	Karl Freund, The Good Earth
1930	Joseph T. Rucker, Willard Van Der Veer, With Byrd at the South Pole	1938	Joseph Ruttenberg, The Great Waltz
1931	Floyd Crosby, Tabu	1939	Gregg Toland, Wuthering Heights
1932	Lee Garmes, Shanghai Express		Ernest Haller, Ray Rennahan, Gone With the Wind
1933	Charles Bryant Lang Jr., A Farewell to Arms	1940	George Barnes, Rebecca
1934	Victor Milner, Cleopatra		George Perinal, Thief of Baghdad

Year	Cinematographer, Film	Year	Cinematographer, Film
1941	Arthur Miller, *How Green Was My Valley*		Freddie Young, *Lawrence of Arabia*
	Ernest Palmer, Ray Rennahan, *Blood & Sand*	1963	James Wong Howe, *Hud*
1942	Joseph Ruttenberg, *Mrs. Miniver*		Leon Shamroy, *Cleopatra*
	Leon Shamroy, *The Black Swan*	1964	Walter Lassally, *Zorba the Greek*
1943	Arthur Miller, *The Song of Bernadette*		Harry Stradling, *My Fair Lady*
	Hal Mohr, W. Howard Greene, *The Phantom of the Opera*	1965	Ernest Laszlo, *Ship of Fools*
			Freddie Young, *Dr. Zhivago*
1944	Joseph LaShelle, *Laura*	1966	Haskell Wexler, *Who's Afraid of Virginia Woolf?*
	Leon Shamroy, *Wilson*		Ted Moore, *A Man for All Seasons*
1945	Harry Stradling, *The Picture of Dorian Gray*	1967	Burnett Guffey, *Bonnie and Clyde*
	Leon Shamroy, *Leave Her to Heaven*	1968	Pasqualino De Santis, *Romeo and Juliet*
1946	Arthur Miller, *Anna and the King of Siam*	1969	Conrad Hall, *Butch Cassidy and the Sundance Kid*
	Charles Rosher, Leonard Smith, Arthur Arling, *The Yearling*	1970	Freddie Young, *Ryan's Daughter*
1947	Guy Green, *Great Expectations*	1971	Oswald Morris, *Fiddler on the Roof*
1948	William Daniels, *The Naked City*	1972	Geoffrey Unsworth, *Cabaret*
	Joseph Valentine, William V. Skall, Winton Hoch, *Joan of Arc*	1973	Sven Nykvist, *Cries and Whispers*
		1974	Fred Koenekamp, Joseph Biroc, *The Towering Inferno*
1949	Paul C. Vogel, *Battleground*		
	Winton Hoch, *She Wore a Yellow Ribbon*	1975	John Alcott, *Barry Lyndon*
1950	Robert Krasker, *The Third Man*	1976	Haskell Wexler, *Bound for Glory*
	Robert Surtees, *King Solomon's Mines*	1977	Vilmos Zsigmond, *Close Encounters of the Third Kind*
1951	William C. Mellor, *A Place in the Sun*		
	Alfred Gilks, John Alton (ballet), *An American in Paris*	1978	Nestor Almendros, *Days of Heaven*
		1979	Vittorio Storaro, *Apocalypse Now*
1952	Robert Surtees, *The Bad and the Beautiful*	1980	Geoffrey Unsworth, Ghislain Cloquet, *Tess*
	Winton Hoch, Archie Stout, *The Quiet Man*	1981	Vittorio Storaro, *Reds*
1953	Burnett Guffey, *From Here to Eternity*	1982	Billy Williams, Ronnie Taylor, *Gandhi*
	Loyal Griggs, *Shane*	1983	Sven Nykvist, *Fanny & Alexander*
1954	Boris Kaufman, *On the Waterfront*	1984	Chris Menges, *The Killing Fields*
	Milton Krasner, *Three Coins in the Fountain*	1985	David Watkin, *Out of Africa*
1955	James Wong Howe, *The Rose Tattoo*	1986	Chris Menges, *The Mission*
	Robert Burks, *To Catch a Thief*	1987	Vittorio Storaro, *The Last Emperor*
1956	Joseph Ruttenberg, *Sombody Up There Likes Me*	1988	Peter Biziou, *Mississippi Burning*
		1989	Freddie Francis, *Glory*
	Lionel Lindon, *Around the World in 80 Days*	1990	Dean Semler, *Dances With Wolves*
1957	Jack Hildyard, *The Bridge on the River Kwai*	1991	Robert Richardson, *JFK*
1958	Sam Leavitt, *The Defiant Ones*	1992	Philippe Rousselot, *A River Runs Through It*
	Joseph Ruttenberg, *Gigi*	1993	Janusz Kaminski, *Schindler's List*
1959	William C. Mellor, *The Diary of Anne Frank*	1994	John Toll, *Legends of the Fall*
	Robert L. Surtees, *Ben-Hur*	1995	John Toll, *Braveheart*
1960	Freddie Francis, *Sons and Lovers*	1996	John Seale, *The English Patient*
	Russell Metty, *Spartacus*	1997	Russell Carpenter, *Titanic*
1961	Eugene Shuftan, *The Hustler*	1998	Janusz Kaminski, *Saving Private Ryan*
	Daniel L. Fapp, *West Side Story*	1999	Conrad L. Hall, *American Beauty*
1962	Jean Bourgoin, Walter Wottitz, *The Longest Day*	2000	Peter Pau, *Crouching Tiger, Hidden Dragon*

Academy Awards for Best Foreign Language Film, 1956–2000

Year	Film, Country	Director	Year	Film, Country	Director
1956	*La Strada*, Italy	Federico Fellini	1967	*Closely Watched Trains*, Czechoslovakia	Jiri Menzel
1957	*The Nights of Cabiria*, Italy	Federico Fellini			
1958	*Mon Oncle*, France	Jacques Tati	1968	*War and Peace*, USSR	Sergei Bondarchuk
1959	*Black Orpheus*, France/Italy/Brazil	Marcel Camus			
			1969	*Z*, France/Algeria	Constantin Costa-Gavras
1960	*The Virgin Spring*, Sweden	Ingmar Bergman	1970	*Investigation of a Citizen Above Suspicion*, Italy	Elio Petri
1961	*Through A Glass Darkly*, Sweden	Ingmar Bergman	1971	*The Garden of the Finzi-Continis*, Italy	Vittorio de Sica
1962	*Sundays and Cybele*, France	Serge Bourgignon	1972	*The Discreet Charm of the Bourgeoisie*, France	Luis Buñuel
1963	*8½*, Italy	Federico Fellini			
1964	*Yesterday, Today, and Tomorrow*, Italy/France	Vittorio de Sica	1973	*Day For Night*, France/Italy	François Truffaut
			1974	*Amarcord*, Italy/France	Federico Fellini
1965	*The Shop on Main Street*, Czechoslovakia	Jan Kadar	1975	*Dersu Uzala*, USSR/Japan	Akira Kurosawa
1966	*A Man and a Woman* France	Claude Lelouch	1976	*Black and White in Color*, France/Switzerland/Ivory Coast	Jean-Jacques Annaud

Year	Film, Country	Director	Year	Film, Country	Director
1977	*Madame Rosa,* France	Moshe Mizrahi	1989	*Cinema Paradiso,* Italy	Giuseppe
1978	*Get Out Your Handkerchiefs,*	Bertrand Blier			Tornatore
	France		1990	*Journey of Hope,* Switzerland	Xavier Koller
1979	*The Tin Drum,* Germany	Volker	1991	*Mediterraneo,* Italy	Gabriel
		Scholondorff			Salvatores
1980	*Moscow Does Not Believe*	Vladimir	1992	*Indochine,* France	Regis Wargnier
	in Tears, USSR	Menshov	1993	*Belle Époque,* Spain	Fernando
1981	*Mephisto,* Austria/ Germany/	Istvan Szabo			Trueba
	Hungary		1994	*Burnt by the Sun,* Russia	Nikita
1982	*To Begin Again,* Spain	Jose Luis Garcia			Mikhalkov
1983	*Fanny and Alexander,*	Ingmar	1995	*Antonia's Line,* Netherlands	Marlene Gorris
	Sweden	Bergman	1996	*Kolya,* Czech Republic	Jan Sverak
1984	*Dangerous Moves,* France	Richard Dembo	1997	*Character,* Netherlands	Mike van Diem
1985	*The Official Story,* Argentina	Luis Puenzo	1998	*Life is Beautiful,* Italy	Roberto Benigni
1986	*The Assault,* Netherlands	Fons	1999	*All About My Mother,*	Pedro
		Rademakers		Spain	Almodóvar
1987	*Babette's Feast,* Denmark	Gabriel Axel	2000	*Crouching Tiger, Hidden*	Ang Lee
1988	*Pelle the Conqueror,*	Bille August		*Dragon,* China	
	Denmark				

Cannes Film Festival Best Film Awards, 1946–2001

The Festival International du Film was first held in 1946. The official name for the best film award was the Grand Prix (1949–54, 1964–74) and the Palme d'Or (1955–63, 1975–present)

Year	Film and director	Year	Film and director
1946	*La Bataille du Rail,* René Clément[1]	1976	*Taxi Driver,* Martin Scorsese
1949[2]	*The Third Man,* Carol Reed	1977	*Padre Padrone,* Paolo and Vittorio Taviani
1951	*Miracle in Milan,* Vittorio De Sica	1978	*The Tree of Wooden Clogs,* Ermanno Olmi
	Miss Julie, Alf Sjöberg	1979	*The Tin Drum,* Volker Schlöndorff
1952	*Two Cents Worth of Hope,* Renato Castellani	1980	*Kagemusha,* Akira Kurosawa
	Othello, Orson Welles	1981	*Man of Iron,* Andrzej Wajda
1953	*The Wages of Fear,* Georges Clouzot	1982	*Missing,* Costa-Gavras
1954	*Gate of Hell,* Teinosuke Kinugasa		*Yol,* Yilmar Güney
1955	*Marty,* Delbert Mann	1983	*The Ballad of Narayama,* Shohei Imamura
1956	*The Silent World,* Jacques Cousteau, Louis Malle	1984	*Paris, Texas,* Wim Wenders
1957	*Friendly Persuasion,* William Wyler	1985	*When Father Was Away on Business,*
1958	*The Cranes are Flying,* Mikhail Kalatozov		Emir Kusturica
1959	*Black Orpheus,* Marcel Camus	1986	*The Mission,* Roland Joffé
1960	*La Dolce Vita,* Federico Fellini	1987	*Under Satan's Sun,* Maurice Pialat
1961	*Viridiana,* Luis Buñuel	1988	*Pelle the Conqueror,* Bille August
1962	*The Given Word,* Anselmo Duarte	1989	*sex, lies and videotape,* Steven Soderbergh
1963	*The Leopard,* Luchino Visconti	1990	*Wild at Heart,* David Lynch
1964	*The Umbrellas of Cherbourg,* Jacques Demy	1991	*Barton Fink,* Joel Coen
1965	*The Knack, and How to Get It,* Richard Lester	1992	*The Best Intentions,* Bille August
1966	*A Man and a Woman,* Claude Lelouch	1993	*The Piano,* Jane Campion
1967	*Blow-Up,* Michelangelo Antonioni		*Farewell My Concubine,* Chen Kaige
1969	*If . . . ,* Lindsay Anderson	1994	*Pulp Fiction,* Quentin Tarantino
1970	*M*A*S*H,* Robert Altman	1995	*Underground,* Emir Kusturica
1971	*The Go-Between,* Joseph Losey	1996	*Secrets and Lies,* Mike Leigh
1972	*The Working Class Goes to Heaven,* Elio Petri	1997	*Taste of Cherries,* Abbas Kiarostami
	The Mattei Affair, Francesco Rosi		*Unagi (The Eel),* Shohei Imamura
1973	*Scarecrow,* Jerry Schatzberg	1998	*Eternity and a Day,* Theo Angelopoulos
	The Hireling, Alan Bridges	1999	*Rosetta,* Jean-Pierre and Luc Dardenne
1974	*The Conversation,* Francis Ford Coppola	2000	*Dancer in the Dark,* Lars von Trier
1975	*Chronique des Années de Braise,*	2001	*The Son's Room,* Nanni Moretti
	M. Lakhdar Hamina		

1. Winner of the International Jury Prize. 2. In 1947, there was no "best film" award as such, but prizes were given instead to outstanding works in several categories, including "Psychological and Love Films," "Adventure and Police Films," and so on. The festival was cancelled in 1948 and 1950. **Source:** www.festival-cannes.org.

American Film Institute Life Achievement Awards, 1973–2001

Awarded to individuals whose "talent has fundamentally advanced the art of American film or television . . . and whose work has withstood the test of time."

Year	Recipient	Year	Recipient	Year	Recipient	Year	Recipient
1973	John Ford	1981	Fred Astaire	1989	Gregory Peck	1997	Martin Scorsese
1974	James Cagney	1982	Frank Capra	1990	David Lean	1998	Robert Wise
1975	Orson Welles	1983	John Huston	1991	Kirk Douglas	1999	Dustin Hoffman
1976	William Wyler	1984	Lillian Gish	1992	Sidney Poitier	2000	Harrison Ford
1977	Henry Fonda	1985	Gene Kelly	1993	Elizabeth Taylor	2001	Barbra Streisand
1978	Bette Davis	1986	Billy Wilder	1994	Jack Nicholson		
1979	Alfred Hitchcock	1987	Barbara Stanwyck	1995	Steven Spielberg		
1980	James Stewart	1988	Jack Lemmon	1996	Clint Eastwood		

Source: American Film Institute. www.afionline.org

The National Film Registry

In 1988, the Library of Congress established the National Film Preservation Board to preserve 25 films each year to add to a National Film Registry. Films selected must be culturally, historically, or aesthetically significant, and they must be at least 10 years old. Films are not limited to Hollywood movie releases; they include documentaries and other noncommercial films such as the Abraham Zapruder film of John F. Kennedy's assassination.

Film (Year)	Film (Year)	Film (Year)
Adam's Rib (1949)	Citizen Kane (1941)	42nd Street (1933)
The Adventures of Robin Hood (1938)	The City (1939)	The Four Horsemen of the Apocalypse (1921)
The African Queen (1951)	City Lights (1931)	Frank Film (1973)
All About Eve (1950)	Civilization (1916)	Frankenstein (1931)
All Quiet on the Western Front (1930)	The Conversation (1974)	Freaks (1932)
All That Heaven Allows (1955)	Cops (1922)	The Freshman (1925)
American Graffiti (1973)	A Corner in Wheat (1909)	From the Manger to the Cross (1912)
An American in Paris (1951)	The Cool World (1963)	Fury (1936)
Annie Hall (1977)	The Crowd (1928)	The General (1927)
The Apartment (1960)	Czechoslovakia 1968 (1968)	Gerald McBoing Boing (1951)
Apocalypse Now (1979)	David Holzman's Diary (1968)	Gertie the Dinosaur (1914)
The Awful Truth (1937)	The Day the Earth Stood Still (1951)	Gigi (1958)
Badlands (1973)	Dead Birds (1964)	The Godfather (1972)
The Band Wagon (1953)	The Deer Hunter (1978)	The Godfather, Part II (1974)
The Bank Dick (1940)	Destry Rides Again (1939)	The Gold Rush (1925)
The Battle of San Pietro (1945)	Detour (1946)	Gone With the Wind (1939)
Ben-Hur (1926)	Do the Right Thing (1989)	Goodfellas (1990)
The Best Years of Our Lives (1946)	The Docks of New York (1928)	The Graduate (1967)
Big Business (1929)	Dodsworth (1936)	The Grapes of Wrath (1940)
The Big Parade (1925)	Dog Star Man (1964)	Grass (1925)
The Big Sleep (1946)	Don't Look Back (1967)	The Great Dictator (1940)
The Birth of a Nation (1915)	Double Indemnity (1944)	The Great Train Robbery (1903)
The Black Pirate (1926)	Dr. Strangelove (or, How I	Greed (1924)
Blacksmith Scene (1893)	Learned To Stop Worrying and	Gun Crazy (1949)
Blade Runner (1982)	Love the Bomb) (1964)	Gunga Din (1939)
The Blood of Jesus (1941)	Dracula (1931)	Harlan County, U.S.A. (1976)
Bonnie and Clyde (1967)	Duck Amuck (1953)	Harold and Maude (1972)
Bride of Frankenstein (1935)	Duck Soup (1933)	The Heiress (1949)
The Bridge on the River Kwai (1957)	E.T. The Extra-Terrestrial (1982)	Hell's Hinges (1916)
Bringing Up Baby (1938)	Easy Rider (1969)	Hindenburg disaster footage (1937)
Broken Blossoms (1919)	Eaux d'artifice (1953)	High School (1968)
Cabaret (1972)	El Norte (1983)	High Noon (1952)
Carmen Jones (1954)	The Emperor Jones (1933)	His Girl Friday (1940)
Casablanca (1942)	The Exploits of Elaine (1914)	The Hitch-hiker (1953)
Castro Street (1966)	The Fall of the House of Usher (1928)	Hospital (1970)
Cat People (1942)	Fantasia (1940)	The Hospital (1971)
Chan Is Missing (1982)	Fatty's Tintype Tangle (1915)	How Green Was My Valley (1941)
The Cheat (1915)	Five Easy Pieces (1970)	How the West Was Won (1962)
Chinatown (1974)	Flash Gordon Serial (1936)	The Hustler (1961)
Chulas Fronteras (1976)	Footlight Parade (1933)	I Am a Fugitive From a Chain Gang (1932)
	Force of Evil (1948)	
	The Forgotten Frontier (1931)	

Film (Year)	Film (Year)	Film (Year)
The Immigrant (1917)	The Music Box (1932)	Shock Corridor (1963)
In the Land of the Head-hunters (1914)	My Darling Clementine (1946)	The Shop Around the Corner (1940)
Intolerance (1916)	My Man Godfrey (1936)	Show Boat (1936)
Invasion of the Body Snatchers (1956)	The Naked Spur (1953)	Singin' in the Rain (1952)
It Happened One Night (1934)	Nanook of the North (1922)	Sky High (1922)
It's A Wonderful Life (1946)	Nashville (1975)	Snow White (1933)
The Italian (1915)	Network (1976)	Snow White and the Seven Dwarfs (1937)
Jammin' the Blues (1944)	A Night at the Opera (1935)	Some Like it Hot (1959)
Jazz on a Summer's Day (1959)	The Night of the Hunter (1955)	Stagecoach (1939)
The Jazz Singer (1927)	Night of the Living Dead (1968)	A Star is Born (1954)
Killer of Sheep (1977)	Ninotchka (1939)	Star Wars (1977)
King: A Filmed Record. . . Montgomery to Memphis (1970)	North by Northwest (1959)	Steamboat Willie (1928)
King Kong (1933)	Nothing but a Man (1964)	A Streetcar Named Desire (1951)
The Kiss (1896)	On the Waterfront (1954)	Sullivan's Travels (1941)
Kiss Me Deadly (1955)	One Flew Over the Cuckoo's Nest (1975)	Sunrise (1927)
Knute Rockne, All American (1940)	Out of the Past (1947)	Sunset Boulevard (1950)
Koyaanisqatsi (1983)	The Ox-Bow Incident (1943)	Sweet Smell of Success (1957
The Lady Eve (1941)	The Outlaw Josey Wales (1976)	Tabu (1931)
Lambchops (1929)	Pass the Gravy (1928)	Tacoma Narrows Bridge Collapse (1940)
The Land Beyond the Sunset (1912)	Paths of Glory (1957)	The Tall T (1957)
Lassie Come Home (1943)	Peter Pan (1924)	Taxi Driver (1976)
The Last of the Mohicans (1920)	Phantom of the Opera (1925)	The Ten Commandments (1956)
The Last Picture Show (1972)	The Philadelphia Story (1940)	Tevye (1939)
Laura (1944)	Pinocchio (1940)	The Thief of Bagdad (1924)
Lawrence of Arabia (1962)	A Place in the Sun (1951)	The Thin Man (1934)
The Learning Tree (1969)	The Plow that Broke the Plains (1936)	To Be or Not to Be (1942)
Let's All Go to the Lobby (1957)	Point of Order (1964)	To Fly (1976)
Letter From an Unknown Woman (1948)	The Poor Little Rich Girl (1917)	To Kill a Mockingbird (1962)
The Life and Death of 9413—a Hollywood Extra (1927)	Porky in Wackyland (1938)	Tootsie (1982)
The Life and Times of Rosie the Riveter (1980)	Powers of Ten (1978)	Top Hat (1935)
The Life of Emile Zola (1937)	President McKinley Inauguation Footage (1901)	Topaz (home movie footage taken at Japanese-American internment camp, the Topaz War Relocation Authority Center) (1943–45)
Little Caesar (1930)	Primary (1960)	Touch of Evil (1958)
The Little Fugitive (1953)	The Prisoner of Zenda (1937)	Trance and Dance in Bali (1938-39)
Little Miss Marker (1934)	The Producers (1968)	The Treasure of the Sierra Madre (1948)
The Living Desert (1953)	Psycho (1960)	Trouble in Paradise (1932)
The Lost World (1925)	The Public Enemy (1931)	Tulips Shall Grow (1942)
Louisiana Story (1948)	Pull My Daisy (1959)	Twelve O'Clock High (1949)
Love Finds Andy Hardy (1938)	Raging Bull (1980)	2001: A Space Odyssey (1968)
Love Me Tonight (1932)	Raiders of the Lost Ark (1981)	Verbena Tragica (1939)
M*A*S*H (1970)	Rear Window (1954)	Vertigo (1958)
Magical Maestro (1952)	Rebel Without a Cause (1955)	West Side Story (1961)
The Magnificent Ambersons (1942)	Red River (1948)	Westinghouse Works, 1904 (1904)
The Maltese Falcon (1941)	Regeneration (1915)	What's Opera, Doc? (1957)
The Manchurian Candidate (1962)	Republic Steel Strike Riot Newsreel Footage (1937)	Where Are My Children? (1916)
Manhatta (1921)	Return of the Secaucus 7 (1980)	Why We Fight (series) (1943-45)
March of Time: Inside Nazi Germany—1938 (1938)	Ride the High Country (1962)	The Wild Bunch (1969)
Marty (1955)	Rip van Winkle (1896)	Will Success Spoil Rock Hunter? (1957)
Master Hands (1936)	The River (1937)	The Wind (1928)
Mean Streets (1973)	Road to Morocco (1942)	Wings (1927)
Meet Me in St. Louis (1944)	Roman Holiday (1953)	Within Our Gates (1920)
Meshes of the Afternoon (1943)	Safety Last (1923)	The Wizard of Oz (1939)
Midnight Cowboy (1969)	Salesman (1969)	Woman of the Year (1942)
Mildred Pierce (1945)	Salome (1922)	A Woman Under the Influence (1974)
Modern Times (1936)	Salt of the Earth (1954)	Woodstock (1970)
Modesta (1956)	Scarface (1932)	Yankee Doodle Dandy (1942)
Morocco (1930)	The Searchers (1956)	Zapruder film (1963)
Motion Painting No. 1 (1947)	Seventh Heaven (1927)	
A Movie (1958)	Shadow of a Doubt (1943)	
Mr. Smith Goes to Washington (1939)	Shadows (1959)	
Multiple Sidosis (1970)	Shaft (197__)	
	Shane (1953)	
	She Done Him Wrong (1933)	
	Sherlock, Jr. (1924)	
	Sherman's March (1986)	

The Emmy Awards, 1951–2000

The Academy of Television Arts and Sciences, formed in 1946, presented the first Emmy Awards in 1949. The number and names of awards have changed over the years, but since 1965, the Academy has recognized an outstanding comedy and drama, as well as an actor and an actress in a comedy and in a drama.

Year	Comedy	Drama	Comedy Actor	Comedy Actress	Drama Actor	Drama Actress
1951	The Red Skelton Show (CBS)	Studio One (CBS)	Sid Caesar (NBC)	Imogene Coca (NBC)	(1)	(1)
1952	I Love Lucy (CBS)	Robert Montgomery Presents (NBC)	Thomas Mitchell	Helen Hayes	(1)	(1)
1953	I Love Lucy (CBS)	The U.S. Steel Hour (ABC)	Donald O'Connor, Colgate Comedy Hour (NBC)	Eve Arden, Our Miss Brooks (CBS)	(1)	(1)
1954	Make Room for Daddy (ABC)	The U.S. Steel Hour (ABC)	Danny Thomas, Make Room for Daddy (ABC)	Loretta Young, The Loretta Young Show (NBC)	(1)	(1)
1955	The Phil Silvers Show (CBS)	Producers' Showcase (NBC)	Phil Silvers, The Phil Silvers Show (CBS)	Lucille Ball, I Love Lucy (CBS)	(1)	(1)
1956	The Phil Silvers Show (CBS)	Requiem for a Heavyweight (CBS)	Sid Caesar, Caesar's Hour (NBC)	Nanette Fabray, Caesar's Hour (NBC)	Robert Young, Father Knows Best (NBC)	Loretta Young, The Loretta Young Show (NBC)
1957	The Phil Silvers Show (CBS)	Gunsmoke (CBS)	Robert Young, Father Knows Best (NBC)	Jane Wyatt, Father Knows Best (NBC)	(1)	(1)
1958 –59	The Jack Benny Show (CBS)	(2)	Jack Benny, The Jack Benny Show (CBS)	Jane Wyatt, Father Knows Best (NBC and CBS)	Raymond Burr, Perry Mason (CBS)	Loretta Young, The Loretta Young Show (NBC)
1959 –60	"Art Carney Special" (NBC)	Playhouse 90 (CBS)	Robert Stack, The Untouchables (ABC)	Jane Wyatt, Father Knows Best (CBS)	(1)	(1)
1960 –61	The Jack Benny Show (CBS)	"Macbeth," Hallmark Hall of Fame (NBC)	Raymond Burr, Perry Mason (CBS)	Barbara Stanwyck, The Barbara Stanwyck Show (NBC)	(1)	(1)
1961 –62	The Bob Newhart Show (CBS)	The Defenders (CBS)	E.G. Marshall, The Defenders (CBS)	Shirley Booth, Hazel (NBC)	(1)	(1)
1962 –63	The Dick Van Dyke Show (CBS)	The Defenders (CBS)	E.G. Marshall, The Defenders (CBS)	Shirley Booth, Hazel (NBC)	(1)	(1)
1963 –64	The Dick Van Dyke Show (CBS)	The Defenders (CBS)	Dick Van Dyke, The Dick Van Dyke Show (CBS)	Mary Tyler Moore, The Dick Van Dyke Show (CBS)	(1)	(1)
1964 –65	(3)	(3)	(3)	(3)	(3)	(3)
1965 –66	The Dick Van Dyke Show (CBS)	The Fugitive (ABC)	Dick Van Dyke, The Dick Van Dyke Show (CBS)	Mary Tyler Moore, The Dick Van Dyke Show (CBS)	Bill Cosby, I Spy (NBC)	Barbara Stanwyck, The Big Valley (ABC)
1966 –67	The Monkees (NBC)	Mission: Impossible (CBS)	Don Adams, Get Smart (NBC)	Lucille Ball, The Lucy Show (CBS)	Bill Cosby, I Spy (NBC)	Barbara Bain, Mission: Impossible (CBS)
1967 –68	Get Smart (NBC)	Mission: Impossible (CBS)	Don Adams, Get Smart (NBC)	Lucille Ball, The Lucy Show (CBS)	Bill Cosby, I Spy (NBC)	Barbara Bain, Mission: Impossible (CBS)
1968 –69	Get Smart (NBC)	NET Playhouse (NET)	Don Adams, Get Smart (NBC)	Hope Lange, The Ghost and Mrs. Muir (NBC)	Carl Betz, Judd for the Defense (ABC)	Barbara Bain, Mission: Impossible (CBS)
1969 –70	My World & Welcome to It (NBC)	Marcus Welby, M.D. (ABC)	William Windom, My World & Welcome to It (NBC)	Hope Lange, The Ghost and Mrs. Muir (ABC)	Robert Young, Marcus Welby, M.D. (ABC)	Susan Hampshire The Forsyte Saga (NET)

Year	Comedy	Drama	Comedy Actor	Comedy Actress	Drama Actor	Drama Actress
1970 –71	All in the Family (CBS)	The Senator (segment), The Bold Ones (NBC)	Jack Klugman, The Odd Couple (ABC)	Jean Stapleton, All in the Family (CBS)	Hal Holbrook, The Senator (segment), The Bold Ones (NBC)	Susan Hampshire, The First Churchills (PBS)
1971 –72	All in the Family (CBS)	"Elizabeth R" Masterpiece Theatre (PBS)	Carroll O'Connor, All in the Family (CBS)	Jean Stapleton, All in the Family (CBS)	Peter Falk, Columbo (NBC)	Glenda Jackson, "Elizabeth R" Masterpiece Theatre (PBS)
1972 –73	All in the Family (CBS)	The Waltons (CBS)	Jack Klugman, The Odd Couple (ABC)	Mary Tyler Moore, The Mary Tyler Moore Show (CBS)	Richard Thomas, The Waltons (CBS)	Michael Learned, The Waltons (CBS)
1973 –74	M*A*S*H (CBS)	"Upstairs, Downstairs," Masterpiece Theatre (PBS)	Alan Alda, M*A*S*H (CBS)	Mary Tyler Moore, The Mary Tyler Moore Show (CBS)	Telly Savalas, Kojak (CBS)	Michael Learned, The Waltons (CBS)
1974 –75	The Mary Tyler Moore Show (CBS)	"Upstairs, Downstairs," Masterpiece Theatre (PBS)	Tony Randall, The Odd Couple (ABC)	Valerie Harper, Rhoda (CBS)	Robert Blake, Baretta (ABC)	Jean Marsh, "Upstairs, Downstairs," Masterpiece Theater (PBS)
1975 –76	The Mary Tyler Moore Show (CBS)	Police Story (NBC)	Jack Albertson, Chico & the Man (NBC)	Mary Tyler Moore, The Mary Tyler Moore Show (CBS)	Peter Falk, Columbo (NBC)	Michael Learned, The Waltons (CBS)
1977 –78	All in the Family (CBS)	The Rockford Files (NBC)	Carroll O'Connor, All in the Family (CBS)	Jean Stapleton, All in the Family (CBS)	Edward Asner, Lou Grant (CBS)	Sada Thompson, Family (ABC)
1978 –79	Taxi (ABC)	Lou Grant (CBS)	Carroll O'Connor, All in the Family (CBS)	Ruth Gordon, Taxi (ABC)	Ron Leibman, Kaz (CBS)	Mariette Hartley, The Incredible Hulk (CBS)
1979 –80	Taxi (ABC)	Lou Grant (CBS)	Richard Mulligan, Soap (ABC)	Cathryn Damon, Soap (ABC)	Ed Asner, Lou Grant (CBS)	Barbara Bel Geddes, Dallas (CBS)
1980 –81	Taxi (ABC)	Hill Street Blues (NBC)	Judd Hirsch, Taxi (ABC)	Isabel Sanford, The Jeffersons (CBS)	Daniel Travanti, Hill Street Blues (NBC)	Barbara Babcock Hill Street Blues (NBC)
1981 –82	Barney Miller (ABC)	Hill Street Blues (NBC)	Alan Alda, M*A*S*H (CBS)	Carol Kane, Taxi (ABC)	Daniel Travanti, Hill Street Blues (NBC)	Michael Learned, Nurse (CBS)
1982 –83	Cheers (NBC)	Hill Street Blues (NBC)	Judd Hirsch, Taxi (NBC)	Shelley Long, Cheers (NBC)	Ed Flanders, St. Elsewhere (NBC)	Tyne Daly, Cagney &Lacey (CBS)
1983 –84	Cheers (NBC)	Hill Street Blues (NBC)	John Ritter, Three's Company (ABC)	Jane Curtin, Kate & Allie (CBS)	Tom Selleck, Magnum P.I. (CBS)	Tyne Daly, Cagney &Lacey (CBS)
1984 –85	The Cosby Show (NBC)	Cagney & Lacey (CBS)	Robert Guillaume, Benson (ABC)	Jane Curtin, Kate & Allie (CBS)	William Daniels, St. Elsewhere (NBC)	Tyne Daly, Cagney &Lacey (CBS)
1985 –86	The Golden Girls (NBC)	Cagney & Lacey (CBS)	Michael J. Fox, Family Ties (NBC)	Betty White, The Golden Girls (NBC)	William Daniels, St. Elsewhere (NBC)	Sharon Gless, Cagney &Lacey (CBS)
1986 –87	The Golden Girls (NBC)	L.A. Law (NBC)	Michael J. Fox, Family Ties (NBC)	Rue McClanahan, The Golden Girls (NBC)	Bruce Willis, Moonlighting (ABC)	Sharon Gless, Cagney &Lacey (CBS)
1987 –88	The Wonder Years (ABC)	thirtysomething (ABC)	Michael J. Fox, Family Ties (NBC)	Beatrice Arthur, The Golden Girls (NBC)	Richard Kiley, A Year in the Life (NBC)	Tyne Daly, Cagney &Lacey (CBS)
1988 –89	Cheers (NBC)	L.A. Law (NBC)	Richard Mulligan, Empty Nest (NBC)	Candice Bergen, Murphy Brown (CBS)	Carroll O'Connor, In the Heat of the Night (NBC)	Dana Delany, China Beach, (ABC)
1989 –90	Murphy Brown (CBS)	L.A. Law (NBC)	Ted Danson, Cheers (NBC)	Candice Bergen, Murphy Brown (CBS)	Peter Falk, Columbo (ABC)	Patricia Wettig, thirtysomething (ABC)

Year	Comedy	Drama	Comedy Actor	Comedy Actress	Drama Actor	Drama Actress
1990 –91	Cheers (NBC)	L.A. Law (NBC)	Burt Reynolds, Evening Shade (CBS)	Kirstie Alley, Cheers (NBC)	James Earl Jones, Gabriel's Fire (ABC)	Patricia Wettig, thirtysomething (ABC)
1991 –92	Murphy Brown (CBS)	Northern Exposure (CBS)	Craig T. Nelson, Coach (ABC)	Candice Bergen, MurphyBrown (CBS)	Christopher Lloyd, Avonlea (Disney)	Dana Delany, China Beach, (ABC)
1992 –93	Seinfeld (NBC)	Picket Fences (CBS)	Ted Danson, Cheers (NBC)	Roseanne Arnold, Roseanne (ABC)	Tom Skerritt, Picket Fences (CBS)	Kathy Baker, Picket Fences (CBS)
1993 –94	Frasier (NBC)	Picket Fences (CBS)	Kelsey Grammer, Frasier (NBC)	Candice Bergen, Murphy Brown (CBS)	Dennis Franz, NYPD Blue (ABC)	Sela Ward, Sisters (NBC)
1994 –95	Frasier (NBC)	NYPD Blue (ABC)	Kelsey Grammer, Frasier (NBC)	Candice Bergen, Murphy Brown (CBS)	Mandy Patinkin, Chicago Hope (CBS)	Kathy Baker, Picket Fences (CBS)
1995 –96	Frasier (NBC)	E.R. (NBC)	John Lithgow, Third Rock From the Sun (NBC)	Helen Hunt, Mad About You (NBC)	Dennis Franz, NYPD Blue (ABC)	Kathy Baker, Picket Fences (CBS)
1996 –97	Frasier (NBC)	Law & Order (NBC)	John Lithgow, Third Rock From the Sun (NBC)	Helen Hunt, Mad About You (NBC)	Dennis Franz, NYPD Blue (ABC)	Gillian Anderson, The X-Files (FOX)
1997 –98	Frasier (NBC)	The Practice (ABC)	Kelsey Grammer, Frasier (NBC)	Helen Hunt, Mad About You (NBC)	Andre Braugher, Homicide (NBC)	Christine Lahti, Chicago Hope (CBS)
1998 –99	Ally McBeal (FOX)	The Practice (ABC)	John Lithgow, Third Rock From the Sun (NBC)	Helen Hunt, Mad About You (NBC)	Dennis Franz, NYPD Blue (ABC)	Edie Falco, The Sopranos (HBO)
1999 –2000	Will and Grace (NBC)	The West Wing (NBC)	Michael J. Fox, Spin City (ABC)	Patricia Heaton, Everybody Loves Raymond (CBS)	James Gandolfini, The Sopranos (HBO)	Sela Ward, Once and Again (ABC)
2000 –01[4]	—	—	—			

Notes: 1. Before 1965, the Academy did always not give separate acting awards for comedy and drama. 2. *Playhouse 90* (CBS) was best drama of one hour or longer; *Alcoa-Goodyear Theatre* (NBC) was best drama of less than one hour. 3. In 1964, the Academy gave acting awards to Dick Van Dyke for *The Dick Van Dyke Show* (CBS), Lynn Fontaine and Alfred Lunt for *"The Magnificent Yankee" Hallmark Hall of Fame* (NBC), and Barbra Streisand for *My Name is Barbra* (CBS). It also gave Achievements in Entertainment awards to these programs 4. The 2001 Emmy Awards presentation was cancelled after the U.S. began military action in Afghanistan. At press time, winners had not yet been announced. www.emmys.tv

Emmy Awards for Variety Shows, 1951–2000

Year	Show	Year	Show
1951	Your Show of Shows (NBC)	1976–77	Van Dyke & Company (NBC)
1952	Your Show of Shows (NBC)	1977–78	The Muppet Show (syndicated)
1953	Omnibus (CBS)	1978–79	"Steve & Eydie Celebrate Irving Berlin" (NBC)
1954	Disneyland (ABC)	1979–80	"IBM Presents Baryshnikov on Broadway" (ABC)
1955	The Ed Sullivan Show (CBS)	1980–81	"Lily: Sold Out "(CBS)
1956	Caesar's Hour (NBC)	1981–82	"Night of 100 Stars" (ABC)
1957	The Dinah Shore Show (NBC)	1982–83	"Motown 25: Yesterday, Today, Forever" (NBC)
1958–59	The Dinah Shore Chevy Show (NBC)	1983–84	"The 6th Annual Kennedy Center Honors" (CBS)
1959–60	"The Fabulous '50s" (CBS)	1984–85	"Motown Returns to the Apollo" (NBC)
1960–61	"Astaire Time" (NBC)	1985–86	"The Kennedy Center Honors" (CBS)
1962–63	The Andy Williams Show (NBC)	1986–87	"The 1987 Tony Awards" (CBS)
1963–64	The Danny Kaye Show (CBS)	1987–88	"Irving Berlin's 100th Birthday Celebration" (CBS)
1964–65	My Name is Barbra (CBS).	1988–89	The Tracey Ullman Show (FOX)
1965–66	The Andy Williams Show (NBC)	1989–90	In Living Color (FOX)
1966–67	The Andy Williams Show (NBC)	1990–91	"The 63rd Annual Academy Awards" (ABC)
1967–68	Rowan & Martin's Laugh-In (NBC)	1991–92	The Tonight Show Starring Johnny Carson (NBC)
1968–69	Rowan & Martin's Laugh-In (NBC)	1992–93	Saturday Night Live (NBC)
1969–70	The David Frost Show (syndicated)	1993–94	Late Show with David Letterman (CBS)
1970–71	The Flip Wilson Show (NBC)	1994–95	The Tonight Show with Jay Leno (NBC)
1971–72	Music: The Carol Burnett Show (CBS) Talk: The Dick Cavett Show (ABC)	1995–96	Dennis Miller Live (HBO)
		1996–97	Tracey Takes On . . . (HBO)
1972–73	The Julie Andrews Hour (ABC)	1997–98	Late Show with David Letterman (CBS)
1973–74	The Carol Burnett Show (CBS)	1998–99	Late Show with David Letterman (CBS)
1974–75	The Carol Burnett Show (CBS)	1999-2000	Late Show with David Letterman (CBS)
1975–76	NBC's Saturday Night (NBC)		

Source: Academy of Television Arts and Sciences. www.emmys.tv

The Tony Awards, 1947-2000

The Tony Awards are presented each year by the American Theatre Wing for distinguished achievement in the Broadway theater. Named for Antoinette Perry, an actress, producer, director, and chairman of the American Theatre Wing who died in 1946, the Tonys were first presented in 1947. Awards are given to performers, authors, producers, directors, composers, and choreographers, and scenic, costume, and lighting designers. Listed here is a selection of major awards for each year: best play (author), performance by an actor in a play, performance by an actress in a play, best musical (composer and lyricist), performance by an actor in a musical, performance by an actress in a musical. In 2001, *The Producers* won 12 Tony Awards, breaking the previous record of 10 set by *Hello, Dolly!* in 1964.

PLAYS

Year	Best Play	Best Actor	Best Actress
1947	no award	José Ferrer, *Cyrano de Bergerac* Fredric March, *Years Ago*	Ingrid Bergman, *Joan of Lorraine* Helen Hayes, *Happy Birthday*
1948	*Mister Roberts,* Thomas Heggen and Joshua Logan	Henry Fonda, *Mister Roberts* Paul Kelly, *Command Decision* Basil Rathbone, *The Heiress*	Judith Anderson, *Medea;* Katharine Cornell, *Antony and Cleopatra;* Jessica Tandy, *A Streetcar Named Desire*
1949	*Death of a Salesman,* Arthur Miller	Rex Harrison, *Anne of the Thousand Days*	Martita Hunt, *The Madwoman of Chaillot*
1950	*The Cocktail Party,* T. S. Eliot	Sidney Blackmer, *Come Back, Little Sheba*	Shirley Booth, *Come Back, Little Sheba*
1951	*The Rose Tattoo,* Tennessee Williams	Claude Rains, *Darkness at Noon*	Uta Hagen, *The Country Girl*
1952	*The Fourposter,* Jan de Hartog	José Ferrer, *The Shrike*	Julie Harris, *I Am a Camera*
1953	*The Crucible,* Arthur Miller	Tom Ewell, *The Seven Year Itch*	Shirley Booth, *Time of the Cuckoo*
1954	*The Teahouse of the August Moon,* John Patrick	David Wayne, *The Teahouse of the August Moon*	Audrey Hepburn, *Ondine*
1955	*The Desperate Hours,* Joseph Hayes	Alfred Lunt, *Quadrille*	Nancy Kelly, *The Bad Seed*
1956	*The Diary of Anne Frank,* Frances Goodrich and Albert Hackett	Paul Muni, *Inherit the Wind*	Julie Harris, *The Lark*
1957	*Long Day's Journey Into Night,* Eugene O'Neill	Fredric March, *Long Day's Journey Into Night*	Margaret Leighton, *Separate Tables*
1958	*Sunrise at Campobello,* Dore Schary	Ralph Bellamy, *Sunrise at Campobello*	Helen Hayes, *Time Remembered*
1959	*J.B.,* Archibald Macleish	Jason Robards, *The Disenchanted*	Gertrude Berg, *A Majority of One*
1960	*The Miracle Worker,* William Gibson	Melvyn Douglas, *The Best Man*	Anne Bancroft, *The Miracle Worker*
1961	*Becket,* Jean Anouilh	Zero Mostel, *Rhinoceros*	Joan Plowright, *A Taste of Honey*
1962	*A Man for All Seasons,* Robert Bolt	Paul Scofield, *A Man for All Seasons*	Margaret Leighton, *Night of the Iguana*
1963	*Who's Afraid of Virginia Woolf,* Edward Albee	Arthur Hill, *Who's Afraid of Virginia Woolf*	Uta Hagen, *Who's Afraid of Virginia Woolf*
1964	*Luther,* John Osborne	Alec Guiness, *Dylan*	Sandy Dennis, *Any Wednesday*
1965	*The Subject Was Roses,* Frank Gilroy	Walter Matthau, *The Odd Couple*	Irene Worth, *Tiny Alice*
1966	*Marat/Sade,* Peter Weiss	Hal Holbrook, *Mark Twain Tonight!*	Rosemary Harris, *The Lion in Winter*
1967	*The Homecoming,* Harold Pinter	Paul Rogers, *The Homecoming*	Beryl Reid, *The Killing of Sister George*
1968	*Rosencrantz and Guildenstern Are Dead,* Tom Stoppard	Martin Balsam, *You Know I Can't Hear You When the Water's Running*	Zoe Caldwell, *The Prime of Miss Jean Brodie*
1969	*The Great White Hope,* Howard Sackler	James Earl Jones, *The Great White Hope*	Julie Harris, *Forty Carats*
1970	*Borstal Boy,* Frank McMahon	Fritz Weaver, *Child's Play*	Tammy Grimes, *Private Lives (R)*
1971	*Sleuth,* Anthony Shaffer	Brian Bedford, *The School for Wives*	Maureen Stapleton, *Gingerbread Lady*
1972	*Sticks and Bones,* David Rabe	Cliff Gorman, *Lenny*	Sada Thompson, *Twigs*
1973	*That Championship Season,* Jason Miller	Alan Bates, *Butley*	Julie Harris, *The Last of Mrs. Lincoln*
1974	*The River Niger,* Joseph A. Walker	Michael Moriarty, *Find Your Way Home*	Colleen Dewhurst, *A Moon for the Misbegotten (R)*
1975	*Equus,* Peter Shaffer	John Kani, *Sizwe Banzi Is Dead* Winston Ntshona, *The Island*	Ellen Burstyn, *Same Time, Next Year*
1976	*Travesties,* Tom Stoppard	John Wood, *Travesties*	Irene Worth, *Sweet Bird of Youth (R)*

Year	Best Play	Best Actor	Best Actress
1977	The Shadow Box, Michael Cristofer	Al Pacino, The Basic Training of Pavlo Hummel	Julie Harris, The Belle of Amherst
1978	Da, Hugh Leonard	Barnard Hughes, Da	Jessica Tandy, The Gin Game
1979	The Elephant Man, Bernard Pomerance	Tom Conti, Whose Life Is It Anyway?	Constance Cummings, Wings Carole Shelley, The Elephant Man
1980	Children of a Lesser God, Mark Medoff	John Rubinstein, Children of a Lesser God	Phyllis Frelich, Children of a Lesser God
1981	Amadeus, Peter Shaffer	Ian McKellen, Amadeus	Jane Lapotaire, Piaf
1982	The Life and Adventures of Nicholas Nickleby, David Edgar	Roger Rees, The Life and Adventures of Nicholas Nickleby	Zoe Caldwell, Medea (R)
1983	Torch Song Trilogy, Harvey Fierstein	Harvey Fierstein, Torch Song Trilogy	Jessica Tandy, Foxfire
1984	The Real Thing, Tom Stoppard	Jeremy Irons, The Real Thing	Glenn Close, The Real Thing
1985	Biloxi Blues, Neil Simon	Derek Jacobi, Much Ado About Nothing (R)	Stockard Channing, Joe Egg (R)
1986	I'm Not Rappaport, Herb Gardner	Judd Hirsch, I'm Not Rappaport	Lily Tomlin, The Search for Signs of Intelligent Life in the Universe
1987	Fences, August Wilson	James Earl Jones, Fences	Linda Lavin, Broadway Bound
1988	M. Butterfly, David Henry Hwang	Ron Silver, Speed-The-Plow	Joan Allen, Burn This
1989	The Heidi Chronicles, Wendy Wasserstein	Philip Bosco, Lend Me a Tenor	Pauline Collins, Shirley Valentine
1990	The Grapes of Wrath, Frank Galati	Robert Morse, Tru	Maggie Smith, Lettice and Lovage
1991	Lost in Yonkers, Neil Simon	Nigel Hawthorne, Shadowlands	Mercedes Ruhl, Lost in Yonkers
1992	Dancing at Lughnasa, Brian Friel	Judd Hirsch, Conversations with My Father	Glenn Close, Death and the Maiden
1993	Angels in America: Millennium Approaches, Tony Kushner	Ron Leibman, Angels in America: Millennium Approaches	Madeline Kahn, The Sisters Rosensweig
1994	Angels in America: Perestroika, Tony Kushner	Stephen Spinella, Angels in America: Perestroika	Diana Rigg, Medea (R)
1995	Love! Valour! Compassion!, Terrence McNally	Ralph Fiennes, Hamlet	Cherry Jones, The Heiress
1996	Master Class, Terrence McNally	George Grizzard, A Delicate Balance (R)	Zoe Caldwell, Master Class
1997	Last Night of Ballyhoo, Alfred Uhry	Christopher Plummer, Barrymore	Janet McTeer, A Doll's House
1998	Art, Yasmina Reza	Anthony La Paglia, A View From the Bridge	Marie Mullen, The Beauty Queen of Leenane
1999	Side Man, Warren Leight	Brian Dennehy, Death of a Salesman	Judi Dench, Amy's View
2000	Copenhagen, Michael Frayn	Stephen Dillane, The Real Thing	Jennifer Ehle, The Real Thing
2001	Proof, David Auburn	Richard Easton, The Invention of Love	Mary-Louise Parker, Proof

MUSICALS

Year	Best Musical	Best Actor	Best Actress
1947	no award	no award	no award
1948	no award	Paul Hartman, Angel in the Wings	Grace Hartman, Angel in the Wings
1949	Kiss Me Kate, Cole Porter (M&L)	Ray Bolger, Where's Charley?	Nanette Fabray, Love Life
1950	South Pacific, Richard Rodgers (M), Oscar Hammerstein (L)	Ezio Pinza, South Pacific	Mary Martin, South Pacific
1951	Guys and Dolls, Frank Loesser (M&L)	Robert Alda, Guys and Dolls	Ethel Merman, Call Me Madam
1952	The King and I, Richard Rodgers (M), Oscar Hammerstein (L)	Phil Silvers, Top Banana	Gertrude Lawrence, The King and I
1953	Wonderful Town, Leonard Bernstein (M), Betty Comden and Adolph Green (L)	Thomas Mitchell, Hazel Flagg	Rosalind Russell, Wonderful Town
1954	Kismet, Alexander Borodin (M), adapted by Robert Wright and George Forrest (L)	Alfred Drake, Kismet	Dolores Gray, Carnival in Flanders
1955	The Pajama Game, Richard Adler and Jerry Ross (M&L)	Walter Slezak, Fanny	Mary Martin, Peter Pan
1956	Damn Yankees, Richard Adler and Jerry Ross (M&L)	Ray Walston, Damn Yankees	Gwen Verdon, Damn Yankees
1957	My Fair Lady, Frederick Loewe (M), Alan Jay Lerner (L)	Rex Harrison, My Fair Lady	Judy Holliday, Bells Are Ringing

Year	Best Musical	Best Actor	Best Actress
1958	*The Music Man,* Meredith Willson (M&L)	Robert Preston, *The Music Man*	(tie) Thelma Ritter, Gwen Verdon, *New Girl in Town*
1959	*Redhead,* Albert Hague (M), Dorothy Fields (L)	Richard Kiley, *Redhead*	Gwen Verdon, *Redhead*
1960	(tie) *Fiorello,* Jerry Bock (M), Sheldon Harnick (L); *The Sound of Music,* Richard Rodgers (M), Oscar Hammerstein (L)	Jackie Gleason, *Take Me Along*	Mary Martin, *The Sound of Music*
1961	*Bye, Bye, Birdie,* Charles Strouse (M), Lee Adams (L)	Richard Burton, *Camelot*	Elizabeth Seal, *Irma la Douce*
1962	*How to Succeed in Business Without Really Trying,* Frank Loesser (M&L)	Robert Morse, *How to Succeed in Business Without Really Trying*	(tie) Anna Maria Alberghetti, *Carnival;* Diahann Carroll, *No Strings*
1963	*A Funny Thing Happened on the Way to the Forum,* Stephen Sondheim (M&L)	Zero Mostel, *A Funny Thing Happened on the Way to the Forum,*	Vivien Leigh, *Tovarich*
1964	*Hello, Dolly!* Jerry Herman (M&L)	Bert Lahr, *Foxy*	Carol Channing, *Hello, Dolly!*
1965	*Fiddler on the Roof,* Jerry Bock (M), Sheldon Harnick (L)	Zero Mostel, *Fiddler on the Roof*	Liza Minnelli, *Flora, the Red Menace*
1966	*Man of La Mancha,* Mitch Leigh (M), Joe Darion (L)	Richard Kiley, *Man of La Mancha*	Angela Lansbury, *Mame*
1967	*Cabaret,* John Kander (M), Fred Ebb (L)	Robert Preston, *I Do! I Do!*	Barbara Harris, *The Apple Tree*
1968	*Hallelujah, Baby!* Jule Styne (M), Betty Comden & Adolph Green (L)	Robert Goulet, *The Happy Time*	Patricia Routledge, *Darling of the Day* Leslie Uggams, *Hallelujah, Baby!*
1969	*1776,* Sherman Edwards (M&L)	Jerry Orbach, *Promises, Promises*	Angela Lansbury, *Dear World*
1970	*Applause,* Charles Strouse (M), Lee Adams (L)	Cleavon Little, *Purlie*	Lauren Bacall, *Applause*
1971	*Company,* Stephen Sondheim (M&L)	Hal Linden, *The Rothschilds*	Helen Gallagher, *No, No Nannette (R)*
1972	*Two Gentlemen of Verona* [best score: *Follies,* Stephen Sondheim (M&L)]	Phil Silvers, *A Funny Thing Happened on the Way to the Forum (R)*	Alexis Smith, *Follies*
1973	*A Little Night Music,* Stephen Sondheim (M&L)	Ben Vereen, *Pippin*	Glynis Johns, *A Little Night Music*
1974	*Raisin,* [best score: *Gigi,* Frederick Loewe (M), Alan Jay Lerner (L)]	Christopher Plummer, *Cyrano*	Virginia Capers, *Raisin*
1975	*The Wiz,* Charlie Smalls (M&L)	John Cullum, *Shenandoah*	Angela Lansbury, *Gypsy (R)*
1976	*A Chorus Line,* Marvin Hamlisch (M), Edward Kleban (L)	George Rose, *My Fair Lady (R)*	Donna McKechnie, *A Chorus Line*
1977	*Annie,* Charles Strouse (M), Martin Charnin (L)	Barry Bostwick, *The Robber Bridegroom*	Dorothy Loudon, *Annie*
1978	*Ain't Misbehavin'* [best score: *On the Twentieth Century,* Cy Coleman (M) Betty Comden and Adolph Green (L)]	John Cullum, *On the Twentieth Century*	Liza Minnelli, *The Act*
1979	*Sweeney Todd,* Stephen Sondheim	Len Cariou, *Sweeney Todd*	Angela Lansbury, *Sweeney Todd*
1980	*Evita,* Andrew Lloyd Webber (M), Tim Rice (L)	Jim Dale, *Barnum*	Patti LuPone, *Evita*
1981	*42nd Street,* [best score: *Woman of the Year,* John Kander (M), Fred Ebb (L)]	Kevin Kline, *The Pirates of Penzance*	Lauren Bacall, *Woman of the Year*
1982	*Nine,* Maury Yeston (M&L)	Ben Harney, *Dreamgirls*	Jennifer Holliday, *Dreamgirls*
1983	*Cats,* Andrew Lloyd Webber (M), T.S. Eliot (L)	Tommy Tune, *My One and Only*	Natalia Makarova, *On Your Toes*
1984	*La Cage Aux Folles,* Jerry Herman (M&L)	George Hearn, *La Cage Aux Folles*	Chita Rivera, *The Rink*
1985	*Big River,* Roger Miller (M&L)	No award	No award
1986	*The Mystery of Edwin Drood,* Rupert Holmes (M&L)	George Rose, *The Mystery of Edwin Drood*	Bernadette Peters, *Song and Dance*
1987	*Les Misérables,* Claude-Michel Schönberg (M); Herbert Kretzmer & Alain Boublil (L)	Robert Lindsay, *Me and My Girl*	Maryann Plunkett, *Me and My Girl*
1988	*The Phantom of the Opera* [best score: *Into the Woods,* Stephen Sondheim (M&L)]	Michael Crawford, *The Phantom of the Opera*	Joanna Gleason, *Into the Woods*
1989	*Jerome Robbins' Broadway* [best score: no award]	Jason Alexander, *Jerome Robbins' Broadway*	Ruth Brown, *Black and Blue*
1990	*City of Angels,* Cy Coleman (M) David Zippel (L)	James Naughton, *City of Angels*	Tyne Daly, *Gypsy (R)*

Year	Best Musical	Best Actor	Best Actress
1991	*The Will Rogers Follies,* Cy Coleman (M); Betty Comden and Adolph Green (L)	Jonathan Pryce, *Miss Saigon*	Lea Salonga, *Miss Saigon*
1992	*Crazy for You,* [best score: *Falsettos,* William Finn (M&L)]	Gregory Hines, *Jelly's Last Jam*	Faith Prince, *Guys and Dolls* (R)
1993	*Kiss of the Spider Woman* [best score: (tie) *Kiss of the Spider Woman,* John Kander (M) and Fred Ebb (L)' *Tommy,* Pete Townshend (M&L)]	Brent Carver, *Kiss of the Spider Woman*	Chita Rivera, *Kiss of the Spider Woman*
1994	*Passion,* Stephen Sondheim (M&L)	Boyd Gaines, *She Loves Me* (R)	Donna Murphy, *Passion*
1995	*Sunset Boulevard,* Andrew Lloyd Webber (M&L)	Matthew Broderick, *How to Succeed in Business Without Really Trying* (R)	Glenn Close, *Sunset Boulevard*
1996	*Rent,* Jonathan Larson (M&L)	Nathan Lane, *A Funny Thing Happened on the Way to the Forum* (R)	Donna Murphy, *The King and I* (R)
1997	*Titanic,* Maury Yeston (M&L)	James McNaughton, *Chicago* (R)	Bebe Neuwirth, *Chicago* (R)
1998	*The Lion King,* [best score: *Ragtime,* Stephen Flaherty & Lynn Ahrens (M&L)]	Alan Cumming, *Cabaret* (R)	Natasha Richardson, *Cabaret* (R)
1999	*Fosse,* [best score: *Parade,* Jason Robert Brown (M&L)]	Martin Short, *Little Me*	Bernadette Peters, *Annie Get Your Gun* (R)
2000	*Contact* [best score: *Aida,* Elton John (M) and Tim Rice (L)]	Brian Stokes Mitchell, *Kiss Me Kate*	Heather Headley, *Aida*
2001	*The Producers,* Mel Brooks (M&L)	Nathan Lane, *The Producers*	Christine Ebersole, *42nd Street* (R)

M = music; L = lyrics, R = revival. **Note:** Since 1971 "Musical" and "Score" have been separate categories. However, the winner of the Tony for Best Musical usually wins the award for Best Score, except where otherwise indicated.

Source: Isabelle Stevenson, *The Tony Award* 1989; American Theatre Wing.

The Grammys, 1958–2000

The "Grammys" are officially known as the National Academy of Recording Arts and Sciences Awards. Winners (in almost 70 categories) are selected yearly by the 6,000 or so voting members of the academy. The five award categories listed below have remained fairly constant over the years, although the overall "Best Vocal Performance" awards were phased out in 1968. From that year on, we list "Best Pop Vocal Performance" (male and female), except where indicated.

Year	Record of the year	Album of the year	Song of the year	Best male vocal performance	Best female vocal performance
1958	Domenico Modugno, *Nel Blu Dipinto di Blu (Volare)*	Henry Mancini, *The Music from Peter Gunn*	Domenico Modugno, "Nel Blu Dipinto di Blu *(Volare)*"	Perry Como, *Catch a Falling Star*	Ella Fitzgerald, *Ella Fitzgerald Sings the Irving Berlin Songbook*[2]
1959	Bobby Darin, *Mack the Knife*	Frank Sinatra, *Come Dance with Me*	Jimmy Driftwood, "The Battle of New Orleans"	Frank Sinatra, *Come Dance with Me*	Ella Fitzgerald, *But Not for Me*
1960	Percy Faith, *Theme from a Summer Place*	Bob Newhart, *Button-Down Mind*	Ernest Gold, "Theme from Exodus"	Ray Charles, *Georgia on My Mind*	Ella Fitzgerald, *Mack the Knife*
1961	Henry Mancini, *Moon River*	Judy Garland, *Judy at Carnegie Hall*	Henry Mancini, Johnny Mercer, "Moon River"	Jack Jones, *Lollipops and Roses*	Judy Garland, *Judy at Carnegie Hall*[2]
1962	Tony Bennett, *I Left My Heart in San Francisco*	Vaughn Meader, *The First Family*	Leslie Bricusse, Anthony Newley, "What Kind of Fool Am I?"	Tony Bennett, *I Left My Heart in San Francisco*[2]	Ella Fitzgerald, *Ella Swings Brightly with Nelson Riddle*[2]
1963	Henry Mancini, *The Days of Wine and Roses*	Barbra Streisand, *The Barbra Streisand Album*	Henry Mancini, Johnny Mercer, "The Days of Wine and Roses"	Jack Jones, *Wives and Lovers*	Barbra Streisand, *The Barbra Streisand Album*[2]
1964	Stan Getz, Astrud Gilberto, *The Girl from Ipanema*	Stan Getz, Astrud Gilberto, *Getz/Gilberto*	Jerry Herman, "Hello, Dolly!"	Louis Armstrong, *Hello, Dolly!*	Barbra Streisand, *People*
1965	Herb Alpert & the Tijuana Brass, *A Taste of Honey*	Frank Sinatra, *September of My Years*	Paul Francis Webster, Johnny Mandel, "The Shadow of Your Smile"	Frank Sinatra, *It Was a Very Good Year*	Barbra Streisand, *My Name is Barbra*[2]
1966	Frank Sinatra, *Strangers in the Night*	Frank Sinatra, *A Man and His Music*	John Lennon, Paul McCartney, "Michelle"	Frank Sinatra, *Strangers in the Night*	Eydie Gorme, *If He Walked into My Life*

Year	Record of the year	Album of the year	Song of the year	Best male vocal performance	Best female vocal performance
1967	5th Dimension, *Up, Up and Away*	The Beatles, *Sgt. Pepper's Lonely Hearts Club Band*	Jim Webb, "Up, Up, and Away"	Glen Campbell, *By the Time I Get to Phoenix*	Bobbie Gentry, *Ode to Billie Joe*
1968	Simon & Garfunkel, *Mrs. Robinson*	Glen Campbell, *By the Time I Get to Phoenix*	Bobby Russell, "Little Green Apples"	Jose Feliciano[3], *Light My Fire*	Dionne Warwick[3], *Do You Know the Way to San Jose?*
1969	5th Dimension, *Aquarius/Let the Sunshine In*	Blood, Sweat & Tears, *Blood, Sweat & Tears*	Joe South, "Games People Play"	Harry Nilsson[4], *Everybody's Talkin'*	Peggy Lee[4], *Is That All There Is?*
1970	Simon & Garfunkel, *Mrs. Robinson*	Simon & Garfunkel, *Bridge over Troubled Water*	Paul Simon, "Bridge over Troubled Water"	Ray Stevens[4], *Everything is Beautiful*	Dionne Warwick[4], *I'll Never Fall in Love Again*[2]
1971	Carole King, *It's Too Late*	Carole King, *Tapestry*	Carole King, "You've Got a Friend"	James Taylor[5], *You've Got a Friend*	Carole King[5], *Tapestry*[2]
1972	Roberta Flack, *The First Time Ever I Saw Your Face*	George Harrison, Ravi Shankar, Bob Dylan et al, *Concert for Bangladesh*	Ewan McColl, "The First Time Ever I Saw Your Face"	Harry Nilsson, *Without You*	Helen Reddy, *I Am Woman*
1973	Roberta Flack, *Killing Me Softly with His Song*	Stevie Wonder, *Innervisions*	Norman Gimbel, Charles Fox, "Killing Me Softly with His Song"	Stevie Wonder, *You Are the Sunshine of My Life*	Roberta Flack, *Killing Me Softly with His Song*
1974	Olivia Newton-John, *I Honestly Love You*	Stevie Wonder, *Fulfillingness' First Finale*	Marilyn & Alan Bergman, Marvin Hamlisch, "The Way We Were"	Stevie Wonder, *Fulfillingness' First Finale*[2]	Olivia Newton-John, *I Honestly Love You*
1975	Captain & Tennille, *Love Will Keep Us Together*	Paul Simon, *Still Crazy After All These Years*	Stephen Sondheim, "Send in the Clowns"	Paul Simon, *Still Crazy after All These Years*[2]	Janis Ian, *At Seventeen*
1976	George Benson, *This Masquerade*	Stevie Wonder, *Songs in the Key of Life*	Bruce Johnston, "I Write the Songs"	Stevie Wonder, *Songs in the Key of Life*[2]	Linda Ronstadt, *Hasten Down the Wind*[2]
1977	The Eagles, *Hotel California*	Fleetwood Mac, *Rumours*	Barbra Streisand, Paul Williams, "Evergreen"	James Taylor, *Handy Man*	Barbra Streisand, *Evergreen*
1978	Billy Joel, *Just the Way You Are*	Various Artists, *Saturday Night Fever*	Billy Joel, "Just the Way You Are"	Barry Manilow, *Copacabana (At the Copa)*	Anne Murray, *You Needed Me*
1979	The Doobie Brothers, *What a Fool Believes*	Billy Joel, *52nd Street*	Kenny Loggins, Michael McDonald, "What a Fool Believes"	Billy Joel, *52nd Street*[2]	Dionne Warwick, *I'll Never Love This Way Again*
1980	Christopher Cross, *Sailing*	Christopher Cross, *Christopher Cross*	Christopher Cross, "Sailing"	Kenny Loggins, *This Is It*	Bette Midler, *The Rose*
1981	Kim Carnes, *Bette Davis Eyes*	John Lennon/Yoko Ono, *Double Fantasy*	Donna Weiss, Jackie DeShannon, "Bette Davis Eyes"	Al Jarreau, *Breakin' Away*[2]	Lena Horne, *The Lady and Her Music Live on Broadway*[2]
1982	Toto, *Rosanna*	Toto, *Toto IV*	Johnny Christopher, Mark James, Wayne Carson, "Always on My Mind"	Lionel Richie, *Truly*	Melissa Manchester, *You Should Hear How She Talks About You*
1983	Michael Jackson, *Beat It*	Michael Jackson, *Thriller*	Sting, "Every Breath You Take"	Michael Jackson, *Thriller*[2]	Irene Cara, *Flashdance . . . What a Feeling*
1984	Tina Turner, *What's Love Got to Do with It?*	Lionel Richie, *Can't Slow Down*	Graham Lyle, Terry Britten, "What's Love Got to Do with It?"	Phil Collins, *Against All Odds (Take a Look at Me Now)*	Tina Turner, *What's Love Got to Do with It?*
1985	USA for Africa, *We Are the World*	Phil Collins, *No Jacket Required*	Michael Jackson, Lionel Richie, "We Are the World"	Phil Collins, *No Jacket Required*[2]	Whitney Houston, *Saving All My Love for You*
1986	Steve Winwood, *Higher Love*	Paul Simon, *Graceland*	Various Artists, "That's What Friends Are For"	Steve Winwood, *Higher Love*	Barbra Streisand, *The Broadway Album*[2]

Year	Record of the year	Album of the year	Song of the year	Best male vocal performance	Best female vocal performance
1987	Paul Simon, *Graceland*	U2, *The Joshua Tree*	Linda Ronstadt, James Ingram, "Somewhere Out There"	Sting, *Bring on the Night*[2]	Whitney Houston, *I Wanna Dance with Somebody (Who Loves Me)*
1988	Bobby McFerrin, *Don't Worry, Be Happy*	George Michael, *Faith*	Bobby McFerrin, "Don't Worry, Be Happy"	Bobby McFerrin, *Don't Worry, Be Happy*	Tracy Chapman, *Fast Car*
1989	Bette Midler, *Wind Beneath My Wings*	Bonnie Rait, *Nick of Time*	Bette Midler, "Wind Beneath My Wings"	Michael Bolton, *How Am I Supposed to Live Without You*	Bonnie Raitt, *Nick of Time*
1990	Phil Collins, *Another Day in Paradise*	Quincy Jones, *Back on the Block*	Julie Gold, "From a Distance"	Roy Orbison, *Oh, Pretty Woman*	Mariah Carey, *Vision of Love*
1991	Natalie Cole, *Unforgettable*	Natalie Cole, *Unforgettable*	Irving Gordon, "Unforgettable"	Michael Bolton , *When a Man Loves a Woman*	Bonnie Raitt, *Something to Talk About*
1992	Eric Clapton, *Tears in Heaven*	Eric Clapton, *Unplugged*	Eric Clapton, "Tears in Heaven"	Eric Clapton, *Tears in Heaven*	k.d. Lang, *Constant Craving*
1993	Whitney Houston, *I Will Always Love You*	Whitney Houston, *The Bodyguard*	Alan Menken and Tim Rice, " A Whole New World (Aladdin's Theme)"	Sting, *If I Ever Lose My Faith in You*	Whitney Houston, *I Will Always Love You*
1994	Sheryl *Crow*, *All I Wanna Do*	Tony Bennett, *MTV Unplugged*	Bruce Springsteen, "Streets of Philadelphia"	Elton John, *Can You Feel the Love Tonight*	Sheryl Crow, *All I Wanna Do*
1995	Seal, *Kiss From a Rose*	Alanis Morissette, *Jagged Little Pill*	Seal, "Kiss From a Rose"	Seal, *Kiss From a Rose*	Annie Lennox, *No More "I Love Yous"*
1996	Eric Clapton, *Change the World*	Celine Dion, *Falling Into You*	Wayne Kirkpatrick and Tommy Sims, "Change the World"	Eric Clapton, *Change the World*	Toni Braxton, *Unbreak My Heart*
1997	Shawn Colvin, *Sunny Came Home*	Bob Dylan, *Time Out of Mind*	Shawn Colvin and John Leventhal, "Sunny Came Home"	Elton John, *Candle in the Wind, 1997*	Sarah McLachlan, *Building a Mystery*
1998	Celine Dion, *My Heart Will Go On*	Lauryn Hill, *The Miseducation of Lauryn Hill*	James Horner and Will Jennings, "My Heart Will Go On"	Eric Clapton, *My Father's Eyes*	Celine Dion, *My Heart Will Go On*
1999	Santana, *Smooth*	Santana, *Supernatural*	Itaal Shur and Rob Thomas, "Smooth"	Sting, *Brand New Day*	Sara McLachlan, *I Will Remember You*
2000	U2, *Beautiful Day*	Steely Dan, *Two Against Nature*	U2 *Beautiful Day*	Sting, *She Walks This Earth*	Macy Gray, *I Try*

1. Awarded to the composer, rather than the performer, of the song. 2. Awarded for an album, rather than an individual song. 3. Award given for "Best Contemporary Pop Vocal Performance." 4. Award given for "Best Vocal Performance Contemporary." 5. From 1971 on, all awards are for "Best Pop Vocal Performance."   **Source:** National Academy of Recording Arts and Sciences; www.grammy.com.

MTV Video Music Awards, 1984–2001

Each year MTV Networks recognizes outstanding achievement in the field of video music with the MTV Video Music Awards. In addition to those listed below, there are categories for rap, heavy metal and dance videos, as well as achievement in choreography, cinematography, and direction.

Year	Best video	Best male video	Best female video	Best group video	Best new artist
1984	The Cars, *You Might Think*	David Bowie, *China Girl*	Cyndi Lauper, *Girls Just Want to Have Fun*	ZZ Top, *Legs*	Eurythmics, *Sweet Dreams (are Made of This)*
1985	Don Henley, *The Boys of Summer*	Bruce Springsteen, *I'm on Fire*	Tina Turner, *What's Love Got to Do With It?*	USA for Africa, *We Are the World*	til' tuesday, *Voices Carry*
1986	Dire Straits, *Money for Nothing*	Robert Palmer, *Addicted to Love*	Whitney Houston, *How Will I Know?*	Dire Straits, *Money for Nothing*	a-Ha, *Take On Me*
1987	Peter Gabriel, *Sledgehammer*	Peter Gabriel, *Sledgehammer*	Madonna, *Papa Don't Preach*	Talking Heads, *Wild Wild Life*	Crowded House, *Don't Dream it's Over*
1988	INXS, *Need You Tonight/Mediate*	Prince, *U Got the Look*	Suzanne Vega, *Luka*	INXS, *Need You Tonight/Mediate*	Guns N' Roses, *Welcome to the Jungle*

Year	Best video	Best male video	Best female video	Best group video	Best new artist
1989	Neil Young, *This Note's for You*	Elvis Costello, *Veronica*	Paula Abdul, *Straight Up*	Living Color, *Cult of Personality*	Living Color, *Cult of Personality*
1990	Sinead O'Connor, *Nothing Compares to You*	Don Henley, *End of the Innocence*	Sinead O'Connor, *Nothing Compares to You*	B-52s, *Love Shack*	Michael Penn, *No Myth*
1991	R.E.M., *Losing My Religion*	Chris Isaak, *Wicked Game*	Janet Jackson, *Love Will Never Do Without You*	R.E.M., *Losing My Religion*	Jesus Jones, *Right Here, Right Now*
1992	Van Halen, *Right Now*	Eric Clapton, *Tears in Heaven*	Annie Lennox, *Why*	U2, *Even Better Than the Real Thing*	Nirvana, *Smells Like Teen Spirit*
1993	Pearl Jam, *Jeremy*	Lenny Kravitz, *Are You Gonna Go My Way*	k.d. lang, *Constant Craving*	Pearl Jam, *Jeremy*	Stone Temple Pilots, *Plush*
1994	Aerosmith, *Cryin'*	Tom Petty and the Heartbreakers, *Mary Jane's Last Dance*	Janet Jackson, *If*	Aerosmith, *Cryin'*	Counting Crows, *Mr. Jones*
1995	TLC, *Waterfalls*	Tom Petty and the Heartbreakers, *You Don't Know How it Feels*	Madonna, *Take a Bow*	TLC, *Waterfalls*	Hootie & the Blowfish, *Hold My Hand*
1996	Smashing Pumpkins *Tonight, Tonight*	Beck, *Where It's At*	Alanis Morissette, *Ironic*	Foo Fighters, *Big Me*	Alanis Morissette, *Ironic*
1997	Jamiroquai, *Virtual Insanity*	Beck, *Devil's Haircut*	Jewel, *You Were Meant For Me*	No Doubt, *Don't Speak*	Fiona Apple, *Sleep to Dream*
1998	Madonna, *Ray of Light*	Will Smith, *Just the Two of Us*	Madonna, *Ray of Light*	Backstreet Boys, *Everybody (Backstreet's Back)*	Natalie Imbruglia, *Torn*
1999	Lauryn Hill, *Doo-Wop*	Will Smith, *Miami*	Lauryn Hill, *Doo-Wop*	TLC, *No Scrubs*	Eminem, *My Name Is*
2000	Eminem, *The Real Slim Shady*	Eminem, *The Real Slim Shady*	Aaliyah, *Try Again*	Blink-182, *All The Small Things*	Macy Gray, *I Try*
2001	Various Artists, *Lady Marmalade*	Moby *South Side*	Eve, *Let Me Blow Ya Mind*	'N SYNC *Pop*	Alicia Keys *Fallin'*

Source: Press Department, MTV Networks. www.mtv.com.

The National Book Awards, 1950-2000

The National Book Awards are given annually for outstanding literary works by American citizens. The number of prizes awarded has varied, including categories such as poetry, fiction, biography, science, philosophy, religion, and history.

FICTION

Year	Author, Title
1950	Nelson Algren, *The Man with the Golden Arm*
1951	William Faulkner, *The Collected Stories*
1952	James Jones, *From Here to Eternity*
1953	Ralph Ellison, *Invisible Man*
1954	Saul Bellow, *The Adventures of Augie March*
1955	William Faulkner, *A Fable*
1956	John O'Hara, *Ten North Frederick*
1957	Wright Morris, *Field of Vision*
1958	John Cheever, *The Wapshot Chronicle*
1959	Bernard Malamud, *The Magic Barrel*
1960	Philip Roth, *Goodbye, Columbus*
1961	Conrad Richter, *The Waters of Kronos*
1962	Walker Percy, *The Moviegoer*
1963	J. F. Powers, *Morte d'Urban*
1964	John Updike, *The Centaur*
1965	Saul Bellow, *Herzog*
1966	Katherine Anne Porter, *The Collected Stories*
1967	Bernard Malamud, *The Fixer*
1968	Thornton Wilder, *The Eighth Day*
1969	Jerzy Kosinski, *Steps*
1970	Joyce Carol Oates, *Them*
1971	Saul Bellow, *Mr. Sammler's Planet*
1972	Flannery O'Connor, *The Complete Stories*
1973	John Barth, *Chimera*
1974	Thomas Pynchon, *Gravity's Rainbow* / Isaac Bashevis Singer, *A Crown of Feathers & Other Stories*
1975	Robert Stone, *Dog Soldiers* / Thomas Williams, *The Hair of Harold Roux*
1976	William Gaddis, *JR*
1977	Wallace Stegner, *The Spectator Bird*
1978	Mary Lee Settle, *Blood Ties*
1979	Tim O'Brien, *Going After Cacciato*
1980	William Styron, *Sophie's Choice*
1981	Wright Morris, *Plains Song*
1982	John Updike, *Rabbit Is Rich*
1983	Alice Walker, *The Color Purple*
1984	Ellen Gilchrist, *Victory Over Japan*
1985	Don DeLillo, *White Noise*
1986	E. L. Doctorow, *World's Fair*
1987	Larry Heinemann, *Paco's Story*
1988	Pete Dexter, *Paris Trout*
1989	John Casey, *Spartina*
1990	Charles Johnson, *Middle Passage*
1991	Norman Rush, *Mating*
1992	Cormac McCarthy, *All the Pretty Horses*
1993	E. Annie Proulx, *The Shipping News*
1994	William Gaddis, *A Frolic of His Own*
1995	Philip Roth, *Sabbath's Theater*
1996	Andrea Barrett, *Ship Fever and Other Stories*
1997	Charles Frazier, *Cold Mountain*
1998	Alice McDermott, *Charming Billy*
1999	Ha Jin, *Waiting*
2000	Susan Sontag, *In America*

NONFICTION

Year	Author, Title
1950	Ralph L. Rusk, *Ralph Waldo Emerson*
1951	Newton Arvin, *Herman Melville*
1952	Rachel Carson, *The Sea Around Us*
1953	Bernard De Voto, *Course of Empire*
1954	Bruce Catton, *A Stillness at Appomattox*
1955	Joseph Wood Krutch, *The Measure of Man*
1956	Herbert Kubly, *An American in Italy*
1957	George F. Kennan, *Russia Leaves the War*
1958	Catherine Drinker Bowen, *The Lion and the Throne*
1959	J. Christopher Herold, *Mistress to an Age*
1960	Richard Ellman, *James Joyce*
1961	William L. Shirer, *The Rise and Fall of the Third Reich*
1962	Lewis Mumford, *The City in History*
1963	Leon Edel, *Henry James, vols. 2 and 3*
1964	Aileen Ward, *John Keats: The Making of a Poet*
1965	Louis Fisher, *The Life of Lenin*
1966	Arthur M. Schlesinger Jr., *A Thousand Days: JFK in the White House*
1967	Justin Kaplan, *Mr. Clemens and Mark Twain*
1968	Jonathan Kozol, *Death at an Early Age*
1969	Norman Mailer, *The Armies of the Night*
1970	Lillian Hellman, *An Unfinished Woman, a Memoir*
1971	James MacGregor Burns, *Roosevelt: The Soldier of Freedom*
1972	Joseph P. Lash, *Eleanor and Franklin*
1973	Frances Fitzgerald, *Fire in the Lake: The Vietnamese and the Americans in Vietnam*
1974	Pauline Kael, *Deeper into the Movies*
1975	Richard B. Sewall, *The Life of Emily Dickinson* Lewis Thomas, *The Lives of a Cell*
1976	Paul Fussell, *The Great War and Modern Memory*
1977	Bruno Bettelheim, *The Uses of Enchantment: The Meaning and Importance of Fairy Tales*

Year	Author, Title
1978	Walter Jackson Bate, *Samuel Johnson*
1979	Arthur M. Schlesinger Jr., *Robert Kennedy and His Times*
1980	Tom Wolfe, *The Right Stuff*
1981	Maxine Hong Kingston, *China Men*
1982	Tracy Kidder, *The Soul of a New Machine*
1983	Fox Butterfield, *China: Alive in the Bitter Sea*
1984	Robert V. Remini, *Andrew Jackson and the Course of American Democracy, 1833–45*
1985	J. Anthony Lukas, *Common Ground: A Turbulent Decade in the Lives of Three American Families*
1986	Barry Lopez, *Arctic Dreams*
1987	Richard Rhodes, *The Making of the Atom Bomb*
1988	Neil Sheehan, *A Bright and Shining Lie: John Paul Vann and America in Vietnam*
1989	Thomas L. Friedman, *From Beirut to Jerusalem*
1990	Ron Chernow, *The House of Morgan*
1991	Orlando Patterson, *Freedom*
1992	Paul Monette, *Becoming a Man: Half a Life*
1993	Gore Vidal, *United States: Essays 1952-1992*
1994	Sherwin B. Nuland, *How We Die: Reflections on Life's Final Chapter*
1995	Tina Rosenberg, *The Haunted Land: Facing Europe's Ghosts After Communism*
1996	James Carroll, *An American Requiem: God, My Father and the War That Came Between Us*
1997	Joseph J. Ellis, *American Sphinx: The Character of Thomas Jefferson*
1998	Edward Ball, *Slaves in the Family*
1999	John W. Dower, *Embracing Defeat: Japan in the Wake of World War II*
2000	Nathaniel Philbrick, *In the Heart of the Sea: The Tragedy of the Whaleship Essex*

POETRY

Year	Author, Title
1950	William Carlos Williams, *Paterson: Book III* and *Selected Poems*
1951	Wallace Stevens, *The Auroras of Autumn*
1952	Marianne Moore, *Collected Poems*
1953	Archibald MacLeish, *Collected Poems 1917–52*
1954	Conrad Aiken, *Collected Poems*
1955	Wallace Stevens, *The Collected Poems*
1956	W. H. Auden, *The Shield of Achilles*
1957	Richard Wilbur, *Things of This World*
1958	Robert Penn Warren, *Promises: Poems, 1954–56*
1959	Theodore Roethke, *Words for the Wind*
1960	Robert J. Lowell, *Life Studies*
1961	Randall Jarrell, *The Woman at the Washington Zoo*
1962	Alan Dugan, *Poems*
1963	William Stafford, *Traveling Through the Dark*
1964	John Crowe Ransom, *Selected Poems*
1965	Theodore Roethke, *The Far Field*
1966	James Dickey, *Buckdancer's Choice*
1967	James Merrill, *Nights and Days*
1968	Robert Bly, *The Light Around the Body*
1969	John Berryman, *His Toy, His Dream, His Rest*
1970	Elizabeth Bishop, *The Complete Poems*
1971	Mona Van Duyn, *To See, To Take*
1972	Howard Moss, *Selected Poems*
1973	A. R. Ammons, *Collected Poems: 1951–71*

Year	Author, Title
1974	Allen Ginsberg, *The Fall of America: Poems of These States, 1965–71* Adrienne Rich, *Diving into the Wreck: Poems, 1971–72*
1975	Marilyn Hacker, *Presentation Piece*
1976	John Ashbery, *Self-Portrait in a Convex Mirror*
1977	Richard Eberhart, *Collected Poems, 1930–1976*
1978	Howard Nemerov, *The Collected Poems*
1979	James Merrill, *Mirabell: Books of Number*
1980	Philip Levine, *Ashes*
1981	Lisel Mueller, *The Need to Hold Still*
1982	William Bronk, *Life Supports*
1983	Galway Kinnell, *Selected Poems*
1984	Charles Wright, *Country Music*
1991	Philip Levine, *What Work Is*
1992	Mary Oliver, *New and Selected Poems*
1993	A. R. Ammons, *Garbage*
1994	James Tate, *Worshipful Company of Fletchers*
1995	Stanley Kunitz, *Passing Through*
1996	Hayden Carruth, *Scrambled Eggs and Whiskey: Poems 1991–1995*
1997	William Meredith, *Effort at Speech: New and Selected Poems*
1998	Gerald Stern, *This Time: New and Selected Poems*
1999	Ai, *New and Selected Poems*
2000	Lucille Clifton, *Blessing the Boats: New and Selected Poems 1988-2000*

YOUNG PEOPLE'S LITERATURE

Year	Author, Title	Year	Author, Title
1996	Victor Martinez, *Parrot in the Oven: Mi Vida*	1999	Kimberly Willis Holtt, *When Zachary Beaver Came to Town*
1997	Han Nolan, *Dancing on the Edge*		
1998	Louis Sachar, *Holes*	2000	Gloria Whelan, *Homeless Bird*

Note: No award was given in poetry from 1985 to 1990. **Source:** National Book Awards, Inc.

The National Book Critics Circle Award, 1975–2000

Selected by a 24-member board of critics (who serve 3-year terms) from around the country, this award has been increasingly important in the last few years. Books are often recommended to the board by the more than 500 general members of the Circle.

FICTION

Year	Author, Title	Year	Author, Title
1975	E.L. Doctorow, *Ragtime*	1989	E.L. Doctorow, *Billy Bathgate*
1976	John Gardner, *October Light*	1990	John Updike, *Rabbit at Rest*
1977	Toni Morrison, *Song of Solomon*	1991	Jane Smiley, *A Thousand Acres*
1978	John Cheever, *The Stories of John Cheever*	1992	Cormac McCarthy, *All the Pretty Horses*
1979	Thomas Flanagan, *The Year of the French*	1993	Ernest J. Gaines, *A Lesson Before Dying*
1980	Shirley Hazzard, *The Transit of Venus*	1994	Carol Shields, *The Stone Diaries*
1981	John Updike, *Rabbit is Rich*	1995	Stanley Elkin[1], *Mrs. Ted Bliss*
1982	Stanley Elkin, *George Mills*	1996	Gina Berriault, *Women in Their Beds*
1983	William Kennedy, *Ironweed*	1997	Penelope Fitzgerald, *The Blue Flower*
1984	Louise Erdrich, *Love Medicine*	1998	Alice Munro, *The Love of a Good Woman*
1985	Anne Tyler, *The Accidental Tourist*		
1986	Reynolds Price, *Kate Vaiden*	1999	Jonathan Lethem, *Motherless Brooklyn*
1987	Phillip Roth, *The Counterlife*	2000	Jim Crace, *Being Dead*
1988	Bharati Mukherjee, *The Middleman and Other Stories*		

GENERAL NONFICTION

Year	Author, Title	Year	Author, Title
1975	R.W.B. Lewis, *Edith Wharton*	1989	Michael Dorris, *The Broken Cord*
1976	Maxine Hong Kingston, *The Woman Warrior: Memoirs of a Girlhood Among Ghosts*	1990	Shelby Steele, *The Content of Our Character: A New Vision of Race in America*
1977	Walter Jackson Bate, *Samuel Johnson*	1991	Susan Faludi, *Backlash*
1978	Maureen Howard, *Facts of Life*	1992	Norman Maclean, *Young Men and Fire*
1979	Telford Taylor, *Munich: The Price of Peace*	1993	Alan Lomax, *The Land Where Blues Began*
1980	Ronald Steel, *Walter Lippmann and the American Century*	1994	Lynn H. Nicholas, *The Rape of Europa: The Fate of Europe's Treasures in the Third Reich and the Second World War*
1981	Stephen Jay Gould, *The Mismeasure of Man*		
1982	Robert A. Caro, *The Path of Power: The Years of Lyndon Johnson*	1995	Jonathan Harr, *A Civil Action*
		1996	Jonathan Raban, *Bad Land: An American Romance*
1983	Seymour M. Hersh, *The Price of Power: Kissinger and the Nixon White House*	1997	Anne Fadiman, *The Spirit Catches You and You Fall Down*
1984	Freeman Dyson, *Weapons and Hope*		
1985	J. Anthony Lukas, *Common Ground: A Turbulent Decade in the Lives of Three Americans*	1998	Philip Gourevitch, *We Wish to Inform You That Tomorrow We Will Be Killed With Our Familes*
1986	John W. Dower, *War Without Mercy: Race and Power in the Pacific War*	1999	Jonathan Weiner, *Time, Love, and Memory, A Great Biologist and His Quest for the Origins of Behavior*
1987	Richard Rhodes, *The Making of the Atomic Bomb*	2000	Ted Conover, *Newjack: Guarding Sing Sing*
1988	Taylor Branch, *Parting the Waters: America in the King Years, 1954–63*		

BIOGRAPHY/AUTOBIOGRAPHY

Year	Author, Title	Year	Author, Title
1983	Joyce Johnson, *Minor Characters*	1992	Carol Brightman, *Writing Dangerously: Mary McCarthy and Her World*
1984	Joseph Frank, *Dostoevsky: The Years of Ordeal. 1850–1859*	1993	Edmund White, *Genet*
1985	Leon Edel, *Henry James: A Life*	1994	Mikal Gilmore, *Shot in the Heart*
1986	Theodore Rosengarten, *Tombee: Portrait of a Cotton Planter*	1995	Robert Polito, *Savage Art: A Biography of Jim Thompson*
1987	Donald R. Howard, *Chaucer: His Life, His Works, His World*	1996	Frank McCourt, *Angela's Ashes*
1988	Richard Ellman, *Oscar Wilde*	1997	James Tobin, *Ernie Pyle's War: America's Eyewitness to World War II*
1989	Geoffrey C. Ward, *A First-Class Temperament: The Emergence of Franklin Roosevelt*	1998	Sylvia Nasar, *A Beautiful Mind*
1990	Robert A. Caro, *Means of Ascent: The Years of Lyndon Johnson, Vol. 2*	1999	Henry Wiencek, *The Hairstons: An American Family in Black and White*
1991	Philip Roth, *Patrimony*	2000	Herbert P. Bix, *Hirohito and the Making of Modern Japan*

CRITICISM

Year	Author, Title	Year	Author, Title
1975	Paul Fussell, *The Great War and Modern Memory*	1987	Edwin Denby, *Dance Writings*
1976	Bruno Bettelheim, *The Uses of Enchantment: The Meaning and Importance of Fairy Tales*	1988	Clifford Geertz, *Works and Lives: The Anthropologist as Author*
1977	Susan Sontag, *On Photography*	1989	John Clive, *Not by Fact Alone: Essays on the Writing and Reading of History*
1978	Meyer Schapiro, *Modern Art: 19th and 20th Centuries, Selected Papers*	1990	Arthur C. Danto, *Encounters and Reflections: Art in the Historical Present*
1979	Elaine Pagels, *The Gnostic Gospels*	1991	Lawrence L. Langer, *Holocaust Testimonies*
1980	Helen Vendler, *Part of Nature, Part of Us: Modern American Poets*	1992	Garry Wills, *Lincoln At Gettysburg: The Words That Remade America*
1981	Virgil Thompson, *A Virgil Thompson Reader*	1993	John Dizikes, *Opera in America*
1982	Gore Vidal, *The Second American Revolution and Other Essays, 1976–82*	1994	Gerald Early, *The Culture of Bruising: Essays on Prizefighting, Literature and Modern American Culture*
1983	John Updike, *Hugging the Shore*	1995	Robert Darnton, *The Forbidden Best-Sellers of Pre-Revolutionary France*
1984	Robert Hass, *Twentieth Century Pleasures: Prose on Poetry*	1996	William Gass, *Finding a Form*
1985	William H. Gass, *Habitations of the Word: Essays*	1997	Mario Vargas Llosa, *Making Waves*
1986	Joseph Brodsky, *Less Than One: Selected Essays*	1998	Gary Giddins, *Visions of Jazz*
		1999	Jorge Luis Borges[1], *Selected Non-Fictions*
		2000	Cynthia Ozick, *Quarrel & Quandary*

POETRY

Year	Author, Title	Year	Author, Title
1975	John Ashbery, *Self-Portrait in a Convex Mirror*	1986	Edward Hirsch, *Wild Gratitude*
1976	Elizabeth Bishop, *Geography III*	1987	C.K. Williams, *Flesh and Blood*
1977	Robert Lowell, *Day by Day*	1988	Donald Hall, *The One Day*
1978	L.E. Sissman, *Hello Darkness: The Collected Poems of L.E. Sissman*	1989	Rodney Jones, *Transparent Gestures*
1979	Philip Levine, *Ashes and Seven Years from Somewhere*	1990	Amy Gerstler, *Bitter Angel*
		1991	Albert Goldbarth, *Heaven and Earth*
1980	Frederick Seidel, *Sunrise*	1992	Hayden Carruth, *Collected Shorter Poems*
1981	A.R. Ammons, *A Coast of Trees*	1993	Mark Doty, *My Alexandria*
1982	Katha Pollitt, *Antarctic Traveler*	1994	Mark Rudman, *Rider*
1983	James Merrill, *The Changing Light at Sandover*	1995	William Matthews, *Time & Money*
		1996	Robert Hass, *Sun Under Wood*
1984	Sharon Olds, *The Dead and the Living*	1997	Charles Wright, *Black Zodiac*
1985	Louise Gluck, *The Triumph of Achilles*	1998	Marie Ponsot, *The Bird Catcher*
		1999	Ruth Stone, *Ordinary Words*
		2000	Judy Jordan, *Carolina Ghost Woods*

1. Awarded posthumously. **Source:** The National Book Critics Circle.

Bollingen Prize for Poetry, 1949–2001

First awarded annually, and biennially since 1965, the Bollingen Prize for Poetry is offered by Yale University to an American citizen for a distinguished book of poetry, or in recognition of a poet's entire achievement.

Year	Recipient	Year	Recipient	Year	Recipient
1949	Wallace Stevens	1961	Richard Eberhart	1983	Anthony E. Hecht
1950	John Crowe		John Hall Wheelock		John Hollander
	Ransom	1962	Robert Frost	1985	John Ashbery
1951	Marianne Moore	1965	Horace Gregory		Fred Chappel
1952	Archibald MacLeish	1967	Robert Penn Warren	1987	Stanley Kunitz
	William Carlos Williams	1969	John Berryman	1989	Edgar Bowers
1953	W. H. Auden		Karl Shapiro	1991	Laura Riding
1954	Leonie Adams	1971	Richard Wilbur		Jackson
	Louise Bogan		Mona Van Duyn		Donald Justice
1955	Conrad Aiken	1973	James Merrill	1993	Mark Strand
1956	Allen Tate	1975	A. R. Ammons	1995	Kenneth Koch
1957	e.e. cummings	1977	David Ignatow	1997	Gary Snyder
1958	Theodore Roethke	1979	W. S. Merwin	1999	Robert W. Creeley
1959	Delmore Schwartz	1981	May Swenson	2001	Louise Glück
1960	Ivor Winters		Howard Nemerov		

Source: Yale University.

The Newbery Medal, 1922–2001

The Newbery Medal, presented by the American Library Association, is awarded annually to the author of the most distinguished contribution to American literature for children published in the United States during the previous year. The award is named in honor of John Newbery (1713–67), the first English publisher of books for children.

Year	Author, Title	Year	Author, Title
1922	Willem Van Loon, *The Story of Mankind*	1957	Virginia Sorensen, *Miracles on Maple Hill*
1923	Hugh Lofting, *The Voyages of Doctor Dolittle*	1958	Harold Keith, *Rifles for Watie*
1924	Charles Hawes, *The Dark Frigate*	1959	Elizabeth George Speare, *The Witch of Blackbird Pond*
1925	Charles Finger, *Tales from Silver Lands*	1960	Joseph Krumgold, *Onion John*
1926	Arthur Bowie Chrisman, *Shen of the Sea*	1961	Scott O'Dell, *Island of the Blue Dolphins*
1927	Will James, *Smoky, The Cowhorse*	1962	Elizabeth George Speare, *The Bronze Bow*
1928	Dhan Gopal Mukerji, *Gayneck, The Story of a Pigeon*	1963	Madeleine L'Engle, *A Wrinkle in Time*
1929	Eric P. Kelly, *The Trumpeter of Krakow*	1964	Emily Cheney Neville, *It's Like This, Cat*
1930	Rachel Field, *Hitty, Her First Hundred Years*	1965	Maia Wojciechowska, *Shadow of a Bull*
1931	Elizabeth Coatsworth, *The Cat Who Went to Heaven*	1966	Elizabeth Borten de Trevino, *I, Juan de Pareja*
1932	Laura Adams Armer, *Waterless Mountain*	1967	Irene Hunt, *Up a Road Slowly*
1933	Elizabeth Foreman Lewis, *Young Fu of the Upper Yangtze*	1968	E.L. Konigsburg, *From the Mixed-up Files of Mrs. Basil E. Frankweiler*
1934	Cornelia Meigs, *Invincible Louisa*	1969	Lloyd Alexander, *The High King*
1935	Monica Shannon, *Dobry*	1970	William H. Armstrong, *Sounder*
1936	Carol Brink, *Caddie Woodlawn*	1971	Betsy Byars, *Summer of the Swans*
1937	Ruth Sawyer, *Roller Skates*	1972	Robert C. O'Brien, *Mrs. Frisby and the Rats of NIMH*
1938	Kate Seredy, *The White Stag*	1973	Jean George, *Julie of the Wolves*
1939	Elizabeth Enright, *Thimble Summer*	1974	Paula Fox, *The Slave Dancer*
1940	James Daugherty, *Daniel Boone*	1975	Virginia Hamilton, *M.C. Higgins the Great*
1941	Armstrong Sperry, *Call It Courage*	1976	Susan Cooper, *The Grey King*
1942	Walter D. Edmonds, *The Matchlock Gun*	1977	Mildred D. Taylor, *Roll of Thunder, Hear My Cry*
1943	Elizabeth Janet Gray, *Adam of the Road*		
1944	Esther Forbes, *Johnny Tremain*	1978	Katherine Paterson, *Bridge to Terabithia*
1945	Robert Lawson, *Rabbit Hill*	1979	Ellen Raskin, *The Westing Game*
1946	Lois Lenski, *Strawberry Girl*	1980	Joan Blos, *A Gathering of Days: A New England Girl's Journal, 1830–32*
1947	Carolyn Sherwin Bailey, *Miss Hickory*		
1948	William Pène du Bois, *The 21 Balloons*	1981	Katherine Paterson, *Jacob Have I Loved*
1949	Marguerite Henry, *King of the Wind*	1982	Nancy Willard, *A Visit to William Blake's Inn: Poems for Innocent and Experienced Travelers*
1950	Marguerite de Angeli, *The Door in the Wall*		
1951	Elizabeth Yates, *Amos Fortune, Free Man*		
1952	Eleanor Estes, *Ginger Pye*	1983	Cynthia Voigt, *Dicey's Song*
1953	Ann Nolan Clark, *Secret of the Andes*	1984	Beverly Cleary, *Dear Mr. Henshaw*
1954	Joseph Krumgold, *. . . And Now Miguel*	1985	Robin McKinley, *The Hero and the Crown*
1955	Meindert DeJong, *The Wheel on the School*	1986	Patricia MacLachlan, *Sarah, Plain and Tall*
1956	Jean Lee Latham, *Carry On, Mr. Bowditch*	1987	Sid Fleischman, *The Whipping Boy*

Year	Author, Title	Year	Author, Title
1988	Russell Freedman, *Lincoln: A Photo-biography*	1994	Lois Lowry, *The Giver*
		1995	Sharon Creech, *Walk Two Moons*
1989	Paul Fleischman, *Joyful Noise: Poems for Two Voices*	1996	Karen Cushman, *The Midwife's Apprentice*
		1997	Elaine Konigsburg, *The View From Saturday*
1990	Lois Lowry, *Number the Stars*	1998	Karen Hesse, *Out of the Dust*
1991	Jerry Spinelli, *Maniac Magee*	1999	Louis Sachar, *Holes*
1992	Phyllis Reynolds Naylor, *Shiloh*	2000	Christopher Paul Curtis, *Bud, Not Buddy*
1993	Cynthia Rylant, *Missing May*	2001	Richard Peck, *A Year Down Yonder*

Source: American Library Association.

The Caldecott Medal, 1938–2001

The Caldecott Medal, presented by the American Library Association, is awarded annually to the illustrator of the most distinguished picture book for children published in the United States during the preceding year. The award is named in honor of the English illustrator Randolph Caldecott (1846–1886). In cases where only one name is given, the book was written and illustrated by the same person.

Year	Illustrator/Author/Title	Year	Illustrator/Author/Title
1938	Dorothy Lathrop; Helen Dean Fish, *Animals of the Bible*	1970	William Steig, *Sylvester and the Magic Pebble*
1939	Thomas Handforth, *Mei Li*	1971	Gail E. Haley, *A Story—A Story*
1940	Ingri and Edgar Parin d'Aulaire, *Abraham Lincoln*	1972	Nonny Hogrogian, *One Fine Day*
1941	Robert Lawson, *They Were Strong and Good*	1973	Blair Lent; retold by Arlene Mosel, *The Funny Little Woman*
1942	Robert McCloskey, *Make Way for Ducklings*	1974	Margot Zemach; Harve Zemach, *Duffy and the Devil*
1943	Virginia Lee Burton, *The Little House*		
1944	Louis Slobodkin; James Thurber, *Many Moons*	1975	Gerald McDermott, *Arrow to the Sun*
1945	Elizabeth Orton Jones; Rachel Jones, *Prayer for a Child*	1976	Leo and Diane Dillon; retold by Verna Aardema, *Why Mosquitoes Buzz in People's Ears*
1946	Maude and Miska Petersham, *The Rooster Crows* (traditional Mother Goose)	1977	Leo & Diane Dillon; Margaret Musgrove, *Ashanti to Zulu: African Traditions*
1947	Leonard Weisgard; Golden MacDonald, *The Little Island*	1978	Peter Spier, *Noah's Ark*
1948	Roger Duvoisin; Alvin Tresselt, *White Snow, Bright Snow*	1979	Paul Goble, *The Girl Who Loved Wild Horses*
1949	Bert and Elmer Hader, *The Big Snow*	1980	Barbara Cooney; Donald Hall, *Ox-Cart Man*
1950	Leo Politi, *Song of the Swallows*	1981	Arnold Lobel, *Fables*
1952	Nicolas Mordvinoff; Will Mordvinoff, *Finders Keepers*	1983	Marcia Brown, *Shadow*
		1984	Martin and Alice Provensen, *The Glorious Flight*
1953	Lynd Ward, *The Biggest Bear*		
1954	Ludwig Bemelmans, *Madeline's Rescue*	1985	Trina Schart Hyman, *Saint George and the·
	or the Little Glass Slipper	1986	Chris Van Allsburg, *The Polar Express*
1956	Feodor Rojankovsky; John Langstaff, *Frog Went A-Courtin'*	1987	Richard Egielski; Arthur Yorinks, *Hey, Al*
		1988	John Schoenherr, *Owl Moon*
1957	Marc Simont; Janice May Udry, *A Tree is Nice*	1989	Stephen Gammell; Karen Ackerman, *Song*
1959	Barbara Cooney (adapted from Geoffrey Chaucer), *Chanticleer and the Fox*	1990	Paul Fleischman, *Lon Po Po: A Red-Riding Hood Story from China*
1960	Marie Hall Ets and Aurora Labastida, *Nine Days to Christmas*	1991	David Macaulay, *Black and White*
		1992	David Wiesner, *Tuesday*
1961	Nicolas Sidjakov; Ruth Robbins, *Baboushka and the Three Kings*	1993	Emily Arnold McCully, *Mirette on the High Wire*
1962	Marcia Brown, *Once a Mouse . . .*	1994	Allen Say, *Grandfather's Journey*
1963	Ezra Jack Keats, *The Snowy Day*	1995	David Diaz; Eve Bunting, *Smoky Night*
1964	Maurice Sendak, *Where the Wild Things Are*	1996	Peggy Rathman, *Officer Buckle and Gloria*
1965	Beni Montresor; Beatrice Schenk de Regniers, *May I Bring a Friend?*	1997	David Wisniewski, *Golem*
		1998	Paul O. Zelinsky, *Rapunzel*
1966	Nonny Hogrogian; Sorche Nic Leodhas, *Always Room for One More*	1999	Mary Azarian; Jacqueline Briggs Martin, *Snowflake Bentley*
1967	Evaline Ness, *Sam, Bangs & Moonshine*	2000	Simms Taback, *Joseph Had a Little Overcoat*
1968	Ed Emberley; Barbara Emberley, *Drummer Hoff*	2001	David Small, *So You Want to Be President?*
1969	Uri Shulevitz; Arthur Ransome, *The Fool of the World and the Flying Ship*		

Source: American Library Association.

American Institute of Architects Gold Medalists, 1907–2001

The AIA medal recognizes outstanding lifetime achievement in architecture. It is not awarded every year.

Year	Medalist, Country	Year	Medalist, Country
1907	Sir Aston Webb, U.K.	1963	Alvar Aalto, Finland
1909	Charles Follen McKim, U.S.	1964	Pier Luigi Nervi, Italy
1911	George B. Post, U.S.	1966	Kenzo Tange, Japan
1914	Jean Louis Pascal, France	1967	Wallace K. Harrison, U.S.
1922	Victor Laloux, France	1968	Marcel Breuer, U.S.
1923	Henry Bacon, U.S.	1969	William Wilson Wurster, U.S.
1925	Bertram Grosvenor Goodhue, U.S.	1970	Richard Buckminster Fuller, U.S.
1925	Sir Edwin Landseer Lutyens, London	1971	Louis I. Kahn, U.S.
1927	Howard Van Doren Sha w, U.S.	1972	Pietro Belluschi, U.S.
1929	Milton Bennett Medary, U.S.	1977	Richard Joseph Neutra, U.S.[1]
1933	Ragnar Ostberg, Stockholm	1978	Philip Johnson, U.S.
1938	Paul Philippe Cret, U.S.	1979	Ieoh Ming Pei, U.S.
1944	Louis Henri Sullivan, U.S.	1981	Josep Lluis Sert, U.S.
1947	Eliel Saarinen, U.S.	1982	Romaldo Giurgola, U.S.
1948	Charles Donagh Maginnis, U.S.	1983	Nathaniel A. Owings, U.S.
1949	Frank Lloyd Wright, U.S.	1985	William Caudill, U.S.[1]
1950	Sir Patrick Abercrombie, U.K.	1986	Arthur Erickson, Canada
1951	Bernard Ralph Maybeck, U.S.	1989	Joseph Esherick, U.S.
1952	Auguste Perret, France	1990	Fay Jones, U.S.
1953	William Adams Delano, U.S.	1991	Charles Willard Moore, U.S.
1955	Willem Marinus Dudock, Netherlands	1992	Benjamin Thompson, U.S.
1956	Clarence S. Stein, U.S.	1993	Kevin Roche, U.S.
1957	Louis Skidmore, U.S.		Thomas Jefferson, U.S.[1]
1957	Ralph Walker, U.S.	1994	Sir Norman Foster, U.K.
1958	John Wellborn Root, U.S.	1995	Cesar Pelli, U.S.
1959	Walter Gropius, U.S.	1997	Richard Meier, U.S.
1960	Ludwig Mies van der Rohe, U.S.	1998	No Award
1961	Le Corbusier (Charles Edouard	1999	Frank Gehry, U.S.
	Jeanneret-Gris), France	2000	Ricardo Legorreta, Mexico
1962	Eero Saarinen, U.S.[1]	2001	Michael Graves, U.S.

1. Awarded posthumously.   **Source:** American Institute of Architects.

Pritzker Prize Winners, 1979–2001

Recognized as the most prestigious award in architecture, the Pritzker Prize is given annually by the Hyatt Hotel Foundation, and is named for its chairman, Jay Pritzker. The selection process is modeled after the Nobel Prizes, with secret voting by an international jury.

Year	Medalist, Country	Year	Medalist, Country
1979	Philip Johnson, U.S.	1991	Robert Venturi, U.S.
1980	Luis Barragan, Mexico	1992	Alvaro Siza, Portugal
1981	James Stirling, U.K.	1993	Fumihiko Maki, Japan
1982	Kevin Roche, U.S.	1994	Christian de Portzamparc, France
1983	I.M. Pei, U.S.	1995	Tadao Ando, Japan
1984	Richard Meier, U.S.	1996	Rafael Moneo, Spain
1985	Hans Hollein, Austria	1997	Sverre Fehn, Norway
1986	Gottfried Boehm, Germany	1998	Renzo Piano, Italy
1987	Kenzo Tange, Japan	1999	Norman Foster, U.K.
1988	Gordon Bunshaft, U.S.	2000	Rem Koolhaas, Netherlands
	Oscar Niemeyer, Brazil	2001	Jacques Herzog, Switzerland
1989	Frank O. Gehry, U.S.		Pierre de Meuron, Switzerland
1990	Aldo Rossi, Italy		

Templeton Prize Winners, 1973-2001

Believing that religion had been unfairly excluded from consideration by the Nobel Prize committee, John Marks Templeton in 1972 established the Templeton Prize for Progress in Religion for "those who seek new and different paths in advancing the world's understanding of God and/or spirituality." Templeton, a Tennessee-born financier who became one of Wall Street's most successful fund managers, decreed that the monetary value of his prize should always exceed that of the Nobel Prize. The 2001 Prize was worth 700,000 pounds sterling, or approximately $1 million.

Year	Recipient

1973   Mother Teresa, for her "efforts to help the homeless and neglected children of Calcutta."

1974   Brother Roger. He harbored Jewish refugees in Nazi-occupied France, then later established the Taize Community, which aided orphaned children in France.

1975   Sarvepalli Radhakrishnan, President of India (1962-67), and Oxford Professor of Eastern Religions and Ethics, for his advocacy of "a non-aggressive, defensive military posture during India's conflicts with Pakistan." His writings made India's religious heritage accessible to both Eastern and Western audiences.

1976   Leon Joseph Cardinal Suenens, Archbishop of Malines-Brussles, for his pioneering work in the Charismatic Renewal Movement, which gained popularity in the early 1970s.

1977   Chiara Lubich, founder of Italy's Focolare Movement, for developing "an alternative to a cloistered existence for women who decided to become nuns." The movement eventually expanded to include men and married people and to communities in Europe, the U.S., and Japan.

1978   Thomas F. Torrance, former Moderator of the Church of Scotland, "one of the first religious thinkers to win the respect of both theologians and scientists for his work on the relationship between science and religion."

1979   Rev. Nikkyo Niwano, founder of Rissho Kosei-Kai in Japan and the World Conference on Religion and Peace. The Buddhist group he co-founded with Masa Naganuma literally means "establishing the teaching of the true Law in the world, mutual exchange of thought among people of faith and the perfection of the personality."

1980   Ralph Wendell Burhoe, founder and editor of *Zygon, Journal of Religion and Science*, for providing enlightenment in understanding similarities and differences between theology and science, and for providing neutral ground for discussion.

1981   Dame Cecily Saunders, founder of the Hospice and Palliative Care Movement, which helps terminally ill patients express their physical, psycho-social and spiritual pain.

1982   The Rev. Billy Graham, televangelist, for keeping his Gospel message "pure, simple and authentic, yet tailored to address the problems and pressures of today."

1983   Aleksandr Solzhenitsyn, Soviet dissident whose "struggle to speak and think freely [gives] renewed vitality to the Orthodox tradition of spirituality and provides evidence of the strength of profound Christian faith."

1984   The Rev. Michael Bourdeaux, founder of Keston College in England, for his "long, sometimes singular struggle to reveal the systematic destruction of religion in communist countries during the Cold War."

1985   Sir Alister Hardy, founder of the Sir Alister Hardy Research Centre at Oxford, which used scientific methods to investigate religious experience.

1986   The Rev. James McCord, Chancellor of the Center of Theological Inquiry in Princeton, N.J., for his lifelong study of the relationship between science and religion through his studies of the nature of reality.

1987   The Rev. Stanley L. Jaki, professor of Astrophysics at Seton Hall University, N.J. A Benedictine monk and the author of more than two dozen books, who carefully emphasized the differences as well as similarities between science and religion.

1988   Dr. Inamullah Khan, founder and Secretary-General of the Modern World Muslim Congress in Karachi, Pakistan, for his tireless work in establishing harmony among Muslims, Christians, and Jews.

1989   The very Rev. Lord MacLeod, founder of the Iona Community, a monastic island off the west coast of Scotland, for building a prayer-centered spiritual movement dedicated to peacemaking and simplicity. **Professor Carl Friedrich von Weizsacker**, for his exploration of inter-relationships of physics, cosmology, and theology.

1990   Baba Amte, a wealthy Hindu lawyer who left a comfortable life behind to help modern communities deal with India's lepers and other so-called "untouchable" social problems. Amte's community brought "employment, education, health, and other services to citizens long denied compassion." **L. Charles Birch**, professor of biology at the University of Sydney, for his "search for spiritual meaning in the realms of specialized knowledge."

1991   Lord Jakobovits, Chief Rabbi of Great Britain (1967-91), for over half a century of spiritual leadership. His steadfast principles and unwavering integrity made him a rock of unyielding ethics whose moral authority extended far beyond the Jewish community.

1992   Rev. Dr. Kyung-Chik Han, founder of Seoul's 60,000-member Young Nak Presbyterian Church, the world's largest Presbyterian congregation, with more than 500 churches worldwide. His work on behalf of refugees and the poor attracted the world's attention to the growth of Christianity in Korea.

1993   Charles W. Colson, founder of the Prison Fellowship. A former Special Counsel to U.S. President Richard M. Nixon, Colson spent time in federal prison for Watergate-related crimes before founding the largest prison outreach program in the world. It has succeeded in reducing recidivism among criminals.

1994   Michael Novak, author, journalist, professor, and diplomat, for his "revolutionary insights into the spiritual foundations of economic and political systems." A pioneer in the discipline in the theology of economics.

1995   Paul Charles William Davies, a mathematical physicist whose "inquiries into the workings of the universe have breached the barrier between science and religion." He contended that humanity's

| Year | Recipient | | Year | Recipient |

ability to calculate the physical universe evidences purpose and design to human existence.

1996   William R. "Bill" Bright, founder of Campus Crusade for Christ, which revived biblical study on the campuses of more than 1,000 colleges worldwide.

1997   Pandurang Shastri Athavale, founder of the Bhagavad Gita–based self-study known as *swadhyaya*, which is credited with liberating close to 20 million people in India from poverty and other social ills.

1998   Sir Sigmund Sternberg, a Hungarian-born British philanthropist, for his tireless promotion of interfaith dialogue, especially between Catholics and Jews.

1999   Ian Barbour, professor emeritus at Carleton College in Northfield, Minn., for promoting "scrutiny of areas where science and religion might meet." An outspoken advocate for ethics in technology, energy policy, and genetic engineering.

2000   Freeman J. Dyson, Princeton Univ. physicist, "whose futurist views have consistently challenged humankind to reconcile technology and social justice."

2001   Arthur Peacocke, Oxford Univ. physical biochemist and Anglican priest, founder of the Society of Ordained Scientists (S.O.Sc.), which seeks to foster the spirituality of those working as scientists and as ordained persons and to act as a bridge between the Church and science.

Source: John Marks Templeton Foundation. **www.templeton.org.**

Fields Medal Winners, 1936-98

The Fields Medal, named for Canadian mathematician J. D. Fields, is often described as the Nobel Prize for Mathematics. In agreement with Fields's wish that the awards recognize both existing work and the promise of future achievement, the medals are awarded to mathematicians no older than 40. Since 1950, medals have been awarded every four years.

Year	Winners
1936	**Lars Ahlfors**, Harvard Univ.; **Jesse Douglas**, MIT
1950	**Laurent Schwartz**, Universite de Nancy; **Atle Selberg**, Princeton/IAS
1954	**Kunihiko Kodaira**, Princeton Univ.; **Jean-Pierre Serre**, College de France
1958	**Klaus Roth**, Univ. of London; **Rene Thom**, Univ. of Strasbourg
1962	**Lars Hormander**, Univ. of Stockholm; **John Milnor**, Princeton Univ.
1966	**Michael Atiyah**, Oxford Univ.; **Paul Cohen**, Stanford Univ.; **Alex Grothendieck**, Univ. of Paris; **Stephen Smale**, Univ. of California
1970	**Alan Baker**, Cambridge Univ.; **Heisuke Hironaka**, Harvard Univ.; **Serge Novikov**, Moscow Univ.; **John Thompson**, Univ. of Chicago
1974	**Enrico Bombieri**, Univ. of Pisa; **David Mumford**, Harvard Univ.
1978	**Pierre Deligne**, IHES; **Charles Fefferman**, Princeton Univ.; **Gregori Margulis**, Moscow Univ.; **Daniel Quillen**, MIT
1982	**Alain Connes**, IHES; **William Thurston**, Princeton Univ.; **Shing-Tung Yau**, IAS
1986	**Simon Donaldson**, Oxford Univ.; **Gerd Faltings**, Princeton Univ.; **Michael Freedman**, Univ. of California at San Diego
1990	**Vladimir Drinfeld**, Phys.Inst.Kharkov; **Vaughan Jones**, Univ. of California; **Shigefumi Mori**, Univ. of Kyoto; **Edward Witten**, Princeton/IAS
1994	**Pierre-Louis Lions**, Universite de Paris-Dauphine; **Jean-Chrisophe Yoccoz**, Universite de Paris-Sud; **Jean Bourgain**, Princeton/IAS; **Efim Zelmanov**, Univ. of Wisconsin
1998	**Richard E. Borcherds**, Cambridge Univ.; **William T. Gowers**, Cambridge Univ.; **Maxim Kontsevich**, IHES and Rutgers Univ.; **Curtis T. McMullen**, Harvard Univ.

Note: IAS= Institute of Advanced Study. IHES=Institut des Hautes Etudes Scientifiques.
Source: Fields Institute for Research in Mathematical Sciences. **www.fields.toronto.edu**

Pulitzer Prizes

PULITZER PRIZES IN JOURNALISM

The Pulitzer Prize for Reporting is the oldest given in journalism and was first awarded in 1917 together with the Pulitzer Prizes for History and Biography. The changing nature and public perception of reporting can be seen in the various categories established over the years. Originally, the prize recognized excellence irrespective of the journalist's beat; it could be local, national or international, and it could be either reporting for a deadline or investigative reporting carried out over a longer period. In 1929 a Correspondence category was created to distinguish correspondents stationed either in Washington or abroad from local journalists. Separate categories for National and International Reporting were added in 1942, and the Correspondence category was absorbed by these categories in 1947.

Meritorious Public Service, 1918–2001

Year	Paper, Distinction

1918 New York Times, Reports, documents, and speeches relating to World War I.
1919 Milwaukee Journal, Campaign for Americanism.
1920 No award
1921 Boston Post, Articles exposing operations and leading to arrest of Charles Ponzi.
1922 New York World, Articles exposing operations of Ku Klux Klan.
1923 Memphis Commercial Appeal, News and cartoons about Ku Klux Klan.
1924 New York World, Exposure of Florida peonage evil.
1925 No award
1926 Columbus (Ga.) Enquirer Sun, Articles decrying Ku Klux Klan, dishonest public officials, lynching, and a law barring the teaching of evolution.
1927 Canton (Ohio) Daily News, Articles about collusion between city government and organized crime, resulting in assassination of editor, Don R. Mellett.
1928 Indianapolis Times, Exposure of political corruption in Indiana.
1929 New York Evening World, Campaign to correct evil and corruption in administration of justice.
1930 No award
1931 Atlanta Constitution, Municipal graft exposure leading to convictions.
1932 Indianapolis News, Campaign to eliminate waste in city management and reduce tax levy.
1933 New York World-Telegram, Series of articles on veterans' relief, real estate bond evil, and articles exposing lottery schemes of fraternal organizations.
1934 Medford (Oreg.) Mail Tribune, Campaign against unscrupulous politicians in Jackson County, Oreg.
1935 Sacramento Bee, Campaign against political machine influence in appointment of two federal judges in Nevada.
1936 Cedar Rapids Gazette, Crusade against corruption and misgovernment in state of Iowa.
1937 St. Louis Post-Dispatch, Exposure of registration fraud in St. Louis, resulting in invalidation of more than 40,000 fraudulent ballots and appointment of new election board.
1938 Bismarck (N.D.) Tribune, News reports and editorials entitled "Self Help in the Dust Bowl."
1939 Miami Daily News, Campaign for recall of Miami City Commission.
1940 Waterbury (Conn.) Republican & American, Campaign exposing municipal graft.
1941 St. Louis Post-Dispatch, Campaign against city smoke nuisance.
1942 Los Angeles Times, Campaign resulting in clarification and confirmation of freedom of press rights for all American newspapers.
1943 Omaha (Nebr.) World-Herald, Campaign for collection of scrap metal for war effort.

Year	Paper, Distinction

1944 New York Times, Survey of teaching of American history.
1945 Detroit Free Press, Investigation of legislative graft and corruption at Lansing, Mich.
1946 Scranton (Pa.) Times, Fifteen-year investigation of judicial practices in U.S. District Court, resulting in removal of the district judge and indictment of many others.
1947 Baltimore Sun, Series of articles by Howard M. Norton dealing with administration of unemployment compensation in Maryland, resulting in 93 criminal convictions and/or guilty pleas.
1948 St. Louis Post-Dispatch, Coverage of Centralia, Ill. mine disaster and follow-up articles resulting in reforms in mine safety laws and regulations.
1949 Nebraska State Journal, Campaign establishing "Nebraska All-Star Primary" that called attention to issues early in presidential campaign.
1950 Chicago Daily News and St. Louis Post-Dispatch, Work of George Thiem and Roy J. Harris, respectively, in exposing presence of 37 Illinois newspapermen on an Illinois state payroll.
1951 Miami Herald and Brooklyn Eagle, Crime reporting during the year.
1952 St. Louis Post-Dispatch, Investigation and disclosures of corruption in Internal Revenue Bureau and other government departments.
1953 Whiteville (N.C.) News Reporter and Tabor City (N.C.) Tribune, Campaign against Ku Klux Klan, culminating in the conviction of more than 100 Klansman and an end to terrorism in their communities.
1954 Newsday (Garden City, N.Y.), Exposé of New York State's racetrack scandals and labor racketeering, leading to imprisonment of racketeer William C. DeKooonig Sr.
1955 Columbus (Ga.) Ledger and Sunday Ledger-Enquirer, News coverage and editorial attack on corruption in neighboring Phenix City, leading to destruction of racket-ridden city government.
1956 Watsonville (Calif.) Register-Pajaronion, Exposure of corruption in public office leading to resignation of a district attorney and conviction of one of his associates.
1957 Chicago Daily News, Exposure of $2.5 million fraud in office of Illinois state auditor, resulting in his conviction.
1958 Arkansas Gazette, Civic leadership, journalistic responsibility, and moral courage during school integration crisis.
1959 Utica Observer-Dispatch and Utica Daily Press (N.Y.), Campaign against corruption, gambling, and vice.
1960 Los Angeles Times, Attack on narcotics traffic; reporting of Gene Sherman, which led to opening of negotiations between U.S. and Mexico to halt the flow of illegal drugs into California and other border states.

Year   Paper, Distinction

Year   Paper, Distinction

1961   Amarillo (Tex.) Globe-Times, Exposure of lax law enforcement resulting in punitive action sweeping officials from their posts and creating election of reform slate.
1962   Panama City (Fla.) News-Herald, Three-year campaign against entrenched power and corruption, resulting in reforms in Panama City and Bay County.
1963   Chicago Daily News, Articles calling public attention to providing birth control services in public health programs.
1964   St. Petersburg Times, Investigation of illegal activity within Florida Turnpike Authority, resulting in major reorganization state's road construction program.
1965   Hutchinson (Kans.) News, Campaign for more equitable reapportionment of Kansas legislature.
1966   Boston Globe, Campaign to prevent confirmation of Francis X. Morrissey as federal district judge in Massachusetts.
1967   Louisville Courier Journal and Milwaukee Journal, Campaign to control Kentucky strip-mining industry; campaign to stiffen water pollution laws in Wisconsin.
1968   Riverside (Calif.) Press-Enterprise, Exposure of corruption in courts in connection with handling of property and estates of an Indian tribe in California.
1969   Los Angeles Times, Exposure of wrongdoing within Los Angeles city government commissions, resulting in criminal convictions, resignations, and sweeping reforms.
1970   Newsday (Garden City, N.Y.), Three-year investigation and exposure of secret land deals in eastern Long Island, leading to criminal convictions, resignations, and discharges among public and political officials.
1971   Winston-Salem Journal and Sentinel, Coverage of environmental problems, as exemplified by campaign to block a strip-mining operation that would have caused irreparable damage to northwest North Carolina hill country.
1972   New York Times, Publication of Pentagon Papers.
1973   Washington Post, Investigation of Watergate case.
1974   Newsday (Garden City, N.Y.), Definitive report on illicit narcotics traffic in U.S. and abroad, entitled "The Heroin Trail."
1975   Boston Globe, Coverage of Boston school desegregation crisis.
1976   Anchorage Daily News, Disclosures of impact and influence of Teamsters Union on Alaska's economy and politics.
1977   Lufkin (Tex.) News, Obituary of local men who died in Marine training camp, which grew into investigation of that death and fundamental reform in Marine Corps' recruiting and training practices.
1978   Philadelphia Inquirer, Series of articles showing abuses of power by Philadelphia police.
1979   Point Reyes (Calif.) Light, Investigation of Synanon.
1980   Gannett News Service, Series on financial contributions to Pauline Fathers.
1981   Charlotte Observer, Series called "Brown Lung: A Case of Deadly Neglect."
1982   Detroit News, Series by Sydney P. Freedberg and David Ashenfelter exposing U.S. Navy's cover-up of circumstances surrounding deaths of seamen aboard ship and leading to significant reforms in naval procedures.

1983   Jackson (Miss.) Clarion-Ledger, Campaign supporting Gov. Winter in his legislative battle for reform of Mississippi's public education system.
1984   Los Angeles Times, In-depth examination of southern California's growing Latino community.
1985   Fort Worth Star-Telegram, Reporting by Mark J. Thompson revealing that nearly 250 U.S. servicemen died because of a design problem in helicopters built by Bell Helicopter—causing the army to ground almost 600 Huey helicopters pending their modification.
1986   Denver Post, In-depth study of "missing children," revealing that most are involved in custody disputes or are runaways, and helping to mitigate national fears stirred by exaggerated statistics.
1987   Pittsburgh Press, Reporting by Andrew Schneider and Matthew Brelis, revealing inadequacy of FAA's medical screening of airline pilots, and leading to reform.
1988   Charlotte Observer, Revealing misuse of funds by the PTL television ministry, despite massive campaign by PTL to discredit the newspaper.
1989   Anchorage Daily News, For series revealing high incidence of alcoholism and suicide among Native Alaskans.
1990   Philadelphia Inquirer, For series by Gilbert M. Gaul disclosing shortcomings in federal regulation of the nation's blood banks.
Washington (N.C.) Daily News, For series by Betty Gray and Mike Voss revealing contamination of the municipal water supply in the town of 9,000 and the eight-year cover-up by elected officials.
1991   Des Moines Register, For series by Jane Schorer about a rape and its aftermath that reopened debate over whether rape victims should be identified by name.
1992   Sacramento Bee, For series by Tom Knudson about pollution, overdevelopment and overpopulation along the Sierra Nevada mountain range.
1993   Miami Herald, For helping readers cope with Hurricane Andrew's devastation and for showing "how lax zoning, inspection and building codes had contributed to the destruction."
1994   Akron Beacon Journal, For two-part examination of race relations.
1995   Virgin Islands Daily News, For 10-part series on crime that examined crime on the islands and ultimately led to major reforms.
1996   Raleigh News and Observer, For stories revealing how agricultural corporations, unfettered by government regulation, were elbowing out small family hog farms and polluting the environment in the process.
1997   New Orleans Times-Picayune, For series analyzing the environmental, commercial, political, and social conditions that threaten the world's fish supply. It affected changes in Federal fisheries laws.
1998   Grand Forks (N.D.) Herald, For its coverage of the blizzard, flood, and fire that devastated the city and the newspaper's own plant.
1999   Washington Post, For its series that identified and analyzed patterns of reckless gunplay by city police officers who had little training or supervision.
2000   Washington Post, For a series by Katherine Boo about gross mistreatment of mentally retarded patients in District of Columbia group homes. The series prompted the city government to reform the system.
2001   The Oregonian (Portland, Ore.), For a series on inefficiency, misconduct and other systemic problems in the Immigration and Naturalization Service.

Pulitzer Prizes for National Reporting, 1942–2001

Year	Winner, Newspaper	Year	Winner, Newspaper
1942	Louis Stark, *New York Times*	1973	Robert Boyd and Clark Hoyt, Knight Newspapers
1943	No award	1974	James R. Polk, *Washington Star-News*
1944	Dewey L. Fleming, *Baltimore Sun*		Jack White, *Providence Journal and Evening*
1945	James B. Reston, *New York Times*		*Bulletin*
1946	Edward A. Harris, *St. Louis Post-Dispatch*	1975	Donald L. Bartlett and James B. Steele,
1947	Edward T. Folliard, *Washington Post*		*Philadelphia Inquirer*
1948	Bert Andrews, *New York Herald Tribune*	1976	James Risser, *Des Moines Register*
	Nat S. Finney, *Minneapolis Tribune*	1977	Walter Mears, Associated Press
1949	C.P. Trussell, *New York Times*	1978	Gaylord D. Shaw, *Los Angeles Times*
1950	Edwin O. Guthman, *Seattle Times*	1979	James Risser, *Des Moines Register*
1951	No award[1]	1980	Bette Swenson Orsini and Charles Stafford,
1952	Anthony Leviero, *New York Times*		*St. Petersburg Times*
1953	Don Whitehead, Associated Press	1981	John M Crewdson, *New York Times*
1954	Richard Wilson, *Des Moines Register and*	1982	Rick Atkinson, *Kansas City Times*
	Tribune	1983	Staff, *Boston Globe*
1955	Anthony Lewis, *Washington Daily News*	1984	John Noble Wilford, *New York Times*
1956	Charles L. Bartlett, *Chattanooga Times*	1985	Thomas J. Knudson, *Des Moines Register*
1957	James B. Reston, *New York Times*	1986	Arthur Howe, *Philadelphia Inquirer*
1958	Relman Morin, Associated Press		Craig Flournoy and George Rodrigues,
	Clark Mollenhoff, *Des Moines Register and*		*Dallas Morning News*
	Tribune	1987	Staff, *Miami Herald*
1959	Howard Van Smith, *Miami News*		Staff, *New York Times*
1960	Vance Trimble , Scripps-Howard	1988	Tim Weiner, *Philadelphia Inquirer*
	Newspaper Alliance	1989	Donald L. Bartlett and James B. Steele,
1961	Edward R. Cony, *Wall Street Journal*		*Philadelphia Inquirer*
1962	Nathan G. Caldwell and Gene S. Graham,	1990	Ross Anderson, Bill Dietrich, Mary Ann
	Nashville Tennessean		Gwinn, and Eric Nalder, *Seattle Times*
1963	Anthony Lewis, *New York Times*	1991	Marji Lundstrom and Rochelle Sharpe,
1964	Merriman Smith, United Press International		Gannet News Service
1965	Louis M. Kohlmeier, *Wall Street Journal*	1992	Jeff Taylor and Mike McGraw, *Kansas City Star*
1966	Haynes Johnson, *Washington Evening Star*	1993	David Maraniss, *Washington Post*
1967	Stanley Penn and Monroe Karmin, *Wall*	1994	Eileen Welsome, *Albuquerque Tribune*
	Street Journal	1995	Tony Horwitz, *Wall Street Journal*
1968	Howard James, *Christian Science Monitor*	1996	Alix M. Freedman, *Wall Street Journal*
	Nathan K. (Nick) Kotz, *Des Moines*	1997	Staff, *Wall Street Journal*
	Register and *Minneapolis Tribune*	1998	Russell Carollo and Jeff Nesmith, *Dayton*
1969	Robert Cahn, *Christian Science Monitor*		*(Ohio) Daily News*
1970	William J. Eaton, *Chicago Daily News*	1999	Staff, *New York Times*
1971	Lucinda Franks and Thomas Powers, United	2000	Staff, *Wall Street Journal*
	Press International	2001	Staff, *New York Times*
1972	Jack Anderson, (Syndicated columnist)		

1. The board decided that Arthur Krock of The *New York Times* deserved the prize but he could not accept because he was a board member.

Pulitzer Prizes for International Reporting, 1942–2001

Year	Winner, Newspaper	Year	Winner, Newspaper
1942	Lawrence Edmund Allen, Associated Press	1955	Harrison E. Salisbury, *New York Times*
1943	Ira Wolfert, North American Newspaper	1956	William Randolph Hearst Jr., Kingsbury
	Alliance, Inc.		Smith, and Frank Conniff, International
1944	Daniel DeLuce, Associated Press		News Service
1945	Mark S. Watson, *Baltimore Sun*	1957	Russell Jones, United Press
1946	Homer William Bigart, *New York Herald Tribune*	1958	Staff, *New York Times*
1947	Eddy Gilmore, Associated Press	1959	Joseph Martin and Philip Santora,
1948	Paul W. Ward, *Baltimore Sun*		*New York Daily News*
1949	Price Day, *Baltimore Sun*	1960	A.M. Rosenthal, *New York Times*
1950	Edmund Stevens, *Christian Science Monitor*	1961	Lynn Heinzerling, Associated Press
1951	Keyes Beech, *Chicago Daily News*	1962	Walter Lippmann, *New York Herald*
	Homer William Bigart, *New York Herald Tribune*		*Tribune Syndicate*
	Marguerite Higgins, *New York Herald Tribune*	1963	Hal Hendrix, *Miami News*
	Relman Morin, Associated Press	1964	Malcolm W. Browne, Associated Press
	Fred Sparks, *Chicago Daily News*		David Halberstam, *New York Times*
	Don Whitehead, Associated Press	1965	J. A. Livingston, *Philadelphia Bulletin*
1952	John M. Hightower, Associated Press	1966	Peter Arnett, Associated Press
1953	Austin Wehrwien, *Milwaukee Journal*	1967	R. John Hughes, *Christian Science Monitor*
1954	Jim G. Lucas, Scripps-Howard Newspaper	1968	Alfred Friendly, *Washington Post*
	Alliance	1969	William Tuohy, *Los Angeles Times*

Year	Winner, Newspaper	Year	Winner, Newspaper
1970	Seymour M. Hersh, Dispatch News Service	1986	Lewis M. Simons, Pete Carey, and
1971	Jimmie Lee Hoagland, Washington Post		Katherine Ellison, San Jose Mercury News
1972	Peter R. Kann, Wall Street Journal	1987	Michael Parks, Los Angeles Times
1973	Max Frankel, New York Times	1988	Thomas L. Friedman, New York Times
1974	Hedrick Smith, New York Times	1989	Glenn Frankel, Washington Post
1975	William Mullen (reporter), Ovie Carter		Bill Keller, New York Times
	(photographer), Chicago Tribune	1990	Nicholas D. Kristof and Sheryl WuDunn,
1976	Sydney H. Schanberg, New York Times		New York Times
1977	No award	1991	Caryle Murphy, Washington Post
1978	Henry Kamm, New York Times		Serge Schmemann, New York Times
1979	Richard Ben Cramer, Philadelphia Inquirer	1992	Patrick J. Sloyan, Newsday (Garden City, N.Y.)
1980	Joel Brinkley (reporter), Jay Mather	1993	John F. Burns, New York Times
	(photographer), Louisville Courier-Journal		Roy Gutman, Newsday (Garden City, N.Y.)
1981	Shirley Christian, Miami Herald	1994	Team of reporters, Dallas Morning News
1982	John Darnton, New York Times	1995	Mark Fritz, Associated Press
1983	Thomas L. Friedman, New York Times	1996	David Rohde, Christian Science Monitor
	Loren Jenkins, Washington Post	1997	John F. Burns, New York Times
1984	Karen Elliott House, Wall Street Journal	1998	Staff, New York Times
1985	Josh Friedman and Dennis Bell (reporters)	1999	Staff, Wall Street Journal
	and Ozier Muhammad (photographer),	2000	Mark Schoofs, The Village Voice (N.Y. City)
	Newsday (Garden City, N.Y.)	2001	Ian Johnson, Wall Street Journal
			Paul Salopek, Chicago Tribune

Pulitzer Prizes for Editorial Writing, 1917–2001

Year	Winner, Newspaper	Year	Winner, Newspaper
1917	Lusitania editorial article, New York Tribune		Herbert Elliston, Washington Post
1918	War editorials and articles, Louisville	1950	Carl M. Saunders, Jackson (Mich.) Citizen
	Courier Journal		Patriot
1919	No award	1951	William Harry Fitzpatrick, New Orleans
1920	Harvey E. Newbranch, Evening World Herald		States
1921	No award	1952	Louis LaCoss, St. Louis Globe Democrat
1922	Frank M. O'Brien, New York Herald	1953	Vermont Connecticut Royster, Wall Street
1923	William Allen White, Emporia (Kans.) Gazette		Journal
1924[1]	Coolidge editorial, Boston Herald	1954	Don Murray, Boston Herald
1925	"Plight of the South" editorial, Charleston	1955	Royce Howes, Detroit Free Press
	(S.C.) News and Courier	1956	Lauren K. Soth, Des Moines Register and
1926	Edward M. Kingsbury, New York Times		Tribune
1927	F. Lauriston Bullard, Boston Herald	1957	Buford Boone, Tuscaloosa News
1928	Grover Cleveland Hall, Montgomery	1958	Harry S. Ashmore, Arkansas Gazette
	Advertiser	1959	Ralph McGill, Atlanta Constitution
1929	Louis Isaac Jaffe, Norfolk Virginian-Pilot	1960	Lenoir Chambers, Norfolk Virginian-Pilot
1930	No award	1961	William J. Dorvillier, San Juan (Puerto Rico)
1931	Charles S. Ryckman, Fremont (Nebr.) Tribune		Star
1932	No award	1962	Thomas M. Storke, Santa Barbara (Calif.)
1933	series of editorials, Kansas City Star		News Press
1934	E.P. Chase, Atlantic (Iowa) News-Telegraph	1963	Ira B. Harkey Jr., Pascagoula (Miss.) U.
1935	No award		Chronicle
1936	Felix Morley, Washington Post	1964	Hazel Brannon Smith, Lexington (Miss.)
	George B. Parker, Scripps-Howard		Advertiser
	Newspapers	1965	John R. Harrison, Gainesville (Fla.) Daily Sun
1937	John W. Owens, Baltimore Sun	1966	Robert Lasch, St. Louis Post-Dispatch
1938	William Wesley Waymack, Des Moines	1967	Eugene Patterson, Atlanta Constitution
	Register and Tribune	1968	John S. Knight, Knight Newspapers
1939	Ronald G. Callvert, Portland Oregonian	1969	Paul Greenberg, Pine Bluff (Ark.)
1940	Bart Howard, St. Louis Post-Dispatch		Commercial
1941	Reuben Maury, New York Daily News	1970	Philip L. Geyelin, Washington Post
1942	Geoffrey Parsons, New York Herald Tribune	1971	Horance G. Davis Jr., Gainesville (Fla.) Daily
1943	Forrest W. Seymour, Des Moines Register		Sun
	and Tribune	1972	John Strohmeyer, Bethlehem (Pa.) Globe-Times
1944	Henry J. Haskell, Kansas City Star	1973	Roger B. Linscott, Berkshire Eagle (Pittsfield,
1945	George W. Potter, Providence Journal-		Mass.)
	Bulletin	1974	F. Gilman Spencer, Trentonian (Trenton, N.J.)
1946	Hodding Carter, Delta Democrat-Times	1975	John D. Maurice, Charleston (W.V.) Daily Mail
	(Greenville, Miss.)	1976	Philip P. Kerby, Los Angeles Times
1947	William H. Grimes, Wall Street Journal	1977	Warren L. Lerude, Foster Church and
1948	Virginius Dabney, Richmond Times-Dispatch		Norman F. Cardoza, Reno Evening Gazette
1949	John H. Crider, Boston Herald		and Nevada State Journal

Year	Winner, Newspaper	Year	Winner, Newspaper
1978	Meg Greenfield, *Washington Post*	1991	Ron Casey, Harold Jackson, and Joey
1979	Edwin M. Yoder Jr., *Washington Star*		Kennedy, *Birmingham News*
1980	Robert L. Bartley, *Wall Street Journal*	1992	Maria Henson, *Lexington Herald-Leader*
1981	No award	1993	No award
1982	Jack Rosenthal, *New York Times*	1994	R. Bruce Dold, *Chicago Tribune*
1983	Editorial Board, *Miami Herald*	1995	Jeffrey Good, *St. Petersburg Times*
1984	Albert Scardino, *Georgia Gazette*	1996	Robert B. Semple, Jr., *New York Times*
1985	Richard Aregood, *Philadelphia Daily News*	1997	Michael G. Gartner, *Daily Tribune* (Ames,
1986	Jack Fuller, *Chicago Tribune*		Iowa)
1987	Jonathan Freedman, *San Diego Tribune*	1998	Bernard L. Stein, *Riverdale* (N.Y.) *Press*
1988	Jane Healy, *Orlando Sentinel*	1999	Editorial Board, *N.Y. Daily News*
1989	Lois Wille, *Chicago Tribune*	2000	John C. Bersia, *Orlando Sentinel*
1990	Thomas J. Hylton, *Pottstown* (Pa.) *Mercury*	2001	David Moats, *Rutland* (Vt.) *Herald*

1. A special prize was awarded to the widow of the late Frank I. Cobb of *The New York World* in recognition of his lifetime of editorial writing and service.

Pulitzer Prizes for Editorial Cartooning, 1922–2001

Year	Winner, Newspaper	Year	Winner, Newspaper
1922	Rollin Kirby, *New York World*	1963	Frank Miller, *Des Moines Register*
1923	No award	1964	Paul Conrad, *Denver Post*
1924	Jay Norwood Darling, *Des Moines Register*	1965	No award
	and Tribune	1966	Don Wright, *Miami News*
1925	Rollin Kirby, *New York World*	1967	Patrick Oliphant, *Denver Post*
1926	Daniel R. Fitzpatrick, *St. Louis Post-Dispatch*	1968	Eugene Gray Payne, *Charlotte Observer*
1927	Nelson Harding, *Brooklyn Daily Eagle*	1969	John Fischettii, *Chicago Daily News*
1928	Nelson Harding, *Brooklyn Daily Eagle*	1970	Thomas F. Darcy, *Newsday* (Garden City,
1929	Rollin Kirby, *New York World*		N.Y.)
1930	Charles R. Macauley, *Brooklyn Daily Eagle*	1971	Paul Conrad, *Los Angeles Times*
1931	Edmund Duffy, *Baltimore Sun*	1972	Jeffrey K. MacNelly, *Richmond News-Leader*
1932	John T. McCutcheon, *Chicago Tribune*	1973	No award
1933	H.M. Talburt, *Washington Daily News*	1974	Paul Szep, *Boston Globe*
1934	Edmund Duffy, *Baltimore Sun*	1975	Garry Trudeau, Universal Press Syndicate
1935	Ross A. Lewis, *Milwaukee Journal*	1976	Tony Auth, *Philadelphia Inquirer*
1936	No award	1977	Paul Szep, *Boston Globe*
1937	C.D. Batchelor, *New York Daily News*	1978	Jeffrey K. MacNelly, *Richmond News-Leader*
1938	Vaughn Shoemaker , *Chicago Daily News*	1979	Herbert L. Block (Herblock), *Washington*
1939	Charles G. Werner, *Daily Oklahoman*		*Post*
1940	Edmund Duffy, *Baltimore Sun*	1980	Don Wright, *Miami News*
1941	Jacob Burck, *Chicago Times*	1981	Mike Peters, *Dayton* (Ohio) *Daily News*
1942	Herbert L. Block (Herblock), NEA Service	1982	Ben Sargent, *Austin* (Tex.) *American-*
1943	Jay Norwood Darling, *Des Moines Register*		*Statesman*
	and Tribune	1983	Richard Locher, *Chicago Tribune*
1944	Clifford K. Berryman, *Washington Evening*	1984	Paul Conrad, *Los Angeles Times*
	Star	1985	Jeff MacNelly , *Chicago Tribune*
1945	Sergeant Bill Mauldin, United Feature	1986	Jules Feiffer, *Village Voice* (New York City)
	Syndicate, Inc	1987	Berke Breathed, Washington Post Writers
1946	Bruce Alexander Russell, *Los Angeles Times*		Group
1947	Vaughn Shoemaker , *Chicago Daily News*	1988	Doug Marlette, *Atlanta Constitution* and
1948	Reuben L. Goldberg, *New York Sun*		*Charlotte Observer*
1949	Lute Pease, *Newark Evening News*	1989	Jack Higgins, *Chicago Sun-Times*
1950	James T. Berryman, *Washington Evening Star*	1990	Tom Toles, *Buffalo News*
1951	Reg Manning, *Arizona Republic*	1991	Jim Borgman, *Cincinnati Enquirer*
1952	Fred L. Packer, *New York Mirror*	1992	Signe Wilkinson, *Philadelphia Daily News*
1953	Edward D. Kuekes, *Cleveland Plain Dealer*	1993	Stephen R. Benson, *Arizona Republic*
1954	Herbert L. Block (Herblock), *Washington*	1994	Michael P. Ramirez, *Commercial Appeal*
	Post & Times Herald		(Memphis)
1955	Daniel R. Fitzpatrick, *St. Louis Post-Dispatch*	1995	Mike Luckovich, *Atlanta Constitution*
1956	Robert York, *Lousiville Times*	1996	Jim Morin, *Miami Herald*
1957	Tom Little, *Nashville Tennessean*	1997	Walt Handelsman, *New Orleans Times-*
1958	Bruce M. Shanks, *Buffalo Evening News*		*Picayune*
1959	Bill Mauldin, *St. Louis Post-Dispatch*	1998	Stephen P. Breen, *Asbury Park* (N.J.) *Press*
1960	No award	1999	David Horsey, *Seattle Post-Intelligencer*
1961	Carey Orr, *Chicago Tribune*	2000	Joel Pett, *Lexington Herald-Leader*
1962	Edmund S. Valtman, *Hartford Times*	2001	Ann Telnaes, *Los Angeles Times* Syndicate

Pulitzer Prizes for Photography

The **photography** category began in 1942 and was divided into spot news and feature categories in 1968.

PHOTOGRAPHY, 1942–67

Year	Winner, Newspaper	Year	Winner, Newspaper
1942	Milton Brooks, *Detroit News*	1955	John L. Gaunt Jr., *Los Angeles Times*
1943	Frank Noel, *Associated Press*	1956	Photography staff, *New York Daily News*
1944	Frank Filan, *Associated Press*	1957	Harry A. Trask, *Boston Traveler*
	Earle L. Bunker, *World-Herald* (Omaha, Neb.)	1958	William C. Beall, *Washington Daily News*
1945	Joe Rosenthal, *Associated Press*	1959	William Seaman, *Minneapolis Star*
1946	No award	1960	Andrew Lopez, United Press International
1947	Arnold Hardy, Amateur; photo distributed by Associated Press	1961	Yasushi Nago, *Manichi* (Tokyo); photo distributed by United Press International
1948	Frank Cushing, *Boston Traveler*	1962	Paul Vathis, Associated Press
1949	Nathaniel Fein, *New York Herald Tribune*	1963	Hector Rondon, *La Republica* (Caracas,
1950	Bill Crouch, *Oakland Tribune*		Venezuela); photo distributed by
1951	Max Desfor, *Associated Press*		Associated Press
1952	John Robinson and Don Ultang, *Des Moines Register and Tribune*	1964	Robert H. Jackson, *Dallas Times-Herald*
1953	William M. Gallagher, *Flint* (Mich.) *Journal*	1965	Horst Faas, Associated Press
1954	Mrs. Walter M. Schau, Amateur; photo published by *Akron Beacon Journal*	1966	Kyoichi Sawada, United Press International
		1967	Jack R. Thornell, Associated Press

SPOT NEWS PHOTOGRAPHY: 1968–2001

Year	Winner, Newspaper
1968	Rocco Morabito, *Jacksonville Journal*
1969	Edward T. Adams, Associated Press
1970	Steve Starr, Associated Press
1971	John Paul Filo, *Valley Daily News* and *Daily Dispatch*, (New Kensington, Pa.)
1972	Horst Faas and Michael Laurent, Associated Press
1973	Hyunh Cong Ut, Associated Press
1974	Anthony K. Roberts, freelancer, Beverly Hills, Calif.
1975	Gerald H. Gay, *Seattle Times*
1976	Stanley Forman, *Boston Herald American*
1977	Neal Ulevich, Associated Press
	Stanley Forman, *Boston Herald American*
1978	John H. Blair, United Press International
1979	Thomas J. Kelly III, *Pottstown* (Pa.) *Mercury*
1980	Unnamed photographer, United Press International
1981	Larry C. Price, *Fort Worth Star-Telegram*
1982	Ron Edmonds, Associated Press
1983	Bill Foley, Associated Press
1984	Stan Grossfeld, *Boston Globe*
1985	Photography Staff, *Register* (Santa Ana, Calif.)
1986	Carol Guzy and Michael duCille, *Miami Herald*
1987	Kim Komenich, *San Francisco Examiner*
1988	Scott Shaw, *Odessa* (Tex.) *American*
1989	Ron Olshwanger, freelancer, *St. Louis Post-Dispatch*
1990	Photography Staff, *Oakland Tribune*
1991	Greg Marinovich, Associated Press
1992	Photography Staff, Associated Press
1993	William Snyder and Ken Geiger, *Dallas Morning News*
1994	Paul Watson, *Toronto Star*
1995	Carol Guzy, *Washington Post*
1996	Charles Porter 4th, freelancer, Associated Press
1997	Annie Wells, *Press Democrat* (Santa Rosa, Calif.)
1998	Martha Rial, *Pittsburgh Post-Gazette*
1999	John McConnico, Associated Press
2000	Photography Staff, *Rocky Mountain News*
2001	Alan Diaz, Associated Press

FEATURE PHOTOGRAPHY: 1968–2001

Year	Winner, Newspaper
1968	Toshio Sakai, United Press International
1969	Moneta Sleet Jr., *Ebony* Magazine
1970	Dallas Kinney, *Palm Beach Post* (West Palm Beach, Fla.)
1971	Jack Dykinga, *Chicago Sun-Times*
1972	Dave Kennerly, United Press International
1973	Brian Lanker, *Topeka Capital-Journal*
1974	Slava Veder, Associated Press
1975	Matthew Lewis, *Washington Post*
1976	Photography Staff, *Louisville Courier Journal and Times*
1977	Robin Hood, *Chattanooga News-Free Press*
1978	J. Ross Baughman, Associated Press
1979	Photography Staff, *Boston Herald American*
1980	Erwin H. Hagler, *Dallas Times Herald*
1981	Taro M. Yamasaki, *Detroit Free Press*
1982	John H. White, *Chicago Sun-Times*
1983	James B. Dickman, *Dallas Times Herald*
1984	Anthony Suau, *Denver Post*
1985	Stan Grossfeld, *Boston Globe*
	Larry C. Price, *Philadelphia Inquirer*
1986	Tom Gralish, *Philadelphia Inquirer*
1987	David Peterson, *Des Moines Register*
1988	Michael duCille, *Miami Herald*
1989	Manny Crisostomo, *Detroit Free Press*
1990	David C. Turnley, *Detroit Free Press*
1991	William Snyder, *Dallas Morning News*
1992	John Kaplan, *Pittsburgh Post-Gazette*, Block Newspapers
1993	Staff, Associated Press
1994	Kevin Carter, freelancer, *New York Times*
1995	Staff, Associated Press
1996	Stephanie Welsh, freelancer, Newhouse News Service
1997	Alexander Zemlianichenko, Associated Press
1998	Clarence Williams, *Los Angeles Times*
1999	Susan Walsh, Associated Press
2000	Carol Guzy, Michael S. Williamson, and Lucian Perkins, *Washington Post*
2001	Matt Rainey, *Star-Ledger* (N.J.)

Pulitzer Prizes for Commentary, 1970–2001

Year	Winner, Newspaper	Year	Winner, Newspaper
1970	Marquis W. Childs, *St. Louis Post-Dispatch*	1985	Murray Kempton, *Newsday* (Garden City, N.Y.)
1971	William A. Caldwell, *The Record* (Hackensack, N.J.)	1986	Jimmy Breslin, *New York Daily News*
1972	Mike Royko, *Chicago Daily News*	1987	Charles Krauthammer, *Washington Post*
1973	David S. Broder, *Washington Post*	1988	Dave Barry, *Miami Herald*
1974	Edwin A. Roberts Jr., *National Observer*	1989	Clarence Page, *Chicago Tribune*
1975	Mary McGrory, *Washington Star*	1990	Jim Murray, *Los Angeles Times*
1976	Walter (Red) Smith, *New York Times*	1991	Jim Hoagland, *Washington Post*
1977	George F. Will, Washington Post Writers Group	1992	Anna Quindlen, *New York Times*
		1993	Liz Balmaseda, *Miami Herald*
1978	William Safire, *New York Times*	1994	William Raspberry, *Washington Post*
1979	Russell Baker, *New York Times*	1995	Jim Dwyer, *New York Newsday*
1980	Ellen H. Goodman, *Boston Globe*	1996	E.R. Shipp, *New York Daily News*
1981	Dave Anderson, *New York Times*	1997	Eileen McNamara, *Boston Globe*
1982	Art Buchwald, *Los Angeles Times* Syndicate	1998	Mike McAlary, *New York Daily News*
		1999	Maureen Dowd, *New York Times*
1983	Claude Sitton, *Raleigh* (N.C.) *News & Observer*	2000	Paul A. Gigot, *Wall Street Journal*
		2001	Dorothy Rabinowitz, *Wall Street Journal*
1984	Vermont Royster, *Wall Street Journal*		

Pulitzer Prizes for Criticism, 1970–2001

Year	Winner, Newspaper	Year	Winner, Newspaper
1970	Ada Louise Huxtable, *New York Times*	1987	Richard Eder, *Los Angeles Times*
1971	Harold C. Schonberg, *New York Times*	1988	Tom Shales, *Washington Post*
1972	Frank Peters, *St. Louis Post-Dispatch*	1989	Michael Skube, *Raleigh (N.C.) News and Observer*
1973	Ronald Powers, *Chicago Sun-Times*		
1974	Emily Genauer, *Newsday* Syndicate	1990	Allan Temko, *San Francisco Chronicle*
1975	Roger Ebert, *Chicago Sun-Times*	1991	David Shaw, *Los Angeles Times*
1976	Alan M. Kriegsman, *Washington Post*	1992	No award
1977	William McPherson, *Washington Post*	1993	Michael Dirda, *Washington Post*
1978	Walter Kerr, *New York Times*	1994	Lloyd Schwartz, *Boston Phoenix*
1979	Paul Gapp, *Chicago Tribune*	1995	Margo Jefferson, *New York Times*
1980	William A. Henry III, *Boston Globe*	1996	Robert Campbell, *Boston Globe*
1981	Jonathan Yardley, *Washington Star*	1997	Tim Page, *Washington Post*
1982	Martin Bernheimer, *Los Angeles Times*	1998	Michiko Kakutani, *New York Times*
1983	Manuela Hoelterhoff, *Wall Street Journal*	1999	Blair Kamin, *Chicago Tribune*
1984	Paul Goldberger, *New York Times*	2000	Henry Allen, *Washington Post*
1985	Howard Rosenberg, *Los Angeles Times*	2001	Gail Caldwell, *Boston Globe*
1986	Donal Henahan, *New York Times*		

Pulitzer Prizes for Feature Writing, 1979–2001

Year	Winner, Newspaper	Year	Winner, Newspaper
1979	Jon D. Franklin, *Baltimore Evening Sun*	1991	Sheryl James, *St. Petersburg Times*
1980	Madeline Blais, *Miami Herald*	1992	Howell Raines, *New York Times*
1981	Teresa Carpenter, *Village Voice* (New York)	1993	George Lardner, Jr., *Washington Post*
1982	Saul Pett, Associated Press	1994	Isabel Wilkerson, *New York Times*
1983	Nan Robertson, *New York Times*	1995	Ron Suskind, *Wall Street Journal*
1984	Peter Mark Rinearson, *Seattle Times*	1996	Rick Bragg, *New York Times*
1985	Alice Steinbach, *Baltimore Sun*	1997	Lisa Pollak, *Baltimore Sun*
1986	John Camp, *St. Paul Pioneer Press Dispatch*	1998	Thomas French, *St. Petersburg (Fla.) Times*
1987	Steve Twomey, *Philadelphia Inquirer*	1999	Angelo B. Henderson, *Wall Street Journal*
1988	Jacqui Banaszynski, *St. Paul Pioneer Press Dispatch*	2000	J.R. Moehringer, *Los Angeles Times*
		2001	Tom Hallman Jr., *Oregonian* (Portland, Ore.)
1989	David Zucchino, *Philadelphia Inquirer*		
1990	Dave Curtin, *Colorado Springs Gazette Telegram*		

Special Awards and Citations

Year	Winner, Newspaper	Year	Winner, Newspaper
1930	William O. Dapping, *Auburn* (N.Y.) *Citizen*, Prison reporting	1951	Cyrus L. Sulzberger, *New York Times*, Interview with Archbishop Stepinac
1938	*Edmonton* (Alberta) *Journal*, Freedom of the Press editorials	1952	Max Kase, *New York Journal-American*, Corruption in basketball
1941	*New York Times*, Foreign news reporting	1953	*New York Times*, Sunday *Review of the Week* section
1944	Byron Price, Director of the Office of Censorship, Creation and administration of newspaper and radio codes.	1958	Walter Lippman, *New York Herald Tribune*, Lifetime achievement
1944	Mrs. William Allen White, Services to Advisory Board Graduate School of Journalism, Columbia Univ.	1964	Gannett Newspapers, "Road to Integration" program
1945	American press cartographers, Maps of war fronts	1976	Professor John Hohenberg, Administration of Pulitzer Prizes
1947	Columbia University and Graduate School of Journalism, Governing Pulitzer Prize awards	1978	Richard Lee Strout, *Christian Science Monitor*, Lifetime achievement
1947	*St. Louis Post Dispatch*, Adherence to ideals of journalism	1987	Joseph Pulitzer Jr., Lifetime services to Pulitzer Board
1948	Dr. Frank Diehl Fackenthal, Interest and Service	1996	Herb Caen, *San Francisco Chronicle*, Lifetime achievement

PULITZER PRIZES IN LETTERS

The Pulitzer Prize for Fiction, 1918–2001

Year	Author, Title	Year	Author, Title
1918	Ernest Poole, *His Family*	1954	No award
1919	Booth Tarkington, *The Magnificent Ambersons*	1955	William Faulkner, *A Fable*
1920	No award	1956	MacKinlay Kantor, *Andersonville*
1921	Edith Wharton, *The Age of Innocence*	1957	No award
1922	Booth Tarkington, *Alice Adams*	1958	James Agee, *A Death in the Family*
1923	Willa Cather, *One of Ours*	1959	Robert Lewis Taylor, *The Travels of Jaimie McPheeters*
1924	Margaret Wilson, *The Able McLaughlins*		
1925	Edna Ferber, *So Big*	1960	Allen Drury, *Advise and Consent*
1926	Sinclair Lewis, *Arrowsmith*	1961	Harper Lee, *To Kill a Mockingbird*
1927	Louis Bromfield, *Early Autumn*	1962	Edwin O'Connor, *The Edge of Sadness*
1928	Thornton Wilder, *The Bridge of San Luis Rey*	1963	William Faulkner, *The Reivers*
1929	Julia Peterkin, *Scarlet Sister Mary*	1964	No award
1930	Oliver LaFarge, *Laughing Boy*	1965	Shirley Ann Grau, *The Keepers of the House*
1931	Margaret Ayer Barnes, *Years of Grace*	1966	Katherine Anne Porter, *Collected Stories*
1932	Pearl S. Buck, *The Good Earth*	1967	Bernard Malamud, *The Fixer*
1933	T.S. Stribling, *The Store*	1968	William Styron, *The Confessions of Nat Turner*
1934	Caroline Miller, *Lamb in His Bosom*		
1935	Josephine Winslow Johnson, *Now in November*	1969	N. Scott Momaday, *House Made of Dawn*
		1970	Jean Stafford, *Collected Stories*
1936	Harold L. Davis, *Honey in the Horn*	1971	No award
1937	Margaret Mitchell, *Gone With the Wind*	1972	Wallace Stegner, *Angle of Repose*
1938	John Phillips Marquand, *The Late George Apley*	1973	Eudora Welty, *The Optimist's Daughter*
		1974	No award
1939	Marjorie Kinnan Rawlings, *The Yearling*	1975	Michael Shaara, *The Killer Angels*
1940	John Steinbeck, *The Grapes of Wrath*	1976	Saul Bellow, *Humboldt's Gift*
1941	No award	1977	No award
1942	Ellen Glasgow, *In This Our Life*	1978	James Alan McPherson, *Elbow Room*
1943	Upton Sinclair, *Dragon's Teeth*	1979	John Cheever, *The Stories of John Cheever*
1944	Martin Flavin, *Journey in the Dark*	1980	Norman Mailer, *The Executioner's Song*
1945	John Hersey, *A Bell for Adano*	1981	John Kennedy Toole[2], *A Confederacy of Dunces*
1946	No award		
1947	Robert Penn Warren, *All the King's Men*	1982	John Updike, *Rabbit Is Rich*
1948[1]	James A. Michener, *Tales of the South Pacific*	1983	Alice Walker, *The Color Purple*
		1984	William Kennedy, *Ironweed*
1949	James Gould Cozzens, *Guard of Honor*	1985	Alison Lurie, *Foreign Affairs*
1950	A.B. Guthrie Jr., *The Way West*	1986	Larry McMurtry, *Lonesome Dove*
1951	Conrad Richter, *The Town*	1987	Peter Taylor, *A Summons to Memphis*
1952	Herman Wouk, *The Caine Mutiny*	1988	Toni Morrison, *Beloved*
1953	Ernest Hemingway, *The Old Man and the Sea*	1989	Anne Tyler, *Breathing Lessons*

Year	Author, Title	Year	Author, Title
1990	Oscar Hijuelos, *The Mambo Kings Play Songs of Love*	1996	Richard Ford, *Independence Day*
1992	Jane Smiley, *A Thousand Acres*	1997	Steven Millhauser, *Martin Dressler: The Tale of an American Dreamer*
1991	John Updike, *Rabbit at Rest*	1998	Philip Roth, *American Pastoral*
1993	Robert Olen Butler, *A Good Scent From a Strange Mountain*	1999	Michael Cunningham, *The Hours*
1994	E. Annie Proulx, *The Shipping News*	2000	Jhumpa Lahiri, *Interpreter of Maladies*
1995	Carol Shields, *The Stone Diaries*	2001	Michael Chabon, *The Amazing Adventures of Kavalier & Clay*

1. In 1948, the name of the category was changed from "The Novel" to "Fiction." 2. Awarded posthumously.

The Pulitzer Prize for Drama, 1918–2001

Year	Author, Title	Year	Author, Title
1918	Jesse Lynch Williams, *Why Marry*	1961	Tad Mosel, *All the Way Home*
1919	No award	1962	Frank Loesser and Abe Burrows, *How to Succeed in Business Without Really Trying*
1920	Eugene O'Neill, *Beyond the Horizon*		
1921	Zona Gale, *Miss Lulu Bett*	1963	No award
1922	Eugene O'Neill, *Anna Christie*	1964	No award
1923	Owen Davis, *Icebound*	1965	Frank D. Gilroy, *The Subject Was Roses*
1924	Hatcher Hughes, *Hell-Bent Fer Heaven*	1966	No award
1925	Sidney Howard, *They Knew What They Wanted*	1967	Edward Albee, *A Delicate Balance*
1926	George Kelly, *Craig's Wife*	1968	No award
1927	Paul Green, *In Abraham's Bosom*	1969	Howard Sackler, *The Great White Hope*
1928	Eugene O'Neill, *Strange Interlude*	1970	Charles Gordone, *No Place to Be Somebody*
1929	Elmer L. Rice, *Street Scene*		
1930	Marc Connelly, *The Green Pastures*	1971	Paul Zindel, *The Effect of Gamma Rays on Man-in-the-Moon Marigolds*
1931	Susan Glaspell, *Alison's House*		
1932	George S. Kaufman, Morrie Ryskind, and Ira Gershwin, *Of Thee I Sing*	1972	No award
		1973	Jason Miller, *That Championship Season*
1933	Maxwell Anderson, *Both Your Houses*	1974	No award
1934	Sidney Kingsley, *Men in White*	1975	Edward Albee, *Seascape*
1935	Zoe Akins, *The Old Maid*	1976	Michael Bennett; Nicholas Dante & James Kirkwood (book); Marvin Hamlisch (music); and Edward Kleban (lyrics), *A Chorus Line*
1936	Robert E. Sherwood, *Idiot's Delight*		
1937	Moss Hart and George S. Kaufman, *You Can't Take It With You*		
1938	Thornton Wilder, *Our Town*	1977	Michael Cristofer, *The Shadow Box*
1939	Robert E. Sherwood, *Abe Lincoln in Illinois*	1978	Donald L. Coburn, *The Gin Game*
1940	William Saroyan, *The Time of Your Life*	1979	Sam Shepard, *Buried Child*
1941	Robert E. Sherwood, *There Shall Be no Night*	1980	Lanford Wilson, *Talley's Folly*
1942	No award	1981	Beth Henley, *Crimes of the Heart*
1943	Thornton Wilder, *The Skin of Our Teeth*	1982	Charles Fuller, *A Soldier's Play*
1944	No award	1983	Marsha Norman, *'night Mother*
1945	Mary Chase, *Harvey*	1984	David Mamet, *Glengarry Glen Ross*
1946	Russel Crouse and Howard Lindsay, *State of the Union*	1985	Stephen Sondheim (music and lyrics); James Lapine (book), *Sunday in the Park With George*
1947	No award		
1948	Tennessee Williams, *A Streetcar Named Desire*	1986	No award
		1987	August Wilson, *Fences*
1949	Arthur Miller, *Death of a Salesman*	1988	Alfred Uhry, *Driving Miss Daisy*
1950	Richard Rodgers, Oscar Hammerstein II, and Joshua Logan, *South Pacific*	1989	Wendy Wasserstein, *The Heidi Chronicles*
		1990	August Wilson, *The Piano Lesson*
1951	No award	1991	Neil Simon, *Lost in Yonkers*
1952	Joseph Kramm, *The Shrike*	1992	Robert Schenkkan, *The Kentucky Cycle*
1953	William Inge, *Picnic*	1993	Tony Kushner, *Angels in America: Millennium Approaches*
1954	John Patrick, *The Teahouse of the August Moon*		
		1994	Edward Albee, *Three Tall Women*
1955	Tennessee Williams, *Cat on a Hot Tin Roof*	1995	Horton Foote, *The Young Man From Atlanta*
1956	Albert Hackett and Frances Goodrich, *The Diary of Anne Frank*	1996	Jonathan Larson, *Rent*
		1997	No award
1957	Eugene O'Neill, *Long Day's Journey Into Night*	1998	Paula Vogel, *How I Learned to Drive*
		1999	Margaret Edson, *Wit*
1958	Ketti Frings, *Look Homeward, Angel*	2000	Donald Margulies, *Dinner With Friends*
1959	Archibald MacLeish, *J.B.*	2001	David Auburn, *Proof*
1960	Jerome Weidman and George Abbott (book); Jerry Bock (music); and Sheldon Harnick (lyrics), *Fiorello!*		

The Pulitzer Prize for History, 1917–2001

Year	Author, Title	Year	Author, Title
1917	J.J. Jusserand, *With Americans of Past and Present Days*	1959	Leonard D. White, with Miss Jean Schneider, *The Republican Era: 1869–1901*
1918	James Ford Rhodes, *A History of the Civil War*	1960	Margaret Leech, *In the Days of McKinley*
1919	No award	1961	Herbert Feis, *Between War and Peace: The Potsdam Conference*
1920	Justin H. Smith, *The War with Mexico*	1962	Lawrence H. Gipson, *The Triumphant Empire: Thunder Clouds in the West*
1921	William Sowden Sims, with Burton J. Hendrick, *The Victory at Sea*		
1922	James Truslow Adams, *The Founding of New England*	1963	Constance McLaughlin Green, *Washington, Village and Capital, 1800–1878*
1923	Charles Warren, *The Supreme Court in United States History*	1964	Sumner Chilton Powell, *Puritan Village*
1924	Charles Howard McIlwain, *The American Revolution*	1965	Irwin Unger, *The Greenback Era*
		1966	Perry Miller[1], *Life of the Mind in America*
1925	Frederic L. Paxson, *A History of the American Frontier*	1967	William H. Goetzmann, *Exploration and Empire*
1926	Edward Channing, *The History of the United States*	1968	Bernard Bailyn, *The Ideological Origins of the American Revolution*
1927	Samuel Flagg Bemis, *Pinckney's Treaty*	1969	Leonard W. Levy, *Origins of the Fifth Amendment*
1928	Vernon Louis Parrington, *Main Currents in American Thought*	1970	Dean Acheson, *Present at the Creation*
1929	Fred Albert Shannon, *The Organization and Administration of the Union Army, 1861–1865*	1971	James MacGregor Burns, *Roosevelt, The Soldier of Freedom*
1930	Claude H. Van Tyne, *The War of Independence*	1972	Carl N. Degler, *Neither Black Nor White*
1931	Bernadotte E. Schmitt, *The Coming of the War: 1914*	1973	Michael Kammen, *People of Paradox*
		1974	Daniel J. Boorstin, *The Americans: The Democratic Experience*
1932	John J. Pershing, *My Experiences in the World War*	1975	Dumas Malone, *Jefferson and His Time*
1933	Frederick J. Turner, *The Significance of Sections in American History*	1976	Paul Horgan, *Lamy of Santa Fe*
		1977	David M. Potter[1] *The Impending Crisis*
1934	Herbert Agar, *The People's Choice*	1978	Alfred D. Chandler Jr., *The Visible Hand: The Managerial Revolution in American Business*
1935	Charles McLean Andrews, *The Colonial Period of American History*	1979	Don E. Fehrenbacher, *The Dred Scott Case*
1936	Andrew C. McLaughlin, *The Constitutional History of the United States*	1980	Leon F. Litwack, *Been in the Storm So Long*
		1981	Lawrence A. Cremin, *American Education*
1937	Van Wyck Brooks, *The Flowering of New England*	1982	C. Vann Woodward (ed.), *Mary Chesnut's Civil War*
1938	Paul Herman Buck, *The Road to Reunion 1856–1900*	1983	Rhys L. Isaac, *The Transformation of Virginia, 1740–1790*
1939	Frank Luther Mott, *A History of American Magazines*	1984	No award
		1985	Thomas K. McCraw, *Prophets of Regulation*
1940	Carl Sandburg, *Abraham Lincoln: The War Years*	1986	Walter A. McDougall, *. . .the Heavens and the Earth*
1941	Marcus Lee Hansen, *The Atlantic Migration, 1607–1860*	1987	Bernard Bailyn, *Voyagers to the West*
		1988	Robert V. Bruce, *The Launching of Modern American Science 1846–1876*
1942	Margaret Leech, *Reveille in Washington*	1989	Taylor Branch, *Parting the Waters*
1943	Esther Forbes, *Paul Revere and the World He Lived In*		James M. McPherson, *Battle Cry of Freedom: The Civil War Era*
1944	Merle Curti, *The Growth of American Thought*	1990	Stanley Karnow, *In Our Image*
1945	Stephen Bonsal, *Unfinished Business*	1991	Laurel Thatcher Ulrich, *A Midwife's Tale*
1946	Arthur Meier Schlesinger Jr., *The Age of Jackson*	1992	Mark E. Neely Jr., *The Fate of Liberty*
		1993	Gordon S. Wood, *The Radicalism of the American Revolution*
1947	James Phinney Baxter III, *Scientists Against Time*	1994	No award
1948	Bernard DeVoto, *Across the Wide Missouri*	1995	Doris Kearns Goodwin, *No Ordinary Time: Franklin and Eleanor Roosevelt*
1949	Roy Franklin Nichols, *The Disruption of American Democracy*	1996	Alan Taylor, *William Cooper's Town*
1950	Oliver W. Larkin, *Art and Life in America*	1997	Jack N. Rakove, *Original Meanings: Politics and Ideas in the Making of the Constitution*
1951	R. Carlyle Buley, *The Old Northwest*		
1952	Oscar Handlin, *The Uprooted*		
1953	George Dangerfield, *The Era of Good Feelings*	1998	Edward J. Larson, *Summer for the Gods: The Scopes Trial and America's Continuing Debate Over Science and Religion*
1954	Bruce Catton, *A Stillness at Appomattox*		
1955	Paul Horgan, *Great River: The Rio Grande in North American History*	1999	Edwin G. Burrows and Mike Wallace, *Gotham: A History of New York City to 1898*
1956	Richard Hofstadter, *The Age of Reform*		
1957	George F. Kennan, *Russia Leaves the War: Soviet American Relations, 1917–1920*	2000	David M. Kennedy, *Freedom From Fear: The American People in Depression*
1958	Bray Hammond, *Banks and Politics in America*	2001	Joseph P. Ellis, *Founding Brothers: The Revolutionary Generation*

1. Awarded posthumously.

The Pulitzer Prize for Biography/Autobiography, 1917–2001

Year	Author, Title
1917	Laura E. Richards and Maude Howe Elliott, with Florence Howe Hall, *Julia Ward Howe*
1918	William Cabell Bruce, *Benjamin Franklin, Self-Revealed*
1919	Henry Adams, *The Education of Henry Adams*
1920	Albert J. Beveridge, *The Life of John Marshall*
1921	Edward Bok, *The Americanization of Edward Bok*
1922	Hamlin Garland, *A Daughter of the Middle Border*
1923	Burton J. Hendrick, *The Life and Letters of Walter H. Page*
1924	Michael Idvorsky Pupin, *From Immigrant to Inventor*
1925	M.A. DeWolfe Howe, *Barrett Wendell and His Letter*
1926	Harvey Cushing, *The Life of Sir William Osler*
1927	Emory Holloway, *Whitman*
1928	Charles Edward Russell, *The American Orchestra and Theodore Thomas*
1929	Burton J. Hendrick, *The Training of an American. The Earlier Life and Letters of Walter H.Page*
1930	Marquis James, *The Raven*
1931	Henry James, *Charles W. Eliot*
1932	Henry F. Pringle, *Theodore Roosevelt*
1933	Allan Nevins, *Grover Cleveland*
1934	Tyler Dennett, *John Hay*
1935	Douglas S. Freeman, *R.E. Lee*
1936	Ralph Barton Perry, *The Thought and Character of William James*
1937	Allan Nevins, *Hamilton Fish*
1938	Odell Shepard, *Pedlar's Progress* Marquis James, *Andrew Jackson*
1939	Carl Van Doren, *Benjamin Franklin*
1940	Ray Stannard Baker, *Woodrow Wilson, Life and Letters*, vols. 7 & 8
1941	Ola Elizabeth Winslow, *Jonathan Edwards*
1942	Forrest Wilson, *Crusader in Crinoline*
1943	Samuel Eliot Morison, *Admiral of the Ocean Sea*
1944	Carleton Mabee, *The American Leonardo: The Life of Samuel F.B. Morse*
1945	Russell Blaine Nye, *George Bancroft*
1946	Linnie Marsh Wolfe, *Son of the Wilderness*
1947	William Allen White, *The Autobiography of William Allen White*
1948	Margaret Clapp, *Forgotten First Citizen: John Bigelow*
1949	Robert E. Sherwood, *Roosevelt and Hopkins*
1950	Samuel Flagg Bemis, *John Quincy Adams and the Foundations of American Foreign Policy*
1951	Margaret Louise Coit, *John C. Calhoun*
1952	Merlo J. Pusey, *Charles Evan Hughes*
1953	David J. Mays, *Edmund Pendleton 1721-1803*
1954	Charles A. Lindbergh, *The Spirit of St. Louis*
1955	William S. White, *The Taft Story*
1956	Talbot Faulkner Hamlin, *Benjamin Henry Latrobe*
1957	John F. Kennedy, *Profiles in Courage*
1958	Douglas Southall Freeman[1], John Alexander Carroll, Mary Wells Ashworth, *George Washington*, vols. 1–4; and vol. 7, written after Dr. Freeman's death in 1953.
1959	Arthur Walworth, *Woodrow Wilson, American Prophet*
1960	Samuel Eliot Morison, *John Paul Jones*
1961	David Donald, *Charles Sumner and the Coming of the Civil War*
1962	No award
1963	Leon Edel, *Henry James*
1964	Walter Jackson Bate, *John Keats*
1965	Ernest Samuels, *Henry Adams*
1966	Arthur M. Schlesinger Jr., *A Thousand Days*
1967	Justin Kaplan, *Mr. Clemens and Mark Twain*
1968	George F. Kennan, *Memoirs*
1969	Benjamin Lawrence Reid, *The Man From New York: John Quinn and His Friends*
1970	T. Harry Williams, *Huey Long*
1971	Lawrance Thompson, *Robert Frost*
1972	Joseph P. Lash, *Eleanor and Franklin*
1973	W.A. Swanberg, *Luce and His Empire*
1974	Louis Sheaffer, *O'Neill, Son and Artist*
1975	Robert A. Caro, *The Power Broker*
1976	R.W.B. Lewis, *Edith Wharton: A Biography*
1977	John E. Mack, *A Prince of Our Disorder: The Life of T.E. Lawrence*
1978	Walter Jackson Bate, *Samuel Johnson*
1979	Leonard Baker, *Days of Sorrow and Pain*
1980	Edmund Morris, *The Rise of Theodore Roosevelt*
1981	Robert K. Massie, *Peter the Great*
1982	William S. McFeely, *Grant: A Biography*
1983	Russell Baker, *Growing Up*
1984	Louis R. Harlan, *Booker T. Washington*
1985	Kenneth Silverman, *The Life and Times of Cotton Mather*
1986	Elizabeth Frank, *Louise Bogan: A Portrait*
1987	David J. Garrow, *Bearing the Cross: Martin Luther King, Jr. and the Southern Christian Leadership Conference*
1988	David Herbert Donald, *Look Homeward: A Life of Thomas Wolfe*
1989	Richard Ellmann[1], *Oscar Wilde*
1990	Sebastian de Grazia, *Machiavelli in Hell*
1991	Steven Naifeh, Gregory White Smith, *Jackson Pollock*
1992	Lewis B. Puller Jr., *Fortunate Son*
1993	David McCullough, *Truman*
1994	David Levering Lewis, *W.E.B. DuBois*
1995	Joan D. Hedrick, *Harriet Beecher Stowe*
1996	Jack Miles, *God: A Biography*
1997	Frank McCourt, *Angela's Ashes*
1998	Katharine Graham, *Personal History*
1999	A. Scott Berg, *Lindbergh*
2000	Stacy Schiff, *Véra (Mrs. Vladimir Nabokov)*
2001	David Levering Lewis, *W.E.B. DuBois (vol. 2)*

1. Awarded posthumously.

The Pulitzer Prize for Poetry, 1922–2001

Pulitzer Prizes in poetry were first awarded in 1922. The Poetry Society awarded prizes in 1918 to Sara Teasdale for *Love Songs*, and in 1919 to Margaret Widdemer for *Old Road to Paradise* and to Carl Sandburg for *Corn Huskers*.

Year	Author, Title
1922	Edward Arlington Robinson, *Collected Poems*
1923	Edna St. Vincent Millay, *The Ballad of the Harp-Weaver; A Few Figs from Thistles; Eight Sonnets in American Poetry, 1922, A Miscellany*
1924	Robert Frost, *New Hampshire: A Poem with Notes and Grace Notes*
1925	Edward Arlington Robinson, *The Man Who Died Twice*
1926	Amy Lowell[1], *What's O'Clock*
1927	Leonora Speyer, *Fiddler's Farewell*
1928	Edward Arlington Robinson, *Tristram*
1929	Stephen Vincent Benét, *John Brown's Body*
1930	Conrad Aiken, *Selected Poems*
1931	Robert Frost, *Collected Poems*
1932	George Dillon, *The Flowering Stone*
1933	Archibald MacLeish, *Conquistador*
1934	Robert Hillyer, *Collected Verse*
1935	Audrey Wurdemann, *Bright Ambush*
1936	Robert P. Tristram Coffin, *Strange Holiness*
1937	Robert Frost, *A Further Range*
1938	Marya Zaturenska, *Cold Morning Sky*
1939	John Gould Fletcher, *Selected Poems*
1940	Mark Van Doren, *Collected Poems*
1941	Leonard Bacon, *Sunderland Capture*
1942	William Rose Benét, *The Dust Which Is God*
1943	Robert Frost, *A Witness Tree*
1944	Stephen Vincent Benét[1], *Western Star*
1945	Karl Shapiro, *V-Letter and Other Poems*
1946	No award
1947	Robert Lowell, *Lord Weary's Castle*
1948	W.H. Auden, *The Age of Anxiety*
1949	Peter Viereck, *Terror and Decorum*
1950	Gwendolyn Brooks, *Annie Allen*
1951	Carl Sandburg, *Complete Poems*
1952	Marianne Moore, *Collected Poems*
1953	Archibald MacLeish, *Collected Poems 1917–1952*
1954	Theodore Roethke, *The Waking*
1955	Wallace Stevens, *Collected Poems*
1956	Elizabeth Bishop, *Poems—North & South*
1957	Richard Wilbur, *Things of This World*
1958	Robert Penn Warren, *Promises: Poems 1954–1956*
1959	Stanley Kunitz, *Selected Poems 1928–1958*
1960	W.D. Snodgrass, *Heart's Needle*
1961	Phyllis McGinley, *Times Three: Selected Verse From Three Decades*
1962	Alan Dugan, *Poems*
1963	William Carlos Williams[1], *Pictures from Breughel*
1964	Louis Simpson, *At the End of the Open Road*
1965	John Berryman, *77 Dream Songs*
1966	Richard Eberhart, *Selected Poems*
1967	Anne Sexton, *Live or Die*
1968	Anthony Hecht, *The Hard Hours*
1969	George Oppen, *Of Being Numerous*
1970	Richard Howard, *Untitled Subjects*
1971	William S. Merwin, *The Carrier of Ladders*
1972	James Wright, *Collected Poems*
1973	Maxine Kumin, *Up Country*
1974	Robert Lowell, *The Dolphins*
1975	Gary Snyder, *Turtle Island*
1976	John Ashberry, *Self-Portrait in a Convex Mirror*
1977	James Merrill, *Divine Comedies*
1978	Howard Nemerov, *Collected Poems*
1979	Robert Penn Warren, *Now and Then*
1980	Donald Justice, *Selected Poems*
1981	James Schuyler, *The Morning of the Poem*
1982	Sylvia Plath[1], *The Collected Poems*
1983	Galway Kinnell, *Selected Poems*
1984	Mary Oliver, *American Primitive*
1985	Carolyn Kizer, *Yin*
1986	Henry Taylor, *The Flying Change*
1987	Rita Dove, *Thomas and Beulah*
1988	William Meredith, *Partial Accounts: New and Selected Poems*
1989	Richard Wilbur, *New and Collected Poems*
1990	Charles Simic, *The World Doesn't End*
1991	Mona Van Duyn, *Near Changes*
1992	James Tate, *Selected Poems*
1993	Louise Gluck, *The Wild Iris*
1994	Yusef Komunyakaa, *Neon Vernacular*
1995	Philip Levine, *Simple Truth*
1996	Jorie Graham, *The Dream of the Unified Field*
1997	Lisel Mueller, *Alive Together: New and Selected Poems*
1998	Charles Wright, *Black Zodiac*
1999	Mark Strand, *Blizzard of One*
2000	C.K. Williams, *Repair*
2001	Stephen Dunn, *Different Hours*

1. Awarded posthumously.

The Pulitzer Prize for General Nonfiction, 1962–2001

Year	Author, Title
1962	Theodore H. White, *The Making of the President, 1960*
1963	Barbara W. Tuchman, *The Guns of August*
1964	Richard Hofstadter, *Anti-Intellectualism in American Life*
1965	Howard Mumford Jones, *O Strange New World*
1966	Edwin Way Teal, *Wandering Through Winter*
1967	David Brion Davis, *The Problem of Slavery in Western Culture*
1968	Will and Ariel Durant, *Rousseau and Revolution*
1969	René Jules Dubos, *So Human An Animal* Norman Mailer, *The Armies of the Night*
1970	Erik H. Erikson, *Gandhi's Truth*
1971	John Toland, *The Rising Sun*
1972	Barbara W. Tuchman, *Stilwell and the American Experience in China, 1911–45*
1973	Robert Coles, *Children of Crisis, vols.2 & 3* Frances Fitzgerald, *Fire in the Lake*
1974	Ernest Becker[1], *The Denial of Death*

Year	Author, Title	Year	Author, Title
1975	Annie Dillard, *Pilgrim at Tinker Creek*	1989	Neil Sheehan, *A Bright and Shining Lie*
1976	Robert N. Butler, *Why Survive? Being Old in America*	1990	Dale Maharidge, Michael Williamson, *And Their Children After Them*
1977	William N. Warner, *Beautiful Swimmers*	1991	Bert Holldobler, Edward O. Wilson, *The Ants*
1978	Carl Sagan, *The Dragons of Eden*	1992	Daniel Yergin, *The Prize: The Epic Quest for Oil, Money and Power.*
1979	Edward O. Wilson, *On Human Nature*	1993	Garry Wills, *Lincoln at Gettysburg*
1980	Douglas R. Hofstadter, *Gödel, Escher, Bach: an Eternal Golden Braid*	1994	David Remnick, *Lenin's Tomb: The Last Days of the Soviet Empire*
1981	Carl E. Schorske, *Fin-de Siècle Vienna: Politics and Culture*	1995	Jonathan Weiner, *The Beak of the Finch*
1982	Tracy Kidder, *The Soul of A New Machine*	1996	Tina Rosenberg, *The Haunted Land*
1983	Susan Sheehan, *Is There No Place on Earth for Me?*	1997	Richard Kluger, *Ashes to Ashes*
		1998	Jared Diamond, *Guns, Germs, and Steel: The Fates of Human Societies*
1984	Paul Starr, *The Social Transformation of American Medicine*	1999	John McPhee, *Annals of the Former World*
1985	Studs Terkel, *The Good War*	2000	John W. Dower, *Embracing Defeat: Japan in the Wake of World War II*
1986	Joseph Lelyveld, *Move Your Shadow* J. Anthony Lukas, *Common Ground*	2001	Herbert P. Bix, *Hirohito and the Making of Modern Japan*
1987	David K. Shipler, *Arab and Jew*		
1988	Richard Rhodes, *The Making of the Atomic Bomb*		

1. Awarded posthumously.

The Pulitzer Prize for Music, 1943–2001

Year	Author, Title	Year	Author, Title
1943	William Schuman, Secular Cantata No. 2, *A Free Song*	1974	Donald Martino, *Notturno* (chamber music piece)
1944	Howard Hanson, Symphony No. 4, Opus 34	1975	Dominick Argento, *From the Diary of Virginia Woolf*
1945	Aaron Copland, *Appalachian Spring*	1976	Ned Rorem, *Air Music: Ten Etudes for Orchestra*
1946	Leo Sowerby, *The Canticle of the Sun*		
1947	Charles Ives, Symphony No. 3	1977	Richard Wernick, *Visions of Terror and Wonder*
1948	Walter Piston, Symphony No. 3		
1949	Virgil Thomson, Music for the film, *Louisiana Story*	1978	Michael Colgrass, *Deja Vu* for Percussion Quartet and Orchestra
1950	Gian-Carlo Menotti, Music for the opera *The Consul*	1979	Joseph Schwantner, *Aftertones of Infinity*
		1980	David Del Tredici, *In Memory of a Summer Day*
1951	Douglas S. Moore, Music for the opera, *Giants in the Earth*	1981	No award
1952	Gail Kubik, *Symphony Concertante*	1982	Roger Sessions, Concerto for Orchestra
1953	No award	1983	Ellen Taaffe Zwilich, Symphony No. 1
1954	Quincy Porter, Concerto for Two Pianos and Orchestra	1984	Bernard Rands, "Canti del Sole" for Tenor and Orchestra
1955	Gian-Carlo Menotti, *The Saint of Bleecker Street* (opera)	1985	Stephen Albert, Symphony *RiverRun*
1956	Ernest Toch, Symphony No. 3	1986	George Perle, Wind Quintet IV
1957	Norman Dello Joio, *Meditations on Ecclesiastes*	1987	John Harbison, *The Flight Into Egypt*
		1988	William Bolcom, 12 New Etudes for Piano
1958	Samuel Barber, *Vanessa* (opera)	1989	Roger Reynolds, *Whispers Out of Time*
1959	John LaMontaine, Concerto for Piano and Orchestra	1990	Mel Powell, *Duplicates: A Concerto for Two Pianos and Orchestra*
1960	Elliott Carter, Second String Quartet	1991	Shulammit Ran, *Symphony*
1961	Walter Piston, Symphony No. 7	1992	Wayne Peterson, *The Face of the Night, The Heart of the Dark*
1962	Robert Ward, *The Crucible* (opera)		
1963	Samuel Barber, Piano Concerto No. 1	1993	Christopher Rouse, *Trombone Concerto*
1964	No award	1994	Gunther Schuller, *Of Reminiscences and Reflections*
1965	No award		
1966	Leslie Bassett, Variations for Orchestra	1995	Morton Gould, *Stringmusic*
1967	Leon Kirchner, Quartet No. 3	1996	George Walker, *Lilacs*
1968	George Crumb, *Echoes of Time and the River* orchestral suite	1997	Wynton Marsalis, *Blood on the Fields*
		1998	Aaron Jay Kernis, *String Quartet No.2*
1969	Karel Husa, String Quartet No. 3	1999	Melinda Wagner, *Concerto for Flute, Strings, and Percussion*
1970	Charles Wuorinen, *Time's Encomium*		
1971	Mario Davidovsky, Synchronisms No. 6 for Piano and Electronic Sound	2000	Lewis Spratalan, *Life is a Dream, Opera in Three Acts: Act II, Convert Version*
1972	Jacob Druckman, *Windows*	2001	John Corigliano, *Symphony No. 2 for String Orchestra*
1973	Elliott Carter, String Quartet No. 3		

Pulitzer Special Citations

Year	SPECIAL CITATIONS IN LETTERS Recipient
1944	Richard Rodgers and Oscar Hammerstein II, *Oklahoma!*
1957	Kenneth Roberts, for his historical novels
1960	Garret Mattingly, *The Armada*
1961	Publishers, *The American Heritage Picture History of the Civil War*
1973	James Flexner, *George Washington*, vols. 1–4
1977	Alex Haley, *Roots*
1978	E.B. White, Lifetime achievement
1984	Theodore Seuss Geisel (Dr. Seuss), Lifetime achievement
1992	Art Speigelman, *Maus*

Year	SPECIAL CITATIONS IN MUSIC Recipient
1974	Roger Sessions, Lifetime achievement
1976	Scott Joplin[1], Contributions to American music
1982	Milton Babbitt, Lifetime achivement
1985	William Schuman, Lifetime achievement
1998	George Gershwin[1], Contributions to American music
1999	Edward "Duke" Ellington[1], Contributions to American music

1. Awarded posthumously.   **Source:** Columbia University.

The Nobel Prizes

First awarded in 1901, the Nobel Prizes were established through a bequest of $9.2 million from Alfred Bernhard Nobel (1833–1896), a Swedish chemical engineer and the inventor of dynamite and other explosives, and by a gift from the Bank of Sweden. Nobel's will directed that the interest from the fund be divided annually among people who have made significant discoveries or inventions in the fields of chemistry, physics, and physiology or medicine, as well as to that author who has "produced in the field of literature the most outstanding work of an idealistic tendency," and to that individual or group that has "done the most or the best work for fraternity between nations, for the abolition or reduction of standing armies and for the holding and promotion of peace congresses." In 1968, the 300th anniversary of the Bank of Sweden, an additional prize for outstanding work in the economic sciences was established; it was first granted the following year.

Today, all of the prizes are funded with the help of the Bank of Sweden. Final decisions are made for physics, chemistry and economics by the Royal Swedish Academy of Sciences, Stockholm; for physiology or medicine by the Nobel Assembly at the Karolinska Institute, Stockholm; for literature by the Swedish Academy, Stockholm; and for peace by the Norwegian Nobel Committee, Oslo.

The prizes are awarded annually on December 10, the anniversary of Nobel's death. The peace prize is presented in Oslo and other awards are given in Stockholm, by the king of Sweden. The amount of each prize varies according to the interest from the fund. In 2001, the award was worth 10 million Swedish crowns (approximately $1.33 million), up from $362,500 in 1987. No prizes were awarded between 1940 and 1942.

Note: For winners of the 2001 Nobel Prizes in all categories, see "Part I: The Almanac of the Year," or the Nobel Foundation web site: www.nobel.se/.

Nobel Peace Prize Recipients

1901   Jean-Henri Dunant (Switzerland) Founder of International Committee of the Red Cross; **Frédéric Passy** (France) Founder of first French peace society.
1902   Elie Ducommun (Switzerland) Director of Permanent International Peace Bureau; **Charles Albert Gobat** (Switzerland) Secretary-General of Inter-Parliamentary Union.
1903   Sir William R. Cremer (Great Britain) Founder of International Arbitration League.
1904   Institute of International Law Founded in 1873.
1905   Baroness Bertha S.F. von Suttner (Austria) Author of antiwar novel *Lay Down Your Arms.*
1906   Theodore Roosevelt (U.S.) President; mediated Russo-Japanese War.
1907   Ernesto T. Moneta (Italy) Founder of Lombard League of Peace; **Louis Renault** (France) Professor of International Law at Hague Peace Conference.
1908   Klas P. Arnoldson (Sweden) Founder of Swedish Peace and Arbitration League; **Fredrik Bajer** (Denmark) Writer and peace activist, Danish parliament member.
1909   Auguste M.F. Beernaert (Belgium) Prime minister and peace activist; **Paul H.B.B. D'Estournelles de Constant** (Baron Constant de Rebecque) (France)

Founder of French parliamentary group for voluntary arbitration.
1910   Permanent International Peace Bureau Founded 1891.
1911   Tobias M.C. Asser (Netherlands) A founder of Institute of International Law; **Alfred H. Fried** (Austria) Journalist and founder of many peace publications.
1912   Elihu Root (U.S.) Secretary of state and originator of several arbitration treaties.
1913   Henri Lafontaine (Belgium) President of Permanent International Peace Bureau in Bern.
1914–1916   No awards given.
1917   International Committee of the Red Cross Founded 1863.
1918   No award.
1919   Thomas Woodrow Wilson (U.S.) President; instrumental in establishing League of Nations.
1920   Léon Victor A. Bourgeois (France) Drafted framework for League of Nations.
1921   Karl H. Branting (Sweden) Prime minister and pacifist; **Christian L. Lange** (Norway) A founder of Inter-Parliamentary Union.
1922   Fridtjof Nansen (Norway) Scientist; explorer; originator of "Nansen passports" for refugees.

1923–24   No award.

1925   Sir Austen Chamberlain (Great Britain) Foreign secretary; worked for Locarno Pact; **Charles G. Dawes** (U.S.) Vice president; drafted Dawes Plan settling German reparations issue.

1926   Aristide Briand (France) and **Gustav Stresemann** (Germany) Creators of Locarno Pact.

1927   Ferdinand Buisson (France) Human rights advocate; **Ludwig Quidde** (Germany) Peace activist.

1928   No award.

1929   Frank B. Kellogg (U.S.) Secretary of state; a creator of Kellogg-Briand Pact.

1930   L.O. Nathan Söderblom (Sweden) Archbishop; leader in the ecumenical movement.

1931   Jane Addams (U.S.) President of Women's International League for Peace and Freedom; **Nicholas M. Butler** (U.S.) Promoter of Kellogg-Briand Pact.

1932   No award.

1933   Sir Norman Angell (Ralph Lane) (Great Britain) Author of antiwar book *The Great Illusion.*

1934   Arthur Henderson (Great Britain) President of League of Nations World Disarmament Conference 1932.

1935   Carol von Ossietzky (Germany) Journalist and pacifist.

1936   Carlos Saavedra Lamas (Argentina) Secretary of state; president of League of Nations and mediator in conflict between Paraguay and Bolivia.

1937   Lord Edgar Algernon R.G. Cecil (Great Britain) An architect of League of Nations.

1938   Nansen International Office for Refugees Founded 1921.

1939–1943   No awards given.

1944   International Committee of the Red Cross Founded 1863.

1945   Cordell Hull (U.S.) Secretary of state; instrumental in creating United Nations.

1946   Emily G. Balch (U.S.) Leader of international women's movement for peace; **John R. Mott** (U.S.) Leader of Christian ecumenical movement.

1947   The Friends Service Council and The American Friends Service Committee (The Quakers)

1948   No award.

1949   Lord John Boyd Orr (Great Britain) Nutritionist; worked to eliminate world hunger.

1950   Ralph Bunche (U.S.) Mediator in Middle East war.

1951   Léon Jouhaux (France) Advocate of improved working-class conditions.

1952   Albert Schweitzer (France) Missionary surgeon/founder of Lambarene Hospital in Africa.

1953   George C. Marshall (U.S.) General; originator of Marshall Plan, which provided recovery loans and technical aid to European nations after World War II.

1954   Office of the U.N. High Commissioner for Refugees for their aid work for European refugees.

1955–1956   No awards given.

1957   Lester B. Pearson (Canada) Secretary of state; worked to resolve Suez Canal Crisis of 1956.

1958   George Pire (Belgium) Dominican priest and leader of relief organization for refugees, l'Europe du Coeur au Service du Monde.

1959   Philip J. Noel-Baker (Great Britain) Lifelong worker for international peace through disarmament.

1960   Albert J. Lutuli (South Africa) President of the African National Congress; led peaceful resistance to apartheid.

1961   Dag Hammarskjöld (Sweden) United Nations Secretary General; worked for peace in the Congo.

1962   Linus C. Pauling (U.S.) Chemist; warned against dangers of radioactive fallout in nuclear weapons testing and war.

1963   International Committee of the Red Cross and League of Red Cross Societies

1964   Martin Luther King, Jr. (U.S.) Leader of American civil rights movement.

1965   United Nations Children's Fund (UNICEF).

1966–1967   No awards given.

1968   René Cassin (France) President of European Court for Human Rights.

1969   International Labour Organization United Nations agency involved in improving worldwide working and social conditions.

1970   Norman Borlaug (U.S.) Agricultural scientist and developer of high-yield grains credited with helping to alleviate world hunger.

1971   Willy Brandt (Federal Republic of Germany) Chancellor; champion of East-West détente.

1972   No award

1973   Henry A. Kissinger (U.S.) Secretary of state and **Le Duc Tho** (Democratic Republic of Viet Nam) Foreign minister; negotiated Vietnam cease-fire agreement. Mr. Tho declined the prize.

1974   Seán MacBride (Ireland) President of International Peace Bureau and United Nations commissioner for Namibia; **Eisaku Sato** (Japan) Prime minister of Japan and campaigner against nuclear weapons.

1975   Andrei Sakharov (USSR) Nuclear physicist and human rights campaigner.

1976   Betty Williams and Mairead Corrigan (Northern Ireland) Founder of Northern Ireland Peace Movement.

1977   Amnesty International for human rights work.

1978   Anwar el-Sadat (Egypt) President, and **Menachem Begin** (Israel) Prime minister; negotiated Israeli-Egyptian peace accord.

1979   Mother Teresa (India) Worker for the poor in Calcutta.

1980   Adolfo Pérez Esquivel (Argentina) Architect, sculptor, and human rights leader.

1981   Office of the United Nations High Commissioner for Refugees for aid work with Asian refugees.

1982   Alva Myrdal (Sweden) and **Alfonso Garcia Robles** (Mexico) Campaigners for disarmament.

1983   Lech Walesa (Poland) Leader of the Solidarity trade union federation.

1984   Desmond M. Tutu (South Africa) Bishop of Johannesburg; a leader of the anti-apartheid movement.

1985   International Physicians for the Prevention of Nuclear War Organization jointly headed by a Soviet and an American doctor.

1986   Elie Wiesel (U.S.) Writer on the Holocaust and Nazi death camp survivor.

1987   Oscar Arias Sánchez (Costa Rica) President of Costa Rica; creator of a peace plan for Central America.

1988   United Nations Peacekeeping Forces

1989   Dalai Lama (Tibet) Exiled religious and political leader of Tibet for his nonviolent campaign to end China's domination of his country.

1990   Mikhail Gorbachev (USSR) President of the Soviet Union, "for his role in the peace process which today characterizes important parts of the international community."

1991   Aung San Suu Kyi (Myanmar), leader of opposition National League for Democracy (under house arrest at the time) "for her nonviolent struggle for democracy and human rights."

1992   Rigoberta Menchú (Guatemala) A Quiché Indian and an outspoken advocate of human rights during the civil war in her country.

1993   Pres. F. W. de Klerk of South Africa and **Nelson Mandela,** black leader of the opposition African National Congress, for negotiating an end to the apartheid policies of the state and their collaboration on the formation of a democracy not based on race.

1994 Yitzhak Rabin (Israel) Prime Minister, **Shimon Peres** (Israel) Foreign Minister, and **Yasir Arafat,** leader of the Palestinian Liberation Organization, for negotiating the historic peace pact allowing Palestinian self-rule in the West Bank and Gaza Strip.

1995 Joseph Rotblat (U.K. b. Poland), Pugwash Conferences on Science and World Affairs. A former Manhattan Project physicist who spent 40 years campaigning to eliminate nuclear weapons.

1996 Bishop Carlos Ximenes Belo (Australia, b. East Timor) and **Jose Ramos-Horta** (East Timor) for "sustained and self-sacrificing contributions for a small but oppressed people" in East Timor, a former Portuguese colony invaded by Indonesia in the 1970s.

1997 The International Campaign to Ban Landmines and its 47-year-old coordinator, **Jody Williams** (U.S.), for their efforts to outlaw land mines worldwide. The Nobel committee admitted that it was openly trying to persuade the U.S. to sign the international treaty banning landmines.

1998 John Hume (Ireland) and **David Trimble** (Ireland) respectively the leaders of the largest Roman Catholic and Protestant political parties in Northern Ireland who brought about a peace agreement in April 1998.

1999 Doctors Without Borders (Médecins Sans Frontières), whose foudning principle is that all disaster victims have a right to quick, efficient, professional assistance, without regard to the origin of the disaster, national boundaries, or political circumstances. Its independence and rapid intervention have helped " to form bodies of public opinion opposed to violations and abuses of power."

2000 Kim Dae Jung, President of South Korea, "for his work for democracy and human rights in South Korea and in East Asia in general, and for peace and reconciliation with North Korea in particular."

2001 See Part I: "The Almanac of the Year."

Nobel Prizes in Physiology or Medicine

1901 Emil A. von Behring (Germany) Marburg Univ. "for his work on serum therapy, especially its application against diphtheria, by which he has opened a new road in the domain of medical science and thereby placed in the hands of the physician a victorious weapon against illness and deaths."

1902 Sir Ronald Ross (Great Britain) University College "for his work on malaria, by which he has shown how it enters the organism and thereby has laid the foundation for successful research on this disease and methods of combating it."

1903 Niels R. Finsen (Denmark) Finsen Medical Light Institute "in recognition of his contribution to the treatment of diseases, especially lupus vulgaris, with concentrated light radiation, whereby he has opened a new avenue for medical science."

1904 Ivan P. Pavlov (Russia) Military Medical Academy "in recognition of his work on the physiology of digestion."

1905 Robert Koch (Germany) Institute for Infectious Diseases "for his investigations and discoveries in relation to tuberculosis."

1906 Camillio Golgi (Italy) Pavia Univ., and **Santiago Ramon Y Cajal** (Spain) Madrid Univ. for "their work on the structure of the nervous system."

1907 Charles L.A. Laveran (France) Institute Pasteur "in recognition of his work on the role played by protozoa in causing diseases."

1908 Il'ja I. Mecnikov (Russia) Institut Pasteur (Paris), and **Paul Ehrlich** (Germany) Goettingen Univ. and Royal Institute for Experimental Therapy "in recognition of their work on immunity."

1909 Emil R. Kocher (Switzerland) Berne Univ. "for his work on the physiology, pathology, and surgery of the thyroid gland."

1910 Albrecht Kossel (Germany) Heidelberg Univ. "in recognition of the contributions to our knowledge of cell chemistry made through his work on proteins, including the nucleic substances."

1911 Allvar Gullstrand (Sweden) Uppsala Univ. "for his work on the dioptrics of the eye."

1912 Alexis Carrel (France) Rockefeller Institute for Medical Research (New York) "in recognition of his work on vascular suture and the transplantation of blood vessels and organs."

1913 Charles R. Richet (France) Sorbonne Univ. "in recognition of his work on anaphylaxis."

1914 Robert Bárány (Austria) Vienna Univ. "for his work on the physiology and pathology of the vestibular apparatus."

1915–1918 No awards given.

1919 Jules Bordet (Belgium) Brussels Univ. "for his discoveries relating to immunity."

1920 Schack A.S. Krogh (Denmark) Copenhagen Univ. "for his discoveries of the capillary motor regulating mechanism."

1921 No award

1922 Sir Archibald V. Hill (Great Britain) London Univ. "for his discovery relating to the production of heat in the muscle"; **Otto F. Meyerhof** (Germany) Kiel Univ. "for his discovery of the fixed relationship between the consumption of oxygen and the metabolism of lactic acid in the muscle."

1923 Sir Frederick G. Banting (Canada) Toronto Univ. and **John J.R. Macleod** (Canada) Toronto Univ. "for the discovery of insulin."

1924 Willem Einthoven (Netherlands) Leyden Univ. "for his discovery of the mechanism of the electrocardiogram."

1925 No award

1926 Johannes A.G. Fibiger (Denmark) Copenhagen Univ. "for his discovery of the Spiroptera carcinoma."

1927 Julius Wagner-Jauegg (Austria) Vienna Univ. "for his discovery of the therapeutic value of malaria inoculation in the treatment of dementia paralytica."

1928 Charles J.H. Nicolle (France) Institut Pasteur "for his work on typhus."

1929 Christiaan Eijkman (Netherlands) Utrecht Univ. "for his discovery of the antineuritic vitamin"; **Sir Frederick G. Hopkins** (Great Britain) Cambridge Univ. "for his discovery of the growth-stimulating vitamins."

1930 Karl Landsteiner (Austria) Rockefeller Institute of Medical Research (New York) "for his discovery of human blood groups."

1931 Otto H. Warburg (Germany) Kaiser-Wilhelm Institut "for his discovery of the nature and mode of action of the respiratory enzyme."

1932 Sir Charles S. Sherrington (Great Britain) Oxford Univ. and **Lord Edgar D. Adrian** (Great Britain) Cambridge Univ. "for their discoveries regarding the functions of neurons."

1933   Thomas H. Morgan (U.S.) California Institute of Technology "for his discoveries concerning the role played by the chromosome in heredity."
1934   George H. Whipple (U.S.) Rochester Univ., **George R. Minot** (U.S.) Harvard Univ., and **William P. Murphy** (U.S.) Harvard Univ. "for their discoveries concerning liver therapy in cases of anaemia."
1935   Hans Spemann (German) Univ. of Freiburg "for his discovery of the organizer effect in embryonic development."
1936   Sir Henry H. Dale (Great Britain) National Institute for Medical Research, and **Otto Loewi** (Austria) Graz Univ. "for their discoveries relating to chemical transmission of nerve impulses."
1937   Albert Szent-Györgyi von Nagyrapolt (Hungary) Szeged Univ. "for his discoveries in connection with the biological combustion processes, with special reference to vitamin C and the catalysis of fumaric acid."
1938   Corneille J.F. Heymans (Belgium) Ghent Univ. "for the discovery of the role played by the sinus and aortic mechanisms in the regulation of respiration."
1939   Gerhard Domagk (Germany) Munster Univ. for "discovery of the antibacterial effects of prontosil."
1940–1942   No awards given.
1943   Henrik C.P. Dam (Denmark) Polytechnic Institut "for his discovery of vitamin K"; **Edward A. Doisy** (U.S.) St. Louis Univ. "for his discovery of the chemical nature of vitamin K."
1944   Joseph Erlanger (U.S.) Washington Univ. and **Herbert S. Gasser** (U.S.) Rockefeller Institute for Medical Research "for their discoveries relating to the highly differentiated functions of single nerve fibers."
1945   Sir Alexander Fleming (Great Britain) London Univ., **Sir Ernst B. Chain** (Great Britain) Oxford Univ., and **Lord Howard W. Florey** (Great Britain) Oxford Univ. "for their discovery of penicillin and its curative effect in various infectious diseases."
1946   Hermann J. Muller (U.S.) Indiana Univ. "for his discovery of the production of mutations by means of X-ray irradiation."
1947   Carl F. Cori (U.S.) Washington Univ. and his wife **Gerty T. Cori** (U.S.) Washington Univ. "for their discovery of the course of the catalytic conversion of glycogen"; **Bernardo A. Houssay** (Argentina) Institute of Biology and Experimental Medicine "for his discovery of the part played by the hormone of the anterior pituitary lobe in the metabolism of sugar."
1948   Paul H. Müller (Switzerland) Laboratory of the J.R. Geigy Dye-Factory Co. "for his discovery of the high efficiency of DDT as a contact poison against several arthropods."
1949   Walter R. Hess (Switzerland) Zurich Univ. "for his discovery of the functional organization of the interbrain as a coordinator of the activities of the internal organs; **Antonio Caetano de Abreu F.E. Moniz** (Portugal) Univ. of Lisbon "for his discovery of the therapeutic value of leucotomy in certain psychoses."
1950   Edward C. Kendall (U.S.) Mayo Clinic, **Tadeus Reichstein** (Switzerland) Basel Univ., and **Philip S. Hench** (U.S.) Mayo Clinic "for their discoveries relating to the hormones of the adrenal cortex, their structure, and biological effects."
1951   Max Theiler (Union of South Africa) Laboratories Division of Medicine and Public Health, Rockefeller Foundation (New York) "for his discoveries concerning yellow fever and how to combat it."
1952   Selman A. Waksman (U.S.) Rutgers Univ. "for his discovery of streptomycin, the first antibiotic effective against tuberculosis."
1953   Sir Hans A. Krebs (Great Britain) Sheffield Univ. "for his discovery of the citric acid cycle"; **Fritz A. Lip-**

mann (U.S.) Harvard Medical School and Massachusetts General Hospital "for his discovery of coenzyme A and its importance for intermediary metabolism."
1954   John F. Enders (U.S.) Harvard Medical School and Research Division of Infectious Diseases, Children's Medical Center; **Thomas H. Weller** (U.S.) Research Division of Infectious Diseases, Children's Medical Center; and **Frederick C. Robbins** (U.S.) Western Reserve Univ. "for their discovery of the ability of poliomyelitis viruses to grow in cultures of various types of tissue."
1955   Axel H.T. Theorell (Sweden) Nobel Medical Institute "for his discoveries concerning the nature and mode of action of oxidation enzymes."
1956   Andre F. Cournand (U.S.) Cardio-Pulmonary Laboratory, Columbia Univ. Division. Bellevue Hospital; **Werner Forssman** (Germany) Mainz Univ. and Bad Kreuznach; and **Dickinson W. Richards** (U.S.) Columbia Univ. "for their discoveries concerning heart catheterization and pathological changes in the circulatory system."
1957   Daniel Bovet (Italy) Chief Institute of Public Health "for his discoveries relating to synthetic compounds that inhibit the action of certain body substances, and especially their action on the vascular system and the skeletal muscles."
1958   George W. Beadle (U.S.) California Institute of Technology, and **Edward L. Tatum** (U.S.) Rockefeller Institute for Medical Research "for their discovery that genes act by regulating definite chemical events"; **Joshua Lederberg** (U.S.) Wisconsin Univ. "for his discoveries concerning genetic recombination and the organization of the genetic material of bacteria."
1959   Severo Ochoa (U.S.) New York Univ. College of Medicine, and **Arthur Kornberg** (U.S.) Stanford Univ. "for their discovery of the mechanisms in the biological synthesis of ribonucleic acid and deoxyribonucleic acid."
1960   Sir Frank M. Burnet (Australia) Walter and Eliza Hall Institute for Medical Research, and **Sir Peter B. Medawar** (Great Britain) Univ. College "for discovery of acquired immunological tolerance."
1961   Georg von Békésy (U.S.) Harvard Univ. "for his discoveries of the physical mechanism of stimulation within the cochlea."
1962   Francis H.C. Crick (Great Britain) Institute of Molecular Biology, **James D. Watson** (U.S.) Harvard Univ., and **Maurice H.F. Wilkins** (Great Britain) University of London "for their discoveries concerning the molecular structure of nuclear acids and its significance for information transfer in living material."
1963   Sir John E. Eccles (Australia) Australian National Univ. **Sir Alan L. Hodgkin** (Great Britain) Cambridge Univ., and **Sir Andrew F. Huxley** (Great Britain) University of London :for their discoveries concerning the ionic mechanisms involved in excitation and inhibition in the peripheral and central portions of the nerve cell membrane."
1964   Konrad Block (U.S.) Harvard Univ. and **Feodor Lymen** (Germany) Man-Planck-Institut fur Zellchemie "for their discoveries concerning the mechanism and regulation of the cholesterol and fatty acid metabolism."
1965   Francois Jacob (France) Institut Pasteur, **André Lwoff** (France) Institut Pasteur, and **Jacques Monod** (France) Institut Pasteur "for their discoveries concerning genetic control of enzyme and virus synthesis."
1966   Peyton Rous (U.S.) Rockefeller Univ. "for his discovery of tumor-inducing viruses"; **Charles B. Huggins** (U.S.) Ben May Laboratory for Cancer Research, Univ. of Chicago "for his discoveries concerning hormonal treatment of prostatic cancer."

1967 Ragnar Granit (Sweden) Karolinska Institutet, **Haldan K. Hartline** (U.S.) Rockefeller Univ., and **George Wald** (U.S.) Harvard Univ. "for their discoveries concerning the primary physiological and chemical visual processes in the eye."

1968 Robert W. Holley (U.S.) Cornell Univ., **Har G. Khorana** (U.S.) Univ. of Wisconsin, and **Marshall W. Nirenberg** (U.S.) National Institutes of Health "for their interpretation of the genetic code and its functions in protein synthesis."

1969 Max Delbrück (U.S.) California Institute of Technology, **Alfred D. Hershey** (U.S.) Carnegie Institution of Washington, and **Salvador Luria** (U.S.) M.I.T. for their discoveries concerning the replication mechanism and the genetic structure of viruses."

1970 Sir Bernard Katz (Great Britain) University College, **Ulf von Euler** (Sweden) Karolinska Institutet, and **Julius Axelrod** (U.S.) National Institutes of Health "for their discoveries concerning the humoral transmittors in the nerve terminals and the mechanism for their storage, release, and inactivation."

1971 Earl W. Sutherland, Jr. (U.S.) Vanderbilt Univ. "for his discoveries concerning the mechanisms of the action of hormones."

1972 Gerald M. Edelman (U.S.) Rockefeller Univ. and **Rodney R. Porter** (Great Britain) Oxford Univ. "for their discoveries concerning the chemical structure of antibodies."

1973 Karl von Frisch (W. Germany) Zoologisches Institut der Universitat Munchen; **Konrad Lorenz** (Austria) Osterreichische Akademie der Wissenschaften, Institut fur vergleichende Verhaltensforschung, and **Nikolaas Tinbergen** (Great Britain) University Museum for their discoveries concerning organization and elicitation of individual and social behavior patterns."

1974 Albert Claude (Belgium) Université Catholique de Louvain, **Christian de Duve** (Belgium) Rockefeller Univ. (New York), and **George E. Palade** (U.S.) Yale Univ. "for their discoveries concerning the structural and functional organization of the cell."

1975 David Baltimore (U.S.) M.I.T., **Renato Dulbecco** (U.S.) Imperial Cancer Research Fund Laboratory (London), and **Howard M. Temin** (U.S.) Univ. of Wisconsin "for their discoveries concerning the interaction between tumor viruses and the genetic material of the cell."

1976 Baruch S. Blumberg (U.S.) Institute for Cancer Research, and **D. Carleton Gajdusek** (U.S.) National Institutes of Health "for their discoveries concerning new mechanism for the origin and dissemination of infectious diseases."

1977 Roger Guillemin (U.S.) Salk Institute, and **Andrew V. Schally** (U.S.) Veterans Administration Hospital, New Orleans "for their discoveries concerning the peptide hormone production of the brain"; **Rosalyn Yalow** (U.S.) Veterans Administration Hospital, Bronx "for the development of radioimmunoassays of peptide hormones."

1978 Werner Arber (Switzerland) Biozentrum der Universitat, **Daniel Nathans** (U.S.) John Hopkins Univ., and **Hamilton O. Smith** (U.S.) John Hopkins Univ. "for the discovery of restriction enzymes and their application to problems of molecular genetics."

1979 Alan M. Cormack (U.S.) Tufts Univ., and **Sir Godfrey N. Hounsfield** (Great Britain) Central Research Laboratories, EMI, "for the development of computer assisted tomography."

1980 Baruj Benacerraf (U.S.) Harvard Medical School; **Jean Dausset** (France) Université de Paris, Laboratoire Immuno-Hemetologie; and **George D. Snell** (U.S.) Jackson Laboratory "for their discoveries concerning genetically determined structures on the cell surface that regulate immunological reactions."

1981 Roger W. Sperry (U.S.) California Institute of Technology "for his discoveries concerning the functional specialization of the cerebral hemispheres"; **David H. Hubel** (U.S.) Harvard Medical School, and **Torsten T. Wiesel** (Sweden) Harvard Medical School "for their discoveries concerning information processing in the visual system."

1982 Sune K. Bergström (Sweden) Karolinska Institute, **Bengt I. Samuelsson** (Sweden) Karolinska Institute, and **Sir John R. Vane** (Great Britain) Wellcome Research Laboratories "for their discoveries concerning prostaglandins and related biologically active substances."

1983 Barbara McClintock (U.S.) Cold Spring Harbor Laboratory "for her discovery of mobile genetic elements."

1984 Niels K. Jerne (Denmark) and **Georges J.F. Köhler** (W. Germany) of the Basel Institute for Immunology; and **César Milstein** (Great Britain and Argentina) Medical Research Council Laboratory of Molecular Biology (Cambridge) for theories concerning the specificity in development and controls of the immune system and the discovery of the principle for production of monoclonal antibodies."

1985 Michael S. Brown (U.S.), and **Joseph L. Goldstein** (U.S.) both of the Univ. of Texas Health Science Center at Dallas "for their discoveries concerning the regulation of cholesterol metabolism."

1986 Stanley Cohen (U.S.) Vanderbilt Univ., and **Rita Levi-Montalcini** (Italy and U.S.) Institute of Cell Biology of the C.N.R. (Rome) "for their discoveries of growth factors."

1987 Susumu Tonegawa (U.S.) MIT "for discovery of the genetic principle for generation of antibody diversity."

1988 Sir James W. Black (U.K.) King's College Hospital Medical School, **Gertrude B. Elion** (U.S.) Welcome Research Laboratories, and **George H. Hitchings** (U.S.) Wellcome Research Laboratories "for their discoveries of Important Principles for Drug Treatment."

1989 J. Michael Bishop and **Harold E. Varmus** (U.S.) Univ. of California, San Francisco "for their discovery of the Cellular Origin of Retroviral Oncogenes."

1990 Joseph E. Murray (U.S.) Brigham and Women's Hospital (Boston) who performed the first kidney transplant (1954), and **E. Donnall Thomas** (U.S.), Fred Hutchinson Cancer Research Center (Seattle), who performed the first successful bone marrow transplant between two people who were not twins (1979).

1991 Erwin Neher (Germany) Max-Planck Institute for Biophysical Chemistry, Göttingen, and **Bert Sakmann** (Germany) Max-Planck Institute for Medical Research, Heidelberg, for establishing existence of ion channels by developing technique that allows detection of "incredibly small electrical currents that pass through a single ion channel."

1992 Edmond H. Fischer (U.S.) and **Edwin G. Krebs** (U.S.), both of the Univ. of Washington for a discovery in the 1950s of a regulatory mechanism in almost all human cells linked to some cancers, to the rejection of transplanted organs, and many other processes.

1993 Richard J. Roberts (U.K.), New England Bio Labs, and **Phillip A. Sharp** (U.S.), MIT, for their discovery in the 1970s that the composition of genes is of several segments, which led to gene splicing and to a better understanding of hereditary diseases and cancer.

1994 Alfred G. Gilman (U.S.) Univ. of Texas Southwestern Medical Center, and **Martin Rodbell**

(U.S.) National Institute of Environmental Health Sciences, for their discovery of natural substances known as G-proteins and for showing how they help cells respond to stimuli like light and odors.

1995   Edward B. Lewis (U.S.) California Institute of Technology, **Eric F. Wieschaus** (U.S.) Princeton Univ., and **Christiane Nüsslein-Volhard** (Germany) Max-Planck Institute in Tübingen, for their discovery of how genes control structural development of the body. Their research, performed on fruit flies, helps explain birth defects in humans.

1996   Peter C. Doherty (Australia) St. Jude's Medical Center in Memphis, and **Rolf Zinkernagel** (Switzerland) University of Zurich, for their discovery of how the immune system recognizes and kills virus-infected cells. Their work required more than a decade of study to be proved correct.

1997   Stanley B. Prusiner (U.S.), for his discovery of particles called prions, which he and others claim are disease-causing proteins that can be linked to Creutzfeldt-Jakob disease (mad cow disease) and other degenerative brain diseases.

1998   Robert F. Furchgott (U.S.), State Univ. of New York Health Science Center; **Louis J. Ignarro** (U.S.), UCLA School of Medicine; and **Ferid Murad** (U.S.), Univ. of Texas, for their discovery of nitric oxide (NO) as a signalling molecule in the cardiovascular system.

1999   Günter Blobel (Germany) for his discovery that "proteins have intrinsic signals that govern their transport and localization in the cell." Blobel also found that many hereditary diseases are caused by mistakes in these signals.

2000   Arvid Carlsson (Sweden), Univ. of Gothenburg; **Paul Greengard** (U.S.), Rockefeller Univ., N.Y.; and **Eric Kandel** (U.S.), Columbia Univ., "for their discoveries concerning signal transduction in the nervous system," leading to greater understanding of how variations from the brain's normal functioning patterns can lead to neurological and psychiatric diseases like Parkinson's.

2001   See Part I: "The Almanac of the Year."

Nobel Prizes in Economic Sciences

1969   Ragnar Frisch (Norway) Oslo Univ. and **Jan Tinbergen** (Netherlands) Netherlands School of Economics "for having developed and applied dynamic models for the analysis of economic processes."

1970   Paul A. Samuelson (U.S.) M.I.T. "for the scientific work through which he has developed static and dynamic economic theory and actively contributed to raising the level of analysis in economic science."

1971   Simon Kuznets (U.S.) Harvard Univ. "for his empirically founded interpretation of economic growth which has led to new and deepened insight into the economic and social structure and process of development."

1972   Sir John R. Hicks (U.K.) All Souls College, and **Kenneth J. Arrow** (U.S.) Harvard Univ. "for their pioneering contributions to general economic equilibrium theory and welfare theory."

1973   Wassily Leontief (U.S.) Harvard Univ. "for the development of the input-output method and for its application to important economic problems."

1974   Gunnar Mydal (Sweden), **Friedrich A. von Hayek** (U.K.) "for their pioneering work in the theory of money and economic fluctuations and for their penetrating analysis of the interdependence of economic, social and institutional phenomena."

1975   Leonid Kantorovich (USSR) Academy of Sciences, and **Tjalling C. Koopmans** (U.S.) Yale Univ. "for their contributions to the theory of optimum allocation of resources."

1976   Milton Friedman (U.S.) Univ. of Chicago for "achievements in the fields of consumption analysis, monetary history and theory, and for his demonstration of the complexity of stabilization policy."

1977   Bertil Ohlin (Sweden) Stockholm School of Economics, and **James E. Meade** (U.K.) Cambridge Univ. "for their pathbreaking contribution to the theory of international trade and international capital movements."

1978   Herbert A. Simon (U.S.) Carnegie-Mellon Univ. "for his pioneering research into the decision-making process within economic organizations."

1979   Theodore W. Schultz (U.S.) Univ. of Chicago, and **Sir Arthur Lewis** (U.K.) Princeton Univ. "for their pioneering research into economic development research with particular consideration of the problems of developing countries."

1980   Lawrence R. Klein (U.S.) Univ. of Pennsylvania "for the creation of econometric models and their application to the analysis of economic fluctuations and economic policies."

1981   James Tobin (U.S.) Yale Univ. "for his analysis of financial markets and their relations to expenditure decisions, employment, production, and prices."

1982   George J. Stigler (U.S.) Univ. of Chicago "for his seminal studies of industrial structures, functioning markets, and causes and effects of public regulation."

1983   Gerard Debreu (U.S.) Univ. of California, "for having incorporated new analytical methods into economic theory and for his rigorous reformulation of the theory of general equilbrium."

1984   Sir Richard Stone (U.K.) Cambridge Univ. "for having made fundamental contributions to the development of systems of national accounts and hence greatly improved [sic]the basis for empirical economic analysis."

1985   Franco Modigliani (U.S.) M.I.T. "for his pioneering analyses of saving and of financial markets.

1986   James M Buchanan Jr. (U.S.) Center for Study of Public Choice "for his development of the contractual and constitutional bases for the theory of economic and political decision-making."

1987   Robert M. Solow (U.S.) M.I.T. "for his contributions to the theory of economic growth."

1988   Maurice Allais (France) Centre d'analyse économique "for his pioneering contributions to the theory of markets and efficient utilization of resources."

1989   Trygve Haavelmo (Norway) Univ. of Oslo "for his clarification of the probability theory foundations of econometircs and his analyses of simultaneous economic structures."

1990   Harry Markowitz (U.S.) Baruch College (of the City Univ. of New York, for his Portfolio Theory; **William F. Sharpe** (U.S.) Stanford Univ., for his Capital Asset Pricing Model, and **Merton Miller** (U.S.) Univ. of Chicago, for his work on the Miller-Modigliani Theory. Together, their work revolutionized the financial/business industries.

1991 Ronald H. Coase (U.K.) Univ. of Chicago Law School, for his work on the role of firms in the economy and on social cost of industry, notably his articles "The Theory of the Firm" (1937) and "The Problem of Social Cost" (1960).

1992 Gary S. Becker (U.S.), Univ. of Chicago, for "having extended the domain of economic theory to aspects of human behavior . . ." including crime, family life, and racial bias. His book on education, *Human Capital* (1964), was cited by the Academy.

1993 Robert W. Fogel (U.S.), Univ. of Chicago, and **Douglass C. North** (U.S.), Washington Univ., for "applying economic theory and quarantine methods to historical puzzles." Fogel's work on slavery as an efficient economic system caused great controversy.

1994 John F. Nash (U.S.) Princeton Univ., **John C., Harsanyi** (U.S., b. Hungary) Univ. of California, and **Reinhard Selten** (Germany) Univ. of Bonn, for their separate contributions to the field of game theory, which is used to predict how information and competition affect economic outcomes.

1995 Robert E. Lucas, Jr., (U.S.) Univ. of Chicago, "the economist who has had the greatest influence on macroeconomic research since 1970." His work challenges the Keynesian belief that the government is able to fine-tune the economy.

1996 James A. Mirrlees (U.K.) Cambridge, Univ. and **William Vickrey** (U.S., b. Canada), Columbia Univ. for "their fundamental contributions to the economic theory of incentives" in situations when participants have different information. Their theories have been used in designing more efficient tax codes and eliciting the highest bids at auctions. Vickrey died three days after winning the award.

1997 Robert Merton (U.S.), Harvard University, and **Myron Scholes** (U.S.), Stanford University, for their work in creating "a pioneering formula for the valuation of stock options" and other derivatives. The Nobel committee cited their research as one of the principal reasons for the success of the derivatives markets.

1998 Amartya Sen (India), Cambridge Univ. and Harvard Univ., for his work on human rights, poverty, and inequality that has changed the way governments deal with famines, and for restoring "an ethical dimension to the discussion of vital economics problems."

1999 Robert A. Mundell (U.S.,b. Canada), Columbia University, "for his analysis of monetary and fiscal policy under different exchange rate regimes and his analysis of optimum currency areas." Although his work dates back several decades, "Mundell's contributions remain outstanding and constitute the core of teaching in international macroeconomics."

2000 James J. Heckman (U.S.), Univ. of Chicago "for his development of theory and methods for analyzing selective samples," and **Daniel L. McFadden** (U.S.), Univ. of California, "for his development of theory and methods for analyzing discrete choice."

2001 See Part I: "The Almanac of the Year."

Nobel Prizes in Chemistry

1901 Jacobus H. Van't Holt (Netherlands) Berlin Univ. (Germany) for "the extraordinary services he has rendered by the discovery of the laws of chemical dynamics and osmotic pressure in solutions."

1902 Hermann E. Fischer (Germany) "in recognition of the extraordinary services he has rendered by his work on sugar and purine synthesis."

1903 Svante A. Arrhenius (Sweden) Stockholm Univ. "in recognition of the extraordinary services he has rendered to the advancement of chemistry by his electrolytic theory of dissociation."

1904 Sir William Ramsay (Great Britain) London Univ. "in recognition of his services in the discovery of the inert gaseous elements in air; and his determination of their place in the periodic system."

1905 Johann F.W.A. von Baeyer (Germany) Munich Univ. "in recognition of his services in the advancement of organic chemistry and the chemical industry, through his work on organic dyes and hydroaromatic compounds."

1906 Henri Moissan (France) Sorbonne Univ. "in recognition of the great services rendered by him in his investigation and isolation of the element fluorine, and for the adoption in the service of science of the electric furnace called after him."

1907 Eduard Buchner (Germany) Agricultural College "for his biochemical researches and his discovery of cell-free fermentation."

1908 Lord Ernest Rutherfold (Great Britain) Victoria Univ. "for his investigation into the disintegration of the elements, and the chemistry of radioactive substances."

1909 Wilhelm Ostwald (Germany) Leipzig Univ. "in recognition of his work on catalysis, and for his investigations into the fundamental principles governing chemical equilibria and rates of reaction."

1910 Otto Wallach (Germany) Goettingen Univ. "in recognition of his services to organic chemistry and the chemical industry by his pioneer work in the field of alicyclic compounds."

1911 Marie Curie (France) Sorbonne Univ. "in recognition of her services to the advancement of chemistry by the discovery of the elements radium and polonium, by the isolation of radium and the study of the nature and compounds of this remarkable element."

1912 Victor Grignard (France) Nancy Univ. "for the discovery of the so-called Grignard reagent, which in recent years has greatly advanced the progress of organic chemistry"; **Paul Sabatier** (France) Toulouse Univ., "for his method of hydrogenating organic compounds in the presence of finely disintegrated metals whereby the progress of organic chemistry has been greatly advanced in recent years."

1913 Alfred Werner (Switzerland) Zurich Univ. "in recognition of his work on the linkage of atoms in molecules by which he has thrown new light on earlier investigations and opened up new fields of research especially in inorganic chemistry."

1914 Theodore W. Richards (U.S.) Harvard Univ. for "his accurate determinations of the atomic weight of a large number of chemical elements."

1915 Richard M. Willstätter (Germany) Munich Univ. "for his researches on plant pigments, especially chlorophyll."

1916–1917 No awards given.

1918 Fritz Haber (Germany) Kaiser-Wilhelm Institut "for the synthesis of ammonia from its elements."

1919 No award

1920 Walther H. Nernst (Germany) Berlin Univ. "in recognition of his work in thermochemistry."

1921 Frederick Soddy (Great Britain) Oxford Univ. "for his contributions to our knowledge of the chemistry of radioactive substances, and his investigations into the origin and nature of isotopes."

1922 Francis W. Aston (Great Britain) Cambridge Univ. "for his discovery, by means of his mass spectrograph, of isotopes in a large number of nonradioactive elements, and for his enunciation of the whole-number rule."

1923 Fritz Pregl (Austria) Graz Univ. "for his invention of the method of microanalysis of organic substances."

1924 No award

1925 Richard A. Zsigmondy (Germany) Goettingen Univ. "for his demonstration of the heterogeneous nature of colloid solutions."

1926 The (Theodor) Svedberg (Sweden) Uppsala Univ. "for his work on disperse systems."

1927 Heinrich O. Wieland (Germany) Munich Univ. "for his investigations of the constitution of the bile acids and related substances."

1928 Adolf O.R. Windaus (Germany) Goettingen Univ. "for the services rendered through his research into the constitution of the sterols and their connection with the vitamins."

1929 Sir Arthur Harden (Great Britain) London Univ., Hans K.A. von Euler-Chelpin (Sweden) "for their investigations on the fermentation of sugar and fermentative enzymes."

1930 Hans Fischer (Germany) Institute of Technology "for his researches into the constitution of haemin and chlorophyll, and especially for his synthesis of haemin."

1931 Carl Bosch (Germany) Heidelberg Univ. I.G. Farbenindustrie A.G., and **Fredrich Bergius** (Germany) Heidelberg Univ. and I.G. Farbenindustrie A.G. for "their contributions to the invention and development of chemical high pressure methods."

1932 Irving Langmuir (U.S.) General Electric Co., "for his discoveries and investigations in surface chemistry."

1933 No award

1934 Harold C. Urey (U.S.) Columbia Univ. "for his discovery of heavy hydrogen."

1935 Frédéric Joliot (France) Institut du Radium and his wife, **Iréne Joliot-Curie**, (France) Institut du Radium "in recognition of their synthesis of new radioactive elements."

1936 Petrus (Peter) J.W. Debye (Netherlands) Berlin Univ. and Kaiser-Wilhelm-Institut (now Max-Planck-Institut) "for his contributions to our knowledge of molecular structure through his investigations on dipole moments and on the diffraction of X-rays and electrons in gases."

1937 Sir Walter N. Haworth (Great Britain) Birmingham Univ. "for his investigations on carbohydrates and vitamin C"; **Paul Karrer** (Switzerland) Zurich Univ. "for his investigations on carotenoids, flavins, and vitamins A and B-2."

1938 Richard Kuhn (Germany) Heidelberg Univ. and Kaiser-Wilhelm-Institut (now Max-Planck-Institut) "for his work on carotenoids and vitamins. (Compelled by the authorities of his country to decline the award, but later received diploma and medal.)

1939 Adolf F.J. Butenandt (Germany) Berlin Univ. and Kaiser-Wilhelm-Institut (now Max-Planck-Institut) "for his work on sex hormones. (Compelled by his country to decline the award, but later received diploma and medal); **Leopold Ruzicka** (Switzerland) Federal Institute of Technology "for his work on polymethylenes and higher terpenes."

1940–1942 No awards

1943 George de Hevesy (Hungary) Stockholm Univ. "for his work on the use of isotopes as tracers in the study of chemical processes."

1944 Otto Hahn (Germany) Kaiser-Wilhelm-Institut (now Max-Planck-Institut) "for his discovery of the fission of heavy nuclei."

1945 Artturi I. Virtanen (Finland) Helsinki Univ. "for his research and inventions in agricultural and nutrition chemistry, especially for his fodder preservation method."

1946 James B. Sumner (U.S.) Cornell Univ. "for his discovery that enzymes can be crystallized"; **John H. Northrop** (U.S.) Rockefeller Institute for Medical Research "for their preparation of enzymes and virus proteins in a pure form."

1947 Sir Robert Robinson (Great Britain) Oxford Univ. "for his investigations on plant products of biological importance, especially alkaloids."

1948 Arne W.K. Tiselius (Sweden) Uppsala Univ. "for his research on electrophoresis and adsorption analysis, especially for his discoveries concerning the complex nature of the serum proteins."

1949 William F. Giauque (U.S.) Univ. of California, "for his contributions in the field of chemical thermodynamics, particularly concerning the behavior of substances at extremely low temperatures."

1950 Otto P.H. Diels (Germany) Kiel Univ. and **Kurt Alder** (Germany) Cologne Univ. "for their discovery and development of the diene synthesis."

1951 Edwin M. McMillan (U.S.) and **Glenn T. Seaborg** (U.S.) both of Univ. of California, "for their discoveries in the chemistry of the transuranium elements."

1952 Archer J.P. Martin (Great Britain) Nations Institute for Medical Research, and **Richard L.M. Synge** (Great Britain) Rowett Research Institute (Scotland) "for their invention of partition chromatography."

1953 Herman Staudinger (Germany) State Research Institute for Macromolecular Chemistry "for his discoveries in the field of macromolecular chemistry."

1954 Linus C. Pauling (U.S.) California Institute of Technology "for his research into the nature of the chemical bond and its application to the elucidation of the structure of complex substances."

1955 Vincent du Vigneaud (U.S.) Cornell Univ. "for his work on biochemically important sulphur compounds, especially for the first synthesis of a polypeptide hormone."

1956 Sir Cyril N. Hinshelwood (Great Britain) Oxford Univ. and **Nikolaj N. Semenov** (USSR) Institute for Chemical Physics of the Academy of Sciences of the USSR "for their researches into the mechanism of chemical reactions."

1957 Lord Alexander R. Todd (Great Britain) Cambridge Univ. "for his work on nucleotides and nucleotide co-enzymes."

1958 Frederick Sanger (Great Britain) Cambridge Univ. "for his work on the structure of proteins, especially that of insulin."

1959 Jaroslav Heyrovsky (Czechoslovakia) Polaro-Institute of the Czechoslovakia Academy of Science for his discovery and development of the polarographic methods of analysis."

1960 Willard F. Libby (U.S.) Univ. of California, Los Angeles "for his method to use carbon-14 for age determination in archaeology, geology, geophysics, and other branches of science."

1961 Melvin Calvin (U.S.) Univ. of California, for research on carbon dioxide assimilation in plants."

1962 Max F. Perutz (Great Britain) Laboratory of Molecular Biology, and **Sir John C. Kendrew** (Great

Britain) Laboratory of Molecular Biology, "for their studies on the structures of globular proteins."

1963   Karl Ziegler (Germany) Max-Planck-Institute for Carbon Research, and **Giulio Natta** (Italy) Institute of Technology "for their discoveries in the field of the chemistry and technology of high polymers."

1964   Dorothy C. Hodgkin (Great Britain) Royal Society, Oxford Univ. "for her determinations by X-ray techniques of the structures of important biochemical substances."

1965   Robert B. Woodward (U.S.) Harvard Univ. "for his outstanding achievements in the art of organic synthesis."

1966   Robert S. Mulliken (U.S.) Univ. of Chicago "for his fundamental work concerning chemical bonds and the electronic structure of molecules by the molecular orbital method."

1967   Manfred Eigen (W. Germany) Max-Planck-Institut, **Ronald G.W. Norrish** (U.K.) Institute of Physical Chemistry, and **Sir George Porter** (U.K.) The Royal Institution "for their studies of extremely fast chemical reactions, effected by disturbing the equilibrium by means of very short pulses of energy."

1968   Lars Onsager (U.S.) Yale Univ. "for the discovery of the reciprocal relations bearing his name, which are fundamental for the thermodynamics of irreversible processes."

1969   Sir Derek H.R. Barton (Great Britain) Imperial College of Science and Technology, and **Odd Hassel** (Norway) Kjemisk Institut "for their contributions to the development of the concept of conformation and its application in chemistry."

1970   Luis F. Leloir (Argentina) Institute for Biochemical Research for his discovery of sugar nucleotides and their role in the biosynthesis of carbohydrates."

1971   Gerhard Herzberg (Canada) National Research Council of Canada "for his contributions to the knowledge of electronic structure and geometry of molecules, particularly free radicals."

1972   Christian B. Anfinsen (U.S.) National Institutes of Health "for his work on ribonuclease, especially concerning the connection between the amino acid sequence and the biologically active conformation"; **Stanford Moore** (U.S.) Rockefeller Univ. and **William H. Stein** (U.S.) Rockefeller Univ. "for their contribution to the understanding of the connection between chemical structure and catalytic activity of the active center of the ribonuclease molecule."

1973   Ernst O. Fischer (W. Germany) Technical Univ. of Munich, and **Sir Geoffrey Wilkinson** (Great Britain) Imperial College "for their pioneering work, performed independently, on the chemistry of the organometallic, so-called sandwich compounds."

1974   Paul J. Flory (U.S.) Stanford Univ. "for his fundamental achievements, both theoretical and experimental, in the physical chemistry of the macromolecules."

1975   Sir John W. Cornforth (Australia and Great Britain) Univ. of Sussex "for his work on the stereochemistry of enzyme-catalyzed reactions"; **Vladimir Prelog** (Switzerland) Eidgenossische Technische Hochschule "for his research into the sterochemistry of organic molecules and reactions."

1976   William N. Lipscomb (U.S.) Harvard Univ. "for his studies on the structure of boranes illuminating problems of chemical bonding."

1977   Ilya Prigogine (Belgium) Université Libre de Bruxelles, (Univ. of Texas, U.S.) "for his contributions to nonequilibrium thermodynamics, particularly the theory of dissipative structures."

1978   Peter D. Mitchell (Great Britain) Glynn Research Laboratories "for his contribution to the understanding of biological energy transfer through the formulation of the chemiosmotic theory."

1979   Herbert C. Brown (U.S.) Purdue Univ., and **Georg Wittig** (Germany) Univ. of Heidelberg "for their development of the use of boron-and-phosphorus-containing compounds, respectively, into important reagents in organic synthesis."

1980   Paul Berg (U.S.) Stanford Univ. "for his fundamental studies of the biochemistry of nucleic acids, with particular regard to recombinant-DNA"; **Walter Gilbert** (U.S.) Biological Laboratories, and **Frederick Sanger** (Great Britain) MRC Laboratory of Molecular Biology "for their contributions concerning the determination of base sequences in nucleic acids."

1981   Kenichi Fukui (Japan) Kyoto Univ. and **Roald Hoffman** (U.S.) Cornell Univ. "for their theories, developed independently, concerning the course of chemical reactions."

1982   Aaron Klug (Great Britain) MRC Laboratory of Molecular Biology "for his development of crystallographic electron microscopy and his structural elucidation of biologically important nucleic acid-protein complexes."

1983   Henry Taube (U.S.) Stanford Univ. "for his work on the mechanisms of electron transfer reactions, especially in metal complexes."

1984   Robert B. Merrifield (U.S.) Rockefeller Univ. "for his development of methodology for chemical synthesis on solid matrix."

1985   Herbert A. Hauptman (U.S.) Medical Foundation of Buffalo, and **Jerome Karle** (U.S.) U.S. Naval Research Laboratory "for their outstanding achievements in the development of direct methods for the determination of crystal structures."

1986   Dudley R. Herschbach (U.S.) Harvard Univ., **Yuan T. Lee** (U.S.) Univ. of California, and **John C. Polanyi** (Canada) Univ. of Toronto, "for their contributions concerning the dynamics of chemical elementary processes."

1987   Donald J. Cram (U.S.) University of California, Los Angeles, **Jean-Marie Lehn** (France) Université Louis Pasteur, and **Charles J. Pedersen** (U.S.) Du Pont Laboratory "for their development and use of molecules with structure-specific interactions of high selectivity."

1988   Johann Deisenhofer (U.S.) Howard Hughes Medical Institute, Robert Huber (W. Germany) Max-Planck-Institut, and **Hartmut Michel** (W. Germany) Max-Planck-Institut, "for their determination of the three-dimensional structure of a photosynthetic reaction centre."

1989   Sidney Altman (U.S.) Yale Univ., and **Thomas Cech** (U.S.) Univ. of Colorado for their separate discoveries of the catalytic properties of RNA.

1990   Elias James Corey (U.S.) Harvard Univ. for developing new ways to synthesize complex molecules ordinarily found in nature, work that has contributed to "the high standard of living and health, and the longevity enjoyed at least in the Western world."

1991   Richard R. Ernst (Switzerland) Eidgenössische Technische Hochschule, Zurich, for his work in refining nuclear magnetic resonance spectroscopy for use in chemical analysis.

1992   Rudolph A. Marcus (U.S., b. Canada), Cal Tech., for his mathematical explanation of chemical interactions involving the transfer of electrons between molecules.

1993   Kary B. Mullis (U.S.) for his discovery, in the 1970s, of the polymerase chain reaction (PCR) that allowed scientists to make trillions of copies of DNA. **Michael Smith** (Canada), Univ. of British Columbia, for developing the technique that alters the code of genetic molecules that will facilitate new medical therapies and plants that resist disease.

1994   George A. Olah (U.S., b. Hungary) Univ. of Southern California, for his discovery of new ways of breaking apart and rebuilding carbon and hydrogen compounds. He opened a wholly new field of hydrocarbon research, leading to improved fuels based on coal, methane, and petroleum.

1995   F. Sherwood Roland (U.S.) Univ. of California-Irvine, **Mario Molina** (U.S.) M.I.T., and **Paul Crutzen** (Netherlands) Max Planck Institute for Chemistry in Mainz, Germany, for their pioneering work in explaining how production and use of refrigerants and other chlorofluorocarbons deplete the ozone layer, thus increasing the risk of skin cancer, cataracts, and damage to human immune systems.

1996   Robert F. Curl, Jr., (U.S.) and **Richard E. Smalley** (U.S.), of Rice University, and **Harold W. Kroto** (U.K.) of Univ. of Sussex, for their 1985 discovery of buckminsterfullerene, or "buckyballs": a carbon molecule containing 60 atoms arranged like a soccer ball in a geodesic sphere. Their work opened an entirely new branch of chemistry and gve scientists a greater understanding on how nature bonds carbon atoms together.

1997   Paul D. Boyer (U.S.), UCLA and **John E. Walker** (U.K.), Medical Research Council Laboratory of Molecular Biology, for demonstrating how all living things create adenosine triphosphate, a tiny molecule that stores energy and builds proteins, transmits nerve impulses, and contracts muscles. **Jens C. Skou** (Denmark), Aarhus Univ., for his discovery of sodium-potassium-stimulated adenosine triphosphate, an enzyme that maintains the balance of sodium and potassium ions in living cells.

1998   Walter Kohn (U.S., b. Austria), Univ. of California, Santa Barbara; **John A. Pople** (U.S., b U.K.), Northwestern Univ. Their achievements helped extend the mathematics of quantum mechanics to predicting specific chemical reactions and designing molecules for use in medicine and other applications.

1999   Ahmed H. Zewail (U.S., b. Egypt), CalTech, "for showing that it is possible with rapid laser technique to see how atoms in a molecule move during a chemical reaction." His discovery of the field of femtochemistry, the scientific equivalent of super slow-motion, has allowed scientists to study chemical reactions in extremely intricate detail.

2000   Alan J. Heeger (U.S.), Univ. of California at Santa Barbara; **Alan G. MacDiarmid** (U.S.), Univ. of Pennsylvania; and **Hideki Shirakawa** (Japan), Univ. of Tsukuba, for their discovery and development of a plastic that conducts electricity like a metal and may be used to increase the speed and decrease the size of computers.

2001   See Part I: "The Almanac of the Year."

Nobel Prizes in Physics

1901   Wilhelm C. Röntgen (Germany) Munich Univ. "in recognition of the extraordinary services he has rendered by the discovery of remarkable rays subsequently named after him."

1902   Hendrik A. Lorentz (Netherlands) Leyden Univ., and **Pieter Zeeman** (Netherlands) Amsterdam Univ. "in recognition of the extraordinary service they rendered by their researches into the influence of magnetism upon radiation phenomena."

1903   Antoine H. Becquerel (France) Ecole Polytechnique "in recognition of the extraordinary services he has rendered by the discovery of spontaneous radioactivity"; **Pierre Curie** (France) Municipal School of Industrial Physics and Chemistry and his wife, **Marie Curie,** (France) (born in Poland) "in recognition of the extraordinary services they have rendered by their joint researches on the radiation phenomena discovered by Professor Henri Becquerel."

1904   Lord Rayleigh (John W. Strutt) (Great Britain) Royal Institution of Great Britain "for his investigations of the densities of the most important gases and for his discovery of argon in connection with these studies."

1905   Philipp E.A. Lenard (Germany) Kiel Univ. "for his work on cathode rays."

1906   Sir Joseph J. Thomas (Great Britain) Cambridge Univ. "in recognition of the great merits of his theoretical and experimental investigations on the conduction of electricity by gases."

1907   Albert A. Michelson (U.S.) Univ. of Chicago "for his optical precision instruments and the spectroscopic and meteorological investigations carried out with their aid."

1908   Gabriel Lippman (France) Sorbonne Univ. "for his method of reproducing colours photographically based on the phenomenon of interference."

1909   Guglielmo Marconi (Italy) Marconi Wireless Telegraph Co., Ltd., and **Carl F. Braun** (Germany) Strasbourg Univ. "in recognition of their contributions to the development of wireless telegraphy."

1910   Johannes D. van der Waals (Netherlands) Amsterdam Univ. "for his work on the equation of state for gases and liquids."

1911   Wilhelm Wien (Germany) Würzburg Univ. "for his discoveries regarding the laws governing the radiation of heat."

1912   Nils G. Dalén (Sweden) Swedish Gas-Accumulator Co. "for his invention of automatic regulators for use in conjunction with gas accumulators for illuminating lighthouses and buoys."

1913   Heike Kamerlingh-Onnes (Netherlands) Leyden Univ. "for his investigations on the properties of matter at low temperatures which led, inter alia, to the production of liquid helium."

1914   Max von Laue (Germany) Frankfurt-am-Main Univ. "for his discovery of the diffraction of X-rays by crystals."

1915   Sir William Henry Gragg (Great Britain) London Univ. and his son **Sir William Lawrence Bragg** (Great Britain) Victoria Univ. "for their services in the analysis of crystal structure by means of X-rays."

1916   No award.

1917   Charles G. Barkla (Great Britain) Edinburgh Univ. "for his discovery of the characteristic Röntgen radiation of the elements."

1918   Max K.E.L. Planck (Germany) Berlin Univ. "in recognition of the services he rendered to the advancement of Physics by his discovery of energy quanta."

1919   Johannes Stark (Germany) Greifswald Univ. "for his discovery of the Doppler effect in canal rays and the splitting of spectral lines in electric fields."

1920   Charles E. Guillaume (Switzerland) International Bureau of Weights and Measurers "in recognition of the service he has rendered to precision measurements in physics by his discovery of anomalies in nickel steel alloys."

1921 Albert Einstein (Germany) Kaiser-Wilhelm-Institut für Physik (now Max-Panck-Institut) "for his services to theoretical physics, and especially for his discovery of the law of the photoelectric effect."

1922 Niels Bohr (Denmark) Copenhagen Univ. "for his services in the investigation of the structure of atoms and of the radiation emanating from them."

1923 Robert A. Millikan (U.S.) California Institute of Technology "for his work on the elementary charge of electricity and on the photoelectric effect."

1924 Karl M.G. Siegbahn (Sweden) Uppsala Univ. "for his discoveries and research in the field of X-ray spectroscopy."

1925 James Franck (Germany) Goettingen Univ., and **Gustav Hertz** (Germany) Halle Univ. "for their discovery of the laws of governing the impact of an electron upon an atom."

1926 Jean B. Perrin (France) Sorbonne Univ. "for his work on the discontinuous structure of matter, and especially for his discovery of sedimentation equilibrium."

1927 Arthur H. Compton (U.S.) Univ. of Chicago "for his discovery of the effect named after him"; **Charles T.R. Wilson** (Great Britain) Cambridge Univ. "for his method of making the paths of electrically charged particles visible by condensation of vapor."

1928 Sir Own W. Richardson (Great Britain) London Univ. "for his work on the thermionic phenomenon and especially for the discovery of the law named after him."

1929 Prince Louis-Victor de Broglie (France) Sorbonne Univ. "for his discovery of the wave nature of electrons."

1930 Sir Chandrasekhara V. Raman (India) Calcutta Univ. "for his work on the scattering of light and for the discovery of the effect names after him."

1931 No award.

1932 Werner Heisenberg (Germany) Leipzig Univ. "for the creation of quantum mechanics, the application of which, has, inter alia, led to the discovery of the allotropic forms of hydrogen."

1933 Edwin Schrödinger (Austria) Berlin Univ. and **Paul A.M. Dirac** (Great Britain) Cambridge Univ. "for the discovery of new productive forms of atomic theory."

1934 No award

1935 Sir James Chadwick (Great Britain) Liverpool Univ. "for his discovery of the neutron."

1936 Victor F. Hess (Austria) Innsbruck Univ. "for his discovery of cosmic radiation"; **Carl D. Anderson** (U.S.) California Institute of Technology "for his discovery of the positron."

1937 Clinton J. Davisson (U.S.) Bell Telephone Laboratories, and **Sir George P. Thomson** (Great Britain) London Univ. "for their experimental discovery of the diffraction of electrons by crystals."

1938 Enrico Fermi (Italy) Rome Univ. "for his demonstration of the existence of new radioactive elements produced by neutron irradiation, and for his related discovery of nuclear reactions brought about by slow neutrons."

1939 Ernest O. Lawrence (U.S.) Univ. of California, Berkeley "for the invention and development of the cyclotron and for results obtained with it, especially with regard to artificial redioactive elements."

1940–1942 No awards given.

1943 Otto Stern (U.S.) Carnegie Institute of Technology "for his contribution to the development of the molecular ray method and his discovery of the magnetic moment of the proton."

1944 Isidor I. Rabi (U.S.) Columbia Univ. "for his resonance method for recording the magnetic properties of atomic nuclei."

1945 Wolfgang Pauli (Austria) Princeton Univ. "for the discovery of the Exclusion Principle, also called the Pauli Principle."

1946 Percy W. Bridgman (U.S.) Harvard Univ. "for the invention of an apparatus to produce extremely high pressures, and for the discoveries he made therewith in the field of high-pressure physics."

1947 Sir Edward V. Appleton (Great Britain) Dept. of Scientific and Industrial Research "for his investigations of the physics of the upper atmosphere, especially the so-called Appleton layer."

1948 Lord Patrick M.S. Blackett (Great Britain) Victoria Univ. "for his development of the Wilson cloud chamber method, and his discoveries therewith in the fields of nuclear physics and cosmic radiation."

1949 Hideki Yukawa (Japan) Kyoto Imperial Univ. "for his prediction of the existence of mesons on the basis of theoretical work on nuclear forces."

1950 Cecil F. Powell (Great Britain) Bristol Univ. "for his development of the photographic method of studying nuclear processes and his discoveries regarding mesons made with this method."

1951 Sir John D. Cockcroft (Great Britain) Atomic Energy Research Establishment, and Ernest T.S. Walton (Ireland) Dublin Univ. "for their pioneer work on the transmutation of atomic nuclei by artificially accelerated atomic particles."

1952 Felix Block (U.S.) Stanford Univ., and **Edward M. Purcell** (U.S.) Harvard Univ. "for their development of new methods for nuclear magnetic precision measurements and discoveries in connection therewith."

1953 Frits (Frederik) Zernike (Netherlands) Groningern Univ. "for his demonstration of the phase contrast method, especially for his invention of the phase contrast microscope."

1954 Max Born (Great Britain) Edinburgh Univ. "for his fundamental research in quantum mechanics, especially for his statistical interpretation of the wave-function"; **Walther Bothe** (Germany) Heidelbery Univ., Max-Planck-Institut "for the coincidence method and his discoveries made therewith."

1955 Willis E. Lamb (U.S.) Stanford Univ. "for his discoveries concerning the fine structure of the hydrogen spectrum"; **Polykarp Kusch** (U.S.) Columbia Univ. "for his precision determination of the magnetic moment of the electron."

1956 William Shockley (U.S. Semiconductor Laboratory of Beckman Instruments, Inc., **John Bardeen** (U.S.) Univ. of Illinois, and **Walter H. Brattain** (U.S.) Bell Telephone Laboratories on research on semiconductors and discovery of "the transistor effect."

1957 Chen N. Yang (China) Institute for Advanced Study (Princeton, NJ) and **Tsung-Dao Lee** (China) Columbia Univ. "for their penetrating investigation of the so-called parity laws which has led to important discoveries regarding the elementary particles."

1958 Pavel A. Cherenkov (USSR) Physics Institute of USSR Academy of Sciences, **Il'ja M.Frank** (USSR) Academy of Sciences, and **Igor J. Tamm** (USSR) Univ. of Moscow and Physics Institute of USSR Academy of Sciences "for their discovery and the interpretation of the Cherenkov effect."

1959 Emilio G. Segrè (U.S.) Univ. of California, Berkeley, and **Owen Chamberlain** (U.S.) Univ. of California, Berkeley "for their discovery of the antiproton."

1960　Donald A. Glaser (U.S.) Univ. of California, Berkeley "for the invention of the bubble chamber."
1961　Robert Hofstadter (U.S.) Stanford Univ. "for his pioneering studies of electron scattering in atomic nuclei and for his thereby achieved discoveries concerning the structure of the nucleons"; **Rudolf L. Mössbauer** (Germany) Technische Hochschule (Munich), and California Institute of Technology "for his researches concerning the resonance absorption of gamma radiation and his discovery in this connection of the effect which bears his name."
1962　Lev D. Landau (USSR) Academy of Sciences "for his pioneering theories for condensed matter, especially liquid helium."
1963　Eugene P. Wigner (U.S.) Princeton Univ. "for his contributions to the theory of the atomic nucleus and the elementary particles, particularly through the discovery and application of fundamental symmetry principles"; **Maria Goeppert-Mayer** (U.S.) Univ. of California, La Jolla, and **J. Hans D. Jensen** (Germany) Univ. of Heidelberg "for their discoveries concerning nuclear shell structure."
1964　Charles H. Townes (U.S.) M.I.T., **Nikolai G. Basov** (USSR) Lebedev Institute for Physics, and **Aleksandre M. Prochorov** (USSR) Lebedev Institute for Physics "for fundamental work in the field of quantum electronics, which has led to the construction of oscillators and amplifiers based on the maser-laser-principle."
1965　Schin'ichiro Tomonaga (Japan) Toyko Univ., **Julian Schwinger** (U.S.) Harvard Univ., and **Richard P. Feynman** (U.S.) California Institute of Technology "for their fundamental work in quantum electrodynamcis, with deep-ploughing consequences for the physics of elementary particles."
1966　Alfred Kastier (France) Ecole Normale Supérieure, Université de Paris "for the discovery and development of optical methods for studying hertzian resonance in atoms."
1967　Hans A. Bethe (U.S.) Cornell Univ. "for his contributions to the theory of nuclear reactions, especially his discoveries concerning the energy production in stars."
1968　Luis W. Alvarez (U.S.) Univ. of California, Berkeley "for his decisive contributions to elementary particle physics, in particular the discovery of a large number of resonance states, made possible through his development of the technique of using hydrogen bubble chamber and data analysis."
1969　Murray Gell-Mann (U.S.) California Institute of Technology "for his contributions and discoveries concerning the classification of elementary particles and their interactions."
1970　Hannes Alfvén (Sweden) Royal Institute of Technology "for fundamental work and discoveries in magneto-hydrodynamics with fruitful applications in different parts of plasma physics"; **Louis Neel** (France) Univ. of Grenoble "for fundamental work and discoveries concerning antiferromagnetism and ferrimagetism which have led to important applications in solid-state physics."
1971　Dennis Gabor (Great Britain) Imperial College of Science and Technology "for his invention and development of the holographic method."
1972　John Bardeen (U.S.) Univ. of Illinois, **Leon N. Cooper** (U.S.) Brown Univ., and **J. Robert Schrieffer** (U.S.) Univ. of Pennsylvania "for their jointly developed theory of superconductivity, usually called the BCS-theory."
1973　Leo Esaki (Japan) IBM Thomas J. Watson Research Center (New York), and **Ivar Giaever** (U.S.) General Electric Co. "for their experimental discoveries regarding tunneling phenomena in semicon-

ductors and superconductors, respectively"; **Brian D. Josephson** (U.K.) Cambridge Univ. "for his theoretical predictions of the properties of a supercurrent through a tunnel barrier, in particular those phenomena which are generally known as the Josephson effects."
1974　Sir Martin Ryle (U.K.) and **Antony Hewish** (U.K.), both of Cambridge Univ., "for their pioneering research in radio astrophysics: Ryle for his observations and inventions, in particular of the aperture synthesis technique, and Hewish for his decisive role in the discovery of pulsars."
1975　Aage Bohr (Denmark) Niels Bohr Institute, **Ben Mottelson** (Denmark) Nordita, and **James Rainwater** (U.S.) Columbia Univ. "for the discovery of the connection between collective motion and particle motion in atomic nuclei and the development of the theory of the structure of the atomic nucleus based on this connection."
1976　Burton Richter (U.S.) Stanford Linear Accelerator Center, and **Samuel C.C. Ting** (U.S.) M.I.T. "for their pioneering work in the discovery of a heavy elementary particle of a new kind."
1977　Philip W. Anderson (U.S.) Bell Laboratories, **Sir Nevill F. Mott** (U.K.) Cambridge Univ. and **John H. van Vleck** (U.S.) Harvard Univ. "for their fundamental theoretical investigations of the electronic structure of magnetic and disordered systems."
1978　Peter L. Kapitsa (USSR) Academy of Sciences "for his basic inventions and discoveries in the area of low-temperature physics, **Arno A. Penzias** (U.S.) Bell Laboratories, and **Robert W. Wilson** (U.S.) Bell Laboratories "for their discovery of cosmic microwave background radiation."
1979　Sheldon L. Glashow (U.S.) Lyman Laboratory, Harvard Univ., **Abdus Salam** (Pakistan) International Centre for Theoretical Physics (Italy) and Imperial College of Science and Technology (London), and **Steven Weinberg** (U.S.) Harvard Univ. "for their contributions to the theory of the unified weak and electromagnetic interaction between elementary particles, including, inter alia, the predictions of the weak neutral current."
1980　James W. Cronin (U.S.) Univ. of Chicago, and **Val L. Fitch** (U.S.) Princeton Univ. "for the discovery of violations of fundamental symmetry principles in the decay of neutral K-mesons."
1981　Nicolaas Bloembergen (U.S.) Harvard Univ., and **Arthur L. Schawlow** (U.S.) Stanford Univ. "for their contributions to the development of laser spectroscopy"; **Kai M. Siegbahn** (Sweden) Uppsala Univ. "for his contribution to the development of high-resolution election spectroscopy."
1982　Kenneth G. Wilson (U.S.) Cornell Univ. "for his theory for critical phenomena in connection with phase transitions."
1983　Subrahmanyan Chandrasekhar (U.S.) Univ. of Chicago "for his theoretical studies of the physical processes of importance to the structure and evolution of the stars"; **William A. Fowler** (U.S.) California Institute of Technology for his "studies of the nuclear reactions of importance in the formation of the chemical elements in the universe."
1984　Carlo Rubbia (Italy) CERN (Switzerland), and **Simon van der Meer** (Netherlands) CERN (Switzerland) "for their decisive contributions to the discovery of the field particles W and Z, communicators of weak interaction."
1985　Klaus von Klitzing (W. Germany) Max-Planck-Institut for Solid State Research "for the discovery of the quantized Hall effect."
1986　Ernst Ruska (W. Germany) Fritz-Haber-Institut der Max-Planck-Gesellschaft "for his fundamen-

tal work in electron optics, and for the design of the first electron microscope"; **Gerd Binnig** (W. Germany) IBM Zurich Research Laboratory and **Heinrich Rohrer** (Switzerland) IBM Zurich Research Laboratory "for their design of the scanning tunneling microscope."

1987 Georg J. Bednorz (Switzerland) IBM Zurich research Laboratory, and **Dr. K. Alex Müller** (Switzerland) IBM Zurich Research Laboratory "for the discovery of new superconducting materials."

1988 Leon M. Lederman (U.S.) Fermi National Accelerator Laboratory, **Melvin Schwartz** (U.S.) Digital Pathways, Inc., and **Jack Steinberger** (Switzerland) "for the neutrino beam method and the demonstration of the doublet structure of the leptons through the discovery of the muon neutrino."

1989 Norman R. Ramsey (U.S.) Harvard Univ. "for the invention of the separated oscillatory fields method and its use in . . . atomic clocks"; **Hans G. Dehmelt** (U.S.) Univ. of Washington, and **Wolfgang Paul** (W. Germany) Univ. of Bonn "for the development of the ion trap technique," which allows detailed study of subatomic particles."

1990 Richard E. Taylor (Can.), Stanford U.; **Jerome I. Friedman** (U.S.) MIT; and **Henry W. Kendall** (U.S.) MIT, whose experiments between 1967 and 1973 confirmed the existence of quarks, the fundamental building blocks of matter.

1991 Pierre-Gilles de Gennes (France), Collège de France, Paris, for his discoveries about the ordering of molecules in a variety of substances but especially liquid crystals, where his work has helped in understanding superconductivity.

1992 George Charpak (France, b. Poland), affiliated with CERN, the accelerator complex, where he developed electronic detectors that traced the paths of subatomic particles with lightning speed.

1993 Joseph H. Taylor (U.S.), Princeton Univ., and **Russel A. Hulse** (U.S.), Princeton Plasma Physics Laboratory, for their discovery of a binary pulsar and their later success in measuring its pulse rate.

1994 Clifford G. Shull (U.S.) MIT, and **Bertram N. Brockhouse** (Canada) McMaster Univ., for experiments in the 1940s and '50s that exploited the penetrating power of low-energy neutron beams produced by nuclear reactors. Neutron beams are more powerful than other forms of radiation, and are now widely used to explore the atomic structure of matter.

1995 Martin L. Perl, (U.S.) Stanford Univ. Linear Accelerator Center, and **Frederick Reines** (U.S.) Los Alamos National Laboratory, for their separate discoveries of "two of nature's most remarkable subatomic particles." Perl's discovery of the tau in the 1970s and Reines discovery of the neutrino in the 1950s are watershed events in scientists' understanding of elementary particle physics.

1996 Robert C. Richardson (U.S.) and **David M. Lee** (U.S.) of Cornell Univ., and **Douglas S. Osheroff** (U.S.) Stanford Univ., for their 1972 discovery of superfluiditiy in a rare form of helium. The superfluid helium evidences surprising magnetic properties, and may offer insights into the formation of galaxies and the rotational behavior of neutron stars.

1997 Steven Chu (U.S.) Stanford Univ., **Claude Cohen-Tannoudji** (France), Collège de France, and **William D. Phillips** (U.S.), National Institute of Standards and Technology, for development of a method to trap individual atoms, which allow them to be studied in greater detail.

1998 Robert B. Laughlin (U.S.), Stanford Univ., **Horst L. Störmer** (U.S.), Bell Laboratories; **Daniel Tsui** (U.S.), Princeton Univ., for their discovery of the fractional quantum Hall effect, the culmination of studies of magnetic fields dating back to 1897.

1999 Gerardus 't Hooft (Netherlands), Univ. of Utrecht, and **Martinus J.G. Veltman** (Netherlands) Univ. of Michigan, for placing the theory of particle physics on firm mathematical ground by showing how the theory "may be used for precise calculations of physical quantities."

2000 Jack S. Kilby (U.S.), Texas Instruments, for his contribution to the invention of the integrated circuit, a.k.a. the computer chip; **Zhores I. Alferov** (Russia), A.F. Ioffe Physico-Technical Institute, St. Petersburg, and **Herbert Kroemer,** (U.S.), Univ. of California at Santa Barbara, for their invention of components called heterostructures, which are used in high-speed electronic devices like CD players, bar-code readers, and laser pointers.

2001 See Part I: "The Almanac of the Year."

Nobel Prizes in Literature

1901 Sully Prudhomme (pen name of René F.A. Prudhomme) (France) "in special recognition of his poetic composition."

1902 Christian M.T. Mommsen (Germany) "the greatest living master of the art of historical writing, with special reference to his monumental work, *A History of Rome.*

1903 Bjørstjerne M. Bjørnson (Norway) for "his noble, magnificent, and versatile poetry which has always been distinguished by both the freshness of its inspiration and the rare purity of its spirit."

1904 Frederic Mistral (France) "in recognition of the fresh originality and true inspiration of his poetic production, which faithfully reflects the natural scenery and native spirit of his people, and, in addition, his significant work as a Provençal philologist." **José Echegaray y Eizaguirre** (Spain) "in recognition of the numerous and brilliant compositions which, in an individual and original manner, have revived the great traditions of the Spanish drama."

1905 Henryk Sienkiewicz (Poland) "because of his outstanding merits as an epic writer.

1906 Giosué Carducci (Italy) "as a tribute to the creative energy, freshness of style, and lyrical force which characterize his poetic masterpieces."

1907 Rudyard Kipling (Great Britain) "in consideration of the power of observation, originality of imagination, virility of ideas, and remarkable talent for narration which characterize the creations of this world-famous author."

1908 Rudolf C. Eucken (Germany) "in recognition of his earnest search for truth, his penetrating power of thought, his wide range of vision, and the warmth and strength in presentation with which in his numerous works he had vindicated and developed an idealistic philosophy of life."

1909 Selma O.L. Lagerlöf (Sweden) "in appreciation of the lofty idealism, vivid imagination, and spiritual perception that characterize her writings."

1910 Paul J.L. Heyse (Germany) "as a tribute to the consummate artistry, permeated with idealism, which he has demonstrated during his long productive career as lyric poet, dramatist, novelist, and writer of world-renowned short stories."

1911 Count Maurice (Mooris) P.M.B. Maeterlinck (Belgium) "in appreciation of his many-sided literary activities, and especially of his dramatic works, which are distinguished by a wealth of imagination and by a poetic fancy."

1912   Gerhart J.R. Hauptmann (Germany) "primarily in recognition of his fruitful, varied, and outstanding production in the realm of dramatic art."
1913   Rabindranath Tagore (India) "because of his profoundly sensitive, fresh, and beautiful verse, by which, with consummate skill, he has made his poetic thought, expressed in his own English words, a part of the literature of the West."
1914   No award
1915   Romain Rolland (France) "as a tribute to the lofty idealism of his literary production and to the sympathy and love of truth with which he has described different types of human beings."
1916   Carl G.V. von Heidenstam (Sweden) "in recognition of his significance as the leading representative of a new era in our literature."
1917   Karl A. Gjellerup (Denmark) "for his varied and rich poetry, which is inspired by lofty ideals"; **Henrik Pontoppidan** (Denmark) "for his authentic descriptions of presentday life in Denmark."
1918   No award
1919   Carl F.G. Spitteler (Switzerland) "in special appreciation of his epic, 'Olympian Spring'"
1920   Knut P. Hamsun (Norway) "for his monumental work, *Growth of the Soil.*"
1921   Antole France (*pen name of Jacques A. Thibault*) (France) "in recognition of his brilliant literary achievements, characterized as they are by a nobility of style, a profound human sympathy, grace, and a true Gallic temperament."
1922   Jacinto Benavent (Spain) "for the happy manner in which he has continued the illustrious traditions of the Spanish drama."
1923   William B. Yeats (Ireland) "for his always inspired poetry, which in a highly artistic form gives expression to the spirit of a whole nation."
1924   Wladyslaw S. Reymont (pen name of Reyment) (Poland) "for his great national epic, *The Peasants.*"
1925   George B. Shaw (Great Britain) "for his work which is marked by both idealism and humanity, its stimulating satire often being infused with a singular poetic beauty."
1926   Grazia Deledda (pen name of Grazia Madesani (Italy) "for her idealistically inspired writings, which picture the life on her native island and with depth and sympathy deal with human problems."
1927   Henri Bergson (France) "in recognition of his rich and vitalizing ideas."
1928   Sigrid Undset (Norway) "principally for her powerful descriptions of Northern life during the Middle Ages."
1929   Thomas Mann (Germany) "principally for his great novel *Buddenbrooks.*"
1930   Sinclair Lewis (U.S.) "for his vigorous and graphic art of description and his ability to create, with wit and humor, new types of characters."
1931   Erik A. Karlfeldt (Sweden) for his poetry.
1932   John Galsworthy (Great Britain) "for his distinguished art of narration which takes its highest form in *The Forsyte Saga.*"
1933   Ivan A. Bunin (stateless domicile in France) "for the strict artistry with which he has carried on the classical Russian traditions in prose writing."
1934   Luigi Pirandello (Italy) "for his bold and ingenious revival of dramatic art."
1935   No award
1936   Eugene G. O'Neill (U.S.) "for the power, honesty, and deep-felt emotions of his dramatic works, which embody an original concept of tragedy."
1937   Roger Martin du Gard (France) "for the artistic power and truth with which he has depicted human conflict as well as some fundamental aspects of contemporary life in his novel-cycle *Les Thibault.*"
1938   Pearl Buck (pen name of Pearl Walsh) (U.S.) "for her rich and truly epic descriptions of peasant life in China and for her biographical masterpieces."
1939   Frans E. Sillanpää (Finland) "for his deep understanding of his country's peasantry and the exquisite art with which he has portrayed their way of life and their relationship with Nature."
1940–1943   No awards given.
1944   Johannes V. Jensen (Denmark) "for the rare strength and fertility of his poetic imagination."
1945   Gabriela Mistral (*pen name of Lucila Godoy y Alcayaga*) (Chile) "for her lyric poetry which, has made her name a symbol of the idealistic aspirations of the entire Latin American world."
1946   Hermann Hesse (Switzerland) "for his inspired writings which exemplify the classical humanitarian ideals and high qualities of style."
1947   André P.G. Gide (France) "for his writings in which human problems and conditions have been presented with a fearless love of truth and keen psychological insight."
1948   Thomas S. Eliot (Great Britain) for his "outstanding, pioneer contribution to present-day poetry."
1949   William Faulkner (U.S.) ":for his powerful and artistically unique contribution to the modern American novel."
1950   Earl (Bertrand) Russell (Great Britain) "in recognition of his varied and significant writings in which he champions humanitarian ideals and freedom of thought."
1951   Pär G. Lägerkvist (Sweden) "for the artistic vigour and true independence of mind with which he endeavours in his poetry to find answers to the eternal questions confronting mankind."
1952   François Mauriac (France) "for the deep spiritual insight and the artistic intensity with which he has in his novels penetrated the drama of human life."
1953   Sir Winston L.S. Churchill (Great Britain) "for his mastery of historical and biographical description as well as for brilliant oratory in defending exalted human values."
1954   Ernest M. Hemingway (U.S.) "for his mastery of the art of narrative, most recently demonstrated in *The Old Man and the Sea,* and for the influence that he has exerted on contemporary style."
1955   Halldór K. Laxness (Iceland) "for his vivid epic power which has renewed the great narrative art of Iceland."
1956   Juan R. Jiménez (Puerto Rico, b. Spain) "for his lyrical poetry, which in Spanish language constitutes an example of high spirit and artistic purity."
1957   Albert Camus (France) "for his important literary production, which with clearsighted earnestness illuminates the problems of the human conscience in our times."
1958   Boris L. Pasternak (USSR) "for his important achievement both in contemporary lyrical poetry and in the field of the great Russian epic tradition." (Declined the prize).
1959   Salvatore Quasimodo (Italy) "for his lyrical poetry, which with classical fire expresses the tragic experience of life in our own times."
1960   Saint-John Perse (pen name of Alexis Léger) (France) "for the soaring flight and the evocative imagery of his poetry which in a visionary fashion reflects the conditions of our time."
1961   Ivo Andric (Yugoslavia) "for the epic force with which he has traced themes and depicted human destinies drawn from the history of his country."

1962 John Steinbeck (U.S.) "for his realistic and imaginative writings, combining as they do sympathetic humour and keen social perception."

1963 Giorgos Seferis (pen name of Giogos Seferiades) (Greece) "for his eminent lyrical writing, inspired by a deep feeling for the Hellenic world of culture."

1964 Jean-Paul Sartre (France) "for his work which, rich in ideas and filled with the spirit of freedom and the quest for truth, has exerted a far-reaching influence on our age." (Declined the prize.)

1965 Michail A. Solochov (USSR) "for the artistic power and integrity with which, in his epic of the Don, he has given expression to a historic phase in the life of the Russian people."

1966 Shmuel U. Agnon (Israel) "for his profoundly characteristic narrative art with motifs from the life of the Jewish people; **Nelly Sachs** (Germany) (domiciled in Sweden) " for her outstanding lyrical and dramatic writing, which interprets Israel's destiny with touching strength."

1967 Miguel A. Asturias (Guatemala) "for his vivid literary achievement, deep-rooted in the national traits and traditions of Indian peoples of Latin America."

1968 Yasunari Kawabata (Japan) "for his narrative mastery, which with great sensibility expresses the essence of the Japanese mind."

1969 Samuel Beckett (Ireland) "for his writing, which—in new forms for the novel and drama—in the destitution of modern man acquires its elevation."

1970 Alexander Solzhenitsyn (USSR) "for the ethical force with which he has pursued the indispensable traditions of Russian literature."

1971 Pablo Neruda (Chile) "for a poetry that brings alive a continent's destiny and dreams."

1972 Heinrich Böll (W. Germany) "for his writing which through its combination of a broad perspective on his time and a sensitive skill in characterization has contributed to a renewal of German literature."

1973 Patrick White (Australia) "for an epic and psychological narrative art which has introduced a new continent into literature."

1974 Eyvind Johnson (Sweden) "for a narrative art, far-seeing in lands and ages, in the service of freedom"; **Harry Martinson** (Sweden) "for writings that catch the dewdrop and reflect the cosmos."

1975 Eugenio Montale (Italy) "for his distinctive poetry which, with great artistic sensitivity, has interpreted human values under the sign of an outlook on life with no illusions."

1976 Saul Bellow (U.S.) "for the human understanding and subtle analysis of contemporary culture."

1977 Vincente Aleixandre (Spain) "for a creative poetic writing which illuminates man's condition in the cosmos and in present-day society, at the same time representing the great renewal of the traditions of Spanish poetry between the wars."

1978 Isaac Bashevis Singer (U.S.) "for his impassioned narrative art which, with roots in a Polish-Jewish cultural tradition, brings universal human conditions to life."

1979 Odysseus Elytis (pen name of Odysseus Alepoudhelis) (Greece) "for his poetry, which against the background of Greek tradition, depicts man's struggle for freedom and creativeness."

1980 Czeslaw Milosz (U.S. and Poland) "who with uncompromising clear-sightedness voices man's exposed condition in a world of severe conflicts."

1981 Elias Canetti (Great Britain) "for writings marked by a broad outlook, a wealth of ideas, and artistic power."

1982 Gabriel García Marquez (Colombia) "for his novels and short stories, in which the fantastic and the realistic are combined in a richly composed world of imagination, reflecting a continent's life and conflicts."

1983 William Golding (Great Britain) "for his novels, which illuminate the human condition in the world of today."

1984 Jaroslav Seifert (Czechoslovakia) "for his poetry which, endowed with freshness, sensuality, and rich inventiveness, provides a liberating image of the indomitable spirit and versatility of man."

1985 Claude Simon (France) "who in his novel combines the poet's and the painter's creativeness with a deepened awareness of time in the depiction of the human condition."

1986 Wole Soyinka (Nigeria) "who in a wide cultural perspective and with poetic overtones fashions the drama of existence."

1987 Joseph Brodsky (U.S.) "for his all-embracing authorship imbued with clarity of thought and poetic intensity."

1988 Naguib Mahfouz (Egypt) "who through works rich in nuance, has formed an Arabian narrative art that applies to all mankind."

1989 Camilo José Cela (Spain) a novelist whose "rich and inventive prose, forms a challenging vision of man's vulnerability." His most famous work is *The Family of Pascual Duarte* (1942).

1990 Octavio Paz (Mexico) poet and social essayist. Volumes include *The Labyrinth of Solitude* (1950), *Sunstone* (1957), and *Sor Juana: Or, the Traps of Faith* (1990).

1991 Nadine Gordimer (South Africa) for her "involvement on behalf of literature and free speech in a police state where censorship and persecution of books and people exist."

1992 Derek Walcott (West Indies, b. St. Lucia), poet and playwright whose works evoke the cultural diversity of the Carribean "but through them he speaks to each and every one of us."

1993 Toni Morrison (U.S.), whose novels about racial prejudice are "characterized by visionary force and poetic import."

1994 Kenzaburo Oe (Japan), best known for his accounts of the atomic bombing of Hiroshima. The poetic force of his writing "creates an imagined world where life and myth condense to form a disconcerting picture of the human predicament."

1995 Seamus Heaney (Ireland), poet and essayist, "for works of lyrical beauty and ethical depth, which exalt everyday miracles and the living past."

1996 Wislawa Szymborska (Poland), a poet whose work contemplates the oddities of daily life.

1997 Dario Fo, (Italy), a leftist playwright, best known for biting political satires (*Can't Pay, Won't Pay* and *Accidental Death of an Anarchist*), which brought threats of censure and condemnation from the Italian government and the Catholic Church.

1998 José Saramago (Portugal), for his richly imaginative works that often use the supernatural and irrational to address questions of faith. Best known novels include: *Baltasar and Blimunda* (1982), *The Year of the Death of Ricardo Reis* (1984).

1999 Günter Grass (Germany) "whose frolicsome black fables portray the forgotten face of history." His epic 1959 novel, *The Tin Drum* addressed the uncomfortable issue of the German national identity through the Nazi era.

2000 Gao Xingjian (France, b. China), one of the most important Chinese dramatists of the 20th century, whose most significant works have been banned in China since the 1980s.

2001 See Part I: "The Almanac of the Year."

VI SPORTS
College Sports

THE NCAA

The NCAA acts as the governing body of intercollegiate athletics, setting the playing rules for each sport, and eligibility standards for participating athletes. Its other major functions are to conduct championships and maintain historical records.

The organization grew out of a series of meetings convened by President Theodore Roosevelt, who was concerned about the number serious injuries and deaths in college football games. In 1905 alone, 18 players died.

National Collegiate Athletic Association (NCAA)
One NCAA Place
700 W. Washington St.
Indianapolis, Ind. 46204
(317) 917–6222
www.ncaa.org

COLLEGE FOOTBALL

NCAA National Football Champions

For many years, college football selected its national champion through an arcane structure of bowl games and two press association polls (one of coaches, the other of writers), which often did not agree with each other, creating co-champions and arguments about which was the better team.

But in 1998, the NCAA adopted the Bowl Alliance, in which the top two teams (as determined by the same two polls) meet in a national championship game that rotates annually among the Rose, Fiesta, Orange, and Sugar Bowls. (Teams ranked 3–8 in the polls fill out the other bowl games).

Year	Team	Year	Team	Year	Team	Year	Team	Year	Team
1936	Minnesota	1951	Tennessee	1964	Alabama	1976	Oklahoma	1990	Colorado and
1937	Pittsburgh	1952	Michigan St.	1965	Alabama and	1977	Notre Dame		Georgia Tech
1938	TCU	1953	Maryland		Michigan St.	1978	Alabama	1991	Miami and
1939	Texas A&M	1954	Ohio State	1966	Notre Dame		and USC		Washington
1940	Minnesota		and UCLA	1967	USC	1979	Alabama	1992	Alabama
1941	Minnesota	1955	Oklahoma	1968	Ohio State	1980	Georgia	1993	Florida State
1942	Ohio State	1956	Oklahoma	1969	Texas	1981	Clemson	1994	Nebraska
1943	Notre Dame	1957	Auburn and	1970	Nebraska	1982	Penn State	1995	Nebraska
1944	Army		Ohio State		and Texas	1983	Miami (Fla.)	1996	Florida
1945	Army	1958	Louisiana St.	1971	Nebraska	1984	BYU	1997	Michigan
1946	Notre Dame	1959	Syracuse	1972	USC	1985	Oklahoma		and Nebraska
1947	Notre Dame	1960	Minnesota	1973	Notre Dame	1986	Penn State	1998	Tennessee
1948	Michigan	1961	Alabama		and Alabama	1987	Miami (Fla.)	1999	Florida State
1949	Notre Dame	1962	USC	1974	USC	1988	Notre Dame	2000	Oklahoma
1950	Oklahoma	1963	Texas	1975	Oklahoma	1989	Miami (Fla.)		

Source: NCAA.

NCAA Football–Major Bowl Games, 1902-2001

ROSE BOWL (Pasadena, California)

1902	Michigan 49, Stanford 0	1932	USC 21, Tulane 12
1916	Washington St. 14, Brown 0	1933	USC 35, Pittsburgh 0
1917	Oregon 14, Pennsylvania 0	1934	Columbia 7, Stanford 0
1918	Mare Island 19, Camp Lewis 7	1935	Alabama 29, Stanford 13
1919	Great Lakes 17, Mare Island 0	1936	Stanford 7, Southern Methodist 0
1920	Harvard 7, Oregon 6	1937	Pittsburgh 21, Washington 0
1921	California 28, Ohio State 0	1938	California 13, Alabama 0
1922	Washington and Jefferson 0, Cal. 0	1939	USC 7, Duke 0
1923	USC 14, Penn State 3	1940	USC 14, Tennessee 0
1924	Navy 14, Washington 14	1941	Stanford 21, Nebraska 13
1925	Notre Dame 27, Stanford 10	1942	Oregon State 20, Duke 16 (at Durham)
1926	Alabama 20, Washington 19	1943	Georgia 9, UCLA 0
1927	Alabama 7, Stanford 7	1944	USC 29, Washington 0
1928	Stanford 7, Pittsburgh 6	1945	USC 25, Tennessee 0
1929	Georgia Tech 8, California 7	1946	Alabama 34, USC 14
1930	USC 47, Pittsburgh 14	1947	Illinois 45, UCLA 14
1931	Alabama 24, Washington State 0	1948	Michigan 49, USC 0
		1949	Northwestern 20, California 14

1950	Ohio State 17, California 14
1951	Michigan 14, California 6
1952	Illinois 40, Stanford 7
1953	USC 7, Wisconsin 0
1954	Michigan State 28, UCLA 20
1955	Ohio State 20, USC 7
1956	Michigan State 17, UCLA 14
1957	Iowa 35, Oregon State 19
1959	Iowa 38, California 12
1960	Washington 44, Wisconsin 8
1961	Washington 17, Minnesota 7
1962	Minnesota 21, UCLA 3
1963	USC 42, Wisconsin 37
1964	Illinois 17, Washington 7
1965	Michigan 34, Oregon State7
1966	UCLA 14, Michigan State 12
1967	Purdue 14, USC 13
1968	USC 14, Indiana 3
1969	Ohio State 27, USC 16
1970	USC 10, Michigan 3
1971	Stanford 27, Ohio State 17
1972	Stanford 13, Michigan 12
1973	USC 42, Ohio State 17
1974	Ohio State 42, USC 21
1975	USC18, Ohio State 17
1976	UCLA 23, Ohio State 10
1977	USC 14, Michigan 6
1978	Washington 27, Michigan 20
1979	USC 17, Michigan 10
1980	USC 17, Ohio State 16
1981	Michigan 23, Washington 6
1982	Washington 28, Iowa 0
1983	UCLA 24, Michigan 14
1984	UCLA 45, Illinois 9
1985	USC 20, Ohio State 17
1986	UCLA 45, Iowa 28
1987	Arizona State 22, Michigan 15
1988	Michigan State 20, USC 17
1989	Michigan 22, USC 14
1990	USC 17, Michigan 10
1991	Washington 46, Iowa 34
1992	Washington 34, Michigan 14
1993	Michigan 38, Washington 31
1994	Wisconsin 21, UCLA 16
1995	Penn State 38, Oregon 20
1996	USC 41, Northwestern 32
1997	Ohio State 20, Arizona State 17
1998	Michigan 21, Washington State 16
1999	Wisconsin 38, UCLA 31
2000	Wisconsin 17, Stanford 9
2001	Washington 34, Purdue 24

COTTON BOWL (Dallas, Texas)

1937	Texas Christian 16, Marquette 6
1938	Rice 28, Colorado 14
1939	St. Mary's 20, Texas Tech 13
1940	Clemson 6, Boston College 3
1941	Texas A&M 13, Fordham 12
1942	Alabama 29, Texas A&M 21
1943	Texas 14, Georgia Tech 7
1944	Texas 7, Randolph Field 7
1945	Oklahoma A&M 34, Texas Christian 0
1946	Texas 40, Missouri 27
1947	Arkansas 0, Louisiana State 0
1948	Southern Methodist 13, Penn State 13
1949	Southern Methodist 21, Oregon 13
1950	Rice 27, North Carolina 13
1951	Tennessee 20, Texas 14
1952	Kentucky 20, Texas Christian 7
1953	Texas 16, Tennessee 0
1954	Rice 28, Alabama 0
1955	Georgia Tech 14, Arkansas 6

1956	Mississippi 14, Texas Christian 13
1957	Texas Christian 28, Syracuse 27
1958	Navy 20, Rice 7
1959	Texas Christian 0, Air Force 0
1960	Syracuse 23, Texas 14
1961	Duke 7, Arkansas 6
1962	Texas 12, Mississippi 7
1963	Louisiana State 13, Texas 0
1964	Texas 28, Navy 6
1965	Arkansas 10, Nebraska 7
1966	Louisiana State 14, Arkansas 7
1967	Georgia 24, Southern Methodist 9
1968	Texas A&M 20, Alabama 16
1969	Texas 36, Tennessee 13
1970	Texas 21, Notre Dame 17
1971	Notre Dame 24, Texas 11
1972	Penn State 30, Texas 6
1973	Texas 17, Alabama 13
1974	Nebraska 19, Texas 3
1975	Penn State 41, Baylor 20
1976	Arkansas 31, Georgia 10
1977	Houston 30, Maryland 21
1978	Notre Dame 38, Texas 10
1979	Notre Dame 35, Houston 34
1980	Houston 17, Nebraska 14
1981	Alabama 30, Baylor 2
1982	Texas 14, Alabama 12
1983	Southern Methodist 7, Pittsburgh 3
1984	Georgia 10, Texas 9
1985	Boston College 45, Houston 28
1986	Texas A&M 36, Auburn 16
1987	Ohio State 28, Texas A&M 12
1988	Texas A&M 35, Notre Dame 10
1989	UCLA 17, Arkansas 3
1990	Tennessee 31, Arkansas 27
1991	Miami (Fla.) 46, Texas 3
1992	Florida St. 10, Texas A&M 2
1993	Notre Dame 28, Texas A&M 3
1994	Notre Dame 24, Texas A&M 21
1995	USC 55, Texas Tech 14
1996	Colorado 38, Oregon 6
1997	Brigham Young 19, Kansas State 15
1998	UCLA 29, Texas A&M 23
1999	Texas 38, Mississippi State 11
2000	Arkansas 27, Texas 6
2001	Kansas St. 35, Tennessee 21

ORANGE BOWL (Miami, Florida)

1935	Bucknell 26, Miami (Fla.) 0
1936	Catholic U. 20, Mississippi 19
1937	Duquesne 13, Mississippi State 12
1938	Auburn 6, Michigan State 0
1939	Tennessee 17, Oklahoma 0
1940	Georgia Tech 21, Misouri 7
1941	Mississippi State 14, Georgetown 7
1942	Georgia 40, Texas Christian 26
1943	Alabama 37, Boston College 21
1944	Louisiana State 19, Texas A&M 14
1945	Tulsa 26, Georgia Tech 12
1946	Miami (Fla.)13, Holy Cross 6
1947	Rice 8, Tennessee 0
1948	Georgia Tech 20, Kansas 14
1949	Texas 41, Georgia 28
1950	Santa Clara 21, Kentucky 13
1951	Clemson 15, Miami (Fla.)14
1952	Georgia Tech 20, Baylor 14
1953	Alabama 61, Syracuse 6
1954	Oklahoma 7, Maryland 0
1955	Duke 34, Nebraska 7
1956	Oklahoma 20, Maryland 6
1957	Colorado 27, Clemson 21
1958	Oklahoma 48, Duke 21

1959	Oklahoma 21, Syracuse 6
1960	Georgia 14, Missouri 0
1961	Missouri 21, Navy 14
1962	Louisiana State 25, Colorado 7
1963	Alabama 17, Oklahoma 0
1964	Nebraska 13, Auburn 7
1965	Texas 21, Alabama 17
1966	Alabama 39, Nebraska 28
1967	Florida 27, Georgia Tech 12
1968	Oklahoma 26, Tennessee 24
1969	Penn State 15, Kansas 14
1970	Penn State 10, Missouri 3
1971	Nebraska 17, Louisiana State 12
1972	Nebraska 38, Alabama 6
1973	Nebraska 40, Notre Dame 6
1974	Penn State 16, Louisiana State 9
1975	Notre Dame 13, Alabama 11
1976	Oklahoma 14, Michigan 6
1977	Ohio State 27, Colorado 10
1978	Arkansas 31, Oklahoma 6
1979	Oklahoma 31, Nebraska 21
1980	Oklahoma 24, Florida State 7
1981	Oklahoma 18, Florida State 17
1982	Clemson 22, Nebraska 15
1983	Nebraska 21, Louisiana State 20
1984	Miami (Fla.) 31, Nebraska 30
1985	Washington 28, Oklahoma 17
1986	Oklahoma 25, Penn State 10
1987	Oklahoma 42, Arkansas 8
1988	Miami (Fla.) 20, Oklahoma 14
1989	Miami (Fla.) 23, Nebraska 3
1990	Notre Dame 21, Colorado 6
1991	Colorado 10, Notre Dame 9
1992	Miami (Fla.) 22, Nebraska 0
1993	Florida State 27, Nebraska 14
1994	Florida State 18, Nebraska 16
1995	Nebraska 24, Miami 17
1996	Florida State 31, Notre Dame 26
1997	Nebraska 41, Virginia Tech 21
1998	Nebraska 42, Tennessee 17
1999	Florida 31, Syracuse 10
2000	Michigan 35, Alabama 34
2001	Oklahoma 13, Florida State 2

SUGAR BOWL (New Orleans, Louisiana)

1935	Tulane 20, Temple 14
1936	Texas Christian 3, Louisiana State 2
1937	Santa Clara 21, Louisiana State 14
1938	Santa Clara 6, Louisiana State 0
1939	Texas Christian 15, Carnegie Tech 7
1940	Texas A&M 14, Tulane 13
1941	Boston College 19, Tennessee 13
1942	Fordham 2, Missouri 0
1943	Tennessee 14, Tulsa 7
1944	Georgia Tech 20, Tulsa 18
1945	Duke 29, Alabama 26

1946	Oklahoma A&M 33, St. Mary's (Colo.) 13
1947	Georgia 20, North Carolina 10
1948	Texas 27, Alabama 7
1949	Oklahoma 14, North Carolina 6
1950	Oklahoma 35, Louisiana State 0
1951	Kentucky 13, Oklahoma 7
1952	Maryland 28, Tennessee 13
1953	Georgia Tech 24, Mississippi 7
1954	Georgia Tech 42, West Virginia 19
1955	Navy 21, Mississippi 0
1956	Georgia Tech 7, Pittsburgh 0
1957	Baylor 13, Tennessee 7
1958	Mississippi 39, Texas 7
1959	Louisiana State 7, Clemson 0
1960	Mississippi 21, Louisiana State 0
1961	Mississippi 14, Rice 6
1962	Alabama 10, Arkansas 3
1963	Mississippi 17, 13
1964	Alabama 12, Mississippi 7
1965	Louisiana State 13, Syracuse 10
1966	Missouri 20, Florida 18
1967	Alabama 34, Nebraska 7
1968	Louisiana State 20, Wyoming 13
1969	Arkansas 16, Georgia 2
1970	Mississippi 27, Arkansas 22
1971	Tennessee 34, Air Force 13
1972	Oklahoma 40, Auburn 22
1973	Oklahoma 14, Penn State 0
1974	Notre Dame 24, Alabama 23
1975	Nebraska 13, Florida 10
1976	Alabama 13, Penn State 7
1977	Pittsburgh 27, Georgia 3
1978	Alabama 35, Ohio State 6
1979	Alabama 14, Penn State
1980	Alabama 24, Arkansas 9
1981	Georgia 17, Notre Dame 10
1982	Pittsburgh 24, Georgia 20
1983	Penn State 27, Georgia 23
1984	Auburn 9, Michigan 7
1985	Nebraska 28, Louisiana State 10
1986	Tennessee 35, Miami (Fla.) 7
1987	Nebraska 30, Louisiana State 15
1988	Syracuse 16, Auburn 16
1989	Florida State 13, Auburn 7
1990	Miami (Fla.) 33, Alabama 25
1991	Tennesee 23, Virginina 22
1992	Notre Dame 39, Florida 28
1993	Alabama 34, Miami 13
1994	Florida 41, West Virginia 7
1995	Florida State 23, Florida 17
1996	Virginia Tech 28, Texas 10
1997	Florida 52, Florida State 20
1998	Florida State 31, Ohio State 14
1999	Ohio State 24, Texas A&M 14
2000	Florida State 46, Virginia Tech 29
2001	Miami 37, Florida 20

NCAA Football Career Leaders

Player, Team	Years	PASSING, Career yards Att.	Comp.	Int.	Pct.	Yards	TD
Ty Detmer, Brigham Young	1988-91	1,530	958	65	.626	15,031	121
Tim Rattay, Louisiana Tech	1997-99	1,552	1,015	35	.654	12,746	115
Chris Redman, Louisville	1996-99	1,679	1,031	51	.614	12,541	84
Todd Santos, San Diego State	1984-87	1,484	910	57	.613	11,425	70
Tim Lester, Western Michigan	1996-99	1,507	875	49	.581	11,299	87
Peyton Manning, Tennessee	1994-97	1,381	863	33	.625	11,201	89
Eric Zeier, Georgia	1991-94	1,402	838	37	.598	11,153	67
Alex Van Pelt, Pittsburgh	1989-92	1,463	845	59	.578	10,913	64
Drew Brees, Purdue	1997-2000	1,525	942	41	.618	10,909	81
Danny Wuerffel, Florida	1994-96	1,170	708	42	.605	10,875	114

CAREER POINTS (Nonkickers)

Player, Team	Years	TD	Pts.
Travis Prentice, Miami (Ohio)	1996-99	78	468
Ricky Williams, Texas	1995-98	75	452
Anthony Thomson, Indiana	1968-69	65	394
Ron Dayne, Wisconsin	1996-99	63	378
Marshall Faulk, San Diego St.	1991-93	62	376
Tony Dorsett, Pittsburgh	1973-76	59	356
Glenn Davis, Army	1943-46	59	354
Troy Edwards, La. Tech.	1996-98	57	344
Art Luppino, Arizona	1953-56	48	337
Chris Lemon, Nevada	1996-99	56	336
Steve Owens, Oklahoma	1967-69	56	336

CAREER POINTS (Kickers)

Player, Team	Years	PAT	FG	Pts.
Roman Anderson, Houston	1988-91	213	70	423
Carlos Huerta, Miami (Fla.)	1988-91	178	73	397
Jason Elam, Hawaii	1988-92	158	79	395
Derek Schmidt, Florida St.	1984-87	174	73	393
Kris Brown, Nebraska	1995-98	217	57	388
Shayne Graham, Virginia Tech.	1996-99	167	68	371
Jeff Hall, Tennessee	1995-98	188	61	371
Luis Zendejas, Arizona St.	1981-84	134	78	368
Jeff Jaeger, Washington	1983-86	118	80	358
John Lee, UCLA	1982-85	116	79	353
Max Zendejas, Arizona	1982-85	122	77	353
Kevin Butler, Georgia	1981-84	122	77	353

RUSHING, Career yards

Player, Team	Years	Carries	Yards
Ron Dayne, Wisconsin	1996-99	1,115	63,97
Ricky Williams, Texas	1995-98	1,011	6,279
Tony Dorsett, Pittsburgh	1973-76	1,074	6,082
Charles White, USC	1976-79	1,023	5,598
Travis Prentice, Miami (Ohio)	1996-99	1,138	5,596
LaDainian Tomlinson, TCU	1997-2000	907	5,263
Herschel Walker, Georgia	1980-82	994	5,259
Archie Griffin, Ohio State	1972-75	845	5,177
Darren Lewis, Texas A&M	1987-90	909	5,012
Anthony Thomson, Indiana	1986-89	1,089	4,965

RECEIVING, Career catches

Player, Team	Years	Catches	Yards
Arnold Jackson, Louisville	1997-2000	300	3,670
Trevor Insley, Nevada	1996-99	298	5,005
Geoff Noisy, Nevada	1995-98	295	4,249
Troy Edwards, Lousiana Tech.	1996-98	280	4,352
Aaron Turner, Pacific (Calif.)	1988-91	266	4,345
Chad Mackey, Lousiana Tech.	1988-91	264	3,789
Terance Mathis, New Mexico	1988-92	263	4,254
Mark Templeton, Long Beach St.	1984-87	262	1,969
Howard Twilley, Tulsa	1981-84	261	3,343
Marcus Harris, Wyoming	1983-86	259	4,518

Heisman Memorial Trophy

The Heisman Trophy honors the outstanding college football player in the U.S. Presented by the Downtown Athletic Club of New York, the award is named for John Heisman, former player, coach, and club director.

Year	Player	College	Pos.
1935	Jay Berwanger	Chicago	HB
1936	Larry Kelley	Yale	E
1937	Clint Frank	Yale	HB
1938	Davey O'Brien	Texas Christian	QB
1939	Nile Kinnick	Iowa	HB
1940	Tom Harmon	Michigan	HB
1941	Bruce Smith	Minnesota	HB
1942	Frank Sinkwich	Georgia	HB
1943	Angelo Bertelli	Notre Dame	QB
1944	Les Horvath	Ohio State	QB
1945	Doc Blanchard	Army	FB
1946	Glenn Davis	Army	HB
1947	John Lujack	Notre Dame	E
1948	Doak Walker	SMU	HB
1949	Leon Hart	Notre Dame	E
1950	Vic Janowicz	Ohio State	HB
1951	Dick Kazmaier	Princeton	HB
1952	Billy Vessels	Oklahoma	HB
1953	John Lattner	Notre Dame	HB
1954	Alan Ameche	Wisconsin	FB
1955	Howard Cassady	Ohio State	HB
1955	Paul Hornung	Notre Dame	QB
1957	John David Crow	Texas A&M	HB
1958	Pete Dawkins	Army	HB
1959	Billy Cannon	Louisiana State	HB
1960	Joe Bellino	Navy	HB
1961	Ernie Davis	Syracuse	HB
1962	Terry Baker	Orgeon State	QB
1963	Roger Staubach	Navy	QB
1964	John Huarte	Notre Dame	QB
1965	Mike Garrett	USC	HB
1966	Steve Spurrier	Florida	QB
1967	Gary Beban	UCLA	QB
1968	O.J. Simpson	USC	HB
1969	Steve Owens	Oklahoma	HB
1970	Jim Plunkett	Stanford	QB
1971	Pat Sullivan	Auburn	QB
1972	Johnny Rodgers	Nebraska	QB
1973	John Cappelletti	Penn State	HB
1974	Archie Griffin	Ohio State	HB
1975	Archie Griffin	Ohio State	HB
1976	Tony Dorsett	Pittsburgh	HB
1977	Earl Campbell	Texas	HB
1978	Billy Sims	Oklahoma	HB
1979	Charles White	USC	HB
1980	George Rogers	South Carolina	HB
1981	Marcus Allen	USC	HB
1982	Herschel Walker	Georgia	HB
1983	Mike Rozier	Nebraska	HB
1984	Doug Flutie	Boston College	QB
1985	Bo Jackson	Auburn	HB
1986	Vinny Testaverde	Miami (Fla.)	QB
1987	Tim Brown	Notre Dame	WR
1988	Barry Sanders	Oklahoma State	RB
1989	Andre Ware	Houston	QB
1990	Ty Detmer	Brigham Young	QB
1991	Desmond Howard	Michigan	WR
1992	Gino Toretta	Miami (Fla.)	QB
1993	Charlie Ward	Florida State	QB
1994	Rashaan Salaam	Colorado	RB
1995	Eddie George	Ohio State	RB
1996	Danny Wuerffel	Florida	QB
1997	Charles Woodson	Michigan	CB
1998	Ricky Williams	Texas	RB
1999	Ron Dayne	Wisconsin	RB
2000	Chris Weinke	Florida State	QB

COLLEGE BASKETBALL

NCAA Division I Men's Basketball Championship Final Four Results

Year	Champion	Score	Runner-up	Third place	Fourth place	Champion coach
1939	Oregon	46–33	Ohio State	Oklahoma[1]	Villanova[1]	Howard Hobson
1940	Indiana	60–42	Kansas	Duquesne[1]	USC [1]	Branch McCracken
1941	Wisconsin	39–34	Washington St.	Pittsburgh[1]	Arkansas[1]	Harold Foster
1942	Stanford	53–38	Dartmouth	Colorado[1]	Kentucky[1]	Everett Dean
1943	Wyoming	46–34	Georgetown	Texas[1]	DePaul[1]	Everett Shelton
1944	Utah	42–40[2]	Dartmouth	Iowa State[1]	Ohio State [1]	Vadal Peterson
1945	Oklahoma State	49–45	NYU	Arkansas[1]	Ohio State[1]	Henry Iba
1946	Oklahoma State	43–40	North Carolina	Ohio St.	California	Henry Iba
1947	Holy Cross	58–47	Oklahoma	Texas	CCNY	Alvin Julian
1948	Kentucky	58–42	Baylor	Holy Cross	Kansas State	Adolph Rupp
1949	Kentucky	46–36	Oklahoma State	Illinois	Oregon State	Adolph Rupp
1950	CCNY	71–68	Bradley	North Carolina State	Baylor	Nat Holman
1951	Kentucky	68–58	Kansas State	Illinois	Oklahoma State	Aldolph Rupp
1952	Kansas	80–63	St. John's	Illinois	Santa Clara	Forrest Allen
1953	Indiana	69–68	Kansas	Washington	Louisiana State	Branch McCracken
1954	LaSalle	92–76	Bradley	Penn State	USC	Kenneth Loeffler
1955	San Francisco	77–63	La Salle	Colorado	Iowa	Phil Woolpert
1956	San Francisco	83–71	Iowa	Temple	Southern Methodist	Phil Woolpert
1957	North Carolina	54–53[3]	Kansas	San Francisco	Michigan State	Frank McGuire
1958	Kentucky	84–72	Seattle	Temple	Kansas State	Adolph Rupp
1959	California	71–70	West Virginia	Cincinnati	Louisville	Pete Newell
1960	Ohio State	75–55	California	Cincinnati	NYU	Fred Taylor
1961	Cincinnati	70–65[2]	Ohio State	St. Joe's[4]	Utah	Edwin Jucker
1962	Cincinnati	71–59	Ohio State	Wake Forest	UCLA	Edwin Jucker
1963	Loyola (Ill.)	60–58[2]	Cincinnati	Duke	Utah	George Ireland
1964	UCLA	98–83	Duke	Michigan	Kansas State	John Wooden
1965	UCLA	91–80	Michigan	Princeton	Wichita State	John Wooden
1966	UTEP	72–65	Kentucky	Duke	Utah	Don Haskins
1967	UCLA	79–64	Dayton	Houston	North Carolina	John Wooden
1968	UCLA	78–55	North Carolina	Ohio State	Houston	John Wooden
1969	UCLA	92–72	Purdue	Drake	North Carolina	John Wooden
1970	UCLA	80–69	Jacksonville	New Mexico St.	St. Bonaventure	John Wooden
1971	UCLA	68–62	Villanova[4]	Western Kentucky[4]	Kansas	John Wooden
1972	UCLA	81–76	Florida State	North Carolina	Louisville	John Wooden
1973	UCLA	87–66	Memphis State	Indiana	Providence	John Wooden
1974	North Carolina State	76–64	Marquette	UCLA	Kansas	Norm Sloan
1975	UCLA	92–85	Kentucky	Louisville	Syracuse	John Wooden
1976	Indiana	86–68	Michigan	UCLA	Rutgers	Bob Knight
1977	Marquette	67–59	North Carolina	UNLV	UNC-Charlotte	Al McGuire
1978	Kentucky	94–88	Duke	Arkansas	Notre Dame	Joe Hall
1979	Michigan State	75–64	Indiana State	DePaul	Pennsylvania	Jud Heathcote
1980	Louisville	59–54	UCLA[4]	Purdue	Iowa	Denny Crum
1981	Indiana	63–50	North Carolina	Virginia	Louisiana State	Bob Knight
1982	North Carolina	63–62	Georgetown	Houston[1]	Louisville[1]	Dean Smith
1983	North Carolina State	54–52	Houston	Georgia[1]	Louisville[1]	Jim Valvano
1984	Georgetown	84–75	Houston	Kentucky[1]	Virginia[1]	John Thompson
1985	Villanova	66–64	Georgetown	St. John's[1]	Memphis[1,4]	Rollie Massimino
1986	Louisville	72–69	Duke	Kansas[1]	Louisiana State[1]	Denny Crum
1987	Indiana	74–73	Syracuse	UNLV[1]	Providence[1]	Bob Knight
1988	Kansas	83–79	Oklahoma	Arizona[1]	Duke[1]	Larry Brown
1989	Michigan	80–79[2]	Seton Hall	Illinois[1]	Duke[1]	Steve Fisher
1990	UNLV	103–73	Duke	Georgia Tech[1]	Arkansas[1]	Jerry Tarkanian
1991	Duke	72–65	Kansas	UNLV[1]	North Carolina[1]	Mike Krzyzewski
1992	Duke	71–51	Michigan	Cincinnati[1]	Indiana[1]	Mike Krzyzewski
1993	North Carolina	77–71	Michigan	Kansas[1]	Kentucky[1]	Dean Smith
1994	Arkansas	76–70	Duke	Arizona[1]	Florida[1]	Nolan Richardson
1995	UCLA	89–78	Arkansas	North Carolina[1]	Oklahoma State[1]	Jim Harrick
1996	Kentucky	76–67	Syracuse	Massachusetts[1,4]	Mississippi State[1]	Rick Pitino
1997	Arizona	84–79	Kentucky	Minnesota[1]	North Carolina[1]	Lute Olson
1998	Kentucky	78–69	Utah	North Carolina[1]	Stanford[1]	Tubby Smith
1999	Connecticut	77–74	Duke	Michigan State[1]	Ohio State[1]	Jim Calhoun
2000	Michigan State	89–76	Florida	North Carolina[1]	Wisconsin[1]	Tom Izzo
2000	Duke [1]	82–72	Arizona	Maryland[1]	Michigan State[1]	Mike Krzyzewski

1. Tied for third place. 2. Overtime. 3. Triple overtime. 4. Later declared ineligible.

National Invitation Tournament Champions

Year	Champion	Year	Champion	Year	Champion	Year	Champion	Year	Champion
1938	Temple	1951	BYU	1964	Bradley	1977	St. Bonaventure	1990	Vanderbilt
1939	Long Island	1952	LaSalle	1965	St. John's	1978	Texas	1991	Stanford
1940	Colorado	1953	Seton Hall	1966	BYU	1979	Indiana	1992	Virginia
1941	Long Island	1954	Holy Cross	1967	So. Illinois	1980	Virginia	1993	Minnesota
1942	West Virginia	1955	Duquesne	1968	Dayton	1981	Tulsa	1994	Villanova
1943	St. John's	1956	Louisville	1969	Temple	1982	Bradley	1995	Virginia Tech
1944	St. John's	1957	Bradley	1970	Marquette	1983	Fresno State	1996	Nebraska
1945	DePaul	1958	Xavier (Ohio)	1971	North Carolina	1984	Michigan	1997	Michigan
1946	Kentucky	1959	St. John's	1972	Maryland	1985	UCLA	1998	Minnesota
1947	Utah	1960	Bradley	1973	Virginia Tech	1986	Ohio State	1999	California
1948	St. Louis	1961	Providence	1974	Purdue	1987	So. Mississippi	2000	Wake Forest
1949	San Francisco	1962	Dayton	1975	Princeton	1988	Connecticut	2001	Tulsa
1950	CCNY	1963	Providence	1976	Kentucky	1989	St. John's		

NCAA Basketball Career Leaders

SCORING

Player, Team	Points
Pete Maravich, Louisiana State	3,667
Freeman Williams, Portland State	3,249
Lionel Simmons, LaSalle	3,217
Alphonzo Ford, Mississippi Valley	3,165
Harry Kelly, Texas Southern	3,066
Hersey Hawkins, Bradley	3,008
Oscar Robertson, Cincinnati	2,973
Danny Manning, Kansas	2,951
Alfredrick Hughes, Loyola (Ill.)	2,914
Elvin Hayes, Houston	2,884

ASSISTS

Player, Team	Assists
Bobby Hurley, Duke	1,076
Chris Corchiani, N.Carolina State	1,038
Ed Cota, North Carolina	1,030
Keith Jennings, East Tennessee St.	983
Sherman Douglas, Syracuse	960
Tony Miller, Marquette	956
Greg Anthony, Portland/UNLV	950
Doug Gottlieb, Notre Dame/Oklahoma State	947
Gary Payton, Oregon State	938
Orlando Smart, San Francisco	902

REBOUNDS

Player, team	Rebounds
Tom Gola, LaSalle	2,201
Joe Holup, George Washington	2,030
Charlie Slack, Marshall	1,916
Ed Conlin, Fordham	1,884
Dickie Hemric, Wake Forest	1,802
Paul Silas, Creighton	1,751
Art Quimby, Connecticut	1,716
Jerry Harper, Alabama	1,688
Jeff Cohen, William and Mary	1,679
Steve Hamilton, Morehead State	1,675

FIELD GOAL PERCENTAGE[1]

Player, team	Pct.
Steve Johnson, Oregon State	67.8
Michael Bradley, Kentucky/Villanova	67.7
Murray Brown, Florida State	66.8
Lee Campbell, Southwest Mo. St.	66.5
Warren Kidd, Middle Tenn. State	66.4
Todd MacCulloch, Univ. of Washington	66.4
Joe Senser, West Chester	66.2
Kevin Magee, Univ. of California, Irvine	65.6
Orlando Phillips, Pepperdine	65.4
Bill Walton, UCLA	65.1

1. Minimum 400 made and 4 made per game.

OTHER MEN'S NCAA CHAMPIONS

CROSS COUNTRY

Year	Champion	Year	Champion	Year	Champion	Year	Champion
1938	Indiana	1961	Oregon State	1985	Wisconsin	1965	St. Louis	1987	Clemson
1939	Michigan State	1962	San Jose State	1986	Arkansas	1966	San Franciso	1988	Indiana
1940	Indiana	1963	San Jóse State	1987	Arkansas	1967	Michigan State,	1989	Santa Clara,
1941	Rhode Island	1964	W. Michigan	1988	Wisconsin		St. Louis		Virginia
1942	Indiana	1965	W. Michigan	1989	Iowa State	1968	Maryland	1990	UCLA
1943	No Meet	1966	Villanova	1990	Arkansas		Michigan State	1991	Virginia
1944	Drake	1967	Villanova	1991	Arkansas	1969	St. Louis	1992	Virginia
1945	Drake	1968	Villanova	1992	Arkansas	1970	St. Louis	1993	Virginia
1946	Drake	1969	UTEP	1993	Arkansas	1971	Vacated	1994	Virginia
1947	Penn State	1970	Villanova	1994	Iowa State	1972	St. Louis	1995	Wisconsin
1948	Michigan State	1971	Oregon	1995	Arkansas	1973	St. Louis	1996	St. John's (N.Y.)
1949	Michigan State	1972	Tennessee	1996	Stanford	1974	Howard	1997	UCLA
1950	Penn State	1973	Oregon	1997	Stanford	1975	San Francisco	1998	Indiana
1951	Syracuse	1974	Oregon	1998	Arkansas	1976	San Francisco	1999	Indiana
1952	Michigan State	1975	UTEP	1999	Arkansas	1977	Hartwick	2000	Connecticut
1953	Kansas	1976	UTEP	2000	Arkansas	1978	Vacated		
1954	Oklahoma State	1977	Oregon			1979	SIU Edwardsville	**WATER POLO**	
1955	Michigan State	1978	UTEP	**SOCCER**		1980	San Francisco	1969	UCLA
1956	Michigan State	1979	UTEP	1959	St. Louis	1981	Connecticut	1970	UC Irvine
1957	Notre Dame	1980	UTEP	1960	St. Louis	1982	Indiana	1971	UCLA
1958	Michigan State	1981	UTEP	1961	West Chester	1983	Indiana	1972	UCLA
1959	Michigan State	1982	Wisconsin	1962	St. Louis	1984	Clemson	1973	California
1960	Houston	1983	Vacated	1963	St. Louis	1985	UCLA	1974	California
		1984	Arkansas	1964	Navy	1986	Duke	1975	California

1976 Stanford	1951 Florida State	1983 Wisconsin	1930 Oklahoma State[1]	1979 Villanova
1977 California	1952 Florida State	1984 Bowling Green	1931 Oklahoma State[1]	1980 UTEP
1978 Stanford	1953 Penn State	1985 Rensselaer	1932 Indiana	1981 UTEP
1979 UC Santa Barbara	1954 Penn State	1986 Michigan State	1933 Oklahoma State[1],	1982 UTEP
1980 Stanford	1955 Illinois	1987 North Dakota	Iowa State[1]	1983 SMU
1981 California	1956 Illinois	1988 Lake Superior St.	1934 Oklahoma State	1984 Arkansas
1982 UC Irvine	1957 Penn State	1989 Harvard	1935 Oklahoma State	1985 Arkansas
1983 California	1958 Michigan State,	1990 Wisconsin	1936 Oklahoma	1986 Arkansas
1984 California	Illinois	1991 N. Michigan	1937 Oklahoma State	1987 Arkansas
1985 Stanford	1959 Penn State	1992 Lake Superior St.	1938 Oklahoma State	1988 Arkansas
1986 Stanford	1960 Penn State	1993 Maine	1939 Oklahoma State	1989 Arkansas
1987 California	1961 Penn State	1994 Lake Superior St.	1940 Oklahoma State	1990 Arkansas
1988 California	1962 USC	1995 Boston University	1941 Oklahoma State	1991 Arkansas
1989 California	1963 Michigan	1996 Michigan	1942 Oklahoma State	1992 Arkansas
1990 California	1964 Southern Illinois	1997 North Dakota	1943 No Tournament	1993 Arkansas
1991 California	1965 Southern Illinois	1998 Michigan	1944 No Tournament	1994 Arkansas
1992 California	1966 Southern Illinois	1999 Maine	1945 No Tournament	1995 Arkansas
1993 Stanford	1967 Southern Illinois	2000 North Dakota	1946 Oklahoma State	1996 George Mason
1994 Stanford	1968 California	2001 Boston College	1947 Cornell College	1997 Arkansas
1995 UCLA	1969 Iowa		1948 Oklahoma State	1998 Arkansas
1996 UCLA	1970 Michigan	**SWIMMING**	1949 Oklahoma State	1999 Arkansas
1997 Pepperdine	1971 Iowa State	1937 Michigan	1950 Northern Iowa	2000 Arkansas
1998 USC	1972 Southern Illinois	1938 Michigan	1951 Oklahoma	2001 Louisiana State
1999 UCLA	1973 Iowa State	1939 Michigan	1952 Oklahoma	
2000 UCLA	1974 Iowa State	1940 Michigan	1953 Penn State	**OUTDOOR TRACK**
	1975 California	1941 Michigan	1954 Oklahoma State	1921 Illinois
FENCING*	1976 Penn State	1942 Yale	1955 Oklahoma State	1922 California
1941 Northwestern	1977 Indiana State,	1943 Ohio State	1956 Oklahoma State	1923 Michigan
1942 Ohio State	Oklahoma	1944 Yale	1957 Oklahoma	1924 No Meet
1943 No Meet	1978 Oklahoma	1945 Ohio State	1958 Oklahoma State	1925 Stanford
1944 No Meet	1979 Nebraska	1946 Ohio State	1959 Oklahoma State	1926 USC
1945 No Meet	1980 Nebraska	1947 Ohio State	1960 Oklahoma	1927 Illinois
1946 No Meet	1981 Nebraska	1948 Michigan	1961 Oklahoma State	1928 Stanford
1947 NYU	1982 Nebraska	1949 Ohio State	1962 Oklahoma State	1929 Ohio State
1948 CCNY	1983 Nebraska	1950 Ohio State	1963 Oklahoma	1930 USC
1949 Army, Rutgers	1984 UCLA	1951 Yale	1964 Oklahoma State	1931 USC
1950 Navy	1985 Ohio State	1952 Ohio State	1965 Iowa State	1932 Indiana
1951 Columbia	1986 Arizona State	1953 Yale	1966 Oklahoma State	1933 Louisiana State
1952 Columbia	1987 UCLA	1954 Ohio State	1967 Michigan State	1934 Stanford
1953 Pennsylvania	1988 Nebraska	1955 Ohio State	1968 Oklahoma State	1935 USC
1954 Columbia, NYU	1989 Illinois	1956 Ohio State	1969 Iowa State	1936 USC
1955 Columbia	1990 Nebraska	1957 Michigan	1970 Iowa State	1937 USC
1956 Illinois	1991 Oklahoma	1958 Michigan	1971 Oklahoma State	1938 USC
1957 NYU	1992 Stanford	1959 Michigan	1972 Iowa State	1939 USC
1958 Illinois	1993 Stanford	1960 USC	1973 Iowa State	1940 USC
1959 Navy	1994 Nebraska	1961 Michigan	1974 Oklahoma	1941 USC
1960 NYU	1995 Stanford	1962 Ohio State	1975 Iowa	1942 USC
1961 NYU	1996 Ohio State	1963 USC	1976 Iowa	1943 USC
1962 Navy	1997 California	1964 USC	1977 Iowa State	1944 Illinois
1963 Columbia	1998 California	1965 USC	1978 Iowa	1945 Navy
1964 Princeton	1999 Michigan	1966 USC	1979 Iowa	1946 Illinois
1965 Columbia	2000 Penn State	1967 Stanford	1980 Iowa	1947 Illinois
1966 NYU	2001 Ohio State	1968 Indiana	1981 Iowa	1948 Minnesota
1967 NYU		1969 Indiana	1982 Iowa	1949 USC
1968 Columbia	**ICE HOCKEY**	1970 Indiana	1983 Iowa	1950 USC
1969 Pennsylvania	1948 Michigan	1971 Indiana	1984 Iowa	1951 USC
1970 NYU	1949 Boston College	1972 Indiana	1985 Iowa	1952 USC
1971 NYU, Columbia	1950 Colorado College	1973 Indiana	1986 Iowa	1953 USC
1972 Detroit	1951 Michigan	1974 USC	1987 Iowa State	1954 USC
1973 NYU	1952 Michigan	1975 USC	1988 Arizona State	1955 USC
1974 NYU	1953 Michigan	1976 USC	1989 Oklahoma State	1956 UCLA
1975 Wayne State	1954 Rensselaer	1977 USC	1990 Oklahoma State	1957 Villanova
1976 NYU	1955 Michigan	1978 Tennessee	1991 Iowa	1958 USC
1977 Notre Dame	1956 Michigan	1979 California	1992 Iowa	1959 Kansas
1978 Notre Dame	1957 Colorado College	1980 California	1993 Iowa	1960 Kansas
1979 Wayne State	1958 Denver	1981 Texas	1994 Oklahoma State	1961 USC
1980 Wayne State	1959 North Dakota	1982 UCLA	1995 Iowa	1962 Oregon
1981 Pennsylvania	1960 Denver	1983 Florida	1996 Iowa	1963 USC
1982 Wayne State	1961 Denver	1984 Florida	1997 Iowa	1964 Oregon
1983 Wayne State	1962 Michigan Tech.	1985 Stanford	1998 Iowa	1965 Oregon, USC
1984 Wayne State	1963 North Dakota	1986 Stanford	1999 Iowa	1966 UCLA
1985 Wayne State	1964 Michigan	1987 Stanford	2000 Iowa	1967 USC
1986 Notre Dame	1965 Michigan Tech	1988 Texas	2001 Minnesota	1968 USC
1987 Columbia	1966 Michigan State	1989 Texas	1. Unofficial champions.	1969 San Jose State
1988 Columbia	1967 Cornell	1990 Texas		1970 BYU, Kansas
1989 Columbia	1968 Denver	1991 Texas	**INDOOR TRACK**	1971 UCLA
1.For champions after	1969 Denver	1992 Stanford	1965 Missouri	1972 UCLA
1989, see "Men's and	1970 Cornell	1993 Stanford	1966 Kansas	1973 UCLA
Women's Titles."	1971 Boston University	1994 Stanford	1967 USC	1974 Tennessee
	1972 Boston University	1995 Michigan	1968 Villanova	1975 UTEP
GYMNASTICS	1973 Wisconsin	1996 Texas	1969 Kansas	1976 USC
1938 Chicago	1974 Minnesota	1997 Auburn	1970 Kansas	1977 Arizona State
1939 Illinois	1975 Michigan Tech	1998 Stanford	1971 Villanova	1978 UCLA, UTEP
1940 Illinois	1976 Minnesota	1999 Auburn	1972 USC	1979 UTEP
1941 Illinois	1977 Wisconsin	2000 Texas	1973 Manhattan	1980 UTEP
1942 Illinois	1978 Boston University	2001 Texas	1974 UTEP	1981 UTEP
1943-47 No Meet	1979 Minnesota		1975 UTEP	1982 UTEP
1948 Penn State	1980 North Dakota	**WRESTLING**	1976 UTEP	1983 SMU
1949 Temple	1981 Wisconsin	1928 Oklahoma State[1]	1977 Washington St.	1984 Oregon
1950 Illinois	1982 North Dakota	1929 Oklahoma State	1978 UTEP	1985 Arkansas

1986	SMU
1987	UCLA
1988	UCLA
1989	Louisiana State
1990	Louisiana State
1991	Tennessee
1992	Arkansas
1993	Arkansas
1994	Arkansas
1995	Arkansas
1996	Arkansas
1997	Arkansas
1998	Arkansas
1999	Arkansas
2000	Stanford
2001	Tennessee

BASEBALL

1947	California
1948	USC
1949	Texas
1950	Texas
1951	Oklahoma
1952	Holy Cross
1953	Michigan
1954	Missouri
1955	Wake Forest
1956	Minnesota
1957	California
1958	USC
1959	Oklahoma State
1960	Minnesota
1961	USC
1962	Michigan
1963	USC
1964	Minnesota
1965	Arizona State
1966	Ohio State
1967	Arizona State
1968	USC
1969	Arizona State
1970	USC
1971	USC
1972	USC
1973	USC
1974	USC
1975	Texas
1976	Arizona
1977	Arizona State
1978	USC
1979	Cal St. Fullerton
1980	Arizona
1981	Arizona State
1982	Miami (Fla.)
1983	Texas
1984	Cal St. Fullerton
1985	Miami (Fla.)
1986	Arizona
1987	Stanford
1988	Stanford
1989	Wichita State
1990	Georgia
1991	Louisiana State
1992	Pepperdine
1993	Louisiana State
1994	Oklahoma
1995	Cal St. Fullerton
1996	Louisiana State
1997	Louisiana State
1998	USC
1999	Miama (Fla.)
2000	Louisiana State
2001	Miami (Fla.)

GOLF

1897	Yale
1898	Harvard (spring)
1898	Yale (fall)
1899	Harvard
1900	no tournament
1901	Harvard
1902	Yale (spring)
1903	Harvard
1904	Harvard
1905	Yale
1906	Yale
1907	Yale
1908	Yale
1909	Yale
1910	Yale
1911	Yale
1912	Yale
1913	Yale
1914	Princeton
1915	Yale
1916	Princeton
1917	no tournament
1918	no tournament
1919	Princeton
1920	Princeton
1921	Dartmouth
1922	Princeton
1923	Princeton
1924	Yale
1925	Yale
1926	Yale
1927	Princeton
1928	Princeton
1929	Princeton
1930	Princeton
1931	Yale
1932	Yale
1933	Yale
1934	Michigan
1935	Michigan
1936	Yale
1937	Princeton
1938	Stanford
1939	Stanford
1940	Princeton, Louisiana State
1941	Stanford
1942	Louisiana State, Stanford
1943	Yale
1944	Notre Dame
1945	Ohio State
1946	Stanford
1947	Louisiana State
1948	San Jose State
1949	North Texas
1950	North Texas
1951	North Texas
1952	North Texas
1953	Stanford
1954	SMU
1955	Louisiana State
1956	Houston
1957	Houston
1958	Houston
1959	Houston
1960	Houston
1961	Purdue
1962	Houston
1963	Oklahoma State
1964	Houston
1965	Houston
1966	Houston
1967	Houston
1968	Florida
1969	Houston
1970	Houston
1971	Texas
1972	Texas
1973	Florida
1974	Wake Forest
1975	Wake Forest
1976	Oklahoma
1977	Houston
1978	Oklahoma State
1979	Ohio State
1980	Oklahoma State
1981	Brigham Young
1982	Houston
1983	Oklahoma State
1984	Houston
1985	Houston
1986	Wake Forest
1987	Oklahoma State
1988	UCLA
1989	Oklahoma
1990	Arizona
1991	Oklahoma State
1992	Arizona
1993	Florida
1994	Stanford
1995	Oklahoma State
1996	Arizona State
1997	Pepperdine
1998	UNLV
1999	Georgia
2000	Oklahoma State
2001	Florida

LACROSSE

1971	Cornell
1972	Virginia
1973	Maryland
1974	Johns Hopkins
1975	Maryland
1976	Cornell
1977	Cornell
1978	Johns Hopkins
1979	Johns Hopkins
1980	Johns Hopkins
1981	North Carolina
1982	North Carolina
1983	Syracuse
1984	Johns Hopkins
1985	Johns Hopkins
1986	North Carolina
1987	Johns Hopkins
1988	Syracuse
1989	Syracuse
1990	Syracuse
1991	North Carolina
1992	Princeton
1993	Syracuse
1994	Princeton
1995	Syracuse
1996	Princeton
1997	Princeton
1998	Princeton
1999	Virginia
2000	Syracuse
2001	Princeton

TENNIS

1946	USC
1947	William & Mary
1948	William & Mary
1949	San Francisco
1950	UCLA
1951	USC
1952	UCLA
1953	UCLA
1954	UCLA
1955	USC
1956	UCLA
1957	Michigan
1958	USC
1959	Notre Dame, Tulane
1960	UCLA
1961	UCLA
1962	USC
1963	USC
1964	USC
1965	UCLA
1966	USC
1967	USC
1968	USC
1969	USC
1970	UCLA
1971	UCLA
1972	Trinity (Tex.)
1973	Stanford
1974	Stanford
1975	UCLA
1976	USC, UCLA
1977	Stanford
1978	Stanford
1979	UCLA
1980	Stanford
1981	Stanford
1982	UCLA
1983	Stanford
1984	UCLA
1985	Georgia
1986	Stanford
1987	Georgia
1988	Stanford
1989	Stanford
1990	Stanford
1991	USC
1992	Stanford
1993	USC
1994	USC
1995	Stanford
1996	Stanford
1997	Stanford
1998	Stanford
1999	Georgia
2000	Stanford
2001	Georgia

VOLLEYBALL

1970	UCLA
1971	UCLA
1972	UCLA
1973	San Diego State
1974	UCLA
1975	UCLA
1976	UCLA
1977	USC
1978	Pepperdine
1979	UCLA
1980	USC
1981	UCLA
1982	UCLA
1983	UCLA
1984	UCLA
1985	Pepperdine
1986	Pepperdine
1987	UCLA
1988	USC
1989	UCLA
1990	USC
1991	Cal State Long Beach
1992	Pepperdine
1993	UCLA
1994	Penn State
1995	UCLA
1996	UCLA
1997	Stanford
1998	UCLA
1999	Brigham Young
2000	UCLA
2001	Brigham Young

Men's and Women's Titles

FENCING

1990	Penn State
1991	Penn State
1992	Columbia
1993	Columbia
1994	Notre Dame
1995	Penn State
1996	Penn State
1997	Penn State
1998	Penn State
1999	Penn State
2000	Penn State
2001	St. John's (N.Y.)

RIFLE

1954	Seattle
1955	Dartmouth
1956	Dartmouth
1957	Colorado
1958	Denver
1959	Denver
1960	Denver
1961	Middlebury
1962	Colorado
1963	Colorado
1964	Dartmouth
1965	Utah
1966	W. Colorado
1967	Wyoming
1968	Denver
1969	Dartmouth
1970	Dartmouth
1971	Colorado
1972	Denver
1973	Wyoming
1974	Wyoming
1975	Vermont
1976	Colorado
1977	Wyoming
1978	Wyoming
1979	Utah
1980	Tennessee Tech
1981	Tennessee Tech
1982	Tennessee Tech
1983	West Virginia
1984	West Virginia
1985	Murray State
1986	West Virginia
1987	Murray State
1988	West Virginia
1989	West Virginia
1990	West Virginia
1991	West Virginia
1992	West Virginia
1993	West Virginia
1994	Alaska Fairbanks
1995	West Virginia
1996	West Virginia
1997	West Virginia
1998	West Virginia
1999	Alaska Fairbanks
2000	Alaska Fairbanks
2001	Alaska Fairbanks

SKIING

1954	Denver
1955	Denver
1956	Denver
1957	Denver
1958	Dartmouth
1959	Colorado
1960	Colorado
1961	Denver
1962	Denver
1963	Denver
1964	Denver
1965	Denver
1966	Denver
1967	Denver
1968	Wyoming
1969	Denver
1970	Denver
1971	Denver
1972	Colorado
1973	Colorado
1974	Colorado
1975	Colorado
1976	Dartmouth
1977	Colorado
1978	Colorado
1979	Colorado
1980	Vermont
1981	Utah
1982	Colorado
1983	Utah
1984	Utah
1985	Wyoming
1986	Utah
1987	Utah
1988	Utah
1989	Vermont
1990	Vermont
1991	Colorado
1992	Vermont
1993	Utah
1994	Vermont
1995	Colorado
1996	Utah
1997	Utah
1998	Colorado
1999	Colorado
2000	Denver
2001	Denver

NCAA WOMEN'S MAJOR SPORTS

Division I Women's Basketball Championship

Year	Champion	Coach	Outstanding player	Score	Runner-Up
1982	Louisiana Tech	Sonja Hogg	Janice Lawrence	76–62	Cheyney
1983	USC	Linda Sharp	Cheryl Miller	69–67	Louisiana Tech
1984	USC	Linda Sharp	Cheryl Miller	72–61	Tennessee
1985	Old Dominion	Marianne Stanley	Tracy Claxton	70–65	Georgia
1986	Texas	Jody Conradt	Clarissa Davis	97–81	USC
1987	Tennessee	Pat Summitt	Tonya Edwards	67–44	Louisiana Tech
1988	Louisiana Tech	Leon Barmore	Erica Westbrooks	56–54	Auburn
1989	Tennessee	Pat Summitt	Brigitte Gordon	76–60	Auburn
1990	Stanford	Tara VanderVeer	Jennifer Azzi	88–81	Auburn
1991	Tennessee	Pat Summitt	Dawn Staley	70–67	Virginia
1992	Stanford	Tara VanderVeer	Molly Goodenbour	78–62	Western Kentucky
1993	Texas Tech	Marcia Sharp	Sheryl Swoopes	84–82	Ohio State
1994	North Carolina	Sylvia Hatchell	Charlotte Smith	60–59	Louisiana Tech
1995	Connecticut	Geno Auriemma	Rebecca Lobo	70–64	Tennessee
1996	Tennessee	Pat Summitt	Michelle Marciniak	83–65	Georgia
1997	Tennessee	Pat Summitt	Chamique Holdsclaw	68–59	Old Dominion
1998	Tennessee	Pat Summitt	Chamique Holdsclaw	93–75	Louisiana Tech
1999	Purdue	Carolyn Peck	Ukari Figgs	62–45	Duke
2000	Connecticut	Geno Auriemma	Shea Ralph	71-52	Tennessee
2001	Notre Dame	Muffet McGraw	Ruth Riley	68-66	Purdue

Other Women's Champions

Year	Cross-Country	Field Hockey	Soccer	Volleyball	Indoor Track	Outdoor Track
1981	Virginia	Connecticut	N.A.	USC	N.A.	N.A.
1982	Virginia	Old Dominion	North Carolina	Hawaii	N.A.	UCLA
1983	Oregon	Old Dominion	North Carolina	Hawaii	Nebraska	UCLA
1984	Wisconsin	Old Dominion	North Carolina	UCLA	Nebraska	Florida State
1985	Wisconsin	Connecticut	George Mason	Pacific	Florida State	Oregon
1986	Texas	Iowa	North Carolina	Pacific	Texas	Texas
1987	Oregon	Maryland	North Carolina	Hawaii	Louisiana State	Louisiana State
1988	Kentucky	Old Dominion	North Carolina	Texas	Texas	Louisiana State
1989	Villanova	North Carolina	North Carolina	Cal St. Long Beach	Louisiana State	Louisiana State
1990	Villanova	Old Dominion	North Carolina	UCLA	Texas	Louisiana State
1991	Villanova	Old Dominion	North Carolina	UCLA	Louisiana State	Louisiana State
1992	Villanova	Old Dominion	North Carolina	Stanford	Florida	Louisiana State
1993	Villanova	Maryland	North Carolina	Long Beach State	Louisiana State	Louisiana State
1994	Villanova	James Madison	North Carolina	Stanford	Louisiana State	Louisiana State
1995	Providence	North Carolina	Notre Dame	Nebraska	Louisiana State	Louisiana State
1996	Stanford	North Carolina	North Carolina	Stanford	Louisiana State	Louisiana State
1997	BYU	North Carolina	North Carolina	Stanford	Louisiana State	Louisiana State
1998	Villanova	Old Dominion	Florida	Long Beach State	Texas	Texas
1999	BYU	Maryland	North Carolina	Penn State	Texas	Texas
2000	Colorado	Old Dominion	North Carolina	Nebraska	UCLA	Louisiana State
2001	N.A.	N.A.	N.A.	N.A.	UCLA	USC

Year	Golf	Gymnastics	Lacrosse	Softball	Swimming	Tennis	Fencing[1]
1982	Tulsa	Utah	Massachusetts	UCLA	Florida	Stanford	N.A.
1983	Texas Christian	Utah	Delaware	Texas A&M	Stanford	USC	Wayne State
1984	Miami (Fla.)	Utah	Temple	UCLA	Texas	Stanford	Penn State
1985	Florida	Utah	New Hampshire	UCLA	Texas	USC	Yale
1986	Florida	Utah	Maryland	Cal State Fullerton	Texas	Stanford	Yale
1987	San Jose State	Georgia	Penn State	Texas A&M	Texas	Stanford	Pennsylvania
1988	Tulsa	Alabama	Temple	UCLA	Texas	Stanford	Notre Dame
1989	San Jose State	Georgia	Penn State	UCLA	Stanford	Stanford	Wayne State
1990	Arizona State	Utah	Harvard	UCLA	Texas	Stanford	Wayne State
1991	UCLA	Alabama	Virginia	Arizona	Texas	Stanford	1.For champions
1992	San Jose State	Utah	Maryland	UCLA	Stanford	Florida	since 1990, see
1993	Arizona State	Georgia	Virginia	Arizona	Stanford	Texas	"Men's and
1994	Arizona State	Utah	Princeton	Arizona	Stanford	Georgia	Women's Title.s"
1995	Arizona State	Utah	Maryland	UCLA	Stanford	Texas	
1996	Arizona	Alabama	Maryland	Arizona	Stanford	Florida	
1997	Arizona State	UCLA	Maryland	Arizona	USC	Stanford	
1998	Arizona State	Georgia	Maryland	Fresno State	Stanford	Florida	
1999	Duke	Georgia	Maryland	UCLA	Georgia	Stanford	
2000	Arizona	UCLA	Maryland	Oklahoma	Georgia	Georgia	Water Polo
2001	Georgia	UCLA	Maryland	Arizona	Georgia	Stanford	UCLA

International Sports

THE WORLD CUP

From its origins in various "football" games dating back to ancient Greece and China, soccer (as it is called in the U.S.) has become the world's most popular sport. The World Cup championship, modern soccer's most spectacular event, is staged every four years by the Federation Internationale de Football Association (FIFA). The first World Cup in 1930 attracted a mere 13 nations. In 1998, 173 nations competed for a bid to the 32-team tournament. The top 16 teams among those 32 (as decided during a 48-game round-robin first round) advance to a single-elimination tournament until a single winner is crowned. Players must represent their home country, regardless of where they regularly play. Millions attend the Cup's many contests and the televised final is viewed by over a billion people worldwide.

The World Cup, 1930–98

Year	Final Score	Golden Boot Award: Leading scorer, country (goals)	Host country	Participating nations
1930	Uruguay 4, Argentina 2	Stabile, Argentina (8)	Uruguay	13
1934	Italy 2, Czechoslovakia 1 (OT)	Conen, Germany Nejedly, Czechoslovakia Schiavo, Italy (4)	Italy	31
1938	Italy 4, Hungary 2	Leonidas, Brazil (8)	France	36
1942	No tournament—World War II			
1946	No tournament—World War II			
1950	Uruguay 2, Brazil 1	Ademir, Brazil (7)	Brazil	33
1954	West Germany 3, Hungary 2	Kocsis, Hungary (11)	Switzerland	38
1958	Brazil 5, Sweden 2	Fontaine, France (13)	Sweden	53
1962	Brazil 3, Czechoslovakia 1	Jerkovic, Yugoslavia (5)	Chile	56
1966	England 4, West Germany 2 (OT)	Eusebio, Portugal (9)	England	71
1970	Brazil 4, Italy 1	Muller, West Germany (10)	Mexico	71
1974	West Germany 2, Netherlands 1	Lato, Poland (7)	West Germany	98
1978	Argentia 3, Netherlands 1 (OT)	Kempes, Argentina (6)	Argentina	106
1982	Italy 3, West Germany 1	Rossi, Italy (6)	Spain	109
1986	Argentina 3, West Germany 2	Lineker, England (6)	Mexico	121
1990	West Germany 1, Argentina 0	Schilacci, Italy (6)	Italy	112
1994	Brazil 0, Italy 0 (Brazil won 3-2 on penalty kicks)	Stoichkov, Bulgaria (6)	United States	144
1998	France 3, Brazil 0	Suker, Croatia (6)	France	173

Source: FIFA

The World Cup, 1998

When the 1998 World Cup began in June, France hardly seemed to acknowledge that it was hosting the world's largest sporting event. But the French soccer team aroused an indifferent nation and on July 12 won its first World Cup title 3–0 over Brazil, with the championship game providing the most unexpected upset in the final in nearly five decades. Zinedine Zidane, France's exquisite playmaker, scored two goals in the championship game, heading in a pair of corner kicks, to provide the home team with its first World Cup title since Argentina prevailed in 1978.

The 1998 World Cup provided a moment of sweet symmetry for the French. It was a Frenchman, Jules Rimet, who conceived of a world championship for soccer. Only seven teams have won the Cup since the tournament, held every four years, began play in 1930. France joined an exclusive club that includes four-time champion Brazil, Germany, Argentina, Italy, Uruguay and England.

France's victory over Brazil was the largest margin ever in a championship game and the biggest upset since Brazil lost 2–1 at home to Paraguay in 1950. Ronaldo, the 21-year-old Brazilian forward considered to be the best player in the world, played a listless game against France. It was later revealed that Ronaldo had suffered convulsions in the hours prior to the game.

France was the dominant squad in this 32-team tournament, allowing only two goals in seven matches. The biggest disappointments were Spain, an early favorite which did not advance beyond the first round, and the United States, which scored only one goal and lost all three of its first-round matches. Coach Steve Sampson resigned immediately after the Americans exited, and several of the team's most experienced players, including Eric Wynalda, Tab Ramos and Alexi Lalas, further shamed themselves by harshly criticizing Sampson without taking any responsibility for the total collapse.

—Jere Longman, *The New York Times*

1998 World Cup, First Round

Group A	Wins-Losses-Ties	Points
1. Brazil	2–1–0	6
2. Norway	1–0–2	5
3. Scotland	1–1–1	4
4. Morocco	0–2–1	1

Brazil 2, Scotland	1	Morocco 2, Norway	2
Scotland 1, Norway	1	Brazil 3, Morocco	0
Norway 2, Brazil	1	Morocco 3, Scotland	1

Group E	Wins-Losses-Ties	Points
1. Netherlands	1–0–2	5
2. Mexico	1–0–2	5
3. Belgium	0–0–3	3
4. South Korea	0–2–1	1

Mexico 3, S. Korea	1	Netherlands 0, Belgium	0
Netherlands 5, S. Korea	0	Belgium 2, Mexico	2
Netherlands 2, Mexico	2	Belgium 1, S. Korea	1

Group B	Wins-Losses-Ties	Points
1. Italy	2–0–1	7
2. Chile	0–0–3	3
3. Austria	0–1–2	2
4. Cameroon	0–1–2	2

Chile 2, Italy	2	Cameroon 1, Austria	1
Chile 1, Austria	1	Italy 3, Cameroon	0
Italy 2, Austria	1	Cameroon 1, Chile	1

Group F	Wins-Losses-Ties	Points
1. Germany	2–0–1	7
2. Yugoslavia	2–0–1	7
3. Iran	1–2–0	3
4. United States	0–3–0	0

Yugoslavia 1, Iran	0	Germany 2, United States	0
Germany 2, Yugoslavia	2	Iran 2, United States	1
Germany 2, Iran	0	Yugoslavia 1, United States	0

Group C	Wins-Losses-Ties	Points
1. France	3–0–0	9
2. Denmark	1–1–1	4
3. South Africa	0–1–2	2
4. Saudi Arabia	0–2–1	1

Denmark 1, Saudi Arabia	0	France 3, South Africa	0
Denmark 1, South Africa	1	France 4, Saudi Arabia	0
France 2, Denmark	1	Saudi Arabia 2, S. Africa	2

Group G	Wins-Losses-Ties	Points
1. Romania	2–0–1	7
2. England	2–1–0	6
3. Colombia	1–2–0	3
4. Tunisia	0–2–1	1

England 2, Tunisia	0	Romania 1, Colombia	0
Colombia 1, Tunisia	0	Romania 2, England	1
Romania 1, Tunisia	1	England 2, Colombia	0

Group D	Wins-Losses-Ties	Points
1. Nigeria	2–1–0	6
2. Paraguay	1–0–2	5
3. Spain	1–1–1	4
4. Bulgaria	0–2–1	1

Paraguay 0, Bulgaria	0	Nigeria 3, Spain	2
Nigeria 1, Bulgaria	0	Paraguay 0, Spain	0
Spain 6, Bulgaria	1	Paraguay 3, Nigeria	1

Group H	Wins-Losses-Ties	Points
1. Argentina	3–0–0	9
2. Croatia	2–1–0	6
3. Jamaica	1–2–0	3
4. Japan	0–3–0	0

Argentina 1, Japan	0	Croatia 3, Jamaica	1
Croatia 1, Japan	0	Argentina 5, Jamaica	0
Argentina 1, Croatia	0	Jamaica 2, Japan	1

Note: A win is worth three points and a tie is worth one point. The top two teams in each group advance to the second round.

1998 World Cup, Second Round

1. Argentina beat England 4-3 on penalty kicks. 2. France beat Italy 4-3 on penalty kicks. 3. Brazil beat the Netherlands 4-2 on penalty kicks.

The Women's World Cup, 1999

The U.S. women's soccer team won the 1999 World Cup, battling China to a 0-0 tie that wasn't decided until the penalty kick round, which the U.S. won by a narrow 5-4 margin. Goalkeeper Briana Scurry made a crucial save to give the U.S. the lead, and Brandi Chastain booted home the game-winner. More surprising than the outcome (the U.S. and China were the two favorites to win the Cup) was the popularity of the sport. Many of the early round games sold out football stadiums seating in excess of 70,000 people, and the finale, held in the cavernous Rose Bowl, drew more than 90,000 spectators. Television ratings were equally strong. The U.S.-Brazil semifinal game garnered a 3.78 Nielsen rating (or 2.9 million households), ESPN's highest rating ever for soccer, men's or women's. The rating for ABC's coverage of the championship game was an astounding 13.3, more even than 11.3 average for the five games of the NBA finals, and nearly double the 6.9 rating earned by the 1998 Men's World Cup Final between France and Brazil. Those numbers were all the more surprising coming just three years after NBC failed to air live the gold medal game at the 1996 Olympics, which the U.S. women also won on penalty kicks.

FIRST ROUND

Group A	Wins-Losses-Ties	Points
x-USA	3–0–0	9
x-Nigeria	2–1–0	6
N. Korea	1–2–0	3
Denmark	0–3–0	0

USA 3, N. Korea 1	Nigeria 2, N. Korea 1
Nigeria 2, Denmark 0	USA 7, Nigeria 1
USA 3, Denmark 0	N. Korea 3, Denmark 1

Group B	Wins-Losses-Ties	Points
x-Brazil	2–1–0	7
x-Germany	1–0–2	5
Italy	1–1–1	4
Mexico	0–3–0	0

Brazil 3, Germany 3	Germany 1, Italy 1
Italy 2, Mexico 0	Brazil 2, Italy 0
Brazil 7, Mexico 1	Germany 6, Mexico 0

Group C	Wins-Losses-Ties	Points
x-Norway	3–0–0	9
x-Russia	2–1–0	6
Japan	0–2–1	1
Canada	0–2–1	1

Canada 1, Japan 1	Norway 7, Canada 1
Norway 2, Russia 1	Russia 4, Canada 1
Russia 5, Japan 0	Norway 4, Japan 0

Group D	Wins-Losses-Ties	Points
x-China	3–0–0	9
x-Sweden	2–1–0	6
Australia	0–2–1	1
Ghana	0–2–1	1

China 2, Sweden 1	China 7, Ghana 1
Australia 1, Ghana 1	China 3, Australia 1
Sweden 3, Australia 1	Sweden 2, Ghana 0

Note: A win is worth three points, and a tie is worth one point. The top two teams in each group advance to the second round.

1999 Women's World Cup, Second Round

USA 3 — USA 2 — Semifinals

Germany 2

Nigeria 3 — Brazil 0

Brazil 4 (OT)

World Cup Final
USA 0 (5–4)[1] China 0[1]

Semifinals — China 5 — China 2

Russia 0

Sweden 1 — Norway 0

Norway 3

Third Place Game
Brazil 0 (5–4)[2] Norway 0[2]

1. The U.S won the championship 5–4 on penalty kicks. 2. Brazil beat Norway 5–4 on penalty kicks for third place.

CHESS

World Chess Champions

Year	Name	Country	Year	Name	Country
1886–94	Wilhelm Steinitz	Austria	1960–61	Mikhail Tal	USSR
1894–1921	Emanuel Lasker	Germany	1961–63	Mikhail Botvinnik	USSR
1921–27	José R. Capablanca	Cuba	1963–69	Tigran Petrosian	USSR
1927–35	Alexander A. Alekhine	France	1969–72	Boris Spassky	USSR
1935–37	Max Euwe	Netherlands	1972–75	Bobby Fischer	USA
1937–48	Alexander A. Alekhine	France	1975–85	Anatoly Karpov	USSR
1948–57	Mikhail Botvinnik	USSR	1985–2000[1]	Garry Kasparov	USSR/Russia
1957–58	Vassily Smyslov	USSR	1993[1]–	Anatoly Karpov	Russia
1958–60	Mikhail Botvinnik	USSR	2000[1]–	Vladimir Kramnik	Russia

1. In 1993, Kasparov started his own chess sanctioning body, the Professional Chess Association, leaving his World Chess Federation (FIDE) championship vacant, whereupon FIDE awarded the title to Karpov. **Source:** U.S. Chess Federation

U.S. Chess Champions

Years	Name	Years	Name	Years	Name
1845–57	Charles Henry Stanley	1960–61	Bobby Fischer	1985	Lev Alburt
1857–71	Paul Morphy	1961–62	Larry Evans	1986	Yasser Seirawan
1871–90	Capt. George Mackenzie	1962–63	Bobby Fischer	1987	(tie) Joel Benjamin
1890–91	Jackson Showalter	1963–64	Bobby Fischer		Nick deFirmian
1891–94	Solomon Lipschutz	1965	Bobby Fischer	1988	Michael Wilder
1894	Jackson Showalter	1966	Bobby Fischer	1989	(tie) Roman
1894-95	Albert Hodges	1968	Larry Evans		Dzindzichashvili
1895–97	Jackson Showalter	1969	Samuel Reshevksy		Yasser Seirawan
1897–1906	Harry Nelson Pillsbury	1972	Robert Byrne		Stuart Rachels
1906–09	Jackson Showalter	1973	(tie) John Grefe	1990	Lev Alburt
1909–36	Frank J. Marshall		Lubomir Kavalek	1991	Gata Kamsky
1936	Samuel Reshevsky	1974	Walter Browne	1992	Patrick Wolff
1938	Samuel Reshevsky	1975	Walter Browne	1993	(tie) Alexander Shabalov
1940	Samuel Reshevsky	1977	Walter Browne		Alex Yermolinsky
1942	Samuel Reshevsky	1978	Lubomir Kavalek	1994	Boris Gulko
1944	Arnold Denker	1980	(tie)Walter Browne	1995	(tie) Nick deFirmian,
1946	Samuel Reshevsky		Larry Evans		Alexander Ivanov,
1948	Herman Steiner		Larry Christiansen		Patrick Wolf
1951	Larry Evans	1981	(tie) Walter Browne	1996	Alex Yermolinski
1952	Larry Evans		Yasser Seirawan	1997	Joel Benjamin
1954	Arthur Bisguier	1983	(tie) Walter Browne	1998	Nick deFirmian
1957–58	Bobby Fischer		Larry Christiansen	1999	Boris Gulko
1958–59	Bobby Fischer		Roman Dzindzichashvili	2000	Joel Benjamin
1959-60	Bobby Fischer	1984	Lev Alburt		

Note: The U.S. championship is not held every year. **Source:** U.S. Chess Federation

CYCLING

The Tour De France

Year	Champion	Year	Champion	Year	Champion	Year	Champion
1903	Maurice Garin	1929	Maurice Dewaele	1958	Charly Gaul	1980	Joop Zoetemelk
1904	Henri Cornet	1930	Andre Leducq	1959	Federico Bahamontes	1981	Bernard Hinault
1905	Louis Trousselier	1931	Antonin Magne	1960	Gastone Nencini	1982	Bernard Hinault
1906	Rene Pottier	1932	Andre Leducq	1961	Jacques Anquetil	1983	Laurent Fignon
1907	Lucien Petit-Breton	1933	Georges Speicher	1962	Jacques Anquetil	1984	Laurent Fignon
1908	LucienPetit-Breton	1934	Antonin Magne	1963	Jacques Anquetil	1985	Bernard Hinault
1909	Francois Faber	1935	Romain Maes	1964	Jacques Anquetil	1986	Greg LeMond
1910	Octave Lapize	1936	Sylvere Maes	1965	Felice Gimondi	1987	Stephen Roche
1911	Gustave Garrigou	1937	Roger Lapebie	1966	Lucien Aimar	1988	Pedro Delgado
1912	Odile Defraye	1938	Gino Bartali	1967	Roger Pingeon	1989	Greg LeMond
1913	Philippe Thijs	1939	Sylvere Maes	1968	Jan Janssen	1990	Greg LeMond
1914	Philippe Thijs	1947	Jean Robic	1969	Eddy Merckx	1991	Miguel Indurain
1919	Firmin Lambot	1948	Gino Bartali	1970	Eddy Merckx	1992	Miguel Indurain
1920	Philippe Thijs	1949	Fausto Coppi	1971	Eddy Merckx	1993	Miguel Indurain
1921	Leon Scieur	1950	Ferdi Kubler	1972	Eddy Merckx	1994	Miguel Indurain
1922	Firmin Lambot	1951	Hugo Koblet	1973	Luis Ocana	1995	Miguel Indurain
1923	Henri Pelissier	1952	Fausto Coppi	1974	Eddy Merckx	1996	Bjarne Riis
1924	Ottavio Bottecchia	1953	Louison Bobet	1975	Bernard Thevenet	1997	Jan Ullrich
1925	Ottavio Bottecchia	1954	Louison Bobet	1976	Lucien Van Impe	1998	Marco Pantini
1926	Lucien Buysse	1955	Louison Bobet	1977	Bernard Thevenet	1999	Lance Armstrong
1927	Nicolas Frantz	1956	Roger Walkowiak	1978	Bernard Hinault	2000	Lance Armstrong
1928	Nicolas Frantz	1957	Jacques Anquetil	1979	Bernard Hinault	2001	Lance Armstrong

FIGURE SKATING

U.S. Figure Skating Champions

Year	Men	Women	Year	Men	Women
1952	Richard Button	Tenley Albright	1977	Charles Tickner	Linda Fratianne
1953	Hayes Jenkins	Tenley Albright	1978	Charles Tickner	Linda Fratianne
1954	Hayes Jenkins	Tenley Albright	1979	Charles Tickner	Linda Fratianne
1955	Hayes Jenkins	Tenley Albright	1980	Charles Tickner	Linda Fratianne
1956	Hayes Jenkins	Tenley Albright	1981	Scott Hamilton	Elaine Zayak
1957	Dave Jenkins	Carol Heiss	1982	Scott Hamilton	Rosalynn Sumners
1958	Dave Jenkins	Carol Heiss	1983	Scott Hamilton	Rosalynn Sumners
1959	Dave Jenkins	Carol Heiss	1984	Scott Hamilton	Rosalynn Sumners
1960	Dave Jenkins	Carol Heiss	1985	Brian Boitano	Tiffany Chin
1961	Bradley Lord	Laurence Owen	1986	Brian Boitano	Debi Thomas
1962	Monty Hoyt	Barbara Roles Pursley	1987	Brian Boitano	Jill Trenary
1963	Tommy Litz	Lorraine Hanlon	1988	Brian Boitano	Debi Thomas
1964	Scott Allen	Peggy Fleming	1989	Christopher Bowman	Jill Trenary
1965	Gary Visconti	Peggy Fleming	1990	Todd Eldredge	Jill Trenary
1966	Scott Allen	Peggy Fleming	1991	Todd Eldredge	Tonya Harding
1967	Gary Visconti	Peggy Fleming	1992	Christopher Bowman	Kristi Yamaguchi
1968	Tim Wood	Peggy Fleming	1993	Scott Davis	Nancy Kerrigan
1969	Tim Wood	Janet Lynn	1994	Scott Davis	Tonya Harding[1]
1970	Tim Wood	Janet Lynn	1995	Todd Eldredge	Nicole Bobek
1971	John Misha Petkevich	Janet Lynn	1996	Rudy Galindo	Michelle Kwan
1972	Ken Shelley	Janet Lynn	1997	Todd Eldredge	Tara Lipinski
1973	Gordon McKellen Jr.	Janet Lynn	1998	Todd Eldredge	Michelle Kwan
1974	Gordon McKellen Jr.	Dorothy Hamill	1999	Michael Weiss	Michelle Kwan
1975	Gordon McKellen Jr.	Dorothy Hamill	2000	Michael Weiss	Michelle Kwan
1976	Terry Kubicka	Dorothy Hamill	2001	Tim Goebel	Michelle Kwan

1. Later stripped of title.

World Figure Skating Champions

Year	Men	Women	Year	Men	Women
1952	Richard Button, U.S.	Jacqueline du Bief, France	1974	Jan Hoffmann, East Germany	Christine Errath, East Germany
1953	Hayes Jenkins, U.S.	Tenley Albright, U.S.	1975	Sergei Volkov, USSR	Dianne de Leeuw, Netherlands-U.S.
1954	Hayes Jenkins, U.S.	Gundi Busch, W. Germany	1976	John Curry, Great Britain	Dorothy Hamill, U.S.
1955	Hayes Jenkins, U.S.	Tenley Albright, U.S.	1977	Vladimir Kovalev, USSR	Linda Fratianne, U.S.
1956	Hayes Jenkins, U.S.	Carol Heiss, U.S.	1978	Charles Tickner, U.S.	Anett Potzsch, East Germany
1957	Dave Jenkins, U.S.	Carol Heiss, U.S.	1979	Vladimir Kovalev, USSR	Linda Fratianne, U.S.
1958	Dave Jenkins, U.S.	Carol Heiss, U.S.	1980	Jan Hoffmann, East Germany	Anett Potzsch, East Germany
1959	Dave Jenkins, U.S.	Carol Heiss, U.S.	1981	Scott Hamilton, U.S.	Denise Biellmann, Switzerland
1960	Alain Giletti, France	Carol Heiss, U.S.	1982	Scott Hamilton, U.S.	Elaine Zayak, U.S.
1961	No champion	No champion	1983	Scott Hamilton, U.S.	Rosalynn Sumners, U.S.
1962	Don Jackson, Canada	Sjoukje Dijkstra, Netherlands	1984	Scott Hamilton, U.S.	Katarina Witt, E. Germany
1963	Don McPherson, Canada	Sjoukje Dijkstra, Netherlands	1985	Aleksandr Fadeev, USSR	Katarina Witt, E. Germany
1964	Manfred Schnelldorfer, W. Germany	Sjoukje Dijkstra, Netherlands	1986	Brian Boitano, U.S.	Debi Thomas, U.S.
1965	Alain Calmat, France	Petra Burka, Canada	1987	Brian Orser, Canada	Katarina Witt, E. Germany
1966	Emmerich Danzer, Austria	Peggy Fleming, U.S.	1988	Brian Boitano, U.S.	Katarina Witt, E. Germany
1967	Emmerich Danzer, Austria	Peggy Fleming, U.S.	1989	Kurt Browning, Canada	Midori Ito, Japan
1968	Emmerich Danzer, Austria	Peggy Fleming, U.S.	1990	Kurt Browning, Canada	Jill Trenary, U.S.
1969	Tim Wood, U.S.	Gabriele Seyfert, East Germany	1991	Kurt Browning, Canada	Kristi Yamaguchi, U.S.
1970	Tim Wood, U.S.	Gabriele Seyfert, East Germany	1992	Victor Petrenko, Russia	Kristi Yamaguchi, U.S.
1971	Ondrej Nepela, Czechoslovakia	Beatrix Schuba, Austria	1993	Kurt Browning, Canada	Oksana Baiul, Ukraine
1972	Ondrej Nepela, Czechoslovakia	Beatrix Schuba, Austria	1994	Elvis Stojko, Canada	Yuka Sato, Japan
1971	Ondrej Nepela, Czechoslovakia	Karen Magnussen, Canada	1995	Elvis Stojko, Canada	Lu Chen, China
			1996	Todd Eldredge, U.S.	Michelle Kwan, U.S.
			1997	Elvis Stojko, Canada	Tara Lipinski, U.S.
			1998	Alexi Yagudin, Russia	Michelle Kwan, U.S.
			1999	Alexi Yagudin, Russia	Maria Butyrskaya, Russia
			2000	Alexi Yagudin, Russia	Michelle Kwan, U.S.
			2001	Evgeni Plushenko, Russia	Michelle Kwan, U.S.

MARATHON RUNNING

Marathons are 26 miles, 385 yards long, the distance purportedly run by the Athenian messenger who announced his city-state's victory over the Persian Empire on the Plains of Marathon in 490 B.C. The oldest U.S. marathon covers a route from Hopkinton, Mass. to Boston. For many years, the winners received only a laurel wreath and the traditional pot of beef stew.

Boston Marathon

Year	Winner	Time	Year	Winner	Time
	MEN		1965	Morio Shigematsu	2:16:33
1897	John J. McDermott	2:55:10	1966	Kenji Kimihara	2:17:11
1898	Ronald J. McDonald	2:42:00	1967	David McKenzie	2:15:45
1899	Lawrence J. Brignolia	2:54:38	1968	Ambrose Burfoot	2:22:17
1900	James J. Caffrey	2:39:44	1969	Yoshiaki Unetani, Japan	2:13:49
1901	James J. Caffrey	2:29:23	1970	Ron Hill	2:10:30
1902	Samuel A. Mellor, Yonkers	2:43:12	1971	Alavaro Mejia	2:18:45
1903	John C. Lorden	2:41:29	1972	Olavi Suomalainen	2:15:39
1904	Michael Spring	2:38:04	1973	Jon Anderson	2:16:03
1905	Fred Lorz	2:38:25	1974	Neil Cusack	2:13:39
1906	Timothy Ford	2:45:45	1975	Bill Rodgers	2:09:55
1907	Thomas Longboat	2:24:24	1976	Jack Fultz	2:20:19
1908	Thomas P. Morrissey	2:25:43	1977	Jerome Drayton	2:14:46
1909	Henri Renaud	2:53:36	1978	Bill Rodgers	2:10:13
1910	Fred L. Cameron	2:28:52	1979	Bill Rodgers	2:09:27
1911	Clarence H. DeMar	2:21:39	1980	Bill Rodgers	2:12:11
1912	Michael J. Ryan	2:21:18	1981	Toshihiko Seko	2:09:26
1913	Fritz Carlson	2:25:14	1982	Alberto Salazar	2:08:52
1914	James Duffy	2:25:01	1983	Gregory A. Meyer	2:09:00
1915	Edouard Fabre	2:31:41	1984	Geoff Smith	2:10:34
1916	Arthur V. Roth	2:27:16	1985	Geoff Smith	2:14:05
1917	William K. Kennedy	2:28:37	1986	Robert de Castella	2:07:51
1918	Service team race won by Camp Devens		1987	Toshihiko Seko	2:11:50
1919	Carl W. A. Linder	2:29:13	1988	Ibrahim Hussein	2:08:43
1920	Peter Trivoulidas	2:29:31	1989	Abebe Mekonnen	2:09:06
1921	Frank Zuna	2:18:57	1990	Gelindo Bordin	2:08:20
1922	Clarence H. DeMar	2:18:10	1991	Ibrahim Hussein	2:11:06
1923	Clarence H. DeMar	2:23:37	1992	Ibrahim Hussein	2:08:14
1924	Clarence H. DeMar	2:29:40	1993	Cosmas N'Deti	2:09:33
1925	Charles L. Mellor	2:33:00	1994	Cosmas N'Deti	2:07:15
1926	John C. Miles	2:25:40	1995	Cosmas N'Deti	2:09:22
1927	Clarence H. DeMar	2:40:22	1996	Moses Tanui	2:09:16
1928	Clarence H. DeMar	2:37:07	1997	Lameck Aguta	2:10:34
1929	John C. Miles	2:33:08	1998	Moses Tanui	2:07:34
1930	Clarence H. DeMar	2:34:48	1999	Joseph Chebet	2:09:52
1931	James P. Henigan	2:46:45	2000	Elijah Lagat	2:09:47
1932	Paul deBruyn	2:33:36	2001	Lee Bong-ju	2:09:43
1933	Leslie Pawson	2:33:01			
1934	Dave Komonen	2:32:53		**WOMEN**	
1935	John A. Kelley	2:32:07	1972	Nina Kuscsik	3:10:26
1936	Ellison M. (Tarzan) Brown	2:33:40	1973	Jacqueline Hansen	3:05:59
1937	Walter Young, Verdun	2:33:20	1974	Miki Gorman	2:47:11
1938	Leslie Pawson	2:35:34	1975	Liane Winter	2:42:24
1939	Ellison M. (Tarzan) Brown	2:28:51	1976	Kim Merritt	2:47:10
1940	Gerard Cote	2:33:20	1977	Miki Gorman	2:46:22
1941	Leslie Pawson	2:30:38	1978	Gayle Barron	2:44:52
1942	Bernard Joe Smith	2:26:51	1979	Joan Benoit	2:35:15
1943	Gerard Cote	2:28:25	1980	Jacqueline Gareau	2:34:28
1944	Gerard Cote	2:31:50	1981	Allison Roe	2:26:46
1945	John A. Kelley	2:30:40	1982	Charlotte Teske	2:29:33
1946	Stylianos Kyriakides	2:29:27	1983	Joan Benoit	2:22:43
1947	Yun Bok Suh	2:25:39	1984	Lorraine Moller	2:29:28
1948	Gerard Cote	2:31:02	1985	Lisa Larsen-Weidenbach	2:34:06
1949	Karle Gosta Leandersson	2:31:50	1986	Ingrid Kristiansen	2:24:55
1950	Kee Yong Ham	2:32:39	1987	Rosa Mota	2:25:21
1951	Shigeki Tanaka	2:27:45	1988	Rosa Mota	2:24:30
1952	Doroteo Flores	2:31:53	1989	Ingrid Kristiansen	2:24:33
1953	Keizo Yamada	2:18:51	1990	Rosa Mota	2:25:24
1954	Veikko L. Karvonen	2:20:39	1991	Wanda Panfil	2:24:18
1955	Hideo Hamamura	2:18:22	1992	Olga Markova	2:23:43
1956	Antti Viskari	2:14:14	1993	Olga Markova	2:25:27
1957	John J. Delley	2:20:05	1994	Uta Pippig	2:21:45
1958	Franjo Mihalic	2:25:54	1995	Uta Pippig	2:25:11
1959	Eino Oksanen	2:22:42	1996	Uta Pippig	2:27:12
1960	Paavo Kotila	2:20:54	1997	Fatuma Roba	2:28:03
1961	Eino Oksanen	2:23:39	1998	Fatuma Roba	2:23:21
1962	Eino Oksanen	2:23:48	1999	Fatuma Roba	2:23:25
1963	Aurele Vandendriessche	2:18:58	2000	Catherine Ndereba	2:26:11
1964	Aurele Vandendriessche	2:19:59	2001	Catherine Ndereba	2:21:50

New York Marathon

Year	Winner	Time
	MEN	
1970	Gary Muhrcke	2:31:39
1971	Norman Higgins	2:22:55
1972	Sheldon Karlin	2:27:53
1973	Tom Fleming	2:21:55
1974	Norbert Sander	2:26:31
1975	Tom Fleming	2:19:27
1976	Bill Rodgers	2:10:10
1977	Bill Rodgers	2:11:28
1978	Bill Rodgers	2:12:12
1979	Bill Rodgers	2:11:42
1980	Alberto Salazar	2:09:41
1981	Alberto Salazar	2:08:13
1982	Alberto Salazar	2:09:29
1983	Rod Dixon	2:08:59
1984	Orlando Pizzolato	2:14:53
1985	Orlando Pizzolato	2:11:34
1986	Gianni Poli	2:11:06
1987	Ibrahim Hussein	2:11:01
1988	Steve Jones	2:08:20
1989	Jumo Ikangaa	2:08:01
1990	Douglas Waikihuri	2:12:39
1991	Salvador Garcia	2:09:28
1992	Willie Mtolo	2:09:29
1993	Andres Espinosa	2:10:04
1994	German Silva	2:11:21
1995	German Silva	2:11:00
1996	Giacomo Leone	2:10:09
1997	John Kagwe	2:08:12
1998	John Kagwe	2:08:45
1999	Joseph Chebet	2:09:14
2000	Abdelkhader el-Mouaziz	2:10:09
	WOMEN	
1970	No Finisher	—
1971	Beth Bonner	2:55:22
1972	Nina Kuscsik	3:08:42
1973	Nina Kuscsik	2:57:08
1974	Katherine Switzer	3:07:29
1975	Kim Merritt	2:46:15
1976	Miki Gorman	2:39:11
1977	Miki Gorman	2:43:10
1978	Grete Waitz	2:32:30
1979	Grete Waitz	2:27:33
1980	Grete Waitz	2:25:41
1981	Allison Roe	2:25:29
1982	Grete Waitz	2:27:14
1983	Grete Waitz	2:27:00
1984	Grete Waitz	2:29:30
1985	Grete Waitz	2:28:34
1986	Grete Waitz	2:28:06
1987	Priscilla Welch	2:30:17
1988	Grete Waitz	2:28:07
1989	Ingrid Kristiansen	2:25:30
1990	Wanda Panfil	2:30:45
1991	Liz McColgan	2:27:32
1992	Lisa Ondieki	2:24:40
1993	Uta Pippig	2:26:24
1994	Tegla Loroupe	2:27:37
1995	Tegla Loroupe	2:28:06
1996	Anuta Catuna	2:28:18
1997	Franziska Rochat-Moser	2:28:43
1998	Franca Fiacconi	2:25:17
1999	Adriana Fernandez	2:25:06
2000	Lyudmila Petrova	2:25:45

TRACK AND FIELD

Track and Field World Records (as of August 22, 2001)

These are the recognized records of the IAAF (International Amateur Athletic Federation). All walk records must have been made on a track, and all relay records must be made by teams composed of individuals from the same country. Indoor records must be performed on tracks no larger than 200m in circumference, and the meet must be subject to drug testing. Awards awaiting ratification are not shown.

MEN, OUTDOOR

Event	(min./sec.)	Record holder (country)	Date
100 m	9.79	Maurice Greene (U.S.)	6/16/99
200 m	19.32	Michael Johnson (U.S.)	8/1/96
400 m	43.18	Michael Johnson (U.S.)	8/26/99
800 m	1:41.11	Wilson Kipketer (Denmark)	8/24/97
1,000 m	2:11.96	Noah Ngeny (Kenya)	9/5/99
1,500 m	3:26.00	Hicham el-Guerrouj (Morocco)	7/14/98
Mile	3:43.13	Hicham el-Guerrouj (Morocco)	7/7/99
2,000 m	4:44.79	Hicham el-Guerrouj (Morocco)	9/7/99
3,000m	7:20.67	Daniel Komen (Kenya)	9/1/96
Steeplechase	7:55.72	Bernard Barmasai (Kenya)	8/24/97
5,000 m	12:39.36	Haile Gebrselassie (Ethiopia)	6/13/98
10,000 m	26:22.75	Haile Gebrselassie (Ethiopia)	6/1/98
Marathon	2:05:42	Khalid Khannouchi (Morocco)	10/24/99
110 m hurdles	12.91	Colin Jackson (U.K.)	8/20/93
400 m hurdles	46.78	Kevin Young (U.S.)	8/6/92
20 km walk	1:17:25.60	Bernardo Segura (Mexico)	5/7/94
50 km walk	3:40:57.90	Thierry Toutain (France)	9/29/96
4 x 100m	37.40	United States	8/8/92
	37.40	United States	8/21/93
4x200m	1:18.68	Santa Monica Track Club (US)	4/17/94
4 x 400m	2:54.20	United States	7/22/98

Event	Meters	Ft./In.	Recordholder (country)	Date
High jump	2.45	8–0.5	Javier Sotomayor (Cuba)	7/27/93
Pole vault	6.14	20–1.75	Sergey Bubka (Ukraine)	7/31/94
Long jump	8.95	29–4.5	Mike Powell (U.S.)	8/30/91
Triple jump	18.29	60–0	Jonathan Edwards (Britain)	8/7/95
Shot put	23.12	75–10.25	Randy Barnes (U.S.)	5/20/90
Discus	74.08	243–0	Jurgen Schult (E. Germany)	6/6/86
Hammer	86.74	284–7	Yuriy Syedikh (USSR)	8/30/86
Javelin	98.48	323–1	Jan Zelezny (Czech Rep.)	5/25/96
Decathlon		9,026 points	Roman Sebrle (Czech Rep.)	5/27/01

MEN, INDOOR

Event	(min./sec.)	Record holder (country)	Date
50m	5.56	Donovan Bailey (Canada)	2/6/96
60m	6.39	Maruice Green (U.S.)	2/3/98
200m	19.92	Frank Fredericks (Namibia)	2/18/96
400m	44.63	Michael Johnson (U.S.)	3/4/95
800m	1:42.67	Wilson Kipketer (Denmark)	3/9/97
1,000 m	2:14.96	Wilson Kipketer (Denmark)	2/20/00
1,500 m	3:31.18	Hicham el-Guerrouj (Morocco)	2/2/97
Mile	3:48.45	Hicham el-Guerrouj (Morocco)	2/12/97
3,000 m	7:24.90	Daniel Komen (Kenya)	2/6/98
5,000 m	12:50.38	Haile Gebrselassie (Ethiopia)	2/14/99
50 m hurdles	6.25	Mark McKoy (Canada)	3/5/86
60 m hurdles	7.30	Colin Jackson (Great Britain)	3/6/94
5,000 m walk	18:07.08	Mikhail Shchennikov (Russia)	2/14/95
4 x 200 m	1:22.11	Great Britain	3/3/91
4 x 400 m	3:02.83	United States	3/7/99
4 x 800 m	7:13.94	United States	2/6/00

Event	Meters	Ft./In.	Recordholder (country)	Date
High jump	2.43	7–11.5	Javier Sotomayor (Cuba)	3/4/89
Pole vault	6.15	20–2	Sergey Bubka (Ukraine)	2/21/93
Long jump	8.79	28–10.25	Carl Lewis (U.S.)	1/27/84
Triple jump	17.83	58–6	Eliecer Urrutia (Cuba)	3/1/97
Shot put	22.66	74–4.25	Randy Barnes (U.S.)	1/20/89
Heptathlon		6,476 points	Dan O' Brien (U.S.)	3/14/93

WOMEN, OUTDOOR

Event	(min./sec.)	Record holder (country)	Date
100 m	10.49	Florence Griffith Joyner (U.S.)	7/16/88
200 m	21.34	Florence Griffith Joyner (U.S.)	9/29/88
400 m	47.60	Marita Koch (E. Germany)	10/6/85
800 m	1:53.28	Jarmila Kratochvilova (Czech.)	7/26/83
1,000 m	2:28.98	Svetlana Masterkova (Russia)	8/23/96
1,500 m	3:50.46	Yunxia Qu (China)	9/11/93
Mile	4:12.56	Svetlana Masterkova (Russia)	8/14/96
2,000 m	5:25.36	Sonia O'Sullivan (Ireland)	7/9/94
3,000 m	8:06.11	Junxia Wang (China)	9/13/93
5,000 m	14:28.09	Bo Jiang (China)	10/23/97
10,000 m	29:31.78	Junxia Wang (China)	9/8/93
Marathon	2:20:43	Tegla Loroupe (Kenya)	9/26/99
100 m hurdles	12.21	Yordanka Donkova (Bulgaria)	8/20/88
400 m hurdles	52.61	Kim Batten (U.S.)	8/11/95
5 km walk	20:13.26	Kerry Saxby (Australia)	2/25/96
10 km walk	41:56.23	Nadezhda Ryashkina (USSR)	7/4/90
4 x 100m	41.37	East Germany	10/6/85
4 x 200m	1:27.46	United States	4/29/00
4 x 400m	3:15.17	Soviet Union	10/1/88

Event	Meters	Ft./In.	Recordholder (country)	Date
High jump	2.09	6–10.25	Stefka Kostadinova (Bulgaria)	8/30/87
Pole vault	4.62	15–1	Stacy Dragila (U.S.)	5/27/00
Long jump	7.52	24–8.25	Galina Chistyakova (USSR)	6/11/88
Triple jump	15.50	50–10.25	Inessa Kravets (Ukraine)	7/10/95
Shot put	22.63	74–3	Natalya Lisovskaya (USSR)	6/7/87
Discus	76.80	252–0	Gabriele Reinsch (E. Germany)	7/9/88
Hammer	76.07	249-7.25	Michaela Melinte (Romania)	8/29/99
Javelin	80.00	262–5	Petra Felke (East Germany)	9/9/88
Heptathlon		7,291 points	Jackie Joyner-Kersee (U.S.)	9/24/88

WOMEN, INDOOR

Event	(min./sec.)	Record holder (country)	Date
50 m	5.96	Irina Privalova (Russia)	2/9/95
60 m	6.92	Irina Privalova (Russia)	2/9/95
200 m	21.87	Merlene Ottey (Jamaica)	2/13/93
400 m	49.59	Jarmila Kratochvilova (Czech.)	3/7/82
800 m	1:56.40	Christine Wachtel (E. Germany)	2/13/88
1,000 m	2:30.94	Maria Mutola (Mozambique)	2/25/99
1,500 m	4:00.27	Doina Melinte (Romania)	2/9/90
Mile	4:17.14	Doina Melinte (Romania)	2/9/90
3,000 m	8:32.88	Gabriela Szabo (Romania)	2/18/01
5,000 m	14:47.35	Gabriela Szabo (Romania)	2/13/99
50 m hurdles	6.58	Cornelia Oschkenat (E. Germany)	2/20/88
60 m hurdles	7.69	Lyudmila Narozhilenko (USSR)	2/4/90
3,000 m walk	11:40.33	Claudia Iovan (Romania)	1/30/99
4 x 200 m	1:32.55	Germany	2/21/99
4 x 400 m	3:24.25	Russia	3/7/99
4x800m	8:18.71	Russia	2/4/94

Event	Meters	Ft./In.	Record Holder (country)	Date
High jump	2.07	6–9.5	Heike Henkel (Germany)	2/8/92
Pole vault	4.70	15-5	Stacy Dragila (U.S.)	2/17/01
Long jump	7.37	24–2.25	Heike Drechsler (E. Germany)	2/13/88
Triple jump	15.16	49–8.75	Ashia Hansen (Britain)	2/28/98
Shot put	22.50	73–10	Helena Fibingerova (Czech.)	2/19/77
Pentathlon		4,991 points	Irina Belova (Unified Team)	2/15/92

Source: International Amateur Athletic Federation.

Olympic Sports

The 2000 Summer Olympics at Sydney, Australia
September 15–October 1, 2000

Event	Gold	Silver	Bronze
ARCHERY, MEN			
Individual	Simon Fairweather, Australia	Victor Wunderle, United States	Wietsevan Alten, Netherlands
Team	Korea	Italy	United States
ARCHERY, WOMEN			
Individual	Mi-Jin Yun, South Korea	Nam-Soon Kim, South Korea	Soo-Nyung Kim, South Korea
Team	Korea	Ukraine	Germany
BADMINTON			
Men's Singles	Xinpeng Ji, China	Hendrawan, Indonesia	Xuanze Xia, China
Men's Doubles	Indonesia	South Korea	South Korea
Women's Singles	Zhichao Gong, China	Camilla Martin, Denmark	Zhaoying Ye, China
Women's Doubles	China	China	China
Mixed Doubles	China	Indonesia	Great Britain
BASEBALL	United States	Cuba	Korea
BASKETBALL,			
Men	United States	France	Lithuania
Women	United States	Australia	Brazil
BOXING			
Light Flyweight 48 kg (106 lbs.)	Brahim Asloum, France	Rafael Lozano Muñoz, Spain	Un Chol Kim, North Korea/ Maikro Romero Esquirol, Cuba
Flyweight 51 kg (112 lbs.)	Wijan Ponlid, Thailand	Bulat Jumadilov, Kazakhstan	Vladimir Sidorenko, Ukraine/ Jerome Thomas, France
Bantamweight 54 kg (119 lbs.)	Guillermo Rigondeaux Ortiz, Cuba	Raimkoul Malakhbekov, Russia	Serguey Daniltchenko, Ukraine/ Clarence Vinson, United States
Featherweight 57 kg (126 lbs.)	Bekzat Sattarkhanov, Kazakhstan	Ricardo Juarez, United States	Kamil Dzamalutdinov, Russia/ Tahar Tamsamani, Morocco
Lightweight 60 kg (132 lbs.)	Mario Kindelan, Cuba	Andriy Kotelnyk, Ukraine	Cristian Bejarano Benitez, Mexico/ Alexandr Maletin, Russia
Light Welterweight 63.5 kg (140 lbs.)	Mahamadkadyz Abdullaev, Uzbekistan	Ricardo Williams, United States	Mohamed Allalou, Algeria/ Diogenes Luna Martinez, Cuba
Welterweight 67 kg (148 lbs.)	Oleg Saitov, Russia	Sergey Dotsenko, Ukraine	Vitalii Grusac, Moldova/ Dorel Simion, Romania
Light Middleweight 71 kg (156 lbs.)	Yermakhan Ibraimov, Kazakhstan	Marin Simion, Romania	Jermain Taylor, United States/ Pornchai Thongburan, Thailand
Middleweight 75 kg (165 lbs.)	Jorge Gutierrez, Cuba	Gaidarbek Gaidarbekov, Russia	Vugar Alekperov, Azerbaijan/ Zsolt Erdei, Hungary
Light Heavyweight 81 kg (179 lbs.)	Alexander Lebziak, Russia	Rudolf Kraj, Czech Republic	Andri Fedtchouk, Ukraine/ Sergei Mikhailov, Uzbekistan
Heavyweight 91 kg (201 lbs.)	Felix Savon, Cuba	Sultanahmed Ibzagimov, Russia	Sebastian Kober, Germany/ Vladimir Tchantouria, Georgia
Super Heavyweight 91+ kg (201+ lbs.)	Audley Harrison, Great Britain	Mukhtarkhan Dildabekov, Kazakhstan	Rustam Saidov, Uzbekistan/ Paolo Vidoz, Italy
CANOE/KAYAK, MEN			
Canoe 500m singles	Gyorgy Kolonics, Hungary	Maksim Opalev, Russia	Andreas Dittmer, Germany
Canoe 1,000m singles	Andreas Dittmer, Germany	Ledys Frank Balceiro, Cuba	Steve Giles, Canada
Canoe 500m pairs	Hungary	Poland	Romania
Canoe 1,000m pairs	Romania	Cuba	Germany
Canoe slalom singles	Tony Estanguet, France	Michal Martikan, Slovakia	Juraj Mincik, Slovakia
Canoe slalom pairs	Slovakia	Poland	Czech Republic
Kayak 500m singles	Knut Holmann, Norway	Petar Merkov, Bulgaria	Michael Kolganov, Israel
Kayak 1,000m singles	Knut Holmann, Norway	Petar Merkov, Bulgaria	Tim Brabants, Great Britain
Kayak 500m pairs	Hungary	Australia	Germany
Kayak 1,000m pairs	Italy	Sweden	Hungary
Kayak 1,000m fours	Hungary	Germany	Poland
Kayak slalom singles	Thomas Schmidt, Germany	Paul Ratcliffe, Great Britain	Pierpaolo Ferrazzi, Italy

Event	Gold	Silver	Bronze
KAYAK, WOMEN			
500 meter singles	Josefa Idem Guerrini, Italy	Caroline Brunet, Canada	Katrin Borchert, Australia
500 meter pairs	Germany	Hungary	Poland
500 meter fours	Germany	Hungary	Romania
Slalom singles	Stepanka Hilgertova, Czech Republic	Brigitte Guibal, France	Anne-Lise Bardet, France
CYCLING, MEN			
Road race	Jan Ullrich, Germany	Alexandre Vinokourov, Kazakhstan	Andreas Kloeden, Germany
Road time trial	Viacheslav Ekimov, Russia	Jan Ullrich, Germany	Lance Armstrong, United States
Ikm time trial	Jason Queally, Great Britain	Stefan Nimke, Germany	Shane Kelly, Australia
Individual pursuit	Robert Bartko, Germany	Jens Lehmann, Germany	Brad McGee, Australia
Team pursuit	Germany	Ukraine	Great Britain
Sprint	Marty Nothstein, U.S.	Florian Rousseau, France	Jens Fiedler, Germany
Olympic sprint	France	Great Britain	Australia
Points race	Juan Llaneras, Spain	Miolton Wynants, Uruguay	Alexey Markov, Russia
Madison 60-km relay	Australia	Belgium	Italy
Keirin	Florian Rousseau, France	Gary Neiwand, Australia	Jens Fiedler, Germany
Mountain bike	Miguel Martinez, France	Filip Meirhaeghe, Belgium	Christoph Sauser, Switzerland
CYCLING, WOMEN			
Road race	Leontien Zijlaard, Netherlands	Hanka Kupfernagel, Germany	Diana Ziliute, Lithuania
Road time trial	Leontien Zijlaard, Netherlands	Mari Holden, United States	Jeannie Longo-Ciprelli, France
500-meter time trial	Felicia Ballanger, France	Michelle Ferris, Australia	Cuihua Jiang, China
Individual pursuit (3,000 meters)	Leontien Zijlaard, Netherlands	Marion Clignet, France	Yvonne McGregor, Great Britain
Sprint	Felicia Ballanger, France	Oxana Grichina, Russia	Iryna Yanovych, Ukraine
Points race	Antonella Bellutti, Italy	Leontien Zijlaard, Netherlands	Olga Slioussareva, Russia
Mountain bike	Paola Pezzo, Italy	Barbara Blatter, Switzerland	Margarita Fullana, Spain
DIVING, MEN			
Platform	Liang Tian, China	Jia Hu, China	Dmitri Saoutine, Russia
Springboard	Ni Xiong, China	Fernando Platas, Mexico	Dmitri Saoutine, Russia
Synchronized platform	Russia	China	Germany
Synchronized springboard	China	Russia	Australia
DIVING, WOMEN			
Platform	Laura Wilkinson, U.S.	Na Li, China	Anne Montminy, Canada
Springboard	Mingxia Fu, China	Jingjing Guo, China	Doerte Lindner, Germany
Synchronized platform	China	Canada	Australia
Synchronized springboard	Russia	China	Ukraine
EQUESTRIAN			
Individual 3-day event	David O'Connor, U.S.	Andrew Hoy, Australia	Mark Todd, New Zealand
Individual dressage	Anky van Grunsven, Netherlands	Isabell Werth, Germany	Ulla Salzberger, Germany
Individual jumping	Jeroen Dubbeldam, Netherlands	Albert Voorn, Netherlands	Khaled Aleid, Saudi Arabia
Team 3-day event	Australia	Great Britain	United States
Team dressage	Germany	Netherlands	United States
Team jumping	Germany	Switzerland	Brazil
FENCING, MEN			
Individual epee	Pavel Kolobkov, Russia	Hugues Obry, France	Sang-Ki Lee, South Korea
Individual foil	Young-Ho Kim, Korea	Ralf Bissdorf, Germany	Dmitri Chevtchenko, Russia
Individual sabre	Mihai Claudiu Covaliu, Romania	Mathieu Gourdain, France	Wiradech Kothny, Germany
Team epee	Italy	France	Cuba
Team foil	France	China	Italy
Team sabre	Russia	France	Germany
FENCING, WOMEN			
Individual epee	Timea Nagy, Hungary	Gianna Habluetzel-Buerki, Switzerland	Laura Flessel-Colovic, France
Individual foil	Valentina Vezzali, Italy	Rita Koenig, Germany	Giovanna Trillini, Italy
Team epee	Russia	Switzerland	China
Team foil	Italy	Poland	Germany

Event	Gold	Silver	Bronze

FIELD HOCKEY

Event	Gold	Silver	Bronze
Men	Netherlands	South Korea	Australia
Women	Australia	Argentina	Netherlands

GYMNASTICS, MEN

Event	Gold	Silver	Bronze
Individual all-around	Alexei Nemov, Russia	Wei Yang, China	Oleksandr Beresh, Ukraine
Floor exercise	Igors Vihrovs, Latvia	Alexei Nemov, Russia	Iordan Iovtchev, Bulgaria
Horizontal bar	Alexei Nemov, Russia	Benjamin Varonian, France	Joo-Hyung Lee, S. Korea
Parallel bars	Xiaopeng Li, China	Joo-Hyung Lee, S. Korea	Alexei Nemov, Russia
Pommel horse	Marius Urzica, Romania	Eric Poujade, France	Alexei Nemov, Russia
Rings	Szilveszter Csollany, Hungary	Dimosthenis Tampakos, Greece	Iordan Iovtchev, Bulgaria
Trampoline	Alexandre Moskalenko, Russia	Ji Wallace, Australia	Mathieu Turgeon, Canada
Vault	Gervasio Deferr, Spain	Alexey Bondarenko, Russia	Leszek Blanik, Poland
Team	China	Ukraine	Russia

GYMNASTICS, WOMEN

Event	Gold	Silver	Bronze
Individual all-around	Simona Amanar, Romania*	Maria Olaru, Romania	Xuan Liu, Romania
Balance beam	Xuan Liu, China	Ekaterina Lobazniouk, Russia	Elena Prodounova, Russia
Floor exercise	Elena Zamolodtchikova, Russia	Svetlana Khorkina, Russia	Simona Amanar, Romania
Trampoline	Irina Karavaeva, Russia	Oxana Tsyhuleva, Ukraine	Karen Cockburn, Canada
Uneven bars	Svetlana Khorkina, Russia	Jie Ling, China	Yun Yang, China
Vault	Elena Zamolodtchikova, Russia	Andreea Raducan, Romania	Ekaterina Lobazniouk, Russia
Team	Romania	Russia	China
Rhythmic, individual	Yulia Barsukova, Russia	Yulia Raskina, Belarus	Alina Kabaeva, Russia
Rhythmic, group	Russia	Belarus	Greece

HANDBALL

Event	Gold	Silver	Bronze
Men	Russia	Sweden	Spain
Women	Denmark	Hungary	Norway

JUDO, MEN

Event	Gold	Silver	Bronze
Extra lightweight 60 kg (132 lbs.)	Tadahiro Nomura, Japan	Bu-Kyung Jung, South Korea	Manolo Poulot, Cuba/ Aidyn Smagulov, Kyrgyzstan
Half lightweight 66 kg (145 lbs.)	Huseyin Ozkan, Turkey	Larbi Benboudaoud France	Giroalmo Giovinazzo, Italy/ Georgi Vazagashvilli, Georgia
Lightweight 73 kg (161 lbs.)	Giuseppe Maddaloni, Italy	Tiago Camilo, Brazil	Anatoly Laryukov, Belarus/ Vsevolods Zelonijs, Latvia
Half middleweight 81 kg (178 lbs.)	Makoto Takimoto, Japan	In-Chul Cho, South Korea	Aleksei Budolin, Estonia/ Nuno Delgado, Portugal
Middleweight 90 kg (198 lbs.)	Mark Huizinga, Netherlands	Carlos Honorato, Brazil	Frederic Demontfaucon, France/ Ruslan Mashurenko, Ukraine
Half heavyweight 100 kg (220 lbs.)	Kosei Inoue, Japan	Nicolas Gill, Canada	Iouri Stepkine, Russia/ Stephane Traineau, France
Heavyweight 100+ kg (220+ lbs.)	David Douillet, France	Shinichi Shinohara, Japan	Indrek Pertelson, Estonia/ Tamerlan Tmenov, Russia

JUDO, WOMEN

Event	Gold	Silver	Bronze
Extra lightweight 48 kg (106 lbs.)	Ryoko Tamura, Japan	Lioubov Brouletova, Russia	Anna-Maria Gradante, Germany/ Ann Simons, Belgium
Half lightweight 52 kg (114 lbs.)	Legna Verdecia, Cuba	Noriko Narazaki, Japan	Sun Hui Kye, N. Korea and Yuxiang Liu, China
Lightweight 57 kg (125 lbs.)	Isabel Fernandez, Spain	Driulys Gonzalez, Cuba	Kie Kusakabe, Japan/ Maria Pekli, Australia
Half middleweight 63 kg (139 lbs.)	Severine Vandenhende, France	Shufang Li, China	Sung-Sook Jung, South Korea/ Gella Vandecaveye, Belgium
Middleweight 70 kg (154 lbs.)	Sibelis Veranes, Cuba	Kate Howey, Great Britain	Min-Sun Cho, South Korea/ Ylenia Scapin, Italy
Half heavyweight 78 kg (172 lbs.)	Lin Tang, China	Celine Lebrun, France	Emanuela Pierantozzi, Italy/ Simona Richter, Romania
Heavyweight 78+ kg (172+ lbs.)	Hua Yuan, China	Daima Mayelis Beltran, Cuba	Seon-Young Kim, South Korea/ Mayumi Yamashita, Japan

MODERN PENTATHLON

Event	Gold	Silver	Bronze
Men	Dmitry Svatkovsky, Russia	Gabor Balogh, Hungary	Pavel Dovgal, Belarus
Women	Stephanie Cook, Great Britain	Emily deRiel, United States	Kate Allenby, Great Britain

Event	Gold	Silver	Bronze

ROWING, MEN

Event	Gold	Silver	Bronze
Single sculls	Rob Waddell, New Zealand	Xeno Mueller, Switzerland	Marcel Hacker, Germany
Double sculls	Slovenia	Norway	Italy
Ltwght. double sculls	Poland	Italy	France
Pair w/o coxswain	France	United States	Australia
Quad sculls	Italy	Netherlands	Germany
Four w/o coxswain	Great Britain	Italy	Australia
Ltwght. fours w/o cox	France	Australia	Denmark
Eights	Great Britain	Australia	Croatia

ROWING, WOMEN

Event	Gold	Silver	Bronze
Single sculls	Ekaterina Karsten, Belarus	Rumyana Neykova, Bulgaria	Katrin Rutschow-Stomporowski, Germany
Double sculls	Germany	Netherlands	Lithuania
Ltwght. double sculls	Romania	Germany	United States
Pair w/o coxswain	Romania	Australia	United States
Quad sculls	Germany	Great Britain	Russia
Eights	Romania	Netherlands	Canada

SAILING

Event	Gold	Silver	Bronze
Men's 470	Australia	United States	Argentina
Men's Finn	Iain Percy, Great Britain	Luca Devoti, Italy	Fredrik Loof, Sweden
Men's Mistral	Christoph Sieber, Austria	Carlos Espinola, Argentina	Aaron McIntosh, New Zealand
Women's 470	Australia	United States	Ukraine
Women's Europe	Shirley Robertson, Great Britain	Margriet Matthysse, Netherlands	Serena Amato, Argentina
Women's Mistral	Alessandra Sensini, Italy	Amelie Lux, Germany	Barbara Kendall, New Zealand
Open 49er	Finland	Great Britain	United States
Open Laser	Ben Ainslie, Great Britain	Robert Scheidt, Brazil	Michael Blackburn, Australia
Open Soling	Denmark	Germany	Norway
Open Star	United States	Great Britain	Brazil
Open Tornado Class	Austria	Australia	Germany

SHOOTING, MEN

Event	Gold	Silver	Bronze
10-m air pistol	Franck Dumoulin, France	Yifu Wang, China	Igor Basinsky, Belarus
25-m rapid-fire pistol	Serguei Alifirenko, Russia	Michel Ansermet, Switzerland	Iulian Raicea, Romania
50-m pistol	Tanyu Kiriakov, Bulgaria	Igor Basinsky, Belarus	Martin Tenk, Czech Republic
10-m running target	Ling Yang, China	Oleg Moldovan, Moldova	Zhiyuan Niu, China
10-m air rifle	Yalin Cai, China	Artem Khadjibekov, Russia	Evgueni Aleinikov, Russia
50-m rifle, 3 positions	Rajmond Debevec, Slovenia	Juha Hirvi, Finland	Harald Stenvaag, Norway
50-m rifle, prone pos.	Jonas Edman, Sweden	Torben Grimmel, Denmark	Sergei Martynov, Belarus
Trap	Michael Diamond, Australia	Ian Peel, Great Britain	Giovanni Pellielo, Italy
Double trap	Richard Faulds, Great Britain	Russell Mark, Australia	Fehaid al-Deehani, Kuwait
Skeet	Mykola Milchev, Ukraine	Petr Malek, Czech Republic	James Graves, United States

SHOOTING, WOMEN

Event	Gold	Silver	Bronze
10-m air pistol	Luna Tao, China	Jasna Sekaric, Yugoslavia	Annemarie Forder, Australia
25-m pistol	Maria Grozdeva, Bulgaria	Luna Tao, China	Lolita Evglevskaya, Belarus
10-m air rifle	Nancy Johnson, U.S.	Cho-Hyun Kang, S. Korea	Jing Gao, China
50-m rifle, 3 positions	Renata Mauer-Rozanska, Poland	Tatiana Goldobina, Russia	Maria Feklistova, Russia
Trap	Daina Gudzineviciute, Lithuania	Delphine Racinet, France	E Gao, China
Double trap	Pia Hansen, Sweden	Deborah Gelisio, Italy	Kim Rhode, United States
Skeet	Zemfira Meftakhetdinova, Azerbaijan	Svetlana Demina, Russia	Diana Igaly, Hungary

SOCCER

Event	Gold	Silver	Bronze
Men	Cameroon	Spain	Chile
Women	Norway	United States	Germany

SOFTBALL

Event	Gold	Silver	Bronze
SOFTBALL	United States	Japan	Australia

SWIMMING, MEN

Event	Gold	Silver	Bronze
50-meter freestyle	(tie) Anthony Ervin, United States, and Gary Hall Jr., United States, 21.98		Pieter van den Hoogenband, Netherlands, 22.03
100-meter freestyle	Pieter van den Hoogenband, Netherlands, 48.30	Alexander Popov, Russia, 48.69	Gary Hall Jr., United States, 48.73
200-meter freestyle	Pieter van den Hoogenband, Netherlands, 1:45.35	Ian Thorpe, Australia, 1:45.83	Massimiliano Rosolino, Italy, 1:46.65

Event	Gold	Silver	Bronze
400-meter freestyle	Ian Thorpe, Australia, 3:40.59	Massimiliano Rosolino, Italy, 3:43.40	Klete Keller, United States, 3:47.00
1,500-meter freestyle	Grant Hackett, Australia, 14:48.33	Kieren Perkins, Australia, 14:53.59	Chris Thompson, United States, 14:56.81
100-meter backstroke	Lenny Krayzelburg, United States, 53.72	Matthew Welsh, Australia, 54.07	Stev Theloke, Germany, 54.82
200-meter backstroke	Lenny Krayzelburg, United States, 1:56.76	Aaron Peirsol, United States, 1:57.35	Matthew Welsh, Australia, 1:57.59
100-meter breaststroke	Domenico Fioravanti, Italy, 1:00.46	Ed Moses, United States, 1:00.73	Roman Sloudnov, Russia, 1:00.91
200-meter breaststroke	Domenico Fioravanti, Italy, 2:10.87	Terence Parkin, South Africa, 2:12.50	Davide Rummolo, Italy, 2:12.73
100-meter butterfly	Lars Froelander, Sweden, 52.00	Michael Klim, Australia, 52.18	Geoff Huegill, Australia, 52.22
200-meter butterfly	Tom Malchow, United States, 1:55.35	Denys Sylant'yev, Ukraine, 1:55.76	Justin Norris, Australia, 1:56.17
200-meter individual medley	Massimiliano Rosolino, Italy, 1:58.98	Tom Dolan, United States, 1:59.77	Tom Wilkens, United States, 2:00.87
400-meter individual medley	Tom Dolan, United States, 4:11.76	Erik Vendt, United States, 4:14.23	Curtis Myden, Canada, 4:15.33
4x100m medley relay	United States, 3:33.73	Australia, 3:35.27	Germany, 3:35.88
4x100m free relay	Australia, 3:13.67	United States, 3:13.86	Brazil, 3:17.40
4x200m free relay	Australia, 7:07.05	United States, 7:12.64	Netherlands, 7:12.70

SWIMMING, WOMEN

Event	Gold	Silver	Bronze
50-meter freestyle	Inge de Bruijn, Netherlands, 24.32	Therese Alshammar, Sweden, 24.51	Dara Torres, United States, 24.63
100-meter freestyle	Inge de Bruijn, Netherlands, 53.83	Therese Alshammar Sweden, 54.33	(tie) Jenny Thompson, U.S. & Dara Torres, U.S. 54.43
200-meter freestyle	Susie O'Neill, Australia, 1:58.24	Martina Moravcova, Slovakia, 1:58.32	Claudia Poll, Costa Rica, 1:58.81
400-meter freestyle	Brooke Bennett, United States, 4:05.80	Diana Munz, United States, 4:07.07	Claudia Poll, Costa Rica, 4:07.83
800-meter freestyle	Brooke Bennett, United States, 8:19.67	Yana Klochkova, Ukraine, 8:22.66	Kaitlin Sandeno, United States, 8:24.29
100-meter backstroke	Diana Mocanu, Romania, 1:00.21	Mai Nakamura, Japan, 1:00.55	Nina Zhivanevskaya, Spain, 1:00.89
200-meter backstroke	Diana Mocanu, Romania, 2:08.16	Roxana Maracineanu, France, 2:10.25	Miki Nakao, Japan, 2:11.05
100-meter breaststroke	Megan Quann, United States, 1:07.05	Leisel Jones, Australia, 1:07.49	Penny Heyns, South Africa, 1:07.55
200-meter breaststroke	Agnes Kovacs, Hungary, 2:24.35	Kristy Kowal, United States, 2:24.56	Amanda Beard, United States, 2:25.35
100-meter butterfly	Inge de Bruijn, Netherlands, 56.61	Martina Moravcova, Slovakia, 57.97	Dara Torres, United States, 58.20
200-meter butterfly	Misty Hyman, United States, 2:05.88	Susie O'Neill, Australia, 2:06.58	Petria Thomas, Australia, 2:07.12
200-meter individual medley	Yana Klochkova, Ukraine, 2:10.68,	Beatrice Caslaru, Romania, 2:12.57	Cristina Teuscher, United States, 2:13.32
400-meter individual medley	Yana Klochkova, Ukraine, 4:33.59	Yasuko Tajima, Japan, 4:35.96	Beatrice Caslaru, Romania, 4:37.18
4x100m medley relay	United States, 3:58.30	Australia, 4:01.59	Japan, 4:04.16
4x100m free relay	United States, 3:36.61	Netherlands, 3:39.83	Sweden, 3:40.30
4x200m free relay	United States, 7:57.80	Australia, 7:58.52	Germany, 7:58.64
Synchronized, duet	Russia	Japan	France
Synchronized, team	Russia	Japan	Canada

TABLE TENNIS

Event	Gold	Silver	Bronze
Men's singles	Linghui Kong, China	Jan-Ove Waldner, Sweden	Guoliang Liu, China
Men's doubles	China	China	France
Women's singles	Nan Wang, China	Ju Li, China	Jing Chen, Taiwan
Women's doubles	China	China	South Korea

TAEKWONDO, MEN

Event	Gold	Silver	Bronze
58 kg (128 lbs.)	Michail Mouroutsos, Greece	Gabriel Esparza, Spain	Chih-Hsiung Huang, Taiwan
68 kg (150 lbs.)	Steven Lopez, United States	Joon-Sik Sin, South Korea	Hadi Saeibonehkohal, Iran
80 kg (176 lbs.)	Angel Valodia Matos Fuentes, Cuba	Faissal Ebnoutalib, Germany	Victor Manuel Estrada Garibay, Mexico
80+ kg (176+ lbs.)	Kyong-Hun Kim, South Korea	Daniel Trenton, Australia	Pascal Gentil, France

Event	Gold	Silver	Bronze
TAEKWONDO, WOMEN			
49 kg (108 lbs.)	Lauren Burns, Australia	Urbia M. Rodriguez, Cuba	Shu-Ju Chi, Taiwan
57 kg (126 lbs.)	Jae-Eun Jung, South Korea	Hieu Ngan Tran, Vietnam	Hamide Bikcin, Turkey
67 kg (148 lbs.)	Sun-Hee Lee, South Korea	Trude Gundersen, Norway	Yoriko Okamoto, Japan
67+ kg (148+ lbs.)	Zhong Chen, China	Natalia Ivanova, Russia	Dominique Bosshart, Canada
TENNIS			
Men's Singles	Yevgeny Kafelnikov, Russia	Tommy Haas, Germany	Arnaud Di Pasquale, France
Men's Doubles	Sebastien Lareau/Daniel Nestor, Canada	Todd Woodbridge/Mark Woodforde, Australia	Alex Corretja/Alberto Costa, Spain
Women's Singles	Venus Williams, United States	Elena Dementieva, Russia	Monica Seles, United States
Women's Doubles	Serena and Venus Williams, United States	Kristie Boogert/ Miriam Oremans, Netherlands	Els Callens/Dominique van Roost, Belgium
TRACK & FIELD, MEN			
100 meters	Maurice Greene, United States, 9.87	Ato Boldon, Trinidad & Tobago, 9.99	Obadele Thompson, Barbados, 10.04
200 meters	Konstantinos Kenteris, Greece, 20.09	Darren Campbell, Great Britain, 20.14	Ato Boldon, Trinidad & Tobago, 20.20
400 meters	Michael Johnson, United States, 43.84	Alvin Harrison, United States, 44.40	Gregory Haughton, Jamaica, 44.70
800 meters	Nils Schumann, Germany, 1:45.08	Wilson Kipketer, Denmark, 1:45.14	Aissa Djabir Said-Guerni, Algeria, 1:45.16
1,500 meters	Noah Ngeny, Kenya, 3:32.07	Hicham El-Guerrouj, Morocco, 3:32.32	Bernard Lagat, Kenya, 3:32.44
5,000 meters	Millon Wolde, Ethiopia, 13:35.49	Ali Saidi-Sief, Algeria, 13:36.20	Brahim Lahlafi, Morocco, 13:36.47
10,000 meters	Haile Gebrselassie, Ethiopia, 27:18.20	Paul Tergat, Kenya, 27:18.29	Assefa Mezgebu, Ethiopia, 27:19.75
Marathon	Gezahgne Abera, Ethiopia, 2:10:11	Eric Wainaina, Kenya, 2:10:31	Tesfaye Tola, Ethiopia, 2:11:10
110-meter hurdles	Anier Garcia, Cuba, 13.00	Terrence Trammell, United States, 13.16	Mark Crear, United States, 13.22
400-meter hurdles	Angelo Taylor, United States, 47.50	Hadi Souan Somayli, Saudi Arabia, 47.53	Llewellyn Herbert, South Africa, 47.81
20 km walk	Robert Korzeniowski, Poland, 1:18:59	Noe Hernandez, Mexico, 1:19:03	Vladimir Andreyev, Russia, 1:19:27
50 km walk	Robert Korzeniowski, Poland, 3:42:22	Aigars Fadejevs, Latvia, 3:43:40	Joel Sanchez, Mexico, 3:44:36
3000 meter steeplechase	Reuben Kosgei, Kenya, 8:21.43	Wilson Kipketer, Kenya, 8:21.77	Ali Ezzine, Morocco, 8:22.15
4 x 100 meter relay	United States, 37.61	Brazil, 37.90	Cuba, 38.04
4 x 400 meter relay	United States, 2:56.35	Nigeria, 2:58.68	Jamaica, 2:58.78
Discus	Virgilijus Alekna, Lithuania, 69.30m	Lars Riedel, Germany, 68.50m	Frantz Krugermany, South Africa, 68.19m
Hammer throw	Szymon Ziolkowski, Poland, 80.02m	Nicola Vizzoni, Italy, 79.64m	Igor Astapkovich, Belarus, 79.17m
High jump	Sergey Kliugin, Russia, 2.35m	Javier Sotomayor, Cuba, 2.32m	Abderrahmane Hammad, Algeria, 2.32m
Javelin	Jan Zelezny, Czech Republic, 90.17m	Steve Backley, Great Britain, 89.85m	Sergey Makarov, Russia, 88.67m
Long jump	Ivan Pedroso, Cuba, 8.55m	Jai Taurima, Australia, 8.49m	Roman Schurenko, Ukraine, 8.31m
Pole vault	Nick Hysong, United States, 5.90m	Lawrence Johnson, United States, 5.90m	Maksim Tarasov, Russia, 5.90m
Shotput	Arsi Harju, Finland, 21.29m	Adam Nelson, United States, 21.21m	John Godina, United States, 21.20m
Triple jump	Jonathan Edwards, Great Britain, 17.71m	Yoel Garcia, Cuba, 17.47m	Denis Kapustin, Russia, 17.46m
Decathlon	Erki Nool, Estonia, 8,641 points	Roman Sebrle, Czech Republic, 8,606 points	Chris Huffins, United States, 8,595 points
TRACK & FIELD, WOMEN			
100 meters	Marion Jones, United States, 10.75	Ekaterini Thanou, Greece, 11.12	Tanya Lawrence, Jamaica, 11.18
200 meters	Marion Jones, United States, 21.84	Pauline Davis-Thompson, Bahamas, 22.27	Susanthika Jayasinghe, Sri Lanka, 22.28
400 meters	Cathy Freeman, Australia, 49.11	Lorraine Graham, Jamaica, 49.58	Katharine Merry, Great Britain, 49.72
800 meters	Maria Mutola, Mozambique, 1:56.15	Stephanie Graf, Austria, 1:56.64	Kelly Holmes, Great Britain, 1:56.80

Event	Gold	Silver	Bronze
1,500 meters	Nouria Merah-Bbenida, Algeria, 4:05.10	Violeta Szekely, Romania, 4:05.15	Gabriela Szabo, Romania, 4:05.27
5,000 meters	Gabriela Szabo, Romania, 14:40.79	Sonia O'Sullivan, Ireland, 14:41.02	Gete Wami, Ethiopia, 14:42.23
10,000 meters	Derartu Tulu, Ethiopia, 30:17.49	Gete Wami, Ethiopia, 30:22.48	Fernanda Ribeiro, Portugal, 30:22.88
Marathon	Naoko Takahashi, Japan, 2:23:14	Lidia Simon, Romania, 2:23:22	Joyce Chepchumba, Kenya, 2:24:45
100-meter hurdles	Olga Shishigina, Kazakhstan, 12.65	Glory Alozie, Nigeria, 12.68	Melissa Morrison, United States, 12.76
400-meter hurdles	Irina Privalova, Russia, 53.02	Deon Hemmings, Jamaica, 53.45	Nouzha Bidouane, Morocco, 53.57
20 km walk	Liping Wang, China, 1:29:05	Kjersti Plaetzer, Norway, 1:29:33	Maria Vasco, Spain, 1:30:23
4 x 100 meter relay	Bahamas, 41.95	Jamaica, 42.13	United States, 42.20
4 x 400 meter relay	United States, 3:22.62	Jamaica, 3:23.25	Russia, 3:23.46
Discus	Ellina Zvereva, Belarus, 68.40m	Anastasia Kelesidou, Greece, 65.71m	Irina Yatchenko, Belarus, 65.20m
Hammer throw	Kamila Skolimowska, Poland, 71.16m	Olga Kuzenkova, Russia, 69.77m	Kirsten Muenchow, Germany, 69.28m
High jump	Yelena Yelesina, Russia, 2.01m	Hestrie Cloete, South Africa, 2.01m	Kajsa Bergqvist, Sweden, 1.99m
Javelin	Trine Hattestad, Norway, 68.91m	Mirella Maniani-Tzelili, Greece, 67.51m	Osleidys Menendez, Cuba, 66.18m
Long jump	Heike Drechsler, Germany, 6.99m	Fiona May, Italy, 6.92m	Marion Jones, United States, 6.92m
Pole vault	Stacy Dragila, United States, 4.60m	Tatiana Grigorieva, Australia, 4.55m	Vala Flosadottir, Iceland, 4.50m
Shotput	Yanina Korolchik, Belarus, 20.56m	Larisa Peleshenko, Russia, 19.92m	Astrid Kumbernuss, Germany, 19.62m
Triple jump	Tereza Marinova, Bulgaria, 15.20m	Tatyana Lebedeva, Russia, 15.00m	Olena Hovorova, Ukraine, 14.96m
Heptathlon	Denise Lewis, Great Britain, 6,584 points	Yelena Prokhorova, Russia, 6,531 points	Natalya Sazanovich, Belarus, 6,527 points

TRIATHLON

	Gold	Silver	Bronze
Men	Simon Whitfield, Canada, 1:48:24.02	Stephan Vuckovic, Germany, 1:48:37.58	Jan Rehula, Czech Republic, 1:48:46.64
Women	Brigitte McMahon, Switzerland, 2:00:40.52	Michellie Jones, Australia, 2:00:42.55	Magali Messmer, Switzerland, 2:01:08.83

VOLLEYBALL

	Gold	Silver	Bronze
Men's Beach	United States	Brazil	Germany
Men's Indoor	Yugoslavia	Russia	Italy
Women's Beach	Australia	Brazil	Brazil
Women's Indoor	Cuba	Russia	Brazil

WATER POLO

	Gold	Silver	Bronze
Men	Hungary	Russia	Yugoslavia
Women	Australia	United States	Russia

WEIGHTLIFTING, MEN

	Gold	Silver	Bronze
56 kg (123 lbs)	Halil Mutlu, Turkey	Wenxiong Wu, China	Xiangxiang Zhang, China
62 kg (137 lbs)	Nikolay Pechalov, Croatia	Leonidas Sabanis, Greece	Gennady Oleshchuk, Belarus
69 kg (152 lbs)	Galabin Boevski, Bulgaria	Georgi Markov, Bulgaria	Sergei Lavrenov, Belarus
77 kg (170 lbs)	Xugang Zhan, China	Viktor Mitrou, Greece	Arsen Melikyan, Armenia
85 kg (187 lbs)	Pyrros Dimas, Greece	Marc Huster, Germany	George Asanidze, Georgia
94 kg (207 lbs)	Akakios Kakiasvilis, Greece	Szymon Kolecki, Poland	Alexei Petrov, Russia
105 kg (231.5 lbs)	Hossein Tavakoli, Iran	Alan Tsagaev, Bulgaria	Said S Asaad, Qatar
105+ kg (231.5+ lbs)	Hossein Rezazadeh, Iran	Ronny Weller, Germany	Ashot Danielyan, Armenia

WEIGHTLIFTING, WOMEN

	Gold	Silver	Bronze
48 kg (106 lbs.)	Tara Nott, United States	Raema Lisa Rumbewas, Indonesia	Sri Indriyani, Indonesia
53 kg (117 lbs)	Xia Yang, China	Feng-Ying Li, Taiwan	Winarni Binti Slamet, Indonesia
58 kg (128 lbs)	Soraya Jimenez Mendivil, Mexico	Song Hui Ri, North Korea	Khassaporn Suta, Thailand
63 kg (139 lbs)	Xiaomin Chen, China	Valentina Popova, Russia	Ioanna Chatziioannou, Greece
69 kg (152 lbs)	Weining Lin, China	Erzsebet Markus, Hungary	Karnam Malleswari, India
75 kg (165 lbs)	Maria Isabel Urrutia, Colombia	Ruth Ogbeifo, Nigeria	Yi-Hang Kuo, Taiwan
75+ kg (165+ lbs)	Meiyuan Ding, China	Agata Wrobel, Poland	Cheryl Haworth, United States

Event	Gold	Silver	Bronze

WRESTLING, FREESTYLE

Event	Gold	Silver	Bronze
54 kg (119 lbs)	Namig Abdullayev, Azerbaijan	Samuel Henson, United States	Amiran Karntanov, Greece
58 kg (128 lbs)	Alireza Dabir, Iran	Yevgen Buslovych, Ukraine	Terry Brands, United States
63 kg (139 lbs)	Mourad Oumakhanov, Russia	Serafim Barzakov, Bulgaria	Jae Sung Jang, South Korea
69 kg (152 lbs)	Daniel Igali, Canada	Arsen Gitinov, Russia	Lincoln Mcilravy, United States
76 kg (167.5 lbs)	Alexander Leipold, Germany	Brandon Slay, United States	Eui Jae Moon, South Korea
85 kg (187 lbs)	Adam Saitiev, Russia	Yoel Romero, Cuba	Mogamed Ibragimov, Macedonia
97 kg (214 lbs)	Saghid Mourtasaliyev, Russia	Islam Bairamukov, Kazakhstan	Eldar Kurtanidze, Georgia
130 kg (287 lbs)	David Moussoulbes, Russia	Artur Taymazov, Uzbekistan	Alexis Rodriguez, Cuba

WRESTLING, GRECO-ROMAN

Event	Gold	Silver	Bronze
54 kg (119 lbs)	Kwon Ho Sim, South Korea	Lazaro Rivas, Cuba	Yong Gyun Kang, North Korea
58 kg (128 lbs)	Armen Nazarian, Bulgaria	In-Sub Kim, South Korea	Zetian Sheng, China
63 kg (139 lbs)	Varteres Samourgachev, Russia	Juan Luis Maren, Cuba	Akaki Chachua, Georgia
69 kg (152 lbs)	Filiberto Azcuy, Cuba	Katsuhiko Nagata, Japan	Alexei Glouchkov, Russia
76 kg (167.5 lbs)	Mourat Kardanov, Russia	Matt Lindland, U.S.	Marko Yli-hannuksela, Finland
85 kg (187 lbs)	Hamza Yerlikaya, Turkey	Sandor Istvan Bardosi, Hungary	Mukhran Vakhtangadze, Georgia
97 kg (214 lbs)	Mikael Ljungberg, Sweden	Davyd Saldadze, Ukraine	Garrett Lowney, United States
130 kg (287 lbs)	Rulon Gardner, United States	Alexandre Kareline, Russia	Dmitry Debelka, Belarus

* Andreea Raducan of Romania placed first, but was later disqualified for using a cold medicine that contained a banned substance.

Medal Count by Nation, 2000

Country	Gold	Silver	Bronze	Total	Country	Gold	Silver	Bronze	Total
United States	39	25	33	97	Uzbekistan	1	1	2	4
Russia	32	28	28	88	Latvia	1	1	1	3
China	28	16	15	59	Yugoslavia	1	1	1	3
Australia	16	25	17	58	Bahamas	1	1	0	2
Germany	14	17	26	57	New Zealand	1	0	3	4
France	13	14	11	38	Estonia	1	0	2	3
Italy	13	8	13	34	Thailand	1	0	2	3
Netherlands	12	9	4	25	Croatia	1	0	1	2
Cuba	11	11	7	29	Cameroon	1	0	0	1
Great Britain	11	10	7	28	Colombia	1	0	0	1
Romania	11	6	9	26	Mozambique	1	0	0	1
South Korea	8	9	11	28	Brazil	0	6	6	12
Hungary	8	6	3	17	Jamaica	0	4	3	7
Poland	6	5	3	14	Nigeria	0	3	0	3
Japan	5	8	5	18	Belgium	0	2	3	5
Bulgaria	5	6	2	13	South Africa	0	2	3	5
Greece	4	6	3	13	Argentina	0	2	2	4
Sweden	4	5	3	12	Morocco	0	1	4	5
Norway	4	3	3	10	Taiwan	0	1	4	5
Ethiopia	4	1	3	8	North Korea	0	1	3	4
Ukraine	3	10	10	23	Saudi Arabia	0	1	1	2
Kazakhstan	3	4	0	7	Moldova	0	1	1	2
Belarus	3	3	11	17	Trinidad & Tobago	0	1	1	2
Canada	3	3	8	14	Ireland	0	1	0	1
Spain	3	3	5	11	Uruguay	0	1	0	1
Iran	3	0	1	4	Vietnam	0	1	0	1
Turkey	3	0	1	4	Georgia	0	0	6	6
Czech Republic	2	3	3	8	Costa Rica	0	0	2	2
Kenya	2	3	2	7	Portugal	0	0	2	2
Denmark	2	3	1	6	Armenia	0	0	1	1
Finland	2	1	1	4	Barbados	0	0	1	1
Austria	2	1	0	3	Chile	0	0	1	1
Lithuania	2	0	3	5	India	0	0	1	1
Azerbaijan	2	0	1	3	Iceland	0	0	1	1
Slovenia	2	0	0	2	Israel	0	0	1	1
Switzerland	1	6	2	9	Kyrgyzstan	0	0	1	1
Indonesia	1	3	2	6	Kuwait	0	0	1	1
Slovakia	1	3	1	5	Macedonia	0	0	1	1
Mexico	1	2	3	6	Qatar	0	0	1	1
Algeria	1	1	3	5	Sri Lanka	0	0	1	1

The Summer Olympics

Olympiad	Year	Place	Competitors		Nations represented	Events
			Men	Women		
I	1896	Athens, Greece	311	—	13	43
II	1900	Paris, France	1,319	11	21	85
III	1904	St. Louis, U.S.	681	6	13	96
IV	1908	London, U.K.	1,999	36	22	110
V	1912	Stockholm, Sweden	2,490	57	29	102
VI	1916	Berlin, Germany	—Canceled due to War—			
VII	1920	Antwerp, Belgium	2,543	64	29	152
VIII	1924	Paris, France	2,956	136	45	126
IX	1928	Amsterdam, Holland	2,724	290	46	109
X	1932	Los Angeles, U.S.	1,281	127	37	117
XI	1936	Berlin, Germany	3,738	328	49	129
XII[2]	1940	Tokyo, Japan	—Canceled due to War—			
XIII[2]	1944	London, Great Britain	—Canceled due to War—			
XIV	1948	London, Great Britain	3,714	385	59	136
XV	1952	Helsinki, Finland	4,407	518	69	149
XVI	1956	Melbourne, Australia	2,958	384	67	145
XVII	1960	Rome, Italy	4,738	610	84	150
XVIII	1964	Tokyo, Japan	4,457	683	94	163
XIX	1968	Mexico City, Mexico	4,750	781	113	172
XX	1972	Munich, W. Germany	6,659	1,171	122	195
XXI	1976	Montreal, Canada	4,915	1,274	93	198
XXII	1980	Moscow, USSR	4,265	1,192	81	203
XXIII	1984	Los Angeles, U.S.	5,458	1,620	140	221
XXIV	1988	Seoul, South Korea	7,105	2,438	160	237
XXV	1992	Barcelona, Spain	7,555	3,008	171	257
XXVI	1996	Atlanta, U.S.	7,006	3,684	197	271
XXVII	2000	Sydney, Australia	6,593	4,072	199	300
XXVIII	2004	Athens, Greece				
XXVIII	2008	Beijing, China				

Source: United States Olympic Committee.

The Winter Olympics

Olympiad	Year	Place	Competitors		Nations represented	Events
			Men	Women		
I	1924	Chamonix, France	281	13	16	13
II	1928	St. Moritz, Switzerland	366	27	25	13
III	1932	Lake Placid, U.S.	277	30	17	14
IV	1936	Garmisch-Partenkirchen, Germany	680	76	28	17
V	1948	St. Moritz, Switzerland	636	77	28	24
VI	1952	Oslo, Norway	624	108	30	22
VII	1956	Cortina D'Ampezzo, Italy	687	132	32	24
VIII	1960	Squaw Valley, U.S.	502	146	30	27
IX	1964	Innsbruck, Austria	758	175	36	34
X	1968	Grenoble, France	1,063	230	37	35
XI	1972	Sapporo, Japan	927	218	36	35
XII	1976	Innsbruck, Austria	1,013	248	37	37
XIII	1980	Lake Placid, U.S.	1,012	271	37	39
XIV	1984	Sarajevo, Yugoslavia	1,127	283	49	40
XV	1988	Calgary, Canada	1,270	364	57	46
XVI	1992	Albertville, France	1,313	488	64	57
XVII	1994	Lillehammer, Norway	1,216	522	66	61
XVIII	1998	Nagano, Japan	1,389	788	72	68
XIX	2002	Salt Lake City, Utah				

SUMMER OLYMPIC CHAMPIONS

Swimming and Diving, Men

50m Freestyle

		Time
1904	Zoltán Halmay, Hungary	0:28.00
1988	Matt Biondi, U.S.	0:22.14
1992	Aleksandr Popov, Unified Team	0:21.91
1996	Aleksandr Popov, Russia	0:22.13

100m Freestyle

		Time
1896	Alfréd Hajós, Hungary	1:22.20
1904	Zoltán Halmay, Hungary (100 yds.)	1:02.80
1908	Charles Daniels, U.S.	1:05.60
1912	Duke Paoa Kahanamoku, U.S.	1:03.40
1920	Duke Paoa Kahanamoku, U.S.	1:00.40

1924	Johnny Weissmuller, U.S.	0:59.00
1928	Johnny Weissmuller, U.S.	0:58.60
1932	Yasuji Miyazaki, Japan	0:58.20
1936	Ferenc Csík, Hungary	0:57.60
1948	Walter Ris, U.S.	0:57.30
1952	Clarke Scholes, U.S.	0:57.40
1956	Jon Henricks, Australia	0:55.40
1960	John Devitt, Australia	0:55.20
1964	Donald Schollander, U.S.	0:53.40
1968	Michael Wenden, Australia	0:52.20
1972	Mark Spitz, U.S.	0:51.22
1976	Jim Montgomery, U.S.	0:49.99
1980	Jörg Woithe, E. Germany	0:50.40
1984	Rowdy Gaines, U.S.	0:49.80
1988	Matt Biondi, U.S.	0:48.63
1992	Aleksandr Popov, Unified Team	0:49.02
1996	Aleksandr Popov, Russia	0:48.74

200m Freestyle		**Time**
1900	Frederick Lane, Austria	2:25.20
1904	Charles Daniels, U.S.	2:44.20
1968	Michael Wenden, Australia	1:55.20
1972	Mark Spitz, U.S.	1:52.78
1976	Bruce Furniss, U.S.	1:50.29
1980	Sergei Kopliakov, U.S.S.R.	1:49.81
1984	Michael Gross, W. Germany	1:47.44
1988	Duncan Armstrong, Australia	1:47.25
1992	Evgueni Sadovyi, Unified Team	1:46.70
1996	Danyon Loader, New Zealand	1:47.63

400m Freestyle		**Time**
1896	Paul Neumann, Austria (500m)	8:12.60
1904	Charles Daniels, U.S. (440 yds.)	6:16.20
1908	Henry Taylor, Great Britain (440 yds.)	5:36.80
1912	George Hodgson, Canada	5:24.40
1920	Norman Ross, U.S.	5:26.80
1924	Johnny Weissmuller, U.S.	5:04.20
1928	Alberto Zorilla, Argentina	5:01.60
1932	Clarence "Buster" Crabbe, U.S.	4:48.40
1936	Jack Medica, U.S.	4:44.50
1948	William Smith, U.S.	4:41.00
1952	Jean Boiteux, France	4:30.70
1956	Murray Rose, Australia	4:27.30
1960	Murray Rose, Australia	4:18.30
1964	Donald Schollander, U.S.	4:12.20
1968	Michael Burton, U.S.	4:09.00
1972	Bradford Cooper, Australia	4:00.27
1976	Brian Goodell, U.S.	3:51.93
1980	Vladimir Salnikov, U.S.S.R.	3:51.31
1984	George DiCarlo, U.S.	3:51.23
1988	Ewe Dassler, E. Germany	3:46.95
1992	Evgueni Sadovyi, Unified Team	3:45.00
1996	Danyon Loader, New Zealand	3:47.97

1,500m Freestyle		**Time**
1896	Alfréd Hajós, Hungary (1200m)	18:22.20
1900	John Arthur Jarvis, Great Britain (1,000 m)	13:40.20
1904	Emil Rausch, Germany (1,609 m)	27:18.20
1908	Henry Taylor, Great Britain	22:48.40
1912	George Hodgson, Canada	22:00.00
1920	Norman Ross, U.S.	22:23.20
1924	Andrew "Boy" Charlton, Australia	20:06.60
1928	Arne Borg, Sweden	19:51.80
1932	Kusuo Kitamura, Japan	19:12.40
1936	Noboru Terada, Japan	19:13.70
1948	James McLane, U.S.	19:18.50
1952	Ford Konno, U.S.	18:30.30
1956	Murray Rose, Australia	17:58.90
1960	John Konrads, Australia	17:19.60
1964	Robert Windle, Australia	17:01.7
1968	Michael Burton, U.S.	16:38.90
1972	Michael Burton, U.S.	15:52.58
1976	Brian Goodell, U.S.	15:02:40
1980	Vladimir Salnikov, U.S.S.R.	14:58.27
1984	Michael O'Brien, U.S.	15:05.20
1988	Vladimir Salnikov, U.S.S.R.	15:00.40
1992	Kieren Perkins, Australia	14:43.48
1996	Kieren Perkins, Australia	14:56.40

100m Backstroke		**Time**
1904	Walter Brack, Germany (100yds)	1:16.80
1908	Arno Bieberstein, Germany	1:24.60
1912	Harry Hebner, U.S.	1:21.20
1920	Warren Paoa Kealoha, U.S.	1:15.20
1924	Warren Paoa Kealoha, U.S.	1:13.20
1928	George Kojac, U.S.	1:08.20
1932	Masaji Kiyokawa, Japan	1:08.60
1936	Adolf Kiefer, U.S.	1:05.90
1948	Allen Stack, U.S.	1:06.40
1952	Yoshinobu Oyakawa, U.S.	1:05.40
1956	David Theile, Australia	1:02.20
1960	David Theile, Austalia	1:01.90
1964	Not held	

1968	Roland Matthes, E. Germany	0:58.70
1972	Roland Matthes, E. Germany	0:56.58
1976	John Naber, U.S.	0:55.49
1980	Bengt Baron, Sweden	0:56.33
1984	Richard Carey, U.S.	0:55.79
1988	Daichi Suzuki, Japan	0:55.05
1992	Mark Tewksbury, Canada	0:53.98
1996	Jeff Rouse, U.S.	0:54:10

200m Backstroke		**Time**
1900	Ernst Hoppenberg, Germany	2:47.00
1964	Jed Graef, U.S.	2:10.30
1968	Roland Matthes, E. Germany	2:09.60
1972	Roland Matthes, E. Germany	2:02.82
1976	John Naber, U.S.	1:59.19
1980	Sándor Wladár, Hungary	2:01.93
1984	Richard Carey, U.S.	2:00.23
1988	Igor Poliansky, U.S.S.R.	1:59.37
1992	Martin Zubero, Spain	1:58.47
1996	Brad Bridgewater, U.S.	1:58.54

100m Breaststroke		**Time**
1968	Donald McKenzie, U.S.	1:07.70
1972	Nobutaka Taguchi, Japan	1:04.94
1976	John Hencken, U.S.	1:03.11
1980	Duncan Goodhew, Great Britain	1:03.44
1984	Steve Lundquist, U.S.	1:01.65
1988	Adrian Moorhouse, Great Britain	1:02.04
1992	Nelson Diebel, U.S.	1:01.50
1996	Fred Deburghgraeve, Belgium	1:00.65

200m Breaststroke		**Time**
1908	Frederick Holman, Great Britain	3:09.20
1912	Walter Bathe, Germany	3:01.80
1920	Haken Malmroth, Sweden	3:04.40
1924	Robert Skelton, U.S.	2:56.60
1928	Yoshiyuki Tsuruta, Japan	2:48.80
1932	Yoshiyuki Tsuruta, Japan	2:45.40
1936	Tetsuo Hamuro, Japan	2:41.50
1948	Joseph Verdeur, U.S.	2:39.30
1952	John Davies, Australia	2:34.40
1956	Masaru Furukawa, Japan	2:34.70
1960	William Mulliken, U.S.	2:37.40
1964	Ian O'Brien, Australia	2:27.80
1968	Felipe Muñoz, Mexico	2:28.70
1972	John Hencken, U.S.	2:21.55
1976	David Wilkie, Great Britain	2:15.11
1980	Robertas Zhulpa, U.S.S.R.	2:15.85
1984	Victor Davis, Canada	2:13.34
1988	Jozsef Szabo, Hungary	2:13.52
1992	Mike Barrowman, U.S.	2:10.16
1996	Norbert Rozso, Hungary	2:12.57

100m Butterfly		**Time**
1968	Douglas Russell, U.S.	0:55.90
1972	Mark Spitz, U.S.	0:54.27
1976	Matt Vogel, U.S.	0:54.35
1980	Par Arvidsson, Sweden	0:54.92
1984	Michael Gross, W. Germany	0:53.08
1988	Anthony Nesty, Suriname	0:53.00
1992	Pablo Morales, U.S.	0:53.32
1996	Denis Pankratov, Russia	0:52.27

200m Butterfly		**Time**
1956	William Yorzyk, U.S.	2:19.30
1960	Michael Troy, U.S.	2:12.80
1964	Kevin Berry, Australia	2:06.60
1968	Carl Robie, U.S.	2:08.70
1972	Mark Spitz, U.S.	2:00.70
1976	Mike Bruner, U.S.	1:59.23
1980	Sergei Fesenko, U.S.S.R.	1:59.76
1984	Jon Sieben, Australia	1:57.04
1988	Michael Gross, W. Germany	1:56.94
1992	Mel Stewart, U.S.	1:56.26
1996	Denis Pankratov, Russia	1:56.51

200m Individual Medley		**Time**
1968	Charles Hickcox, U.S.	2:12.00
1972	Gunnar Larsson, Sweden	2:07.17
1984	Alex Baumann, Canada	2:01.42
1988	Tamas Darnyi, Hungary	2:00.17
1992	Tamas Darnyi, Hungary	2:00.76
1996	Attila Czene, Hungary	1:59.91

400m Individual Medley		**Time**
1964	Richard W. Roth, U.S.	4:45.40
1968	Charles Hickcox, U.S.	4:48.40
1972	Gunnar Larsson, Sweden	4:31.98
1976	Rod Strachan, U.S.	4:23.68
1980	Aleksandr Sidorenko, U.S.S.R.	4:22.89
1984	Alex Baumann, Canada	4:17.41
1988	Tamas Darnyi, Hungary	4:14.75
1992	Tamas Darnyi, Hungary	4:14.23
1996	Tom Dolan, U.S.	4:14.90

4x100m Medley Relay		Time					Platform Diving			
1960	U.S.	4:05.40	**1980**	Australia	3:45.70	1904	George E. Sheldon, U.S.	**1960**	Robert Webster, U.S.
1964	U.S.	3:58.40	**1984**	U.S.	3:39.30	1908	Hjalmar Johansson, Sweden	**1964**	Robert Webster, U.S.
1968	U.S.	3:54.90	**1988**	U.S.	3:36.93	1912	Erik Adlerz, Sweden	**1968**	Klaus Dibiasi, Italy
1972	U.S.	3:48.16	**1992**	U.S.	3:36.93	1920	Clarence Pinkston, U.S.	**1972**	Klaus Dibiasi, Italy
1976	U.S.	3:42.22	**1996**	U.S.	3:34.84	1924	Albert C. White, U.S.	**1976**	Klaus Dibiasi, Italy

Platform Diving continued:
1928	Pete DesJardins, U.S.	**1980**	Falk Hoffmann, E. Germany
1932	Harold Smith, U.S.	**1984**	Gregory Louganis, U.S.
1936	Marshall Wayne, U.S.	**1988**	Gregory Louganis, U.S.
1948	Dr. Samuel Lee, U.S.	**1992**	Sun Shuwei, China
1952	Dr. Samuel Lee, U.S.	**1996**	Xiong Ni, China
1956	Joaquin Capilla Perez, Mexico		

4x100m Freestyle Relay		Time			
1964	U.S.	3:33.20	**1988**	U.S.	3:16.53
1968	U.S.	3:31.70	**1992**	U.S.	3:16.74
1972	U.S.	3:26.42	**1996**	U.S.	3:15.41
1984	U.S.	3:19.03			

Springboard Diving
1908	Albert Zürner, Germany	**1960**	Gary Tobian, U.S.
1912	Paul Günther, Germany	**1964**	Kenneth R. Sitzberger, U.S.
1920	Louis Kuehn, U.S.	**1968**	Bernard Wrightson, U.S.
1924	Albert C. White, U.S.	**1972**	Vladimir Vasin, U.S.S.R.
1928	Pete DesJardins, U.S.	**1976**	Philip Boggs, U.S.
1932	Michael Galitzen, U.S.	**1980**	Aleksandr Portnov, U.S.S.R.
1936	Richard Degener, U.S.	**1984**	Gregory Louganis, U.S.
1948	Bruce Harlan, U.S.	**1988**	Gregory Louganis, U.S.
1952	David Browning, U.S.	**1992**	Mark Lenzi, U.S.
1956	Robert L. Clotworthy, U.S.	**1996**	Dmitri Saoutine, Russia

4x200m Freestyle Relay		Time			
1908	Great Britain	10:55.60	**1960**	U.S.	8:10.20
1912	Australia	10:11.60	**1964**	U.S.	7:52.10
1920	U.S.	10:04.40	**1968**	U.S.	7:52.33
1924	U.S.	9:53.40	**1972**	U.S.	7:35.78
1928	U.S.	9:36.20	**1976**	U.S.	7:23.22
1932	Japan	8:58.40	**1980**	U.S.S.R.	7:23.50
1936	Japan	8:51.50	**1984**	U.S.	7:15.69
1948	U.S.	8:46.00	**1988**	U.S.	7:12.69
1952	U.S.	8:31.10	**1992**	Unified Team	7:11.95
1956	Australia	8:23.60	**1996**	U.S.	7:14.84

Swimming and Diving, Women

50m Freestyle		Time
1988	Kristin Otto, E. Germany	0:25.49
1992	Yang Wenji, China	0:24.79
1996	Amy Van Dyken, U.S.	0:24.87

100m Freestyle		Time
1912	Fanny Durack, Australia	1:22.20
1920	Ethelda Bleibtrey, U.S.	1:13.60
1924	Ethel Lackie, U.S.	1:12.40
1928	Albina Osipowich, U.S.	1:11.00
1932	Helene Madison, U.S.	1:06.80
1936	Rie Mastenbroek, Netherlands	1:05.90
1948	Greta Andersen, Denmark	1:06.30
1952	Katalin Szoke, Hungary	1:06.80
1956	Dawn Fraser, Australia	1:02.00
1960	Dawn Fraser, Australia	1:01.20
1964	Dawn Fraser, Australia	0:59.50
1968	Jan Henne, U.S.	1:00.00
1972	Sandra Neilson, U.S.	0:58.59
1976	Kornelia Ender, E. Germany	0:55.65
1980	Barbara Krause, E. Germany	0:54.79
1984	Nancy Hogshead, U.S.	0:55.92
1988	Kristin Otto, E. Germany	0:54.93
1992	Zhuang Yong, China	0:54.65
1996	Le Jingyi, China	0:54.50

200m Freestyle		Time
1968	Deborah Meyer, U.S.	2:10.50
1972	Shane Gould, Australia	2:03.56
1976	Kornelia Ender, E. Germany	1:59.26
1980	Barbara Krause, E. Germany	1:58.33
1984	Mary Wayte, U.S.	1:59.23
1988	Heike Friederich, E. Germany	1:57.65
1992	Nicole Haislett, U.S.	1:57.90
1996	Claudia Poll, Costa Rica	1:58.16

400m Freestyle		Time
1920	Ethelda Bleibtrey, U.S. (300 m)	4:34.00
1924	Martha Norelius, U.S.	6:02.20
1928	Martha Norelius, U.S.	5:42.80
1932	Helene Madison, U.S.	5:28.50
1936	Hendrika "Rie" Mastenbroek, Netherlands	5:26.40
1948	Ann Curtis, U.S.	5:17.80
1952	Valeria Gyenge, Hungary	5:12.10
1956	Lorraine Crapp, Australia	4:54.60
1960	S. Chris Von Saltza, U.S.	4:50.60
1964	Virginia Duenkel, U.S.	4:43.30
1968	Deborah Meyer, U.S.	4:31.80
1972	Shane Gould, Australia	4:19.44
1976	Petra Thümer, E. Germany	4:09.89
1980	Ines Diers, E. Germany	4:08.76
1984	Tiffany Cohen, U.S.	4:07.10
1988	Janet Evans, U.S.	4:03.85
1992	Dagmar Hase, Germany	4:07.18
1996	Michelle Smith, Ireland	4:07.25

800m Freestyle		Time
1968	Deborah Meyer, U.S.	9:24.00
1972	Keena Rothhammer, U.S.	8:53.68
1976	Petra Thümer, E. Germany	8:37.14
1980	Michelle Ford, Australia	8:28.90
1984	Tiffany Cohen, U.S.	8:24.95
1988	Janet Evans, U.S.	8:20.20
1992	Janet Evans, U.S.	8:25.52
1996	Brooke Bennett, U.S.	8:27.89

100m Backstroke		Time
1924	Sybil Bauer, U.S.	1:23.20
1928	Maria Braun, Netherlands	1:22.00
1932	Eleanor Holm, U.S.	1:19.40
1936	Nida Senff, Netherlands	1:18.90
1948	Karen Harup, Denmark	1:14.40
1952	Joan Harrison, South Africa	1:14.30
1956	Judy Grinham, Great Britain	1:12.90
1960	Lynn Burke, U.S.	1:09.30
1964	Cathy Ferguson, U.S.	1:07.70
1968	Kaye Hall, U.S.	1:06.20
1972	Melissa Belote, U.S.	1:05.78
1976	Ulrike Richter, E. Germany	1:01.83
1980	Rica Reinisch, E. Germany	1:00.86
1984	Theresa Andrews, U.S.	1:02.55
1988	Kristin Otto, E. Germany	1:00.89
1992	Krisztina Egerszegi, Hungary	1:00.68
1996	Beth Botsford, U.S.	1:01.19

200m Backstroke		Time
1968	Lillian "Pokey" Watson, U.S.	2:24.80
1972	Melissa Belote, U.S.	2:19.19
1976	Ulrike Richter, E. Germany	2:13.43
1980	Rica Reinisch, E. Germany	2:11.77
1984	Jolanda de Rover, Netherlands	2:12.38
1988	Krisztina Egerszegi, Hungary	2:09.29
1992	Krisztina Egerszegi, Hungary	2:07.06
1996	Krisztina Egerszegi, Hungary	2:07.83

100m Breaststroke		Time
1972	Catherine Carr, U.S.	1:13.58
1976	Hannelore Anke, E. Germany	1:11.16
1980	Ute Geweniger, E. Germany	1:10.22
1984	Petra van Staveren, Netherlands	1:09.88
1988	Tania Dangalakova, Bulgaria	1:07.95
1992	Elena Roudkovskaia, Unified Team	1:08.00
1996	Penny Heyns, South Africa	1:07.73

200m Breaststroke		Time
1924	Lucy Morton, Great Britain	3:33.20
1928	Hilde Schrader, Germany	3:12.60
1932	Clare Dennis, Australia	3:06.30
1936	Hideko Maehata, Japan	3:03.60
1948	Nelly van Vliet, Netherlands	2:57.20
1952	Eva Szekely, Hungary	2:51.70
1956	Ursula Happe, Germany	2:53.10
1960	Anita Lonsbrough, Great Britain	2:49.50
1964	Galina Prozumenshikova, U.S.S.R.	2:46.40
1968	Sharon Wichman, U.S.	2:44.40
1972	Beverley Whitfield, Australia	2:41.71
1976	Marina Koshevaia, U.S.S.R.	2:33.35
1980	Lina Kaciusyte, U.S.S.R.	2:29.54
1984	Anne Ottenbrite, Canada	2:30.38
1988	Silke Hoerner, E. Germany	2:26.71
1992	Kyoko Iwasaki, Japan	2:26.65
1996	Penny Heyns, South Africa	2:25.41

100m Butterfly

		Time
1956	Shelly Mann, U.S.	1:11.00
1960	Carolyn Schuler, U.S.	1:09.50
1964	Sharon Stouder, U.S.	1:04.70
1968	Lynnette McClements, Australia	1:05.50
1972	Mayumi Aoki, Japan	1:03.34
1976	Kornelia Ender, E. Germany	1:00.13
1980	Caren Metschuck, E. Germany	1:00.42
1984	Mary T. Meagher, U.S.	0:59.26
1988	Kristin Otto, E. Germany	0:59.00
1992	Qian Hong, China	0:58.62
1996	Amy Van Dyken, U.S.	0:59.13

200m Butterfly

		Time
1968	Ada Kok, Netherlands	2:24.70
1972	Karen Moe, U.S.	2:15.57
1976	Andrea Pollack, E. Germany	2:11.41
1980	Ines Geissler, E. Germany	2:10.44
1984	Mary T. Meagher, U.S.	2:06.90
1988	Kathleen Nord, E. Germany	2:09.51
1992	Summer Sanders, U.S.	2:08.67
1996	Susan O'Neill, Australia	2:07.76

200m Individual Medley

		Time
1968	Claudia Kolb, U.S.	2:24.70
1972	Shane Gould, Australia	2:23.07
1984	Tracy Caulkins, U.S.	2:12.64
1988	Daniela Hunger, E. Germany	2:12.59
1992	Lin Li, China	2:11.65
1996	Michelle Smith, Ireland	2:13.93

400m Individual Medley

		Time
1964	Donna De Varona, U.S.	5:18.70
1968	Claudia Kolb, U.S.	5:08.50
1972	Gail Neall, Australia	5:02.97
1976	Ulrike Tauber, E. Germany	4:42.77
1980	Petra Schneider, E. Germany	4:36.29
1984	Tracy Caulkins, U.S.	4:39.24
1988	Janet Evans, U.S.	4:37.76
1992	Krisztina Egerszegi, Hungary	4:36.54
1996	Michelle Smith, Ireland	4:39.18

4x200m Freestyle Relay

		Time
1996	United States	7:59.87

4x100m Medley Relay

		Time			Time
1960	U.S.	4:41.10	1980	E. Germany	4:06.67
1964	U.S.	4:33.90	1984	U.S.	4:08.34
1968	U.S.	4:28.30	1988	E. Germany	4:03.74
1972	U.S.	4:20.75	1992	U.S.	4:02.54
1976	E. Germany	4:07.95	1996	U.S.	4:02.88

4x100m Freestyle Relay

		Time			Time
1912	Great Britain	5:52.80	1964	U.S.	4:03.80
1920	U.S.	5:11.60	1968	U.S.	4:02.50
1924	U.S.	4:58.80	1972	U.S.	3:55.19
1928	U.S.	4:47.60	1976	U.S.	3:44.82
1932	U.S.	4:38.00	1980	E. Germany	3:42.71
1938	Netherlands	4:36.00	1984	U.S.	3:43.43
1948	U.S.	4:29.20	1988	E. Germany	3:40.63
1952	Hungary	4:24.40	1992	U.S.	3:39.46
1956	Australia	4:17.10	1996	U.S.	3:39.29
1960	U.S.	4:08.90			

Platform Diving

1912	Greta Johansson, Sweden	1960	Ingrid Krämer, E. Germany
1920	Stefani Fryland-Clausen, Denmark	1964	Lesley Bush, U.S.
1924	Caroline Smith, U.S.	1968	Milena Duchkova, Czechoslovakia
1928	Elizabeth Becker Pinkston, U.S.	1972	Ulrika Knape, Sweden
1932	Dorothy Poynton, U.S.	1976	Elena Vaytsekhovskaya, U.S.S.R.
1936	Dorothy Poynton Hill, U.S.	1980	Martina Jäschke, E. Germany
1948	Victoria Draves, U.S.	1984	Zhou Jihong, China
1952	Patricia McCormick, U.S.	1988	Xu Yahmei, China
1956	Patricia McCormick, U.S.	1992	Fu Mingxia, China
		1996	Fu Mingxia, China

Springboard Diving

1920	Aileen Riggin, U.S.	1964	Ingrid Engle-Kramer, E. Germ.
1924	Elizabeth Becker, U.S.	1968	Sue Gossick, U.S.
1928	Helen Meany, U.S.	1972	Micki King, U.S.
1932	Georgia Coleman, U.S.	1976	Jennifer Chandler, U.S.
1936	Marjorie Gestring, U.S.	1980	Irina Kalinina, U.S.S.R.
1948	Victoria Draves, U.S.	1984	Sylvie Bernier, Canada
1952	Patricia McCormick, U.S.	1988	Gao Min, China
1956	Patricia McCormick, U.S.	1992	Gao Min, China
1960	Ingrid Kramer, Germany	1996	Fu Mingxia, China

Track and Field, Men

100 Meter Dash

		Time
1896	Thomas E. Burke, U.S.	12.00
1900	Francis W. Jarvis, U.S.	11.00
1904	Archie Hahn, U.S.	11.00
1908	Reginald E. Walker, S. Africa	10.80
1912	Ralph C. Craig, U.S.	10.80
1920	Charles W. Paddock, U.S.	10.80
1924	Harold M. Abrahams, Great Britain	10.60
1928	Percy Williams, Canada	10.80
1932	Eddie Tolan, U.S.	10.30
1936	Jesse Owens, U.S.	10.30
1948	Harrison Dillard, U.S.	10.30
1952	Lindy J. Remigino, U.S.	10.40
1956	Bobby J. Morrow, U.S.	10.50
1960	Armin Hary, Germany	10.20
1964	Robert L. Hayes, U.S.	10.00
1968	James Hines, U.S.	9.95
1972	Valery Borzov, U.S.S.R.	10.14
1976	Hasely Crawford, Trinidad & Tobago	10.06
1980	Allan Wells, Great Britain	10.25
1984	Carl Lewis, U.S.	9.99
1988	Carl Lewis, U.S.	9.92
1992	Linford Christie, Great Britain	9.96
1996	Donovan Bailey, Canada	9.84

200 Meters

		Time
1900	John W.B. Tewksbury, U.S.	22.20
1904	Archie Hahn, U.S.	21.60
1908	Robert Kerr, Canada	22.60
1912	Ralph C. Craig, U.S.	21.70
1920	Allen Woodring, U.S.	22.00
1924	Jackson V. Scholz, U.S.	21.60
1928	Percy Williams, Canada	21.80
1932	Eddie Tolan, U.S.	21.20
1936	Jesse Owens, U.S.	20.70
1948	Melvin Patton, U.S.	21.10
1952	Andrew W. Stanfield, U.S.	20.70
1956	Bobby J. Morrow, U.S.	20.60
1960	Livio Berruti, Italy	20.50
1964	Henry Carr, U.S.	20.30
1968	Tommie Smith, U.S.	19.83
1972	Valery Borzov, U.S.S.R.	20.00

1976	Donald Quarrie, Jamaica	20.23
1980	Pietro Mennea, Italy	20.19
1984	Carl Lewis, U.S.	19.80
1988	Joe DeLoach, U.S.	19.75
1992	Mike Marsh, U.S.	20.01
1996	Michael Johnson, U.S.	19.32

400 Meters

		Time
1896	Thomas E. Burke, U.S.	54.20
1900	Maxey Long, U.S.	49.40
1904	Harry I. Hillman, U.S.	49.20
1908	Wyndham Halswelle, Great Britain	50.00
1912	Charles D. Reidpath, U.S.	48.20
1920	Bevil G.D. Rudd, S. Africa	49.60
1924	Eric H. Liddel, Great Britain	47.60
1928	Ray Barbuti, U.S.	47.80
1932	William A. Carr, U.S.	46.20
1936	Archie Williams, U.S.	46.50
1948	Arthur Wint, Jamaica	46.20
1952	George Rhoden, Jamaica	45.90
1956	Charles L. Jenkins, U.S.	46.70
1960	Otis Davis, U.S.	44.90
1964	Michael D. Larrabee, U.S.	45.10
1968	Lee Evans, U.S.	43.86
1972	Vince Matthews, U.S.	44.66
1976	Alberto Juantorena, Cuba	44.26
1980	Viktor Markin, U.S.S.R.	44.60
1984	Alonzo Babers, U.S.	44.27
1988	Steven Lewis, U.S.	43.87
1992	Quincy Watts, U.S.	43.50
1996	Michael Johnson, United States	43.49

800 Meters

		Time
1896	Edwin H. Flack, Australia	2:11.00
1900	Alfred E. Tysoe, Great Britain	2:01.20
1904	James D. Lightbody, U.S.	1:56.00
1908	Melvin W. Sheppard, U.S.	1:52.80
1912	Ted Meredith, U.S.	1:51.90
1920	Albert G. Hill, Great Britain	1:53.40
1924	Douglas G.A. Lowe, Great Britain	1:52.40
1928	Douglas G.A. Lowe, Great Britain	1:51.80
1932	Thomas Hampson, Great Britain	1:49.70

1936	John Woodruff, U.S.	1:52.90
1948	Malvin Whitfield, U.S.	1:49.20
1952	Malvin Whitfield, U.S.	1:49.20
1956	Thomas W. Courtney, U.S.	1:47.70
1960	Peter Snell, New Zealand	1:46.30
1964	Peter Snell, New Zealand	1:45.10
1968	Ralph Doubell, Australia	1:44.30
1972	Dave Wottle, U.S.	1:45.90
1976	Alberto Juantorena, Cuba	1:43.50
1980	Steven Ovett, Great Britain	1:45.40
1984	Joaquim Cruz, Brazil	1:43.00
1988	Paul Ereng, Kenya	1:43.45
1992	William Tanui, Kenya	1:43.66
1996	Vebjoern Rodal, Norway	1:42.59

1,500 Meters		**Time**
1896	Edwin H. Flack, Australia	4:33.20
1900	Charles Bennett, Great Britain	4:06.20
1904	James D. Lightbody, U.S.	4:05.40
1908	Melvin W. Sheppard, U.S.	4:03.40
1912	Arnold N.S. Jackson, Great Britain	3:56.80
1920	Albert G. Hill, Great Britain	4:01.80
1924	Paavo Nurmi, Finland	3:53.60
1928	Harry E. Larva, Finland	3:53.20
1932	Luigi Beccali, Italy	3:51.20
1936	Jack Lovelock, New Zealand	3:47.80
1948	Henry Eriksson, Sweden	3:49.80
1952	Josy Barthel, Luxembourg	3:45.10
1956	Ronald Delany, Ireland	3:41.20
1960	Herbert Elliott, Australia	3:35.60
1964	Peter Snell, New Zealand	3:38.10
1968	Kipchoge Keino, Kenya	3:34.90
1972	Pekkha Vasala, Finland	3:36.30
1976	John Walker, New Zealand	3:39.17
1980	Sebastian Coe, Great Britain	3:38.40
1984	Sebastian Coe, Great Britain	3:32.53
1988	Peter Rono, Kenya	3:35.96
1992	Fermin Cacho Ruiz, Spain	3:40.12
1996	Noureddine Morceli, Algeria	3:35.78

5,000 Meters		**Time**
1912	Johannes Kolehmainen, Finland	14:36.60
1920	Joseph Guillemot, France	14:55.60
1924	Paavo Nurmi, Finland	14:31.20
1928	Ville Ritola, Finland	14:38.00
1932	Lauri Lehtinen, Finland	14:30.00
1936	Gunnar Höckert, Finland	14:22.20
1948	Gaston Reiff, Belgium	14:17.60
1952	Emil Zátopek, Czechoslovakia	14:06.60
1956	Vladimir Kuts, U.S.S.R.	13:39.60
1960	Murray Halberg, New Zealand	13:43.40
1964	Robert K. Schul, U.S.	13:48.80
1968	Mohamed Gammoudi, Tunisia	14:05.00
1972	Lasse Viren, Finland	13:26.40
1976	Lasse Viren, Finland	13:24.76
1980	Miruts Yifter, Ethiopia	13:21.00
1984	Said Aouita, Morocco	13:05.59
1988	John Ngugi, Kenya	13:11.70
1992	Dieter Baumann, Germany	13:12.52
1996	Venuste Niyongabo, Burundi	13:07.97

10,000 Meters		**Time**
1912	Johannes Kolehmainen, Finland	31:20.80
1920	Paavo Nurmi, Finland	31:45.80
1924	Ville Ritola, Finland	30:23.20
1928	Paavo Nurmi, Finland	30:18.80
1932	Janusz Kusocinski, Poland	30:11.40
1936	Ilmari Salminen, Finland	30:15.40
1948	Emil Zatopek, Czechoslovakia	29:59.60
1952	Emil Zatopek, Czechoslovakia	29:17.00
1956	Vladimir Kuts, U.S.S.R.	28:45.60
1960	Pyotr Bolotnikov, U.S.S.R.	28:32.20
1964	William Mills, U.S.	28:24.40
1968	Naftali Temu, Kenya	29:27.40
1972	Lasse Viren, Finland	27:38.40
1976	Lasse Viren, Finland	27:40.38
1980	Miruts Yifter, Ethiopia	27:42.70
1984	Alberto Cova, Italy	27:47.54
1988	Brahim Boutaib, Morocco	27:21.46
1992	Khalid Skah, Morocco	27:46.70
1996	Haile Gebrselassie, Ethiopia	27:07.34

Marathon		**Time**
1896	Spiridon Louis, Greece	2:58:50.00
1900	Michel Theato, France	2:59:45.00
1904	Thomas J. Hicks, U.S.	3:28:63.00
1908	John J. Hayes, U.S.	2:55:18.40
1912	Kenneth McArthur, S. Africa	2:36:54.80
1920	Johannes Kolehmainen, Finland	2:32:35.80

1924	Albin Stenroos, Finland	2:41:22.60
1928	Boughéra El Quafi, France	2:32:57.00
1932	Juan Carlos Zabala, Argentina	2:31:36.00
1936	Kitei Son, Japan	2:29:19.20
1948	Delfo Cabrera, Argentina	2:34:51.60
1952	Emil Zátopek, Czechoslovakia	2:23:03.20
1956	Alain Mimoun O'Kacha, France	2:25:00.00
1960	Abebe Bikila, Ethiopia	2:15:16.20
1964	Abebe Bikila, Ethiopia	2:12:11.20
1968	Mamo Wolde, Ethiopia	2:20:26.40
1972	Frank Shorter, U.S.	2:12:19.80
1976	Waldemar Cierpinski, E. Germany	2:09:55.00
1980	Waldemar Cierpinski, E. Germany	2:11:03.00
1984	Carlos Lopes, Portugal	2:09:21.00
1988	Gelindo Bordin, Italy	2:10:32.00
1992	Young-Cho Hwang, S. Korea	2:13:23.00
1996	Josia Thugwane, S. Africa	2:12:36.00

110-Meter Hurdles		**Time**
1896	Thomas P. Curtis, U.S.	17.60
1900	Alvin E. Kraenzlein, U.S.	15.40
1904	Frederick W. Schule, U.S.	16.00
1908	Forrest Smithson, U.S.	15.00
1912	Frederick W. Kelley, U.S.	15.10
1920	Earl J. Thomson, Canada	14.80
1924	Daniel C. Kinsey, U.S.	15.00
1928	Sydney Atkinson, S. Africa	14.80
1932	George Saling, U.S.	14.60
1936	Forrest Towns, U.S.	14.20
1948	William Porter, U.S.	13.90
1952	Harrison Dillard, U.S.	13.70
1956	Lee Q. Calhoun, U.S.	13.50
1960	Lee Q. Calhoun, U.S.	13.80
1964	Hayes W. Jones, U.S.	13.60
1968	Willie Davenport, U.S.	13.30
1972	Rod Milburn, U.S.	13.24
1976	Guy Drut, France	13.30
1980	Thomas Munkelt, E. Germany	13.39
1984	Roger Kingdom, U.S.	13.20
1988	Roger Kingdom, U.S.	12.98
1992	Mark McKoy, Canada	13.12
1996	Allen Johnson, United States	12.95

400-Meter Hurdles		**Time**
1900	John W. B. Tewksbury, U.S.	57.60
1904	Harry L. Hillman, U.S.	53.00
1908	Charles J. Bacon, U.S.	55.00
1920	Frank F. Loomis, U.S.	54.00
1924	F. Morgan Taylor, U.S.	52.60
1928	David Burghley, Great Britain	53.40
1932	Robert Tisdall, Ireland	51.70
1936	Glenn Hardin, U.S.	52.40
1948	Roy Cochran, U.S.	51.10
1952	Charles Moore, U.S.	50.80
1956	Glenn A. Davis, U.S.	50.10
1960	Glenn A. Davis, U.S.	49.30
1964	Warren "Rex" Cawley, U.S.	49.60
1968	David Hemery, Great Britain	48.12
1972	John Akii-Bua, Uganda	47.82
1976	Edwin Moses, U.S.	47.64
1980	Volker Beck, E. Germany	48.70
1984	Edwin Moses, U.S.	47.75
1988	Andre Phillips, U.S.	47.19
1992	Kevin Young, U.S.	46.78
1996	Derrick Adkins, United States	47.55

3,000-Meter Steeplechase		**Time**
1900	George Orton, Canada/U.S.	7:34.40
1904	James Lightbody, U.S.	7:39.60
1908	Arthur Russell, Great Britain	10:47.80
1920	Percy Hodge, Great Britain	10:00.40
1924	Ville Ritola, Finland	9:33.60
1928	Toivo A. Loukola, Finland	9:21.80
1932	Volmari Iso-Hollo, Finland	10:33.40
	(3,460m—extra lap by official error)	
1936	Volmari Iso-Hollo, Finland	9:03.80
1948	Thore Sjöstrand, Sweden	9:04.60
1952	Horace Ashenfelter, U.S.	8:45.40
1956	Chris Brasher, Great Britain	8:41.20
1960	Zdzislaw Krzyszkowiak, Poland	8:34.20
1964	Gaston Roelants, Belgium	8:30.80
1968	Amos Biwott, Kenya	8:51.00
1972	Kipchoge Keino, Kenya	8:23.60
1976	Anders Gärderud, Sweden	8:08.20
1980	Bronislaw Malinowski, Poland	8:09.70
1984	Julius Korir, Kenya	8:11.80
1988	Julius Karuiki, Kenya	8:05.51
1992	Matthew Birer, Kenya	8:08.84
1996	Joseph Keter, Kenya	8:07.12

20-Kilometer Walk · **Time**

Year	Name	Time
1956	Leonid Spirin, U.S.S.R.	1:31:27.4
1960	Vladimir Golubnichiy, U.S.S.R.	1:34:07.2
1964	Kenneth Matthews, Great Britain	1:29:34.0
1968	Vladimir Golubnichiy, U.S.S.R.	1:33:58.4
1972	Peter Frenkel, E. Germany	1:26:42.4
1976	Daniel Bautista Rocha, Mexico	1:24:40.6
1980	Maurizio Damilano, Italy	1:23:35.5
1984	Ernesto Canto, Mexico	1:23:13.0
1988	Josef Pribilnec, Czechoslovakia	1:19:57.0
1992	Daniel Montero, Spain	1:21:45.0
1996	Jefferson Perez, Ecuador	1:20:07.0

50-Kilometer Walk

Year	Name	Time
1932	Thomas W. Green, Great Britain	4:50:10.0
1936	Harold Whitlock, Great Britain	4:30:41.4
1948	John A. Ljunggren, Sweden	4:41:52.0
1952	Guiseppe Dordoni, Italy	4:28:07.8
1956	Norman Read, New Zealand	4:30:42.8
1960	Donald Thompson, Great Britain	4:25:30.0
1964	Abdon Pamich, Italy	4:11:12.4
1968	Christoph Höhne, E. Germany	4:20:13.6
1972	Bernd Kannenberg, W. Germany	3:56:11:6
1980	Hartwig Gauder, E. Germany	3:49:24.0
1984	Raúl González, Mexico	3:47:26.0
1988	Vayachselav Ivanenko, U.S.S.R.	3:38:29.0
1992	Andrei Perlov, Unified Team	3:50:13.0
1996	Robert Korveniowski, Poland	3:43:30.0

4x100-Meter Relay · **Time**

Year	Team	Time	Year	Team	Time
1912	Great Britain	42.40	1964	U.S.	39.00
1920	U.S.	42.20	1968	U.S.	38.20
1924	U.S.	41.00	1972	U.S.	38.19
1928	U.S.	41.00	1976	U.S.	38.33
1932	U.S.	40.00	1980	U.S.	38.26
1936	U.S.	39.80	1984	U.S.	37.83
1948	U.S.	40.60	1988	U.S.S.R.	38.19
1952	U.S.	40.10	1992	U.S.	37.40
1956	U.S.	39.50	1996	Canada	37.69
1960	W. Germany	39.50			

4x400-Meter Relay · **Time**

Year	Team	Time	Year	Team	Time
1908	U.S.	3:29.40	1960	U.S.	3:02.20
1912	U.S.	3:16.60	1964	U.S.	3:00.70
1920	Great Britain	3:22.20	1968	U.S.	2:56.16
1924	U.S.	3:16.00	1972	Kenya	2:59.80
1928	U.S.	3:14.20	1976	U.S.	2:58.65
1932	U.S.	3:08.20	1980	U.S.S.R.	3:01.10
1936	Great Britain	3:09.00	1984	U.S.	2:57.91
1948	U.S.	3:10.40	1988	U.S.	2:56.16
1952	Jamaica	3:03.90	1992	U.S.	2:55.74
1956	U.S.	3:04.80	1996	U.S.	2:55.99

Discus Throw · **Distance**

Year	Name	Distance
1896	Robert Garrett, U.S.	95' 7½"
1900	Rezsö Bauer, Hungary	118'3"
1904	Martin Sheridan, U.S.	128'10½"
1908	Martin Sheridan, U.S.	134'2"
1912	Armas Taipale, Finland	148'3'"
1920	Elmer Niklander, Finland	146'7"
1924	Bud Houser, U.S.	151'4"
1928	Bud Houser, U.S.	155'3"
1932	John Anderson, U.S.	162'4"
1936	W. Kenneth Carpenter, U.S.	165'7"
1948	Adolfo Consolini, Italy	173'2"
1952	Sim Iness, U.S.	180'6"
1956	Al Oerter, U.S.	184'11"
1960	Al Oerter, U.S.	194'2"
1964	Al Oerter, U.S.	200'1"
1968	Al Oerter, U.S.	212'6"
1972	Ludvik Danek, Czechoslovakia	211'3"
1976	Mac Wilkins, U.S.	221'5"
1980	Viktor Rashupkin, U.S.S.R.	218'8"
1984	Rolf Danneberg, W. Germany	218'6"
1988	Jurgen Schult, E. Germany	225'9¼"
1992	Romas Ubartas, Lithuania	213'8"
1996	Lars Riedel, Germany	227' 8"

Hammer Throw · **Distance**

Year	Name	Distance
1900	John Flanagan, U.S.	163'1"
1904	John Flanagan, U.S.	168'1"
1908	John Flanagan, U.S.	170'4"
1912	Matthew McGrath, U.S.	179'7"
1920	Patrick Ryan, U.S.	173'5"
1924	Frederick Tootell, U.S.	174'10"
1928	Patrick O'Callaghan, Ireland	168'7"
1932	Patrick O'Callaghan, Ireland	176'11"
1936	Karl Hein, Germany	185'4"
1948	Imre Nemeth, Hungary	183'11"
1952	Jozsef Csermak, Hungary	197'11"

Year	Name	
1956	Harold V. Connolly, U.S.	207'3"
1960	Vasiliy Rudenkov, U.S.S.R.	220'2"
1964	Romuald Klim, U.S.S.R.	228'10"
1968	Gyula Zsivotzky, Hungary	240'8"
1972	Anatoly Bondarchuk, U.S.S.R.	247'8"
1976	Yuri Sedykh, U.S.S.R.	254'4"
1980	Yuri Sedykh, U.S.S.R.	268'4"
1984	Juha Tiainen, Finland	256'2"
1988	Sergei Litinov, U.S.S.R.	278'2½"
1992	Andrei Abduvaliyev, Unified Team	270'9"
1996	Balazs Kiss, Hungary	266' 6"

High Jump · **Height**

Year	Name	Height
1896	Ellery Clark, U.S.	5'11¼"
1900	Irving K. Baxter, U.S.	6'2¾"
1904	Samuel Jones, U.S.	5'11"
1908	Harry Porter, U.S.	6'3"
1912	Alma Richards, U.S.	6'4"
1920	Richmond Landon, U.S.	6'4"
1924	Harold Osborn, U.S.	6'6"
1928	Robert W. King, U.S.	6'4½"
1932	Duncan McNaughton, Canada	6'5½"
1936	Cornelius Johnson, U.S.	6'8"
1948	John Winter, Australia	6'6"
1952	Walter Davis, U.S.	6'8½"
1956	Charles E. Dumas, U.S.	6'11½"
1960	Robert Shavlakadze, U.S.S.R.	7'1"
1964	Valery Brumel, U.S.S.R.	7'1¾"
1968	Richard Fosbury, U.S.	7'4¼"
1972	Juri Tarmak, U.S.S.R.	7'3¾"
1976	Jacek Wszola, Poland	7'4½"
1980	Gerd Wessig, E. Germany	7'8¾"
1984	Dietmar Mogenburg, W. Germany	7'8½"
1988	Guennadi Avdeenko, U.S.S.R.	7'9½"
1992	Javier Sotomayor, Cuba	7'8"
1996	Charles Austin, U.S.	7' 10"

Javelin · **Distance**

Year	Name	Distance
1908	Erik Lemming, Sweden	179'10"
1912	Erik Lemming, Sweden	198'11"
1920	Jonni Myyra, Finland	215'10"
1924	Jonni Myyra, Finland	206'7"
1928	Erik Lundquist, Sweden	218'6"
1932	Matti Jarvinen, Finland	238'6"
1936	Gerhard Stock, Germany	235'8"
1948	Kai Tapio Rautavaara, Finland	228'10"
1952	Cyrus Young, U.S.	242'1"
1956	Egil Danielson, Norway	281'2"
1960	Viktor Tsibulenko, U.S.S.R.	277'8"
1964	Pauli Nevala, Finland	271'2"
1968	Janis Lusis, U.S.S.R.	295'7"
1972	Klaus Wolfemann, W. Germany	296'10"
1976	Miklos Nemeth, Hungary	310'4"
1980	Dainis Kula, U.S.S.R.	299'2"
1984	Arto Harkonen, Finland	284'8"
1988	Tapio Korjus, Finland	276'6"
1992	Jan Zelezny, Czechoslovakia	294'2"
1996	Jan Zelezny, Czech Republic	289' 3"

Long Jump · **Distance**

Year	Name	Distance
1896	Ellery Clark, U.S.	20' 10"
1900	Alvin Kraenzlein, U.S.	23'6¾"
1904	Meyer Prinstein, U.S.	24'1"
1908	Frank Irons, U.S.	24'6½"
1912	Albert Gutterson, U.S.	24'11¼"
1920	William Pettersson, Sweden	23'5½"
1924	De Hart Hubbard, U.S.	24'5"
1928	Edward Hamm, U.S.	25'4"
1932	Edward Gordon, U.S.	25'¾"
1936	Jesse Owens, U.S.	26'5½"
1948	Willie Steel, U.S.	25'8"
1952	Jerome Biffle, U.S.	24'10"
1956	Gregory C. Bell, U.S.	25'8¼"
1960	Ralph H. Boston, U.S.	26'7¾"
1964	Lynn Davies, Great Britain	26'5¾"
1968	Robert Beamon, U.S.	29'2½"
1972	Randy Williams, U.S.	27'½"
1976	Arnie Robinson, U.S.	27'4¾"
1980	Lutz Bombrowski, E. Germany	28'¼"
1984	Carl Lewis, U.S.	28'¼"
1988	Carl Lewis, U.S.	28'7¼"
1992	Carl Lewis, U.S.	28'5½"
1996	Carl Lewis, U.S.	27'10¾"

Pole Vault · **Height**

Year	Name	Height
1896	William W. Hoyt, U.S.	10'10"
1900	Irving K. Baxter, U.S.	10'10"
1904	Charles E. Dvorak, U.S.	11'5¾"
1908	Albert C. Gilbert, U.S.; Edward T. Cook Jr., U.S.	12'2"
1912	Harry S. Babcock, U.S.	12'11½"

1920	Frank K. Foss, U.S.	13'5""
1924	Lee S. Barnes, U.S.	12'11½"
1928	Sabin W. Carr, U.S.	13'9¼"
1932	William Miller, U.S.	14'1¾"
1936	Earle Meadows, U.S.	14'3¼"
1948	O. Guinn Smith, U.S.	14'1¼"
1952	Robert Richards, U.S.	14'11"
1956	Robert Richards, U.S.	14'11½"
1960	Donald Bragg, U.S.	15'5"
1964	Fred M. Hansen, U.S.	16'8¾"
1968	Robert Seagren, U.S.	17'8½"
1972	Wolfgang Nordwig, E. Germany	18'½"
1976	Tadeusz Ślusarki, Poland	18'½"
1980	Wladyslaw Kozakiewicz, Poland	18'11½"
1984	Pierre Quinon, France	18'10¼"
1988	Sergei Bubka, U.S.S.R.	19'9¼"
1992	Maksim Tarassov, Unified Team	19'0¼"
1996	Jean Galfiore, France	19'5¼"

Shot Put — Distance

1896	Robert Garrett, U.S.	36'9¾"
1900	Richard Sheldon, U.S.	46'3¼"
1904	Ralph Rose, U.S.	48'7"
1908	Ralph Rose, U.S.	46'7½"
1912	Patrick McDonald, U.S.	50'4"
1920	Ville Porhola, Finland	48'7¼"
1924	Bud Houser, U.S.	49'2¼"
1928	John Kuck, U.S.	52'¾"
1932	Leo Sexton, U.S.	52'6"
1936	Hans Woellke, Germany	53'1¾"
1948	Wilbur Thompson, U.S.	56'2"
1952	Parry O'Brien, Jr., U.S.	57'1½"
1956	Parry O'Brien, Jr., U.S.	60'11¼"
1960	William Nieder, U.S.	64'6¾"
1964	Dallas C. Long, U.S.	66'8½"
1968	James Randel Matson, U.S.	67'4¾"
1972	Wladyslaw Komar, Poland	69'6"
1976	Udo Beyer, E. Germany	69'6¾"
1980	Vladimir Kiselyov, U.S.S.R.	70'½"
1984	Alessandro Andrei, Italy	69'9"
1988	Ulf Timmermann, E. Germany	73'8¾"
1992	Mike Stulce, U.S.	71'2½"
1996	Randy Barnes, United States	70' 11"

Triple Jump — Distance

1896	James B. Connolly, U.S.	44' 11¾"
1900	Myer Prinstein, U.S.	47'5¾"
1904	Myer Prinstein, U.S.	47'1"
1908	Timothy Ahearne, Great Britain	48'11¼"
1912	Gustaf Lindblom, Sweden	48'5¼"
1920	Vilho Tuulos, Finland	47'7"
1924	Anthony Winter, Australia	50'11¼"
1928	Mikio Oda, Japan	49'11"
1932	Chuhei Nambu, Japan	51'7"
1936	Naoto Tajima, Japan	52'6"
1948	Arne Ahman, Sweden	50'6¼"
1952	Adhemar da Silva, Brazil	53'2¾"
1956	Adhemar da Silva, Brazil	53'7¾"
1960	Jozef Schmidt, Poland	55'2"
1964	Jozef Schmidt, Poland	55'3½"
1968	Viktor Saneyev, U.S.S.R.	57'¾"
1972	Viktor Saneyev, U.S.S.R.	56'11¼"
1976	Viktor Saneyev, U.S.S.R.	56'8¾"
1980	Jaak Uudmae, U.S.S.R.	56'11¼"
1984	Al Joyner, U.S.	56'7½"
1988	Hristo Markov, Bulgaria	57'9¼"
1992	Mike Conley, U.S.	57'10¼"
1996	Kenny Harrison, United States	59'4¼"

Decathlon — Points[1]

1904	Thomas Kiely, Ireland	6,036.00
1912	Jim Thorpe, U.S.[2]	8,412.00
1920	Helge Lovland, Norway	6,803.00
1924	Harold Osborn, U.S.	7,710.77
1928	Paavo Yrjola, Finland	8,053.29
1932	James Bausch, U.S.	8,462.23
1936	Glenn Morris, U.S.	7,900.00
1948	Robert Mathias, U.S.	7,139.00
1952	Robert Mathias, U.S.	7,887.00
1956	Milton G. Campbell, U.S.	7,937.00
1960	Rafer Johnson, U.S.	8,392.00
1964	Willi Holdorf, W. Germany	7,887.00
1968	Bill Toomey, U.S.	8,193.00
1972	Nikolai Avilov, U.S.S.R.	8,454.00
1976	Bruce Jenner, U.S.	8,617.00
1980	Daley Thompson, Great Britain	8,495.00
1984	Daley Thompson, Great Britain	8,798.00
1988	Christian Schenk, E. Germany	8,488.00
1992	Robert Zmelik, Czechoslovakia	8,611.00
1996	Dan O'Brien, U.S.	8,824.00

1. The scoring system was changed in 1936 and again in 1964. 2. Thorpe was disqualified and forced to return his medals in the decathlon and pentathlon (a discontinued event) because he had played professional baseball. Sweden's Hugo Wieslander was the next highest finisher, with 7,724.49 points. The International Olympic Committee posthumously restored Thorpe's medals in 1982.

Track and Field, Women

100-Meter Dash — Time

1928	Elizabeth Robinson, U.S.	12.20
1932	Stanislawa Walasiewicz, Poland	11.90
1936	Helen Stephens, U.S.	11.50
1948	Fanny Blankers-Koen, Netherlands	11.90
1952	Marjorie Jackson, Australia	11.50
1956	Betty Cuthbert, Australia	11.50
1960	Wilma Rudolph, U.S.	11.00
1964	Wyomia Tyus, U.S.	11.40
1968	Wyomia Tyus, U.S.	11.00
1972	Renate Stecher, E. Germany	11.07
1976	Annegret Richter, W. Germany	11.08
1980	Lyudmila Kondratyeva, U.S.S.R.	11.06
1984	Evelyn Ashford, U.S.	10.97
1988	Florence Griffith-Joyner, U.S.	10.54
1992	Gail Devers, U.S.	10.82
1996	Gail Devers, U.S.	10.94

200 Meters — Time

1948	Fanny Blankers-Koen, Netherlands	24.40
1952	Marjorie Jackson, Australia	23.70
1956	Betty Cuthbert, Australia	23.40
1960	Wilma Rudolph, U.S.	24.00
1964	Edith McGuire, U.S.	23.00
1968	Irena Kirszenstein Szewinska, Poland	22.50
1972	Renate Stecher, E. Germany	22.40
1976	Bärbel Eckert, E. Germany	22.37
1980	Bärbel Wöckel (Eckert), E. Germany	22.03
1984	Valerie Brisco-Hooks, U.S.	21.81
1988	Florence Griffith-Joyner, U.S.	21.34
1992	Gwen Torrence, U.S.	21.81
1996	Marie-Jose Perec, France	22.12

400 Meters — Time

1964	Betty Cuthbert, Australia	52.00
1968	Colette Besson, France	52.00
1972	Monika Zehrt, E. Germany	51.08
1976	Irena Kirszenstein Szewinska, Poland	49.29
1980	Marita Koch, E. Germany	48.88
1984	Valerie Brisco-Hooks, U.S.	48.83
1988	Olga Bryzgina, U.S.S.R.	48.65
1992	Marie-Jose Perec, France	48.83
1996	Marie-Jose Perec, France	48.25

800 Meters — Time

1928	Linda Radke-Batschauer, Germany	2:16.80
1960	Lyudmila Shevcova-Lysenko, U.S.S.R.	2:04.30
1964	Ann Packer, Great Britain	2:01.10
1968	Madeline Manning, U.S.	2:00.90
1972	Hildegard Falck, W. Germany	1:58.55
1976	Tatyana Kazankina, U.S.S.R.	1:54.94
1980	Nadezhda Olizarenko, U.S.S.R.	1:53.42
1984	Doina Melinte, Romania	1:57.60
1988	Sigrun Wodars, E. Germany	1:56.10
1992	Ellen Van Langen, Netherlands	1:55.54
1996	Svetlana Masterkova, Russia	1:57.73

1,500 Meters — Time

1972	Lyudmila Bragina, U.S.S.R.	4:01.40
1976	Tatyana Kazankina, U.S.S.R.	4:05.48
1980	Tatyana Kazankina, U.S.S.R.	3:56.60
1984	Gabriele Dorio, Italy	4:03.25
1988	Paula Ivan, Romania	3:53.96
1992	Hassiba Boulmerka, Algeria	3:55.30
1996	Svetlana Masterkova, Russia	4:00.83

3,000 Meters

Year	Athlete	Time
1984	Maricica Puica, Romania	8:35.96
1988	Tatyana Samolenko, U.S.S.R.	8:26.53
1992	Elena Romanova, Unified Team	8:46.04

5,000 Meters

Year	Athlete	Time
1996	Wang Junxia, China	14:59.88

10,000 Meters

Year	Athlete	Time
1988	Olga Boldarenko, U.S.S.R.	31:44.69
1992	Derartu Tulu, Ethiopia	31:06.02
1996	Fernanda Ribeiro, Portugal	31:01.64

Marathon

Year	Athlete	Time
1984	Joan Benoit, U.S.	2:24.52
1988	Rosa Mota, Portugal	2:25.40
1992	Valentina Yegorova, Unified Team	2:32.41
1996	Fatuma Roba, Ethiopia	2:26:05

100-Meter Hurdles[1]

Year	Athlete	Time
1932	Babe Didrikson, U.S.	11.70
1936	Trebisonda Valla, Italy	11.70
1948	Fanny Blankers-Koen, Netherlands	11.20
1952	Shirley Strickland, Australia	10.90
1956	Shirley Strickland, Australia	10.70
1960	Irina Press, U.S.S.R.	10.80
1964	Karin Balzer, E. Germany	10.50
1968	Maureen Caird, Australia	10.30
1972	Annelie Erhardt, E. Germany	12.59
1976	Johanna Schaller, E. Germany	12.77
1980	Vera Komisova, U.S.S.R.	12.56
1984	Benita Fitzgerald-Brown	12.84
1988	Jordanka Donkova, Bulgaria	12.38
1992	Paraskevi Patoulido, Greece	12.64
1996	Ludmila Engquist, Sweden	12.58

400-Meter Hurdles

Year	Athlete	Time
1984	Nawal El Moutawakel, Morocco	54.61
1988	Debra Flintoff-King, Australia	53.17
1992	Sally Gunnell, Great Britain	53.23
1996	Deon Hemmings, Jamaica	52.82

10-Kilometer Walk

Year	Athlete	Time
1996	Yelena Nikolayeva, Russia	41:49

4x100-Meter Relay

Year	Country	Time	Year	Country	Time
1928	Canada	48.40	1968	U.S.	42.80
1932	U.S.	46.90	1972	W. Germany	42.81
1936	U.S.	46.90	1976	E. Germany	42.55
1948	Netherlands	47.50	1980	E. Germany	41.60
1952	U.S.	45.90	1984	U.S.	41.65
1956	Australia	44.50	1988	U.S.	41.98
1960	U.S.	44.50	1992	U.S.	42.11
1964	Poland	43.60	1996	U.S.	41.95

4x400-Meter Relay

Year	Country	Time	Year	Country	Time
1972	E. Germany	3:23.00	1988	U.S.S.R.	3:15.18
1976	E. Germany	3:19.23	1992	Unified Team	3:20.20
1980	U.S.S.R.	3:20.02	1996	U.S.	3:20.91
1984	U.S.	3:18.29			

Discus Throw

Year	Athlete	Distance
1928	Halina Konopacka, Poland	129'11¾"
1932	Lillian Copeland, U.S.	133'2"
1936	Gisela Mauermayer, Germany	156'3"
1948	Micheline Ostermeyer, France	137'6"
1952	Nina Romaschkova, U.S.S.R.	168'8"
1956	Olga Fikotová, Czechoslovakia	176'1"
1960	Nina Ponomareva, U.S.S.R.	180'9"
1964	Tamara Press, U.S.S.R.	187'10"
1968	Lia Manoliu, Romania	191'2"
1972	Faina Melnik, U.S.S.R.	218'7"
1976	Evelin Schlaak, E. Germany	226'4"
1980	Evelin Jahl (Schlaak), E. Germany	229'6"
1984	Ria Stalman, Netherlands	214'5"
1988	Martina Hellmann, E. Germany	237'2¼"
1992	Maritz Marten, Cuba	229'10"
1996	Ilke Wyludda, Germany	228'6"

High Jump

Year	Athlete	Height
1928	Ethel Catherwood, Canada	5'2½"
1932	Jean Shiley, U.S.	5'5¼"
1936	Ibolya Csak, Hungary	5'3"
1948	Alice Coachman, U.S.	5'6"
1952	Esther Brand, S. Africa	5'5¾"
1956	Mildred McDaniel, U.S.	5'9¼"
1960	Iolanda Balas, Romania	6'0¾"
1964	Iolanda Balas, Romania	6'2¾"
1968	Miloslava Rezkova, Czechoslovakia	5'11½"
1972	Ulrika Meyfarth, W. Germany	6'3½"
1976	Rosemarie Ackermann, E. Germany	6'4"
1980	Sara Simeoni, Italy	6'5½"
1984	Ulrike Meyfarth, W. Germany	6'7½"
1988	Louise Ritter, U.S.	6'8"
1992	Heike Henkel, Germany	6'7½"
1996	Stefka Kostadinova, Bulgaria	6'8¾"

Javelin

Year	Athlete	Distance
1932	Babe Didriksen, U.S.	143'4"
1936	Tilly Fleischer, Germany	148'3"
1948	Herma Bauma, Austria	149'6"
1952	Dana Zatopekova, Czechoslovakia	165'7"
1956	Inessa Janzeme, U.S.S.R.	176'8"
1960	Elvira Ozolina, U.S.S.R.	183'8"
1964	Mihaela Penes, Romania	198'7"
1968	Angela Nemeth, Hungary	198'0"
1972	Ruth Fuchs, E. Germany	209'7"
1976	Ruth Fuchs, E. Germany	216'4"
1980	Maria Colon Rueñes, Cuba	224'5"
1984	Theresa Sanderson, Great Britain	228'2"
1988	Petra Felke, E. Germany	245'0"
1992	Silke Renke, Germany	224'2"
1996	Heli Rantanen, Finland	222'11"

Long Jump

Year	Athlete	Distance
1948	Olga Gyarmati, Hungary	18'8¼"
1952	Yvette Williams, New Zealand	20'5¾"
1956	Elizbieta Krzesinska, Poland	20'10"
1960	Vyera Krepkina, U.S.S.R.	20'10¾"
1964	Mary Rand, Great Britain	22'2¼"
1968	Viorica Viscopoleanu, Romania	22'4½"
1972	Heidemarie Rosendahl, W. Germany	22'3"
1976	Angela Voigt, E. Germany	22'2¾"
1980	Tatiana Kolpakova, U.S.S.R.	23'0¾"
1984	Anisoara Cusmir-Stanciu, Romania	22'10"
1988	Jackie Joyner-Kersee, U.S.	24'3½"
1992	Heike Drechsler, Germany	23'5¼"
1996	Chioma Ajunwa, Nigeria	23'4½"

Shot Put

Year	Athlete	Distance
1948	Micheline Ostermeyer, France	45'1½"
1952	Galina Zybina, U.S.S.R.	50'1¾"
1956	Tamara Tyshkevich, U.S.S.R.	54'5"
1960	Tamara Press, U.S.S.R.	56'10"
1964	Tamara Press, U.S.S.R.	59'6¼"
1968	Margitta Gummel, E. Germany	64'4"
1972	Nadezhda Chizhova, U.S.S.R.	69'0"
1976	Ivanka Hristova, Bulgaria	69'5¾"
1980	Ilona Slupianek, E. Germany	73'6¼"
1984	Claudia Losch, W. Germany	67'2¼"
1988	Natalya Lisovskaya, U.S.S.R.	72'11½"
1992	Svetlana Krivaleva, Unified Team	69'1¼"
1996	Astrid Kumbernuss, Germany	67'5½"

Triple Jump

Year	Athlete	Distance
1996	Inessa Kravets, Ukraine	50'3½"

Pentathlon/Heptathlon[2]

Year	Athlete	Points
1964	Irina Press, U.S.S.R.	5,246
1968	Ingrid Becker, W. Germany	5,098
1972	Mary Peters, Great Britain	4,801
1976	Siegrun Siegl, E. Germany	4,745
1980	Nadezhda Tkachenko, U.S.S.R.	5,083
1984	Glynis Nunn, Australia	6,390
1988	Jackie Joyner-Kersee, U.S.	7,215
1992	Jackie Joyner-Kersee, U.S.	7,044
1996	Ghada Shouaa, Syria	6,780

1. 80 meters until 1972. 2. In 1984, two additional events were added: the 800-meter run and the javelin throw.

Gymnastics-Men

All-Around
1900 Gustave Sandras, France
1904 Julius Lenhart, Austria
1908 Alberto Braglia, Italy
1912 Alberto Braglia, Italy
1920 Giorgio Zampori, Italy
1924 Leon Stukelj, Yugoslavia
1928 Georges Miez, Switzerland
1932 Romeo Neri, Italy
1936 Alfred Schwarzmann, Germany
1948 Veikko Huhtanen, Finland
1952 Viktor Chukarin, USSR
1956 Viktor Chukarin, USSR
1960 Boris Shakhlin, USSR
1964 Yukio Endo, Japan
1968 Sawao Kato, Japan
1972 Sawao Kato, Japan
1976 Nikolai Andrianov, USSR
1980 Aleksandr Dityatin, USSR
1984 Koji Gushiken, Japan
1988 Vladimir Artemov, USSR
1992 Vitali Scherbo, Unified Team
1996 Li Xiaoshuang, China

Floor Exercises
1932 István Pelle, Hungary
1936 Georges Miez, Switzerland
1948 Ferenc Pataki, Hungary
1952 K. William Thoresson, Sweden
1956 Valentin Muratov, USSR
1960 Nobuyuki Aihara, Japan
1964 Franco Menichelli, Italy
1968 Sawao Koto, Japan
1972 Nikolai Andrianov, USSR
1976 Nikolai Andrianov, USSR
1980 Roland Brückner, E. Germany
1984 Li Ning, China
1988 Sergei Kharikov, USSR
1992 Xiaoshuang Li, China
1996 Ioannis Melissanidis, Greece

Horizontal Bar
1896 Herman Weingärtner, Germany
1904 Anton Heida, U.S.
       Edward Hennig, U.S. (tie)
1924 Leon Stukelj, Yugoslavia
1928 Georges Miez
1932 Dallas Bixler, U.S.
1936 Aleksanteri Saarvala, Finland
1948 Josef Stalder, Switzerland
1952 Jack Günthard, Switzerland
1956 Takashi Ono, Japan
1960 Takashi Ono, Japan
1964 Boris Shakhlin, USSR
1968 Akinori Nakayama, Japan

1972 Mitsuo Tsukahara, Japan
1976 Mitsuo Tsukahara, Japan
1980 Stoyan Deltchev, Bulgaria
1984 Shinji Morisue, Japan
1988 Vladimir Artemov, USSR
       Valeri Lioukine, USSR (tie)
1992 Trent Dimas, U.S.
1996 Andreas Wecker, Germany

Long Horse Vault
1896 Karl Schumann, Germany
1904 George Eyser, U.S.
       Anton Heida, U.S. (tie)
1924 Frank Kriz, U.S.
1928 Eugen Mack, Switzerland
1932 Savino Guglielmetti, Italy
1936 Alfred Schwarzmann, Germany
1948 Paavo Aaltonen, Finland
1952 Viktor Chukarin, USSR
1956 Helmut Bantz, West Germany
1960 Takashi Ono, Japan
1964 Haruhiro Yamashita, Japan
1968 Mikhail Voronin, USSR
1972 Klaus Köste, East Germany
1976 Nikolai Andrianov, USSR
1980 Nikolai Andrianov, USSR
1984 Lou Yun, China
1988 Lou Yun, China
1992 Vitali Scherbo, Unified Team
1996 Alexei Nemov, Russia

Parallel Bars
1896 Alfred Flatow, Germany
1904 George Eyser, U.S.
1924 August Güttinger, Switzerland
1928 Ladislav Vácha, Czechoslovakia
1932 Romeo Neri, Italy
1936 Konrad Frey, Germany
1948 Michael Reusch, Switzerland
1952 Hans Eugster, Switzerland
1956 Viktor Chukarin, USSR
1960 Boris Shakhlin, USSR
1964 Yukio Endo, Japan
1968 Akinori Nakayama, Japan
1972 Sawao Koto, Japan
1976 Sawao Koto, Japan
1980 Aleksandr Tkachyov, USSR
1984 Bart Conner, U.S.
1988 Vladimir Artemov, USSR
1992 Vitali Scherbo, Unified Team
1996 Rustam Sharipov, Ukraine

Rings
1896 Ioannis Mitropoulos, Greece
1904 Hermann Glass, U.S.

1924 Francesco Martino, Italy
1928 Leon Stukelj, Yugoslavia
1932 George Gulack, U.S.
1936 Alois Hudec, Czechoslovakia
1948 Karl Frei, Switzerland
1952 Grant Shaginyan, USSR
1956 Albert Azaryan, USSR
1960 Albert Azaryan, USSR
1964 Takuji Haytta, Japan
1968 Akinori Nakayama, Japan
1972 Akinori Nakayama, Japan
1976 Nikolai Andrianov, USSR
1980 Aleksandr Dityatin, USSR
1984 Koji Gushiken, Japan
1988 Holger Behrendt, E. Germany
       Dmitri Bilozertchev, USSR
1992 Vitali Scherbo, Unified Team
1996 Yuri Chechi, Italy

Side (Pommel) Horse
1896 Jules Zutter, Switzerland
1904 Anton Heida, U.S.
1924 Josef Wilhelm, Switzerland
1928 Hermann Hänggi, Switzerland
1932 István Pelle, Hungary
1936 Konrad Frey, Germany
1948 Paavo Aaltonen, Finland
1952 Viktor Chukarin, USSR
1956 Boris Shakhlin, USSR
1960 Eugene Ekman, Finland
1964 Miroslav Cerar, Yugoslavia
1968 Miroslav Cerar, Yugoslavia
1972 Viktor Klimenko, USSR
1976 Zoltán Magyar, Hungary
1980 Zoltán Magyar, Hungary
1984 Li Ning, China
1988 Lyubomir Gueraskov, Bulgaria
       Dmitri Bilozertchev, USSR
       Zsolt Borkai, Hungary
1992 Vitali Scherbo, Unified Team
       Gil Su Pae, North Korea
1996 Li Donghua, Switzerland

Team Combined

1908	Sweden	1964	Japan
1912	Italy	1968	Japan
1920	Italy	1972	Japan
1928	Switzerland	1976	Japan
1932	Italy	1980	USSR
1936	Germany	1984	USA
1948	Finland	1988	USSR
1952	USSR	1992	Unified Team
1956	USSR	1996	Russia
1960	Japan		

Gymnastics-Women

All-Around
1952 Maria Gorokhovskaya, USSR
1956 Larissa Latynina, USSR
1960 Larissa Latynina, USSR
1964 Vera Cáslavská, Czechoslovakia
1968 Vera Cáslavská, Czechoslovakia
1972 Lyudmila Tourischeva, USSR
1976 Nadia Comaneci, Romania
1980 Yelena Davydova, USSR
1984 Mary Lou Retton, U.S.
1988 Elena Shushunova, USSR
1992 Tatiana Goutsou, Unified Team
1996 Lilia Popkopayeva, Ukraine

Floor Exercises
1952 Agnes Keleti, Hungary
1956 Agnes Keleti, Hungary
1960 Larissa Latynina, U.S.S.R.
1964 Larissa Latynina, U.S.S.R.
1968 Vera Cáslavská, Czechoslovakia
1972 Olga Korbut, U.S.S.R.
1976 Nelli Kim, U.S.S.R.
1980 Nadia Comaneci, Rom.
1984 Ecaterina Szabó, Romania
1988 Daniela Silivas, Romania
1992 Lavina Milosovici, Rom.
1996 Lillia Podkopayeva, Ukraine

Balance Beam
1952 Nina Bocharova, U.S.S.R.
1956 Agnes Keleti, Hungary
1960 Eva Bosáková, Czechoslovakia
1964 Vera Cáslavská, Czechoslovakia
1968 Natalya Kuchinskaya, U.S.S.R.
1972 Olga Korbut, U.S.S.R.
1976 Nadia Comaneci, Romania
1980 Nadia Comaneci, Romania
1984 Simona Pauca, Romania
1988 Daniela Silivas, Romania
1992 Tatiana Lyssenko, UnifiedTeam
1996 Shannon Miller, United States

Uneven Bars
1952 Margit Korondi, Hungary
1956 Agnes Keleti, Hungary
1960 Polina Astakhova, U.S.S.R.
1964 Polina Astakhova, U.S.S.R.
1968 Vera Cáslavská, Czechoslovakia
1972 Karin Janz, East Germany
1976 Nadia Comaneci, Romania
1980 Maxi Gnauck, East Germany
1984 Ma Yanhong, China
1988 Daniela Silivas, Romania
1992 Li Lu, China
1996 Svetlana Chorkina, Russia

Vault
1952 Yekaterina Kalinchuk
1956 Larissa Latynina, U.S.S.R.
1960 Margarita Nikolayeva, U.S.S.R.
1964 Vera Cáslavská, Czechoslovakia
1968 Vera Cáslavská, Czechoslovakia
1972 Karin Janz, East Germany
1976 Nelli Kim, U.S.S.R.
1980 Natalya Shaposhnikova, U.S.S.R.
1984 Ecaterina Szabó, Romania
1988 Svetlana Boguinskaya, U.S.S.R.
1992 Henrietta Onodi, Hungary
       Lavinia Milosovici, Romania
1996 Simona Amanar, Romania

Team Combined

1928	Holland	1968	U.S.S.R.
1936	W. Germany	1972	U.S.S.R.
1948	Czecho-	1976	U.S.S.R.
	slovakia	1980	U.S.S.R.
1952	U.S.S.R.	1984	Romania
1956	U.S.S.R.	1988	U.S.S.R.
1960	U.S.S.R.	1992	Unified Team
1964	U.S.S.R.	1996	United States

Team Sports

Baseball		Basketball-Women		1964	Hungary		1980	U.S.S.R.		1912	Great Britain
1988	U.S.	1976	U.S.S.R.	1968	Hungary		1984	U.S.		1920	Great Britain/
1992	Cuba	1980	U.S.S.R.	1972	Poland		1988	U.S.			Ireland
1996	Cuba	1984	U.S.	1976	E. Germany		1992	Brazil		1924	France
		1988	U.S.	1980	Czechoslovakia		1996	Netherlands		1928	Germany
Basketball-Men		1992	Unified Team	1984	France					1932	Hungary
1936	U.S.	1996	U.S.	1988	U.S.S.R.		Volleyball-Women			1936	Germany
1948	U.S.			1992	Spain		1964	Japan		1948	Italy
1952	U.S.	Soccer-Men		1996	Nigeria		1968	U.S.S.R.		1952	Hungary
1956	U.S.	1900	Great Britain				1972	U.S.S.R.		1956	Hungary
1960	U.S.	1904	Canada	Soccer-Women			1976	Japan		1960	Italy
1964	U.S.	1908	Great Britain	1996	U.S.		1980	U.S.S.R.		1964	Hungary
1968	U.S.	1912	Great Britain				1984	China		1968	Yugoslavia
1972	U.S.S.R.	1920	Belgium	Softball			1988	U.S.S.R.		1972	U.S.S.R.
1976	U.S.	1924	Uruguay	1996	U.S.		1992	Cuba		1976	Hungary
1980	Yugoslavia	1928	Uruguay				1996	Cuba		1980	U.S.S.R.
1984	U.S.	1936	Italy	Volleyball-Men						1984	Yugoslavia
1988	U.S.S.R.	1948	Sweden	1964	U.S.S.R.		Water Polo			1988	Yugoslavia
1992	U.S.	1952	Hungary	1968	U.S.S.R.		1900	Great Britain		1992	Italy
1996	U.S.	1956	U.S.S.R.	1972	Japan		1904	U.S.		1996	Spain
		1960	Yugoslavia	1976	Poland		1908	Great Britain			

WINTER OLYMPIC CHAMPIONS

Biathlon
(Cross-country skiing and riflery)

Men's 10-Kilometer (6.2 Miles)

		Time
1980	Frank Ulrich, East Germany	32:10.69
1984	Eirik Kvalfoss, Norway	30:53.80
1988	Frank-Peter Roetsch, E. Germany	25:08.10
1992	Mark Kirchner, Germany	26:02.30
1994	Sergei Tchepikov, Russia	28:07.00
1998	Ole Bjorndalen, Norway	27:16.20

Men's 20-Kilometer (12.4 miles)

		Time
1960	Klas Lestander, Sweden	1:33:21.60
1964	Vladimir Melanin, U.S.S.R.	1:20:26.80
1968	Magnar Solberg, Norway	1:13:45.90
1972	Magnar Solberg, Norway	1:15:55.50
1976	Nikolai Kruglov, U.S.S.R.	1:14:12.26
1980	Anatoli Alabyev, U.S.S.R.	1:08:16.31
1984	Peter Angerer, West Germany	1:11:52.70
1988	Frank-Peter Roetsch, E. Germany	0:56:33.33
1992	Evgueni Redkine, Unified Team	0:57:34.04
1994	Sergei Tarasov, Russia	0:57:25.30
1998	Halvard Hanevold, Norway	56:16.40

Men's 4x7.5 Kilometer (18.6 mile) Relay [1]

		Time
1968	U.S.S.R., Norway, Sweden	2:13:02.40
1972	U.S.S.R., Finland, East Germany	1:51:44.92
1976	U.S.S.R., Finland, East Germany	1:57:55.64
1980	U.S.S.R., E. Germany, W. Germany	1:34:03.27
1984	U.S.S.R., Norway, West Germany	1:38:51.70
1988	U.S.S.R., West Germany, Italy	1:22:30.00
1992	Germany, Unified Team, Sweden	1:24:43.50
1994	Germany, Russia, France	1:30:22.10
1998	Germany, Norway, Russia	1:19:43.30

Women's 7.5 Kilometer (4.6 miles)

		Time
1992	Anfissa Restzova, Unified Team	24:29.2
1994	Myriam Bedard, Canada	26:08.8
1998	Galina Kukleva, Russia	23:08.0

Women's 15 Kilometer (9.3 miles)

		Time
1992	Antje Misersky, Germany	51:47.2
1994	Myriam Bedard, Canada	52:06.6
1998	Yekaterina Dafovska, Bulgaria	54:52.0

Women's 4x7.5 Kilometer (18.6 mile) Relay

		Time
1992	France, Germany, Unified Team[2]	1:15:55.6
1994	Russia, Germany, France	1:47:19.5
1998	Germany, Russia, Norway	1:40:13.6

1. 4x10km until 1980. 2. 22.5km (3x7.5km) in 1992 only.

Bobsled

Two Man		Time	Four Man		Time
1932	U.S.	8:14.74	1924	Switzerland	5:45.54
1936	U.S.	5:29.29	1928	U.S. (5-man)	3:20.50
1948	Switzerland	5:29.20	1932	U.S.	7:53.68
1952	Germany	5:24.54	1936	Switzerland	5:19.85
1956	Italy	5:30.14	1948	U.S.	5:20.10
1964	Great Britain	4:21.90	1952	Germany	5:07.84
1968	Italy	4:41.54	1956	Switzerland	5:10.44
1972	W. Germany	4:57.07	1964	Canada	4:14.46
1976	E. Germany	3:44.42	1968	Italy	2:17.39
1980	Switzerland	4:09.36	1972	Switzerland	4:43.07
1984	E. Germany	3:25.56	1976	E. Germany	3:40.43
1988	U.S.S.R.	3:54.19	1980	E. Germany	3:59.42
1992	Switzerland	4:03.26	1984	E. Germany	3:20.22
1994	Switzerland	3:30.81	1988	Switzerland	3:47.51
1998	Canada, Italy	3:37.24	1992	Austria	3:53.90
			1994	Germany	3:27.78
			1998	Germany	2:39.41

Luge

Singles (Men)

		Time
1964	Thomas Köhler, East Germany	3:26.77
1968	Manfred Schmid, Austria	2:52.48
1972	Wolfgang Scheidel, East Germany	3:27.58
1976	Dettlef Günther, East Germany	3:27.68
1980	Bernhard Glass, East Germany	2:54.79
1984	Paul Hildgartner, Italy	3:04.25
1988	Jens Mueller, East Germany	3:05.54
1992	Georg Hackl, Germany	3:02.36
1994	Georg Hackl, Germany	3:21.57
1998	Georg Hackl, Germany	3:18.44

Two-seater (Men)		Time	Year	Winner	Time
1964	Austria	1:41.62	1984	W. Germany	1:23.62
1968	E. Germany	1:35.85	1988	E.	1:31.94
1972	Italy, (tie)	1:28.35	1992	Germany	1:32.05
	E. Germany		1994	Italy	1:36.72
1976	E. Germany	1:25.60	1998	Germany	1:41.10
1980	E. Germany	1:19.33			

Singles (Women)

		Time
1964	Ortrun Enderlein, East Germany	3:24.67
1968	Erica Lechner, Italy	2:28.66
1972	Anna M. Müller, East Germany	2:59.18
1976	Margit Schumann, East Germany	2:50.62
1980	Vera Zozulya, U.S.S.R.	2:36.53
1984	Steffi Martin, East Germany	2:46.57
1988	Steffi Walter (Martin), East Germany	3:03.97
1992	Doris Neuner, Austria	3:06.69
1994	Gerda Weissensteiner, Italy	3:15.52
1998	Silke Kraushaar, Germany	3:23.78

Alpine Skiing (Men)

Downhill		Time
1948	Henri Oreiller, France	2:55.00
1952	Zeno Colo, Italy	2:30.80
1956	Anton Sailer, Austria	2:52.20
1960	Jean Vuarnet, France	2:06.00
1964	Egon Zimmerman, Austria	2:18.16
1968	Jean-Claude Killy, France	1:59.85
1972	Bernhard Russi, Switzerland	1:51.43
1976	Franz Klammer, Austria	1:45.73
1980	Leonhard Stock, Austria	1:45.50
1984	William Johnson, United States	1:45.59
1988	Pirmin Zurbriggen, Switzerland	1:59.63
1992	Patrick Ortlieb, Austria	1:50.37
1994	Tommy Moe, United States	1:45.75
1998	Jean-Luc Cretier, France	1:50.11

Slalom		Time
1948	Edi Reinalter, Switzerland	2:10.30
1952	Othmar Schneider, Austria	2:00.00
1956	Anton Sailer, Austria	3:14.70
1960	Ernst Hinterseer, Austria	2:08.90
1964	Josef Stiegler, Austria	2:11.13
1968	Jean Claude Killy, France	1:39.73
1972	Francisco Fernandez Ochoa, Spain	1:39.73
1976	Piero Gros, Italy	2:03.29
1980	Ingemar Stenmark, Sweden	1:44.26
1984	Philip Mahre, United States	1:39.41
1988	Alberto Tomba, Italy	1:39.47
1992	Finn Christian Jagge, Norway	1:44.39
1994	Thomas Stangassinger	2:02.02
1998	Hans-Petter Buraas, Norway	1:49.31

Giant Slalom		Time
1952	Stein Eriksen, Norway	2:25.00
1956	Anton Sailer, Austria	3:00.10
1960	Roger Staub, Switzerland	1:48.30
1964	Francois Bonlieu, France	1:46.71
1968	Jean Claude Killy, France	3:29.28
1972	Gustavo Thöni, Italy	3:09.62
1976	Heini Hemmi, Switzerland	3:26.97
1980	Ingemar Stenmark, Sweden	2:40.74
1984	Max Julen, Switzerland	2:41.18
1988	Alberto Tomba, Italy	2:06.37
1992	Alberto Tomba, Italy	2:06.98
1994	Markus Wasmeier, Germany	2:52.46
1998	Hermann Maier, Austria	2:38.51

Super Giant Slalom		Time
1988	Frank Piccard, France	1:39.66
1992	Kjetil Andre Aamodt, Norway	1:13.04
1994	Markus Wasmeier, Germany	1:32.53
1998	Hermann Maier, Austria	1:34.82

Combined (Downhill/Slalom)	
1988	Hubert Strolz, Austria
1992	Josef Polig, Italy
1994	Lasse Kjus, Norway
1998	Mario Reiter, Austria

Alpine Skiing (Women)

Downhill		Time
1948	Hedi Schlunegger, Switzerland	2:28.30
1952	Trude Jochum-Beiser, Austria	1:47.10
1956	Madeleine Berthod, Switzerland	1:40.70
1960	Heidi Biebl, Germany	1:37.60
1964	Christl Haas, Austria	1:55.39
1968	Olga Pall, Austria	1:40.87
1972	Marie-Theres Nadig, Switzerland	1:36.68
1976	Rosi Mittermaier, West Germany	1:46.16
1980	Annemarie Moser-Pröll, Austria	1:37.52
1984	Michela Figini, Switzerland	1:13.36[1]
1988	Marina Kiehl, West Germany	1:25.86
1992	Kerrin Lee-Gartner, Canada	1:52.55
1994	Katja Seizinger, Germany	1:35.93
1998	Katja Seizinger, Germany	1:28.89

Slalom		Time
1948	Gretchen Fraser, United States	1:57.20
1952	Andrea Mead Lawrence, United States	2:10.60
1956	Renée Colliard, Switzerland	1:52.30
1960	Anne Heggtveigt, Canada	1:49.60
1964	Christine Goitschel, France	1:29.86
1968	Marielle Goitschel, France	1:25.86
1972	Barbara Cochran, United States	1:31.24
1976	Rosi Mittermaier, West Germany	1:30.54
1980	Hanni Wenzel, Liechtenstein	1:25.09
1984	Paoletta Magoni, Italy	1:36.47
1988	Vreni Schneider, Switzerland	1:36.69
1992	Petra Kronberger, Austria	1:32.68
1994	Vreni Schneider, Switzerland	1:56.01
1998	Hilde Gerg, Germany	1:32.40

Giant Slalom		Time
1952	Andrea Mead Lawrence, United States	2:06.80
1956	Ossi Reichert, Germany	1:56.50
1960	Yvonne Rüegg, Switzerland	1:39.90
1964	Marielle Goitschel, France	1:52.24
1968	Nancy Greene, Canada	1:51.97
1972	Marie-Theres Nadig, Switzerland	1:29.90
1976	Kathy Kreiner, Canada	1:29.13
1980	Hanni Wenzel, Liechtenstein	2:41.66
1984	Debbie Armstrong, United States	2:20.98
1988	Vreni Schneider, Switzerland	2:06.49
1992	Pernilla Wiberg, Sweden	2:12.74
1994	Deborah Compagnoni, Italy	2:30.97
1998	Deborah Compagnoni, Italy	2:50.59

Super Giant Slalom		Time
1988	Sigrid Wolf, Austria	1:19.03
1992	Deborah Compagnoni, Italy	1:21.22
1994	Diann Roffe-Steinrotter, United States	1:22.15
1998	Picabo Street, United States	1:18.02

Combined (Downhill/Slalom)	
1988	Anita Wachter, Austria
1992	Petra Kronberger, Austria
1994	Pernilla Wiberg, Sweden
1998	Katja Seizinger, Germany

1. Race shortened by weather conditions

Ice Hockey

Year	Gold, Silver, Bronze
1920	Canada, United States Czechoslovakia
1924	Canada, United States, Great Britain
1928	Canada, Sweden, Switzerland
1932	Canada, United States, Germany
1936	Great Britain, Canada, United States
1948	Canada, Czechoslovakia, Switzerland
1952	Canada, United States, Sweden
1956	U.S.S.R., United States, Canada
1960	U.S., Canada, U.S.S.R.
1964	U.S.S.R., Sweden, Czechoslovakia
1968	U.S.S.R., Czechoslovakia, Canada
1972	U.S.S.R., United States, Czechoslovakia
1976	U.S.S.R., Czechoslovakia, West Germany
1980	U.S., U.S.S.R., Sweden
1984	U.S.S.R., Czechoslovakia, Sweden
1988	U.S.S.R., Finland, Sweden
1992	Unified Team, Canada, Czechoslovakia
1994	Sweden, Canada, Finland
1998	Czech Republic, Russia, Finland

Freestyle Skiing–Men

Aerials		Points
1994	Andreas Schoenbaechler, Switzerland	234.67
1998	Eric Bergoust, United States	255.64

Moguls		Points
1992	Edgar Grospiron, France	25.81
1994	Jean-Luc Brassard, Canada	27.24
1998	Jonny Moseley, United States	26.93

Freestyle Skiing–Women

Aerials		Points
1994	Lina Cherjazova, Uzbekistan	166.84
1998	Nikki Stone, United States	193.00

Moguls		Points
1992	Donna Weinbrecht, United States	23.69
1994	Stine Lise Hattestad, Norway	25.97
1998	Tae Satoya, Japan	25.06

Nordic Skiing and Jumping (Men)

10-Kilometer (6.2 Miles) Cross-Country	Time
1992 Vegard Ulvang, Norway	27:36.00
1994 Bjorn Dahlie, Norway	24:20.10
1998 Bjorn Dahlie, Norway	27:24.50

15-Kilometer (9.3 Miles) Pursuit Method[1]	Time
1924 Thorleif Haug, Norway	1:14:31.00
1928 Johan Gröttumsbraaten, Norway	1:37:01.00
1932 Sven Utterstrom, Sweden	1:23:07.00
1936 Erik-August Larsson, Sweden	1:14:38.00
1948 Martin Lundström, Sweden	1:13:50.70
1952 Hallgeir Brenden, Norway	1:01:34.00
1956 Hallgeir Brenden, Norway[1]	0:49:39.00
1960 Hakon Brusveen, Norway	0:51:55.50
1964 Eero Mäntyranta, Finland	0:50:54.10
1968 Harald Grönningen, Norway	0:47:54.20
1972 Sven-Ake Lundbäck, Sweden	0:45:28.24
1976 Nikolai Bazhukov, U.S.S.R.	0:43:58.47
1980 Thomas Wassberg, Sweden	0:41:57.63
1984 Gunde Svan, Sweden	0:41:25.60
1988 Mikhail Deviatiarov, U.S.S.R.	0:41:18.90
1992 Bjorn Dahlie, Norway	0:38:01.90
1994 Bjorn Dahlie, Norway	0:35:48.80
1998 Thomas Alsgaard, Norway	1:07:01.70

1. Until 1956, 18 km

30-Kilometer (18.6 Miles) Cross-Country	Time
1956 Veikko Hakulinen, Finland	1:44:06.00
1960 Sixten Jernberg, Sweden	1:51:03.90
1964 Eero Mäntyranta, Finland	1:30:50.70
1968 Franco Nones, Italy	1:35:39.20
1972 Vyacheslav Vedenin, U.S.S.R.	1:36:31.15
1976 Sergei Saveliev, U.S.S.R.	1:30:29.38
1980 Nikolai Zimyatov, U.S.S.R.	1:27:02.80
1984 Nikolai Zimyatov, U.S.S.R.	1:28:56.30
1988 Aleksei Prokourorov, U.S.S.R.	1:24:26.30
1992 Vegard Ulvang, Norway	1:22:27.80
1994 Thomas Alsgaard, Norway	1:12:26.40
1998 Mika Myllylae, Finland	1:33.55.80

50-Kilometer (31.2 Miles) Cross-Country	Time
1924 Thorleif Haug, Norway	3:44:32.00
1928 Per Erik Hedlund, Sweden	4:52:03.00
1932 Veli Saarinen, Finland	4:28:00.00
1936 Elis Viklund, Sweden	3:30:11.00
1948 Nils Karlsson, Sweden	3:47:48.00
1952 Veikko Hakulinen, Finland	3:33:33.00
1956 Sixten Jernberg, Sweden	2:50:27.00
1960 Kalevi Hamalainen, Finland	2:59:06.30
1964 Sixten Jernberg, Sweden	2:43:52.60
1968 Ole Ellefsaeter, Norway	2:28:45.80
1972 Pål Tyldum, Norway	2:43:14.75
1976 Ivar Formo, Norway	2:37:30.05
1980 Nikolai Zimyatov, U.S.S.R.	2:27:24.60
1984 Thomas Wassberg, Sweden	2:15:55.80
1988 Gunde Svan, Sweden	2:04:30.90
1992 Bjorn Dahlie, Norway	2:03:41.50
1994 Vladimir Smirnov, Kazakhstan	2:07:20.30
1998 Bjorn Dahlie, Norway	2:05:08.20

40-Kilometer (24.8 Miles) Relay (4x10)	Time
1936 Finland, Norway, Sweden	2:41:33.00
1948 Sweden, Finland, Norway	2:32:08.00
1952 Finland, Norway, Sweden	2:20:16.00
1956 U.S.S.R., Finland Sweden	2:15:30.00
1960 Finland, Norway, U.S.S.R.	2:18:45.60
1964 Sweden, Finland, U.S.S.R.	2:18:34.60
1968 Norway, Sweden, Finland	2:08:33.50
1972 U.S.S.R., Norway, Switzerland	2:04:47.94
1976 Finland, Norway, U.S.S.R.	2:07:59.72
1980 U.S.S.R., Norway, Finland	1:57:03.46
1984 Sweden, U.S.S.R., Finland	1:55:06.30

1988 Sweden, U.S.S.R., Czechoslovakia	1:43:58.60
1992 Norway, Italy, Finland	1:39:26.00
1994 Italy, Norway, Finland	1:41:15.00
1998 Norway, Italy, Finland	1:40:55.70

Nordic Combined
(15 km Cross-Country and 70-Meter Ski Jump[1])

1924 Thorleif Haug, Norway	18.906
1928 Johan Gröttumsbraaten, Norway	17.833
1932 Johan Gröttumsbraaten, Norway	446.00
1946 Oddbjörn Hagen, Norway	430.30
1952 Simon Slåttvik, Norway	451.62
1956 Sverre Stenersen, Norway	455.00
1960 George Thoma, West Germany	457.95
1964 Tormod Knutsen, Norway	469.28
1968 Franz Keller, West Germany	449.04
1972 Ulrich Wehling, East Germany	413.34
1976 Ulrich Wehling, East Germany	423.39
1980 Ulrich Wehling, East Germany	432.20
1984 Torn Sandberg, Norway	422.59
1988 Hippolyt Kempf Switzerland	235.80
1992 Fabrice Guy, France	426.47
1994 Fred Lundberg, Norway	—
1998 Bjarte Engen Vik, Norway	—

1. Until 1956, 18 km

Nordic Combined, Team

1988 W. Germany, Switzerland, Austria	1:20:46.00
1992 Japan, Norway, Austria	1:23:36.50
1994 Japan, Norway, Switzerland	—
1998 Norway, Finland, France	—

90-Meter (293.5 ft.) Jump	Points
1964 Veikko Kankkonen, Finland	229.90
1968 Jiri Raska, Czechoslovakia	216.50
1972 Yukio Kasaya, Japan	244.20
1976 Hans-Georg Aschenbach, E. Germany	252.00
1980 Anton Innauer, Austria	266.30
1984 Jens Weissflog, East Germany	215.20
1988 Matti Nykänen, Finland	229.10
1992 Ernst Vettori, Austria	222.80
1994 Espen Bredesen, Norway	282.00
1998 Jani Soininen, Finland	234.50

1. Until 1992, 70 meters

120-Meter (393.7 ft.) Jump[1]	Points
1924 Jacob Tullin Thambs, Norway	18.960
1928 Alf Andersen, Norway	19.208
1932 Birger Ruud, Norway	228.10
1936 Birger Ruud, Norway	232.00
1948 Petter Hugsted, Norway	228.10
1952 Arnfinn Bergmann, Norway	226.00
1956 Antti Hyvarinen, Finland	227.00
1960 Helmut Recknagel, Germany	227.20
1964 Toralf Engan, Norway	230.70
1968 Vladimir Beloussov, U.S.S.R.	231.30
1972 Wojiech Fortuna, Poland	219.90
1976 Karl Schnabl, Austria	234.80
1980 Jouko Tormanen, Finland	271.00
1984 Matti Nykänen, Finland	231.20
1988 Matti Nykänen, Finland	224.00
1992 Toni Nieminen, Finland	239.50
1994 Jens Weissflog, Germany	274.50
1998 Kazuyoshi Funaki, Japan	272.30

1. Until 1992, 90 meters.

120-Meter (393.7 ft.) Jump, Team[1]	Points
1988 Finland, Yugoslavia, Norway	634.40
1992 Finland, Austria, Czechoslovakia	644.40
1994 Germany, Japan, Austria	970.10
1998 Japan, Germany, Austria	933.00

1. Until 1992, 90 meters.

Nordic Skiing (Women)

5-Kilometer (3.1 Miles) Cross-Country		Time
1964	Claudia Boyarskikh, U.S.S.R.	17:50.50
1968	Toini Gustafsson, Sweden	16:45.20
1972	Galina Kulakova, U.S.S.R.	17:00.50
1976	Helena Takalo, Finland	15:48.69
1980	Raisa Smetanina, U.S.S.R.	15:06.92
1984	Marja-Liisa Hämäläinen, Finland	17:04.00
1988	Marjo Matikainen, Finland	15:04.00
1992	Marjut Lukkarinen, Finland	14:13.80
1994	Lyubov Egorova, Russia	14:08.80
1998	Larissa Lazutina, Russia	17:39.90

10-Kilometer (6.2 Miles) Pursuit Method		Time
1952	Lydia Wideman, Finland	41:40.00
1956	Lyubov Kosyreva, U.S.S.R.	38:11.00
1960	Maria Gusakova, U.S.S.R.	39:46.60
1964	Claudia Boyarskikh, U.S.S.R.	40:24.30
1968	Toini Gustafsson, Sweden	36:46.50
1972	Galina Kolakova, U.S.S.R.	34:17.82
1976	Raisa Smetanina, U.S.S.R.	30:31.54
1980	Barbara Petzold, East Germany	30:31.54
1984	Marja-Liisa Hämäläinen, Finland	31:44.20
1988	Vida Ventsene, U.S.S.R.	30:08.20
1992	Lyubov Egorova, Unified Team	40:07.70
1994	Lyubov Egorova, Russia	41:38.10
1998	Larissa Lazutina, Russia	46:06.90

15-Kilometer (9.3 Miles) Cross-Country		Time
1992	Lyubov Egorova, Unified Team	42:20.80
1994	Manuela Di Centa, Italy	39:44.50
1998	Olga Danilova, Russia	46:55.40

30-Kilometer (18.6 Miles) Cross-Country[1]		Time
1984	Marja Liisa Hämäläinen, Finland	1:01:45.0
1988	Tamara Tikhonova, U.S.S.R.	55:53.6
1992	Stefania Belmondo, Italy	1:22:30.10
1994	Manuela Di Centa, Italy	1:25:41.60
1998	Yuliya Chepalova, Russia	1:22:01.50

20-Kilometer (12.4 Miles) Cross-Country Relay[2] (4x5Km)	
1956	Finland	1:09:01.00
1960	Sweden	1:04.21.00
1964	U.S.S.R.	0:59:20.00
1968	Norway	0:57:30.00
1972	U.S.S.R.	0:48:46.15
1976	U.S.S.R.	1:07:49.75
1980	East Germany	1:02:11.10
1984	Norway	1:06:49.70
1988	U.S.S.R.	0:59:51.10
1992	Unified Team	0:59:34.80
1994	Russia	0:57:12.50
1998	Russia, Norway, Italy	0:55:13.50

1. 20 Km until 1992.   2. 15 km (3 x 5 km) until 1976.

Figure Skating

MEN

1908	Ulrich Salchow, Sweden
1920	Gillis Grafstrom, Sweden
1924	Gillis Grafstrom Sweden
1928	Gillis Grafstrom, Sweden
1932	Karl Schafer, Austria
1936	Karl Schafer, Austria
1948	Richard Button, United States
1952	Richard Button, United States
1956	Hayes Alan Jenkins, United States
1960	David W. Jenkins, United States
1964	Manfred Schnelldorfer, Germany
1968	Wolfgang Schwartz, Austria
1972	Ondrej Nepela, Czechoslovakia
1976	John Curry, Great Britain
1980	Robin Cousins, Great Britain
1984	Scott Hamilton, United States
1988	Brian Boitano, United States
1992	Viktor Petrenko, Unified Team
1994	Aleksei Urmanov, Russia
1998	Ilya Kulik, Russia

WOMEN

1908	Madge Syers, Great Britain
1920	Magda Julin-Mauroy, Sweden
1924	Herma von Szabo-Planck, Austria
1928	Sonja Henie, Norway
1932	Sonja Henie, Norway
1936	Sonja Henie, Norway
1948	Barbara Ann Scott, Canada
1952	Jeanette Altwegg, Great Britain
1956	Tenley Albright, United States
1960	Carol Heiss, United States
1964	Sjoukje Dijkstra, Netherlands
1968	Peggy Fleming, United States
1972	Beatrix Schuba, Austria
1976	Dorothy Hamill, United States
1980	Annett Pötzsch, East Germany
1984	Katarina Witt, East Germany
1988	Katarina Witt, East Germany
1992	Kristi Yamaguchi, United States
1994	Oksana Baiul, Ukraine
1998	Tara Lipinski, United States

PAIRS

1908	Germany—Anna Hubler, Heinrich Burger
1920	Finland—Ludovika & Walter Jakobsson
1924	Austria—Helene Engelman, Alfred Berger
1928	France—Andree Joly, Pierre Brunet
1932	France—Andree & Pierre Brunet
1936	Germany—Maxie Herber, Ernst Baier
1948	Belgium—Micheline Lannoy, Pierre Baugniet
1952	Germany—Ria & Paul Falk
1956	Austria—Elisabeth Schwartz, Kurt Oppelt
1960	Canada—Barbara Wagner, Robert Paul
1964	U.S.S.R.—Ludmila Beloussova, Oleg Protopopov
1968	U.S.S.R.—Ludmila Beloussova, Oleg Protopopov
1972	U.S.S.R.—Irina Rodnina, Alexei Ulanov
1976	U.S.S.R.—Irina Rodnina, Aleksandr Zaitsev
1980	U.S.S.R.—Irina Rodnina, Aleksandr Zaitsev
1984	U.S.S.R.—Elena Valova, Oleg Vassiliev
1988	U.S.S.R.—Ekaterina Gordeeva, Sergei Grinkov
1992	Unified Team—Natalya Mishkutienok, Artur Dmitriev
1994	Russia—Ekaterina Gordeeva, Sergei Grinkov
1998	Russia—Oksana Kazakova, Artur Dmitriev

ICE DANCING

1976	U.S.S.R.—Lyudmila Pakhomova, Aleksandr Gorshkov
1980	U.S.S.R.—Natalia Linichuk, Gennadi Karponosov
1984	Great Britain—Jayne Torvill, Christopher Dean
1988	U.S.S.R.—Natalia Bestemianova, Andrei Bukin
1992	Unified Team—Marina Kimova, Sergei Ponomarenko
1994	Russia—Pasha Grishuk, Yevgeny Platov
1998	Russia—Pasha Grishuk, Yevgeny Platov

Speed Skating, Men

500 Meters (1,641 Ft.)		Time
1924	Charles Jewtraw, U.S	0:44.00
1928	Clas Thunberg, Finland	0:43.40
	Bernst Evensen, Norway (tie)	
1932	John A. Shea, United States	0:43.40
1936	Ivar Ballangrud, Norway	0:43.40
1948	Finn Helgesen, Norway	0:43.10
1952	Ken Henry, United States	0:43.20
1956	Yevgeny Grishin, U.S.S.R.	0:40.20
1960	Yevgeny Grishin, U.S.S.R.	0:40.20
1964	Terry McDermott, United States	0:40.10
1968	Erhard Keller, West Germany	0:40.30
1972	Erhard Keller, West Germany	0:39.44
1976	Yergeny Kulikov, U.S.S.R.	0:39.17
1980	Eric Heiden, United States	0:38.03
1984	Sergei Fokichev, U.S.S.R.	0:38.19
1988	Uwe-Jens Mey, East Germany	0:36.45
1992	Uwe-Jens Mey, Germany	0:37.14
1994	Aleksandr Golubev, Russia	0:36.33
1998	Hiroyasu Shimizu, Japan	1:11.35

1,000 Meters (3,281 Ft.)		Time
1976	Peter Mueller, United States	1:19.32
1980	Eric Heiden, United States	1:15.18
1984	Gaétan Boucher, Canada	1:15.80
1988	Nikolai Guiliaev, U.S.S.R.	1:13.03
1992	Olaf Zinke, Germany	1:14.85
1994	Dan Jansen, United States	1:12.43
1998	Ids Postma, Netherlands	1:10.64

1,500 Meters (4,922 Ft.)		Time
1924	Clas Thunberg, Finland	2:20.80
1928	Clas Thunberg, Finland	2:21.10
1932	John A. Shea, United States	2:57.50
1936	Charles Mathisen, Norway	2:19.20
1948	Sverre Farstad, Norway	2:17.60
1952	Hjalmar Andersen, Norway	2:20.40
1956	Yevgeni Grishin	2:08.60
	Yuri Mikhailov, U.S.S.R. (tie)	
1960	Roald Aas, Norway	2:10.40
	Yevgeni Grishin, U.S.S.R. (tie)	
1964	Ants Anston, U.S.S.R.	2:10.30
1968	Cornelis Verkerk, Netherlands	2:03.40
1972	Ard Schenk, Netherlands	2:02.96
1976	Jan Egil Storholt, Norway	1:59.38
1980	Eric Heiden, United States	1:55.44
1984	Gaétan Boucher, Canada	1:58.36
1988	Andre Hoffmann, East Germany	1:52.06
1992	Johann Olav Koss, Norway	1:54.81
1994	Johann Olav Koss, Norway	1:51.29
1998	Aadne Sondral, Norway	1:47.87

5,000 Meters (16,405 Ft.)		Time
1924	Clas Thunberg, Finland	8:39.00
1928	Ivar Ballangrud, Norway	8:50.50
1932	Irving Jaffee, United States	9:40.80
1936	Ivar Ballangrud, Norway	8:19.60
1948	Reidar Liaklev, Norway	8:29.40
1952	Hjalmar Andersen, Norway	8:10.60
1956	Boris Shilkov, U.S.S.R.	7:48.70
1960	Viktor Kosichkin, U.S.S.R.	7:51.30
1964	Knut Johannesen, Norway	7:38.40
1968	F. Anton Maier, Norway	7:22.40
1972	Ard Schenk, Netherlands	7:23.61
1976	Sten Stensen, Norway	7:24.48
1980	Eric Heiden, United States	7:02.29
1984	Sven Tomas Gustafson, Sweden	7:12.28
1988	Tomas Gustafson, Sweden	6:44.63
1992	Geir Karlstad, Sweden	6:59.97
1994	Johann Olav Koss, Norway	6:34.96
1998	Gianni Romme, Netherlands	6:22.20

10,000 Meters (32,810 Ft.)		Time
1924	Julien Skutnabb, Finland	18:04.80
1928	(ice thawed, event cancelled)	
1932	Irving Jaffee, United States	19:13.60
1936	Ivan Ballangrud, Norway	17:24.30
1948	Ake Seyffarth, Sweden	17:26.30
1952	Hjalmar Andersen, Norway	16:45.80
1956	Sigvard Ericsson, Sweden	16:35.90
1960	Knut Johannessen, Norway	15:46.60
1964	Jonny Nilsson, Sweden	15:50.10
1968	Johnny Hoeglin, Sweden	15:23.60
1972	Ard Schenk, Netherlands	15:01.35
1976	Piet Kleine, Netherlands	14:50.59
1980	Eric Heiden, United States	14:28.13
1984	Igor Malikov, U.S.S.R.	14:39.90
1988	Tomas Gustafson, Sweden	13:48.20
1992	Bart Veldkamp, Netherlands	14:12.12
1994	Johann Olav Koss, Norway	13:30.55
1998	Gianni Romme, Netherlands	13:15.33

Speed Skating, Women

500 Meters (1,641 Ft.)		Time
1960	Helga Haase, Germany	0:45.90
1964	Lydia Skoblikova, U.S.S.R.	0:45.00
1968	Ludmila Titova, U.S.S.R.	0:46.10
1972	Anne Henning, United States	0:43.30
1976	Sheila Young, United States	0:42.76
1980	Karin Enke, East Germany	0:41.78
1984	Christa Rothenburger, East Germany	0:41.02
1988	Bonnie Blair, United States	0:39.10
1992	Bonnie Blair, United States	0:40.33
1994	Bonnie Blair, United States.	0:39.25
1998	Catriona Le May-Doan, Canada	1:16.60

1,000 Meters (3,281 Ft.)		Time
1960	Klara Guseva, U.S.S.R.	1:34.10
1964	Lydia Skoblikova, U.S.S.R.	1:33.20
1968	Carolina Geiissen, Netherlands	1:32.60
1972	Monika Pflug, West Germany	1:31.40
1976	Tatiana Averina, U.S.S.R.	1:28.43
1980	Natalia Petruseva, U.S.S.R.	1:24.10
1984	Karin Enke, East Germany	1:21.61
1988	Christa Rothenburger, East Germany	1:17.65
1992	Bonnie Blair, United States	1:21.90
1994	Bonnie Blair, United States	1:18.74
1998	Marianne Timmer, Netherlands	1:16.51

1,500 Meters (4,922 Ft.)		Time
1960	Lydia Skoblikova, U.S.S.R.	2:25.20
1964	Lydia Skoblikova, U.S.S.R.	2:22.60
1968	Kaija Mustonen, Finland	2:22.40
1972	Dianne Holum, United States	2:20.80
1976	Galina Stepanskaya, U.S.S.R.	2:16.58
1980	Annie Borchink, Netherlands	2:10.95
1984	Karin Enke, East Germany	2:03.42
1988	Yvonne Van Gennip, Netherlands	2:00.68
1992	Jacqueline Boerner, Germany	2:05.87
1994	Emese Hunyady, Austria	2:02.19
1998	Marianne Timmer, Netherlands	1:57.58

3,000 Meters (9,843 Ft.)		Time
1960	Lydia Skoblikova, U.S.S.R.	5:14.30
1964	Lydia Skoblikova, U.S.S.R.	5:14.90
1968	Johanna Schut, Netherlands	4:56.20
1972	Christina Baas-Kaiser, Netherlands	4:52.14
1976	Tatiana Averina, U.S.S.R.	4:45.19
1980	Bjoerg Eva Jensen, Norway	4:32.13
1984	Andrea Schöne, East Germany	4:24.79
1988	Yvonne Van Gennip, Netherlands	4:11.94
1992	Gunda Niemann, Germany	4:19.90
1994	Svetlana Bazhanova, Russia	4:17.43
1998	Gunda Niemann-Stirnemann, Germany	4:07.29

5,000 Meters (16,405 Ft.)		Time
1988	Yvonne Van Gennip, Netherlands	7:14.13
1992	Gunda Niemann, Germany	7:31.57
1994	Claudia Pechstein, Germany	7:14.37
1998	Claudia Pechstein, Germany	6:59.61

PROFESSIONAL SPORTS

AUTOMOBILE RACING

A number of U.S. states and cities banned automobile racing on public roads during the early 1900s, leading to the development of closed-circuit courses. The Indianapolis Motor Speedway, a 2.5 mile macadam oval, was built in 1909. It was paved with brick in 1911, when the first Indy 500 was run. The American Automobile Association, troubled by a series of fatal crashes, stopped sanctioning races in 1956, whereupon the United States Auto Club (USAC) took over the Indy 500.

Indianapolis 500 Winners, 1911–2001

Year	Winner	Time	MPH	Year	Winner	Time	MPH
Under AAA Sanction				1958	Jim Bryan	3:44:13	133.791
1911	Ray Harroun	6:42.08	74.602	1959	Rodger Ward	3:40:49	135.857
1912	Joe Dawson	6:21.06	78.719	1960	Jim Rathmann	3:36:11	138.767
1913	Juses Goux	6:35:05	75.933	1961	A.J. Foyt, Jr.	3:35:37	139.131
1914	Rene Thomas	6:03:45	82.474	1962	Roger Ward	3:33:50	140.293
1915	Ralph DePalma	5:33:55	89.840	1963	Parnelli Jones	3:29:35	143.137
1916	Dario Resta	3:34:17	84.001	1964	A.J. Foyt, Jr.	3:23:35	147.350
1919	Howard Wilcox	5:40:42	88.050	1965	Jim Clark	3:19:05	150.686
1920	Gaston Chevrolet	5:38:32	88.618	1966	Graham Hill	3:27:52	144.317
1921	Tommy Milton	5:34:34	89.621	1967	A.J. Foyt, Jr.	3:18:14	151.207
1922	Jimmy Murphy	5:17:30	94.484	1968	Bobby Unser	3:16:13	152.882
1923	Tommy Milton	5:29:50	90.954	1969	Mario Andretti	3:11:14	156.867
1924	L.L. Corum, Joe Boyer	5:05:23	98.234	1970	Al Unser	3:12:37	155.749
1925	Peter DePaolo	4:56:39	101.127	1971	Al Unser	3:10:11	157.735
1926	Peter Lockhart	4:10:14	95.904	1972	Mark Donohue	3:04:05	162.962
1927	George Souders	5:07:33	97.545	1973	Gordon Johncock	2:05:264	159.036
1928	Louis Meyer	5:01:33	99.482	1974	Johnny Rutherford	3:09:10	158.589
1929	Ray Keech	5:07:25	97.585	1975	Bobby Unser	2:54:555	149.213
1930	Billy Arnold	4:58:39	100.448	1976	Johnny Rutherford	1:42:526	148.725
1931	Louis Schneider	5:10:27	96.629	1977	A.J. Foyt, Jr.	3:05:57	161.331
1932	Fred Frame	4:48:03	104.144	1978	Al Unser	3:05:54	161.363
1933	Louis Meyer	4:48:00	104.162	1979	Rick Mears	3:08:47	158.899
1934	William Cummings	4:46:05	104.863	1980	Johnny Rutherford	3:29:59	142.862
1935	Kelly Petillo	4:42:22	106.240	1981	Bobby Unser	3:35:41	139.084
1936	Louis Meyer	4:35:03	109.069	1982	Gordon Johncock	3:05:09	162.029
1937	Wilbur Shaw	4:24:07	113.580	1983	Tom Sneva	3:05:03	162.117
1938	Floyd Roberts	4:15:58	117.200	1984	Rick Mears	3:30:21	163.612
1939	Wilbur Shaw	4:20:47	115.035	1985	Danny Sullivan	3:16:06	152.982
1940	Wilbur Shaw	4:22:31	114.277	1986	Bobby Rahal	2:55:43	170.722
1941	Floyd Davis, Mauri Rose	4:20:36	115.117	1987	Al Unser	3:04:59	162.175
1946	George Robson	4:21:16	114.820	1988	Rick Mears	3:27:10	144.809
1947	Mauri Rose	4:17:52	116.338	1989	Emerson Fittipaldi	2:59:01	167.581
1948	Mauri Rose	4:10:23	119.814	1990	Arie Luyendyk	2:41:18	185.984[7]
1949	Bill Holland	4:07:15	121.327	1991	Rick Mears	2:50:01	176.457
1950	Johnnie Parsons	2:46:55	124.002	1992	Al Unser, Jr.	3:43:05	134.477
1951	Lee Wallard	3:57:38	126.244	1993	Emerson Fittipaldi	3:10:50	157.207
1952	Troy Tuttman	3:52:41	128.922	1994	Al Unser, Jr.	3:06:29	160.872
1953	Bill Vukovich	3:53:01	128.740	1995	Jacques Villeneuve	3:15:18	153.616
1954	Bill Vukovich	3:49:17	130.840	1996	Buddy Lazier	3:22:46	147.956
1955	Bob Sweikert	3:53:59	128.209	1997	Arie Luyendyk	3:25:43	145.827
				1998	Eddie Cheever	3:26:40	145.155
Under USAC Sanction				1999	Kenny Brack	3:15:51	153.176
1956	Pat Flaherty	3:53.28	128.490	2000	Juan Montoya	2:58.59	167.607
1957	Sam Hanks	3:41.14	135.601	2001	Helio Castroneves	3:31.54	141.574

1. 300 miles (scheduled). 2. 400 miles (rain). 3. 345 miles (rain). 4. 332.5 miles (rain). 5. 435 miles (rain). 6. 255 miles (rain). 7. Track record. **Source:** Indianapolis Motor Speedway Hall of Fame and Museum.

Daytona 500 Winners, 1959–2001

Year	Driver	Avg.	Year	Driver	Avg.	Year	Driver	Avg.
1959	Lee Petty	135.521	1962	Fireball Roberts	152.529	1965	Fred Lorenzen	141.539
1960	Junior Johnson	124.740	1963	Tiny Lund	151.566	1966	Richard Petty	160.627
1961	Marvin Panch	149.601	1964	Richard Petty	154.334	1967	Mario Andretti	146.926

Year	Driver	Avg.	Year	Driver	Avg.	Year	Driver	Avg.
1968	Cale Yarborough	143.251	1979	Richard Petty	143.977	1991	Ernie Irvan	148.148
1969	LeeRoy Yarbrough	157.950	1980	Buddy Baker	177.602	1992	Davey Allison	160.260
1970	Pete Hamilton	149.601	1981	Richard Petty	169.651	1993	Dale Jarrett	154.972
1971	Richard Petty	144.462	1982	Bobby Allison	153.991	1994	Sterling Marlin	156.931
1972	A.J. Foyt Jr.	161.550	1983	Cale Yarborough	155.979	1995	Sterling Marlin	141.710
1973	Richard Petty	157.205	1984	Cale Yarborough	150.994	1996	Dale Jarrett	154.308
1974	Richard Petty	140.894	1985	Bill Elliott	172.265	1997	Jeff Gordon	148.295
1975	Benny Parsons	153.649	1986	Geoff Bodine	148.124	1998	Dale Earnhardt	172.712
1976	David Pearson	152.181	1987	Bill Elliott	176.263	1999	Jeff Gordon	161.551
1977	Cale Yarborough	153.218	1988	Bobby Allison	137.531	2000	Dale Jarrett	155.669
1978	Bobby Allison	159.730	1989	Darrell Waltrip	148.466	2001	Michael Waltrip	161.783
Source: NASCAR.			1990	Derrike Cope	165.761			

Winston Cup Winners 1959–2000

Year	Driver	Year	Driver	Year	Driver	Year	Driver	Year	Driver
1959	Lee Petty	1968	David Pearson	1977	Cale Yarborough	1986	Dale Earnhardt	1995	Jeff Gordon
1960	Rex White	1969	David Pearson	1978	Cale Yarborough	1987	Dale Earnhardt	1996	Terry Labonte
1961	Ned Jarrett	1970	Bobby Isaac	1979	Richard Petty	1988	Bill Elliott	1997	Jeff Gordon
1962	Joe Weatherly	1971	Richard Petty	1980	Dale Earnhardt	1989	Rusty Wallace	1998	Jeff Gordon
1963	Joe Weatherly	1972	Richard Petty	1981	Darrell Waltrip	1990	Dale Earnhardt	1999	Dale Jarrett
1964	Richard Petty	1973	Benny Parsons	1982	Darrell Waltrip	1991	Dale Earnhardt	2000	Bobby Labonte
1965	Ned Jarrett	1974	Richard Petty	1983	Bobby Allison	1992	Alan Kulwicki		
1966	David Pearson	1975	Richard Petty	1984	Terry Labonte	1993	Dale Earnhardt		
1967	Richard Petty	1976	Cale Yarborough	1985	Darrell Waltrip	1994	Dale Earnhardt		

Source: NASCAR.

BOWLING

PBA Leading Money Winners, 1959–2000

Year	Name	Amount	Year	Name	Amount	Year	Name	Amount
1959	Dick Weber	$ 7,672	1975	Earl Anthony	$107,585	1990	Aurelio Monacelli	$204,775
1960	Don Carter	22,525	1976	Earl Anthony	110,833	1991	David Ozio	225,585
1961	Dick Weber	26,280	1977	Mark Roth	105,583	1992	Marc McDowell	174,215
1962	Don Carter	49,972	1978	Mark Roth	134,500	1993	Walter Ray. Williams Jr.	296,370
1963	Dick Weber	46,333	1979	Mark Roth	124,517			
1964	Bob Strampe	33,592	1980	Wayne Webb	116,700	1994	Norm Duke	273,753
1965	Dick Weber	47,675	1981	Earl Anthony	164,735	1995	Mike Aulby	219,792
1966	Wayne Zahn	54,720	1982	Earl Anthony	134,760	1996	Walter Ray. Williams Jr,	241,330
1967	Dave Davis	54,165	1983	Earl Anthony	135,605			
1968	Jim Stefanich	67,375	1984	Mark Roth	158,712	1997	Walter Ray. Williams Jr	240,544
1969	Billy Hardwick	64,160	1985	Mike Aulby	201,200			
1970	Mike McGrath	52,049	1986	Walter Ray Williams Jr.	145,550	1998	Walter Ray Williams Jr.	238,225
1971	Johnny Petraglia	85,065						
1972	Don Johnson	56,648	1987	Pete Weber	179,516	1999	Parker Bohn III	240,912
1973	Don McCune	69,000	1988	Brian Voss	225,485	2000	Norm Duke	136,900
1974	Earl Anthony	99,585	1989	Mike Aulby	298,237			
Source: Professional Bowlers Association.								

Professional Women's Bowling Association, Career Money Leaders

Rank, Bowler	Earnings	Rank, Bowler	Earnings	Rank, Bowler	Earnings
1. Aleta Sill	$1,061,159	8. Kim Adler	$ 723,282	15. Marianne DiRupo	$565,713
2. Wendy Macpherson	1,038,385	9. Carolyn Dorin-Ballard	719,379	16. Carol Norman	560,504
3. Tish Johnson	998,440	10. Robin Mossontte	714,304	17. Cindy Coburn-Carroll	551,808
4. Anne Marie Duggan	876,648	11. Cheryl Daniels	706,102	18. Kim Terrell	547,584
5. Leanne Barrette	861,358	12. Dede Davidson	660,467	19. Jeanne Naccarato	541,402
6. Carol Gianotti-Block	852,232	13. Dana Miller-Mackie	633,577	20. Lorrie Nichols	485,644
7. Lisa Wagner	846,281	14. Nikki Gianulias	612,165		

Note: Career figures as of July 3, 2001. Earnings do not include TV incentives. Source: Professional Women's Bowling Association.

BOXING

Although many governing bodies now issue and certify their own boxing championships, the three most widely accepted are the World Boxing Association (WBA), World Boxing Council (WBC), and the International Boxing Federation (IBF). Years given indicate the year the championship belt changed hands in a title bout. Champions who were awarded belts without a championship bout are not shown. Current champions (as of October 3, 2001) are shown in **boldface type.**

Heavyweights (over 190 lbs.)

Year	Name
1885	John L. Sullivan
1892	James J. Corbett
1897	Robert Fitzsimmons
1899	James J. Jeffries
1905	Marvin Hart
1906	Tommy Burns
1908	Jack Johnson
1915	Jess Willard
1919	Jack Dempsey
1926	Gene Tunney[1]
1928–30	vacant
1930	Max Schmeling
1932	Jack Sharkey
1933	Primo Carnera
1934	Max Baer
1935	James J. Braddock
1937	Joe Louis[1]
1949	Ezzard Charles
1951	Jersey Joe Walcott
1952	Rocky Marciano[1]
1956	Floyd Patterson
1959	Ingemar Johansson
1960	Floyd Patterson
1962	Sonny Liston
1964	Cassius Clay[1] (Muhammad Ali)
1965	Ernie Terrell (WBA)
1967	Muhammad Ali (unifies world title)
1968	Jimmy Ellis (WBA)
1970	Joe Frazier (unifies world title)
1973	George Foreman
1974	Muhammad Ali
1978	Leon Spinks, Larry Holmes[1], Muhammad Ali[1] (WBA)
1979	John Tate (WBA)
1980	Mike Weaver (WBA)
1982	Michael Dokes (WBA)
1983	Gerrie Coetzee (WBA)
1984	Tim Witherspoon (WBC), Pinklon Thomas (WBC),Greg Page (WBA)
1985	Tony Tubbs (WBA)
1986	Tim Witherspoon (WBA), Trevor Berbick (WBC), Mike Tyson (WBC), James "Bonecrusher" Smith (WBA)
1987	Mike Tyson (WBA), Tony Tucker (IBF)
1990	Buster Douglas (unifies world title), Evander Holyfield
1992	Riddick Bowe
1993	Evander Holyfield (WBA, IBF)
1994	George Foreman (WBA, IBF), Bruce Seldon (WBA), Frank Bruno[1] (WBC)
1996	Mike Tyson (WBC), Michael Moorer (IBF), Mike Tyson (WBA), Evander Holyfield (WBA)
1997	Lennox Lewis (WBC), Evander Holyfield (IBF)
1999	Lennox Lewis (WBA[1], IBF)
2001	**Hasim Rahman (WBC, IBF), John Ruiz (WBA)**

Light Heavyweights (169–175 lbs.)

Year	Name
1903	Jack Root, George Gardner
1903	Bob Fitzsimmons
1905	Philadelphia Jack O'Brien[1]
1912	Jack Dillon
1916	Battling Levinsky
1920	George Carpentier
1922	Battling Siki
1923	Mike McTigue
1925	Paul Berlenbach
1926	Jack Delaney[1]
1927	Tommy Loughran[1]
1930	Maxey Rosenbloom
1934	Bob Olin
1935	John Henry Lewis[1]
1939	Billy Conn[1]
1941	Gus Lesnevich
1948	Freddie Mills
1950	Joey Maxim
1952	Archie Moore[1]
1960	*Vacant*
1962	Harold Johnson
1963	Willie Pastrano
1965	Jose Torres
1966	Dick Tiger
1968	Bob Foster
1971	Vicente Rondon (WBA)
1972	Bob Foster (unifies world title)
1974	John Conteh (WBC),Victor Galindez (WBA)
1977	Miguel Angel Cuello (WBC)
1978	Mate Parlov (WBC), Mike Rossman (WBA), Marvin Johnson (WBC)
1979	Matthew Franklin (Matthew Saad Muhammad) (WBC), Marvin Johnson (WBA)
1980	Eddie Gregory (Eddie Mustafa Muhammad) (WBA)
1981	Michael Spinks (WBA), Dwight Braxton (Dwight Muhammad Qawi) (WBC)
1983	Michael Spinks (unifies world title)
1985	J.B. Williamson (WBC),Slobodan Kacar (IBF)
1986	Marvin Johnson (WBA), Dennis Andries (WBC), Bobby Czyz (IBF)
1987	Thomas Hearns[1] (WBC), Leslie Stewart (WBA), Virgil Hill (WBA), Prince Charles Williams (IBF), Don Lalonde (WBC)
1988	Sugar Ray Leonard (WBC)
1989	Dennis Andries (WBC), Jeff Harding (WBC)
1990	Dennis Andries (WBC)
1991	Thomas Hearns (WBA),Jeff Harding (WBC)
1992	Iran Barkley[1] (WBA), Virgil Hill (WBA)
1993	Henry Maske (IBF)
1994	Mike McCallum (WBC)
1995	Fabrice Tiozzo (WBC)
1996	Roy Jones Jr.[1] (WBC),Virgil Hill[1] (IBF)
1997	William Guthrie (IBF), Dariusz Michalczewski[1] (WBA), Lou Del Valle (WBA)
1998	Reggie Johnson (IBF), Graciano Rocchigiani (WBC), **Roy Jones Jr. (WBA, WBC)**
1999	**Roy Jones Jr. (IBF)**

Note: WBC = World Boxing Council. WBA = World Boxing Association. IBF= International Boxing Federation.

Middleweights (155–160 lbs.)

Year	Name
1884	"Nonpareil" Jack Dempsey
1891	Bob Fitzsimmons[1]
1897	Kid McCoy[1], Tommy Ryan[1]
1907	Stanley Ketchel
1908	Billy Papke, Stanley Ketchel[1]
1911	*Vacant*
1913	Frank Klaus, George Chip
1914	Al McCoy
1917	Mike O'Dowd
1920	Johnny Wilson
1921	William Bryan Downey[1]
1923	Harry Greb
1926	Tiger Flowers, Mickey Walker
1931	Gorilla Jones
1932	Marcel Thil
1937	Fred Apostoli
1939	Ceferino Garcia
1940	Ken Overlin
1941	Billy Soose[1], Tony Zale
1947	Rocky Graziano
1948	Tony Zale, Marcel Cerdan
1949	Jake LaMotta
1951	Sugar Ray Robinson, Randy Turpin, Sugar Ray Robinson[1]
1953	Bobo Olson
1955	Sugar Ray Robinson
1957	Gene Fullmer (NBA), Sugar Ray Robinson, Carmen Basilio
1958	Sugar Ray Robinson
1960	Paul Pender
1961	Terry Downes
1962	Paul Pender
1963	Dick Tiger
1963	Joey Giardello
1965	Dick Tiger
1966	Emile Griffith
1967	Nino Benvenuti, Emile Griffith
1968	Nino Benvenuti
1970	Carlos Monzon
1977	Rodrigo Valdez
1978	Hugo Corro
1979	Vito Antuofermo
1980	Alan Minter, Marvin Hagler[1]
1987	Ray Leonard[1] (WBC), Frank Tate (IBF), Sumbo Kalambay (WBA), Thomas Hearns (WBC)
1988	Iran Barkley (WBC), Michael Nunn (IBF)
1989	Roberto Duran[1] (WBC), Mike McCallum[1] (WBA)
1990	Julian Jackson (WBC), James Toney[1] (IBF)
1991	Reggie Johnson[1] (WBA)
1993	Gerald McClellan[1] (WBC), Roy Jones[1] (IBF), John David Jackson (WBA)
1994	Jorge Castro (WBA)
1995	Julian Jackson (WBC), **Bernard Hopkins (IBF)**, Quincy Taylor (WBC), Shinij Takehara (WBA)
1996	Keith Holmes (WBC), William Joppy (WBA)
1997	Julio Cesar Green (WBA)
1996	William Joppy (WBA), Hassine Cherifi (WBC)
1999	Keith Holmes (WBC)
2001	Felix Trinidad (WBA), **Bernard Hopkins (WBA, WBC)**

Welterweights (141–147 lbs.)

Year	Name
1888	Paddy Duffy
1892	Mysterious Billy Smith
1894	Tommy Ryan[1]
1896	Kid McCoy[1]
1898	Mysterious Billy Smith
1900	Matty Matthews, Eddie Connolly, Rube Ferns, Matty Matthews
1901	Rube Ferns, Joe Walcott
1904	Dixie Kid[1]
1906	Honey Mellody
1907	Frank Mantell
1908	Harry Lewis[1]
1911–13	Vacant
1914	Waldemar Holberg, Tom McCormick, Matt Wells
1915	Mike Glover, Jack Britton, Ted (Kid) Lewis
1916	Jack Britton
1917	Ted (Kid) Lewis
1919	Jack Britton
1922	Mickey Walker
1926	Pete Latzo
1927	Joe Dundee
1929	Jackie Fields
1930	Young Jack Thompson, Tommy Freeman
1931	Young Jack Thompson, Lou Brouillard
1932	Jackie Fields
1933	Young Corbett, Jimmy McLarnin
1934	Barney Ross, Jimmy McLarnin
1935	Barney Ross
1938	Henry Armstrong
1940	Fritzie Zivic
1941	Fred Cochrane
1946	Marty Servo[1], Ray Robinson[1]
1951	Kid Gavilan
1954	Johnny Saxton
1955	Tony De Marco, Carmen Basilio
1956	Johnny Saxton, Carmen Basilio
1957	Carmen Basilio[1]
1958	Virgil Akins, Don Jordan
1960	Benny Paret
1961	Emile Griffith, Benny Paret
1962	Emile Griffith
1963	Luis Rodriguez, Emile Griffith[1]
1966	Curtis Cokes
1969	Jose Napoles
1970	Billy Backus
1971	Jose Napoles
1975	Angel Espada (WBA), John Stracey (WBC)
1976	Carlos Palomino (WBC), Jose Cuevas (WBA)
1979	Wilfredo Benitez (WBC), Sugar Ray Leonard (WBC)
1980	Roberto Duran (WBC), Thomas Hearns (WBA) Sugar Ray Leonard (WBC)
1981	Sugar Ray Leonard[1] (unifies world title)
1983	Donald Curry (WBA), Milton McCrory (WBC)
1985	Donald Curry (unifies world title)
1986	Lloyd Honeyghan[1]
1987	Mark Breland (WBA), Marlon Starling (WBA), Jorge Vaca (WBC)
1988	Simon Brown[1] (IBF), Thomas Molinares[1] (WBA)
1989	Marlon Starling (WBC), Mark Breland (WBA)
1990	Aaron Davis (WBA), Maurice Blocker (WBC)
1991	Meldrick Taylor (WBA), Simon Brown (WBC), Maurice Blocker (IBF), Buddy McGirt (WBC)
1992	Crisanto Espana (WBA)
1993	Pernell Whitaker (WBC), Felix Trinidad (IBF)
1994	Ike Quartey[1] (WBA)
1997	Oscar de la Hoya (WBC)
1998	**James Page (WBA)**
1999	**Felix Trinidad (WBC)**
2001	**Vernon Forrest (IBF)**

Lightweights (131–135 lbs.)

Year	Name
1896	Jack McAuliffe[1], Kid Lavigne
1899	Frank Erne
1902	Joe Gans[1]
1904	Jimmy Britt
1905	Battling Nelson
1906	Joe Gans
1908	Battling Nelson
1910	Ad Wolgast
1912	Willie Ritchie
1914	Freddie Welsh
1917	Benny Leonard[1]
1925	Jimmy Goodrich, Rocky Kansas
1926	Sammy Mandell
1930	Al Singer, Tony Canzoneri
1933	Barney Ross[1]
1935	Tony Canzoneri
1936	Lou Ambers
1938	Henry Armstrong
1939	Lou Ambers
1940	Lew Jenkins
1941	Sammy Angott
1942	Beau Jack
1943	Bob Montgomery, Beau Jack
1944	Bob Montgomery, Juan Zurita
1945	Ike Williams
1951	Jimmy Carter
1952	Lauro Salas, Jimmy Carter
1954	Paddy De Marco, Jimmy Carter
1955	Bud Smith
1956	Joe Brown
1962	Carlos Ortiz
1965	Ismael Laguna, Carlos Ortiz
1968	Teo Cruz
1969	Mando Ramos
1970	Ismael Laguna, Ken Buchanan[1]
1971	Pedro Carrasco (WBC)
1972	Mando Ramos (WBC), Roberto Duran[1] (WBA) Chango Carmona (WBC), Rodolfo Gonzalez (WBC)
1974	Ishimatsu Suzuki (WBC)
1976	Esteban De Jesus[1] (WBC)
1979	Jim Watt (WBC), Ernesto España (WBA)
1980	Hilmer Kenty (WBA)
1981	Sean O'Grady (WBA), Alexis Arguello (WBC), Claude Noel (WBA), Arturo Frias (WBA)
1982	Ray Mancini (WBA)
1983	Edwin Rosario (WBC)
1984	Charlie (Choo Choo) Brown (IBF), Livingstone Bramble (WBA), Jose Luis Ramirez (WBC)
1985	Jimmy Paul (IBF), Hector (Macho) Camacho[1] (WBC)
1986	Edwin Rosario (WBA), Greg Haugen (IBF)
1987	Vinny Pazienza (IBF), Jose Luis Ramirez (WBC), Julio Cesar Chavez[1] (WBA)
1988	Greg Haugen (IBF), Julio Cesar Chavez[1] (WBC)
1989	Pernell Whitaker (IBF), Edwin Rosario (WBA), Pernell Whitaker (WBC)
1990	Juan Nazario (WBA), Pernell Whitaker[1] (unifies world title)
1991	Vacant
1992	Tony Lopez (WBA)
1993	Fred Pendleton (IBF), Dingaan Thobela (WBA), Orzubek Nazarov (WBA)
1994	Rafael Ruelas (IBF)
1995	Oscar de la Hoya[1] (IBF), Phillip Holiday (IBF)
1996	Jean-Baptiste Mendy (WBC)
1997	Steve Johnston (WBC), Shane Mosley (IBF)
1998	Jean-Baptiste Mendy (WBA), Cesar Bazan (WBC)
1999	Julian Lorcy Fra (WBA), **Steve Johnston (WBC)**, Stefano Zoff (WBA), **Paul Spadafora (IBF)**, **Gilberto Serrano (WBA)**

Featherweights (123–126 lbs.)

Year	Name
1900	Terry McGovern, Young Corbett[1]
1901	Abe Attell
1904	Tommy Sullivan[1]
1906	Abe Attell
1912	Johnny Kilbane
1923	Eugene Criqui, Johnny Dundee[1]
1925	Kid Kaplan[1]
1927	Benny Bass, Ton Canzoneri
1928	Andre Routis
1929	Battling Battalino[1]
1932	Tommy Paul
1933	Freddie Miller
1936	Petey Sarron
1937	Henry Armstrong[1]
1938	Joey Archibald
1940	Harry Jeffra, Joey Archibald
1941	Chalky Wright
1942	Wilie Pep
1948	Sandy Saddler
1949	Willie Pep
1950	Sandy Saddler[1]
1957	Hogan (Kid) Bassey
1959	Davey Moore
1963	Sugar Ramos
1964	Vicente Saldivar[1]
1968	Jose Legra[1] (WBA), Shojo Saijo (WBA)
1969	Johnny Famechon (WBC)
1970	Vicente Saldivar (WBC), Kuniaki Shibata (WBC)
1971	Antonio Gomez (WBA
1972	Clemente Sanchez (WBC), Ernesto Marcel[1] (WBA), Jose Legra (WBC)
1973	Eder Jofre[1] (WBC)
1974	Ruben Olivares (WBA), Bobby Chacon (WBC), Alexis Arguello[1] (WBA)
1975	Ruben Olivares (WBC), David Kotey (WBC)
1976	Danny Lopez (WBC)
1977	Rafael Ortega (WBA), Cecillio Lastra (WBA)
1978	Eusebio Pedrosa (WBA)
1980	Salvador Sanchez[1] (WBC)
1982	Juan LaPorte (WBC)
1984	Min Keun Oh (IBF), Wilfredo Gomez (WBC), Azumah Nelson (WBC)
1985	Barry McGuigan (WBA), Ki Yung Chung[1] (IBF)
1986	Steve Cruz (WBA)
1987	Antonio Esparragoza (WBA)
1988	Calvin Grove (IBF), Jeff Fenech[1] (WBC), Jorge Paez (IBF)
1990	Marcos Villasana (WBC)
1991	Yung Kyun Park (WBA)
1992	Troy Dorsey (IBF), Manuel Medina (IBF), Paul Hodkinson (WBC)
1993	Tom Johnson (IBF), Goyo Vargas (WBC), Kevin Kelley (WBC), Eloy Rojas (WBA)
1995	Alejandro Gonzalez (WBC), Manuel Medina (WBC), Luisito Espinosa (WBC)
1996	Wilfredo Vasquez[1] (WBA)
1997	Naseem Hamed (IBF), Hector Lizarraga (IBF)
1998	Fred Norwood (WBA), Manuel Medina (IBF), Antonio Cermeño Ven (WBA)
1999	Cesar Soto (WBC), Paul Ingle (IBF), **Fred Norwood (WBA)**
2001	**Frankie Toledo (IBF) Vacant (WBC)**

1. Stripped of title or abandoned belt.
Source: International Boxing Hall of Fame.

GOLF

▶THE FOUR MAJOR TOURNAMENTS

No golfer has ever won the four major tournaments—the Masters, the U.S. Open, the British Open, and the PGA—in the same calendar year. The players to come closest were Ben Hogan, who won the first three tournaments in 1953, and Tiger Woods, who won them consecutively, but not in the same calendar year –he won the last three in 2000 and the Masters in 2001. Five players have won each of the four majors at least once over their entire careers: Hogan, Woods, Jack Nicklaus (who won each at least three times), Gary Player, and Gene Sarazen.

The Senior Tour began with two tournaments in 1980, which offered a total of $250,000 in prize money to qualified PGA members over the age of 50. By 1984, the tour had spiralled to 24 tournaments with prize money totalling $5 million. The arrival in 1990 of Jack Nicklaus and Lee Trevino on the senior tour helped propel the 50-and-over tour to unprecedented popularity, surpassing the Ladies' Professional Tour in both prize money and television ratings. That was also the year that Trevino became the first player to win more than $1 million in prize money on the senior tour.

The Masters

Year	Winner	Year	Winner	Year	Winner	Year	Winner
1934	Horton Smith	1951	Ben Hogan	1968	Bob Goalby	1985	Bernhard Langer
1935	Gene Sarazen	1952	Sam Snead	1969	George Archer	1986	Jack Nicklaus
1936	Horton Smith	1953	Ben Hogan	1970	Billy Casper	1987	Larry Mize
1937	Byron Nelson	1954	Sam Snead	1971	Charles Coody	1988	Sandy Lyle
1938	Henry Picard	1955	Cary Middlecoff	1972	Jack Nicklaus	1989	Nick Faldo
1939	Ralph Guldahl	1956	Jack Burke Jr.	1973	Tommy Aaron	1990	Nick Faldo
1940	Jimmy Demaret	1957	Doug Ford	1974	Gary Player	1991	Ian Woosnam
1941	Craig Wood	1958	Arnold Palmer	1975	Jack Nicklaus	1992	Fred Couples
1942	Byron Nelson	1959	Art Wall Jr.	1976	Ray Floyd	1993	Bernhard Langer
1943	Not held	1960	Arnold Palmer	1977	Tom Watson	1994	José María Olazábal
1944	Not held	1961	Gary Player	1978	Gary Player	1995	Ben Crenshaw
1945	Not held	1962	Arnold Palmer	1979	Fuzzy Zoeller	1996	Nick Faldo
1946	Herman Keiser	1963	Jack Nicklaus	1980	Seve Ballesteros	1997	Tiger Woods
1947	Jimmy Demaret	1964	Arnold Palmer	1981	Tom Watson	1998	Mark O'Meara
1948	Claude Harman	1965	Jack Nicklaus	1982	Craig Stadler	1999	José María Olazábal
1949	Sam Snead	1966	Jack Nicklaus	1983	Seve Ballesteros	2000	Vijay Singh
1950	Jimmy Demaret	1967	Gay Brewer Jr.	1984	Ben Crenshaw	2001	Tiger Woods

The U.S. Open

Year	Winner	Year	Winner	Year	Winner	Year	Winner
1895	Horace Rawlins	1922	Gene Sarazen	1949	Cary Middlecoff	1976	Jerry Pate
1896	James Foulis	1923	Robert T. Jones Jr.	1950	Ben Hogan	1977	Hubert Green
1897	Joe Lloyd	1924	Cyril Walker	1951	Ben Hogan	1978	Andy North
1898	Fred Herd	1925	W. MacFarlane	1952	Julius Boros	1979	Hale Irwin
1899	Willie Smith	1926	Robert T. Jones Jr.	1953	Ben Hogan	1980	Jack Nicklaus
1900	Harry Vardon	1927	Tommy Armour	1954	Ed Furgol	1981	David Graham
1901	Willie Anderson	1928	Johnny Farrell	1955	Jack Fleck	1982	Tom Watson
1902	Laurie Auchterlonie	1929	Robert T. Jones Jr.	1956	Cary Middlecoff	1983	Larry Nelson
1903	Willie Anderson	1930	Robert T. Jones Jr.	1957	Dick Mayer	1984	Fuzzy Zoeller
1904	Willie Anderson	1931	Billy Burke	1958	Tommy Bolt	1985	Andy North
1905	Willie Anderson	1932	Gene Sarazen	1959	Billy Casper	1986	Ray Floyd
1906	Alex Smith	1933	Johnny Goodman	1960	Arnold Palmer	1987	Scott Simpson
1907	Alex Ross	1934	Olin Dutra	1961	Gene Littler	1988	Curtis Strange
1908	Fred McLeod	1935	Sam Parks, Jr.	1962	Jack Nicklaus	1989	Curtis Strange
1909	George Sargent	1936	Tony Manero	1963	Julius Boros	1990	Hale Irwin
1910	Alex Smith	1937	Ralph Guldahl	1964	Ken Venturi	1991	Payne Stewart
1911	John McDermott	1938	Ralph Guldahl	1965	Gary Player	1992	Tom Kite
1912	John McDermott	1939	Byron Nelson	1966	Billy Casper	1993	Lee Janzen
1913	Francis Ouimet	1940	Lawson Little	1967	Jack Nicklaus	1994	Ernie Els
1914	Walter Hagen	1941	Craig Wood	1968	Lee Trevino	1995	Corey Pavin
1915	Jerome Travers	1942	Not held	1969	Orville Moody	1996	Steve Jones
1916	Charles Evans Jr.	1943	Not held	1970	Tony Jacklin	1997	Ernie Els
1917	Not held	1944	Not held	1971	Lee Trevino	1998	Lee Janzen
1918	Not held	1945	Not held	1972	Jack Nicklaus	1999	Payne Stewart
1919	Walter Hagen	1946	Lloyd Mangrum	1973	Johnny Miller	2000	Tiger Woods
1920	Edward Ray	1947	Lew Worsham	1974	Hale Irwin	2001	Retief Goosen
1921	James M. Barnes	1948	Ben Hogan	1975	Lou Graham		

The British Open

Year	Winner	Year	Winner	Year	Winner	Year	Winner
1860	Willie Park	1895	John H. Taylor	1931	Tommy D. Armour	1967	Roberto DeVicenzo
1861	Tom Morris Sr.	1896	Harry Vardon	1932	Gene Sarazen	1968	Gary Player
1862	Tom Morris Sr.	1897	Harold H. Hilton	1933	Denny Shute	1969	Tony Jacklin
1863	Willie Park	1898	Harry Vardon	1934	Henry Cotton	1970	Jack Nicklaus
1864	Tom Morris Sr.	1899	Harry Vardon	1935	Alfred Perry	1971	Lee Trevino
1865	Andrew Strath	1900	John H. Taylor	1936	Alfred Padgham	1972	Lee Trevino
1866	Willie Park	1901	James Braid	1937	Henry Cotton	1973	Tom Weiskopf
1867	Tom Morris Sr.	1902	Alexander Herd	1938	R.A. Whitcombe	1974	Gary Player
1868	Tom Morris Jr.	1903	Harry Vardon	1939	Richard Burton	1975	Tom Watson
1869	Tom Morris Jr.	1904	Jack White	1940	Not held	1976	Johnny Miller
1870	Tom Morris Jr.	1905	James Braid	1941	Not held	1977	Tom Watson
1871	Not held	1906	James Braid	1942	Not held	1978	Jack Nicklaus
1872	Tom Morris Jr.	1907	Arnaud Massy	1943	Not held	1979	Seve Ballesteros
1873	Tom Kidd	1908	James Braid	1944	Not held	1980	Tom Watson
1874	Mungo Park	1909	John H. Taylor	1945	Not held	1981	Bill Rogers
1875	Willie Park	1910	James Braid	1946	Sam Snead	1982	Tom Watson
1876	Bob Martin	1911	Harry Vardon	1947	Fred Daly	1983	Tom Watson
1877	Jamie Anderson	1912	Edward (Ted) Ray	1948	Henry Cotton	1984	Seve Ballesteros
1878	Jamie Anderson	1913	John H. Taylor	1949	Bobby Locke	1985	Sandy Lyle
1879	Jamie Anderson	1914	Harry Vardon	1950	Bobby Locke	1986	Greg Norman
1880	Robert Ferguson	1915	Not held	1951	Max Faulkner	1987	Nick Faldo
1881	Robert Ferguson	1916	Not held	1952	Bobby Locke	1988	Seve Ballesteros
1882	Robert Ferguson	1917	Not held	1953	Ben Hogan	1989	Mark Calcavecchia
1883	Willie Fernie	1918	Not held	1954	Peter Thomson	1990	Nick Faldo
1884	Jack Simpson	1919	Not held	1955	Peter Thomson	1991	Ian Baker-Finch
1885	Bob Martin	1920	George Duncan	1956	Peter Thomson	1992	Nick Faldo
1886	David Brown	1921	Jock Hutchison	1957	Bobby Locke	1993	Greg Norman
1887	Willie Park Jr.	1922	Walter Hagen	1958	Peter Thomson	1994	Nick Price
1888	Jack Burns	1923	Arthur G. Havers	1959	Gary Player	1995	John Daly
1889	Willie Park Jr.	1924	Walter Hagen	1960	Kel Nagle	1996	Tom Lehman
1890	John Ball	1925	James M. Barnes	1961	Arnold Palmer	1997	Justin Leonard
1891	Hugh Kirkaldy	1926	Robert T. Jones Jr.	1962	Arnold Palmer	1998	Mark O'Meara
1892	Harold H. Hilton[1]	1927	Robert T. Jones Jr.	1963	Bob Charles	1999	Paul Lawrie
1893	William Auchterlonie	1928	Walter Hagen	1964	Tony Lema	2000	Tiger Woods
		1929	Walter Hagen	1965	Peter Thomson	2001	David Duval
1894	John H. Taylor	1930	Robert T. Jones Jr.	1966	Jack Nicklaus		

PGA Championship

Year	Winner	Year	Winner	Year	Winner	Year	Winner
1916	James M. Barnes	1938	Paul Runyan	1960	Jay Hebert	1982	Raymond Floyd
1917	Not held	1939	Henry Picard	1961	Jerry Barber	1983	Hal Sutton
1918	Not held	1940	Byron Nelson	1962	Gary Player	1984	Lee Trevino
1919	James M. Barnes	1941	Vic Ghezzi	1963	Jack Nicklaus	1985	Hubert Green
1920	Jock Hutchison	1942	Sam Snead	1964	Bobby Nichols	1986	Bob Tway
1921	Walter Hagen	1943	Not held	1965	Dave Marr	1987	Larry Nelson
1922	Gene Sarazen	1944	Bob Hamilton	1966	Al Geiberger	1988	Jeff Sluman
1923	Gene Sarazen	1945	Byron Nelson	1967	Don January	1989	Payne Stewart
1924	Walter Hagen	1946	Ben Hogan	1968	Julius Boros	1990	Wayne Grady
1925	Walter Hagen	1947	Jim Ferrier	1969	Ray Floyd	1991	John Daly
1926	Walter Hagen	1948	Ben Hogan	1970	Dave Stockton	1992	Nick Price
1927	Walter Hagen	1949	Sam Snead	1971	Jack Nicklaus	1993	Paul Azinger
1928	Leo Diegel	1950	Chandler Harper	1972	Gary Player	1994	Nick Price
1929	Leo Diegel	1951	Sam Snead	1973	Jack Nicklaus	1995	Steve Elkington
1930	Tommy Armour	1952	Jim Turnesa	1974	Lee Trevino	1996	Mark Brooks
1931	Tom Creavy	1953	Walter Burkemo	1975	Jack Nicklaus	1997	Davis Love III
1932	Olin Dutra	1954	Chick Harbert	1976	Dave Stockton	1998	Vijay Singh
1933	Gene Sarazen	1955	Doug Ford	1977	Lanny Wadkins	1999	Tiger Woods
1934	Paul Runyan	1956	Jack Burke	1978	John Mahaffey	2000	Tiger Woods
1935	Johnny Revolta	1957	Lionel Hebert	1978	David Graham	2001	David Toms
1936	Denny Shute	1958	Dow Finsterwald	1980	Jack Nicklaus		
1937	Denny Shute	1959	Bob Rosburg	1981	Larry Nelson		

PGA Leading Money Winners, 1934–2000

Year	Name	Winnings	Year	Name	Winnings	Year	Name	Winnings
1934	Paul Runyan	$6,767	1957	Dick Mayer	$65,835	1980	Tom Watson	$530,808
1935	Johnny Revolta	9,543	1958	Arnold Palmer	42,607	1981	Tom Kite	375,698
1936	Horton Smith	7,682	1959	Art Wall	53,167	1982	Craig Stadler	446,462
1937	Harry Cooper	14,138	1960	Arnold Palmer	75,262	1983	Hal Sutton	426,668
1938	Sam Snead	19,534	1961	Gary Player	64,540	1984	Tom Watson	476,260
1939	Henry Picard	10,303	1962	Arnold Palmer	81,448	1985	Curtis Strange	542,321
1940	Ben Hogan	10,655	1963	Arnold Palmer	128,230	1986	Greg Norman	653,296
1941	Ben Hogan	18,358	1964	Jack Nicklaus	113,284	1987	Curtis Strange	925,941
1942	Ben Hogan	13,143	1965	Jack Nicklaus	140,752	1988	Curtis Strange	1,147,644
1943	No statistics compiled		1966	Billy Casper	121,944	1989	Tom Kite	1,395,278
1944	Byron Nelson	37,967[1]	1967	Jack Nicklaus	188,998	1990	Greg Norman	1,165,477
1945	Byron Nelson	63,335[1]	1968	Billy Casper	205,168	1991	Corey Pavin	979,430
1946	Ben Hogan	42,556	1969	Frank Beard	164,707	1992	Fred Couples	1,344,188
1947	Jimmy Demaret	27,936	1970	Lee Trevino	157,037	1993	Nick Price	1,478,557
1948	Ben Hogan	32,112	1971	Jack Nicklaus	244,490	1994	Nick Price	1,499,927
1949	Sam Snead	31,593	1972	Jack Nicklaus	320,542	1995	Greg Norman	1,654,959
1950	Sam Snead	35,758	1973	Jack Nicklaus	308,362	1996	Tom Lehman	1,780,159
1951	Lloyd Mangrum	26,088	1974	Johnny Miller	353,021	1997	Tiger Woods	2,066,833
1952	Julius Boros	37,032	1975	Jack Nicklaus	298,149	1998	David Duval	2,591,031
1953	Lew Worsham	34,002	1976	Jack Nicklaus	266,438	1999	Tiger Woods	6,616,585
1954	Bob Toski	65,819	1977	Tom Watson	310,653	2000	Tiger Woods	9,188,321
1955	Julius Boros	63,121	1978	Tom Watson	362,428			
1956	Ted Kroll	72,835	1979	Tom Watson	462,636			

1. Paid in War Bonds. **Source:** Professional Golfers' Association. www.pgatour.com

PGA Leading Money Winners, 2001 and Career

2001			Career					
Rank, Golfer		Earnings	Career Rank, Golfer		Earnings	Rank, Golfer		Earnings
1.	Tiger Woods	$4,383,591	1.	Tiger Woods	$24,887,040	11.	Fred Couples	$12,628,350
2.	Phil Mickelson	3,569,724	2.	Phil Mickelson	17,003,839	12.	Payne Stewart	11,737,008
3.	Vijay Singh	2,691,146	3.	Davis Love III	16,527,533	13.	Mark O'Meara	11,695,108
4.	Joe Durant	2,233,674	4.	Nick Price	13,994,795	14.	Tom Lehman	11,497,782
5.	Sergio Garcia	2,191,741	5.	Vijay Singh	13,774,770	15.	Paul Azinger	11,321,336
6.	Scott Hoch	1,856,686	6.	David Duval	13,699,986	16.	Ernie Els	10,978,813
7.	Davis Love III	1,702,305	7.	Hal Sutton	13,632,952	17.	Tom Kite	10,865,959
8.	Frank Lickliter II	1,621,707	8.	Scott Hoch	13,534,569	18.	Jim Furyk	10,336,264
9.	Mark Calcavecchia	1,621,419	9.	Greg Norman	13,272,444	19.	Justin Leonard	9,872,936
10.	David Toms	1,614,866	10.	Mark Calcavecchia	13,039,192	20.	Jeff Sluman	9,826,032

Note: Figures are as of July 1, 2001. **Source:** Professional Golfers' Association (www.pga.com).

LPGA Leading Money Winners 1956–2000

Year	Player	Winnings	Year	Player	Winnings	Year	Player	Winnings
1956	Marlene Hagge	$20,235	1971	Kathy Whitworth	$41,181	1986	Pat Bradley	$492,021
1957	Patty Berg	16,272	1972	Kathy Whitworth	65,063	1987	Ayako Okamoto	466,034
1958	Beverly Hanson	12,629	1973	Kathy Whitworth	82,864	1988	Sherri Turner	350,851
1959	Betsy Rawls	26,774	1974	JoAnne Carner	87,094	1989	Betsy King	654,132
1960	Louise Suggs	16,892	1975	Sandra Palmer	76,374	1990	Beth Daniel	863,578
1961	Mickey Wright	22,238	1976	Judy T. Rankin	150,734	1991	Pat Bradley	763,118
1962	Mickey Wright	21,654	1977	Judy T. Rankin	122,890	1992	Dottie Mochrie	693,335
1963	Mickey Wright	31,269	1978	Nancy Lopez	189,813	1993	Betsy King	595,992
1964	Mickey Wright	29,800	1979	Nancy Lopez	197,488	1994	Laura Davies	687,201
1965	Kathy Whitworth	28,658	1980	Beth Daniel	231,000	1995	Annika Sorenstam	666,533
1966	Kathy Whitworth	33,517	1981	Beth Daniel	206,977	1996	Karrie Webb	1,002,000
1967	Kathy Whitworth	32,937	1982	JoAnne Carner	310,399	1997	Annika Sorenstam	1,236,789
1968	Kathy Whitworth	48,379	1983	JoAnne Carner	291,404	1998	Annika Sorenstam	1,092,748
1969	Carol Mann	49,152	1984	Betsy King	266,771	1999	Karrie Webb	1,591,959
1970	Kathy Whitworth	30,235	1985	Nancy Lopez	416,472	2000	Karrie Webb	1,876,853

Source: Ladies Professional Golfers' Association. www.lpga.com

LPGA Leading Money Winners

	2001			Career			
Rank, Golfer	Earnings	Rank, Golfer	Earnings		Rank, Golfer	Earnings
1. Annika Sorenstam	1,144,324	**1.** Annika Sorenstam	$7,344,920		**11.** Nancy Lopez	$5,303,297
2. Karrie Webb	1,112,128	**2.** Karrie Webb	7,275,023		**12.** Rosie Jones	5,289,524
3. Se Ri Pak	808,992	**3.** Betsy King	7,074,886		**13.** Liselotte Neumann	4,191,104
4. Dottie Pepper	688,344	**4.** Dottie Pepper	6,570,475		**14.** Kelly Robbins	4,174,612
5. Maria Hjorth	629,165	**5.** Juli Inkster	6,437,887		**15.** Jane Geddes	3,726,116
6. Lorie Kane	548,208	**6.** Beth Daniel	6,367,143		**16.** Sherri Steinhauer	3,712,836
7. Catriona Matthew	523,690	**7.** Pat Bradley	5,743,605		**17.** Tammie Green	3,456,866
8. Rachel Teske	486,527	**8.** Meg Mallon	5,709,478		**18.** Brandie Burton	3,413,540
9. Sophie Gustafson	468,159	**9.** Laura Davies	5,531,176		**19.** Chris Johnson	3,391,123
10. Laura Diaz	437,524	**10.** Patty Sheehan	5,504,005		**20.** Amy Alcott	3,373,273

Note: As of July 2, 2001.   Source: Ladies' Professional Golfers' Association.   www.lpga.com

U.S. Women's Grand Slam Champions, 1972–2001

Until 1979, women's golf had two major championships: The LPGA and the U.S. Women's Open. The duMaurier Classic became the third major in 1979, and the Nabisco Championship was added in 1983. In 2001, the Women's British Open replaced the duMaurier. In the table below, names in italics show the tournament winner before it became a major.

Year	Nabisco Dinah Shore[1]	LPGA Championship	U.S. Women's Open	Women's British Open[2]
1972	*Jane Blalock*	Kathy Ahern	Susie Berning	N.A.
1973	*Mickey Wright*	Mary Mills	Susie Berning	*Jocelyne Bourasa*
1974	*JoAnn Prentice*	Sandra Haynie	Sandra Haynie	*Carole Jo Callison*
1975	*Sandra Palmer*	Kathy Whitworth	Sandra Palmer	*JoAnne Carner*
1976	*Judy Rankin*	Betty Burfeindt	JoAnne Carner	*Donna Caponi*
1977	*Kathy Whitworth*	Chako Higuchi	Hollis Stacy	*Judy Rankin*
1978	*Sandra Post*	Nancy Lopez	Hollis Stacy	*JoAnne Carner*
1979	*Sandra Post*	Donna Caponi	Jerilyn Britz	Amy Alcott
1980	*Donna Caponi*	Sally Little	Amy Alcott	Pat Bradley
1981	*Nancy Lopez*	Donna Caponi	Pat Bradley	Jan Stephenson
1982	*Sally Little*	Jan Stephenson	Janet Anderson	Sandra Haynie
1983	Amy Alcott	Patty Sheehan	Jan Stephenson	Hollis Stacy
1984	Juli Inkster	Patty Sheehan	Hollis Stacy	Juli Inkster
1985	Alice Miller	Nancy Lopez	Kathy Baker	Pat Bradley
1986	Pat Bradley	Pat Bradley	Jane Geddes	Pat Bradley
1987	Betsy King	Jane Geddes	Laura Davies	Jody Rosenthal
1988	Amy Alcott	Sherri Turner	Liselotte Neumann	Sally Little
1989	Juli Inkster	Nancy Lopez	Betsy King	Tammie Green
1990	Betsy King	Beth Daniel	Betsy King	Cathy Johnston
1991	Amy Alcott	Meg Mallon	Meg Mallon	Nancy Scranton
1992	Dottie Pepper	Betsy King	Patty Sheehan	Sherri Steinhauer
1993	Helen Alfredsson	Patty Sheehan	Lauri Merten	Brandie Burton
1994	Donna Andrews	Laura Davies	Patty Sheehan	Martha Nause
1995	Nanci Bowen	Kelly Robbins	Annika Sorenstam	Jenny Lidback
1996	Patty Sheehan	Laura Davies	Annika Sorenstam	Laura Davies
1997	Betsy King	Chris Johnson	Alison Nicholas	Colleen Walker
1998	Pat Hurst	Se Ri Pak	Se Ri Pak	Brandie Burton
1999	Dottie Pepper	Juli Inkster	Juli Inkster	Karrie Webb
2000	Karrie Webb	Juli Inkster	Karrie Webb	Meg Mallon
2001	Annika Sorenstam	Karrie Webb	Karrie Webb	Se Ri Pak

1. The Nabisco Championship was not a major until 1983. 2. From 1972–2000, names are winners of the duMaurier Classic.
Source: Ladies' Professional Golf Association. www.lpga.com

U.S. Women's Open Champions, 1946–71

Year	Champion	Year	Champion	Year	Champion	Year	Champion
1946	Patty Berg	1953	Betsy Rawls	1960	Betsy Rawls	1967	Catherine LaCoste
1947	Betty Jameson	1954	Babe Zaharias	1961	Mickey Wright	1968	Susie Berning
1948	Babe Zaharias	1955	Fay Crocker	1962	Murle Breer	1969	Donna Caponi
1949	Louise Suggs	1956	Kathy Cornelius	1963	Mary Mills	1970	Donna Caponi
1950	Babe Zaharias	1957	Betsy Rawls	1964	Mickey Wright	1971	JoAnne Carner
1951	Betsy Rawls	1958	Mickey Wright	1965	Carol Mann		
1952	Louise Suggs	1959	Mickey Wright	1966	Sandra Spuzich		

TENNIS

►THE GRAND SLAM CHAMPIONSHIPS

The four tournaments that constitute the Grand Slam are the Australian, French, Wimbledon (officially known as the All-England Club's Lawn Tennis Championships), and U.S. championships. A challenge round system, in which the defending champion automatically qualified for the following year's final, was used at Wimbledon from 1877-1921 and at the U.S. Championships from 1884-1911. Prior to 1925, entry to the French Open was restricted to members of French clubs, and from 1941-45, the French tournament was closed to all foreigners. Wimbledon, the French, and U.S. Championships became open to amateurs and pros in 1968; the Australian championships joined the open era a year later. Five players have completed the Grand Slam, winning all four championships in the same year: Don Budge (1938), Maureen Connolly (with straight set victories in all four finals in 1953), Rod Laver (1962 and 1969), Margaret Court (1970) and Steffi Graf (1988). Martina Navratilova won the four tournaments consecutively, but not in the same calendar year; she won the French Open in 1984, following 1983 victories in the other three.

Men's Grand Slam Champions 1920-2001

Year	Australian Champion	French Champion	Wimbledon Champion	U.S. Champion
1920	Pat O'Hara Wood	—	Bill Tilden	Bill Tilden
1921	Rhys H. Gemmell	—	Bill Tilden	Bill Tilden
1922	Pat O'Hara Wood	—	Gerald L. Patterson	Bill Tilden
1923	Pat O'Hara Wood	—	William M. Johnston	Bill Tilden
1924	James Anderson	—	Jean Borotra	Bill Tilden
1925	James Anderson	Rene Lacoste	Rene Lacoste	Bill Tilden
1926	John Hawkes	Henri Cochet	Jean Borotra	Rene Lacoste
1927	Gerald Patterson	Rene Lacoste	Henri Cochet	Rene Lacoste
1928	Jean Borotra	Henri Cochet	Rene Lacoste	Henri Cochet
1929	John C. Gregory	Rene Lacoste	Henri Cochet	Bill Tilden
1930	Gar Moon	Henri Cochet	Bill Tilden	John H. Doeg
1931	Jack Crawford	Jean Borotra	Sidney B. Wood Jr.	H. Ellsworth Vines
1932	Jack Crawford	Henri Cochet	Ellsworth Vines	H. Ellsworth Vines
1933	Jack Crawford	John H. Crawford	Jack Crawford	Fred Perry
1934	Fred J. Perry	Gottfried von Cramm	Fred Perry	Fred Perry
1935	Jack Crawford	Fred J. Perry	Fred Perry	Wilmer L. Allison
1936	Adrian Quist	Gottfried von Cramm	Fred Perry	Fred Perry
1937	Vivian B. McGrath	Henner Henkel	Don Budge	Don Budge
1938[1]	Don Budge	Don Budge	Don Budge	Don Budge
1939	John Bromwich	W. Donald McNeill	Bobby Riggs	Bobby Riggs
1940	Adrian Quist	No competition	Not Held	Donald McNeill
1941	Foreigners excluded	Bernard Destremau	Not Held	Bobby Riggs
1942	Foreigners excluded	Bernard Destremau	Not Held	Frederick Schroeder
1943	Foreigners excluded	Yvon Petra	Not Held	Joseph R. Hunt
1944	Foreigners excluded	Yvon Petra	Not Held	Frank Parker
1945	Foreigners excluded	Yvon Petra	Not Held	Frank Parker
1946	John Bromwich	Marcel Bernard	Yvon Petra	Jack Kramer
1947	Dinny Pails	Joseph Asboth	Jack Kramer	Jack Kramer
1948	Adrian Quist	Frank Parker	Bob Falkenburg	Pancho Gonzales
1949	Frank Sedgman	Frank Parker	Ted Schroeder	Pancho Gonzales
1950	Frank Sedgman	Budge Patty	Budge Patty	Arthur Larsen
1951	Richard Savitt	Jaroslav Drobny	Dick Savitt	Frank Sedgman
1952	Ken McGregor	Jaroslav Drobny	Frank Sedgman	Frank Sedgman
1953	Ken Rosewall	Ken Rosewall	Vic Seixas	Tony Trabert
1954	Mervyn Rose	Tony Trabert	Jaroslav Drobny	E. Victor Seixas Jr.
1955	Ken Rosewall	Tony Trabert	Tony Trabert	Tony Trabert
1956	Lew Hoad	Lew Hoad	Lew Hoad	Ken Rosewall
1957	Ashley Cooper	Sven Davidson	Lew Hoad	Malcolm Anderson
1958	Ashley Cooper	Mervyn Rose	Ashley Cooper	Ashley J. Cooper
1959	Alex Olmedo	Nicola Pietrangeli	Alex Olmedo	Neale Fraser
1960	Rod Laver	Nicola Pietrangeli	Neale Fraser	Neale Fraser
1961	Roy Emerson	Manuel Santana	Rod Laver	Roy Emerson
1962[1]	Rod Laver	Rod Laver	Rod Laver	Rod Laver
1963	Roy Emerson	Roy Emerson	Chuck McKinley	Rafael Osuna
1964	Roy Emerson	Manuel Santana	Roy Emerson	Roy Emerson
1965	Roy Emerson	Fred Stolle	Roy Emerson	Manuel Santana
1966	Roy Emerson	Tony Roche	Manuel Santana	Fred Stolle
1967	Roy Emerson	Roy Emerson	John Newcombe	John Newcombe
1968	Bill Bowrey	Ken Rosewall	Rod Laver	Arthur Ashe

Year	Australian Champion	French Champion	Wimbledon Champion	U.S. Champion
1969[1]	Rod Laver	Rod Laver	Rod Laver	Rod Laver
1970	Arthur Ashe	Jan Kodes	John Newcombe	Ken Rosewall
1971	Ken Rosewall	Jan Kodes	John Newcombe	Stan Smith
1972	Ken Rosewall	Andres Gimeno	Stan Smith	Ilie Nastase
1973	John Newcombe	Ilie Nastase	Jan Kodes	John Newcombe
1974	Jimmy Connors	Bjorn Borg	Jimmy Connors	Jimmy Connors
1975	John Newcombe	Bjorn Borg	Arthur Ashe	Manuel Orantes
1976	Mark Edmondson	Adriano Panatta	Bjorn Borg	Jimmy Connors
1977	Roscoe Tanner[2]	Guillermo Vilas	Bjorn Borg	Guillermo Vilas
	Vitas Gerulaitis[2]			
1978	Guillermo Vilas	Bjorn Borg	Bjorn Borg	Jimmy Connors
1979	Guillermo Vilas	Bjorn Borg	Bjorn Borg	John McEnroe
1980	Brian Teacher	Bjorn Borg	Bjorn Borg	John McEnroe
1981	Johan Kriek	Bjorn Borg	John McEnroe	John McEnroe
1982	Johan Kriek	Mats Wilander	Jimmy Connors	Jimmy Connors
1983	Mats Wilander	Yannick Noah	John McEnroe	Jimmy Connors
1984	Mats Wilander	Ivan Lendl	John McEnroe	John McEnroe
1985	Stefan Edberg	Mats Wilander	Boris Becker	Ivan Lendl
1986	Moved to Jan. 1987	Ivan Lendl	Boris Becker	Ivan Lendl
1987	Stefan Edberg	Ivan Lendl	Pat Cash	Ivan Lendl
1988	Mats Wilander	Mats Wilander	Stefan Edberg	Mats Wilander
1989	Ivan Lendl	Michael Chang	Boris Becker	Boris Becker
1990	Ivan Lendl	Andrés Gomez	Stefan Edberg	Pete Sampras
1991	Boris Becker	Jim Courier	Michael Stich	Stefan Edberg
1992	Jim Courier	Jim Courier	Andre Agassi	Stefan Edberg
1993	Jim Courier	Sergi Bruguera	Pete Sampras	Pete Sampras
1994	Pete Sampras	Sergi Bruguera	Pete Sampras	Andre Agassi
1995	Andre Agassi	Thomas Muster	Pete Sampras	Pete Sampras
1996	Boris Becker	Yevgeny Kafelnikov	Richard Krajicek	Pete Sampras
1997	Pete Sampras	Gustavo Kuerten	Pete Sampras	Patrick Rafter
1998	Petr Korda	Carlos Moya	Pete Sampras	Patrick Rafter
1999	Yevgeny Kafelnikov	Andre Agassi	Pete Sampras	Andre Agassi
2000	Andre Agassi	Gustavo Kuerten	Pete Sampras	Marat Safin
2001	Andre Agassi	Gustavo Kuerten	Goran Ivanisevic	Lleyton Hewitt

1. Grand Slam winner. 2. Two tournaments were held in 1977, the first in January, the second in December.

Women's Grand Slam Champions, 1920–2001

Year	Australian Champion	French Champion	Wimbledon Champion	U.S. Champion
1920	Not held	Suzanne Lenglen	Suzanne Lenglen	Molla Bjurstedt Mallory
1921	Not held	Suzanne Lenglen	Suzanne Lenglen	Molla Bjurstedt Mallory
1922	Margaret Molesworth	Suzanne Lenglen	Suzanne Lenglen	Molla Bjurstedt Mallory
1923	Margaret Molesworth	Suzanne Lenglen	Suzanne Lenglen	Helen Wills
1924	Sylvia Lance	Diddie Vlasto	Kathleen McKane	Helen Wills
1925	Daphne Akhurst	Suzanne Lenglen	Suzanne Lenglen	Helen Wills
1926	Daphne Akhurst	Suzanne Lenglen	Kathleen McKane Godfree	Molla Bjurstedt Mallory
1927	Edna Boyd	Kea Bouman	Helen Wills	Helen Wills
1928	Daphne Akhurst	Helen Wills	Helen Wills	Helen Wills
1929	Daphne Akhurst	Helen Wills	Helen Wills	Helen Wills
1930	Daphne Akhurst	Helen Wills Moody	Helen Wills Moody	Betty Nuthall
1931	Coral Buttsworth	Cilly Aussem	Cilly Aussem	Helen Wills Moody
1932	Coral Buttsworth	Helen Wills Moody	Helen Wills Moody	Helen Jacobs
1933	Joan Hartigan	Margaret Scriven	Helen Wills Moody	Helen Jacobs
1934	Joan Hartigan	Margaret Scriven	Dorothy Round	Helen Jacobs
1935	Dorothy Round	Hilde Sperling	Helen Wills Moody	Helen Jacobs
1936	Joan Hartigan	Hilde Sperling	Helen Jacobs	Alice Marble
1937	Nancye Wynne Bolton	Hilde Sperling	Dorothy Round	Anita Lizane
1938	Dorothy Bundy	Simone Mathieu	Helen Wills Moody	Alice Marble
1939	Emily Westacott	Simone Mathieu	Alice Marble	Alice Marble
1940	Nancye Wynne Bolton	Not Held	Not Held	Alice Marble
1941	Not Held	Not Held	Not Held	Sarah Palfrey Cooke
1942	Not Held	Not Held	Not Held	Pauline Betz
1943	Not Held	Not Held	Not Held	Pauline Betz
1944	Not Held	Not Held	Not Held	Pauline Betz Cooke

Year	Australian Champion	French Champion	Wimbledon Champion	U.S. Champio
1945	Not Held	Not Held	Not Held	Sarah Palfrey Cooke
1946	Nancye Wynne Bolton	Margaret Osborne	Pauline Betz	Pauline Betz
1947	Nancye Wynne Bolton	Patricia Todd	Margaret Osborne	Louise Brough
1948	Nancye Wynne Bolton	Nelly Landry	Louise Brough	Margaret Osborne duPont
1949	Doris Hart	Margaret Osborne duPont	Louise Brough	Margaret Osborne duPont
1950	Louise Brough	Doris Hart	Louise Brough	Margaret Osborne duPont
1951	Nancye Wynne Bolton	Shirley Fry	Doris Hart	Maureen Connolly
1952	Thelma Long	Doris Hart	Maureen Connolly	Maureen Connolly
1953[1]	Maureen Connolly	Maureen Connolly	Maureen Connolly	Maureen Connolly
1954	Thelma Long	Maureen Connolly	Maureen Connolly	Doris Hart
1955	Beryl Penrose	Angela Mortimer	Louise Brough	Doris Hart
1956	Mary Carter	Althea Gibson	Shirley Fry	Shirley Fry
1957	Shirley Fry	Shirley Bloomer	Althea Gibson	Althea Gibson
1958	Angela Mortimer	Zsuzsi Kormoczy	Althea Gibson	Althea Gibson
1959	Mary Carter Reitano	Christine Truman	Maria Bueno	Maria Bueno
1960	Margaret Smith	Darlene Hard	Maria Bueno	Darlene Hard
1961	Margaret Smith	Ann Haydon	Angela Mortimer	Darlene Hard
1962	Margaret Smith	Margaret Smith	Karen Hantze Susman	Margaret Smith
1963	Margaret Smith	Lesley Turner	Margaret Smith	Maria Bueno
1964	Margaret Smith	Margaret Smith	Maria Bueno	Maria Bueno
1965	Margaret Smith	Lesley Turner	Margaret Smith	Margaret Smith
1966	Margaret Smith	Ann Jones	Billie Jean King	Maria Bueno
1967	Nancy Richey	Francoise Durr	Billie Jean King	Billie Jean King
1968	Billie Jean King	Nancy Richey	Billie Jean King	Virginia Wade
1969	Margaret Smith Court	Margaret Smith Court	Ann Jones	Margaret Smith Court
1970[1]	Margaret Smith Court	Margaret Smith Court	Margaret Smith Court	Margaret Smith Court
1971	Margaret Smith Court	Evonne Goolagong	Evonne Goolagong	Billie Jean King
1972	Virginia Wade	Billie Jean King	Billie Jean King	Billie Jean King
1973	Margaret Smith Court	Margaret Smith Court	Billie Jean King	Margaret Smith Court
1974	Evonne Goolagong	Chris Evert	Chris Evert	Billie Jean King
1975	Evonne Goolagong	Chris Evert	Billie Jean King	Chris Evert
1976	Evonne Goolagong Cawley	Sue Barker	Chris Evert	Chris Evert
1977	Kerry Melville Reid[2] Evonne Goolagong Cawley[2]	Mima Jasuovec	Virginia Wade	Chris Evert
1978	Chris O'Neil	Virginia Ruzici	Martina Navratilova	Chris Evert
1979	Barbara Jordan	Chris Evert Lloyd	Martina Navratilova	Tracy Austin
1980	Hana Mandlikova	Chris Evert Lloyd	Evonne Goolagong Cawley	Chris Evert Lloyd
1981	Martina Navratilova	Hana Mandlikova	Chris Evert Lloyd	Tracy Austin
1982	Chris Evert Lloyd	Martina Navratilova	Martina Navratilova	Chris Evert Lloyd
1983	Martina Navratilova	Chris Evert Lloyd	Martina Navratilova	Martina Navratilova
1984	Chris Evert Lloyd	Martina Navratilova	Martina Navratilova	Martina Navratilova
1985	Martina Navratilova	Chris Evert Lloyd	Martina Navratilova	Hana Mandlikova
1986	Moved to Jan. 1987	Chris Evert Lloyd	Martina Navratilova	Martina Navratilova
1987	Hana Mandlikova	Steffi Graf	Martina Navratilova	Martina Navratilova
1988[1]	Steffi Graf	Steffi Graf	Steffi Graf	Steffi Graf
1989	Steffi Graf	Arantxa Sanchez	Steffi Graf	Steffi Graf
1990	Steffi Graf	Monica Seles	Martina Navratilova	Gabriela Sabatini
1991	Monica Seles	Monica Seles	Steffi Graf	Monica Seles
1992	Monica Seles	Monica Seles	Steffi Graf	Monica Seles
1993	Monica Seles	Steffi Graf	Steffi Graf	Steffi Graf
1994	Steffi Graf	Arantxa Sánchez Vicario	Conchita Martinez	Arantxa Sánchez Vicario
1995	Mary Pierce	Steffi Graf	Steffi Graf	Steffi Graf
1996	Monica Seles	Steffi Graf	Steffi Graf	Steffi Graf
1997	Martina Hingis	Iva Majoli	Martina Hingis	Martina Hingis
1998	Martina Hingis	Arantxa Sánchez Vicario	Jana Novotna	Lindsay Davenport
1999	Martina Hingis	Steffi Graf	Lindsay Davenport	Serena Williams
2000	Lindsay Davenport	Mary Pierce	Venus Williams	Venus Williams
2001	Jennifer Capriati	Jennifer Capriati	Venus Williams	Venus Williams

1. Grand Slam winner. 2. Two tournaments were held in 1977, the first in January, the second in December.

THOROUGHBRED RACING

Thoroughbred Horse of the Year (Eclipse Award)

Year	Horse	Year	Horse	Year	Horse	Year	Horse
1936	Granville	1953	Tom Fool	1970	Personality	1987	Ferdinand
1937	War Admiral	1954	Native Dancer	1971	Ack Ack	1988	Alysheba
1938	Seabiscuit	1955	Nashua	1972	Secretariat	1989	Sunday Silence
1939	Challedon	1956	Swaps	1973	Secretariat	1990	Criminal Type
1940	Challedon	1957	Bold Ruler	1974	Forego	1991	Black Tie Affair
1941	Whirlaway	1958	Round Table	1975	Forego	1992	A.P. Indy
1942	Whirlaway	1959	Sword Dancer	1976	Forego	1993	Kotashaan
1943	Count Fleet	1960	Kelso	1977	Seattle Slew	1994	Holy Bull
1944	Twilight Tear	1961	Kelso	1978	Affirmed	1995	Cigar
1945	Busher	1962	Kelso	1979	Affirmed	1996	Cigar
1946	Assault	1963	Kelso	1980	Spectacular Bid	1997	Favorite Trick
1947	Armed	1964	Kelso	1981	John Henry	1998	Skip Away
1948	Citation	1965	Moccasin	1982	Conquistador Cielo	1999	Charismatic
1949	Capot	1966	Buckpasser	1983	All Along	2000	Tiznow
1950	Hill Prince	1967	Damascus	1984	John Henry		
1951	Counterpoint	1968	Dr. Fager	1985	Spend a Buck		
1952	Native Dancer	1969	Arts and Letters	1986	Lady's Secret		

Source: *The Jockey Club*

The Triple Crown Winners

Only 11 horses have won the Kentucky Derby, the Preakness, and the Belmont Stakes in the same year.

Year	Horse	Year	Horse	Year	Horse	Year	Horse
1919	Sir Barton	1937	War Admiral	1946	Assault	1977	Seattle Slew
1930	Gallant Fox	1941	Whirlaway	1948	Citation	1978	Affirmed
1935	Omaha	1943	Count Fleet	1973	Secretariat		

The Breeders' Cup

Thoroughbred racing's richest, most glamorous, and most exciting day of the year attracts the finest horses in the world for record purses as high as $4 million. The site changes from year to year.

Year	Winner	Jockey	Time	Year	Winner	Jockey	Time
	BREEDER'S CUP JUVENILE				**BREEDER'S CUP JUVENILE FILLIES**		
	Purse: $1 million	**Distance: 1¹/₁₆ miles**			**Purse: $1 million**	**Distance: 1¹/₁₆ miles**	
1984¹	Chief's Crown	D. MacBeth	1:36.1	1984¹	Outstandingly	W. Guerra	1:37.4
1985¹	Tasso	L. Pincay Jr.	1:36.1	1985¹	Twilight Ridge	J. Velasquez	1:35.4
1986	Capote	L. Pincay Jr.	1:43.4	1986	Brave Raj	P. Valenzuela	1:43.1
1987¹	Success Express	J. Santos	1:35.1	1987¹	Epitome	P. Day	1:36.2
1988¹	Is It True	L. Pincay Jr.	1:36.3	1988	Open Mind	A. Cordero Jr.	1:46.3
1989	Rhythm	C. Perret	1:43.3	1989	Go For Wand	R. Romero	1:44.1
1990	Fly So Free	J. Santos	1:43.2	1990	Meadow Star	J. Santos	1:44.0
1991	Arazi	P. Valenzuela	1:44.78	1991	Pleasant Stage	E. Delahoussaye	1:46.48
1992	Gilded Time	C. McCarron	1:43.43	1992	Eliza	P. Valenzuela	1:42.93
1993	Brocco	G. Stevens	1:42.99	1993	Phone Chatter	L. Pincay Jr.	1:43.08
1994	Timber Country	P. Day	1:44.55	1994	Flanders	P. Day	1:45.28
1995	Unbridled's Song	M. Smith	1:41.60	1995	My Flag	J. Bailey	1:42.55
1996	Boston Harbor	J. Bailey	1:43.40	1996	Storm Song	C. Perret	1:43.60
1997	Favorite Trick	P. Day	1:41.47	1997	Countess Diana	S. Sellers	1:42.11
1998	Answer Lively	J. Bailey	1:44.00	1998	Silverbulletday	G. Stevens	1:43.68
1999	Anees	G. Stevens	1:42.29	1999	Cash Run	J. Bailey	1:36.32
2000	Macho Uno	J. Bailey	1:42.05	2000	Caressing	J. Velasquez	1:42.77

Year	Winner	Jockey	Time	Year	Winner	Jockey	Time

BREEDER'S CUP SPRINT

Purse: $1 million   Distance: 6 furlongs

BREEDER'S CUP TURF

Purse: $2 milion   Distance: 1½ miles

Year	Winner	Jockey	Time	Year	Winner	Jockey	Time
1984	Eillo	C. Perret	1:10.1	1984	Lashkari	Y. Saint-Martin	2:25.1
1985	Precisionist	C. McCarron	1:08.2	1985	Pebbles	P. Eddery	2:27.0
1986	Smile	J. Vasquez	1:08.2	1986	Manila	J. Santos	2:25.2
1987	Very Subtle	P. Valenzuela	1:08.4	1987	Theatrical	P. Day	2:24.2
1988	Gulch	A. Cordero Jr.	1:10.2	1988	Great Communicator	R. Sibille	2:35.1
1989	Dancing Spree	A. Cordero Jr.	1:09.0	1989	Prized	E. Delahoussaye	2:28.0
1990	Safely Kept	C. Perret	1:09.3	1990	In the Wings	G. Stevens	2:29.3
1991	Sheik Albadou	P. Eddery	1:09.36	1991	Miss Alleged	E. Legrix	2:30.95
1992	30 Slews	E. Delahoussaye	1:08.21	1992	Fraise	P. Valenzuela	2:24.08
1993	Cardmania	E. Delahoussaye	1:08.76	1993	Kotashaan	K. Desormeaux	2:25.16
1994	Cherokee Run	M. Smith	1:09.54	1994	Tikkanen	M. Smith	2:26.50
1995	Desert Stormer	K. Desormeaux	1:09.14	1995	Northern Spur	C. McCarron	2:42.07
1996	Lit de Justice	C. Nakatani	1:08.60	1996	Pilsudski	W. Swinburn	2:30.20
1997	Elmhurst	C. Nakatani	1:08.01	1997	Chief Bearhart	J. Santos	2:23.92
1998	Reraise	C. Nakatani	1:09.07	1998	Buck's Boy	S. Sellers	2:28.74
1999	Artax	J. Chavez	1:07.89	1999	Daylami	L. Dettori	2:24.73
2000	Kona Gold	A. Solis	1:07.77	2000	Kalanisi	J. Murtagh	2:26.96

BREEDER'S CUP MILE

Purse: $1 million   Distance: 1 mile, turf.

BREEDER'S CUP CLASSIC

Purse: $4 million   Distance: 1¼ miles

Year	Winner	Jockey	Time	Year	Winner	Jockey	Time
1984	Royal Heroine	F. Toro	1:32.3	1984	Wild Again	P. Day	2:03.2
1985	Cozzene	W. Guerra	1:35.0	1985	Proud Truth	J. Velasquez	2:00.4
1986	Last Tycoon	Y. Saint-Martin	1:35.1	1986	Skywalker	L. Pincay Jr.	2:00.2
1987	Miesque	F. Head	1:32.4	1987	Ferdinand	B. Shoemaker	2:01.2
1988	Miesque	F. Head	1:38.3	1988	Alysheba	C. McCarron	2:04.4
1989	Steinlen	J. Santos	1:37.1	1989	Sunday Silence	C. McCarron	2:00.1
1990	Royal Academy	L. Piggott	1:35.1	1990	Unbridled	P. Day	2:02.1
1991	Opening Verse	P. Valenzuela	1:37.59	1991	Black Tie Affair	J. Bailey	2:02.95
1992	Lure	M. Smith	1:32.90	1992	A.P. Indy	E. Delahoussaye	2:00.20
1993	Lure	M. Smith	1:33.58	1993	Arcangues	J. Bailey	2:00.83
1994	Barathea	L. Dettori	1:34.50	1994	Concern	P. Day	2:02.41
1995	Ridgewood Pearl	J. Murtagh	1:43.65	1995	Cigar	J. Bailey	1:59.58
1996	Da Hoss	G. Stevens	1:35.80	1996	Alphabet Soup	C. McCarron	2:01.00
1997	Spinning World	C. Asmussen	1:32.77	1997	Skip Away	M. Smith	1:59.16
1998	Da Hoss	J. Velazquez	1:35.27	1998	Awesome Again	P. Day	2:02.16
1999	Silic	C. Nakatani	1:34.26	1999	Cat Thief	P. Day	1:59.52
2000	War Chant	G. Stevens	1:34.67	2000	Tiznow	C. McCarron	2:00.75

BREEDER'S CUP DISTAFF

Purse: $2 million   Distance: 1⅛ miles

BREEDER'S CUP FILLIES AND MARES TURF

Purse: $1 million   Distance: 1⅜ miles

Year	Winner	Jockey	Time	Year	Winner	Jockey	Time
1984[2]	Princess Rooney	E. Delahoussaye	2:02.2	1999	Soaring Softly	J. Bailey	2:13.89
1985[2]	Life's Magic	A. Cordero Jr.	2:02.0	2000	Perfect Sting	J. Bailey	2:13.07
1986[2]	Lady's Secret	P. Day	2:01.1				
1987[2]	Sacahuista	R. Romero	2:02.4				
1988	Personal Ensign	R. Romero	1:52.0				
1989	Bayakoa	L. Pincay Jr.	1:47.2				
1990	Bayakoa	L. Pincay Jr.	1:49.1				
1991	Dance Smartly	P. Day	1:50.95				
1992	Paseana	C. McCarron	1:48.17				
1993	Hollywood Wildcat	E. Delahoussaye	1:48.35				
1994	One Dreamer	G. Stevens	1:50.70				
1995	Inside Information	M. Smith	1:46.15				
1996	Jewel Princess	C. Nakatani	1:48.40				
1997	Ajina	M. Smith	1:47.20				
1998	Escena	G. Stevens	1:49.89				
1999	Beautiful Pleasure	J. Chavez	1:47.56				
2000	Spain	V. Espinoza	1:47.66				

BREEDER'S CUP LOCATIONS

1984	Hollywood	1993	Santa Anita
1985	Aqueduct	1994	Churchill Downs
1986	Santa Anita	1995	Belmont Park
1987	Hollywood	1996	Woodbine
1988	Churchill Downs	1997	Hollywood
1989	Gulfstream	1998	Churchill Downs
1990	Belmont Park	1999	Gulfstream
1991	Churchill Downs	2000	Churchill Downs
1992	Gulfstream	2001	Belmont Park

Note: Before 1991, decimals refer to fifths of a second. 1. One mile. 2. 1¼ miles. **Source:** Breeder's Cup Ltd., www.breederscup.com

Kentucky Derby, 1875–2001

Thoroughbred racing's most celebrated event was first run in 1875. The distance was 1½ miles until 1896, when it was shortened to 1¼ miles. "The Run for the Roses," is the first leg of racing's Triple Crown for three-year-olds. It is always held the first Saturday in May. **Site: Churchill Downs,** Louisville, Kentucky.

Year	Horse	Jockey	Time	Year	Horse	Jockey	Time
1875	Aristides	O. Lewis	2:37¾	1938	Lawrin	E. Arcaro	2:04.4
1876	Vagrant	R. Swim	2:38¼	1939	Johnston	J. Stout	2:03.2
1877	Baden-Baden	W. Walker	2:38.0	1940	Gallahadion	C. Bierman	2:05.0
1878	Day Star	J. Carter	2:37¼	1941	**Whirlaway**	E. Arcaro	2:01.2
1879	Lord Murphy	C. Shauer	2:37.0	1942	Shut Out	W. D. Write	2:04.2
1880	Fonso	G. Lewis	2:37½	1943	**Count Fleet**	J. Longden	2:04.0
1881	Hindoo	J. McLaughlin	2:40.0	1944	Pensive	C. McCreary	2:04.1
1882	Apollo	B. Hurd	2:40¼	1945	Hoop Jr.	E. Arcaro	2:07.0
1883	Leonatus	W. Donohue	2:43.0	1946	**Assault**	W. Mehrtens	2:06.3
1884	Buchanan	I. Murphy	2:40¼	1947	Jet Pilot	E. Guerin	2:06.3
1885	Joe Cotton	E. Henderson	2:37¼	1948	**Citation**	E. Arcaro	2:05.2
1886	Ben Ali	P. Duffy	2:36½	1949	Ponder	S. Brooks	2:04.1
1887	Montrose	I. Lewis	2:39¼	1950	Middleground	W. Boland	2:01.3
1888	MacBeth II	G. Covington	2:38¼	1951	Count Turf	C. McCreary	2:02.3
1889	Spokane	T. Kiley	2:34½	1952	Hill Gail	E. Arcaro	2:01.3
1890	Riley	I. Murphy	2:45.0	1953	Dark Star	H. Moreno	2:02.0
1891	Kingman	I. Murphy	2:52¼	1954	Determine	R. York	2:03.0
1892	Azra	A. Clayton	2:41½	1955	Swaps	W. Shoemaker	2:01.4
1893	Lookout	E. Kunze	2:39¼	1956	Needles	D. Erb	2:03.2
1894	Chant	F. Goodale	2:41.0	1957	Iron Liege	W. Hartack	2:02.1
1895	Halma	J. Perkins	2:37½	1958	Tim Tam	I. Valenzuela	2:05.0
1896	Ben Brush	W. Simms	2:07¾	1959	Tommy Lee	W. Shoemaker	2:02.1
1897	Typhoon II	F. Garner	2:12½	1960	Venetian Way	W. Hartack	2:02.2
1898	Plaudit	W. Simms	2:09.0	1961	Carry Back	J. Sellers	2:04.0
1899	Manuel	F. Taral	2:12.0	1962	Decidedly	W. Hartack	2:00.2
1900	Lieut.Gibson	J. Boland	2:06¼	1963	Chateaugay	B. Baeza	2:01.4
1900	Lieut. Gibson	J. Boland	2:06¼	1964	Northern Dancer	W. Hartack	2:00.0
1901	His Eminence	J. Winkfield	2:07¾	1965	Lucky Debonair	W. Shoemaker	2:01.1
1902	Alan-a-Dale	J. Winkfield	2:08¼	1966	Kauai King	D. Brumfield	2:02.0
1903	Judge Himes	H. Booker	2:09.0	1967	Proud Clarion	R. Ussery	2:00.3
1904	Elwood	F. Prior	2:08½	1968	Forward Pass[1]	R. Ussery	2:02.1
1905	Agile	J. Martin	2:10¾	1969	Majestic Prince	W. Hartack	2:01.4
1906	Sir Huon	R. Troxler	2:08.4	1970	Dust Commander	M. Manganello	2:03.2
1907	Pink Star	A. Minder	2:12.3	1971	Canonero II	G. Avila	2:03.1
1908	Stone Street	A. Pickens	2:15.1	1972	Riva Ridge	R. Turcotte	2:01.4
1909	Wintergreen	V. Powers	2:08.1	1973	**Secretariat**[2]	R. Turcotte	1:59.2
1910	Donau	F. Herbert	2:06.2	1974	Cannonade	A. Cordero	2:04.0
1911	Meridian	G. Archibald	2:05.0	1975	Foolish Pleasure	J. Vasquez	2:02.0
1912	Worth	C. H. Shilling	2:09.2	1976	Bold Forbes	A. Cordero	2:01.3
1913	Donerail	R. Goose	2:04.4	1977	**Seattle Slew**	J. Cruquet	2:02.1
1914	Old Rosebud	J. McCabe	2:03.2	1978	**Affirmed**	S. Cauthen	2:01.1
1915	Regret	J. Notter	2:05.2	1979	Spectacular Bid	R. Franklin	2:02.2
1916	George Smith	J. Loftus	2:04.3	1980	Genuine Risk	J. Vasquez	2:02.0
1917	Omar Khayyam	C. Borel	2:04.0	1981	Pleasant Colony	J. Velasquez	2:02.0
1918	Exterminator	W. Knapp	2:10.4	1982	Gato Del Sol	E. Delahoussaye	2:02.2
1919	**Sir Barton**	J. Loftus	2:09.4	1983	Sunny's Halo	E. Delahoussaye	2:02.1
1920	Paul Jones	T. Rice	2:09.0	1984	Swale	L. Pincay	2:02.2
1921	Behave Yourself	C. Thompson	2:04.1	1985	Spend A Buck	A. Cordero	2:00.1
1922	Morvich	A. Johnson	2:04.3	1986	Ferdinand	W. Shoemaker	2:02.4
1923	Zev	E. Sande	2:05.2	1987	Alysheba	C. McCarron	2:03.2
1924	Black Gold	J. D. Mooney	2:05.1	1988	Winning Colors	G. Stevens	2:02.2
1925	Flying Ebony	E. Sande	2:07.3	1989	Sunday Silence	P. Valenzuela	2:05.0
1926	Bubbling Over	A. Johnson	2:03.4	1990	Unbridled	C. Perret	2:02.0
1927	Whiskery	L. McAtee	2:06.0	1991	Strike the Gold	C. Antley	2:03.0
1928	Reigh Count	C. Lang	2:10.2	1992	Lil E. Tee	P.Day	2:03.0
1929	Clyde Van Dusen	L. McAtee	2:10.4	1993	Sea Hero	J. Bailey	2:02.42
1930	**Gallant Fox**	E. Sande	2:07.3	2001	Go for Gin	C. McCarron	2:03.72
1931	Twenty Grand	C. Kurtsinger	2:01.4	2001	Thunder Gulch	G. Stevens	2:01.27
1932	Burgoo King	E. James	2:05.1	2001	Grindstone	J. Bailey	2:01.60
1933	Brokers Tip	D. Meade	2:06.4	2001	Silver Charm	G. Stevens	2:02.59
1934	Cavalcade	M. Garner	2:04.0	2001	Real Quiet	K. Desormeaux	2:02.38
1935	**Omaha**	W. Saunders	2:05.0	2001	Charismatic	C. Antley	2:03.29
1936	Bold Venture	I. Hanford	2:03.3	2001	Fusaichi Pegasus	K. Desormeaux	2:01.12
1937	**War Admiral**	C. Kurtsinger	2:03.1	2001	Monarchos	J. Chavez	1:59.97

Note: Names in bold indicate Triple Crown winners. Before 1993, decimals refer to fifths of a second. 1. In 1968, Dancer's Image finished first, but was later disqualified from the purse money, and Forward Pass was declared winner. 2. Record. **Source:** *Daily Racing Form.*

Preakness Stakes Winners 1873–2001

The Preakness was first run in 1873, and the distance varied from 1 mile 70 yards to 1½ miles until 1925, when it was standardized at 1³⁄₁₆ miles. **Site: Pimlico Racetrack,** Baltimore, Maryland.

Year	Horse	Jockey	Time	Year	Horse	Jockey	Time
1873	Survivor	G. Barbee	2:43.0	1938	Dauber	M. Peters	1:59.4
1874	Culpepper	Donohue	2:56½	1939	Challedon	G. Seabo	1:59.4
1875	Tom Ochiltree	L. Hughes	2:43½	1940	Bimelech	F. A. Smith	1:58.3
1876	Shirley	Barbee	2:44¾	1941	**Whirlaway**	E. Arcaro	1:58.4
1877	Cloverbrook	Holloway	2:45½	1942	Alsab	B. James	1:57.0
1878	Duke of Magenta	Holloway	2:41¾	1943	**Count Fleet**	J. Longden	1:57.2
1879	Harold	Hughes	2:40½	1944	Pensive	C. McCreary	1:59.1
1880	Grenada	L. Hughes	2:40½	1945	Polynesian	W. D. Wright	1:58.4
1881	Saunterer	Costello	2:40½	1946	**Assault**	W. Mehrtens	2:01.2
1882	Vanguard	Costello	2:44½	1947	Faultless	D. Dodson	1:59.0
1883	Jacobus	Barbee	2:42½	1948	**Citation**	E. Arcaro	2:02.2
1884	Knight of Ellerslie	Fisher	2:39½	1949	Capot	T. Atkinson	1:56.0
1885	Tecumseh	M. McLaughlin	2:49.0	1950	Hill Prince	E. Arcaro	1:59.1
1886	The Bard	Fisher	2:45.0	1951	Bold	E. Arcaro	1:56.2
1887	Dunboyne	W. Donohue	2:39½	1952	Blue Man	C. McCreary	1:57.2
1888	Refund	Littlefield	2:49.0	1953	Native Dancer	E. Guerin	1:57.4
1889	Buddhist	Anderson	2:17½	1954	Hasty Road	J. Adams	1:57.2
1890	Montague	W. Martin	2:36¾	1955	Nashua	E. Arcaro	1:54.3
1891–93	Not run			1956	Fabius	W. Hartack	1:58.2
1894	Assignee	F. Taral	1:49¼	1957	Bold Ruler	E. Arcaro	1:56.1
1895	Belmar	F. Taral	1:50½	1958	Tim Tam	I. Valenzuela	1:57.1
1896	Margrave	H. Griffin	1:51.0	1959	Royal Orbit	W. Harmatz	1:57.0
1897	Paul Kauver	Thorpe	1:51¼	1960	Bally Ache	R. Ussery	1:57.3
1898	Sly Fox	W. Simms	1:49¾	1961	Carry Back	J. Sellers	1:57.3
1899	Half Time	R. Clawson	1:47.0	1962	Greek Money	J. L. Rotz	1:56.1
1900	Hindus	H. Spencer	1:48.2	1963	Candy Spots	W. Shoemaker	1:56.1
1901	The Parader	F. Landry	1:47.1	1964	Northern Dancer	W. Hartack	1:56.4
1902	Old England	L. Jackson	1:45.4	1965	Tom Rolfe	R. Turncotte	1:56.1
1903	Flocarline	W. Gannon	1:44.4	1966	Kauai King	D. Brumfield	1:55.2
1904	Bryn Mawr	E. Hildebrand	1:44.1	1967	Damascus	W. Shoemaker	1:55.1
1905	Cairngorm	W. Davis	1:45.4	1968	Forward Pass	I. Valenzuela	1:56.4
1906	Whimsical	W. Miller	1:45.0	1969	Majestic Prince	W. Hartack	1:55.3
1907	Don Enrique	G. Mountain	1:45.2	1970	Personality	E. Belmonte	1:56.1
1908	Royal Tourist	E. Dugan	1:46.2	1971	Canonero II	G. Avila	1:54.0
1909	Effendi	W. Doyle	1:39.4	1972	Bee Bee Bee	E. Nelson	1:55.3
1910	Layminister	R. Estep	1:40.3	1973	**Secretariat**	R. Turcotte	1:54.2
1911	Watervale	E. Dugan	1:51.0	1974	Little Current	M. Rivera	1:54.3
1912	Colonel Holloway	C. Turner	1:56.3	1975	Master Derby	D. McHargue	1:56.2
1913	Buskin	J. Butwell	1:53.2	1976	Elocutionist	J. Lively	1:55.0
1914	Holiday	A. Schuttinger	1:53.4	1977	**Seattle Slew**	J. Cruguet	1:54.2
1915	Rhine Maiden	D. Hoffman	1:58.0	1978	**Affirmed**	S. Cauthen	1:54.2
1916	Damrosch	L. McAtee	1:54.4	1979	Spectacular Bid	R. Franklin	1:54.1
1917	Kalitan	E. Haynes	1:54.2	1980	Codex	A. Cordero	1:54.1
1918	Jack Hare Jr.	C. Peak	1:53.2	1981	Pleasant Colony	J. Valasquez	1:54.3
	War Cloud	J. Loftus	1:53.3	1982	Aloma's Ruler	J. Kaenel	1:55.2
1919	**Sir Barton**	J. Loftus	1:53.0	1983	Deputed Testamony	D. Miller	1:55.2
1920	Man o'War	C. Kummer	1:51.3	1984	Gate Dancer	A. Cordero	1:53.3
1921	Broomspun	F. Coltiletti	1:54.1	1985	Tank's Prospect	P. Day	1:53.2
1922	Pillory	L. Morris	1:51.3	1986	Snow Chief	A. Solls	1:54.4
1923	Vigil	B. Marinelli	1:53.3	1987	Alysheba	C. McCarron	1:55.4
1924	Nellie Morse	J. Merimee	1:57.1	1988	Risen Star	E. Delahoussaye	1:56.1
1925	Coventry	C. Kummer	1:59.0	1989	Sunday Silence	P. Valenzuela	1:53.4
1926	Display	J. Maiben	1:59.4	1990	Summer Squall	P. Day	1:53.3
1927	Bostonian	A. Abel	2:01.3	1991	Hansel	J. Bailey	1:54.0
1928	Victorian	R. Workman	2:00.1	1992	Pine Bluff	C. McCarron	1:55.3
1929	Dr. Freeland	L. Schaefer	2:01.3	1993	Prairie Bayou	M. Smith	1:56.3
1930	**Gallant Fox**	E. Sande	2:00.3	1994	Tabasco Cat	P. Day	1:56.2
1931	Mate	G. Ellis	1:59.0	1995	Timber Country	P. Day	1:54.2
1932	Burgoo King	E. James	1:59.4	1996	Louis Quatorze	P. Day	1:53.4
1933	Head Play	C. Kurtsinger	2:02.0	1997	Silver Charm	G. Stevens	1:54.4
1934	High Quest	R. Jones	1:58.1	1998	Real Quiet	K. Desormeaux	1:54.75
1935	**Omaha**	W. Saunders	1:58.2	1999	Charismatic	C. Antley	1:55.32
1936	Bold Venture	G. Woolf	1:59.0	2000	Red Bullet	J. Bailey	1:56.04
1937	**War Admiral**	C. Kurtsinger	1:58.2	2001	Point Given	G. Stevens	1:56.51

Note: Names in **bold** indicate Triple Crown winners. Before 1998, decimals refer to fifths of a second. **Source:** *Daily Racing Form*

Belmont Stakes Winners 1880–2001

The **Belmont Stakes** was first run in 1867. The distance of the race varied from 1¹⁄₁₈ miles to 1⅜ miles until 1926, when it was standardized at 1½ miles. **Site: Belmont Park,** New York. (The race was held at Jerome Park prior to 1890, at Morris Park from 1890 to 1904, at Aqueduct from 1963 to 1967.)

Year	Horse	Jockey	Time
1880	Grenada	L. Hughes	2:47.0
1881	Saunterer	T. Costello	2:47.0
1882	Forester	J. McLaughlin	2:43.0
1883	George Kinney	J. McLaughlin	2:42.2
1884	Panique	J. McLaughlin	2:42.0
1885	Tyrant	P. Duffy	2:43.0
1886	Inspector B.	J. McLaughlin	2:41.0
1887	Hanover	J. McLaughlin	2:43.2
1888	Sir Dixon	J. McLaughlin	2:40.2
1889	Eric	W. Hayward	2:47.0
1890	Burlington	S. Barnes	2:07.6
1891	Foxford	E. Garrison	2:08.6
1892	Patron	W. Hayward	2:17.0
1893	Comanche	W. Simms	1:53.2
1894	Henry of Navarre	W. Simms	1:56.2
1895	Belmar	F. Taral	2:11.2
1896	Hastings	H. Griffin	2:24.2
1897	Scottish Chieftain	J. Scherrer	2:32.2
1898	Bowling Brook	F. Littlefield	2:32.0
1899	Jean Bereaud	R.R. Clawson	2:23.0
1900	Ildrim	N. Turner	2:21½
1901	Commando	H. Spencer	2:21.0
1902	Masterman	J. Bullman	2:22½
1903	Africander	J. Bullman	2:23.1
1904	Delhi	G. Odom	2:06.3
1905	Tanya	E. Hildebrand	2:08.0
1906	Burgomaster	L. Lyne	2:20.0
1907	Peter Pan	G. Mountain	No Time
1908	Colin	J. Notter	No Time
1909	Joe Madden	E. Dugan	2:21.3
1910	Sweep	J. Butwell	2:22.0
1911–12	Not run		
1913	Prince Eugene	R. Troxler	2:18.0
1914	Luke McLuke	M. Buxton	2:20.0
1915	The Finn	G. Byrne	2:18.2
1916	Friar Rock	E. Haynes	2:22.0
1917	Hourless	J. Butwell	2:17.4
1918	Johren	F. Robinson	2:20.2
1919	**Sir Barton**	J. Loftus	2:17.2
1920	Man o'War	C. Kummer	2:14.1
1921	Grey Lag	E. Sande	2:16.4
1922	Pillory	C. H. Miller	2:18.4
1923	Zev	E. Sande	2:19.0
1924	Mad Play	E. Sande	2:18.4
1925	American Flag	A. Johnson	2:16.4
1926	Crusader	A. Johnson	2:32.1
1927	Chance Shot	E. Sande	2:32.2
1928	Vito	C. Kummer	2:33.1
1929	Blue Larkspur	M. Garner	2:32.4
1930	**Gallant Fox**	E. Sande	2:31.1
1931	Twenty Grand	C. Kurtsinger	2:29.3
1932	Faireno	T. Malley	2:32.4
1933	Hurryoff	M. Garner	2:32.3
1934	Peace Chance	W. D. Wright	2:29.5
1935	**Omaha**	W. Saunders	2:30.3
1936	Granville	J. Stout	2:30.0
1937	**War Admiral**	C. Kurtsinger	2:28.3
1938	Pasteurized	J. Stout	2:29.2
1939	Johnstown	J. Stout	2:29.2
1940	Bimelech	F. A. Smith	2:29.3
1941	**Whirlaway**	E. Arcaro	2:31.0

Year	Horse	Jockey	Time
1942	Shut Out	E. Arcaro	2:29.1
1943	**Count Fleet**	J. Longden	2:28.1
1944	Bounding Home	G. L. Smith	2:32.1
1945	Pavot	E. Arcaro	2:30.1
1946	**Assault**	W. Mehrtens	2:30.4
1947	Phalanx	R. Donoso	2:29.2
1948	**Citation**	E. Arcaro	2:28.1
1949	Capot	T. Atkinson	2:30.1
1950	Middleground	W. Boland	2:28.3
1951	Counterpoint	D. Gorman	2:29.0
1952	One Count	E. Arcaro	2:30.1
1953	Native Dancer	E. Guerin	2:28.3
1954	High Gun	E. Guerin	2:30.4
1955	Nashua	E. Arcaro	2:29.0
1956	Needles	D. Erb	2:29.4
1957	Gallant Man	W. Shoemaker	2:26.3
1958	Cavan	P. Anderson	2:30.1
1959	Sword Dancer	W. Shoemaker	2:28.2
1960	Celtic Ash	W. Hartack	2:29.3
1961	Sherluck	B. Baeza	2:29.1
1962	Jaipur	W. Shoemaker	2:28.4
1963	Chateaugay	B. Baeza	2:30.1
1964	Quadrangle	M. Ycaza	2:28.2
1965	Hail To All	J. Sellers	2:28.2
1966	Amberoid	W. Boland	2:29.3
1967	Damascus	W. Shoemaker	2:28.4
1968	Stage Door Johnny	H. Gustines	2:27.1
1969	Arts and Letters	B. Baeza	2:28.4
1970	High Echelon	J. L. Rotz	2:34.0
1971	Pass Catcher	W. Blum	2:30.2
1972	Riva Ridge	R. Turcotte	2:28.0
1973	**Secretariat**	R. Turcotte	2:24.0
1974	Little Current	M. Rivera	2:29.1
1975	Avatar	W. Shoemaker	2:28.1
1976	Bold Forbes	A. Cordero	2:29.0
1977	**Seattle Slew**	Jean Cruguet	2:29.3
1978	**Affirmed**	S. Cauthen	2:26.4
1979	Coastal	R. Hernandez	2:28.3
1980	Temperance Hill	E. Maple	2:29.4
1981	Summing	G. Martens	2:29.0
1982	Conquistador Cielo	L. Pincay	2:28.1
1983	Caveat	L. Pincay	2:27.4
1984	Swale	L. Pincay	2:27.1
1985	Creme Fraiche	E. Maple	2:27.0
1986	Danzig Connection	C. McCarron	2:29.4
1987	Bet Twice	C. Perret	2:28.1
1988	Risen Star	E. Delahoussaye	2:26.1
1989	Easy Goer	P. Day	2:26.0
1990	Go and Go	M. Kinane	2:27.1
1991	Hansel	J. Bailey	2:28.0
1992	A.P. Indy	E. Delahoussaye	2:26.0
1993	Colonial Affair	J. Krone	2:29.4
1994	Tabasco Cat	P. Day	2:26.4
1995	Thunder Gulch	G. Stevens	2:32.0
1996	Editor's Note	R. Douglas	2:28.4
1997	Touch Gold	C. McCarron	2:28.4
1998	Victory Gallop	G. Stevens	2:29.16
1999	Lemon Drop Kid	J. Santos	2:27.88
2000	Commendable	P. Day	2:31.19
2001	Point Given	G. Stevens	2:26.56

Note: Names in **bold** indicate Triple Crown winners. Before 1998, decimals refer to fifths of a second. **Source:** *Daily Racing Form.*

FOOTBALL

National Football League
410 Park Avenue
New York, NY 10022
(212) 450-2000

www.nfl.com
Commissioner: Paul Tagliabue
Founded 1920.
Number of Teams: 31

2000 NFL Regular Season Final Standings

AMERICAN FOOTBALL CONFERENCE	W-L-T	PCT.	PTS.	OPP.
Eastern Division				
Miami[1]	11-5-0	.688	323	226
Indianapolis[2]	10-6-0	.625	429	326
New York Jets	9-7-0	.562	321	321
Buffalo	8-8-0	.500	315	350
New England	5-11-0	.312	276	338
Central Division				
Tennessee[1]	13-3-0	.812	346	191
Baltimore[2]	12-4-0	.750	333	165
Pittsburgh	9-7-0	.562	321	255
Jacksonville	7-9-0	.438	367	327
Cincinnati	4-12-0	.250	185	359
Cleveland	3-13-0	.188	161	419
Western Division				
Oakland[1]	12-4-0	.750	479	299
Denver[2]	11-5-0	.688	485	369
Kansas City	7-9-0	.438	355	354
Seattle	6-10-0	.375	320	405
San Diego	1-15-0	.062	269	440

NATIONAL FOOTBALL CONFERENCE	W-L-T	PCT.	PTS.	OPP.
Eastern Division				
N.Y. Giants[1]	12-4-0	.750	328	246
Philadelphia[2]	11-5-0	.688	351	245
Washington	8-8-0	.500	281	269
Dallas	5-11-0	.312	294	361
Arizona	3-13-0	.188	210	443
Central Division				
Minnesota[1]	11-5-0	.688	397	371
Tampa Bay[2]	10-6-0	.625	388	269
Green Bay	9-7-0	.562	353	323
Detroit	9-7-0	.562	307	307
Chicago	5-11-0	.312	216	355
Western Division				
New Orleans[1]	10-6-0	.625	354	305
St. Louis[2]	10-6-0	.625	540	471
Carolina	7-9-0	.438	310	310
San Francisco	6-10-0	.375	388	422
Atlanta	4-12-0	.250	252	413

1. Division champion. 2. Wild Card for playoffs.

2000 NFL Post-Season Playoff Results

AFC Wild Card Playoff
MIAMI 23, Indianapolis 17 (OT)
BALTIMORE 21, Denver 3
AFC Divisional Playoff
OAKLAND 27, Miami 0
Baltimore 24, TENNESSEE 10
AFC Championship Game
Baltimore 16, OAKLAND 3

NFC Wild Card Playoff
NEW ORLEANS 31, St. Louis 28
PHILADELPHIA 21, Tampa Bay   3
NFC Divisional Playoff
MINNESOTA 34, New Orleans   16
NEW YORK GIANTS 20, Philadelphia 10
NFC Championship Game
NEW YORK GIANTS 41, Minnesota 0

Super Bowl XXXV at Raymond James Stadium, Tampa, Fla. (January 28, 2001)
BALTIMORE 34, New York Giants 7

Note: Home team in CAPITAL LETTERS.

NFL First Round Draft Choices, 2001

Team	Selection, Position	School
1. Atlanta	Michael Vick, QB	Virginia Tech
2. Arizona	Leonard Davis, OT	Texas
3. Cleveland	Gerard Warren, DT	Florida
4. Cincinnati	Justin Smith, DE	Missouri
5. San Diego	LaDainian Tomlinson, RB	Texas Christian
6. New England	Richard Seymour, DL	Georgia
7. San Francisco	Andre Carter, DE	California
8. Chicago	David Terrell, WR	Michigan
9. Seattle	Koren Robinson, WR	North Carolina St.
10. Green Bay	Jamal Reynolds, DE	Florida State
11. Carolina	Dan Morgan, LB	Miami (Fla.)
12. St. Louis	Damione Lewis, DT	Miami (Fla.)
13. Jacksonville	Marcus Stroud, DT	Georgia
14. Tampa Bay	Kenyatta Walker, OT	Florida
15. Washington	Rod Gardner, WR	Clemson

Team	Selection, Position	School
16. N.Y. Jets	Santana Moss, WR	Miami (Fla.)
17. Seattle	Steve Hutchinson, G	Michigan
18. Detroit	Jeff Backus, OT	Michigan
19. Pittsburgh	Casey Hampton, DT	Texas
20. St. Louis	Adam Archuleta, S	Arizona St.
21. Buffalo	Nate Clements, CB	Ohio State
22. N.Y. Giants	Will Allen, CB	Syracuse
23. New Orleans	Deuce McAllister, RB	Mississippi
24. Denver	Willie Middlebrooks, CB	Minnesota
25. Philadelphia	Freddie Mitchell, WR	UCLA
26. Miami	Jamar Fletcher, CB	Wisconsin
27. Minnesota	Michael Bennett, RB	Wisconsin
28. Oakland	Derrick Gibson, S	Florida State
29. St. Louis	Ryan Pickett, DT	Ohio State
30. Indianapolis	Reggie Wayne, WR	Miami (Fla.)
31. Baltimore	Todd Heap, TE	Arizona St.

NFL Leaders, 2000

RUSHING

AFC	No.	Yds.	Avg.	TDs
Edgerrin James, Indianapolis	387	1,709	4.4	13
Eddie George, Tennessee	403	1,509	3.7	14
Mike Anderson, Denver	297	1,500	5.1	15
Corey Dillon, Cincinnati	315	1,435	4.6	7
Fred Taylor, Jacksonville	292	1,399	4.8	12
Jamal Lewis, Baltimore	309	1,364	4.4	6
Jerome Bettis, Pittsburgh	355	1,341	3.8	8
Ricky Watters, Seattle	278	1,242	4.5	7
Curtis Martin, New York Jets	316	1,204	3.8	9
Lamar Smith, Miami	309	1,139	3.7	14

NFC	No.	Yds.	Avg.	TDs
Robert Smith, Minnesota	295	1,521	5.2	7
Marshall Faulk, St. Louis	253	1,359	5.4	18
Stephen Davis, Washington	332	1,318	4.0	11
Emmitt Smith, Dallas	294	1,203	4.1	9
James Stewart, Detroit	339	1,184	3.5	10
Ahman Green, Green Bay	263	1,175	4.5	10
Charlie Garner, San Francisco	258	1,142	4.4	7
Warrick Dunn, Tampa Bay	248	1,133	4.6	8
James Allen, Chicago	290	1,120	3.9	2
Jamal Anderson, Atlanta	282	1,024	3.6	6

RECEIVING

AFC	No.	Yds.	Avg.	TDs
Marvin Harrison, Indianapolis	102	1,413	13.9	14
Ed McCaffrey, Denver	101	1,317	13.0	9
Rod Smith, Denver	100	1,602	16.0	8
Keenan McCardell, Jacksonville	94	1,207	12.8	5
Eric Moulds, Buffalo	94	1,326	14.1	5
Tony Gonzalez, Kansas City	93	1,203	12.9	9
Jimmy Smith, Jacksonville	91	1,213	13.3	8
Richie Anderson, N.Y. Jets	88	853	9.7	2
Troy Brown, New England	83	944	11.4	4
Terry Glenn, New England	79	963	12.2	6

NFC	No.	Yds.	Avg.	TDs
Muhsin Muhammad, Carolina	102	1,183	11.6	6
Terrell Owens, San Francisco	97	1,451	15.0	13
Cris Carter, Minnesota	96	1,274	13.3	9
Joe Horn, New Orleans	94	1,340	14.3	8
Isaac Bruce, St. Louis	87	1,471	16.9	9
Torry Holt, St. Louis	82	1,635	19.9	6
Larry Centers, Washington	81	600	7.4	3
Marshall Faulk, St. Louis	81	830	10.2	8
Amani Toomer, N.Y. Giants	78	1,094	14.0	7
Randy Moss, Minnesota	77	1,437	18.7	15

PASSING RATING

AFC	Att.	Comp.	Pct.	Yds.	Avg.	TDs	Int.	Rating
Brian Griese, Denver	336	216	64.3	2,688	8.0	19	4	102.9
Peyton Manning, Indianapolis	571	357	62.5	4,413	7.7	33	15	94.7
Rich Gannon, Oakland	473	284	60.0	3,430	7.3	28	11	92.4
Elvis Grbac, Kansas City	547	326	59.6	4,169	7.6	28	14	89.9
Doug Flutie, Buffalo	231	132	57.1	1,700	7.4	8	3	86.5
Mark Brunell, Jacksonville	512	311	60.7	3,640	7.1	20	14	84.0
Steve McNair, Tennessee	396	248	62.6	2,847	7.2	15	13	83.2
Rob Johnson, Buffalo	306	175	57.2	2,125	6.9	12	7	82.2
Gus Frerotte, Denver	232	138	59.5	1,776	7.7	9	8	82.1
Drew Bledsoe, New England	531	312	58.8	3,291	6.2	17	13	77.3

NFC	Att.	Comp.	Pct.	Yds.	Avg.	TDs	Int.	Rating
Trent Green, St. Louis	240	145	60.4	2,063	8.6	16	5	101.8
Kurt Warner, St. Louis	347	235	67.7	3,429	9.9	21	18	98.3
Daunte Culpepper, Minnesota	474	297	62.7	3,937	8.3	33	16	98.0
Jeff Garcia, San Francisco	561	355	63.3	4,278	7.6	31	10	97.6
Kerry Collins, N.Y. Giants	529	311	58.8	3,610	6.8	22	13	83.1
Jeff Blake, New Orleans	302	184	60.9	2,025	6.7	13	9	82.7
Steve Beuerlein, Carolina	533	324	60.8	3,730	7.0	19	18	79.7
Brett Favre, Green Bay	580	338	58.3	3,812	6.6	20	16	78.0
Donovan McNabb, Philadelphia	569	330	58.0	3,365	5.9	21	13	77.8
Shaun King, Tampa Bay	428	233	54.4	2,769	6.5	18	13	75.8

Source: National Football League. www.nfl.com

NFL Number One Draft Picks, 1936-2001

Year	Player	Team	Pos.	College
1936	Jay Berwanger	Philadelphia Eagles	RB	Chicago
1937	Sam Francis	Philadelphia Eagles	RB	Nebraska
1938	Corbett Davis	Cleveland Rams	RB	Indiana
1939	Charles Aldrich	Chicago Cardinals	OL	Texas Christian
1940	George Cafego	Chicago Cardinals	QB	Tennessee
1941	Tom Harmon	Chicago Bears	RB	Michigan
1942	Bill Dudley	Pittsburgh Steelers	RB	Virginia
1943	Frank Sinkwich	Detroit Lions	RB	Georgia
1944	Angelo Bertelli	Boston Yanks	QB	Notre Dame
1945	Charley Trippi	Chicago Cardinals	RB	Georgia
1946	Frank Dancewicz	Boston Yanks	QB	Notre Dame
1947	Bob Fenimore	Chicago Bears	RB	Oklahoma A&M
1948	Harry Gilmer	Washington Redskins	QB	Alabama
1949	Chuck Bednarik	Philadelphia Eagles	OL	Pennsylvania
1950	Leon Hart	Detroit Lions	RB	Notre Dame
1951	Kyle Rote	New York Giants	E/K	Southern Methodist
1952	Bill Wade	Los Angeles Rams	QB	Vanderbilt
1953	Harry Babcock	San Francisco 49ers	E	Georgia
1954	Bobby Garrett	Cleveland Browns	QB	Stanford
1955	George Shaw	Baltimore Colts	QB	Oregon
1956	Gary Glick	Pittsburgh Steelers	QB	Colorado State
1957	Paul Hornung	Green Bay Packers	RB	Notre Dame
1958	King Hill	St. Louis Cardinals	QB	Rice
1959	Randy Duncan	Green Bay Packers	QB	Iowa
1960	Billy Cannon	Los Angeles Rams	RB	Louisiana State
1961	Tommy Mason	Minnesota Vikings	RB	Tulane
1962	Ernie Davis	Washington Redskins	RB	Syracuse
1963	Terry Baker	Los Angeles Rams	QB	Oregon State
1964	Dave Parks	San Francisco 49ers	E	Texas Tech.
1965	Tucker Frederickson	New York Giants	RB	Auburn
1966	Tommy Nobis	Atlanta Falcons	LB	Texas
1967	Bubba Smith	Baltimore Colts	DL	Michigan State
1968	Ron Yary	Minnesota Vikings	OL	USC
1969	O.J. Simpson	Buffalo Bills	RB	USC
1970	Terry Bradshaw	Pittsburgh Steelers	QB	Louisiana Tech.
1971	Jim Plunkett	Boston Patriots	QB	Stanford
1972	Walt Patulski	Buffalo Bills	DL	Notre Dame
1973	John Matuzak	Houston Oilers	DL	Tampa
1974	Ed Jones	Dallas Cowboys	DL	Tampa
1975	Steve Bartkowski	Atlanta Falcons	QB	California
1976	Lee Roy Selmon	Tampa Bay Buccaneers	DL	Oklahoma
1977	Ricky Bell	Tampa Bay Buccaneers	RB	USC
1978	Earl Campbell	Houston Oilers	RB	Texas
1979	Tom Cousineau	Buffalo Bills	LB	Ohio State
1980	Billy Sims	Detroit Lions	RB	Oklahoma
1981	George Rogers	New Orleans Saints	RB	South Carolina
1982	Kenneth Sims	New England Patriots	DL	Texas
1983	John Elway	Baltimore Colts	QB	Stanford
1984	Irving Fryar	New England Patriots	WR	Nebraska
1985	Bruce Smith	Buffalo Bills	DL	Virginia Tech.
1986	Bo Jackson	Tampa Bay Buccaneers	RB	Auburn
1987	Vinny Testaverde	Tampa Bay Buccaneers	QB	Miami
1988	Aundray Bruce	Atlanta Falcons	LB	Auburn
1989	Troy Aikman	Dallas Cowboys	QB	UCLA
1990	Jeff George	Indianapolis Colts	QB	Illinois
1991	Russell Maryland	Dallas Cowboys	DT	Miami (Fla.)
1992	Steve Emtman	Indianapolis Colts	DT	Washington
1993	Drew Bledsoe	New England Patriots	QB	Washington State
1994	Dan Wilkinson	Cincinnati Bengals	DT	Ohio State
1995	Ki-Jana Carter	Cincinnati Bengals	RB	Penn State
1996	Keyshawn Johnson	New York Jets	WR	Southern California
1997	Orlando Pace	St. Louis Rams	OT	Ohio State
1998	Peyton Manning	Indianapolis Colts	QB	Tennessee
1999	Tim Couch	Cleveland Browns	QB	Kentucky
2000	Courtney Brown	Cleveland Browns	DL	Penn State
2001	Michael Vick	Atlanta Falcons	QB	Virginia Tech.

The Sporting News' NFL Rookie of the Year, 1955–2000

Year	Player	Pos.	Team	Year	Player	Pos.	Team
1955	Alan Ameche	FB	Baltimore Colts	1977	NFC: Tony Dorsett	RB	Dallas Cowboys
1956	J.C. Caroline	HB	Chicago Bears		AFC: A.J. Duhe	DT	Miami Dolphins
1957	Jim Brown	FB	Cleveland Browns	1978	NFC: Al Baker	DE	Detroit Lions
1958	Bobby Mitchell	HB	Cleveland Browns		AFC: Earl Campbell	RB	Houston Oilers
1959	Nick Pietrosante	FB	Detroit Lions	1979	NFC: Ottis Anderson	RB	St. Louis Cardinals
1960	Gail Codgill	E	Detroit Lions		AFC: Jerry Butler	WR	Buffalo Bills
1961	Mike Ditka	E	Chicago Bears	1980	Billy Sims	RB	Detroit Lions
1962	Ronnie Bull	HB	Chicago Bears	1981	George Rogers	RB	New England Patriots
1963	Paul Flatley	WR	Minnesota Vikings	1982	Marcus Allen	RB	Los Angeles Raiders
1964	Charley Taylor	HB	Washington Redskins	1983	Dan Marino	QB	Miami Dolphins
1965	Gale Sayers	RB	Chicago Bears	1984	Louis Lipps	WR	Pittsburgh Steelers
1966	Tommy Nobis	LB	Atlanta Falcons	1985	Eddie Brown	WR	Cincinnati Bengals
1967	Mel Farr	RB	Detroit Lions	1986	Rueben Mayes	RB	New Orleans Saints
1968	Earl McCullouch	WR	Detroit Lions	1987	Robert Awalt	TE	St. Louis Cardinals
1969	Calvin Hill	RB	Dallas Cowboys	1988	Keith Jackson	TE	Philadelphia Eagles
1970	NFC: Bruce Taylor	CB	San Francisco 49ers	1989	Barry Sanders	RB	Detroit Lions
	AFC: Dennis Shaw	QB	Buffalo Bills	1990	Richmond Webb	OL	Miami Dolphins
1971	NFC: John Brockington	RB	Green Bay Packers	1991	Mike Croel	LB	Denver Broncos
	AFC: Jim Plunkett	QB	New England Patriots	1992	Santana Dotson	DE	Tampa Bay Buccaneers
1972	NFC: Chester Marcol	PK	Green Bay Packers				
	AFC: Franco Harris	RB	Pittsburgh Steelers	1993	Jerome Bettis	RB	Los Angeles Rams
1973	NFC: Chuck Foreman	RB	Minnesota Vikings	1994	Marshall Faulk	RB	Indianapolis Colts
	AFC: Boobie Clark	RB	Cincinnati Bengals	1995	Curtis Martin	RB	New England
1974	NFC: Wilbur Jackson	RB	San Francisco 49ers	1996	Eddie George	RB	Houston Oilers
	AFC: Don Woods	RB	San Diego Chargers	1997	Warrick Dunn	RB	Tampa Bay Buccaneers
1975	NFC: Steve Bartkowski	QB	Atlanta Falcons				
	AFC: Robert Brazile	LB	Houston Oilers	1998	Randy Moss	WR	Minnesota Vikings
1976	NFC: Sammy White	WR	Minnesota Vikings	1999	Edgerrin James	RB	Indianapolis Colts
	AFC: Mike Haynes	CB	New England Patriots	2000	Brian Urlacher	LB	Chicago Bears

Note: The NFL does not officially honor a rookie of the year. From 1970–79, separate players were chosen for each conference.
Source: *The Sporting News.*

NFL Most Valuable Player, 1957–2000

Year	Player,	Pos.	Team	Year	Player,	Pos.	Team
1957	Jim Brown	RB	Cleveland Browns	1979	Earl Campbell	RB	Houston Oilers
1958	Gino Marchetti	DE	Baltimore Colts	1980	Brian Sipe	QB	Cleveland Browns
1959	Charley Conerly	QB	New York Giants	1981	Ken Anderson	QB	Cincinnati Bengals
1960	Norm Van Brocklin	QB	Philadelphia Eagles	1982	Mark Moseley	PK	Washington Redskins
	Joe Schmidt	LB	Detroit Lions	1983	Joe Theismann	QB	Washington Redskins
1961	Paul Hornung	RB	Green Bay Packers	1984	Dan Marino	QB	Miami Dolphins
1962	Jim Taylor	RB	Green Bay Packers	1985	Marcus Allen	RB	Los Angeles Raiders
1963	Y.A. Tittle	QB	New York Giants	1986	Lawrence Taylor	LB	New York Giants
1964	Johnny Unitas	QB	Baltimore Colts	1987	John Elway	QB	Denver Broncos
1965	Jim Brown	RB	Cleveland Browns	1988	Boomer Esiason	QB	Cincinnati Bengals
1966	Bart Starr	QB	Green Bay Packers	1989	Joe Montana	QB	San Francisco 49ers
1967	Johnny Unitas	QB	Baltimore Colts	1990	Joe Montana	QB	San Francisco 49ers
1968	Earl Morrall	QB	Baltimore Colts	1991	Thurman Thomas	RB	Buffalo Bills
1969	Roman Gabriel	QB	Los Angeles Rams	1992	Steve Young	QB	San Francisco 49ers
1970	John Brodie	QB	San Francisco 49ers	1993	Emmitt Smith	RB	Dallas Cowboys
1971	Alan Page	DT	Minnesota Vikings	1994	Steve Young	QB	San Francisco 49ers
1972	Larry Brown	RB	Washington Redskins	1995	Brett Favre	QB	Green Bay Packers
1973	O.J. Simpson	RB	Buffalo Bills	1996	Brett Favre	QB	Green Bay Packers
1974	Ken Stabler	QB	Oakland Raiders	1997	Brett Favre	QB	Green Bay Packers
1975	Fran Tarkenton	QB	Minnesota Vikings		Barry Sanders	RB	Detroit Lions
1976	Bert Jones	RB	Baltimore Colts	1998	Terrell Davis	RB	Denver Broncos
1977	Walter Payton	RB	Chicago Bears	1999	Kurt Warner	QB	St. Louis Rams
1978	Terry Bradshaw	QB	Pittsburgh Steelers	2000	Marshall Faulk	RB	St. Louis Rams

Source: National Football League

All-Time Pro Football Records

SCORING (Total Points)	Years	Points	Touchdowns	PATs	Field Goals
1. Gary Anderson[1]	19	2,059	0	676	461
2. George Blanda	26	2,002	9	943	335
3. Morten Andersen[1]	19	1,938	0	615	441
4. Norm Johnson	18	1,736	0	638	366
5. Nick Lowery	18	1,711	0	562	383
6. Jan Stenerud	19	1,699	0	580	373
7. Eddie Murray	18	1,563	0	501	344
8. Al Del Greco[1]	17	1,584	0	543	347
9. Pat Leahy	18	1,470	0	558	304
10. Jim Turner	16	1,439	1	521	304

RUSHING (Yards)	Years	Rushes	Yards	Avg.	TD	RECEPTIONS	Years	Receptions	Yards	Avg.	TD
1. Walter Payton	13	3,838	16,726	4.4	110	1. Jerry Rice[1]	16	1,281	19,247	15.0	176
2. Barry Sanders	10	3,062	15,269	5.0	99	2. Cris Carter[1]	14	1,020	12,962	12.7	123
3. Emmitt Smith[1]	11	3,537	15,166	4.3	145	3. Andre Reed[1]	16	951	13,198	13.9	87
4. Eric Dickerson	11	2,996	13,259	4.4	90	4. Art Monk	16	940	12,721	13.5	68
5. Tony Dorsett	12	2,936	12,739	4.3	77	5. Irving Fryar[1]	17	851	12,785	15.0	84
6. Jim Brown	9	2,359	12,312	5.2	106	6. Tim Brown[1]	13	846	12,072	14.3	86
7. Marcus Allen	16	3,022	12,243	4.1	123	7. Steve Largent	14	819	13,089	16.0	100
8. Franco Harris	13	2,949	12,120	4.1	91	8. Henry Ellard	16	814	13,777	16.9	65
9. Thurman Thomas[1]	13	2,877	12,074	4.2	65	9. James Lofton	16	764	14,004	18.3	75
10. John Riggins	14	2,916	11,352	3.9	104	10. Michael Irvin	12	750	11,904	15.9	65

QUARTERBACK RATING	Yrs.	Attempts	Completions	Yards	TDs	Interceptions	Rating
1. Steve Young	15	4,149	2,667	33,124	232	107	96.8
2. Joe Montana	15	5,391	3,409	40,551	273	139	92.3
3. Dan Marino	17	8,358	4,967	61,361	420	252	86.4
4. Brett Favre[1]	10	4,932	2,997	34,706	255	157	86.0
5. Peyton Manning[1]	3	1,679	1,014	12,287	85	58	85.4
6. Mark Brunell[1]	7	2,672	1,608	19,212	106	66	85.1
7. Brad Johnson[1]	7	1,821	1,126	12,973	79	57	84.7
8. Jim Kelly	11	4,779	2,874	35,467	237	175	84.4
9. Roger Staubach	11	2,958	1,685	22,700	153	109	83.4
10. Neil Lomax	8	3,153	1,817	22,771	136	90	82.7

Passes Completed		Yards Passing		Touchdown Passes	
1. Dan Marino	4,967	1. Dan Marino	61,361	1. Dan Marino	420
2. John Elway	4,123	2. John Elway	51,475	2. Fran Tarkenton	342
3. Warren Moon[1]	3,988	3. Warren Moon[1]	49,325	3. John Elway	300
4. Fran Tarkenton	3,686	4. Fran Tarkenton	47,003	4. Warren Moon[1]	291
5. Joe Montana	3,409	5. Dan Fouts	43,040	5. Johnny Unitas	290
6. Dan Fouts	3,297	6. Joe Montana	40,551	6. Joe Montana	273
7. Dave Krieg	3,105	7. Johnny Unitas	40,239	7. Dave Krieg	261
8. Brett Favre[1]	2,997	8. Dave Krieg	38,147	8. Brett Favre[1]	255
9. Boomer Esiason	2,969	9. Boomer Esiason	37,920	8. Sonny Jurgensen	255
10. Troy Aikman[1]	2,898	10. Vinny Testaverde[1]	36,307	10. Dan Fouts	254
11. Vinny Testaverde[1]	2,897	11. Jim Kelly	35,467	11. Boomer Esiason	247
12. Steve DeBerg	2,874	12. Jim Everett	34,837	12. John Hadl	244
12. Jim Kelly	2,874	13. Brett Favre[1]	34,706	13. Len Dawson	239
14. Jim Everett	2,841	14. Jim Hart	34,665	14. Jim Kelly	237
15. Johnny Unitas	2,830	15. Steve DeBerg	34,241	15. George Blanda	236

Note: Through end of 2000 season. Includes players who played a portion of their careers in the American Football League. Quarterback rating is based on a combination of performances in the following four categories: percentage of completions, percentage of touchdown passes, percentage of interceptions and average gain per pass attempts. Minimum 1,500 attempts; through end of 2000 season. 1. Player active in 2000. **Source:** National Football League *2001 Record and Fact Book*.

NFL Champions, 1921–66

Year	Team (record)	Year	Team (record)	Year	Team (record)
1921	Chicago Staleys[1] (10-1-1)	1937	Washington Redskins (8-3-0)	1952	Detroit Lions (9-3-0)
1922	Canton Bulldogs (10-0-2)	1938	New York Giants (8-2-1)	1953	Detroit Lions (10-2-0)
1923	Canton Bulldogs (11-0-1)	1939	Green Bay Packers (9-2-0)	1954	Cleveland Browns (9-3-0)
1924	Cleveland Bulldogs[2] (7-1-1)	1940	Chicago Bears (8-3-0)	1955	Cleveland Browns (9-2-1)
1925	Chicago Cardinals (11-2-1)	1941	Chicago Bears (10-1-1)	1956	New York Giants (8-3-1)
1926	Frankford Yellowjackets (14-1-1)	1942	Washington Redskins (10-1-1)	1957	Detroit Lions (8-4-0)
1927	New York Giants (11-1-1)	1943	Chicago Bears (8-1-1)	1958	Baltimore Colts (9-3-0)
1928	Providence Steamrollers (8-1-2)	1944	Green Bay Packers (8-2-0)	1959	Baltimore Colts (9-3-0)
1929	Green Bay Packers (12-0-1)	1945	Cleveland Rams (9-1-0)	1960	Philadelphia Eagles (10-2-0)
1930	Green Bay Packers (10-3-1)	1946	Chicago Bears (8-2-1)	1961	Green Bay Packers (11-3-0)
1931	Green Bay Packers (12-2-0)	1947	Chicago Cardinals (9-3-0)	1962	Green Bay Packers (13-1-0)
1932	Chicago Bears (7-1-6)	1948	Philadelphia Eagles (9-2-1)	1963	Chicago Bears (11-1-2)
1933	Chicago Bears (10-2-1)	1949	Philadelphia Eagles (11-1-0)	1964	Cleveland Browns (10-3-1)
1934	New York Giants (8-5-0)	1950	Cleveland Browns (10-2-0)	1965	Green Bay Packers (10-3-1)
1935	Detroit Lions (7-3-2)	1951	Los Angeles Rams (8-4-0)	1966	Green Bay Packers (12-2-0)
1936	Green Bay Packers (10-1-1)				

1. Later called the Chicago Bears. 2. Franchise moved from Canton.

Super Bowl Results

SUPER BOWL I
Jan. 15, 1967 Memorial Coliseum, Los Angeles
Green Bay Packers 35   Kansas City Chiefs 10
Green Bay's Max McGee was a surprise star, filling in for ailing Boyd Dowler. McGee had caught only four passes all year, but in Super Bowl I he caught seven for 138 yards and two touchdowns. Quarterback Bart Starr was the game's MVP, as he completed 16 of 23 passes for 250 yards and two touchdowns. Green Bay broke up the game with three second-half touchdowns, the first of which was set up by safety Willie Wood's 45-yard interception return.

SUPER BOWL II
Jan. 14, 1968, Orange Bowl, Miami
Green Bay Packers 33   Oakland Raiders 14
Bart Starr again dominated proceedings with 13 completions in 24 attempts, for 202 yards and a touchdown, winning his second straight MVP award. The Pack attack was in control all the way after building a 16–7 halftime lead. Don Chandler kicked four field goals and all-pro cornerback Herb Adderley capped the Green Bay scoring with a 60-yard interception return.

SUPER BOWL III
Jan. 12, 1969, Orange Bowl, Miami
New York Jets 16   Baltimore Colts 7
Quarterback Joe Namath guaranteed victory before the game and then he and the upstart AFL Jets easily dispatched the heavily favored Colts. Namath won MVP honors by completing 17 of 28 passes for 206 yards and directing a steady attack that racked up 337 total yards. Three times in the first half, the Jet defense intercepted Colts quarterback Earl Morrall, who was playing for an injured Johnny Unitas. With the Jets ahead 13–0 in the third quarter, Unitas came off the bench and later orchestrated Baltimore's sole touchdown.

SUPER BOWL IV
Jan. 11, 1970, Tulane Stadium, New Orleans
Kansas City Chiefs 23   Minnesota Vikings 7
MVP quarterback Len Dawson called a nearly flawless game for Kansas City, completing 12 of 17 passes and hitting Otis Taylor on a 46-yard pass for the final Chiefs touchdown. The Kansas City defense limited Minnesota's strong rushing game to 67 yards and had three interceptions and two fumble recoveries. The second consecutive victory by an AFL team proved that AFL teams could compete with NFL franchises, and assured a smooth merger between the two leagues.

SUPER BOWL V
Jan. 17, 1971, Orange Bowl, Miami
Baltimore Colts 16   Dallas Cowboys 13
Rookie Jim O'Brien's 32-yard field goal in the closing seconds broke a 13–13 tie and gave the Colts their first Super Bowl victory. Dallas led 13–6 at halftime, but two Colt interceptions set up a Baltimore touchdown and O'Brien's crucial kick. Baltimore's first touchdown came when a Johnny Unitas pass caromed off receiver Eddie Hinton's fingertips, bounced off Dallas defensive back Mel Renfro and finally settled into the grasp of tight end John Mackey, who went 47 yards for the score. Dallas linebacker Chuck Howley was the MVP, the only time the MVP came from the losing team.

SUPER BOWL VI
Jan. 16, 1972, Tulane Stadium, New Orleans
Dallas Cowboys 24   Miami Dolphins 3
The Cowboys rushed for 252 yards and their defense limited the Dolphins to 185 total yards and no touchdowns. Dallas converted Chuck Howley's recovery of Larry Csonka's first fumble of the season into a 3–0 advantage. At halftime, Dallas led 10–3. An eight-play, 71-yard march made it a 17–3 game. Cowboys' quarterback Roger Staubach was voted MVP for his 12 completions in 19 attempts, 119 yards passing and two touchdowns.

SUPER BOWL VII
Jan. 14, 1973, Memorial Coliseum, Los Angeles
Miami Dolphins 14   Washington Redskins 7
In a game that wasn't as close as the score, the Dolphins thoroughly dominated the Redskins to complete the NFL's only undefeated season. Quarterback Bob Griese hit Paul Warfield for 18 yards, then delivered a 28-yard strike to Howard

Twilley for the Dolphins' first score. Just before the half, Dolphins linebacker Nick Buoniconti intercepted a Billy Kilmer pass and returned it to the Washington 27, setting up Miami's second touchdown. Safety Jake Scott led the Dolphin defense with two interceptions (one in the end zone killing a Redskin scoring drive) and was the MVP. The Redskins' sole touchdown resulted when Dolphin kicker Garo Yepremian tried to turn a botched field goal into a forward pass. Washington's Mike Bass picked the ball out of the air and returned it 49 yards for the score.

SUPER BOWL VIII
Jan. 13, 1974, Rice Stadium, Houston
Miami Dolphins 24   Minnesota Vikings 7
Miami scored on its first two possessions, on 62- and 56-yard marches. The initial 10-play drive was climaxed by a Larry Csonka touchdown bolt through right guard. Four plays later, Miami's Jim Kiick burst one yard through the middle for the second touchdown. By halftime Miami led 17–0. The Dolphins defense held off the Vikings on a crucial fourth-and-one play from the Miami 6-yard-line when middle linebacker Nick Buoniconti jarred the ball loose from Minnesota running back Oscar Reed and Jake Scott recovered for Miami. Csonka rushed 33 times for 145 yards, winning the MVP.

SUPER BOWL IX
Jan, 12, 1975, Tulane Stadium, New Orleans
Pittsburgh Steelers 16   Minnesota 6
Steeler Dwight White tackled Minnesota quarterback Fran Tarkenton in the end zone for a safety to put the Steelers on the board in the second quarter. They took advantage of another break in the second half, when Minnesota's Bill Brown fumbled the kickoff and Marv Kellum recovered for Pittsburgh on the Vikings' 30. From there, Franco Harris carried three straight times for the game's first touchdown. Minnesota blocked a Bobby Walden punt and Terry Brown recovered the ball for a touchdown to cut the lead to 9–6, but the Steelers roared back with a 66-yard march, climaxed by Terry Bradshaw's 4-yard scoring pass to Larry Brown. Pittsburgh's defense controlled the game, permitting Minnesota only 119 yards total offense. Franco Harris rushed 34 times for 158 yards to win MVP honors.

SUPER BOWL X
Jan. 18, 1976, Orange Bowl, Miami
Pittsburgh Steelers 21   Dallas Cowboys 17
Steeler quarterback Terry Bradshaw hurled a 64-yard touchdown pass to Lynn Swann to win the game, while the Steel Curtain defense stopped the Cowboys' last rally with an end-zone interception in the game's final play. It was a battle of quarterbacks with Bradshaw and Cowboy Roger Staubach each hurling two touchdowns. Swann earned MVP honors with 161 yards on four receptions. The Steelers blasted out in front with a 14-point fourth quarter.

SUPER BOWL XI
Jan. 9, 1977, Rose Bowl, Pasadena,California
Oakland Raiders 32   Minnesota Vikings 14
A record 81 million TV viewers watched the Raiders gain a record-breaking 429 yards, including running back Clarence Davis' 137 yards rushing. Wide receiver Fred Biletnikoff made four key receptions, which earned him the game's MVP trophy. Oakland scored on three successive pos-sessions in the second quarter to build a 16–0 halftime lead. Minnesota's Fran Tarkenton passed for a touchdown in the third to cut the deficit, but two fourth-quarter interceptions clinched the title for the Raiders. One set up Pete Banaszak's second touchdown run, the other resulted in cornerback Willie Brown's 75-yard interception return.

SUPER BOWL XII
Jan. 15, 1978, Louisiana Superdome, New Orleans
Dallas Cowboys 27   Denver Broncos 10
The TV audience climbed to 102 million, as Dallas converted two interceptions into 10 points and a 13–0 Dallas halftime lead. Butch Johnson made a spectacular diving catch in the end zone of a Roger Staubach pass to make it 20–3. Dallas clinched the victory when running back Robert Newhouse threw a 29-yard touchdown pass to Golden Richards. Co-MVP's Harvey Martin and Randy White led the Cowboys' defense, which recovered four fumbles and intercepted four passes.

SUPER BOWL XIII
Jan, 21, 1979, Orange Bowl, Miami
Pittsburgh Steelers 35   Dallas Cowboys 31
MVP Terry Bradshaw hurled four touchdown passes to lead the Steelers to victory, making them the first team to win three Super Bowls. Bradshaw completed 17 of 30 passes for 318 yards. In the fourth quarter, the Steelers broke open the contest with two touchdowns in 19 seconds. Franco Harris rambled 22 yards up the middle to put Pittsburgh in front 28–17. The Steelers got the ball right back when Randy White fumbled the kickoff and Dennis Winston recovered. On first down, Bradshaw hit Lynn Swann with an 18-yard scoring pass to boost the lead to 35–17. The Cowboys came back with a Roger Staubach touchdown pass to Billy Joe DuPree and then recovered an onside kick, which led to another Staubach touchdown pass, this time to Butch Johnson. But Rocky Bleier smothered an onside kick with 17 seconds remaining to seal the victory.

SUPER BOWL XIV
Jan. 20, 1980, Rose Bowl, Pasadena, California
Pittsburgh Steelers 31   Los Angeles Rams 19
It was all Terry Bradshaw again as he completed 14 of 21 passes for 309 records, and set two passing records as the Steelers became the first team to win four Super Bowls. Despite three interceptions by the Rams, Bradshaw brought the Steelers back from behind twice in the second half. On Pittsburgh's first possession of the final period, Bradshaw lofted a 73-yard scoring pass to John Stallworth to put the Steelers in front to stay, 24–19. Franco Harris scored on a one-yard run later to seal the verdict. Bradshaw was the MVP for the second straight Super Bowl.

SUPER BOWL XV
Jan. 25, 1981, Louisiana Superdome, New Orleans
Oakland Raiders 27   Philadelphia Eagles 10
Jim Plunkett threw three touchdown passes, including an 80-yarder to Kenny King, to give Oakland a decisive 14-0 advantage nine seconds before halftime. Oakland linebacker Rod Martin intercepted three passes as the Raiders completely stifled Eagle quarterback Ron Jaworski's offense. Jaworski managed an 8-yard touchdown pass in the fourth quarter, but the issue had been decided by Plunkett, who completed 13 of the 21 pass attempts for 261 yards and was named MVP.

SUPER BOWL XVI

Jan. 24, 1982, Pontiac Silverdome, Pontiac, Mich.
San Francisco 49ers 26   Cincinnati Bengals 21
The 49ers led 20-0 at halftime, but barely hung on
for the win. Ray Wersching kicked four field goals
for San Francisco and quarterback Joe Montana
engineered two touchdown drives, passing for
one and scoring the other himself on a one-yard
dive. The Bengals rebounded in the second half
as quarterback Ken Anderson ran in a touchdown
and passed for another. With 16 seconds remaining, the Bengals scored again, on a 3-yard pass to
Dan Ross, but couldn't get the ball back a final
time. Ross set a Super Bowl record with 11 receptions for 104 yards. Montana, the MVP, completed
14 of 22 passes for 157 yards.

SUPER BOWL XVII

Jan. 30, 1983, Rose Bowl, Pasadena, California
Washington Redskins 27   Miami Dolphins 17
Washington fullback John Riggins carried the ball
for 166 yards on 38 carries to lead Washington to
their first NFL title since 1942. Riggins, the MVP,
and quarterback Joe Theismann, who passed 23
times for 15 completions, 143 yards, and two
touchdowns paced the Redskins to 400 total yards
of offense. Riggin's 43-yard touchdown run on
fourth-and-one was the gamebreaker.

SUPER BOWL XVIII

Jan, 22, 1984, Tampa Stadium, Tampa, Florida
Los Angeles Raiders 38   Washington Redskins 9
This hopelessly lopsided victory set records.
Raider reserve linebacker Jack Squirek intercepted a Joe Theismann pass at the Redskins five-
yard line and ran the ball in for a touchdown with
seven seconds left in the first half. Raiders' Marcus
Allen rushed for 191 yards on 20 carries, including
two touchdowns, one on a 74-yard run. Allen was
voted game MVP.

SUPER BOWL XIX

Jan. 20, 1985, Stanford Stadium, Stanford, Calif.
San Francisco 49ers 38   Miami Dolphins 16
The Dolphins led 10-7 at the end of the first period, but 49er running back Roger Craig came
back with three touchdowns. Joe Montana dominated the game with an MVP performance: 24 of
35 passes for yards and three touchdowns. He
also rushed five times for 59 yards and a touchdown. Craig had 58 yards on 15 carries and
caught seven passes for 77 yards. Wendell Tyler
rushed 13 times for 65 yards, as San Francisco's
running game racked up 211 yards..

SUPER BOWL XX

Jan 26, 1986 Louisiana Superdome, New Orleans
Chicago Bears 46   New England Patriots 10
The Patriots took a quick 3-0 lead on Tony
Franklin's 36-yard field goal with 1:19 elapsed in
the first period. But the Bears rebounded by
mauling the Pats. Chicago tied the record for
sacks (7), and limited the Pats to 7 yards rushing.
Total yardage at intermission told the story:
Chicago 236, New England -19. The Bears ran up a
fat 23-3 lead in the first half. In the second, the
Bears marched 96 yards in nine plays, capped by
quarterback Jim McMahon's one-yard rush for a
touchdown. Bears defensive end Richard Dent
won the MVP after contributing 1/2 sacks, and
leading the ferocious Chicago defense.

SUPER BOWL XXI

Jan. 25, 1987, Rose Bowl, Pasadena, California
New York Giants 39   Denver Broncos 20
The Broncos held a 10–9 lead at halftime, backed
by the passing of John Elway. He capped a 58 yard
scoring drive on six plays with a four yard touchdown run. But in the second half, the Giants' defense took over, sacking Elway in his end zone for
a safety. The Broncos had a first and goal, but
failed to score on three plays and a field goal attempt. After that the Giants' offense rebounded,
scoring 30 points in the second half. Giant quarterback Phil Simms passed for 268 yards and three
touchdowns, and was named MVP.

SUPER BOWL XXII

Jan 31, 1988, Jack Murphy Stadium, San Diego
Washington Redskins 42   Denver Broncos 10
The Broncos jumped in front early as John Elway
hurled a 56-yard touchdown pass to wide receiver
Ricky Nattiel on the Broncos' first play from
scrimmage. But the Redskins erupted for 35
points on five straight possessions. Redskins'
quarterback Doug Williams led the assault, hurling four touchdown passes, including 80- and 50-
yarders to wide receiver Rick Sanders.
Washington scored five touchdowns in 18 plays in
5:47 of possession. MVP Williams completed 18 of
29 passes for 340 yards. Rookie running back
Timmy Smith ran 22 times for 204 yards.

SUPER BOWL XXIII

Jan. 22, 1989, Joe Robbie Stadium, Miami
San Francisco 49ers 20   Cincinnati Bengals 16
San Francisco became the first NFC team to win
three Super Bowls by defeating the Bengals in a
rematch of Super Bowl XVI. Even though San
Francisco held an advantage in total yards (453 vs.
229), they found themselves trailing when Jim
Breech's field goal gave Cincinnati a 16-13 lead
with 3:20 left in the game. The 49ers started their
winning drive at their own 8-yard line. Over the
next 11 plays, they drove 92 yards to the winning
score, a 10-yard touchdown pass from Joe Montana to John Taylor with 34 seconds left. San Francisco's Jerry Rice won the MVP after catching 11
passes for 215 yards. Montana completed 23 of
36 passes for 357 yards and two touchdowns.

SUPER BOWL XXIII

Jan. 28,1990, Louisiana Superdome, New Orleans
San Francisco 49ers 55   Denver Broncos 10
San Francisco demolished the Broncos and became the first team to repeat as champions since
the 1979–80 Steelers. Quarterback Joe Montana
orchestrated the 49ers' diverse offense, completing 22 of 29 passes for 297 yards and five touchdowns, en route to winning the MVP. Montana
raised his record to 122 straight Super Bowl pass
attempts without an interception. His primary
receiver was Jerry Rice, who hauled in seven
passes for 148 yards and three touchdowns. Running backs Tom Rathman and Roger Craig ran for
three more touchdowns. Meanwhile, the San
Francisco defense completely dominated Denver's offense, limiting them to 167 total yards
while sacking quarterback John Elway six times
and intercepting two passes.

SUPER BOWL XXV
Jan. 27, 1991, Tampa Stadium, Tampa, Florida
New York Giants 20   Buffalo Bills, 19
The Giants edged the Bills in a nearly error-free game that was decided only when the Bills' Scott Norwood missed a field goal with eight seconds to play. Backup quarterback Jeff Hostetler and veteran running back Ottis Anderson directed the Giants' ball-control offense, holding the ball for a stunning 40:33. Anderson carried the ball 21 times for 102 yards and was named the MVP. After falling behind 12–3, the veteran Giants team refused to panic. Their defense slowed Buffalo's "hurry-up" offense to a crawl, surrounding Jim Kelly's receivers with extra defensive backs and linebackers. Kelly finished the day with 18 completions in 30 attempts for 205 yards, but could rarely convert on crucial third down opportunities. Hostetler, substituting for the injured Phil Simms, led the Giants on touchdown drives of 75 and 87 yards, while completing 20 of 32 passes for 214 yards and no turnovers.

SUPER BOWL XXVI
Jan. 26, 1992, The Metrodome, Minneapolis
Washington Redskins 37   Buffalo Bills 24
Washington jumped out to a 17-0 lead in the first half and never looked back. MVP quarterback Mark Rypien completed 18 of 33 passes for 292 yards and two touchdowns. Meanwhile, the blitzing Redskin defense intercepted Buffalo quarterback Jim Kelly four times and sacked the Bills' signal-caller five times. Buffalo's no-huddle offense was also plagued by several dropped passes, including two that would have gone for touchdowns. In all, Kelly threw a record 58 passes, 30 of which went incomplete. Brad Edwards, Washington's free safety, had two interceptions and broke up five passes, while linebacker Wilber Marshall forced two fumbles. Bills running back Thurman Thomas, the NFL's regular season MVP, was limited to 13 yards on 10 rushes.

SUPER BOWL XXVII
Jan. 31, 1993, Rose Bowl, Pasadena, California
Dallas Cowboys 52   Buffalo Bills 17
Buffalo lost its third straight Super Bowl and the second consecutive rout. The game's turning point came early in the second quarter, when Buffalo drove inside the Dallas five-yard-line twice but came away with only three points, and lost starting quarterback Jim Kelly in the process. Inspired by its defense's two goal line stands, the Cowboys' offense, which had been fairly inept up to this point, came alive for a long scoring drive. The Bills fumbled their first play from scrimmage on the ensuing drive, and one play later, the Cowboys had scored again, this time on a strike from Troy Aikman to Michael Irvin, giving Dallas a 28–10 halftime lead. Aikman passed for four touchdowns and was named MVP.

SUPER BOWL XXVIII
Jan. 30, 1994, Georgia Dome, Atlanta
Dallas Cowboys 30   Buffalo Bills 13
Buffalo became the first team in U.S. professional sports history to lose four consecutive championship games. The Bills actually led at halftime 13–6 on the strength of Thurman Thomas's 37 yards rushing and 54- and 28-yard field goals by Steve Christie. But Thomas fumbled on the opening drive of the second half and Dallas safety James Washington returned it 46 yards for a touchdown, tying the game at 13. Dallas then drove the length of the field on its next drive, with running back Emmitt Smith grinding out 61 yards. The Cowboys added another

touchdown and a field goal to secure the victory. Smith, the league's regular season MVP, was named MVP of the Super Bowl as well.

SUPER BOWL XXIX
Jan. 29, 1995, Joe Robbie Stadium, Miami
San Francisco 49ers 49   San Diego Chargers 26
Favored by 20 points, (the largest margin in Super Bowl history), San Francisco scored early and often to capture a fifth Super Bowl championship. On the third play from scrimmage, Steve Young found Jerry Rice wide open inside the San Diego 10-yard line. Young threw six touchdowns and ran for 49 yards, making him the 49ers' leading rusher as well. Rice and running back Ricky Watters each scored three touchdowns. Young was named MVP for his 24-for-36 for 325 yard performance.

SUPER BOWL XXX
Jan. 28, 1996, Sun Devil Stadium, Tempe, Ariz.
Dallas Cowboys 27   Pittsburgh Steelers 17
Dallas scored on its first three possessions, but failed to dominate the game, and led only 13–7 at halftime. In the second half, the Steelers threatened to close the gap, but quarterback Neil O'Donnell stunted the drive by throwing an interception to Cowboy cornerback Larry Brown. Pittsburgh rallied again in the fourth quarter to cut Dallas' lead to 20–17. But O'Donnell threw another interception to Brown, who returned it to the Steeler 6-yard line, setting up the Cowboys' final touchdown. Brown was the obvious MVP choice.

SUPER BOWL XXXI
Jan. 26, 1997, Louisiana Superdome, New Orleans,
Green Bay Packers 35   New England Patriots 21
Packer quarterback Bret Favre hit Andre Rison for a 54-yard touchdown pass on Green Bay's second play from scrimmage, but the Patriots rallied for a 14-10 first quarter lead. The Packers recaptured the lead with a 17-points in the second quarter. In the second half, New England running back Curtis Martin scored to cut the lead to 27-21, but Desmond Howard returned the ensuing kickoff 99 yards for a touchdown. Howard's 154 yards on four kickoff returns and 90 yards on six punt returns earned him MVP honors.

SUPER BOWL XXXII
Jan. 25, 1998, Qualcomm Stadium, San Diego
Denver Broncos 31   Green Bay Packers 24
The victory was Denver's first in five tries, and the AFC's first in 13 years. With the game tied at 24 late in the fourth quarter, Denver took over at midfield. A penalty and a pass moved the Broncos closer, and then running back Terrell Davis ran 17 yards to the one-yard-line. On the next play, he punched it in for his third touchdown. With less than two minutes left, the Packers drove into Denver territory but could not convert a 4th and 6. Davis earned MVP honors for his 30 carries, 157 yards, and three touchdowns.

SUPER BOWL XXXIII
Jan. 31, 1999, Pro Player Stadium, Miami
Denver Broncos 34   Atlanta Falcons 19
Denver quarterback John Elway completed 18 of 29 passes for 336 yards and MVP honors, as the Broncos cruised to their second straight Super Bowl victory. Broncos running back Terrell Davis added 102 yards rushing, and cornerback Darrien Gordon had interception returns of 50 and 58 yards, each setting up a Denver touchdown. Atlanta scored first on a Morten Andersen field goal

to take a brief 3–0 lead. But despite driving deep into Denver territory several times, they could not crack the end zone until the fourth quarter, when the outcome was already decided.

SUPER BOWL XXXIV
Jan. 30, 2000, Georgia Dome, Atlanta
St. Louis Rams 23   Tennessee Titans 16

St. Louis dominated the first half, moving at will into Tennessee territory, but came away with only three field goals to show for it. The Rams extended their lead to 16-0 in the third quarter before the Titans put together three long scoring drives that tied the game with 2:12 remaining. On the very next play from scrimmage, quarterback Kurt Warner hit Isaac Bruce for a 73-yard touchdown pass to put St. Louis back up 23-16. With time running out, Tennessee quarterback Steve McNair engineered an 87-yard drive, but his last completion to Kevin Dyson left the Titans a yard short of a game-tying touchdown as time expired. Warner was named MVP on the strength of his 414 yards passing.

SUPER BOWL XXXV
Jan. 28, 2001, Raymond James Stadium, Tampa
Baltimore Ravens 34, New York Giants 7

Baltimore's vaunted defense pitched a shutout, as the Giants' only points came on special teams. The Ravens stymied New York's offense, constantly pinning the Giants deep inside their own territory, and creating five turnovers. Jermaine Lewis's 34-yard punt return set up Baltimore's first touchdown in the first quarter, and Duane Starks's interception return gave the Ravens a 17-0 lead late in the third quarter. Ron Dixon returned the ensuing kickoff 97 yards for the Giants' to cut the score to 17-7, but Lewis put the game out of reach on the very next play with an 84-yard kickoff return of his own. Middle linebacker Ray Lewis, the heart and soul of the Ravens defense, was the MVP.

Pro Football Hall of Fame Members

Alphabetical listing of the members of the Professional Football Hall of Fame. Listing includes enshrinee's name, year of enshrinement, position, and the teams he played for.

Herb Adderley (1980) CB, Packers, Cowboys.
Lance Alworth (1978) WR, Chargers, Cowboys.
Doug Atkins (1982) DE, Browns, Bears, Saints.
Morris (Red) Badgro (1981) E, Yankees, Giants, Dodgers.
Lem Barney (1992) CB, Lions.
Cliff Battles (1968) RB, QB Braves, Redskins.
Sammy Baugh (1963) QB, Redskins.
Chuck Bednarik (1967) C, LB, Eagles.
Bert Bell (1963 Charter) Commissioner, NFL. Founder/coach, Eagles, Steelers.
Bobby Bell (1983) LB, DE, Chiefs.
Raymond Berry (1973) E, Colts.
Charles W. Bidwill, Sr. (1967) Owner/president, Cardinals.
Fred Biletnikoff (1988) WR, Raiders.
George Blanda (1981) QB, PK, Bears, Colts, Oilers, Raiders.
Mel Blount (1989) CB, Steelers.
Terry Bradshaw (1989) QB, Steelers.
Jim Brown (1971) FB, Browns.
Paul E. Brown (1967) Coach and GM, Browns, Bengals.
Roosevelt Brown (1975) OT, Giants.
Willie Brown (1984) CB, Broncos, Raiders.
Buck Buchanan (1990) DT, Chiefs.
Nick Buoniconti (2001) LB, Patriots, Dolphins.
Dick Butkus (1979) LB, Bears.
Earl Campbell (1991) RB, Oilers, Saints.
Tony Canadeo (1974) RB, Packers.
Joe Carr (1963) NFL President.
Guy Chamberlin (1965) E, Bulldogs, Staleys, Yellowjackets, Cardinals. Coach, Bulldogs, Yellowjackets, Cardinals.
Jack Christiansen (1970) DB, Spartans, Lions.
Earl (Dutch) Clark (1970) DB, Spartans, Lions, Rams.
George Connor (1975) OT, DT, LB, Bears.
Jimmy Conzelman (1964) QB, Staleys, Independents, Badgers, Panthers. Owner, Steamrollers, Cardinals.
Lou Creekmur, (1996) OL, Lions.
Larry Csonka (1987) RB, Dolphins, Giants.

Al Davis (1992) President, Owner, General Manager, Coach, Raiders. Commissioner, American Football League.
Willie Davis (1981) DE, Browns, Packers.
Len Dawson (1987) QB, Steelers, Browns, Texans, Chiefs.
Eric Dickerson, (1999) RB, Rams, Colts, Raiders, Falcons.
Dan Dierdorf, (1996) OT, Cardinals
Mike Ditka (1988) TE, Bears, Eagles, Cowboys.
Art Donovan (1968) DT, Colts, Yankees, Texans.
Tony Dorsett (1994) RB, Cowboys, Broncos.
John (Paddy) Driscoll (1965) QB, Pros, Staleys, Cardinals, Bears.
Bill Dudley (1966) RB, Steelers, Lions, Redskins.
Albert Glen (Turk) Edwards (1969) OT, Braves, Redskins.
Weeb Ewbank (1978) Coach, Colts, Jets.
Tom Fears (1970) E, Rams.
Jim Finks (1995) President, Vikings, Bears, Saints.
Ray Flaherty (1976) Coach, Redskins, Yankees.
Len Ford (1976) DE, E, Dons, Browns, Packers.
Dan Fortmann (1965) G, Bears.
Dan Fouts (1993) QB, Chargers.
Frank Gatski (1985) C, Browns, Lions.
Bill George (1974) LB, Bears, Rams.
Joe Gibbs (1996) Coach, Chargers, Redskins.
Frank Gifford (1977) RB, Giants.
Sid Gillman (1983) Coach, Rams, Chargers, Oilers.
Otto Graham (1965) QB, Browns.
Harold (Red) Grange (1963 Charter) RB, Bears, Yankees.
Bud Grant (1994) Coach, Vikings.
(Mean) Joe Greene (1987) DT, Steelers.
Forrest Gregg (1977) OL, Packers, Cowboys.
Bob Griese (1990) QB, Dolphins.
Lou Groza (1974) OT, PK Browns.
Joe Guyon (1966) RB, Bulldogs, Indians, Independents, Cowboys, Giants.
George Halas (1963) Founder, Coach, player, Staleys. President, Coach, player, Bears.
Jack Ham (1988) LB, Steelers.
John Hannah (1991) G, Patriots.
Franco Harris (1990) RB, Steelers, Seahawks.
Mike Haynes (1997) CB, Patriots, Raiders.

Ed Healey (1964) OT, Independents, Bears.
Mel Hein (1963) C, Giants. Coach, Dons.
Ted Hendricks (1990) LB, Colts, Packers, Raiders
Wilbur (Pete) Henry (1963) OT, Bulldogs, Giants, Maroons.
Arnie Herber (1966) QB, Packers, Giants.
Bill Hewitt (1971) E, Bears, Eagles.
Clarke Hinkle (1964) RB, Packers.
Elroy (Crazylegs) Hirsch (1968) HB, E, Rockets, Rams.
Paul Hornung (1986) HB, Packers.
Ken Houston (1986) S, Oilers, Redskins.
Cal Hubbard (1963) OT, Giants, Packers, Pirates.
Sam Huff (1982) LB, Giants, Redskins.
Lamar Hunt (1972) Founder, AFL; Owner Texans, Chiefs.
Don Hutson (1963) E, Packers.
Jimmy Johnson (1994) CB, 49ers.
John Henry Johnson (1987) RB, 49ers, Lions, Steelers, Oilers.
Charlie Joiner (1996), WR, Oilers, Bengals, Chargers.
David (Deacon) Jones (1980) DE, Rams, Chargers, Redskins.
Stan Jones (1991) G, DT, Bears, Redskins.
Henry Jordan (1995) DT, Packers.
Sonny Jurgensen (1983) QB, Eagles, Redskins.
Leroy Kelly (1994) RB, Browns.
Walt Kiesling (1966) G, Eskimos, Maroons, Cardinals, Bears, Packers, Pirates. Coach, Pirates, Steelers.
Frank (Bruiser) Kinard (1971) OT, Dodgers, Yankees.
Paul Krause (1998) S, Vikings, Redskins.
Early (Curly) Lambeau (1963) Founder, Packers. Coach, Packers, Cardinals, Redskins.
Jack Lambert (1990) LB, Steelers.
Tom Landry (1990) Coach, Cowboys.
Dick (Night Train) Lane (1974). DB, Rams, Cardinals, Lions.
Jim Langer (1987) C, Dolphins, Vikings.
Willie Lanier (1986) LB, Chiefs.
Steve Largent (1995) WR, Seahawks.
Yale Lary (1979) DB, Lions.
Dante Lavelli (1975) E, Browns.
Bobby Layne (1967) QB, Bears, Bulldogs, Lions, Steelers.
Alphonse (Tuffy) Leemans (1978) RB, Giants.
Marv Levy (2001) Coach, Chiefs, Bills.
Bob Lilly (1980) DT, Cowboys.
Larry Little (1993) G, Chargers, Dolphins.
Vince Lombardi (1971) Coach, GM, Packers, Redskins.
Howie Long (2000) DL, Raiders.
Ronnie Lott (2000) DB, 49ers, Raiders, Jets.
Sid Luckman (1965) QB, Bears.
William Roy (Link) Lyman (1964) T, Bulldogs, Yellowjackets, Bears.
Tom Mack (1999) OG, Rams.
John Mackey (1992) TE, Colts, Chargers.
Tim Mara (1963) Founder, President, Giants.
Wellington Mara (1997) Owner, Giants
Gino Marchetti (1972) DE, Texans, Colts.
George Preston Marshall (1963) Founder, President, Braves (Redskins).
Ollie Matson (1972) RB, Cardinals, Rams, Lions, Eagles.
Don Maynard (1987) WR, Giants, Titans, Jets, Cardinals.
George McAfee (1966) RB, Bears.
Mike McCormack (1984) OT, Yankees, Browns.
Tommy McDonald (1988) WR, Eagles, Cowboys, Rams, Falcons, Browns.

Hugh McElhenny (1970) RB, 49ers Vikings, Giants, Lions.
John (Blood) McNally (1963) RB, Badgers, Eskimos, Maroons, Packers, Pirates Packers.
Mike Michalske (1964) G, Yankees, Packers.
Wayne Millner (1968) E, Redskins. Coach Eagles.
Bobby Mitchell (1983) WR, RB Browns, Redskins.
Ron Mix (1979) OT, Chargers, Raiders.
Joe Montana (2000) QB, 49ers, Chiefs.
Lenny Moore (1975) WR, RB, Colts.
Marion Motley (1968) RB, Browns, Steelers.
Mike Munchak (2001) G, Oilers.
Anthony Muñoz (1998) T, Bengals.
George Musso (1982) OT, G, Bears.
Bronko Nagurski (1963) RB, Bears.
Joe Namath (1985) QB, Jets, Rams.
Earle (Greasy) Neale (1969) Coach, Eagles.
Ernie Nevers (1963) RB, Eskimos, Cardinals.
Ozzie Newsome (1999) TE, Browns.
Ray Nitschke (1978) LB, Packers.
Chuck Noll (1993) Coach, Steelers.
Leo Nomellini (1969) DT, 49ers.
Merlin Olsen (1982) DT, Rams.
Jim Otto (1980) C, Raiders.
Steve Owen (1966) T, Cowboys, Giants. Coach, Giants.
Alan Page (1988) DT, Vikings, Bears.
Clarence (Ace) Parker (1972) QB, Dodgers, Yankees.
Jim Parker (1973) OL, Colts.
Walter Payton (1993) RB, Bears.
Joe Perry (1969) RB, 49ers, Colts.
Pete Pihos (1970) E, Eagles.
Hugh (Shorty) Ray Supervisor of Officials.
Dan Reeves (1967) Owner, Rams.
Mel Renfro (1996), CB, Cowboys.
John Riggins (1992) RB, Jets, Redskins.
Jim Ringo (1981) C, Packers, Eagles.
Andy Robustelli (1971) DE, Rams, Giants.
Art Rooney (1964) Founder, President, Pirates, Steelers.
Dan Rooney (2000) President, Steelers.
Pete Rozelle (1985) Commissioner, NFL.
Bob St. Clair (1990) OT, 49ers.
Gale Sayers (1977) RB, Bears.
Joe Schmidt (1973) LB, Lions. Coach, Lions.
Tex Schramm (1991) GM, Cowboys.
Lee Roy Selmon (1995) DE, Buccaneers.
Billy Shaw (1999) OG, Bills.
Art Shell (1989) OT, Raiders.
Don Shula (1997) Coach, Colts, Dolphins.
Mike Singletary (1998) LB, Bears.
O.J. Simpson (1985) RB, Bills, 49ers.
Jackie Slater (2001) OT, Rams.
Jackie Smith (1994) TE, Cardinals, Cowboys.
Bart Starr (1977) QB, Packers.
Roger Staubach (1985) QB, Cowboys.
Ernie Stautner (1969) DT, Steelers.
Jan Stenerud (1991) PK, Chiefs, Packers, Vikings.
Dwight Stephenson (1998) C, Dolphins.
Ken Strong (1967) RB, Stapletons, Giants, Yankees.
Joe Stydahar (1967) OT, Bears.
Lynn Swann (2001) WR, Steelers.
Fran Tarkenton (1986) QB, Giants, Vikings.
Charley Taylor (1984) WR, RB, Redskins.
Jim Taylor (1976) RB, Packers, Saints.
Lawrence Taylor (1999) LB, Giants.
Jim Thorpe (1963) RB, Bulldogs, Indians, Maroons, Independents, Giants, Bulldogs, Cardinals.
Y.A. Tittle (1971) QB, Colts 49ers, Giants.
George Trafton (1964) C, Staleys, Bears.
Charley Trippi (1968) RB, QB, Cardinals.
Emlen Tunnell (1967) DB, Giants, Packers.
Clyde (Bulldog) Turner (1966) C, LB, Bears.

Johnny Unitas (1979) QB, Colts, Chargers.
Gene Upshaw (1987) G, Raiders.
Norm Van Brocklin (1971) QB, Rams, Eagles
Steve Van Buren (1965) RB, Eagles.
Doak Walker (1986) RB, Lions.
Bill Walsh (1993) Coach, 49ers.
Paul Warfield (1983) WR, Browns, Dolphins.
Bob Waterfield(1965) QB, Coach, Rams.
Mike Webster (1997) C, Steelers.
Arnie Weinmeister, (1984) DT, Yankees, Giants.

Randy White (1994) DT, Cowboys.
Dave Wilcox (2000) LB, 49ers.
Bill Willis (1977) G, MG, Browns.
Larry Wilson (1978) DB, Cardinals.
Kellen Winslow (1995) TE, Chargers.
Alex Wojciechowicz (1968) C, LB, Lions, Eagles.
Willie Wood (1989) S, Packers.
Ron Yary (2001) OT, Vikings.
Jack Youngblood (2001) DE, Rams.

BASKETBALL

National Basketball Association

Olympic Tower
645 Fifth Avenue
New York, NY 10022
(212) 826-7000

www.nba.com
Commissioner: David Stern
Founded: 1946
Number of teams: 29

Dr. James Naismith invented basketball in 1891, only after his indoor versions of lacrosse, rugby, and soccer proved too violent for the intended use in a YMCA fitness program. Yet even his "noncontact" amateur sport proved too rough for many YMCAs, which dropped basketball. Teams were forced to rent halls; they charged an admission fee to pay the rent, and split any leftover cash among the players.

The first pro game was played in 1896 in Trenton, N.J., and by 1898, the fledgling National Basketball League and several others were organized. The Buffalo Germans were the first powerhouse, winning 792 games against only 86 losses from 1895 to 1925. In 1914, the New York Celtics (later renamed the Original Celtics) were organized, playing a "modern" style of basketball using zone defenses, the fast break, and a pivot man.

Other "ethnic" teams dominated in the 1930s, including the Philadelphia SPHAs (South Philadelphia Hebrew Association) under Eddy Gottlieb, and the black barnstorming New York Rens. Several weak leagues continued to compete until the end of World War II. The Basketball Association of America was formed in 1946 by hockey arena managers seeking additional tenants. By 1949, it had merged with its biggest rival to form the modern NBA.

The American Basketball Association, an alternative pro league known for its three-point shots and its red, white and blue ball, lasted for nine seasons (1968–76) and featured such future NBA All-Stars as Julius Erving and Artis Gilmore. When the league folded after the 1975–76 season, four of its teams, the Denver Nuggets, Indiana Pacers, New York (now New Jersey) Nets, and San Antonio Spurs were admitted into the NBA.

The NBA expanded cautiously in the 1970s. Cleveland joined the league in 1970 along with Portland and the Buffalo Braves (now the Los Angeles Clippers); New Orleans received a franchise in 1974 but lost it to Utah in 1979; and in 1980, the NBA expanded to Dallas. Charlotte and Miami joined in 1988, followed by Orlando and Minnesota in 1989. The two Canadian expansion teams, Vancouver and Toronto, joined in 1995. The Vancouver franchise will move to Memphis for the 2001-02 season.

Under the current collective bargaining agreement, which is in effect until 2003–2004, player salaries are capped at 48 percent of gross income ($30 million per team in 1998–99; $34 million per team in 1999–2000), individual salaries may not exceed $14 million per year ($9 million for players with less than 6 years experience; $11 million for players with 7–9 years service), and players in their first three years of service have severely limited contracts.

NBA Final Standings, 2000–01

EASTERN CONFERENCE	W-L	Pct.	Home	Away	WESTERN CONFERENCE	W-L	Pct.	Home	Away
Atlantic Division					**Midwest Division**				
Philadelphia 76ers (1)	56-26	.683	29-12	27-14	San Antonio Spurs (1)	58-24	.707	33-8	25-16
Miami Heat (3)	50-32	.610	29-12	21-20	Utah Jazz (4)	53-29	.646	28-13	25-16
New York Knicks (4)	48-34	.585	30-11	18-23	Dallas Mavericks (5)	53-29	.646	28-13	25-16
Orlando Magic (7)	43-39	.524	26-15	17-24	Minnesota Timberwolves (8)	47-35	.573	30-11	17-24
Boston Celtics	36-46	.439	20-21	16-25	Houston Rockets	45-37	.549	24-17	21-20
New Jersey Nets	26-56	.317	18-23	8-33	Denver Nuggets	40-42	.488	29-12	11-30
Washington Wizards	19-63	.232	12-29	7-34	Vancouver Grizzlies	23-59	.280	15-26	8-33
Central Division					**Pacific Division**				
Milwaukee Bucks (2)	52-30	.634	31-10	21-20	Los Angeles Lakers (2)	56-26	.683	31-10	25-16
Toronto Raptors (5)	47-35	.573	27-14	20-21	Sacramento Kings (3)	55-27	.671	33-8	22-19
Charlotte Hornets (6)	46-36	.561	28-13	18-23	Phoenix Suns (6)	51-31	.622	31-10	20-21
Indiana Pacers (8)	41-41	.500	26-15	15-26	Portland Trail Blazers(7)	50-32	.610	28-13	22-19
Detroit Pisons	32-50	.390	18-23	14-27	Seattle SuperSonics	44-38	.537	26-15	18-23
Cleveland Cavaliers	30-52	.366	20-21	10-31	Los Angeles Clippers	31-51	.378	22-19	9-32
Atlanta Hawks	25-57	.305	18-23	7-34	Golden State Warriors	17-65	.207	11-30	6-35
Chicago Bulls	15-67	.183	10-31	5-36					

Note: The numbers in parentheses reflect the team's seed for the playoffs. **Source:** NBA.

NBA Playoff Results, 2000-01

FIRST ROUND

EASTERN CONFERENCE

Philadelphia (1) v. Indiana (8)
Indiana Pacers 79, PHILADELPHIA 76ERS 78
PHILADELPHIA 76ERS 116, Indiana Pacers 98
Philadelphia 76ers 92, INDIANA PACERS 87
Philadelphia 76ers 88, INDIANA PACERS 85
(Philadelphia wins series 3-1)

Milwaukee (2) v. Orlando (7)
MILWAUKEE BUCKS 103, Orlando Magic 90
MILWAUKEE BUCKS 103, Orlando Magic 96
ORLANDO MAGIC 121, Milwaukee Bucks 116
MILWAUKEE BUCKS 112, Orlando Magic 104
(Milwaukee wins series 3-1)

Miami (3) v. Charlotte (6)
Charlotte Hornets 106, MIAMI HEAT 80
Charlotte Hornets 102, MIAMI HEAT 78
CHARLOTTE HORNETS 94, Miami Heat 79
(Charlotte wins series 3-0)

New York (4) v. Toronto (5)
NEW YORK KNICKS 92, Toronto Raptors 85
Toronto Raptors 94, NEW YORK KNICKS 74
New York Knicks 97, TORONTO RAPTORS 89
TORONTO RAPTORS 100, New York Knicks 93
Toronto Raptors 93, NEW YORK KNICKS 89
(Toronto wins series 3-2)

WESTERN CONFERENCE

San Antonio (1) v. Minnesota (8)
SAN ANTONIO SPURS 87, Minnesota Timberwolves 82
SAN ANTONIO SPURS 86, Minnesota Timberwolves 69
MINNESOTA TIMBERWOLVES 93, San Antonio Spurs 84
San Antonio Spurs 97, MINNESOTA TIMBERWOLVES 84
(San Antonio wins series 3-1)

Los Angeles Lakers (2) v. Portland (7)
LOS ANGELES LAKERS 106, Portland Trail Blazers 93
LOS ANGELES LAKERS 106, Portland Trail Blazers 88
Los Angeles Lakers 99, PORTLAND TRAIL BLAZERS 86
(Los Angeles Lakers win series 3-0)

Sacramento (3) v. Phoenix (6)
Phoenix Suns 86, SACRAMENTO KINGS 83
SACRAMENTO KINGS 116, Phoenix Suns 90
Sacramento Kings 104, PHOENIX SUNS 96
Sacramento Kings 89, PHOENIX SUNS 82
(Sacramento wins series 3-1)

Utah (4) v. Dallas (5)
UTAH JAZZ 88, Dallas Mavericks 86
UTAH JAZZ 109, Dallas Mavericks 98
DALLAS MAVERICKS 94, Utah Jazz 91
DALLAS MAVERICKS 107, Utah Jazz 77
Dallas Mavericks 84, UTAH JAZZ 83
(Dallas wins series 3-2)

CONFERENCE SEMIFINALS

Philadelphia (1) v. Toronto (5)
Toronto Raptors 96, PHILADELPHIA 76ERS 93
PHILADELPHIA 76ERS 97, Toronto Raptors 92
TORONTO RAPTORS 102, Sixers 78
Philadelphia 76ers 84, TORONTO RAPTORS 79
PHILADELPHIA 76ERS 121, Toronto Raptors 88
TORONTO RAPTORS 101, Philadelphia 76ers 89
PHILADELPHIA 76ERS 88, Toronto Raptors 87
(Philadelphia wins series 4-3)

Milwaukee (2) v. Charlotte (6)
MILWAUKEE BUCKS 104, Charlotte Hornets 92
MILWAUKEE BUCKS 91, Charlotte Hornets 90
CHARLOTTE HORNETS 102, Milwaukee Bucks 92
CHARLOTTE HORNETS 85, Milwaukee Bucks 78
Charlotte Hornets 94, MILWAUKEE BUCKS 86
Milwaukee Bucks 104, CHARLOTTE HORNETS 97
MILWAUKEE BUCKS 104, Charlotte Hornets 95
(Milwaukee wins series 4-3)

San Antonio (1) v. Dallas (5)
SAN ANTONIO SPURS 94, Dallas Mavericks 78
SAN ANTONIO SPURS 100, Dallas Mavericks 86
San Antonio Spurs 104, DALLAS MAVERICKS 90
DALLAS MAVERICKS 112, San Antonio Spurs 108
SAN ANTONIO SPURS 105, Dallas Mavericks 87
(San Antonio wins series 4-1)

Los Angeles Lakers (2) v. Sacramento (3)
LOS ANGELES LAKERS 108, Sacramento Kings 105
LOS ANGELES LAKERS 96, Sacramento Kings 90
Los Angeles Lakers 103, SACRAMENTO KINGS 81
Los Angeles Lakers 119, SACRAMENTO KINGS 113
(Los Angeles Lakers win series 4-0)

CONFERENCE FINALS

Philadelphia (1) v. Milwaukee (2)
PHILADELPHIA 76ERS 93, Milwaukee Bucks 85
Milwaukee Bucks 92, PHILADELPHIA 76ERS 78
MILWAUKEE BUCKS 80, Philadelphia 76ers 74
Philadelphia 76ers 89, MILWAUKEE BUCKS 83
PHILADELPHIA 76ERS 89, Milwaukee Bucks 88
MILWAUKEE BUCKS 110, Philadelphia 76ers 100
PHILADELPHIA 76ERS 108, Milwaukee Bucks 91
(Philadelphia wins series 4-3)

San Antonio (1) v. Los Angeles Lakers (2)
Los Angeles Lakers 104, SAN ANTONIO SPURS 90
Los Angeles Lakers 88, SAN ANTONIO SPURS 81
LOS ANGELES LAKERS 111, San Antonio Spurs 72
LOS ANGELES LAKERS 111, San Antonio Spurs 82
(Los Angeles Lakers win series 4-0)

NBA CHAMPIONSHIP SERIES
L.A. Lakers v. Philadelphia 76ers

Game 1: Philadelphia 76ers 107, L.A. LAKERS 101 (OT)
Game 2: L.A. LAKERS 98, Philadelphia 76ers 89
Game 3: L.A. Lakers 96, PHILADELPHIA 76ERS 91
Game 4: L.A. Lakers 100, PHILADELPHIA 76ERS 86
Game 5: L.A. Lakers 108, PHILADELPHIA 76ers 96
(Los Angeles Lakers win series 4-1)

Note: Home team in CAPS. Numbers in parentheses reflect team's playoff seed.

NBA Leaders, 2000–01

SCORING	G	Pts.	Avg.
Allen Iverson, Philadelphia	71	2,207	31.1
Jerry Stackhouse, Detroit	80	2,380	29.8
Shaquille O'Neal, L.A. Lakers	74	2,125	28.7
Kobe Bryant, L.A. Lakers	68	1,938	28.5
Vince Carter, Toronto	75	2,070	27.6
Chris Webber, Sacramento	70	1,898	27.1
Tracy McGrady, Orlando	77	2,065	26.8
Paul Pierce, Boston	82	2,071	25.3
Antawn Jamison, Golden State	82	2,044	24.9
Stephon Marbury, New Jersey	67	1,598	23.9
Antoine Walker, Boston	81	1,892	23.4
Karl Malone, Utah	81	1,878	23.2
Gary Payton, Seattle	79	1,823	23.1
Tim Duncan, San Antonio	82	1,820	22.2
Glenn Robinson, Milwaukee	76	1,674	22.0
Kevin Garnett, Minnesota	81	1,784	22.0
Ray Allen, Milwaukee	82	1,806	22.0
Dirk Nowitzki, Dallas	82	1,784	21.8
Michael Finley, Dallas	82	1,765	21.5
Antonio McDyess, Denver	70	1,458	20.8

REBOUNDS	G	Reb.	Avg.
Dikembe Mutombo, Philadelphia	75	1,015	13.5
Ben Wallace, Detroit	80	1,052	13.2
Shaquille O'Neal, L.A. Lakers	74	940	12.7
Tim Duncan, San Antonio	82	997	12.2
Antonio McDyess, Denver	70	845	12.1
Kevin Garnett, Minnesota	81	921	11.4
Chris Webber, Sacramento	70	777	11.1
Shawn Marion, Phoenix	79	848	10.7
Antonio Davis, Toronto	78	787	10.1
Elton Brand, Chicago	74	746	10.1

ASSISTS	G	No.	Avg.
Jason Kidd, Phoenix	77	753	9.8
John Stockton, Utah	82	713	8.7
Nick Van Exel, Denver	71	600	8.5
Mike Bibby, Vancouver	82	685	8.4
Gary Payton, Seattle	79	642	8.1
Andre Miller, Cleveland	82	657	8.0
Mark Jackson, New York	83	661	8.0
Sam Cassell, Milwaukee	76	580	7.6
Stephon Marbury, New Jersey	67	506	7.6
Terrell Brandon, Minnesota	78	583	7.5

BLOCKED SHOTS	G	No.	Avg.
Theo Ratliff, Atlanta	50	187	3.74
Jermaine O'Neal, Indiana	81	228	2.81
Shawn Bradley, Dallas	82	228	2.78
Shaquille O'Neal, L.A. Lakers	74	204	2.76
Dikembe Mutombo, Philadelphia	75	203	2.71
Adonal Foyle, Golden State	58	156	2.69
Raef LaFrentz, Denver	78	206	2.64
David Robinson, San Antonio	80	197	2.46
Tim Duncan, San Antonio	82	192	2.34
Ben Wallace, Detroit	80	186	2.33

STEALS	G	No.	Avg.
Allen Iverson, Philadelphia	71	178	2.51
Mookie Blaylock, Golden State	69	163	2.36
Doug Christie, Sacramento	81	183	2.26
Jason Kidd, Phoenix	77	166	2.16
Baron Davis, Charlotte	82	170	2.07
Terrell Brandon, Minnesota	78	161	2.06
Ron Artest, Chicago	76	152	2.00
Darrell Armstrong, Orlando	75	135	1.80
Steve Francis, Houston	80	141	1.76
Antoine Walker, Boston	81	138	1.70

3-PT. FIELD GOALS	FGM	FGA	Pct.
Brent Barry, Seattle	109	229	.476
John Stockton, Utah	61	132	.462
Shammond Williams, Seattle	61	133	.459
Hubert Davis, Washington	78	171	.456
Danny Ferry, San Antonio	70	156	.449
Toni Kukoc, Atlanta	70	157	.446
Pat Garrity, Orlando	97	224	.433
Ray Allen, Milwaukee	202	467	.433
Rashard Lewis, Seattle	123	285	.432
Dell Curry, Toronto	62	145	.428

MINUTES PER GAME	G	Min.	Avg.
Michael Finley, Dallas	82	3,443	42.0
Allen Iverson, Philadelphia	71	2,979	42.0
Antoine Walker, Boston	81	3,396	41.9
Ron Mercer, Chicago	61	2,535	41.6
Antawn Jamison, Golden State	82	3,394	41.4
Gary Payton, Seattle	79	3,244	41.1
Kobe Bryant, L.A. Lakers	68	2,783	40.9
Jalen Rose, Indiana	72	2,943	40.9
Anthony Mason, Miami	80	3,254	40.7
Chris Webber, Sacramento	70	2,836	40.5

FIELD GOAL PERCENTAGE	FGM	FGA	Pct.
Shaquille O'Neal, L.A. Lakers	813	1,422	.572
Bonzi Wells, Portland	387	726	.533
Marcus Camby, New York	304	580	.524
Kurt Thomas, New York	314	614	.511
Wally Szczerbiak, Minnesota	469	920	.510
Darius Miles, L.A. Clippers	318	630	.505
John Stockton, Utah	328	651	.504
Donyell Marshall, Utah	427	849	.503
Corliss Williamson, Detroit	325	647	.502
Clarence Weatherspoon, Cleveland	347	692	.501
Rasheed Wallace, Portland	590	1,178	.501

FREE THROW PERCENTAGE	FTM	FTA	Pct.
Reggie Miller, Indiana	323	348	.928
Allan Houston, New York	279	307	.909
Doug Christie, Sacramento	280	312	.897
Steve Nash, Dallas	231	258	.895
Mitch Richmond, Washington	143	160	.894
Steve Smith, Portland	309	347	.890
Ray Allen, Milwaukee	348	392	.888
Darrell Armstrong, Orlando	220	249	.884
Eric Piatkowski, L.A. Clippers	158	181	.873
Terrell Brandon, Minnesota	195	224	.871

NBA World Championship Series

Year	Winner	Loser	Games	Year	Winner	Loser	Games
1947	Philadelphia Warriors	Chicago Stags	4-1	1975	Golden State Warriors	Washington Bullets	4-0
1948	Baltimore Bullets	Philadelphia Warriors	4-2	1976	Boston Celtics	Phoenix Suns	4-2
1949	Minneapolis Lakers	Washington Capitols	4-2	1977	Portland Trail Blazers	Philadelphia 76ers	4-2
1950	Minneapolis Lakers	Syracuse Nationals	4-2	1978	Washington Bullets	Seattle SuperSonics	4-3
1951	Rochester Royals	New York Knicks	4-3	1979	Seattle SuperSonics	Washington Bullets	4-1
1952	Minneapolis Lakers	New York Knicks	4-3	1980	Los Angeles Lakers	Philadelphia 76ers	4-2
1953	Minneapolis Lakers	New York Knicks	4-1	1981	Boston Celtics	Houston Rockets	4-2
1954	Minneapolis Lakers	Syracuse Nationals	4-3	1982	Los Angeles Lakers	Philadelphia 76ers	4-2
1955	Syracuse Nationals	Fort Wayne Pistons	4-3	1983	Philadelphia 76ers	Los Angeles Lakers	4-0
1956	Philadelphia Warriors	Fort Wayne Pistons	4-1	1984	Boston Celtics	Los Angeles Lakers	4-3
1957	Boston Celtics	St. Louis Hawks	4-3	1985	Los Angeles Lakers	Boston Celtics	4-2
1958	St. Louis Hawks	Boston Celtics	4-2	1986	Boston Celtics	Houston Rockets	4-2
1959	Boston Celtics	Minneapolis Lakers	4-0	1987	Los Angeles Lakers	Boston Celtics	4-2
1960	Boston Celtics	St. Louis Hawks	4-3	1988	Los Angeles Lakers	Detroit Pistons	4-3
1961	Boston Celtics	St. Louis Hawks	4-1	1989	Detroit Pistons	Los Angeles Lakers	4-0
1962	Boston Celtics	Los Angeles Lakers	4-3	1990	Detroit Pistons	Portland Trail Blazers	4-1
1963	Boston Celtics	Los Angeles Lakers	4-2	1991	Chicago Bulls	Los Angeles Lakers	4-1
1964	Boston Celtics	San Francisco Warriors	4-1	1992	Chicago Bulls	Portland Trail Blazers	4-2
1965	Boston Celtics	Los Angeles Lakers	4-1	1993	Chicago Bulls	Phoenix Suns	4-2
1966	Boston Celtics	Los Angeles Lakers	4-3	1994	Houston Rockets	New York Knicks	4-3
1967	Philadelphia	San Francisco Warriors	4-2	1995	Houston Rockets	Orlando Magic	4-0
1968	Boston Celtics	Los Angeles Lakers	4-2	1996	Chicago Bulls	Seattle SuperSonics	4-2
1969	Boston Celtics	Los Angeles Lakers	4-3	1997	Chicago Bulls	Utah Jazz	4-2
1970	New York Knicks	Los Angeles Lakers	4-3	1998	Chicago Bulls	Utah Jazz	4-2
1971	Milwaukee Bucks	Baltimore Bullets	4-0	1999	San Antonio Spurs	New York Knicks	4-1
1972	Los Angeles Lakers	New York Knicks	4-1	2000	Los Angeles Lakers	Indiana Pacers	4-2
1973	New York Knicks	Los Angeles Lakers	4-1	2001	Los Angeles Lakers	Philadelphia 76ers	4-1
1974	Boston Celtics	Milwaukee Bucks	4-3				

2001 NBA First Round Draft Picks

Rank, Team	Player	College	Position
1. Washington	Kwame Brown	Glynn Academy	F
2. L.A. Clippers[1]	Tyson Chandler	Dominguez H.S.	F
3. Atlanta	Pau Gasol	Barcelona	F
4. Chicago	Eddy Curry	Thornwood (Ill.) H.S.	F/C
5. Golden State	Jason Richardson	Michigan State	G/F
6. Memphis	Shane Battier	Duke	F
7. New Jersey[2]	Eddie Griffin	Seton Hall	F
8. Cleveland	DeSagana Diop	Oak Hill Academy (Va.)	C
9. Detroit	Rodney White	Charlotte	F
10. Boston	Joe Johnson	Arkansas	G/F
11. Boston	Kedrick Brown	Okaloosa-Walton CC (Fla.)	F
12. Seattle	Vladimir Radmanovic	FMP Zeleznik (Yugoslavia)	F/C
13. Houston[2]	Richard Jefferson	Arizona	F
14. Golden State	Troy Murphy	Notre Dame	F
15. Orlando	Steven Hunter	DePaul	C
16. Charlotte	Kirk Haston	Indiana	F
17. Toronto	Michael Bradley	Villanova	F
18. Houston[2]	Jason Collins	Stanford	C
19. Portland	Zach Randolph	Michigan State	F
20. Cleveland[3]	Brendan Haywood	North Carolina	C
21. Boston	Joseph Forte	North Carolina	G
22. Orlando	Jeryl Sasser	Southern Methodist	G
23. Houston[2]	Brandon Armstrong	Pepperdine	G
24. Utah	Raul Lopez	Real Madrid (Spain)	G
25. Sacramento	Gerald Wallace	Alabama	F
26. Philadelphia	Samuel Dalembert	Seton Hall	C
27. Memphis[4]	Jamaal Tinsley	Iowa State	G
28. San Antonio	Tony Parker	Paris Basket Racing (Paris)	G

1. Los Angeles traded Chandler to Chicago for Brian Skinner and Elton Brand. 2. New Jersey traded Griffin to Houston for Richard Jefferson, Jason Collins, and Brandon Armstrong. 3. Cleveland traded Haywood to Orlando. 4. Memphis (formerly Vancouver) traded Tinsley to Indiana. **Source:** National Basketball Association. www.nba.com

NBA Most Valuable Players and Rookies of the Year, 1952-2001

Year	Most Valuable Player	Team	Rookie of the Year	Team
1952-53			Don Meineke	Fort Wayne Pistons
1953-54			Ray Felix	Baltimore Bullets
1954-55			Bob Pettit	Milwaukee Hawks
1955-56	Bob Pettit	St. Louis Hawks	Maurice Stokes	Rochester Royals
1956-57	Bob Cousy	Boston Celtics	Tom Heinsohn	Boston Celtics
1957-58	Bill Russell	Boston Celtics	Woody Sauldsberry	Philadelphia Warriors
1958-59	Bob Pettit	St. Louis Hawks	Elgin Baylor	Minneapolis Lakers
1959-60	Wilt Chamberlain	Philadelphia Warriors	Wilt Chamberlain	Philadelphia Warriors
1960-61	Bill Russell	Boston Celtics	Oscar Robertson	Cincinnati Royals
1961-62	Bill Russell	Boston Celtics	Walt Bellamy	Chicago Bulls
1962-63	Bill Russell	Boston Celtics	Terry Dischinger	Chicago Bulls
1963-64	Oscar Robertson	Cincinnati Royals	Jerry Lucas	Cincinnati Royals
1964-65	Bill Russell	Boston Celtics	Willis Reed	New York Knicks
1965-66	Wilt Chamberlain	Philadelphia 76ers	Rick Barry	San Francisco Warriors
1966-67	Wilt Chamberlain	Philadelphia 76ers	Dave Bing	Detroit Pistons
1967-68	Wilt Chamberlain	Philadelphia 76ers	Earl Monroe	Baltimore Bullets
1968-69	Wes Unseld	Baltimore Bullets	Wes Unseld	Baltimore Bullets
1969-70	Willis Reed	New York Knicks	Kareem Abdul-Jabbar	Milwaukee Bucks
1970-71	Kareem Abdul-Jabbar	Milwaukee Bucks	Dave Cowens	Boston Celtics
			Geoff Petrie	Portland Trail Blazers
1971-72	Kareem Abdul-Jabbar	Milwaukee Bucks	Sidney Wicks	Portland Trail Blazers
1972-73	Dave Cowens	Boston Celtics	Bob McAdoo	Buffalo Braves
1973-74	Kareem Abdul-Jabbar	Milwaukee Bucks	Ernie DiGregorio	Buffalo Braves
1974-75	Bob McAdoo	Buffalo Braves	Keith Wilkes	Golden State Warriors
1975-76	Kareem Abdul-Jabbar	Los Angeles Lakers	Alvin Adams	Phoenix Suns
1976-77	Kareem Abdul-Jabbar	Los Angeles Lakers	Adrian Dantley	Buffalo Braves
1977-78	Bill Walton	Portland Trail Blazers	Walter Davis	Phoenix Suns
1978-79	Moses Malone	Houston Rockets	Phil Ford	Kansas City Kings
1979-80	Kareem Abdul-Jabbar	Los Angeles Lakers	Larry Bird	Boston Celtics
1980-81	Julius Erving	Philadelphia 76ers	Darrell Griffith	Utah Jazz
1981-82	Moses Malone	Houston Rockets	Buck Williams	New Jersey Nets
1982-83	Moses Malone	Philadelphia 76ers	Terry Cummings	San Diego Clippers
1983-84	Larry Bird	Boston Celtics	Ralph Sampson	Houston Rockets
1984-85	Larry Bird	Boston Celtics	Michael Jordan	Chicago Bulls
1985-86	Larry Bird	Boston Celtics	Patrick Ewing	New York Knicks
1986-87	Magic Johnson	Los Angeles Lakers	Chuck Person	Indiana Pacers
1987-88	Michael Jordan	Chicago Bulls	Mark Jackson	New York Knicks
1988-89	Magic Johnson	Los Angeles Lakers	Mitch Richmond	Golden State Warriors
1989-90	Magic Johnson	Los Angeles Lakers	David Robinson	San Antonio Spurs
1990-91	Michael Jordan	Chicago Bulls	Derrick Coleman	New Jersey Nets
1991-92	Michael Jordan	Chicago Bulls	Larry Johnson	Charlotte Hornets
1992-93	Charles Barkley	Phoenix Suns	Shaquille O'Neal	Orlando Magic
1993-94	Hakeem Olajuwon	Houston Rockets	Chris Webber	Golden State Warriors
1994-95	David Robinson	San Antonio Spurs	Grant Hill	Detroit Pistons
			Jason Kidd	Dallas Mavericks
1995-96	Michael Jordan	Chicago Bulls	Damon Stoudamire	Toronto Raptors
1996-97	Karl Malone	Utah Jazz	Allen Iverson	Philadelphia 76ers
1997-98	Michael Jordan	Chicago Bulls	Tim Duncan	San Antonio Spurs
1998-99	Karl Malone	Utah Jazz	Vince Carter	Toronto Raptors
1999-2000	Shaquille O'Neal	Los Angeles Lakers	Elton Brand	Chicago Bulls
			Steve Francis	Houston Rockets
2000-01	Allen Iverson	Philadelphia 76ers	Mike Miller	Orlando Magic

WNBA Final Standings, 2001

East	W-L	Pct.	West	W-L	Pct.	Playoffs
Cleveland	22-10	.688	Los Angeles	28-4	.875	**First Round**
New York	21-11	.656	Sacramento	20-12	.625	Charlotte Sting 2, Cleveland Rockers 1
Miami	20-12	.625	Utah	19-13	.594	New York Liberty 2, Miami Sol 1
Charlotte	18-14	.563	Houston	19-13	.594	Los Angeles Sparks 2, Houston Comets 0
Orlando	13-19	.406	Phoenix	13-19	.406	Sacramento Monarchs 2, Utah Starzz 0
Indiana	10-22	.313	Minnesota	12-20	.375	**Conference Semifinals**
Detroit	10-22	.313	Portland	11-21	.344	Charlotte Sting 2, New York Liberty 1
Washington	10-22	.313	Seattle	10-22	.313	Los Angeles Sparks 2, Sacramento Monarchs 1

Note: The top four teams in each division made the playoffs.

Source: WNBA. www.wnba.com.

WNBA CHAMPIONSHIP
Los Angeles Sparks 2, Charlotte Sting 0.

NBA All-Time Career Leaders

Games		Points		Scoring average (min. 400 games)	
Robert Parish	1,611	Kareem Abdul-Jabbar	38,387	Michael Jordan	31.5
Kareem Abdul-Jabbar	1,560	Karl Malone[1]	32,919	Wilt Chamberlain	30.1
John Stockton[1]	1,340	Wilt Chamberlain	31,419	Shaquille O'Neal[1]	27.7
Moses Malone	1,329	Michael Jordan	29,277	Elgin Baylor	27.4
Buck Williams	1,307	Moses Malone	27,409	Jerry West	27.0
Elvin Hayes	1,303	Elvin Hayes	27,313	Bob Pettit	26.4
Sam Perkins[1]	1,286	Oscar Robertson	26,710	George Gervin	26.2
A.C. Green[1]	1,278	Dominique Wilkins	26,668	Karl Malone[1]	25.9
Karl Malone[1]	1,273	Hakeem Olajuwon[1]	26,511	Oscar Robertson	25.7
John Havlicek	1,270	John Havlicek	26,395	Dominique Wilkins	24.8

Assists		Rebounds		Free throw percentage (min. 1,200 made)	
John Stockton[1]	14,503	Wilt Chamberlain	23,924	Mark Price	.904
Magic Johnson	10,141	Bill Russell	21,620	Rick Barry	.893
Oscar Robertson	9,887	Kareem Abdul-Jabbar	17,440	Calvin Murphy	.892
Mark Jackson[1]	9,235	Elvin Hayes	16,279	Scott Skiles	.889
Isiah Thomas	9,061	Moses Malone	16,212	Larry Bird	.886
Maurice Cheeks	7,392	Robert Parish	14,715	Reggie Miller[1]	.884
Len Wilkens	7,211	Nate Thurmond	14,464	Bill Sharman	.883
Rod Strickland[1]	7,026	Walt Bellamy	14,241	Jeff Hornacek[1]	.877
Bob Cousy	6,955	Wes Unseld	13,769	Ray Allen[1]	.876
Terry Porter[1]	6,955	Hakeem Olajuwon[1]	13,282	Ricky Pierce	.875

Note: Does not include statistics compiled in the ABA. Totals are as of the end of 2000-01 season. 1. Player active in 2000-01. **Source:** NBA.

Naismith Memorial Basketball Hall of Fame

The Basketball Hall of Fame elected its first members (including Dr. James Naismith, the game's originator) in 1959, but it did not have a physical home until February 17, 1968. In 1985 the Hall of Fame moved to larger quarters in Springfield, Mass. The Basketball Hall of Fame includes players from all basketball levels, including college, women's, and foreign leagues. Career statistics are given only for players who played some portion of their career in the NBA.

Player (Year Elected)	Games	Points	FG%	FT%	Rebs.	Assts.
Archibald, Nate (Tiny) (1991)	876	16,481	.467	.810	2,046	6,476
Averaged 18.8 ppg over 13 seasons; six-time All-Star.						
Arizin, Paul J. (1977)	713	16,266	.421	.810	6,129	1,665
NBA scoring leader in 1952 (25.4 ppg) and 1957 (25.6 ppg).						
Barry, Rick (1987)	794	18,395	.449	.900	5,168	4,017
(ABA)	226	6,884	.477	.880	1,695	935
NBA all-time free-throw percentage leader.						
Baylor, Elgin (1976)	846	23,149	.431	.780	11,463	3,650
Named to NBA All-Star First Team 10 times.						
Bellamy, Walt (1993)	1,043	20,941	.516	.632	14,241	2,544
NBA Rookie of the Year in 1962.						
Bing, Dave (1990)	901	18,327	.441	.775	3,420	5,397
NBA Rookie of the Year 1967, MVP 1976.						
Bird, Larry (1998)	897	21,791	.496	.886	8,974	5,695
NBA Rookie of the Year 1980. NBA MVP 1984, 1985, and 1986. 12-time All-star.						
Bradley, Bill (1982)	742	9,217	.448	.840	2,533	2,363
Averaged 30.2 ppg in 83 games at Princeton University.						
Chamberlain, Wilt (1978)	1045	31,419	.540	.511	23,924	4,643
Holds NBA single-game records for points (100) and rebounds (55); led league in scoring 1959-66.						
Cousy, Bob (1970)	924	16,960	.375	.803	4,786	6,955
Led NBA in assists eight consecutive seasons (1953-60)						
Cowens, Dave (1991)	766	13,516	.460	.783	10,444	2,950
Seven-time All-star; three-time All-defensive team						
Cunningham, Billy (1986)	654	13,626	.446	.720	6,638	2,625
(ABA)	116	2,684	.483	.791	1,343	680
Coached Philadelphia 76ers to 454-196 record in eight years						
Davies, Bob (1969)	462	6,594	.378	.759	980[1]	2,050
NBL MVP, 1947	(NBL)[2]	107	1177		.747	
DeBusschere, Dave (1982)	875	14,053	.432	.699	9,618	2,497
NBA All-Defensive team six consecutive seasons (1969-74)						

Player (Year Elected)	Games	Points	FG%	FT%	Rebs.	Assts.
English, Alex (1997)	1,193	25,613	.507	.832	6,538	4,351
Eight-time all-star; Averaged 21.5 points per game over 15 seasons						
Erving, Julius (Dr. J) (1993)	836	18,364	.507	.777	5,601	3,224
(ABA)	407	11,662	.504	.778	4,924	1,952
ABA MVP 1974-76; NBA MVP, 1981.						
Frazier, Walt (Clyde) (1987)	825	15,581	.490	.786	4,830	5,040
NBA All-Defensive team seven consecutive seasons (1969-75)						
Fulks, Joe (1977)	489	8,003	.302	.766	1,382[1]	587
NBA scoring leader in 1947 (23.2 ppg)						
Gallatin, Harry (1991)	682	8,843	.398	.773	6,684	1,208
Seven-time All-Star						
Gervin, George (Iceman) (1996)	791	20,708	.511	.844	3,607	2,214
(ABA)	269	5,887	.480	.831	1,995	584
All-NBA team five years in a row (1978-82).						
Gola, Tom (1975)	698	7,871	.431	.760	5,605	2,953
One of only two major-college players with over 2,000 points and 2,000 rebounds in career						
Goodrich, Gail (1996)	1,031	19,181	.456	.807	3,279	4,805
Scored 42 points in 1965 NCAA Final; averaged 18.6 points per game over 14 years in NBA						
Greer, Harold (Hal) (1981)	1,122	21,586	.452	.801	5,665	4,540
Scored 19 points in one quarter of 1968 All-Star game						
Hagan, Cliff (1977)	746	13,447	.450	.798	5,019	2,236
(ABA)	94	1,423	.496	.807	436	398
Helped St. Louis to 1958 championship with 27.7 ppg in playoffs						
Havlicek, John J. (Hondo) (1983)	1,270	26,395	.439	.815	8,007	6,114
Averaged 20.8 ppg; Member of 8 NBA championship teams						
Hawkins, Connie (1992)	499	8,233	.467	.785	3,971	2,052
(ABA)	117	3,295	.515	.765	1,479	504
Four-time All-Star; ABA MVP 1969						
Hayes, Elvin (1990)	1,303	27,313	.452	.670	16,279	2,398
Led league in scoring (1969) and rebounds per game (1970,1974)						
Heinsohn, Tom (1986)	654	12,194	.405	.790	5,749	1,318
Played for eight NBA championship teams and coached two others						
Houbregs, Robert J. (1987)	281	2,611	.404	.721	1,552	500
NCAA Player of the Year, 1953						
Issel, Dan (1993)	718	14,659	.506	.797	5,707	1,804
(ABA)	500	12,823	.488	.786	5,426	1,103
Averaged 33.7 points per game in senior year at Kentucky, 1969-70						
Jabbar, Kareem Abdul (1995)	1,560	38,387	.559	.721	17,440	5,660
Six-time NBA MVP. All-time NBA leader in scoring, games, minutes, field goals						
Jeannette, Buddy (1994) (BAA-NBA)	139	997	.341	.781	N.A.	287
Won NBL MVP three times						
Johnston, Neil (1990)	516	10,023	.444	.768	5,856	1,269
Named to four straight all-NBA First Teams (1953-56)						
Jones, K.C. (1989)	676	5,011	.387	.647	2,399	2,908
High scorer in 1955 NCAA finals (24 pts); held Tom Gola scoreless for 21 mins.						
Jones, Sam (1983)	871	15,411	.456	.803	4,305	2,209
Member of 10 NBA championship teams						
Lanier, Bob (1992)	959	19,248	.514	.767	9,698	3,007
Eight-time All-Star; NBA MVP, 1974						
Lovellette, Clyde (1988)	704	11,947	.443	.756	6,663	1,165
Three-time All-American at University of Kansas (1950-52)						
Lucas, Jerry Ray (Luke) (1979)	829	14,053	.499	.783	12,942	2,730
NBA Rookie of the Year and field-goal percentage leader (.527) in 1964						
Macauley, Edward (Easy Ed) (1960)	641	11,234	.436	.761	2,079	1,667
NBA All-Star Game MVP, 1951						
Malone, Moses (2001)	1,329	27,409	.491	.769	16,212	1,796
Three-time MVP, 12-time All-Star. Averaged 20 points per game 11 straight seasons.						
Maravich, Pete (Pistol) (1987)	658	15,948	.441	.820	2,747	3,563
NCAA career record holder for points scored (3667) and scoring avg. (44.2 ppg)						
Martin, Slater (1981)	745	7,337	.364	.762	2,302[1]	3,160
Played in seven straight All-Star Games, 1953-59						
McAdoo, Bob (2000)	852	18,787	.503	.754	8,048	1,951
NBA Rookie of the Year (1973); led league in scoring 1974, 1975, and 1976.						
McGuire, Dick (1993)	738	5,921	.389	.644	2,784	4,205
Averaged 8.0 ppg.						
McHale, Kevin (1999)	971	17,335	.554	.798	7,122	1,670
Seven-time All-Star; won Sixth Man Award twice; won 3 NBA Championships: 1981, 1984, 1986						
Mikan, George L. (1959)	439	10,156	.404	.782	4,167[1]	1,245
Three-time NBA scoring leader (1949, 1950, 1952).						
Mikkelson, Vern (1995)	699	10,063	.403	.766	5,940[1]	1,515
Six-time NBA All-Star; won 4 NBA Championships: 1950, 1952, 1953, & 1954						

Player (Year Elected)	Games	Points	FG%	FT%	Rebs.	Assts.
Monroe, Earl (The Pearl) (1990)	926	17,454	.464	.807	2,796	3,594
NBA Rookie of the Year, 1968.						
Murphy, Calvin (1993)	1,002	17,949	.482	.892	2,103	4,402
Set single-season free throw percentage record with .958 in 1980-81.						
Pettit, Bob (1970)	792	20,880	.436	.761	12,849	2,369
Led NBA in scoring (25.7 ppg) and rebounds (1164) in 1956.						
Phillip, Andy (1961)	701	6,384	.368	.695	2,395[1]	3,759
Led NBA in assists, 1951 and 1952						
Pollard, Jim (1977)	438	5,762	.360	.750	2,487[1]	1,417
Started four NBA All-Star Games						
Ramsey, Frank (1981)	623	8,378	.402	.804	3,410	1,136
Member of seven NBA championship teams						
Reed, Willis (1981)	650	12,183	.476	.747	8,414	1,186
1970 NBA Most Valuable Player, All-Star Game MVP and Playoff MVP						
Risen, Arnie (1998)	637	7,633	.381	.699	5,011	1,058
Three-time NBA All-star (1953, 1954,and 1955)						
Robertson, Oscar (1979)	1,040	26,710	.485	.838	7,804	9,887
NBA MVP 1964; Member of All-NBA First team, 1961-69						
Russell, Bill (1974)	963	14,522	.440	.561	21,620	4,100
Five-time NBA Most Valuable Player; 32 rebounds in one half vs. Philadelphia, 1957						
Schayes, Adolph (Dolph) (1972)	996	18,438	.380	.849	11,256[1]	3,072
NBA Coach of the Year (1966)						
Sharman, Bill (1974)	711	12,665	.426	.883	2,779	2,101
Led NBA in free-throw percentage seven seasons						
Thomas, Isiah, (2000)	979	18,822	.452	.759	3,478	9,061
NBA Rookie of the Year (1982); 12-time All-Star; MVP of the 1990 Finals.						
Thompson, David (1996)	509	11,264	.504	.778	1,921	1,631
(ABA)	83	2,158	.515	.794	525	308
NCAA player of the year 1974 and 1975; ABA Rookie of the Year, 1976.						
Thurmond, Nate (1984)	964	14,437	.421	.667	14,464	2,575
1,000+ rebounds 1964-69, 1970-73						
Twyman, Jack (1982)	823	15,840	.450	.778	5,421	1,969
Led NBA in field-goal percentage, 1958 (.452)						
Unseld, Wes (1988)	984	10,624	.509	.633	13,769	3,822
Named NBA Most Valuable Player and Rookie of the Year in same year (1969)						
Walton, Bill (1993)	468	6,215	.521	.660	4,923	1,590
MVP in 1976.						
Wanzer, Robert (1987)	502	5,891	.388	.800	1,652[1]	1,575
Free-throw percentage leader, 1952 (.904)						
West, Jerry Alan (1979)	932	25,192	.474	.814	5,376	6,238
NBA MVP in 1970; .805 free throw percentage in 13 years in the playoffs						
Wilkens, Lenny (1989)	1,077	17,772	.432	.774	5,030	7,211
600+ assists 6 consecutive seasons						
Yardley, George (1996)	472	9,063	.422	.780	4,220	815
First player in NBA history to score 2,000 points in a season						

Note: All statistics for NBA career unless otherwise noted. NBL = National Basketball League. ABA = American Basketball Association. NCAA (National Collegiate Athletic Association) 1. Does not include seasons played prior to 1950-51 when the NBA first began keeping statistics for rebounds. 2. The National Basketball League did not keep statistics for field-goal percentage, rebounds, or assists.

COACHES

Anderson, W. Harold 1984
Auerbach, Arnold J. "Red" 1968
Barry, Justin "Sam" 1978
Blood, Ernest A. 1960
Cann, Howard G. 1967
Carlson, Dr. H. Clifford 1959
Carnesecca, Lou 1992
Carnevale, Ben 1969
Carril, Pete 1997
Case, Everett 1981
Chaney, John 2001
Conradt, Jody 1998
Crum, Denny, 1994
Daly, Chuck, 1994
Dean, Everett S. 1966
Diddle, Edgar A. 1971
Drake, Bruce 1972
Gaines, Clarence 1981
Gardner, James H. "Jack" 1983

Gill, Amory T. "Slats" 1967
Hannum, Alex 1998
Harshman, Marv 1984
Haskins, Don 1997
Hickey, Edgar S. 1978
Hobson, Howard A. 1965
Holzman, William "Red" 1985-86
Iba, Henry P. "Hank" 1968
Julian, Alvin "Doggie" 1967
Keaney, Frank W. 1960
Keogan, George E. 1961
Knight, Bob 1991
Krzyzewski, Mike 2001
Kundla, John 1995
Lambert, Ward L. 1960
Litwack, Harry 1975
Loeffler, Kenneth D. 1964
Lonborg, Arthur C. 1972
McCutchan, Arad A. 1980
McGuire, Al 1992
McGuire, Frank J. 1976

Meanwell, Dr. Walter E. 1959
Meyer, Raymond J. 1978
Miller, Ralph 1987
Moore, Billie 1999
Nikolic, Aleksandar 1998
Ramsay, Jack 1992
Rupp, Adolph F. 1968
Sachs, Leonard D. 1961
Shelton, Everett F. 1979
Smith, Dean 1982
Summitt, Pat, 2000
Taylor, Fred R. 1985-86
Teague, Bertha 1984
Thompson, John 1999
Wade, L. Margaret 1984
Watts, Stanley H. 1985-86
Wilkens, Lenny, 1998
Wooden, John R. 1972
Woolpert, Phil 1992
Wootten, Morgan, 2000

ICE HOCKEY

National Hockey League
www.nhl.com
Commissioner: Gary Bettman
Founded: 1917
Number of Teams: 30

The NHL started with six franchises, and nearly went bankrupt in the 1970s due to lack of interest and financial mismanagement. But the sport and the league are thriving in the 1990s, winning national television broadcast deals and expanding rapidly to warm-weather cities like San Jose and Tampa Bay. Franchise relocation has also become common, as teams from Minnesota, Quebec, Winnipeg, and Hartford have moved, respectively, to Dallas, Colorado, Phoenix, and North Carolina.

At the start of the 1998-99 season, the NHL expanded to Nashville. And in 1999, Atlanta took its second crack at an expansion franchise (its first, the Atlanta Flames, now plays in Calgary). In 2000, expansion teams were added in St. Paul, Minnesota and Columbus, Ohio. The new franchises each paid an $80 million entry fee.

NHL Standings, 2000-01

EASTERN CONFERENCE

Northeast Division	W	L	T	OTL	Pts.
Ottawa Senators	48	21	9	4	109
Buffalo Sabres	46	30	5	1	98
Toronto Maple Leafs	37	29	11	5	90
Boston Bruins	36	30	8	8	88
Montreal Canadiens	28	40	8	6	70

Atlantic Division	W	L	T	OTL	Pts.
New Jersey Devils	48	19	12	3	111
Philadelphia Flyers	43	25	11	3	100
Pittsburgh Penguins	42	28	9	3	96
N.Y. Rangers	33	43	5	1	72
N.Y. Islanders	21	51	7	3	52

Southeast Division	W	L	T	OTL	Pts.
Washington Capitals	41	27	10	4	96
Carolina Hurricanes	38	32	9	3	88
Florida Panthers	22	38	13	9	66
Atlanta Thrashers	23	45	12	2	60
Tampa Bay Lightning	24	47	6	5	59

WESTERN CONFERENCE

Central Division	W	L	T	OTL	Pts.
Detroit Red Wings	49	20	9	4	111
St. Louis Blues	43	22	12	5	103
Nashville Predators	34	36	9	3	80
Columbus Blue Jackets	28	39	9	6	71
Chicago Blackhawks	29	40	8	5	71

Northwest Division	W	L	T	OTL	Pts.
Colorado Avalanche	52	16	10	4	118
Edmonton Oilers	39	28	12	3	93
Vancouver Canucks	36	28	11	7	90
Calgary Flames	27	36	15	4	73
Minnesota Wild	25	39	13	5	68

Pacific Division	W	L	T	OTL	Pts.
Dallas Stars	48	24	8	2	106
San Jose Sharks	40	27	12	3	95
Los Angeles Kings	38	28	13	3	92
Phoenix Coyotes	35	27	17	3	90
Anaheim Mighty Ducks	25	41	11	5	66

Source: National Hockey League

Stanley Cup Playoffs 2000-01

(All rounds are seven-game series)

EASTERN CONFERENCE				WESTERN CONFERENCE		

ROUND 1

New Jersey Devils	4	Carolina Hurricanes	2	Colorado Avalanche	4	Vancouver Canucks	0
Toronto Maple Leafs	4	Ottawa Senators	0	Los Angeles Kings	4	Detroit Red Wings	2
Pittsburgh Penguins	4	Washington Capitals	2	Dallas Stars	4	Edmonton Oilers	2
Buffalo Sabres	4	Philadelphia Flyers	2	St. Louis Blues	4	San Jose Sharks	2

ROUND 2

New Jersey Devils	4	Toronto Maple Leafs	3	Colorado Avalanche	4	Los Angeles Kings	3
Pittsburgh Penguins	4	Buffalo Sabres	3	St. Louis Blues	4	Dallas Stars	0

CONFERENCE CHAMPIONSHIPS

New Jersey Devils	4	Pittsburgh Penguins	1	Colorado Avalanche	4	St. Louis Blues	1

STANLEY CUP CHAMPIONSHIP
Colorado Avalanche 4, New Jersey Devils 3

The Stanley Cup

The oldest trophy competed for by professional athletes in North America, the Stanley Cup was donated by Frederick Arthur, Lord Stanley of Preston, in 1893. Lord Stanley purchased the trophy for 10 guineas (about $50) for presentation to the amateur hockey champions of Canada. Since 1910, when the National Hockey Association took possession of the Stanley Cup, the trophy has been the symbol of professional hockey supremacy. The National Hockey League took exclusive control of the cup in 1946, and now awards it annually to the team that wins the league's best-of-seven final playoff series.

Season	Champion	Finalist	GP in final	Season	Champion	Finalist	GP in final
1917–18	Toronto Arenas	Vancouver Millionaires	5	1959–60	Montreal Canadiens	Toronto Maple Leafs	4
1918–19	No decision[1]	No decision	5	1960–61	Chicago Blackhawks	Detroit Red Wings	6
1919–20	Ottawa Senators	Seattle Millionaires	5	1961–62	Toronto Maple Leafs	Chicago Blackhawks	6
1920–21	Ottawa Senators	Vancouver Millionaires	5	1962–63	Toronto Maple Leafs	Detroit Red Wings	5
1921–22	Toronto St. Pats	Vancouver Millionaires	5	1963–64	Toronto Maple Leafs	Detroit Red Wings	7
1922–23	Ottawa Senators	Edmonton	2	1964–65	Montreal Canadiens	Chicago Blackhawks	7
1923–24	Montreal Canadiens	Calgary	2	1965–66	Montreal Canadiens	Detroit Red Wings	6
1924–25	Victoria Cougars	Montreal Canadiens	4	1966–67	Toronto Maple Leafs	Montreal Canadiens	6
1925–26	Montreal Maroons	Victoria Cougars	4	1967–68	Montreal Canadiens	St. Louis Blues	4
1926–27	Ottawa Senators	Boston Bruins	4	1968–69	Montreal Canadiens	St. Louis Blues	4
1927–28	New York Rangers	Montreal Canadiens	5	1969–70	Boston Bruins	St. Louis Blues	4
1928–29	Boston Bruins	New York Rangers	2	1970–71	Montreal Canadiens	Chicago Blackhawks	7
1929–30	Montreal Canadiens	Boston Bruins	2	1971–72	Boston Bruins	New York Rangers	6
1930–31	Montreal Canadiens	Chicago Blackhawks	5	1972–73	Montreal Canadiens	Chicago Blackhawks	6
1931–32	Toronto Maple Leafs	New York Rangers	3	1973–74	Philadelphia Flyers	Boston Bruins	6
1932–33	New York Rangers	Toronto Maple Leafs	4	1974–75	Philadelphia Flyers	Buffalo Sabres	6
1933–34	Chicago Blackhawks	Detroit Red Wings	4	1975–76	Montreal Canadiens	Philadelphia Flyers	4
1934–35	Montreal Maroons	Toronto Maple Leafs	3	1976–77	Montreal Canadiens	Boston Bruins	4
1935–36	Detroit Red Wings	Toronto Maple Leafs	4	1977–78	Montreal Canadiens	Boston Bruins	6
1936–37	Detroit Red Wings	New York Rangers	5	1978–79	Montreal Canadiens	New York Rangers	5
1937–38	Chicago Blackhawks	Toronto Maple Leafs	4	1979–80	New York Islanders	Philadelphia Flyers	6
1938–39	Boston Bruins	Toronto Maple Leafs	5	1980–81	New York Islanders	Minnesota North Stars	5
1939–40	New York Rangers	Toronto Maple Leafs	6	1981–82	New York Islanders	Vancouver Canucks	4
1940–41	Boston Bruins	Detroit Red Wings	4	1982–83	New York Islanders	Edmonton Oilers	4
1941–42	Toronto Maple Leafs	Detroit Red Wings	7	1983–84	Edmonton Oilers	New York Islanders	5
1942–43	Detroit Red Wings	Boston Bruins	4	1984–85	Edmonton Oilers	Philadelphia Flyers	5
1943–44	Montreal Canadiens	Chicago Blackhawks	4	1985–86	Montreal Canadiens	Calgary Flames	5
1944–45	Toronto Maple Leafs	Detroit Red Wings	7	1986–87	Edmonton Oilers	Philadelphia Flyers	7
1945–46	Montreal Canadiens	Boston Bruins	5	1987–88	Edmonton Oilers	Boston Bruins	4
1946–47	Toronto Maple Leafs	Montreal Canadiens	6	1988–89	Calgary Flames	Montreal Canadiens	6
1947–48	Toronto Maple Leafs	Detroit Red Wings	4	1989–90	Edmonton Oilers	Boston Bruins	5
1948–49	Toronto Maple Leafs	Detroit Red Wings	4	1990–91	Pittsburgh Penguins	Minnesota North Stars	5
1949–50	Detroit Red Wings	New York Rangers	7	1991–92	Pittsburgh Penguins	Chicago Blackhawks	4
1950–51	Toronto Maple Leafs	Montreal Canadiens	5	1992–93	Montreal Canadiens	Los Angeles Kings	5
1951–52	Detroit Red Wings	Montreal Canadiens	4	1993–94	New York Rangers	Vancouver Canucks	7
1952–53	Montreal Canadiens	Boston Bruins	5	1994–95[3]	New Jersey Devils	Detroit Red Wings	4
1953–54	Detroit Red Wings	Montreal Canadiens	7	1995–96	Colorado Avalanche	Florida Panthers	4
1954–55	Detroit Red Wings	Montreal Canadiens	7	1996–97	Detroit Red Wings	Philadelphia Flyers	4
1955–56	Montreal Canadiens	Detroit Red Wings	5	1997–98	Detroit Red Wings	Washington Capitals	4
1956–57	Montreal Canadiens	Boston Bruins	5	1998–99	Dallas Stars	Buffalo Sabres	6
1957–58	Montreal Canadiens	Boston Bruins	6	1999-2000	New Jersey Devils	Dallas Stars	6
1958–59	Montreal Canadiens	Toronto Maple Leafs	5	2000-01	Colorado Avalanche	New Jersey Devils	7

1. In the spring of 1919 the Montreal Canadiens traveled to Seattle to meet Seattle, champs of the Pacific Coast Hockey League. After five games had been played—teams were tied at 2 wins and 1 tie—the series was called off by the local Department of Health because of the influenza epidemic. 3. Strike-shortened season. **Source:** National Hockey League.

Top Scorers, 2000–01

Player, Team	POINTS	Player, Team	GOALS	Player, Team	ASSISTS
Jaromir Jagr, Pittsburgh	121	Pavel Bure, Florida	59	Jaromir Jagr, Pittsburgh	69
Joe Sakic, Colorado	118	Joe Sakic, Colorado	54	Adam Oates, Washington	69
Patrik Elias, New Jersey	96	Jaromir Jagr, Pittsburgh	52	Martin Straka, Pittsburgh	68
Jason Allison, Boston	95	Peter Bondra, Washington	45	Doug Weight, Edmonton	65
Alexei Kovalev, Pittsburgh	95	Alexei Kovalev, Pittsburgh	44	Joe Sakic, Colorado	64
Martin Straka, Pittsburgh	95	Alexander Mogilny, New Jersey	43	Peter Forsberg, Colorado	62
Pavel Bure, Florida	92	Jeff O'neill, Carolina	41	Jason Allison, Boston	59
Doug Weight, Edmonton	90	Milan Hejduk, Colorado	41	Brian Leetch, N. Y. Rangers	58
Peter Forsberg, Colorado	89	Markus Naslund, Vancouver	41	Nicklas Lidstrom, Detroit	56
Zigmund Palffy, Los Angeles	89	Three tied with	40	Patrik Elias, New Jersey	56

Source: National Hockey League.

Top 10 All-Time NHL Scoring Leaders

Player	GOALS Seasons	Games	Goals	Goals/ Game	Player	ASSISTS Seasons	Games	Assists	Assists/ Game
Wayne Gretzky	20	1,487	894	.601	Wayne Gretzky	20	1,487	1,963	1.320
Gordie Howe	26	1,767	801	.453	Ray Bourque[1]	22	1,612	1,169	.725
Marcel Dionne	18	1,348	731	.542	Ron Francis[1]	20	1,489	1,137	.764
Phil Esposito	18	1,282	717	.559	Paul Coffey[1]	21	1,409	1,135	.806
Mike Gartner	19	1,432	708	.494	Mark Messier[1]	22	1,561	1,130	.724
Mark Messier[1]	22	1,561	651	.417	Gordie Howe	26	1,767	1,049	.594
Brett Hull[1]	16	1019	649	.637	Marcel Dionne	18	1,348	1,040	.772
Mario Lemieux[1]	13	788	648	.822	Steve Yzerman[1]	18	1,310	969	.740
Steve Yzerman[1]	18	1,310	645	.492	Adam Oates	16	1,130	963	.852
Bobby Hull	16	1,063	610	.574	Larry Murphy[1]	21	1,615	929	.575

POINTS

Player	Seasons	Games	Goals	Assists	Points	Player	Seasons	Games	Goals	Assists	Points
Wayne Gretzky	20	1,487	894	1,963	2,857	Steve Yzerman[1]	18	1,310	645	969	1,614
Gordie Howe	26	1,767	801	1,049	1,850	Phil Esposito	18	1,282	717	873	1,590
Mark Messier[1]	22	1,561	651	1,130	1,781	Ray Bourque[1]	22	1,612	410	1,169	1,579
Marcel Dionne	18	1,348	731	1,040	1,771	Mario Lemieux	13	788	648	922	1,570
Ron Francis[1]	20	1,489	487	1,137	1,624	Paul Coffey[1]	21	1,409	396	1,135	1,531

Note: As of end of 2000-01 season. 1. Player active in 2000-01.   Source: NHL.

Hart Trophy Winners, 1924–2001

The league's most valuable player is chosen by a poll of the Professional Hockey Writers' Association.

Season	Player	Team	Season	Player	Team
1924	Frank Nighbor	Ottawa Senators	1963	Gordie Howe	Detroit
1925	Billy Burch	New York Americans	1964	Jean Béliveau	Montreal
1926	Nels Stewart	Montreal Maroons	1965	Bobby Hull	Chicago
1927	Herb Gardiner	Montreal	1966	Bobby Hull	Chicago
1928	Howie Morenz	Montreal	1967	Stan Mikita	Chicago
1929	Roy Worters	New York Americans	1968	Stan Mikita	Chicago
1930	Nels Stewart	Montreal Maroons	1969	Phil Esposito	Boston
1931	Howie Morenz	Montreal	1970	Bobby Orr	Boston
1932	Howie Morenz	Montreal	1971	Bobby Orr	Boston
1933	Eddie Shore	Boston	1972	Bobby Orr	Boston
1934	Aurel Joliat	Montreal	1973	Bobby Clarke	Philadelphia
1935	Eddie Shore	Boston	1974	Phil Esposito	Boston
1936	Eddie Shore	Boston	1975	Bobby Clarke	Philadelphia
1937	Babe Siebert	Montreal	1976	Bobby Clarke	Philadelphia
1938	Eddie Shore	Boston	1977	Guy Lafleur	Montreal
1939	Toe Blake	Montreal	1978	Guy Lafleur	Montreal
1940	Ebbie Goodfellow	Detroit	1979	Bryan Trottier	New York Islanders
1941	Bill Cowley	Boston	1980	Wayne Gretzky	Edmonton
1942	Tom Anderson	New York Americans	1981	Wayne Gretzky	Edmonton
1943	Bill Cowley	Boston	1982	Wayne Gretzky	Edmonton
1944	Babe Pratt	Toronto	1983	Wayne Gretzky	Edmonton
1945	Elmer Lach	Montreal	1984	Wayne Gretzky	Edmonton
1946	Max Bentley	Toronto	1985	Wayne Gretzky	Edmonton
1947	Maurice Richard	Montreal	1986	Wayne Gretzky	Edmonton
1948	Buddy O'Connor	New York Rangers	1987	Wayne Gretzky	Edmonton
1949	Sid Abel	Detroit	1988	Mario Lemieux	Pittsburgh
1950	Charlie Rayner	New York Rangers	1989	Wayne Gretzky	Los Angeles
1951	Milt Schmidt	Boston	1990	Mark Messier	Edmonton
1952	Gordie Howe	Detroit	1991	Bret Hull	St. Louis
1953	Gordie Howe	Detroit	1992	Mark Messier	New York Rangers
1954	Al Rollins	Toronto	1993	Mario Lemieux	Pittsburgh
1955	Ted Kennedy	Toronto	1994	Sergei Fedorov	Detroit
1956	Jean Béliveau	Montreal	1995	Eric Lindros	Philadelphia
1957	Gordie Howe	Detroit	1996	Mario Lemieux	Pittsburgh
1958	Gordie Howe	Detroit	1997	Dominik Hasek	Buffalo
1959	Andy Bathgate	New York Rangers	1998	Dominik Hasek	Buffalo
1960	Gordie Howe	Detroit	1999	Jaromir Jagr	Pittsburgh
1961	Bernie Geoffrion	Montreal	2000	Chris Pronger	St. Louis
1962	Jacques Plante	Montreal	2001	Joe Sakic	Colorado

Art Ross Trophy Winners, 1918–2001

The Art Ross Trophy goes "to the player who leads the league in scoring at the end of the regular season."

Season	Player	Team	Season	Player	Team
1918	Joe Malone	Montreal	1960	Bobby Hull	Chicago
1919	Newsy Lalonde	Montreal	1961	Bernie Geoffrion	Montreal
1920	Joe Malone	Quebec	1962	Bobby Hull	Chicago
1921	Newsy Lalonde	Montreal	1963	Gordie Howe	Detroit
1922	Punch Broadbent	Ottawa	1964	Stan Mikita	Chicago
1923	Babe Dye	Toronto	1965	Stan Mikita	Chicago
1924	Cye Denneny	Ottawa	1966	Bobby Hull	Chicago
1925	Babe Dye	Toronto	1967	Stan Mikita	Chicago
1926	Nels Stewart	Montreal Maroons	1968	Stan Mikita	Chicago
1927	Bill Cook	New York Rangers	1969	Phil Esposito	Boston
1928	Howie Morenz	Montreal	1970	Bobby Orr	Boston
1929	Ace Bailey	Toronto	1971	Phil Esposito	Boston
1930	Cooney Weiland	Boston	1972	Phil Esposito	Boston
1931	Howie Morenz	Montreal	1973	Phil Esposito	Boston
1932	Harvey Jackson	Toronto	1974	Phil Esposito	Boston
1933	Bill Cook	New York Rangers	1975	Bobby Orr	Boston
1934	Charlie Conacher	Toronto	1976	Guy Lafleur	Montreal
1935	Charlie Conacher	Toronto	1977	Guy Lafleur	Montreal
1936	Dave Shriner	New York Americans	1978	Guy Lafleur	Montreal
1937	Dave Shriner	New York Americans	1979	Bryan Trottier	New York Islanders
1938	Gordie Drillon	Toronto	1980	Marcel Dionne	Los Angeles
1939	Toe Blake	Montreal	1981	Wayne Gretzky	Edmonton
1940	Milt Schmidt	Boston	1982	Wayne Gretzky	Edmonton
1941	Bill Cowley	Boston	1983	Wayne Gretzky	Edmonton
1942	Bryan Hextall	New York Rangers	1984	Wayne Gretzky	Edmonton
1943	Doug Bentley	Chicago	1985	Wayne Gretzky	Edmonton
1944	Herbie Cain	Boston	1986	Wayne Gretzky	Edmonton
1945	Elmer Lach	Montreal	1987	Wayne Gretzky	Edmonton
1946	Max Bentley	Chicago	1988	Mario Lemieux	Pittsburgh
1947	Max Bentley	Chicago	1989	Mario Lemieux	Pittsburgh
1948	Elmer Lach	Montreal	1990	Wayne Gretzky	Los Angeles
1949	Roy Conacher	Chicago	1991	Wayne Gretzky	Los Angeles
1950	Ted Lindsay	Detroit	1992	Mario Lemieux	Pittsburgh
1951	Gordie Howe	Detroit	1993	Mario Lemieux	Pittsburgh
1952	Gordie Howe	Detroit	1994	Wayne Gretzky	Los Angeles
1953	Gordie Howe	Detroit	1995	Jaromir Jagr	Pittsburgh
1954	Gordie Howe	Detroit	1996	Mario Lemieux	Pittsburgh
1955	Bernie Geoffrion	Montreal	1997	Mario Lemieux	Pittsburgh
1956	Jean Béliveau	Montreal	1998	Jaromir Jagr	Pittsburgh
1957	Gordie Howe	Detroit	1999	Jaromir Jagr	Pittsburgh
1958	Dickie Moore	Montreal	2000	Jaromir Jagr	Pittsburgh
1959	Dickie Moore	Montreal	2001	Jaromir Jagr	Pittsburgh

Conn Smythe Trophy Winners, 1965–2001

The Conn Smythe Trophy is awarded to the most valuable player in the playoffs.

Season	Player, Team	Season	Player, Team	Season	Player, Team
1965	Jean Béliveau, Montreal	1978	Larry Robinson, Montreal	1991	Mario Lemieux, Pittsburgh
1966	Roger Crozier, Detroit	1979	Bob Gainey, Montreal	1992	Mario Lemieux, Pittsburgh
1967	Dave Keon, Toronto	1980	Bryan Trottier, N.Y. Islanders	1993	Patrick Roy, Montreal
1968	Glenn Hall, St. Louis	1981	Butch Goring, N.Y. Islanders	1994	Brian Leetch, N.Y. Rangers
1969	Serge Savard, Montreal	1982	Mike Bossy, N.Y. Islanders	1995	Claude Lemieux, New Jersey
1970	Bobby Orr, Boston	1983	Bill Smith, N.Y. Islanders	1996	Joe Sakic, Colorado
1971	Ken Dryden, Montreal	1984	Mark Messier, Edmonton	1997	Mike Vernon, Detroit
1972	Bobby Orr, Boston	1985	Wayne Gretzky, Edmonton	1998	Steve Yzerman, Detroit
1973	Yvan Cournoyer, Montreal	1986	Patrick Roy, Montreal	1999	Joe Nieuwendyk, Dallas
1974	Bernie Parent, Philadelphia	1987	Ron Hextall, Philadelphia	2000	Scott Stevens, New Jersey
1975	Bernie Parent, Philadelphia	1988	Wayne Gretzky, Edmonton	2001	Patrick Roy, Colorado
1976	Reggie Leach, Philadelphia	1989	Al MacInnis, Calgary		
1977	Guy Lafleur, Montreal	1990	Bill Ranford, Edmonton		

James Norris Memorial Trophy, 1954-2001

The James Norris Memorial Trophy for the league's best defenseman is awarded by the Professional Hockey Writers' Association. The winner receives $10,000.

Season	Player, Team	Season	Player, Team	Season	Player, Team
1954	Red Kelly, Detroit	1970	Bobby Orr, Boston	1986	Paul Coffey, Edmonton
1955	Doug Harvey, Montreal	1971	Bobby Orr, Boston	1987	Ray Bourque, Boston
1956	Doug Harvey, Montreal	1972	Bobby Orr, Boston	1988	Ray Bourque, Boston
1957	Doug Harvey, Montreal	1973	Bobby Orr, Boston	1989	Chris Chelios, Montreal
1958	Doug Harvey, Montreal	1974	Bobby Orr, Boston	1990	Ray Bourque, Boston
1959	Tom Johnson, Montreal	1975	Bobby Orr, Boston	1991	Ray Bourque, Boston
1960	Doug Harvey, Montreal	1976	Denis Potvin, N.Y. Islanders	1992	Brian Leetch, N.Y. Rangers
1961	Doug Harvey, Montreal	1977	Larry Robinson, Montreal	1993	Chris Chelios, Chicago
1962	Doug Harvey, N.Y. Rangers	1978	Denis Potvin, N.Y. Islanders	1994	Ray Bourque, Boston
1963	Pierre Pilote, Chicago	1979	Denis Potvin, N.Y. Islanders	1995	Paul Coffey, Detroit
1964	Pierre Pilote, Chicago	1980	Larry Robinson, Montreal	1996	Chris Chelios, Chicago
1965	Pierre Pilote, Chicago	1981	Randy Carlyle, Pittsburgh	1997	Brian Leetch, N.Y. Rangers
1966	Jacques Laperrière, Montreal	1982	Doug Wilson, Chicago	1998	Rob Blake, Los Angeles
1967	Harry Howell, N.Y. Rangers	1983	Rod Langway, Washington	1999	Al MacInnis, St. Louis
1968	Bobby Orr, Boston	1984	Rod Langway, Washington	2000	Chris Pronger, St. Louis
1969	Bobby Orr, Boston	1985	Paul Coffey, Edmonton	2001	Nicklas Lidstrom, Detroit

Vezina Trophy Winners, 1927-2001

The Vezina Trophy is awarded to the league's best goalkeeper and is selected by a poll of the league's general managers. The winner receives $10,000.

Season	Player	Team	Season	Player	Team
1927	George Hainsworth	Montreal	1966	Lorne Worsley/Charlie Hodge	Montreal
1928	George Hainsworth	Montreal	1967	Glenn Hall/ Denis Dejordy	Chicago
1929	George Hainsworth	Montreal	1968	Lorne Worsley/Rogie Vachon	Montreal
1930	Tiny Thompson	Boston	1969	Jacques Plante/Glenn Hall	St. Louis
1931	Roy Worters	N.Y. Americans	1970	Tony Esposito	Chicago
1932	Charlie Gardiner	Chicago	1971	Ed Giacomin/Gilles Villemure	N.Y. Rangers
1933	Tiny Thompson	Boston	1972	Tony Esposito/Gary Smith	Chicago
1934	Charlie Gardiner	Chicago	1973	Ken Dryden	Montreal
1935	Lorne Chabot	Chicago	1974	Bernie Parent	Philadelphia
1936	Tiny Thompson	Boston		Tony Esposito	Chicago
1937	Normie Smith	Detroit	1975	Bernie Parent	Philadelphia
1938	Tiny Thompson	Boston	1976	Ken Dryden	Montreal
1939	Frank Brimsek	Boston	1977	Ken Dryden/Michel Larocque	Montreal
1940	Dave Kerr	N.Y. Rangers	1978	Ken Dryden/Michel Larocque	Montreal
1941	Turk Broda	Toronto	1979	Ken Dryden/Michel Larocque	Montreal
1942	Frank Brimsek	Boston	1980	Bob Sauvé/Don Edwards	Buffalo
1943	Johnny Mowers	Detroit	1981	Richard Sevigny/Denis	Montreal
1944	Bill Durnan	Montreal		Herron/ Michel Larocque	
1945	Bill Durnan	Montreal	1982	Bill Smith	N.Y. Islanders
1946	Bill Durnan	Montreal	1983	Pete Peeters	Boston
1947	Bill Durnan	Montreal	1984	Tom Barrasso	Buffalo
1948	Turk Broda	Toronto	1985	Pele Lindbergh	Philadelphia
1949	Bill Durnan	Montreal	1986	John Vanbiesbrouck	N.Y. Rangers
1950	Bill Durnan	Montreal	1987	Ron Hextall	Philadelphia
1951	Al Rollins	Toronto	1988	Grant Fuhr	Edmonton
1952	Terry Sawchuk	Detroit	1989	Patrick Roy	Montreal
1953	Terry Sawchuk	Detroit	1990	Patrick Roy	Montreal
1954	Harry Lumley	Toronto	1991	Ed Belfour	Chicago
1955	Terry Sawchuk	Detroit	1992	Patrick Roy	Montreal
1956	Jacques Plante	Montreal	1993	Ed Belfour	Chicago
1957	Jacques Plante	Montreal	1994	Dominik Hasek	Buffalo
1958	Jacques Plante	Montreal	1995	Dominik Hasek	Buffalo
1959	Jacques Plante	Montreal	1996	Jim Carey	Washington
1960	Jacques Plante	Montreal	1997	Dominik Hasek	Buffalo
1961	Johnny Bower	Toronto	1998	Dominik Hasek	Buffalo
1962	Jacques Plante	Montreal	1999	Dominik Hasek	Buffalo
1963	Glenn Hall	Chicago	2000	Olaf Kolzig	Washington
1964	Charlie Hodge	Montreal	2001	Dominik Hasek	Buffalo
1965	Terry Sawchuk/Johnny Bower	Toronto			

Calder Memorial Trophy Winners, 1933–2001

The NHL rookie of the year, chosen by the Professional Hockey Writers' Association, receives $10,000.

Season	Player	Team	Season	Player	Team
1933	Carl Voss	Detroit	1967	Bobby Orr	Boston
1934	Russ Blinko	Montreal Maroons	1968	Derek Sanderson	Boston
1935	Dave Schriner	New York Americans	1969	Danny Grant	Minnesota
1936	Mike Karakas	Chicago	1970	Tony Esposito	Chicago
1937	Syl Apps	Toronto	1971	Gilbert Perreault	Buffalo
1938	Cully Dahlstrom	Chicago	1972	Ken Dryden	Montreal
1939	Frank Brimsek	Boston	1973	Steve Vickers	New York Rangers
1940	Kilby MacDonald	New York Rangers	1974	Denis Potvin	New York Islanders
1941	Johnny Quilty	Montreal	1975	Eric Vail	Atlanta
1942	Grant Warwick	New York Rangers	1976	Bryan Trottier	New York Islanders
1943	Gaye Stewart	Toronto	1977	Willie Plett	Atlanta
1944	Gus Bodnar	Toronto	1978	Mike Bossy	New York Islanders
1945	Frank McCool	Toronto	1979	Bobby Smith	Minnesota
1946	Edgar Laprade	New York Rangers	1980	Ray Bourque	Boston
1947	Howie Meeker	Toronto	1981	Peter Stastny	Quebec
1948	Jim McFadden	Detroit	1982	Dale Hawerchuk	Winnipeg
1949	Pentti Lund	New York Rangers	1983	Steve Larmer	Chicago
1950	Jack Gelineau	Boston	1984	Tom Barrasso	Buffalo
1951	Terry Sawchuk	Detroit	1985	Mario Lemieux	Pittsburgh
1952	Bernie Geoffrion	Montreal	1986	Gary Suter	Calgary
1953	Lorne Worsley	New York Rangers	1987	Luc Robitaille	Los Angeles
1954	Camille Henry	New York Rangers	1988	Joe Nieuwendyk	Calgary
1955	Ed Litzenberger	Chicago	1989	Brian Leetch	New York Rangers
1956	Glenn Hall	Detroit	1990	Sergei Makarov	Calgary
1957	Larry Regan	Boston	1991	Ed Belfour	Chicago
1958	Frank Mahovlich	Toronto	1992	Pavel Bure	Vancouver
1959	Ralph Backstrom	Montreal	1993	Teemu Selanne	Winnipeg
1960	Bill Hay	Chicago	1994	Martin Brodeur	New Jersey
1961	Dave Keon	Toronto	1995	Petr Forsberg	Quebec
1962	Bobby Rousseau	Montreal	1996	Daniel Alfredsson	Ottawa
1963	Kent Douglas	Toronto	1997	Bryan Berard	New York Islanders
1964	Jacques Laperriere	Montreal	1998	Sergei Samsonov	Boston
1965	Roger Crozier	Detroit	1999	Chris Drury	Colorado
1966	Brit Selby	Toronto	2000	Scott Gomez	New Jersey

BASEBALL

Major League Baseball,
245 Park Avenue
New York, N.Y. 10167
(212)-931-7800
www.mlb.com
Commissioner: Allan "Bud" Selig
Number of teams: 30

►THE 2001 BASEBALL SEASON

Several significant major league records were set in 2001. Two of them, the single season home run mark, and total victories by an American League team, had stood for more than 35 years before they were both broken, in 1998. Barry Bonds's 73 homers topped Mark McGwire just three years after McGwire had shattered Roger Maris's 61 in 1961. But while Bonds did not go on to up the record by 15 percent (as McGwire did with his 70 in 1998), he had arguably the single greatest offensive season in baseball history. His .863 slugging percentage easily topped Babe Ruth's .847, a record that had stood since 1920. And Bonds also set the single-season record for walks, with 177. Like McGwire in 1998, he also finished with more home runs than singles (49), and was on base more than half the time (his on-base average was .515, the highest in more than 40 years).

Bonds wasn't the only record-breaker in 2001. Rickey Henderson finished the season with 2,248 career runs, three more than the former record of 2,245 set by Ty Cobb. Henderson also got his 3,000th hit on the final day of the season. Sammy Sosa became the first player to hit 60 home runs three times, though oddly, each time he did it, he came in second in homers for the year.

The Seattle Mariners amassed a whopping 116 victories, breaking by two the previous American League record set by the New York Yankees in 1998, and tying the major league record set by the Chicago Cubs in 1906. The Atlanta Braves won an unprecedented 10th-straight division title.

Major League Baseball All-Time Career Leaders

Hits (3,000 or more)
1.	Pete Rose	4,256
2.	Ty Cobb	4,191
3.	Hank Aaron	3,771
4.	Stan Musial	3,630
5.	Tris Speaker	3,515
6.	Carl Yastrzemski	3,419
7.	Honus Wagner	3,418
8.	Paul Molitor	3,319
9.	Eddie Collins	3,311
10.	Willie Mays	3,283
11.	Eddie Murray	3,255
12.	Nap Lajoie	3,244
13.	Cal Ripken Jr.[1]	3,184
14.	George Brett	3,154
15.	Paul Waner	3,152
16.	Robin Yount	3,142
17.	Tony Gwynn[1]	3,141
18.	Dave Winfield	3,110
19.	Rod Carew	3,053
20.	Cap Anson	3,041
21.	Lou Brock	3,023
22.	Wade Boggs	3,010
23.	Al Kaline	3,007
24.	Roberto Clemente	3,000
25.	Rickey Henderson[1]	3,000

Home Runs (450 or more)
1.	Hank Aaron	755
2.	Babe Ruth	714
3.	Willie Mays	660
4.	Frank Robinson	586
5.	Mark McGwire[1]	583
6.	Harmon Killebrew	573
7.	Barry Bonds[1]	567
8.	Reggie Jackson	563
9.	Mike Schmidt	548
10.	Mickey Mantle	536
11.	Jimmie Foxx	534
12.	Ted Williams	521
12.	Willie McCovey	521
14.	Eddie Mathews	512
14.	Ernie Banks	512
16.	Mel Ott	511
17.	Eddie Murray	504
18.	Lou Gehrig	493
19.	Stan Musial	475
19.	Willie Stargell	475
21.	Dave Winfield	465
22.	Jose Canseco[1]	462
23.	Ken Griffey Jr.[1]	460
24.	Carl Yastrzemski	452
25.	Sammy Sosa[1]	450

Runs Batted In
1.	Hank Aaron	2,297
2.	Babe Ruth	2,211
3.	Lou Gehrig	1,990
4.	Ty Cobb	1,961
5.	Stan Musial	1,951
6.	Jimmie Foxx	1,921
7.	Eddie Murray	1,917
8.	Willie Mays	1,903
9.	Mel Ott	1,861
10.	Carl Yastrzemski	1,844

Runs
1.	Rickey Henderson[1]	2,248
2.	Ty Cobb	2,245
3.	Babe Ruth	2,174
3.	Hank Aaron	2,174
5.	Pete Rose	2,165
6.	Willie Mays	2,062
7.	Cap Anson	1,996

8.	Stan Musial	1,949
9.	Lou Gehrig	1,888
10.	Tris Speaker	1,881

Average (minimum 4,000 at bats)
1.	Ty Cobb	.367
2.	Rogers Hornsby	.358
3.	Joe Jackson	.356
4.	Ed Delahanty	.346
5.	Ted Williams	.344
6.	Tris Speaker	.344
7.	Billy Hamilton	.344
8.	Willie Keeler	.343
9.	Dan Brouthers	.342
10.	Babe Ruth	.342

Stolen Bases
1.	Rickey Henderson[1]	1,395
2.	Lou Brock	938
3.	Ty Cobb	892
4.	Tim Raines[1]	808
5.	Vince Coleman	752
6.	Eddie Collins	743
7.	Max Carey	738
8.	Honus Wagner	703
9.	Joe Morgan	689
10.	Willie Wilson	668

Total Bases
1.	Hank Aaron	6,856
2.	Stan Musial	6,134
3.	Willie Mays	6,066
4.	Ty Cobb	5,863
5.	Babe Ruth	5,793
6.	Pete Rose	5,752
7.	Carl Yastrzemski	5,539
8.	Eddie Murray	5,397
9.	Frank Robinson	5,373
10.	Dave Winfield	5,221

Slugging Percentage (total bases divided by minimum 400 at-bats.)
1.	Babe Ruth	.690
2.	Ted Williams	.634
3.	Lou Gehrig	.632
4.	Jimmie Foxx	.609
5.	Hank Greenberg	.605
6.	Mark McGwire[1]	.588
7.	Barry Bonds[1]	.585
8.	Joe DiMaggio	.579
9.	Frank Thomas[1]	.577
9.	Rogers Hornsby	.577

Extra Base Hits
1.	Hank Aaron	1,477
2.	Stan Musial	1,377
3.	Babe Ruth	1,356
4.	Willie Mays	1,323
5.	Lou Gehrig	1,190
6.	Frank Robinson	1,186
7.	Carl Yastrzemski	1,157
8.	Ty Cobb	1,139
9.	Tris Speaker	1,132
10.	Barry Bonds[1]	1,121

Games Played
1.	Pete Rose	3,562
2.	Carl Yastrzemski	3,308
3.	Hank Aaron	3,298
4.	Ty Cobb	3,034
5.	Stan Musial	3,026
6.	Eddie Murray	3,026
7.	Cal Ripken[1]	3,001
8.	Willie Mays	2,992
9.	Rickey Henderson[1]	2,979
10.	Dave Winfield	2,972

Pitching-Wins
1.	Cy Young	511
2.	Walter Johnson	416
3.	Christy Mathewson	373
4.	Grover Alexander	373
5.	Warren Spahn	363
6.	Pud Galvin	361
7.	Kid Nichols	361
8.	Tim Keefe	342
9.	Steve Carlton	329
10.	Eddie Plank	327
11.	John Clarkson	326
12.	Don Sutton	324
13.	Nolan Ryan	324
14.	Phil Niekro	318
15.	Gaylord Perry	314
16.	Charles "Old Hoss" Radbourne	311
17.	Tom Seaver	311
18.	Mickey Welch	308
19.	Lefty Grove	300
20.	Early Wynn	300

Strikeouts
1.	Nolan Ryan	5,714
2.	Steve Carlton	4,136
3.	Roger Clemens[1]	3,717
4.	Bert Blyleven	3,701
5.	Tom Seaver	3,640
6.	Don Sutton	3,574
7.	Gaylord Perry	3,534
8.	Walter Johnson	3,508
9.	Randy Johnson[1]	3,412
10.	Phil Niekro	3,342

Earned run average
1.	Ed Walsh	1.82
2.	Addie Joss	1.88
3.	Mordecai "Three Finger" Brown	2.06
4.	Christy Mathewson	2.13
5.	Rube Waddell	2.16
6.	Walter Johnson	2.17
7.	Orval Overall	2.24
8.	Ed Reulbach	2.28
9.	Jim Scott	2.32
10.	Eddie Plank	2.34

Innings Pitched
1.	Cy Young	7,356
2.	Pud Galvin	5,941
3.	Walter Johnson	5,923
4.	Phil Niekro	5,403
5.	Nolan Ryan	5,387
6.	Gaylord Perry	5,351
7.	Don Sutton	5,280
8.	Warren Spahn	5,244
9.	Steve Carlton	5,217
10.	Grover Cleveland Alexander	5,189

Shutouts
1.	Walter Johnson	110
2.	Grover Cleveland Alexander	90
3.	Christy Mathewson	80
4.	Cy Young	76
5.	Eddie Plank	69
6.	Warren Spahn	63
7.	Nolan Ryan	61
8.	Tom Seaver	61
9.	Bert Blyleven	60
10.	Don Sutton	58

Note: As of the end of the 2001 season. 1. Active during the 2001 season. **Source:** Major League Baseball.

Triple Crown Winners

Only 11 players have led their league in home runs, runs batted in, and batting average in one season.

Player	Club	Year	HR	RBI	AVG.
Ty Cobb	Detroit Tigers	1909	9	115	.377
Henry Zimmerman	Chicago Cubs	1912	14	98	.372
Rogers Hornsby	St. Louis Cardinals	1922	42	152	.401
Rogers Hornsby	St. Louis Cardinals	1925	39	143	.403
Chuck Klein	Philadelphia Phillies	1933	28	120	.368
Jimmie Foxx	Philadelphia A's	1933	48	163	.356
Lou Gehrig	New York Yankees	1934	49	165	.363
Joe Medwick	St. Louis Cardinals	1937	31	154	.374
Ted Williams	Boston Red Sox	1942	36	137	.356
Ted Williams	Boston Red Sox	1947	32	114	.343
Mickey Mantle	New York Yankees	1956	52	130	.353
Frank Robinson	Baltimore Orioles	1966	49	122	.316
Carl Yastrzemski	Boston Red Sox	1967	44	121	.326

Batting Champions 1876–2001

NATIONAL LEAGUE

Year	Name	Team	Avg.	Year	Name	Team	Avg.
1876	Roscoe Barnes	Chicago Cubs	.403	1889	Dan Brouthers	Boston Braves	.373
1877	James White	Boston Braves	.385	1890	Jack Glasscock	N.Y. Giants	.336
1878	Abner Dalrymple	Milwaukee Brewers	.356	1891	Billy Hamilton	Philadelphia Phillies	.338
1879	Cap Anson	Chicago Cubs	.407	1892	"Cupid" Childs	Cleveland Spiders	.335
1880	George Gore	Chicago Cubs	.365		Dan Brouthers	Brooklyn Dodgers	.335
1881	Cap Anson	Chicago Cubs	.399	1893	Hugh Duffy	Boston Braves	.378
1882	Dan Brouthers	Buffalo Bisons	.367	1894	Hugh Duffy	Boston Braves	.438
1883	Dan Brouthers	Buffalo Bisons	.371	1895	Jesse Burkett	Cleveland Spiders	.423
1884	Jim O'Rourke	Buffalo Bisons	.350	1896	Jesse Burkett	Cleveland Spiders	.410
1885	Roger Connor	N.Y. Giants	.371	1897	Willie Keeler	Baltimore Orioles	.432
1886	Mike Kelly	Chicago Cubs	.388	1898	Willie Keeler	Baltimore Orioles	.379
1887	Cap Anson	Chicago Cubs	.421	1899	Ed Delahanty	Philadelphia Phillies	.408
1888	Cap Anson	Chicago Cubs	.343	1900	Honus Wagner	Pittsburgh Pirates	.380

	NATIONAL LEAGUE				AMERICAN LEAGUE		
Year	Name	Team	Avg.		Name	Team	Avg.
1901	Jesse Burkett	St. Louis Cardinals	.382		Nap Lajoie	Philadelphia Athletics	.422
1902	C.H. Beaumont	Pittsburgh Pirates	.357		Ed Delahanty	Washington Senators	.376
1903	Honus Wagner	Pittsburgh Pirates	.355		Nap Lajoie	Cleveland Indians	.355
1904	Honus Wagner	Pittsburgh Pirates	.349		Nap Lajoie	Cleveland Indians	.381
1905	J. Bentley Seymour	Cincinnati Reds	.377		Elmer Flick	Cleveland Indians	.306
1906	Honus Wagner	Pittsburgh Pirates	.339		George Stone	St. Louis Browns	.358
1907	Honus Wagner	Pittsburgh Pirates	.350		Ty Cobb	Detroit Tigers	.350
1908	Honus Wagner	Pittsburgh Pirates	.354		Ty Cobb	Detroit Tigers	.324
1909	Honus Wagner	Pittsburgh Pirates	.339		Ty Cobb	Detroit Tigers	.377
1910	Sherwood Magee	Philadelphia Phillies	.331		Ty Cobb	Detroit Tigers	.385
1911	Honus Wagner	Pittsburgh Pirates	.334		Ty Cobb	Detroit Tigers	.420
1912	Heinie Zimmerman	Chicago Cubs	.372		Ty Cobb	Detroit Tigers	.410
1913	Jake Daubert	Brooklyn Dodgers	.350		Ty Cobb	Detroit Tigers	.390
1914	Jake Daubert	Brooklyn Dodgers	.329		Ty Cobb	Detroit Tigers	.368
1915	Larry Doyle	New York Giants	.320		Ty Cobb	Detroit Tigers	.370
1916	Hal Chase	Cincinnati Reds	.339		Tris Speaker	Cleveland Indians	.386
1917	Edd Roush	Cincinnati Reds	.341		Ty Cobb	Detroit Tigers	.383
1918	Zack Wheat	Brooklyn Dodgers	.335		Ty Cobb	Detroit Tigers	.382
1919	Edd Roush	Cincinnati Reds	.321		Ty Cobb	Detroit Tigers	.407
1920	Rogers Hornsby	St. Louis Cardinals	.370		George Sisler	St. Louis Browns	.407
1921	Rogers Hornsby	St. Louis Cardinals	.397		Harry Heilmann	Detroit Tigers	.394
1922	Rogers Hornsby	St. Louis Cardinals	.401		George Sisler	St. Louis Browns	.420
1923	Rogers Hornsby	St. Louis Cardinals	.384		Harry Heilmann	Detroit Tigers	.403
1924	Rogers Hornsby	St. Louis Cardinals	.424		Babe Ruth	New York Yankees	.378
1925	Rogers Hornsby	St. Louis Cardinals	.403		Harry Heilmann	Detroit Tigers	.393
1926	Bubbles Hargrave	Cincinnati Reds	.353		Heinie Manush	Detroit Tigers	.377
1927	Paul Waner	Pittsburgh Pirates	.380		Harry Heilmann	Detroit Tigers	.398
1928	Rogers Hornsby	Boston Braves	.387		Goose Goslin	Washington Senators	.379
1929	Lefty O'Doul	Philadelphia Phillies	.398		Lew Fonseca	Cleveland Indians	.369
1930	Bill Terry	New York Giants	.401		Al Simmons	Philadelphia Athletics	.381

		NATIONAL LEAGUE			AMERICAN LEAGUE	
Year	Name	Team	Avg.	Name	Team	Avg.
1931	Chick Hafey[1]	St Louis Cardinals	.349	Al Simmons	Philadelphia Athletics	.390
1932	Lefty O'Doul	Brooklyn Dodgers	.368	Dale Alexander	Detroit-Boston	.367
1933	Chuck Klein	Philadelphia Phillies	.368	Jimmie Foxx	Philadelphia Athletics	.356
1934	Paul Waner	Pittsburgh Pirates	.362	Lou Gehrig	New York Yankees	.363
1935	Arky Vaughan	Pittsburgh Pirates	.385	Buddy Myer	Washington Senators	.349
1936	Paul Waner	Pittsburgh Pirates	.373	Luke Appling	Chicago White Sox	.388
1937	Joe Medwick	St. Louis Cardinals	.374	Charlie Gehringer	Detroit Tigers	.371
1938	Ernie Lombardi	Cincinnati Reds	.342	Jimmie Foxx	Boston Red Sox	.349
1939	Johnny Mize	St. Louis Cardinals	.349	Joe DiMaggio	New York Yankees	.381
1940	Debs Garms	Pittsburgh Pirates	.355	Joe DiMaggio	New York Yankees	.352
1941	Pete Reiser	Brooklyn Dodgers	.343	Ted Williams	Boston Red Sox	.406
1942	Ernie Lombardi	Boston Braves	.330	Ted Williams	Boston Red Sox	.356
1943	Stan Musial	St. Louis Cardinals	.357	Luke Appling	Chicago White Sox	.328
1944	Dixie Walker	Brooklyn Dodgers	.357	Lou Boudreau	Cleveland Indians	.327
1945	Phil Cavarretta	Chicago Cubs	.355	Snuffy Stirnweiss	New York Yankees	.309
1946	Stan Musial	St. Louis Cardinals	.365	Mickey Vernon	Washington Senators	.352
1947	Harry Walker	St. Louis-Philadelphia	.363	Ted Williams	Boston Red Sox	.343
1948	Stan Musial	St. Louis Cardinals	.376	Ted Williams	Boston Red Sox	.369
1949	Jackie Robinson	Brooklyn Dodgers	.342	George Kell	Detroit Tigers	.343
1950	Stan Musial	St. Louis Cardinals	.346	Billy Goodman	Boston Red Sox	.354
1951	Stan Musial	St. Louis Cardinals	.355	Ferris Fain	Philadelphia Athletics	.344
1952	Stan Musial	St. Louis Cardinals	.336	Ferris Fain	Philadelphia Athletics	.327
1953	Carl Furillo	Brooklyn Dodgers	.344	Mickey Vernon	Washington Senators	.337
1954	Willie Mays	New York Giants	.345	Bobby Avila	Cleveland Indians	.341
1955	Richie Ashburn	Philadelphia Phillies	.338	Al Kaline	Detroit Tigers	.340
1956	Hank Aaron	Milwaukee Braves	.328	Mickey Mantle	New York Yankees	.353
1957	Stan Musial	St. Louis Cardinals	.351	Ted Williams	Boston Red Sox	.388
1958	Richie Ashburn	Philadelphia Phillies	.350	Ted Williams	Boston Red Sox	.328
1959	Hank Aaron	Milwaukee Braves	.355	Harvey Kuenn	Detroit Tigers	.353
1960	Dick Groat	Pittsburgh Pirates	.325	Pete Runnels	Boston Red Sox	.320
1961	Roberto Clemente	Pittsburgh Pirates	.351	Norm Cash	Detroit Tigers	.361
1962	Tommy Davis	Los Angeles Dodgers	.346	Pete Runnels	Boston Red Sox	.326
1963	Tommy Davis	Los Angeles Dodgers	.326	Carl Yastrzemski	Boston Red Sox	.321
1964	Roberto Clemente	Pittsburgh Pirates	.339	Tony Oliva	Minnesota Twins	.323
1965	Roberto Clemente	Pittsburgh Pirates	.329	Tony Oliva	Minnesota Twins	.321
1966	Matty Alou	Pittsburgh Pirates	.342	Frank Robinson	Baltimore Orioles	.316
1967	Roberto Clemente	Pittsburgh Pirates	.357	Carl Yastrzemski	Boston Red Sox	.326
1968	Pete Rose	Cincinnati Reds	.335	Carl Yastrzemski	Boston Red Sox	.301
1969	Pete Rose	Cincinnati Reds	.348	Rod Carew	Minnesota Twins	.332
1970	Rico Carty	Atlanta Braves	.366	Alex Johnson	California Angels	.329
1971	Joe Torre	St. Louis Cardinals	.363	Tony Oliva	Minnesota Twins	.337
1972	Billy Williams	Chicago Cubs	.333	Rod Carew	Minnesota Twins	.318
1973	Pete Rose	Cincinnati Reds	.338	Rod Carew	Minnesota Twins	.350
1974	Ralph Garr	Atlanta Braves	.353	Rod Carew	Minnesota Twins	.364
1975	Bill Madlock	Chicago Cubs	.354	Rod Carew	Minnesota Twins	.359
1976	Bill Madlock	Chicago Cubs	.339	George Brett	Kansas City Royals	.333
1977	Dave Parker	Pittsburgh Pirates	.338	Rod Carew	Minnesota Twins	.388
1978	Dave Parker	Pittsburgh Pirates	.334	Rod Carew	Minnesota Twins	.333
1979	Keith Hernandez	St. Louis Cardinals	.344	Fred Lynn	Boston Red Sox	.333
1980	Bill Buckner	Chicago Cubs	.324	George Brett	Kansas City Royals	.390
1981[2]	Bill Madlock	Pittsburgh Pirates	.341	Carney Lansford	Boston Red Sox	.336
1982	Al Oliver	Montreal Expos	.331	Willie Wilson	Kansas City Royals	.332
1983	Bill Madlock	Pittsburgh Pirates	.323	Wade Boggs	Boston Red Sox	.361
1984	Tony Gwynn	San Diego Padres	.351	Don Mattingly	New York Yankees	.343
1985	Willie McGee	St. Louis Cardinals	.353	Wade Boggs	Boston Red Sox	.368
1986	Tim Raines	Montreal Expos	.334	Wade Boggs	Boston Red Sox	.357
1987	Tony Gwynn	San Diego Padres	.370	Wade Boggs	Boston Red Sox	.363
1988	Tony Gwynn	San Diego Padres	.313	Wade Boggs	Boston Red Sox	.366
1989	Tony Gwynn	San Diego Padres	.336	Kirby Puckett	Minnesota Twins	.339
1990	Willie McGee	St. Louis Cardinals	.335	George Brett	Kansas City Royals	.329
1991	Terry Pendleton	Atlanta Braves	.319	Julio Franco	Texas Rangers	.341
1992	Gary Sheffield	San Diego Padres	.330	Edgar Martinez	Seattle Mariners	.343
1993	Andres Galarraga	Colorado Rockies	.370	John Olerud	Toronto Blue Jays	.363
1994[2]	Tony Gwynn	San Diego Padres	.394	Paul O'Neill	New York Yankees	.359
1995[2]	Tony Gwynn	San Diego Padres	.368	Edgar Martinez	Seattle Mariners	.356
1996	Ellis Burks	Colorado Rockies	.344	Alex Rodriguez	Seattle Mariners	.358
1997	Tony Gwynn	San Diego Padres	.372	Frank Thomas	Chicago White Sox	.347
1998	Larry Walker	Colorado Rockies	.363	Bernie Williams	New York Yankees	.339
1999	Larry Walker	Colorado Rockies	.379	Nomar Garciaparra	Boston Red Sox	.357
2000	Todd Helton	Colorado Rockies	.372	Nomar Garciaparra	Boston Red Sox	.372
2001	Larry Walker	Colorado Rockies	.350	Ichiro Suzuki	Seattle Mariners	.350

1. Hafey led with .3489, Bill Terry, N.Y., second with .3486, Jim Bottomley, St. Louis, third with .3482. 2. Strike-shortened season.

Home Run Champions, 1938–2001

	NATIONAL LEAGUE		AMERICAN LEAGUE	
Year	Name, Team	HRs	Name, Team	HRs
1938	Mel Ott, New York	36	Hank Greenberg, Detroit	58
1939	Johnny Mize, St. Louis	28	Jimmie Foxx, Boston	35
1940	Johnny Mize, St. Louis	43	Hank Greenberg, Detroit	41
1941	Dolph Camillia, Brooklyn	34	Ted Williams, Boston	37
1942	Mel Ott, New York	30	Ted Williams, Boston	36
1943	Bill Nicholson, Chicago	29	Rudy York, Detroit	34
1944	Bill Nicholson, Chicago	33	Nick Etten, New York	22
1945	Tommy Holmes, Boston	28	Vern Stephens, St. Louis	24
1946	Ralph Kiner, Pittsburgh	23	Hank Greenberg, Detroit	44
1947	Ralph Kiner, Pittsburgh; Johnny Mize, New York	51	Ted Williams, Boston	32
1948	Ralph Kiner, Pittsburgh; Johnny Mize, New York	40	Joe DiMaggio, New York	39
1949	Ralph Kiner, Pittsburgh	54	Ted Williams, Boston	43
1950	Ralph Kiner, Pittsburgh	47	Al Rosen, Cleveland	37
1951	Ralph Kiner, Pittsburgh	42	Gus Zernial, Chicago-Philadelphia	33
1952	Ralph Kiner, Pittsburgh; Hank Sauer, Chicago	37	Larry Doby, Cleveland	32
1953	Eddie Mathews, Milwaukee	47	Al Rosen, Cleveland	43
1954	Ted Kluszewski, Cincinnati	49	Larry Doby, Cleveland	32
1955	Willie Mays, New York	51	Mickey Mantle, New York	37
1956	Duke Snider, Brooklyn	43	Mickey Mantle, New York	52
1957	Hank Aaron, Milwaukee	44	Roy Sievers, Washington	42
1958	Ernie Banks, Chicago	47	Mickey Mantle, New York	42
1959	Eddie Mathews, Milwaukee	46	Rocky Colavito, Cleveland; Harmon Killebrew, Washington	42
1960	Ernie Banks, Chicago	41	Mickey Mantle, New York	40
1961	Orlando Cepeda, San Francisco	46	Roger Maris, New York	61
1962	Willie Mays, San Francisco	49	Harmon Killebrew, Minnesota	48
1963	Hank Aaron, Milwaukee; Willie McCovey, San Francisco	44	Harmon Killebrew, Minnesota	45
1964	Willie Mays, San Francisco	47	Harmon Killebrew, Minnesota	49
1965	Willie Mays, San Francisco	52	Tony Conigliaro, Boston	32
1966	Hank Aaron, Atlanta	44	Frank Robinson, Baltimore	49
1967	Hank Aaron, Atlanta	39	Harmon Killebrew, Minnesota; Carl Yastrzemski, Boston	44
1968	Willie McCovey, San Francisco	36	Frank Howard, Washington	44
1969	Willie McCovey, San Francisco	45	Harmon Killebrew, Minnesota	49
1970	Johnny Bench, Cincinnati	45	Frank Howard, Washington	44
1971	Willie Stargell, Pittsburgh	48	Bill Melton, Chicago	33
1972	Johnny Bench, Cincinnati	40	Dick Allen, Chicago	37
1973	Willie Stargell, Pittsburgh	44	Reggie Jackson, Oakland	32
1974	Mike Schmidt, Philadelphia	36	Dick Allen, Chicago	32
1975	Mike Schmidt, Philadelphia	38	Reggie Jackson, Oakland; George Scott, Milwaukee	36
1976	Mike Schmidt, Philadelphia	38	Graig Nettles, New York	32
1977	George Foster, Cincinnati	52	Jim Rice, Boston	39
1978	George Foster, Cincinnati	40	Jim Rice, Boston	46
1979	Dave Kingman, Chicago	48	Gorman Thomas, Milwaukee	45
1980	Mike Schmidt, Philadelphia	48	Reggie Jackson, New York; Ben Oglivie, Milwaukee	41
1981[1]	Mike Schmidt, Philadelphia	31	Tony Armas, Boston; Dwight Evans, Boston; Bobby Grich, California; Eddie Murray, Baltimore	22
1982	Dave Kingman, New York	37	Reggie Jackson, California; Gorman Thomas, Milwaukee	39
1983	Mike Schmidt, Philadelphia	40	Jim Rice, Boston	39
1984	Dale Murphy, Atlanta; Mike Schmidt, Philadelphia	36	Tony Armas, Boston	50
1985	Dale Murphy, Atlanta	37	Darrell Evans, Detroit	40
1986	Mike Schmidt, Philadelphia	37	Jesse Barfield, Toronto	40
1987	Andre Dawson, Chicago	49	Mark McGwire, Oakland	49
1988	Darryl Strawberry, New York Mets	39	Jose Canseco, Oakland	42
1989	Kevin Mitchell, San Francisco	47	Fred McGriff, Toronto	36
1990	Ryne Sandberg, Chicago	40	Cecil Fielder, Detroit	51
1991	Howard Johnson, New York Mets	38	Jose Canseco, Oakland	44
1992	Fred McGriff, San Diego	35	Juan Gonzalez, Texas	43
1993	Barry Bonds, San Francisco	46	Juan Gonzalez, Texas	46
1994[1]	Matt Williams, San Francisco	43	Ken Griffey Jr., Seattle	40
1995[1]	Dante Bichette, Colorado	40	Albert Belle, Cleveland	50
1996	Andres Galarraga, Colorado	47	Mark McGwire, Oakland	52
1997	Larry Walker, Colorado[2]	49	Ken Griffey Jr., Seattle[2]	56
1998	Mark McGwire, St. Louis	70	Ken Griffey Jr., Seattle	56
1999	Mark McGwire, St. Louis	65	Ken Griffey Jr., Seattle	48
2000	Sammy Sosa, Chicago Cubs	50	Troy Glaus, Anaheim	47
2001	Barry Bonds, San Francisco	73	Alex Rodriguez, Texas	52

1. Strike-shortened season 2. Mark McGwire hit 34 home runs with Oakland and 24 with St. Louis for a major-league-leading total of 58. **Source:** Major League Baseball.

Rookie of the Year

NATIONAL LEAGUE			AMERICAN LEAGUE		
Year	Name	Team	Year	Name	Team
1947[1]	Jackie Robinson	Brooklyn Dodgers			
1948[1]	Alvin Dark	Boston Braves			
1949	Don Newcombe	Brooklyn Dodgers	1949	Roy Sievers	St. Louis Browns
1950	Sam Jethroe	Boston Braves	1950	Walt Dropo	Boston Red Sox
1951	Willie Mays	New York Giants	1951	Gil McDougald	New York Yankees
1952	Joe Black	Brooklyn Dodgers	1952	Harry Byrd	Philadelphia Athletics
1953	Junior Gilliam	Brooklyn Dodgers	1953	Harvey Kuenn	Detroit Tigers
1954	Wally Moon	St. Louis Cardinals	1954	Bob Grim	New York Yankees
1955	Bill Virdon	St. Louis Cardinals	1955	Herb Score	Cleveland Indians
1956	Frank Robinson	Cincinnati Reds	1956	Luis Aparicio	Chicago White Sox
1957	Jack Sanford	Philadelphia Phillies	1957	Tony Kubek	New York Yankees
1958	Orlando Cepeda	San Francisco Giants	1958	Albie Pearson	Washington Senators
1959	Willie McCovey	San Francisco Giants	1959	Bob Allison	Washington Senators
1960	Frank Howard	Los Angeles Dodgers	1960	Ron Hansen	Baltimore Orioles
1961	Billy Williams	Chicago Cubs	1961	Don Schwall	Boston Red Sox
1962	Ken Hubbs	Chicago Cubs	1962	Tom Tresh	New York Yankees
1963	Pete Rose	Cincinnati Reds	1963	Gary Peters	Chicago White Sox
1964	Richie Allen	Philadelphia Phillies	1964	Tony Oliva	Minnesota Twins
1965	Jim Lefebvre	Los Angeles Dodgers	1965	Curt Blefary	Baltimore Orioles
1966	Tommy Helms	Cincinnati Reds	1966	Tommie Agee	Chicago White Sox
1967	Tom Seaver	New York Mets	1967	Rod Carew	Minnesota Twins
1968	Johnny Bench	Cincinnati Reds	1968	Stan Bahnsen	New York Yankees
1969	Ted Sizemore	Los Angeles Dodgers	1969	Lou Piniella	Kansas City Royals
1970	Carl Morton	Montreal Expos	1970	Thurman Munson	New York Yankees
1971	Earl Williams	Atlanta Braves	1971	Chris Chambliss	Cleveland Indians
1972	Jon Matlack	New York Mets	1972	Carlton Fisk	Boston Red Sox
1973	Gary Matthews	San Francisco Giants	1973	Al Bumbry	Baltimore Orioles
1974	Bake McBride	St. Louis Cardinals	1974	Make Hargrove	Texas Rangers
1975	John Montefusco	San Francisco Giants	1975	Fred Lynn	Boston Red Sox
1976	Pat Zachry	Cincinnati Reds	1976	Mark Fidrych	Detroit Tigers
	Butch Metzger	San Diego Padres	1977	Eddie Murray	Baltimore Orioles
1977	Andre Dawson	Montreal Expos	1978	Lou Whitaker	Detroit Tigers
1978	Bob Horner	Atlanta Braves	1979	John Castino	Minnesota Twins
1979	Rick Sutcliffe	Los Angeles Dodgers		Alfredo Griffin	Toronto Blue Jays
1980	Steve Howe	Los Angeles Dodgers	1980	Joe Charboneau	Cleveland Indians
1981	Fernando Valenzuela	Los Angeles Dodgers	1981	Dave Righetti	New York Yankees
1982	Steve Sax	Los Angeles Dodgers	1982	Cal Ripken Jr.	Baltimore Orioles
1983	Darryl Strawberry	New York Mets	1983	Ron Kittle	Chicago White Sox
1984	Dwight Gooden	New York Mets	1984	Alvin Davis	Seattle Mariners
1985	Vince Coleman	St. Louis Cardinals	1985	Ozzie Guillen	Chicago White Sox
1986	Todd Worrell	St. Louis Cardinals	1986	Jose Canseco	Oakland Athletics
1987	Benito Santiago	San Diego Padres	1987	Mark McGwire	Oakland Athletics
1988	Chris Sabo	Cincinnati Reds	1988	Walt Weiss	Oakland Athletics
1989	Jerome Walton	Chicago Cubs	1989	Greg Olson	Baltimore Orioles
1990	Dave Justice	Atlanta Braves	1990	Sandy Alomar Jr.	Cleveland Indians
1991	Jeff Bagwell	Houston Astros	1991	Chuck Knoblauch	Minnesota Twins
1992	Eric Karros	Los Angeles Dodgers	1992	Pat Listach	Milwaukee Brewers
1993	Mike Piazza	Los Angeles Dodgers	1993	Tim Salmon	California Angels
1994	Raul Mondesi	Los Angeles Dodgers	1994	Bob Hamelin	Kansas City Royals
1995	Hideo Nomo	Los Angeles Dodgers	1995	Marty Cordoba	Minnesota Twins
1996	Todd Hollandsworth	Los Angeles Dodgers	1996	Derek Jeter	New York Yankees
1997	Scott Rolen	Philadelphia Phillies	1997	Nomar Garciaparra	Boston Red Sox
1998	Kerry Wood	Chicago Cubs	1998	Ben Grieve	Oakland Athletics
1999	Scott Williamson	Cincinnati Reds	1999	Carlos Beltran	Kansas City Royals
2000	Rafael Furcal	Atlanta Braves	2000	Kazuhiro Sasaki	Seattle Mariners

1. One player selected as Major League Rookie of the Year. Policy of naming a player from each league was inaugurated in 1949.
Source: Baseball Writer's Association.

Cy Young Award Winners

BOTH LEAGUES

Year	Name, Team	W–L,	ERA	Year	Name, Team	W–L,	ERA
1956	Don Newcombe, Brooklyn Dodgers	27– 7	3.06	1962	Don Drysdale, Los Angeles Dodgers	25– 9,	2.83
1957	Warren Spahn, Milwaukee Braves	21–11	2.69	1963	Sandy Koufax, Los Angeles Dodgers	25– 5,	1.88
1958	Bob Turley, New York Yankees	21– 7	2.97	1964	Dean Chance, Los Angeles Angels	20– 9,	1.65
1959	Early Wynn, Chicago White Sox	22–10	3.17	1965	Sandy Koufax, Los Angeles Dodgers	26– 8,	2.04
1960	Vernon Law, Pittsburgh Pirates	20– 9	3.08	1966	Sandy Koufax, Los Angeles Dodgers	27– 9,	1.73
1961	Whitey Ford, New York Yankees	25– 4	3.21				

NATIONAL LEAGUE

Year	Name, Team	W–L	ERA
1967	Mike McCormick, San Francisco Giants	22–10	2.85
1968	Bob Gibson, St. Louis Cardinals	22– 9	1.12
1969	Tom Seaver, New York Mets	25– 7	2.21
1970	Bob Gibson, St. Louis Cardinals	23– 7	3.12
1971	Ferguson Jenkins, Chicago Cubs	24–13	2.77
1972	Steve Carlton, Philadelphia Phillies	27–10	1.97
1973	Tom Seaver, New York Mets	19–10	2.08
1974	Mike Marshall[1], Los Angeles Dodgers	15–12	2.42
1975	Tom Seaver, New York Mets	22– 9	2.38
1976	Randy Jones, San Diego Padres	22–1	2.74
1977	Steve Carlton, Philadelphia Phillies	23–10	2.64
1978	Gaylord Perry, San Diego Padres	21– 6	2.72
1979	Bruce Sutter[2], Chicago Cubs	6– 6	2.23
1980	Steve Carlton, Philadelphia Phillies	24– 9	2.34
1981	Fernando Valenzuela[3], Los Angeles Dodgers	13– 7	2.48
1982	Steve Carlton, Philadelphia Phillies	23–11	3.10
1983	John Denny, Philadelphia Phillies	19– 6	2.37
1984	Rick Sutcliffe, Chicago Cubs	20– 6	3.64
1985	Dwight Gooden, New York Mets	24– 4	1.53
1986	Mike Scott, Houston Astros	18–10	2.22
1987	Steve Bedrosian[4], Philadelphia Phillies	5– 3	2.83
1988	Orel Hershiser, Los Angeles Dodgers	23– 8	2.26
1989	Mark Davis[5], San Diego Padres	4– 3	1.85
1990	Doug Drabek, Pittsburgh Pirates	22– 6	2.76
1991	Tom Glavine, Atlanta Braves	20–11	2.55
1992	Greg Maddux, Chicago Cubs	20–11	2.18
1993	Greg Maddux, Atlanta Braves	20–10	2.36
1994	Greg Maddux[3], Atlanta Braves	16– 6	1.56
1995	Greg Maddux[3], Atlanta Braves	19– 2	1.53
1996	John Smoltz, Atlanta Braves	24– 8	2.94
1997	Pedro Martinez, Montreal Expos	17– 8	1.90
1998	Tom Glavine, Atlanta Braves	20– 6	2.47
1999	Randy Johnson, Arizona Diamondbacks	17 – 9	2.48
2000	Randy Johnson, Arizona Diamondbacks	19 – 7	2.64

AMERICAN LEAGUE

Year	Name, Team	W–L	ERA
1967	Jim Lonborg, Boston Red Sox	22– 9	3.16
1968	Denny McLain, Detroit Tigers	31– 6	1.96
1969	Mike Cuellar, Baltimore Orioles	23–11	2.38
1970	Jim Perry, Minnesota Twins	24–12	3.03
1971	Vida Blue, Oakland Athletics	24– 8	1.82
1972	Gaylord Perry, Cleveland Indians	24–16	1.92
1973	Jim Palmer, Baltimore Orioles	22– 9	2.40
1974	Catfish Hunter, Oakland Athletics	25–12	2.49
1975	Jim Palmer, Baltimore Orioles	23–11	2.09
1976	Jim Palmer, Baltimore Orioles	22–13	2.51
1977	Sparky Lyle[6], New York Yankees	13– 5	2.17
1978	Ron Guidry, New York Yankees	25– 3	1.74
1979	Mike Flanagan, Baltimore Orioles	23– 9	3.08
1980	Steve Stone, Baltimore Orioles	25– 7	3.23
1981	Rollie Fingers[3,7], Milwaukee Brewers	6– 3	1.04
1982	Pete Vuckovich, Milwaukee Brewers	18– 6	3.34
1983	LaMarr Hoyt, Chicago White Sox	24–10	3.66
1984	Willie Henandez[8], Detroit Tigers	9– 3	1.92
1985	Bret Saberhagen, Kansas City Royals	20– 6	2.87
1986	Roger Clemens, Boston Red Sox	24– 4	2.48
1987	Roger Clemens, Boston Red Sox	20– 9	2.97
1988	Frank Viola, Minnesota Twins	24– 7	2.64
1989	Bret Saberhagen, Kansas City Royals	23– 6	2.16
1990	Bob Welch, Oakland Athletics	27– 6	3.06
1991	Roger Clemens, Boston Red Sox	18–10	3.06
1992	Dennis Eckersley[9], Oakland Athletics	7– 1	1.91
1993	Jack McDowell, Chicago White Sox	22–10	3.37
1994	David Cone[3], Kansas City Royals	16– 5	2.94
1995	Randy Johnson[3], Seattle Mariners	18– 2	2.48
1996	Pat Hentgen, Toronto Blue Jays	20–10	3.22
1997	Roger Clemens, Toronto Blue Jays	21 – 7	2.05
1998	Roger Clemens, Toronto Blue Jays	20 – 6	2.65
1999	Pedro Martinez, Boston Red Sox	23 – 4	2.07
2000	Pedro Martinez, Boston Red Sox	18 – 6	1.74

1. 21 saves in 1974. 2. 37 saves in 1979. 3. Strike-shortened season. 4. 40 saves in 1987. 5. 44 saves in 1989. 6. 26 saves in 1977. 7. 28 saves in 1981. 8. 32 saves in 1984. 9. 51 saves in 1992.

Most Valuable Player Award Winners

Between 1911 and 1914 the Chalmers Award was given to the player judged to be the most valuable in each league. It was not until 1922 that the American League began to select a league MVP. The National League began to do so as well two years later. By the end of the decade , though, both leagues failed to select an MVP. In 1931 the Baseball Writers Association of America began to select the league MVP's and has continued to do so through today.

NATIONAL LEAGUE

Year	Name	Team	HRs	RBIs	Avg.
1911	Frank Schulte	Chicago Cubs	21	121	.300
1912	Larry Doyle	New York Giants	10	90	.330
1913	Jake Daubert	Brooklyn Dodgers	2	52	.350
1914	Johnny Evers	Chicago Cubs	1	40	.279
1924	Dazzy Vance (P)	Brooklyn Dodgers	28W	6L	2.16 ERA
1925	Rogers Hornsby	St. Louis Cardinals	29	143	.403
1926	Bob O'Farrell	St. Louis Cardinals	7	68	.293
1927	Paul Waner	Pittsburgh Pirates	9	131	.380
1928	Jim Bottomley	St. Louis Cardinals	31	136	.325
1929	Rogers Hornsby	St. Louis Cardinals	39	149	.380
1931	Frankie Frisch	St. Louis Cardinals	4	82	.311
1932	Chuck Klein	Philadelphia Phillies	38	137	.348
1933	Carl Hubbell (P)	New York Giants	23W	12L	1.66 ERA
1934	Dizzy Dean (P)	St. Louis Cardinals	30W	7L	2.66 ERA
1935	Gabby Hartnett	Chicago Cubs	13	91	.344
1936	Carl Hubbell (P)	New York Giants	26W	6L	2.31 ERA
1937	Joe Medwick	St. Louis Cardinals	31	154	.374
1938	Ernie Lombardi	Cincinnati Reds	19	95	.342
1939	Bucky Walters (P)	Cinncinati Reds	27W	11L	2.29 ERA
1940	Frank McCormick	Cinncinati Reds	19	127	.309
1941	Dolph Camilli	Brooklyn Dodgers	34	120	.285
1942	Mort Cooper (P)	St. Louis Cardinals	22W	7L	1.78 ERA
1943	Stan Musial	St. Louis Cardinals	13	81	.357
1944	Marty Marion	St. Louis Cardinals	6	63	.267
1945	Phil Cavarretta	Chicago Cubs	6	97	.355
1946	Stan Musial	St. Louis Cardinals	16	103	.365
1947	Bob Elliott	Boston Braves	22	113	.317
1948	Stan Musial	St. Louis Cardinals	39	131	.376
1949	Jackie Robinson	Brooklyn Dodgers	16	124	.342
1950	Jim Konstanty (P)[1]	Philadelphia Phillies	16W	7L	2.66 ERA
1951	Roy Campanella	Brooklyn Dodgers	33	108	.325
1952	Hank Sauer	Chicago Cubs	37	121	.270
1953	Roy Campanella	Brooklyn Dodgers	41	142	.312
1954	Willie Mays	New York Giants	41	110	.345
1955	Roy Campanella	Brooklyn Dodgers	32	107	.318
1956	Don Newcombe (P)	Brooklyn Dodgers	27W	7L	3.06 ERA
1957	Hank Aaron	Milwaukee Braves	44	132	.322
1958	Ernie Banks	Chicago Cubs	47	129	.313
1959	Ernie Banks	Chicago Cubs	45	143	.304
1960	Dick Groat	Pittsburgh Pirates	2	50	.325
1961	Frank Robinson	Cincinnati Reds	37	124	.323
1962	Maury Wills	Los Angeles Dodgers	6	48	.299
1963	Sandy Koufax (P)	Los Angeles Dodgers	25W	5L	1.88 ERA
1964	Ken Boyer	St. Louis Cardinals	24	119	.295
1965	Willie Mays	San Francisco Giants	52	112	.317
1966	Roberto Clemente	Pittsburgh Pirates	29	119	.317
1967	Orlando Cepeda	San Francisco Giants	25	111	.325
1968	Bob Gibson (P)	St. Louis Cardinals	22W	9L	1.12 ERA
1969	Willie McCovey	San Francisco Giants	45	126	.320
1970	Johnny Bench	Cincinnati Reds	45	148	.293
1971	Joe Torre	St. Louis Cardinals	45	137	.363
1972	Johnny Bench	Cincinnati Reds	40	125	.270
1973	Pete Rose	Cincinnati Reds	5	64	.338
1974	Steve Garvey	Los Angeles Dodgers	21	111	.312
1975	Joe Morgan	Cincinnati Reds	17	94	.327
1976	Joe Morgan	Cincinnati Reds	27	111	.320
1977	George Foster	Cincinnati Reds	52	149	.320
1978	Dave Parker	Pittsburgh Pirates	30	117	.334
1979	Keith Hernandez	St. Louis Cardinals	11	105	.344
	Willie Stargell	Pittsburgh Pirates	32	82	.281

NATIONAL LEAGUE

Year	Name	Team	HRs	RBIs	Avg.
1980	Mike Schmidt	Philadelphia Phillies	48	121	.286
1981	Mike Schmidt[2]	Philadelphia Phillies	31	91	.316
1982	Dale Murphy	Atlanta Braves	36	109	.281
1983	Dale Murphy	Atlanta Braves	36	121	.302
1984	Ryne Sandberg	Chicago Cubs	19	84	.314
1985	Willie McGee	St. Louis Cardinals	10	82	.353
1986	Mike Schmidt	Philadelphia Phillies	37	119	.290
1987	Andre Dawson	Chicago Cubs	49	137	.287
1988	Kirk Gibson	Los Angeles Dodgers	25	76	.290
1989	Kevin Mitchell	San Francisco Giants	47	125	.291
1990	Barry Bonds	Pittsburgh Pirates	33	114	.301
1991	Terry Pendleton	Atlanta Braves	22	86	.319
1992	Barry Bonds	Pittsburgh Pirates	34	103	.311
1993	Barry Bonds	San Francisco Giants	46	123	.336
1994	Jeff Bagwell[2]	Houston Astros	39	116	.368
1995	Barry Larkin[2]	Cincinnati Reds	15	66	.319
1996	Ken Caminiti	San Diego Padres	40	130	.326
1997	Larry Walker	Colorado Rockies	49	130	.366
1998	Sammy Sosa	Chicago Cubs	66	158	.308
1999	Chipper Jones	Atlanta Braves	45	110	.319
2000	Jeff Kent	San Francisco Giants	33	125	.334

1. 22 saves in 1950. 2. Strike-shortened season. **Source:** Baseball Writers' Association.

AMERICAN LEAGUE

Year	Player	Team	HRs	RBIs	Avg.
1911	Ty Cobb	Detroit Tigers	8	144	.420
1912	Tris Speaker	Boston Red Sox	10	98	.383
1913	Walter Johnson (P)	Washington Senators	36W	7L	1.09 ERA
1914	Eddie Collins	Philadelphia Athletics	2	85	.344
1922	George Sisler	St. Louis Browns	8	105	.420
1923	Babe Ruth	New York Yankees	41	131	.393
1924	Walter Johnson (P)	Washington Senators	23W	7L	2.72 ERA
1925	Roger Peckinpaugh	Washington Senators	4	64	.294
1926	George Burns	Cleveland Indians	4	114	.358
1927	Lou Gehrig	New York Yankees	47	175	.373
1928	Mickey Cochrane	Philadelphia Athletics	10	57	.293
1931	Lefty Grove (P)	Philadelphia Athletics	31W	4L	2.06 ERA
1932	Jimmie Foxx	Philadelphia Athletics	58	169	.364
1933	Jimmie Foxx	Philadelphia Athletics	48	163	.356
1934	Mickey Cochrane	Detroit Tigers	2	76	.320
1935	Hank Greenberg	Detroit Tigers	36	170	.328
1936	Lou Gehrig	New York Yankees	49	152	.354
1937	Charley Gehringer	Detroit Tigers	14	96	.371
1938	Jimmie Foxx	Boston Red Sox	50	175	.349
1939	Joe DiMaggio	New York Yankees	30	126	.381
1940	Hank Greenberg	Detroit Tigers	30	125	.357
1941	Joe DiMaggio	New York Yankees	30	125	.357
1942	Joe Gordon	New York Yankees	18	103	.322
1943	Spud Chandler (P)	New York Yankees	20W	4L	1.64 ERA
1944	Hal Newhouser (P)	Detroit Tigers	29W	9L	2.22 ERA
1945	Hal Newhouser (P)	Detroit Tigers	25W	9L	1.81 ERA
1946	Ted Williams	Boston Red Sox	38	123	.342
1947	Joe DiMaggio	New York Yankees	20	97	.315
1948	Lou Boudreau	Cleveland Indians	18	106	.355
1949	Ted Williams	Boston Red Sox	43	159	.343
1950	Phil Rizzuto	New York Yankees	7	66	.324
1951	Yogi Berra	New York Yankees	27	88	.294
1952	Bobby Shantz (P)	Philadelphia Athletics	24W	7L	2.48 ERA
1953	Al Rosen	Cleveland Indians	43	145	.336
1954	Yogi Berra	New York Yankees	22	125	.307
1955	Yogi Berra	New York Yankees	27	108	.272
1956	Mickey Mantle	New York Yankees	52	130	.353
1957	Mickey Mantle	New York Yankees	34	94	.365
1958	Jackie Jensen	Boston Red Sox	35	122	.286
1959	Nelson Fox	Chicago White Sox	2	70	.306
1960	Roger Maris	New York Yankees	39	112	.283

AMERICAN LEAGUE

Year	Player	Team	HRs	RBIs	Avg.
1961	Roger Maris	New York Yankees	61	142	.269
1962	Mickey Mantle	New York Yankees	30	89	.321
1963	Elston Howard	New York Yankees	28	85	.287
1964	Brooks Robinson	Baltimore Orioles	28	118	.317
1965	Zoilo Versalles	Minnesota Twins	19	77	.273
1966	Frank Robinson	Baltimore Orioles	49	122	.316
1967	Carl Yastrzemski	Boston Red Sox	44	121	.326
1968	Dennis McLain (P)	Detroit Tigers	31W	6L	1.96ERA
1969	Harmon Killebrew	Minnesota Twins	49	140	.276
1970	Boog Powell	Baltimore Orioles	35	114	.297
1971	Vida Blue (P)	Oakland Athletics	24W	8L	1.82ERA
1972	Dick Allen	Chicago White Sox	37	113	.308
1973	Reggie Jackson	Oakland Athletics	32	117	.293
1974	Jeff Burroughs	Texas Rangers	25	118	.301
1975	Fred Lynn	Boston Red Sox	21	105	.331
1976	Thurman Munson	New York Yankees	17	105	.302
1977	Rod Carew	Minnesota Twins	14	100	.388
1978	Jim Rice	Boston Red Sox	46	139	.315
1979	Don Baylor	California Angels	36	139	.296
1980	George Brett	Kansas City Royals	24	118	.390
1981	Rollie Fingers (P)[1, 2]	Milwaukee Brewers	6W	3L	1.04 ERA
1982	Robin Yount	Milwaukee Brewers	29	114	.331
1983	Cal Ripken Jr.	Baltimore Orioles	27	102	.318
1984	Willie Hernandez (P)[3]	Detroit Tigers	9W	3L	2.48 ERA
1985	Don Mattingly	New York Yankees	35	145	.324
1986	Roger Clemens (P)	Boston Red Sox	24W	4L	2.48 ERA
1987	George Bell	Toronto Blue Jays	47	134	.308
1988	Jose Canseco	Oakland Athletics	42	124	.307
1989	Robin Yount	Milwaukee Brewers	21	103	.318
1990	Rickey Henderson	Oakland Athletics	28	61	.325
1991	Cal Ripken Jr.	Baltimore Orioles	34	114	.323
1992	Dennis Eckersley (P)[4]	Oakland Athletics	7W	1L	1.91 ERA
1993	Frank Thomas	Chicago White Sox	41	128	.317
1994	Frank Thomas[1]	Chicago White Sox	38	101	.353
1995	Mo Vaughn[1]	Boston Red Sox	39	126	.300
1996	Juan Gonzalez	Texas Rangers	47	144	.314
1997	Ken Griffey Jr.	Seattle Mariners	56	147	.304
1998	Juan Gonzalez	Texas Rangers	45	157	.318
1999	Ivan Rodriguez	Texas Rangers	35	113	.332
2000	Jason Giambi	Oakland Athletics	43	137	.333

1. Strike-shortened season. 2. 28 saves in 1981. 3. 32 saves in 1984. 4. 51 saves in 1992. **Source:** Baseball Writers' Association.

All Star Game Results, 1933–2001

Year	Winner, Score	Year	Winner, Score	Year	Winner, Score	Year	Winner, Score
1933	American, 4–2	1950	National, 4–3	1965	National, 6–5	1984	National, 3–1
1934	American, 9–7	1951	National, 8–3	1966	National, 2–1	1985	National , 6–1
1935	American, 4–1	1952	National, 3–2	1967	National, 2–1	1986	American, 3–2
1936	National, 4–3	1953	National, 5–1	1968	National, 1–0	1987	National, 2–0 (10)
1937	American, 8–3	1954	American, 11–9	1969	National, 9–3	1988	American, 2–1
1938	National, 4–1	1955	National, 6–5	1970	National, 5–4	1989	American, 5–3
1939	American, 3–1	1956	National, 7–3	1971	American, 6–4	1990	American, 2–0
1940	National, 4–0	1957	American, 6–5	1972	National, 4–3	1991	American, 4–2
1941	American, 7–5	1958	American, 4–3	1973	National, 7–1	1992	American, 13–6
1942	American, 3–1	1959(1)[1]	National, 5–4	1974	National , 7–2	1993	American, 9–3
1943	American, 5–3	1959(2)	American, 5–3	1975	National, 6–3	1994	National, 8–7 (10)
1944	National, 7–1	1960(1)	National, 5–3	1976	National , 7–1	1995	National, 3–2
1945	No game due to wartime travel restrictions	1960(2)	National , 6–0	1977	National, 7–5	1996	National, 6–0
		1961(1)	National, 5–4	1978	National, 7–3	1997	American, 3–1
		1961(2)	Tie[2], 1–1	1979	National, 7–6	1998	American, 13–8
1946	American, 12–0	1962(1)	National, 3–1	1980	National, 4–2	1999	American, 4–1
1947	American, 2–1	1962(2)	American, 9–4	1981	National, 5–4	2000	American, 6-3
1948	American, 5–2	1963	National, 5–3	1982	National, 4–1	2001	American, 4–1
1949	American, 11–7	1964	National, 7–4	1983	American, 13–3		

1. Two All Star games were played 1959–62. 2. Game was called because of rain after nine innings.

The Baseball Hall of Fame

National Baseball Hall of Fame and Museum
Main Street, Cooperstown, NY 13326.
(607) 547-9988; www.baseballhalloffame.org
Hours: From May 1 to Sept. 30—9:00 a.m. to 9:00 p.m.
From Oct. 1 to April 30—9:00 a.m. to 5:00 p.m. (Closed Thanksgiving, Christmas and New Year's.)

The **Hall of Fame** was established in 1936 and opened in Cooperstown, N.Y. in 1939. From the start, there were two ways to be elected: by receiving 75 percent of the votes cast by the Baseball Writers Association of America or 75 percent of the votes cast by a Committee on Old Timers. In the first year, the writers picked the top five players of the post-1900 era: Ty Cobb, Walter Johnson, Christy Mathewson, Babe Ruth, and Honus Wagner. To be elected, a player must have played at least 10 years in the major leagues and been retired for at least five years. The Committee on Old Timers, originally created to consider 19th Century players, was replaced by a Special Veterans Committee whose scope includes all players retired for a minimum of 25 years who may have been overlooked when they were first eligible. In 1971 a Special Committee on the Negro Leagues was set up to consider ballplayers who played in the old Negro Leagues.

Player/Position/Year Inducted	Games	At Bats	HRs	Avg.	Hits	RBIs
Aaron, Henry (Hank) OF 1982	3,298	12,364	755	.305	3,771	2,297
All-time leader in home runs and RBI						
Anson, Adrian (Cap) 1B 1939	2,276	9,108	96	.334	3,041	1,715
Managed 20 years, 1879-98, winning five pennants						
Aparicio, Luis SS 1984	2,599	10,230	83	.262	2,677	791
Led AL in stolen bases nine years in a row (1955–64)						
Appling, Luke SS 1964	2,422	8,857	45	.310	2,749	1,116
Batted .388 in 1936						
Ashburn, Richie OF 1995	2,189	8,365	29	.308	2,574	586
Hit .300 or more nine times						
Averill, Earl OF 1975	1,669	6,358	238	.318	2,020	1,165
232 hits in 1936						
Baker, Frank (Home Run) 3B 1955	1,575	5,985	96	.307	1,838	1,013
Batted .363 in six World Series						
Bancroft, Dave SS 1971	1,913	7,182	32	.279	2,004	591
Handled 984 chances in 1922						
Banks, Ernie SS, 1B 1977	2,528	9,421	512	.274	2,583	1,636
Consecutive MVP awards, 1958–59						
Beckley, Jake 1B 1971	2,386	9,527	88	.308	2,931	1,575
244 career triples, mostly in 19th Century						
Bench, Johnny C 1989	2,158	7,658	389	.267	2,048	1,376
Hit .529 in 1976 World Series; NL MVP 1970, 1972						
Berra, Lawrence (Yogi) C, OF 1972	2,120	7,555	358	.285	2,150	1,430
Three MVP awards, 1951, 1954, 1955						
Bottomley, Jim 1B 1974	1,991	7,471	219	.310	2,313	1,422
12 RBI in one game, 1924						
Boudreau, Lou SS 1970	1,646	6,030	68	.295	1,779	789
MVP in 1948; managed 16 years						
Bresnahan, Roger C, OF 1945	1,430	4,478	26	.279	1,251	530
212 stolen bases; first catcher elected to Hall of Fame						
Brett, George 3B, 1B 1999	2,707	10,349	317	.305	3,154	1,595
Hit .300 11 times; 13-time all-star; hit .390 in 1980.						
Brock, Lou OF 1985	2,616	10,332	149	.293	3,023	900
938 stolen bases; batted .391 in three World Series						
Brouthers, Dan 1B 1945	1,673	6,716	106	.343	2,304	1,056
Seven slugging and five batting titles during 19th Century						
Burkett, Jesse OF 1946	2,072	8,430	75	.341	2,873	952
Led NL in batting three times and in hits four times						
Campanella, Roy C 1969	1,215	4,205	242	.276	1,161	856
Three MVP awards, 1951, 1953, 1955						
Carey, Max OF 1961	2,476	9,363	69	.285	2,665	800
738 stolen bases						
Cepeda, Orlando 1B 1999	2,124	7,927	379	.297	2,351	1,365
Seven-time All-star; NL MVP 1967; .499 career slugging percentage						
Chance, Frank 1B 1946	1,286	4,295	20	.297	1,274	596
Managed Chicago (NL) to four pennants in five years, 1906–10						
Clarke, Fred OF 1945	2,245	8,588	67	.315	2,708	1,015
223 career triples, hit .300 or better 11 times						
Clemente, Roberto OF 1973	2,433	9,454	240	.317	3,000	1,305
Career average of over 18 outfield assists per season						
Cobb, Ty OF 1936	3,034	11,429	118	.367	4,191	1,961
Batted .320 or better in 23 straight years						
Cochrane, Micky C 1947	1,482	5,169	119	.320	1,652	832
Two MVP awards, 1928 and 1934						

Player/Position/Year Inducted	Games	At Bats	HRs	Avg.	Hits	RBIs
Collins, Eddie 2B 1939	2,826	9,949	47	.333	3,311	1,299
Hit .340 or better 10 times; led AL in fielding nine times						
Collins, Jimmy 3B 1945	1,728	6,796	64	.294	1,997	982
Led NL in home runs, 1898						
Combs, Earle OF 1970	1,454	5,748	58	.325	1,866	629
Averaged 127 runs scored per season						
Connor, Roger 1B 1976	1,998	7,798	136	.318	2,480	1,078
Held all-time HR record before Babe Ruth						
Crawford, Sam OF 1957	2,517	9,580	97	.309	2,964	1,525
312 triples, best ever						
Cronin, Joe SS 1956	2,124	7,579	170	.301	2,285	1,424
MVP in 1930; managed 1933-47						
Cuyler, Hazen (Kiki) OF 1968	1,879	7,161	127	.321	2,299	1,065
Led NL in runs scored twice, stolen bases four times						
Davis, George SS 1998	2,376	9,035	73	.295	2,665	1,435
Hit over .300 nine years in a row (1893–1901)						
Delahanty, Ed IF, OF 1945	1,834	7,502	100	.345	2,591	1,464
Batted .408 in 1899						
Dickey, Bill C 1954	1,789	6,300	202	.313	1,969	1,209
Catcher on eight AL-pennant-winning teams						
DiMaggio, Joe OF 1955	1,736	6,821	361	.325	2,214	1,537
56 game hitting streak in 1941						
Doby, Larry OF 1998	1,533	5,348	253	.283	1,515	969
Led AL in HR twice; seven-time all-star (1949–55); first black man to play in AL						
Doerr, Bobby 2B 1986	1,865	7,093	223	.288	2,042	1,247
Led AL in slugging 1944						
Duffy, Hugh OF 1945	1,736	7,062	103	.328	2,314	1,299
Batted .438 in 1894						
Evers, Johnny 2B 1946	1,783	6,134	12	.270	1,658	538
NL MVP in 1914						
Ewing, Buck C, IF, OF 1939	1,315	5,363	70	.303	1,625	733
Regarded as the greatest player of the 19th Century						
Ferrell, Rick C 1984	1,884	6,028	28	.281	1,692	734
Led AL catchers at times in putouts, assists, fielding average, and double plays						
Fisk, Carlton C 2000	2,499	8,756	376	.269	2,356	1,330
Hit 20 or more home runs 8 times						
Flick, Elmer OF 1963	1,484	5,603	47	.315	1,767	756
Led AL in triples 1905–07						
Fox, Nellie 2B 1997	2,367	9,232	35	.288	2,663	790
Led AL in putouts, 1951–60						
Foxx, Jimmie 1B, 3B 1951	2,317	8,134	534	.325	2,646	1,921
Slugged over .700 three seasons						
Frisch, Frank 2B, 3B 1947	2,311	9,112	105	.316	2,880	1,244
Hit .300 or better 11 years in a row (1921–31)						
Gehrig, Lou 1B 1939	2,164	8,001	493	.340	2,721	1,990
Played in 2,130 consecutive games; first player to hit 4 HRs in one game						
Gehringer, Charlie 2B 1949	2,323	8,860	184	.320	2,839	1,427
60 doubles in 1936						
Goslin, Leon (Goose) OF 1968	2,287	8,655	248	.316	2,735	1,609
100+ RBI 11 years						
Greenberg, Hank 1B 1956	1,394	5,193	331	.313	1,628	1,276
58 home runs in 1938; 63 doubles in 1934						
Hafey, Charles (Chick) OF 1971	1,283	4,625	164	.317	1,466	833
NL batting title (.349) in 1931						
Hamilton, Billy OF 1961	1,593	6284	40	.344	2,163	736
Scored 196 runs in 1894, with a .509 on-base average and 99 stolen bases						
Hartnett, Charles (Gabby) C 1955	1,990	6,432	236	.297	1,912	1,179
Played on four NL pennant winners, managed one						
Heilmann, Harry OF, 1B 1952	2,146	7,787	183	.342	2,660	1551
Batted .403 in 1923						
Herman, Billy 2B 1975	1,922	7,707	47	.304	2,345	839
57 doubles in 1935						
Hooper, Harry OF 1971	2,308	8,785	75	.281	2,466	817
375 career stolen bases						
Hornsby, Rogers 2B, IF 1942	2,259	8,173	301	.358	2,930	1584
Batted .402 in years 1921–25; nine slugging titles						
Jackson, Reggie 1993	2,820	9,864	563	.262	2,584	1,702
Played in 5 World Series and 11 divisional playoffs in 21 years; World Series MVP 1977						
Jackson, Travis SS 1982	1,656	6,086	135	.291	1,768	929
Batted over .300 six times in 1920's and 1930's						
Jennings, Hugh SS 1945	1,285	4,905	18	.312	1,531	840
Batted .398 in 1896						
Kaline, Al OF 1980	2,834	10,116	399	.297	3,007	1,583
3,007 career hits						

Player/Position/Year Inducted	Games	At Bats	HRs	Avg.	Hits	RBIs
Keeler, Willie OF 1939	2,124	8,591	34	.345	2,962	810
Batted .432 in 1897; 495 career stolen bases						
Kell, George 3B 1983	1,795	6,702	78	.306	2,054	870
AL batting champ (.343) in 1949						
Kelley, Joe OF 1971	1,845	7,018	65	.319	2,242	1,193
Averaged 151 runs scored, 1894–96						
Kelly, George 1B 1973	1,622	5,993	148	.297	1,778	1,020
Led NL in RBI, 1920 and 1925						
Kelly, Mike (King) OF, C 1945	1,463	5,923	69	.307	1,820	794
Two batting titles, 1884 and 1886; 315 career stolen bases						
Killebrew, Harmon 1B, 3B, OF 1984	2,435	8,147	573	.256	2,086	1,584
40+ home runs eight years						
Kiner, Ralph OF 1975	1,472	5,205	369	.279	1,451	1,015
Second highest home run per at bat ratio of all-time						
Klein, Chuck OF 1980	1,753	6,486	300	.320	2,076	1,201
44 outfield assists in 1930						
Lajoie, Napoleon (Larry) 2B 1937	2,475	9,589	82	.339	3,251	1,599
Batted .422 in 1901						
Lazerri, Tony IF 1991	1,740	6,297	178	.292	1,840	1,191
Batted .300 or better five times; clutch hitter in World Series						
Lindstrom, Fred 3B, OF 1976	1,438	5,611	103	.311	1,747	779
231 hits in 1928						
Lombardi, Ernie C 1986	1,853	5,855	190	.306	1,792	990
Two NL batting titles, 1938 and 1942						
Mantle, Mickey OF 1974	2,401	8,102	536	.298	2,415	1,509
52 home runs in 1956, 54 in 1961						
Manush, Heinie OF 1964	2,009	7,653	110	.330	2,524	1,173
Hit .378 in 1926						
Maranville, Rabbit SS, 2B 1954	2,670	10,078	28	.258	2,605	884
23 year career; hit .308 in two World Series						
Mathews, Eddie 3B 1978	2,388	8,537	512	.271	2,315	1,453
1,444 career walks						
Mays, Willie OF 1979	2,992	10,881	660	.302	3,283	1,903
Slugged over .600 six seasons						
Mazeroski, Bill 2B 2001	2,163	7,775	138	.260	2,016	853
Eight-time gold glove winner. Turned a record 1,706 double plays.						
McCarthy, Tommy OF 1946	1,275	5,128	44	.292	1,496	666
Averaged 122 runs scored, 1888–94						
McCovey, Willie 1B, OF 1986	2,588	8,197	521	.270	2,211	1,555
Hit 18 career grand slams						
McPhee, Bid 2B 2000	2,135	8,291	53	.279	2,250	727
Considered greatest second baseman of the 19th century, though he played without a glove						
Medwick, Joe OF 1968	1,984	7,635	205	.324	2,471	1,383
Won NL triple crown in 1937						
Mize, Johnny 1B 1981	1,884	6,443	359	.312	2,011	1,337
Four-time NL home run champ						
Morgan, Joe 2B 1990	2,649	9,277	268	.271	2,517	1,133
Won back-to-back MVP Awards (1975–76)						
Musial, Stan OF, 1B 1969	3,026	10,972	475	.331	3,630	1,951
725 doubles and 177 triples						
O'Rourke, Jim OF 1945	1,774	7,435	51	.310	2,304	830
Batted .300+ eleven times in the 19th Century						
Ott, Mel OF 1951	2,732	9,456	511	.304	2,876	1,860
Averaged 121 RBI 1929–38						
Perez, Tony 1B 2000	2,777	9,778	379	.279	2,732	1,652
His 1,652 RBIs are the most ever by a Latin player.						
Puckett, Kirby OF 2001	1,783	7,244	207	.318	2,304	1,085
Led Minnesota Twins to World Series wins in 1987 and 1991. Won AL batting title in 1989.						
Reese, Harold (Pee Wee) SS 1984	2,166	8,058	126	.269	2,170	885
Finished in the top ten of MVP ballotting nine times						
Rice, Sam OF 1963	2,404	9,269	34	.322	2,987	1,078
Only 18 strikeouts per 154 games						
Rizzuto, Phil SS 1994	1,661	5,816	38	.273	1,588	563
AL MVP in 1950; Played in 9 World Series						
Robinson, Brooks 3B 1983	2,896	10,654	268	.267	2,848	1357
16 consecutive Gold Gloves, 1960–75						
Robinson, Frank OF 1982	2,808	10,006	586	.294	2,943	1812
MVP in both leagues; AL triple crown in 1966						
Robinson, Jackie 2B 1962	1,382	4,877	137	.311	1,518	734
First black player in MLB; Rookie of the Year 1947; MVP and batting champ 1949						
Roush, Edd OF 1962	1,967	7,363	68	.323	2,376	981
Two NL batting titles, 1917 and 1919						
Ruth, George (Babe) OF, P 1936	2,503	8,399	714	.342	2,873	2211
Slugged .847 1920–21						

Player/Position/Year Inducted	Games	At Bats	HRs	Avg.	Hits	RBIs
Schalk, Ray C 1955	1,760	5,306	12	.253	1,345	594
176 stolen bases						
Schmidt, Mike 3B 1995	2,404	8,352	548	.267	2,234	1,595
Led NL in homers 8 times; won 10 Gold Gloves						
Schoendienst, Albert (Red) 1989	2,216	8,479	84	.289	2,449	773
Managed Cardinals to two pennants and 1967 World Series crown						
Sewell, Joe SS, 3B 1977	1,902	7,132	49	.312	2,226	1,051
Only 22 strikeouts in his last 2,500 at bats, 1929–33						
Simmons, Al OF 1953	2,215	8,761	307	.334	2,927	1,827
Drove in over 100 runs in each of his first 11 years, 1924–34						
Sisler, George 1B 1939	2,055	8,267	100	.340	2,812	1,175
Batted .400 1920–22						
Slaughter, Enos OF 1985	2,380	7,946	169	.300	2,383	1,304
52 doubles in 1939						
Snider, Edwin (Duke) OF 1980	2,143	7,161	407	.295	2,116	1,333
Averaged 41 home runs, 1953–57						
Speaker, Tris OF 1937	2,789	10,208	117	.344	3,515	1,559
Led AL in doubles eight times						
Stargell, Willie OF, 1B 1988	2,360	7,927	475	.282	2,232	1,540
MVP in 1979						
Terry, Bill 1B 1954	1,721	6,428	154	.341	2,193	1,078
Hit .401 in 1930						
Thompson, Sam OF 1974	1,410	6,005	128	.331	1,986	1,299
166 RBI in 1887, 165 in 1895						
Tinker, Joe SS 1946	1,805	6,441	31	.263	1,695	782
Played in four World Series with Chicago Cubs						
Traynor, Pie 3B 1948	1,941	7,559	58	.320	2,416	1,273
100+ RBI seven years						
Vaughan, Joseph (Arky) SS 1985	1,817	6,622	96	.318	2,103	926
.385 in 1935						
Wagner, Honus SS 1936	2786	10,427	101	.329	3,430	1,732
Eight batting titles, four in a row 1906–09						
Wallace, Bobby SS 1953	2,386	8,652	35	.267	2,314	1,121
Handled 6.1 chances per game at shortstop.						
Waner, Lloyd OF 1967	1,992	7,772	28	.316	2,459	598
234 hits in 1929						
Waner, Paul OF 1952	2,549	9,459	112	.333	3,152	1,309
62 doubles in 1932						
Wheat, Zack OF 1959	2,410	9,106	132	.317	2,884	1,261
Batted .375 at age 36 in 1924						
Williams, Billy OF 1987	2,488	9,350	426	.290	2,711	1,475
30+ home runs in five seasons						
Williams, Ted OF 1966	2,292	7,706	521	.344	2,654	1,839
Last .400 hitter in majors, .406 in 1941						
Wilson, Lewis (Hack) OF 1979	1,348	4,760	244	.307	1,461	1,062
56 home runs and 190 RBI in 1930						
Winfield, Dave OF 2001	2,973	11,003	465	.283	3,110	1,833
Member of both the 3,000-hit and 400-home run club.						
Yastrzemski, Carl (Yaz) OF, 1B 1989	3,308	11,988	452	.285	3,419	1,844
Won Triple Crown in 1967; won batting titles in 1963, 1967, and 1968						
Youngs, Ross OF 1972	1,211	4,627	42	.322	1,491	592
Killed at age 30; .398 on-base average in four World Series, 1921–24.						
Yount, Robin SS, OF 1999	2,856	11,008	251	.285	3,142	1,406
Won AL MVP awards at shortstop (1982) and center field (1989), the only player ever to do so.						

Source: Major League Baseball.

▶FUTURE HALL OF FAMERS

While there are no specific criteria for election to the Hall of Fame, certain benchmark numbers almost guarantee enshrinement. For many years, those numbers were 3,000 hits or 400 home runs. Every eligible player with 3,000 hits—Pete Rose, banned for life from baseball, is ineligible—and all but two (Dave Kingman and Darrell Evans) of the eligible players with 400 home runs are in the Hall of Fame. Although given the ease with which players are hitting homers these days, the bar may have to be raised to 500 homers.

Assuming the status quo, however, the following players who have retired in the past several years should start booking hotel reservations in Cooperstown: **Paul Molitor** (3,319 hits), **Eddie Murray** (3,255 hits and 504 home runs) and **Wade Boggs** (3,010 hits). Two other members of the 3,000- hit club, **Tony Gwynn**, and **Cal Ripken Jr.**, both retired at the end of the 2001 season.

Rickey Henderson, the all-time leader in runs scored and stolen bases, will ultimately make the Hall, but he has to retire first: the 42-year-old outfielder was still contributing for the San Diego Padres in 2001.

Lee Smith, the all-time leader in saves with 473, may join Hoyt Wilhelm and Rollie Fingers as the only relievers in the Hall. The only active pitchers likely to be enshrined are **Roger Clemens** with five Cy Young awards, and **Greg Maddux**, with four (as of October, 2001).

Hall of Fame Pitchers

Player/Year Inducted	W	L	ERA	Games	Innings	Strikeouts
Alexander, Grover Cleveland 1938	373	208	2.56	696	5,189	2,199
Won 30 games three years; led NL in ERA five times						
Bender, Charles (Chief) 1953	210	127	2.46	459	3,017	1,711
Led AL in winning percentage three seasons						
Brown, Mordecai (Three-Finger) 1949	239	129	2.06	481	3,172	1,375
1.04 ERA in 1906						
Bunning, Jim 1996	224	184	3.27	591	3,760	2,855
Struck out 1,000 batters in each league						
Carlton, Steve (Lefty) 1994	329	244	3.22	741	5,217	4,136
Four-time Cy Young Award winner (1972, 1977, 1980, 1982)						
Chesbro, Jack 1946	198	132	2.68	392	2,897	1,265
41 wins in 1904						
Clarkson, John 1963	326	177	2.81	531	4,536	2,015
53 wins in 1885, with 623 innings pitched						
Coveleski, Stan 1969	215	142	2.88	450	3,093	981
Led AL in ERA in 1925, 2.84						
Cummings, Williams (Candy) 1939	21	22	2.78	43	372	37
Inventor of the curveball						
Dean, Jay (Dizzy) 1953	150	83	3.03	317	1,966	1,155
30 wins in 1934						
Drysdale, Don 1984	209	166	2.95	518	3,432	2,486
56 2/3 consecutive scoreless innings, 1968						
Faber, Urban (Red) 1964	254	212	3.15	669	4,088	1,471
Led AL in ERA in 1921 and 1922						
Feller, Bob 1962	266	162	3.25	570	3,827	2,581
Led AL in wins six times, in shutouts seven						
Rollie Fingers 1992	114	118	2.90	944	1,701	1,299
341 saves over 17 years; AL MVP in 1981						
Ford, Edward (Whitey) 1974	236	106	2.75	498	3,170	1,956
25–4 in 1961, 24–7 in 1963						
Galvin, James (Pud) 1965	361	310	2.87	697	5,941	1,799
46 wins in 1883 and 1884						
Gibson, Bob 1981	251	174	2.91	528	3,885	3,117
1.12 ERA in 1968, seven straight wins in World Series play						
Gomez, Vernon (Lefty) 1972	189	102	3.34	368	2,503	1,468
Led AL in shutouts three years						
Grimes, Burleigh 1964	270	212	3.53	617	4,180	1,512
Last legal spitball pitcher, he won 20+ five times						
Grove, Robert (Lefty) 1947	300	141	3.06	616	3,941	2,266
Led AL in ERA nine times, in strikeouts seven						
Haines, Jesse 1970	210	158	3.64	555	3,209	981
Twice led NL in shutouts, 1921 and 1927						
Hoyt, Waite 1969	237	182	3.59	674	3,763	1,206
1.83 in 84 World Series innings						
Hubbell, Carl 1947	253	154	2.97	535	3,589	1,678
26–6 in 1936; 1.66 ERA in 1933						
Hunter, Jim (Catfish) 1987	224	166	3.26	500	3,448	2,012
21 or more wins, 1971–75						
Jenkins, Ferguson 1991	284	226	3.34	664	4,499	3,192
Cy Young Award winner in 1971; three-time all-star						
Johnson, Walter 1936	416	279	2.17	802	5,924	3,508
36–7, 1.09 ERA in 1913						
Joss, Addie 1978	160	97	1.88	286	2,336	926
Averaged 21–11, 1.66 ERA in years 1904–08						
Keefe, Tim 1964	344	225	2.62	601	5,072	2,533
Averaged 37 wins 1883–85						
Koufax, Sandy 1972	165	87	2.76	397	2,324	2,396
95–27, 1.85 ERA for seasons 1963-66						
Lemon, Bob 1976	207	128	3.23	460	2,850	1,277
Won 20 or more seven times						
Lyons, Ted 1955	260	230	3.67	594	4,161	1,073
Pitched 27 shutouts, but never won 20 games.						
Marichal, Juan 1983	243	142	2.89	471	3,509	2,303
Only 1.8 walks per nine innings over career						
Marquard, Richard (Rube) 1971	201	177	3.08	536	3,307	1,593
73–23 in years 1911–13						
Mathewson, Christy 1936	373	188	2.13	636	4,782	2,502
80 career shutouts						
McGinnity, Joe 1946	247	144	2.64	466	3,459	1,068
35–8 in 1904, with an ERA of 1.61						
Newhouser, Hal 1992	207	150	3.06	488	2,993	1,796
Led AL in victories three years in a row (1944–46)						

Player/Year Inducted	W	L	ERA	Games	Innings	Strikeouts
Nichols, Charles (Kid) 1949	360	203	2.94	621	5,084	1,885
Won 30 or more games seven straight seasons, 1891–1897						
Niekro, Phil 1997	318	274	3.35	864	5,404	3,342
Knuckleballer pitched until age 48; five-time all-star						
Palmer, Jim 1990	268	152	2.86	558	3,948	2,212
Won Cy Young Award 1973, 1975, 1976						
Pennock, Herb 1948	240	162	3.61	617	3,558	1,227
162–90 as a New York Yankee, 1923–33						
Perry, Gaylord 1991	314	265	3.10	777	5,352	3,534
Won Cy Young Award in both leagues						
Plank, Eddie 1946	327	193	2.34	622	4,505	2,246
1.32 ERA in seven World Series games						
Radbourn, Charles (Old Hoss) 193	308	191	2.67	528	4,535	1,830
60–12 in 1884, with 679 innings pitched						
Rixey, Eppa 1963	266	251	3.15	692	4,495	1,350
Won 25 games in 1922						
Roberts, Robin 1976	286	245	3.41	676	4,689	2,357
28–7 in 1952; five-time NL leader in complete games						
Ruffing, Charles (Red) 1967	273	225	3.80	624	4,344	1,987
.645 winning percentage as a New York Yankee						
Rusie, Amos 1977	243	160	3.07	462	3,770	1,957
Won 30+ games three years						
Ryan, Nolan 1999	324	292	3.19	807	5,386	5,714
Threw seven no-hitters; struck out 300 or more six times; struck out 200 or more 15 times						
Seaver, Tom 1992	311	205	2.86	656	4,782	3,640
Won 20 or more games five times; won Cy Young Award 1969, 1973, 1975						
Spahn, Warren 1973	363	245	3.09	750	5,244	2,583
Won 20 or more games 13 times, including 23 at age 42						
Sutton, Don 1998	324	256	3.26	774	5,280	3,574
Won 15 or more games eight years in a row (1969–76)						
Vance, Clarence (Dazzy) 1955	197	140	3.24	442	2,697	2,045
60–15 over two years—1924, 1925						
Waddell, George (Rube) 1946	191	145	2.16	407	2,961	2,316
349 strikeouts in 1904						
Walsh, Ed 1946	195	126	1.82	430	2,964	1,736
40–15 in 1908 with 11 shutouts; all-time ERA leader						
Ward, Monte 1964	161	101	2.10	291	2,462	920
47 wins in 1879; 40 wins in 1880; played 1,825 games as a hitter						
Welch, Mickey 1973	311	207	2.71	564	4,802	1,850
44–11 in 1885						
Wilhelm, Hoyt 1985	143	122	2.52	1070	2,254	1,610
227 career saves; first relief pitcher elected to Hall of Fame						
Willis, Vic 1995	249	205	2.63	513	3,996	1,651
Won 20 games eight times; 45 complete games in 1902						
Wynn, Early 1972	300	244	3.54	691	4,564	2,334
Led AL in shutouts at age 40 in 1960						
Young, Cy 1937	511	313	2.63	906	7,359	2,799
All-time leader in wins, losses, complete games, and innings pitched.						

Managers
Alston, Walter 1983
Anderson, Sparky 2000
Durocher, Leo 1994
Hanlon, Ned 1996
Harris, Bucky 1975
Huggins, Miller 1964
Lasorda, Tommy 1997
Lopez, Al 1977
Mack, Connie 1937
McCarthy, Joe 1957
McGraw, John 1937
McKechnie, Bill 1962
Robinson, Wilbert 1945
Selee, Frank, 1999
Stengel, Casey 1966
Weaver, Earl 1996

Umpires
Barlick, Al 1989
Chylak, Nestor, 1999
Conlan, Jocko 1974
Connolly, Tom 1953
Evans, Billy 1973

Hubbard, Cal 1976
Klem, Bill 1953
McGowan, Bill 1992

Pioneers and Executives
Barrow, Ed 1953
Bulkeley, Morgan 1937
Cartwright, Alexander 1938
Chadwick, Henry 1938
Chandler, Happy 1982
Comiskey, Charles 1939
Foster, Andrew (Rube) 1981
Frick, Ford 1970
Giles, Warren 1979
Griffith, Clark 1946
Harridge, William 1972
Hulbert, William 1995
Johnson, Ban 1937
Landis, Kenesaw Mountain 1944
MacPhail, Larry 1978
MacPhail, Lee 1998
Rickey, Branch 1967
Spalding, Albert Goodwill 1939
Veeck, Bill 1991

Weiss, George 1971
Wright, George 1937
Wright, Harry 1953
Yawkey, Tom 1980

Negro Leaguers
Bell, James "Cool Papa" 1974
Charleston, Oscar 1976
Dandridge, Ray 1987
Day, Leon 1995
Dihigo, Martin 1977
Foster, Bill 1996
Gibson, Josh 1972
Irvin, Monte 1973
Johnson, Judy 1975
Leonard, William "Buck" 1972
Lloyd, Pop 1977
Paige, Satchel 1971
Rogan, "Bullet" Joe 1998
Smith, Hilton 2001
Stearnes, Turkey 2000
Wells, Willie 1997
Williams, "Smokey Joe", 1999

Major League Baseball League Championship Series Results

AMERICAN LEAGUE

Year	Winner	Loser	MVP
1969	Baltimore Orioles-3	Minnesota Twins-0	
1970	Baltimore Orioles-3	Minnesota Twins-0	
1971	Baltimore Orioles-3	Oakland A's-0	
1972	Oakland A's-3	Detroit Tigers-2	
1973	Oakland A's-3	Baltimore Orioles-2	
1974	Oakland A's-3	Baltimore Orioles-1	
1975	Boston Red Sox-3	Oakland A's-0	
1976	New York Yankees-3	Kansas City Royals-2	
1977	New York Yankees-3	Kansas City Royals-2	
1978	New York Yankees-3	Kansas City Royals-1	
1979	Baltimore Orioles-3	California Angels-1	
1980	Kansas City Royals-3	New York Yankees-0	Frank White, Kansas City
1981	New York Yankees-3	Oakland A's-0	Graig Nettles, New York
1982	Milwaukee Brewers-3	California Angels-2	Fred Lynn, California
1983	Baltimore Orioles-3	Chicago White Sox-1	Mike Boddicker, Baltimore
1984	Detroit Tigers-3	Kansas City Royals-0	Kirk Gibson, Detroit
1985[1]	Kansas City Royals-4	Toronto Blue Jays	George Brett, Kansas City
1986	Boston Red Sox-4	California Angels-3	Marty Barrett, Boston
1987	Minnesota Twins-4	Detroit Tigers-1	Gary Gaetti, Minnesota
1988	Oakland A's-4	Boston Red Sox-0	Dennis Eckersley, Oakland
1989	Oakland A's-4	Toronto Blue Jays-1	Rickey Henderson, Oakland
1990	Oakland A's-4	Boston Red Sox-0	Dave Stewart, Oakland
1991	Minnesota Twins-4	Toronto Blue Jays-1	Kirby Puckett, Minnesota
1992	Toronto Blue Jays-4	Oakland Athletics-2	Roberto Alomar, Toronto
1993	Toronto Blue Jays-4	Chicago White Sox-2	Dave Stewart, Toronto
1994	No League Championship Series		
1995	Cleveland Indians-4	Seattle Mariners-2	Orel Hershiser, Cleveland
1996	New York Yankees-4	Baltimore Orioles-1	Bernie Williams, New York
1997	Cleveland Indians-4	Baltimore Orioles-2	Marquis Grissom, Cleveland
1998	New York Yankees-4	Cleveland Indians-2	David Wells, New York
1999	New York Yankees-4	Boston Red Sox-1	Orlando Hernandez, New York
2000	New York Yankees-4	Seattle Mariners-2	David Justice, New York
2001	New York Yankees-4	Seattle Mariners-1	Andy Pettitte, New York

NATIONAL LEAGUE

Year	Winner	Loser	MVP
1969	New York Mets-3	Atlanta Braves-0	
1970	Cincinnati Reds-3	Pittsburgh Pirates-0	
1971	Pittsburgh Pirates-3	San Francisco Giants-1	
1972	Cincinnati Reds-3	Pittsburgh Pirates-2	
1973	New York Mets-3	Cincinnati Reds-2	
1974	Los Angeles Dodgers-3	Pittsburgh Pirates-1	
1975	Cincinnati Reds-3	Pittsburgh Pirates-0	
1976	Cincinnati Reds-3	Philadelphia Phillies-0	
1977	Los Angeles Dodgers-3	Philadelphia Phillies-1	Dusty Baker, Los Angeles
1978	Los Angeles Dodgers-3	Philadelphia Phillies-1	Steve Garvey, Los Angeles
1979	Pittsburgh Pirates-3	Cincinnati Reds-0	Willie Stargell, Pittsburgh
1980	Philadelphia Phillies-3	Houston Astros-2	Manny Trillo, Philadelphia
1981	Los Angeles Dodgers-3	Montreal Expos-2	Burt Hooton, Los Angeles
1982	St. Louis Cardinals-3	Atlanta Braves-0	Darrell Porter, St. Louis
1983	Philadelphia Phillies-3	Los Angeles Dodgers-1	Gary Mathews, Philadelphia
1984	San Diego Padres-3	Chicago Cubs-2	Steve Garvey, San Diego
1985[1]	St. Louis Cardinals-4	Los Angeles Dodgers-2	Ozzie Smith, St. Louis
1986	New York Mets-4	Houston Astros-2	Mike Scott, Houston
1987	St. Louis Cardinals-4	San Francisco Giants-3	Jeff Leonard, San Francisco
1988	Los Angeles Dodgers-4	New York Mets-3	Orel Hershiser, Los Angeles
1989	San Francisco Giants-4	Chicago Cubs-1	Will Clark, San Francisco
1990	Cincinnati Reds-4	Pittsburgh Pirates-2	Rob Dibble, Rany Myers, Cincinnati
1991	Atlanta Braves-4	Pittsburgh Pirates-3	Steve Avery, Atlanta
1992	Atlanta Braves-4	Pittsburgh Pirates-3	John Smoltz, Atlanta
1993	Philadelphia Phillies-4	Atlanta Braves-2	Curt Schilling, Philadelphia
1994	No League Championship Series		
1995	Atlanta Braves-4	Cincinnati Reds-0	Mike Devereaux, Atlanta
1996	Atlanta Braves-4	St. Louis Cardinals-3	Javier Lopez, Atlanta
1997	Florida Marlins-4	Atlanta Braves-2	Livan Hernández, Florida
1998	San Diego Padres-4	Atlanta Braves-2	Sterling Hitchcock, San Diego
1999	Atlanta Braves-4	New York Mets-2	Eddie Perez, Atlanta
2000	New York Mets-4	St. Louis Cardinals-1	Mike Hampton, New York
2001	Arizona Diamondbacks-4	Atlanta Braves-1	Craig Counsell, Arizona

1. In 1985 the League Championship Series was switched to a best-of-seven format.

The World Series

A championship series between the winners of two leagues had been instituted in 1882 between the National League and the American Association, and was played at the end of each season until the A.A. folded in 1890. Following this, the top two N.L. clubs played each other for the "Temple Cup", but the idea never really caught on with the public. When the American League began operations in 1901, there was great animosity between the two circuits due to bidding wars for the services of star players. Peace was established before the 1903 season, and when it became clear that Pittsburgh would win the NL and Boston the AL, the owners of each club reached a private agreement to hold a "World Series" in October. Many were surprised that the newer American League won the title.

There was no agreement to play such a series every year, however, and in 1904 the New York Giants refused to meet the Boston club, probably due to John McGraw's dislike of American League President Ban Johnson. But the baseball public wanted a championship series, and by 1905 Giants owner John Brush proposed rules governing a mandatory series to be played every year. With minute changes, those rules stand to this day.

1903 Boston (A) over Pittsburgh (N), 5–3. The upstart American league emerged victorious in the first World Series, a best of nine affair. The "Pilgrims" (Red Sox) staged one of the greatest comebacks in history by sweeping the final four games. Bill Dineen won three and Cy Young won two for Boston, and held Pirate immortal Honus Wagner to a .222 average.

1904 No series. New York Giant owner John T. Brush and manager John McGraw refused to play the World Champion Boston club, dismissing them as representative of an "inferior league."

1905 New York (N) over Philadelphia (A), 4–1. Every game was a shutout, with Cristy Mathewson throwing three for the Giants. In 27 innings, he allowed 14 hits, striking out 18 and walking one. The Athletics committed five errors in Game 3, the pivotal contest.

1906 Chicago (A) over Chicago (N), 4–2. The first "subway series" was a stunning upset. The "Hitless Wonders" White Sox had batted .230 with 7 home runs during the season, while the Cubs were winning 116 games, still the all-time record. Utilityman George Rohe hit two game-winning triples for the Sox and Ed Walsh pitched two of their wins.

1907 Chicago (N) over Detroit (A), 4–0. The Cubs shut down Ty Cobb, Sam Crawford et al, behind a superb four-man pitching performance, and the hitting of Harry Steinfeldt (.471) and Johnny Evers (.350).

1908 Chicago (N) over Detroit (A), 4–1. Only a little closer this year. Johnny Evers repeated his .350 average of 1907, joining player-manager Frank Chance (.421) and outfielder Wildfire Schulte (.389) in the Cub attack. Ty Cobb led Detroit (.368), to no avail.

1909 Pittsburgh (N) over Detroit (A), 4–3. The Tigers lost their third straight series, as Honus Wagner won the Battle of the Titans with Ty Cobb. The Pirate shortstop hit .333 with six RBI and six stolen bases, and Babe Adams pitched in with three complete game victories.

1910 Philadelphia (A) over Chicago (N), 4–1. Connie Mack's infielders combined to bat .364 as the A's rolled to an easy title. Jack Coombs pitched three wins and tossed in a .385 batting average. The great Cubs pitching staff was growing old.

1911 Philadelphia (A) over New York (N), 4–2. Regarded by some as the greatest team ever, the A's wrestled down a strong New York club featuring Christy Mathewson and Rube Marquard. Frank "Home Run" Baker got his nickname from game-winning blasts in Games Two and Three.

1912 Boston (A) over New York (N), 4–3. This thrill-a-minute series featured an 11-inning tie in Game Two, and an extra-inning final game. Errors by Giants Fred Merkle and Fred Snodgrass enabled Boston to score two runs in the bottom of the tenth inning of the final contest.

1913 Philadelphia (A) over New York (N), 4–1. Home Run Baker again hammered Giant pitching, batting .450 with seven RBI. Eddie Collins also starred for the A's, hitting .421 with three stolen bases.

1914 Boston (N) over Philadelphia (A), 4–0. The red-hot "Miracle Braves" swept the heavily favored Athletics, who scored only six runs in the four games. Catcher Hank Gowdy (.545) and second baseman Johnny Evers (.438) led the Boston offense.

1915 Boston (A) over Philadelphia (N), 4–1. The famous Red Sox outfield of Speaker, Lewis, and Hooper combined to bat .364 while Rube Foster pitched two complete game wins. Foster also batted .500 driving in the winning run in Game Two.

1916 Boston (A) over Brooklyn (N), 4–1. After three one-run games, Boston took charge with 6–2 and 4–1 victories. A young lefthander named Babe Ruth twirled a 14-inning six hitter in Game Two.

1917 Chicago (A) over New York (N), 4–2. The pitching of Red Faber (3-1, 2.33) and the hitting of Eddie Collins, Buck Weaver, and Joe Jackson were too much for the Giants in a sloppy (23 errors) series.

1918 Boston (A) over Chicago (N), 4–2. Every game was a pitchers' duel. The losing Cubs posted a 1.04 ERA over the six games. The Boston staff allowed but nine runs in the series, led by Babe Ruth who extended his consecutive scoreless inning streak to 29⅔.

1919 Cincinnati (N) over Chicago (A), 5–3. The results of this surprising World Series were declared invalid after eight members of the "Black Sox," including Shoeless Joe Jackson, were accused of throwing games for money. A court later found the Chicago players not guilty (most of them never even received the money from the gamblers with whom they conspired), but commissioner Kenesaw Mountain Landis nonetheless barred them from baseball forever.

1920 Cleveland (A) over Brooklyn (N), 5–2. Game Five was surely the most freakish in series history. It featured a) the first World Series grand slam (Indians rightfielder Elmer Smith), b) the first World Series home run by a pitcher (Indians Jim Bagby), and c) the first and only unassisted triple play in series action (Indians second baseman Billy Wambsganss).

1921 New York (N) over New York (A), 5–3. Six Giants batted over .300, and their pitchers held Babe Ruth to a .500 slugging average. Giant hurler Jesse Barnes won two games and batted .444.

1922 New York (N) over New York (A), 4–0. The result was said to be final proof that "brains beat brawn." Giant pitching shut down Babe Ruth, allowing only 11 runs in the five contests (one tie).

1923 New York (A) over New York (N), 4–2. The Yankees took the last three to break the spell of their cross-river rivals, behind Babe Ruth's three homers and .368 average. Casey Stengel hit two home runs for the losers.

1924 Washington (A) over New York (N), 4–3. A 12-inning seventh game won by Walter Johnson in relief capped an exciting affair. Player-manager Bucky Harris starred for the Senators (.333, 7 RBIs), as did outfielder Goose Goslin (.344, 7 RBIs).

1925 Pittsburgh (N) over Washington (A), 4–3. Pirate centerfielder Max Carey had 11 hits and three stolen bases, as Pittsburgh became the first team since 1903 to come back from a three games to one deficit.

1926 St. Louis (N) over New York (A), 4–3. Babe Ruth hit three homers in Game 4, but in the seventh inning of the seventh contest, Grover Cleveland Alexander struck out Tony Lazzeri with the bases loaded, saving the game and the series for the Cardinals.

1927 New York (A) over Pittsburgh (N), 4–0. Generally regarded as the greatest team of all time, the "Murderers Row" Yankees disposed of the Pirates behind two Babe Ruth homers, plus the pitching of Wilcy Moore, Herb Pennock, and George Pipgras.

1928 New York (A) over St. Louis (N), 4–0. Another Yankee sweep. Ruth and Lou Gehrig combined to bat .593, with seven home runs and 13 RBI. Waite Hoyt pitched two complete game victories.

1929 Philadelphia (A) over Chicago (N), 4–1. Trailing 8-0 in Game 4, the A's roared back to score 10 runs in the seventh inning. In the next contest, the Mackmen took the series with a three-run ninth inning.

1930 Philadelphia (A) over St. Louis (N), 4–2. Lefty Grove and George Earnshaw pitched well, while Al Simmons, Jimmie Foxx, and Mickey Cochrane combined for 11 extra-base hits. Cardinal regulars batted only .185 in the six games.

1931 St. Louis (N) over Philadelphia (A), 4–3. Cardinal centerfielder Pepper Martin set a record that stood for 33 years with his 12 hits. Martin also stole five bases and hit a home run. Bill Hallahan and Burleigh Grimes handled the pitching, combining for a 4–0, 1.25 ERA.

1932 New York (A) over Chicago (N), 4–0. The Yankees completed a streak of 12 straight World Series victories in sweeping the Cubs. Babe Ruth and Lou Gehrig combined to bat .438, with five homers and 14 RBI.

1933 New York (N) over Washington (A), 4–1. Bill Terry's Giants defeated Joe Cronin's Senators in a battle of player-managers. Carl Hubbell won two for New York and did not allow an earned run.

1934 St. Louis (N) over Detroit (A), 4–3. Dizzy and Paul Dean hurled the Cardinals to the title, winning all four Redbird victories. A bad defensive series, with 27 errors and 13 unearned runs.

1935 Detroit (A) over Chicago (N), 4–2. The Cubs won 21 straight games in September, but came up short against Mickey Cochrane's Tigers. Charlie Gehringer and Tommy Bridges starred for Detroit, while Lou Warneke (2–0, 0.54) was superb for the losers.

1936 New York (A) over New York (N), 4–2. The Yankees hammered Giant pitching in Games 2 and 6, ending with 43 runs for the series. Tony Lazzeri and Bill Dickey each drove in five runs in the second contest, when Joe McCarthy's "Windowbreakers" scored 18 times to set a record.

1937 New York (A) over New York (N), 4–1. Lefty Gomez pitched two of the Yankee wins and drove in the winning run with a single in the final game. The Yanks scored seven runs in the sixth inning of Game 1, then coasted to an easy championship.

1938 New York (A) over Chicago (N), 4–0. In a replay of 1932, the Bronx Bombers blew out an overmatched Cub squad. Cub fans are still waiting for their team's first series victory over the Yankees.

1939 New York (A) over Cincinnati (N), 4–0. New York won its fourth straight World Championship the same way they won the first three—easily. Charlie Keller batted .438 with three homers, and scored as many runs as the entire Reds team, eight.

1940 Cincinnati (N) over Detroit (A), 4–3. The Reds repeated as NL champs, then prevailed over the Tigers when Paul Derringer beat Bobo Newsome 2–1 in the seventh game. Derringer and Bucky Walters each won two games.

1941 New York (A) over Brooklyn (N), 4–1. With two outs in the ninth inning of Game Four, Dodger catcher Mickey Owen dropped a third strike on Tommy Henrich, allowing him to reach first base. The Yankees then scored four times to win the ballgame, and finished Brooklyn off the next day.

1942 St. Louis (N) over New York (A), 4–1. The Cardinals, winners of 106 games during the regular season, lost Game 1 with the tying run at bat. They then swept four in a row, behind the pitching of Johnny Beazley (2–0, 2.50) and Ernie White's shutout in Game 3.

1943 New York (A) over St. Louis (N), 4–1. In a turnaround from 1942, the Yanks held St. Louis to nine runs in the five games. Joe Gordon and Bill Dickey homered, while third baseman Billy Johnson drove in three runs for New York.

1944 St. Louis (N) over St. Louis (A), 4–2. The Browns struggled valiantly in their only World Series appearance, but fell short against a strong Cardinal club left relatively intact by World War II. Ten Browns errors gave the Redbirds 7 unearned runs.

1945 Detroit (A) over Chicago (N), 4–3. Tiger ace Hal Newhouser was hit hard in Game 1, but he bounced back to win Games 5 and 7. Doc Cramer (.379) and Hank Greenberg (2 HR, 7 RBIs) led the Detroit offense.

1946 St. Louis (N) over Boston (A), 4–3 Enos Slaughter scored from first on a base-hit by Harry Walker in the eighth inning of Game 7, giving St. Louis its third title in five years. Harry Brecheen won three games for the Cardinals, allowing but one run.

1947 New York (A) over Brooklyn (N), 4–3. Yankee pitcher Bill Bevens had a no-hitter for 8⅔ innings in Game 4, but lost the game on a double by Cookie Lavagetto. Tommy Henrich (.323) had the game winning RBI in Games 1, 2, and 7.

1948 Cleveland (A) over Boston (N), 4–2. The series featured fine pitching on both sides, including the first game, when Boston's Johnny Sain beat Bob Feller 1–0. Cleveland's Gene Beardon did not allow a run in 10⅔ innings.

1949 New York (A) over Brooklyn (N), 4–1. Game 1 was 0–0 until Tommy Henrich led off the bottom of the ninth with a home run off Don Newcombe. Bobby Brown batted .500 with five RBIs.

1950 New York (A) over Philadelphia (N), 4–0. New York struggled to win the first three contests by scores of 1-0, 2-1, and 3–2, in a series that was closer than it looks. The "Whiz Kid" Phillies held the Yanks to a .222 batting average, but managed to hit only .203 themselves.

1951 New York (A) over New York (N), 4–2. A tired Giant pitching staff held the Yankees in check for three games, but the AL champs broke out to score 23 runs in the final three. Eddie Lopat (2–0, 0.50) starred for the winners.

1952 New York (A) over Brooklyn (N), 4–3. Allie Reynolds and Vic Raschi each won two games, combining for a 1.69 ERA. Johnny Mize hit three homers, and Mickey Mantle and Yogi Berra each hit two. Duke Snider batted .345 with four homers in a losing cause.

1953 New York (A) over Brooklyn (N), 4–2. The Yankees won their fifth straight World Championship as second baseman Billy Martin tied a record with 12 hits. Martin slugged .958 and drove in eight runs.

1954 New York (N) over Cleveland (A), 4–0. The Indians won 111 games during the season, still an AL record. But the Giants, sparked by a spectacular Willie Mays catch in Game 1, went on to defeat Cleveland easily. Pinch hitter-outfielder Dusty Rhodes drove in seven runs on two homers and two singles in six at bats.

1955 Brooklyn (N) over New York (A), 4–3. The Dodgers finally won a World Series in their eighth try, behind the pitching of series MVP Johnny Podres (2–0, 1.00). Duke Snider hit four homers in a series for the second time, and Dodger leftfielder Sandy Amoros made a game-saving catch in Game 7.

1956 New York (A) over Brooklyn (N), 4–3. Yankee righthander and series MVP Don Larsen pitched a perfect game in the fifth contest, while Mickey Mantle and Yogi Berra each hit three homers for New York.

1957 Milwaukee (N) over New York (A), 4–3. Lew Burdette won three times for the Braves, allowing but two runs in 27 innings and won the MVP. Milwaukee's hitting was led by Hank Aaron (.393, 3 HR, 7 RBIs).

1958 New York (A) over Milwaukee (N), 4–3. Yankees Hank Bauer and Moose Skowron combined for six homers and 15 RBI as the Bronx Bombers came back from a 3–1 deficit. Yankee pitcher "Bullet" Bob Turley earned MVP honors.

1959 Los Angeles (N) over Chicago(A), 4–2. Los Angeles enjoyed its first World Championship as the transplanted Dodgers prevailed, aided by the relief pitching of MVP Larry Sherry (two wins, two saves). Ted Kluszewski of the "Go-Go White Sox hit .391, with three homers and 10 RBI.

1960 Pittsburgh (N) over New York (A), 4–3. Pirate second baseman Bill Mazeroski's home run in the bottom of the ninth in Game 7 capped one of the most exciting contests in history. In the 10–9 ballgame, 10 of the runs were scored in the last two innings. Yankee second baseman Bobby Richardson, a hitting star throughout the series, was named MVP.

1961 New York (A) over Cincinnati (N),4–1. Whitey Ford tossed two shutouts in winning the MVP, and the Yankee offense pounded out 16 extra-base hits in the five games. Bobby Richardson (.391) and John Blanchard (.400, 2 HR) starred for New York.

1962 New York (A) over San Francisco (N), 4–3. Ralph Terry's four-hit shutout won the seesaw affair for the Yanks, and earned him the MVP. Whitey Ford completed his series record 33⅔ consecutive scoreless innings in the first game, and for the Giants, Chuck Hiller hit the first National League series grand slam in Game 4.

1963 Los Angeles (N) over New York (A), 4–0. Dodger pitchers held New York to four runs, led by Sandy Koufax's two wins and 23 strikeouts, including a record-breaking 15 in the first game. Koufax was the runaway choice for MVP.

1964 St. Louis (N) over New York (A), 4–3. Ten Yankee home runs were not enough to beat the Cardinals. Bob Gibson was the series MVP, and Tim McCarver (.478) also starred. Highlights included Ken Boyer's game-winning grand slam in Game 4, and Bobby Richardson's record 13 hits.

1965 Los Angeles (N) over Minnesota (A), 4–3. As in 1963, MVP Sandy Koufax again excelled for the Dodgers, allowing only two runs in 24 innings, striking our 29. Jim "Mudcat" Grant won two games and hit a three-run homer for the Twins.

1966 Baltimore (A) over Los Angeles (N), 4–0. The Orioles made the most of their first World Series appearance, as their young pitchers did not allow a run after the third inning of the first game. Slugger Frank Robinson capped a great year with the series MVP award.

1967 St. Louis (N) over Boston (A), 4–3. Bob Gibson pitched three complete game victories, added a home run in Game Seven, and was named MVP. Lou Brock batted .414 and stole seven bases, tying Eddie Collins' record and pacing the Cards.

1968 Detroit (A) over St. Louis (N), 4–3. the Cardinals were rolling behind Bob Gibson's record 17 strikeouts in Game 1 and his record seventh straight series win in Game 4. Again Lou Brock joined him in the record books with 13 hits and seven stolen bases. But their feats couldn't stop the Tigers, led by the MVP pitching of Mickey Lolich (3–0, 1.67).

1969 New York (N) over Baltimore (A), 4–1. The Mets stunned the baseball world by winning four in a row after dropping the opener. Their young pitchers held the Orioles to only nine runs, aided by the great outfield catches of Ron Swoboda and Tommy Agee. Series MVP Donn Clendenon (.357, 3 HR) and Al Weis (.455, 1 HR) led the Met attack.

1970 Baltimore (A) over Cincinnati, 4–1. Brooks Robinson almost singlehandedly beat the Reds with spectacular defense at third base and a .429 average with two homers and two doubles. His dominance of the series earned the MVP. Also chipping in for the O's were Paul Blair (.474), Frank Robinson, and Boog Powell (two homers each).

1971 Pittsburgh (N) over Baltimore (A), 4–3. Roberto Clemente played in 14 World Series games and hit safely in every one. Here he batted .414, slugged .759, and won MVP honors. Steve Blass, Nelson Briles, and Bruce Kison won all the Pirate victories with a combined ERA of 0.54.

1972 Oakland (A) over Cincinnati (N), 4–3. A's backup catcher Gene Tenace hit home runs in his first two series at bats, then went on to hit two more, becoming the surprise star and MVP selection. Rollie Fingers relieved in six of the contests, winning one and saving two.

1973 Oakland (A) over New York (N), 4–3. The Mets had the worst record of any pennant winner ever (82–79), but they lasted till the seventh game in a sloppy (19 errors) affair. Darold Knowles pitched in all seven games for the A's, saving two. Reggie Jackson slugged his way to the first of his two series MVP awards.

1974 Oakland (A) over Los Angeles (N), 4–1. The A's won their third straight World Championship behind the two saves and one win of MVP Rollie Fingers. Joe Rudi (.333) and Bert Campaneris (.353) starred with the bats.

1975 Cincinnati (N) over Boston (A), 4–3. Five of the seven games were decided by one run, including Game 6, a memorable 12-inning contest decided by Carlton Fisk's famous home run. Cincinnati used 23 relief pitchers. Pete Rose, the heart and soul of the Big Red Machine, hustled his way to MVP honors.

1976 Cincinnati (N) over New York (A), 4–0. The Big Red Machine drove over the Yankees, slugging .522 as a team. Seven Reds hitters batted over .300, led by MVP Johnny Bench's .533 (1.133 slugging average).

1977 New York (A) over Los Angeles (N), 4–2. Reggie Jackson hit five homers, including three in the final game, to equal records set by Babe Ruth, and win the MVP for the second time. Mike Torrez won two for the Yankees.

1978 New York (A) over Los Angeles (N), 4–2. Shortstop Bucky Dent and backup infielder Brian Doyle batted .417 and .438 respectively, pacing New York in its second straight six-game triumph. Dent was named MVP. In the last four contests, the Yankees outscored L.A. 28–8.

1979 Pittsburgh (N) over Baltimore (A), 4–3. The Pirates overcame a three games to one deficit as Earl Weaver's Orioles waited for three-run homers that never came. Led by Willie Stargell (.400, 3 HR) and Phil Garner (.500), Pittsburgh batted .323 as a team. "Pops" Stargell's on-field performance and team leadership of the Pirates' "family" was honored with the MVP.

1980 Philadelphia (N) over Kansas City (A), 4–2. The two teams batted .292 in a series decided largely by the relief pitching of Tug McGraw (1–1, 2 saves) vs. Dan Quisenberry (1–2, 1 save). Mike Schmidt took MVP honors with a .381 average and 7 RBI.

1981 Los Angeles (N) over New York (A), 4–2. Many observers called this sloppy series a fitting end to this strike-stricken 1981 season. Even the MVP award proved impossible to settle, as Pedro Guerrero, Steve Yeager, and Ron Cey shared the honor.

1982 St. Louis (N) over Milwaukee (A), 4–3. Joaquin Andujar won two games for the Cardinals, and Willie McGee had perhaps the greatest single series game by a rookie, with two homers and two great catches in Game 3. American League MVP Robin Yount batted .414 for the losers, but St. Louis' Darrell Porter won MVP honors for his clutch hitting and 5 RBI.

1983 Baltimore (A) over Philadelphia (N), 4–1. The Phillies couldn't hit Orioles' pitching, scoring but nine runs in the five games. Catcher Rick Dempsey hit four doubles and a home run, held the Phils to one stolen base, and was named MVP.

1984 Detroit (A) over San Diego (N), 4–1. The Tigers belted seven homers and backed them up with the pitching of Jack Morris (2–0, 2.00). Sparky Anderson become the first manager to win World Championships in both leagues. Alan Trammell, the Tigers' sure-handed shortstop, hit two home runs to earn MVP honors.

1985 Kansas City (A) over St. Louis (N), 4–3. The Cards were one inning away from the title, but a disputed call at first base opened the door for the Royals in Game 6. They won that contest, then blew St. Louis away 11–0 in the finale. Bret Saberhagen won two for Kansas City, and the MVP.

1986 New York (N) over Boston (A), 4–3. The Red Sox were one out away from winning it all, when Bob Stanley's wild pitch let in the tying run, and Mookie Wilson's grounder slipped between Bill Buckner's legs to score the winning run in Game 6. MVP Ray Knight hit a tie-breaking homer in Game 7 to send Boston to its fourth straight seven-game beating.

1987 Minnesota (A) over St. Louis (N), 4–3. The Twins won their first championship by taking all four games in their exotic home park, the Metrodome. Cardinal pitching held them to five runs in the three games in St. Louis, but in Minnesota the Twins could not be contained, scoring 33 times. Frank Viola (2–1,3.72) was the MVP.

1988 Los Angeles (A) over Oakland (A), 4–1. Series MVP Orel Hershiser (2–0, 17 K's) dazzled the powerful A's. Injured Dodger Kirk Gibson's dramatic two-out home run in the bottom of the ninth in Game 1 set the tone for the unexpected L.A. triumph.

1989 Oakland (A) over San Francisco (N), 4–0. The A's thoroughly dominated a weak Giants' pitching staff, pounding out 32 runs, 44 hits (including nine home runs) in only four games. Series MVP Dave Stewart and reliever Dennis Eckersley led the Oakland staff. This series will be long remembered for the major earthquake that struck the Bay area just before Game 3 and delayed the contest for 12 days.

1990 Cincinnati (N) over Oakland (A), 4–0. Cincinnati dominated the heavily favored A's in a stunning series sweep. The Reds hit .317 as a team, while their pitchers, led by MVP José Rijo, held Oakland's vaunted offense to a mere .207 series average. Billy Hatcher broke Babe Ruth's World Series record by hitting .750, with seven consecutive hits and four doubles.

1991 Minnesota (A) over Atlanta (N), 4–3. No team in baseball had ever gone from worst to first. In 1991, it happened twice, as the Twins and Braves, both of whom had finished last in their divisions, the year before met in one of the most exciting fall classics ever. Five games were decided by one run, three went into extra innings, and four were decided on the last at bat. Perhaps the best of all was Game 7, a scoreless affair until the bottom of the 10th inning, when the Twins finally scored a run. Jack Moris went the distance for Minnesota and earned MVP honors.

1992 Toronto (A) over Atlanta (N), 4–2. The Blue Jays became the first non-American team to win (or play in) the World Series. Braves closer Jeff Reardon gave up the winning hits in games 2 and 3, making Atlanta manager Bobby Cox reluctant to use him the rest of the series. Dave Winfield's first extra-base hit in World Series play broke a 2–2 tie in the 11th-inning of game 6 to send the Braves to their second straight World Series defeat. Toronto catcher Pat Borders was the MVP with a .450 average.

1993 Toronto (A) over Philadelphia (N), 4–2. The Blue Jays became the first team since the 1977–78 Yankees to repeat as World Series champions, battering the Phillies pitching staff for 45 runs (despite being shut out in Game 5). Toronto outfielder Joe Carter's home run in the bottom of the ninth in Game 6 marked only the second time the World Series had ended on a home run (Bill Mazeroski's Game 7 shot in 1960 was the other). Toronto DH Paul Molitor went 12 for 24 with six extra-base hits to win World Series honors.

1994 World Series canceled. The longest work stoppage in professional sports history, a 232-day dispute between players and owners over a cap on player salaries, forced the cancellation of the World Series and playoffs for the first time in baseball history.

1995 Atlanta (N) over Cleveland (A), 4–2. Good pitching beats good hitting as evidenced by this dramatic series. Baseball's best pitching staff (the Braves) held the game's most explosive offense (the Indians) to a .179 average, five home runs, and 19 runs. Five of the six games were decided by one run, including the clincher: a dazzling 1–0 one-hitter by the Atlanta's Tom Glavine. Glavine won two games and the MVP.

1996 New York (A) over Atlanta (N), 4–2. The Braves shellacked the Yankees 12–1 and 4–0 in the first two games in New York. But the Yankees struck back and won the next four in a row. The turning point came in Game 4, when the Yankees rallied from a 6–0 deficit to win the game 8–6 in 10 innings. Jim Leyritz provided the crushing blow: a three-run homer off Mark Wohlers to tie the game at 6–6. Yankee closer John Wetteland saved all four wins and was the MVP.

1997 Florida (N) over Cleveland (A), 4–3. This sloppy series was marked by hot bats, cold weather, porous defense, and poor relief pitching. Game 3 alone involved 17 walks and 6 errors. Cleveland was two outs away from winning it all in Game 7, when Craig Counsell's sacrifice fly tied the game at 2–2. In the bottom of the 11th, Edgar Renteria singled home the deciding run. Florida's rookie pitcher Livan Hernandez, winner of Games 1 and 5, was the MVP.

1998 New York (A) over San Diego (N), 4–0. The Yankees completed one of the greatest seasons in baseball history with a four-game sweep that gave them a combined record of 125–50 and a .714 winning percentage. Home runs from Chuck Knoblauch and Tino Martinez helped the Yankees come from behind in Game 1, while Scott Brosius's three-run blast off San Diego closer Trevor Hoffman in Game 3 broke the Padres' back. Brosius, who had hit .203 the year before, hit .471 in the series and was named MVP.

1999 New York (A) over Atlanta (N), 4–0. The Yankees ran their World Series winning streak to 12 games in a row with their second-straight sweep. They beat the Braves every which way: pitching, hitting and fielding. Atlanta errors opened the door to big innings for New York in Games 1 and 2; and the Yankees used four home runs in Game 3 to turn a 5-1 deficit into a 10-inning, 6-5 win. Mariano Rivera, who won Game 3 in relief and saved Games 1 and 4 (and did not give up a run after July) won the MVP award.

2000 New York (A) over New York (N), 4-1. Every game of the first Subway Series in 45 years was decided by one or two runs. The Yankees entered the ninth inning of Game 1 down by a run, but tied the game on a bases-loaded sacrifice fly and won it in the 12th inning. Derek Jeter hit the first pitch of Game 4 over the center field fence to give the Yankees a lead they would never relinquish. Jeter, who hit another home run in Game 5, batted .409, and was the MVP. **2001** See Page 972 for results and game-by-game summaries of the 2001 World Series.

World Series MVP Winners

Year	Name	Team
1955	Johnny Podres	Brooklyn Dodgers
1956	Don Larsen	New York Yankees
1957	Lew Burdette	Milwaukee Braves
1958	Bob Turley	New York Yankees
1959	Larry Sherry	Los Angeles Dodgers
1960	Bobby Richardson	New York Yankees
1961	Whitey Ford	New York Yankees
1962	Ralph Terry	New York Yankees
1963	Sandy Koufax	Los Angeles Dodgers
1964	Bob Gibson	St. Louis Cardinals
1965	Sandy Koufax	Los Angeles Dodgers
1966	Frank Robinson	Baltimore Orioles
1967	Bob Gibson	St. Louis Cardinals
1968	Mickey Lolich	Detroit Tigers
1969	Donn Clendenon	New York Mets
1970	Brooks Robinson	Baltimore Orioles
1971	Roberto Clemente	Pittsburgh Pirates
1972	Gene Tenace	Oakland A's
1973	Reggie Jackson	Oakland A's
1974	Rollie Fingers	Oakland A's
1975	Pete Rose	Cincinnati Reds
1976	Johnny Bench	Cincinnati Reds
1977	Reggie Jackson	New York Yankees
1978	Bucky Dent	New York Yankees

Year	Name	Team
1979	Willie Stargell	Pittsburgh Pirates
1980	Mike Schmidt	Philadelphia Philles
1981	Ron Cey, Pedro Guerrero, Steve Yeager	Los Angeles Dodgers
1982	Darrell Porter	St. Louis Cardinals
1983	Rick Dempsey	Baltimore Orioles
1984	Alan Trammell	Detroit Tigers
1985	Bret Saberhagen	Kansas City Royals
1986	Ray Knight	New York Mets
1987	Frank Viola	Minnesota Twins
1988	Orel Hershiser	Los Angeles Dodgers
1989	Dave Stewart	Oakland Athletics
1990	José Rijo	Cincinnati Reds
1991	Jack Morris	Minesota Twins
1992	Pat Borders	Toronto Blue Jays
1993	Paul Molitor	Toronto Blue Jays
1994	No World Series	
1995	Tom Glavine	Atlanta Braves
1996	John Wetteland	New York Yankees
1997	Livan Hernández	Florida Marlins
1998	Scott Brosius	New York Yankees
1999	Mariano Rivera	New York Yankees
2000	Derek Jeter	New York Yankees
2001	See page 972	

World Series Records

Total Hits		Total Home runs		Total Runs batted in		Total Runs scored	
Yogi Berra	71	Mickey Mantle	18	Mickey Mantle	40	Mickey Mantle	42
Mickey Mantle	59	Babe Ruth	15	Yogi Berra	39	Yogi Berra	41
Frankie Frisch	58	Yogi Berra	12	Lou Gehrig	35	Babe Ruth	37

Most hits in one series		Most home runs in one series		Most runs batted in in one series	
Bobby Richardson, 1964	13	Reggie Jackson, 1977	5	Bobby Richardson, 1960	12
Lou Brock, 1968	13				
Marty Barrett, 1986	13				

Most Wins by Managers

	Manager	Wins	Losses	Pct.
1.	Connie Mack	3,776	4,025	.484
2.	John McGraw	2,840	1,984	.589
3.	Sparky Anderson	2,194	1,834	.545
4.	Bucky Harris	2,159	2,219	.493
5.	Joe McCarthy	2,126	1,335	.614
6.	Walter Alston	2,040	1,613	.558
7.	Leo Durocher	2,010	1,710	.540
8.	Casey Stengel	1,926	1,867	.508
9.	Gene Mauch	1,901	2,037	.483
10.	Bill McKechnie	1,898	1,724	.524

A Most Valuable Team

Only eleven players have won the Most Valuable Player Award in consecutive seasons; oddly enough there is at least one from each fielding position.

Position	Player, Team	Years
1B	Jimmie Foxx, Philadelphia A's	1932–33
1B	Frank Thomas, Chicago White Sox	1993–94
2B	Joe Morgan, Reds	1975–76
3B	Mike Schmidt, Phillies	1980–81
SS	Ernie Banks, Cubs	1958–59
OF	Mickey Mantle, Yankees	1956–57
OF	Roger Maris, Yankees	1960–61
OF	Dale Murphy, Braves	1982–83
OF	Barry Bonds, Pirates/Giants	1992–93
C	Yogi Berra, Yankees	1954–55
P	Hal Newhouser, Tigers	1944–45

2001 Individual Leaders

AMERICAN LEAGUE

Batting average (min. 500 plate appearances)		Home runs		Runs batted in	
Ichiro Suzuki, Seattle	.350	Alex Rodriguez, Texas	52	Bret Boone, Seattle	141
Jason Giambi, Oakland	.342	Jim Thome, Cleveland	49	Juan Gonzalez, Cleveland	140
Roberto Alomar, Cleveland	.336	Rafael Palmeiro, Texas	47	Alex Rodriguez, Texas	135
Bret Boone, Seattle	.331	Troy Glaus, Anaheim	41	Manny Ramirez, Boston	125
Frank Catalanotto, Texas	.330	Manny Ramirez, Boston	41	Jim Thome, Cleveland	124
Juan Gonzalez, Cleveland	.325	Carlos Delgado, Toronto	39	Garret Anderson, Anaheim	123
Alex Rodriguez, Texas	.318	Jason Giambi, Oakland	38	Rafael Palmeiro, Texas	123
Shannon Stewart, Toronto	.316	Bret Boone, Seattle	37	Jason Giambi, Oakland	120
Jeff Conine, Baltimore	.311	Juan Gonzalez, Cleveland	35	Edgar Martinez, Seattle	116
Derek Jeter, New York	.311	Jose Cruz Jr., Toronto	34	Eric Chavez, Oakland	114
		Tino Martinez, New York	34		

Pitching-wins		Earned run average (min. 162 innings)		Strikeouts	
Mark Mulder, Oakland	21- 8	Freddy Garcia, Seattle	3.05	Hideo Nomo, Boston	220
Roger Clemens, New York	20- 3	Mike Mussina, New York	3.15	Mike Mussina, New York	214
Jamie Moyer, Seattle	20- 6	Joe Mays, Minnesota	3.16	Roger Clemens, New York	213
Freddy Garcia, Seattle	18- 6	Mark Buehrle, CWS	3.29	Barry Zito, Oakland	205
Tim Hudson, Oakland	18- 9	Tim Hudson, Oakland	3.37	Bartolo Colon, Cleveland	201
Paul Abbott, Seattle	17- 4	Jamie Moyer, Seattle	3.43	Tim Hudson, Oakland	181
Joe Mays, Minnesota	17-13	Mark Mulder, Oakland	3.45	C.C. Sabathia, Cleveland	171
Mike Mussina, New York	17-11	Barry Zito, Oakland	3.49	Andy Pettitte, New York	164
C.C. Sabathia, Cleveland	17- 5	Roger Clemens, New York	3.51	Freddy Garcia, Seattle	163
Barry Zito, Oakland	17- 8	Cory Lidle, Oakland	3.59	Pedro Martinez, Boston	163

NATIONAL LEAGUE

Batting average (min. 500 plate appearances)		Home runs		Runs batted in	
Larry Walker, Colorado	.350	Barry Bonds, San Francisco	73	Sammy Sosa, Chicago	160
Todd Helton, Colorado	.336	Sammy Sosa, Chicago	64	Todd Helton, Colorado	146
Moises Alou, Houston	.331	Luis Gonzalez, Arizona	57	Luis Gonzalez, Arizona	142
Lance Berkman, Houston	.331	Shawn Green, Los Angeles	49	Barry Bonds, San Francisco	137
Chipper Jones, Atlanta	.330	Todd Helton, Colorado	49	Jeff Bagwell, Houston	130
Albert Pujols, St. Louis	.329	Richie Sexson, Milwaukee	45	Albert Pujols, St. Louis	130
Barry Bonds, San Francisco	.328	Phil Nevin, San Diego	41	Lance Berkman, Houston	126
Sammy Sosa, Chicago	.328	Jeff Bagwell, Houston	39	Phil Nevin, San Diego	126
Juan Pierre, Colorado	.327	Chipper Jones, Atlanta	38	Shawn Green, Los Angeles	125
Luis Gonzalez, Arizona	.325	Larry Walker, Colorado	38	Richie Sexson, Milwaukee	125

Pitching-wins		Earned run average (min. 162 innings)		Strikeouts	
Curt Schilling, Arizona	22- 6	Randy Johnson, Arizona	2.49	Randy Johnson, Arizona	372
Matt Morris, St. Louis	22- 8	Curt Schilling, Arizona	2.98	Curt Schilling, Arizona	293
Randy Johnson, Arizona	21- 6	John Burkett, Atlanta	3.04	Chan Ho Park, Los Angeles	218
Jon Lieber, Chicago	20- 6	Greg Maddux, Atlanta	3.05	Kerry Wood, Chicago	217
Ramon Ortiz, San Francisco	17- 9	Darryl Kile, St. Louis	3.09	Javier Vazquez, Montreal	208
Greg Maddux, Atlanta	17-11	Matt Morris, St. Louis	3.16	John Burkett, Atlanta	187
Tom Glavine, Atlanta	16- 7	Ramon Ortiz, San Francisco	3.29	Matt Morris, St. Louis	185
Wade Miller, Houston	16- 8	Al Leiter, New York Mets	3.31	Wade Miller, Houston	183
Darryl Kile, St. Louis	16-11	Kerry Wood, Chicago	3.36	Robert Person, Philadelphia	183
Javier Vazquez, Montreal	16-11	Wade Miller, Houston	3.40	Darryl Kile, St. Louis	179

Major League Baseball Final Standings, 2001

Division/Team	W	L	Pct.	GB	Division/Team	W	L	Pct.	GB
American League East					**National League East**				
New York Yankees[1]	95	65	.594	–	Atlanta[1]	88	74	.543	–
Boston	82	79	.509	13½	New York	86	76	.531	2
Toronto	80	82	.494	16	Florida	82	80	.506	6
Baltimore	63	98	.391	32½	Montreal	76	86	.469	12
Tampa Bay	62	100	.383	34	Philadelphia	68	94	.420	20
American League Central					**National League Central**				
Cleveland[1]	91	71	.562	–	Houston[1]	93	69	.574	–
Minnesota	85	77	.525	6	St. Louis[2]	93	69	.574	–
Chicago	83	79	.512	8	Chicago	88	74	.543	5
Detroit	66	96	.407	25	Milwaukee	68	94	.420	25
Kansas City	65	97	.401	26	Cincinnati	66	96	.407	27
					Pittsburgh	62	100	.383	31
American League West					**National League West**				
Seattle[1]	116	46	.716	–	Arizona[1]	92	70	.568	–
Oakland[2]	102	60	.630	14	San Francisco	90	72	.556	2
Anaheim	75	87	.463	41	Los Angeles	86	76	.531	6
Texas	73	89	.451	43	San Diego	79	83	.488	13
					Colorado	73	89	.451	19

1. Division champion. 2. Wild card for playoffs.

2001 Division Series

AMERICAN LEAGUE

Seattle defeats Cleveland, 3 games to 2
Cleveland 5, SEATTLE 0
Bartolo Colon struck out 10 Mariners over eight innings. Cleveland scored three runs on a double by Roberto Alomar and three bloop singles.
SEATTLE 5, Cleveland 1
Mike Cameron and Edgar Martinez each launched two-run homers before Cleveland retired a single batter. Jamie Moyer changed speeds and painted corners for six innings for the win.
CLEVELAND 17, Seattle 2
Cleveland scored two in the first, two in the second, and four in the third, and the rout was on. C. C. Sabathia cruised for the victory.
Seattle 6, CLEVELAND 2
Trailing 1-0 in the seventh, the Mariners finally scored off Bartolo Colon with three runs on two walks and three hits.
SEATTLE 3, Cleveland 1
Jamie Moyer again limited Cleveland to one run over six innings. Mark McLemore's bases-loaded single in the second gave Seattle a 2-0 lead and the bullpen again held the Indians scoreless.

New York Yankees defeat Oakland, 3 games to 2
Oakland 5, NEW YORK 3
Terrence Long homered twice to power the Oakland offense, while Mark Mulder held New York to one run in 6⅔ innings for the win.
Oakland 2, NEW YORK 0
Tim Hudson bested Andy Pettitte in this classic pitcher's duel. Ron Gant's solo homer in the fourth inning was all the offense Oakland needed.
New York 1, OAKLAND 0
Barry Zito limited the Yankees to two hits, but one of them was a Jorge Posada homer. Mike Mussina and Mariano Rivera combined on a shutout. Derek Jeter's backhanded flip to Posada nailed Jeremy Giambi at home plate and saved the game.
New York 9, OAKLAND 2
The Yankees scored twice after F.P. Santangelo's error, then pounded Cory Lidle for four more runs. Orlando Hernandez struggled for the win.
Note: Home teams in CAPITAL LETTERS.

NEW YORK 5, Oakland 3
The Yankees became the first team to win a five-game series after losing the first two at home. They again capitalized on A's miscues to score unearned runs in the third and fourth innings

NATIONAL LEAGUE

Arizona defeats St. Louis 3 games to 2
ARIZONA 1, St. Louis 0
Curt Schilling limited the Cardinals to three hits over nine innings. In the fifth, Steve Finley singled home Damian Miller, who had been hit by a pitch.
St. Louis 4, ARIZONA 1
Albert Pujols got St. Louis on the board in the first inning, with a two-run homer off Arizona's Randy Johnson, and the Cardinals never looked back.
Arizona 5, ST. LOUIS 3
With the score tied at 2-2 in the seventh, light-hitting Craig Counsell tagged a three-run homer off reliever Mike Matthews to give Arizona the lead.
ST. LOUIS 4, Arizona 1
Jim Edmonds hit a solo homer in the second inning and Fernando Viña hit a two-run shot in the third to power the St. Louis offense.
ARIZONA 2, St. Louis 1
With runners at first and third and one out in the ninth, Tony Womack botched the suicide squeeze, and Midre Cummings was an easy out at home plate. But later in the same at-bat, Womack blooped a single that scored the winning run.

Atlanta defeats Houston, 3 games to 0
Atlanta 7, HOUSTON 4
Houston's bullpen couldn't hold a 3-2 lead. Mike Jackson gave up the tying run in the eighth and Chipper Jones launched Billy Wagner's first pitch over the left field wall to give the Braves a 6-3 lead.
Atlanta 1, HOUSTON 0
Tom Glavine threw eight shutout innings and John Smoltz pitched a scoreless ninth. The Braves scored on Julio Lugo's error in the second inning.
ATLANTA 6, Houston 2
Backup catcher Paul Bako homered for two runs and drove in a third with a squeeze bunt. John Burkett held Houston to two runs in 6¼ innings.

New York Yankees defeat Seattle Mariners, 4 games to 1

New York 4, SEATTLE 2

Yankee starter Andy Pettitte didn't give up a hit until the fifth inning, and held Seattle to three hits and one run over eight innings. Mariano Rivera gave up a run in the ninth, but held on for the save. Paul O'Neill sparked New York's offense with a two-run homer in the fourth inning off Seattle starter Aaron Sele, who ran his postseason record against the Yankees to 0-4.

New York 3, SEATTLE 2

Freddy Garcia, pitching on three days' rest, settled down after a rocky start, but not before giving up all three runs in the second inning. Scott Brosius's double drove in the first two runs; Chuck Knoblauch followed it with a single that Mike Cameron trapped in centerfield, then tried to convince the umpires that he caught it while Brosius scored. New York starter Mike Mussina labored through six innings, surrendering a two-run homer to Stan Javier. But Ramiro Mendoza ($1^1/_3$ innings) and Mariano Rivera ($1^2/_3$ innings) held onto the lead for the last three innings.

Seattle 14, NEW YORK 3

The Yankees jumped out to a 2-0 lead in the first on Bernie Williams's two-run homer off Jamie Moyer. But Seattle tied it in the fifth on walks to Ichiro Suzuki and Mark McLemore and Bret Boone's sinking line drive, which Chuck Knoblauch caught and then dropped. John Olerud homered to lead off the sixth, and the

Mariners jumped all over Orlando Hernandez and two relievers for six more runs. Moyer held New York to four hits over seven innings for the victory.

NEW YORK 3, Seattle 1

Neither starter gave up a run, but they both walked so many batters that they were gone by the sixth inning. Roger Clemens walked four, but gave up only one hit; Paul Abbott didn't give up any hits, but walked eight Yankees. Seattle finally scored on Bret Boone's solo homer in the eighth against Ramiro Mendoza. But the Yankees answered back in their half of the inning when Bernie Williams went deep off Arthur Rhodes. In the ninth, both managers brought in their closers, with drastically different results. Mariano Rivera retired the Mariners on three pitches; Kazuhiro Sasaki gave up a single to Scott Brosius, and then a game-winning home run by Alfonso Soriano.

NEW YORK 12, Seattle 3

The Yankees pounced on Aaron Sele for the second time in a week, tagging him for four unearned runs in the third inning. Third baseman David Bell booted a grounder to let the leadoff man on base, and the Yankees followed with a single, a sacrifice bunt, a sacrifice fly, a double, and a two-run homer by Bernie Williams. The game was never close after that, as New York cruised to its fourth straight World Series. Andy Pettitte again shut down the Seattle offense and was named the series MVP.

Arizona Diamondbacks defeat Atlanta Braves , 4 games to 1

ARIZONA 2, Atlanta 0

Diamondbacks ace Randy Johnson stopped his postseason losing streak at seven with a three-hit, ten-strikeout, complete game performance. He held Atlanta to one hit over the first eight innings: a infield single off the glove of Matt Williams in the first inning. Braves starter Greg Maddux pitched in and out of trouble for seven innings, but induced timely double play grounders to keep Atlanta in contention. Atlanta put the tying run on base in the ninth inning, but Johnson struck out Brian Jordan to end the game. Craig Counsell scored both of Arizona's runs.

Atlanta 8, ARIZONA 1

Javy Lopez, who did not play in the Division Series because of an ankle injury, broke open a 1-1 game in the seventh inning with a two-out, two-run homer off Miguel Batista. The Braves scored five more runs against Arizona's bullpen after two were out in the eighth inning. Up until the seventh, the game was a pitcher's duel between Batista and Atlanta's Tom Glavine, who allowed Arizona to tie the game in the bottom of the sixth but still got the win.

Arizona 5, ATLANTA 1

Curt Schilling continued his postseason domination, pitching his third straight complete game victory. He held Atlanta to one run on four hits and struck out 12. Steve Finley doubled home Craig Counsell and Matt Williams in the third

inning to give Arizona all the offense it needed. Schilling singled and scored in his own cause in the fifth, when the Diamondbacks added three insurance runs on two walks, three weak singles, and an error by Javy Lopez.

Arizona 11, ATLANTA 4

Atlanta jumped out to a 2-0 lead on a Chipper Jones RBI double in the first and a solo homer by Andruw Jones in the second. But the Braves made three errors and botched a fielder's choice in the third inning, and Arizona took advantage, scoring four runs on four hits. The Diamondbacks added two more runs in the fourth on Craig Counsell's double. The Braves brought the tying run to the plate in both the seventh and eighth innings, but each time came away with only one run. Arizona blew the game open in the ninth with four runs.

Arizona 3, ATLANTA 2

Randy Johnson wasn't as good as in his first start, but he pitched well enough for the win. He held Atlanta to two runs and seven hits over seven innings, and escaped a seventh inning jam by striking out Brian Jordan with the bases loaded. Erubiel Durazo entered the game in the fifth after Mark Grace hurt his hamstring, and promptly hit a two-run homer that was the difference. Byung Hyun Kim pitched the final two innings for the save, sending Arizona to its first World Series ever. Craig Counsell hit .381 and scored five runs over the five games, and was named series MVP.

The 2001 World Series

Game 1   ARIZONA 9   New York 1
Curt Schilling was masterful again, holding the Yankees to three hits over seven innings. He only refrained from pitching his fourth straight complete game of the postseason so that he could throw Game Four on three days' rest. New York took the early lead when Schilling hit Derek Jeter with a pitch, and Bernie Williams' bloop double brought him home. But the Diamondbacks responded in their half of the first on Craig Counsell's homer, and blew the game open with four runs in the third and four more in the fourth against Mike Mussina. Luis Gonzalez's two-run homer in the third was the crowning blow.

	123	456	789	R	H	E
New York	100	000	000	1	3	2
Arizona	104	400	00x	9	10	0

WP: Curt Schilling (1-0). LP: Mike Mussina (0-1)

Game 2   ARIZONA 4   New York 0
The Yankees stacked their lineup with righthanded hitters against lefty Randy Johnson, but with no more success than they had the night before against Schilling. Johnson threw a shutout, striking out 11, and limiting New York to three hits for the second straight night. Andy Pettitte kept the game close for six innings, but surrendered a three-run home run to Matt Williams in the seventh that put the game out of reach.

	123	456	789	R	H	E
New York	000	000	000	0	3	0
Arizona	010	000	30x	4	5	0

WP: Randy Johnson (1-0). LP: Andy Pettitte (0-1)

Game 3   NEW YORK 2   Arizona 1
The Yankees relied on their usual formula to fight their way back into the series: strong starting pitching, timely hitting, and Mariano Rivera. Roger Clemens gave up one run over seven innings before giving way to Rivera, who pitched a scoreless eighth and ninth. Jorge Posada's solo homer gave the Yankees the early lead, and Scott Brosius's double in the 6th drove home Bernie Williams with the deciding run. Arizona loaded the bases with one out in the 4th, but came away with only one run; Brian Anderson was the hard-luck loser for the Diamondbacks.

	123	456	789	R	H	E
Arizona	000	100	000	1	3	3
New York	010	001	00x	2	7	1

WP: Roger Clemens (1-0). LP: Brian Anderson (0-1)

Game 4   NEW YORK 4   Arizona 3 (10 innings)
This was an instant classic, marked by close plays at the plate, escape-artist pitching, second-guessable managerial decisions, and dramatic home runs. The Yankees were down to their last out in the ninth inning when Tino Martinez hit a game-tying two-run homer off Diamondback closer Byung-Hun Kim. In the 10th, Kim gave up the game-winning run on a Derek Jeter homer. Curt Schilling, pitching on three days' rest, again stymied the New York offense for seven innings, but left the game with a 3-1 lead after Erubiel Durazo's RBI double broke a 1-1 tie. Orlando "El Duque" Hernandez loaded the bases in the first, but wriggled out of trouble and pitched 6 1/3 strong innings of one-run ball. Mariano Rivera pitched a scoreless 10th for the win.

	123	456	789	10	R	H	E
Arizona	000	100	020	0	3	6	0
New York	001	000	002	1	4	7	0

WP: Mariano Rivera (1-0). LP: Byung-Hyun Kim (0-1)

Game 5   NEW YORK 3   Arizona 2 (12 innings)
If this game had been a Hollywood script, it would have been ridiculed. For the second night in a row, the Yankees were down to their last out in the ninth, when Scott Brosius hit a two-run homer off Byung-Hyun Kim to tie the game. After Mariano Rivera wriggled out of a bases-loaded, one-out jam in the top of the 11th, New York rallied in the 12th on a Chuck Knoblauch single, a sacrifice by Brosius, and Alfonso Soriano's game-winning single. Arizona scored both of their runs in the 5th against Mike Mussina on home runs by Steve Finley and backup catcher Rod Barajas. The unprecedented comeback spoiled a stunning effort by Diamondback starter Miguel Batista, who shut out the Yankee bats for 7 2/3 innings.

	123	456	789	10 11 12	R	H	E
Arizona	000	020	000	0 0 0	2	8	0
New York	000	000	002	0 0 1	3	9	1

WP: Sterling Hitchcock (1-0). LP: Albie Lopez (0-1)

Game 6   ARIZONA 15   New York 2
The home team held sway again, as Arizona pounded Yankee starter Andy Pettitte for six runs over two innings. His replacement, Jay Witasick, was even worse, giving up nine runs on 10 hits, while retiring only four batters. Every Diamondback starter, including pitcher Randy Johnson, had a hit, and the team's total of 22 set a World Series Record. Johnson struck out seven over seven innings, and left the game after 101 pitches in case he was needed in Game Seven.

	123	456	789	R	H	E
New York	000	002	000	2	7	1
Arizona	138	300	00x	15	22	0

WP: Randy Johnson (2-0). LP: Andy Pettitte (0-2)

Game 7   ARIZONA 3   New York 2
This time, it was Arizona's turn for an unlikely comeback. The Yankees held a 2-1 lead in the ninth inning, and with Mariano Rivera on the mound, they seemed poised for their fourth straight championship. But the Diamondbacks rallied behind a Mark Grace single, an error by Rivera, and a double by Tony Womack that scored the tying run and put the winning run at third. Luis Gonzalez's bloop single brought home the game-winner. Curt Schilling left the game trailing 2-1 after 7 1/3 innings, but Randy Johnson held the Yankees scoreless for the last 1 2/3 innings. The two pitchers shared MVP honors.

	123	456	789	R	H	E
New York	000	000	110	2	6	3
Arizona	000	001	002	3	11	0

WP: Randy Johnson (3-0). LP: Mariano Rivera (1-1)